Recent Developments in the Econometrics of Panel Data
Volume II

The International Library of Critical Writings in Econometrics

Series Editors: Mark Blaug

Professor Emeritus, University of London, UK
Professor Emeritus, University of Buckingham, UK
Visiting Professor, University of Amsterdam, The Netherlands
Visiting Professor, Erasmus University of Rotterdam, The Netherlands

Adrian C. Darnell

Professor and Principal, George Stephenson College,
University of Durham, UK

1. The Econometrics of Panel Data (Volumes I and II)
   G.S. Maddala
2. Macroeconometric Modelling (Volumes I and II)
   Kenneth F. Wallis
3. Simultaneous Equation Estimation
   Carl F. Christ
4. The History of Econometrics (Volumes I and II)
   Adrian C. Darnell
5. Time Series (Volumes I and II)
   Andrew Harvey
6. The Methodology of Econometrics (Volumes I and II)
   Dale J. Poirier
7. Bayesian Inference (Volumes I and II)
   Nicholas G. Polson and George C. Tiao
8. Nonlinear Models (Volumes I and II)
   Herman J. Bierens and A. Ronald Gallant
9. Recent Developments in the Econometrics of Panel Data (Volumes I and II)
   Badi H. Baltagi

Future titles will include:

Recent Developments in Time Series
Paul Newbold and Stephen J. Leybourne

General to Specific Modelling
David F. Hendry, Neil R. Ericsson and Julia Campos

Selection Bias and Program Evaluation
James J. Heckman

Wherever possible, the articles in these volumes have been reproduced as originally published using facsimile reproduction, inclusive of footnotes and pagination to facilitate ease of reference.

For a list of all Edward Elgar published titles visit our site on the World Wide Web at
http://www.e-elgar.co.uk

Recent Developments in the Econometrics of Panel Data Volume II

Edited by

Badi H. Baltagi

Professor of Economics and George Summey, Jr. Chair in Liberal Arts
Texas A&M University, USA

THE INTERNATIONAL LIBRARY OF CRITICAL WRITINGS IN ECONOMETRICS

An Elgar Reference Collection
Cheltenham, UK • Northampton, MA, USA

Published by
Edward Elgar Publishing Limited
Glensanda House
Montpellier Parade
Cheltenham
Glos GL50 1UA
UK

Edward Elgar Publishing, Inc.
136 West Street
Suite 202
Northampton
Massachusetts 01060
USA

A catalogue record for this book is available from the British Library

Library of Congress Cataloguing in Publication Data

Recent developments in the econometrics of panel data / edited by Badi H. Baltagi.
p. cm. — (International library of critical writings in econometrics ; 9)
Includes bibliographical references and index.
1. Panel analysis. 2. Econometrics. I. Baltagi, Badi H. (Badi Hani) II. Series.

H61.26 .R4 2003
330'.01'5195—dc21

2002029825

ISBN 1 84064 967 4 (2 volume set)

Printed and bound in Great Britain by MPG Books Ltd, Bodmin, Cornwall

Contents

Acknowledgements

The editor and publishers wish to thank the authors and the following publishers who have kindly given permission for the use of copyright material.

American Statistical Association for article: Michael Lechner (1995), 'Some Specification Tests for Probit Models Estimated on Panel Data', *Journal of Business and Economic Statistics*, **13** (4), October, 475–88.

Blackwell Publishing Ltd for article: David J. McKenzie (2001), 'Estimation of AR(1) Models with Unequally Spaced Pseudo-Panels', *Econometrics Journal*, **4** (1), 89–108.

Cambridge University Press for article: Badi H. Baltagi and Ping X. Wu (1999), 'Unequally Spaced Panel Data Regressions with AR (1) Disturbances', *Econometric Theory*, **15**, 814–23.

Econometric Society for articles: Bo E. Honoré (1992), 'Trimmed LAD and Least Squares Estimation of Truncated and Censored Regression Models with Fixed Effects', *Econometrica*, **60** (3), May, 533–65; Michael P. Keane (1994), 'A Computationally Practical Simulation Estimator for Panel Data', *Econometrica*, **62** (1), January, 95–116; Ekaterini Kyriazidou (1997), 'Estimation of a Panel Data Sample Selection Model', *Econometrica*, **65** (6), November, 1335–64; Myoung-jae Lee (1999), 'A Root-N Consistent Semiparametric Estimator for Related-Effect Binary Response Panel Data', *Econometrica*, **67** (2), March, 427–33; Bo E. Honoré and Ekaterini Kyriazidou (2000), 'Panel Data Discrete Choice Models with Lagged Dependent Variables', *Econometrica*, **68** (4), July, 839–74.

Elsevier Science for articles: Robert Moffitt (1993), 'Identification and Estimation of Dynamic Models with a Time Series of Repeated Cross-Sections', *Journal of Econometrics*, **59**, 99–123; Jeffrey M. Wooldridge (1995), 'Selection Corrections for Panel Data Models under Conditional Mean Independence Assumptions', *Journal of Econometrics*, **68**, 115–32; Badi H. Baltagi and Qi Li (1995), 'Testing AR(1) against MA(1) Disturbances in an Error Component Model, *Journal of Econometrics*, **68**, 133–51; Gilbert E. Metcalf (1996), 'Specification Testing in Panel Data with Instrumental Variables', *Journal of Econometrics*, **71**, 291–307; Badi H. Baltagi, Javier Hidalgo and Qi Li (1996), 'A Nonparametric Test for Poolability Using Panel Data', *Journal of Econometrics*, **75**, 345–67; M. Dolores Collado (1997), 'Estimating Dynamic Models from Time Series of Independent Cross-Sections', *Journal of Econometrics*, **82**, 37–62; Q. Li and C. Hsiao (1998), 'Testing Serial Correlation in Semiparametric Panel Data Models', *Journal of Econometrics*, **87**, 207–37; Jeffrey M. Wooldridge (1999), 'Distribution-free Estimation of Some Nonlinear Panel Data Models', *Journal of Econometrics*, **90**, 77–97; Francis Vella and Marno Verbeek (1999), 'Two-step Estimation of Panel Data Models with Censored Endogenous Variables and Selection Bias', *Journal of Econometrics*, **90**, 239–63; Jason Abrevaya (1999), 'Leapfrog Estimation of a Fixed-Effects Model with Unknown Transformation of the Dependent Variable', *Journal of Econometrics*, **93**, 203–28; Sourafel Girma (2000), 'A Quasi-Differencing Approach to Dynamic Modelling from a Time Series of Independent Cross-Sections', *Journal of Econometrics*, **98**, 365–83; Anil K. Bera, Walter Sosa-Escudero and Mann Yoon (2001), 'Tests for the Error Component Model in the Presence of Local Misspecification', *Journal of Econometrics*, **101**, 1–23; Werner Antweiler (2001), 'Nested Random Effects Estimation in Unbalanced Panel Data', *Journal of Econometrics*, **101**, 295–313; Badi H. Baltagi, Seuck Heun Song and Byoung Cheol Jung (2001), 'The Unbalanced Nested Error Component Regression Model', *Journal of Econometrics*, **101**, 357–81; Peter Davis (2002), 'Estimating Multi-way Error Components Models with Unbalanced Data Structures', *Journal of Econometrics*, **106** (1), 67–95.

Every effort has been made to trace all the copyright holders but if any have been inadvertently overlooked the publishers will be pleased to make the necessary arrangement at the first opportunity.

In addition the publishers wish to thank the Marshall Library of Economics, Cambridge University and the Library of the University of Warwick for their assistance in obtaining these articles.

Part I
Limited Dependent Variables

[1]

Econometrica, Vol. 60, No. 3 (May, 1992), 533–565

TRIMMED LAD AND LEAST SQUARES ESTIMATION OF TRUNCATED AND CENSORED REGRESSION MODELS WITH FIXED EFFECTS

BY BO E. HONORÉ[1]

This paper considers estimation of truncated and censored regression models with fixed effects in panel data. Up until now, no estimator has been shown to be consistent as the cross section dimension increases with the time dimension fixed. Trimmed least absolute deviations (LAD) and trimmed least squares estimators are proposed for the case where the panel is of length two, and it is proven that they are consistent and asymptotically normal under suitable regularity conditions. It is not necessary to maintain parametric assumptions on the error terms to obtain this result. Because three of the four estimators are defined as minimizers of nondifferentiable functions, traditional methods cannot be used to establish asymptotic normality. Instead, the approach of Pakes and Pollard (1989) is used. A small scale Monte Carlo study demonstrates that these estimators can perform well in small samples. Despite their nonlinear nature, the estimators are easy to calculate in practice, as are consistent estimators of their asymptotic variances. Generalization of the estimators to panels of arbitrary length is briefly discussed.

KEYWORDS: Panel data, fixed effects, truncated and censored regression.

1. INTRODUCTION

FIXED EFFECTS PLAY AN IMPORTANT ROLE in the analysis of panel data. If the econometric specification has the fixed effects entering linearly, then the remaining parameters of the model can be estimated by differencing the estimating equations.[2] However, fixed effects can also be of importance in nonlinear models. For example, Heckman and MaCurdy's (1980) labor supply model implies that the decision of whether or not to work can be modelled as a discrete choice model with fixed effects, and that the actual labor supply will be a limited dependent variable with fixed effects. It is therefore of interest to study estimators of these models. As panel data are characterized by having many individuals observed over few time periods, it is most useful to consider the asymptotic properties of these estimators as the number of individuals increases with the number of observations per individual fixed. Estimation schemes that require estimation of the fixed effects will, in general, be inconsistent in this sense.

[1] This research was supported by NSF Grants No. SES-8809352 and SES-9009879. Steve Cameron, Jeff Campbell, Tom Downes, Debbie Garvey, Jim Heckman, Charles Manski, Bruce Meyer, Whitney Newey, Rob Porter, Jim Powell, Richard Spady, two anonymous referees and the co-editor, Lars Hansen, made valuable comments on this paper, as did workshop participants at the University of Chicago, Northwestern University, University of Wisconsin, University of Minnesota, Indiana University, Carnegie Mellon University, Princeton University, New York University, Queens University, Cornell University, Harvard University, and Massachusetts Institute of Technology.

[2] Throughout the paper, it is assumed that the parameter of interest is the vector of "remaining parameters." The fixed effects are treated as nuisance parameters.

Estimation of discrete choice models with fixed effects has been considered in the literature. If the underlying errors are independent with logistic distribution, then a conditional maximum likelihood estimator will be consistent and asymptotically normal (see Chamberlain (1984) for a discussion of this approach and for additional references). Manski (1987) has proposed a conditional maximum score estimator for the same model. The advantage of Manski's estimator is that it is consistent under assumptions that are much weaker than those needed for the conditional maximum likelihood estimator.

This paper proposes estimators for limited dependent variable models with fixed effects. These models are usually estimated by maximizing a likelihood function over all the parameters, including the fixed effects. As mentioned, these estimators will generally not have the desired asymptotic properties. In contrast, the estimators proposed here are consistent and asymptotically normal as the number of individuals approaches infinity with the number of observations per individual fixed. The idea behind the estimators can be thought of as a bivariate generalization of the idea behind Powell's (1986) trimmed least squares estimators for Tobit models (without fixed effects). Like Powell's estimators, the estimators presented here are semiparametric. It is not necessary to assume a parametric form for the disturbances. Nor is it necessary to assume homoskedasticity across individuals.

The problems with estimating limited dependent variable models with fixed effects from panel data are most acute when the time dimension of the panel is low. For the greater part of this paper, we therefore restrict attention to the case with two time periods. The notation for this case is also simpler. In Section 7, we briefly discuss extensions of the estimators to more than two periods.

Section 2 of this paper defines the estimators and explains why they might work. Consistency and asymptotic normality of the estimators are investigated in Sections 3 and 4, respectively. The asymptotic variances derived in Section 4 will, in practice, have to be estimated. In Section 5, we suggest consistent estimators of these variances. Section 6 presents the results of a small scale Monte Carlo experiment, which illustrates that the large sample properties of the estimators can provide good approximations in small samples and that it is feasible computationally to calculate the estimators. The latter is of interest because it can be cumbersome to estimate a large number of fixed effects. Extensions of the estimators to the case where there are more than two observations for each individual, are discussed in Section 7, which concludes the paper. All proofs are in the appendices.

2. THE ESTIMATORS

It is useful to think about the data being generated as transformations of unobserved latent variables Y_1^* and Y_2^* given by

$$Y_t^* = \alpha + X_t\beta + \varepsilon_t \quad \text{for} \quad t = 1, 2, \tag{2.1}$$

where X_1 and X_2 are K-dimensional (row-)vectors of explanatory variables, β is the parameter (column-)vector of interest, and α is the fixed effect. ε_1 and ε_2 are the error terms.

Two sampling schemes are considered. For the *truncated* regression model, the observations $\{(Y_{i1}, X_{i1}, Y_{i2}, X_{i2})$: $i=1,\dots,n\}$ are a random sample from the distribution of $\{(Y_1^*, X_1, Y_2^*, X_2)$: $i=1,\dots,n\}$ induced by conditioning on the event $\{Y_1^*>0$ and $Y_2^*>0\}$. For the *censored* regression model, we observe $\{(Y_{it}, X_{it})$: $t=1,2,\ i=1,\dots,n\}$ where $Y_{it}=\max\{0, Y_{it}^*\}$, and Y_{it}^* and X_{it} are distributed as in (2.1). In terms of Heckman and MaCurdy's (1980) labor supply model, the truncated model would be relevant if the sample consists of continuously working individuals, whereas the censored model is appropriate if the sample consists of a random sample of individuals, with hours worked reported as 0 if the individual does not work. From a practical point of view, the latter is the more interesting model, but since the truncated sampling is more extreme, it is also of interest to consider this model. The notation will be simplified if we define $\Delta X = X_1 - X_2$ and $\Delta Y = Y_1 - Y_2$.

To fix ideas, assume for the moment that ε_1 and ε_2 in (2.1) are independent and identically distributed conditional on (X_1, X_2, α). This implies that (Y_1^*, Y_2^*), conditional on (X_1, X_2, α), will be distributed symmetrically around the 45°-degree line through $(X_1\beta, X_2\beta)$ (or equivalently around the 45°-degree line through $(\Delta X\beta, 0)$). As this is true for any value of α, the same statement is true for the distribution of (Y_1^*, Y_2^*) conditional on (X_1, X_2).

To facilitate the exposition, this is stated as a proposition.

PROPOSITION 1: *If ε_1 and ε_2 in* (2.1) *are independent and identically distributed conditional on (X_1, X_2, α), then the distribution of (Y_1^*, Y_2^*) conditional on (X_1, X_2) is symmetric around the* 45°*-line through $(\Delta X\beta, 0)$.*

The purpose of this section is to point out that the symmetry in Proposition 1 suggests orthogonality conditions that must hold at the true parameter values. These in turn suggest objective functions that can be used to estimate β in (2.1) when the data are either censored or truncated, as described above. The idea of using the symmetry of (Y_1^*, Y_2^*) around the 45°-line through $(\Delta X\beta, 0)$ can be thought of as a two-dimensional extension of Powell's (1986) idea of using symmetry of Y around $X\beta$ to construct an estimator of β in an ordinary Tobit model. In Powell's work it is assumed that the distribution of the errors is symmetric. This is not the case here. The symmetry is a consequence of the assumption that ε_1 and ε_2 are independent and identically distributed.

It is easiest to illustrate the ideas graphically. Let (x_1, x_2) be arbitrary. The distribution of (Y_1^*, Y_2^*) conditional on $(X_1, X_2)=(x_1, x_2)$ is then symmetric around the line LL' in Figures 1A and 1B (in Figure 1A, it is assumed that $\Delta x\beta \geqslant 0$, where Figure 1B illustrates the situation $\Delta x\beta < 0$).

Consider first the truncated case. The symmetry of the distribution of (Y_1^*, Y_2^*) around LL' means that the probability that (Y_1^*, Y_2^*) falls in the region A_1 equals the probability that it falls in the region B_1 (the sets A_1, A_2, B_1, and B_2 are all defined in Figures 1A and 1B). Observations in the regions A_1 and B_1

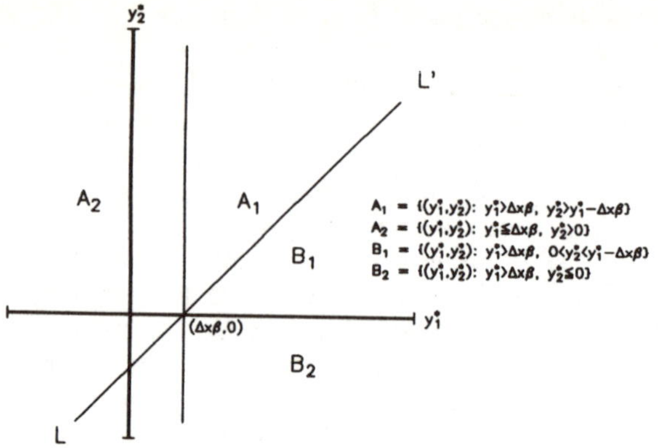

FIGURE 1A

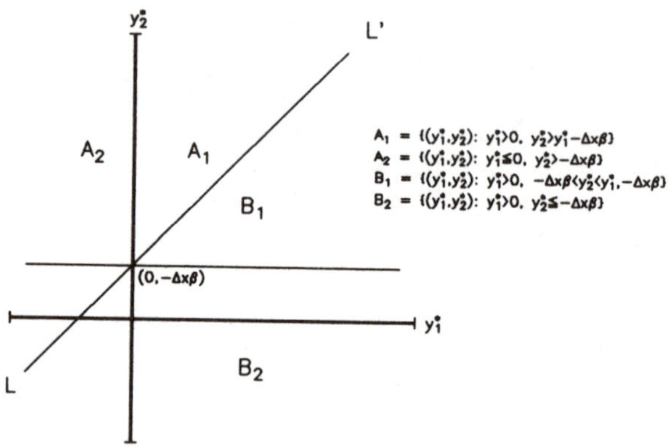

FIGURE 1B

are not affected by the truncation, so the same statement is true for the observed variables, (Y_1, Y_2). Therefore[3]

$$(2.2)\qquad E\big[\big(1\{(Y_1,Y_2)\in A_1\} - 1\{(Y_1,Y_2)\in B_1\}\big)\,\Delta X\big]$$
$$= E\big[\big(P((Y_1,Y_2)\in A_1 | X_1, X_2)$$
$$- P((Y_1,Y_2)\in B_1 | X_1, X_2)\big)\,\Delta X\big] = 0,$$

where $1\{\cdot\}$ represents the indicator function.

Using the same argument as above, the expected vertical distance from (Y_1^*, Y_2^*) in A_1 to the line LL' equals the expected horizontal distance from (Y_1^*, Y_2^*) in B_1 to the line LL', where both expectations are conditional on (X_1, X_2). For (Y_1^*, Y_2^*) in A_1, the vertical distance to LL' can be written as $-(Y_1^* - Y_2^* - \Delta x\,\beta)$ whereas for (Y_1^*, Y_2^*) in B_1 the horizontal distance to LL'

[3] The moment condition in (2.2) is also the basis for the estimator of the truncated regression model (without fixed effects) proposed by Bhattacharya, Chernoff, and Yang (1983).

is $Y_1^* - Y_2^* - \Delta x\,\beta$. Therefore

$$\begin{aligned}(2.3)\quad & E\left[1\{(Y_1,Y_2)\in A_1\cup B_1\}(Y_1-Y_2-\Delta X\beta)\,\Delta X\right]\\ &= E\left[\left(E\left[1\{(Y_1,Y_2)\in A_1\}(Y_1-Y_2-\Delta X\beta)|X_1,X_2\right]\right.\right.\\ &\qquad \left.\left.+E\left[1\{(Y_1,Y_2)\in B_1\}(Y_1-Y_2-\Delta X\beta)|X_1,X_2\right]\right)\Delta X\right]\\ &= 0.\end{aligned}$$

The two estimators for the truncated regression model, $\hat{\beta}_1$ and $\hat{\beta}_2$, are defined by minimization of objective functions that have as first order conditions that the sample analogs of (2.2) and (2.3), respectively, are satisfied. Specifically, $\hat{\beta}_1$ and $\hat{\beta}_2$ are defined by minimization of $Q_n(b)$ and $R_n(b)$, where

$$\begin{aligned}Q_n(b) &= \sum_{i=1}^{n} |\Delta Y_i - \Delta X_i b| 1\{Y_{i1} \geqslant \Delta X_i b, Y_{i2} \geqslant -\Delta X_i b\}\\ &\quad + |Y_{i1}| 1\{Y_{i1} \geqslant \Delta X_i b, Y_{i2} < -\Delta X_i b\}\\ &\quad + |Y_{i2}| 1\{Y_{i1} < \Delta X_i b, Y_{i2} \geqslant -\Delta X_i b\}\\ &= \sum_{i=1}^{n} \psi(Y_{i1}, Y_{i2}, \Delta X_i b)\end{aligned}$$

and

$$\begin{aligned}R_n(b) &= \sum_{i=1}^{n} (\Delta Y_i - \Delta X_i b)^2 1\{Y_{i1} \geqslant \Delta X_i b, Y_{i2} \geqslant -\Delta X_i b\}\\ &\quad + Y_{i1}^2 1\{Y_{i1} \geqslant \Delta X_i b, Y_{i2} < -\Delta X_i b\}\\ &\quad + Y_{i2}^2 1\{Y_{i1} < \Delta X_i b, Y_{i2} \geqslant -\Delta X_i b\}\\ &= \sum_{i=1}^{n} \psi(Y_{i1}, Y_{i2}, \Delta X_i b)^2,\end{aligned}$$

where the function $\psi(z_1, z_2, \delta)$ is defined for $z_1 > 0$ and $z_2 > 0$ by

$$\psi(z_1, z_2, \delta) = \begin{cases} z_1, & \text{for } \delta \leqslant -z_2;\\ |z_1 - z_2 - \delta|, & \text{for } -z_2 < \delta < z_1;\\ z_2, & \text{for } z_1 \leqslant \delta.\end{cases}$$

Now turn to the censored regression model. By the same argument that led to (2.2), the probability of (Y_1^*, Y_2^*) falling in $A = A_1 \cup A_2$ equals the probability that it will fall in $B = B_1 \cup B_2$ (where both probabilities are conditional on (X_1, X_2)). As neither of these probabilities is affected by censoring, the same is true in the censored sample. This implies

$$(2.4)\quad E\left[\left(1\{(Y_1,Y_2)\in A_1\cup A_2\} - 1\{(Y_1,Y_2)\in B_1\cup B_2\}\right)\Delta X\right] = 0.$$

As in the truncated model, the expected vertical distance from a (Y_1^*, Y_2^*) in A to the boundary of A, equals the expected horizontal distance from a

(Y_1^*, Y_2^*) in B to the boundary of B (again these expectations are conditional on (X_1, X_2)). As neither of these distances is affected by censoring, the same is true for the distribution of the censored observations (Y_1, Y_2). Therefore

$$\begin{aligned}(2.5)\qquad E\big[(&1\{(Y_1,Y_2)\in A_1\}(Y_1 - Y_2 - \Delta X\beta) - 1\{(Y_1,Y_2)\in A_2\}\\ &\times (Y_2 - \max\{0, -\Delta X\beta\})\\ &+ 1\{(Y_1,Y_2)\in B_1\}(Y_1 - Y_2 - \Delta X\beta)\\ &+ 1\{(Y_1,Y_2)\in B_2\}(Y_1 - \max\{0, \Delta X\beta\}))\,\Delta X\big] = 0.\end{aligned}$$

The proposed estimators for the censored regression model, $\hat{\beta}_3$ and $\hat{\beta}_4$, are defined by minimization of objective functions that have as first order conditions that the sample analogs of (2.4) and (2.5), respectively, are satisfied. $\hat{\beta}_3$ and $\hat{\beta}_4$ are defined by minimization of $S_n(b)$ and $T_n(b)$, where

$$\begin{aligned}S_n(b) &= \sum_{i=1}^{n} (1 - 1\{Y_{i1} \leqslant \Delta X_i b, Y_{i2} \leqslant 0\})\\ &\qquad \times (1 - 1\{Y_{i2} \leqslant -\Delta X_i b, Y_{i1} \leqslant 0\})|Y_{i1} - Y_{i2} - \Delta X_i b|\\ &= \sum_{i=1}^{n} \varphi(Y_{i1}, Y_{i2}, \Delta X_i b),\end{aligned}$$

where

$$\varphi(z_1, z_2, \delta) = \begin{cases} 0, & \text{for } z_1 \leqslant \max\{0, \delta\} \text{ and } z_2 \leqslant \max\{0, -\delta\},\\ |z_1 - z_2 - \delta|, & \text{otherwise,}\end{cases}$$

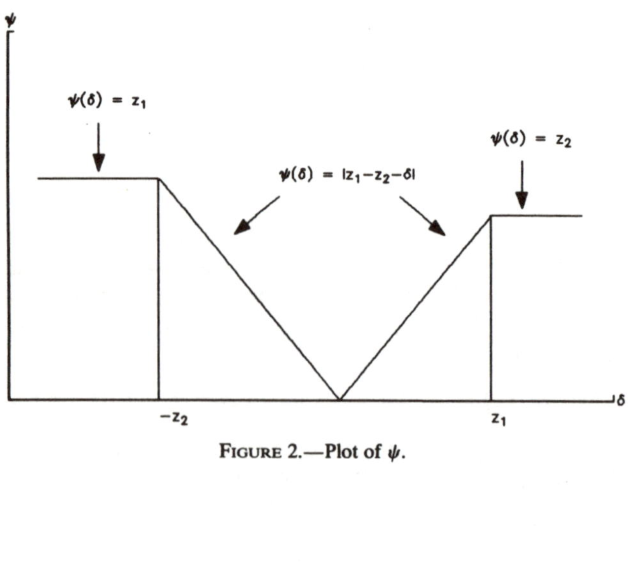

FIGURE 2.—Plot of ψ.

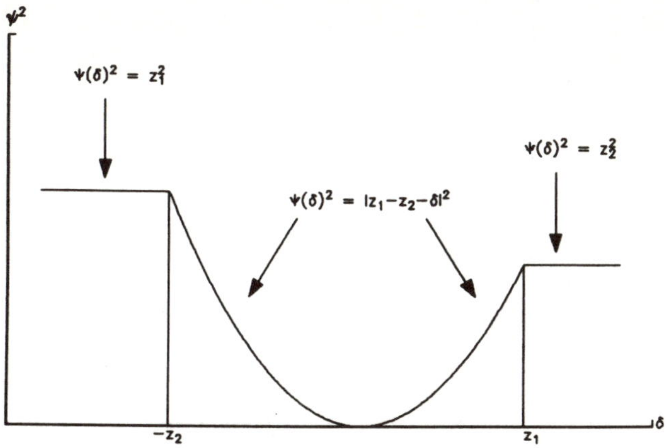

FIGURE 3.—Plot of ψ^2.

and

$$
\begin{aligned}
T_n(b) = \sum_{i=1}^{n} & \left(\max\{Y_{i1}, \Delta X_i b\} - \max\{Y_{i2}, -\Delta X_i b\} - \Delta X_i b\right)^2 \\
& + 2 \times 1\{Y_{i1} < \Delta X_i b\}(\Delta X_i b - Y_{i1}) Y_{i2} \\
& + 2 \times 1\{Y_{i2} < -\Delta X_i b\}(-\Delta X_i b - Y_{i2}) Y_{i1} \\
= \sum_{i=1}^{n} & \chi(Y_{i1}, Y_{i2}, \Delta X_i b),
\end{aligned}
$$

where

$$
\chi(z_1, z_2, \delta) = \begin{cases} z_1^2 + 2 z_1(-z_2 - \delta), & \text{for } \delta \leqslant -z_2, \\ (z_1 - z_2 - \delta)^2, & \text{for } -z_2 < \delta < z_1, \\ z_2^2 + 2 z_2(\delta - z_1), & \text{for } z_1 \leqslant \delta. \end{cases}
$$

Figures 2–5 graph the functions ψ, ψ^2, φ, and χ.

Note that S_n is piecewise linear and convex. T_n is continuously differentiable and convex and twice differentiable except at a finite number of points. This implies that $\hat{\beta}_3$ and especially $\hat{\beta}_4$ are very easy to calculate. The objective functions for the truncated case, Q_n and R_n, are not convex, and it is clear from Figures 2 and 3 that they are likely to have numerous local minima.

3. CONSISTENCY

In this section, we study the consistency of the estimators defined in the previous section. First, the two models considered in this paper are formally stated.

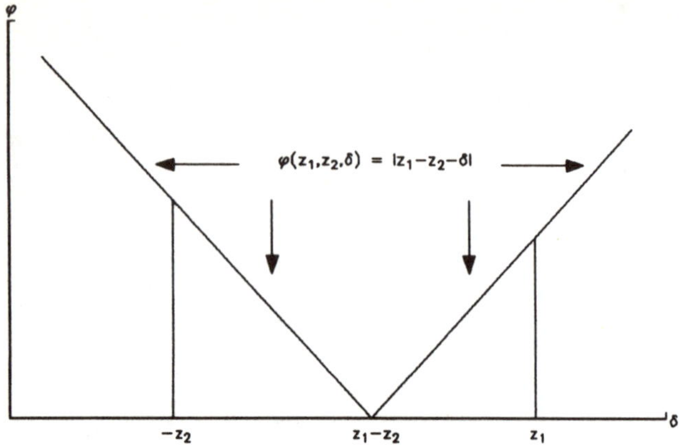

FIGURE 4A.—Plot of φ when $z_1 > 0$, $z_2 > 0$.

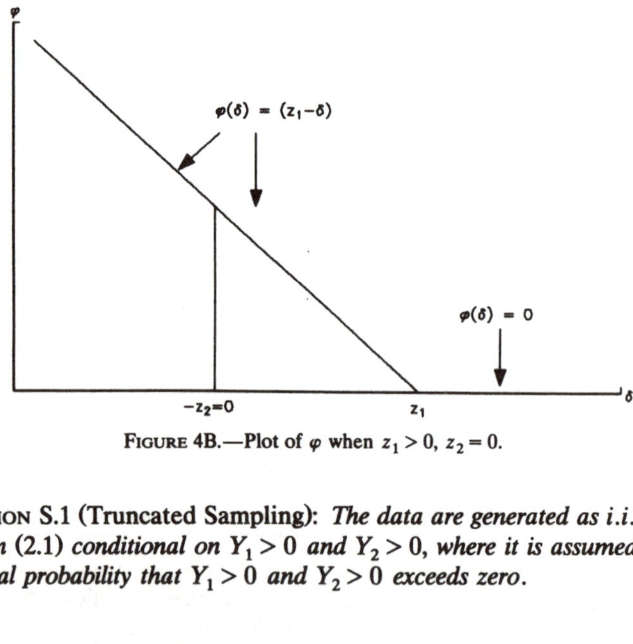

FIGURE 4B.—Plot of φ when $z_1 > 0$, $z_2 = 0$.

ASSUMPTION S.1 (Truncated Sampling): *The data are generated as i.i.d. observations from* (2.1) *conditional on* $Y_1 > 0$ *and* $Y_2 > 0$, *where it is assumed that the unconditional probability that* $Y_1 > 0$ *and* $Y_2 > 0$ *exceeds zero.*

ASSUMPTION S.2 (Censored Sampling): *The data are generated as i.i.d. observations from* (2.1), *except that* $Y_1 = \max\{0, Y_1^*\}$ *and* $Y_2 = \max\{0, Y_2^*\}$ *are observed rather than* Y_1^* *and* Y_2^*. *It is assumed that* $P(Y_1 > 0, Y_2 > 0) > 0$.

In addition to defining the models, Assumptions S.1 and S.2 also requires random sampling. This assumption is made for convenience and is not essential.

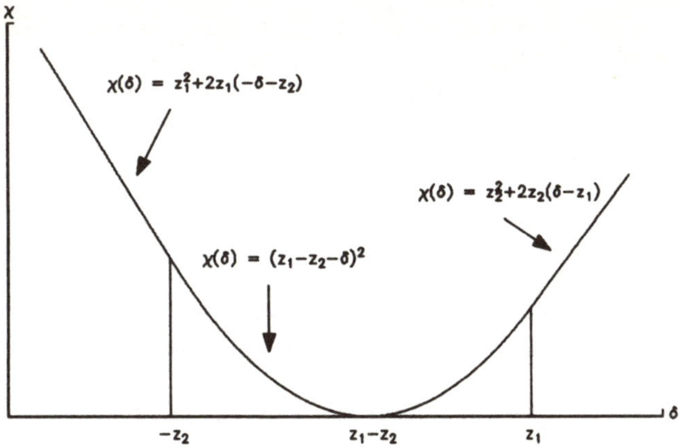

FIGURE 5A.—Plot of χ when $z_1 > 0$, $z_2 > 0$.

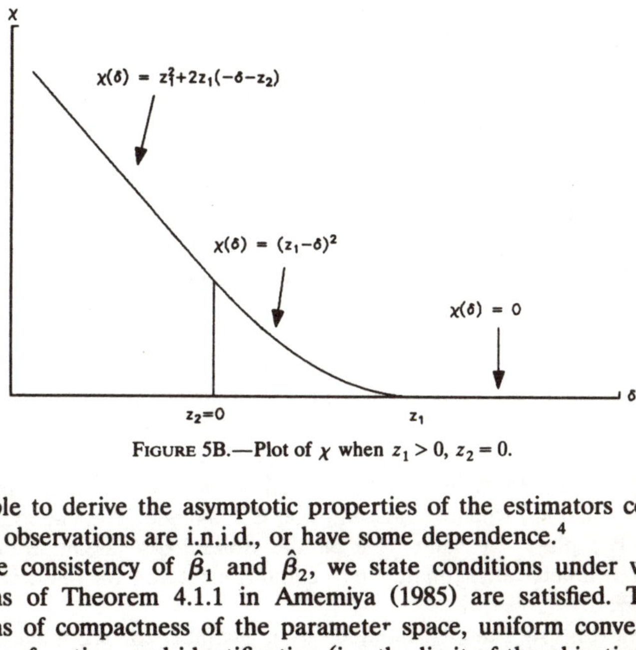

FIGURE 5B.—Plot of χ when $z_1 > 0$, $z_2 = 0$.

It is possible to derive the asymptotic properties of the estimators considered here if the observations are i.n.i.d., or have some dependence.[4]

To prove consistency of $\hat{\beta}_1$ and $\hat{\beta}_2$, we state conditions under which the assumptions of Theorem 4.1.1 in Amemiya (1985) are satisfied. These are assumptions of compactness of the parameter space, uniform convergence of the objective function, and identification (i.e. the limit of the objective function is uniquely minimized at the true parameter value, β). Newey and Powell (1987) have demonstrated that if an estimator is defined by minimization of a convex function, then the assumption that the parameter space is compact can be

[4] Pakes and Pollard's (1989) result cannot be used to prove asymptotic normality without the i.i.d. assumption. However, generalizations of Huber's (1965) papers (see Powell (1984) and Weiss (1991) or the results in Andrews (1991a, b)) could be used.

eliminated. The consistency of $\hat{\beta}_3$ and $\hat{\beta}_4$ is therefore proven by satisfying the conditions of that paper.

For the truncated case, compactness of the parameter space is assumed and, in anticipation of the discussion of asymptotic normality, it is also assumed that β is in the interior of the parameter space:

ASSUMPTION P.1 (Compact Parameter Space): *The parameter space, $\boldsymbol{B}$, is compact, and the true value of the parameter is an interior point of $\boldsymbol{B}$, $\beta \in \operatorname{int} \boldsymbol{B}$.*

Uniform convergence of the objective function obtains under the right uniform law of large numbers. We will make use of the following assumptions.

ASSUMPTION M.1 (Moment Condition): *$E[X_1]$ and $E[X_2]$ are finite.*

ASSUMPTION M.2 (Moment Condition): *$E[\|X_1\|^2]$, $E[\|X_2\|^2]$, $E[\alpha\|\Delta X\|]$, $E[\varepsilon_1\|\Delta X\|]$, and $E[\varepsilon_2\|\Delta X]\|$ are all finite.*

LAD-type estimators are, in general, not identified unless it is assumed that the observations are continuously distributed. For $\hat{\beta}_1$ and $\hat{\beta}_3$ we therefore make the following assumption.

ASSUMPTION E.1: *The conditional distribution of $(\varepsilon_1, \varepsilon_2)$ given (α, X_1, X_2) is continuous with finite density.*

To prove identification for the truncated model, the following assumption is made.

ASSUMPTION E.2 (Symmetry and Unimodality): *The distribution of $\varepsilon_1 - \varepsilon_2$ conditional on $\varepsilon_1 + \varepsilon_2$ and on (α, X_1, X_2) is strictly unimodal*[5] *and symmetric around* 0.

For the unimodality in Assumption E.2 to be well-defined, Assumption E.1 will be maintained whenever Assumption E.2 is made. The unimodality assumption in E.2 plays the same role as the unimodality assumption needed for Powell's symmetrically trimmed least squares estimator for the truncated regression model.

For the censored model, unimodality is not needed. We make the following assumption.[6]

ASSUMPTION E.3 (Symmetry): *The distribution of $\varepsilon_1 - \varepsilon_2$ conditional on $\varepsilon_1 + \varepsilon_2$ and on (α, X_1, X_2), is symmetric around* 0.

[5] We say that a continuous distribution is strictly unimodal, if its density has a unique maximum, and if it is monotone on either side of the maximum with strict monotonicity in a neighborhood around the maximum. This is the definition used by Powell (1986).

[6] Assumption E.3 can be restated as an assumption that ε_1 and ε_2 are exchangeable.

More readily interpreted conditions implying E.2 and E.3, are given later in this section. We also need to make an assumption about the rank of the regressors:

ASSUMPTION R.1 (Full Rank of Regressors): *There is no proper linear subspace of R^K containing the random variable* $1\{P(Y_1 > 0, Y_2 > 0 | X_1, X_2) > 0\} \Delta X$ *with probability* 1.

With these assumptions, the consistency result can be stated.

THEOREM 1 (Consistency): *The estimators* $\hat{\beta}_1$, $\hat{\beta}_2$, $\hat{\beta}_3$, *and* $\hat{\beta}_4$ *are consistent under the following conditions*:

(i) $\hat{\beta}_1$ *defined by minimization of* $Q_n(b)$ *is strongly consistent under Assumptions P.*1, *S.*1, *M.*1, *E.*1, *E.*2, *and R.*1.

(ii) $\hat{\beta}_2$ *defined by minimization of* $R_n(b)$ *is strongly consistent under Assumptions P.*1, *S.*1, *M.*2, *E.*1, *E.*2, *and R.*1.

(iii) $\hat{\beta}_3$ *defined by minimization of* $S_n(b)$ *is strongly consistent under Assumptions S.*2, *M.*1, *E.*1, *E.*3, *and R.*1.

(iv) $\hat{\beta}_3$ *defined by minimization of* $T_n(b)$ *is strongly consistent under Assumptions S.*2, *M.*2, *E.*3, *and R.*1.

We now return to the interpretation of Assumptions E.2 and E.3. It is not clear, a priori, whether these assumptions are reasonable. The following lemma states conditions that imply that Assumptions E.2 and E.3 are satisfied.

LEMMA 1: *If, conditional on* (α, X_1, X_2), ε_1 *and* ε_2 *are independent, and identically and continuously distributed, then Assumption E.*3 *is satisfied. If, in addition, the (common) marginal density of* ε_1 *and* ε_2 *is strictly log-concave (i.e., the logarithm of the density is strictly concave), then Assumption E.*2 *is also satisfied.*

The assumption that ε_1 and ε_2 are independent in Lemma 1 is less restrictive than it may seem. The fixed effect can capture some dependence between the error terms. For example, the assumptions of Lemma 1 are satisfied if the error terms are jointly normal, with equal variance but arbitrary positive correlation. Dependent normals with positive correlation can be written as a (normal) fixed effect plus independent normals—the dependence can be captured in the fixed effect.

The assumptions of Lemma 1 allow for heteroskedasticity across individuals, but homoskedasticity is assumed over time (for a given individual). This is not just a technical assumption. Without it, the estimators in this paper would be inconsistent.

4. ASYMPTOTIC NORMALITY

The objective functions Q_n, R_n, S_n, and T_n are not twice differentiable. This means that standard results (see, for example, Amemiya (1985)) cannot be used to prove asymptotic normality of $\hat{\beta}_1$, $\hat{\beta}_2$, $\hat{\beta}_3$, and $\hat{\beta}_4$. Powell (1984, 1986) proves asymptotic normality for closely related estimators by verifying the conditions of Huber (1965). In this paper, the approach of Pakes and Pollard (1989) is adopted. This choice is made for convenience—it certainly seems possible to verify the conditions of Huber (1965) for the estimators defined in this paper, but it is easier to verify the conditions in Pakes and Pollard (1989). Alternatively, the results of Pollard (1985) or Andrews (1991a, b) could have been used.

In order to prove asymptotic normality of $\hat{\beta}_1$, $\hat{\beta}_2$, $\hat{\beta}_3$, and $\hat{\beta}_4$ we make the following definitions:

$$V_1 = E\left[1\{-Y_2 < \Delta X\beta < Y_1\}\,\Delta X'\Delta X\right],$$

$$V_2 = E\left[1\{-Y_2 < \Delta X\beta < Y_1\}(\Delta Y - \Delta X\beta)^2\,\Delta X'\Delta X\right],$$

$$V_3 = E\big[1\{\{Y_1 < Y_2 + \Delta X\beta,\, Y_2 > \max\{0, -\Delta X\beta\}\}$$
$$\cup\{Y_1 > Y_2 + \Delta X\beta,\, Y_1 > \max\{0, \Delta X\beta\}\}\}\,\Delta X'\Delta X\big],$$

$$V_4 = E\big[\big(Y_2^2 1\{Y_1 \leqslant \Delta X\beta\} + Y_1^2 1\{\Delta X\beta \leqslant -Y_2\}$$
$$+(Y_1 - Y_2 - \Delta X\beta)^2 1\{-Y_2 < \Delta X\beta < Y_1\}\big)\,\Delta X'\Delta X\big],$$

$$\Gamma_1 = E\big[\big(2f_{Y_1-Y_2}(\Delta X\beta|X_1, X_2, \alpha) - 1\{\Delta X\beta \geqslant 0\}f_{Y_1}(\Delta X\beta|X_1, X_2, \alpha)$$
$$-1\{\Delta X\beta < 0\}f_{Y_2}(-\Delta X\beta|X_1, X_2, \alpha)\big)\,\Delta X'\Delta X\big],$$

$$\Gamma_2 = E\big[\big(1\{\Delta X\beta \geqslant 0\}f_{Y_1}(\Delta X\beta|X_1, X_2, \alpha)E[Y_2|Y_1 = \Delta X\beta, X_1, X_2, \alpha]$$
$$+1\{\Delta X\beta < 0\}f_{Y_2}(-\Delta X\beta|X_1, X_2, \alpha)$$
$$\times E[Y_1|Y_2 = -\Delta X\beta, X_1, X_2, \alpha]$$
$$-P(Y_1 > \Delta X\beta, Y_2 > -\Delta X\beta|X_1, X_2, \alpha)\big)\,\Delta X'\Delta X\big],$$

$$\Gamma_3 = E\big[\big(2f_{Y_1-Y_2}(\Delta X\beta|X_1, X_2, \alpha, Y_1 > 0, Y_2 > 0)$$
$$+1\{\Delta X\beta \geqslant 0\}P(Y_2 \leqslant 0|\alpha, X_1, X_2)$$
$$\times f_{Y_1}(\Delta X\beta|X_1, X_2, \alpha, Y_2 \leqslant 0)$$
$$+1\{\Delta X\beta < 0\}P(Y_1 \leqslant 0|\alpha, X_1, X_2)$$
$$\times f_{Y_2}(-\Delta X\beta|X_1, X_2, \alpha, Y_1 \leqslant 0)\big)\,\Delta X'\Delta X\big],$$

$$\Gamma_4 = E\left[1\{-Y_2 < \Delta X\beta < Y_1\}\,\Delta X'\Delta X\right].$$

The following assumptions will be used to prove asymptotic normality of the estimators.

ASSUMPTION V (Rank of Covariance Matrices): (1) *The expectations in* V_1 *and* Γ_1 *are finite and* V_1 *and* Γ_1 *are of full rank.* (2) *The expectations in* V_2 *and* Γ_2 *are finite and* V_2 *and* Γ_2 *are of full rank.* (3) *The expectations in* V_3 *and* Γ_3 *are finite and* V_3 *and* Γ_3 *are of full rank.* (4) *The expectations in* V_4 *and* Γ_4 *are finite and* V_4 *and* Γ_4 *are of full rank.*

ASSUMPTION M.3 (Moment Condition): $E[\|X_1\|^4]$, $E[\|X_2\|^4]$, $E[\alpha^2\|\Delta X\|^2]$, $E[\varepsilon_1^2\|\Delta X\|^2]$, *and* $E[\varepsilon_2^2\|\Delta X\|^2]$ *are all finite.*

ASSUMPTION E.4: *There exists a number* $M<\infty$ *such that* $f_{\varepsilon_1-\varepsilon_2}(\cdot\,|X_1,X_2,\alpha)<M$, $f_{\varepsilon_1}(\cdot\,|X_1,X_2,\alpha)<M$, *and* $f_{\varepsilon_2}(\cdot\,|X_1,X_2,\alpha)<M$ *for almost all* (X_1,X_2,α).

ASSUMPTION E.5: *There exists an* $M<\infty$ *such that* $f_{\varepsilon_1}(\cdot\,|,\varepsilon_2,X_1,X_2,\alpha)<M$ *for almost all* $(\varepsilon_2,X_1,X_2,\alpha)$ *and* $f_{\varepsilon_2}(\cdot\,|,\varepsilon_1,X_1,X_2,\alpha)<M$ *for almost all* $(\varepsilon_1,X_1,X_2,\alpha)$. *In addition,*

$$\int_{-\infty}^{\infty}|\varepsilon_1|f_{\varepsilon_1,\varepsilon_2}(\varepsilon_1,\eta\,|X_1,X_2,\alpha)\,d\varepsilon_1<M \qquad \text{and}$$

$$\int_{-\infty}^{\infty}|\varepsilon_2|f_{\varepsilon_1,\varepsilon_2}(\eta,\varepsilon_2|X_1,X_2,\alpha)\,d\varepsilon_2<M$$

for all η *and for almost all* (X_1,X_2,α).

With these assumptions, we can derive the asymptotic distributions of the estimators defined in Section 2.

THEOREM 2 (Asymptotic Normality):

(i) $\hat{\beta}_1$ *is asymptotically normal under Assumptions P.1, S.1, M.2, E.1, E.2, R.1, V.1, and E.4:*

$$\sqrt{n}\,(\hat{\beta}_1-\beta)\xrightarrow{d}N(0,\Gamma_1^{-1}V_1\Gamma_1^{-1}).$$

(ii) $\hat{\beta}_2$ *is asymptotically normal under Assumptions P.1, S.1, M.3, E.1, E.2, R.1, V.2, and E.5:*

$$\sqrt{n}\,(\hat{\beta}_2-\beta)\xrightarrow{d}N(0,\Gamma_2^{-1}V_2\Gamma_2^{-1}).$$

(iii) $\hat{\beta}_3$ *is asymptotically normal under Assumptions S.2, M.2, E.1, E.3, R.1, V.3, and E.4:*

$$\sqrt{n}\,(\hat{\beta}_3-\beta)\xrightarrow{d}N(0,\Gamma_3^{-1}V_3\Gamma_3^{-1}).$$

(iv) $\hat{\beta}_4$ *is asymptotically normal under Assumptions S.2, M.3, E.1, E.3, V.4, and R.1:*

$$\sqrt{n}\,(\hat{\beta}_4-\beta)\xrightarrow{d}N(0,\Gamma_4^{-1}V_4\Gamma_4^{-1}).$$

Assumptions E.4 and E.5 guarantee that the expectations of the objective functions (evaluated at β) are twice differentiable and that the second derivative can be found by interchanging differentiation and expectation. The latter is not necessary and Assumptions E.4 and E.5 could be replaced by alternative assumptions that will make the expected objective functions twice differentiable.

5. ESTIMATING THE ASYMPTOTIC VARIANCES

For the asymptotic distributions in Theorem 2 to be useful in practice, we must be able to consistently estimate V_1, V_2, V_3, V_4, Γ_1, Γ_2, Γ_3, and Γ_4. This section presents one set of consistent estimators for these matrices.

The estimators for V_1, V_2, V_3, V_4, and Γ_4 are straightforward, whereas the estimators for Γ_1, Γ_2, and Γ_3 are more complicated because they involve estimation of densities.

V_1, V_2, V_3, V_4, and Γ_4 can be estimated by their sample analogs:

$$\hat{V}_1 = \frac{1}{n} \sum_{i=1}^{n} 1\{-Y_{i2} < \Delta X_i \hat{\beta}_1 < Y_{i1}\} \Delta X_i' \Delta X_i,$$

$$\hat{V}_2 = \frac{1}{n} \sum_{i=1}^{n} 1\{-Y_{i2} < \Delta X_i \hat{\beta}_2 < Y_{i1}\} (\Delta Y_i - \Delta X_i \hat{\beta}_2)^2 \Delta X_i' \Delta X_i,$$

$$\hat{V}_3 = \frac{1}{n} \sum_{i=1}^{n} 1\Big\{\{\Delta Y_i < \Delta X_i \hat{\beta}_3, Y_{i2} > \max\{0, -\Delta X_i \hat{\beta}_3\}\} \\ \cup \{\Delta Y_i > \Delta X_i \hat{\beta}_3, Y_{i1} > \max\{0, \Delta X_i \hat{\beta}_3\}\}\Big\} \Delta X_i' \Delta X_i,$$

$$\hat{V}_4 = \frac{1}{n} \sum_{i=1}^{n} \big(Y_{i2}^2 1\{Y_{i1} \leqslant \Delta X_i \hat{\beta}_4\} + Y_{i1}^2 1\{\Delta X_i \hat{\beta}_4 \leqslant -Y_{i2}\} \\ + (Y_{i1} - Y_{i2} - \Delta X_i \beta)^2 1\{-Y_{i2} < \Delta X_i \beta < Y_{i1}\}\big) \Delta X_i' \Delta X_i$$

and

$$\hat{\Gamma}_4 = \frac{1}{n} \sum_{i=1}^{n} 1\{-Y_{i2} < \Delta X_i \hat{\beta}_4 < Y_{i1}\} \Delta X_i' \Delta X_i.$$

It is less obvious how to construct sample analogs of Γ_1, Γ_2, and Γ_3 because they involve the densities and conditional expectations. In general, these can be estimated by the method of kernels. Using uniform kernels, Powell (1984, 1986) constructed consistent estimators of the variances of estimators similar to those considered in this paper. It is possible (see Honoré (1989)) to use the same approach to form consistent estimators of Γ_l $(l = 1,2,3)$, but the proof of Theorem 2 suggests estimators that are simpler to analyze.

Consider, for example, Γ_3. From the proof of Theorem 2, it is clear that Γ_3 is constructed in such a way that it equals the derivative of the expected values of the "first order conditions" for minimization of S_n, evaluated at the true parameter value. In other words, the (j,k)th element of Γ_3 is

$$\Gamma_3^{(j,k)} = \frac{d}{db_k} E\big[(1\{Y_2 > 0, Y_2 > Y_1 - \Delta X b\} \\ - 1\{Y_1 > 0, Y_1 > Y_2 + \Delta X b\})\, \Delta X^{(j)}\big]$$

evaluated at $b = \beta$, where $\Delta X^{(j)}$ is the jth coordinate of ΔX. One "natural" estimator of Γ_3 is one that modifies this expression by replacing β by $\hat{\beta}_3$, replacing the expectation by a sample average, and by replacing the differentiation by a finite difference which decreases with sample size. This suggests estimating $\Gamma_3^{(j,k)}$ by

$$\hat{\Gamma}_3^{(j,k)} = \frac{1}{\omega_n}\Bigg(\frac{1}{n}\sum_{i=1}^{n}\Big(1\big\{Y_{i2} > 0, Y_{i2} > Y_{i1} - \Delta X_i\big(\hat{\beta}_3 + \omega_n u_k\big)\big\} \\ - 1\big\{Y_{i1} > 0, Y_{i1} > Y_{i2} + \Delta X\big(\hat{\beta}_3 + \omega_n u_k\big)\big\}\Big)\,\Delta X_i^{(j)} \\ - \frac{1}{n}\sum_{i=1}^{n}\Big(1\big\{Y_{i2} > 0, Y_{i2} > Y_{i1} - \Delta X_i \hat{\beta}_3\big\} \\ - 1\big\{Y_{i1} > 0, Y_{i1} > Y_{i2} + \Delta X \hat{\beta}_3\big\}\Big)\,\Delta X_i^{(j)}\Bigg)$$

where u_k is a unit vector with 1 in its kth place and ω_n decreases to 0 with sample size.

Estimators of Γ_1 and Γ_2 can be constructed in the same way:

$$\hat{\Gamma}_1^{(j,k)} = \frac{1}{\omega_n}\Bigg(\frac{1}{n}\sum_{i=1}^{n}\Big(-1\big\{-Y_{i2} < \Delta X_i\big(\hat{\beta}_1 + \omega_n u_k\big) < \Delta Y_i\big\} \\ + 1\big\{\Delta Y_i < \Delta X_i\big(\hat{\beta}_1 + \omega_n u_k\big) < Y_{i1}\big\}\Big)\,\Delta X_i^{(j)} \\ - \frac{1}{n}\sum_{i=1}^{n}\Big(-1\big\{-Y_{i2} < \Delta X_i \hat{\beta}_1 < \Delta Y_i\big\} \\ + 1\big\{\Delta Y_i < \Delta X_i \hat{\beta}_1 < Y_{i1}\big\}\Big)\,\Delta X_i^{(j)}\Bigg),$$

and

$$\hat{\Gamma}_2^{(j,k)} = \frac{1}{\omega_n}\Bigg(\frac{1}{n}\sum_{i=1}^{n} 1\big\{-Y_{i2} < \Delta X_i\big(\hat{\beta}_2 + \omega_n u_k\big) < Y_{i1}\big\} \\ \times\big(Y_{i1} - Y_{i2} - \Delta X_i\big(\hat{\beta}_2 + \omega_n u_k\big)\big)\,\Delta X_i^{(j)} \\ - \frac{1}{n}\sum_{i=1}^{n} 1\big\{-Y_{i2} < \Delta X_i \hat{\beta}_2 < Y_{i1}\big\} \\ \times\big(Y_{i1} - Y_{i2} - \Delta X_i \hat{\beta}_2\big)\,\Delta X_i^{(j)}\Bigg).$$

If ω_n goes to zero too quickly, the term $1/\omega_n$ will prevent the estimators of Γ_1, Γ_2, and Γ_3 from being consistent. The following assumption prevents this.

ASSUMPTION W.1: *The sequences* $\{\omega_n\}_{n=1}^{\infty}$ *converges to* 0 *in probability and* $n^{-1/2}\omega_n^{-1} = O_p(1)$.

THEOREM 3: *For* $l = 1, \ldots, 4$, V_l *and* Γ_l *are consistent under Assumption W.*1 *and the assumptions made for* β_l *in Theorem* 2.

It is clear that ω_n need not be the same for different columns of Γ_l. Furthermore, ω_n can be arbitrarily data-dependent, as long as Assumption W.1 is satisfied.

6. MONTE CARLO INVESTIGATION

In this section, we summarize a small scale Monte Carlo study designed to illustrate the small sample properties of the estimators defined in Section 2 and the computational feasibility of the estimators. Only $\hat{\beta}_4$ is considered.[7] As noted earlier, the censored regression model is probably more interesting from an applied point of view than the truncated regression model. And since $\hat{\beta}_4$ is defined in terms of minimizing a differentiable function, it is simpler to calculate than $\hat{\beta}_3$. By considering only $\hat{\beta}_4$, we also avoid making arbitrary decisions about ω_n, when studying the small sample behavior of the "*t* statistics" implied by the large sample distributions.

All the results presented in this paper are based on 1000 replications from the model[8]

$$Y_{it} = \max\left\{0, \alpha_i + \sum_{k=1}^{K} X_{kit}\beta_k + \varepsilon_{it}\right\} \qquad \text{for} \quad t = 1,2; \quad i = 1, \ldots, n.$$

The first three specifications take $K = 2$ and $X_{1it} = \alpha_i + \eta_{it}$. The three specifications illustrate the behavior of the estimator for different sample sizes and differ only in their distributional assumptions. The results from these specifications are given in Table I. The table reports the true parameter values, the estimated bias and root mean squared error of $\hat{\beta}_4$, as well as the root mean squared error implied by the asymptotic distribution in Theorem 2. As the estimators may not have finite moments in any sample size, we also report the quartiles and the median absolute error (MAE) of the estimator, as well as the median absolute error predicted by the asymptotic distribution (AMAE).

In Specification 1, the random variables α_i η_{i1}, η_{i2}, X_{2i1}, X_{2i2}, ε_{i1}, and ε_{i2} are independent and normally distributed with mean 0 and variance 1. The true value of β is $(1,1)$. With this specification $P(Y_{i1} > 0, Y_{i2} > 0) = 0.35$, $P(Y_{i1} > 0,$

[7] Honoré (1989) reports the results of similar experiments for $\hat{\beta}_1$ and $\hat{\beta}_2$.

[8] All the calculations reported in this section were performed in GAUSS386. The pseudo-random generators in GAUSS were used to generate the samples.

TABLE I

RESULTS FOR DIFFERENT SAMPLE SIZES

		True	Bias	RMSE	ARMSE	LQ	Median	QU	MAE	AMAE
				Specification 1.						
$n = 20$	b_1	1.000	0.051	0.485	0.366	0.754	1.008	1.289	0.271	0.247
	b_2	1.000	0.033	0.505	0.365	0.735	0.987	1.268	0.266	0.247
$n = 50$	b_1	1.000	0.011	0.252	0.232	0.829	0.997	1.161	0.167	0.156
	b_2	1.000	0.025	0.250	0.231	0.855	1.015	1.176	0.164	0.156
$n = 200$	b_1	1.000	−0.003	0.123	0.116	0.915	0.998	1.083	0.084	0.078
	b_2	1.000	0.001	0.113	0.116	0.924	0.999	1.078	0.077	0.078
$n = 500$	b_1	1.000	0.006	0.073	0.073	0.956	1.005	1.055	0.048	0.049
	b_2	1.000	0.007	0.072	0.073	0.962	1.006	1.051	0.045	0.049
$n = 2000$	b_1	1.000	−0.000	0.037	0.037	0.974	0.999	1.025	0.026	0.025
	b_2	1.000	0.002	0.036	0.037	0.977	1.003	1.027	0.025	0.025
				Specification 2.						
$n = 20$[a]	b_1	1.000	0.057	0.648	0.403	0.721	0.984	1.307	0.292	0.272
	b_2	1.000	0.078	0.766	0.398	0.694	1.011	1.331	0.319	0.268
$n = 50$	b_1	1.000	0.025	0.285	0.255	0.845	0.998	1.185	0.164	0.172
	b_2	1.000	0.025	0.283	0.252	0.838	0.999	1.171	0.166	0.170
$n = 200$	b_1	1.000	0.006	0.134	0.127	0.918	1.002	1.096	0.089	0.086
	b_2	1.000	0.006	0.135	0.126	0.917	1.004	1.097	0.089	0.085
$n = 500$	b_1	1.000	0.003	0.082	0.081	0.950	1.001	1.055	0.052	0.054
	b_2	1.000	0.004	0.079	0.080	0.954	1.002	1.053	0.049	0.054
$n = 2000$	b_1	1.000	−0.002	0.041	0.040	0.969	0.998	1.026	0.028	0.027
	b_2	1.000	0.001	0.042	0.040	0.973	1.002	1.028	0.027	0.027
				Specification 3.						
$n = 20$[b]	b_1	1.000	0.116	1.356	0.350	0.752	0.996	1.320	0.292	0.236
	b_2	1.000	0.075	0.589	0.354	0.765	1.026	1.327	0.273	0.239
$n = 50$	b_1	1.000	0.025	0.252	0.221	0.852	1.013	1.186	0.166	0.149
	b_2	1.000	0.018	0.259	0.224	0.851	1.002	1.182	0.164	0.151
$n = 200$	b_1	1.000	0.006	0.118	0.111	0.920	1.010	1.084	0.081	0.075
	b_2	1.000	0.005	0.115	0.112	0.927	1.003	1.078	0.076	0.076
$n = 500$	b_1	1.000	0.002	0.073	0.070	0.950	1.002	1.048	0.050	0.047
	b_2	1.000	−0.001	0.073	0.071	0.951	1.000	1.048	0.048	0.048
$n = 2000$	b_1	1.000	−0.000	0.037	0.035	0.973	0.998	1.025	0.026	0.024
	b_2	1.000	−0.001	0.035	0.035	0.976	1.000	1.021	0.023	0.024

[a] The results exclude three cases in which the objective function did not have a unique minimum.
[b] The results exclude two cases in which the objective function did not have a unique minimum.

$Y_{i2} = 0) = 0.15$, $P(Y_{i1} = 0, Y_{i2} > 0) = 0.15$, and $P(Y_{i1} = 0, Y_{i2} = 0) = 0.35$. Except where explicitly noted, these are approximately the censoring probabilities for all the specifications considered here. In the first panel of Table I, it is seen that with this specification, the asymptotic distribution provides a fairly good approximation to the first two moments of the exact distribution of $\hat{\beta}_4$ for sample sizes greater than 200. For a sample size of 20, $\hat{\beta}_4$ is biased (though close to median-unbiased) and its variance and median absolute error are much larger than that suggested by its asymptotic distribution.

The discrepancy between the exact distribution of $\hat{\beta}_4$ and the distribution implied by Theorem 2 is due largely to the finite distribution of $\hat{\beta}_4$ being asymmetric. Consider, for example, the first coefficient of $\hat{\beta}_4$. The 10th, 25th, 50th, 75th, and 90th percentiles of $\hat{\beta}_4$ (with those suggested by the asymptotic distribution in parentheses) are: 0.52 (0.53), 0.75 (0.75), 1.01 (1.00), 1.29 (1.25), and 1.64 (1.47). These suggest that with Specification 1, the asymptotic distribution of $\hat{\beta}_4$ provides a good approximation for the left half of the exact distribution of (the first coefficient of) $\hat{\beta}_4$, whereas the right half of the exact distribution is much thicker than the asymptotic distribution.

The asymmetry of the finite sample distribution of $\hat{\beta}_4$ is to be expected. Chesher and Spady (1990) have shown by Monte Carlo experimentation and asymptotic expansions, that the exact distribution of Powell's trimmed least squares estimator is skewed in small samples. As $\hat{\beta}_4$ can be thought of as a bivariate generalization of Powell's estimator, it is not surprising that the finite sample characteristics of the two estimators are similar.

There are (at least) two reasons to be skeptical about the results from Specification 1. First, it is possible that the normality of the error terms will make $\hat{\beta}_4$ look "too good." If no observations are censored, then $\hat{\beta}_4$ reduces to the OLS estimator on the first differences of the observations. As OLS is equivalent to maximum likelihood estimation under normality, this may lead to a performance of $\hat{\beta}_4$ that is better than that under other different distributional assumptions. Secondly, joint normality of regressors and error terms in some cases gives consistency and asymptotic normality, where this would otherwise not be the case. Specifications 2 and 3, therefore, make different distributional assumptions.

Specification 2 differs from Specification 1 in the distribution of the errors as well as the regressors. The random variables α_i, η_{i1}, η_{i2}, X_{2i1}, X_{2i2}, ε_{i1}, and ε_{i2} are independent and all distributed gamma with three degrees of freedom (standardized to have mean 0 and variance 1). The true value of β is $(1,1)$. The censoring probabilities with this specification are $P(Y_{i1}>0,\ Y_{i2}>0)=0.30$, $P(Y_{i1}>0,\ Y_{i2}=0)=0.16$, $P(Y_{i1}=0,\ Y_{i2}>0)=0.16$, and $P(Y_{i1}=0,\ Y_{i2}=0)=$ 0.39. In Specification 3, α_i, η_{i1}, η_{i2}, X_{2i1}, X_{2i2}, ε_{i1}, and ε_{i2} are independent. ε_{i1} and ε_{i2} are normally distributed with mean 0 and variance 1. The remainder are distributed gamma with three degrees of freedom (standardized to have mean 0 and variance 1). Again, the true value of β is $(1,1)$. The censoring probabilities under Specification 3 equal those under Specification 2.

With the exception that the small sample biases seem to be more severe under Specifications 2 and 3, the results do not differ substantially from the results from Specification 1.

Most of the results in Specifications 1 to 3 are for samples that are "unrealistically" large compared to the number of parameters. In Specification 4, we modify Specification 1 by adding three more regressors. The three regressors all have true coefficients of 0, and hence do not change the "R^2" of the model. The random variables α_i, η_{i1}, η_{i2}, X_{ki1}, X_{ki2} for $k=2,\dots,5$, ε_{i1}, and ε_{i2} are all independent and normally distributed with mean 0 and variance 1. The true value of β is $(1,1,0,0,0)$. The results of Specification 4 (Table II) are similar to those of Specifications 1, 2, and 3.

TABLE II

RESULTS FOR DIFFERENT SPECIFICATIONS

	True	Bias	RMSE	ARMSE	LQ	Median	QU	MAE	AMAE
					Specification 4.				
b_1	1.000	0.005	0.121	0.115	0.925	0.997	1.083	0.079	0.078
b_2	1.000	0.001	0.122	0.115	0.916	1.001	1.078	0.080	0.078
b_3	0.000	−0.004	0.111	0.106	−0.078	−0.004	0.070	0.073	0.071
b_4	0.000	0.003	0.108	0.107	−0.063	0.004	0.071	0.068	0.072
b_5	0.000	−0.003	0.114	0.106	−0.082	−0.003	0.070	0.076	0.072
					Specification 5.				
b_1	1.000	0.009	0.134	0.135	0.919	1.002	1.099	0.087	0.091
b_2	1.000	0.008	0.139	0.135	0.913	1.005	1.093	0.090	0.091
b_3	0.000	−0.008	0.123	0.117	−0.086	−0.003	0.078	0.081	0.079
b_4	0.000	−0.004	0.122	0.117	−0.083	−0.008	0.080	0.081	0.079
b_5	0.000	−0.005	0.120	0.116	−0.084	−0.004	0.074	0.079	0.078
					Specification 6.				
b_1	1.000	0.011	0.122	0.114	0.929	1.008	1.090	0.081	0.077
b_2	1.000	0.007	0.134	0.133	0.914	1.007	1.092	0.088	0.089
b_3	0.000	−0.004	0.105	0.104	−0.074	−0.003	0.069	0.072	0.070
b_4	0.000	0.001	0.105	0.105	−0.062	−0.003	0.064	0.062	0.071
b_5	0.000	0.001	0.108	0.105	−0.065	0.003	0.073	0.069	0.071
					Specification 7.				
b_1	1.000	0.008	0.120	0.117	0.930	1.003	1.084	0.077	0.079
b_2	1.000	0.001	0.161	0.160	0.893	0.992	1.105	0.107	0.108
b_3	0.000	0.008	0.107	0.108	−0.063	0.002	0.079	0.070	0.073
b_4	0.000	0.003	0.109	0.107	−0.071	0.004	0.072	0.071	0.072
b_5	0.000	−0.002	0.111	0.107	−0.081	−0.001	0.073	0.075	0.072

In many Monte Carlo studies of nonlinear models, it is found that heteroskedasticity can severely contaminate the estimators. In Specifications 5 and 6, the design in Specification 4 is modified by letting the variance of the error depend on the fixed effect and on one of the regressors, respectively. Specification 5 differs from Specification 4 in that the variances of ε_1 and ε_2 are $(1/2)+(\alpha_i^2/2)$. In Specification 6 they are $(1/2)+(X_{2i1}^2/2)$. This makes the unconditional variances of the error terms 1, as in Specification 4.

The results presented in Table II indicate that $\hat{\beta}_4$ behaves well under heteroskedasticity, and that Theorem 2 provides a good approximation to the small sample distribution of $\hat{\beta}_4$ (when the sample size is 200).

Comparing the results of Specifications 1 and 4, the small sample properties of the estimators of the first two elements of β do not seem to depend on the presence of the additional regressors. This may be because the additional regressors are independent of the first two regressors. In Specification 7, we repeat the experiment in Specification 4, but with the additional regressors not being independent of the first two regressors. The difference between Specification 7 and Specification 4 is that in Specification 7, $X_{3ij}=\nu_{1ij}+\alpha_i$ (so the third

TABLE III

T STATISTICS BASED ON $\hat{\beta}_4$; $n = 200$

Specification 4.

	b_1	b_2	b_3	b_4	b_5
Size (0.20)	0.238	0.223	0.221	0.222	0.246
Size (0.10)	0.125	0.134	0.131	0.115	0.142
Size (0.05)	0.072	0.078	0.068	0.060	0.084

Specification 5.

	b_1	b_2	b_3	b_4	b_5
Size (0.20)	0.209	0.226	0.240	0.211	0.227
Size (0.10)	0.119	0.118	0.137	0.127	0.112
Size (0.05)	0.070	0.072	0.077	0.068	0.059

Specification 6.

	b_1	b_2	b_3	b_4	b_5
Size (0.20)	0.216	0.204	0.223	0.211	0.214
Size (0.10)	0.114	0.110	0.114	0.122	0.117
Size (0.05)	0.072	0.073	0.068	0.065	0.064

Specification 7.

	b_1	b_2	b_3	b_4	b_5
Size (0.20)	0.224	0.207	0.219	0.218	0.217
Size (0.10)	0.133	0.117	0.121	0.124	0.112
Size (0.05)	0.066	0.063	0.058	0.060	0.056

regressor depends on the fixed effect, and hence is correlated with the first regressor) and $X_{4ij} = \nu_{2ij} + X_{2ij}$ (so the fourth regressor depends on the second regressor but not on the fixed effect). The random variables ν_{kij} are independent with standard normal distributions. The censoring probabilities equal those in Specification 4.

The results for Specification 7 are given in the fourth panel of Table II. There is almost no effect on the first and third coefficients. This is not surprising, as the dependence between the regressors is "differenced out" (though it still might have an effect through the dependent variables). As expected, the estimates of the second coefficient are less precise than in Specification 4. We have no good intuition as to why the precision of the estimates of the fourth coefficient seem to be unchanged from Specification 4 to Specification 7.

Theorems 2 and 3 are of interest mostly because they imply that the usual t statistics are asymptotically normally distributed. For each of the samples used to construct Table II, the estimator of the variance of $\hat{\beta}_4$ was calculated. Based on this, a t statistic that tests whether each coefficient of β equals its true value, was calculated. The three lines of each panel of Table III give the fraction of samples for which the true value was rejected at a 20%, 10%, and 5% asymptotic level. These fractions are in the 21–25% range when the asymptotic level is 20%, 11–14% when the asymptotic level is 10%, and between 6 and 8% when the tests are performed at the 5% level. The size of the test exceeds the asymptotic level in all cases. This is due partly to the estimation error in the variance of $\hat{\beta}_4$ and partly to the small sample distribution of $\hat{\beta}_4$ having tails that are heavier than the asymptotic distribution. For example, when the true (unknown) asymptotic variance of $\hat{\beta}_4$ is used to calculate the t statistic for $\beta_k = 1$, the rejection frequency falls in all of the cases considered in Table III, but it remains above the asymptotic level in 53 out of the 60 cases.

7. CONCLUDING REMARKS

This paper has suggested estimators of truncated and censored regression models with fixed effects. The idea behind the estimators is to exploit a symmetry in the distribution of the latent variables. If the true value of the parameter was known, then trimming could introduce the same symmetry in the distribution of the observed variables. This suggests orthogonality conditions which must hold at the true value of the parameter. These orthogonality conditions are the asymptotic first order conditions for minimization of the objective functions used to define the estimators in this paper.

The estimators are proved to be consistent and asymptotically normal, and consistent estimators of the asymptotic variances are presented. A small Monte Carlo experiment investigates the small sample distribution of one of the estimators. The results give some indication that the asymptotic distribution is a good approximation of the small sample distribution when the sample size is 200 or larger, but that the small sample distribution of the estimator is skewed when the sample size is small.

The estimators presented in this paper all assume that the data consist of a panel of n individuals, each observed at two points in time. However, most panel data sets have more than two observations per individual. The estimators presented here can easily be modified to cover this case as well. Suppose that we want to use $\hat{\beta}_4$ in a case where there are $T \geqslant 2$ observations for each individual (for simplicity assume that T is nonrandom and constant across individuals). If $\{\varepsilon_{i,t}\}_{t=1}^{T}$ are i.i.d., then equation (2.5) must hold for all pairs of observations s, t (because T_n is convex, β will be the unique vector that satisfies the orthogonality conditions). This gives $KT(T-1)/2$ orthogonality conditions that can be used to estimate β. Theorem 3.2 of Hansen (1982) can be used to construct the optimal weights to give to the orthogonality conditions. The optimal weights will depend on the true value of β, and an initial estimator will, therefore, be needed. One possible choice of initial estimator is one that gives equal weight to all the pairs of observations:

$$\hat{\beta}_4^* = \underset{b \in B}{\arg\min} \sum_{i=1}^{n} \sum_{s<t} \chi(Y_{is}, Y_{it}, (X_{is} - X_{it})b)$$

It is clear that the symmetry exploited in Section 2 can be used to derive an infinite number of orthogonality conditions. For example, for the censored regression model, (2.2)–(2.5) must all hold. Theorem 3.2 of Hansen (1982) can be used to optimally combine a finite number of these orthogonality conditions. In future research, we plan to explore estimation strategies that use all information contained in Proposition 1. It is also clear that it is possible to derive estimators based on loss functions other than the absolute or quadratic loss. A library of GAUSS-routines that calculates the estimators for the censored regression model with fixed effects from a panel data set of arbitrary length is available from the author.

Another topic with which we have not dealt here, is the question of lagged endogenous variables. In the Monte Carlo study cited in the Introduction, Heckman (1979) found that the fixed effects probit estimator performs much worse when there are lagged endogenous variables. It would therefore be interesting to investigate whether "trimmed" estimators like those in this paper can be constructed for models with lagged endogenous variables. This issue is pursued in Honoré (1990).

Department of Economics, Northwestern University, Evanston, IL 60208, U.S.A.

Manuscript received June, 1989; final revision received August, 1991.

APPENDIX 1: LAD INTERPRETATION OF $\hat{\beta}_1$

In this appendix, we show that the estimator $\hat{\beta}_1$ can be interpreted as a least absolute deviations estimator. Suppose that the data are from the truncated model, and that we are to estimate β and $\{\alpha_i\}_{i=1}^n$ by Powell's least absolute deviations estimator for censored regression:

$$\min_{b,\{a_i:\, i=1,\ldots,n\}} \sum_{i=1}^{n} \sum_{t=1}^{2} |Y_{it} - \max\{0, a_i + X_{it}b\}|.$$

Below, it is proved that the solution for b would be given by minimization of Q_n. Note that this is the minimization used to find the least absolute deviations estimator for the censored regression model—not for the truncated regression model.

It will be proved that

$$\min_a \sum_{t=1}^{2} |Y_{it} - \max\{0, a + X_{it}b\}| = \psi(Y_{i1}, Y_{i2}, (X_{i1} - X_{i2})b),$$

which establishes the desired result.

Let b be given, and consider the ith individual. Without loss of generality, assume that $Y_{i1} - X_{i1}b > Y_{i2} - X_{i2}b$. There are two cases to be considered.

First, consider the case where $Y_{i2} - X_{i2}b \geqslant -X_{i1}b$. The function

$$g(a,b) = \sum_{t=1}^{2} |Y_{it} - \max\{0, a + X_{it}b\}|$$

is then continuous and piecewise linear with slope

$$\frac{\partial g}{\partial a} = \begin{cases} 0 & \text{for } a < \min\{-X_{i1}b, -X_{i2}b\}, \\ -1 & \text{for } \min\{-X_{i1}b, -X_{i2}b\} < a < \max\{-X_{i1}b, -X_{i2}b\} \\ -2 & \text{for } \max\{-X_{i1}b, -X_{i2}b\} < a < Y_{i2} - X_{i2}b, \\ 0 & \text{for } Y_{i2} - X_{i2}b < a < Y_{i1} - X_{i2}b, \\ 2 & \text{for } a > Y_{i1} - X_{i1}b. \end{cases}$$

The minimum is therefore attained in the interval $Y_{i2} - X_{i2}b < a < Y_{i1} - X_{i1}b$, and the minimized value is $(Y_{i1} - X_{i1}b) - (Y_{i2} - X_{i2}b)$, as was to be shown.

Second, consider the case where $Y_{i2}-X_{i2}b<-X_{i1}b$. The function

$$g(a,b)=\sum_{t=1}^{2}|Y_{it}-\max\{0,a+X_{it}b\}|$$

is then again continuous and piecewise linear. Its slope

$$\frac{\partial g}{\partial a}=\begin{cases}0 & \text{for } a<-X_{i2}b,\\ -1 & \text{for } -X_{i2}b<a<Y_{i2}-X_{i2}b,\\ 1 & \text{for } Y_{i2}-X_{i2}b<a<-X_{i1}b,\\ 0 & \text{for } -X_{i1}b<a<Y_{i1}-X_{i1}b,\\ 2 & \text{for } a>Y_{i1}-X_{i1}b.\end{cases}$$

The minimum of $\Sigma_{t=1}^{2}|Y_{it}-\max\{0,a+X_{it}b\}|$ is then attained at $a=Y_{i2}-X_{i2}b$, and the value is then Y_{i1}.

APPENDIX 2: SOME USEFUL LEMMAS

This Appendix states and proves a number of lemmas which will be used to prove the theorems stated in the text.

Let

$$\psi^{\circ}(z_1,z_2,\delta,\delta_0)=1\{z_1>0,\ z_2>0\}(\psi(z_1,z_2,\delta)-\psi(z_1,z_2,\delta_0)),$$

$$\xi^{\circ}(z_1,z_2,\delta,\delta_0)=1\{z_1>0,\ z_2>0\}(\psi(z_1,z_2,\delta)^2-\psi(z_1,z_2,\delta_0)^2),$$

$$\varphi^{\circ}(z_1,z_2,\delta,\delta_0)=\varphi(\max\{0,z_1\},\max\{0,z_2\},\delta)-\varphi(\max\{0,z_1\},\max\{0,z_2\},\delta_0)$$

and

$$\chi^{\circ}(z_1,z_2,\delta,\delta_0)=\chi(\max\{0,z_1\},\max\{0,z_2\},\delta)-\chi(\max\{0,z_1\},\max\{0,z_2\},\delta_0).$$

Also let

$$Q_n^{\circ}(b)=\frac{1}{n}(Q_n(b)-Q_n(\beta))=\frac{1}{n}\sum_{i=1}^{n}\psi^{\circ}(Y_{i1},Y_{i2},\Delta X_i b,\Delta X_i\beta),$$

$$R_n^{\circ}(b)=\frac{1}{n}(R_n(b)-R_n(\beta))=\frac{1}{n}\sum_{i=1}^{n}\xi^{\circ}(Y_{i1},Y_{i2},\Delta X_i b,\Delta X_i\beta),$$

$$S_n^{\circ}(b)=\frac{1}{n}(S_n(b)-S_n(\beta))=\frac{1}{n}\sum_{i=1}^{n}\varphi^{\circ}(Y_{i1},Y_{i2},\Delta X_i b,\Delta X_i\beta),$$

and

$$T_n^{\circ}(b)=\frac{1}{n}(T_n(b)-T_n(\beta))=\frac{1}{n}\sum_{i=1}^{n}\chi^{\circ}(Y_{i1},Y_{i2},\Delta X_i b,\Delta X_i\beta).$$

$\hat\beta_1$, $\hat\beta_2$, $\hat\beta_3$, and $\hat\beta_4$ are then defined as the minimizers of Q_n°, R_n°, and T_n°, respectively. There are two reasons for working with Q_n° through T_n°, rather than Q_n through T_n. The first is that the assumptions needed for existence of moments of Q_n° through T_n° are weaker than those needed for existence of moments of Q_n through T_n. The second reason is that ψ° through χ° are defined for negative values of z_1 and z_2 in such a way that the minimizations of Q_n° through T_n° are unchanged if the truncated or censored observations are replaced with their latent counterparts.

LEMMA A.1: *Let* (Z_1, Z_2) *be continuously distributed with density* f. *Then*

$$\frac{\partial E[\psi^\circ(Z_1,Z_2,\delta,\delta_0)]}{\partial\delta} = E[1\{Z_1 - Z_2 < \delta < Z_1, Z_1 > 0, Z_2 > 0\}] - E[1\{Z_2 - Z_1 < -\delta < Z_2, Z_1 > 0, Z_2 > 0\}]$$

and

$$\frac{\partial E[\varphi^\circ(Z_1,Z_2,\delta)]}{\partial\delta} = E[1\{Z_2 > 0, Z_2 > \max\{0, Z_1\} - \delta\}] - E[1\{Z_1 > 0, Z_1 > \max\{0, Z_2\} + \delta\}].$$

If, in addition, (Z_1, Z_2) *has finite first moments, then*

$$\frac{\partial E[\xi^\circ(Z_1,Z_2,\delta,\delta_0)]}{\partial\delta} = -2E[1\{Z_1 > 0, Z_2 > 0, -Z_2 < \delta < Z_1\}(Z_1 - Z_2 - \delta)]$$

and

$$\frac{\partial E[\chi^\circ(Z_1,Z_2,\delta,\delta_0)]}{\partial\delta} = 2E\big[1\{\delta \geqslant \max\{0,Z_1\}\}\max\{0,Z_2\} - 1\{\delta \leqslant -\max\{0,Z_2\}\}\max\{0,Z_1\} + 1\{-\max\{0,Z_2\} < \delta < \max\{0,Z_1\}\}(\max\{0,Z_2\} - \max\{0,Z_1\} + \delta)\big].$$

The last statement is true, even if (Z_1, Z_2) *is not continuously distributed.*

PROOF: In all cases, use the Lebesque dominated convergence theorem to justify differentiation under expectation. *Q.E.D.*

LEMMA A.2: *Assume that* (Z_1, Z_2) *is a continuously distributed random vector, such that* $P(Z_1 > 0, Z_2 > 0) > 0$ *and the distribution of* $Z_1 - Z_2 - \delta_0$ *conditional on* $Z_1 + Z_2$ *is symmetric around* 0 *for some real number* δ_0.

(a) *If the density of* $Z_1 - Z_2 - \delta_0$ *conditional on* $Z_1 + Z_2$ *is strictly unimodal, then* $E[\psi^\circ(Z_1, Z_2, \delta, \delta_0)]$ *is uniquely minimized at* $\delta = \delta_0$.

(b) *If the density of* $Z_1 - Z_2 - \delta_0$ *conditional on* $Z_1 + Z_2$ *is strictly unimodal, and* (Z_1, Z_2) *has finite first moments, then* $E[\xi^\circ(Z_1, Z_2, \delta, \delta_0)]$ *is uniquely minimized at* $\delta = \delta_0$.

(c) $E[\varphi^\circ(Z_1, Z_2, \delta, \delta_0)]$ *is uniquely minimized at* $\delta = \delta_0$.

(d) *If* (Z_1, Z_2) *has finite first moments, then* $E[\chi^\circ(Z_1, Z_2, \delta, \delta_0)]$ *is uniquely minimized at* $\delta = \delta_0$ (*this is true even if* (Z_1, Z_2) *is not continuously distributed*).

If $P(Z_1 > 0, Z_2 > 0) = 0$, *then* (a)–(d) *still hold, except that the* $\delta = \delta_0$ *need not be the unique minimizer*.

PROOF: Let δ_0 be given as in the statement of the lemma and let δ be an arbitrary real number. Define W_1 and W_2, by $W_1 = Z_1 - Z_2 - \delta_0$ and $W_2 = Z_1 + Z_2 - |\delta|$. Also define $\eta = \delta_0 - \delta$.

We can then write

$$\begin{aligned}\frac{\partial E[\psi^\circ(Z_1,Z_2,\delta,\delta_0)]}{\partial\delta} &= E[1\{W_2 > 0, -W_2 < W_1 + \eta < 0\}] - E[1\{W_2 > 0, 0 < W_1 + \eta < W_2\}] \\ &= E[1\{W_2 > 0, -W_2 - \eta < W_1 < -\eta\}] - E[1\{W_2 > 0, -\eta < W_1 < W_2 - \eta\}] \\ &= E[1\{W_2 > 0\}(P(-W_2 - \eta < W_1 < -\eta \mid W_2) - P(-\eta < W_1 < W_2 - \eta \mid W_2))].\end{aligned}$$

As the conditional distribution of W_1 given W_2 is unimodal and symmetric around 0, this is negative for $\delta < \delta_0$ $(\eta > 0)$, 0 at $\delta = \delta_0$ $(\eta = 0)$, and positive for $\delta > \delta_0$ $(\eta < 0)$. Therefore, $E[\psi^\circ(Z_1, Z_2, \delta, \delta_0)]$ is minimized at $\delta = \delta_0$. This proves (a).

By the same line of reasoning

$$\frac{\partial E[\xi^{\circ}(Z_1, Z_2, \delta, \delta_0)]}{\partial \delta} = -2E[1\{-W_2 < W_1 + \eta < W_2\}(W_1 + \eta)].$$

As $W_1 + \eta$ is unimodal and symmetric around η, this is negative for $\delta < \delta_0$ ($\eta > 0$), 0 at $\delta = \delta_0$ ($\eta = 0$), and positive for $\delta > \delta_0$ ($\eta < 0$). Therefore $E[\xi^{\circ}(Z_1, Z_2, \delta, \delta_0)]$ is minimized at $\delta = \delta_0$.

This proves (b).

To prove (c) and (d), note that the assumptions of the lemma imply that $(Z_1, Z_2 + \delta_0)$ is distributed like $(Z_2 + \delta_0, Z_1)$. This, in turn, implies that

$$\left.\frac{\partial E[\varphi^{\circ}(Z_1, Z_2, \delta, \delta_0)]}{\partial \delta}\right|_{\delta=\delta_0} = 0 \quad \text{and} \quad \left.\frac{\partial E[\chi^{\circ}(Z_1, Z_2, \delta, \delta_0)]}{\partial \delta}\right|_{\delta=\delta_0} = 0.$$

Since both of these derivatives are increasing as a function of δ, it follows that $E[\varphi^{\circ}(Z_1, Z_2, \delta, \delta_0)]$ and $E[\chi^{\circ}(Z_1, Z_2, \delta, \delta_0)]$ are minimized at $\delta = \delta_0$. This completes the proof. *Q.E.D.*

LEMMA A.3: *Assume that* (Z_1, Z_2) *is distributed symmetrically around the 45°-line through* $(\delta_0, 0)$ (*or, equivalently, through* $(0, -\delta_0)$).

If (Z_1, Z_2) *is continuously distributed with density f then*

$$\left.\frac{\partial^2 E[\psi^{\circ}(Z_1, Z_2, \delta, \delta_0)]}{\partial \delta^2}\right|_{\delta=\delta_0} = \begin{cases} P(Z_1 > 0, Z_2 > 0)\big(2f_{Z_1 - Z_2}(\delta_0 | Z_1 > 0, Z_2 > 0) - f_{Z_1}(\delta_0 | Z_1 > 0, Z_2 > 0)\big) & \text{for } \delta_0 \geqslant 0, \\ P(Z_1 > 0, Z_2 > 0)\big(2f_{Z_1 - Z_2}(\delta_0 | Z_1 > 0, Z_2 > 0) - f_{Z_2}(-\delta_0 | Z_1 > 0, Z_2 > 0)\big) & \text{for } \delta_0 < 0, \end{cases}$$

and

$$\left.\frac{\partial^2 E[\varphi^{\circ}(Z_1, Z_2, \delta, \delta_0)]}{\partial \delta^2}\right|_{\delta=\delta_0} = \begin{cases} 2\int_0^{\infty} f(\delta_0 + z_2, z_2)\, dz_2 + \int_{-\infty}^{0} f(\delta_0, z_2)\, dz_2, & \text{for } \delta_0 \geqslant 0, \\ 2\int_0^{\infty} f(z_1, z_1 - \delta_0)\, dz_1 + \int_{-\infty}^{0} f(z_1, -\delta_0)\, dz_1, & \text{for } \delta_0 < 0. \end{cases}$$

If (Z_1, Z_2) *is continuously distributed with density f and finite first moments, then*

$$\left.\frac{\partial^2 E[\xi^{\circ}(Z_1, Z_2, \delta, \delta_0)]}{\partial \delta^2}\right|_{\delta=\delta_0} = \begin{cases} 2P(Z_1 > \delta_0, Z_2 > 0) - 2\int_0^{\infty} z_2 f(\delta_0, z_2)\, dz_2 & \text{for } \delta_0 \geqslant 0, \\ 2P(Z_2 > -\delta_0, Z_1 > 0) - 2\int_0^{\infty} z_1 f(z_1, -\delta_0)\, dz_1 & \text{for } \delta_0 < 0, \end{cases}$$

and

$$\left.\frac{\partial^2 E[\chi^{\circ}(Z_1, Z_2, \delta, \delta_0)]}{\partial \delta^2}\right|_{\delta=\delta_0} = 2P(-\max\{0, Z_2\} < \delta_0 < \max\{0, Z_1\}).$$

PROOF: It is simple to find the second derivative of $E[\chi^{\circ}(Z_1, Z_2, \delta, \delta_0)]$ and the second derivatives of $E[\psi^{\circ}(Z_1, Z_2, \delta, \delta_0)]$, $E[\varphi^{\circ}(Z_1, Z_2, \delta, \delta_0)]$, and $E[\xi^{\circ}(Z_1, Z_2, \delta, \delta_0)]$ evaluated at any point except 0. The difficulty in the proof arises because the second derivatives might not exist at $\delta = 0$. However, the first derivatives (given in Lemma A.1) have right and left derivatives given by[9]

$$\left[\frac{\partial^2 E[\psi^\circ(Z_1, Z_2, \delta, \delta_0)]}{\partial \delta^2}\right]_+ = \begin{cases} P(Z_1 > 0, Z_2 > 0)\big(2f_{Z_1 - Z_2}(\delta | Z_1 > 0, Z_2 > 0) - f_{Z_1}(\delta | Z_1 > 0, Z_2 > 0)\big) & \text{for } \delta \geqslant 0, \\ P(Z_1 > 0, Z_2 > 0)\big(2f_{Z_1 - Z_2}(\delta | Z_1 > 0, Z_2 > 0) - f_{Z_2}(-\delta | Z_1 > 0, Z_2 > 0)\big) & \text{for } \delta < 0, \end{cases}$$

$$\left[\frac{\partial^2 E[\psi^\circ(Z_1, Z_2, \delta, \delta_0)]}{\partial \delta^2}\right]_- = \begin{cases} P(Z_1 > 0, Z_2 > 0)\big(2f_{Z_1 - Z_2}(\delta | Z_1 > 0, Z_2 > 0) - f_{Z_1}(\delta | Z_1 > 0, Z_2 > 0)\big) & \text{for } \delta > 0, \\ P(Z_1 > 0, Z_2 > 0)\big(2f_{Z_1 - Z_2}(\delta | Z_1 > 0, Z_2 > 0) - f_{Z_2}(-\delta | Z_1 > 0, Z_2 > 0)\big) & \text{for } \delta \leqslant 0, \end{cases}$$

$$\left[\frac{\partial^2 E[\varphi^\circ(Z_1, Z_2, \delta, \delta_0)]}{\partial \delta^2}\right]_+ = \begin{cases} 2\int_0^\infty f(\delta + z_2, z_2)\, dz_2 + \int_{-\infty}^0 f(\delta, z_2)\, dz_2, & \text{for } \delta \geqslant 0, \\ 2\int_0^\infty f(z_1, z_1 - \delta)\, dz_1 + \int_{-\infty}^0 f(z_1, -\delta)\, dz_1, & \text{for } \delta < 0, \end{cases}$$

$$\left[\frac{\partial^2 E[\varphi^\circ(Z_1, Z_2, \delta, \delta_0)]}{\partial \delta^2}\right]_- = \begin{cases} 2\int_0^\infty f(\delta + z_2, z_2)\, dz_2 + \int_{-\infty}^0 f(\delta, z_2)\, dz_2, & \text{for } \delta > 0, \\ 2\int_0^\infty f(z_1, z_1 - \delta)\, dz_1 + \int_{-\infty}^0 f(z_1, -\delta)\, dz_1, & \text{for } \delta \leqslant 0, \end{cases}$$

$$\left[\frac{\partial^2 E[\xi^\circ(Z_1, Z_2, \delta, \delta_0)]}{\partial \delta^2}\right]_+ = \begin{cases} 2P(Z_1 > \delta, Z_2 > 0) - 2\int_0^\infty z_2 f(\delta, z_2)\, dz_2 & \text{for } \delta \geqslant 0, \\ 2P(Z_2 > -\delta, Z_1 > 0) - 2\int_0^\infty z_1 f(z_1, -\delta)\, dz_1 & \text{for } \delta < 0, \end{cases}$$

$$\left[\frac{\partial^2 E[\xi^\circ(Z_1, Z_2, \delta, \delta_0)]}{\partial \delta^2}\right]_- = \begin{cases} 2P(Z_1 > \delta, Z_2 > 0) - 2\int_0^\infty z_2 f(\delta, z_2)\, dz_2 & \text{for } \delta > 0, \\ 2P(Z_2 > -\delta, Z_1 > 0) - 2\int_0^\infty z_1 f(z_1, -\delta)\, dz_1 & \text{for } \delta \leqslant 0. \end{cases}$$

The left and right derivatives will, in general, be different at $\delta = 0$. However, if $\delta_0 = 0$, $f(z_1, z_2) = f(z_2, z_1)$ and the left and right derivatives agree at $\delta = 0$. *Q.E.D.*

LEMMA B.1 (Uniform Convergence): *Let* $\boldsymbol{B}$ *be a compact set with the true parameter value,* β, *in the interior (for* $\hat{\beta}_1$ *and* $\hat{\beta}_2$, $\boldsymbol{B}$ *can be thought of as the parameter space). Under the assumptions of Theorem* 1, Q_n°, R_n°, S_n°, *and* T_n° *converge to their expectations uniformly in* $b \in \boldsymbol{B}$.

[9] I thank an anonymous referee for pointing out a flaw in the use of an earlier version of this lemma, and for suggesting the current version.

PROOF: First, notice that $\psi^\circ(Y_1, Y_2, \Delta Xb, \Delta X\beta)$, $\xi^\circ(Y_1, Y_2, \Delta Xb, \Delta X\beta)$, $\varphi^\circ(Y_1, Y_2, \Delta Xb, \Delta X\beta)$, and $\chi^\circ(Y_1, Y_2, \Delta Xb, \Delta X\beta)$ are measurable functions of (Y_1, Y_2, X_1, X_2) for a given b, and continuous functions of b given (Y_1, Y_2, X_1, X_2).

From the definitions of ψ, φ, and χ (see also Figures 2–5, which makes the following expressions trivial), it follows that

$$|\psi(z_1, z_2, \delta_1) - \psi(z_1, z_2, \delta_2)| \leqslant |\delta_1 - \delta_2|,$$

$$|\psi(z_1, z_2, \delta_1)^2 - \psi(z_1, z_2, \delta_2)^2| \leqslant 2\max\{z_1, z_2\}|\delta_1 - \delta_2|,$$

$$|\varphi(z_1, z_2, \delta_1) - \varphi(z_1, z_2, \delta_2)| \leqslant |\delta_1 - \delta_2|,$$

$$|\chi(z_1, z_2, \delta_1) - \chi(z_1, z_2, \delta_2)| \leqslant 2\max\{z_1, z_2\}|\delta_1 - \delta_2|.$$

This implies that

$$E\Big[\sup_{b\in B} |\psi^\circ(Y_{i1}, Y_{i2}, \Delta X_i b, \Delta X_i \beta)|\Big] \leqslant E\Big[\sup_{b\in B} |\Delta X(b-\beta)|\Big] < \infty,$$

$$E\Big[\sup_{b\in B} |\xi^\circ(Y_{i1}, Y_{i2}, \Delta X_i b, \Delta X_i \beta)|\Big] \leqslant E\Big[\sup_{b\in B} 2(Y_1+Y_2)|\Delta X(b-\beta)|\Big] < \infty,$$

$$E\Big[\sup_{b\in B} |\varphi^\circ(Y_{i1}, Y_{i2}, \Delta X_i b, \Delta X_i \beta)|\Big] \leqslant E\Big[\sup_{b\in B} |\Delta X(b-\beta)|\Big] < \infty,$$

and

$$E\Big[\sup_{b\in B} |\chi^\circ(Y_{i1}, Y_{i2}, \Delta X_i b, \Delta X_i \beta)|\Big] \leqslant E\Big[\sup_{b\in B} 2(Y_1+Y_2)|\Delta X(b-\beta)|\Big] < \infty,$$

where Assumption M.1 is used in the first and third equations, and Assumption M.2 is used in the second and fourth equations.

The result now follows from a standard uniform law of large numbers (for example, Amemiya (1985), Theorem 4.2.1). *Q.E.D.*

LEMMA B.2 (Identification): *Under the assumptions of Theorem* 1, $E[Q_n^\circ(b)]$, $E[R_n^\circ(b)]$, $E[S_n^\circ(b)]$, *and* $E[T_n^\circ(b)]$ *are uniquely minimized at* $b = \beta$.

PROOF: First notice that

$$E[\psi^\circ(Y_1, Y_2, \Delta Xb, \Delta X\beta)] = E\big[E[\psi^\circ(Y_1, Y_2, \Delta Xb, \Delta X\beta)|\alpha, X_1, X_2]\big].$$

Consider a, x_1, x_2 in the support of α, X_1, X_2 and let $\delta_0 = (x_1 - x_2)\beta$. Lemma A.2 then implies that $E[\psi^\circ(Y_1, Y_2, \Delta Xb, \Delta X\beta)]$ is minimized at a b such that $\Delta Xb = \Delta X\beta$ with probability 1. Assumption R.1 implies that the only b satisfying this is $b = \beta$. This proves the first statement of the lemma. The remaining statements can be proved in exactly the same way. *Q.E.D.*

APPENDIX 3: PROOFS OF THEOREMS AND LEMMAS IN THE TEXT

PROOF OF THEOREM 1: Rather than proving that $\hat\beta_1$ and $\hat\beta_2$ are consistent as the number of observations for which $Y_1^* > 0$ and $Y_2^* > 0$ approaches infinity, we will prove that they are consistent as the number of latent observations increases (the latter clearly implies the former). In this proof, n will therefore denote the number of observations in the latent sample. This makes the notation a little clearer, because it will not be necessary to work with distributions conditional on $Y_1^* > 0$ and $Y_2^* > 0$. As $\psi^\circ(z_1, z_2, \delta, \delta_0) = 0$, whenever either $z_1 \leqslant 0$ or $z_2 \leqslant 0$, the estimators will not change, if the observations for which either $Y_1^* \leqslant 0$ or $Y_2^* \leqslant 0$ are included in the definition of Q_n° and R_n°.

To prove consistency of $\hat\beta_1$ and $\hat\beta_2$, we will verify the conditions of Theorem 4.1.1 in Amemiya (1985). Assumption A (compactness) is satisfied by Assumption P.1; Assumption B (continuity and measurability) is trivially satisfied; finally, Assumption C (uniform convergence and identification) is satisfied by Lemmas B.1 and B.2.

For $\hat{\beta}_3$ and $\hat{\beta}_4$, it suffices to verify the conditions of Lemma A in Newey and Powell (1987). Assumption A (uniform convergence) is satisfied by Lemma B.1, Assumption B (identification) is satisfied by Lemma B.2, and Assumption C (convexity) is trivially verified. This proves that $\hat{\beta}_3$ and $\hat{\beta}_4$ are consistent. *Q.E.D.*

Proof of Lemma 1: The symmetry part is obvious. The unimodality is proved as follows: Let f be the (common) marginal density for ε_1 and ε_2. The unimodality in the statement of the Lemma is then implied by $f(e-v)f(e+v)$ being strictly increasing for $v<0$ (and hence decreasing for $v>0$) for all e, or

$$f(e-v_1)f(e+v_1)<f(e-v_2)f(e+v_2)$$

or

$$\log(f(e-v_1))+\log(f(e+v_1))<\log(f(e-v_2))+\log(f(e+v_2))$$

for all e and $|v_2|<|v_1|$ such that $e-v_1$, $e+v_1$, $e-v_2$, and $e+v_2$ are in the support of f. It is easily seen that this is true if $\log f$ is strictly concave. *Q.E.D.*

Proof of Theorem 2: For notational convenience let $Z=(\varepsilon_1,\varepsilon_2,X_1,X_2,\alpha)$. Define $V_1^*=P(Y_1>0,\ Y_2>0)V_1$, $V_2^*=P(Y_1>0,\ Y_2>0)V_2$, $\Gamma_1^*=P(Y_1>0,\ Y_2>0)\Gamma_1$, and $\Gamma_2^*=P(Y_1>0,\ Y_2>0)\Gamma_2$. The statements in (i) and (ii) are then implied by

$$\sqrt{n}\left(\hat{\beta}_1-\beta\right)\xrightarrow{d}N\left(0,\Gamma_1^{*-1}V_1^*\Gamma_1^{*-1}\right)$$

and

$$\sqrt{n}\left(\hat{\beta}_2-\beta\right)\xrightarrow{d}N\left(0,\Gamma_2^{*-1}V_2^*\Gamma_2^{*-1}\right),$$

where n now denotes the number of observations in the latent sample.

First, note that the assumptions of Theorem 1 are satisfied, so $\hat{\beta}_l$, $l=1,\dots,4$, are consistent. Asymptotic normality will be proved by defining functions, $f_l(Z,b)$, and then verifying that for $l=1,\dots,4$, G_l and G_{ln} defined by

$$G_l(b)=E[f_l(Z,b)]\quad\text{and}\quad G_{ln}(b)=\frac{1}{n}\sum_{i=1}^{n}f_l(Z_i,b)$$

satisfy:

(i) $\|G_{ln}(\hat{\beta}_l)\|=o_p(n^{-1/2})$.

(ii) $G_l(\cdot)$ is differentiable at β with derivative matrix Γ_l (Γ_l^* for $l=1,2$) of full rank.

(iii) For any sequence $\{\delta_n\}$ of positive numbers such that $\delta_n\to 0$ as $n\to\infty$,

$$\sup_{\|b-\beta\|<\delta_n}\|G_{ln}(b)-G_l(b)-G_{ln}(\beta)\|=o_p(n^{-1/2}).$$

(iv) $\sqrt{n}\,G_{ln}(\beta)\xrightarrow{d}N(0,V_l)$ ($N(0,V_l^*)$ for $l=1,2$).

(v) β is an interior point of the parameter space.

We can then use Theorem 3.3 of Pakes and Pollard (1989) (and the consistency of $\hat{\beta}_l$) to conclude that

$$\sqrt{n}\left(\hat{\beta}_l-\beta\right)\xrightarrow{d}N\left(0,(\Gamma_l'\Gamma_l)^{-1}\Gamma_l'V_l\Gamma_l(\Gamma_l'\Gamma_l)^{-1}\right).$$

Under our assumptions, Γ_l is symmetric and of full rank, so this expression reduces to

$$\sqrt{n}\left(\hat{\beta}_l-\beta\right)\xrightarrow{d}N\left(0,\Gamma_l^{-1}V_l\Gamma_l^{-1}\right).$$

Define

$$\begin{aligned}
f_1(Z,b)&=1\{Y_1^*>0,Y_2^*>0\}(1\{\Delta Y^*<\Delta Xb<Y_1^*\}-1\{-Y_2^*<\Delta Xb<\Delta Y^*\})\,\Delta X,\\
f_2(Z,b)&=-1\{Y_1^*>0,Y_2^*>0\}1\{-Y_2^*<\Delta Xb<Y_1^*\}(Y_1^*-Y_2^*-\Delta Xb)\,\Delta X,\\
f_3(Z,b)&=(1\{Y_2^*>0,Y_2^*>\max\{0,Y_1^*\}-\Delta Xb\}\\
&\qquad-1\{Y_1^*>0,Y_1^*>\max\{0,Y_2^*\}+\Delta Xb\})\,\Delta X,\\
f_4(b,Z)&=(1\{\Delta Xb\geqslant\max\{0,Y_1^*\}\}\max\{0,Y_2^*\}\\
&\qquad-1\{\Delta Xb\leqslant-\max\{0,Y_2^*\}\}\max\{0,Y_1^*\}\\
&\qquad+1\{-\max\{0,Y_2^*\}<\Delta Xb<\max\{0,Y_1^*\}\}\\
&\qquad\times(\max\{0,Y_2^*\}-\max\{0,Y_1^*\}+\Delta Xb))\,\Delta X.
\end{aligned}$$

With these definitions, f_1, f_2, f_3, and f_4 are the derivatives of $\psi^\circ(Y_1^*, Y_2^*, \Delta Xb, \Delta X\beta)$, $\xi^\circ(Y_1^*, Y_2^*, \Delta Xb, \Delta X\beta)/2$, $\varphi^\circ(Y_1^*, Y_2^*, \Delta Xb, \Delta X\beta)$, and $\chi^\circ(Y_1^*, Y_2^*, \Delta Xb, \Delta X\beta)/2$ respectively, at all points at which these are differentiable. Therefore G_{ln} ($l = 1, \ldots, 4$) are the derivatives (at all points of differentiability) of $Q_n(b)$, $R_n(b)$, $T_n(b)$, and $S_n(b)$.

As noted earlier, S_n is everywhere differentiable so $G_{4n}(\hat\beta_4) = 0$. This proves (i) for $\hat\beta_4$. To prove (i) for $\hat\beta_1$, observe that the left and right derivatives of $Q_n(b)$ with respect to the kth coordinate of b, $Q_{k,n}^-(b)$ and $Q_{k,n}^+(b)$, must satisfy $Q_{k,n}^-(\hat\beta_1) \leqslant 0$ and $Q_{k,n}^+(\hat\beta_1) \geqslant 0$. But $Q_{k,n}^-(\hat\beta_1)$ and $Q_{k,n}^+(\hat\beta_1)$ equal the kth coordinate of $G_{1n}(\hat\beta_1), G_{k,1n}(\hat\beta_1)$, plus the contribution to the left and right derivatives from observations that are located at the kinks of $\psi(Y_1^*, Y_2^*, \Delta X\hat\beta_1)$. Hence, the absolute value of the kth coordinate of $G_{1n}(\hat\beta_1)$ cannot exceed the absolute value of the maximum contribution of the observations at the kinks to the left and right derivatives of $Q_n(\hat\beta_1)$. Therefore

$$\left|G_{k,1n}(\hat\beta_1)\right| \leqslant \max_{1\leqslant i\leqslant n}\{\|\Delta X_i\|\} \times \frac{1}{n}\sum_{i=1}^{n}\Big(1\{\Delta X_i\hat\beta_1 = -Y_{i2}^*, \Delta X_i \neq 0\}$$
$$+1\{\Delta X_i\hat\beta_1 = Y_{i1}^*, \Delta X_i \neq 0\} + 1\{\Delta X_i\hat\beta_1 = \Delta Y_i^*, \Delta X_i \neq 0\}\Big).$$

By the same argument

$$\left|G_{k,2n}(\hat\beta_2)\right| \leqslant \max_{1\leqslant i\leqslant n}\{Y_{i1}^*\|\Delta X_i\|\} \times \frac{1}{n}\sum_{i=1}^{n}1\{\Delta X_i\hat\beta_2 = -Y_{i2}^*, \Delta X_i \neq 0\}$$
$$+ \max_{1\leqslant i\leqslant n}\{Y_{i2}^*\|\Delta X_i\|\} \times \frac{1}{n}\sum_{i=1}^{n}1\{\Delta X_i\hat\beta_2 = Y_{i1}^*, \Delta X_i \neq 0\}$$

and

$$\left|G_{k,3n}(\hat\beta_3)\right| \leqslant \max_{1\leqslant i\leqslant n}\{\|\Delta X_i\|\} \times \frac{1}{n}\sum_{i=1}^{n}\Big(1\{Y_{i1}^* > 0, \Delta X_i\hat\beta_3 = Y_{i1}^* - \max\{0, Y_{i2}^*\}\}$$
$$+1\{Y_{i2}^* > 0, -\Delta X_i\hat\beta_3 = Y_{i2}^* - \max\{0, Y_{i1}^*\}\}\Big).$$

To see that (i) is satisfied, observe that (a) the sums on the right-hand side of these inequalities are all $O_p(1)$ (because (Y_1^*, Y_2^*) is continuously distributed), and (b) $\max_{1\leqslant i\leqslant n}\{\|\Delta X_i\|\} = o_p(\sqrt{n})$ (because $E[\|\Delta X\|^2] < \infty$) and $\max_{1\leqslant i\leqslant n}\{Y_{it}^*\|\Delta X_i\|\} = o_p(\sqrt{n})$ (because $E[Y_t^{*2}\|\Delta X\|^2] < \infty$). This completes the proof on (i).[10]

To verify (ii) for $\hat\beta_1$, note that

(A1) $$G_1(b) = E\big[\big(P(\Delta Y^* < \Delta Xb < Y_1^*, Y_1^* > 0, Y_2^* > 0 | X_1, X_2, \alpha)$$
$$-P(-Y_2^* < \Delta Xb < \Delta Y^*, Y_1^* > 0, Y_2^* > 0 | X_1, X_2, \alpha)\big)\Delta X\big].$$

Using Lemma A.3, we have for almost all (X_1, X_2, α)

$$\Bigg|\frac{\partial}{\partial b_j}\big(P(\Delta Y < \Delta Xb < Y_1^*, Y_1^* > 0, Y_2^* > 0 | X_1, X_2, \alpha)$$
$$-P(-Y_2^* < \Delta Xb < \Delta Y, Y_1^* > 0, Y_2^* > 0 | X_1, X_2, \alpha)\big)\Delta X_k\Bigg|$$
$$\leqslant \big|\big(2f_{Y_1^*-Y_2^*}(\Delta Xb | X_1, X_2, \alpha) + f_{Y_1^*}(\Delta Xb | X_1, X_2, \alpha)$$
$$+f_{Y_2^*}(-\Delta Xb | X_1, X_2, \alpha)\big)\Delta X_j \Delta X_k\big|$$
$$= \big|\big(2f_{\varepsilon_1-\varepsilon_2}(\Delta X(b-\beta) | X_1, X_2, \alpha) + f_{\varepsilon_1}(X_1(b-\beta) - X_2 b - \alpha | X_1, X_2, \alpha)$$
$$+f_{\varepsilon_2}(X_2(b-\beta) - X_1 b - \alpha | X_1, X_2, \alpha)\big)\Delta X_j \Delta X_k\big|$$
$$\leqslant |K\Delta X_j \Delta X_k|$$

[10] The proof of (i) for $l = 1, 2, 3$ is similar to the proofs in Ruppert and Carroll (1980) and in Powell (1984, 1986).

for some constant K (by Assumption E.4). This means that we can find the derivative of G by differentiating under the expectation on the right-hand side of (A1) (see Cramér (1945, pp. 67–68)):

$$\begin{aligned}\frac{\partial G_{k,1}(\beta)}{\partial \beta_j} &= E\big[P(Y_1^*>0, Y_2^*>0|X_1,X_2,\alpha)\\ &\quad\times\big(2f_{Y_1^*-Y_2^*}(\Delta X\beta|X_1,X_2,\alpha,Y_1^*>0,Y_2^*>0)\\ &\quad-1\{\Delta X\beta\geqslant 0\}f_{Y_1^*}(\Delta X\beta|X_1,X_2,\alpha,Y_1^*>0,Y_2^*>0)\\ &\quad-1\{\Delta X\beta<0\}f_{Y_2^*}(-\Delta X\beta|X_1,X_2,\alpha,Y_1^*>0,Y_2^*>0)\big)\,\Delta X_j\Delta X_k\big]\\ &=P(Y_1^*>0,Y_2^*>0)\times E\big[\big(2f_{Y_1^*-Y_2^*}(\Delta X\beta|X_1,X_2,\alpha,Y_1^*>0,Y_2^*>0)\\ &\quad-1\{\Delta X\beta\geqslant 0\}f_{Y_1^*}(\Delta X\beta|X_1,X_2,\alpha,Y_1^*>0,Y_2^*>0)\\ &\quad-1\{\Delta X\beta<0\}f_{Y_2^*}(-\Delta X\beta|X_1,X_2,\alpha,Y_1^*>0,Y_2^*>0)\big)\\ &\quad\times\Delta X_j\Delta X_k|Y_1^*>0,Y_2^*>0\big].\end{aligned}$$

Therefore, (ii) is satisfied and Γ_1^* has full rank by Assumption V.1. This proves (ii) for $l=1$. For $l=2$ note that

(A2) $$\begin{aligned}G_2(b) = -E\big[&P(-Y_2^*<\Delta Xb<Y_1^*, Y_1^*>0, Y_2^*>0|X_1,X_2,\alpha)\\ &\times E\big[Y_1^*-Y_2^*-\Delta Xb|-Y_2^*<\Delta Xb<Y_1^*,Y_1^*>0,Y_2^*>0,X_1,X_2,\alpha\big]\Delta X\big]\end{aligned}$$

and that, using Lemma A.3 and Assumption E.5,

$$\begin{aligned}&\Big|\frac{\partial}{\partial b_j}P(-Y_2^*<\Delta Xb<Y_1^*,Y_1^*>0,Y_2^*>0|X_1,X_2,\alpha)\\ &\quad\times E\big[Y_1^*-Y_2^*-\Delta Xb|-Y_2^*<\Delta Xb<Y_1^*,Y_1^*>0,Y_2^*>0,X_1,X_2,\alpha\big]\\ &\quad\times 1\{Y_1^*>0,Y_2^*>0\}\Delta X_k\Big|\\ &\leqslant\Big|\Big(1+1\{\Delta Xb\geqslant 0\}\int_0^\infty y_2 f_{Y_1^*,Y_2^*}(\Delta Xb,y_2|X_1,X_2,\alpha)\,dy_2\\ &\quad+1\{\Delta Xb<0\}\int_0^\infty y_1 f_{Y_1^*,Y_2^*}(y_1,-\Delta Xb|X_1,X_2,\alpha)\,dy_1\Big)\Delta X_j\Delta X_k\Big|\\ &=\Big|\Big(1+1\{\Delta Xb\geqslant 0\}\int_{-X_2\beta-\alpha}^\infty (X_2\beta+\alpha+\varepsilon_2)\\ &\quad\times f_{\varepsilon_1,\varepsilon_2}(\Delta Xb-X_1\beta-\alpha,\varepsilon_2|X_1,X_2,\alpha)\,d\varepsilon_2\\ &\quad+1\{\Delta Xb<0\}\int_{-X_1\beta-\alpha}^\infty (X_1\beta+\alpha+\varepsilon_1)\\ &\quad\times f_{\varepsilon_1,\varepsilon_2}(\varepsilon_1,-\Delta Xb-X_2\beta-\alpha|X_1,X_2,\alpha)\,d\varepsilon_1\Big)\Delta X_j\Delta X_k\Big|\\ &\leqslant H(X,\alpha)\end{aligned}$$

for some continuous and integrable function H (this follows from Assumptions M.3 and E.5). This means that we can find the derivative of G by differentiating under the expectation on the right-hand side of (A2):

$$\begin{aligned}\frac{\partial G_{2,k}(\beta)}{\partial \beta_j} = -E\Big[& P(Y_1^* > 0, Y_2^* > 0 | X_1, X_2, \alpha) \\ & \times\big(1\{\Delta X\beta \geqslant 0\} f_{Y_1^*}(\Delta X\beta | X_1, X_2, \alpha, Y_1^* \geqslant 0, Y_2^* > 0) \\ & \times E[Y_2^* | Y_1^* = \Delta X\beta, X_1, X_2, \alpha, Y_1^* > 0, Y_2^* > 0] \\ & + 1\{\Delta X\beta < 0\} f_{Y_2^*}(-\Delta X\beta | X_1, X_2, \alpha, Y_1^* > 0, Y_2^* > 0) \\ & \times E[Y_1^* | Y_2^* = \Delta X\beta, X_1, X_2, \alpha, Y_1^* > 0, Y_2 > 0] \\ & - P(Y_1^* > \Delta X\beta > -Y_2^* | X_1, X_2, \alpha, Y_1^* > 0, Y_2^* > 0)\big)\, \Delta X_j \Delta X_k\Big] \\ = & -P(Y_1^* > 0, Y_2^* > 0) \\ & \times E\Big[\big(1\{\Delta X\beta \geqslant 0\} f_{Y_1^*}(\Delta X\beta | X_1, X_2, \alpha, Y_1^* > 0, Y_2^* > 0) \\ & \times E[Y_2^* | Y_1^* = \Delta X\beta, X_1, X_2, \alpha, Y_1^* > 0, Y_2^* > 0] \\ & + 1\{\Delta X\beta < 0\} f_{Y_2^*}(-\Delta X\beta | X_1, X_2, \alpha, Y_1^* > 0, Y_2^* > 0) \\ & \times E[Y_1^* | Y_2^* = \Delta X\beta, X_1, X_2, \alpha, Y_1^* > 0, Y_2^* > 0] \\ & - P(Y_1^* > \Delta X\beta > -Y_2^* | X_1, X_2 \alpha, Y_1^* > 0, Y_2^* > 0)\big) \\ & \times \Delta X_j \Delta X_k | Y_1^* > 0, Y_2^* > 0\Big].\end{aligned}$$

Therefore, (ii) is satisfied and Γ_2^* has full rank by Assumption V.2. This proves (ii) for $l = 2$.

To verify (iii) for $\hat{\beta}_3$, write

$$\text{(A3)} \qquad \begin{aligned} G_3(b) = E\big[\big(& P(Y_2^* > 0, Y_2^* > \max\{0, Y_1^*\} - \Delta Xb | X_1, X_2, \alpha) \\ & - P(Y_1^* > 0, Y_1^* > \max\{0, Y_2^*\} + \Delta Xb | X_1, X_2, \alpha)\big)\, \Delta X\big].\end{aligned}$$

Using Lemma A.3, we have for almost all (X_1, X_2, α):

$$\begin{aligned} & \Big| \frac{\partial}{\partial b_j}\big(P(Y_2^* > 0, Y_2^* > \max\{0, Y_1^*\} - \Delta Xb | X_1, X_2, \alpha) \\ & \qquad - P(Y_1^* > 0, Y_1^* > \max\{0, Y_2^*\} + \Delta Xb | X_1, X_2, \alpha)\big)\, \Delta X_k \Big| \\ & \leqslant \big|\big(2 f_{\varepsilon_1 - \varepsilon_2}(\Delta X(b-\beta) | X_1, X_2, \alpha) + f_{\varepsilon_1}(X_1(b-\beta) - X_2 b - \alpha | X_1, X_2, \alpha) \\ & \qquad + f_{\varepsilon_2}(X_2(b-\beta) - X_1 b - \alpha | X_1, X_2, \alpha)\big)\, \Delta X_j \Delta X_k\big| \\ & \leqslant |K \Delta X_j \Delta X_k| \end{aligned}$$

for some constant K (by Assumption E.4).

Differentiation under the expectation on the right-hand side of (A3) gives

$$\begin{aligned} \frac{\partial G_{k,3}(\beta)}{\partial \beta_j} & \\ = E\Big[\big(& 2 f_{Y_1^* - Y_2^*}(\Delta X\beta | X_1, X_2, \alpha, Y_1^* > 0, Y_2^* > 0) \\ & + 1\{\Delta X\beta \geqslant 0\} P(Y_2^* \leqslant 0 | \alpha, X_1, X_2) f_{Y_1^*}(\Delta X\beta | X_1, X_2, \alpha, Y_2^* \leqslant 0) \\ & + 1\{\Delta X\beta < 0\} P(Y_1^* \leqslant 0 | \alpha, X_1, X_2) f_{Y_2^*}(-\Delta X\beta | X_1, X_2, \alpha, Y_1^* \leqslant 0)\big) \\ & \times \Delta X_j \Delta X_k\Big].\end{aligned}$$

Therefore, (ii) is satisfied and Γ_3 has full rank by Assumption V.3. This proves (iii) for $l = 3$.

(ii) is trivially satisfied for $l=4$ (use Lebesque dominated convergence theorem to justify differentiation under expectation).

The results from the empirical processes literature, summarized in Pakes and Pollard (1989), can be used to verify (iii). First, notice that it suffices to prove that for $l=1,\ldots,4$, $k=1,\ldots,K$,

$$\begin{aligned}
&\sup_{\|b-\beta\|<\delta_n} |G_{k,ln}(b)-G_{k,l}(b)-G_{k,ln}(\beta)| \\
&\quad= \sup_{\|b-\beta\|<\delta_n} |(G_{k,ln}(b)-G_{k,l}(b))-(G_{k,ln}(\beta)-G_{k,l}(\beta))| \\
&\quad= n^{-1/2} \sup_{\|b-\beta\|<\delta_n} |\nu_n f_{k,l}(\cdot,b)-\nu_n f_{k,l}(\cdot,\beta)| \\
&\quad= o_p(n^{-1/2})
\end{aligned}$$

where we have used the linear operator notation of Pakes and Pollard (1989), with ν_n denoting the standardized empirical process $\sqrt{n}(P_n-P)$.

It follows from Lemma 2.17 of Pakes and Pollard, that it is sufficient to demonstrate that (a) $\mathscr{F}_{k,l} \overset{\text{def}}{=} \{f_{k,l}(\cdot,b): b\in \boldsymbol{B}\}$ ($f_{k,l}$ is the kth coordinate of f_l) is a Euclidian class with an envelope $F_{k,l}$ for which $E[F_{k,l}(Z)^2]<\infty$, and (b) $E[f_{k,l}(Z,b)^2]$ is continuous at $b=\beta$.

Clearly, $\mathscr{F}_{k,l}$ ($l=1,3$) and $\mathscr{F}_{k,l}$ ($l=2,4$) are bounded in absolute value by $|\Delta X_k|$ and by $(|Y_1^*|+|Y_2^*|)|\Delta X_k|$, respectively. These are squared integrable by Assumptions M.2 and M.3. It is also clear that $E[f_{k,l}(Z,b)^2]$ ($l=1,\ldots,4$) are continuous at $b=\beta$ (see the expression for V_l). Therefore, it only remains to be shown that $\mathscr{F}_{k,l}$ are Euclidian.

To see that this is the case, note that for each $f_{k,l}\in\mathscr{F}_{k,l}$ ($l=1,3$; $k=1,\ldots,K$), there is a partition of R^{K+2} into L regions, all of which are finite intersections of a finite number of halfplanes, such that on each of the regions, $f_{k,l}$ is linear. We can, therefore, mimic the argument leading to Example 2.11 in Pakes and Pollard to show that $\mathscr{F}_{k,1}$ and $\mathscr{F}_{k,3}$ are Euclidian.

For $l=2$, notice that $f_{k,l}$ can be written as

$$\begin{aligned}
f_{k,l}(Z,b) = {}& 1\{-\Delta X_k Y_2^* < \Delta X_k\, \Delta X b < \Delta X_k Y_1^*,\ \Delta X_k>0\} \\
&\times(\Delta X_k Y_1^* - \Delta X_k Y_2^* - \Delta X_k\, \Delta X b) \\
&+1\{-\Delta X_k Y_2^* > \Delta X_k\, \Delta X b > \Delta X_k Y_1^*,\ \Delta X_k>0\} \\
&\times(\Delta X_k Y_1^* - \Delta X_k Y_2^* - \Delta X_k\, \Delta X b).
\end{aligned}$$

Now consider this a function of ΔX_k, $\Delta X_k\, Y_1^*$, $\Delta X_k\, Y_2^*$, and $\Delta X_k\, \Delta X$. As a function of $\Delta X_k\, Y_1^*$, $\Delta X_k\, Y_2^*$, and $\Delta X_k\, \Delta X$, there is a partition of R^{K+3} into at most L regions (for some finite L depending only on K), such that on each of the regions, f_k is linear. It therefore follows by the same argument as above, that $\mathscr{F}_{k,2}$ is Euclidian.

$\mathscr{F}_{k,4}$ is Euclidian by Lemma 2.13 of Pakes and Pollard.

Condition (iv) is a direct consequence of the Central Limit Theorem.

Part (v) follows from Assumption P.1 (for $l=1,2$) and is trivial for $l=3,4$ (for which the parameter space is R^K). *Q.E.D.*

PROOF OF THEOREM 3: Proof follows immediately from the discussion in Pakes and Pollard (1989, page 1043). *Q.E.D.*

REFERENCES

AMEMIYA, T. (1985): *Advanced Econometrics*. Cambridge: Harvard University Press.

ANDREWS, D. W. K. (1991a): "Asymptotics for Semiparametric Econometric Models: I. Estimation and Testing," Cowles Foundation Discussion Paper No. 908, Yale University.

—— (1991b): "Asymptotics for Semiparametric Econometric Models: II. Stochastic Equicontinuity and Nonparametric Kernel Estimation," Cowles Foundation Discussion Paper No. 909, Yale University.

BHATTACHARYA, P. K., H. CHERNOFF, AND S. S. YANG (1983): "Nonparametric Estimation of the Slope of a Truncated Regression," *Annals of Statistics*, 11, 505–514.

CHAMBERLAIN, G. (1984): "Panel Data," Chapter 22 of *Handbook of Econometrics*, Volume II, edited by Z. Griliches and M. Intriligator. Amsterdam: North Holland.

CHESHER, A. D., AND R. H. SPADY (1990): "Asymptotic Approximations to the Small-Sample Distribution of Estimators of the Censored Regression Model," unpublished manuscript.

CRAMÉR, H. (1945): *Mathematical Methods of Statistics*. Princeton: Princeton University Press.

HANSEN, L. P. (1982): "Large Sample Properties of Generalized Methods of Moments Estimators," *Econometrica*, 50, 1029–1054.

HECKMAN, J. J. (1979): "The Incidental Parameter Problem and the Problem of Initial Conditions in Estimating a Discrete Time-Discrete Data Stochastic Process and Some Monte Carlo Evidence," in *Structural Analysis of Discrete Data*, ed. by D. McFadden and C. Manski. Cambridge, Mass.: MIT Press.

HECKMAN, J. J., AND T. E. MACURDY (1980): "A Life Cycle Model of Female Labour Supply," *Review of Economic Studies*, 47, 47–74.

HONORÉ, B. E. (1989): "Trimmed LAD and Least Squares Estimation of Truncated and Censored Regression Models with Fixed Effects," unpublished manuscript.

——— (1990): "Orthogonality Conditions for Tobit Models with Fixed Effects and Lagged Dependent Variables," unpublished manuscript.

HUBER, P. (1965): "The Behavior of Maximum Likelihood Estimates under Nonstandard Conditions," *Proceedings of the Fifth Berkeley Symposium*, 1, 221–233.

MANSKI, C. (1987): "Semiparametric Analysis of Random Effects Linear Models from Binary Panel Data," *Econometrica*, 55, 357–362.

NEWEY, W. K., AND J. L. POWELL (1987): "Asymmetric Least Squares Estimation and Testing," *Econometrica*, 55, 819–847.

POWELL, J. (1984): "Least Absolute Deviations Estimation for the Censored Regression Model," *Journal of Econometrics*, 25, 303–325.

——— (1986): "Symmetrically Trimmed Least Squares Estimation for Tobit Models," *Econometrica*, 54, 1435–1460.

PAKES, A., AND D. POLLARD (1989): "Simulation and the Asymptotics of Optimization Estimators," *Econometrica*, 57, 1027–1057.

POLLARD, D. (1985): "New Ways to Prove Central Limit Theorems," *Econometric Theory*, 1, 295–314.

RUPPERT, D., AND R. J. CARROLL (1980): "Trimmed Least Squares Estimation in the Linear Model," *Journal of the American Statistical Association*, 75, 825–838.

WEISS, A. A. (1991): "Estimating Nonlinear Dynamic Models Using Least Absolute Error Estimation," *Econometric Theory*, 7, 46–68.

[2]

Econometrica, Vol. 68, No. 4 (July, 2000), 839–874

PANEL DATA DISCRETE CHOICE MODELS WITH LAGGED DEPENDENT VARIABLES

BY BO E. HONORÉ AND EKATERINI KYRIAZIDOU[1]

In this paper, we consider identification and estimation in panel data discrete choice models when the explanatory variable set includes strictly exogenous variables, lags of the endogenous dependent variable as well as unobservable individual-specific effects. For the binary logit model with the dependent variable lagged only once, Chamberlain (1993) gave conditions under which the model is not identified. We present a stronger set of conditions under which the parameters of the model are identified. The identification result suggests estimators of the model, and we show that these are consistent and asymptotically normal, although their rate of convergence is slower than the inverse of the square root of the sample size. We also consider identification in the semiparametric case where the logit assumption is relaxed. We propose an estimator in the spirit of the conditional maximum score estimator (Manski (1987)), and we show that it is consistent. In addition, we discuss an extension of the identification result to multinomial discrete choice models, and to the case where the dependent variable is lagged twice. Finally, we present some Monte Carlo evidence on the small sample performance of the proposed estimators for the binary response model.

KEYWORDS: Dynamic discrete choice, panel data.

1. INTRODUCTION

IN MANY SITUATIONS, such as in the study of labor force and union participation, accident occurrence, unemployment, purchase decisions, etc., it is observed that an individual who has experienced an event in the past is more likely to experience the event in the future than an individual who has not experienced the event. Heckman (1981a, b) discusses two explanations for this phenomenon. The first explanation is the presence of "true state dependence," in the sense that the lagged choice/decision enters the model in a structural way as an explanatory variable. The second is the presence of serial correlation in the unobserved transitory errors that underlie the threshold-crossing econometric specification of the model. A case that has received considerable attention in the literature is the case where this serial correlation is due to the presence of unobservable permanent individual specific heterogeneity, i.e. to different propensities across individuals to experience the event. Heckman calls the latter source of serial correlation "spurious state dependence." Distinguishing between these two explanations is important, for example, in evaluating the effect of economic policies that aim to alleviate short-term unemployment (see Phelps (1972)), or the effect of training programs on the future employment of trainees

[1] Both authors gratefully acknowledge financial support from the National Science Foundation. Honoré in addition acknowledges support from the Alfred P. Sloan Foundation. We thank a co-editor, three anonymous referees, Luojia Hu, Manuel Arellano, and seminar participants at many institutions for helpful comments. All errors are our responsibility.

(see Card and Sullivan (1988)). As pointed out by Heckman, longitudinal data on individual histories are required in order to discriminate between true and spurious state dependence. This paper presents methods for discrete choice models with structural state dependence that allow for the presence of unobservable individual heterogeneity in panels with a large number of individuals observed over a small number of time periods.

Specifically, we consider discrete choice models of the form:

$$y_{it} = 1\{x_{it}\beta + \gamma y_{it-1} + \alpha_i + \varepsilon_{it} > 0\}$$

where x_{it} is a vector of exogenous variables, ε_{it} is an unobservable error term, α_i is an unobservable individual-specific effect, and β and γ are the parameters of interest to be estimated. In addition to the basic structure of the model, a key assumption is that ε_{it} is serially independent over time. Generally, one would like to distinguish between dynamic responses to the exogenous variables (through lagged dependent variables), unobserved heterogeneity, and serial correlation. This paper takes a step in this direction by proposing a method for distinguishing between the first two in a model that explicitly rules out serial correlation. In a recent paper, Chintagunta, Kyriazidou, and Perktold (1998) motivate the econometric model above in the context of consumer choice across different brands of non-durable goods. They set up a dynamic model where each consumer maximizes expected lifetime utility. The period utility function depends on which brand is consumed in the previous period (which renders lifetime utility non-separable over time), on (possibly time-varying) brand and consumer characteristics, on unobserved (to the econometrician) permanent heterogeneity in preferences for the different brands, as well as on unobservable transitory taste shocks. Chintagunta, Kyriazidou, and Perktold (1998) show that it is possible to derive the optimal decision rule for each period's brand choice as described by the econometric model above, provided that the consumer cannot forecast future prices, shocks, or the other state variables of the model (for example, firms' promotional efforts). Thus, their model rules out serial dependence in the transitory errors in line with the assumption of the econometric model studied here.

It is well-known[2] that nonlinear panel data models with individual-specific effects, such as discrete choice, censored and truncated, sample selection models, etc., may be estimated by the "random effects" approach. See Arellano and Carrasco (1996) for an example. This approach requires the specification of the statistical relationship between the observed covariates and the unobservable permanent individual effect. Furthermore, it requires distributional assumptions on the initial conditions of the process, if there is serial correlation in the unobserved transitory error components and/or if lags of the dependent variable are used as explanatory variables. The problems associated with misspecification of these distributions are partly overcome in the "fixed effects"

[2] For this and other results concerning panel data models, see the survey articles by Chamberlain (1984, 1985), Hsiao (1986), and Maddala (1983).

approach. Below we discuss existing estimators for panel data discrete choice models. Estimators for the fixed effects censored and truncated regression models with strictly exogenous regressors have been proposed by Honoré (1992). Honoré (1993) considered the case where the explanatory variable set also includes lags of the dependent variable. Kyriazidou (1997a) proposed estimators for the panel data sample selection model assuming strictly exogenous regressors in both the main equation and the binary sample selection equation. In Kyriazidou (1997b), the main equation is also allowed to contain lags of the continuous dependent variable, while the selection equation may have lags of the endogenous selection indicator.

In the absence of state dependence (that is, with only strictly exogenous regressors), the parametric "fixed effects" approach for the discrete choice model assumes that the time-varying errors are independent of all the other covariates and that they are i.i.d. over time with a logistic distribution. No assumptions are made on the distribution of the individual effects conditional on the observed explanatory variables. As Rasch (1960) and Andersen (1970) have shown, the model may then be estimated by conditional maximum likelihood. In the case of binary choice, the model has the form:

$$(1)\qquad P(y_{it}=1\,|\,x_i,\alpha_i,y_{i0},\ldots,y_{it-1})=\frac{\exp(x_{it}\beta+\alpha_i)}{1+\exp(x_{it}\beta+\alpha_i)}$$

$$(t=1,\ldots,T;T\geq 2),$$

where β is the parameter of interest, α_i is an individual-specific effect that may depend on the exogenous explanatory variables $x_i \equiv (x_{i1},\ldots,x_{iT})$ in an arbitrary way, and where y_{i0} may or may not be observed. (Throughout, $i=1,\ldots,n$ indicates the identity of the individual.) In the case where $T=2$, inference concerning β is based on the observation that $P(y_{it}=1\,|\,\alpha_i,x_i,y_{i0},y_{i1}+y_{i2}=1)$ is independent of α_i.

As Manski (1987) has shown, it is possible to relax the logistic assumption as well as to allow for certain forms of serial correlation in the underlying time-varying errors in (1) above. In the special case where the errors are independent, the model takes the form

$$P(y_{it}=1\,|\,x_i,\alpha_i,y_{i0},\ldots,y_{it-1})=F_i(x_{it}\beta+\alpha_i)\qquad(t=1,\ldots,T;T\geq 2),$$

where F_i is a strictly increasing distribution function with full support on $\Re$ that is allowed to differ across individuals, but not over time for a given individual. In the case where $T=2$, identification of β is based on the fact that, under certain regularity conditions on the distribution of the exogenous variables, $\text{sgn}(P(y_{i2}=1\,|\,x_{i1},x_{i2},\alpha_i)-P(y_{i1}=1\,|\,x_{i1},x_{i2},\alpha_i))=\text{sgn}((x_{i2}-x_{i1})\beta)$. This implies that Manski's (1975, 1985) maximum score estimator can be applied to the first differences of the data in the subsample for which $y_{i1}\neq y_{i2}$.

The parametric "fixed effects" approach may be also used to estimate panel data logit models with individual effects and lags of the dependent variable, provided that there are no other explanatory variables and that there are at least four observations per individual (see Chamberlain (1985) and Magnac (1997)). In the binary choice case with the dependent variable lagged once, the model is

$$P(y_{i0}=1 \mid \alpha_i)=p_0(\alpha_i),$$

$$P(y_{it}=1 \mid \alpha_i, y_{i0},\ldots,y_{it-1})=\frac{\exp(\gamma y_{it-1}+\alpha_i)}{1+\exp(\gamma y_{it-1}+\alpha_i)} \tag{2}$$

$$t=1,\ldots,T;T\geq 3,$$

where y_{i0} is assumed to be observed, although the model is not specified in the initial period. When $T=3$, inference on γ is based on the observation that $P(y_{i0}=d_0, y_{i1}=0,\ y_{i2}=1,\ y_{i3}=d_3 \mid y_{i1}+y_{i2}=1,\alpha_i)$ is independent of α_i. (Here $d_0, d_3 \in \{0,1\}$.)

In this paper, we consider identification and estimation in panel data discrete choice models when the explanatory variable set includes strictly exogenous variables, lags of the endogenous dependent variable, as well as unobservable individual-specific effects that may be correlated with the observed covariates in an unspecified way. For the binary logit model with the dependent variable lagged only once, Chamberlain (1993) has shown that, if individuals are observed in three time periods, then the parameters of the model are not identified. In this paper, we demonstrate that β and γ are both identified (subject to regularity conditions) if the econometrician has access to four or more observations per individual. The identification result suggests estimators of the model. We show that these are consistent and asymptotically normal, although their rate of convergence is not the inverse of the square root of the sample size. This result is in line with recent findings by Hahn (1997) that suggest that it may not be possible to estimate the model at the standard $n^{-1/2}$ rate.

We also consider identification in the semiparametric case where the logit assumption is relaxed. We propose an estimator in the spirit of Manski's (1987) conditional maximum score estimator. For this estimator, we only show consistency. The results by Kim and Pollard (1990) suggest that the estimator will not have a limiting normal distribution and that its rate of convergence will be slower than $n^{-1/3}$.

The paper is organized as follows. Section 2 presents our identification and estimation methods for the case where the panel contains only four observations per individual. Section 3 states the assumptions and derives the asymptotic properties for the estimators proposed in Section 2. Section 4 discusses generalizations and extensions of the estimators to the case of longer panels, to the case where the dependent variable is lagged twice, and to the multinomial choice case. Section 5 presents the results of a small Monte Carlo study investigating the small sample properties of the estimators proposed in Section 2. Section 6 concludes the paper. The proofs of the theorems are in the Appendix.

2. IDENTIFICATION AND MOTIVATION OF THE ESTIMATORS

2.1. *The Logit Case*

We consider the following fixed effects logit model which combines the features of (1) and (2):

$$P(y_{i0}=1\mid x_i,\alpha_i)=p_0(x_i,\alpha_i),$$

$$(3)\qquad P(y_{it}=1\mid x_i,\alpha_i,y_{i0},\dots,y_{it-1})=\frac{\exp(x_{it}\beta+\gamma y_{it-1}+\alpha_i)}{1+\exp(x_{it}\beta+\gamma y_{it-1}+\alpha_i)}$$

$$(t=1,\dots,T),$$

where $x_i\equiv(x_{i1},\dots,x_{iT})$. Throughout this section $T=3$. Here, the logit specification is imposed for periods one to three. The model is left unspecified in the initial period, since the value of the dependent variable is not assumed to be known in periods prior to the sample. We assume that y_{i0} is observed, but it is not necessary to assume that the explanatory variables are observed in the initial period. It is important to note the implicit assumption that the errors in a threshold-crossing model leading to (3) are i.i.d. over time with logistic distributions and independent of (x_i,α_i,y_{i0}) in all time periods. While the independence over time assumption is fairly standard (it is also implicitly assumed in (1) and (2)), it is certainly a weakness of the approach taken here (as well as those taken to derive (1) and (2)).

Our identification scheme follows the intuition of the conditional logit approach.[3] The aim is to derive a set of probabilities that do not depend on the individual effect. Following Chamberlain (1985), we consider the events:

$$A=\{y_{i0}=d_0,y_{i1}=0,y_{i2}=1,y_{i3}=d_3\},$$

$$B=\{y_{i0}=d_0,y_{i1}=1,y_{i2}=0,y_{i3}=d_3\},$$

where d_0 and d_3 are either 0 or 1. A straightforward calculation yields:

$$P(A\mid x_i,\alpha_i)=p_0(x_i,\alpha_i)^{d_0}(1-p_0(x_i,\alpha_i))^{1-d_0}$$
$$\times\frac{1}{1+\exp(x_{i1}\beta+\gamma d_0+\alpha_i)}$$
$$\times\frac{\exp(x_{i2}\beta+\alpha_i)}{1+\exp(x_{i2}\beta+\alpha_i)}\times\frac{\exp(d_3x_{i3}\beta+d_3\gamma+d_3\alpha_i)}{1+\exp(x_{i3}\beta+\gamma+\alpha_i)}$$

[3] Jones and Landwehr (1988) attempt to use the conditional logit approach to estimate the model considered in this paper. However, their calculation does not allow for exogenous explanatory variables.

and

$$P(B \mid x_i, \alpha_i) = p_0(x_i, \alpha_i)^{d_0}(1 - p_0(x_i, \alpha_i))^{1-d_0}$$
$$\times \frac{\exp(x_{i1}\beta + \gamma d_0 + \alpha_i)}{1 + \exp(x_{i1}\beta + \gamma d_0 + \alpha_i)}$$
$$\times \frac{1}{1 + \exp(x_{i2}\beta + \alpha_i + \gamma)} \times \frac{\exp(d_3 x_{i3}\beta + d_3\alpha_i)}{1 + \exp(x_{i3}\beta + \alpha_i)}.$$

In general, the probabilities $P(A \mid x_i, \alpha_i, A \cup B)$ and $P(B \mid x_i, \alpha_i, A \cup B)$, which are conditional on the event that the dependent variable changes sign between periods one and two, will depend on α_i. This is the reason why a conditional likelihood approach will not eliminate the fixed effect. Our identification scheme rests on the observation that, if $x_{i2} = x_{i3}$, then the conditional probabilities

$$P(A \mid x_i, \alpha_i, A \cup B, x_{i2} = x_{i3}) = \frac{1}{1 + \exp((x_{i1} - x_{i2})\beta + \gamma(d_0 - d_3))} \tag{4}$$

and

$$P(B \mid x_i, \alpha_i, A \cup B, x_{i2} = x_{i3}) = \frac{\exp((x_{i1} - x_{i2})\beta + \gamma(d_0 - d_3))}{1 + \exp((x_{i1} - x_{i2})\beta + \gamma(d_0 - d_3))} \tag{5}$$

do *not* depend on α_i. This observation is the key to all the results presented in this paper. In the special case where all the explanatory variables are discrete and the x_{it} process satisfies $P(x_{i2} = x_{i3}) > 0$, one can use (4) and (5) to make inference about β and γ. In particular, one may estimate β and γ by maximizing the weighted likelihood function:

$$\sum_{i=1}^{n} 1\{y_{i1} + y_{i2} = 1\} 1\{x_{i2} - x_{i3} = 0\}$$
$$\times \ln\left(\frac{\exp((x_{i1} - x_{i2})b + g(y_{i0} - y_{i3}))^{y_{i1}}}{1 + \exp((x_{i1} - x_{i2})b + g(y_{i0} - y_{i3}))}\right).$$

The resulting estimator will have all the usual properties (consistency and root-n asymptotic normality under standard assumptions).

While inference based only on observations for which $x_{i2} = x_{i3}$ may be reasonable in some cases (in particular, experimental cases where the distribution of x_i is in the control of the researcher), there are many economic applications where it is not useful. The idea then is to replace the indicator functions $1\{x_{i2} - x_{i3} = 0\}$ in the objective function above with weights that depend inversely on the magnitude of the difference $x_{i2} - x_{i3}$, giving more weight to observations for which x_{i2} is "close" to x_{i3}. Specifically, we propose estimating β and γ by maximizing

$$\sum_{i=1}^{n} 1\{y_{i1}+y_{i2}=1\}K\left(\frac{x_{i2}-x_{i3}}{\sigma_n}\right) \times \ln\left(\frac{\exp((x_{i1}-x_{i2})b+g(y_{i0}-y_{i3}))^{y_{i1}}}{1+\exp((x_{i1}-x_{i2})b+g(y_{i0}-y_{i3}))}\right) \tag{6}$$

with respect to b and g over some compact set. Here $K(\cdot)$ is a kernel density function that gives appropriate weight to observation i, while σ_n is a bandwidth that shrinks as n increases. The asymptotic theory will require that $K(\cdot)$ be chosen so that a number of regularity conditions, such as $K(\nu)\to 0$ as $\|\nu\|\to\infty$, are satisfied.

Note that the proposed estimators are maximum-likelihood-type (or extremum or M-) estimators. The key idea behind the estimation is that the limit of the objective function above (as well as of the objective function in the semiparametric case, discussed below), is uniquely maximized at the true parameter values, under appropriate assumptions. It is clear that identification of the model will require that $x_{i2}-x_{i3}$ be continuously distributed with support in a neighborhood of 0, and that $x_{i1}-x_{i2}$ have sufficient variation conditional on the event that $x_{i2}-x_{i3}=0$.

The asymptotic properties of the estimators may be derived in a manner similar to that underlying local likelihood estimation (see, for example, Staniswalis (1989), and Tibshirani and Hastie (1987)) and robust regression function estimation (see, for example, Härdle (1984), Robinson (1984), and Härdle and Tsybakov (1988)). Section 3 states conditions under which the estimators maximizing (6) are consistent and asymptotically normal, although their rate of convergence will be slower than $n^{-1/2}$ and will depend on the number of continuous covariates in x_{it}.

2.2. *The Semiparametric Case*

In this section, we will use Manski's (1987) insight to relax the logit assumption on the distribution of the time-varying errors underlying a threshold-crossing specification of the model in (3). The independence over time assumption of the previous section will be maintained. Suppose[4] that

$$\begin{aligned} &P(y_{i0}=1\,|\,x_i,\alpha_i)=p_0(x_i,\alpha_i),\\ &P(y_{it}=1\,|\,x_i,\alpha_i,y_{i0},\dots,y_{it-1})=F(x_{it}\beta+\gamma y_{it-1}+\alpha_i) \quad (t=1,\dots,T), \end{aligned} \tag{7}$$

[4] It is possible to generalize the results in the remainder of this section to allow the distribution function, F, to differ across individuals, provided that it does not differ over time for a given individual.

where y_{i0} is assumed to be observed and F is a strictly increasing function that has full support on $\Re$. As before, we will focus on the case where there are four observations per individual, i.e. $T = 3$. With A and B defined as in the previous section, we have:

$$\begin{aligned}
&P(A \mid x_i, \alpha_i, x_{i2} = x_{i3}) \\
&\quad = p_0(x_i, \alpha_i)^{d_0}(1 - p_0(x_i, \alpha_i))^{1-d_0} \times (1 - F(x_{i1}\beta + \gamma d_0 + \alpha_i)) \\
&\qquad \times F(x_{i2}\beta + \alpha_i) \times (1 - F(x_{i2}\beta + \gamma + \alpha_i))^{(1-d_3)} \\
&\qquad \times F(x_{i2}\beta + \gamma + \alpha_i)^{d_3}
\end{aligned}$$

and

$$\begin{aligned}
&P(B \mid x_i, \alpha_i, x_{i2} = x_{i3}) \\
&\quad = p_0(x_i, \alpha_i)^{d_0}(1 - p_0(x_i, \alpha_i))^{1-d_0} \times F(x_{i1}\beta + \gamma d_0 + \alpha_i) \\
&\qquad \times (1 - F(x_{i2}\beta + \gamma + \alpha_i)) \times (1 - F(x_{i2}\beta + \alpha_i))^{(1-d_3)} \\
&\qquad \times F(x_{i2}\beta + \alpha_i)^{d_3}.
\end{aligned}$$

If $d_3 = 0$, then

$$\begin{aligned}
&\frac{P(A \mid x_i, \alpha_i, x_{i2} = x_{i3})}{P(B \mid x_i, \alpha_i, x_{i2} = x_{i3})} \\
&\quad = \frac{(1 - F(x_{i1}\beta + \gamma d_0 + \alpha_i))}{(1 - F(x_{i2}\beta + \alpha_i))} \times \frac{F(x_{i2}\beta + \alpha_i)}{F(x_{i1}\beta + \gamma d_0 + \alpha_i)} \\
&\quad = \frac{(1 - F(x_{i1}\beta + \gamma d_0 + \alpha_i))}{(1 - F(x_{i2}\beta + \gamma d_3 + \alpha_i))} \times \frac{F(x_{i2}\beta + \gamma d_3 + \alpha_i)}{F(x_{i1}\beta + \gamma d_0 + \alpha_i)}
\end{aligned}$$

where the second equality follows from the fact that d_3 is zero. If $d_3 = 1$, then

$$\begin{aligned}
&\frac{P(A \mid x_i, \alpha_i, x_{i2} = x_{i3})}{P(B \mid x_i, \alpha_i, x_{i2} = x_{i3})} \\
&\quad = \frac{(1 - F(x_{i1}\beta + \gamma d_0 + \alpha_i))}{(1 - F(x_{i2}\beta + \gamma + \alpha_i))} \times \frac{F(x_{i2}\beta + \gamma + \alpha_i)}{F(x_{i1}\beta + \gamma d_0 + \alpha_i)} \\
&\quad = \frac{(1 - F(x_{i1}\beta + \gamma d_0 + \alpha_i))}{(1 - F(x_{i2}\beta + \gamma d_3 + \alpha_i))} \times \frac{F(x_{i2}\beta + \gamma d_3 + \alpha_i)}{F(x_{i1}\beta + \gamma d_0 + \alpha_i)}
\end{aligned}$$

where the second equality follows from the fact that $d_3 = 1$, so that $\gamma d_3 = \gamma$. In either case, the monotonicity of F implies that

$$\text{(8)} \qquad \operatorname{sgn}(P(A \mid x_i, \alpha_i, x_{i2} = x_{i3}) - P(B \mid x_i, \alpha_i, x_{i2} = x_{i3})) = \operatorname{sgn}((x_{i2} - x_{i1})\beta + \gamma(d_3 - d_0)).$$

If $P(x_{i2} = x_{i3}) > 0$, a maximum score estimator may therefore be applied to the observations satisfying $A \cup B$ and $x_{i2} = x_{i3}$. That is, β and γ may be estimated by maximizing

$$\sum_{i=1}^{n} 1\{x_{i2} - x_{i3} = 0\}(y_{i2} - y_{i1})\operatorname{sgn}((x_{i2} - x_{i1})b + g(y_{i3} - y_{i0}))$$

with respect to b and g over some compact set. It is obvious from the expression above that only observations that satisfy $y_{i1} + y_{i2} = 1$ are used in the estimation.

Similar to the logistic case, when $x_{i2} - x_{i3}$ is continuously distributed with support in a neighborhood of 0, we propose to estimate β and γ (up to scale) by maximizing the score function

$$\text{(9)} \qquad \sum_{i=1}^{n} K\left(\frac{x_{i2} - x_{i3}}{\sigma_n}\right)(y_{i2} - y_{i1})\operatorname{sgn}((x_{i2} - x_{i1})b + g(y_{i3} - y_{i0}))$$

with respect to b and g over some compact set. In Section 3, we show consistency of this estimator. We do not derive its asymptotic distribution, but in view of existing results on the maximum score estimator for the cross-sectional binary response model, we expect the limiting distribution to be nonnormal and the rate of convergence to be slower than $n^{-1/3}$.

In both the logistic and the semiparametric case, the main limitations of our approach are (i) the assumption that the errors in the underlying threshold-crossing model are independent over time, and (ii) the assumption that $x_{i2} - x_{i3}$ has support in a neighborhood of 0. The latter restriction rules out time dummies. In the analysis above we have assumed that all explanatory variables are continuous. The estimators may be modified in a straightforward manner to account for discreteness of some variables in x_{it}, namely multiply the objective functions (6) and (9) by indicators that restrict the discrete regressors to be equal in periods 2 and 3.

3. ASYMPTOTIC PROPERTIES OF ESTIMATORS

In this section, we discuss the asymptotic properties of the estimators proposed in the previous section. The following notation will be useful:

$$\theta = (b', g')', \qquad \theta_0 = (\beta', \gamma')',$$

$$x_{23} = x_2 - x_3, \qquad x_{12} = x_1 - x_2, \qquad x_{21} = x_2 - x_1,$$

$$y_{03} = y_0 - y_3, \qquad y_{30} = y_3 - y_0, \qquad \text{and} \qquad y_{21} = y_2 - y_1.$$

3.1. *The Logit Case*

We first consider the estimator defined by maximizing (6). It will be useful to define the (random) functions:

$$h(\theta) = 1\{y_1 \neq y_2\}\ln\left(\frac{\exp(z\theta)^{y_1}}{1+\exp(z\theta)}\right),$$

$$h^{(1)}(\theta) = \frac{\partial h}{\partial \theta} = 1\{y_1 \neq y_2\}\left(y_1 - \frac{\exp(z\theta)}{1+\exp(z\theta)}\right)z',$$

$$h^{(2)}(\theta) = \frac{\partial^2 h}{\partial\theta\,\partial\theta'} = -1\{y_1 \neq y_2\}\frac{\exp(z\theta)}{(1+\exp(z\theta))^2}z'z,$$

where $z \equiv (x_{12}, y_{03})$. The following theorem gives sufficient conditions for consistency of the estimator proposed in (6). For simplicity, we will focus on the case where all the exogenous variables are continuously distributed.

THEOREM 1 (Consistency): *Let the following assumptions hold*:

(C1) $\{(y_{i0}, y_{i1}, y_{i2}, y_{i3}, x_{i1}, x_{i2}, x_{i3})\}_{i=1}^{n}$ *is a random sample of n observations from a distribution satisfying* (3).

(C2) $\theta_0 \in \Theta$, *a compact subset of* $\Re^{k+1}$.

(C3) *The random vector* $x_{23} \in X \subseteq \Re^k$ *is absolutely continuously distributed with density* $f(\cdot)$ *that is bounded from above on its support, and strictly positive and continuous in a neighborhood of zero.*

(C4) *The function* $E[\|x_{12}\|^2 \mid x_{23} = \cdot]$ *is bounded on its support.*

(C5) *The function* $E[h(\theta) \mid x_{23} = \cdot]$ *is continuous in a neighborhood of zero for all* $\theta \in \Theta$.

(C6) *The function* $E[x_{12}' x_{12} \mid x_{23} = \cdot]$ *has full column rank k in a neighborhood of zero.*

(C7) K: $\Re^k \to \Re$ *is a function of bounded variation that satisfies*: (i) $\sup_{\nu \in \Re}|K(\nu)| < \infty$, (ii) $\int|K(\nu)|\,d\nu < \infty$, *and* (iii) $\int K(\nu)\,d\nu = 1$.

(C8) σ_n *is a sequence of positive numbers that satisfies*: $\sigma_n \to 0$ *as* $n \to \infty$.

Let $\hat{\theta}_n \equiv (\hat{\beta}_n, \hat{\gamma}_n)$ *be a sequence of solutions to the problem*

$$\max_{\theta \in \Theta} \sum_i K\left(\frac{x_{i23}}{\sigma_n}\right)h_i(\theta). \qquad (10)$$

Then, $\hat{\theta}_n \xrightarrow{p} \theta_0$.

Assumptions (C7) and (C8) are standard in kernel density and regression function estimation. The strict positiveness of f and the full rank condition of Assumption (C6) are required for identification of θ_0. The rest of the assumptions are regularity conditions that permit the application of a uniform law of large numbers to show convergence of the objective function to a nonstochastic limit that is uniquely maximized at θ_0. Note that, in some cases, the boundedness condition of Assumption (C4) may be restrictive. However, it is clear from the proof of the theorem that it may be relaxed. In particular, we only need to assume that the product $f(\cdot)E[\|x_{12}\| \,|\, x_{23} = \cdot]$ is bounded on its support. The same comment applies to similar conditions in the theorems that follow. Finally, the compactness of the parameter space (Assumption (C2)) may also be relaxed if $K(\cdot) > 0$, in which case the object function is strictly concave (see, e.g., Newey and Powell (1987)).

We next present conditions that are sufficient for asymptotic normality of the proposed estimators. Apart from the usual strengthening of regularity conditions on the existence and finiteness of moments higher than those required for consistency, additional smoothness is imposed on the model that allows convergence at a faster rate.

THEOREM 2 (Asymptotic Normality): *Let Assumptions* (C1)–(C8) *hold and* $\hat{\theta}_n$ *be a solution to* (10). *In addition assume*:

(N1) $\theta_0 \in \operatorname{int}(\Theta)$.

(N2) $f(\cdot)$ *is* s $(s \geq 1)$ *times continuously differentiable on its support and has bounded derivatives*.

(N3) *The function* $E[h^{(1)}(\theta_0) \,|\, x_{23} = \cdot]$ *is* s *times continuously differentiable on its support and has bounded derivatives*.

(N4) *The function* $E[h^{(2)}(\theta) \,|\, x_{23} = \cdot]$ *is continuous in a neighborhood of zero for all* $\theta \in \Theta$.

(N5) *The function* $E[\|x_{12}\|^6 \,|\, x_{23} = \cdot]$ *is bounded on its support*.

(N6) *The function* $E[h^{(1)}(\theta_0)h^{(1)}(\theta_0)' \,|\, x_{23} = \cdot]$ *is continuous in a neighborhood of zero*.

(N7) $K\colon \Re^k \to \Re$ *is an s'th order bias-reducing kernel that satisfies*:

(i)

$$\int |\nu|^i |K(\nu)| \, d\nu < \infty, \qquad \text{for } i = 0 \text{ and } i = s, \text{ where } s \geq 1,$$

(ii)

$$\int \nu_1^{i_1} \nu_2^{i_2} \cdots \nu_k^{i_k} K(\nu_1, \nu_2, \ldots, \nu_k) \, d\nu_1 \, d\nu_2 \ldots d\nu_k$$

$$= \begin{cases} 1 & \text{if } i_1 = i_2 = \cdots = i_k = 0, \\ 0 & \text{if } 0 < i_1 + i_2 + \cdots + i_k < s. \end{cases}$$

Let $\sqrt{n\sigma_n^k}\,\sigma_n^s \to 0$. *Then*

$$\sqrt{n\sigma_n^k}\left(\hat{\theta}_n - \theta_0\right) \tilde{\to} N(0, J^{-1}VJ^{-1})$$

where

$$J \equiv J(\theta_0) \equiv -f(0)\cdot E\left[h^{(2)}(\theta_0) \mid x_{23}=0\right],$$

$$V \equiv V(\theta_0) \equiv f(0)\cdot E\left[h^{(1)}(\theta_0)h^{(1)}(\theta_0)' \mid x_{23}=0\right]\cdot \int K^2(\nu)\,d\nu.$$

REMARK: Note that the rate of convergence of the proposed estimator is maximized for $\sqrt{n\sigma_n^k}\,\sigma_n^s \to \sigma \neq 0$. However, in this case the estimator is asymptotically biased. It may be easily shown that in this case, $\sqrt{n\sigma_n^k}(\hat{\theta}_n - \theta_0) \overset{\sim}{\to} N(\sigma J^{-1}B, J^{-1}VJ^{-1})$, where B is a function of the s'th order derivative of $f(\cdot)\times E[h^{(1)}(\theta_0) \mid x_{23}=\cdot]$. Although it is possible to eliminate the asymptotic bias in the manner suggested, for example, by Horowitz (1992), we have found that the asymptotic bias correction is not effective in reducing the small sample bias in our Monte Carlo experiments.

The next theorem provides consistent estimators of the two components of the asymptotic variance-covariance matrix.

THEOREM 3 (Asymptotic Variance Estimation): *Let Assumptions* (C1)–(C8) *and* (N1)–(N7) *hold and* $\hat{\theta}_n$ *be a consistent estimator of* θ_0.

(i) *Define*

$$J_n(\theta) \equiv -\frac{1}{n\sigma_n^k}\sum_i K\left(\frac{x_{i23}}{\sigma_n}\right)h_i^{(2)}(\theta).$$

Then, $J_n(\hat{\theta}_n) \overset{p}{\to} J(\theta_0)$, *where* $J(\theta_0)$ *is defined in Theorem* 2.

(ii) *Define*

$$V_n(\theta) \equiv \frac{1}{n\sigma_n^k}\sum_i K^2\left(\frac{x_{i23}}{\sigma_n}\right)h_i^{(1)}(\theta)h_i^{(1)}(\theta)'.$$

If $E[h^{(1)}(\theta)h^{(1)}(\theta)' \mid x_{23}=\cdot]$ *is continuous in a neighborhood of zero as a function of* x_{23} *for all* $\theta \in \Theta$, *then* $V_n(\hat{\theta}_n) \overset{p}{\to} V(\theta_0)$, *where* $V(\theta_0)$ *is defined in Theorem* 2.

3.2. *The Semiparametric Case*

In this section, we present conditions that are sufficient to identify and consistently estimate θ_0 when the logit assumption on the distribution of the underlying time-varying errors is relaxed. We define the function

$$h(\theta) = y_{21}\,\mathrm{sgn}(z\theta)$$

where now $z \equiv (x_{21}, y_{30})$.

THEOREM 4 (Identification and Consistency): *Let the following conditions hold*:

(CS1) $\{(y_{i0}, y_{i1}, y_{i2}, y_{i3}, x_{i1}, x_{i2}, x_{i3})\}_{i=1}^{n}$ *is a random sample of n observations from a distribution satisfying* (7).

(CS2) *F is strictly increasing on* $\Re$ *for almost all* (x_i, α_i).

(CS3) *There exists at least one* $\kappa \in \{1, \ldots, k\}$, *such that* $\beta_\kappa \neq 0$, *and such that, for almost all* $\tilde{x}_{21} \equiv (x_{21,1}, \ldots, x_{21,\kappa-1}, x_{21,\kappa+1}, \ldots, x_{21,k})$, *the random variable* $x_{21,\kappa}$ *has everywhere positive Lebesgue density conditional on* $\tilde{x}_{21}$ *and conditional on* x_{23} *in a neighborhood of* x_{23} *near zero.*

(CS4) *The support of* x_{12} *conditional on* x_{23} *in a neighborhood of* x_{23} *near zero is not contained in any proper linear subspace of* $\Re^k$.

(CS5) *The random vector* $x_{23} \in X \subseteq \Re^k$ *is absolutely continuously distributed with density* $f(\cdot)$ *that is bounded from above on its support and strictly positive in a neighborhood of zero.*

(CS6) *For all* $\theta \in \Theta$, $f(\cdot)$ *and* $E[h(\theta)\,|\,x_{23} = \cdot]$ *are continuously differentiable on their support with bounded first-order derivatives.*

(CS7) K: $\Re^k \to \Re$ *is a function of bounded variation that satisfies*: (i) $\sup_{\nu \in \Re}|K(\nu)| < \infty$, (ii) $\int |K(\nu)|\,d\nu < \infty$, *and* (iii) $\int K(\nu)\,d\nu = 1$.

(CS8) σ_n *is a sequence of positive numbers that satisfies*: (i) $\sigma_n \to 0$ *as* $n \to \infty$, *and* (ii) $n\sigma_n^k/\ln n \to \infty$ *as* $n \to \infty$.

Then:

(i) θ_0 *is identified* (*up to scale*) *relative to all* $\theta \in \Re^{k+1}$ *such that* $\theta/\|\theta\| \neq \theta_0/\|\theta_0\| \equiv \theta_0^*$.

(ii) *Let* $\hat{\theta}_n \equiv (\hat{\beta}_n, \hat{\gamma}_n)$ *be a sequence of solutions to the problem*

$$\max_{\theta \in \Theta} \sum_i K\left(\frac{x_{i23}}{\sigma_n}\right) h_i(\theta) \tag{11}$$

where $\Theta \equiv \{\theta \in \Re^{k+1}: \|\theta\| = 1 \cap |b_\kappa| \geq \eta\}$ *and* η *is a known positive constant such that* $|\beta_\kappa|/\|\theta_0\| \geq \eta$. *Then*, $\hat{\theta}_n \xrightarrow{p} \theta_0^*$.

Assumptions (CS1)–(CS4) are analogous to Manski's (1987) Assumptions 1 and 2. The rest of the assumptions of the theorem are similar to the assumptions in the logit case. Here, however, we strengthen the continuity assumption on $f(\cdot)$ and $E[h(\theta)\,|\,x_{23} = \cdot]$ to first order differentiability, in order to show uniform convergence of the objective function to its population analog. This is a consequence of the fact that, in the semiparametric case, the summands in the objective function are not continuous in the parameter, although they are uniformly bounded.

4. EXTENSIONS

4.1. *Identification with More than Four Observations per Individual*

The identification and estimation approach described in Section 2 extends to the case of longer panels. Note that in the case where $T = 4$, the idea behind the identification for the logit model (3) follows Chamberlain's (1985) intuition, namely that conditional on a switch between periods 1 and 2 (and in our case, conditional also on $x_{i2} = x_{i3}$), the probability of a sequence of choices (a "string") does not depend on the individual effect. For general T, identification in the dynamic logit model (2), which has only one lag of the dependent variable and no other explanatory variables, relies on the fact that conditional on the initial and the last observation, and conditional on $\Sigma_t y_{it}$, the probability of a string is independent of the individual effect. To investigate whether the same intuition holds in the general T case for the model that also contains exogenous variables, we consider $T = 4$. In this case, it is possible to show that the same statement holds, namely that conditional on the initial and the last observation, and conditional on $\Sigma_t y_{it}$, the probability of a string is independent of the individual effect, provided that we also condition on $x_{i2} = x_{i3} = x_{i4}$. This implies that the rate of convergence would be $\sqrt{n\sigma_n^{2k}}$, i.e. slower than the rate we obtain for $T = 3$. However, as will become clear below, it is possible to retain the same rate of convergence as in the $T = 3$ case, namely $\sqrt{n\sigma_n^{k}}$, if we instead use a pairwise approach that is based on considering all possible pairs of observations in a string that display a switch in the sign of the dependent variable.

Suppose that individuals are observed for $T + 1$ periods, where $T \geq 3$. In either the logistic or the semiparametric case, identification is based on sequences for which $y_{it} + y_{is} = 1$ for some $1 \leq t < s \leq T - 1$. Consider the event

$$A = \{y_{i0} = d_0, \ldots, y_{it-1} = d_{t-1}, y_{it} = 0, y_{it+1} = d_{t+1}, \ldots, y_{is-1} = d_{s-1}, y_{is} = 1, y_{is+1} = d_{s+1}, \ldots, y_{iT} = d_T\}$$

and its counterpart,

$$B = \{y_{i0} = d_0, \ldots, y_{it-1} = d_{t-1}, y_{it} = 1, y_{it+1} = d_{t+1}, \ldots, y_{is-1} = d_{s-1}, y_{is} = 0, y_{is+1} = d_{s+1}, \ldots, y_{iT} = d_T\}.$$

It is not difficult to show that for the logit model (3),

$$\Pr(B \mid x_i, \alpha_i, A \cup B, x_{it+1} = x_{is+1}) = \frac{\exp((x_{it} - x_{is})\beta + \gamma(d_{t-1} - d_{s+1}) + (d_{t+1} - d_{s-1})1\{s - t > 1\})}{1 + \exp((x_{it} - x_{is})\beta + \gamma(d_{t-1} - d_{s+1}) + \gamma(d_{t+1} - d_{s-1})1\{s - t > 1\})}$$

which does *not* depend on α_i. This suggests estimating β and γ by maximizing

$$\sum_{i=1}^{n} \sum_{1 \leq t < s \leq T-1} 1\{y_{it} + y_{is} = 1\} K\left(\frac{x_{it+1} - x_{is+1}}{\sigma_n}\right) \times \ln\left(\frac{\exp((x_{it} - x_{is})b + g(y_{it-1} - y_{is+1}) + g(y_{it+1} - y_{is-1})1\{s - t > 1\})^{y_{it}}}{1 + \exp((x_{it} - x_{is})b + g(y_{it-1} - y_{is+1}) + g(y_{it+1} - y_{is-1})1\{s - t > 1\})}\right).$$

For the semiparametric model (7), we consider two cases depending on whether periods t and s are adjacent or not. For $s = t + 1$, it is easily verified that whether $d_{t+2}=0$ or $d_{t+2}=1$,

$$\frac{\Pr(A\,|\,x_i,\alpha_i,x_{it+1}=x_{it+2})}{\Pr(B\,|\,x_i,\alpha_i,x_{it+1}=x_{it+2})} = \frac{1-F(x_{it}\beta+\alpha_i+\gamma d_{t-1})}{1-F(x_{it+1}\beta+\alpha_i+\gamma d_{t+2})}\,\frac{F(x_{it+1}\beta+\alpha_i+\gamma d_{t+2})}{F(x_{it}\beta+\alpha_i+\gamma d_{t-1})}$$

and therefore,

$$\operatorname{sgn}\{\Pr(A\,|\,x_i,\alpha_i,x_{it+1}=x_{it+2})-\Pr(B\,|\,x_i,\alpha_i,x_{it+1}=x_{it+2})\} = \operatorname{sgn}\{(x_{it+1}-x_{it})\beta+\gamma(d_{t+2}-d_{t-1})\}.$$

If t and s are not adjacent (so that $s>t+1$), then

$$\frac{\Pr(A\,|\,x_i,\alpha_i,x_{it+1}=x_{is+1},y_{it+1}=y_{is+1})}{\Pr(B\,|\,x_i,\alpha_i,x_{it+1}=x_{is+1},y_{it+1}=y_{is+1})} = \frac{1-F(x_{it}\beta+\alpha_i+\gamma d_{t-1})}{1-F(x_{is}\beta+\alpha_i+\gamma d_{s-1})}\,\frac{F(x_{is}\beta+\alpha_i+\gamma d_{s-1})}{F(x_{it}\beta+\alpha_i+\gamma d_{t-1})},$$

which implies that

$$\begin{aligned}\operatorname{sgn}\{&\Pr(A\,|\,x_i,\alpha_i,x_{it+1}=x_{is+1},y_{it+1}=y_{is+1})\\ &-\Pr(B\,|\,x_i,\alpha_i,x_{it+1}=x_{is+1},y_{it+1}=y_{is+1})\}\\ &=\operatorname{sgn}\{(x_{is}-x_{it})\beta+\gamma(d_{s-1}-d_{t-1})\}.\end{aligned}$$

This suggests estimating β and γ by maximizing:

$$\begin{aligned}\sum_{i=1}^{n}\Bigg(&\sum_{t=1}^{T-3}1\{y_{it}+y_{it+1}=1\}K\left(\frac{x_{it+1}-x_{it+2}}{\sigma_n}\right)\operatorname{sgn}(y_{it+1}-y_{it})\\ &\times\operatorname{sgn}((x_{it+1}-x_{it})b+g(y_{it+2}-y_{it-1}))\\ &+\sum_{t=1}^{T-2}\sum_{s=t+2}^{T-1}1\{y_{it}+y_{is}=1\}1\{y_{it+1}=y_{is+1}\}\\ &\times K\left(\frac{x_{it+1}-x_{is+1}}{\sigma_n}\right)\operatorname{sgn}(y_{is}-y_{it})\\ &\times\operatorname{sgn}((x_{is}-x_{it})b+g(y_{is-1}-y_{it-1}))\Bigg).\end{aligned}$$

It is interesting that although in general time dummies are ruled out in either the logistic or the semi-parametric case, it is possible to allow for seasonal effects in the case of quarterly data and at least seven observations per individual (i.e. $T=6$).

4.2. *Identification with More than One Lag of the Dependent Variable*

As noted by Chamberlain (1985), for the logit model without exogenous regressors, it is possible to test for the presence of the endogenous dependent variable lagged twice, when there are at least six observations per individual.[5] The same is true in the presence of exogenous variables for the model

$$P(y_{i0}=1\mid x_i,\alpha_i)=p_0(x_i,\alpha_i),$$

$$P(y_{i1}=1\mid x_i,\alpha_i,y_{i0})=p_1(x_i,\alpha_i,y_{i0}),$$

$$P(y_{it}=1\mid x_i,\alpha_i,y_{i0},\dots,y_{it-1})$$

$$=\frac{\exp(x_{it}\beta+\gamma_1 y_{it-1}+\gamma_2 y_{it-2}+\alpha_i)}{1+\exp(x_{it}\beta+\gamma_1 y_{it-1}+\gamma_2 y_{it-2}+\alpha_i)}\qquad (t=2,\dots,T;T\geq 5),$$

where $x_i\equiv(x_{i2},\dots,x_{iT})$. It is assumed that (y_{i0},y_{i1}) is observed although the model is not specified for these time periods. For $T=5$, inference on β and γ_2 can be based on pairs of sequences (strings) that satisfy $\{x_{i3}=x_{i4}=x_{i5},y_{i2}+y_{i3}=1\}$ and either $\{y_{i0}\neq y_{i1},y_{i1}=y_{i4}=y_{i5}\}$ or $\{y_{i4}\neq y_{i5},y_{i0}=y_{i1}=y_{i4}\}$ (there are four such pairs of strings). Consider, for example, the pair $A=(1,0,0,1,0,0)$ and $B=(1,0,1,0,0,0)$. It is straightforward to establish that

$$\Pr(A\mid x_i,\alpha_i,A\cup B,x_{i3}=x_{i4}=x_{i5})=\frac{1}{1+\exp(\gamma_2+(x_{i2}-x_{i3})\beta)}$$

and

$$\Pr(B\mid x_i,\alpha_i,A\cup B,x_{i3}=x_{i4}=x_{i5})=\frac{\exp(\gamma_2+(x_{i2}-x_{i3})\beta)}{1+\exp(\gamma_2+(x_{i2}-x_{i3})\beta)},$$

which does not depend on α_i.

For the semiparametric case, where

$$P(y_{it}=1\mid \alpha_i,x_i,y_{i0},\dots,y_{i,t-1})=F(x_{it}\beta+\gamma_1 y_{i,t-1}+\gamma_2 y_{i,t-2}+\alpha_i)$$
$$(t=2,\dots,T;T\geq 5)$$

and where y_{i0} and y_{i1} are given as above, it is easy to establish that for $T=5$,

$$\frac{\Pr(A\mid x_i,\alpha_i,x_{i3}=x_{i4}=x_{i5})}{\Pr(B\mid x_i,\alpha_i,x_{i3}=x_{i4}=x_{i5})}$$

$$=\frac{F(x_{i2}\beta+\gamma_2+\alpha_i)}{F(x_{i3}\beta+\alpha_i)}\,\frac{1-F(x_{i3}\beta+\alpha_i)}{1-F(x_{i2}\beta+\gamma_2+\alpha_i)}.$$

[5] As noted by Chamberlain, it is possible in the dynamic logit model with two lags of the dependent variable and without exogenous regressors to allow the coefficient of the first lag to be individual-varying. The same observation applies to the model considered in this section, in both the logistic and in the semiparametric case. We are grateful to one of the referees for pointing this out to us.

Thus,

$$\operatorname{sgn}(\Pr(A \mid x_i, \alpha_i, x_{i3} = x_{i4} = x_{i5}) - \Pr(B \mid x_i, \alpha_i, x_{i3} = x_{i4} = x_{i5}))$$
$$= \operatorname{sgn}((x_{i2} - x_{i3})\beta + \gamma_2).$$

The analysis above suggests estimators of β and γ_2 analogous to (6) and (9) provided that $(x_{i3} - x_{i4}, x_{i4} - x_{i5})$ has support in a neighborhood of (0,0). It may be possible to generalize the preceding identification results for general T and for an arbitrary (but finite) number of included lags. Magnac (1997) provides such results for the dynamic logit model when no exogenous covariates are present.

4.3. *Identification in Multinomial Logit Models*

We next consider the case where the individual chooses among M alternatives. The model is

$$\Pr(y_{i0} = m \mid x_i, \alpha_i) = p_{mi0}(x_i, \alpha_i)$$

$$\Pr(y_{it} = m \mid x_i, \alpha_i, y_{it-1} = j) = \frac{\exp(x_{mit}\beta_m + \alpha_{mi} + \gamma_{jm})}{\sum_{h=1}^{M} \exp(x_{hit}\beta_h + \alpha_{hi} + \gamma_{jh})}$$

$$(t = 1, \ldots, T; T \geq 3),$$

where $\alpha_i \equiv \{\alpha_{mi}\}_{m=1}^{M}$ and $x_i \equiv \{\{x_{mit}\}_{m=1}^{M}\}_{t=1}^{T}$. The model above is obtained if we assume that the underlying errors in the well known random utility maximization framework are independent across alternatives and over time conditional on (x_i, α_i, y_{i0}), and identically distributed according to the Type 1 extreme value distribution, and hence independent of (x_i, α_i, y_{i0}). Note that we now model individual heterogeneity as depending also on the choice, i.e. each individual has a specific taste for each alternative, α_{ji}, where $j \in \{1, \ldots, M\}$. Furthermore, the coefficient γ on the lagged endogenous variable is now allowed to depend upon both the past choice and the current choice, so that there are in total M^2 feedback parameters. Thus, γ_{jm} is the feedback effect when a choice of alternative j at $t-1$ is followed by choice m at time t, where $j, m \in \{1, \ldots, M\}$.

For the model above, identification of $\{\beta_m\}_{m=1}^{M}$ and $\{\gamma_{jm}\}_{j,m=1}^{M}$ is based on sequences of choices where the individual switches between alternatives at least once during the periods 1 through $T-1$. Out of all possible M^{T+1} sequences of choices among the M alternatives in the $T+1$ periods, there are $(M^{T+1} - M^3)$ such sequences. However, similar to the dynamic multinomial logit model without time-varying exogenous regressors (see Magnac (1997)), only $(M^2 - (2M-1))$ feedback parameters γ are identified.

Consider the events:

$$A = \{y_{i0} = d_0, \ldots, y_{it-1} = j, y_{it} = m, y_{it+1} = q, \ldots, y_{is-1} = p, y_{is} = l, y_{is+1} = r, \ldots, y_{iT} = d_T\}$$

and

$$B = \{y_{i0} = d_0, \ldots, y_{it-1} = j, y_{it} = l, y_{it+1} = q, \ldots, y_{is-1} = p, y_{is} = m, y_{is+1} = r, \ldots, y_{iT} = d_T\}$$

where $1 \leq t < s \leq T-1$, and $j, m, q, p, l, r, d_0, d_T \in \{1, \ldots, M\}$ with $m \neq l$. It is possible to verify that, if $x_{mit+1} = x_{mis+1}$ for all $m \in \{1, \ldots, M\}$, then

$$\Pr\left(A \mid x_i, \alpha_i, A \cup B, \{x_{mit+1} = x_{mis+1}\}_{m=1}^{M}\right) = \frac{\left(\begin{array}{l}\exp\big((x_{mit} - x_{mis})\beta_m + (x_{lis} - x_{lit})\beta_l \\ \quad + (\gamma_{jm} + \gamma_{ml} + \gamma_{lr}) - (\gamma_{jl} + \gamma_{lm} + \gamma_{mr})\big)\end{array}\right)}{\left(\begin{array}{l}1 + \exp\big((x_{mit} - x_{mis})\beta_m + (x_{lis} - x_{lit})\beta_l \\ \quad + (\gamma_{jm} + \gamma_{ml} + \gamma_{lr}) - (\gamma_{jl} + \gamma_{lm} + \gamma_{mr})\big)\end{array}\right)}$$

if $s - t = 1$, whereas if $s - t > 1$, then

$$\Pr\left(A \mid x_i, \alpha_i, A \cup B, \{x_{mit+1} = x_{mis+1}\}_{m=1}^{M}\right) = \frac{\left(\begin{array}{l}\exp\big((x_{mit} - x_{mis})\beta_m + (x_{lis} - x_{lit})\beta_l \\ \quad + (\gamma_{jm} + \gamma_{mq} + \gamma_{pl} + \gamma_{lr}) - (\gamma_{jl} + \gamma_{lq} + \gamma_{pm} + \gamma_{mr})\big)\end{array}\right)}{\left(\begin{array}{l}1 + \exp\big((x_{mit} - x_{mis})\beta_m + (x_{lis} - x_{lit})\beta_l \\ \quad + (\gamma_{jm} + \gamma_{mq} + \gamma_{pl} + \gamma_{lr}) - (\gamma_{jl} + \gamma_{lq} + \gamma_{pm} + \gamma_{mr})\big)\end{array}\right)}.$$

Defining the binary variables $y_{hit} = 1$ if alternative $h \in \{1, \ldots, M\}$ is chosen in period t and 0 otherwise, estimation may be based on maximization of

$$\sum_{i=1}^{n} \sum_{1 \leq t < s \leq T-1} \sum_{m \neq l} 1\{y_{mit} + y_{lis} = 1\} K\left(\frac{x_{it+1} - x_{is+1}}{\sigma_n}\right) \times 1\{s - t = 1\}$$
$$\times \ln\left(\frac{\exp(D_1)^{y_{mit}}}{1 + \exp(D_1)}\right)$$
$$+ \sum_{i=1}^{n} \sum_{1 \leq t \leq s \leq T-1} \sum_{m \neq l} 1\{y_{mit} + y_{lis} = 1\} K\left(\frac{x_{it+1} - x_{is+1}}{\sigma_n}\right) \times 1\{s - t > 1\}$$
$$\times \ln\left(\frac{\exp(D_2)^{y_{mit}}}{1 + \exp(D_2)}\right)$$

where

$$D_1 = (x_{mit} - x_{mis})b_m + (x_{lis} - x_{lit})b_l + g_{y_{it-1},m} + g_{m,y_{it+1}} + g_{l,y_{is+1}} - g_{y_{it-1},l} - g_{l,y_{it+1}} - g_{m,y_{is+1}}$$

and

$$D_2 = (x_{mit} - x_{mis})b_m + (x_{lis} - x_{lit})b_l + g_{y_{it-1},m} + g_{m,y_{it+1}} + g_{y_{is-1},l} + g_{l,y_{is+1}} - g_{y_{it-1},l} - g_{l,y_{it+1}} - g_{y_{is-1},m} - g_{m,y_{is+1}}.$$

In the objective function above, $x_{it} \equiv (x_{1it}, \ldots, x_{Mit})$ and the necessary $2M-1$ restrictions on the g's have been imposed (for example, $g_{j1} = g_{1j} = 0$ for all $j = 1, \ldots, M$).

5. SOME MONTE CARLO EVIDENCE

In this section, we summarize the main results from a small Monte Carlo experiment designed to illustrate the finite sample properties of the estimators defined in Section 2. All the results presented in this section are based on 1000 replications of the model:

$$y_{i0} = 1\{x_{it}\beta + \alpha_i + \varepsilon_{i0} \geq 0\},$$
$$y_{it} = 1\{x_{it}\beta + \gamma y_{it-1} + \alpha_i + \varepsilon_{it} \geq 0\} \qquad (t = 1, \ldots, T-1).$$

We consider several designs that differ on the length of the panel, the relative magnitudes of β and γ, on the number of variables in x_{it} and on the data generating process for x_{it}. In all designs, ε_{it} is i.i.d. logistically distributed over time. The benchmark design has $T = 4$, $\gamma = 0.5$, $\beta = 1$, and only one exogenous variable x_{it} which is i.i.d. over time with distribution $N(0, \pi^2/3)$. This makes the variance of $x_{it}\beta$ equal to the variance of ε_{it}. The fixed effect is generated as $\alpha_i = (x_{i0} + x_{i1} + x_{i2} + x_{i3})/4$. Recall that the estimators proposed in Section 2 use only the observations for which $y_{i1} \neq y_{i2}$. For this design, the "effective" sample size is reduced to about 37%. We consider sample sizes of 250, 500, 1000, 2000, and 4000.

We first focus on the finite sample performance of the estimator proposed for the logit case, which maximizes (6). Given that the distribution of the underlying errors is correctly specified, this estimator is consistent and asymptotically normal. To implement the estimator, one must choose a kernel as well as a bandwidth. All the results presented in this section use a normal kernel. This means that s in Theorem 2 is equal to 2. Since there is only one regressor in the benchmark design, the rate of convergence is maximized by setting $\sigma_n = c \cdot n^{-1/5}$, for some constant c. However, in this case the estimator is asymptotically biased (see the Remark following Theorem 2). In Table I, we present results for $c = 1$, 2, 4, 8, 16, 32, and 64. For each bandwidth and for each sample size, we present the mean bias and the root mean squared error (RMSE) of the estimator. Since these measures can be sensitive to outliers, we also present the median bias and the median absolute error (MAE) of the estimator. In what follows, we focus on these robust measures of bias and precision.

TABLE I

BENCHMARK DESIGN ($\gamma = 0.5, \beta = 1, x_{it} \sim N(0, \pi^2/3), \alpha_i = \Sigma_{t=0}^3 x_{it}/4$)

		Results for $\hat{\beta}_n$				Results for $\hat{\gamma}_n$			
	Sample Size	Mean Bias	RMSE	Median Bias	MAE	Mean Bias	RMSE	Median Bias	MAE
$\sigma_n = 1 \cdot n^{-1/5}$	250	1.393	5.631	0.284	0.450	0.890	6.642	0.103	1.106
	500	0.421	1.479	0.140	0.296	0.054	1.371	0.017	0.670
	1000	0.148	0.445	0.081	0.207	0.047	0.829	0.029	0.448
	2000	0.065	0.259	0.035	0.147	0.025	0.524	−0.007	0.350
	4000	0.037	0.182	0.017	0.109	0.015	0.405	0.006	0.264
$\sigma_n = 2 \cdot n^{-1/5}$	250	0.323	0.891	0.127	0.269	0.166	1.331	0.059	0.688
	500	0.144	0.431	0.075	0.205	−0.005	0.686	−0.007	0.412
	1000	0.073	0.255	0.044	0.148	0.022	0.506	−0.009	0.327
	2000	0.033	0.175	0.019	0.109	0.003	0.356	−0.007	0.242
	4000	0.019	0.120	0.010	0.079	0.011	0.277	0.013	0.192
$\sigma_n = 4 \cdot n^{-1/5}$	250	0.165	0.423	0.080	0.183	0.036	0.787	0.018	0.487
	500	0.085	0.264	0.049	0.144	−0.019	0.467	−0.013	0.295
	1000	0.049	0.173	0.035	0.108	−0.006	0.351	−0.022	0.221
	2000	0.024	0.123	0.019	0.076	−0.015	0.256	−0.024	0.170
	4000	0.015	0.086	0.010	0.053	−0.003	0.196	0.001	0.134
$\sigma_n = 8 \cdot n^{-1/5}$	250	0.137	0.335	0.076	0.154	−0.015	0.645	−0.039	0.403
	500	0.075	0.207	0.044	0.113	−0.044	0.382	−0.052	0.256
	1000	0.049	0.137	0.038	0.086	−0.038	0.282	−0.035	0.178
	2000	0.032	0.098	0.028	0.063	−0.041	0.207	−0.042	0.143
	4000	0.022	0.069	0.019	0.044	−0.031	0.151	−0.035	0.102
$\sigma_n = 16 \cdot n^{-1/5}$	250	0.138	0.320	0.088	0.152	−0.035	0.611	−0.069	0.367
	500	0.078	0.192	0.051	0.102	−0.063	0.361	−0.070	0.255
	1000	0.058	0.130	0.049	0.077	−0.062	0.264	−0.064	0.168
	2000	0.044	0.092	0.040	0.058	−0.065	0.196	−0.065	0.135
	4000	0.035	0.066	0.031	0.043	−0.058	0.141	−0.059	0.098
$\sigma_n = 32 \cdot n^{-1/5}$	250	0.141	0.320	0.090	0.152	−0.042	0.607	−0.068	0.363
	500	0.081	0.190	0.055	0.102	−0.070	0.359	−0.074	0.244
	1000	0.063	0.130	0.052	0.077	−0.071	0.263	−0.069	0.173
	2000	0.050	0.093	0.046	0.058	−0.075	0.197	−0.069	0.134
	4000	0.043	0.069	0.039	0.046	−0.072	0.144	−0.076	0.100
$\sigma_n = 64 \cdot n^{-1/5}$	250	0.142	0.320	0.092	0.156	−0.043	0.607	−0.072	0.359
	500	0.082	0.190	0.056	0.102	−0.072	0.359	−0.077	0.243
	1000	0.064	0.131	0.054	0.077	−0.074	0.264	−0.071	0.176
	2000	0.051	0.094	0.048	0.058	−0.079	0.199	−0.073	0.134
	4000	0.046	0.071	0.042	0.047	−0.076	0.146	−0.079	0.103

By the Remark following Theorem 2, the estimator converges at rate $n^{-2/5}$. The results in Table I suggest that for this design, the theoretical rate of convergence gives a fairly good approximation to the finite sample behavior of the estimator. For example, when we regress the logarithm of the median absolute error of $\hat{\gamma}_n$ on the logarithm of sample size (and allowing for bandwidth-specific intercept), we get a coefficient of -0.47, which is fairly close to the predicted value of -0.4. If we exclude the samples of size 250, then the coefficient is -0.41.

When $\gamma = 0$ or $\beta = 0$, the estimator defined by minimization of (6) is consistent and root-n asymptotically normal if the bandwidth is fixed, i.e., does not shrink to 0. The reason for this is that, when $\gamma = 0$ or $\beta = 0$, the terms in (6) are the same terms that would enter into a correctly specified conditional likelihood function.[6] It therefore seems likely that the small-sample performance of the estimator depends on the relative magnitudes of γ and β. In particular, if γ is small, one would expect the estimator to perform well even if the bandwidth is large. In order to investigate the sensitivity of our results to the value of γ, we consider designs with γ equal to 0.25, 1.0, and 2.0. For these designs, the effect of the lagged dependent variable on the first order serial correlation of y_{it} ranges from being smaller, to being greater than the effect of the permanent error component.[7] The results for the alternative values of γ are given in Tables II (to conserve space, we present only the results for $\sigma_n = 8 \cdot n^{-1/5}$). Our findings confirm that as γ increases, the bias increases dramatically.[8] Intuitively, we would expect that longer panels would dramatically improve the performance of the estimator for γ. Table II therefore also presents results for $T = 8$. Since the same bandwidth is used for the two sample sizes, it is not surprising that the bias is of approximately the same magnitude, but the median absolute errors do decrease dramatically. Interestingly, the gains seem to be about the same for both $\hat{\beta}$ and $\hat{\gamma}$.

It is difficult to interpret Monte Carlo results like the ones presented here without a comparison to competing estimators. Because there is no other consistent (as $n \to \infty$) estimator for the dynamic panel data logit model considered here, we will compare our estimator to the maximum likelihood estimator that estimates all the fixed effects. This estimator is consistent as $T \to \infty$ with n fixed, which suggests that its behavior will depend crucially on the number of time periods. We therefore report results for $T = 4$, 8, and 16 (to conserve space, we consider only $n = 250$). As this estimator will be inconsistent (as $n \to \infty$) but converge at rate $n^{-1/2}$ to its probability limit, we expect this estimator to have larger bias but less variability than the estimator proposed here. Columns three through six of Table III give the results for this estimator

[6] This observation also suggests that it is possible to test for true state dependence by considering (6) with a fixed bandwidth. Investigation of such a test, which would be in the same spirit as the test proposed by Heckman (1978), is left for future research.

[7] Specifically, if there is no fixed effect and no exogenous explanatory variables in the model, then the first order serial correlation of y_{it}, due entirely to the presence of the lagged dependent variable, is approximately 0.06, 0.12, 0.23, and 0.41, for γ equal to 0.25, 0.5, 1.0, and 2.0, respectively. If only the fixed effect is present in the model, then the first order serial correlation is 0.15. Including the term $x_{it}\beta$, and when there are no individual effects, the corresponding calculations yield first order serial correlation of 0.04, 0.07, 0.15, and 0.29 for the four values of γ. In the absence of the lagged dependent variable, and with the inclusion of the exogenous variable, the first order serial correlation resulting from the fixed effect is 0.16.

[8] In simulations not reported here, we found that this is especially true for large bandwidths. This suggests that it might be important to let the bandwidth be data-dependent.

TABLE II

BENCHMARK DESIGN WITH DIFFERENT VALUES OF γ

		$T=4$				$T=8$			
		Results for $\hat{\beta}_n$		Results for $\hat{\gamma}_n$		Results for $\hat{\beta}_n$		Results for $\hat{\gamma}_n$	
	n	Bias	MAE	Bias	MAE	Bias	MAE	Bias	MAE
$\gamma=0.25$	250	0.060	0.155	−0.027	0.354	0.010	0.049	−0.026	0.124
	500	0.029	0.106	−0.033	0.239	0.005	0.038	−0.025	0.081
	1000	0.028	0.082	−0.019	0.174	0.007	0.027	−0.019	0.062
	2000	0.018	0.060	−0.027	0.133	0.004	0.020	−0.018	0.045
	4000	0.008	0.039	−0.011	0.091	0.003	0.015	−0.018	0.034
$\gamma=0.5$	250	0.076	0.154	−0.039	0.403	0.014	0.050	−0.053	0.131
	500	0.044	0.113	−0.052	0.256	0.007	0.037	−0.054	0.098
	1000	0.038	0.086	−0.035	0.178	0.009	0.027	−0.041	0.075
	2000	0.028	0.063	−0.042	0.143	0.007	0.020	−0.036	0.051
	4000	0.019	0.044	−0.035	0.102	0.005	0.015	−0.033	0.039
$\gamma=1$	250	0.121	0.187	−0.028	0.454	0.021	0.054	−0.095	0.152
	500	0.076	0.126	−0.072	0.312	0.014	0.041	−0.092	0.113
	1000	0.062	0.095	−0.085	0.225	0.012	0.029	−0.080	0.098
	2000	0.045	0.072	−0.075	0.167	0.010	0.021	−0.074	0.077
	4000	0.036	0.051	−0.058	0.119	0.007	0.016	−0.064	0.065
$\gamma=2.0$	250	0.196	0.251	−0.056	0.620	0.016	0.064	−0.195	0.227
	500	0.139	0.181	−0.117	0.417	0.014	0.044	−0.179	0.197
	1000	0.113	0.136	−0.148	0.321	0.016	0.034	−0.160	0.164
	2000	0.087	0.102	−0.142	0.241	0.009	0.023	−0.133	0.134
	4000	0.063	0.074	−0.118	0.163	0.006	0.017	−0.116	0.116

TABLE III

ALTERNATIVE ESTIMATORS FOR BENCHMARK DESIGN ($n=250$)

		Estimating the Fixed Effects				Estimator Proposed Here				Infeasible MLE			
		$\hat{\beta}_n$		$\hat{\gamma}_n$		$\hat{\beta}_n$		$\hat{\gamma}_n$		$\hat{\beta}_n$		$\hat{\gamma}_n$	
γ	T	Bias	MAE	Bias	MAE	Bias	MAE	Bias	MAE	Bias	MAE	Bias	MAE
0.25	4	0.796	0.796	−2.663	2.663	0.066	0.161	−0.022	0.341	0.008	0.060	−0.006	0.099
	8	0.263	0.263	−0.760	0.760	0.011	0.051	−0.024	0.131	0.005	0.036	0.003	0.065
	16	0.010	0.010	−0.307	0.307	0.003	0.028	−0.022	0.067	0.001	0.024	−0.003	0.041
0.5	4	0.787	0.787	−2.577	2.577	0.086	0.170	−0.039	0.360	0.009	0.058	−0.006	0.100
	8	0.257	0.257	−0.745	0.745	0.014	0.050	−0.053	0.131	0.003	0.035	0.005	0.062
	16	0.101	0.101	−0.298	0.298	0.005	0.029	−0.053	0.074	0.003	0.024	−0.000	0.040
1.0	4	0.772	0.772	−2.355	2.355	0.107	0.191	−0.057	0.402	−0.001	0.006	−0.011	0.101
	8	0.259	0.259	−0.700	0.700	0.021	0.054	−0.093	0.152	0.001	0.036	−0.000	0.062
	16	0.104	0.104	−0.291	0.291	0.005	0.028	−0.105	0.109	0.003	0.024	0.003	0.040
2.0	4	0.740	0.740	−2.054	2.054	0.195	0.260	−0.074	0.579	0.003	0.068	0.005	0.120
	8	0.268	0.268	−0.636	0.636	0.018	0.062	−0.190	0.222	0.006	0.039	0.008	0.079
	16	0.109	0.109	−0.289	0.289	−0.003	0.034	−0.200	0.201	0.001	0.028	−0.004	0.051

TABLE IV

BENCHMARK DESIGN WITH VARIOUS DESIGNS FOR x_{it}

	$\chi^2(1)$-Regressors, $\sigma_n = 8 \cdot n^{-1/5}$				Additional Regressors, $\sigma_n = 8 \cdot n^{-1/8}$			
	Results for $\hat{\beta}_n$		Results for $\hat{\gamma}_n$		Results for $\hat{\beta}_{1n}$		Results for $\hat{\gamma}_n$	
n	Bias	MAE	Bias	MAE	Bias	MAE	Bias	MAE
250	0.090	0.171	−0.011	0.309	0.143	0.186	−0.041	0.431
500	0.052	0.128	−0.010	0.222	0.094	0.141	−0.037	0.273
1000	0.038	0.085	−0.034	0.161	0.070	0.099	−0.026	0.197
2000	0.037	0.071	−0.032	0.117	0.051	0.068	−0.063	0.155
4000	0.032	0.053	−0.021	0.081	0.041	0.056	−0.050	0.116
	Trending Regressor, $T = 4$, $\sigma_n = 8 \cdot n^{-1/5}$				Trending Regressor, $T = 8$, $\sigma_n = 8 \cdot n^{-1/5}$			
	Results for $\hat{\beta}_n$		Results for $\hat{\gamma}_n$		Results for $\hat{\beta}_n$		Results for $\hat{\gamma}_n$	
n	Bias	MAE	Bias	MAE	Bias	MAE	Bias	MAE
250	0.089	0.184	−0.013	0.385	0.008	0.060	−0.049	0.136
500	0.036	0.127	−0.035	0.260	0.004	0.045	−0.055	0.099
1000	0.040	0.093	−0.046	0.196	−0.002	0.031	−0.040	0.071
2000	0.020	0.066	−0.055	0.141	0.001	0.021	−0.034	0.056
4000	0.015	0.050	−0.039	0.092	−0.001	0.015	−0.030	0.043

for the four values of γ considered earlier, whereas the results for the estimator proposed in this paper (with $\sigma_n = 8 \cdot n^{-1/5}$) are presented in columns seven through ten. The most striking feature of these results is that the maximum likelihood estimator that estimates all the fixed effects is inferior in terms of median absolute error to the estimator proposed here for all the values of γ and T, although the results for $\hat{\gamma}$ are close when $\gamma = 2$ and $T = 16$.

It is not too surprising that our estimator performs better than an estimator that is inconsistent. We therefore also compare the estimator to the infeasible maximum likelihood estimator that uses the fixed effect as one of the explanatory variables (treating its coefficient as an unknown parameter to be estimated). As expected, this estimator performs better than the one proposed here, with the relative performance of our estimator being worse when γ is larger and when T is smaller.

It is well understood that the design of the regressors in Monte Carlo studies may have a large effect on the results. For example, normally distributed regressors often make estimators look better than they are for other distributions of the regressors. In order to investigate this issue, we modify the benchmark design by changing the distribution of x_{it} to a $\chi^2(1)$ random variable, normalized to have the same mean and variance as the regressor in the benchmark design (see the upper left hand corner of Table IV). The results are quite similar to those presented in Table I. To conserve space, we present only the results for $\sigma_n = 8 \cdot n^{-1/5}$. Another problem with the choice of design is that the rate of convergence of the proposed estimators decreases as the number of regressors increases. In order to obtain information about the finite sample behavior of the estimator when there are more explanatory variables, we add three regressors to the benchmark design. All three are generated as $N(0, \pi^2/3)$

independently of each other and of all the other variables. The true values of the coefficients on the additional regressors are all zero, i.e. $\beta_2 = \beta_3 = \beta_4 = 0$, so the data-generating process is the same as for the benchmark case and the only difference is that three additional regressors are used in the estimation. The results from this experiment are given in the upper right-hand corner of Table IV. To conserve space we report only the results for β_1 and for γ and for one of the bandwidth sequences (note that the rate at which the bandwidths decrease is slower as a result of the additional regressors). The results suggest that the cost of adding the additional parameters is not high in terms of the median absolute error of the estimator of the two original parameters, β_1 and γ.

Since γ is essentially identified from the time series behavior of y_{it}, one might worry that the i.i.d. design of the regressors biases the results in favor of our estimator. To investigate this, we change the benchmark design to allow for serial correlation and a time trend in x. Specifically we generate x_{it} as

$$x_{it} = c \cdot (\zeta_{it} + a + 0.1 \cdot t)$$

where ζ_{it} is an AR(1) with standard normal innovations and autoregressive coefficient equal to 0.5. We choose a so that $a + 0.1 \cdot t$ averages 0 over the sample, and c is chosen so that the variance of the marginal distribution of x_{it} is the same as in the benchmark design. This design was chosen because it is very close to that used in Heckman (1981b). The fixed effect is constructed as the average of the first four realizations of $c \cdot \zeta_{it}$. The results of this experiment for $T = 4$ and $T = 8$ are given in the lower part of Table IV. A comparison between the results in Table IV and the corresponding results in Table II suggests that the i.i.d. property of the explanatory variable in the benchmark design is favorable to the estimator proposed here, although the difference is surprisingly small. As one might expect, the difference is more pronounced when T is larger, presumably because the time trend in the regression is more important with many time periods.

The asymptotic normality of the estimator may be used to conduct asymptotically valid inference. To investigate how well the asymptotic results approximate the finite sample properties of the resulting confidence intervals, we calculate 80% and 95% confidence intervals for each of the two parameters of the benchmark design. In Table V, we present the percentage of times that these confidence intervals cover the true parameter values. The results suggest that for the benchmark design, the asymptotics provide a fairly good approximation of the finite sample distribution of the estimator (and the estimator of its variance), although it seems that the confidence intervals have coverage probabilities that are slightly smaller than the asymptotic theory would predict. This is consistent with the fact that the confidence intervals are not centered correctly (due to the asymptotic bias). We expect this problem to be more severe if γ is big, and the sample size and bandwidth are both large, because in this case the bias will be more important relative to the variance of the estimator. Indeed, in

TABLE V

COVERAGE PROBABILITIES OF CI'S FOR BENCHMARK DESIGN

		Results for $\hat{\beta}_n$		Results for $\hat{\gamma}_n$	
	n	95% CI	80% CI	95% CI	80% CI
$\sigma_n = 2 \cdot n^{-1/5}$	250	0.911	0.720	0.874	0.679
	500	0.911	0.749	0.927	0.772
	1000	0.929	0.754	0.937	0.773
	2000	0.934	0.778	0.949	0.794
	4000	0.956	0.809	0.940	0.774
$\sigma_n = 8 \cdot n^{-1/5}$	250	0.943	0.786	0.926	0.751
	500	0.933	0.776	0.952	0.795
	1000	0.944	0.765	0.944	0.784
	2000	0.945	0.790	0.939	0.784
	4000	0.941	0.788	0.938	0.785
$\sigma_n = 32 \cdot n^{-1/5}$	250	0.949	0.766	0.935	0.759
	500	0.941	0.763	0.948	0.802
	1000	0.934	0.753	0.941	0.791
	2000	0.928	0.753	0.923	0.748
	4000	0.900	0.695	0.900	0.721

additional experiments (not reported in Table V), we found that, with 4000 observations, $\gamma = 1$, and $\sigma_n = 64 \cdot n^{-1/5}$, the coverage probabilities for the 80% and 95% confidence intervals were approximately 47% and 74% for β and 57% and 80% for γ, respectively.

We finally turn to examine the small sample properties of the maximum score estimator obtained by maximizing (9). In Table VI, we present the results for the benchmark design. Because the assumptions maintained for the maximum score estimator do not identify the scale of the parameter vector, we consider γ/β as the parameter of interest.[9] A priori, we expect the maximum score estimator to perform worse than the estimator that imposes the logit assumption. We also expect the rate of convergence to be slower than that of the logit estimator, because, for the panel data binary response model with only exogenous regressors, the maximum score estimator is known to converge at rate $n^{-1/3}$, as opposed to the $n^{-1/2}$ rate of convergence of the logit maximum likelihood estimator. The results in Table VI confirm this. The median absolute error of the maximum score estimator is larger than that of the logit estimator in all cases, and the relative difference is larger for larger sample sizes.

[9] The objective function for the maximum score estimator is not differentiable, and is therefore potentially difficult to maximize. We calculate the estimator by performing a grid search over 600 equally spaced points on the unit circle. If more than one point achieves the maximum value of the objective function, then the estimate is calculated as the average value of those different point estimates of γ/β.

TABLE VI

MAXIMUM SCORE ESTIMATION FOR BENCHMARK DESIGN

	n	$\hat{\beta}_n/\hat{\gamma}_n$ (MS) Bias	MAE	$\hat{\beta}_n/\hat{\gamma}_n$ (Logit) Bias	MAE
$\sigma_n = 2 \cdot n^{-1/5}$	250	−0.059	0.674	0.015	0.591
	500	−0.138	0.593	−0.041	0.397
	1000	−0.044	0.483	−0.025	0.334
	2000	−0.015	0.421	−0.025	0.239
	4000	−0.022	0.330	0.002	0.187
$\sigma_n = 8 \cdot n^{-1/5}$	250	−0.126	0.539	−0.078	0.365
	500	−0.113	0.451	−0.062	0.254
	1000	−0.066	0.354	−0.046	0.177
	2000	−0.072	0.303	−0.060	0.133
	4000	−0.054	0.212	−0.040	0.105
$\sigma_n = 32 \cdot n^{-1/5}$	250	−0.125	0.525	−0.091	0.347
	500	−0.109	0.431	−0.104	0.237
	1000	−0.084	0.339	−0.096	0.175
	2000	−0.109	0.277	−0.090	0.132
	4000	−0.103	0.214	−0.093	0.107

6. CONCLUDING REMARKS

In this paper, we consider discrete choice models that allow for both unobserved individual heterogeneity (Heckman's "spurious" state dependence) and "true" state dependence. We show that it is possible to identify such models within the logit framework, and we propose an estimator that is consistent and asymptotically normal, although the rate of convergence is slower than the usual inverse of the square root of the sample size. The results of a small Monte Carlo study suggest that the estimator performs well (for the very simple designs considered), and that the asymptotics provide a reasonable approximation to the finite sample behavior of the estimator. The paper also proposes an estimator of the semiparametric version of the model. That estimator, which is an adaptation of Manski's maximum score estimator, is consistent, but we do not derive its asymptotic distribution. In future research, we plan to investigate whether it is possible to obtain an asymptotically normal distribution (under a stronger set of regularity conditions), by applying Horowitz's (1992) approach to smooth the objective function (9) above. This suggests estimating β and γ by maximizing

$$\sum_{i=1}^{n} K\left(\frac{x_{i2}-x_{i3}}{\sigma_n}\right)(y_{i2}-y_{i1})L\left(\frac{(x_{i2}-x_{i1})b+g(y_{i3}-y_{i0})}{h_n}\right),$$

where L is a kernel function that satisfies: $L(\nu) \xrightarrow{v \to -\infty} 0$ and $L(\nu) \xrightarrow{v \to \infty} 1$, and h_n is another bandwidth sequence that tends to 0 as n increases.

Dept. of Economics, Princeton University, Princeton, NJ 08544, U.S.A.

and

Dept. of Economics, University of Chicago, Chicago, IL 60637, U.S.A.

Manuscript received April, 1997; final revision received March, 1999.

APPENDIX

Logit Case

The ideas behind the proofs of Theorems 1 and 2 are very closely related to those underlying local likelihood estimation (Staniswalis (1989), and Tibshirani and Hastie (1987)) and robust regression function estimation (Härdle (1984), Robinson (1984), and Härdle and Tsybakov (1988)). The difference is that the object of interest here is a finite dimensional vector, whereas in those papers it is an unknown function.

PROOF OF THEOREM 1: After re-scaling by $1/n\sigma_n^k$, the objective function (6), can be written as:

$$Q_n(\theta) = \frac{1}{n\sigma_n^k}\sum_i K\left(\frac{x_{i23}}{\sigma_n}\right)h_i(\theta).$$

To show consistency of the maximizer of $Q_n(\theta)$, we will use Theorem 4.1.1 in Amemiya (1985). The theorem requires that the following conditions hold: (A1) Θ is compact, (A2) $Q_n(\theta)$ is continuous in $\theta \in \Theta$, (A3) $Q_n(\theta)$ is measurable for all $\theta \in \Theta$, (A4) $Q_n(\theta)$ converges to a nonstochastic function $Q(\theta)$ in probability uniformly in $\theta \in \Theta$ and (A5) $Q(\theta)$ is uniquely maximized at θ_0.

Notice that (A1) is satisfied by Assumption C2, while (A2) and (A3) are trivially satisfied.

To verify (A4) we will use Lemma 2.9 in Newey and McFadden (1994), which requires that Θ be compact (satisfied by Assumption C2), that $Q_n(\theta)$ converge to $Q(\theta)$ in probability for all θ, where $Q(\theta)$ is continuous in θ, and that there exist $\alpha > 0$ and $Z_n = O_p(1)$ such that for all $\theta, \tilde{\theta} \in \Theta, |Q_n(\theta) - Q_n(\tilde{\theta})| \le Z_n \|\theta - \tilde{\theta}\|^{\alpha}$.

Note that by standard arguments (bounded convergence) and under our assumptions,

$$E[Q_n(\theta)] = E\left[\frac{1}{\sigma_n^k}K\left(\frac{x_{23}}{\sigma_n}\right)h(\theta)\right] \to f(0)E[h(\theta)\,|\,x_{23} = 0] = Q(\theta)$$

and

$$\operatorname{Var}[Q_n(\theta)] = O\left(\frac{1}{n\sigma_n^k}\right) = o(1),$$

which by Chebyshev's theorem imply that $Q_n(\theta) \xrightarrow{p} Q(\theta)$ for all $\theta \in \Theta$. Continuity of $Q(\theta)$ may be easily established by dominated convergence arguments using the fact that $|h(\theta)| \le \ln 2 + 2\|z\|\,\|\theta\|$, and that under our assumption $E[\|z\| | x_{23}] < \infty$. Next, note that by the multivariate mean value theorem and by the triangular inequality,

$$|Q_n(\theta) - Q_n(\tilde{\theta})| \le \|\theta - \tilde{\theta}\| \frac{1}{n\sigma_n^k}\sum_i \left|K\left(\frac{x_{i23}}{\sigma_n}\right)\right| \|h_i^{(1)}(\theta^*)\|$$

$$\le 2\|\theta - \tilde{\theta}\| \frac{1}{n\sigma_n^k}\sum_i \left|K\left(\frac{x_{i23}}{\sigma_n}\right)\right| \|z_i\|$$

where θ^* lies between θ and $\tilde{\theta}$, and where the second inequality follows from the fact that

$$\|h_i^{(1)}(\theta^*)\| \le \left(1 + \frac{\exp(z\theta)}{1 + \exp(z\theta)}\right)\|z_i\| \le 2\|z_i\|.$$

Let $Z_n = (1/n\sigma_n^k)\Sigma_i |K(\frac{x_{i23}}{\sigma_n})|\,\|z_i\|$. It is straightforward to show that under our assumptions, $E[Z_n] = O(1)$ and $\operatorname{Var}[Z_n] = O(1/n\sigma_n^k)$, which imply that $Z_n = O_p(1)$ as required.

Finally, to complete the proof of the theorem we need to show (A5), i.e. that $Q(\theta)$ is uniquely maximized at θ_0. Recall that $\theta = (b, g)'$. By assumption, $Q(b, g)$ is well-defined and finite for all b

and g, and

$$Q(b,g) = f(0)E[h(b,g)\,|\,x_{23}=0]$$
$$= f(0)E[P(y_1 \neq y_2\,|\,x_{23}=0, y_0, y_3)$$
$$\times E[\tilde{h}(b,g)\,|\,x_{23}=0, y_0, y_3, y_1 \neq y_2]\,|\,x_{23}=0]$$

where

$$\tilde{h}(b,g) \equiv \ln\left(\frac{\exp(x_{12}b + y_{03}g)^{y_1}}{1+\exp(x_{12}b + y_{03}g)}\right).$$

The logit assumption implies that $P(y_1 \neq y_2\,|\,x_{23}=0, y_0, y_3) > 0$. Next note that conditional on $(x_{23}=0, y_0, y_3, y_1 \neq y_2), \tilde{h}(b,g)$ is the log-likelihood of a logit model with explanatory variables x_{12} and y_{03}. If $y_3 = y_0$, then $E[\tilde{h}(\theta)\,|\,x_{23}=0, y_0, y_3, y_1 \neq y_2]$ does not depend on g, but as a function of b, it is uniquely maximized at $b=\beta$ provided that x_{12} is not contained in a proper linear subspace of $\mathscr{R}^k$ with probability 1, conditional on $(x_{23}=0, y_0, y_3, y_1 \neq y_2)$ (this follows from standard proofs of consistency of the maximum likelihood estimator of a logit model). By the maintained logit assumption, this "full-rank" condition follows from (C6). If $y_3 \neq y_0$, then $E[\tilde{h}(\theta)\,|\,x_{23}=0, y_0, y_3, y_1 \neq y_2]$ depends on both g and b, and it is uniquely maximized at $b=\beta$ and $g=\gamma$ provided that (x_{12}, y_{03}) is not contained in a proper linear subspace of $\mathscr{R}^{k+1}$ with probability 1 conditional on $(x_{23}=0, y_0, y_3, y_1 \neq y_2)$. Again, the latter will be true by the logit assumption under assumption (C6). This implies that $Q(b,g)$ is uniquely maximized at $b=\beta$ and $g=\gamma$.

PROOF OF THEOREM 2: The asymptotic normality of the proposed estimator is derived in a standard way. Since the objective function is differentiable, $\theta_0 \in \text{int}(\Theta)$, and $\hat{\theta}_n$ is a consistent estimator of θ_0, then for n large enough the estimator satisfies the first order conditions:

$$\frac{1}{\sqrt{n\sigma_n^k}}\sum_i K\left(\frac{x_{i23}}{\sigma_n}\right)h_i^{(1)}(\hat{\theta}_n) = 0.$$

An expansion of these around θ_0 yields

$$0 = \frac{1}{\sqrt{n\sigma_n^k}}\sum_i\left(K\left(\frac{x_{i23}}{\sigma_n}\right)h_i^{(1)}(\theta_0) - E\left[K\left(\frac{x_{i23}}{\sigma_n}\right)h_i^{(1)}(\theta_0)\right]\right)$$
$$+\sqrt{n\sigma_n^k}\,\frac{1}{n\sigma_n^k}\sum_i E\left[K\left(\frac{x_{i23}}{\sigma_n}\right)h_i^{(1)}(\theta_0)\right]$$
$$+\frac{1}{n\sigma_n^k}\sum_i K\left(\frac{x_{i23}}{\sigma_n}\right)h^{(2)}(\theta_n^*)\cdot\sqrt{n\sigma_n^k}\,(\hat{\theta}_n - \theta_0)$$
$$= Z_n(\theta_0) + \sqrt{n\sigma_n^k}\,E[B_n(\theta_0)] - J_n(\theta_n^*)\cdot\sqrt{n\sigma_n^k}\,(\hat{\theta}_n - \theta_0)$$

where θ_n^* (which may be different for different rows of $J_n(\cdot)$) lies between $\hat{\theta}_n$ and θ_0 and therefore converges in probability to θ_0. The asymptotic normality of $\sqrt{n\sigma_n^k}\,(\hat{\theta}_n - \theta_0)$ will follow from $Z_n(\theta_0 \xrightarrow{d} N(0,V)$, $\sqrt{n\sigma_n^k}\,EB_n(\theta_0) \to 0$, and $J_n(\theta) \xrightarrow{p} J(\theta)$ uniformly in $\theta \in \Theta$ where $J(\theta)$ is a non-stochastic function that is continuous at θ_0. This last result will imply (by Theorem 4.1.5 in Amemiya (1985)) that $J_n(\theta_n^*) \xrightarrow{p} J(\theta_0) \equiv J$.

We will first show that $Z_n(\theta_0) \xrightarrow{d} N(0, V)$.

Let c be a $(k+1) \times 1$ vector of finite constants such that $c'c = 1$. To show the claim it suffices to show that $c'Z_n(\theta_0) \xrightarrow{d} N(0, c'Vc)$. Write

$$c'Z_n(\theta_0) \equiv \frac{1}{\sqrt{n\sigma_n^k}} \sum_i c'(q_i^{(1)}(\theta_0) - E[q_i^{(1)}(\theta_0)]) = \frac{1}{\sqrt{n}} \sum_i \xi_{in}$$

where $\{\xi_{in}\}_{i=1}^n$ is an independent sequence of scalar random variables. We will verify that $\{\xi_{in}\}_{i=1}^n$ satisfies the conditions of the Lyapunov CLT for double arrays (see Theorem 7.1.2 in Chung (1974) and comment on page 209). We need $E[\xi_{in}] = 0, \text{var}[\xi_{in}] < \infty$, $V \equiv \lim_{n\to\infty} \text{var}[\xi_{in}] < \infty$, and $\Sigma_{i=1}^n E[|\xi_{in}/\sqrt{n}|^{2+\delta}] \to 0$ for some $\delta \in (0,1)$. Indeed,

$$E[\xi_{in}] = c'E\left[\frac{1}{\sqrt{\sigma_n^k}} q_i^{(1)}(\theta_0) - E\left[\frac{1}{\sqrt{\sigma_n^k}} q_i^{(1)}(\theta_0)\right]\right] = 0,$$

$$\text{var}[\xi_{in}] = c'E[\xi_{in}\xi_{in}']c = c'E\left[\frac{1}{\sigma_n^k} q_i^{(1)}(\theta_0) q_i^{(1)}(\theta_0)'\right]c$$
$$- \frac{1}{\sigma_n^k} c'E[q^{(1)}(\theta_0)]E[q^{(1)}(\theta_0)]'c.$$

Note that under our assumptions (see Assumptions (N5) and (C7)) both terms of $\text{var}[\xi_{in}]$ are finite. Now, for the first term of the variance, bounded convergence yields

$$E\left[\frac{1}{\sigma_n^k} q^{(1)}(\theta_0) q^{(1)}(\theta_0)'\right] = E\left[\frac{1}{\sigma_n^k} K\left(\frac{x_{23}}{\sigma_n}\right)^2 E[h^{(1)}(\theta_0)h^{(1)}(\theta_0)' \mid x_{23}]\right]$$
$$\to f(0)E[h^{(1)}(\theta_0)h^{(1)}(\theta_0)' \mid x_{23} = 0] \int K(\nu)^2 \, d\nu$$

since $f(\cdot)$ and $E[h^{(1)}(\theta_0)h^{(1)}(\theta_0)' \mid x_{23} = \cdot]$ are continuous in a neighborhood of zero (Assumptions (C3) and (N6)). The second component of $\text{var}[\xi_{in}]$ goes to 0 since $E[q^{(1)}(\theta_0)] = O(\sigma_n^k)$. Therefore,

$$\lim_{n\to\infty} \text{var}[\xi_{in}] = c'\left\{f(0)E[h^{(1)}(\theta_0)h^{(1)}(\theta_0)' \mid x_{23} = 0] \int K^2(\nu)\, d\nu\right\}c = c'Vc,$$

which under our assumptions is bounded away from infinity. Finally, for any $\delta \in (0,1)$,

$$\sum_{i=1}^n E\left[\left|\frac{\xi_{in}}{\sqrt{n}}\right|^{2+\delta}\right]$$
$$\leq 2^{2+\delta}\left(\frac{1}{\sqrt{n\sigma_n^k}}\right)^\delta E\left[\frac{1}{\sigma_n^k}\left|K\left(\frac{x_{23}}{\sigma_n}\right)\right|^{2+\delta} \|h^{(1)}(\theta_0)\|^{2+\delta}\right]$$
$$= 2^{2+\delta}\left(\frac{1}{\sqrt{n\sigma_n^k}}\right)^\delta \int |K(\nu)|^{2+\delta} E[\|h^{(1)}(\theta_0)\|^{2+\delta} \mid x_{23} = \nu\sigma_n] f(\nu\sigma_n)\, d\nu$$
$$\leq 2^{2+\delta}\left(\frac{1}{\sqrt{n\sigma_n^k}}\right)^\delta \int |K(\nu)|^{2+\delta} E[\|z\|^{2+\delta} \mid x_{23} = \nu\sigma_n] f(\nu\sigma_n)\, d\nu$$
$$= O\left(\frac{1}{\sqrt{n\sigma_n^k}}\right)^\delta = o(1),$$

since $\int|K(\nu)|^{2+\delta}\,d\nu$ is finite by the finiteness and absolute integrability of the kernel, and $E[\|z\|^{2+\delta}|x_{23}=\cdot]f(\cdot)$ is bounded for all x_{23} under (C3) and (N5).

We will next show that $\sqrt{n\sigma_n^k}\,EB_n(\theta_0)\to 0$.

By Assumptions (N2) and (N3), $E[h^{(1)}(\theta_0)|x_{23}=\cdot]f(\cdot)\equiv\varphi(\cdot)$ is s times continuously differentiable. A Taylor expansion around $x_{23}=0$ yields

$$
\begin{aligned}
E[B_{n,j}(\theta_0)] &= E\left[\frac{1}{\sigma_n^k}K\left(\frac{x_{23}}{\sigma_n}\right)h_j^{(1)}(\theta_0)\right]\\
&=\int\frac{1}{\sigma_n^k}E[h_j^{(1)}(\theta_0)|x_{23}]f(x_{23})K\left(\frac{x_{23}}{\sigma_n}\right)dx_{23}\\
&=\int\frac{1}{\sigma_n^k}\varphi_j(x_{23})K\left(\frac{x_{23}}{\sigma_n}\right)dx_{23}\\
&=\int\frac{1}{\sigma_n^k}\left[\varphi_j(0)+\varphi_j^{(1)}(0)x_{23}+\cdots+\frac{1}{s!}\varphi_j^{(s)}(\hat{x}_{23})(x_{23},\ldots,x_{23})\right]K\left(\frac{x_{23}}{\sigma_n}\right)dx_{23}\\
&=\varphi_j(0)\int K(\nu)\,d\nu+\sigma_n\varphi_j^{(1)}(0)\int\nu K(\nu)\,d\nu+\cdots\\
&\quad+\sigma_n^{(s-1)}\frac{1}{(s-1)!}\varphi^{(s-1)}(0)\int(\nu,\ldots,\nu)K(\nu)\,d\nu\\
&\quad+\sigma_n^s\frac{1}{s!}\int\varphi_j^{(s)}(c_n)(\nu,\ldots,\nu)K(\nu)\,d\nu\\
&=0+\cdots+0+\sigma_n^s\frac{1}{s!}\int\varphi_j^{(s)}(c_n)(\nu,\ldots,\nu)K(\nu)\,d\nu
\end{aligned}
$$

for any $j=1,\ldots,k$, since $\varphi(0)\equiv f(0)\cdot E[h^{(1)}(\theta_0)|x_{23}=0]=f(0)\cdot 0=0$ by the first order conditions of the limiting maximization problem, and K is an s'th order kernel (Assumption N7). Here, c_n is a $(k\times 1)$ vector whose elements lie between 0 and $\nu\sigma_n$. Now, under our assumptions $(1/s!)\int\varphi^{(s)}(c_n)(\nu,\ldots,\nu)K(\nu)\,d\nu=O(1)$. Therefore, since $\sqrt{n\sigma_n^k}\,\sigma_n^s\to 0$, we obtain

$$
\sqrt{n\sigma_n^k}\,E[B_{n,j}(\theta_0)]=\sqrt{n\sigma_n^k}\,\sigma_n^s\frac{1}{s!}\int\varphi_j^{(s)}(c_n)(\nu,\ldots,\nu)K(\nu)\,d\nu\to 0.
$$

Finally, we will show that $\sup_{\theta\in\Theta}\|J_n(\theta)-J(\theta)\|=o_p(1)$ where $J(\theta)\equiv -f(0)\cdot E[h^{(2)}(\theta)|x_{23}=0]$ is continuous at θ_0.

First note that $J(\theta)$ is continuous in θ for all θ (and hence at θ_0). This may be easily verified using dominated convergence arguments and the proof is omitted. To verify the uniform convergence, we will use Lemma 2.9 of Newey and McFadden (1994).

Note that by standard arguments (bounded convergence) and under our assumptions,

$$
E[J_n(\theta)]=-E\left[\frac{1}{\sigma_n^k}K\left(\frac{x_{23}}{\sigma_n}\right)h^{(2)}(\theta)\right]\to -f(0)E[h^{(2)}(\theta)|x_{23}=0]\equiv J(\theta)
$$

since $f(\cdot)$ and $E[h^{(2)}(\theta)|x_{23}=\cdot]$ are continuous in a neighborhood of zero, and for the jl'th component of $J_n(\theta)$,

$$
\mathrm{var}[J_n(\theta)_{jl}]\le\frac{1}{n\sigma_n^k}E\left[\frac{1}{\sigma_n^k}K\left(\frac{x_{23}}{\sigma_n}\right)^2h^{(2)}(\theta)_{jl}^2\right]=O\left(\frac{1}{n\sigma_n^k}\right)=o(1),
$$

which by Chebyshev's theorem imply that $J_n(\theta)\xrightarrow{p}J(\theta)$ for all $\theta\in\Theta$. Next, note that by the multivariate mean value theorem and by the triangular inequality,

$$
\|J_n(\theta)-J_n(\tilde{\theta})\|\le\|\theta-\tilde{\theta}\|\frac{1}{n\sigma_n^k}\sum_i\left|K\left(\frac{x_{i23}}{\sigma_n}\right)\right|\|h_i^{(3)}(\theta^*)\|
$$

$$\leq \|\theta - \tilde{\theta}\| \frac{1}{n\sigma_n^k} \sum_i \left| K\left(\frac{x_{i23}}{\sigma_n}\right) \right| \|z_i\|^3$$

where θ^* lies between θ and $\tilde{\theta}$, and where the second inequality follows from the fact that

$$\|h_i^{(3)}(\theta^*)\| \leq \left| \frac{\exp(z_i\theta^*)(1 - \exp(z_i\theta^*))}{(1 + \exp(z_i\theta^*))^3} \right| \|z_i\|^3 \leq \|z_i\|^3.$$

Let $Z_n = (1/n\sigma_n^k)\Sigma_i |K(x_{i23}/\sigma_n)| \|z_i\|^3$. It is straightforward to show that $E[Z_n] = O(1)$ and $\text{var}[Z_n] \leq O(1/n\sigma_n^k)$, since by Assumption (N5) $E[\|z\|^6 | x_{23} = \cdot] < \infty$, which imply that $Z_n = O_p(1)$ as required.

PROOF OF THEOREM 3: The proofs of the two parts of the theorem rely on the fact that, under the assumptions, $\hat{\theta}_n \overset{p}{\to} \theta_0$ and on the fact that the proposed estimators of the asymptotic variance components converge in probability uniformly in $\theta \in \Theta$ to nonstochastic limit functions that are continuous at θ_0. Uniform convergence in probability of $J_n(\theta)$ to $J(\theta)$ was established above. The proof that $V_n(\theta)$ converges in probability to $V(\theta)$ uniformly in $\theta \in \Theta$ follows exactly the same arguments and it is omitted.

Semiparametric Case

The following result on uniform rates of convergence, adapted from Pollard (1995) to the multivariate case, will be useful (see also Theorem 37, Chapter 2 in Pollard (1984)). We will denote by P_n the empirical measure generated by independent sampling from a probability distribution P. Following the empirical process literature, we will also use P to denote the expectation operator.

LEMMA 5 (Uniform Rates of Convergence): *Let $\mathcal{F}_n$ be a subclass of a fixed Euclidean class of functions $\mathcal{F}$ that has envelope F. Suppose there exist constants $\sigma_n \to 0$ such that $\sup_{\mathcal{F}_n} P|\chi| = O(\sigma_n^k)$. If F is constant and $n\sigma_n^k/\ln n \to \infty$, then:*

$$\sup_{\mathcal{F}_n} |P_n\chi - P\chi| = O_p\left(\sqrt{\frac{\sigma_n^k \ln n}{n}}\right) = o_p(\sigma_n^k).$$

Note that $n\sigma_n^k/\ln n \to \infty$ implies that $\ln n/n = o(\sigma_n^k)$. Hence, if $a_n = O_p(\sqrt{(\sigma_n^k \ln n)/n})$, then $a_n = o_p(\sqrt{(\sigma_n^k)^2}) = o_p(\sigma_n^k)$.

Define

$$Q_n(\theta) = \frac{1}{\sigma_n^k} \cdot \frac{1}{n} \sum_i K\left(\frac{x_{i23}}{\sigma_n}\right) h_i(\theta) = \frac{1}{\sigma_n^k} \cdot \frac{1}{n} \sum_i q_i(\theta) = \frac{1}{\sigma_n^k} P_n q$$

where now $h(\theta) = y_{21}\,\text{sgn}(z\theta)$ with $z \equiv (x_{21}, y_{30})$. As we show below, $Q_n(\theta)$ converges in probability uniformly in $\theta \in \Theta$ to the nonstochastic function: $Q(\theta) = f(0)E[h(\theta) | x_{23} = 0]$.

PROOF OF THEOREM 4: Note that in the semiparametric case the objective function is no longer continuous in θ. To show consistency we will use Theorem 9.6.1 in Amemiya (1985), which requires that the following conditions hold: (A1) Θ is a compact set, (A2) $Q_n(\theta)$ is a measurable function for all $\theta \in \Theta$, (A3) $Q_n(\theta)$ converges in probability to a nonstochastic function $Q(\theta)$ uniformly in $\theta \in \Theta$, and (A4) $Q(\theta)$ is continuous in θ and is uniquely maximized at θ_0.

The first condition is satisfied by construction of Θ. Condition (A2) is trivially satisfied. For condition (A3) we need to verify that $\sup_{\theta\in\Theta}|Q_n(\theta)-Q(\theta)|=o_p(1)$, which follows from $\sup_{\theta\in\Theta}|Q_n(\theta)-EQ_n(\theta)|=o_p(1)$ and $\sup_{\theta\in\Theta}|EQ_n(\theta)-Q(\theta)|=o(1)$.

Note that $\sup_{\theta\in\Theta}|Q_n(\theta)-EQ_n(\theta)|=o_p(1)\Leftrightarrow \sup_{\mathscr{F}_n}|P_nq-Pq|=o_p(\sigma_n^{\ k})$ where

$$\mathscr{F}_n\equiv\left\{K\left(\frac{x_{23}}{\sigma_n}\right)h(\theta):\ \theta\in\Theta\right\}$$

with $\sigma_n>0$ and $\sigma_n\to 0$. $\mathscr{F}_n$ is a subclass of the fixed class $\mathscr{F}=\{K(x_{23}/\sigma)h(\theta):\ \theta\in\Theta,\sigma>0\}=\mathscr{F}_\sigma\mathscr{F}_\theta$, with $\mathscr{F}_\sigma\equiv\{K(x_{23}/\sigma):\ \sigma>0\}$, which is Euclidean for the constant envelope $\sup|K|$ (see Lemma 22(ii) in Nolan and Pollard (1987)) and $\mathscr{F}_\theta\equiv\{h(\theta)=y_{21}\operatorname{sgn}(z\theta):\ \theta\in\Theta\}$. Note that $h(\theta)$ is uniformly bounded by the constant envelope $F_\theta=1$. Furthermore, it is easy to see that there is a partition of $\Re$ into $k+1$ intervals on each of which $h(\theta)$ is linear. This implies that $\mathscr{F}$ is Euclidean for the constant envelope $F=\sup|K|$ (see Example 2.11 in Pakes and Pollard (1989)). Next, note that

$$\begin{aligned}\sup_{\mathscr{F}_n}P|q|&\le\sup_{\mathscr{F}_n}\sigma_n^{\ k}\int|K(\nu)|E[|y_{21}\operatorname{sgn}(z\theta)|\,|\,x_{23}=\nu\sigma_n]f(\nu\sigma_n)\,d\nu\\&\le\sup_{\mathscr{F}_n}\sigma_n^{\ k}\int|K(\nu)|f(\nu\sigma_n)\,d\nu=O(\sigma_n^{\ k}).\end{aligned}$$

Applying Lemma 5 we obtain that

$$\sup_{\mathscr{F}_n}|P_nq-Pq|=O_p\left(\sqrt{\frac{\sigma_n^{\ k}\ln n}{n}}\right)=o_p(\sigma_n^{\ k})$$

by Assumption (CS8).

We next show that $\sup_{\theta\in\Theta}|EQ_n(\theta)-Q(\theta)|=o(1)$. Let $\varphi(\cdot)\equiv E[h(\theta)\,|\,x_{23}=\cdot]f(\cdot)$. Notice that by Assumption (CS6) we can write:

$$\begin{aligned}\sup_{\theta\in\Theta}|EQ_n(\theta)-Q(\theta)|&=\sup_{\theta\in\Theta}\left|E\left[\frac{1}{\sigma_n^{\ k}}K\left(\frac{x_{23}}{\sigma_n}\right)h(\theta)\right]-f(0)E[h(\theta)\,|\,x_{23}=0]\right|\\&=\sup_{\theta\in\Theta}\left|\int\frac{1}{\sigma_n^{\ k}}K\left(\frac{x_{23}}{\sigma_n}\right)\varphi(x_{23})\,dx_{23}-\varphi(0)\right|\\&=\sup_{\theta\in\Theta}\left|\int\frac{1}{\sigma_n^{\ k}}K\left(\frac{x_{23}}{\sigma_n}\right)[\varphi(0)+\varphi^{(1)}(\tilde{x}_{23})x_{23}]\,dx_{23}-\varphi(0)\right|\\&=\sup_{\theta\in\Theta}\left|\varphi(0)\int K(\nu)\,d\nu+\sigma_n\int\nu K(\nu)\varphi^{(1)}(c_n)\,d\nu-\varphi(0)\right|\\&=\sup_{\theta\in\Theta}\left|\sigma_n\int\nu K(\nu)\varphi^{(1)}(c_n)\,d\nu\right|\\&\le\sigma_n\int|\nu K(\nu)|\sup_{\theta\in\Theta}|\varphi^{(1)}(c_n)|\,d\nu\\&=O(\sigma_n)\\&=o(1)\end{aligned}$$

and the desired result follows.

To show that the identification condition (A4) holds, we will follow Manski (1985, 1987). Let

$$Z_\theta\equiv\{z:\ \operatorname{sgn}(z\theta)\neq\operatorname{sgn}(z\theta_0)\}$$

and

$$R(\theta) \equiv \int_{Z_\theta} dF_{z \mid x_{23}=0}.$$

Lemma 6 establishes that $R(\theta) > 0$ for all $\theta \in \Re^{k+1}$ such that $\theta/\|\theta\| \neq \theta_0^*$. Lemma 7 uses this result to establish the desired result, namely that $Q(\theta_0^*) > Q(\theta)$. We will assume throughout that all distributions that are conditional on the event that $x_{23} = 0$ are well defined.

LEMMA 6: *Let Assumptions* (CS2)–(CS4) *hold. Then* $R(\theta) > 0$ *for all* $\theta \in \Re^{k+1}$ *such that* $\theta/\|\theta\| \neq \theta_0^*$.

PROOF: The claim follows from Lemma 2 of Manski (1985) provided that we can show that

(i) $\Pr(x_{21,\kappa} \in N \mid \tilde{x}_{21}, y_0 = d_0, y_3 = d_3, x_{23} = 0) > 0$ for any subset N of $\Re$, and

(ii) $\Pr(\tilde{x}_{21}\tilde{b} + y_{30}g = 0 \mid x_{23} = 0) < 1$ for all $(\tilde{b}, g)$.

(i) Note that for any subset N of $\Re$:

$$\begin{aligned}
&\Pr(x_{21,\kappa} \in N \mid \tilde{x}_{21}, y_0 = d_0, y_3 = d_3, x_{23} = 0)\\
&= \frac{\Pr(x_{21,\kappa} \in N, y_0 = d_0, y_3 = d_3 \mid \tilde{x}_{21}, x_{23} = 0)}{\Pr(y_0 = d_0, y_3 = d_3 \mid \tilde{x}_{21}, x_{23} = 0)}\\
&= \frac{\Pr(x_{21,\kappa} \in N \mid \tilde{x}_{21}, x_{23} = 0) \cdot \Pr(y_0 = d_0, y_3 = d_3 \mid x_{21,\kappa} \in N, \tilde{x}_{21}, x_{23} = 0)}{\Pr(y_0 = d_0, y_3 = d_3 \mid \tilde{x}_{21}, x_{23} = 0)}\\
&= \frac{\Pr(x_{21,\kappa} \in N \mid \tilde{x}_{21}, x_{23} = 0) \cdot \int \Pr(y_0 = d_0, y_3 = d_3 \mid x, \alpha, x_{23} = 0)\, dF_{x,\alpha \mid x_{23}=0, \tilde{x}_{21}, x_{21,\kappa} \in N}}{\Pr(y_0 = d_0, y_3 = d_3 \mid \tilde{x}_{21}, x_{23} = 0)}.
\end{aligned}$$

By Assumption (CS3) $x_{21,\kappa}$ has positive density on $\Re$ for almost all $\tilde{x}_{21}$ and conditional on $x_{23} = 0$, so that $\Pr(x_{21,\kappa} \in N \mid \tilde{x}_{21}, x_{23} = 0) > 0$. Next, note that

$$\begin{aligned}
&\int \Pr(y_0 = d_0, y_3 = d_3 \mid x, \alpha, x_{23} = 0)\, dF_{x,\alpha \mid x_{23}=0, \tilde{x}_{21}, x_{21,\kappa} \in N}\\
&= \int \Pr(y_3 = d_3 \mid x, \alpha, y_0 = d_0, x_{23} = 0)\\
&\quad \times \Pr(y_0 = d_0 \mid x, \alpha, x_{23} = 0)\, dF_{x,\alpha \mid x_{23}=0, \tilde{x}_{21}, x_{21,\kappa} \in N}\\
&= \int \sum_{d_1, d_2 \in \{0,1\}} \Pr(y_3 = d_3 \mid x, \alpha, y_0 = d_0, y_2 = d_2, y_1 = d_1, x_{23} = 0)\\
&\quad \times \Pr(y_2 = d_2 \mid x, \alpha, y_0 = d_0, y_1 = d_1, x_{23} = 0)\\
&\quad \times \Pr(y_1 = d_1 \mid x, \alpha, y_0 = d_0, x_{23} = 0)\\
&\quad \times \Pr(y_0 = d_0 \mid x, \alpha, x_{23} = 0)\, dF_{x,\alpha \mid x_{23}=0, \tilde{x}_{21}, x_{21,\kappa} \in N}
\end{aligned}$$

where the integrand is strictly positive by Assumption (CS2), and from the fact that $\Pr(y_0 = d_0 \mid x, \alpha, x_{23} = 0)$ will be always positive even if $y_0 = 1$ (or 0) with probability one conditional on (x, α).

Hence, $\Pr(y_0 = d_0, y_3 = d_3 \mid x_{21,\kappa} \in N, \tilde{x}_{21}, x_{23} = 0) > 0$ and therefore $\Pr(y_0 = d_0, y_3 = d_3 \mid \tilde{x}_{21}, x_{23} = 0) > 0$.

(ii) Note that for $g=0$, $\Pr(\tilde{x}_{21}\tilde{b}+y_{30}g=0\,|\,x_{23}=0)=\Pr(\tilde{x}_{21}\tilde{b}=0\,|\,x_{23}=0)<1$ by the full rank condition in Assumption (CS4). Now, for $g\neq 0$

$$\Pr(\tilde{x}_{21}\tilde{b}+y_{30}g=0\,|\,x_{23}=0)=\int \Pr(y_{30}g=-\tilde{x}_{21}\tilde{b}\,|\,\tilde{x}_{21},x_{23}=0)\,dF_{\tilde{x}_{21}|x_{23}=0}$$

$$=\int \sum_{d_0\in\{0,1\}} \Pr(y_3 g=d_0 g-\tilde{x}_{21}\tilde{b}\,|\,y_0=d_0,\tilde{x}_{21},x_{23}=0)$$

$$\times \Pr(y_0=d_0\,|\,\tilde{x}_{21},x_{23}=0)\,dF_{a\tilde{x}_{21}|x_{23}=0}.$$

By Assumption (CS2), $\Pr(y_3 g=d_0 g-\tilde{x}_{21}\tilde{b}\,|\,y_0=d_0,\tilde{x}_{21},x_{23}=0)<1$, and the desired result follows.

LEMMA 7: *Let Assumptions* (CS2)–(CS5) *hold. Then* $Q(\theta_0^*)>Q(\theta)$ *for all* $\theta\in\Re^{k+1}$ *such that* $\theta/\|\theta\|\neq\theta_0^*$.

PROOF: For all $\theta\in\Re^{k+1}$,

$$Q(\theta_0^*)-Q(\theta)$$

$$=f(0)E[y_{21}(\operatorname{sgn}(z\theta_0^*)-\operatorname{sgn}(z\theta))\,|\,x_{23}=0]$$

$$=2f(0)\int_{Z_\theta}\operatorname{sgn}(z\theta_0)E[y_2-y_1\,|\,z,x_{23}=0]\,dF_{z|x_{23}=0}$$

$$=2f(0)\int_{Z_\theta}\operatorname{sgn}(z\theta_0)E[E[y_2-y_1\,|\,x,\alpha,y_0=d_0,y_3=d_3,x_{23}=0]\,|\,z,x_{23}=0]\,dF_{z|x_{23}=0}$$

$$=2f(0)\int \operatorname{sgn}(z\theta_0)E[\Pr(y_1=0,y_2=1\,|\,x,\alpha,y_0=d_0,y_3=d_3,x_{23}=0)$$

$$-\Pr(y_1=1,y_2=0\,|\,x,\alpha,y_0=d_0,y_3=d_3,x_{23}=0)\,|\,z,x_{23}=0]\,dF_{z|x_{23}=0}$$

$$=2f(0)\int_{Z_\theta}\operatorname{sgn}(z\theta_0)E[\Pr(A\,|\,x,\alpha,y_0=d_0,y_3=d_3,x_{23}=0)$$

$$-\Pr(B\,|\,x,\alpha,y_0=d_0,y_3=d_3,x_{23}=0)\,|\,z,x_{23}=0]\,dF_{z|x_{23}=0}$$

$$=2f(0)\int_{Z_\theta}E\left[\operatorname{sgn}(z\theta_0)\left(\frac{\Pr(A\,|\,x,\alpha,x_{23}=0)-\Pr(B\,|\,x,\alpha,x_{23}=0)}{\Pr(y_0=d_0,y_3=d_3\,|\,x,\alpha,x_{23}=0)}\right)\right|$$

$$\left. z,x_{23}=0\right]dF_{z|x_{23}=0}.$$

As we have shown in Section 2, $\operatorname{sgn}(\Pr(A\,|\,x,\alpha,x_{23}=0)-\Pr(B\,|\,x,\alpha,x_{23}=0))=\operatorname{sgn}(z\theta_0)$, so that the integrand above is nonnegative, which implies that $\operatorname{sgn}(z\theta_0)E[y_2-y_1\,|\,z,x_{23}=0]=|E[y_2-y_1\,|\,z,x_{23}=0]|$. Therefore,

$$Q(\theta_0^*)-Q(\theta)=2f(0)\int_{Z_\theta}|E[y_2-y_1\,|\,z,x_{23}=0]|\,dF_{z|x_{23}=0}\geq 0.$$

Now, $E[y_2-y_1\,|\,z,x_{23}=0]\neq 0$ for almost all z since $E[y_2-y_1\,|\,z,x_{23}=0]=0$ if and only if $\operatorname{sgn}(z\theta_0)=0$, or equivalently $z\theta_0=0$, an event that has zero probability measure under our assumptions. It then follows from Lemma 6 and from Assumption (CS5) that $Q(\theta_0^*)-Q(\theta)>0$ whenever $\theta/\|\theta\|\neq\theta_0^*$.

Finally, to show continuity of the limiting objective function with respect to θ, we follow Lemma 5 of Manski (1985). From the proof of that Lemma, it is clear that we need to establish continuity of terms of the form:

$$\Pr(y_1 = d_1, y_2 = d_2, x_{21,\kappa} b_\kappa > -g(y_3 - y_0) - \bar{x}_{21}\tilde{b} \mid x_{23} = 0)$$

$$= \sum_{d_0, d_3 \in \{0,1\}} \Pr(y_1 = d_1, y_2 = d_2, x_{21,\kappa} b_\kappa > -g(d_3 - d_0) - \bar{x}_{21}\tilde{b} \mid x_{23} = 0, y_0 = d_0, y_3 = d_3) \Pr(y_0 = d_0, y_3 = d_3 \mid x_{23} = 0)$$

$$= \sum_{d_0, d_3 \in \{0,1\}} \int_{\bar{x}_{21}} \left[\int_{-g(d_3 - d_0) - \bar{x}_{21}\tilde{b}} \Pr(y_1 = d_1, y_2 = d_2 \mid x, x_{23} = 0, y_0 = d_0, y_3 = d_3) \times f_{x_{21,\kappa} \mid x_{23} = 0, y_0 = d_0, y_3 = d_3, \bar{x}_{21}}(x_{21,\kappa})\, dx_{21,\kappa} \right] dF_{\bar{x}_{21} \mid x_{23} = 0, y_0 = d_0, y_3 = d_3} \times \Pr(y_0 = d_0, y_3 = d_3 \mid x_{23} = 0).$$

Note that in order to establish continuity of the last expression above with respect to $\theta = (\tilde{b}, g)$ it is sufficient that $f_{x_{21,\kappa} \mid x_{23} = 0, y_0 = d_0, y_3 = d_3}(x_{21,\kappa})$ does not have any mass points. This will be true given our Assumption (CS3) on $f_{x_{21,\kappa} \mid x_{23} = 0, \bar{x}_{21}}(x_{21,\kappa})$.

REFERENCES

AMEMIYA, T. (1985): *Advanced Econometrics*. Cambridge, MA: Harvard University Press.

ANDERSEN, E. (1970): "Asymptotic Properties of Conditional Maximum Likelihood Estimators," *Journal of the Royal Statistical Society*, Series B, 32, 283–301.

ARELLANO, M., AND R. CARRASCO (1996): "Binary Choice Panel Data Models with Predetermined Variables," unpublished manuscript, CEMFI, Madrid.

CARD, D., AND D. SULLIVAN (1988): "Measuring the Effects of Subsidized Training Programs on Movements In and Out of Employment," *Econometrica*, 56, 497–530.

CHAMBERLAIN, G. (1984): "Panel Data," in *Handbook of Econometrics*, Vol. II, edited by Z. Griliches and M. Intriligator. Amsterdam: North Holland.

——— (1985): "Heterogeneity, Omitted Variable Bias, and Duration Dependence," in *Longitudinal Analysis of Labor Market Data*, edited by J. J. Heckman and B. Singer. Cambridge: Cambridge University Press.

——— (1993): "Feedback in Panel Data Models," unpublished manuscript, Department of Economics, Harvard University.

CHINTAGUNTA, P., E. KYRIAZIDOU, AND J. PERKTOLD (1998): "Panel Data Analysis of Household Brand Choices," unpublished manuscript, Department of Economics, University of Chicago.

CHUNG, K. L. (1974): *A Course in Probability Theory*. New York: Academic Press.

HAHN, J. (1997): "Information Bound of the Dynamic Panel Logit Model with Fixed Effects," unpublished manuscript, Department of Economics, University of Pennsylvania.

HÄRDLE, W. (1984): "Robust Regression Function Estimation," *Journal of Multivariate Analysis*, 14, 169–180.

HÄRDLE, W., AND A. B. TSYBAKOV (1988): "Robust Nonparametric Regression with Simultaneous Scale Curve Estimation," *The Annals of Statistics*, 16, 120–135.

HECKMAN, J. J. (1978): "Simple Statistical Models for Discrete Panel Data Developed and Applied to Tests of the Hypothesis of True State Dependence against the Hypothesis of Spurious State Dependence," *Annales de l'INSEE*, 30–31, 227–269.

——— (1981a): "Statistical Models for Discrete Panel Data," in *Structural Analysis of Discrete Panel Data with Econometric Applications*, edited by C. F. Manski and D. McFadden. Cambridge, MA: MIT Press.

——— (1981b): "Heterogeneity and State Dependence," in *Studies of Labor Markets*, edited by S. Rosen. Chicago: The National Bureau of Economic Research, The University of Chicago Press.

HONORÉ, B. E. (1992): "Trimmed LAD and Least Squares Estimation of Truncated and Censored Regression Models with Fixed Effects," *Econometrica*, 60, 533–565.

——— (1993): "Orthogonality Conditions for Tobit Models with Fixed Effects and Lagged Dependent Variables," *Journal of Econometrics*, 59, 35–61.

HOROWITZ, J. L. (1992): "A Smoothed Maximum Score Estimator for the Binary Response Model," *Econometrica*, 60, 505–531.

HSIAO, C. (1986): *Econometric Analysis of Panel Data*. Cambridge: Cambridge University Press.

JONES, J. M., AND T. J. LANDWEHR (1988): "Removing Heterogeneity Bias from Logit Model Estimation," *Marketing Science*, 7, 41–59.

KIM, J., AND D. POLLARD (1990): "Cube Root Asymptotics," *Annals of Statistics*, 18, 191–219.

KYRIAZIDOU, E. (1997a): "Estimation of a Panel Data Sample Selection Model," *Econometrica*, 65, 1335–1364.

——— (1997b): "Estimation of Dynamic Panel Data Sample Selection Models," unpublished manuscript, Department of Economics, University of Chicago.

MADDALA, G. S. (1983): "*Limited Dependent and Qualitative Variables in Econometrics*," Cambridge: Cambridge University Press.

MAGNAC, T. (1997): "State Dependence and Heterogeneity in Youth Employment Histories," Working Paper, INRA and CREST, Paris.

MANSKI, C. (1975): "The Maximum Score Estimation of the Stochastic Utility Model of Choice," *Journal of Econometrics*, 3, 205–228.

——— (1985): "Semiparametric Analysis of Discrete Response: Asymptotic Properties of the Maximum Score Estimator," *Journal of Econometrics*, 27, 313–333.

——— (1987): "Semiparametric Analysis of Random Effects Linear Models from Binary Panel Data," *Econometrica*, 55, 357–362.

NEWEY, W. K., AND D. MCFADDEN (1994): "Large Sample Estimation and Hypothesis Testing," in *Handbook of Econometrics*, Volume IV, edited by R. F. Engle and D. McFadden. Amsterdam: North Holland, pp. 2113–2245.

NEWEY, W. K., AND J. L. POWELL (1987): "Asymmetric Least Squares Estimation and Testing," *Econometrica*, 55, 819–847.

NOLAN, D., AND D. POLLARD (1987): "U-Processes: Rates of Convergence," *The Annals of Statistics*, 16, 780–799.

PAKES, A., AND D. POLLARD (1989): "Simulation and the Asymptotics of Optimization Estimators," *Econometrica*, 57, 1027–1057.

PHELPS, E. (1972): *Inflation Policy and Unemployment Theory*. New York: Norton.

POLLARD, D. (1984): *Convergence of Stochastic Processes*. New York: Springer-Verlag.

——— (1995): "Uniform Ratio Limit Theorems for Empirical Processes," *Scandinavian Journal of Statistics*, 22, 271–278.

RASCH, G. (1960): *Probabilistic Models for Some Intelligence and Attainment Tests*. Copenhagen: Denmark Pædagogiske Institut.

ROBINSON, P. M. (1984): "Robust Nonparametric Autoregression," in *Robust and Nonlinear Time Series Analysis*, Lecture Notes in Statistics, edited by J. Franke, W. Härdle, and D. Martin. Heidelberg: Springer-Verlag.

STANISWALIS, J. G. (1989): "The Kernel Estimate of a Regression Function in Likelihood-Based Models," *Journal of the American Statistical Association*, 84, 276–283.

TIBSHIRANI, R., AND T. HASTIE (1987): "Local Likelihood Estimation," *Journal of the American Statistical Association*, 82, 559–567.

[3]

Econometrica, Vol. 62, No. 1 (January, 1994), 95–116

A COMPUTATIONALLY PRACTICAL SIMULATION ESTIMATOR FOR PANEL DATA

BY MICHAEL P. KEANE[1]

In this paper I develop a practical extension of McFadden's method of simulated moments estimator for limited dependent variable models to the panel data case. The method is based on a factorization of the MSM first order condition into transition probabilities, along with the development of a new highly accurate method for similating these transition probabilities. A series of Monte-Carlo tests show that this MSM estimator performs quite well relative to quadrature-based ML estimators, even when large numbers of quadrature points are employed. The estimator also performs well relative to simulated ML, even when a highly accurate method is used to simulate the choice probabilities. In terms of computational speed, complex panel data models involving random effects and ARMA errors may be estimated via MSM in times similar to those necessary for estimation of simple random effects models via ML-quadrature.

KEYWORDS: Method of simulated moments, panel data, limited dependent variables, equicorrelation, importance sampling, multinomial probit.

1. INTRODUCTION

AN IMPORTANT PROBLEM in the panel data literature is the estimation of limited dependent variable (LDV) models in the presence of serially correlated errors. Maximum likelihood estimation (ML) of these models generally requires the evaluation of choice probabilities which are multivariate integrals—with the order of integration proportional to the number of time periods in the panel. In order to make estimation practical, it is typically assumed that the covariance matrix of the errors has some simple form which allows the order of integration to be reduced. In particular, it is generally assumed that the errors are i.i.d. or that they are equicorrelated. The latter assumption leads to the popular random effects model (see Heckman (1981)) which is practical to estimate using the Gaussian quadrature procedure described by Butler and Moffitt (1982).

The assumption that errors are either equicorrelated or i.i.d. can be undesirable in many situations. Economic theory often suggests of serially correlated error components. Furthermore, if we wish to use an LDV model for prediction purposes, it is important to determine the error structure which gives the best fit to the data, rather than imposing a particular structure a priori.

[1] I would like to thank the Alfred P. Sloan Foundation, the Federal Reserve Bank of Minneapolis, and the Institute for Empirical Macroeconomics for their support of this research. This paper is taken from the first chapter of my Ph.D. dissertation at Brown University. I thank my dissertation committee of Robert Moffitt, Tony Lancaster, and David Runkle for their advice and comments. The comments of Daniel McFadden, Ariel Pakes, John Geweke, and seminar particpants at the 1988 Winter meetings of the Econometric Society, the University of Chicago, the University of Minnesota, the University of Rochester, and the 1990 Banff Invitational Symposium on Consumer Decision Making and Choice Behavior are also greatly appreciated. All errors are of course the responsibility of the author.

The views expressed herein are those of the author and not necessarily those of the Federal Reserve Bank of Minneapolis or the Federal Reserve System.

An additional problem with the a priori assumption of a particular error structure in LDV models is that, due to the nonlinearity of these models, the ML estimator is not in general consistent when the error structure is misspecified. For example, if one falsely assumes equicorrelated errors when there is an AR(1) error component, the ML estimator of the regressor coefficients may be inconsistent. If one assumes i.i.d. errors, the ML estimator will be consistent in the presence of any type of serial correlation so long as the errors are normally distributed (see Robinson (1982)). However the resultant estimator is inefficient if serial correlation is present, and the resultant model will not predict as well as one which accounts for serial correlation.

The method of simulated moments (MSM), a new estimation technique developed by McFadden (1989) and Pakes and Pollard (1989), provides a practical method for estimating LDV models in which the choice probabilities are cumbersome multivariate integrals. The idea is to perform Monte-Carlo simulations of these integrals rather than evaluating them numerically. If the simulations are unbiased, the simulation errors tend to cancel out of the first order conditions of a method of moments estimator (MOM) when one sums over observations. Both McFadden and Pakes and Pollard (1989) prove that an MSM estimator based on unbiased simulators is consistent and asymptotically normal, as well as being asymptotically (in simulation size) as efficient as ML, given the optimal choice of the MOM weighting matrix. If an MSM estimator is constructed using simulators that are only asymptotically (in simulation size) unbiased, these consistency and asymptotic normality results continue to hold if simulation size is increased with sample size at a sufficient rate (see also McFadden and Ruud (1991)). When importance sampling or other similar techniques are used to construct simulators which are smooth functions of the model parameters, standard gradient methods can be used to obtain MSM estimates.

Thus, the MSM estimator provides a potential means for estimating LDV models with complex patterns of serial correlation. However, the discussion of LDV models in McFadden is limited largely to the estimation of multinomial probits involving many choices on cross-sectional data. Here the order of integration is equal to $M-1$, where M is the number of possible choices. Application of the MSM to panel data is a difficult problem for the following reason: with T time periods and M possible choices, there are M^T possible choice sequences. The probability of each sequence must be simulated in order to apply MSM directly, and this quickly becomes impractical as T increases.

In this paper, I develop a practical extension of the MSM estimator to the panel data case. This estimator avoids the problem of having to simulate the probabilities of M^T possible choice sequences by expressing the objective function in terms of transition probabilities. A practical method for simulating transition probabilities is developed by using importance sampling techniques. This probability simulator is smooth in the model parameters, so that standard gradient methods of optimization work well.

Unfortunately, for large T, practical simulators of transition probabilities that are smooth functions of the model parameters can be only asymptotically unbiased in the number of random draws used in simulation. As a result, the simulation estimator proposed here can only be made asymptotically unbiased in simulation size when $T \geqslant 4$. To assess the importance of the bias that exists for finite simulation size, I perform a series of Monte-Carlo repeated sampling experiments. These Monte-Carlo experiments are of additional interest, because they are the first repeated sampling experiments for any simulation estimator to be reported in the econometrics literature. Even for large T and small sized simulations, the Monte-Carlo tests indicate that the bias in the MSM estimator is negligible.

The method for simulating probabilities developed in this paper is also of interest in its own right. The method is often referred to as the Geweke-Hajivassiliou-Keane, or GHK, simulator, because simultaneous and independent work by Geweke (1991) and Hajivassiliou led to the development of the same method. Hajivassiliou, McFadden, and Ruud (1991), in an extensive study of alternative methods for the simulation of probabilities, find that the GHK simulator is extremely accurate even for small numbers of Monte-Carlo draws, and that it outperforms all the other methods considered.

In addition to the present paper, other attempts to develop simulation estimators for panel data LDV models have been made by Hajivassiliou and McFadden (1990) and by McFadden and Ruud (1987). These approaches are described in detail in Section 3.2. But basically, the preferred approach of these authors is to use the highly accurate GHK simulator to implement simulated maximum likelihood (SML) or to find the roots of the simulated score (also using GHK). In this paper, I also present the first repeated sampling experiments for the SML estimator based on GHK. The results indicate that SML based on a small number of draws works reasonably well, but that its estimates of serial correlation parameters suffer from substantial biases when serial correlation is strong. These biases are not present with the MSM estimator, and hence SML is clearly dominated by MSM in my experiments.

Besides these alternative simulation estimators, several authors have devised practical non-ML estimators for LDV models with dependent observations which are more efficient than ML estimators that assume i.i.d. errors, but which remain consistent in the presence of serially correlated errors. These include the "orthogonality condition" estimators of Avery, Hansen, and Hotz (1983), the minimum distance method of Chamberlain (1985), the "nonlinear IV" estimators of Bates and White (1987), and the quasi-ML estimator of Poirier and Ruud (1988). However, none of these estimators is as efficient as ML, and their extension to systems of equations or multinomial probit models is computationally burdensome. The simulation estimator for panel data proposed here thus has three important advantages over these procedures. First, it is asymptotically (in simulation size) as efficient as ML; second, being a simulation estimator, it can readily handle multinomial probit situations; and third, it can be readily extended to estimate nonlinear systems of equations which would be impractical to estimate by ML.

The outline of the paper is as follows. Section 2 describes the probit model. Section 3.1 describes the MSM estimator and Section 3.2 explains the difficulties involved in applying it to panel data. The key section of the paper is 3.3 which presents the construction of the simulation estimator for panel data. Section 3.4 contains the details of the construction of smooth simulators for transition probabilities, and contains a discussion of the asymptotic properties of the MSM estimator based on this simulation procedure. Section 4 presents the Monte-Carlo test results. Section 5 concludes the paper.

2. THE PROBIT MODEL

Although the simulation estimator which I will describe has more general application, I will follow McFadden (1989) and restrict my exposition to the multinomial probit model. The probit model has the following form. An individual chooses from the set S of M mutually exclusive choices that choice which gives greatest utility. The utility of choice j to person i at time t is given by:

$$\mu_{ijt} = X_{it}\beta_j + \varepsilon_{ijt} \qquad (j = 1, \ldots, M-1; t = 1, \ldots, T), \tag{1}$$

where X_{it} is a row vector of exogenous regressors and β_j is a vector of coefficients possibly specific to choice j. μ_{iMt} is normalized to 0 for identification. ε_{ijt} is a disturbance which is independent across individuals but has a multivariate normal distribution over choices and time, $\varepsilon_i \sim N(0, \Sigma)$. Here, and below, the suppression of subscripts indicates that a variable becomes a vector including elements for all values of the subscripts. The covariance matrix Σ has the Cholesky decomposition $A'A$, so that $\varepsilon_i = A'\eta_i$ where η_i is i.i.d. We do not observe μ_{ijt} directly, but instead observe only the indicator d_{ijt}, where

$$d_{ijt} = \begin{cases} 1 & \text{if } \mu_{ijt} \geqslant \mu_{ij't} \ \forall j' \in S, \\ 0 & \text{otherwise.} \end{cases} \tag{2}$$

Let the $K \times 1$ parameter vector θ contain the elements of β and the parameters of the error processes that generate Σ. Thus θ denotes the true parameter vector. Letting j_t be the index of the choice actually made at time t, define $J_{it} = \{j_1, \ldots, j_t\}_i$ as the sequence of choices actually made by person i in periods 1 through t. Then, maximum likelihood estimation of the probit model requires that one calculate the choice probabilities $E(d_{ijt}|J_{i,t-1}, \hat{\theta}, X_i)$ for a large number of trial parameter values $\hat{\theta}$. The problem with the probit model in the panel data case is that, for unrestricted Σ, the time T choice probabilities are $T \cdot (M-1)$ variate integrals. Even in the single period case, estimation is prohibitively expensive for $M \geqslant 4$ (see Kahaner (1991)).

The required order of integration may exceed $T \cdot (M-1)$ if the history of the choice process begins prior to $t = 1$, the first period of observed data. Then, consistent estimation requires that the past history of the (X, ε) process be "integrated out" of the likelihood function (see Heckman (1981)). This problem is simplified if X is exogenous. Then it is only necessary to integrate over the history of the ε process prior to $t=1$ to form the appropriate marginal density $f(\varepsilon_{i1},\ldots,\varepsilon_{iT}|\hat{\theta})$. For many stochastic processes a closed form exists for this marginal density. Examples are when ε_{it} is a sum of an individual random effect plus a stationary invertible ARMA process, as in the probit models I consider in Section 4. In such cases, where a closed form for the marginal density exists, the order of integration remains $T\cdot(M-1)$ despite the existence of an unobserved past history of the ε_{it} process.

3. THE METHOD OF SIMULATED MOMENTS AND PANEL DATA

3.1. *Background on the Method of Simulated Moments*

The idea of simulation estimation is to simulate integrals like $E(d_{ijt}|J_{i,t-1},\hat{\theta},X_i)$ via inexpensive Monte-Carlo methods, rather than evaluate them accurately via expensive numerical methods. For example, consider the integral $P=\int_R f(\mu|\hat{\theta})d\eta$ where $f(\mu|\hat{\theta})$ is the density of the random variable μ given a trial parameter value $\hat{\theta}$ and R is a region in the support of μ. The value of P can be simulated by taking one or more draws from the density $f(\mu|\hat{\theta})$ and calculating the fraction of these draws which fall in the region R. For example, referring to the probit model in equation (1), one could draw values for μ_{ijt}, $j=1,\ldots,M$, $t=1,\ldots,T$ from the multivariate normal distribution determined by $X_i\beta$ and Σ and count the percentage that generate a particular choice sequence. This is called a "frequency" simulator. The resulting estimate of P is unbiased even if only one draw from $f(\mu|\hat{\theta})$ is used.[2]

McFadden proposes the use of simulation in the context of method of moments (MOM) estimation to solve the problem of high order multivariate integration in the probit model. In the single period case on which McFadden concentrates, the vector of first order conditions for an MOM estimator is given by:

$$(3)\qquad \sum_{i=1}^{N} W_i\left(d_i - E\left(d_i|\hat{\theta}_{\mathrm{MOM}},X_i\right)\right)=0$$

where $\hat{\theta}_{\mathrm{MOM}}$ is the MOM estimator of θ, d_i is an $M\times 1$ column vector of indicator variables for person i, $E(d_i|\hat{\theta},X_i)$ is an $M\times 1$ column vector of expected values of the elements of d_i conditional on $\hat{\theta}$ and X_i, and W_i is a $K\times M$ weighting matrix. The optimal MOM weights are obtained if the (k,j)th element of W_i is chosen to be $E(d_{ij}|\hat{\theta}_c,X_i)^{-1}\ \partial E(d_{ij}|\hat{\theta}_c,X_i)/\partial\hat{\theta}_{ck}$ for each j and k where $\hat{\theta}_c$ is a consistent (but inefficient) initial estimate of θ. Then the

[2] Frequency simulation has been used to evaluate choice probabilities in the context of ML estimation by Albright, Lerman, and Manski (1977), Lerman and Manski (1981), and Pakes (1986). Note, however, that if one simulates a probability P in a log likelihood function, the resulting estimate of $\ln P$ will be biased because of the nonlinearity of the logarithmic transformation (i.e., $E\ln(P+s)\neq\ln E(P+s)=\ln P$, where s is a mean zero random simulation error). Thus, simulations of P must be very precise in order to keep the bias in simulating $\ln P$ small.

FOC for the MOM estimator are (asymptotically) equivalent to the derivatives of the log-likelihood function, and the estimator is asymptotically efficient.

The important aspect of the MOM estimator is that the $E(d_{ij}|\hat{\theta}, X_i)$, which are the difficult quantities to evaluate, enter *linearly* into the FOC of the estimator. The MSM estimator replaces the difficult to evaluate $E(d_{ij}|\hat{\theta}, X_i)$ by simulators $\hat{E}(d_{ij}|\hat{\theta}, X_i)$. Because these simulators enter the FOC linearly, the simulation errors enter the FOC linearly as well, and simulation error tends to cancel across observations i. Both McFadden and Pakes-Pollard have independently proved that the MSM estimator based on unbiased simulators is consistent and asymptotically normal and that, if frequency simulation is used, it has a covariance matrix which is $(1 + 1/r)$ times that of the MOM estimator, where r is the number of draws used in the simulation. If the optimal MOM weights are consistently simulated, the estimator is asymptotically as efficient as ML. It generally will not be possible to simulate the weights consistently (for fixed r) because of denominator bias, so the MSM estimator will approach the efficiency of ML only as the number of random draws used to simulate the denominators of the weights grows large. McFadden and Ruud (1991) show that these asymptotic results continue to hold for MSM estimators based on biased simulators, so long as the simulation bias converges to zero in probability as sample size increases at a sufficient rate (see Section 3.4).

As a practical matter it may not be desirable to use frequency simulators to evaluate choice probabilities. If $E(d_{ij}|\hat{\theta}, X_i)$ is evaluated using a frequency simulator, $\partial\hat{E}(d_{ij}|\hat{\theta}, X_i)/\partial\hat{\theta}$ is not continuous. In fact, $\hat{E}(d_{ij}|\hat{\theta}, X_i)$ is piecewise constant in $\hat{\theta}$ with discrete jumps at values of $\hat{\theta}$ which produce ties among alternatives. Hence, conventional gradient methods cannot be used to minimize the objective, and random search or pseudo-gradient methods must be used instead.

As discussed in McFadden, it is often more practical to use a techniques such as "importance sampling" to construct "smooth" simulators. Returning to the equation for P we see it can be rewritten as $P = \int_R[f(\mu|\hat{\theta})/\gamma(\mu)]\gamma(\mu)\,d\mu$ where $\gamma(\mu)$ is any density function such that $f(\mu|\hat{\theta})/\gamma(\mu)$ is finite almost everywhere in region R. By definition, this integral is the expectation of the quantity $f(\mu|\hat{\theta})/\gamma(\mu)$. Thus, P can be simulated by evaluating $f(\mu|\hat{\theta})/\gamma(\mu)$ at one or more draws from the "importance sampling" density $\gamma(\mu)$ that fall in the region R. This method is inexpensive because $\gamma(\mu)$ can be chosen in such a way that most or all the μ drawn will fall in the region R. Such a simulator is called "smooth" because, for a given $\mu = \mu^*$, the derivative of $f(\mu^*|\hat{\theta})/\gamma(\mu^*)$ with respect to $\hat{\theta}$ is continuous.[3] Hence standard gradient methods can be used to minimize objectives with respect to $\hat{\theta}$. For stability of the optimization process it is essential that the draws from $\gamma(\mu)$ be held fixed as we iterate on $\hat{\theta}$.

[3] As discussed by Geweke (1987) and McFadden, smooth simulators are often more efficient than frequency simulators. Thus, an MSM estimator based on smooth simulators may have an asymptotic covariance matrix less than $(1 + 1/r)$ times that of the MOM estimator. The smooth simulators described here are a form of importance sampling because the simulator is a weighted sum of the $f(\mu|\hat{\theta})$ with the weights being $\gamma(\mu)^{-1}$

3.2. *The Problem of Applying the Method of Simulated Moments to Panel Data*

This section describes the difficulties inherent in applying MSM to panel data. In McFadden's original formulation, the FOC for the MSM estimator are constructed in terms of unconditional choice probabilities. In the panel data case, this is only possible if we treat *sequences* of states as the objects of choice. For this purpose, let $j \in \{1, \ldots, M^T\}$ index alternative sequences. Then the d_{ij} become indicators for certain sequences of events, and the $E(d_{ij}|\hat{\theta}, X_i)$ become the probabilities of observing these sequences. Since there are M^T possible sequences of choices, the residual vector $[d_i - E(d_i|\hat{\theta}, X_i)]$ in equation (3) is M^T elements long. To utilize a smooth simulator, it is necessary to calculate the probability of observing each possible sequence for each person. As M and T increase, this will quickly require an impractical number of calculations.

McFadden discusses two ways around this problem, neither of which is adopted here. The first, investigated by McFadden and Ruud, is to construct a frequency simulator based on only r draws from the density $f(\mu|\hat{\theta})$ of random variables μ that determine the sequence of states chosen. This frequency simulator will give nonzero values for the probabilities of at most r of the possible sequences. McFadden shows that an MSM estimator utilizing residuals $[d_{ij} - \hat{E}(d_{ij}|\hat{\theta}, X_i)]$ only for these few sequences, plus that for the observed sequence if it is not among them, has a covariance matrix which is still only $(1 + 1/r)$ times as large as that for the MOM estimator. The drawback of this approach is that the simulator is not smooth, so that costly random search or pseudo-gradient procedures must be employed in estimation. To my knowledge this method has not yet been successfully applied, although advances in non-smooth hill climbing algorithms may make it more appealing.

The second approach, investigated by Hajivassiliou and McFadden, is to simulate directly, via a smooth simulator, the score of the log-likelihood function, which is

$$\sum_{j=1}^{MT} d_{ij}\,\partial \ln E\left(d_{ij}|\hat{\theta}, X_i\right)/\partial\hat{\theta} = \sum_{j=1}^{MT} d_{ij} E\left(d_{ij}|\hat{\theta}, X_i\right)^{-1} \partial E\left(d_{ij}|\hat{\theta}, X_i\right)/\partial\hat{\theta}.$$

Since $d_{ij} = 0$ for all sequences except that which is observed, the score need only be simulated for the particular observed sequence and the problem of having an enormous number of possible sequences is avoided. However, such a simulator is biased because the term $E(d_{ij}|\hat{\theta}, X_i)$ is simulated and the nonlinear transformation $1/E$ taken. Note that this method of simulated scores, or MSS, procedure is essentially identical to SML, so long as the same smooth probability simulator is used in each case, because any trial value $\hat{\theta}$ that gives a local maximum of the simulated log likelihood function is also a root of the simulated score.

Despite the biases involved in these procedures, Hajivassiliou and McFadden and Borsch-Supan and Hajivassiliou (1990) argue that SML or MSS based on the highly accurate GHK simulator performs well using very small numbers of draws. However, extensive repeated sampling studies of such estimators have not yet been performed.[4] In this paper I present the first such study. I find that SML based on the GHK simulator does perform reasonably well using only small numbers of draws. However, in my Monte-Carlo experiments this SML procedure is dominated by the MSM estimator I describe in the next section.

In addition to these approaches, van Praag and Hop (1987) and Ruud (1992) point out that the score also can be written in terms of the latent vector μ rather than in terms of choice probabilities. Then, it is possible to form unbiased simulators of the score if it is feasible to draw the μ from their conditional distribution determined by agents' observed choices d. This idea forms the basis of "simulated EM algorithm" and "Gibbs sampling" approaches to estimation of LDV models (see Albert and Chib (1993) and McCulloch and Rossi (1992)). Monte-Carlo analysis of the performance of these procedures relative to MSM or SML based on GHK do not yet exist for the panel data case. Geweke, Keane, and Runkle (1992) compare the performance of all these approaches in a cross-section case. An important avenue for future research is to perform Monte-Carlo studies of the simulated EM and Gibbs sampling approaches in the panel data case.

3.3. *Construction of the Simulation Estimator for Panel Data*

The solution to the problem of applying MSM estimation to panel data that is proposed in this section involves two parts. First, to circumvent the problem of having M^T possible sequences of choices, the MOM first order condition is rewritten in terms of transition probabilities. Second, a method for obtaining computationally efficient smooth simulators of these transition probabilities is devised.

Recalling that J_{it} is the sequence of observed choices for person i in periods 1 through t, the MOM first order condition written in terms of transition probabilities has the form:

$$(4) \qquad \sum_{i=1}^{N} \sum_{t=1}^{T} \sum_{j=1}^{M} W_{ijt}\left[d_{ijt} - E\left(d_{ijt} | J_{i,t-1}, \hat{\theta}_{\text{MOM}}, X_i\right)\right] = 0.$$

Now, rather than M^T, there are only $M \cdot T$ probabilities to be simulated. However, expressing the FOC in this way creates an important new problem—from the second period onward, the transition probabilities $E(d_{ijt}|J_{i,t-1}, \hat{\theta}, X_i)$ must be simulated. In most circumstances, it is either impossible or extremely difficult to construct unbiased smooth simulators of transition probabilities. This is because transition probabilities are generally ratios of two integrals, and simulating a denominator produces bias.

Unbiased frequency simulators of transition probabilities can be constructed using the acceptance-rejection method (henceforth A/R). In the probit model

[4] Borsch-Supan and Hajivassiliou study the performance of SML based on the GHK simulator in a cross-section trinomial probit model using a single Monte-Carlo data set. They do not do a repeated sampling experiment or consider the panel data case.

of Section 2 we see that, for given values of θ and X_i, a draw for the vector of i.i.d. errors η will generate a particular sequence of states. In the simplest A/R method, random vectors η are drawn from a standard normal distribution with density $f(\eta_{i1},\ldots,\eta_{1,t-1})$ until one or more which generate the sequence of states $J_{i,t-1}$ actually chosen by individual i up through period $t-1$ are obtained. I will refer to such sequences of i.i.d. errors η which generate the observed sequence of choices $J_{i,t-1}$ as "accepted conditioning sequences." When such a sequence is obtained by the A/R method, it will have the correct density $f(\eta_{i1},\ldots,\eta_{i,t-1}|J_{i,t-1},\hat{\theta},X_i)$.[5] If we randomly draw from $f(\eta_{it})$ values for the time t elements of η (i.e., the η_{ijt} for $j=1,\ldots,M-1$), then the fraction of these draws which, conditional on a particular accepted conditioning sequence, imply the choice of state j at time t, is an unbiased frequency simulator of $E(d_{ijt}|J_{i,t-1},\hat{\theta},X_i)$.

Unfortunately, the simple A/R method is not practical. An enormous number of draws may be necessary to obtain just one accepted sequence if M^{t-1} is large, making the A/R method extremely expensive.[6] An important innovation in my approach is the use of an alternative method that generates accepted conditioning sequences at low cost. This method involves drawing sequences very inexpensively from an importance sampling distribution, say with density $\phi(\eta_{i1},\ldots,\eta^*_{i,t-1}|J_{i,t-1},\hat{\theta},X_i)$, chosen so that sequences drawn from it are likely to be accepted. Denote by $(\eta^*_{i,1},\ldots,\eta^*_{i,t-1})$ a *particular* sequence drawn from $\phi(\cdot|\cdot)$ that generates the observed set of choices $J_{i,t-1}$. Of course, since $(\eta^*_{it},\ldots,\eta_{i,t-1})$ is not drawn from $f(\eta_{i,1},\ldots,\eta_{i,t-1}|J_{i,t-1},\hat{\theta},X_i)$ we have, letting E_ϕ denote the expectation over all $(\eta^*_{i,t},\ldots,\eta^*_{i,t-1})$ sequences obtained from ϕ, that $E_\phi\{\hat{E}(d_{ijt}|(\eta^*_{i,1},\ldots,\eta^*_{i,t-1}),\hat{\theta},X_i)\}\neq E(d_{ijt}|J_{i,t-1},\hat{\theta},X_i)$. However, an *unbiased* simulator of the transition probability $E(d_{ijt}|J_{i,t-1},\hat{\theta},X_i)$ may be formed as a weighted sum of transition probabilities conditional on each of several such sequences $(\eta^*_{i,1},\ldots,\eta^*_{i,t-1})_s$ for $s=1,\ldots,S$ as follows:

$$(5)\qquad \hat{E}\left(d_{ijt}|J_{i,t-1},\hat{\theta},X_i\right)=\frac{1}{S}\sum_{s=1}^{S}\omega_s\hat{E}\left(d_{ijt}|(\eta^*_{i,1},\ldots,\eta^*_{i,t-1})_s,\hat{\theta},X_i\right).$$

Here the "sequence weights" ω_s are ratios of the correct joint density

[5] Note, as was mentioned in Section 2, that since the history of ε prior to $t=1$ is assumed unobserved, $f(\cdot|\cdot)$ must be an appropriate marginal density with respect to ε dated prior to $t=1$. If the ε_{it} process is ergodic Markov and has been operating since the indefinite past, then it is stationary and it is appropriate to draw from the ergodic distribution. For example, if $\varepsilon_{it}=\rho\varepsilon_{i,t-1}+v_{it}$ where $|\rho|<1$ and $v_{it}\sim N(0,1-\rho^2)$ then draw ε_{i1} from the $N(0,1)$ distribution. If the ε_{it} process started in the recent past one cannot draw from the ergodic distribution. For example, if ε_{it} is as above, but the process started K periods prior to $t=1$, then draw ε_{i1} from the $N(0,(1-\rho^2)\Sigma_{q=0}^{K}\rho^{2q})$ distribution. Since $\varepsilon_i=A'\eta_i$, simple mappings exist from these ε distributions to the approximate η distributions. Note that there may be processes for which integration over the past history does not lead to a closed form for the marginal distribution of ε_{it} for $t=1,T$. In such cases, one must simulate the whole history of the ε_{it} process in order to obtain draws from the appropriate marginal distribution.

[6] As discussed in Hajivassiliou and McFadden, more elaborate A/R methods have been devised which reduce the number of draws needed to obtain accepted sequences. However, they find that even the more sophisticated A/R methods are prohibitively expensive in practice.

$f(\eta^*_{i,1}, \ldots, \eta^*_{i,t-1} | J_{i,t-1}, \hat{\theta}, X_i)$ to the importance sampling joint density $\phi(\eta^*_{i,1}, \ldots, \eta^*_{i,t-1} | J_{i,t-1}, \hat{\theta}, X_i)$ of sequence s. Thus the ω_s are importance sampling weights.

Different choices of the importance sampling density ϕ and the method for forming the $\hat{E}$ lead to different estimators. Section 3.4 describes the details of the particular procedure used here to form $\hat{E}$ and to construct accepted conditioning sequences (i.e., the particular importance sampling distribution from which the sequences are drawn), and derives the correct form of the sequence weights corresponding to this procedure. In this procedure, ϕ is specified as the density of sequences constructed by drawing recursively (i.e., one component of η at a time) until a complete η vector implying a person's choice history is obtained, and $\hat{E}$ is also formed using such recursive draws. This amounts to using the GHK method to simulate the transition probabilities. It is important to note, however, that other choices of ϕ and $\hat{E}$ could potentially dominate this procedure. This is an important avenue for future research.

3.4. *Asymptotically Unbiased Simulation of Transition Probabilities via Importance Sampling*

To simulate a time t transition probability we must construct conditioning sequences that generate the observed set of choices up through period $t-1$, denoted $J_{i,t-1}$. Rather than drawing entire vectors $(\eta^*_{i,1}, \ldots, \eta^*_{i,t-1})$ from the unconditional density $f(\cdot)$ and accepting only those vectors for which *all* $\eta_{i\tau}$ for $\tau = 1, t-1$ are accepted (i.e., those that generate the entire set of observed choices $J_{i,t-1}$), the inexpensive method of sequence construction used in this paper is to build up sequences on an element-by-element basis. Specifically, using the $M = 2$ case (where there is only one error per period) to illustrate, the procedure works as follows. A value for η_{i1} is drawn from the truncated standard normal distribution from which *all* draws generate the state actually chosen in period one. This value, call it η^*_{i1}, is retained and a value of η_{i2} is drawn from the truncated normal distribution conditional on η^*_{i1}, all draws from which generate the state actually chosen in period two. The vector $(\eta^*_{i1}, \eta^*_{i2})$ is then an accepted conditioning sequence for periods 1 and 2. Repeating this for $t-1$ periods we obtain one conditioning sequence η for the first $t-1$ time periods.[7]

[7] To draw from the truncated univariate normal, let Y^* be a particular draw from a univariate standard uniform distribution, $Y \in [0, 1]$. Let $F(\cdot)$ be the standard normal distribution function. Then, $F(\eta_{it} | a \leqslant \eta_{it} \leqslant b) = (F(\eta_{it}) - F(a))/(F(b) - F(a))$. Letting $F(\eta^*_{it} | a \leqslant \eta_{it} \leqslant b)$ equal Y^*, we have $\eta^*_{it} = F^{-1}\{(F(b) - F(a))Y^* + F(a)\}$, where $F^{-1}(\cdot)$ is the inverse distribution function. In the probit model, the values of a and b may be simply calculated given knowledge of X_i, $\hat{\theta}$ and the previous period draws $(\eta^*_{i,1}, \ldots, \eta^*_{i,t-1})$. As $\hat{\theta}$ is varied in optimization, the draws from the uniform distribution are held fixed. Then, the values of a and b, and hence the draws η^*_{it}, vary smoothly with $\hat{\theta}$. The weights ω_s also vary smoothly with $\hat{\theta}$. It will, therefore, be possible to construct smooth simulators of transition probabilities using formula (5).

Given this method of constructing conditioning sequences, the proper sequence weights are constructed as follows. Begin with the 3-period case. Recalling that j_t denotes the choice actually made at time t, while $J_{i,t} \equiv \{j_1,\ldots,j_t\}$, and suppressing all individual subscripts i, define the sets:

$$A = \{\eta_1 | d_{j1} = 1 \text{ for } j = j_1\},$$

$$B = \{\eta_1, \eta_2 | d_{j1} = 1 \text{ for } j = j_1, d_{j2} = 1 \text{ for } j = j_2\},$$

$$B(\eta_1^*) = \{\eta_2 | d_{j2} = 1 \text{ for } j = j_2 \text{ given } \eta_1 = \eta_1^* \in A\},$$

where η_1^* is the particular value of η_1 drawn from the truncated standard normal distribution. It is clear that $f(\eta_1^*, \eta_2^* | (\eta_1, \eta_2) \in B)$, the joint density of a particular vector (η_1^*, η_2^*) obtained by an unbiased A/R method, does not equal $f(\eta_2^* | \eta_2 \in B(\eta_1^*)) f(\eta_1^* | \eta_1 \in A)$, the importance sampling density obtained when the η^* vector is constructed on an element-by-element basis. Notice, however, that:

$$(6) \qquad f(\eta_1^*, \eta_2^* | (\eta_1, \eta_2) \in B) = \frac{f(\eta_1^*) f(\eta_2^*)}{\int_A \int_{B(\eta_1)} f(\eta_1) f(\eta_2)\, d\eta_2\, d\eta_1},$$

$$f(\eta_1^* | \eta_1 \in A) = \frac{f(\eta_1^*)}{\int_A f(\eta_1)\, d\eta_1},$$

$$f(\eta_2^* | \eta_2 \in B(\eta_1^*)) = \frac{f(\eta_2^*)}{\int_{B(\eta_1^*)} f(\eta_2)\, d\eta_2}.$$

Therefore, defining $\omega(\eta_1^*)$ as the ratio of the correct to the importance sampling density, we have:

$$(7) \qquad \omega(\eta_1^*) = \frac{f(\eta_1^*, \eta_2^* | (\eta_1, \eta_2) \in B)}{f(\eta_2^* | \eta_2 \in B(\eta_1^*)) f(\eta_1^* | \eta_1 \in A)} = \frac{\text{prob}\,(\eta_2 \in B(\eta_1) | \eta_1 = \eta_1^*)}{\text{prob}\,(\eta_2 \in B(\eta_1) | \eta_1 \in A)}$$

where $\text{prob}(\cdot | \cdot)$ denotes integration over a conditional normal density. Hence, $\omega(\eta_1^*)$ is the proper weight to apply to simulated probabilities conditional on sequences (η_1^*, η_2^*) in order for the simulations to be unbiased. To see this, consider simulating the probability of a certain event in period 3, $d_{ij3} = 1$ for some $j \in \{1,\ldots,M\}$, conditional on $(\eta_1^*, \eta_2^*) \in B$. Describe this event as $(\eta_1, \eta_2, \eta_3) \in C_j$ where C_j is a subset of B. Define

$$C_j(\eta_1^*, \eta_2^*) = \{\eta_3 | d_{ij3} = 1 \text{ for } j \in \{1,\ldots,M\} \text{ given } (\eta_1^*, \eta_2^*) \in B\},$$

$$\chi_{C_j(\eta_1^*, \eta_2^*)}(\eta_3) = \begin{cases} 1 & \text{if } \eta_3 \in C_j(\eta_1^*, \eta_2^*), \\ 0 & \text{otherwise;} \end{cases}$$

then:

$$(8)\qquad \text{prob}\left[(\eta_1,\eta_2,\eta_3)\in C_j|(\eta_1,\eta_2)\in B\right]$$
$$=\int_A\int_{B(\eta_1)}\int_{-\infty}^{\infty}\chi_{C_j(\eta_1,\eta_2)}(\eta_3)$$
$$\times f(\eta_3)f(\eta_1,\eta_2|(\eta_1,\eta_2)\in B)\,d\eta_3\,d\eta_2\,d\eta_1$$
$$=\int_A\int_{B(\eta_1)}\int_{-\infty}^{\infty}\chi_{C_j(\eta_1,\eta_2)}(\eta_3)f(\eta_3)\omega(\eta_1)$$
$$\times f(\eta_2|\eta_2\in B(\eta_1))f(\eta_1|\eta_1\in A)\,d\eta_3\,d\eta_2\,d\eta_1.$$

Thus, the quantity $\omega(\eta_1^*)\chi_{C_j(\eta_1^*,\eta_2^*)}(\eta_3^*)$ evaluated at a particular draw $(\eta_1^*,\eta_2^*,\eta_3^*)$ from the importance sampling density $f(\eta_3)f(\eta_2|\eta_2\in B(\eta_1))f(\eta_1|\eta_2\in A)$, which is what we have when we obtain draws for η_1 and η_2 on an element-by-element basis and draw η_3 randomly, is an unbiased simulator of the desired transition probability. Here $\omega(\eta_{1s}^*)$ is the importance sampling weight.

Since the sequence weights and the sequences themselves are smooth functions of the model parameters (see footnote 7), the construction of a smooth simulator by a further application of importance sampling to $f(\eta_3)$ is straightforward. Simply rewrite equation (8) as:

$$(9)\qquad \int_A\int_{B(\eta_1)}\int_{C_j(\eta_1,\eta_2)}\left[\frac{f(\eta_3)}{\gamma(\eta_3)}\omega(\eta_1)\right]\gamma(\eta_3)$$
$$\times f(\eta_2|\eta_2\in B(\eta_1))f(\eta_1|\eta_1\in A)\,d\eta_3\,d\eta_2\,d\eta_1.$$

An unbiased smooth simulator is obtained by evaluating the quantity $f(\eta_3)\omega(\eta_1)/\gamma(\eta_3)$ at a draw from the importance sampling density $\gamma(\eta_3)f(\eta_2|\eta_2\in B(\eta_1))f(\eta_1|\eta_1\in A)$. $\gamma(\eta_3)$ is chosen so that most or all random draws for η_3 fall in the region $C_j(\eta_1,\eta_2)$.

To form a more accurate smooth simulator, we may take an average of simulated transition probabilities over several conditioning sequences (as in equation (5)). Additionally, we may also average over several different draws from the importance sampling density $\gamma(\eta_3)$. Letting S be the number of conditioning sequences and R be the number of importance sampling draws, we obtain:

$$(10)\qquad \hat{E}\left(d_{ij3}|J_{i2},\hat{\theta},X_i\right)=\frac{1}{S}\sum_{s=1}^{S}\omega_s(\eta_{1s}^*)$$
$$\times\frac{1}{R}\sum_{r=1}^{R}\hat{E}\left(d_{ij3}|\eta_{i3sr},(\eta_{i1s}^*,\eta_{i2s}^*),\hat{\theta},X_i\right)$$
$$=\frac{1}{S}\sum_{s=1}^{S}\omega_s(\eta_{1s}^*)$$
$$\times\frac{1}{R}\sum_{r=1}^{R}\left[f\left(\eta_{i3sr}|\eta_{i3sr}\in C_j(\eta_{i1s}^*,\eta_{i2s}^*)\right)/\gamma(\eta_{i3sr})\right]$$

where η_{i3sr} is the value of η_{i3} generated by the sth conditioning sequence and the rth importance sampling draw.

Turning from the three-period example to the general case, the proper weights for t element conditioning sequences can be constructed recursively. Define $\eta(t) = (\eta_1, \dots, \eta_t)$ and define $\eta(J_t)$ as the set of sequences that generate the observed set of choices through the first t periods. Then $\omega(\eta_1^*, \dots, \eta_1^*)$, the weight that corresponds to any $t+1$ element accepted conditioning sequence $\eta^*(t+1) = (\eta_1^*, \dots, \eta_t^*, \eta_{t+1}^*)$ that begins with the elements $(\eta_1^*, \dots, \eta_t^*)$, is defined recursively as:

$$\text{(11)} \qquad \omega(\eta^*(t)) = \frac{\omega(\eta^*(t-1))\,\text{prob}\,(\eta_{t+1} \in \eta(J_{t+1}) | \eta(t) = \eta^*(t))}{\text{prob}\,(\eta_{t+1} \in \eta(J_{t+1}) | \eta(t) \in \eta(J_t))}$$

which is obtained by the same type of algebraic manipulations used to obtain equation (7).

Finally, it is important to note that Monte-Carlo simulation of choice probabilities conditional on accepted conditioning sequences, as in equation (10), may be unnecessary. Choice probabilities conditional on accepted conditioning sequences are integrals over only the time t values of the η_{ijt}. Thus, in multinomial probit with $M \leqslant 3$, direct numerical evaluation is feasible, since the order of integration involved is only $M-1$. In the case where $M \geqslant 3$, one possible choice for forming $\hat{E}$ is to use a recursive simulation procedure like that used to construct the conditioning sequences. Note that a time t choice probability may be written as:

$$\begin{aligned}
&\hat{E}\left(d_{ijt} | \eta^*(t-1), \hat{\theta}, X_i\right) \\
&\quad = \text{prob}\left(\mu_{ikt} < \mu_{ijt} \,\forall k \neq j | \eta^*(t-1), \hat{\theta}, X_i\right) \\
&\quad = \text{prob}\left(\{\eta_{ikt}\}_{k=1, M-1} \in \eta(J_t) | \eta^*(t-1), \hat{\theta}, X_i\right).
\end{aligned}$$

This probability may be simulated recursively using a procedure that has the same mathematical form as the procedure for generating accepted conditioning sequences. First, draw from a truncated normal an η_{i1t} that belongs to the set $\eta(J_t)$ conditional on $\eta^*(t-1)$. Then this value, call it η_{i1t}^*, is retained and a value of η_{i2t} is drawn from a truncated normal distribution such that $(\eta_{i1t}^*, \eta_{i2t}) \in \eta(J_t)$ conditional on $\eta^*(t-1)$. This is repeated until the whole η_{it} vector is constructed. Then, an unbiased simulator of the choice j probability is given by:

$$\begin{aligned}
\text{(12)} \quad &\hat{E}\left(d_{ijt} | \eta^*(t-1), \hat{\theta}, X_i\right) \\
&\quad = \text{prob}\left(\eta_{i1t} \in \eta(J_t) | \eta^*(t-1), \hat{\theta}, X_i\right) \\
&\quad \cdot \text{prob}\left(\eta_{i2t} \in \eta(J_t) | \eta_{i1t}^*, \eta^*(t-1), \hat{\theta}, X_i\right) \\
&\quad \cdots\cdot \text{prob}\left(\eta_{i,M-1,t} \in \eta(J_t) | \eta_{i1t}^*, \dots, \eta_{i,M-2,t}^*, \eta^*(t-1), \hat{\theta}, X_t\right).
\end{aligned}$$

This procedure for simulating choice probabilities is referred to as the Geweke-Hajivassiliou-Keane (or GHK) simulator in the paper by Hajivassiliou, McFadden, and Ruud (1991), who compare its performance to many alternative probability simulators and find that it is the most accurate of those considered. It is important to note that the GHK simulator has an importance sampling interpretation, where the importance sampling density $\gamma(\cdot)$ for η_{it} is chosen to be of the same form $\phi(\cdot)$ that was used to draw accepted conditioning sequences, and the importance sampling weights are of a form analogous to that given in equation (11). Thus, the GHK procedure for simulating within period choice probabilities may be integrated with the recursive procedure for constructing conditioning sequences. Specifically, the conditioning sequences may be constructed element-by-element *within* each period, as in (12), and the sequence weights for transition probability simulation will continue to have a structure similar to (11), except that they will be a product of within period weights.

The drawback of my importance sampling technique for simulating transition probabilities is that the denominators of the sequence weights involve multiple integrals. Observe that in (12) the denominator of the weight for a t period sequence is a t variate integral. Simulation of tth period transition probabilities thus requires evaluation of sequence weights that involve $T-1$ variate integrals. Thus, the denominators of the weights must be simulated when $T \geqslant 4$ in order to avoid cumbersome 3-variate or higher numerical integration.

Note that the denominators of the sequence weights equal the expected value of the numerators over all possible sequences. Thus, given S sequences, an unbiased simulator of their sequence weight denominators is given by the mean of their sequence weight numerators. Such simulation of the sequence weight denominators induces denominator bias. This leads to biased simulators of transition probabilities when simulated sequence weights $\hat{\omega}(\eta_s^*(t-1))$ are substituted for the $\omega(\eta_s^*(t-1))$ in equation (10). In the case of biased simulation, McFadden and Ruud (1991) show that if the difference between the simulated MOM first order condition $W(d-\hat{E}(d|J,\hat{\theta},X))$ and the exact MOM first order condition $W(d-E(d|J,\hat{\theta},X))$ is $O_p(S^{-1/2})$ uniformly in $\hat{\theta}$, and if $S/\sqrt{N}\to\infty$, then the asymptotic bias of the MSM estimator converges to zero in probability uniformly in $\hat{\theta}$, and McFadden's (1989) consistency and asymptotic normality results continue to hold. This $O_p(S^{-1/2})$ condition is simple to verify in the present case. Define:

$$(13)\qquad \omega_{Ast} \equiv \omega_A(\eta_s^*(t)) = \text{prob}\,(\eta_{t+1} \in \eta(J_{t+1})|\eta(t) = \eta^*(t)) \cdot \text{prob}\,(\eta_t \in \eta(J_t)|\eta(t-1) = \eta^*(t-1)) \cdot \cdots \cdot \text{prob}\,(\eta_1 \in \eta(J_1)).$$

Then, defining $\hat{\omega}_{BSt} = S^{-1}\Sigma_{s=1}^{S}\omega_{Ast}$, the simulated sequence weights may be written as $\hat{\omega}(\eta_s^*(t)) = \omega_{Ast}/\hat{\omega}_{BSt}$. For person i, alternative j and time t, the difference between the simulated and exact FOC contributions is:

$$(14)\qquad W_{ijt}\left[E\left(d_{ijt}|J_{i,t-1},\hat{\theta},X_i\right)-S^{-1}\sum_{s=1}^{S}\frac{\omega_{As,t-2}}{\hat{\omega}_{BS,t-2}}\hat{E}\left(d_{ijt}|\eta_s^*(t-2),\hat{\theta},X_i\right)\right]$$

$$=W_{ijt}\left[E\left(d_{ijt}|J_{i,t-1},\hat{\theta},X_i\right)-S^{-1}\sum_{s=1}^{S}\frac{\omega_{As,t-2}}{\omega_{B,t-2}}\hat{E}\left(d_{ijt}|\eta_s^*(t-2),\hat{\theta},X_i\right)\right]$$

$$+W_{ijt}\left[S^{-1}\sum_{s=1}^{S}\left[\frac{\omega_{As,t-2}}{\omega_{B,t-2}}-\frac{\omega_{As,t-2}}{\hat{\omega}_{BS,t-2}}\right]\hat{E}\left(d_{ijt}|\eta_s^*(t-2),\hat{\theta},X_i\right)\right].$$

The first term on the right has expectation zero. The second term is the source of bias. Since W_{ijt} and $\hat{E}(d_{ijt}|\eta_s^*(t-2),\hat{\theta},X_i)$ are bounded, it is sufficient to show that $S^{-1}\Sigma_{s=1}^{S}(\omega_{As,t-2}/\omega_{B,t-2}-\omega_{As,t-2}/\hat{\omega}_{BS,t-2})$ is $O_p(S^{-1/2})$. Suppressing the time subscript, the first order Taylor expansion with remainder of $S^{-1}\Sigma_{s=1}^{S}\omega_{As}/\hat{\omega}_{BS}$ around $S^{-1}\Sigma_{s=1}^{S}\omega_{As}/\omega_B$ is (after some algebraic manipulation):

$$(15)\qquad S^{-1}\sum_{s=1}^{S}\frac{\omega_{As}}{\hat{\omega}_{BS}}=S^{-1}\sum_{s=1}^{S}\frac{\omega_{As}}{\omega_B}-S^{-1}\sum_{s=1}^{S}\frac{\omega_{As}}{\hat{\omega}_{BS}}\times\left[\frac{\hat{\omega}_{BS}-\omega_B}{\omega_B}\frac{\hat{\omega}_{BS}}{\omega_B}+\frac{\omega_B^2-\hat{\omega}_{BS}^2}{\omega_B^2}-2\frac{\omega_B-\hat{\omega}_{BS}}{\omega_B}\right].$$

The terms $(\hat{\omega}_B-\omega_B)\hat{\omega}_{BS}/\omega_B^2$ and $(\omega_B^2-\hat{\omega}_{BS}^2)/\omega_B^2$ and $(\omega_B-\hat{\omega}_{BS})/\omega_B$ can all be shown to be $O_p(S^{-1/2})$ by simple applications of the Chebyshev inequality. The quantity $S^{-1}\Sigma_{s=1}^{S}(\omega_{As}/\hat{\omega}_{BS})$ is one by construction. Thus the $O_p(S^{-1/2})$ condition holds.

Despite the fact that $S/\sqrt{N}$ must go to infinity as N increases for the simulation estimator proposed here to be consistent and asymptotically normal, the Monte-Carlo results in Section 4 show little evidence of bias in the proposed estimator, even for small S. I believe the reason that simulation bias is relatively unimportant in the present case is that all time t transition probabilities for person i are simulated conditional on the same set of conditioning sequences, all of which have the same simulated denominator. Thus, all are biased by the same proportion. It is simple to show that any proportional bias of all time t transition probabilities will have no affect asymptotically (in N) on the MOM first order conditions if the optimal MOM weights are used. Of course the optimal weights are only simulated, but if the simulated optimal weights are highly correlated with the true optimal weights there should be a strong tendency for this proportional bias to cancel out of the MSM first order conditions.

Finally, a referee has observed that, using a technique due to McFadden and Ruud (1991), one may, after substituting the biased simulators (equation (5)) into the MOM first order condition (equation (4)), multiply through by the simulated sequence weight denominators $\hat{\omega}_{BS}$ to obtain the expression:

$$\text{(19)} \quad \sum_{i=1}^{N} \sum_{t=1}^{T} \sum_{j=1}^{M} \frac{W_{ijt}}{\hat{\omega}_{BSi,t-2}} \times \left[d_{ijt} \hat{\omega}_{BSi,t-2} - \frac{1}{S} \sum_{s=1}^{S} \omega_{Asi,t-2} \hat{E}\left(d_{ijt} | \eta_s^*(t-2), \hat{\theta}_{\text{MSM}}, X_i \right) \right] \approx 0.$$

Here the term in brackets is a mean zero residual. Thus, the usual consistency and asymptotic normality results hold for this MSM estimator with *fixed* simulation size. Since this alternative estimator involves different simulated moments and weights than are given by equation (5), it will in general have different small sample properties. An important avenue for future research is to compare the small sample properties of these two estimators.

4. MONTE-CARLO TESTS

This section contains three Monte-Carlo tests of the proposed simulation estimator for panel data. Three types of Monte-Carlo data sets are created using different values for the true model parameters. For each parameter vector, 1,000 Monte-Carlo data sets are created, and a repeated sampling experiment is performed in which MSM estimates are obtained for each data set. For each estimation, a different seed for the probability simulator is used. The Monte-Carlo data for the tests are constructed using the latent variable model of Section 2, with the number of alternatives $M = 2$. The independent variables in all three models are a constant and a variable X that is normally distributed with a mean of 6, an across individual variance of 3, and a within individual variance of 2. Each individual is observed over 8 time periods. Thus, the simulation estimator is required to simulate 8-variate integrals. The number of people N is set to 500. Two types of models are considered in the experiments: a random effects model, so that comparisons can be made with ML, and a random effects plus AR(1) error model that is not feasible to estimate by ML. For comparison purposes, I have also included the SML estimator based on the GHK simulator in all three experiments.

The computational speed of both simulation estimators is such that repeated sampling experiments are feasible. For MSM, I have set the number of conditioning sequences S at 10. Since $M = 2$, the choice probabilities conditional on these sequences are evaluated numerically. For SML the number of draws used to form the GHK simulator is also set to 10. For the random effects model, ML-quadrature estimates are obtained using 16 quadrature points. For MSM, a single estimation of the random effects plus AR(1) error model on the 500 individual, 4,000 observation size data sets typically requires approximately 1.5 cpu minutes on an IBM 3090 computer, while runs on an IBM 486 PC

TABLE I

REPEATED SAMPLING EXPERIMENT—1,000 REPLICATIONS—RANDOM EFFECTS MODEL

		MSM—10 Draws			
Parameter	True Value	Mean $\hat{\beta}$	Std$(\hat{\beta})$	Mean $\hat{\text{Std}}(\hat{\beta})$	t-Stat Bias
ρ	.600	.60603	.02903	.03304	6.55
Constant	−.900	−.89991	.08861	.08750	.03
X	.250	.24936	.01386	.01443	−1.45
		ML-Quadrature—16 Points			
Parameter	True Value	Mean $\hat{\beta}$	Std$(\hat{\beta})$	Mean $\hat{\text{Std}}(\hat{\beta})$	t-Stat Bias
ρ	.600	.59628	.02635	.02668	−4.46
Constant	−.900	−.91017	.08149	.08293	−3.95
X	.250	.25152	.01310	.01332	3.67
		Simulated ML-GHK—10 Draws			
Parameter	True Value	Mean $\hat{\beta}$	Std$(\hat{\beta})$	Mean $\hat{\text{Std}}(\hat{\beta})$	t-Stat Bias
ρ	.600	.57954	.02826	.02518	−22.99
Constant	−.900	−.90126	.08267	.07987	−.48
X	.250	.24952	.01331	.01289	−1.14

Note: 1,000 Monte-Carlo data sets were created using the true parameter values shown. Each data set consisted of 500 individuals and 4,000 person year observations. Mean $\hat{\beta}$ refers to mean of the estimated parameters over all 1,000 data sets. Std$(\hat{\beta})$ refers to the sample standard deviation of the estimated parameters. Mean $\hat{\text{Std}}(\hat{\beta})$ refers to the mean of the estimated parameter standard errors over all 1,000 data sets. Typical times for a single estimation of the random effects model on an IBM 3090 are 1.2 cpu minutes for MSM and 0.8 cpu minutes for ML-quadrature.

(without math coprocessor) require an average of only 4.5 minutes. The SML runs typically require about 30% more time than the MSM runs. MSM requires that the probabilities of choosing all alternatives be simulated, while SML requires only that the probabilities of the chosen alternatives be simulated. However, this computational advantage for SML is counterbalanced by the fact that SML requires derivative calculations on each iteration, while MSM only requires that derivatives be calculated once to form the initial weighting matrix.

The results from the first repeated sampling experiment are reported in Table I. In this experiment, a random effects model is used. The true parameter values are $\rho = 0.60$, constant $= -0.90$, and X coefficient $= 0.25$, where ρ denotes the fraction of variance due to the individual effect. The mean and empirical standard deviation of the MSM, SML, and ML-quadrature estimates, along with the mean of the estimated standard errors, are reported. Also reported are t statistics for the statistical significance of the biases, based on the empirical standard errors. The mean MSM estimates of the constant and X coefficient are extremely close to the true values (e.g., 0.24936 vs. 0.250 for the X coefficient) and the estimated biases in these coefficients are insignificant. The mean MSM estimate of the fraction of variance due to the random effect is significantly larger than the true value (0.60603 vs. 0.6000 with a t statistic of 6.55 for the bias) but obviously the magnitude of the bias is small. The ML-quadrature estimates all suffer from biases that are significant but negligible in magnitude. (In an earlier version of this paper, I found that ML-quadrature estimates suffer from serious bias in these types of models when serial correlation is of this magnitude and conventional numbers of quadrature points—3 to 9—are used.) The sample standard deviations of the MSM estimates range from 5.3 percent higher than that of ML-quadrature for the X coefficient (0.01386 vs. 0.01310) to 10.2 percent higher for ρ. Given the use here of a smooth simulator with simulation size 10 and of (simulated) optimal weights, these results conform well with the MSM to MOM asymptotic covariance matrix ratio of $(1+1/R)$ that obtains when frequency simulation is used (more efficient smooth simulators being expected to improve on this ratio). The only drawback in these results is that the mean estimated standard deviation of the ρ estimates is 13.8 percent larger than the empirical standard deviation (0.03304 vs. 0.02903), but the empirical and mean estimated standard deviations are quite close for the constant and X coefficient.

The SML estimates in Table I also appear acceptable. The biases in the estimates of the intercept and slope coefficient are insignificant. The estimate of ρ is very significantly biased downward, and the magnitude of this bias is more than three times greater than the magnitude of the bias in $\hat{\rho}$ for MSM. However, the magnitude of the bias still appears negligible. The empirical standard errors for the SML estimates are very close to those for MSM, and in all cases slightly smaller. The estimated SML standard errors are slightly downward biased.

The second repeated sampling experiment involves 1,000 replications of data constructed to have random effects plus an AR(1) error component ($\rho = 0.20$, AR(1) = 0.60, giving a first lagged autocorrelation of 0.68). The results are reported in Table II. Only MSM and SML results are reported, because ML by quadrature is not feasible for this model. The MSM results are again very

TABLE II

REPEATED SAMPLING EXPERIMENT—1,000 REPLICATIONS—RANDOM EFFECTS + AR(1) ERROR MODEL

		MSM—10 Draws			
Parameter	True Value	Mean $\hat{\beta}$	Std$(\hat{\beta})$	Mean $\hat{\text{Std}}(\hat{\beta})$	t-Stat Bias
ρ	.200	.19401	.06970	.07065	−2.72
AR(1)	.600	.60421	.04713	.04816	2.83
Constant	−.900	−.90041	.08449	.08431	−.15
X	.250	.24998	.01348	.01404	−.05
		Simulated ML-GHK—10 Draws			
Parameter	True Value	Mean $\hat{\beta}$	Std$(\hat{\beta})$	Mean $\hat{\text{Std}}(\hat{\beta})$	t-Stat Bias
ρ	.200	.21915	.05368	.04838	11.26**
AR(1)	.600	.53747	.04183	.03922	−47.37**
Constant	−.900	−.90298	.08123	.07703	1.16
X	.250	.24984	.01329	.01251	−.38

Note: 1,000 Monte-Carlo data sets were created using the true parameter values shown. Each data set consisted of 500 individuals and 4,000 person year observations. Mean $\hat{\beta}$ refers to mean of the estimated parameters over all 1,000 data sets. Std$(\hat{\beta})$ refers to the sample standard deviation of the estimated parameters. Mean $\hat{\text{Std}}(\hat{\beta})$ refers to the mean of the estimated parameter standard errors over all 1,000 data sets. Typical times for a single MSM estimation of the random effects plus AR(1) error model are 1.5 cpu minutes on an IBM 3090 and 4.5 minutes on an IBM 486 PC.

impressive. Bias is insignificant for the estimates of the intercept and X coefficient. Bias in the estimates of ρ and the AR(1) coefficient are significant but very small in magnitude. In fact, the mean estimated parameter values are all within 0.09 empirical standard errors of the true values, and the mean estimated standard errors are all within 4.2 percent of the empirical standard errors. The SML estimates of the intercept and X coefficient also exhibit no significant bias. However, the SML estimator has some difficulty in uncovering the true correlation structure in this example. In particular, the estimates of the AR(1) parameter are significantly biased downward (0.53747 vs. 0.60 with a t statistic of -47.37 for the bias), and the magnitude of this bias exceeds 10% of the true value.

In the third experiment, I have set $\rho = 0.20$, AR(1) = 0.90, constant = -0.600, and X coefficient = 0.10. Thus, the first lagged autocorrelation is 0.92. Despite this high degree of serial correlation, the MSM estimator continues to perform well. All four parameter estimates are significantly biased, but in each case the magnitude of the bias is negligible. The SML estimator, on the other hand, has severe difficulty in uncovering the true error structure in this example. It greatly overestimates the fraction of variance due to the random effect (43.8% vs. a true value of 20%) and substantially understates the AR(1) parameter (0.8007 vs. a true value of 0.90). Note that although the bias in $\hat{\rho}$ may appear small in percentage terms (only 11%), an AR(1) parameter of 0.8 implies serial correlation that dies out much more quickly than if the AR(1) parameter were 0.9. Thus, the SML estimates imply less short run persistence and more very long run persistence in choice behavior than does the true model. The SML estimates of the intercept and slope also show significant bias, but again, as in experiments 1 and 2, this bias is negligible in magnitude. Finally, note that in experiment 3 both the MSM and SML estimators have difficulty in estimating the standard errors of the correlation structure parameters. For SML the means of the estimated standard errors for $\hat{\rho}$ and $\widehat{\text{AR}}(1)$ are 30% and 25% below the empirical standard errors, respectively. For MSM, they are both over 3 times larger than the empirical standard errors. This may be because with such strong serial correlation the effective sample size is small, causing the asymptotic distribution of the estimators to be a poor approximation to the finite sample distribution.

A note of caution is in order with regard to using empirical means and standard deviations to characterize the small sample distributions of these estimators. Although the MSM, SML, and ML-quadrature estimators are all aysmptotically normal, they may depart substantially from normality in small samples—in which case the empirical mean and standard deviation do not adequately characterize their distributions. Furthermore, the first and second moments of the estimators for the AR(1) parameter, constant, and X coefficient are not finite in finite samples. In practice, this may cause empirical means and standard deviations to be dominated by extreme outlier estimates.

To address these problems, I also calculated the 1st, 2nd, and 3rd quantiles of the parameter estimates for all the Monte-Carlo experiments in Tables I–III. Looking at quantiles does not affect the ranking of performance of the estima-

TABLE III

REPEATED SAMPLING EXPERIMENT—1,000 REPLICATIONS—RANDOM EFFECTS + AR(1) ERROR MODEL

		MSM—10 Draws			
Parameter	True Value	Mean $\hat{\beta}$	Std($\hat{\beta}$)	Mean $\hat{\text{Std}}(\hat{\beta})$	t-Stat Bias
ρ	.200	.19248	.12484	.42393	−1.90
AR(1)	.900	.90473	.01949	.05903	7.63
Constant	−.600	−.59245	.07496	.07572	3.19
X	.100	.09882	.00923	.01036	−4.07
		Simulated ML-GHK—10 Draws			
Parameter	True Value	Mean $\hat{\beta}$	Std($\hat{\beta}$)	Mean $\hat{\text{Std}}(\hat{\beta})$	t-Stat Bias
ρ	.200	.43922	.13932	.10036	54.24
AR(1)	.900	.80070	.05027	.03752	−64.45
Constant	−.600	−.61785	.07034	.06648	−8.41
x	.100	.10292	.00885	.00899	10.43

Note: 1,000 Monte-Carlo data sets were created using the true parameter values shown. Each data set consisted of 500 individuals and 4,000 person year observations. Mean $\hat{\beta}$ refers to mean of the estimated parameters over all 1,000 data sets. Std($\hat{\beta}$) refers to the sample standard deviation of the estimated parameters. Mean $\hat{\text{Std}}(\hat{\beta})$ refers to the mean of the estimated parameter standard errors over all 1,000 data sets. Typical times for a single MSM estimation of the random effects plus AR(1) error model are 1.5 cpu minutes on an IBM 3090 and 4.5 minutes on an IBM 486 PC.

tors. In all cases, except for the parameter ρ in Table III, the actual quantiles were negligibly different from those that would be predicted based on normality (a table of these results is available on request). For the MSM estimates of ρ in Table III, the 1st, 2nd, and 3rd quantiles are 0.08989, 0.14948, and 0.30745. Given the mean and empirical standard deviation of the estimates and assuming normality, one would predict these quantiles to be 0.10822, 0.19248, and 0.27675 respectively. For the SML estimates of ρ the quantiles are 0.36737, 0.46609, and 0.54078 respectively, while given normality one would predict 0.34518, 0.43922, and 0.53326. Although the distributions of both estimators depart substantially from normality, there were no extreme outliers influencing the first two moments in either case. Since the true value of ρ is 0.200, while the mean MSM estimate is 0.19248 and the median MSM estimate is 0.14948, MSM does not perform as well under a median criterion. However, it continues to dominate SML, for which the median is 0.46609 and all but 72 of the 1,000 estimates exceed the true value.

5. CONCLUSION

In this paper I have used a factorization of the MSM first order condition into transition probabilities in order to construct a practical MSM estimator for panel data. The key problem in constructing such an estimator is the inexpensive simulation of transition probabilities without the introduction of substantial bias. I develop a particular very inexpensive importance sampling technique for simulation of transition probabilities which is asymptotically unbiased in simulation size. This simulation method is of interest in its own right, since Hajivassiliou, McFadden, and Ruud, who call it the GHK simulator, find that this method outperforms all other probability simulators from a large set of alternative methods they consider. A battery of Monte-Carlo tests reveal no significant bias in an MSM estimator that utilizes this method to simulate transition probabilities, even for small simulation sizes. For models in which ML is feasible, the MSM estimator performs well relative to quadrature-based methods using many more quadrature points than are typically used in practice. For models in which ML is not feasible, the MSM estimator outperforms SML based on the highly accurate GHK probability simulator. Specifically, when serial correlation is very strong I find that SML produces severely biased estimates of the serial correlation structure, while the MSM estimator does not. The computational speed of the MSM estimator is such that it is possible to estimate panel data models with complex error structures involving random effects and ARMA errors in times similar to those necessary for estimation of simple random effects models by quadrature.

I motivated this paper by arguing that the ability to deal with complex patterns of serial correlation in LDV models may be important for out-of-sample prediction purposes. As an example, Elrod and Keane (1992) have applied the method developed in this paper to estimate detergent choice models with eight alternatives and 30 time periods. We find that a probit model that allows for a rich pattern of serial correlation outperforms all competing choice models in terms of accuracy in forecasting agents' future purchases.

Industrial Relations Center and Dept. of Economics, University of Minnesota, Minneapolis, MN 55455, U.S.A.

Manuscript received August, 1990; final revision received April, 1993.

REFERENCES

ALBERT, J., AND S. CHIB (1993): "Bayesian Analysis of Binary and Polychotomous Data," forthcoming, *Journal of the American Statistical Association*.

ALBRIGHT, R., S. LERMAN, AND C. MANSKI (1977): "Report on the Development of an Estimation Program for the Multinomial Probit Model," Report prepared by Cambridge Systematics for the Federal Highway Administration.

AVERY, R., L. HANSEN, AND V. J. HOTZ (1983): "Multiperiod Probit Models and Orthogonality Condition Estimation," *International Economic Review*, 24, 21–35.

BATES, C., AND H. WHITE (1987): "Efficient Instrumental Variable Estimation of Systems of Equations with Nonspherical Errors," UCSD Discussion Paper #87–14.

BORSCH-SUPAN, A., AND V. HAJIVASSILIOU (1990): "Smooth Unbiased Multivariate Probability Simulators for Maximum Likelihood Estimation of Limited Dependent Variable Models," Cowles Foundation Discussion Paper 960.

BUTLER, J. S., AND R. MOFFITT (1982): "A Computationally Efficient Quadrature Procedure for the One-Factor Multinomial Probit Model," *Econometrica*, 50, 761–764.

CHAMBERLAIN, G. (1985): "Panel Data," in *Handbook of Econometrics*, ed. by Z. Griliches and M. D. Intrilligator. Amsterdam: North-Holland Publishing Co.

ELROD, T., AND M. KEANE (1992): "A Factor-Analytic Probit Model for Estimating Market Structure in Panel Data," forthcoming, *Journal of Marketing Research*.

GEWEKE, J. (1987): "Bayesian Inference in Econometric Models using Monte-Carlo Integration," *Econometrica*, 57, 1317–1340.

——— : "Efficient Simulation from the Multivariate Normal and Student-*t* Distributions Subject to Linear Constraints," *Computing Science and Statistics: Proceedings of the Twenty-third Symposium on the Interface*, forthcoming.

GEWEKE, J., M. KEANE, AND D. RUNKLE (1992): "Alternative Computational Approaches to Statistical Inference in the Multinomial Probit Model," University of Minnesota manuscript.

HAJIVASSILIOU, V., AND D. MCFADDEN (1990): "The Method of Simulated Scores for the Estimation of LDV Models with an Application to External Debt Crisis," Cowles Foundation Discussion Paper 967.

HAJIVASSILIOU, V., D. MCFADDEN, AND P. RUUD (1991): "Simulation of Multivariate Normal Orthant Probabilities: Methods and Programs," Working Paper, Yale University.

HECKMAN, J. (1981): "Statistical Models for Discrete Panel Data," in *Structural Analysis of Discrete Data with Econometric Applications*, ed. by C. Manski and D. McFadden. Cambridge: MIT Press.

KAHANER, D. K. (1991): "A Survey of Existing Multinomial Quadrature Routines," in *Statistical Multiple Integration: Proceedings of the AMS-IMS-SIAM Joint Summer Research Conference*, ed. by N. Flournoy and R. K. Tsutakawa. Providence, RI: American Mathematical Society.

LERMAN, S., AND C. MANSKI (1981): "On the Use of Simulated Frequencies to Approximate Choice Probabilities," in *Structural Analysis of Discrete Data with Econometric Applications*, ed. by C. Manski and D. McFadden. Cambridge: MIT Press.

MCCULLOCH, R., AND P. ROSSI (1992): "An Exact Likelihood Analysis of the Multinomial Probit Model," Working Paper, University of Chicago.

MCFADDEN, D. (1989): "A Method of Simulated Moments for Estimation of Discrete Response Models without Numerical Integration," *Econometrica*, 57, 995–1026.

MCFADDEN, D., AND P. RUUD (1987): "Estimation of Limited Dependent Variable Models from the Regular Exponential Family by the Method of Simulated Moments," Working Paper, University of California, Berkeley.

——— : "Estimation by Simulation," Working Paper, University of California, Berkeley.

PAKES, A. (1986): "Patents as Options: Some Estimates of the Value of Holding European Patent Stocks," *Econometrica*, 54, 755–784.

PAKES, A., AND D. POLLARD (1989): "Simulation and the Asymptotics of Optimization Estimators," *Econometrica*, 57, 1027–1058.

POIRIER, D., AND P. RUUD (1988): "Probit with Dependent Observations," *Review of Economic Studies*, 55, 593–614.

ROBINSON, P. (1982): "On the Asymptotic Properties of Models Containing Limited Dependent Variables," *Econometrica*, 50, 27–41.

RUUD, P. (1992): "Extensions of Estimation Methods using the EM Algorithm," forthcoming in *Journal of Econometrics*.

VAN PRAAG, B. M. S., AND J. P. HOP (1987): "Estimation of Continuous Models on the Basis of Set-valued Observations," manuscript, Erasmus University, Rotterdam.

[4]

Econometrica, Vol. 65, No. 6 (November, 1997), 1335–1364

ESTIMATION OF A PANEL DATA SAMPLE SELECTION MODEL

BY EKATERINI KYRIAZIDOU[1]

We consider the problem of estimation in a panel data sample selection model, where both the selection and the regression equation of interest contain unobservable individual-specific effects. We propose a two-step estimation procedure, which "differences out" both the sample selection effect and the unobservable individual effect from the equation of interest. In the first step, the unknown coefficients of the "selection" equation are consistently estimated. The estimates are then used to estimate the regression equation of interest. The estimator proposed in this paper is consistent and asymptotically normal, with a rate of convergence that can be made arbitrarily close to $n^{-1/2}$, depending on the strength of certain smoothness assumptions. The finite sample properties of the estimator are investigated in a small Monte Carlo simulation.

KEYWORDS: Sample selection, panel data, individual-specific effects.

1. INTRODUCTION

SAMPLE SELECTION IS A PROBLEM frequently encountered in applied research. It arises as a result of either self-selection by the individuals under investigation, or sample selection decisions made by data analysts. A classic example, studied in the seminal work of Gronau (1974) and Heckman (1976), is female labor supply, where hours worked are observed only for those women who decide to participate in the labor force. Failure to account for sample selection is well known to lead to inconsistent estimation of the behavioral parameters of interest, as these are confounded with parameters that determine the probability of entry into the sample. In recent years a vast amount of econometric literature has been devoted to the problem of controlling for sample selectivity. The research however has almost exclusively focused on the cross-sectional data case. See Powell (1994) for a review of this literature and for references. In contrast, this paper focuses on the case where the researcher has panel or longitudinal data available.[2] Sample selectivity is as acute a problem in panel as in cross section data. In addition, panel data sets are commonly characterized by nonrandomly missing observations due to sample attrition.

[1] This paper is based on Chapter 1 of my thesis completed at Northwestern University, Evanston, Illinois. I wish to thank my thesis advisor Bo Honoré for invaluable help and support during this project. Many individuals, among them a co-editor and two anonymous referees, have offered useful comments and suggestions for which I am very grateful. Joel Horowitz kindly provided a computer program used in this study. An earlier version of the paper was presented at the North American Summer Meetings of the Econometric Society, June, 1994. Financial support from NSF through Grant No. SES-9210037 to Bo Honoré is gratefully acknowledged. All remaining errors are my responsibility. An Appendix which contains a proof of a theorem not included in the paper may be obtained at the world wide web site: http://www.spc.uchicago.edu/E-Kyriazidou.

[2] Obviously, the analysis is similar for any kind of data that have a group structure.

The most typical concern in empirical work using panel data has been the presence of unobserved heterogeneity. Heterogeneity across economic agents may arise for example as a result of different preferences, endowments, or attributes. These permanent individual characteristics are commonly unobservable, or may simply not be measurable due to their qualitative nature. Failure to account for such individual-specific effects may result in biased and inconsistent estimates of the parameters of interest. In linear panel data models, these unobserved effects may be "differenced" out, using the familiar "within" ("fixed-effects") approach. This method is generally not applicable in limited dependent variable models. Exceptions include the discrete choice model studied by Rasch (1960, 1961), Anderson (1970), and Manski (1987), and the censored and truncated regression models (Honoré (1992, 1993)). See also Chamberlain (1984), and Hsiao (1986) for a discussion of panel data methods.

The simultaneous presence of sample selectivity and unobserved heterogeneity has been noted in empirical work (as for example in Hausman and Wise (1979), Nijman and Verbeek (1992), and Rosholm and Smith (1994)). Given the pervasiveness of either problem in panel data studies. it appears highly desirable to be able to control for both of them simultaneously. The present paper is a step in this direction.

In particular, we consider the problem of estimating a panel data model, where both the sample selection rule, assumed to follow a binary response model, and the (linear) regression equation of interest contain additive permanent unobservable individual-specific effects that may depend on the observable explanatory variables in an arbitrary way. In this type 2 Tobit model (in the terminology of Amemiya (1985)), sample selectivity induces a fundamental nonlinearity in the equation of interest with respect to the unobserved characteristics, which, in contrast to linear panel data models, cannot be "differenced away." This is because the sample selection effect, which enters additively in the main equation, is a (generally unknown) nonlinear function of both the observed time-varying regressors and the unobservable individual effects of the selection equation, and is therefore not constant over time.

Furthermore, even if one were willing to specify the distribution of the underlying time-varying errors (for example normal) in order to estimate the model by maximum likelihood, the presence of unobservable effects in the selection rule would require that the researcher also specify a functional form for their statistical dependence on the observed variables. Apart from being nonrobust to distributional misspecification, this fully parametric "random effects" approach is also computationally cumbersome, as it requires multiple numerical integration over both the unobservable effects and the entire length of the panel. Heckman's (1976, 1979) two-step correction, although computationally much more tractable, also requires full specification of the underlying distributions of the unobservables, and is therefore susceptible to inconsistencies due to misspecification. Thus, the results of this paper will be important even if the distribution of the individual effects is the only nuisance parameter in the model.

Panel data selection models with latent individual effects have been most recently considered by Verbeek and Nijman (1992), and Wooldridge (1995), who proposed methods for testing and correcting for selectivity bias. A crucial assumption underlying these methods is the parameterization of the sample selection mechanism. Specifically, these authors assume that both the unobservable effect and the idiosyncratic errors in the selection process are normally distributed. The present paper is an important departure from this work, in the sense that the distributions of all unobservables are left unspecified.

We focus on the case where the data consist of a large number of individuals observed through a small number of time periods, and analyze asymptotics as the number of individuals (n) approaches infinity. Short-length panels are not only the most relevant for practical purposes, they also pose problems in estimation. In such cases, even if the individual effects are treated as parameters to be estimated, a parametric maximum likelihood approach yields inconsistent estimates, the well known "incidental parameters problem."

Our method for estimating the main regression equation of interest follows the familiar two-step approach proposed by Heckman (1974, 1976) for parametric selection models, which has been used in the construction of most semiparametric estimators for such models. In the first step, the unknown coefficients of the "selection" equation are consistently estimated. In the second step, these estimates are used to estimate the equation of interest by a weighted least squares regression: The fixed effect from the main equation is eliminated by taking time differences on the observed selected variables, while the first-step estimates are used to construct weights, whose magnitude depends on the magnitude of the sample selection bias. For a fixed sample size, observations with less selectivity bias are given more weight, while asymptotically, only those observations with zero bias are used. This idea has been used by Powell (1987), and Ahn and Powell (1993) for the estimation of cross sectional selection models. The intuition is that, for an individual that is selected into the sample in two time periods, it is reasonable to assume that the magnitude of the selection effect in the main equation will be the same if the observed variables determining selection remain constant over time. Therefore, time differencing the outcome equation will eliminate not only its unobservable individual effect but also the sample selection effect. In fact, by imposing a linear regression structure on the latent model underlying the selection mechanism, the above argument will also hold if only the linear combination of the observed selection covariates, known up to a finite number of estimable parameters, remains constant over time. Under appropriate assumptions on the rate of convergence of the first step estimator, the proposed estimator of the main equation of interest is shown to be consistent and asymptotically normal, with a rate of convergence that can be made arbitrarily close to $n^{-1/2}$. In particular, by assuming that the selection equation is estimated at a "faster" rate than the main equation, we obtain a limiting distribution which does not depend on the distribution of the first step estimator.

The first step of the proposed estimation method requires that the discrete choice selection equation be estimated consistently and at a sufficiently fast rate. To this end, we propose using a "smoothed" version of Manski's (1987) conditional maximum score estimator,[3] which follows the approach taken by Horowitz (1992) for estimating cross section discrete choice models. Under appropriate assumptions, stronger than those in Manski (1987), the smoothed estimator improves on the rate of convergence of the original estimator, and also allows standard statistical inference. Furthermore, it dispenses with parametric assumptions on the distribution of the errors, required for example by the conditional maximum likelihood estimator proposed by Rasch (1960, 1961) and Andersen (1970).

Although our analysis is based on the assumption of a censored panel, with only two observations per individual, it easily generalizes to the case of a longer and possibly unbalanced panel, and may be also modified to accommodate truncated samples, in which case estimation of the selection equation is infeasible. Extensions of our estimation method to cover these situations are discussed at the end of the next section.

The paper is organized as follows. Section 2 describes the model and motivates the proposed estimation procedure. Section 3 states the assumptions and derives the asymptotic properties of the estimator. Section 4 presents the results of a Monte Carlo study investigating the small sample performance of the proposed estimator. Section 5 offers conclusions and suggests topics for future research. The proofs of theorems and lemmata are given in the Appendix.

2. THE MODEL AND THE PROPOSED ESTIMATOR

We consider the following model:

$$y_{it} = d_{it} \cdot y_{it}^* = d_{it} \cdot (x_{it}^* \beta + \alpha_i^* + \varepsilon_{it}^*) = x_{it} \beta + \alpha_{it} + \varepsilon_{it} \quad (i = 1, \ldots, n;\ t = 1, 2), \tag{2.1}$$

$$d_{it} = 1\{w_{it}\gamma + \eta_i - u_{it} \geq 0\}. \tag{2.2}$$

Here, $\beta \in \Re^k$ and $\gamma \in \Re^q$ are unknown parameter vectors which we wish to estimate,[4] x_{it}^* and w_{it} are vectors of explanatory variables (with possibly common elements), α_i^* and η_i are unobservable time-invariant individual-specific effects[5] (possibly correlated with the regressors and the errors), ε_{it}^* and u_{it} are unobserved disturbances (not necessarily independent of each other), while $y_{it}^* \in \Re$ is a latent variable whose observability depends on the outcome of the indicator

[3] The smoothed conditional maximum score estimator for binary response panel data models, along with its asymptotic properties and necessary assumptions, is presented in an earlier version of this paper (Kyriazidou (1994)). See also Charlier, Melenberg, and van Soest (1995).

[4] Obviously constants cannot be identified in either equation, since they would be absorbed in the individual effects.

[5] These will be treated as nuisance parameters and will not be estimated. Our analysis also applies to the case where $\alpha_i^* \equiv \eta_i$.

variable $d_{it} \in \{0,1\}$. In particular, it is assumed that, while (d_{it}, w_{it}) is always observed, (y_{it}^*, x_{it}^*) is observed only[6] if $d_{it} = 1$. In other words, the "selection" variable d_{it} determines whether the itth observation in equation (2.1) is censored or not. Thus, our problem is to estimate β and γ from a sample consisting of quadruples $(d_{it}, w_{it}, y_{it}, x_{it})$. We will denote the vector of (observed and unobserved) explanatory variables by $\zeta_i \equiv (w_{i1}, w_{i2}, x_{i1}^*, x_{i2}^*, \alpha_i^*, \eta_i)$. Notice that, without the "fixed effects" α_i^* and η_i, our model becomes a panel data version of the well known sample selection model considered in the literature, and could be estimated by any of the existing methods. Without sample selectivity, that is with $d_{it} = 1$ for all i and t, equation (2.1) is the standard panel data linear regression model.

In our setup, it is possible to estimate γ in the discrete choice "selection" equation (2.2) using either the conditional maximum likelihood approach proposed by Rasch (1960, 1961) and Andersen (1970), or the conditional maximum score method proposed by Manski (1987). On the other hand, estimation of β based on the main equation of interest (2.1) is confronted with two problems: first, the presence of the unobservable effect $\alpha_{it} = d_{it} \cdot \alpha_i^*$, and second and more fundamental, the potential "endogeneity" of the regressors $x_{it} = d_{it} \cdot x_{it}^*$, which arises from their dependence on the selection variable d_{it}, and which may result in "selection bias."

The first problem is easily solved by noting that for those observations that have $d_{i1} = d_{i2} = 1$, time differencing will eliminate the effect α_{it} from equation (2.1). This is analogous to the "fixed-effects" approach taken in linear panel data models. In general though, application of standard methods, e.g., OLS, on this first-differenced subsample will yield inconsistent estimates of β, due to sample selectivity. This may be seen from the population regression function for the first-differenced subsample:

$$E(y_{i1} - y_{i2} | d_{i1} = 1, d_{i2} = 1, \zeta_i)$$
$$= (x_{i1}^* - x_{i2}^*)\beta + E(\varepsilon_{i1}^* - \varepsilon_{i2}^* | d_{i1} = 1, d_{i2} = 1, \zeta_i).$$

In general, there is no reason to expect that $E(\varepsilon_{it}^* | d_{i1} = 1, d_{i2} = 1, \zeta_i) = 0$, or that $E(\varepsilon_{i1}^* | d_{i1} = 1, d_{i2} = 1, \zeta_i) = E(\varepsilon_{i2}^* | d_{i1} = 1, d_{i2} = 1, \zeta_i)$. In particular, for each time period the "sample selection effect" $\lambda_{it} \equiv E(\varepsilon_{it}^* | d_{i1} = 1, d_{i2} = 1, \zeta_i)$ depends not only on the (partially unobservable) conditioning vector ζ_i, but also on the (generally unknown) joint conditional distribution of $(\varepsilon_{it}^*, u_{i1}, u_{i2})$, which may differ across individuals, as well as over time for the same individual:

$$\lambda_{it} \equiv E(\varepsilon_{it}^* | d_{i1} = 1, d_{i2} = 1, \zeta_i)$$
$$= E(\varepsilon_{it}^* | u_{i1} \leq w_{i1}\gamma + \eta_i, u_{i2} \leq w_{i2}\gamma + \eta_i, \zeta_i)$$
$$= \Lambda(w_{i1}\gamma + \eta_i, w_{i2}\gamma + \eta_i; F_{it}(\varepsilon_{it}^*, u_{i1}, u_{i2} | \zeta_i))$$
$$= \Lambda_{it}(w_{i1}\gamma + \eta_i, w_{i2}\gamma + \eta_i, \zeta_i).$$

[6] Obviously, the analysis carries through to the case where x_{it}^* is always observed, which is the case most commonly treated in the literature.

It is convenient to rewrite the main equation (2.1) as a "partially linear regression:"

$$(2.1')\qquad y_{it} = x_{it}\beta + \alpha_{it} + \lambda_{it} + v_{it}$$

where $v_{it} \equiv \varepsilon_{it} - \lambda_{it}$ is a new error term, which by construction satisfies $E(v_{it}|d_{i1} = 1, d_{i2} = 1, \zeta_i) = 0$. The idea of our scheme for estimating β is to "difference out" the nuisance terms α_{it} and λ_{it} from the equation above.

As a motivation of our estimation procedure, consider the case where $(\varepsilon_{it}^*, u_{it})$ is independent and identically distributed over time and across individuals, and is independent of ζ_i. Under these assumptions, it is easy to see that

$$\lambda_{it} = E(\varepsilon_{it}^*|d_{it} = 1) = E(\varepsilon_{it}^*|u_{it} \le w_{it}\gamma + \eta_i) = \Lambda(w_{it}\gamma + \eta_i)$$

where $\Lambda(\cdot)$ is an unknown function, the same over time and across individuals, of the single index $w_{it}\gamma + \eta_i$. Obviously in general, $\lambda_{i1} \ne \lambda_{i2}$, unless $w_{i1}\gamma = w_{i2}\gamma$. In other words, for an individual i that has $w_{i1}\gamma = w_{i2}\gamma$ and $d_{i1} = d_{i2} = 1$, the sample selection effect λ_{it} will be the same in the two periods. Thus, for this particular individual, applying first-differences in equation (2.1′) will eliminate both the unobservable effect α_{it} and the selection effect λ_{it}. At this point it is important to notice that, even if the functional form of Λ were known (as for example in the case of a bivariate normal distribution—see Heckman (1976)), it would still involve the unobservable effect η_i. This suggests that it would be generally infeasible to consistently estimate β from (2.1′) even in the absence of the effect α_{it}, and with knowledge of γ, unless a parametric form for the distribution of η_i conditional on the observed exogenous variables were also specified.

The preceding argument for "differencing out" both nuisance terms from equation (2.1′) will hold under much weaker distributional assumptions. In particular, since first-differences are taken on an individual basis, it is not required that $(\varepsilon_{it}^*, u_{it})$ be i.i.d. across individuals nor that it be independent of the individual-specific vector ζ_i. In other words, we may allow the functional form of Λ to vary across individuals. It is also possible to allow for serial correlation in the errors. Consider for example the case where $(\varepsilon_{i1}^*, \varepsilon_{i2}^*, u_{i1}, u_{i2})$ and $(\varepsilon_{i2}^*, \varepsilon_{i1}^*, u_{i2}, u_{i1})$ are identically distributed conditional on ζ_i, i.e. $F(\varepsilon_{i1}^*, \varepsilon_{i2}^*, u_{i1}, u_{i2}|\zeta_i) = F(\varepsilon_{i2}^*, \varepsilon_{i1}^*, u_{i2}, u_{i1}|\zeta_i)$. Under this *conditional exchangeability* assumption, it is easy to see that for an individual i that has $w_{i1}\gamma = w_{i2}\gamma$,

$$\begin{aligned}\lambda_{i1} &= E(\varepsilon_{i1}^*|u_{i1} \le w_{i1}\gamma + \eta_i, u_{i2} \le w_{i2}\gamma + \eta_i, \zeta_i)\\ &= E(\varepsilon_{i2}^*|u_{i2} \le w_{i1}\gamma + \eta_i, u_{i1} \le w_{i2}\gamma + \eta_i, \zeta_i)\\ &= \lambda_{i2}.\end{aligned}$$

Notice that in general, it is not sufficient to assume joint conditional stationarity of the errors. An extreme example is the case where ε_{i1}^*, ε_{i2}^*, and u_{i1} are i.i.d. $N(0,1)$ and independent of ζ_i, while $u_{i2} = \varepsilon_{i1}^*$. Then, $\lambda_{i1} = E(\varepsilon_{i1}^*|\varepsilon_{i1}^* \le w_{i2}\gamma + \eta_i) \ne \lambda_{i2} = E(\varepsilon_{i2}^*)$, regardless of whether $w_{i1}\gamma = w_{i2}\gamma$.

The above discussion, which presumes knowledge of the true γ, suggests estimating β by OLS from a subsample that consists of those observations that have $w_{i1}\gamma = w_{i2}\gamma$ and $d_{i1} = d_{i2} = 1$. Defining $\Psi_i \equiv 1\{w_{i1}\gamma = w_{i2}\gamma\}$, $\Phi_i \equiv 1\{d_{i1} = d_{i2} = 1\} \equiv d_{i1}d_{i2}$, and with Δ denoting first differences, the OLS estimator is of the form $\check{\beta}_n = [\Sigma_{i=1}^n \Delta x_i' \Delta x_i \Psi_i \Phi_i]^{-1}[\Sigma_{i=1}^n \Delta x_i' \Delta y_i \Psi_i \Phi_i]$. Under appropriate regularity conditions, this estimator will be consistent and root-n asymptotically normal. An obvious requirement is that $\Pr(\Delta w_i \gamma = 0) > 0$, which may be satisfied for example when all the random variables in w_{it} are discrete, or in experimental cases where the distribution of w_{it} is in the control of the researcher, situations that are rare in economic applications.

Of course, this estimation scheme cannot be directly implemented since γ is unknown. Furthermore, as argued above, it may be the case that $\Psi_i = 0$ (i.e. $\Delta w_i \gamma \neq 0$) for all individuals in our sample. Notice though that, if Λ is a sufficiently "smooth" function, and $\hat{\gamma}_n$ is a consistent estimate of γ, observations for which the difference $\Delta w_i \hat{\gamma}_n$ is close to zero should also have $\Delta\lambda_i \cong 0$, and the preceding arguments would hold approximately.

We therefore propose the following two-step estimation procedure, which is in the spirit of Powell (1987), and Ahn and Powell (1993): In the first step, γ is consistently estimated based on equation (2.2) alone. In the second step, the estimate $\hat{\gamma}_n$ is used to estimate β, based on those pairs of observations for which $w_{i1}\hat{\gamma}_n$ and $w_{i2}\hat{\gamma}_n$ are "close." Specifically, we propose

$$\text{(2.3)} \qquad \hat{\beta}_n = \left[\sum_{i=1}^{n} \hat{\psi}_{in} \Delta x_i' \Delta x_i \Phi_i\right]^{-1} \left[\sum_{i=1}^{n} \hat{\psi}_{in} \Delta x_i' \Delta y_i \Phi_i\right]$$

where $\hat{\psi}_{in}$ is a weight that declines to zero as the magnitude of the difference $|w_{i1}\hat{\gamma}_n - w_{i2}\hat{\gamma}_n|$ increases. We choose "kernel" weights of the form:

$$\text{(2.4)} \qquad \hat{\psi}_{in} \equiv \frac{1}{h_n} K\left(\frac{\Delta w_i \hat{\gamma}_n}{h_n}\right)$$

where K is a "kernel density" function, and h_n is a sequence of "bandwidths" which tends to zero as $n \to \infty$. Thus, for a fixed (nonzero) magnitude of the difference $|\Delta w_i \hat{\gamma}_n|$, the weight $\hat{\psi}_{in}$ shrinks as the sample size increases, while for a fixed n, a larger $|\Delta w_i \hat{\gamma}_n|$ corresponds to a smaller weight.

It is interesting to note that the arguments used in estimating the main regression equation may be modified to accommodate the case of a truncated sample, that is when we only observe those individuals that have $d_{it} = 1$ for all time periods. Recall that our method for eliminating the sample selection effect from equation (2.1′) is based on the fact that, under certain distributional assumptions, $\Delta w_i \gamma = 0$ implies $\Delta\lambda_i = 0$. However, $\Delta w_i = 0$ also implies $\Delta\lambda_i = 0$. In other words, we might dispense altogether with the first step of estimating γ, and estimate β from those observations for which w_{i1} and w_{i2} are "close," which would suggest using the weights: $\tilde{\psi}_{in} \equiv (1/h_n^q)K(\Delta w_i/h_n)$. Although this approach would imply a slower rate of convergence for the resulting estimator, this estimation scheme may be used for estimating β from a truncated sample, in which case estimation of the selection equation is infeasible. An obvious drawback in this method is that, in order to consistently estimate the entire parameter vector β, we would have to impose the restriction that w_{it} and x_{it}^{*} do not contain any elements in common.

The above analysis extends naturally to the case of a longer (and possibly unbalanced) panel, that is when $T_i \geq 2$. Then β could be estimated from those observations that have $d_{it} = d_{is} = 1$, and for which $w_{it}\hat{\gamma}_n$ and $w_{is}\hat{\gamma}_n$ are "close," for all $s, t = 1 \ldots, T_i$. The estimator is of the form

$$\hat{\beta}_n = \left[\sum_{i=1}^{n} \frac{1}{T_i - 1} \sum_{s<t} \hat{\psi}_{in}(x_{it} - x_{is})'(x_{it} - x_{is})\, d_{it} d_{is} \right]^{-1} \times \left[\sum_{i=1}^{n} \frac{1}{T_i - 1} \sum_{s<t} \hat{\psi}_{in}(x_{it} - x_{is})'(y_{it} - y_{is})\, d_{it} d_{is} \right],$$

where

$$\hat{\psi}_{in} \equiv \frac{1}{h_n} K\left(\frac{(w_{it} - w_{is})\hat{\gamma}_n}{h_n} \right).$$

In the following section we derive the asymptotic properties of our proposed estimator for the main equation of interest, under the assumption that γ has been consistently estimated. At the end of the section, we examine the applicability of existing estimators for obtaining first-step estimates of the selection equation.

3. ESTIMATION OF THE MAIN EQUATION

3.1. *Asymptotic Properties of the Estimator*

The derivation of the large sample properties of $\hat{\beta}_n$ of equations (2.3) and (2.4) proceeds in two steps. First, the asymptotic behavior of the infeasible estimator which uses the true γ in the construction of the kernel weights, denoted by $\tilde{\beta}_n$, is analyzed. Then the large sample behavior of the difference $(\hat{\beta}_n - \tilde{\beta}_n)$ is investigated.

It will be useful to define the scalar index $W_i \equiv \Delta w_i \gamma$ and its estimated counterpart $\hat{W}_i \equiv \Delta w_i \hat{\gamma}_n$, along with the following quantities:

$$S_{xx} \equiv \frac{1}{n} \sum_{i=1}^{n} \frac{1}{h_n} K\left(\frac{W_i}{h_n} \right) \Delta x_i' \Delta x_i \Phi_i,$$

$$\hat{S}_{xx} \equiv \frac{1}{n} \sum_{i=1}^{n} \frac{1}{h_n} K\left(\frac{\hat{W}_i}{h_n} \right) \Delta x_i' \Delta x_i \Phi_i,$$

$$S_{xv} \equiv \frac{1}{n} \sum_{i=1}^{n} \frac{1}{h_n} K\left(\frac{W_i}{h_n} \right) \Delta x_i' \Delta v_i \Phi_i,$$

$$\hat{S}_{xv} \equiv \frac{1}{n}\sum_{i=1}^{n}\frac{1}{h_n}K\left(\frac{\hat{W}_i}{h_n}\right)\Delta x_i' \,\Delta v_i\, \Phi_i,$$

$$S_{x\lambda} \equiv \frac{1}{n}\sum_{i=1}^{n}\frac{1}{h_n}K\left(\frac{W_i}{h_n}\right)\Delta x_i' \,\Delta \lambda_i\, \Phi_i,$$

$$\hat{S}_{x\lambda} \equiv \frac{1}{n}\sum_{i=1}^{n}\frac{1}{h_n}K\left(\frac{\hat{W}_i}{h_n}\right)\Delta x_i' \,\Delta \lambda_i\, \Phi_i.$$

With these definitions we can write: $\tilde{\beta}_n - \beta = S_{xx}^{-1}(S_{xv} + S_{x\lambda})$ and $\hat{\beta}_n - \beta = \hat{S}_{xx}^{-1}(\hat{S}_{xv} + \hat{S}_{x\lambda})$.

Our asymptotic results for the infeasible estimator are based on the following assumptions.[7] From Section 2, $\Phi_i \equiv d_{i1}d_{i2}$, $\zeta_i \equiv (w_{i1}, w_{i2}, x_{i1}^*, x_{i2}^*, \alpha_i^*, \eta_i)$, and $v_{it} \equiv d_{it}\varepsilon_{it}^* - E(\varepsilon_{it}^*|d_{i1} = 1, d_{i2} = 1, \zeta_i)$.

ASSUMPTION R1: *$(\varepsilon_{i1}^*, \varepsilon_{i2}^*, u_{i1}, u_{i2})$ and $(\varepsilon_{i2}^*, \varepsilon_{i1}^*, u_{i2}, u_{i1})$ are identically distributed conditional on ζ_i. That is, $F(\varepsilon_{i1}^*, \varepsilon_{i2}^*, u_{i1}, u_{i2}|\zeta_i) = F(\varepsilon_{i2}^*, \varepsilon_{i1}^*, u_{i2}, u_{i1}|\zeta_i)$.*

As discussed in Section 2, this conditional exchangeability assumption is crucial to our method for eliminating the sample selection effect. Although in principle we could allow F to vary across individuals, it will be convenient for our analysis to assume that cross-section sampling is random:

ASSUMPTION R2: *An i.i.d. sample, $\{(x_{it}^*, \varepsilon_{it}^*, \alpha_i^*, w_{it}, u_{it}, \eta_i); t = 1, 2\}_{i=1}^n$ is drawn from the population. For each $i = 1, \ldots, n$, and each $t = 1, 2$, we observe $(d_{it}, w_{it}, y_{it}, x_{it})$.*

With this assumption, we may from now on drop the subscripts i that denote the identity of each panel member.

ASSUMPTION R3: *$E(\Delta x' \Delta x\, \Phi|W = 0)$ is finite and nonsingular.*

Note that this assumption implicitly imposes an exclusion restriction on the set of regressors, namely that at least one of the variables in the selection equation, w_{it}, is not contained in x_{it}^*.

ASSUMPTION R4: *The marginal distribution of the index function $W \equiv \Delta w\, \gamma$ is absolutely continuous, with density function f_W which is bounded from above on its support and strictly positive at zero, i.e. $f_W(0) > 0$. In addition, f_W is almost everywhere r times ($r \geq 1$) continuously differentiable and has bounded derivatives.*[8]

[7] Observe that by definition, $\Phi_t \Delta x_t = \Phi_t \Delta x_t^*$. Thus, although certain assumptions are stated in terms of the observed regressors x_{it}, they also hold for the latent (possibly unobserved) x_{it}^*.

[8] It is possible to relax certain smoothness assumptions so that they hold only in a neighborhood of W near zero, at the cost though of more technical detail.

ASSUMPTION R5: *The unknown function*[9] $\Lambda(w_t\gamma+\eta, w_\tau\gamma+\eta, \zeta) \equiv E(\varepsilon_t^*|d_t = 1, d_\tau = 1, \zeta) = E(\varepsilon_t^*|u_t \leq w_t\gamma+\eta, u_\tau \leq w_\tau\gamma+\eta, \zeta)$ *satisfies*: $\Lambda(s_t, s_\tau, \zeta) - \Lambda(s_\tau, s_t, \zeta) = \tilde{\Lambda}\cdot(s_t - s_\tau)$ *for* $t,\tau = 1,2$, *where* $\tilde{\Lambda}$ *is a function of* (s_t, s_τ, ζ), *i.e.*, $\tilde{\Lambda} \equiv \tilde{\Lambda}(s_t, s_\tau, \zeta)$, *which is bounded*[10] *on its support.*

This assumption is crucial to our analysis. It will be satisfied, for example, if Λ is continuously differentiable with respect to its first two arguments, with bounded first-order partial derivatives (as, for example, when the errors are jointly normally distributed), in which case we may apply the multivariate mean-value theorem:

$$\Delta\lambda = (\Lambda^{(1)}(c_1^*) - \Lambda^{(2)}(c_2^*))W.$$

Here $\Lambda^{(j)}$ $(j = 1,2)$ denotes the first-order partial derivative of Λ with respect to its first and second argument respectively, and c_j^* lies on the line segment connecting $(w_1\gamma+\eta, w_2\gamma+\eta, \zeta)$ and $(w_2\gamma+\eta, w_1\gamma+\eta, \zeta)$. Thus, in this case, $\tilde{\Lambda} = \Lambda^{(1)}(c_1^*) - \Lambda^{(2)}(c_2^*)$, and by assumption will be bounded.

ASSUMPTION R6: (a) x_t^* *and* ε_t^* *have bounded* $4+2\delta$ *moments conditional on* W, *for any* $\delta \in (0,1)$.

(b) $E(\Delta x'\,\Delta x\,\Phi|W)$ *and* $E(\Delta x'\,\Delta x\,\Delta v^2\,\Phi|W)$ *are continuous at* $W = 0$ *and do not vanish.*

(c) $E(\Delta x'\,\tilde{\Lambda}\Phi|W)$ *is almost everywhere r times continuously differentiable as a function of* W, *and has bounded derivatives.*

ASSUMPTION R7: *The function* $K: \Re \to \Re$ *satisfies*: (a) $\int K(\nu)\,d\nu = 1$, (b) $\int |K(\nu)|\,d\nu < \infty$, (c) $\sup_\nu |K(\nu)| < \infty$, (d) $\int |\nu|^{r+1}|K(\nu)|\,d\nu < \infty$, *and* (e) $\int \nu^j K(\nu)\,d\nu = 0$ *for all* $j = 1,\ldots,r$.

ASSUMPTION R8: $h_n \to 0$ *and* $nh_n \to \infty$ *as* $n \to \infty$.

From our analysis in Section 2, it is easy to see that Assumptions R1–R3 would suffice to identify β for known γ. An identification scheme in the spirit of our discussion in Section 2 would obviously require support of W at zero, as well as nonsingularity of the matrix Σ_{xx}, imposed by Assumption R3, analogous to the familiar full rank assumption.

The continuity of the distribution of the index W, imposed in Assumption R4, is a regularity condition, common in kernel estimation of density and regression functions. It is precisely this continuity that renders the estimator $\breve{\beta}_n$ of Section 2 infeasible, even if γ were known.

[9] Notice that by Assumption R1, the functional form of Λ is the same over time for the same individual, while by Assumption R2, it is also the same across individuals.

[10] In principle, we could dispense with the assumption that $\tilde{\Lambda}$ is bounded, by assuming that $\tilde{\Lambda}$ has finite fourth moment conditional on W.

Since our estimation scheme is based on pairs of observations for which $W_i \equiv \Delta w_i \gamma \cong 0$, it is obvious that additional smoothness conditions are required. These are imposed by Assumptions R4–R8. Notice, in particular, Assumption R5, which imposes a Lipschitz continuity property on the selection correction function $\Lambda(\ )$. It is easy to see that simple continuity will not be sufficient to guarantee that $\Delta\lambda_i \to 0$ as $W_i \to 0$, since $\Delta\lambda_i$ is not a function of W_i. Furthermore, similarly to kernel density and regression estimation, a high order of differentiability r for certain functions of the index W, along with the appropriate choice of the kernel function and the bandwidth sequence, imply a faster rate of convergence in distribution for $\tilde{\beta}_n$. Specifically, we choose a "$(r+1)$th order bias-reducing" kernel, which by Assumption R7(e) is required to be negative in part of its domain.

The next lemma establishes the asymptotic properties of the infeasible estimator $\hat{\beta}_n$.

LEMMA 1: *Let Assumptions R1–R8 hold. Define*

$$\Sigma_{xx} \equiv f_W(0)\cdot E(\Delta x'\,\Delta x\,\Phi | W=0),$$

$$\Sigma_{xv} \equiv f_W(0) E(\Delta x'\,\Delta x\,\Delta v^2\,\Phi | W=0)\int K(\nu)^2\,d\nu,$$

$$\Sigma_{x\lambda} \equiv g^{(r)}(0)\cdot\frac{1}{r!}\int \nu^{r+1}K(\nu)\,d\nu,$$

where $g^{(r)}(0)$ is the $(k\times 1)$ vector of rth*-order derivatives of*

$$g(W) \equiv E(\Delta x\,\tilde{\Lambda}\Phi | W)\cdot f_W(W)$$

evaluated at $W=0$. Then,

(a) $S_{xx} \xrightarrow{p} \Sigma_{xx}$.

(b) *If* $\sqrt{nh_n}\,h_n^{r+1} \to \tilde{h}$ *with* $0 \le \tilde{h} < \infty$, *then* (i) $\sqrt{nh_n}\,S_{xv} \xrightarrow{\sim} N(0, \Sigma_{xv})$, *and* (ii) $\sqrt{nh_n}\,S_{x\lambda} \xrightarrow{p} \tilde{h}\,\Sigma_{x\lambda}$.

(c) *If* $\sqrt{nh_n}\,h_n^{r+1} \to \infty$, *then* (i) $h_n^{-(r+1)}S_{xv} \xrightarrow{p} 0$ *and* (ii) $h_n^{-(r+1)}S_{x\lambda} \xrightarrow{p} \Sigma_{x\lambda}$.

The asymptotic properties of $\tilde{\beta}_n$ easily follow from the previous Lemma: If $\sqrt{nh_n}\,h_n^{r+1} \to \tilde{h}$, then $\sqrt{nh_n}\,(\tilde{\beta}_n - \beta) \xrightarrow{\sim} N(\tilde{h}\,\Sigma_{xx}^{-1}\Sigma_{x\lambda},\ \Sigma_{xx}^{-1}\Sigma_{xv}\,\Sigma_{xx}^{-1})$, while if $\sqrt{nh_n}\,h_n^{r+1} \to \infty$, then $h_n^{-(r+1)}(\tilde{\beta}_n - \beta) \xrightarrow{p} \Sigma_{xx}^{-1}\Sigma_{x\lambda}$.

In order to derive the asymptotic properties of the feasible estimator $\hat{\beta}_n$, we will make the following additional assumptions:

ASSUMPTION R9: *In addition to the conditions of Assumption R7, the kernel function satisfies*: (a) $K(\nu)$ *is three times continuously differentiable with bounded derivatives, and* (b) $\int|K'(\nu)|\,d\nu$, $\int|K''(\nu)|\,d\nu$, $\int\nu^2K'(\nu)^2\,d\nu$, *and* $\int\nu^2K''(\nu)^2\,d\nu$ *are finite.*

The conditions of Assumption R9 are satisfied, for example, for $K(\nu)$ being the standard normal density function, which is a second order kernel.

ASSUMPTION R10: *x_t^*, ε_t^*, and w_t have bounded $8+4\delta$ moments conditional on W, for some $\delta \in (0,1)$. In addition, $E(\Delta x^l\, \Delta v\, \Delta w^j\, \Phi | W)$ and $E(\Delta x^l\, \Delta v\, \Delta w^j\, \Delta w^m\, \Phi | W)$ are continuous at $W=0$ for all $l=1,\dots,k$ and $j,m=1,\dots,q$.*

ASSUMPTION R11: *The parameter vector γ in the selection equation lies in a compact*[11] *set, and $\hat{\gamma}_n$ is a consistent estimator that satisfies: $\hat{\gamma}_n - \gamma = O_p(n^{-p})$, where $2/5 < p \le 1/2$.*

For example, $p = 1/2$, if γ is estimated by maximizing the conditional likelihood function.

ASSUMPTION R12: *$h_n = h \cdot n^{-\mu}$, where $0 < h < \infty$, and $1 - 2p < \mu < p/2$.*

Assumption R12 is crucial for establishing the result that follows. This result states that $\hat{S}_{xx}$, $\hat{S}_{xv}$, and $\hat{S}_{x\lambda}$ have the same probability limits as their infeasible counterparts S_{xx}, S_{xv}, and $S_{x\lambda}$, provided that the bandwidth sequence h_n is chosen appropriately for any given rate of convergence of the first-step estimator, that is for any given p, and for any degree of smoothness r.

LEMMA 2: *Let Assumptions R1–R12 hold. Then:*

(a) $\hat{S}_{xx}^{-1} - S_{xx}^{-1} = o_p(1)$.

(b) *If* $\sqrt{nh_n}\, h_n^{r+1} \to \tilde{h}$ *with* $0 \le \tilde{h} < \infty$, *then* (i) $\sqrt{nh_n}\,(\hat{S}_{xv} - S_{xv}) = o_p(1)$ *and* (ii) $\sqrt{nh_n}\,(\hat{S}_{x\lambda} - S_{x\lambda}) = o_p(1)$.

(c) *If* $\sqrt{nh_n}\, h_n^{r+1} \to \infty$, *then* (i) $h_n^{-(r+1)}(\hat{S}_{xv} - S_{xv}) = o_p(1)$ *and* (ii) $h_n^{-(r+1)}(\hat{S}_{x\lambda} - S_{x\lambda}) = o_p(1)$.

Lemma 2 readily implies that, if $\sqrt{nh_n}\, h_n^{r+1} \to \tilde{h}$ then $\sqrt{nh_n}\,(\hat{\beta}_n - \tilde{\beta}_n) = o_p(1)$, while if $\sqrt{nh_n}\, h_n^{r+1} \to \infty$, then $h_n^{-(r+1)}(\hat{\beta}_n - \tilde{\beta}_n) = o_p(1)$. Since $(\hat{\beta}_n - \beta) = (\hat{\beta}_n - \tilde{\beta}_n) + (\tilde{\beta}_n - \beta)$, we have the following theorem:

THEOREM 1: *Let Assumptions R1–R12 hold.*

(a) *If* $\sqrt{nh_n}\, h_n^{r+1} \to \tilde{h}$, *with* $0 \le \tilde{h} < \infty$, *then* $\sqrt{nh_n}\,(\hat{\beta}_n - \beta) \xrightarrow{d} N(\tilde{h}\, \Sigma_{xx}^{-1}\Sigma_{x\lambda}, \Sigma_{xx}^{-1}\Sigma_{xv}\Sigma_{xx}^{-1})$.

(b) *If* $\sqrt{nh_n}\, h_n^{r+1} \to \infty$, *then* $h_n^{-(r+1)}(\hat{\beta}_n - \beta) \xrightarrow{p} \Sigma_{xx}^{-1}\Sigma_{x\lambda}$.

[11] Compactness of the parameter space is required for consistency of both Manski's estimator and the smoothed conditional maximum score estimator, while it is not required for the conditional maximum likelihood estimator. Notice though, that since γ can only be estimated up to scale, we can always normalize it so that it lies on the unit circle. Thus the compactness assumption is not restrictive.

Thus, in the limit, the fact we are using $\hat{\gamma}_n$ to estimate β does not affect the asymptotic distribution of $\tilde{\beta}_n$. The lower bound on μ, imposed by Assumption R12, is the key for this result to hold. In words, this bound implies that β is estimated at a rate slower than γ. Indeed, from Theorem 1, the rate of convergence of $\hat{\beta}_n$ is $(nh_n)^{-1/2} = n^{-1/2+\mu/2}$, which is obviously slower than n^{-p}, since $\mu > 1 - 2p$. Thus in effect, Assumption R12 requires that $\sqrt{nh_n}(\hat{\gamma}_n - \gamma) = o_p(1)$.

In principle, we could allow β to be estimated at the same rate as γ. Thus, if $\sqrt{nh_n}(\hat{\gamma}_n - \gamma) = O_p(1)$ for $\sqrt{nh_n}h_n^{r+1} \to \tilde{h}$, we obtain the following asymptotic representation, which may be easily derived from the analysis of Lemma 2(b) in the Appendix:

$$\sqrt{nh_n}\left(\hat{\beta}_n - \beta\right) = \Sigma_{xx}^{-1}\sqrt{nh_n}\,S_{xv} + \Sigma_{xx}^{-1}\Omega\sqrt{nh_n}\,(\hat{\gamma}_n - \gamma) + o_p(1)$$

where

$$\Omega = \operatorname{plim}_{n\to\infty}(1/n)\sum_{i=1}^{n}(1/h_n^2)K'(W_i/h_n)\,\Delta x_i'\,\Delta w_i\,\Delta\lambda_i\,\Phi_i$$

$$= -f_W(0)E(\Delta x'\,\Delta w\,\tilde{\Lambda}\Phi|W=0),$$

provided that $E(\Delta x'\,\Delta w\,\tilde{\Lambda}\Phi|W)$ is continuous at $W=0$ and $\nu K(\nu) \to 0$ as $|\nu| \to \infty$. Asymptotic normality of $\hat{\beta}_n$ may still be established if $\sqrt{nh_n}(\hat{\gamma}_n - \gamma)$ has an asymptotic representation of the form: $\sqrt{nh_n}(\hat{\gamma}_n - \gamma) = 1/\sqrt{nh_n}\sum_{i=1}^{n} g(\Delta w_i, \Delta d_i, \gamma) + o_p(1)$.[12]

At first glance it looks attractive to eliminate the asymptotic bias of $\hat{\beta}_n$ by choosing h_n so that $\sqrt{nh_n}h_n^{r+1} \to \tilde{h} = 0$, or equivalently by setting $\mu > (1/(2(r+1)+1))$. In that case, however, the rate of convergence of $\hat{\beta}_n$ is lower than when $\tilde{h} > 0$. Indeed, the rate of convergence in distribution of $\hat{\beta}_n$ is maximized by making μ as small as possible, that is by setting $\mu = 1/(2(r+1)+1)$, in which case it becomes $n^{-(r+1)/(2(r+1)-1)}$. Thus, for r large enough, the estimator converges at a rate that can be arbitrarily close to $n^{-1/2}$, provided also that γ is estimated fast enough, that is provided $p > (r+1)/(2(r+1)+1)$.

Although the proposed estimator is asymptotically biased, it is possible to eliminate the asymptotic bias while maintaining the maximal rate of convergence, in the manner suggested by Bierens (1987).

COROLLARY: *Let $\hat{\beta}_n$ be the estimator with window width $h_n = h\cdot n^{-1/(2(r+1)+1)}$, and $\hat{\beta}_{n,\delta}$ the estimator with window width $h_{n,\delta} = h\cdot n^{-\delta/(2(r+1)+1)}$, where $\delta \in (0,1)$.*

[12] We can also derive an asymptotic representation for $\hat{\beta}_n$ in the case where γ is estimated at rate n^{-p} that is slower than $1/\sqrt{nh_n}$. In this case we obtain $n^p(\hat{\beta}_n - \beta) = \Sigma_{xx}^{-1}\Omega\cdot n^p(\hat{\gamma}_n - \gamma) + o_p(1)$, which implies that $\hat{\beta}_n$ converges at the same rate as $\hat{\gamma}_n$, which is slower than the "optimal" rate obtained for the infeasible estimator $\tilde{\beta}_n$, that is when γ is known.

Define

$$\hat{\hat{\beta}}_n \equiv \frac{\hat{\beta}_n - n^{-(1-\delta)(r+1)/(2(r+1)+1)}\hat{\beta}_{n,\delta}}{1 - n^{-(1-\delta)(r+1)/(2(r+1)+1)}}.$$

Then, $n^{(r+1)/(2(r+1)+1)}(\hat{\hat{\beta}}_n - \beta) \xrightarrow{d} N(0, h^{-1}\Sigma_{xx}^{-1}\Sigma_{x\varepsilon}\Sigma_{xx}^{-1})$.

3.2. *Practical Issues*

In order to compute $\hat{\beta}_n$ or $\hat{\hat{\beta}}_n$ in an application, one needs to choose the kernel function K, and to assign a numerical value to the bandwidth parameter h_n. Results on kernel density and regression function estimation suggest that the asymptotic performance of the estimator will be likely more sensitive to the choice of the window width than to the choice of the kernel. Furthermore, the asymptotic normality result of the Corollary above shows that the variance of the limiting distribution depends crucially on the choice of the constant h. We will thus focus here on the problem of bandwidth selection. Bierens (1987) discusses the construction of high order bias-reducing kernels.

For a given order of differentiability r, and a given sample size n, the results of Theorem 1 suggest that $h_n = h \cdot n^{-\mu}$ be chosen so that $\mu = 1/(2(r+1)+1)$. So the problem of bandwidth selection reduces to the problem of choosing the constant h. A natural way to proceed (see Horowitz (1992) and Härdle (1990)), is to choose h so as to minimize some kind of measure of the "distance" of the estimator from the true value, based on the asymptotic result of Theorem 1. Consider for example minimizing the asymptotic mean squared error of the estimator, defined as:

$$\begin{aligned} MSE &= E\left(\left(\hat{\beta}_n - \beta\right)' A\left(\hat{\beta}_n - \beta\right)\right) = \text{trace}\left[AE\left(\left(\hat{\beta}_n - \beta\right)\left(\hat{\beta}_n - \beta\right)'\right)\right] \\ &= n^{-2(r+1)/(2(r+1)+1)}\,\text{trace}\left[A\,\Sigma_{xx}^{-1}\left(h^{-1}\Sigma_{x\varepsilon} + h^{2(r+1)}\Sigma_{x\lambda}\Sigma_{x\lambda}'\right)\Sigma_{xx}^{-1}\right] \end{aligned}$$

for any nonstochastic positive semidefinite matrix A that satisfies $\Sigma_{x\lambda}'\Sigma_{xx}^{-1}A\,\Sigma_{xx}^{-1}\Sigma_{x\lambda} \neq 0$. It is straightforward to show that MSE is minimized by setting

$$h = h^* = \left(\frac{\text{trace}\left[\Sigma_{xx}^{-1}A\,\Sigma_{xx}^{-1}\Sigma_{x\varepsilon}\right]}{2(r+1)\,\Sigma_{x\lambda}'\Sigma_{xx}^{-1}A\,\Sigma_{xx}^{-1}\Sigma_{x\lambda}}\right)^{1/(2(r+1)+1)}. \tag{3.2.1}$$

This last expression suggests that we may construct a consistent estimate of h^* if consistent estimates of Σ_{xx}, $\Sigma_{x\varepsilon}$, and $\Sigma_{x\lambda}$ are available. By part (a) of Lemmata 1 and 2, $\hat{S}_{xx}$ consistently estimates S_{xx} for any h_n that satisfies $h_n \to 0$ and $nh_n \to \infty$. In the next theorem, we provide consistent estimators of $\Sigma_{x\varepsilon}$ and $\Sigma_{x\lambda}$.

THEOREM 2:[13] Assume that Assumptions R1–R12 hold. (a) Let $\hat{\beta}_n$ be a consistent estimator of β based on $h_n = h \cdot n^{-1/(2(r+1)+1)}$, and define $\hat{\varepsilon}_{it} \equiv y_{it} - x_{it}\hat{\beta}_n$.

[13] The proof of Theorem 2 is omitted here to conserve space. It is available at the author's world wide web page.

Then

$$\hat{\Sigma}_{xv} \equiv \frac{1}{n}\sum_{i=1}^{n}\frac{1}{h_n}K\left(\frac{\Delta w_i\hat{\gamma}_n}{h_n}\right)^2 \Delta x_i' \, \Delta x_i \, \Delta\hat{\varepsilon}_i^2 \, \Phi_i \xrightarrow{p} \Sigma_{xv}.$$

(b) Let $h_{n,\delta} = h \cdot n^{-\delta/(2(r+1)+1)}$, where $0 < \delta < 1$. Then, for $\hat{\varepsilon}_{it}$ defined as in part (a),

$$\hat{\Sigma}_{x\lambda} \equiv h_{n,\delta}^{-(r+1)}\frac{1}{n}\sum_{i=1}^{n}\frac{1}{h_{n,\delta}}K\left(\frac{\Delta w_i\hat{\gamma}_n}{h_{n,\delta}}\right) \Delta x_i' \, \Delta\hat{\varepsilon}_i \, \Phi_i \xrightarrow{p} \Sigma_{x\lambda}.$$

Returning to our discussion about the construction of the estimator of β in practice, we propose the following method (see also Horowitz (1992)). In the first stage, for a given r and n, choose any $h_n = h \cdot n^{-1/(2(r+1)+1)}$ and any $h_{n,\delta} = h \cdot n^{-\delta/(2(r+1)+1)}$, with h an arbitrary positive constant, and $0 < \delta < 1$. Compute $\hat{\beta}_n$ based on h_n, and construct $\hat{\varepsilon}_{it}$ as defined in Theorem 2. Use $\hat{\beta}_n$ to compute the estimates of Σ_{xx}, Σ_{xv}, and $\Sigma_{x\lambda}$ as discussed above. Then estimate h^* by $\hat{h}$, using equation (3.2.1) with Σ_{xx}, Σ_{xv}, and $\Sigma_{x\lambda}$ replaced by their consistent estimates. In the second stage, compute the asymptotic bias-corrected estimates as in the Corollary using $\hat{h}$ as the constant in the definition of h_n and $h_{n,\delta}$.

This two-stage procedure is similar to the "plug-in" method used in kernel density and regression function estimation, and it shares the same disadvantages: First, it involves the choice of a smoothing parameter in the first stage, namely choosing the initial constant h. Second, by specifying the order of differentiability r, the researcher is restricted to a certain smoothness class.

It is interesting to note that standard statistical software may be used for computing estimates for the main equation and their standard errors: Given a consistent estimate $\hat{\gamma}_n$ for the selection equation, and a bandwidth $h_n = h \cdot n^{-1/(2(r+1)+1)}$, run OLS regression of $\hat{Y}_i \equiv \sqrt{K(\Delta w_i \hat{\gamma}_n / h_n)}\, \Delta y_i \Phi_i$ on $\hat{X}_i \equiv \sqrt{K(\Delta w_i \hat{\gamma}_n / h_n)}\, \Delta x_i \Phi_i$, and compute the (asymptotically biased) estimate $\hat{\beta}_n$. Standard errors are obtained from the Eicker-White covariance matrix:

$$\left(\sum_{i=1}^{n}\hat{X}_i'\hat{X}_i\right)^{-1}\sum_{i=1}^{n}\hat{X}_i'\hat{X}_i\hat{e}_i^2\left(\sum_{i=1}^{n}\hat{X}_i'\hat{X}_i\right)^{-1} \tag{3.2.2}$$

using the residuals from the regression, $\hat{e}_i \equiv \hat{Y}_i - \hat{X}_i\hat{\beta}$. The bias-corrected estimate $\hat{\hat{\beta}}_n$ is obtained as a linear combination of $\hat{\beta}_n$ and $\hat{\beta}_{n,\delta}$ as described in the Corollary of Theorem 1, where $\hat{\beta}_{n,\delta}$ comes from the auxiliary OLS regression of $\hat{Y}_i$ on $\hat{X}_i$ with bandwidth $h_{n,\delta} = h \cdot n^{-\delta/(2(r+1)+1)}$.

We next turn to the problem of estimating the unknown parameter vector γ in the selection equation. As we established, the asymptotic results obtained for the proposed estimator of β depend crucially on the rate of convergence of the first-step estimator of γ. In particular, it is straightforward to establish consistency[14] of $\hat{\beta}_n$ if $h_n^{-2}(\hat{\gamma}_n - \gamma) = o_p(1)$, for any h_n that satisfies Assumption R8, i.e. for $h_n \to 0$ and $nh_n \to \infty$. On the other hand, the asymptotic normality result of Theorem 1 requires that $\sqrt{nh_n}(\hat{\gamma}_n - \gamma) = o_p(1)$, for any h_n that satisfies $\sqrt{nh_n} h_n^{r+1} \to \tilde{h}$, with $0 \leq \tilde{h} < \infty$.

The conditions for obtaining consistency and asymptotic normality of $\hat{\beta}_n$ are satisfied by the conditional maximum likelihood estimator proposed by Rasch (1960, 1961) and Andersen (1970), which is consistent and root-n asymptotically normal, under the assumption that the errors in the selection equation are white noise with a logistic distribution and independent of the regressors and the individual effects. In fact, as Chamberlain (1992) has shown, if the support of the predictor variables in the selection equation is bounded, then identification of γ is possible only in the logistic case. Furthermore, even if the support is unbounded, in which case γ may be identified and thus consistently estimated, consistent estimation at rate $n^{-1/2}$ is possible only in the logistic case. As is well known though, if the distribution of the errors is misspecified, the conditional maximum likelihood approach will in general produce inconsistent estimators.

Another possible choice for estimating γ is the conditional maximum score estimator, proposed by Manski (1987). Under fairly weak distributional assumptions, this estimator consistently estimates γ up to scale. However, the results of Cavanagh (1987), and Kim and Pollard (1990) for the maximum score estimator proposed by Manski (1975, 1985) for the cross section binary response model, namely that it converges at the slow rate of $n^{-1/3}$ to a non-normal random variable, suggest that these properties carry through to its panel data analog, the conditional maximum score estimator. Thus, if $(\hat{\gamma}_n - \gamma) = O_p(n^{-1/3})$, it is possible to consistently estimate β by choosing h_n to satisfy $n^{1/3}h_n^2 \to \infty$. In this case though, the analysis for obtaining the asymptotic distribution for $\hat{\beta}_n$ is not applicable.

It is possible, however, to modify Manski's conditional maximum score estimator and obtain control over both its rate of convergence and its limiting distribution, by imposing sufficient smoothness on the distribution of the errors and the explanatory variables in the selection equation. Specifically, following the approach taken by Horowitz (1992) for estimating the cross section binary response model, we can construct a "smoothed conditional maximum score" estimator, which under weak (but stronger than Manski's) assumptions, is consistent and asymptotically normally distributed, with a rate of convergence that can be arbitrarily close to $n^{-1/2}$, depending on the amount of smoothness

[14] Consistency of $\hat{\beta}_n$ may be established under the weaker restriction that $h_n^{-4}\|\hat{\gamma}_n - \gamma\|^3 = o_p(1)$. The proof of Lemma 2(a) would then have to be modified, by taking a third instead of a first order Taylor series expansion. This modification does not alter the basic restriction for obtaining an asymptotic distribution for $\hat{\beta}_n$ which does not depend on the estimation of γ in the first step, namely that γ has to be estimated at a faster rate than β. Notice that in this case, the upper bound on μ in Assumption R12 would have to be replaced by $(6p-1)/7$. However, this modification would affect the proof of Theorem 2, which would become unnecessarily complicated and long.

we are willing to assume for the underlying distributions. This estimator is considered in an earlier version of the paper (Kyriazidou (1994)) and also in Charlier et al. (1995).

4. MONTE CARLO EVIDENCE

In this section we illustrate certain finite sample properties of the proposed estimator. The Monte Carlo results presented here are in no sense representative of the estimator's sampling behavior since only one experimental design is considered. Further, there is little justification for the choice of the particular design, except that it is simple to set up and that, in the absence of sample selectivity, ordinary least squares on the first differences would perform quite well. The simulation study of this section is intended more as an investigation of the sensitivity of the estimator to the choice of bandwidth, the order of the kernel, the proposed asymptotic bias correction, the first step estimation method, the performance in practice of the proposed plug-in method for estimating the bandwidth constant, and finally the practical usefulness of the proposed covariance matrix estimator in testing hypotheses about the main regression equation coefficients.

Data for the Monte Carlo experiments are generated according to the model:

$$y_{it} = d_{it} \cdot (x_{it}\beta^0 + \alpha_i + \varepsilon_{it}) \qquad (i = 1, \ldots, n;\ t = 1, 2), \tag{5.1}$$

$$d_{it} = 1\{w_{1,it}\gamma_1 + w_{2,it}\gamma_2 + \eta_i - u_{it} \geq 0\}, \tag{5.2}$$

where $\beta^0 = 1$, $\gamma_1 = \gamma_2 = 1$, $w_{1,it}$ and $w_{2,it}$ are independent $N(-1,1)$ variables, $\eta_i = (w_{1,i1} + w_{1,i2})/2 + 2\xi_1$, with ξ_1 an independent variable distributed uniformly over the interval $(0,1)$, u_{it} is logistically distributed normalized to have variance equal to 1, $x_{it} = w_{1,it}$, $\alpha_i = (w_{2,i1} + w_{2,i2})/2 + \xi_2$, with ξ_2 an independent $N(0,2)$ variable, and $\varepsilon_{it} = 0.8\xi_3 + 0.6u_{it}$, with ξ_3 an independent standard normal variable. All data are generated i.i.d. across individuals and over time. This design implies that $\Pr(d_1 + d_2 = 1) \approx 0.37$, and $\Pr(d_1 = d_2 = 1) \approx 0.31$, so that approximately 37 percent of each sample is used in the first step estimation of the selection equation and approximately 31 percent in the second step. Each Monte Carlo experiment is performed 1000 times, while the same pseudorandom number sequences are used for each one of three different sample sizes n: 250, 1000, and 4000.

Table I presents the finite sample properties of the "naive" estimator, denoted by $\hat{\beta}_{\text{NAIVE}}$, that ignores sample selectivity and is therefore inconsistent. This estimator is obtained by applying OLS on the first differences using only those individuals that are selected into the sample both time periods, i.e. those that have $d_{i1} = d_{i2} = 1$. This estimator may be viewed as a limiting case of our proposed estimator with bandwidth equal to infinity. Panel A reports the estimated mean bias and root mean squared error (RMSE) for this estimator over 1000 replications for different sample sizes n. As the estimator may not have a finite mean or variance in any finite sample, we also report its median

TABLE I

	Panel A: Finite Sample Properties of $\hat{\beta}_{NAIVE}$ Mean Bias	Median Bias	RMSE	MAD
$n = 250$	0.1033	0.1032	0.1588	0.1149
$n = 1000$	0.1044	0.1055	0.1205	0.1055
$n = 4000$	0.1083	0.1088	0.1123	0.1088
	Panel B: Sizes of t tests			
	0.01	0.05	0.10	0.20
$n = 250$	0.0490	0.1510	0.2300	0.3860
$n = 1000$	0.2300	0.4250	0.5470	0.6770
$n = 4000$	0.8510	0.9550	0.9810	0.9910

bias and the median absolute deviation (MAD). Panel B reports the number of rejections of the null hypothesis that β is equal to its true value $\beta^0 = 1$ at the 1, 5, 10, and 20 percent significance levels. Both panels confirm that the estimator is inconsistent.

Table II presents the finite sample properties of the proposed two-step estimator. The left-hand-side panels are for $\hat{\beta}_n$ obtained by specifying $r = 1$ and using $K(\nu) = \phi(\nu)$, where ϕ is the density of the standard normal distribution,

TABLE II

FINITE SAMPLE PROPERTIES OF $\hat{\beta}_n$ AND $\hat{\hat{\beta}}_n$: $h_n = n^{-1/5}$, $K(\nu) = \phi(\nu)$

	$\hat{\beta}_n$ (Without Asymptotic Bias Correction)				$\hat{\hat{\beta}}_n$ (With Asymptotic Bias Correction)			
	Mean Bias	Median Bias	RMSE	MAD	Mean Bias	Median Bias	RMSE	MAD
	Panel A: True γ							
$n = 250$	0.0090	0.0131	0.2427	0.1625	0.0018	0.0105	0.2623	0.1723
$n = 1000$	0.0118	0.0072	0.1368	0.0924	0.0078	0.0034	0.1439	0.0971
$n = 4000$	0.0051	0.0085	0.0792	0.0511	0.0024	0.0062	0.0820	0.0525
	Panel B: $\hat{\gamma}_L$							
$n = 250$	0.0224	0.0312	0.2076	0.1438	0.0145	0.0245	0.2230	0.1500
$n = 1000$	0.0167	0.0140	0.1169	0.0778	0.0117	0.0072	0.1222	0.0795
$n = 4000$	0.0093	0.0116	0.0672	0.0455	0.0059	0.0081	0.0693	0.0457
	Panel C: $\hat{\gamma}_{CMS}$							
$n = 250$	0.0060	0.0196	0.2592	0.1725	−0.0021	0.0088	0.2815	0.1831
$n = 1000$	0.0022	0.0008	0.1435	0.0950	−0.0026	−0.0037	0.1516	0.1002
$n = 4000$	0.0023	0.0099	0.0826	0.0544	−0.0005	0.0073	0.0857	0.0563
	Panel D: $\hat{\gamma}_{SCMS,4}$							
$n = 250$	0.0403	0.0480	0.1780	0.1255	0.0327	0.0408	0.1878	0.1318
$n = 1000$	0.0170	0.0156	0.1063	0.0703	0.0106	0.0093	0.1108	0.0743
$n = 4000$	−0.0088	−0.0083	0.0629	0.0410	−0.0139	−0.0136	0.0661	0.0434
	Panel E: $\hat{\gamma}_{SCMS,2}$							
$n = 250$	0.0433	0.0482	0.1765	0.1242	0.0361	0.0384	0.1854	0.1309
$n = 1000$	0.0207	0.0177	0.1071	0.0721	0.0146	0.0118	0.1115	0.0764
$n = 4000$	−0.0048	−0.0066	0.0659	0.0416	−0.0098	−0.0119	0.0689	0.0438

which is a second order bias-reducing kernel. The bandwidth sequence is $h_n = h \cdot n^{-1/(2(r+1)+1)} = h \cdot n^{-1/5}$ with $h = 1$. The panels on the right-hand side present the results for $\hat{\hat{\beta}}_n$, the estimator of the Corollary of Theorem 1 which corrects for asymptotic bias, where we use $\delta = 0.1$. Going from top to bottom of Table II, Panel A reports the results for the proposed estimator using the true γ in the construction of the kernel weights.[15] In Panel B, γ is estimated by conditional logit, denoted by $\hat{\gamma}_L$, which in this case will be consistent since all of the assumptions underlying the approach hold in our Monte Carlo design. In Panel C, γ is estimated using the conditional maximum score estimator,[16] denoted by $\hat{\gamma}_{CMS}$, and in Panels D and E we use the smoothed conditional maximum score estimator, denoted by $\hat{\gamma}_{SCMS}$. In Panel D, γ is estimated at a rate faster than β, while in Panel E both β and γ are estimated at the same rate.[17]

From Table II we see that the propose estimator is less biased than the "naive" OLS estimator both with and without the asymptotic bias correction. Furthermore, this bias decreases with sample size since the estimator is consistent, at rate slower than $n^{-1/2}$, as predicted by the asymptotic theory. This may be seen by the fact that the RMSE decreases by less than half when we quadruple the sample size. Notice that the results do not change substantially whether we use the true γ or we estimate it for the construction of the kernel weights, except when the smoothed maximum score approach is used. In the latter case (Panels D and E), the estimator is significantly more biased, although its RMSE is lower than in the other panels. This may be due to the relatively large finite sample bias of the smoothed maximum score estimates (see also Horowitz (1992)), which may be thought of as increasing the effective window

[15] In the construction of the kernel weights of both the infeasible estimator $\tilde{\beta}_n$ of Panel A and the feasible estimators of Panels B–E, the norm of γ is set equal to one so that the results across panels are comparable.

[16] The CMS estimates are computed by maximizing the objective function $(1/n)\Sigma_{i=1}^{n} \Delta d_i \cdot 1\{\Delta w_{i1} g_1 + \Delta w_{i2} g_2 \geq 0\}$ (see also equation (7) in Manski (1987)) over $g_1 = \sin(g)$ and $g_2 = \cos(g)$ with g ranging in a 2,000-point equispaced grid from 0 to 2π.

[17] The SCMS estimates are computed by maximizing

$$\frac{1}{n} \sum_{i=1}^{n} \Delta d_i \cdot L(\Delta w_{i1} g_1 + \Delta w_{i2} g_2 / \sigma_n)$$

over all $g \in \Re^2$ that have $|g_1| = 1$ and g_2 in a compact subset of $\Re$ by the method of fast simulated annealing. Joel Horowitz kindly provided the optimization routine. In Panel D, we set $L(\nu) = K_4(\nu)$ of Horowitz (1992, page 516), which implies that the estimator, denoted by $\hat{\gamma}_{SCMS,4}$, converges in distribution at rate $n^{-4/9}$ (faster than the rate of $\hat{\beta}_n$ which in the case of a second order kernel is $n^{-2/5}$), so that the asymptotic theory of Section 3.1 is valid. In Panel E, we use $L(\nu) = \Phi(\nu)$ where Φ is the standard normal cumulative distribution function. In this case the estimator, denoted by $\hat{\gamma}_{SCMS,2}$, converges in distribution at the same rate as $\hat{\beta}_n$, $n^{-2/5}$. The SCMS estimates used in the construction of the kernel weights are corrected for asymptotic bias using $\delta = 0.1$ and are obtained by the two stage "plug-in" procedure, where in the first stage the bandwidth sequence is $\sigma_n = 0.5 n^{-(1/(2m+1))}$ $(m = 2$ or $4)$, while the second stage uses the estimated optimal constant in the construction of the bandwidth. For details, see Horowitz (1992) and Kyriazidou (1994).

width used in the estimation of β. Furthermore, we notice that the results are very similar when γ is estimated at the same rate as β (Panel E) relative to the case where it is estimated faster than β (Panel D). Comparing the right and left sides of Table II, we see that the asymptotic bias correction does decrease the estimated (mean and median) bias of the estimator, it invariably however increases its variability.

In Table III we investigate the sensitivity of the (infeasible) estimator with respect to the choice of the bandwidth constant and the choice of the kernel function. Panels A and B present the results for $\hat{\beta}_n$ and $\hat{\hat{\beta}}_n$ using a bandwidth constant h equal to 0.5 and 3, respectively, and a second order bias-reducing kernel. As expected the estimator's bias increases as we increase the bandwidth while the RMSE decreases. The increase in both mean and median bias appears quite large, which indicates that point estimates may be quite sensitive to the choice of bandwidth. In order to give a sense of the precision with which these biases are estimated, we provide at the bottom of Table III their estimated standard errors for the two sets of experiments that use 0.5 and 3 as bandwidth constant (Panels A and B).[18]

In Panels C and D we use a fourth and a sixth order bias-reducing kernel[19] and set $h_n = n^{-1/(2(r+1)-1)}$ with $r = 3$ and $r = 5$, respectively. A comparison of Panels II-A and III-C and III-D suggests that the use of higher order kernels speeds up the rate of convergence of the estimator, although there does not appear to be much gain from increasing the order of the kernel from four to six.

Table IV explores the properties of the proposed estimator when the "plug-in" method described in Section 3.2 is used. The specification is the same as in Table II. Comparing Panels A–D in Tables II and IV, we see that the bias of the estimates increases when the optimal bandwidth constant $\hat{h}^*$ is used while their RMSE decreases (except in Panel IV-D). This is because, in general, $\hat{h}^*$ is larger than the initial constant (here the initial bandwidth constant is set equal to one[20]). Table V displays the mean of $\hat{h}^*$ across 1000 replications for different specifications of the initial constant for the case of the infeasible estimator. We find that the means of the estimates are increasing in the initial bandwidth constant (although this is not necessarily true for all 1000 samples). Our finding may be interpreted by the asymptotic bias term being in general poorly estimated in the particular Monte Carlo design used in this study. Indeed, we find that, for the sample sizes considered here, the estimated asymptotic bias of the estimator decreases with the bandwidth constant h contrary to the asymptotic

[18] To estimate the standard errors for the median bias we need to calculate the estimator's density. This is estimated using a normal kernel and the rule-of-thumb bandwidth suggested by Silverman (1986, equation 3.28).

[19] The fourth-order kernel is $K_4(v) = 1.1\exp(-v^2/2) - 0.1\exp(-v^2/2\cdot 11)(1/\sqrt{11})$, and the sixth-order kernel is $K_6(v) = 1.5\exp(-v^2/2) + 0.1\exp(-v^2/2\cdot 9)(1/\sqrt{9}) - 0.6\exp(-v^2/2\cdot 4)(1/\sqrt{4})$. See Bierens (1987).

[20] We chose the initial h equal to one as the mean squared error of the distribution of the (infeasible) estimator in the 1000 replications was found to be minimized in that neighborhood when a rough search over a 10-point grid from 0.5 to 10 was performed for a sample size $n = 100{,}000$.

TABLE III

FINITE SAMPLE PROPERTIES OF $\hat{\beta}_n$ AND $\hat{\hat{\beta}}_n$: TRUE γ[a,b]

	$\hat{\beta}_n$ (Without Asymptotic Bias Correction)				$\hat{\hat{\beta}}_n$ (With Asymptotic Bias Correction)			
	Mean Bias	Median Bias	RMSE	MAD	Mean Bias	Median Bias	RMSE	MAD
	Panel A: $K(\nu)=\phi(\nu), h_n=0.5\cdot n^{-1/5}$							
$n=250$	0.0012	0.0040	0.3463	0.2140	−0.0017	0.0065	0.3761	0.2289
$n=1000$	0.0069	0.0064	0.1930	0.1308	0.0053	0.0023	0.2038	0.1378
$n=4000$	0.0006	−0.0002	0.1119	0.0752	−0.0005	−0.0014	0.1161	0.0772
	Panel B: $K(\nu)=\phi(\nu), h_n=3\cdot n^{-1/5}$							
$n=250$	0.0597	0.0631	0.1550	0.1097	0.0542	0.0566	0.1586	0.1126
$n=1000$	0.0478	0.0459	0.0933	0.0626	0.0435	0.0426	0.0936	0.0626
$n=4000$	0.0349	0.0351	0.0565	0.0418	0.0316	0.0321	0.0556	0.0402
	Panel C: $K(\nu)=K_4(\nu), h_n=n^{-1/9}$							
$n=250$	0.0234	0.0246	0.1966	0.1390	0.0080	0.0121	0.2259	0.1548
$n=1000$	0.0216	0.0159	0.1067	0.0723	0.0099	0.0003	0.1181	0.0797
$n=4000$	0.0151	0.0159	0.0582	0.0397	0.0051	0.0054	0.0627	0.0417
	Panel D: $K(\nu)=K_6(\nu), h_n=n^{1/13}$							
$n=250$	0.0220	0.0269	0.1973	0.1362	0.0002	0.0030	0.2401	0.1594
$n=1000$	0.0209	0.0144	0.1041	0.0719	0.0032	−0.0031	0.1213	0.0826
$n=4000$	0.0156	0.0170	0.0560	0.0391	−0.0006	−0.0002	0.0633	0.0429

[a] The estimated standard errors of the mean bias estimates for n = 250, 1000, and 4000 are 0.0110, 0.0061, 0.0035 for Panel A, and 0.0045, 0.0026, and 0.0014 for Panel B, respectively.

[b] The estimated standard errors of the median bias estimates for n = 250, 1000, and 4000 are 0.0136, 0.0077, and 0.0044 for Panel A, and 0.0059, 0.0033, and 0.0018 for Panel B, respectively.

TABLE IV

FINITE SAMPLE PROPERTIES OF $\hat{\beta}_n$ AND $\hat{\hat{\beta}}_n$: $h_n=\hat{h}^* n^{-1/5}$, INITIAL $h=1$, $K(\nu)=\phi(\nu)$

	$\hat{\beta}_n$ (Without Asymptotic Bias Correction)				$\hat{\hat{\beta}}_n$ (With Asymptotic Bias Correction)			
	Mean Bias	Median Bias	RMSE	MAD	Mean Bias	Median Bias	RMSE	MAD
	Panel A: True γ							
$n=250$	0.0341	0.0476	0.1919	0.1287	0.0261	0.0416	0.2046	0.1347
$n=1000$	0.0378	0.0434	0.1053	0.0700	0.0330	0.0387	0.1079	0.0711
$n=4000$	0.0308	0.0370	0.0653	0.0507	0.0273	0.0333	0.0655	0.0499
	Panel B: $\hat{\gamma}_L$							
$n=250$	0.0519	0.0658	0.1703	0.1191	0.0454	0.0597	0.1778	0.1226
$n=1000$	0.0507	0.0543	0.1000	0.0693	0.0465	0.0512	0.1009	0.0689
$n=4000$	0.0416	0.0453	0.0654	0.0504	0.0385	0.0428	0.0647	0.0493
	Panel C: $\hat{\gamma}_{CMS}$							
$n=250$	0.0309	0.0491	0.2117	0.1329	0.0221	0.0397	0.2282	0.1407
$n=1000$	0.0301	0.0364	0.1114	0.0718	0.0246	0.0315	0.1154	0.0739
$n=4000$	0.0282	0.0354	0.0671	0.0507	0.0246	0.0319	0.0676	0.0505
	Panel D: $\gamma_{SCMS,4}$							
$n=250$	0.0743	0.0818	0.1543	0.1086	0.0705	0.0803	0.1563	0.1100
$n=1000$	0.0637	0.0645	0.1004	0.0740	0.0604	0.0616	0.1003	0.0743
$n=4000$	0.0432	0.0449	0.0658	0.0488	0.0401	0.0421	0.0650	0.0482

TABLE V

MEAN OF $\hat{h}^*$: TRUE γ

	Initial $h = 0.5$	Initial $h = 1$	Initial $h = 2$	Initial $h = 3$
$n = 250$	1.3743	2.8938	6.3115	11.2053
$n = 1000$	1.6314	3.3807	6.6703	11.0386
$n = 4000$	2.0264	3.6447	5.9648	8.8710

result of Theorem 1. It thus appears that, for the particular design, small sample bias is more important than asymptotic bias. The sensitivity of the optimal constant estimate $\hat{h}^*$ to the choice of the initial constant suggests that further research on alternative methods for choosing the bandwidth may be warranted.

We next investigate whether normality might be a good approximation to the finite sample distribution of the proposed estimator. In Figure 1 we plot the quantiles of $\hat{\beta}_n$ against those of a normal random variable with the same mean and variance as the sample mean and sample variance of $\hat{\beta}_n$. Such quantile-quantile plots are provided for different sample sizes, and for the true and the

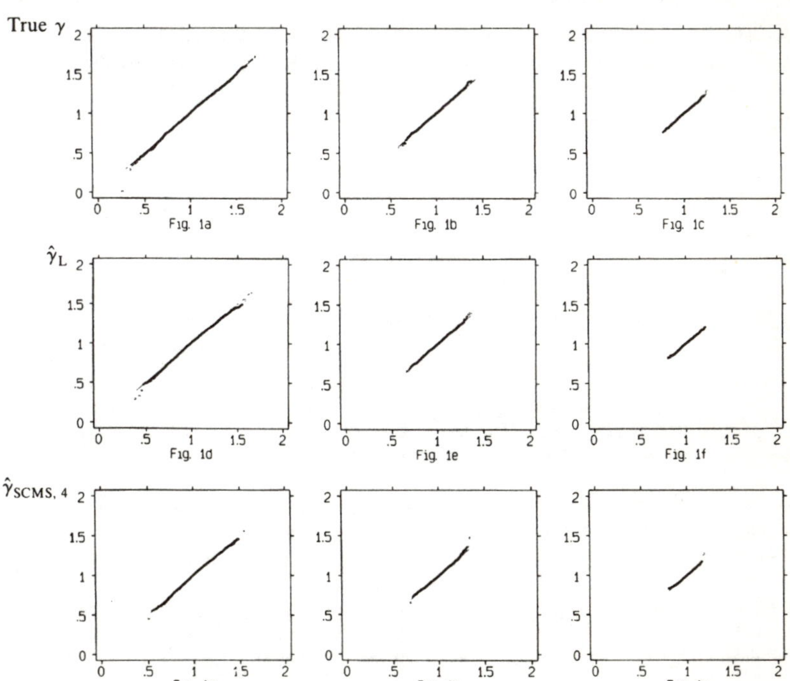

Note: Figures 1a, 1d, 1g: $n = 250$. Figures 1b, 1e, 1h: $n = 1000$. Figures 1c, 1f, 1i: $n = 4000$.

FIGURE 1.—Quantile-quantile plots of $\hat{\beta}_n$ against a Normal: $h_n = n^{-1/5}$, $K(\nu) = \phi(\nu)$.

estimated values of γ, using the specification of Table II (that is, using a second order kernel and $h_n = n^{-1/5}$). We find that, for the experimental design used in this study, the small sample distribution of the proposed estimator is well approximated by a normal distribution. The plots for the asymptotic bias-corrected estimator are very similar, albeit displaying a larger dispersion, and are not given here.

Finally, we examine the size of "t tests" where the test statistics use the asymptotic covariance matrix estimator proposed in Theorem 2. Specifically, in Table VI we test the null hypothesis that β is equal to its true value $\beta^0 = 1$. To this end, we construct t statistics for $\hat{\beta}_n$ and $\hat{\hat{\beta}}_n$ for the specification of Table II (that is, using a second order kernel and $h_n = n^{-1/5}$). Standard errors are constructed using the estimator given by equation (3.2.2). The table presents the fraction of samples for which the null hypothesis is rejected at the 1, 5, 10, and 20 percent statistical significance level. We find that the actual levels of the tests are not far from the nominal levels, especially for larger sample sizes, and that they are closer for the estimates without the asymptotic bias correction. Note that, although we report the results of the t tests for $\hat{\beta}_n$ using Manski's CMS estimator in the first step (Panel VI-C), the standard errors calculated for the two-step estimator of the main equation are only heuristic, since as discussed in Section 3.2 the asymptotic normality of $\hat{\beta}_n$ (and $\hat{\hat{\beta}}_n$) does not obtain in this case due to the slow rate of convergence of $\hat{\gamma}_{CMS}$. However, the levels of the tests even in this case are reasonable. Alternatively, we could have used bootstrap standard errors.

TABLE VI

SIZE OF t TESTS USING $\hat{\beta}_n$ AND $\hat{\hat{\beta}}_n$: $h_n = n^{-1/5}$, $K(\nu) = \phi(\nu)$

	$\hat{\beta}_n$ (Without Asymptotic Bias Correction)				$\hat{\hat{\beta}}_n$ (With Asymptotic Bias Correction)			
	0.0	0.05	0.10	0.20	0.01	0.05	0.10	0.20
				Panel A: True γ				
$n = 250$	0.0370	0.0940	0.1610	0.2530	0.0590	0.1200	0.1800	0.2800
$n = 1000$	0.0200	0.0680	0.1240	0.2180	0.0260	0.0820	0.1410	0.2400
$n = 4000$	0.0180	0.0560	0.1120	0.2260	0.0210	0.0660	0.1270	0.2370
				Panel B: $\hat{\gamma}_L$				
$n = 250$	0.0330	0.0930	0.1580	0.2680	0.0450	0.1140	0.1850	0.2940
$n = 1000$	0.0210	0.0660	0.1160	0.2140	0.0230	0.0760	0.1370	0.2210
$n = 4000$	0.0100	0.0630	0.1140	0.2250	0.0180	0.0690	0.1260	0.2380
				Panel C: $\hat{\gamma}_{CMS}$				
$n = 250$	0.0440	0.1050	0.1600	0.2720	0.0610	0.1300	0.1830	0.3070
$n = 1000$	0.0260	0.0760	0.1170	0.2160	0.0350	0.0860	0.1370	0.2410
$n = 4000$	0.0200	0.0610	0.1180	0.2390	0.0240	0.0730	0.1290	0.2590
				Panel D: $\hat{\gamma}_{SCMS,4}$				
$n = 250$	0.0200	0.0850	0.1430	0.2570	0.0280	0.1010	0.1640	0.2860
$n = 1000$	0.0190	0.0630	0.1220	0.2250	0.0190	0.0730	0.1450	0.2480
$n = 4000$	0.0170	0.0590	0.1230	0.2430	0.0250	0.0730	0.1430	0.2630

5. CONCLUSIONS

This paper proposed estimators for a sample selection model from panel data with individual-specific effects. We developed a two-step estimation procedure for the parameters of the regression equation of interest, which exploits a conditional exchangeability assumption on the errors to "difference out" both the unobservable individual effect and the sample selection effect, in a manner similar to the "fixed-effects" approach taken in linear panel data models. The Monte Carlo results indicate that the estimator may work well in practice with sufficiently large data sets. However it is quite sensitive to the choice of the bandwidth parameter, which suggests that further research on this issue may be warranted. Two more issues will be also left for future investigation:

First, notice that the exchangeability assumption (Assumption R1) underlying the proposed estimator implies a conditional symmetry restriction for the first-differenced errors of the main equation, which could be used to develop a Least Absolute Deviations-type estimator. This estimator might then be combined optimally with the Least-Squares-type estimator proposed in this paper for efficiency considerations. Furthermore, LAD estimators might be preferable in the case of heavy-tailed distributions, but they do not have closed-form solutions and their asymptotic properties are more difficult to derive.

Second, although the analysis rested on the strict exogeneity of the explanatory variables in both equations, it is possible to allow for lagged endogenous variables in the set of regressors. Honoré and Kyriazidou (1997) propose estimators for discrete choice panel data models with exogenous regressors, individual effects, and lags of the dependent discrete variable. Kyriazidou (1997) proposes estimators for dynamic sample selection models where the latent equations contain strictly exogenous regressors, individual effects, and lags of the dependent endogenous variables.

Department of Economics, University of Chicago, 1126 E. 59th St., Chicago, Illinois 60637, U.S.A.

Manuscript received May, 1994; final revision received January, 1997.

APPENDIX

The proofs of the results in the main text make use of the following two lemmas, which maintain Assumptions R4 and R8 of Section 3.

LEMMA A1: *Let* $S = (1/n)\sum_{i=1}^{n}(1/h_n)L(W_i/h_n)Z_iW_i^s$, $s \geq 0$, *where* $\{(Z_i, W_i)\}_{i=1}^{n}$ *is a random sample from a distribution that has* $E(|Z|^2|W) < M < \infty$ *for almost all* W, *and the function* L *satisfies:* $\int |\nu^s L(\nu)|^2\, d\nu < \infty$. *Then,* $E(S) = O(h_n^s)$ *and* $\mathrm{var}(S) = O(h_n^{2s}/nh_n)$. *Thus, for* $s \geq 1$, $S \xrightarrow{p} 0$, *while for* $s = 0$, $S \xrightarrow{p} f_W(0)E(Z|W = 0)\int L(\nu)\, d\nu$, *provided that* $E(Z|W)$ *is continuous at* $W = 0$.

PROOF: Random sampling implies that

$$E(S) = \int E(Z|W)\frac{1}{h_n}L\left(\frac{W}{h_n}\right)W^s f_W(W)\,dW$$

$$= h_n^s \int E(Z|W = \nu h_n)L(\nu)\nu^s f_W(\nu h_n)\,d\nu = O(h_n^s),$$

$$\operatorname{var}(S) \leq \frac{1}{nh_n}\int E(Z^2|W)\frac{1}{h_n}L\left(\frac{W}{h_n}\right)^2 W^{2s} f_W(W)\,dW$$

$$= \frac{h_n^{2s}}{nh_n}\int E(Z^2|W = \nu h_n)L(\nu)^2 \nu^{2s} f_W(\nu h_n)\,d\nu = O(h_n^{2s}/nh_n) = o(1).$$

Under our assumptions and by bounded convergence we obtain:

$$E(S) \to \begin{cases} f_W(0)E(Z|W=0)\int L(\nu)\,d\nu & \text{if } s = 0, \\ 0 & \text{if } s \geq 1. \end{cases}$$

The stated probability limits then obtain by Chebyshev's theorem.

LEMMA A2 (Liapounov CLT for double arrays): *Let $\sqrt{nh_n}\,S = (1/\sqrt{n})\Sigma_{i=1}^n \xi_{in}$, where $\{\xi_{in}\}_{i=1}^n$ is an independent sequence of scalar random variables that satisfies: $E(\xi_{in}) = 0$, $\operatorname{var}(\xi_{in}) < \infty$, $\operatorname{var}(\xi_{in}) \to V < \infty$, and $\Sigma_{i=1}^n E|\xi_{in}/\sqrt{n}|^{2+\delta} \to 0$ for some $\delta \in (0,1)$ as $n \to \infty$. Then $\sqrt{nh_n}\,S \xrightarrow{d} N(0, V)$.*

PROOF: See Theorem 7.1.2 and comment on page 209 in Chung (1974).

COROLLARY A1: *Let $\xi_{in} = (1/\sqrt{h_n})L(W_i/h_n)Z_i$ where $\{(Z_i, W_i)\}_{i=1}^n$ is a random sample from a distribution such that $E(Z|W) = 0$ and $E(|Z|^{2+\delta}|W) < M < \infty$ for almost all W, $E(Z^2|W)$ is continuous at $W = 0$, and the function L satisfies: $\int |L(\nu)|^{2+\delta}\,d\nu < \infty$. Then, $\sqrt{nh_n}\,S \equiv (1/\sqrt{n})\Sigma_{i=1}^n \xi_{in} \xrightarrow{d} N(0, f_W(0)E(Z^2|W=0)\int L(\nu)^2\,d\nu)$.*

PROOF OF LEMMA 1: (a) Apply Lemma A1 with $Z_i \equiv \Delta x_i^l\, \Delta x_i^j\, \Phi_i$ $(l, j = 1, \ldots, k)$, $s = 0$, and $L(\nu) \equiv K(\nu)$.

(b-i) Apply Lemma A2 with $\xi_{in} \equiv c'(1/\sqrt{h_n})K(W_i/h_n)\,\Delta x_i\, \Delta v_i\, \Phi_i$, where c is a $k \times 1$ vector of constants such that $c'c = 1$.

(b-ii) Note that, by Assumption R5, $\Delta\lambda_i = \tilde{\lambda}_i \cdot W_i$. Thus, we may write

$$S_{x\lambda} = (1/n)\Sigma_{i=1}^n (1/h_n)K(W_i/h_n)\,\Delta x_i'\, \tilde{\lambda}_i W_i \Phi_i.$$

Therefore, $E(S_{x\lambda}) = \int (1/h_n)K(W/h_n)Wg(W)\,dW$, where $g(W) \equiv E(\Delta x'\, \tilde{\Lambda}\Phi|W)f_W(W)$ is by assumption r times continuously differentiable, with derivatives that are bounded on the support of W, and has $g(0) < \infty$. A Taylor series expansion of $g(\cdot)$ around 0, and a change of variables $W = \nu h_n$ lead to

$$E(S_{x\lambda}) = h_n \int g(\nu h_n)\nu K(\nu)\,d\nu$$

$$= h_n \int g(0)\nu K(\nu)\,d\nu + h_n^2 \int g^{(1)}(0)\nu^2 K(\nu)\,d\nu + \cdots$$

$$+ h_n^{r+1}\frac{1}{r!}\int g^{(r)}(c_n^*)\nu^{r+1}K(\nu)\,d\nu$$

$$= 0 + \cdots + 0 + h_n^{r+1}\frac{1}{r!}\int g^{(r)}(c_n^*)\nu^{r+1}K(\nu)\,d\nu$$

for some c_n^* lying between 0 and W, since $\int \nu^j K(\nu)\,d\nu = 0$ for $j = 1,\ldots,r$. Therefore, by bounded convergence,

$$E\left(\sqrt{nh_n}\, S_{x\lambda}\right) \to \bar{h} \cdot \frac{1}{r!} g^{(r)}(0) \int \nu^{r-1} K(\nu)\, d\nu$$

since under our assumptions $\int |\nu|^{r-1} |K(\nu)|\, d\nu < \infty$, and by assumption, $\sqrt{nh_n}\, h_n^{r+1} \to \bar{h}$. Furthermore, by Lemma A1, $\operatorname{var}(S_{x\lambda}) = O(h_n^2/nh_n)$, which implies that $\operatorname{var}(\sqrt{nh_n}\, S_{x\lambda}) = O(nh_n)O(h_n/n) = O(h_n^2) = o(1)$. Hence, $\sqrt{nh_n}\, S_{x\lambda} \xrightarrow{p} \bar{h}\, \Sigma_{x\lambda}$.

(c-i) Note that,

$$E(S_{xv}) = E\left(\frac{1}{h_n} K\left(\frac{W}{h_n}\right) \Delta x'\, E(\Delta v\, \Phi | d_1 = 1, d_2 = 1, \zeta)\right) = 0,$$

while by Lemma A1, $\operatorname{var}(S_{xv}) = O((nh_n)^{-1})$. Therefore, $E(h_n^{-(r-1)} S_{xv}) = 0$ and $\operatorname{var}(h_n^{-(r-1)} S_{xv}) = O(h_n^{-2(r+1)})$. Since by assumption $\sqrt{nh_n}\, h_n^{r-1} \to \infty$ as $n \to \infty$, $(nh_n)^{-1}) = O((nh_n^{2(r+1)+1})^{-1}) = o(1)$. Thus, $h_n^{-(r+1)} S_{xv} \xrightarrow{p} 0$.

(c-ii) From part (b-ii) above,

$$E(h_n^{-(r+1)} S_{x\lambda}) \to \frac{1}{r!} g^{(r)}(0) \int \nu^{r-1} K(\nu)\, d\nu$$

and

$$\operatorname{var}(h_n^{-(r+1)} S_{x\lambda}) = O(h_n^{-2(r-1)} \cdot h_n n^{-1}) = O\left((nh_n^{2r-1})^{-1}\right) = o(1)$$

since $nh_n^{2(r+1)+1} \to \infty$ implies that $nh_n^{2r+1} \to \infty$. Thus, $h_n^{-(r+1)} S_{x\lambda} \xrightarrow{p} \Sigma_{x\lambda}$.

REMARKS: (i) In what follows, M stands for a generic constant which is the upper bound of certain quantities.

(ii) We define the matrix norm $\|A\| = \sqrt{\operatorname{trace}(A'A)}$.

(iii) In the Taylor series expansions, c_{in}^* stands for a generic value between W_i and $\hat{W}_i$.

PROOF OF LEMMA 2: (a) By a Taylor series expansion, we can write

$$\hat{S}_{xx} - S_{xx} = \frac{1}{n} \sum_{i=1}^{n} \frac{1}{h_n} \left[K\left(\frac{\Delta w_i \hat{\gamma}_n}{h_n}\right) - K\left(\frac{\Delta w_i \gamma}{h_n}\right) \right] \Delta x_i' \Delta x_i \Phi_i$$

$$= \frac{1}{n} \sum_{i=1}^{n} \frac{1}{h_n^2} K'\left(\frac{c_{in}^*}{h_n}\right) \Delta w_i (\hat{\gamma}_n - \gamma)\, \Delta x_i' \Delta x_i \Phi_i.$$

Therefore,

$$\|\hat{S}_{xx} - S_{xx}\| \le \frac{1}{n} \sum_{i=1}^{n} \frac{1}{h_n^2} \left| K'\left(\frac{c_{in}^*}{h_n}\right) \right| \|\Delta w_i\| \|(\hat{\gamma}_n - \gamma)\| \|\Delta x_i\|^2$$

$$\le M \frac{1}{h_n^2} \|(\hat{\gamma}_n - \gamma)\| \cdot \frac{1}{n} \sum_{i=1}^{n} \|\Delta w_i\| \|\Delta x_i\|^2$$

$$= O(n^{2\mu}) O_p(n^{-p}) \cdot O_p(1) = o_p(1)$$

since by assumption $\mu < p/2$, $|K'(\nu)| < \infty$, and $E(\|\Delta w\| \|\Delta x\|^2) < \infty$.

(b-i) Let $\hat{S}^l_{xv}$ and S^l_{xv} denote the lth ($l = 1, \ldots, k$) elements of $\hat{S}_{xv}$ and S_{xv} respectively. A third order Taylor series expansion yields:

$$\sqrt{nh_n}\,(\hat{S}^l_{xv} - S^l_{xv})$$

$$= \sqrt{nh_n}\frac{1}{n}\sum_{i=1}^{n}\frac{1}{h_n}\left[K\left(\frac{\Delta w_i \hat{\gamma}_n}{h_n}\right) - K\left(\frac{\Delta w_i \gamma}{h_n}\right)\right]\Delta x^l_i\, \Delta v_i\, \Phi_i$$

$$= \left(\frac{1}{\sqrt{nh_n}}\sum_{i=1}^{n}K'\left(\frac{W_i}{h_n}\right)\Delta x^l_i\, \Delta v_i\, \Phi_i\, \Delta w_i\right)\cdot\frac{1}{h_n}(\hat{\gamma}_n - \gamma)$$

$$+ \frac{1}{2h_n}(\hat{\gamma}_n - \gamma)'\cdot\left(\frac{1}{\sqrt{nh_n}}\sum_{i=1}^{n}K''\left(\frac{W_i}{h_n}\right)\Delta x^l_i\, \Delta v_i\, \Phi_i\, \Delta w'_i\, \Delta w_i\right)\cdot\frac{1}{h_n}(\hat{\gamma}_n - \gamma)$$

$$+ \sqrt{n}\frac{1}{h_n^{7/2}}\frac{1}{6n}\sum_{i=1}^{n}K'''\left(\frac{c^*_{in}}{h_n}\right)\Delta x^l_i\, \Delta v_i\, \Phi_i(\Delta w_i(\hat{\gamma}_n - \gamma))^3$$

$$= A_1\cdot\frac{1}{h_n}(\hat{\gamma}_n - \gamma) + \frac{1}{2h_n}(\hat{\gamma}_n - \gamma)'\cdot A_2\cdot\frac{1}{h_n}(\hat{\gamma}_n - \gamma) + A_3.$$

We will show that A_1 and A_2 are $O_p(1)$, while $A_3 = o_p(1)$. The desired result will then follow from the fact that $\mu < p/2$ implies that $h_n^{-1}(\hat{\gamma}_n - \gamma) = O_p(n^{\mu - p}) = o_p(1)$.

Let A^j_1 be the jth element ($j = 1, \ldots, q$) of the $(1 \times q)$ vector A_1. Write $A^j_1 = 1/\sqrt{n}\sum^n_{i=1}\xi_{in}$, where $\xi_{in} \equiv (1/\sqrt{h_n})K'(W_i/h_n)\,\Delta x^l_i\, \Delta v_i\, \Phi_i\, \Delta w^j_i$. Note that $\{\xi_{in}\}^n_{i=1}$ is a sequence of scalar random variables that satisfies the requirements of Lemma A2, since under our assumptions, $E(|\Delta x^l\, \Delta w^j\, \Delta v|^{2+\delta}|W) < \infty$ for almost all W, while $|K'(\nu)| < \infty$ and $\int|K'(\nu)|\,d\nu < \infty$ imply that $\int|K'(\nu)|^{2+\delta}\,d\nu < \infty$. Therefore, A_1 is bounded in probability.

Similarly, we can show that the jmth element ($j, m = 1, \ldots, q$) of the $(q \times q)$ matrix A_2 is also bounded in probability, by defining $\xi_{in} \equiv (1/\sqrt{h_n})K''(W_i/h_n)\,\Delta x^l_i\, \Delta v_i\, \Phi_i\, \Delta w^j_i\, \Delta w^m_i$, since $E(|\Delta x^l\, \Delta w^j\, \Delta w^m\, \Delta v|^{2+\delta}|W) < \infty$ for almost all W, and the boundedness and absolute integrability of $K''(\nu)$ implies that $\int|K''(\nu)|^{2+\delta}\,d\nu < \infty$.

Next, observe that, since $p > 2/5$ and $\mu < p/2$ imply that $(1/2) + (7\mu/2) - 3p < 0$,

$$\|A_3\| \le M\sqrt{n}\frac{1}{h_n^{7/2}}\|\hat{\gamma}_n - \gamma\|^3\cdot\frac{1}{n}\sum_{i=1}^{n}\|\Delta x^l_i\|\,\|\Delta w_i\|^3|\Delta v_i|$$

$$= O_p(n^{1/2 + (7\mu/2) - 3p}) = o_p(1).$$

(b-ii) Let $\hat{S}^l_{x\lambda}$ and $S^l_{x\lambda}$ denote the lth ($l = 1, \ldots, k$) elements of $\hat{S}_{x\lambda}$ and $S_{x\lambda}$ respectively. A third order Taylor series expansion yields:

$$\sqrt{nh_n}\,(\hat{S}^l_{x\lambda} - S^l_{x\lambda})$$

$$= \left(\frac{1}{n}\sum_{i=1}^{n}\frac{1}{h_n^2}K'\left(\frac{W_i}{h_n}\right)\Delta x^l_i\, \Delta\lambda_i\, \Phi_i\, \Delta w_i\right)\cdot\sqrt{nh_n}\,(\hat{\gamma}_n - \gamma)$$

$$+ \frac{1}{2h_n}(\hat{\gamma}_n - \gamma)'\cdot\left(\frac{1}{n}\sum_{i=1}^{n}\frac{1}{h_n^2}K''\left(\frac{W_i}{h_n}\right)\Delta x^l_i\, \Delta\lambda_i\, \Phi_i\, \Delta w'_i\, \Delta w_i\right)\cdot\sqrt{nh_n}\,(\hat{\gamma}_n - \gamma)$$

$$+ \sqrt{n}\frac{1}{h_n^{7/2}}\frac{1}{6n}\sum_{i=1}^{n}K'''\left(\frac{c^*_{in}}{h_n}\right)\Delta x^l_i\, \Delta\lambda_i\, \Phi_i(\Delta w_i(\hat{\gamma}_n - \gamma))^3$$

$$= B_1\cdot\sqrt{nh_n}\,(\hat{\gamma}_n - \gamma) + \frac{1}{2h_n}(\hat{\gamma}_n - \gamma)'\cdot B_2\cdot\sqrt{nh_n}\,(\hat{\gamma}_n - \gamma) + B_3.$$

We will show that B_1 and B_2 are $O_p(1)$, while $B_3 = o_p(1)$. The desired result will then follow from the fact that $1 - 2p < \mu < p/2$ implies that $h_n^{-1}(\hat{\gamma}_n - \gamma) = O_p(n^{\mu - p}) = o_p(1)$, and $\sqrt{nh_n}\,(\hat{\gamma}_n - \gamma) = O_p(n^{1/2 - (\mu/2) - p}) = o_p(1)$.

Note that B_1 is a $(1 \times q)$ row-vector. For its jth element,

$$B_1^j = \frac{1}{n}\sum_{i=1}^{n}\frac{1}{h_n^2}K'\left(\frac{W_i}{h_n}\right)\Delta x_i^l\,\Delta\lambda_i\,\Phi_i\,\Delta w_i^j = \frac{1}{h_n}\cdot\frac{1}{n}\sum_{i=1}^{n}\frac{1}{h_n}K'\left(\frac{W_i}{h_n}\right)\Delta x_i^l\,\tilde{\Lambda}_i W_i \Phi_i\,\Delta w_i^j,$$

application of Lemma A1 with $s = 1$, $Z_i \equiv \Delta x_i^l\,\tilde{\Lambda}_i\Phi_i\,\Delta w_i^j$, and $L(\nu) \equiv K'(\nu)$, yields

$$E(B_1^j) = \frac{1}{h_n}\cdot O(h_n) = O(1) \quad \text{and}$$

$$\operatorname{var}(B_1^j) = \frac{1}{h_n^2}\cdot O(h_n^2/nh_n) = O(1/nh_n) = o(1)$$

since $E(\Delta x^{l^2}\,\tilde{\Lambda}^2\Phi\,\Delta w^{j^2}\,|\,W) < \infty$ for almost all W, and $\int|\nu K'(\nu)|^2\,d\nu < \infty$.

Similarly, we can show that the jmth element $(j, m = 1,\ldots,q)$ of the $(q \times q)$ matrix B_2,

$$B_2^{jm} = \frac{1}{n}\sum_{i=1}^{n}\frac{1}{h_n^2}K''\left(\frac{W_i}{h_n}\right)\Delta x_i^l\,\Delta\lambda_i\,\Phi_i\,\Delta w_i^j\,\Delta w_i^m$$

is also bounded in probability, since $E(\Delta x^{l^2}\,\tilde{\Lambda}^2\Phi\,\Delta w^{j^2}\,\Delta w^{m^2}\,|\,W) < \infty$ for almost all W, and $\int|\nu K''(\nu)|\,d\nu < \infty$.

Next, observe that

$$\|B_3\| \le \sqrt{n}\,\frac{1}{h_n^{7/2}}\|\hat{\gamma}_n - \gamma\|^3\cdot\frac{1}{n}\sum_{i=1}^{n}\left|K'''\left(\frac{c_{in}^*}{h_n}\right)\right|\|\Delta x_i^l\|\,|\tilde{\Lambda}_i|\,\|\Delta w_i\|\,\|\gamma\|\,\|\Delta w_i\|^3$$

$$\le M\sqrt{n}\,\frac{1}{h_n^{7/2}}\|\hat{\gamma}_n - \gamma\|^3\cdot\frac{1}{n}\sum_{i=1}^{n}\|\Delta x_i^l\|\,\|\Delta w_i\|^4 = O_p(n^{(1/2)+(7\mu/2)-3p}) = o_p(1)$$

since under assumptions, $(1/2) + (7\mu/2) - 3p < 0$, γ lies in a compact set, and $E(\|\Delta x\|\,\|\Delta w\|^4) < \infty$.

(c-i) Note that, with $h_n = h\cdot n^{-\mu}$, the condition $nh_n^{2(r+1)+1} \to \infty$ implies that $\mu < 1/(2(r+1)+1)$. In what follows, we will use the fact that, for $r \ge 1$,

(1) $$\mu < \frac{1}{2(r+1)+1} \Rightarrow \mu < \frac{p}{r+1}.$$

(2) $$\mu < \frac{p}{r+1} \Rightarrow \mu < \frac{3p}{r+5}.$$

Define $\hat{S}_{xt}^l$ and S_{xt}^l as before. A third order Taylor series expansion yields:

$$\frac{1}{h_n^{r+1}}(\hat{S}_{xt}^l - S_{xt}^l)$$

$$= \left(\frac{1}{\sqrt{nh_n}}\sum_{i=1}^{n}K'\left(\frac{W_i}{h_n}\right)\Delta x_i^l\,\Delta v_i\,\Phi_i\,\Delta w_i\right)\cdot\frac{1}{\sqrt{nh_n}\,h_n^{r+1}}\cdot\frac{1}{h_n}(\hat{\gamma}_n - \gamma)$$

$$+\frac{1}{2h_n}(\hat{\gamma}_n-\gamma)'\left(\frac{1}{\sqrt{nh_n}}\sum_{i=1}^{n}K''\left(\frac{W_i}{h_n}\right)\Delta x_i^l\,\Delta v_i\,\Phi_i\,\Delta w_i'\,\Delta w_i\right)\frac{1}{\sqrt{nh_n}\,h_n^{r+1}}\,\frac{1}{h_n}(\hat{\gamma}_n-\gamma)$$

$$+\frac{1}{h_n^{r-1}}\,\frac{1}{h_n^4}\,\frac{1}{3n}\sum_{i=1}^{n}K'''\left(\frac{c_{in}^*}{h_n}\right)\Delta x_i^l\,\Delta v_i\,\Phi_i(\Delta w_i(\hat{\gamma}_n - \gamma))^3$$

$$= A_1\cdot\frac{1}{\sqrt{nh_n}\,h_n^{r+1}}\cdot\frac{1}{h_n}(\hat{\gamma}_n-\gamma) + \frac{1}{2h_n}(\hat{\gamma}_n-\gamma)'\cdot A_2\cdot\frac{1}{\sqrt{nh_n}\,h_n^{r+1}}\cdot\frac{1}{h_n}(\hat{\gamma}_n - \gamma) + A_4$$

where A_1 and A_2 are defined as in the proof of part (b-1). As we showed there, both these quantities are bounded in probability for any h_n that satisfies $h_n \to 0$ and $nh_n \to \infty$ as n increases. Furthermore, from (1) above, $h_n^{-1}(\hat{\gamma}_n - \gamma) = O_p(n^{\mu - p}) = o_p(1)$. Thus, the first two terms of the sum above are $o_p(1)$. Now, by (2),

$$\|A_4\| \leq M \frac{1}{h_n^{r+1}} \frac{1}{h_n^4} \|\hat{\gamma}_n - \gamma\|^3 \frac{1}{n} \sum_{i=1}^{n} \|\Delta x_i'\| \, |\Delta v_i| \, \|\Delta w_i\|^3 = O_p(n^{\mu(r+5)-3p}) = o_p(1).$$

(c-ii) Let $\hat{S}^l_{x\lambda}$ and $S^l_{x\lambda}$ be defined as before. A third order Taylor series expansion yields:

$$\frac{1}{h_n^{r+1}}(\hat{S}^l_{x\lambda} - S^l_{x\lambda})$$

$$= \left(\frac{1}{n} \sum_{i=1}^{n} \frac{1}{h_n^2} K'\left(\frac{W_i}{h_n}\right) \Delta x_i' \, \Delta\lambda_i \Phi_i \, \Delta w_i \right) \cdot \frac{1}{h_n^{r+1}} (\hat{\gamma}_n - \gamma)$$

$$+ \frac{1}{2h_n} (\hat{\gamma}_n - \gamma)' \cdot \left(\frac{1}{n} \sum_{i=1}^{n} \frac{1}{h_n^2} K''\left(\frac{W_i}{h_n}\right) \Delta x_i' \, \Delta\lambda_i \, \Phi_i \, \Delta w_i' \, \Delta w_i \right) \cdot \frac{1}{h_n^{r+1}} (\hat{\gamma}_n - \gamma)$$

$$+ \frac{1}{h_n^{r+1}} \frac{1}{h_n^4} \frac{1}{6n} \sum_{i=1}^{n} K'''\left(\frac{c^*_{in}}{h_n}\right) \Delta x_i' \, \Delta\lambda_i \, \Phi_i (\Delta w_i (\hat{\gamma}_n - \gamma))^3$$

$$= B_1 \cdot \frac{1}{h_n^{r+1}} (\hat{\gamma}_n - \gamma) + \frac{1}{2h_n} (\hat{\gamma}_n - \gamma)' \cdot B_2 \cdot \frac{1}{h_n} (\hat{\gamma}_n - \gamma) + B_4$$

where B_1 and B_2 are defined as in the proof of part (b-ii), and as we showed there, they are bounded in probability for any h_n that satisfies $nh_n \to \infty$ as n increases. Thus, the first two terms of the sum above are $o_p(1)$. Furthermore,

$$\|B_4\| \leq M \frac{1}{h_n^{r+1}} \frac{1}{h_n^4} \|\hat{\gamma}_n - \gamma\|^3 \frac{1}{n} \sum_{i=1}^{n} \|\Delta x_i'\| \, \|\Delta w_i\|^4 = O_p(n^{\mu(r+5)-3p}) = o_p(1).$$

REFERENCES

AHN, H., AND J. L. POWELL (1993): "Semiparametric Estimation of Censored Selection Models with a Nonparametric Selection Mechanism," *Journal of Econometrics*, 58, 3–29.

AMEMIYA, T. (1985): *Advanced Econometrics*. Cambridge: Harvard University Press.

ANDERSEN, E. (1970): "Asymptotic Properties of Conditional Maximum Likelihood Estimators," *Journal of the Royal Statistical Society*, Series B, 32, 283–301.

BIERENS, H. J. (1987): "Kernel Estimators of Regression Functions," in *Advances in Econometrics: Fifth World Congress*, Vol. 1, ed. by T. F. Bewley. Cambridge: Cambridge University Press.

CAVANAGH, C. L. (1987): "Limiting Behavior of Estimators Defined by Optimization," unpublished manuscript.

CHAMBERLAIN, G. (1984): "Panel Data," *Handbook of Econometrics*, Volume II, edited by Z. Griliches and M. Intriligator. Amsterdam: North-Holland, Ch. 22.

——— (1992): "Binary Response Models for Panel Data: Identification and Information," unpublished manuscript. Department of Economics, Harvard University.

CHARLIER, E., B. MELENBERG, AND A. H. O. VAN SOEST (1995): "A Smoothed Maximum Score Estimator for the Binary Choice Panel Data Model with an Application to Labour Force Participation," *Statistica Nederlandica*, 49, 324–342.

CHUNG, K. L. (1974): *A Course in Probability Theory*. New York: Academic Press.

GRONAU, R. (1974): "Wage Comparisons—A Selectivity Bias," *Journal of Political Economy*, 82, 1119–1144.

HÄRDLE, W. (1990): *Applied Nonparametric Regression*. Cambridge: Cambridge University Press.

HAUSMAN, J. A., AND D. WISE (1979): "Attrition Bias in Experimental and Panel Data: The Gary Income Maintenance Experiment," *Econometrica*, 47, 455–473.

HECKMAN, J. J. (1974): "Shadow Prices, Market Wages, and Labor Supply," *Econometrica*, 42, 679–694.

——— (1976): "The Common Structure of Statistical Models of Truncation, Sample Selection and Limited Dependent Variables, and a Simple Estimator for Such Models," *Annals of Economic and Social Measurement*, 15, 475–492.

——— (1979): "Sample Selection Bias as a Specification Error," *Econometrica*, 47, 153–161.

HONORÉ, B. E. (1992): "Trimmed LAD and Least Squares Estimation of Truncated and Censored Regression Models with Fixed Effects," *Econometrica*, 60, 533–565.

——— (1993): "Orthogonality Conditions for Tobit Models with Fixed Effects and Lagged Dependent Variables," *Journal of Econometrics*, 59, 35–61.

HONORÉ, B. E., AND E. KYRIAZIDOU (1997): "Panel Data Discrete Choice Models with Lagged Dependent Variables," unpublished manuscript.

HOROWITZ, J. (1992): "A Smoothed Maximum Score Estimator for the Binary Response Model," *Econometrica*, 60, 505–531.

HSIAO, C. (1986): *Analysis of Panel Data*. Cambridge: Cambridge University Press.

KIM, J., AND D. POLLARD (1990): "Cube Root Asymptotics," *Annals of Statistics*, 18, 191–219.

KYRIAZIDOU, E. (1994): "Estimation of A Panel Data Sample Selection Model," unpublished manuscript, Northwestern University.

——— (1997): "Estimation of Dynamics Panel Data Sample Selection Models," unpublished manuscript, University of Chicago.

MANSKI, C. (1975): "Maximum Score Estimation of the Stochastic Utility Model of Choice," *Journal of Econometrics*, 3, 205–228.

——— (1985): "Semiparametric Analysis of Discrete Response: Asymptotic Properties of Maximum Score Estimation," *Journal of Econometrics*, 27, 313–334.

——— (1987): "Semiparametric Analysis of Random Effects Linear Models from Binary Panel Data," *Econometrica*, 55, 357–362.

NIJMAN, T., AND M. VERBEEK (1992): "Nonresponse in Panel Data: The Impact on Estimates of a Life Cycle Consumption Function," *Journal of Applied Econometrics*, 7, 243–257.

POWELL, J. L. (1987): "Semiparametric Estimation of Bivariate Latent Variable Models," Working Paper No. 8704, Social Systems Research Institute, University of Wisconsin-Madison.

——— (1994): "Estimation of Semiparametric Models," *Handbook of Econometrics*, Vol. 4, 2444–2521.

RASCH, G. (1960): *Probabilistic Models for Some Intelligence and Attainment Tests*. Copenhagen: Denmarks Paedagogiske Institut.

——— (1961): "On General Laws and the Meaning of Measurement in Psychology," *Proceedings of the Fourth Berkeley Symposium on Mathematical Statistics and Probability*, Vol. 4. Berkeley and Los Angeles: University of California Press.

ROSHOLM, M., AND N. SMITH (1994): "The Danish Gender Wage Gap in the 1980s: A Panel Data Study," Working Paper 94-2, Center for Labour Market and Social Research, University of Aarhus and Aarhus School of Business.

SILVERMAN, B. W. (1986): *Density Estimation for Statistics and Data Analysis*. New York: Chapman and Hall.

VERBEEK, M., AND T. NIJMAN (1992): "Testing for Selectivity Bias in Panel Data Models," *International Economic Review*, 33, 681–703.

WOOLDRIDGE, J. M. (1995): "Selection Corrections for Panel Data Models under Conditional Mean Independence Assumptions," *Journal of Econometrics*, 68, 115–132.

[5]

Journal of Business & Economic Statistics, October 1995, Vol. 13, No. 4

Some Specification Tests for Probit Models Estimated on Panel Data

Michael LECHNER
Institut für Volkswirtschaftslehre und Statistik, Universität Mannheim, D-68131 Mannheim, Germany

Generalized score and Wald tests are proposed to examine certain aspects of the specification of panel probit models. The procedures used to detect misspecifications, such as omitted and superfluous variables, heteroscedasticity, nonnormality, and random-coefficient variations, are designed specifically for the case in which the model is estimated by sequential methods. The finite-sample distributions of the test statistics in correctly and incorrectly specified models are investigated by a Monte Carlo study. Applying the proposed procedures to the analysis of the determinants of self-employment in Germany shows that the suggested specification checks are useful instruments in applied work.

KEY WORDS: Binary choice models; Limited dependent variable models; Longitudinal data; Nonlinear models; Random-effects models; Testing.

In the last few years, the use of panel data has become increasingly popular among microeconometricians. Panel-data sets allow the estimation of more realistic behavioral models, which might not be identified using a single cross-section or time series data set alone. Furthermore, the efficiency gains from using the restrictions implied by the panel structure of the data can be substantial. This article focuses on probit models estimated on samples with a large number (N) of independent units, such as firms or individuals, which are observed over a certain period of time (T).

In this framework, fixed effects (in dimension N) estimators, which allow for an arbitrary correlation of the regressors with the time constant part of the error term, are generally—with some exceptions, which have other drawbacks—inconsistent, as a result of the incidental parameter problem (see the survey by Maddala 1987). On the other hand, random-effects models require additional distributional assumptions that may not be satisfied by the data. Thus, specification testing is particularly important.

In cross-sections with independent observations, probit and related models are typically estimated by maximum likelihood (ML) (see the survey by Maddala 1983). Given the known sensitivity of the results to the correct specification of the model, a battery of specification tests exists. Because, however, observations for a single unit in different points of time are generally not independent in panel-data sets, ML estimation is less attractive. It requires either the computation of multivariate cumulative distribution functions, which can consume a large amount of computer time, or the imposition of restrictions on the intertemporal covariances of the error terms.

Chamberlain (1980, 1984) proposed a sequential estimator that incorporates many of the desirable features for panel estimators. It is easy to compute because it avoids the evaluation or approximation of high-dimensional integrals. It allows for a potential correlation of time-constant error components (individual effects) and regressors, and it does not require specific assumptions about the intertemporal correlation structure of the error terms, which is left unspecified. The drawbacks of this approach are that, first, it is not efficient when the error terms are correlated over time and, second, that the complete error distribution cannot be identified. For the validity of this simple and convenient approach it is nevertheless essential that certain rather stringent statistical assumptions are appropriate. Testing these assumptions for the panel probit model is the topic of this article. Although the focus is on the probit model, the estimation and test methods could be adjusted to accommodate other limited dependent variable models as well.

The article is organized as follows: Sections 1 and 2 introduce the model and discuss a sequential procedure to estimate its coefficients. Section 3 contains a brief review of some existing general test procedures and then formulates some hypotheses that are important and testable in this particular framework. Section 4 investigates the small-sample behavior of the proposed tests by a Monte Carlo study. Section 5 discusses an application of the tests to an empirical study—namely, the analysis of "Income, Uncertainty and the Probability of Self-Employment" (Pfeiffer and Pohlmeier 1992). The sample used in this study contains almost 2,000 individuals, who are observed for six years. Section 6 draws conclusions. Appendix A gives additional formulas for the computation of the test statistics and Appendix B contains descriptions of the variables used in the application.

1. PANEL PROBIT MODEL

The panel probit model is an important model in applied microeconometrics. For example, it is the base of the econometric analysis in the already-mentioned article by Pfeiffer and Pohlmeier (1992), which serves as an empirical example to illustrate the econometric discussions in this article. The authors investigate the individual determinants of self-employment within a structural model of discrete choice under uncertainty. The choice equations are derived from the assumption that agents maximize a Von Neuman–Morgenstern utility function. The empirical part is based on an (approximately) random sample of 1,926 (N) working men selected from the German Socio-Economic Panel (GSOEP). All individuals are observed yearly from 1984 to 1989 ($T = 6$). For each individual the observed information (the data) is captured by the vector (y_n, X_n, Z_n). The equation of major interest is a binary panel probit of the following form:

$$y_{tn}^* = X_{tn}\beta + Z_n\delta + \epsilon_{tn}$$
$$y_{tn} = 1(y_{tn}^* > 0), \qquad t = 1, \ldots, T; \quad n = 1, \ldots, N. \quad (1)$$

In the example the vector of unobserved variables $y_n^* = (y_{1n}^*, \ldots, y_{Tn}^*)$ is related to the utility differences of the two possible employment choices. The observed dependent variables $y_n = (y_{1n}, \ldots, y_{Tn})$ indicate whether individual n is self-employed in period $t(y_{tn} = 1)$ or not $(y_{tn} = 0)$. This is explained by economic variables measuring expected relative risks (unemployment and bankruptcy) and expected relative incomes in self-employment versus dependent work. Additionally, individual heterogeneity may influence this choice. The observed components of the heterogeneity include human-capital-type variables, social and family-background variables, and variables taking account of regional and institutional aspects. Those of the explanatory variables that vary over time are denoted by $X_n = (X_{1n}, \ldots, X_{Tn})$, those that are constant over time are denoted by Z_n. β and δ are coefficient vectors to be estimated.

The authors of that study argued that it is important to allow for time-specific constant terms (for notational convenience, they are contained in X_n) and an unrestricted intertemporal covariance matrix of the error terms $\epsilon_n = (\epsilon_{1n}, \ldots, \epsilon_{Tn})$, which capture the unobserved part of the heterogeneity. Each component ϵ_{tn} is assumed to be independently distributed of all elements of (X_{tn}, Z_n). Its marginal distribution is assumed to be normal with mean 0 and variance σ_t^2. To identify the model, one of the T variances is set to unity. The other components of the joint distribution of ϵ_n remain unspecified. In the following, this model is called the uncorrelated random-effects (URE) model.

The assumption of independence of regressors and error terms may not be tenable, however; an example in the analysis of self-employment is the potential correlation of (individually predicted) income in the specific employment states with unobserved managerial skills. The latter, which can be reasonably assumed to be approximately time constant at least over short periods, is captured by the error term, whereas the former is part of the observed explanatory variables. Before discussing a way to tackle such a problem the error term is decomposed in a time-constant part denoted by c_n and a remaining part denoted by $u_n = (u_{1n}, \ldots, u_{Tn})$. Let the time-varying regressors be partitioned such that $X_n = (X_n^i, X_n^c)$, and denote the dimension of X_{tn}^i and X_{tn}^c by K^i and K^c. To relax the independence assumption without estimating a fixed-effects model, Chamberlain (1984) proposed to parameterize a possible dependence between the time-constant part of the error term and time-varying explanatory variables $X_n^c = (X_{1n}^c, \ldots, X_{Tn}^c)$ as

$$\epsilon_{tn} = (c_n + u_{tn})$$
$$c_n = \sum_{t=1}^{T} (X_{tn}^c \lambda_t) + v_n, \quad (2)$$

where $\lambda = (\lambda_1', \ldots \lambda_T')'$ denotes a coefficient vector and v_n an unobserved error term. In this model, called a correlated random-effects (CRE) model in the following, it is assumed that the error term $\tilde{\epsilon}_{tn} = v_n + u_{tn}$ is distributed independently of all elements of (X_{tn}^i, X_n^c, Z_n). This assumption requires X_n^c to be strictly exogenous. The marginal distribution of $\tilde{\epsilon}_{tn}$ is assumed to be normal with mean 0 and variance σ_t^2. As in the URE model, one of the T variances is set to unity and the remaining components of the joint distribution of the elements of $\tilde{\epsilon}_n = (\tilde{\epsilon}_{1n}, \ldots, \tilde{\epsilon}_{Tn})$ remain unspecified. Note that the error components specification is not used to impose equicorrelated errors but only to model the potential correlation of time-constant error components with regressors.

2. SEQUENTIAL ESTIMATION

For the discussion of sequential estimation and testing procedures, it is useful to obtain similar reduced forms for both models by combining the preceding equations (for the CRE model only) and allow for period-specific coefficients. The reduced form of the URE model is given by

$$y_{tn}^* = X_{tn}\gamma_t^X + Z_n\gamma_t^Z + \omega_{tn}. \quad (3)$$

With $\omega_{tn} = \epsilon_{tn}$ and $\gamma = (\gamma_1', \ldots, \gamma_T')', \gamma_t = (\gamma_t^{X'}, \gamma_t^{Z'})'$ are vectors of parameters to be estimated. The dimension of γ is $K = T(K^X + K^Z)$. K^X and K^Z denote the dimension of X_{tn} and Z_n, respectively. The CRE model defined by Equations (1) and (2) leads to a similar reduced form:

$$y_{tn}^* = \sum_{\tau=1}^{T} (X_{\tau n}^c \gamma_{\tau t}^{xc}) + X_{tn}^i \gamma_t^{x^i} + Z_n \gamma_t^z + \omega_{tn}, \quad (4)$$

where $\gamma_t = (\gamma_{1t}^{X^{c\prime}}, \ldots, \gamma_{Tt}^{X^{c\prime}}, \gamma_t^{X^{i\prime}}, \gamma_t^{Z'})'$ is a $K[= T(TK^c + K^i + K^z)]$-dimensional vector of coefficients to be estimated and $\omega_{tn} = v_n + u_{tn}$ denotes the reduced-form error term.

Relative variances of the reduced-form error term $\omega_n = (\omega_{1n}, \ldots, \omega_{Tn})$ cannot be identified, because all coefficients vary over time. The reduced-form coefficients of Equations (3) and (4) are related to the structural coefficients of Equations (1) and (2), denoted by θ, such that the true coefficients γ^0 and θ^0 fulfill the identity $\gamma^0 = g(\theta^0)$ for an appropriately defined function $g(\cdot)$.

A sequential estimation strategy (Chamberlain 1984), which is also used in the empirical example, is as follows: In a first step, the coefficients of (3) or (4) are estimated by the maximum likelihood estimator (MLE) of the marginal distribution of $(y_{tn} \mid X_{tn}, Z_n; \gamma_t)$ or $(y_{tn} \mid X_n^c, X_{tn}^i, Z_n; \gamma_t)$. This is identical to cross-section probit analysis but with additional regressors for the CRE model. In the following, the estimator is abbreviated as *marginal MLE*. In the second step a minimum distance estimator [MDE, asymptotic least squares (Kodde, Palm, and Pfann 1990)] is used to estimate the structural coefficients θ—for example, β, δ, λ (for the CRE model only) and some elements of the covariance matrix of the error terms. The asymptotically best MDE estimator, which depends on a consistent estimate of the joint covariance matrix of the first-step coefficient estimates (see Chamberlain 1984), denoted by $\text{var}(\widehat{\gamma})$ is given by

$$\widehat{\theta} = \arg\min_{\theta\in\Theta} D(\widehat{\gamma}, \theta),$$

$$D(\widehat{\gamma}, \theta) = [\widehat{\gamma} - g(\theta)]'\text{var}(\widehat{\gamma})^{-1}[\widehat{\gamma} - g(\theta)], \quad (5)$$

where Θ denotes the parametric space of θ. When the model is correctly specified, the distance $D(\widehat{\theta}, \widehat{\gamma})$ is distributed as a central χ^2 distribution with degrees of freedom equal to the number of overidentifying restrictions.

Generally, this approach is not efficient. It is computationally less burdensome, however, than full information ML estimation, which may require the evaluation of a T-dimensional integral of the multivariate normal probability distribution function either by numerical approximation methods for small T or by simulation method (see the surveys by Hajivassiliou 1993; Keane 1993). Both methods are expensive in terms of computer time necessary to obtain good approximations. The alternative to restrict the covariance matrix of the error terms to an equicorrelation structure to simplify the computation of the MLE (Butler and Moffitt 1982) is not attractive because to the best of my knowledge there are no consistency results available for the case in which this assumption is incorrect. Furthermore, there is no need to parameterize and estimate the off-diagonal elements of the covariance matrix of the error terms. Finally, the sequential estimator is very convenient for specification testing. Note that the first-step estimates are obtained without imposing typical panel restrictions, such as constant coefficients over time. Therefore, tests of assumptions used to obtain consistent first-step estimates are not influenced by the validity of these restrictions. When the specification tests of the first step reveal no problems, in the second step different specifications of the structural coefficients, which can be obtained from the same reduced-form estimates, can be compared. In this respect the sequential approach is more flexible than related generalized method of moments procedures suggested by Avery, Hansen, and Hotz (1983). Applications of the sequential estimation method can be found, for example, in works by Chamberlain (1984), Jakubson (1988), Laisney, Lechner, van Soest, and Wagenhals (1993), or Hujer and Schnabel (in press).

Because most of the specification tests are concerned with the reduced-form estimation, it is useful to formalize the first-step estimator in a general way. Suppose that the consistent estimate $\widehat{\gamma}$ of γ^0 is obtained by

$$\widehat{\gamma} = \arg\max_{\gamma\in\Gamma} L_N(\gamma), \qquad L_N(\gamma) = \sum_{n=1}^{N}\sum_{t=1}^{T} l_{tn}(\gamma_t),$$

where Γ denotes the parametric space of γ and $l_{tn}(\gamma_t)$ is the contribution of individual n in period t to the quasi log-likelihood function. As noted previously, $l_{tn}(\gamma_t)$ is the same as the likelihood contribution in a cross-section analysis.

It is assumed that a sequence of $N^{-1/2}$ times the scores of $L_N(\gamma^0)$ converges for $N \to \infty$ in distribution to a normal distribution with mean 0 and covariance matrix $I(\gamma^0)$. Under mild regularity conditions this assumption is satisfied when the individual cross-sectional units are independent. Furthermore, it is assumed that a sequence of $1/N$ times the matrix of second derivatives and outer products of $L_N(\gamma^0)$ converges almost surely to deterministic, symmetric, and positive-definite matrix $-J(\gamma^0)$ and $I(\gamma^0)$. The estimated coefficients obey

$$N^{1/2}(\widehat{\gamma} - \gamma^0) \underset{N\to\infty}{\overset{d}{\to}} N[0, J(\gamma^0)^{-1}I(\gamma^0)J(\gamma^0)^{-1}].$$

$J(\gamma^0)$ and $I(\gamma^0)$ can be consistently estimated by the average (N) of their respective sample analogs, evaluated at $\widehat{\gamma}$ and denoted by $\widehat{J}$ and $\widehat{I}$ (for details, see Gouriéroux and Monfort 1989).

The first-step estimator need not be the marginal MLE, but it can be another of the existing parametric (see Maddala 1983) or semiparametric estimators (see Horowitz 1993) for binary-choice models on cross-sections. The prerequisite to obtain consistent and asymptotic normal estimates in the second step is that the estimates are $\sqrt{N}$-consistent and converge to a normal distribution. Performing the estimations with more robust semiparametric methods, however, might be computationally cumbersome and involve possibly a further loss of efficiency. The typical parametric methods—like probit—that are generally much easier to use have the drawback that they involve stringent statistical assumptions, such as homoscedasticity and normality of the reduced-form error terms. A violation of these assumptions generally leads to inconsistent estimates of the parameters of interest (see Horowitz 1993). Therefore, performing specification tests becomes a necessity, especially when the convenient methods are used.

3. SPECIFICATION TESTS

3.1 Generalized Score and Wald Tests

This section gives the formulas of the generalized score and Wald tests for nested models. These tests are generalizations of the classical score, Lagrange multiplier, and Wald tests to the case in which the objective function of the estimation problem is not a correctly specified likelihood function. The reader is referred, for example, to White (1982) or Gouriéroux and Monfort (1989) for any details.

The restrictions to be tested are given in the implicit form by a multidimensional function $h(\gamma^0) = 0$. Let the rank of $\partial h(\gamma)/\partial\gamma'$ be r, and let $\widetilde{\gamma}$ denote the constraint and $\widehat{\gamma}$ the unconstrained estimate of γ^0. The expressions for the generalized Wald and score statistics are

$$W = Nh(\widehat{\gamma})'\left[\frac{\partial h}{\partial\gamma'}(\widehat{\gamma})\widehat{J}^{-1}\widehat{I}\widehat{J}^{-1}\frac{\partial h'}{\partial\gamma}(\widehat{\gamma})\right]^{-1}h(\widehat{\gamma}),$$

$$S = \frac{1}{N}\frac{\partial L_N}{\partial\gamma'}(\widetilde{\gamma})\widetilde{J}^{-1}\frac{\partial h}{\partial\gamma'}(\widetilde{\gamma})\left[\frac{\partial h}{\partial\gamma'}(\widetilde{\gamma})\widetilde{J}^{-1}\widetilde{I}\widetilde{J}^{-1}\frac{\partial h'}{\partial\gamma}(\widetilde{\gamma})\right]^{-1} \times \frac{\partial h'}{\partial\gamma}(\widetilde{\gamma})\widetilde{J}^{-1}\frac{\partial L_N}{\partial\gamma}(\widetilde{\gamma}).$$

Under the null hypothesis, W and S are asymptotically equivalent and follow a χ^2 distribution with r df. Under alternatives of misspecifications, which lead to inconsistent estimates or nonzero scores, both statistics tend to infinity when N increases. The score test has the advantage that it is not necessary to estimate the model under the alternative, which could be burdensome. The equivalence property of these statistics with the likelihood ratio statistic is not valid when the objective function is no proper likelihood function, except in the special case when $I(\gamma^0) \equiv -J(\gamma^0)$. In the probit model, this identity holds when the error terms are homoscedastic and uncorrelated over time.

The information matrix test (White 1982) is a useful tool to detect misspecifications in models estimated by maximum likelihood. Although it can be modified to fit in the marginal ML framework outlined in Section 2, it is difficult to find forms of this test that have small-sample distributions close to the respective asymptotic approximations. The reason is that the complete distribution of the error terms cannot be identified with the marginal MLE. Indeed the small-sample performance is so poor (Lechner 1992) that these tests are omitted from the rest of the discussion in this article.

3.2 Applications of the Test Principles and Formulation of Alternative Hypotheses

3.2.1 Omitted and Superfluous Variables, Dynamics, Correlated Random Effects, and Functional Form. The omission of important variables from the regression function has serious consequences in probit models even when they are uncorrelated with the other explanatory variables of the model because the error terms (a sum of the original error terms and the omitted variables) may become nonnormal and heteroscedastic. Both problems could lead to inconsistent estimates. In the empirical example, such an omitted (unobserved) variable could be the amount of financial assets an individual holds. The inclusion of superfluous variables that otherwise fulfill the necessary regularity conditions results in an efficiency loss.

A generalized score test can be used to detect omitted variables that are observed in the data. For unobserved variables, either general specification tests may have power against that problem or the (possible) consistency property of the score test eventually detects the misspecification. To test whether some variables are superfluous, the joint covariance matrix computed after the first step [var($\hat{\gamma}$)] can be used to conduct Wald or t tests.

Aside from testing whether current-period variables are omitted or superfluous, it is useful to test whether lagged explanatory variables should be included. If so, this points to a possible misspecification of the dynamic structure of the model, which may be due to lagged explanatory variables or lagged dependent variables. This is a concern in the empirical example because high costs of a change of the employment status may lead to state dependence, which implies that the current employment status is explained additionally by the lagged employment status.

To find possible correlations of the random individual effects with some explanatory variables, test in particular whether the coefficients of future realizations of these variables are jointly 0. The idea behind using only future realizations is to separate this problem from the dynamic one that implies nonzero coefficients on lagged realizations, too. This test should also reject, however, if the strict exogeneity assumption is violated.

The same procedures can be applied to check the functional form by testing the significance of powers, cross-products, or other transformations of the explanatory variables. The relevant formulas to compute the components of this and all the following tests are contained in Appendix A.

3.2.2 Heteroscedasticity. Davidson and MacKinnon (1984) introduced the following procedure to detect heteroscedasticity in logit and probit models: Suppose that a vector $\widetilde{X}_{tn}$ of exogenous variables is suspected of influencing second moments of the error term such that the error term of the reduced form as defined by Equation (3) or (4) obtains the following form: $\omega_{tn} = \widetilde{\omega}_{tn}\exp(\widetilde{X}_{tn}\widetilde{\gamma}_t)$, where $\widetilde{\gamma}_t$ denotes a vector of unknown coefficients and $\widetilde{\omega}_n = (\widetilde{\omega}_{1n}, \ldots, \widetilde{\omega}_{Tn})'$ are idd (in dimension N) normal error terms with mean 0 and variance $\sigma^2 = (\sigma_1^2, \ldots, \sigma_T^2)$. The reduced-form coefficients can be rescaled $[\gamma_t/\exp(\widetilde{X}_{tn}\widetilde{\gamma}_t)]$, and an observationally equivalent form is obtained. The coefficients vary across observations, but the variance is homoscedastic (in dimension N).

Under the null, all elements of $\widetilde{\gamma}_t$ are 0. A score test is most convenient to check these conditions because it avoids the estimation of a model that is nonlinear in parameters. Furthermore, the functional-form assumption is less restrictive because the scores are identical for various specifications under the null. The same variables that are part of the explanatory variables may also appear in $\widetilde{X}_{tn}$, but it may as well contain other exogenous variables or variables from other periods. In the Monte Carlo study and the empirical example the statistics are computed for the variables (X_{tn}, Z_n) for the URE model and $(X_{tn}^i, X_{1n}^c, \ldots, X_{Tn}^c, Z_n)$ for the CRE model only.

3.2.3 Nonnormality. The assumption of normality of the error terms can rarely be motivated by a behavioral economic model. Furthermore, in contrast to aggregate data, the error term is not even approximately an arithmetic mean of many different independent components for which a law of large numbers applies. Because an incorrect normality assumption can lead to inconsistent estimates (e.g., Horowitz 1993), a nonnormality test is important. Two generalized score tests are suggested, a test against seminonparametric (SNP) alternatives and a RESET-like test.

The test against SNP alternatives uses a flexible functional form, proposed by Gallant and Nychka (1987), for the density of the error terms. It was made operational for testing and estimation in binary-choice models by Gabler, Laisney, and Lechner (1993). Laisney, Lechner, and Pohlmeier (1992) discussed panel estimation using an SNP density. The density of the error term in period t is given by

$$f(\omega_t) = \alpha_t' M(\omega_t)\alpha_t \Big/ \int_{-\infty}^{+\infty} \alpha_t' M(\omega)\alpha_t d\omega,$$

where $\alpha_t = [(2\pi)^{-1/4}, \alpha_{1,t}, \ldots, \alpha_{H,t}]'$ is a coefficient vector, $M(\omega)$ denotes the matrix with j, ith element $\omega^{i+j}\exp(\omega^2/2)$, and H is a constant chosen to allow for the desired flexibility of the approximation. There is almost no smooth density that is excluded from the specified family. It nests the normal, and therefore it can be used to check the conditions normality imposes on its coefficients. Following the results obtained by Gabler et al. (1993), $\alpha_{3,t}$, $\alpha_{4,t}$, and $\alpha_{5,t}$ are tested jointly and separately for nullity in the Monte Carlo study and the empirical example. $\alpha_{3,t}$ and $\alpha_{5,t}$ have power against skewed alternatives, whereas $\alpha_{4,t}$ has power against symmetric departures from the normal. The respective formulas for the computation of the tests were given in detail in appendix B of Gabler et al. (1993).

The use of RESET tests (Ramsey 1969) as general specification tests is frequently discussed in the regression literature—for example, by Thursby and Schmidt (1977) and Thursby (1985). The test principle is to include additional variables in the regression function and to test their significance. These variables may be powers or cross-products of regressors, powers of the predicted left-side variable, or something different, depending on the particular alternatives of interest. In the Monte Carlo study and the empirical example, the square, the cubic, and the fourth power of the mean function are included. A score test is used to check whether their coefficients are individually as well as jointly 0. As noted by Newey (1985), a joint test of the coefficients related to the squared and cubic mean is identical to a score test against the Pearson family of distributions; hence the Bera–Jarque–Lee test (Bera, Jarque, and Lee 1984) is not computed explicitly.

3.2.4 Random-Coefficient Variation. Ignoring random-coefficient variation leads to an error term that could be heteroscedastic and nonnormal. In a Monte Carlo study by Lechner (1991) the information matrix test (IMT) appears as the most powerful test against that problem. Due to the small-sample problems with the IMT in the framework used here, however, one has to rely on the already-mentioned heteroscedasticity and nonnormality tests. In the empirical example, random-coefficient variation could be a problem when the influence of explanatory variables, such as the expected income difference of the employment states or the expected bankruptcy risk, vary across individuals in a random manner.

3.2.5 Strict Exogeneity. The CRE model tackles the problem of correlations of regressors and individual effects in a way that is not valid when the explanatory variables are not strictly exogenous. Because it appears to be difficult to devise tests that are particularly sensitive to this misspecification within a CRE probit model, the power of some more indirect tests are studied. For example, the realizations from other periods of the potentially correlated explanatory variables $(\ldots, X^c_{t-1n}, X^c_{t+1n}, \ldots)$ can be used in constructing the matrix $\tilde{X}_{tn}$ for the heteroscedasticity test. Furthermore, a RESET test that includes only the variables $(\ldots, X^c_{t-1n}, X^c_{t+1n}, \ldots)$ could be useful.

4. MONTE CARLO STUDY

4.1 Design

The purpose of the Monte Carlo study is obtain insights about the finite-sample behavior of the suggested procedures. The data-generating process (DGP) under the two null hypotheses considered, with and without correlated random effects, is as follows:

$$y_{tn} = (X_{N,tn}\beta_N + X_{D,tn}\beta_D + d_t + c_n + u_{tn}) > 0$$

$$c_n = \sum_{t=1}^{T} X_{N,tn}\lambda_{N,t} + v_n, \qquad t = 1, \ldots, T; \quad n = 1, \ldots, N,$$

where $X_{D,tn}$ is a dummy variable that equals 1 with probability .5. The elements of $X_{N,n} = (X_{N,1n}, \ldots, X_{N,Tn})'$ are correlated over time. This is modeled by a Nerlove (1971) process—a time trend (starting with 1 and divided by 10) plus a uniform random number in the interval $[-.5, .5]$ plus half of the realized value of the previous period, starting with 0 for $X_{N,0n}$. Both error terms (c_n, u_{tn}) are independently drawn from a normal distribution with mean 0 and variance .5. For the URE DGP's the coefficient vector $\lambda_N = (\lambda_{N,1}, \ldots, \lambda_{N,T})'$ is 0; otherwise it equals $(1, .5, .2, 0, -.4)'$. The β-coefficients are set to 1 and the time effects (d_t) to -1 for all periods. These coefficient values are chosen to obtain a mean of y_{tn} close to .5. An additional design is used to check the sensitivity of the results with respect to a correlation of the regressors within the same period: $X_{N,tn}$ is substituted by $X^{(2)}_{N,tn} = X_{N,tn} + .5X_{D,tn}$. Furthermore, the sensitivity with respect to a larger influence of the error term is investigated by decreasing the absolute value of the coefficients of the URE model from 1 to .7. The expected values of the R^2's of the latent linear model are on average (over time) about .27/.40/.16 for the three URE DGP's and .40 for the CRE DGP. Sample sizes of $N = 250$ or $N = 1{,}000$ with $T = 5$ are considered. In particular with respect to sample sizes and types of regressors used the preceding setting mimics crudely samples often found in applied microeconometric work. One thousand replications are performed for the simulations under the null and five hundred for the various misspecifications and sensitivity checks. The estimated models are a URE model and a CRE model. For the latter only the continuous variable (X_N) is specified to be correlated with the random effect.

The following statistics are considered. The score tests against omitted variables test whether both regressors for URE, or only X_D for CRE, are omitted in period t $(t = 1, \ldots, T)$. Based on the following alternatives, three different statistics are computed: (1) All lagged realizations of a single regressor $(X_\tau, \tau < t)$ omitted (10 df), (2) all future realizations $(X_\tau, \tau > t)$ omitted (10 df), (3) lagged and future realizations omitted (20 df). The score tests against heteroscedasticity use both regressors separately $[\tilde{X}_{tn} = X_{D,tn}$, 5 df; $\tilde{X}_{tn} = X_{N,tn}$, 5 df for URE; or $\tilde{X}_{tn} = (X_{N,1n}, \ldots, X_{N,Tn})$, 25 df for CRE]. The score tests against the SNP distributions and the RESET tests have 5, 10, or 15 df. The distance $D(\hat{\gamma}, \hat{\theta})$ for the model with free time effects and free intertemporal variances has 4 df (URE) or 19 df (CRE).

4.2 Results

4.2.1 Correctly Specified Models. Tables 1–4 contain the results of the simulations based on the smaller sample $(N = 250)$. The results for $N = 1{,}000$ are available on request from the author. Tables 1 and 2 refer to the estimation

Table 1. Uncorrelated Random Effects: Data-Generating Process and Coefficient Estimates

Coefficients		d_1	d_2	d_3	d_4	d_5	β_N	β_D	$\lambda_{N,1}$	$\lambda_{N,2}$	$\lambda_{N,3}$	$\lambda_{N,4}$	$\lambda_{N,5}$	σ_1^{-1}	σ_2^{-1}	σ_3^{-1}	σ_4^{-1}
True value	(1, 2)	−1	−1	−1	−1	−1	1	1	0	0	0	0	0	1	1	1	1
Bias (std. dev.)	(1)	−.02(.19)	−.01(.18)	−.02(.18)	−.01(.19)	−.01(.22)	.01(.19)	.01(.15)	—	—	—	—	—	.03(.24)	.02(.22)	.02(.23)	.02(.23)
Bias (std. dev.)	(2)	−.02(.18)	−.02(.17)	−.01(.17)	−.01(.16)	−.01(.19)	.01(.19)	.01(.16)	—	—	—	—	—	.02(.18)	.02(.18)	.01(.18)	.01(.18)
True value	(3)	−.7	−.7	−.7	−.7	−.7	.7	.7	0	0	0	0	0	1	1	1	1
Bias (std. dev.)	(3)	−.03(.20)	−.02(.18)	−.02(.18)	−.01(19)	−.02(.22)	.01(.19)	.01(.15)	—	—	—	—	—	.03(.35)	.03(.32)	.04(.32)	.04(.33)

NOTE: $\lambda_N = 0, \lambda_D = 0$; $N = 250$; $T = 5$; replications: 1,000 (1), 500 (2, 3). (1) "Standard" DGP; (2) $X_{N,tn}^{(2)} = X_{N,tn} + .5X_{D,tn}$; (3) lower R^2.

Table 3. Correlated Random Effects: Data-Generating Process and Coefficient Estimates

Coefficients		d_1	d_2	d_3	d_4	d_5	β_N	β_D	$\lambda_{N,1}$	$\lambda_{N,2}$	$\lambda_{N,3}$	$\lambda_{N,4}$	$\lambda_{N,5}$	σ_1^{-1}	σ_2^{-1}	σ_3^{-1}	σ_4^{-1}
True value	(1)	−1	−1	−1	−1	−1	1	1	1	.5	.2	0	−.4	1	1	1	1
Bias (std. dev.)	(1)	−.02(.24)	−.02(.24)	−.02(.24)	−.02(.24)	−.02(.26)	.02(.23)	.01(.17)	.02(.27)	.01(.26)	.01(.24)	−.00(.24)	.00(.23)	.02(.21)	.02(.21)	.01(.22)	.01(.21)
True value	(2)	−1	−1	−1	−1	−1	1	1	0	0	0	0	0	1	1	1	1
Bias (std. dev.)	(2)	−.01(.25)	−.01(.24)	−.01(.23)	−.01(.23)	−.02(.25)	.01(.20)	.00(.18)	.00(.23)	.01(.24)	−00(.23)	−00(.24)	.00(.21)	.02(.27)	.02(.25)	.03(.24)	.04(.25)

NOTE: λ_N free, $\lambda_D = 0$, $N = 250$; $T = 5$; replications:1,000. (1) True model is CRE. (2) True model is URE.

Table 2. Uncorrelated Random Effects: Tests

Test	df	5% (1)	10% (1)	10% (2)	10% (3)
		Empirical rejection probability at theoretical quantile of			
Score test against omitted variables					
$X_{N,\tau n}, \tau < t$	10	3.6	8.7	10.6	11.2
$X_{D,\tau n}, \tau < t$	10	4.2	9.8	11.0	8.2
$X_{N,\tau n}, \tau > t$	10	5.1	9.5	12.4	8.2
$X_{D,\tau n}, \tau > t$	10	4.7	9.0	11.4	8.2
$X_{N,\tau n}, \tau \neq t$	20	3.6	8.5	10.6	9.4
$X_{D,\tau n}, \tau \neq t$	20	4.3	10.1	12.0	7.8
Score test against heteroscedasticity					
$\tilde{X}_{tn} = X_{N,tn}$	5	5.6	10.2	10.2	8.0
$\tilde{X}_{tn} = X_{D,tn}$	5	5.8	10.7	10.4	9.4
Score test against SNP distribution					
$\alpha_{3,t}$	5	3.1	6.9	9.6	.4
$\alpha_{4,t}$	5	3.3	6.1	9.8	.0
$\alpha_{5,t}$	5	2.6	6.5	10.8	.0
$\alpha_{3,t}, \alpha_{4,t}$	10	2.1	4.0	7.2	.0
$\alpha_{3,t}, \alpha_{4,t}, \alpha_{5,t}$	15	1.6	2.7	5.0	.0
RESET—mean function					
$(X_{tn}\gamma_t)^2$	5	5.7	10.7	11.0	8.6
$(X_{tn}\gamma_t)^3$	5	7.0	13.8	12.8	10.2
$(X_{tn}\gamma_t)^4$	5	5.5	11.7	13.2	9.0
$(\cdot)^2, (\cdot)^3$	10	7.7	14.6	13.4	9.6
$(\cdot)^2, (\cdot)^3, (\cdot)^4$	15	6.6	13.3	14.0	11.2
Distance	4	5.4	10.7	9.0	9.0

NOTE: See note to Table 1.

of a URE model with a URE DGP. The results for the "standard" DGP given in Section 4.1 are denoted by (1); (2) and (3) denote the results for the sensitivity analysis with respect to a correlation of the regressors within each period [about .6, (2)] and a larger influence of the error term (3). Tables 3 and 4 present the results of a CRE model with a CRE DGP and of a CRE model with a URE DGP. The latter is included to study the behavior of the tests in an overparameterized model.

Tables 1 and 3 contain the true values of the coefficients and the empirical biases and standard deviations of the estimates. To identify the model, σ_ζ^2 is set to 1 in the estimations. In Tables 2 and 4 the degrees of freedom of the χ^2 statistics and the empirical probabilities of the null rejected at asymptotic critical values related to the 5% and 10% quantile are given. The values for the 5% quantile are omitted for the sensitivity analysis (Tables 1 and 2) because only 500 replications are used. In the following discussion the same statistics are compared across both tables.

All coefficient estimates are nearly unbiased. The pseudo-R^2's, which estimate the expected R^2 of the latent linear model, are between about .19 (Efron)/.27 (McKelvey–Zavoina) for the URE DGP and .25/.40 for the CRE DGP. In DGP (3) of Tables 1 and 2 the pseudo-R^2's are about .1/.15. Comparing these estimates with the true expected R^2 confirms previous findings (Veall and Zimmermann 1992) that the McKelvey–Zavoina version of the pseudo-R^2 is a nearly unbiased estimate of the true R^2, but that Efron's version is downward biased.

Table 4. Correlated Random Effects: Tests

Test	df	5% (1)	10% (1)	5% (2)	10% (2)
		Empirical rejection probability at theoretical quantile of			
Score test against omitted variables					
$X_{D,\tau n}, \tau < t$	10	5.5	12.3	4.8	11.2
$X_{D,\tau n}, \tau > t$	10	6.0	10.6	5.7	10.8
$X_{D,\tau n}, \tau \neq t$	20	4.5	10.8	4.5	9.8
Score test against heteroscedasticity					
$\tilde{X}_{tn} = (X_{N,1n}, \ldots, X_{N,Tn})'$	25	2.9	7.3	4.2	8.9
$\tilde{X}_{tn} = X_{D,tn}$	5	6.3	12.0	5.8	9.6
Score test against SNP—distribution					
$\alpha_{3,t}$	5	9.1	15.8	2.6	5.1
$\alpha_{4,t}$	5	20.2	27.8	2.7	5.6
$\alpha_{5,t}$	5	8.9	17.3	2.4	4.6
$\alpha_{3,t}, \alpha_{4,t}$	10	30.3	41.4	2.9	4.7
$\alpha_{3,t}, \alpha_{4,t}, \alpha_{5,t}$	15	33.3	42.6	1.3	3.3
RESET—mean function					
$(X_{tn}\gamma_t)^2$	5	4.1	9.5	5.2	10.2
$(X_{tn}\gamma_t)^3$	5	6.7	14.9	6.7	14.4
$(X_{tn}\gamma_t)^4$	5	3.2	7.4	5.4	12.0
$(\cdot)^2, (\cdot)^3$	10	6.5	13.8	7.3	13.2
$(\cdot)^2, (\cdot)^3, (\cdot)^4$	15	2.8	8.1	5.5	12.4
RESET—only λ-related part					
$(\sum_{\tau \neq t} X_{N,\tau n}\lambda_{N,\tau})^2$	5	4.4	9.4	5.4	9.3
$(\sum_{\tau \neq t} X_{N,\tau n}\lambda_{N,\tau})^3$	5	6.0	12.4	4.7	9.0
$(\sum_{\tau \neq t} X_{N,\tau n}\lambda_{N,\tau})^4$	5	5.1	9.7	3.9	9.8
$(\cdot)^2, (\cdot)^3$	10	6.0	12.2	5.5	10.7
$(\cdot)^2, (\cdot)^3, (\cdot)^4$	15	3.3	9.1	3.7	9.5
Distance	19	9.7	17.1	10.1	16.2

NOTE: See note to Table 3.

The score tests against omitted variables and heteroscedasticity closely approximate their asymptotic distributions. Note that a smaller number of expected realizations in the tail of the distribution (50 for the 5% quantile and 1,000 replications) leads to not-so-precise estimates of these quantiles. As expected, the approximation of the asymptotic distribution is better the larger the sample.

The tests against the SNP distribution perform worse. For the URE DGP's they are undersized in the small samples, and this remains a problem for the joint tests even for the larger samples. There is also a particular problem for the DGP with a lower R^2. The problem is reversed for the CRE DGP. The tests, especially the joint tests, are oversized even for the larger samples. This instability casts serious doubt on the usefulness of the joint tests in applied work. At least SNP (α_3) approximates its asymptotic distribution fairly well for the larger samples with larger R^2's.

Some of the RESET statistics are oversized, others are undersized. Although these problems diminish for the larger samples, they still exist to some extent. Those forms of the tests that use quadratic terms only, however, are very close to their asymptotic distributions for all sample sizes.

The distances are close to their asymptotic distributions for the larger samples, but those based on many degrees of freedom are oversized for the smaller samples.

Table 5. Comparisons of the Power: Data-Generating Processes and Coefficient Estimates

Coefficient		β_N		β_D		$\lambda_{N,1}$		$\lambda_{N,2}$		$\lambda_{N,3}$		$\lambda_{N,4}$		$\lambda_{N,5}$	
True value	(1, 2)		1		1		1		.5		.2		0		−.4
Bias	(1)	.06	*.04*	−.35	*−.34*		—		—		—		—		—
Bias	(2)	−.61	*.62*	−.31	*−.30*	−.37	*−.37*	.10	*.11*	.16	*.18*	.11	*.11*	.26	*.27*
True value	(3–8)		1		1	—	0		0		0		0		0
Bias	(3)	.02	*.00*	.03	*.01*		—		—		—		—		—
Bias	(4)	.01	*.00*	−.01	*−.02*		—		—		—		—		—
Bias	(5)	−.01	*.00*	−.07	*−.06*		—		—		—		—		—
Bias	(6)	−.27	*−.27*	−.24	*−.25*		—		—		—		—		—
Bias	(7)	−.24	*−.22*	−.42	*−.42*		—		—		—		—		—
Bias	(8)	−.44	*−.43*	−.40	*−.39*	.18	*.20*	.12	*.12*	.01	*.02*	.13	*.12*	−.05	*−.01*

NOTE: $\lambda_N$free, $\lambda_D = 0$; $N = 250$, *1,000*; $T = 5$; replications: 500. Numbers in italics relate to $N = 1,000$. (1) DGP is CRE, URE estimated. (2) DGP is CRE without strict exogeneity; CRE with strict exogeneity estimated. (3) DGP is URE with heteroscedasticity: $\omega_{tn} = \tilde{\omega}_{tn} \exp(X_{N,tn}.2)$; URE estimated. (4) DGP is URE with Burr II (.2) distribution; URE estimated. (5) DGP is URE with $\chi^2(2)$ distribution; URE estimated. (6) DGP is URE with $\beta_N \sim N(1, 1)$; URE estimated. (7) DGP is URE and dynamic ($y^*_{tn} = .5y^*_{t-1n} + \cdots$); static URE estimated. (8) DGP is URE and dynamic ($y^*_{tn} = .5y^*_{t-1n} + \cdots$); static CRE estimated.

4.2.2 Misspecified Models. Tables 5 and 6 briefly summarize power properties for some misspecifications. Comparing the results for different sample sizes of $N = 250$ and $N = \mathit{1,000}$ (in italics) indicates if and for what sample sizes the different procedures detect these misspecifications. As before, Table 5 gives the true coefficients and the biases of the estimates. The latter are a possible measure for the distance of the alternative to the null, but note that even when coefficient estimates are almost unbiased, the same need not be true for the estimated asymptotic standard errors. The alternatives are chosen "close" enough to the null so that differences between the tests are visible when the null is rejected at asymptotic critical values related to the 5% level. Table 6 gives the corresponding empirical rejection probabilities.

Table 6. Comparisons of the Power: Tests

		Empirical rejection probability at theoretical quantile of 5%															
Test	df	(1)	(2)	(3)	(4)	(5)	(6)	(7)	(8)	(1)	(2)	(3)	(4)	(5)	(6)	(7)	(8)
Score test against omitted variables																	
$X_{N,\tau n}, \tau < t$	10	100	—	5	4	6	4	45	—	100	—	5	6	9	5	100	—
$X_{D,\tau n}, \tau < t$	10	4	5	4	5	5	4	77	77	27	8	6	6	6	5	100	100
$X_{N,\tau n}, \tau > t$	10	100	—	4	5	6	6	25	—	100	—	4	6	4	5	86	—
$X_{D,\tau n}, \tau > t$	10	25	3	5	5	3	5	15	20	88	7	6	6	8	6	69	78
$X_{N,\tau n}, \tau \neq t$	20	100	—	4	5	6	5	32	—	100	—	4	5	8	5	99	—
$X_{D,\tau n}, \tau \neq t$	20	4	4	5	5	5	4	75	76	32	8	4	6	6	5	100	100
Score test against heteroscedasticity																	
$\widetilde{X}_{tn} = X_{N,tn}$	5	4	—	7	58	27	12	4	—	19	—	24	100	96	45	6	—
$\widetilde{X}_{tn} = (X_{N,1n}, \ldots, X_{N,Tn})'$	25	—	1	—	—	—	—	—	2	—	7	—	—	—	—	—	8
$\widetilde{X}_{tn} = X_{D,tn}$	5	6	4	7	63	26	12	5	5	19	7	19	100	90	34	6	6
Score test against SNP—distribution																	
$\alpha_{3,t}$	5	5	11	4	67	7	2	0	0	19	8	23	100	96	34	3	1
$\alpha_{4,t}$	5	14	33	2	31	2	1	1	1	17	34	9	87	20	5	2	2
$\alpha_{5,t}$	5	5	10	3	63	2	1	1	0	19	9	23	100	95	30	2	1
$\alpha_{3,t}, \alpha_{4,t}$	10	16	51	2	58	1	1	0	0	31	43	13	100	91	10	1	1
$\alpha_{3,t}, \alpha_{4,t}, \alpha_{5,t}$	15	17	63	1	49	2	1	0	0	29	60	8	99	81	8	1	1
RESET—mean function																	
$(X_{tn}\gamma_t)^2$	5	5	4	8	67	31	14	5	5	22	5	26	100	97	43	7	5
$(X_{tn}\gamma_t)^3$	5	9	5	7	33	16	9	6	8	16	22	15	89	42	16	6	6
$(X_{tn}\gamma_t)^4$	5	5	1	6	59	22	13	3	5	15	5	24	99	93	37	6	7
$(\cdot)^2, (\cdot)^3$	10	11	5	10	60	34	10	7	7	36	24	23	100	97	37	8	9
$(\cdot)^2, (\cdot)^3, (\cdot)^4$	15	10	1	7	48	28	10	6	4	39	25	20	99	96	29	11	12
RESET—only λ-related part																	
$(\sum_{\tau \neq t} X_{N,\tau n}\lambda_{N,\tau})^2$	5	—	4	—	—	—	—	—	8	—	6	—	—	—	—	—	9
$(\sum_{\tau \neq t} X_{N,\tau n}\lambda_{N,\tau})^3$	5	—	5	—	—	—	—	—	7	—	11	—	—	—	—	—	9
$(\sum_{\tau \neq t} X_{N,\tau n}\lambda_{N,\tau})^4$	5	—	5	—	—	—	—	—	7	—	13	—	—	—	—	—	8
$(\cdot)^2, (\cdot)^3$	10	—	5	—	—	—	—	—	7	—	21	—	—	—	—	—	10
$(\cdot)^2, (\cdot)^3, (\cdot)^4$	15	—	3	—	—	—	—	—	5	—	23	—	—	—	—	—	10
Dist. URE, CRE	4,19	82	100	6	5	6	6	6	28	100	100	6	9	3	7	8	97

NOTE: Numbers in italics relate to $N = 1000$. See notes on Table 5.

When a URE model is estimated and the DGP is CRE (1), the tests explicitly designed against that alternative (omitted variables) as well as the distance are most powerful. But at least for the larger sample all the other tests have some power.

A necessary assumption for the CRE approach to give a valid correction for a correlation between the random effects and explanatory variables is strict exogeneity of the latter. The following DGP (2) violates this assumption: $\widetilde{X}_{N,tn} = X_{N,tn} + .7u_{t-1n} + .3u_{t-2n}$, where $\widetilde{X}_{N,tn}$ is included in the DGP instead of $X_{N,tn}$. This misspecification leads to severely biased coefficient estimates. In the empirical example, this kind of feedback from the error terms to the explanatory variables could occur when some unobserved factors influence future values of variables, which are independent of the error term of the current period. The distance appears as the most powerful test. Other powerful tests include some of the RESET tests and the SNP tests. It is a surprising feature of the latter, however, that their power seems not to increase with sample size.

In Specification (3) the DGP possesses a heteroscedastic error term with a variance that depends on an explanatory variable of the model $[\omega_{tn} = \widetilde{\omega}_{tn}\exp(X_{N,tn}.2)]$. At least for the larger sample all tests but the one against omitted variables and the distance are more or less equally powerful. Similarly the distance also has no power for the following misspecifications (4) to (7).

The feature that the behavior of the test against omitted variables is entirely different from the other tests based on the first-step estimates is repeated for all remaining misspecifications. The reason could stem from the problem of identification in the binary-choice model. Different transformations of the model are not observationally distinguishable, as long as the sign is preserved (see Manski 1988 for the implications). Hence the RESET test, the SNP test, and the heteroscedasticity test can all be seen as checking different types of nonlinearities of the mean function, whereas the test against omitted variables checks for additional linear elements in the mean-function. Therefore it is not surprising that the test against omitted variables has almost no power for the misspecifications (2) to (6).

Two DGP's with skewed distributions are considered, (1) Burr II (.2) [1 is the logistic distribution; see Johnson and Kotz (1970, p. 31)], (4), and (2) a $\chi^2(2)$ distribution, (5). The means and variances of the disturbances are normalized to 0 and unity. Heteroscedasticity, SNP, and RESET tests are almost equally powerful. The exceptions are the SNP (α_4) and the RESET $[(\cdot)^3]$ tests, which have significantly less power. They are known to be particularly sensitive, however, to symmetric departure from normality, which is not considered here because asymmetric departures from normality are generally far more harmful to the probit estimates (see Gabler et al. 1993) than symmetric ones. Taking into account the results of Table 2, the RESET $[(\cdot)^2]$ is the most powerful test for both misspecifications and both sample sizes. For the Burr II distribution the SNP (α_3) test is equally powerful. For the case of a $\chi^2(2)$ distribution, however, the RESET as well as the heteroscedasticity test clearly outperform the SNP tests at least for the small sample. This illustrates the point that a rejection of a model based on a test constructed against a specific alternative (here heteroscedasticity) can result because of a violation of a different assumption (here nonnormality).

When a coefficient varies randomly (6), the results are very similar to those for Specifications (3)–(5). This is not surprising because this DGP leads to a heteroscedastic and nonnormal error term.

The score tests against the omission of lagged explanatory variables are by far the most powerful for two dynamic DGP's (7, 8). The fact that the distance is powerful only when a CRE model is estimated (8) can be explained as follows: When all leads and lags are omitted from the model (URE, 7) the distance has no power, because there are no restrictions—except equality restrictions over time, which are not violated—which could be enforced (and checked for their validity) in the second step. Once the lags and the leads are included (CRE) the minimum-distance procedure imposes incorrect restrictions because the difference in the coefficients of lags versus leads as implied by the dynamic model is ignored. The power of all the other tests is very low, although even the CRE model does not lead to consistent estimates of the reduced-form coefficients because the lags of X_D are not included in the CRE model. The extremely small values for the SNP statistics are yet another undesirable feature of these tests.

5. EMPIRICAL EXAMPLE: RESULTS

As already explained in Section 1, the equation of major interest in the empirical example is a binary panel probit with free time effects and an unrestricted intertemporal covariance matrix of the error terms. The latter are assumed to be uncorrelated with the regressors (URE). Specification (1) in Table 7 reproduces estimates of this model from Pfeiffer and Pohlmeier (1992). Specifications (2) and (3) will be discussed later. The results for the constant terms, the variance, shares, and the λ coefficients for the CRE model (3) are suppressed. The estimated pseudo-R^2's are in the same range as in the Monte Carlo study [.2 /.3 for the URE models (1–2), .25/.45 for the CRE model]. The estimated asymptotic t values in Specification (1) do not take account of the prediction of the variable *income difference*. The other specifications do not contain predicted variables.

Definitions of the variables used in the estimation and some descriptive statistics can be found in Appendix B. For all further details concerning the economic model and the estimations performed, the reader is referred to Pfeiffer and Pohlmeier (1992).

The specification tests already used in the Monte Carlo study are applied to check the reliability of the results and possibly to suggest improvements. These improvements have to be of a limited nature, however, because, first, there are no other variables outside the current model available, and second, it is beyond the scope of this article to suggest and estimate entirely different models for the determinants of self-employment. Furthermore, sequential testing and estimation procedures are subject to pre-test problems, and the derivation of the appropriate pre-test distributions is also beyond

Table 7. Selected Estimates of the Minimum Distance Step of the Random-Effects Probit Model With Free Time Effects and Heteroscedasticity Over Time (self-employment probit)

Model: random effects variable				*Structural uncorrelated (1)*		*Reduced form uncorrelated (2)*		*Reduced form correlated (3)*	
				Coef.	*t val.*	*Coef.*	*t val.*	*Coef.*	*t val.*
Variables appearing only in employment status equation									
Bankruptcy			TV	−.02	−.2	−.12	−1.5	−.06	−2.1
Income difference/10			TV	.83	1.7	—	—	—	—
Divorced			TV	.39	3.2	.37	3.4	.50	4.3
Inheritance			TV	−.02	−.2	−.04	−.8	−.02	−.6
Subsidy			TV	.06	.7	−.07	−.8	.02	.3
Unemployment			TV	−.00	−.1	−.00	−.1	.01	.7
No training			TV	.36	5.7	.23	3.6	.36	5.9
No degree			TC	−.22	−2.2	−.53	−4.6	−.61	−5.5
Variables appearing in employment status equation and income equations									
Age/10	S	E	TV	.93	2.2	1.12	3.0	.91	2.1
$Age^2/10$		E	TV	.04	.2	.11	.6	−.04	−.3
Big city		E	TV	.26	2.6	.11	1.3	.17	1.8
Small city		E	TV	.39	3.4	.33	3.3	.30	2.9
Village		E	TV	.42	3.3	.39	3.2	.30	2.4
Handicapped	S	E	TV	−.14	−2.6	−.19	−3.8	−.19	−4.2
Father self-employed	S	E	TC	.88	9.6	.78	8.8	.78	8.8
Schooling	S	E	TC	.03	1.4	.01	.6	.03	1.3
Foreign		E	TC	−.10	−.8	.01	.1	−.13	−1.2
EC, EFTA		E	TC	−.02	−.2	.18	1.5	.31	2.6
Variables appearing only in income equations									
Agriculture	S	E	TV	—		1.48	7.2	.70	3.4
Manufacturing		E	TV	—		−.28	−4.9	−.35	−5.2
Banking, insurance		E	TV	—		.27	2.2	.49	3.8

NOTE: Sample: GSOEP, $N = 1926$, $T = 6$, balanced panel, working men, age: 25–60 in 1984. Dependent variable: 1: individual is self-employed; 0 otherwise. S: regressor of income equation for self-employed. E: regressor of income equation for employees. TV: regressor varies over time. TC: regressor is constant over time.

the scope of this article. The results of the tests are contained in Table 8. Only those results that are significant at the 10% level in one of the specifications are given, but because no score tests against omitted variables and heteroscedasticity using variables outside the model are performed, the reader can unambiguously infer which tests are not significant at this level. Given the large sample, it seems reasonable to choose the 1% level for the tests to indicate severe rejection (numbers in bold letters).

The rejection of specification (1) is clear-cut. The tests point especially to the variables *bankruptcy* (sectoral bankruptcy growth rates) and *income difference* (predicted income difference between being self-employed and being an employee) as well as to an overall misspecification of the model.

The tests do not account for the fact that *income difference* is predicted and therefore a reduced-form model is estimated in which the predicted (ln) income difference is substituted by the two linear equations explaining it (2). To keep the estimation tractable with a personal computer, joint Wald tests are used after the first step to eliminate completely insignificant additional regressors from these equations. The final reduced form contains three additional sector-specific variables. The interpretation of the coefficients changes for the variables that are included in the income as well as the self-employment equations; these variables are marked with an *S* if they are included in the equation for the self-employment income and with an *E* if they are included in the income equation for an employee. The tests reject the model again. It seems that the problem with the variable *income difference* stems from its explaining component, which indicates whether the individual works in the sector *manufacturing*.

Finally, a CRE model (*bankruptcy* correlated with the random effect) is estimated (3) because the score tests against omitted variables clearly point in this direction. Although there are still rejections of several tests at the 5% level, only three rejections occur at the 1% level, two joint RESET tests of the λ-related part and the distance. The latter may also indicate that the assumption of time-constant coefficients, or the assumption of strict exogeneity of the variable *bankruptcy*, is doubtful. Given the test results, the CRE model seems to be more parsimonious than the URE model. The Wald statistic in the last line of Table 8 shows that the estimates of λ coefficients are highly significant. The change in the other coefficients due to the CRE specification is also important (Table 7). For example the impact of *bankruptcy* becomes significantly negative, as suggested by economic theory, and other coefficients change as well.

There remain considerable doubts, however, about the validity of all specifications, and more general respecifications might be considered. One of the possibilities is suggested

Table 8. Selected Results of Specification Tests for the Self-employment Probit

Model: random effects test	df	Structural uncorrelated (1) χ^2	Structural uncorrelated (1) Prob. in %	Reduced form uncorrelated (2) χ^2	Reduced form uncorrelated (2) Prob. in %	Reduced form correlated (3) χ^2	Reduced form correlated (3) Prob. in %
Score test against omitted variables							
Bankruptcy $X_{\tau n}, \tau < t$	15	**104**	.0	**88**	.0	—	—
Bankruptcy $X_{\tau n}, \tau > t$	15	**96**	.0	**76**	.0	—	—
Bankruptcy $X_{\tau n}, \tau \neq t$	30	**120**	.0	**106**	.0	—	—
Income difference $X_{\tau n}, \tau < t$	15	**61**	.0	—	—	—	—
Income difference $X_{\tau n}, \tau > t$	15	**62**	.0	—	—	—	—
Income difference $X_{\tau n}, \tau \neq t$	30	**82**	.0	—	—	—	—
Manufacturing $X_{\tau n}, \tau > t$	15	—	—	29	1.5	26	3.7
Manufacturing $X_{\tau n}, \tau \neq t$	30	—	—	**64**	.0	41	9.2
No training $X_{\tau n}, \tau \neq t$	30	45	3.9	39	13	19	22
Score test against heteroscedasticity							
Bankruptcy	6,6,36	12	5.4	**17**	.8	52	3.9
Income difference	6	**29**	.0	—	—	—	—
Father self-employed	6	**21**	.2	**17**	.9	9	20
Age	6	12	5.5	10	14	10	13
Age²	6	16	1.6	11	9.1	10	11
No training	6	14	2.6	14	2.7	17	1.0
Small city	6	13	3.8	5	62	9	19
Village	6	13	3.9	5	61	3	77
Manufacturing	6	—	—	**24**	.1	15	2.3
Score test against SNP distribution							
$\alpha_{3,t}$	6	**18**	.7	**18**	.7	11	10
$\alpha_{4,t}$	6	**19**	.5	**18**	.6	11	8.1
$\alpha_{5,t}$	6	**17**	.9	15	2.0	10	12
$\alpha_{3,t}, \alpha_{4,t}$	12	**20**	7.3	20	6.0	12	43
$\alpha_{3,t}, \alpha_{4,t}, \alpha_{5,t}$	18	25	13	**37**	.5	19	37
RESET—mean function							
$(X_{tn}\gamma_t)^2$	6	**19**	.4	**17**	.9	12	7.3
$(X_{tn}\gamma_t)^3$	6	**18**	.6	**19**	.5	13	3.8
$(X_{tn}\gamma_t)^4$	6	**17**	.9	**18**	.7	13	4.3
$(\cdot)^2, (\cdot)^3$	12	23	2.5	24	2.3	17	15
$(\cdot)^2, (\cdot)^3, (\cdot)^4$	18	29	4.5	**36**	.8	28	6.9
RESET—only λ-related part							
$(\sum_{\tau \neq t} X_{N,\tau n}\lambda_{N,\tau})^2$	6	—	—	—	—	11	10
$(\sum_{\tau \neq t} X_{N,\tau n}\lambda_{N,\tau})^3$	6	—	—	—	—	11	8.1
$(\sum_{\tau \neq t} X_{N,\tau n}\lambda_{N,\tau})^4$	6	—	—	—	—	12	6.2
$(\cdot)^2, (\cdot)^3$	12	—	—	—	—	**35**	.0
$(\cdot)^2, (\cdot)^3, (\cdot)^4$	18	—	—	—	—	**38**	.4
Tests based on minimum distance estimation							
Distance	85,95,119	**229**	.0	**232**	.0	**202**	.0
Wald: CRE vs. URE	6	—	—	—	—	**119**	.0

by the tests because some important problematic variables are sector specific. In general the choice of a sector of employment and the choice between self-employment and being an employee may be simultaneous. This suggests that a correlated random-effects model may not be sufficient. Instead a simultaneous model explaining sector choice and self-employment may be required, but other models may be plausible as well.

In concluding I stress that the article by Pfeiffer and Pohlmeier (1992) presented an innovative and very interesting microeconometric approach to analyzing the determinants of the individual probability of self-employment. This section shows, however, that the proposed specification tests, which were not available to them, can add information about the "fit" of the model and the data that is important to have. On the one hand the tests may—or may not—cast some doubts on the results obtained and lead to more cautious interpretations of the results, but on the other hand they may also give some additional ideas about ways to set up alternative models (although the latter might result in pre-test problems).

The GAUSS program used for the Monte Carlo study and the application is available on request from the author.

6. CONCLUSIONS

Several methods to test the specification of panel probit models are proposed in this article. The tests are constructed to have high power against alternatives that lead to the inconsistency of the probit estimator, such as omitted variables, incorrect functional form, neglected dynamics, heteroscedasticity, random-coefficient variation, and nonnormality. Some of those proposed may also serve as omnibus tests against several misspecifications.

The small-sample distributions of the test statistics are investigated by a Monte Carlo study. The performance under the null hypothesis is acceptable for most of the tests even for a moderate sample size. Whenever the bias of the estimated coefficients is substantial, at least some of the tests reject the specification.

The tests are applied to an empirical analysis of the individual probability of self-employment in West Germany. The results indicate that the chosen specification may not be flexible enough and suggest possible directions for respecifications.

ACKNOWLEDGMENTS

Financial support by the Deutsche Forschungsgemeinschaft (DFG) and the Center for European Economic Studies (ZEW), Mannheim, is gratefully acknowledged. A previous version was presented at the Fourth Conference on Panel Data in Budapest, 1992, and at the European Meeting of the Econometric Society in Brussels, 1992. I thank the DIW for providing the data of the GSOEP, Yvonne Gintz for able research assistance, Crystal Petty and Nadine Riede for carefully reading the manuscript, and Jörg Breitung, François Laisney, Viktor Steiner, the editor, an associate editor, and two anonymous referees of this journal for helpful comments and suggestions. My special thanks go to Friedhelm Pfeiffer and Winfried Pohlmeier for allowing and helping me to test their model.

APPENDIX A: FORMULAS OF THE COMPONENTS OF SOME TEST STATISTICS

For the sake of brevity the following additional notation is useful. All explanatory variables that enter the reduced form in period t under the null are collected in the K-dimensional vector X_{tn} and the respective coefficients in γ_t. In the cases in which additional variables enter the test statistics, they are collected in the $\widetilde{K}$-dimensional vector $\widetilde{X}_{tn}$. Under the null $(X_{tn}, \widetilde{X}_{tn})$ is assumed to be independent of ω_{tn}. The vector of additional coefficients under the alternative is denoted by $\widetilde{\gamma}_t$. Under the null, all elements of $\widetilde{\gamma}_t$ are 0. Furthermore, let Φ_{tn} and ϕ_{tn} denote the cumulative distribution function and the probability density of the standard normal distribution evaluated at $X_{tn}\gamma_t$. All expectations are taken with respect to the distribution under the null conditional on $(X_{tn}, \widetilde{X}_{tn})$.

The alternative model for testing against omitted variables and incorrect functional form is given by $y^*_{tn} = X_{tn}\gamma_t + \widetilde{X}_{tn}\widetilde{\gamma}_t + \omega_{tn}$.

The score vector and expected Hessian, both evaluated under the null, are given by

$$s_{tn.\widetilde{\gamma}_{t,j}} = \frac{(y_{tn} - \Phi_{tn})\phi_{tn}}{\Phi_{tn}(1 - \Phi_{tn})}\widetilde{X}_{tn.j}$$

$$E(h_{tn.\gamma_{t,i}.\widetilde{\gamma}_{t,j}}) = \frac{-\phi^2_{tn}}{\Phi_{tn}(1 - \Phi_{tn})}X_{tn,i}\widetilde{X}_{tn,j}$$

$$E(h_{tn.\widetilde{\gamma}_{t,l}.\widetilde{\gamma}_{t,j}}) = \frac{-\phi^2_{tn}}{\Phi_{tn}(1 - \Phi_{tn})}\widetilde{X}_{tn,l}\widetilde{X}_{tn,j},$$

$$i = 1, \ldots, K; \quad j, l = 1, \ldots, \widetilde{K}; \quad t = 1, \ldots, T; \quad n = 1, \ldots, N.$$

The alternative model and the main components of the score test against heteroscedasticity, evaluated under the null, are as follows:

$$y^*_{tn} = \frac{X_{tn}\gamma_t}{\exp(\widetilde{X}_{tn}\widetilde{\gamma}_t)} + \widetilde{\omega}_{tn}$$

$$s_{tn.\widetilde{\gamma}_{t,j}} = \frac{(y_{tn} - \Phi_{tn})\phi_{tn}}{\Phi_{tn}(1 - \Phi_{tn})}(-X_{tn}\gamma_t)\widetilde{X}_{tn,i}$$

$$E(h_{tn.\widetilde{\gamma}_{t,i}.\gamma_{t,j}}) = \frac{-\phi^2_{tn}}{\Phi_{tn}(1 - \Phi_{tn})}(-X_{tn}\gamma_t)\widetilde{X}_{tn,j}X_{tn,i}$$

$$E(h_{tn.\widetilde{\gamma}_{t,i}.\widetilde{\gamma}_{t,j}}) = \frac{-\phi^2_{tn}}{\Phi_{tn}(1 - \Phi_{tn})}(X_{tn}\gamma_t)^2\widetilde{X}_{tn,l}\widetilde{X}_{tn,i},$$

$$i = 1, \ldots, K; \quad j, l = 1, \ldots, \widetilde{K}; \quad t = 1, \ldots, T; \quad n = 1, \ldots, N.$$

The alternative model and the main components of the RESET test, evaluated under the null, are given by

$$y^*_{tn} = X_{tn}\gamma_t + \sum_{m=1}^{M}\widetilde{\gamma}_{t,m}(X_{tn}\gamma_t)^m + \omega_{tn}$$

$$s_{tn}, \widetilde{\gamma}_{t,m} = \frac{(y_{tn} - \Phi_{tn})\phi_{tn}}{\Phi_{tn}(1 - \Phi_{tn})}(X_{tn}\gamma_t)^m$$

$$E(h_{tn.\gamma_{t,i}.\widetilde{\gamma}_{t,m}}) = \frac{-\phi^2_{tn}}{\Phi_{tn}(1 - \Phi_{tn})}X_{tn,i}(X_{tn}\gamma_t)^m$$

$$E(h_{tn.\widetilde{\gamma}_{t,j}.\widetilde{\gamma}_{t,m}}) = \frac{-\phi^2_{tn}}{\Phi_{tn}(1 - \Phi_{tn})}(X_{tn}\gamma_t)^j(X_{tn}\gamma_t)^m,$$

$$i = 1, \ldots, K; \quad j, m = 1, \ldots, M; \quad t = 1, \ldots, T; \quad n = 1, \ldots, N.$$

Under the null, $\widetilde{\gamma}_{t,m}$ is 0.

APPENDIX B: DESCRIPTION OF THE VARIABLES USED IN THE APPLICATION

In Tables B.1 and B.2 the definitions of the variables and some descriptive statistics are reproduced from Pfeiffer and

Table B.1. Sample Size and Dependent Variable

Year	Sample size	Self-employed workers
1984	1926	162
1985	1926	172
1986	1926	184
1987	1926	186
1988	1926	188
1989	1926	184

Table B.2. Definition, Means, and Standard Deviations of Explanatory Variables

Variable	Definition	Mean	Std.
Income difference	predicted ln (real monthly income for the self-employed) minus predicted ln (real monthly income for employees)	.16	.27
Age	(age in years − 40)/2	.28	.88
Age^2	(age in years − 40)^2/100	.86	.98
Schooling	number of years spent at school	9.9	1.5
Divorced	=1, individual is divorced	.06	
Big city	=1, community has more than 500,000 inhabitants	.48	
Small city	=1, community has 5,000 to 50,000 inhabitants	.22	
Village	=1, community has less than 50,000 inhabitants	.12	
Inheritance	sum of inheritances received in the last five years/50,000	.041	.55
Subsidy	=1, state of residency provides specific subsidies for new-firm formation	.26	
Handicapped	officially handicapped: 0 = no handicap; 1 = up to 30%; 2 = 31 to 50%; 3 = 51 to 75%; 4 = 76 to 100%	.18	.70
Unemployment	federal state unemployment rate from last year	8.8	2.4
No training	=1, current job requires no vocational degree	.31	
Father self.	=1, father was self-employed	.12	
No degree	=1, no vocational or professional degree	.19	
EC, EFTA	=1, citizenship of EC or EFTA country (except Germany)	.13	
Foreign	=1, citizenship of other country (except EC, EFTA)	.13	
Bankruptcy	sectoral bankruptcy growth rate, t, $t-1$, of 20 sectors	−.03	.11
Agriculture	=1, working in agriculture	.015	
Manufacturing	=1, working in manufacturing	.44	
Banking, insurance	=1, working in banking or insurance	.037	

Pohlmeier (1992). For more details, the reader is referred to their article.

[*Received June 1993. Revised January 1994.*]

REFERENCES

Avery, R., Hansen, L. P., and Hotz, V. J. (1983), "Multiperiod Probit Models and Orthogonality Condition Estimation," *International Economic Review*, 25, 563–578.

Bera, A., Jarque, C., and Lee, L. F. (1984), "Testing the Normality Assumption in Limited Dependent Variable Models," *International Economic Review*, 25, 563–578.

Butler, J. S., and Moffitt, R. (1982), "A Computationally Efficient Quadrature Procedure for the One-factor Multinomial Probit Model," *Econometrica*, 50, 761–764.

Chamberlain, G. (1980), "Analysis of Covariance With Qualitative Data," *The Review of Economic Studies*, 47, 225–238.

——— (1984), "Panel Data," in *Handbook of Econometrics* (Vol. II.), eds. Z. Griliches and M. D. Intriligator, Amsterdam: North-Holland, pp. 1247–1318.

Davidson, R., and MacKinnon, J. G. (1984), "Convenient Specification Tests for Logit and Probit Models," *Journal of Econometrics*, 25, 241–262.

Gabler, S., Laisney, F., and Lechner, M. (1993), "Seminonparametric Estimation of Binary Choice Models With an Application to Labor Force Participation," *Journal of Business & Economic Statistics*, 11, 61–80.

Gallant, A. R., and Nychka, D. N. (1987), "Semi-Nonparametric Maximum Likelihood Estimation," *Econometrica*, 55, 363–390.

Gouriéroux, C., and Monfort, A. (1989), *Statistique et Modèles Économétriques*, Paris: Économica.

Hajivassiliou, V. A. (1993), "Simulation Estimation Methods for Limited Dependent Variable Models," in *Handbook of Statistics, Vol. 11: Econometrics*, eds. G. S. Maddala, C. R. Rao, and H. D. Vinod, Amsterdam: North-Holland, pp. 519–543.

Horowitz, J. L. (1993), "Semiparametric and Nonparametric Estimation of Quantal Response Models," in *Handbook of Statistics, Vol. 11: Econometrics*, eds. G. S. Maddala, C. R. Rao, and H. D. Vinod, Amsterdam: North-Holland, pp. 45–72.

Hujer, R., and Schnabel, R. (in press), "The Impact of Regional and Sectoral Labor Market Conditions on Wages and Labor Supply—An Empirical Analysis for Married Women Using West-German Panel Data," *Empirical Economics*, 19.

Johnson, N. L., and Kotz, S. (1970), *Continuous Univariate Distributions-1*, Boston: Houghton Mifflin.

Jakubson, G. (1988), "The Sensitivity of Labor Supply Parameter Estimates to Unobserved Individual Effects: Fixed- and Random-Effects Estimates in a Nonlinear Model Using Panel Data," *Journal of Labor Economics*, 6, 302–329.

Keane, M. (1993), "Simulation Estimation for Panel Data Models With Limited Dependent Variables," in *Handbook of Statistics, Vol. 11: Econometrics*, eds. G. S. Maddala, C. R. Rao, and H. D. Vinod, Amsterdam: North-Holland, pp. 545–571.

Kodde, D. A., Palm, F. C., and Pfann, G. A. (1990), "Asymptotic Least-Squares Estimation Efficiency Considerations and Applications," *Journal of Applied Econometrics*, 5, 229–243.

Laisney, F., Lechner, M., and Pohlmeier, W. (1992), "Semi-Nonparametric Estimation of Binary Choice Models Using Panel Data: An Application to the Innovation Activity of German Firms," *Recherches Economiques de Louvain*, 58, 329–343.

Laisney, F., Lechner, M., van Soest, A., and Wagenhals, G. (1993), "A Life Cycle Labor Supply Model With Taxes Estimated on German Panel Data: The Case of Parallel Preferences," *The Social and Economic Review*, 24, 335–368.

Lechner, M. (1991), "Testing Logit Models in Practice," *Empirical Economics*, 16, 177–198.

——— (1992), "Some Specification Tests for Static Limited Dependent Variable Models Estimated on Panel Data," Discussion Paper 474-92, University of Mannheim, Dept. of Economics and Statistics.

Maddala G. S. (1983), *Limited Dependent and Qualitative Variables in Econometrics*, Cambridge, U.K.: Cambridge University Press.

——— (1987),"Limited Dependent Variable Models Using Panel Data," *Journal of Human Resources*, 22, 307–338.

Manski, C. F. (1988), "Identification of Binary Response Models," *Journal of American Statistical Association*, 83, 729–738.

Nerlove, M. (1971), "Further Evidence on the Estimation of Dynamic Economic Relations From a Time Series of Cross Sections," *Econometrica*, 39, 359–382.

Newey, W. (1985), "Maximum Likelihood Specification Testing and Conditional Moment Tests," *Econometrica*, 53, 1047–1070.

Pfeiffer, F., and Pohlmeier, W. (1992), "Income, Uncertainty and the Probability of Self-employment," *Recherches Economiques de Louvain*, 58, 265–281.

Ramsey, J. B. (1969), "Tests for Specification Errors in Classical Linear Least Squares Regression Analysis," *Journal of the Royal Statistical Society*, Ser. B, 31, 350–371.

Thursby, J. G. (1985), "The Relationship Among the Specification Tests of Hausman, Ramsey, and Chow," *Journal of the American Statistical Association*, 80, 926–928.

Thursby, J. G., and Schmidt, P. (1977), "Some Properties of Tests for Specification Error in a Linear Mode," *Journal of the American Statistical Association*, 72, 635–641.

Veall, M. R., and Zimmermann, K. F. (1992), "Pseudo-R^2 in the Ordinal Probit Model," *Journal of Mathematical Sociology*, 16, 333–342.

White, H. (1982), "Maximum Likelihood Estimation of Misspecified Models," *Econometrica*, 50, 1–25 (Corrigendum, 1993, 51, 513).

[6]

Econometrica, Vol. 67, No. 2 (March, 1999), 427–433

A ROOT-N CONSISTENT SEMIPARAMETRIC ESTIMATOR FOR RELATED-EFFECT BINARY RESPONSE PANEL DATA

BY MYOUNG-JAE LEE

1. INTRODUCTION

CONSIDER "RELATED-EFFECT" binary response panel data $(y_{it}, x'_{it})'$:

$$y_{it} = 1[y^*_{it} > 0], \qquad y^*_{it} = x'_{it}\beta + \alpha_i + u_{it} \qquad (i = 1, \ldots, N, t = 1, 2) \tag{1.1}$$

where $1[A] = 1$ if the event A holds and 0 otherwise, x_{it} is a $k \times 1$ regressor vector, α_i is a unit-specific error term possibly related with $x_i \equiv (x'_{i1}, x'_{i2})'$, and u_{it} is an error term varying across i and t. Manski (1987) proposed a semiparametric "panel maximum score estimator" for β that is likely to be $N^{1/3}$-consistent. Charlier et al. (1995) and Kyriazidou (1997) smooth the panel maximum score estimator adopting Horowitz' (1992) idea; the resulting estimator can converge at a rate close to but yet slower than $\sqrt{N}$.

In this paper, we propose a $\sqrt{N}$-consistent semiparametric estimator for (1.1). In Section 2, the estimator is introduced and its consistency is proven. In Section 3, the asymptotic distribution is derived. In Section 4, conclusions are drawn.

2. THE ESTIMATOR

Define

$$\Delta y_i \equiv y_{i2} - y_{i1} \quad \text{and} \quad \Delta x_i \equiv x_{i2} - x_{i1}. \tag{2.1}$$

The panel maximum score estimator is obtained by maximizing

$$(1/N) \sum_i \text{sgn}(\Delta x'_i b) \cdot \Delta y_i \tag{2.2}$$

with respect to (wrt) b, and its consistency is based upon

$$\text{med}(\Delta y_i | x_i, \Delta y_i \neq 0) = \text{sgn}(\Delta x'_i \beta) \tag{2.3}$$

where $\text{med}(y|A)$ is the median of the distribution of y given A, and $\text{sgn}(H) = 1$ if $H > 0$, 0 if $H = 0$, and -1 if $H < 0$.

Our estimator, say b_N, is obtained by maximizing

$$\{N(N-1)\}^{-1} \sum_{i \neq j} \text{sgn}(\Delta x'_i b - \Delta x'_j b) \cdot (\Delta y_i - \Delta y_j) \cdot \Delta y_i^2 \Delta y_j^2 \tag{2.4}$$

$$= \binom{N}{2}^{-1} \sum_{i<j,\, \Delta y_i \neq \Delta y_j,\, \Delta y_i \neq 0,\, \Delta y_j \neq 0} \text{sgn}(\Delta x'_i b - \Delta x'_j b) \cdot (\Delta y_i - \Delta y_j) \tag{2.5}$$

wrt b, and its consistency is based on the following key equation:

$$\text{med}(\Delta y_i - \Delta y_j | \Delta x_i, \Delta x_j, \Delta y_i \neq \Delta y_j, \Delta y_i \neq 0, \Delta y_j \neq 0) = 2 \cdot \text{sgn}(\Delta x'_i \beta - \Delta x'_j \beta). \tag{2.6}$$

Although $\Delta y_i - \Delta y_j$ can take five values $(0, \pm 1, \pm 2)$, the conditioning event in (2.6) excludes $(0, \pm 1)$ to make $\Delta y_i - \Delta y_j$ binary. The main impetus for $\sqrt{N}$-consistency of our estimator is the double sums where one sum turns the nonsmooth optimand into the smooth function

(2.7) $$E\{\text{sgn}(\Delta x'b - \Delta x_j'b)\cdot(\Delta y - \Delta y_j)\cdot \Delta y^2 \Delta y_j^2 | \Delta x_j, \Delta y_j\};$$

then the other sum with this smooth summand leads to $\sqrt{N}$-consistency.

Define $\beta_c \equiv (\beta_1, \ldots, \beta_{k-1})'$ to get $\beta = (\beta_c', \beta_k)'$; a generic element of the parameter space will be denoted as $b \equiv (b_c', b_k)'$. Since β is identified only up to an unknown positive scale, replace β by $\beta/|\beta_k| = (\beta_c'/|\beta_k|, \text{sgn}(\beta_k))'$ assuming $\beta_k \neq 0$. But when we discuss asymptotic distribution later, since $\text{sgn}(\beta_k)$ is to be estimated at a rate faster than $\sqrt{N}$, we will set $\beta_k = 1$ without loss of generality; of course, both $b_k = 1$ and $\beta_k = -1$ should be tried in practice.

Define Δx_{ic} as the components of Δx_i other than the last one Δx_{ik}: $\Delta x_i = (\Delta x_{ic}', \Delta x_{ik})'$. Time-invariant variables (e.g. intercept) drop out in Δx_i, and time-variant but "unit-invariant" variables (e.g. time dummies and macro-economic shocks common to all individuals) drop out in $\Delta x_i - \Delta x_j$, reducing the dimension of the parameters further; to simplify notations, however, we will ignore this. Let $|H|^2 \equiv \Sigma_i \Sigma_j h_{ij}^2$ for a matrix $H = [h_{ij}]$. Often the index i for individuals will be omitted.

ASSUMPTION 1:

(a) *The parameter space B for β_c is a compact subset of R^{k-1}.*

(b) $(y_{i1}, y_{i2}, x_{i1}', x_{i2}')'$, $i = 1, \ldots, N$, *are iid.*

(c) $E\{(\Delta x - E\Delta x)(\Delta x - E\Delta x)\}'$ *is p.d.*, $\beta_k \neq 0$, *and* $\Delta x_k | \Delta x_c$ *has an everywhere positive Lebesque density for a.e.* Δx_c.

(d) $(u_1, u_2)|\alpha$ *is independent of* $(x_1', x_2')|\alpha$, *and the support of* $(u_1, u_2)|\alpha$ *is* R^2 *for a.e.* α.

(e) $P(\Delta y = 1|\Delta x'\beta)$ *is an increasing function of* $\Delta x'\beta$ *and* $P(\Delta y = -1|\Delta x'\beta)$ *is a decreasing function of* $\Delta x'\beta$.

(f) *"Index increment sufficiency" of* $(x_1'\beta, \alpha)$:

$$P(x_1'\beta, \alpha|\Delta x) = P(x_1'\beta, \alpha|\Delta x'\beta) \quad \textit{for a.e. } \Delta x$$

where $P(\cdot|\cdot)$ *denotes the conditional distribution function.*

Assumption (d) allows relation between u_1 and u_2 as well as between $(u_1, u_2)'$ and α; (u_1, u_2) can have heteroskedasticity of an unknown form where the conditional variance depends only on α. (d) does not allow the lagged dependent variable as a regressor.

For (the first part of) (e), observe that

(2.8) $$P(\Delta y = 1|x_1'\beta, \Delta x'\beta, \alpha)$$
$$= P(u_1 \langle -x_1'\beta - \alpha, u_2 \rangle -x_1'\beta - \Delta x'\beta - \alpha | x_1'\beta, \Delta x'\beta, \alpha)$$

is an increasing function of $\Delta x'\beta$ for a given $x_1'\beta$ and α. Integrate this wrt $(x_1'\beta, \alpha)|\Delta x'\beta$ to get the weighted average $P(\Delta y = 1|\Delta x'\beta)$:

(2.9) $$\int P(\Delta y = 1|x_1'\beta, \Delta x'\beta, \alpha)\cdot f_{x_1'\beta|(\alpha, \Delta x'\beta)}(x_1'\beta)\cdot F_{\alpha|\Delta x'\beta}(d\alpha)\cdot d(x_1'\beta)$$

where the weight is the product of $f_{x_1'\beta|(\alpha, \Delta x'\beta)}$ and $F_{\alpha|\Delta x'\beta}$, a conditional density for $x_1'\beta|(\alpha, \Delta x'\beta)$ and the conditional distribution for $\alpha|\Delta x'\beta$ respectively. Since (2.8) is an increasing function of $\Delta x'\beta$ for a given $(x_i\,\beta, \alpha)$, satisfaction of (e) depends on the form of the weight as a function of $\Delta x'\beta$. Note that $(x_1'\,\beta, \Delta x'\beta)$ is one-to-one to $(x_1'\,\beta, x_2'\,\beta)$, and a relation between $x_1'\,\beta$ and $x_2'\,\beta$ is allowed as long as (2.9) is increasing in $\Delta x'\beta$.

Since x_{it} is one-to-one to $(x_{itc}', x_{it}'\,\beta)'$, $t = 1,2$, where $x_{it} = (x_{itc}', x_{itk})'$, rewrite (f) as

$$(2.10) \qquad P(x_1'\,\beta|\alpha, \Delta x_c, \Delta x'\beta)\cdot P(\alpha|\Delta x_c, \Delta x'\beta) = P(x_1'\,\beta|\alpha, \Delta x'\beta)\cdot P(\alpha|\Delta x'\beta).$$

Thus, a sufficient condition for (f) is:

(g) *α is independent of Δx_c given $\Delta x'\beta$, and*
(h) *$x_1'\,\beta$ is independent of Δx_c given $(\alpha, \Delta x'\beta)$.*

Since α is time-invariant, (g) is not so restrictive. Although (h) is restrictive, independence between an unobserved variable $(x_1'\,\beta)$ and observed ones (Δx_c) is nothing new in econometrics. One example where Assumptions 1 (e) and (f) are satisfied is: generate (u_1,u_2) and $(\alpha, x_1'\,\beta, \Delta x'\beta)$ subject to (2.9) first, and then generate x_{1c} and x_{2c} independently of $(\alpha, x_1'\,\beta, \Delta x'\beta)$. Both (e) and (f) with α integrated out are testable once b_N is obtained. Due to (e) and (f), our related-effect is not "pure" and does not contradict the impossibility result of Chamberlain (1992) on $\sqrt{N}$-consistency for (1.1).

LEMMA 1: *Under Assumption* 1, *Δy is independent of Δx_c given $\Delta x'\beta$*:

$$(2.11) \qquad P(\Delta y|\Delta x_c, \Delta x'\beta) = P(\Delta y|\Delta x'\beta) \quad \textit{for a.e. } \Delta x,$$

and (2.6) *holds.*

(2.11) is a panel analog of index (increment) sufficiency: with $\Delta x'\beta$ given, Δx_c is not informative for Δy.

In essence, (2.6) "identifies" $(\Delta x_i - \Delta x_j)'\beta$. To separate β from $\Delta x_i - \Delta x_j$, $P(X_{id}) > 0$ is sufficient where, with $\bar{B} \equiv B \times \{-1, 1\}$,

$$X_{id} \equiv \big\{(x_i', x_j'): \operatorname{sgn}(\Delta x_i'\,\beta - \Delta x_j'\,\beta) \neq \operatorname{sgn}(\Delta x_i'b - \Delta x_j'b) \text{ for any } b \neq \beta,\, b \in \bar{B}\big\}.$$

$P(X_{id}) > 0$ can be proven under Assumption 1, following Manski (1985). With the identification established, the a.s. consistency follows from the uniform convergence of U-processes in Sherman (1994) and the continuity of the population version of (2.5).

3. THE ASYMPTOTIC DISTRIBUTION

The asymptotic distribution of our estimator b_{cN} for β_c is derived following Sherman (1993); see also Arcones et al. (1994). Define

$$w_i \equiv \Delta x_i \quad \text{and} \quad z_i \equiv \Delta y_i.$$

The key expression for the asymptotic distribution is

$$\tau(z_j, w_j, b_c) \equiv E_{i|j}\{\operatorname{sgn}(w_i'b - w_j'b)\cdot(z_i - z_j)\cdot z_i^2 z_j^2\}, \quad i \neq j,$$

where $i|j$ means that the integral is wrt (z_i, w_i') conditional on (z_j, w_j'). Denote the gradient of $\tau(z_j, w_j, b_c)$ wrt b_c as $\nabla_1\tau(z_j, w_j, b_c)$. Denote the second order derivative matrix wrt b_c as $\nabla_2\tau(z_j, w_j, b_c)$.

ASSUMPTION 2:

(a) $\nabla_2 \tau(z_j, w_j, b_c)$ *exists for a.e.* $(z_j, w_j')'$ *in a neighborhood* N_β *of* β_c.
(b) *There is an integrable function* $M(z_j, w_j)$ *such that for all* $b_c \in N_\beta$

$$|\nabla_2 \tau(z_j, w_j, b_c) - \nabla_2 \tau(z_j, w_j, \beta_c)| \leq M(z_j, w_j) \cdot |b_c - \beta_c|.$$

(c) $E|\nabla_1 \tau(z_j, w_j, \beta_c)|^2 < \infty$.
(d) $E\nabla_2 \tau(z_j, w_j, \beta_c)$ *is n.d.*

Later, we provide a more primitive Assumption 3 that implies Assumption 2. Let $E^{-1}(\lambda) \equiv \{E(\lambda)\}^{-1}$. The following is proven in the Appendix.

THEOREM 1: *Under Assumptions* 1 *and* 2, $\sqrt{N}(b_{cN} - \beta_c)$ *is asymptotically normal with the variance matrix* $4 \cdot E^{-1}\nabla_2 \tau \cdot E(\nabla_1 \tau \nabla_1 \tau') \cdot E^{-1}\nabla_2 \tau$,

$$E\nabla_2 \tau = -8 \cdot E[\{w_c - E(w_c|w'\beta)\}\{w_c - E(w_c|w'\beta)\}' \cdot g_0(w'\beta) \cdot \eta(w'\beta)],$$

$$E(\nabla_1 \tau \nabla_1 \tau') = 16 \cdot E\Big[\{w_c - E(w_c|w'\beta)\}\{w_c - E(w_c|w'\beta)\}' \cdot g_0(w'\beta)^2$$
$$\cdot P(z = -1|w'\beta) P(z = 1|w'\beta) \cdot \{P(z = -1|w'\beta) + P(z = 1|w'\beta)\}\Big]$$

where $g_0(\cdot)$ *is a Lebesque density of* $w'\beta$,

$$\eta(w'\beta) \equiv P'(z = 1|w'\beta) \cdot P(z = -1|w'\beta) - P'(z = -1|w'\beta) \cdot P(z = 1|w'\beta),$$

and $P'(z = 1|w'\beta) = dP(z = 1|w'\beta)/d(w'\beta)$.

$E\nabla_2 \tau$ is n.d. because $P'(z = 1|w'\beta) > 0 > P'(z = -1|w'\beta)$ using Assumption 1(e). A consistent estimator for the asymptotic variance can be obtained using nonparametric techniques. The following Assumption 3 implies Assumption 2; the proof is omitted.

ASSUMPTION 3:

(a) *There exists a Lebesque density* $h(w_k|w_c, z)$ *for* $w_k|(w_c, z)$ *that is everywhere positive for a.e.* (w_c', z), *and* $\partial h(w_k|w_c, z)/\partial w_k$ *and* $\partial^2 h(w_k|w_c, z)/\partial w_k^2$ *exist for a.e.* (w_c', z).
(b) $h(w_k|w_c, z)$, $|\partial h(w_k|w_c, z)/\partial w_k|$, *and* $|\partial^2 h(w_k|w_c, z)/\partial w_k^2|$ *are bounded by constants* M_0, M_1, *and* M_2, *respectively, for a.e.* (w_c', z).
(c) $|\partial h(w_k|w_c, z)/\partial w_k| < h(w_k|w_c, z)\zeta_1$ *for a constant* ζ_1 *a.e.* (w_c', z).
(d) $|\partial h^2(w_k|w_c, z)/\partial w_k^2| < h(w_k|w_c, z)\zeta_2$ *for a constant* ζ_2 *a.e.* (w_c', z).
(e) $E|w|^4 < \infty$.

4. CONCLUSIONS

We proposed a semiparametric $\sqrt{N}$-consistent estimator for "related-effect" binary response panel data. The estimator does not depend on a smoothing parameter and is asymptotically normal with a simple asymptotic variance. It is straightforward to extend the estimator to related-effect ordered discrete response panel data.

Institute of Policy and Planning Sciences, University of Tsukuba, Tsukuba, Ibaraki 305, Japan

Manuscript received October, 1995; final revision received January, 1998.

APPENDIX

PROOF OF LEMMA 1: (x_1', x_2') is one-to-one to $(x_{1c}', x_1'\beta, x_{2c}', x_2'\beta)$ which is in turn one-to-one to $(x_{1c}', x_1'\beta, \Delta x_c', \Delta x'\beta)$. Observe

$$\text{(a.1)} \qquad P(\Delta y = 1|x, \alpha) = P(u_1 \langle -x_1'\beta - \alpha, u_2 \rangle - x_1'\beta - \Delta x'\beta - \alpha | x_{1c}', x_1'\beta, \Delta x_c', \Delta x'\beta, \alpha).$$

Under the independence of $(u_1, u_2)|\alpha$ from $(x_1', x_2')|\alpha$, this becomes

$$\text{(a.2)} \qquad P(\Delta y = 1|x_1'\beta, \Delta x'\beta, \alpha) = P(u_1 \langle -x_1'\beta - \alpha, u_2 \rangle - x_1'\beta - \Delta x'\beta - \alpha | x_1'\beta, \Delta x'\beta, \alpha).$$

Integrate (a.1) and (a.2) wrt the distribution of $(x_{1c}', x_1'\beta, \alpha)|(\Delta x_c, \Delta x'\beta)$ and invoke Assumption 1(f) for the integration of (a.2) to get the first part of Lemma 1.

With $C \equiv \{\Delta x_i, \Delta x_j, \Delta y_i \neq 0, \Delta y_j \neq 0, \Delta y_i \neq \Delta y_j\}$, we need to prove

$$\text{(a.3)} \qquad P(\Delta y_i > \Delta y_j|C) > (<)\ P(\Delta y_i < \Delta y_j|C) \quad \text{iff} \quad \Delta x_i'\beta > (<)\ \Delta x_j'\beta.$$

$P(\Delta y_i > \Delta y_j|C)$ is

$$\text{(a.4)} \qquad P(\Delta y_i = 1, \Delta y_j = -1|C)$$
$$= P(\Delta y_i = 1, \Delta y_j = -1, \Delta y_i \neq \Delta y_j | \Delta x_i, \Delta x_j, \Delta y_i \neq 0, \Delta y_j \neq 0)/\pi$$
$$\text{(a.5)} \qquad = P(\Delta y_i = 1|\Delta x_i, \Delta y_i \neq 0) \cdot P(\Delta y_j = -1|\Delta x_j, \Delta y_j \neq 0)/\pi;$$

$\pi = P(\Delta y_i \neq \Delta y_j | \Delta x_i, \Delta x_j, \Delta y_i \neq 0, \Delta y_j \neq 0) > 0$ due to Assumption 1(d). Likewise,

$$\text{(a.6)} \qquad P(\Delta y_i < \Delta y_j|C) = P(\Delta y_i = -1|\Delta x_i, \Delta y_i \neq 0) \cdot P(\Delta y_j = 1|\Delta x_j, \Delta y_j \neq 0)/\pi.$$

Since π appears in both (a.5) and (a.6), it can be ignored. Also instead of comparing (a.5) and (a.6), we can compare

$$\text{(a.7)} \qquad P(\Delta y_i = 1|\Delta x_i) \cdot P(\Delta y_j = -1|\Delta x_j) \quad \text{vs.} \quad P(\Delta y_i = -1|\Delta x_i) \cdot P(\Delta y_j = 1|\Delta x_j)$$

due to $P(\Delta y_i = 1|\Delta x_i, \Delta y_i \neq 0) = P(\Delta y_i = 1|\Delta x_i)/P(\Delta y_i \neq 0|\Delta x_i)$. Furthermore, due to the first part of Lemma 1, we can compare as well

$$\text{(a.8)} \qquad P(\Delta y_i = 1|\Delta x_i'\beta) \cdot P(\Delta y_j = -1|\Delta x_j'\beta) \quad \text{vs.} \quad P(\Delta y_i = -1|\Delta x_i'\beta) \cdot P(\Delta y_j = 1|\Delta x_j'\beta).$$

Owing to Assumption 1(e), (a.3) (and hence (2.6)) holds.

PROOF FOR THEOREM 1: Using $w_k = w'\beta - w_c'\beta_c$, rewrite $\tau(z_j, w_j, b_c)$ as

$$\text{(b.1)} \qquad E_{w|j}[1[w_c'(b_c - \beta_c) + w'\beta > w_{jc}'(b_c - \beta_c) + w_j'\beta] \cdot E(z_j^2 z - z_j z^2|w, z_j)$$
$$- 1[w_c'(b_c - \beta_c) + w'\beta < w_{jc}'(b_c - \beta_c) + w_j'\beta] \cdot E(z_j^2 z - z_j z^2|w, z_j)]$$

$$\text{(b.2)} \qquad = E_{w_c|j}\left[\int_{(w_{jc} - w_c)'(b_c - \beta_c) + w_j'\beta}^{\infty} E(z_j^2 z - z_j z^2|w'\beta, z_j) \cdot g(w'\beta|w_c)\, d(w'\beta)\right.$$
$$\left. - \int_{-\infty}^{(w_{jc} - w_c)'(b_c - \beta_c) + w_j'\beta} E(z_j^2 z - z_j z^2|w'\beta, z_j) \cdot g(w'\beta|w_c)\, d(w'\beta)\right]$$

where $(z - z_j) \cdot z^2 z_j^2 = z_j^2 z - z_j z^2$, $g(\cdot|\cdot)$ is a density for $w'\beta|w_c$ and "$\cdot|j$" means that z_j and w_j are conditioned upon. Differentiating this wrt b_c,

$$\text{(b.3)} \qquad \nabla_1 \tau(z_j, w_j, b_c) = 2 \cdot E_{w_c|j}[E\{z_j^2 z - z_j z^2|(w_{jc} - w_c)'(b_c - \beta_c) + w_j'\beta, z_j\}$$
$$\cdot g\{(w_{jc} - w_c)'(b_c - \beta_c) + w_j'\beta|w_c\} \cdot (w_c - w_{jc})]$$
$$\Rightarrow \nabla_1 \tau(z_j, w_j, \beta_c) = 2 \cdot E_{w_c|j}[E(z_j^2 z - z_j z^2|w_j'\beta, z_j) \cdot g(w_j'\beta|w_c)(w_c - w_{jc})]$$
$$\text{(b.4)} \qquad = 2 \cdot E_{w_c|j}[\{E(z|w_j'\beta) z_j^2 - z_j E(z^2|w_j'\beta)\} \cdot g(w_j'\beta|w_c) w_c]$$
$$\text{(b.5)} \qquad - 2 \cdot E_{w_c|j}[\{E(z|w_j'\beta) z_j^2 - z_j E(z^2|w_j'\beta)\} \cdot g(w_j'\beta|w_c) w_{jc}].$$

In view of $g(w_j'\beta|w_c)\cdot F(dw_c)=F(dw_c|w_j'\beta)\cdot g_0(w_j'\beta)$ where $F(\cdot|\cdot)$ is the distribution function for $w_c|w'\beta$ and $F(\cdot)$ is the distribution function for w_c, $E_{w_c|j}g(w_j'\beta|w_c)=g_0(w_j'\beta)$. Thus rewrite (b.5) as

(b.6) $$-2\cdot\{E(z|w_j'\beta)z_j^2-z_jE(z^2|w_j'\beta)\}\cdot g_0(w_j'\beta)\cdot w_{jc}.$$

Examine (b.4). Multiplying and dividing by $g_0(w_j'\beta)$, the first term is

$$=2z_j^2g_0(w_j'\beta)\cdot E(z|w_j'\beta)\cdot\int w_cg(w_j'\beta|w_c)\,dF(w_c)/g_0(w_j'\beta)$$

$$=2z_j^2g_0(w_j'\beta)E(z|w_j'\beta)\int w_c\,dF(w_c|w_j'\beta)=2z_j^2g_0(w_j'\beta)E(z|w_j'\beta)E(w_c|w_j'\beta).$$

Doing analogously for the second term of (b.4), (b.4) becomes

(b.7) $$2\cdot\{E(z|w_j'\beta)z_j^2-z_jE(z^2|w_j'\beta)\}\cdot g_0(w_j'\beta)\cdot E(w_c|w_j'\beta).$$

Thus, putting (b.6) to (b.7) together, $\nabla_1\tau(z_j,w_j,\beta_c)$ becomes

(b.8) $$-2\cdot\{w_{jc}-E(w_{jc}|w_j'\beta)\}\cdot g_0(w_j'\beta)\cdot\{z_j^2E(z|w_j'\beta)-z_jE(z^2|w_j'\beta)\}.$$

Note that

(b.9) $$E(z|w'\beta)=P(z=1|w'\beta)-P(z=-1|w'\beta)\quad\text{and}\quad E(z^2|w'\beta)=P(z=\pm1|w'\beta).$$

From (b.8) (now drop the subscript j and denote $\{E(\lambda)\}^2$ as $E^2(\lambda)$)

$$E(\nabla_1\tau\nabla_1\tau')=E[4\{g_0(w'\beta)\}^2\cdot\{w_c-E(w_c|w'\beta)\}\{w_c-E(w_c|w'\beta)\}'$$
$$\cdot\{z^2E^2(z|w'\beta)+z^2E^2(z^2|w'\beta)-2zE(z|w'\beta)E(z^2|w'\beta)\}]$$

for z takes only 0 and ±1. Define W, a function of w_c and $w'\beta$, as

$$W\equiv4\{g_0(w'\beta)\}^2\cdot\{w_c-E(w_c|w'\beta)\}\{w_c-E(w_c|w'\beta)\}'.$$

Then, defining $P_{-1}\equiv P(z=-1|w'\beta)$, $P_1\equiv P(z=1|w'\beta)$, and $P_{\pm1}\equiv P_{-1}+P_1$,

(b.10) $$\begin{aligned}E(\nabla_1\tau\nabla_1\tau'|w'\beta)&=E(z^2W|w'\beta)\cdot E^2(z|w'\beta)+E(z^2W|w'\beta)\cdot E^2(z^2|w'\beta)\\&\quad-2E(zW|w'\beta)\cdot E(z|w'\beta)\cdot E(z^2|w'\beta)\\&=E(W|w'\beta)\cdot E(z^2|w'\beta)\cdot E^2(z|w'\beta)+E(W|w'\beta)\cdot E^3(z^2|w'\beta)\\&\quad-2E(W|w'\beta)\cdot E(z^2|w'\beta)\cdot E^2(z|w'\beta)\quad\text{due to Lemma 1}\\&=E(W|w'\beta)\cdot\{E^3(z^2|w'\beta)-E(z^2|w'\beta)\cdot E^2(z|w'\beta)\}\\&=E(W|w'\beta)\cdot\{P_{\pm1}^3-P_{\pm1}(P_1-P_{-1})^2\}=E(W|w'\beta)\cdot4\cdot P_{\pm1}P_1P_{-1}.\end{aligned}$$

Substitute this into $E\{E(\nabla_1\tau\nabla_1\tau'|w'\beta)\}$ to get the desired $E(\nabla_1\tau\nabla_1\tau')$.

Turning to $E\nabla_2\tau$, observe that $\nabla_2\tau(z_j,w_j,b_c)$ is

(b.11) $$\begin{aligned}&-2\cdot E_{w_c|j}[\partial E\{z_j^2z-z_jz^2|w'\beta=(w_{jc}-w_c)'(b_c-\beta_c)+w_j'\beta,z_j\}/\partial(w'\beta)\\&\cdot g\{(w_{jc}-w_c)'(b_c-\beta_c)+w_j'\beta|w_c\}\cdot(w_c-w_{jc})(w_c-w_{jc})'\\&+E\{z_j^2z-z_jz^2|w'\beta=(w_{jc}-w_c)'(b_c-\beta_c)+w_j'\beta,z_j\}\\&\cdot\partial g\{w'\beta=(w_{jc}-w_c)'(b_c-\beta_c)+w_j'\beta|w_c\}/\partial(w'\beta)\cdot(w_c-w_{jc})(w_c-w_{jc})']\end{aligned}$$

(b.12) $$\begin{aligned}&\Rightarrow\nabla_2\tau(z_j,w_j,\beta_c)\\&=-2E_{w_c|j}[\partial E(z_j^2z-z_jz^2|w'\beta=w_j'\beta,z_j)/\partial(w'\beta)\cdot g(w_j'\beta|w_c)\cdot(w_c-w_{jc})(w_c-w_{jc})'\\&\quad+E(z_j^2z-z_jz^2|w_j'\beta,z_j)\cdot\partial g(w'\beta=w_j'\beta|w_c)/\partial(w'\beta)\cdot(w_c-w_{jc})(w_c-w_{jc})'].\end{aligned}$$

Ignore the second term that becomes zero for $E\nabla_2\tau$. The first term is

$$-2\cdot\partial E(z_j^2 z - z_j z^2|w'\beta = w_j'\beta, z_j)/\partial(w'\beta)\cdot E_{w_c|j}\{g(w_j'\beta|w_c)\cdot(w_c - w_{jc})(w_c - w_{jc})'\}.$$

Taking $E_{z_j|w_j'\beta}$ on this, the second term that depends only on $w_j'\beta$ can be taken out of the expectation. As for the first term, we get

(b.13) $$-2\cdot P_{\pm 1}\cdot\partial E(z|w'\beta = w_j'\beta)/\partial(w'\beta) + 2(P_1 - P_{-1})\cdot\partial E(z^2|w'\beta = w_j'\beta)/\partial(w'\beta)$$

(b.14) $$= -2\cdot P_{\pm 1}(P_1' - P_{-1}') + 2\cdot(P_1 - P_{-1})\cdot(P_1' + P_{-1}') = -4\cdot(P_{-1}P_1' - P_1P_{-1}')$$

which is $-4\eta(w_j'\beta)$ where P_m' denotes the derivative, $m = -1, 1$. Hence

(b.15) $$E_{z_j|w_j'\beta}\{(\text{b.12})\} = -4\eta(w_j'\beta)\cdot E_{w_c|j}\{g(w_j'\beta|w_c)\cdot(w_c - w_{jc})(w_c - w_{jc})'\}.$$

Rewrite $E_{w_c|j}\{\cdot\}$ in (b.15) as

(b.16) $$E_{w_c|w_j'\beta}\{g(w_j'\beta|w_c)\cdot(w_cw_c' - w_{jc}w_c' - w_cw_{jc}' + w_{jc}w_{jc}')\}$$

which has four terms. The first term of (b.16) is

(b.17) $$\int w_cw_c'g(w_j'\beta|w_c)\cdot F(dw_c) = g_0(w_j'\beta)\int w_cw_c'g(w_j'\beta|w_c)\cdot F(dw_c)/g_0(w_j'\beta)$$

$$= g_0(w_j'\beta)\cdot\int w_cw_c'F(dw_c|w_j'\beta)$$

$$= g_0(w_j'\beta)\cdot E(w_cw_c'|w_j'\beta).$$

Analogously, the last three terms in (b.16) are respectively

$$-g_0(w_j'\beta)\cdot w_{jc}E(w_c'|w_j'\beta),\quad -g_0(w_j'\beta)\cdot E(w_c|w_j'\beta)w_{jc}',\quad g_0(w_j'\beta)\cdot w_{jc}w_{jc}'.$$

Insert these and (b.17) into (b.15) and take $E_{w_j'\beta}$ on (b.15) to get

(b.18) $$E\nabla_2\tau = -8\cdot E[\eta(w'\beta)g_0(w'\beta)\cdot\{E(w_cw_c'|w'\beta) - E(w_c|w'\beta)E(w_c'|w'\beta)\}],$$

which is the same as $E\nabla_2\tau$ in Theorem 1; 4 in (b.15) is replaced by 8 at this step.

REFERENCES

ARCONES, M. A., Z. CHEN, AND E. GINÉ (1994): "Estimators Related to U-Processes with Applications to Multivariate Medians: Asymptotic Normality," *Annals of Statistics*, 22, 1460–1477.

CHAMBERLAIN, G. (1992): "Binary Response Models for Panel Data: Identification and Information," Harvard Univ., unpublished paper.

CHARLIER, E., B. MELENBERG, AND A. VAN SOEST (1995): "A Smoothed Maximum Score Estimator for the Binary Choice Panel Data Model with an Application to Labor Force Participation," *Statistica Neerlandica*, 49, 324–343.

HOROWITZ, J. (1992): "A Smoothed Maximum Score Estimator for the Binary Response Model," *Econometrica*, 60, 505–531.

KYRIAZIDOU, E. (1997): "Estimation of a Panel Data Sample Selection Model," *Econometrica*, 65, 1335–1364.

MANSKI, C. F. (1985): "Semiparametric Analysis of Discrete Response: Asymptotic Properties of the Maximum Score Estimator," *Journal of Econometrics*, 27, 313–333.

——— (1987): "Semiparametric Analysis of Random Effects Linear Models from Binary Panel Data," *Econometrica*, 55, 357–362.

SHERMAN, R. P. (1993): "The Limiting Distribution of the Maximum Rank Correlation Estimator," *Econometrica*, 61, 123–137.

——— (1994): "Maximal Inequalities for Degenerate U-Processes with Applications to Optimization Estimators," *Annals of Statistics*, 22, 439–459.

[7]

ELSEVIER Journal of Econometrics 90 (1999) 239–263

JOURNAL OF Econometrics

Two-step estimation of panel data models with censored endogenous variables and selection bias

Francis Vella[a], Marno Verbeek[b,*]

[a] *Rutgers University, Department of Economics, New Jersey Hall, New Brunswick, NJ 08903-5055, USA and I.F.S.*

[b] *Center for Economic Studies, K.U. Leuven, Naamsestraat 69, B-3000 Leuven, Belgium and Tilburg University, Tilburg, The Netherlands*

Received 1 February 1996; received in revised form 1 March 1998

Abstract

This paper presents some two-step estimators for a wide range of parametric panel data models with censored endogenous variables and sample selection bias. Our approach is to derive estimates of the unobserved heterogeneity responsible for the endogeneity/selection bias to include as additional explanatory variables in the primary equation. These are obtained through a decomposition of the reduced form residuals. The panel nature of the data allows adjustment, and testing, for two forms of endogeneity and/or sample selection bias. Furthermore, it incorporates roles for dynamics and state dependence in the reduced form. Finally, we provide an empirical illustration which features our procedure and highlights the ability to test several of the underlying assumptions.

JEL classification: C23; C33; C34

Keywords: Two-step estimation; Panel data; Endogenous regressors; Sample selection; Conditional maximum likelihood

1. Introduction

Despite the frequent use of panel data in empirical work there are few suitable estimators for panel data models with sample selection, truncation and limited dependent variables. While maximum likelihood can, under appropriate

* Corresponding author. E-mail: marno.verbeek@econ.kuleuven.ac.be

PII: S0304-4076(98)00043-8

distributional assumptions, provide consistent estimators, its empirical use is hampered by computational complexities such as local maxima and multi-dimensional integrals. This paper proposes some two-step estimators, for a range of parametric panel data models, which avoid these problems. The models comprise a primary equation with an endogeneous explanatory variable, or selection bias, and a reduced form for the endogenous explanator or selection process. Following Heckman (1979), we argue that endogeneity and sample selection bias result from the failure to account for unobserved heterogeneity in the primary equation. We derive estimates of this heterogeneity from the reduced form residuals, to include as additional explanatory variables.

We examine two classes of models. The first is characterized by a primary equation with an uncensored dependent variable and an endogenous censored explanator. This case includes the sample selection model. Given estimates of the reduced form parameters, the primary equation parameters can be estimated by ordinary least squares, based upon a conditional expectation, and we refer to this as *conditional moment estimation*. The second class features a primary equation with a censored dependent variable and an uncensored endogenous explanatory variable. As the primary equation is estimated by maximum likelihood, where the likelihood function corresponds to the conditional density given the endogenous explanatory variable, we assign it an interpretation of *conditional maximum likelihood* (Smith and Blundell, 1986).

Many panel data estimators assume that the endogeneity or selection bias is due to time-invariant individual effects (see, for example, Hausman and Taylor, 1981; Amemiya and MaCurdy, 1986; Honoré, 1992, Honoré, 1993).[1] We, however, also incorporate endogeneity/selectivity through an individual time specific component. This extends cross-sectional estimators (see, for example, Heckman, 1978, Heckman, 1979; Smith and Blundell, 1986; Rivers and Vuong, 1988; Vella, 1993) by separating the individual effects from these individual specific/time effects. We also capture state dependence in the process generating the endogeneity/selection bias. Our approach also encompasses existing panel data procedures for sample selection and attrition bias (see, for example, Ridder, 1990; Nijman and Verbeek, 1992).

Two-step procedures are generally inefficient (see, for example, Newey, 1987) and thus the attraction of our approach, in contrast to maximum likelihood, is its relative computational ease. In some instances, however, our two-step estimator is asymptotically efficient within a limited information framework (LIML). Our method provides initial consistent estimators for a LIML

[1] A recent exception is Kyriazidou (1997) who provides a semi-parametric estimator for the panel data sample selection model in which the selection bias also operates through time-varying effects.

approach so that asymptotically efficient estimators can be obtained in one iteration.[2]

The following two sections consider conditional moment and conditional maximum likelihood estimation, respectively. Section 4 presents an empirical example, featuring the wage–hours relationship, which illustrates a non-conventional form of sample selection bias where the endogenous explanatory variable, which is also the basis of the selection rule, enters the conditional mean non-linearly. This empirical example illustrates our procedure and highlights how many of our assumptions can be tested. Concluding comments are contained in Section 5.

2. Conditional moment estimation

Consider the following model where the parameters of Eq. (1) are of primary focus while Eq. (2) is the reduced form for the explanatory variable which is endogenous and/or the basis of the selection rule. The censoring and selection rules are in Eqs. (3) and (4):

$$y_{it}^* = m_1(x_{it}, z_{it}; \theta_1) + \mu_i + \eta_{it}, \tag{1}$$

$$z_{it}^* = m_2(x_{it}, z_{i,t-1}; \theta_2) + \alpha_i + v_{it}, \tag{2}$$

$$z_{it} = h(z_{it}^*; \theta_3), \tag{3}$$

$$\begin{aligned} y_{it} &= y_{it}^* \quad \text{if } g_t(z_{i1}, \ldots, z_{iT}) = 1, \\ &= 0 \text{ (unobserved)} \quad \text{if } g_t(z_{i1}, \ldots, z_{iT}) = 0, \end{aligned} \tag{4}$$

where i indexes individuals ($i = 1, \ldots, N$) and t indexes time ($t = 1, \ldots, T$); y_{it}^* and z_{it}^* are latent endogenous variables with observed counterparts y_{it} and z_{it}; m_1 and m_2 denote general functions characterized by the unknown parameters in θ_1 and θ_2, respectively. This allows a non-linear relationship between z_{it} and y_{it}^*. The mapping from the latent to the observed form is through the censoring functions h and g_t noting that the former may depend on the unknown parameter vector θ_3. The function g_t indicates that y_{it} is only observed for certain values of $z_{i1}, \ldots, z_{iT}$. This includes sample selection where y_{it} is only observed if, for example, $z_{it} = 1$ or, alternatively in the balanced subsample case, if $z_{i1} = \cdots = z_{iT} = 1$.

The equations' errors comprise random individual effects, μ_i and α_i, and random individual specific time effects, η_{it} and v_{it}, which are assumed to be

[2] A potentially computationally attractive alternative is simulate maximum likelihood, in which the integrals in the log-likelihood function are replaced by simulators (see Gourieroux and Monfort, 1993). Nevertheless, the use of consistent starting values reduces computational costs substantially.

independent across individuals. Denote $\varepsilon_{it} = \mu_i + \eta_{it}$; $u_{it} = \alpha_i + v_{it}$; and u_i as the T vector of u_{it}'s for individual i. Writing $X_i = [x_{i1}, \ldots, x_{iT}]'$, we assume

$$u_i|_{X_i} \sim N.I.D.(0, \sigma_\alpha^2 \iota\iota' + \sigma_v^2 I), \tag{5}$$

$$E\{\varepsilon_{it} | X_i, u_i\} = \tau_1 u_{it} + \tau_2 \bar{u}_i, \tag{6}$$

where ι is a T vector of ones; $\bar{u}_i = T^{-1}\sum_{t=1}^{T} u_{it}$; and τ_1 and τ_2 are unknown constants. Eq. (5) imposes normality and a strict error components structure on the reduced form and excludes any form of autocorrelation in v_{it}. Eq. (6) allows for heteroskedasticity and autocorrelation in η_{it} but imposes the strict exogeneity of x_{it}.

The model features a potential role for state dependence in the reduced form. This ensures that the error components do not incorrectly capture the dynamics which should be attributed to lagged dependent variables. Unfortunately, we are unable to incorporate dynamics operating through the lagged dependent variable in the primary equation.[3] To estimate this model we first consider condition (1) on the T vector of outcomes, $z_i = (z_{i1}, \ldots, z_{iT})'$, and $g_t(z_i) = 1$, to get

$$E\{y_{it} | X_i, z_{i0}, z_i\} = m_1(x_{it}, z_{it}, \theta_1) + E\{\varepsilon_{it} | X_i, z_{i0}, z_i\}. \tag{7}$$

If m_2 does not depend on $z_{i,t-1}$, and sample selection only depends on the current z_{it}, it is possible to condition upon z_{it} only, rather than z_i, and base estimators on the corresponding conditional moments (see Wooldridge, 1995). In this case z_{i0} drops from the conditioning set.

Eq. (6) implies that the conditional expectation of ε_{it} in Eq. (7) is a linear function of the conditional expectation of u_{it}. To derive this latter expectation we use:

$$E\{u_{it} | X_i, z_{i0}, z_i\} = \int [\alpha_i + E\{v_{it} | X_i, z_{i0}, z_i, \alpha_i\}] f(\alpha_i | X_i, z_{i0}, z_i)\, d\alpha_i, \tag{8}$$

where $f(\alpha_i | X_i, z_{i0}, z_i)$ denotes the conditional density of α_i. The conditional expectation of v_{it} given X_i, z_{i0}, z_i and α_i is the cross-sectional generalized residual (see Gourieroux et al., 1987) from Eq. (2) as, conditional on α_i, the errors from Eq. (2) are independent across observations. The conditional distribution of α_i can be derived using the result[4]

$$f(\alpha_i | X_i, z_{i0}, z_i) = \frac{f(z_i, z_{i0} | X_i, \alpha_i) f(\alpha_i)}{f(z_i, z_{i0} | X_i)}, \tag{9}$$

[3] Arellano et al. (1997) present an estimator that allows for the lagged *latent* dependent variables to enter both equations linearly. This approach is restricted to models with tobit types of censoring.

[4] We use $f(.)$ as generic notation for any density/mass function.

where we have used that α_i is independent of X_i and

$$f(z_i, z_{i0} \mid X_i) = \int f(z_i, z_{i0} \mid X_i, \alpha_i) f(\alpha_i)\, d\alpha_i \tag{10}$$

is the likelihood contribution of individual i in Eq. (2). Finally,

$$f(z_i, z_{i0} \mid X_i, \alpha_i) = \left[\prod_{t=1}^{T} f(z_{it} \mid X_i, z_{i,t-1}, \alpha_i) \right] f(z_{i0} \mid X_i, \alpha_i), \tag{11}$$

where $f(z_{it} \mid X_i, z_{i,t-1}, \alpha_i)$ has the form of the likelihood contribution in the cross-sectional case.

If we assume that $f(z_{i0} \mid X_i, \alpha_i)$ does not depend upon α_i and any of the other error components, z_{i0} is strictly exogenous and $f(z_{i0} \mid X_i, \alpha_i) = f(z_{i0} \mid X_i)$. Thus we can condition upon z_{i0} in Eqs. (10) and (11) and obtain valid inferences neglecting its distribution. In general, however, we require an expression for the distribution of the initial value conditional on the exogenous variables and α_i. For most applications, the only practical solution will be a methodology, suggested by Heckman (1981) for the random effects probit model, in which the reduced form for z_{i0} is approximated using all pre-sample information on the exogenous variables. Apart from its dependence upon the unobserved component α_i, the specification of $f(z_{i0}|X_i, \alpha_i)$ can be tested separately from the rest of the model (see Labeaga, 1996).

The unknown parameters in Eq. (2) can be estimated consistently by maximum likelihood under the usual regularity conditions. With these values we can estimate Eq. (8), which requires an expression for the likelihood contribution in an i.i.d. context, the corresponding generalized residual, and the numerical evaluation of two one-dimensional integrals.[5] The estimate of Eq. (8) and its average over time provide two additional terms to be included in the primary equation, with coefficients τ_1 and τ_2. These parameters can be estimated jointly with θ_1 in the second step from conditional moment restrictions such as least squares based on Eq. (7). Under the null hypothesis of no endogeneity $\tau_1 = \tau_2 = 0$ standard errors can be computed in the usual way. Consequently, the standard Wald test of the significance of the additional terms is an endogeneity test. In general, standard errors should be adjusted for heteroskedasticity, autocorrelation, and for the estimation of the correction terms. This is discussed in Appendix A. In the sample selection model the second step is estimated using the subsample based upon $g_t(z_i) = 1$ and the t-statistics on the correction terms provide tests for sample selection bias.

[5] Evaluation of these integrals is straightforward using, for example, results from Butler and Moffitt (1982).

The model, in theory, can be estimated by maximum likelihood if we complement Eqs. (5) and (6) with additional distributional assumptions. If all error components are assumed to be homoskedastic and jointly normal, excluding autocorrelation in the time-varying components, it follows that Eq. (6) holds with $\tau_1 = \sigma_{\eta v}/\sigma_\eta^2$ and $\tau_2 = T(\sigma_{\mu\alpha} - \sigma_{\eta v}\sigma_\alpha^2/\sigma_\eta^2)/(\sigma_v^2 + T\sigma_\alpha^2)$, where $\sigma_{\eta v}$ and $\sigma_{\mu\alpha}$ denote the covariances between the corresponding terms. This shows that τ_2 is non-zero even when the individual effects α_i and μ_i are uncorrelated. In contrast, the two-step approach readily allows for heteroskedasticity and autocorrelation in the primary equation. Moreover, the assumption in Eq. (6) can easily be relaxed to, for example,

$$\mathrm{E}\{\varepsilon_{it} \mid u_i\} = \lambda_{1t}u_{i1} + \lambda_{2t}u_{i2} + \cdots + \lambda_{Tt}u_{iT}. \tag{12}$$

By altering Eq. (6) our approach can be extended to multiple endogenous regressors or sample selection rules. With two endogenous variables, $z_{1,it}$ and $z_{2,it}$, say, with reduced form errors $u_{1,it}$ and $u_{2,it}$, respectively, Eq. (6) is replaced by

$$\mathrm{E}\{\varepsilon_{it} \mid u_{1,i}, u_{2,i}\} = \tau_{11}u_{1,it} + \tau_{12}\bar{u}_{1,i} + \tau_{21}u_{2,it} + \tau_{22}\bar{u}_{2,i}. \tag{13}$$

Computation of the generalized residuals, however, now requires the evaluation of $\mathrm{E}\{u_{j,it} \mid X_i, z_{1,i}, z_{2,i}\}$ for $j = 1, 2$. Unless $z_{1,i}$ and $z_{2,i}$ are independent, conditional upon X_i, the required expressions are different from those obtained from Eqs. (8) and (9) and generally involve multi-dimensional numerical integration.

Many of the above assumptions can be tested empirically. While relaxing normality in the reduced form is computationally difficult, except in special cases for the h function, it is possible to test for departures from normality. It is also possible to test for serial correlation and heteroskedasticity using conditional moment tests. Also, we assume that the variables in X_i are strictly exogenous. This assumption excludes lagged dependent variables in the primary equation as well as feedback from lagged values of y to current x's. If components of X_i are not strictly exogenous they should be included in z and excluded from the reduced form. The conditional moment restriction given in Eq. (7) would typically then be changed to

$$\mathrm{E}\{(y_{it} - \mathrm{E}\{y_{it} \mid X_i, z_i, z_{io}\})\zeta(x_{it}, z_{it})\} = 0 \tag{14}$$

for a vectorial instrument function ζ, depending upon the functional form of m_1. Consequently, strict exogeneity of x_{it} could be tested through, for example, the following moment condition:

$$\mathrm{E}\{(y_{it} - \mathrm{E}\{y_{it} \mid X_i, z_i, z_{io}\})x_{i,t+1}\} = 0. \tag{15}$$

That is, if the last period's values of y influence current x's the strict exogeneity condition would be violated.

An important issue is identification. As in the standard non-linear regression model we require that the matrix of first derivatives of m_j with respect to θ_j, evaluated at the observation points, has full column rank ($j = 1,2$). Then, non-linearities in m_1 or m_2, or a non-linear mapping from the reduced form variables to the correction terms will identify the model. However, in instances where we do not wish to rely on such an identification scheme we need an exclusion restriction in m_1 for every endogenous variable. If the endogeneity is restricted to the time-invariant component ($\tau_1 = 0$) no exclusion restrictions are required as, in the spirit of Hausman and Taylor (1981), the time variation in the exogenous regressors is exploited.

The contribution of our approach is the following. First, it extends many available cross-sectional estimators (see, for example Heckman, 1978; Heckman, 1979; Vella, 1993) by exploiting the panel nature of the data to isolate the form of heterogeneity responsible for the endogeneity/selection bias. Second, while our treatment of the sample selection model is not new (see Ridder, 1990; Nijman and Verbeek, 1992), we generalize it to a wide range of selection rules. We also extend the panel data dummy endogenous regressor model in Vella and Verbeek (1998) by allowing for other forms of censored endogenous regressors. Finally, our estimator represents first attempt to introduce dynamics into panel data models involving general forms of sample selection and/or censored endogenous regressors. This is particularly important as it exploits the panel nature of the data and enables isolation of the individual effects from state dependence.

Our analysis also indicates how the estimation procedures proposed by Wooldridge (1995) for the sample selection model, can be applied to more general specifications. For example, one can estimate the primary equation while allowing for fixed individual effects. This relaxes Eq. (6) to

$$E\{\varepsilon_{it} \mid X_i, u_i\} = \tau u_{it} + \xi_i, \tag{16}$$

for some ξ_i which may be a function of X_i. If $E\{u_{it} \mid X_i, z_{i0}, z_i\} = u_{it}$, as for tobit-type sample selection rules, the resulting two-step estimator is essentially the same as that in Wooldridge (1995).[6] Wooldridge also considers assumptions of the form

$$E\{\varepsilon_{it} \mid X_i, u_{it}\} = \tau_t u_{it} + X_i \psi. \tag{17}$$

As the conditioning set in Eq. (17) is smaller than in Eq. (16), u_{it} is no longer strictly exogenous in the second step and using a fixed effects or GLS estimator is generally inconsistent (for fixed T). Thus a correlated random effects approach (see Chamberlain, 1980) is required where the second step would include all

[6] Wooldridge only imposes that $u_{it} \mid X_i \sim N.I.D.(0, \sigma_t^2)$ for each t, leaving the temporal dependence in u_{it} unrestricted. The reduced form is estimated cross-section by cross-section. Clearly, this does not allow for dynamics in the reduced form specification.

exogenous variables from all periods as additional regressors. While Wooldridge restricts attention to sample selection models with tobit- or probit-type censoring, the approach would be more generally valid. For general h functions, $E\{u_{it} | X_i, z_{it}\}$ is the cross-sectional generalized residual from the reduced form model, which can be included as additional regressor. Note that the assumption in Eq. (17) excludes cases where attention is restricted to a balanced sub-panel of the original data (the conditioning set is larger than z_{it}), and when lagged dependent variables appear in the reduced form.

Arellano et al. (1997) also discuss estimation of panel data models which allow for lagged latent dependent variables in both equations, though only in a linear additive way. They derive orthogonality conditions, based on first-differencing the primary equation, that can be exploited in estimation provided there exist subsets of the data for which the latent variables are observed. Obviously, this seriously restricts the form of the censoring function h, and the functions m_1 and m_2.

3. Conditional maximum-likelihood estimation

We now consider where the dependent variable in the primary equation is censored while the endogenous explanatory variable is fully observed. The model has the following general form:

$$y_{it}^* = m_1(x_{it}, z_{it}; \theta_1) + \mu_i + \eta_{it}, \tag{18}$$

$$z_{it}^* = m_2(x_{it}, z_{i,t-1}; \theta_2) + \alpha_i + v_{it}, \tag{19}$$

$$y_{it} = h(y_{it}^*; \theta_3), \tag{20}$$

$$z_{it} = z_{it}^*, \tag{21}$$

where h is a function mapping the latent y_{it}^* into the observed y_{it}. The assumptions on the unobservables are stronger than before and given by

$$\begin{pmatrix} \mu_i\iota + \eta_i \\ \alpha_i\iota + v_i \end{pmatrix}\Bigg|_{X_i} \sim N.I.D.\left(\begin{pmatrix} 0 \\ 0 \end{pmatrix}, \begin{pmatrix} \sigma_\mu^2 \iota\iota' + \sigma_\eta^2 I & \sigma_{\mu\alpha}\iota\iota' + \sigma_{\eta v} I \\ & \sigma_\alpha^2 \iota\iota' + \sigma_v^2 I \end{pmatrix}\right) \tag{22}$$

which implies Eq. (6) with $\tau_1 = \sigma_{\eta v}/\sigma_\eta^2$ and $\tau_2 = T(\sigma_{\mu\alpha} - \sigma_{\eta v}\sigma_\alpha^2/\sigma_\eta^2)/(\sigma_v^2/T\sigma_\alpha^2)$.

When $y_{it} \neq y_{it}^*$ the model's parameters cannot be estimated by exploiting the conditional expectations of the random components only and the conditional moment approach is not applicable. However, as the endogenous explanator is fully observed the conditional distribution of the error terms in Eq. (18) given z_i is still normal and the error components structure is preserved. Thus we can estimate the model in Eqs. (18) and (20) conditional on the estimated parameters from Eq. (19) using the random effects likelihood function, after making appropriate adjustments for the mean and noting that the variances now reflect the conditional variances.

Write the joint density of $y_i = (y_{i1}, \ldots, y_{iT})'$ and z_i given X_i as[7]

$$f(y_i \mid z_i, X_i; \theta^{(1)}, \theta^{(2)}) f(z_i \mid X_i; \theta^{(2)}), \tag{23}$$

where $\theta^{(1)}$ denotes $(\theta_1, \theta_3, \sigma_\mu^2, \sigma_\eta^2, \sigma_{\mu\alpha}, \sigma_{\eta v})$ and $\theta^{(2)}$ denotes $(\theta_2, \sigma_\alpha^2, \sigma_v^2)$. We first estimate $\theta^{(2)}$ by maximizing the marginal likelihood function of the z_i's. Subsequently, the conditional likelihood function

$$\prod_i f(y_i \mid z_i, X_i; \theta^{(1)}, \hat{\theta}^{(2)}) \tag{24}$$

is maximized with respect to $\theta^{(1)}$. The conditional distribution of y_i given z_i is multivariate normal with an error components structure. The conditional expectation can be derived directly from Eq. (6), substituting $u_{it} = z_{it} - m_2(x_{it}, z_{i,t-1}; \theta_2)$, while the covariance structure corresponds to that of $v_{1i} + v_{2,it}$, where v_{1i} and $v_{2,it}$ are zero mean normal variables with zero covariance and variances

$$\sigma_1^2 := V\{v_{1i}\} = \sigma_\eta^2 - \sigma_{\eta v}^2 \sigma_v^{-2}, \tag{25}$$

$$\sigma_2^2 := V\{v_{2,it}\} = \sigma_\mu^2 - \frac{T\sigma_{\mu\alpha}^2\sigma_v^2 + 2\sigma_{\mu\alpha}\sigma_{\eta v}\sigma_v^2 - \sigma_{\eta v}^2\sigma_\alpha^2}{\sigma_v^2(\sigma_v^2 + T\sigma_\alpha^2)}. \tag{26}$$

These follow from straightforward matrix manipulations and show that the error components structure is preserved and the conditional likelihood function of Eqs. (18) and (20) has the same form as the marginal likelihood function without endogenous explanatory variables.[8] The asymptotic variance of the conditional ML estimator, and the efficiency loss compared to the LIML estimator, is provided in Appendix A.

The conditional maximum likelihood estimator can be easily extended to account for multiple endogenous variables. For two endogenous regressors, for example, this implies the imposition of Eq. (13), the conditional expectation of which is easily obtained as all endogenous regressors are continuously observed. Even if the reduced form errors of the endogenous regressors are correlated,

[7] When Eq. (19) is dynamic with an exogenous initial value z_{i0}, Eq. (23) is valid if z_{i0} is included in X_i. When the initial value is endogenous, we need to include z_{i0} in z_i.

[8] The algebraic manipulations are simplified if σ_1^2 and σ_2^2 replace the unconditional variances σ_η^2 and σ_μ^2 in $\theta^{(1)}$. In this case, estimates for the latter two variances are easily obtained in a third step from the estimates from the first stage for σ_v^2 and σ_α^2, and the estimated covariances from the mean function, using the equalities in Eqs. (25) and (26).

provided they are characterized by an error components structure it can be shown that the conditional distribution of $\mu_i + \eta_{it}$ also has an error components structure. Time-specific heteroskedasticity in η_{it} does not affect the conditional expectations and can be incorporated by having σ_1^2 vary over time. The model can also be estimated, along the lines suggested above, over subsets of the data chosen on the basis of z_{it}.

In general the conditional maximum-likelihood estimator cannot be employed when $z_{it} \neq z_{it}^*$. Thus the family of sample selection models considered in the conditional moment section cannot be estimated by conditional maximum likelihood. One exception is when the primary equation is estimated over the subsample of individuals that have $z_{is} = z_{is}^*$, for all $s = 1, \ldots, T$.[9] This follows from the result that the error components structure is preserved when the reduced form dependent variables are observed.

Once again it is important to consider identification. In these models there is no non-linearity induced in the correction terms, but the non-linearity of m_1 or m_2 will identify the model. In the linear case, or if one does not want to rely on non-linearities for identification, exclusion restrictions are required. More explicitly, for each endogenous explanatory variable we need one exclusion restriction in the primary equation, unless, as before, the endogeneity can be restricted to be related to the time-invariant components only ($\sigma_{\eta v} = 0$).

This conditional maximum-likelihood approach generalizes the cross-sectional estimators of Smith and Blundell (1986) and Rivers and Vuong (1988) to panel data. As in the previous section the use of panel data allows the separation of the error into two components and the incorporation of dynamics in the reduced form. By excluding dynamics and assuming that there is a single-error component one obtains the models considered by Smith and Blundell (1986) and Rivers and Vuong (1988) as special cases.

4. Empirical example

We now provide an empirical example estimating the impact of weekly hours worked on the offered hourly wage rate while accounting for the endogeneity of hours. This issue has attracted attention in the labor economics literature (see, for example, Moffitt, 1984; and Biddle and Zarkin, 1989). The model has the form

$$w_{it} = x'_{1,it}\beta_1 + x'_{2,it}\beta_2 + m(\text{hours}_{it}; \beta_3) + \mu_i + \eta_{it}, \tag{27}$$

$$\text{hours}^*_{it} = x'_{3,it}\theta_1 + \text{hours}_{i,t-1}\theta_2 + \alpha_i + v_{it}, \tag{28}$$

[9] A similar argument is exploited in Arellano et al. (1997).

$$\text{hours}_{it} = \text{hours}^*_{it} \quad \text{if hours}^*_{it} > 0, \tag{29}$$

$$\text{hours}_{it} = 0,\ w_{it} \text{ not observed if hours}^*_{it} \leqslant 0,$$

where w_{it} represents the log of the hourly wage of individual i in time period t; $x_{1,it}$ and $x_{3,it}$ are variables representing individual characteristics; $x_{2,it}$ are characteristics of the individual's work place; hours^*_{it} and hours_{it} represent desired and observed number of hours worked, respectively; m denotes a polynomial of known length with unknown coefficients β_3, while $\beta' = (\beta'_1, \beta'_2, \beta'_3)$ and $\theta' = (\theta'_1, \theta'_2)$ are parameters to be estimated. The assumptions on the unobservables are given in Eqs. (5) and (6) above. This example highlights several aspects of our approach. First, as the wage equation is estimated over the sub-sample reporting positive hours it illustrates our ability to control for selection bias. Second, the inclusion of the correction terms enables the identification of the form of the endogeneity while their inclusion also corrects for the endogeneity of experience via past labor supply. Finally, the inclusion of a lagged dependent variable in the reduced form isolates the role of dynamics and state dependence.

Note that the model is not easily estimated by existing procedures. First, as the wage equation is only estimated over those reporting positive hours it is not possible to use instrumental variables. Second, as the reduced form includes a role for dynamics it is not appropriate to employ cross-sectional procedures nor apply panel data estimators which ignore the presence of state dependence. Third, as the primary equation is non-linear in hours, the approach of Arellano et al. (1997) cannot be employed. Fourth, even with stronger distributional assumptions (as given in Eq. (22)), non-linearities due to both the sample selection problem and the non-linear appearance of hours in the wage equation, substantially complicate analytical expressions for the joint likelihood function (see Davidson and Mackinnon, 1993, Section 18.7). As two-dimensional numerical integrals are involved, maximum likelihood does not appear to be a viable approach. Moreover, the number of parameters in our most general specification equals 79, so that the risk of computational problems will be high for any one-step procedure.

To estimate the model we employ data for young females from the National Longitudinal Survey (Youth Sample) for the period 1980–1987. For the period examined there were 2300 observations for each of the eight years. From these 18,400 total observations there were 12,039 observations reporting positive hours of work in a given period.[10] The summary statistics are reported in Table 1.

[10] Only 481 women report positive hours of work over all eight years.

Table 1
Variable definitions and means

SCHOOL	Years of schooling	11.91	1.55	11.67
HISP	Dummy, 1 if hispanic	0.126	0.331	0.132
BLACK	Dummy, 1 if black	0.189	0.189	0.208
AGE	Age in years	24.08	2.73	23.89
MAR	Dummy, 1 if married	0.386	0.487	0.415
WAGE	Log of real hourly wage	1.285	0.640	—
EXPER	Actual exp. in yr.	5.22	2.45	4.95
EX2	Actual exp. squared	33.27	29.09	30.33
HLTH	Dummy, 1 if health disability	0.038	0.191	0.047
HOURS	Hours of work per week	33.98	11.82	—
UNION	Dummy, 1 if wage set by collective bargaining	0.168	0.374	—
RUR	Dummy, 1 if rural area	0.181	0.385	0.192
S	Dummy, 1 if lives in South	0.370	0.483	0.370
NC	Dummy, 1 if Northern Central	0.240	0.427	0.248
NE	Dummy, 1 if North East	0.204	0.403	0.187
Industry dummies				
PUB	Public sector	0.048	0.215	—
AG	Agricultural	0.008	0.087	—
MIN	Mining	0.003	0.057	—
CON	Construction	0.008	0.087	—
MAN	Manufacturing	0.159	0.366	—
TRA	Transportation	0.040	0.195	—
TRAD	Trade	0.237	0.425	—
FIN	Finance	0.097	0.296	—
BUS	Business and repair service	0.045	0.206	—
PER	Personal service	0.061	0.240	—
ENT	Entertainment	0.013	0.115	—
PRO	Professional and related services	0.281	0.450	—

Note: Averages in column 3 are based on observations over 2300 women over eight years (1980–1987); averages and standard deviations in columns 1 and 2 are for the subsample of observations with positive hours only (12,039 cases).

We estimate three variants of the random effects tobit model in Eq. (28). To highlight the differences which may arise from misspecifying the dynamics we estimate the model with and without the lagged dependent variable. Given the presence of the individual effects α_i it is unlikely that one can validly assume that hours worked in the first period are truly exogenous. Therefore, the dynamic model is estimated either treating initial hours worked as exogenous, which ignores the initial conditions problem, or modelling the initial value in the spirit of Heckman (1981). For this last approach, we approximated the reduced form for hours_{io} by a tobit function using all pre-sample information on the exogenous variables.[11] The results of all three specifications are presented in Table 2. Column 1 represents the specification without the lagged dependent variable while Columns 2 and 3 include it. The specification does not include any work-related variables as these characteristics are not recorded for the non-participants and their inclusion, while assigning values of zero for the non-participants, would produce a spurious statistical relationship between these characteristics and hours of work.

Several points are worth noting. First, the parameter estimates in all columns are generally in keeping with expectations and most variables have a statistically significant impact on hours worked. Second, the impact of lagged hours of work, in Columns 2 and 3, is highly significant and indicates the presence of 'state' dependence. The inclusion of this variable has a relatively small impact on the coefficients of the other variables although it generally reduces their magnitude. This is expected as their effect now partially operates through lagged hours. Third, the coefficients on the time dummies indicate an increasing trend in hours worked over the period examined in both specifications. Comparing the columns with the exogenous [A] and endogenous [B] treatment of the initial value, we see that exogeneity of initial hours of work is strongly rejected. The parameter ξ measures to what extent the individual-specific heterogeneity enters the initial equation's error, given by $\xi\alpha_i + v_{i0}$, and does not differ significantly from unity. We found no statistical evidence that ξ varies with age.[12] Despite the rejection of exogeneity, the estimates of the tobit coefficients do not appear to be very sensitive with respect to the treatment of the initial condition. A final point is related to the contribution of the error components to the total variance. The model which omits a lagged dependent variable attributes approximately 39% of the total variance to the individual effects. The specifications in columns 2 and 3, where the contribution of the individual effects reduces to approximately 13 percent, indicate that this may be due to the failure to account for dynamics.

We noted above that many of the assumptions of the model are testable. The first we consider is normality of the two error components. We test this via Lagrange Multiplier tests using a parameterization suggested by Ruud (1984). Unfortunately, these tests reject normality of both the individual specific component and the idiosyncratic component for each of the specifications.[13] This is

[11] More details of treatment of the initial value are provided in Appendix B. The estimation results for the initial period are not presented here.

[12] A likelihood ratio test against the alternative that ξ is a linear function of age produced a test statistic of 0.02.

[13] The LM test statistics (χ^2_2) for testing normality of α_i and η_{it} in Column 3 are 119.52 and 535.28, respectively. For Column 2 they are 244.64 and 436.60, while the corresponding values for the Column 1 specification are 297.6 and 814.5.

Table 2
Maximum likelihood estimation results hours of work equation

		Dynamic model	
Variable	Static model	[A]	[B]
Dummy 1981	1.816	4.549	4.483
	(0.777)	(0.646)	(0.650)
Dummy 1982	1.697	3.457	3.436
	(0.845)	(0.736)	(0.739)
Dummy 1983	3.807	5.505	5.476
	(1.017)	(0.817)	(0.822)
Dummy 1984	6.561	7.205	7.238
	(1.241)	(0.923)	(0.931)
Dummy 1985	8.592	8.029	8.124
	(1.475)	(1.036)	(1.047)
Dummy 1986	11.849	10.300	10.418
	(1.679)	(1.121)	(1.136)
Dummy 1987	14.313	11.016	11.188
	(1.922)	(1.245)	(1.268)
Age	13.368	6.073	6.297
	(0.796)	(0.988)	(0.982)
Age-squared	− 0.291	− 0.139	− 0.143
	(0.015)	(0.020)	(0.020)
Married	− 5.682	− 4.737	− 4.946
	(0.384)	(0.398)	(0.396)
Black	− 6.419	− 4.016	− 4.154
	(0.940)	(0.578)	(0.591)
Hispanic	− 0.510	− 0.349	− 0.350
	(1.113)	(0.679)	(0.694)
Rural	− 1.893	− 1.289	− 1.434
	(0.534)	(0.495)	(0.493)
Health	− 3.870	− 4.760	− 4.783
	(0.285)	(0.752)	(0.749)
School	4.172	2.481	2.546
	(0.285)	(0.168)	(0.172)
Lagged hours	—	0.616	0.594
		(0.014)	(0.013)
σ_α^2	259.09	55.406	60.81
	(12.36)	(4.53)	(4.74)
σ_v^2	402.87	398.32	395.51
	(4.93)	(5.78)	(5.69)
ξ		0	0.939
			(0.099)
Loglikelihood	− 59,856.13	− 58,731.91	
with initial period		− 66,074.19	− 66,019.24

Note: Models also include regional dummies. Dynamic Model [A] assumes exogenous initial labor supply, while [B] employs a specification for the initial distribution.

not surprising given the large number of observations. However, as this example is primarily illustrative we continue despite this rejection.

Before focusing on the primary equation consider our exclusion restrictions. First, given the form of the correction terms we are unable to estimate the model unless we exclude at least one variable from the wage equation which appears in the hours equation. The variables we employ are the health measure and lagged hours. Health is excluded on the basis that while health will influence one's ability to seek employment it is increasingly difficult for employers to offer different wage levels on the basis of an individual's health. The lagged hours variable is excluded on the basis that we believe that the variable has no direct effect but rather operates through its impact on current hours. As this implies that the model is overidentified, we can test this latter restriction.

We estimate the wage equation for the subsample of working women, specifying m as a fourth order polynomial. The order of the polynomial is guided by the results of Newey et al. (1998) which provides a semi-parametric estimate of the wage/hours profile. Using this result as a starting point we were unable to identify a dominating alternative specification. The OLS results reported in Column 1 of Table 3, without corrections for the potential endogeneity of hours, reveal a significant non-linear relationship between the number of weekly hours worked and the weekly wage rate. The remaining coefficients in this column are reasonable in sign and magnitude although the coefficient reflecting the returns to schooling is rather high. As it is well known that wage inequality increased over this period it is likely that the error terms are heteroskedastic. The estimated standard errors in Table 3 allow for unknown forms of time-related heteroskedasticity.

Column 2 of Table 3 reports the results from estimating the wage equation while correcting for the endogeneity of hours and sample selection through the inclusion of correction terms based upon the static hours model. The results in Columns 3 and 4 incorporate a role for dynamics in the reduced form hours equation, treating the initial value as exogeneous or endogeneous, respectively. The inclusion of the correction terms simultaneously accounts for the endogeneity of the participation decision and hours worked. As the decision to not participate corresponds to a zero value for hours_{it}, the inclusion of the correction terms also account for the selection bias from estimating over the subsample of workers.

A number of features are worth noting from a comparison of the unadjusted estimates, in Column 1, to those from our preferred specification in Column 4.[14] Both correction terms are statistically significant indicating that the two forms

[14] We refer to the specification in Column 4 as preferred in spite of the evidence of non-normality in the reduced form. We choose this specification on the basis of the statistically significant role of lagged hours and the strong rejection of exogeneity of the initial value.

Table 3
Wage equation results

Method	OLS	OLS	OLS	OLS
Correction	No	Yes	Yes	Yes
Hours equation	—	Static	Dynamic	Dynamic
Initial value	—	—	Exogenous	Endogenous
Married	− 0.018	0.043	0.017	0.025
	(0.011)	(0.018)	(0.011)	(0.011)
Black	− 0.147	− 0.103	− 0.133	− 0.124
	(0.015)	(0.022)	(0.015)	(0.015)
Hispanic	− 0.029	− 0.024	− 0.024	− 0.023
	(0.017)	(0.017)	(0.017)	(0.017)
Rural	− 0.116	− 0.102	− 0.111	− 0.109
	(0.014)	(0.015)	(0.014)	(0.04)
School	0.096	0.064	0.080	0.076
	(0.004)	(0.010)	(0.004)	(0.004)
Union	0.116	0.120	0.118	0.118
	(0.013)	(0.013)	(0.013)	(0.013)
Exper	0.037	0.009	− 0.009	− 0.010
	(0.009)	(0.009)	(0.009)	(0.009)
Exper2	− 0.0010	− 0.0005	0.0004	0.0006
	(0.0007)	(0.0007)	(0.0007)	(0.0007)
Hours/100	− 5.062	− 4.130	− 4.474	− 4.334
	(1.378)	(1.379)	(1.360)	(1.360)
$(\text{Hours}/100)^2$	31.925	30.509	30.296	30.206
	(6.118)	(6.017)	(6.000)	(6.006)
$(\text{Hours}/100)^3$	− 61.275	− 58.647	− 58.780	− 58.672
	(10.986)	(10.755)	(10.710)	(10.720)
$(\text{Hours}/100)^4$	34 586	33.383	33.742	33.688
	(6.835)	(6.658)	(6.621)	(6.627)
u_{it}	—	− 0.0121	− 0.0084	− 0.0095
		(0.0022)	(0.0006)	(0.0006)
$\bar{u}_i$	—	− 0.0016	0.0145	0.0109
		(0.0087)	(0.0018)	(0.0016)
adj R^2	0.249	0.271	0.279	0.279
Observations	12,039	12,039	12,039	12,039

Note: All specifications also include regional, industry and time dummies.

of endogeneity/selectivity are present. The positive coefficient on the individual effect indicates that the time-invariant unobserved individual effects which increase the number of hours worked also increase the wage level. In constrast, the time varying effects generating the simultaneity of wages to hours appears to increase hours and decrease wages. Note, however, that as the reduced form is estimated by tobit it is possible that the unobserved effects are affecting the probability of participation in addition to the number of hours worked. The inclusion of the correction terms induces a number of changes in the results. First, the time effects, which are not reported, appear to be much stronger in this adjusted equation in comparison to the unadjusted equation. However, this increased time effect is partially due to the reduced experience effects. Second, the inclusion of the correction terms substantially reduces the impact of schooling from almost 10% to a more reasonable 7.6%. Finally, the hours/wage profile appears to have noticeably changed from that implied in the Column 1.

For our preferred specification in column 4 we tested the assumption in Eq. (6) against several alternatives. In particular, we tested whether τ_1 and τ_2 were time-invariant. Both tests resulting in a marginal rejection without noticeable changes in the estimated coefficients of the model. Further, we tested Eq. (6) against a restricted version of Eq. (12) which specifies

$$E\{\varepsilon_{it} \mid u_i\} = \tau_1 u_{it} + \lambda_1 u_{i1} + \cdots + \lambda_T u_{iT}.$$

The Wald test statistic for the hypothesis $\lambda_1 = \cdots = \lambda_T$ resulted in a value of 60.52, which is highly significant for a χ^2 distribution with seven degrees of freedom. Despite this rejection, the estimated coefficients were only marginally different from those for our preferred specification in column 4 of Table 3 and we choose not to report them.[15]

Human capital accumulation suggests that lagged hours of work positively affect current wages. As our model conditions upon the entire vector of labor supply, this hypothesis can be directly tested by our two-step procedure by including lagged hours as additional explanatory variables in columns 1 to 4. This resulted in t-ratios of 15.3, 11.2, -0.18 and -3.16, respectively.[16] These results indicate that ignoring the endogeneity of hours or incorrectly imposing a static hours equation, lead to a spurious finding of a statistically significant human capital accumulation effect. Apparently, the effect of lagged hours upon current wages operates through its effect on current hours. This provides support for our exclusion restriction.

Our approach assumes strict exogeneity of the explanatory variables. For time-varying variables this can be tested by including values of the particular exogeneous variable from other time periods in the mean function, and testing for a zero coefficient. This is restricted to time-varying variables as those which are time invariant are imposed to be uncorrelated with the error components in estimation. For the current application union status is a natural candidate of a time-varying regressor which may violate the strict exogeneity assumption.

---

[15] The estimated coefficients for the hours variables in this specification were -4.339, 30.282, -58.870, 33.831, respectively, implying a very similar wage-hours profile.

[16] The estimated coefficients ranged from -0.004 to 0.006 indicating that the lagged hours effect was small.

We tested its strict exogeneity by including next period's union status in the wage equation. The coefficient on this lead value of the variable had a *t*-statistic of 7.29 leading one to reject that union status is strictly exogenous. Another candidate is the schooling variable but as this is time invariant in our sample we cannot test its exogeneity. Recall that we allow experience to be endogenous through lagged hours and that age and age-squared are included in the reduced form.

It is also useful to contrast our preferred estimates to those in Column 2 to highlight the effect of including a lagged dependent variable in the reduced form. First, the failure to account for dynamics in Column 2 has led to the inclusion of the incorrect correction terms. This has resulted in an incorrect inference regarding the presence of individual effects. Second, the inclusion of dynamics in the reduced form has resulted in more precise estimates for a number of the regressors. Third, while the estimates across the two columns are generally similar the coefficient capturing the returns to schooling is quite different. This coefficient is expected to be affected by the treatment of the individual effects as it is likely to be sensitive to unobserved ability. Also note that the estimate of this coefficient, in our preferred specification, is notably more precise than its counterpart in Column 2. Finally, despite the differences across Columns 2 and 4 the coefficients on the hours variables appear to be similar.

To examine the effect of weekly hours worked on the wage rate we employ the wage equation estimates to plot the implied relationships. We do this by plotting the hours effect, relative to the sample average of 34 h per week in 1987, against hours worked. The four plots corresponding to the results from columns 1–4 are shown in Fig. 1. Several important points are worth noting. First, all of the profiles indicate that the hourly wage rate is responsive to changes in the hours of weekly work. For each of the profiles the wage rate appears to either initially slightly increase or slightly decrease before showing a notable increase in the range of around 15 to approximately 42 to 45 h. The point at which the wage rate stops increasing depends on the specification. After wages peak they tend to show a dramatic decrease. Note, however, that the profile at higher hours is dominated by relatively few observations.[17] Second, for the values of hours at which the majority of the observations are located, the unadjusted figure clearly reveals less response in wages to changes in hours worked. This suggests that the impact of endogeneity is reducing the estimated hours effect on wages. Third, the adjusted profiles peak to the right of that for the unadjusted equation. While the unadjusted results suggest that hours peak in the 35–40 range the adjusted

[17] The hours distribution in the sample of workers is as follows: 0–10 h (4.4%); 10–20 h (10.7%); 20–30 h (15.0%); 30–40 h (49.9%); 40–50 h (15.6%); 50 + h (4.4%).

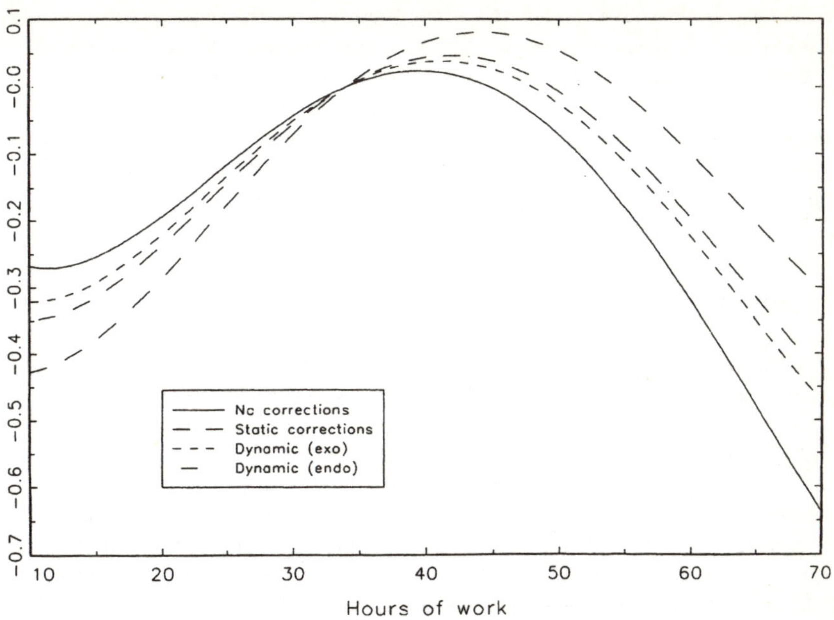

Fig. 1. The Estimated effect of hours on wages, relative to average of 34 hours.

results indicate that the overtime effects are stronger and lead to wages peaking at approximately 42 h per week, for the dynamic specifications, and at approximately 45 h for the static model. Fig. 1 reveals that the profiles for the two dynamic specifications are located between the OLS and adjusted static model. This highlights the importance of incorporating dynamics. In the absence of the lagged dependent variable we are assigning too much importance to the error components. This results in overadjusting for endogeneity. Finally, consider the implied increase in wages over the interval revealed by our preferred specification to feature an increasing effect of hours. Over the hours interval 10–41, comprising 82% of the data, the unadjusted estimates imply a wage increase of 34%. The corresponding increase implied by our preferred specification is 43%, while correcting with a static labor supply equation produces a number of almost 65%.

Ideally we would estimate the model by maximum likelihood to explore the efficiency loss that occurs in this particular example by employing our two step approach. Unfortunately, the complicated form of the likelihood function made such a comparison impractical. While this failure to make efficiency comparisons is disappointing it highlights a major attraction of our approach, namely the ability to estimate models which would otherwise not be estimable. We also considered other methods of obtaining asymptotically efficient standard errors in order to make comparisons. However, due to the complicated nature of the model we were unable to do so. The one piece of information we are able to provide is how much the standard errors increased in the second step by having to estimate the parameters in the first step. We found that, depending on the specification employed, the standard errors increased by up to 10%.

5. Concluding remarks

This paper presents a two-step approach to estimating panel data models with censored endogenous variables and sample selection. In contrast to maximum likelihood estimation our procedure is computationally simple because only one-dimensional numerical integration is required, while a closed-form solution for the second step estimator is available. The cost is a loss of efficiency, which partially depends upon the magnitude of the covariances responsible for the endogeneity/selectivity. Our approach can handle a large variety of models. In particular it allows for truncation, censoring and sample selection. In addition, it is straightforward to extend the current framework to switching regressions models with endogenous switching and observed regimes. Moreover, the two-step method identifies an additional number of parameters that may have economic appeal, including two potential sources of endogeneity/selectivity and state dependence. Direct test for endogeneity/selectivity are also provided.

Acknowledgements

This paper was partially written while the authors were visitors in the Department of Economics, Research School of Social Sciences and the Department of Statistics, The Faculties at the Australian National University, Canberra, and while Vella was visiting the CentER for Economic Research at Tilburg University. An earlier version of this paper was circulated under the title 'Estimating and Testing Simultaneous Equations Panel Data Models with Censored Endogenous Variables'. Helpful comments by Bertrand Melenberg, Robin Sickles, Jeffrey Wooldridge and seminar participants at the University of Groningen, Australian National University, Texas A&M University, Southern Methodist University, Nuffield College, Tilburg University and the London School of Economics are gratefully acknowledged. We are also grateful for detailed comments from Richard Blundell and two anonymous referees. We alone are responsible for any remaining errors.

Appendix A. Covariance matrix estimation

First consider conditional moment estimation. The estimator is $\sqrt{N}$ consistent and asymptotically normal under weak regularity conditions. The asymptotic covariance matrix can be obtained using the results in Newey (1984). Let $\theta^{(2)}$ denote the parameter vector from the reduced form (2) and (3) and let its $\sqrt{N}$ consistent estimator be given by $\hat{\theta}^{(2)}$ with asymptotic covariance matrix V_2. Furthermore, let $\theta^{(1)}$ denote the vector of parameters characterizing the conditional mean in the second step, i.e:

$$\theta^{(1)} = (\theta_1', \tau')',$$

with $\tau = (\tau_1, \tau_2)'$. In vector notation, write

$$y_i = m_1(x_i, z_i; \theta_1) + Z_i(\theta^{(2)})\tau + e_i,$$

where $Z_i(\theta^{(2)})$ denotes the generated regressors and where e_i is an error term vector corresponding to the conditional distribution of ε_i. Let Ω_i denote the variance of e_i for individual i and let

$$G_i = \frac{\partial m_1(x_i, z_i; \theta_1)}{\partial \theta_1}.$$

Defining:

$$M_N = \frac{1}{N}\sum_{i=1}^{N} \mathrm{E}\{[G_i\ Z_i(\theta^{(2)})]'[G_i\ Z_i(\theta^{(2)})]\},$$

$$V_N = \frac{1}{N}\sum_{i=1}^{N} \mathrm{E}\{[G_i\ Z_i(\theta^{(2)})]'\Omega_i[G_i\ Z_i(\theta^{(2)})]\},$$

$$D_N = \frac{1}{N}\sum_{i=1}^{N} \mathrm{E}\left\{[G_i\ Z_i(\theta^{(2)})]'\frac{\partial Z_i(\theta^{(2)})\theta_2^{(1)}}{\partial \theta^{(2)\prime}}\right\},$$

the asymptotic covariance matrix of the second step estimator for $\theta^{(1)}$ is given by

$$V_1 = \lim_{N\to\infty} M_N^{-1}(V_N + D_N V_2 D_N')M_N^{-1},$$

which can be consistently estimated by replacing expectations with sample moments and unknown parameters by their estimators. The second part within brackets for V_1 is due to the generated regressors problem and equals zero if $\tau = 0$. A heteroskedasticity- and autocorrelation-consistent estimator for V_N is given by

$$\hat{V}_N = \frac{1}{N}\sum_{i=1}^{N} [\hat{G}_i\ Z_i(\hat{\theta}^{(2)})]'\hat{e}_i\hat{e}_i'[\hat{G}_i\ Z_i(\hat{\theta}^{(2)})],$$

where $\hat{e}_i$ is the T-dimensional vector of residuals.

Finally, if conditioning upon z_i implies that certain observations are excluded from the second stage estimation, the dimensions of all vectors and matrices should be adjusted to include only those observations used in estimation.

Now consider conditional maximum likelihood estimation. Let $\hat{\theta}^{(2)}$ denote the (marginal) ML estimator for $\theta^{(2)}$ with asymptotic covariance matrix V_2 and $\hat{\theta}^{(1)}$ the conditional ML estimator obtained from maximizing Eq. (24). Let f_1 denote the conditional density of y_i given z_i. Define

$$F_{11} = \mathrm{E}\left\{ -\frac{\partial^2 \ln f_1}{\partial\theta^{(1)}\partial\theta^{(1)\prime}} \right\}, \qquad F_{12} = \mathrm{E}\left\{ \frac{\partial^2 \ln f_1}{\partial\theta^{(1)}\partial\theta^{(2)\prime}} \right\}.$$

Then, it is easily verified from Taylor expansions that

$$\sqrt{N}(\hat{\theta}^{(1)} - \theta^{(1)}) = F_{11}^{-1}\left[\frac{1}{\sqrt{N}}\sum_{i=1}^{N} \frac{\partial \ln f_1}{\partial\theta^{(1)}} + F_{12}\sqrt{N}(\hat{\theta}^{(2)} - \theta^{(2)}) \right] + \mathrm{o}_p(1).$$

Using the result that the two terms in square brackets are asymptotically independent (see Pierce, 1982; Parke, 1986) it follows that the conditional ML estimator is asymptotically normal with covariance matrix:

$$V_1 = F_{11}^{-1}[F_{11} + F_{12}V_2F_{12}']F_{11}^{-1}.$$

F_{11}^{-1} is estimated by standard ML programs. In two cases $\hat{\theta}^{(1)}$ attains the Cramér–Rao lower bound. The first corresponds to the null hypothesis of exogeneity ($\sigma_{\mu\alpha} = \sigma_{\eta v} = 0$) and is characterized by $F_{12} = 0$. The second case is given by

$$J = F_{22} - F_{12}'F_{11}^{-1}F_{12} = 0,$$

where

$$F_{22} = \mathrm{E}\left\{ -\frac{\partial^2 \ln f_1}{\partial\theta^{(2)}\partial\theta^{(2)\prime}} \right\}.$$

Note that J summarizes all information on $\theta^{(2)}$ contained in the conditional distribution f_1. We refer to $J = 0$ as the exactly identified case (see Rivers and Vuong, 1988, for an example). In general, the efficiency loss due to the two-step nature is given by

$$F_{11}^{-1}F_{12}(V_2 - [V_2^{-1} + J]^{-1})F_{12}'F_{11}^{-1}.$$

Appendix B. Treatment of initial conditions

As the hours process for different individuals may have different starting dates, and as some of the explanatory variables are likely to be non-stationary, it is not tractable to derive an exact and estimable form of the marginal distribution of hours_{i0} consistent with the conditional model in Eq. (28) (see Heckman, 1981). Our first approach ignores this problem and assumes that the initial value hours_{i0} can be treated as exogenous, i.e. independent of all error components in the model (including the unobserved heterogeneity (α_i) in the hours process for $t = 1$ onwards). In this case, all inferences are conditional upon hours_{i0}, the marginal distribution of which is not needed for consistency. In our second approach we approximate the distribution of hours_{i0} by a reduced form tobit using presample (1979) information. With different starting dates, as indicated by different levels of age or experience, it can be expected that the tobit parameters are heterogeneous with respect to these two variables. Similarly, the error terms are likely to exhibit heteroskedasticity. The specification of this reduced form is determined, and empirically tested, independently of the rest of the model.

Starting from a linear additive specification with the explanatory variables from Table 2, we experimented with interaction terms and heteroskedasticity. We arrived at a specification for initial hours that included, besides the exogenous variables from Table 2, age-cubed and age interacted with years schooling and the two racial dummies. For this specification there was no statistical evidence of omitted interaction terms or heteroskedasticity related to age. Normality, however, was rejected. This is similar to the finding for the other periods. In the next step, this specification for the initial period was estimated jointly with the dynamic model for the other periods. This requires one to specify how the error terms are related. We chose to allow for different error variances for this initial period. In particular, we modelled the initial error as $\xi\alpha_i + v_{i0}$, where v_{i0} is i.i.d. normal with unrestricted variance and ξ is an unknown parameter.

References

Amemiya, T, MaCurdy, T, 1986. Instrumental-variable estimation of an error-components model. Econometrica 54, 869–881.

Arellano, M., Bover, O., Labeaga, J.M., 1997. Autoregressive models with sample selectivity for panel data. Working paper 9706, CEMFI, Madrid.

Biddle, J, Zarkin, G, 1989. Choice among wage-hours packages: An empirical investigation of male labor supply. Journal of Labor Economics 7, 415–437.

Butler, J, Moffitt, R, 1982. A computationally efficient quadrature procedure for the one-factor multinomial probit model. Econometrica 50, 761–764.

Chamberlain, G, 1980. Analysis of covariance with qualitative data. Review of Economic Studies 47, 225–238.

Davidson, R, MacKinnon, J.G, 1993. Estimation and Inference in Econometrics. Oxford University Press, Oxford.

Gourieroux, C, Monfort, A, 1993. Simulation-based inference. A survey with special reference to panel data models. Journal of Econometrics 59, 5–33.

Gourieroux, C, Monfort, A, Renault, E, Trognon, A, 1987. Generalized residuals. Journal of Econometrics 34, 5–32.

Hausman, J, Taylor, W, 1981. Panel data and unobservable individual effects. Econometrica 49, 1377–1398.

Heckman J.J., 1978. Dummy endogenous variables in a simultaneous equation system. Econometrica 931–959.

Heckman, J.J, 1979. Sample selection bias as a specification error. Econometrica 47, 153–161.

Heckman, J.J., 1981. The incidental parameters problem and the problem of initial conditions in estimating a discrete-time-discrete-data stochastic process. In: Manski, C.F., McFadden, D. (Eds.), Structural Analysis of Discrete Data with Econometric Applications. MIT Press, Cambridge, MA.

Honoré, B, 1992. Trimmed LAD and least squares estimation of truncated and censored regression models with fixed effects. Econometrica 60, 533–565.

Honoré, B, 1993. Orthogonality conditions for tobit models with fixed effects and lagged dependent variables. Journal of Econometrics 59, 35–61.

Kyriazidou, E, 1997. Estimation of a panel data sample selection model. Econometrica 65, 1335–1364.

Labeaga, J.M., 1996. A dynamic panel data model with limited-dependent variables: An application to the demand for tobacco. Working paper, Universitat Pompeu Fabra.

Moffitt, R, 1984. The estimation of a joint wage-hours labor supply model. Journal of Labor Economics 2, 550–566.

Newey, W, 1984. A method of moments interpretation of sequential estimators. Economics Letters 14, 201–206.

Newey, W, 1987. Efficient estimation of limited dependent variable models with endogenous explanatory variables. Journal of Econometrics 36, 231–250.

Newey, W., Powell, J., Vella, F., 1998. Nonparametric instrumental variables estimation of triangular simultaneous equations models. Econometrica, forthcoming.

Nijman, T, Verbeek, M, 1992. Nonresponse in panel data: The impact on estimates of a life cycle consumption function. Journal of Applied Econometrics 7, 243–257.

Parke, W.R, 1986. Pseudo maximum likelihood estimation: The asymptotic distribution. Annals of Statistics 14, 355–357.

Pierce, D.A, 1982. The asymptotic effect of substituting estimators for parameters in certain types of statistics. Annals of Statistics 10, 475–478.

Ridder, G., 1990. Attrition in multi-wave panel data. In: Hartog, J., Ridder, G., Theeuwes, J. (Eds.), Panel Data and Labor Market Studies. Elsevier, North-Holland, Amsterdam.

Rivers, D, Vuong, Q, 1988. Limited information estimators and exogeneity tests for simultaneous probit models. Journal of Econometrics 39, 347–366.

Ruud, P.A, 1984. Tests for specification in econometrics. Econometric Reviews 3, 221–242.

Smith, R.J, Blundell, R, 1986. An exogeneity test for a simultaneous equation Tobit model with an application to labor supply. Econometrica 54, 679–685.

Vella, F, 1993. A simple estimator for simultaneous models with censored endogenous regressors. International Economic Review 34, 441–457.

Vella, F., Verbeek, M., 1998. Whose wages do unions raise? A dynamic model of unionism and wage rate determination for young men. Journal of Applied Econometrics, 13, 163–168.

Wooldridge, J, 1995. Selection corrections for panel data models under conditional mean independence assumptions. Journal of Econometrics 68, 115–132.

[8]

ELSEVIER Journal of Econometrics 68 (1995) 115–132

JOURNAL OF Econometrics

Selection corrections for panel data models under conditional mean independence assumptions

Jeffrey M. Wooldridge

Department of Economics, Michigan State University, East Lansing, MI 48824-1038, USA

Abstract

Some new methods for testing and correcting for sample selection bias in panel data models are proposed. The assumptions allow the unobserved effects in both the regression and selection equations to be correlated with the observed variables; the error distribution in the regression equation is unspecified; arbitrary serial dependence in the idiosyncratic errors of both equations is allowed; and all idiosyncratic errors can be heterogeneously distributed. Compared with maximum likelihood and other estimators derived under fully parametric assumptions, the new estimators are much more robust and have significant computational advantages.

Key words: Panel data; Sample selection; Fixed effects; Conditional mean independence; Two-step estimation
JEL classification: C23

1. Introduction

This paper offers some new methods for testing and correcting for selection bias in linear unobserved components panel data models. The model studied is of the fixed effects (FE) variety in the sense that the unobserved component is allowed to be correlated with the observable explanatory variables, and we impose no distributional assumptions on the unobserved effect. In addition, we do not require the idiosyncratic errors in the regression equation to have a known distribution, and they can have serial dependence of unspecified form.

Tom Mroz, Peter Schmidt, Jeff Zabel, and two anonymous referees provided very helpful comments. Financial support from a Sloan Foundation Research Fellowship is gratefully acknowledged.

SSDI 0304407694 01645 G

These features distinguish the paper from other recent work on correcting for selection bias in linear panel data models. Verbeek and Nijman (1992) (hereafter VN) consider a random effects (RE) model under the assumptions of normality and serial independence of the idiosyncratic errors in both the selection and regression equations, and the time-constant unobserved effects in the selection and regression equations are assumed to be normally distributed. Nijman and Verbeek (1992) (hereafter NV) and Zabel (1992) study almost the same model except they allow both unobserved effects to be correlated with the observables. Vella and Verbeek (1992) extend NV to allow for functions of the endogenous censoring variable to appear among the explanatory variables.

In order to make the selection equation simple to estimate we make a normality assumption on the errors in the selection equation; but we allow these errors to display arbitrary serial correlation and unconditional heteroskedasticity. The key assumptions that lead to estimable equations that identify the structural parameters – the conditional mean independence assumptions – are much weaker than full joint distributional assumptions on the time-constant unobservables and the idiosyncratic errors.

In addition to their wide array of applicability, the new procedures are relatively computationally simple. Current corrections for the fully parametric model require bivariate numerical integration due to the time dimension and the integrating out of the unobserved effect. Allowing for even simple forms of serial correlation would make the parametric approach almost prohibitively difficult. The methods offered here require a standard probit or Tobit regression for each time period followed by a multivariate linear regression, regardless of the time series properties of the errors.

In Section 3 we offer some variable addition tests for selection bias based on fixed effects estimation using the unbalanced panel. These tests have some advantages over the variable addition tests suggested by VN (1992). In addition to the absence of selection bias, the latter tests maintain a null hypothesis of no correlation between the unobserved effect and the regressors. Such tests could reject even in the absence of selection bias if the unobserved effect and the regressors are correlated, or if selection is based on the unobserved effect. Here, the unobserved effect and regressors are allowed to be arbitrarily correlated and selection may depend on the unobserved effect, so in this sense the tests are complementary to the Hausman test proposed by VN that compares the fixed effects estimators from the balanced and unbalanced panels. Our variable addition tests are easily computable after probit or Tobit estimation for each time period followed by fixed effects estimation, and they are explicitly robust to arbitrary dependence and heterogeneity in the errors of the regression equation.

In what follows we cover two cases that arise in practice. The first is when the selection variable is partially observed. The leading application of this case is to labor studies where the regression equation is, say, a wage equation, and selection depends on whether or not individuals are working. If a person is working, then her/his hours are recorded, and selection is determined by nonzero hours worked. The other case is the more widely applicable one, where only a binary selection indicator is observed. One might expect that more flexibility is available in the first case because more information is known, and we show here that this is the case.

A final note on the sampling assumption. Throughout we assume that the cross-section observations are independent, identically distributed. The independence assumption is crucial but the identical distribution assumption is mostly for notational ease. Unless otherwise stated there is no assumption on the dependence across time. This is possible because the asymptotic analysis is for fixed T and N going to infinity.

2. Consistency of fixed effects under exogenous selection

We first briefly investigate assumptions under which the usual fixed effects estimator on the unbalanced panel is consistent. The model is the usual linear, unobserved effects model for i.i.d. cross-section observations: for any i,

$$y_{it} = \alpha_i + \boldsymbol{x}_{it}\beta + u_{it}, \quad t = 1, \dots, T, \tag{2.1}$$

where $\boldsymbol{x}_{it}$ is $1 \times K$ and β is the $K \times 1$ vector of interest. We assume that N cross-section observations are available and the asymptotic analysis is as $N \to \infty$. We explicitly cover the case where α_i is allowed to be correlated with $\boldsymbol{x}_{it}$, so that all elements of $\boldsymbol{x}_{it}$ are time-varying; this allows for time dummies and interactions of time dummies with time-constant variables.

If all T periods are available for any cross-section drawn from the population, then a sufficient condition for fixed effects (and a variety of other procedures) to be consistent as $N \to \infty$ is:

Asuumption 1. $\mathrm{E}(u_{it} | \alpha_i, \boldsymbol{x}_{i1}, \dots, \boldsymbol{x}_{iT}) = 0, \quad t = 1, 2, \dots, T.$ ■

Under Assumption 1, fixed effects is consistent and $\sqrt{N}$-asymptotically normal. Since the regressors for *all* time periods are in the conditioning set at any time t, the assumption implies that the $\boldsymbol{x}_{it}$ are *strictly exogenous conditional* on the latent effect α_i (see, for example, Chamberlain, 1982). Technically speaking, Assumption 1 is more restrictive than needed for fixed effects to be consistent, but it gives a natural interpretation for β and it extends in a straightforward manner to the sample selection case.

For the usual FE standard errors and test statistics to be valid we should add to Assumption 1 the assumption

$$\mathrm{E}(\boldsymbol{u}_i \boldsymbol{u}_i' | \alpha_i, \boldsymbol{x}_i) = \sigma^2 \boldsymbol{I}_T, \tag{2.2}$$

where $\boldsymbol{u}_i = (\boldsymbol{u}_{i1}, \ldots, \boldsymbol{u}_{iT})'$ and $\boldsymbol{x}_i \equiv (\boldsymbol{x}_{i1}, \ldots, \boldsymbol{x}_{iT})$. Alternatively, we could relax (2.2) by replacing $\sigma^2 \boldsymbol{I}_T$ with Ω, a positive definite $T \times T$ matrix. Then, as in Kiefer (1980), fixed effects GLS can be applied. We will not use GLS-type procedures because we make *no* assumptions about $\mathrm{E}(\boldsymbol{u}_i \boldsymbol{u}_i' | \alpha_i, \boldsymbol{x}_i)$.

We will not cover the random effects case in detail, except to occasionally note how the assumptions would have to be strengthened. In addition to Assumption 1, random effects add the assumption

$$\mathrm{E}(\alpha_i | \boldsymbol{x}_{i1}, \ldots, \boldsymbol{x}_{iT}) = \mathrm{E}(\alpha_i). \tag{2.3}$$

This is too restrictive for many applications, so we will not impose it here.

Now consider the fixed effects estimator on the unbalanced panel. The vector of selection indicators for each i is denoted $\boldsymbol{s}_i = (s_{i1}, \ldots, s_{iT})'$, and for now we assume only that $(\boldsymbol{x}_{it}, y_{it})$ is observed if $s_{it} = 1$. The FE estimator can be written

$$\hat{\beta} = \left(N^{-1} \sum_{i=1}^{N} \sum_{t=1}^{T} s_{it} \ddot{\boldsymbol{x}}_{it}' \ddot{\boldsymbol{x}}_{it} \right)^{-1} \left(N^{-1} \sum_{i=1}^{N} \sum_{t=1}^{T} s_{it} \ddot{\boldsymbol{x}}_{it}' \ddot{y}_{it} \right), \tag{2.4}$$

where, for $s_{it} = 1$,

$$\ddot{\boldsymbol{x}}_{it} \equiv \boldsymbol{x}_{it} - T_i^{-1} \sum_{r=1}^{T} s_{ir} \boldsymbol{x}_{ir}, \tag{2.5}$$

$$\ddot{y}_{it} \equiv y_{it} - T_i^{-1} \sum_{r=1}^{T} s_{ir} y_{ir}, \tag{2.6}$$

$$T_i = \sum_{t=1}^{T} s_{it}. \tag{2.7}$$

Expanding (2.4) shows that the following is sufficient for FE on the selected subsample to be consistent and asymptotically normal (as $N \to \infty$):

Assumption 1'. $\mathrm{E}(u_{it} | \alpha_i, \boldsymbol{x}_i, \boldsymbol{s}_i) = 0, \quad t = 1, 2, \ldots, T.$ ■

Note that – just as it is not sufficient to put only $\boldsymbol{x}_{it}$ in the conditioning set at time t – it is not sufficient to put only s_{it} in the conditioning set at time t. In other words, under Assumption 1' the selection process is *strictly* exogenous conditional on α_i and x_i. As with Assumption 1, this assumption allows for arbitrary serial correlation and heteroskedasticity in the (u_{it}).

Technically, Assumption 1' is more restrictive than the exogeneity assumptions used by VN in their analysis of the fixed effects estimator. (VN state conditions directly in terms of $\ddot{u}_{it} \equiv u_{it} - T_i^{-1} \sum_{r=1}^{T} s_{ir} u_{ir}$.) But Assumption 1' is simple to state and is less cumbersome to apply to cases where selection is based on the exogenous variables. In fact, because Assumption 1' puts no restrictions on how $\boldsymbol{s}_i$ relates to $(\alpha_i, \boldsymbol{x}_i)$, it follows that selection can depend on $(\alpha_i, \boldsymbol{x}_i)$ in an arbitrary fashion (contrast VN, 1992, fn. 5).

For the usual fixed effects variance–covariance matrix and inference to be valid an additional assumption is needed. Sufficient is

$$\mathrm{E}(\boldsymbol{u}_i\boldsymbol{u}_i'|\alpha_i, \boldsymbol{x}_i, \boldsymbol{s}_i) = \sigma^2 \boldsymbol{I}_T. \tag{2.8}$$

If (2.8) does not hold we can obtain a robust variance–covariance matrix estimator by applying the results from the appendix: let $\boldsymbol{w}_{it} = \ddot{\boldsymbol{x}}_{it}$, $\hat{e}_{it} = \ddot{y}_{it} - \ddot{\boldsymbol{x}}_{it}\hat{\beta}$, and set $\hat{\boldsymbol{D}} = \boldsymbol{0}$ in Appendix equations (A.3)–(A.5).

Consistency of random effects estimation using the unbalanced or balanced panel requires an additional assumption. The most natural is

$$\mathrm{E}(\alpha_i|\boldsymbol{x}_i, \boldsymbol{s}_i) = \mathrm{E}(\alpha_i). \tag{2.9}$$

An important limitation of (2.9) is that it rules out selection that depends on the unobserved effect α_i. Tests that maintain Assumption 1′ and (2.9) under H_0 cannot distinguish between selection that depends on α_i and selection that does not. Because fixed effects is consistent under Assumption 1′ only, the tests we derive in the next section maintain only that assumption – or its natural variant when the selection variable is partially observed – under H_0.

3. Some variable addition tests for selection bias

We now derive some simple variable addition tests of selection bias. There are unlimited tests one can derive that have the proper size under the null, but one must be guided by power and computational considerations. Here we use variable addition tests similar in spirit to VN (1992), but our auxiliary regressors are either Tobit residuals or inverse Mills ratios, and we explicitly allow for serial correlation and heteroskedasticity of unknown form in $\{u_{it}\}$.

3.1. Testing when the selection variable is partially observed

We first obtain a test under the assumption that the (latent) variable determining selection can be observed whenever it is nonnegative. To motivate the test we write down a particular selection mechanism, but it should be remembered that the selection mechanism need not be correctly specified in any sense; it is simply a vehicle for obtaining a sensible test. In Section 4 we formalize the assumptions on the selection mechanism.

Unless otherwise stated we assume that the explanatory variables $\boldsymbol{x}_{it}$ are observed for all $t = 1, 2, \ldots, T$. The variable y_{it} is observed if $s_{it} = 1$ and not otherwise. For each $t = 1, 2, \ldots, T$, define a latent variable

$$h_{it}^* = \delta_{t0} + \boldsymbol{x}_{i1}\delta_{t1} + \cdots + \boldsymbol{x}_{iT}\delta_{tT} + v_{it}, \tag{3.1}$$

where v_{it} is independent of $(\alpha_i, \boldsymbol{x}_i)$, $v_{it} \sim$ Normal $(0, \sigma_t^2)$, and δ_{tr} is a $K \times 1$ vector of unknown parameters, $r = 1, 2, \ldots, T$. At this point it should be mentioned that independence between v_{it} and α_i is often too strong an assumption for deriving selection *corrections*, so we will not impose such an assumption in Section 4. Here we are only deriving a test of selection bias, and because it is convenient to do so, we proceed as if v_{it} and α_i are independent. As will be seen in Section 4, the test we derive here also falls out under much less restrictive assumptions.

The binary selection indicator is defined as $s_{it} \equiv 1[h_{it}^* > 0]$. In this subsection we also assume that, for all t, the censored variable $h_{it} \equiv \max(0, h_{it}^*)$ is observed; this is what we mean by partial observability of the selection variable. Technically, the null hypothesis is a strengthened version of Assumption 1′, where $\boldsymbol{h}_i \equiv (h_{i1}, h_{i2}, \ldots, h_{iT})'$ replaces $\boldsymbol{s}_i$ in the conditioning set; but the interpretation of the assumption is essentially the same.

Note that we use $\boldsymbol{x}_{it}$ as the explanatory variables in both (2.1) and (3.1). Technically this does not affect our ability to carry out testing and correcting for selection bias, but it helps if one has exclusion restrictions in (2.1). This is accomplished in what follows by simply omitting the appropriate elements from $\boldsymbol{x}_{it}$ in (2.1). We do not show this explicitly to keep the notation as simple as possible.

The mechanism described by (3.1) is the reduced form for many popular selection equations. For example, consider the structural selection equation

$$h_{it}^* = \xi_i + \boldsymbol{x}_{it}\delta + a_{it}, \tag{3.2}$$

where (ξ_i, a_{it}) is jointly normally distributed with $\mathrm{E}(a_{it}) = 0$ and a_{it} independent of $\boldsymbol{x}_i$; ξ_i is a time-constant unobserved effect. If ξ_i is independent of $\boldsymbol{x}_i$, as in a random effects-type specification, then (3.1) holds with $\delta_{t0} = \delta_0 \equiv \mathrm{E}(\xi_i)$, $\delta_{tr} \equiv 0$, $r \neq t$, and $\delta_{tt} \equiv \delta$. Note that $v_{it} = (\xi_i - \delta_0) + a_{it}$ in this case, so the v_{it} are probably serially dependent.

To allow ξ_i to be correlated with $\boldsymbol{x}_i$ we can specify, as in Chamberlain (1980) and VN (1992),

$$\xi_i = \eta_0 + \boldsymbol{x}_{i1}\eta_1 + \cdots + \boldsymbol{x}_{iT}\eta_T + c_i, \tag{3.3}$$

where c_i is independent of $\boldsymbol{x}_i$ with a zero mean normal distribution. Then (3.1) holds with $\delta_{t0} \equiv \eta_0$, $\delta_{tr} \equiv \eta_r$, $r \neq t$, $\delta_{tt} \equiv \eta_t + \delta$, and

$$v_{it} \equiv c_i + a_{it}. \tag{3.4}$$

Again, unless a_{it} has a very specific type of autocorrelation, v_{it} is serially correlated. Also, $\mathrm{var}(v_{it})$ can change over time if $\mathrm{var}(a_{it})$ does.

Another model that can be expressed as in (3.1) is the dynamic model

$$h_{it}^* = \delta_0 + \rho h_{i,t-1}^* + \boldsymbol{x}_{it}\delta + a_{it}, \tag{3.5}$$

where a_{it} is a mean zero normal random variable independent of $\boldsymbol{x}_i$. Then, assuming that h_{i0}^* given $\boldsymbol{x}_i$ is normally distributed with linear conditional expectation, (3.5) can be written as in (3.1). The same conclusion holds if a time-constant unobserved effect of the form (3.3) is added to (3.5).

We now derive a conditional expectation that leads to a test for selection bias. Because $\boldsymbol{s}_i$ is a function of $(\boldsymbol{x}_i, \boldsymbol{v}_i)$, where $\boldsymbol{v}_i \equiv (v_{i1}, \dots, v_{iT})'$, a sufficient condition for Assumption 1′ – with $\boldsymbol{h}_i$ or $\boldsymbol{s}_i$ in the conditioning set – is

$$\mathrm{E}(u_{it} \mid \alpha_i, \boldsymbol{x}_i, \boldsymbol{v}_i) = 0, \qquad t = 1, 2, \dots, T. \tag{3.6}$$

This equation also suggests useful alternatives that imply selectivity bias. The simplest such alternative is

$$\mathrm{E}(u_{it} \mid \alpha_i, \boldsymbol{x}_i, \boldsymbol{v}_i) = \mathrm{E}(u_{it} \mid v_{it}) = \rho v_{it}, \qquad t = 1, 2, \dots, T, \tag{3.7}$$

for some unknown scalar ρ. Later we will use assumptions similar to, but not nearly as restrictive as, (3.7) when correcting for selection bias. For now, note that it states that u_{it} is mean independent of $(\alpha_i, \boldsymbol{x}_i, v_{i1}, \dots, v_{i,t-1}, v_{i,t+1}, \dots, v_{iT})$, conditional on v_{it}. In addition, the regression of u_{it} on v_{it} is linear and constant across t.

Under the alternative (3.7) we have

$$\mathrm{E}(y_{it} \mid \alpha_i, \boldsymbol{x}_i, \boldsymbol{v}_i, \boldsymbol{s}_i) = \mathrm{E}(y_{it} \mid \alpha_i, \boldsymbol{x}_i, \boldsymbol{v}_i) = \alpha_i + \boldsymbol{x}_{it}\beta + \rho v_{it}. \tag{3.8}$$

From (3.8) it follows that, if we could observe v_{it} when $s_{it} = 1$, then we could test H_0 by including the v_{it} as an additional regressor in fixed effects estimation and testing $\mathrm{H}_0\colon \rho = 0$ using standard methods. While v_{it} cannot be observed, it can be estimated whenever $s_{it} = 1$ because v_{it} is simply the error in a Tobit model. Thus, we propose the following test for selection bias when h_{it} is observed.

Procedure 3.1 (h_{it} is observed; valid under Assumption 1′ with $\boldsymbol{h}_i$ replacing $\boldsymbol{s}_i$):

(i) For each t, estimate the equation

$$h_{it} = \max(0, \boldsymbol{x}_i\delta_t + v_{it})$$

by standard Tobit, where now $\boldsymbol{x}_i = (1, \boldsymbol{x}_{i1}, \boldsymbol{x}_{i2}, \dots, \boldsymbol{x}_{iT})$ and $\delta_t \equiv (\delta_{t0}, \delta'_{t1}, \dots, \delta'_{tT})'$. (Henceforth, for notational simplicity, $\boldsymbol{x}_i$ is defined to have unity as its first element.) For $s_{it} = 1$, define $\hat{v}_{it} = h_{it} - \boldsymbol{x}_i\hat{\delta}_t$.

(ii) Estimate the equation

$$\ddot{y}_{it} = \ddot{\boldsymbol{x}}_{it}\beta + \rho\ddot{v}_{it} + \mathrm{error}_{it} \tag{3.9}$$

by pooled OLS using those observations for which $s_{it} = 1$, where $\ddot{\boldsymbol{x}}_{it}$ and $\ddot{y}_{it}$ are defined in (2.5) and (2.6), and

$$\ddot{v}_{it} \equiv \hat{v}_{it} - T_i^{-1} \sum_{r=1}^{T} s_{ir}\hat{v}_{ir}.$$

(iii) Test H_0: $\rho = 0$ using the t-statistic for $\hat{\rho}$. Unless assumption (2.8) is maintained under H_0, a serial correlation and heteroskedasticity-robust standard error should be computed for $\hat{\rho}$. The robust variance matrix for $\hat{\theta} \equiv (\hat{\beta}', \rho)'$ is obtained by setting $w_{it} \equiv (\ddot{x}_{it}, \ddot{v}_{it})$ and $\hat{e}_{it} \equiv \ddot{y}_{it} - \ddot{x}_{it}\hat{\beta} - \hat{\rho}\ddot{v}_{it}$ and using these in Appendix equations (A.3)–(A.5); under H_0 one can take $\boldsymbol{D} \equiv \boldsymbol{0}$ in (A.4). ■

Rather than unconstrained Tobit estimation for each t one might prefer to impose restrictions on the δ_{tr} derived from one of the structural selection models mentioned earlier. For example, under (3.2), (3.3), and a homoskedasticity assumption on the a_{it},

$$h_{it}^* = \eta_0 + x_{i1}\eta_1 + \cdots + x_{iT}\eta_T + x_{it}\delta + v_{it}, \tag{3.10}$$

and $v_{it}|x_i \sim \text{Normal}(0, \sigma_v^2)$, $t = 1, 2, \ldots, T$. Even though the v_{it} are *not* serially independent, one can use pooled Tobit to estimate $(\eta_0, \eta_1, \ldots, \eta_T)$, δ, and σ_v^2. Simply define $w_{it} \equiv (1, x_{i1}, \ldots, x_{iT}, x_{it})$ and $\theta \equiv (\eta_0, \eta_1', \ldots, \eta_T', \delta')$, and estimate the equations $h_{it} = \max(0, w_{it}\ \theta + v_{it})$ as if on one long cross-section. Because the h_{it} are not independent across t given x_i, the usual Tobit standard errors and test statistics are inappropriate, but the estimators are still consistent and $\sqrt{N}$-asymptotically normal. The consistency proof is quite simple and is based on the Kullback–Leibler information criterion, as in White (1994); a proof is available upon request.

Another popular simplification – see for example Mundlak (1978), NV (1992), and Zabel (1992) – is to assume that ξ_i depends only on the time average of x_{it}, in which case (3.10) can be replaced by

$$h_{it}^* = \eta_0 + \bar{x}_i\eta + x_{it}\delta + v_{it}, \tag{3.11}$$

where η is a $K \times 1$ vector of parameters. Again, (η_0, η, δ) can be consistently estimated by pooled Tobit, ignoring the serial dependence in v_{it}.

Simplest of all is to carry out the test assuming that ξ_i is independent of x_i and obtaining the $\hat{v}_{it}$ from pooled Tobit estimation on the equations $h_{it} = \max(0, \delta_0 + x_{it}\delta + v_{it})$. In thinking about these alternative procedures one should remember that the method for obtaining $\hat{v}_{it}$ does not affect the asymptotic size of the test, but it should affect the power.

A final comment before turning to the case where only s_{it} is observed. As noted earlier, many variable addition tests are valid tests of Assumption 1′. The test in Procedure 3.1 seems reasonable because the alternative (3.7) can be derived from a standard model of sample selection. Also, as we show in Section 4.1, under certain assumptions this procedure produces consistent estimates of β under sample selection. Nevertheless, for testing it is just as legitimate to replace $\hat{v}_{it}$ with h_{it} in Procedure 3.1. This approach does have two advantages: it circumvents having to do the T cross-section Tobits to obtain $\hat{v}_{it}$, and it can be used when x_{it} is observed only when $s_{it} = 1$.

3.2. *Testing when only the selection indicator is observed*

An alternative to Procedure 3.1 is needed when h_{it} is not observed. The starting point is still Eq. (3.8), but we must now condition only on $\mathbf{s}_i$ rather than $\mathbf{v}_i$. Using iterated expectations, this gives

$$\begin{aligned} \mathrm{E}(y_{it}|\alpha_i, \mathbf{x}_i, \mathbf{s}_i) &= \alpha_i + \mathbf{x}_{it}\beta + \rho \mathrm{E}(v_{it}|\alpha_i, \mathbf{x}_i, \mathbf{s}_i) \\ &= \alpha_i + \mathbf{x}_{it}\beta + \rho \mathrm{E}(v_{it}|\mathbf{x}_i, \mathbf{s}_i), \end{aligned} \tag{3.12}$$

under the assumption – used for deriving the test – that $\mathbf{v}_i$ is independent of $(\alpha_i, \mathbf{x}_i)$. If the v_{it} were independent across t then $\mathrm{E}(v_{it}|\mathbf{x}_i, \mathbf{s}_i) = \mathrm{E}(v_{it}|\mathbf{x}_i, s_{it})$. As mentioned earlier, this is unrealistic when a structural selection equation contains an unobserved effect. Still, it is computationally much easier to replace $\mathrm{E}(v_{it}|\mathbf{x}_i, \mathbf{s}_i)$ with $\mathrm{E}(v_{it}|\mathbf{x}_i, s_{it})$, so we do that here for the purposes of obtaining a simple test. Then the conditional expectation we need to estimate is

$$\mathrm{E}(v_{it}|\mathbf{x}_i, s_{it} = 1) = \mathrm{E}(v_{it}|\mathbf{x}_i, v_{it} > -\mathbf{x}_i\delta_t). \tag{3.13}$$

Assuming now that the variance of v_{it} is unity, we have

$$\mathrm{E}(v_{it}|\mathbf{x}_i, v_{it} > -\mathbf{x}_i\delta_t) = \lambda(\mathbf{x}_i\delta_t), \tag{3.14}$$

where $\lambda(\cdot)$ denotes the inverse Mills ratio. This leads to the following procedure:

Procedure 3.2 (s_{it} is observed; valid under Assumption 1′):

(i) For each t, estimate the equation

$$\mathrm{P}(s_{it} = 1|\mathbf{x}_i) = \Phi(\mathbf{x}_i\delta_t), \tag{3.15}$$

using standard probit. For $s_{it} = 1$, compute $\hat{\lambda}_{it} \equiv \lambda(\mathbf{x}_i\hat{\delta}_t)$.

(ii) Estimate Eq. (3.9) with $\ddot{\lambda}_{it} = \hat{\lambda}_{it} - T_i^{-1}\sum_{r=1}^{T} s_{ir}\hat{\lambda}_{ir}$ in place of $\ddot{v}_{it}$, again using only those observations for which $s_{it} = 1$.

(iii) Test H_0: $\rho = 0$ using the t-statistic for ρ. Again, a serial correlation and heteroskedasticity-robust standard error is warranted unless (2.8) is maintained under H_0. ■

The same remarks concerning restricting the δ_{tr} – in this case using pooled probit – hold here as in the case where h_{it} is observed.

This procedure is different from the ones proposed by VN (1992). VN suggest variable addition tests in a random effects framework using the variables T_i, $\prod_{r=1}^{T} s_{ir}$, and $s_{i,t-1}$. The first two of these could not be implemented in a fixed effects framework because the added variables have no time variation. The third of these could be after dropping the first time period. There are other possibilities that can be used in place of $\hat{\lambda}_{it}$ in a variable addition test during fixed effects estimation; for example, $\sum_{r \neq t}^{T} s_{ir}$ and $\prod_{r \neq t}^{T} s_{ir}$. Such tests have the advantage of computational simplicity and the need to only observe $\boldsymbol{x}_{it}$ when $s = 1$. Procedure 3.2 can be viewed as an extension of Heckman's (1976) procedure to an unobserved effects framework.

4. Correcting for sample selection bias

We now consider correcting for selection bias, and again we consider the two cases that h_{it}^* is partially observed and that only s_{it} is observed. In the former case two different corrections are offered. The first is obtained directly from the testing Procedure 3.1 in Section 3, and it has the advantage of not specifying how α_i depends on $(\boldsymbol{x}_i, \boldsymbol{v}_i)$. The second procedure relaxes (implicit) assumptions on the errors in the selection equation by imposing a linearity assumption on the regression of α_i on $(\boldsymbol{x}_i, v_{it})$.

The regression equation is still given by (2.1). For interpretive reasons it is useful to think of Assumption 1 as also holding, but it is not directly assumed in what follows. We first formalize the selection mechanism.

Assumption 2. Define h_{it}^* as in (3.1), where v_{it} is independent of $\boldsymbol{x}_i$ and $v_{it} \sim \text{Normal}(0, \sigma_t^2)$. Let $h \equiv \max(0, h_{it}^*)$, $s_{it} \equiv 1[h_{it}^* > 0]$, $t = 1, \ldots, T$. ■

Assumption 2 was one of the assumptions used to motivate the tests for selection bias in Section 3; unlike there, we must now take this assumption seriously. Further, we now need to be very careful with our assumptions about relationships among α_i, u_{it}, and v_{it} so as not to rule out structural selection equations of the type covered in Section 3.

Although we assume normality of v_{it} in Assumption 2, the temporal dependence in $\{v_{it}\colon t = 1, 2, \ldots, T\}$ is entirely unrestricted. This is important for examples like (3.2) and (3.5) because – whether or not the a_{it} are independent across t – the v_{it} can never be counted on to be serially independent. Note also that the v_{it} are allowed to have different variances in different time periods.

4.1. Selection corrections when the selection variable is partially observed

We begin with an assumption that allows us to correct for selection bias in a fixed effects estimation framework. It is a combination of a conditional mean independence assumption and a linearity assumption.

Assumption 3. For some zero-mean random variable ζ_i and all $t = 1, 2, \ldots, T$,

$$\mathrm{E}(u_{it} | \alpha_i, \zeta_i, \boldsymbol{x}_i, \boldsymbol{v}_i) = \mathrm{E}(u_{it} | \zeta_i, v_{it}) = \zeta_i + \rho v_{it}. \quad ■ \tag{4.1}$$

The first equality in (4.1) is a particular conditional mean independence assumption. Namely, Assumption 3 implies that there is a latent variable ζ_i such that, conditional on ζ_i, u_{it} is mean independent of $\boldsymbol{x}_i$ and v_{ir}, $r \neq t$. This assumption is aimed at the leading case of the structural selection model (3.2), where the errors a_{it} in the structural selection equation are zero-mean normally distributed, $(\boldsymbol{u}_i, \boldsymbol{a}_i)$ is independent of $(\alpha_i, \xi_i, \boldsymbol{x}_i)$, ξ_i has the representation in (3.3), and

$$\mathrm{E}(u_{it} | \boldsymbol{a}_i) = \rho a_{it}. \tag{4.2}$$

Then $\rho a_{it} = \mathrm{E}(u_{it} | \alpha_i, \xi_i, \boldsymbol{x}_i, \boldsymbol{a}_i) = \mathrm{E}(u_{it} | \alpha_i, c_i, \boldsymbol{x}_i, \boldsymbol{v}_i)$, or $\mathrm{E}(u_{it} | \alpha_i, c_i, \boldsymbol{x}_i, \boldsymbol{v}_i) = -\rho c_i + \rho v_{it}$. Thus, Assumption 3 holds by taking $\zeta_i = -\rho c_i$.

The linearity in v_{it} assumed in (4.1) can be relaxed by adding, for example, polynomials in v_{it}. This gives even more flexibility – and explicitly allows the joint distribution of (u_{it}, v_{it}) to be nonnormal – but we focus on the linear case for simplicity.

The limitations of Assumption 3 can be seen by studying (4.2) a little more closely. A sufficient condition for (4.2) with linear conditional expectations is that (u_{it}, a_{it}) is uncorrelated with a_{ir}, $r \neq t$ (although serial correlation in $\{u_{it}\}$ is unrestricted). Unfortunately, (4.2) can fail if there is serial correlation in $\{a_{it}\}$; below we offer a different assumption that explicitly allows such serial correlation.

Under Assumptions 2 and 3 we have

$$\mathrm{E}(y_{it} | \alpha_i, \zeta_i, \boldsymbol{x}_i, \boldsymbol{v}_i) = \omega_i + \boldsymbol{x}_{it}\beta + \rho v_{it}, \tag{4.3}$$

where $\omega_i \equiv \alpha_i + \zeta_i$. Arguments similar to this have appeared in Smith and Blundell (1986) and Vella (1992) in the context of limited dependent variable models in pure cross-section contexts under distributional assumptions. Here we derive it in a selection context under weaker conditions and, more importantly, without making restrictive assumptions on the unobserved components or the time series properties of $\{u_{it}: t = 1, 2, \ldots, T\}$.

The strategy for the selection correction follows from (4.3). Because $\boldsymbol{s}_i$ is a function of $(\boldsymbol{x}_i, \boldsymbol{v}_i)$, (4.3) implies that

$$\mathrm{E}(y_{it} | \omega_i, \boldsymbol{x}_i, \boldsymbol{v}_i, \boldsymbol{s}_i) = \omega_i + \boldsymbol{x}_{it}\beta + \rho v_{it}, \tag{4.4}$$

which means that $\boldsymbol{x}_{it}$ and v_{it} are strictly exogenous conditional on ω_i. Estimation of β and ρ proceeds *exactly* as in Procedure 3.1. But, because ρ is generally different from zero, the asymptotic variance of $\hat{\theta} \equiv (\hat{\beta}', \hat{\rho})'$ needs to be adjusted due to the preliminary estimation of δ.

Procedure 4.1.1 (h_{it} observed; valid under Assumptions 2 and 3):

Steps (i) and (ii) are carried out exactly as in Procedure 3.1.

(iii) To estimate the asymptotic variance of $\hat{\theta}$ using the results in the Appendix, define $\hat{\boldsymbol{w}}_{it} = (\ddot{\boldsymbol{x}}_{it}, \ddot{v}_{it})$ and $\hat{e}_{it} \equiv \ddot{y}_{it} - \ddot{\boldsymbol{x}}_{it}\hat{\beta} - \hat{\rho}\ddot{v}_{it}$. Define a $(K+1)\times$

$T(1 + TK)$ matrix by $\boldsymbol{G}_{it} \equiv (\boldsymbol{0}'\ z'_{it})'$, where $\boldsymbol{0}$ is a $K \times T(1 + TK)$ matrix of zeros and the $1 \times T(1 + TK)$ vector z_{it} is defined as

$$z_{it} \equiv \frac{1}{T_i}(s_{i1}\boldsymbol{x}_i, \ldots, s_{i,t-1}\boldsymbol{x}_i, -(T_i - 1)\boldsymbol{x}_i, s_{i,t+1}\boldsymbol{x}_i, \ldots, s_{iT}\boldsymbol{x}_i).$$

Then

$$\hat{\boldsymbol{D}} \equiv N^{-1} \sum_{i=1}^{N} \sum_{t=1}^{T} s_{it}\hat{\boldsymbol{w}}'_{it}\hat{\theta}'\boldsymbol{G}_{it}. \tag{4.5}$$

Next, for each t, let $\hat{\boldsymbol{r}}_{it}$ be minus the inverse of the average estimated Hessian (over the entire cross-section) times the estimated score of the Tobit log-likelihood function for observation i; delete the last element of this vector because $\hat{\sigma}_t^2$ does not appear in $\hat{v}_{it}$. Thus, $\hat{\boldsymbol{r}}_{it}$ is a $(1 + TK) \times 1$ vector for each i and t. The expressions for the average Hessian and score for each i, evaluated at $\hat{\delta}_t$, are given in Maddala (1983, Sect. 6.3). Form the $T(1 + TK) \times 1$ vector $\hat{\boldsymbol{r}}_i$ by stacking $\{\hat{\boldsymbol{r}}_{i1}, \hat{\boldsymbol{r}}_{i2}, \ldots, \hat{\boldsymbol{r}}_{iT}\}$. Obtain $\hat{\boldsymbol{A}}$ as in the Appendix equation (A.3), define $\hat{\boldsymbol{q}}_i$ and $\hat{\boldsymbol{p}}_i$ as in (A.4), and use these to construct $\hat{\boldsymbol{B}}$ in (A.5). Then $\text{Av\^{a}r}(\hat{\theta}) = \hat{\boldsymbol{A}}^{-1}\hat{\boldsymbol{B}}\hat{\boldsymbol{A}}^{-1}/N$. ■

Procedure 4.1.1 is useful when h_{it} is observed and heterogeneity and serial correlation in the errors of a structural selection model such as (3.2) can be ruled out. If the expected value of u_{it} given $\boldsymbol{v}_i$ depends on v_{ir}, $r \neq t$, even after conditioning on a time-constant effect, then Procedure 4.1.1 does not generally produce a consistent estimator of β. If we are willing to make an assumption about α_i, then we can replace (4.1) with an assumption that allows for heterogeneity and unrestricted serial correlation in the errors of both the selection and regression equations.

Assumption 3'. For $t = 1, 2, \ldots, T$,

(i) $$\mathrm{E}(u_{it}|\boldsymbol{x}_i, v_{it}) = \mathrm{E}(u_{it}|v_{it}) = \mathrm{L}(u_{it}|v_{it}), \tag{4.6}$$

(ii) $$\mathrm{E}(\alpha_i|\boldsymbol{x}_i, v_{it}) = \mathrm{L}(\alpha_i|1, \boldsymbol{x}_{i1}, \ldots, \boldsymbol{x}_{iT}, v_{it}), \tag{4.7}$$

where $\mathrm{L}(\cdot|\cdot)$ denotes the linear projection operator. ■

Consider first Assumption 3'(i). The first equality in (4.6) states that u_{it} is mean independent of $\boldsymbol{x}_i$ conditional on v_{it}. The key observation is that, unlike in (4.1), the entire history $(v_{i1}, \ldots, v_{iT})$ does *not* appear in the first conditioning set in (4.6); this is done on purpose so that the nature of any serial dependence in the v_{it} is entirely unrestricted. The conditional mean independence assumption (4.6) always holds if (u_{it}, v_{it}) is independent of $\boldsymbol{x}_i$, something usually maintained in selection contexts. (Recall that we have already assumed that v_{it} is independent of $\boldsymbol{x}_i$ in Assumption 2, but we have not required u_{it} to be independent of $\boldsymbol{x}_i$.) Also,

(4.6) imposes no restriction on the temporal dependence of $\{u_{it}\}$, or on how u_{it} relates to v_{ir}, $r \neq t$.

The second equality in (4.6) is much less important, and could be relaxed. For simplicity, and because it is the leading case, we have assumed that $\mathrm{E}(u_{it} | v_{it})$ is linear, which allows us to write

$$\mathrm{E}(u_{it} | v_{it}) = \rho_t v_{it}, \tag{4.8}$$

for some scalar ρ_t. We can allow for more flexibility by, say, adding to (4.8) the quadratic term $v_{it}^2 - \sigma_t^2$. For simplicity we focus on (4.8).

Practically speaking, Assumption 3′(i) is much weaker than Assumption 3. Apparently, this comes at the cost of needing an assumption on the unobserved effect α_i, given here by Assumption 3′(ii). Without the term v_{it}, that assumption is similar to an assumption used by Chamberlain (1980) in the context of unobserved component probit models. Here, except for linearity of $\mathrm{E}(\alpha_i | \boldsymbol{x}_i, v_{it})$, the distribution of α_i given $(\boldsymbol{x}_i, v_{it})$ is otherwise unrestricted for all t; for example, conditional heteroskedasticity of unknown form is allowed. Assumption 3′(ii) is hardly for free, but it is notably less restrictive than – and implied by – the assumptions made in previous work on sample selection with panel data. In particular, Assumption 3′(ii) always holds when (α_i, v_{it}) conditional on $\boldsymbol{x}_i$ is bivariate normal with constant variance matrix and expectation linear in $\boldsymbol{x}_i$ (recall that $\mathrm{E}(v_{it} | \boldsymbol{x}_i) = 0$ and $\mathrm{E}(v_{it}^2 | \boldsymbol{x}_i) = \sigma_t^2$ already hold under Assumption 3). Unlike a random effects specification, Assumption 3′(ii) allows α_i to be correlated with $\boldsymbol{x}_i$. Also, that assumption places no restrictions on the serial dependence of $\{v_{it}\}$, and so it applies to all structural selection models discussed in Section 3 with arbitrary serial correlation in $\{a_{it}\}$.

To see how Assumption 3′ allows us to correct for selection bias, first note that for each t the linear predictor in (4.7) can always be written as

$$\mathrm{L}(\alpha_i | \boldsymbol{x}_i, v_{it}) = \psi_{t0} + \boldsymbol{x}_{i1}\psi_{t1} + \boldsymbol{x}_{i2}\psi_{t2} + \cdots + \boldsymbol{x}_{iT}\psi_{tT} + \phi_t v_{it}, \tag{4.9}$$

where ψ_{t0} is a scalar and ψ_{tr}, $r = 1, \ldots, T$, are $K \times 1$ vectors. This representation turns out to be too general for identifying the vector β. The key point is that, under Assumptions 2 and 3′, the ψ_{tr} are necessarily *constant* across t; that is, the coefficients on the $\boldsymbol{x}_{ir}$ are the same regardless of which v_{it} is also being conditioned on. This is crucial to the approach and it is a simple application of the law of iterated expecations: for any t,

$$\begin{aligned}\mathrm{E}(\alpha_i | \boldsymbol{x}_{i1}, \ldots, \boldsymbol{x}_{iT}) &= \psi_{t0} + \boldsymbol{x}_{i1}\psi_{t1} + \boldsymbol{x}_{i2}\psi_{t2} + \cdots + \boldsymbol{x}_{iT}\psi_{tT} + \phi_t \mathrm{E}(v_{it} | \boldsymbol{x}_i) \\ &= \psi_{t0} + \boldsymbol{x}_{i1}\psi_{t1} + \boldsymbol{x}_{i2}\psi_{t2} + \cdots + \boldsymbol{x}_{iT}\psi_{tT} \qquad (4.10) \\ &= \psi_0 + \boldsymbol{x}_{i1}\psi_1 + \boldsymbol{x}_{i2}\psi_2 + \cdots + \boldsymbol{x}_{iT}\psi_T. \qquad (4.11)\end{aligned}$$

Eq. (4.10) follows because $\mathrm{E}(v_{it} | \boldsymbol{x}_i) = 0$ under Assumption 2, and Eq. (4.11) is just the fact that the coefficients in the linear projection of α_i onto $\boldsymbol{x}_i$ are necessarily time-invariant. Thus, we have established the important conclusion that the vector of coefficients appearing on $\boldsymbol{x}_i$ in $\mathrm{E}(\alpha_i|\boldsymbol{x}_i, v_{it})$ is the same for all t.

Given Assumptions 2 and 3′ we can easily identify β. Write

$$\mathrm{E}(y_{it}|\boldsymbol{x}_i, v_{it}) = \boldsymbol{x}_i\psi + \boldsymbol{x}_{it}\beta + \gamma_t v_{it}, \tag{4.12}$$

where $\gamma_t = \rho_t + \phi_t$. Thus, for each t we are left with a population regression that contains a linear combination of the explanatory variables from all time periods, the term $\boldsymbol{x}_{it}\beta$, and the additional term $\gamma_t v_{it}$. Without the term $\gamma_t v_{it}$, (4.12) is similar to Chamberlain (1982). The important difference is that Chamberlain can work with the linear projection $\mathrm{L}(y_{it}|\boldsymbol{x}_i)$, while here, because of the sample selection problem, we need (4.12) to be a conditional expectation. Still, we do not need to assume a particular conditional distribution or a constant conditional second moment for α_i.

We could extend (4.7) by adding a quadratic term, $v_{it}^2 - \sigma_t^2$, and even interaction terms such as $v_{it}\boldsymbol{x}_i$. It is easily shown using iterated expectations that these modifications for $\mathrm{E}(\alpha_i|\boldsymbol{x}_i, v_{it})$ are entirely consistent with Assumptions 2 and 3′(i).

We can also assume that α_i depends on $\boldsymbol{x}_i$ only through the time average. In this case, $\boldsymbol{x}_i$ would be replaced with $(1, \bar{\boldsymbol{x}}_i)$ in (4.12). This conserves on parameters but also imposes restrictions on the relationship between α_i and $\boldsymbol{x}_i$ that could be violated, especially if the $\boldsymbol{x}_{it}$ are trending.

In using (4.12) to motivate estimators for β it is important to remember that v_{ir} for $r \neq t$ is not included in the conditioning set (remember we did this on purpose to place as few restrictions as possible on time dependence in the idiosyncratic errors). This means that v_{it} is not strictly exogenous in (4.12). Consequently, estimators such as feasible GLS applied to (4.12) are generally inconsistent for β. Although other procedures could be used – such as minimum distance estimation – we will focus on the simplest consistent estimator, pooled OLS.

Because s_{it} is a function of $(\boldsymbol{x}_i, v_{it})$, (4.12) implies that

$$\mathrm{E}(y_{it}|\boldsymbol{x}_i, v_{it}, s_{it} = 1) = \boldsymbol{x}_i\psi + \boldsymbol{x}_{it}\beta + \gamma_t v_{it}. \tag{4.13}$$

This makes it clear that a pooled OLS procedure consistently estimates β.

Procedure 4.1.2 (h_{it} observed; valid under Assumptions 2 and 3′):

(i) Obtain $\hat{v}_{it}$ when $s_{it} = 1$ from T separate Tobit equations, just as in Procedure 3.1. For $s_{it} = 1$ define the $1 \times (1 + TK + K + T)$ vector

$$\hat{\boldsymbol{w}}_{it} = (1, \boldsymbol{x}_{i1}, \ldots,, \boldsymbol{x}_{iT}, \boldsymbol{x}_{it}, 0, \ldots, 0, \hat{v}_{it}, 0, \ldots, 0).$$

(ii) Obtain $\hat{\theta} = (\hat{\psi}', \hat{\beta}', \hat{\gamma}')'$ as the pooled OLS estimator in the equation

$$y_{it} = \hat{\boldsymbol{w}}_{it}\theta + \mathrm{error}_{it}, \qquad s_{it} = 1. \tag{4.14}$$

This yields

$$\hat{\theta} \equiv \left(\sum_{i=1}^{N} \sum_{t=1}^{T} s_{it} \hat{w}_{it}' \hat{w}_{it} \right)^{-1} \left(\sum_{i=1}^{N} \sum_{t=1}^{T} s_{it} \hat{w}_{it}' y_{it} \right), \tag{4.15}$$

which will be consistent and $\sqrt{N}$-asymptotically normal under Assumptions 2 and 3′, and standard regularity conditions.

(iii) Estimate Avar$(\hat{\theta})$ as follows: define the OLS residuals $\hat{e}_{it} = y_{it} - \hat{w}_{it}\hat{\theta}$, $s_{it} = 1$. Define the matrix $\hat{D}$ as in (4.5) except now G_{it} is the $(1 + TK + K + T) \times T(1 + TK)$ matrix

$$G_{it} = \begin{pmatrix} 0 \; 0 \dots 0 & 0 & 0 \dots 0 \\ 0 \; 0 \dots 0 & Z_{it} & 0 \dots 0 \end{pmatrix}; \tag{4.16}$$

each zero in the first row block of G_{it} is a $(1 + TK + K) \times (1 + TK)$ matrix and each zero in the second row block is a $T \times (1 + TK)$ matrix. (The matrix Z_{it} is in the tth column block of this matrix.) The $T \times (1 + TK)$ matrix Z_{it} is defined as

$$Z_{it} = (0' \; 0' \dots 0' \; -x_i' \; 0' \dots 0')', \tag{4.17}$$

where each zero in Z_{it} is a $1 \times (1 + TK)$ vector and the $1 \times (1 + TK)$ vector $-x_i$ is in the t row. Now finish exactly as in Procedure 4.1.1 (that is, first form the $T(1 + TK) \times 1$ vector $\hat{r}_i$, then construct $\hat{q}_i$, $\hat{p}_i$, $\hat{A}$, and $\hat{B}$). ■

Note that a test of the T restrictions H_0: $\gamma = 0$ is easily carried out by constructing a Wald statistic. This can be used as a test for selection bias, but it has a drawback compared with the test in Section 3. Namely, the test would maintain Assumption 3′(ii) under H_0 even though we know this assumption is not needed for fixed effects to consistently estimate β.

4.2. A selection correction when only the selection indicator is observed

If h_{it} is not observed then the fixed effects approach to the selection correction is not available, even under Assumptions 2 and 3. Nevertheless, Procedure 4.1.2 is easily modified to handle the case where only s_{it} is observed. Thus, we impose Assumptions 2 and 3′ in this subsection. Without loss of generality we now assume that $E(v_{it}^2) = 1$.

In place of (4.13) we must find the expectation of y_{it} given $(x_i, s_{it} = 1)$. This yields

$$E(y_{it} | x_i, s_{it} = 1) = x_i\psi + x_{it}\beta + \gamma_t \lambda(x_i\delta_t), \tag{4.18}$$

leading to the following procedure.

Procedure 4.2 (s_{it} observed; valid under Assumptions 2 and 3′):

(i) For each $t = 1, 2, \ldots, T$ estimate Eq. (3.15) by standard probit. For $s_{it} = 1$ obtain the inverse Mills ratio $\lambda(\boldsymbol{x}_i\hat{\boldsymbol{\delta}}_t)$. For $s_{it} = 1$ define $\hat{\boldsymbol{w}}_{it} \equiv (1, \boldsymbol{x}_{i1}, \ldots, \boldsymbol{x}_{iT}, \boldsymbol{x}_{it}, 0, \ldots, 0, \hat{\lambda}_{it}, 0, \ldots, 0)$.

(ii) Obtain $\hat{\theta} \equiv (\hat{\psi}', \hat{\beta}', \hat{\gamma}')'$ as the pooled OLS estimator in Eq. (4.14).

(iii) Estimate $\text{Avar}(\hat{\theta})$ as follows: first define the OLS residuals $\hat{e}_{it} \equiv y_{it} - \hat{\boldsymbol{w}}_{it}\hat{\theta}$, $s_{it} = 1$. Define the matrix $\hat{\boldsymbol{D}}$ as in (4.5), where $\boldsymbol{G}_{it}$ is defined as in (4.16) but $\boldsymbol{Z}_{it}$ is now defined by replacing $-\boldsymbol{x}_i$ with $\hat{v}_{it}\boldsymbol{x}_i$ in (4.17), where $\hat{v}_{it}$ is the derivative of $\lambda(\cdot)$ evaluated at $\boldsymbol{x}_i\hat{\boldsymbol{\delta}}_t$. For each t let $\hat{\boldsymbol{r}}_{it}$ be the $(1 + TK) \times 1$ vector equal to minus the inverse of the average estimated Hessian times the estimated score of the probit log-likelihood function for observation i; these are given in Maddala (1983, Sect. 2.5). Now proceed exactly as in Procedure 4.1.1. ■

5. Concluding remarks

The selection corrections proposed in this paper have been derived for an unobserved effects linear model under the assumption of strict exogeneity of the regressors conditional on the unobserved effect. We used the strict exogeneity assumption to allow α_i to be correlated with $(\boldsymbol{x}_{i1}, \boldsymbol{x}_{i2}, \ldots, \boldsymbol{x}_{iT})$. If a random effects type specification is preferred, then one can simply replace $\boldsymbol{x}_i\psi$ in (4.12) and (4.18) with a constant; Procedure 4.1.2 or 4.2 can then be applied to the simplified equation. Even in a random effects framework the assumptions used here are much weaker than usual: the u_{it} can be arbitrarily heterogeneous and serially dependent.

A more difficult case to handle is when (2.1) contains a lagged dependent variable, which is necessarily correlated with α_i and is only observed for a subset of time periods. Such an extension would allow estimation of dynamic wage equations with unobserved effects while accounting for the sample selection bias due to current and lagged wage being observed for only those working in two consecutive periods. Preliminary work shows that, under reasonable extensions of the current assumptions, it is possible to allow for variables in (2.1) that are not strictly exogenous and that are observed for only a selected subset of time periods.

Appendix

In Sections 3 and 4 we rely on some general results concerning pooled OLS estimation using a selected sample. For brevity we present only the formulas for the asymptotic variance; derivations are available on request.

For each i let $\{(\boldsymbol{w}_{it}, y_{it}, s_{it})\colon t = 1, \ldots, T\}$ be a random draw from some population, where $\boldsymbol{w}_{it}$ is $1 \times \boldsymbol{G}$ and y_{it} and s_{it} are scalars. The pair $(\boldsymbol{w}_{it}, y_{it})$ is observed only if the selection indicator is unity: $s_{it} = 1$. Suppose that

$$\mathrm{E}(y_{it}|\boldsymbol{w}_{it}, s_{it} = 1) = \boldsymbol{w}_{it}\theta, \tag{A.1}$$

where θ is a $\boldsymbol{G} \times 1$ vector. Then, we can write (A.1) in error form as

$$y_{it} = \boldsymbol{w}_{it}\theta + e_{it}, \quad \mathrm{E}(e_{it}|\boldsymbol{w}_{it}, s_{it} = 1) = 0, \qquad t = 1, 2, \ldots, T.$$

The pooled OLS estimator on the selected sample can be written as

$$\hat{\theta} = \left(N^{-1} \sum_{i=1}^{N} \sum_{t=1}^{T} s_{it}\boldsymbol{w}_{it}'\boldsymbol{w}_{it} \right)^{-1} \left(N^{-1} \sum_{i=1}^{N} \sum_{t=1}^{T} s_{it}\boldsymbol{w}_{it}' y_{it} \right),$$

and this is easily shown to be consistent. In the applications here we need to obtain the asymptotic variance of $\sqrt{N}(\hat{\theta} - \theta)$ when some elements of $\boldsymbol{w}_{it}$ are estimated in a preliminary stage, as in Newey (1984) and Pagan (1984). Suppose that $\boldsymbol{w}_{it} = \boldsymbol{w}_{it}(\delta)$, where δ is a $Q \times 1$ vector of unknown parameters (typically only a subset of $\boldsymbol{w}_{it}$ will actually depend on δ). Let $\hat{\delta}$ be a $\sqrt{N}$-asymptotically normal estimator of δ with representation

$$\sqrt{N}(\hat{\delta} - \delta) = N^{-1/2} \sum_{i=1}^{N} \boldsymbol{r}_i + \mathrm{o}_p(1), \tag{A.2}$$

where $\{\boldsymbol{r}_i\}$ is a $Q \times 1$ i.i.d. sequence with $\mathrm{E}(\boldsymbol{r}_i) = \boldsymbol{0}$. Typically, $\boldsymbol{r} = \boldsymbol{r}_i(\delta)$, and we estimate this as $\hat{\boldsymbol{r}}_i = \hat{\boldsymbol{r}}_i(\hat{\delta})$. A simplifying assumption that holds in our applications is that $\mathrm{E}[s_{it} \nabla_\delta \boldsymbol{w}_{it}(\delta)' e_{it}] = \boldsymbol{0}$, where $\nabla_\delta \boldsymbol{w}_{it}(\delta)'$ is the $G \times Q$ gradient of $\boldsymbol{w}_{it}(\delta)'$; this simplifies estimation of the asymptotic variance.

Let $\hat{\theta}$ now denote the OLS estimator from the regression on the selected sample, but where $\hat{\boldsymbol{w}}_{it} \equiv \boldsymbol{w}_{it}(\hat{\delta})$ is used in place of $\boldsymbol{w}_{it}$. It can be shown that

$$\sqrt{N}(\hat{\theta} - \theta) \xrightarrow{d} \mathrm{Normal}(\boldsymbol{0}, \boldsymbol{A}^{-1}\boldsymbol{B}\boldsymbol{A}^{-1}),$$

where

$$\boldsymbol{A} \equiv \mathrm{E}\left(\sum_{t=1}^{T} s_{it}\boldsymbol{w}_{it}'\boldsymbol{w}_{it} \right) \quad \text{and} \quad \boldsymbol{B} = \mathrm{var}(\boldsymbol{p}_i) = \mathrm{E}(\boldsymbol{p}_i\boldsymbol{p}_i');$$

the $G \times 1$ vector $\boldsymbol{p}_i$ is defined as $\boldsymbol{p}_i = \boldsymbol{q}_i - \boldsymbol{D}\boldsymbol{r}_i$. where $\boldsymbol{r}_i$ is from (A.2), $\boldsymbol{q}_i \equiv \sum_{t=1}^{T} s_{it}\boldsymbol{w}_{it}' e_{it}$ is a $G \times 1$ vector, and $\boldsymbol{D} \equiv \mathrm{E}(\sum_{t=1}^{T} s_{it}\boldsymbol{w}_{it}'\theta' \nabla_\delta \boldsymbol{w}_{it}(\delta)')$ is a $G \times Q$ matrix.

To estimate $\mathrm{Avar}(\hat{\theta}) \equiv \boldsymbol{A}^{-1}\boldsymbol{B}\boldsymbol{A}^{-1}/N$, first define

$$\hat{\boldsymbol{A}} \equiv N^{-1} \sum_{i=1}^{N} \sum_{t=1}^{T} s_{it}\hat{\boldsymbol{w}}_{it}'\hat{\boldsymbol{w}}_{it} \quad \text{and} \quad \hat{\boldsymbol{D}} \equiv N^{-1} \sum_{i=1}^{N} \sum_{t=1}^{T} s_{it}\hat{\boldsymbol{w}}_{it}'\hat{\theta}' \nabla_\delta \boldsymbol{w}_{it}(\hat{\delta})', \tag{A.3}$$

where $\nabla_\delta \boldsymbol{w}_{it}(\hat{\delta})'$ is the $G \times Q$ gradient of $\hat{\boldsymbol{w}}_{it}(\delta)'$ evaluated at $\hat{\delta}$. Let $\hat{\boldsymbol{r}}_i \equiv \boldsymbol{r}_i(\hat{\delta})$ be estimates of $\hat{\boldsymbol{r}}_i$, and let $\hat{e}_{it} = y_{it} - \hat{\boldsymbol{w}}_{it}\hat{\theta}$ be the OLS residuals for all i and t such that $s_{it} = 1$. Then for each $i = 1, 2, \dots, N$, define

$$\hat{\boldsymbol{q}}_i = \sum_{t=1}^{T} s_{it}\hat{\boldsymbol{w}}'_{it}\hat{e}_{it} \quad \text{and} \quad \hat{\boldsymbol{p}}_i = \hat{\boldsymbol{q}}_i - \hat{\boldsymbol{D}}\hat{\boldsymbol{r}}_i, \qquad i = 1, \dots, N. \tag{A.4}$$

A consistent estimator of $\boldsymbol{B}$ is

$$\hat{\boldsymbol{B}} \equiv N^{-1} \sum_{i=1}^{N} \hat{\boldsymbol{p}}_i\hat{\boldsymbol{p}}'_i. \tag{A.5}$$

The asymptotic variance of $\hat{\theta}$ is estimated as $\text{Av}\hat{\text{a}}\text{r}(\hat{\theta}) = \hat{\boldsymbol{A}}^{-1}\hat{\boldsymbol{B}}\hat{\boldsymbol{A}}^{-1}/N$, and the asymptotic standard errors are obtained as the square roots of the diagonal elements of this matrix. If the elements of $\hat{\boldsymbol{w}}_{it}$ depending on $\hat{\delta}$ have coefficients in θ equal to zero – as when testing for exclusion of the generated regressors – then $\boldsymbol{D} = \boldsymbol{0}$ and one can take $\hat{\boldsymbol{D}} \equiv \boldsymbol{0}$.

References

Chamberlain, G., 1980, Analysis of covariance with qualitative data, Review of Economic Studies 47, 225–238.

Chamberlain, G., 1982, Multivariate regression models for panel data, Journal of Econometrics 18, 5–46.

Heckman, J., 1976, The common structure of statistical models of truncation, sample selection and limited dependent variables and a simple estimator for such models, Annals of Economic and Social Measurement 5, 475–492.

Kiefer, N.M., 1980, Estimation of fixed effect models for time series of cross-sections with arbitrary intertemporal covariance, Journal of Econometrics 14, 195–202.

Maddala, G.S., 1983, Limited dependent and qualitative variables in econometrics (Cambridge University Press, Cambridge).

Mundlak, Y., 1978, On the pooling of time series and cross section data, Econometrica 46, 69–85.

Newey, W.K., 1984, A method of moments interpretation of sequential estimators, Economics Letters 14, 201–206.

Nijman, T. and M. Verbeek, 1992, Nonresponse in panel data: the impact on estimates of a life cycle consumption function, Journal of Applied Econometrics 7, 243–257.

Pagan, A., 1984, Econometric issues in the analysis of regressions with generated regressors, International Economic Review 25, 221–247.

Smith, R. and R. Blundell, 1986, An exogeneity test for a simultaneous Tobit model with an application to labor supply, Econometrica 54, 679–685.

Verbeek, M. and T. Nijman, 1992, Testing for selectivity bias in panel data models, International Economic Review 33, 681–703.

Vella, F., 1992, Simple tests for sample selection bias in censored and discrete choice models, Journal of Applied Econometrics 7, 413–421.

Vella, F. and M. Verbeek, 1992, Estimating and testing simultaneous equation panel data models with censored endogenous variables. Unpublished manuscript (Department of Economics, Rice University, Houston, TX).

White, H., 1994, Estimation, inference and specification analysis (Cambridge University Press, Cambridge).

Zabel, J.E., 1992, Estimating fixed and random effects with selectivity, Economics Letters 40, 269–272.

Part II
Non-linear Panel Models

[9]

ELSEVIER

Journal of Econometrics 93 (1999) 203–228

JOURNAL OF Econometrics

www.elsevier.nl/locate/econbase

Leapfrog estimation of a fixed-effects model with unknown transformation of the dependent variable☆

Jason Abrevaya*

University of Chicago, Graduate School of Business, 1101 East 58 Street, Chicago, IL 60637, USA

Received 1 November 1996; accepted 1 December 1998

Abstract

This paper considers a fixed-effects panel version of the linear transformation model, in which the dependent variable is $h(y_t)$ for an unspecified, strictly monotonic h. Examples of the model include the multiple-spell proportional hazards model and dependent-variable transformation models (e.g., the Box–Cox model) with fixed effects. A semiparametric estimator, called the *leapfrog estimator*, is introduced and shown to be $\sqrt{n}$-consistent and asymptotically normal. The leapfrog estimator allows for h to vary over time and for heteroskedasticity across observational units. Related semiparametric estimators are considered, and a general covariance result for estimators based on second-order U-processes is presented. © 1999 Elsevier Science S.A. All rights reserved.

JEL classification: C14; C23; C41

Keywords: Semiparametric estimation; Fixed-effects models; Transformation models; Multiple-spell duration models

* Corresponding author. Tel.: 001-773-834-0721; fax: 001-773-702-0458.

E-mail address: jason.abrevaya@gsb.uchicago.edu (J. Abrevaya)

☆ This paper is a revised version of the first chapter of the author's Ph.D. dissertation at the MIT Department of Economics. Thanks to Jerry Hausman, Bo Honoré, Ekaterini Kyriazidou, M.J. Lee, Whitney Newey, and Robert Sherman as well as seminar participants at Berkeley, Caltech, Duke, Princeton, Stanford GSB, University of Chicago GSB, and Yale for their valuable comments. The comments of two anonymous referees and an Associate Editor substantially improved this paper. Financial support from the National Science Foundation (graduate fellowship and SBR-9730155) and the University of Chicago GSB Faculty Research Fund is gratefully acknowledged.

PII: S0304-4076(99)00009-3

1. Introduction

The *linear transformation model* has received a great deal of attention in the statistics and econometrics literature. Most research has focused on the non-panel model

$$h(y_i) = x_i'\beta + \varepsilon_i \quad (i = 1, \ldots, n), \tag{1}$$

where h is a strictly increasing function.[1] When h is left unspecified, several $\sqrt{n}$-consistent semiparametric estimators of β exist (see, for example, Cavanagh and Sherman, 1998; Han, 1987;[2] Horowitz and Härdle, 1996; Ichimura, 1993; Powell et al., 1989). Since h is unspecified, these estimators estimate β up-to-scale (and without a location parameter). With an i.i.d. assumption on ε, the function h and the distribution of ε can be non-parametrically estimated using the techniques of Horowitz (1996) or Ye and Duan (1997). See Horowitz (1996) for a thorough survey and discussion of this model.

This paper considers the fixed-effects version of (1):

$$h(y_{it}) = x_{it}'\beta + \gamma_t + \alpha_i + \varepsilon_{it} \quad (i = 1, \ldots, n;\ t = 1, \ldots, T), \tag{2}$$

where α is a fixed effect (possibly correlated with the covariates), γ is a time effect, $n \to \infty$, and T is fixed.[3] Time-invariant covariates are not included explicitly since they can be thought of as being part of the fixed effect. The focus of this paper is on estimation of β, the coefficient vector for the time-varying covariates. Since h is left unspecified, the goal is to estimate β up-to-scale. The two-period model ($T = 2$) is considered in detail, with extension to larger T discussed in Section 3. The standard differencing notation used is $\Delta x \equiv x_2 - x_1$, and similarly for other variables.

Several interesting econometric models are described by the fixed-effects model in (1). The first important example is the multiple-spell proportional hazards model (where h is the log-integrated baseline hazard function). Most of the literature on proportional hazards models, in both the single- and multiple-spell models, uses a random-effects approach to model heterogeneity. The drawback of this approach is that the heterogeneity is assumed to be independent of the covariates. For multiple-spell models, panel data allow the possibility of using a fixed-effects approach where heterogeneity can be correlated with

---

[1] Of course, h could be strictly decreasing; define $\tilde{h} \equiv -h$ so that $\tilde{h}$ satisfies (1) with $-\beta$ as the parameter vector.

[2] Sherman (1993) makes inference possible with the estimator of Han (1987).

[3] A location normalization $h(0) = c_0$ is required for identification of the time effect relative to $x'\beta$.

the covariates.[4] Examples of multiple-spell models which have been studied in the fixed-effects framework are consumer purchasing behavior (Gönül and Srinivasan, 1993; Jain and Vilcassim, 1991), child mortality (Olsen and Wolpin, 1983); and timing of births, (Newman and McCulloch, 1984). The existing fixed-effects estimation techniques require some specification of the baseline hazard. Chamberlain (1985), for instance, considers marginal and conditional-likelihood methods for eliminating the fixed effect in models with Weibull, lognormal, or gamma specifications. Gönül and Srinivasan (1993) propose a concentrated-likelihood method which can be used regardless of the functional form of the baseline hazard, but the chosen baseline enters into the concentrated-likelihood function. The estimators of this paper effectively eliminate the fixed effect without having to make any assumptions about the baseline hazard.

A second example of interest is that the model in (2) can be used as a flexible alternative to dependent-variable transformation models like the Box–Cox model.[5] When a parametrized family of transformation functions is used, the transformation parameter(s) and the coefficient vector β are jointly estimated (using maximum-likelihood estimation or non-linear instrumental variables). If the true transformation function does not belong to the specified family of transformation functions, the resulting estimators can be biased and inconsistent. Semiparametric estimation of the more flexible model avoids this potential problem. In addition, the semiparametric estimator of β can be used to conduct a specification test against the parametric estimator.

The semiparametric estimators of β for the non-panel model in (1) are not applicable to the panel model in (2) due to the possible correlation between the fixed effect α and the regressors. The first-differencing method used to remove the fixed effect in the linear panel model cannot be used since first-differencing the model in (2) removes the fixed effect but leaves $h(y_2) - h(y_1)$ as the dependent variable. For unknown h, the value of the dependent variable is unknown, making standard "within" estimation impossible.

This sort of problem is common in non-linear fixed-effects models. In these models, the "latent" dependent variable is not observed; instead, only some transformation of the "latent" dependent variable is observed. For instance, in the binary choice model, we observe $1(y^* > 0)$ rather than y^*; in the linear censored model, we observe $y^* \cdot 1(y^* > 0)$ rather than y^*. In our model, we observe y rather than the "latent" $h(y)$. In the literature on non-linear fixed-effects models, some estimators are based on a parametric assumption on the

[4] Honoré (1993a) shows that it is possible to identify multiple-spell duration models with fixed effects and no covariates. This identification result implies that it is possible to identify such models with covariates (since all features of the model are identified conditional on the covariates).

[5] For more details on these (and other) examples, see Abrevaya (1996).

error disturbances which allows for cancellation of the fixed effects in some models – e.g., the conditional logit model for binary data, the Poisson model for count data, and certain parametric models for duration data. Semiparametric estimators, which do not require parametric assumptions on the error term, exist for consistent estimation of the coefficient vector in the binary choice model (Manski, 1987), the linear censored and truncated models (Honoré, 1992), and the sample-selection model (Kyriazidou, 1997a).

Before discussing the leapfrog estimator, consider the following simple semiparametric estimation method. If $\Delta\varepsilon$ is i.i.d., note that $\Pr(\Delta y > 0|\Delta x) = F(\Delta x'\beta + \Delta\gamma)$, where F is the c.d.f. of $-\Delta\varepsilon$. Defining $d \equiv 1(\Delta y > 0)$, one can estimate a binary response model with dependent variable d, independent variables Δx, and an unspecified increasing $F:\mathscr{R} \to [0,1]$. If one is willing to assume the form of F, an efficient estimator (within the class of estimators using binary data for the dependent variable) is the maximum-likelihood estimator. Otherwise, many semiparametric $\sqrt{n}$-consistent estimators of β exist, including those developed by Han (1987), Horowitz and Härdle (1996), Ichimura (1993), Klein and Spady (1993), and Powell et al. (1989). A drawback of this "binary-choice approach" is that consistency requires that the error disturbances have the same distribution across observational units. Consistency also requires that h does not change over time, which may be a concern in particular applications.[6] The leapfrog estimator of this paper is consistent in the presence of heteroskedastic errors across observational units (as well as time-varying h). In cases where both the binary-choice approach and leapfrog estimation are consistent, the distribution of the data will determine their relative efficiencies.[7]

In Section 2, the leapfrog estimator is introduced. Identification and consistency are proven using standard asymptotic results. Asymptotic normality of the estimator follows directly from the U-statistic asymptotic theory in Sherman (1993). In Section 3, estimators similar to the leapfrog estimator are introduced. In this section, extension to $T > 2$ is considered. Also, a new semiparametric estimator (based on a fourth-order U-process) of the cross-sectional model (1) is considered. Section 4 presents some Monte Carlo evidence, and Section 5 concludes.

---

[6] For instance, Abrevaya (1996) discusses repeated-ratings data where y_{it} is a rating (or test score) and h would be expected to vary if a different rating system (or exam) is used in successive periods. Also, in the multiple-spell hazard model, the baseline hazard can be allowed to vary over spells (as discussed in Honoré, 1993a), though the resulting model implies that the fixed effect enters multiplicatively in each spell.

[7] If there is a significant time trend (i.e., $\Delta\gamma$ has low variance), the binary-choice approach will be relatively inefficient. On the other hand, if the distribution of fixed effects has a large variance, the leapfrog estimator will be relatively inefficient. See Section 4 for some discussion.

2. Leapfrog estimation

In this section, a semiparametric estimator for (2) is proposed. First, the objective function(s) is introduced. Then, the technical assumptions and theorems for consistency and asymptotic normality are given.

The basic idea behind the proposed estimator is to compare dependent variables of a given time period across different observational units. For any pair of observational units indexed i and j (with $i \neq j$) at time t,

$$h_t(y_{it}) - h_t(y_{jt}) = (x_{it} - x_{jt})'\beta + (\alpha_i - \alpha_j) + (\varepsilon_{it} - \varepsilon_{jt}). \tag{3}$$

Note that the transformation h has a time subscript. allowing for a different strictly monotonic transformation h_t in each time period. Eq. (3) yields

$$\Pr(y_{it} > y_{jt}|x_{i1}, x_{i2}, \alpha_i, x_{j1}, x_{j2}, \alpha_j) = \Pr(\varepsilon_{jt} - \varepsilon_{it} < (x_{it} - x_{jt})'\beta + (\alpha_i - \alpha_j)) \tag{4}$$

Also, note that

$$\Delta x_i'\beta > \Delta x_j'\beta \Leftrightarrow (x_{i2} - x_{j2})'\beta + (\alpha_i - \alpha_j) > (x_{i1} - x_{j1})'\beta + (\alpha_i - \alpha_j). \tag{5}$$

If $(\varepsilon_{i1} - \varepsilon_{j1})$ and $(\varepsilon_{i2} - \varepsilon_{j2})$ have the same marginal distribution (conditional on $(x_{i1}, x_{i2}, \alpha_i, x_{j1}, x_{j2}, \alpha_j)$), combining (4) and (5) yields

$$\begin{aligned}\Delta x_i'\beta > \Delta x_j'\beta \Rightarrow &\Pr(y_{i2} > y_{j2}|x_{i1}, x_{i2}, \alpha_i, x_{j1}, x_{j2}, \alpha_j)\\ &\geqslant \Pr(y_{i1} > y_{j1}|x_{i1}, x_{i2}, \alpha_i, x_{j1}, x_{j2}, \alpha_j).\end{aligned} \tag{6}$$

If the common marginal density of $(\varepsilon_{i1} - \varepsilon_{j1})$ and $(\varepsilon_{i2} - \varepsilon_{j2})$ is positive everywhere along the real line, the weak inequality in (6) becomes a strict inequality,

$$\begin{aligned}\Delta x_i'\beta > \Delta x_j'\beta \Rightarrow &\Pr(y_{i2} > y_{j2}|x_{i1}, x_{i2}, \alpha_i, x_{j1}, x_{j2}, \alpha_j)\\ &> \Pr(y_{i1} > y_{j1}|x_{i1}, x_{i2}, \alpha_i, x_{j1}, x_{j2}, \alpha_j).\end{aligned} \tag{7}$$

From either (6) or (7), the function

$$S(b) \equiv \mathrm{E}[\mathrm{sign}((\Delta x_i - \Delta x_j)'b)(1(y_{i2} > y_{j2}) - 1(y_{i1} > y_{j1}))], \tag{8}$$

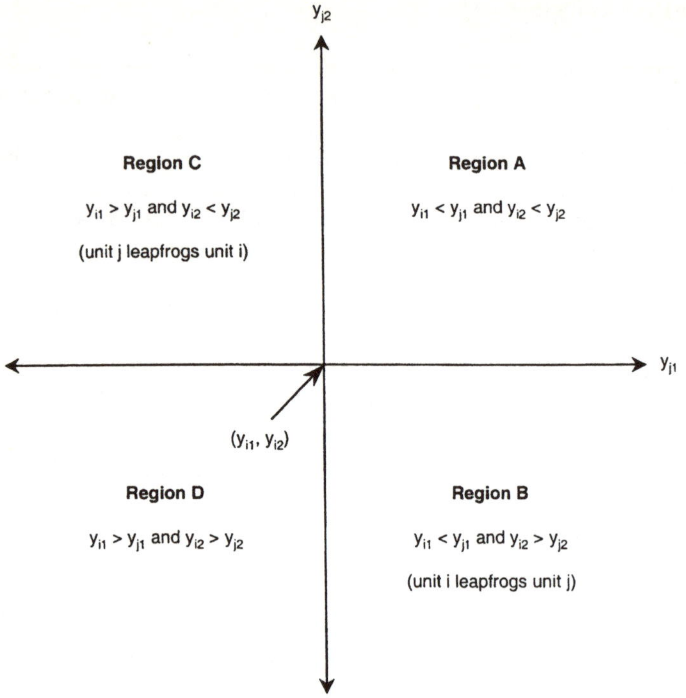

Fig. 1. Graphical Intuition for Leapfrogging.

where $\text{sign}(v) = 1$ if $v \geqslant 0$ and -1 if $v < 0$, is maximized at $b = \beta$.[8] An estimator of β maximizes the sample analogue of (8),

$$S_n(b) \equiv \frac{1}{n(n-1)} \sum_{i \neq j} \text{sign}((\Delta x_i - \Delta x_j)'b)(1(y_{i2} > y_{j2}) - 1(y_{i1} > y_{j1})). \tag{9}$$

To develop a bit more intuition for this estimator, consider the diagram in Fig. 1 which considers the possible relative values for (y_{i1}, y_{i2}) and (y_{j1}, y_{j2}). Observational unit i, with its values (y_{i1}, y_{i2}), is located at the origin. The four quadrants (labeled A–D) correspond to possible values of y_{j1} and y_{j2} (relative to y_{i1} and y_{i2}). For $\Delta x_i'\beta > \Delta x_j'\beta$, Eq. (7) says that

$$\Pr((y_{j1}, y_{j2}) \in B \cup D) > \Pr((y_{j1}, y_{j2}) \in C \cup D)$$

[8] When $\Delta x_i'\beta = \Delta x_j'\beta$, the probabilities in (6) or (7) are equal.

(with the conditioning arguments suppressed). Since the region D is in both probabilities, it follows that $\Pr((y_{j1}, y_{j2}) \in B) > \Pr((y_{j1}, y_{j2}) \in C)$. Region B corresponds to a pair of observational units for which i has a lower dependent variable than j in the first time period and a higher dependent variable than j in the second time period. For such a pair of observational units, we say that unit i *leapfrogs* unit j. Similarly, region C corresponds to a pair of observational units for which unit j leapfrogs unit i. Viewed in this way, the source of identification of the estimator based on (9) becomes clear; only those pairs of observational units which leapfrog each other contribute to the objective function. If $\Delta x_i'\beta$ is larger than $\Delta x_j'\beta$, it is more likely that unit i leapfrogs unit j than vice versa. An objective function with the same maximizer as (9) is[9]

$$T_n(b) \equiv \frac{1}{n(n-1)} \sum_{i \neq j} 1(\Delta x_i' b > \Delta x_j' b) \cdot$$

$$(1(y_{i1} < y_{j1}, y_{i2} > y_{j2}) - 1(y_{i1} > y_{j1}, y_{i2} < y_{j2})). \tag{10}$$

The estimator maximizing (9) or (10) is called the *leapfrog estimator* (LFE, hereafter).

This objective function bears resemblance to that of the *maximum rank correlation* estimator (MRCE, hereafter). Though the objective function is a double sum, the MRCE algorithm of Abrevaya (1999a) can be used to compute the LFE objective function in $O(n \log n)$ computations (rather than $O(n^2)$ computations).[10] Since the objective function is not a smooth function, standard gradient-based optimization techniques cannot be used. The Nelder–Mead simplex method, which does not require smoothness, seems to work quite well in practice. Before optimization, one can calculate the percentage of observation-pairs that leapfrog each other to get a sense of how well the LFE will perform.

2.1. Consistency

The following assumptions are made to establish strong consistency of the LFE.

Assumption 1 (*Parameter vector*). β is an interior element of the parameter space $\mathscr{B}$, a compact subset of $\{b \in \mathscr{R}^k\colon |b_k| = 1\}$.

---

[9] Abrevaya (1996) formally shows the equivalence between $S_n(b)$ and $T_n(b)$.

[10] Note that $S_n(b)$ is the difference of two functions which are identical in form to the MRCE objective function.

Normalization is required since β is only identified up-to-scale. Compactness is required for consistency, and β an interior element is required for asymptotic normality.[11]

Assumption 2 (*Sampling*). A sample of n i.i.d. realizations $\{(y_{i1}, y_{i2}, x_{i1}, x_{i2}, \alpha_i, \varepsilon_{i1}, \varepsilon_{i2})\}_{i=1}^{n}$, is drawn from the population, satisfying the model in (2). The observed sample is $\{(y_{i1}, y_{i2}, x_{i1}, x_{i2})\}_{i=1}^{n}$.

Assumption 3 (*Covariates*). Δx is an i.i.d. k-dimensional random variable s.t.: (i) The support of Δx is not contained in a proper linear subspace of $\mathscr{R}^k$; and (ii) the kth component of Δx has everywhere positive Lebesgue density, conditional on the other components.

Assumption 3(i) is the standard full-rank assumption, and Assumption 3(ii) is a familiar continuity condition in the semiparametric literature required for identification.

Assumption 4 (*Error disturbances*). (i) For all i, ε_{i1} and ε_{i2} have the same marginal distribution, conditional on $(x_{i1}, x_{i2}, \alpha_i)$. (ii) The common marginal density function is positive everywhere along the real line.

This assumption is the same as Manski (1987) and the weakest condition required for consistency of the estimators in Honoré (1992) (see Honoré, 1993b for a discussion). The assumption requires stationarity of the disturbances within an observational unit but allows for heteroskedasticity across observational units. Since only the marginal distributions need be the same, the assumption also allows for certain forms of serial correlation of the error disturbances. The obvious weakness of Assumption 4 is that strict exogeneity of the regressors is required; for instance, the dependent variable from the first time period cannot be a regressor in the second time period.

The key importance of Assumption 4 is given in the following lemma:

Lemma 1. Assumption 4 implies that condition (7) holds for any $i \neq j$.

The proof of this lemma is trivial since Assumption 4(i) implies that $(\varepsilon_{i1} - \varepsilon_{j1})$ and $(\varepsilon_{i2} - \varepsilon_{j2})$ have the same marginal density (conditional on $(x_{i1}, x_{i2}, \alpha_i, x_{j1}, x_{j2}, \alpha_j)$), and Assumption 4(ii) implies that this density is positive everywhere.

[11] Alternatively, the normalization $\|\beta\| = 1$ *implies* compactness. This normalization would require the additional assumption that the kth component of β is non-zero (see, e.g., the proof of consistency in Han, 1987).

With Lemma 1 established, the consistency result follows easily (see the appendix for proof).

Theorem 1. Let $\hat{\beta}$ be a value that maximizes $T_n(b)$ over the parameter space $\mathscr{B}$. If Assumptions 1–4 hold , then $\hat{\beta}$ is strongly consistent for β.

2.2. Asymptotic normality

For asymptotic normality, some additional notation (following Sherman, 1993 where possible) is required. Let $z \equiv (y_1, y_2, \Delta x)$ denote an observation from the set $\mathscr{S} \subseteq \mathscr{R} \times \mathscr{R} \times \mathscr{R}^k$. For each $z \in \mathscr{S}$ and $b \in \mathscr{B}$, define

$$H(y_1, y_2, v) \equiv \Pr_Z[y_1 < Y_1, y_2 > Y_2 | \Delta X'\beta = v] \\ - \Pr_Z[y_1 > Y_1, y_2 < Y_2 | \Delta X'\beta = v] \tag{11}$$

and

$$\tau_t(z, b) \equiv E_Z[1(\Delta x'b > \Delta X'b) \cdot (1(y_1 < Y_1, y_2 > Y_2) \\ - 1(y_1 > Y_1, y_2 < Y_2))] \tag{12}$$

where $Z \equiv (Y_1, Y_2, \Delta X)$. Write ∇_m for the mth partial derivative operator applied to the first $k-1$ components of b.

Since asymptotic normality follows directly from Sherman (1993), the additional technical assumption required (that allows for the Taylor expansion of $\tau_t(z, \cdot)$ about β) is stated in the appendix. We say that "$\tau_t(z, \cdot)$ *is Taylor-expandable*" if it satisfies this assumption. The asymptotic normality result is as follows.

Theorem 2. Let $\hat{\beta}$ be a value that maximizes $T_n(b)$ over the parameter space $\mathscr{B}$. If Assumptions 1–4 hold and $\tau_t(z, \cdot)$ is Taylor-expandable, then

$$\sqrt{n}(\hat{\beta} - \beta) \xrightarrow{d} \begin{pmatrix} W \\ 0 \end{pmatrix},$$

where $W \sim N(0, V^{-1}\Delta V^{-1})$, *with* $\Delta = E[\nabla_1 \tau_t(\cdot, \beta)(\nabla_1 \tau_t(\cdot, \beta))']$ *and* $2V = E[\nabla_2 \tau_t(\cdot, \beta)]$.

As in Section 7 of Sherman (1993), numerical derivatives can be used to consistently estimate Δ and V. In practice, however, these estimates seem to be sensitive to bandwidth choice. An alternative approach to consistent estimation of the covariance matrix involves deriving closed-form expressions for V and Δ and non-parametrically estimating the expressions. Under some additional smoothness assumptions, the closed-form expressions are given by the following theorem:

Theorem 3. Let $g(\cdot)$ denote the marginal density function of $\Delta x'\beta$, and let $\Delta\tilde{x}$ denote the first $k-1$ components of Δx. If g is differentiable, H is differentiable with respect to its third argument (let H_3 denote this partial derivative), and Δx has finite second moments, then

$$\Delta = \mathrm{E}[(\Delta\tilde{x} - \mathrm{E}(\Delta\tilde{x}|\Delta x'\beta))(\Delta\tilde{x} - \mathrm{E}(\Delta\tilde{x}|\Delta x'\beta))' g(\Delta x'\beta)^2 H(y_1, y_2, \Delta x'\beta)^2] \tag{13}$$

and

$$V = \mathrm{E}[(\Delta\tilde{x} - \mathrm{E}(\Delta\tilde{x}|\Delta x'\beta))(\Delta\tilde{x} - \mathrm{E}(\Delta\tilde{x}|\Delta x'\beta))' g(\Delta x'\beta) H_3(y_1, y_2, \Delta x'\beta)]. \tag{14}$$

Consistent estimates of Δ and V can be obtained by (i) plugging in $\hat{\beta}$ for β, (ii) estimating the functionals $\mathrm{E}(\Delta\tilde{x}|\cdot)$, $g(\cdot)$, $H(y_1, y_2, \cdot)$, and $H_3(y_1, y_2, \cdot)$ by kernel regression on $\Delta x'\hat{\beta}$, and (iii) evaluating the sample analogues of (13) and (14). For kernel bandwidth $h \to 0$, Abrevaya (1999b) shows that the resulting estimator of Δ is consistent if $nh^3 \to \infty$ and the resulting estimator of V is consistent if $nh^5 \to \infty$.[12]

The bootstrap may also be useful for estimation of standard errors. Theoretical justification of the bootstrap for estimators based on U-statistics has yet to be developed, but Cavanagh and Sherman (1998) find that the bootstrap is quite accurate for monotone rank estimators. Future research might extend Horowitz (1997), which justifies use of the bootstrap for the smoothed maximum score estimator, to estimators based on U-statistics.

3. Related estimators

In this section, several estimators similar to the LFE are considered. First, we consider alternative estimators of the transformation model with fixed effects

[12] These rates for h are slower than usually required for consistency of kernel estimates since $\hat{\beta}$ is used in place of the true β. Some additional assumptions are required, including the existence of the third moments of Δx and boundedness of the marginal densities of $\Delta x'\beta$ and $\Delta x'\hat{\beta}$. See Section 2 of Abrevaya (1999b) for complete details.

when h is time-invariant. Second, we consider estimators for the case of more than two time periods ($T > 2$). Finally, we consider an estimator of the transformation model (1) (without fixed effects) that is based on the same insight used to construct the LFE.

3.1. Estimation when h is time-invariant

If the transformation h does not change over time, note that we can write versions of (3) and (4) using observations of different time periods $s \neq t$ as follows:

$$h(y_{is}) - h(y_{jt}) = (x_{is} - x_{jt})'\beta + (\gamma_s - \gamma_t) + (\alpha_i - \alpha_j) + (\varepsilon_{is} - \varepsilon_{jt}) \tag{15}$$

and

$$\begin{aligned} &\Pr(y_{is} > y_{jt} | x_{i1}, x_{i2}, \alpha_i, x_{j1}, x_{j2}, \alpha_j) \\ &\quad = \Pr(\varepsilon_{jt} - \varepsilon_{is} < (x_{is} - x_{jt})'\beta + (\gamma_s - \gamma_t) + (\alpha_i - \alpha_j)). \end{aligned} \tag{16}$$

Notice that the time trend is identified by condition (16). To simplify notation, let the covariates have an additional component to account for the time trend, so that

$$\Pr(y_{is} > y_{jt} | x_{i1}, x_{i2}, \alpha_i, x_{j1}, x_{j2}, \alpha_j) = \Pr(\varepsilon_{jt} - \varepsilon_{is} < (x_{is} - x_{jt})'\beta + (\alpha_i - \alpha_j)). \tag{17}$$

Assumption 4 yields

$$\begin{aligned} (\Delta x_i + \Delta x_j)'\beta > 0 \Rightarrow &\Pr(y_{i2} > y_{j1} | x_{i1}, x_{i2}, \alpha_i, x_{j1}, x_{j2}, \alpha_j) \\ &> \Pr(y_{i1} > y_{j2} | x_{i1}, x_{i2}, \alpha_i, x_{j1}, x_{j2}, \alpha_j), \end{aligned} \tag{18}$$

meaning that

$$\tilde{S}(b) \equiv E[\text{sign}((\Delta x_i + \Delta x_j)'b)(1(y_{i2} > y_{j1}) - 1(y_{i1} > y_{j2}))] \tag{19}$$

is maximized at $b = \beta$. An estimator of β (call it LFE2) is defined to maximize the sample analogue of (19),

$$\tilde{S}_n(b) \equiv \frac{1}{n(n-1)} \sum_{i \neq j} \text{sign}((\Delta x_i + \Delta x_j)'b)(1(y_{i2} > y_{j1}) - 1(y_{i1} > y_{j2})). \tag{20}$$

The LFE2 is strongly consistent and asymptotically normal under the same assumptions as the LFE. Since the theorems are the same as Theorems 1 and 2 (with $\tau(z, b)$ appropriately defined), the details are omitted.

There are two alternative methods of combining LFE and LFE2. The first method is to incorporate the two conditions underlying LFE and LFE2 into a single objective function. For instance, one possible estimator of β would maximize the sum of the objective functions, $(S_n(b) + \tilde{S}_n(b))$; the asymptotic properties of this estimator would be similar to Theorems 1 and 2 (again, with $\tau(z, b)$ appropriately defined). The second method is to use a classical minimum-distance (CMD) framework (see, e.g., Chamberlain, 1984; Newey and McFadden, 1994) in which LFE and LFE2 are used to get initial estimates, $\hat{\beta}_1$ and $\hat{\beta}_2$, respectively. Then, the efficient CMD estimator $\hat{\beta}$ minimizes the objective function

$$\left[\begin{pmatrix} b \\ b \end{pmatrix} - \begin{pmatrix} \hat{\beta}_1 \\ \hat{\beta}_2 \end{pmatrix}\right]' \hat{V}^- \left[\begin{pmatrix} b \\ b \end{pmatrix} - \begin{pmatrix} \hat{\beta}_1 \\ \hat{\beta}_2 \end{pmatrix}\right], \tag{21}$$

where $\hat{V}$ is a consistent estimate of the covariance matrix of $\binom{\hat{\beta}_1}{\hat{\beta}_2}$ and $\hat{V}^-$ is its generalized inverse. Appendix B contains general results on the covariances between estimators based on second-order U-processes. These results can be used in order to obtain $\hat{V}$ and the asymptotically efficient CMD estimator.

3.2. Estimation when $T > 2$

With more than two time periods, any pair of time periods can be used to construct a leapfrog estimator as in Section 2, yielding $\binom{T}{2}$ different leapfrog estimators. If h is time-invariant, estimators based on Section 3.1 can also be constructed, yielding an additional $\binom{T}{2}$ possible estimators. As in Section 3.1, these estimators can be combined either explicitly in a single objective function or by using CMD estimation. (The covariance results of Appendix B are used for CMD estimation.)

3.3. Pairwise-difference estimation of the transformation model

The LFE approach can be applied to the cross-sectional transformation model in (1). Consider four different observations (indexed i, j, k, l). Then,

$$\Pr(y_i > y_j | x_i, x_j) = \Pr(\varepsilon_j - \varepsilon_i < (x_i - x_j)'\beta) \tag{22}$$

implies

$$(x_i - x_j)'\beta > (x_k - x_l)'\beta \Rightarrow \Pr(y_i > y_j | x_i, x_j, x_k, x_l) > \Pr(y_k > y_l | x_i, x_j, x_k, x_l), \tag{23}$$

if the error disturbances are i.i.d. with positive density everywhere. Thus, the function

$$U(b) \equiv \mathrm{E}[\mathrm{sign}(((x_i - x_j) - (x_k - x_l))'b)(1(y_i > y_j) - 1(y_k > y_l))] \tag{24}$$

is maximized at $b = \beta$. An estimator of β (call it PDE, for "pairwise-difference estimator") is defined to maximize the sample analogue of (24),

$$U_n(b) \equiv \frac{1}{n(n-1)(n-2)(n-3)} \sum_{\mathscr{C}_4} \mathrm{sign}(((x_i - x_j) - (x_k - x_l))'b)(1(y_i > y_j) - 1(y_k > y_l)), \tag{25}$$

where

$$\mathscr{C}_4 \equiv \{(i, j, k, l): i, j, k, l \in \{1, \ldots, n\}, \quad i \neq j, i \neq k, i \neq l, j \neq k, j \neq l, k \neq l\} \tag{26}$$

is the set of distinct quadruples from the set $\{1, \ldots, n\}$. For each b, $U_n(b)$ is a fourth-order U-statistic. The brute-force approach to computation of this objective function would require $O(n^4)$ operations since the number of comparisons in (25) is of this order. Instead, consider the sample of $n(n-1)/2$ observation pairs. The objective function (25) has the same maximizer(s) as

$$\sum_{i \neq j} \mathrm{Rank}_{i,j}((x_i - x_j)'b) \cdot 1(y_i > y_j), \tag{27}$$

where $\mathrm{Rank}_{i,j}(\cdot)$ gives the rank of the pairwise difference among the $(n-2)(n-3)$ pairwise differences with indices other than i and j. Computation of (27) requires $O(n^2 \log n)$, rather than $O(n^4)$, operations since the number of terms is $O(n^2)$ and the fastest sorting algorithms require $O(N \log N)$ operations (where N is the number of items to be sorted).[13]

Assumptions 2–4 are replaced by the following three assumptions.

Assumption 5. A sample of n i.i.d. realizations, $\{(y_i, x_i, \varepsilon_i)\}_{i=1}^n$, is drawn from the population, satisfying the model in (1). The observed sample is $\{(y_i, x_i)\}_{i=1}^n$.

---

[13] This same idea has been used to show that the MRCE can be computed in $O(n \log n)$, rather than $O(n^2)$, operations for the binary choice model.

Assumption 6. x is an i.i.d. k-dimensional random variable s.t.: (i) The support of x is not contained in a proper linear subspace of $\mathscr{R}^k$; and, (ii) the kth component of x has everywhere positive Lebesgue density, conditional on the other components.

Assumption 7. The random variables $\varepsilon_1, \dots, \varepsilon_n$ are independent of $\{x_1, \dots, x_n\}$ and have a common density function which is positive everywhere along the real line.

Consistency and asymptotic normality are direct consequences of Sherman (1994), which generalizes the results of Sherman (1993) to estimators based on U-processes of order greater than two. Let $z \equiv (y, x)$ denote an observation from the set $\mathscr{S} \subseteq \mathscr{R} \times \mathscr{R}^k$. For each $z \in \mathscr{S}$ and $b \in \mathscr{B}$, define

$$\tau_p(z, b) \equiv \mathrm{E}_{Z_1, Z_2, Z_3}[1((x - X_1)'b > (X_2 - X_3)'b) \cdot (1(y > Y_1) - 1(Y_2 > Y_3))], \tag{28}$$

where $Z_j \equiv (Y_j, X_j)$ for $j = 1, 2, 3$ are random variables drawn from $\mathscr{S}$. The following theorem gives the asymptotic properties:

Theorem 4. Let $\hat{\beta}$ be a value that maximizes $U_n(b)$ over the parameter space $\mathscr{B}$. If Assumptions 1 and 5–7 hold, then $\hat{\beta}$ is strongly consistent for β. If, in addition, $\tau_p(z, \cdot)$ is Taylor-expandable, then

$$\sqrt{n}(\hat{\beta} - \beta) \xrightarrow{d} \begin{pmatrix} W \\ 0 \end{pmatrix}$$

where $W \sim \mathrm{N}(0, V^{-1}\Delta V^{-1})$, *with* $\Delta = \mathrm{E}[\nabla_1 \tau_p(\cdot, \beta)(\nabla_1 \tau_p(\cdot, \beta))']$ *and* $4V = \mathrm{E}[\nabla_2 \tau_p(\cdot, \beta)]$.

The proof is given in Appendix A. The $4V$ in Theorem 4 (rather than $2V$) reflects the fact that the PDE is based on a fourth-order U-process (rather than a second-order U-process).

The slow computation speed for the PDE objective function is unattractive, when compared with the alternative single-index semiparametric estimators available for estimating β in (1). An advantage of the PDE (shared with the rank estimators of Han, 1987 and Cavanagh and Sherman, 1998) is that no subjective bandwidth choice is necessary for estimation of β. In preliminary research, the author finds that the PDE objective function is much smoother than the objective functions for alternative rank estimators (even for samples as small as

50 observations). This smoothness makes optimization a bit more reliable (i.e., reducing local optima) and allows the use of numerical differentiation for computation of covariance matrices. Further investigation of the properties of the PDE, including its relative efficiency, will be considered in future research.

4. Monte Carlo results

In this section, we report results from Monte Carlo simulations with the proposed estimators. For comparison, we study the least-squares within estimator to see the effect of misspecification. We consider the power transformation family studied by Bickel and Doksum (1981), which allows for negative y values unlike the Box–Cox family:

$$h(y, \lambda) \stackrel{\smile}{=} \frac{|y|^{\lambda}\mathrm{sgn}(y) - 1}{\lambda} \text{ for positive } \lambda.$$

We consider three values for λ (0.6, 0.8, and 1), where $\lambda = 1$ corresponds to the linear model. The associated transformations are shown in Fig. 2 for the range of y used in the simulations. As the figure shows, the value of $\lambda = 0.8$ corresponds to a rather mild non-linear transformation, whereas the value of $\lambda = 0.6$ corresponds to a more significant departure from linearity.

We consider the following specification for the Monte Carlo design:

$$h(y_{i1}) = 1 + x_{1i1} - 2x_{2i1} + 4x_{3i1} + \alpha_i + \varepsilon_{i1},$$

$$h(y_{i2}) = x_{1i2} - 2x_{2i2} + 4x_{3i2} + \alpha_i + \varepsilon_{i2},$$

where x_{1i1} and x_{1i2} are lognormally distributed, x_{2i1} and x_{2i2} are uniformly distributed, x_{3i1} and x_{3i2} are dummy variables (equal to one with probability 0.3), ε_{i1} and ε_{i2} are normally distributed, and the fixed effect is

$$\alpha_i = 0.5(x_{2i1} + x_{2i2}) + \eta_i,$$

where η_i is normally distributed. Aside from the fixed effect, there is no additional correlation between any of the random variables. The true coefficient vector for this design, including an intercept term, is $\beta = (\beta_0, \beta_1, \beta_2, \beta_3) = (1, 1, -2, 4)$.

We report the results from four different estimators: (1) the LFE from Section 2, (2) the LFE2 from Section 3, (3) the probit estimator of $1(\Delta y > 0)$ on Δx, and (4) the ordinary least-squares (OLS) estimator. The probit estimator is the most

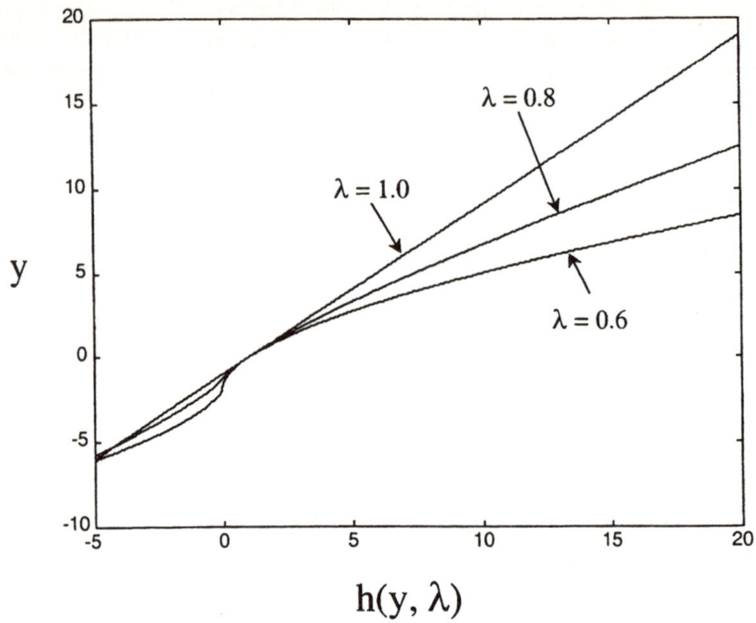

Fig. 2. Bickel–Doksum transformations.

efficient estimator that uses only within-unit comparisons of the dependent variable (see Introduction for the discussion). Of the four estimators, only the OLS estimator is sensitive to the choice of λ. Tables 1 and 2 report the results from 200 simulations using sample sizes of $n = 100$ and 200, respectively. For comparability, the ratios of the coefficient estimates (relative to β_3) are shown. The first four rows report the mean, median, root-mean square error (RMSE), and mean absolute deviation (MAD) for the 200 simulations. The last row reports the percentage of observations that fall outside 2/1.645/1 "asymptotic" standard errors of the true value, as computed from the asymptotic (normal) distribution of the associated estimator. The values in this row should be compared to the percentages 5.0/10.0/32.0.

For the sample sizes considered, there is no evidence of serious bias in either LFE or LFE2.[14] Their RMSE and MAD values are about half of those of the probit estimates for $n = 100$ and about two-thirds for $n = 200$. It is important to note, however, that a different Monte Carlo design could yield different

[14] Combining LFE and LFE2 together (as described in Section 3) did not seem to improve efficiency very much in the design considered here, which is probably due to the fact that the covariates are independent and stationary over time (with the exception of the slight time trend).

Table 1
Simulation results ($n = 100$)

		LFE	LFE2	Probit	OLS $\lambda = 1.0$	OLS $\lambda = 0.8$	OLS $\lambda = 0.6$
β_0/β_3	MEAN	-	0.2415	0.2364	0.2442	0.2390	0.2128
	MEDIAN		0.2457	0.2395	0.2379	0.2364	0.2114
	RMSE	–	0.0482	0.0887	0.0369	0.0431	0.0601
	MAD	—	0.0380	0.0678	0.0294	0.0329	0.0495
	Asymp. coverage	—	5.5/9.0/35.5	9.5/12.5/29.0	5.0/11.5/29.5	6.0/11.0/30.5	6.5/9.0/33.5
β_1/β_3	MEAN	0.2522	0.2502	0.2588	0.2502	0.2849	0.3295
	MEDIAN	0.2515	0.2470	0.2607	0.2512	0.2822	0.3156
	RMSE	0.0367	0.0345	0.0745	0.0157	0.0479	0.1013
	MAD	0.0291	0.0270	0.0523	0.0127	0.0385	0.0803
	Asymp. coverage	6.5/10.5/35.0	4.0/7.5/28.0	4.0/8.5/30.5	4.0/8.5/32.0	8.0/11.0/24.0	8.5/27.0/50.5
β_2/β_3	MEAN	– 0.4979	– 0.4979	– 0.4855	– 0.5086	– 0.4988	– 0.4544
	MEDIAN	– 0.4985	– 0.5094	– 0.4974	– 0.5010	– 0.5048	– 0.4552
	RMSE	0.1303	0.1066	0.2107	0.0910	0.0950	0.1289
	MAD	0.0941	0.0829	0.1671	0.0694	0.0792	0.0950
	Asymp. coverage	6.0/12.5/30.0	5.0/9.0/27.5	7.0/9.0/26.0	4.5/9.5/32.0	3.0/15.5/30.5	10.5/19.0/31.0

Table 2
Simulation results ($n = 200$)

		LFE	LFE2	Probit	OLS $\lambda = 1.0$	OLS $\lambda = 0.8$	OLS $\lambda = 0.6$
β_0/β_3	MEAN	—	0.2490	0.2415	0.2497	0.2314	0.2203
	MEDIAN	—	0.2486	0.2414	0.2501	0.2324	0.2211
	RMSE	—	0.0372	0.0570	0.0295	0.0358	0.0495
	MAD	—	0.0305	0.0448	0.0242	0.0292	0.0404
	Asymp. coverage	—	4.0/9.0/33.0	5.0/12.5/31.0	5.0/9.5/33.0	8.5/18.5/39.5	10.5/19.0/45.5
β_1/β_3	MEAN	0.2494	0.2489	0.2449	0.2502	0.2796	0.3626
	MEDIAN	0.2482	0.2463	0.2413	0.2493	0.2774	0.3440
	RMSE	0.0259	0.0279	0.0356	0.0142	0.0381	0.1336
	MAD	0.0209	0.0213	0.0274	0.0113	0.0309	0.1126
	Asymp. coverage	4.5/12.0/33.0	4.0/10.5/30.0	6.0/10.5/29.0	4.5/9.0/32.0	19.5/31.0/53.5	25.0/35.0/67.0
β_2/β_3	MEAN	− 0.5012	− 0.5025	− 0.5071	− 0.4977	− 0.4765	− 0.4457
	MEDIAN	− 0.5072	− 0.5052	− 0.5132	− 0.5011	− 0.4750	− 0.4421
	RMSE	0.0944	0.0917	0.1558	0.0680	0.0681	0.1084
	MAD	0.0734	0.0715	0.1185	0.0542	0.0552	0.0880
	Asymp. coverage	4.5/11.0/31.5	5.5/10.5/29.0	6.0/11.0/30.0	5.5/9.0/32.5	6.5/13.5/38.0	9.0/11.0/37.5

conclusions about the relative efficiency of LFE versus probit, for instance. In the design considered, about 60% of the observations have $\Delta y > 0$ and about 20% of the observation pairs leapfrog each other. In a design where the fixed effect has greater variance (so that leapfrogging is less prevalent), the probit estimator could be more efficient. For $\lambda = 0.6$, the bias of the OLS estimates results in larger RMSE values than LFE and LFE2. For $\lambda = 0.8$, the RMSE values for OLS are larger than LFE and LFE2 for β_1/β_3 but not β_2/β_3. The coverage probabilities for LFE and LFE2 are rather encouraging, with the asymptotic coverage slightly better when $n = 200$.[15] Notice that the coverage probabilities for the biased OLS estimators gets worse for $n = 200$ since the estimates are more precise but are centered around the wrong value. Again, the results are significantly worse for β_1/β_3 than for β_2/β_3.

5. Conclusions and extensions

The estimators proposed in this paper represent a first step in the semiparametric approach to the linear transformation panel model. An obvious question is, given estimates of β, how can we nonparametrically estimate the transformation function h? One possible approach is to use series estimation of h via polynomial and spline approximations. It would be preferable to have a more efficient estimation strategy as is the case for the non-panel case, where Horowitz (1996) and Ye and Duan (1997) obtain $\sqrt{n}$-consistent estimates of h.

A shortcoming of the estimators considered in this paper is that strict exogeneity of the explanatory variables is crucial for identification and consistency. This shortcoming is shared by many semiparametric estimators of nonlinear fixed-effects models, though some progress has been made for estimation in the presence of lagged dependent variables as explanatory variables. For instance, Honoré (1993b) gives orthogonality conditions for estimation of the linear censored and truncated models (although identification is not guaranteed), Honoré and Kyriazidou (1996) develop a modified version of the maximum score estimator for the binary choice model (which requires $T \geqslant 4$), and Kyriazidou (1997b) develops moment-based estimators for the sample selection model (which requires $T \geqslant 3$). Estimation of (2) with lagged dependent variables is an interesting topic for future research.

Finally, the issue of efficiency has been mostly ignored in this paper. Since efficiency is being sacrificed for flexibility, it may be important to re-weight estimators. For the LFE, the intuition for re-weighting is that observation-pairs

[15] Comparing the distribution of estimates to the normal distribution yields similar conclusions. The asymptotic normal distribution fits very closely for $n = 200$ and slightly less so for $n = 100$.

(i, j) with larger $|\Delta x_i'\beta - \Delta x_j'\beta|$ should be weighted more heavily in the objective function since the direction of leapfrogging for these pairs is more predictable than for pairs with lower $|\Delta x_i'\beta - \Delta x_j'\beta|$. A Monte Carlo investigation of the efficiency gains from using such re-weighting would be interesting. Also, a general theory concerning optimal weighting of estimators based on U-statistics would be an interesting area for future research.

Appendix A. Proofs of theorems

Proof of Theorem 1. The proof is based on $S_n(b)$ (which has the same maximizer(s) as $T_n(b)$). The kernel function of $S_n(b)$ is

$$p(z_i, z_j, b) \equiv \text{sign}((\Delta x_i - \Delta x_j)'b)(1(y_{i2} > y_{j2}) - 1(y_{i1} > y_{j1})).$$

where $z_i \equiv (x_{i1}, x_{i2}, y_{i1}, y_{i2}, \alpha_i)$. The limiting objective function is

$$S(b) = \text{E}[\text{sign}((\Delta x_i - \Delta x_j)'b)(1(y_{i2} > y_{j2}) - 1(y_{i1} > y_{j1}))].$$

Define $f(z_i, z_j, b) \equiv p(z_i, z_j, b) - S(b)$. Then,

$$S_n(b) - S(b) = \frac{1}{n(n-1)} \sum_{i \neq j} f(z_i, z_j, b) = U_n f(\cdot, \cdot, b),$$

where U_n places mass $[n(n-1)]^{-1}$ at each (z_i, z_j) (adopting the notation of Sherman, 1993, 1994). Note that $\{U_n f(\cdot, \cdot, b) : b \in \mathscr{B}\}$ is a zero-mean empirical process.

The following conditions are sufficient for strong consistency:[16] (i) $\mathscr{B}$ compact; (ii) $S(b)$ continuous; (iii) $S_n(b)$ converges uniformly almost surely to $S(b)$ (i.e., $\sup_{b \in \mathscr{B}} |S_n(b) - S(b)| \overset{\text{a.s.}}{\to} 0$); and, (iv) $S(b)$ uniquely maximized at β.

Condition (i) holds by Assumption 1. Assumption 3(ii) and $b_k \neq 0$ (from Assumption 1) imply that $\Delta x'b$ is continuously distributed for each $b \in \mathscr{B}$, which means $\text{sign}((\Delta x_i - \Delta x_j)'b)$ (and thus $p(z_i, z_j, b)$) will be continuous at each $b \in \mathscr{B}$ with probability one. Then, condition (ii) holds by the dominated convergence theorem since the sign function and indicator functions are trivially bounded. For condition (iii), note that the class of functions $\mathscr{F} \equiv \{p(\cdot, \cdot, b) : b \in \mathscr{B}\}$ is

[16] See, for example, Theorem 2.1 of Newey and McFadden (1994). These conditions are the same, except that uniform convergence in probability is replaced by almost-sure uniform convergence.

Euclidean for a constant envelope (see Pakes and Pollard, 1989, ex. 2.11).[17] Almost-sure convergence follows directly from Corollary 9 of Sherman (1994). For condition (iv), note that β maximizes $S(b)$ by Lemma 1. For any $b \in \mathscr{B}$ s.t. $b \neq \beta$, Assumption 3 implies that there is a region of positive probability (w.r.t. Lebesgue measure) on which the sign of $(\Delta x_i - \Delta x_j)'b$ and $(\Delta x_i - \Delta x_j)'\beta$ differ. Denote this region by $\mathscr{Z}_b$. Then,

$$\begin{aligned} S(b) &= \mathrm{E}_{(z_i,z_j)\notin\mathscr{Z}_b}[p(z_i, z_j, b)] + \mathrm{E}_{(z_i,z_j)\in\mathscr{Z}_b}[p(z_i, z_j, b)] \\ &= \mathrm{E}_{(z_i,z_j)\notin\mathscr{Z}_b}[p(z_i, z_j, \beta)] + \mathrm{E}_{(z_i,z_j)\in\mathscr{Z}_b}[p(z_i, z_j, b)] \\ &< \mathrm{E}_{(z_i,z_j)\notin\mathscr{Z}_b}[p(z_i, z_j, \beta)] + \mathrm{E}_{(z_i,z_j)\in\mathscr{Z}_b}[p(z_i, z_j, \beta)] = S(\beta). \end{aligned}$$

The strict inequality follows from Lemma 1 since $\mathscr{Z}_b$ has positive Lebesgue measure. Thus, β is the unique maximizer of $S(b)$ on the compact set $\mathscr{B}$, which completes the proof of strong consistency.

Technical assumption for asymptotic normality: Define

$$|\nabla_m|\sigma(b) \equiv \sum_{i_1,\ldots,i_m} \left| \frac{\partial^m}{\partial b_{i_1} \cdots \partial b_{i_m}} \sigma(b) \right|.$$

The symbol $\|\cdot\|$ denotes the matrix norm: $\|(a_{ij})\| \equiv (\sum_{i,j} a_{ij}^2)^{1/2}$. Then, corresponding to Assumption A4 of Sherman (1993), say that "$\tau(z,\cdot)$ *is Taylor-expandable*" if, for $\mathscr{N}$ a neighborhood of β,

(i) *For each* $z \in \mathscr{S}$, *all mixed second partial derivatives of* $\tau(z,\cdot)$ *exist on* $\mathscr{N}$.
(ii) *There is an integrable function* $\Gamma(z)$ *such that for all* $z \in \mathscr{S}$ *and* $b \in \mathscr{N}$,

$$\|\nabla_2\tau(z, b) - \nabla_2\tau(z, \beta)\| \leqslant \Gamma(z)|b - \beta|.$$

(iii) $\mathrm{E}[|\nabla_1\tau(\cdot, \beta)|^2] < \infty$.
(iv) $\mathrm{E}[|\nabla_2|\tau(\cdot, \beta)] < \infty$.
(v) *The* $(k-1)\times(k-1)$ *matrix* $\mathrm{E}[\nabla_2\tau(\cdot,\beta)]$ *is negative definite.*

Proof of Theorem 2. The proof is nearly identical to Theorem 4 of Sherman (1993). The only difference is that the kernel function is given by $p(z_1, z_2, b)$, defined above. With $\mathscr{F} \equiv \{ p(\cdot,\cdot,b)\colon b \in \mathscr{B}\}$ Euclidean, Assumptions 1–4, and $\tau(z,\cdot)$ Taylor-expandable, the proof follows Sherman (1993, pp. 130–131).

[17] Thanks to a referee who pointed out the application of the example from Pakes and Pollard (1989).

Proof of Theorem 3. The results of Section 6 of Sherman (1993) apply. Note that

$$\tau_t(z, b) = \int_{\Delta X'b < \Delta x'b} H(y_1, y_2, \Delta X'b)G(\mathrm{d}\Delta X) + \int \rho(y_1, y_2, \Delta X'\beta)G(\mathrm{d}\Delta X),$$

where $G(\cdot)$ is the distribution of Δx and $\rho(y_1, y_2, v) = \Pr_Z[y_1 > Y_1, y_2 < Y_2|\Delta X'\beta = v]$. The second integral does not depend on b, so $\nabla_1\tau_t(z, \beta) = (\Delta\tilde{x} - \mathrm{E}(\Delta\tilde{x}|\Delta x'\beta))g(\Delta x'\beta)H(y_1, y_2, \Delta x'\beta)$. Taking an outer product and taking expectations gives Δ. Evaluation of the second derivative, using

$$\frac{\partial}{\partial v}[H(y_1, y_2, v)g(v)]|_{v=\Delta x'\beta} = H_3(y_1, y_2, \Delta x'\beta)g(\Delta x'\beta)$$

$$+ H(y_1, y_2, \Delta x'\beta)g'(\Delta x'\beta),$$

gives V.[18]

Proof of Theorem 4. The proof of strong consistency is similar to the proof of Theorem 1. For asymptotic normality, the kernel function is

$$p(z_1, z_2, z_3, z_4, b) = 1((x_1 - x_2)'b > (x_3 - x_4)'b)\cdot(1(y_1 > y_2)$$

$$- 1(y_3 - y_4))$$

for each $(z_1, z_2, z_3, z_4) \in \mathscr{S} \times \mathscr{S} \times \mathscr{S} \times \mathscr{S}$ (for $z_i \equiv (y_i, x_i)$) and $b \in \mathscr{B}$, and the class of functions

$$\mathscr{F} = \{ p(\cdot,\cdot,\cdot,\cdot,b) \colon b \in \mathscr{B}\},$$

is Euclidean for a constant envelope. Then, the proof in Section 7.3 of Sherman (1994) applies (with the decomposition applied to a fourth-order U-statistic instead of a third-order U-statistic).

Appendix B. Covariances of estimators based on second-order U-processes

This appendix presents results for determining the covariance between estimators based on U-processes of order two. As discussed in Section 3, the

[18] Note that the $2V$ in the statement of Theorem 4 on p. 133 of Sherman (1993) should be V instead. See Abrevaya (1999b) for the details of computation of the second derivative for a similar estimator.

covariance(s) can be used to combine several different estimators of β in the classical-mininum distance framework. Theorem 5, stated below, gives the covariance matrix of two estimators (and can be extended to more than two estimators trivially):

Theorem 5. *Let $\Gamma_{1n}(\cdot)$ and $\Gamma_{2n}(\cdot)$ be objective functions which are sample analogues of $\Gamma_1(\cdot)$ and $\Gamma_2(\cdot)$, based on the i.i.d. sample $\{z_1, \ldots, z_n\}$. Both $\Gamma_1(\cdot)$ and $\Gamma_2(\cdot)$ are maximized at θ_0, whereas the sample analogues are maximized at θ_{1n} and θ_{2n}, respectively. Suppose θ_{1n} and θ_{2n} are $\sqrt{n}$-consistent estimates of θ_0, an interior point of Θ. Suppose that, uniformly over $O_p(1/\sqrt{n})$ neighborhoods of θ_0,*

$$\Gamma_{1n}(\theta) = \frac{1}{2}(\theta - \theta_0)'V_1(\theta - \theta_0) + \frac{1}{\sqrt{n}}(\theta - \theta_0)'W_{1n} + o_p(1/n),$$

$$\Gamma_{2n}(\theta) = \frac{1}{2}(\theta - \theta_0)'V_2(\theta - \theta_0) + \frac{1}{\sqrt{n}}(\theta - \theta_0)'W_{2n} + o_p(1/n),$$

where V_1 and V_2 are negative-definite matrices and

$$W_{1n} = \frac{1}{\sqrt{n}}\sum_{i=1}^{n} \nabla_1\tau_1(z_i, \theta_0), \qquad W_{2n} = \frac{1}{\sqrt{n}}\sum_{i=1}^{n} \nabla_1\tau_2(z_i, \theta_0),$$

where both $\tau_1(z,\cdot)$ and $\tau_2(z,\cdot)$ are Taylor-expandable.[19] *Then,*

$$\sqrt{n}\begin{pmatrix}\theta_{1n} - \theta_0 \\ \theta_{2n} - \theta_0\end{pmatrix} \xrightarrow{d} N\left(0, \begin{pmatrix} V_1^{-1}\Delta_1 V_1^{-1} & V_1^{-1}\Delta_{12}V_2^{-1} \\ V_2^{-1}\Delta_{12}'V_1^{-1} & V_2^{-1}\Delta_2 V_2^{-1}\end{pmatrix}\right),$$

where

$$\Delta_1 = E[\nabla_1\tau_1(\cdot,\theta_0)(\nabla_1\tau_1(\cdot,\theta_0))']$$

$$\Delta_2 = E[\nabla_1\tau_2(\cdot,\theta_0)(\nabla_1\tau_2(\cdot,\theta_0))']$$

and

$$\Delta_{12} = E[\nabla_1\tau_1(\cdot,\theta_0)(\nabla_1\tau_2(\cdot,\theta_0))'].$$

---

[19] Note that θ is not a normalized parameter. For instance, it can be thought of as the first $k - 1$ components of β from the previous sections. As a result, ∇_m is the mth partial derivative applied to *all* components of θ. Likewise, Taylor-expandability is defined in this way.

Proof of Theorem 5. Let

$$\Gamma_n\begin{pmatrix}\theta_1\\ \theta_2\end{pmatrix} \equiv \Gamma_{1n}(\theta_1) + \Gamma_{2n}(\theta_2).$$

By definition, $\binom{\theta_1}{\theta_2}$ maximizes $\Gamma_n(\cdot)$. Also, $\binom{\theta_0}{\theta_0}$ maximizes the sample analogue of $\Gamma_n(\cdot)$ since expectation is a linear operator. Uniformly over $O_p(1/\sqrt{n})$ neighborhoods of $\binom{\theta_0}{\theta_0}$, we have

$$\Gamma_n\begin{pmatrix}\theta_1\\ \theta_2\end{pmatrix} = \frac{1}{2}(\theta_1-\theta_0)'V_1(\theta_1-\theta_0) + \frac{1}{\sqrt{n}}(\theta_1-\theta_0)'W_{1n}$$

$$+\frac{1}{2}(\theta_2-\theta_0)'V_2(\theta_2-\theta_0) + \frac{1}{\sqrt{n}}(\theta_2-\theta_0)'W_{2n} + o_p(1/n)$$

$$=\frac{1}{2}\begin{pmatrix}\theta_1-\theta_0\\ \theta_2-\theta_0\end{pmatrix}'\begin{pmatrix}V_1 & 0\\ 0 & V_2\end{pmatrix}\begin{pmatrix}\theta_1-\theta_0\\ \theta_2-\theta_0\end{pmatrix}$$

$$+\frac{1}{\sqrt{n}}\begin{pmatrix}\theta_1-\theta_0\\ \theta_2-\theta_0\end{pmatrix}'\begin{pmatrix}W_{1n}\\ W_{2n}\end{pmatrix} + o_p(1/n).$$

Since $E[\nabla_1\tau_1(\cdot,\theta_0)] = E[\nabla_1\tau_2(\cdot,\theta_0)] = 0$ and $\tau_1(z,\cdot)$ and $\tau_2(z,\cdot)$ are Taylor-expandable, we have

$$\begin{pmatrix}W_{1n}\\ W_{2n}\end{pmatrix} \xrightarrow{d} N\left(0, \begin{pmatrix}\Delta_1 & \Delta_{12}\\ \Delta_{12}' & \Delta_2\end{pmatrix}\right).$$

Also, $\begin{pmatrix}V_1 & 0\\ 0 & V_2\end{pmatrix}$ is negative definite since V_1 and V_2 are. Applying Theorem 2 of Sherman (1993) and multiplying out gives the desired result.

To make Theorem 5 useful in practice, a specific expression for Δ_{12} (which can be estimated using kernel techniques, like Theorem 2 for the LFE) is given below for estimators that maximize objective functions of the form $\sum_{i\neq j}1(w_i'b > w_j'b)\cdot(\cdots)$:

Theorem 6. Let θ_{1n} and θ_{2n} be estimates satisfying the conditions of Theorem 5. Suppose that θ_{1n} and θ_{2n} are the first $k-1$ components of $\hat{\beta}_1$ and $\hat{\beta}_2$ (elements of

$\mathscr{B}$), respectively. Suppose also that

$$\tau_1(z_1, b) = \int_{W'_1 b < w'_1 b} S(y_1, W'_1\beta) G_1(\mathrm{d}W_1) + \int \rho(y_1, W'_1\beta) G_1(\mathrm{d}W_1),$$

$$\tau_2(z_2, b) = \int_{W'_2 b < w'_2 b} T(y_2, W'_2\beta) G_2(\mathrm{d}W_2) + \int \nu(y_2, W'_2\beta) G_2(\mathrm{d}W_2),$$

where $z_i = (y_i, w_i)$, $Z_i = (Y_i, W_i)$, and $G_i(\cdot)$ is the distribution of w_i for $i = 1, 2$. If $\mathrm{E}|w_1 w'_2| < \infty$, then

$$\Delta_{12} = \mathrm{E}[(\tilde{w}_1 - \mathrm{E}(\tilde{w}_1|w'_1\beta))(\tilde{w}_2 - \mathrm{E}(\tilde{w}_2|w'_2\beta))' g_1(w'_1\beta) g_2(w'_2\beta)$$

$$S(y_1, w'_1\beta) T(y_2, w'_2\beta)],$$

where $\tilde{w}_i$ denotes the first $k-1$ components of w_i and $g_i(\cdot)$ is the marginal density of $w'_i\beta$ for $i = 1, 2$.

Proof of Theorem 6. Similar to proof of Theorem 3.

The estimators in Section 2 and Section 3.1 have $w_1 = w_2 = \Delta x$ and $y_1 = y_2 = (y_1, y_2)$, but Theorem 6 is stated more generally so that it can be applied for different w_i and y_i (e.g., estimators discussed in Section 3.2 for $T > 2$). Abrevaya (1996) also discusses how Theorems 5 and 6 can be used to construct certain specification tests, like testing the assumption of correlated fixed effects or testing a specific h transformation.

References

Abrevaya, J., 1996. Semiparametric estimation methods for nonlinear panel data models and mismeasured dependent variables. Ph.D. Thesis, MIT Department of Economics.

Abrevaya, J., 1999a. Computation of the maximum rank correlation estimator. Economics Letters, forthcoming.

Abrevaya, J., 1999b. Rank regression for current-status data: asymptotic normality. Statistics and Probability Letters, forthcoming.

Bickel, P.J., Doksum, K.A., 1981. An analysis of transformations revisited. Journal of the American Statistical Association 76, 296–311.

Cavanagh, C., Sherman, R.P., 1998. Rank estimators for monotonic index models. Journal of Econometrics 84, 351–381.

Chamberlain, G., 1984. Panel data. In: Griliches, Z., Intriligator, M. (Eds.), Handbook of Econometrics, vol. II. North-Holland, Amsterdam, pp. 1247–1318.

Chamberlain, G., 1985. Heterogeneity, omitted variable bias, and duration dependence. In: Heckman, J.J., Singer, B. (Eds.), Longitudinal Analysis of Labor Market Data. Cambridge University Press, New York, pp. 3–38.

Gönül, F., Srinivasan, K., 1993. Consumer purchase behavior in a frequently bought product category: estimation issues and managerial insights from a hazard function model with heterogeneity. Journal of the American Statistical Association 88, 1219–1227.

Han, A.K., 1987. Non-parametric analysis of a generalized regression model: the maximum rank correlation estimator. Journal of Econometrics 35, 303–316.

Honoré, B., 1992. Trimmed LAD and least squares estimation of truncated and censored regression models with fixed effects. Econometrica 60, 533–565.

Honoré, B., 1993a. Identification results for duration models with multiple spells. Review of Economic Studies 60, 241–246.

Honoré, B., 1993b. Orthogonality conditions for Tobit models with fixed effects and lagged dependent variables. Journal of Econometrics 59, 35–61.

Honoré, B., Kyriazidou, E., 1996. Panel data discrete choice models with lagged dependent variables. Mimeo.

Horowitz, J.L., 1996. Semiparametric estimation of a regression model with an unknown transformation of the dependent variable. Econometrica 64, 103–137.

Horowitz, J.L., 1997. Bootstrap critical values for the smoothed maximum score estimator. Mimeo.

Horowitz, J.L., Härdle, W., 1996. Direct semiparametric estimation of single-index models with discrete covariates. Journal of the American Statistical Association 91, 1632–1640.

Ichimura, H., 1993. Semiparametric least squares (SLS) and weighted SLS estimation of single-index models. Journal of Econometrics 58, 71–120.

Jain, D.J., Vilcassim, N.J., 1991. Investigating household purchase timing decisions: a conditional hazard function approach. Marketing Science 10, 1–23.

Klein, R.W., Spady, R.H., 1993. An efficient semiparametric estimator for binary response models. Econometrica 61, 387–421.

Kyriazidou, E., 1997a. Estimation of a panel data sample selection model. Econometrica 65, 1335–1364.

Kyriazidou, E., 1997b. Estimation of dynamic panel data sample selection models. Mimeo.

Manski, C.F., 1987. Semiparametric analysis of random effects linear models from binary panel data. Econometrica 55, 357–362.

Newey, W.K., McFadden, D.L., 1994. Large sample estimation and hypothesis testing. In: Engle, R.F., McFadden, D.L. (Eds.), Handbook of Econometrics, vol. IV. North-Holland, Amsterdam, pp. 2111–2245.

Newman, J.L., McCulloch, C.E., 1984. A hazard rate approach to the timing of births. Econometrica 52, 939–961.

Olsen, R.J., Wolpin, K.I., 1983. The impact of exogenous child mortality on fertility: a waiting time regression with dynamic regressors. Econometrica 51, 731–751.

Pakes, A., Pollard, D., 1989. Simulation and the asymptotics of optimization estimators. Econometrica 57, 1027–1057.

Powell, J.L., Stock, J.H., Stoker, T.M., 1989. Semiparametric estimation of index coefficients. Econometrica 57, 474–523.

Sherman, R.P., 1993. The limiting distribution of the maximum rank correlation estimator. Econometrica 61, 123–137.

Sherman, R.P., 1994. Maximal inequalities for degenerate U-processes with applications to optimization estimators. Annals of Statistics 22, 439–459.

Ye, J., Duan, N., 1997. Nonparametric $n^{-1/2}$-consistent estimation for the general transformation model. Annals of Statistics 25, 2682–2717.

ELSEVIER Journal of Econometrics 90 (1999) 77–97

JOURNAL OF Econometrics

Distribution-free estimation of some nonlinear panel data models

Jeffrey M. Wooldridge*

Department of Economics, Michigan State University, East Lansing, MI 48824-1038, USA

Received 1 October 1996; received in revised form 1 January 1998

Abstract

This paper studies distribution-free estimation of some multiplicative unobserved components panel data models. One class of estimators requires only specification of the conditional mean; in particular, the multinomial quasi-conditional maximum likelihood estimator is shown to be consistent when only the conditional mean in the unobserved effects model is correctly specified. Additional orthogonality conditions can be used in a method of moments framework. A second class of problems specifies the conditional mean, conditional variances, and conditional covariances. Using the notion of a conditional linear predictor, it is shown that specification of conditional second moments implies further orthogonality conditions in the observable data that can be exploited for efficiency gains. This has applications to both count and gamma-type panel data regression models. © 1999 Elsevier Science S.A. All rights reserved.

JEL classification: C23

Keywords: Fixed effects Poisson model; Panel data; Robustness; Quasi-conditional maximum likelihood; Generalized method of moments

1. Introduction

In the standard linear unobserved effects model, popular estimators are consistent under correct specification of the conditional mean and strict exogeneity of the explanatory variables, conditional on the latent individual

* E-mail: wooldri1@pilot.msu.edu

0304-4076/99/$ – see front matter
PII: S0304-4076(98)00033-5

effect. The usual fixed effects (within) estimator is consistent, as is the minimum chi-square estimator proposed by Chamberlain (1982).

Less has been written on distribution-free estimation of nonlinear unobserved effects models. Most of the work on nonlinear panel data methods relies on the method of conditional maximum likelihood (CML), where a sufficient statistic (the sum of the explained variable across time) is conditioned on to remove the unobserved effect. Examples include Chamberlain (1980,1984) for binary responses and Hausman et al. (1984) (hereafter HHG) for count data. The robustness properties of these CMLEs to misspecification of the initially specified joint distribution have not been investigated. It is important to stress that, even though the resulting conditional density (e.g., the multinomial) is typically in the linear exponential family (LEF), the robustness of the quasi-CMLE (QCMLE) in the LEF, e.g., Gourieroux et al. (1984) (hereafter GMT), cannot be appealed to. This is because, except in special cases, the expectation associated with the LEF conditional density is misspecified if the initial joint distribution in the unobserved components model is misspecified.

For models of nonnegative variables, we would like to have a class of estimators that requires minimal distributional assumptions while further relaxing the first two moment assumptions appearing in the literature. In independent work, Chamberlain (1992a) has offered a method of moments approach to nonlinear unobserved components models that applies to multiplicative models as a special case. All that is the required is the specification of the mean conditional on the exogenous variables and the latent effects.

This paper reports on results first derived in Wooldridge (1990b), and derives consistent estimators of multiplicative unobserved effects models under two kinds of assumptions. The first class of models specifies only the conditional mean, as in Chamberlain (1992a). However, I offer a direct proof that the multinomial QCMLE, also known as the fixed effects Poisson (FEP) estimator, consistently estimates the conditional mean parameters, and this leads naturally into method of moments estimators that could improve on the efficiency of the FEP estimator. Second, I consider models that specify the conditional variances and covariances in addition to the conditional means. For a count model with individual-specific dispersion and an unobserved effects gamma-type regression model, further orthogonality conditions are implied that can be exploited in estimation.

Section 2 introduces the count model that motivated this research, and discusses the assumptions that have been imposed in previous work. Section 3 discusses the estimation of models that specify only the conditional mean, and shows that the fixed effects Poisson estimator is consistent very generally. Conditional linear predictors are introduced in Section 4. Section 5 analyzes a count-type model, where the conditional variance is proportional to the conditional mean, and the conditional covariances are zero. Section 6 covers the case where the variance is proportional to the square of the mean, and models with parametric serial correlation are discussed briefly in Section 7.

2. Motivation: An unobserved effects model for count panel data

Let $\{(\boldsymbol{y}_i, \boldsymbol{x}_i, \phi_i): i = 1, 2, \ldots\}$ be a sequence of i.i.d. random variables, where $\boldsymbol{y}_i \equiv (y_{i1}, \ldots, y_{iT})'$ is an observable $T \times 1$ vector of counts, $\boldsymbol{x}_i \equiv (\boldsymbol{x}_{i1}', \boldsymbol{x}_{i2}', \ldots, \boldsymbol{x}_{iT}')'$ is a $T \times K$ matrix of observable conditioning variables ($\boldsymbol{x}_{it}$ is $1 \times K$, $t = 1, \ldots, T$), and ϕ_i is an unobservable random scalar. The fixed effects Poisson model analyzed by HHG assumes that

$$y_{it}|\boldsymbol{x}_i, \phi_i \sim \text{Poisson}(\phi_i \mu(\boldsymbol{x}_{it}, \boldsymbol{\beta}_0)), \quad t = 1, \ldots, T \tag{2.1}$$

and

$$y_{it}, y_{ir} \text{ are independent conditional on } \boldsymbol{x}_i, \phi_i, \quad t \neq r, \tag{2.2}$$

where

$$\mathrm{E}(y_{it}|\boldsymbol{x}_i, \phi_i) = \mathrm{E}(y_{it}|\boldsymbol{x}_{it}, \phi_i) = \phi_i \mu(\boldsymbol{x}_{it}, \boldsymbol{\beta}_0), \tag{2.3}$$

and $\boldsymbol{\beta}_0$ is a $P \times 1$ vector of unknown parameters. Actually, HHG take $\mu(\boldsymbol{x}_{it}, \boldsymbol{\beta}) \equiv \exp(\boldsymbol{x}_{it}\boldsymbol{\beta})$, but there is no need to use this particular functional form. It is convenient to choose μ so that $\mu(\boldsymbol{x}_{it}, \boldsymbol{\beta})$ is well-defined and positive for all $\boldsymbol{x}_{it}$ and $\boldsymbol{\beta}$. Assumptions (2.1) and (2.2) incorporate strict exogeneity of $\boldsymbol{x}_{it}$ conditional on ϕ_i, independence of y_{it} and y_{ir} conditional on $\boldsymbol{x}_i$ and ϕ_i, and the Poisson distributional assumption.

HHG use Andersen's (1970) conditional ML methodology to estimate $\boldsymbol{\beta}_0$ under Eqs. (2.1) and (2.2). Let $n_i \equiv \sum_{t=1}^{T} y_{it}$ denote the sum across time of the explained variable. Then HHG show (see also Palmgren, 1981) that

$$\boldsymbol{y}_i|n_i, \boldsymbol{x}_i, \phi_i \sim \text{Multinomial}(n_i, p_1(\boldsymbol{x}_i, \boldsymbol{\beta}_0), \ldots, p_T(\boldsymbol{x}_i, \boldsymbol{\beta}_0)), \tag{2.4}$$

where

$$p_t(\boldsymbol{x}_i, \boldsymbol{\beta}_0) \equiv \mu(\boldsymbol{x}_{it}, \boldsymbol{\beta}_0) \Big/ \left(\sum_{r=1}^{T} \mu(\boldsymbol{x}_{ir}, \boldsymbol{\beta}_0) \right). \tag{2.5}$$

Because this distribution does not depend on ϕ_i, Eq. (2.4) is also the distribution of $\boldsymbol{y}_i$ conditional on n_i and $\boldsymbol{x}_i$. Therefore, $\boldsymbol{\beta}_0$ can be estimated by standard conditional ML techniques. For later use, the conditional log-likelihood for observation i, apart from terms not depending on $\boldsymbol{\beta}$, is

$$\ell_i(\boldsymbol{\beta}) = \sum_{t=1}^{T} y_{it} \log[p_t(\boldsymbol{x}_i, \boldsymbol{\beta})]. \tag{2.6}$$

Because the multinomial distribution is in the LEF, the results of GMT imply a certain amount of robustness of the QCMLE. *If*

$$E(y_{it}|n_i, \boldsymbol{x}_i) = p_t(\boldsymbol{x}_i, \boldsymbol{\beta}_0)n_i \tag{2.7}$$

then the multinomial QCMLE is consistent and asymptotically normal, even if the multinomial distribution is misspecified. Other than the FEP model (2.1) and (2.2), there is another interesting case where Eq. (2.7) holds: HHG's fixed effects negative binomial (FENB) model. Let $\delta_i > 0$ be the unobserved effect. If

$$y_{it}|\boldsymbol{x}_i, \delta_i \sim \text{ Negative Binomial}(\mu(\boldsymbol{x}_{it}, \boldsymbol{\beta}_0), \delta_i) \tag{2.8}$$

(parameterized as in HHG so that $E(y_{it}|\boldsymbol{x}_i, \delta_i) = \mu(\boldsymbol{x}_{it}, \boldsymbol{\beta}_0)/\delta_i$) and

$$y_{it}, y_{ir} \text{ are independent conditional on } (\boldsymbol{x}_i, \delta_i), \quad t \neq r, \tag{2.9}$$

then Eq. (2.7) can be shown to hold. (This is asserted in HHG, p. 935, based on features of the negative hypergeometric distribution, which is not quite general enough; in fact, y_{it} given $(n_i, \boldsymbol{x}_i, \delta_i)$ has a binomial-beta distribution with parameters $(\mu(\boldsymbol{x}_{it}, \boldsymbol{\beta}_0), \sum_{r=1}^{T} \mu(\boldsymbol{x}_{ir}, \boldsymbol{\beta}_0), n_i)$. Then Eq. (2.7) follows from Johnson and Kotz (1969), p. 231). A complete proof is available on request from the author.) By the results of GMT, the QCMLE based on the multinomial distribution provides consistent estimates of $\boldsymbol{\beta}_0$ under Eqs. (2.8) and (2.9). This is a useful result but, as shown in the next section, is much more restrictive than necessary.

A robust approach consists of specifying at most a couple of low-order conditional moments. Chamberlain (1992a) offers a transformation that eliminates ϕ_i, resulting in orthogonality conditions that allow estimation of $\boldsymbol{\beta}_0$ by the method of moments. The next section takes a different approach to this problem, starting by showing that the multinomial QCMLE is consistent and asymptotically normal under just the conditional mean assumption (2.3). This analysis leads to additional orthogonality conditions that can improve efficiency if the full set of assumptions listed in Eqs. (2.1) and (2.2) do not hold. Section 5 examines a model that is more general than Eqs. (2.1) and (2.2) in the first two moments, and suggests methods of estimation.

3. Estimation under conditional mean assumptions

3.1. *The quasi-conditional maximum likelihood estimator*

Let $\{(\boldsymbol{y}_i, \boldsymbol{x}_i, \phi_i): i = 1, 2, \ldots\}$ be a sequence of i.i.d. random variables, where $\boldsymbol{y}_i$ is $T \times 1$, $\boldsymbol{x}_i$ is $T \times K$, and ϕ_i is an unobserved scalar effect. Consider the model

$$E(y_{it}|\boldsymbol{x}_i, \phi_i) = \phi_i \mu(\boldsymbol{x}_{it}, \boldsymbol{\beta}_0), \quad t = 1, \ldots, T, \tag{3.1}$$

where $\boldsymbol{\beta}_0$ is a $P \times 1$ unknown vector. Suppose that $\boldsymbol{\beta}_0$ is estimated by maximizing the log-likelihood associated with the multinomial density, given for each i by Eq. (2.6). It is important to see that this does not require $\boldsymbol{y}_i$ to be a vector of counts. For example, y_{it} could be a binary variable – in which case $0 < \phi_i < 1$ and $\mu(\boldsymbol{x}_{it},\boldsymbol{\beta})$ could be the logit or probit response probability – or a nonnegative continuous variable – in which case a popular choice of $\mu(\boldsymbol{x}_{it}, \boldsymbol{\beta})$ is the exponential function.

We now show that the multinomial QCMLE is consistent for $\boldsymbol{\beta}_0$ under Eq. (3.1) only. There are two ways to establish the consistency of the QCMLE. The first is to show that $\mathrm{E}[\ell_i(\boldsymbol{\beta})]$ is maximized at $\boldsymbol{\beta}_0$, for which we use the following lemma.

Lemma 3.1. Let $y_1, y_2, \ldots, y_T$ be nonnegative random variables with finite, nonzero means $\mu_1^0, \mu_2^0, \ldots, \mu_T^0$, and let $\mathbb{R}^T_{++}$ denote the subset of T-dimensional Euclidean space with strictly positive elements. Then $\mu_0 \equiv (\mu_1^0, \mu_2^0, \ldots, \mu_T^0)$ is the unique solution to

$$\max_{\mu \in \mathbb{R}^T_{++}} \sum_{t=1}^{T} \mu_t^0 \log\left(\mu_t \Big/ \left(\sum_{r=1}^{T} \mu_r\right)\right). \tag{3.2}$$

Proof. Dividing Eq. (3.2) by $\sum_{r=1}^{T} \mu_r^0$ does not change the problem. Thus, write $p_t^0 = \mu_t^0/(\sum_{r=1}^{T} \mu_r^0)$ and $p_t = \mu_t/(\sum_{r=1}^{T} \mu_r)$. Then, it suffices to show that

$$\sum_{t=1}^{T} p_t^0 \log(p_t^0) > \sum_{t=1}^{T} p_t^0 \log(p_t), \tag{3.3}$$

for all $\boldsymbol{p} = (p_1, \ldots, p_T)' \neq \boldsymbol{p}^0 = (p_1^0, \ldots, p_T^0)'$. But this follows immediately from the Kullback–Leibler information inequality (see, for example, Rao, 1973, p. 59), because the left-hand side is the expected value of the log density that puts mass p_t^0 at point t, and the right-hand side is the expected value of the log of another candidate density over the points $\{1, 2, \ldots, T\}$. □

How does this lemma apply to the QCMLE estimator? From Eq. (2.6) we have $\mathrm{E}[\ell_i(\boldsymbol{\beta})|\boldsymbol{x}_i, \phi_i] = \phi_i \sum_{t=1}^{T} \mu(\boldsymbol{x}_{it}, \boldsymbol{\beta}_0) \log[p_t(\boldsymbol{x}_i, \boldsymbol{\beta})]$, and so, by Lemma 3.1, $\boldsymbol{\beta}_0$ maximizes $\mathrm{E}[\ell_i(\boldsymbol{\beta})|\boldsymbol{x}_i, \phi_i]$ for any $(\boldsymbol{x}_i, \phi_i)$. The law of iterated expectations then shows that $\boldsymbol{\beta}_0$ maximizes $\mathrm{E}[\ell_i(\boldsymbol{\beta})]$ over the parameter space. Consistency then follows under a standard identification assumption and regularity conditions that ensure the uniform weak law of large numbers holds (see, for example. Newey and McFadden, 1994, Section 2).

A second approach is to show that the score of the QCMLE log-likelihood has a zero expectation when evaluated at $\boldsymbol{\beta}_0$. Because we will need this score for inference and for motivating additional orthogonality conditions, we sketch the derivation:

$$\begin{aligned} s_i(\beta) = \nabla_\beta \ell_i(\beta) &= \sum_{t=1}^{T} y_{it}[\nabla_\beta p_t(x_i, \beta)'/p_t(x_i, \beta)] \\ &= \sum_{t=1}^{T} [\nabla_\beta p_t(x_i, \beta)'/p_t(x_i, \beta)]\{y_{it} - p_t(x_i, \beta)n_i\} \qquad (3.4) \\ &\equiv \nabla_\beta p(x_i, \beta)' W(x_i, \beta)\{y_i - p(x_i, \beta)n_i\} \\ &\equiv \nabla_\beta p(x_i, \beta)' W(x_i, \beta) u_i(\beta), \qquad (3.5) \end{aligned}$$

where $W(x_i, \beta) \equiv [\text{diag}\{p_1(x_i, \beta), \ldots, p_T(x_i, \beta)\}]^{-1}$, $u_i(\beta) \equiv y_i - p(x_i, \beta)n_i$, $p(x_i, \beta) \equiv [p_1(x_i, \beta), \ldots, p_T(x_i, \beta)]'$, and $p_t(x_i, \beta)$ is given by Eq. (2.5). Eq. (3.4) follows from the fact that $\sum_{t=1}^{T} p_t(x_i, \beta) = 1$ for all β, so that $\sum_{t=1}^{T} \nabla_\beta p_t(x_i, \beta) = 0$ for all β.

The expectation of $s_i(\beta_0)$ conditional on x_i can be found by computing $\text{E}[u_i(\beta_0)|x_i]$. Let $\mu(x_i, \beta) \equiv [\mu(x_{i1}, \beta), \ldots, \mu(x_{iT}, \beta)]'$ be the $T \times 1$ vector of conditional means. Then

$$\begin{aligned} \text{E}[u_i(\beta_0)|x_i, \phi_i] &= \text{E}(y_i|x_i, \phi_i) - p(x_i, \beta_0)\text{E}(n_i|x_i, \phi_i) \\ &= \phi_i \mu(x_i, \beta_0) - \left[\mu(x_i, \beta_0) \Big/ \sum_{t=1}^{T} \mu(x_{it}, \beta_0)\right]\left[\phi_i \sum_{t=1}^{T} \mu(x_{it}, \beta_0)\right] \\ &= \phi_i \mu(x_i, \beta_0) - \phi_i \mu(x_i, \beta_0) = 0. \qquad (3.6) \end{aligned}$$

Thus, $\text{E}[u_i(\beta_0)|x_i] = 0$ and therefore $\text{E}[s_i(\beta_0)|x_i] = 0$; by iterated expectations,

$$\text{E}[s_i(\beta_0)] = 0, \qquad (3.7)$$

so that the score evaluated at β_0 has zero mean under Eq. (3.1) only.

We have effectively shown that the multinomial QCMLE – which is derived from a nominal Poisson assumption – is generally consistent for β_0 provided only that the conditional mean assumption (3.1) holds. We do not need to assume Eq. (2.4) or make any assumptions about the temporal dependence of the y_{it}. This is a useful result, as multinomial QCMLE is a popular method of estimating fixed effects count models. It also shows that the multinomial QCMLE can be used to obtain consistent estimates of β_0 under Eq. (3.1) whether or not y_i is a vector of counts. The response y_{it} could be a binary variable, a proportion, a nonnegative continuously distributed random variable, or could have discrete and continuous characteristics: its distribution is not restricted, nor is its temporal dependence.

Unless assumptions (2.1) and (2.2) hold, the usual inverse of the estimated information matrix is not a valid estimator of the asymptotic variance of $\hat{\beta}$.

Generally,

$$\sqrt{N}(\hat{\boldsymbol{\beta}} - \boldsymbol{\beta}_0) \overset{a}{\sim} N(\boldsymbol{0}, \boldsymbol{A}_0^{-1}\boldsymbol{B}_0\boldsymbol{A}_0^{-1}), \tag{3.8}$$

where $\boldsymbol{A}_0$ is the expected value of the Hessian of $\ell_i(\boldsymbol{\beta}_0)$ and $\boldsymbol{B}_0$ is the expected value of $\boldsymbol{s}_i(\boldsymbol{\beta}_0)\boldsymbol{s}_i(\boldsymbol{\beta}_0)'$. A consistent estimator of $\boldsymbol{A}_0$ (as $N \to \infty$ with T fixed) is easily seen to be

$$\hat{\boldsymbol{A}} \equiv \left(N^{-1}\sum_{i=1}^{N} n_i \nabla_\beta \boldsymbol{p}(\boldsymbol{x}_i,\hat{\boldsymbol{\beta}})'\boldsymbol{W}(\boldsymbol{x}_i,\hat{\boldsymbol{\beta}})\nabla_\beta \boldsymbol{p}(\boldsymbol{x}_i,\hat{\boldsymbol{\beta}})\right) \equiv \left(N^{-1}\sum_{i=1}^{N} \nabla_\beta \hat{\boldsymbol{m}}_i'\hat{\boldsymbol{V}}_i^{-1}\nabla_\beta \hat{\boldsymbol{m}}_i\right), \tag{3.9}$$

where $\hat{\boldsymbol{m}}_i \equiv n_i \boldsymbol{p}(\boldsymbol{x}_i, \hat{\boldsymbol{\beta}})$ and $\hat{\boldsymbol{V}}_i \equiv \boldsymbol{V}(n_i, \boldsymbol{x}_i, \hat{\boldsymbol{\beta}}) \equiv \text{diag}\{p_{i1}(\hat{\boldsymbol{\beta}})n_i, \ldots, p_{iT}(\hat{\boldsymbol{\beta}})n_i\}$. When Eq. (3.9) is multiplied by N and inverted, we obtain the usual maximum likelihood estimate of Avar($\hat{\boldsymbol{\beta}}$), which is familiar from standard likelihood theory involving the multinomial distribution.

A consistent estimator of $\boldsymbol{B}_0$ is

$$\hat{\boldsymbol{B}} \equiv N^{-1}\sum_{i=1}^{N} \boldsymbol{s}_i(\hat{\boldsymbol{\beta}})\boldsymbol{s}_i(\hat{\boldsymbol{\beta}})' = N^{-1}\sum_{i=1}^{N} \nabla_\beta \boldsymbol{p}(\boldsymbol{x}_i, \hat{\boldsymbol{\beta}})'\boldsymbol{W}(\boldsymbol{x}_i, \hat{\boldsymbol{\beta}})\hat{\boldsymbol{u}}_i\hat{\boldsymbol{u}}_i'\boldsymbol{W}(\boldsymbol{x}_i, \hat{\boldsymbol{\beta}})\nabla_\beta \boldsymbol{p}(\boldsymbol{x}_i, \hat{\boldsymbol{\beta}})$$

$$\equiv N^{-1}\sum_{i=1}^{N} \nabla_\beta \hat{\boldsymbol{m}}_i'\hat{\boldsymbol{V}}_i^{-1}\hat{\boldsymbol{u}}_i\hat{\boldsymbol{u}}_i'\hat{\boldsymbol{V}}_i^{-1}\nabla_\beta \hat{\boldsymbol{m}}_i. \tag{3.10}$$

A fully robust asymptotic variance estimator of $\hat{\boldsymbol{\beta}}$ is

$$\hat{\boldsymbol{A}}^{-1}\hat{\boldsymbol{B}}\hat{\boldsymbol{A}}^{-1}/N. \tag{3.11}$$

This can be used to compute robust standard errors and asymptotic t-statistics.

One important feature of Eq. (3.11) is that it is robust to arbitrary (conditional) serial correlation in $\{u_{it}: t = 1, 2, \ldots, T\}$. By definition, $\sum_{t=1}^{T} u_{it} \equiv 0$, so that the u_{it} might generally be expected to exhibit negative serial correlation. In fact, from McCullagh and Nelder, 1989, p. 165), it follows that, under Eqs. (2.1) and (2.2), the correlation between u_{it} and u_{ir}, conditional on $(n_i, \boldsymbol{x}_i)$, is

$$-p_{it}(\boldsymbol{\beta}_0)p_{ir}(\boldsymbol{\beta}_0)/[p_{it}(\boldsymbol{\beta}_0)\{1 - p_{it}(\boldsymbol{\beta}_0)\}p_{ir}(\boldsymbol{\beta}_0)\{1 - p_{ir}(\boldsymbol{\beta}_0)\}]^{1/2}.$$

This particular negative correlation, which is used implicitly in the estimator $\hat{\boldsymbol{A}}^{-1}N$ of the asymptotic variance of $\hat{\boldsymbol{\beta}}$, need not hold under Eq. (3.1). Consequently, the robust covariance matrix estimator should always be computed; it can produce standard errors smaller or larger than those obtained from $\hat{\boldsymbol{A}}^{-1}/N$.

3.2. Generalized method of moments estimation

In showing that the score of the QCMLE objective function has zero mean conditional on $\boldsymbol{x}_i$ under Eq. (3.1), the key step was to show that $\boldsymbol{u}_i(\boldsymbol{\beta}_0)$ has zero mean conditional on $\boldsymbol{x}_i$. This implies innumerable orthogonality conditions. Let $\boldsymbol{D}(\boldsymbol{x}_i)$ be any $T \times L$ function of $\boldsymbol{x}_i$. Then, assuming the existence of appropriate moments,

$$E[\boldsymbol{D}(\boldsymbol{x}_i)'\boldsymbol{u}_i(\boldsymbol{\beta}_0)] = \boldsymbol{0}; \tag{3.12}$$

this immediately suggests a generalized method of moments (GMM) approach. Actually, in order to obtain estimators that are asymptotically no less efficient than the QCMLE, one must allow $\boldsymbol{D}$ to depend on $\boldsymbol{\beta}$: $\boldsymbol{D}(\boldsymbol{x}_i, \boldsymbol{\beta})$. If $\tilde{\boldsymbol{\beta}}$ is a preliminary consistent estimator of $\boldsymbol{\beta}_0$ – such as the QCMLE – then a minimum chi-square estimator of $\boldsymbol{\beta}_0$ minimizes

$$\left(N^{-1}\sum_{i=1}^{N} \tilde{\boldsymbol{D}}_i'\boldsymbol{u}_i(\boldsymbol{\beta})\right)'\left(N^{-1}\sum_{i=1}^{N} \tilde{\boldsymbol{D}}_i'\tilde{\boldsymbol{u}}_i\tilde{\boldsymbol{u}}_i'\tilde{\boldsymbol{D}}_i\right)^{-1}\left(N^{-1}\sum_{i=1}^{N} \tilde{\boldsymbol{D}}_i'\boldsymbol{u}_i(\boldsymbol{\beta})\right),$$

where '$\sim$' denotes evaluation at the initial estimate $\tilde{\boldsymbol{\beta}}$. This is the efficient estimator given the choice of the matrix $\boldsymbol{D}(\boldsymbol{x}_i, \boldsymbol{\beta})$.

Since the mechanics of GMM estimation are by now well known, I will not go through the details here. The reader is referred to Newey and McFadden (1994) for a general treatment and Wooldridge (1990b) for the specifics of the current application.

It is important to choose $\boldsymbol{D}(\boldsymbol{x}_i, \boldsymbol{\beta})$ so that the GMM estimator is no less efficient than the QCMLE. This is ensured by including $\boldsymbol{W}(\boldsymbol{x}_i, \boldsymbol{\beta})\nabla_{\beta}\boldsymbol{p}(\boldsymbol{x}_i, \boldsymbol{\beta})$ as part of $\boldsymbol{D}(\boldsymbol{x}_i, \boldsymbol{\beta})$, so that the first-order condition for the QCMLE is among the orthogonality conditions for the GMM estimator. The difficulty lies in choosing additional elements of $\boldsymbol{D}(\boldsymbol{x}_i, \boldsymbol{\beta})$ that will produce nontrivial efficiency gains. One possibility is the partitioned matrix

$$\boldsymbol{D}(\boldsymbol{x}_i, \boldsymbol{\beta}) = [\boldsymbol{W}(\boldsymbol{x}_i, \boldsymbol{\beta})\nabla_{\beta}\boldsymbol{p}(\boldsymbol{x}_i, \boldsymbol{\beta}) | \nabla_{\beta}\boldsymbol{p}(\boldsymbol{x}_i, \boldsymbol{\beta})],$$

so that $\boldsymbol{D}(\boldsymbol{x}_i, \boldsymbol{\beta})$ is a $T \times 2P$ matrix. This adds the orthogonality condition $\mathrm{E}[\nabla_{\beta}\boldsymbol{p}(\boldsymbol{x}_i, \boldsymbol{\beta}_0)'\boldsymbol{u}_i(\boldsymbol{\beta}_0)] = \boldsymbol{0}$ to the QCMLE first-order condition (giving P overidentifying restrictions), but there is no reason to think this choice is somehow optimal.

An ad hoc approach to choosing additional orthogonality conditions can be avoided by finding the optimal set of instruments. Chamberlain (1992a) studies this problem for a class of unobserved effects models that contains Eq. (3.1) as a special case. Chamberlain's moment conditions are of the form

$$\mathrm{E}[\boldsymbol{Q}(\boldsymbol{x}_i, \boldsymbol{\beta}_0)'\boldsymbol{y}_i|\boldsymbol{x}_i] = \boldsymbol{0}, \tag{3.13}$$

where $\boldsymbol{Q}(\boldsymbol{x}_i, \boldsymbol{\beta}_0)$ is a $T \times L$ matrix such that

$$\boldsymbol{Q}(\boldsymbol{x}_i, \boldsymbol{\beta}_0)'\boldsymbol{\mu}(\boldsymbol{x}_i, \boldsymbol{\beta}_0) \equiv \boldsymbol{0}.$$

Chamberlain characterizes the optimal choice of $\boldsymbol{Q}(\boldsymbol{x}_i, \boldsymbol{\beta}_0)$. Choosing $\boldsymbol{Q}(\boldsymbol{x}_i, \boldsymbol{\beta}) \equiv \boldsymbol{W}(\boldsymbol{x}_i, \boldsymbol{\beta})\nabla_{\beta}\boldsymbol{p}(\boldsymbol{x}_i, \boldsymbol{\beta})$ puts the multinomial QCMLE first-order conditions in the form of Eq. (3.13).

3.3. Specification testing

Testing the conditional mean specification (3.1) can be carried out by testing

$$\mathrm{H}_0\colon \mathrm{E}[\boldsymbol{u}_i(\boldsymbol{\beta}_0)|\boldsymbol{x}_i] = \boldsymbol{0}. \tag{3.14}$$

This is straightforward in a minimum chi-square setting with overidentifying restrictions: one simply uses Hansen's (1982) overidentification test statistic (see also Davidson and MacKinnon, 1993, Section 17.6; and Newey and McFadden, 1994, Section 9.5).

Since the QCMLE is easy to obtain, one may want to obtain relatively simple tests of Eq. (3.1) after QCMLE estimation. Such tests can be obtained along the lines of Newey (1985) and Wooldridge (1990a). If $\boldsymbol{\Lambda}(\boldsymbol{x}_i, \boldsymbol{\beta})$ is a $T \times Q$ matrix depending on $\boldsymbol{x}_i$ and $\boldsymbol{\beta}$, a general class of tests is based on the sample moment

$$N^{-1}\sum_{i=1}^{N} \boldsymbol{\Lambda}(\boldsymbol{x}_i, \hat{\boldsymbol{\beta}})'\boldsymbol{u}_i(\hat{\boldsymbol{\beta}}), \tag{3.15}$$

which should not be statistically different from zero if Eq. (3.1) is true. (The function Λ can also depend on other estimated nuisance parameters, but we do not show that here; see Wooldridge (1990b) for details.)

Under H_0, the following expansions are easily seen to hold (for similar reasoning, see Wooldridge, 1990a):

$$\begin{aligned} N^{-1/2}\sum_{i=1}^{N} \boldsymbol{\Lambda}(\boldsymbol{x}_i, \hat{\boldsymbol{\beta}})'\boldsymbol{u}_i(\hat{\boldsymbol{\beta}}) &= N^{-1/2}\sum_{i=1}^{N} \boldsymbol{\Lambda}_i(\boldsymbol{\beta}_0)'\boldsymbol{u}_i(\boldsymbol{\beta}_0) \\ &\quad - \mathrm{E}[\boldsymbol{\Lambda}_i(\boldsymbol{\beta}_0)'\nabla_{\beta}\boldsymbol{m}_i(\boldsymbol{\beta}_0)]\sqrt{N}(\hat{\beta} - \boldsymbol{\beta}_0) + \mathrm{o_p}(1) \\ &= N^{-1/2}\sum_{i=1}^{N} \{\boldsymbol{\Lambda}_i(\boldsymbol{\beta}_0) - \boldsymbol{W}(\boldsymbol{x}_i,\boldsymbol{\beta}_0)\nabla_{\beta}\boldsymbol{p}(\boldsymbol{x}_i,\boldsymbol{\beta}_0)\boldsymbol{A}_0^{-1}\boldsymbol{K}_0'\}' \\ &\quad \times \boldsymbol{u}_i(\boldsymbol{\beta}_0) + \mathrm{o_p}(1), \end{aligned}$$

where $\boldsymbol{A}_0 = \mathrm{E}[n_i \nabla_\beta \boldsymbol{p}(\boldsymbol{x}_i, \boldsymbol{\beta}_0)' \boldsymbol{W}(\boldsymbol{x}_i, \boldsymbol{\beta}_0) \nabla_\beta \boldsymbol{p}(\boldsymbol{x}_i, \boldsymbol{\beta}_0)]$, $\boldsymbol{\Lambda}_i(\boldsymbol{\beta}_0) \equiv \boldsymbol{\Lambda}(\boldsymbol{x}_i, \boldsymbol{\beta}_0)$, and $\boldsymbol{K}_0 \equiv \mathrm{E}[\boldsymbol{\Lambda}_i(\boldsymbol{\beta}_0)' \nabla_\beta \boldsymbol{m}_i(\boldsymbol{\beta}_0)]$. Thus, let

$$\hat{\boldsymbol{K}} \equiv N^{-1} \sum_{i=1}^{N} \boldsymbol{\Lambda}_i(\hat{\boldsymbol{\beta}})' \nabla_\beta \boldsymbol{m}_i(\hat{\boldsymbol{\beta}}) \tag{3.16}$$

and

$$\hat{\boldsymbol{r}}_i \equiv \hat{\boldsymbol{u}}_i'(\hat{\boldsymbol{\Lambda}}_i - \hat{\boldsymbol{W}}_i \nabla_\beta \hat{\boldsymbol{p}}_i \hat{\boldsymbol{A}}^{-1} \hat{\boldsymbol{K}}'), \quad i = 1, \ldots, N \tag{3.17}$$

(note that $\hat{\boldsymbol{r}}_i$ is a $1 \times Q$ vector). A valid test statistic is obtained as $N - \mathrm{SSR}$ from the auxiliary regression

$$1 \text{ on } \hat{\boldsymbol{r}}_i, \quad i = 1, \ldots, N, \tag{3.18}$$

where SSR is just the usual sum of squared residuals. Under the null hypothesis (3.14), $N - \mathrm{SSR} \stackrel{a}{\sim} \chi^2_Q$, provided there are no redundant columns in $\boldsymbol{\Lambda}_i(\boldsymbol{\beta}_0) - \boldsymbol{W}(\boldsymbol{x}_i, \boldsymbol{\beta}_0) \nabla_\beta \boldsymbol{p}(\boldsymbol{x}_i, \boldsymbol{\beta}_0) \boldsymbol{A}_0^{-1} \boldsymbol{K}_0'$.

For example, if we want to test Eq. (3.14) using the extra orthogonality conditions $\mathrm{E}[\nabla_\beta \boldsymbol{p}(\boldsymbol{x}_i, \boldsymbol{\beta}_0)' \boldsymbol{u}_i(\boldsymbol{\beta}_0)] = \boldsymbol{0}$, then $Q = P$ and $\hat{\boldsymbol{\Lambda}}_i \equiv \nabla_\beta \boldsymbol{p}_i(\hat{\boldsymbol{\beta}})$ in Eqs. (3.16) and (3.17).

4. Conditional linear predictors

This section defines the notion of a conditional linear predictor (or conditional linear projection, CLP) and derives some simple properties; these are convenient for analyses in Sections 5–7. Conditional linear predictors were introduced by Hansen and Richard (1987) in the context of asset pricing relationships; see also Hansen et al. (1988). Here, we use CLPs to obtain orthogonality conditions in the context of certain unobserved effects models.

Unsurprisingly, much of the intuition about linear predictors in an unconditional setting generally carries over to the conditional case. Let $\boldsymbol{y}$ be $J \times 1$, $\boldsymbol{z}$ be $K \times 1$, and $\boldsymbol{w}$ be $I \times 1$. In what follows, $\boldsymbol{z}$ may or may not contain unity as one of its elements. This distinction turns out to be important in the applications. In Section 5, it is inconsequential whether or not unity is included in $\boldsymbol{z}$; in the example of Section 6, unity must be excluded from $\boldsymbol{z}$.

Throughout this section, without stating it explicitly, an expectation is assumed to exist whenever it is written down. Define the following conditional moments:

$$\boldsymbol{\Sigma}_{yz}(\boldsymbol{w}) = \mathrm{E}(\boldsymbol{y}\boldsymbol{z}'|\boldsymbol{w}), \qquad \boldsymbol{\Sigma}_{zz}(\boldsymbol{w}) \equiv \mathrm{E}(\boldsymbol{z}\boldsymbol{z}'|\boldsymbol{w}). \tag{4.1}$$

Assume that $\Sigma_{zz}(w)$ is positive definite with probability one (w.p.1.). The following definition holds only w.p.1., but this is left implicit throughout.

Definition 4.1. Let y, z, and w be defined as above. The *linear predictor of y on z, conditional on w*, is defined to be

$$L(y|z;\, w) \equiv \Sigma_{yz}(w)\Sigma_{zz}^{-1}(w)z \equiv C_0(w)z, \tag{4.2}$$

where $C_0(w)$ is the $J \times K$ matrix $C_0(w) \equiv \Sigma_{yz}(w)\Sigma_{zz}^{-1}(w)$. □

Note that $L(y|z;\, w)$ is always linear in z, but is generally a nonlinear function of w. When the context is clear, $L(y|z;\, w)$ is simply called a conditional linear predictor. The difference between y and its CLP has zero orthogonality properties that are immediate extensions from unconditional linear predictor theory.

Lemma 4.1. Let y, z, and w be as in Definition 4.1. Define

$$u \equiv y - L(y|z;\, w) = y - C_0(w)z. \tag{4.3}$$

Then

$$\mathrm{E}(uz'|w) = 0. \tag{4.4}$$

Proof. $uz' = [y - C_0(w)z]z' = yz' - C_0(w)zz'$, so that

$$\mathrm{E}(uz'|w) = \mathrm{E}(yz'|w) - C_0(w)\mathrm{E}(zz'|w) = \Sigma_{yz}(w) - \Sigma_{yz}(w)\Sigma_{zz}^{-1}(w)\Sigma_{zz}(w) = 0. \quad \square$$

The next corollary formalizes the class of orthogonality conditions that can be used in estimating the parameters of a conditional linear predictor. It is a simple application of the law of iterated expectations.

Corollary 4.1. Let y, z, w, and u be as in Lemma 4.1, and let $D(w)$ be a $JK \times L$ random matrix. Then

$$\mathrm{E}[D(w)'(z \otimes I_J)u] = \mathrm{E}[D(w)' \operatorname{vec}\{uz'\}] = 0. \tag{4.5}$$

Suppose now that $C_0(w) \equiv C(w, \theta_0)$, where $C(w, \theta)$ is a known function of w and the $P \times 1$ parameter vector $\theta \in \Theta$. Then, for a matrix function $D(w)$ as defined in Corollary 4.1, θ_0 solves (perhaps not uniquely) the system of equations

$$\mathrm{E}[D(w)'(z \otimes I_J)\{y - C(w, \theta)\}] \equiv 0. \tag{4.6}$$

Eq. (4.6) can be exploited to obtain a variety of consistent estimators of $\boldsymbol{\theta}_0$. In the applications in Sections 5–7, not all of the vector $\boldsymbol{w}$ is observed (in particular, $\boldsymbol{w}$ contains unobserved effects as well as observed conditioning variables). The CLP is useful for estimating $\boldsymbol{\theta}_0$ only if $\boldsymbol{C}(\boldsymbol{w}, \boldsymbol{\theta}_0)$ does not depend on the unobserved elements of $\boldsymbol{w}$, as in the subsequent examples.

5. A count-type model under mean and variance assumptions

The methods in Section 3 require only that the conditional mean in the latent variable model be correctly specified. These estimators have satisfying robustness properties, but may have large asymptotic variances. As mentioned earlier, Chamberlain (1992a) derives the variance lower bound of estimators that use only Eq. (3.1). But achieving this lower bound via optimal instrumental variables estimation generally requires nonparametric estimation of a very high dimensional conditional expectation.

A different way to improve efficiency is to make conditional variance and covariance assumptions in the unobserved effects model and use these assumptions in estimating $\boldsymbol{\beta}_0$. If y_{it} is a count variable, we might wish to impose a constant variance–mean ratio, as is popular in the count data literature. Nonlinear unobserved effects models that use full distributional assumptions assume conditional independence in the y_{it} across time, something we might want to exploit in estimation without making full distributional assumptions.

The following model is motivated by, but certainly not restricted to, count data. For $t = 1, \ldots, T$, assume that

$$\mathrm{E}(y_{it}|\boldsymbol{x}_i, \phi_i, \psi_i) = \phi_i \mu(\boldsymbol{x}_{it}, \boldsymbol{\beta}_0), \tag{5.1}$$

$$\mathrm{Var}(y_{it}|\boldsymbol{x}_i, \phi_i, \psi_i) = \psi_i \mathrm{E}(y_{it}|\boldsymbol{x}_i, \phi_i, \psi_i) = \psi_i \phi_i \mu(\boldsymbol{x}_{it}, \boldsymbol{\beta}_0), \tag{5.2}$$

$$\mathrm{Cov}(y_{it}, y_{ir}|\boldsymbol{x}_i, \phi_i, \psi_i) = 0, \quad t \neq r. \tag{5.3}$$

This model has two unobserved effects, one that multiplies the mean and the other that determines the variance-to-mean ratio:

$$\mathrm{Var}(y_{it}|\boldsymbol{x}_i, \phi_i, \psi_i)/\mathrm{E}(y_{it}|\boldsymbol{x}_i, \phi_i, \psi_i) = \psi_i. \tag{5.4}$$

Models with a constant variance-to-mean ratio are known as *log-linear models* in the generalized linear models literature (e.g. McCullagh and Nelder, 1989, Chapter 6). Assumption (5.2) relaxes this assumption by allowing the variance-to-mean ratio to be different for each i. This means that some cross-section units can display underdispersion and others overdispersion.

Assumptions (5.1)–(5.3) are notably more flexible than the first two moments of all of the fixed effects models estimated by HHG. The fixed effects Poisson model imposes $\psi_i \equiv 1$. The fixed effects negative binomial model of HHG, mentioned in Section 2, imposes $\psi_i = 1 + \phi_i$, which rules out underdispersion for all individuals and ties the amount of overdispersion directly to the mean effect. HHG introduced two unobserved effects in their negative binomial model, μ_i and ϕ_i, but it is easily seen that only the ratio $1/\delta_i \equiv \exp(\mu_i)/\phi_i$ actually appears in their model. In addition, Eq. (5.3) is weaker than the independence assumption imposed by HHG, and no distributional assumption is made.

The variance assumption (5.2) is also more general than that implied by a common parameterization of the gamma distribution (for example, Rao, 1973, p. 164); in this case, $\psi_i = \phi_i$. Therefore, this model can be usefully applied to continuous, nonnegative responses.

The orthogonality condition

$$\mathrm{E}[\boldsymbol{u}_i(\boldsymbol{\beta}_0)|\boldsymbol{x}_i] = \boldsymbol{0}, \tag{5.5}$$

where $\boldsymbol{u}_i(\boldsymbol{\beta}) \equiv \boldsymbol{y}_i - \boldsymbol{p}(\boldsymbol{x}_i, \boldsymbol{\beta})n_i$, was derived under Eq. (3.1) only. Therefore, the additional assumptions (5.2) and (5.3) are useful only if they imply orthogonality conditions in addition to Eq. (5.5). In fact, assumptions (5.1)–(5.3) also imply that

$$\mathrm{E}[n_i\boldsymbol{u}_i(\boldsymbol{\beta}_0)|\boldsymbol{x}_i] = \boldsymbol{0}, \tag{5.6}$$

where $n_i \equiv \sum_{t=1}^{T} y_{it}$, as before. Condition (5.6) is a simple consequence of the form of the linear predictor of y_{it} on $(1, n_i)'$, conditional on $(\boldsymbol{x}_i, \phi_i, \psi_i)$. From Definition 4.1, for each t

$$L(y_{it}|1, n_i; \boldsymbol{x}_i, \phi_i, \psi_i) = \mathrm{E}(y_{it}|\boldsymbol{x}_i, \phi_i, \psi_i) + \frac{\mathrm{Cov}(y_{it}, n_i|\boldsymbol{x}_i, \phi_i, \psi_1)}{\mathrm{Var}(n_i|\boldsymbol{x}_i, \phi_i, \psi_i)} \times (n_i - \mathrm{E}(n_i|\boldsymbol{x}_i, \phi_i, \psi_i)) \tag{5.7}$$

$$= \mathrm{E}(y_{it}|\boldsymbol{x}_i, \phi_i, \psi_i) + \frac{\mathrm{Var}(y_{it}|\boldsymbol{x}_i, \phi_i, \psi_i)}{\mathrm{Var}(n_i|\boldsymbol{x}_i, \phi_i, \psi_i)}(n_i - \mathrm{E}(n_i|\boldsymbol{x}_i, \phi_i, \psi_i))$$

$$= \phi_i\mu(\boldsymbol{x}_{it}, \boldsymbol{\beta}_0)\frac{\psi_i\phi_i\mu(\boldsymbol{x}_{it}, \boldsymbol{\beta}_0)}{\sum_{r=1}^{T}\psi_i\phi_i\mu(\boldsymbol{x}_{ir}, \boldsymbol{\beta}_0)}\left(n_i - \sum_{r=1}^{T} \phi_i\mu(\boldsymbol{x}_{ir}, \boldsymbol{\beta}_0)\right)$$

$$= \frac{\mu(\boldsymbol{x}_{it}, \boldsymbol{\beta}_0)}{\sum_{r=1}^{T}\mu(\boldsymbol{x}_{ir}, \boldsymbol{\beta}_0)}n_i, \tag{5.8}$$

which does not depend on ϕ_i or ψ_i. It follows from Lemma 4.1 that $\mathrm{E}[n_i\{\boldsymbol{y}_i - \boldsymbol{p}(\boldsymbol{x}_i, \boldsymbol{\beta}_0)n_i\}|\boldsymbol{x}_i, \phi_i, \psi_i] = 0$, which implies Eq. (5.6). It is important to see that, as in Section 3, Eq. (5.8) does *not* generally equal $\mathrm{E}(y_{it}|n_i, \boldsymbol{x}_i, \phi_i, \psi_i)$.

Eqs. (5.5) and (5.6) imply orthogonality conditions of the form

$$\mathrm{E}[\boldsymbol{D}(\boldsymbol{x}_i)'\{(1, n_i)' \otimes \boldsymbol{I}_T\}\boldsymbol{u}_i(\boldsymbol{\beta}_0)] = \boldsymbol{0}, \tag{5.9}$$

where $\boldsymbol{D}(\boldsymbol{x}_i)$ is any $2T \times L$ matrix function of $\boldsymbol{x}_i$. These orthogonality conditions can be used in GMM estimation.

Interestingly, the multivariate nonlinear least-squares (MNLS) estimator $\hat{\boldsymbol{\beta}}$, which solves

$$\min_{\boldsymbol{\beta}} \sum_{i=1}^{N} \{\boldsymbol{y}_i - \boldsymbol{p}(\boldsymbol{x}_i, \boldsymbol{\beta})n_i\}'\{\boldsymbol{y}_i - \boldsymbol{p}(\boldsymbol{x}_i, \boldsymbol{\beta})n_i\}/2, \tag{5.10}$$

has a first-order condition of the form (5.9): $\mathrm{E}[n_i \nabla_{\beta}\boldsymbol{p}(\boldsymbol{x}_i, \boldsymbol{\beta}_0)'\boldsymbol{u}_i(\boldsymbol{\beta}_0)] = \boldsymbol{0}$. Therefore, under Eqs. (5.1)–(5.3) and standard regularity conditions, $\hat{\boldsymbol{\beta}}$ is consistent for $\boldsymbol{\beta}_0$ and asymptotically normally distributed. This estimator is *not* generally consistent for $\boldsymbol{\beta}_0$ under the conditional mean assumption (5.1) only. This is because Eq. (5.1) alone does not imply Eq. (5.6), which is the basis for the MNLS consistency result. The asymptotic variance of $\sqrt{N}(\hat{\boldsymbol{\beta}} - \boldsymbol{\beta}_0)$ takes the form $\boldsymbol{A}_0^{-1}\boldsymbol{B}_0\boldsymbol{A}_0^{-1}$, with consistent estimators of $\boldsymbol{A}_0$ and $\boldsymbol{B}_0$ given by

$$\hat{\boldsymbol{A}} \equiv N^{-1}\sum_{i=1}^{N} \nabla_{\beta}\hat{\boldsymbol{m}}_i' \nabla_{\beta}\hat{\boldsymbol{m}}_i \tag{5.11}$$

and

$$\hat{\boldsymbol{B}} \equiv N^{-1}\sum_{i=1}^{N} \nabla_{\beta}\hat{\boldsymbol{m}}_i'\hat{\boldsymbol{u}}_i\hat{\boldsymbol{u}}_i' \nabla_{\beta}\hat{\boldsymbol{m}}_i, \tag{5.12}$$

where $\nabla_{\beta}\hat{\boldsymbol{m}}_i \equiv \nabla_{\beta}\boldsymbol{m}_i(\hat{\boldsymbol{\beta}}) \equiv \nabla_{\beta}\boldsymbol{p}_i(\hat{\boldsymbol{\beta}})n_i$. This is easily extended to weighted least squares with $T \times T$ weighting matrix $\hat{\boldsymbol{G}}_i(\boldsymbol{x}_i) \equiv \boldsymbol{G}(\boldsymbol{x}_i, \hat{\boldsymbol{\gamma}})$, which can depend on $\boldsymbol{x}_i$ (and some estimated parameters $\hat{\boldsymbol{\gamma}}$) but not n_i; see Wooldridge (1990b) for details.

Because Eq. (5.6) does not generally hold under Eq. (5.1), these additional orthogonality conditions can be used to test the variance and covariance assumptions (5.2) and (5.3). One simple way to do this is to compare the multinomial QCMLE and the MNLS estimator via a Hausman (1978) test. However, neither estimator is relatively efficient under Eqs. (5.1)–(5.3), so a robust form of the test is needed. A regression-based approach, which requires estimation of the QCMLE only, is obtained from Wooldridge (1991). Let $\hat{\boldsymbol{u}}_i, \nabla_{\beta}\hat{\boldsymbol{m}}_i$, and $\hat{\boldsymbol{V}}_i$ be defined as in Section 3, evaluated at the QCMLE, $\hat{\boldsymbol{\beta}}$.

Define the weighted quantities $\tilde{u}_i \equiv \hat{V}_i^{-1/2}\hat{u}_i, \nabla_\beta \tilde{m}_i \equiv \hat{V}_i^{-1/2}\nabla_\beta \hat{m}_i$, and $\tilde{\Lambda}_i \equiv \hat{V}_i^{1/2}\nabla_\beta \hat{m}_i$. The robust Hausman test is easily computed by first orthogonalizing $\tilde{\Lambda}_i$ with respect to $\nabla_\beta \tilde{m}_i$. Let $\tilde{E}_i$ be the $T \times P$ matrix residuals from the matrix regression

$$\tilde{\Lambda}_i \text{ on } \nabla_\beta \tilde{m}_i, \quad i = 1, \ldots, N. \tag{5.13}$$

Then compute $H \equiv N -$ SSR from the regression

$$1 \text{ on } \tilde{u}_i' \tilde{E}_i, \quad i = 1, \ldots, N; \tag{5.14}$$

under Eqs. (5.5) and (5.6), $H \overset{a}{\sim} \chi^2_P$. If the specification tests in Section 3 fail to reject Eq. (3.1), but Eq. (5.14) rejects Eqs. (5.1)–(5.3), this can be taken as evidence that at least one of the second moment assumptions (5.2) and (5.3) is violated.

If a minimum chi-square approach is used, specification tests are available from the overidentification test statistics. A useful GMM estimator stacks the orthogonality conditions of QCMLE and MNLS, and then the overidentification test can be used to test assumptions (5.1)–(5.3) (see Wooldridge, 1990b for details).

It is important to remember that the moment assumptions (5.1)–(5.3) encompass HHG's fixed effects negative binomial model. Consequently, a rejection of either Eqs. (5.5) and (5.6) based on H or any other test statistic necessarily implies misspecification of the FENB specification. A rejection implies some failure of Eqs. (5.1)–(5.3), so one needs to work harder in specifying $\mathrm{E}(y_i|x_i, \phi_i, \psi_i)$ or $\mathrm{Var}(y_i|x_i, \phi_i, \psi_i)$.

6. A gamma-type model under mean and variance assumptions

The variance assumption (5.2) is known to fail for some popular continuous distributions. For example, the parameterization of the gamma distribution used in the quasi-likelihood literature (for example, GMT, p. 685) implies that the conditional variance of y_{it} is proportional to the *square* of the conditional mean. This is also true for a natural parameterization of the lognormal distribution. This motivates the following model for all t:

$$\mathrm{E}(y_{it}|x_i, \phi_i) = \phi_i \mu(x_{it}, \beta_0), \tag{6.1}$$

$$\mathrm{Var}(y_{it}|x_i, \phi_i) = \sigma_0^2[\mathrm{E}(y_{it}|x_i, \phi_i)]^2 = \sigma_0^2[\phi_i \mu(x_{it}, \beta_0)]^2, \tag{6.2}$$

$$\mathrm{Cov}(y_{it}, y_{ir}|x_i, \phi_i) = 0, \quad t \neq r. \tag{6.3}$$

Assumption (6.1) is essentially the same as Eq. (5.1), while Eq. (6.3) is essentially Eq. (5.3). Eq. (6.2) corresponds to what is sometimes referred to as a *constant coefficient of variation model* (e.g. McCullagh and Nelder, 1989, Chapter 8) because the ratio of the standard deviation to the mean is constant. Ideally, the parameter σ_0^2 could be replaced by an unobserved effect that depends on i, but I do not know how to do that using the conditional linear predictor approach.

As before, under Eq. (6.1) $\boldsymbol{\beta}_0$ can be estimated using the methods in Section 3. However, assumptions (6.2) and (6.3) expand the list of orthogonality conditions. As far as I know, there has been no work analyzing models such as Eqs. (6.1)–(6.3) in an unobserved components, panel data setting, with or without distributional assumptions. This is probably because, when y_{it} is a non-negative continuous random variable, most researchers use $\log(y_{it})$ in a linear fixed effects model.

Define $\boldsymbol{p}(\boldsymbol{x}_i, \boldsymbol{\beta}), n_i$, and $\boldsymbol{u}_i(\boldsymbol{\beta})$ as in the previous sections. Additional orthogonality conditions are obtained by computing the linear predictor of y_{it} on n_i, conditional on $(\boldsymbol{x}_i, \phi_i)$. For each $t = 1, \ldots, T$,

$$L(y_{it}|n_i; \boldsymbol{x}_i, \phi_i) \equiv \frac{\mathrm{E}(y_{it}n_i|\boldsymbol{x}_i, \phi_i)}{\mathrm{E}(n_i^2|\boldsymbol{x}_i, \phi_i)} n_i. \tag{6.4}$$

To show that Eq. (6.4) does not depend on ϕ_i, note that

$$\begin{aligned}\mathrm{E}(y_{it}n_i|\boldsymbol{x}_i, \phi_i) &= \mathrm{Cov}(y_{it}, n_i|\boldsymbol{x}_i, \phi_i) + \mathrm{E}(y_{it}|\boldsymbol{x}_i, \phi_i)\mathrm{E}(n_i|\boldsymbol{x}_i, \phi_i) \\ &= \mathrm{Var}(y_{it}|\boldsymbol{x}_i, \phi_i) + [\phi_i\mu(\boldsymbol{x}_{it}, \boldsymbol{\beta}_0)]\left(\sum_{r=1}^{T} \phi_i\mu(\boldsymbol{x}_{ir}, \boldsymbol{\beta}_0)\right) \\ &= \phi_i^2\left(\sigma_0^2[\mu(\boldsymbol{x}_{it}, \boldsymbol{\beta}_0)]^2 + \mu(\boldsymbol{x}_{it}, \boldsymbol{\beta}_0)\left(\sum_{r=1}^{T} \mu(\boldsymbol{x}_{ir}, \boldsymbol{\beta}_0)\right)\right).\end{aligned}$$

Similarly,

$$\begin{aligned}\mathrm{E}(n_i^2|\boldsymbol{x}_i, \phi_i) &= \mathrm{Var}(n_i|\boldsymbol{x}_i, \phi_i) + [\mathrm{E}(n_i|\boldsymbol{x}_i, \phi_i)]^2 \\ &= \phi_i^2\left(\sigma_0^2 \sum_{r=1}^{T} [\mu(\boldsymbol{x}_{ir}, \boldsymbol{\beta}_0)]^2 + \left(\sum_{r=1}^{T} \mu(\boldsymbol{x}_{ir}, \boldsymbol{\beta}_0)\right)^2\right).\end{aligned}$$

Therefore,

$$L(y_{it}|n_i; \boldsymbol{x}_i, \phi_i) \equiv q_t(\boldsymbol{x}_i, \boldsymbol{\theta}_0)n_i, \tag{6.5}$$

where $\boldsymbol{\theta}_0 \equiv (\boldsymbol{\beta}_0', \sigma_0^2)'$ and

$$q_t(\boldsymbol{x}_i,\boldsymbol{\theta}_0) \equiv \frac{\sigma_0^2[\mu(\boldsymbol{x}_{it},\boldsymbol{\beta}_0)]^2 + \mu(\boldsymbol{x}_{it},\boldsymbol{\beta}_0)\ (\sum_{r=1}^T \mu(\boldsymbol{x}_{ir},\boldsymbol{\beta}_0))}{\sigma_0^2 \sum_{r=1}^T\ [\mu(\boldsymbol{x}_{ir},\boldsymbol{\beta}_0)]^2 + (\sum_{r=1}^T \mu(\boldsymbol{x}_{ir},\boldsymbol{\beta}_0))^2}. \tag{6.6}$$

Note that, for all $\boldsymbol{\theta}$, $\sum_{t=1}^T q_t(\boldsymbol{x}_i,\boldsymbol{\theta}) = 1$.

In terms of the vector $\boldsymbol{y}_i$, Eq. (6.5) is expressed as

$$L(\boldsymbol{y}_i|n_i; \boldsymbol{x}_i, \phi_i) = \boldsymbol{q}(\boldsymbol{x}_i,\boldsymbol{\theta}_0)n_i, \tag{6.7}$$

where $\boldsymbol{q}(\boldsymbol{x}_i,\boldsymbol{\theta}) \equiv [q_1(\boldsymbol{x}_i,\boldsymbol{\theta}),\ldots,q_T(\boldsymbol{x}_i,\boldsymbol{\theta})]'$ is $T \times 1$. Let $\boldsymbol{v}_i(\boldsymbol{\theta}) \equiv \boldsymbol{y}_i - \boldsymbol{q}(\boldsymbol{x}_i,\boldsymbol{\theta})n_i$. Then Eqs. (6.1), (6.2) and (6.3) imply joint orthogonality conditions of the form

$$\mathrm{E}[\boldsymbol{D}_1(\boldsymbol{x}_i)'\boldsymbol{u}_i(\boldsymbol{\beta}_0)] = \boldsymbol{0}, \tag{6.8}$$

$$\mathrm{E}[\boldsymbol{D}_2(\boldsymbol{x}_i)'n_i\boldsymbol{v}_i(\boldsymbol{\theta}_0)] = \boldsymbol{0}, \tag{6.9}$$

where $\boldsymbol{D}_1(\boldsymbol{x}_i)$ is $T \times L_1$ and $\boldsymbol{D}_2(\boldsymbol{x}_i)$ is $T \times L_2$.

For example, weighted MNLS estimators, which solve

$$\min_{\boldsymbol{\theta}} \sum_{i=1}^{N} \{\boldsymbol{y}_i - \boldsymbol{q}(\boldsymbol{x}_i,\boldsymbol{\theta})n_i\}'\boldsymbol{G}(\boldsymbol{x}_i,\hat{\boldsymbol{\gamma}})\{\boldsymbol{y}_i - \boldsymbol{q}(\boldsymbol{x}_i,\boldsymbol{\theta})n_i\}, \tag{6.10}$$

are generally consistent and asymptotically normally distributed for $\boldsymbol{\beta}_0$ and σ_0^2. Further, given one such estimator, it is straightforward to stack WMNLS orthogonality conditions along with the multinomial QCMLE orthogonality conditions to obtain a more efficient minimum chi-square estimator. The details are omitted.

7. Models with parametric serial correlation

For some applications, the zero covariance assumptions (5.3) and (6.3) might be too restrictive (but one should remember that these are conditional on latent effects; conditional on $\boldsymbol{x}_i$ only, the y_{it} are correlated). The methods of Section 3 are available without any assumptions on the variances and covariances, but sometimes we might want to model the serial correlation parametrically and use this information in estimating $\boldsymbol{\beta}_0$.

For the model in Section 6, it is straightforward to relax the zero covariance assumption. In fact. Eqs. (6.2) and (6.3) can be replaced with the more general assumption

$$\mathrm{Var}(\boldsymbol{y}_i|\boldsymbol{x}_i, \phi_i) = \phi_i^2\boldsymbol{\Omega}(\boldsymbol{x}_i,\boldsymbol{\delta}_0), \tag{7.1}$$

where $\boldsymbol{\Omega}(\mathbf{x}_i,\boldsymbol{\delta})$ is a $T \times T$ positive-definite variance function. The conditional linear prediction argument used in Section 6 still eliminates ϕ_i. In fact, letting $\boldsymbol{\Omega}_t(\mathbf{x}_i,\boldsymbol{\delta})$ denote the tth row of $\boldsymbol{\Omega}(\mathbf{x}_i,\boldsymbol{\delta})$ and $\mathbf{j}_T \equiv (1,1,\ldots,1)'$, $L(y_{it}|n_i; \mathbf{x}_i, \phi_i)$ is given by Eq. (6.6) with

$$q_t(\mathbf{x}_i, \boldsymbol{\theta}_0) \equiv \frac{\boldsymbol{\Omega}_t(\mathbf{x}_i,\boldsymbol{\delta}_0)\,\mathbf{j}_T + \mu(\mathbf{x}_{it}, \boldsymbol{\beta}_0)(\sum_{r=1}^{T}\mu(\mathbf{x}_{ir}, \boldsymbol{\beta}_0))}{\mathbf{j}'_T\boldsymbol{\Omega}(\mathbf{x}_i, \boldsymbol{\delta}_0)\,\mathbf{j}_T + (\sum_{r=1}^{T}\mu(\mathbf{x}_{ir}, \boldsymbol{\beta}_0))^2}. \tag{7.2}$$

The model that combines Eqs. (6.1) and (7.1) allows for serial correlation and a variety of variance functions. For example, a gamma-type model with constant AR(1) serial correlation would take

$$\boldsymbol{\Omega}(\mathbf{x}_i, \boldsymbol{\delta}_0) \equiv \sigma_0^2\boldsymbol{\Delta}(\mathbf{x}_i, \boldsymbol{\beta}_0)\mathbf{R}_T(\rho_0)\boldsymbol{\Delta}(\mathbf{x}_i, \boldsymbol{\beta}_0), \tag{7.3}$$

where

$$\boldsymbol{\Delta}(\mathbf{x}_i, \boldsymbol{\beta}_0) \equiv \mathrm{diag}\{\mu(\mathbf{x}_{i1}, \boldsymbol{\beta}_0), \ldots, \mu(\mathbf{x}_{iT}, \boldsymbol{\beta}_0)\} \tag{7.4}$$

and $\mathbf{R}_T(\rho)$ is the $T \times T$ matrix with (r,t)th element $\rho^{|r-t|}$. This model maintains Eq. (6.2) but relaxes Eq. (6.3) to $\mathrm{Cov}(y_{it}, y_{ir}|\mathbf{x}_i, \phi_i) = \phi_i^2\sigma_0^2\rho_0^{|r-t|}\mu(\mathbf{x}_{it}, \boldsymbol{\beta}_0)\mu(\mathbf{x}_{ir}, \boldsymbol{\beta}_0)$.

We can also allow for serial correlation in models where the variance is proportional to the mean (as in Section 5), but the individual dispersion is restricted in this case. A model with constant AR(1) serial correlation chooses $\boldsymbol{\Omega}(\mathbf{x}_i,\boldsymbol{\delta}_0)$ as in Eq. (7.3), except that

$$\boldsymbol{\Delta}(\mathbf{x}_i, \boldsymbol{\beta}_0) \equiv \mathrm{diag}\{[\mu(\mathbf{x}_{i1}, \boldsymbol{\beta}_0)]^{1/2}, \ldots, [\mu(\mathbf{x}_{iT}, \boldsymbol{\beta}_0)]^{1/2}\}. \tag{7.5}$$

In terms of model (5.1)–(5.3), Eq. (5.2) has been maintained and Eq. (5.3) has been relaxed at the cost of imposing $\psi_i \equiv \sigma_0^2\phi_i$.

The identification issue in these more complicated models warrants some attention. For example, in Eqs. (6.1), (7.3) and (7.5), it can be seen that σ_0^2 is not identified if $\rho_0 = 0$. In this case the model of Section 5 applies, and a separate variance effect ψ_i can vary independently of ϕ_i.

8. Concluding remarks

This paper offers some distribution-free estimators for multiplicative panel data models. The estimators of Section 3 require only a conditional mean assumption. Perhaps the most practical result is that the fixed effects Poisson estimator is fully robust in the sense that only the structural conditional mean assumption, given in Eq. (3.1), is needed for consistency and asymptotic normality. The robust variance matrix estimate is easy to obtain, and specification testing is fairly straightforward. These results have already been used in several published and unpublished studies, including Papke (1991), Hausman et al. (1995), Page (1995), Gordy (1996), and Crépon and Duguet (1997). The recent proof by Hahn (1997) that the FEP estimator achieves the semiparametric efficiency bound under Eqs. (2.1) and (2.2) provides further justification for the FEP estimator.

A GMM approach that adds orthogonality conditions to the FEP orthogonality conditions might prove useful in future studies, both for enhancing efficiency and providing convenient specification testing.

Sections 5–7 demonstrate how additional orthogonality conditions can be derived from certain models that specify the conditional second moments in addition to the conditional mean. The model in Section 5 extends the mean and variance assumptions for well-known count distributions, and Section 6 studies a variance assumption suited to nonnegative, continuously distributed response variables. Section 7 shows how parametric models of serial correlation can be used in estimation. In each section, no distributional assumptions are needed for consistent estimation: the estimators are robust to assumptions not explicitly imposed.

Chamberlain's (1992a) approach for deriving efficiency bounds can apparently be applied to models such as Eqs. (5.1)–(5.3) by augmenting his orthogonality conditions with orthogonality conditions for the squares and cross products of the explained variable. We leave this to future research.

Finally, the models in Sections 3, 5–7 assume that $\boldsymbol{x}_{it}$ is strictly exogenous conditional on the latent variable or variables. This can be violated especially when there is feedback from y_{it} to $\boldsymbol{x}_{ir}$, $r > t$ (that is, if $\{y_{it}\}$ Granger-causes $\{\boldsymbol{x}_{it}\}$). While strict exogeneity is natural for certain explanatory variables, it is difficult to justify in general. For example, in HHG's patents-R&D application, the number of patents awarded in one year could affect subsequent R&D expenditures. If $\boldsymbol{x}_{it}$ is not strictly exogenous, all of the estimators offered here are inconsistent. In the case of a conditional mean specification, Chamberlain (1992b) and Wooldridge (1997) suggest orthogonality conditions that can be used in method of moments procedures.

Acknowledgements

This is a revised version of MIT Department of Economics Working Paper No. 564. I am grateful to two anonymous referees, an associate editor, Zvi Griliches, Lars Hansen, Jerry Hausman, Danny Quah, Tom Stoker, and especially Gary Chamberlain and Whitney Newey for very helpful comments, suggestions, and extensions.

References

Andersen, E.B., 1970. Asymptotic properties of conditional maximum likelihood estimators. Journal of the Royal Statistical Society Series B 32, 283–301.

Chamberlain, G., 1980. Analysis of covariance with qualitative data. Review of Economic Studies 47, 225–238.

Chamberlain, G., 1982. Multivariate regression models for panel data. Journal of Econometrics 18, 5–46.

Chamberlain, G., 1984. Panel data. In: Griliches, Z., Intriligator, M. (Eds.). Handbook of Econometrics, vol. I, North-Holland, Amsterdam.

Chamberlain, G., 1992a. Efficiency bounds for semiparametric regression. Econometrica 60, 567–596.

Chamberlain, G., 1992b. Comment: sequential moment restrictions in panel data. Journal of Business and Economic Statistics 10, 20–26.

Crépon, B., Duguet, E., 1997. Estimating the innovation function from patent numbers: GMM on count panel data. Journal of Applied Econometrics 12, 243–263.

Davidson, R., MacKinnon, J.G., 1993. Estimation and Inference in Econometrics. Oxford University Press, New York.

Gordy, M.B., 1996. Hedging winner's curse with multiple bids: evidence from the portuguese treasury bill auction. Mimeo. Division of Research and Statistics, Federal Reserve Board, Washington, DC.

Gourieroux, C., Monfort, A., Trognon, C., 1984. Pseudo-maximum likelihood Methods: theory. Econometrica 52, 681–700.

Hahn, J., 1997. A note on efficient semiparametric estimation of some exponential panel models. Econometric Theory 13, 583–588.

Hansen, L.P., 1982. Large sample properties of generalized method of moments estimators. Econometrica 50, 1029–1054.

Hansen, L.P., Richard, S.F., 1987. The role of conditioning information in deducing testable restrictions implied by dynamic asset pricing models. Econometrica 55, 587–613.

Hansen, L.P., Heaton, J., Ogaki, M., 1988. Efficiency bounds implied by multiperiod conditional moment restrictions. Journal of the American Statistical Association 83, 663–871.

Hausman, J.A., 1978. Specification tests in econometrics. Econometrica 46, 1251–1271.

Hausman, J.A., Hall, B.H., Griliches, Z., 1984. Econometric models for count data with an application to the patents-R&D relationship. Econometrica 52, 909–938.

Hausman, J.A., Leonard, G., McFadden. D.L., 1995. A utility-consistent, combined discrete choice and count data model. Assessing recreational use losses due to natural resource damage. Journal of Public Economics 56, 1–30.

Johnson, N.L., Kotz, S., 1969. Discrete Distributions. Wiley, New York.

McCullagh P., Nelder, J.A., 1989. Generalized Linear Models. Chapman & Hall, New York.

Newey, W.K., 1985. Maximum likelihood specification testing and conditional moment tests. Econometrica 53, 1047–1070.

Newey, W.K., McFadden, D.L., 1994. Large sample estimation and hypothesis testing. In: Engle, R.F., McFadden, D.L. (Eds.), Handbook of Econometrics, vol. 4. North-Holland, Amsterdam, pp. 2111–2245.

Page, M., 1995. Racial and ethnic discrimination in urban housing markets: evidence from a recent audit study. Journal of Urban Economics 38, 183–206.

Palmgren, J., 1981. The Fisher information matrix for log-linear models arguing conditionally in the observed explanatory variables. Biometrika 68, 563–566.

Papke, L.E., 1991. Interstate business tax differentials and new firm location. Journal of Public Economics 45, 47–68.

Rao, C.R., 1973. Linear Statistical Inference and its Applications, 2nd Ed. Wiley, New York.

Wooldridge, J.M., 1990a. A unified approach to robust, regression-based specification tests. Econometric Theory 6, 17–43.

Wooldridge, J.M., 1990b. Distibution-free estimation of some nonlinear panel data models. MIT Department of Economics working paper No. 564.

Wooldridge, J.M., 1991. Specification testing and quasi-maximum likelihood estimation. Journal of Econometrics 48, 29–55.

Wooldridge, J.M., 1997. Multiplicative panel data models without the strict exogeneity assumption. Econometric Theory, 13, 667–678.

Part III
Unbalanced Panels

[11]

ELSEVIER

Journal of Econometrics 101 (2001) 295–313

JOURNAL OF Econometrics

www.elsevier.nl/locate/econbase

Nested random effects estimation in unbalanced panel data

Werner Antweiler*

Faculty of Commerce, The University of British Columbia, 2053 Main Mall, Vancouver, BC Canada V6T 1Z2

Received 27 October 1997; received in revised form 26 July 2000; accepted 2 October 2000

Abstract

Panel data in many econometric applications exhibit a nested (hierarchical) structure. For example, data on firms may be grouped by industry, or data on air pollution may be grouped by observation station within a city, city within a country, and by country. In these cases, one can control for unobserved group and sub-group effects using a nested-error component model. A double-nested unbalanced panel is examined and a corresponding maximum likelihood estimator is derived. A generalization to even higher-order nesting is feasible. A practical example and a Monte-Carlo simulation compare the new estimator against the non-nested ML estimator. The style of presentation is intended to aid applied econometricians in implementing the new ML estimator. © 2001 Elsevier Science S.A. All rights reserved.

JEL classification: C13; C23

Keywords: Panel data; Nested effects; Error component model; Econometrics

1. Introduction and motivation

Data often exhibit a nested (or hierarchical) structure. For example, firms may be grouped by industry. This is a single-nested structure. Data on air pollution

* Corresponding author. Tel.: + 1-604-822-8484; fax: + 1-604-822-8477.
E-mail address: werner.antweiler@ubc.ca (W. Antweiler).

PII: S0304-4076(00)00086-5

may be grouped by observation station within a city and city within a country. This is a double-nested structure. Although there can be any number of nestings, most applications will be of the single-or double-nested type. This paper explores the double-nested error component model, but estimators for higher-order nestings can be obtained using the methodology presented here. This paper is aimed at the econometric practitioner. Therefore, care has been taken to use notation that will allow the practitioner to implement the methods described in this paper into suitable econometric software. In what follows, Section 2 provides a brief overview of the literature on nested panels and motivates the analysis by presenting the case of balanced panels. Section 3 addresses the more complex case of unbalanced panels and introduces a suitable maximum likelihood (ML) estimator. A concrete example is provided in Section 4 where this new ML estimator for double-nested panels is compared to the non-nested panel ML estimator. Section 5 concludes with a small Monte-Carlo study of the new ML estimator.

While the problem of hierarchical panels appears to be one of great practical importance, not much work has been published on this topic. Early work on balanced panels include Ghosh (1976), who developed an ANOVA-type estimator for single-nested panels, and Fuller and Battese (1973), who investigated the error structure of double-nested data sets with cross-sectional data but no time dimension. This was later improved upon by Baltagi (1987). Pakes (1983) discusses regression analysis where populations are grouped. Searle (1987, Chapter 3) discusses nested data structures in a variance analysis context. It appears that Baltagi (1993) first proposed the term "nested effects," adapting the term "nested-error structure" by Fuller and Battese (1973) to the context of panel data.

New and complementary work to this paper appears in Baltagi et al. (1999a, b) and Davis (1999).

One econometric problem in data sets with a nested structure relates to the possibility that individual effects may be associated with each level. For example, in a model with cities and countries there can be city-specific effects as well as country-specific effects. Using country-specific effects alone would exclude the possibility of city-specific effects, and vice versa.[1]

Another econometric problem is introduced by estimating a nested panel with a non-nested error structure. This leads to a phenomenon similar to the

[1] For single-nested panels one alternative is the estimation of 'mixed effects' where a fixed-effects approach is used for the top-level group (e.g. countries) and a random-effects approach is used for the low-level group (e.g. cities). This method may be appropriate in cases where the top level covers an entire population (such as all industries in an economy or all countries in the world); in other cases, however, this method may be inappropriate.

well-known *Moulton bias* in standard errors.[2] There are two issues. First, the standard errors computed under the assumption that the error term is i.i.d. will be biased (downward if the error terms are positively correlated). Second, the assumption of independence is unlikely to be satisfied when aggregate (macro) data are merged with micro data. For example, it is common in labour economics to merge micro data on individual workers with macro data on industry, occupation, or geographic location. More concretely, estimation of a wage equation for individual workers could involve characteristics of the individual worker as well as aggregate (e.g., state or country) unemployment rates.

Consider a regression equation

$$y_{ijkt} = x'_{ijkt}\beta + u_{ijkt}, \tag{1}$$

for $i = 1,\ldots,L$; $j = 1,\ldots,M_i$; $k = 1,\ldots,N_{ij}$ and $t = 1,\ldots,T_{ijk}$. For example, the dependent variable y_{ijkt} could denote the air pollution measured at station k in city j of country i in time period t. This means that there are L countries, and each country i has M_i cities in which N_{ij} observation stations are located. At such a station, air pollution is observed during T_{ijk} periods. The x_{ijkt} denotes a vector of K explanatory variables, and the disturbance is given by

$$u_{ijkt} = \lambda_i + \mu_{ij} + \nu_{ijk} + \varepsilon_{ijkt}, \tag{2}$$

where $\lambda_i \sim \mathrm{IID}(0, \sigma_\lambda^2)$, $\mu_{ij} \sim \mathrm{IID}(0, \sigma_\mu^2)$, $\nu_{ijk} \sim \mathrm{IID}(0, \sigma_\nu^2)$, and $\varepsilon_{ijkt} \sim \mathrm{IID}(0, \sigma_\varepsilon^2)$, are independent of each other and among themselves. When considering the ML estimator, the assumption of normality will be added.

2. Nested balanced panels

The first reference of a nested error structure can be found in Ghosh (1976). This study considers a balanced panel with a single-nested (e.g., country and region) structure as well as individual time effects. Baltagi (1987), using methodology developed by Wansbeek and Kapteyn (1982), provides a more rigorous algebraic derivation of this type of estimator based on the spectral decomposition of the variance–covariance matrix Ω.

Xiong (1995) elegantly derives a nested-effects estimator for single-nested balanced panels (without separate time effects). I generalize this estimator to the double-nested case to provide a reference point for the discussion of the double-nested unbalanced panel in Section 3. To begin with, let I_s be an identity matrix of dimension s, and let J_s be a square matrix of dimension s with all elements 1, and for convenience of algebraic manipulation, introduce $P_s \equiv J_s/s$ and

[2] See Moulton (1986, 1987, 1990).

$Q_s \equiv I_s - P_s$. Also note that $I_{rs} = I_r \otimes I_s$ and $P_{rs} = P_r \otimes P_s$ for any positive integers r and s. Expressing (2) in matrix form and computing $\Omega = E(uu')$, it follows that

$$\Omega = \sigma_\lambda^2(I_L \otimes J_{MNT}) + \sigma_\mu^2(I_{LM} \otimes J_{NT}) + \sigma_\nu^2(I_{LMN} \otimes J_T) + \sigma_\varepsilon^2 I_{LMNT}. \tag{3}$$

First transforming the J matrices into P matrices, then recursively expanding the multi-group I matrices into the sum of P and Q matrices, collapsing contiguous P matrices, and finally collecting terms, yields

$$\begin{aligned}\Omega &= MNT\sigma_\lambda^2(I_L \otimes P_{MNT}) + NT\sigma_\mu^2(I_{LM} \otimes P_{NT}) + T\sigma_\nu^2(I_{LMN} \otimes P_T) + \sigma_\varepsilon^2 I_{LMNT} \\ &= (MNT\sigma_\lambda^2 + NT\sigma_\mu^2 + T\sigma_\nu^2 + \sigma_\varepsilon^2)(I_L \otimes P_{MNT}) \\ &\quad + (NT\sigma_\mu^2 + T\sigma_\nu^2 + \sigma_\varepsilon^2)(I_L \otimes Q_M \otimes P_{NT}) \\ &\quad + (T\sigma_\nu^2 + \sigma_\varepsilon^2)(I_{LM} \otimes Q_N \otimes P_T) + \sigma_\varepsilon^2(I_{LMN} \otimes Q_T) \\ &= \sigma_\varepsilon^2(I_{LMN} \otimes Q_T) + \sigma_1^2(I_{LM} \otimes Q_N \otimes P_T) + \sigma_2^2(I_L \otimes Q_M \otimes P_{NT}) \\ &\quad + \sigma_3^2(I_L \otimes P_{MNT}),\end{aligned} \tag{4}$$

where in the last line σ_ε^2, σ_1^2, σ_2^2, and σ_3^2 were introduced as the characteristic roots of the spectral decomposition of Ω. They are defined as follows:

$$\sigma_1^2 \equiv T\sigma_\nu^2 + \sigma_\varepsilon^2, \tag{5}$$

$$\sigma_2^2 \equiv NT\sigma_\mu^2 + T\sigma_\nu^2 + \sigma_\varepsilon^2, \tag{6}$$

$$\sigma_3^2 \equiv MNT\sigma_\lambda^2 + NT\sigma_\mu^2 + T\sigma_\nu^2 + \sigma_\varepsilon^2. \tag{7}$$

As the terms with the Kronecker products are all orthogonal to each other and sum to I_{LMNT}, it follows that[3]

$$\begin{aligned}\Omega^{-1/2} &= \sigma_\varepsilon^{-1}(I_{LMN} \otimes Q_T) + \sigma_1^{-1}(I_{LM} \otimes Q_N \otimes P_T) \\ &\quad + \sigma_2^{-1}(I_L \otimes Q_M \otimes P_{NT}) + \sigma_3^{-1}(I_L \otimes P_{MNT}).\end{aligned} \tag{8}$$

Now expand all the Q matrices as the difference of I and P, multiply both sides of the equation by σ_ε, and collect terms

$$\begin{aligned}\sigma_\varepsilon \Omega^{-1/2} &= I_{LMNT} - \left(1 - \frac{\sigma_\varepsilon}{\sigma_1}\right)(I_{LMN} \otimes P_T) \\ &\quad - \left(\frac{\sigma_\varepsilon}{\sigma_1} - \frac{\sigma_\varepsilon}{\sigma_2}\right)(I_{LM} \otimes P_{NT}) - \left(\frac{\sigma_\varepsilon}{\sigma_2} - \frac{\sigma_\varepsilon}{\sigma_3}\right)(I_L \otimes P_{MNT}).\end{aligned} \tag{9}$$

[3] For scalars ζ_i and an arbitrary scalar r, it holds that $\Omega^r = \sum_i \zeta_i^r Z_i$ when the matrices Z_i are pairwise orthogonal to each other and sum to the identity matrix, and each Z_i is symmetric and idempotent with its rank equal to its trace. See Nerlove (1971b).

To perform generalized least squares, the following transformed system of y (and likewise x) is estimated via OLS:

$$y^*_{ijkt} = y_{ijkt} - \left(1 - \frac{\sigma_\varepsilon}{\sigma_1}\right)\bar{y}_{ijk\bullet} - \left(\frac{\sigma_\varepsilon}{\sigma_1} - \frac{\sigma_\varepsilon}{\sigma_2}\right)\bar{y}_{ij\bullet\bullet} - \left(\frac{\sigma_\varepsilon}{\sigma_2} - \frac{\sigma_\varepsilon}{\sigma_3}\right)\bar{y}_{i\bullet\bullet\bullet}, \tag{10}$$

where $\bar{y}_{ijk\bullet}$, $\bar{y}_{ij\bullet\bullet}$, and $\bar{y}_{i\bullet\bullet\bullet}$ indicate group averages. The pattern exhibited in Eq. (10) is suggestive of solutions for higher-order nested panels. For feasible generalized least squares, estimates of the variances can be obtained from the three group-wise between estimators and the within estimator for the innermost group.

3. An ML estimator for unbalanced panels

Unbalanced panels cannot be handled easily in the framework developed in the previous section. The Kronecker product can only be used in the case of balanced panels. Thus, unbalanced panels introduce quite a bit of notational inconvenience into the algebra.[4] At the same time, it will become apparent that unbalanced panels cannot be easily moulded into a feasible generalized least squares (FGLS) transformation for OLS estimation. Provided that introducing the normality assumption on the error structure is unproblematic in the given application, maximum likelihood estimation provides a suitable alternative.[5] Two other points make ML estimation appealing: the variances are estimated directly, and ML generally performs well for unbalanced panels.[6]

In deriving a practical estimator for nested panels, the key challenge is finding an expression for Ω^{-1} that is computationally feasible. The expression I derive below turns out to be just that, and by exploiting the recursive nature of the panel's hierarchic structure it suggests an immediate generalization to arbitrary orders of nesting.

I begin by introducing some notation and defining certain types of matrices that are used in the derivation of an inverse and determinant of Ω. An unbalanced panel is made up of L top level groups, each containing M_i second-level groups. The second-level groups contain the innermost N_{ij} subgroups, which in turn contain T_{ijk} observations. The number of observations in the higher-level groups are thus $T_{ij} \equiv \sum_{k=1}^{N_{ij}} T_{ijk}$ and $T_i \equiv \sum_{j=1}^{M_i} T_{ij}$, and the total number of

[4] For a discussion, see Baltagi (1995, Chapter 9), and in particular, Wansbeek and Kapteyn (1989).

[5] Computational cost is hardly a consideration anymore.

[6] For the latter, see Maddala and Mount (1973). Also see Section 5 below.

observations is $H \equiv \sum_{i=1}^{L} T_i$. The number of top-level groups is L, the number of second-level groups is $F \equiv \sum_{i=1}^{L} M_i$, and the number of bottom-level groups is $G \equiv \sum_{i=1}^{L} \sum_{j=1}^{M_i} N_{ij}$.

For balanced panels it was possible to neatly stack the J matrices of all '1's using $I \otimes J$ products. For unbalanced panels I redefine the J matrices to be blockdiagonal of size $H \times H$, corresponding in structure to the groups or subgroups they represent. They can be constructed explicitly by using "group membership" matrices consisting of ones and zeros that uniquely assign each of the H observations to one of the G (or F or L) groups. Let R_ν be such an $H \times G$ matrix corresponding to the innermost group level. Then the blockdiagonal $H \times H$ matrix J_ν can be expressed as the outer product of its membership matrices: $J_\nu = R_\nu R'_\nu$. Further note that the inner product $R'_\nu R_\nu$ produces a diagonal matrix $\tilde{T}_\nu$ of size $G \times G$ that contains the number of observations for each group. Similarly, $\tilde{T}_\mu = R'_\mu R_\mu$. In what follows the tilde accent will always denote such an "interior" matrix corresponding to the "exterior" $H \times H$ matrix of the same name. Define T_ν as an $H \times H$ matrix of observations with elements $T_{\nu,ijkt} = T_{ijk}$, and then it is apparent that $R_\nu \tilde{T}_\nu = T_\nu R_\nu$. Define T_μ analogously as the $H \times H$ matrix corresponding to the $F \times F$ matrix $\tilde{T}_\mu$. The properties of the T and J matrices can be exploited advantageously. Note that $J_\nu J_\nu = R_\nu (R'_\nu R_\nu) R'_\nu = R_\nu \tilde{T}_\nu R'_\nu = T_\nu J_\nu$. Similarly, $J_\mu J_\mu = T_\mu J_\mu$.

The mapping from groups to subgroups can also be captured through membership matrices. Let $R_\mu^\nu \equiv R'_\mu R_\nu \tilde{T}_\nu^{-1}$ be an $F \times G$ matrix mapping F groups to G subgroups. Define R_λ^μ correspondingly as an $L \times F$ matrix. Also note the recursive nature of the mapping process: $R_\mu = R_\nu (R_\mu^\nu)'$.

Similar to the P matrices that were defined for balanced panels, projection matrix $P_\nu \equiv R_\nu \tilde{T}_\nu^{-1} R'_\nu = T_\nu^{-1} J_\nu$ is idempotent: $P_\nu P_\nu = R_\nu \tilde{T}_\nu^{-1} R'_\nu R_\nu \tilde{T}_\nu^{-1} R'_\nu = R_\nu (\tilde{T}_\nu^{-1} \tilde{T}_\nu) \tilde{T}_\nu^{-1} R'_\nu = P_\nu$. The second property of this projection matrix establishes that such a matrix can be pre- or post-multiplied with a J or P matrix of *equal* nesting without changing it, for example, $P_\nu J_\nu = R_\nu \tilde{T}_\nu^{-1} R'_\nu R_\nu R'_\nu = R_\nu \tilde{T}_\nu^{-1} \tilde{T}_\nu R'_\nu = R_\nu R'_\nu = J_\nu$. Using this second property I establish the third property which allows a projection matrix to be applied to a J or P of *higher-order* nesting without changing it: $P_\nu J_\mu = P_\nu P_\mu J_\mu = (R_\nu \tilde{T}_\nu^{-1} R'_\nu)(R_\mu \tilde{T}_\mu^{-1} R'_\mu) J_\mu = T_\nu^{-1} (R_\nu R'_\nu)(R_\mu R'_\mu) T_\mu^{-1} J_\mu = (T_\nu^{-1} T_\nu)(T_\mu^{-1} T_\mu) J_\mu = J_\mu$. Now it is apparent that $J_\nu J_\mu = T_\nu J_\mu$, and analogously, $J_\mu J_\nu = J_\mu T_\nu$. To see this, observe that by construction $J_\nu = T_\nu P_\nu$, and that $P_\nu J_\mu = J_\mu$ by property 3 of the projection matrix.

In the next step I introduce a further type of matrix. It will turn out that the diagonal S matrices introduced here are made up of eigenvalues of yet another type of matrix (the Z matrices) introduced later. Let

$$S_\nu \equiv I + \rho_\nu T_\nu, \tag{11}$$

$$S_\mu \equiv I + \rho_\mu \Phi_\mu, \tag{12}$$

$$S_\lambda \equiv I + \rho_\lambda \Phi_\lambda, \tag{13}$$

where Φ_μ and Φ_λ are diagonal matrices with elements $\Phi_{\mu,ijkt} = \phi_{ij}$ and $\Phi_{\lambda,ijkt} = \phi_i$. The elements of the S and Φ matrices are defined recursively

$$\theta_{ijk} \equiv 1 + \rho_v T_{ijk}, \quad \phi_{ij} \equiv \sum_{k=1}^{N_{ij}} \frac{T_{ijk}}{\theta_{ijk}}, \quad \theta_{ij} \equiv 1 + \rho_\mu \phi_{ij}, \quad \phi_i \equiv \sum_{j=1}^{M_i} \frac{\phi_{ij}}{\theta_{ij}},$$

$$\theta_i \equiv 1 + \rho_\lambda \phi_i$$

where $\rho_v \equiv \sigma_v^2/\sigma_\varepsilon^2$, $\rho_\mu \equiv \sigma_\lambda^2/\sigma_\varepsilon^2$, and $\rho_\lambda \equiv \sigma_\lambda^2/\sigma_\varepsilon^2$ are variance ratios.

For the following proofs it is helpful to consider the $G \times G$, $F \times F$, and $L \times L$ "interior" counterparts of the S and Φ matrices; they are indicated again by a tilde accent on their top.[7] Corresponding to (11)–(13) are $\tilde{S}_v = I_G + \rho_v \tilde{T}_v$; $\tilde{S}_\mu = I_F + \rho_\mu \tilde{\Phi}_\mu$; and $\tilde{S}_\lambda = I_L + \rho_\lambda \tilde{\Phi}_\lambda$. The $\tilde{\Phi}$ matrices can then be derived as follows:

$$\tilde{\Phi}_\mu = R_\mu^v \tilde{S}_v^{-1} \tilde{T}_v R_\mu^{v\prime} = R_\mu' R_v \tilde{S}_v^{-1} \tilde{T}_v^{-1} R_v' R_\mu = R_\mu' S_v^{-1} R_\mu, \tag{14}$$

$$\begin{aligned} \tilde{\Phi}_\lambda &= R_\lambda^\mu \tilde{S}_\mu^{-1} \tilde{\Phi}_\mu R_\lambda^{\mu\prime} = R'_\lambda R_\mu T_\mu^{-1} (R_\mu' S_v^{-1} R_\mu) \tilde{S}_\mu^{-1} T_\mu^{-1} R_\mu' R_\lambda \\ &= R'_\lambda S_\mu^{-1} S_v^{-1} R_\lambda. \end{aligned} \tag{15}$$

In the above simplifications it should be noted that $R_v \tilde{S}_v = S_v R_v$, $R_\mu \tilde{S}_\mu = S_\mu R_\mu$, and $R_\lambda \tilde{S}_\lambda = S_\lambda R_\lambda$. Also remember that $R_\mu \tilde{T}_\mu^{-1} R_\mu'$ is an idempotent matrix and that $P_\mu R_\mu = R_\mu$. S matrices and J matrices commute in one special case: if S can be represented by an "interior" matrix S that corresponds to the nesting level of J. This means that the commutativity holds only when for each block in the J matrix the corresponding elements in the S matrix are all the same. Thus it is true that $S_\mu J_\mu = J_\mu S_\mu$, but note that $S_v J_\mu \neq J_\mu S_v$. Also, $S_\mu J_v = J_v S_\mu$. To see this, consider the case where $S_\mu J_\mu = S_\mu R_\mu R_\mu' = R_\mu \tilde{S}_\mu R_\mu' = R_\mu R_\mu' S_\mu = J_\mu S_\mu$. As long as S of size $H \times H$ is reducible to $\tilde{S}$ of size $F \times F$ corresponding to R, commutativity is guaranteed.

Having dealt with these preliminaries, the variance–covariance matrix for an unbalanced panel can be written as

$$\Omega = \sigma_e^2 [I + \rho_v J_v + \rho_\mu J_\mu + \rho_\lambda J_\lambda]. \tag{16}$$

The log-likelihood function $\mathscr{L}$ corresponding to the error structure given in (2) is[8]

$$\mathscr{L} = -\tfrac{1}{2}\{H \ln(2\pi) + \ln|\Omega| + u'\Omega^{-1}u\}. \tag{17}$$

[7] By comparison, the matrices with the tilde accent contain one unique value for each group, while the matrices without a tilde accent replicate the value from each group for all observations in that group.

[8] See also Baltagi (1995, Chapters 2.4 and 3.4) and Hsiao (1986, Chapter 3.3.3).

There are thus two challenges: computing the determinant $|\Omega|$ and the inverse Ω^{-1}. The following technique can be used to tackle these two challenges. Introduce

$$Z_\nu \equiv I + \rho_\nu J_\nu, \tag{18}$$

$$Z_\mu \equiv I + Z_\nu^{-1}\rho_\mu J_\mu = I + S_\nu^{-1}\rho_\mu J_\mu, \tag{19}$$

$$Z_\lambda \equiv I + Z_\mu^{-1}Z_\nu^{-1}\rho_\lambda J_\lambda = I + S_\mu^{-1}S_\nu^{-1}\rho_\lambda J_\lambda, \tag{20}$$

so that instead of writing (16) as a sum it can be written as the product $\Omega = Z_\nu Z_\mu Z_\lambda$, which is verified by substituting (18)–(20) into this expression and expanding. Notice the introduction of the S matrices in (19)–(20). They are direct counterparts to the Z matrices, but unlike these, the S matrices are diagonal and made up of eigenvalues of the corresponding Z matrices. Proving the equality parts of (19)–(20) is the primary challenge. It is now apparent that

$$|\Omega| = (\sigma_\varepsilon^2)^{\mathrm{H}}|Z_\nu||Z_\mu||Z_\lambda|, \tag{21}$$

$$\Omega^{-1} = Z_\lambda^{-1}Z_\mu^{-1}Z_\nu^{-1}/\sigma_\varepsilon^2, \tag{22}$$

and it needs to be shown that[9]

$$Z_\nu^{-1} = I - Z_\nu^{-1}\rho_\nu J_\nu = I - S_\nu^{-1}\rho_\nu J_\nu, \tag{23}$$

$$Z_\mu^{-1} = I - Z_\mu^{-1}Z_\nu^{-1}\rho_\mu J_\mu = I - S_\mu^{-1}S_\nu^{-1}\rho_\mu J_\mu, \tag{24}$$

$$Z_\lambda^{-1} = I - Z_\lambda^{-1}Z_\mu^{-1}Z_\nu^{-1}\rho_\lambda J_\lambda = I - S_\lambda^{-1}S_\mu^{-1}S_\nu^{-1}\rho_\lambda J_\lambda. \tag{25}$$

It is easily verified that the left and middle expressions in (23)–(25) are identical. By construction $Z_\nu^{-1}Z_\nu = I$, $Z_\mu^{-1}Z_\mu = I$, and $Z_\lambda^{-1}Z_\lambda = I$. In the first case, rearranging expressions yields $Z_\nu^{-1}(I + \rho_\nu J_\nu) = I$, where the part in parenthesis is of course Z_ν. The other two cases work analogously. The remaining task is to show the equality of the middle and right parts of (23)–(25). I will only show the most difficult case (25); the two simpler cases are embedded within. Proving (25) is equivalent to demonstrating that

$$\begin{aligned} J_\lambda &= Z_\nu Z_\mu Z_\lambda S_\lambda^{-1}S_\mu^{-1}S_\nu^{-1}J_\lambda, \\ &= [I + \rho_\nu J_\nu + \rho_\mu J_\mu + \rho_\lambda J_\lambda]S_\lambda^{-1}S_\mu^{-1}S_\nu^{-1}J_\lambda, \\ &= S_\lambda^{-1}[S_\mu^{-1}(S_\nu^{-1}(J_\lambda + \rho_\nu J_\nu J_\lambda) + \rho_\mu J_\mu S_\nu^{-1}J_\lambda) + \rho_\lambda J_\lambda S_\mu^{-1}S_\nu^{-1}J_\lambda], && (26) \\ &= S_\lambda^{-1}[S_\mu^{-1}(S_\nu^{-1}(J_\lambda + \rho_\nu T_\nu J_\lambda) + \rho_\mu \Phi_\mu J_\lambda) + \rho_\lambda \Phi_\lambda J_\lambda], && (27) \end{aligned}$$

[9] Note that the following is a highly specialized version of rule 19.18 in Sydsæter et al. (1999, p. 125).

$$= S_\lambda^{-1}[S_\mu^{-1}(S_v^{-1}(I + \rho_v T_v) + \rho_\mu \Phi_\mu) + \rho_\lambda \Phi_\lambda]J_\lambda,$$

$$= S_\lambda^{-1}[S_\mu^{-1}(I + \rho_\mu \Phi_\mu) + \rho_\lambda \Phi_\lambda]J_\lambda,$$

$$= S_\lambda^{-1}[I + \rho_\lambda \Phi_\lambda]J_\lambda,$$

$$= J_\lambda.$$

Arriving at step (26) simply makes use of the commutativity of the S and J matrices. The crucial step from (26) to (27) makes use of three equalities. First, it was shown earlier that $J_v J_v = T_v J_v$. Second, using the simplification from (14), it is true that $J_\mu S_v^{-1} J_\lambda = R_\mu(R'_\mu S_v^{-1} R_\mu)\tilde{T}_\mu^{-1} R'_\mu J_\lambda = R_\mu \tilde{\Phi}_\mu \tilde{T}_\mu^{-1} R'_\mu J_\lambda = \Phi_\mu P_\mu J_\lambda = \Phi_\mu J_\lambda$. And third, $J_\lambda S_\mu^{-1} S_v^{-1} J_\lambda = \Phi_\lambda J_\lambda$ is trivially true from (15).

The above proof is also helpful in the following step. Using the same technique it can be shown that $J_\lambda Z_\mu^{-1} Z_v^{-1} = J_\lambda S_\mu^{-1} S_v^{-1}$ and $J_\mu Z_v^{-1} = J_\mu S_v^{-1}$. I use these equalities below in proceeding from steps (28) to (29) when I expand and simplify $\sigma_\varepsilon^2 \Omega^{-1}$:

$$Z_\lambda^{-1} Z_\mu^{-1} Z_v^{-1} = Z_\mu^{-1} Z_v^{-1} - S_\lambda^{-1} S_\mu^{-1} S_v^{-1} J_\lambda Z_\mu^{-1} Z_v^{-1},$$

$$= Z_v^{-1} - S_\mu^{-1} S_v^{-1} \rho_\mu J_\mu Z_v^{-1} - S_\lambda^{-1} S_\mu^{-1} S_v^{-1} J_\lambda Z_\mu^{-1} Z_v^{-1},$$

$$= I - S_v^{-1} \rho_v J_v - S_\mu^{-1} S_v^{-1} \rho_\mu J_\mu Z_v^{-1} - S_\lambda^{-1} S_\mu^{-1} S_v^{-1} J_\lambda Z_\mu^{-1} Z_v^{-1}, \tag{28}$$

$$= I - S_v^{-1} \rho_v J_v - S_\mu^{-1} S_v^{-1} \rho_\mu J_\mu S_v^{-1} - S_\lambda^{-1} S_\mu^{-1} S_v^{-1} J_\lambda S_\mu^{-1} S_v^{-1}. \tag{29}$$

In passing I note the difficulty of finding a simple projection matrix C satisfying $C'C = \Omega^{-1}$ that would produce an observation-by-observation GLS-to-OLS transformation. The J_μ and J_λ matrices are bordered on both sides by some non-commutable S matrices. Thus, an observation-by-observation transformation cannot be obtained from (29) except in the non-nested case where $\rho_\mu = \rho_\lambda = 0$.

In the next step I derive the determinant of Ω. The following lemma applies to the sum of the identity matrix and the product of an arbitrary diagonal matrix D and a block-diagonal J matrix stacked with $k = 1, \ldots, N$ blocks of 1's with size $T_k \times T_k$.

$$|I + \rho DJ| = \prod_{k=1}^{N} \left(1 + \rho \sum_{t=1}^{T_k} d_{kt}\right). \tag{30}$$

This lemma can be applied immediately to (18). In the case of (19) and (20), it is true that $Z_v^{-1} J_\mu = S_v^{-1} J_\mu$ and $Z_\mu^{-1} Z_v^{-1} J_\lambda = S_\mu^{-1} S_v^{-1} J_\lambda$. Then $|\Omega|$ can be written as follows:

$$|\Omega| = (\sigma_\varepsilon^2)^{\mathrm{H}} \prod_{i=1}^{L} \theta_i \prod_{j=1}^{M_i} \theta_{ij} \prod_{k=1}^{N_{ij}} \theta_{ijk}. \tag{31}$$

In the case of a balanced panel, $|\Omega|$ simplifies to

$$|\Omega| = (\sigma_\varepsilon^2)^H (1 + \rho_\nu T)^{LM(N-1)} (1 + \rho_\nu T + \rho_\mu NT)^{L(M-1)}$$

$$(1 + \rho_\nu T + \rho_\mu NT + \rho_\lambda MNT)^L. \tag{32}$$

Having dealt with these lengthy preliminaries, the log-likelihood function (17) can now be fully expanded by taking the log of (31), using (29) in $u'\Omega^{-1}u$, and rearranging. In order to simplify the resulting expression, I abbreviate the residual sum of squares as $V_{ijk} \equiv \sum_{t=1}^{T_{ijk}} u_{ijkt}^2$, and further define recursively

$$U_{ijk} \equiv \sum_{t=1}^{T_{ijk}} u_{ijkt}, \quad U_{ij} \equiv \sum_{k=1}^{N_{ij}} \frac{U_{ijk}}{\theta_{ijk}}, \quad U_i \equiv \sum_{j=1}^{M_i} \frac{U_{ij}}{\theta_{ij}}.$$

Thus,

$$\mathscr{L} = -\frac{1}{2}\left[H \ln(2\pi\sigma_\varepsilon^2) + \sum_{i=1}^{L} \left\{ \ln\theta_i + \sum_{j=1}^{M_i} \left\{ \ln\theta_{ij} + \sum_{k=1}^{N_{ij}} \left\{ \ln\theta_{ijk} + \frac{V_{ijk}}{\sigma_\varepsilon^2} \right.\right.\right.\right.$$

$$\left.\left.\left.\left. - \frac{\rho_\nu}{\theta_{ijk}} \frac{U_{ijk}^2}{\sigma_\varepsilon^2} \right\} - \frac{\rho_\mu}{\theta_{ij}} \frac{U_{ij}^2}{\sigma_\varepsilon^2} \right\} - \frac{\rho_\lambda}{\theta_i} \frac{U_i^2}{\sigma_\varepsilon^2} \right\}\right]. \tag{33}$$

The solution for a single-nested unbalanced panel is obtained by setting $L = 1$ and $\rho_\lambda = 0$. A gradient of this log-likelihood function can be obtained analytically (see the appendix), but it can also be obtained through numeric approximation.[10] Using a set of suitable starting values (for example, OLS or non-nested-panel GLS estimates combined with setting the variance ratios equal to values so that their sum is less than one), convergence can be achieved reasonably fast. A technical concern in carrying out the maximization is that the variances must not become negative. It is thus necessary to constrain the optimization such that the variance σ_ε^2 remains positive and that the variance ratios ρ_λ, ρ_μ, and ρ_ν remain non-negative.

[10] While an analytic gradient is not strictly necessary for computational purposes (as many software packages provide numeric approximations), they significantly speed up computations. Even with an analytic gradient, however, the Hessian matrix Ψ is typically obtained through numeric approximation methods. Ψ is used to obtain standard errors s_b for the estimates of the B regressors. The diagonal elements of the inverse of the Hessian, corrected for the degrees of freedom, are approximately following a t-distribution with $H - G - B$ degrees of freedom. More formally, this can be expressed as $s_b = \sqrt{\text{abs}([\Psi^{-1}H/(H-G-B)]_{bb})} \sim t(H-G-B)$.

4. Empirical example

To illustrate the practical value of the method introduced in Section 3, Table 1 compares the estimates from a conventional non-nested random effects ML estimation with those from a nested-effects ML estimation.

The example is a constant-elasticity closed-economy version of the regression model in Antweiler et al. (1998). The original model passed a number of standard robustness and specification checks. The dependent variable in this model is the log of atmospheric sulfuric dioxide concentration at observation stations around the world. A total of 2621 observations are obtained from 293 observation stations located in 44 countries, spanning a time period (not necessarily continuous) from 1971 to 1996. In this highly unbalanced panel, about a third of the observations are from stations in the United States. The second column in Table 1 indicates the dimensions of the independent variables. The indicators 'C', 'S', and 'T' symbolize the dimensions country, observation station and time; a dot indicates that the variable does not vary over this dimension. The three key regressors in the model are the log of economic intensity (measured as GDP per square kilometer) at a particular location, the

Table 1
Example regression: Simple vs. Nested[a]

Dep. Var. $\log(SO_2)$	Dim.	Simple		Nested	
Intercept		− 10.787***	(12.037)	− 7.103***	(5.613)
log(GDP/km²)	C S T	0.445***	(7.921)	0.202*	(2.531)
$\log(K/L)$	C . T	0.255*	(1.999)	0.371*	(2.345)
log(Income)	C . T	− 0.714***	(5.004)	− 0.477**	(2.620)
Suburban location	C S T	− 0.627***	(3.685)	− 0.720***	(4.531)
Rural location	C S T	− 0.834*	(2.181)	− 1.061***	(3.439)
Communist country	C . .	0.471*	(2.241)	0.613	(1.443)
log(Oilprice)	. . T	− 0.083*	(2.267)	− 0.089*	(2.410)
Average temperature	C S T	− 0.045***	(4.299)	− 0.044***	(3.719)
Time trend	. . T	− 0.043***	(11.666)	− 0.046***	(10.927)
σ_ε^2		0.330***	(31.992)	0.329***	(31.986)
ρ_ν		1.807***	(9.389)	1.017***	(8.243)
ρ_μ				1.347**	(3.229)
$\log(\mathscr{L})$		− 2645.4		− 2608.0	

[a] T ratios are given in parenthesis. The second column indicates over which dimensions the variable varies: 'C' indicates country, 'S' indicates observation station, and 'T' indicates time.
*Significance at 95% confidence level.
**Significance at 99% confidence level.
***Significance at 99.9% confidence level.

log of a country's capital abundance, and the log of its lagged 3-year moving income per capita. These regressors correspond (in that order) to the scale, composition, and technique effect that determine pollution concentration. Additional regressors are station-specific factors such as average temperature and the geographic proximity to urban centres (suburban and rural location dummies). A communist-country dummy, a time series for the real price of crude oil, and a time trend conclude the set of regressors for this model.

The results of this comparison shed some light on the problems with nested and highly unbalanced panels. First, the magnitudes of the estimates of the key regressors are noticeably different across the two models. The scale elasticity is only one-half the value from the non-nested panel estimation, while the importance of the composition effect has increased, and the income effect has decreased. While these results still (and strongly) support the conclusions in Antweiler et al. (1998), they cast doubt on the reliability of the point estimates. Second, the decomposition of the error term permits a clearer view on the aggregation level where the disturbances are introduced. In the simple model, the station and country variations are lumped together. When they are disaggregated it appears that more variation is at the country level than at the station level. Third, insofar as the simple model can be viewed as being nested within the more general nested-panel model, a likelihood ratio test between the two models with a test statistic of 74.8 is highly significant and favours the nested-panel model.

5. Monte-Carlo simulation

Comparing variance components estimators for unbalanced panel data requires comparison under a variety of panel patterns and true values of the variance components. An early Monte-Carlo study by Maddala and Mount (1973) evaluated the performance of different estimators for panel data. A recent and very thorough study by Baltagi and Chang (1994) comes to the conclusion that the ML estimator performs better than ANOVA-type estimators in severely unbalanced panels and when variance component ratios are large. The Baltagi and Chang study also introduces important concepts for the design of a Monte-Carlo study for such unbalanced panels which I will follow in this section. Here I investigate the performance of the new ML estimator for a double-nested panel and compare its performance with the conventional non-nested random-effects ML estimator.

The degree of "unbalancedness" of a panel can be captured through a generalization of the Ahrens and Pincus (1981) statistic $0 < \omega \leqslant 1$ which captures the ratio of harmonic to arithmetic mean of the number of observations (or subgroups) in a group, and which is equal to one if the panel is completely balanced.

A generalization of this concept to nested panels is as follows:

$$\omega_v \equiv \frac{G/\sum_{i=1}^{L}\sum_{j=1}^{M_i}\sum_{k=1}^{N_{ij}}(1/T_{ijk})}{H/G}, \quad \omega_\mu \equiv \frac{F/\sum_{i=1}^{L}\sum_{j=1}^{M_i}(1/N_{ij})}{G/F}$$

$$\omega_\lambda \equiv \frac{L/\sum_{i=1}^{L}(1/M_i)}{F/L}.$$

I consider two degrees of unbalancedness: strong unbalancedness (U) corresponds to a pattern of seven groups with $\{16, 11, 10, 7, 3, 1, 1\}$ subgroups (implying $\omega = 0.366$), while weak unbalancedness (u) corresponds to a pattern of seven groups with a uniform $\{2, \ldots, 12\}$ distribution of subgroups (implying an average of $\omega = 0.827$). In all cases, groups have an average of seven subgroups, which implies a sample size of $H = 7^4 = 2{,}401$ observations. In varying the degree of unbalancedness over the three hierarchical levels in the panel, I consider the six patterns Uuu, uUu, uuU, UUu, UuU, and uUU.

The variance decomposition will be measured by the familiar ρ_v, ρ_μ, and ρ_λ variance ratios, fixing σ_ε^2 at 5. I consider 10 permutations of the variance ratios 0.1, 0.4, and 0.7 for each of the three ρ's that satisfy $1 - \rho_\lambda - \rho_\mu - \rho_v > 0$. With H and σ_ε^2 fixed, the parameter space $(\omega_v, \omega_\mu, \omega_\lambda, \rho_v, \rho_\mu, \rho_\lambda)$ encompasses 60 different models. The Monte-Carlo simulation was conducted with 500 replications of each model, making use of the analytic gradient for the log-likelihood function documented in the appendix. The true model is assumed to be

$$y_{ijkt} = \beta_0 + \beta_1 x_{1,ijkt} + \beta_2 x_{2,ijt} + \beta_3 x_{3,it} + \lambda_i + \mu_{ij} + v_{ijk} + \varepsilon_{ijt}, \tag{34}$$

with x_3 varying only at the top (e.g., country) level, x_2 varying at the mid (e.g., province) level, and x_1 available for all observations at the most detailed (e.g., city) level.[11]

Results of the simulation are shown in Table 2. The first group (six columns) in the table identifies the parameter space (suppressing the fixed H and σ_ε^2). The second group – consisting of the $\hat{\sigma}_\varepsilon^2$ and $\hat{\rho}_u$ columns – shows results for the simple non-nested model, while the third group – consisting of the $\hat{\sigma}_\varepsilon^2$, $\hat{\rho}_v$, $\hat{\rho}_\mu$ and $\hat{\rho}_\lambda$ columns – contains the results from the double-nested model. All results in these six columns are ratios of the estimated variance relative to the true

---

[11] The data generation process (DGP) is an adaptation from Nerlove (1971a); see also Baltagi et al. (1999b). Here, $x_{1,ijkt} = 0.2t + 0.9x_{1,ijk,t-1} w_{ijt}$, $x_{2,ijt} = 0.3t + 0.8x_{2,ij,t-1} + w_{ij}$, and $x_{3,it} = 0.3t + 0.8x_{3,ij,t-1} + w_i$, where the w_{ijk}, w_{ij} and w_i are uniformly distributed on the interval $[-z, +z]$ with z equal to 0.5, 5, and 1, respectively. The initial observations are defined as $x_{1,ijk0} = 4 + 2w_{ij0}$, $x_{2,ij0} = 40 + 20w_{ij0}$, and $x_{3,i0} = 8 + 5w_{i0}$. The true β is [10,3,0.2, − 1.5]. Starting values for the ML routine are OLS estimates for the non-nested ML, and estimates from the non-nested ML were used in turn as starting values for the nested ML.

Table 2
Monte-Carlo simulation results

ω_v	ω_μ	ω_λ	ρ_v	ρ_μ	ρ_λ	$\hat{\sigma}^2_e$	$\hat{\rho}_u$	$\hat{\sigma}^2_\varepsilon$	$\hat{\rho}_v$	$\hat{\rho}_\mu$	$\hat{\rho}_\lambda$	s_{β_1}	s_{β_2}	s_{β_3}
0.819	0.819	0.366	0.1	0.1	0.1	1.01	0.28	1.00	0.88	0.89	0.69	1.10	1.25	1.11
0.819	0.366	0.827	0.1	0.1	0.1	1.01	0.29	1.00	0.90	0.85	0.73	1.10	1.27	1.16
0.366	0.821	0.823	0.1	0.1	0.1	1.01	0.28	1.00	0.89	0.88	0.70	1.10	1.22	1.10
0.819	0.366	0.366	0.1	0.1	0.1	1.01	0.25	1.00	0.95	0.86	0.62	1.11	1.30	1.11
0.366	0.822	0.366	0.1	0.1	0.1	1.01	0.28	1.00	0.83	0.89	0.69	1.09	1.22	1.09
0.366	0.366	0.826	0.1	0.1	0.1	1.01	0.30	1.00	0.86	0.90	0.70	1.10	1.25	1.10
0.820	0.819	0.366	0.4	0.1	0.1	1.08	0.15	1.00	0.99	0.78	0.60	1.13	1.36	1.08
0.819	0.366	0.822	0.4	0.1	0.1	1.08	0.16	1.00	1.00	0.74	0.69	1.12	1.40	1.09
0.366	0.820	0.826	0.4	0.1	0.1	1.08	0.16	1.00	0.99	0.83	0.64	1.10	1.30	1.07
0.819	0.366	0.366	0.4	0.1	0.1	1.08	0.15	1.00	0.99	0.79	0.56	1.13	1.39	1.12
0.366	0.821	0.366	0.4	0.1	0.1	1.08	0.17	1.00	1.00	0.76	0.63	1.10	1.29	1.07
0.366	0.366	0.825	0.4	0.1	0.1	1.08	0.17	1.00	0.99	0.79	0.62	1.12	1.31	1.09
0.820	0.822	0.366	0.7	0.1	0.1	1.22	0.12	1.00	0.99	0.79	0.55	1.06	1.43	1.04
0.819	0.366	0.824	0.7	0.1	0.1	1.22	0.12	1.00	0.99	0.74	0.58	1.07	1.43	1.03
0.366	0.820	0.827	0.7	0.1	0.1	1.22	0.12	1.00	0.99	0.83	0.57	1.03	1.29	1.00
0.819	0.366	0.366	0.7	0.1	0.1	1.22	0.12	1.00	1.00	0.75	0.58	1.07	1.44	1.05
0.366	0.820	0.366	0.7	0.1	0.1	1.22	0.14	1.00	1.00	0.88	0.50	1.04	1.29	1.02
0.366	0.366	0.825	0.7	0.1	0.1	1.22	0.13	1.00	1.00	0.77	0.62	1.04	1.29	1.01
0.819	0.819	0.366	0.1	0.4	0.1	1.07	0.33	1.00	0.91	0.97	0.51	1.09	1.78	1.11
0.819	0.366	0.832	0.1	0.4	0.1	1.06	0.30	1.00	0.91	0.97	0.54	1.09	1.72	1.07
0.366	0.818	0.827	0.1	0.4	0.1	1.07	0.27	1.00	0.87	0.98	0.55	1.07	1.50	1.06
0.819	0.366	0.366	0.1	0.4	0.1	1.07	0.27	1.00	0.91	0.97	0.50	1.08	1.74	1.08
0.366	0.819	0.366	0.1	0.4	0.1	1.07	0.33	1.00	0.85	0.98	0.60	1.07	1.51	1.05
0.366	0.366	0.827	0.1	0.4	0.1	1.06	0.32	1.00	0.89	0.98	0.63	1.07	1.48	1.05
0.818	0.817	0.366	0.4	0.4	0.1	1.13	0.21	1.00	0.99	0.97	0.52	1.10	1.66	1.06
0.818	0.366	0.825	0.4	0.4	0.1	1.13	0.20	1.00	1.00	0.96	0.65	1.10	1.65	1.03
0.366	0.819	0.822	0.4	0.4	0.1	1.13	0.18	1.00	0.99	0.97	0.61	1.08	1.47	1.05
0.820	0.366	0.366	0.4	0.4	0.1	1.13	0.19	1.00	0.99	0.96	0.57	1.09	1.72	1.05
0.366	0.821	0.366	0.4	0.4	0.1	1.13	0.22	1.00	1.00	0.97	0.59	1.08	1.47	1.05
0.366	0.366	0.824	0.4	0.4	0.1	1.13	0.21	1.00	1.00	0.95	0.59	1.10	1.47	1.06
0.819	0.819	0.366	0.1	0.7	0.1	1.19	0.36	1.00	0.87	0.97	0.71	0.98	1.69	0.94
0.819	0.366	0.825	0.1	0.7	0.1	1.17	0.30	1.00	0.87	0.97	0.69	1.00	1.67	0.97
0.366	0.819	0.833	0.1	0.7	0.1	1.19	0.26	1.00	0.89	0.97	0.63	0.97	1.43	0.95
0.819	0.366	0.366	0.1	0.7	0.1	1.19	0.29	1.00	0.94	0.98	0.61	0.97	1.69	0.95
0.366	0.818	0.366	0.1	0.7	0.1	1.19	0.34	1.00	0.86	0.98	0.65	0.96	1.43	0.95
0.366	0.366	0.823	0.1	0.7	0.1	1.17	0.31	1.00	0.92	0.97	0.62	0.98	1.41	0.96
0.819	0.821	0.366	0.1	0.1	0.4	1.01	0.58	1.00	0.89	0.88	0.87	1.10	1.25	1.09
0.819	0.366	0.828	0.1	0.1	0.4	1.01	0.57	1.00	0.82	0.88	0.86	1.10	1.28	1.08
0.366	0.818	0.827	0.1	0.1	0.4	1.01	0.60	1.00	0.92	0.87	0.89	1.10	1.22	1.09
0.819	0.366	0.366	0.1	0.1	0.4	1.01	0.57	1.00	0.91	0.85	0.85	1.10	1.28	1.08
0.366	0.819	0.366	0.1	0.1	0.4	1.01	0.60	1.00	0.87	0.86	0.89	1.09	1.22	1.09
0.366	0.366	0.824	0.1	0.1	0.4	1.01	0.57	1.00	0.88	0.90	0.85	1.10	1.24	1.09
0.819	0.821	0.366	0.4	0.1	0.4	1.08	0.37	1.00	1.00	0.81	0.85	1.12	1.38	1.06
0.819	0.366	0.827	0.4	0.1	0.4	1.08	0.37	1.00	1.00	0.82	0.88	1.12	1.39	1.05
0.366	0.819	0.823	0.4	0.1	0.4	1.08	0.38	1.00	0.99	0.83	0.89	1.10	1.30	1.08

Table 2 (*continued*)

ω_ν	ω_μ	ω_λ	ρ_ν	ρ_μ	ρ_λ	$\hat{\sigma}_e^2$	$\hat{\rho}_u$	$\hat{\sigma}_\varepsilon^2$	$\hat{\rho}_\nu$	$\hat{\rho}_\mu$	$\hat{\rho}_\lambda$	s_{β_1}	s_{β_2}	s_{β_3}
0.819	0.366	0.366	0.4	0.1	0.4	1.08	0.37	1.00	0.99	0.86	0.83	1.12	1.41	1.05
0.366	0.822	0.366	0.4	0.1	0.4	1.08	0.37	1.00	0.99	0.79	0.84	1.11	1.30	1.08
0.366	0.366	0.830	0.4	0.1	0.4	1.08	0.39	1.00	1.00	0.84	0.90	1.10	1.31	1.08
0.818	0.822	0.366	0.1	0.4	0.4	1.07	0.42	1.00	0.93	0.99	0.80	1.07	1.72	1.04
0.818	0.366	0.832	0.1	0.4	0.4	1.06	0.41	1.00	0.87	0.99	0.82	1.08	1.71	1.05
0.366	0.818	0.827	0.1	0.4	0.4	1.07	0.40	1.00	0.92	0.99	0.83	1.06	1.51	1.05
0.819	0.366	0.366	0.1	0.4	0.4	1.07	0.41	1.00	0.87	1.00	0.80	1.08	1.75	1.05
0.366	0.819	0.366	0.1	0.4	0.4	1.07	0.42	1.00	0.86	0.99	0.82	1.06	1.51	1.05
0.366	0.366	0.825	0.1	0.4	0.4	1.06	0.42	1.00	0.90	0.99	0.82	1.07	1.49	1.05
0.819	0.820	0.366	0.1	0.1	0.7	1.01	0.66	1.00	0.87	0.89	0.85	1.10	1.26	1.08
0.819	0.366	0.824	0.1	0.1	0.7	1.01	0.69	1.00	0.86	0.91	0.89	1.10	1.29	1.08
0.366	0.822	0.827	0.1	0.1	0.7	1.01	0.69	1.00	0.83	0.91	0.90	1.09	1.22	1.09
0.819	0.366	0.366	0.1	0.1	0.7	1.01	0.67	1.00	0.88	0.89	0.86	1.10	1.31	1.08
0.366	0.821	0.366	0.1	0.1	0.7	1.01	0.68	1.00	0.85	0.86	0.87	1.09	1.22	1.09
0.366	0.366	0.834	0.1	0.1	0.7	1.01	0.70	1.00	0.85	0.90	0.90	1.10	1.24	1.09

variance; in the case of $\hat{\rho}_u$ the ratio is relative to $\rho_\lambda + \rho_\mu + \rho_\nu$. The last group of three columns shows the standard errors obtained for the parameter estimates β_1, β_2, and β_3, where each is expressed as the ratio of the standard error from the nested-effects estimation relative to the standard error from the non-nested-effects estimation. For brevity, information on bias of the regressor estimates is not included as they were found to be negligible.

The Monte-Carlo simulation provides several interesting results. First, the use of the non-nested panel estimation for a nested panel does not deliver a clear picture of the variance decomposition. When estimating a nested model with the conventional non-nested random-effects ML estimator, $\hat{\sigma}_\varepsilon^2$ is biased slightly upwards and $\rho_u = \rho_\nu + \rho_\mu + \rho_\lambda$ is biased downwards. The bias seems to be more pronounced when the variance ratio ρ_ν is relatively large compared to ρ_μ and ρ_λ. The degree of unbalancedness only has a modest impact. Second, using the nested-effects estimator for a nested panel delivers much superior estimates of the variance terms.[12] Third, the standard errors of parameter estimates obtained from the non-nested estimation appear to be biased. For the estimate of the standard error of β_2 (corresponding to the variable x_2 which varies only over mid-groups), the non-nested panel estimator introduces a downward bias with a sizeable magnitude, indicating a problem resembling

[12] There appears to be a downward bias in the estimates of ρ_μ, and more pronounced, ρ_λ. While this appears puzzling at first sight, closer inspection of the simulation results reveals that the estimates of ρ_μ and ρ_λ are in some cases approaching zero, while in other cases, there are right on target. The average shown in the table reflects the mixing of these cases. This peculiarity may be attributed to the high degree of non-linearity of the log-likelihood function (and its partial derivatives) which in turn may lead to numerical instability in the maximization routine.

the *Moulton bias*. This downward bias is persistent over the entire parameter space and is relevant for all three types of variables. The effect is noticeably pronounced in the case of β_2 when either ρ_μ or ρ_ν are large, or when a large ρ_μ coincides with the corresponding panel level being highly unbalanced. In conclusion, the Monte-Carlo results suggest that inferences drawn from a non-nested estimation of a nested panel may be inaccurate because the standard errors are downward biased.

6. Conclusions

Hierarchically structured panel data are a common feature in many econometric studies. This paper has argued that a nested structure for the error term is a suitable way to deal with related pertinent econometric problems. In particular, nested-effects models provide a method for addressing the problem of merging micro and macro data. This paper has focused on unbalanced panels, acknowledging their pervasiveness in applied work. The maximum-likelihood estimator introduced in this paper provides a convenient estimation method. The double-nested error structure discussed here also provides the basis for generalizations to higher-order nested error structures.

I have compared the performance of the double-nested ML estimator with the performance of the conventional non-nested ML estimator. The results from the corresponding Monte-Carlo simulation reveal a downward bias in the standard errors of the regressors when the conventional (non-nested) random-effects estimator is applied to a nested panel. This key finding, along with illustrating the comparative performance of the estimator in a practical application, make a solid case for using the nested-effects ML estimator.

A caveat applies to the exclusion of separate time effects in this model. One way to deal with possible time effects is to introduce fixed time effects or a time trend variable. It appears that extending the present model to a "two-way" model with random time effects is very challenging because the time effects and hierarchical individual effects overlap in a non-trivial manner.

The discussion of the nested-effects ML estimator in this paper is directed at applied econometricians. Researchers interested in using this estimator can obtain the software developed for this paper by sending an e-mail request to the author.

Acknowledgements

The idea for this paper originated in a joint project with Scott Taylor and Brian Copeland on international trade and the environment where we were dealing with hierarchically-structured environmental data as well as the problem of merging micro and macro data. I would like to thank Badi Baltagi, John

DiNardo and David Green for helpful comments. I am particularly grateful for the suggestions and comments from one very helpful anonymous referee. This project was supported, directly or indirectly, by grants from the Social Sciences and Humanities Research Council of Canada, UBC's Centre for International Business Studies, and UBC's Entrepreneurship and Venture Capital Research Centre.

Appendix. Derivation of $\nabla\mathscr{L}$

In what follows I derive the analytic gradient $\nabla\mathscr{L}$ of the log-likelihood function. The derivatives are highly non-linear. For notational convenience let

$$\Psi_{ij} \equiv \sum_{k=1}^{N_{ij}} \left(\frac{T_{ijk}}{\theta_{ijk}}\right)^2, \quad \Psi_i \equiv \sum_{j=1}^{M_i} \left(\frac{\phi_{ij}}{\theta_{ij}}\right)^2,$$

$$V_{ij} \equiv \sum_{k=1}^{N_{ij}} \left(\frac{U_{ijk}}{\theta_{ijk}}\right)^2, \quad V_i \equiv \sum_{j=1}^{M_i} \left(\frac{U_{ij}}{\theta_{ij}}\right)^2,$$

$$\Xi_{ij} \equiv \sum_{k=1}^{N_{ij}} \frac{U_{ijk} T_{ijk}}{\theta_{ijk}^2}, \quad \Xi_i \equiv \sum_{j=1}^{M_i} \frac{U_{ij}\phi_{ij}}{\theta_{ij}^2},$$

$$\tilde{\Psi}_i \equiv \sum_{j=1}^{M_i} \frac{\Psi_{ij}}{\theta_{ij}^2}, \quad \tilde{\Xi}_i \equiv \sum_{j=1}^{M_i} \left\{\frac{\Xi_{ij}}{\theta_{ij}} - \frac{\rho_\mu}{\theta_{ij}} U_{ij} \frac{\Psi_{ij}}{\theta_{ij}}\right\},$$

$$X_{f,ijk} \equiv \sum_{t=1}^{T_{ijk}} x_{f,ijkt}, \quad X_{f,ij} \equiv \sum_{k=1}^{N_{ij}} \frac{X_{f,ijk}}{\theta_{ijk}},$$

$$X_{f,i} \equiv \sum_{j=1}^{M_i} \frac{X_{f,ij}}{\theta_{ij}}, \quad W_{f,ijk} \equiv \sum_{t=1}^{T_{ijk}} u_{f,ijkt} x_{f,ijkt}.$$

Then,

$$\frac{\partial\mathscr{L}}{\partial\beta_f} = \frac{1}{\sigma_\varepsilon^2} \sum_{i=1}^{L} \left\{ \sum_{j=1}^{M_i} \left\{ \sum_{k=1}^{N_{ij}} \left\{ W_{f,ijk} - \frac{\rho_\nu}{\theta_{ijk}} X_{f,ijk} U_{ijk} \right\} - \frac{\rho_\mu}{\theta_{ij}} X_{f,ij} U_{ij} \right\} - \frac{\rho_\lambda}{\theta_i} X_{f,i} U_i \right\},$$

$$\frac{\partial\mathscr{L}}{\partial\sigma_\varepsilon^2} = -\frac{1}{2\sigma_\varepsilon^2} \left[H - \frac{1}{\sigma_\varepsilon^2} \sum_{i=1}^{L} \left\{ \sum_{j=1}^{M_i} \left\{ \sum_{k=1}^{N_{ij}} \left\{ V_{ijk} - \frac{\rho_\nu}{\theta_{ijk}} U_{ijk}^2 \right\} - \frac{\rho_\mu}{\theta_{ij}} U_{ij}^2 \right\} - \frac{\rho_\lambda}{\theta_i} U_i^2 \right\} \right],$$

$$\frac{\partial\mathscr{L}}{\partial\rho_\lambda} = \frac{1}{2} \sum_{i=1}^{L} \frac{1}{\theta_i} \left\{ \frac{U_i^2}{\theta_i \sigma_\varepsilon^2} - \phi_i \right\},$$

$$\frac{\partial \mathscr{L}}{\partial \rho_\mu} = \frac{1}{2}\sum_{i=1}^{L}\left\{\frac{V_i}{\sigma_\varepsilon^2} - \phi_i + \frac{\rho_\lambda}{\theta_i}\left[\frac{U_i}{\sigma_\varepsilon^2}\left(\frac{\rho_\lambda}{\theta_i}U_i\Psi_i - 2\Xi_i\right) + \Psi_i\right]\right\},$$

$$\frac{\partial \mathscr{L}}{\partial \rho_\nu} = \frac{1}{2}\sum_{i=1}^{L}\left\{\sum_{j=1}^{M_i}\left\{\frac{V_{ij}}{\sigma_\varepsilon^2} - \phi_{ij} + \frac{\rho_\mu}{\theta_{ij}}\left[\frac{U_{ij}}{\sigma_\varepsilon^2}\left(\frac{\rho_\mu}{\theta_{ij}}U_{ij}\Psi_{ij} - 2\Xi_{ij}\right) + \Psi_{ij}\right]\right\}\right.$$

$$\left. + \frac{\rho_\lambda}{\theta_i}\left[\frac{U_i}{\sigma_\varepsilon^2}\left(\frac{\rho_\lambda}{\theta_i}U_i\tilde{\Psi}_i - 2\tilde{\Xi}_i\right) + \tilde{\Psi}_i\right]\right\}.$$

where β_f is the estimate corresponding to the fth regressor in the model.

References

Ahrens, H., Pincus, R., 1981. On two measures of unbalancedness in a one-way model and their relation to efficiency. Biometric Journal 23, 227–235.

Antweiler, W., Copeland, B., Taylor, M.S., 1998. Is free trade good for the environment? National Bureau of Economic Research Working Paper Series #6707. Forthcoming, American Economic Review.

Baltagi, B.H., 1987. On estimating from a more general time-series cum cross-section data structure. The American Economist 31, 69–71.

Baltagi, B.H., 1993. Nested effects (Problem 93.4.2). Econometric Theory 9, 687–688.

Baltagi, B.H., 1995. Econometric Analysis of Panel Data. Wiley, Chichester, UK.

Baltagi, B.H., Chang, Y.-J., 1994. Incomplete panels: a comparative study of alternative estimators for the unbalanced one-way error component regression model. Journal of Econometrics 62 (2), 67–89.

Baltagi, B.H., Song, S.H., Jung, B.C., 1999a. Further evidence on the unbalanced two-way error component regression model. Discussion paper, Texas A&M University.

Baltagi, B.H., Song, S.H., Jung, B.C., 1999b. The unbalanced nested error component regression model. Discussion paper, Texas A&M University.

Davis, P., 1999. Estimating multi-way error components models with unbalanced data structures. Mimeo, MIT Sloan School.

Fuller, W.A., Battese, G.E., 1973. Transformations for estimation of linear models with nested error structures. Journal of the American Statistical Association 68 (343), 626–632.

Ghosh, S.G., 1976. Estimating from a more general time-series cum cross-section data structure. The American Economist 20, 15–21.

Hsiao, C., 1986. Analysis of Panel Data. Cambridge University Press, Cambridge, MA.

Maddala, G.S., Mount, T.D., 1973. A comparative study of alternative estimators for variance components models used in econometric applications. Journal of the American Statistical Association 68, 324–328.

Moulton, B.R., 1986. Random group effects and the precision of regression estimates. Journal of Econometrics 32, 385–397.

Moulton, B.R., 1987. Diagnostics for group effects in regression analysis. Journal of Business and Economic Statistics 5, 275–282.

Moulton, B.R., 1990. An illustration of a pitfall in estimating the effects of aggregate variables on micro units. Review of Economics and Statistics 72 (2), 334–338.

Nerlove, M., 1971a. Further evidence on the estimation of dynamic economic relations from a time-series of cross-sections. Econometrica 39 (2), 359–382.

Nerlove, M., 1971b. A note on error components models. Econometrica 39, 383–396.

Pakes, A., 1983. On group effects and errors in variables in aggregation. Review of Economics and Statistics 65, 168–173.

Searle, S.R., 1987. Linear Models for Unbalanced Data. Wiley, New York.

Sydsæter, K., Strøm, A., Berck, P., 1999. Economists' Mathematical Manual, 3rd Edition. Springer, Berlin.

Wansbeek, T., Kapteyn, A., 1982. A class of decompositions of the variance-covariance matrix of a generalized error components model. Econometrica 50 (3), 713–724.

Wansbeek, T., Kapteyn, A., 1989. Estimation of the error-components model with incomplete panels. Journal of Econometrics 41, 341–361.

Xiong, W., 1995. Nested effects (Solution 93.4.2). Econometric Theory 11, 658–659.

[12]

Econometric Theory, **15**, 1999, 814–823. Printed in the United States of America.

UNEQUALLY SPACED PANEL DATA REGRESSIONS WITH AR(1) DISTURBANCES

BADI H. BALTAGI
Texas A&M University

PING X. WU
University of Melbourne

This paper deals with the estimation of unequally spaced panel data regression models with AR(1) remainder disturbances. A feasible generalized least squares (GLS) procedure is proposed as a weighted least squares that can handle a wide range of unequally spaced panel data patterns. This procedure is simple to compute and provides natural estimates of the serial correlation and variance components parameters. The paper also provides a locally best invariant test for zero first-order serial correlation against positive or negative serial correlation in case of unequally spaced panel data.

1. INTRODUCTION

Some panel data sets cannot be collected every period as a result of lack of resources or cut in funding. Instead, these panels are collected over unequally spaced time intervals. For example, a panel of households could be collected over unequally spaced years rather than annually. This is also likely when collecting data on countries, states, or firms where in certain years, the data are not recorded, are hard to obtain, or are simply missing. Other common examples are panel data sets using daily data from the stock market, including stock prices, commodity prices, futures, etc. These panel data sets are unequally spaced when the market closes on weekends and holidays. The model considered in this paper allows for unequally spaced time-series data for each country, individual, or firm. This is particularly useful for housing resale data where the pattern of resales for each house occurs at different time periods and the panel is unbalanced because we observe different number of resales for each house.

Panel data with missing observations have been studied by Wansbeek and Kapteyn (1989) and Baltagi and Chang (1994). However, none of these studies consider the problem of serial correlation with unequally spaced panels. Estima-

We thank three anonymous referees and the editor for helpful comments and suggestions. We also thank Dong Li for his research assistance. An earlier version of this paper was given at the North American summer meetings of the Econometric Society held in Montreal, Canada, June 1998. Address correspondence to: Badi H. Baltagi, Department of Economics, Texas A&M University, College Station, TX 77843-4228, USA; e-mail: Badi@econ.tamu.edu.

  0266-4666/99 $9.50

tion of AR(1) disturbances in time-series regressions with missing observations has been studied by Wansbeek and Kapteyn (1985), whereas testing for AR(1) disturbances in this context has been considered by Shively (1993), Robinson (1985), Dufour and Dagenais (1985), and Savin and White (1978). This paper proposes a simple, feasible generalized least squares (GLS) estimation method for unbalanced panels that allows for a variety of patterns of missing data and serially correlated errors of the AR(1) type. In addition, this paper provides a locally best invariant (LBI) test for zero first-order serial correlation against positive or negative serial correlation. This extends the work of King (1985), Dufour and Dagenais (1985), and Shively (1993) to the context of an unequally spaced panel. In particular, we consider a random error component regression model with AR(1) disturbances (see Lillard and Willis, 1978; Bhargava, Franzini, and Narendranathan, 1982, Baltagi and Li, 1991). However, we allow for unequally spaced patterns for each individual in the time series dimension. Savin and White (1978) allowed for a gap of m consecutive observations in time-series data. Here, we allow for a general type of unequally spaced panel data for each individual of the type considered by Shively (1993) in a time-series context.

2. THE MODEL

Consider the following unbalanced panel data regression model (see Wansbeek and Kapteyn, 1989):

$$y_{it} = x_{it}'\beta + u_{it} \qquad i = 1,\dots,N; \qquad t = 1,\dots,T_i, \tag{1}$$

where β is a $K \times 1$ vector of regression coefficients including the intercept and x_{it} is a $K \times 1$ vector of nonstochastic regressors. The disturbances follow a one-way error component model $u_{it} = \mu_i + \nu_{it}$ with individual effects $\mu_i \sim \text{IID}(0,\sigma_\mu^2)$ and the remainder disturbances ν_{it} following a stationary AR(1), i.e., $\nu_{it} = \rho\nu_{i,t-1} + \epsilon_{it}$ with $|\rho| < 1$ and ϵ_{it} is $\text{IID}(0,\sigma_\epsilon^2)$. The μ_i's are independent of the ν_{it}'s, and $\nu_{i0} \sim (0,\sigma_\epsilon^2/(1-\rho^2))$. Each individual i observes data at times $t_{i,j}$ for $j = 1,\dots,n_i$ with $1 = t_{i,1} < \cdots < t_{i,n_i} = T_i$ with $n_i > K$ for $i = 1,2,\dots,N$. For estimation of the equally spaced panel data regression model with AR(1) disturbances and no missing observations, see Baltagi and Li (1991). Note that the typical covariance element of ν_{it} for the observed periods $t_{i,j}$ and $t_{i,\ell}$ is given by $\text{cov}(\nu_{i,t_{i,j}},\nu_{i,t_{i,\ell}}) = \sigma_\epsilon^2\rho^{|t_{i,j}-t_{i,\ell}|}/(1-\rho^2)$ for $\ell, j = 1,\dots,n_i$. In fact, by continuous substitution over the AR(1) process, one can show that

$$\nu_{i,t_{i,j}} = \rho^{t_{i,j}-t_{i,j-1}}\nu_{i,t_{i,j-1}} + \epsilon_{i,t_{i,j}} + \rho\epsilon_{i,t_{i,j}-1} + \cdots + \rho^{t_{i,j}-t_{i,j-1}-1}\epsilon_{i,t_{i,j-1}+1}. \tag{2}$$

Define $S_{i,t_{i,j}} = \nu_{i,t_{i,j}} - \rho^{t_{i,j}-t_{i,j-1}}\nu_{i,t_{i,j-1}} = \epsilon_{i,t_{i,j}} + \rho\epsilon_{i,t_{i,j}-1} + \cdots + \rho^{t_{i,j}-t_{i,j-1}-1} \times \epsilon_{i,t_{i,j-1}+1}$ for $j = 2,\dots,n_i$, and let $S_{i,t_{i,1}} = (1-\rho^2)^{1/2}\nu_{i,t_{i,1}}$. For equally spaced data, with no missing observations, $S_{i,t_{i,j}}$ is equivalent to the Prais–Winsten transformation for the AR(1) model. In fact, for $\nu_i' = (\nu_{i,t_{i,1}},\dots,\nu_{i,t_{i,n_i}})$

and $S_i' = (S_{i,t_{i,1}},\ldots,S_{i,t_{i,n_i}})$, this transformation can be written in matrix form as $S_i(\rho) = C_i(\rho)\nu_i$ where

$$C_i(\rho) = \begin{bmatrix} (1-\rho^2)^{1/2} & 0 & 0 & \ldots & 0 & 0 & 0 \\ -\rho^{t_{i,2}-t_{i,1}} & 1 & 0 & \ldots & 0 & 0 & 0 \\ \vdots & \vdots & \vdots & \ldots & \vdots & \vdots & \vdots \\ 0 & 0 & 0 & \ldots & -\rho^{t_{i,n_i-1}-t_{i,n_i-2}} & 1 & 0 \\ 0 & 0 & 0 & \ldots & 0 & -\rho^{t_{i,n_i}-t_{i,n_i-1}} & 1 \end{bmatrix} \quad (3)$$

However, for the unequally spaced data the transformed disturbances are still heteroskedastic. In fact, $\text{var}(S_{i,t_{i,1}}) = \sigma_\epsilon^2$ whereas $\text{var}(S_{i,t_{i,j}}) = \sigma_\epsilon^2(1 + \rho^2 + \cdots + \rho^{2(t_{i,j}-t_{i,j-1}-1)}) = \sigma_\epsilon^2(1 - \rho^{2(t_{i,j}-t_{i,j-1})})/(1-\rho^2)$ for $j = 2,\ldots,n_i$. Note that for the no missing observations case with $t_{i,j} - t_{i,j-1} = 1$ for all $j = 1,2,\ldots,n_i$, $\text{var}(S_{i,t_{i,j}}) = \sigma_\epsilon^2$ for all j. In general, the vector of disturbances S_i can be easily made homoskedastic by premultiplying S_i by a diagonal matrix

$$D_i(\rho) = \begin{bmatrix} 1 & 0 & 0 & \ldots & 0 & 0 \\ 0 & \left(\dfrac{1-\rho^2}{1-\rho^{2(t_{i,2}-t_{i,1})}}\right)^{1/2} & 0 & \ldots & 0 & 0 \\ \vdots & \vdots & \vdots & & \vdots & \vdots \\ \vdots & \vdots & \vdots & & \vdots & \vdots \\ 0 & 0 & 0 & \ldots & 0 & \left(\dfrac{1-\rho^2}{1-\rho^{2(t_{i,n_i}-t_{i,n_i-1})}}\right)^{1/2} \end{bmatrix}. \quad (4)$$

Hence, if we let $C_i^*(\rho) = D_i(\rho)C_i(\rho)$, and define $\nu_i^* = C_i^*(\rho)\nu_i$ then $\nu_i^* \sim (0,\sigma_\epsilon^2 I_{n_i})$. Note that for equally spaced data with no missing observations, the diagonal matrix $D_i(\rho)$ reverts back to the identity matrix as expected. The $n_i \times n_i$ matrix $C_i^*(\rho) = D_i(\rho)C_i(\rho)$ is given by[1]

$$C_i^*(\rho) = (1-\rho^2)^{1/2} \begin{bmatrix} 1 & 0 & \ldots & 0 & 0 \\ -\left(\dfrac{\rho^{2(t_{i,2}-t_{i,1})}}{1-\rho^{2(t_{i,2}-t_{i,1})}}\right)^{1/2} & \left(\dfrac{1}{1-\rho^{2(t_{i,2}-t_{i,1})}}\right)^{1/2} & \ldots & \vdots & \vdots \\ \vdots & \vdots & \ldots & \vdots & \vdots \\ \vdots & \vdots & \ldots & \vdots & \vdots \\ 0 & 0 & \ldots & -\left(\dfrac{\rho^{2(t_{i,n_i}-t_{i,n_i-1})}}{1-\rho^{2(t_{i,n_i}-t_{i,n_i-1})}}\right)^{1/2} & \left(\dfrac{1}{1-\rho^{2(t_{i,n_i}-t_{i,n_i-1})}}\right)^{1/2} \end{bmatrix}. \quad (5)$$

Premultiply the panel data regression given in equation (1) by $\text{diag}[C_i^*(\rho)]$, which is a block-diagonal matrix with $C_i^*(\rho)$ in the ith block. This transforms the disturbances as follows:

$$u^* = \text{diag}[C_i^*(\rho)]u = \text{diag}[C_i^*(\rho)]\,\text{diag}(\iota_{n_i})\mu + \text{diag}[C_i^*(\rho)]\nu, \quad (6)$$

where ι_{n_i} is a vector of ones of dimension n_i, $u' = (u_1',\ldots,u_N')$, $\mu' = (\mu_1,\ldots,\mu_N)$, and $\nu' = (\nu_1',\ldots,\nu_N')$. Note that ν_i' was defined following (2) and u_i' is similarly defined. It can be easily verified that

$$g_i = [C_i^*(\rho)]\iota_{n_i} = (1-\rho^2)^{1/2}\left(1, \frac{1-\rho^{(t_{i,2}-t_{i,1})}}{(1-\rho^{2(t_{i,2}-t_{i,1})})^{1/2}}, \ldots, \frac{1-\rho^{(t_{i,n_i}-t_{i,n_i-1})}}{(1-\rho^{2(t_{i,n_i}-t_{i,n_i-1})})^{1/2}}\right)'. \quad (7)$$

Therefore, $u^* = \mathrm{diag}(g_i)\mu + \mathrm{diag}[C_i^*(\rho)]\nu$, and $\Omega^* = E(u^*u^{*\prime}) = \sigma_\mu^2\,\mathrm{diag}(g_ig_i') + \sigma_\epsilon^2\,\mathrm{diag}(I_{n_i})$, because $\mathrm{diag}[C_i^*(\rho)]E(\nu\nu')\mathrm{diag}[C_i^*(\rho)]' = \sigma_\epsilon^2\,\mathrm{diag}(I_{n_i})$. This can be rewritten as

$$\Omega^* = \sigma_\mu^2\,\mathrm{diag}(g_i'g_i)\mathrm{diag}(P_{g_i}) + \sigma_\epsilon^2\,\mathrm{diag}(P_{g_i} + Q_{g_i}),$$

where $P_{g_i} = g_i(g_i'g_i)^{-1}g_i'$, $Q_{g_i} = I_{n_i} - P_{g_i}$, $g_i'g_i = \sum_{j=1}^{n_i} g_{i,j}^2 = (1-\rho^2) + (1-\rho^2) \times \sum_{j=2}^{n_i}(1-\rho^{(t_{i,j}-t_{i,j-1})})^2/(1-\rho^{2(t_{i,j}-t_{i,j-1})})$, and $g_{i,j}$ is the jth element of $g_i = [C_i^*(\rho)]\iota_{n_i}$ given in (7) for $j = 1,2,\ldots,n_i$. This replaces I_{n_i} by $(Q_{g_i} + P_{g_i})$ (see Wansbeek and Kapteyn, 1982). Collecting terms with the same matrices, one obtains

$$\Omega^* = \mathrm{diag}(\omega_i^2)\mathrm{diag}(P_{g_i}) + \sigma_\epsilon^2\,\mathrm{diag}(Q_{g_i}), \quad (8)$$

where $\omega_i^2 = g_i'g_i\sigma_\mu^2 + \sigma_\epsilon^2$. Note that P_{g_i} and Q_{g_i} are idempotent, are orthogonal to each other, and sum to the identity matrix. Therefore,

$$\sigma_\epsilon\Omega^{*-1/2} = \sigma_\epsilon\,\mathrm{diag}(1/\omega_i)\mathrm{diag}(P_{g_i}) + \mathrm{diag}(Q_{g_i}) = \mathrm{diag}(I_{n_i}) - \mathrm{diag}(\theta_i P_{g_i}), \quad (9)$$

where $\theta_i = 1 - (\sigma_\epsilon/\omega_i)$. For equally spaced panel data with no missing observations and no serial correlation, i.e., $\rho = 0$, this reduces to the familiar Fuller and Battese (1974) transformation. Premultiplying $y^* = \mathrm{diag}[C_i^*(\rho)]y$ by $\sigma_\epsilon\Omega^{*-1/2}$ one gets $y^{**} = \sigma_\epsilon\Omega^{*-1/2}y^*$. The typical elements of y^{**} are given by

$$y_{i,t_{i,j}}^{**} = y_{i,t_{i,j}}^* - \theta_i g_{i,j}\left(\sum_{s=1}^{n_i} g_{i,s}y_{i,t_{i,s}}^*\right)\Big/\left(\sum_{s=1}^{n_i} g_{i,s}^2\right). \quad (10)$$

Quadratic unbiased estimators of the variance components arise naturally from (8) (for the balanced panel data case, see Baltagi and Li, 1991). In fact, $\mathrm{diag}(P_{g_i})u^* \sim (0, \mathrm{diag}(\omega_i^2 P_{g_i}))$ and $\mathrm{diag}(Q_{g_i})u^* \sim (0, \sigma_\epsilon^2\,\mathrm{diag}(Q_{g_i}))$. Therefore, quadratic unbiased estimators of $\sigma_\omega^2 = \sum_{i=1}^N \omega_i^2$ and σ_ϵ^2 are given by

$$\hat\sigma_\omega^2 = u^{*\prime}\,\mathrm{diag}(P_{g_i})u^* \quad \text{and} \quad \hat\sigma_\epsilon^2 = u^{*\prime}\,\mathrm{diag}(Q_{g_i})u^*\Big/\sum_{i=1}^N (n_i - 1), \quad (11)$$

where $\mathrm{tr}(P_{g_i}) = 1$ and $\mathrm{tr}(Q_{g_i}) = n_i - 1$. Using $\sum_{i=1}^N \omega_i^2 = \sum_{i=1}^N g_i'g_i\sigma_\mu^2 + N\sigma_\epsilon^2$, an estimator for σ_μ^2 can be obtained as follows:

$$\hat\sigma_\mu^2 = (u^{*\prime}\,\mathrm{diag}(P_{g_i})u^* - N\hat\sigma_\epsilon^2)\Big/\sum_{i=1}^N g_i'g_i. \quad (12)$$

Using a consistent estimate of ρ, one can estimate this model by feasible GLS using the following steps.

Step 1. Perform the diag$[C_i^*(\rho)]$ transformation given in (5) on equation (1) to get rid of serial correlation and ensure homoskedasticity. This yields $y_i^* = [C_i^*(\rho)]y_i$, where $y_i' = (y_{it_{i,1}}, \ldots, y_{it_{i,n_i}})$.

Step 2. Compute the residuals $\hat{u}^*$ obtained from the ordinary least squares (OLS) regression of y^* on X^* in step 1. Using these $\hat{u}^*$'s, compute estimates of σ_μ^2 and σ_ϵ^2 from (11) and (12). Deduce $\hat{\theta}_i = 1 - (\hat{\sigma}_\epsilon/\hat{\omega}_i)$, where $\hat{\omega}_i^2 = g_i' g_i \hat{\sigma}_\mu^2 + \hat{\sigma}_\epsilon^2$.

Step 3. Obtain y^{**} as described in (10) using the y^*'s in step 1 and $\hat{\theta}_i$ from step 2. Perform OLS of y^{**} on X^{**} to obtain the feasible GLS estimate of β. In the next section, we consider the problem of testing for zero first-order serial correlation and in the process provide a natural estimator for ρ.

3. LOCALLY BEST INVARIANT (LBI) TEST

In this section, we derive a locally best invariant (LBI) test for H_0; $\rho = 0$ versus H_a^+; $\rho > 0$ or H_a^-; $\rho < 0$, for the unequally spaced panel data regression model described in Section 2. We assume normality of the disturbances and rewrite (1) in matrix form as

$$y = X\beta + \text{diag}(\iota_{n_i})\mu + \nu, \tag{13}$$

where ι_{n_i}, μ, and ν have been defined following (6). Also $\Sigma_\nu(\rho) = E(\nu\nu') = \sigma_\epsilon^2 \text{diag}(V_i) = \sigma_\epsilon^2 \Omega_\nu(\rho)$, where $\sigma_\epsilon^2 V_i$ has a typical element given preceding (2). Consider the orthogonal matrix O_{n_i} of dimension n_i and let $O_{n_i} = (\iota_{n_i}/\sqrt{n_i}, B_i)$, where B_i is an $n_i \times (n_i - 1)$ matrix that by definition satisfies the following properties: $B_i'\iota_{n_i} = 0$, $B_i'B_i = I_{n_i-1}$, and $B_iB_i' = I_{n_i} - \bar{J}_{n_i}$, where $\bar{J}_{n_i} = J_{n_i}/n_i$ and J_{n_i} is a matrix of ones of dimension n_i. Premultiplying the preceding model by diag(B_i') yields diag$(B_i')y = $ diag$(B_i')X\beta + $ diag$(B_i')\nu$. Note that μ is swept away because $B_i'\iota_{n_i} = 0$. If we let $\tilde{y} = $ diag$(B_i')y$, $\tilde{X} = $ diag$(B_i')X$, and $\tilde{\nu} = $ diag$(B_i')\nu$, then this transformed model can be rewritten as

$$\tilde{y} = \tilde{X}\beta + \tilde{\nu}, \tag{14}$$

where $\Sigma_{\tilde{\nu}}(\rho) = E(\tilde{\nu}\tilde{\nu}') = \sigma_\epsilon^2 \text{diag}(B_i' V_i B_i) = \sigma_\epsilon^2 \Omega_{\tilde{\nu}}(\rho)$. Under H_0; $\rho = 0$, we have $V_i = I_{n_i}$, and $\Sigma_{\tilde{\nu}}(\rho)$ reduces to σ_ϵ^2 diag(I_{n_i-1}). This means that under H_0, $\tilde{\nu} \sim N(0, \sigma_\epsilon^2 I_{\Sigma n_i - N})$.

This testing problem is invariant to transformations of the form $y \to \gamma_0 y + X\gamma$, where γ_0 is a positive scalar and γ is $K \times 1$. This means that if we change the scale of y and add a known linear combination of the regressors to the rescaled y, this does not change the truth of either H_0 or H_a. This is the transformation used by Durbin and Watson (1971) to establish optimal properties of the Durbin–Watson test (see Dufour and King, 1991). Let $m = \sum_{i=1}^N (n_i - 1) - K$, $\bar{P}_{\tilde{X}} = I_{\Sigma(n_i-1)} - P_{\tilde{X}}$, where $P_{\tilde{X}} = \tilde{X}(\tilde{X}'\tilde{X})^{-1}\tilde{X}'$, and $z = \bar{P}_{\tilde{X}}\tilde{y}$ be the OLS residuals from $\tilde{y}$ on $\tilde{X}$. Let R be the $m \times \Sigma(n_i - 1)$ matrix such that $RR' = I_m$ and $R'R = \bar{P}_{\tilde{X}}$. Note that the $m \times 1$ vector Rz is a linear unbiased residual vector with a scalar covariance matrix (see Theil, 1971, Ch. 5) with zero mean and variance-covariance matrix $\sigma_\epsilon^2 I_m$ under H_0. As noted by King and Hillier (1985), the vector $s = Rz/(z'R'Rz)^{1/2}$ is a maximal invariant under the preceding group of transformations for our testing problem. Also, the LBI test, which is also known as the locally most powerful invariant test, is of the form $d = z'A_0z/z'z < c_\alpha$, where $A_0 = \{\partial\Omega_{\bar{\nu}}^{-1}(\rho)/\partial\rho\}|_{\rho=0} = -(\partial\Omega_{\bar{\nu}}(\rho)/\partial\rho)|_{\rho=0}$ and c_α is the α-level critical value of d. This test has the steepest sloping power curve at H_0; $\rho = 0$ within the class of invariant tests of the same significance level. It can also be viewed as the test that has optimal power within the neighborhood of H_0. King and Hillier (1985) also demonstrated the equivalence of this test to a one-sided version of the Lagrange multiplier test. Note that the denominator of the test statistic d is easy to compute. In fact, $z'z = \bar{y}'\bar{P}_{\bar{X}}\bar{y} = \bar{y}'\bar{y} - \bar{y}'P_{\bar{X}}\bar{y} = y'Qy - y'QX(X'QX)^{-1}X'Qy$, where $Q = \mathrm{diag}(I_{n_i} - \bar{J}_{n_i})$. This is the within residuals sum of squares obtained from the fixed effects model, i.e., assuming the μ_i's are fixed parameters to be estimated. It can be obtained from the OLS residuals sum of squares of (13) or in case N is large from the regression of $(y_{i,t_{i,j}} - \bar{y}_{i.})$ on $(X_{i,t_{i,j},k} - \bar{X}_{i.,k})$ for $k = 2, \ldots, K$. In this case, $\bar{y}_{i.} = \sum_{j=1}^{n_i} y_{i,t_{i,j}}/n_i$ and $\bar{X}_{i.,k}$ is defined similarly.

For the numerator of d, we note that $\partial V_i/\partial\rho|_{\rho=0} = V_i^0$, where the typical elements of V_i^0 are

$$V_i^0(j,\ell) = \begin{cases} 1 & \text{if } |t_{i,j} - t_{i,\ell}| = 1 \\ 0 & \text{if } |t_{i,j} - t_{i,\ell}| > 1 \end{cases} \quad \text{or} \quad \text{if } j = \ell \quad \text{for } j,\ell = 1,\ldots,n_i, \tag{15}$$

so that $z'A_0z = -z'\,\mathrm{diag}(B_i'V_i^0B_i)z$. Let $\tilde{z} = \mathrm{diag}(B_i)z$; then $z'A_0z = \tilde{z}'\,\mathrm{diag}(V_i^0)\tilde{z}$. It can be easily shown that OLS on (14) yields $\tilde{\beta} = (X'QX)^{-1}X'Qy$, the within estimator of β, and $z = \bar{y} - \bar{X}\tilde{\beta} = \mathrm{diag}(B_i')(y - X\tilde{\beta})$. This means that $\tilde{z} = \mathrm{diag}(B_iB_i')(y - X\tilde{\beta}) = Qy - QX\tilde{\beta}$, which is exactly the within residuals described previously using the deviation from individual means regression. This also proves that $z'z = \tilde{z}'\tilde{z}$. Therefore, the LBI test statistic can be written as

$$d^* = d + 2 = \tilde{z}'\,\mathrm{diag}(2I_{n_i} - V_i^0)\tilde{z}/\tilde{z}'\tilde{z}, \tag{16}$$

and our test statistic can be expressed as the sum of four terms:

$$d_1 = \sum_{i=1}^{N}\sum_{j=1}^{n_i}[\tilde{z}_{i,t_{i,j}} - \tilde{z}_{i,t_{i,j-1}}I(t_{i,j} - t_{i,j-1} = 1)]^2 \Big/ \sum_{i=1}^{N}\sum_{j=1}^{n_i}\tilde{z}_{i,t_{i,j}}^2,$$

$$d_2 = \sum_{i=1}^{N}\sum_{j=1}^{n_i-1}\tilde{z}_{i,t_{i,j}}^2[1 - I(t_{i,j+1} - t_{i,j} = 1)] \Big/ \sum_{i=1}^{N}\sum_{j=1}^{n_i}\tilde{z}_{i,t_{i,j}}^2,$$

$$d_3 = \sum_{i=1}^{N}\tilde{z}_{i,t_{i,1}}^2 \Big/ \sum_{i=1}^{N}\sum_{j=1}^{n_i}\tilde{z}_{i,t_{i,j}}^2 \quad \text{and} \quad d_4 = \sum_{i=1}^{N}\tilde{z}_{i,t_{i,n_i}}^2 \Big/ \sum_{i=1}^{N}\sum_{j=1}^{n_i}\tilde{z}_{i,t_{i,j}}^2,$$

where $I(t_{i,j} - t_{i,j-1} = 1)$ is the indicator function that takes the value 1 when the proposition in parentheses is true and zero elsewhere. In the time-series context, d^* reduces to the LBI test suggested by Dufour and Dagenais (1985). Some comments are in order: (i) When there are no missing observations, i.e., $t_{i,n_i} - t_{i,n_i-1} = t_{i,n_i-1} - t_{i,n_i-2} = \cdots = t_{i,2} - t_{i,1} = 1$, then $d_2 = 0$ and our test statistic reduces to $d_1 + d_3 + d_4$. Note that in this case, d_1 reduces to the Durbin–Watson test statistic proposed by Bhargava et al. (1982, p. 535) for the fixed effect AR(1) model. Bhargava et al. claimed that d_1 is a locally most powerful invariant test in the neighborhood of $\rho = 0$. They argued that exact critical values for d_1 are both impractical and unnecessary because they involve the computation of nonzero eigenvalues of a large $NT \times NT$ matrix. Instead, the 5% upper and lower bounds for d_1 were tabulated for various values of N, T, and K. Note that the Bhargava et al. test statistic ignores d_3 and d_4 and is therefore approximately locally best invariant. This is the same criticism for the Durbin–Watson statistic in the time-series context pointed out by King (1981). Whereas terms such as d_3 and d_4 are negligible when T is very large, they are less likely to be so in typical panels where T is usually small. (ii) In practice, one can insert zeros in between $\tilde{z}_{i,t_{i,j}}$ and $\tilde{z}_{i,t_{i,j+1}}$ if $t_{i,j+1} - t_{i,j} > 1$. Then one gets a new residuals series that may look like $e_i' = (\tilde{z}_{i,t_{i,1}}, 0, 0, \tilde{z}_{i,t_{i,2}}, 0, \ldots, \tilde{z}_{i,t_{i,j}}, \ldots, \tilde{z}_{i,t_{i,n_i}})$ if $t_{i,1} = 1$, $t_{i,2} = 4, \ldots$, and $t_{i,n_i} = T$ (see Dufour and Dagenais, 1985, p. 375; Shively, 1993, p. 248). The term e_i is a $T \times 1$ vector of within residuals for the ith individual whose element is zero if the data for that period are not available. Now it is easy to compute the test statistic in the usual way, $d_c = \sum_{i=1}^{N}\sum_{t=2}^{T}(e_{i,t} - e_{i,t-1})^2/\sum_{i=1}^{N}\sum_{t=1}^{T}e_{i,t}^2$. This also suggests a natural estimator of ρ, i.e., $\hat{\rho} = (\sum_{i=1}^{N}\sum_{t=2}^{T} e_{i,t}e_{i,t-1}/m_c)/(\sum_{i=1}^{N}\sum_{t=1}^{T} e_{i,t}^2/n)$, where m_c is the number of consecutive pairs of nonzero e_{it}'s. (iii) Note that our test statistic d^* in (16) can be rewritten as $d^* = 2 - \tilde{z}'\,\mathrm{diag}(V_i^0)\tilde{z}/\tilde{z}'\tilde{z} = 2 - z'\,\mathrm{diag}(B_i'V_i^0B_i)z/z'z$ where $z = \bar{P}_{\tilde{X}}\tilde{y} = \bar{P}_{\tilde{X}}\tilde{\nu}$ from (14) with $\tilde{\nu} \sim N(0, \sigma_\epsilon^2 I_{\Sigma(n_i-1)})$ under H_0; $\rho = 0$. Substituting this in the test statistic, we get $d^* = 2 - (\tilde{\nu}'\bar{P}_{\tilde{X}}A\bar{P}_{\tilde{X}}\tilde{\nu}/\tilde{\nu}'\bar{P}_{\tilde{X}}\tilde{\nu})$, where $A = \mathrm{diag}(B_i'V_i^0B_i)$. This statistic is in the form of a ratio of quadratic forms of normal variates ($\tilde{\nu}$). For a given A, bounds for critical values can be constructed just like the Bhargava et al. or Durbin–Watson test statistics. However, different patterns of missing observations imply a different V_i^0 matrix and therefore a different A matrix.[2] A reasonable and practical way to approximate these critical values is to standardize this test statistic. Using the results in Evans and King (1985), we compute $E(d^*) = 2 - \mathrm{tr}(\bar{P}_{\tilde{X}}A)/m$ and $\mathrm{var}(d^*) = 2[m\,\mathrm{tr}(\bar{P}_{\tilde{X}}A)^2 - \{\mathrm{tr}(\bar{P}_{\tilde{X}}A)\}^2]/m^2(m+2)$, where $m = \sum_{i=1}^{N}(n_i - 1) - K$, and then use the test statistic

$$d_s^* = [d^* - E(d^*)]\big/\sqrt{\mathrm{var}(d^*)}. \qquad \textbf{(17)}$$

For testing H_0; $\rho = 0$ versus H_a; $\rho > 0$ (or $\rho < 0$), one compares d^* to the critical value from the lower (upper) tail of an $N(0,1)$ distribution. Although B_i appears in the preceding standardized test statistic, this matrix is not needed for the actual computations. In fact,

$$\begin{aligned}\mathrm{tr}(\bar{P}_{\tilde{X}}A) &= \mathrm{tr}[\bar{P}_{\tilde{X}}\,\mathrm{diag}(B_i')\mathrm{diag}(V_i^0)\mathrm{diag}(B_i)] \\ &= \mathrm{tr}\{[Q - QX(X'QX)^{-1}X'Q]\mathrm{diag}(V_i^0)\}.\end{aligned}$$

A weakness of the preceding LBI test is that for unequally spaced observations that are two or more periods apart, the LBI test statistic in (16) degenerates to 2 because $\partial V_i'/\partial\rho$ evaluated at the maximum likelihood estimator (MLE) under H_0 is equal to zero. Even in situations that are not as extreme as this, if a big portion of the sample has observations that are two or more periods apart, then the LBI test will still be ineffective because it ignores these observations in the computations. Clearly, this difficulty can be removed if we do not evaluate $\partial V_i/\partial\rho$ at the null hypothesis in the test construction. A test that is particularly suitable for this situation is the POI test suggested by King (1985). In fact, King's point optimal invariant test for the AR(1) case has been generalized to the missing data case in time-series regressions by Shively (1993). This POI test can be easily generalized for the unequally spaced panel data model and is available upon request from the authors. Also, our proposed estimator of ρ breaks down if there are no consecutive observations. In this case, one may want to use maximum likelihood methods that do not throw away nonconsecutive observations (for MLE in the serially correlated time-series model with missing observations, see Wansbeek and Kapteyn, 1985).

4. EMPIRICAL ILLUSTRATION

Table 1 applies the LBI test statistic given by d^* in (16) and the Bhargava et al. modified Durbin–Watson test statistic given by d_1 following (16) to the Grunfeld data on investment. This is the same data set used for time-series illustration by Wansbeek and Kapteyn (1985). It consists of 10 large U.S. manufacturing firms observed from 1935 to 1954. Real gross investment of firm i in year t (I_{it}) is regressed on the real value of the firm (F_{it}) and the real value of the capital stock (C_{it}):

$$I_{it} = \alpha + \beta_1 F_{it} + \beta_2 C_{it} + u_{it}. \tag{18}$$

The assumption of normality of the disturbances and nonstochastic regressors may be untenable for this empirical example, but we use these data for illustrative purposes. The null hypothesis is H_0; $\rho = 0$ versus H_a^+; $\rho > 0$, and various patterns of missing observations are considered. As clear from the table, the LBI statistic is greater than the Bhargava et al. statistic for all patterns considered. The difference between the LBI and BFN test statistics highlights the contributions of d_2, d_3, and d_4 defined following (16) to the LBI statistic. This difference is substantial depending on the pattern of missing observations. Table 1 also gives the standardized LBI statistic given by d_s^* defined in (17). The null hypothesis of no serial correlation is rejected in all cases.

5. SUMMARY AND CONCLUSION

This paper derives a simple method of correcting for serial correlation and random individual effects in the context of unequally spaced panel data models. It

TABLE 1. Testing for Zero Serial Correlation in Unequally Spaced Panels: Grunfeld Data[a]

Pattern	Missing periods								LBI	Bhargava et al.	d_s^*	n
A	9	10							1.022	0.706	−7.870	180
B	17	18							1.139	0.807	−6.994	180
C	3	4	5						1.162	0.738	−6.751	170
D	7	8	9						1.013	0.701	−7.796	170
E	13	14	15						0.982	0.674	−7.986	170
F	3	4	5	6					1.188	0.733	−6.455	160
G	12	13	14	15					0.920	0.612	−8.254	160
H	2	4	5	14					1.237	0.694	−6.493	160
I	8	9	16	17	19				1.499	0.968	−4.447	150
J	2	3	15	16	17	19			1.580	0.911	−3.842	140
K	2	3	15	18	19	20			1.174	0.813	−6.471	140
L	2	3	5	7	15	20			1.330	0.689	−5.899	140
M	3	5	8	9	16	17	19		1.807	1.031	−2.290	130
N	2	4	5	14	15	16	19		1.641	0.901	−3.459	130
O	2	3	4	8	9	16	17	19	1.709	1.005	−2.998	120
P	2	3	5	7	15	18	19	20	1.589	0.866	−3.881	120
Q	2	4	5	8	14	15	16	19	1.656	0.873	−3.430	120

[a]This tests H_0; $\rho = 0$ versus H_a; $\rho > 0$. The LBI statistic is given in (16). The Bhargava et al. statistic is given by d_1 following (16). The term d_s^* is given in (17). Here n denotes the total number of observations in the panel.

also provides an LBI test for zero first-order serial correlation against positive or negative serial correlation. Although exact critical values can be computationally prohibitive with panel data, advances in computing exact critical values following Shively et al. (1990) can be used. Alternatively, one can approximate these critical values by standardizing the LBI statistic using the results of Evans and King (1985) on quadratic normals. Finally, the LBI test statistic is illustrated for various missing observations panels using the Grunfeld investment data. Future work should generalize the results to allow for stochastic regressors.

NOTES

1. An alternative derivation of this matrix in a time-series context is given by Wansbeek and Kapteyn (1985).

2. To take advantage of the power optimality of the LBI test (d^*), one should compute the exact critical values. Unfortunately, this needs the nonzero eigenvalues of $AP_{\bar{X}}$, which is a large $\Sigma(n_i - 1) \times \Sigma(n_i - 1)$ matrix. This requires $O([\Sigma(n_i - 1)]^3)$ operations. Here, advances in computing exact critical values by Shively, Ansley, and Kohn (1990) can be used. Alternatively, one can easily compute bounds for the exact critical values as described in the Appendix that is available upon request from the authors.

REFERENCES

Baltagi, B.H. & Y.J. Chang (1994) Incomplete panels: A comparative study of alternative estimators for the unbalanced one-way error component regression model. *Journal of Econometrics* 62, 67–89.

Baltagi, B.H. & Q. Li (1991) A transformation that will circumvent the problem of autocorrelation in an error component model. *Journal of Econometrics* 48, 385–393.

Bhargava, A., L. Franzini, & W. Narendranathan (1982) Serial correlation and the fixed effects model. *Review of Economic Studies* 49, 533–549.

Dufour, J.M. & M.G. Dagenais (1985) Durbin-Watson tests for serial correlation in regressions with missing observations. *Journal of Econometrics* 27, 371–381.

Dufour, J.M. & M. King (1991) Optimal invariant tests for the autocorrelation coefficient in linear regressions with stationary and nonstationary AR(1) errors. *Journal of Econometrics* 47, 115–143.

Durbin, J. & G.S. Watson (1971) Testing for serial correlation in least squares regression III. *Biometrika* 58, 1–19.

Evans, M.A. & M.L. King (1985) Critical value approximations for tests of linear regression disturbances. *Australian Journal of Statistics* 27, 68–83.

Fuller, W.A. & G.E. Battese (1974) Estimation of linear models with cross-error structure. *Journal of Econometrics* 2, 67–78.

King, M.L. (1981) The alternative Durbin-Watson test: An assessment of Durbin and Watson's choice of test statistic. *Journal of Econometrics* 17, 51–66.

King, M.L. (1985) A point optimal test for autoregressive disturbances. *Journal of Econometrics* 27, 21–37.

King, M.L. & G.H. Hillier (1985) Locally best invariant tests of the error covariance matrix of the linear regression model. *Journal of the Royal Statistical Society, Series B* 47, 98–102.

Lillard, L.A. & R.J. Willis (1978) Dynamic aspects of earning mobility. *Econometrica* 46, 985–1012.

Robinson, P.M. (1985) Testing for serial correlation in regression with missing observations. *Journal of the Royal Statistical Society, Series B* 47, 429–437.

Savin, N.E. & K.J. White (1978) Testing for autocorrelation with missing observations. *Econometrica* 46, 59–67.

Shively, T.S. (1993) Testing for autoregressive disturbances in a time series regression with missing observations. *Journal of Econometrics* 57, 233–255.

Shively, T.S., C.F. Ansley, & R. Kohn (1990) Fast evaluation of the distribution of the Durbin-Watson and other invariant test statistics in time series regression. *Journal of the American Statistical Association* 85, 676–685.

Theil, H. (1971) *Principles of Econometrics*. New York: Wiley.

Wansbeek, T. & A. Kapteyn (1982) A simple way to obtain the spectral decomposition of variance components models for balanced data. *Communications in Statistics A* 11, 2105–2112.

Wansbeek, T. & A. Kapteyn (1985) Estimation in a linear model with serially correlated errors when observations are missing. *International Economic Review* 26, 469–490.

Wansbeek, T. & A. Kapteyn (1989) Estimation of the error components model with incomplete panels. *Journal of Econometrics* 41, 341–361.

[13]

ELSEVIER

Journal of Econometrics 101 (2001) 357–381

JOURNAL OF
Econometrics

www.elsevier.nl/locate/econbase

The unbalanced nested error component regression model

Badi H. Baltagi[a,*], Seuck Heun Song[b], Byoung Cheol Jung[b]

[a]*Department of Economics, Texas A&M University, College Station, TX 77843-4228, USA*
[b]*Department of Statistics, Korea University, Sungbuk-Ku, Seoul 136-701, South Korea*

Received 1 December 1998; received in revised form 31 August 2000; accepted 2 October 2000

Abstract

This paper considers a nested error component model with unbalanced data and proposes simple analysis of variance (ANOVA), maximum likelihood (MLE) and minimum norm quadratic unbiased estimators (MINQUE)-type estimators of the variance components. These are natural extensions from the biometrics, statistics and econometrics literature. The performance of these estimators is investigated by means of Monte Carlo experiments. While the MLE and MINQUE methods perform the best in estimating the variance components and the standard errors of the regression coefficients, the simple ANOVA methods perform just as well in estimating the regression coefficients. These estimation methods are also used to investigate the productivity of public capital in private production. © 2001 Published by Elsevier Science S.A.

JEL: C23

Keywords: Panel data; Nested error component; Unbalanced ANOVA; MINQUE; MLE; Variance components

1. Introduction

The analysis of panel data in econometrics have relied on the error component regression model which has its origin in the statistics and biometrics

* Corresponding author. Tel.: + 1-979-845-7380; fax: + 1-979-847-8757.
E-mail address: badi@econ.tamu.edu (B.H. Baltagi).

0304-4076/01/$ - see front matter © 2001 Published by Elsevier Science S.A.
PII: S0304-4076(00)00089-0

literature, see Hsiao (1986), Baltagi (1995) and Mátyás and Sevestre (1996). A huge bulk of this econometrics literature focuses on the complete or balanced panels, yet the empirical applications face missing observations or incomplete panels. Exceptions are Baltagi (1985), Wansbeek and Kapteyn (1989) and Baltagi and Chang (1994). This paper considers the incomplete panel data regression model in which the economic data has a natural nested groupings. For example, data on firms may be grouped by industry, data on states by region and data on individuals by profession. In this case, one can control for unobserved industry and within industry firm effects using a nested error component model. See Montmarquette and Mahseredjian (1989) for an empirical application of the nested error component model to study whether schooling matters in educational achievements in Montreal's Francophone public elementary schools. More recently, see Antweiler (1999) for an application of the determinants of pollution concentration as measured by observation stations in various countries over time.

This paper proposes natural extensions of the analysis of variance (ANOVA), maximum likelihood (MLE) and minimum norm quadratic unbiased estimators (MINQUE) and compares their performance by means of Monte Carlo experiments. Statisticians and biometricians are more interested in the estimates of the variance components per se, see Harville (1969, 1977), Hocking (1985), LaMotte (1973a, b), Rao (1971a, b), Searle (1971, 1987) and Swallow and Monahan (1984) to mention a few. Econometricians, on the other hand, are more interested in the regression coefficients, see Hsiao (1986) and Baltagi (1995). Monte Carlo results on the balanced error component regression model include Nerlove (1971), Maddala and Mount (1973) and Baltagi (1981). For the unbalanced error component regression model, see Wansbeek and Kapteyn (1989) and Baltagi and Chang (1994). None of these studies deal with the nested and unbalanced error component model. The only exception is Fuller and Battese (1973). This paper generalizes several estimators in the literature to the nested unbalanced setting and reports the results of Monte Carlo experiments comparing the performance of these proposed estimators. The type of unbalancedness considered in this paper allows for unequal number of firms in each industry as well as different number of time periods across industries. Section 2 describes the model and the estimation methods to be compared. Section 3 gives the design of the Monte Carlo experiment and summarizes the results, while Section 4 gives an empirical illustration applying these estimation methods to the study of productivity of public capital in private production. Section 5 gives our conclusion.

2. The model

We consider the following unbalanced panel data regression model:

$$y_{ijt} = x'_{ijt}\beta + u_{ijt}, \quad i = 1,\ldots,M, \quad j = 1,\ldots,N_i \text{ and } t = 1,\ldots,T_i, \tag{1}$$

where y_{ijt} could denote the output of the jth firm in the ith industry for the tth time period. x_{ijt} denotes a vector of k nonstochastic inputs. The disturbance of (1) is given by

$$u_{ijt} = \mu_i + \nu_{ij} + \varepsilon_{ijt}, \quad i = 1, \ldots, M, \quad j = 1, \ldots, N_i \text{ and } t = 1, \ldots, T_i, \tag{2}$$

where μ_i denotes the ith unobservable industry specific effect which is assumed to be i.i.d. $(0, \sigma_\mu^2)$,ν_{ij} denotes the nested effect of the jth firm within the ith industry which is assumed to be i.i.d. $(0, \sigma_\nu^2)$ and ε_{ijt} denotes the remainder disturbance which is also assumed to be i.i.d. $(0, \sigma_\varepsilon^2)$. The μ_i's, ν_{ij}'s and ε_{ijt}'s are independent of each other and among themselves. This is a nested classification in that each successive component of the error term is imbedded or 'nested' within the preceding component, see Graybill (1961, p. 350). This model allows for unequal number of firms in each industry as well as different number of observed time periods across industries. Model (1) can be rewritten in matrix notation as

$$y = X\beta + u, \tag{3}$$

where y is a $\sum_{i=1}^{M} N_i T_i \times 1$, X is a $\sum_{i=1}^{M} N_i T_i \times k$, β is a $k \times 1$ parameter vector, and u is a $\sum_{i=1}^{M} N_i T_i \times 1$ disturbance vector. Eq. (2) in vector form yields

$$u = Z_\mu \mu + Z_\nu \nu + \varepsilon, \tag{4}$$

where $\mu' = (\mu_1, \ldots, \mu_M)$, $\nu' = (\nu_{11}, \ldots, \nu_{1N_1}, \ldots, \nu_{MN_M})$, $\varepsilon' = (\varepsilon_{111}, \ldots, \varepsilon_{11T_1}, \ldots, \varepsilon_{MN_MT_M})$, $Z_\mu = diag(\iota_{N_i} \otimes \iota_{T_i})$, $Z_\nu = diag(I_{N_i} \otimes \iota_{T_i})$, ι_{N_i} and ι_{T_i} are vectors of ones of dimension N_i and T_i, respectively. By $diag(\iota_{N_i} \otimes \iota_{T_i})$ we mean $diag(\iota_{N_1} \otimes \iota_{T_1}, \ldots, \iota_{N_M} \otimes \iota_{T_M})$. I_{N_i} is an identity matrix of dimension N_i, and $\otimes$ denotes the Kronecker product. Note that the observations are stacked such that the slowest running index is the industry index i, the next slowest running index is the firm index j and the fastest running index is time.

Under these assumptions, the disturbance covariance matrix $E(uu')$ can be written as

$$\begin{aligned} \Omega &= \sigma_\mu^2 Z_\mu Z_\mu' + \sigma_\nu^2 Z_\nu Z_\nu' + \sigma_\varepsilon^2\, diag(I_{N_i} \otimes I_{T_i}) \\ &= diag[\sigma_\mu^2 (J_{N_i} \otimes J_{T_i}) + \sigma_\nu^2 (I_{N_i} \otimes J_{T_i}) + \sigma_\varepsilon^2 (I_{N_i} \otimes I_{T_i})], \end{aligned} \tag{5}$$

where $J_{N_i} = \iota_{N_i} \iota_{N_i}'$ and $J_{T_i} = \iota_{T_i} \iota_{T_i}'$ are matrices of ones of dimension N_i and T_i. It is clear from Eq. (5) that Ω is a block diagonal matrix with the ith block given by

$$\Lambda_i = \sigma_\mu^2 (J_{N_i} \otimes J_{T_i}) + \sigma_\nu^2 (I_{N_i} \otimes J_{T_i}) + \sigma_\varepsilon^2 (I_{N_i} \otimes I_{T_i}), \quad i = 1, \ldots, M. \tag{6}$$

Replacing J_{T_i} by its idempotent counterpart $T\bar{J}_{T_i}$ where $\bar{J}_{T_i} = J_{T_i}/T_i$ and J_{N_i} by $N_i \bar{J}_{N_i}$ where $\bar{J}_{N_i} = J_{N_i}/N_i$, we get

$$\Lambda_i = N_i T_i \sigma_\mu^2 (\bar{J}_{N_i} \otimes \bar{J}_{T_i}) + T_i \sigma_\nu^2 (I_{N_i} \otimes \bar{J}_{T_i}) + \sigma_\varepsilon^2 (I_{N_i} \otimes I_{T_i}). \tag{7}$$

Replacing I_{N_i} by $E_{N_i} + \bar{J}_{N_i}$ and I_{T_i} by $E_{T_i} + \bar{J}_{T_i}$, where $E_{N_i} = I_{N_i} - \bar{J}_{N_i}$ and $E_{T_i} = I_{T_i} - \bar{J}_{T_i}$ and collecting terms with the same matrices, see Wansbeek and Kapteyn (1982, 1983), one gets the spectral decomposition of Λ_i:

$$\Lambda_i = \lambda_{1i}Q_{1i} + \lambda_{2i}Q_{2i} + \lambda_{3i}Q_{3i}, \tag{8}$$

where $\lambda_{1i} = \sigma_\varepsilon^2$, $\lambda_{2i} = T_i\sigma_v^2 + \sigma_\varepsilon^2$ and $\lambda_{3i} = N_iT_i\sigma_\mu^2 + T_i\sigma_v^2 + \sigma_\varepsilon^2$. Correspondingly, $Q_{1i} = I_{N_i} \otimes E_{T_i}$, $Q_{2i} = E_{N_i} \otimes \bar{J}_{T_i}$ and $Q_{3i} = \bar{J}_{N_i} \otimes \bar{J}_{T_i}$. The λ_{pi}, $p = 1, 2, 3$, are the distinct characteristic roots of Λ_i of multiplicity $N_i(T_i - 1)$, $N_i - 1$ and 1, respectively. Note that each Q_{pi}, for $p = 1, 2, 3$ is symmetric, idempotent with its rank equal to its trace. Moreover, the Q_{pi}'s are pairwise orthogonal and sum to the identity matrix. The advantages of this spectral decomposition are that

$$\Lambda_i^p = \lambda_{1i}^p Q_{1i} + \lambda_{2i}^p Q_{2i} + \lambda_{3i}^p Q_{3i}, \tag{9}$$

where p is an arbitrary scalar, see Baltagi (1993). Therefore, we can easily obtain Ω^{-1} as

$$\Omega^{-1} = diag[\Lambda_i^{-1}] = diag[\lambda_{1i}^{-1}Q_{1i} + \lambda_{2i}^{-1}Q_{2i} + \lambda_{3i}^{-1}Q_{3i}] \tag{10}$$

and

$$\begin{aligned} \sigma_\varepsilon\Omega^{-1/2} &= diag\left[\frac{\sigma_\varepsilon}{\sqrt{\lambda_{1i}}}Q_{1i} + \frac{\sigma_\varepsilon}{\sqrt{\lambda_{2i}}}Q_{2i} + \frac{\sigma_\varepsilon}{\sqrt{\lambda_{3i}}}Q_{3i}\right] \\ &= diag[I_{N_i} \otimes I_{T_i}] - diag[\theta_{1i}(I_{N_i} \otimes \bar{J}_{T_i})] - diag[\theta_{2i}(\bar{J}_{N_i} \otimes \bar{J}_{T_i})], \end{aligned} \tag{11}$$

where $\theta_{1i} = 1 - \sigma_\varepsilon/\sqrt{\lambda_{2i}}$ and $\theta_{2i} = \sigma_\varepsilon/\sqrt{\lambda_{2i}} - \sigma_\varepsilon/\sqrt{\lambda_{3i}}$. This allows us to obtain GLS on (3) as an ordinary least squares (OLS) of $y^* = \sigma_\varepsilon\Omega^{-1/2}y$ on $X^* = \sigma_\varepsilon\Omega^{-1/2}X$. The typical element of y^* is given by $(y_{ijt} - \theta_{1i}\bar{y}_{ij.} - \theta_{2i}\bar{y}_{i..})$ where $\bar{y}_{ij.} = \sum_{t=1}^{T_i} y_{ijt}/T_i$ and $\bar{y}_{i..} = \sum_{j=1}^{N_i}\sum_{t=1}^{T_i} y_{ijt}/N_iT_i$. This is known in the econometrics literature as the Fuller and Battese (1973) transformation.

Note that the OLS estimator is given by

$$\hat{\beta}_{OLS} = (X'X)^{-1}X'y. \tag{12}$$

This is the best linear unbiased estimator when the variance components σ_μ^2 and σ_v^2 are both equal to 0. Even when these variance components are positive, the OLS estimator is still unbiased and consistent, but its standard errors are biased, see Moulton (1986). The OLS residuals are denoted by $\hat{u}_{OLS} = y - X\hat{\beta}_{OLS}$.

The within estimator in this case can be obtained by transforming the model in (3) by $Q_1 = diag(I_{N_i} \otimes E_{T_i})$ and then applying OLS. Note that $Q_1Z_\mu = Q_1Z_v = 0$ because $E_{T_i}\iota_{T_i} = 0$. Therefore, Q_1 sweeps away the μ_i's and v_{ij}'s whether they are fixed or random effects. This yields

$$\tilde{\beta}_s = (X_s'Q_1X_s)^{-1}X_s'Q_1y, \tag{13}$$

where X_s denotes the exogenous regressors excluding the intercept and β_s denotes the corresponding $(k-1)$ vector of slope coefficients. $\beta' = (\alpha, \beta_s')$ and the estimate of the intercept can be retrieved as follows: $\tilde{\alpha} = (\bar{y}_{...} - \bar{X}_{s...}\tilde{\beta}_s)$, where the dots indicate summation and the bar indicates averaging. Following Amemiya (1971), the within residuals $\tilde{u}_{WTN}$ for the unbalanced nested effect model are given by

$$\tilde{u}_{WTN} = y - \tilde{\alpha}\iota_m - X_s\tilde{\beta}_s \tag{14}$$

where $m = \sum_{i=1}^{M} N_i T_i$.

Next, we consider methods of estimating the variance components.

2.1. Analysis of variance methods

These are methods of moments-type estimators that equate quadratic sums of squares to their expectations and solve the resulting equations for the unknown variance components. These ANOVA estimators are best quadratic unbiased (BQU) estimators of the variance components in the balanced error component model case, see Graybill (1961). Under normality of the disturbances they are even minimum variance unbiased. However, for the unbalanced model, BQU estimators of the variance components are a function of the variance components themselves, see Searle (1987). Unbalanced ANOVA methods are available but optimal properties beyond unbiasedness are lost. We consider four ANOVA-type methods which are natural extensions of those proposed in the balanced error component literature:

(1) A modified Wallace and Hussain (WH) estimator: Consider the three quadratic forms of the disturbances using the Q_1, Q_2 and Q_3 matrices obtained from the spectral decomposition of Ω in (8):

$$q_1 = u'Q_1u, \quad q_2 = u'Q_2u, \quad q_3 = u'Q_3u, \tag{15}$$

where $Q_1 = diag(Q_{1i})$, $Q_2 = diag(Q_{2i})$ and $Q_3 = diag(Q_{3i})$. Substituting OLS residuals $\hat{u}_{OLS}$ for u in (15) we get $\hat{q}_1$, $\hat{q}_2$ and $\hat{q}_3$, see Wallace and Hussain (1969) and Baltagi and Chang (1994). Taking expected values, we obtain

$$E(\hat{q}_1) = E(\hat{u}_{OLS}'Q_1\hat{u}_{OLS}) = \delta_{11}\sigma_\varepsilon^2 + \delta_{12}\sigma_\mu^2 + \delta_{13}\sigma_v^2,$$

$$E(\hat{q}_2) = E(\hat{u}_{OLS}'Q_2\hat{u}_{OLS}) = \delta_{21}\sigma_\varepsilon^2 + \delta_{22}\sigma_\mu^2 + \delta_{23}\sigma_v^2,$$

$$E(\hat{q}_3) = E(\hat{u}_{OLS}'Q_3\hat{u}_{OLS}) = \delta_{31}\sigma_\varepsilon^2 + \delta_{32}\sigma_\mu^2 + \delta_{33}\sigma_v^2, \tag{16}$$

where the δ_{ij}'s are given by

$$\delta_{11} = m - n - tr(X'Q_1X(X'X)^{-1}),$$

$$\delta_{12} = tr[(X'Z_\mu Z_\mu' X)(X'X)^{-1}(X'Q_1X)(X'X)^{-1}],$$

$$\delta_{13} = tr[(X'Z_v Z_v' X)(X'X)^{-1}(X'Q_1X)(X'X)^{-1}],$$

$$\delta_{21} = n - M - tr(X'Q_2X(X'X)^{-1}),$$
$$\delta_{22} = tr[(X'Z_\mu Z'_\mu X)(X'X)^{-1}(X'Q_2X)(X'X)^{-1}],$$
$$\delta_{23} = m - t - 2tr[(X'Z_v Z'_v Q_2 X)(X'X)^{-1}] + tr[(X'Z_v Z'_v X)(X'X)^{-1}(X'Q_2X)(X'X)^{-1}],$$
$$\delta_{31} = M - tr(X'Q_3X(X'X)^{-1}),$$
$$\delta_{32} = m - 2tr[(X'Z_\mu Z'_\mu X)(X'X)^{-1}] + tr[(X'Z_\mu Z'_\mu X)(X'X)^{-1}(X'Q_3X)(X'X)^{-1}],$$
$$\delta_{33} = t - 2tr[(X'Z_v Z'_v Q_3 X)(X'X)^{-1}] + tr[(X'Z_v Z'_v X)(X'X)^{-1}(X'Q_3X)(X'X)^{-1}], \quad (17)$$

with $m = \sum_{i=1}^M N_i T_i$, $n = \sum_{i=1}^M N_i$ and $t = \sum_{i=1}^M T_i$. Equating the $\hat{q}_i$'s to their expected values $E(\hat{q}_i)$ in (16) and solving the system of equations, one gets the Wallace and Hussain (1969)-type estimators of the variance components.[1] These are denoted by WH.

(2) A modified Wansbeek and Kapteyn (WK) estimator: Alternatively, one can substitute within residuals in the quadratic forms given by (15) to get $\tilde{q}_1$, $\tilde{q}_2$ and $\tilde{q}_3$, see Amemiya (1971) and Wansbeek and Kapteyn (1989). Taking expected values of $\tilde{q}_1$, $\tilde{q}_2$ and $\tilde{q}_3$ we get

$$E(\tilde{q}_1) = E(\tilde{u}'_{\text{WTN}} Q_1 \tilde{u}_{\text{WTN}}) = (m - n - k + 1)\sigma_\varepsilon^2,$$
$$E(\tilde{q}_2) = E(\tilde{u}'_{\text{WTN}} Q_2 \tilde{u}_{\text{WTN}}) = [n - M + tr\{(X'_s Q_1 X_s)^{-1} X'_s Q_2 X_s\}]\sigma_\varepsilon^2 + (m - t)\sigma_v^2,$$
$$E(\tilde{q}_3) = E(\tilde{u}'_{\text{WTN}} Q_3 \tilde{u}_{\text{WTN}}) = [M - 1 + tr\{(X'_s Q_1 X_s)^{-1} X'_s Q_3 X_s\} - tr\{(X'_s Q_1 X_s)^{-1} X'_s \bar{J}_m X_s\}]\sigma_\varepsilon^2 + [t - \textstyle\sum N_i T_i^2/m]\sigma_v^2 + [m - \textstyle\sum N_i^2 T_i^2/m]\sigma_\mu^2. \quad (18)$$

Equating $\tilde{q}_i$ to its expected value $E(\tilde{q}_i)$ in (18) and solving the system of equations, we get the following Wansbeek and Kapteyn-type estimator of the variance components which we denote by WK:

$$\tilde{\sigma}_\varepsilon^2 = \tilde{u}'_{\text{WTN}} Q_1 \tilde{u}_{\text{WTN}}/(m - n - k + 1),$$
$$\tilde{\sigma}_v^2 = \frac{\tilde{u}'_{\text{WTN}} Q_2 \tilde{u}_{\text{WTN}} - [n - M + tr\{(X'_s Q_1 X_s)^{-1}(X'_s Q_2 X_s)\}\tilde{\sigma}_\varepsilon^2]}{m - t},$$

[1] Most of the algebra involved is simple but tedious and all proofs are available upon request from the authors.

$$\tilde{\sigma}_\mu^2 = (\tilde{u}'_{\text{WTN}} Q_3 \tilde{u}_{\text{WTN}} - [M - 1 + tr\{(X'_s Q_1 X_s)^{-1} X'_s Q_3 X_s\} - tr\{(X'_s Q_1 X_s)^{-1} X'_s \bar{J}_m X_s\}]\tilde{\sigma}_\varepsilon^2 - [t - \textstyle\sum N_i T_i^2/m]\tilde{\sigma}_v^2)/[m - \textstyle\sum N_i^2 T_i^2/m]. \quad (19)$$

(3) A Modified Swamy and Arora (SA) estimator: Following Swamy and Arora (1972), we transform the regression model in (3) by premultiplying it by Q_1, Q_2 and Q_3 and we obtain the transformed residuals $\tilde{u}_1$, $\tilde{u}_2$ and $\tilde{u}_3$, respectively. Let $\tilde{q}_1^+ = \tilde{u}'_1 Q_1 \tilde{u}_1$, $\tilde{q}_2^+ = \tilde{u}'_2 Q_2 \tilde{u}_2$ and $\tilde{q}_3^+ = \tilde{u}'_3 Q_3 \tilde{u}_3$. Since $\tilde{q}_1^+$ is exactly the same as $\tilde{q}_1$ the resulting expected value of $\tilde{q}_1^+$ is the same as that given in (18). The expected values of $\tilde{q}_2^+$ and $\tilde{q}_3^+$ are

$$E(\tilde{q}_2^+) = E(\tilde{u}'_2 Q_2 \tilde{u}_2) = (n - M - k + 1)\sigma_\varepsilon^2 + [m - t - tr\{(X'_s Z_v Z'_v Q_2 X_s)(X'_s Q_2 X_s)^{-1}\}]\sigma_v^2,$$

$$E(\tilde{q}_3^+) = E(\tilde{u}'_3 Q_3 \tilde{u}_3) = (M - k)\sigma_\varepsilon^2 + [t - tr\{(X' Z_v Z'_v Q_3 X)(X' Q_3 X)^{-1}\}]\sigma_v^2 + [m - tr\{(X' Z_\mu Z'_\mu X)(X' Q_3 X)^{-1}\}]\sigma_\mu^2. \quad (20)$$

Equating $\tilde{q}_i^+$ to its expected value $E(\tilde{q}_i^+)$ and solving the system of equations, we get the following Swamy and Arora-type estimators of the variance components which we denote by SA:

$$\tilde{\sigma}_\varepsilon^2 = \tilde{u}'_{\text{WTN}} Q_1 \tilde{u}_{\text{WTN}}/(m - n - k + 1),$$

$$\tilde{\sigma}_v^2 = \frac{\tilde{u}'_2 Q_2 \tilde{u}_2 - (n - M - k + 1)\tilde{\sigma}_\varepsilon^2}{m - t - tr\{(X'_s Z_v Z'_v Q_2 X_s)(X'_s Q_2 X_s)^{-1}\}},$$

$$\tilde{\sigma}_\mu^2 = \frac{\tilde{u}'_3 Q_3 \tilde{u}_3 - (M - k)\tilde{\sigma}_\varepsilon^2 - [t - tr\{(X' Z_v Z'_v Q_3 X)(X' Q_3 X)^{-1}\}]\tilde{\sigma}_v^2}{m - tr\{(X' Z_\mu Z'_\mu X)(X' Q_3 X)^{-1}\}}. \quad (21)$$

(4) Henderson Method III: Fuller and Battese (1973) suggest an estimation of the variance components using the fitting constants methods. This method uses the within residual sums of squares given by $\tilde{q}_1^* = \tilde{u}'_{\text{WTN}} \tilde{u}_{\text{WTN}}$. Also, the residual sum of squares obtained by transforming the regression in (3) by $(Q_1 + Q_2)$ (i.e., the regression of $y_{ijt} - \bar{y}_{i..}$ on $x_{ijtl} - \bar{x}_{i..l}$, for $l = 1, \ldots, k$). This is denoted by $\tilde{q}_2^* = \tilde{u}_2^{*\prime} \tilde{u}_2^*$ where $\tilde{u}_2^*$ is the residual vector of the $(Q_1 + Q_2)$ transformed regression. Finally, this method uses the conventional OLS residual sum of squares denoted by $\tilde{q}_3^* = \hat{u}'_{\text{OLS}} \hat{u}_{\text{OLS}}$. If the x variables do not have constant values for measurement of group and nested subgroups, $\tilde{q}_1^*$ is exactly the same as that for

the WK method, the resulting expected value of $\tilde{q}_1^*$ is the same as that given in (18). Also, the expected value of $\tilde{q}_2^*$ and $\tilde{q}_3^*$ are given by

$$\begin{aligned} E(\tilde{q}_2^*) &= \sigma_\varepsilon^2[m - M - k + 1] \\ &\quad + \sigma_v^2[m - t - tr\{(X_s'Z_vZ_v'Q_2X_s)(X_s'(Q_1 + Q_2)X_s)^{-1}\}], \\ E(\tilde{q}_3^*) &= \sigma_\varepsilon^2[m - k] + \sigma_v^2[m - tr\{(X'Z_vZ_v'X)(X'X)^{-1}\}] \\ &\quad + \sigma_\mu^2[m - tr\{(X'Z_\mu Z_\mu' X)(X'X)^{-1}\}]. \end{aligned} \tag{22}$$

Equating $\tilde{q}_i^*$, for $i = 1, 2, 3$ to its expected value $E(\tilde{q}_i^*)$ in (22), we obtain the Henderson Method III estimator of the variance components, see Fuller and Battese (1973). These are denoted by HFB:

$$\begin{aligned} \tilde{\sigma}_\varepsilon^2 &= \tilde{u}_{\mathrm{WTN}}'Q_1\tilde{u}_{\mathrm{WTN}}/(m - n - k + 1), \\ \tilde{\sigma}_v^2 &= \frac{\tilde{u}_2^{*\prime}\tilde{u}_2^* - (m - M - k + 1)\tilde{\sigma}_\varepsilon^2}{m - t - tr\{(X_s'Z_vZ_v'Q_2X_s)(X_s'(Q_1 + Q_2)X_s)^{-1}\}}, \\ \tilde{\sigma}_\mu^2 &= \frac{\hat{u}_{\mathrm{OLS}}'\hat{u}_{\mathrm{OLS}} - (m - k)\tilde{\sigma}_\varepsilon^2 - [m - tr\{(X'diag(I_{N_i} \otimes J_{T_i})X)(X'X)^{-1}\}\tilde{\sigma}_v^2]}{m - tr\{(X'Z_\mu Z_\mu'X)(X'X)^{-1}\}}. \end{aligned} \tag{23}$$

2.2. *Maximum likelihood estimator*

Since λ_{pi}, for $p = 1, 2, 3$ are the distinct characteristic roots of Λ_i then $|\Lambda_i| = (\lambda_{3i})(\lambda_{2i}^{N_i - 1})(\lambda_{1i}^{N_i(T_i - 1)})$. Let $\rho_1 = \sigma_\mu^2/\sigma_\varepsilon^2$, $\rho_2 = \sigma_v^2/\sigma_\varepsilon^2$ and $\Omega = \sigma_\varepsilon^2\Sigma$, then the log-likelihood function can be written as

$$\begin{aligned} \log L &= C - \frac{m}{2}\log\sigma_\varepsilon^2 - \frac{1}{2}\sum_{i=1}^{M}\log(N_iT_i\rho_1 + T_i\rho_2 + 1) \\ &\quad - \frac{1}{2}\sum_{i=1}^{M}(N_i - 1)\log(T_i\rho_2 + 1) - \frac{1}{2}u'\Sigma^{-1}u/2\sigma_\varepsilon^2. \end{aligned} \tag{24}$$

The first-order conditions give closed form solutions for β and σ_ε^2 conditional on ρ_1 and ρ_2:

$$\hat{\beta}_{ML} = (X'\hat{\Sigma}^{-1}X)^{-1}X'\hat{\Sigma}^{-1}y, \tag{25}$$

$$\hat{\sigma}_\varepsilon^2 = (y - X\beta)'\hat{\Sigma}^{-1}(y - X\beta)/m. \tag{26}$$

However, the first-order conditions based on $\hat{\rho}_1$ and $\hat{\rho}_2$ are nonlinear in ρ_1 and ρ_2 even for known values of β and σ_ε^2. Following Hemmerle and Hartley (1973), we get

$$\frac{\partial \log L}{\partial \rho_1} = -\frac{1}{2}tr[Z_\mu'\Sigma^{-1}Z_\mu] + \frac{1}{2\sigma_\varepsilon^2}(y - X\beta)'\Sigma^{-1}Z_\mu Z_\mu'\Sigma^{-1}(y - X\beta),$$

$$\frac{\partial \log L}{\partial \rho_2} = -\frac{1}{2}\, tr[Z_v'\Sigma^{-1}Z_v] + \frac{1}{2\sigma_\varepsilon^2}\,(y - X\beta)'\Sigma^{-1}Z_vZ_v'\Sigma^{-1}(y - X\beta). \quad (27)$$

Therefore, a numerical solution by means of iteration is needed. The Fisher scoring procedure is used to estimate ρ_1 and ρ_2. The partition of the information matrix corresponding to ρ_1 and ρ_2 is given by

$$E\left[-\frac{\partial^2 \log L}{\partial \rho_1^2}\right] = \frac{1}{2}\sum_{i=1}^{M}\frac{(N_iT_i)^2}{(1+\rho_2T_i+\rho_1N_iT_i)^2},$$

$$E\left[-\frac{\partial^2 \log L}{\partial \rho_1 \partial \rho_2}\right] = \frac{1}{2}\sum_{i=1}^{M}\frac{N_iT_i^2}{(1+\rho_2T_i+\rho_1N_iT_i)^2},$$

$$E\left[-\frac{\partial^2 \log L}{\partial \rho_2^2}\right] = \frac{1}{2}\sum_{i=1}^{M}\frac{(N_i-1)T_i^2}{(1+\rho_2T_i)^2} + \frac{1}{2}\sum_{i=1}^{M}\frac{T_i^2}{(1+\rho_2T_i+\rho_1N_iT_i)^2}, \quad (28)$$

see Harville (1977). Starting with an initial value, the $(r+1)$th updated value of ρ_1 and ρ_2 is given by

$$\begin{bmatrix}\hat\rho_1\\ \hat\rho_2\end{bmatrix}_{r+1} = \begin{bmatrix}\hat\rho_1\\ \hat\rho_2\end{bmatrix}_{r} + \begin{bmatrix} E\left[-\frac{\partial^2 \log L}{\partial \rho_1^2}\right] & E\left[-\frac{\partial^2 \log L}{\partial \rho_1\partial\rho_2}\right] \\ E\left[-\frac{\partial^2 \log L}{\partial \rho_1\partial\rho_2}\right] & E\left[-\frac{\partial^2 \log L}{\partial \rho_2^2}\right]\end{bmatrix}_r^{-1} \begin{bmatrix}\frac{\partial \log L}{\partial \rho_1}\\ \frac{\partial \log L}{\partial \rho_2}\end{bmatrix}_r, \quad (29)$$

where at each step, $\partial \log L/\partial\rho_1$ and $\partial \log L/\partial\rho_2$ are obtained from Eq. (27), $\hat\beta$ and $\hat\sigma_\varepsilon^2$ are obtained from (25) and (26), the information matrix is obtained from Eq. (28). The subscript r means this is evaluated at the rth iteration. For a review of the advantages and disadvantages of MLE, see Harville (1977).

2.3. Restricted maximum likelihood estimator

Patterson and Thompson (1971) suggested a restricted maximum likelihood (REML) estimation method that takes into account the loss of degrees of freedom due to the regression coefficients in estimating the variance components. REML is based on a transformation that partitions the likelihood function into two parts, one being free of the fixed regression coefficients. Maximizing this part yields REML. Patterson and Thompson (1971) suggest the singular transformation $y'[C \,\vdots\, \Sigma^{-1}X/\sigma_\varepsilon^2]$, where $C = I - X(X'X)^{-1}X'$. Cy is distributed as $N(0, C\Sigma C'/\sigma_\varepsilon^2)$, and from the fact that $CX = 0$, it is independent of $X'\Sigma^{-1}y/\sigma_\varepsilon^2$ which is also distributed as $N(X'\Sigma^{-1}X\beta/\sigma_\varepsilon^2, X'\Sigma^{-1}X/\sigma_\varepsilon^2)$. It is clear that Cy does not depend on β. Since C is an idempotent matrix of rank $m-k$, there exists an $(m-k)\times m$ matrix A such that

$$A'A = C, \quad AA' = I. \quad (30)$$

Using the $A'y$ transformation instead of $C'y$, we get

$$\begin{bmatrix} A'y \\ X'\Sigma^{-1}y/\sigma_\varepsilon^2 \end{bmatrix} \sim \mathrm{N}\left(\begin{bmatrix} 0 \\ X'\Sigma^{-1}X\beta/\sigma_\varepsilon^2 \end{bmatrix}, \begin{bmatrix} \sigma_\varepsilon^2 A\Sigma A' & 0 \\ 0 & X'\Sigma^{-1}X/\sigma_\varepsilon^2 \end{bmatrix}\right). \tag{31}$$

Following Corbeil and Searle (1976), the log-likelihood function of $A'y$ and $X'\Sigma^{-1}y/\sigma_\varepsilon^2$ are given by $\log L_1$ and $\log L_2$, respectively:

$$\begin{aligned} \log L_1 &= -\frac{m-k}{2}\log(2\pi) - \frac{m-k}{2}\log(\sigma_\varepsilon^2) - \frac{1}{2}\log|A\Sigma A'| \\ &\quad - \frac{1}{2\sigma_\varepsilon^2}\, y'[A'(A\Sigma A')^{-1}A]y, \\ \log L_2 &= -\frac{k}{2}\log(2\pi) - \frac{1}{2}\log(\sigma_\varepsilon^2) - \log|X'\Sigma^{-1}X| \\ &\quad - \frac{1}{2\sigma_\varepsilon^2}(y - X\beta)'\Sigma^{-1}X(X'\Sigma^{-1}X)^{-1}X'\Sigma^{-1}(y - X\beta). \end{aligned} \tag{32}$$

Using the results of Hocking (1985) and Corbeil and Searle (1976), we obtain

$$A'(A\Sigma A')^{-1}A = \Sigma^{-1}[I - X(X'\Sigma^{-1}X)^{-1}X'\Sigma^{-1}] = \Sigma^{-1}(I - M), \tag{33}$$

where $M = X(X'\Sigma^{-1}X)^{-1}X'\Sigma^{-1}$.

Using $\log L_1$ which is free from β, the first-order derivatives of $\log L_1$ with respect to σ_ε^2, ρ_1 and ρ_2 are given by

$$\begin{aligned} \frac{\partial \log L_1}{\partial \sigma_\varepsilon^2} &= -\frac{m-k}{2\sigma_\varepsilon^2} + \frac{1}{2\sigma_\varepsilon^4}\, y'A'(A\Sigma A')^{-1}Ay \\ &= -\frac{m-k}{2\sigma_\varepsilon^2} + \frac{1}{2\sigma_\varepsilon^4}\, y'\Sigma^{-1}(I - M)y, \\ \frac{\partial \log L_1}{\partial \rho_1} &= -\frac{1}{2}\, tr[Z_\mu' A'(A\Sigma A')^{-1}AZ_\mu] \\ &\quad + \frac{1}{2\sigma_\varepsilon^2}\, y'[A'(A\Sigma A')^{-1}AZ_\mu Z_\mu' A'(A\Sigma A')^{-1}A]y, \\ \frac{\partial \log L_1}{\partial \rho_2} &= -\frac{1}{2}\, tr[Z_\nu' A'(A\Sigma A')^{-1}AZ_\nu] \\ &\quad + \frac{1}{2\sigma_\varepsilon^2}\, y'[A'(A\Sigma A')^{-1}AZ_\nu Z_\nu' A'(A\Sigma A')^{-1}A]y. \end{aligned} \tag{34}$$

Equating the equations in (34) to 0's yield the REML estimates. For example, solving $\partial \log L_1/\partial\sigma_\varepsilon^2 = 0$ conditional on ρ_1 and ρ_2, we obtain

$$\hat{\sigma}_\varepsilon^2 = y'A'(A\hat{\Sigma}A')^{-1}Ay/(m-k) = y'[\hat{\Sigma}^{-1}(I - M)]y/(m-k). \tag{35}$$

But there are no closed-form solutions on ρ_1 and ρ_2. Thus a numerical solution by means of iteration is needed. The Fisher scoring procedure is used to estimate ρ_1 and ρ_2. Using the results of Harville (1977) and Eq. (33), the information matrix with respect to ρ_1 and ρ_2 is given by

$$E\left[-\frac{\partial^2 \log L_1}{\partial \rho_1^2}\right] = \frac{1}{2}\, tr[Z_\mu Z_\mu' \Sigma^{-1}(I-M) Z_\mu Z_\mu' \Sigma^{-1}(I-M)],$$

$$E\left[-\frac{\partial^2 \log L_1}{\partial \rho_1 \partial \rho_2}\right] = \frac{1}{2}\, tr[Z_\mu Z_\mu' \Sigma^{-1}(I-M) Z_\nu Z_\nu' \Sigma^{-1}(I-M)],$$

$$E\left[-\frac{\partial^2 \log L_1}{\partial \rho_2^2}\right] = \frac{1}{2}\, tr[Z_\nu Z_\nu' \Sigma^{-1}(I-M) Z_\nu Z_\nu' \Sigma^{-1}(I-M)]. \quad (36)$$

The updated values of ρ_1 and ρ_2 can be obtained as in (29).

2.4. MINQUE and MIVQUE

Rao (1971a) proposed a general procedure for variance components estimation which requires no distributional assumptions other than the existence of the first four moments. This procedure yields MINQUE of the variance components. Under normality of the disturbances, MINQUE and minimum variance quadratic unbiased estimators (MIVQUE) are identical. Since we assume normality, we will focus on MIVQUE. Let

$$R = \Sigma^{-1}[I - X(X'\Sigma^{-1}X)^{-1}X'\Sigma^{-1}]/\sigma_\varepsilon^2, \quad (37)$$

$$S = \{s_{ij}\} = \{tr(V_i R V_j R)\}, \quad i, j = 1, 2, 3 \quad (38)$$

and

$$u = \{u_i\} = \{y' R V_i R y\}, \quad i = 1, 2, 3, \quad (39)$$

where $V_1 = I_m$, $V_2 = Z_\mu Z_\mu'$ and $V_3 = Z_\nu Z_\nu'$. Rao (1971b) shows that the vector of MIVQUEs is given by

$$\hat{\theta} = S^{-1} u, \quad (40)$$

where $\hat{\theta}' = (\hat{\sigma}_\varepsilon^2, \hat{\sigma}_\mu^2, \hat{\sigma}_\nu^2)$. However, MIVQUE requires a priori values of the variance components. Therefore, MIVQUE is only 'locally minimum variance', see LaMotte (1973a, b), and 'locally best', see Harville (1969). Three priors of the MIVQUE estimator are considered in our Monte Carlo study: (1) the identity matrix, which we denote by MV1, and (2) all values of the variance components equal to 1, see Swallow and Searle (1978) which we denote by MV2, and (3) the ANOVA estimator of WK, which we denote by MV3. Note that the MIVQUE estimator can produce negative estimates of the variance components. In this case, we replace the negative variance estimate by 0.

3. Monte Carlo results

3.1. Design of the Monte Carlo study

We consider the following simple regression equation:

$$y_{ijt} = \alpha + x_{ijt}\beta + u_{ijt}, \quad i = 1, \dots, M, \quad j = 1, \dots, N_i, \quad t = 1, \dots, T_i, \tag{41}$$

with $u_{ijt} = \mu_i + \nu_{ij} + \varepsilon_{ijt}$. The exogenous variable x_{ijt} was generated by a similar method to that of Nerlove (1971). In fact, $x_{ijt} = 0.3t + 0.8x_{ij,t-1} + w_{ijt}$, where w_{ijt} is uniformly distributed on the interval $[-0.5, 0.5]$. The initial values x_{ij0} were chosen as $(100 + 250w_{ij0})$. Throughout the experiment $\alpha = 5$ and $\beta = 2$. For generating the u_{ijt} disturbances, we let $\mu_i \sim \text{IIN}(0, \sigma_\mu^2)$, $\nu_{ij} \sim \text{IIN}(0, \sigma_\nu^2)$ and $\varepsilon_{ijt} \sim \text{IIN}(0, \sigma_\varepsilon^2)$. We fix $\sigma^2 = \sigma_\mu^2 + \sigma_\nu^2 + \sigma_\varepsilon^2 = 20$ and define $\gamma_1 = \sigma_\mu^2/\sigma^2$ and $\gamma_2 = \sigma_\nu^2/\sigma^2$. These are varied over the set (0, 0.2, 0.4, 0.6, 0.8) such that $(1 - \gamma_1 - \gamma_2)$ is always positive. Extending a measure of unbalancedness given by Ahrens and Pincus (1981) to the unbalanced nested model, we define

$$c_1 = M/\bar{N} \textstyle\sum(1/N_i) \quad \text{where } \bar{N} = \textstyle\sum N_i/M,$$
$$c_2 = M/\bar{T} \textstyle\sum(1/T_i) \quad \text{where } \bar{T} = \textstyle\sum T_i/M,$$
$$c_3 = M/\overline{NT} \textstyle\sum(1/N_iT_i) \quad \text{where } \overline{NT} = \textstyle\sum N_iT_i/M, \tag{42}$$

where c_1, c_2 and c_3 denote the measures of subgroup unbalancedness, observed time unbalancedness and group unbalancedness due to each group size. Note that c_1, c_2 and c_3 take the value 1 when the data are balanced but take smaller values than 1 as the data pattern gets more unbalanced. Table 1 gives the (N_i, T_i) pattern used along with the corresponding unbalancedness measures for $M = 10$. The first parentheses gives the N_i pattern, while the second parentheses below it gives the corresponding T_i pattern. For example, P_1 observes the first grouping of eight individuals over six time periods and the last grouping of 12 individuals over four time periods. The sample size is fixed at 500 for every pattern. Two other values of M are used, $M = 6$ and 15. For each experiment, 1000 replications are performed. For each replication, we calculate OLS, WTN, WH, SA, WK, HFB, ML, REML, MV1, MV2, MV3 and true GLS. The last estimator is obtained for comparison purposes.

3.2. A comparison of regression coefficient estimates

Table 2 gives the mean square error (MSE) of the estimate of $\hat{\beta}$ relative to that of true GLS for the case when $M = 10$.[2] From this table it is clear that OLS is

[2] Similar MSE tables for the regression coefficients and the variance components estimates are generated for $M = 6$ and 15, but they are not produced here to save space. These tables are available upon request from the authors.

Table 1
(N_i, T_i) patterns considered and their corresponding unbalancedness measures when $M = 10$

Pattern	$(N_1, N_2, \ldots, N_{10})$[a] $(T_1, T_2, \ldots, T_{10})$	c_1	c_2	c_3
P_1	(8,8,8,10,10,10,10,12,12,12) (6,6,6,5,5,5,5,5,4,4)	0.976	0.980	0.996
P_2	(6,6,6,10,10,10,10,12,12,12) (9,9,9,9,8,3,3,3,3,3)	0.925	0.757	0.8238
P_3	(5,5,5,10,10,10,10,11,11,11) (2,2,3,3,3,6,7,8,8,9)	0.893	0.734	0.504
P_4	(4,4,4,5,5,9,9,10,10,10) (14,15,15,15,15,3,3,4,4,4)	0.854	0.619	0.881
P_5	(3,3,3,3,3,8,8,8,8,8) (2,2,2,3,3,11,11,12,12,12)	0.793	0.550	0.258
P_6	(2,2,6,6,6,10,10,10,13,13) (16,16,16,16,16,2,2,3,3,3)	0.656	0.465	0.718
P_7	(2,2,2,10,10,10,10,13,13,13) (2,1,1,1,8,8,8,8,8,8)	0.552	0.424	0.133
P_8	(20,20,15,15,15,3,3,3,2,2) (1,1,6,6,6,10,10,10,25,25)	0.444	0.347	0.732
P_9	(16,16,16,16,16,2,2,2,2,2) (2,2,3,3,3,28,28,30,30,30)	0.395	0.290	0.949
P_{10}	(20,20,20,20,20,2,2,2,2,1) (2,2,2,3,3,25,30,30,30,30)	0.282	0.272	0.945
P_{11}	(1,1,1,1,5,5,25,25,25,25) (1,2,2,35,35,2,2,3,3,3)	0.192	0.280	0.091
P_{12}	(1,1,1,1,5,5,30,30,30,30) (27,27,28,28,28,2,2,2,2,2)	0.165	0.252	0.626

[a]The first parentheses gives the N_i pattern, while the parentheses below it gives the corresponding T_i pattern.

inferior to true GLS, ML-type (ML, REML) estimators and all feasible GLS-type estimators except when $\gamma_1 = \gamma_2 = 0$. For all experiments, the effect of an increase in γ_1 on the MSE of OLS is much larger than that of an increase in γ_2. This is because γ_1 affects the primary group while γ_2 affects only the nested subgroup. The WTN estimator performs poorly for small γ_1 and γ_2 values. The performance of WTN is in some cases worse than OLS if either γ_1 or γ_2 is 0. However, its performance improves as γ_1 and γ_2 increase and the unbalancedness pattern gets more severe. The ANOVA-type (WH, WK, SA and HFB)

Table 2
MSE of $\hat{\beta}$ relative to that of true GLS when $M = 10$

	γ_1	γ_2	OLS	WTN	WH	WK	SA	HFB	MLE	REML	MV1	MV2	MV3
P_1	0.0	0.0	1.000	4.864	0.998	1.006	0.996	0.999	0.998	0.999	0.998	0.999	0.999
	0.0	0.2	1.069	2.732	1.014	1.016	1.011	1.014	1.012	1.015	1.017	1.013	1.014
	0.0	0.4	1.396	1.985	1.008	1.011	1.009	1.009	1.008	1.009	1.010	1.009	1.009
	0.0	0.6	2.073	1.406	1.000	1.001	1.001	1.000	0.999	0.999	1.000	1.001	1.000
	0.0	0.8	4.341	1.212	1.000	1.000	1.001	1.000	1.000	1.000	1.004	0.999	0.999
	0.2	0.0	1.649	3.979	1.003	1.001	1.003	1.002	1.003	1.004	1.002	1.002	1.004
	0.2	0.2	1.633	2.333	1.002	0.998	1.002	1.001	1.001	1.001	0.999	1.000	1.001
	0.2	0.4	2.274	1.549	1.010	1.011	1.014	1.011	1.011	1.010	1.014	1.010	1.010
	0.2	0.6	4.358	1.219	1.011	1.010	1.017	1.010	1.011	1.010	1.015	1.010	1.010
	0.4	0.0	3.537	4.149	1.001	0.998	1.004	0.999	1.001	1.000	1.004	0.999	1.000
	0.4	0.2	2.748	2.049	1.004	1.008	1.006	1.006	1.006	1.007	1.012	1.007	1.007
	0.4	0.4	4.407	1.276	1.000	0.998	1.001	1.000	0.999	0.999	1.003	0.999	0.999
	0.6	0.0	6.235	4.077	1.003	1.004	1.007	1.005	1.005	1.005	1.036	1.004	1.005
	0.6	0.2	5.673	1.555	1.000	0.998	1.003	0.998	0.998	0.998	1.013	0.998	0.998
	0.8	0.0	13.606	4.473	1.007	1.011	1.004	1.006	1.006	1.006	1.135	1.006	1.006
P_3	0.0	0.0	1.000	3.578	1.003	1.013	1.002	1.004	0.998	1.002	1.001	1.016	1.004
	0.0	0.2	1.236	2.233	1.025	1.024	1.022	1.025	1.021	1.025	1.020	1.031	1.025
	0.0	0.4	1.653	1.735	1.009	1.009	1.005	1.010	1.009	1.011	1.008	1.011	1.010
	0.0	0.6	2.590	1.296	0.999	1.000	1.002	0.998	1.000	0.999	1.003	0.999	0.999
	0.0	0.8	5.815	1.133	1.015	1.012	1.014	1.015	1.011	1.012	1.026	1.014	1.012
	0.2	0.0	1.970	3.400	1.001	1.007	1.004	1.001	1.006	1.005	1.002	1.006	1.004
	0.2	0.2	2.106	1.816	1.016	1.010	1.025	1.014	1.016	1.016	1.024	1.014	1.016
	0.2	0.4	3.005	1.508	1.015	1.016	1.022	1.014	1.011	1.011	1.035	1.011	1.011
	0.2	0.6	6.389	1.097	1.018	1.011	1.023	1.014	1.010	1.008	1.040	1.009	1.008
	0.4	0.0	3.932	3.022	1.003	1.004	1.001	1.001	1.000	0.999	1.012	1.002	0.999
	0.4	0.2	3.467	1.605	1.004	1.003	1.003	1.003	1.005	1.004	1.016	1.004	1.004
	0.4	0.4	6.324	1.180	1.004	1.003	1.009	1.004	1.001	1.001	1.038	1.001	1.001
	0.6	0.0	8.675	3.474	1.011	1.010	1.012	1.007	1.008	1.008	1.028	1.006	1.008
	0.6	0.2	7.699	1.433	1.017	1.015	1.017	1.016	1.017	1.017	1.048	1.017	1.017
	0.8	0.0	19.474	3.528	1.028	1.026	1.015	1.016	1.011	1.011	1.054	1.023	1.012
P_5	0.0	0.0	1.000	2.541	1.020	1.029	1.013	1.023	1.014	1.020	1.017	1.046	1.021
	0.0	0.2	1.473	1.560	1.020	1.019	1.021	1.019	1.019	1.021	1.020	1.031	1.020
	0.0	0.4	2.237	1.328	1.007	1.009	1.006	1.009	1.009	1.011	1.005	1.014	1.011
	0.0	0.6	4.354	1.127	1.005	1.004	1.004	1.005	1.004	1.005	1.005	1.006	1.005
	0.0	0.8	9.091	1.056	1.004	1.002	1.003	1.003	1.003	1.003	1.005	1.002	1.003
	0.2	0.0	1.979	2.066	1.018	1.021	1.021	1.017	1.015	1.012	1.028	1.014	1.014
	0.2	0.2	2.374	1.212	1.028	1.027	1.033	1.029	1.026	1.022	1.039	1.017	1.024
	0.2	0.4	3.961	1.162	1.019	1.018	1.022	1.018	1.015	1.015	1.024	1.014	1.016
	0.2	0.6	8.756	1.047	1.008	1.006	1.008	1.007	1.005	1.004	1.013	1.004	1.004
	0.4	0.0	3.404	1.922	1.011	1.014	1.014	1.011	1.012	1.011	1.021	1.015	1.011
	0.4	0.2	4.385	1.174	1.030	1.022	1.036	1.025	1.021	1.018	1.040	1.017	1.019
	0.4	0.4	9.748	1.094	1.005	1.004	1.005	1.004	1.006	1.005	1.015	1.004	1.004
	0.6	0.0	6.053	1.918	1.009	1.010	1.009	1.007	1.006	1.006	1.014	1.020	1.006
	0.6	0.2	9.692	1.093	1.018	1.014	1.021	1.016	1.013	1.012	1.035	1.011	1.012
	0.8	0.0	17.824	1.893	1.020	1.020	1.018	1.017	1.008	1.008	1.041	1.030	1.010
P_7	0.0	0.0	1.000	2.894	1.010	1.016	1.008	1.011	1.009	1.012	1.011	1.020	1.012
	0.0	0.2	1.293	1.806	1.008	1.010	1.007	1.010	1.005	1.006	1.006	1.012	1.006
	0.0	0.4	2.008	1.470	1.015	1.013	1.016	1.014	1.015	1.014	1.017	1.014	1.014

Table 2 (Continued)

	γ_1	γ_2	OLS	WTN	WH	WK	SA	HFB	MLE	REML	MV1	MV2	MV3
	0.0	0.6	3.153	1.298	1.001	1.001	1.002	1.001	1.001	1.002	1.001	1.002	1.001
	0.0	0.8	6.276	1.156	1.012	1.012	1.011	1.012	1.010	1.010	1.016	1.011	1.010
	0.2	0.0	1.916	2.684	1.012	1.015	1.019	1.012	1.016	1.015	1.021	1.014	1.015
	0.2	0.2	1.910	1.644	1.014	1.017	1.015	1.014	1.010	1.008	1.026	1.003	1.010
	0.2	0.4	3.302	1.300	1.022	1.020	1.023	1.021	1.015	1.014	1.035	1.008	1.015
	0.2	0.6	7.084	1.140	1.012	1.011	1.017	1.011	1.006	1.006	1.019	1.006	1.006
	0.4	0.0	3.178	3.043	1.037	1.045	1.045	1.037	1.028	1.027	1.065	1.034	1.029
	0.4	0.2	3.232	1.535	1.010	1.014	1.013	1.012	1.012	1.012	1.014	1.013	1.012
	0.4	0.4	7.325	1.225	1.005	1.001	1.005	1.002	1.003	1.002	1.012	1.003	1.003
	0.6	0.0	6.502	2.779	1.018	1.026	1.020	1.018	1.008	1.009	1.024	1.032	1.009
	0.6	0.2	7.435	1.296	1.010	1.007	1.008	1.009	1.011	1.010	1.030	1.009	1.010
	0.8	0.0	16.032	2.662	1.034	1.035	1.028	1.028	1.019	1.019	1.104	1.039	1.019
P_9	0.0	0.0	1.000	5.028	1.033	1.045	1.027	1.037	1.022	1.032	1.028	1.048	1.031
	0.0	0.2	1.254	3.273	1.014	1.025	1.013	1.017	1.008	1.011	1.014	1.021	1.015
	0.0	0.4	1.939	2.228	1.035	1.033	1.034	1.035	1.016	1.019	1.069	1.027	1.024
	0.0	0.6	2.871	1.670	1.014	1.016	1.014	1.015	1.010	1.012	1.075	1.014	1.012
	0.0	0.8	5.502	1.340	1.013	1.011	1.012	1.013	1.007	1.007	1.120	1.007	1.009
	0.2	0.0	3.053	4.067	1.009	1.010	1.014	1.006	1.008	1.006	1.024	1.012	1.007
	0.2	0.2	3.198	2.904	1.012	1.024	1.013	1.012	1.018	1.014	1.037	1.012	1.011
	0.2	0.4	4.132	2.137	1.044	1.038	1.049	1.037	1.018	1.019	1.134	1.019	1.018
	0.2	0.6	8.514	1.348	1.044	1.035	1.048	1.038	1.011	1.007	1.251	1.015	1.007
	0.4	0.0	8.563	4.782	1.004	1.007	1.012	1.000	1.001	1.000	1.083	1.004	1.000
	0.4	0.2	6.631	2.555	1.007	1.006	1.014	1.006	1.001	1.002	1.174	1.000	1.003
	0.4	0.4	10.603	1.568	1.032	1.027	1.040	1.030	1.015	1.014	1.355	1.014	1.015
	0.6	0.0	14.027	4.090	1.014	1.008	1.016	1.007	1.009	1.008	1.187	1.007	1.008
	0.6	0.2	14.553	1.899	1.022	1.019	1.030	1.021	1.010	1.011	1.267	1.011	1.011
	0.8	0.0	37.097	4.310	1.018	1.009	1.007	1.007	1.007	1.007	1.396	1.012	1.008
P_{11}	0.0	0.0	1.000	8.900	1.061	1.091	1.054	1.063	1.035	1.048	1.047	1.092	1.054
	0.0	0.2	1.489	4.513	1.014	1.009	1.012	1.014	1.008	1.007	1.034	1.015	1.007
	0.0	0.4	1.821	3.154	1.007	1.012	1.005	1.010	1.002	1.005	1.050	1.007	1.005
	0.0	0.6	2.856	2.322	1.032	1.033	1.030	1.033	1.016	1.017	1.159	1.017	1.017
	0.0	0.8	4.494	1.455	1.036	1.036	1.032	1.039	1.014	1.016	1.366	1.021	1.016
	0.2	0.0	4.970	6.283	1.011	1.019	1.032	1.010	1.010	1.007	1.023	1.027	1.007
	0.2	0.2	5.078	3.682	1.016	1.013	1.042	1.011	1.010	1.006	1.052	1.015	1.006
	0.2	0.4	5.933	2.392	1.033	1.025	1.037	1.033	1.017	1.013	1.238	1.013	1.011
	0.2	0.6	8.409	1.643	1.007	1.008	1.003	1.008	1.003	1.003	1.253	1.008	1.002
	0.4	0.0	13.184	7.260	1.001	1.009	1.012	1.003	1.002	1.001	1.050	1.002	1.001
	0.4	0.2	10.965	3.193	1.005	1.006	1.009	1.006	1.006	1.006	1.079	1.006	1.006
	0.4	0.4	14.110	1.818	1.009	1.007	1.015	1.007	1.004	1.003	1.227	1.002	1.004
	0.6	0.0	28.659	6.450	1.017	1.007	1.012	1.007	1.004	1.004	1.268	1.006	1.005
	0.6	0.2	21.438	2.374	1.024	1.021	1.031	1.019	1.008	1.008	1.218	1.007	1.008
	0.8	0.0	73.642	5.963	1.009	1.000	1.009	1.001	0.998	0.998	1.142	1.000	0.999

estimators, the ML-type and MV2 and MV3 estimators all perform well relative to true GLS. See also Fig. 1 which plots the MSE of $\hat{\beta}$ relative to that of true GLS for the 12 unbalanced patterns for $M = 10$ and $\gamma_1 = \gamma_2 = 0.4$. It is important to point out that the simple ANOVA-type estimators compare well in

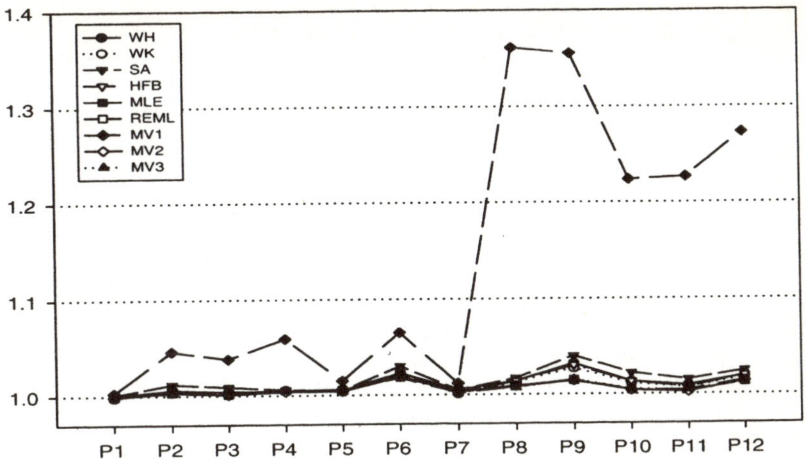

Fig. 1. MSE of $\hat{\beta}$ relative to that of true GLS when $M = 10$, $\gamma_1 = \gamma_2 = 0.4$.

MSE performance to the ML- and MIVQUE-type estimators which are relatively more difficult to compute. They have at most 9.1% higher MSE than true GLS, see the WK estimator for pattern P_{11} when $\gamma_1 = \gamma_2 = 0$. MV1 performs well for $\gamma_1 < 0.4$ and $\gamma_2 < 0.4$. This is to be expected since the prior values for MV1 are $\gamma_1 = 0$ and $\gamma_2 = 0$. As γ_1 and γ_2 increase or the degree of unbalancedness gets large, the performance of MV1 deteriorates relative to the other estimators, see Fig. 1.

To summarize, for the regression parameters, the computationally simple ANOVA estimators compare well with the more complicated estimators such as ML, REML, MV2 and MV3 in terms of MSE criteria. Also, MV1 is not recommended when the primary group effects or nested subgroup effects are suspected to be large or the unbalanced pattern is severe.

3.3. A comparison of variance components estimates

Tables 3–5 report the MSE of the variance components relative to that of MLE for the 12 unbalancedness patterns for $M = 10$ and $\gamma_1 = \gamma_2 = 0.4$. Similar tables for other values of $M = 6$ and 15 and various values of γ_1 and γ_2 are available upon request from the authors. These tables are plotted in Figs. 2–4 for ease of comparison.

For the estimation of σ_μ^2, see Table 3 or Fig. 2, MLE ranks first; REML, MV2 and MV3 rank second and the ANOVA methods rank third by the MSE criteria. MV1 does well only when γ_1 and γ_2 are close to 0. For $\gamma_1 = \gamma_2 = 0.4$, MV1 performs the worst. The ANOVA methods yield almost twice the MSE of

Table 3
MSE of $\hat{\sigma}_\mu^2$ relative to that of MLE when $M = 10$, $\gamma_1 = \gamma_2 = 0.4$

	WH	WK	SA	HFB	REML	MV1	MV2	MV3
P_1	1.170	1.170	1.302	1.168	1.158	1.204	1.160	1.157
P_2	1.284	1.267	1.448	1.274	1.170	1.669	1.165	1.170
P_3	1.523	1.487	1.722	1.512	1.183	2.175	1.176	1.173
P_4	1.307	1.295	1.413	1.297	1.140	1.602	1.133	1.134
P_5	1.866	1.855	1.951	1.863	1.140	2.244	1.156	1.140
P_6	1.814	1.750	2.022	1.779	1.170	3.124	1.162	1.159
P_7	1.897	1.885	2.034	1.891	1.178	2.216	1.202	1.159
P_8	1.473	1.476	1.558	1.472	1.189	2.196	1.183	1.169
P_9	1.446	1.362	1.579	1.402	1.159	1.407	1.159	1.146
P_{10}	1.427	1.360	1.585	1.383	1.177	1.459	1.179	1.170
P_{11}	1.680	1.863	1.787	1.755	1.211	2.558	1.171	1.129
P_{12}	1.338	1.379	1.465	1.336	1.165	2.170	1.074	1.100

Table 4
MSE of $\hat{\sigma}_\nu^2$ relative to that of MLE when $M = 10$, $\gamma_1 = \gamma_2 = 0.4$

	WH	WK	SA	HFB	REML	MV1	MV2	MV3
P_1	1.010	1.010	1.012	1.004	0.999	1.312	0.997	0.998
P_2	1.205	1.181	1.194	1.179	0.999	2.514	1.012	0.998
P_3	1.116	1.115	1.117	1.104	1.000	1.450	1.001	1.002
P_4	1.458	1.428	1.430	1.412	0.999	3.224	1.002	0.990
P_5	1.086	1.066	1.096	1.065	0.995	1.181	0.989	1.015
P_6	1.584	1.566	1.567	1.549	0.999	3.563	1.015	0.993
P_7	1.105	1.103	1.110	1.092	0.999	1.333	1.024	1.007
P_8	1.475	1.453	1.466	1.442	0.998	16.188	1.039	0.985
P_9	2.615	2.561	2.581	2.551	0.993	13.130	0.998	0.977
P_{10}	2.717	2.672	2.681	2.650	1.000	21.473	1.021	0.992
P_{11}	2.694	2.583	2.583	2.559	1.001	20.234	1.001	1.004
P_{12}	2.863	2.697	2.692	2.667	1.000	23.894	1.000	0.989

MLE for patterns P_5, P_6 and P_7. On the other hand, REML, MV2 and MV3 have MSE that are only 14–20% higher than that of MLE. MV1 has 2–3 times the MSE of MLE for these patterns and is not included in Fig. 2.

For the estimation of σ_ν^2, see Table 4 or Fig. 3, REML, MLE, MV2 and MV3 rank first by the MSE criteria. They are followed by the ANOVA methods with MV1 performing the worst. For patterns P_9, P_{10}, P_{11} and P_{12}, these ANOVA methods yield more than 2.5 times the MSE of MLE. In contrast, MV1 yields 13–23 times the MSE of MLE and is not included in Fig. 3.

For the estimation of σ_ε^2, there is not much difference among WK, SA, HFB, REML, MV2 and MV3. However, WH performs slightly worse than the other

Table 5
MSE of $\hat{\sigma}_\varepsilon^2$ relative to that of MLE when $M = 10$, $\gamma_1 = \gamma_2 = 0.4$

	WH	WK	SA	HFB	REML	MV1	MV2	MV3
P_1	1.038	1.001	1.001	1.001	1.001	5.190	1.004	1.002
P_2	1.053	1.005	1.005	1.005	1.002	34.983	0.999	1.003
P_3	1.050	1.000	1.000	1.000	1.000	27.465	1.002	1.000
P_4	1.202	1.004	1.004	1.004	1.002	54.860	1.002	1.003
P_5	1.201	1.006	1.006	1.006	1.006	8.669	1.012	1.010
P_6	1.173	1.005	1.005	1.005	1.002	58.511	1.009	1.003
P_7	1.078	1.000	1.000	1.000	1.000	6.469	1.012	1.001
P_8	1.126	1.004	1.004	1.004	1.002	124.852	1.018	1.005
P_9	1.121	1.000	1.000	1.000	1.002	124.467	1.010	1.006
P_{10}	1.128	1.003	1.003	1.003	1.001	154.966	1.006	1.005
P_{11}	1.193	1.004	1.004	1.004	1.002	144.898	1.006	1.004
P_{12}	1.148	1.001	1.001	1.001	0.997	119.133	0.994	1.000

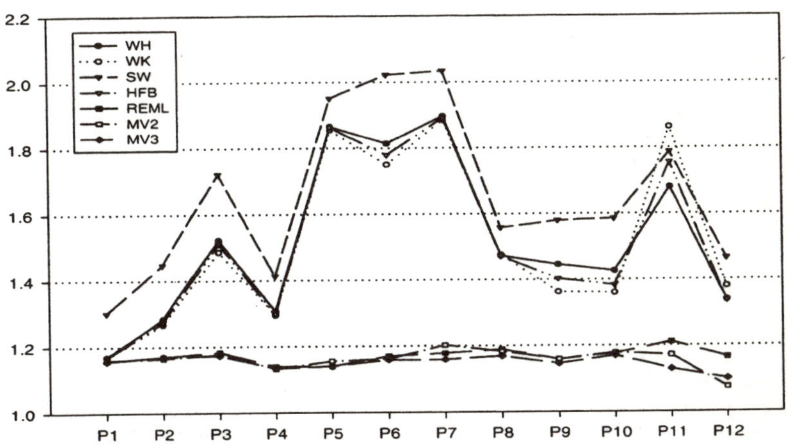

Fig. 2. MSE of $\hat{\sigma}_\mu^2$ relative to that of MLE when $M = 10$, $\gamma_1 = \gamma_2 = 0.4$.

ANOVA methods yielding 3.8–20% higher MSE than that of MLE. MV1 performs the worst yielding MSE that is 5–154 times that of MLE and is therefore not included in Fig. 4.

This confirms that if one is interested in the estimates of the variance components per se one is better off with MLE, REML or MV2 and MV3-type estimators. The ANOVA methods suggested here are second best. MV1 is not recommended unless one suspects γ_1 and γ_2 are close to 0. However, for the estimation of the regression coefficients, the ANOVA methods compare well and are recommended.

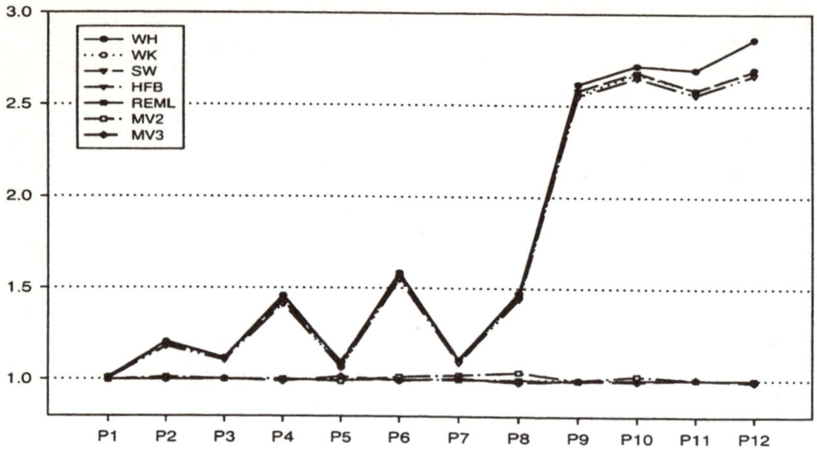

Fig. 3. MSE of $\hat{\sigma}_v^2$ relative to that of MLE when $M = 10$, $\gamma_1 = \gamma_2 = 0.4$.

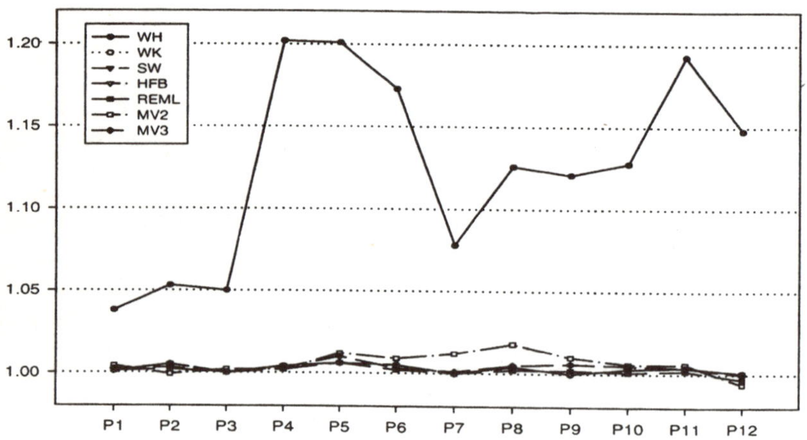

Fig. 4. MSE of $\hat{\sigma}_\varepsilon^2$ relative to that of MLE when $M = 10$, $\gamma_1 = \gamma_2 = 0.4$.

For ANOVA and MIVQUE-type estimators, negative estimates of σ_μ^2 or σ_v^2 occur in about 50% of the replications when $\gamma_1 = 0$ or $\gamma_2 = 0$. When the negative estimates of variance components are replaced by 0, the corresponding estimator forfeits its unbiasedness property. But, replacing these negative estimates by 0 did not lead to much loss in efficiency using the MSE criterion.

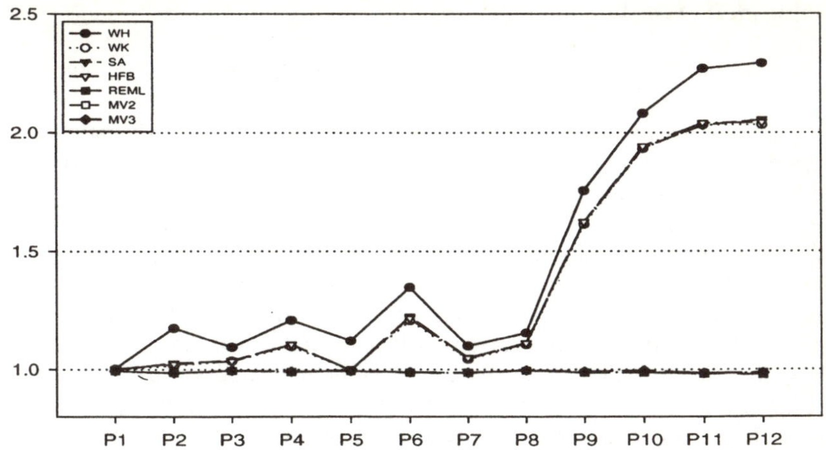

Fig. 5. MSE of standard errors of $\hat{\beta}$ relative to that of MLE when $M = 10$, $\gamma_1 = \gamma_2 = 0.4$.

Finally, better estimates of the variance components by the MSE criterion, do not necessarily imply better estimates of the regression coefficients. A similar result was obtained by Baltagi and Chang (1994) for the unbalanced one way model and by Taylor (1980) and Baltagi (1981) for the balanced error component model. However, MV1 has worse relative MSE performance than other ANOVA, ML, REML and MIVQUE-type estimators of the variance components when γ_1 and γ_2 are large and the pattern is severely unbalanced and this clearly translates into a corresponding worse relative MSE performance of the regression coefficients. Similar conclusions can be drawn for $M = 6$ and 15 and are not produced here to save space.

3.4. A comparison of standard errors of the regression coefficients

Fig. 5 plots the MSE of the standard error of $\hat{\beta}$ relative to that of MLE for the 12 unbalanced patterns for $M = 10$ and $\gamma_1 = \gamma_2 = 0.4$. Besides the relative efficiency of the parameter estimates, one is also interested in proper inference on the parameter values. This is where the computationally involved estimators (like MV2, MV3 and REML) perform well producing a MSE for the standard error of $\hat{\beta}$ that is close to that of MLE. The computationally simple ANOVA methods (WH, WK, SA, HFB) have MSE for the standard error of $\hat{\beta}$ that are 2 times that of MLE for severely unbalanced patterns like P_{10}, P_{11} and P_{12}. However, these ANOVA methods perform reasonably well in patterns P_1–P_8 giving MSEs of the standard error of $\hat{\beta}$ that are no more than 30% higher than that of MLE.

4. Empirical example

Baltagi and Pinnoi (1995) estimated a Cobb–Douglas production function investigating the productivity of public capital in each state's private output. This is based on a panel of 48 states over the period 1970–1986. The data were provided by Munnell (1990). These states can be grouped into nine regions with the Middle Atlantic region for example containing three states: New York, New Jersey and Pennsylvania and the Mountain region containing eight states: Montana, Idaho, Wyoming, Colorado, New Mexico, Arizona, Utah and Nevada. The primary group would be the regions, the nested group would be the states and these are observed over 17 years. The dependent variable y is the gross state product and the regressors include the private capital stock (K) computed by apportioning the Bureau of Economic Analysis (BEA) national estimates. The public capital stock is measured by its components: highways and streets (KH), water and sewer facilities (KW), and other public buildings and structures (KO), all based on the BEA national series. Labor (L) is measured by the employment in nonagricultural payrolls. The state unemployment rate is included to capture the business cycle in a given state. See Munnell (1990) for details on the data series and their construction. All variables except the unemployment rate are expressed in natural logarithm

$$\begin{aligned} y_{ijt} &= \alpha + \beta_1 K_{ijt} + \beta_2 \mathrm{KH}_{ijt} + \beta_3 \mathrm{KW}_{ijt} + \beta_4 \mathrm{KO}_{ijt} \\ &\quad + \beta_5 L_{ijt} + \beta_6 \,\mathrm{Unemp}_{ijt} + u_{ijt}, \end{aligned} \tag{43}$$

where $i = 1, 2, \ldots, 9$ regions, $j = 1, \ldots, N_i$ with N_i equaling 3 for the Middle Atlantic region and 8 for the Mountain region and $t = 1, 2, \ldots, 17$. The data is unbalanced only in the differing number of states in each region. The disturbances follow the nested error component specification given by (2).

Table 6 gives the OLS, WTN, ANOVA, MLE, REML and MIVQUE-type estimates using this unbalanced nested error component model. The OLS estimates show that the highways and streets and water and sewer components of public capital have a positive and significant effect upon private output whereas that of other public buildings and structures is not significant. Because OLS ignores the state and region effects, the corresponding standard errors and t-statistics are biased, see Moulton (1986). The within estimator shows that the effect of KH and KW are insignificant whereas that of KO is negative and significant. The primary region and nested state effects are significant using several LM tests developed in Baltagi et al. (1999). This justifies the application of the feasible GLS, MLE and MIVQUE methods. For the variance components estimates, there are no differences in the estimate of σ_ε^2. But estimates of σ_μ^2 and σ_ν^2 vary. $\hat{\sigma}_\mu^2$ is as low as 0.0015 for SA and MLE and as high as 0.0029 for HFB. Similarly, $\hat{\sigma}_\nu^2$ is as low as 0.0043 for SA and as high as 0.0069 for WK. This variation had little effect on estimates of the regression coefficients or their

Table 6
Cobb–Douglas production function estimates with unbalanced nested error components 1970–1986, Nine regions, 48 states[a]

Variable	OLS	WTN	WH	WK	SA	HFB	MLE	REML	MV1	MV2	MV3
Intercept	1.926	--	2.082	2.131	2.089	2.084	2.129	2.127	2.083	2.114	2.127
	(0.053)		(0.152)	(0.160)	(0.144)	(0.150)	(0.154)	(0.157)	(0.152)	(0.154)	(0.156)
K	0.312	0.235	0.273	0.264	0.274	0.272	0.267	0.266	0.272	0.269	0.267
	(0.011)	(0.026)	(0.021)	(0.022)	(0.020)	(0.021)	(0.021)	(0.022)	(0.021)	(0.021)	(0.021)
L	0.550	0.801	0.742	0.758	0.740	0.743	0.754	0.756	0.742	0.750	0.755
	(0.016)	(0.030)	(0.026)	(0.027)	(0.025)	(0.026)	(0.026)	(0.026)	(0.026)	(0.026)	(0.026)
KH	0.059	0.077	0.075	0.072	0.073	0.075	0.071	0.072	0.075	0.072	0.072
	(0.015)	(0.031)	(0.023)	(0.024)	(0.022)	(0.022)	(0.023)	(0.023)	(0.023)	(0.023)	(0.023)
KW	0.119	0.079	0.076	0.076	0.076	0.076	0.076	0.076	0.076	0.076	0.076
	(0.012)	(0.015)	(0.014)	(0.014)	(0.014)	(0.014)	(0.014)	(0.014)	(0.014)	(0.014)	(0.014)
KO	0.009	−0.115	−0.095	−0.102	−0.094	−0.096	−0.100	−0.101	−0.095	−0.098	−0.100
	(0.012)	(0.018)	(0.017)	(0.017)	(0.017)	(0.017)	(0.017)	(0.017)	(0.017)	(0.017)	(0.017)
Unemp	−0.007	−0.005	−0.006	−0.006	−0.006	−0.006	−0.006	−0.006	−0.006	−0.006	−0.006
	(0.001)	(0.001)	(0.001)	(0.001)	(0.001)	(0.001)	(0.001)	(0.001)	(0.001)	(0.001)	(0.001)
σ_ε^2	0.0073	0.0013	0.0014	0.0014	0.0014	0.0014	0.0013	0.0014	0.0014	0.0014	0.0014
σ_μ^2	—	--	0.0027	0.0022	0.0015	0.0029	0.0015	0.0019	0.0027	0.0017	0.0017
σ_ν^2	--		0.0045	0.0069	0.0043	0.0044	0.0063	0.0064	0.0046	0.0056	0.0063

[a]The dependent variable is log of gross state product. Standard errors are given in parentheses.

standard errors. For all estimators of the random effects model, the highways and streets and water and sewer components of public capital had a positive and significant effect, while the other public buildings and structures had a negative and significant effect upon private output.

5. Conclusion

For the regression coefficients of the nested unbalanced error component model, the simple ANOVA methods proposed in this paper performed well in Monte Carlo experiments as well as in the empirical example and are recommended. However, for the variance components estimates themselves, as well as the standard errors of the regression coefficients, the computationally more demanding MLE, REML or MIVQUE (MV2 and MV3) estimators are recommended especially if the unbalanced pattern is severe. Further research should extend the unbalanced nested error component model considered in this paper to allow for endogeneity of the regressors, a dynamic specification, ignorability of the sample selection and serial correlation in the disturbances.

Acknowledgements

The authors would like to thank two anonymous referees and an Associate Editor for their helpful comments and suggestions. A preliminary version of this paper was presented at the European meetings of the Econometric Society held in Santiago de Compostela, Spain, August, 1999. Also, at the University of Chicago, University of Pennsylvania and the University of Rochester. Baltagi would like to thank the Texas Advanced Research Program and the Bush Program in economics of public policy for their financial support.

References

Ahrens, H., Pincus, R., 1981. On two measures of unbalancedness in a one-way model and their relation to efficiency. Biometric Journal 23, 227–235.

Amemiya, T., 1971. The estimation of variances in a variance components model. International Economic Review 12, 1–13.

Antweiler, W., 1999. Nested random effects estimation in unbalanced panel data. Working Paper, University of British Columbia.

Baltagi, B.H., 1981. Pooling: an experimental study of alternative testing and estimation procedures in a two-way error components model. Journal of Econometrics 17, 21–49.

Baltagi, B.H., 1985. Pooling cross-sections with unequal time series lengths. Economics Letters 18, 133–136.

Baltagi, B.H., 1993. Useful matrix transformations for panel data analysis: a survey. Statistical Papers 34, 281–301.

Baltagi, B.H., 1995. Econometric Analysis of Panel Data. Wiley, New York.

Baltagi, B.H., Chang, Y.J., 1994. Incomplete panels: a comparative study of alternative estimators for the unbalanced one-way error component regression model. Journal of Econometrics 62, 67–89.

Baltagi, B.H., Pinnoi, N., 1995. Public capital stock and state productivity growth: further evidence from an error component model. Empirical Economics 20, 351–359.

Baltagi, B.H., Song, S.H., Jung, B.C., 1999. Simple LM tests for the unbalanced nested error component regression model. Working Paper, Texas A&M University, Department of Economics, College Station, TX.

Corbeil, R.R., Searle, S.R., 1976. Restricted maximum likelihood (REML) estimation of variance components in the mixed model. Technometrics 18, 31–38.

Fuller, W.A., Battese, G.E., 1973. Transformations for estimation of linear models with nested error structure. Journal of the American Statistical Association 68, 626–632.

Graybill, F.A., 1961. An Introduction to Linear Statistical Models. McGraw-Hill, New York.

Harville, D.A., 1969. Quadratic unbiased estimation of variance component for the one-way classification. Biometrika 56, 313–326.

Harville, D.A., 1977. Maximum likelihood approaches to variance component estimation and to related problems. Journal of the American Statistical Association 72, 320–340.

Hemmerle, W.J., Hartley, H.O., 1973. Computing maximum likelihood estimate of the mixed A.O.V. model using the W-transformation. Technometrics 15, 819–831.

Hocking, R.R., 1985. The Analysis of Linear Model. Brooks Cole, Monterey.

Hsiao, C., 1986. Analysis of Panel Data. Cambridge University Press, Cambridge.

LaMotte, L.R., 1973a. On non-negative quadratic unbiased estimation of variance components. Journal of the American Statistical Association 68, 728–730.

LaMotte, L.R., 1973b. Quadratic estimation of variance components. Biometrics 29, 311–330.

Maddala, G.S., Mount, T.D., 1973. A comparative study of alternative estimators for variance components models used in econometric applications. Journal of the American Statistical Association 68, 324–328.

Mátyás, L., Sevestre, P., 1996. The Econometrics of Panel Data: Handbook of Theory and Application. Kluwer Academic Publishers, Dordrecht.

Montmarquette, C., Mahseredjian, S., 1989. Does school matter for educational achievement? A two-way nested-error components analysis. Journal of Applied Econometrics 4, 181–193.

Moulton, B.R., 1986. Random group effects and the precision of regression estimates. Journal of Econometrics 32, 385–397.

Munnell, A., 1990. Why has productivity growth declined? Productivity and public investment. New England Economic Review 3-22.

Nerlove, M., 1971. Further evidence on the estimation of dynamic economic relations from a time-series of cross-sections. Econometrica 39, 359–382.

Patterson, H.D., Thompson, R., 1971. Recovery of inter-block information when block sizes are unequal. Biometrika 58, 545–554.

Rao, C.R., 1971a. Estimation of variance and covariance components – MINQUE theory. Journal of Multivariate Analysis 1, 257–275.

Rao, C.R., 1971b. Minimum variance quadratic unbiased estimation of variance components. Journal of Multivariate Analysis 1, 445–456.

Searle, S.R., 1971. Linear Models. Wiley, New York.

Searle, S.R., 1987. Linear Models for Unbalanced Data. Wiley, New York.

Swallow, W.H., Monahan, J.F., 1984. Monte Carlo comparison of ANOVA, MIVQUE, REML and ML estimators of variance components. Technometrics 26, 47–57.

Swallow, W.H., Searle, S.R., 1978. Minimum variance quadratic unbiased estimation (MIVQUE) of variance components. Technometrics 20, 265–272.

Swamy, P.A.V.B., Arora, A.A., 1972. The exact finite sample properties of the estimators of coefficients in the error components regression models. Econometrica 40, 261–275.

Taylor, W.E., 1980. Small sample considerations in estimation from panel data. Journal of Econometrics 13, 203–223.

Wallace, T.D., Hussain, A., 1969. The use of error components models in combining cross-section and time-series data. Econometrica 37, 55–72.

Wansbeek, T., Kapteyn, A., 1982. A simple way to obtain the spectral decomposition of variance components models for balanced data. Communications in Statistics – Theory and Method 11, 2105–2111.

Wansbeek, T., Kapteyn, A., 1983. A note on spectral decomposition and maximum likelihood estimation of ANOVA models with balanced data. Statistics and Probability Letters 1, 213–215.

Wansbeek, T., Kapteyn, A., 1989. Estimation of the error components model with incomplete panels. Journal of Econometrics 41, 341–361.

[14]

ELSEVIER

Journal of Econometrics 106 (2002) 67–95

JOURNAL OF Econometrics

www.elsevier.com/locate/econbase

Estimating multi-way error components models with unbalanced data structures

Peter Davis*

MIT Sloan School of Management, Room E52-449, 50 Memorial Drive, Cambridge, MA 02142-1347, USA

Received 11 February 1999; revised 11 February 2001; accepted 30 April 2001

Abstract

I develop simple matrix algebra techniques that simplify and unify much of the previous literature on estimating error components models (ECMs). In fact, the simple analytic results provided here are useful for analyzing a very broad set of models with complex error structures. To illustrate the techniques, I develop the algebra for three- and four-way ECMs explicitly. In addition, I provide Monte Carlo simulation evidence on the performance of several estimators for the three-way ECM and estimate the model using data from a retail market where the three dimensions of data variation are products selling in many locations over time. © 2002 Elsevier Science S.A. All rights reserved.

JEL classification: C13; C23

Keywords: Unbalanced panel data; Instrumental variables; Error component models

1. Introduction

The error components model (ECM) is one of the most frequently used econometric models for panel data. Work by Balestra and Nerlove (1973), Wallace and Hussain (1969), Amemiya (1971), Nerlove (1971a, b), Mazodier (1972), and Fuller and Batese (1974) among others, provide a comprehensive analysis of the one- and two-way ECM for balanced panels. In practice, researchers often have to deal with missing observations. Consequently,

* Corresponding author. Tel.: +1-617-253-1277; fax: +1-617-258-6855.
E-mail address: pjdavis@mit.edu (P. Davis).

PII: S0304-4076(01)00087-2

Baltagi (1985) and Wansbeek and Kapteyn (1989) (henceforth WK), respectively, developed the one- and two-way ECM for unbalanced data.

In a related literature, the nested ECM has also been developed. Most recently, Baltagi et al. (2001) and Antweiler (2001), respectively, develop the two- and three-way nested ECM for unbalanced panels, building on earlier work by Fuller and Battesse (1973). The nested ECM has proven particularly useful for datasets with a natural grouping structure. For example, data on firms may be grouped by industry.

The aim of this paper is to extend the literature in a number of directions. First, I provide a series of mathematical results which allow an elegant analysis of the ECM for unbalanced panel data with an *arbitrary* number of error components.[1] I illustrate the results by developing estimators for the three-way ECM in the text while results for the four-way model are presented in the appendix.[2] By developing the paper's results as recurrence relations, the extensions to the five- or more-way ECMs are easily developed, while the one- and two-way ECMs are observed as special cases.

Second, I show that the standard and nested ECMs have the same mathematical structure and therefore the results I present can be applied to both. In fact, the results are useful for estimating a broad array of models with complex error structures. In each case, modeling the correlation structure among the errors is important because it allows efficient estimation of the parameters of interest and consistent estimates of the standard errors of the parameters. Naturally, the latter is crucially important for performing inference correctly.

Third, whenever possible, I relax WK's assumption that all regressors are exogenous, thereby allowing estimation of the general ECM using instrumental variables. Applied demand analysis motivated these extensions of the literature and this aspect of the results is particularly important in that and other contexts.[3]

---

[1] Datasets with three or more dimensions of data variation are now commonly available to applied researchers in fields such as marketing and industrial organization. For example, when estimating differentiated product demand systems, perhaps using the techniques developed by Berry (1994) and Berry et al. (1995), observations on a cross-section of products, sold in many locations over time are frequently available. Disaggregated data sets are usually unbalanced. Fortunately, the ideas and models developed for panel data can be extended to allow for these richer data structures and using them makes it possible to empirically distinguish between models which could not be differentiated using only panel data (see Pakes (1983) for example).

[2] Ghosh (1976) develops the three-way ECM for balanced panels. See also Baltagi (1987).

[3] The previous literature on instrumental variable estimation of ECMs has emphasized two other important contexts: dynamic panel data and simultaneous equation ECMs. Instrumental variable estimation of the one-way ECM with lagged endogenous variable is considered by Hausman and Taylor (1981), Arellano and Bond (1991) and Arellano and Bover (1995) among others. Baltagi (1981) and Amemiya and MaCurdy (1986) consider instrumental variable estimation of the simultaneous equation ECM. The reader is directed to Baltagi (1995) and the references therein for further details.

The paper proceeds as follows: Sections 2 and 3 develop the multi-way fixed- and random-effects models, respectively, for given estimates of the variance of each error component. In Section 4 quadratic unbiased estimators (QUEs), minimum norm quadratic unbiased estimators (MINQUEs) and maximum likelihood estimators (MLEs) of the variance of each error component are developed. Section 5 provides Monte Carlo evidence on estimators of the three-way ECM. In Section 6, I apply the results by estimating a differentiated product demand equation using a new dataset from a retail market. Section 7 concludes.

2. The fixed effects model

Consider the three-way error components linear regression model:

$$y_{ijk} = X_{ijk}\beta + u_{ijk} \quad \text{where } u_{ijk} = \mu_i + \lambda_j + \gamma_k + v_{ijk} \tag{1}$$

and $i = 1,\ldots,N_1$ might index products selling in location $j = 1,\ldots,N_2$ at date $k = 1,\ldots,N_3$. In that case, N_1 would denote the total number of different products ever observed being sold at any location in any time period. Similarly, N_2 and N_3 would denote the number of locations and time periods for which data are available. Let n denote the total number of observations in the dataset.

Using matrix notation, the three-way ECM may be written

$$y = X\beta + u \quad \text{where } u = \Delta_1\mu + \Delta_2\lambda + \Delta_3\gamma + v, \tag{2}$$

$\mu' = (\mu_1,\ldots,\mu_{N_1})$, $\lambda' = (\lambda_1,\ldots,\lambda_{N_2})$ and $\gamma' = (\gamma_1,\ldots,\gamma_{N_3})$ are parameters in the fixed effects model, Δ_s for $s = 1, 2, 3$ are $n \times N_s$ matrices of indicator variables denoting observations on products, locations and time periods, respectively, and v is the vector of econometric unobservables.

The three-way nested ECM is

$$y_{ijkl} = X_{ijkl}\beta + u_{ijkl} \quad \text{where } u_{ijkl} = \mu_i + \lambda_{ij} + \gamma_{ijk} + v_{ijkl} \tag{3}$$

with $i = 1,\ldots,N_1$, $j = 1,\ldots,N_2$, $k = 1,\ldots,N_3$ and $l = 1,\ldots,N_4$. Writing the model in matrix form also yields Eq. (2), but with $\mu = (\mu_1,\ldots,\mu_{N_1})$, $\lambda = (\lambda_{11},\ldots,\lambda_{1N_2},\ldots,\lambda_{N_1N_2})$, $\gamma = (\gamma_{111},\ldots,\gamma_{N_1,N_2,N_3})$, and Δ_s $s = 1,\ldots,3$ are matrices of zeros and ones denoting inclusion of the observation in the relevant group.[4]

[4] Clearly, the appropriate definition of Δ_s will change between the conventional ECM and the nested ECM. However, the mathematical results provided below do not rely on the detailed structure of these inclusion matrices, so I shall consider the two classes of models together. This fact also means that many other error component structures, such as combinations of nested and non-nested ECMs, can be considered using the same analytic framework. In addition, the same feature of the results also implies that the ordering of the data is immaterial provided that the inclusion matrices are appropriately defined.

When μ, λ, and γ are parameters and the data set is large, direct estimation of either model is often infeasible. For example, OLS requires the inverse of a matrix which grows with the number of columns in the entire data and indicator variable matrix, $(X, \Delta_1, \Delta_2, \Delta_3)$. To circumvent this familiar difficulty, we may use the "within" transformation to obtain estimates of the parameters of interest. [5]

Developing an expression for the within transformation requires various projection arguments. Throughout, I follow the convention that $P_{[A]} = A(A'A)^{-}A'$ is a matrix (or corresponding linear transformation) which projects onto the range of A, denoted $R(A)$. Similarly, denote the orthogonal projection onto the null space of the matrix A, $N(A)$, by $Q_{[A]} = I - P_{[A]}$. First, I establish that the orthogonal projection onto the columns of an arbitrary matrix X may be performed in stages. This result allows the within transformation to be performed in stages, reducing the computational burden substantially.

Lemma 1. *Let* $X = (X_1, X_2)$, *and* $P_{[\cdot]}$ *denote an orthogonal projection onto* $R(\cdot)$, *then* $P_{[X]} = P_{[X_1]} + P_{[Q_{[X_1]}X_2]}$.

Proof. See Appendix A. □

Clearly, with $X = (\Delta_2, \Delta_1)$ this lemma corresponds to the lemma in WK, p. 344. Applying the lemma to cover the three- or four-way models is simple. Here I present the results for the three-way ECM.

Corollary 1. *Let* $Y = (Y_1, Y_2, Y_3)$, *then* $P_{[Y]} = P_{[A]} + P_{[B]} + P_{[C]}$ *where*

$$A = Y_3, \quad B = Q_{[A]}Y_2 \quad \text{and} \quad C = Q_{[B]}Q_{[A]}Y_1. \tag{4}$$

Proof. Let $X_1 = (Y_1, Y_2)$ and $X_2 = Y_3 = A$. By Lemma 1, $P_{[X]} = P_{[X_2]} + P_{[Q_{[X_2]}X_1]} = P_{[A]} + P_{[Q_{[X_2]}X_1]}$. Next define $\tilde{Y}_1 = Q_{[Y_3]}Y_1$ and $B = Q_{[Y_3]}Y_2$. Applying Lemma 1 a second time yields $P_{[\tilde{Y}_1, B]} = P_{[B]} + P_{[Q_{[B]}\tilde{Y}_1]}$. Hence, $P_{[Y]} = P_{[A]} + P_{[B]} + P_{[C]}$. □

Defining the matrix $\Delta = (\Delta_1, \Delta_2, \Delta_3)$, the within transformation of the three-way error components model is, therefore, given by $Q_{[\Delta]} = Q_{[A]} - P_{[B]} - P_{[C]}$, where [6,7]

$$Q_{[A]} = I - \Delta_3(\Delta_3'\Delta_3)^{-}\Delta_3',$$

[5] Recall that OLS estimates of β from the full model are equivalently provided by transforming y and X using the within transformation and performing OLS on the transformed regression.

[6] Note that $Q_{[A]}Q_{[B]} = Q_{[A]} - P_{[B]} = Q_{[B]}Q_{[A]}$ and $P_{[B]}Q_{[A]} = P_{[B]}$ so $Q_{[A]}Q_{[B]}Q_{[A]} = Q_{[A]}Q_{[B]}$.

[7] Since the only requirement is that each matrix represent an orthogonal projection, any generalized inverse may be used.

$$P_{[B]} = Q_{[\Delta_3]}\Delta_2(\Delta_2' Q_{[\Delta_3]}\Delta_2)^- \Delta_2' Q_{[\Delta_3]},$$

$$P_{[C]} = Q_{[\Delta]}Q_{[B]}\Delta_1(\Delta_1'(Q_{[\Delta]}Q_{[B]})\Delta_1)^- \Delta_1' Q_{[\Delta]}Q_{[B]}.$$

The parameters of the transformed model $Q_{[\Delta]}y = Q_{[\Delta]}X\beta + Q_{[\Delta]}v$ can be consistently estimated as $n \to \infty$ using any standard instrumental variable estimator, such as two-stage least squares, provided the researcher has a sufficient number of within transformed instrumental variables $Q_{[\Delta]}Z$ to identify the parameters on the transformed regressors $Q_{[\Delta]}X$. The within two stage least squares estimator is

$$\hat{\beta}^{\text{W2SLS}} = (X'P_{QZ}X)^{-1}X'P_{QZ}y,$$

where $P_{QZ} = Q_{[\Delta]}Z(Z'Q_{[\Delta]}Z)^{-1}Z'Q_{[\Delta]}$.[8] Special cases of this estimator include the single equation variant of the error component two stage least squares estimator derived in Baltagi (1981) and WK's within estimator which takes $Z = X$ in the two-way model.

3. The random effects model

Eq. (2) describes the error structure of the three-way random effects model, when μ, λ, γ and v are random vectors. I assume μ, λ, γ and v are independent of each other and among themselves with zero means and variances σ_1^2, σ_2^2, σ_3^2 and σ_0^2, respectively. Thus, $\Omega \equiv \text{E}[uu'] = \sigma_0^2 I_n + \sigma_1^2\Delta_1\Delta_1' + \sigma_2^2\Delta_2\Delta_2' + \sigma_3^2\Delta_3\Delta_3'$.

Given a consistent estimate of Ω^{-1}, a set of instruments Z and the identification condition that $\text{E}[u(X, y; \beta_0)|Z, \Delta] = 0$ at the true parameter β_0, we may use the GMM framework developed by Hansen (1982) to provide an estimator for β. Specifically, defining $\hat{\beta}$ as the solution to the minimum distance problem

$$\min_{\beta\in\Theta} ||G_n(\beta)||_A \quad \text{where } G_n(\beta) = \frac{1}{n}Z'\Omega^{-1}u \text{ and } A = \text{Var}\left[\lim_{n\to\infty}\sqrt{n}G_n(\beta)\right],$$

it is easy to show that

$$\hat{\beta} = (X'\Omega^{-1/2}P_{[\Omega^{-1/2}Z]}\Omega^{-1/2}X)^{-1}X'\Omega^{-1/2}P_{[\Omega^{-1/2}Z]}\Omega^{-1/2}y,$$

and

$$\text{Var}(\hat{\beta}) = (X'\Omega^{-1/2}P_{[\Omega^{-1/2}Z]}\Omega^{-1/2}X)^{-1}.$$

[8] Naturally, we may not wish to explicitly calculate the $(n \times n)$ matrix P_{QZ}. Fortunately, for arbitrary matrices A and B with dimensions $(a \times n)$ and $(n \times b)$, respectively, the matrix $AP_{QZ}B = (AQ_{[\Delta]}Z)(Z'Q_{[\Delta]}Z)^{-1}(Z'Q_{[\Delta]}B)$. Similarly $AQ_{[\Delta]}B = AB - AP_{[\Delta]}B = AB - (A\Delta)(\Delta'\Delta)^{-1}(\Delta'B)$. By grouping the matrices before multiplication, in the way indicated by the parentheses, the evaluation of all $(n \times n)$ matrices is avoided.

Conceptually therefore, efficient estimation of an ECM with unbalanced data using instrumental variables poses no new problems. In practice, two problems remain. First, to provide a practical technique for calculating Ω^{-1} for given values of the variances associated with each error component, $(\sigma_0^2, \sigma_1^2, \sigma_2^2, \sigma_3^2)$. This is a non-trivial task since Ω is $n \times n$ and n is typically too large for a direct numerical calculation of the inverse to be feasible. The second remaining problem is to provide consistent estimates of the variance components. I postpone the latter to Section 4.

Notice that, however, many error components there are, the variance–covariance matrix of the composite error term always has the form $\Omega = \sigma_0^2(I + XX')$. Thus, $\Omega^{-1} = \sigma_0^{-2}(I + XX')^{-1}$. In fact, *any* variance–covariance matrix may always be written in this form, provided only that there is at least one idiosyncratic component which is uncorrelated across observations. Lemma 2 provides an expression for the inverse of a matrix of the general form $I + XX'$.

Lemma 2. If $|I+XX'| \neq 0$, *then* $(I+XX')^{-1} = \tilde{Q}_{[X_2]} - \tilde{Q}_{[X_2]}X_1 S_1^{-1} X_1' \tilde{Q}_{[X_2]}$ *where* $X = (X_1, X_2)$ *and*

$$\tilde{Q}_{[X_2]} = I - X_2(I + X_2'X_2)^{-1}X_2' = (I + X_2X_2')^{-1}$$

$$\text{and} \quad S_1 = I + X_1'\tilde{Q}_{[X_2]}X_1.$$

Proof. See Appendix A. □

By implicitly applying this lemma once, with $X = (\sigma_1/\sigma_0 \Delta_1, \sigma_2/\sigma_0 \Delta_2)$, WK provide an analytic expression for the two-way error components model. Now suppose $X_1 = Y_1$ and $X_2 = (Y_2, Y_3)$. Since $\tilde{Q}_{[X_2]} = I - X_2(I + X_2'X_2)^{-1}X_2' = (I + X_2X_2')^{-1}$, Lemma 2 may be applied a second time to provide an analytic expression for $\tilde{Q}_{[X_2]} = \tilde{Q}_{[Y_2,Y_3]}$.

Corollary 2. If $Y = (Y_1, Y_2, Y_3)$ *and* $\Omega = \sigma_0^2(I + YY')$, *then* $\Omega^{-1} = \sigma_0^{-2}(I + YY')^{-1}$ *where* $(I + YY')^{-1} = \tilde{Q}_{[Y_2,Y_3]} - \tilde{Q}_{[Y_2,Y_3]}Y_1 S_1^{-1} Y_1' \tilde{Q}_{[Y_2,Y_3]}$ *and*

$$\tilde{Q}_{[Y_2,Y_3]} = \tilde{Q}_{[Y_3]} - \tilde{Q}_{[Y_3]}Y_2 S_2^{-1} Y_2' \tilde{Q}_{[Y_3]}, \quad \tilde{Q}_{[Y_3]} = I - Y_3(I + Y_3'Y_3)^{-1}Y_3'$$

$$S_1 = I + Y_1'\tilde{Q}_{[Y_2,Y_3]}Y_1, \qquad S_2 = I + Y_2'\tilde{Q}_{[Y_3]}Y_2.$$

Proof. Apply Lemma 2, twice. □

Notice that the inverses of three matrices remain to be calculated: S_1, S_2 and $(I + Y_3'Y_3)$. These matrices have dimensions that are the number of columns of Y_1, Y_2 and Y_3, respectively. Moreover, if the columns of Y_3 are a collection of indicator variables representing mutually exclusive groupings of the data,

$Y_3'Y_3$ will be diagonal and consequently, this third inversion can be performed analytically.[9]

Applying Lemma 2 multiple times, expressions for Ω^{-1} are easily obtained for the four- and five-way ECMs. In each case, the variance–covariance matrix is of the form $(I+XX')$. Indeed, since the lemma may be applied any number of times, models with an arbitrary number of error components can easily be developed. In each case, inversions of $n \times n$ matrices are avoided entirely and numerical inversion is avoided entirely in one dimension of the data.

4. Estimation of the variance components

The expression for Ω^{-1} reduces computational time considerably relative to inverting Ω numerically given any specified values of the variances of the error components. Various methods are available to estimate the variance components themselves. In this section, I develop analysis of variance type Quadratic Unbiased Estimators (QUEs) analogous to WK's QUEs for the two-way model. Then I present the Minimum Norm Quadratic Unbiased Estimator (MINQUE) developed by Rao (1971) and finally Maximum Likelihood Estimators (MLE).

4.1. Quadratic unbiased estimators

Define $e = y - X\hat{\beta}^{\mathrm{W2SLS}}$, $q_n = e'Q_{[\Delta]}e$ and $q_i = e'P_{[\Delta_i]}e$ for $i = 1,2,3$. In Lemma 3, I provide expressions for the expected values of q_n, q_1, q_2, and q_3. QUEs are obtained by solving the four equations that result from equating the observed quadratic forms q_n, q_1, q_2 and q_3 to their expectations for the parameters σ_0^2, σ_1^2, σ_2^2, and σ_3^2.

Lemma 3.

$$\mathrm{E}[q_n] = (n - t_1 - t_2 - t_3 + k_n)\sigma_0^2,$$

$$\mathrm{E}[q_1] = (N_1 + k_1)\sigma_0^2 + n\sigma_1^2 + k_{12}\sigma_2^2 + k_{13}\sigma_3^2,$$

$$\mathrm{E}[q_2] = (N_2 + k_2)\sigma_0^2 + k_{21}\sigma_1^2 + n\sigma_2^2 + k_{23}\sigma_3^2,$$

$$\mathrm{E}[q_3] = (N_3 + k_3)\sigma_0^2 + k_{31}\sigma_1^2 + k_{32}\sigma_2^2 + n\sigma_3^2,$$

[9] Judicious choice of Y_3 will minimize the dimension of the numerical inversions required. For example, in the application presented in Section 6, N_2 and N_3 are small relative to N_1, thus the required computational resources are minimized by setting $Y = (\sigma_2/\sigma_0\Delta_2, \sigma_3/\sigma_0\Delta_3, \sigma_1/\sigma_0\Delta_1)$ before applying the lemma.

where $k_n = tr\{(X'P_{[QZ]}X)^{-1}X'Q_{[\Delta]}X\}$, $k_i = tr\{(X'P_{[QZ]}X)^{-1}X'P_{[\Delta_i]}X\}$, $k_{ij} = tr\{\Delta_j'P_{[\Delta_i]}\Delta_j\}$ *for* $i,j = 1,2,3$, $t_1 = tr\{(A'A)^{-}A'A)\} = rank(A)$, $t_2 = tr\{(B'B)^{-}B'B\} = rank(B)$ *and* $t_3 = tr\{(C'C)^{-}C'C\} = rank(C)$,[10] *where* A, B, C *are defined as in corollary* 1.[11]

Proof. Let $M \equiv I_n - X(X'P_{QZ}X)^{-1}X'P_{QZ}$, then by definition $e = My = Mu$. Since $Q_{[\Delta]}\Delta_i = 0$ for $i = 1,2,3$, $Q_{[\Delta]}\Omega = \sigma_0^2 Q_{[\Delta]}$, $M\Omega = \Omega - \sigma_0^2 X(X'P_{QZ}X)^{-1}X'P_{QZ}$ and $M\Omega M' = \Omega - \sigma_0^2 X(X'P_{QZ}X)^{-1}X'P_{QZ} - \sigma_0^2 P_{QZ}X(X'P_{QZ}X)^{-1}X' + \sigma_0^2 X(X'P_{QZ}X)^{-1}X'$.

Since $P_{[\Delta_i]}P_{[QZ]} = 0$, $tr\{P_{[\Delta_i]}M\Omega M'\} = tr\{P_{[\Delta_i]}\Omega\} + \sigma_0^2 tr\{P_{[\Delta_i]}X(X'P_{QZ}X)^{-1}X'\} = tr\{P_{[\Delta_i]}\Omega\} + \sigma_0^2 k_i$. Hence,

$$E[q_i] = E[e'P_{[\Delta_i]}e] = tr\{P_{[\Delta_i]}M\Omega M'\} = tr\{P_{[\Delta_i]}\Omega\} + \sigma_0^2 k_i,$$

$$E[q_n] = E[e'Q_{[\Delta]}e] = tr\{Q_{[\Delta]}M\Omega M'\} = \sigma_0^2 tr\{Q_{[\Delta]}\} + \sigma_0^2 k_n.$$

The results follow immediately from these expressions since $tr\{P_{[\Delta_i]}\Delta_i\Delta_i'\} = n$, $tr\{P_{[\Delta_i]}\} = N_i$, and $tr\{Q_{[\Delta]}\} = tr\{I_n - P_{[A]} - P_{[B]} - P_{[C]}\} = n - t_1 - t_2 - t_3$. □

4.2. MINQUE estimation of the variance components

The MINQUE of a general error component model is developed in Rao (1971). Let

$$R = \Omega^{-1}[I_n - X(X'\Omega^{-1}X)^{-1}X'\Omega^{-1}]$$

$$S = \{s_{i+1,j+1}\} = \{tr\{V_iRV_jR\}\}, \quad i,j = 0,\dots,3 \text{ where}$$

$$u = \{u_{i+1}\} = \{y'RV_iRy\} \quad i = 0,\dots,3 \text{ with}$$

$$V_i = \Delta_i\Delta_i' \quad i = 0,\dots,3 \text{ and } \Delta_0 \equiv I_n.$$

Rao (1971) shows that the vector of MINQUEs is given by $\hat{\theta} = S^{-1}u$ where $\hat{\theta}' = (\hat{\sigma}_0^2, \hat{\sigma}_1^2, \hat{\sigma}_2^2, \hat{\sigma}_3^2)$. Clearly, an initial estimate of Ω is required to compute the matrix R, which is required to compute the MINQUE. The WK estimators provided in the previous sections provide one way to construct the required initial estimate of Ω. Appendix D provides the computational details.

---

[10] For any matrix A, $trace((A'A)^{-}A'A) = rank(A'A) = rank(A)$. The first equality follows since $(A'A)^{-}A'A$ is a projection matrix and the latter since the $range(A) = range(A'A)$. See, for example, Lancaster and Tismenetsky (1985, p. 430) and Ostaszewski (1990, p. 41), respectively.

[11] Notice that the constants k_{ij} just represent average sums of squares. For example, in the conventional error components model if Δ_1 and Δ_2 contain the indicator variable structure for products and locations, respectively, n_i denotes the total number of observations available on product i, and n_{ij} denotes the total number of observations available on product i at location j, then $k_{12} = tr\{\Delta_2'P_{[\Delta_1]}\Delta_2\} = \sum_{i=1}^{N_1} 1/n_i \sum_{j=1}^{N_2} n_{ij}^2$.

4.3. MLE and the information matrix

Amemiya (1971) studied maximum likelihood estimation of complete data ECMs. Applying the general results obtained by Magnus (1978), the first order conditions for ML estimation of β and the parameters in Ω are

$$\hat{\beta}=(X'\hat{\Omega}^{-1}X)^{-1}X'\hat{\Omega}^{-1}y, \tag{5}$$

$$tr\{\hat{\Omega}_{\theta}^{-1}\Omega\}=e'\hat{\Omega}_{\theta}^{-1}e, \quad \text{for } \theta=\sigma_0^2,\sigma_1^2,\sigma_2^2 \text{ and } \sigma_3^2 \tag{6}$$

with $e=y-X\hat{\beta}$ and Ω_{θ}^{-1} the partial derivative of Ω^{-1} with respect to θ. A well known result in matrix differentiation is that $\Omega_{\theta}^{-1}=-\Omega^{-1}\Omega_{\theta}\Omega^{-1}$ (see Magnus and Neudecker (1999) for example). Defining $\Delta_0\equiv I_n$, it follows immediately that

$$e'\Omega_{\theta}^{-1}e=-e'\Omega^{-1}\Omega_{\theta}\Omega^{-1}e=-e'\Omega^{-1}\Delta_i\Delta_i'\Omega^{-1}e \quad \text{if } \theta=\sigma_i^2,\ i=0,\ldots,3 \tag{7}$$

while

$$tr\{\Omega_{\theta}^{-1}\Omega^{-1}\}=-tr\{\Omega^{-1}\Omega_{\theta}\}=-tr\{\Delta_i'\Omega^{-1}\Delta_i\} \quad \text{if } \theta=\sigma_i^2,\ i=0,\ldots,3. \tag{8}$$

These expressions allow both sides of the first order conditions for the ML estimators of the variance components to be evaluated for each proposed value of the four parameters $(\sigma_0^2,\sigma_1^2,\sigma_2^2,\sigma_3^2)$. In Appendix C, I demonstrate that each of these expressions may easily be evaluated without explicitly calculating any $n\times n$ matrices. Thus, finding the MLEs amounts to finding a solution of these four equations in the four unknowns.[12] As usual, the recursive structure of the matrix algebra ensures that this is will also be true for the fourth or higher variance component models. In each case, good initial values are available from the QUE estimators derived previously.

Following Magnus (1978), the information matrix of the log-likelihood function is given by the $(k+4)\times(k+4)$ matrix

$$\Phi=\begin{bmatrix} X'\Omega^{-1}X & 0 \\ 0 & \frac{1}{2}\Phi_{\theta} \end{bmatrix},$$

where $(\Phi_{\theta})_{i+1,j+1}=tr\{\Omega_{\theta_i}^{-1}\Omega\Omega_{\theta_j}^{-1}\Omega\}=tr\{\Delta_i'\Omega^{-1}\Delta_j\Delta_j'\Omega^{-1}\Delta_i\}$ for $i,j=0,\ldots,3$, $\theta_i=\sigma_i^2$ and $\theta_j=\sigma_j^2$.

[12] In fact, by transforming the parameters of the model, the non-analytic dimensions of the first order conditions can be reduced to only three. Specifically, by writing the likelihood function in terms of β, σ_0^2 and the transformed parameters $\rho_i=\sigma_i^2/\sigma_0^2$, the MLE of σ_0^2 is available analytically for each value of β, ρ_1, ρ_2, ρ_3: $\hat{\sigma}_0^2=e'(I+\sum_{i=1}^{3}\rho_i\Delta_i\Delta_i')^{-1}e/n$.

In Appendix C, I demonstrate that each element in the information matrix may be calculated without explicitly evaluating any $(n \times n)$ matrices. In Appendix D, I provide an alternative method for directly evaluating the likelihood function.[13]

5. Monte Carlo simulations

5.1. *Design of the Monte Carlo study*

While previous Monte Carlo studies of ECMs with unbalanced data have considered designs which emphasize the traditional panel data context with observations missing in only one dimension (individuals are only observed in some time periods), I consider the simplest possible regression model with a three-way error component structure and data sets which are symmetrically unbalanced in multiple dimensions. Specifically, I use the data generating process

$$y_{ijk} = x_{ijk}\beta + \mu_i + \lambda_j + \gamma_k + v_{ijk},$$

where the exogenous variable $x_{ijt} \sim IIN(0,1)$, β is fixed at 1, $\mu_i \sim IIN(0,\sigma_1^2)$, $\lambda_j \sim IIN(0,\sigma_2^2)$, $\gamma_k \sim IIN(0,\sigma_3^2)$, and $v_{ijk} \sim IIN(0,\sigma_0^2)$. I fix the total variance of the error term to be $\sigma_0^2 + \sigma_1^2 + \sigma_2^2 + \sigma_3^2 = 1$ vary each σ_i^2 over the set $\{0, 0.2, 0.4, 0.6, 0.8\}$ such that $\sigma_0^2 = 1 - \sum_{i=1}^{3} \sigma_i^2 > 0$. Following Ahrens and Pincus (1981), I define the three, one-way, measures of unbalancedness

$$r_i = \frac{N_i^2}{tr\{(\Delta_i'\Delta_i)^{-1}\} tr\{\Delta_i'\Delta_i\}}, \quad i = 1,2,3.$$

Note that r_i takes the value 1 when the data are balanced in *both* of the other two dimensions, but takes on smaller values as the data pattern becomes more unbalanced. In contrast to the Monte Carlo studies for the two-way model reported in Baltagi and Chang (1994) and Baltagi et al. (1999a), who use an asymmetric design with unbalancedness in one dimension, I consider a

[13] Having provided an expression for the likelihood function and information matrix, Lagrange multiplier and likelihood ratio test statistics can easily be computed using the results developed in this section and Appendix C. The availability of likelihood ratio tests obviously follow directly from the ability to evaluate the likelihood function for any number of error components, while Lagrange multiplier tests require the derivative of the likelihood and the relevant component of the information matrix evaluated at the restricted parameter point:

$$\frac{\partial L}{\partial \theta} = -\frac{1}{2} tr\{\Omega^{-1}\Omega_\theta\} + \frac{1}{2} u'\Omega^{-1}\Omega_\theta\Omega^{-1}u \tag{9}$$

while

$$\mathrm{E}\left[-\frac{\partial^2 L}{\partial\theta_i \partial\theta_j}\right] = \frac{1}{2} tr\{\Omega^{-1}\Omega_{\theta_i}\Omega^{-1}\Omega_{\theta_j}\}. \tag{10}$$

symmetrically unbalanced design with unbalancedness in multiple dimensions and with $r_1 = r_2 = r_3$.[14] This difference reflects the differences in typical data sets; three dimensional data structures are often multi-dimensionally unbalanced while panel data unbalancedness arises from not observing all individuals in every time period (while some data is usually observed each time period.)

A symmetrically unbalanced data pattern with three dimensions of data variation can be described by the matrix $\{(a,b,c),(b,c,a),(c,a,b)\}$ where the first vector (a,b,c) denotes the data pattern: observe a products at b stores for c time periods. The second vector denotes observe b products at c stores for a time periods and so forth. Thus, the matrix generates a data set with $3 \times a \times b \times c$ observations. I report this symmetric pattern using the shorthand notation, (a,b,c). The advantage of this symmetric approach is that it provides a single index of unbalancedness while, at the same time, allowing multiple dimensions of unbalancedness.

I consider three unbalancedness patterns $(4,4,4)$, $(4,8,2)$ and $(2,16,2)$. The first is clearly a balanced data pattern, while the others are increasingly unbalanced. The AP statistics for these three patterns are 1, 0.777 and 0.505, respectively. For each case, I compute estimates of the variance components using the Wansbeek and Kapteyn (WK) method, the maximum likelihood estimator (MLE), and three types of MINQUE estimators corresponding to three initial values. MV_1 reports MINQUE taking the initial value of the variance components to each be equal to zero and the initial value of $\sigma_0^2 = 1$. MV_2 takes the initial value of $\sigma_i^2 = 1$, $i = 0,1,2,3$ and MV_3 takes the computationally more intensive approach of using the WK estimates as initial values. The results for the linear parameters also report OLS and the within (WTN) estimators for completeness.

5.2. *Comparison of the estimators*

Table 1 reports the mean square error (MSE) of the various estimators of β relative to that of true GLS. The results are relatively similar to those presented by Baltagi et al. (1999a) for the linear parameters in the two-way model. Specifically, OLS is inferior to GLS, MLE, MV_1, MV_2, and MV_3 unless $\sigma_1^2 = \sigma_2^2 = \sigma_3^2 = 0$, while it will be superior to the WTN estimator if the σ_i^2's are all sufficiently close to zero since OLS is equivalent to MLE in that case. The WK and MV estimators perform well relative to true GLS for a correctly specified three-way model and are much simpler to compute. Even when the model is misspecified, the simpler ANOVA methods

---

[14] In terms of the AP unbalancedness statistics, Baltagi and Chang (1994) and Baltagi et al. (1999a) consider designs which allow r_1 to vary, but constrain $r_2 = 1$. The symmetric design in the two-way case would consider the case where both r_1 and r_2 decrease, but do so with $r_1 = r_2$.

Table 1
Regression coefficient estimates[a]

Pattern	σ_1^2	σ_2^2	σ_3^2	GLS	OLS	WTN	WK	MLE	MV_1	MV_2	MV_3
(4,4,4)	0.00	0.00	0.00	1.00	1.00	1.19	1.01	1.01	1.01	1.01	1.01
(4,4,4)	0.00	0.00	0.20	1.00	1.14	1.14	1.02	1.01	1.02	1.02	1.01
(4,4,4)	0.00	0.00	0.40	1.00	1.86	1.13	0.99	0.98	0.99	0.99	0.99
(4,4,4)	0.00	0.00	0.60	1.00	2.39	1.17	1.04	0.99	1.05	1.02	1.01
(4,4,4)	0.00	0.00	0.80	1.00	3.85	1.06	1.02	0.99	1.02	1.00	0.98
(4,4,4)	0.00	0.20	0.20	1.00	1.58	1.03	1.01	1.00	1.01	1.00	1.00
(4,4,4)	0.00	0.20	0.40	1.00	2.57	1.08	0.99	0.99	1.00	0.99	0.99
(4,4,4)	0.00	0.20	0.60	1.00	4.02	1.07	1.08	1.03	1.12	1.03	1.02
(4,4,4)	0.00	0.40	0.40	1.00	4.80	1.00	1.00	1.00	1.01	0.99	1.00
(4,4,4)	0.20	0.20	0.20	1.00	2.11	1.02	1.04	1.04	1.05	1.00	1.00
(4,4,4)	0.20	0.40	0.20	1.00	5.36	1.01	1.04	1.05	1.04	1.00	1.00
(4,8,2)	0.00	0.00	0.00	1.00	1.00	1.26	1.01	1.02	1.02	1.01	1.02
(4,8,2)	0.00	0.00	0.20	1.00	1.21	1.18	1.01	1.01	1.01	1.02	1.02
(4,8,2)	0.00	0.00	0.40	1.00	1.27	1.17	1.01	1.01	1.02	1.00	1.00
(4,8,2)	0.00	0.00	0.60	1.00	2.48	1.07	1.02	1.01	0.98	1.01	1.00
(4,8,2)	0.00	0.00	0.80	1.00	4.94	1.27	1.08	1.01	1.11	1.04	1.04
(4,8,2)	0.00	0.20	0.20	1.00	1.28	1.13	1.00	0.99	1.03	0.98	0.98
(4,8,2)	0.00	0.20	0.40	1.00	1.94	1.05	1.03	1.02	1.07	1.01	1.01
(4,8,2)	0.00	0.20	0.60	1.00	5.12	1.14	1.06	1.03	1.14	1.03	1.02
(4,8,2)	0.00	0.40	0.40	1.00	3.97	1.03	1.04	1.01	1.12	1.01	1.00
(4,8,2)	0.20	0.20	0.20	1.00	1.72	1.05	1.01	1.02	0.99	1.01	1.01
(4,8,2)	0.20	0.40	0.20	1.00	4.16	1.01	1.07	1.04	1.17	1.00	1.00
(2,16,2)	0.00	0.00	0.00	1.00	1.00	1.36	1.01	1.00	1.00	1.03	1.01
(2,16,2)	0.00	0.00	0.20	1.00	1.18	1.14	0.99	0.99	0.98	1.01	0.98
(2,16,2)	0.00	0.00	0.40	1.00	1.48	1.18	1.02	1.01	1.05	1.01	1.00
(2,16,2)	0.00	0.00	0.60	1.00	2.36	1.20	1.02	1.01	1.07	1.03	1.02
(2,16,2)	0.00	0.00	0.80	1.00	4.24	1.35	1.04	1.00	1.11	1.00	1.01
(2,16,2)	0.00	0.20	0.20	1.00	1.65	1.20	1.06	1.03	1.11	1.04	1.05
(2,16,2)	0.00	0.20	0.40	1.00	2.11	1.00	0.99	0.98	1.07	0.99	0.97
(2,16,2)	0.00	0.20	0.60	1.00	4.12	1.15	1.01	1.02	1.20	0.99	0.99
(2,16,2)	0.00	0.40	0.40	1.00	5.27	1.15	1.06	1.02	1.28	1.01	1.00
(2,16,2)	0.20	0.20	0.20	1.00	2.02	1.13	0.98	0.95	1.10	0.99	0.98
(2,16,2)	0.20	0.40	0.20	1.00	4.30	1.03	1.07	1.04	1.38	1.01	1.02

[a]The table reports the mean squared error of the linear parameters, β, achieved by each estimation technique relative to the mean squared error achieved by GLS evaluated at the true parameter values. The Monte Carlo experiment uses 200 repetitions of each estimation procedure for each value of the parameters and each data unbalancedness pattern.

demonstrate relatively good performance. The only exception is MV_1 which performs poorly relative to the other estimators when the data is highly unbalanced. In contrast, if the data pattern is sufficiently unbalanced, the WTN estimator can suffer from non-trivial increases in MSE over GLS. For example, with the unbalanced data pattern 3, $\sigma_1^2=\sigma_2^2=0$, and $\sigma_3^2=0.8$ the WTN increase in MSE reaches 35%. Clearly, over-transforming the data in this way can lead to poor small sample performance of the within estimator.

Table 2
The ratio of the mean squared error of $\hat{\sigma}_0^2$, $\hat{\sigma}_1^2, \hat{\sigma}_2^2$ and $\hat{\sigma}_3^2$ from each estimation method relative to the mean squared error provided by MLE. All methods except MV_1 perform relatively well, but WK, MV_2 and MV_3 can perform better than MLE when most of the variance in the residual is coming from the error components rather than the idiosyncratic component of the error term. The Monte Carlo experiment uses 200 repetitions of each estimation procedure for each value of the parameters and each data unbalancedness pattern.

				$MSE(\hat{\sigma}_0^2)/MSE^{MLE}$				$MSE(\hat{\sigma}_1^2)/MSE^{MLE}$				$MSE(\hat{\sigma}_2^2)/MSE^{MLE}$				$MSE(\hat{\sigma}_3^2)/MSE^{MLE}$			
Pattern	σ_1^2	σ_2^2	σ_3^2	WK	MV_1	MV_2	MV_3	WK	MV_1	MV_2	MV_3	WK	MV_1	MV_2	MV_3	WK	MV_1	MV_2	MV_3
(4,4,4)	0	0	0	1.1	1.1	1.1	1.1	1.3	1.3	1.6	1.2	1.4	1.4	1.5	1.3	1.2	1.2	1.4	1.1
(4,4,4)	0	0	0.2	1.1	1.9	1.1	1.1	3.7	4.2	1.1	1.3	3.1	3.5	1.1	1.2	1.0	1.0	1.2	0.9
(4,4,4)	0	0	0.4	1.2	3.8	1.2	1.1	22.5	26.0	2.0	2.0	15.4	17.7	1.5	1.5	1.1	1.0	1.3	1.0
(4,4,4)	0	0	0.6	1.1	16.3	1.1	1.1	108.1	121.7	6.4	3.0	154.5	175.2	8.9	4.4	1.1	1.1	1.3	1.0
(4,4,4)	0	0	0.8	1.1	62.7	1.1	1.1	1617.3	1866.3	73.5	10.5	1418.4	1634.4	64.4	9.4	1.0	1.0	1.1	0.9
(4,4,4)	0	0.2	0.2	1.1	4.7	1.0	1.0	25.2	28.6	2.3	1.6	1.1	1.1	1.0	0.9	1.2	1.2	0.9	0.9
(4,4,4)	0	0.2	0.4	1.1	12.1	1.1	1.1	93.1	107.2	5.2	2.6	1.4	1.5	0.9	0.9	1.0	1.0	1.0	0.9
(4,4,4)	0	0.2	0.6	0.4	19.5	0.3	0.3	483.4	554.0	22.8	4.3	1.4	1.5	0.8	0.8	1.0	1.0	1.3	1.0
(4,4,4)	0	0.4	0.4	1.0	54.4	1.0	1.0	708.7	818.7	35.2	7.2	1.1	1.1	1.0	0.9	1.1	1.1	1.0	0.9
(4,4,4)	0.2	0.2	0.2	0.9	11.4	0.9	0.9	1.3	1.3	0.9	0.8	1.3	1.3	1.0	0.8	1.3	1.4	0.9	0.8
(4,4,4)	0.2	0.4	0.2	0.4	14.3	0.4	0.4	1.7	1.8	0.9	0.9	1.1	1.1	1.1	0.9	1.7	1.8	0.9	0.9
(4,8,2)	0	0	0	1.1	1.0	1.1	1.0	1.4	0.8	2.9	1.3	1.2	0.8	2.1	1.2	1.3	0.9	2.6	1.2
(4,8,2)	0	0	0.2	1.1	2.1	1.1	1.1	8.5	7.2	2.3	1.6	3.8	4.0	1.4	1.1	1.1	1.9	1.2	1.0
(4,8,2)	0	0	0.4	1.1	6.2	1.1	1.1	20.2	16.6	2.2	1.4	15.6	30.5	1.5	1.1	1.1	2.1	1.2	1.0
(4,8,2)	0	0	0.6	1.2	20.2	1.1	1.1	163.0	135.9	5.9	2.9	319.5	438.5	8.6	3.6	1.3	2.8	1.1	1.0
(4,8,2)	0	0	0.8	1.1	97.6	1.1	1.1	764.7	546.0	16.9	3.8	732.2	815.2	15.8	4.4	1.0	1.8	1.2	1.0
(4,8,2)	0	0.2	0.2	1.1	5.4	1.0	1.1	15.9	16.9	2.5	1.6	1.2	2.4	1.0	0.9	1.3	2.5	1.0	0.9
(4,8,2)	0	0.2	0.4	1.1	14.3	1.1	1.1	61.2	85.3	3.6	1.8	1.8	3.7	0.9	1.0	1.2	2.3	1.1	1.0
(4,8,2)	0	0.2	0.6	0.6	34.3	0.6	0.5	1220.6	1141.0	23.7	5.0	2.1	4.4	0.8	0.8	1.3	3.1	1.1	0.9
(4,8,2)	0	0.4	0.4	1.1	70.3	1.0	1.0	1066.7	2124.2	36.3	9.8	1.3	2.2	1.0	0.9	1.6	3.3	1.0	0.9
(4,8,2)	0.2	0.2	0.2	0.9	11.9	0.9	0.9	1.5	3.0	0.9	0.9	1.4	2.8	1.0	0.9	1.5	2.9	1.0	0.9
(4,8,2)	0.2	0.4	0.2	0.5	18.2	0.4	0.5	2.2	3.2	0.8	0.8	1.3	3.1	1.0	0.9	2.2	4.1	0.9	0.9

Table 2 (*continued*)

				$MSE(\hat{\sigma}_0^2)/MSE^{MLE}$				$MSE(\hat{\sigma}_1^2)/MSE^{MLE}$				$MSE(\hat{\sigma}_2^2)/MSE^{MLE}$				$MSE(\hat{\sigma}_3^2)/MSE^{MLE}$			
Pattern	σ_1^2	σ_2^2	σ_3^2	WK	MV_1	MV_2	MV_3	WK	MV_1	MV_2	MV_3	WK	MV_1	MV_2	MV_3	WK	MV_1	MV_2	MV_3
(2, 16, 2)	0	0	0	1.3	0.9	1.3	1.0	2.4	1.1	7.5	1.9	1.5	0.5	5.3	1.5	1.9	0.5	7.3	1.5
(2, 16, 2)	0	0	0.2	1.1	1.9	1.1	1.0	2.6	6.7	3.9	1.3	4.0	6.1	5.0	1.2	1.4	2.4	1.3	1.0
(2, 16, 2)	0	0	0.4	1.1	5.1	1.1	1.0	11.1	33.4	3.5	1.1	10.9	20.5	3.0	1.4	1.4	2.9	1.2	1.0
(2, 16, 2)	0	0	0.6	1.2	23.0	1.2	1.2	53.5	102.1	3.5	1.9	43.5	115.4	3.8	1.5	1.9	3.8	1.2	1.0
(2, 16, 2)	0	0	0.8	1.2	76.4	1.2	1.1	975.5	1804.3	15.4	3.6	650.3	1693.0	16.9	4.4	2.3	4.8	1.1	1.0
(2, 16, 2)	0	0.2	0.2	1.0	4.1	1.0	1.0	7.5	18.2	2.3	1.1	1.4	2.7	1.0	0.9	1.6	3.1	1.1	1.0
(2, 16, 2)	0	0.2	0.4	1.1	13.0	1.0	1.0	59.2	128.4	4.6	2.4	1.9	4.5	0.9	0.9	1.7	4.1	1.0	1.0
(2, 16, 2)	0	0.2	0.6	0.4	23.1	0.4	0.5	1367.9	3252.6	29.4	6.9	3.7	7.2	0.7	0.8	2.1	5.0	1.1	1.0
(2, 16, 2)	0	0.4	0.4	0.6	31.7	0.6	0.6	789.2	899.2	9.1	3.0	2.6	6.5	1.0	1.0	2.8	7.6	1.0	0.9
(2, 16, 2)	0.2	0.2	0.2	0.8	8.3	0.7	0.9	1.7	3.0	0.9	0.9	1.6	3.1	0.9	0.8	2.3	4.2	0.9	0.9
(2, 16, 2)	0.2	0.4	0.2	0.3	13.1	0.3	0.6	2.7	5.2	0.7	0.8	2.2	5.0	0.9	1.0	2.1	4.2	0.8	0.8

Table 2 reports the MSE of the variance components relative to that of MLE for the three unbalanced patterns considered. Not much difference between the WK, MV_2 and MV_3 estimates of σ_0^2 is evident in the table; however, all three show MSE performance which is significantly better than MLE when the true value of σ_0^2 generates 20% or less of the total variance in the error term and all the variance components are non-zero. Since MV_1 and MV_2 both use biased initial estimators of the variance components, one might expect both of these estimators to show poorer performance when the true values of the variance components differ substantially from the initial estimates. Somewhat surprisingly however, MV_1 performs poorly relative to MV_2 generally and demonstrates consistently worse performance and as σ_0^2 decreases toward zero.

The remaining columns report the MSE of the various estimators of σ_i^2 for $i = 1,\dots,3$ relative to the MSE of MLE. The most striking pattern in the table is that the WK, MV_1, MV_2, and MV_3 estimators are evidently not robust to the model misspecification when some, but not all, variance components in the data generating process are truthfully zero.

In contrast, the estimators each generally perform well whenever the *i*th variance component is truly non-zero. This is most clearly seen in the final four columns of the table since $\sigma_3^2 \neq 0$ in most of the table entries. Evidently, there are some efficiency losses due to WK and MV_1 since Table 2 shows that MV_2 and MV_3 estimators can benefit from as much as a 20–30% reduction in MSE relative to MLE, even when some of the random components are zero, *provided that the true value of* σ_i^2 *is non-zero.* However, these potential gains are very small relative to the potential for huge MSE losses incurred by not using MLE when the true σ_i^2 is in fact zero.

Qualitatively, these results are similar to those provided by Baltagi et al. (1999a) and indicate substantial gains from the computationally more intensive MLE estimator. Quantitatively however, the results are much less favorable for the WK estimator when the true value of the variance component is in fact zero; WK can have a MSE of more than a thousand times that of the MLE. The potential losses in MSE from using WK instead of MLE dwarf the magnitudes of the effects reported in Baltagi et al. (1999a).

6. Application: the demand for retail products

Berry (1994) demonstrates that discrete choice random utility models of differentiated product demand may be estimated from the linear equation[15]

$$y_{jht} = x'_{jht}\beta + \psi \ln(s_{jht|g}) + u_{jht}, \tag{11}$$

[15] The reader is directed to Davis (2000) and the references provided therein for a full discussion of this class of differentiated product demand models.

where $y_{jht} = \ln(s_{jht}/s_{ot})$, with s_{jht} the observed market share of product j selling at location h on date t, s_{ot} is the fraction of people choosing not to consume any of the products in the market on day t and x_{jht} represents the observed characteristics of the product, location and day. Berry (1994) demonstrates that if $\psi = 0$, the model corresponds to the multinomial logit model, while if $\psi \neq 0$, this corresponds to the nested multinomial logit model where $s_{jht|g}$ is the observed market share of jht given that one of the products in nest $g = 1, \ldots, G$ is purchased. In either case, the error term u_{jht} represents the unobserved (to the econometrician, but observed by the consumer) quality of the product and location on that day.

I estimate the demand model using data from a retail market, the motion picture exhibition market, in order to determine the between theater cross-price elasticity of demand.[16] The dataset consists of sales, price, and theater characteristics for six movie theaters, located near New Haven CT, from the six-week period (4/17/1998 to 5/28/1998.) This period coincides with a major marketing experiment undertaken by the Hoyts theater chain: for 3 weeks, during the middle of the sample period, Hoyts substantially reduced adult evening admission prices (from $7.75 to $5), and subsequently raised the adult admission price to $8. Several other local movie theaters immediately responded, reducing their prices for the same period. Daily sales data for each film playing in each theater during the period were obtained from *Entertainment Data Inc.* The number of weeks the film has played at a particular theater is also observed, while price and theater characteristics data were obtained separately by surveying individual theaters repeatedly during the six-week experiment.[17] Table 3 reports the theaters in the sample, the

[16] One particularly high profile issue in this market is the appropriate treatment of mergers between theater chains in highly concentrated local markets. For example, in the recent Sony Theaters and Cineplex–Odeon merger, antitrust concern resulted in forced divestiture of individual theaters in New York and Chicago on the presumption that these divestitures would sustain competition in the post-merger market. Obviously, determining appropriate regulatory treatment of proposed mergers requires an understanding of the substitutability of theaters in a market and for that reason determining own- and cross-price elasticities of demand in this market is a useful activity. Since admission prices rarely vary substantially either across films within a theater, or across theaters, either within or across theater chains, this marketing experiment provides a rare opportunity to observe demand responses to variation in prices in this market.

[17] On average, a film playing in a single location achieved revenues of $647 each day over the sample, but the data are highly skewed with one film achieving a daily box office of $13,608 in a single location. The number of weeks the film has played at the theater is also available. The average film plays for only 3–4 weeks; however, some films play for an extremely long time with one film in the sample achieving a run of 22 weeks at the same theater.

Table 3
Theaters in the sample

Theater	Chain	Pricing strategy during sample
1 Branford 12	HOYTS	$5 for 3 weeks
2 Milford Quad	National Amusements	No price change
3 Showcase Orange	National Amusements	$4.50 for 3 weeks
4 Showcase 5 Milford	National Amusements	No price change
5 Showcase 8 North Haven	National Amusements	$4.50 for 3 weeks
6 New Haven	York Square Cinema	No price change

theater chain which owned the theater, and their pricing strategy in response to Hoyts marketing experiment. [18]

Table 4 reports a selection of the 47 films in the sample and illustrates the major sources of unbalancedness in the dataset. First, not all films are shown in all locations. Second, films start and stop being shown at theaters during the sample period. This pattern is described in the table entries which are the number of days a film played at the theater during the sample period. In addition some revenue data are missing because of data reporting failures. [19] The Ahrens–Pincus unbalancedness statistics are $(r_{\text{time}}, r_{\text{theater}}, r_{\text{films}}) = (0.97, 0.72, 0.44)$, indicating that the data is approximately balanced in terms of number of observations for each day of data. In contrast, the data are substantially more unbalanced across theater locations and extremely unbalanced across films. Evidently, the Branford 12 theater is much larger than the Milford 4, hence we tend to see many more observations from the Branford 12 than from the smaller theaters. Similarly, some films show in more locations or for a longer time period than others.

The estimation results are reported in Table 5. The first five columns report various estimators of the multinomial logit demand equation, while the last three columns report nested multinomial logit results. The first column

[18] The pricing response of theaters provides important additional identifying information about the extent of substitution between the movie theaters. No price response by theater A to a price decrease at theater B indicates that the owners of theater A expect very little substitution will occur. This is useful information that can be incorporated into the demand model by using it to form groups or nests of products. Specifically, the two National Amusement theaters in Milford did not respond to Hoyts price experiment, therefore they are placed in one nest. In contrast, the National Amusement theaters in Orange and North Haven did change their prices in response to Hoyts's experiment. Thus, the Hoyts Branford 12 and these two National Amusement theaters are placed in a second nest. The York Square art house in downtown New Haven did not respond, so it is given its own nest. Finally, the fourth nest is the outside good.

[19] Each evening, *Entertainment Data* attempt to contact each theater either electronically or via telephone. Despite multiple attempts to contact the theater, inevitably some data are missing. Reasons that the sales data are missing include: the figures were not ready, only a recording could be reached, no one at the theater answered the phone and so forth.

Table 4
Data unbalancedness due to films only playing in some locations[a]

FILM	Theater no.						Total
	1	2	3	4	5	6	
AS GOOD AS IT GETS	14	0	7	0	0	21	42
BARNEYS GREAT ADVENTURE	35	0	35	0	0	0	70
BLACK DOG	21	14	0	0	14	0	49
BULWORTH	7	0	7	0	0	0	14
CHINESE BOX	0	0	0	0	0	7	7
CITY OF ANGELS	42	0	42	0	0	0	84
LOST IN SPACE	28	28	0	0	28	0	84
PAULIE	42	42	0	0	28	0	112
THE BIG HIT	28	7	0	21	21	0	77
TITANIC	42	0	21	21	21	0	105
TWO GIRLS AND A GUY	0	0	0	0	0	14	14
WOO	0	14	0	0	7	0	21
Total	588	196	350	119	273	147	1673

[a]This table reports the number of days a selection of films played at each location during the sample. The final row of the table reports total numbers of observations in the sample broken down by theater. Thus, the dataset provides a total of 1673 observations on 47 films that play in at least one theater during the six-week data period. The regression results use 1478 observations because sales figures are sometimes not observed as a result of electronic reporting failures.

reports the naive, inefficient, OLS estimator of the random effects model.[20] This naive estimator ignores the correlation structure in the errors, does not use all of the information in the sample optimally[21] and nicely illustrates the problems that result: the parameters of particular interest for the calculation of price elasticities are not well determined. The second column reports the estimates that would be obtained using the within regression.[22] The point estimates of the linear parameters obtained from the WK, MV_1, MV_2, and[23] MV_3

[20] Irrespective of the correlation structure, provided $E[u(\beta_0)|Z,\Delta]=0$, a standard instrumental variables estimator, $\beta^{\text{inefficient}}=(X'P_{[Z]}X)^{-}X'P_{[Z]}y$, provides a consistent estimator of the linear parameters. In this specification, all variables are assumed exogenous.

[21] Consistent estimates of the standard errors are reported, using the MLE estimates of the error components.

[22] These results are actually calculated using OLS on the full fixed effects model. To ensure comparability across the specifications, the R-squared reported in this column is the proportion of variance explained by the full model relative to a model with just film, time, and theater fixed effects.

[23] The estimates for MV_1 and MV_2 are not reported due to space limitations. The estimates of the linear parameters are quantitatively virtually identical to those obtained by MV_3. The vector of variance component estimates for MV_1 and MV_2 are $(0.092, 0.041, 0.407, 0.673)$ and $(0.499, 0.101, 1.665, 0.324)$, respectively.

Table 5

Parameter	OLS(1)		OLS(2)		WK		MV_3		MLE		WTN		2SLS		WK	
Const	−8.91**	(0.92)	−6.99**	(0.32)	−7.91**	(0.45)	−8.00**	(0.45)	−7.98**	(0.40)	.	.	−5.18**	(0.37)	−5.81**	(0.55)
Week	−0.21	(0.20)	0.01	(0.03)	−0.04	(0.03)	−0.01	(0.03)	−0.01	(0.03)	0.00	(0.03)	0.00	(0.03)	−0.01	(0.01)
Week2	0.01	(0.01)	−0.00	(0.00)	−0.00	(0.00)	−0.00	(0.00)	−0.00	(0.00)	−0.00	(0.00)	−0.00	(0.00)	−0.00	(0.00)
Sat	0.41	(0.43)	.	.	0.43	(0.51)	0.43	(0.44)	0.43	(0.42)	.	.	.	.	0.40	(0.49)
Sun	0.09	(0.43)	.	.	0.12	(0.51)	0.12	(0.44)	0.12	(0.42)	.	.	.	.	0.05	(0.49)
Mon	−1.06*	(0.43)	.	.	−1.11*	(0.51)	−1.11*	(0.44)	−1.11**	(0.42)	.	.	.	.	−1.14*	(0.49)
Tue	−1.39**	(0.43)	.	.	−1.50**	(0.51)	−1.50**	(0.44)	−1.51**	(0.42)	.	.	.	.	−1.52**	(0.49)
Wed	−1.32**	(0.43)	.	.	−1.51**	(0.51)	−1.51**	(0.44)	−1.52**	(0.42)	.	.	.	.	−1.38**	(0.49)
Thu	−1.33**	(0.43)	.	.	−1.49**	(0.51)	−1.50**	(0.44)	−1.50**	(0.42)	.	.	.	.	−1.40**	(0.49)
Prices	−0.03	(0.11)	−0.23**	(0.03)	−0.23**	(0.03)	−0.23**	(0.03)	−0.26**	(0.02)	−0.16**	(0.03)	−0.16**	(0.03)	−0.16**	(0.01)
$p * th2$	−0.04	(0.05)	0.04**	(0.01)	0.01	(0.05)	0.01	(0.05)	0.04**	(0.01)	−0.10	(0.40)	−0.11**	(0.02)	−0.11	(0.10)
$p * th3$	0.08	(0.05)	0.01	(0.03)	0.02	(0.03)	0.02	(0.03)	0.10**	(0.01)	0.01	(0.02)	0.01	(0.02)	0.01	(0.01)
$p * th4$	0.12	(0.07)	0.08**	(0.01)	0.06	(0.05)	0.05	(0.05)	0.08**	(0.01)	−0.07	(0.45)	−0.09**	(0.03)	−0.09	(0.10)
$p * th5$	0.10*	(0.04)	0.07*	(0.03)	0.07**	(0.03)	0.07**	(0.03)	0.08**	(0.01)	0.04	(0.03)	0.04	(0.03)	0.04**	(0.01)
$p * th6$	−0.01	(0.08)	0.13**	(0.03)	0.03	(0.06)	0.06	(0.07)	0.09**	(0.03)	−0.27	(2.04)	−0.23**	(0.06)	−0.24*	(0.12)
$\ln(sh_{jht\|\|g})$	.	.	.	.	.	.	.	.	.	.	0.66**	(0.09)	0.66**	(0.09)	0.64**	(0.05)
R^2	0.39		0.27		0.25		0.22		0.22		0.10		0.27		0.39	
Num.	1478.00		1478.00		1478.00		1478.00		1478.00		1478.00		1478.00		1478.00	
Estimated variance components																
σ^2_{time}					0.777		0.568		0.521**	(0.29)					0.731	
$\sigma^2_{theater}$					0.093		0.102		0.000	(0.04)					0.426	
σ^2_{film}					0.601		1.853		1.952**	(0.41)					0.211	
σ^2_{v}					0.313		0.319		0.317**	(0.01)					0.0.54	

**and * denote statistically different from zero at the 1% and 5% level of significance, respectively. All standard errors are computed assuming that the true data generating process corresponds to the three-way error components model. The variable "Price" is the adult evening admission price to the theater. "Weeks at theater" corresponds to the number of weeks the film had played at that particular theater. $p * th2$, say, denotes an interaction between price and a dummy variable indicating that the observation is from theater two. Day of the week fixed effects are included in each of the specifications but are collinear with time fixed effects included in the full fixed effects specification reported in OLS(2), in the 2SLS specification and are annihiliated by the within transformation so do not appear in those columns. The variance components modelled are: (i) A time random effect. This effect allows correlation in the error term across theaters and films within the time period that the data were observed. (ii) A "theater" random effect. This effect allows correlation in the errors across time and films for a given theater. (iii) A "film" random effect. This final effect allows errors to be correlated across theaters and time for a given film. The sixth column reports regression estimates from two-stage least-squares estimation of the within regression. The seventh column reports two-stage least-squares estimation of the full regression equation allowing for film, theater, and time fixed effects. The final column reports instrumental variable WK estimates of the random effects model. In the last three sets of estimates, $\ln(sh_{jht||g})$ is instrumented using the set of films playing in *other* theaters in the same group as theater h. All R^2 reported are the appropriate generalized R^2 for instrumental variable regressions, while for conformity, the 2SLS column reports the proportion of variance explained relative to a model which includes only fixed film, theater, and time effects.

estimators are similar to each other, but all perform poorly for correct inference about the price coefficients relative to MLE or the fixed effects estimator. In contrast, the estimates from OLS(2) and MLE are very similar except that the coefficient on $p * th3$ is larger and statistically significant in the MLE results. In this dataset, modeling the error components results in substantial increases in the precision with which the linear parameters are estimated relative to the naive estimator.

The estimates from the full model are also useful because they determine the correlation structure in the residuals and therefore provide relative contributions that each source of variance makes toward the total variance of the error term. While MV_2, MV_3 and MLE each provide similar estimates of the variance components, the WK and MV_1 estimates are quite different. This is precisely as the Monte Carlo simulations predicted; the true value of the theater random effect is evidently close to zero in the non-nested multinomial logit specifications.

Instrumental variable estimates of the nested multinomial logit are reported in the final three columns of the table.[24] First the within equation, then two stage least squares performed with film theater and time fixed effects and finally WK estimates are provided.[25] The general pattern of the estimates is similar to those found for the multinomial logit model. However, the additional parameter, ψ, representing the level of correlation between utilities within a group is also statistically highly significant in both specifications.[26]

Table 6 reports the estimated elasticities of demand between theaters in the sample for the nested multinomial model with three-way error components. Notice that the estimated cross-price elasticity between theaters not in the same group is essentially zero. Within group elasticities are always of the right sign and several are large. The predicted theater cross elasticities

[24] Berry (1994) argues that $\ln(s_{jht|g})$ will likely be high when the unobserved quality of product jht is high, hence an instrument for $\ln(s_{jht|g})$ must be constructed. The films that are playing at other theaters within the same nest will be correlated with $s_{jht|g}$, but are assumed uncorrelated with the unobserved quality of the film playing at that theater, u_{jht}. Consequently, they provide valid instruments to identify ψ. This identification assumption is standard in the differentiated product demand literature, but is certainly mildly troubling since there is a market which determines the way films are allocated to theaters. In the absence of obvious alternatives I follow the literature.

[25] Neither MV nor MLE estimators are provided for the nested model since, unfortunately, these estimators are not easily generalized to allow for instrumental variable estimation, although the former could probably be with some considerable effort.

[26] A Hausman misspecification test of the WK estimates relative to the within estimator is easily accepted indicating the random effects specification is not misspecified. The within estimator is consistent whether the effects are random or fixed, but inefficient if they are random. In contrast, the WK estimator is efficient if the effects are random but inconsistent if they are fixed. The Hausman statistic yields a value of 0.4, but is distributed as a $\chi^2(9)$ under the null hypothesis. Thus the null of correct specification cannot be rejected.

Table 6
Estimates of theater own and cross price elasticities[a]

	1	2	3	4	5	6
1	−2.78	0.002	0.683	0.003	0.545	0.004
2	0.005	−4.11	0.008	1.597	0.002	0.004
3	1.094	0.002	−2.26	0.003	0.823	0.004
4	0.005	2.033	0.008	−3.53	0.002	0.004
5	0.451	0.002	0.425	0.003	−2.30	0.004
6	0.004	0.002	0.006	0.002	0.002	−2.61

[a]Diagonal elements correspond to estimated own theater price elasticities of demand, while non-diagonal elements are theater cross-price elasticities of demand. The element $(h.k)$ in the table reports the elasticity of demand at theater h in response to a change in price at theater k. The table is not symmetric since these are theater cross-price elasticities of demand and the size of theaters and movies playing at each theater differs across theaters.

are asymmetric. For example, an increase in price at Hoyts 12 screen theater in Branford is found to have a significantly bigger impact on demand at National Amusement's showcase Orange than vice versa. This is intuitive since the latter is only an 8 screen theater. The estimates show that the art house theater is essentially a monopoly but one whose own-price elasticity is substantial. The theater facing the highest price elasticity of demand is the National Amusement Milford Quad, which would see a 4% decline in demand in response to a 1% increase in the admission price. The sister theater in Milford, also owned by National Amusements, would see a 2% rise in demand. Consistent with the observed price responses to Hoyts experiment, the estimates reveal little evidence of substitution between the groups of theaters, but considerable evidence of substitution within each of the groups.

7. Conclusions

In this paper I show that the econometric techniques required to construct efficient estimators allowing for instrumental variable estimation of multi-way error components models in unbalanced data structures involves simple and elegant generalizations of the panel data methods developed by Wansbeek and Kapteyn (1989). By presenting the results in terms of recurrence relations, feasible estimators for models with an arbitrary number of error components can be easily developed. In addition, the approach allows the analysis of the standard- and nested error component models to be unified, in contrast to their treatment to date. In fact, the inverse provided for the variance–covariance matrix is useful quite generally for estimating regression models with complex error structures. Where possible, I also generalize the results available from the literature by allowing for instrumental variable estimation of the linear parameters.

Monte Carlo simulation results for the three-way model yield three main conclusions. First, the mean-squared error of the linear parameters does not differ dramatically across the different error component estimation methods. Second, MLE performs considerably better than all the other suggested methods whenever the model is misspecified in the sense that at least one variance component is truthfully zero. Finally, when all variance components are truly non-zero, the various ANOVA methods appear to perform at least as well as the more computationally burdensome MLE.

I estimate a three-way error components version of the nested and non-nested multinomial logit model of demand for differentiated products with unobserved product characteristic using the formulation developed in Berry (1994). I use a new dataset constructed during a major marketing experiment in the motion picture exhibition market to estimate the parameters of the model and to provide estimates of the cross-price elasticity of demand between a group of geographically differentiated movie theaters. The estimates reveal a complex set of asymmetric cross-theater price elasticities of demand. These estimates are particularly useful for strategic decision making by the theater chains, for analysis of the impact of mergers on prices and for determining the appropriate extent of geographic market definition in these markets. The extent of appropriate geographic market definition is strikingly evident from Table 6. Further evaluation of these issues is beyond the scope of this paper, but several are explored further using a related dataset in Davis (1998).

Acknowledgements

Thanks are due to Steve Berry, Ariel Pakes, Nadia Soboleva, and Tom Stoker for helpful comments and suggestions. This paper is a substantially revised version of Chapter 3 of my Ph.D. dissertation which has benefited greatly from the suggestions of two anonymous referees and an associate editor of this journal. Financial Support from Yale University and the Robert M. Leyian Doctoral Fellowship Fund is gratefully acknowledged.

Appendix A. Proofs

Proof of Lemma 1. Partition the matrix X, so that $X = (X_1, X_2)$. Searle (1982, p. 263) shows that a generalized inverse of the matrix $X'X$ is given by

$$(X'X)^{-} = \begin{bmatrix} (X_1'X_1)^{-} & 0 \\ 0 & 0 \end{bmatrix} + \begin{bmatrix} -(X_1'X_1)^{-}X_1'X_2 \\ I \end{bmatrix}$$

$$\times (X_2'Q_{[X_1]}X_2)^{-} \begin{bmatrix} -X_2'X_1(X_1'X_1)^{-} & I \end{bmatrix}.$$

The lemma follows immediately by pre-multiplying this expression by X and post-multiplying by X'. □

Proof of Lemma 2. If A is $n\times m$ and B is $m\times n$, then $(I_n+AB)^{-1}=I_n-A(I_m+BA)^{-1}B$ provided $|I_m+AB|\neq 0$. Thus, $(I_n+XX')^{-1}=I_n-X(I+X'X)^{-1}X'$ (see for example Berk and Sydsæter (1993, p. 100)). Applying the partitioned inverse formula for matrices yields

$$(I+X'X)^{-1}=$$

$$\begin{pmatrix} S^{-1}, & -S^{-1}X_1'X_2(I+X_2'X_2)^{-1} \\ -(I+X_2'X_2)^{-1}X_2'X_1S^{-1}, & (I+X_2'X_2)^{-1}[I+X_2'X_1S^{-1}X_1'X_2(I+X_2'X_2)^{-1}] \end{pmatrix},$$

where $S=I+X_1'X_1-X_1'X_2(I+X_2'X_2)^{-1}X_2'X_1=I+X_1'\tilde{Q}_{[X_2]}X_1$. Consequently,

$$\begin{aligned} X[I+X'X]^{-1}X' &= X_1S^{-1}X_1'\tilde{Q}_{[X_2]}-\tilde{P}_{[X_2]}X_1S^{-1}X_1' \\ &\quad +\tilde{P}_{[X_2]}+\tilde{P}_{[X_2]}X_1S^{-1}X_1'\tilde{P}_{[X_2]} \\ &= \tilde{P}_{[X_2]}+\tilde{Q}_{[X_2]}X_1S^{-1}X_1'\tilde{Q}_{[X_2]} \end{aligned}$$

and hence $(I+XX')^{-1}=\tilde{Q}_{[X_2]}-\tilde{Q}_{[X_2]}X_1S^{-1}X_1'\tilde{Q}_{[X_2]}$. □

Appendix B. Results for the four-way model

Proof of Lemma 2. In the four-way model, $u=\Delta_1\mu+\Delta_2\lambda+\Delta_3\gamma+\Delta_4\delta+v$ and $\Omega=E[uu']=\sigma_0^2I_n+\sum_{s=1}^{4}\sigma_s^2\Delta_s\Delta_s'$. In this appendix I present three sets of results. Proofs are simple applications of the results provided in the paper and are consequently left to the reader.

Corollary 3 (Within transformation). *Let* $Y=(Y_1,Y_2,Y_3,Y_4)$, *then* $P_{[Y]}=P_{[A]}+P_{[B]}+P_{[C]}+P_{[D]}$ *where* $A=Y_4$, $B=Q_{[A]}Y_3$, $C=Q_{[B]}Q_{[A]}Y_2$ *and* $D=Q_{[C]}Q_{[B]}Q_{[A]}Y_1$.

Corollary 4 (Expression for Ω^{-1}). *If* $Y=(Y_1,Y_2,Y_3,Y_4)$ *and* $\Omega=\sigma_0^2(I+YY')$, *then* $\Omega^{-1}=\sigma_0^{-2}(I+YY')^{-1}$ *where* $(I+YY')^{-1}=\tilde{Q}_{[Y_2,Y_3,Y_4]}-\tilde{Q}_{[Y_2,Y_3,Y_4]}Y_1S_1^{-1}Y_1'\tilde{Q}_{[Y_2,Y_3,Y_4]}$, $\tilde{Q}_{[Y_2,Y_3,Y_4]}=\tilde{Q}_{[Y_3,Y_4]}-\tilde{Q}_{[Y_3,Y_4]}Y_2S_2^{-1}Y_2'\tilde{Q}_{[Y_3,Y_4]}$, $\tilde{Q}_{[Y_3,Y_4]}=$

$\tilde{Q}_{[Y_4]} - \tilde{Q}_{[Y_4]} Y_3 S_3^{-1} Y_3' \tilde{Q}_{[Y_4]}$, $\tilde{Q}_{[Y_4]} = I - Y_4(I + Y_4'Y_4)^{-1} Y_4'$, $S_1 = I + Y_1' \tilde{Q}_{[Y_2,Y_3,Y_4]} Y_1$, $S_2 = I + Y_2' \tilde{Q}_{[Y_3,Y_4]} Y_2$ *and* $S_3 = I + Y_3' \tilde{Q}_{[Y_4]} Y_3$.

Lemma 4 (QUE's of the variance components). *If* $e = y - X\hat{\beta}^{\text{W2SLS}}$, $q_n = e' Q_{[\Delta]} e$ *and* $q_i = e' P_{[\Delta_i]} e$, *for* $i = 1,2,3,4$. *Then,*

$$\mathrm{E}[q_n] = (n - t_1 - t_2 - t_3 - t_4 + k_n)\sigma_0^2,$$

$$\mathrm{E}[q_1] = (N_1 + k_1)\sigma_0^2 + n\sigma_1^2 + k_{12}\sigma_2^2 + k_{13}\sigma_3^2 + k_{14}\sigma_4^2,$$

$$\mathrm{E}[q_2] = (N_2 + k_2)\sigma_0^2 + k_{21}\sigma_1^2 + n\sigma_2^2 + k_{23}\sigma_3^2 + k_{24}\sigma_4^2,$$

$$\mathrm{E}[q_3] = (N_3 + k_3)\sigma_0^2 + k_{31}\sigma_1^2 + k_{32}\sigma_2^2 + n\sigma_3^2 + k_{34}\sigma_4^2,$$

$$\mathrm{E}[q_4] = (N_4 + k_4)\sigma_0^2 + k_{41}\sigma_1^2 + k_{42}\sigma_2^2 + k_{43}\sigma_3^2 + n\sigma_4^2,$$

where $k_n = tr\{(X'P_{[QZ]}X)^{-1} X' Q_{[\Delta]} X\}$, $k_i = tr\{(X'P_{[QZ]}X)^{-1} X' P_{[\Delta_i]} X\}$, $k_{ij} = tr\{P_{[\Delta_i]} \Delta_j \Delta_j',\}$ *for* $i,j = 1,2,3,4$, $t_1 = rank(A)$, $t_2 = rank(B)$, $t_3 = rank(C)$ *and* $t_4 = rank(D)$, *where* A, B, C, D *are defined in Corollary* 3.

Appendix C. Some useful matrix algebra

To calculate the MLE and MINQUE estimators, we would like to evaluate the matrix expressions developed above without ever explicitly calculating any $(n \times n)$ matrices. First, consider the matrix calculation $A\Omega^{-1}B$ for an arbitrary pair of matrices A and B, where A is $(a \times n)$ and B is $(n \times b)$. Applying the results and notation from the previous sections, in particular $X_1 = Y_1$, $X_2 = (Y_2, Y_3)$, we may recursively write

$$A\tilde{Q}_{[Y_3]}B = AB - (AY_3)(I + Y_3'Y_3)^{-1}(Y_3'B), \text{ while}$$

$$A\tilde{Q}_{[X_2]}B = A\tilde{Q}_{[Y_3]}B - (A\tilde{Q}_{[Y_3]}Y_2)S_2^{-1}(Y_2'\tilde{Q}_{[Y_3]}B), \text{ and therefore}$$

$$\sigma_0^2 A\Omega^{-1}B = A\tilde{Q}_{[X_2]}B - (A\tilde{Q}_{[X_2]}X_1)S_1^{-1}(X_1'\tilde{Q}_{[X_2]}B).$$

Since $A\tilde{Q}_{[Y_3]}B$ and $A\tilde{Q}_{[X_2]}B$ are $(a \times b)$ matrices that may be constructed without calculating any $(n \times n)$ matrices directly, so can any matrix of the form $A\Omega^{-1}B$. This approach can also be used for the other expressions we require for the maximum likelihood or MINQUE estimators, such as $tr\{\Omega^{-1}\}$, $e'\Omega^{-2}e$, $tr\{\Omega^{-2}\}$, $tr\{\Delta_j'\Omega^{-2}\Delta_j\}$, $\sigma_0^6 tr\{\Omega^{-3}\}$ and $A\Omega^{-3}B$. Let $\tilde{Q}_3 \equiv \tilde{Q}_{[Y_3]}$, $\tilde{Q}_2 \equiv \tilde{Q}_{[X_2]}$ and $\phi_1 = X_1 S_1^{-1} X_1'$. Then

$$\sigma_0^4 A\Omega^{-2}B = A(I + XX')^{-2}B = A(\tilde{Q}_2 - \tilde{Q}_2\phi_1\tilde{Q}_2)^2 B$$

$$= A\tilde{Q}_2^2 B - A\tilde{Q}_2^2\phi_1\tilde{Q}_2 B - A\tilde{Q}_2\phi_1\tilde{Q}_2^2 B + A\tilde{Q}_2\phi_1\tilde{Q}_2^2\phi_1\tilde{Q}_2 B, \text{ while}$$

$$\begin{aligned}\sigma_0^6 A\Omega^{-3}B &= A(I+XX')^{-3}B = A(\tilde{Q}_2 - \tilde{Q}_2 X_1 S_1^{-1} X_1' \tilde{Q}_2)^3 B \\ &= A\tilde{Q}_2^3 B - A\tilde{Q}_2^2\phi_1\tilde{Q}_2^2 B - A\tilde{Q}_2\phi_1\tilde{Q}_2^3 B + A\tilde{Q}_2\phi_1\tilde{Q}_2^2\phi_1\tilde{Q}_2^2 B \\ &\quad - A\tilde{Q}_2^3\phi_1\tilde{Q}_2 B + A\tilde{Q}_2^2\phi_1\tilde{Q}_2^2\phi_1\tilde{Q}_2 B + A\tilde{Q}_2\phi_1\tilde{Q}_2^3\phi_1\tilde{Q}_2 B \\ &\quad - A\tilde{Q}_2\phi_1\tilde{Q}_2^2\phi_1\tilde{Q}_2^2\phi_1\tilde{Q}_2 B.\end{aligned}$$

First note that any matrix with one of A, B, or ϕ_1 on either side is not a large $n \times n$ matrix and will be amenable to the bracketing technique. For instance, $A\tilde{Q}_2\phi_1\tilde{Q}_2^3\phi_1\tilde{Q}_2 B = (A\tilde{Q}_2 X_1)S_1^{-1}(X_1'\tilde{Q}_2^3 X_1)S_1^{-1}(X_1'\tilde{Q}_2 B)$.

Second, note that $A\tilde{Q}_2^m B = A\tilde{Q}_2^{m-1} B - (A\tilde{Q}_2^{m-1} X_2)(I + X_2'X_2)^{-1}(X_2'B)$ for all integers, $m \geqslant 0$ when $\tilde{Q}_2^0 \equiv I_n$. Then, since $A\tilde{Q}_2^1 B$ can be evaluated without explicitly evaluating any $n \times n$ matrices, by induction so can $A\tilde{Q}_2^m B$ for all integers $m \geqslant 1$ and hence each term in the expressions for $A\Omega^{-2}B$ and $A\Omega^{-3}B$ can be calculated numerically without ever evaluating any $n \times n$ matrices explicitly.

The trace expressions required are computable using the identical technique, viz., $\sigma_0^2 tr\{\Omega^{-1}\} = tr\{\tilde{Q}_2\} - tr\{S_1^{-1}X_1'\tilde{Q}_2^2 X_1\}$, where $tr\{\tilde{Q}_2\} = n - tr\{(I + X_2'X_2)^{-1}X_2'X_2\}$.

These calculations do require matrices of the form $(I_{dim\{X_2\}} + X_2'X_2)^{-1}$ to be numerically invertible, or else diagonal. However, if the number of columns of X_2 remains too large for this inverse to be computable, the inversion formula may easily be applied a second time to each expression involving $\tilde{Q}_2$. Specifically, $\tilde{Q}_2^s = (\tilde{Q}_3 - \tilde{Q}_3 Y_2 S_2^{-1} Y_2' \tilde{Q}_3)^s$ can be expanded by direct multiplication for any integer required $s = 1,2,3,4$ (or indeed beyond.) Each term in the expansion has the form $\tilde{Q}_3^m Y_2 S_2^{-1} Y_2' \tilde{Q}_3^2 Y_2 S_2^{-1} Y_2' \tilde{Q}_3^2 Y_2 S_2^{-1} Y_2' \ldots Y_2' \tilde{Q}_3^2 Y_2 S_2^{-1} Y_2' \tilde{Q}_3^r$ for some integers $r, m \geqslant 1$. Then any matrix of the form $A\tilde{Q}_2^s B$ can be written as the sum of products of matrices of the form $A\tilde{Q}_3^m Y_2$, $Y_2'\tilde{Q}_3^2 Y_2$ and $Y_2'\tilde{Q}_3^r B$ which may each be calculated without explicitly evaluating any $n \times n$ matrices and requiring only numerical or analytic inversion of a matrix of the form $(I_{dim\{Y_3\}} + Y_3'Y_3)^{-1}$ which has dimension of the columns of Y_3.

Appendix D. MINQUE

Construction of the matrix $S = \{s_{i+1,j+1}\} = tr\{V_i R V_j R\}$ involves

$$s_{i+1,j+1} = \begin{cases} tr\{RR\} & \text{if } i,j=0, \\ tr\{\Delta_j' R R \Delta_j\} & \text{if } i=0 \text{ and } j=1,\ldots,3, \\ tr\{\Delta_i' R \Delta_j \Delta_j' R \Delta_i\} & \text{if } i,j=1,\ldots,3, \end{cases} \tag{D.1}$$

while the vector u requires components $y'RRy$ and $y'R\Delta_i\Delta_i'Ry$ for $i = 1,\ldots,3$.

Given the matrix expressions provided in Appendix C, these matrix calculations are entirely straightforward. Let A and B denote arbitrary $(a \times n)$ and $(n \times b)$ matrices, then $ARB = A\Omega^{-1}B - A\Omega^{-1}X(X'\Omega^{-1}X)^{-1}X'\Omega^{-1}B$ and

$$\begin{aligned} ARRB &= A\Omega^{-2}B - A\Omega^{-1}X(X'\Omega^{-1}X)^{-1}X'\Omega^{-2}B \\ &\quad - A\Omega^{-1}X(X'\Omega^{-1}X)^{-1}X'\Omega^{-2}B + A\Omega^{-1}X(X'\Omega^{-1}X)^{-1} \\ &\quad \times X'\Omega^{-2}X(X'\Omega^{-1}X)^{-1}X'\Omega^{-1}B, \text{ hence} \\ tr\{RR\} &= tr\{\Omega^{-2}\} - 2tr\{(X'\Omega^{-1}X)^{-1}X'\Omega^{-3}X\} \\ &\quad + tr\{(X'\Omega^{-1}X)^{-1}X'\Omega^{-2}X(X'\Omega^{-1}X)^{-1}X'\Omega^{-2}X\}, \text{ while} \\ tr\{\Delta_i'RR\Delta_i\} &= tr\{\Delta_i'\Omega^{-2}\Delta_i - \Delta_i'\Omega^{-1}X(X'\Omega^{-1}X)^{-1}X'\Omega^{-2}\Delta_i \\ &\quad - \Delta_i'\Omega^{-1}X(X'\Omega^{-1}X)^{-1}X'\Omega^{-2}\Delta_i + \Delta_i'\Omega^{-1}X(X'\Omega^{-1}X)^{-1} \\ &\quad \times X'\Omega^{-2}X(X'\Omega^{-1}X)^{-1}X'\Omega^{-1}\Delta_i\} \end{aligned}$$

while $tr\{\Delta_i'R\Delta_j\Delta_j'R\Delta_i\}$ may be directly computed using ARB with $A = \Delta_i'$ and $B = \Delta_j$.

Appendix E. Maximum likelihood estimation

An alternative method for obtaining the ML estimators involves directly numerically maximizing the log likelihood function, $L = -\frac{n}{2}\ln 2\pi + \frac{1}{2}\ln|\Omega^{-1}| - \frac{1}{2}u'\Omega^{-1}u$. I have already provided a computationally efficient expression for the term $u'\Omega^{-1}u$. It remains to provide a convenient expression for $|\Omega^{-1}|$ using the well known matrix result that for any $(n \times m)$ matrix A and $(m \times n)$ matrix B, $|I_n + AB| = |I_m + BA|$ (see Berk and Sydsæter (1993, p. 95)). Specifically, $|\Omega^{-1}| = \sigma_0^{-2n}|(I + XX')^{-1}|$, so

$$\begin{aligned} |(I + XX')^{-1}| &= |\tilde{Q}_{[X_2]}|.|I_n - X_1S_1^{-1}X_1'\tilde{Q}_{[X_2]}| \\ &= |\tilde{Q}_{[X_2]}|.|I_{N_1} - S_1^{-1}X_1'\tilde{Q}_{[X_2]}X_1|, \text{ where} \end{aligned}$$

$$\begin{aligned} |Q_{[X_2]}| &= |(I_n + X_2X_2')^{-1}| = |I_n - X_2(I + X_2'X_2)^{-1}X_2'| \\ &= |I_{\dim\{X_2\}} - (I + X_2'X_2)^{-1}X_2'X_2|. \end{aligned}$$

As usual, if $\dim\{X_2\}$ remains too large for computational convenience, the same process may once again be repeated, viz.,

$$|\tilde{Q}_{[X_2]}| = |\tilde{Q}_{[Y_3]}|.|I_n - Y_2S_2^{-1}Y_2'\tilde{Q}_{[Y_3]}| = |\tilde{Q}_{[Y_3]}|.|I_{dim\{Y_2\}} - S_2^{-1}Y_2'\tilde{Q}_{[Y_3]}Y_2| \text{ where}$$

$$|\tilde{Q}_{[Y_3]}| = |I_{dim\{Y_3\}} - (I + Y_3'Y_3)^{-1}Y_3'Y_3|.$$

Appendix F. Modified Wallace and Hussain (WH) estimators

Wallace and Hussain (1969) suggest using the OLS residuals instead of the true disturbances to estimate the variance components in a balanced two-way model. Baltagi and Chang (1994) extend the approach to consider the one-way unbalanced model. More generally, allowing for a two-stage least squares estimator, the approach leads to the quadratic forms

Lemma 5. If $q_n = \hat{u}'_{2SLS} Q_{[\Delta]} \hat{u}_{2SLS}$ *and* $q_i = \hat{u}'_{2SLS} P_{[\Delta_i]} \hat{u}_{2SLS}$ *for* $i = 1,2,3$. *Then,*

$$E[q_n] = \left(n - \sum_{s=1}^{3} t_s - 2tr\{Q_{[\Delta]}\psi\} + tr\{\psi' Q_{[\Delta]}\psi\} \right) \sigma_0^2 + \sum_{j=1}^{3} \sigma_j^2 tr\{\Delta_j' \psi' Q_{[\Delta]} \psi \Delta_j\},$$

$$E[q_i] = (N_i - 2tr\{P_{[\Delta_i]}\psi\} + tr\{\psi' P_{[\Delta_i]}\psi\})\sigma_0^2 + \sum_{j=1}^{3} \sigma_j^2 (k_{ij} - 2a_{ij} + b_{ij}),$$

where $k_{ij} = tr\{P_{[\Delta_i]}\Delta_j \Delta_j'\}$, $a_{ij} = tr\{\Delta_j' P_{[\Delta_i]} \psi \Delta_j\}$, $b_{ij} = tr\{\Delta_j' \psi' P_{[\Delta_i]} \psi \Delta_j\}$, $\psi = X(X'P_{[Z]}X)^{-1}X'P_{[Z]}$, $t_1 = rank(A)$, $t_2 = rank(B)$ *and* $t_3 = rank(C)$, *where A, B, C are defined in Corollary* 1.

Proof. Let $M = I - X(X'P_{[Z]}X)^{-1}X'P_{[Z]}$ so that $\hat{u}_{2SLS} = My = Mu$. Notice that $tr\{Q_{[\Delta]}\} = n - t_1 - t_2 - t_3$, $tr\{P_{[\Delta_i]}\} = N_i$ and

$$E[q_n] = E[u'M'Q_{[\Delta]}Mu] = tr\{M'Q_{[\Delta]}M\Omega\}$$

$$= \sigma_0^2 tr\{M'Q_{[\Delta]}M\} + \sum_{j=1}^{3} \sigma_i^2 tr\{\Delta_j' M' Q_{[\Delta]} M \Delta_j\}, \text{ while}$$

$$E[q_i] = E[u'M'P_{[\Delta_i]}Mu] = tr\{M'P_{[\Delta_i]}M\Omega\}$$

$$= \sigma_0^2 tr\{M'P_{[\Delta_i]}M\} + \sum_{j=1}^{3} \sigma_j^2 tr\{\Delta_j' M' P_{[\Delta_i]} M \Delta_j\}, \text{ where}$$

$$tr\{M'P_{[\Delta_i]}M\} = tr\{P_{[\Delta_i]}\} - 2tr\{P_{[\Delta_i]}\psi\} + tr\{\psi' P_{[\Delta_i]}\psi\},$$

$$tr\{M'Q_{[\Delta]}M\} = tr\{Q_{[\Delta]}\} - 2tr\{Q_{[\Delta]}\psi\} + tr\{\psi' Q_{[\Delta]}\psi\},$$

$$tr\{\Delta_j' M' P_{[\Delta_i]} M \Delta_j\} = k_{ij} - 2a_{ij} + b_{ij} \quad \text{and}$$

$$tr\{\Delta_j' M' Q_{[\Delta]} M \Delta_j\} = tr\{\Delta_j' \psi' Q_{[\Delta]} \psi \Delta_j\}.$$

References

Ahrens, H., Pincus, R., 1981. On two measures of unbalancedness in a one-way model and their relation to efficiency. Biometric Journal 23, 227–235.

Amemiya, T., 1971. The estimation of the variances in a variance–covariance model. International Economic Review 12, 1–13.

Amemiya, T., MaCurdy, T.E., 1986. Instrumental-variable estimation of an error components model. Econometrica 54 (4), 869–880.

Antweiler, W., 2001. Nested random effects estimation in unbalanced panel data. Journal of Econometries 101 (2), 295–313.

Arellano, M., Bond, S., 1991. Some tests of specification for panel data: Monte Carlo evidence and an application to employment equations. Review of Economic Studies 58, 277–297.

Arellano, M., Bover, O., 1995. Another look at the instrumental variable estimation of error-components models. Journal of Econometrics 68 (1), 29–51.

Balestra, P., Nerlove, M., 1973. Pooling cross section and time series data in the estimation of a dynamic model: the demand for natural gas. Journal of Econometrics 1, 17–28.

Baltagi, B.H., 1981. Simultaneous equations with error components. Journal of Econometrics 17, 189–200.

Baltagi, B.H., 1985. Pooling cross-sections with unequal time series lengths. Economics Letters 18, 133–136.

Baltagi, B.H., 1987. On Estimating from a more general time series cum cross-section data structure. The American Economist.

Baltagi, B.H., 1995. Econometric Analysis of Panel Data. Wiley, Chichester, UK.

Baltagi, B.H., Chang, Y.J., 1994. Incomplete panels: a comparative study of alternative estimators for the unbalanced one-way error component regression model. Journal of Econometrics 62, 67–89.

Baltagi, B.H., Song, S.H., Jung, B.C., 1999a. Further evidence on the unbalanced nested error component regression model. Discussion paper, Texas A&M University.

Baltagi, B.H., Song, S.H., Jung, B.C., 2001. The unbalanced nested error component regression model. Journal of Econometrics 101 (2), 357–381.

Berk, P., Sydsæter, K., 1993. Economists' Mathematical Manual. Springer, Germany.

Berry, S., 1994. Estimating discrete-choice models of product differentiation. Rand Journal of Economics 25, 242–262.

Berry, S., Levinsohn, J., Pakes, A., 1995. Automobile prices in market equilibrium. Econometrica 63, 841–890.

Davis, P., 1998. Spatial competition in retail markets: movie theaters. Mimeo, MIT, Cambridge, MA.

Davis, P., 2000. Empirical models of demand for differentiated products. European Economic Review (papers and proceedings) 44 (4–6), 993–1005.

Fuller, W.A., Batese, G.E., 1974. Estimation of linear functions with crossed-error structure. Journal of Econometrics 2, 67–78.

Fuller, W.A., Battesse, G.E., 1973. Transformations for estimation of linear models with nested error structures. Journal of the American Statistical Association 68, 626–632.

Ghosh, S.K., 1976. Estimating from a more general time series cum cross-section data structure. The American Economist 20, 15–21.

Hansen, L., 1982. Large sample properties of generlized method of moment estimators. Econometrica 50, 1029–1954.

Hausman, J., Taylor, W., 1981. Panel data and unobservable individual effects. Econometrica 49 (6), 1377–1398.

Lancaster, P., Tismenetsky, M., 1985. The Theory of Matrices, 2nd Edition. Computer Science and Applied Mathematics. Academic Press, New York.

Magnus, J.R., 1978. Maximum likelihood estimation of the GLS model with unknown parameters in the disturbance covariance matrix. Journal of Econometrics 7 (3), 281–312.

Magnus, J.R., Neudecker, H., 1999. Matrix Differential Calculus with Applications in Statistics and Econometrics. Wiley, New York.

Mazodier, P., 1972. l'Estimation des modèles à erreurs composées. Annales de l'INSEE 7, 43–72.

Nerlove, A., 1971a. Further evidence on the estimation of dynamic economic relations from a time series of cross sections. Econometrica 39, 359–382.

Nerlove, M., 1971b. A note on error components models. Econometrica 39, 383–396.

Ostaszewski, A., 1990. Advanced Mathematical Methods. Cambridge University Press, Cambridge, UK.

Pakes, A., 1983. On group effects and errors in variables in aggregation. Review of Economics and Statistics 65 (1), 168–173.

Rao, R.C., 1971. Estimation of variance and covariance components-MINQUE theory. Journal of Multivariate Analysis 1, 257–275.

Searle, S.R., 1982. Matrix Algebra Useful for Statistics. Wiley, New York.

Wallace, T.D., Hussain, A., 1969. The use of error components models in combining cross-section and time-series data. Econometrica 37, 55–72.

Wansbeek, T., Kapteyn, A., 1989. Estimation of the error-components model with incomplete panels. Journal of Econometrics 41 (3), 341–361.

Part IV
Pseudo-Panels

[15]

ELSEVIER

Journal of Econometrics 82 (1997) 37–62

JOURNAL OF
Econometrics

Estimating dynamic models from time series of independent cross-sections

M. Dolores Collado*

Universidad Carlos III de Madrid, Calle Madrid 126, 28903 Getafe (Madrid), Spain

Received 1 September 1992; final version received 1 August 1996

Abstract

The purpose of this paper is to analyze the estimation of dynamic models from time series of independent cross-sections. The population is divided into groups with fixed membership (cohorts) and the cohort sample means are used as a panel subject to measurement errors. We propose measurement-error corrected estimators and analyze their asymptotic properties. We also calculate the asymptotic biases of the non-corrected estimators for the AR(1) model to check up to what extent the measurement-error correction is needed. Finally, we carry out the Monte Carlo simulations to evaluate the performance of our estimators in finite samples. © 1997 Elsevier Science S.A.

Keywords: Time series of cross-sections; Cohorts; Measurement errors; Asymptotic bias
JEL classification: C23

1. Introduction

The advantages of using panel data to estimate models of individual behaviour have been repeatedly stressed in the literature and are well known. However, for many countries there are no panel data sets available with the information required to estimate some of these models. For example, in the UK there is no panel data on household expenditures and labour supply. However,

* Tel.: 341-6249861; fax: 341-6429849; e-mail: collad@eco.uc3m.es

I would like to thank Manuel Arellano, Steve Bond, Martin Browning, Danny Quah and four anonymous referees for helpful comments. I also acknowledge the financial support from the Bank of Spain, and the research facilities provided by the Centre for Economic Performance at the LSE and CEMFI (Madrid).

PII S0304-4076(97)00015-8

a large survey on consumer expenditures and labour supply (The Family Expenditure Survey) is carried out with a regular periodicity. The pioneer work of Deaton (1985) opens an alternative possibility to estimate models of individual behaviour using micro data. If we have time series of independent cross-sections, that is, if we observe independent samples of individuals for different periods of time, we can divide the population into groups (cohorts) so that each group contains the same individuals over time. Then, we can calculate the sample means for each group on each time period, and we can use the sample means as a panel subject to measurement errors.[1]

The cohort population means have a genuine panel structure given that at the population level the groups contain the same individuals over time. However, the sample means are only consistent estimators of the true cohort population means, and therefore, when we work with the sample means we will have a measurement error problem.[2] The advantage in this case is that we can estimate the variance of the measurement errors using the individual survey data. Then, we can use these estimates to correct the classical estimators for panel data. Deaton (1985) proposes a measurement-error corrected within-groups estimator for the static model with individual effects, which is consistent for a fixed number of observations per cohort. He analyzes the asymptotic properties of this estimator. Verbeek and Nijman (1993) modify Deaton's estimator to achieve consistency for a fixed number of time periods and a fixed number of individuals per cohort.

Obviously, the larger the number of observations per cohort the less severe the measurement error problem will be. However since, in practice, the cross-section dimension is finite there is a trade off between the number of observations per group and the number of groups.[3] In applied studies with cohort data (see Browning et al., 1985; Attanasio and Weber, 1993; Blundell et al., 1994), the population is normally divided into small number of groups with quite a large number of observations in each, and the sample means are treated as a genuine panel. Verbeek and Nijman (1992) study under which conditions this approach would be valid. They also consider the impact of the cohort sizes on the bias of the classical within-groups estimator for the static model with individual effects.

---

[1] Notice that a model with lagged endogenous variables or a model with unobservable individual effects correlated with the explanatory variables is not identified on the basis of a single cross-section.

[2] The standard linear regression model aggregates exactly and therefore the measurement error problem is irrelevant in such a case. However, in a model with lagged endogenous variables or fixed effects the measurement error problem can be rather serious.

[3] The cross-section sizes of the most widely used data sets are around 2000–6000 observations. If we want to have groups of about 200 observations we will only have 10–30 groups.

In this paper, we deal with the estimation of a dynamic model with individual effects using time series of cross-sections. We propose a generalized method of moments (GMM) estimator corrected for measurement errors. This estimator is consistent as the number of cohorts tends to infinity, for a fixed number of time periods and a fixed number of individuals per cohort. We derive the asymptotic distribution of our estimator. We also consider a measurement-error corrected within-groups estimator, which is consistent as the number of time periods tends to infinity. Moffitt (1993) also considers the estimation of a dynamic model from time series of cross-sections. However, his approach is different, and the estimator that he proposes is consistent only if the number of observations per cohort tends to infinity and there are no cohort effects, while in our approach the number of observations per cohort is fixed and the individual effects do not cancel out at the cohort level. Despite the differences in the asymptotics and the assumptions in the underlying model, it is of interest to compare both approaches in our context, so that we have included Moffitt's estimator in our Monte Carlo experiments.[4] We do not attempt to analyze the influence of the cohort design on the performance of the estimators proposed. This topic is very interesting and relevant for practical applications but it is left for further research.

The paper is organized as follows. In Section 2 we construct a measurement-error corrected GMM estimator for the static regression model which sets the framework that we are going to use in the rest of the paper. In Section 3, we extend this procedure to deal with dynamic models. In Section 4, we calculate analytic formulae for the asymptotic bias of different estimators for the AR(1) model, and analyze the size of the biases for different values of the parameters of the model. In Section 5, we carry out Monte Carlo simulations, and discuss the performance in finite samples of the estimators proposed.

2. Errors-in-variable estimator for the static model

Consider the static regression model with individual effects

$$y_{it} = x'_{it}\beta + \theta_i + v_{it} \qquad v_{it} \sim \text{iid}(0, \sigma^2) \quad \theta_i \sim \text{iid}(0, \sigma_\theta^2), \tag{2.1}$$

where y_{it} is the dependent variable for individual i at time t, x_{it} is a vector of explanatory variables, θ_i is the individual effect, and v_{it} is the disturbance term. We assume that $\mathrm{E}(x_{it}v_{is}) = 0 \ \forall t, s$. If the individual effects are correlated with

---

[4] Notice that, as explained above, Moffitt's estimator was proposed for a model without cohort effects. Therefore, since our model do have cohort effects, we may expect Moffitt's estimator to be biased in our simulations.

the explanatory variables, the model cannot be identified with a single cross-section, unless external instruments are available. If the data available are time series of independent cross-sections the model cannot be directly estimated using panel data techniques, since the individuals are different from period to period. However, the population can be divided into groups with fixed membership over time (cohorts) according to a certain characteristic. Let g be a random variable which determines the cohort membership for each individual (i.e. for any individual $i \in c$ if and only if $g_i \in I_c$). Taking expectations conditional on g_i in model (2.1), we have

$$\mathrm{E}(y_{it}/g_i \in I_c) = \mathrm{E}(x_{it}/g_i \in I_c)'\beta + \mathrm{E}(\theta_i/g_i \in I_c) + \mathrm{E}(v_{it}/g_i \in I_c) \qquad \begin{matrix} c = 1,\dots,C, \\ t = 1,\dots,T. \end{matrix} \tag{2.2}$$

A necessary condition for identification is that the cohort population means of all the explanatory variables do vary across cohorts and over time.

We can rewrite (2.2) using a simple notation as

$$y_{ct}^{*} = x_{ct}^{*\prime}\beta + \theta_c^{*} + v_{ct}^{*} \qquad \begin{matrix} c = 1,\dots,C & v_{ct}^{*} \sim \mathrm{iid}(0, \sigma_{v^*}^2), \\ t = 1,\dots,T & \theta_c^{*} \sim \mathrm{iid}(0, \sigma_{\theta^*}^2). \end{matrix} \tag{2.3}$$

where $y_{ct}^{*} = \mathrm{E}(y_{it}/g_i \in I_c)$, $x_{ct}^{*} = \mathrm{E}(x_{it}/g_i \in I_c)$, etc. We assume that the v_{ct}^{*}s are uncorrelated with the explanatory variables, while the cohort effects are potentially correlated.

Model (2.3) cannot be directly estimated because we do not observe the cohort population means. However, we do observe a certain number of individuals on each group for each time period. We can assume that for any individual in a given cohort c

$$\begin{matrix} y_{it} = y_{ct}^{*} + \zeta_{it} \\ x_{it} = x_{ct}^{*} + \eta_{it} \end{matrix} \qquad \begin{pmatrix} \zeta_{it} \\ \eta_{it} \end{pmatrix} \Big/ g_i \in I_c \sim \mathrm{iid}\left(\begin{pmatrix} 0 \\ 0 \end{pmatrix}, \begin{pmatrix} \sigma_\zeta^2 & \sigma_{\zeta\eta}' \\ \sigma_{\zeta\eta} & \Sigma_\eta \end{pmatrix} \right).$$

Then, we can consider the sample mean of the observations for each cohort in each time period

$$\frac{1}{nc}\sum_{i \in c} y_{it} = y_{ct}^{*} + \frac{1}{nc}\sum_{i \in c} \zeta_{it} \qquad y_{ct} = y_{ct}^{*} + \zeta_{ct}$$

$$\frac{1}{nc}\sum_{i \in c} x_{it} = x_{ct}^{*} + \frac{1}{nc}\sum_{i \in c} \eta_{it} \qquad x_{ct} = c_{ct}^{*} + \eta_{ct}$$

$$\begin{pmatrix} \zeta_{ct} \\ \eta_{ct} \end{pmatrix} \sim \mathrm{iid}\left(\begin{pmatrix} 0 \\ 0 \end{pmatrix}, \frac{1}{nc}\begin{pmatrix} \sigma_\zeta^2 & \sigma_{\zeta\eta}' \\ \sigma_{\zeta\eta} & \Sigma_\eta \end{pmatrix} \right), \tag{2.4}$$

where nc is the number of individuals per cohort.[5] The sample means can be used as a panel subject to measurement errors.

The covariance matrix of $(\zeta_{it}, \eta_{it})'/g_i \in I_c$ and the variance of the v^*s can and will normally depend on the choice of the cohorts. The only assumption we are making here is that the cohorts are chosen so that, the covariance matrix of $(\zeta_{it}, \eta_{it})'/g_i \in I_c$ does not depend on the particular cohort to which the individual belongs.[6] The validity of this assumption will rely on the homogeneity of the cohorts chosen. The measurement error covariance matrix in (2.4) will in general be unknown, but it can be estimated using the micro survey data.

Using (2.4), we can rewrite (2.3) in terms of the cohort sample means as

$$\begin{aligned} y_{ct} &= x'_{ct}\beta + \theta^*_c + u_{ct} \qquad & c = 1,\dots,C, \\ u_{ct} &= v^*_{ct} + \zeta_{ct} - \eta'_{ct}\beta \qquad & t = 1,\dots,T. \end{aligned} \tag{2.5}$$

As mentioned earlier, the cohort effects in (2.5) are potentially correlated with the explanatory variables in the model. However, when we work with genuine panel data, we can easily eliminate those effects using any operator orthogonal to the unity vector (e.g. first differences, deviations from time means, etc.).

Let us consider model (2.5) in first differences as a system of equations

$$\begin{matrix} \Delta y_{c2} = \Delta x'_{c2}\beta + \Delta u_{c2} \\ \cdots\cdots\cdots\cdots\cdots\cdots \\ \Delta y_{cT} = \Delta x'_{cT}\beta + \Delta u_{cT} \end{matrix} \qquad c = 1,\dots,C. \tag{2.6}$$

Contrary to the genuine panel case, the explanatory variables in model (2.6) are correlated with the error terms through the measurement errors. However, the matrix

$$Z_c = \begin{bmatrix} x'_{c1},\dots,x'_{cT} & & \\ & \ddots & \\ & & x'_{c1},\dots,x'_{cT} \end{bmatrix}$$

can be used as a matrix of instruments for the system. The moment restrictions are given by $E(Z'_c \Delta u_c) = \Psi\beta + \psi$, where $\Delta u_c = (\Delta u_{c2},\dots,;\Delta u_{cT})'$. Ψ and ψ depend on the covariance matrix of the measurement errors. If the covariance matrix is known, the measurement-error corrected GMM estimator of

[5] nc is assumed to be constant across cohorts and over time to simplify notation. This assumption can be easily relaxed.

[6] The homoscedasticity assumption can be relaxed and assume that the measurement error covariance matrix is constant for each cohort, but it may vary across cohorts. However, to be able to obtain consistent estimates of the covariance matrices in such cases, a long time series dimension is needed.

β (GMMC) is obtained by minimizing

$$\sum_{c=1}^{C} (Z_c'\Delta u_c - \Psi\beta - \psi)' A_c \sum_{c=1}^{C} (Z_c'\Delta u_c - \Psi\beta - \psi),$$

and the optimal choice of A_c is any consistent estimator of the inverse of the covariance matrix of $Z_c'\Delta u_c$ (cf. Hansen (1982)). The GMMC estimator is consistent for fixed T when C goes to infinity and is given by

$$\hat{\beta} = \left[\sum_{c=1}^{C} (\Delta X_c' Z_c + \Psi') A_c \sum_{c=1}^{C} (Z_c'\Delta X_c + \Psi) \right]^{-1} * \left[\sum_{c=1}^{C} (\Delta X_c' Z_c + \Psi') A_c \sum_{c=1}^{C} (Z_c'\Delta X_c - \psi) \right]^{-1}, \quad (2.7)$$

where $\Delta y_c = (\Delta y_{c2}, \dots, \Delta y_{cT})'$, and $\Delta X_c = (\Delta x_{c2}, \dots, \Delta x_{cT})'$. If the covariance matrix of the measurement errors is unknown, the GMMC estimator in (2.7) is not feasible. However, we can replace Ψ and ψ by consistent estimators based on the survey data.[7] The GMM estimator (2.7) would also be trivially consistent if the number of observations per cohort goes to infinity.

Notice that the corresponding GMM estimator for the true panel coincides with the within-groups estimator (see Arellano and Bover (1995)). However, this is no longer the case when we are using cohort data, and this estimator does not coincide with any of the estimators proposed by Deaton (1985). Deaton's within-groups estimator is based on the following set of moment restrictions

$$\mathrm{E}(\tilde{x}_{ct}\tilde{u}_{ct} - A\beta - a) = 0,$$

where the tildes denote deviations from time means, and A and a depend on the covariance matrix of the measurement errors. Deaton's first differences estimator is based on

$$\mathrm{E}(\Delta x_{ct}\Delta u_{ct} - B\beta - b) = 0,$$

where B and b depend on the covariance matrix of the measurement errors. Thus, Deaton's estimators are based on a linear combination of the moment restrictions that we use, and therefore, the GMM estimator in (2.7) is at least as efficient as the estimators proposed by Deaton.

---

[7] Notice that replacing Ψ and ψ by consistent estimates alters the asymptotic variance of the GMM estimator. In the appendix we obtain its asymptotic distribution for the dynamic model when the covariance matrix of the measurement errors is unknown. For the static model this distribution can be derived analogously.

3. Estimation of a dynamic model using cohort data

Consider the following dynamic model with individual effects

$$y_{it} = \alpha y_{it-1} + x'_{it}\beta + \theta_i + v_{it} \qquad v_{it} \sim \text{iid}(0, \sigma^2) \quad \theta_i \sim \text{iid}(0, \sigma^2_\theta). \tag{3.1}$$

We will assume that the individual effects are potentially correlated with all the explanatory variables in the model, and that $\text{E}(x_{it} v_{is}) = 0 \; \forall \, t,s$. If the data available are independent cross-sections, as we said earlier, we can divide the population in C cohorts containing the same individuals over time. Taking expectations conditional on the cohort the individual belongs to, and proceeding in a similar way as we did above for the static model, we can write the cohort population version of model (3.1) as

$$y^*_{ct} = \alpha y^*_{ct-1} + x^{*\prime}_{ct}\beta + \theta^*_c + v^*_{ct} \qquad \begin{matrix} c = 1, \dots, C & \theta^*_c \sim \text{iid}(0, \sigma^2_{\theta*}) \\ t = 2, \dots, T & v^*_{ct} \sim \text{iid}(0, \sigma^2_{v*}) \end{matrix}. \tag{3.2}$$

The cohort population means are unobservable but they can be estimated by the cohort sample means. Using (2.4), we can write (3.2) in terms of the observables as

$$\begin{matrix} y_{ct} = \alpha y_{ct-1} + x'_{ct}\beta + \theta^*_c + u_{ct} & c = 1, \dots, C \\ u_{ct} = v^*_{ct} + \zeta_{ct} - \alpha\zeta_{ct-1} - \eta'_{ct}\beta & t = 2, \dots, T \end{matrix}. \tag{3.3}$$

In the work with time series of cross-sections it is very important to establish the properties for different estimators under alternative asymptotics. Depending on the data available and on the size of the cohorts that we have chosen, some estimators will lead to better estimates than others. In what follows we present different types of estimators for the first order autoregressive model with explanatory variables, and we will discuss their applicability depending on the sample size.

First we consider a measurement-error corrected within-groups estimator. Even for the true panel, the within-groups estimator for the dynamic model is consistent only when $T \to \infty$ (see Nickell (1981)). In the case of cohort data we can achieve consistency (as $T \to \infty$) correcting the within-groups estimator taking into account the measurement error variances.

The model in deviations from time means is

$$\tilde{y}_{ct} = \alpha \tilde{y}_{ct-1} + \tilde{x}'_{ct}\beta + \tilde{u}_{ct}. \tag{3.4}$$

When $T \to \infty$, all the variables on the right hand side of (3.4) are correlated with the error term only through the measurement errors in the following way

$$\text{E}\left[\begin{pmatrix} \tilde{y}_{ct-1} \\ \tilde{x}_{ct} \end{pmatrix} \tilde{u}_{ct}\right] \to \frac{1}{n_c}\begin{bmatrix} -\alpha\sigma^2_\zeta \\ \sigma_{\zeta\eta} - \Sigma_\eta \beta \end{bmatrix} \qquad \text{as } T \to \infty$$

and the measurement-error corrected within-groups estimator (WGC) is given by

$$\begin{pmatrix}\hat{\alpha}_{\text{wgc}}\\ \hat{\beta}_{\text{wgc}}\end{pmatrix} = \left[\frac{1}{C(T-1)}\sum_{c=1}^{C}\sum_{t=2}^{T}\begin{pmatrix}\tilde{y}_{ct-1}^2 & \tilde{y}_{ct-1}\tilde{x}'_{ct}\\ \tilde{x}_{ct}\tilde{y}_{ct-1} & \tilde{x}_{ct}\tilde{x}'_{ct}\end{pmatrix} - \frac{1}{nc}\begin{pmatrix}\sigma_{\varsigma}^2 & 0\\ 0 & \Sigma_{\eta}\end{pmatrix}\right]^{-1}$$

$$* \left[\frac{1}{C(T-1)}\sum_{c=1}^{C}\sum_{t=2}^{T}\begin{pmatrix}\tilde{y}_{ct-1}\tilde{y}_{ct}\\ \tilde{x}_{ct}\tilde{y}_{ct}\end{pmatrix} - \frac{1}{nc}\begin{pmatrix}0\\ \sigma_{\varsigma\eta}\end{pmatrix}\right]. \quad (3.5)$$

In applied work we do not always have data for a large number of time periods, and in this case within-groups would not be an appropriate technique. Hence, we are going to study an alternative estimator which is consistent for finite T when C is large.

Let us consider model (3.3) in first differences as a system of equations

$$\begin{matrix}\Delta y_{c3} = \alpha\Delta y_{c2} + \Delta x'_{c3}\beta + \Delta u_{c3}\\ \cdots\cdots\cdots\cdots\cdots\cdots\cdots\cdots\cdots\cdots,\\ \Delta y_{cT} = \alpha\Delta y_{cT-1} + \Delta x'_{cT}\beta + \Delta u_{cT}\end{matrix} \qquad c = 1, \ldots, C.$$

If the x^*s are strictly exogenous, i.e. $E(x^*_{ct} v^*_{cs}) = 0$; $t,s = 1, \ldots, T$, the matrix;

$$Z_c = \begin{bmatrix} y_{c1}x'_{c1}, \ldots, x'_{cT} & & \\ & \ddots & \\ & & y_{c1}, \ldots, y_{cT-2}x'_{c1}, \ldots, x'_{cT}\end{bmatrix}$$

can be used as a matrix of instruments for the system (see Arellano and Bond (1991) for the genuine panel case). In our case, the moment restrictions are given by $E(Z'_c\Delta u_c) = \Lambda\delta + \lambda$, where $\Delta u_c = (\Delta u_{c3}, \ldots, \Delta u_{cT})'$, and $\delta = (\alpha, \beta')'$. Λ and λ depend on the covariance matrix of the measurement errors. The measurement-error corrected GMM estimator of δ (GMMC) is obtained by minimizing

$$\sum_{c=1}^{C}(Z'_c\Delta u_c - \Lambda\delta - \lambda)' A_c \sum_{c=1}^{C}(Z'_c\Delta u_c - \Lambda\delta - \lambda),$$

and is given by

$$\hat{\delta} = [\textstyle\sum(\Delta W'_c Z_c + \Lambda')A_c\sum(Z'_c\Delta W_c + \Lambda)]^{-1}$$

$$* [\textstyle\sum(\Delta W'_c Z_c + \Lambda')A_c\sum(Z'_c\Delta y_c - \lambda)], \quad (3.6)$$

where $W_c = (y_{c(-1)}, X_c)$, $y_{c(-1)} = (y_{c2}, \ldots, y_{cT-1})'$, $X_c = (x_{c3}, \ldots, x_{cT})'$.

The asymptotic distribution of the GMMC estimator when Λ and λ are assumed to be known can be easily derived using standard assumptions and

GMM theory

$$\sqrt{C}(\hat{\delta} - \delta) \rightarrow_d \mathrm{N}(0, (D_0' A_0 D_0)^{-1} D_0' A_0 V_0 A_0 D_0 (D_0' A_0 D_0)^{-1}), \qquad (3.7)$$

where

$$A_0 = \operatorname{plim} A_c,$$

$$D_0 = \operatorname{plim} \frac{\partial}{\partial \delta'} \sum_c (Z_c' \Delta u_c - \Lambda \delta - \lambda) = -(\mathrm{E}(Z_c' \Delta W_c) + \Lambda),$$

$$V_0 = \mathrm{E}[(Z_c' \Delta u_c - \Lambda \delta - \lambda)(Z_c' \Delta u_c - \Lambda \delta - \lambda)'].$$

We can obtain a consistent estimator of the asymptotic covariance matrix in (3.7) by replacing A_0 by A_c and D_0, V_0 by

$$\hat{D} = -\frac{1}{C} \sum_{c=1}^{C} Z_c' \Delta W_c - \Lambda$$

$$\hat{V} = \frac{1}{C} \sum_{c=1}^{C} (Z_c' \Delta \hat{u}_c - \Lambda \hat{\delta} - \lambda)(Z_c \Delta \hat{u}_c - \Lambda \hat{\delta} - \lambda)'$$

where $\Delta \hat{u}_c$ is the vector of residuals.

The GMMC estimator in (3.6) is consistent as $C \rightarrow \infty$ for any choice of the weighting matrix. For example, we could use

$$A_c = \left[\frac{1}{C} \sum_{c=1}^{C} Z_c' H Z_c \right]^{-1}, \qquad H = \begin{bmatrix} 2 & -1 & \dots & 0 \\ -1 & 2 & \dots & 0 \\ & \dots & \dots & \\ 0 & \dots & -1 & 2 \end{bmatrix}.$$

Notice that in the genuine panel case, this matrix is a natural choice for the one step GMM and it is optimal if the disturbances in model (3.1) are serially uncorrelated and homoscedastic.

We can obtain a more efficient estimator in a second step using, as weighting matrix, a consistent estimator of V_0^{-1}. Once we have a preliminary consistent estimate $\hat{\delta}$, the two step GMMC is obtained using

$$A_c = \left[\frac{1}{C} \sum_{c=1}^{C} (Z_c' \Delta \hat{u}_c - \Lambda \hat{\delta} - \lambda)(Z_c' \Delta \hat{u}_c - \Lambda \hat{\delta} - \lambda)' \right]^{-1}.$$

When the covariance matrix of the measurement errors is unknown, it has to be estimated using the micro survey data. Λ and λ are replaced by consistent estimates, and the asymptotic variance of the GMMC estimator has a more complicated expression (see Appendix A).

4. Asymptotic biases in the AR(1) model

In Section 3 we have considered different types of measurement-error corrected estimators for a dynamic model with individual effects that are consistent under different kinds of asymptotics. The corresponding noncorrected estimators are not consistent with the same type of asymptotics, and it is interesting to know the size of their asymptotic biases, in order to get an idea about the sample sizes for which it is worth to use the measurement-error correction for particular models. Furthermore, the within-groups estimators are not consistent as $C \to \infty$ for fixed T. However, in order to compare their behaviour with the GMM type estimators that rely on C asymptotics, we will calculate the asymptotic biases of the within-groups estimators as $C \to \infty$ for fixed T.

In this section we concentrate on the AR(1) model with individual effects

$$y_{it} = \alpha y_{it-1} + \theta_i + v_{it} \qquad v_{it} \sim \text{iid}(0,\sigma^2) \quad \theta_i \sim \text{iid}(0,\sigma_\theta^2). \tag{4.1}$$

This model has received a great deal of attention in the literature and it has the advantage of its simplicity. The alternative estimators for model (4.1) can be derived as in Section 3.

Let us first consider the classical within-groups estimator (WG) without correcting for measurement errors and the measurement-error corrected within-groups estimator (WGC). Their asymptotic biases for fixed T are (see Appendix B)

$$\text{plim}_{C\to\infty}(\hat{\alpha}_{wg} - \alpha) = -\frac{h_T\phi + [(T/(T-1)) + (T-2)\alpha]}{[(T-2)/(1-\alpha^2)]\,\phi - [2\alpha/(1-\alpha^2)]\,h_T\phi + T - 2}, \tag{4.2}$$

and

$$\text{plim}_{C\to\infty}(\hat{\alpha}_{wgc} - \alpha) = -\frac{h_T\phi + [(T/(T-1) - \alpha]}{[(T-2)/(1-\alpha^2)]\,\phi - [2\alpha/(1-\alpha^2)]\,h_T\phi - 1},$$

where

$$h_T = \frac{1}{1-\alpha}\left[1 - \frac{1}{T-1}\,\frac{1-\alpha^{T-1}}{1-\alpha}\right] \quad \text{and} \quad \phi = \frac{nc\sigma_{v^*}^2}{\sigma_\zeta^2}. \tag{4.3}$$

The asymptotic bias of the GMM estimator without correcting for measurement errors is (see Appendix C)

$$\text{plim}_{C\to\infty}(\hat{\alpha} - \alpha) = -\frac{\left[\nu\dfrac{1}{1+\alpha}\phi + \mu\right]' A_0\mu\alpha}{\left[\nu\dfrac{1}{1+\alpha}\phi + \mu\right]' A_0\left[\nu\dfrac{1}{1+\alpha}\phi + \mu\right]}, \tag{4.4}$$

where

$$A_0 = \text{plim}\, A_c,$$

$$\mu = (1, 0, 1, 0, 0, 1, \ \dots)',$$

$$v = (1, \alpha, 1, \alpha^2, \alpha, 1, \ \dots)'.$$

The asymptotic bias in (4.4) depends also on $\rho = nc\sigma_0^2/\sigma_\xi^2$ through the matrix A_0.[8]

When $0 \leq a < 1$ the asymptotic biases are negative. In Fig. 1 we present the absolute value of the biases for $T = 5$.[9] The biases are increasing in α, and the asymptotic bias of the GMM estimator is smaller than the asymptotic biases of the within-groups estimators, unless α is close to 1.[10] The asymptotic bias of the WGC estimator can be larger or smaller than the noncorrected WG depending on the parameters of the model. This is due to the fact that the measurement-error correction is appropriate only if T is large.

The biases are decreasing in ϕ, which implies that the smaller the measurement error variance, the smaller are the biases. However, when the measurement error variance approaches zero (i.e. $\phi \to \infty$), the bias of the GMM estimator vanishes, whereas the bias of the WG estimator approaches the asymptotic bias for the true panel which is not zero for finite T. The asymptotic biases depend also on the time series dimension, as T increases the biases decrease, and this effect is stronger for the within-groups estimators.

5. Monte Carlo simulations

In Section 4 we obtained analytic formulae for the asymptotic biases of different estimators for the AR(1) model without explanatory variables. However, it is also interesting to know to what extent the asymptotic behaviour approximates the actual behaviour observed in finite samples.

To investigate the finite sample performance of the different estimators for the AR(1) model, we have carried out Monte Carlo simulations for different values of the parameters of the model.

---

[8] We are considering the two step GMM estimator and hence A_0 is the inverse of the covariance matrix of $Z_c'\Delta u_c$ which depends on ρ.

[9] We have chosen both ϕ and ρ equal to 12.5. In the Monte Carlo simulations in Section 5, we have considered $nc = 25$ which implies that the ratios σ_ϵ^2 σ_ξ^2 and σ_0^2/σ_ξ^2 are both equal to 0.5.

[10] The asymptotic bias of the GMM estimator is large when α is very close to 1. The reason is that the A_0 matrix that we are using is close to be singular when α is close to 1.

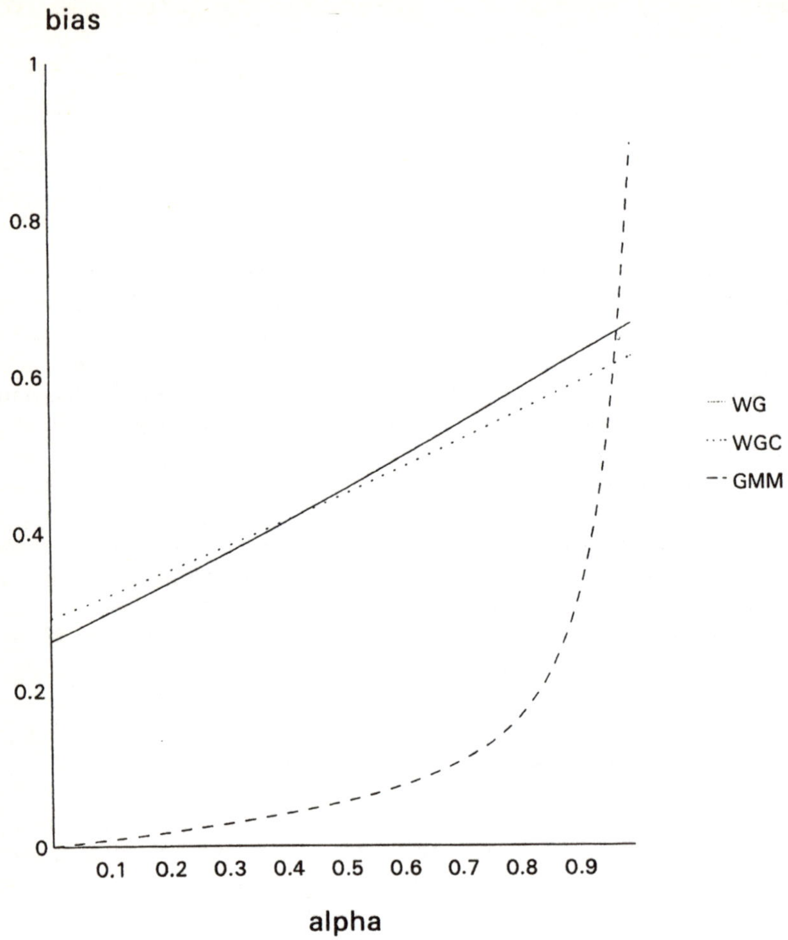

Fig. 1. Estimating dynamic models from time series of independent cross-sections.

The data were generated using the following model. First, the cohort population means were constructed using an AR(1) model

$$y^*_{ct} = \alpha y^*_{ct-1} + \theta^*_c + v^*_{ct} \qquad v^*_{ct} \sim \text{iid } N(0,\sigma^2_{v^*}) \quad \theta^*_c \sim \text{iid } N(0,\sigma^2_{\theta^*}).$$

The initial values were obtained from $y^*_{c0} = \theta^*_c/(1-\alpha) + v^*_{c0}/(1-\alpha^2)^{1/2}$, and the first ten cross-sections were discarded. Then, the individual observations on each cohort were generated as $y_{it} \sim \text{iid}\, N(y^*_{ct}, \sigma^2_\zeta)$, and the cohort sample means and variances were calculated.[11]

Using the model above, the variance of y can be decomposed as follows

$$\sigma^2_y = \sigma^2_\zeta + \frac{\sigma^2_{v*}}{1-\alpha^2} + \frac{\sigma^2_{\theta*}}{(1-\alpha)^2}\,.$$

i.e.,

$$\begin{matrix}\textit{total} \\ \textit{variance}\end{matrix} = \begin{matrix}\textit{within} \\ \textit{cohort} \\ \textit{variance}\end{matrix} + \begin{matrix}\textit{time-varying} \\ \textit{between cohorts} \\ \textit{variance}\end{matrix} + \begin{matrix}\textit{time-invariant} \\ \textit{between cohorts} \\ \textit{variance}\end{matrix}.$$

It is clear that the performance of the estimators will depend on the proportion of the variance due to the different components. In order to compare the behaviour of the estimators for different values of the autoregressive parameter, without having the additional effect of a change in the composition of the variance, we have chosen, for each α, the appropriate values of σ^2_{v*} and $\sigma^2_{\theta*}$ to keep this proportion constant.

We have performed experiments for different time dimensions, $T = 5$, 7, 10, 15, different values of the autoregressive parameter, $\alpha = 0.1, 0.5, 0.9$, and different proportions on the composition of the variance of y. The size of the cross-sections is 2000. The results from 1000 replications are summarized in Tables 1–4. In Tables 1–3 cross-sections are divided into 80 cohorts of 25 individuals, and in Table 4 they are divided into 10 cohorts of 200 individuals.

The estimators considered are: the non-corrected within-groups, the measurement-error corrected within-groups, the non-corrected GMM, the measurement-error corrected GMM, and Moffitt's estimator (MOF). In the absence of any sample information on time-invariant variables (different from the cohort defining variable) or time-varying variables observed over time for every individual, Moffitt suggests to use, as a proxy for y_{it-1}, the sample average of those individuals in the same cohort than i in $t-1$. This is equal to OLS in levels using cohort means of the variables. Such estimator would only be consistent in the absence of cohort effects (although one could have individual effects that cancel out at the cohort level). Since in our sample design there are cohort effects, we may expect Moffitt's estimator to be upward biased, with the size of the bias depending on the autoregressive coefficient and the variance of the cohort effects.

---

[11] Notice that this data generating procedure is equivalent to that of generating the samples according to the AR(1) model (4.1) at the individual level. The advantage is that we just need to generate $n_c * C$ observations per period, while if we had generated the individual data on the basis of the model we would have needed to generate $n_c * C * T$ observations per period, in order to keep in the sample $n_c * C$ observations corresponding to different individuals on each period.

Let us first comment the results in Tables 1–3. As we can see, the bias of the within-groups and GMM estimators increases as α increases, while the bias of Moffitt's estimator decreases with α, and it is larger than the bias of the GMMC estimator for $\alpha = 0.1$, 0.5 and smaller for large α.

Another interesting feature is that the behaviour of the within-groups and GMM estimators depend on the time series dimension of the data. For all these estimators, both the bias and the standard deviation decrease as T increases, whereas the bias of Moffitt's estimator does not depend on T.

The bias of the estimators depend also on the composition of the variance of y. The larger the ratio of the time-varying component of the between-cohort variance to the within-cohort variance, the smaller the bias of the estimators

Table 1
Mean and standard deviation of the estimators. (Within cohort variance: 50%, between cohorts variance (time invariant component): 25%, between cohorts variance (time varying component): 25%)

	WG[a]	WGC[b]	GMM[c]	GMMC[d]	MOF[e]
			$\alpha = 0.1$		
$T = 5$					
Mean	−0.1858	−0.2076	0.0680	0.0718	0.5264
St. dev.	0.0584	0.0655	0.1070	0.1161	0.0577
$T = 7$					
Mean	−0.0936	−0.1031	0.0723	0.0766	0.5223
St. dev.	0.0461	0.0509	0.0752	0.0813	0.0498
$T = 10$					
Mean	−0.0303	−0.0331	0.0803	0.0854	0.5245
St. dev.	0.0380	0.0416	0.0552	0.0598	0.0466
$T = 15$					
Mean	0.0150	0.0163	0.0823	0.0877	0.5247
St. dev.	0.0311	0.0339	0.0422	0.0456	0.0429
			$\alpha = 0.5$		
$T = 5$					
Mean	0.0507	0.0592	0.3873	0.4329	0.7186
St. dev.	0.0644	0.0755	0.1455	0.1648	0.0411
$T = 7$					
Mean	0.1843	0.2089	0.4057	0.4506	0.7161
St. dev.	0.0481	0.0539	0.0921	0.1016	0.0352
$T = 10$					
Mean	0.2790	0.3105	0.4249	0.4699	0.7175
St. dev.	0.0395	0.0430	0.0656	0.0712	0.0315
$T = 15$					
Mean	0.3479	0.3827	0.4323	0.4769	0.7182
St. dev.	0.0297	0.0317	0.0463	0.0497	0.0283

Table 1 (continued)

	WG[a]	WGC[b]	GMM[c]	GMMC[d]	MOF[e]
		$\alpha = 0.9$			
$T = 5$					
Mean	0.1425	0.2583	0.3453	0.4963	0.9115
St. dev.	0.0698	0.1239	0.2391	0.3762	0.0210
$T = 7$					
Mean	0.3207	0.4789	0.4220	0.5989	0.9105
St. dev.	0.0513	0.0704	0.1601	0.2298	0.0176
$T = 10$					
Mean	0.4637	0.6176	0.5078	0.7077	0.9110
St. dev.	0.0421	0.0475	0.1159	0.1427	0.0155
$T = 15$					
Mean	0.5853	0.7215	0.5714	0.7819	0.9117
St. dev.	0.0308	0.0302	0.0778	0.0827	0.0133

Notes: $C = 80$. $nc = 25$, where C is the number of cohorts on the population and nc is the number of individuals per cohort. The estimators are based on 1000 replications and cross-sections of 2000 individuals. The AR(1) model is with individuals effects.

[a] WG: within-groups estimator.

[b] WGC: measurement-error corrected within-groups.

[c] GMM: Generalized method of moments estimator.

[d] GMMC: measurement-errors corrected GMM. Matrix of instruments used

$$Z_c = \begin{bmatrix} y_{c1} & & & & & & \\ & y_{c1} & y_{c2} & & & & \\ & & & \ddots & & & \\ & & & & y_{cT-4} & y_{cT-3} & y_{cT-2} \end{bmatrix}$$

[e] MOF: Moffitt's estimator.

(compare Tables 1 and 2). As stated above, the within-groups estimator does not depend on the ratio of the time-invariant component of the between-cohort variance to the within-cohort variance, while the bias of the GMM and Moffitt's estimators increases with this ratio (compare Tables 1 and 3).

If we look at the results for the measurement-error corrected estimators, we can see that the GMMC leads to less biased estimates than the GMM estimator, with a small increase, in most of the cases, of the standard deviation. The performance of the WGC estimator is worse than the non-corrected WG for small values of α. However, when α is large the bias of the WGC estimator is smaller than the WG. The reason is that the correction is appropriate for large values of T and we are considering relatively small values of T. Finally, when we compare GMMC, WGC and MOF estimators we can see that the GMMC

Table 2
Mean and standard deviation of the estimators. (Within cohort variance: 40% between cohorts variance (time invariant component): 20%. between cohorts variance (time varying component): 40%)

	WG[a]	WGC[b]	GMM[c]	GMMC[d]	MOF[e]
			$\alpha = 0.1$		
$T = 5$					
Mean	−0.1830	−0.1936	0.0748	0.0771	0.3876
St. dev.	0.0581	0.0616	0.0983	0.1025	0.0611
$T = 7$					
Mean	−0.0907	−0.0953	0.0785	0.0810	0.3835
St. dev.	0.0462	0.0486	0.0708	0.0738	0.0518
$T = 10$					
Mean	−0.0271	−0.0283	0.0859	0.0888	0.3861
St. dev.	0.0380	0.0398	0.0527	0.0549	0.0466
$T = 15$					
Mean	0.0184	0.0192	0.0871	0.0900	0.3869
St. dev.	0.0312	0.0326	0.0411	0.0428	0.0423
			$\alpha = 0.5$		
$T = 5$					
Mean	0.0684	0.0741	0.4255	0.4506	0.6467
St. dev.	0.0641	0.0695	0.1317	0.1399	0.0449
$T = 7$					
Mean	0.2023	0.2157	0.4395	0.4636	0.6441
St. dev.	0.0480	0.0508	0.0851	0.0893	0.0378
$T = 10$					
Mean	0.2976	0.3143	0.4546	0.4786	0.6459
St. dev.	0.0391	0.0407	0.0610	0.0635	0.0330
$T = 15$					
Mean	0.3664	0.3846	0.4589	0.4825	0.6471
St. dev.	0.0293	0.0302	0.0440	0.0456	0.0290
			$\alpha = 0.9$		
$T = 5$					
Mean	0.2215	0.3033	0.5193	0.6432	0.9071
St. dev.	0.0692	0.0919	0.2500	0.3224	0.0222
$T = 7$					
Mean	0.3980	0.4922	0.5893	0.7145	0.9062
St. dev.	0.0500	0.0578	0.1535	0.1760	0.0182
$T = 10$					
Mean	0.5355	0.6228	0.6615	0.7867	0.9066
St. dev.	0.0398	0.0411	0.1047	0.1099	0.0159
$T = 15$					
Mean	0.6484	0.7232	0.7069	0.8314	0.9075
St. dev.	0.0280	0.0268	0.0650	0.0640	0.0134

Notes: See notes to Table 1.

Table 3
Mean and standard deviation of the estimators. (Within cohort variance: 40%, between cohorts variance (time invariant component): 40%, between cohorts variance (time varying component): 20%)

	WG[a]	WGC[b]	GMM[c]	GMMC[d]	MOF[e]
			$\alpha = 0.1$		
$T = 5$					
Mean	−0.1858	−0.2076	0.0641	0.0672	0.6792
St. dev.	0.0584	0.0655	0.1168	0.1269	0.0477
$T = 7$					
Mean	−0.0936	−0.1031	0.0688	0.0725	0.6759
St. dev.	0.0461	0.0509	0.0841	0.0882	0.0418
$T = 10$					
Mean	−0.0303	−0.0331	0.0772	0.0818	0.6774
St. dev.	0.0380	0.0416	0.0594	0.0643	0.0399
$T = 15$					
Mean	0.0150	0.0163	0.0804	0.0855	0.6772
St. dev.	0.0311	0.0339	0.0444	0.0480	0.0372
			$\alpha = 0.5$		
$T = 5$					
Mean	0.0507	0.0592	0.3702	0.4136	0.8096
St. dev.	0.0644	0.0755	0.1649	0.1889	0.0332
$T = 7$					
Mean	0.1843	0.2089	0.3918	0.4357	0.8076
St. dev.	0.0481	0.0539	0.1038	0.1154	0.0284
$T = 10$					
Mean	0.2790	0.3105	0.4156	0.4603	0.8084
St. dev.	0.0395	0.0430	0.0728	0.0793	0.0258
$T = 15$					
Mean	0.3479	0.3827	0.4271	0.4716	0.8087
St. dev.	0.0297	0.0317	0.0502	0.0538	0.0236
			$\alpha = 0.9$		
$T = 5$					
Mean	0.1425	0.2583	0.2863	0.3942	0.9402
St. dev.	0.0698	0.1239	0.2603	0.4087	0.0167
$T = 7$					
Mean	0.3207	0.4789	0.3662	0.5138	0.9393
St. dev.	0.0513	0.0704	0.1788	0.2726	0.0139
$T = 10$					
Mean	0.4637	0.6176	0.4611	0.6458	0.9397
St. dev.	0.0421	0.0475	0.1332	0.1750	0.0119
$T = 15$					
Mean	0.5853	0.7215	0.5399	0.7448	0.9402
St. dev.	0.0308	0.0302	0.0940	0.1042	0.0102

Notes: See notes to Table 1.

Table 4
Mean and standard deviation of the estimators. (Within cohort variance: 50%, between cohorts variance (time invariant component): 25%, between cohorts variance (time varying component): 25%)

	WG[a]	WGC[b]	GMM[c]	GMMC[d]	MOF[e]
			$\alpha=0.1$		
$T=5$					
Mean	−0.1848	−0.1877	−0.0276	−0.0293	0.5134
St. dev.	0.1556	0.1581	0.2727	0.2753	0.1651
$T=7$					
Mean	−0.0790	−0.0801	−0.0040	−0.0054	0.5210
St. dev.	0.1335	0.1353	0.1882	0.1897	0.1459
$T=10$					
Mean	−0.0270	−0.0274	−0.0006	−0.0018	0.5224
St. dev.	0.1120	0.1134	0.1474	0.1486	0.1322
$T=15$					
Mean	0.0121	0.0123	0.0167	0.0157	0.5219
St. dev.	0.0857	0.0867	0.1079	0.1087	0.1205
			$\alpha=0.5$		
$T=5$					
Mean	0.0684	0.0696	0.2352	0.2336	0.7172
St. dev.	0.1708	0.1749	0.3629	0.3662	0.1202
$T=7$					
Mean	0.2154	0.2189	0.2846	0.2842	0.7252
St. dev.	0.1395	0.1417	0.2313	0.2337	0.1000
$T=10$					
Mean	0.3018	0.3060	0.3146	0.3152	0.7274
St. dev.	0.1121	0.1134	0.1773	0.1790	0.0895
$T=15$					
Mean	0.3684	0.3731	0.3660	0.3677	0.7290
St. dev.	0.0834	0.0840	0.1267	0.1279	0.0771
			$\alpha=0.9$		
$T=5$					
Mean	0.2858	0.3113	0.2676	0.2644	0.9353
St. dev.	0.1791	0.1946	0.4766	0.4847	0.0571
$T=7$					
Mean	0.4571	0.4843	0.3807	0.3738	0.9371
St. dev.	0.1413	0.1463	0.3269	0.3327	0.0468
$T=10$					
Mean	0.5896	0.6144	0.4639	0.4614	0.9379
St. dev.	0.1054	0.1059	0.2512	0.2542	0.0395
$T=15$					
Mean	0.6930	0.7139	0.5845	0.5858	0.9387
St. dev.	0.0743	0.0731	0.1945	0.1983	0.0301

Notes: $C=10$, $nc=200$. (See also notes to Table 1).

estimator leads to better results than the WGC, specially for small values of T, whereas GMMC is better than Moffitt's estimator for small α, but it leads to worse results when α is large.

Now compare the results in Tables 1 and 4. When the number of observation per cohort is large, the measurement-error correction becomes irrelevant, however, there is a loss of efficiency due to the fact that the number of cohorts is small. If we now compare the performance of the GMM and the within-groups estimators, we can see that, when α is large, the bias of the WGC estimator is smaller than the bias of the GMMC. However, the way of grouping the data is chosen by the researcher, and even for large α the GMMC estimator in Table 1 is less biased than the corresponding WGC in Table 4.

6. Conclusions

The problem analyzed in this paper is the estimation of dynamic models with individual effects using time series of independent cross-sections. As it happens when we work with panel data, we can consider different types of estimators which are consistent with different types of asymptotics (cross-section or time series). We propose a measurement-error corrected within-groups estimator which is consistent as the number of time periods tends to infinity, and a measurement-error corrected GMM estimator which is consistent as the number of cohorts tends to infinity. We also calculate the asymptotic biases of the non-corrected estimators for the AR(1) model, and analyze the size of the biases depending on the parameters of the model.

In Section 5, the Monte Carlo simulations are carried out to study the small sample properties of the estimators proposed. The conclusions derived from the simulations reinforce the asymptotic results. The measurement-error correction appears to be important, and the corrected estimators lead to less biased results. Furthermore, for small values of T, GMM estimators are better than within-groups estimators.

Appendix A. Asymptotic distribution of the GMM estimator when the covariance matrix of the measurement errors is unknown

Let $\hat{\Lambda}$ and $\hat{\lambda}$ be consistent estimators of Λ and λ, respectively. Here, the criterion function we have to minimize is

$$s(\delta) = \frac{1}{C}\sum_{c=1}^{C}(Z_c'\Delta u_c - \hat{\Lambda}\delta - \hat{\lambda})' A_c \frac{1}{C}\sum_{c=1}^{C}(Z_c'\Delta u_c - \hat{\Lambda}\delta - \hat{\lambda}).$$

Let

$$b_c(\delta) = \frac{1}{C}\sum_{c=1}^{C}(Z_c'\Delta u_c - \hat{\Lambda}\delta - \hat{\lambda})$$

$$= \frac{1}{C}\sum_{c=1}^{C}(Z_c'\Delta u_c - \Lambda\delta - \lambda) - [(\hat{\Lambda}\delta + \hat{\lambda}) - (\Lambda\delta + \lambda)]. \quad \text{(A.1)}$$

The elements of $\hat{\Lambda}$ and $\hat{\lambda}$ are either zero or else estimates of the variances and covariances of the measurement errors, and given that we are assuming that they are constant across cohorts and over time the elements of $\hat{\Lambda}$ and $\hat{\lambda}$ are calculated as follows

$$\hat{\sigma}_\zeta^2 = \frac{1}{C}\sum_{c=1}^{C}\frac{1}{(nc-1)T}\sum_{t=1}^{T}\sum_{i\in c,t}(y_{it} - y_{ct})^2 = \frac{1}{C}\sum_{c=1}^{C}\hat{\sigma}_\zeta^c.$$

Analogously we construct $\hat{\sigma}_{\zeta\eta}$ and $\hat{\Sigma}_\eta$.

Using the definition of the vec operator and the Kronecker product

$$(\hat{\Lambda}\delta + \hat{\lambda}) - (\Lambda\delta + \lambda) = (\delta'\otimes I)(\operatorname{vec}\hat{\Lambda} - \operatorname{vec}\Lambda) + (\hat{\lambda} - \lambda)$$

$$= (\delta'\otimes I : I)\frac{1}{C}\sum_{c=1}^{C}\begin{pmatrix}\operatorname{vec}\hat{\Lambda}_c - \operatorname{vec}\Lambda \\ \hat{\lambda}_c - \lambda\end{pmatrix},$$

where $\hat{\Lambda}_c$ and $\hat{\lambda}_c$ are obtained using the individuals in cohort c. Substituting in (A.1) we get

$$b_c(\delta) = (I : -\delta'\otimes I : -I)\frac{1}{C}\sum_{c=1}^{C}\begin{pmatrix}Z_c'\Delta u_c - \Lambda\delta - \lambda \\ \operatorname{vec}\hat{\Lambda}_c - \operatorname{vec}\Lambda \\ \hat{\lambda}_c - \lambda\end{pmatrix} = H\frac{1}{C}\sum_{c=1}^{C}(\hat{\psi}_c - \psi).$$

The $\hat{\psi}_c$s are iid with mean and covariance matrix $V_\psi = \mathrm{E}(\hat{\psi}_c - \psi)(\hat{\psi}_c - \psi)'$. Then, using a central limit theorem

$$\sqrt{C}\,b_c(\delta) \to_{\mathrm{d}} \mathrm{N}(0, V_0), \quad \text{where } V_0 = HV_\psi H'.$$

The asymptotic distribution of the GMMC estimator is given by

$$\sqrt{C}(\hat{\delta} - \delta) \to_{\mathrm{d}} \mathrm{N}(0, (D_0'A_0D_0)^{-1}D_0'A_0V_0A_0D_0(D_0'A_0D_0)^{-1}),$$

where

$$A_0 = \operatorname{plim} A_c,$$

$$D_0 = \operatorname{plim}\frac{\partial}{\partial\delta'}\sum_c(Z_c'\Delta u_c - \hat{\Lambda}\delta - \hat{\lambda}) = -(\mathrm{E}(Z_c'\Delta W_c) + \Lambda).$$

A consistent estimator of the asymptotic covariance matrix is obtained by replacing A_0 by A_c and D_0, V_0 by

$$\hat{D} = -\frac{1}{C}\sum_{c=1}^{C} Z_c'\Delta W_c - \hat{\Lambda},$$

$$\hat{V} = \hat{H}\hat{V}_\psi\hat{H}',$$

where

$$\hat{H} = (I{:} - \hat{\delta}'\otimes I{:} - I)$$

$$\hat{V}_\psi = \frac{1}{C}\sum_{c=1}^{C}\hat{\psi}_c\hat{\psi}_c' - \left(\frac{1}{C}\sum_{c=1}^{C}\hat{\psi}_c\right)\left(\frac{1}{C}\sum_{c=1}^{C}\hat{\psi}_c'\right),$$

Δu_c has to be replaced by $\Delta\hat{u}_c$ the vector of residuals.

Appendix B. Asymptotic bias of the within-groups estimator

Let us consider the model in deviations from time means

$$\tilde{y}_{ct} = \alpha\tilde{y}_{ct-1} + \tilde{u}_{ct}.$$

The OLS estimator of α in the model above is the within-groups estimator. Consider now the within-groups estimator obtained using the tth cross-section

$$\hat{\alpha}_{\mathrm{wgt}} = \frac{\frac{1}{C}\sum_{c=1}^{C}\tilde{y}_{ct-1}\tilde{y}_{ct}}{\frac{1}{C}\sum_{c=1}^{C}\tilde{y}_{ct-1}^2} = \alpha + \frac{\frac{1}{C}\sum_{c=1}^{C}\tilde{y}_{ct-1}\tilde{u}_{ct}}{\frac{1}{C}\sum_{c=1}^{C}\tilde{y}_{ct-1}^2},$$

and

$$\mathrm{plim}_{C\to\infty}(\hat{\alpha}_{\mathrm{wgt}} - \alpha) = \frac{\mathrm{plim}\frac{1}{C}\sum_{c=1}^{C}\tilde{y}_{ct-1}\tilde{u}_{ct}}{\mathrm{plim}\frac{1}{C}\sum_{c=1}^{C}\tilde{y}_{ct-1}^2} = \frac{A_t}{B_t}.$$

We are going to calculate A_t and B_t

$$A_t = \mathrm{E}[\tilde{y}_{ct-1}\tilde{u}_{ct}] = \mathrm{E}[\tilde{y}_{ct-1}^{*}\tilde{u}_{ct}] + \mathrm{E}[\tilde{\zeta}_{ct-1}\tilde{u}_{ct}]. \tag{B.1}$$

The second term in (B.1) can be obtained as follows:

$$
\begin{aligned}
\mathrm{E}[\tilde{\zeta}_{ct-1}\tilde{u}_{ct}] &= \mathrm{E}[\tilde{\zeta}_{ct-1}(\tilde{v}^*_{ct} + \tilde{\zeta}_{ct} - \alpha\tilde{\zeta}_{ct-1})] \\
&= \mathrm{E}(\tilde{\zeta}_{ct-1}\tilde{\zeta}_{ct}) - \alpha\mathrm{E}(\tilde{\zeta}^2_{ct-1}) \\
&= -\frac{T}{(T-1)^2}\frac{\sigma^2_\zeta}{nc} - \alpha\frac{T-2}{T-1}\frac{\sigma^2_\zeta}{nc}.
\end{aligned} \tag{B.2}
$$

Following Nickell (1981), we can calculate the first term in (B.1)

$$
\begin{aligned}
\mathrm{E}(\tilde{y}^*_{ct-1}\tilde{u}_{ct}) &= \mathrm{E}(\tilde{y}^*_{ct-1}\tilde{v}^*_{ct}) \\
&= -\frac{\sigma^2_{v^*}}{(T-1)(1-\alpha)}\left[1-\alpha^{t-2}-\alpha^{T-t}+\frac{1}{T-1}\frac{1-\alpha^{T-1}}{1-\alpha}\right],
\end{aligned} \tag{B.3}
$$

substituting (B.2) and (B.3) in (B.1) we get

$$
\begin{aligned}
A_t = &-\frac{\sigma^2_{v^*}}{(T-1)(1-\alpha)}\left[1-\alpha^{t-2}-\alpha^{T-t}+\frac{1}{T-1}\frac{1-\alpha^{T-1}}{1-\alpha}\right] \\
&-\left[\frac{T}{(T-1)^2}+\frac{T-2}{T-1}\alpha\right]\frac{\sigma^2_\zeta}{nc},
\end{aligned} \tag{B.4}
$$

analogously we can obtain

$$
\begin{aligned}
B_t &= \mathrm{E}(\tilde{y}^2_{ct-1}) = \mathrm{E}(\tilde{y}^{*2}_{ct-1}) + \mathrm{E}(\tilde{\zeta}^2_{ct-1}) \\
&= \frac{\sigma^2_{v^*}}{1-\alpha^2}\frac{T-2}{T-1} - \frac{2\alpha}{1-\alpha^2}\frac{\sigma^2_{v^*}}{(T-1)(1-\alpha)} \\
&\quad\times\left[1-\alpha^{t-2}-\alpha^{T-t}+\frac{1}{T-1}\frac{1-\alpha^{T-1}}{1-\alpha}\right]+\frac{T-2}{T-1}\frac{\sigma^2_\zeta}{nc},
\end{aligned} \tag{B.5}
$$

using the whole sample

$$
\begin{aligned}
\hat{\alpha}_{\mathrm{wg}} &= \frac{(1/C(T-1))\sum_{t=2}^{T}\sum_{c=1}^{C}\tilde{y}_{ct-1}\tilde{y}_{ct}}{(1/C(T-1))\sum_{t=2}^{T}\sum_{c=1}^{C}\tilde{y}^2_{ct-1}} \\
&= \alpha + \frac{(1/C(T-1))\sum_{t=2}^{T}\sum_{c=1}^{C}\tilde{y}_{ct-1}\tilde{u}_{ct}}{(1/C(T-1))\sum_{t=2}^{T}\sum_{c=1}^{C}\tilde{y}^2_{ct-1}},
\end{aligned}
$$

and

$$
\operatorname{plim}_{C\to\infty}(\hat{\alpha}_{\mathrm{wg}}-\alpha) = \frac{(1/(T-1))\sum_{t=2}^{T}A_t}{(1/(T-1))\sum_{t=2}^{T}B_t}
$$

adding up the expressions for A_t and B_t in (B.4) and (B.5) and substituting we obtain

$$\operatorname{plim}_{C\to\infty}(\hat{\alpha}_{\mathrm{wg}}-\alpha)$$

$$= -\frac{\dfrac{1}{(T-1)(1-\alpha)}\left[1-\dfrac{1}{T-1}\dfrac{1-\alpha^{T-1}}{1-\alpha}\right]\dfrac{nc\sigma_{r^*}^2}{\sigma_\zeta^2}+\left[\dfrac{T}{(T-1)^2}+\dfrac{T-2}{T-1}\alpha\right]}{\dfrac{1}{1-\alpha^2}\left[1-\dfrac{1}{T-1}\right]\dfrac{nc\sigma_{r^*}^2}{\sigma_\zeta^2}-\dfrac{2\alpha}{1-\alpha^2}\dfrac{1}{(T-1)(1-\alpha)}\left[1-\dfrac{1}{T-1}\dfrac{1-\alpha^{T-1}}{1-\alpha}\right]\dfrac{nc\sigma_{r^*}^2}{\sigma_\zeta^2}+\dfrac{T-2}{T-1}}.$$

Rearranging terms and defining h_T and ϕ as in (4.3) we obtain (4.2). Analogously we obtain the asymptotic bias of the measurement-error corrected within-groups estimator WGC.

Appendix C. Asymptotic bias of the GMM estimator

Let us consider the model in first differences as a system of equations

$$\begin{array}{c}\Delta y_{c3}=\alpha\Delta y_{c2}+\Delta u_{c3}\\ \cdots\cdots\cdots\cdots\cdots\cdots\\ \Delta y_{cT}=\alpha\Delta y_{cT-1}+\Delta u_{cT}\end{array},\qquad c=1,\ldots,C.$$

We can use the matrix

$$Z_c=\begin{bmatrix} y_{c1} & & & & & \\ & y_{c1} & y_{c2} & & & \\ & & & \ddots & & \\ & & & & y_{c1} & \cdots\; y_{cT-1}\end{bmatrix},$$

as a matrix of instruments for the system. The GMM estimator without correcting for measurement errors is given by

$$\hat{\alpha}=\frac{\left(\sum_{c=1}^{C}Z_c'\Delta y_{c(-1)}\right)'A_c\sum_{c=1}^{C}Z_c'\Delta y_c}{\left(\sum_{c=1}^{C}Z_c'\Delta y_{c(-1)}\right)'A_c\sum_{c=1}^{C}Z_c'\Delta y_{c(-1)}}$$

$$=\alpha+\frac{\left(\sum_{c=1}^{C}Z_c'\Delta y_{c(-1)}\right)'A_c\sum_{c=1}^{C}Z_c'\Delta u_c}{\left(\sum_{c=1}^{C}Z_c'\Delta y_{c(-1)}\right)'A_c\sum_{c=1}^{C}Z_c'\Delta y_{c(-1)}},$$

$$\operatorname{plim}_{C\to\infty}(\hat{\alpha}-\alpha)=\frac{\operatorname{plim}\frac{1}{C}\sum_{c=1}^{C}\Delta y_{c(-1)}Z_c \operatorname{plim} A_c \operatorname{plim}\frac{1}{C}\sum_{c=1}^{C}Z_c'\Delta u_c}{\operatorname{plim}\frac{1}{C}\sum_{c=1}^{C}\Delta y_{c(-1)}Z_c \operatorname{plim} A_c \operatorname{plim}\frac{1}{C}\sum_{c=1}^{C}Z_c'\Delta y_{c(-1)}}. \tag{C.1}$$

Let us now calculate the different probability limits in the expression above

$$\operatorname{plim}\frac{1}{C}\sum_{c=1}^{C}Z_c'\Delta y_{c(-1)}=\mathrm{E}(Z_c'\Delta y_{c(-1)})$$

$$=\mathrm{E}(Z_c^{*\prime}\Delta y_{c(-1)}^{*})+\mathrm{E}\begin{bmatrix}\zeta_{c1} & & \\ & \zeta_{c1} & \\ & \zeta_{c2} & \\ & & \ddots \\ & & \cdots \\ & & \zeta_{c1} \\ & & \vdots \\ & & \zeta_{cT-2}\end{bmatrix}\begin{bmatrix}\Delta\zeta_{c2}\\ \vdots \\ \Delta\zeta_{c(T-1)}\end{bmatrix}, \tag{C.2}$$

$$=\mathrm{E}(Z_c^{*\prime}\Delta y_{c(-1)}^{*})-\mu\frac{\sigma_\zeta^2}{nc},$$

$$\operatorname{plim}\frac{1}{C}\sum_{c=1}^{C}Z_c'\Delta u_c=\mathrm{E}(Z_c'\Delta u_c)=\alpha\frac{\sigma_\zeta^2}{nc}\mu, \tag{C.3}$$

$$\operatorname{plim} A_c = A_0\,, \tag{C.4}$$

where $\mu=(1,0,1,0,0,1,\ \ldots\ )'$. Assuming that the process is stationary

$$y_{ct}^{*}=\frac{1}{1-\alpha}\theta_c^{*}+\sum_{j=0}^{\infty}\alpha^j v_{ct-j}^{*}$$

$$\Delta y_{ct}^{*}=\sum_{j=0}^{\infty}\alpha^j\Delta v_{ct-j}^{*}$$

$$\mathrm{E}[Z_c^{*\prime}\Delta y_{c(-1)}^*] = \mathrm{E}\begin{bmatrix} y_{c1}^* & & & \\ & y_{c1}^* & & \\ & y_{c2}^* & & \\ & & \ddots & \\ & & & y_{c1}^* \\ & & & \vdots \\ & & & y_{cT-2}^* \end{bmatrix}\begin{bmatrix} y_{c2}^* \\ \ddots \\ y_{cT-1}^* \end{bmatrix}$$

$$= -\begin{bmatrix} \frac{1}{\alpha} \\ \frac{1}{\alpha^2} \\ \alpha \\ \frac{1}{\vdots} \end{bmatrix}\frac{\sigma_{\varepsilon*}^2}{1+\alpha} = -v\frac{\sigma_{\varepsilon*}^2}{1+\alpha}.$$

Then substituting in (C.2) we get

$$\operatorname{plim}_{C\to\infty}\frac{1}{C}\sum_{c=1}^{C} Z_c'\Delta y_{c(-1)} = -v\frac{\sigma_{\varepsilon*}^2}{1+\alpha} = -\mu\frac{\sigma_\varepsilon^2}{nc}. \tag{C.5}$$

and substituting (C.3), (C.4) and (C.5) in (C.1) we obtain the expression for the asymptotic bias in (4.4).

References

Arellano, M., Bond, S.R., 1991. Some test of specification for panel data: Monte Carlo evidence and an application to employment equations. Review of Economic Studies 58, 277–297.

Arellano, M., Bover, O., 1995. Another look at the instrumental-variable estimation of error-components models. Journal of Econometrics 68, 29–51.

Attanasio, O.P., Weber, G., 1993. Consumption growth, the interest rate and aggregation. Review of Economic Studies 60, 631–649.

Blundell, R., Browning M., Meghir, C., 1994. Consumer demand and the life-cycle allocation of household expenditures. Review of Economic Studies 61, 57–80.

Browning, M., Deaton A., Irish, M., 1985. A profitable approach to labour supply and commodity demand over the life-cycle. Econometrica 53, 503–543.

Deaton, A., 1985. Panel data from time series of cross-sections. Journal of Econometrics 30, 109–126.

Hansen, L.P., 1982. Large sample properties of generalized method of moments estimators. Econometrica 50, 1029–1054.

Moffitt, R., 1993. Identification and estimation of dynamic models with a time series of repeated cross-sections. Journal of Econometrics 59, 99–123.

Nickell, S., 1981. Biases in dynamic models with fixed effects. Econometrica 49, 1417–1426.

Verbeek, M., Nijman, T., 1992. Can cohort data be treated as genuine panel data? Empirical Economics 17, 9–23.

Verbeek, M., Nijman, T., 1993. Minimum MSE estimation of a regression model with fixed effects from a series of cross-sections. Journal of Econometrics 59, 125–136.

[16]

ELSEVIER

Journal of Econometrics 98 (2000) 365–383

JOURNAL OF Econometrics

www.elsevier.nl/locate/econbase

A quasi-differencing approach to dynamic modelling from a time series of independent cross-sections

Sourafel Girma*

School of Economics, University of Nottingham, Nottingham NG7 2RD, UK

Received 4 May 1998; received in revised form 10 March 2000; accepted 13 March 2000

Abstract

We motivate and describe a GMM method of estimating linear dynamic models from a time series of independent cross-sections. This involves subjecting the model to a quasi-differencing transformation across pairs of individuals that belong to the same group. Desirable features of the model include the fact that: (i) no aggregation is involved, (ii) dynamic response parameters can vary across groups, (iii) the presence of unobserved individual specific heterogeneity is explicitly allowed for, and (iv) the GMM estimators are derived by realistically assuming group size asymptotics. The Monte Carlo experiments conducted to assess the finite sample performances of the proposed estimators provide us with encouragement. © 2000 Elsevier Science S.A. All rights reserved.

JEL classification: C23

Keywords: Time series of cross sections; Panel data; GMM

1. Introduction

In this paper we propose a new method of using data from a time series of independent cross-sections (abbreviated to TISICS in what follows) in fitting

* Corresponding author. Tel.: + 44-115-951-4733; fax: + 44-115-951-4159.
E-mail address: sourafel.girma@nottingham.ac.uk (S. Girma).

PII: S0304-4076(00)00024-5

linear dynamic models such as

$$y_{it} = \alpha y_{it-1} + \beta x_{it} + f_i + \varepsilon_{it}, \tag{1}$$

where i and t index individual units and time periods, respectively, f is an individual effect and ε is a disturbance term. The main problem is the fact that such data sets do not track the same group of individuals over time, whereas the econometric models of interest require some information on intra-individual differences. Thus, it is not possible to consistently estimate the parameters of interest unless additional information in the shape of instrumental variables is available or further identifying restrictions are imposed on the model.

Deaton (1985) proposes a pseudo-panel approach to circumvent the identification problem caused by the absence of repeated observations on individual units. This involves placing individuals into distinct groups or cohorts, say G_c, for $c = 1, \ldots, C$ and working with the expectation of model (1) at each point in time conditional on cohort membership. Thus taking $E\{y_{it} | i(t) \in G_c\}$, we have

$$y^*_{ct} = \alpha y^*_{ct-1} + \beta x^*_{ctit} + f^*_{ct} + \varepsilon^*_{ct} \tag{2}$$

where superscripts asterisk denote the conditional expectations.

Eq. (2) is a model of the average behaviour of a cohort, much in the spirit of the 'representative agent' construction. Since cohort averages are effectively the units of analysis and the number of cross-sections is often small in practice, one might have to assume asymptotics on C to derive large-sample properties of the ensuing econometric estimators. On the other hand as y^*_{ct-1} and f^*_{ct} are correlated by construction, it is desirable to difference the latter out of the model. This requires that f^*_{ct} be invariant over time. One way to force this condition is to assume that all individuals within a cohort are homogeneous with respect to the unobserved heterogeneity factors. It will then be possible to apply standard dynamic panel data techniques by treating sample cohort averages as error-ridden observations on typical individuals (Collado, 1997).

Notwithstanding the fact that the pseudo-panel approach offers a framework for making joint use of independent cross-sectional information, there are problems with some of its features. Firstly the assertion of intra-cohort homogeneity seems too strong. It is indeed difficult to assume away unobserved individual heterogeneity away in micro data. Secondly the aggregation framework might not be desirable. An estimation method that is based on individual level data can make a more efficient use of the available information and potential problems of interpretation arising out of aggregation are likely to be mitigated. Thirdly, the practice of establishing the large-sample properties of econometric estimators and test statistics by driving the number of cohorts to infinity is not satisfactory. There is often a physical limit beyond which one cannot increase the number of cohorts. The oft-cited example of date of birth cohorts is a case in point. Finally, and this pertains to dynamic modelling in particular, standard pooling estimators will lead to invalid inference if the response parameters are characterised by cohort-wise heterogeneity. This follows from Pesaran and Smith (1995) who showed that dynamic modelling from pooled heterogeneous panels is not trivial. Given that cohorts should be chosen so that they are as distinct from each other as possible (cf. Deaton, 1985), it is important to have a framework which allows for some sort of response heterogeneity.

The above discussion demonstrates that there is clearly scope for studying alternative estimators for dynamic models from TISICS. In a contribution to the literature Moffit (1993) suggests a two-stage least-squares approach where the regressor y_{it-1} in (1) is instrumented by the predicted value $\hat{y}_{it-1}$ from a linear projection of the dependent variable on a vector of time-varying and time-invariant variables, say S_{it} and Z_i, respectively. To make this operational, one needs knowledge of S_{it-1}. But it is not always clear where this information is going to come from as TISICS data sets do not typically contain the history of the variables for the cross-sectional units. Moreover two-stage least squares is potentially problematic in that the fitted instruments (which need to be correlated with y_{it-1}) will also have a non-zero correlation with the individual effect f_i, since the two quantities are statistically related. The only obvious exception is if S_{it} is a function of time alone, hence uncorrelated with the time invariant f_i. But this will result in instruments that do not have much variation across individuals in the likely case where the number of cross-sections is much smaller than the cross-sectionals units. As a result the ensuing instrumental variables estimators will be highly inaccurate. So, although Moffit's (1993) paper generalises Deaton (1985) in the sense that the possibility of instrumentation procedures other than grouping is discussed, it does not seem to be too promising due to its rather strong informational requirement (Verbeek, 1992). In this paper we explore the possibility of making inference on model (1) from individual level data, by performing pair-wise quasi-differences across different observed individuals within the same group. This produces the following regression function at each time period and for all i and j: $\mathrm{E}\{y_{it}|y_{jt-1}, x_{it}\}$. This is potentially estimable since $\mathrm{Cov}\{y_{it}, y_{jt-1}\}$ can be identified from the data as long there are group-wise cross-sectional correlations.

The plan for the rest of the paper is as follows. In Section 2 we formally describe the quasi-differenced model along with the maintained assumptions. We identify the maximum number of linearly independent quasi-differences that are available and those will be used as a basis for estimation. In Section 3 we generate some population moment restrictions implied by the quasi-differenced model and suggest a generalised method of moments (GMM) estimation framework. The asymptotic properties of the GMM estimators are realistically based on having a large number of individuals per group-time cell. This compares favourably to the Deaton-type estimators in which the number of group/time periods is required to grow without limit. Another important advantage of the quasi-differencing approach is that slope parameter heterogeneity across groups can easily be allowed since the method can be applied on a single group. In Section 4 we conduct some Monte Carlo experiments to assess the finite sample performances of the proposed estimators. Section 5 concludes.

2. Model description

2.1. Basic identifying assumptions

We focus on the estimation of the following class of models form TISICS:

$$y_{i(t)t} = \alpha_{i(t)} y^{*}_{i(t)t-1} + \beta'_{i(t)} x_{i(t)t} + f_{i(t)} + \varepsilon_{i(t)t}$$
$$t = 2, T;\ i(t) = 1, \ldots, N_t. \tag{3}$$

Here x is a k-dimensional vector of control variables, f represents individual-specific effects and the ε's are time-varying disturbances. The time index in parentheses is used to emphasise the non-panel nature of the data. However, when no ambiguity is apparent, we will sometimes drop this index for the sake of notational elegance. It is assumed that we have cross-sectional observations for $t = 1, \ldots, T$, with $T \geqslant 2$. Notice that for $y^{*}_{i(t)t-1}$ the time index on the individual does not match to the (proper) time index. Such variables are not observed and they will often be denoted by a superscript asterisk. We will next discuss some of the basic identifying assumptions of the model.

H.1: The population is partitioned into a finite set of mutually exclusive and exhaustive groups G_c, $c = 1, \ldots, C$. Groups may be based on one or more underlying observed variables that are constant over time for all individuals. Without loss of generality, we assume that at each point in time n members are drawn at random from G_c, $\forall c$.

H.2: $\alpha_i = \alpha_j = \alpha_c$ and $\beta_i = \beta_j = \beta_c$ for $\forall (i,j) \in G_c$.

This assumption restricts the individual level heterogeneity in response parameters by stating that those parameters are identical within a group, but we do the next best thing by allowing for the possibility of group-wise heterogeneity.

H.3: $|\alpha_c| < 1$, $\forall c$.

H.4: $y_{i(t)0} = k_1 f_c + k_2 \varepsilon_{i(t)0}$, where the k's are constants and f_c is a random group specific effect.

The above assumption implies that the initial (unobserved) conditions are random draws from possibly different populations, but share a common component in the specification of a conditional mean. Assumption H.4 has an important implication: $\mathrm{Cov}\{y_{i(t)t}, y_{j(s)s}\} \neq 0$ for $\forall (i(t), j(s)) \in G_c$ and $\forall t, s$. That is, different individuals within the same group exhibit nonzero correlations. The information obtained from this source of correlations will prove useful in identifying the dynamic response parameters. While H.4 may not be an easily testable restriction, it is not without its justifications. It has been noted in the econometric literature that group structures are a common feature of many cross-sectional data sets (e.g., Frees, 1995). Researchers working with TISICS data often assume that each member of the group has some information about the average group value (Blundell et al., 1994).

H.5: $x_{i(t)t} = \upsilon_{i(t)} + \lambda' x_{i(t)t-1} + \theta_{ct} + w_{i(t)t}$ where the eigenvectors of λ lie within the unit circle, $\upsilon_{i(t)}$ is a k-dimensional vector of individual specific drift and θ_{ct} is group-time specific error component which can come about due to some shared characteristics between individuals within a group-time cell. It can be seen that θ_{ct} is a further source of within group correlations. From the above two assumptions, it is clear that intra-group correlation is directly proportional to the variances of f_c and θ_{ct}.Further assumptions are:

H.6: $\mathrm{Cov}\{f_i, \varepsilon_{ti}\} = 0, \forall i$ and t.

H.7:$f_i, f_c, f_{ct}, \theta_{ct}$ and ε_{it} are all mutually, independently distributed with mean zero and nonzero and finite variances.

The above assumption allows for purely individual-specific heterogeneity, even if individuals within a group share a common effect. This is in contrast to Deaton's (1985) approach where within-group heterogeneity is not explicitly allowed for.

H.8: $\mathrm{Cov}\,\{x_{i(t)t}, f_{j(s)}\} = 0$.

This is an innocuous assumption since $f_{j(s)}$ is specific to individual $j(s)$.

Making use of the above assumptions, we can show that $\mathrm{Cov}\{y_{i(t)t}, y_{j(s)s}\} \neq 0$ and equal $\forall (i,j) \in G_c$. In other words, our assumptions imply an equicorrelation structure within a group-time cell. Intuitively, without equicorrelation there would not be enough independent information to estimate $O(n^2)$ covariances per cell from just n observations. We like to note that in one form or another, the assumption of equicorrelation amongst the units of analysis is prevalent in econometric modelling. For example, the two-way panel estimation relies on equicorrelation between individuals observed during the same time period (e.g., Hsiao, 1986). The covariance stationarity assumption employed in time series models is also a case in point.

2.2. A quasi-differencing approach

We begin by writing (3) in its reduced-form representation as[1]

$$y_{i(t)t} = \pi_{t1} x^*_{i(t)1} + \cdots + \pi_{t(t-1)} x^*_{i(t)t-1} + \pi_{tt} x_{i(t)t} + \pi_{t0} y^*_{i(t)0} + v_{i(t)t} \tag{4}$$

with

$$v_{i(t)t} = \sum_{s=0}^{t-1} \alpha^s \varepsilon_{i(t)(t-s)} + \frac{1-\alpha^t}{1-\alpha} f_{i(t)} \pi_{ts}$$

$$= \beta' \alpha^{t-s} \quad \text{for } 1 \leqslant s \leqslant t,$$

[1] As the estimator proposed in this section deals with a single group, the index on α and β is dropped.

and

$$\pi_{t0} = \alpha^t.$$

Quasi-differencing the model as $\{y_{i(t)t} - \alpha y_{j(t-1)t-1};\ \forall[i(t), j(t-1)] \text{ and } \forall t \geqslant 2\}$, we obtain the following potentially estimable model:

$$y_{i(t)t} = \alpha y_{j(t-1)t-1} + \beta' x_{i(t)t} + \eta_{ijt} \tag{5}$$

where

$$\eta_{ijt} = \alpha^t[y_{i(t)0} - y_{j(t-1)0}] + \Delta f_{ijt} + \Delta x_{ijt} + \Delta\varepsilon_{ijt}$$

with

$$\Delta f_{ijt} = \frac{1-\alpha^t}{1-\alpha} f_{i(t)} - \frac{\alpha - \alpha^t}{1-\alpha} f_{j(t-1)},$$

$$\Delta x_{ijt} = \beta' \sum_{r=0}^{t-2} \alpha^{r+1}\{x^*_{i(t)(t-1-r)} - x^*_{j(t-1)(t-1-r)}\}^2$$

and

$$\Delta\varepsilon_{ijt} = \sum_{r=1}^{t-1} \alpha^r\{\varepsilon_{i(t)t-r} - \varepsilon_{j(t-1)t-r}\} + \varepsilon_{i(t)t}.$$

Let $D_1 = [0_{(T-1)\times 1} : I_{T-1}]$; $D_2 = [I_{T-1} : 0_{(T-1)\times 1}]$ and $A_2 = D_2 \otimes l_n \otimes I_n$, where 0_a; I_a *and* l_a are the null matrix, the identity matrix and the vector of ones of dimension a, respectively. When all observations within a group are arranged first by individuals and then by time periods, and the transformation matrix $B(\alpha) = A_1 - \alpha A_2$ is applied to the resulting $nT \times 1$ vector, it can be checked that the pairwise quasi-differenced model of Eq. (4) will be produced. Since the $n^2(T-1) \times nT$ matrix $B(\alpha)$ has rank equal to $nT - 1$, the transformed error covariance matrix will be singular because $r = n^2(T-1) - (nT-1)$ equations in the quasi-differenced model are redundant. Consequently, any estimation strategy has to make due allowance for the singularity of the disturbance covariance matrix. There are two main ways of dealing with this (e.g., Judge et al., 1985): (a) the use of appropriate generalised inverse estimators, and (b) the elimination of the redundant equations prior to estimation. Employing generalised inverses does not seem to be a terribly attractive alternative in our framework. This is because it involves a multiple of n^4 terms and with possibly large n, this will pose awkward computational problems. We thus attempt to identify $nT - 1$ linearly independent pairwise quasi-differences within each group. To

[2] Although $x_{j(t-1)t-1}$ is observed, it is left in the disturbances for reasons that will shortly become apparent.

do so we first consider the following set of quasi-differences within each group between individuals with the same ordering in their respective time domains: $L_1 = \{y_{i(t)t} - \alpha y_{i(t-1)t-1};\ \forall i(t),\ i(t-1) \text{ and } t \geqslant 2\}$.

Note that $i(t) = i(t-1)$ is to be understood that as the case where individual i at time t and individual i at time $(t-1)$ correspond to the same ordering within their respective time domains. It can be verified that L_1 consists of $n(T-1)$ linearly independent quasi-differenced equations. By augmenting L_1 by the following $n-1$ quasi-differences between the first observation at time $t = 2$ and all observations bar the first one at time $t = 1$, $L_2 = \{y_{1(2)2} - \alpha y_{j(1)1};\ \forall j \geqslant 2 \in G_{c1}\}$, it can be checked that $L = L_1 \cup L_2$ will produce the desired full set of $nT - 1$ linearly independent quasi-differences. As a result L will exhaust all information contained in the pairwise quasi-differenced model. Of course this is not the only set of linearly independent quasi-differences. However, since any other such set is a nonsingular transformation of L, the same information will be preserved.

Let $W_{ijt} = [y_{j(t-1)t-1}, x'_{i(t)t}]'$ and define $\gamma_0 = [\alpha, \beta']'$ as the true parameter vector. When the above transformations are applied to Eq. (3), the following model will then be available for estimation for

$$\forall [i(t), j(t-1)] \in S \equiv S_1 \cup S_2$$

$$y_{i(t)t} = \alpha y_{j(t-1)t-1} + \beta' x_{i(t)t} + \eta_{ijt} \equiv \gamma_0' W_{ijt} + \eta_{ijt}, \tag{6}$$

where $S_1 = \{[i(t), i(t-1)] \text{ and } t \geqslant 2\}$; $S_2 = \{\forall [1(2), j(1)], j(1) \geqslant 2)\}$.

3. Inference

3.1. Identification

OLS on model (6) would produce inconsistent estimators because η_{ijt} is correlated with both $y_{j(t-1)t-1}$ and $x_{i(t)t}$. This can easily be checked using the underlying assumptions of the model. Fortunately, these assumptions also imply that the composite error term η^{t}_{cij} satisfies the following two sets of linear moment conditions:

$$\mathrm{E}\{y_{g(t-s,t-s)}\eta_{ijt}\} = 0;\ t = 2, \ldots, T;\ s = 1, \ldots, t-1;\ \forall g(t-1) \neq j(t-1)$$

and

$$\mathrm{E}\{x_{g(t-s)t-s}\eta_{ijt}\} = 0;\ t = 2, \ldots, T;\ s = 0, \ldots, t-1;$$

$$\forall g(t-s) \mid g(t-s) \neq i(t) \text{ or } g(t-1) = j(t-1).$$

That is past and present values of the dependent and explanatory variables within the same group can be used as instruments. Because of assumptions H.4 and H.5, a nonzero IV-regressor correlation is ensured. Notice that since the correlations in the x's between the different individuals comes from the θ_{ct}'s, leaving the observable $x_{j(t-1)t-1}$ in the composite disturbance term ensures that the latter does not contain a θ term. Also notice that since η_{ijt} contains $y_{i(t)0} - y_{j(t-1)0}$, any $y_{g(t-s)(t-s)}$ will not be correlated with it because of the equicorrelation assumption imposed on the model.

A problem that we face is the possibility of an infinite number of instruments, given that the number of observations per group-time cell is allowed to grow. For example, $X_{i(t-2)t-2}; i = 1, \ldots, n$ can be used as instruments for the regressors in the quasi-differenced model. Since standard optimality results for GMM estimators (e.g., Hansen, 1982) are not trivially applicable when the vector of conditioning variables is infinite dimensional, it pays to look for some ways to economise on the number of instruments to be used. One apparent solution might be to average the instruments over cells. In this case there would not be enough internal variation in the instruments set, unless the number of groups grows with n at a suitable rate. This is bound to adversely affect the precision of the resulting estimators. In this paper we restrict ourselves to a set of finite orthogonality conditions by the simple, albeit ad hoc, device of using just one orthogonality condition within each subset of the moment restrictions. For example in the Monte Carlo experiments conducted in the next section, the following moment restrictions are chosen to be the basis for estimating γ: $E\{Z_{ijt}\eta_{ijt}\} = 0$ with $Z_{ijt} = \{y_{g(t-1)t-1}, x'_{g(t-1)t-1}, x'_{g(t)t}\}$, where g is made to correspond to $j-1$.[3] We have to emphasise, however, that this is entirely arbitrary. All that is needed is to assign distinct instruments to each observation.

3.2. GMM inference

GMM estimation proceeds by forming sample analogs of those population moment conditions. The sample analogs are usually sample averages of $Z_{ijt}\eta_{ijt}$ (also known as the disturbances of GMM) and the latter are expected to satisfy appropriate laws of large numbers (LLNs) for all admissible points in the parameter space. As far as justifying the use of LLNs is concerned, the simplest case occurs when the random variables under consideration are independently and identically distributed. In our case, however, there is some dependence across observations due to the assumptions we employed and the quasi-differencing transformation of the data. In fact the disturbances of the model exhibit contemporaneous as well as temporal correlations within groups. They are also heterogeneous across time as can be verified by inspecting the structure of η^t_{cij}. Alternative approaches to deriving LLNs that are applicable to a variety of non i.i.d environments are proposed by several authors (e.g., White, 1984). These

[3] We adopt the convention of putting $g = n$ for $j = 1$

laws of large numbers typically place some restrictions on the dependence, heterogeneity and moments of the data process.

The main problem in the present context is the contemporaneous within group dependence introduced by the transformation function L_2. One practical solution may be to average all quasi-differences produced by L_2 and assume that as n grows the dependence will become negligible (and accept the risk of any finite sample bias). In the sequel we work with the model produced by L_1 alone, because the large sample argument with a fixed number of groups and time periods is neater and the computations involved are simpler. Thus we have, for $i = 1, \ldots, n$ and $t = 2, \ldots, T$

$$y_{i(t)} = \alpha y_{i(t-1)(t-1)} + \beta' x_{i(t)t} + \eta_{iit} \equiv \gamma_0' W_{iit} + \eta_{iit}$$

and the resulting orthogonality conditions can be expressed as $\mathrm{E}\{Z_{iit}\eta_{iit}\} \equiv \mathrm{E}\{h_{it}\} = 0$, with $Z_{iit} = \{y_{i-1(t-1)t-1}, x'_{i-1(t-1)t-1}, x'_{i-1(t)t}\}$ In the Appendix A we prove that the following proposition holds:

Proposition 1.

$$\frac{1}{n(T-1)} \sum_{it-2}^{T} \sum_{i=1}^{n} h_{it} \xrightarrow{\mathrm{P}} 0$$

as $n \to \infty$ with T fixed.

Defining S_{nT} to be a sequence of weight matrices, the GMM estimator of γ_0 can thus be obtained upon solving

$$\operatorname{argmin}_{\gamma} \left[\frac{1}{n(T-1)} \sum_{i,t} h_{it} \right]' S_{nT} \left[\frac{1}{n(T-1)} \sum_{i,t} h_{it} \right].$$

The optimal GMM estimator of γ is obtained by setting the weight matrix in the GMM minimand function to the inverse of

$$\Omega \equiv \mathrm{Cov}\left[\frac{1}{n(T-1)} \sum_{i,t} h_{it} \right]$$

and it is given as $\hat{\gamma} = [W'Z\Omega^{-1}Z'W]^{-1}[W'Z\Omega^{-1}Z'y]$, where the data and instruments matrices are constructed in an obvious way. In Appendix B we show that the following proposition holds under the assumptions of the model:

Proposition 2.

$$\frac{1}{\sqrt{n(T-1)}} \sum_{t=2}^{T} \sum_{i}^{n} h_{it} \xrightarrow{\mathrm{d}} \mathrm{N}(0, \Omega)$$

as $n \to \infty$ with T fixed.

Thus under some regularity conditions (White, 1984), $\hat{\gamma}_c$ will be asymptotically normally distributed as

$$\sqrt{L}(\hat{\gamma} - \gamma_0) \rightarrow \mathrm{N}(0, V), \tag{7}$$

with

$$V = \left[\left(\frac{1}{n(T-1)} Z'W\right)\Omega^{-1}\left(\frac{1}{n(T-1)} Z'W\right)\right]^{-1}.$$

Obviously $\hat{\gamma}$ is not feasible since Ω is unknown, but the latter can be replaced by a consistent estimator without affecting the asymptotic properties of $\hat{\gamma}$ (Hansen, 1982). A Newey–West (1987)-type estimator for Ω can be constructed nonparametrically as

$$\hat{\Omega} = \frac{1}{n(T-1)}\left[\sum_{i,t} h_{it}h'_{it} + \left(\sum_{i,t} h_{it}h'_{i(t-1)} + h_{i(t-1)}h'_{it}\right)\right].$$

An advantage of this approach is that it can be implemented with only two cross-sections. And when we have more than one group and the parameters of the model are heterogeneous across these groups and the equation errors are not related, it can be implemented separately for each group without loss of efficiency. If the groups share a common parameter, however, a joint estimation can enhance efficiency. For example, with $C < \infty$ groups and only α varying across groups, the model can be estimated within a system of instrumental variables method by stacking the observation by groups.

3.3. A simpler estimator

For some M in each time period, randomly divide observations within a group into M groups. Let $\bar{y}_{mt}$ be the sample mean across all observations in subgroup $m, m = 1, M$. Now consider the quasi-differenced equations: $\{y_{it} - \alpha\bar{y}_{mt-1}\}$ which gives rise to the following estimable model: $y_{it} = \alpha\bar{y}_{mt-1} + \beta' x_{it} + \bar{\eta}_{imt}$. One can then implement the GMM estimation strategy of this paper by using $[\bar{y}_{(m-1)t-1}\bar{x}_{(m-1)t}\bar{x}_{(m-1)t-1}]$ as instrumental variables.[4] The advantage of this approach is that for fixed M, the asymptotic of the resulting estimator is much simpler since for *sufficiently large n*. M the disturbance of the quasi-differenced equation are asymptotically uncorrelated. As a result GMM can be routinely implemented. The disadvantage of this approach is that using instruments based on sub-group averages might throw away information contained in the separately lagged individual instruments. In Section 4 we assess the

---

[4] As an anonymous referee noted, the pairwise quasi-differencing estimators proposed in this paper can be seen as the limiting case of this simpler estimator as M approaches the sample size.

relative merits of these alternative estimators by conducting some simulation experiments.

3.4. Some extensions to the basic model

The study of the effects of observed time-invariant variables such as sex, region and other socio-economic background variables (assuming that they are not used to define groups) could be important in practice. To see how such variables fit into the quasi-differencing framework, define by W the vector of observed time-invariant regressors and consider the following model:

$$y_{i(t)t} = \alpha y^{*}_{i(t)t-1} + \varphi W_{i(t)} + \varepsilon_{i(t)t}. \tag{8}$$

Pairwise quasi-differencing Eq. (8) would yield

$$y_{i(t)t} = \alpha y_{j(t-1)t-1} + \rho_1 W_{i(t)} + \rho_2 W_{j(t-1)} + q^{t}_{ij} \tag{9}$$

where

$$q^{t}_{ij} = \alpha^{t} \lfloor y_{0i} - y_{0j} \rfloor + \Delta f^{t}_{ij} + \Delta f^{t}_{ij};$$

$$\rho_1 = \frac{1-\alpha^{t}}{1-\alpha}\varphi \quad \text{and} \quad \rho_2 = -\frac{\alpha-\alpha^{t}}{1-\alpha}\varphi.$$

The identification of φ from (9) would be greatly simplified if $W_{i(t)} = W_{j(t-1)}$, that is if individuals $i(t)$ and $j(t-1)$ exhibit the same time-invariant characteristics. Eq. (9) then simplifies to $y_{ti} = \alpha y_{j(t-1)t-1} + \rho W_{i(t)} + q^{t}_{cij}$.

Thus a suitable choice of pairs for differencing would ease the estimation of φ, a parameter which is not identifiable in first-differenced dynamic (pseudo) panel models.

The model we have considered in this paper can also be easily extended to include lagged regressors of higher orders. For example, to estimate the pure AR(2) model $y_{i(t)t} = \alpha_1 y_{i(t)t-1} + \alpha_2 y_{i(t)t-2} + \varepsilon_{it}$, we need to perform the following transformation to the data:

$$\{y_{i(t)t} - \alpha_1 y_{j(t-1)(t-1)} - \alpha_2 y_{k(t-2)(t-2)};\ \forall i(t), j(t-1) \text{ and } k(t-2) \in G_c\}.$$

4. Monte Carlo simulations

To get a feel for how the GMM estimators based on the pairwise quasi-differences (PQD) and the simpler average quasi-differences (AQD) perform in practice, we conducted some Monte Carlo simulations. We are mainly concerned with the consistency of the estimators and their respective standard errors. We examine two combinations of parameters, $(\alpha, \beta) = (0.8, -0.5)$, $(0.3, 0.8)$, to explore the possible sensitivity of the results to parameter values.

Since an important factor affecting the behaviour of the estimators is the magnitude of IV-regressor correlation, we consider alternative data generating mechanism in which 25%, 50% and 75% of the total variability in the (scalar) exogenous variable and the initial values is attributed to a common group component. In each of these cases, the individual-specific variance is taken to be unity. Fixing the number of groups and cross sections to 1 and 5 respectively, we experimented with three different group-time cell sizes, 100, 200 and 400, which we think are not unrealistic. For each of the resulting 18 configurations, one hundred Monte Carlo experiments are conducted. For the AQD estimators the observations are randomly assigned to 10 subgroups.

Tables 1 and 2 summarise the results from the experiments. The means and standard deviations are computed over the 100 replications and the figures in parentheses represent the percentage biases from the true values. The sample means of the asymptotic standard errors calculated from the GMM formula are also reported, with the percentage deviation of these asymptotic values from the respective across replication standard deviations of estimated values given in parentheses.

A noteworthy result from the experiments is that the finite sample bias of the GMM estimator is more pronounced when the relative variance of the group effect (say ζ) is small. For example in Table 1, the bias in the estimator for $\alpha(\beta)$ decreases from 3.6% (3.8%) to 1.5% (1.8%) when $n = 100$ as ζ increases from 25% to 50%. But, it is encouraging to note that this bias seems to be tolerable for all sample sizes.

When it comes to the efficiency of the GMM estimators as measured by the across-simulation standard deviations, the role of ζ is more crucial. For given sample size, efficiency improves dramatically as ζ increases. For example, in Table 2 the standard deviations of the estimators is divided by a factor of 3 as ζ doubles to 50%, for $n = 200$. A marked gain in efficiency is also observed as ζ increases to 75%.

A worrying aspect of the results is the absolute magnitude of the standard deviations (and asymptotic standard errors) when ζ is small, irrespective of the sample sizes. Assuming that the estimators will be deemed precise enough if the margin of error at 5% level is within 20% for the true parameter value, the standard deviation should be less than a tenth of the corresponding parameter. Using this rough guide most estimates based on $n = 100$ and 200 are disappointing when $\zeta = 25\%$. In general good precision is obtained when ζ is set to 75%, although some reasonably precise estimates emerge with $\zeta = 50\%$.

Another important issue to be addressed is whether the asymptotic standard errors are consistently estimated. The only clue to this comes from a comparison with the simulated standard deviations of the estimators, which themselves are subject to error. Following the argument of Crepon and Mairesse (1996) we conclude that the estimated asymptotic standard errors and the simulated standard deviations are not significantly different at the 5% level as they are

Table 1
Mean (% bias), standard deviation and asymptotic standard error of the estimators for $\alpha = 0.8$; $\beta = -0.5$

	Relative variance of group effect					
	25%		50%		75%	
	PQD	AQD	PQD	AQD	PQD	AQD
$n = 100$, α						
Mean	0.771 (3.6%)	0.358 (55.2%)	0.812 (1.5%)	0.539 (32.6%).	0.810 (1.3%)	0.669 (16.4%)
Std deviation	0.294	0.078	0.209	0.087	0.071	0.046
Asym s.error	0.297 (1%)	0.034 (56.4%)	0.175 (16.3%)	0.037 (47.5%)	0.070 (1.4%)	0.026 (43.5%)
β						
Mean	− 0.519 (3.8%)	− 0.796 (59.2%)	− 0.491 (1.8%)	− 0.665 (33%)	− 0.494 (1.2%)	− 0.589 (17.8%)
Std deviation	0.211	0.06	0.135	0.062	0.057	0.042
Asym s.error	0.213 (1%)	0.034 (43.3%)	0.122 (9.6%)	0.034 (45.1%)	0.054 (5.3%)	0.023 (45.2%)
$n = 200$, α						
α						
Mean	0.818 (2.2%)	0.462 (42.2%)	0.805 (0.6%)	0.623 (22.2%)	0.786 (1.8%)	0.717 (10.4%)
Std deviation	0.439	0.090	0.151	0.073	0.049	0.041
Asym s.error	0.421 (4.1%)	0.042 (53.3%)	0.131 (13.2%)	0.029 (61.3%)	0.050 (2%)	0.019 (53.6%)
β						
Mean	− 0.463 (7.4%)	− 0.714 (42.8%)	− 0.496 (1%)	− 0.616 (23.2%)	− 0.506 (1%)	− 0.559 (11.8%)
Std deviation	0.342	0.085	0.112	0.057	0.040	0.029
Asym s.error	0.299 (12.6%)	0.039 (54.1%)	0.094 (16.1%)	0.026 (54.4%)	0.038 (5%)	0.017 (41.4%)
$n = 400$, α						
α						
Mean	0.764 (4.5%)	0.574 (28.2%)	0.801 (0%)	0.695 (13.1%)	0.803 (0%)	0.754 (5.7%)
Std deviation	0.247	0.084	0.099	0.043	0.038	0.028
Asym s.error	0.238 (3.6%)	0.032 (62%)	0.091 (8.1)%	0.022 (48.9%)	0.037 (2.6%)	0.014 (50%)
β						
Mean	− 0.546 (9.2%)	− 0.663 (32.6%)	− 0.504 (1%)	− 0.569 (13.8%)	− 0.498 (0.4%)	− 0.532 (6.4%)
Std deviation	0.196	0.063	0.059	0.037	0.026	0.019
Asym s.error	0.182 (7.2%)	0.030 (52.4%)	0.065 (10.2%)	0.019 (48.6%)	0.029 (11.5%)	0.013 (31.6%)

Table 2
Mean (% bias), standard deviation and asymptotic standard error of the estimators for $\alpha = 0.3$; $\beta = -0.8$

	Relative variance of group effect					
	25%		50%		75%	
	PQD	AQD	PQD	AQD	PQD	AQD
$n = 100$, α						
Mean	0.340 (13%)	0.121 (60%)	0.299 (0%)	0.185 (38%)	0.304 (1.3%)	0.242 (19%)
Std deviation	0.221	0.029	0.107	0.028	0.042	0.024
Asym s.error	0.251 (13.6%)	0.023 (20%)	0.105 (1.9%)	0.024 (14.3%)	0.041 (2.4%)	0.016 (33.3%)
β						
Mean	0.769 (3.9%)	0.934 (16.8%)	0.800 (0%)	0.888 (11.1%)	0.798 (0%)	0.846 (5.75%)
Std deviation	0.188	0.027	0.086	0.026	0.035	0.022
Asym s.error	0.211 (12.2%)	0.022 (19.5%)	0.089 (3.48%)	0.022 (15.4%)	0.034 (2.8%)	0.014 (36.3%)
$n = 200$, α						
α						
Mean	0.290 (3.3%)	0.164 (45.3%)	0.308 (2.6%)	0.230 (23%)	0.301 (0%)	0.267 (11%)
Std deviation	0.242	0.046	0.66	0.026	0.031	0.019
Asym s.error	0.206 (14.9%)	0.027 (41.3%)	0.071 (7.6%)	0.018 (31.8%)	0.030 (3.3)	0.12 (36.8%)
β						
Mean	0.815 (1.88%)	0.902 (12.8%)	0.791 (1.12%)	0.854 (6.8%)	0.799 (0%)	0.826 (3.25%)
Std deviation	0.177	0.033	0.063	0.023	0.025	0.016
Asym s.error	0.166 (6.2%)	0.025 (24.2%)	0.060 (4.8%)	0.016 (23.1%)	0.025 (0%)	0.011 (31.3%)
$n = 400$, α						
α						
Mean	0.324 (8%)	0.208 (30.6%)	0.294 (2%)	0.258 (14%)	0.297 (0%)	0.279 (7%)
Std deviation	0.164	0.032	0.049	0.020	0.029	0.013
Asym s.error	0.170 (3.7%)	0.022 (31.2%)	0.046 (6.1)%	0.014 (30%)	0.021 (27.6%)	0.010 (27.6%)
β						
Mean	0.789 (1.4%)	0.871 (8.9%)	0.805 (0.6%)	0.832 (0.4%)	0.803 (0.4%)	0.817 (2.1%)
Std deviation	0.146	0.029	0.039	0.017	0.020	0.010
Asym s.error	0.139 (4.8%)	0.020 (31%)	0.040 (2.6%)	0.013 (23.5%)	0.017 (15%)	0.007 (30%)

mostly within 20% of each other. We thus find it encouraging that the nonparametric covariance matrix estimator performs quite well in small samples.

The above discussion has highlighted the desirability of having a reasonably high level of relative variation in the group-specific component (and hence a high degree of correlation between individuals within the same group) for the success of the quasi-differencing method proposed in this paper. This is not a surprising result in view of recent work which emphasises the pitfalls of IV-type estimators when the instrument-regressor correlation is low (Staiger and Stock, 1997). So an important implication for applied work is to routinely examine the correlations between the regressors and the instrumental variables candidates and exercise caution when these values are low.

The small sample performance of the simpler AQD proposed in Section 3.3 proves to be disappointing, except when the sample size is quite large ($n = 400$) and most of the variation in the data comes from the group specific effect ($\zeta = 75\%$). A large number of observation per sub-group is needed to guarantee that the AQD disturbances are not correlated; while the consequences of throwing some individual specific information following the aggregation procedure is not serious if only a small part of the sample variation is due to individual-specific effects.

5. Concluding remarks

In this paper we motivated and described a new method of estimating linear dynamic models from a time series of independent cross-sections. Some of the desirable features of the method include the fact that no aggregation is involved; the response parameters can freely vary across groups; the presence of unobserved individual specific heterogeneity is explicitly allowed for and the large-sample results are derived by realistically assuming group size asymptotics. Moreover the Monte Carlo experiments conducted to assess the finite sample performances of the proposed estimators provide us with some encouragement. For these reasons, we think that it can be considered as a feasible alternative in applied work.

Acknowledgements

I want to thank Len Gill for motivating this paper, Tae-Hwan Kim for his help and two anonymous referees for their constructive suggestions. I also acknowledge the support of David Greenaway. Finally, financial support from the Leverhulme Trust under Programme Grant F114/BF is gratefully acknowledged.

Appendix A. Proof of consistency

Proposition A.1.

$$\frac{1}{nT}\sum_{t=1}^{T}\sum_{i=1}^{n} h_{it} \xrightarrow{p} \mathrm{E}(h_{it}) = 0$$

as $n \to \infty$ with T fixed.

For the sake of notational elegance we pretend that t runs from 1 to T and for ease of exposition we assume that h is scalar. We want to show that the sequence of random vector $\{h_{it}; t = 1, \ldots, T; n = 1, 2, \ldots\}$ satisfies a Weak Law of Large Numbers (WLLN). Using the assumptions of the model and further assuming that the various fourth-order moments exist and are finite, it can be established that the covariance of the GMM disturbances have the following general structure:

$$\mathrm{E}[h_{it}h_{jt}] = \begin{cases} f_1(t) < \infty & \text{if } i = j \text{ and } t = s, \\ f_2(t, s) < \infty & \text{if } i = j \text{ and } |t - s| = 1, \\ f_3(t, s) < \infty & \text{if } i = j - 1 \text{ and } |t - s| = 1, \\ 0 & \text{else.} \end{cases}$$

Here $f_1(t)$ denotes the variance terms which is a function of time; $f_2(t, s)$ represents covariance terms between two individuals which correspond to the same ordering within adjacent time periods, and $f_3(t, s)$ is the result of using the stochastic $y_{i-1(t-1)t-1}$ as an instrument. Thus we have a zero-mean random variable which is heterogeneous across time but whose covariance structure is independent of the individual index.

Now re-write

$$\frac{1}{nT}\sum_{t=1}^{T}\sum_{i=1}^{n} h_{it}$$

as

$$\frac{1}{T}\left\{\frac{1}{n}\sum_{i=1}^{n} h_{i1} + \frac{1}{n}\sum_{i=1}^{n} h_{i2} + \cdots + \frac{1}{n}\sum_{i=1}^{n} h_{iT}\right\}$$

and consider the tth term $(1/n)\sum_{i=1}^{n} h_{it}$. Since $\mathrm{E}((1/n)\sum_{i=1}^{n} h_{it}) = 0$ and by Chebyshev inequality, for $\varepsilon > 0$

$$P\left(\left|\frac{1}{n}\sum_{i=1}^{n} h_{it}\right| > \varepsilon\right) \leqslant \frac{\mathrm{Var}\,[1/n\sum_{i=1}^{n} h_{it}]}{\varepsilon^2}.$$

Now, since $\mathrm{E}(h_{it}h_{jt}) = 0$

$$\mathrm{Var}\left[\frac{1}{n}\sum_{i=1}^{n} h_{it}\right] = \frac{1}{n^2}\left[\sum_{i=1}^{n} \mathrm{Var}(h_{it})\right] = \frac{1}{n^2}\sum_{i=1}^{n} f_1(t) \to 0 \text{ as } n \to \infty .$$

Hence $(1/n)\sum_{i=1}^{n} h_{it} \xrightarrow{p} 0$ as $n \to \infty$, for a given t. It then follows that the $T \times 1$ vector

$$H_n = \begin{bmatrix} \frac{1}{n}\sum_{i=1}^{n} h_{i1} \\ \vdots \\ \frac{1}{n}\sum_{i=1}^{n} h_{iT} \end{bmatrix} \xrightarrow{p} H = \begin{bmatrix} 0 \\ \vdots \\ 0 \end{bmatrix} \text{as } n \to \infty .$$

Now let $g(H_n) = (1/T)H_n' i_T$, where i_T is the $T \times 1$ vector of ones. Since $g(.)$ is a continuous function, we use Proposition 6.1.4 in Brockwell and Davis (1991) to establish that $g(H_n) = H_n' i_T = (1/nT)\sum_{t=1}^{T}\sum_{i=1}^{n} h_{it} \xrightarrow{p} g(H) = 0$ as $n \to \infty$ with T fixed. □.

Further assume that

(a) the IV-regressor product matrix satisfies $(1/nT)\sum_{t=1}^{T}\sum_{i=1}^{n} z_{it}w_{it} - Q_{nT} \xrightarrow{p} = 0$, where $\{Q_{nT}\}$ is O(1) and has uniformly full rank and (b) The GMM weighting matrix S_{nT} converges in probability to S which is O(1) and uniformly positive definite.Then it follows from the theorem in White (1984, p. 25) that $\hat{\gamma}$, which is the solution to establish that

$$\mathrm{argmin}_{\gamma}\left[\frac{1}{n(T-1)}\sum_{i,t} h_{it}\right]' S_{nT}\left[\frac{1}{n(T-1)}\sum_{i,t} h_{it}\right]$$

exists in probability and $\hat{\gamma} \xrightarrow{p} \gamma_0$.

Appendix B. Proof of asymptotic normality

Proposition B.1.i$(1/\sqrt{nT})\sum_{t=1}^{T}\sum_{i}^{n} h_{it} \xrightarrow{d} \mathrm{N}(0, \Omega)$ as $n \to \infty$ with T fixed.

Proof. Rewrite $(1/\sqrt{nT})\sum_{t=1}^{T}\sum_{i}^{n} h_{it}$ as $(1/\sqrt{T})\, 1/\sqrt{n}\sum_{i=1}^{n} H_i$, where $H_i \equiv \sum_{t=1}^{T} h_{it} = [h_{i1}, \ldots, h_{iT}]i_T \equiv h_i' i_T$.

Consider $(1/\sqrt{n})\sum_{i=1}^{n} H_i$ with $E(H_i) = 0$, by the orthogonality conditions. The variance of H_i can be written as

$$\mathrm{Var}(H_i) = i'_T \, \mathrm{Var}(h_i) i_T = i'_T = \begin{bmatrix} E(h_{i1}h_{i1}) & E(h_{i1}h_{i2}) & \cdots & E(h_{i1}h_{iT}) \\ E(h_{i2}h_{i1}) & E(h_{i2}h_{i2}) & \cdots & E(h_{12}h_{iT}) \\ \vdots & \vdots & \ddots & \vdots \\ E(h_{iT}h_{i1}) & E(h_{iT}h_{i2}) & \vdots & E(h_{iT}h_{iT}) \end{bmatrix} i_T$$

$$= i'_T \begin{bmatrix} f_1(1) & f_2(1,2) & 0 & \cdots & \cdots & 0 \\ f_2(2,1) & f_1(2) & f_2(2,3) & 0 & \cdots & 0 \\ 0 & f_2(3,2) & f_1(3) & \ddots & 0 & \vdots \\ \vdots & 0 & & \ddots & \ddots & 0 \\ \vdots & \vdots & & & f_1(T-1) & f_2(T-1,T) \\ 0 & 0 & \cdots & 0 & f_2(T,T-1) & f_1(T) \end{bmatrix} \kappa_T$$

$$= \sum_{t=1}^{T} f_1 + \sum_{t=1}^{T-1} [f_2(t,t+1) + f_2(t+1,t)] \equiv \Omega_1.$$

Similarly we establish that $E(H_i H_{i-1}) = \sum_{t=1}^{T-1}[f_3(t,t+1) + f_3(t+1,t)] \equiv \Omega_2$. By assumption $E(H_i H_{i-j}) = 0$ if $j \geqslant 2$, implying that $\{H_i\}_{i=1}^{\infty}$ is 'covariance stationary'. Thus we can use Wold's decomposition theorem to write $H_i = \mu + \lambda_i + \theta\lambda_{i-1}$, where $\lambda_i \sim n(0, \sigma^2)$;

$$E(H_i) = \mu = 0 \quad \text{and} \quad \theta = \frac{\Omega_1 \pm \sqrt{\Omega_1^2 - 4\Omega_2^2}}{2\Omega_2}.$$

Then by the theorem in Anderson (1971, p. 429), $\sqrt{n}(\bar{H} - \mu) \overset{a}{\to} N(0, \sum_{j=-\infty}^{j=\infty}\sigma_j)$ as $n \to \infty$, where $\sigma_j = E\{(H_i - \mu)(H_{i-j} - \mu)\}$ and $\bar{H} = (1/n)\sum_{i=1}^{n} H_i$. Since $\sigma_j = 0$ *for* $|j| > 1$, we have $(1/\sqrt{n}\sum_{i=1}^{n} H_i \overset{a}{\to} N(0, \Omega_1 + 2\Omega_2)$.

Hence

$$\left(\frac{1}{\sqrt{nT}}\right)\sum_{i=1}^{n} H_i \equiv \frac{1}{\sqrt{nT}}\sum_{t=1}^{T}\sum_{i=1}^{n} h_{it} \overset{a}{\to} N\left(0, \frac{1}{T}(\Omega_1 + 2\Omega_2)\right)$$

$$\equiv N(0, \Omega) \text{ as } n \to \infty \text{ with } T \text{ fixed.} \quad \square.$$

If Ω is uniformly positive definite and O(1) and assumptions (a) and (b) of Appendix A hold, we can use the theorem in White (1984, p. 69) to establish that

$$D^{-1/2}\sqrt{nT}(\hat{\gamma} - \gamma_0) \overset{a}{\sim} N(0, I),$$

where $D \equiv (Q'_{nT}S_{nT}Q_{nT})^{-1}Q'_{nT}S_{nT}\Omega S_{nT}Q_{nT}(Q'_{nT}S_{nT}Q_{nT})^{-1}$. In practice, the asymptotic covariance matrix Ω is substituted by its positive semidefinite consistent estimator and Q_{nT} is replaced by $Z'W/nT$, where Z and W are the matrices of instruments and regressors, respectively. Since $\{H_i\}_{i=1}^{\infty}$ is 'covariance stationary', the nonparametric estimators of asymptotic covariance matrices in the econometric literature (e.g., Newey and West, 1987) should work under some regularity conditions regarding the underlying error terms.

References

Anderson, T.W., 1971. The Statistical Analysis Time Series. Wiley, New York.

Brockwell, P.J., Davis, R.A., 1991. Time Series: Theory and Methods. Springer, New York.

Blundell, R., Browning, M., Meghir, C., 1994. Consumer demand and the life-cycle allocation of household expenditure. Review of Economic Studies 61, 57–80.

Crepon, B., Mairesse, J., 1996. The Chamberlain approach. In: Matyas, L., Sevestre, P. (Eds.), The Econometrics of Panel Data: Handbook of Theory and Applications. Kluwer Academic Publishers, Dordrecht, pp. 323–395.

Collado, M.D., 1997. Estimating dynamic models from time series of independent cross sections. Journal of Econometrics 82, 37–62.

Deaton, A., 1985. Panel data from time series of cross sections. Journal of Econometrics 30, 109–126.

Frees, E.D., 1995. Assessing cross-sectional correlation in panel data. Journal of Econometrics 69, 393–414.

Hansen, L.P., 1982. Large sample properties of generalised method of moments estimators. Econometrica 50, 1029–1054.

Hsiao, C., 1986. Analysis of Panel Data. Cambridge University Press, Cambridge.

Judge, G., Griffiths, W., Hill, W., Lutkepohl, R.C., Lee, T.C., 1985. The Theory and Practice of Econometrics. Wiley, New York.

Moffitt, R., 1993. Identification and estimation of dynamic models with time series of repeated cross sections. Journal of Econometrics 59, 99–123.

Newey, W.K., West, K.D., 1987. A simple, positive definite, heteroskedasticity and autocorrelation consistent covariance matrix. Econometrica 55, 703–708.

Pesaran, M.H., Smith, R., 1995. Estimating long-run relationship from dynamic heterogeneous panels. Journal of Econometrics 68, 79–112.

Staiger, D., Stock, J.H., 1997. Instrumental variables regression with weak instruments. Econometrica 65, 557–586.

Verbeek, M., 1992. Pseudo Panel Data. In: Matyas, L., Sevestre, P. (Eds.), The Econometrics of Panel Data: Handbook of Theory and Applications. Kluwer Academic Publishers, Dordrecht, pp. 303–315.

White, H., 1984. Asymptotic Theory for Econometricians. Academic Press, New York.

[17]

Econometrics Journal (2001), volume **4**, pp. 89–108.

Estimation of AR(1) models with unequally spaced pseudo-panels

DAVID J. MCKENZIE

Economics Department, Yale University, P.O. Box 208268, New Haven, CT 06511, USA
E-mail: david.mckenzie@yale.edu

Received: October 2000

Summary Surveys in developing countries are often taken at unequally spaced intervals. This paper provides for the estimation of dynamic pseudo-panel models with such data. Non-linear least squares, minimum distance, and one-step estimators are used to impose the non-linear parameter restrictions which occur in dynamic models over unequally spaced periods. Consistency and asymptotic normality of the estimators is established. A small-scale Monte Carlo simulation study corroborates the results. The paper also shows how these methods can be applied to allow estimation of dynamic models with irregularly spaced genuine panel data.

Keywords: *Pseudo-panel, Repeated cross-sections, Synthetic cohorts, Irregular sampling, Unequal-spacing.*

1. INTRODUCTION

Despite the creation of a considerable number of panel data sets over the past few decades, genuine panel data is still relatively rare. This is particularly true for developing countries, but even in developed nations the high cost of panel surveys limits their use. Deaton (1985) suggested that a feasible alternative is to use regular cross-sectional surveys to construct a time-series of repeated cross-sections or 'pseudo-panel'. Moffitt (1993) and Collado (1997) showed that dynamic models may be consistently estimated using such data. A problem which can arise in practice is that various factors, such as funding cuts and political disturbances, can result in the cross-sectional surveys being taken at irregular intervals. This paper considers estimation of AR(1) models with unequally spaced pseudo-panel data.

In the panel data literature a distinction can be made between unbalanced and unequally spaced panels. Both constitute examples of incomplete panels, which we define to be panels defined over N individuals and T time periods, for which the full NT observations are not available. Arellano and Bond (1991, p. 281) define an unbalanced panel to be 'a sample in which consecutive observations on individual units are available, but the number of time periods available may vary from unit to unit as well as the historical points to which observations correspond'. Arellano and Bond remark that nothing fundamental changes in the econometric methods provided a minimum number of continuous time periods are available for each unit. In contrast, some observations are non-consecutive in an unequally spaced panel, and no observations may be available for the entire cross-section in certain periods. Baltagi and Wu (1999) study the estimation of non-dynamic panel data regression models with AR(1) disturbances using unequally spaced panels.[1] The estimation of dynamic models with unequally spaced data introduces additional complications. The differencing approach used in the dynamic panel data literature to remove the individual effects can no longer be directly applied and, furthermore, unequal spacing in a dynamic model imposes nonlinear restrictions on the parameters.

The emphasis of this paper is on pseudo-panels, rather than genuine panels, although we also show how the methods considered in this paper can be used to estimate dynamic models with genuine panel data. The paper shows that consistent and asymptotically normal parameter estimates can be obtained for AR(1) pseudo-panel models with unequally spaced data, as the cross-sectional dimension of the data passes to infinity for finite T. We allow for parameter heterogeneity across cohorts and give results for the nonlinear least squares (NLS) and optimal minimum distance (OMD) estimators in a simple AR(1) model. One-step efficient NLS and OMD estimators are also provided. A consistent estimator of the covariance matrix is obtained using sample cross-sectional variances and covariances. Results for the equally spaced dynamic pseudo-panel model studied in McKenzie (2000) arise as a special case of these results. The NLS results are then extended to allow for estimation of a general model with cohort-specific intercepts, common deterministic trends and stochastic regressors. A small simulation study is used to examine the finite-sample performance of these estimators.

Irregularly spaced observations can occur for several reasons, and different techniques may be required according to context. Our focus is on large N, small T pseudo-panels constructed from several surveys. It is assumed that data exist for the intervening periods, but are simply not collected. Examples include surveys of consumption, income, fertility, expectations and production. These can be contrasted with stock market data, whereby market closures over weekends and holidays result in irregular spacing of asset price data.[2] Our methods are also not intended for the case of irregular spacing in ultra-high frequency data, studied recently by Engle (2000). Table 1 details some examples of unequally spaced surveys which motivate this paper. A considerable number of the household surveys used for studying income, consumption and poverty in developing countries are unequally spaced. For example, the Mexican ENIGH surveys of income and expenditure were taken in 1984, 1989, 1992, 1994 and 1996. Even when surveys are initially planned to be regular, unforeseen problems may cause the delay of a survey. This was the case with the CASEN surveys in Chile, where the 1989 survey was not taken until 1990, resulting in a 3-year interval in the otherwise biennial data. Surveys in developed countries are more likely to be regularly spaced, but again budgetary considerations and a desire to change the frequency at which data are obtained can lead to unequally spaced pseudo-panels. For example, the General Social Survey, a major sociological survey intended to study trends in American attitudes and practices, was previously an annual survey which became biennial in 1994.

The remainder of this paper is structured as follows. Section 2 introduces the notation and derives results for AR(1) models with unequally spaced pseudo-panels. Section 3 extends these results to a general dynamic model with cohort-specific intercepts, individual effects, a deterministic time trend, and stochastic regressors. In Section 4 we show how the methods in this paper can be applied to genuine panel data, and in Section 5 we present results from a small-scale simulation study. Conclusions are made in Section 6 and mathematical proofs are contained in Section 7.

[1] Baltagi and Wu (1999) allow for the panel to be both unbalanced and unequally spaced. As a new random sample is drawn each sampling period, a pseudo-panel is by construction balanced, and so for this reason and notational ease we consider balanced, unequally spaced data in this study.

[2] See Campbell *et al.* (1997, Chapter 3) for an introduction to the finance literature on nonsynchronous trading.

Table 1. Some examples of unequally spaced surveys.

Country	*Survey*	*Survey periods*
Panel A: household surveys for monitoring poverty in developing countries[a]		
Bolivia	Encuesta Integrada de Hogares (EIH)	Mar 89, Nov 89, Sept 90, Nov 91, Nov 92, July–Dec 93, July–Dec 94, June 95
Brazil	Pesquisa Nacional por Amostra de Domicillios (PNAD)	Annual surveys since 1971, but surveys not taken in census years 1980 and 1991
Chile	Caracterización Socioeconómica Nacional (CASEN)	1985, 87, 90, 92, 94, 96
Ethiopia	Welfare monitoring survey	1995, 97, 98
Ghana	Ghana living standards survey	1987, 88, 91, 98
Kenya	Welfare monitoring survey	1992, 94, 97
Kyrgyz Republic	Poverty monitoring survey	1993, 96, 96, 97, 98
Mexico	Encuesta nacional de Ingreso-Gasto de los hogares (ENIGH)	1984, 89, 92, 94, 96
Nigeria	National consumer survey	1980, 85, 92, 96
Panama	Encuesta de Hogares–Mano de Obra (EMO)	1979, 89, 91, 95, 96
Peru	Encuesta Nacional de Hogares Sobre Medición de Niveles de Vida (ENNIV)	1985, 90, 91, 94
Senegal	Enquête Démographique et de Santé	1986, 92, 97
Thailand	Thailand Socio-Economic Survey (SES)	1975, 81, 86, 88, 90, 92, 94, 96, 98
Panel B: fertility studies		
Taiwan[b]	Knowledge, attitudes and practices (KAP) surveys	1965, 67, 70, 73, 80, 86
Panel C: some unequally spaced surveys in the USA		
USA[c]	Adult eduction and lifelong learning surveys	1991, 95, 99, 2001
USA[c]	Early childhood program participation surveys	1991, 95, 99, 2001
USA[d]	General Social Survey (GSS)	1972–78, 80, 82–84, 96,98
USA[e]	Survey of small business finances	1987, 93, 98

Sources:
[a] The World Bank PovertyNet Inventory of household surveys:
`http://www.worldbank.org/poverty/data/index.htm`
[b] Academia Sinica Survey Research Data Archive:
`http://www.sinica.edu.tw/as/survey/srda/english/tot_list.htm`
[c] National Center for Education Statistics: `http://nces.ed.gov/surveys/`
[d] National Opinion Research Center (NORC): `http://www.norc.uchicago.edu/gss/homepage.htm`
[e] The Federal Reserve Board: `http://www.federalreserve.gov/ssbf/`

2. THE AR(1) MODEL

Consider the latent data generating process:

$$\begin{aligned} y_{i,t} &= \beta y_{i,t-1} + u_{i,t} \\ u_{i,t} &= \mu_i + \nu_{i,t} \end{aligned} \tag{1}$$

Assumption 1. *The data generating process is given by* (1) *with* $\mu_i \sim i.i.d.\ (0, \sigma_\mu^2)$, $\nu_{it} \sim i.i.d.\ (0, \sigma_\nu^2)$ *and* $y_{i0} \sim i.i.d.\ \{E(y_0), \sigma_y^2\}$ $\forall i, t$, *with* $E(y_0) \neq 0$.

We consider balanced unequally spaced pseudo-panels and panels, in which no observations are present for all individuals in certain periods. The irregular spacing is presumed to arise from the surveys being taken at irregular intervals, so that the same data generating process applies over the missing time periods as it does for the observed time periods. Data are observed at times t_j for $j = 1, 2, \ldots, \tau$, with $1 = t_1 < t_2 < \cdots < t_\tau = T$ and $t_j \in \mathbb{Z}_+ \ \forall j$. That is, we observe data in τ time periods, which in general are unequally spaced over the T periods. Let S be the number of distinct spacing intervals, so that if $S = 1$ the data are equally spaced.

Writing equation (1) in terms of observed time periods gives

$$y_{i,t_j} = \beta^{(t_j - t_{j-1})} y_{i,t_{j-1}} + \sum_{h=0}^{t_j - t_{j-1} - 1} \beta^h u_{i,t_j - h}. \tag{2}$$

From (2) it can easily be seen that the standard differencing transformation used to remove individual fixed effects does not work with unequally spaced data. In particular, differencing based on observed time periods gives

$$\begin{aligned} y_{i,t_j} - y_{i,t_{j-1}} &= \beta^{(t_j - t_{j-1})} y_{i,t_{j-1}} - \beta^{(t_{j-1} - t_{j-2})} y_{i,t_{j-2}} \\ &+ \sum_{h=0}^{t_j - t_{j-1} - 1} \beta^h v_{i,t_j - h} - \sum_{h=0}^{t_{j-1} - t_{j-2} - 1} \beta^h v_{i,t_{j-1} - h} \\ &+ \sum_{h=\min\{t_j - t_{j-1}, t_{j-1} - t_{j-2}\}}^{\max\{t_j - t_{j-1} - 1, t_{j-1} - t_{j-2} - 1\}} \beta^h \mu_i \end{aligned} \tag{3}$$

The last term in (3) is present only when the data are unequally spaced, in which case the differencing transformation does not eliminate the individual effect.

2.1. Pseudo-panel estimation

The distinguishing feature of a pseudo-panel is that at each time t_j, a different sample of individuals is observed. We follow Moffitt (1993) in making this explicit through the use of the subscript $i(t_j)$, which denotes the ith individual observed in period t_j. In (2) we therefore have that $y_{i(t_j),t_j}$ is observed, but that $y_{i(t_j),t_{j-1}}$ is not. A solution to this problem is to divide the population into C groups, or cohorts, with fixed memberships over time, such as birth cohorts. Let n_c be the number of individuals in cohort c, which for notational ease we assume to be the same over the observed time periods. Taking sample means of (2) over individuals in cohort c gives

$$\bar{y}_{c,t_j}^{i(t_j)} = \beta^{(t_j - t_{j-1})} \bar{y}_{c,t_{j-1}}^{i(t_j)} + \sum_{h=0}^{t_j - t_{j-1} - 1} \beta^h \bar{u}_{c,t_j - h}^{i(t_j)} \quad c = 1, \ldots, C; \quad j = 2, \ldots, \tau, \tag{4}$$

where $\bar{y}_{c,t_j}^{i(t_j)} = \frac{1}{n_c} \sum_{i=1}^{n_c} y_{i(t_j),t_j}$ is the sample mean over the $y_{i(t_j),t_j}$ in cohort c at time t_j. The $i(t_j)$ superscript makes explicit the fact the mean is taken over individuals observed at time t_j. The resulting data set is a pseudo-panel over C cohorts and T unequally spaced time periods. The mean $\bar{y}_{c,t_{j-1}}^{i(t_j)}$ is not observed, and so is replaced with the sample mean over the individuals which are observed at time t_{j-1}, resulting in the regression model

$$\overline{y}_{c,t_j}^{i(t_j)} = \beta^{(t_j-t_{j-1})}\overline{y}_{c,t_{j-1}}^{i(t_{j-1})} + \varepsilon_{c,t_j} \quad c = 1, \ldots, C; \; j = 2, \ldots, \tau$$

$$\varepsilon_{c,t_j} = \sum_{h=0}^{t_j-t_{j-1}-1} \beta^h \overline{u}_{c,t_j-h}^{i(t_j)} + \beta^{(t_j-t_{j-1})}\left(\overline{y}_{c,t_{j-1}}^{i(t_j)} - \overline{y}_{c,t_{j-1}}^{i(t_{j-1})}\right) \tag{5}$$

The regression error contains the true averaged error, which in addition to the period t_j error contains the errors for all missing periods between time t_{j-1} and time t_j, and a term which arises from observing a different sample of individuals at time t_j to those observed at time t_{j-1}. In the case of equally spaced time intervals, equation (5) is a linear regression model, which can be estimated by least squares or instrumental variables, as in Moffitt (1993) and Collado (1997), respectively. McKenzie (2000) allows for parameter heterogeneity amongst cohorts, and shows consistency of least squares depends on $n_c \to \infty$, $\frac{T}{n_c} \to 0$, and that instrumental variables estimators are consistent under weaker conditions.

For unequally spaced time intervals, (5) is a linear regression model subject to nonlinear parameter restrictions. To be explicit, denote the S separate spacing intervals by $s = s_1, \ldots, s_S$. For $s = t_j - t_{j-1}$, let α_s be the parameter relating observations in time t_j to those in time t_{j-1}. Then the restrictions can be expressed as

$$\alpha_s = \beta^s \quad \forall \quad s = s_1, \ldots, s_S. \tag{6}$$

If the intervals are equally spaced, $S = 1$ and (6) does not impose any restrictions, in which case linear regression methods can be used. For unequally spaced data, stack the data by time period, so that

$$y = \left(\overline{y}_{1,t_2}^{i(t_2)}, \ldots, \overline{y}_{C,t_2}^{i(t_2)}, \ldots, \overline{y}_{1,t_\tau}^{i(t_\tau)}, \ldots, \overline{y}_{C,t_\tau}^{i(t_\tau)}\right)'$$

is the $C(\tau - 1) \times 1$ vector of dependent variables and $\widetilde{X}$ denotes the $C(\tau - 1) \times S$ matrix which has non-zero elements in column m for $m = 1, \ldots, S$ consisting of the $\overline{y}_{c,t_k}^{i(t_k)}$ that are spaced s_m time periods before the corresponding element in y. Letting $\alpha(\beta) = (\alpha_{s_1}, \ldots, \alpha_{s_S})'$ be the $S \times 1$ parameter vector and ε the stacked vector of error terms, the model in (5) can be expressed as

$$y = \widetilde{X}\alpha(\beta) + \varepsilon \tag{7}$$

Under the restrictions in (6), $\alpha(\beta)$ is a $S \times 1$ vector of smooth functions of the scalar parameter β. For $S \geq 2$, the expression is nonlinear in the parameter β.[3]

We consider several alternatives for estimating β from (7). Firstly we show that under Assumption 1, applying least squares to (7) yields consistent estimates of the α_s, from which one can obtain consistent estimates of β, denoted $\widehat{\beta}_s = \widehat{\alpha}_s^{1/s}$. These initial consistent estimates can be used as starting values for nonlinear least squares estimation. For practical purposes, it can be computationally more convenient to use the one-step estimation method outlined in Davidson and MacKinnon (1993, pp. 196–198). The one-step estimates are obtained from the Gauss–Newton regression (GNR) with parameter β evaluated at $\widehat{\beta}_s$:

$$y - \widetilde{X}\alpha(\widehat{\beta}_s) = \widetilde{X}^*c + \text{residuals} \tag{8}$$

[3]Of course if $S = 1$, but the observations are spaced more than one time period apart, then $\alpha(\beta)$ will also be nonlinear in β. This can be easily solved or avoided altogether by redefining the base time period.

Where the $C(\tau - 1) \times 1$ vector $\widetilde{X}^*$ is defined by

$$\widetilde{X}^* \equiv \widetilde{X} \left. \frac{\partial \alpha(\beta)}{\partial \beta} \right|_{\beta=\widehat{\beta}_s} \tag{9}$$

The one-step estimate is $\widetilde{\beta}_{\text{OSNLS}} = \widehat{\beta}_s + \widehat{c}$, which will be asymptotically equivalent to the nonlinear least squares estimator, and is easier to compute.

Wansbeek and Kapteyn (1989) note that a possible approach to estimation of incomplete panel data models is the EM algorithm for obtaining maximum-likelihood estimates. They consider models without the lagged dependent variable, and remark that working out the EM approach involves a lot of messy algebra. It would be possible to use the EM algorithm on the pseudo-panel to 'fill in' the missing years. However, this approach becomes even more complicated when a lagged dependent variable is included as a regressor and would introduce additional uncertainty into the model. Furthermore, aside from the much lower computational complexity, our approach also has the advantage of not requiring distributional assumptions for the error components.

Given that $\alpha(\beta)$ is $S \times 1$, we can recover S initial estimates of β from the least squares estimator $\widehat{\alpha}$. The optimal minimum distance estimator of β, denoted $\widehat{\beta}_{\text{OMD}}$ is the solution to the problem

$$\min_{\beta} Q_n(\beta) = \{\widehat{\alpha} - \alpha(\beta)\}' \widehat{\Omega}^{-1} \{\widehat{\alpha} - \alpha(\beta)\}, \tag{10}$$

where Ω is defined in Theorem 1. As with the nonlinear least squares estimator, there is an asymptotically equivalent one-step estimator. Let $\widehat{G} = \frac{\partial \alpha(\beta)}{\partial \beta} \big|_{\beta=\widehat{\beta}_s}$ be the $S \times 1$ vector of derivatives of $\alpha(\beta)$ evaluated at $\widehat{\beta}_s = \widehat{\alpha}_s^{\frac{1}{s}}$, the initial estimate of β_0. Then Newey and McFadden (1994)'s one-step minimum distance estimator is

$$\widetilde{\beta}_{\text{OMD}} = \widehat{\beta}_s + (\widehat{G}'\widehat{\Omega}^{-1}\widehat{G})^{-1}\widehat{G}'\widehat{\Omega}^{-1}\{\widehat{\alpha} - \alpha(\widehat{\beta}_s)\} \tag{11}$$

We make the following assumption on relative divergence rates of the different cohort sample sizes.

Assumption 2. *Assume that $n_c = \delta_c n_1$ for $0 < \delta_c < \infty$ for all c, so that as $n_1 \to \infty$, $n_c \to \infty$ at the same rate up to a constant scaling factor.*

We also require the following identification condition for consistency of the NLS and OMD estimators.

Assumption 3. *$\alpha(\beta) \neq \alpha(\beta_0)$ for all $\beta \neq \beta_0$, where β_0 is the true value of β.*

This assumption is satisfied provided at least one of the S spacing intervals is odd. Otherwise if all the restrictions are of the form $\alpha_k = \beta_0^{2k}$ for k even, we can only identify β_0^2. This case can be easily handled by either rescaling the time dimension so that the basic time unit becomes two time periods, or by restricting the parameter space so that $\beta_0 \geq 0$.

The following result then provides for the consistency and asymptotic normality of the estimators of β considered above.

Theorem 1. *Under Assumptions* 1, 2 *and* 3, *as $n_1 \to \infty$ for fixed T and fixed C,*

(a) $\widehat{\alpha} \xrightarrow{p} \alpha(\beta_0)$ *and* $\sqrt{n_1}\{\widehat{\alpha} - \alpha(\beta_0)\} \xrightarrow{d} N(0, \Omega)$
where $\widetilde{X} \xrightarrow{p} X$, *where* X *has non-zero elements* $\beta^{t_j-1}E(y_0)$ *in the cells corresponding to those where* $\widetilde{X}$ *has elements* $\overline{y}_{c,t_{j-1}}^{i(t_{j-1})}$, *and* $\Omega = (X'X)^{-1}X'VX(X'X)^{-1}$ *with the elements of* V *given in part (c).*

(b) *Each of the S initial estimates for* β, *obtained as* $\widehat{\beta}_s = (\widehat{\alpha}_s)^{\frac{1}{s}}$ *are consistent for* β, *and* $\sqrt{n_1}(\widehat{\beta}_s - \beta_0) \xrightarrow{d} \frac{1}{s}\beta_0^{1-s}N(0, \Omega_s)$ *where* Ω_s *is the submatrix of* Ω *which gives the variance of* $\sqrt{n_1}(\widehat{\alpha}_s - \beta_0^s)$.

(c) $\widehat{\Omega} = (\widetilde{X}'\widetilde{X})^{-1}\widetilde{X}'\widehat{V}\widetilde{X}(\widetilde{X}'\widetilde{X})^{-1} \xrightarrow{p} \Omega$, *where* $\widehat{V}$ *has elements:*

(i) $\widehat{\text{var}}\left(\sqrt{n_1}\varepsilon_{c,t_j}\right) = \delta_c^{-1}\overline{\text{var}}_i(y_{i,t_j}) + \delta_c^{-1}\overline{\beta}^{2(t_j-t_{j-1})}\overline{\text{var}}_i(y_{i,t_{j-1}})$;

(ii) $\widehat{\text{cov}}\left(\sqrt{n_1}\varepsilon_{c,t_j}, \sqrt{n_1}\varepsilon_{c,t_{j-1}}\right) = -\delta_c^{-1}\overline{\beta}^{(t_j-t_{j-1})}\overline{\text{var}}_i(y_{i,t_{j-1}})$;

(iii) $\widehat{\text{cov}}\left(\sqrt{n_1}\varepsilon_{c,t_j}, \sqrt{n_1}\varepsilon_{c',t_b}\right) = 0\ \forall c' \neq c,\ \forall j, b$;

(iv) $\widehat{\text{cov}}\left(\sqrt{n_1}\varepsilon_{c,t_j}, \sqrt{n_1}\varepsilon_{c,t_b}\right) = 0$ *for all* $b : |b - j| > 1$.

Where $\overline{\text{var}}_i(y_{i,t_j}) = \frac{1}{n_c-1}\sum_{i=1}^{n_c}(y_{i(t_j)t_j} - \overline{y}_{c,t_j}^{i(t_j)})^2$ *is the cross-sectional sample variance over the individuals in cohort* c *at time* t_j *and* $\overline{\beta}$ *is any consistent estimator of* β. *The matrix* V *replaces sample variances with population variances and* $\overline{\beta}$ *with the true value* β.

(d) *The one-step nonlinear least squares estimator* $\widetilde{\beta}_{\text{OSNLS}}$ *is consistent and* $\sqrt{n_1}(\widetilde{\beta}_{\text{OSNLS}} - \beta_0) \xrightarrow{d} N\{0, (X_0^{*\prime}X_0^*)^{-1}X_0^{*\prime}VX_0^*(X_0^{*\prime}X_0^*)^{-1}\}$ *where* $X_0^* = X\left.\frac{\partial\alpha(\beta)}{\partial\beta}\right|_{\beta=\beta_0}$

(e) $\widetilde{\beta}_{\text{OSNLS}}$ *is asymptotically equivalent to the nonlinear least squares estimator in equation* (7).

(f) *The minimum distance estimator* $\widehat{\beta}_{\text{OMD}}$ *and efficient one-step minimum distance estimator* $\widetilde{\beta}_{\text{OMD}}$ *are both consistent and asymptotically normal estimators of* β, *with asymptotic variance* $(G'\Omega^{-1}G)^{-1}$ *where* $G = \left.\frac{\partial\alpha(\beta)}{\partial\beta}\right|_{\beta=\beta_0}$.

Remarks 1.

(a) β can be allowed to differ across cohorts simply by carrying out the estimation process for each cohort separately. If the data are equally spaced and observed every period, the asymptotic distribution given in (b), and the covariance estimator in (c) reduce to those given in McKenzie (2000) for the OLS estimator.

(b) The assumptions made in Assumption 1 are stronger than needed to establish consistency, but simplify the notation and work needed in proving the results above. Our asymptotic theory holds the time dimension fixed and lets $n_c \to \infty$, using laws of large numbers and central limit theorems in the cross-sectional dimension. One can therefore allow for quite general forms of weak temporal dependence in the $\nu_{i(t_j),t_j}$, and provided we still assume cross-sectional independence, all of the above results will still hold. This is because each individual is observed only once with repeated cross-sections, and so $\nu_{i(t_j),t_j}$ and $\nu_{i(t_j-1),t_j-1}$ will still be uncorrelated, even if $\nu_{i(t_j),t_j}$ and $\nu_{i(t_j),t_j-1}$ are correlated. It is usual in this literature to assume cross-sectional independence, and no well-developed theory for general forms of spatial dependence currently exists. If the form which the spatial dependence takes is known, due to geographic clustering for example, one can explicitly allow for this as a regressor in the general model in the next section. If the $u_{i(t_j),t_j}$ display weak spatial dependence of an unknown form, the above parameter estimators will still be consistent, but the covariance estimates will no longer be valid in this case. Further discussion of these issues for equally spaced pseudo-panel data can be found in McKenzie (2000).

(c) Although the OLS estimator $\widehat{\alpha}$ of $\alpha(\beta)$ is consistent as $n_1 \to \infty$ for fixed T, in finite-samples it will be biased towards zero due to the correlation between $\overline{y}_{c,t_{j-1}}^{i(t_{j-1})}$ and ε_{c,t_j}. As in the equally spaced case, one could use instrumental variables methods to estimate $\alpha(\beta)$ and thereby obtain improved initial estimates of β.
(d) The covariance matrix $\widehat{\Omega}$ is $S \times S$, so that there are $(S+1)S/2$ elements to estimate. If there are a large number of distinct spacing intervals between the data, it is possible that the estimated matrix may be nearly singular. In such situations, the reader should be cautious about unrestricted estimation of this covariance matrix, and consider suitable cross-restrictions on the elements of $\widehat{V}$.

3. GENERAL MODEL

A more general model which allows for cohort-specific intercepts, individual effects, a deterministic time trend, and stochastic regressors is

$$y_{i,t} = \alpha_c + \beta_c y_{i,t-1} + \gamma z_t + x_{i,t}'\psi + u_{i,t} \tag{12}$$
$$u_{i,t} = \mu_i + v_{i,t} \tag{13}$$

where ψ is a $K \times 1$ vector of regression coefficients, $x_{i,t}$ is a $K \times 1$ vector of stochastic regressors and z_t is a common deterministic time trend.[4] We assume that for all individuals i in cohort c at time t, $x_{i,t}' \sim i.i.d.\{E(x_{c,t}'), \Omega_x\}$. As before the data are observed at irregular intervals. Expressing (12) in terms of observed time periods, taking cohort means, and replacing the unobserved $\overline{y}_{c,t_{j-1}}^{i(t_j)}$ with $\overline{y}_{c,t_{j-1}}^{i(t_{j-1})}$ gives the following model to be estimated:

$$\begin{aligned}\overline{y}_{c,t_j}^{i(t_j)} &= \beta_c^{(t_j-t_{j-1})}\overline{y}_{c,t_{j-1}}^{i(t_{j-1})} \\ &\quad + \sum_{h=0}^{t_j-t_{j-1}-1} \beta_c^h\left(\alpha_c + \gamma z_{t_j-h} + \overline{x}_{c,t_j-h}^{i(t_j)\prime}\psi\right) + \varepsilon_{c,t_j}\end{aligned} \tag{14}$$

$$\varepsilon_{c,t_j} = \beta_c^{(t_j-t_{j-1})}\left(\overline{y}_{c,t_{j-1}}^{i(t_j)} - \overline{y}_{c,t_{j-1}}^{i(t_{j-1})}\right) + \sum_{h=0}^{t_j-t_{j-1}-1} \beta_c^h \overline{u}_{c,t_j-h}^{i(t_j)} \tag{15}$$

Observe that this nonlinear regression requires that z_t and $\overline{x}_{c,t}^{i(t_j)\prime}$ are known in every period $t = 1, \ldots, T$, not just in the observed time periods. This is certainly true of deterministic time trends, but will generally restrict the $x_{i,t}$ regressors to aggregate variables which can be obtained each period from sources outside of the survey, time-invariant variables such as sex and race, and deterministic time-varying variables such as age. For a given spacing $s = t_j - t_{j-1}$, (14) requires the estimation of C cohort-specific intercepts $\alpha_c \sum_{h=0}^{s-1} \beta_c^h$, C coefficients β_c^s on the lagged variable, s coefficients on the trend and sK coefficients on the $x_{i,t}$ regressors. In many applications this will result in more terms than there are observations with spacing s, so that one cannot simply apply unrestricted least squares to obtain initial consistent estimates as was done for the AR(1) model. However, provided that the number of observations in our pseudo-panel, $C(\tau - 1)$, exceeds the number of parameters to be estimated, $2C + K + 1$, one can proceed using nonlinear least squares.

[4]More generally one can allow for parameter heterogeneity in γ and ψ, although this may not be feasible for the sample sizes found in many developing country applications.

Let $\theta = (\alpha_{c_1}, \ldots, \alpha_{c_C}, \beta_{c_1}, \ldots, \beta_{c_C}, \gamma, \psi')$ be the vector of parameters to be estimated. Stack the data by cohort and then time, to form y as for the AR(1) case and let $h(\theta)$ be the $D \times 1$ vector consisting of the nonlinear functions of θ to be estimated in equation (14). Denote by $\widetilde{X}$ the corresponding $C(\tau - 1) \times D$ matrix of regressors in the stacked data, where D is chosen so that $\widetilde{X}$ has full rank as $n_c \to \infty$. The nonlinear least squares model is

$$y = \widetilde{X}h(\theta) + \varepsilon \tag{16}$$

An example is given for the model with an intercept and drift in Section 5. As in the AR(1) model, we show that as $n_1 \to \infty$ for fixed T and C, we have $\varepsilon \xrightarrow{p} 0$ and $\sqrt{n_1}\varepsilon \xrightarrow{d} N(0, V)$. We assume that the identification condition $h(\theta) \neq h(\theta_0)$ for all $\theta \neq \theta_0$ is met, which is quite easily checked and as with Assumption 3 will be true provided at least one of the spacing intervals is odd. The following result then gives the consistency and asymptotic normality of the nonlinear least squares estimator.

Theorem 3. *Assume that as $n_1 \to \infty$ for fixed T and C, $\overline{x}_{c,t}^{i(t_j)\prime} \xrightarrow{p} E(x_{c,t}')$ $\forall c, j, t$ and that the identification condition $h(\theta) \neq h(\theta_0)$ $\forall \theta \neq \theta_0$ is met. Then under Assumptions* 1 *and* 2, *as $n_1 \to \infty$ for fixed T and C,*

(a) the nonlinear least squares estimator $\widehat{\theta}_{NLS}$ in (16) *is consistent for θ, and*

$$\sqrt{n_1}(\widehat{\theta}_{NLS} - \theta_0) \xrightarrow{d} N\{0, (X_0^{*\prime}X_0^*)^{-1}X_0^{*\prime}VX_0^*(X_0^{*\prime}X_0^*)^{-1}\}$$

where $X_0^* = X \left.\frac{\partial h(\theta)}{\partial \theta'}\right|_{\theta=\theta_0}$ and $\widetilde{X} \xrightarrow{p} X$, a full rank matrix.

(b) The covariance matrix V can be consistently estimated by $\widehat{V}$ with elements:

(i)

$$\begin{aligned}\widehat{\text{var}}\left(\sqrt{n_1}\varepsilon_{c,t_j}\right) = {} & \delta_c^{-1}\overline{\text{var}}_i(y_{i,t_j}) + \delta_c^{-1}\widehat{\beta}_c^{2(t_j - t_{j-1})}\overline{\text{var}}_i(y_{i,t_{j-1}}) \\ & -\delta_c^{-1}\sum_{h=0}^{t_j - t_{j-1} - 1}\widehat{\beta}_c^{2h}\widehat{\psi}'\overline{\text{var}}_i(x_{i,t_j})\widehat{\psi} \\ -\delta_c^{-1}\sum_{l \neq h}^{t_j - t_{j-1} - 1}\sum_{h=0}^{t_j - t_{j-1} - 1} & \beta_c^{h+l}\widehat{\psi}'\overline{\text{cov}}_i(x_{i,t_{j-h}}, x_{i,t_{j-l}})\widehat{\psi}\end{aligned}$$

(ii)

$$\begin{aligned}\widehat{\text{cov}}\left(\sqrt{n_1}\varepsilon_{c,t_j}, \sqrt{n_1}\varepsilon_{c,t_{j-1}}\right) = {} & -\delta_c^{-1}\widehat{\beta}_c^{(t_j - t_{j-1})}\overline{\text{var}}_i(y_{i,t_{j-1}}) \\ +\delta_c^{-1}\widehat{\beta}_c^{(t_j - t_{j-1})}\sum_{h=0}^{t_{j-1} - t_{j-2} - 1} & \widehat{\beta}_c^h\widehat{\psi}'\overline{\text{cov}}_i(y_{i,t_{j-1}}, x_{i,t_j - h})\end{aligned}$$

(iii) $\widehat{\text{cov}}\left(\sqrt{n_1}\varepsilon_{c,t_j}, \sqrt{n_1}\varepsilon_{c',t_b}\right) = 0\ \forall c' \neq c, \forall j, b.$

(iv) $\widehat{\text{cov}}\left(\sqrt{n_1}\varepsilon_{c,t_j}, \sqrt{n_1}\varepsilon_{c,t_b}\right) = 0$ *for all $b : |b - j| > 1$,*

where

$$\overline{\text{cov}}_i(y_{i,t_{j-1}}, x_{i,t_j-h})$$

$$= \frac{1}{n_c} \sum_{i(t_{j-1})=1}^{n_c} \left(y_{i(t_{j-1}),t_{j-1}} - \overline{y}_{c,t_{j-1}}^{i(t_{j-1})} \right) \left(x_{i(t_{j-1}),t_j-h} - \overline{x}_{c,t_j-h}^{i(t_{j-1})} \right)$$

is the cross-sectional sample covariance over the individuals in cohort c at time t_{j-1}.

Remarks 2.

(a) If sufficient observations are available, one-step efficient NLS and OMD estimates can be obtained by a simple generalization of the results given for the AR(1) model.
(b) If the x_{i,t_j} are the same for all i in cohort c, as is the case with aggregate variables, the form of the covariance estimator simplifies to that given for the AR(1) model.
(c) The inclusion of an intercept or additional variables means that one can relax the initialization condition $E(y_0) \neq 0$ made for the AR(1) model, and, in particular, one could set the initial values to zero, or allow for remote past initializations.

4. UNEQUALLY SPACED GENUINE PANEL DATA

Differencing fails to remove all individual effects from a dynamic panel when the data are unequally spaced. The procedures detailed above for pseudo-panels can also be used to estimate dynamic models with unequally spaced genuine panel data. One choice is to consider the entire population as a single cohort, so that $C = 1$, and then take means over the entire sample at each point in time. Equation (1) becomes

$$\overline{y}_{t_j} = \beta^{(t_j - t_{j-1})} \overline{y}_{t_{j-1}} + \eta_{t_j} \quad j = 2, \ldots, \tau$$

$$\eta_{t_j} = \sum_{h=0}^{t_j - t_{j-1} - 1} \beta^h \overline{u}_{c,t_j - h}. \tag{17}$$

As $N \to \infty$ for fixed T, $\eta_{t_j} \xrightarrow{p} 0$ under Assumption 1, and hence the one-step estimates will be consistent, as in the pseudo-panel case. Likewise one can obtain convergence in distribution to a normally distributed limiting variable. The estimator for the covariance matrix will differ as a consequence of having the same individuals each period in the sample. In finite samples η_{t_j} will be correlated with $\overline{y}_{t_{j-1}}$ due to the individual effects, and so the estimates will be biased.

A problem with this procedure is that by averaging over the entire sample, the estimate of β is based on only the $\tau - 1$ observations in the averaged model (17). Moreover, births and mortality will mean that the overall population is changing in a nonrandom manner over time. An alternative approach which makes greater use of the data is to employ the idea of cohorts, used extensively in pseudo-panel analysis. Cohorts can be defined according to criterion such as birth year and education level, as with pseudo-panels. However as the individuals in a genuine panel are the same from year to year, cohorts could also be formed by arbitrary methods, such as the cohort of all individuals in the first tenth of the sample. The key condition for consistency is then that the number of individuals in each cohort, n_c, goes to infinity. With C cohorts, this gives $C(\tau - 1)$ observations with which to estimate β. The downside of this approach is that the rate of convergence is slower, and the finite sample bias arising from the correlation between the η_{t_j} and $\overline{y}_{c,t_{j-1}}$ will be higher. The optimal choice of cohorts is thus an important topic for future research.

5. SIMULATIONS

A small simulation study was carried out to investigate the finite-sample performance of the one-step, NLS and OMD estimators.[5] We simulated an unequally spaced pseudo-panel with data observed in periods 1, 6, 9, 11 and 13: the spacing scheme found in the Mexican ENIGH surveys. We let $y_{i(t)0} \sim i.i.d.\ N(2, 0.5^2)$, $u_{i(t)t} \sim i.i.d.\ N(0, 0.5^2)$ and $v_{i(t)} \sim i.i.d.\ N(0, 0.3^2)$. Experiments were carried out for a range of values of n_c and β_c. Ten thousand replications were carried out for each n_c and β_c combination.[6] Three models were considered. We first simulated a pseudo-panel for the AR(1) model discussed in Section 2. The second model studied is an AR(1) model with an intercept, which is a simple case of the more general model of Section 3. For cohort c the model to be estimated is written in the form $y = \widetilde{X}h(\theta) + \varepsilon$ as

$$\begin{bmatrix} \overline{y}^{i(6)}_{c,6} \\ \overline{y}^{i(9)}_{c,9} \\ \overline{y}^{i(11)}_{c,11} \\ \overline{y}^{i(13)}_{c,13} \end{bmatrix} = \begin{bmatrix} \overline{y}^{i(1)}_{c,1} & 0 & 0 & 1 & 1 & 1 \\ 0 & \overline{y}^{i(6)}_{c,6} & 0 & 1 & 1 & 0 \\ 0 & 0 & \overline{y}^{i(9)}_{c,9} & 1 & 0 & 0 \\ 0 & 0 & \overline{y}^{i(11)}_{c,11} & 1 & 0 & 0 \end{bmatrix} \begin{bmatrix} \beta_c^5 \\ \beta_c^3 \\ \beta_c^2 \\ \alpha_c(1+\beta_c) \\ \alpha_c\beta_c^2 \\ \alpha_c\beta_c^3(1+\beta_c) \end{bmatrix} + \begin{bmatrix} \varepsilon_{c,6} \\ \varepsilon_{c,9} \\ \varepsilon_{c,11} \\ \varepsilon_{c,13} \end{bmatrix}$$

Note that the vector $h(\theta)$ is written so that the matrix $\widetilde{X}$ has full rank. Finally, the AR(1) model for genuine panel data given in Section 4 was also simulated. The use of the same parameters and initializations enables us to compare the relative performance of the pseudo-panel to a genuine panel in this setting.

Table 2 presents the mean and standard deviation of the estimates of β_c obtained from an AR(1) regression with unequally spaced pseudo-panel data. The spacing of the data enables one to obtain three separate OLS (and one-step) estimates for each replication. Table 2 gives the mean and standard deviation over all 30 000 estimates for these estimators. The simulation results corroborate the asymptotic theory, with the point estimates approaching the true value as the cross-sectional sample size gets larger, and the standard deviations approaching zero. In small samples there is a downward bias, due to the correlation between the error term and regressor in finite samples. The NLS and minimum distance (MD) estimators have lower mean squared error than their one-step equivalents, and than the OLS estimators in small samples. In particular, the one-step MD estimator performs poorly in small samples, showing that inaccurate OLS estimates can lead to even less accurate one-step MD estimates.

Means and standard deviations of the NLS estimates of α_c and β_c in the AR(1) model with drift are presented in Table 3. Again the results suggest convergence to the true values as n_c gets large, with a small sample downward bias for β_c. Table 4 gives results for an AR(1) model with genuine panel data, using the same data generating process as in Table 2. Once again the NLS and MD estimators have lower mean squared error than their one-step versions, and than the OLS estimator, in small samples. The individual effects cause a downward bias in the estimates of β_c, even when we have the same individuals in the sample each period. However, the mean squared errors are lower with genuine panel data than with pseudo-panel data, showing that a pseudo-panel gives less accurate results than a genuine panel for a given finite sample of data.

[5]Simulations were carried out in GAUSS using the OPTMUM add-on package to carry out NLS and OMD estimation.
[6]Simulation results did not differ much using one thousand replications, and are available from the author upon request.

Table 2. Simulation results for AR(1) model with unequally spaced pseudo-panel data. Results shown are from 10 000 replications drawn from the AR(1) pseudo-panel model. $y_{i(t),t} = \beta y_{i(t),t-1} + u_{i(t),t}, u_{i(t),t} = \mu_{i(t)} + \nu_{i(t),t}$, where $\nu_{i(t),t} \sim i.i.d.\ N(0, 0.5^2)$, $\mu_{i(t)} \sim i.i.d.\ N(0, 0.3^2)$ and $y_{i(t),0} \sim i.i.d.\ N(2, 0.5^2)$. Observations are made in time periods 1, 6, 9, 11 and 13.

Mean estimate (standard deviation) of autoregressive parameter beta.

	Sample size						
	10	20	30	50	100	250	500
Beta = 0.95							
OLS	0.838	0.901	0.919	0.934	0.942	0.947	0.949
	(0.439)	*(0.250)*	*(0.182)*	*(0.116)*	*(0.074)*	*(0.045)*	*(0.031)*
One-step NLS	0.862	0.934	0.949	0.954	0.953	0.951	0.950
	(0.457)	*(0.209)*	*(0.127)*	*(0.051)*	*(0.021)*	*(0.011)*	*(0.007)*
NLS	0.826	0.911	0.930	0.940	0.945	0.948	0.949
	(0.282)	*(0.115)*	*(0.058)*	*(0.025)*	*(0.016)*	*(0.010)*	*(0.007)*
One-step MD	0.745	0.852	0.887	0.920	0.937	0.945	00.948
	(1.246)	*(0.543)*	*(0.333)*	*(0.173)*	*(0.085)*	*(0.048)*	*(0.033)*
Minimum distance	0.872	0.931	0.944	0.948	0.949	0.950	0.950
	(0.316)	*(0.139)*	*(0.070)*	*(0.028)*	*(0.018)*	*(0.011)*	*(0.008)*
Beta = 1							
OLS	0.943	0.976	0.985	0.992	0.996	0.998	0.999
	(0.326)	*(0.164)*	*(0.119)*	*(0.084)*	*(0.057)*	*(0.035)*	*(0.025)*
One-step NLS	0.958	0.991	0.997	0.999	0.999	1.000	1.000
	(0.311)	*(0.110)*	*(0.049)*	*(0.024)*	*(0.015)*	*(0.009)*	*(0.006)*
NLS	0.924	0.973	0.984	0.991	0.995	0.998	0.999
	(0.184)	*(0.061)*	*(0.031)*	*(0.021)*	*(0.014)*	*(0.008)*	*(0.006)*
One-step MD	0.878	0.948	0.968	0.984	0.992	0.997	0.999
	(0.580)	*(0.292)*	*(0.160)*	*(0.106)*	*(0.064)*	*(0.039)*	*(0.027)*
Minimum distance	0.969	0.995	0.999	0.999	1.000	1.000	1.000
	(0.184)	*(0.061)*	*(0.031)*	*(0.021)*	*(0.014)*	*(0.008)*	*(0.006)*
Beta = 1.05							
OLS	1.020	1.037	1.042	1.046	1.048	1.049	1.050
	(0.209)	*(0.120)*	*(0.093)*	*(0.068)*	*(0.047)*	*(0.030)*	*(0.021)*
One-step NLS	1.026	1.041	1.044	1.047	1.048	1.049	1.050
	(0.175)	*(0.063)*	*(0.033)*	*(0.023)*	*(0.015)*	*(0.009)*	*(0.006)*
NLS	0.999	1.028	1.039	1.042	1.046	1.048	1.049
	(0.114)	*(0.042)*	*(0.030)*	*(0.022)*	*(0.015)*	*(0.009)*	*(0.006)*
One-step MD	0.979	1.021	1.031	1.040	1.045	1.048	1.049
	(0.358)	*(0.159)*	*(0.114)*	*(0.078)*	*(0.053)*	*(0.033)*	*(0.023)*
Minimum distance	1.040	1.049	1.050	1.050	1.050	1.050	1.050
	(0.106)	*(0.038)*	*(0.026)*	*(0.019)*	*(0.013)*	*(0.008)*	*(0.006)*

Table 2. Continued.

Mean estimate (standard deviation) of autoregressive parameter beta.

	Sample size						
	10	20	30	50	100	250	500
Beta = 1.10							
OLS	1.084	1.093	1.095	1.097	1.098	1.100	1.100
	(0.158)	*(0.099)*	*(0.079)*	*(0.059)*	*(0.041)*	*(0.026)*	*(0.018)*
One-step NLS	1.082	1.091	1.094	1.097	1.098	1.099	1.100
	(0.099)	*(0.045)*	*(0.034)*	*(0.025)*	*(0.017)*	*(0.010)*	*(0.007)*
NLS	1.061	1.082	1.088	1.093	1.096	1.099	1.099
	(0.079)	*(0.042)*	*(0.033)*	*(0.024)*	*(0.017)*	*(0.010)*	*(0.007)*
One-step MD	1.057	1.081	1.087	1.093	1.097	1.099	1.100
	(0.227)	*(0.121)*	*(0.094)*	*(0.067)*	*(0.046)*	*(0.029)*	*(0.020)*
Minimum distance	1.098	1.100	1.100	1.100	1.100	1.100	1.100
	(0.062)	*(0.029)*	*(0.023)*	*(0.017)*	*(0.012)*	*(0.008)*	*(0.005)*

Table 3. Simulation results for NLS estimation of AR(1) model with drift with unequally spaced pseudo-panels. Results shown are from 10 000 replications drawn from the AR(1) with drift pseudo-panel model. $y_{i(t),t} = \alpha + \beta y_{i(t),t-1} + u_{i(t),t}, u_{i(t),t} = \mu_{i(t)} + v_{i(t),t}$, where $v_{i(t),t} \sim i.i.d.\ N(0, 0.5^2)$, $\mu_{i(t)} \sim i.i.d.\ N(0, 0.3^2)$ and $y_{i(t),0} \sim i.i.d.\ N(2, 0.5^2)$. Observations are made in time periods 1, 6, 9,11 and 13.

Mean estimate (standard deviation) of parameter estimates.

	Cross-sectional sample size			
	10	50	100	500
Beta= 0.30, Alpha = 2				
Alpha	2.039	2.002	1.999	1.999
	(0.101)	*(0.042)*	*(0.024)*	*(0.005)*
Beta	0.286	0.299	0.300	0.300
	(0.035)	*(0.016)*	*(0.012)*	*(0.002)*
Beta = 0.95, Alpha = 2				
Alpha	2.058	2.011	2.006	2.000
	(0.357)	*(0.152)*	*(0.109)*	*(0.049)*
Beta	0.946	0.949	0.949	0.950
	(0.032)	*(0.014)*	*(0.010)*	*(0.005)*
Beta = 1, Alpha = 2				
Alpha	2.058	2.014	2.005	2.001
	(0.352)	*(0.157)*	*(0.112)*	*(0.048)*
Beta	0.996	0.999	0.999	1.000
	(0.029)	*(0.013)*	*(0.010)*	*(0.004)*
Beta = 1.05, Alpha = 2				
Alpha	2.054	2.002	2.007	2.001
	(0.350)	*(0.155)*	*(0.106)*	*(0.051)*
Beta	1.046	1.050	1.051	1.050
	(0.027)	*(0.012)*	*(0.008)*	*(0.004)*

Table 4. Simulation results for AR(1) model with unequally spaced genuine panel data. Results shown are from 10 000 replications drawn from the AR(1) genuine panel model. $y_{i,t} = \beta y_{i,t-1} + u_{i,t}, u_{i,t} = \mu_i + \nu_{i,t}$ where $\nu_{i,t} \sim i.i.d.\ N(0, 0.5^2)$, $\mu_i \sim i.i.d.\ N(0, 0.3^2)$ and $y_{i,0} \sim i.i.d.\ N(2, 0.5^2)$. Observations are made in time periods 1, 6, 9,11 and 13.

Mean estimate (standard deviation) of autoregressive parameter beta.

	Sample size						
	10	20	30	50	100	250	500
Beta = 0.95							
OLS	0.889	0.918	0.932	0.939	0.946	0.948	0.949
	(0.332)	*(0.176)*	*(0.107)*	*(0.064)*	*(0.033)*	*(0.019)*	*(0.013)*
One-step NLS	0.919	0.945	0.949	0.948	0.948	0.949	0.950
	(0.313)	*(0.170)*	*(0.096)*	*(0.063)*	*(0.022)*	*(0.014)*	*(0.010)*
NLS	0.921	0.938	0.943	0.945	0.948	0.949	0.950
	(0.162)	*(0.064)*	*(0.043)*	*(0.033)*	*(0.022)*	*(0.014)*	*(0.010)*
One-step MD	0.866	0.901	0.922	0.934	0.945	0.948	0.949
	(0.539)	*(0.329)*	*(0.291)*	*(0.151)*	*(0.037)*	*(0.020)*	*(0.014)*
Minimum distance	0.888	0.928	0.940	0.944	0.948	0.949	0.950
	(0.293)	*(0.139)*	*(0.067)*	*(0.038)*	*(0.023)*	*(0.014)*	*(0.010)*
Beta = 1							
OLS	0.965	0.985	0.992	0.995	0.998	0.999	1.000
	(0.209)	*(0.093)*	*(0.052)*	*(0.033)*	*(0.021)*	*(0.013)*	*(0.009)*
One-step NLS	0.981	0.993	0.996	0.997	0.998	0.999	1.000
	(0.199)	*(0.084)*	*(0.039)*	*(0.025)*	*(0.017)*	*(0.011)*	*(0.008)*
NLS	0.981	0.991	0.995	0.996	0.998	0.999	1.000
	(0.099)	*(0.044)*	*(0.034)*	*(0.026)*	*(0.017)*	*(0.011)*	*(0.008)*
One-step MD	0.948	0.977	0.989	0.994	0.997	0.999	1.000
	(0.407)	*(0.215)*	*(0.087)*	*(0.035)*	*(0.021)*	*(0.013)*	*(0.009)*
Minimum distance	0.969	0.990	0.995	0.997	0.999	1.000	1.000
	(0.188)	*(0.066)*	*(0.040)*	*(0.027)*	*(0.018)*	*(0.011)*	*(0.008)*
Beta = 1.05							
OLS	1.032	1.043	1.047	1.048	1.049	1.050	1.050
	(0.126)	*(0.048)*	*(0.029)*	*(0.022)*	*(0.015)*	*(0.009)*	*(0.006)*
One-step NLS	1.037	1.044	1.047	1.048	1.049	1.050	1.050
	(0.110)	*(0.039)*	*(0.025)*	*(0.019)*	*(0.013)*	*(0.008)*	*(0.006)*
NLS	0.037	1.043	1.046	1.047	1.049	1.050	1.050
	(0.059)	*(0.033)*	*(0.025)*	*(0.019)*	*(0.013)*	*(0.008)*	*(0.006)*
One-step MD	1.025	1.040	1.045	1.047	1.049	1.049	1.050
	(0.193)	*(0.083)*	*(0.030)*	*(0.022)*	*(0.014)*	*(0.009)*	*(0.006)*
Minimum distance	1.036	1.045	1.048	1.048	1.049	1.050	1.050
	(0.112)	*(0.045)*	*(0.028)*	*(0.021)*	*(0.014)*	*(0.009)*	*(0.006)*

Table 4. Continued.

Mean estimate (standard deviation) of autoregressive parameter beta.

	Sample size						
	10	20	30	50	100	250	500
Beta = 1.10							
OLS	1.092	1.096	1.098	1.099	1.099	1.100	1.100
	(0.090)	*(0.029)*	*(0.021)*	*(0.016)*	*(0.011)*	*(0.007)*	*(0.005)*
One-step NLS	1.091	1.096	1.098	1.098	1.099	1.100	1.100
	(0.083)	*(0.025)*	*(0.018)*	*(0.014)*	*(0.009)*	*(0.006)*	*(0.004)*
NLS	1.090	1.095	1.097	1.098	1.099	1.100	1.100
	(0.049)	*(0.024)*	*(0.018)*	*(0.014)*	*(0.009)*	*(0.006)*	*(0.004)*
One-step MD	1.088	1.095	1.097	1.098	1.099	1.100	1.100
	(0.121)	*(0.027)*	*(0.020)*	*(0.015)*	*(0.010)*	*(0.007)*	*(0.005)*
Minimum distance	1.093	1.097	1.099	1.099	1.099	1.100	1.100
	(0.070)	*(0.031)*	*(0.023)*	*(0.018)*	*(0.012)*	*(0.008)*	*(0.005)*

6. CONCLUSIONS

We have shown that consistent estimation of AR(1) models with unequally spaced pseudo-panel or genuine panel data is possible provided that the number of individuals per cohort is allowed to pass to infinity. Although one-step nonlinear least squares and minimum distance estimators are asymptotically equivalent to the full NLS and MD estimators, they do not perform as well in the sample sizes likely to be encountered in practice. The computational simplicity of the one-step and OLS estimators should therefore be sacrificed for the greater accuracy of the nonlinear least squares estimator.

In light of the prevalence of unequally spaced surveys in many developing nations, we believe the methods given here will be of practical relevance in studies of consumption, income and the labour market in developing nations. More generally, the methods developed in this paper can be used to obtain consistent estimates for any dynamic pseudo-panel model with nonlinear parameter restrictions, not just those with unequal spacing.

Although consistency and asymptotic normality were shown in this paper, the estimators studied suffer from a finite-sample bias. The nonlinear nature of the problem prevents simple application of the instrumental variables methods used by Collado (1997) and McKenzie (2000) to eliminate this bias in equally spaced pseudo-panels. We leave the adaption of these techniques to the unequally spaced case as an area for future research. The optimal choice of the number of cohorts to divide genuine panel data into is also an important topic for future research.

7. PROOFS

7.1. Proof of Theorem 1

Convergence in probability and in distribution are for fixed T and fixed C, as $n_1 \rightarrow \infty$. To prove consistency in (a) we show that $\varepsilon \xrightarrow{p} 0$ and $\widetilde{X}$ converges to a full rank matrix X. Consider the behaviour of the ε_{c,t_j} as $n_c \rightarrow \infty$ for fixed T:

$$\varepsilon_{c,t_j} = \sum_{h=0}^{t_j-t_{j-1}-1} \beta^h \overline{u}^{i(t_j)}_{c,t_j-h} + \beta^{(t_j-t_{j-1})}\left(\overline{y}^{i(t_j)}_{c,t_{j-1}} - \overline{y}^{i(t_{j-1})}_{c,t_{j-1}}\right) \tag{18}$$

Application of the ergodic theorem under Assumption 1 gives that

$$\overline{u}^{i(t_j)}_{c,t_j-h} = \frac{1}{n_c}\sum_{i=1}^{n_c}\mu_{i(t_j)} + \frac{1}{n_c}\sum_{i=1}^{n_c}\nu_{i(t_j)t_j-h} \xrightarrow{p} E(\mu_{i(t_j)}) + E(\nu_{i(t_j)t_j-h}) = 0$$

and

$$\overline{y}^{i(t_j)}_{c,t_{j-1}} = \sum_{k=1}^{t_{j-1}} \beta^{t_{j-1}-k}\overline{u}^{i(t_j)}_{c,k} + \beta^{t_{j-1}}\overline{y}^{i(t_j)}_{c0} \xrightarrow{p} 0 + \beta^{t_{j-1}}E(y_0)$$

Likewise, $\overline{y}^{i(t_{j-1})}_{c,t_{j-1}} \xrightarrow{p} \beta^{t_{j-1}}E(y_0)$. Hence $\varepsilon_{c,t_j} \xrightarrow{p} 0$ as $n_c \to \infty$ for fixed T. Furthermore the result that $\overline{y}^{i(t_{j-1})}_{c,t_{j-1}} \xrightarrow{p} \beta^{t_{j-1}}E(y_0)$ gives that $\widetilde{X} \xrightarrow{p} X$, where X has non-zero elements $\beta^{t_{j-1}}E(y_0)$ in the cells where $\widetilde{X}$ has elements $\overline{y}^{i(t_{j-1})}_{c,t_{j-1}}$. Under the assumption that $E(y_0) \neq 0$, X has full rank.

The least squares estimator of α_s, $s = s_1, \ldots, s_S$, in (7) is

$$\widehat{\alpha}_s = \alpha_s + \frac{\sum_{j:t_j-t_{j-1}=s}^{\tau}\sum_{c=1}^{C}\overline{y}^{i(t_{j-1})}_{c,t_{j-1}}\varepsilon_{c,t_j}}{\sum_{j:\,t_j-t_{j-1}=s}^{\tau}\sum_{c=1}^{C}(\overline{y}^{i(t_{j-1})}_{c,t_{j-1}})^2} \to^p \alpha_s + \frac{0}{C\sum_{j:\,t_j-t_{j-1}=s}^{\tau}\beta^{2t_{j-1}}E(y_0)^2}$$

Thus the least squares estimator $\widehat{\alpha}_s$ provides a consistent estimator of $\alpha_s = \beta^s$ and $\widehat{\alpha} \xrightarrow{p} \alpha(\beta_0)$.

To show asymptotic normality we use Assumption 2, according to which $n_1 \to \infty$, $n_c \to \infty$ at the same rate up to a constant scaling factor. Then

$$\sqrt{n_1}\{\widehat{\alpha} - \alpha(\beta_0)\} = (\widetilde{X}'\widetilde{X})^{-1}\widetilde{X}'\sqrt{n_1}\varepsilon$$

From (18) we have

$$\sqrt{n_c}\varepsilon_{c,t_j} = \sum_{h=0}^{t_j-t_{j-1}-1}\beta^h\sqrt{n_c}\overline{u}^{i(t_j)}_{c,t_j-h} + \beta^{(t_j-t_{j-1})}\sqrt{n_c}(\overline{y}^{i(t_j)}_{c,t_{j-1}} - \overline{y}^{i(t_{j-1})}_{c,t_{j-1}})$$

Application of the Lindeberg central limit theorem under Assumption 1 gives

$$\sqrt{n_c}\overline{u}^{i(t_j)}_{c,t_j-h} \xrightarrow{d} N\{0, (\sigma_\mu^2 + \sigma_\nu^2)\} \text{ and}$$
$$\sqrt{n_c}\{\overline{y}^{i(t_j)}_{c,t_{j-1}} - \beta^{t_{j-1}}E(y_0)\} \xrightarrow{d} N(0, \sigma_{cy}^2),$$

where

$$\sigma_{cy}^2 = \sum_{k=1}^{t_{j-1}}\beta^{2(t_{j-1}-k)}\sigma_\nu^2 + \beta^{2t_{j-1}}\sigma_y^2 + \sum_{k=1}^{t_{j-1}}\sum_{q=1}^{t_{j-1}}\beta^{2t_{j-1}-k-q}\sigma_\mu^2$$

Also, $\text{cov}\left(\sqrt{n_c}\overline{u}^{i(t_j)}_{c,t_j-h}, \sqrt{n_c}\overline{y}^{i(t_j)}_{c,t_{j-1}}\right) = \sum_{k=1}^{t_{j-1}}\beta^{t_{j-1}-k}\sigma_\mu^2$, and so $\sqrt{n_c}\varepsilon_{c,t_j} \xrightarrow{d} N(0, \sigma_j^2)$ with

$$\sigma_j^2 = \sum_{h=0}^{t_j-t_{j-1}-1}\beta^{2h}\sigma_\nu^2 + \sum_{h=0}^{t_j-t_{j-1}-1}\sum_{q=0}^{t_j-t_{j-1}-1}\beta^{h+q}\sigma_\mu^2 + 2\beta^{2(t_j-t_{j-1})}\sigma_{cy}^2$$

$$+ 2\beta^{(t_j - t_{j-1})} \sum_{h=0}^{t_j - t_{j-1} - 1} \beta^h \sum_{k=1}^{t_{j-1}} \beta^{t_{j-1}-k} \sigma_\mu^2$$

The cross-sectional independence assumptions made in Assumption 1 ensure that ε_{c,t_j} and ε_{c,t_b} are independent for all $b : |b - j| > 1$, and that for all j, b the terms $\varepsilon_{c.t_j}$ and ε_{c',t_b} are independent for all $c \neq c'$. This is because under these conditions each error term is an average over completely different independent samples of individuals. Consider then the covariance between $\sqrt{n_1}\varepsilon_{c,t_j}$ and $\sqrt{n_1}\varepsilon_{c,t_{j-1}}$. We have from (18) and (5) that

$$\begin{aligned} \operatorname{cov}\left(\sqrt{n_1}\varepsilon_{c,t_j}, \sqrt{n_1}\varepsilon_{c,t_{j-1}}\right) &= -\beta^{(t_j - t_{j-1})}\delta_c^{-1} \operatorname{cov}\left(\sqrt{n_c}\overline{y}_{c,t_{j-1}}^{i(t_{j-1})}, \sqrt{n_c}\overline{y}_{c,t_{j-1}}^{i(t_{j-1})}\right) \\ &= -\beta^{(t_j - t_{j-1})}\delta_c^{-1} \operatorname{var}\left(\sqrt{n_c}\overline{y}_{c,t_{j-1}}^{i(t_{j-1})}\right) = -\beta^{(t_j - t_{j-1})}\delta_c^{-1}\sigma_{cy}^2 \end{aligned}$$

Therefore

$$\begin{aligned} \operatorname{var}\left(\sqrt{n_1}\varepsilon_{c,t_j}\right) &= \delta_c^{-1}\sigma_j^2 \\ \operatorname{cov}\left(\sqrt{n_1}\varepsilon_{c,t_j}, \sqrt{n_1}\varepsilon_{c',t_b}\right) &= 0 \ \forall c' \neq c, \forall j, b \\ \operatorname{cov}\left(\sqrt{n_1}\varepsilon_{c,t_j}, \sqrt{n_1}\varepsilon_{c.t_{j-1}}\right) &= -\beta^{(t_j - t_{j-1})}\delta_c^{-1}\sigma_{cy}^2 \\ \operatorname{cov}\left(\sqrt{n_1}\varepsilon_{c,t_j}, \sqrt{n_1}\varepsilon_{c,t_b}\right) &= 0 \qquad \text{for all } b : |b - j| > 1. \end{aligned} \tag{19}$$

Consequently, we have $\sqrt{n_1}\varepsilon \xrightarrow{d} N(0, V)$, where V has elements as given in (19). We have shown $\widetilde{X} \xrightarrow{p} X$, and hence

$$\sqrt{n_1}(\widehat{\alpha} - \alpha(\beta_0)) \xrightarrow{d} N\{0, (X'X)^{-1}X'VX(X'X)^{-1}\}$$

Part (b) follows from part (a) as from Slutsky's Theorem $\widehat{\beta}_s = \widehat{\alpha}_s^{\frac{1}{s}}$ is a consistent estimator of β and application of the delta method gives asymptotic normality.

To prove (c), let $\operatorname{var}_i(z_{it})$ denote the population cross-sectional variance of variable $z_{i(t)t}$ across the individuals in cohort c at time t. Then, writing

$$\begin{aligned} \sqrt{n_c}\varepsilon_{c.t_j} &= \sum_{h=0}^{t_j - t_{j-1} - 1} \beta^h \sqrt{n_c}\overline{u}_{c,t_j - h}^{i(t_j)} + \beta^{(t_j - t_{j-1})}\sqrt{n_c}\left(\overline{y}_{c,t_{j-1}}^{i(t_j)} - \overline{y}_{c,t_{j-1}}^{i(t_{j-1})}\right) \\ &= \frac{1}{\sqrt{n_c}} \sum_{i(t_j)=1}^{n_c} \sum_{h=0}^{t_j - t_{j-1} - 1} \beta^h u_{i(t_j),t_j - h} + \frac{1}{\sqrt{n_c}} \sum_{i(t_j)=1}^{n_c} \beta^{(t_j - t_{j-1})} y_{i(t_j),t_{j-1}} \\ &\quad - \frac{1}{\sqrt{n_c}} \sum_{i(t_{j-1})=1}^{n_c} \beta^{(t_j - t_{j-1})} y_{i,t_{j-1}} \end{aligned}$$

and, taking variances gives by cross-sectional independence, we have

$$\begin{aligned} \operatorname{var}\left(\sqrt{n_c}\varepsilon_{c,t_j}\right) &= \operatorname{var}_i\left(\sum_{h=0}^{t_j - t_{j-1} - 1} \beta^h u_{i,t_j - h}\right) + 2\beta^{2(t_j - t_{j-1})} \operatorname{var}_i(y_{i,t_{j-1}}) \\ &\quad + 2\beta^{(t_j - t_{j-1})} \operatorname{cov}_i\left(\sum_{h=0}^{t_j - t_{j-1} - 1} \beta^h u_{i,t_j - h}, y_{i,t_{j-1}}\right) \end{aligned}$$

Taking cross-sectional variances over the data generating process given in (2) gives

$$\operatorname{var}_i(y_{i,t_j}) = \beta^{2(t_j-t_{j-1})}\operatorname{var}_i(y_{i,t_{j-1}}) + \operatorname{var}_i\left(\sum_{h=0}^{t_j-t_{j-1}-1}\beta^h u_{i,t_j-h}\right) + 2\beta^{(t_j-t_{j-1})}\operatorname{cov}_i\left(\sum_{h=0}^{t_j-t_{j-1}-1}\beta^h u_{i,t_j-h}, y_{i,t_{j-1}}\right)$$

Hence, $\operatorname{var}(\sqrt{n_c}\varepsilon_{c,t_j}) = \operatorname{var}_i(y_{i(t_j),t_j}) + \beta^{2(t_j-t_{j-1})}\operatorname{var}_i(y_{i(t_{j-1}),t_{j-1}})$. This can be estimated using the sample covariances and a consistent estimator of β. Assumption 2 gives that

$$\operatorname{var}(\sqrt{n_1}\varepsilon_{c,t_j}) = \delta_c^{-1}\operatorname{var}(\sqrt{n_c}\varepsilon_{c,t_j}), \qquad \text{and similarly,}$$
$$\operatorname{cov}(\sqrt{n_1}\varepsilon_{c,t_j}, \sqrt{n_1}\varepsilon_{c,t_{j-1}}) = -\delta_c^{-1}\beta^{(t_j-t_{j-1})}\operatorname{var}_i(y_{i(t_{j-1}),t_{j-1}})$$

Assumption 1 is sufficient to ensure that the sample cross-sectional variances converge to their population quantities, and together with the consistency of the estimator of β, this gives convergence of $\widehat{V}$ to V.

Any of the S estimators $\widehat{\beta}_s$ are $\sqrt{n_1}-$ consistent for β and can be used to show part (d). The proofs of (d) and (e) follow those given in Davidson and MacKinnon (1993, p. 196–97) after making the appropriate rescalings required by the use of pseudo-panel data.

To prove part (f) we note that by the consistency of $\widehat{\beta}_s$ we have $\widehat{G} \xrightarrow{p} G$ and from parts (a) and (c) we have that $\widehat{\Omega} \xrightarrow{p} \Omega$. The conditions of Theorem 3.5 in Newey and McFadden (1994, p. 2151) are then satisfied, giving the stated result.

7.2. *Proof of Theorem* 3

To prove consistency we first show that ε converges uniformly to zero. Write

$$\overline{y}_{c,t}^{i(t)} = \alpha_c\sum_{j=0}^{t-1}\beta_c^j + \gamma\sum_{j=0}^{t-1}\beta_c^j z_{t-j} + \sum_{j=0}^{t-1}\beta_c^j\overline{x}_{c,t-j}^{i(t)\prime}\psi + \beta_c^t\overline{y}_{c,0}^{i(t)} + \sum_{j=0}^{t-1}\beta_c^j\overline{u}_{c,t-j}^{i(t)}$$

Under the *i.i.d.* assumptions made, $\overline{y}_{c,t}^{i(t)}$ converges uniformly to

$$\alpha_c\sum_{j=0}^{t-1}\beta_c^j + \gamma\sum_{j=0}^{t-1}\beta_c^j z_{t-j} + \sum_{j=0}^{t-1}\beta_c^j E(x_{c,t}')\psi + \beta_c^t E(y_{c0})$$

as $n_1 \to \infty$ for fixed T. Therefore $\overline{y}_{c,t_{j-1}}^{i(t_j)} - \overline{y}_{c,t_{j-1}}^{i(t_{j-1})}$ converges uniformly to zero, as does $\overline{u}_{c,t_j-h}^{i(t_j)}$. Hence $\sup_\theta|\varepsilon_{c,t_j}| \xrightarrow{p} 0$. The matrix $\widetilde{X}$ has non-zero elements of the forms 1, $\overline{y}_{c,t_{j-1}}^{i(t_{j-1})}$, z_{t_j-h} and $\overline{x}_{c,t_j-h}^{i(t_j)\prime}$. Each element therefore converges in probability, and thus $\widetilde{X} \xrightarrow{p} X$, a full-rank matrix. Under the *i.i.d.* assumptions made, this convergence will also be uniform, i.e. $\sup_\theta|\widetilde{X} - X| \xrightarrow{p} 0$. We then have uniform convergence of the criterion function to $\{Xh(\theta_0) - Xh(\theta)\}'\{Xh(\theta_0) -$

$Xh(\theta)\}$, which is uniquely minimized at θ_0 provided that the identification condition $h(\theta_0) \neq h(\theta)$ $\forall\theta \neq \theta_0$ is met.

Asymptotic normality of the nonlinear least squares estimator follows from standard results for extremum estimators, such as Theorem 3.1 in Newey and McFadden (1994), provided that one can show that $\sqrt{n_1}\varepsilon \xrightarrow{d} N(0, V)$. As in the AR(1) case the ε_{c,t_j}'s are functions of means of *i.i.d.* random variables, so that standard central limit theory for these components gives convergence in distribution of the standardized quantities. It remains to determine the exact form of V, which can be used for consistent estimation. Taking cross-sectional variances of the ε_{c,t_j} as in the Proof of Theorem 1 gives

$$\operatorname{var}\left(\sqrt{n_c}\varepsilon_{c,t_j}\right) = \operatorname{var}_i\left(\sum_{h=0}^{t_j-t_{j-1}-1} \beta_c^h u_{i,t_j-h}\right) + 2\beta_c^{2(t_j-t_{j-1})}\operatorname{var}_i(y_{i,t_{j-1}}) + 2\beta_c^{(t_j-t_{j-1})}\operatorname{cov}_i\left(\sum_{h=0}^{t_j-t_{j-1}-1} \beta_c^h u_{i,t_j-h}, y_{i,t_{j-1}}\right) \quad (20)$$

Taking cross-sectional variances of the data generating process gives

$$\operatorname{var}_i(y_{i,t_j}) = \beta_c^{2(t_j-t_{j-1})}\operatorname{var}_i(y_{i,t_{j-1}}) + \operatorname{var}_i\left(\sum_{h=0}^{t_j-t_{j-1}-1} \beta_c^h u_{i,t_j-h}\right) + 2\beta_c^{(t_j-t_{j-1})}\operatorname{cov}_i\left(\sum_{h=0}^{t_j-t_{j-1}-1} \beta_c^h u_{i,t_j-h}, y_{i,t_{j-1}}\right) + \sum_{h=0}^{t_j-t_{j-1}-1} \beta_c^{2h}\psi'\operatorname{var}_i(x_{i,t_j})\psi + \sum_{l\neq h}^{t_j-t_{j-1}-1}\sum_{h=0}^{t_j-t_{j-1}-1} \beta_c^{h+l}\psi'\operatorname{cov}_i(x_{i,t_{j-h}}, x_{i,t_{j-l}})\psi \quad (21)$$

Comparing the terms in (21) and (20), we therefore have

$$\operatorname{var}\left(\sqrt{n_c}\varepsilon_{c,t_j}\right) = \operatorname{var}_i(y_{i,t_j}) + \beta_c^{2(t_j-t_{j-1})}\operatorname{var}_i(y_{i,t_{j-1}}) - \sum_{h=0}^{t_j-t_{j-1}-1} \beta_c^{2h}\psi'\operatorname{var}_i(x_{i,t_j})\psi - \sum_{l\neq h}^{t_j-t_{j-1}-1}\sum_{h=0}^{t_j-t_{j-1}-1} \beta_c^{h+l}\psi'\operatorname{cov}_i(x_{i,t_{j-h}}, x_{i,t_{j-l}})\psi$$

Similarly, under cross-sectional independence, algebraic manipulation gives the covariance formulae.

ACKNOWLEDGEMENTS

I thank Peter Phillips, Donald Andrews, Karim Abadir and two referees for their helpful comments and suggestions. Financial assistance from a Cowles Foundation Prize and Sasakawa Fellowship is gratefully acknowledged.

REFERENCES

Arellano, M. and S. Bond (1991). Some tests of specification for panel data: Monte Carlo evidence and an application to employment equations. *Review of Economic Studies 58*, 277–97.

Baltagi, B. H. and P. X. Wu (1999). Unequally spaced panel data regressions with AR(1) disturbances. *Econometric Theory 15*, 814–23.

Campbell, J. Y., A. W. Lo and A. C. MacKinlay (1997). *The Econometrics of Financial Markets*. Princeton, NJ: Princeton University Press.

Collado, M. D. (1997). Estimating dynamic models from time series of independent cross-sections. *Journal of Econometrics 82*, 37–62.

Davidson, R. and J. G. MacKinnon (1993). *Estimation and Inference in Econometrics*. New York: Oxford University Press

Deaton, A. (1985). Panel data from time series of cross-sections. *Journal of Econometrics 30*, 109–26.

Engle, R. F. (2000). The econometrics of ultra-high frequency data. *Econometrica 68*, 1–22.

McKenzie, D. J. (2000). Estimation of heterogeneous stationary and non-stationary pseudopanels. mimeo. Yale University.

Moffitt, R. (1993). Identification and estimation of dynamic models with a time series of repeated cross-sections. *Journal of Econometrics 59*, 99–123.

Newey, W. K. and D. McFadden (1994). Large sample estimation and hypothesis testing. In Engle. R. F. and D. L. McFadden (eds), *Handbook of Econometrics*, vol. 4, pp. 2111–2245. New York: Elsevier Science.

Wansbeek, T. and A. Kapteyn (1989). Estimation of the error-components model with incomplete panels. *Journal of Econometrics 41*, 341–61.

Journal of Econometrics 59 (1993) 99–123. North-Holland

Identification and estimation of dynamic models with a time series of repeated cross-sections*

Robert Moffitt*

Brown University, Providence, RI 02912, USA

Repeated cross-sectional data contain information on independent cross-sections of individual units at two or more points in time. Estimation of dynamic models with such data is made difficult by the general lack of information on lagged dependent and independent variables and the consequent unobservability of the intertemporal covariances needed to identify and estimate dynamic models. It is demonstrated here that the parameters of such models, both linear and nonlinear, both with and without fixed individual effects, are identified and can be consistently estimated with the imposition of certain restrictions. The paper includes an examination of the identification and estimation with repeated cross-sectional data of dynamic discrete dependent variable models, which can be parameterized in terms of transition rates between the different cross-sections.

1. Introduction

Repeated cross-sectional (RCS) data contain information from independently drawn sets of cross-sections of a population at two or more points in time. While such data obviously provide more information than data from a single cross-section, RCS data are generally regarded as inferior to true panel data – that is, data on the same cross-sectional units over time – for the estimation of dynamic models. However, it has been pointed out previously that at least one class of models – linear with fixed effects – is identified and can be consistently estimated with RCS data [Browning et al. (1985), Deaton (1985)].[1] The present paper extends this point in several ways: (1) the identification conditions for the

Correpondence to: Robert Moffitt, Department of Economics, Brown University, Providence, RI 02912, USA.

*The author would like to thank Christopher Flinn, James Heckman, Franco Peracchi, Marno Verbeek, and the participants of seminars at several universities for comments. The comments of three anonymous referees were also helpful. This paper was presented at the August 1990 World Congress of the Econometric Society in Barcelona and the CIDE Conference on 'The Econometrics of Panels and Pseudo Panels' in Venice in October 1990.

[1]It has also been shown by Heckman and Robb (1985) that certain classes of models for the impact of interventions can be consistently estimated with RCS data.

linear fixed effects model are stated explicitly; (2) estimation methods for the linear fixed effects model are demonstrated which make use of the individual micro data and which economize on parameters; (3) autoregressive linear models are considered; and (4) the methods are extended to models with discrete dependent variables, both with and without fixed effects. It is shown that the dynamic models in all cases are identified and that consistent estimating techniques are available from RCS data with the imposition of certain restrictions.

Efficiency questions are not considered in the paper nor is any direct consideration of the relative efficiency of true panel data and RCS data considered. That is an important topic but one left for future work. The analysis raises a number of other important questions as well which are left for future investigation; these are discussed at the end of the paper.

The availability of methods for the estimation of dynamic models with RCS data is important for applied work in countries without panel data, as is the situation in many Western European countries and many developing countries. However, it is also important even in countries, such as the U.S., where panel data are often available, for the available panels are often inferior to the available cross-sections in some respects. For example, the U.S. Current Population Survey (CPS) has larger samples, more representative samples over time because they are unaffected by attrition, and more consistently-defined questions over time than the available U.S. panels. While a direct comparison of this pe will not be made in the paper, it is worth noting that the relative desirability of the particular panels and RCS data sets that may be available in a country may not be clearcut.

The analysis of RCS data is also of interest because such data provide a connecting link between micro and aggregate data. As will become clear below, the methods for estimating dynamic models with RCS data are explicitly or implicitly grouping methods akin to those used to generate aggregate data series. A comparison of estimates from RCS data and from true panel data would shed light on, for example whether the commonly observed differences in parameter estimates from aggregate data and panel data in some areas of research (e.g., of life cycle models) are the result of the panel nature of the latter or simply their individual micro nature.

Section 2 of the paper outlines the classes of models to be considered. Linear models are discussed in section 3 and discrete-dependent-variable models are discussed in section 4. Section 5 reports two empirical illustrations, and a summary and set of conclusions follows in section 6.

2. Classes of models considered

The classes of models considered in the paper are specializations of the general model:

$$y_{it}^* = \alpha y_{i,t-1} + x_{it}'\beta + f_i + \varepsilon_{it}, \qquad i = 1, \ldots, N, \quad t = 1, \ldots, T, \tag{1}$$

$$E(\varepsilon_{it}^2) = \sigma^2, \quad E(\varepsilon_{it}\varepsilon_{j\tau}) = 0, \qquad \forall i, j, t \neq \tau, \tag{2}$$

where y_{it}^* is a latent endogenous continuous variable for cross-sectional unit i at time t, y_{it} is its (possibly dichotomous) realization, $\boldsymbol{x}_{it}$ is a $(K \times 1)$ vector of strictly exogenous (w.r.t. ε_{it}) variables for i at t, $\boldsymbol{\beta}$ is its associated coefficient vector, f_i is a fixed effect orthogonal to ε_{it} but not to $\boldsymbol{x}_{it}$ and $y_{i,t-1}$, and ε_{it} is an error term with scalar covariance matrix. The dynamics in the model arise both from the presence of the fixed effect and from the lagged endogenous variable. Fixed effects rather than random effects are considered because the latter, at least if orthogonal to $\boldsymbol{x}_{it}$, are less likely to raise issues of consistency (e.g., if $\alpha = 0$, then consistent estimates in the presence of orthogonal random effects can be obtained by pooling the cross-sections).[2] Only first-order lags in y_{it} are considered for simplicity; generalization to higher-order lags is straightforward. A nonscalar covariance matrix of ε_{it} is also not considered because serial correlation parameters in that matrix will generally not be identified with RCS data, and identification of the other parameters in the model will generally not hinge on the absence of such correlation in any case. Finally, it is assumed for simplicity that the cross-sections at each t are of the same size (N), that the population is closed with respect to in- and out-migration, and that there are no births or deaths.

Letting y_{it} denote the observed value of the endogenous variable for unit i at time t, the critical characteristic of RCS data is that y_{it} is observed but $y_{i,t-1}$ is not. Thus no estimate of $\text{cov}(y_{it}, y_{i,t-1})$ is available in the data. Covariances are needed to estimate (1) not only because of the presence of $y_{i,t-1}$ as a regressor but also because of the presence of the fixed effect. The question of the paper is the nature of the restrictions that must be imposed to estimate such models in the absence of information on the covariances.

Four special cases will be separately considered:

I. *Linear Models* $(y_{it} = y_{it}^*)$

(A) $\alpha = 0$ (fixed effects model),

(B) $f_i = 0$ (autoregressive model).

II. *Binary Choice Limited Dependent Variable Models*

$(y_{it} = 1 \quad \text{if} \quad y_{it}^* \geq 0; \qquad y_{it} = 0 \quad \text{otherwise})$

[2]The 'fixed effect' in this model can be considered to be either a fixed unknown constant or a stochastic term possibly correlated with X_{it} (i.e., a 'correlated random effect'). The distinction will have no operational content for the analysis below.

(A) $\alpha = 0$ (binary choice fixed effects model),

(B) $f_i = 0$ (Markov model).

Extensions to cases which are combinations of these are straightforward and not discussed.[3]

3. Linear models

3.1. Fixed effects models

To keep matters simple we shall initially consider a model with a single regressor. In addition, we shall henceforth make explicit the nonpanel nature of the data by indexing individuals in each cross-section by $i(t)$, for in RCS data the individuals are potentially different in each cross-section. We therefore have

$$y_{i(t)t} = \beta_0 + \beta_1 x_{i(t)t} + f_{i(t)} + \varepsilon_{i(t)t}, \quad i(t) = 1, \ldots, N, \quad t = 1, \ldots, T. \tag{3}$$

Estimation of (3) by least squares on the pooled RCS data set will yield inconsistent estimates for β_1 if $x_{i(t)t}$ and $f_{i(t)}$ are correlated, since the latter is unobserved and hence must be omitted from the regression. Considering identification indirectly by search for a consistent estimator, we seek an instrumental variables (IV) estimator that yields a consistent estimate of β_1, and hopefully an estimator for which identification conditions are well-known. For this we require an instrument for $x_{i(t)t}$ that will, among other things, be asymptotically uncorrelated with $f_{i(t)}$.

The most important class of instruments is that consisting of functions of t. Let us specify a linear projection of $x_{i(t)t}$ onto K such functions as follows:

$$x_{i(t)t} = \sum_{k=1}^{K} \delta_k g_k(t) + \omega_{i(t)t}, \tag{4}$$

where g_k are known functions and where $\omega_{i(t)t}$ is a residual orthogonal to those functions by construction. Using a function of t as an instrument is sensible because $x_{i(t)t}$ presumably varies with t; if it did not, β_1 could not be identified

[3]In the binary choice model the lagged dependent variable could be in latent form rather than in the form of the observable. The analysis would be simpler in that case because an analytic reduced form could be derived and because instrumental variables could be used, as it cannot be in the case actually considered here (see below).

even with true panel data.[4] Also, functions of t should be uncorrelated with true fixed effects because the latter are time-invariant and hence must be uncorrelated with functions of t.

Formally, let $\hat{x}_t$ be the least squares prediction from (4). Then consistency of the IV estimator of β_1 requires that at least one element of the set $\{\delta_k\}$ be nonzero and that $\text{plim}\,[(1/NT)\sum_{i(t),t}\hat{x}_t f_{i(t)}] = 0$.[5] The first of these conditions should hold if $\hat{x}_t$ varies with t, as just noted. Whether the second condition will hold is more questionable, for the nature of the RCS data implies that the fixed effects in the sample will differ in each cross-section (t) because there are potentially different individuals in each.

The fixed effect $f_{i(t)}$ can be decomposed into its sample mean at each t ($\bar{f}_t$) and its deviation from that mean ($v_{i(t)}$):

$$f_{i(t)} = \bar{f}_t + v_{i(t)}. \tag{5}$$

The former can be further decomposed into the true mean fixed effect in the total population ($\bar{f}^*$), which is time-invariant by necessity – here the assumption of a closed population is important – and a deviation from that mean arising from sampling error in the data (v'_t):

$$\bar{f}_t = \bar{f}^* + v'_t. \tag{6}$$

Thus we have

$$f_{i(t)} = \bar{f}^* + v'_t + v_{i(t)}. \tag{7}$$

Consistency of the IV estimator requires that $\hat{x}_t$ be asymptotically uncorrelated with $\bar{f}^*$, v'_t, and $v_{i(t)}$. Since $\bar{f}^*$ is a constant, this condition must be met. However, it is met for the latter two variables as well as $N \rightarrow \infty$, though not as $T \rightarrow \infty$. As $N \rightarrow \infty$, the sampling error v'_t goes to 0; further, the distribution of $v_{i(t)}$ becomes independent of t (and hence of $\hat{x}_t$) because the sample of individuals in each successive cross-section becomes identical when the total population is sampled, even if their identities are not known.

Remark 1. The two conditions for consistency are stronger than what is required for true panel data. With panel data, β_1 can be identified even if $\delta_k = 0$ $\forall k$ because $\omega_{i(t)t}$ still provides variation over t conditional on $i(t)$. Furthermore, since $f_{i(t)} = f_i$ $\forall t$, unbiased estimates of β_1 can be obtained even at finite N by conditioning on f_i.

[4]However, variation in $x_{i(t)t}$ over t could arise from $\omega_{i(t)t}$ only; see below.

[5]By assumption, $x_{i(t)t}$ is asymptotically uncorrelated with $\varepsilon_{i(t)t}$.

Remark 2. The restrictions necessary for identification and estimation with RCS data are needed to circumvent what is a type of missing data problem, namely, that the past and future values of y_{it} and x_{it} for the same individual i are missing. But the lack of data on x_{it} at different t for the same i is more serious than the lack of data on similar y_{it}. With true panel data the conventional within estimator for β_1 can be written as an instrumental variables estimator with $(x_{it} - x_{i.})$ as instrument ($x_{i.}$ = mean over t for each i):

$$\hat{\beta}_1(\text{within}) = \frac{\sum_i \sum_t y_{it}(x_{it} - x_{i.})}{\sum_i \sum_t x_{it}(x_{it} - x_{i.})}. \tag{8}$$

If the available RCS data contained information on histories of the x_{it} of the individuals in the sample, even if not the y_{it} histories, the right-hand side of (8) could be computed even for such data. The resulting estimator would be consistent under the same conditions as is the within estimator because they are identical.

The model thus far requires time series aggregation – the instrument $\hat{x}_t$ varies only with t, not with $i(t)$.[6] More efficient estimates can be obtained if the micro data contain information on exogenous time-invariant characteristics which are determinants of x. In many models of individual behavior, year of birth qualifies as such as a variable. If there are 'cohort' effects in x, then an instrument for $x_{i(t)t}$ can be based on a linear projection onto functions of both t and $c_{i(t)}$, the year of birth of individual $i(t)$:

$$x_{i(t)t} = \sum_{k=1}^{K} \delta_{1k} g_{1k}(t) + \sum_{m=1}^{M} \delta_{2m} g_{2m}(c_{i(t)}, t) + \sum_{j=1}^{J} \delta_{3j} g_{3j}(c_{i(t)}) + \omega_{i(t)t}, \tag{9}$$

where g_{1k}, g_{2m}, and g_{3j} are known functions. Unfortunately, an instrument based on (9) is likely to be correlated with $f_{i(t)}$ because the fixed effect is likely to be correlated with cohort as well (indeed, this may be one source of the covariation between $x_{i(t)t}$ and $f_{i(t)}$). Denoting $\bar{f}_{c(t)}$ as the mean fixed effect for those sampled at t who were born in year c; $v_{i(t)}$ as the deviation of $f_{i(t)}$ from that mean; $\bar{f}_c^*$ as the true mean for cohort c in the total population; and $v'_{c(t)}$ as the deviation of $\bar{f}_{c(t)}$ from $\bar{f}_c^*$, we have

$$f_{i(t)} = \bar{f}_c^* + v'_{c(t)} + v_{i(t)}, \tag{10}$$

[6]The left-hand side need not be grouped w.r.t. (i.e., aggregated over) t for consistent estimation. See footnote 8 below.

in analogy with (7). Since $\bar{f}_c^*$ can be represented with cohort dummies explicitly in the main equation (3), consistency again requires that $\hat{x}_{i(t)t}$ be asymptotically uncorrelated with $v'_{c(t)}$ and $v_{i(t)}$. Consistency follows in this case as $N \to \infty$, holding T and the number of cohorts fixed. The reasoning is identical to that given previously with the modification that the number of observations in each cohort–t cell goes to infinity.[7]

Remark 3. Browning et al. (1985) computed group means of $y_{i(t)t}$ and $x_{i(t)t}$ within cohort–age cells and regressed the y means on the x means and cohort dummies. This procedure is a special case of the one outlined here, with a full set of age, cohort, and cohort–age interaction dummies appearing in (9). It is well-known that grouping methods are instrumental variables methods, with cohort and age serving as the grouping criteria in this case. Only age (t) is excluded from the main equation and hence it serves as the identifying grouping variable, just as in the simpler model.[8]

It may be noted that a full set of cohort dummies may not be required in the main equation. The equation

$$y_{i(t)t} = \beta_0 + \beta_1 x_{i(t)t} + \sum_{j=1}^{J} \gamma_j h_j(c_{i(t)}) + \varepsilon'_{i(t)t}, \tag{11}$$

where h_j are known functions, has as a special case equation (3) with (10) substituted in and with cohort dummies used for the $\bar{f}_c^*$. In most applications, it is likely that y will vary smoothly with cohort effects and, hence, those effects will be representable with fewer parameters than would be required with a full set of cohort dummies. Efficiency gains could thus result. An example of the degree to which such parsimony can be achieved in one application is given in the empirical section below.[9]

Remark 4. Deaton (1985) noted an errors-in-variables problem with the Browning et al. procedure that arises because the means of $x_{i(t)t}$ for each cohort–age cell are error-filled measures of true cohort–age means. In the model here that problem appears in the terms $v'_{c(t)}$ and $v_{i(t)}$. Those terms represent errors

[7]See Verbeek and Nijman (1992) and Angrist (1991) for a discussion of this condition as well.

[8]Grouping the dependent variable, $y_{i(t)t}$, is unnecessary for identification and point estimation. It is straightforward to show that a least squares regression of the cell means of y on the cell means of x yields estimates identical to those of a regression of the individual $y_{i(t)t}$ on the cell means of x. However, standard errors may be more accurate if y is grouped. The efficiency and optimality of IV methods is not discussed here, only their identification.

[9]Parsimony in (9) is not particularly desirable asymptotically. There is no large-sample efficiency loss from including all possible functions of t and $c_{i(t)}$ in the instrument. However, there may be small-sample losses.

in the cohort dummies for $\bar{f}_c^*$ which arise because those dummies imperfectly proxy the cross-section-specific means $\bar{f}_{c(t)}$. Those errors may be correlated with $\hat{x}_{i(t)t}$ in small samples, but this correlation disappears as $N \to \infty$, as noted previously.

Moving to the general case, new issues are raised. The general case can be written

$$y_{i(t)t} = X'_{i(t)t}\beta + f_{i(t)} + \varepsilon_{i(t)t}, \tag{12}$$

where $X_{i(t)}$ is now a $(K \times 1)$ vector of regressors potentially correlated with $f_{i(t)}$. Assume that there exists an $(L \times 1)$ vector $Z_{i(t)}$ of time-invariant variables [for individual $i(t)$] including not only cohort but also, for example, sex, race, years of education (if schooling has been completed), and residential location (if mobility can be ignored). Also let $W_{i(t)t}$ be an $(M \times 1)$ vector of time-varying variables uncorrelated with $f_{i(t)}$, which may consist only of functions of t. Then the linear projections upon which the IV method is based can be written as

$$X_{i(t)t} = \delta_1 W_{i(t)t} + \delta_2 Z_{i(t)} + \omega_{i(t)t}, \tag{13}$$

$$f_{i(t)} = Z'_{i(t)}\gamma + v_{i(t)}, \tag{14}$$

where δ_1 is a $(K \times M)$ matrix of coefficients, δ_2 is a $(K \times L)$ matrix of coefficients, $\omega_{i(t)t}$ is a $(K \times 1)$ vector of errors, γ is a $(L \times 1)$ vector of coefficients, and $v_{i(t)}$ represents the remaining individual effect conditional on $Z_{i(t)}$. Eq. (14) is a generalization of (10), with $Z'_{i(t)}\gamma$ capturing the effects of all time-invariant variables, not just cohort, and with $v_{i(t)}$ in (14) representing both errors in (10) combined. Letting y, X, Z, and v be the stacked NT vectors for all i and t and letting $U = [X\ Z]$ and $\hat{U} = [\hat{X}\ Z]$, where $\hat{X}$ is the matrix of least squares predictions from (13), the IV estimator for β and γ is $(\hat{U}'U)^{-1}\hat{U}'y$ and consistency requires that $\text{plim}[(1/NT)\hat{U}'v] = 0$ and that $\hat{U}$ be of full column rank, $(K + L)$. As in the simpler case, consistency is achievable only as $N \to \infty$ holding T fixed.[10]

Remark 5. This generalization permits 'grouping' conditional on any set of time-invariant variables, not just cohort. The sample sizes in most data sets would not permit literal grouping by cells of $Z_{i(t)}$. The regression-based procedure proposed here is one method for dealing with this problem (literal grouping by sufficiently large cells is still an alternative).[11]

[10] Also required is $\text{plim}[(1/NT)\hat{U}'\varepsilon] = 0$; this is assumed throughout. If this assumption fails, e.g., because of time-specific shocks, different instruments may be needed. See below.

[11] Time-specific variables such as the aggregate unemployment rate may also be entered and used to 'group' in this regression sense.

Remark 6. There may be difficulties in meeting the rank condition if the dimension of $\boldsymbol{X}_{i(t)t}$ is high and if $\boldsymbol{W}_{i(t)t}$ only contains functions of t, for identification in this case requires an additional independent function of t for each additional variable in $\boldsymbol{X}_{i(t)t}$. The problem is likely to be especially severe if functions of t are included themselves in $\boldsymbol{X}_{i(t)t}$, for, while they can serve as their own instruments, they will make it more difficult to identify the coefficients of other variables in $\boldsymbol{X}_{i(t)t}$ because additional functions of t will be required.

Remark 7. If $\boldsymbol{X}_{i(t)t}$ is redefined to include time-invariant variables for which 'structural' coefficients in the $\boldsymbol{\beta}$ vector are defined, their coefficients cannot be identified if those variables are allowed to be correlated with $f_{i(t)}$. This result is similar to the nonidentification of the coefficients on time-invariant variables in the panel data model with fixed effects.

Remark 8. If $X_{i(t)t}$ is not strictly exogenous w.r.t. $\varepsilon_{i(t)t}$, then additional restrictions on the choice of instruments may result. For example, if aggregate or individual shocks affect both $\boldsymbol{X}_{i(t)t}$ and $\varepsilon_{i(t)t}$, instruments which use only variables in an information set at some prior time may appear in (13). More generally, whatever orthogonality conditions are suggested by theory may be used to generate the instruments. See Blundell et al. (1989) for a discussion of this issue in the context of the Browning et al. grouping estimator.

3.2. Autoregressive models

The autoregressive model is

$$y_{i(t)t} = \alpha y_{i(t),t-1} + \boldsymbol{X}'_{i(t)t}\boldsymbol{\beta} + \boldsymbol{Z}'_{i(t)}\gamma + \varepsilon_{i(t)t}, \qquad \begin{matrix} i = 1, \ldots, N, \\ t = 2, \ldots, T, \end{matrix} \tag{15}$$

where all variables are as defined previously, but where $\boldsymbol{X}_{i(t)t}$ is defined to include only time-varying variables distinct from the vector of time-invariant variables $\boldsymbol{Z}_{i(t)}$. Estimation of the autoregressive model with RCS data can be achieved with methods similar to the IV methods used for the fixed effects model if an instrument for $y_{i(t),t-1}$ can be constructed, though here it must be 2SLS since the true value of $y_{i(t),t-1}$ is not observed. Consider a linear projection using the observations at $t-1$ on $y_{i(t-1),t-1}$:

$$y_{i(t-1),t-1} = \boldsymbol{W}'_{i(t-1),t-1}\delta_1 + \boldsymbol{Z}'_{i(t-1)}\delta_2 + \omega_{i(t-1),t-1}, \tag{16}$$

where $\boldsymbol{W}_{i(t-1),t-1}$ is a vector of time-varying variables. The vector of time-invariant variables is assumed to be identical in (15) and (16) although it is conceivable that they may differ.

Inserting a predicted variable $\hat{y}_{i(t),t-1}$ obtained from least-squares estimation of (16) (using $\boldsymbol{W}_{i(t),t-1}$ and $\boldsymbol{Z}_{i(t)}$) into (15) in place of $y_{i(t),t-1}$ and applying least squares will yield consistent estimates of $\boldsymbol{\beta}$ and γ provided that $\hat{y}_{i(t),t-1}$ is asymptotically uncorrelated with $\varepsilon_{i(t)t}$. Identification of the coefficients requires that the stacked matrix $[\boldsymbol{y}\,\boldsymbol{X}\,\boldsymbol{Z}]$ be of full column rank.

Remark 1. As in the simple case considered in the fixed effects model, the $\boldsymbol{Z}_{i(t)}$ could consist of cohort functions and the $\boldsymbol{W}_{i(t)t}$ vector could consist of functions of t alone. The model would then be clearly identified by the variation in t in the instrument. Inserting the mean $\bar{y}_{i(t-1),t-1}$ of the sample at $t-1$ in the same cohort as that at t is a simple example of such an instrument. But (15) and (16) generalize that method to one permitting regression-based 'grouping' on any other set of time-invariant variables $\boldsymbol{Z}_{i(t)}$ and any other time-varying variables that may be available. Indeed, even a single cross-section may be used to estimate the model if there are no cohort effects if t is defined as age and if $y_{i(t),t-1}$ is constructed from the units aged $t-1$ in the same cross-section.

Remark 2. Construction of an instrument $\hat{y}_{i(t),t-1}$ using variables in $\boldsymbol{W}_{i(t)t}$ other than t itself requires knowing the history of those variables for the cross-sectional units at t. This is a strong data requirement unlikely to be satisfied by most RCS data sets. Variables that may be thought to be in $\boldsymbol{W}_{i(t)t}$ but which are not observed must themselves be projected onto functions of t and whatever time-varying variables are observed in much the same manner as $x_{i(t)t}$ was projected in the fixed effects model.[12] The rank condition for identification may be difficult to meet in this circumstance if $\boldsymbol{X}_{i(t)t}$ itself contains time-varying functions of t or functions of t itself.

Remark 3. A more formal approach to the problem may be taken by imposing the structure (15) on all previous t and by constructing an instrument for $y_{i(t),t-1}$ from the reduced form of the equation. For illustration, assume that the process has a finite start date and that the initial value of $y_{i(t)t}$ is determined by the function

$$y_{i(t)1} = \boldsymbol{X}'_{i(t)1}\boldsymbol{\beta} + \boldsymbol{Z}'_{i(t)}\gamma + \varepsilon_{i(t)1}, \tag{17}$$

which is simply (15) evaluated at $y_{i(t)0} = 0$. A more general formulation could be given in which the variables, coefficients, and error variance in (17) are less

[12] It should be noted that some time-varying variables like the number and ages of children may be backcast with considerable accuracy, and that aggregate variables such as the unemployment rate will presumably also be measurable in the past.

strictly tied to those in (15). The reduced form of (15) can be shown to be

$$y_{i(t),t-1} = \sum_{\tau=1}^{t-1} \alpha^{t-\tau} X'_{i(t)\tau}\beta + Z'_{i(t)}\gamma\left(\frac{1-\alpha^{t-1}}{1-\alpha}\right) + v_{i(t),t-1}, \tag{18}$$

where

$$v_{i(t),t-1} = \sum_{\tau=1}^{t-1} \alpha^{t-\tau} \varepsilon_{i(t)\tau}, \tag{19}$$

which can be estimated on the $t-1$ sample and used to construct an instrument for the t sample. Note that in this case the absence of any time-varying variables $X_{i(t)t}$ in the model still permits identification because the autoregressive structure implies that the cumulative effects of $Z_{i(t)}$ on $y_{i(t),t-1}$ vary with t, thus permitting the construction of an instrument not linearly dependent on $Z_{i(t)}$ in (15). More flexible specifications of the autoregressive structure of the model would generate less rigid forms of the t-dependence of the effect of $Z_{i(t)}$ in (18).

Remark 4. It may be of interest to note that least squares estimates of (15) on true panel data using the observed values of $y_{i(t),t-1}$ will generate inconsistent estimates of the parameters if there is individual-specific serial correlation in $\varepsilon_{i(t)t}$ (e.g., from 'unobserved heterogeneity'). But this problem does not appear with RCS data because IV methods are used by necessity. These methods are consistent in the presence of such heterogeneity.[13]

4. Discrete dependent variables

4.1. Fixed effects models

Only binary choice models will be considered; extensions to other discrete models and to limited dependent variable models is straightforward. Write the fixed effects model as

$$y^*_{i(t)t} = X'_{i(t)t}\beta + f_{i(t)} + \varepsilon_{i(t)t}, \tag{20}$$

$$\begin{aligned} y_{i(t)t} &= 1 \quad \text{if} \quad y^*_{i(t)t} \geq 0, \\ &= 0 \quad \text{otherwise.} \end{aligned} \tag{21}$$

[13]Note that one cannot used the lagged $y_{i(t),t-1}$ as an instrument – that is not observable. Using it in true panel data would be erroneous if there is first-order serial correlation. Instead, lagged $y_{i(t-1),t-1}$ must be used, but that variable is identical for all individuals $i(t)$ who are of the same age or cohort.

Assuming $\varepsilon_{i(t)t} \sim N(0, 1)$, the issue is whether the IV or 2SLS methods discussed in section 3.1 can be applied here. 2SLS methods for limited dependent variable models without fixed effects were first used by Nelson and Olsen (1978), who simply estimated a Tobit model with predicted regressors. Amemiya (1979) demonstrated the consistency of the estimator and derived its asymptotic covariance matrix. A number of other consistent 2SLS and IV methods for probit and Tobit have since been developed; Newey (1987) considers their relative efficiencies. Thus consistency of 2SLS in such models has been established. Identification requires meeting the same conditions as in the linear model.

Relatively little is altered when the fixed effects model in (20)–(21) is considered, although an additional normality assumption is required. In the case where there are no cohort effects, insertion of (7) into (20) generates a composite error term $v_t' + v_{i(t)} + \varepsilon_{i(t)t}$. As $N \to \infty$, $v_t' \to 0$, as before, and, further, the distribution of the within-period individual fixed effects $v_{i(t)}$ converges to a distribution uncorrelated with the instruments for $X_{i(t)t}$. With the additional (not necessarily innocuous) assumption of normality of $v_{i(t)} + \varepsilon_{i(t)t}$, the consistency results in the articles cited in the previous paragraph are immediately applicable. Unlike the case with true panel data, where large T is required for consistent estimation of logit and probit fixed effects models [Chamberlain (1980), Heckman (1981a)], here the individual fixed effects are not estimated and hence no inconsistency in their estimates at finite T is transmitted to $\boldsymbol{\beta}$.

If cohort fixed effects are estimated, consistency of the 2SLS-estimator-plus-cohort-dummies requires that $N \to \infty$ while the number of cohorts is held fixed, or, alternatively, that $N/N_c \to \infty$, where N_c is the number of cohorts. However, this requirement is present even in the linear model, where the cohort dummies are already error-filled proxies for true mean cohort fixed effects in finite-N samples. Thus we have consistency only with $N \to \infty$ in both the linear and probit models. The same applies for the general case shown in (20) using (13) to construct instruments.

4.2. Markov models

A first-order autoregressive model between binary outcome variables is equivalent to a first-order Markov model.[14] That model can be characterized by two transition rates, one each for the probabilities of inflow and outflow from

[14]If the lagged endogenous variable is $y^*_{i,t-1}$ rather than $y_{i,t-1}$, simpler methods more directly analogous to those in the linear autoregressive model can be used.

each of the two states. Define the model as follows:[15]

$$p_{it} = \text{Prob}(y_{it} = 1), \tag{22}$$

$$\mu_{it} = \text{Prob}(y_{it} = 1 \mid y_{i,t-1} = 0), \tag{23}$$

$$\lambda_{it} = \text{Prob}(y_{it} = 0 \mid y_{i,t-1} = 1). \tag{24}$$

Then we have the accounting identity

$$p_{it} = \mu_{it}(1 - p_{i,t-1}) + (1 - \lambda_{it})(1 - p_{i,t-1}) = \mu_{it} + \eta_{it} p_{i,t-1}, \tag{25}$$

where $\eta_{it} = 1 - \lambda_{it} - \mu_{it}$. Eq. (25), a standard flow equation in the literature on Markov processes, relates the two marginal probabilities at t and $t-1$ to the two transition rates.

That the parameters of (25) are identified with panel data in cases in which they are not with RCS data is intuitive and forms the basis for a fundamental nonidentification result for RCS data. For example, reinterpreting the cross-sectional index i as indexing groups of cross-sectional units within which frequency estimates of μ and λ can be estimated with a given panel sample, nonidentification in the RCS case can be seen from (25) by merely noting that the two parameters μ_{it} and λ_{it} for group i at period t cannot be identified solely from knowledge of p_{it} and $p_{i,t-1}$. Thus a model with μ_{it} and λ_{it} completely unrestricted with respect to i and t cannot be estimated with RCS data.[16]

Identification is possible with restrictions imposed over i and/or t, however. Consider two examples.

Example 1: *Time-homogeneous and unit-homogeneous hazards.* If $\mu_{it} = \mu$ and $\lambda_{it} = \lambda$ for all i and t, then, letting $\eta = 1 - \lambda - \mu$, we have

$$p_{it} = \mu + \eta p_{i,t-1}, \tag{26}$$

with reduced form

$$p_{it} = \mu\left(1 + \sum_{\tau=1}^{t-1} \eta^{t-\tau}\right) = \mu\frac{1-\eta^t}{1-\eta}, \tag{27}$$

[15]The notation for $i(t)$ is not used in this section for simplicity.

[16]More generally, in a transition model with L possible states rather than 2, the $L(L-1)$ unique elements of a $L \times L$ transition matrix cannot be estimated from the marginal probabilities at $t-1$ and t alone.

assuming $p_{i0} = 0$.[17] Thus the profile of $p_{it} = p_t$ over t is a two-parameter function; hence both μ and λ are identified provided estimates on p_t at two different t are available. This result obviously generalizes to cases in which the hazards are homogeneous w.r.t. t but only within groups defined over i.

Models with this type of homogeneity imposed have been studied extensively in the statistical literature, where the predominant approach considers least squares estimation of (26) using aggregate frequency estimates of the $p_{it} = p_t$, thus identifying the hazards from an estimated slope and intercept [Miller (1952), Madansky (1959), Lee et al. (1970), Lawless and McLeish (1984), Kalbfleish and Lawless (1985)]. These studies typically ignore the boundedness of the variable p_t as well as the presence of sampling error in the frequency estimates and consequent errors-in-variables difficulties in least squares estimation.[18]

Example 2: Linear probability model for hazards. Let $\mu_{it} = \boldsymbol{X}'_{it}\boldsymbol{\theta}_1$ and $\lambda_{it} = \boldsymbol{X}'_{it}\boldsymbol{\theta}_2$, where $\boldsymbol{X}_{it}$ is a vector of observables for unit i at time t (perhaps including independent functions of t). Then we have

$$p_{it} = \boldsymbol{X}'_{it}\boldsymbol{\theta}_1 + (\boldsymbol{X}'_{it}\boldsymbol{\theta}_2)p_{i,t-1}. \tag{28}$$

Estimation of (28) can be considered using methods analogous to the 2SLS methods proposed for the autoregressive linear model. Construction of a predicted value of $\hat{p}_{i,t-1}$, possibly by explicit calculation of the reduced form for (28), and substitution of the dichotomous y_{it} and $y_{i,t-1}$ for p_{it} and $p_{i,t-1}$ leads to the same identification condition as that for the linear model, namely, that the predicted value $\hat{p}_{i,t-1}$ have sufficient variation independent of $\boldsymbol{X}_{it}$ to meet the rank condition, which will often mean variation over t.[19] The rank condition will involve interactions of $\hat{p}_{i,t-1}$ and x_{it} as well since the parameters $\boldsymbol{\theta}_2$ are identified from such interactions.[20]

This example demonstrates that the proportionality restrictions inherent in the index functions $\boldsymbol{X}'_{it}\boldsymbol{\theta}_1$ and $\boldsymbol{X}'_{it}\boldsymbol{\theta}_2$ are themselves sufficient for identification of transition rates from RCS data. However, while such restrictions are not

[17]The value of p_{i0} is not the first observed outcome of the process – that is p_{i1} – but is instead the value of the state prior to the beginning of the process. As most outcome variables are defined, p_{i0} will be zero – an individual is unemployed at the beginning of an unemployment spell, not working prior to entering the labor force, unmarried at the beginning of the lifetime, and so on.

[18]However, some authors consider ML estimation to address the first problem, though still taking the sample estimate of p_{t-1} as exogenous and error-free.

[19]Note that this implies that the parameters of transition rates cannot be identified for steady state processes.

[20]As in the linear case, it can also be shown that the predicted value $\hat{p}_{i,t-1}$ will vary with t even if all the $\boldsymbol{X}_{it}$ are time-invariant.

necessary with true panel data, in practice most studies using panel data nevertheless impose such index function restrictions in the specification of their transition rates.

Imposing the index function restriction in a proper model of binary choice requires leaving the linear probability model. The specification and estimation of a probit model illustrates such a proper probability model identifiable with RCS data. Let

$$y_{it}^* = X_{it}'\theta_1 + (X_{it}'\theta_2)y_{i,t-1} + \varepsilon_{it}, \tag{29}$$

$$\begin{aligned} y_{it} &= 1 \quad \text{if} \quad y_{it} \geq 0, \\ &= 0 \quad \text{otherwise,} \end{aligned} \tag{30}$$

where $\varepsilon_{it} \sim N(0, 1)$. The hazard rates are

$$\mu_{it} = F[X_{it}'\theta_1], \tag{31}$$

$$\lambda_{it} = 1 - F[X_{it}'(\theta_1 + \theta_2)], \tag{32}$$

where F is the unit normal c.d.f. Consistent instrumental variable and two-stage estimation methods are not available for this model because of the nonlinear errors-in-variables problem that would be created by instrumenting $y_{i,t-1}$. However, the reduced form can be estimated directly. Letting $p_{it} = \text{Prob}(y_{it} = 1)$, the reduced form for p_{it} can be shown to be

$$p_{it} = \mu_{it} + \sum_{\tau=1}^{t-1} \mu_{i\tau}\left(\prod_{s=\tau+1}^{t} \eta_{is}\right), \tag{33}$$

where $\eta_{is} = 1 - \lambda_{is} - \mu_{is}$. Consistent estimates of θ_1 and θ_2 can be obtained by maximization of

$$L = \sum_i \sum_t [y_{it}\log(p_{it}) + (1 - y_{it})\log(1 - p_{it})], \tag{34}$$

using (31) and (32) in (33).[21]

Computing p_{it} by means of (33) is equivalent to integrating out all possible histories for each individual i at time t to derive an expression for the marginal probabilities that are observed. This integration over histories is identical to the formal solution to the initial conditions problem in panel data [Heckman

[21]Including fixed effects in the model cannot be addressed with predicted values of X as discussed previously because of similar nonlinear errors-invariables problems. In this case the function in (13) could be estimated jointly with (29)–(30) using FIML.

(1981b, pp. 181–185)]. The problem in that case arises when several periods of a process are observed for an agent but the beginning of the process is not; hence the unobserved history must be integrated out. The situation here is identical except that there is only a single observed time period.

It may be noted that the assumption of a scalar covariance matrix for ε_{it} is less innocuous in this model than in the linear autoregressive model. Whereas the presence of serial correlation in the linear model, such as that generated by unobserved heterogeneity, only affects the variance of the reduced form error term in (18), in the probit model it affects the form of the reduced form expression (33), where the elements of the covariance matrix of ε_{it} would enter nonlinearly with the regressor variables in X_{it} because the complete distribution of ε_{it} would have to be integrated out. No simple identification restrictions can be derived guaranteeing separation of the elements of the covariance matrix and the parameters of the transition function in this case.[22]

5. Empirical illustrations

The major issue raised by the discussion is whether the identification restrictions necessary for the estimation of the various dynamic models with RCS data are indeed met in common areas of application. That exercise requires the use of panel data and therefore will be conducted in future work. Instead, this section provides two illustrations of the estimation of dynamic models with RCS data, one a linear fixed effects model and one a Markov model. The first is treated only briefly since it is less novel than the latter.

5.1. Linear fixed effects

To illustrate the IV method for the linear fixed effects model, the life cycle model of labour supply of Browning et al. (1985) is estimated with U.S. RCS data (Browning et al. used U.K. data). In the model, y_{it} is hours of work and x_{it} is the log of the real discounted hourly wage rate. The fixed effects are given a specific interpretation, as including the marginal utility of wealth, and the coefficient on x_{it} is interpreted as an intertemporal substitution effect of this wage. The data set is the U.S. Current Population Survey (CPS) and the sample includes white males 20–59 from 21 annual waves, 1968 to 1988.[23]

[22]A less severe problem also arises with incomplete panel data when the covariance matrix estimated for the included periods must be extrapolated to unobserved pre-sample periods.

[23]Only the March files are used. Hours of work are measured as the annual amount over the year prior to the survey and the wage rate is measured as the ratio of earnings in the prior year to hours worked. The wage is discounted with annualized three-month T-bill rates using a 1978 base. To keep the estimation problem manageable and to make the sample size roughly the same as that used by Browning et al., the data are randomly subsampled down to a total of 15,500 over the years.

Table 1 shows IV estimates of eq. (3) with f_i projected onto cohort and individual characteristics for education, number of children, family size, and regional location, and with x_{it} projected onto these same variables plus age.[24] Year dummies are also included in both hours and wage equations for consistency with Browning et al. Columns (1) and (2) show wage and hours estimates, respectively, with a relatively unrestricted age and cohort specification, and columns (3) and (4) show estimates after a specification search on the form of the age and cohort effects. F-tests on the age, cohort, year effects, and on the seven individual characteristics are also shown.

Two conclusions can be drawn from the results. First, a considerable amount of parsimony is achieved in the specification of age and cohort effects. The unrestricted specification in the first two columns contains 27 parameters for age and cohort effects in the wage equation and 12 parameters for cohort effects in the hours equation. Although this is much more restricted than a full specification of all single-year cohort and age effects and interactions (the sample size is insufficient for such a specification in any case), most of the age and cohort parameters are insignificant. The more restrictive model shown in the table, which has quadratic age and cohort effects in the wage equation and cubic cohort effects in the hours equation, cannot be rejected at the 10 percent level but only contains seven age–cohort parameters in the wage equation and three cohort parameters in the hours-worked equation.

Second, the relative sizes of the F-statistics imply that the presence of the individual characteristics is considerably more important than either age, cohort, or year effects. Thus the IV procedure proposed in section 3 above, which makes full use of the individual micro data and of the cross-sectional variation in individual characteristics within age–cohort cells, significantly improves the fit of the model.[25]

5.2. Markov model

To illustrate the Markov model the CPS data are used to estimate a model of female labor supply. The dependent variable y_{it} is defined to equal 1 if the individual is employed and 0 if not. The model in (29)–(30) is estimated with ML by maximizing the likelihood function in (34). The sample includes white married women 20–59 in the 21 years 1968–1988.

[24]Some of the individual characteristics are time-varying, inconsistent with an interpretation as fixed effects. They may alternatively be considered as time-varying variables in X_{it} in (12) for which no instruments are needed.

[25]The wage coefficient in column (4) implies an intertemporal wage elasticity of 0.68, considerably larger than that obtained by Browning et al. or, for example, MaCurdy (1981). It appears to be a result neither of the parsimony of the age and cohort effects or the inclusion of the individual characteristics: the difference seems to arise from the differences in the data sets used. However, the year effects are still significant.

Table 1

Labor supply and wage estimates for white males; n = 15,500.[a]

	Unrestricted age and cohort effects[b]		Restricted age and cohort effects[c]	
	Log discounted hourly wage (1)	Annual hours worked (2)	Log discounted hourly wage (3)	Annual hours worked (4)
Log discounted hourly wage[d]	—	964.6[e] (139.1)	—	1037.3[e] (142.7)
Individual characteristics				
Education	0.056[e] (0.002)	– 28.0[e] (8.1)	0.056[e] (0.002)	– 32.3[e] (8.3)
No. children < 6	0.011 (0.012)	6.7 (11.2)	0.010 (0.012)	4.9 (11.2)
No. children 6–17	0.002 (0.010)	12.8 (9.3)	– 0.001 (0.010)	12.9 (9.3)
Family size	0.006 (0.008)	– 6.0 (7.9)	0.008 (0.008)	– 6.4 (7.9)
Northeast	0.116[e] (0.016)	– 159.0[e] (22.2)	0.116[e] (0.016)	– 167.9[e] (22.5)
North central	0.062[e] (0.015)	– 38.0[e] (16.8)	0.063[e] (0.015)	– 43.4[e] (17.0)
West	0.074[e] (0.015)	– 119.2[e] (18.1)	0.075[e] (0.015)	– 125.6[e] (18.3)
F-statistics				
Age effects	6.4[e] (8)	—	10.0[e] (5)	—
Cohort effects	4.2[e] (12)	2.7[e] (12)	7.3[e] (5)	9.2[e] (3)
Year effects	1.9[e] (20)	5.5[e] (20)	1.8[e] (20)	5.9[e] (20)
Individual characteristics	151.1[e] (7)	14.3[e] (7)	151.8[e] (7)	15.1[e] (7)
R-squared	0.123	0.032	0.122	0.031

[a]Standard errors in parentheses; for F-statistics, number of parameters in parentheses.

[b]*Wage equation*: Piecewise-linear age splines at five-year intervals from age 20 to 59; piecewise-linear cohort splines at five-year intervals from 1908 to 1967; interactions of linear cohort variable with all age splines; year dummies. *Labor supply equation*: Same but without age-related variables.

[c]*Wage equation*: Age, age squared, cohort, cohort squared, age × cohort, age × cohort squared, cohort × age squared, year dummies. *Labor supply equation*: cohort, cohort squared, cohort cubed, year dummies.

[d]Predicted from wage equation.

[e]Significant at 10% level.

Table 2 shows the results of three specifications of the hazards of varying degrees of simplicity. Column (1) presents estimates of a model with constant hazards and implies transition rates of $\mu = 0.43$ and $\lambda = 0.35$ [see (31)–(32) for definitions]. These annual transition rates are implausibly high and exceed those typically found in panel data, for example, by Heckman and Willis (1977) who found $\mu = 0.139$ and $\lambda = 0.144$.[26] However, a model with constant hazards is a gross violation of the data, for it implies a monotonically rising lifecycle profile of employment rates [see (27)], contrary to the actual shapes of such profiles (see below).

The second column shows an expanded version of this model with two time-invariant variables, education and cohort, and one time-varying variable, the U.S. unemployment rate for prime-age males, which can be backcast over the past periods of the life cycle for each observation in the data.[27] The parameters are again well-determined, with entry rates positively affected by education and cohort and with exit rates negatively affected by education and positively affected by cohort. Higher unemployment rates lower entry rates, but lower exit rates as well, a result to be discussed more momentarily.

Column (3) shows the most well-specified model, including quadratic age terms in both hazards (age can be perfectly backcast), variables for children (backcast from current numbers and ages of children in the household), and three initial conditions variables. The initial conditions variables permit the first transition in the process, μ_1 (i.e., entry starting from $p_{i0} = 0$ at age 19 to some positive value at age 20), to differ from the rest of the profile of entry rates by an amount varying by education and cohort. Most of the parameters of the model are fairly precisely determined. Moreover, the results are consistent with findings from panel data: both entry and exit are concave in age and are affected by children of different ages in the expected directions. The unemployment rate decreases the exit rate, consistent with added-worker behavior.

Fig. 1 shows the actual and fitted employment probabilities in the data as well as the estimated transition rates. The model fits the actual profile reasonably well except at the very beginning of the life cycle, where an initial rise and subsequent fall in actual employment rates is not fully captured; the introduction of more age terms would improve this fit. More interesting are the estimated transition rates shown in the figure, which 'explain' the employment profile by the pattern of entry and exit rates shown. Both entry and exit rates rise initially though the former eventually dominates and employment probabilities rise, but entry rates are forced down and exit rates forced up (by rising numbers

[26]These estimates are averages over the four transition rates between their five years, 1967–1971, shown in their fig. 2, pp. 46–47. The estimates are based on a sample of 1583 white women in the Panel Study of Income Dynamics.

[27]Given the ages of the women in the data, this requires the use of unemployment rates back to 1928.

Table 2

Markov estimates for employment status for white females; $n = 19{,}892$.[a]

	(1)	(2)	(3)
		$\theta_1(\mu)$	
Intercept	− 0.308[c] (0.070)	− 2.649[c] (0.137)	− 3.649[c] (0.566)
Education	—	0.041[c] (0.011)	0.043[c] (0.008)
Cohort	—	0.043[c] (0.002)	0.013[c] (0.005)
Unemployment rate	—	− 0.185[c] (0.026)	− 0.012 (0.019)
Age	—	—	0.085[c] (0.026)
Age squared/100	—	—	− 0.120[c] (0.035)
No. children < 6	—	—	− 0.774[c] (0.052)
No. children 6–17	—	—	0.099[c] (0.022)
D_{20}[b]	—	—	− 0.273 (0.504)
D_{20} × Education	—	—	0.026[c] (0.007)
D_{20} × Cohort	—	—	0.035[c] (0.021)
		$\theta_2(\eta)$	
Intercept	0.476[c] (0.149)	3.986[c] (0.347)	5.570[c] (1.121)
Education	—	− 0.007 (0.027)	− 0.025 (0.016)
Cohort	—	− 0.103[c] (0.007)	− 0.023[c] (0.013)
Unemployment rate	—	0.647[c] (0.073)	0.134[c] (0.045)
Age	—	—	− 0.113[c] (0.047)
Age squared/100	—	—	0.142[c] (0.062)
No. children < 6	—	—	0.366[c] (0.072)
No. children 6–17	—	—	0.091[c] (0.050)
Log likelihood	− 13734.3	− 13263.9	− 12606.5

[a]Asymtotic standard errors in parentheses.
[b]Equals 1 if age = 20, 0 if not.
[c]Significant at 10% level.

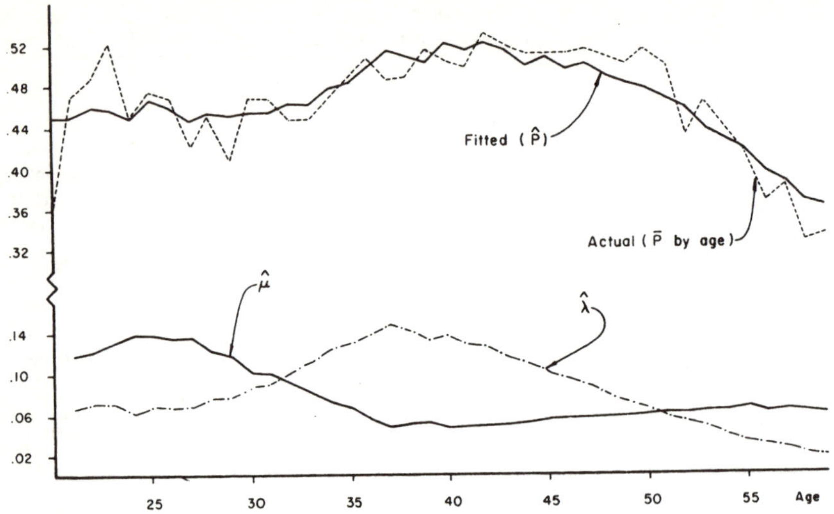

Fig. 1. Actual and fitted employment probabilities, and fitted transition rates, by age.

of young children), eventually reaching levels that begin pulling down the employment rate. As the children age, entry rates are pulled back up slowly and exit rates are pushed down, but the direct effects of age in the hazards slow this process by exerting an upward effect on exit and a downward effect on entry. As a result, the exit effect continues to dominate and employment rates continue to decline. These life cycle profiles of entry and exit, and the reasons for their patterns, are quite consistent with those found in the literature using panel data even though transitions are not directly observed in the RCS data used here.

It is of some interest in the application at hand to note the difference between the profiles shown in fig. 1, which confound true within-cohort profiles with across-cohort profiles, and those for a single woman or group of women from the same cohort and with the same characteristics. Fig. 2 shows the simulated profile for a woman aged 45 and with the mean values of the other variables in the data. The employment profile has the same general shape as that in fig. 1 but shows much more curvature, implying that the quasi-cross-sectional profiles in fig. 1 were too flat if taken as true cohort profiles. This is again a finding commonly reported in other such comparisons in the literature. The shapes of all three curves in fig. 2 are explained by the same forces discussed for the profiles in fig. 1, although the trends are more dramatic in fig. 2.

Finally, table 3 provides a comparison of the fitted model with a conventional cross-sectional probit model in which employment status is made a function of only contemporaneous characteristics of the observation. To date, such probit

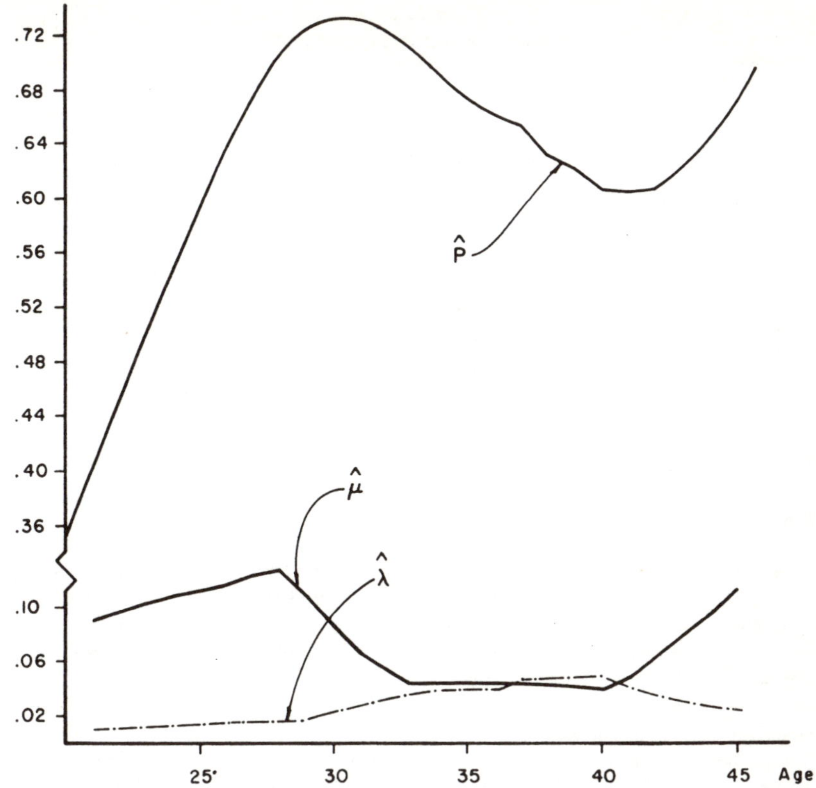

Fig. 2. Simulated life cycle profile of employment and transition rates for women with mean values of the characteristics.

models have been the predominant type of model estimated with RCS data. The probit coefficients are shown in the first column and the effects of a unit change in each of the regressors on the employment probability is shown in the next two columns for both the cross-sectional and the Markov model (standard errors are obtained with the delta method). For the Markov model, the effects shown represent those resulting from a unit change in each regressor variable in both the $X_{it}\theta_1$ and $X_{it}\theta_2$ vectors, and thus represent the combined effect of each variable on the employment rate working through the lagged distribution of entry and exit. As the table shows, the probit and Markov estimates are close for the estimates of education and children but less so for the other variables. The age effect in the Markov model is lower than that in the probit model, but this

Table 3
Comparisons with cross-sectional probit.[a]

	Cross-sectional probit coefficients (1)	$\partial p/\partial X$[b] Markov model (2)	Cross-sectional probit (3)
Intercept	− 3.297[d] (0.216)	—	—
Education	0.072[d] (0.004)	0.030[d] (0.002)	0.029[d] (0.001)
Cohort	0.026[d] (0.003)	0.003 (0.002)	0.010[d] (0.001)
Unemployment rate	− 0.007 (0.008)	0.044[d] (0.010)	− 0.003 (0.003)
Age	0.079[d] (0.008)	− 0.001 (0.002)	0.005[d] (0.001)
Age squared/100[c]	− 0.087[d] (0.010)	—	—
No. children < 6	− 0.516[d] (0.015)	− 0.172[d] (0.009)	− 0.197[d] (0.005)
No. children 6–17	− 0.101[d] (0.009)	− 0.053[d] (0.005)	− 0.040[d] (0.004)
Log likelihood	− 12635.7	—	—

[a]Standard errors in parentheses.
[b]p = probability of employment. In the Markov model, $\partial p/\partial X$ is the derivative of eq. (33) w.r.t. elements of X common to μ and η. In the cross-sectional probit model, $\partial p/\partial X = f(X\beta)X$, where $X\beta$ is the probit index. All effects are evaluated at the means of the data.
[c]In columns (2) and (3), a unit change in age squared is not separately shown; its effect is captured in the prior row.
[d]Significant at 10% level.

difference arises because a one-year increase in the age of an observation in the Markov model implies a different history of the children variables. In particular, if the same number and ages of children are observed for the older woman, the children must therefore have been born later in her life cycle and, in this case, to have pushed down her employment rate history and therefore her contemporaneous employment rate.[28] The unemployment rate shows no effect in the

[28]The age effects for the Markov model could be estimated, alternatively, by holding the children history fixed, although some assumption about new births at the higher age would have to be assumed. However, this would still not be comparable to the cross-sectional probit coefficients because the contemporaneous numbers and ages of children would not be held constant. Thus it is not possible to obtain completely comparable age effects in the two models. The same obtains for the unemployment rate (see below).

probit model but a positive one in the Markov model, consistent with an added-worker effect for married women. The difference is in part a result of the differing amounts of information used in the two estimation procedures, for the Markov model uses the entire life cycle history of unemployment rates for each observation while the probit model uses only the contemporaneous unemployment rate. However, there is also a lack of strict comparability between the two estimated effects, for the Markov coefficient is obtained by shifting the entire history of unemployment rates up by one unit.[29]

The differences in the two models are not surprising since the Markov model contains a formal lag structure. Also not surprisingly, comparison of the likelihood functions for the two models indicates that the Markov model provides a better fit even after adjustment for the number of parameters using the Akaike criterion. Nevertheless, it does confirm that a dynamic model fit to RCS data is superior in many respects to the cross-section models usually estimated.

6. Summary and conclusions

The results of this analysis suggest that many dynamic models are identified with repeated cross-sectional data under what appear to be relatively mild restrictions. This raises a number of questions and issues for future work. The most important is whether the identification conditions do indeed hold, an issue that can be investigated with panel data. Such an investigation is not entirely straightforward, however, if the panel data suffer from measurement error with well-known deleterious consequences for fixed-effects estimators. Conditional on identification, the relative efficiencies of panel and RCS estimators of dynamic models could be considered as a second issue. Other issues worth examination are (1) the importance of serial correlation and unobserved heterogeneity in the Markov model and (2) means of incorporating the effects of migration, mortality, and birth rates into RCS estimates.

References

Amemiya, T., 1979, The estimation of a simultaneous-equation Tobit model, International Economic Review 20, 169–181.

Angrist, J., 1991, Grouped-data estimation and testing in simple labor supply models, Journal of Econometrics 47, 243–266.

Blundell, R., M. Browning, and C. Meghir, 1989, A microeconometric model of intertemporal substitution and consumer demand, Discussion paper no. 89–11 (University College London, London).

Browning, M., A. Deaton, and M. Irish, 1985, A profitable approach to labor supply and commodity demands over the life cycle, Econometrica 53, 503–544.

[29]The Markov model permits the estimation of the effect of any alteration in the time pattern of historical unemployment rates.

Chamberlain, G., 1980, Analysis of covariance with qualitative data, Review of Economic Studies 47, 225–238.

Deaton, A., 1985, Panel data from time series of cross sections, Journal of Econometrics 30, 109–126.

Heckman, J., 1981a, Statistical models for discrete panel data, in: C. Manski and D. McFadden, eds., Structural analysis of discrete data with econometric applications (MIT, Cambridge, MA) 114–178.

Heckman, J., 1981b, The incidental parameters problem and the problem of initial conditions in estimating a discrete time–discrete data stochastic process, in: C. Manski and D. McFadden, eds., Structural analysis of discrete data with econometric application (MIT, Cambridge, MA) 179–195.

Heckman, J. and R. Robb, 1985, Alternative methods for evaluating the impact of interventions, in: J. Heckman and B. Singer, eds., Longitudinal analysis of labor market data (Cambridge University, Cambridge) 156–245.

Heckman, J. and R. Willis, 1977, A beta-logistic model for the analysis of sequential labor force participation by married women, Journal of Political Economy 85, 27–58.

Kalbfleish, J.D. and J.F. Lawless, 1985, The analysis of panel data under a Markov assumption, Journal of the American Statistical Association 80, 863–871.

Lawless, J.F. and D.L. McLeish, 1984, The information in aggregate data from Markov chains, Biometrika 71, 419–430.

Lee, T.C., G.C. Judge, and A. Zellner, 1970, Estimating the parameters of the Markov probability model from aggregate time series data (North-Holland, Amsterdam).

MaCurdy, T., 1981, An empirical model of labor supply in a life-cycle setting, Journal of Political Economy 89, 1059–1085.

Madansky, A., 1959, Least squares estimation in finite Markov processes, Psychometrika 24, 137–144.

Miller, G., 1952, Finite Markov processes in psychology, Psychometrika 17, 149–167.

Nelson, F.D. and L. Olson, 1978, Specification and estimation of a simultaneous-equation model with limited dependent variables, International Economic Review 19, 695–709.

Newey, W., 1987, Efficient estimation of limited dependent variable models with endogenous explanatory variables, Journal of Econometrics 36, 231–250.

Verbeek, M. and T. Nijman, 1992, Can cohort data be treated as genuine panel data?, Empirical Economics 17, 9–23.

Part V
Specification Tests in Panels

[19]

ELSEVIER

Journal of Econometrics 75 (1996) 345–367

JOURNAL OF Econometrics

A nonparametric test for poolability using panel data

Badi H. Baltagi [*,a], Javier Hidalgo [b], Qi Li [c]

[a] *Department of Economics, Texas A&M University, College Station, TX 77843, USA*
[b] *London School of Economics, London WC2A 2AE, UK*
[c] *Department of Economics, University of Guelph, Guelph, Ont. N1G 2W1, Canada*

(Received February 1993; final version received May 1995)

Abstract

This paper derives a nonparametric procedure for testing poolability in a panel data framework. This is contrasted with alternative parametric tests which are not robust to functional misspecification. This test is illustrated with an earning equation using data from the Panel Study of Income Dynamics (PSID).

Key words: Panel data; Poolability; Nonparametric; Hypothesis testing
JEL classification: C12; C14; C23

1. Introduction

Panel data availability is on the rise in economics, and the benefit and limitation of using panel data as compared to strictly time-series or cross-section data are given in Hsiao (1986) and Klevmarken (1989). A major concern for panel data users is whether the data is poolable. The main literature in this area assumes a specific parametric form, usually linear, and tests the constancy of parameters over time. In contrast to this approach, this paper tests the constancy of an unspecified nonparametric relationship over time for a group of individuals. The most popular test for pooling time-series of cross-section data is the Chow (1960) test. Since the number of individuals in a typical panel is very large, a cross-section regression relationship is estimated for each year in the sample and the constancy of the parameters is tested over time. This is also known in the

*Corresponding author.
We would like to thank Richard Blundell, Yanqin Fan, and anonymous referees for many helpful comments. Q. Li would like to thank the Social Sciences and Humanities Research Council of Canada for financial support.

SSDI 0304-4076(95)01779-9

literature as the stability of the regression relationship over time.[1] The Chow test has been generalized (i) to take advantage of the trade-off between bias and variance, see the MSE criteria introduced by Wallace (1972), and (ii) to allow for a general variance–covariance matrix Ω on the disturbances, see Zellner (1962) and Baltagi (1981) in the context of an error component model.

The Chow test, in its spherical as well as nonspherical disturbances form, assumes a correct underlying parametric specification and one cannot tell whether rejection of poolability is due to nonparameter constancy or a more fundamental misspecification, such as incorrect functional form, omitted variables, etc., see Dufour (1982) and Hidalgo (1995).[2] For example, suppose that the true model is nonlinear and stable over time, so that the data is poolable. However, the researcher assumes a linear model and fails the poolability test. In this case, rejection of poolability is indicating functional misspecification. The reverse is also possible, i.e., the data is not poolable but a misspecified functional form can lead to an acceptance of the poolability test. Hidalgo (1995) showed, both theoretically and through Monte Carlo simulations, that when the model is misspecified, the test for structural change can reject the null hypothesis (of no structural change, when in fact it is true) with probability tending to one as the sample size increases. Also, the power of the test can tend to its size as the sample size gets large. In order to avoid this 'lack of robustness' to correct functional form, we propose a nonparametric test which is free of any particular parametric specification of the regression function.

Section 2 gives the model and derives the nonparametric test for poolability. Section 3 applies this test to an earning equation using data from the Panel Study of Income Dynamics (PSID). Section 4 gives our conclusion.

2. The model and the test statistic

Consider the following nonparametric panel data model:

$$y_{it} = g_t(x_{it}) + \varepsilon_{it}, \qquad i = 1, \dots, N, \quad t = 1, \dots, T, \tag{1}$$

where $g_t(\cdot)$ is an unspecified functional form that may vary over time. x_{it} is a $q \times 1$ column vector of predetermined explanatory variables with $p(\geqslant 1)$ variables being continuous and $q - p(\geqslant 0)$ discrete.

---

[1] For a recent survey of the structural change literature, see the annotated bibliography by Hackl and Westlund (1989), and the recent monograph on the econometrics of structural change by Krämer (1989). Also, for a test of time-varying parameters, see Hidalgo (1995).

[2] Other tests for structural change include the CUSUM and CUSUM of Square tests proposed by Brown, Durbin, and Evans (1975) and extended from time-series to panel data by Han and Park (1989).

An important question that the researcher faces with panel data is whether the data is poolable, i.e., is $g_t(x) = g_s(x)$ almost everywhere (a.e.) for all t and s? More precisely, the econometrician faces the following competing hypotheses:

$$\begin{aligned} \mathrm{H}_0: &\quad g_t(x) = g_s(x) \quad \text{(a.e.) for all } t \text{ and } s, \\ \mathrm{H}_1: &\quad g_t(x) \neq g_s(x) \quad \text{for some } t \neq s \text{ with probability greater than zero.} \end{aligned}$$

Let $g(x) \equiv (1/T)\sum_s g_s(x)$. Then the null and the alternative hypotheses can be equivalently written as

$$\begin{aligned} \mathrm{H}_0: &\quad g_t(x) = g(x) \quad \text{(a.e.) for all } t, \\ \mathrm{H}_1: &\quad g_t(x) \neq g(x) \quad \text{for some } t \text{ with probability greater than zero.} \end{aligned}$$

In Section 1, we reviewed some of the test statistics available in the literature to test H_0 versus H_1. All the tests considered are based on a specific form of $g(x_{it}, \beta_t)$ and reduce to a test of equality of the parameters β_t, $t = 1, \ldots, T$. These tests are not robust, i.e., they depend heavily on the correct specification of the regression function $g_t(\cdot)$. In fact, it may be possible that if the $g_t(\cdot)$ function is misspecified, the hypothesis of poolability will be rejected when in fact the data is poolable. The reverse is also likely, i.e., due to functional misspecification, we may not reject the hypothesis of poolability based on a misspecified $g_t(\cdot)$ function when the data is in fact not poolable. To avoid this 'lack of robustness' we propose a test that is free of any particular specification for the regression function.

In the parametric setup, the test of hypothesis of H_0 versus H_1 is based upon the difference between the restricted residuals sum of squares and the unrestricted residuals sum of squares. One could also construct a nonparametric poolability test based on the nonparametric pooled and unpooled sum of squares residuals. However, such an approach will lead to very complicated derivations. Also the conditions on the smoothing parameter are likely to be restrictive. In this paper we will take a different approach. Let $u_{it} = y_{it} - g(x_{it})$, then under H_0, model (1) can be equivalently written as

$$y_{it} = g(x_{it}) + u_{it}. \tag{2}$$

Define the pooled kernel estimator of $\mathrm{E}(y_{it}|x_{it})$ by

$$\hat{y}_{it} = \frac{1}{NTa^p}\sum_j \sum_s y_{js} K_{it,js} / \hat{f}_{it}, \tag{3}$$

where

$$\hat{f}_{it} = \frac{1}{NTa^p}\sum_j \sum_s K_{it,js}$$

is the pooled kernel estimator of the density function of x_{it}.

$$K_{it,js} = K\left(\frac{x_{it} - x_{js}}{a}\right)$$

is the kernel function that is used for the pooled estimator and a is the corresponding smoothing parameter. We use product kernel

$$K(v) = \prod_{l=1}^{p} k^c(v_l) \prod_{l=p+1}^{q} k^d(v_l),$$

where v_l is the lth component of v, and k^c and k^d are univariate kernels for the continuous and the discrete variables respectively. Then it is easy to see that, if $n \to \infty$ and the conditions stated before Theorem 1 are satisfied, that $\hat{y}_{it}$ converges to $g_t(x_{it})$ under H_0 and to $g(x_{it})$ under H_1. The nonparametric residual from the pooled model $\tilde{u}_{it} \equiv y_{it} - \hat{y}_{it}$ will converge to $u_{it} = y_{it} - g(x_{it}) = y_{it} - g_t(x_{it}) = \varepsilon_{it}$ under H_0, and to $u_{it} = y_{it} - g(x_{it}) = y_{it} - g_t(x_{it}) + g_t(x_{it}) - g(x_{it}) = \varepsilon_{it} + g_t(x_{it}) - g(x_{it})$ under H_1. Thus $E(u_{it}|x_{it}) = 0$ a.e. under H_0 and $E(u_{it}|x_{it}) = g_t(x_{it}) - g(x_{it}) = (1/T)\sum_s [g_t(x_{it}) - g_s(x_{it})]$ under H_1, which is not a.e. equal to zero under H_1. Hence we can construct a consistent test for poolability based on $E(uE(u|x))$ because $E[uE(u|x)] = E\{[E(u|x)]^2\} \geqslant 0$ and the equality holds if and only if H_0 is true. To avoid the random denominator problem in the nonparametric kernel estimation, similar to Powell, Stock, and Stoker (1989), we choose to estimate a density-weighted version of $E[uE(u|x)]$. We estimate $u_{it} f_{it}$ by $\tilde{u}_{it} \hat{f}_{it} \equiv (y_{it} - \hat{y}_{it})\hat{f}_{it}$, and $E(\tilde{u}_{it} \hat{f}_{it}|x_{it}) f(x_{it})$ by $(1/(N-1)h^p) \times \sum_{j \neq i} \tilde{u}_{jt} \hat{f}_{jt} \bar{K}_{it,jt}$, using N cross-sectional data for a fixed value of t. In this case,

$$\bar{K}_{it,jt} = \bar{K}\left(\frac{x_{it} - x_{jt}}{h}\right), \qquad \bar{K}(v) = \prod_{l=1}^{p} \bar{k}^c(v_l) \prod_{l=p+1}^{q} \bar{k}^d(v_l)$$

is the kernel function used for a fixed t, and h is the smoothing parameter associated with the kernel $\bar{K}$. Hence our test statistic is

$$J_N = \frac{1}{NT} \sum_i \sum_t (\tilde{u}_{it} \hat{f}_{it}) \left\{ \frac{1}{(N-1)h^p} \sum_{j \neq i} (\tilde{u}_{jt} \hat{f}_{jt}) \bar{K}_{it,jt} \right\}$$

$$= \frac{1}{N(N-1)Th^p} \sum_i \sum_t \sum_{j \neq i} (\tilde{u}_{it} \hat{f}_{it})(\tilde{u}_{jt} \hat{f}_{jt}) \bar{K}_{it,jt}. \tag{4}$$

Using $\tilde{u}_{it} \hat{f}_{it} = y_{it} \hat{f}_{it} - \hat{y}_{it} \hat{f}_{it} = (g(x_{it}) - \hat{g}(x_{it}))\hat{f}_{it} + u_{it} \hat{f}_{it} - \hat{u}_{it} \hat{f}_{it}$, where $\hat{g}(x_{it})$ and $\hat{u}_{it}$ are defined similarly as $\hat{y}_{it}$, i.e., they are obtained by replacing y_{js} in (3) by $g(x_{js})$ and u_{js} respectively. Eq. (5) can be written as

$$J_N = \frac{1}{N(N-1)Th^p}\sum_i\sum_t\sum_{j\neq i}\{(g_{it}-\hat{g}_{it})\hat{f}_{it}(g_{jt}-\hat{g}_{jt})\hat{f}_{jt}$$
$$+u_{it}u_{jt}\hat{f}_{it}\hat{f}_{jt}+\hat{u}_{it}\hat{f}_{it}\hat{u}_{jt}\hat{f}_{jt}+2u_{it}\hat{f}_{it}(g_{jt}-\hat{g}_{jt})\hat{f}_{jt}$$
$$-2\hat{u}_{it}\hat{f}_{it}(g_{jt}-\hat{g}_{jt})\hat{f}_{jt}-2u_{it}\hat{f}_{it}\hat{u}_{jt}\hat{f}_{jt}\}\bar{K}_{it,jt}$$
$$\equiv J_{N1}+J_{N2}+J_{N3}+2J_{N4}-2J_{N5}-2J_{N6}. \tag{5}$$

To derive the asymptotic distribution of J_{Ns} (for $s = 1,\dots,6$), the following conditions are needed:

We will use the definitions given in Robinson (1988) for the class of kernel functions $\mathscr{K}_l$ ($l \geqslant 1$ is an integer) and the class of functions $\mathscr{G}^{\alpha}_{\mu}$, $\alpha > 0$ and $\mu > 0$. Also we will use $\mathscr{K}^d_l$ ($l \geqslant 0$ is an integer) to denote the class of kernel functions, such that if $k^d \in \mathscr{K}^d_l$, then k^d: $R \to R$ is an even *nonnegative* function with $k^d(0) = 1$ and $k^d(v) = O((1+|v|)^{-(l+1)})$. Note that the class of functions of $\mathscr{K}^d_l$ belong to the *second*-order kernel. The l subscript here denotes the tail property of the kernel functions $k^d \in \mathscr{K}^d_l$, not the order of kernels.

(C1) (x_{it}, y_{it}) are i.i.d. in the i subscript. There is no restriction placed on the t subscript.

(C2) For those continuous variables, $g \in \mathscr{G}^4_v$ and the joint p.d.f. $f(x_{11},\dots,x_{1s}) \in \mathscr{G}^{\infty}_{v-1}$ $(1 \leqslant s \leqslant T)$ where $v \geqslant 2$ is an integer. For all $1 \leqslant t \leqslant T$, $E|\varepsilon^4_{1t}| < \infty$, $\sigma^2(x_{1t}) \equiv E[\varepsilon^2_{1t}|x_{1t}]$, and $m_4(x_{1t}) \equiv E[\varepsilon^4|x]$ are continuous for those continuous variables; $f(x_{1t})\sigma^2(x_{1t})$ and $f(x_{1t})m_4(x_{1t})$ are bounded in R^p.

(C3) As $N \to \infty$, (i) $Nh^p \to \infty$, $a \to 0$, $Na^{2v}h^{p/2} \to 0$, $h/a^2 \to 0$; (ii) $k^c \in \mathscr{K}_v$ and $k^d \in \mathscr{K}^d_v$; (iii) $\bar{k}^c \in \mathscr{K}_2$ and $\bar{k}^d \in \mathscr{K}^d_0$.

(C2) is quite standard, it imposes some smoothness (for those continuous variables) and moments conditions on the unknown regression function and imposes some mild restrictions on $f(x)$, $\sigma^2(x)$, and $m_4(x)$.

(C3) (i) implies that $h \to 0$ and $Na^p \to \infty$. These conditions ensure the kernel estimators are consistent. The last two conditions in (ii) ensure that the asymptotic mean square error of the pooled kernel estimator $\tilde{u}_{it}\hat{f}_{it}$ is of smaller order than $(Nh^{p/2})^{-1}$, i.e., $Nh^{p/2}(a^{2v}+(Na^p)^{-1}) = o(1)$. This condition ensures that our test statistic will be centered at zero under H_0. Otherwise the test statistic will involve some center terms which in turn need to be estimated, and hence may introduce finite-sample bias to the test statistic.

Assumption (C1) implies that the error ε_{it} is i.i.d. in the i subscript but no restriction is placed on the t subscript. Hence it allows the error $\varepsilon_{it} = y_{it} - g(x_{it})$ to have an arbitrary form of serial correlation and/or conditional heteroskedasticity. For example, the popular one-way error component structure $\varepsilon_{it} = \mu_i + v_{it}$ with μ_i i.i.d. $(0, \sigma_\mu^2)$ and v_{it} i.i.d. $(0, \sigma_v^2)$, is included in our specification, where μ_i denotes the 'individual' time-invariant effects and v_{it} denotes the remainder disturbance. We also allow the correlated 'fixed effects' case,[3] i.e., $\mathrm{E}(\mu_i|x_{it}) = m_t(x_{it}) \neq 0$. Then $m_t(x_{it})$ will be incorporated into the unknown function $g_t(x_{it})$. In practice, one may be interested in testing the poolability of regression functions that is devoid of the (fixed) individual effects. In a linear regression model, this is usually done by estimating a first-differenced model or by performing a within transformation to wipe out the individual effects. However, this approach does not work for a nonparametric model. To see this, let us consider the following correlated 'fixed effects' model:

$$y_{it} = G_t(x_{it}) + \varepsilon_{it}, \tag{6}$$

where $\varepsilon_{it} = \mu_i + v_{it}$, and $\mathrm{E}(\varepsilon_{it}|x_{it}) = \mathrm{E}(\mu_i|x_{it}) = m_t(x_{it}) \neq 0$. Let $g_t(x_{it}) = G_t(x_{it}) + m_t(x_{it})$ and $u_{it} = \varepsilon_{it} - m_t(x_{it})$, then (6) becomes

$$y_{it} = g_t(x_{it}) + u_{it}, \tag{7}$$

where $g_t(x_{it}) = \mathrm{E}(y_{it}|x_{it})$ and u_{it} is the error that is orthogonal to x_{it}. Note that (7) is exactly the same as (1). Moreover given that both $m_t(\cdot)$ and $G_t(\cdot)$ are of unknown functional forms, it is not possible to distinguish between (1) and (7). In contrast to the conventional parametric (usually linear) regression model, one cannot distinguish between random and fixed individual effects in a nonparametric regression model.

Although one cannot identify $G_t(x_{it})$ in a nonparametric regression model, one can still test the poolability of $G_t(\cdot)$ given an additional jointly stationary assumption on (μ_i, x_{it}). Since $m_t(x_{it}) = \mathrm{E}(\mu_i|x_{it})$, by stationarity, we know that the functional form of $m_t(\cdot)$ is independent of t, hence we have $m_t(x) = m(x)$ for all t. Thus we have $g_t(x_{it}) = G_t(x_{it}) + m(x_{it})$. Hence $g_t(x) = g_s(x)$ (a.e.) for all t and s, if and only if $G_t(x) = G_s(x)$ (a.e.) for all t and s. Therefore the same poolability test applies to testing the poolability of the $G_t(\cdot)$ function. However, one should keep in mind that in order to estimate $G_t(\cdot)$, one needs to assume a parametric functional form for $G_t(\cdot)$. Nonparametric methods guard against such functional form misspecification.

Theorem 1. Under (C1) to (C3), we have:

(i) $\quad Nh^{p/2}J_N \to \mathrm{N}(0, 2\sigma_0^2)$ *under* H_0,

[3] By calling μ_i a fixed individual effect we mean that the random individual effect term μ_i is correlated with x_{it}.

where

$$\sigma_0^2 = \left[\int \bar{K}^2(u)\mathrm{d}u\right]\left\{\frac{1}{T^2}\sum_t \mathrm{E}[\sigma^4(x_{1t})f^5(x_{1t})]\right\},$$

σ_0^2 *can be consistently estimated by* $\hat{\sigma}_0^2$, *where*

$$\hat{\sigma}_0^2 = \frac{1}{T^2}\sum_t\left[\frac{1}{N(N-1)h^p}\sum_i\sum_{j\neq i}(\tilde{u}_{it}\hat{f}_{it})^2(\tilde{u}_{jt}\hat{f}_{jt})^2\bar{K}^2_{it,js}\right].$$

Hence

(ii) $\qquad Nh^{p/2}(J_N/\sqrt{2\hat{\sigma}_0^2}) \xrightarrow{d} \mathrm{N}(0,1)$ *under* H_0.

The proof of Theorem 1 is given in the Appendix.

The consistency of our test is given in the next theorem.

Theorem 2. Under (C1) to (C3), we have

$$\mathrm{Prob}\left[Nh^{p/2}(J_N/\sqrt{2\hat{\sigma}_0^2}) > B_N\right] \to 1 \quad \textit{under } H_1,$$

where B_N *is any nonstochastic sequence with* $B_N = \mathrm{o}(Nh^{p/2})$.

The proof of Theorem 2 is sketched as follows: It is easy to show that $\tilde{u}_{it}\hat{f}_{it} \to \varepsilon_{it}f_{it} + [g_t(x_{it}) - g(x_{it})]f_{it}$. Also using similar arguments as in the proof of Theorem 1, one can show that

$$\begin{aligned}
\mathrm{E}(J_N) &= \frac{1}{N(N-1)Th^p}\sum_i\sum_t\sum_{j\neq i}\mathrm{E}\{[\varepsilon_{it} + g_t(x_{it}) - g(x_{it})] \\
&\quad \times[\varepsilon_{jt} + g_t(x_{jt}) - g(x_{jt})]f_{it}f_{jt}\bar{K}_{it,jt}\} + \mathrm{o}(1) \\
&= \frac{1}{N(N-1)Th^p}\sum_i\sum_t\sum_{j\neq i}\mathrm{E}\{[g_t(x_{it}) - g(x_{it})] \\
&\quad \times[g_t(x_{jt}) - g(x_{jt})]f_{it}f_{jt}\bar{K}_{it,jt}\} + \mathrm{o}(1) \\
&= \frac{1}{NT}\sum_i\sum_t\mathrm{E}\{[g_t(x_{it}) - g(x_{it})]^2 f_{it}^3\} + \mathrm{o}(1) \\
&\equiv \frac{1}{T}\sum_t\mathrm{E}\left\{\left[g_t(x_{1t}) - \frac{1}{T}\sum_s g_s(x_{1t})\right]^2 f_{1t}^3\right] + \mathrm{o}(1) \\
&\equiv J_0 + \mathrm{o}(1)
\end{aligned}$$

(under H_1), and that

$$\mathrm{var}(J_N) = \mathrm{o}(1).$$

This implies that $J_N \xrightarrow{p} J_0 (> 0)$ under H_1. Finally, it is easy to show that $\hat{\sigma}_0^2 = O_p(1)$ under H_1. Hence $\text{Prob}[Nh^{p/2}(J_N/\sqrt{2\hat{\sigma}_0^2}) \geq B_N] \to 1$ for any nonstochastic sequence $B_N = o(Nh^{p/2})$ under H_1 .

3. An empirical example

We apply our nonparametric poolability test to a simple earnings equation which measures the returns to schooling and experience for a panel of 595 heads of households over the period 1976–1982.[4] The data are drawn from the non-Survey of Economic Opportunity portion of the Panel Study of Income Dynamics (PSID), see Cornwell and Rupert (1988). The dependent variable is log(*wage*) and the independent variables are years of full-time work experience (*EXP*) and years of education (*ED*). We perform the Chow poolability tests for the following parametric specifications:

(F1) $\log(wage)_{it} = \beta_{t1} + \beta_{t2}(EXP)_{it} + \beta_{t3}(EXP)_{it}^2 + \beta_{t4}(ED)_{it} + \varepsilon_{it}$ with ε_{it} i.i.d. $(0, \sigma_\varepsilon^2)$,

(F2) $\log(wage)_{it} = \beta_{t1} + \beta_{t2}(EXP)_{it} + \beta_{t3}(EXP)_{it}^2 + \beta_{t4}(ED)_{it} + \varepsilon_{it}$ with $\varepsilon_{it} = \mu_i + v_{it}$, where $\mu_i \sim$ i.i.d. $(0, \sigma_\mu^2)$ and $v_{it} \sim$ i.i.d. $(0, \sigma_v^2)$, and μ_i and v_{js} are independent.

The null hypothesis for models (F1) and (F2) is H_0: $\beta_{tk} = \beta_k$ for all $t = 1, ..., T$ and $k = 1, 2, 3, 4$. The nonparametric regression model is

(F3) $\log(wage)_{it} = g_t(EXP_{it}, ED_{it}) + \varepsilon_{it}$.

We only need to assume that the ε_{it} are independent in the i subscript. The test statistic $Nh^{p/2}J_N/\sqrt{2\hat{\sigma}_0^2}$ is asymptotically distributed as N(0, 1) under H_0.

In this example, although both *EXP* and *ED* take only integer values, their ranges are quite wide. The range for *EXP* is from 1 to 51, and the range for *ED* is from 4 to 17. Hence we will treat them as continuous variables in computing the kernel estimators. We use both a normal kernel and a uniform kernel to compute our nonparametric test statistic. The normal kernel is $k(v) = (1/\sqrt{2\pi})\exp(-v^2/2)$ and the uniform kernel is defined as

$$k(v) = \begin{cases} 1 & |v| < 0.5, \\ 0 & \text{otherwise.} \end{cases}$$

For the smoothing parameter choices, we use $a = c\, x_{sd} N^{-1/\alpha}$ and $h = c\, x_{sd} N^{-1/\alpha'}$, where x_{sd} is the sample standard deviation of x_{it}'s ($x_{it} = EXP_{it}$ or ED_{it}), c, α, and

[4]These individuals were between the ages of 18 and 65 in 1976 and reported positive wage in some private, nonfarm employment for the duration of the sample.

Table 1
Parametric and nonparametric tests for poolability

	$T = 7$	$T = 5$	$T = 3$
Chow test	38.25	25.96	13.11
Roy–Zellner test	124.07	103.89	62.66
N(0.8,0.8)	76.99	45.58	15.62
N(0.9,0.9)	81.01	47.71	16.28
N(1.0,1.0)	84.75	49.75	16.98
N(1.1,1.1)	88.43	51.74	17.55
N(1.2,1.2)	92.04	53.70	18.17
U(0.8,0.8)	55.56	34.97	12.44
U(0.9,0.9)	58.14	34.97	12.44
U(1.0,1.0)	58.14	34.97	12.44
U(1.1,1.1)	58.14	34.97	12.44
U(1.2,1.2)	76.37	45.99	15.58

α' are constants. For our case $p = 2$ and $\nu = 2$ (because we use a second-order kernel), and condition (C3) implies that $Nh^2 \to \infty$, $h^2/a \to 0$, and $Na^4h \to 0$. This in turn implies that we need to choose $\alpha > 2$, $\alpha' > 2\alpha$, and $1-4/\alpha-1/\alpha' < 0$. Hence we choose $\alpha = 3$ and $\alpha' = 7$, i.e., we choose $a_1 = c_1 EXP_{sd} N^{-1/7}$, $a_2 = c_2 ED_{sd} N^{-1/7}$, $h_1 = c_1 EXP_{sd} N^{-1/3}$, and $h_2 = c_2 ED_{sd} N^{-1/3}$. We denote these cases by N(c_1, c_2) and U(c_1, c_2), where N$(1,1)$, for example, means normal kernel with $(c_1, c_2) = (1,1)$. To check the sensitivity of the testing results on different choices of a's and h's, we varied c_1, and c_2 in the ranges of $[0.8, 1.2]$. The results for both the parametric and the nonparametric tests are given in Table 1 above.

Our nonparametric test is one-sided. Therefore, we reject the null hypothesis H_0 at the 5% level if $Nh^{p/2}(J_N/\sqrt{2\hat{\sigma}_0^2}) > 1.645$. Table 1 tests the stability over the entire period 1976–1982 ($T = 7$), over the first five years 1976–1980 ($T=5$), and over the first three years 1976–1979 ($T=3$). The results in Table 1 show that for all choices of the bandwidth, the nonparametric test statistic yields values that are much larger than 1.645. In other words, these test statistics have p-values that are smaller than 0.05 and we reject the null hypothesis of poolability for $T = 7$, $T = 5$. and $T = 3$.

Let us contrast these nonparametric testing results with the usual panel data parametric tests. For $T = 7$, $T = 5$, and $T = 3$, the Chow test for model (F1) gives observed F-statistics of 38.25, 25.96, and 13.11, which are much larger than the corresponding critical values of $F(24, 4137) = 1.52$, $F(16, 2995) = 1.64$, and $F(8, 1773) = 1.94$ at the 5% level. Therefore the Chow test rejects poolability for $T = 7$, $T = 5$, and $T = 3$. Similarly the Roy–Zellner test also decisively reject the poolable null hypothesis.

In this case we have an agreement between parametric and nonparametric testing results. Thus we feel more confident that the data is not poolable. The results also tell us that there is no need to search for a more flexible functional form in the hope that the data may be poolable.

4. Conclusion

In this paper, we derived a nonparametric poolability test for panel data. The nonparametric test has the advantage over the conventional parametric tests in that it is robust to regression functional form misspecification. The test statistic is shown to be consistent and asymptotically normal. We apply this nonparametric test to a panel data set on earnings. In practice, the nonparametric test may agree or disagree with the corresponding popular parametric tests. In case of agreement, one feels more confident about whether the data is poolable or not. In case of conflict, one should recheck the model specification.

Appendix A

Proof of Theorem 1 (i)

The proof is similar to the proof of Theorem 5.1 (a consistent nonparametric test for omitted variables) of Fan and Li (1994). The detailed proof will be extremely tedious. We sketch the proof in Propositions 1 to 6 below. Let $\mathscr{X}_i = (u_i, x_i)$, where $u_i = (u_{i1}, \ldots, u_{iT})$ and $x_i = (x_{i1}, \ldots, x_{iT})$. Whenever we write double subscripts, the first one always refers to the individual index and the second one refers to the time index. Also we will let $A_N \sim B_N$ denote that A_N has an order at most as large as B_N.

Proposition 1. $J_{N1} = o_p((Nh^{p/2})^{-1})$.

Proof.

$$J_{N1} = \frac{1}{T}\sum_t \left\{ \frac{1}{N(N-1)h^p} \sum_i \sum_{j \neq i} (g_{it} - \hat{g}_{it}) \hat{f}_{it} (g_{jt} - \hat{g}_{jt}) \hat{f}_{jt} \right\}$$

$$= \frac{1}{T^3}\sum_t \sum_s \sum_r \left\{ \frac{1}{N(N-1)^3 h^p a^{2p}} \sum_i \sum_{j \neq i} \sum_{l \neq i} \sum_{k \neq j} (g_{it} - g_{ls}) \right.$$

$$\left. \times K_{it,ls} (g_{jt} - g_{kr}) K_{jt,kr} \bar{K}_{it,jt} \right\}$$

$$\sim \frac{1}{T^3}\sum_t \sum_s \sum_r \left\{ \frac{1}{N(N-1)^3 h^p a^{2p}} \sum_i \sum_{j \neq i} \sum_{l \neq i} \sum_{k \neq j} (g_{it} - g_{lt}) \right.$$

$$\left. \times K_{it,lt} (g_{jt} - g_{kt}) K_{jt,kt} \bar{K}_{it,jt} \right\}$$

$$\equiv \frac{1}{T}\sum_t \left\{ \frac{1}{N(N-1)h^p} \sum_i \sum_{j \neq i} (g_{it} - \hat{g}_{it,t}) \hat{f}_{it,t} (g_{jt} - \hat{g}_{jt,t}) \hat{f}_{jt,t} \bar{K}_{it,jt} \right\}$$

$$\equiv \frac{1}{T}\sum_t J_{1t},$$

where

$$J_{1t} = \frac{1}{N(N-1)^3 a^{2p} h^p} \sum_i \sum_{j \neq i} \sum_{l \neq i} \sum_{k \neq j} (g_{it} - g_{lt}) K_{it,lt} (g_{jt,t} - g_{kt}) K_{jt,kt} \bar{K}_{it,jt}.$$

Below, we show that $\mathrm{E}(J_{1t}) = o((Nh^{p/2})^{-1})$. First we use $J_{1t(0)}$ to denote the case that i, j, l, k are all different from each other. Using Lemmas B.2 and B.3, it is easy to see that

$$\begin{aligned} \mathrm{E}(J_{1t(0)}) &= a^{-2p} h^{-p} \mathrm{E}\{[\mathrm{E}_{1t}(g_{1t} - g_{2t}) K_{1t,2t}][\mathrm{E}_{3t}(g_{3t} - g_{4t}) K_{3t,4t}] \bar{K}_{1t,3t}\} \\ &\leqslant a^{2v} h^{-p} \mathrm{E}\{D_g(x_{1t}) D_g(x_{3t}) \bar{K}_{1t,3t}\} \\ &= O(a^{2v}) = o((nh^{p/2})^{-1}). \end{aligned}$$

Next we consider the case that i, j, l, k take exactly three different values. There are three possibilities: (i) $l = k$, (ii) $i = k$, and (iii) $j = k$. We use $J_{1t(i)}$, $J_{1t(ii)}$, and $J_{1t(iii)}$ to denote these cases.

$$\begin{aligned} \mathrm{E}(J_{1t(i)}) &= \frac{1}{Na^{2p}h^p} \sum_t \mathrm{E}\{(g_{1t} - g_{3t}) K_{1t,3t} (g_{2t} - g_{3t}) K_{2t,3t} \bar{K}_{1t,2t}\} \\ &= \frac{1}{Na^{2p}h^p} \sum_t \{\textstyle\int f(x_{1t}, x_{2t}, x_{3t})(g_{1t} - g_{3t}) \\ &\quad \times K_{1t,3t}(g_{2t} - g_{3t}) K_{2t,3t} \bar{K}_{1t,2t} \mathrm{d}x_{1t} \mathrm{d}x_{2t} \mathrm{d}x_{3t}\} \\ &= \frac{1}{Na^{2p}} \sum_t \left\{ \int f(x_{1t}, x_{1t} + bu, x_{3t})(g_{1t} - g_{3t}) \right. \\ &\quad \left. \times K_{1t,3t}(g(x_{1t} + au) - g_{3t}) K\left(\frac{x_{1t} - x_{3t} + bu}{a}\right) \bar{K}(u) \mathrm{d}x_{1t} \mathrm{d}u \mathrm{d}x_{3t} \right\} \\ &= \frac{1}{Na^p} \sum_t \left\{ \int f(x_{1t}, x_{1t} + bu, x_{1t} + av)(g_{1t} - g(x_{1t} + av)) \right. \\ &\quad \left. \times K(v)(g(x_{1t} + bu) - g(x_{1t} + av)) K\left(\frac{bu}{a} - v\right) \bar{K}(u) \mathrm{d}x_{1t} \mathrm{d}u \mathrm{d}v \right\} \\ &= O(N^{-1} a^{-p}) = o((Nh^{p\,2})^{-1}). \end{aligned}$$

$$\begin{aligned}
E(J_{1t(ii)}) &= \frac{1}{Na^{2p}h^p}\sum_t E\{[E_1(g_{1t}-g_{3t})K_{1t,3t}](g_{2t}-g_{1t})K_{2t,1t}\bar{K}_{1t,2t}\} \\
&\leqslant \frac{Ca^{v}}{Na^p h^p}\sum_t E\{|D_g(x_{1t})(g_{2t}-g_{1t})K_{1t,2t}\bar{K}_{1t,2t}|\} \\
&= O(a^{v}(Na^p)^{-1}) = o((Nh^{p/2})^{-1}).
\end{aligned}$$

Similarly, one can show that $E(J_{1t(iii)}) = O(a^{v}(Na^p)^{-1}) = o((Nh^{p/2})^{-1})$.

Let $J_{1t(iv)}$ denote the case that i,j,l,k take no more than two different values. It is easy to see that $E(J_{1t(iv)}) = O(N^{-2}a^{-2p}) = o((Nh^{p/2})^{-1})$. Thus we have proved that $E(J_{1t}) = o((Nh^{p/2})^{-1})$. Similarly it is straightforward, though tedious, to show that $\mathrm{var}(Nh^{p/2}J_{1t}) = o(1)$. Hence $J_{1t} = o_p((Nh^{p/2})^{-1})$ and, as a result, $J_{N1} = o_p((Nh^{p/2})^{-1})$ because T is finite.

Proposition 2. $Nh^{p/2}J_{N2} \to N(0, 2\sigma_0^2)$,

where

$$\sigma_0^2 = \frac{1}{T^2}\sum_t E[\sigma^4(x_{1t})f^5(x_{1t})][\textstyle\int \bar{K}^2(u)du].$$

Proof.

$$\begin{aligned}
J_{N2} &= \frac{1}{N(N-1)Th^p}\sum_i\sum_t\sum_{j\neq i} u_{it}\hat{f}_{it}u_{jt}\hat{f}_{jt}\bar{K}_{it,jt} \\
&= \frac{1}{N(N-1)^3T^3a^{2p}h^p}\sum_i\sum_t\sum_{j\neq i}\sum_{l\neq i}\sum_s\sum_{k\neq j}\sum_r u_{it}u_{jt}K_{it,ls}K_{jt,kr}\bar{K}_{it,jt} \\
&= \frac{1}{N(N-1)^3T^3a^{2p}h^p}\sum\sum\sum\sum_{i\neq j\neq l\neq k}\{\sum_t\sum_s\sum_r u_{it}u_{jt}K_{it,ls}K_{jt,kr}\bar{K}_{it,jt}\} \\
&\quad + J_2R \\
&\equiv J_2U + J_2R,
\end{aligned}$$

where J_2U denotes the case that all individual summation indices i,j,l,k are different from each other and J_2R denotes the remaining summation terms. Rewriting J_2U as a U-statistic, we get

$$\begin{aligned}
J_2U &= \binom{N}{4}\frac{1}{N(N-1)^3T^3a^{2p}h^p} \\
&\quad \times\left[\binom{N}{4}^{-1}\sum\sum\sum\sum_{1\leqslant i<j<l<k\leqslant N} P_n(\mathscr{Z}_i,\mathscr{Z}_j,\mathscr{Z}_l,\mathscr{Z}_k)\right],
\end{aligned}$$

where

$$P_n(\mathscr{Z}_i,\mathscr{Z}_j,\mathscr{Z}_l,\mathscr{Z}_k) = \sum_{4!}\left\{\sum_t\sum_s\sum_r u_{it}u_{jt}K_{it,ls}K_{jt,kr}\bar{K}_{it,jt}\right\},$$

and $\sum_{4!}$ denotes a summation over all the $4! = 24$ different permutations of i,j,l,k.

Define

$$P_n(\mathscr{X}_i,\mathscr{X}_j)=\mathrm{E}[P_n(\mathscr{X}_i,\mathscr{X}_j,\mathscr{X}_l,\mathscr{X}_k)|\mathscr{X}_i,\mathscr{X}_j],$$

then we have

$$\begin{aligned}P_n(\mathscr{X}_i,\mathscr{X}_j)&=2\sum_t\sum_s\sum_r\{u_{it}u_{jt}\bar{K}_{it,jt}\mathrm{E}[K_{it,ls}K_{jt,kr}|\mathscr{X}_i,\mathscr{X}_j]\\&\quad+u_{it}u_{jt}\bar{K}_{it,jt}\mathrm{E}[K_{it,ls}K_{jt,kr}|\mathscr{X}_i,\mathscr{X}_j]\}\\&=4\left\{\sum_t\sum_s\sum_r u_{it}u_{jt}\bar{K}_{it,jt}\mathrm{E}[K_{it,ls}K_{jt,kr}|\mathscr{X}_i,\mathscr{X}_j]\right\}.\end{aligned}$$

Thus

$$\begin{aligned}\mathrm{E}[P_n^2(\mathscr{X}_1,\mathscr{X}_2)]&=16\sum_t\sum_s\sum_r\sum_{t'}\sum_{s'}\sum_{r'}\mathrm{E}\{u_{1t}u_{2t}u_{1t'}u_{2t'}\bar{K}_{1t,2t}\bar{K}_{1t',2t'}\\&\quad\times\mathrm{E}[K_{1t,ls}K_{2t,kr}|\mathscr{X}_1,\mathscr{X}_2]\mathrm{E}[K_{1t',ls'}K_{2t',kr'}|\mathscr{X}_1,\mathscr{X}_2]\}.\end{aligned}$$

Note that

$$\begin{aligned}\mathrm{E}[K_{1t,ls}K_{2t,kr}|\mathscr{X}_1,\mathscr{X}_2]&=\int f(x_{ls})f(x_{kr})K_{1t,ls}K_{2t,kr}\mathrm{d}x_{ls}\mathrm{d}x_{kr}\\&=a^{2p}\int f(x_{1t}+au)f(x_{2t}+av)K(u)K(v)\mathrm{d}u\mathrm{d}v\\&=a^{2p}[\int f(x_{1t})f(x_{2t})+\mathrm{o}(1)],\end{aligned}$$

similarly,

$$\begin{aligned}\mathrm{E}[K_{1t',ls'}K_{2t',kr'}|\mathscr{X}_1,\mathscr{X}_2]&=\int f(x_{ls'})f(x_{kr'})K_{1t',ls'}K_{2t',kr'}\mathrm{d}x_{ls'}\mathrm{d}x_{kr'}\\&=a^{2p}\int f(x_{1t'}+au)f(x_{2t'}+av)K(u)K(v)\mathrm{d}u\mathrm{d}v\\&=a^{2p}[f(x_{1t'})f(x_{2t'})+\mathrm{o}(1)].\end{aligned}$$

Hence

$$\begin{aligned}\mathrm{E}[P_n^2(\mathscr{X}_1,\mathscr{X}_2)]&=16a^{4p}\sum_t\sum_s\sum_r\sum_{s'}\sum_{r'}\mathrm{E}\{\sigma^2(X_{1t})\sigma^2(X_{2t})\\&\quad\times\bar{K}^2_{1t,2t}\,[f^2(x_{1t})f^2(x_{2t})+\mathrm{o}(1)]\}\\&\quad+16a^{4p}\sum_t\sum_s\sum_r\sum_{t'\neq t}\sum_{s'}\sum_{r'}\mathrm{E}\{\rho(x_{1t},x_{1t'})\rho(x_{2t},x_{2t'})\\&\quad\times\bar{K}_{1t,2t}\bar{K}_{1t',2t'}[f(x_{1t})f(x_{2t})f(x_{1t'})f(x_{2t'})+\mathrm{o}(1)]\}\\&\equiv S_1+S_2,\end{aligned}$$

where S_1 denotes the case $t=t'$ and S_2 denotes the case $t \neq t'$. Also $\rho(x_{1t}, x_{1t'}) \equiv \mathrm{E}(u_{1t}u_{1t'}|x_1)$.

$$S_1 = 16a^{4p}T^4\sum_t\{\int f(x_{1t})f(x_{2t})\sigma^2(x_{1t})\sigma^2(x_{2t})\bar{K}^2_{1t,2t}$$

$$\times[f^2(x_{1t})f^2(x_{2t}) + \mathrm{o}(1)]\mathrm{d}x_{1t}\mathrm{d}x_{2t}$$

$$= 16a^{4p}h^qT^4\sum_t\{\int\sigma^2(x_{1t})\sigma^2(x_{1t}+bu)\bar{K}^2(u)$$

$$\times[f^3(x_{1t})f^3(x_{1t}+bu) + \mathrm{o}(1)]\mathrm{d}x_{1t}\mathrm{d}w$$

$$= 16a^{4p}h^p\sum_t\sum_s\sum_r\sum_{s'}\sum_{r'}\{[\int\sigma^4(x_{1t})f^6(x_{1t})][\int\bar{K}^2(u)\mathrm{d}u] + \mathrm{o}(1)\}$$

$$= 16a^{4p}h^pT^4\{\sum_t\{\mathrm{E}[\sigma^4(x_{1t})f^5(x_{1t})][\int\bar{K}^2(u)\mathrm{d}u] + \mathrm{o}(1)\}$$

$$\equiv 16a^{4p}h^p\{\sigma_0^2 + \mathrm{o}(1)\},$$

$$S_2 = 16a^{4p}T^4\sum_t\sum_{t'\neq t}\{\int f(x_{1t},x_{1t'})f(x_{2t},x_{2t'})\rho(x_{1t},x_{1t'})\rho(x_{2t},x_{2t'})\bar{K}_{1t,2t}$$

$$\times\bar{K}_{1t',2t'}[f(x_{1t})f(x_{2t})f(x_{1t'})f(x_{2t'}) + \mathrm{O}(a^p)]\mathrm{d}x_{1t}\mathrm{d}x_{2t}\mathrm{d}x_{1t'}\mathrm{d}x_{2t'}\}$$

$$= 16a^{4p}h^{2p}T^4\sum_t\sum_{t'\neq t}\{\int f(x_{1t},x_{1t'})f(x_{1t}+bu, x_{1t'}+bv)$$

$$\times\rho(x_{1t}+bu, x_{1t'}+bv)\rho(x_{1t},x_{1t'})\bar{K}(u)\bar{K}(v)$$

$$\times[f(x_{1t})f(x_{1t}+bu)f(x_{1t'})f(x_{1t'}+bv) + \mathrm{O}(a^p)]\mathrm{d}x_{1t}\mathrm{d}u\mathrm{d}x_{1t'}\mathrm{d}v\}$$

$$= 16a^{4p}h^{2p}T^4\sum_t\sum_{t'\neq t}\{\int f^2(x_{1t},x_{1t'})\rho^2(x_{1t},x_{1t'})$$

$$\times[f^2(x_{1t})f^2(x_{1t'}) + \mathrm{O}(a^p)]\mathrm{d}x_{1t}\mathrm{d}x_{1t'}\}$$

$$= \mathrm{O}(a^{4p}h^{2p}).$$

Hence S_2 has a smaller order of magnitude than S_1.

Thus

$$\mathrm{E}[P_n^2(\mathscr{X}_1, \mathscr{X}_2)] = 16a^{4p}h^p\{\sigma_0^2 + \mathrm{o}(1)\},$$

and one can verify that the condition of Lemma B.1 holds. Denote

$$U_N = \binom{N}{4}^{-1}\sum\sum\sum_{1\leqslant i<j<l<k\leqslant N}\sum P_n(\mathscr{X}_i, \mathscr{X}_j, \mathscr{X}_l, \mathscr{X}_k),$$

then

$$Nh^{p/2}J_2U \equiv \binom{N}{4} \frac{1}{N(N-1)^3h^{p/2}a^{2p}}[NU_N]$$

$$\xrightarrow{d} \binom{N}{4} \frac{1}{N(N-1)^3h^{p/2}a^{2p}} \mathrm{N}(0, \tfrac{1}{2}4^2(4-1)^2[16a^{4p}h^p\sigma_0^2])$$

$$\xrightarrow{d} \mathrm{N}\left(0, \binom{N}{4}^2 \frac{1}{N^2(N-1)^6h^pa^{4p}} 2^{-1}4^2(4-1)^2[16a^{4p}h^p\sigma_0^2]\right)$$

$$\xrightarrow{d} \mathrm{N}(0, 2\sigma_0^2).$$

One can easily see that

$$J_2R = \frac{1}{N(N-1)^3a^{2p}h^p} \mathrm{O}_p(N^3h^pa^p) = \mathrm{O}_p((Na^p)^{-1}) = \mathrm{o}_p((Nh^{p/2})^{-1}).$$

Hence

$$Nh^{p/2}J_{N2} \xrightarrow{d} \mathrm{N}(0, 2\sigma_0^2).$$

Proposition 3. $J_{N3} = \mathrm{o}_p((Nh^{p/2})^{-1})$.

Proof.

$$J_{N3} = \frac{1}{N(N-1)Th^p} \sum_i \sum_t \sum_{j \neq i} \hat{u}_{it}\hat{u}_{jt}\hat{f}_{it}\hat{f}_{jt}\bar{K}_{it,jt}$$

$$= \frac{1}{N(N-1)^3T^3h^pa^{2p}} \sum_i \sum_t \sum_{j \neq i} \sum_{l \neq i} \sum_s \sum_{k \neq j} \sum_r u_{ls}u_{kr}K_{it,ls}K_{jt,kr}\bar{K}_{it,jt}$$

$$\sim \frac{1}{N^4Th^pa^{2p}} \sum_i \sum_t \sum_{j \neq i} \sum_{l \neq i} \sum_{k \neq j} u_{lt}u_{kt}K_{it,lt}K_{jt,kt}\bar{K}_{it,jt}$$

$$\equiv \frac{1}{T}\sum_t J_{3t},$$

where

$$J_{3t} = \frac{1}{N^4h^pa^{2p}} \sum_i \sum_{j \neq i} \sum_{l \neq i} \sum_{k \neq j} u_{lt}u_{kt}K_{it,lt}K_{jt,kt}\bar{K}_{it,jt}.$$

Below we show that $J_{3t} = \mathrm{o}_p((Nh^{p/2})^{-1})$. We consider (i) $l = k$ and (ii) $l \neq k$ separately, we use $J_{3t(i)}$ and $J_{3t(ii)}$ to denote these two cases.

Case (*i*) $l = k$

$$
\begin{aligned}
E(J_{3t(i)}) &= \frac{1}{N^4 h^p a^{2p}} \sum_i \sum_{j \neq i} \sum_{l \neq i,j} E[u_{lt}^2 K_{it,lt} K_{jt,lt} \bar{K}_{it,jt}] \\
&= \frac{1}{Nh^p a^{2p}} E\{\sigma^2(x_{3t}) K_{1t,3t} K_{2t,3t} \bar{K}_{1t,2t}\} \\
&= \frac{1}{Nh^p a^{2p}} E\{\bar{K}_{1t,2t} E[\sigma^2(x_{3t}) K_{1t,3t} K_{2t,3t} | \mathscr{Z}_1, \mathscr{Z}_2]\} \\
&= \frac{1}{Nh^p a^{2p}} E\{\bar{K}_{1t,2t} [\textstyle\int f(x_{3t}) \sigma^2(x_{3t}) K_{1t,3t} K_{2t,3t} dx_{3t}]\} \\
&= \frac{1}{Nh^p a^p} \textstyle\int f(x_{1t}) f(x_{2t}) \bar{K}_{1t,2t} \int f(x_{1t} + au) \sigma^2(x_{1t} + au) \\
&\quad \times K(u) K\left(\frac{x_{2t} - x_{1t}}{a} - u\right) dx_{1t} dx_{2t} du \\
&= \frac{1}{Na^p} \left\{ \textstyle\int f(x_{1t}) f(x_{1t} + bv) \bar{K}(v) \int f(x_{1t} + au) \sigma^2(x_{1t} + au) \right. \\
&\quad \left. \times K(u) K\left(\frac{b}{a} v - u\right) dx_{1t} du dv \right\} \\
&= \frac{1}{Na^p} \left\{ [\textstyle\int f^3(x_{1t}) \sigma^2(x_{1t}) dx_{1t}] \left[\int K(u) K\left(\frac{b}{a} \Delta v - u\right) du \right] + o(1) \right\} \\
&= \frac{1}{Na^p} \{E[f^2(x_{1t}) \sigma^2(x_{1t})][\textstyle\int K^2(u) du] + o(1)\} \\
&= O(N^{-1} a^{-p}) = o((Nh^{p/2})^{-1}).
\end{aligned}
$$

It is easy to see that $\mathrm{var}(J_{3t(i)}) = o_p(N^{-2} h^{-p})$, hence $J_{3t(i)} = o_p((Nh^{p/2})^{-1})$.

Case (*ii*) $l \neq k$

$$
\begin{aligned}
J_{3t(ii)} &= \frac{1}{N(N-1)^3 h^p a^{2p}} \sum_i \sum_{j \neq i} \sum_{l \neq i} \sum_{k \neq j,l} u_{lt} u_{kt} K_{it,lt} K_{jt,kt} \bar{K}_{it,jt} \\
&= \frac{1}{N(N-1)^3 h^p a^{2p}} \sum_{i \neq j \neq l \neq k} \sum \sum \sum u_{lt} u_{kt} K_{it,lt} K_{jt,kt} \bar{K}_{it,jt} + J_{3t(ii)} S \\
&\equiv J_{3t(ii)} F + J_{3t(ii)} S,
\end{aligned}
$$

where $J_{3t(ii)}F$ denotes the case that all summation indices i, j, l, k are different and $J_{3t(ii)}S$ denotes the remaining summation terms.

$$
\begin{aligned}
E[(J_{3t(ii)}F)^2] &= \frac{1}{N^8 h^{2p} a^{4p}} \sum_{i \neq j \neq l \neq k} \sum \sum \sum \sum_{i' \neq l,k} \sum_{j' \neq i',l,k} E[u_{lt}^2 u_{kt}^2 K_{it,lt} \\
&\quad \times K_{jt,kt} \bar{K}_{it,jt} K_{i't,lt} K_{j't,kt} \bar{K}_{i't,j't}]
\end{aligned}
$$

$$= \frac{1}{N^6 h^{2p} a^{4p}} \sum_{i \neq 1} \sum_{j \neq i,2} \sum_{i' \neq 1} \sum_{j' \neq i',2} \mathrm{E}[u_{1t}^2 u_{2t}^2 K_{it,1t}$$

$$\times K_{jt,2t} \bar{K}_{it,jt} K_{i't,1t} K_{j't,2t} \bar{K}_{i't,j't}]$$

$$\equiv AA.$$

The leading term in AA is the case that i, j, i', j' are all different; in this case,

$$AA = \frac{1}{N^2 h^{2p} a^{4p}} \mathrm{E}[\sigma^2(x_{1t})\sigma^2(x_{2t}) K_{3t,1t} K_{4t,2t} \bar{K}_{3t,4t} K_{5t,1t} K_{6t,2t} \bar{K}_{5t,6t}]$$

$$= \frac{1}{N^2 h^{2p} a^{4p}} \mathrm{E}\{\sigma^2(x_{1t})\sigma^2(x_{2t})(\mathrm{E}[K_{3t,1t} K_{4t,2t} \bar{K}_{3t,4t} | x_{1t}, x_{2t}])^2\}$$

$$= \frac{1}{N^2 h^{2p} a^{4p}} \mathrm{E}\{\sigma^2(x_{1t})\sigma^2(x_{2t})[\textstyle\int f(x_{3t}, x_{4t} | x_{1t}, x_{2t}) K_{3t,1t} K_{4t,2t} \bar{K}_{3t,4t} \mathrm{d}u \mathrm{d}v]^2\}$$

$$= \frac{h^{2p}}{N^2 a^{4p}} \mathrm{E}\left\{ \sigma^2(x_{1t})\sigma^2(x_{2t}) \left[\int f(x_{1t} + bu, x_{2t} + bv | x_{1t}, x_{2t}) \right.\right.$$

$$\left.\left. \times K\left(\frac{bu}{a}\right) K\left(\frac{bv}{a}\right) \bar{K}\left(\frac{x_1 - x_2}{b} + (u - v)\right)\right]^2 \right\}$$

$$= \frac{h^{2p}}{N^2 a^{4p}} \mathrm{O}(h^p) = \mathrm{O}(N^{-2} h^{3p} a^{-4p}) = \mathrm{o}(N^{-2} h^{-p}).$$

It is easy to see that when some of the i, j, i', j' take the same values,

$$AA = \frac{1}{N^6 a^{4p} h^{2p}} \mathrm{O}(N^2 a^{2p} h^{2p}) = \mathrm{O}(N^{-3} a^{-2p}) = \mathrm{o}(N^{-2} h^{-p}).$$

Hence

$$J_{3t(ii)} F = \mathrm{o}_p((N h^{p/2})^{-1}).$$

Also, one can verify that $J_{3t(ii)} S$ is

$$\frac{1}{N^3 a^p h^p} \mathrm{O}_p(N^3 a^p h^p) = \mathrm{O}_p(N^{-1} a^{-p}) = \mathrm{o}_p((N h^{p/2})^{-1}).$$

Hence

$$J_{3t(ii)} = \mathrm{o}_p((N h^{p/2})^{-1}).$$

We have shown that $J_{3t} = \mathrm{o}_p((N h^{p/2})^{-1})$ which implies $J_{N3} = \mathrm{o}_p((N h^{p/2})^{-1})$ because T is finite.

Proposition 4. $J_{N4} = \mathrm{o}_p((N h^{p/2})^{-1})$.

Proof.

$$J_{N4} = \frac{1}{T}\sum_t \left\{ \frac{1}{N(N-1)h^p} \sum_i \sum_{j \neq i} u_{it} \hat{f}_{it}(g_{jt} - \hat{g}_{jt}) \hat{f}_{jt} \bar{K}_{it,jt} \right\}$$

$$= \frac{1}{T^3}\sum_t \sum_s \sum_r \left\{ \frac{1}{N^4 h^p a^{2p}} \sum_i \sum_{j \neq i} \sum_{l \neq i} \sum_{k \neq j} u_{it} K_{it,ls}(g_{jt} - g_{kr}) K_{jt,kr} \bar{K}_{it,jt} \right\}$$

$$\sim \frac{1}{T}\sum_t \left\{ \frac{1}{N^3 h^p a^{2p}} \sum_i \sum_{j \neq i} \sum_{l \neq i} \sum_{k \neq j} u_{it}(g_{jt} - g_{kt}) K_{it,lt} K_{jt,kt} \bar{K}_{it,jt} \right\}$$

$$\equiv \frac{1}{T}\sum_t J_{4t},$$

where

$$J_{4t} = \frac{1}{N^3 h^p a^{2p}} \sum_i \sum_{j \neq i} \sum_{l \neq i} \sum_{k \neq j} u_{it}(g_{jt} - g_{kt}) K_{it,lt} K_{jt,kt} \bar{K}_{it,jt}$$

$$\equiv \frac{1}{\sqrt{N}} \sum_i u_{it} S_{it},$$

with

$$S_{it} \equiv \frac{1}{N^{5/2} h^p a^{2p}} \sum_{j \neq i} \sum_{l \neq i} \sum_{k \neq j} (g_{jt} - g_{kt}) K_{it,lt} K_{jt,kt} \bar{K}_{it,jt}.$$

Because T is finite, it suffices to show that $J_{4t} = o_p((Nh^{p/2})^{-1})$ for all $1 \leqslant t \leqslant T$.

$$\mathrm{E}[(J_{4t})^2] = \frac{1}{N}\sum_i \mathrm{E}[u_{it}^2 S_{it}^2]$$

$$= \mathrm{E}[u_{1t}^2 S_{1t}^2] = \frac{1}{N^7 h^{2p} a^{4p}} \sum_{j \neq 1} \sum_{l \neq 1} \sum_{k \neq j} \sum_{j' \neq 1} \sum_{l' \neq 1} \sum_{k' \neq j'} \mathrm{E}[u_{1t}^2 (g_{jt} - g_{kt})$$

$$\times K_{1t,lt} K_{jt,kt} \bar{K}_{1t,jt} (g_{j't} - g_{k't}) K_{1t,l't} K_{j't,k't} \bar{K}_{1t,j't}]$$

$$\equiv BB.$$

If $1, j, l, k, j', l', k'$ are all different from each other, using Lemma B.1, it is easy to see that BB is $O(N^{-1}a^{2\nu}) = o(N^{-2}h^{-p})$.

Next we consider the case that $j, l, k, j', l', k', 1$ take six different values. By symmetry, we only need to consider (i) j equals one of the other indices, (ii) l equals one of the other indices, (iii) k equals one of the other indices. It is straightforward to show that all these three cases are $O(N^{-2}a^{-p}) = o(N^{-2}h^{-p})$.

Finally it is easy to see that when $1, j, l, k, j', l', k'$ take no more than five different values, BB has an order of $O(N^{-3}a^{-2p}) = o(N^{-2}h^{-p})$. Hence

$$J_{4t} = o_p((Nh^{p/2})^{-1}).$$

Proposition 5. $J_{N5} = o_p((Nh^{p/2})^{-1})$.

Proof. First observe that

$$J_{N5} = \frac{1}{N(N-1)h^{(p+q)}} \sum_i \sum_t \sum_{j \neq i} \hat{u}_i \hat{f}_i (g_{jt} - \hat{g}_{jt}) \hat{f}_{jt} \bar{K}_{it,jt}$$

$$= \frac{1}{T^3} \sum_t \sum_s \sum_r \frac{1}{N(N-1)^3 h^p a^{2p}} \sum_i \sum_{j \neq i} \sum_{l \neq i} \sum_{k \neq j} u_{ls} (g_{jt} - g_{kr})$$

$$\times K_{it,lt} K_{jt,kr} \bar{K}_{it,jt}$$

$$\sim \frac{1}{T^3} \sum_t \sum_s \sum_r \frac{1}{N(N-1)^3 h^p a^{2p}} \sum_i \sum_{j \neq i} \sum_{l \neq i} \sum_{k \neq j} u_{lt} (g_{jt} - g_{kt})$$

$$\times K_{it,lt} K_{jt,kt} \bar{K}_{it,jt}$$

$$\equiv \frac{1}{T} \sum_t J_{5t},$$

where

$$J_{5t} = \frac{1}{N(N-1)^3 h^p a^{2p}} \sum_i \sum_{j \neq i} \sum_{l \neq i} \sum_{k \neq j} u_{lt} (g_{jt} - g_{kt}) K_{it,lt} K_{jt,kt} \bar{K}_{it,jt}.$$

Then using similar arguments as we did in the proof of Proposition 4, one can show that $J_{5t} = o_p((Nh^{p/2})^{-1})$.

Proposition 6. $J_{N6} = o_p((Nh^{p/2})^{-1})$.

Proof.

$$J_{N6} = \frac{1}{N(N-1)Th^p} \sum_i \sum_t \sum_{j \neq i} u_i \hat{f}_i \hat{u}_{jt} \hat{f}_{jt} \bar{K}_{it,jt}$$

$$= \frac{1}{N(N-1)^3 T^3 h^p a^{2p}} \sum_i \sum_t \sum_{j \neq i} \sum_{l \neq i} \sum_s \sum_{k \neq j} \sum_r u_{it} u_{kr} K_{it,ls} K_{jt,kr} \bar{K}_{it,jt}$$

$$\sim \frac{1}{T} \sum_t \left\{ \frac{1}{N^4 h^p a^{2p}} \sum_i \sum_{j \neq i} \sum_{l \neq i} \sum_{k \neq j} u_{it} u_{kt} K_{it,lt} K_{jt,kt} \bar{K}_{it,jt} \right\}$$

$$\equiv \frac{1}{T} \sum_t J_{6t}.$$

We consider two cases, (i) $i = k$ and (ii) $i \neq k$, we use $J_{6t(i)}$ and $J_{6t(ii)}$ to denote these two cases.

Case (i) $i = k$

$$\begin{aligned}
\mathrm{E}[J_{6t(i)}] &= \frac{1}{N^4 h^p a^{2p}} \sum_i \sum_{j \neq i} \sum_{l \neq i} \mathrm{E}[u_{it}^2 K_{it,lt} K_{jt,it} \bar{K}_{it,jt}] \\
&= \frac{1}{N^4 h^p a^{2p}} \sum_i \sum_{j \neq i} \mathrm{E}[u_{it}^2 K_{it,jt} K_{jt,it} \bar{K}_{it,jt}] \\
&\quad + \frac{1}{N^4 h^p a^{2p}} \sum_i \sum_{j \neq i} \sum_{l \neq i, l \neq j} \mathrm{E}[u_{it}^2 K_{it,lt} K_{jt,it} \bar{K}_{it,jt}] \\
&= \frac{1}{N^4 h^p a^{2p}} \mathrm{O}(N^2 h^p) + \frac{1}{N^4 h^p a^{2p}} \mathrm{O}(N^3 a^p h^p) \\
&= \mathrm{O}(N^{-1} a^{-p}) = \mathrm{o}((N h^{p/2})^{-1})
\end{aligned}$$

and

$$\mathrm{var}(J_{6t(i)}) = \mathrm{o}(N^{-2} h^{-p}).$$

Hence

$$J_{6t(i)} = \mathrm{o}_p((N h^{p/2})^{-1}).$$

Case (ii): $i \neq k$

$$\begin{aligned}
I_{6t(ii)} &= \frac{1}{N(N-1)^3 a^{2p} h^p} \sum_i \sum_{j \neq i} \sum_{k \neq j, k \neq i} u_{it} u_{kt} K_{it,lt} K_{jt,kt} \bar{K}_{it,jt} \\
&\equiv \frac{1}{N(N-1)^3 a^{2p} h^p} \sum\sum\sum_{i \neq j \neq k \neq l}\sum u_{it} u_{kt} K_{it,lt} K_{jt,kt} \bar{K}_{it,jt} + J_{6t(ii)S} \\
&\equiv J_{6t(ii)F} + J_{6t(ii)S},
\end{aligned}$$

$$\begin{aligned}
\mathrm{E}[(I_{6t(ii)F})^2] &= \frac{1}{N^6 a^{4p} h^{2p}} \sum \sum_{j \neq l = 3} \sum \sum_{j' \neq l' = 3} \mathrm{E}[u_{1t}^2 u_{2t}^2 \\
&\quad \times K_{1t,lt} K_{jt,2t} \bar{K}_{1t,jt} K_{1t,l't} K_{j't,2t} \bar{K}_{1t,j't}] \\
&\equiv CC.
\end{aligned}$$

Obviously the leading term of CC is the case when j, l, j', l' are all different. In this case

$$\begin{aligned}
CC &= \frac{1}{N^6 a^{4p} h^{2p}} N^4 \mathrm{E}[u_{1t}^2 u_{2t}^2 K_{1t,4t} K_{3t,2t} \bar{K}_{1t,3t} K_{1t,6t} K_{5t,2t} \bar{K}_{1t,5t}] \\
&= \mathrm{O}(N^{-2} a^{-q}) = \mathrm{o}(N^{-2} h^{-p}).
\end{aligned}$$

Finally, one can show that

$$J_{6t(ii)}S = \frac{1}{N^4 a^{2p} h^p} \mathrm{O}_p(N^3 a^p h^p)$$
$$= \mathrm{O}_p(N^{-1} a^{-p}) = \mathrm{o}_p((Nh^{p/2})^{-1}).$$

Hence

$$J_{6t(ii)} = \mathrm{o}_p((Nh^{p/2})^{-1}) \quad \text{and} \quad J_{6t} = \mathrm{o}_p((Nh^{p/2})^{-1}).$$

Proof of Theorem 1 (ii)

It suffices to show that $\hat{\sigma}_0^2 = \sigma_0^2 + \mathrm{o}_p(1)$. Using the fact that $\tilde{u}_{it}\hat{f}_{it} = u_{it} f_{it} + \mathrm{o}_p(1)$, it is easy to show that

$$\mathrm{E}(\hat{\sigma}_0^2) = \frac{1}{T^2}\sum_t \left\{ \frac{1}{N(N-1)h^p} \sum_i \sum_{j \neq i} \mathrm{E}[u_{it}^2 u_{js}^2 f_{it}^2 f_{jt}^2 \bar{K}_{it,js}^2] \right\} + \mathrm{o}(1)$$
$$= \frac{1}{T^2 h^p} \sum_t \int f(x_{1t}) f(x_{2t}) \sigma^2(x_{1t}) \sigma^2(x_{2t}) f^2(x_{1t}) f^2(x_{2t})$$
$$\times \bar{K}^2\left(\frac{x_{1t} - x_{2t}}{a}\right) \mathrm{d}x_{1t} \mathrm{d}x_{2t} + \mathrm{o}(1)$$
$$= \frac{1}{T^2} \sum_t \mathrm{E}[\sigma^4(x_{1t}) f^5(x_{1t})][\int \bar{K}^2(v)\mathrm{d}v] + \mathrm{o}(1)$$
$$\equiv \sigma_0^2 + \mathrm{o}(1).$$

One can easily show that $\mathrm{var}(\hat{\sigma}_0^2) = \mathrm{o}(1)$. Hence

$$\hat{\sigma}_0^2 = \sigma_0^2 + \mathrm{o}_p(1).$$

Appendix B

Lemma B.1. Let U_N be a U-statistic of order k given by

$$U_N = \binom{N}{k}^{-1} \sum_{(N,k)} \phi_N(Z_{i_1}, \ldots, Z_{i_k}),$$

where ϕ_N is a symmetric function that depends on N, $Z_1, \ldots, Z_k$ are independent and identically distributed random variables (or vectors), and the sum $\sum_{(N,k)}$ is taken over all subsets $1 \leqslant i_1 < \ldots < i_k \leqslant N$ of $\{1, 2, \ldots, N\}$. Define, for $c = 1, \ldots, k$, the conditional expectations

$$\phi_{Nc}(z_1, \ldots, z_c) = \mathrm{E}[\phi_N(Z_1, \ldots, Z_k) | (Z_1, \ldots, Z_c) = (z_1, \ldots, z_c)],$$

and their variances

$$\sigma_{Nc}^2 = \mathrm{var}[\phi_{Nc}(X_1, ..., X_c)].$$

Assume ϕ_N *is symmetric,* $\mathrm{E}[\phi_N(X_1, ..., X_k)|X_1] = 0$ *almost surely, and* $\mathrm{E}[\phi_N^2(Z_1, ..., Z_k)] < \infty$ *for each* N. *If* $\sigma_{Nc}^2/\sigma_{N2}^2 = o(N^{(c-2)})$ *for* $c = 3, ..., k$ *and*

$$\frac{\mathrm{E}[G_N^2(Z_1, Z_2)] + N^{-1}\mathrm{E}[\phi_{N2}^4(Z_1, Z_2)]}{\{\mathrm{E}[\phi_{N2}^2(Z_1, Z_2)]\}^2} \to 0$$

as $N \to \infty$, *then* (NU_N) *is asymptotically distributed with zero mean and variance given by* $\frac{1}{2}k^2(k-1)^2\sigma_{N2}^2$, *where* $G_N(x, y) \equiv \mathrm{E}[\phi_N(Z_1, x)\phi_N(Z_1, y)]$.

Proof: This is Lemma B.4 of Fan and Li (1994).

Lemma B.2. $f(x) \in \mathcal{G}_{\lambda}^{\infty}$, $k^c \in \mathcal{K}_{\lambda}$, *where* $\lambda \geqslant 1$ *is an integer,* $k^d \in \mathcal{K}_0^d$. *Then* $\mathrm{E}_{1t}(K_{1t,2t}) = O(a^p)$.

Proof.

$$\begin{aligned}\mathrm{E}_{1t}(K_{1t,2t}) &= \int K_{1t,2t} f(x_{2t})\mathrm{d}x_{2t} \\ &= a^p K^d(0) \int K^c(v) f(x_{1t}^c + av|x_{1t}^d)P(x_{1t}^d)\mathrm{d}v \\ &\quad + a^p {\textstyle\sum}' K^d\left(\frac{x_{1t}^d - x_{2t}^d}{a}\right)\int K^c(v) f^c(x_{1t}^c + av|x_{2t}^d)P(x_{2t}^d)\mathrm{d}v,\end{aligned}$$

where $v = (x_{1t} - x_{2t}/a)$, $\sum'$ denotes the sum for those $x_{2t}^d \neq x_{1t}^d$. The first term is $O(a^p)$ by Robinson's (1988) Lemma 1. The second term is $o(a^p)$ because

$$K^d\left(\frac{x_{1t}^d - x_{2t}^d}{a}\right) = o(1) \quad \text{for} \quad x_{2t}^d \neq x_{1t}^d.$$

Lemma B.3. $f(x) \in \mathcal{G}_{v-1}^{\infty}$ *and* $g(x) \in \mathcal{G}_v^{\alpha}$ *for those continuous variables, and* $k^c \in \mathcal{K}_v$, *where* $v \geqslant 2$ *is an integer,* $k^d \in \mathcal{K}_v^d$. *Then*

$$\mathrm{E}|\mathrm{E}_{1t}\{[g(x_{1t}) - g(x_{2t})]K_{1t,2t}\}| \leqslant D_g(x_{1t})a^{p+v},$$

where $D_g(\cdot)$ *has* α *finite moment.*

Proof.

$$\begin{aligned}&\mathrm{E}|\mathrm{E}_{1t}\{[g(x_{1t}) - g(x_{2t})]K_{1t,2t}\}| \\ &= K^d(0)a^p \int K^c(v) f(x_{1t}^c + av|x_{1t}^d)P(x_{1t}^d)\{g(x_{1t}^c, x_{1t}^d) - g(x_{1t}^c + av, x_{1t}^d)\}\mathrm{d}v \\ &\quad + a^p {\textstyle\sum}' K_{1t,2t}^d \int K^c(v) f(x_{1t}^c + av|x_{2t}^d)P(x_{2t}^d)\{g(x_{1t}^c, x_{1t}^d) - g(x_{1t}^c + av, x_{2t}^d)\}\mathrm{d}v,\end{aligned}$$

where $\sum'$ has the same meaning as in Lemma B.2. The first term, by Robinson's (1988) Lemma 5 and the dominated convergence theorem, is less or equal to $D_g(x_{1t})a^{p+v}$, where $D_g(x_{1t})$ has finite α moments. The second term is $o(a^{p+v})$ because

$$K^d\left(\frac{x_{1t}-x_{2t}}{a}\right) = o(a^v) \quad \text{for} \quad x_{2t}^d \neq x_{1t}^d.$$

References

Baltagi, B.H., 1981, Pooling: An experimental study of alternative testing and estimation procedure in a two-way error component model, Journal of Econometrics 17, 21–49.

Brown, R.L., J. Durbin, and J.M. Evans, 1975, Techniques for testing the constancy of regression relationships over time, Journal of the Royal Statistical Society 37, 149–192.

Chow, G.C., 1960, Tests of equality between sets of coefficients in two linear regressions, Econometrica 28, 591–605.

Cornwell, C. and P. Rupert, 1988, Efficient estimation with panel data: An empirical comparison of instrumental variables estimators, Journal of Applied Econometrics 3, 149–155.

Dufour, J.M., 1982, Recursive stability analysis of linear regression relationships: An exploratory methodology, Journal of Econometrics 19, 31–76.

Fan, Y. and Q. Li, 1994, Consistent model specification tests: Omitted variables and semiparametric functional forms, Econometrica, forthcoming.

Hackl, P. and A.H. Westlund, 1989, Statistical analysis of 'structural change': An annotated bibliography, Empirical Economics 14, 103–128.

Han, A.K. and D. Park, 1989, Testing for structural change in panel data: application to a study of US foreign trade in manufacturing goods, Review of Economics and Statistics 71, 135–142.

Hidalgo, J., 1995, A nonparametric conditional moment test for structural stability, Econometric Theory, forthcoming.

Hsiao, C., 1986, Analysis of panel data (Cambridge University Press, Cambridge).

Klevmarken, N.A., 1989, Panel studies: What can we learn from them? Introduction, European Economic Review 33, 523–529.

Krämer, W., 1989, Econometrics of structural change (Physica-Verlag, Heidelberg).

Powell, J.L., H. Stock, and T.M. Stoker, 1989, Semiparametric estimation of index coefficients, Econometrica 57, 1403–1430.

Robinson, P., 1988, Root-N-consistent semiparametric regression, Econometrica 156, 931–954.

Wallace, T.D., 1972, Weaker criteria and tests for linear restrictions in regression, Econometrica 40, 689–698.

Zellner, A., 1962, An efficient method of estimating seemingly unrelated regression and tests for aggregation bias, Journal of the American Statistical Association 57, 348–368.

JOURNAL OF
Econometrics

ELSEVIER Journal of Econometrics 68 (1995) 133–151

Testing AR(1) against MA(1) disturbances in an error component model

Badi H. Baltagi*[,a], Qi Li[b]

[a]*Department of Economics, Texas A&M University, College Station, TX 77843-4228, USA*
[b]*Department of Economics, University of Guelph, Guelph, Ont. N1G 2W1, Canada*

Abstract

This paper derives three LM statistics for an error component model with first-order serially correlated errors. The first LM statistic jointly tests for zero first-order serial correlation and random individual effects, the second LM statistic tests for zero first-order serial correlation assuming fixed individual effects, and the third LM statistic tests for zero first-order serial correlation assuming random individual effects. In *all* three cases, the corresponding LM statistic is the *same* whether the alternative is AR(1) or MA(1). This paper also derives two extensions of the Burke, Godfrey, and Termayne (1990) test from the time-series to the panel data literature. The first tests the null of AR(1) disturbances against MA(1) disturbances, and the second tests the null of MA(1) disturbances against AR(1) disturbances in an error component model. These tests are computationally simple requiring only OLS or within residuals. The small sample performance of these tests are studied using Monte Carlo experiments.

Key words: Error components; Serial correlation; Lagrange multiplier; Random and fixed effects
JEL classification: C23

* Corresponding author.

The authors would like to thank Richard Blundell and two anonymous referees for their helpful comments and suggestions. Baltagi was funded by the Advanced Research Progam, Texas Higher Education Board, while Li was funded by the Social Sciences of Humanities Research Council of Canada.

SSDI 0304407694 01646 H

1. Introduction

A random or fixed effects error component model is by far the most widely used specification in panel data econometrics.[1] The error component model was extended to take into account first-order serial correlation in the remainder disturbances by Lillard and Willis (1978) for the random effects model and by Bhargava, Franzini, and Narendranathan (1982) for the fixed effects model. Both studies considered the AR(1) specification on the remainder disturbances. However, the MA(1) model is a viable alternative; see Nicholls, Pagan, and Terrell (1975). In fact, in the time-series literature, it is well known that the same Lagrange Multiplier test statistic is obtained for testing the null hypothesis of zero first-order serial correlation whether the alternative is AR(1) or MA(1); see Breusch and Godfrey (1981). This paper demonstrates that this result extends to the error component model with serial correlation. In Section 2, we derive three LM test statistics:[2] the first LM test statistic *jointly* tests for zero first-order serial correlation and random individual effects. The second LM test statistic tests for zero first-order serial correlation assuming a fixed effects model, and the third LM test statistic tests for zero first-order serial correlation assuming a random effects model. In *all* three cases, the corresponding LM statistic is the *same* whether the alternative is AR(1) or MA(1).

Section 3 deals with the problem of testing AR(1) against MA(1) in an error component model. This problem has been extensively studied in the time-series framework; see Walker (1967), King (1983), and more recently King and McAleer (1987), King (1988), and Burke, Godfrey, and Termayne (1990). For panel data, this paper proposes two extensions of the Burke, Godfrey, and Termayne (1990) test to the error component model: The first test assumes that the null is AR(1) while the alternative is MA(1). It is computationally simple using only the within residuals and performs well when T is large. However, for typical labor panels, N is large and T is small. Hence, we propose an alternative BGT-type test which relies on N large to achieve its asymptotic distribution. This test switches the hypotheses so that the null is MA(1) while the alternative is AR(1). It is also computationally simple, requiring only ordinary least squares residuals. Section 4 gives the Monte Carlo design along with the results of the experiments, while Section 5 gives our summary and conclusion.

2. Testing for first-order serial correlation in an error component model

Consider the following panel data regression:

$$y_{it} = x'_{it}\beta + u_{it}, \quad i = 1, 2, \ldots, N, \quad t = 1, 2, \ldots, T, \tag{1}$$

---

[1] See Hsiao (1986) and the references cited there.

[2] See Breusch and Pagan (1980), Engle (1984), and the recent monograph by Godfrey (1989) for the advantages of the LM test and its application to several econometric examples.

where β is a $K \times 1$ vector of regression coefficients including the intercept, i denoting individuals and t denoting time-periods. x_{it} is a $K \times 1$ vector of observations on K strictly exogenous explanatory variables. The composite disturbance is

$$u_{it} = \mu_i + v_{it}, \tag{2}$$

where $\mu_i \sim \text{IIN}(0, \sigma_\mu^2)$ and the remainder disturbances follow a stationary AR(1) process: $v_{it} = \rho v_{i,t-1} + \varepsilon_{it}$ with $|\rho| < 1$, or a MA(1) process: $v_{it} = \varepsilon_{it} + \lambda \varepsilon_{i,t-1}$ with $|\lambda| < 1$. In both cases, we assume $\varepsilon_{it} \sim \text{IIN}(0, \sigma_\varepsilon^2)$. In the next section, we will show that the joint LM test statistic for $\text{H}_1^{\text{a}}: \sigma_\mu^2 = 0; \lambda = 0$ is the same as the joint LM test statistic for $\text{H}_1^{\text{b}}: \sigma_\mu^2 = 0; \rho = 0$.

2.1. A joint LM test for serial correlation and random individual effects

Let us consider the LM test for the error component model where the remainder disturbances follow a MA(1) process. Writing the error term in vector form,

$$u = (I_N \otimes e_N)\mu + v, \tag{3}$$

where $\mu' = (\mu_1, \ldots, \mu_N)$ and $v' = (v_{11}, \ldots, v_{1T}, \ldots, v_{N1}, \ldots, v_{NT})$. e_T is a vector of ones of dimension T and I_N is an identity matrix of dimension N. The variance–covariance matrix for this model is

$$\Sigma = \text{E}(uu') = \sigma_\mu^2 I_N \otimes J_T + \sigma_\varepsilon^2 I_N \otimes V_\lambda, \tag{4}$$

where

$$J_T = e_T e_T' \quad \text{and} \quad V_\lambda = \begin{bmatrix} 1+\lambda^2 & \lambda & 0 & \cdots & 0 & 0 \\ \lambda & 1+\lambda^2 & \lambda & \cdots & 0 & 0 \\ \vdots & \vdots & \vdots & \ddots & \vdots & \vdots \\ 0 & 0 & 0 & \cdots & \lambda & 1+\lambda^2 \end{bmatrix}.$$

The log-likelihood function is

$$l(\beta, \theta) = \text{const.} - \tfrac{1}{2}\log|\Sigma| - \tfrac{1}{2}u'\Sigma^{-1}u, \tag{5}$$

where $\theta = (\lambda, \sigma_\mu^2, \sigma_\varepsilon^2)'$. In order to construct the LM test statistic for $\text{H}_1^{\text{a}}: \sigma_\mu^2 = 0$; $\lambda = 0$, one needs $D(\theta) = \partial l(\theta)/\partial\theta$ and the information matrix $J(\theta) = \text{E}[\partial^2 l(\theta)/\partial\theta\,\partial\theta']$ evaluated at the restricted maximum likelihood estimator $\hat{\theta}$. Following Hartley and Rao (1967) and Harville (1977), one can derive the following LM statistic for the null hypothesis H_1^{a}:

$$\text{LM}_1 = \hat{D}'\hat{J}^{-1}\hat{D} = \frac{NT^2}{2(T-1)(T-2)}[A^2 - 4AB + 2TB^2], \tag{6}$$

where $A = [\hat{u}(I_N \otimes J_T)\hat{u}/(\hat{u}'\hat{u}) - 1]$, $B = (\hat{u}'\hat{u}_{-1}/\hat{u}'\hat{u})$, and $\hat{u}$ denotes the OLS residuals. This is asymptotically distributed (for large N) as χ^2_2 under H^a_1. LM_1 is exactly the same as the joint test statistic derived by Baltagi and Li (1991) for AR(1) residual disturbances and random individual effects. In fact, one can repeat the above derivation for H^b_1: $\sigma^2_\mu = 0$; $\rho = 0$, by replacing the V_λ matrix by its AR(1) counterpart

$$V_\rho = \frac{1}{1-\rho^2}\begin{bmatrix} 1 & \rho & \cdots & \rho^{T-1} \\ \rho & 1 & \cdots & \rho^{T-2} \\ \vdots & \vdots & \ddots & \vdots \\ \rho^{T-1} & \rho^{T-2} & \cdots & 1 \end{bmatrix}.$$

Note that under the null hypothesis, we have $(V_\rho)_{\rho=0} = I_T = (V_\lambda)_{\lambda=0}$ and $(\partial V_\rho/\partial\rho)_{\rho=0} = G = (\partial V_\lambda/\partial\lambda)_{\lambda=0}$, where G is the bi-diagonal matrix with bi-diagonal elements all equal to one. Then it is easy to show that the same joint LM test statistic results whether the residual disturbances follow an AR(1) or a MA(1) process.

Note that the A^2 term in (6) is the basis for the LM test statistic for H_2: $\sigma^2_\mu = 0$ assuming there is no serial correlation (see Breusch and Pagan, 1980). In fact, $LM_2 = \sqrt{NT/2(T-1)}A$ is asymptotically distributed (for large N) as N(0,1) under H_2 against the one-sided alternative H'_2: $\sigma^2_\mu > 0$. Also, the B^2 term in (6) is the basis for the LM test statistic for H_3: $\rho(\lambda = 0)$ assuming there are no individual effects (see Breusch and Godfrey, 1981). In fact, $LM_3 = \sqrt{NT^2/(T-1)}B$ is asymptotically distributed (for large N) as N(0,1) under H_3 against the one-sided alternative H'_3: $\rho(\lambda) > 0$. The presence of an interaction term in the joint LM test statistic emphasizes the importance of the joint test when both serial correlation and random individual effects are suspected. However, when T is large the interaction term becomes negligible.

Note that all the LM tests considered assume that the underlying null hypothesis is that of white noise disturbances. However, in panel data applications, especially with large labor panels, one is concerned with individual effects and is guaranteed their existence. In this case, it is inappropriate to test for serial correlation assuming no individual effects as is done in H_3. In fact, if one uses LM_3 to test for serial correlation, one is very likely to reject the null hypothesis of H_3 even if the null is true. This is because the μ_i's are correlated for the same individual across time and this will contribute to rejecting the null of no serial correlation. Section 2.2 derives the appropriate LM test statistic in case of random individual effects, while Section 2.3 derives the appropriate LM test statistic in case of fixed individual effects.

2.2. An LM test for first-order serial correlation in a random effects model

Case 1: Let us start with the AR(1) model. The null hypothesis is H_4^b: $\rho = 0$ (given $\sigma_\mu^2 > 0$) vs. $H_4^{b'}$: $\rho \neq 0$ (given $\sigma_\mu^2 > 0$). The variance–covariance matrix (under the alternative) is

$$\Sigma_1 = \sigma_\mu^2(I_N \otimes J_T) + \sigma_\nu^2(I_N \otimes V_\rho).$$

Under the null hypothesis H_4^b, we have

$$\begin{aligned} D_\rho &= (\partial l/\partial \rho)|_{\rho=0} \\ &= [N(T-1)/T]\frac{\sigma_1^2 - \sigma_\varepsilon^2}{\sigma_1^2} \\ &\quad + (\sigma_\varepsilon^2/2)u'\{I_N \otimes [(\bar{J}_T/\sigma_1^2 + E_T/\sigma_\varepsilon^2)G(\bar{J}_T/\sigma_1^2 + E_T/\sigma_\varepsilon^2)]\}u, \end{aligned}$$

where $\bar{J}_T = e_T e_T'/T$, $E_T = I_T - \bar{J}_T$, G is the bi-diagonal matrix defined above, and $\sigma_1^2 = T\sigma_\mu^2 + \sigma_\varepsilon^2$. The information matrix,[3] when evaluated under the null hypothesis ($\rho = 0$), is

$$\hat{J} = \begin{bmatrix} \hat{J}_{\rho\rho} & N(T-1)\hat{\sigma}_\varepsilon^2/\hat{\sigma}_1^4 & \dfrac{N(T-1)}{T}\hat{\sigma}_\varepsilon^2[1/\hat{\sigma}_1^4 - 1/\hat{\sigma}_\varepsilon^4] \\ & (NT^2/2\hat{\sigma}_1^4) & NT/2\hat{\sigma}_1^4 \\ & & \dfrac{N}{2}\left[\dfrac{1}{\hat{\sigma}_1^4} + \dfrac{T-1}{\hat{\sigma}_\varepsilon^4}\right] \end{bmatrix},$$

where $\hat{J}_{\rho\rho} = N[2a^2(T-1)^2 + 2a(2T-3) + (T-1)]$ and $a = [(\hat{\sigma}_\varepsilon^2 - \hat{\sigma}_1^2)/T\hat{\sigma}_1^2]$. Thus the LM test statistic is

$$LM = \hat{D}'\hat{J}^{-1}D = (\hat{D}_\rho)^2\hat{J}^{11}, \tag{7}$$

where $\hat{J}^{11} = N^2T^2(T-1)/\det(\hat{J})4\hat{\sigma}_1^4\hat{\sigma}_\varepsilon^4$. Under the null hypothesis, LM is asymptotically distributed (for large N) as χ_1^2. $\hat{\sigma}_\varepsilon^2 = \hat{u}'(I_N \otimes E_T)\hat{u}/N(T-1)$ and $\hat{\sigma}_1^2 = \hat{u}'(I_N \otimes \bar{J}_T)\hat{u}/N$, where $\hat{u}$ denotes the maximum likelihood residuals under the null hypothesis. The one-sided LM test for the hypothesis H_4^b (corresponding to the alternative $\rho > 0$) is

$$LM_4 = \hat{D}_\rho\sqrt{\hat{J}^{11}}, \tag{8}$$

and this is asymptotically distributed (for large N) as N(0, 1).

Case 2: MA(1) model; H_4^a: $\lambda = 0$ (given $\sigma_\mu^2 > 0$) vs. $H_4^{a'}$: $\lambda \neq 0$ (given $\sigma_\mu^2 > 0$). The variance–covariance matrix is

$$\Sigma_2 = \sigma_\mu^2(I_N \otimes J_T) + \sigma_\varepsilon^2(I_N \otimes V_\lambda).$$

[3] Detailed derivation of the information matrix J is available upon request from the authors.

Note that under the null hypothesis H_4^a,

$$(\Sigma_2^{-1})|_{\lambda=0} = (\Sigma_1^{-1})|_{\rho=0},$$

$$(\partial\Sigma_2/\partial\lambda)|_{\lambda=0} = (\partial\Sigma_1/\partial\rho)|_{\rho=0},$$

$$(\partial\Sigma_2/\partial\sigma_\mu^2)|_{\lambda=0} = (\partial\Sigma_1/\partial\sigma_\mu^2)|_{\rho=0},$$

$$(\partial\Sigma_2/\partial\sigma_\varepsilon^2)|_{\lambda=0} = (\partial\Sigma_1/\partial\sigma_\varepsilon^2)|_{\rho=0}.$$

Therefore, it is easy to show that the LM test statistic for H_4^a is the same as that given in (7).

2.3. An LM test for first-order serial correlation in a fixed effects model

The model is the same as (1), and the null hypothesis is H_5^b: $\rho = 0$, given that the μ_i's are fixed parameters.[4] Writing each individual's variables in a $T \times 1$ vector form, we have

$$y_i = x_i\beta + \mu_i e_T + v_i, \tag{9}$$

where $y_i = (y_{i1}, y_{i2}, \dots, y_{iT})'$, x_i is $T \times K$, and v_i is $T \times 1$. $v_i \sim N(0, \Omega_\rho)$, where $\Omega_\rho = \sigma_\varepsilon^2 V_\rho$ for the AR(1) disturbances. The log-likelihood function is

$$l(\beta, \rho, \mu, \sigma_\varepsilon^2) = \text{const.} - \tfrac{1}{2}\log|\Sigma| - \frac{1}{2\sigma_\varepsilon^2}\sum_{i=1}^{N}[(y_i - x_i\beta - \mu_i e_T)' V_\rho^{-1}(y_i - x_i\beta - \mu_i e_T)], \tag{10}$$

where $\Sigma = I_N \otimes \Omega_\rho$ is the variance–covariance matrix of $v = (v'_1, \dots, v'_N)'$. One can easily verify that the LM test statistic for testing H_5^b is

$$LM = [NT^2/(T-1)](\tilde{v}'\tilde{v}_{-1}/\tilde{v}'\tilde{v})^2, \tag{11}$$

where $\tilde{v}$ denote the usual within residuals. This LM statistic is asymptotically distributed (for large T) as χ_1^2 under the null hypothesis H_5^b. The one-sided test for H_5^b (corresponding to the alternative $\rho > 0$) is

$$LM_5 = \sqrt{NT^2/(T-1)}(\tilde{v}'\tilde{v}_{-1}/\tilde{v}'\tilde{v}), \tag{12}$$

which is asymptotically distributed (for large T) as N(0, 1). By a similar argument, one can show that the LM test statistic for H_5^a: $\lambda = 0$, in a fixed effects model with MA(1) residual disturbances is identical to LM_5. Note also that LM_5 differs from LM_3 only by the fact that the within residuals $\tilde{v}$ (in LM_5)

[4] It is important to note that Bhargava, Franzini, and Narendranathan (1982), hereafter BFN, modified the Durbin–Watson statistic to test for serial correlation of the AR(1) type when the individual effects are assumed fixed. BFN provide tables for the lower and upper bounds of their modified Durbin–Watson statistic for $N \geqslant 50$ and $T \leqslant 20$.

replace the OLS residuals $\hat{u}$ (in LM_3). Since the within transformation wipes out the individual effects whether fixed or random, one can also use (12) to test for serial correlation in the random effects models.

3. Testing AR(1) against MA(1) in an error component model

We now turn to the discussion of testing AR(1) against MA(1) in the random effects model.[5] Testing AR(1) against MA(1) in a time-series framework has been extensively studied; see King and McAleer (1987) for a Monte Carlo comparison of nonnested, approximate point optimal, as well as Lagrange Multiplier tests. In fact, King and McAleer (1987) found that the nonnested tests perform poorly in small samples, while King's (1983) point optimal test performs the best. Also, Godfrey's (1978a, 1978b) LM test for testing AR(1) against ARMA(1,1) is quite powerful even when testing AR(1) against MA(1). For the error component model, one can derive a corresponding LM test for testing AR(1) against ARMA(1,1). However, such a test is computationally burdensome. In this section, we propose two extensions of the Burke, Godfrey, and Termayne (1990) test (hereafter BGT) to the error component model. These tests are simple to implement requiring within or OLS residuals.

The basic idea of the BGT test is as follows: Under the null hypothesis of an AR(1) process, the remainder error term v_{it} satisfies

$$\mathrm{corr}(v_{it}, v_{i,t-\tau}) = \rho_\tau = (\rho_1)^\tau, \quad \tau = 1, 2, \ldots, \tag{13}$$

and, therefore, under the null hypothesis

$$\rho_2 - (\rho_1)^2 = 0. \tag{14}$$

Under the alternative hypothesis of an MA(1) process on v_{it}, $\rho_2 = 0$ and hence $\rho_2 - (\rho_1)^2 < 0$. Therefore, BGT recommends a test statistic based on (14) using estimates of ρ's obtained from OLS residuals. One problem remains. King (1983) suggest that any 'good' test should have a size which tends to zero, asymptotically, for $\rho_1 > 0.5$. The test based on (14) does not guarantee this property. To remedy this, BGT proposed supplementing (14) with the decision to accept the null hypothesis of AR(1) if $\hat{\rho}_1 > \frac{1}{2} + 1/\sqrt{T}$.

In an error component model, the within transformation wipes out the individual effects, and one can use the within residuals $\tilde{u}_{it}(= \tilde{v}_{it})$ instead of OLS

[5] A test that helps distinguish between the AR(1) and MA(1) process will be useful in obtaining a pre-test estimator that may be more efficient than the 'pure' estimators; see Griffiths and Beesley (1984) for a Monte Carlo study that compares pre-test and pure estimators in the time-series literature.

residuals $\hat{u}_{it}$ to construct the BGT test. Let

$$(\tilde{\rho}_1)_i = \sum_{t=2}^{T} \tilde{u}_{it}\tilde{u}_{i,t-1} \Big/ \sum_{t=1}^{T} \tilde{u}_{it}^2, \quad (\tilde{\rho}_2)_i = \sum_{t=3}^{T} \tilde{u}_{it}\tilde{u}_{i,t-2} \Big/ \sum_{t=1}^{T} \tilde{u}_{it}^2$$

$$\text{for} \quad i = 1, \ldots, N.$$

The following test statistic, based on (14),

$$\tilde{\gamma}_i = \sqrt{T}((\tilde{\rho}_2)_i - (\tilde{\rho}_1^2)_i)/(1 - (\tilde{\rho}_2)_i), \tag{15}$$

is asymptotically distributed (for large T) as N(0,1) under the null hypothesis of an AR(1). Using the data on all N individuals, we can construct a generalized BGT test statistic for the error component model,

$$\tilde{\gamma} = \sqrt{N}\left(\sum_{i=1}^{N} \tilde{\gamma}_i/N\right) = \sqrt{NT} \sum_{i=1}^{N} \left[\frac{(\tilde{\rho}_2)_i - (\tilde{\rho}_1^2)_i}{1 - (\tilde{\rho}_2)_i}\right] \Big/ N. \tag{16}$$

$\tilde{\gamma}_i$'s are independent for different i since the $\tilde{u}_i$'s are independent. Hence $\tilde{\gamma}$ is also asymptotically distributed (for large T) as N(0, 1) under the null hypothesis of an AR(1) process. The test statistic (16) is supplemented by

$$\tilde{\rho}_1 = \sum_{i=1}^{N} (\tilde{\rho}_1)_i/N \equiv \frac{1}{N} \sum_{i=1}^{N} \left[\sum_{t=2}^{T} \tilde{u}_{it}\tilde{u}_{i,t-1} \Big/ \sum_{t=1}^{T} \tilde{u}_{it}^2\right], \tag{17}$$

and our proposed BGT_1 test can be summarized as follows:

1) Use the within residuals $\tilde{u}_{it}$ to calculate $\tilde{\gamma}$ and $\tilde{\rho}_1$ from (16) and (17).

2) Accept the AR(1) model if $\tilde{\gamma} > c_\alpha$ or $\tilde{\rho}_1 > \frac{1}{2} + 1/\sqrt{T}$, where Prob [N(0, 1) $\leqslant c_\alpha] = \alpha$.

The bias in estimating ρ_s ($s = 1, 2$) by using within residuals is of $O(1/T)$ as $N \to \infty$ (see Nickell, 1981). Therefore, BGT_1 may not perform well for small T. Since for typical labor panels, N is large and T is small, we turn next to an alternative extension of the BGT test which performs well for large N rather than large T.

An alternative BGT-type test for testing AR(1) vs. MA(1)

Let the null hypothesis be H_7: $\nu_{it} = \varepsilon_{it} + \lambda\varepsilon_{i,t-1}$ and the alternative be H_7': $\nu_{it} = \rho\nu_{i,t-1} + \varepsilon_{it}$, where $\varepsilon_{it} \sim N(0, \sigma_\varepsilon^2)$. Note that this test differs from the BGT_1 test in that the null hypothesis is MA(1) rather than AR(1).[6] The alternative

[6] In the time-series literature, Walker (1967) derived nonnested tests for the AR(1) against the MA(1) as well as for the case where the null and alternative are interchanged.

BGT-type test uses autocorrelation estimates derived from OLS residuals and can be motivated as follows:

Let $Q_0 = \sum\sum u_{it}^2/NT = u'u/NT$ and $Q_s = \sum\sum u_{it}u_{i,t-s}/N(T-s) = u'(I_N \otimes G_s)u/N(T-s)$ for all $s = 1, \ldots, S$, where $G_s = \frac{1}{2}\,\text{Toeplitz}\,(\iota_s)$, ι_s is a vector of zeros with the $(s+1)$th element being 1. $s = 1, \ldots, S$ with $S \leqslant (T-1)$ and S is finite.[7] Given the true residuals (the u's), and assuming $[u'Au/n - \text{E}(u'Au/n)] \xrightarrow{\text{P}} 0$, where $n = NT$ and A is an arbitrary symmetric matrix, it is straightforward to show the following:[8]

(i) For the MA(1) model,

$$\text{plim}\, Q_0 = \sigma_\mu^2 + \sigma_v^2 + \text{o}_p(1) = \sigma_\mu^2 + \sigma_\varepsilon^2(1+\lambda^2) + \text{o}_p(1),$$

$$\text{plim}\, Q_1 = \sigma_\mu^2 + \lambda\sigma_\varepsilon^2 + \text{o}_p(1),$$

$$\text{plim}\, Q_s = \sigma_\mu^2 + \text{o}_p(1) \quad \text{for} \quad s = 2, \ldots, S.$$

(ii) For the AR(1) model,

$$\text{plim}\, Q_0 = \sigma_\mu^2 + \sigma_v^2 + \text{o}_p(1),$$

$$\text{plim}\, Q_s = \sigma_\mu^2 + \rho^s\sigma_v^2 + \text{o}_p(1) \quad \text{for} \quad s = 1, \ldots, S.$$

We only give the proof for the MA(1) case since the AR(1) case can be similarly shown.

Proof. For the MA(1) case, we have plim $Q_0 = \lim \text{E}(u'u)/(NT) = \lim \text{tr}(\Sigma)/(NT) = (\sigma_\mu^2 + \sigma_v^2)$. Similarly, we have

$$\begin{aligned}\text{plim}\, Q_1 &= \lim \text{E}(u'(I_N \otimes G_1)u)/N(T-1) = \lim \text{tr}\,[\Sigma(I_N \otimes G_1)]/N(T-1)\\ &= \text{tr}\,[\sigma_\mu^2 J_T G_1 + \sigma_\varepsilon^2 V_\lambda G_1]/(T-1)\\ &= [\sigma_u^2(T-1) + \sigma_\varepsilon^2\lambda(T-1)]/(T-1)\\ &= (\sigma_u^2 + \sigma_\varepsilon^2\lambda).\end{aligned}$$

The third equality uses the fact that $\text{tr}(J_T G_1) = (T-1)$ and $\text{tr}(V_\lambda G_1) = \lambda(T-1)$.

$$\begin{aligned}\text{plim}\, Q_s &= \lim \text{E}(u'(I_N \otimes G_s)u)/N(T-s) = \lim \text{tr}[\Sigma(I_N \otimes G_s)]/N(T-s)\\ &= \text{tr}[\sigma_\mu^2 J_T G_s + \sigma_\varepsilon^2 V_\lambda G_s]/(T-s) = [\sigma_\mu^2(T-s)]/(T-s) = \sigma_\mu^2\\ &\quad \text{for} \quad s = 2, \ldots, S.\end{aligned}$$

[7] Let $a = (a_1, a_2, \ldots, a_n)'$ denote an arbitrary $n \times 1$ vector, then Toeplitz(a) is an $n \times n$ symmetric matrix generated from the $n \times 1$ vector a with the diagonal elements all equal to a_1, second diagonal elements equal to a_2, etc. For example, Toeplitz(ι_1) is the G matrix defined in Section 2.1.

[8] Unless otherwise stated, plim is taken as $N \to \infty$.

The third equality uses the fact that $\mathrm{tr}(J_T G_s) = (T - s)$ and $\mathrm{tr}(V_\lambda G_s) = 0$ for $s = 2, \ldots, S$.

The inclusion of the individual effects μ_i makes the composite error term $u_{it} = \mu_i + v_{it}$ correlated across time, even for more than one period apart from the MA(1) model. Therefore, a direct comparison of the $\mathrm{corr}(u_{it}, u_{i,t-s})$ cannot distinguish the AR(1) process from the MA(1) process. However, if we take differences of $Q_s - Q_{s+l}$ for $s \geqslant 2$ and $l \geqslant 1$, we can see that $\mathrm{plim}(Q_s - Q_{s+l}) = 0$ for the MA(1) process and $\mathrm{plim}(Q_s - Q_{s+l}) = \sigma_v^2 \rho^s (1 - \rho^l) > 0$ for the AR(1) process. Hence for N very large we should be able to distinguish these two processes based on the information obtained from $Q_s - Q_{s+l}$.

Take $s = 2$ and $l = 1$, an asymptotic test of H_7 against H'_7 could, therefore, be based upon $(Q_2 - Q_3)$ with significantly small positive values leading to the rejection of H_7. Under the standard assumptions, an appropriate test statistic is

$$\gamma = \sqrt{N/V}\,(Q_2 - Q_3), \tag{18}$$

where $V = 2\mathrm{tr}\{[(\sigma_\mu^2 J_T + \sigma_\varepsilon^2 V_\lambda)(G_2/(T-2) - G_3/(T-3))]^2\}$. It can be shown, under some regularity condition, that γ is asymptotically distributed (for large N) as N(0, 1) under the null hypothesis of an MA(1) process.[9] Obviously, there are many different ways to construct such a test. For example, we can use $Q_2 + Q_3 - 2Q_4$ instead of $Q_2 - Q_3$ to define the γ test. In this case, $V = 2\mathrm{tr}\{[(\sigma_\mu^2 J_T + \sigma_\varepsilon^2 V_\lambda)(G_2/(T-2) + G_3/(T-3) - 2G_4/(T-4))]^2\}$. In order to calculate V, we need to know σ_μ^2, σ_ε^2, and λ. We make the following simple but important observation which enables us to compute the test statistic γ using only OLS residuals. Under the null hypothesis, v_{it} follows an MA(1) process. By noting the fact that $\sigma_\varepsilon^2(1 + \lambda^2) = \sigma_v^2$, we can write $\sigma_\varepsilon^2 V_\lambda = \sigma_v^2 I_T + (\sigma_\varepsilon^2 \lambda) G$. Thus we do not need to estimate λ in order to compute the test statistic γ, all we need to get are some consistent estimators for σ_v^2, $(\lambda\sigma_\varepsilon^2)$, and σ_μ^2. These are obtained as follows:

$$\hat{\sigma}_v^2 = \hat{Q}_0 - \hat{Q}_2, \quad (\lambda\hat{\sigma}_\varepsilon^2) = \hat{Q}_1 - \hat{Q}_2, \quad \hat{\sigma}_\mu^2 = \hat{Q}_2,$$

where $\hat{Q}_s$ are obtained from Q_s by replacing u_{it} by the OLS residuals $\hat{u}_{it}$.

It is easy to show that $\hat{Q}_s - Q_s = O_p(1/N)$, hence $\hat{Q}_s$ and Q_s are asymptotically equivalent estimators for the test statistic γ. Substituting these consistent estimators into V we get $\hat{V}$, and the test statistic γ becomes

$$\hat{\gamma} = \sqrt{N/\hat{V}}\,(\hat{Q}_2 - \hat{Q}_3), \tag{19}$$

[9] A derivation of this result is available upon request from the authors.

where

$$(\hat{Q}_2 - \hat{Q}_3) = \sum_{i=1}^{N}\sum_{t=3}^{T} \hat{u}_{it}\hat{u}_{i,t-2}/N(T-2) - \sum_{i=1}^{N}\sum_{t=4}^{T} \hat{u}_{it}\hat{u}_{i,t-3}/N(T-3)$$

and

$$\hat{V} = 2\,\mathrm{tr}\{[(\hat{\sigma}_\mu^2 J_T + \hat{\sigma}_v^2 I_T + \sigma_\varepsilon^2 \hat{\lambda} G)(G_2/(T-2) + G_3/(T-3))]^2\}.$$

$\hat{\gamma}$ is asymptotically distributed (for large N) as N(0, 1) under the null hypothesis H_7, and is referred to as the BGT_2 test.

4. Monte Carlo results

The model is set as follows:

$$Y_{it} = 5 + 0.5X_{it} + \mu_i + v_{it}, \qquad i = 1, \ldots, N, \quad t = 1, \ldots, T, \tag{20}$$

where $X_{it} = 0.1t + 0.5X_{i,t-1} + \omega_{it}$, with ω_{it} uniformly distributed on the interval $[-0.5, 0.5]$. X_{i0} is chosen as $(5 + 10\omega_{i0})$; see Nerlove (1971). $\mu_i \sim \mathrm{IIN}(0, \sigma_\mu^2)$. $\sigma^2 = \sigma_\mu^2 + \sigma_v^2$ is fixed at 20 and $\omega = \sigma_\mu^2/\sigma^2$ takes five different values, $\omega = (0.2, 0.4, 0.6, 0.8, 0.9)$.[10] The v_{it}'s follow an AR(1) process, or an MA(1) process, see (2), where both ρ and λ take five different values (0.2, 0.4, 0.6, 0.8, 0.9). We use three different combinations of $(N, T) = (10, 20), (20, 20), (50, 10)$ for all the tests considered in this paper (see Table 1 for a summary). In order to study the asymptotic behavior of the BGT_1 and BGT_2 test statistics, we conduct additional Monte Carlo experiments for large $T = 30, 60, 100$ for the BGT_1 test with $N = 10, 20, 30$. For the BGT_2 test, we choose large $N = 50, 100, 150$ with $T = 10, 20, 30$.

For the various null hypotheses listed in Table 1, Table 2 gives the corresponding number of rejections of that null in 1000 replications for $(N, T) = (10, 20)$.[11] The main results can be summarized as follows:

(i) The joint LM_1 test performs well in testing the null of H_1: $\rho = \sigma_\mu^2 = 0$. Its estimated size is not statistically different from its nominal size. In the presence of large individual effects ($\omega > 0.2$) or high serial correlation $\rho(\lambda) > 0.2$, this test has high power rejecting the null in 99 to 100% of the cases. It only has low power when $\omega = 0$ and $\rho(\lambda) = 0.2$ or $\omega = 0.2$ and $\rho(\lambda) = 0$.

(ii) The test statistic LM_2 for testing H_2: $\sigma_\mu^2 = 0$ implicitly assumes that $\rho(\lambda) = 0$. When ρ is indeed equal to zero, this test performs well. However, as

[10] The Monte Carlo results are invariant to the choice of α, β, and σ^2 (see Breusch, 1980).

[11] Results for $(N, T) = (20, 20)$ and $(50, 10)$ are similar and are available upon request from the authors.

Table 1
Summary of the tests considered

	Null hypothesis H_0	Alternative hypothesis H_A	Test statistic	Asymptotic distribution under H_0
(1a)	H_1^a: $\sigma_\mu^2 = 0$; $\lambda = 0$	σ_μ^2 or $\lambda \neq 0$	LM_1	χ_2^2
(1b)	H_1^b: $\sigma_\mu^2 = 0$; $\rho = 0$	σ_μ^2 or $\rho \neq 0$	LM_1	χ_2^2
(2)	H_2: $\sigma_\mu^2 = 0$	$\sigma_\mu^2 > 0$	LM_2	N(0, 1)
(3a)	H_3^a: $\lambda = 0$	$\lambda > 0$	LM_3	N(0, 1)
(3b)	H_3^b: $\rho = 0$	$\rho > 0$	LM_3	N(0, 1)
(4a)	H_4^a: $\lambda = 0$ $(\sigma_\mu^2 > 0)$	$\lambda > 0$ $(\sigma_\mu^2 > 0)$	LM_4	N(0, 1)
(4b)	H_4^b: $\rho = 0$ $(\sigma_\mu^2 > 0)$	$\rho > 0$ $(\sigma_\mu^2 > 0)$	LM_4	N(0, 1)
(5a)	H_5^a: $\lambda = 0$ (μ_i's fixed)	$\lambda > 0$ (μ_i's fixed)	LM_5	N(0, 1)
(5b)	H_5^b: $\rho = 0$ (μ_i's fixed)	$\rho > 0$ (μ_i's fixed)	LM_5	N(0, 1)
(6)	H_6: AR(1)	MA(1)	BGT_1	N(0, 1)
(7)	H_7: MA(1)	AR(1)	BGT_2	N(0, 1)

Row (5b): For H_5^b we also consider the modified Durbin–Watson test considered by Bhargava, Franzini, and Narendranathan (1982).

ρ moves away from zero and increases, this test tends to be biased in favor of rejecting the null. This is because a large serial correlation coefficient (i.e., large ρ) contributes to a large correlation among the individuals in the sample, even though $\sigma_\mu^2 = 0$. The first block corresponds to $\sigma_\mu^2 = 0$, i.e., the null is true. In this case, the number of rejections of the null are monotonically increasing as ρ increases, and for $\rho = 0.9$, LM_2 rejects in 100% of the cases. Similar results are obtained in case v_{it} follows an MA(1) process. The other blocks correspond to $\omega > 0$, i.e., the null is false, and LM_2 performs well when $\rho(\lambda) = 0$. As $\rho(\lambda)$ increases, this helps LM_2 even more in rejecting the null hypothesis of $\sigma_\mu^2 = 0$. In general, the presence of positive serial correlation tend to bias the case in favor of finding nonzero individual effects.

(iii) Similarly, the LM_3 test for testing H_3: $\rho = 0$ implicitly assumes $\sigma_\mu^2 = 0$. This test performs well when $\sigma_\mu^2 = 0$. However, as σ_μ^2 increases, the performance of this test deteriorates when the null ($\rho = 0$) is true. For example, when $\omega = 0.9$ and $\rho = 0$, it rejects the null hypothesis, when it is true, 100% of the time. The large correlation among the μ_i's contribute to the rejection of null hypothesis of no serial correlation. These results strongly indicate that one should not ignore the individual effects when testing for serial correlation.

Table 2
Testing for serial correlation and/or individual effects; number of rejections in 1000 replications; $N = 10$, $T = 20$

Null hypothesis		H_1	H_2	H_3	H_4	H_5	H_6	H_7
ω	$\rho(\lambda)$	LM_1	LM_2	LM_3	LM_4	LM_5	BGT_1	BGT_2
0	$\rho = \lambda = 0$	39[c]	45	37	34	10	223[a]	54[b]
	$\rho = 0.2$	657	207	825	790	539	217	116
	0.4	1000	530	1000	1000	996	225	350
	0.6	1000	876	1000	1000	1000	231	780
	0.8	1000	988	1000	1000	1000	290	951
	0.9	1000	1000	1000	1000	1000	288	984
	$\lambda = 0.2$	643	279	802	770	523	367	65
	0.4	995	293	1000	997	992	809	52
	0.6	1000	358	1000	1000	1000	987	60
	0.8	1000	392	1000	1000	1000	999	56
	0.9	1000	405	1000	1000	1000	1000	45
0.2	$\rho = \lambda = 0$	898	941	639	47	10	223	42
	$\rho = 0.2$	983	968	983	790	539	217	108
	0.4	1000	977	1000	999	996	225	306
	0.6	1000	993	1000	1000	1000	231	770
	0.8	1000	1000	1000	1000	1000	290	961
	0.9	1000	1000	1000	1000	1000	288	975
	$\lambda = 0.2$	985	971	986	807	523	367	61
	0.4	1000	981	1000	1000	992	809	45
	0.6	1000	969	1000	1000	1000	987	50
	0.8	1000	973	1000	1000	1000	999	42
	0.9	1000	975	1000	1000	1000	1000	38
0.4	$\rho = \lambda = 0$	997	999	947	36	10	223	49
	$\rho = 0.2$	1000	999	999	796	539	217	104
	0.4	1000	996	1000	999	996	225	314
	0.6	1000	999	1000	1000	1000	231	745
	0.8	1000	1000	1000	1000	1000	290	946
	0.9	1000	1000	1000	1000	1000	288	973
	$\lambda = 0.2$	997	995	999	811	523	367	55
	0.4	1000	1000	1000	1000	992	809	44
	0.6	1000	999	1000	1000	1000	987	45
	0.8	1000	999	1000	1000	1000	999	48
	0.9	1000	999	1000	1000	1000	1000	40
0.6	$\rho = \lambda = 0$	999	999	996	33	10	223	41
	$\rho = 0.2$	1000	1000	1000	817	539	217	95
	0.4	1000	1000	1000	999	996	225	309
	0.6	1000	1000	1000	1000	1000	231	686
	0.8	1000	1000	1000	1000	1000	290	895
	0.9	1000	1000	1000	1000	1000	288	911

Table 2 (continued)

Null hypothesis		H_1	H_2	H_3	H_4	H_5	H_6	H_7
ω	$\rho(\lambda)$	LM_1	LM_2	LM_3	LM_4	LM_5	BGT_1	BGT_2
0.6	$\lambda = 0.2$	1000	1000	1000	796	523	367	50
	0.4	1000	1000	1000	999	992	809	55
	0.6	1000	1000	1000	1000	1000	987	48
	0.8	1000	1000	1000	1000	1000	999	45
	0.9	1000	1000	1000	1000	1000	1000	65
0.8	$\rho = \lambda = 0$	999	1000	999	52	10	223	59
	$\rho = 0.2$	1000	1000	1000	812	539	217	113
	0.4	1000	1000	1000	1000	996	225	260
	0.6	1000	1000	1000	1000	1000	231	627
	0.8	1000	1000	1000	1000	1000	290	770
	0.9	1000	1000	1000	1000	1000	288	784
	$\lambda = 0.2$	1000	1000	1000	817	523	367	63
	0.4	1000	1000	1000	1000	992	809	57
	0.6	1000	1000	1000	1000	1000	987	60
	0.8	1000	1000	1000	1000	1000	999	61
	0.9	1000	1000	1000	1000	1000	1000	54
0.9	$\rho = \lambda = 0$	1000	1000	1000	39	10	223	52
	$\rho = 0.2$	1000	1000	1000	808	539	217	106
	0.4	1000	1000	1000	1000	996	225	244
	0.6	1000	1000	1000	1000	1000	231	481
	0.8	1000	1000	1000	1000	1000	290	632
	0.9	1000	1000	1000	1000	1000	288	712
	$\lambda = 0.2$	1000	1000	1000	816	523	367	68
	0.4	1000	1000	1000	999	992	809	62
	0.6	1000	1000	1000	1000	1000	987	59
	0.8	1000	1000	1000	1000	1000	999	61
	0.9	1000	1000	1000	1000	1000	1000	61

[a]The null hypothesis is AR(1).
[b]The null hypothesis, is MA(1).
[c]Counts between 37 and 63 are not statistically different from 50 at the 0.05 level.

(iv) In contrast to LM_3, both LM_4 and LM_5 take into account the presence of individual effects. Recall that LM_5 tests H_5: $\rho = 0$ (assuming the μ_i's are fixed effects). The performance of this test is independent of the values of σ_μ^2 (i.e., independent of the value of ω). This is because the within transformation wipes out the individual effects even if they are random. For large values of ρ or λ (ρ or λ greater than 0.4), both LM_4 and LM_5 have high power, rejecting the null more than 99% of the time. However, the estimated size of LM_4 is closer to the 5% nominal value than that of LM_5. In addition, for $N = 50$ and $T = 10$, our results show that the Bhargava, Franzini, and Narendranathan (1982) modified Durbin–Watson statistic has similar performance to that of LM_4 and is closer to its nominal size than LM_5.[12]

Now let us turn to the results of the tests of AR(1) against MA(1) specification in an error component model. Recall that for BGT_1, the null hypothesis is an AR(1) model, while for the BGT_2 test, the null hypothesis is an MA(1) model. From Table 2, the performance of BGT_1 is not satisfactory when the true model is AR(1) or MA(1) with small λ, while the performance of BGT_2 is not satisfactory when the true model is AR(1) with small ρ. These results suggest that $T = 20$ and $N = 10$ are not large enough for the BGT_1 and BGT_2 tests to achieve their asymptotic distribution. We therefore conduct additional Monte Carlo experiments with larger values of T for BGT_1 and larger values of N for BGT_2 (see Tables 3 and 4 below).

Table 3 reports the estimated power and size functions for BGT_1 for three values of $T = 30$, 60, 100. Note that this test is independent of the value of ω since the within transformation wipes out the individual effects. Overall, the BGT_1 test performs well if $T \geqslant 60$ and $T > N$. However, when T is small, or T is of moderate size but N is large, this test will tend to overreject the AR(1) process and therefore is not recommended in these cases.

Table 4 reports the estimated power and size function for BGT_2 for $N = 50$, 100, 150 and $T = 10$, 20, 30. Recall that for BGT_2 the null hypothesis is that of

Table 3
Estimated size and power functions of BGT_1 test; number of rejections of H_6 in 1000 replications

	$T = 30$			$T = 60$			$T = 100$		
$\rho(\lambda)$	$N = 10$	$N = 20$	$N = 30$	$N = 10$	$N = 20$	$N = 30$	$N = 10$	$N = 20$	$N = 30$
$\rho = \lambda = 0$	169	231	315	132	151	193	92	127	152
$\rho = 0.2$	165	244	310	135	142	193	103	127	149
0.4	181	255	316	125	155	205	102	122	155
0.6	185	276	354	117	166	205	87	119	152
0.8	134	214	300	1	0	0	0	0	0
0.9	22	11	3	0	0	0	0	0	0
$\lambda = 0.2$	363	523	583	376	596	745	435	670	821
0.4	849	984	1000	1000	1000	1000	1000	1000	1000
0.6	999	1000	1000	1000	1000	1000	1000	1000	1000
0.8	1000	1000	1000	1000	1000	1000	1000	1000	1000
0.9	1000	1000	1000	1000	1000	1000	1000	1000	1000

[12] $N = 50$ is the smallest N for which the upper and lower limits of the modified Durbin–Watson statistic are reported by Bhargava, Franzini, and Narendranathan (1982).

Table 4
Estimated size and power functions of BGT_2 test; number of rejections of H_7 in 1000 replications

		$T = 10$			$T = 20$			$T = 30$		
ω	$\rho(\lambda)$	$N = 50$	$N = 100$	$N = 150$	$N = 50$	$N = 100$	$N = 150$	$N = 50$	$N = 100$	$N = 150$
0.2	$\rho = 0.2$	134	182	258	228	331	306	272	417	548
	0.4	613	828	951	913	993	1000	982	1000	1000
	0.6	987	1000	1000	1000	1000	1000	1000	10000	1000
	0.8	1000	1000	1000	1000	1000	1000	1000	10000	1000
	0.9	1000	1000	1000	1000	1000	1000	1000	10000	1000
	$\lambda = 0.2$	54	53	52	52	47	51	49	50	49
	0.4	65	44	42	43	49	49	46	47	64
	0.6	52	41	42	57	52	50	40	52	49
	0.8	46	59	47	43	53	46	58	64	45
	0.9	56	53	45	43	40	52	60	46	54
0.4	$\rho = 0.2$	122	181	225	218	331	404	262	426	550
	0.4	582	828	935	890	989	999	979	1000	1000
	0.6	973	1000	1000	1000	1000	1000	1000	10000	1000
	0.8	1000	1000	1000	1000	1000	1000	1000	10000	1000
	0.9	1000	1000	1000	1000	1000	1000	1000	10000	1000
	$\lambda = 0.2$	40	49	48	69	54	57	46	55	47
	0.4	41	44	55	53	44	64	46	44	49
	0.6	49	52	48	56	48	49	39	56	57
	0.8	43	44	40	46	57	48	47	45	40
	0.9	53	57	45	40	47	44	52	69	55
0.6	$\rho = 0.2$	135	181	202	203	301	394	234	425	542
	0.4	553	780	923	869	988	999	977	1000	1000
	0.6	952	999	1000	1000	1000	1000	1000	10000	1000
	0.8	997	1000	1000	1000	1000	1000	1000	10000	1000
	0.9	1000	1000	1000	1000	1000	1000	1000	10000	1000
	$\lambda = 0.2$	50	49	50	62	50	48	37	54	51
	0.4	57	48	64	51	66	56	52	48	54
	0.6	41	41	50	56	46	51	54	60	55
	0.8	55	47	44	39	51	47	54	40	48
	0.9	51	57	62	48	45	45	63	45	41
0.8	$\rho = 0.2$	107	131	180	185	257	355	242	352	506
	0.4	464	711	834	824	979	994	961	998	1000
	0.6	886	993	1000	999	1000	1000	1000	10000	1000
	0.8	976	1000	1000	1000	1000	1000	1000	10000	1000
	0.9	984	1000	1000	1000	1000	1000	1000	10000	1000
	$\lambda = 0.2$	46	53	47	52	56	39	48	40	48
	0.4	49	57	50	45	53	61	56	45	61
	0.6	57	51	62	61	44	54	51	63	60
	0.8	50	48	47	56	47	53	43	45	53
	0.9	69	44	59	51	46	55	51	34	47

Table 4 (continued)

		$T = 10$			$T = 20$			$T = 30$		
ω	$\rho(\lambda)$	$N = 50$	$N = 100$	$N = 150$	$N = 50$	$N = 100$	$N = 150$	$N = 50$	$N = 100$	$N = 150$
0.9	$\rho = 0.2$	105	164	152	167	253	297	230	336	428
	0.4	389	559	663	750	920	988	929	988	1000
	0.6	743	935	986	986	1000	1000	1000	10000	1000
	0.8	884	985	998	996	1000	1000	1000	10000	1000
	0.9	870	993	999	991	1000	1000	1000	10000	1000
	$\lambda = 0.2$	60	65	53	55	58	43	59	44	49
	0.4	68	50	48	49	52	46	61	62	53
	0.6	46	63	63	60	51	53	61	53	53
	0.8	57	52	57	67	60	53	41	36	62
	0.9	49	64	65	56	49	37	56	43	45

an MA(1) process and the alternative is an AR(1) process. If the true model is MA(1), the performance of the BGT_2 is satisfactory, with its size close to 5% for all cases considered. When the true model is an AR(1) process, we observe the following: (i) For each fixed T, the performance of BGT_2 improves as N increases. (ii) For each fixed N, the performance of BGT_2 improves as T increases. This is in sharp contrast to the BGT_1 test where, when AR(1) is the true model, the performance of the test deteriorates as N increases for fixed T. Overall, BGT_2's performance is good except when the true model is AR(1) with small ρ.

5. Summary and conclusions

This paper recommends testing jointly for serial correlation and random individual effects in panel data applications. Rejecting the null, one can test for individual effects assuming serial correlation. Most likely, in labor panels, the presence of individual effects will not be rejected. In addition, one can test for serial correlation assuming fixed or random individual effects. This paper focuses on the latter tests, and shows that the resulting LM statistics are invariant to the form of the first-order serial correlation whether AR(1) or MA(1). This extends the Breusch and Godfrey (1981) result from time-series regressions to panel data regressions with individual effects. The Monte Carlo results show that tests for first-order serial correlation, assuming individual effects (whether fixed or random) perform better than those ignoring them. Of these tests, LM_4 and BFN give better estimated size than LM_5 and are therefore recommended.

This paper also derives two test statistics that extend the Burke, Godfrey, and Termayne (1990) test for the AR(1) against MA(1) disturbances from the time-series regressions to panel data regressions with individual effects. The first statistic, named the BGT_1 test, uses within residuals and tests the null of an AR(1) against the alternative of an MA(1). This test performs well if $T \geqslant 60$ and $T > N$. However, when T is small, or T is of moderate size but N is large, BGT_1 will tend to overreject the null hypothesis. Therefore BGT_1 is not recommended for these cases. For typical labor panels, N is large and T is small. For these cases, this paper recommends the BGT_2 test, which uses OLS residuals and tests the null of an MA(1) against the alternative of an AR(1). This test performs well when N is large and does not rely on T to achieve its asymptotic distribution. Our Monte Carlo results show that BGT_2's performance improves as either N or T increases.

References

Baltagi, B.H. and Q. Li, 1991, A joint test for serial correlation and random individual effects, Statistics and Probability Letters 11, 277-280.

Bhargava, A., L. Franzini, and W. Narendranathan, 1982, Serial correlation and the fixed effects model, Review of Economic Studies 49, 533–549.

Breusch, T.S., 1980, Useful invariance results for generalized regression models, Journal of Econometrics 13, 327–340.

Breusch, T.S. and L.G. Godfrey, 1981, A review of recent work on testing for autocorrelation in dynamic simultaneous models, in: D.A. Currie, R. Nobay, and D. Peel, eds., Macroeconomic analysis: Essays in macroeconomics and economics (Croom Helm, London).

Breusch, T.S. and A.R. Pagan, 1980, The Lagrange multiplier test and its applications to model specification, Review of Economic Studies 47, 225–238.

Burke, S.P., L.G. Godfrey, and A.R. Termayne, 1990, Testing AR(1) against MA(1) disturbances in the linear regression model: An alternative procedure, Review of Economic Studies 57, 135–145.

Engle, R.F., 1984, Wald, likelihood ratio, and Lagrange multiplier tests in econometrics, in: Z. Griliches and M.D. Intriligator, eds., Handbook of econometrics (North-Holland, Amsterdam).

Godfrey, L.G., 1978a, Testing against general autoregressive and moving average error models when the regressors include lagged dependent variables, Econometrica 46, 1293–1302.

Godfrey, L.G., 1978b, Testing for higher order serial correlation in regression equations when the regressors include lagged dependent variables, Econometrica 46, 1303–1310.

Godfrey, L.G., 1987, Discriminating between autocorrelation and misspecification in regression analysis: An alternative strategy, Review of Economics and Statistics 69, 128–134.

Godfrey, L.G., 1989, Misspecification tests in econometrics (Cambridge University Press, Cambridge).

Griffiths, W.E. and P.A.A. Beesley, 1984, The small-sample properties of some preliminary test estimators in a linear model with autocorrelated errors, Journal of Econometrics 25, 49–61.

Hartley, H.O. and J.N.K. Rao, 1967, Maximum likelihood estimation for the mixed analysis of variance model, Biometrika 54, 93–108.

Harville, D.A., 1977, Maximum likelihood approaches to variance component estimation and to related problems, Journal of the American Statistical Association 72, 320–338.

Hsiao, C., 1986, Analysis of panel data (Cambridge University Press, Cambridge).

King, M.L., 1983, Testing for autoregressive against moving average errors in the linear regression model, Journal of Econometrics 21, 35–51.

King, M.L., 1988, Towards a theory of point optimal testing, Econometric Reviews 6, 169–218.

King, M.L. and M. McAleer, 1987, Further results on testing AR(1) against MA(1) disturbances in the linear regression model, Review of Economic Studies 54, 649–636.

Lillard, L.A. and R.J. Willis, 1978, Dynamic aspects of learning mobility, Econometrica 46, 985–1012.

Nerlove, M., 1971, Further evidence of the estimation of dynamic economic relations from a time-series of cross-sections, Econometrica 39, 359–382.

Nicholls, D.F., A.R. Pagan, and R.D. Terrell, 1975, The estimation and use of models with moving average disturbance terms: A survey, International Economic Review 16, 113–134.

Nickell, S., 1981, Biases in dynamic models with fixed effects, Econometrica 49, 1417–1426.

Walker, A.M., 1967, Some tests of separate families of hypotheses in time series analysis, Biometrika 54, 39–68.

ELSEVIER

Journal of Econometrics 101 (2001) 1–23

JOURNAL OF
Econometrics

www.elsevier.nl/locate/econbase

Tests for the error component model in the presence of local misspecification

Anil K. Bera[a,*], Walter Sosa-Escudero[b], Mann Yoon[c]

[a]*Department of Economics, University of Illinois, 1206 S. Sixth Street, Champaign, IL 61820, USA*
[b]*Department of Economics, National University of La Plata, Calle 48 No. 555, Of. 516, (1900) La Plata, Argentina*
[c]*Department of Economics and Statistics, California State University at Los Angeles, 5151 State University Drive, Los Angeles, CA 90032, USA*

Received 1 February 1998; received in revised form 1 March 2000; accepted 5 July 2000

Abstract

It is well known that most of the standard specification tests are not valid when the alternative hypothesis is misspecified. This is particularly true in the error component model, when one tests for either random effects or serial correlation without taking account of the presence of the other effect. In this paper we study the size and power of the standard Rao's score tests analytically and by simulation when the data are contaminated by local misspecification. These tests are adversely affected under misspecification. We suggest simple procedures to test for random effects (or serial correlation) in the presence of local serial correlation (or random effects), and these tests require ordinary least-squares residuals only. Our Monte Carlo results demonstrate that the suggested tests have good finite sample properties for *local* misspecification, and in some cases even for far distant misspecification. Our tests are also capable of detecting the right direction of the departure from the null hypothesis. We also provide some empirical illustrations to highlight the usefulness of our tests. © 2001 Elsevier Science S.A. All rights reserved.

JEL classification: C12; C23; C52

Keywords: Error component model; Testing; Random effects: Serial correlation; Local misspecification

* Corresponding author. Tel.: + 1-217-333-4596; fax: + 1-217-244-6678.
E-mail address: anil@fisher.econ.uiuc.edu (A.K. Bera).

PII: S0304-4076(00)00071-3

1. Introduction

The random error component model introduced by Balestra and Nerlove (1966) was extended by Lillard and Willis (1978) to include serial correlation in the remainder disturbance term. Such an extension, however, raises questions about the validity of the existing specification tests such as the Rao's (1948) score (*RS*) test for random effects assuming no serial correlation as derived in Breusch and Pagan (1980). In a similar way doubts could be raised about tests for serial correlation derived assuming no random effects. Baltagi and Li (1991) proposed a *RS* test that jointly tests for serial correlation and random effects. One problem with the joint test is that, if the null hypothesis is rejected, it is not possible to infer whether the misspecification is due to serial correlation or to random effects. Also, as we will discuss later, because of higher degrees of freedom the joint test will not be optimal if the departure from the null occurs only in *one* direction. More recently, Baltagi and Li (1995) derived *RS* statistics for testing serial correlation assuming fixed/individual effects. These tests require maximum-likelihood estimation of individual effects parameters.

For a long time econometricians have been aware of the problems that arise when the alternative hypothesis used to construct a test deviates from the data-generating process (DGP). As emphasized by Haavelmo (1944, pp. 65–66), in testing any economic relations, specification of a given fixed set of possible alternatives, called the priori admissible hypothesis, Ω^0, is of fundamental importance. Misspecification of the priori admissible hypotheses was termed as type-III error by Bera and Yoon (1993). Welsh (1996, p. 119) also pointed out a similar concept in the statistics literature. Typically, the alternative hypothesis may be misspecified in three different ways. In the first one, which we shall call 'complete misspecification', the set of assumed alternatives, Ω^0, and the DGP, Ω', say, are mutually exclusive. This happens, for instance, if one tests for serial independence when the DGP has random individual effects but no serial dependence. The second case occurs when the alternative is underspecified in that it is a subset of a more general model representing the DGP, i.e., $\Omega^0 \subset \Omega'$. This happens, for example, when both serial correlation and individual effects are present, but are tested separately (one at a time). The last case is 'overtesting' which results from overspecification, that is, when $\Omega^0 \supset \Omega'$. This can happen when, say, Baltagi and Li (1991) joint test for serial correlation and random individual effects is used when only one effect is present. (For a detailed discussion of the concepts of undertesting and overtesting, see Bera and Jarque, 1982.) In this paper, we study analytically the asymptotic effects of misspecifications on the one-directional and joint tests for serial dependence and random individual effects. These results compliment the simulation results of Baltagi and Li (1995). Then, applying the modified *RS* test developed by Bera and Yoon (1993), we derive a test for random effects (serial correlation) in the presence of serial correlation (random effects). Our tests can be easily implemented using ordinary least-squares (OLS) residuals from the standard linear model for panel data. Our testing strategy is close to that of Hillier (1991) in the sense that we try to partition an overall rejection region to obtain evidence about the direction (or directions) in which the model needs revision.

The plan of the paper is as follows. In the next section we review a general theory of the distribution and adjustment of the standard *RS* statistic in the presence of local misspecification. In Section 3, the general results are specialized to the error component model. In Section 4, we present two empirical illustrations. Section 5 reports the results of an extensive Monte Carlo study. These results, along with the empirical examples, clearly demonstrate the inappropriateness of one-directional tests in identifying the specific source of misspecification(s), and highlight the usefulness of our adjusted tests. Section 6 provides some concluding remarks.

2. Effects of misspecification and a general approach to testing in the presence of a nuisance parameter

Consider a general statistical model represented by the log-likelihood $L(\gamma, \psi, \phi)$. Here, the parameters ψ and ϕ are taken as scalars to conform with our error component model, but in general they could be vectors. Suppose an investigator sets $\phi = \phi_0$ and tests H_0: $\psi = \psi_0$ using the log-likelihood function $L_1(\gamma, \psi) = L(\gamma, \psi, \phi_0)$, where ϕ_0 and ψ_0 are known values. The *RS* statistic for testing H_0 in $L_1(\gamma, \psi)$ will be denoted by RS_ψ. Let us also denote $\theta = (\gamma', \psi', \phi')'$ and $\tilde{\theta} = (\tilde{\gamma}', \psi_0', \phi_0')'$, where $\tilde{\gamma}$ is the maximum-likelihood estimator (MLE) of γ when $\psi = \psi_0$ and $\phi = \phi_0$. The score vector and the information matrix are defined, respectively, as

$$d_a(\theta) = \frac{\partial L(\theta)}{\partial a} \quad \text{for } a = \gamma, \psi, \phi$$

and

$$J(\theta) = -E\left[\frac{1}{n}\frac{\partial^2 L(\theta)}{\partial\theta\partial\theta'}\right] = \begin{bmatrix} J_\gamma & J_{\gamma\psi} & J_{\gamma\phi} \\ J_{\psi\gamma} & J_\psi & J_{\psi\phi} \\ J_{\phi\gamma} & J_{\phi\psi} & J_\phi \end{bmatrix},$$

where n denotes the sample size. If $L_1(\gamma, \psi)$ were the true model, then it is well known that under H_0: $\psi = \psi_0$,

$$RS_\psi = \frac{1}{n} d_\psi(\tilde{\theta})' J_{\psi\cdot\gamma}^{-1}(\tilde{\theta}) d_\psi(\tilde{\theta}) \xrightarrow{D} \chi_1^2(0),$$

where $\xrightarrow{D}$ denotes convergence in distribution and $J_{\psi\cdot\gamma}(0) \equiv J_{\psi\cdot\gamma} = J_{\psi} - J_{\psi\gamma}J_{\gamma}^{-1}J_{\gamma\psi}$. Under H_1: $\psi = \psi_0 + \xi/\sqrt{n}$,

$$RS_{\psi} \xrightarrow{D} \chi_1^2(\lambda_1), \tag{1}$$

where the noncentrality parameter λ_1 is given by $\lambda_1 \equiv \lambda_1(\xi) = \xi' J_{\psi\cdot\gamma}\xi$. Given this set-up, asymptotically the test will have correct size and will be locally optimal. Now suppose that the true log-likelihood function is $L_2(\gamma, \phi)$ so that the alternative $L_1(\gamma, \psi)$ becomes *completely* misspecified. Using a sequence of local values $\phi = \phi_0 + \delta/\sqrt{n}$, Davidson and MacKinnon (1987) and Saikkonen (1989) obtained the asymptotic distribution of RS_{ψ} under $L_2(\gamma, \phi)$ as

$$RS_{\psi} \xrightarrow{D} \chi_1^2(\lambda_2), \tag{2}$$

where the non-centrality parameter λ_2 is given by $\lambda_2 \equiv \lambda_2(\delta) = \delta' J_{\phi\psi\cdot\gamma} J_{\psi\cdot\gamma}^{-1} J_{\psi\phi\cdot\gamma}\delta$ with $J_{\psi\phi\cdot\gamma} = J_{\psi\phi} - J_{\psi\gamma}J_{\gamma}^{-1}J_{\gamma\phi}$. Due to this noncentrality parameter, RS_{ψ} will have power in the model $L(\gamma, \psi, \phi)$ even when $\psi = \psi_0$; and, therefore, the test will have incorrect size. Notice that the crucial quantity is $J_{\psi\phi\cdot\gamma}$ which can be interpreted as the partial covariance between d_{ψ} and d_{ϕ} after eliminating the effect of d_{γ} on d_{ψ} and d_{ϕ}. If $J_{\psi\phi\cdot\gamma} = 0$, then the local presence of the parameter ϕ has no effect on RS_{ψ}.

Turning now to the case of *underspecification*, let the true model be represented by the log-likelihood $L(\gamma, \psi, \phi)$. The alternative $L_1(\gamma, \psi)$ is now underspecified with respect to the nuisance parameter ϕ, leading to the problem of undertesting. In order to derive the asymptotic distribution of RS_{ψ} under the true model $L(\gamma, \psi, \phi)$, we again consider the local departures $\phi = \phi_0 + \delta/\sqrt{n}$ together with $\psi = \psi_0 + \xi/\sqrt{n}$. It can be shown that (see Bera and Yoon, 1991)

$$RS_{\psi} \xrightarrow{D} \chi_1^2(\lambda_3), \tag{3}$$

where

$$\begin{aligned}\lambda_3 \equiv \lambda_3(\xi, \delta) &= (\delta' J_{\phi\psi\cdot\gamma} + \xi' J_{\psi\cdot\gamma}) J_{\psi\cdot\gamma}^{-1} (J_{\psi\phi\cdot\gamma}\delta + J_{\psi\cdot\gamma}\xi)\\ &= \lambda_1(\xi) + \lambda_2(\delta) + 2\xi' J_{\psi\phi\cdot\gamma}\delta.\end{aligned}$$

Using this result, we can compare the asymptotic local power of the underspecified test with that of the optimal test. It turns out that the contaminated noncentrality parameter $\lambda_3(\xi, \delta)$ may actually increase or decrease the power depending on the configuration of the term $\xi' J_{\psi\phi\cdot\gamma}\delta$.

The problem of overtesting occurs when multi-directional joint tests are applied based on an overstated alternative model. Suppose we apply a joint test for testing hypothesis of the form H_0: $\psi = \psi_0$ and $\phi = \phi_0$ using the alternative model $L(\gamma, \psi, \phi)$. Let $RS_{\psi\phi}$ be the joint RS test statistic for H_0. To find the asymptotic distribution of $RS_{\psi\phi}$ under overspecification, i.e., when the DGP is represented by the log-likelihood either $L_1(\gamma, \psi)$ or $L_2(\gamma, \phi)$, let us consider the following result, which could be obtained from (1) by replacing ψ with $[\psi', \phi']'$. Assuming correct specification, i.e., under the true model represented by $L(\gamma, \psi, \phi)$ with $\psi = \psi_0 + \xi/\sqrt{n}$ and $\phi = \phi_0 + \delta/\sqrt{n}$,

$$RS_{\psi\phi} \xrightarrow{D} \chi_2^2(\lambda_4), \tag{4}$$

where

$$\lambda_4 \equiv \lambda_4(\xi, \delta) = [\xi' \quad \delta'] \begin{bmatrix} J_{\psi\cdot\gamma} & J_{\psi\phi\cdot\gamma} \\ J_{\phi\psi\cdot\gamma} & J_{\phi\cdot\gamma} \end{bmatrix} \begin{bmatrix} \xi \\ \delta \end{bmatrix}.$$

Using this fact, we can easily find the asymptotic distribution of the overspecified test. Consider testing H_0: $\psi = \psi_0$ and $\phi = \phi_0$ in $L(\gamma, \psi, \phi)$ where $L_1(\gamma, \psi)$ represents the true model. Under $L_1(\gamma, \psi)$ with $\psi = \psi_0 + \xi/\sqrt{n}$, we obtain by setting $\delta = 0$ in (4)

$$RS_{\psi\phi} \xrightarrow{D} \chi_2^2(\lambda_5), \tag{5}$$

where $\lambda_5 \equiv \lambda_5(\xi) = \xi' J_{\psi\cdot\gamma}\xi$.

Note that the noncentrality parameter $\lambda_5(\xi)$ of the overspecified test $RS_{\psi\phi}$ is identical to $\lambda_1(\xi)$ of the optimal test RS_ψ in (1). Although $\lambda_5 = \lambda_1$, some loss of power is to be expected, as shown in Das Gupta and Perlman (1974), due to the higher degrees of freedom of the joint test $RS_{\psi\phi}$.

Using result (2), Bera and Yoon (1993) suggested a modification to RS_ψ so that the resulting test is valid in the *local* presence of ϕ. The modified statistic is given by

$$RS_\psi^* = \frac{1}{n} [d_\psi(\tilde{\theta}) - J_{\psi\phi\cdot\gamma}(\tilde{\theta})J_{\phi\cdot\gamma}^{-1}(\tilde{\theta})d_\phi(\tilde{\theta})]'[J_{\psi\cdot\gamma}(\tilde{\theta}) - J_{\psi\phi\cdot\gamma}(\tilde{\theta})J_{\phi\cdot\gamma}^{-1}(\tilde{\theta})J_{\phi\cdot\psi\cdot\gamma}(\tilde{\theta})]^{-1}$$
$$[d_\psi(\tilde{\theta}) - J_{\psi\phi\cdot\gamma}(\tilde{\theta})J_{\phi\cdot\gamma}^{-1}(\tilde{\theta})d_\phi(\tilde{\theta})]. \tag{6}$$

This new test essentially adjusts the mean and variance of the standard RS_ψ. Bera and Yoon (1993) proved that under $\psi = \psi_0$ and $\phi = \phi_0 + \delta/\sqrt{n}$ RS_ψ^* has a *central* χ_1^2 distribution. Thus, RS_ψ^* has the same asymptotic null distribution as that of RS_ψ based on the correct specification, thereby producing an asymptotically correct size test under locally misspecified model. Bera and Yoon (1993) further showed that for local misspecification the adjusted test is asymptotically equivalent to Neyman's $C(\alpha)$ test and, therefore, shares the optimality properties of the $C(\alpha)$ test. There is, however, a price to be paid for all these benefits. Under the local alternatives $\psi = \psi_0 + \xi/\sqrt{n}$

$$RS_\psi^* \xrightarrow{D} \chi_1^2(\lambda_6), \tag{7}$$

where $\lambda_6 \equiv \lambda_6(\xi) = \xi'(J_{\psi\cdot\gamma} - J_{\psi\phi\cdot\gamma}J_{\phi\cdot\gamma}^{-1}J_{\phi\psi\cdot\gamma})\xi$. Note that $\lambda_1 - \lambda_6 \geqslant 0$, where λ_1 is given in (1). Result (7) is valid both in the presence or absence of the local misspecification $\phi = \phi_0 + \delta/\sqrt{n}$, since the asymptotic distribution of RS_ψ^* is unaffected by the local departure of ϕ from ϕ_0. Therefore, RS_ψ^* will be less powerful than RS_ψ when there is no misspecification. The quantity

$$\lambda_7 = \lambda_1 - \lambda_6 = \xi' J_{\psi\phi\cdot\gamma}J_{\phi\cdot\gamma}^{-1}J_{\phi\cdot\psi\gamma}\xi \tag{8}$$

can be regarded as the premium we pay for the validity of RS_ψ^* under local misspecification. Two other observations regarding RS_ψ^* are also worth noting. First, RS_ψ^* requires estimation only under the joint null, namely $\psi = \psi_0$ and $\phi = \phi_0$. Given the full specification of the model $L(\gamma, \psi, \phi)$ it is, of course, possible to derive a RS test for $\psi = \psi_0$ in the presence of ϕ. However, that requires MLE of ϕ which could be difficult to obtain in some cases. Second, when $J_{\psi\phi\cdot\gamma} = 0$, $RS_\psi^* = RS_\psi$. In practice this is a very simple condition to check. As mentioned earlier, if this condition is true, RS_ψ is an asymptotically valid test in the local presence of ϕ.

3. Tests for error component model

We consider the following one-way error component model introduced by Lillard and Willis (1978), which combines random individual effects and first-order autocorrelation in the disturbance term

$$y_{it} = x_{it}'\beta + u_{it}, \quad i = 1, 2, \ldots, N, \; t = 1, 2, \ldots, T,$$

$$u_{it} = \mu_i + v_{it},$$

$$v_{it} = \rho v_{i,t-1} + \varepsilon_{it}, \quad |\rho| < 1, \tag{9}$$

where β is a $(k \times 1)$ vector of parameters including the intercept, $\mu_i \sim IID\text{N}(0, \sigma_\mu^2)$ is a random individual component, and $\varepsilon_{it} \sim IID\text{N}(0, \sigma_\varepsilon^2)$. The μ_i and v_{it} are assumed to be independent of each other with $v_{i,0} \sim \text{N}(0, \sigma_\varepsilon^2/(1-\rho^2))$. N and T denote the number of individual units and the number of time periods, respectively. For the validity of the tests discussed here, we need to assume that the regularity conditions of Andereson and Hsiao (1982) are satisfied. Also, testing for σ_μ^2 involves the issue of the parameter being at the boundary. Although for the nonregular problem of testing at the boundary value, both the likelihood ratio and Wald test statistics do not have their usual asymptotic chi-squared distribution, the RS test statistic does [see, e.g., Bera et al., 1998].

Let us set $\theta = (\gamma, \psi, \phi)' = (\sigma_\varepsilon^2, \sigma_\mu^2, \rho)'$. Consider the problem of testing for the existence of the random effects (H_0: $\psi = 0$) in the presence of serial correlation ($\phi \neq 0$). To derive our RS_ψ^*, which will now be denoted as RS_μ^*, we note that it is sufficient to consider the scores and the information matrix evaluated at

$\theta_0 = (\gamma_0, \psi_0, \phi_0)' = (\sigma_\varepsilon^2, 0, 0)'$ because of the block-diagonality of the information matrix involving the β and θ parameters. These quantities have been derived in Baltagi and Li (1991):

$$\frac{\partial L}{\partial \sigma_\varepsilon^2} = d_\gamma = -\frac{NT}{2\sigma_\varepsilon^2} + \frac{u'u}{2\sigma_\varepsilon^4},$$

$$\frac{\partial L}{\partial \sigma_\mu^2} = d_\mu \equiv d_\psi = -\frac{NT}{2\sigma_\varepsilon^2}\left[1 - \frac{u'(I_N \otimes e_T e_T')u}{u'u}\right],$$

$$\frac{\partial \mu}{\partial \rho} = d_\rho \equiv d_\phi = NT\left(\frac{u'u_{-1}}{u'u}\right), \tag{10}$$

where I_N is an identity matrix of dimension N, e_T is a vector of ones of dimension T, $u' = (u_{11}, \ldots, u_{1T}, \ldots, u_{N1}, \ldots, u_{NT})$ and u_{-1} is an $(NT \times 1)$ vector containing $u_{i,t-1}$. To simplify notation, here the score for the parameter σ_μ^2 is denoted as d_μ. We will continue to follow this convention for the elements of the information matrix and for expressing our test statistics. Denoting $J = (NT)^{-1}\mathrm{E}(-\partial^2 L/\partial\theta\partial\theta')$ evaluated at θ_0, we have

$$J = \frac{1}{2\sigma_\varepsilon^4}\begin{bmatrix} 1 & 1 & 0 \\ 1 & T & \dfrac{2(T-1)\sigma_\varepsilon^2}{T} \\ 0 & \dfrac{2(T-1)\sigma_\varepsilon^2}{T} & \dfrac{2(T-1)\sigma_\varepsilon^4}{T} \end{bmatrix}.$$

This implies that

$$J_{\mu\rho\cdot\gamma} = J_{\psi\phi\cdot\gamma} = \frac{T-1}{T\sigma_\varepsilon^2},$$

$$J_{\mu\cdot\gamma} = J_{\psi\cdot\gamma} = \frac{T-1}{2\sigma_\varepsilon^4},$$

$$J_{\rho\cdot\gamma} = J_{\phi\cdot\gamma} = \frac{T-1}{T}, \tag{11}$$

where γ stands for the parameter σ_ε^2. Since $J_{\mu\rho\cdot\gamma} > 0$, indicating the asymptotic positive correlation between the scores d_μ and d_ρ, the one-directional test for the random effects reported in Breusch and Pagan (1980) is not valid asymptotically in the presence of serial correlation. For this case our RS_μ^* can be easily constructed, from Eq. (6), as

$$RS_\mu^* = \frac{NT(A+2B)^2}{2(T-1)(1-(2/T))}, \tag{12}$$

where A and B denote, as in Baltagi and Li (1991),

$$A = 1 - \frac{\tilde{u}'(I_N \otimes e_T e_T')\tilde{u}}{\tilde{u}'\tilde{u}}$$

and

$$B = \frac{\tilde{u}'\tilde{u}_{-1}}{\tilde{u}'\tilde{u}}.$$

Note that $\tilde{u}$ are the OLS residuals from the standard linear model $y_{it} = x_{it}'\beta + u_{it}$ without the random effects and serial correlation. Also notice that A and B are closely related to the estimates of the scores d_μ and d_ρ, respectively. It is easy to see that the RS_μ^* adjusts the conventional RS statistic given in Breusch and Pagan (1980), i.e.,

$$RS_\mu = \frac{NTA^2}{2(T-1)}, \tag{13}$$

by correcting the mean and variance of the score d_μ for its asymptotic correlation with d_ρ.

To see the behavior of RS_μ let us first consider the case of complete misspecification, i.e., $\sigma_\mu^2 = 0$ but $\rho \neq 0$. Using (2) and (11), the noncentrality parameter of RS_μ for this case is

$$\lambda_2(\rho) = \delta' J_{\rho\mu\cdot\gamma} J_{\mu\cdot\gamma}^{-1} J_{\mu\rho\cdot\gamma}\delta = 2\rho^2 \frac{T-1}{T^2}, \tag{14}$$

where for simplicity we use ρ in place of δ. In this case, the use or RS_μ will lead to rejection of the null hypothesis $\sigma_\mu^2 = 0$ too often. For local departures RS_μ^* will not have this drawback when $\rho \neq 0$ since under $\sigma_\mu^2 = 0$, RS_μ^* will have a *central* χ^2 distribution. Let us now consider the underspecification situation i.e., when we have both $\sigma_\mu^2 > 0$ and $\rho \neq 0$, and we use RS_μ to test H_0: $\sigma_\mu^2 = 0$. From (1), (3) and (11), we see that the change in the noncentrality parameter of RS_μ due to nonzero ρ is given by

$$\lambda_3(\xi, \delta) - \lambda_1(\xi) = \lambda_2(\rho) + 2\xi' J_{\mu\rho\cdot\gamma}\delta = \rho^2 \frac{2(T-1)}{T^2} + 2\sigma_\mu^2 \rho \frac{T-1}{T\sigma_\varepsilon^2}$$

$$= \frac{2(T-1)}{T}\left[\frac{\rho^2}{T} + \frac{\sigma_\mu^2 \rho}{\sigma_\varepsilon^2}\right], \tag{15}$$

where we use σ_μ^2 in place of ξ. From (15), it is easy to see that when $\rho > 0$, the presence of autocorrelation will add power to RS_μ; but when $\rho < 0$ it can loose power if the individual effect is very high and σ_ε^2 is low. In this situation, the noncentrality parameter of RS_μ^* is not affected. From (7) and (11), the noncentrality parameter of RS_μ^* under $\sigma_\mu^2 > 0$ and $\rho \neq 0$, can be written as

$$\begin{aligned}\lambda_6 \equiv \lambda_6(\sigma_\mu^2) &= \sigma_\mu^4(J_{\mu\cdot\gamma} - J_{\mu\rho\cdot\gamma}J_{\rho\cdot\gamma}^{-1}J_{\rho\mu\cdot\gamma}) \\ &= \sigma_\mu^4\left[\frac{T-1}{2\sigma_\varepsilon^4} - \frac{(T-1)^2}{T^2\sigma_\varepsilon^4}\frac{T}{T-1}\right] \\ &= \frac{\sigma_\mu^4}{\sigma_\varepsilon^4}(T-1)\left(\frac{1}{2}-\frac{1}{T}\right),\end{aligned} \tag{16}$$

which does not depend on ρ. There is, however, a cost in applying RS_μ^* when ρ is indeed zero. From (8) the cost is

$$\lambda_7 \equiv \lambda_7(\sigma_\mu^2) = \sigma_\mu^4 J_{\mu\rho\cdot\gamma}J_{\rho\cdot\gamma}^{-1}J_{\rho\mu\cdot\gamma} = \frac{\sigma_\mu^4}{\sigma_\varepsilon^4}\frac{T-1}{T}. \tag{17}$$

Note that this cost is present only under $\sigma_\mu^2 > 0$. That is, there is a cost only in terms of the power of RS_μ^*; the size is unaffected. Later we will provide an interesting interpretation of this cost of RS_μ^* in terms of the behavior of the unadjusted test RS_ρ under $\sigma_\mu^2 > 0$.

As mentioned before, Baltagi and Li (1995) derived a RS test for serial correlation in the presence of random individual effects. Naturally, the test requires MLE of σ_μ^2. Our procedure gives a simple test for serial correlation in the random effects model. In this situation RS_ρ^* is obtained simply by switching σ_μ^2 and ρ to yield

$$RS_\rho^* = \frac{NT^2(B + (A/T))^2}{(T-1)(1-(2/T))}. \tag{18}$$

If we assume that the random effects are absent throughout, then RS_ρ^* in (18) reduces to

$$RS_\rho = \frac{NT^2B^2}{T-1}. \tag{19}$$

This conventional RS statistic (19) is also given in Baltagi and Li (1991).

As we have done for RS_μ, we can also study the performance of RS_ρ under various misspecifications. When there is complete misspecification, i.e., when $\rho = 0$ but $\sigma_\mu^2 > 0$, the noncentrality parameter of RS_ρ is

$$\lambda_2(\sigma_\mu^2) = \xi' J_{\mu\rho\cdot\gamma}J_{\rho\cdot\gamma}^{-1}J_{\rho\mu\cdot\gamma}\xi = \frac{\sigma_\mu^4}{\sigma_\varepsilon^4}\frac{T-1}{T}, \tag{20}$$

where we have used σ_μ^2 in place of ξ. Therefore, RS_ρ will reject H_0: $\rho = 0$ too often when $\sigma_\mu^2 > 0$. Similarly, when there is underspecification, i.e, $\rho \neq 0$ with $\sigma_\mu^2 > 0$, the change in the noncentrality parameter due to the presence of the random effect, is

$$\lambda_3(\xi,\delta) - \lambda_1(\delta) = \lambda_2(\sigma_\mu^2) + 2\delta' J_{\rho\mu\cdot\gamma}\xi$$
$$= \frac{T-1}{T}\frac{\sigma_\mu^2}{\sigma_\varepsilon^2}\left[\frac{\sigma_\mu^2}{\sigma_\varepsilon^2} + 2\rho\right]. \tag{21}$$

Therefore, we have an increase in (or a possible loss of) power when $\rho > 0$ (or $\rho < 0$). The noncentrality parameter of RS_ρ^* will not be affected at all under $\sigma_\mu^2 > 0$. On the other hand, we do, however, pay a penalty when $\sigma_\mu^2 = 0$ and we use the adjusted test RS_ρ^*. The penalty is

$$\lambda_7(\rho) = \rho^2 J_{\rho\mu\cdot\gamma} J_{\mu\cdot\gamma}^{-1} J_{\mu\rho\cdot\gamma} = 2\rho^2 \frac{T-1}{T^2}. \tag{22}$$

Due to this factor the power of RS_ρ^* will be somewhat less than that of RS_ρ when σ_μ^2 is indeed zero; the size of RS_ρ^*, however, remains unaffected. It is very interesting to note that

$$\lambda_7(\rho) = \lambda_2(\rho), \tag{23}$$

given in (14). Similarly, from (17) and (20)

$$\lambda_7(\sigma_\mu^2) = \lambda_2(\sigma_\mu^2). \tag{24}$$

An implication of (23) is that the cost of using RS_ρ^* when $\sigma_\mu^2 = 0$ is the same as the cost of using RS_μ when $\rho \neq 0$. Similarly, (24) implies that the loss in the noncentrality parameter of RS_μ^* when $\rho = 0$ is equal to the unwanted gain in the noncentrality parameter of RS_ρ when $\sigma_\mu^2 > 0$. We will explain these seemingly unintuitive phenomena after we find a relationship among the four statistics, RS_μ^*, RS_μ, RS_ρ^*, and RS_ρ. It should be noted that the equalities of Eqs. (23) and (24) are not specific for the error component model, and they hold in general. This can be seen by comparing $\lambda_2(\delta)$ below (2) with λ_7 in Eq. (8), where ψ swaps position with ϕ and ξ is replaced by δ.

Baltagi and Li (1991, 1995) derived a joint RS test for serial correlation and random individual effects which is given by

$$RS_{\mu\rho} = \frac{NT^2}{2(T-1)(T-2)}[A^2 + 4AB + 2TB^2]. \tag{25}$$

Under the joint null $\sigma_\mu^2 = \rho = 0$, $RS_{\mu\rho}$ is asymptotically distributed as χ_2^2. Use of this will result in a loss of power compared with the proper one-directional tests when only one of the two forms of misspecification is present, as we noted while discussing (5). For example, when $\rho = 0$ and $\sigma_\mu^2 > 0$, the noncentrality parameter of both RS_μ and $RS_{\mu\rho}$ is (see (1) and (5)).

$$\lambda_1(\sigma_\mu^2) = \sigma_\mu^4 J_{\mu\cdot\gamma} = \frac{\sigma_\mu^4}{\sigma_\varepsilon^4}\frac{T-1}{2}. \tag{26}$$

Since for RS_μ and $RS_{\mu\rho}$ we will use, respectively, χ_1^2 and χ_2^2 critical values, $RS_{\mu\rho}$ will be less powerful. An interesting result follows from (12), (13), (18), (19) and (25), namely,

$$RS_{\mu\rho} = RS_\mu^* + RS_\rho = RS_\mu + RS_\rho^*, \tag{27}$$

i.e., the two directional RS test for σ_μ^2 and ρ can be decomposed into the sum of the adjusted one-directional test of one type of alternative and the unadjusted form for the other one. Using (27) we can easily explain some of our earlier observations. First, consider the identities in (23) and (24). From (27), we have

$$RS_\rho - RS_\rho^* = RS_\mu - RS_\mu^*. \tag{28}$$

Let us consider the case of $\sigma_\mu^2 = 0$ and $\rho \neq 0$. Then the left-hand side of (28) represents the 'penalty' of using RS_ρ^* (instead of RS_ρ) while the right-hand side amounts to the 'cost' of using RS_μ. Eq. (28) implies that these penalty and cost should be the same, as noted in (23). A reverse argument explains (24). Secondly, the local presence of ρ (or σ_μ^2) has no effect on RS_μ^* (or RS_ρ^*); therefore, from (5) and (27), we can clearly see why the noncentrality parameter of $RS_{\mu\rho}$ will be equal to that of RS_ρ (or RS_μ) when $\sigma_\mu^2 = 0$ (or $\rho = 0$).

So far we have considered only two-sided tests for H_0: $\sigma_\mu^2 = 0$. Since $\sigma_\mu^2 \geqslant 0$, it is natural to consider one-sided tests, and it is expected that it will lead to more powerful tests. Within our framework, it is easy to construct appropriate one-sided tests by taking the *signed* square root of our earlier two-sided statistics, RS_μ and RS_μ^*. We will denote these one-sided test statistics as RSO_μ and RSO_μ^*, and they are given by

$$RSO_\mu = -\sqrt{\frac{NT}{2(T-1)}}\,A$$

and

$$RSO_\mu^* = -\sqrt{\frac{NT}{2(T-1)(1-2/T)}}\,(A-2B).$$

The negative sign is due to the fact that $\partial L/\partial\sigma_\mu^2 = -(NT/2\sigma_\varepsilon^2)A$ and the one-sided tests are based on this score function or its adjustment. Under H_0: $\sigma_\mu^2 = 0$, the adjusted test RSO_μ^* will be asymptotically distributed as N(0, 1). The unadjusted RSO_μ will be asymptotically normal but with a nonzero mean $\sqrt{2(T-1)/T^2}\rho$ when $\rho \neq 0$ as can be seen from (14). The statistic RSO_μ^* was first suggested by Honda (1985) and its finite sample properties have been investigated by Baltagi et al. (1992). Similar one-sided versions for RS_ρ and RS_ρ^* can also be used. However, in practice, the direction of serial correlation is rarely known for sure for the one-directional tests to be more powerful. It is easy to see that the one directional tests will not satisfy the equality in (28). In our empirical illustrations below and in the Monte Carlo study we also use these one-sided tests and study their comparative finite sample performance.

4. Empirical illustrations

In this section we present two empirical examples that illustrate the usefulness of the proposed tests. The first is based on a data set used by Greene (1983, 2000). The equation to be estimated is a simple, log-linear cost function:

$$\ln C_{it} = \beta_0 + \beta_1 \ln R_{it} + u_{it},$$

where R_{it} is measured as output of firm i in year t in millions of kilowatt-hours, and C_{it} is the total generation cost in millions of dollars, $i = 1, 2, \ldots, 6$, and $t = 1, 2, 3, 4$. The second example is based on the well-known Grunfeld (1958) and Grunfeld and Griliches (1960) investment data set for five US manufacturing firms measured over 20 years which is frequently used to illustrate panel issues. It has been used in the illustration of misspecification tests in the error-component model in Baltagi et al. (1992), and in recent books such as those by Baltagi (1995, p. 20) and Greene (2000, p. 592). The equation to be estimated is a panel model of firm investment using the real value of the firm and the real value of capital stock as explanatory variables:

$$I_{it} = \beta_0 + \beta_1 F_{it} + \beta_2 C_{it} + u_{it},$$

where I_{it} denotes real gross investment for firm i in period t, F_{it} is the real value of the firm and C_{it} is the real value of the capital stock, $i = 1, 2, \ldots, 5$, and $t = 1, 2, \ldots, 20$.

We estimated the parameters of both models by OLS and implemented the following seven tests based on OLS residuals: the Breusch–Pagan test for random effects (RS_μ), the proposed modified version (RS_μ^*), the LM serial correlation test (RS_ρ), the corresponding modified version (RS_ρ^*), the joint test for serial correlation and random effects ($RS_{\mu\rho}$), and the two one-sided tests for random effects (RSO_μ and RSO_μ^*). The test statistics for both examples are presented in Table 1; the p-values are given in parentheses.

All of the test statistics were computed individually, and the equality in (27) is satisfied for both data sets. In the example based on Greene's data the unmodified tests for serial correlation (RS_ρ) and for random effects (RS_μ to some extent, and RSO_μ quite strongly) reject the respective null hypothesis of no serial correlation and no random effects, and the omnibus test rejects the joint null. But our modified tests suggest that in this example the problem seems to be serial correlation rather the presence of both effects. For Grunfeld's data, applications of our modified tests point to the presence of the other effect. The unmodified tests soundly reject their corresponding null hypotheses. The modified versions of the random effect tests (RS_μ^* and RSO_μ^*) also reject the null but the modified serial correlation test (RS_ρ^*) barely rejects the null at the 5% significance level. It is interesting to note the substantial reduction of the autocorrelation test statistic, from 73.351 to 3.712. So in this example the misspecification can be thought to come from the presence of random effects

Table 1
Empirical illustration. Tests for random effects and serial correlation[a]

Data	RS_μ	RS_μ^*	RS_ρ	RS_ρ^*	$RS_{\mu\rho}$	RSO_μ	RSO_μ^*
Greene	5.872	0.269	15.569	9.966	15.838	2.423	0.518
	(0.015)	(0.604)	(0.000)	(0.002)	(0.000)	(0.007)	(0.3020)
Grunfeld	453.822	384.183	73.351	3.712	457.535	21.303	19.605
	(0.000)	(0.000)	(0.000)	(0.054)	(0.000)	(0.000)	(0.000)

[a] p-values are given in parenthesis.

rather than serial correlation. As expected, the joint test statistic is highly significant.

In spite of the small sample size of the data sets, these examples seem to illustrate clearly the main points of the paper: the proposed modified versions of the test are more informative than a test for serial correlation or random effect that ignores the presence of the other effect. In the first case, serial correlation spuriously induces rejection of the no-random effects hypothesis, and in the second case the opposite happens: the presence of a random effect induces rejection of the no-serial correlation hypothesis. The joint test $RS_{\mu\rho}$ rejects the joint null but is not informative about the direction of the misspecification.

$RS_{\mu\rho}$ provides a correct measure of the joint effects of individual component and serial correlation. The main problem is how to decompose this measure to get an idea about the true departure(s). From a practical standpoint if $RS_{\mu\rho} = RS_\mu + RS_\rho$ does not hold, that should be an indication of the presence of an interaction between random effects and serial correlation; and the unadjusted statistics RS_μ and RS_ρ will be contaminated by the presence of other departures. For example, for the Grunfeld data

$$RS_\mu + RS_\rho - RS_{\mu\rho} = RS_\mu - RS_\mu^* = RS_\rho - RS_\rho^* = 69.638.$$

This provides a measure of the interaction between σ_μ^2 and ρ, and is also equal to the correction needed for each unadjusted test.

It is important to emphasize that the implementation of the modified tests is based solely on OLS residuals. It could be argued that a more efficient test procedure could be based on the estimation of a general model that allows for both serial correlation and random effects, and then the tests of the hypotheses of no-serial correlation and no-random effects as restrictions on this general model (either jointly or individually) could be carried out. But this would require the maximization of a likelihood function whose computational tractability is substantially more involved than computing simple OLS residuals. Hsiao (1986, p. 55) commented that the "computation of the MLE is very complicated". For more on the estimation issues of the error component model with serial correlation see Baltagi (1995, pp. 18–19), Majunder and King (1999) and Phillips (1999).

5. Monte Carlo results

In this section we present the results of a Monte Carlo study to investigate the finite sample behavior of the tests. To facilitate comparison with existing results we follow a structure similar to the one adopted by Baltagi et al. (1992) and Baltagi and Li (1995).

The model was set as a special case of (9):

$$y_{it} = \alpha + \beta x_{it} + u_{it}, \quad i = 1, 2, \ldots, N, \; t = 1, 2, \ldots, T,$$

$$u_{it} = \mu_i + v_{it},$$

$$v_{it} = \rho v_{i,t-1} + \varepsilon_{it}, \quad |\rho| < 1,$$

where $\alpha = 5$ and $\beta = 0.5$. The independent variable x_{it} was generated following Nerlove (1971):

$$x_{it} = 0.1t + 0.5x_{i,t-1} + \omega_{it},$$

where ω_{it} has the uniform distribution on $[-0.5, 0.5]$. Initial values were chosen as in Baltagi et al. (1992). Let σ^2, σ_μ^2, σ_v^2 and σ_ε^2 represent the variances of u_{it}, μ_i, v_{it} and ε_{it}, respectively, and let $\tau = \sigma_\mu^2/\sigma^2$, which represents the "strength" of the random effects. Here, $\sigma^2 = \sigma_\mu^2 + \sigma_v^2$, and we set $\sigma^2 = 20.\tau$ and ρ were allowed to take seven different values (0, 0.05, 0.1, 0.2, 0.4, 0.6, 0.8), and three different sample sizes (N, T) were considered: (25, 10), (25, 20) and (50, 10). Since for each i, v_{it} follows an AR(1) process, $\sigma_v^2 = \sigma_\varepsilon^2/(1-\rho^2)$. Then, according to this structure, the random effect term and the innovation were generated as

$$\mu_i \sim IID\mathrm{N}(0, 20(1-\tau)),$$

$$\varepsilon_{it} \sim IID\mathrm{N}(0, 20(1-\tau)(1-\rho^2)).$$

For each sample size the model described above was generated 1000 times under different parameter settings. Therefore, the maximum standard errors of the estimates of the size and powers would be $\sqrt{0.5(1-0.5)/1000} \simeq 0.015$. In each replication the parameters of the model were estimated using OLS, and seven test statistics, namely, RS_μ, RS_μ^*, RS_ρ, RS_ρ^*, $RS_{\mu\rho}$, RSO_μ and RSO_μ^* were computed. The tables and graphs are based on the nominal size of 0.05. Our simulation study was quite extensive; we carried out experiments for all possible parameter combinations for the three sample sizes. We present here only a portion of our extensive tables and graphs; the rest is available from the authors upon request.

Calculated statistics under $\tau = \rho = 0$ were used to estimate the empirical sizes of the tests and to study the closeness of their distributions to χ^2 through Q–Q plots and the Kolmogorov–Smirnov test. From Table 2 we note that both RS_μ and RS_μ^* have similar empirical sizes, but these are below the nominal size 0.05 for $N = 25$, $T = 10$ and $N = 50$, $T = 10$. The results for RS_ρ, RS_ρ^*, $RS_{\mu\rho}$ are not

Table 2
Empirical size of tests. (nominal size = 0.05)

	Tests						
(N, T)	RS_μ	RS_μ^*	RS_ρ	RS_ρ^*	$RS_{\mu\rho}$	RSO_μ	RSO_μ^*
(25, 10)	0.047	0.048	0.087	0.072	0.062	0.045	0.051
(25, 20)	0.050	0.051	0.060	0.056	0.057	0.052	0.058
(50, 10)	0.043	0.040	0.065	0.062	0.059	0.046	0.053

good. All of them reject the null too frequently, but the empirical sizes improve as we increase N or T. Comparing the performances of RS_ρ and RS_ρ^*, we notice that RS_ρ^* has somewhat better size properties. As expected, the one-sided tests RSO_μ and RSO_μ^* have larger empirical sizes than their two-sided counterparts. Overall, except for a couple of cases, the size performance of all tests are within one standard errors of the nominal size 0.05.

The results of Table 2 are consistent with the Q–Q plots in Fig. 1 for $N = 25$, $T = 10$. To save space figures for the other two combinations of (N, T) are not included. We also do not present the figures for the joint and one-sided tests, since they resemble those reported for the other tests. From the plots note that the empirical distributions of the test statistics diverge from that of the χ_1^2 at the right tail parts. For RS_μ and RS_μ^* the points are below the 45° line, particularly for the high values, and that leads to sizes being *below* 0.05 as we just noted from Table 2. However, the number of points (out of 1000) that are far away from the 45° line at the tail parts are not many. For RS_ρ and RS_ρ^* we observe a higher degree of departure from the 45° line in the opposite direction, and this leads to much higher sizes of the tests. Results from the Kolmogorov–Smirnov test, not reported here, accept the null hypothesis of the *overall* distribution being the same as χ^2 for the first five, and standard normal for the last two statistics. For the true sizes of the tests, however, it is only the tail part, not the overall distribution, that matters.

Let us now turn into the performance of tests in terms of power. For $N = 25$ and $T = 10$, the estimated rejection probabilities of the tests are reported in Table 3, and are also illustrated in Figs. 2(a)–(d). The results for $\tau = \rho = 0.08$ are not reported since in most cases the rejection probabilities were one or very close to one. Moreover, our adjusted tests are designed for locally misspecified alternatives close to $\tau = \rho = 0.0$, and the main objective of our Monte Carlo study is to investigate the performance of our suggested tests in the neighborhood of $\tau = \rho = 0.0$. Let us first concentrate on RS_μ, RS_μ^*, RSO_μ and RSO_μ^* which are designed to test the null hypothesis H_0: $\sigma_\mu^2 = 0$. When $\rho = 0$, RS_μ and RSO_μ are, respectively, the two- and one-sided optimal tests. This is clearly evident looking at all the rows in Table 3 with $\rho = 0$; RSO_μ has the highest

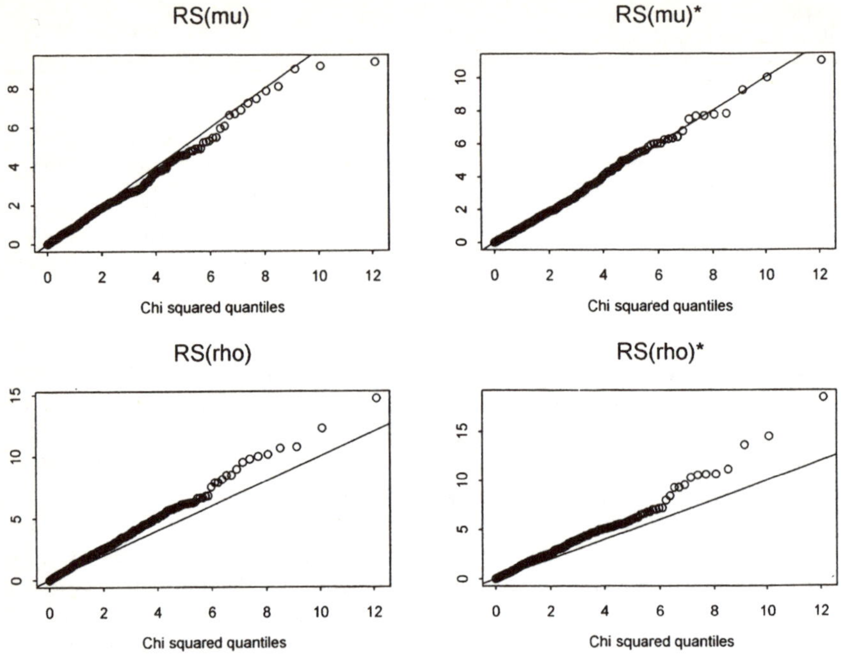

Fig. 1. Q–Q plots. Sample size (25, 10).

powers among all the tests and RS_μ just trails behind it. The power of RS_μ^* is less than that of RS_μ when $\rho = 0$. The losses in power are, however, not very large, as can also be seen from Fig. 2(a). When τ exceeds 0.2 (or σ_μ^2 exceeds 4, since we set $\sigma_\mu^2 = 20\tau$) both tests have power equal to 1. The amount of loss in using RS_μ^* when $\rho = 0$ was characterized by (17) in terms of the decrease in the noncentrality parameter. That loss increases with $\tau(\sigma_\mu^2)$. However, the overall power of RS_μ^* is guided by the noncentrality parameter in (16):

$$\lambda_6(\sigma_\mu^2) = \frac{\sigma_\mu^4}{2\sigma_\varepsilon^4}(T-1) - \frac{\sigma_\mu^4}{\sigma_\varepsilon^4}\frac{T-1}{T},$$

where the second term is the amount of penalty in using RS_μ^* when $\rho = 0$, and it is given in (17). Since the first term dominates, the relative value of the loss is negligible. While RS_μ^* and RSO_μ^* do not sustain much loss in power when $\rho = 0$, we notice some problems in RS_μ and RSO_μ when $\sigma_\mu^2 = 0$ but $\rho \neq 0$. RS_μ and RSO_μ reject H_0: $\sigma_\mu^2 = 0$ too frequently. For example, when $\tau = 0$ (i.e., $\sigma_\mu^2 = 0$) and $\rho = 0.4$, RS_μ and RSO_μ have rejection probabilities 0.847 and 0.888, respectively. For other values of ρ the proportion of rejections of $\sigma_\mu^2 = 0$ (when it is

Table 3
Estimated rejection probabilities of different tests. Sample size: $N = 25$; $T = 10$

τ	ρ	RS_μ	RS_μ^*	RS_ρ	RS_ρ^*	$RS_{\mu\rho}$	RSO_μ	RSO_μ^*
0.00	0.00	0.047	0.048	0.087	0.072	0.062	0.045	0.051
0.00	0.05	0.053	0.050	0.143	0.141	0.122	0.085	0.039
0.00	0.10	0.123	0.080	0.381	0.333	0.342	0.187	0.061
0.00	0.20	0.322	0.158	0.869	0.788	0.818	0.416	0.128
0.00	0.40	0.847	0.325	1.000	0.999	1.000	0.888	0.354
0.00	0.60	0.998	0.776	1.000	1.000	1.000	0.998	0.804
0.05	0.00	0.344	0.298	0.153	0.072	0.308	0.435	0.373
0.05	0.05	0.442	0.301	0.351	0.118	0.423	0.530	0.402
0.05	0.10	0.514	0.296	0.598	0.326	0.605	0.591	0.359
0.05	0.20	0.734	0.364	0.949	0.789	0.932	0.776	0.428
0.05	0.40	0.955	0.576	1.000	1.000	1.000	0.971	0.641
0.05	0.60	0.998	0.867	1.000	1.000	1.000	1.000	0.890
0.10	0.00	0.752	0.691	0.371	0.047	0.702	0.808	0.760
0.10	0.05	0.759	0.630	0.563	0.123	0.728	0.818	0.707
0.10	0.10	0.830	0.644	0.792	0.301	0.852	0.876	0.723
0.10	0.20	0.907	0.648	0.990	0.794	0.980	0.937	0.710
0.10	0.40	0.988	0.790	1.000	0.999	1.000	0.991	0.830
0.10	0.60	1.000	0.933	1.000	1.000	1.000	1.000	0.949
0.20	0.00	0.983	0.968	0.802	0.042	0.977	0.988	0.982
0.20	0.05	0.977	0.962	0.906	0.139	0.981	0.984	0.973
0.20	0.10	0.987	0.967	0.966	0.300	0.988	0.992	0.975
0.20	0.20	0.991	0.942	0.997	0.785	0.998	0.994	0.958
0.20	0.40	0.999	0.954	1.000	0.999	1.000	0.999	0.964
0.20	0.60	1.000	0.990	1.000	1.000	1.000	1.000	0.992
0.40	0.00	1.000	1.000	0.995	0.045	1.000	1.000	1.000
0.40	0.05	0.999	0.999	0.999	0.125	0.999	1.000	0.999
0.40	0.10	1.000	1.000	0.999	0.321	1.000	1.000	1.000
0.40	0.20	1.000	1.000	1.000	0.774	1.000	1.000	1.000
0.40	0.40	1.000	1.000	1.000	0.998	1.000	1.000	1.000
0.40	0.60	1.000	1.000	1.000	1.000	1.000	1.000	1.000
0.60	0.00	1.000	1.000	1.000	0.045	1.000	1.000	1.000
0.60	0.05	1.000	1.000	1.000	0.156	1.000	1.000	1.000
0.60	0.10	1.000	1.000	1.000	0.311	1.000	1.000	1.000
0.60	0.20	1.000	1.000	1.000	0.739	1.000	1.000	1.000
0.60	0.40	1.000	1.000	1.000	0.998	1.000	1.000	1.000
0.60	0.60	1.000	1.000	1.000	1.000	1.000	1.000	1.000

true) for RS_μ can be seen in Fig. 2(b). As we discussed in Section 3, this unwanted rejection probabilities is due to the noncentrality parameter $\lambda_2(\rho)$ in (14), which is "purely" a function of the degree of departure of ρ from zero. RS_μ^* and RSO_μ^* also have some unwanted rejection probabilities but the problem is less severe.

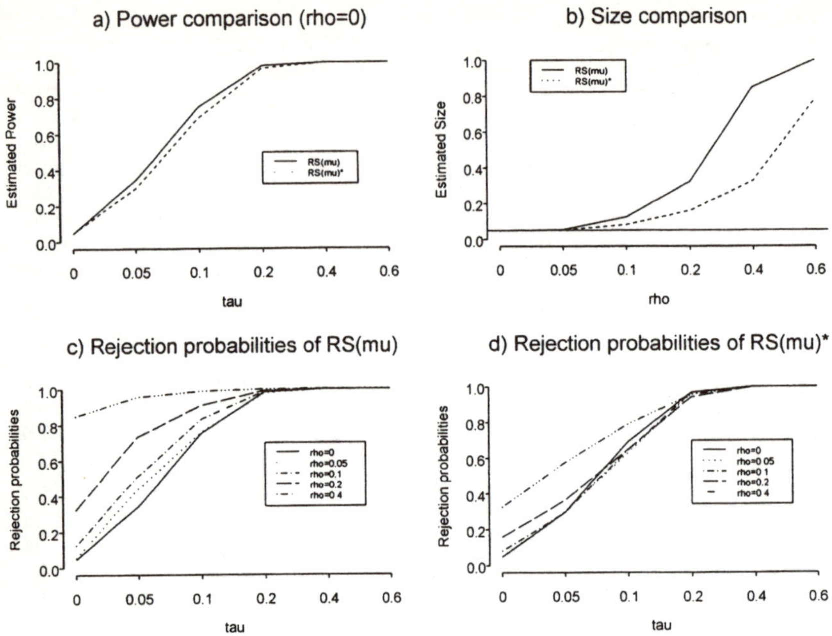

Fig. 2. Tests for random effects. Sample size (25, 10).

For the above case of $\tau = 0$ and $\rho = 0.4$ the rejection probabilities for RS_μ^* and RSO_μ^* are, respectively, 0.325 and 0.354. Fig. 2(b) gives the power of RS_μ^* when $\tau = 0$ for different values of ρ. As we mentioned earlier, RS_μ^* and RSO_μ^* are designed to be robust only under local misspecification, i.e, for low values of ρ. From that point of view, they do a very good job – their performances deteriorate only when ρ takes high values. Now by directly comparing the one- and two-sided tests for H_0: $\sigma_\mu^2 = 0$, we note that the former has higher rejection probabilities except for a few cases when $\tau = 0.0$. For these cases the score $\partial L/\partial \sigma_\mu^2$ takes large negative values and that leads to acceptance of H_0 when one-sided tests are used and rejection of H_0 when we use the two-sided test. Note that $RSO_\mu = \text{sign}\sqrt{RS_\mu}$ rejects H_0 if $RSO_\mu > 1.645$ while using RS_μ rejection occurs if $RS_\mu > 3.84$ which exceeds 1.645^2.

From Table 3 and Fig. 2(c), we note that when $\tau > 0$, an increase in $\rho(> 0)$ enhances the rejection probabilities of RS_μ. For example, when $\tau = 0.05$ the rejection probabilities of RS_μ for $\rho = 0.0$ and 0.2 are, respectively, 0.344 and 0.734. This can be explained using the expression (15), which gives the changes in the noncentrality parameter of RS_μ due to ρ. From (16) we see that the noncentrality parameter of RS_μ^* does not depend on ρ. This result is, of course,

Table 4
Estimated rejection probabilities of different tests for negative ρ

τ	ρ	RS_μ	RS_μ^*	RS_ρ	RS_ρ^*	$RS_{\rho.\mu}$
Sample size: $N = 25$; $T = 10$						
0.00	− 0.05	0.039	0.031	0.173	0.170	0.118
0.00	− 0.10	0.044	0.019	0.396	0.346	0.285
0.00	− 0.20	0.162	0.016	0.902	0.857	0.833
0.00	− 0.40	0.573	0.048	1.000	1.000	1.000
0.05	− 0.05	0.254	0.289	0.097	0.130	0.269
0.05	− 0.10	0.202	0.340	0.184	0.314	0.365
0.05	− 0.20	0.097	0.369	0.680	0.830	0.770
0.05	− 0.40	0.039	0.679	0.997	1.000	1.000
Sample size: $N = 25$; $T = 20$						
0.00	− 0.05	0.041	0.025	0.247	0.217	0.168
0.00	− 0.10	0.049	0.025	0.640	0.600	0.520
0.00	− 0.20	0.136	0.010	0.999	0.999	0.992
0.00	− 0.40	0.610	0.018	1.000	1.000	1.000
0.05	− 0.05	0.652	0.707	0.090	0.200	0.665
0.05	− 0.10	0.613	0.758	0.244	0.557	0.806
0.05	− 0.20	0.507	0.829	0.882	0.987	0.992
0.05	− 0.40	0.303	0.963	1.000	1.000	1.000

valid only asymptotically and for local departures of ρ from zero. Fig. 2(d) shows that there is some uniform gain in rejection probabilities of RS_μ^* only when $\rho = 0.4$. For smaller values of ρ, the rejection probabilities sometimes even decrease but are always close to values for the case $\rho = 0$.

As we indicated earlier there could be some *loss* of power of RS_μ when $\rho < 0$. We performed a small-scale experiment for this case, results of which are reported in Table 4. First note that when $\tau = 0$, an increase in the absolute value of ρ leads to an increase in the size of RS_μ. For example, when $N = 25$, $T = 10$ and $\tau = 0$, the rejection frequencies for $\rho = 0$ and -0.4 are, respectively, 0.047 and 0.573. This is due to the noncentrality parameter (14) which is a function of ρ^2. When $\tau > 0$ ($\sigma_\mu^2 > 0$), the changes in the noncentrality parameter could be negative, and there could be a substantial loss in power of RS_μ. For instance, for the above (25, 10) sample size combinations, and $\tau = 0.05$, the powers of RS_μ, for $\rho = 0.0$ and -0.4 are, respectively, 0.344 and 0.039. RS_μ^* does not suffer from these detrimental effects as we see from Table 4. Its size remains small for all $\rho < 0$, and power even increases as the absolute value of ρ becomes larger.

In a similar way, we can explain the behavior of RS_ρ and RS_ρ^* using Table 3 and Figs. 3(a)–(d). From Table 3 we note that, as expected, when $\sigma_\mu^2 = 0$, RS_ρ has the highest powers among all the tests. The powers of RS_ρ^* are very close to those of RS_ρ. Therefore, the premium we pay for the wider validity of RS_ρ^* is minimal.

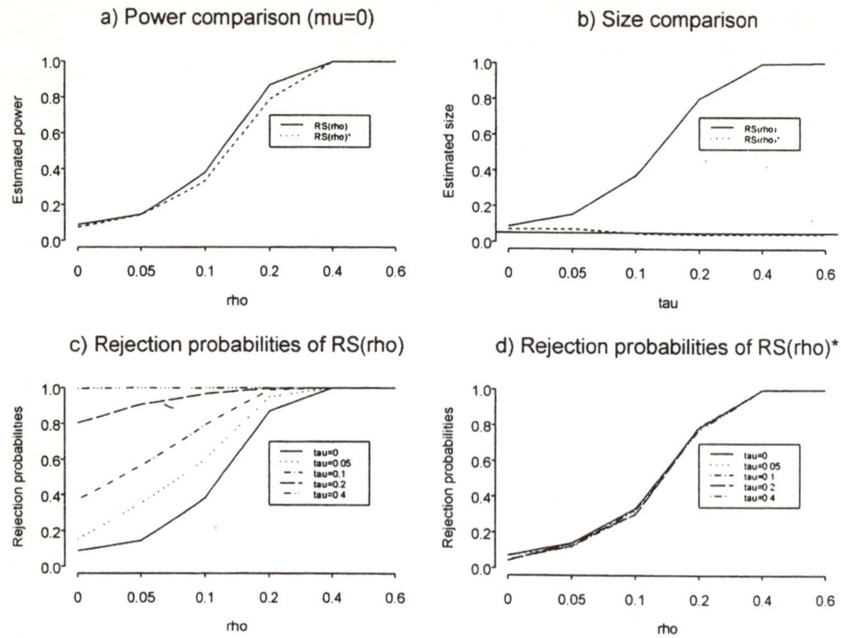

Fig. 3. Tests for serial correlation. Sample size (25, 10).

The real benefit of RS^*_ρ is noticed when $\rho = 0$ but $\tau > 0$; the performance of RS^*_ρ is quite remarkable, as can be seen from Fig. 3(b). RS_ρ rejects H_0: $\rho = 0$ too often, whereas, quite correctly, RS^*_ρ does not reject H_0 so often. For example, when $\tau = 0.2$ and $\rho = 0$, the rejection proportions for RS_ρ and RS^*_ρ are 0.802 and 0.042, respectively. Even when we increase τ to 0.6, the rejection proportion for RS^*_ρ is only 0.045, whereas RS_ρ rejects 100% of the time. In a way, RS^*_ρ is doing more than it is designed to do, that is, not rejecting $\rho = 0$ when ρ is indeed zero even for *large* values of τ.

From Fig. 3(c), we observe that the power of RS_ρ is strongly affected by the presence of random effects, while there is virtually no effect on the power of RS^*_ρ as seen from Fig. 3(d) even for large values of τ. This performance of RS^*_ρ is exceptionally good. For negative values of ρ in Table 4, we see that the presence of τ has a less detrimental effect on RS^*_ρ. For example, when $\rho = -0.10$, the rejection probabilities of RS_ρ are 0.396 and 0.184 for $\tau = 0.0$ and 0.05, respectively; for the same situations, the powers of RS^*_ρ are, respectively, 0.346 and 0.314.

Comparing the performance of RS^*_ρ and RS^*_μ, we see that the former is even more “robust” in the presence of τ, both in terms of size and power, than is the latter in the presence of serial correlation. To see this from a theoretical point of view, let us consider (17) and (22), which are, respectively, the penalties of using RS^*_μ and RS^*_ρ. From (17), $\sigma^4_\mu/\sigma^4_\varepsilon(T-1)/T$, the penalty in using RS^*_μ, also depends on ρ through $\sigma^2_\varepsilon = 20(1-\tau)(1-\rho^2)$, while (22), $2\rho^2(T-1)/T^2$, is a function of ρ only and is of smaller magnitude in terms of T.

Finally, we discuss briefly the performance of the joint statistic $RS_{\mu\rho}$ in the light of our results (4) and (5). This test is optimal when $\sigma^2_\mu > 0$ and $\rho \neq 0$. As we can see from Table 3, in this situation $RS_{\mu\rho}$ has the highest power most of the time. However, when the departure from $\sigma^2_\mu = 0$, $\rho = 0$ is one-directional (say, $\sigma^2_\mu > 0$, $\rho = 0$), RS_μ and $RS_{\mu\rho}$ have the same non-centrality parameter (see (26)). Since $RS_{\mu\rho}$ and RS_ρ use the χ^2_2 and χ^2_1 tests, respectively, there will be a loss of power in using $RS_{\mu\rho}$. For example, when $\tau = 0.10$ and $\rho = 0$, the powers for RS_μ and $RS_{\mu\rho}$ are 0.752 and 0.702, respectively. Similarly, when $\tau = 0$, $\rho = 0.2$, the power of RS_ρ and $RS_{\mu\rho}$ are, respectively, 0.869 and 0.818. These results are consistent with those of Baltagi and Li (1995). Although $RS_{\mu\rho}$ has overall good power, it cannot help to identify the exact source of misspecification when there is only a one-directional departure.

The qualitative performance of all the tests do not change when we increase the sample sizes to $N = 25$, $T = 20$, and $N = 50$, $T = 10$ and they further illustrate the usefulness of our modified tests. These results are not presented but are available from the authors upon request.

6. Conclusions

In this paper we have proposed some simple tests, based on OLS residuals for random effects in the presence of serial correlation, and for serial correlation allowing for the presence of random effects. These tests are obtained by adjusting the existing test procedures. We have investigated the finite sample size and power performance of these and some of the available tests through a Monte Carlo study. We have also provided some empirical examples. The Monte Carlo study, along with the examples, clearly show the usefulness of our procedures to identify the exact source(s) of misspecification. One drawback of our methodology is that we allow for only *local* misspecification. For nonlocal departures, efficient tests could be obtained after estimating full model(s) by maximum likelihood; that, however, will loose the simplicity of our tests using only OLS residuals.

Acknowledgements

We would like to thank the co-editor A. Ronald Gallant, an associate editor and two anonymous referees for many pertinent comments that helped us to improve the paper. Thanks are also due to Miki Naoko for her help in preparing the manuscript. An earlier version of this paper was presented at Texas A&M University, March 1996; the Midwest Econometric Group Meeting, the University of Wisconsin at Madison, November 1996; the Economics seminar at University of San Andres, Argentina, November 1997; and the Annual Meeting of the Argentine Association of Political Economy, Bahia Blanca, Argentina. We wish to thank the participants and Badi Baltagi for helpful comments and discussion. However, we retain responsibility for any remaining errors.

References

Andereson, T.W., Hsiao, C., 1982. Formulation and estimation of dynamic models using panel data. Journal of Econometrics 18, 47–82.

Balestra, P., Nerlove, M., 1966. Pooling cross-section and time-series data in the estimation of a dynamic model: the demand for natural gas. Econometrica 34, 585–612.

Baltagi, B., 1995. Econometric Analysis of Panel Data. Wiley, New York.

Baltagi, B., Chang, Y., Li, Q., 1992. Monte Carlo results on several new and existing tests for the error component model. Journal of Econometrics 54, 95–120.

Baltagi, B., Li, Q., 1991. A joint test for serial correlation and random individual effects. Statistics and Probability Letters 11, 277–280.

Baltagi, B., Li, Q., 1995. Testing AR(1) against MA(1) disturbances in an error component model. Journal of Econometrics 68, 133–151.

Bera, A.K., Jarque, C.M., 1982. Model specification tests: a simultaneous approach. Journal of Econometrics 20, 59–82.

Bera, A.K., Yoon, M.J., 1991. Specification testing with misspecified alternatives. Bureau of Economic and Business Research Faculty Working Paper 91-0123, University of Illinois, presented at the Econometric Society Winter Meeting, Washington, DC, December 1990.

Bera, A.K., Yoon, M.J., 1993. Specification testing with locally misspecified alternatives. Econometric Theory 9, 649–658.

Bera, A.K., Ra, S.S., Sarkar, N., 1998. Hypothesis testing for some nonregular cases in econometrics. In: Chakravorty, S., Coondoo, D., Mukherjee, R. (Eds.), Econometrics: Theory and Practice. Allied Publishers, New Delhi, pp. 319–351.

Breusch, T.S., Pagan, A.R., 1980. The Lagrange multiplier test and its applications to model specification in econometrics. Review of Economic Studies 47, 239–253.

Das Gupta, S., Perlman, M.P., 1974. Power of the noncentral F-test: Effect of additional variate on Hotteling's T^2-test. Journal of the American Statistical Association 69, 174–180.

Davidson, R., MacKinnon, J.G., 1987. Implicit alternatives and local power of test statistics. Econometrica 55, 1305–1329.

Greene, W., 1983. Simultaneous estimation of factor substitution, economies of scale and non-neutral technical change.. In: Dogramaci, A. (Ed.), Econometric Analyses of Productivity. Kluwer-Nijoff, Boston, pp. 121–144.

Greene, W., 2000. Econometric Analysis, 4th Edition. Prentice-Hall, Englewood Cliffs, NJ.

Grunfeld, Y., 1958. The determinants of corporate investment. Unpublished Ph.D. Thesis, Department of Economics, University of Chicago.

Grunfeld, Y., Griliches, Z., 1960. Is aggregation necessarily bad? Review of Economics and Statistics 42, 1–13.

Haavelmo, T., 1944. The probability approach in econometrics. Econometrica(Suppl.) 12, 1–115.

Hillier, G.H., 1991. On multiple diagnostic procedures for the linear model. Journal of Econometrics 47, 47–66.

Honda, Y., 1985. Testing the error component model with non-normal disturbances. Review of Economic Studies 52, 681–690.

Hsiao, C., 1986. Analysis of Panel Data. Cambridge University Press, Cambridge.

Lillard, L.A., Willis, R.J., 1978. Dynamic aspects of earning mobility. Econometrica 46, 985–1012.

Majunder, A.K., King, M.L., 1999. Estimation and testing of a regression with a serially correlated error component. Working paper, Department of Econometrics and Business Statistics, Monash University, Australia.

Nerlove, M., 1971. Further evidence of the estimation of dynamic economic relations from a time-series of cross-sections. Econometrica 39, 359–382.

Phillips, R.F., 1999. Estimation of mixed-effects and error components models with an AR(1) component: some new likelihood maximization procedures and Monte Carlo evidence. Working paper, Department of Economics, George Washington University.

Rao, C.R., 1948. Large sample tests of statistical hypothesis concerning several parameters with applications to problems of estimation. Proceedings of the Cambridge Philosophical Society 44, 50–57.

Saikkonen, P., 1989. Asymptotic relative efficiency of the classical test statistics under misspecification. Journal of Econometrics 42, 351–369.

Welsh, A.H., 1996. Aspects of Statistical Inference. Wiley, New York.

ELSEVIER Journal of Econometrics 87 (1998) 207–237

JOURNAL OF Econometrics

Testing serial correlation in semiparametric panel data models

Q. Li[a,*], C. Hsiao[b]

[a] *Department of Economics, University of Guelph, Guelph, Ontario, Canada N1G 2W1*
[b] *Department of Economics, University of Southern California, Los Angeles, CA 90089, USA*

Received 1 July 1996; received in revised form 1 November 1997

Abstract

We propose three test statistics for testing serial correlation in a semiparametric partially linear panel data model that could allow lagged dependent variables as explanatory variables. The first is for testing zero first-order serial correlation, the second for testing higher-order serial correlations and the third testing for individual effects. The test statistics are shown to have asymptotic normal or chi-square distributions under the null hypothesis of a martingale difference error process. We conduct some Monte Carlo experiments to examine the finite sample performances of the proposed tests. We also discuss the generalization to testing serial correlation in a nonparametric framework.

JEL classification: C12; C14; C52

Keywords: Partially linear model; Dynamic panel data model; Testing serial correlation; Individual effects; Semiparametric estimation

1. Introduction and motivation

This paper proposes three methods to test serial correlation or the presence of the random individual effects in a panel data context when models are only partially specified. Testing for serial correlation has long been a standard practice in applied econometric analysis because if the residuals are serially

* Corresponding author. E-mail: qi@econ.tamu.edu

PII S0304-4076(98)00013-X

correlated, not only the least squares estimator is inefficient, it can be inconsistent if the regressors contain lagged dependent variables. Moreover, strong serial correlation is often an indication of omitting important explanatory variables or functional form misspecification. Testing autocorrelation or random individual effects is important because the choice of an appropriate estimation procedure for a given panel data model crucially depends on the error structure assumed by the model. Panel data studies often simply assume the presence of random individual effects without considering any formal test. For example, a variety of (parametric and nonparametric) GMM estimators have been proposed for dynamic models with random effects or fixed effects. But the estimation of the models could be considerably simplified if the errors are not autocorrelated.

In a time series context with parametric specification, the conventional method to test for the absence of first-order serial correlation is to first estimate the model assuming no serial correlation, then use the estimated residual to construct a Durbin–Watson (1950) statistic when the regressors are exogenous or Durbin (1970) h-statistic when the regressors contain lagged dependent variable. To test higher-order serial correlation, a commonly used test is the LM tests of Breusch (1978) and Godfrey (1978). Although the Q-test of Box and Pierce (1970) is also a commonly used test for testing higher-order serial correlation, the Q-test is not valid when the regressors contain both exogenous and lagged dependent variables. To test for the absence of individual effects in a panel data model, a popular test is the Breusch–Pagan (1980) test. In this paper, we will generalize the Durbin h-statistic, the Breusch (1978) and Godfrey (1978) LM statistics and the Breusch–Pagan (1980) test to the case of a semiparametric partially linear panel data model. When a model is only partially specified, say the partially linear model considered by Engle et al. (1986), and Robinson (1988), we have to appeal to asymptotic theory to justify the validity of the conventional testing procedure. This requires the number of observations to go to infinity and the serial correlation pattern of the explanatory variables to satisfy some kind of mixing conditions for time series data. However, panel data typically contains a large number of individuals, it may not be unreasonable to assume that observations are independently distributed across individuals. Hence, for panels with large N, less restrictive conditions are needed and some (standard) form of the law of large numbers and central limit theorems can be applied to observations across individuals. It not only provides the theoretical basis of deriving the semiparametric tests for serial correlation, but also is empirically feasible.

In Section 2 we set up the basic model. Section 3 proposes a semiparametric test for the absence of first-order serial correlation and discusses its relation to the Durbin–Watson and the Durbin h statistics. Section 4 extends the results of Section 3 to the case of testing higher-order serial correlation. Section 5 provides a test for the absence of individual effects (e.g., Balestra and Nerlove, 1966; Hsiao, 1986). Monte Carlo studies of the size and power of these tests are provided in Section 6. Finally, Section 7 discusses the generalization to testing serial correlation in a nonparametric framework.

2. The model

We consider the following semiparametric partially linear model:

$$y_{it} = z'_{it}\gamma + \theta(w_{it}) + u_{it} \quad (i = 1,\dots,N;\ t = -L+1,\dots,0,1,\dots,T) \tag{1}$$

with u_{it} satisfying

$$\mathrm{E}(u_{it}|w_{it}, z_{it}) = 0, \tag{2}$$

where z_{it} is of dimension $r \times 1$ and w_{it} is of dimension $q \times 1$. We allow the possibility that w_{it} and/or z_{it} contain L ($L \geqslant 0$) lagged values of y_{it}.[1] The functional form of $\theta(\cdot)$ is unknown to the researcher and the functional form of $\sigma^2(z_{it}, w_{it}) = \mathrm{E}(u_{it}^2|z_{it}, w_{it})$ is not specified. We are interested in testing whether the error u_{it} is serially uncorrelated. The case we consider is the panel data with large N and small T. Hence all the asymptotics in this paper are for $N \to \infty$ for a fixed value of T.

In order to test whether u_{it} is serially uncorrelated, we need to get a consistent estimator of γ, which in turn requires some nonparametric estimation techniques either to estimate $\theta(\cdot)$ or to eliminate it from the regression equation. Following Robinson (1988), we will use kernel estimation method to estimate some unknown conditional expectations and then to eliminate $\theta(\cdot)$ before estimating γ. We will use cross-sectional data (for a fixed value of t) to estimate the density of w_{it}, $f_t(w_{it})$,[2] and $\mathrm{E}(A_{it}|w_{it})$. Denote by $\hat{f}_{it}$ and $\hat{A}_{it}$ the kernel estimators of $f_t(w_{it})$ and $\mathrm{E}(A_{it}|w_{it})$, respectively. Then

$$\hat{f}_{it} = \frac{1}{Na^q}\sum_{j \neq i} K_{it,jt}, \tag{3}$$

and

$$\hat{A}_{it} = \frac{1}{Na^q}\sum_{j \neq i} A_{jt}K_{it,\,jt}/\hat{f}_{it}, \tag{4}$$

---

[1] See Kniesner and Li (1994) for an empirical application of using semiparametric partial linear panel data model with w_{it} contains $y_{i,t-1}$. For estimation of a parametric dynamic panel data models, see the pioneering study of Balestra and Nerlove (1966), and the more recent work by Anderson and Hsiao (1982), Ahn and Schmidt (1995), Arellano and Bover (1995), Keane and Runkle (1992), and Pesaran and Smith (1995).

[2] If the data follows a stationary process, then $f_t(\cdot) = f(\cdot)$. We do not require stationary assumption in this paper.

where

$$K_{it,\ jt} = K\left(\frac{w_{it} - w_{jt}}{a}\right)$$

is the kernel function and a is the smoothing parameter. We use product kernel $K(w_{it}) = \prod_{l=1}^{q} k(w_{it,l})$, where k is the univariate kernel and $w_{it,l}$ is the lth component of w_{it}. In this paper A_{it} will be y_{it}, z_{it}, u_{it}, $\theta_{it} \equiv \theta(w_{it})$, $\xi_{it} = \mathrm{E}(z_{it}|w_{it})$ and $v_{it} \equiv z_{it} - \xi_{it}$. Also we use the short-hand notations $\sum_{j \neq i}, \sum_i$ for $\sum_{j=1, j \neq i}^{N}$ and $\sum_{i=1}^{N}$. Similarly we will also use $\sum_t$ and $\sum_{s \neq t}$ to denote $\sum_{t=1}^{T}$ and $\sum_{s=1, s \neq t}^{T}$.

Applying the linear operator $(Na^q)^{-1}\sum_i K_{it,\ jt}/\hat{f}_{jt}$ to Eq. (1) and interchanging i with j, we get

$$\hat{y}_{it} = \hat{z}_{it}'\gamma + \hat{\theta}(w_{it}) + \hat{u}_{it}, \tag{5}$$

where $\hat{y}_{it}$, $\hat{z}_{it}$, $\hat{\theta}(w_{it})$ and $\hat{u}_{it}$ are all defined as the right-hand-side of Eq. (4) with A_{jt} replaced by y_{jt}, z_{jt}, $\theta(w_{jt})$ and u_{jt}, respectively. They are the estimated conditional expectations of y_{it}, z_{it}, $\theta(w_{it})$ and u_{it} given $w = w_{it}$. For example, $\hat{y}_{it} = (Na^q)^{-1}\sum_{j \neq i} y_{jt} K_{it,\ jt}/\hat{f}_{it}$ is a nonparametric kernel estimator of $\mathrm{E}(y_{it}|w_{it})$ based on $(y_{jt}, w_{jt})_{j=1}^{N}$, and $\hat{u}_{it} = (Na^q)^{-1}\sum_{j \neq i} u_{jt} K_{it,\ jt}/\hat{f}_{it}$ is the infeasible kernel estimator of $\mathrm{E}(u_{it}|w_{it}) = 0$ based on $(u_{jt}, w_{jt})_{j=1}^{N}$. Subtracting Eq. (5) from Eq. (1) leads to

$$y_{it} - \hat{y}_{it} = (z_{it} - \hat{z}_{it})'\gamma + (\theta_{it} - \hat{\theta}_{it}) + u_{it} - \hat{u}_{it}. \tag{6}$$

In Eq. (6), $\theta_{it} - \hat{\theta}_{it} = o_p(1)$ and $\hat{u}_{it} = o_p(1)$. Hence, regressing $y_{it} - \hat{y}_{it}$ on $z_{it} - \hat{z}_{it}$ will lead to consistent (in fact $\sqrt{N}$-consistent) estimator of γ. The random denominator $\hat{f}_{it}$ in the kernel estimation will, when $\hat{f}_{it}$ is too small, cause technical difficulties in proving $\sqrt{N}$-consistency of an estimator of γ based on Eq. (6). In the nonparametric kernel estimation literature, two methods are often used to avoid this difficulty. One method is to use density-weighted approach to get rid of the random denominator (e.g., Powell et al., 1989) and the other method is to trim out small values of $\hat{f}_{it}$ (e.g., Robinson, 1988). The advantage of the former method is that no trimming parameter (a nuisance parameter) is needed in the estimation. The disadvantage is that, the proofs usually are more tedious than those based on trimming methods. In this paper we choose to use the density-weighted approach to avoid the issue of using random denominator in the kernel estimation.

We propose to estimate γ by

$$\hat{\gamma} = S_{(z-\hat{z})\hat{f}}^{-1} S_{(z-\hat{z})\hat{f},\,(y-\hat{y})\hat{f}} = \gamma + S_{(z-\hat{z})\hat{f}}^{-1} S_{(z-\hat{z})\hat{f},\,[u-\hat{u}+(\theta-\hat{\theta})]\hat{f}}, \tag{7}$$

where we use notations similar to Robinson (1988), for scalar or column-vector sequences A_{it} and B_{it}, $S_{A\hat{f},\,B\hat{f}} = (1/n)\sum_i\sum_t A_{it}\hat{f}_{it} B'_{it}\hat{f}_{it}$ and $S_{A\hat{f}} = S_{A\hat{f},\,A\hat{f}}$ with $n \equiv NT$.

To derive the asymptotic distribution of $\hat{\gamma}$, we first need some regularity assumptions. We use the definition of Robinson (1988) for the class of kernel functions $\mathscr{K}_l$: $R \to R$, for $l \geqslant 1$ and the class of $\mathscr{G}_v^\alpha$, some $\alpha > 0$ and $v > 0$. These notations represent that, for a positive integer v, if $g \in \mathscr{G}_v^\alpha$, then g is v order differentiable, g and its derivatives (up to the order v) are all bounded by some functions that have finite αth moment. Let y_i denote the $1 \times T$ row vector $(y_{i1}, \dots, y_{iT})$, and z_i and w_i are similarly defined. Also define $\xi_{it} = \mathrm{E}(z_{it}|w_{it})$ and $v_{it} = z_{it} - \xi_{it}$. We assume that

(A1) (i) (y_i, z_i, w_i), $i = 1, 2, \dots, N$, *are independently and identically distributed (i.i.d.) as* (y, z, w). (ii) *For all* t, w_{1t} *admits a density function* $f_t(\cdot) \in \mathscr{G}_{v-1}^{\infty}$, $\theta(\cdot) \in \mathscr{G}_v^4$, *and* $\xi(\cdot) \in \mathscr{G}_v^4$, *where* $v \geqslant 2$ *is an integer.* (iii) $\mathrm{E}(u_{1t}|z_{1t}, w_{1t}) = 0$, *both* u_{1t} *and* v_{1t} *have finite* $(4+\delta)$*th moments for some* $\delta > 0$. $\mathrm{E}(u_{1t}^2|z_{1t}, w_{1t}) = \sigma^2(z_{1t}, w_{1t})$ *is continuous in* w_{1t}.

(A2) *As* $N \to \infty$, *and* $na^{max(2q-4,\, q)} \to \infty$, $na^{2v} \to 0$; $k \in \mathscr{K}_v$, (A2)′ *As* $N \to \infty$, $na^{max(2q-4,\, q)} \to \infty$, $na^{4v} \to 0$; $k \in \mathscr{K}_v$.

Condition (A1)(ii) requires that $f_t(\cdot)$, $\theta(\cdot)$ and $\xi(\cdot)$ all satisfy some moment conditions and are differentiable up to order v. The condition ensures that all these functions admit Taylor expansions up to order v. Together with $k \in \mathscr{K}_v$ (a vth order kernel), they guarantee that the bias in the kernel nonparametric estimation is of the order $\mathrm{O}(a^v)$ (e.g., $\mathrm{E}(\hat{\theta}(z)) - \theta(z) = \mathrm{O}(a^v)$).

We will derive the limiting distributions of our test statistics (which will be given in the next three sections) under the null hypothesis

H_0: The error u_{it} follows a martingale difference process.

The next lemma establishes the asymptotic distribution of $\hat{\gamma}$.

Lemma 1. Under (*A*1), (*A*2)′ *and* H_0, *we have*

(i) $\sqrt{n}(\hat{\gamma} - \gamma) = B^{-1}(1/\sqrt{n})\sum_i\sum_t v_{it}u_{it}f_{it}^2 + o_p(1) \xrightarrow{d} N(0,\Sigma)$, *where* $\Sigma = B^{-1}AB^{-1}$, $A = (1/T)\sum_t \mathrm{E}[v_{1t}v'_{1t}u_{1t}^2 f_{1t}^4]$ *and* $B = (1/T)\sum_t \mathrm{E}[v_{1t}v'_{1t}f_{1t}^2]$.

(ii) $\hat{\Sigma} = \hat{B}^{-1}\hat{A}\hat{B}^{-1}$ *is a consistent estimator for* Σ, *where* $\hat{A} = (1/n)\sum_i\sum_t \tilde{u}_{it}^2(z_{it} - \hat{z}_{it})(z_{it} - \hat{z}_{it})'\hat{f}_{it}^4$, $\hat{B} = (1/n)\sum_i\sum_t(z_{it} - \hat{z}_{it})(z_{it} - \hat{z}_{it})'\hat{f}_{it}^2$ *and* $\tilde{u}_{it} = y_{it} - \hat{y}_{it} - (z_{it} - \hat{z}_{it})'\hat{\gamma}$.

Proof. The proof follows *exactly* the same steps as the proof of Theorem 1 of Li (1996), with the results of Lemma A.3(i)–(iv) of this paper replacing the Lemmas 2–5 of Li (1996) in the proof.

Note that the conditions of Lemma 1 requires $v > \max\{(q/2) - 1, q/4\}$. Hence a second-order kernel ($v = 2$) can be used for $q \leqslant 5$. Li and Stengos (1996) considered the problem of $\sqrt{N}$-consistent estimation of γ under stronger conditions than our (A2)′.

3. Testing zero first-order serial correlation

In this section, we suggest a test statistic for testing the absence of first-order serial correlation. Under the null hypothesis of a martingale difference error, we have $\rho = \mathrm{E}(u_{it}u_{i,t-1}) = 0$ and $\rho_f = \mathrm{E}(u_{it}f_{it}u_{i,t-1}f_{i,t-1}) = 0$. In principle, a test statistic for testing first-order serial correlation can be constructed based on either of the sample analogue of ρ or ρ_f. However, since we consider a semiparametric model and we estimate u_{it} using nonparametric kernel method, it is easier to construct a test statistic based on sample analogue of ρ_f rather than ρ because the former avoids the technical difficulty associated with the use of the random denominator in the kernel estimation. Therefore we shall use ρ_f as the basis to construct our test statistic.

The error u_{it} of the semiparametric model (1) is estimated by

$$\begin{aligned}\tilde{u}_{it} &= y_{it} - \hat{y}_{it} - (z_{it} - \hat{z}_{it})'\hat{\gamma} = y_{it} - \hat{y}_{it} - (z_{it} - \hat{z}_{it})'\gamma - (z_{it} - \hat{z}_{it})'(\hat{\gamma} - \gamma)\\ &= u_{it} - \hat{u}_{it} + (\theta_{it} - \hat{\theta}_{it}) - (z_{it} - \hat{z}_{it})'(\hat{\gamma} - \gamma).\end{aligned} \tag{8}$$

From Eq. (8), it is easy to see that $\tilde{u}_{it} = u_{it} + \mathrm{o_p}(1)$ because $(\hat{\gamma} - \gamma) = \mathrm{O_p}(N^{-1/2})$, $\theta_{it} - \hat{\theta}_{it} = \mathrm{o_p}(1)$ and $\hat{u}_{it} = \mathrm{o_p}(1)$ (recall that $\hat{u}_{it}$ is the kernel estimator of $\mathrm{E}(u_{it}|w_{it}) = 0$). Hence our test statistic for testing zero first-order serial correlation is given by

$$I_n = \sqrt{n}S_{\tilde{u}\hat{f},\,\tilde{u}_{-1}\hat{f}_{-1}} = \frac{1}{\sqrt{n}}\sum_i \sum_t \tilde{u}_{it}\tilde{u}_{i,t-1}\hat{f}_{it}\hat{f}_{i,t-1}. \tag{9}$$

Theorem 1. Under (A1), (A2) and H_0,

(i) $I_n \xrightarrow{d} \mathrm{N}(0, \sigma_0^2)$, where $\sigma_0^2 = (1/T)\sum_t \mathrm{E}[\{(u_{1,t-1}f_{1,t-1} - v'_{1t}f_{1t}B^{-1}\Phi)u_{1t}f_{1t}\}^2]$ *with* $\Phi = \mathrm{E}[v_{1t}f_{1t}u_{1,t-1}f_{1,t-1}]$.

(ii) $\hat{\sigma}_0^2 = (1/n)\sum_i\sum_t\{[\tilde{u}_{i,t-1}\hat{f}_{i,t-1} - (z_{it} - \hat{z}_{it})'\hat{f}_{it}\hat{B}^{-1}\hat{\Phi}]\tilde{u}_{it}\hat{f}_{it}\}^2$ *with* $\hat{\Phi} = (1/n)\sum_i \sum_t (z_{it} - \hat{z}_{it})\hat{f}_{it}\tilde{u}_{i,t-1}\hat{f}_{i,t-1}$, *is a consistent estimator for* σ_0^2. *Hence*

$$S_n \equiv I_n/\hat{\sigma}_0 \xrightarrow{d} \mathrm{N}(0,1).$$

The proof of Theorem 1(i) and (ii) are given by Propositions A.8 and A.9 in the Appendix.

Note that if both w_{it} and z_{it} are strictly exogenous variables, then $\Phi = 0$. The result of Theorem 1 can be simplified. Moreover, condition (A2) can be replaced by (A2)′. Hence from Theorem 1, we immediately have the following corollary.

Corollary 1. Under (A1), (A2)′ *and* H_0, *if in addition,* $\mathrm{E}(u_{1t}|w_{1s}, z_{1s}, w_{1s'}, z_{1s'}) = 0$ *for all t, s and s′. Then*

(i) $I_n \xrightarrow{d} \mathrm{N}(0, \sigma_1^2)$, *where* $\sigma_1^2 = (1/T)\sum_t \mathrm{E}[(u_{1,t-1}f_{1,t-1}u_{1t}f_{1t})^2]$.

(ii) $\hat{\sigma}_1^2 = (1/n)\sum_i\sum_t[\tilde{u}_{i,t-1}\hat{f}_{i,t-1}\tilde{u}_{it}\hat{f}_{it}]^2$ *is a consistent estimator for* σ_1^2. *Hence*

$S_n = I_n/\hat{\sigma}_1 \xrightarrow{d} N(0,1)$.

Proof. The proof follows the same steps as in the proof of Theorem 1 with $\Phi = 0$ since $E(u_{i,t-1}|w_{it}, w_{i,t-1}, z_{it}) = 0$. Moreover, note that when both w_{it} and z_{it} are strictly exogenous variables, the result of Lemma A.6(a) in the appendix can be sharpened to $S_{(\theta-\hat{\theta})\hat{f},u_{-1}\hat{f}_{-1}} = O_p(a^{2v} + N^{-1/2}a^{v/2})$. The proof of this result follows exactly the same steps as in the proof of Lemma A.3(a). This is the reason why we can replace (A2) by a weaker condition (A2)′ in Corollary 1.

Remark 3.1. The conditions of Theorem 1 are different from that of Corollary 1. A stronger condition $Na^{2v} \to 0$ in (A2) is used to prove Theorem 1. This is because in order to prove Theorem 1, we need to show that, among other things, $S_{(\theta-\hat{\theta})\hat{f},\hat{u}_{-1}\hat{f}_{-1}} = o_p(N^{-1/2})$. From Lemma 6(a), we know that $S_{(\theta-\hat{\theta})\hat{f},u_{-1}\hat{f}_{-1}} = O_p(a^v + N^{-1/2}a^{v/2})$. For this to be $o_p(N^{-1/2})$, we need the condition $Na^{2v} \to 0$. Note that (A2) implies that a second-order kernel can be used if $q \leqslant 3$. To see this, note that (A2) requires that $v > \max(q-2, q/2)$. When $v = 2$ (a second-order kernel), this gives $q < 4$ or $q \leqslant 3$ because q is a positive integer.

Remark 3.2. The results of Theorem 1 can be easily understood by noting that the asymptotic null distribution of I_n is identical to the case that $E(y_{it}|w_{it})$ and $E(z_{it}|w_{it})$ are known. To see this, we get from Eq. (1),

$$y_{it} - E(y_{it}|w_{it}) = (z_{it} - E(z_{it}|w_{it}))'\gamma + u_{it} \equiv v'_{it}\gamma + u_{it}. \tag{10}$$

Least squares estimator of γ based on Eq. (10), say $\tilde{\gamma}$, is obviously $\sqrt{N}$-consistent.

$$\sqrt{n}(\tilde{\gamma}-\gamma) = \left[\frac{1}{n}\sum_i\sum_t v_{it}v'_{it}\right]^{-1}\frac{1}{\sqrt{n}}\sum_i\sum_t v_{it}u_{it}$$

$$= [\tilde{B}]^{-1}\frac{1}{\sqrt{n}}\sum_i\sum_t v_{it}u_{it} + o_p(1), \tag{11}$$

where $\tilde{B} = (1/T)\sum_t E[v_{1t}v'_{1t}]$. Then using $\tilde{u}_{it} = u_{it} - z'_{it}(\tilde{\gamma}-\gamma)$, we get

$$\tilde{I}_n \equiv \frac{1}{\sqrt{n}}\sum_i\sum_t \tilde{u}_{it}\tilde{u}_{i,t-1}$$

$$= \frac{1}{\sqrt{n}}\sum_i\sum_t \{u_{it}u_{i,t-1} - (\tilde{\gamma}-\gamma)'v_{it}u_{i,t-1} - u_{it}v_{i,t-1}(\tilde{\gamma}-\gamma)$$

$$+ (\tilde{\gamma}-\gamma)'v_{it}v'_{i,t-1}(\tilde{\gamma}-\gamma)\}$$

$$\equiv C_{1n} - C_{2n}(\tilde{\gamma}-\gamma) - C_{3n}(\tilde{\gamma}-\gamma) + (\tilde{\gamma}-\gamma)'C_{4n}(\tilde{\gamma}-\gamma). \tag{12}$$

It is easy to see that $C_{3n} = O_p(1)$ (because $E(u_{it}|z_{i,t-1}, w_{i,t-1}) = 0$) and $C_{4n} = O_p(N^{1/2})$. Also $(1/\sqrt{n})C_{2n} = (1/n)\sum_i\sum_t v_{it}u_{i,t-1} \xrightarrow{p} (1/T)\sum_t E[v_{1t}u_{1,t-1}] \equiv \tilde{\Phi}$ by a law of large number. Hence

$$\tilde{I}_n = \frac{1}{\sqrt{n}}\sum_i\sum_t \{u_{it}u_{i,t-1} - \sqrt{n}(\hat{\gamma} - \gamma)'\tilde{\Phi} + o_p(1) + \{O_p(N^{-1/2}) + O_p(N^{-1/2})\}$$

$$= \frac{1}{\sqrt{n}}\sum_i\sum_t u_{it}[u_{i,t-1} - v'_{it}\tilde{B}^{-1}\tilde{\Phi}] + o_p(1) \xrightarrow{d} N(0, \tilde{\sigma}_0^2),$$

where the second equality follows from (Eq. (11)), $\tilde{\sigma}_0^2 = (1/T)\sum_t E\{[(u_{1,t-1} - v'_{1t}\tilde{B}^{-1}\tilde{\Phi})u_{1t}]^2\}$, which is the same as our Theorem 1 if one adds the density weight factors.

Remark 3.3. When w and z are strictly exogenous, the I_n test using $\hat{\sigma}_1$ (Corollary 1) is analogous to the Durbin–Watson (1950) test. When z_{it} contains lagged y_{it}, say $y_{i,t-1}$, the I_n test using $\hat{\sigma}_0$ is analogous to the Durbin (1970) h-statistic. This can be seen by noting that in (Eq. (12)), the only term in $(1/\sqrt{n})C_{2n}$ that does not converge to zero is the term $(1/n)\sum_i\sum_t u_{i,t-1}y_{i,t-1}$. Therefore, the variance of I_n will have to be adjusted by the square of this term multiplied by n times the variance of the coefficient estimator of $y_{i,t-1}$.

4. Testing higher-order serial correlation

We show in this section that the results of Section 3 can be easily generalized to the case of testing higher-order serial correlation. Denote $\rho_s = E(u_{it}f_{it}u_{i,t-s}f_{i,t-s})$ $(s = 1,2,\dots,p;\ p < T)$. Obviously, $\rho_s = 0$ under H_0. We are interested in jointly testing: $\rho_1 = \rho_2 = \cdots = \rho_p = 0$. Denotes $\hat{\rho}_s = (1/n)\sum_i\sum_t \tilde{u}_{it}\tilde{u}_{i,t-s}\hat{f}_{it}\hat{f}_{i,t-s}$ $(n = N(T-p))$ and $\hat{\rho} = (\hat{\rho}_1,\dots,\hat{\rho}_p)'$. Let

$$L_{n,p} = \sqrt{n}\hat{\rho}.$$

The next corollary gives the asymptotic distribution of $L_{n,p}$ under H_0.

Corollary 2. Under the same conditions as given in Theorem 1, *we have*

1. $\sqrt{n}L_{n,p} \xrightarrow{d} N(0, \Omega)$, *where* Ω *is a* $p \times p$ *matrix with its* (l, s)*th element given by* $\Omega_{ls} = (1/(T-p)\sum_{t=\max\{l,s\}}^{T} E[u_{1t}^2 f_{1t}^2(u_{1,t-l}f_{1,t-l} - v'_{1t}f_{1t}B^{-1}\Phi_l)(u_{1,t-s}f_{1,t-s} - v'_{1t}f_{1t}B^{-1}\Phi_s)]$, *and* $\Phi_s = \sum_{t=s}^{T} E[v_{1t}f_{1t}u_{1,t-s}f_{1,t-s}]/T$.

2. *Ω can be consistently estimated by $\hat{\Omega}$, where $(\hat{\Omega})_{ls} = (1/n)\sum_i \sum_t \tilde{u}_{it}^2 \hat{f}_{it}^2 (\tilde{u}_{i,t-l}\hat{f}_{i,t-l} - (z_{it} - \hat{z}_{it})' \hat{f}_{it}\hat{B}^{-1}\hat{\Phi}_l)(\tilde{u}_{i,t-s}\hat{f}_{i,t-s} - (z_{it} - \hat{z}_{it})' \hat{f}_{it}\hat{B}^{-1}\hat{\Phi}_s)]$, and $\hat{\Phi}_s = n^{-1}\sum_i\sum_t(z_{it} - \hat{z}_{it})\hat{f}_{it}\tilde{u}_{i,t-s}\hat{f}_{i,t-s}$. Hence*

$$V_{n,p} = nL'_{n,p}(\hat{\Omega})^{-1}L_{n,p} \xrightarrow{d} \chi^2(p).$$

Proof. Similar to the proof of Theorem 1, one can show that $\sqrt{n}\hat{\rho}_s = (1/\sqrt{n})\sum_i\sum_t u_{it} f_{it}(u_{i,t-s} f_{i,t-s} - v'_{it} f_{it} B^{-1}\Phi_s) + o_p(1)$. Hence $\sqrt{n}\hat{\rho}_s \xrightarrow{d} N(0, \Omega_{ss})$ by Lindberg–Levi central limit theorem (because T is finite). The result of Corollary 2(i) follows by a multivariate central limit theorem. Finally the proof that $\hat{\Omega}_{ls} = \Omega_{ls} + o_p(1)$ follows the same arguments as $\hat{\sigma}_0^2 = \sigma_0^2 + o_p(1)$.

Remark 4.1. Similar to the arguments of Remark 3.2, one can easily show that Corollary 2 shows that the asymptotic distribution of the $V_{n,p}$ test is the same as in the case that $E(y_{it}|w_{it})$ and $E(z_{it}|w_{it})$ are known. Hence our $V_{n,p}$ test is similar to the LM type tests of Breusch (1978) and Godfrey (1978). One main difference is that we use residuals from a semiparametric model rather than from a parametric model to construct our test because our model is only partially specified. Also since we do not derive our test from the maximum likelihood principle, we do not need the normality assumption for the error term u_{it}.

5. Testing for individual effects

In this section we show that the test statistic I_n for testing zero first-order serial correlation can be easily generalized to test for the absence of individual effects. In the parametric regression case, the popular Breusch–Pagan (1980) test is often used for testing individual effects in a parametric regression model. The Breusch–Pagan test is based on $\sum_i\sum_t\sum_{s<t}u_{it}u_{is}/\sqrt{NT(T-1)/2}$. Our test will be based on the density weighted version of this quantity:

$$J_n = \frac{\sum_i\sum_t\sum_{s<t}\tilde{u}_{it}\tilde{u}_{is}\hat{f}_{it}\hat{f}_{is}}{\sqrt{NT(T-1)/2}}.$$

Given the results of Theorem 1, it is easy to see that the following corollary holds.

Corollary 3. Under the same conditions as in Theorem 1,

(i) $J_n \xrightarrow{d} N(0, \sigma_2^2)$, *where* $\sigma_2^2 = (2/T(T-1))\sum_t\sum_{s<t}\sum_{s'<t}E[u_{1t}^2 f_{1t}^2(u_{1s}f_{1s} - v'_{1t} f_{1t}B^{-1}\Phi_{t-s})(u_{1s'}f_{1s'} - v'_{1t}f_{1t}B^{-1}\Phi_{t-s'})]$

(ii) $\hat{\sigma}_2^2 = (2/NT(T-1))\sum_i\sum_t\sum_{s<t}\sum_{s'<t}\{\tilde{u}_{it}^2\hat{f}_{it}^2[\tilde{u}_{is}\hat{f}_{is} - (z_{it}-\hat{z}_{it})'\hat{f}_{it}\hat{B}^{-1}\hat{\Phi}_{t-s}]$ $[\tilde{u}_{is'}\hat{f}_{is'} - (z_{it}-\hat{z}_{it})'\hat{f}_{it}\hat{B}^{-1}\hat{\Phi}_{t-s'}]\}$ *is a consistent estimator for* σ_2^2. *Hence*

$$T_n = J_n/\hat{\sigma}_2 \xrightarrow{d} \mathrm{N}(0,1).$$

Proof. Similar to the proof of Theorem 1, one can show that

$$J_n = \sum_i\sum_t\sum_{s<t}\sqrt{2/NT(T-1)}u_{it}f_{it}(u_{is}f_{is} - v_{it}'f_{it}B^{-1}\Phi_{t-s}) + o_p(1).$$

By Lindberg central limit theorem, we have

$$J_n = \frac{1}{\sqrt{N}}\left[\sum_i \eta_i\right] \xrightarrow{d} \mathrm{N}(0,\sigma_2^2)$$

under H_0, where

$$\eta_i = \sum_t\sum_{s<t}\sqrt{2/T(T-1)}u_{it}f_{it}(u_{is}f_{is} - v_{it}'f_{it}B^{-1}\Phi_{t-s})$$

has mean zero and variance

$$\frac{2}{T(T-1)}\sum_t\sum_{s<t}\sum_{s'<t}\mathrm{E}[u_{it}^2f_{it}^2(u_{1s}f_{1s} - v_{1t}'f_{1t}B^{-1}\Phi_{t-s})$$
$$\times(u_{1s'}f_{1s'} - v_{1t}'f_{1t}B^{-1}\Phi_{t-s'})] = \sigma_2^2.$$

The estimator $\hat{\sigma}_2^2 = \sigma_2^2 + o_p(1)$ follows the same arguments as $\hat{\sigma}_0^2 = \sigma_0^2 + o_p(1)$.

Remark 5.1. A popular error structure specification for panel data model is the one-way error components model (e.g., Balestra and Nerlove, 1966; Hsiao, 1986). If the individual effects exist, then the composite error term will exhibit constant serial correlations at different time lags. One would expect the T_n and the $V_{n,p}$ tests to have higher power than the S_n test in rejecting the null of no serial correlation. On the other hand, if the error follows a first-order autoregressive or moving average process, then the higher-order serial correlation coefficients are either zero or quickly converge to zero, one would expect the S_n test to have a higher power in rejecting the null of no serial correlation than the $V_{n,p}$ and the T_n tests.

Remark 5.2. If z_{it} or w_{it} contain lagged dependent variable, one would expect that the I_n, the $V_{n,p}$ and the T_n tests to give the correct size asymptotically under the null hypothesis. However, under the alternative hypothesis, the estimated serial correlation coefficient are likely to be biased toward zero. One would expect this downward bias will reduce the power somewhat under the alternative hypothesis, just like the Durbin h-test in the linear model case. This should be particularly apparent in the one way error component model because conditioning on lagged dependent variable, the serial correlations for all orders will be simultaneously reduced. To see this, consider a parametric specification with the error following an one-way error component structure.

$$y_{it} = z_{it}'\gamma + g(y_{i,t-1}, \beta) + \mu_i + v_{it}, \tag{13}$$

where μ_i is i.i.d. $(0, \sigma_\mu^2)$, v_{it} is i.i.d. $(0, \sigma_v^2)$, and g is a known function with β a unknown (possibly vector) parameter. Assuming that z_{it} is independent of both μ_i and v_{is} for all t and s, then we can rewrite (Eq. (13)) as

$$y_{it} = z_{it}'\gamma + g(y_{i,t-1}, \beta) + h(y_{i,t-1}) + \varepsilon_{it}, \tag{14}$$

where $h(y_{i,t-1}) = \mathrm{E}(\mu_i|z_{it}, y_{i,t-1}) = \mathrm{E}(\mu_i|y_{i,t-1})$ and $\varepsilon_{it} = \mu_i - h(y_{i,t-1}) + v_{it}$. The functional form of h is not specified. Obviously $\mathrm{E}(\varepsilon_{it}|z_{it}, y_{i,t-1}) = 0$. Hence $\mathrm{E}(y_{it}|z_{it}, y_{i,t-1}) = z_{it}'\gamma + g(y_{i,t-1}, \beta) + h(y_{i,\,t-1})$. If we let $w_{it} = y_{i,\,t-1}$ in (Eq. (1)) and define $\theta(y_{i,\,t-1}) = g(y_{i,t-1}, \beta) + h(y_{i,\,t-1})$. Then Eqs. (1) and (14) are not distinguishable because the error ε_{it} in (Eq. (14)) satisfies the same condition (2) as u_{it}. However, the serial correlation coefficient in (Eq. (13)) is equal to $\sigma_\mu^2/(\sigma_\mu^2 + \sigma_v^2)$ and the serial correlation coefficient in (Eq. (14)) is equal to $\sigma_\mu^{*2}/(\sigma_\mu^{*2} + \sigma_v^2)$, where $\sigma_\mu^{*2} = \mathrm{var}[\mu_i - h(y_{i,\,t-1})] < \sigma_\mu^2$.

Remark 5.3. Like the parametric case, if the T_n test fails to reject the null hypothesis, it can be viewed as evidence against one way error components specification of the error process. On the other hand, if the T_n test rejects the null hypothesis, it only rejects the hypothesis that u_{it} is a martingale difference process. To further test whether the serial correlation is due to higher-order serial correlation, or due to unobserved individual effects, is beyond the scope of the present paper. But this is certainly worthy of effort for further research.

6. Monte-Carlo experiments

In this section we report some simulation results to examine the finite sample performance of the test statistics S_n, $V_{n,p}$ and T_n. We use the following data generating processes (DGP):

$$\text{DGP1: } y_{it} = \beta_1 + z_{it}\gamma_1 + x_{it}\beta_2 + u_{it} \equiv z_{it}\gamma_1 + \theta_1(x_{it}) + u_{it},$$

$$\text{DGP2: } y_{it} = \beta_1 + y_{i,t-1}\gamma_2 + x_{it}\beta_3 + u_{it} \equiv y_{i,t-1}\gamma_2 + \theta_2(x_{it}) + u_{it},$$

$$\text{DGP3: } y_{it} = \beta_1 + z_{it}\gamma_3 + y_{i,t-1}\beta_4 + u_{it} \equiv z_{it}\gamma_3 + \theta_3(y_{i,t-1}) + u_{it}.$$

$$\text{DGP4: } y_{it} = \beta_1 + y_{i,t-1}\gamma_4 + x_{it}\beta_5 + x_{it}^2\beta_6 + u_{it} \equiv y_{i,t-1}\gamma_4 + \theta_4(x_{it}) + u_{it}.$$

$$\text{DGP5: } y_{it} = \beta_1 + z_{it}\gamma_5 + y_{i,t-1}\beta_7 + x_{it}\beta_8 + x_{it}y_{i,t-1}\beta_9 + u_{it}$$

$$\equiv z_{it}\gamma_5 + \theta_5(x_{it}, y_{i,t-1}) + u_{it}.$$

We generate six different processes for the error u_{it}:

(a) u_{it}'s are i.i.d. N(0,1); (a white noise error),
(b) $u_{it} = 0.3u_{i,t-1} + \varepsilon_{it}$; (an AR(1) error),
(c) $u_{it} = 0.4\varepsilon_{i,t-1} + \varepsilon_{it}$; (a MA(1) error),
(d) $u_{it} = 0.3u_{i,t-2} + \varepsilon_{it}$; (an AR(2) error),
(e) $u_{it} = 0.4\varepsilon_{i,t-2} + \varepsilon_{it}$; (a MA(2) error),
(f) $u_{it} = \mu_i + v_{it}$. (an one-way EC error).

In (b)–(e), ε_{it}'s are i.i.d. N(0, 1). In (f) μ_i's are i.i.d. N(0,1) and v_{it}'s are i.i.d. N(0,1), also μ_i and v_{jt} are independent. Case (a) corresponds to the null hypothesis H_0. Cases (b) to (f) correspond to the alternatives with $E(u_{it}u_{is}) \neq 0$ for some $s \neq t$. The explanatory variables x_{it}, z_{it}'s and the parameters are chosen as follows:

1. For DGP1, z_{it}'s are i.i.d. N(0, 1), $x_{it} = 0.3x_{i,t-1} + \eta_{it}$ with η_{it} being i.i.d. N(0,1). $(\gamma_1, \beta_1, \beta_2) = (1, 1, 1)$. Also x, z and u are all independent to each other.
2. For DGP2, x_{it} is the same AR(1) process as in (1) above. x and u are independent of each other. $(\gamma_2, \beta_1, \beta_3) = (0.5, 1, 1)$.
3. For DGP3, x_{it} is the same AR(1) process as in (1) above. x and u are independent to each other. $(\gamma_3, \beta_1, \beta_4) = (1, 1, 0.5)$.
4. For DGP4, x_{it} is the same as in DGP3. $(\gamma_4, \beta_1, \beta_5, \beta_6) = (0.5, 1, 1, 1)$.
5. For DGP5, x_{it} and z_{it} are independent i.i.d. N(0, 1) variates. $(\gamma_5, \beta_1, \beta_7, \beta_8, \beta_9) = (1, 1, 0.5, 1, 0.3)$.

We use a standard normal kernel function and the smoothing parameter is chosen via $a_{x,t} = x_{t,sd}N^{-1/5}$ for DGP1, DGP2, DGP4 and DGP5; and $a_{y,t} = 0.5y_{t-1,sd}N^{-1/5}$ for DGP3 and DGP5, where $x_{t,sd}$ and $y_{t-1,sd}$ are the sample standard deviations for $\{x_{it}\}_{i=1}^N$ and $\{y_{i,t-1}\}_{i=1}^N$ respectively. The number of replications are 2000 for size estimation and 1000 for power estimation. We fix $T = 10$. The results for S_n are given in Tables 1–3; the results for $V_{n,p}$ are given in Tables 4–6; and the results for T_n are given in Tables 7–9.

First for the S_n test, Table 1 reports the estimated size for the S_n test. The estimated sizes for DGP1, DGP3 and DGP5 are quite good and it underestimates the sizes for DGP2 and DGP4, perhaps because both cases use lagged

Table 1
S_n-test, case (a): I.I.D. error (estimated size)

DGP1				DGP2			DGP3			DGP4			DGP5		
N	1%	5%	10%	1%	5%	10%	1%	5%	10%	1%	5%	10%	1%	5%	10%
50	0.009	0.056	0.109	0.003	0.021	0.052	0.004	0.037	0.085	0.005	0.029	0.064	0.006	0.048	0.094
100	0.012	0.054	0.106	0.001	0.033	0.068	0.005	0.042	0.090	0.005	0.030	0.069	0.008	0.058	0.104

Table 2
S_n-test, case (b): AR(1) error (estimated power)

DGP1				DGP2			DGP3			DGP4			DGP5		
N	1%	5%	10%	1%	5%	10%	1%	5%	10%	1%	5%	10%	1%	5%	10%
50	1.00	1.00	1.00	0.890	0.979	0.993	0.962	0.996	0.999	0.963	0.994	1.00	0.818	0.954	0.978

Table 3
S_n-test, case (c): MA(1) error (estimated power)

DGP1				DGP2			DGP3			DGP4			DGP5		
N	1%	5%	10%	1%	5%	10%	1%	5%	10%	1%	5%	10%	1%	5%	10%
50	1.00	1.00	1.00	1.00	1.00	1.00	1.00	1.00	1.00	0.999	0.999	1.00	0.966	0.994	0.999

Table 4
$V_{n,2}$-test, case (a): I.I.D. error (estimated size)

DGP1				DGP2			DGP3			DGP4			DGP5		
N	1%	5%	10%	1%	5%	10%	1%	5%	10%	1%	5%	10%	1%	5%	10%
50	0.009	0.055	0.109	0.004	0.023	0.057	0.007	0.036	0.075	0.007	0.034	0.069	0.006	0.037	0.089
100	0.010	0.051	0.107	0.004	0.026	0.058	0.005	0.037	0.081	0.008	0.037	0.074	0.007	0.039	0.091

Table 5
$V_{n,2}$-test, case (d): AR(2) error (estimated power)

DGP1				DGP2			DGP3			DGP4			DGP5		
N	1%	5%	10%	1%	5%	10%	1%	5%	10%	1%	5%	10%	1%	5%	10%
50	1.00	1.00	1.00	0.953	0.984	0.993	0.944	0.988	0.994	0.938	0.988	0.997	0.699	0.890	0.943

Table 6
$V_{n,2}$-test, case (e): MA(2) error (estimated power)

DGP1				DGP2			DGP3			DGP4			DGP5		
N	1%	5%	10%	1%	5%	10%	1%	5%	10%	1%	5%	10%	1%	5%	10%
50	1.00	1.00	1.00	0.995	0.999	1.00	0.996	1.00	1.00	0.995	1.00	1.00	0.858	0.968	0.985

Table 7
T_n-test, case (a): I.I.D. error (estimated size)

DGP1				DGP2			DGP3			DGP4			DGP5		
N	1%	5%	10%	1%	5%	10%	1%	5%	10%	1%	5%	10%	1%	5%	10%
50	0.011	0.044	0.097	0.002	0.024	0.049	0.015	0.055	0.092	0.004	0.035	0.079	0.012	0.054	0.110
100	0.009	0.050	0.094	0.004	0.034	0.062	0.009	0.054	0.106	0.005	0.039	0.081	0.012	0.052	0.107

Table 8
T_n-test, case (b): AR(1) error (estimated power)

DGP1				DGP2			DGP3			DGP4			DGP5		
N	1%	5%	10%	1%	5%	10%	1%	5%	10%	1%	5%	10%	1%	5%	10%
50	1.00	1.00	1.00	0.054	0.161	0.248	0.237	0.418	0.512	0.124	0.268	0.380	0.266	0.432	0.531
100	1.00	1.00	1.00	0.324	0.519	0.638	0.537	0.798	0.808	0.280	0.479	0.605	0.509	0.690	0.776
200	1.00	1.00	1.00	0.669	0.839	0.891	0.854	0.943	0.971	0.608	0.798	0.870	0.838	0.938	0.966

Table 9
T_n-test, case (f): one-way EC (estimated power)

DGP1				DGP2			DGP3			DGP4			DGP5		
N	1%	5%	10%	1%	5%	10%	1%	5%	10%	1%	5%	10%	1%	5%	10%
50	1.00	1.00	1.00	0.585	0.829	0.913	0.995	1.00	1.00	0.959	0.991	0.997	1.00	1.00	1.00
100	1.00	1.00	1.00	0.989	0.998	1.00	1.00	1.00	1.00	1.00	1.00	1.00	1.00	1.00	1.00

dependent variables as explanatory variables in the parametric parts. However, as N increases, the estimated sizes increase toward their nominal sizes. Tables 2 and 3 show that the S_n test is quite powerful in detecting first-order serial correlation for all the DGPs considered.

Secondly for the $V_{n,p}$ test, from Table 4 we see that the estimated size for the $V_{n,p}$ test is similar to Table 1 of the S_n test. It has good estimated size for DGP1, DGP3 and DGP5 and again it underestimates the size for DGP2 and DGP4. Tables 5 and 6 show that the $V_{n,p}$ test is quite powerful for detecting the AR(2) and MA(2) serially correlated errors. Note that for the MA(2) error of case (e), $E(u_{it}u_{i,t-1}) = 0$, hence the S_n test has only trivial power against such a MA(2) process.

Finally for the T_n test, Table 7 gives the estimated sizes for DGP1–DGP5. In general, the size estimation is quite good except that for DGP2, it underestimates the size for DGP2. Tables 8 and 9 report estimated power for the T_n test against an AR(1) and an one-way error component error structure, respectively. The T_n test is quite powerful in detecting one-way error structure, but as expected, it is not very powerful against an AR(1) error process.

The Monte-Carlo simulation results show that our proposed tests perform reasonably well in finite samples for the DGPs we considered. However, the above results are only for conditional homoskedastic normal errors. Also our test statistics depend on the smoothing parameter a. Below we will report simulation results for the S_n test using slightly different smoothing parameters as well as a nonnormal error and some conditional heteroskedastic error cases.

First we increased and decreased the smoothing parameter a by 20% and examine the sensitivity of the estimated sizes of our test statistics to different values of a. In particular, we replace $a_{x,t}$ by $a_{x,t}^{+} \equiv 1.2x_{t,sd}N^{-1/5}$ or $a_{x,t}^{-} \equiv 0.8x_{t,sd}N^{-1/5}$, and replace $a_{y,t}$ by $a_{y,t}^{+} = 0.6y_{t-1,\,sd}N^{-1/5}$ $a_{y,t}^{-} = 0.4y_{t-1,sd}N^{-1/5}$. The results for size estimation for different DGPs are given in Table 10, where a^{+} denotes $a_{x,t}^{+}$ for DGP1, DGP2 and DGP4; $a_{y,t}^{+}$ for DGP3 and $(a_{x,t}^{+}, a_{y,t}^{+})$ for DGP5. a^{-} is similarly defined. The sample size is $N = 50$ and $T = 10$. From Table 10, we observe that for most cases, the estimated sizes only change slightly when the smoothing parameters increased or decreased by 20% except for DGP5. For DGP5 with $a = a^{+}$, the S_n test overestimates the size.

Next, we changed the error term from a normal distribution to a t-distribution with 5 degree of freedom. The estimated sizes for a t_5 error are given in Table 11. We see that the estimated sizes are quite close to their nominal levels for DGP1, DGP3, and DGP5, and the estimated sizes are below their nominal levels for DGP2 and DGP4. These results are quite similar to their corresponding normal disturbance cases.

Finally, we used a conditional heteroskedastic error: $u_{it} = \sigma_{it}\varepsilon_{it}$, where ε_{it} is i.i.d. N(0,1), and $\sigma_{it} = \sqrt{(1 + x_{it}^2 + z_{it}^2)/3}$ for DGP1, $\sigma_{it} = \sqrt{(1 + x_{it}^2 + y_{i,t-1}^2)/10}$ for DGP2, $\sigma_{it} = \sqrt{(1 + z_{it}^2 + y_{i,t-1}^2)/10}$ for DGP3, $\sigma_{it} = \sqrt{(1 + x_{it}^2 + y_{i,t-1}^2)/25}$

Table 10
S_n-test for different smoothing parameter (estimated size, N = 50)

DGP1				DGP2			DGP3			DGP4			DGP5		
a	1%	5%	10%	1%	5%	10%	1%	5%	10%	1%	5%	10%	1%	5%	10%
a^+	0.013	0.059	0.110	0.002	0.019	0.049	0.008	0.047	0.092	0.003	0.027	0.058	0.015	0.068	0.132
a^-	0.009	0.046	0.099	0.003	0.024	0.054	0.005	0.040	0.075	0.004	0.032	0.073	0.004	0.039	0.085

Table 11
S_n-test with t_5 error term (estimated size)

DGP1				DGP2			DGP3			DGP4			DGP5		
N	1%	5%	10%	1%	5%	10%	1%	5%	10%	1%	5%	10%	1%	5%	10%
50	0.004	0.046	0.096	0.002	0.018	0.052	0.005	0.037	0.082	0.003	0.022	0.056	0.007	0.047	0.102

Table 12
S_n-test with conditional heter. error (estimated size)

DGP1				DGP2			DGP3			DGP4			DGP5		
N	1%	5%	10%	1%	5%	10%	1%	5%	10%	1%	5%	10%	1%	5%	10%
50	0.007	0.046	0.093	0.003	0.013	0.037	0.008	0.043	0.092	0.011	0.049	0.101	0.013	0.061	0.119

for DGP4, and $\sigma_{it} = \sqrt{(1 + x_{it}^2 + z_{it} + y_{i,t-1}^2)/14}$ for DGP5. All the errors have unconditional variances close to one. The results is given in Table 12. The estimation results for DGP1, DGP2 and DGP3 are very similar to their corresponding conditional homoskedastic error cases (compare with Table 1). However, for DGP4, the estimated sizes are much closer to their nominal values for this conditional heteroskedastic case, and the S_n test over estimates the sizes for DGP5 in the conditional heteroskedastic error case.

7. The case of nonparametric regression model

In this section we show that our test statistics based on a semiparametric partially linear model can be easily extended to the case of a nonparametric panel data regression model of the form:

$$y_{it} = g(z_{it}, w_{it}) + u_{it} \tag{15}$$

where the functional form of $g(\cdot)$ is not specified. Without loss of generality, we assume that $z_{it} \in R^r$ ($r \geqslant 0$, $r = 0$ is allowed in this section) are discrete variables and $w_{it} \in R^q$ ($q \geqslant 1$) are continuous variables.[3] In this case, we estimate $g(z_{it}, w_{it})$ by

$$\tilde{g}_{it} = (Na^q)^{-1} \sum_{j \neq i} y_{jt} K_{it,jt} P_{it,\, jt} / \hat{f}_{it,1},$$

where $P_{it,\, jt} = \prod_{l=1}^{r} I(z_{l,it} - z_{l,jt})$, $z_{l,it}$ is the lth component of z_{it}, $I(\cdot)$ is the indicator function with $I(0) = 1$ and $I(x) = 0$ for $|x| \neq 0$, and

$$\hat{f}_{it,1} = (Na^q)^{-1} \sum_{j \neq i} K_{it,jt} P_{it,jt}. \tag{16}$$

The nonparametric residual is given by

$$\tilde{u}_{it,1} = y_{it} - \tilde{g}_{it} = g_{it} + u_{it} - \hat{g}_{it,1} - \hat{u}_{it,1}, \tag{17}$$

where $\hat{g}_{it,1}$ and $\hat{u}_{it,1}$ are defined by

$$\hat{g}_{it,1} = (Na^q)^{-1} \sum_{j \neq i} g_{jt} K_{it,jt} P_{it,jt} / \hat{f}_{it,1}, \tag{18}$$

and

$$\hat{u}_{it,1} = (Na^q)^{-1} \sum_{j \neq i} u_{jt} K_{it,jt} P_{it,jt} / \hat{f}_{it,1}. \tag{19}$$

[3] If part of the variables of z_{it} is discrete, say $z_{it} = (z_{1,it}, z_{2,it})$, $z_{1,it}$ is discrete and $z_{2,it}$ is continuous. We can redefine $z_{1,it}$ and $(z_{2,it}, w_{it})$ as the *new* z_{it} and w_{it}, respectively.

The test statistic for testing the absence of first-order serial correlation in a nonparametric regression model becomes

$$I_{n,1} = \frac{1}{\sqrt{n}} \sum_i \sum_t \tilde{u}_{it,1} \tilde{u}_{it-1,1} \hat{f}_{it,1} \hat{f}_{it-1,1}. \tag{20}$$

To derive the asymptotic distribution of $I_{n,1}$, we need some regularity conditions. Let (A1)′ be the same as (A1) with the joint-density function $f_{t,1}(z, w)$ replacing $f_t(w)$ and $g(z, w)$ replacing $\theta(w)$, also all the smoothness conditions in (A1)′ are with respect to w for a fixed value of z, for example $f_t(w) \in \mathscr{G}^{\infty}_{v-1}$ of (A1) becomes, for any fixed value of z, $f_{t,1}(w, z) \in \mathscr{G}^{\infty}_{v-1}$ in (A1)′. Then by the proof of Theorem 1, we immediately have the following corollary.

Corollary 4. Under *(A1)′,(A2)* and H_0, *we have* $I_{n,1}/\hat{\sigma}_{0,1} \xrightarrow{d} N(0,1)$, *where* $\hat{\sigma}^2_{0,1} = n^{-1}\sum_i\sum_t[\tilde{u}_{it,1}\hat{f}_{it,1}\tilde{u}_{it-1,1}\hat{f}_{it-1,1}]^2$ *is a consistent estimator for* $\sigma^2_{0,1} = 1/T\sum_t E[(u_{1t}f_{t,1}(x_{1t})u_{1t-1}f_{t-1,1}(x_{1t-1}))^2]$ *where* $x_{it} = (z_{it}, w_{it})$.

Proof. The proof of Corollary 4 follows from a similar argument as that of the proof of Theorem 1. Hence, we only provide a sketch of the proof below.[4] The $\hat{f}$, $\hat{g}$, $\hat{u}$ below are defined by Eqs. (16), (18) and (19), respectively.

$$\begin{aligned}
I_{n,1} &= n^{1/2} S_{[u-\hat{u}+(g-\hat{g})]\hat{f},[u_{-1}-\hat{u}_{-1}+(g_{-1}-\hat{g}_{-1})]\hat{f}_{-1}} \\
&= n^{1/2} S_{u\hat{f},u_{-1}\hat{f}_{-1}} + n^{1/2}\{S_{u\hat{f},\hat{u}_{-1}\hat{f}_{-1}} + S_{\hat{u}\hat{f},u_{-1}\hat{f}_{-1}} + S_{\hat{u}\hat{f},\hat{u}_{-1}\hat{f}_{-1}}\} \\
&\quad + n^{1/2}\{S_{u\hat{f},(g_{-1}-\hat{g}_{-1})\hat{f}_{-1}} + S_{\hat{u}\hat{f},(g_{-1}-\hat{g}_{-1})\hat{f}_{-1}} + S_{(g-\hat{g})\hat{f},(g_{-1}-\hat{g}_{-1})\hat{f}_{-1}}\} \\
&\quad + n^{1/2}\{S_{(g-\hat{g})\hat{f},u_{-1}\hat{f}_{-1}} + S_{(g-\hat{g})\hat{f},\hat{u}_{-1}\hat{f}_{-1}}\} \\
&\equiv n^{1/2} S_{u\hat{f},u_{-1}\hat{f}_{-1}} + (I) + (II) + (III) \\
&= n^{1/2} S_{uf,\, u_{-1}f_{-1}} + o_p(1),
\end{aligned}$$

where $(I) = o_p(1)$, $(II) = o_p(1)$ and $(III) = o_p(1)$ follow from similar proofs of Lemmas A.4, A.5 and A.6, respectively, and $n^{1/2}S_{u\hat{f},u_{-1}\hat{f}_{-1}} = n^{1/2}S_{uf,u_{-1}f_{-1}} + o_p(1)$ follows from a similar proof as Lemma A.5(a). Now, $n^{1/2}S_{uf,u_{-1}f_{-1}} \xrightarrow{d} N(0, \sigma^2_{0,1})$ by Lindeberg–Levi central limit theorem and $\hat{\sigma}^2_{0,1} = \sigma^2_{0,1} + o_p(1)$ follows the same proof as $\hat{\sigma}^2_0 = \sigma^2_0 + o_p(1)$.

[4] When part of the regressors are discrete and the rest are continuous, the convergence rate of nonparametric kernel estimates is determined by that of the continuous variables, see the pioneer work of Bierens (1983). and the more recent works of Delgado and Mora (1995) and Baltagi et al. (1996). Hence, the proof of Corollary 4 follows the same arguments as in the proof of Theorem 1 where the nonparametric estimation are only associated with continuous variables.

Remark 7.1. An interesting result of Corollary 4 is that $\sigma_{0,1}^2$ has a simple expression whether (z_{it}, w_{it}) is strictly exogenous or not. This is in contrast to the results of Theorem 1 and Corollary 1 where the asymptotic variance of the test statistic depends on whether (z_{it}, w_{it}) and $u_{i,t-1}$ are correlated or not.

Remark 7.2. When $g(\cdot)$ is a linear function, say $g(z_{it}, w_{it}) = z_{it}'\gamma + w_{it}'\beta$, Eq. (15) reduces to a linear model and the appropriate tests for testing first-order serial correlation are the popular Durbin–Watson or Durbin-*h* test when (z_{it}, w_{it}) contains $y_{i,t-1}$. However, Durbin–Watson or Durbin-*h* test is unable to discriminate between serial correlation and regression functional form misspecification. Rejection of no serial correlation by Durbin–Watson or Durbin-*h* test may be due to regression functional form misspecification rather than serial correlation in the error. An important advantage of using a nonparametric functional form of Eq. (15) when testing for serial correlation is that it allows the researchers to separate the issues of functional form misspecification from genuine autocorrelation in the errors. However, nonparametric estimation of Eq. (15) suffers from the well-known curse of dimensionality problem. In this respect, the semiparametric model (1) provides a compromise. It has a more flexible functional form compared with a linear regression model, and the issue of the curse of dimensionality problem is not as serious as a completely nonparametric specification.

Similar generalizations also hold for testing higher-order serial correlation and for testing individual effects. Define $L_{np,1}$ and $J_{n,1}$ the same way as L_{np} and J_n with $\tilde{u}_{it}$ and $\hat{f}_{it}$ replaced by $\tilde{u}_{it,1}$ and $\hat{f}_{it,1}$, respectively. Then we have

Corollary 5. Under (A1)′,(A2) and H_0, we have

(a) $nL_{n,p,1}'(\hat{\Omega}_1)^{-1}L_{n,p,1} \xrightarrow{d} \chi^2(p)$, where the (l, s)*th element of* $\hat{\Omega}_1$ *is given by* $(\hat{\Omega}_1)_{ls} = (1/n)\sum_i\sum_t \tilde{u}_{it,1}\hat{f}_{it,1}\tilde{u}_{it-l,1}\hat{f}_{it-l,1}\tilde{u}_{it-s,1}\hat{f}_{it-s,1}$;

(b) $J_{n,1}/\hat{\sigma}_{2,1} \xrightarrow{d} N(0,1)$, where $\hat{\sigma}_{2,1}^2 = (2/NT(T-1))\sum_i\sum_t\sum_{s<t}\sum_{s'<t}\tilde{u}_{it,1}^2\hat{f}_{it,1}^2\tilde{u}_{is,1}\hat{f}_{is,1}\tilde{u}_{is',1}\hat{f}_{is',1}$.

Note that similar to the result of Corollary 4, both $\hat{\Omega}_1$ and $\hat{\sigma}_2^2$ have simple expressions whether (z_{it}, w_{it}) is strictly exogenous or not.

8. Acknowledgements

We would like to thank two referees and an associate editor for helpful comments that greatly improved the paper. C. Hsiao's research is supported in part by Natural Science Foundation grants SBR 94-09540 and SBR 96-19330.

Q. Li's work is supported by a grant from the Social Sciences and Humanities Research Council of Canada and a grant from the Natural Sciences Engineering Research Council of Canada.

Appendix A. Proof of Theorem 1

We first present some lemmas. In all the lemmas given below, we assume the conditions in Theorem 1 hold. Also $\varepsilon = u$ or v and $g = \theta$ or ξ. Hence $g \in \mathcal{G}_{\nu}^{4}$. Note that both ξ and v are $p \times 1$ vectors. However, when we evaluate the order of some terms, we will often only consider the case of $p = 1$ for ξ and v, because the $p > 1$ vector case follows from the same proof as in the scalar case and the Cauchy inequality.

When we evaluate the order of some terms, if there is no confusion, we will use N, $(N-1)$ and $(N-2)$ interchangeably. We will use $\mathrm{E}_{it}(\cdot)$ and $\mathrm{E}_{it,js}(\cdot)$ to denote conditional expectations $\mathrm{E}(\cdot|w_{it})$ and $\mathrm{E}(\cdot|w_{it},w_{js})$. $w_{\cdot t} \equiv (w_{1t}, \ldots, w_{Nt})$. Also for a $p \times 1$ vector x, we will use $|\cdot|$ to denote its Euclidean norm. The notation $A \sim B$ means $A = \mathrm{O}(B)$. We will write $f(\cdot)$ for $f_t(\cdot)$ to simplify the notation.

Lemma A.1. (a) $|\mathrm{E}_{1t}(g(w_{1t}) - g(w_{2t}))K((w_{1t} - w_{2t})/a)| \leqslant D_g(w_{1t})a^{q+\nu}$,
(b) $|\mathrm{E}_{1t}(g(w_{1t}) - g(w_{2t}))\eta(w_{1t})K((w_{1t} - w_{2t})/a)| \leqslant D_g(w_{1t})\eta(w_{1t})a^{q+\nu}$,
(c) $|\mathrm{E}_{1t}(a^{-q}K((w_{1t} - w_{2t})/a)) - f(w_{1t})| \leqslant D_f(w_{1t})a^{\nu}$,
(d) $|\mathrm{E}[(g_{2t} - g_{1t})^2 K_{1t,2t}^2 \varepsilon_{1t}^2 K_{1t,3t} K_{1t,4t}]| \leqslant C a^{2+3q} \mathrm{E}|H_g^2(w_{1t})\varepsilon_{1t}^2(w_{1t})| = \mathrm{O}(a^{2+3q})$, *where $D_g(\cdot)$ has finite fourth moment and $D_f(\cdot)$ has finite moment of any order. $\varepsilon = u$ or v and $\varepsilon_{1t}^2(w_{1t}) = \mathrm{E}(\varepsilon_{1t}^2|w_{1t})$.*

Proof. See the proof of Lemma 5 of Robinson (1988) for (a). (b) follows directly from (a). (c) is Lemma 4 of Robinson (1988). (d) follows by change-of-variable: $w_{lt} - w_{1t} = a\eta_l$ $(l = 2,3,4)$ and then using $|g(w_{1t} + a\eta_l) - g(w_{1t})| \leqslant aH_g(w_{1t})|\eta_l|$ (see (A2)).

Define $S^t_{A\hat{f},B\hat{f}} = (1/N)\sum_i A_{it}\hat{B}'_{it}\hat{f}^2_{it}$. $S^t_{\hat{A}\hat{f},B\hat{f}}$ and $S^t_{A\hat{f},B\hat{f}}$ are similarly defined.

Lemma A.2.
(a) $S^t_{(g-\hat{g})\hat{f}} = \mathrm{O_p}(a^2(Na^q)^{-1} + a^{2\nu})$, *where* $g = \theta$ or ξ;
(b) $S^t_{(g-\hat{g})\hat{f},\varepsilon\hat{f}} = \mathrm{O_p}(N^{-1/2}a^{\nu} + a(Na^{q/2})^{-1})$, *where $g = \theta$ or ξ and $\varepsilon = u$ or v*;
(c) $S^t_{(g-\hat{g})\hat{f},\varepsilon\hat{f}} = \mathrm{O_p}(a(Na^{q/2})^{-1} + N^{-1/2}a^{\nu})$, *where $g = \theta$ or ξ and $\varepsilon = u$ or v*;
(d) $S^t_{u,\hat{v}} = \mathrm{O_p}(N^{-1}a^{-q/2})$, $S^t_{\hat{u},v} = \mathrm{O_p}(N^{-1}a^{-q/2})$, $S^t_{u,\hat{v}} = \mathrm{O_p}(N^{-1}a^{-q/2})$.

Proof. (a) was proved in the proof of Lemma 1 of Li (1996). The proof of (d) follows exactly the same steps as in the proof of Lemma A.7 of this appendix. The proofs for (b) and (c) are very similar to the proofs of the Lemmas 3 and 4 of Li (1996). Here we will only provide a proof for (b), the proof of (c) is similar to (b).

(b) First we evaluate $\mathrm{E}[S^t_{(g-\hat{g})\hat{f},\varepsilon\hat{f}}]$.

$$\begin{aligned}
\mathrm{E}[S^t_{(g-\hat{g})\hat{f},\varepsilon\hat{f}}]^2 &= \mathrm{E}\left\{\left[\frac{1}{n}\sum_i\sum_t (g_{it}-\hat{g}_{it})\hat{f}_{it}\varepsilon_{it}\hat{f}_{it}\right]\right.\\
&\quad\times\left.\left[\frac{1}{n}\sum_{i'}\sum_{t'}(g_{i't'}-\hat{g}_{i't'})\hat{f}_{i't'}\varepsilon_{i't'}\hat{f}_{i't'}\right]\right\}\\
&= \mathrm{E}\left\{\left[\frac{1}{nN^2a^{2q}}\sum_i\sum_t\sum_{j\neq i}\sum_{l\neq i}(g_{it}-g_{jt})K_{it,jt}\varepsilon_{it}K_{it,lt}\right]\right.\\
&\quad\times\left.\left[\frac{1}{nN^2a^{2q}}\sum_{i'}\sum_{t'}\sum_{j'\neq i'}\sum_{l'\neq i'}(g_{it'}-g_{j't'})K_{it',j't'}\varepsilon_{i't'}K_{i't',l't'}\right]\right\}\\
&\sim \mathrm{E}\left\{\left[\frac{1}{nN^2a^{2q}}\sum_i\sum_t\sum_{j\neq i}\sum_{l\neq i}(g_{it}-g_{jt})K_{it,jt}\varepsilon_{it}K_{it,lt}\right]\right.\\
&\quad\times\left.\left[\frac{1}{N^3a^{2q}}\sum_{i'}\sum_{j'\neq i'}\sum_{l'\neq i'}(g_{i't}-g_{j't})K_{i't,j't}\varepsilon_{i't}K_{i't,l't}\right]\right\}\\
&= \frac{1}{nN^5a^{4q}}\sum_i\sum_t\sum_{j\neq i}\sum_{l\neq i}\sum_{j'\neq i}\sum_{l'\neq i}\mathrm{E}[(g_{it}-g_{jt})\\
&\quad\times K_{it,jt}\varepsilon^2_{it}K_{it,lt}(g_{it}-g_{j't})K_{it,j't}K_{it,l't}]\\
&\equiv \mathrm{RH0}.
\end{aligned}$$

Case (i) i, j, l, j', l' are all different. In this case

$$\mathrm{RH0}_{(\mathrm{i})} = \frac{1}{N^6a^{4q}}\mathrm{O_p}(N^5a^{4q+2v}) = \mathrm{O}(N^{-1}a^{2v})$$

by Lemma A.1(a).

Case (ii) i, j, l, j', l' take four different values. In this case, it has the same order as $j'=j$, which is $(N^2a^{4q})^{-1}|\mathrm{E}[(g_{1t}-g_{2t})^2K^2_{1t,2t}\varepsilon^2_{1t}K_{1t,3t}K_{1t,4t}]| = \mathrm{O}((N^2a^{2-q})^{-1})$ by Lemma A.1(d). Hence $\mathrm{RH0}_{(\mathrm{ii})} = \mathrm{O}((N^2a^{2-q})^{-1})$.

Case (iii) i, j, l, j', l' take at most three different values. Using the same arguments as case (ii) above, it is easy to see that

$$\mathrm{RH0}_{(\mathrm{iii})} = \frac{1}{N^3a^{4q}}\mathrm{O}(a^{2-2q}) = \mathrm{O}((N^3a^{2-2q})^{-1}),$$

which has a smaller order than $\mathrm{RH0}_{(\mathrm{ii})}$. Note that the factor a^2 comes from the fact that $|(g_{it}-g_{jt})(g_{it}-g_{2j'})| \leqslant a^2|\eta_1\eta_2H^2_g(w_{it})|$ by using change-of-variable: $w_{jt}-w_{it}=a\eta_1$ and $w_{j't}-w_{it}=a\eta_2$ (since $j\neq i$ and $j'\neq i$).

We have shown that $\mathrm{RH0} = O(N^{-1}a^{2\nu} + a^2(N^2a^q)^{-1})$. Hence $S^t_{(g-\hat{g})\hat{f},\varepsilon\hat{f}} = O_p(N^{-1/2}a^{\nu} + a(Na^{q/2})^{-1})$.

From Lemma A.2, we immediately have the following lemma.

Lemma A.3.

(a) $S_{g-\hat{g}} = O_p(a^2(Na^q)^{-1} + a^{2\nu})$, *where* $g = \theta$ or ξ;

(b) $S_{(g-\hat{g})\hat{f},\varepsilon\hat{f}} = O_p(a(Na^{q/2})^{-1} + N^{-1/2}a^{\nu})$, *where* $g = \theta$ *or* ξ *and* $\varepsilon = u$ *or* v;

(c) $S_{(g-\hat{g})\hat{f},\hat{\varepsilon}\hat{f}} = O_p(a(Na^{q/2})^{-1} + N^{-1/2}a^{\nu})$, *where* $g = \theta$ *or* ξ *and* $\varepsilon = u$ *or* v;

(d) $S_{u\hat{f},\hat{v}\hat{f}} = O_p(N^{-1}a^{-q/2}b^{-1})$, $S_{\hat{u}\hat{f},v\hat{f}} = O_p(N^{-1}a^{-q/2})$, $S_{u\hat{f},\hat{v}\hat{f}} = O_p(N^{-1}a^{-q/2})$.

Proof. $S_{A\hat{f},B\hat{f}} \equiv (1/T)\sum_t S^t_{A\hat{f},B\hat{f}}$ has the same order as $S^t_{A\hat{f},B\hat{f}}$ (for any $1 \leqslant t \leqslant T$) because T is finite. Lemma A.3 follows directly from Lemma A.2. Note that all the terms in Lemma A.3 are of the order of $o_p(N^{-1/2})$ by (A2).

Lemma A.4.

(a) $S_{u\hat{f},\hat{u}_{-1}\hat{f}_{-1}} = O_p(N^{-1}a^{-q/2})$, (b) $S_{\hat{u}\hat{f},u_{-1}\hat{f}_{-1}} = O_p(N^{-1}a^{-q/2})$, (c) $S_{\hat{u}\hat{f},\hat{u}_{-1}\hat{f}_{-1}} = O_p(N^{-1}a^{-q/2})$.

Proof. (a)

$$
\begin{aligned}
\mathrm{E}[(S_{u\hat{f},\hat{u}_{-1}\hat{f}_{-1}})^2] &= \mathrm{E}\left\{\left[\frac{1}{n}\sum_i\sum_t u_{it}\hat{f}_{it}\hat{u}_{i,t-1}\hat{f}_{i,t-1}\right]^2\right\} \\
&= \mathrm{E}\left\{\left[\frac{1}{n}\sum_i\sum_t u_{it}\hat{f}_{it}\hat{u}_{i,t-1}\hat{f}_{i,t-1}\right]\right. \\
&\quad \times\left.\left[\frac{1}{n}\sum_{i'}\sum_{t'} u_{i't'}\hat{f}_{i't'}\hat{u}_{i',t'-1}\hat{f}_{i',t'-1}\right]\right\} \\
&\sim \mathrm{E}\left[\frac{1}{nN}\sum_i\sum_t\sum_{i'} \mathrm{E}[u_{it}\hat{f}_{it}\hat{u}_{i,t-1}\hat{f}_{i,t-1}u_{i't}\hat{f}_{i't}\hat{u}_{i',t-1}\hat{f}_{i',t-1}]\right] \\
&= \frac{1}{n\ N^5a^{4q}}\sum_i\sum_t\sum_{i'}\sum_{j\neq i}\sum_{l\neq i}\sum_{j'\neq i'}\sum_{l'\neq i'} \\
&\quad \times \mathrm{E}[u_{it}K_{it,jt}u_{l,t-1}K_{i,t-1;l,t-1}u_{i't}K_{i't,j't}u_{l',t-1}K_{i',t-1;l',t-1}] \\
&= \frac{1}{n\ N^5a^{4q}}\sum_i\sum_t\sum_{j\neq i}\sum_{l\neq i}\sum_{j'\neq i}\sum_{l'\neq i} \\
&\quad \times \mathrm{E}[u_{it}^2u_{l,t-1}u_{l',t-1}K_{it,jt}K_{i,t-1;l,t-1}K_{it,j't}K_{i,t-1;l',t-1}] \\
&\equiv \mathrm{RH1},
\end{aligned}
$$

where in the fourth equality, we used the fact that if $i \neq i'$, $\mathrm{E}[u_{it}K_{it,jt}u_{l,t-1} K_{i,t-1;l,t-1}u_{i't}K_{it,j't}u_{l',t-1}K_{i',t-1;l',t-1}] = \mathrm{E}[K_{it,jt}K_{i,t-1;l,t-1}K_{it,j't}K_{i',t-1;l',t-1}\mathrm{E}(u_{it}u_{i't}u_{l,t-1}u_{l',t-1}|w_{\cdot t},w_{\cdot t-1})] = 0$. This is because u_{it} is independent of $u_{i't}$ and $\mathrm{E}(u_{it}|w_{\cdot t},w_{\cdot t-1},u_{\cdot,t-1}) = 0$. This kind of argument will be used several times in this appendix.

We consider RH1 for three different cases: (i) the summation indices i, j, l, j', l' are all different from each other; (ii) i, j, l, j', l' take four different values; and (iii) i, j, l, j', l' take at most three different values.

For case (i), it is easy to see that $\mathrm{RH1}_{(i)} = 0$ because $u_{l,t-1}$ is independent of all the variables in $\mathrm{RH1}_{(i)}$ except $w_{l,t-1}$ and $\mathrm{E}(u_{l,t-1}|w_{l,t-1}) = 0$.

For case (ii), using the same argument as we did in the case (i) above, it is easy to see that $\mathrm{RH1}_{(ii)} \neq 0$ if and only if $l = l'$. In this case, $\mathrm{RH1}_{(ii)}$ becomes

$$\mathrm{RH1}_{(ii)} = \left[\frac{1}{n\ N^5a^{4q}}\sum_i\sum_t\sum_{j\neq i}\sum_{l\neq i}\sum_{j'\neq i}\mathrm{E}[u_{it}^2u_{l,\,t-1}^2K_{it,\,jt}K_{i,\,t-1;\,l,\,t-1}^2K_{it,\,j't}]\right]$$

$$= \frac{1}{nN^5a^{4q}}\mathrm{O}(N^4a^{3q}) = \mathrm{O}((N^2a^q)^{-1}).$$

Finally it is easy to see that $\mathrm{RH1}_{(iii)} = (nN^5a^{4q})^{-1}\mathrm{O}(N^3a^{2q}) = \mathrm{O}(N^{-3}a^{-2q})$.

Summarizing the above, we showed that $\mathrm{RH1} = \mathrm{E}\{[S_{u\hat{f},u_{-1}\hat{f}_{-1}}]^2\} = \mathrm{O}(N^{-2}a^{-q})$. Hence $S_{u\hat{f},u_{-1}\hat{f}_{-1}} = \mathrm{O}_p(N^{-1}a^{-q/2}) = \mathrm{o}_p(N^{-1/2})$.

The proofs of (b) and (c) follow the same arguments as in the proof of (a) and are therefore omitted here. However, these proofs are available from the authors upon request.

Lemma A.5.

(a) $S_{u\hat{f},(\theta_{-1}-\hat{\theta}_{-1})\hat{f}_{-1}} = \mathrm{O}_p(a(Na^{q/2})^{-1} + N^{-1/2}a^{\nu})$,
(b) $S_{\hat{u}\hat{f},(\theta_{-1}-\hat{\theta}_{-1})\hat{f}_{-1}} = \mathrm{O}_p(a(Na^{q/2})^{-1} + N^{-1/2}a^{\nu})$,
(c) $S_{(\theta-\hat{\theta})\hat{f},(\theta_{-1}-\hat{\theta}_{-1})\hat{f}_{-1}} = \mathrm{O}_p(a^2(Na^q)^{-1} + a^{2\nu})$.

Proof. (a) follows the same proof as $S_{u\hat{f},(\theta-\hat{\theta})\hat{f}} = \mathrm{O}_p(a(Na^{q/2})^{-1} + N^{-1/2}a^{\nu})$ of Lemma A.3(b). This is because $\mathrm{E}(u_{it}|w_{i,t-s}) = 0$ for $s \geqslant 0$. Hence replacing $\mathrm{E}(u_{it}|w_{it}) = 0$ in the proof of Lemma A.3(b) by $\mathrm{E}(u_{it}|w_{i,t-1}) = 0$ gives the proof of Lemma A.5(a).

(b) follows the same proof as Lemma A.3(c).

(c) follows from Lemma A.3(a) and the Cauchy's inequality.

Lemma A.6.

(a) $S_{(\theta-\hat{\theta})\hat{f},u_{-1}\hat{f}_{-1}} = \mathrm{O}_p(a^{\nu} + N^{-1/2}a^{\nu/2})$, (b) $S_{(\theta-\hat{\theta})\hat{f},\hat{u}_{-1}\hat{f}_{-1}} = \mathrm{O}_p(N^{-1/2}a^{\nu/2})$.

Proof. (a) We first show that $\mathrm{E}[S_{(\theta-\hat\theta)\hat f, u_{-1}\hat f_{-1}}] = \mathrm{O}(a^{\nu})$.

$$\mathrm{E}[S_{(\theta-\hat\theta)\hat f, u_{-1}\hat f_{-1}}] = \frac{1}{nN^2a^{2q}}\sum_i\sum_t\sum_{j\neq i}\sum_{l\neq i} \times \mathrm{E}[(\theta_{it}-\theta_{jt})K_{it,jt}u_{i,t-1}K_{i,t-1;l,t-1}] \equiv \mathrm{RH2}.$$

We consider RH2 for two different cases: (i) $l \neq j$ and (ii) $l = j$. For case (i), we have

$$\begin{aligned}\mathrm{RH2}_{(\mathrm{i})} &= \frac{1}{Ta^{2q}}\sum_t \mathrm{E}[(\theta_{1t}-\theta_{2t})K_{1t,2t}u_{1,t-1}K_{1,t-1;3,t-1}] \\ &= \frac{1}{Ta^{2q}}\sum_t \mathrm{E}[(\theta_{1t}-\theta_{2t})K_{1t,2t}\eta(w_{1t}, w_{1,t-1})K_{1,t-1;3,t-1}] \\ &\leqslant \frac{a^{\nu}}{Ta^{q}}\sum_t \mathrm{E}[|D_{\theta}(w_{1t})\eta(w_{1t},w_{1,t-1})K_{1,t-1;3,t-1}|] \quad \text{(by Lemma A.1(b))} \\ &= \mathrm{O}(a^{\nu}).\end{aligned}$$

Obviously for case (ii) $\mathrm{RH2}_{(\mathrm{ii})} = (1/Na^{2q})\mathrm{O}_p(a^{2q}) = \mathrm{O}(N^{-1}) = \mathrm{o}(a^{\nu})$. Hence $\mathrm{E}[S_{(\theta-\hat\theta)\hat f, u_{-1}\hat f_{-1}}] = \mathrm{O}(a^{\nu})$.

The second moment of $S_{(\theta-\hat\theta)\hat f, u_{-1}\hat f_{-1}}$ is:

$$\begin{aligned}&\mathrm{E}[S_{(\theta-\hat\theta)\hat f, u_{-1}\hat f_{-1}}]^2 \\ &= \mathrm{E}\left\{\left[\frac{1}{nN^2a^{2q}}\sum_i\sum_t\sum_{j\neq i}\sum_{l\neq i}\mathrm{E}[(\theta_{it}-\theta_{jt})K_{it,jt}u_{i,t-1}K_{i,t-1;l,t-1}\right]^2\right\} \\ &= \frac{1}{n^2N^4a^{4q}}\sum_i\sum_t\sum_{j\neq i}\sum_{l\neq i}\sum_{i'}\sum_{t'}\sum_{j'\neq i'}\sum_{l'\neq i'} \\ &\quad \times \mathrm{E}[(\theta_{it}-\theta_{jt})K_{it,jt}U_{i,t-1}K_{i,t-1;l,t-1}][(\theta_{i't'}-\theta_{j't'}) \\ &\quad \times K_{i't',j't'}u_{i',t'-1}K_{i',t'-1;l',t'-1}] \\ &\sim \frac{1}{n\,N^5a^{4q}}\sum_i\sum_t\sum_{j\neq i}\sum_{l\neq i}\sum_{i'}\sum_{j'\neq i'}\sum_{l'\neq i'} \\ &\quad \times \mathrm{E}\{[(\theta_{it}-\theta_{jt})K_{it,jt}U_{i,t-1}K_{i,t-1;l,t-1}][(\theta_{i't}-\theta_{j't}) \\ &\quad \times K_{i't,j't}u_{i',t-1}K_{i',t-1;l',t-1}]\} \\ &\equiv \mathrm{RH3}.\end{aligned}$$

Case (i) i, j, l, i', j', l' are all different from each other. In this case, the two terms in the two square brackets are independent, we have $\text{RH3}_{(i)} = \text{O}([\text{E}(S_{(\theta-\hat{\theta})\hat{f},u_{-1}\hat{f}_{-1}}]^2) = \text{O}(a^{2\nu})$.

Case (ii) i, j, l, i', j', l' take five different values. It is easy to see that in this case $\text{RH3}_{ii} = (1/N^6a^{4q})\text{O}(N^5a^{2\nu+4q}) = \text{O}(N^{-1}a^{2\nu})$.

Case (iii) i, j, l, i', j', l' take at most four different values. In this case, $\text{RH3}_{(iii)} = (1/N^6a^{4q})\text{O}(N^4a^{3q}) = \text{O}(N^{-2}a^{-q})$.

Thus we have shown that $\text{RH3} = \text{O}(a^{2\nu} + N^{-2}a^{-q})$. Hence $S_{(\theta-\hat{\theta})\hat{f},u_{-1}\hat{f}_{-1}} = \text{O}_p(a^\nu + N^{-1}a^{-q/2})$.

(b) The proof follows the same argument as in the RH3 part of (a). The reason that (b) does not have a $\text{O}(a^\nu)$ order term is that $\text{E}[S_{(\theta-\hat{\theta})\hat{f},u_{-1}\hat{f}_{-1}}] = \text{O}(N^{-1})$ (rather than $\text{O}(a^\nu)$). To see this is indeed the true, we have

$$\text{E}[S_{(\theta-\hat{\theta})\hat{f},\hat{u}_{-1}\hat{f}_{-1}}] = \frac{1}{n\ N^2a^{2q}}\sum_i\sum_t\sum_{j\neq i}\sum_{l\neq i}\text{E}[(\theta_{it}-\theta_{jt})K_{it,\ jt}u_{l,\ t-1}K_{i,\ t-1;\ l,\ t-1}]$$

$$\equiv \text{RH4}.$$

We consider RH4 for two different cases: (i) $l \neq j$ and (ii) $l = j$. For case (i), we have

$$\text{RH4}_{(i)} = \frac{1}{Ta^{2q}}\sum_t\text{E}[(\theta_{1t}-\theta_{2t})K_{1t,\ 2t}u_{3,\ t-1}K_{1,\ t-1;\ 3,\ t-1}] = 0$$

because $u_{3,t-1}$ is independent of all the variables except $w_{3,t-1}$ and $\text{E}(u_{3,t-1}|w_{3,t-1}) = 0$.

Obviously $\text{RH4}_{(ii)} = (1/nN^2a^{2q})\sum_i\sum_t\sum_{j\neq i}\text{E}[(\theta_{1t}-\theta_{2t})K_{1t,\ 2t}u_{2,\ t-1}K_{1,\ t-1;\ 2,\ t-1}] = (1/Na^{2q})\text{O}(a^{2q}) = \text{O}(N^{-1})$. Hence $\text{E}[S_{(\theta-\hat{\theta})\hat{f},u_{-1}\hat{f}_{-1}}] = \text{O}(N^{-1})$.

The second moment of $S_{(\theta-\hat{\theta})\hat{f},\hat{u}_{-1}\hat{f}} = \text{O}(N^{-2}a^{-q})$ by the similar proof as in the proof of (a) $\text{RH3}_{(ii)} + \text{RH3}_{(iii)} = \text{O}(N^{-2}a^{-q})$ above. Hence $S_{(\theta-\hat{\theta})\hat{f},u_{-1}\hat{f}_{-1}} = \text{O}_p(N^{-1}a^{-q/2})$.

Lemma A.7. (a) $S_{u\hat{f},u_{-1}\hat{f}_{-1}} - S_{u\hat{f},u_{-1}f_{-1}} = \text{O}_p(N^{-1/2}a^\nu + N^{-1}a^{-q/2})$.

(b) $S_{u\hat{f},u_{-1}f_{-1}} - S_{uf,u_{-1}f_{-1}} = \text{O}_p(N^{-1/2}a^\nu + N^{-1}a^{-q/2})$.

Proof. (a) $S_{u\hat{f},u_{-1}\hat{f}_{-1}} - S_{u\hat{f},u_{-1}f_{-1}} = (1/n)\sum_i\sum_t u_{it}\hat{f}_{it}u_{i,\ t-1}(\hat{f}_{i,\ t-1} - f_{i,\ t-1}) = (1/nN^2a^q)\sum_i\sum_t\sum_{j\neq i}\sum_{l\neq i}u_{it}K_{it,jt}u_{i,\ t-1}(a^{-q}K_{i,\ t-1;\ l,\ t-1} - f_{i,\ t-1})$. It is easy to see that $S_{u\hat{f},u_{-1}\hat{f}_{-1}} - S_{u\hat{f},u_{-1}f_{-1}}$ has mean zero because $\text{E}(u_{it}|w_{\cdot t},w_{\cdot t-1},u_{i,t-1}) = 0$ (under H_0). Its second moment is

$$\begin{aligned}
&\text{E}[S_{u\hat{f},u_{-1}\hat{f}_{-1}} - S_{u\hat{f},u_{-1}f_{-1}}]^2 \\
&= \frac{1}{n^2N^4a^{2q}}\sum_i\sum_t\sum_{j\neq i}\sum_{l\neq i}\sum_{i'}\sum_{t'}\sum_{j'\neq i'}\sum_{l'\neq i'} \\
&\quad\times\text{E}\{[u_{it}K_{it,\ jt}u_{i,\ t-1}(a^{-q}K_{i,\ t-1;l,\ t-1} - f_{i,\ t-1})] \\
&\quad\times[u_{i't'}K_{i't',\ j't'}u_{i',\ t'-1}(a^{-q}K_{i',\ t'-1;l',\ t'-1} - f_{i',\ t'-1})]\}
\end{aligned}$$

$$\sim \frac{1}{n^2N^4a^{2q}}\sum_i \sum_{j\neq i} \sum_{l\neq i} \sum_{i'} \sum_{j'\neq i'} \sum_{l'\neq i'}$$

$$\times \mathrm{E}\{[u_{it}K_{it,\,jt}u_{i,\,t-1}(a^{-q}K_{i,\,t-1;l,\,t-1} - f_{i,\,t-1})]$$

$$[u_{i't}K_{i't,j't}u_{i',\,t-1}(a^{-q}K_{i',\,t-1;l',\,t-1} - f_{i',\,t-1}))]\}$$

$$= \frac{1}{n^2N^4a^{2q}}\sum_i \sum_{j\neq i} \sum_{l\neq i} \sum_{j'\neq i} \sum_{l'\neq i} \mathrm{E}\{[u_{it}^2K_{it,\,jt}u_{i,\,t-1}(a^{-q}K_{i,\,t-1;l,\,t-1} - f_{i,\,t-1})]$$

$$\times [K_{it,\,j't}u_{i,\,t-1}(a^{-q}K_{i,\,t-1;l',\,t-1} - f_{i,\,t-1}))]\}$$

$$\equiv \mathrm{RH5},$$

because if $i' \neq i$, u_{it} is independent of all the variables except $(w_{it}, w_{i,t-1})$ and $\mathrm{E}(u_{it}|w_{it}, w_{i,t-1}) = 0$.

Case (i) if i, j, l, j', l' are all different from each other, $\mathrm{RH5}_{(i)} = (1/N^6a^{2q})\mathrm{O_p}(N^5a^{2v+2q}) = \mathrm{O}(N^{-1}a^{2v})$ by Lemma A.1(c).

Case (ii) i, j, l, j', l' take four different values. (1) If $l \neq l'$ and both are different from any other indices, we have $\mathrm{RH5}_{(ii),(1)} = (1/N^6a^{2q})\mathrm{O_p}(N^4a^{2v+2q}) = \mathrm{O}(N^{-2}a^{2v})$ by Lemma A.1(c). (2) $l = l'$, $\mathrm{RH5}_{(ii),(2)} = (1/N^6a^{2q})\mathrm{O_p}(N^4a^{q}) = \mathrm{O}(N^{-2}a^{-q})$ by Lemma A.1(d). (3) $l \neq l'$ with l or l' equal one other index. $\mathrm{RH5}_{(ii),(3)} = (1/N^6a^{2q})\mathrm{O}(N^4a^{v+2q}) = \mathrm{O}(N^{-2}a^{v})$. Hence $\mathrm{RH5}_{(ii)} = \mathrm{O}(N^{-2}a^{-q})$.

Case (iii) when i, j, l, j', l' take at most three different values. It is easy to see that $\mathrm{RH5}_{(iii)} = (1/N^6a^{2q})\mathrm{O}(N^3a^{q}) = \mathrm{O}(N^{-3}a^{-q})$.

Summarizing the above, we have shown that $\mathrm{RH5} = \mathrm{O}(N^{-1}a^{2v} + N^{-2}a^{-q})$. Hence $S_{u\hat{f},u_{-1}\hat{f}_{-1}} - S_{u\hat{f},u_{-1}f_{-1}} = \mathrm{O_p}(N^{-1/2}a^{v} + N^{-1}a^{-q/2}) = \mathrm{o_p}(N^{-1/2})$.

(b) $S_{u\hat{f},u_{-1}f_{-1}} - S_{uf,u_{-1}f_{-1}} = (1/n)\sum_i\sum_t u_{it}u_{i,t-1}f_{i,t-1}(\hat{f}_{it} - f_{it}) = (1/nNa^q)\sum_i\sum_t\sum_{j\neq i} u_{it}\, u_{i,t-1}f_{i,t-1}\,(a^{-q}K_{it,jt} - f_{it})$. Obviously $S_{u\hat{f},u_{-1}f_{-1}} - S_{uf,u_{-1}f_{-1}}$ has mean zero and its second moment is

$$\mathrm{E}[S_{u\hat{f},u_{-1}f_{-1}} - S_{uf,u_{-1}f_{-1}}]^2$$

$$= \frac{1}{n^2N^2a^{2q}}\sum_i \sum_t \sum_{j\neq i} \sum_{i'} \sum_{t'} \sum_{j'\neq i'} \mathrm{E}\{[u_{it}u_{i,\,t-1}f_{i,\,t-1}(a^{-q}K_{it,\,jt} - f_{it})]$$

$$\times [u_{i't'}u_{i',t'-1}f_{i',t'-1}(a^{-q}K_{i't',j't'} - f_{i't'})]\}$$

$$= \frac{1}{n^2N^2a^{2q}}\sum_i \sum_t \sum_{j\neq i} \sum_{t'} \sum_{j'\neq i'} \mathrm{E}\{[u_{it}^2u_{i,\,t-1}^2f_{i,\,t-1}(a^{-q}K_{it,\,jt} - f_{it})]$$

$$\times [f_{i,\,t'-1}(a^{-q}K_{it',j't'} - f_{it'})]\}$$

$$\sim \frac{1}{nN^3a^{2q}}\sum_i \sum_t \sum_{j\neq i} \sum_{j'\neq i'} \mathrm{E}\{[u_{it}^2u_{i,\,t-1}^2f_{i,\,t-1}(a^{-q}K_{it,\,jt} - f_{it})]$$

$$\times [f_{i,\,t-1}(a^{-q}K_{it,\,j't} - f_{it})]\}$$

$$\equiv \mathrm{RH6}.$$

Case (i) if i, j, l, j', l' are all different, $\mathrm{RH6}_{(i)} = (1/N^4a^{2q})\mathrm{O}(N^5a^{2q+2\nu}) = \mathrm{O}(N^{-1}a^{2\nu})$.

Case (ii) i, j, l, j', l' take at most four different values, $\mathrm{RH6}_{(ii)} = (1/N^4a^{2q})\mathrm{O}(N^4a^q) = \mathrm{O}(N^{-2}a^{-q})$.

Hence $\mathrm{RH6} = \mathrm{O}(N^{-1}a^{2\nu} + N^{-2}a^{-q})$ and $S_{u\hat{f},u_{-1}f_{-1}} - S_{uf,u_{-1}f_{-1}} = \mathrm{O}_p(N^{-1/2}a^{\nu} + N^{-1}a^{-q/2}) = \mathrm{o}_p(N^{-1/2})$.

Proposition A.8. Under the same conditions as Theorem 1, *then* $I_n \underset{d}{\to} \mathrm{N}(0, \sigma_0^2)$.

Proof. Using Eqs. (8) and (9), we have

$$\begin{aligned} I_n &= n^{1/2}S_{[u-\hat{u}+(\theta-\hat{\theta})-(z-\hat{z})(\hat{\gamma}-\gamma)]\hat{f},[u_{-1}-\hat{u}_{-1}+(\theta_{-1}-\hat{\theta}_{-1})-(z_{-1}-\hat{z}_{-1})(\hat{\gamma}-\gamma)]\hat{f}_{-1}} \\ &= n^{1/2}S_{u\hat{f},u_{-1}-\hat{u}_{-1}+(\theta_{-1}-\hat{\theta}_{-1})-(z_{-1}-\hat{z}_{-1})(\hat{\gamma}-\gamma)]\hat{f}_{-1}} \\ &\quad - n^{1/2}S_{\hat{u}\hat{f},[u_{-1}-\hat{u}_{-1}+(\theta_{-1}-\hat{\theta}_{-1})-(z_{-1}-\hat{z}_{-1})(\hat{\gamma}-\gamma)]\hat{f}_{-1}} \\ &\quad + n^{1/2}S_{(\theta-\hat{\theta})\hat{f},[u_{-1}-\hat{u}_{-1}+(\theta_{-1}-\hat{\theta}_{-1})-(z_{-1}-\hat{z}_{-1})(\hat{\gamma}-\gamma)]\hat{f}_{-1}} \\ &\quad - n^{1/2}S_{(z-\hat{z})(\hat{\gamma}-\gamma)\hat{f},[u_{-1}-\hat{u}_{-1}+(\theta_{-1}-\hat{\theta}_{-1})-(z_{-1}-\hat{z}_{-1})(\hat{\gamma}-\gamma)]\hat{f}_{-1}} \\ &\equiv A_{1n} + A_{2n} + A_{3n} + A_{4n}. \end{aligned}$$

We will first show that $A_{1n} = \sqrt{n}S_{uf,u_{-1}f_{-1}} + \mathrm{o}_p(1)$, $A_{2n} = \mathrm{o}_p(1)$, $A_{3n} = \mathrm{o}_p(1)$, and $A_{4n} = -n^{1/2}S_{v\hat{f},u_{-1}\hat{f}_{-1}}(\hat{\gamma}-\gamma)' + \mathrm{o}_p(1) = -n^{1/2}\Phi(\hat{\gamma}-\gamma)' + \mathrm{o}_p(1)$, where $\Phi = (1/T)\sum_t \mathrm{E}[v_{1t}f_{1t}u_{1,t-1}f_{1,t-1}]$.

Proof of $A_{1n} = \sqrt{n}S_{uf,u_{-1}f_{-1}} + \mathrm{o}_p(1)$: Define B_{1n} from $A_{1n} = \sqrt{n}S_{u\hat{f},u_{-1}\hat{f}_{-1}} + B_{1n}$. $\sqrt{n}S_{u\hat{f},u_{-1}\hat{f}_{-1}} = \sqrt{n}S_{uf,u_{-1}f_{-1}} + \mathrm{o}_p(1)$ follows from $n^{1/2}|S_{u\hat{f},u_{-1}\hat{f}_{-1}} - S_{uf,u_{-1}f_{-1}}| \leqslant n^{1/2}|S_{u\hat{f},u_{-1}\hat{f}_{-1}} - S_{u\hat{f},u_{-1}f_{-1}}| + n^{1/2}|S_{u\hat{f},u_{-1}f_{-1}} - S_{uf,u_{-1}f_{-1}}| = \mathrm{o}_p(1)$ by Lemma A.7.

$$\begin{aligned} B_{1n} &= n^{1/2}S_{u\hat{f},[-\hat{u}_{-1}+(\theta_{-1}-\hat{\theta}_{-1})-(z_{-1}-\hat{z}_{-1})(\hat{\gamma}-\gamma)]\hat{f}_{-1}} \\ &= n^{1/2}\{-S_{u\hat{f},\hat{u}_{-1}\hat{f}_{-1}} + S_{u\hat{f},(\theta_{-1}-\hat{\theta}_{-1})\hat{f}_{-1}} \\ &\quad - (\hat{\gamma}-\gamma)'[S_{u\hat{f},v_{-1}\hat{f}_{-1}} - S_{u\hat{f},\hat{v}_{-1}\hat{f}_{-1}} + S_{u\hat{f},(\xi_{-1}-\hat{\xi}_{-1})\hat{f}_{-1}}]\}. \end{aligned}$$

$S_{u\hat{f},\hat{u}_{-1}\hat{f}_{-1}} = \mathrm{o}_p(N^{-1/2})$ by Lemma A.4 (a) and $S_{u\hat{f},(\theta_{-1}-\hat{\theta}_{-1})\hat{f}_{-1}} = \mathrm{o}_p(N^{-1/2})$ by Lemma A.5 (b). Also $\hat{\gamma}-\gamma = \mathrm{O}_p(N^{-1/2})$. Thus we only need to show $S_{u\hat{f},v_{-1}\hat{f}_{-1}}$, $S_{u\hat{f},\hat{v}_{-1}\hat{f}_{-1}}$ and $S_{u\hat{f},(\xi_{-1}-\hat{\xi}_{-1})\hat{f}_{-1}}$ are all $\mathrm{o}_p(1)$.

By Cauchy's inequality and the facts that $S_{u\hat{f}} = \mathrm{O}_p(1)$, $S_{\hat{v}_{-1}\hat{f}_{-1}} = \mathrm{o}_p(1)$ and $S_{(\xi_{-1}-\hat{\xi}_{-1})\hat{f}_{-1}} = \mathrm{o}_p(1)$, we get $S_{u\hat{f},\hat{v}_{-1}\hat{f}_{-1}}$ and $S_{u\hat{f},(\xi_{-1}-\hat{\xi}_{-1})\hat{f}_{-1}}$ are both $\mathrm{o}_p(1)$. Below we show that $S_{u\hat{f},v_{-1}\hat{f}_{-1}} = \mathrm{o}_p(1)$.

By the fact that $\hat{f}_{it} - f_{it} = \mathrm{o}_p(1)$, it is obvious that $|S_{u\hat{f},v_{-1}\hat{f}_{-1}} - S_{uf,v_{-1}f_{-1}}| \leqslant |S_{u\hat{f},v_{-1}\hat{f}_{-1}} - S_{u\hat{f},v_{-1}f_{-1}}| + |S_{u\hat{f},v_{-1}f_{-1}} - S_{uf,v_{-1}f_{-1}}| = \mathrm{o}_p(1)$. Hence it suffices to show $S_{uf,v_{-1}f_{-1}} = \mathrm{o}_p(1)$. $S_{uf,v_{-1}f_{-1}} = (1/N)\sum_{i=1}^N\{T\sum_{t=1}^T u_{it}f(w_{it})[z_{i,t-1} - \mathrm{E}(z_{i,t-1}|w_{i,t-1})]$ $f(w_{i,t-1})\} \equiv (1/N)\sum_{i=1}^N \eta_i \underset{d}{\to} \mathrm{E}(\eta_1) = 0$ by a law of large number because η_i's are i.i.d. with

$\mathrm{E}(\eta_i) = \mathrm{E}\{u_{it}f(w_{it})[z_{i,t-1} - \mathrm{E}(z_{i,t-1}|w_{i,t-1})]f(w_{i,t-1})\} = \mathrm{E}\{f(w_{it})[z_{i,t-1} - \mathrm{E}(z_{i,t-1}|w_{i,t-1})]f(w_{i,t-1})\,\mathrm{E}(u_{it}|w_{it}, w_{i,t-1}, z_{it}, z_{i,t-1})\} = 0.$

Thus we have shown that $A_{1n} = \sqrt{n}S_{uf,u_{-1}f_{-1}} + o_p(1)$.

Proof of $A_{2n} = o_p(1)$

$$A_{2n} = n^{1/2}S_{\hat{u}\hat{f},[u_{-1}-\hat{u}_{-1}+(\theta_{-1}-\hat{\theta}_{-1})-(z_{-1}-\hat{z}_{-1})(\hat{\gamma}-\gamma)]\hat{f}_{-1}}$$
$$= n^{1/2}\{S_{\hat{u}\hat{f},u_{-1}\hat{f}_{-1}} - S_{\hat{u}\hat{f},\hat{u}_{-1}\hat{f}_{-1}} + S_{\hat{u}\hat{f},(\theta_{-1}-\hat{\theta}_{-1})\hat{f}_{-1}} - S_{\hat{u}\hat{f},z_{-1}-\hat{z}_{-1})\hat{f}_{-1}}(\hat{\gamma}-\gamma)\}.$$

$S_{\hat{u}\hat{f},u_{-1}\hat{f}_{-1}} = o_p(N^{-1/2})$ by Lemma A.4 (b), $S_{\hat{u}\hat{f},\hat{u}_{-1}\hat{f}_{-1}} = o_p(N^{-1/2})$ by Lemma A.4 (c) and $S_{\hat{u}\hat{f},(\theta_{-1}-\hat{\theta}_{-1})\hat{f}_{-1}} = o_p(N^{-1/2})$ by Lemma A.5(b). Finally $S_{(\hat{u}\hat{f},z_{-1}-\hat{z}_{-1})\hat{f}_{-1}} = o_p(1)$ by Cauchy inequality and the facts that $S_{\hat{u}\hat{f}} = o_p(1)$ and $S_{(z_{-1}-\hat{z}_{-1})\hat{f}_{-1}} = O_p(1)$. Hence $S_{\hat{u}\hat{f},z_{-1}-\hat{z}_{-1})\hat{f}_{-1}}(\hat{\gamma}-\gamma) = o_p(N^{-1/2})$ because $\hat{\gamma}-\gamma = O_p(N^{-1/2})$.

Proof of $A_{3n} = o_p(1)$

$$A_{3n} = n^{1/2}S_{(\theta-\hat{\theta})\hat{f},[u_{-1}-\hat{u}_{-1}+(\theta_{-1}-\hat{\theta}_{-1})-(z_{-1}-\hat{z}_{-1})(\hat{\gamma}-\gamma)]\hat{f}_{-1}}$$
$$= n^{1/2}\{S_{(\theta-\hat{\theta})\hat{f},u_{-1}\hat{f}_{-1}} - S_{(\theta-\hat{\theta})\hat{f},\hat{u}_{-1}\hat{f}_{-1}} + S_{(\theta-\hat{\theta})\hat{f},(\theta_{-1}-\hat{\theta}_{-1})\hat{f}_{-1}}$$
$$- S_{(\theta-\hat{\theta})\hat{f},z_{-1}-\hat{z}_{-1})\hat{f}_{-1}}(\hat{\gamma}-\gamma)\}.$$

$S_{(\theta-\hat{\theta})\hat{f},u_{-1}\hat{f}_{-1}} = o_p(N^{-1/2})$ by Lemma A.5(a), $S_{(\theta-\hat{\theta})\hat{f},\hat{u}_{-1}\hat{f}_{-1}} = o_p(N^{-1/2})$ by Lemma A.6(a) and $S_{(\theta-\hat{\theta})\hat{f},(\theta_{-1}-\hat{\theta}_{-1})\hat{f}_{-1}} = o_p(N^{-1/2})$ by Lemma A.5(c). Finally $S_{(\theta-\hat{\theta})\hat{f},z_{-1}-\hat{z}_{-1})\hat{f}_{-1}} = o_p(1)$ by Cauchy inequality and the facts that $S_{(z_{-1}-\hat{z}_{-1})\hat{f}_{-1}} = O_p(1)$ and $S_{(\theta-\hat{\theta})\hat{f}} = o_p(1)$. Hence $S_{(\theta-\hat{\theta})\hat{f},z_{-1}-\hat{z}_{-1})\hat{f}_{-1}}(\hat{\gamma}-\gamma) = o_p(N^{-1/2})$ because $\hat{\gamma}-\gamma = O_p(N^{-1/2})$.

Proof of $A_{4n} = -n^{1/2}\Phi(\hat{\gamma}-\gamma)' + o_p(1)$

$$A_{4n} = -n^{1/2}S_{(z-\hat{z})(\hat{\gamma}-\gamma)\hat{f},[u_{-1}-\hat{u}_{-1}+(\theta_{-1}-\hat{\theta}_{-1})-(z_{-1}-\hat{z}_{-1})(\hat{\gamma}-\gamma)]\hat{f}_{-1}}$$
$$= -n^{1/2}(\hat{\gamma}-\gamma)'\{S_{(z-\hat{z})\hat{f},u_{-1}\hat{f}_{-1}} - S_{(z-\hat{z})\hat{f},\hat{u}_{-1}\hat{f}_{-1}} + S_{(z-\hat{z})\hat{f},(\theta_{-1}-\hat{\theta}_{-1})\hat{f}_{-1}}$$
$$- S_{(z-\hat{z})\hat{f},(z_{-1}-\hat{z}_{-1})\hat{f}_{-1}}(\hat{\gamma}-\gamma)\}.$$

Using the fact that $\hat{\gamma} = O_p(N^{-1/2})$, it sufficies to show that (i) $S_{(z-\hat{z})\hat{f},u_{-1}\hat{f}_{-1}} = \Phi + o_p(1)$, (ii) $S_{(z-\hat{z})\hat{f},\hat{u}_{-1}\hat{f}_{-1}}$ and (iii) $S_{(z-\hat{z})\hat{f},(\theta_{-1}-\hat{\theta}_{-1})\hat{f}_{-1}}$ are both $o_p(1)$, and (iv) $S_{(z-\hat{z})\hat{f},(z_{-1}-\hat{z}_{-1})\hat{f}_{-1}}$ is $O_p(1)$. (iv) is obviously true. Using Cauchy's inequality and the facts that $S_{\hat{u}_{-1}\hat{f}_{-1}} = o_p(1)$, $S_{(\theta_{-1}-\hat{\theta}_{-1})\hat{f}_{-1}} = o_p(1)$ and $S_{(z-\hat{z})\hat{f}} = O_p(1)$, lead to (ii) and (iii). Finally for (i) using $z_{it} - \hat{z}_{it} = (\xi_{it} - \hat{\xi}_{it}) + v_{it} - \hat{v}_{it}$, it is easy to see that $S_{(z-\hat{z})\hat{f},u_{-1}\hat{f}_{-1}} = S_{(\xi-\hat{\xi})\hat{f},u_{-1}\hat{f}_{-1}} + S_{v\hat{f},u_{-1}\hat{f}_{-1}} - S_{\hat{v}\hat{f},u_{-1}\hat{f}_{-1}} = S_{v\hat{f},u_{-1}\hat{f}_{-1}} + o_p(1) = S_{vf,u_{-1}f_{-1}} + o_p(1)$, and that $\mathrm{E}[S_{vf,u_{-1}f_{-1}}] = \Phi$, $\mathrm{var}[S_{vf,u_{-1}f_{-1}}] = o(1)$. Hence (i) also holds.

Now summarizing the above results, we have shown that $I_n = \sqrt{n}S_{uf,u_{-1}f_{-1}} + \sqrt{n}(\hat{\gamma} - \gamma)'\Phi + o_p(1)$. Using Lemma 1(i), we have $\sqrt{n}S_{uf,u_{-1}f_{-1}} - \sqrt{n}(\hat{\gamma} - \gamma)'\Phi = (1/\sqrt{N})\sum_i(1/\sqrt{T})\sum_t[u_{i,t-1}f_{i,t-1} - v'_{it}f_{it}B^{-1}\Phi]u_{it}f_{it} \equiv (1/\sqrt{N})\sum_i\eta_i \xrightarrow{d} N(0,\sigma_0^2)$ by Levi–Lindeberg central limit theorem, because η_i is i.i.d. with zero mean and finite variance $E[\eta_1^2] = (1/T)\sum_t E[(u_{1,t-1}f_{1,t-1} - v'_{1t}f_{1t}B^{-1}\Phi)u_{1t}f_{1t}]^2 = \sigma_0^2$.

Proposition A.9. Under the same conditions as Theorem 1, *then* $\hat{\sigma}_0^2 = \sigma_0^2 + o_p(1)$.

Proof. Using the similar arguments as in the proof of Proposition A.8, it is easy to show that $\hat{B} = B + o_p(1)$, $\hat{\Phi} = \Phi + o_p(1)$. Then it is straightforward to show that $\hat{\sigma}_0^2 = (1/n)\sum_i\sum_t[(u_{i,t-1}f_{i,t-1} - v'_{it}f_{it}B^{-1}\Phi)u_{it}f_{it}]^2 + o_p(1) \equiv (1/N)\sum_i B_i + o_p(1)$, where $B_i = (1/T)\sum_t[(u_{i,t-1}f_{i,t-1} - v'_{it}f_{it}\Phi B^{-1})u_{it}f_{it}]^2$. $(1/N)\sum_i B_i \xrightarrow{p} E[B_1] = \sigma_0^2$ by a law of large number.

References

Ahn, S.C., Schmidt, P., 1995. Efficient estimation of models for dynamic panel data. Journal of Econometrics 68, 5–27.

Anderson, T.W., Hsiao, C., 1982. Formulation and estimation of dynamic models using panel data. Journal of Econometrics 18, 47–82.

Arellano, M., Bover, O., 1995. Another look at the instrumental variables estimation of error-component models. Journal of Econometrics 18, 29–51.

Balestra, P., Nerlove, M., 1966. Pooling cross-section and time-series data in the estimation of a dynamic model: the demand of natural gas. Econometrica 34, 585–612.

Baltagi, B., Hildago, J., Li, Q., 1996. A nonparametric poolability test. Journal of Econometrics 75, 345–367.

Bierens, H., 1983. Uniform consistency of kernel estimators of a regression function under generalized conditions. Journal of American Statistical Association 78, 699–707.

Breusch, T.S., Pagan, A.R., 1980. The lagrange multiplier test and its applications to model specification in econometrics. Review of Economics Studies 47, 239–253.

Box, G., Pierce, D., 1970. Distribution of residual autocorrelations in autoregressive and moving average time series models. Journal of American Statistical Association 65, 1509–1526.

Breusch, T.S., 1978. Testing for autocorrelation in dynamic linear models. Australian Economic Papers 17, 334–355.

Delgado, M., Mora, J., 1995. Nonparametric and semiparametric estimation with discrete regressors.

Durbin, J., 1970. Testing for serial correlation in least squares regression when some of the regressors are lagged dependent variables. Econometrica 38, 410–421.

Durbin, J., Watson, G.S., 1950. Testing serial correlation in least squares regression. Biometrica 37, 409–428.

Engle, R.F., Grange, C.W.J., Rice, J., Weiss, A., 1986. Semiparametric estimates of the relationship between weather and electricity sales. Journal of the American Statistical Association 81, 310–320.

Godfrey, L.G., 1978. Testing for higher order serial correlation in regression equations when the regressors include lagged dependent variables. Econometrica 46, 1303–1310.

Hsiao, C., 1986. Analysis of Panel Data. Cambridge University Press, Cambridge.

Keane, M.P., Runkle, D.E., 1992. On the estimation of panel-data models with serial correlation when instruments are not strictly exogenous. Journal of Business and Economics Statistics 10, 1–9.

Kniesner, T., Li, Q., 1994. Semiparametric panel data models with dynamic adjustment: Theoretical consideration and an application to labor supply. Discussion paper, Department of Economics, Indiana University.

Li, Q., 1996. A note on root-n-consistent semiparametric estimation of partially linear models. Economics Letters 51, 277–285.

Li, Q., Stengos, T., 1996. Semiparametric estimation of partially linear panel data models. Journal of Econometrics 71, 389–397.

Pesaran, M.H., Smith, R., 1995. Estimating long-run relationship from dynamic heterogeneous panels. Journal of Econometrics 68, 79–113.

Powell, J.L., Stock, J.H., Stoker, T.M., 1989. Semiparametric estimation of index coefficients. Econometrica 57, 1043–1430.

Robinson, P., 1988. Root-N consistent semiparametric regression. Econometrica 56, 931–954.

[23]

ELSEVIER

Journal of Econometrics 71 (1996) 291–307

JOURNAL OF Econometrics

Specification testing in panel data with instrumental variables

Gilbert E. Metcalf

Department of Economics, Tufts University, Medford, MA 02155, USA

(Received February 1993; final version received September 1994)

Abstract

I show that specification tests for correlated fixed effects developed by Hausman and Taylor extend in an analogous way to panel data sets with endogenous regressors. Given panel data, different sets of instrumental variables can be used to construct the test. For a simple class of models, the test in many cases is asymptotically more efficient if an incomplete set of instruments is used. However, in small samples one may do better using the complete set of instruments. Monte Carlo results demonstrate the likely gains for different assumptions about the degree of between and within variance in the data.

Key words: Econometrics; Panel data; Instrumental variables; Specification testing
JEL classification: C12; C15; C23

1. Introduction

Following early work by Hausman (1978) and Hausman and Taylor (1981), specification testing for correlated fixed effects in panel data models is now a standard tool for researchers. To date, the test as derived in the latter paper has not allowed for the possibility of endogenous right-hand side variables. In this paper, I extend the results of Hausman and Taylor (1981) to the case where right-hand side variables are assumed to be endogenous (specifically, correlated with the time-varying component of the error structure). It turns out that the IV analogous specification tests for correlated fixed effects given in Hausman and Taylor (1981) are applicable in this context. However, it is important to specify the instrument set appropriately for the test. Perhaps surprisingly, for a simple

My thanks to Jim Powell, Whitney Newey, Gregory Chow, and the referees for helpful advice.

SSDI 0304407694017066

class of models that I consider, the more powerful test statistic in many cases uses an inefficient estimator. Asymptotically, while the variance used to construct the test statistic will be greater than the variance associated with using a more efficient estimator, its asymptotic bias will also be greater as the null hypothesis of no correlation is violated. The increase in bias more than offsets the increase in variance thereby leading to a more powerful test statistic.

The next two sections derive this asymptotic result for a simple model. I then consider the small-sample properties of the different test statistics under different assumptions about the quality of the instrument and the degree of correlation between the fixed effects and the instrument by means of a Monte Carlo experiment. Finally there is a brief conclusion.

2. The model and test

The model under consideration is

$$Y = X\beta + \alpha \otimes e_T + \varepsilon, \tag{1}$$

where Y is an $NT \times 1$ vector, X an $NT \times k$ matrix, α an $N \times 1$ vector of individual effects (α_i i.i.d. with mean 0 and variance σ_α^2), and ε an i.i.d. random vector with mean 0 and covariance matrix $\sigma_\varepsilon^2 I_{NT}$. The vector e_T is a $T \times 1$ vector of ones. The data are stacked by individuals over time. That is, $Y' = [Y_1' \, Y_2' \ldots Y_N']$, where Y_i is a $T \times 1$ vector of observations on the ith individual. This equation is part of a simultaneous system and by assumption some columns of X are correlated with ε. It is assumed that was some (possibly all) columns of X are also correlated with the individual effects. There is a set of instruments Z, a matrix $NT \times L$, $L \geqslant k$, valid in the sense that Z is correlated with X but uncorrelated with ε. It is assumed that columns of X which are uncorrelated with ε are contained in Z. The present purpose is to test whether Z is correlated with the individual effects. Specifically, I consider the hypotheses:[1]

$$\mathrm{H_0}: \quad \operatorname*{plim}_{N\to\infty} \left\{ \sum_{i=1}^{N} Z_{it}' \alpha_i / N \right\} = 0, \quad \forall t,$$

$$\mathrm{H_A}: \quad \operatorname*{plim}_{N\to\infty} \left\{ \sum_{i=1}^{N} Z_{it}' \alpha_i / N \right\} \neq 0, \quad \forall t.$$

[1] An alternative null hypothesis which appears less restrictive is $\operatorname{plim}_{N\to\infty} \sum_{i=1}^{N} \{\bar{Z}_1' \cdot \alpha_i / N\} = 0$ where $\bar{Z}_i$ is the average over time of the observations of Z_{it}. However, Amemiya and McCurdy (1986) note that the assumptions under the two null hypotheses are equivalent if one also assumes that the estimator for β continues to be consistent when estimated using any $T-1$ of the T time periods. While there may be circumstances in which this second set of $T-1$ assumptions fails to hold while the assumption that $\operatorname{plim} \sum_{i=1}^{N} \bar{Z}_i' \cdot \alpha_i / N = 0$ holds, it seems reasonable to believe this is an unusual case. Hence I argue that for our purposes the null hypothesis in the text is not overly restrictive. Whether the additional $T-1$ assumptions implied by this null hypothesis hold or not is in fact an empirical manner. A specification test can easily be constructed to test their validity.

Given the loss of information resulting from the use of the within or first difference estimators to eliminate correlated fixed effects, there is a large gain possible if one can assume the null hypothesis. In this case, the GLS-IV estimator will be more efficient.

Letting $u = \alpha \otimes e_T + \varepsilon$, then

$$E(uu') \equiv \Omega = T\sigma_\alpha^2 P_v + \sigma_\varepsilon^2 I_{NT}, \tag{2}$$

or

$$E(uu') = \sigma_1^2 P_v + \sigma_\varepsilon^2 Q_v, \tag{2'}$$

where $\sigma_1^2 = T\sigma_\alpha^2 + \sigma_\varepsilon^2$, $P_v = (I_N \otimes e_T e_T')/T$, and $Q_v = I - P_v$. For future reference, I use the fact that $\Omega^{-1/2} = \sigma_1^{-1} P_v + \sigma_\varepsilon^{-1} Q_v$ and denote $\Omega^{-1/2}$ by H. $P_v X$ replaces the observations for each column of X by the average of the observations for each individual over time. $Q_v X$ replaces the observations by the deviations from the time averages.

First note that the Hausman-type specification test, comparing the GLS-IV estimator with the fixed effects (within) estimator, can be constructed using the within and the between estimators. Define the operator P_A as the projection operator: $P_A = A(A'A)^{-1}A'$. If Z is a set of variables uncorrelated with ε, there are different possible instrument sets that I can use. Following the general approach of Cornwell, Schmidt, and Wyhowski (1993) (CSW), I consider instrument sets of the form $\tilde{Z} = [Q_v Z, P_v B]$ where B is defined as a matrix of potential instruments. The GLS-IV estimator is given by

$$\hat{\beta}_{\mathrm{GLS}}^{\mathrm{IV}} = (X'H'P_{\tilde{Z}}HX)^{-1}X'H'P_{\tilde{Z}}HY. \tag{3}$$

Some simple algebra (see Appendix A) shows that the GLS-IV estimator is a matrix weighted average of the within IV estimator ($\hat{\beta}_{\mathrm{W}}^{\mathrm{IV}}$) and the between IV estimator ($\hat{\beta}_{\mathrm{B}}^{\mathrm{IV}}$). That is,

$$\hat{\beta}_{\mathrm{GLS}}^{\mathrm{IV}} = \Lambda \hat{\beta}_{\mathrm{W}}^{\mathrm{IV}} + (I - \Lambda)\hat{\beta}_{\mathrm{B}}^{\mathrm{IV}}, \tag{4}$$

where

$$\Lambda = [\sigma_\varepsilon^{-2} X' P_{Q_v Z} X + T\sigma_1^{-2} \bar{X}' P_B \bar{X}]^{-1} \sigma_\varepsilon^{-2} X' P_{Q_v Z} X, \tag{5}$$

$$\hat{\beta}_{\mathrm{W}}^{\mathrm{IV}} = [X' P_{Q_v Z} X]^{-1} [X' P_{Q_v Z} Y], \tag{6}$$

$$\hat{\beta}_{\mathrm{B}}^{\mathrm{IV}} = [\bar{X}' P_B \bar{X}]^{-1} [\bar{X}' P_B \bar{Y}]. \tag{7}$$

In Eqs. (5) and (7), $\bar{X} = [\bar{X}_{1.}' \bar{X}_{2.}' \ldots X_N']'$, where $\bar{X}_{i.}$ is the mean of the T observations on X for the ith individual (and similarly for B, Y, and Z). That Eq. (4) holds should not be surprising as it is simply the IV analog to the result for OLS estimators derived in Maddala (1971).

Under the null hypothesis, $\hat{\beta}_{\mathrm{GLS}}^{\mathrm{IV}}$ and $\hat{\beta}_{\mathrm{W}}^{\mathrm{IV}}$ are consistent estimators of β with $\hat{\beta}_{\mathrm{GLS}}^{\mathrm{IV}}$ the more efficient estimator, while under the alternative, $\hat{\beta}_{\mathrm{W}}^{\mathrm{IV}}$ is consistent and $\hat{\beta}^{IV}_{GLS}$ is inconsistent. A Hausman test statistic of the form

$$m = (\hat{\beta}^{IV}_{GLS} - \hat{\beta}^{IV}_{W})' V(\hat{\beta}^{IV}_{GLS} - \hat{\beta}^{IV}_{W})^{-1}(\hat{\beta}^{IV}_{GLS} - \hat{\beta}^{IV}_{W}) \tag{8}$$

can be constructed. Under the null, m is distributed as a chi-square statistic with k degrees of freedom. Simple algebra using Eq. (4) shows that m can be written as

$$m = (\hat{\beta}^{IV}_{W} - \hat{\beta}^{IV}_{B})'(V_W + V_B)^{-1}(\hat{\beta}^{IV}_{W} - \hat{\beta}^{IV}_{B}). \tag{9}$$

One advantage of the latter formulation of the test statistic is that the covariance matrix of the difference between the between and within estimators is easier to compute. While the $\text{cov}(\hat{\beta}^{IV}_{GLS} - \hat{\beta}^{IV}_{W})$ is equal to $V_W - V_{GLS}$ if $\hat{\beta}^{IV}_{GLS}$ is asymptotically efficient, the estimated difference of the covariance matrices may not be positive definite in small samples. This equivalent formulation of the chi-square test statistic generalizes a result of Hausman and Taylor (1981) to allow for IV estimation.

To this point, I have considered instrument sets of the general form $[Q_v Z, P_v B]$. Now I turn my attention to the choice of B. An obvious choice for B is Z itself. Then $\tilde{Z} = [Q_v Z, P_v Z]$. In other words, the instruments Z are used twice: first as deviations from their time means and then as the time means themselves. This is essentially the Hausman–Taylor (HT) estimator discussed in Breusch, Mizon, and Schmidt (1989) and Cornwall, Schmidt, and Wyhowski (1993). However, since the values of Z_{it} are uncorrelated with the individual effects for each t under H_0, then each of the T $N \times L$ matrices Z_t, where $Z_t = [Z'_{1t}, \ldots, Z'_{Nt}]'$, can be used as instruments for X_t. As a result, more instruments are available which cannot decrease the efficiency of the GLS-IV estimator. Under the null hypothesis that individual values of Z are uncorrelated with the individual effects for all values of t, then the instrument set $B = Z^*$ provides more efficient estimates of β, where Z^* is formed as in Breusch, Mizon, and Schmidt (1989).[2] That is Z^* is an $NT \times TL$ matrix:

$$Z^* = \begin{bmatrix} Z_{11} & \cdots & Z_{1T} \\ Z_{11} & \cdots & Z_{1T} \\ \vdots & & \\ Z_{N1} & \cdots & Z_{NT} \\ Z_{N1} & \cdots & Z_{NT} \end{bmatrix} \Big\} T \text{ times}$$

Note that $Q_v Z^* = 0$ and $P_v Z^* = Z^*$. Hence, $\tilde{Z} = [Q_v Z, Z^*]$ and $\hat{\beta}^{IV}_{GLS}$ constructed using Z^* will be more efficient than if constructed using $P_v Z$. CSW refers to this estimator as the Amemiya–McCurdy (AM) estimator.

[2] Z^* is defined as S^* in Eq. (7) of Breusch, Mizon, and Schmidt (1989). The instrument set $[Q_V Z, Z^*]$ defined below is analogous to set B^0 in Theorem 2 of their paper. While a more efficient instrument set may exist, analogous to the set D in Eq. (8) of B-M-S, for the purposes of this paper all that is needed is that the estimator using Z^* be *more* efficient than the estimator using $P_v Z$.

One might imagine that the appropriate specification test should employ the more efficient GLS estimator to obtain greater power. However, this need not be the case. A reduction in the variance of the difference of the within and between estimators will indeed increase the power of the test. Given the greater efficiency of the between estimator using Z^* rather than Z, the variance will decrease. However, the asymptotic bias may also increase when a less efficient estimator is used. If, for example, the bias increases at the same rate as the variance as the null is violated when using a less efficient estimator, then the power will increase since the test statistic is quadratic in bias but linear in variance. The next section considers the asymptotic efficiency of the test statistic formed with different instrument sets for a particularly simple class of data processes to illustrate this point.

3. Asymptotic efficiency

To illustrate the point that the statistic for testing correlated fixed effects may be more powerful when an inefficient estimator is used, I consider a simple scalar model with one explanatory variable and one instrument:

$$x_{it} = \gamma_x x_{it-1} + v_{it}, \tag{10a}$$

$$z_{it} = \gamma_z z_{it-1} + \eta_{it}, \tag{10b}$$

$$\operatorname*{plim}_{N\to\infty}\left(\frac{1}{NT}v'\eta\right) = \sigma_{v\eta} \neq 0, \tag{10c}$$

$$\operatorname*{plim}_{N\to\infty}\left(\frac{1}{NT}v'v\right) = \sigma_v^2 > 0, \tag{10d}$$

$$\operatorname*{plim}_{N\to\infty}\left(\frac{1}{NT}\eta'\eta\right) = \sigma_\eta^2 > 0, \tag{10e}$$

$$|\gamma_i| < 1, \qquad i = x, z. \tag{10f}$$

I will occasionally refer to σ_x^2 and σ_z^2 which equal $\sigma_v^2/(1-\gamma_x^2)$ and $\sigma_\eta^2/(1-\gamma_z^2)$, respectively. I assume that η is uncorrelated with ε. However, it may be correlated with α:

$$\operatorname*{plim}_{N\to\infty}\left(\frac{1}{N}z_t'\alpha\right) = \sigma_{z\alpha}, \tag{11}$$

when $\sigma_{z\alpha}$ equals zero under the null hypothesis and is nonzero otherwise.[3]

[3] This model easily extends to the matrix case of k explanatory variables and L instruments where the autoregressive parameters γ_x and γ_z are scalar. For details see Metcalf (1992).

This is a particularly simple structure for the data generation process, but it has the appealing property that as γ_i increases from 0 towards 1 an increasing fraction of the variance of the random variable is due to the variation across individuals.[4] Since panel data are often slow-moving over time, the performance of the specification test at high levels of γ_i is of considerable interest. I exclude the possibility that $\gamma_i = 1$. A more general model would allow some variables to be nonstationary. However, the greater model complexity would obscure the essential results without adding much in the way of insights.

Define the between estimator using the mean of the instrument as $\hat{\beta}_{\mathrm{HT}}$ and the between estimator using Z^* as $\hat{\beta}_{\mathrm{AM}}$. Under the null hypothesis, the asymptotic variance of $\sqrt{N}\hat{\beta}_{\mathrm{HT}}$ is given by

$$V_{\mathrm{HT}} = \sigma_u^2 \frac{T^2(2\sum_t b_t - T)}{(\sum(a_t + b_t) - T)^2} \frac{\sigma_z^2}{(\sigma_{xz})^2}, \tag{12}$$

where

$$a_t = \sum_{s=1}^{t} \gamma_x^{s-1} \quad \text{and} \quad b_t = \sum_{s=1}^{t} \gamma_z^{s-1}.$$

The asymptotic variance for $\sqrt{N}\,\hat{\beta}_{\mathrm{AM}}$ is given by

$$V_{\mathrm{AM}} = \sigma_u^2 \frac{T^2}{FB^{-1}F'} \frac{\sigma_z^2}{(\sigma_{xz})^2}, \tag{13}$$

where $F = [a_T + b_1 - 1 \;\; a_{T-1} + b_2 - 1 \; \dots \; a_1 + b_T - 1]$ and B is the $T \times T$ matrix

$$B = \begin{bmatrix} 1 & \gamma_z & \gamma_z^2 & \gamma_z^3 & \cdots & \gamma_z^{T-1} \\ \gamma_z & 1 & \gamma_z & \gamma_z^2 & \cdots & \gamma_z^{T-2} \\ & & \vdots & & & \\ \gamma_z^{T-1} & \gamma_z^{T-2} & \gamma_z^{T-3} & \gamma_z^{T-4} & \cdots & 1 \end{bmatrix}.$$

Consider local alternative of the form $\sigma_{z\alpha} \neq 0$ and $\sqrt{N}\sigma_{z\alpha} \to \psi < \infty$ as N approaches ∞. Under the null hypothesis, the probability limit (as $N \to \infty$) of $\hat{\beta}_{\mathrm{w}}^{\mathrm{IV}} - \hat{\beta}_{\mathrm{b}}^{\mathrm{IV}}$ is zero and m is chi-square with one degree of freedom. Under the alternative hypothesis, m is distributed as a noncentral chi-square random variable with one degree of freedom and noncentrality parameter δ where

[4] For example, the between variance for X as a fraction of the total variance equals $(2\sum_t a_t - T)/T^2$ where $a_t = \sum_{s=1}^{t} \gamma_x^{s-1}$. This fraction varies between $1/T$ and 1 as γ_x increases from 0 to 1.

$\delta^2 = \bar{q}'M^{-1}\bar{q}$, $\bar{q}$ is the probability limit of $\sqrt{N}(\hat{\beta}_{\mathrm{w}}^{\mathrm{IV}} - \hat{\beta}_{\mathrm{b}}^{\mathrm{IV}})$, and M is its asymptotic variance (see Scheff, 1959). Let $\bar{q}_i$ equal $\bar{q}$ with $\hat{\beta}_i$ substituted for $\hat{\beta}_{\mathrm{b}}^{\mathrm{IV}}$ (i = HT, AM). The asymptotic biases for the two estimators using the different set of instruments are

$$\bar{q}_{\mathrm{HT}} = \frac{T^2}{\sum(a_t + b_t) - T}\frac{\sigma_{z\alpha}}{\sigma_{xz}} \tag{14}$$

and

$$\bar{q}_{\mathrm{AM}} = \frac{T \cdot FB^{-1}e_T}{FB^{-1}F'}\frac{\sigma_{z\alpha}}{\sigma_{xz}}. \tag{15}$$

If $\gamma_x = \gamma_z$, it is straightforward to show that $V_{\mathrm{HT}} = V_{\mathrm{AM}}$ and that $\bar{q}_{\mathrm{HT}} = \bar{q}_{\mathrm{AM}}$ leading to the following proposition:

Proposition 1. *Given the model in Eqs. (10)–(11) and the assumption that $\gamma_x = \gamma_z$, the two estimators $\hat{\beta}_{\mathrm{HT}}$ and $\hat{\beta}_{\mathrm{AM}}$ are equally efficient asymptotically and the power of the specification test of the hypothesis that the instrumental variables are uncorrelated with the individual effects is unaffected by the choice of instrument set.*

Proof. See Appendix B.

As $\gamma_x - \gamma_z$ diverges from zero, the variances and power of the specification test begins to differ. Since $V_{\mathrm{HT}} - V_{\mathrm{AM}}$ is positive definite, it would appear that the power of the specification test should increase using Z^* as the set of instruments. However, it will turn out that $\bar{q}_{\mathrm{HT}}$ may also be greater than $\bar{q}_{\mathrm{AM}}$ which will increase the power of the test using the means of Z as instruments. For $\gamma_x > 0$, this result is formalized in the following proposition.

Proposition 2. *If $\gamma_x > 0$ and $\gamma_z = 0$, then the asymptotic power of the test statistic using $\bar{Z}$ as instruments is greater than the power using Z^* as instruments.*

Proof. See Appendix B.

Proposition 2 illustrates very clearly the trade-off between decreased efficiency and greater bias in moving from an efficient to an inefficient set of instruments. Increasing the asymptotic bias ($\bar{q}_i$) will increase the power of the test. With $\gamma_x > \gamma_z = 0$, the bias of each statistic is proportional to the variance ($\bar{q}_i = V_i\lambda$, i = HT, AM, where λ is a $k \times 1$ vector). Since the power of the test statistic is quadratic in bias and linear in the inverse of the variance, the power must increase as the bias and inverse of the variance increase at the same rate.

I now turn my attention to the case where $\gamma_x = 0$ and $\gamma_z > 0$. Some tedious algebra shows that the asymptotic bias for the test statistic under the alternative

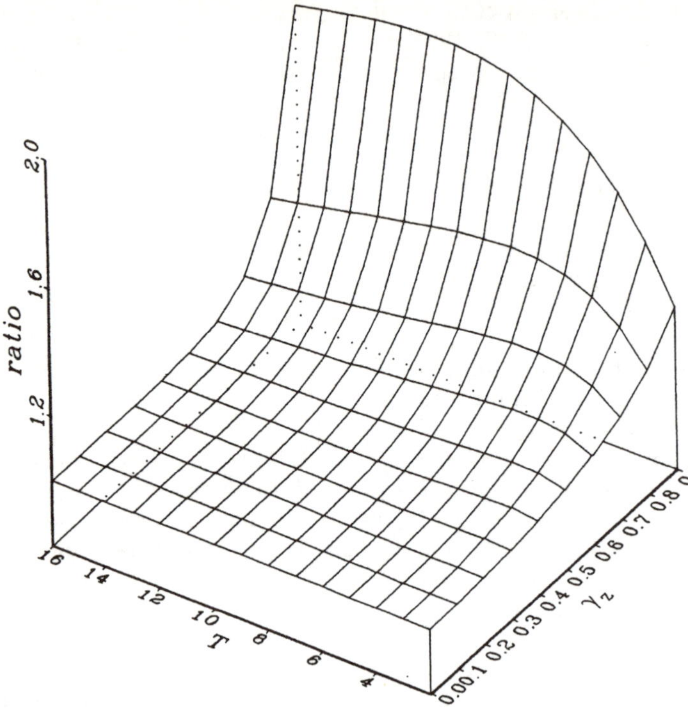

Fig. 1. Power ratio of m_{HT} to m_{AM}.

hypothesis is greater when $\bar{Z}$ is used as the set of instruments. Again, the variance of the between estimator is greater when $\bar{Z}$ is used. In this case it is difficult, however, to show that the power of the test is greater when $\bar{Z}$ is used as the instrument set rather than Z^*. In the simple case where $k = L = 1$ a grid search shows that the test statistic using $\bar{Z}$ is more powerful than when Z^* is used.

The increase in power is quite dramatic as illustrated in Fig. 1. Let the covariance of Z and α be equal to half the variance of Z. At $\gamma_z = 0.8$ and $T = 7$, the increase in the number of rejections is 41% (power equals 0.14 versus 0.10) and declines to 26% at $T = 16$ (power is 0.33 versus 0.26). At $\gamma_z = 0.9$, the test using the mean of the instruments rejects nearly twice as often as when the instruments for each time period are used separately. Note that at $\gamma_z = 0.9$ and $T = 7$, 80% of the variation in the data occurs across individuals rather than for individuals across time. It is quite typical for many panel data applications to lose 80% of the variance in the data when using the fixed effects estimator.

Fig. 2 graphs the efficiency gains from using the means of the instruments when $T = 5$ and γ_x and γ_z vary between 0.1 and 0.9. As pointed out above, the

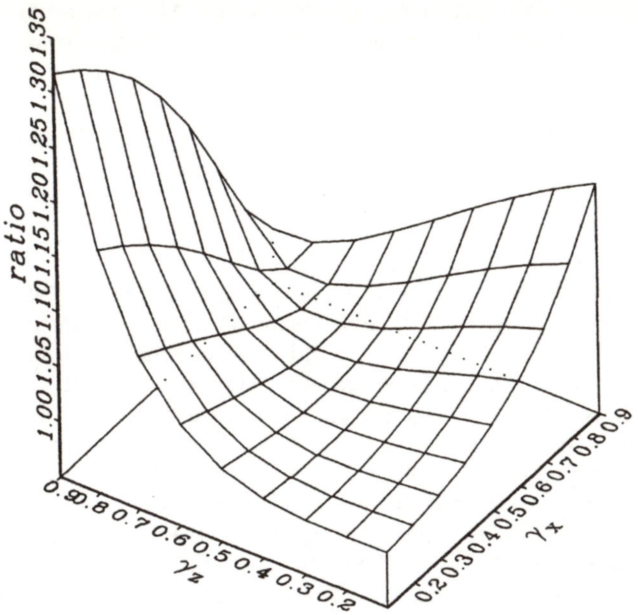

Fig. 2. Power ratio of m_{HT} to m_{AM}.

tests perform equivalently when $\gamma_x = \gamma_z$ and the test using the means of the instruments performs better as the two autocorrelations move apart. However, the improvement is not dramatic with a maximum improvement of less than 32%. This raises the issue of the performance of the tests in small samples. I turn my attention to this issue in the next section.

4. Small-sample characteristics of the test

Specification test statistics in general have been criticized for having low power (e.g., Holly, 1982; Newey, 1985). One might expect that the power of the test would deteriorate further as a result of the additional noise from the instrumenting of variables in X. To consider how well the test works in practice, I present results from a Monte Carlo experiment. I consider a simple model with $k = L = 1$, set β equal to 1 in Eq. (1) and take draws from a normal distribution for X_{it}, Z_{it}, ε_{it}, and α_i, each with mean 0. The first three variables have variance 1 and α_i has variance $1/T$. The covariance of Z and ε is zero while the other covariances vary from experiment to experiment.[5] After generating the data, I compute the within and between estimates of β, their variances, and the chi-square test (which has one degree of freedom).[6] I repeat the process 1000 times for each model.

For the first set of results, I set $\gamma_x = \gamma_z = 0$. With these assumptions, the noncentrality parameter, δ^2, is given by the formula

$$\delta^2 = \psi^2 T^2 \left(\frac{T-1}{2T-1}\right). \tag{16}$$

The asymptotic power of the test increases with more time periods, and with a higher correlation between the time means of the instruments and the individual effects. Note that the tests should perform equally well based on the results from the last section. Table 1 presents Monte Carlo results with $N = 200$ and $T = 5$. $\mathrm{Cov}(X_{it}, \varepsilon_{it}) = 0.4$ and $\sigma_{z\alpha}$ and σ_{xz} vary from 0 to 0.06 and 0.1 to 0.7, respectively. The numbers in each cell show the fraction of times the null hypothesis is rejected due to m in Eq. (9) exceeding the 5% critical value for a chi-square random variable with one degree of freedom. The top number in each cell presents results using the mean of Z as the instrument set, while the bottom number uses the set Z^*. For future reference, call the first test statistic m_{HT} and the second statistic m_{AM}. The first column in the table shows the computed size of the test. Note that neither of these tests has a computed size near 5% at very low levels of correlation between Z and X. This is suggestive of the results of Nelson and Startz (1990a, b) who have shown that the distribution of IV estimators diverges dramatically from the asymptotic distribution in the presence of poor instruments.

The remaining columns in Table 1 show the power of the test in the face of increasing correlation of Z with α. In nearly every case, the power of m_{AM} is higher than that of m_{HT}. The increase in power can be significant, particularly with poor instruments. These results are striking given the number of individuals in the data set ($N = 200$) as well as the fact that m_{AM} has the same distribution asymptotically as m_{HT}. Clearly, in the case where $\gamma_x = \gamma_z = 0$, the main advantage of m_{AM} over m_{HT} lies in its performance in the presence of poor instruments.

These results show that in the case where asymptotically the two formulations of the chi-square test should give equivalent results, the test statistic using the more efficient estimator is a more powerful test statistic. However, Proposition

[5] I have also experimented with varying the variance of α_i. The results are not qualitatively different.

[6] Equivalently, I could take the square root of the statistic and use the standard normal distribution. Constructing the experiment with one degree of freedom allows me to avoid issues of direction in defining the local alternative which affect the power of the test.

Table 1
Computed power and size, $\gamma_x = \gamma_z = 0$

	$\sigma_{z\alpha}$			
σ_{xz}	0.0	0.02	0.04	0.06
0.1	0.004	0.029	0.082	0.146
	0.018	0.058	0.120	0.196
0.3	0.032	0.170	0.457	0.754
	0.044	0.184	0.475	0.744
0.5	0.045	0.174	0.497	0.786
	0.050	0.196	0.512	0.775
0.7	0.051	0.181	0.459	0.803
	0.063	0.205	0.489	0.807

This table presents the fraction of rejections of the null hypothesis that $\sigma_{z\alpha} = 0$ out or 1000 replications. The top entry in each cell uses $\bar{Z}$ as an instrument for $\bar{X}$ while the bottom entry uses Z^*. The covariance of X and ε equals 0.40, N equals 200, and T equals 5. The nominal size of the test is 0.05.

Table 2
Computed power and size, $\gamma_x = 0.9$, $\gamma_z = 0$

	$\sigma_{z\alpha}$			
σ_{xz}	0.0	0.06	0.12	0.18
0.1	0.002	0.007	0.021	0.023
	0.003	0.005	0.012	0.011
0.3	0.026	0.124	0.310	0.362
	0.040	0.101	0.242	0.261
0.5	0.042	0.256	0.514	0.715
	0.058	0.191	0.421	0.639
0.7	0.043	0.328	0.813	0.942
	0.046	0.259	0.608	0.791

This table presents the fraction of rejections of the null hypothesis that $\sigma_{z\alpha} = 0$ out or 1000 replications. The top entry in each cell uses $\bar{Z}$ as an instrument for $\bar{X}$ while the bottom entry uses Z^*. The covariance of X and ε equals 0.40, N equals 200, and T equals 5. The nominal size of the test is 0.05.

2 states that in cases where $\gamma_x > 0$ and $\gamma_z = 0$, then the test statistic using the less efficient estimator is more powerful. Table 2 presents Monte Carlo results in the case that $\gamma_x = 0.9$ and $\gamma_z = 0$. Recall that this implies that 80% of the variance in X is lost when the fixed effects estimator is used. In all other respects, the model is the same as in the first experiment. Table 2 shows the power of the two test

Table 3
Computed power varying γ_x and γ_z

	γ_x				
γ_z	0.00	0.25	0.50	0.75	0.90
0.00	0.979 0.980	0.967 0.962	0.942 0.929	0.837 0.748	0.606 0.430
0.25	0.991 0.990	0.976 0.972	0.969 0.956	0.899 0.847	0.730 0.583
0.50	0.987 0.983	0.981 0.978	0.984 0.973	0.913 0.877	0.806 0.695
0.75	0.975 0.977	0.957 0.963	0.956 0.953	0.879 0.861	0.770 0.682
0.90	0.848 0.961	0.854 0.938	0.814 0.926	0.745 0.821	0.550 0.670

This table presents the fraction of rejections of the null hypothesis that $\sigma_{z\alpha} = 0$ out or 1000 replications. The top entry in each cell uses $\bar{Z}$ as an instrument for $\bar{X}$ while the bottom entry uses Z^*. The covariance of X and ε equals 0.40, N equals 200, and T equals 5. The nominal size of the test is 0.05. $\sigma_{z\alpha} = 0.09$ and $\sigma_{zx} = 0.70$.

statistics. The clear advantage of m_{HT} over m_{AM} is evident here. While both test statistics have the correct size at moderate levels of correlation between Z and X, the power of m_{HT} is greater than the power of m_{AM} in every case conditional on the alternative. The increase in power can be quite substantial even in the presence of good instrumental variables. The power of the test using the inefficient between estimator in the case where $\sigma_{xz} = 0.7$ and $\sigma_{zx} = 0.18$ is 0.942 compared to a power of 0.791 when the efficient between estimator is used to construct the chi-square test. This suggests that in cases where there is significant time variation for the instrumental variable, while there is little time variation for the explanatory variable, one should consider using the inefficient between estimator construct the chi-square statistic to test for correlation between the instrumental variables and the individual effects.

The final sets of Monte Carlo results provide guidelines for generalizing the results of Propositions 1 and 2 along with the Monte Carlo results of Tables 1 and 2. In Table 3, I fix the convariance of Z and α at 0.09, the covariance of Z and X at 0.70 and the covariance of X and ε at 0.40 and vary γ_x and γ_z from 0 to 0.90. In all cases where $\gamma_x > \gamma_z$, m_{HT} has higher power than m_{AM}. Again, the increase in power can be quite dramatic (e.g., $\gamma_x = 0.9, \gamma_z = 0.25$). This suggests that where is more time variation in the instrumental variables than in the explanatory variables, the test statistic should be computed using the inefficient between estimator. Where γ_x equals γ_z, there is no clear result with

Table 4
Computed power when model is overidentified

	γ_1				
γ_2	0.00	0.25	0.50	0.75	0.90
0.00	0.945	0.936	0.951	0.931	0.902
	0.922	0.912	0.941	0.920	0.900
0.25	0.952	0.945	0.958	0.954	0.925
	0.943	0.932	0.937	0.937	0.933
0.50	0.962	0.968	0.958	0.963	0.932
	0.943	0.950	0.944	0.949	0.930
0.75	0.938	0.934	0.941	0.921	0.909
	0.920	0.927	0.936	0.917	0.917
0.90	0.855	0.888	0.852	0.856	0.782
	0.891	0.917	0.910	0.911	0.897

This table presents the fraction of rejections of the null hypothesis that $\sigma_{z\alpha} = 0$ out of 1000 replications. The top entry in each cell uses $\tilde{Z}$ as instruments for $\tilde{X}$ while the bottom entry uses Z^*. The covariance of X and ε equals 0.40, N equals 200, and T equals 5. The nominal size of the test is 0.05. $\sigma_{z\alpha} = 0.05$ and $\sigma_{zx} = 0.50$. There is one explanatory variable (x) with a serial correlation coefficient of 0.5. There are three instrumental variables, two with autoregression coefficient γ_2 and one with coefficient γ_1.

both test statistics performing about the same, as Proposition 1 suggests they should. As γ_z becomes larger than γ_x, it becomes more likely that the m_{AM} outperforms m_{HT} though the improvement is not large until γ_z is much greater than γ_x.

Given the large number of possible configurations to consider, it is difficult to generalize broadly to cases where k and L exceed 1. As a first pass at broadening the findings of the previous tables, Table 4 presents results from a model in which $k = 1$ and $L = 3$. I fix γ_x at 0.5 and range γ for the instrumental variables. The first instrument has an autocorrelation coefficient equal to γ_1 and the next two instruments have a coefficient of γ_2. In cases where both γ_1 and γ_2 are less than γ_x, m_{HT} has higher power than m_{AM}. Similarly, when both γ_1 and γ_2 are greater than γ_x, m_{AM} has higher power than m_{HT} in three of four cases. These results are consistent with the results in Tables 2 and 3. In cases when $\gamma_2 > \gamma_x > \gamma_1$, m_{AM} outperforms m_{HT} when γ_2 is very large (0.9). When $\gamma_1 > \gamma_x > \gamma_2$, m_{HT} tends to outperform m_{AM}, though not by a large margin. These results suggest a tendency for m_{HT} to outperform m_{AM} when there are a number of instrumental variables with a greater fraction of within group variation than between groups variation – again consistent with the results in Tables 2 and 3.

While the results presented here are from a particularly simple model, they illustrate an important point. In certain circumstances one can improve on the power of a specification test for correlated fixed effects by using an inefficient estimator.

5. Conclusion

Testing for correlated individual effects has become increasingly important with the greater use of panel data sets. This paper shows that the type of specification test often employed in models where all the explanatory variables are considered exogenous carries over in a straightforward manner to models with endogenous explanatory variables. However, greater attention must be paid to the quality of the instruments used for the explanatory variables if the actual size and power of the test statistic is to correspond to the theoretical size and power.

The between estimator used in the specification test can be constructed with different sets of instruments. In many cases, a larger set of instruments leads to a more powerful test statistic. However, it is often the case that the more powerful test statistic uses a reduced set of instruments for the between estimator. While the variance of the test statistic is driven up in this case, so is the asymptotic bias which can more than offset the increase in variance. Such a case happens when the explanatory variables are slow moving over time while the instruments are not. In this case, there is a distinct advantage to constructing the specification test using the less efficient estimator to take advantage of its greater asymptotic bias.

These results have been shown in a simple model with one explanatory variable and one instrument. The model is easily extended to the matrix case where the autoregressive parameter is scalar. While the model does not directly generalize to allow for independent autoregressive paramters for individual explanatory variables or instruments or for nonstationary variables, I conjecture (and show in one example) that the basic insight is unchanged: in many cases more powerful statistics for testing correlated fixed effects can be constructed by using less efficient estimators.

Appendix A

Relationship between GLS-IV, within-IV, and between-IV estimators

Define instrument set $\tilde{Z} = [Q_v Z, P_v B]$, where B is an $NT \times M$ matrix with the property that the columns of $P_v B$ are legitimate instruments for the regression in Eq. (1) (i.e., uncorrelated with ε but correlated with X). As noted in the text, the GLS-IV estimator is given by

$$\hat{\beta}^{\mathrm{IV}}_{\mathrm{GLS}} = (X'H'P_{\hat{Z}}HX)^{-1}X'H'P_{\hat{Z}}HY. \tag{A.1}$$

It can easily be shown that $H'P_{\hat{Z}}H = \sigma_\varepsilon^{-2}P_{Q_vZ} + \sigma_1^{-2}P_{P_vB}$ and so

$$\hat{\beta}^{\mathrm{IV}}_{\mathrm{GLS}} = [\sigma_\varepsilon^{-2}X'P_{Q_vZ}X + \sigma_1^{-2}X'P_{P_vB}X]^{-1}$$
$$\times [\sigma_\varepsilon^{-2}X'P_{Q_vZ}Y + \sigma_1^{-2}X'P_{P_vB}Y]. \tag{A.2}$$

If we define the $N \times k$ matrix $\bar{X} = [\bar{X}_1' \bar{X}_2' \dots X_N']'$, where $\bar{X}_i$ is the mean of the T observations on X for the i individual (and similarly for B, Y, and Z), we can rewrite (A.2) using the fact that $P_vB = \bar{B} \otimes e_T$. Making this substitution and some simple algebra leads to

$$\hat{\beta}^{\mathrm{IV}}_{\mathrm{GLS}} = [\sigma_\varepsilon^{-2}X'P_{Q_vZ}X + T\sigma_1^{-2}\bar{X}'P_B\bar{X}]^{-1}$$
$$\times [\sigma_\varepsilon^{-2}X'P_{Q_vZ}Y + T\sigma_1^{-2}\bar{X}'P_B\bar{Y}]. \tag{A.2'}$$

Now the within estimator ($\hat{\beta}^{\mathrm{IV}}_{\mathrm{W}}$) follows first from eliminating α from Eq. (1) in text:

$$Q_vY = Q_vX\beta + Q_v\varepsilon. \tag{A.3}$$

We premultiply this by $P_{\hat{Z}}$ and, noting that $P_{\hat{Z}} = P_{Q_vZ} + P_{P_vB}$, obtain

$$P_{Q_vZ}Y = P_{Q_vZ}X\beta + P_{Q_vZ}\varepsilon, \tag{A.4}$$

and therefore

$$\hat{\beta}^{\mathrm{IV}}_{\mathrm{W}} = [X'P_{Q_vZ}X]^{-1}[X'P_{Q_vZ}Y]. \tag{A.5}$$

This is simply the 2SLS regression of Q_vY on Q_vX using Q_vZ as instruments. The between estimator ($\hat{\beta}^{\mathrm{IV}}_{\mathrm{B}}$) is similarly derived and is given by

$$\hat{\beta}^{\mathrm{IV}}_{\mathrm{B}} = [\bar{X}'P_B\bar{X}]^{-1}[\bar{X}'P_B\bar{Y}]. \tag{A.6}$$

Again, this is simply the 2SLS regression of $\bar{Y}$ and $\bar{X}$ using $\bar{B}$ as instruments. Defining

$$\Lambda = [\sigma_\varepsilon^{-2}X'P_{Q_vZ}X + T\sigma_1^{-2}\bar{X}'P_B\bar{X}]^{-1}\sigma_\varepsilon^{-2}X'P_{Q_vZ}X, \tag{A.7}$$

then it follows immediately that

$$\hat{\beta}^{\mathrm{IV}}_{\mathrm{GLS}} = \Lambda\hat{\beta}^{\mathrm{IV}}_{\mathrm{W}} + (I - \Lambda)\hat{\beta}^{\mathrm{IV}}_{\mathrm{B}}. \tag{A.8}$$

Eq. (A.8) shows that the GLS-IV estimator can be written as a matrix weighted average of the within-IV and the between-IV estimators and is the IV analog to the result for OLS estimators presented in Maddala (1971).

Appendix B

Proof of Proposition 1. Let $\gamma_x = \gamma_z = \gamma < 1$. Therefore $a_t = b_t$ and B^{-1} is given by

$$B^{-1} = (1-\gamma^2)^{-1}\begin{bmatrix} 1 & -\gamma & 0 & & \cdots & 0 \\ -\gamma & 1+\gamma^2 & -\gamma & 0 & \cdots & 0 \\ & & \vdots & & & \\ 0 & \cdots & & -\gamma & & 1 \end{bmatrix}. \tag{B.1}$$

Then

$$FB^{-1} = (1-\gamma^2)^{-1}\,[F_1 - \gamma F_2 (1+\gamma^2)\,F_2 - \gamma(F_1 - F_3) \cdots F_T - \gamma F_{T-1}], \tag{B.2}$$

where F_i is the ith element of F.

Since $a_t = \sum_{s=1}^{t} \gamma^{s-1}$, it is easy to show that $a_t - \gamma a_{t-1} = 1$. Therefore,

$$F_1 - \gamma F_2 = a_T - \gamma(a_{T-1} + \gamma) = 1 - \gamma^2.$$

Similarly,

$$F_T - \gamma F_{T-1} = 1 - \gamma^2.$$

The expression $(1+\gamma^2)F_T - \gamma(F_{t-1} + F_{t-1}), t = 2, \ldots, T-1$, can be written as $-\gamma(a_{T-t+2} - \gamma a_{T-t+1}) + (a_t - \gamma a_{t-1}) + 2\gamma - 1 - \gamma^2 + (a_{T-t+1} - \gamma a_{T-t}) - \gamma(a_{t+1} - \gamma a_t) = 1 - \gamma^2$. Therefore,

$$FB^{-1} = e_T', \tag{B.3}$$

$$FB^{-1}F' = 2\sum_{t=1}^{T} a_t - T, \tag{B.4}$$

$$FB^{-1}e_T = T. \tag{B.5}$$

Substituting Eq. (B.4) into Eq. (13) shows V_{HT} equals V_{AM} and substituting (B.4) and (B.5) into (15) shows $\bar{q}_{\mathrm{HT}}$ equals $\bar{q}_{\mathrm{AM}}$. ■

Proof of Proposition 2. Define δ^2_{HT} as the noncentrality parameter for the test using $\bar{Z}$ as the instrument set. Similarly, define δ^2_{AM} for the test using instrument set Z^*. Let V_W be the variance of the within estimator. First, I note that $V_{\mathrm{HT}} - V_{\mathrm{AM}}$ is a positive definite matrix, assuming $\gamma_x > 0$:

$$V_{\mathrm{HT}} - V_{\mathrm{AM}} = T^3 \sigma^2_{\bar{u}} \frac{\sigma_z^2}{(\sigma_{xz})^2}\left[\frac{1}{(\sum a)_t^2} - \frac{1}{T\sum a_t^2}\right] > 0, \tag{B.6}$$

by Chebyshev's Inequality.

It is easily shown that $V_{\mathrm{HT}}^{-1}\bar{q}_{\mathrm{HT}} = V_{\mathrm{AM}}^{-1}\bar{q}_{\mathrm{AM}} = (\sum a_t/T)(\sigma_{\dot{x}z}\sigma_{z\alpha}/\sigma_z^2) \equiv \lambda$. Therefore,

$$\delta_{\mathrm{HT}}^2 - \delta_{\mathrm{AM}}^2 = \lambda'(R_{\mathrm{HT}} - R_{\mathrm{AM}})\lambda, \tag{B.7}$$

and is greater than zero if $R_{\mathrm{HT}} - R_{\mathrm{AM}}$ is positive definite, where R_i equals $[V_i^{-1}V_w V_i^{-1} + V_i^{-1}]^{-1}$, $i = \mathrm{HT,AM}$. $R_{\mathrm{HT}} - R_{\mathrm{AM}}$ will be positive definite if $R_{\mathrm{AM}}^{-1} - R_{\mathrm{HT}}^{-1}$ is positive definite. But

$$R_{\mathrm{AM}}^{-1} - R_{\mathrm{HT}}^{-1} = (V_{\mathrm{AM}}^{-1} - V_{\mathrm{HT}}^{-1})V_W(V_{\mathrm{AM}}^{-1} - V_{\mathrm{HT}}^{-1}) + (V_{\mathrm{AM}}^{-1} - V_{\mathrm{HT}}^{-1}). \tag{B.8}$$

Each of the bracketed terms in (B.8) is positive definite, so $R_{\mathrm{AM}}^{-1} - R_{\mathrm{HT}}^{-1}$ is positive definite and $\delta_{\mathrm{HT}}^2 > \delta_{\mathrm{AM}}^2$. ■

References

Amemiya, T. and T.E. MaCurdy, 1986, Instrumental variable estimation of an error components model, Econometrica 54, 869–881.

Breusch, T., G. Mizon, and P. Schmidt, 1989, Efficient estimation using panel data, Econometrica 57, 695–700.

Cornwell, C., P. Schmidt, and D. Wyhowski, 1993, Simultaneous equations and panel data, Journal of Econometrics, forthcoming.

Hausman, J.A., 1978, Specification tests in econometrics, Econometrica 46, 1251–1271.

Hausman, J.A. and W.E. Taylor, 1981, Panel data and unobservable individual effects, Econometrica 49, 1377–1398.

Holly, A., 1982, A remark on Hausman's specification test, Econometric 50, 749–760.

Maddala, G.S., 1971, The use of variance components models in pooling cross section and time series data, Econometrica 39, 341–358.

Metcalf, G., 1992, Specification testing in panel data with instrumental variables, NBER technical working paper no. 123.

Nelson, C. and R. Startz, 1990a, The distribution of the instrumental variables estimator and its t-ratio when the instrument is a poor one, Journal of Business 63, S125–S140.

Nelson, C. and R. Startz, 1990b, Some further results on the exact small sample properties of the instrumental variable estimator, Econometrica 58, 967–976.

Newey, W., 1985, Generalized method of moments specification testing, Journal of Econometrics 29, 229–256.

Scheffe, H., 1959, The analysis of variance (Wiley, New York, NY).

Name Index

Recent Developments in the Econometrics of Panel Data
Volume I

The International Library of Critical Writings in Econometrics

Series Editors: Mark Blaug

Professor Emeritus, University of London, UK
Professor Emeritus, University of Buckingham, UK
Visiting Professor, University of Amsterdam, The Netherlands
Visiting Professor, Erasmus University of Rotterdam, The Netherlands

Adrian C. Darnell

Professor and Principal, George Stephenson College,
University of Durham, UK

1. The Econometrics of Panel Data (Volumes I and II)
   G.S. Maddala
2. Macroeconometric Modelling (Volumes I and II)
   Kenneth F. Wallis
3. Simultaneous Equation Estimation
   Carl F. Christ
4. The History of Econometrics (Volumes I and II)
   Adrian C. Darnell
5. Time Series (Volumes I and II)
   Andrew Harvey
6. The Methodology of Econometrics (Volumes I and II)
   Dale J. Poirier
7. Bayesian Inference (Volumes I and II)
   Nicholas G. Polson and George C. Tiao
8. Nonlinear Models (Volumes I and II)
   Herman J. Bierens and A. Ronald Gallant
9. Recent Developments in the Econometrics of Panel Data (Volumes I and II)
   Badi H. Baltagi

Future titles will include:

Recent Developments in Time Series
Paul Newbold and Stephen J. Leybourne

General to Specific Modelling
David F. Hendry, Neil R. Ericsson and Julia Campos

Selection Bias and Program Evaluation
James J. Heckman

Wherever possible, the articles in these volumes have been reproduced as originally published using facsimile reproduction, inclusive of footnotes and pagination to facilitate ease of reference.

For a list of all Edward Elgar published titles visit our site on the World Wide Web at
http://www.e-elgar.co.uk

Recent Developments in the Econometrics of Panel Data Volume I

Edited by

Badi H. Baltagi

Professor of Economics and George Summey, Jr. Chair in Liberal Arts
Texas A&M University, USA

THE INTERNATIONAL LIBRARY OF CRITICAL WRITINGS IN ECONOMETRICS

An Elgar Reference Collection
Cheltenham, UK • Northampton, MA, USA

Published by
Edward Elgar Publishing Limited
Glensanda House
Montpellier Parade
Cheltenham
Glos GL50 1UA
UK

Edward Elgar Publishing, Inc.
136 West Street
Suite 202
Northampton
Massachusetts 01060
USA

A catalogue record for this book is available from the British Library

Library of Congress Cataloguing in Publication Data

Recent developments in the econometrics of panel data / edited by Badi H. Baltagi.
p. cm. — (International library of critical writings in econometrics ; 9)
Includes bibliographical references and index.
1. Panel analysis. 2. Econometrics. I. Baltagi, Badi H. (Badi Hani) II. Series.

H61.26 .R4 2003
330'.01'5195—dc21

2002029825

ISBN 1 84064 967 4 (2 volume set)

Printed and bound in Great Britain by MPG Books Ltd, Bodmin, Cornwall

Contents

Acknowledgements

The editor and publishers wish to thank the authors and the following publishers who have kindly given permission for the use of copyright material.

American Statistical Association for articles: G.S. Maddala, Robert P. Trost, Hongyi Li and Frederick Joutz (1997), 'Estimation of Short-Run and Long-Run Elasticities of Energy Demand from Panel Data Using Shrinkage Estimators', *Journal of Business and Economic Statistics*, **15** (1), January, 90–100; Cheng Hsiao and A. Kamil Tahmiscioglu (1997), 'A Panel Analysis of Liquidity Constraints and Firm Investment', *Journal of the American Statistical Association*, **92** (438), June, 455–65; James P. Ziliak (1997), 'Efficient Estimation with Panel Data when Instruments are Predetermined: An Empirical Comparison of Moment-Condition Estimators', *Journal of Business and Economic Statistics*, **15** (4), October, 419–31; César Alonso-Borrego and Manuel Arellano (1999), 'Symmetrically Normalized Instrumental-Variable Estimation Using Panel Data', *Journal of Business and Economic Statistics*, **17** (1), January, 36–49; M. Hashem Pesaran, Yongcheol Shin and Ron P. Smith (1999), 'Pooled Mean Group Estimation of Dynamic Heterogeneous Panels', *Journal of the American Statistical Association*, **94** (446), June, 621–34.

Blackwell Publishing Ltd for articles: G.S. Maddala and Shaowen Wu (1999), 'A Comparative Study of Unit Root Tests with Panel Data and a New Simple Test', *Oxford Bulletin of Economics and Statistics*, **61**, Special Issue, 631–52; Hyungsik R. Moon and Peter C.B. Phillips (1999), 'Maximum Likelihood Estimation in Panels with Incidental Trends', *Oxford Bulletin of Economics and Statistics*, **61**, Special Issue, 711–47; Kaddour Hadri (2000), 'Testing for Stationarity in Heterogeneous Panel Data', *Econometrics Journal*, **3** (2), 148–61.

Econometric Society for article: Peter C.B. Phillips and Hyungsik R. Moon (1999), 'Linear Regression Limit Theory for Nonstationary Panel Data', *Econometrica*, **67** (5), September, 1057–111.

Elsevier Science for articles and excerpt: Seung C. Ahn and Peter Schmidt (1995), 'Efficient Estimation of Models for Dynamic Panel Data', *Journal of Econometrics*, **68**, 5–27; Manuel Arellano and Olympia Bover (1995), 'Another Look at the Instrumental Variable Estimation of Error-Components Models', *Journal of Econometrics*, **68**, 29–51; Jan F. Kiviet (1995), 'On Bias, Inconsistency, and Efficiency of Various Estimators in Dynamic Panel Data Models', *Journal of Econometrics*, **68**, 53–78; M. Hashem Pesaran and Ron Smith (1995), 'Estimating Long-Run Relationships from Dynamic Heterogeneous Panels', *Journal of Econometrics*, **68**, 79–113; Seung C. Ahn and Peter Schmidt (1997), 'Efficient Estimation of Dynamic Panel Data Models: Alternative Assumptions and Simplified Estimation', *Journal of Econometrics*, **76**, 309–21; Badi H. Baltagi and James M. Griffin (1997), 'Pooled Estimators vs. their Heterogeneous Counterparts in the Context of Dynamic Demand for Gasoline', *Journal of*

Econometrics, **77**, 303–27; Bruno Crepon, Francis Kramarz and Alain Trognon (1997), 'Parameters of Interest, Nuisance Parameters and Orthogonality Conditions: An Application to Autoregressive Error Component Models', *Journal of Econometrics*, **82**, 135–56; Richard Blundell and Stephen Bond (1998), 'Initial Conditions and Moment Restrictions in Dynamic Panel Data Models', *Journal of Econometrics*, **87**, 115–43; Chihwa Kao (1999), 'Spurious Regression and Residual-Based Tests for Cointegration in Panel Data', *Journal of Econometrics*, **90**, 1–44; Richard D.F. Harris and Elias Tzavalis (1999), 'Inference for Unit Roots in Dynamic Panels Where the Time Dimension is Fixed', *Journal of Econometrics*, **91**, 201–26; Jinyong Hahn (1999), 'How Informative is the Initial Condition in the Dynamic Panel Model with Fixed Effects?', *Journal of Econometrics*, **93**, 309–26; Peter Pedroni (2000), 'Fully Modified OLS for Heterogeneous Cointegrated Panels', in Badi H. Baltagi (ed.), *Advances in Econometrics, Volume 15: Nonstationary Panels, Panel Cointegration, and Dynamic Panels*, 93–130; Tom Wansbeek (2001), 'GMM Estimation in Panel Data Models with Measurement Error', *Journal of Econometrics*, **104**, 259–68.

Every effort has been made to trace all the copyright holders but if any have been inadvertently overlooked the publishers will be pleased to make the necessary arrangement at the first opportunity.

In addition the publishers wish to thank the Marshall Library of Economics, Cambridge University and the Library of the University of Warwick for their assistance in obtaining these articles.

Introduction

Badi H. Baltagi

Maddala (1993) defines 'panel data' as data sets on the same individual over several periods of time. This encompasses longitudinal data analysis where the primary focus is on individual histories. Panel data is also used to describe the pooling of time series observations across a variety of cross-sectional units, including countries, regions, states, firms or households. In this introduction, we will also discuss dynamic panels, heterogeneous panels, nonstationary panels, unbalanced panels and pseudo panels.

Some of the benefits and limitations of using panel data sets are given in Hsiao (1986) and Baltagi (2001). Obvious benefits include a much larger data set with more variability and less collinearity among the variables than is typical of cross-sectional or time series data. With more informative data, one can get more reliable estimates and test more sophisticated behavioural models with less restrictive assumptions. Another advantage of panel data sets is their ability to control for individual heterogeneity. Not controlling for these unobserved individual specific effects leads to bias in the resulting estimates. Panel data sets are also better able to identify and estimate effects that are simply not detectable in pure cross-sections or pure time series data. In particular, panel data sets are better able to study complex issues of dynamic behaviour. Limitations of panel data sets include problems of nonresponse and measurement errors. Panel data sets may also exhibit bias due to sample selection problems. For the initial wave of the panel, respondents may refuse to participate or the interviewer may not find anybody at home. This may cause some bias in the inference drawn from this sample. While such nonresponse can also occur in cross-sectional data sets, it is more serious with panels because subsequent waves of the panel are still subject to nonresponse. Respondents may die, or move, or find that the cost of responding is high.

Two well-known examples of US panel data are the Panel Study of Income Dynamics (PSID) collected by the Institute for Social Research at the University of Michigan, and the National Longitudinal Surveys of Labor Market Experience (NLS) from the Center for Human Resource Research at Ohio State University. An inventory of national studies using panel data is given at (http://www.isr.umich.edu/src/psid/panelStudies.html). These include the Belgian Socio-Economic panel, the German Socio-Economic panel, the French household panel, the British Household Panel Survey, the Dutch Socio-Economic Panel, the Luxembourg Panel Socio-Economique and more recently, the European Community Household Panel.

Virtually every graduate text in econometrics contains a chapter on the econometrics of panel data. Classic readings on this subject include Hsiao's (1986) Econometric Society monograph along with Chamberlain's (1984) chapter in the *Handbook of Econometrics* with an updated chapter in Volume V by Arellano and Honoré (2001). There is also a handbook on the econometrics of panel data edited by Mátyás and Sevestre (1996) and a graduate textbook on the subject by Baltagi (2001). Recent special issues of journals on panel data include one in the *Journal of Econometrics*, edited by Baltagi (1995), two volumes of the *Annales D'Economie et de Statistique* edited by Sevestre (1999), a special issue of the *Oxford Bulletin of Economics and Statistics* edited by Banerjee (1999), two special issues of *Econometric Reviews* edited by Maasoumi and Heshmati (2000) and a special issue of the *Advances in Econometrics* edited by Baltagi, Fomby and Hill (2000). The objective of this book is to provide an update of Maddala's (1993) two volumes collecting some of the classic articles on the subject. It is assumed that the reader has read these two volumes and is familiar with the panel data regression model.

Dynamic Panels and GMM

The literature on dynamic panel data models continues to exhibit phenomenal growth. This is understandable given that most of our economic models are implicitly or explicitly dynamic in nature. See, for example, Arellano and Bond (1991) on a dynamic model of employment, Blundell et al. (1992) on a dynamic model of company investment, Islam (1995) on a dynamic model for growth convergence, and Ziliak (Chapter 10, Volume I) on a dynamic life cycle labour supply model. These dynamic relationships are characterized by the presence of a lagged dependent variable among the regressors, that is:

$$y_{it} = \delta y_{i,t-1} + x'_{it}\beta + u_{it} \quad i = 1, \dots, N \quad t = 1, \dots, T \tag{1}$$

where δ is a scalar, x'_{it} is $1 \times K$ and β is $K \times 1$. We will assume that the u_{it} follow a one-way error component model

$$u_{it} = \mu_i + \upsilon_{it} \tag{2}$$

where $\mu_i \sim \text{IID}(0, \sigma^2_\mu)$ and $\upsilon_{it} \sim \text{IID}(0, \sigma^2_\upsilon)$ independent of each other and among themselves. The dynamic panel data regression described in (1) and (2) are characterized by two sources of persistence over time. Autocorrelation due to the presence of a lagged dependent variable among the regressors and individual effects characterizing the heterogeneity among the individuals. For the fixed effects (FE) estimator, the Within transformation wipes out the μ_i, but $(y_{i,t-1} - \bar{y}_{i.-1})$ where $\bar{y}_{i.-1} = \sum_{t=2}^{T} y_{i,t-1}/(T-1)$ will still be correlated with $(\upsilon_{it} - \bar{\upsilon}_{i.})$ even if the υ_{it} are not serially correlated. In fact, the Within estimator will be biased of $O(1/T)$ and its consistency will depend upon T being large; see Nickell (1981). More recently, Kiviet (Chapter 8, Volume I) derives an approximation for the bias of the Within estimator in a dynamic panel data model with serially uncorrelated disturbances and strongly exogenous regressors. Kiviet proposes a corrected Within estimator that subtracts a consistent estimator of this bias from the original Within estimator. Therefore, for the typical labour panel where N is large and T is fixed, the Within estimator is biased and inconsistent. For macro-panels, studying for example long-run growth, the data covers a large number of countries N over a moderate size T, see Islam (1995). In this case, T is not very small relative to N. Hence some researchers may still favour the Within estimator, arguing that its bias may not be large.

The random effects GLS estimator is also biased in a dynamic panel data model. Whether fixed or random, an alternative transformation that wipes out the individual effects is the first difference (FD) transformation. In this case correlation between the predetermined explanatory variables and the remainder error is easier to handle. In fact Anderson and Hsiao (1981) suggested first differencing the model to get rid of the μ_i and then using $\Delta y_{i,t-2} = (y_{i,t-2} - y_{i,t-3})$ or simply $y_{i,t-2}$ as an instrument for $\Delta y_{i,t-1} = (y_{i,t-1} - y_{i,t-2})$. These instruments will not be correlated with $\Delta \upsilon_{it} = \upsilon_{i,t} - \upsilon_{i,t-1}$, as long as the υ_{it} themselves are not serially correlated. This instrumental variable (IV) estimation method leads to consistent but not necessarily efficient estimates of the parameters in the model because it does not make use of all the available moment conditions and it does not take into account the differenced structure on the residual disturbances ($\Delta \upsilon_{it}$). Arellano and Bond proposed a Generalized Method of Moments (GMM) procedure that is more efficient than the Anderson and Hsiao estimator. They argue that additional instruments can be obtained in a dynamic panel data model if one utilizes the orthogonality conditions that exist between lagged values of y_{it} and the disturbances υ_{it}. Let us illustrate this with the simple autoregressive model given by (1) but with no regressors:

$$y_{it} = \delta y_{i,t-1} + u_{it} \qquad i = 1, \ldots, N \qquad t = 1, \ldots, T \tag{3}$$

where u_{it} is given by (2). In order to get a consistent estimate of δ as $N \to \infty$ with T fixed, we first difference (3) to eliminate the individual effects

$$y_{it} - y_{i,t-1} = \delta(y_{i,t-1} - y_{i,t-2}) + (\upsilon_{it} - \upsilon_{i,t-1}) \tag{4}$$

and note that $(\upsilon_{it} - \upsilon_{i,t-1})$ is MA(1) with unit root. For $t = 3$, the first period we observe this relationship, y_{i1} is a valid instrument, since it is highly correlated with $(y_{i2} - y_{i1})$ and not correlated with $(\upsilon_{i3} - \upsilon_{i2})$ as long as the υ_{it} are not serially correlated. But note what happens for $t = 4$, the second period we observe (4). In this case, y_{i2} as well as y_{i1} are valid instruments for $(y_{i3} - y_{i2})$, since both y_{i2} and y_{i1} are not correlated with $(\upsilon_{i4} - \upsilon_{i3})$. One can continue in this fashion, adding an extra valid instrument with each forward period, so that for period T the set of valid instruments becomes $(y_{i1}, y_{i2}, \ldots, y_{i,T-2})$. Arellano and Bond derived a two-step GMM estimator that takes into account the above set of instruments and the MA(1) error structure.

Ahn and Schmidt (Chapter 1, Volume I) show that under the standard assumptions used in a dynamic panel data model, there are additional moment conditions that are ignored by the IV estimators suggested by Anderson and Hsiao (1981). Consider the simple dynamic model with no regressors given in (3) and assume that $y_{i0}, \ldots, y_{iT}$ are observable. The standard assumptions on the dynamic model are that:

A.1 For all i, υ_{it} is uncorrelated with y_{i0} for all t.
A.2 For all i, υ_{it} is uncorrelated with μ_i for all t.
A.3 For all i, the υ_{it} are mutually uncorrelated.

These assumptions on the initial value y_{i0} are weaker than those often made in the literature, see Hsiao (1986). Under these assumptions, one obtains the following $T(T-1)/2$ moment conditions:

$$E(y_{is} \Delta u_{it}) = 0 \qquad t = 2, \ldots, T \qquad s = 0, \ldots, t-2 \tag{5}$$

These are the same moment restrictions exploited by Arellano and Bond (1991). However. Ahn and Schmidt (Chapter 1, Volume I) find $T - 2$ additional moment conditions not implied by (5). These are given by

$$E(u_{iT}\Delta u_{it}) = 0 \qquad t = 2, \ldots, T-1 \tag{6}$$

Therefore, (5) and (6) imply a set of $T(T-1)/2 + (T-2)$ moment conditions which represent all of the moment conditions implied by the assumptions that the υ_{it} are mutually uncorrelated among themselves and with μ_i and y_{i0}. In order to see how these additional moment restrictions are utilized, consider our simple dynamic model in differenced form along with the last period's observation in levels:

$$\Delta y_{it} = \delta\Delta y_{i,t-1} + \Delta u_{it} \qquad t = 2, 3, \ldots, T \tag{7}$$

$$y_{iT} = \delta y_{i,T-1} + u_{iT} \tag{8}$$

The usual IV estimator, utilizing the restrictions in (5), amounts to estimating the first-differenced equations (7) by three-stage least squares, imposing the restriction that δ is the same in every equation, where the instrument set is y_{i0} for $t = 2$; (y_{i0}, y_{i1}) for $t = 3$; . . . ; $(y_{i0}, \ldots, y_{i,T-2})$ for $t = T$. Even though there are no legitimate observable instruments for the levels equation (8), Ahn and Schmidt argue that (8) is still useful in estimation because of the additional covariance restrictions implied by (6), that is, that u_{iT} uncorrelated with Δu_{it} for $t = 2, \ldots, T-1$. Ahn and Schmidt show that any additional covariance restrictions besides (6) are redundant and implied by the basic moment conditions given by (5).

Ahn and Schmidt (Chapter 1, Volume I) and Arellano and Bover (Chapter 4, Volume I) also consider the dynamic version of the Hausman and Taylor (1981) model and show how one can make efficient use of exogenous variables as instruments. In particular, they show that the strong exogeneity assumption implies more orthogonality conditions which lie in the deviations from mean space. These are irrelevant in the static Hausman–Taylor model but are relevant for the dynamic version of that model.

Blundell and Bond (Chapter 5, Volume I) revisit the importance of exploiting the initial condition in generating efficient estimators of the dynamic panel data model when T is small. They consider a simple autoregressive panel data model with no exogenous regressors given in (3). They focus on the case where $T = 3$, that is, where there is only one orthogonality condition given by $E(y_{i1}\Delta u_{i3}) = 0$, so that δ is just-identified. In this case, the first stage IV regression is obtained by running Δy_{i2} on y_{i1}. Note that this regression can be obtained from (3) evaluated at $t = 2$ by subtracting y_{i1} from both sides of this equation, that is:

$$\Delta y_{i2} = (\delta - 1)y_{i,1} + \mu_i + \upsilon_{i2} \tag{9}$$

since we expect $E(y_{i1}\mu_i) > 0$, $(\delta - 1)$ will be biased upwards with

$$\text{plim}\,(\hat{\delta} - 1) = (\delta - 1)\frac{c}{c + (\sigma_\mu^2/\sigma_u^2)} \tag{10}$$

where $c = (1 - \delta)/(1 + \delta)$. The bias term effectively scales the estimated coefficient on the instrumental variable y_{i1} towards zero. They also find that the F-statistic of the first stage IV regression converges to χ_1^2 with noncentrality parameter

$$\tau = \frac{(\sigma_u^2 c)^2}{\sigma_\mu^2 + \sigma_u^2 c} \rightarrow 0 \text{ as } \delta \rightarrow 1 \qquad (11)$$

As $\tau \rightarrow 0$, the instrumental variable estimator performs poorly. Hence Blundell and Bond attribute the bias and the poor precision of the first difference GMM estimator to the problem of weak instruments, and characterize this weak IV by its concentration parameter τ. Next, Blundell and Bond show that an additional mild stationarity restriction on the initial conditions process allows the use of an extended system GMM estimator that uses lagged differences of y_{it} as instruments for equations in levels, in addition to lagged levels of y_{it} as instruments for equations in first differences, see Arellano and Bover (Chapter 4, Volume I). The system GMM estimator is shown to have dramatic efficiency gains over the basic first difference GMM as $\delta \rightarrow 1$ and $(\sigma_\mu^2/\sigma_u^2)$ increases. In fact, for $T = 4$ and $(\sigma_\mu^2/\sigma_u^2) = 1$, the asymptotic variance ratio of the first difference GMM estimator to this system GMM estimator is 1.75 for $\delta = 0$ and increases to 3.26 for $\delta = 0.5$ and 55.4 for $\delta = 0.9$. Hahn (Chapter 7, Volume I) examined the role of the initial condition imposed by the Blundell and Bond estimator. This was done by numerically comparing the semiparametric information bounds for the case that incorporates the stationarity of the initial condition and the case that does not. Hahn finds that the efficiency gain can be substantial.

More recently, Ahn and Schmidt (Chapter 2, Volume I) propose a linearized GMM estimator that is asymptotically as efficient as the nonlinear GMM estimator. They also provide simple moment tests of the validity of these nonlinear restrictions. In addition, they investigate the circumstances under which the optimal GMM estimator is equivalent to a linear instrumental variable estimator. They find that these circumstances are quite restrictive and go beyond uncorrelatedness and homoskedasticity of the errors. Ahn and Schmidt (Chapter 1, Volume I) provide some evidence on the efficiency gains from the nonlinear moment conditions which in turn provide support for their use in practice. By employing all these conditions, the resulting GMM estimator is asymptotically efficient and has the same asymptotic variance as the MLE under normality. In fact, Hahn (1997) shows that GMM based on an increasing set of instruments as $N \rightarrow \infty$ would achieve the semiparametric efficiency bound.

Ziliak (Chapter 10, Volume I) asks the question whether the bias/efficiency trade-off for the GMM estimator for the time series case is still binding in panel data where the sample size is normally larger than 500. This problem becomes more pronounced with panel data, since the number of moment conditions increases dramatically as the number of strictly exogenous variables and the number of time series observations increase. Even though it is desirable from an asymptotic efficiency point of view to include as many moment conditions as possible, it may be infeasible or impractical to do so in many cases. For example, for $T = 10$ and five strictly exogenous regressors, this generates 500 moment conditions for GMM. Ziliak performs an extensive set of Monte Carlo experiments for a dynamic panel data model and finds that the same trade-off between bias and efficiency exists for GMM as the number of moment conditions increase, and that one is better off with sub-optimal instruments. In fact Ziliak finds that GMM performs well with suboptimal instruments, but is not recommended for panel data applications when all the moments are exploited for estimation.

Crépon, Kramarz and Trognon (Chapter 6, Volume I) argue that for the dynamic panel data model, when one considers a set of orthogonal conditions, the parameters can be divided into parameters of interest (like δ) and nuisance parameters (like the second order terms in the autoregressive error component model). They show that the elimination of such nuisance parameters using their empirical counterparts does not entail an efficiency loss when only the parameters of interest are estimated. In fact, Sevestre and Trognon in Chapter 6 of Mátyás and Sevestre (1996) argue that if one is only interested in δ, then one can reduce the number of orthogonality restrictions without loss in efficiency as far as δ is concerned. However the estimates of the other nuisance parameters are not generally as efficient as those obtained from the full set of orthogonality conditions.

The Alonso-Borrego and Arellano (Chapter 3, Volume I) paper is also motivated by the finite sample bias in panel data instrumental variable estimators when the instruments are weak. The dynamic panel model generates many overidentifying restrictions even for moderate values of T. Also the number of instruments increases with T, but the quality of these instruments is often poor because they tend to be only weakly correlated with first differenced endogenous variables that appear in the equation. Limited information maximum likelihood (LIML) is strongly preferred to 2SLS if the number of instruments gets large as the sample size tends to infinity. Hillier (1990) shows that the alternative normalization rules adopted by LIML and 2SLS are at the root of their different sampling behaviour. Hillier also shows that a symmetrically normalized 2SLS estimator has properties similar to those of LIML. Following Hillier, Alonso-Borrego and Arellano derive a symmetrically normalized GMM (SNM) and compare it with ordinary GMM and LIML analogues by means of simulations. Monte Carlo and empirical results show that GMM can exhibit large biases when the instruments are poor, while LIML and SNM remain essentially unbiased. However, LIML and SNM always had a larger interquartile range than GMM. For $T = 4$, $N = 100$, $\sigma^2_\mu = 0.2$ and $\sigma^2_\upsilon = 1$, the bias for $\delta = 0.5$ was 6.9% for GMM, 1.7% for SNM and 1.7% for LIML. This bias increases to 17.8% for GMM, 3.7% for SNM and 4.1% for LIML for $\delta = 0.8$.

Wansbeek and Knaap (1999) consider a simple dynamic panel data model with heterogeneous coefficients on the lagged dependent variable and the time trend, that is:

$$y_{it} = \delta_i y_{i,t-1} + \xi_i t + \mu_i + u_{it} \tag{12}$$

This model results from Islam's (1995) version of Solow's model on growth convergence among countries. Wansbeek and Knaap show that double differencing gets rid of the individual country effects (μ_i) on the first round of differencing and the heterogeneous coefficient on the time trend (ξ_i) on the second round of differencing. Modified OLS, IV and GMM methods are adapted to this model and LIML is suggested as a viable alternative to GMM to guard against the small sample bias of GMM. Simulations show that LIML is the superior estimator for $T \geq 10$ and $N \geq 50$. Macroeconomic data are subject to measurement error and Wansbeek and Knaap show how these estimators can be modified to account for measurement error that is white noise. For example GMM is modified so that it discards the orthogonality conditions that rely on the absence of measurement error. Wansbeek (Chapter 9, Volume I) presents a simple, systematic approach of deriving moment conditions for panel data models with measurement error. This is done by considering the covariances between the dependent variable and regressors, projecting out nuisance parameters. This approach is easily adapted for a variety of assumptions on endogeneity and measurement error structure.

Heterogeneous Panels

Robertson and Symons (1992) study the properties of some panel data estimators when the regression coefficients vary across individuals, that is they are heterogeneous but are assumed homogeneous in estimation. This is done for both stationary and nonstationary regressors. The basic conclusion is that severe biases can occur in dynamic estimation even for relatively small parameter variation.

Pesaran and Smith (Chapter 14, Volume I) consider the problem of estimating a dynamic panel data model when the parameters are individually heterogeneous and illustrate their results by estimating industry-specific UK labour demand functions. They present four different estimation procedures:

1. Aggregate time-series regressions of group averages.
2. Cross-section regressions of averages over time.
3. Pooled regressions allowing for fixed or random intercepts.
4. Separate regressions for each group, where coefficients estimates are averaged over these groups.

They show that when T is small (even if N is large), all the procedures yield inconsistent estimators. When both N and T are large, Pesaran and Smith show that the cross-section regression procedure will yield consistent estimates of the mean values of λ and β. Intuitively, when T is large the individual parameters λ_i and β_i can be consistently estimated using T observations of each individual i, say $\hat{\lambda}_i$ and $\hat{\beta}_i$, then averaging these individual estimators, $\sum_{i=1}^{N} \hat{\lambda}_i/N$ and $\sum_{i=1}^{N} \hat{\beta}_i/N$, which will lead to consistent estimators of the mean values of λ and β. Maddala, Srivastava and Li (1994) argue that shrinkage estimators are superior to either heterogeneous or homogeneous parameter estimates especially for prediction purposes. In fact, Maddala, Trost, Li and Joutz (Chapter 13, Volume I) consider the problem of estimating short-run and long-run elasticities of residential demand for electricity and natural gas for each of 49 states over the period 1970–90. They conclude that individual heterogeneous state estimates were hard to interpret and had the wrong signs. Pooled data regressions were not valid because the hypothesis of homogeneity of the coefficients was rejected. They recommend shrinkage estimators if one is interested in obtaining elasticity estimates for each state since these give more reliable results. Baltagi and Griffin (Chapter 11, Volume I) compare short-run and long-run estimates as well as forecasts for pooled homogeneous, individual heterogeneous and shrinkage estimators of a dynamic demand model for gasoline across 18 OECD countries over the period 1960–90. Based on one, five and ten year forecasts and plausibility of the short-run and long-run elasticity estimates, the results are in favour of pooling. Similar results were obtained for a dynamic model for cigarette demand across 46 states over the period 1963–92, see Baltagi, Griffin and Xiong (2000).

Hsiao and Tahmiscioglu (Chapter 12, Volume I) use a panel of 561 US firms over the period 1971–92 to study the influence of financial constraints on company investment. They find substantial differences across firms in terms of their investment behaviour. When a homogeneous pooled model is assumed, the impact of liquidity on firm investment is seriously underestimated. The authors recommend a mixed fixed and random coefficients framework based on the recursive predictive density criteria.

Non-Stationary Panels

With the growing use of cross-country data over time to study purchasing power parity, growth convergence and international R&D spillovers, the focus of panel data econometrics has shifted towards studying the asymptotics of macro panels with large N (number of countries) and large T (length of the time series) rather than the usual asymptotics of micro panels with large N and small T. The limiting distribution of double indexed integrated processes has been extensively studied by Phillips and Moon (Chapter 22, Volume I; 2000), who argue that the time series components of variables like per capita GDP growth have strong nonstationarity. Some of the distinctive results that are obtained with nonstationary panels are that many test statistics and estimators of interest have Normal limiting distributions. This is in contrast to the nonstationary time series literature where the limiting distributions are complicated functionals of Weiner processes. Several unit root tests applied in the time series literature have been extended to panel data, see Levin and Lin (1992), Im, Pesaran and Shin (1997), Harris and Tzavalis (Chapter 16, Volume I), Maddala and Wu (Chapter 18, Volume I), Choi (2001) and Hadri (Chapter 15, Volume I). However the use of such panel data methods are not without their critics; see Maddala, Wu and Liu (2000) who argue that panel data unit root tests do not rescue purchasing power parity (PPP). In fact the results on PPP with panels are mixed, depending on the group of countries studied, the period of study and the type of unit root test used. More damaging is the argument by Maddala et al. that for PPP, panel data tests are the wrong answer to the low power of unit root tests in single time series. After all, the null hypothesis of a single unit root is different from the null hypothesis of a panel unit root for the PPP hypothesis. Using the same line of criticism Maddala (1999) argues that panel unit root tests did not help settle the question of growth convergence among countries. However it was useful in spurring much needed research into dynamic panel data models.

Quah (1994) suggests a test for unit root in a panel data model without fixed effects where both N and T go to infinity at the same rate such that N/T is constant. Levin and Lin (1992) generalize this model to allow for fixed effects, individual deterministic trends and heterogeneous serially correlated errors. They assume that both N and T tend to infinity. However, T increases at a faster rate than N with $N/T \rightarrow 0$. Harris and Tzavalis (Chapter 16, Volume I) derive panel unit root tests when the time dimension T is *fixed*. This is the typical case for micro panel studies. They show that the assumption that T tends to infinity at a faster rate than N, as in Levin and Lin, rather than T fixed, as in the case of micro panels, yields tests which are substantially undersized and have low power especially when T is small. The Levin and Lin test is restrictive in the sense that it requires ρ to be homogeneous across i. As Maddala (1999) points out, the null may be fine for testing convergence in growth among countries, but the alternative restricts every country to converge at the same rate. Im, Pesaran and Shin (1997) (IPS) allow for a heterogeneous coefficient of y_{it-1} and propose an alternative testing procedure based on averaging individual unit root test statistics.

Maddala and Wu (Chapter 18, Volume I) and Choi (2001) propose a Fisher type test which combines the p-values from unit root tests for each cross-section i to test for unit root in panel data. Hadri (Chapter 15, Volume I) proposes a residual based Lagrange Multiplier (LM) test for the null that the time series for each i are stationary around a deterministic trend against the alternative of a unit root in panel data. Entorf (1997) studies spurious fixed effects regressions when the true model involves independent random walks with and without drifts. Entorf found that for $T \to \infty$ and N finite, the nonsense regression phenomenon holds for spurious fixed effects models and inference based on t-values can be highly misleading. Kao (Chapter 17, Volume I) and Phillips and Moon (Chapter 22, Volume I) derive the asymptotic distributions of the least squares dummy variable estimator and various conventional statistics from the spurious regression in panel data.

Phillips and Moon (Chapter 22, Volume I) study various regressions between two panel vectors that may or may not have cointegrating relations, and present a fundamental framework for studying sequential and joint limit theories in nonstationary panel data. The panel models considered allow for four cases: (i) panel spurious regression, where there is no time series cointegration, (ii) heterogeneous panel cointegration, where each individual has its own specific cointegration relation, (iii) homogeneous panel cointegration where individuals have the same cointegration relation, and (iv) near-homogeneous panel cointegration, where individuals have slightly different cointegration relations determined by the value of a localizing parameter.

Moon and Phillips (Chapter 19, Volume I) investigate the asymptotic properties of the Gaussian MLE of the localizing parameter in local to unity dynamic panel regression models with deterministic and stochastic trends. Moon and Phillips find that for the homogeneous trend model, the Gaussian MLE of the common localizing parameter is $\sqrt{N}$ consistent, while for the heterogeneous trends model, it is inconsistent. The latter inconsistency is due to the presence of an infinite number of incidental parameters (as $N \to \infty$) for the individual trends. Unlike the fixed effects dynamic panel data model, where this inconsistency due to the incidental parameter problem disappears as $T \to \infty$, the inconsistency of the localizing parameter in the Moon and Phillips model persists even when both N and T go to infinity. Moon and Phillips (2000) show that the local to unity parameter in a simple panel near-integrated regression model can be consistently estimated using pooled OLS. When deterministic trends are present, pooled panel estimators of the localizing parameter are asymptotically biased. Some techniques are developed to obtain consistent estimates of this localizing parameter, but only in the region where it is negative. These methods are used to show how to perform efficient trend extraction for panel data. They are also used to deliver consistent estimates of distancing parameters in nonstationary panel models where the initial conditions are in the distant past. The joint asymptotics in the paper rely on $N/T \to 0$, so that the results are most relevant in panels where T is large relative to N.

Pesaran, Shin and Smith (Chapter 21, Volume I) derive the asymptotics of a pooled mean group (PMG) estimator. The PMG estimation constrains the long-run coefficients to be identical, but allow the short-run and adjustment coefficients as the error variances to differ across the cross-sectional dimension. Kao (Chapter 17, Volume I) presents two types of cointegration tests in panel data, the DF and ADF types tests. McCoskey and Kao (1998) derive a residual-based test for the null of cointegration rather than the null of no cointegration in panels. Pedroni (Chapter 20, Volume I) proposes several tests for the null hypothesis of cointegration in a panel data model that allows for considerable heterogeneity. While Pedroni (1999), derives asymptotic distributions and critical values for several residual based tests of the null of no cointegration in panels where there are multiple regressors. The model includes regressions with individual specific fixed effects and time trends. Considerable heterogeneity is allowed across individual members of the panel with regard to the associated cointegrating vectors and the dynamics of the underlying error process. By comparing results from individual countries and the panel as a whole, Pedroni (2001) rejects the strong PPP hypothesis and finds that no degree of cross-sectional dependency would be sufficient to overturn the rejection of strong PPP.

Specification Tests in Panels

Baltagi and Li (Chapter 20, Volume II) derive three LM statistics for an error component model with first-order serially correlated errors. The first LM statistic jointly tests for zero first-order serial correlation and random individual effects. The second LM statistic tests for zero first-order serial correlation assuming fixed individual effects, and the third LM statistic tests for zero first-order serial correlation assuming random individual effects. In all three cases Baltagi and Li show that the corresponding LM statistic is the *same* whether the alternative is AR(1) or MA(1). Also Baltagi and Li derive two extensions of the Burke, Godfrey and Termayne (1990) AR(1) vs MA(1) test from the time-series to the panel data literature. The first extension tests the null of AR(1) disturbances against MA(1) disturbances and the second the null of MA(1) disturbances against AR(1) disturbances in an error component model. These tests are computationally simple requiring only OLS or Within residuals.

Bera, Sosa-Escudero and Yoon (Chapter 21, Volume II) suggest an adjustment of the LM test that is robust to local misspecification. This test essentially modifies the *LM* test by correcting the mean and variance of the score $\partial L/\partial\sigma_\mu^2$ for its asymptotic correlation with $\partial L/\partial\rho$. Under local misspecification, this adjusted test statistic is equivalent to Neyman's $C(\alpha)$ test and shares its optimality properties. Bera et al. argue that these tests use only OLS residuals and are easier to compute than the Baltagi and Li (Chapter 20, Volume II) conditional LM tests. Monte Carlo experiments show the usefulness of these modified Rao-Score tests in guarding against *local* misspecification.

Li and Hsiao (Chapter 22, Volume II) propose three test statistics in the context of a semiparametric partially linear panel data model

$$y_{it} = x'_{it}\beta + \theta(w_{it}) + u_{it}$$

with u_{it} satisfying $E(u_{it}/w_{it}, x_{it}) = 0$. The functional form of $\theta(.)$ is unknown and $E(u_{it}^2/x_{it}, w_{it})$ is not specified. The first test statistic tests the null of zero first order serial correlation. The second tests for the presence of higher order serial correlation and the third tests for the presence of individual effects. The asymptotics are carried out for $N \to \infty$ and fixed T. Monte Carlo experiments are performed to study the finite sample performance of these tests.

Baltagi, Hidalgo and Li (Chapter 19, Volume II) derive a non-parametric test for poolability which is robust to functional form misspecification. In particular, they consider the following nonparametric panel data model

$$y_{it} = g_t(x_{it}) + \varepsilon_{it} \qquad (i = 1, \ldots, N;\ t = 1, \ldots, T)$$

where $g_t(.)$ is an unspecified functional form that may vary over time. x_{it} is a $k \times 1$ column vector of predetermined explanatory variables with ($p \geq 1$) variables being continuous and $k - p$ (≥ 0). Poolability of the data over time is equivalent to testing that $g_t(x) = g_s(x)$ almost everywhere for all t and $s = 1, 2, \ldots, T$; versus $g_t(x) \neq g_s(x)$ for some $t \neq s$ with probability greater than zero. The test statistic is shown to be consistent and asymptotically normal and is applied to an earnings equation using data from the PSID.

For the Hausman and Taylor (1981) model, Metcalf (Chapter 23, Volume II) shows that using less instruments may lead to a more powerful Hausman specification test. Asymptotically, more instruments lead to more efficient estimators. However the asymptotic bias of the less efficient estimator will also be greater as the null hypothesis of no correlation is violated. Metcalf argues that if the bias increases at the same rate as the variance (as the null is violated) for the less efficient estimator, then the power of the Hausman test will increase. This is due to the fact that the test statistic is linear in variance but quadratic in bias.

Limited Dependent Variables and Panel Data

In many economic studies the dependent variable is discrete, indicating for example that a household purchased a car or that an individual is unemployed or that he or she joined the union. Honoré (Chapter 1, Volume II) suggests trimmed least absolute deviations and trimmed least squares estimators for truncated and censored regression models with fixed effects. These are semi-parametric estimators with no distributional assumptions necessary on the error term. The main assumption is that the remainder error υ_{it} is independent and identically distributed conditional on the x_{it} and the μ_i for $t = 1, \ldots, T$. Honoré exploits the symmetry in the distribution of the latent variables and finds that when the true values of the parameters are known, trimming can transmit the same symmetry in distribution to the observed variables. This generates orthogonality conditions which must hold at the true value of the parameters. Therefore the resulting GMM estimator is consistent provided the orthogonality conditions are satisfied at a unique point in the parameter space. Honoré shows that these estimators are consistent and asymptotically normal. Monte Carlo results show that as long as $N \geq 200$, the asymptotic distribution is a good approximation of the small sample distribution. However, if N is small, the small sample distribution of these estimators is skewed.

Honoré and Kyriazidou (2000a) review recent estimators for censored regression and sample selection panel data models with unobserved individual specific effects and show how they can be easily extended to other Tobit-type models. The proposed estimators are semi-parametric and do not require the parametrization of the distribution of the unobservables. However, they do require that the explanatory variables be strictly exogenous. This rules out lags of the dependent variables among the regressors. The general approach exploits stationarity and exchangeability assumptions on the models' transistory error terms in order to construct moment conditions that do not depend on the individual specific effects.

Kyriazidou (Chapter 4, Volume II) studies the panel data sample selection model, also known as the Type 2 Tobit model with

$$y^*_{1it} = x'_{1it}\beta_1 + \mu_{1i} + \upsilon_{1it} \tag{13}$$

$$y^*_{2it} = x'_{2it}\beta_2 + \mu_{2i} + \upsilon_{2it} \tag{14}$$

where

$$\begin{aligned} y_{1it} &= 1 \quad \text{if } y^*_{1it} > 0 \\ &= 0 \quad \text{otherwise} \end{aligned}$$

and

$$\begin{aligned} y_{2it} &= y^*_{2it} \quad \text{if } y_{1it} = 1 \\ &= 0 \quad \text{otherwise} \end{aligned}$$

Kyriazidou suggests estimating β_1 by one of the estimation methods for discrete choice models with individual effects. Next, μ_{2i} is eliminated by first-differencing the data for which y^*_{2it} is observed. With this sample selection, Kyriazidou focuses on individuals for whom $x'_{1it}\beta_1 = x'_{1is}\beta_1$. For these individuals, the same first-differencing that will eliminate the fixed effects will also eliminate the sample selection. This suggests a two-step Heckman procedure where β_1 is estimated in the first step and then β_2 is estimated by applying OLS to the first differences but giving more weight to observations for which $(x_{1it} - x_{1is})'\hat{\beta}_1$ is close to zero. This weighting can be done using a Kernel whose bandwidth h_N shrinks to zero as the sample size increases. The resulting estimator is $\sqrt{Nh_N}$ consistent and asymptotically normal. Monte Carlo results for $N =$ 250, 1000 and 4000 and $T = 2$ indicate that this estimator works well for sufficiently large data sets. However it is quite sensitive to the choice of the bandwidth parameters.

Honoré and Kyriazidou (Chapter 2, Volume II) consider the identification and estimation of panel data discrete choice models with lags of the dependent variable and strictly exogenous variables that allow for unobservable heterogeneity. Honoré and Kyriazidou also consider identification in the semiparametric case where the logit assumption is relaxed. A conditional maximum score estimator à la Manski (1987) is proposed which is shown to be consistent. In addition, Honoré and Kyriazidou discuss an extension of the identification result to multinomial discrete choice models and to the case where the dependent variable is lagged twice.

Keane (Chapter 3, Volume II) derives a computationally practical simulation estimator for the panel data probit model. This sidesteps the problem of having to simulate M^T possible choice sequences by factorizing the method of simulated moments (MSM) first-order conditions into transition probabilities. The latter are simulated using highly accurate importance sampling techniques. Keane performs Monte Carlo experiments and finds that even for large T and small simulation sizes, the bias in the MSM estimator is negligible. When maximum likelihood methods are feasible, the MSM estimator performs well relative to quadrature-based maximum likelihood methods even where the latter are based on a large number of quadrature points. Keane argues that MSM has three advantages over the other practical nonmaximum likelihood estimators. First, MSM is asymptotically as efficient as maximum likelihood (in simulation size) while the other estimators are not. Second, MSM can be easily extended to handle multinomial probit situations, whereas the extension of the other estimators is computationally burdensome. Third, MSM can be extended to handle nonlinear systems of equations which are intractable with maximum likelihood.

Lechner (Chapter 5, Volume II) suggests several specification tests for the panel data probit model. These are generalized score and Wald tests employed to detect omitted variables, neglected dynamics, heteroskedasticity, non-normality and random-coefficient variations. The performance of these tests in small samples is investigated using Monte Carlo experiments. In addition, an empirical example is given on the probability of self-employment in West Germany using a random sample of 1926 working men selected from the German Socio-Economic Panel and observed over the period 1984–89.

Wooldridge (Chapter 8, Volume II) derives some simple variable addition tests of selection bias as well as easy-to-apply estimation techniques that correct for selection bias in linear fixed effects panel data models. The auxiliary regressors are either Tobit residuals or inverse Mill's ratios and the disturbances are allowed to be arbitrarily serially correlated and unconditionally heteroskedastic.

Vella and Verbeek (Chapter 7, Volume II) suggest two-step estimators for a wide range of parametric panel data models with censored endogenous variables and sample selection bias. This generalizes the treatment of sample selection models by Ridder (1990) and Nijman and Verbeek (1992) to a wide range of selection rules. This also generalizes the panel data dummy endogenous regressor model in Vella and Verbeek (1998) by allowing for other forms of censored endogenous regressors. In addition, this analysis shows how Wooldridge's (Chapter 8, Volume II) estimation procedures for sample selection can be applied to more general specifications. The two-step procedure derives estimates of the unobserved heterogeneity responsible for the endogeneity/selection bias in the first step. These in turn are included as additional regressors in the primary equation. This is computationally simple compared to maximum likelihood procedures, since it requires only one-dimensional numerical integration. The panel nature of the data allows adjustment, and testing, for two forms of endogeneity and/or sample selection bias. Furthermore, it allows for dynamics and state dependence in the reduced form.

Charlier, Melenberg and van Soest (1995) provide a smoothed maximum score estimator for the binary choice panel data model which has an asymptotic normal distribution but a convergence rate that is slower than root–N. Lee (Chapter 6, Volume II) proposes a $\sqrt{N}$-consistent semiparametric estimator which does not depend on a smoothing parameter and is asymptotically normal. Lee (2001) proposes a semiparametric first-difference estimator for panel censored-selection models where the selection equation is of the Tobit type. This estimator minimizes a convex function and does not require any smoothing. This estimator is compared with that of Wooldridge (Chapter 8, Volume II) and Honoré and Kyriazidou (2000a) using Monte Carlo experiments. The results show that all three estimators are quite robust to model assumption violation.

Nonlinear Panel Data Models

Abrevaya (Chapter 9, Volume II) proposes a leapfrog estimator for the monotonic transformation panel data model of the type

$$h_t(y_{it}) = x_{it}'\beta + \mu_i + \upsilon_{it}$$

where $h_t(.)$ is assumed to be strictly increasing. The trick here is to difference across pairs of individuals at a given time period, rather than across time periods. This semiparametric estimator is shown to be $\sqrt{N}$-consistent and asymptotically normal. Examples of this model include the multiple-spell proportional hazards model and dependent variable transformation models with fixed effects. Abrevaya (2000) introduces a class of rank estimators that consistently estimate the coefficients of a generalized fixed effects regression model. This model allows for censoring, places no parametric assumptions on the error disturbances and allows the fixed effects to be correlated with the covariates. The maximum score estimator for the binary choice fixed effects model proposed by Manski (1987) is a member of this class of estimators. The class of rank estimators converge at less than $\sqrt{N}$ rate. while smoothed versions of these estimators converge at rates approaching the $\sqrt{N}$ rate. Some of the limitations of this approach are that the estimation relies on a strict exogeneity assumption and does not deal with the inclusion of lagged dependent variables. Also the coefficients of time-invariant covariates are not identified by this class of estimators.

Wooldridge (1997) considers the estimation of multiplicative, unobserved components panel data models without imposing a strict exogeneity assumption on the conditioning variables. A robust method of moments estimator is proposed which requires only a conditional mean assumption. This applies to binary choice models with multiplicative unobserved effects, and models containing parametric nonlinear transformations of the endogenous variables. This model is particularly suited to nonnegative explained variables, including count variables. In addition, it can also be applied to certain nonlinear Euler equations. Wooldridge (Chapter 10, Volume II) offers some distribution-free estimators for multiplicative unobserved components panel data models. Requiring only the correct specification of the conditional mean, the multinomial quasi-conditional MLE is shown to be consistent and asymptotically normal. This estimation method is popular for estimating fixed effects count models, see Hausman, Hall and Griliches (1984). Wooldridge's results show that it can be used to obtain consistent estimates even when the dependent variable y_{it} is not a vector of counts. In fact y_{it} can be a binary response variable, a proportion, a nonnegative continuously distributed random variable, or it can have discrete and continuous characteristics. Neither the distribution of y_{it} nor its temporal dependence are restricted. Additional orthogonality conditions can be used in a GMM framework to improve the efficiency of the estimator. Finally, Wooldridge (2000) proposes a method of estimating very general, nonlinear, dynamic, unobserved effects panel data models with feedback. Wooldridge shows how to construct the likelihood function for the conditional maximum likelihood estimator in dynamic, unobserved effects models where not all conditioning variables are strictly exogenous. A useful innovation is the treatment of the initial conditions which offers a flexible, relatively simple alternative to existing methods.

Unbalanced Panels

Incomplete panels are more likely to be the norm in typical economic empirical settings. For example, in collecting data on US airlines over time, a researcher may find that some firms have dropped out of the market while new entrants have emerged over the sample period observed. Similarly, while using labour or consumer panels on households, one may find that some households have moved and can no longer be included in the panel. These typical scenarios lead to 'unbalanced' or 'incomplete' panels. Wansbeek and Kapteyn (1989), Baltagi and Chang (1994), Baltagi, Song and Jung (2001) and Davis (Chapter 14, Volume II) study various estimation methods used in the literature for the unbalanced error component model including Analysis of Variance, maximum likelihood and MINQUE methods. Antweiler (Chapter 11, Volume II) and Baltagi, Song and Jung (Chapter 13, Volume II) study the imbalanced nested error component model. For this model the incomplete panel data exhibits a natural nested grouping. For example, data on firms may be grouped by industry, data on states by region, data on individuals by profession and data on students by schools. Baltagi, Song and Jung compared the performance of these estimators using Monte Carlo experiments. While the MLE and MIVQUE methods perform the best in estimating the variance components and the standard errors of the regression coefficients, the simple ANOVA methods perform just as well in estimating the regression coefficients. These estimation methods are also used to investigate the productivity of public capital in private production. In a companion paper, Baltagi, Song and Jung (2002) extend the Lagrange Multiplier tests for testing the existence of these effects to this unbalanced nested error component model.

Antweiler (Chapter 11, Volume II) derives the maximum likelihood estimator for an unbalanced nested three-way error component model. This is applied to the problem of explaining the determinants of pollution concentration (measured by the log of atmospheric sulfuric dioxide) at 293 observation stations located in 44 countries over the time period 1971–96. Comparing the results of maximum likelihood for a nested versus a simple (non-nested) unbalanced error component model, Antweiler finds that the scale elasticity coefficient estimate for the nested model is less than half that for the non-nested model. Scale elasticity is the coefficient of log of economic intensity as measured by GDP per square kilometre.

Davis (Chapter 14, Volume II) generalizes the Wansbeek and Kapteyn (1989) results to the three-way, four-way and higher order error component models. Davis shows that the Within transformation can be applied in stages to the variables in the regression. This reduces the computational burden considerably. Davis applies OLS, Within, MIVQUE and MLE procedures to a three-way unbalanced error component model using data on film revenues for six movie theatres near New Haven, CT, observed over a six-week period in 1998. Some of the reasons for unbalancedness in the data occur because (i) not all films are shown at all locations, (ii) films start and stop being shown at theatres during the observation period, and (iii) data on revenues are missing due to nonresponse. The estimates obtained reveal a complex set of asymmetric cross-theatre price elasticities of demand.

Some panel data sets cannot be collected every period due to lack of resources or cut in funding. Instead these panels are collected over unequally spaced time intervals. For example, a panel of households could be collected over unequally spaced years rather than annually. This is also likely when collecting data on countries, states or firms where in certain years the data are not recorded, are hard to obtain, or are simply missing. Other common examples are panel data sets using daily data from the stock market, including stock prices, commodity prices, futures and so on. These panel data sets are unequally spaced when the market closes on weekends and holidays. This is also common for housing resale data, where the pattern of resales for each house occurs at different time periods and the panel is unbalanced because we observe a different number of resales for each house. Baltagi and Wu (Chapter 12, Volume II) extend the Baltagi and Li (1991) results to the estimation of an unequally spaced panel data regression model with AR(1) remainder disturbances. A feasible generalized least squares procedure is proposed as a weighted least square that can handle a wide range of unequally spaced panel data patterns. This procedure is simple to compute and provides natural estimates of the serial correlation and variance components parameters. Baltagi and Wu also provide a locally best invariant test for zero first-order serial correlation against positive or negative serial correlation in case of unequally spaced panel data.

Pseudo-Panels

For some countries panel data may not exist. Instead the researcher may find annual household surveys based on a large random sample of the population. Examples of some of these cross-sectional consumer expenditure surveys include: the British Family Expenditure Survey and the US Current Population Survey. For these repeated cross-section surveys it may be impossible to track the same household over time, as required in a genuine panel. Instead, Deaton (1985) suggests tracking cohorts and estimating economic relationships based on cohort means rather than individual observations. One cohort could be the set of all males born between 1945 and 1950. This age cohort is well defined, and can be easily identified from the data. Deaton argues that these pseudo-panels do not suffer the attrition problem that plagues genuine panels, and may be available over longer time periods compared to genuine panels. Moffitt (Chapter 18, Volume II) extends Deaton's analysis to the estimation of dynamic models with repeated cross-sections. By imposing certain restrictions, Moffitt shows that linear and nonlinear models, with and without fixed effects, can be identified and consistently estimated with pseudo-panels. Collado (Chapter 15, Volume II) proposes measurement-error corrected estimators for dynamic models with individual effects using time-series of independent cross-sections. A GMM estimator corrected for measurement-error is proposed that is consistent, as the number of cohorts tends to infinity for a fixed T and a fixed number of individuals per cohort. In addition a measurement-error corrected within-groups estimator is proposed which is consistent as T tends to infinity. Monte Carlo simulations are performed to study the small sample properties of the estimators proposed. Some of the main results indicate that the measurement-error correction is important, and that corrected estimators reduce the bias obtained. Also, for small T, GMM estimators are better than within-groups estimators. Recently McKenzie (2000) allows for parameter heterogeneity amongst cohorts, and shows that consistency of least squares depends on $n_c \rightarrow \infty$, $(T/n_c) \rightarrow 0$, and that instrumental variables estimators are consistent under weaker conditions. McKenzie (Chapter 17, Volume II) also considers the problem of estimating dynamic models with unequally spaced pseudo panel data. Surveys in developing countries are often taken at unequally-spaced intervals and this unequal spacing, in turn, imposes nonlinear restrictions on the parameters. Nonlinear least squares, minimum distance and one-step estimators are suggested that are consistent and asymptotically normal for finite T as the number of individuals per cohort is allowed to pass to infinity. Girma (Chapter 16, Volume II) suggests an alternative GMM method of estimating linear dynamic models from a time series of independent cross-sections. Unlike the Deaton approach of averaging across individuals in a cohort, Girma suggests a quasi-differencing transformation across pairs of individuals that belong to the same group. The asymptotic properties of the proposed GMM estimators are based upon having a large number of individuals per group-time cell. This is in contrast to the Deaton-type estimator which requires the number of group/time periods to grow without limit. Some of the other advantages of this method include the fact that no aggregation is involved, the dynamic response parameters can freely vary across groups, and the presence of unobserved individual specific heterogeneity is explicitly allowed for.

Conclusion

The panel data econometrics literature has exhibited phenomenal growth since the two Maddala (1993) volumes. One cannot do justice to the many theoretical and empirical contributions to date. Space limitations have prevented the inclusion of many worthy contributions. Some topics are still in their infancy, but growing fast, like nonstationary panels and semi-parametric and nonparametric methods using panel data. Hopefully, this set of papers will whet the reader's appetite and induce him or her to explore this vast literature and use it in their own research.

References

Note: References to papers included in these two volumes are omitted here.

Abrevaya, J. (2000), 'Rank estimation of a generalized fixed-effects regression model', *Journal of Econometrics*, **95**, 1–23.

Anderson, T.W. and C. Hsiao (1981), 'Estimation of dynamic models with error components', *Journal of the American Statistical Association*, **76**, 598–606.

Arellano, M. and S. Bond (1991), 'Some tests of specification for panel data: Monte Carlo evidence and an application to employment equations', *Review of Economic Studies*, **58**, 277–97.

Arellano, M. and B. Honoré (2001), 'Panel data models: Some recent developments', Chapter 53 in J. Heckman and E. Leamer (eds), *Handbook of Econometrics*. Amsterdam: North-Holland.

Baltagi, B.H. (2001), *The Econometrics of Panel Data*. Chichester: Wiley.

Baltagi, B.H. and Y.J. Chang (1994), 'Incomplete panels: A comparative study of alternative estimators for the unbalanced one-way error component regression model', *Journal of Econometrics*, **62**, 67–89.

Baltagi, B.H., T.B. Fomby and R.C. Hill (eds) (2000), 'Nonstationary panels, panel cointegration, and dynamic panels', *Advances in Econometrics*, Vol. 15. Amsterdam: Elsevier Science.

Baltagi, B.H., J.M. Griffin and W. Xiong (2000), 'To pool or not to pool: Homogeneous versus heterogeneous estimators applied to cigarette demand', *Review of Economics and Statistics*, **82**, 117–26.

Baltagi, B.H. and Q. Li (1991), 'A transformation that will circumvent the problem of auto-correlation in an error component model', *Journal of Econometrics*, **48**, 385–93.

Baltagi, B.H., S.H. Song and B.C. Jung (2001), 'A comparative study of alternative estimators for the unbalanced two-way error component regression model', *The Econometrics Journal*, forthcoming.

Baltagi, B.H., S.H. Song and B.C. Jung (2002), 'Simple LM tests for the unbalanced nested error component regression model', *Econometric Reviews*, **21**, 167–87.

Banerjee, A. (1999), 'Panel data unit roots and cointegration: An overview', *Oxford Bulletin of Economics and Statistics*, **61**, 607–29.

Blundell, R., S. Bond, M. Devereux and F. Schiantarelli (1992), 'Investment and Tobin's q: Evidence from company panel data', *Journal of Econometrics*, **51**, 233–57.

Burke, S.P., L.G. Godfrey and A.R. Termayne (1990), 'Testing AR(1) against MA(1) disturbances in the linear regression model: An alternative procedure', *Review of Economic Studies*, **57**, 135–45.

Chamberlain, G. (1984), 'Panel data', Chapter 22 in Z. Griliches and M. Intrilligator (eds), *Handbook of Econometrics*. Amsterdam: North-Holland, 1247–318.

Charlier, E., B. Melenberg and A. van Soest (1995), 'A smoothed maximum score estimator for the binary choice panel data model with an application to labour force participation', *Statistica Neerlandica*, **49**, 324–42.

Choi, I. (2001), 'Unit root tests for panel data', *Journal of International Money and Finance*, **20**, 249–72.

Deaton, A. (1985), 'Panel data from time series of cross-sections', *Journal of Econometrics*, **30**, 109–26.

Entorf, H. (1997), 'Random walks with drifts: Nonsense regression and spurious fixed-effect estimation', *Journal of Econometrics*, **80**, 287–96.

Hahn, J. (1997), 'Efficient estimation of panel data models with sequential moment restrictions', *Journal of Econometrics*, **79**, 1–21.

Hausman, J.A., B.H. Hall and Z. Griliches (1984), 'Econometric models for count data with an application to the patents–R&D relationship', *Econometrica*, **52**, 909–38.

Hausman, J.A. and W.E. Taylor (1981), 'Panel data and unobservable individual effects', *Econometrica*, **49**, 1377–98.

Hillier, G.H. (1990), 'On the normalization of structural equations: Properties of direction estimators', *Econometrica*, **58**, 1181–94.

Honoré, B.E. and E. Kyriazidou (2000a), 'Estimation of Tobit-type models with individual specific effects', *Econometric Reviews*, **19**, 341–66.

Hsiao, C. (1986), *Analysis of Panel Data*. Cambridge: Cambridge University Press.

Im, K.S., M.H. Pesaran and Y. Shin (1997), 'Testing for unit roots in heterogeneous panels', manuscript. Department of Applied Economics, University of Cambridge.

Islam, N. (1995), 'Growth empirics: A panel data approach', *Quarterly Journal of Economics*, **110**, 1127–70.

Lee, M.J. (2001), 'First-difference estimator for panel censored-selection models', *Economics Letters*, **70**, 43–9.

Levin. A. and C.F. Lin (1992), 'Unit root test in panel data: Asymptotic and finite sample properties', discussion paper no. 92–93. University of California at San Diego.

McCoskey, S. and C. Kao (1998), 'A residual-based test of the null of cointegration in panel data', *Econometric Reviews*, **17**, 57–84.

McKenzie, D.J. (2000), 'Estimation of homogeneous stationary and non-stationary pseudopanels', working paper. New Haven, CT: Department of Economics.

Maddala. G.S. (ed.) (1993), *The Econometrics of Panel Data*, Volumes I and II. Cheltenham: Edward Elgar Publishing.

Maddala, G.S. (1999), 'On the use of panel data methods with cross country data', *Annales D'Économie et de Statistique*, **55–56**, 429–48.

Maddala, G.S., V.K. Srivastava and H. Li (1994), 'Shrinkage estimators for the estimation of short-run and long-run parameters from panel data models', working paper. Ohio: Ohio State University.

Maddala, G.S., S. Wu and P.C. Liu (2000), 'Do panel data rescue purchasing power parity (PPP) theory?', Chapter 2 in J. Krishnakumar and E. Ronchetti (eds), *Panel Data Econometrics: Future Directions*. Amsterdam: North-Holland, 35–51.

Manski, C.F. (1987), 'Semiparametric analysis of random effects linear models from binary panel data', *Econometrica*, **55**, 357–62.

Mátyás, L. and P. Sevestre (eds) (1996), *The Econometrics of Panel Data: A Handbook of the Theory With Applications*. Dordrecht: Kluwer Academic Publishers.

Moon, H.R. and P.C.B. Phillips (2000), 'Estimation of autoregressive roots near unity using panel data', *Econometric Theory*, **16**, 927–97.

Nickell, S. (1981), 'Biases in dynamic models with fixed effects', *Econometrica*, **49**, 1417–26.

Nijman, Th.E. and M. Verbeek (1992), 'Nonresponse in panel data: The impact on estimates of a life cycle consumption function', *Journal of Applied Econometrics*, **7**, 243–57.

Pedroni, P. (1999), 'Critical values for cointegration tests in heterogeneous panels with multiple regressors', *Oxford Bulletin of Economics and Statistics*, **61**, 653–78.

Pedroni, P. (2001), 'Purchasing power parity tests in cointegrated panels', *Review of Economics and Statistics*, **83**, 727–31.

Phillips, P.C.B. and H. Moon (2000), 'Nonstationary panel data analysis: An overview of some recent developments', *Econometric Reviews*, **19**, 263–86.

Quah, D. (1994), 'Exploiting cross section variation for unit root inference in dynamic data', *Economics Letters*, **44**, 9–19.

Ridder, G. (1990), 'Attrition in multi-wave panel data', in J. Hartog, G. Ridder and J. Theeuwes (eds), *Panel Data and Labor Market Studies*. Amsterdam: North-Holland, 45–67.

Robertson, D. and J. Symons (1992), 'Some strange properties of panel data estimators', *Journal of Applied Econometrics*, **7**, 175–89.

Sevestre, P. (1999), '1977–1997: Changes and continuities in panel data econometrics', *Annales D'Économie et de Statistique*, **55–56**, 15–25.
Vella, F. and M. Verbeek (1998), 'Whose wages do unions raise? A dynamic model of unionism and wage determination for young men', *Journal of Applied Econometrics*, **13**, 163–8.
Wansbeek, T.J. and A. Kapteyn (1989), 'Estimation of the error components model with incomplete panels', *Journal of Econometrics*, **41**, 341–61.
Wansbeek, T.J. and T. Knapp (1999), 'Estimating a dynamic panel data model with heterogeneous trends', *Annales D'Économie et de Statistique*, **55–56**, 331–49.
Wooldridge, J.M. (1997), 'Multiplicative panel data models without the strict exogeneity assumption', *Econometric Theory*, **13**, 667–78.
Wooldridge, J.M. (2000), 'A framework for estimating dynamic, unobserved effects panel data models with possible feedback to future explanatory variables', *Economics Letters*, **68**, 245–50.

Part I
Dynamic Panels and GMM

[1]

ELSEVIER

Journal of Econometrics 68 (1995) 5–27

JOURNAL OF Econometrics

Efficient estimation of models for dynamic panel data

Seung C. Ahn[a], Peter Schmidt*[,b]

[a]*Department of Economics, Arizona State University, Tempe, AZ 85287-3806, USA*
[b]*Department of Economics, Michigan State University, East Lansing, MI 48824-1038, USA*

Abstract

In this paper we consider a dynamic model for panel data. We show that, under standard assumptions, there are more moment conditions than are currently exploited in the literature. Some of these are linear, but others are quadratic, so that nonlinear GMM is required. We also show that exogenous regressors generate a larger number of relevant moment conditions in a dynamic model than they would in a static model.

Key words: Dynamic model; Panel data; Fixed effects; Random effects
JEL classification: C21, C23

1. Introduction

This paper considers a regression model for dynamic panel data. That is, we assume that we have observations on a large number of individuals, with several observations on each individual, and the model of interest is a regression model in which the lagged value of the dependent variable is one of the explanatory variables. The error in the model is assumed to contain a time-invariant individual effect as well as random noise.

We consider the commonly assumed and empirically relevant case of a large number of individuals (N) and a small number of time series observations per individual (T), and so we study the asymptotic properties of our estimators as $N \to \infty$ for fixed T. Then the basic problem faced in the estimation of this

* Corresponding author.

The second author gratefully acknowledges the financial support of the National Science Foundation. We also thank Trevor Breusch for his help with this paper, and several referees for their helpful comments.

SSDI 0304407694016 41 C

model is that a fixed effects treatment leads to the within estimator (least squares after transformation to deviations from means), which is inconsistent because the within transformation induces a correlation of order $1/T$ between the lagged dependent variable and the error. The currently available response to this problem (e.g., Anderson and Hsiao, 1981; Hsiao, 1986; Holtz-Eakin, 1988; Holtz-Eakin, Newey, and Rosen, 1988; Arellano and Bover, 1990; Arellano and Bond, 1991) is to first difference the equation to remove the effects, and then estimate by instrumental variables (IV), using as instruments values of the dependent variable lagged two or more periods. This treatment leads to consistent estimates, but (under standard assumptions that we will list) not to efficient estimates, because it does not make use of all of the available moment conditions.

In this paper we find the additional moment conditions implied by a standard set of assumptions. Unlike the conditions currently exploited in the literature, some of these conditions are nonlinear. However, they can be easily imposed in a generalized method of moments (GMM) framework. We show that the resulting GMM estimator shares the efficiency properties of Chamberlain's (1982, 1984) minimum distance (MD) estimator if the errors in the model are i.i.d. (independently and identically distributed) across individuals. The GMM estimator is also compatible with a specification of the model in which the unobserved individual effects are independent across individuals but heteroskedastic. For some specific parameter values, we evaluate the relevant asymptotic covariance matrices to show that the additional moment conditions identified in this paper lead to nontrivial gains in asymptotic efficiency.

We also link the literature on the static panel data model (e.g., Mundlak, 1978; Chamberlain, 1980; Hausman and Taylor, 1981; Amemiya and MaCurdy, 1986; Breusch, Mizon, and Schmidt, 1989) with the literature on the dynamic model by showing how to make efficient use of exogenous variables as instruments. The assumption of strong exogeneity implies more orthogonality conditions than current estimators exploit. These additional moment conditions all lie in the 'deviations from means' space and are irrelevant in the case of the static model, but they are relevant in the dynamic model. We show how to categorize and use these conditions.

The plan of the paper is as follows. Section 2 considers the simple dynamic model with no exogenous variables under a standard set of assumptions, and identifies the moment conditions available for estimation. Section 3 considers the same model under some alternative sets of assumptions. Section 4 considers the question of efficiency of estimation, and Section 5 gives some calculations of the gain from using the extra moment conditions we have found. Section 6 considers the model with exogenous regressors, and shows how to categorize the moment conditions that are available and relevant in the dynamic model. Finally, Section 7 contains some concluding remarks.

2. Moment conditions under standard assumptions

We will consider the simple dynamic model

$$y_{it} = \delta y_{i,t-1} + u_{it}, \tag{1}$$

$$u_{it} = \alpha_i + \varepsilon_{it}, \qquad i = 1, \ldots, N, \quad t = 1, \ldots, T.$$

Here i denotes cross-sectional unit (individual) and t denotes time. The error u_{it} contains a time-invariant individual effect α_i and random noise ε_{it}. Note that there are NT observations for the regression and that the initial observed value of y (for individual i) is y_{i0}; assumptions about the generation of y_{i0} are important in this literature. We can also write the T observations for person i as

$$y_i = \delta y_{i,-1} + u_i, \tag{2}$$

where $y_i' = (y_{i1}, \ldots, y_{iT})$ and $y_{i,-1}$ and u_i are defined similarly.

The model (1) does not contain any explanatory variables beyond the lagged dependent variable. The issues raised by the presence of exogenous regressors will be discussed in Section 6.

We assume that α_i and ε_{it} have mean zero for all i and t. (Nonzero mean of α can be handled with an intercept.) We also assume that all observations are independent across individuals. Furthermore, we will begin with the following 'standard assumptions' (SA):

(SA.1) For all i, ε_{it} is uncorrelated with y_{i0} for all t.

(SA.2) For all i, ε_{it} is uncorrelated with α_i for all t.

(SA.3) For all i, the ε_{it} are mutually uncorrelated.

We note that these assumptions are implied by a variety of simple models, such as Chamberlain's (1984) projection model, which asserts that $\text{Proj}(y_{it} \mid \alpha_i, y_{i0}, \ldots, y_{i,t-1}) = \alpha_i + \delta y_{i,t-1}$, where $\text{Proj}(z \mid x)$ represents the population least squares projection of a variable z on a set of variables $x = (x_1, \ldots, x_k)$. We also note that our assumptions on the initial value y_{i0} are weaker than those often made in the literature. See Bhargava and Sargan (1983), Hsiao (1986), and Blundell and Smith (1991) for examples of stronger assumptions about the initial value y_{i0}.

Under SA, it is obvious that the following moment conditions hold:

$$\text{E}(y_{is} \Delta u_{it}) = 0, \qquad t = 2, \ldots, T, \quad s = 0, \ldots, t-2. \tag{3}$$

There are $T(T-1)/2$ such conditions. These are the moment conditions that are currently exploited in the literature. However, under SA there are additional moment conditions beyond those in (3). In particular, the following $T-2$

moment conditions also hold:

$$\mathrm{E}(u_{iT}\Delta u_{it}) = 0, \qquad t = 2, \ldots, T-1. \tag{4}$$

The conditions (3)–(4) are a set of $T(T-1)/2 + (T-2)$ moment conditions that follow directly from the assumptions that the ε_{it} are mutually uncorrelated and uncorrelated with α_i and y_{i0}. Furthermore, they represent *all* of the moment conditions implied by these assumptions. An informal but instructive way to see this is as follows. We cannot observe α_i or ε_{it}, but $u_{it} = (\alpha_i + \varepsilon_{it})$ is 'observable' in the sense that it can be written in terms of data and parameters (which is what is relevant for GMM). The implications of SA for the u_{it} are simply:

$$\mathrm{E}(y_{i0}u_{it}) \text{ is the same for all } t, \tag{5a}$$

$$\mathrm{E}(u_{is}u_{it}) \text{ is the same for all } s \neq t. \tag{5b}$$

This is also a set of $T(T-1)/2 + (T-2)$ moment conditions, and it is easy to show that it is equivalent to the conditions (3)–(4). The main advantage of (3)–(4) over (5) is just that it maximizes the number of *linear* moment conditions.

A more formal proof of the number of restrictions implied by SA can be given as follows. We distinguish those things that we make assumptions about, namely $(\varepsilon_{i1}, \ldots, \varepsilon_{iT}, y_{i0}, \alpha_i)$, from things that we make assumptions about and that are observable in the sense discussed above, namely $(\alpha_i + \varepsilon_{i1}, \ldots, \alpha_i + \varepsilon_{iT}, y_{i0})$. The covariance matrix of the things we make assumptions about will be denoted Σ:

$$\Sigma = \mathrm{cov}\begin{bmatrix} \varepsilon_{i1} \\ \varepsilon_{i2} \\ \vdots \\ \varepsilon_{iT} \\ y_{i0} \\ \alpha_i \end{bmatrix} = \begin{bmatrix} \sigma_{11} & \sigma_{12} & \cdots & \sigma_{1T} & \sigma_{10} & \sigma_{1\alpha} \\ \sigma_{21} & \sigma_{22} & \cdots & \sigma_{2T} & \sigma_{20} & \sigma_{2\alpha} \\ \vdots & \vdots & & \vdots & \vdots & \vdots \\ \sigma_{T1} & \sigma_{T2} & \cdots & \sigma_{TT} & \sigma_{T0} & \sigma_{T\alpha} \\ \sigma_{01} & \sigma_{02} & \cdots & \sigma_{0T} & \sigma_{00} & \sigma_{0\alpha} \\ \sigma_{\alpha 1} & \sigma_{\alpha 2} & \cdots & \sigma_{\alpha T} & \sigma_{\alpha 0} & \sigma_{\alpha\alpha} \end{bmatrix} \tag{6}$$

On the other hand, the covariance matrix of the 'observables' will be denoted Λ:

$$\Lambda = \mathrm{cov}\begin{bmatrix} \alpha_i + \varepsilon_{i1} \\ \alpha_i + \varepsilon_{i2} \\ \vdots \\ \alpha_i + \varepsilon_{iT} \\ y_{i0} \end{bmatrix} = \begin{bmatrix} \lambda_{11} & \lambda_{12} & \cdots & \lambda_{1T} & \lambda_{10} \\ \lambda_{21} & \lambda_{22} & \cdots & \lambda_{2T} & \lambda_{20} \\ \vdots & \vdots & & \vdots & \vdots \\ \lambda_{T1} & \lambda_{T2} & \cdots & \lambda_{TT} & \lambda_{T0} \\ \lambda_{01} & \lambda_{02} & \cdots & \lambda_{0T} & \lambda_{00} \end{bmatrix} \tag{7}$$

$$= \begin{bmatrix} (\sigma_{\alpha\alpha} + \sigma_{11} + 2\sigma_{\alpha 1}) & (\sigma_{\alpha\alpha} + \sigma_{12} + \sigma_{\alpha 1} + \sigma_{\alpha 2}) & \cdots & (\sigma_{\alpha\alpha} + \sigma_{1T} + \sigma_{\alpha 1} + \sigma_{\alpha T}) & (\sigma_{0\alpha} + \sigma_{01}) \\ (\sigma_{\alpha\alpha} + \sigma_{12} + \sigma_{\alpha 1} + \sigma_{\alpha 2}) & (\sigma_{\alpha\alpha} + \sigma_{22} + 2\sigma_{\alpha 2}) & \cdots & (\sigma_{\alpha\alpha} + \sigma_{2T} + \sigma_{\alpha 2} + \sigma_{\alpha T}) & (\sigma_{0\alpha} + \sigma_{02}) \\ \vdots & \vdots & & \vdots & \vdots \\ (\sigma_{\alpha\alpha} + \sigma_{1T} + \sigma_{\alpha 1} + \sigma_{\alpha T}) & (\sigma_{\alpha\alpha} + \sigma_{2T} + \sigma_{\alpha 2} + \sigma_{\alpha T}) & \cdots & (\sigma_{\alpha\alpha} + \sigma_{TT} + 2\sigma_{\alpha T}) & (\sigma_{0\alpha} + \sigma_{0T}) \\ (\sigma_{0\alpha} + \sigma_{01}) & (\sigma_{0\alpha} + \sigma_{02}) & \cdots & (\sigma_{0\alpha} + \sigma_{0T}) & \sigma_{00} \end{bmatrix}.$$

Under SA, we have $\sigma_{\alpha t} = 0$ for all t, $\sigma_{0t} = 0$ for all t, and $\sigma_{ts} = 0$ for all $t \neq s$. Then Λ simplifies as follows:

$$\Lambda = \begin{bmatrix} (\sigma_{\alpha\alpha} + \sigma_{11}) & \sigma_{\alpha\alpha} & \cdots & \sigma_{\alpha\alpha} & \sigma_{0\alpha} \\ \sigma_{\alpha\alpha} & (\sigma_{\alpha\alpha} + \sigma_{22}) & \cdots & \sigma_{\alpha\alpha} & \sigma_{0\alpha} \\ \vdots & \vdots & & \vdots & \vdots \\ \sigma_{\alpha\alpha} & \sigma_{\alpha\alpha} & \cdots & (\sigma_{\alpha\alpha} + \sigma_{TT}) & \sigma_{0\alpha} \\ \sigma_{0\alpha} & \sigma_{0\alpha} & \cdots & \sigma_{0\alpha} & \sigma_{00} \end{bmatrix}. \tag{8}$$

There are $T - 1$ restrictions that λ_{0t} is the same for $t = 1, \ldots, T$, and $T(T-1)/2 - 1$ restrictions that λ_{ts} is the same for $t, s = 1, \ldots, T, t \neq s$. Adding the number of restrictions, we get $T(T-1)/2 + (T-2)$.

An intuitive way to understand the extra moment conditions that we have identified and the efficiency gains that they lead to is as follows. We can rewrite the model (1) as follows:

$$\Delta y_{it} = \delta \Delta y_{i,t-1} + \Delta u_{it}, \qquad t = 2, 3, \ldots, T, \tag{9a}$$

$$y_{iT} = \delta y_{i,T-1} + u_{iT}. \tag{9b}$$

The usual IV estimator amounts to estimating the first-differenced equations (9a) by three-stage least squares, imposing the restriction that δ is the same in every equation, where the instrument set is y_{i0} for $t = 2$, (y_{i0}, y_{i1}) for $t = 3, \ldots, (y_{i0}, \ldots, y_{i,T-2})$ for $t = T$. There are no legitimate observable instruments for the levels equation (9b), but this equation is still useful in estimation because of the covariance restrictions that u_{iT} is uncorrelated with Δu_{it}, $t = 2, \ldots, T-1$. These covariance restrictions are exactly the extra moment conditions identified in (4). Of course, there are additional covariance restrictions in (9a); for example, Δu_4 is uncorrelated with Δu_2. However, these additional covariance restrictions are not useful in estimation because, unlike the covariance restrictions in (4), they are implied by the basic moment conditions in (3).

An interesting sidelight is that the moment conditions (4)–(5) hold under weaker conditions than SA. Define the set of modified assumptions (MA):

(MA.1) For all i, $\text{cov}(\varepsilon_{it}, y_{i0})$ is the same for all t.

(MA.2) For all i, $\text{cov}(\varepsilon_{it}, \alpha_i)$ is the same for all t.

(MA.3) For all i, $\text{cov}(\varepsilon_{it}, \varepsilon_{is})$ is the same for all $t \neq s$.

Note that MA assumes equal covariance where SA assumes zero covariance. Nevertheless, the moment conditions implied by SA are also implied by MA, as is easily checked in the same way as above. Thus we can test whether $\text{cov}(\varepsilon_{it}, \alpha_i)$ is constant over t, but we cannot test whether it is zero. Similarly, we can test constancy of $\text{cov}(\varepsilon_{it}, y_{i0})$ but not whether it is zero.

3. Some alternative assumptions

In this section we briefly consider some alternative sets of assumptions. The first case we consider is the one in which (SA.1)–(SA.3) are augmented by the additional assumption that the ε_{it} are homoskedastic. That is, suppose that we add the assumption:

(AA.4) For all i, $\text{var}(\varepsilon_{it})$ is the same for all t.

(Here 'AA' is short for 'added assumption'.) This assumption, when added to (SA.1)–(SA.3), generates the additional $(T-1)$ moment conditions that

$$E(u_{it}^2) \text{ is the same for } t = 1, \ldots, T. \tag{10}$$

[In terms of (8) above, λ_{tt} is the same for $t = 1, \ldots, T$.] Therefore the total number of moment conditions becomes $T(T-1)/2 + (2T-3)$. These moment conditions can be expressed as (3), (4), and (10). Alternatively, if we wish to maximize the number of linear moment conditions, Ahn and Schmidt (1990) show that these moment conditions can be expressed as (3) plus the additional conditions

$$E(y_{it}\Delta u_{i,t+1} - y_{i,t+1}\Delta u_{i,t+2}) = 0, \qquad t = 1, \ldots, T-2, \tag{11a}$$

$$E(\bar{u}_i \Delta u_{i,t+1}) = 0, \qquad t = 1, \ldots, T-1, \tag{11b}$$

where $\bar{u}_i = T^{-1}\sum_{t=1}^{T} u_{it}$. Comparing this to the set of moment conditions without homoskedasticity [(3)–(4)], we see that homoskedasticity adds $T-1$ moment conditions *and* it allows $T-2$ previously nonlinear moment conditions to be expressed linearly.

Another possible assumption is the 'stationarity' assumption of Arellano and Bover (1990). They assume:

(AA.5) $E(\alpha_i y_{it})$ is the same for all t.

This is equivalent in our framework to asserting that $\sigma_{\alpha\alpha} = (1-\delta)\sigma_{0\alpha}$. If SA and (AA.4) are maintained, (AA.5) adds one moment condition to the set consisting of (3) and (11). However, it also allows all of the moment conditions to be expressed linearly. In particular, given this condition, we can write the set of usable moment conditions as (3) plus

$$E(u_{iT}\Delta y_{it}) = 0, \qquad t = 1, \ldots, T-1, \tag{12a}$$

$$E(u_{it}y_{it} - u_{i,t-1}y_{i,t-1}) = 0, \qquad t = 2, \ldots, T. \tag{12b}$$

This is a set of $T(T-1)/2 + (2T-2)$ moment conditions, all of which are linear in δ.

An interesting question that this paper will not address is how much our assumptions can be weakened without losing all moment conditions. Ahn and Schmidt (1990, App.) give a partial answer by counting the moment conditions implied by many possible combinations of (SA.1), (SA.2), (SA.3), and (A.4). The reader is referred to that paper for details.

4. Asymptotic efficiency

GMM based on the full set of moment conditions (3)–(4) makes efficient use of second moment information, and intuitively we should expect it to be asymptotically equivalent to other estimators that make efficient use of second moment information, notably Chamberlain's (1982, 1984) minimum distance estimator. We now proceed to prove this asymptotic equivalence.

To define some notation, let $\eta_i = (u_{i1}, \ldots, u_{iT}, y_{i0})'$ be the vector of 'observables', with $\mathrm{cov}(\eta_i) = \Lambda$ as given in (7) above, and let $\xi_i = (y_{i0}, y_{i1}, \ldots, y_{iT})'$ be the vector of observed values of y, with covariance matrix Ω. (Recall that η_i is 'observable' in the sense that it can be written as a function of data and δ.) We assume that the η_i (or, equivalently, the ξ_i) are i.i.d. across individuals. The assumption of homoskedasticity is required for the existence of a consistent minimum distance estimator.

The connection between η_i and ξ_i is linear: $\xi_i = D\eta_i$, $\eta_i = D^{-1}\xi_i$, where D is a $(T+1)\times(T+1)$ nonsingular matrix that depends on δ. Specifically, $D_{h,T+1} = \delta^{h-1}$, $h = 1, \ldots, T+1$; for $j = 1, \ldots, T$ and $h = 1, \ldots, T+1$, $D_{hj} = 0$ for $h \leqslant j$ and $D_{hj} = \delta^{|h-j-1|}$ for $h > j$. (If we rearrange η_i so that y_{i0} comes first instead of last, then D is lower triangular and $D_{hj} = \delta^{|h-j|}$ for $h \geqslant j$.) Thus $\Omega = D\Lambda D'$. Define

$$S = N^{-1}\sum_i \xi_i\xi_i', \qquad Z = N^{-1}\sum_i \eta_i\eta_i'; \tag{13}$$

note that $S = DZD'$. Define the vectors of parameters

$$\theta = (\sigma_{00}, \sigma_{\alpha\alpha}, \sigma_{0\alpha}, \sigma_{11}, \ldots, \sigma_{TT})', \qquad \gamma = (\delta, \theta')', \tag{14}$$

so that Λ depends on θ, D depends on δ, and Ω depends on γ. Finally, define $\Delta = \mathrm{cov}[\mathrm{vec}(\eta_i\eta_i')]$, and note that $\mathrm{cov}[\mathrm{vec}(\xi_i\xi_i')] = \psi = (D\otimes D)\Delta(D\otimes D)'$.

In this notation, the basic results of Chamberlain (1984) can be stated as follows. The quasi-maximum likelihood (QML) estimator solves the problem

$$\max_{\gamma} L = (N/2)\ln|\Omega^{-1}| - (N/2)\,\mathrm{trace}(\Omega^{-1}S). \tag{15}$$

Its asymptotic covariance matrix is of the form

$$C_{\mathrm{QML}} = [G'H'(\Omega\otimes\Omega)^{-1}HG]^{-1}G'H'(\Omega\otimes\Omega)^{-1}\psi(\Omega\otimes\Omega)^{-1}HG \times [G'H'(\Omega\otimes\Omega)^{-1}HG]^{-1}. \tag{16}$$

Here $G = \partial v(\Omega)/\partial\gamma'$, where $v(\Omega)$ equals $\mathrm{vec}(\Omega)$ with the above-diagonal elements of Ω deleted, and H is the 'duplication matrix' (e.g., Magnus and Neudecker, 1988, p. 49) such that $Hv(\Omega) = \mathrm{vec}(\Omega)$. The minimum distance (MD) estimator based on the observables ξ_i solves the problem

$$\min_{\gamma}\, [v(S) - v(\Omega)]'A_N[v(S) - v(\Omega)], \tag{17}$$

and its asymptotic covariance matrix is of the form

$$C_{\mathrm{MD}} = (G'AG)^{-1}G'A(J\psi J')^{-1}AG(G'AG)^{-1}, \tag{18}$$

where $J = (H^+)' = (H'H)^{-1}H'$ is the 'elimination matrix' such that $v(\Omega) = J\,\mathrm{vec}(\Omega)$, and where $A = \mathrm{plim}\, A_N$. The QMLE is a MD estimator, with $A = H'(\Omega\otimes\Omega)^{-1}H$. This choice of A is suboptimal except under normality. The optimal minimum distance (OMD) estimator uses $A = (J\psi J')^{-1}$, and its asymptotic covariance matrix is of the form

$$C_{\mathrm{OMD}} = [G'(J\psi J')^{-1}G]^{-1}. \tag{19}$$

The OMD estimator is asymptotically efficient relative to the QML estimator, but they are equally efficient under normality.

Normal quasi-maximum likelihood estimation of the dynamic panel data model has been discussed by Bhargava and Sargan (1983) and Hsiao (1986, Sect. 4.3.2) under a variety of assumptions about the generation of y_{i0}, including assumptions equivalent to ours (y_{i0} correlated with α_i and stationarity not imposed). Chamberlain's results indicate that these estimators are asymptotically dominated by estimators that make efficient use of second moment information but do not impose normality, such as the OMD estimator and (as we shall see) our GMM estimator.

Our GMM estimator is based upon the covariance matrix of the 'observables' η_i instead of the observed ξ_i. Accordingly, we now consider OMD estimation based upon $\Lambda = \mathrm{cov}(\eta_i)$ instead of upon $\Omega = \mathrm{cov}(\xi_i)$, as above; that is, we now consider $Z = N^{-1}\sum_i \eta_i\eta_i'$ instead of $S = N^{-1}\sum_i \xi_i\xi_i'$. This alternative OMD estimator solves the problem

$$\min_{\gamma}\, [v(Z) - v(\Lambda)]'B_N[v(Z) - v(\Lambda)], \tag{20}$$

where plim $B_N = (J\Delta J')^{-1}$, and where it should be remembered that Z depends on δ while Λ depends on θ. Since $S = DZD'$ and $\Omega = D\Lambda D'$, the information contained in $[v(S) - v(\Omega)]$ and $[v(Z) - v(\Lambda)]$ is the same. Thus it is reasonable that the OMD estimators based on (17) and on (20) should be asymptotically equivalent (though they may differ in finite samples due to the way that the weighting matrices are evaluated). We show in Appendix 1 that this is so. Thus it doesn't matter asymptotically whether OMD estimation is based on $\text{cov}(\eta_i)$ or on $\text{cov}(\xi_i)$.

We now wish to show that the OMD estimator based on (20) is asymptotically equivalent to our GMM estimator. Define $m(\gamma) = v[Z(\delta) - \Lambda(\theta)]$, so that the OMD estimator is a GMM estimator based on the moment condition $\mathrm{E}[m(\gamma)] = 0$. Now consider a possible transformation of these moment conditions: $b(\gamma) = Fm(\gamma)$, where F is nonstochastic and nonsingular. Obviously GMM based on $b(\gamma)$ is the same as GMM based on $m(\gamma)$ since we have just taken a nonsingular linear combination of the moment conditions. (In fact, this is essentially the same result as just given in the previous paragraph.) In particular, as discussed in Appendix 1, there exists a matrix F such that

$$b(\gamma) = Fm(\gamma) = [h(\delta)', (p(\delta) - \theta)']', \tag{21}$$

where the first subset of transformed moment conditions, $h(\delta)$, is the set of moment conditions exploited by our GMM estimator, and the second subset of transformed moment conditions, $p(\delta) - \theta$, just determines θ in terms of δ. It follows (see, e.g., Abowd and Card, 1989, App.) that GMM based on $h(\delta)$ only yields the same estimate of δ as GMM based on the entire set of moment conditions $b(\gamma)$ [or $m(\gamma)$].

The fact that our GMM estimator based on the moment conditions (3)–(4) is asymptotically equivalent to Chamberlain's optimal minimum distance estimator confirms the intuition that the GMM estimator is efficient in the class of estimators that make use of second moment information. In this regard, it should be noted explicitly that (SA.1)–(SA.3) are stated in terms of uncorrelatedness only, so that only second moment information is relevant. If we replaced uncorrelatedness with independence, for example, additional moment conditions involving higher-order moments would (at least in principle) be potentially relevant. These additional moment conditions would not lead to gains in asymptotic efficiency when η_i is normal; because our model is linear in η_i, under normality only second moments matter.

The GMM/minimum distance estimator reaches the semiparametric efficiency bound discussed by Newey (1990). A sketch of the proof is given in Appendix 2. This result is intuitively reasonable. The unrestricted estimator of $v(\Omega)$, $v(S)$, reaches the semiparametric efficiency bound $J\psi J'$, using standard results of Chamberlain (1987) and Newey (1990) on the semiparametric efficiency of the sample mean. The minimum distance estimator efficiently imposes the restrictions on $v(\Omega)$, thus preserving semiparametric efficiency. Further discussion can be found in Chamberlain (1987).

Even though under SA the optimal minimum distance estimator shares the asymptotic properties of our GMM estimator, the latter may be preferred for two reasons. First, the GMM estimator of δ can be more easily calculated, because the nuisance parameters $(\sigma_{\alpha\alpha}, \sigma_{00}, \sigma_{0\alpha}, \sigma_{11}, \dots, \sigma_{TT})$ need not be considered in the GMM estimation procedure. Second, the consistency and asymptotic normality of the GMM estimator require only SA and cross-sectional independence of η_i and ξ_i, while cross-sectional homoskedasticity is also required for the consistency of the minimum distance estimator.

5. Calculations of asymptotic variances

In this section we attempt to quantify the gains in asymptotic efficiency that arise from using the extra moment conditions identified in this paper. We consider three estimators. (i) Let $\hat{\delta}_{\text{IV}}$ be GMM using (3) only. This is the estimator suggested in the existing literature. Under homoskedasticity it can be calculated as linear IV on the first-differenced equation. (ii) Let $\hat{\delta}_{\text{GMM1}}$ be GMM using (3) and (4). This estimator exploits the extra nonlinear moment conditions that arise under SA. (iii) Let $\hat{\delta}_{\text{GMM2}}$ be GMM using (3) and (11). This estimator assumes homoskedasticity as well as SA. Asymptotically $\hat{\delta}_{\text{IV}}$ is least efficient and $\hat{\delta}_{\text{GMM2}}$ is most efficient.

We will quantify the differences in efficiency by calculating the asymptotic covariance matrices of the three estimates, for given parameter values. The asymptotic covariance matrices can be found in Ahn (1990) and Ahn and Schmidt (1990). The relevant parameter values are T, δ, σ_{00}, $\sigma_{\alpha\alpha}$, $\sigma_{0\alpha}$, $\sigma_{11}, \dots, \sigma_{TT}$. However, in this section we will consider only the case that the ε_{it} are i.i.d., so that the T variances $\sigma_{11}, \dots, \sigma_{TT}$ can be replaced by a single variance, say $\sigma_{\varepsilon\varepsilon}$. Furthermore, because our results are invariant to scale, a normalization of the variances is possible, and we pick $\sigma_{\varepsilon\varepsilon} = 1$ as our normalization.

In Table 1 we report some results for the case in which y is stationary. Thus the errors are homoskedastic so that the extra moment conditions underlying $\hat{\delta}_{\text{GMM2}}$ are valid. Furthermore, we set σ_{00} and $\sigma_{0\alpha}$ according to the stationarity conditions $\sigma_{0\alpha} = \sigma_{\alpha\alpha}/(1-\delta)$, $\sigma_{00} = \sigma_{\alpha\alpha}/(1-\delta)^2 + \sigma_{\varepsilon\varepsilon}(1-\delta^2)$. This leaves three relevant parameters: T, δ, and $\sigma_{\alpha\alpha}$. We present results for $T = 3$, 4, and 10, for δ ranging from -0.99 to 0.99, and for $\sigma_{\alpha\alpha}$ (to be interpreted as $\sigma_{\alpha\alpha}/\sigma_{\varepsilon\varepsilon}$) ranging from 0 to 4. The results are the ratios of asymptotic variances [e.g., $\text{var}(\hat{\delta}_{\text{IV}})/\text{var}(\hat{\delta}_{\text{GMM2}})$].

The efficiency gains found in Table 1 from using additional moment conditions are certainly nontrivial. They increase as T increases, which is perhaps surprising, since the proportion of extra moment conditions to total moment conditions decreases with T. (The numbers of moment conditions for the three estimators are 3, 4, and 6 for $T = 3$, they are 6, 8, and 11 for $T = 4$, they are and 45, 53, and 62 for $T = 10$.) The efficiency gains also increase as $\sigma_{\alpha\alpha}/\sigma_{\varepsilon\varepsilon}$ increases,

Table 1
Ratios of asymptotic variances; stationarity assumed (to determine σ_{00} and $\sigma_{0\alpha}$)

	var(*IV*)/var(*GMM1*)						var(*IV*)/var(*GMM2*)					
	$\sigma_{\alpha\alpha}/\sigma_{\varepsilon\varepsilon}$						$\sigma_{\alpha\alpha}/\sigma_{\varepsilon\varepsilon}$					
δ	0	0.25	0.5	1	2	4	0	0.25	0.5	1	2	4
$T = 3$												
− 0.99	1.00	1.00	1.01	1.01	1.01	1.01	1.00	1.01	1.01	1.01	1.01	1.01
− 0.9	1.04	1.05	1.05	1.06	1.07	1.10	1.05	1.05	1.06	1.07	1.09	1.12
− 0.8	1.08	1.09	1.10	1.12	1.15	1.21	1.08	1.09	1.11	1.14	1.18	1.25
− 0.5	1.14	1.19	1.23	1.31	1.43	1.61	1.14	1.20	1.26	1.35	1.51	1.72
− 0.3	1.15	1.24	1.31	1.44	1.66	1.94	1.15	1.25	1.35	1.51	1.77	2.11
0	1.14	1.29	1.42	1.67	2.04	2.52	1.14	1.32	1.49	1.80	2.27	2.86
0.3	1.11	1.33	1.54	1.91	2.49	3.20	1.11	1.39	1.67	2.18	2.95	3.91
0.5	1.08	1.35	1.62	2.10	2.82	3.71	1.08	1.45	1.84	2.53	3.58	4.87
0.8	1.03	1.41	1.78	2.42	3.37	4.55	1.03	1.64	2.26	3.34	4.96	6.97
0.9	1.02	1.45	1.85	2.54	3.57	4.85	1.02	1.76	2.49	3.75	5.62	7.96
0.99	1.00	1.48	1.92	2.65	3.76	5.13	1.00	1.94	2.78	4.21	6.35	9.03
$T = 4$												
− 0.99	1.00	1.00	1.00	1.00	1.01	1.01	1.00	1.00	1.00	1.01	1.01	1.01
− 0.9	1.03	1.03	1.04	1.05	1.06	1.09	1.03	1.04	1.04	1.05	1.07	1.10
− 0.8	1.06	1.07	1.08	1.10	1.14	1.19	1.06	1.07	1.09	1.11	1.15	1.21
− 0.5	1.12	1.17	1.22	1.29	1.39	1.52	1.12	1.18	1.23	1.30	1.41	1.55
− 0.3	1.15	1.24	1.32	1.44	1.60	1.79	1.15	1.25	1.34	1.46	1.64	1.84
0	1.17	1.35	1.50	1.73	2.02	2.33	1.17	1.37	1.53	1.78	2.10	2.43
0.3	1.16	1.46	1.72	2.11	2.61	3.11	1.16	1.50	1.79	2.23	2.79	3.35
0.5	1.13	1.55	1.90	2.45	3.13	3.82	1.13	1.61	2.03	2.66	3.46	4.25
0.8	1.06	1.72	2.28	3.13	4.19	5.25	1.06	1.89	2.62	3.74	5.12	6.50
0.9	1.03	1.80	2.45	3.43	4.65	5.86	1.03	2.07	2.96	4.31	6.00	7.67
0.99	1.00	1.91	2.64	3.74	5.11	6.48	1.00	2.33	3.41	5.02	7.03	9.04
$T = 10$												
− 0.99	1.00	1.00	1.00	1.00	1.00	1.01	1.00	1.00	1.00	1.00	1.00	1.01
− 0.9	1.02	1.03	1.03	1.03	1.04	1.05	1.02	1.03	1.03	1.03	1.04	1.05
− 0.8	1.04	1.05	1.06	1.07	1.08	1.10	1.04	1.05	1.06	1.07	1.08	1.10
− 0.5	1.08	1.12	1.15	1.18	1.21	1.24	1.08	1.12	1.15	1.18	1.21	1.25
− 0.3	1.10	1.18	1.22	1.27	1.32	1.37	1.10	1.18	1.22	1.27	1.32	1.37
0	1.15	1.30	1.38	1.46	1.55	1.61	1.15	1.30	1.38	1.47	1.55	1.62
0.3	1.19	1.49	1.64	1.80	1.94	2.04	1.19	1.49	1.65	1.81	1.95	2.05
0.5	1.21	1.70	1.95	2.21	2.41	2.56	1.21	1.71	1.96	2.22	2.43	2.57
0.8	1.17	2.37	3.00	3.61	4.11	4.44	1.17	2.42	3.06	3.71	4.22	4.56
0.9	1.11	2.86	3.76	4.67	5.38	5.86	1.11	2.96	3.92	4.89	5.65	6.16
0.99	1.01	3.65	4.98	6.30	7.36	8.07	1.01	3.94	5.42	6.89	8.07	8.86

which is not surprising. The efficiency gains increase as δ increases toward one, a finding predicted correctly by a referee. When δ is close to unity, the 'first stage regressions' in the calculation of $\hat{\delta}_{IV}$ are essentially regressions of differences on levels and have little explanatory power. Finally, the efficiency gains of $\hat{\delta}_{GMM1}$ over $\hat{\delta}_{IV}$ are often substantial, while the additional efficiency gains of $\hat{\delta}_{GMM2}$ over $\hat{\delta}_{GMM1}$ are usually small. For example, for $T = 4$, $\delta = 0.9$, and $\sigma_{\alpha\alpha}/\sigma_{\varepsilon\varepsilon} = 1$, the asymptotic variance of $\hat{\delta}_{IV}$ is 3.4 times as large as the asymptotic variance of $\hat{\delta}_{GMM1}$ and 4.3 times as large as the asymptotic variance of $\hat{\delta}_{GMM2}$, so the asymptotic variance of $\hat{\delta}_{GMM1}$ is only about 1.3 times as large as the asymptotic variance of $\hat{\delta}_{GMM2}$. Most of our efficiency gains come from imposing the extra moment conditions (4) that follow from SA, not from the moment conditions that follow from the additional assumption of homoskedasticity.

In Table 2 we report results for some cases in which we do not impose stationarity, though we still impose homoskedasticity (with $\sigma_{\varepsilon\varepsilon}$ normalized to unity). We will not discuss these results in detail, but we note that there are

Table 2
Ratios of asymptotic variances; stationarity not assumed

	var(*IV*)/var(*GMM1*)						var(*IV*)/var(*GMM2*)					
$\sigma_{\alpha\alpha}$:	2	2	2	2	2	2	2	2	2	2	2	2
$\sigma_{0\alpha}$:	0.5	0.5	0.5	0	0.5	1	0.5	0.5	0.5	0	0.5	1
σ_{00}:	1	4	7	4	4	4	1	4	7	4	4	4
T:	3	3	3	3	3	3	3	3	3	3	3	3
$\delta = 0$	4.52	1.61	1.33	1.49	1.61	1.73	5.20	1.72	1.39	1.58	1.72	1.87
0.3	32.7	2.23	1.60	1.86	2.23	2.79	40.5	2.51	1.73	2.05	2.51	3.23
0.5	57.3	3.34	2.07	2.39	3.34	5.54	73.	3.97	2.36	2.76	3.97	6.85
0.8	4.86	6.18	4.61	4.18	6.18	6.67	6.28	7.94	5.83	5.24	7.94	8.75
0.9	3.37	5.00	4.94	4.49	5.00	3.91	4.31	6.45	6.36	5.73	6.45	5.06
1	2.58	3.51	3.70	4.00	3.51	2.58	3.26	4.49	4.75	5.14	4.49	3.26
	var(*IV*)/var(*GMM1*)						var(*IV*)/var(*GMM2*)					
$\sigma_{\alpha\alpha}$:	1	2	5	2	2	2	1	2	5	2	2	2
$\sigma_{0\alpha}$:	0.5	0.5	0.5	0.5	0.5	0.5	0.5	0.5	0.5	0.5	0.5	0.5
σ_{00}:	4	4	4	4	4	4	4	4	4	4	4	4
T:	3	3	3	3	4	10	3	3	3	3	4	10
$\delta = 0$	1.31	1.61	2.56	1.61	1.75	1.62	1.38	1.72	2.72	1.72	1.80	1.62
0.3	1.55	2.23	4.20	2.23	2.60	2.45	1.73	2.51	4.57	2.51	2.73	2.46
0.5	2.06	3.34	5.71	3.34	3.91	3.98	2.48	.97	6.33	3.97	4.19	4.00
0.8	6.98	6.18	5.52	6.18	4.76	3.31	10.4	7.94	6.21	7.94	5.29	3.35
0.9	5.64	5.00	4.66	5.00	3.63	2.17	8.56	6.45	5.25	6.45	4.04	2.20
1	2.93	3.51	3.83	3.51	2.67	1.59	4.29	4.49	4.30	4.49	2.96	1.61

exceptions to some of the conclusions from the results in Table 1. However, the gains from our extra moment conditions are, if anything, larger than they were in the stationary case.

This model is heavily overidentifed, in the sense that there are many more moment conditions than parameters to estimate. It is a conventional wisdom that the asymptotic properties of estimators may be a poor guide to their finite sample properties in heavily overidentified models. While we did not conduct any simulations on our model, Arellano and Bond (1991, Sect. 4) provide some relevant Monte Carlo evidence. Their model is the same as ours, except that it contains an exogenous regressor, which was used as a single instrument. Their estimators *GMM1* and *GMM2* correspond to the set of $T(T-1)/2$ moment conditions exploited by our $\hat{\delta}_{IV}$ (they differ in finite samples in the way in which the weighting matrix is evaluated), while their estimators *AHd* and *AH1* follow Anderson and Hsiao (1981) in using only a single moment condition based on lagged y's (using instruments $\Delta y_{i,t-2}$ and $y_{i,t-2}$, respectively). Their results are for $T = 7$ so the model is highly overidentified. They report (p. 284) that the extra instruments result in substantial finite sample efficiency gains, and also (p. 285) that the asymptotic standard errors were close to the finite sample standard deviations of the estimates. Their model and estimation procedures are close enough to ours to hope that their optimistic results would generalize.

6. Moment conditions with exogenous regressors

We now consider the regression model with explanatory variables:

$$y_{it} = \delta y_{i,t-1} + X_{it}\beta + Z_i\gamma + u_{it}, \qquad u_{it} = \alpha_i + \varepsilon_{it}. \tag{22}$$

Here X_{it} is a $1 \times k$ vector of time-varying explanatory variables and Z_i is a $1 \times g$ vector of time-invariant explanatory variables. We create data vectors and matrices by ordering observations first by individual and then by time. Thus, for example,

$$y = (y_{11}, \dots, y_{1T}; \dots; y_{N1}, \dots, y_{NT})'. \tag{23}$$

With this convention the model in matrix form is

$$y = y_{-1}\delta + X\beta + Z\gamma + u = W\xi + u, \tag{24}$$

where

$$u = \alpha + \varepsilon, \qquad W = (y_{-1}, X, Z), \qquad \xi' = (\delta, \beta', \gamma').$$

We adopt the following standard notation for projections. For any matrix A, let P_A be the projection onto the column space of A, so that $P_A = A(A'A)^{-1}A'$ if the inverse exists; let $Q_A = I - P_A$. For any integer m, let e_m be an $m \times 1$ vector of ones, and define $P = e_T e_T'/T$ and $Q = I - P$. Then define

$$V = I_N \otimes e_T, \quad P_V = I_N \otimes e_T e_T'/T = I_N \otimes P, \quad Q_V = I_N - P_V = I_N \otimes Q, \tag{25}$$

so that V is a matrix of individual dummy variables, P_V is the $NT \times NT$ idempotent matrix that converts an $NT \times 1$ vector ordered as in (23) above into a vector of individual means, and Q_V is the $NT \times NT$ idempotent matrix that converts an $NT \times 1$ vector into deviations from individual means. The spaces spanned by Q_V and P_V are orthogonal and exhaustive: $P_V Q_V = 0$, $P_V + Q_V = I_{NT}$.

We assume independence of all variables across individuals (different values of i). We also assume that the regressors X and Z are strongly exogenous with respect to ε; we will later distinguish variables that are or are not correlated with α. We will not make detailed assumptions of regularity conditions on X and Z, but rather simply assume that the relevant second moment matrices converge to nonsingular limits as $N \to \infty$.

In order to explain the efficient use of exogenous variables in the dynamic model, we first give a brief summary of existing results for the static model that does not contain the regressor y_{-1}. We consider the model

$$y = X\beta + Z\gamma + u, \qquad u = \alpha + \varepsilon. \tag{26}$$

For the moment, we maintain assumptions (SA.2), (SA.3), and (AA.4), as is typical in this literature. Under these assumptions,

$$\Phi^{-1} = [\mathrm{cov}(u)]^{-1} = Q_V + \theta^2 P_V, \qquad \Phi^{-1/2} = Q_V + \theta P_V, \tag{27}$$

where Q_V and P_V are defined in (25), $\theta^2 = \sigma_{\varepsilon\varepsilon}/(\sigma_{\varepsilon\varepsilon} + T\sigma_{\alpha\alpha})$, and the equalities in (27) actually hold up to an irrelevant factor of proportionality. Now transform (26) by $\Phi^{-1/2}$:

$$\Phi^{-1/2} y = \Phi^{-1/2} X\beta + \Phi^{-1/2} Z\gamma + \Phi^{-1/2} u, \tag{28}$$

so that the error in (28) is whitened. The estimators that we will generalize are IV estimators of (28), using instruments of the form $G = [Q_V X, P_V J]$, where J is to be defined. As noted by Breusch, Mizon, and Schmidt, IV of (28) using instruments G of this form is equivalent to GMM based on the orthogonality condition $\mathrm{E}(G'u) = 0$, because the optimal weighting matrix in GMM implicitly performs the $\Phi^{-1/2}$ transformation.

The precise form of J in the instrument set varies across authors, and its relationship to exogeneity assumptions is not entirely explicit in the literature. Following Hausman and Taylor, we partition X and Z: $X = [X_1, X_2]$, $Z = [Z_1, Z_2]$, where X_1 and Z_1 are uncorrelated with α but X_2 and Z_2 are correlated with α. As a matter of notation, let the column dimensions of X_1, X_2, Z_1, and Z_2 be k_1, k_2, g_1, and g_2, respectively. We also follow Breusch, Mizon, and Schmidt in defining the following notation. For any (arbitrary) $NT \times h$

matrix S, with representative row S_{it} (of dimension $1 \times h$), define the $N \times ht$ matrix S° as

$$S^{\circ} = \begin{bmatrix} S_{11} & S_{12} & \cdots & S_{1T} \\ S_{21} & S_{22} & \cdots & S_{2T} \\ \vdots & \vdots & & \vdots \\ S_{N1} & S_{N2} & \cdots & S_{NT} \end{bmatrix}, \tag{29}$$

and define the $NT \times hT$ matrix $S^{*} = S^{\circ} \otimes e_T$. (Note that all T values of S_{it} are separate variables in S^{*}.) Then we have the following instrument sets [where HT stands for Hausman and Taylor (1981), BMS stands for Breusch, Mizon, and Schmidt (1989), and AM stands for Amemiya and MaCurdy (1986)]:

$$J_{\mathrm{HT}} = [X_1, Z_1], \quad J_{\mathrm{AM}} = [X_1^{*}, Z_1], \quad J_{\mathrm{BMS}} = [X_1^{*}, (Q_V X_2)^{*}, Z_1]. \tag{30}$$

As in Breusch, Mizon, and Schmidt, $(Q_V X_2)^{*}$ indicates that any $(T-1)$ independent deviations from means of each variable in X_2 are used separately as instruments.

In the set of instruments $G = [Q_V X, P_V J]$, obviously $P_V J$ is in the space spanned by P_V while $Q_V X$ is in the space spanned by Q_V. Hausman and Taylor actually defined their instrument set to be of the form $\bar{G} = [Q_V, J]$, so that all of Q_V was included in the instrument set, not just $Q_V X$. Breusch, Mizon, and Schmidt showed that this did not matter, for the static model. Although the projections onto G and $\bar{G}$ are different, these instrument sets lead to identical estimators for the static model. This is so because, if we conceptually separate the regressors in (28) into $Q_V X$, $P_V X$, and Z, instruments in Q_V space other than $Q_V X$ have no explanatory power in the first-stage regressions. Therefore, *for the static model*, there is no point in looking for additional instruments in the space spanned by Q_V. However, *for the dynamic model*, Q_V is not a legitimate part of the instrument set; this is the reason the within estimator is inconsistent. Therefore functions of X and Z that lie in the space spanned by Q_V can be legitimate instruments and can make a difference to the estimator, by helping to better 'explain' the regressor $Q_V y_{-1}$. As we will see, given strong exogeneity of X and Z with respect to ε, many such instruments exist, in addition to $Q_V X$.

In order to find such instruments, we now make explicit exogeneity assumptions, and make clear how they relate to the existing different treatments of the static model.

(E.1) For all i, X_{it} is uncorrelated with ε_{is} for all t and s.

(E.2) For all i, Z_i is uncorrelated with ε_{it} for all t.

(E.3) For all i, $X_{1,it}$ is uncorrelated with α_i for all t.

(E.4) For all i, $Z_{1,i}$ is uncorrelated with α_i.

(E.5) For all i, $\mathrm{E}(X_{2,it}, \alpha_i)$ is the same for all t.

Assumptions (E.1) and (E.2) say that X and Z are strongly exogenous with respect to the noise ε. Assumptions (E.3) and (E.4) say that X_1 and Z_1 are also uncorrelated with α, but they allow X_2 and Z_2 to be correlated with α. Finally, (E.5) is consistent with the view that the correlation between X_2 and α is due solely to a time-invariant component of X_2 that is correlated with α. The Breusch, Mizon, and Schmidt estimator implicitly depends on all five of these assumptions, while the Amemiya and MaCurdy estimator depends only on the first four. The Hausman and Taylor estimator depends on (E.1), (E.2), (E.4), and a weakened version of (E.3), namely, that $\bar{X}_{1,i}$ is uncorrelated with α_i for all i.

The exogeneity conditions (E.1)–(E.4) immediately imply the following usable moment conditions:

(M.1) $\mathrm{E}(X_{1,it}u_{is}) = 0$ for all t and s.

(M.2) $\mathrm{E}(Z_{1,i}u_{it}) = 0$ for all t.

(M.3) For any t, $\mathrm{E}(X_{2,it}u_{is})$ is the same for all s (it may depend on t).

(M.4) $\mathrm{E}(Z_{2,i}u_i)$ is the same for all t.

In additon, if we add exogeneity condition (E.5), we have the additional moment condition:

(M.5) $\mathrm{E}(X_{2,it}u_{is})$ is the same for all t.

Note that (M.3) and (M.5) imply that $\mathrm{E}(X_{2,it}u_{is})$ is the same for all t and s.

We now proceed to write these conditions in matrix form, and to show that the GMM estimator that imposes these conditions in the static model is equivalent to the Breusch, Mizon, and Schmidt estimator. To do so, we define a little more notation. First, we define the $T \times (T-1)$ (first differencing) matrix L as follows:

$$L = \begin{bmatrix} -1 & 0 & 0 & \cdots & 0 \\ 1 & -1 & 0 & \cdots & 0 \\ 0 & 1 & -1 & \cdots & 0 \\ 0 & 0 & 1 & \cdots & 0 \\ \vdots & \vdots & \vdots & & \vdots \\ 0 & 0 & 0 & \cdots & -1 \\ 0 & 0 & 0 & \cdots & 1 \end{bmatrix}. \tag{31}$$

Second, define the $N \times k_1 T$ matrix X_1° and the $N \times k_2 T$ matrix X_2° as in (29), and define the $N \times g_1$ matrix Z_1° and the $N \times g_2$ matrix Z_2° as follows:

$$Z_1^{\circ} = \begin{bmatrix} Z_{1,1} \\ \vdots \\ Z_{1,N} \end{bmatrix}, \qquad Z_2^{\circ} = \begin{bmatrix} Z_{2,1} \\ \vdots \\ Z_{2,N} \end{bmatrix}. \tag{32}$$

Then, following Schmidt, Ahn, and Wyhowski (1992), we can express the moment conditions (M.1)–(M.4) as follows:

$$\mathrm{E}(R_1'u) = 0, \qquad R_1 = [X_1^{\circ} \otimes I_T, X_2^{\circ} \otimes L, Z_1^{\circ} \otimes I_T, Z_2^{\circ} \otimes L]. \tag{33}$$

Note that each variable in X_1 generates T^2 instruments; each variable in X_2 generates $T(T-1)$ instruments; each variable in Z_1 generates T instruments; and each variable in Z_2 generates $(T-1)$ instruments. Furthermore, if [under exogeneity assumption (E.5)] we add moment condition (M.5), we can express moment conditions (M.1)–(M.5) as follows:

$$\begin{aligned} &\mathrm{E}(R_2'u) = 0, \\ &R_2 = [R_1, (Q_V X_2{}^*)] = [X_1^{\circ} \otimes I_T, X_2^{\circ} \otimes L, Z_1^{\circ} \otimes I_T, Z_2^{\circ} \otimes L, (Q_V X_2)^*]. \end{aligned} \tag{34}$$

To compare GMM based on the instrument sets R_1 and R_2 to the Amemiya and MaCurdy and the Breusch, Mizon, and Schmidt estimators, we use the following notation. We define the relationship '$\overset{P}{=}$' between two matrices to mean that they yield the same projection; that is, $A \overset{P}{=} B$ if $P_A = P_B$. Specifically, we recall the $T \times T$ idempotent matrix $Q = I_T - e_T e_T'/T$, and we note that $P_L \overset{P}{=} P_Q = Q$, $I_T \otimes L \overset{P}{=} Q_V$. We also define the $NT \times k_1 T(T-1)$ matrix $X_1^{**} = X_1^{\circ} \otimes L$, with X_2^{**}, Z_1^{**}, and Z_2^{**} defined similarly. Then we can state the following results:

$$R_1 \overset{P}{=} [X_1^{**}, X_2^{**}, Z_1^{**}, Z_2^{**}; X_1^*, Z_1], \tag{35a}$$

$$R_2 \overset{P}{=} [X_1^{**}, X_2^{**}, Z_1^{**}, Z_2^{**}; X_1^*, (Q_V X_2)^*, Z_1]. \tag{35b}$$

To understand these results, we consider the instruments $X_1^{\circ} \otimes I_T$ that appear in both R_1 and R_2, and which represent the moment conditions (M.1). We can rewrite these as follows: $X_1^{\circ} \otimes I_T = Q_V(X_1^{\circ} \otimes I_T) + P_V(X_1^{\circ} \otimes I_T) \overset{P}{=} [X_1^{\circ} \otimes Q, X_1^*] \overset{P}{=} [X_1^{\circ} \otimes L, X_1^*] = [X_1^{**}, X_1^*]$. Note that there are $k_1 T^2$ instruments, corresponding to the $k_1 T^2$ moment conditions in (M.1), $k_1 T(T-1)$ are in Q_V space and $k_1 T$ are in P_V space.

The remaining moment conditions are similar. The moment conditions (M.2) are represented by the instruments $Z_1^{\circ} \otimes I_T$, which can be rewritten as follows: $Z_1^{\circ} \otimes I_T \overset{P}{=} [Z_1^{\circ} \otimes L, Z_1] = [Z_1^{**}, Z_1]$. There are $g_1 T$ moment conditions in (M.2), and there are $g_1(T-1)$ instruments in Q_V space and g_1 instruments in P_V space. The moment conditions (M.3) are represented by the instruments

$X_2^o \otimes L = X_2^{**}$. There are $k_2T(T-1)$ instruments, all in Q_V space. The moment conditions (M.4) are represented by the instruments $Z_1^o \otimes L = Z_2^{**}$. There are $g_2(T-1)$ instruments, all in Q_V space. Finally, the moment conditions (M.5) add the additional $k_2(T-1)$ instruments $(Q_v X_2)^*$ to R_2; all of these instruments are in P_v space.

From (35a) we can see that the instrument set R_1 is larger than the Amemiya and MaCurdy instrument set $G_{AM} = [Q_v X, X_1^*, Z_1]$ but smaller than the instrument set $\bar{G}_{AM} = [Q_v, X_1^*, Z_1]$. However, for the static model, R_1, G_{AM}, and $\bar{G}_{AM}$ all lead to the same estimator, since additional instruments in Q_v space are irrelevant in the static model. Similarly, from (35b) we see that the instrument set R_2 is larger than the Breusch, Mizon, and Schmidt instrument set $G_{BMS} = [Q_V X, X_1^*, (Q_V X_2)^*, Z_1]$, and not as large as the instrument set $\bar{G}_{BMS} = [Q_V, X_1^*, (Q_V X_2)^*, Z_1]$. However, for the static model, R_2, G_{BMS}, and $\bar{G}_{BMS}$ all lead to the same estimator. Thus, for the static model, GMM based on the moment conditions (M.1)–(M.4) is equivalent to the Amemiya–MaCurdy estimator, and GMM based on the moment conditions (M.1)–(M.5) is equivalent to the Breusch, Mizon, and Schmidt estimator.

We now return to the dynamic model (24) that contains y_{-1} as a regressor, as well as X and Z. Now the extra instruments that are in R_1 but not in G_{AM}, or in R_2 but not in G_{BMS}, are relevant because they help to 'explain' the regressor $(Q_V y_{-1})$. Thus, under assumptions (SA.1)–(SA.3) and (E.1)–(E.4), the available moment conditions are given by (3), (4), and (33). If we add assumption (AA.4), we replace the moment conditions (4) by (11); if we add assumption (E.5), we replace the moment conditions (33) by (34).

Estimation of the model is a straightforward application of GMM. The moment conditions (3) and (33) [or (34)] are linear in the parameters, while the moment conditions (4) are nonlinear. A linearized GMM estimator is possible, along the lines of Newey (1985). Some discussion of computational details is given in Ahn (1990) and Ahn and Schmidt (1990).

7. Concluding remarks

In this paper, we have extended the existing literature on the dynamic panel data model in two directions. First, under standard assumptions, we have counted the additional moment conditions not used by existing estimators, and shown how to exploit these moment conditions efficiently. These extra moment conditions can lead to substantial improvements in the efficiency of estimation, leading to reductions in asymptotic variance on the order of 2 or 3. As a result we expect these extra moment conditions to be of practical importance in empirical work. Second, when the model contains exogenous variables in addition to the lagged dependent variable, we have shown how to exploit the exogeneity assumptions about these variables efficiently. Moment conditions (or instruments) that do not increase the efficiency of estimation in the static model do increase efficiency in the dynamic model.

It is also possible that the analysis of this paper could be extended within the dynamic panel data model. Many of the 'random effects' treatments of this model that are currently found in the literature rely on stronger assumptions than we have made, and they could profitably be recast in terms of the moment conditions that they imply. For example, stationarity of the y process has been considered by Arellano and Bover (1990). It implies that $\mathrm{E}(\alpha_i y_{it})$ is the same for all t, and leads to imposable moment conditions. Stationarity also implies a restriction on the variance of y_{i0} that leads to an imposable moment condition not considered by Arellano and Bover. Presumably other specific assumptions about initial conditions would have similar implications.

Appendix 1

A.1. Equivalence of MD estimators

We wish to show that the OMD estimator based on (17) is asymptotically equivalent to the OMD estimator based on (20). To do so we show that the minimands of the two estimators are asymptotically identical; that is,

$$\begin{aligned}&[v(S)-v(\Omega)]'(J\psi J')^{-1}[v(S)-v(\Omega)]\\&=[v(Z)-v(\Lambda)]'(J\Delta J')^{-1}[v(Z)-v(\Lambda)].\end{aligned}\tag{A.1}$$

To do so, note

$$\begin{aligned}v(S)-v(\Omega)&=J[\mathrm{vec}(S)-\mathrm{vec}(\Omega)]\\&=J(\mathrm{vec}(DZD')-\mathrm{vec}(D\Lambda D')]\\&=J(D\otimes D)[\mathrm{vec}(Z)-\mathrm{vec}(\Lambda)]\\&=J(D\otimes D)H[v(Z)-v(\Lambda)].\end{aligned}\tag{A.2}$$

Similarly, $J\psi J'=J(D\otimes D)\Delta(D\otimes D)'J'$. Therefore the first expression in (A.1) becomes

$$\begin{aligned}&[v(S)-v(\Omega)]'(J\psi J')^{-1}[v(S)-v(\Omega)]\\&=[v(Z)-v(\Lambda)]'H'(D\otimes D)J'[J(D\otimes D)\Delta(D\otimes D)'J']^{-1}\\&\quad\times J(D\otimes D)H[v(Z)-v(\Lambda)].\end{aligned}\tag{A.3}$$

To simplify this, use the fact (Magnus and Neudecker, 1988, p. 50, eq. (14)) that $(D\otimes D)HJ=HJ(D\otimes D)$ and the fact that $JH=I$, which imply that $J(D\otimes D)=JHJ(D\otimes D)=J(D\otimes D)HJ$. With this substitution, the inverse on the right-hand side of (A.3) becomes

$$[J(D\otimes D)HJ\Delta J'H'(D\otimes D)'J']^{-1}$$

$$= [H'(D\otimes D)'J']^{-1}(J\Delta J')^{-1}[J(D\otimes D)H]^{-1}, \tag{A.4}$$

and the right-hand side of (A.3) simplifies to

$$[v(Z)-v(\Lambda)]'(J\Delta J')^{-1}[v(Z)-v(\Lambda)], \tag{A.5}$$

which is the same as the right-hand side of (A.1).

A.2. Explanation of Eq. (21) of the text

There are $(T+1)(T+2)/2$ moment conditions in $m(\gamma)$. The idea of (21) is to split these into the $T(T-1)/2+(T-2)$ moment conditions in $h(\delta)$ plus the additional $(T+3)$ moment conditions in $p(\delta)-\theta$ that determine θ in terms of δ. The choice of $p(\delta)$ is not unique, and we pick $p(\delta)=N^{-1}\sum_i p_i(\delta)$, with

$$p_i(\delta)=[y_{i0}^2, u_{i1}u_{i2}, u_{i1}y_{i0}, u_{i1}^2-u_{i1}u_{i2}, \dots, u_{iT}^2-u_{i1}u_{i2}]'. \tag{A.6}$$

Similarly, let $h(\delta)=N^{-1}\sum_i h_i(\delta)$, $m(\gamma)=N^{-1}\sum_i m_i(\gamma)$. Then we wish to find F such that $Fm_i(\gamma)=[h_i(\delta)', (p_i(\delta)-\theta)']'$. To save space we exhibit this transformation for the simplest possible case, $T=3$. The transformation for $T>3$ is a straightforward extension of the expression in

$$\begin{bmatrix} y_{i0}\Delta u_{i2} \\ y_{i0}\Delta u_{i3} \\ y_{i1}\Delta u_{i3} \\ u_{i3}\Delta u_{i2} \\ y_{i0}^2-\sigma_{00} \\ u_{i1}u_{i2}-\sigma_{\alpha\alpha} \\ u_{i1}y_{i0}-\sigma_{0\alpha} \\ u_{i1}^2-u_{i1}u_{i2}-\sigma_{11} \\ u_{i2}^2-u_{i1}u_{i2}-\sigma_{22} \\ u_{i3}^2-u_{i1}u_{i2}-\sigma_{33} \end{bmatrix} = \begin{bmatrix} 0 & 0 & 0 & -1 & 0 & 0 & 1 & 0 & 0 & 0 \\ 0 & 0 & 0 & 0 & 0 & 0 & -1 & 0 & 1 & 0 \\ 0 & -1 & 1 & 0 & 0 & 0 & -\delta & 0 & \delta & 0 \\ 0 & 0 & -1 & 0 & 0 & 1 & 0 & 0 & 0 & 0 \\ 0 & 0 & 0 & 0 & 0 & 0 & 0 & 0 & 0 & 1 \\ 0 & 1 & 0 & 0 & 0 & 0 & 0 & 0 & 0 & 0 \\ 0 & 0 & 0 & 1 & 0 & 0 & 0 & 0 & 0 & 0 \\ 1 & -1 & 0 & 0 & 0 & 0 & 0 & 0 & 0 & 0 \\ 0 & -1 & 0 & 0 & 1 & 0 & 0 & 0 & 0 & 0 \\ 0 & -1 & 0 & 0 & 0 & 0 & 0 & 1 & 0 & 0 \end{bmatrix}$$

$$\times \begin{bmatrix} u_{i1}^2 - \sigma_{\alpha\alpha} - \sigma_{11} \\ u_{i1}u_{i2} - \sigma_{\alpha\alpha} \\ u_{i1}u_{i3} - \sigma_{\alpha\alpha} \\ u_{i1}y_{i0} - \sigma_{0\alpha} \\ u_{i2}^2 - \sigma_{\alpha\alpha} - \sigma_{22} \\ u_{i2}u_{i3} - \sigma_{\alpha\alpha} \\ u_{i2}y_{i0} - \sigma_{0\alpha} \\ u_{i3}^2 - \sigma_{\alpha\alpha} - \sigma_{33} \\ u_{i3}y_{i0} - \sigma_{0\alpha} \\ y_{i0}^2 - \sigma_{00} \end{bmatrix}. \tag{A.7}$$

Note that the last $T + 3 = 6$ moment conditions on the left-hand side of (A.7) constitute $p_i(\delta) - \theta$. The first $T(T-1)/2 + (T-2) = 4$ moment conditions on the left-hand side of (A.7) constitute $h_i(\delta)$, and are linear combinations of elements of $m_i(\gamma)$. For terms of the form $y_{is}\Delta u_{it}$, $s \geqslant 1$, the linear transformation depends on δ. However, as in the proof above of the equivalence of OMD estimators after a linear transformation involving δ, this does not matter asymptotically.

Appendix 2

We wish to show that the variance of the GMM/OMD estimator is equal to the semiparametric bound. Let ξ be a single observation of i.i.d. data. Define $x = v(\xi\xi')$ with $E(x) = v(\Omega) = \mu(\gamma)$ where the dimensions of μ and γ are p and $q(p > q)$, repectively. Let $f(\xi \mid \rho)$ be a probability density function where ρ is an abstract (infinite-dimensional) parameter vector to which a parametric sub-model corresponds. Then, $\mu(\gamma) = \int x f(\xi \mid \rho) d\xi$. Assuming that γ is differentiable function of ρ, say $\gamma(\rho)$, and defining $G = \partial\mu/\partial\gamma'$ as in the main text, we obtain:

$$G \cdot \partial\gamma/\partial\rho' = \int x S_\rho' f(\xi \mid \rho)\, d\xi = E(x S_\rho'), \tag{A.8}$$

where $S_\rho = \partial \ln(f)/\partial\rho$. Therefore, we have the following equality:

$$\partial\gamma/\partial\rho' = E(d S_\rho'), \tag{A.9}$$

where $d = (G'AG)^{-1}G'Ax$ and A is any nonsingular matrix.

Let $\hat{\delta}$ be an asymptotically linear estimator with influence function d. Then, by Theorem 2.2 of Newey (1990, p. 103), $\hat{\delta}$ is regular. Let $\{(S_\rho)_j\}$ be any sequence of all the possible scores for parametric submodels; and let s be a $q \times 1$ vector such that there exists a sequence of matrices with q rows, $\{A_j\}$, with $\lim_{j\to\infty} E[\, \| s - A_j(S_\rho)_j \|^2] = 0$. We can define the tangent set $\mathscr{L}$ by

$$\mathscr{L} = \{s \mid E(s) = 0 \text{ and } \exists \text{ a matrix } B \text{ with } q \text{ rows} \ni E(xs') = GB\}. \tag{A.10}$$

This conjecture can be verified as follows. Consider any s^t which is a linear combination of the *true* score: $s^t = AS_\rho$. Then, it is obvious that $\mathrm{E}(s^t) = 0$. Also, (A.8) implies that $\mathrm{E}(xs^{t\prime}) = \mathrm{E}(xS_\rho' A) = GB$. Therefore, any $s \in \mathscr{L}$ satisfies the restrictions on the scores implied by the semiparametric model.

Now, define $w = [G'(J\psi J)^{-1}G]^{-1}G'(J\psi J)^{-1}(x - \mu)$. Then, we can easily show that $w \in \mathscr{L}$. Note that

$$d - w = \{(G'AG)^{-1}G'A - [G'(J\psi J')^{-1}G]^{-1}G'(J\psi J')^{-1}\}x$$
$$+ [G'(J\psi J')^{-1}G]^{-1}G'(J\psi J')^{-1}\mu. \tag{A.11}$$

Then, the characteristics of $\mathscr{L}$ imply that $\mathrm{E}[(d - w)s'] = 0$ and therefore $\mathrm{E}[(d - w)'s]$ for any $s \in \mathscr{L}$. By Theorem 3.1 of Newey (1990, p. 106), the semiparametric bound is $\mathrm{E}(ww')$, which is simply the variance of the OMD/GMM estimator. This completes the proof.

References

Abowd, J. and D. Card, 1989, On the covariance structure of earnings and hours changes, Econometrica 57, 411–446.

Ahn, S.C., 1990, Three essays on share contracts, labor supply, and the estimation of models for dynamic panel data, Unpublished Ph.D. dissertation (Michigan State University, East Lansing, MI).

Ahn, S.C. and P. Schmidt, 1990, Efficient estimation of models for dynamic panel data, Unpublished manuscript (Michigan State University, East Lansing, MI).

Amemiya, T. and T.E. MaCurdy, 1986, Instrumental variable estimation of an error components model, Econometrica 54, 869–881.

Anderson, T.W. and C. Hsiao, 1981, Estimation of dynamic models with error components, Journal of the American Statistical Association 76, 598–606.

Arellano, M. and S. Bond, 1991, Tests of specification for panel data: Monte Carlo evidence and an application to employment equations, Review of Economic Studies 58, 277–297.

Arellano, M. and O. Bover, 1990, Another look at the instrumental variables estimation of error-component models, Unpublished manuscript (London School of Economics, London).

Blundell, R. and R.S. Smith, 1991, Conditions initiales et estimation efficace dans les modéles dynamiques sur données de panel, Annales D'Economie et de Statistique, 20–21, 109–123.

Bhargava, A. and J.D. Sargan, 1983, Estimating dynamic random effects models from panel data covering short time periods, Econometrica 51, 1635–1659.

Breusch, T.S., G.E. Mizon, and P. Schmidt, 1989, Efficient estimation using panel data, Econometrica 57, 695–701.

Chamberlain, G., 1980, Analysis of covariance with qualitative data, Review of Economic Studies 47, 225–238.

Chamberlain, G., 1982, Multivariate regression models for panel data, Journal of Econometrics 18, 5–46.

Chamberlain, G., 1984, Panel data, Ch. 22 in: Z. Griliches and M. Intriligator, eds., Handbook of econometrics, Vol. II (North-Holland, Amsterdam).

Hausman, J.A. and W.E. Taylor, 1981, Panel data and unobservable individual effects, Econometrica 49, 1377–1398.

Holtz-Eakin, D., 1988, Testing for individual effects in autoregressive models, Journal of Econometrics 39, 297–308.

Holtz-Eakin, D., W. Newey, and H.S. Rosen, 1988, Estimating vector autoregressions with panel data, Econometrica 56, 1371–1396.

Hsiao, C., 1986, Analysis of panel data (Cambridge University Press, New York, NY).

Mundlak, Y., 1978, On the pooling of time-series and cross-section data, Econometrica 46, 69–86.

Newey, W., 1985, Generalized method of moments specification testing, Journal of Econometrics 29, 229–256.

Newey, W., 1990, Semiparametric efficiency bounds, Journal of Applied Econometrics 5, 99–136.

Schmidt, P., S.C. Ahn, and D. Wyhowski, 1992, Comment, Journal of Business and Economic Statistics 10, 10–14.

[2]

ELSEVIER

Journal of Econometrics 76 (1997) 309–321

JOURNAL OF Econometrics

Efficient estimation of dynamic panel data models: Alternative assumptions and simplified estimation

Seung C. Ahn[a], Peter Schmidt*,[b]

[a]*Department of Economics, Arizona State University, Tempe, AZ 85287, USA*
[b]*Department of Economics, Michigan State University, East Lansing, MI 48824, USA*

(Received July 1994; final version received September 1995)

Abstract

This paper considers the estimation of dynamic models for panel data. It shows how to count and express the moment conditions implied by a variety of covariance restrictions. These conditions can be imposed in a GMM framework. Many of the moment conditions are nonlinear in the parameters. We derive a simple linearized estimator that is asymptotically as efficient as the nonlinear GMM estimator, and convenient tests of the validity of the nonlinear restrictions.

Key words: Panel data; Dynamic models; Stationarity; GMM estimation; Conditional moment tests
JEL classification: C23

1. Introduction

A standard approach to the estimation of the dynamic panel data regression model (e.g., Anderson and Hsiao, 1981; Hsiao, 1986; Holtz-Eakin, 1988; Holtz-Eakin, Newey, and Rosen, 1988; Arellano and Bond, 1991) is to first-difference the equation, and then use instrumental variables (IV). More recent papers (Ahn and Schmidt, 1995b; Arellano and Bover, 1990, 1995) have shown that, under

* Corresponding author.

The first author gratefully acknowledges the financial support of the College of Business, Arizona State University. The second author gratefully acknowledges the financial support of the National Science Foundation. Both authors are grateful for the helpful comments of the editor and two referees.

PII S0304-4076(95)01793-3

certain assumptions, there are additional moment conditions that are not exploited by these IV estimators, and have suggested that the additional moment conditions be imposed in a generalized method of moments (GMM) framework.

In this paper, we extend these analyses in three ways. First, we count and express the moment conditions available under alternative sets of assumptions about initial conditions and the errors. Second, we propose a linearized GMM estimator, starting from an initial consistent estimator such as a linear estimator based on a subset of the moment conditions, and we derive simple moment tests of the nonlinear moment conditions. Third, for the case that only linear moment conditions are used, we investigate the circumstances under which the optimal GMM estimator is equivalent to a linear IV estimator. These circumstances are quite restrictive, and go beyond uncorrelatedness and homoskedasticity of the errors.

The plane of the paper is as follows. Section 2 shows how to count and express the moment conditions available under alternative sets of assumptions. Section 3 considers some implications of assumption of stationarity. Section 4 discusses linearized estimation and conditional moment tests. Finally, Section 5 contains some concluding remarks.

2. Moment conditions under alternative assumptions

In this section, we count and express the moment conditions implied by various sets of assumptions. We consider the simple dynamic panel data model:

$$y_{it} = \delta y_{i,t-1} + u_{it}, \qquad u_{it} = \alpha_i + \varepsilon_{it}. \tag{1}$$

Here $i = 1, \ldots, N$ denotes cross-sectional unit (individual) and $t = 1, \ldots, T$ denotes time. Throughout the paper, we consider the case that N is large and T is small, so that asymptotics will be derived under the assumption that $N \to \infty$ with T fixed. We can also write the T observations on (1) for person i as

$$y_i = \delta y_{i,-1} + u_i, \tag{2}$$

where $y_i' = (y_{i1}, \ldots, y_{iT})$ and $y_{i,-1}$ and u_i are defined similarly. See Ahn and Schmidt (1995b) for more detail on the notation.

This model does not contain any additional regressors beyond the lagged dependent variable, but this is only an expository point. The moment conditions implied by exogeneity assumptions on additional regressors have been identified by Schmidt, Ahn, and Wyhowski (1992), Ahn and Schmidt (1995b), and Arellano and Bover (1995); they can just be added to the sets of moment conditions identified in this section.

We assume independence of all variables across individuals. We will consider various subsets of the following assumptions.

(A.1) *For all i, ε_{it} is uncorrelated with y_{i0} for all t.*

(A.2) *For all i, ε_{it} is uncorrelated with α_i for all t.*

(A.3) *For all i, the ε_{it} are mutually uncorrelated.*

(A.4) *For all i,* var(ε_{it}) *is the same for all t.*

Given the four assumptions (A.1)–(A.4), there are 16 possible cases corresponding to imposing or not imposing each of them. One is the degenerate case of no assumptions. Furthermore, although we have deliberately avoided assumptions about the generation of y_{i0}, it is reasonable to view it as being a linear function of α_i and of $\varepsilon_{i0}, \varepsilon_{i,-1}, \dots$. Therefore we will not impose (A.1) (uncorrelatedness of y_{i0} and ε_{it}, $t = 1, \dots, T$) unless we also impose *both* (A.2) (uncorrelatedness of α_i and the ε_{it}) and (A.3) (mutual uncorrelatedness of the ε_{it}). This leaves nine subsets of assumptions to consider.

We begin with the case in which we assume all of (A.1)–(A.4). We will call this *Case A*, and it is the only case that we will consider in detail. The method by which the moment conditions implied by (A.1)–(A.4) are identified is as follows. Let Σ be the covariance matrix of the things we make assumptions about, namely $(\varepsilon_{i1}, \dots, \varepsilon_{iT}, y_{i0}, \alpha_i)$; see Ahn and Schmidt (1995b, Eq. (6)). Let Λ be the covariance matrix of the 'observables' that can be written in terms of data and parameters, namely $(u_{1i}, \dots, u_{iT}, y_{i0})$; see Ahn and Schmidt (1995b, Eq. (7)). Assumptions (A.1)–(A.4) impose restrictions on Σ and imply restrictions on Λ. For example, under (A.1)–(A.4), we have $\sigma_{\alpha t} \equiv \mathrm{cov}(\varepsilon_{it}, \alpha_i) = 0$ for all t, $\sigma_{0t} \equiv \mathrm{cov}(y_{i0}, \varepsilon_{it}) = 0$ for all t, $\sigma_{ts} \equiv \mathrm{cov}(\varepsilon_{it}, \varepsilon_{is}) = 0$ for all $t \neq s$, and $\sigma_{tt}(\equiv \mathrm{var}(\varepsilon_{it}))$ the same $(\equiv \sigma_{\varepsilon\varepsilon})$ for all t. This implies three types of restrictions on Λ. First, $\lambda_{0t} \equiv \mathrm{cov}(y_{i0}, u_{it})$ is the same for $t = 1, \dots, T$. Second, $\lambda_{tt} \equiv \mathrm{var}(u_{it})$ is the same for $t = 1, \dots, T$. Third, $\lambda_{ts} \equiv \mathrm{cov}(u_{it}, u_{is})$ is the same for $t, s = 1, \dots, T$, $t \neq s$. The total number of restrictions is $(T-1) + (T-1) + [T(T-1)/2 - 1] = T(T-1)/2 + 2T - 3$. The number of restrictions may also be obtained simply by noting that the $(T+1)(T+2)/2$ distinct elements of Λ depend on the four parameters $\sigma_{\alpha\alpha}(\equiv \mathrm{var}(\alpha_i))$, $\sigma_{0\alpha}(\equiv \mathrm{cov}(y_{i0}, \alpha_i))$, $\sigma_{00}(\equiv \mathrm{var}(y_{i0}))$, and $\sigma_{\varepsilon\varepsilon}$. These restrictions correspond to the moment conditions:

$$\mathrm{E}(y_{i0}\Delta u_{it}) = 0, \qquad t = 2, \dots, T, \tag{3a}$$

$$\mathrm{E}(u_{i1}^2 - u_{it}^2) = 0, \qquad t = 2, \dots, T, \tag{3b}$$

$$\mathrm{E}(u_{it}u_{is} - u_{i2}u_{i1}) = 0, \qquad t = 3, \dots, T, \quad s < t. \tag{3c}$$

Tedious but straightforward algebra shows that the conditions (3a)–(3c) are equivalent to

$$\mathrm{E}(y_{is}\Delta u_{it}) = 0, \qquad t = 2, \dots, T, \quad s = 0, \dots, t-2, \tag{4a}$$

$$\mathrm{E}(u_{iT}\Delta u_{it}) = 0, \qquad t = 2, \dots, T-1, \tag{4b}$$

$$\mathrm{E}(\bar{u}_i\Delta u_{it}) = 0, \qquad t = 2, \dots, T, \tag{4c}$$

where $\bar{u}_i = T^{-1}\Sigma_t u_{it}$. The $T(T-1)/2$ moment conditions in (4a) can be motivated by first differencing (1) to get

$$\Delta y_{it} = \delta \Delta y_{i,t-1} + \Delta u_{it}, \qquad t = 2, \dots, T. \tag{5}$$

Holtz-Eakin (1988), Holtz-Eakin, Newey, and Rosen (1988), and Arellano and Bond (1991) have noted that the set of available instruments for (5) is $[y_{i0}, \dots, y_{i,t-2}]$, and the moment conditions (4a) express the validity of these instruments. Given assumptions (A.1)–(A.4), Ahn and Schmidt (1995b) show that conditions in (4b) can be replaced by

$$\mathrm{E}(y_{i,t-2}\Delta u_{i,t-1} - y_{i,t-1}\Delta u_{it}) = 0, \quad t = 3, \dots, T, \tag{6}$$

which are linear in δ.

We now consider the moment conditions that arise under various subsets of (A.1)–(A.4), as discussed above.

Case B. In this case we impose (A.1), (A.2), and (A.3); that is, we impose all of the assumptions except that we do not assume homoskedasticity of the ε_{it}. This is the set of assumptions that the identified as the 'standard assumptions' (SA) in Ahn and Schmidt (1995b). We have the $T-1$ restrictions that λ_{0t} is the same for all t, and the $T(T-1)/2-1$ restrictions that λ_{ts} is the same for all $t \neq s$, just as we did in *Case A*. These restrictions can be expressed as the linear moment conditions in (4a), plus the $T-2$ quadratic moment conditions in (4b).

Case C. In this case we impose (A.2), (A.3), and (A.4). That is, we impose all assumptions except that we do not assume that y_{i0} is uncorrelated with the ε_{it}. This may be arguably a poorly motivated case; however, it has been discussed in the literature as a 'fixed effects' treatment for the initial condition y_{i0}, since it is allowed to be correlated with both α_i and the ε_{it}. The parameters $\sigma_{0\alpha}$ and the σ_{0t} are not separately identified. The elements of Λ depend on the $T+3$ identified parameters $\sigma_{\alpha\alpha}$, σ_{00}, $\sigma_{\varepsilon\varepsilon}$, $(\sigma_{0\alpha}+\sigma_{01}), \dots, (\sigma_{0\alpha}+\sigma_{0T})$, so that the number of restrictions is $(T+1)(T+2)/2-(T+3) = T(T-1)/2+T-2$. We have the $T-1$ restrictions that λ_{tt} is the same for all t, and the $T(T-1)/2-1$ restrictions that λ_{ts} is the same for all $t \neq s$, just as we did in *Case A*. These correspond to the moment conditions in (3b) and (3c).

Case D. In this case we impose (A.2) and (A.3). Thus we assume that the ε_{it} are mutually uncorrelated and uncorrelated with α_i. The elements of Λ depend on the $2T+2$ identified parameters $\sigma_{\alpha\alpha}$, σ_{00}, $(\sigma_{0\alpha}+\sigma_{01}), \ldots, (\sigma_{0\alpha}+\sigma_{0T})$, $\sigma_{11}, \ldots, \sigma_{TT}$, and the total number of moment conditions is $T(T-1)/2-1$. Specifically, λ_{ts} is the same for all $t \neq s$, just as in *Case A* or *Case C*. These restrictions correspond to the moment conditions given in Eq. (3c) above.

Case E. In this case we impose (A.2) and (A.4). Thus we assume only that the ε_{it} are homoskedastic and that they are uncorrelated with α_i. This may be plausible if the ε_{it} are autocorrelated. In this case Λ depends on the $T(T-1)/2+T+2$ identified parameters σ_{00}, $(\sigma_{\alpha\alpha}+\sigma_{\varepsilon\varepsilon})$, $(\sigma_{0\alpha}+\sigma_{01}), \ldots,$ $(\sigma_{0\alpha}+\sigma_{0T})$ and $(\sigma_{\alpha\alpha}+\sigma_{st})$, $s \neq t$. We have only the $T-1$ restrictions that λ_{tt} is the same for all t. They can be expressed as in Eq. (3b) above.

Case F. In this case we impose only (A.3) and (A.4); that is, we assume that the ε_{it} are homoskedastic and mutually uncorrelated, but we make no assumptions about their relationship to y_{i0} or α_i. The elements of Λ depend on the $2T+2$ identified parameters σ_{00}, $\sigma_{\varepsilon\varepsilon}$, $(\sigma_{0\alpha}+\sigma_{01}), \ldots, (\sigma_{0\alpha}+\sigma_{0T})$, $(\sigma_{\alpha\alpha}+2\sigma_{\alpha 1}), \ldots, (\sigma_{\alpha\alpha}+2\sigma_{\alpha T})$. Thus we have $T(T-1)/2-1$ moment conditions. Specifically, we have the restrictions that $\lambda_{tt}+\lambda_{ss}-2\lambda_{ts}$ is the same for all $t, s = 1, \ldots, T$, $t \neq s$. These restrictions correspond to the moment conditions that $E[(u_{it}-u_{is})^2]$ is the same for all $t \neq s$; that is,

$$E[(u_{it}-u_{is})^2-(u_{i2}-u_{i1})^2]=0, \qquad t=3, \ldots, T, \quad s<t. \tag{7}$$

There has always been some question in the dynamic model about what constitutes a 'fixed effects' treatment. So-called 'random effects' treatments of the model have typically imposed stronger assumptions than ours about the generation of y_{i0}, and some treatments have assumed that y_{i0} is uncorrelated with α_i (see, e.g., Hsiao, 1986, Section 4.3.2). The treatments based on the moment conditions (4a) above have sometimes been called fixed-effects treatments, even though they clearly depend on assumptions about y_{i0} and α_i, such as lack of correlation of these quantities with the ε_{it}. The case just considered is arguably as close in spirit as we can get to a fixed effects treatment of this model without literally assuming α_i and y_{i0} to be fixed.

Case G. In this case we assume only (A.2), that α_i is uncorrelated with the ε_{it}. This implies no moment conditions.

Case H. In this case we assume only (A.3), that the ε_{it} are mutually uncorrelated. For $T \geqslant 4$, there are restrictions implied by the fact that the $T(T-1)/2$ off-diagonal elements of Λ corresponding to covariances of the u_{it} depend only on the T identified parameters $(\sigma_{\alpha\alpha}+2\sigma_{\alpha 1}), \ldots, (\sigma_{\alpha\alpha}+2\sigma_{\alpha T})$. Thus we have $T(T-1)/2-T=T(T-3)/2$ restrictions, of the form $\lambda_{qr}+\lambda_{st}=\lambda_{qs}+\lambda_{rt}$ for distinct $q, r, s, t = 1, \ldots, T$. The corresponding moment conditions are

$$E(u_{iq}u_{ir}+u_{is}u_{it}-u_{iq}u_{is}-u_{ir}u_{it})=0 \quad \text{for distinct} \quad q, r, s, t. \tag{8}$$

Case I. In this case we assume only (A.4), homoskedasticity of the ε_{it}. This implies no moment conditions.

3. Assumptions about stationarity

In this section, we consider the implications of two different types of stationarity assumptions. We will first consider the following assumption:

(S.1) *The series* $y_{i0}, \ldots, y_{iT}$ *is covariance-stationary.*

This assumption is made in addition to assumptions (A.1)–(A.4) of the previous section.

Arellano and Bover (1990) discuss the following condition:

$$\text{cov}(\alpha_i, y_{it}) \quad \text{is the same for} \quad t = 0, 1, \ldots, T. \tag{9}$$

This is an assumption of the type made by Breusch, Mizon, and Schmidt (1989); it requires equal covariance between the effects and the variables with which they are correlated. Ahn and Schmidt (1995b) show that, given assumptions (A.1)–(A.4), the condition in (9) corresponds to the restriction that

$$\sigma_{0\alpha} = \sigma_{\alpha\alpha}/(1-\delta), \tag{10}$$

and implies one additional moment restriction. Furthermore, they show that it also allows the entire set of available moment conditions to be written linearly; see their equations (12a)–(12b). An alternative, equivalent set of moment conditions for this case is given by Blundell and Bond (1994).

To see the connection between (S.1) and (9), we use the solution

$$y_{it} = \delta^t y_{i0} + \alpha_i(1-\delta^t)/(1-\delta) + \sum_{j=0}^{t-1} \delta^j \varepsilon_{i,t-j} \tag{11}$$

to calculate

$$\text{var}(y_{it}) = \sigma_{00}\delta^{2t} + \sigma_{0\alpha}2\delta^t(1-\delta^t)/(1-\delta) + \sigma_{\alpha\alpha}[(1-\delta^t)/(1-\delta)]^2 + \sigma_{\varepsilon\varepsilon}(1-\delta^{2t})/(1-\delta^2), \tag{12}$$

where the calculation assumes (A.1)–(A.4). (S1) implies that $\text{var}(y_{it}) = \sigma_{00}$ for all t, which occurs if and only if (10) holds and also

$$\sigma_{00} = \sigma_{\alpha\alpha}/(1-\delta)^2 + \sigma_{\varepsilon\varepsilon}/(1-\delta^2). \tag{13}$$

Thus (S.1) implies (10), which in turn implies (9). However, it also implies the restriction (13) on the variance of the initial observation y_{i0}. Imposing (13) as well as (A.1)–(A.4) and (9) yields one additional, nonlinear moment condition:

$$E[y_{i0}^2 + y_{i1}\Delta u_{i2}/(1-\delta^2) - u_{i2}u_{i1}/(1-\delta)^2] = 0. \tag{14}$$

The assumption (S.1) can be compared to the weaker stationarity assumption:

(S.2) *Conditional* on (α_i, y_{i0}), $(\varepsilon_{i1}, \ldots, \varepsilon_{iT})$ *is stationary.*

This assumption implies the following restrictions on the covariance matrix Λ. First, λ_{tt} is the same for $t = 1, 2, \ldots, T$. Second, λ_{0t} is the same for $t = 1, 2, \ldots, T$. Third, for $j = 1, 2, \ldots, T-2$, $\lambda_{t,t+j}$ is the same for $t = 1, 2, \ldots, T-j$. The total number of moment conditions under (S.2) is $(T-1) + (T-1) + (T-2)(T-1)/2 = (T+2)(T-1)/2$. The moment conditions can be expressed as in (3a)–(3b) above, plus

$$E(u_{it}u_{i,t+j} - u_{i1}u_{i,1+j}) = 0, \quad j = 1, \ldots, T-2, \quad t = 2, \ldots, T-j. \tag{15}$$

4. Estimation and specification testing

In this section we provide some econometric detail on GMM estimation and specification tests. We provide a simple linearized GMM estimator and convenient moment tests of the validity of the moment conditions. We also discuss the relationship between GMM based on the linear moment conditions and IV estimation. Our discussion will proceed under assumptions (A.1)–(A.4), but can easily be modified to accommodate the other cases.

4.1. Notation and general results

We consider the model

$$y = y_{-1}\delta + X\beta + Z\gamma + u = W\xi + u, \tag{16}$$

as given by Ahn and Schmidt (1995b, Eq. (24)). The model may contain time-varying explanatory variables (X) and time-invariant explanatory variables (Z) in addition to the lagged dependent variable. For purposes of GMM it is convenient to focus on the T observations for person i, and we will write

$$u_i(\xi) = y_i - W_i\xi \tag{17}$$

to emphasize the dependence of u_i on ξ.

Exogeneity assumptions on X and Z generate linear moment conditions of the form

$$E[R_i'u_i(\xi)] = 0, \tag{18}$$

where R_i is a function of the exogenous variables. See Ahn and Schmidt (1995b, Eqs. (33) and (34)) for definitions of R_i under different exogeneity assumptions. In addition, the moment conditions given by (4a), (6), and (4c) above are valid. The moment conditions in (4a) above are linear ξ and can be written as $\mathrm{E}[A_i'u_i(\xi)] = 0$, where A_i is the $T \times T(T-1)/2$ matrix

$$A_i = \begin{bmatrix} -y_{i0} & 0 & 0 & \cdots & 0 \\ y_{i0} & -(y_{i0}, y_{i1}) & 0 & \cdots & 0 \\ 0 & (y_{i0}, y_{i1}) & -(y_{i0}, y_{i1}, y_{i2}) & \cdots & 0 \\ 0 & 0 & (y_{i0}, y_{i1}, y_{i2}) & \cdots & 0 \\ \vdots & \vdots & \vdots & & \vdots \\ 0 & 0 & 0 & \cdots & -(y_{i0}, y_{i1}, \ldots, y_{i,T-2}) \\ 0 & 0 & 0 & \cdots & (y_{i0}, y_{i1}, \ldots, y_{i,T-2}) \end{bmatrix}. \tag{19}$$

Similarly, the moment condition in (6) above are also linear in ξ and can be written as $\mathrm{E}[B_{1i}'u_i(\xi)] = 0$, where B_{1i} is the $T \times (T-2)$ matrix defined by

$$B_{1i} = \begin{bmatrix} -y_{i1} & 0 & \cdots & 0 \\ (y_{i1} + y_{i2}) & -y_{i2} & \cdots & 0 \\ -y_{i2} & (y_{i2} + y_{i3}) & \cdots & 0 \\ 0 & -y_{i3} & \cdots & 0 \\ \vdots & \vdots & & \vdots \\ 0 & 0 & \cdots & -y_{i,T-2} \\ 0 & 0 & \cdots & (y_{i,T-2} + y_{i,T-1}) \\ 0 & 0 & \cdots & -y_{i,T-1} \end{bmatrix}. \tag{20}$$

However, the moment conditions in (4c) above are quadratic in ξ.

We will discuss GMM estimation based on all of the available moment conditions and GMM based on a subset (possibly all) of the linear moment conditions. Suppose that l is the total number of moment conditions given in (4a), (6), (4c), and (18). Let $S_i\,(T \times l_1)$ be made up of columns of R_i, A_i, and B_{1i}, so that it represents some or all of the available linear instruments. The corresponding linear moment conditions are $\mathrm{E}[f_i(\xi)] = 0$, with

$$f_i(\xi) = S_i'u_i(\xi) = f_{1i} + f_{2i}\xi, \qquad f_{1i} = S_i'y_i, f_{2i} = -S_i'W_i. \tag{21}$$

If the dimension of ξ is k, we assume $l_1 \geqslant k$ so that the conditions f_i can identify ξ. The remaining $l_2 = l - l_1$ moment conditions will be written as $\mathrm{E}[g_i(\xi)] = 0$.

Since they are at most quadratic, we can write

$$g_i(\xi) = g_{1i} + g_{2i}\xi + (I \otimes \xi')g_{3i}\xi, \tag{22}$$

where g_{1i}, g_{2i}, and g_{3i} are $l_2 \times 1$, $l_2 \times k$, and $l_2k \times k$ matrices of functions of data, respectively, and the dimension of the identity matrix is l_2. An efficient estimator of ξ can be obtained by GMM based on all of the moment conditions:

$$\mathrm{E}[m_i(\xi)] = \mathrm{E}\begin{bmatrix} f_i(\xi) \\ g_i(\xi) \end{bmatrix} = 0. \tag{23}$$

Define $m_N = N^{-1}\sum_i m_i(\xi)$, with f_N, f_{1N}, f_{2N}, g_N, g_{1N}, g_{2N}, and g_{3N} defined similarly; and define $M_N = \partial m_N/\partial\xi' = [\partial f_N'/\partial\xi, \partial g_N'/\partial\xi]' = [F_N', G_N']'$, where $G_N(\xi) = g_{2N} + 2(I \otimes \xi')g_{3N}$ and $F_N = f_{2N}$. Let $M = \text{plim}\, M_N$, with F and G defined similarly. Define the optimal weighting matrix:

$$\Omega = \begin{bmatrix} \Omega_{ff} & \Omega_{fg} \\ \Omega_{gf} & \Omega_{gg} \end{bmatrix} = \lim_{N\to\infty} \text{cov}\left(\sqrt{N}\sum_i m_i\right). \tag{24}$$

Let $\hat{\Omega}$ be a consistent estimate of Ω of the form

$$\hat{\Omega} = \frac{1}{N}\sum_i m_i(\tilde{\xi})m_i(\tilde{\xi})', \tag{25}$$

where $\tilde{\xi}$ is an initial consistent estimate of ξ (perhaps based on the linear moment conditions f_i, as discussed below); partition it similarly to Ω.

In this notation, the efficient GMM estimator $\tilde{\xi}_{\text{GMM}}$ minimizes $Nm_N(\xi)'\hat{\Omega}^{-1}m_N(\xi)$. Using standard results, the asymptotic covariance matrix of $N^{1/2}(\tilde{\xi}_{\text{GMM}} - \xi)$ is $[M'\Omega^{-1}M]^{-1}$. We can also test the validity of the moment conditions $\mathrm{E}[m_i(\xi)] = 0$ using the usual overidentification test statistic $J_N = Nm_N(\tilde{\xi}_{\text{GMM}})'\hat{\Omega}^{-1}m_N(\tilde{\xi}_{\text{GMM}})$. This statistic is asymptotically chi-squared with $(l - k)$ degrees of freedom under the joint hypothesis that all the moment conditions are legitimate.

4.2. Linear moment conditions and IV

Some interesting question arise when we consider GMM based on the linear moment conditions $f_i(\xi)$ only. The optimal GMM estimator based on these conditions is

$$\begin{aligned} \tilde{\xi}_f &= -[f_{2N}'\hat{\Omega}_{ff}^{-1}f_{2N}]^{-1}f_{2N}'\hat{\Omega}_{ff}^{-1}f_{1N} \\ &= \left[\left(\sum_i W_i'S_i\right)\hat{\Omega}_{ff}^{-1}\left(\sum_i S_i'W_i\right)\right]^{-1}\left(\sum_i W_i'S_i\right)\hat{\Omega}_{ff}^{-1}\left(\sum_i S_i'y_i\right). \end{aligned} \tag{26}$$

This GMM estimator can be compared to the linear IV estimator that is of the same form, but with $\hat{\Omega}_{ff}$ replaced by $(\sum_i S_i'S_i)$. The GMM estimator is generally more efficient than the linear IV estimator. They are asymptotically equivalent in the case that Ω_{ff} is proportional to $\mathrm{E}(S_i'S_i)$, which occurs if $\mathrm{E}(S_i'u_iu_i'S_i)$ is proportional to $\mathrm{E}(S_i'S_i)$. For the case that S_i consists only of columns of R_i, so that only the moment conditions (18) based on exogeneity of X and Z are imposed, this equivalence will generally hold. Arellano and Bond (1991) considered the moment conditions (4a), so that S_i also contains A_i, and noted that asymptotic equivalence between the IV and GMM estimates fails if we relax the homoskedasticity assumption (A.4), even though the moment conditions (4a) are still valid under only assumptions (A.1)–(A.3) (our *Case B*). In fact, even the full set of assumptions (A.1)–(A.4) is not sufficient to imply the asymptotic equivalence of the IV and GMM estimates when the moment conditions (4a) are used. Assumptions (A.1)–(A.4) deal only with second moments, whereas asymptotic equivalence of IV and GMM involves restrictions on fourth moments (e.g., $\mathrm{cov}(y_{i0}^2, \varepsilon_{it}^2) = 0$). Ahn (1990) proved the asymptotic equivalence of the IV and GMM estimators based on the moment conditions (4a) for the case that (A.4) is maintained and (A.1)–(A.3) are strengthened by replacing uncorrelatedness with independence. Wooldridge (1996) provides a more general treatment of cases in which IV and GMM are asymptotically equivalent. In the present case, his results indicate that asymptotic equivalence would hold if we rewrite (A.1)–(A.4) in terms of conditional expectations instead of uncorrelatedness; that is, if we assume

$$\mathrm{E}(\varepsilon_{it} \mid y_{i0}, \alpha_i, \varepsilon_{i1}, \ldots, \varepsilon_{i,t-1}) = 0, \tag{A.5}$$

$$\mathrm{E}(\varepsilon_{it}^2 \mid y_{i0}, \alpha_i, \varepsilon_{i1}, \ldots, \varepsilon_{i,t-1}) = \sigma_{\varepsilon\varepsilon}. \tag{A.6}$$

A more novel observation is that the asymptotic equivalence of IV and GMM fails whenever we use the additional linear moment conditions (6). This is so even if assumptions (A.1)–(A.4) are srengthened by replacing uncorrelatedness with independence. When uncorrelatedness in (A.1)–(A.3) is replaced by independence, Ahn (1990, Ch. 3, App. 3) shows that, while $\mathrm{E}(A_i'u_iu_i'A_i) = \sigma_{\varepsilon\varepsilon}\mathrm{E}(A_i'A_i)$ and $\mathrm{E}(A_i'u_iu_i'B_{1i}) = \sigma_{\varepsilon\varepsilon}\mathrm{E}(A_i'B_{1i})$,

$$\mathrm{E}(B_{1i}'u_iu_i'B_{1i}) = \sigma_{\varepsilon\varepsilon}\mathrm{E}(B_{1i}'B_{1i}) + (d + \sigma_{\varepsilon\varepsilon})C, \tag{27}$$

where $d = \mathrm{E}(\varepsilon^4) - 3\sigma_{\varepsilon\varepsilon}^2$ and C is a square matrix of dimension $(T-2)$ with 2 on the diagonal, -1 one position off the diagonal, and 0 elsewhere. Under normality $d = 0$ but the term $\sigma_{\varepsilon\varepsilon}C$ remains.

4.3. Linearized GMM and specification tests

We now consider a linearized GMM estimator. Suppose that $\tilde{\xi}$ is any consistent estimator of ξ; for exmple, $\tilde{\xi}_f$. Following Newey (1985, p. 238), the linearized GMM estimator is of the form

$$\tilde{\xi}_{\mathrm{LGMM}} = \tilde{\xi} - [M_N(\tilde{\xi})'\hat{\Omega}^{-1}M_N(\tilde{\xi})]^{-1}M_N(\tilde{\xi})'\hat{\Omega}^{-1}m_N(\tilde{\xi}). \tag{28}$$

This estimator is consistent and has the same asymptotic distribution as $\tilde{\xi}_{\mathrm{GMM}}$.

When the LGMM estimator is based on the initial estimator $\tilde{\xi}_f$, some further simplification is possible. Applying the usual matrix inversion rule to $\hat{\Omega}$ and using the fact that $f_{2N}'\hat{\Omega}_{ff}^{-1}f_N(\tilde{\xi}_f) = 0$, we can write the LGMM estimator as follows:

$$\tilde{\xi}_{\mathrm{LGMM}} = \tilde{\xi}_f - [\hat{\Gamma} + \tilde{B}_N'\hat{\Omega}_{bb}^{-1}\tilde{B}_N']^{-1}\tilde{B}_N'\hat{\Omega}_{bb}^{-1}\tilde{b}_N. \tag{29}$$

Here $\hat{\Gamma}^{-1} = [f_{2N}'\hat{\Omega}_{ff}^{-1}f_{2N}]^{-1}$ denotes the usual estimate of the asymptotic covariance matrix of $N^{1/2}(\tilde{\xi}_f - \xi)$, $\hat{\Omega}_{bb} = \hat{\Omega}_{gg} - \hat{\Omega}_{gf}\hat{\Omega}_{ff}^{-1}\hat{\Omega}_{fg}$, $b_N(\xi) = g_N(\xi) - \hat{\Omega}_{gf}\hat{\Omega}_{ff}^{-1}f_N(\xi)$, $B_N(\xi) = \partial b_N \partial\xi' = G_N(\xi) - \hat{\Omega}_{gf}\hat{\Omega}_{ff}^{-1}f_{2N}$, and $\tilde{B}_N$ and $\tilde{b}_N$ are shorthand for $B_N(\tilde{\xi}_f)$ and $b^N(\tilde{\xi}_f)$, respectively.

We now consider alternative tests of the validity of the moment conditions. One can of course use J_N to test the joint hypothesis that all the moment conditions are legitimate. We consider an alternative procedure in which we maintain the validity of the moment conditions $\mathrm{E}[f_i(\xi)] = 0$ that yield the linear estimate $\tilde{\xi}_f$, and we test the additional moment conditions $\mathrm{E}[g_i(\xi)] = 0$. This may be a reasonable empirical strategy because the moment conditions based on $f_i(\xi)$ are linear and therefore easy to impose; we can test the validity of the hard-to-impose (nonlinear) restrictions before we impose them. Alternatively, we might choose $f_i(\xi)$ to be only the set of moment conditions based on the exogeneity assumptions (18), and we can test the validity of the further moment conditions based on second-moment assumptions on the errors. Following Newey (1985, p. 243), we can construct the test statistic

$$\begin{aligned} C_N &= N\tilde{b}_N'[\hat{\Omega}_{bb} + \tilde{B}_N\hat{\Gamma}^{-1}\tilde{B}_N']^{-1}\tilde{b}_N \\ &= N\tilde{b}_N'\hat{\Omega}_{bb}^{-1}\tilde{b}_N - N\tilde{b}_N'\hat{\Omega}_{bb}^{-1}\tilde{B}_N[\hat{\Gamma} + \tilde{B}_N'\hat{\Omega}_{bb}^{-1}\tilde{B}_N]^{-1}\tilde{B}_N'\hat{\Omega}_{bb}^{-1}\tilde{b}_N. \end{aligned} \tag{30}$$

This statistic is asymptotically chi-squared with l_2 degrees of freedom under the null hypothesis that the moment conditions based on g_i are legitimate.

We can also construct a modified overidentification test that is closely related to C_N. Letting $\tilde{m}_N = m_N(\tilde{\xi}_f)$ and $\tilde{M}_N = M_N(\tilde{\xi}_f)$, we define

$$\begin{aligned} MJ_N &\equiv N\tilde{m}_N'\hat{\Omega}^{-1}\tilde{m}_N - N\tilde{m}_N'\hat{\Omega}^{-1}\tilde{M}_N[\tilde{M}_N'\hat{\Omega}^{-1}\tilde{M}_N]^{-1}\tilde{M}_N'\hat{\Omega}^{-1}\tilde{m}_N \\ &= C_N + J_N^f, \end{aligned} \tag{31}$$

where $J_N^f = Nf_N(\tilde{\xi}_f)'\hat{\Omega}_{ff}^{-1}f_N(\tilde{\xi}_f)$ is the statistic for testing $\mathrm{E}[f_i(\xi)] = 0$, and the second equality results from the fact that $f_{2N}'\hat{\Omega}_{ff}^{-1}f_N(\tilde{\xi}_f) = 0$. Following Ahn (1955), we can show that MJ_N and J_N are asymptotically identical under the hypothesis that all the moment conditions are valid. In fact MJ_N and J_N are asymptotically equivalent under local alternative hypotheses $H_l^* = \{H_T^*\}_{T=1}^{\infty}$ where H_T^*: $T^{1/2}\mathrm{E}[m_N(\xi)] = \mathrm{O}(1)$. See Ahn (1995, Proposition 1).

An alternative and perhaps more intuitive approach to the estimation and testing problem is as follows. Define $\rho = \mathrm{E}[g_i(\xi)]$, an $l_2 \times 1$ vector of auxiliary parameters; we wish to test the hypothesis $\rho = 0$. Define $\theta = (\xi', \rho')$, and consider the following GMM problem:

$$\min_{\xi} N \begin{bmatrix} f_N(\xi) \\ g_N(\xi) - \rho \end{bmatrix}' \hat{\Omega}^{-1} \begin{bmatrix} f_N(\xi) \\ g_N(\xi) - \rho \end{bmatrix}, \tag{32}$$

for which the solution is $\ddot{\theta} = (\ddot{\xi}', \ddot{\rho}')'$. This problem satisfies the conditions for the 'separability' result of Ahn and Schmidt (1995a) and its solution is simply $\ddot{\xi} = \tilde{\xi}_f$ and $\ddot{\rho} = \tilde{b}_N$. By standard GMM results, the asymptotic covariance matrix of $N^{1/2}(\ddot{\theta} - \theta)$ is given by $\Xi^{-1} = [(M, J)'\Omega^{-1}(M, J)]^{-1}$, where $J' = [0, -I]$, with 0 $l_2 \times l_1$ and I of dimension l_2. It is consistently estimated by

$$\tilde{\Xi}^{-1} = [(M_N(\tilde{\xi}_f), J)'\hat{\Omega}^{-1}(M_N(\tilde{\xi}_f), J)]^{-1}, \tag{33}$$

which is a standard calculation since $\tilde{\Xi}$ is just the Hessian of the GMM minimand in (32). Following Ahn and Schmidt (1995a), the conventional Wald statistic (based on $\ddot{\rho}$ and $\tilde{\Xi}^{-1}$) for the hypothesis $\rho = 0$ is *numerically identical* to C_N, provided that the same weighting matrix is used. The statistic MJ_N can be then obtained by simply adding this Wald statistic and J_N^f.

Once $\ddot{\xi}(= \tilde{\xi}_f)$, $\ddot{\rho}(= \tilde{b}_N)$, and $\tilde{\Xi}^{-1}$ are computed, it is natural to obtain an efficient minimum distance (MD) estimator of ξ. Suppose that $\tilde{\xi}_{\mathrm{MD}}$ solves

$$\min_{\xi} \begin{bmatrix} \ddot{\xi} - \xi \\ \ddot{\rho} \end{bmatrix}' \tilde{\Xi} \begin{bmatrix} \ddot{\xi} - \xi \\ \ddot{\rho} \end{bmatrix}. \tag{34}$$

Then it is straightforward to show that $\tilde{\xi}_{\mathrm{MD}} = \ddot{\xi} + \tilde{\Xi}_{11}^{-1}\tilde{\Xi}_{12}\ddot{\rho}$, where $\tilde{\Xi}_{11} = M_N(\tilde{\xi}_f)'\hat{\Omega}^{-1}M_N(\tilde{\xi}_f)$ and $\tilde{\Xi}_{12} = M_N(\tilde{\xi}_f)'\hat{\Omega}^{-1}J$ are submatrices of $\tilde{\Xi}$. With these substitutions, and substituting $\ddot{\xi} = \tilde{\xi}_f$ and $\ddot{\rho} = \tilde{b}_N = g_N(\tilde{\xi}_f) - \hat{\Omega}_{gf}\hat{\Omega}_{ff}^{-1}f_N(\tilde{\xi}_f)$ as given above, we obtain $\tilde{\xi}_{\mathrm{MD}} = \xi_{\mathrm{LGMM}}$. Unsurprisingly, there is a close link between linearization of the moment conditions $g_i(\xi)$ in estimation and tests of their validity.

5. Concluding remarks

In this paper, we have considered the estimation of dynamic models for panel data. We have counted and expressed the moment conditions implied by a wide variety of different assumptions. These conditions can be imposed in a GMM framework. While many of the moment conditions are nonlinear in the parameters, we derive a very simple linearized estimator that is asymptotically as efficient as the nonlinear GMM estimator, and simple moment tests of the validity of the nonlinear restrictions.

Some evidence on the efficiency gains from using nonlinear moment conditions is given in Ahn and Schmidt (1995b), for one of the sets of assumptions considered in this paper. These efficiency gains appear to be large enough to justify the effort needed to impose the nonlinear moment conditions. Thus the methods developed in this paper to test and impose these conditions should be of practical use.

References

Ahn, S.C., 1990, Three essays on share contracts, labor supply, and the estimation of models for dynamic panel data, Unpublished Ph.D. dissertation (Michigan State University, East Lansing, MI).

Ahn, S.C., 1995, Model specification testing based on root-T consistent estimators, Unpublished manuscript (Arizona State University, Tempe, AZ).

Ahn, S.C. and P. Schmidt, 1995a, A separability result for GMM estimation, with applications to GLS prediction and conditional moment tests, Econometric Reviews 14, 19–34.

Ahn, S.C. and P. Schmidt, 1995b, Efficient estimation of models for dynamic panel data, Journal of Econometrics 68, 5–27.

Anderson, T.W. and C. Hsiao, 1981, Estimation of dynamic models with error components, Journal of the American Statistical Association 76, 598–606.

Arellano, M. and S. Bond, 1991, Tests of specification for panel data: Monte Carlo evidence and an application to employment equations, Review of Economic Studies 58, 277–297.

Arellano, M. and O. Bover, 1990, Another look at the instrumental variables estimation of error-component Models, Unpublished manuscript (London School of Economics, London).

Arellano, M. and O. Bover, 1995, Another look at the instrumental variables estimation of error-component models, Journal of Econometrics 68, 29–51.

Blundell, R. and S. Bond, 1994, The role of initial conditions in GMM and ML estimators for dynamic panel data models, Unpublished manuscript (University College, London).

Breusch, T.S., G.E. Mizon, and P. Schmidt, 1989, Efficient estimation using panel data, Econometrica 57, 695–701.

Holtz-Eakin, D., 1988, Testing for individual effects in autoregressive models, Journal of Econometrics 39, 297–308.

Holtz-Eakin, D., W. Newey, and H.S. Rosen, 1988, Estimating vector autoregressions with panel data, Econometrica 56, 1371–1396.

Hsiao, C., 1986, Analysis of panel data (Cambridge University Press, New York, NY).

Newey, W., 1985, Generalized method of moments specification testing, Journal of Econometrics 29, 229–256.

Schmidt, P., S.C. Ahn, and D. Wyhowski, 1992, Comment, Journal of Business and Economic Statistics 10, 10–14.

Wooldridge, J.M., 1996, Estimating systems of equations with different instruments for different equations, Journal of Econometrics, forthcoming.

[3]

Symmetrically Normalized Instrumental-Variable Estimation Using Panel Data

César ALONSO-BORREGO
Universidad Carlos III de Madrid, 28903 Getafe, Madrid, Spain (alonso1@eco.uc3m.es)

Manuel ARELLANO
CEMFI, 28014 Madrid, Spain (arellano@cemfi.es)

We discuss the estimation of linear panel-data models with sequential moment restrictions using symmetrically normalized generalized method of moments (GMM) estimators (SNM) and limited information maximum likelihood (LIML) analogues. These estimators are asymptotically equivalent to standard GMM but are invariant to normalization and tend to have a smaller finite-sample bias, especially when the instruments are poor. We study their properties in relation to ordinary GMM and minimum distance estimators for AR(1) models with individual effects by mean of simulations. Finally, as empirical illustrations, we estimate by SNM and LIML employment and wage equations using panels of U.K. and Spanish firms.

KEY WORDS: Autoregressive models; Dynamic panel data; Employment equations; Generalized method of moments; Monte Carlo methods; Symmetric normalization.

This work is motivated by a concern with the finite-sample bias in panel data instrumental-variable (IV) estimators when the instruments are weak. A linear panel-data model with predetermined variables [like vector autoregressions (VAR's) or linear Euler equations] is typically estimated by IV techniques in first-differences using all the available lags of the predetermined variables as instruments. The specification of the equation error in first-differences reflects the fact that the analysis is conditional on an unobservable individual effect. Because the number of instruments increases with the time series dimension (T), the model generates many overidentifying restrictions even for moderate values of T, although the quality of these instruments is often poor.

The effect of weak instruments on the distributions of two-stage least squares (2SLS) and limited information maximum likelihood (LIML) differs substantially, despite the fact that both estimators have the same asymptotic distribution. Although the distribution of LIML is centered at the parameter value, 2SLS is biased toward ordinary least squares (OLS), and in the completely unidentified case converges to a random variable with the OLS probability limit as its central value. On the other hand, LIML has no finite moments regardless of the sample size, and as a consequence its distribution has thicker tails than that of 2SLS and a higher probability of extreme values [see Phillips (1983) for a good survey of the literature]. As a result of numerical comparisons of the two distributions involving median bias, interquartile ranges, and rates of approach to normality, Anderson, Kunitomo, and Sawa (1982) concluded that LIML was to be strongly preferred to 2SLS, particularly if the number of instruments is large. Similar conclusions emerge from the results of asymptotic approximations based on an increasing number of instruments as the sample size tends to infinity; under these sequences, LIML is a consistent estimator but 2SLS is inconsistent (Kunitomo 1980; Morimune 1983; and, more recently, Bekker 1994). (In our context, these approximations would amount to allowing T to increase to infinity at a chosen rate as opposed to the standard fixed T, large N asymptotics.)

Despite this favorable evidence, LIML has not been used as much in applications as IV estimators. In the past, LIML was at a disadvantage relative to 2SLS on computational grounds. More fundamentally, applied econometricians have often regarded 2SLS as a more "flexible" choice than LIML from the point of view of the restrictions they were willing to impose on their models. In effect, the IV techniques used for a panel-data model with predetermined instruments are not standard 2SLS estimators because the model gives rise to a system of equations (one for each time period) with a different number of instruments available for each equation. Moreover, concern with heteroscedasticity has led to considering alternative ("two-step") generalized method of moments (GMM) estimators that use as weighting matrix more robust estimators of the variances and covariances of the orthogonality conditions (following the work of Chamberlain 1982; Hansen 1982; White 1982).

In a recent article, Hillier (1990) showed that the alternative normalization rules adopted by LIML and 2SLS are at the root of their different sampling behavior. Hillier also showed that a symmetrically normalized 2SLS estimator has properties similar to those of LIML. This result motivates our focus on symmetrically normalized estimation. Symmetrically normalized 2SLS, unlike LIML, is a GMM estimator based on structural-form orthogonality conditions, and it therefore can be readily extended to two-step weighting matrices and the nonstandard IV situations that are of interest in dynamic panel-data models, while relying on standard GMM asymptotic theory. In this article, we discuss both nonrobust and robust LIML analogues and

Journal of Business & Economic Statistics
January 1999, Vol. 17, No. 1

symmetrically normalized GMM estimates in the panel-data context.

The symmetrically normalized estimator can be described in a simple example as follows. Consider a structural equation with a single endogenous explanatory variable and a matrix of instruments Z,

$$y = \beta_o x + u, \tag{1}$$

with associated reduced-form equations

$$\begin{aligned} y &= Z\pi_o + v_1 \\ x &= Z\gamma_o + v_2. \end{aligned} \tag{2}$$

Both symmetrically normalized 2SLS and LIML are least squares estimators of the reduced form (2) imposing the overidentifying restrictions $\pi = \gamma\beta$. Let us define

$$\begin{aligned} (\tilde{\beta}_V, \tilde{\gamma}_V) &= \arg\min_{\beta,\gamma} \begin{pmatrix} y - Z\gamma\beta \\ x - Z\gamma \end{pmatrix}' \\ &\quad \times (V^{-1} \otimes I) \begin{pmatrix} y - Z\gamma\beta \\ x - Z\gamma \end{pmatrix} \\ &= \arg\min_{\beta,\gamma} \begin{pmatrix} \hat{\pi} - \gamma\beta \\ \hat{\gamma} - \gamma \end{pmatrix}' \\ &\quad \times (V^{-1} \otimes Z'Z) \begin{pmatrix} \hat{\pi} - \gamma\beta \\ \hat{\gamma} - \gamma \end{pmatrix}. \end{aligned} \tag{3}$$

Concentrating γ out of the least squares criterion, we obtain

$$\tilde{\beta}_V = \arg\min_{\beta} \frac{(y - \beta x)' Z (Z'Z)^{-1} Z' (y - \beta x)}{(1, -\beta')V(1, -\beta')'}. \tag{4}$$

LIML is $\tilde{\beta}_V$ with V equal to the reduced-form residual covariance matrix, whereas symmetrically normalized 2SLS is $\tilde{\beta}_V$ with V equal to an identity matrix (Malinvaud 1970; Goldberger and Olkin 1971; Keller 1975; Anderson 1976) so that both LIML and symmetrically normalized 2SLS solve minimum eigenvalue problems. Symmetrically normalized 2SLS can also be described as a GMM estimator based on the unit-length orthogonality conditions

$$E[z_i(y_i - \beta_o x_i)/(1 + \beta_o^2)^{1/2}] = 0. \tag{5}$$

Note that the asymptotic distribution of $\hat{\beta}_V$ does not depend on the choice of V because optimal minimum distance estimators (MDE) of β based on $(\hat{\pi} - \gamma\beta, \hat{\gamma} - \gamma)$ and on $(\hat{\pi} - \hat{\gamma}\beta)$ are asymptotically equivalent. Note also that ordinary and symmetrically normalized 2SLS are given, respectively, by the ordinary and the orthogonal regressions of $\hat{y}$ on $\hat{x}(\hat{y} = Z\hat{\pi}$ and $\hat{x} = Z\hat{\gamma})$, and although the former differs from indirect 2SLS (the inverse regression of $\hat{x}$ on $\hat{y}$), the latter is invariant to normalization.

This article is organized as follows. Section 1 develops the relationship between symmetrically normalized GMM (SNM) and LIML in the context of a linear equation for panel data with sequential moment restrictions. We also present two-step SNM estimators and test statistics of overidentifying restrictions and compare them with robust LIML analogues. The latter are the "continuously updated GMM" estimators considered by Hansen, Heaton, and Yaron (1995). Section 2 compares the finite-sample properties of SNM and LIML to those of ordinary GMM and MDE for first-order autoregressive [AR(1)] models with individual effects. Section 3 reestimates the employment equations for a sample of U.K. firms reported by Arellano and Bond (1991) using SNM, LIML, and indirect GMM estimators. This section further illustrates the techniques by presenting symmetrically normalized estimates and bootstrap confidence intervals of employment and wage VAR's from a larger panel of Spanish firms. Finally, Section 4 concludes.

1. SYMMETRICALLY NORMALIZED IV ESTIMATION

Consider a model with individual effects for panel data given by

$$\begin{aligned} y_{it} &= x'_{it}\delta_o + u_{it}, \qquad t = 1, \ldots, T; i = 1, \ldots, N, \\ u_{it} &= \eta_i + v_{it}. \end{aligned} \tag{6}$$

The model specifies sequential moment conditions of the form $E(v_{it}|z_i^t) = 0$, where $z_i^t = (z'_{i1} \ldots z'_{it})'$ is a vector of instruments, which may include current or lagged values of y_{it} and x_{it}. Thus, this setting is sufficiently general to cover models with strictly exogenous, predetermined, and endogenous explanatory variables. Observations across individuals are assumed to be independent and identically distributed.

Estimation will be based on a sequence of orthogonality conditions of the form

$$E[z_i^t(y_{it}^* - x_{it}^{*\prime}\delta_o)] = 0, \qquad t = 1, \ldots, T-1, \tag{7}$$

where starred variables denote forward orthogonal deviations of the original variables (Arellano and Bover 1995). It is convenient to rewrite the transformed model as

$$y_i^* = X_i^*\delta_o + u_i^*, \tag{8}$$

where $y_i^* = (y_{i1}^* \ldots y_{i(T-1)}^*)'$, and so forth.

The $k \times 1$ parameter vector δ_o is usually estimated by GMM leading to estimators of the form (Holtz-Eakin, Newey, and Rosen 1988; Arellano and Bond 1991; Chamberlain 1992; Arellano and Bover 1995; Ahn and Schmidt 1995)

$$\hat{\delta}_{\text{GMM}} = (X^{*\prime}ZA_NZ'X^*)^{-1}X^{*\prime}ZA_NZ'y^*, \tag{9}$$

where $y^* = (y_1^{*\prime} \ldots y_N^{*\prime})'$, $X^* = (X_1^{*\prime} \ldots X_N^{*\prime})'$, and $Z = (Z'_1 \ldots Z'_N)'$. Z_i is a $(T-1) \times q$ block diagonal matrix whose tth block is z_i^t and an optimal choice of A_N is such that it is a consistent estimate of the inverse of $E(Z'_iu_i^*u_i^{*\prime}Z_i)$. Under "classical" errors [i.e.. when $E(v_{it}^2|z_i^t) = \sigma^2$ and $E(v_{it}v_{i(t+j)}|z_i^t) = 0$ for $j > 0$ and all t], $E(Z'_iu_i^*u_i^{*\prime}Z_i) = \sigma^2E(Z'_iZ_i)$, and hence the "one-step" nonrobust choice $A_N = (\hat{\sigma}^2Z'Z)^{-1}$ is optimal ($\hat{\sigma}^2$, which denotes the residual variance, is irrelevant for estimation, but it is kept here for notational convenience). Alternatively, the standard "two-step" robust choice is $A_N = (\sum_i Z'_i\tilde{u}_i^*\tilde{u}_i^{*\prime}Z_i)^{-1}$, where $\tilde{u}_i^*$ is a vector of residuals evaluated using some preliminary consistent estimate of δ_o. Given identification, $\hat{\delta}_{\text{GMM}}$ is consistent and asymptotically normal as $N \to \infty$ for fixed T. In addition, for either choice of A_N, provided the conditions under which they are optimal choices are satisfied, a consistent estimator of the asymptotic variance of $\hat{\delta}_{\text{GMM}}$ is $\widehat{\text{var}}(\hat{\delta}_{\text{GMM}}) = (X^{*\prime}ZA_NZ'X^*)^{-1}$. Moreover, letting $\hat{u}^* = y^* - X^*\hat{\delta}_{\text{GMM}}$, the Sargan or GMM statistic of overidentifying restrictions is given by

$$S = \hat{u}^{*\prime}ZA_NZ'\hat{u}^* \xrightarrow{d} \chi^2_{q-k}. \tag{10}$$

Now, partition $X^* = (X_1^*, X_2^*)$ and $\delta_o = (\delta_{o1}', \delta_{o2}')'$ to distinguish between nonexogenous and exogenous variables, such that the k_2 columns of X_2^* are linear combinations of those of Z but the k_1 columns of X_1^* are not. SNM is the GMM estimator of δ_o based on the orthogonality conditions

$$E\psi_i(\delta_o) = E\left[\frac{Z_i'(y_i^* - X_i^*\delta_o)}{(1 + \delta_{o1}'\delta_{o1})^{1/2}}\right] = 0. \tag{11}$$

Because $E[\psi_i(\delta_o)\psi_i'(\delta_o)] = E(Z_i'u_i^*u_i^{*\prime}Z_i)/(1 + \delta_{o1}'\delta_{o1})$, a consistent estimate of the inverse of $E(Z_i'u_i^*u_i^{*\prime}Z_i)$ remains an optimal weighting matrix for the SNM estimator. Therefore,

$$\hat{\delta}_{\text{SNM}} = \arg\min_{\delta} \frac{(y^* - X^*\delta)'M(y^* - X^*\delta)}{(1 + \delta_1'\delta_1)}, \tag{12}$$

where $M = ZA_NZ'$. Minimizing the criterion with respect to δ_2 we obtain a concentrated criterion that only depends on δ_1. This gives us

$$\begin{aligned} \hat{\delta}_{1\text{SNM}} &= \arg\min_{\delta_1} d_1'W_1^{*\prime}(M - M_2)W_1^*d_1/d_1'd_1 \\ &= [X_1^{*\prime}(M - M_2)X_1^* - \tilde{\lambda}I]^{-1}X_1^{*\prime}(M - M_2)y^* \end{aligned} \tag{13}$$

and

$$\hat{\delta}_{2\text{SNM}} = (X_2^{*\prime}MX_2^*)^{-1}X_2^{*\prime}M(y^* - X_1^*\hat{\delta}_{1\text{SNM}}), \tag{14}$$

where $W_1^* = (y^*, X_1^*)$, $d_1 = (1, -\delta_1')'$, $M_2 = MX_2^*(X_2^{*\prime}MX_2^*)^{-1}X_2^{*\prime}M$, and $\tilde{\lambda} = \min \text{eigen}[W_1^{*\prime}(M - M_2)W_1^*]$. Notice also that

$$\tilde{\lambda} = \min(y^* - X^*\delta)'M(y^* - X^*\delta)/(1 + \delta_1'\delta_1). \tag{15}$$

Equivalently,

$$\hat{\delta}_{\text{SNM}} = (X^{*\prime}MX^* - \tilde{\lambda}\Delta)^{-1}X^{*\prime}My^* \tag{16}$$

with

$$\Delta = \begin{pmatrix} I_{k_1} & 0 \\ 0 & 0 \end{pmatrix}$$

[if no columns of X^* are perfectly predictable from Z, or if the entire vector of coefficients is normalized to unity, then $\Delta = I$ and $\tilde{\lambda} = \min \text{eigen}(W^{*\prime}MW^*)$, with $W^* = (y^*, X^*)$]. In the just-identified case, $\tilde{\lambda} = 0$, with the result that GMM and SNM coincide.

Because $\hat{\delta}_{\text{GMM}}$ and $\hat{\delta}_{\text{SNM}}$ are asymptotically equivalent, $\widehat{\text{var}}(\hat{\delta}_{\text{GMM}})$ is also a consistent estimate of the asymptotic variance of $\hat{\delta}_{\text{SNM}}$. An alternative natural estimator of $\text{var}(\hat{\delta}_{\text{SNM}})$, however, suggested by the previous expression, is $\widehat{\text{var}}(\hat{\delta}_{\text{SNM}}) = (X^{*\prime}MX^* - \tilde{\lambda}\Delta)^{-1}$. Moreover, because $\tilde{\lambda}$ is a minimized optimal GMM criterion it can be used as an alternative test statistic of overidentifying restrictions. We have that

$$(1 + \hat{\delta}_{1\text{SNM}}'\hat{\delta}_{1\text{SNM}})\tilde{\lambda} \xrightarrow{d} \chi^2_{q-k}, \tag{17}$$

which is asymptotically equivalent to the Sargan test.

Let us now turn to consider LIML analogues or "continuously updated GMM" estimators in the terminology of Hansen et al. (1996). The nonrobust LIML analogue $\hat{\delta}_{\text{LIML1}}$ minimizes a criterion of the form

$$l(\delta) = (y^* - X^*\delta)'ZA_N(\delta)Z'(y^* - X^*\delta) \tag{18}$$

with $A_N(\delta) = (Z'Z)^{-1}/(y^* - X^*\delta)'(y^* - X^*\delta)$. The resulting estimator is

$$\begin{aligned} \hat{\delta}_{\text{LIML1}} &= [X^*Z(Z'Z)^{-1}Z'X^* - \hat{l}X^{*\prime}X^*]^{-1} \\ &\quad \times [X^{*\prime}Z(Z'Z)^{-1}Z'y^* - \hat{l}X^{*\prime}y^*], \end{aligned} \tag{19}$$

where, letting $d = (1, -\delta')'$,

$$\begin{aligned} \hat{l} &= \min d'W^{*\prime}Z(Z'Z)^{-1}Z'W^*d/(d'W^{*\prime}W^*d) \\ &= \min \text{eigen}[W^{*\prime}Z(Z'Z)^{-1}Z'W^*(W^{*\prime}W^*)^{-1}]. \end{aligned} \tag{20}$$

On the other hand, the robust LIML analogue $\hat{\delta}_{\text{LIML2}}$ minimizes a criterion of the same form as (18) with

$$A_N(\delta) = \left(\sum_{i=1}^{N} Z_i'u_i^*(\delta)u_i^*(\delta)'Z_i\right)^{-1}, \tag{21}$$

where $u_i^*(\delta) = y_i^* - X_i^*\delta$. Therefore, LIML2, unlike LIML1 or the SNM estimators, does not solve a simple minimum eigenvalue problem and requires the use of numerical optimization methods.

Both the SNM and the LIML analogues are invariant to normalization, but the ordinary GMM estimator is not. That is, if the equation is solved for an endogenous variable other than y_i, contrary to the case with ordinary GMM, the indirect estimates obtained from SNM or LIML analogues coincide with the direct SNM or LIML estimates, respectively. [Notice that empirical likelihood estimators of the type considered by Qin and Lawless (1994) and Imbens (1997) will also be invariant to normalization due to the invariance property of maximum likelihood estimators.]

Symmetrically normalized estimators are potentially attractive alternatives to ordinary GMM on at least two grounds (aside from the desirability of invariance to normalization in its own right). First, they tend to have a smaller finite-sample bias than the GMM estimators. Hillier (1990) showed that, for the normal case in a standard linear structural equation with two endogenous variables, symmetrically normalized 2SLS and LIML are "spherically unbiased" in finite samples [meaning that the density of $\hat{a} = \hat{d}_1/(\hat{d}_1'\hat{d}_1)^{1/2}$ defined on the unit circle is symmetric about the true points $\pm a = \pm d_1/(d_1'd_1)^{1/2}$ having modes at $\pm a$]. However, 2SLS does not have this property.

Second, the concentration of the densities of the symmetrically normalized estimators depends on the quality of the instruments. In the completely unidentified case, as shown by Hillier, these estimators have a uniform distribution on the unit circle. This is in contrast with 2SLS, which converges to the same limit as OLS and whose distribution is determined exclusively by the normalization adopted. When the instruments are poor, as well as when the number of instruments is large relative to the sample size, 2SLS tends to provide results that are biased in the direction of OLS and also large discrepancies between "direct" and "indirect" 2SLS when using different normalizations. This situation has been stressed in several recent works (Bekker 1994; Bound, Jaeger, and Baker 1995; Angrist and Krueger 1995; Staiger and Stock 1997, among others). In contrast, with poor instruments the distributions of LIML and symmetrically normalized 2SLS accurately reproduce the fact that the information on the structural parameters is very small.

Although the LIML analogues and the SNM estimators are asymptotically equivalent (and in the Hillier setting exhibit similar finite-sample properties as well), SNM has some disadvantages relative to the other estimators. The main one is that in general the results are not independent of the units in which the variables are measured, so that a sensible choice of units may be important. In contrast, ordinary GMM is invariant to units but not to normalization, and LIML is invariant to units and normalization. This problem does not arise in the autoregressive panel-data models discussed later because in that case the SNM estimator is invariant to units and to normalization (just because in the autoregressive case a change in the units of the right-side variable leads trivially to a similar change in the units of the left-side variable). Another disadvantage of SNM is that the distinction between exogenous and nonexogenous variables is relevant for the specification of the estimator. This is so because in the case of SNM only the length of the coefficient vector for the nonexogenous variables is normalized to unity, and, contrary to LIML, this differs from normalizing to unity the entire coefficient vector. SNM, however, does have a computational advantage over LIML when we consider two-step or robust estimators. Indeed, LIML2, or continuously updated GMM, no longer solves a minimum eigenvalue problem, whereas two-step SNM only involves simple calculations that are similar to those performed for two-step ordinary GMM. Of course, SNM is limited to linear models, but in such context it is of interest to see if SNM, which is considerably faster and simpler than LIML2, can provide the benefits of the more complicated estimators and perhaps avoid problems of nonconvergence in the case of LIML2.

Table 1. Model 1: Nonrobust Estimates

		$\alpha = .5$			$\alpha = .8$		
		GMM1	*SNM1*	*LIML1*	*GMM1*	*SNM1*	*LIML1*
				$T = 4$			
$\sigma_\eta^2 = 0$	Median	.49	.50	.50	.76	.80	.80
	% bias	2.5	.3	.6	5.6	.1	.1
	iqr	.18	.19	.19	.28	.29	.29
	iq80	.35	.36	.36	.56	.61	.61
	MAE	.09	.09	.09	.15	.15	.15
$\sigma_\eta^2 = .2$	Median	.47	.49	.49	.66	.77	.77
	% bias	6.9	1.7	1.7	17.8	3.7	4.1
	iqr	.23	.25	.24	.45	.57	.58
	iq80	.44	.47	.47	.93	1.26	1.29
	MAE	.12	.12	.12	.25	.28	.29
$\sigma_\eta^2 = 1$	Median	.43	.48	.48	.44	.65	.61
	% bias	14.8	3.8	3.1	44.7	19.0	23.8
	iqr	.33	.36	.36	.67	.95	1.02
	iq80	.68	.77	.77	1.39	2.81	2.89
	MAE	.18	.18	.18	.44	.50	.53
				$T = 7$			
$\sigma_\eta^2 = 0$	Median	.47	.50	.49	.75	.80	.79
	% bias	5.0	.7	2.0	6.0	.3	1.1
	iqr	.09	.09	.09	.11	.12	.12
	iq80	.16	.17	.17	.22	.23	.24
	MAE	.05	.04	.04	.07	.06	.06
$\sigma_\eta^2 = .2$	Median	.47	.50	.49	.70	.81	.78
	% bias	6.7	.8	1.8	13.0	1.2	2.7
	iqr	.11	.11	.11	.18	.18	.21
	iq80	.20	.21	.21	.34	.39	.45
	MAE	.06	.06	.06	.12	.09	.11
$\sigma_\eta^2 = 1$	Median	.45	.50	.48	.61	.82	.74
	% bias	10.4	1.0	3.3	24.0	3.0	8.1
	iqr	.13	.14	.14	.23	.26	.38
	iq80	.24	.26	.27	.45	.54	.86
	MAE	.07	.07	.07	.20	.13	.19

NOTE 1,000 replications $N = 100$, $\sigma_v^2 = 1$ % bias gives the percentage median bias for all the estimates; iqr is the 75th–25th interquartile range, iq80 is the 90th–10th interquantile range, MAE denotes the median absolute error.

2. EXPERIMENTAL COMPARISONS

The purpose of this section is to study the finite-sample properties of the symmetrically normalized estimators considered previously in relation to ordinary GMM for an AR(1) model with individual effects. The IV restrictions implied by various versions of the model can be represented as simple structures on the covariance matrix of the data, so we can also make comparisons with the MDE of these covariance structures. The emphasis is not on assessing the value of enforcing particular restrictions in the model, as done, for example, by Ahn and Schmidt (1995), Arellano and Bover (1995), and Blundell and Bond (1998). Rather, we wish to evaluate the effects in small samples of using alternative estimating criteria that produce asymptotically equivalent estimators for fixed T and large N. We concentrate on a random-effects AR(1) model because of its simplicity and the fact that it is a case that has received much attention in the literature.

2.1 Models and Estimators

Let us consider a random sample of individual time series of size $T. y_i^T = (y_{i1}, \dots, y_{iT})'(i = 1, \dots, N)$ with second-order moment matrix $E(y_i^T y_{i'}^T) = \Omega = \{\omega_{ts}\}$. We assume that the joint distribution of y_i^T and the unobservable time-invariant effect η_i satisfies Assumption A:

$$y_{it} = \alpha y_{i(t-1)} + \eta_i + v_{it}, \qquad t = 2, \dots, T, \tag{22}$$

$$E(v_{it} | y_i^{t-1}) = 0, \tag{23}$$

where $E(\eta_i) = \gamma, E(v_{it}^2) = \sigma_t^2$, and $\text{var}(\eta_i) = \sigma_\eta^2$.

Notice that the dependence between η_i and v_{it} is not restricted by Assumption A, nor is the possibility of conditional heteroscedasticity ruled out, because $E(v_{it}^2 | y_i^{t-1})$ need not coincide with σ_t^2.

Following Arellano and Bond (1991), Assumption A implies $(T-2)(T-1)/2$ linear moment restrictions of the form

$$E[y_i^{t-2}(\Delta y_{it} - \alpha \Delta y_{i(t-1)})] = 0. \quad (24)$$

These restrictions can also be represented as constraints on the elements of Ω. Multiplying (22) by y_{is} for $s < t$ and taking expectations gives $\omega_{ts} = \alpha\omega_{(t-1)s} + c_s$ ($t = 2, \ldots T; s = 1, \ldots, t-1$), where $c_s = E(y_{is}\eta_i)$. This means that, given Assumption A, the $T(T+1)/2$ different elements of Ω can be written as functions of the $2T \times 1$ parameter vector $\theta = (\alpha, c_1, \ldots, c_{T-1}, \omega_{11}, \ldots, \omega_{TT})'$.

We call this moment structure Model 1. Because it is a special case of the model in Section 1, all the estimators discussed in Section 1 can be particularized to the present case. Here, however, we express the IV restrictions using errors in first-differences as opposed to orthogonal deviations to simplify the mapping with covariance structures. Notice that with $T = 3$ the parameters (α, c_1, c_2) are just-identified as functions of the elements of Ω.

The orthogonality conditions (24) are the only restrictions implied by Assumption A on the second-order moments of the data. They are not the only restrictions available, however, because (23) also implies that nonlinear functions of y_i^{t-2} are uncorrelated with Δv_{it}. The semiparametric efficiency bound for this model can be obtained from the results of Chamberlain (1992). One reason estimators based on (24) may not be fully efficient asymptotically is that the dependence between η_i and y_i^T may be nonlinear. Another reason would be unaccounted conditional heteroscedasticity.

Model 1 is attractive because it is based on minimal assumptions. We may be willing to impose additional structure, however, if this conforms to a priori beliefs. One possibility is to assume that the errors v_{it} are mean independent of the individual effect η_i given y_i^{t-1}. This situation gives rise to Assumption A′:

$$E(v_{it}|y_i^{t-1}, \eta_i) = 0. \quad (25)$$

Note that Assumption A′ is more restrictive than Assumption A. When $T \geq 4$, Assumption A′ implies the following additional $T - 3$ moment restrictions:

$$E[(y_{it} - \alpha y_{i(t-1)})(\Delta y_{i(t-1)} - \alpha \Delta y_{i(t-2)})] = 0, \quad t = 4, \ldots, T. \quad (26)$$

In effect, we can write $E[(y_{it} - \alpha y_{i(t-1)} - \eta_i)(\Delta y_{i(t-1)} - \alpha \Delta y_{i(t-2)})] = 0$ and, because $E(\eta_i \Delta v_{i(t-1)}) = 0$, the result follows.

GMM estimators of α that exploit these restrictions in addition to those in (24) were considered by Ahn and Schmidt (1995), but because the additional restrictions are nonlinear

Table 2. Model 1: Robust Estimates

		$\alpha = .5$				$\alpha = .8$			
		GMM2	SNM2	LIML2	MDE	GMM2	SNM2	LIML2	MDE
				$T = 4$					
$\sigma_\eta^2 = 0$	Median	.49	.50	.51	.51	.76	.80	.81	.80
	% bias	2.1	.2	1.6	2.1	4.9	.3	1.7	.0
	iqr	.19	.19	.19	.12	.29	.30	.31	.10
	iq80	.36	.38	.38	.23	.58	.62	.63	.21
	MAE	.09	.09	.09	.06	.15	.15	.16	.05
$\sigma_\eta^2 = .2$	Median	.47	.49	.50	.51	.65	.76	.84	.71
	% bias	6.5	1.8	.3	1.3	19.0	4.6	5.1	11.3
	iqr	.24	.25	.25	.20	.47	.55	.56	.28
	iq80	.47	.50	.51	.39	.97	1.33	1.23	.58
	MAE	.12	.13	.13	.10	.27	.28	.28	.11
$\sigma_\eta^2 = 1$	Median	.44	.47	.50	.49	.45	.64	.82	.65
	% bias	12.8	5.4	.5	2.2	43.6	19.5	2.9	19.1
	iqr	.35	.38	.38	.82	.70	1.03	.94	.48
	iq80	.75	.80	.80	.56	1.53	2.82	2.22	.94
	MAE	.18	.19	.19	.16	.46	.54	.47	.18
				$T = 7$					
$\sigma_\eta^2 = 0$	Median	.48	.50	.50	.51	.75	.79	.80	.81
	% bias	4.3	.4	.6	2.0	5.7	.8	.1	1.4
	iqr	.10	.10	.10	.09	.13	.13	.14	.10
	iq80	.18	.19	.21	.17	.24	.25	.28	.17
	MAE	.05	.05	.05	.04	.07	.07	.07	.05
$\sigma_\eta^2 = .2$	Median	.47	.50	.50	.50	.69	.79	.81	.74
	% bias	6.2	.5	.4	.1	13.7	1.7	.9	7.8
	iqr	.12	.12	.13	.12	.20	.20	.24	.17
	iq80	.23	.23	.26	.23	.39	.41	.51	.34
	MAE	.06	.06	.06	.06	.13	.10	.12	.09
$\sigma_\eta^2 = 1$	Median	.45	.49	.50	.50	.59	.77	.80	.71
	% bias	9.8	1.5	.0	.2	26.0	3.9	.1	11.1
	iqr	.14	.15	.16	.15	.27	.28	.36	.22
	iq80	.28	.30	.33	.29	.53	.59	.80	.46
	MAE	.08	.07	.08	.08	.22	.15	.18	.11

NOTE. See note to Table 1

we do not simulate them here. An alternative representation of the restrictions in (26) is in terms of a recursion of the coefficients c_t introduced previously. Multiplying (22) by η_i and taking expectations gives $c_t = \alpha c_{t-1} + \phi$ $(t = 2, \ldots, T)$, where $\phi = \gamma^2 + \sigma_\eta^2 = E(\eta_i^2)$ so that $c_1 \ldots c_{T-1}$ can be written in terms of c_1 and ϕ. This gives rise to a covariance structure in which Ω depends on the $(T+3) \times 1$ parameter vector $\theta = (\alpha, \phi, c_1, \omega_{11}, \ldots, \omega_{TT})'$. Notice that with $T = 3$ Assumption A′ does not imply further restrictions in Ω, with the result that α remains just-identified relative to the second-order moments.

Other forms of additional structure that can be imposed are various versions of mean or variance stationarity conditions. Assumption B, which requires the change in y_{it} to be mean independent of the individual effect η_i, is a particularly useful mean stationarity condition:

$$E(y_{it} - y_{i(t-1)} | \eta_i) = 0, \qquad t = 2, \ldots, T. \tag{27}$$

Notice that, given Assumption A, Assumption B implies that $E(y_{it}) = \gamma/(1-\alpha)$. Relative to Assumption A and Model 1, Assumption B adds the following $(T-2)$ moment restrictions on Ω:

$$E[(y_{it} - \alpha y_{i(t-1)}) \Delta y_{i(t-1)}] = 0, \qquad t = 3, \ldots, T, \tag{28}$$

which were proposed by Arellano and Bover (1995), who developed a linear GMM estimator of α on the basis of (24) and (28). Relative to Assumption A′, however, Assumption B only adds one moment restriction, which can be written as $E[(y_{i3} - \alpha y_{i2}) \Delta y_{i2}] = 0$. In terms of the parameters c_t, the implication of Assumption B is that $c_1 = \cdots = c_{T-1}$ if we move from Assumption A or that $c_1 = \phi/(1-\alpha)$ if we move from Assumption A′. This gives rise to Model 2, in which Ω depends on the $(T+2) \times 1$ parameter vector $\theta = (\alpha, \phi, \omega_{11}, \ldots, \omega_{TT})'$. Notice that with $T = 3$, α is overidentified under Assumption B.

The basic specification can be restricted further in various ways. For example, we could consider time series homoscedasticity of the form $E(v_{it}^2) = \sigma^2$ for $t = 2, \ldots, T$ and stationarity of the variance of the initial conditions. The combination of these assumptions with the previous ones would give rise to additional models, some of which were discussed in detail by Ahn and Schmidt (1995). In the simulations, however, we concentrate on Models 1 and 2 because they embody linear IV restrictions that have been found most useful in applications. Although for Model 1 we shall simulate the robust and nonrobust estimators discussed in Section 1, for Model 2 we shall only report robust estimates—that is, the Arellano and Bover (1995) GMM estimator and its symmetrically normalized and continuously

Table 3. Model 2: Robust Estimates

		$\alpha = .5$				$\alpha = .8$			
		GMM2	SNM2	LIML2	MDE	GMM2	SNM2	LIML2	MDE
					$T = 4$				
$\sigma_\eta^2 = 0$	Median	.50	.51	.51	.51	.79	.81	.81	.81
	% bias	.8	2.0	1.9	1.2	.9	1.5	1.7	.7
	iqr	.15	.15	.15	.07	.17	.17	.17	.05
	iq80	.28	.28	.29	.14	.32	.31	.33	.09
	MAE	.07	.07	.08	.03	.08	.08	.09	.02
$\sigma_\eta^2 = .2$	Median	.50	.51	.51	.51	.79	.82	.81	.81
	% bias	.9	2.5	1.9	1.8	.7	2.7	1.5	1.3
	iqr	.17	.17	.19	.19	.20	.19	.22	.21
	iq80	.31	.32	.33	.33	.37	.36	.40	.36
	MAE	.09	.09	.09	.09	.10	.10	.11	.10
$\sigma_\eta^2 = 1$	Median	.52	.54	.51	.51	.85	.87	.81	.82
	% bias	3.1	8.4	1.93	2.3	5.7	9.2	·1.0	2.1
	iqr	.19	.20	.21	.21	.19	.18	.25	.22
	iq80	.36	.37	.39	.39	.38	.37	.43	.40
	MAE	.09	.10	.11	.11	.11	.11	.12	.10
					$T = 7$				
$\sigma_\eta^2 = 0$	Median	.49	.50	.50	.51	.78	.80	.80	.80
	% bias	2.9	.1	.6	1.2	3.0	.5	.6	.4
	iqr	.08	.08	.09	.06	.09	.08	.09	.04
	iq80	.15	.16	.17	.11	.17	.16	.18	.08
	MAE	.04	.04	.04	.03	.05	.04	.05	.02
$\sigma_\eta^2 = .2$	Median	.49	.50	.50	.50	.78	.80	.81	.81
	% bias	2.6	.9	.6	.6	2.4	.5	1.1	1.1
	iqr	.09	.09	.10	.10	.11	.10	.12	.12
	iq80	.18	.18	.20	.20	.20	.19	.22	.22
	MAE	.05	.05	.05	.05	.05	.05	.06	.06
$\sigma_\eta^2 = 1$	Median	.50	.51	.50	.50	.83	.85	.81	.81
	% bias	.7	2.9	.2	.4	3.5	5.7	.7	1.8
	iqr	.10	.11	.11	.11	.12	.11	.14	.13
	iq80	.19	.20	.22	.22	.22	.21	.25	.25
	MAE	.05	.05	.05	.05	.07	.07	.07	.07

NOTE. See note to Table 1

updated counterparts. We do so because the combined set of moments in (24) and (28) lack a sequential structure, with the result that there is no simple optimal one-step estimator under "classical" errors.

The coefficient α together with the other free parameters in the covariance structure representations of the previous models can be jointly estimated by MD on the basis of the matrix of sample second-order moments $\hat{\Omega} = N^{-1}\sum_{i=1}^{N} y_i^T y_i^{T'}$. Such estimates have the same asymptotic distribution as the corresponding GMM estimators but may be cumbersome in more general conditional models because they need to solve a nonlinear optimization problem over a larger parameter space. It is of some interest, however, to compare their finite-sample performance with the SNM and LIML estimates of the random effects AR(1) model. Optimal MDE minimize a criterion of the form

$$c_d(\theta) = [\hat{\omega} - \omega(\theta)]' V_N^{-1} [\hat{\omega} - \omega(\theta)], \qquad (29)$$

where $V_N = N^{-1}\sum_{i=1}^{N} w_i w_i' - \hat{\omega}\hat{\omega}', \hat{\omega} = \text{vech}(\hat{\Omega})$ denotes the $T(T+1)/2$ vector containing the elements in the upper triangle of $\hat{\Omega}$, and similarly $\omega(\theta) = \text{vech}[\Omega(\theta)]$ and $\omega_i = \text{vech}(y_i^T y_i^{T-1'})$.

2.2 Monte Carlo Results

An important issue is how instrument quality affects the estimators. In Model 1, this depends on the values of α and $r = \sigma_\eta^2/\sigma^2$. To see this, note that under stationarity the correlation between Δy_{t-1} and y_{t-2} is $\rho = -(1-\alpha)[2(1-\alpha+(1+\alpha)r)]^{-1/2}$, which is decreasing in α and r. For this reason, we exclude from the simulations models with small values of α, which can be expected to perform relatively well. We consider cases with $\alpha = .5, .8; \sigma_\eta^2 = 0, .2, 1; T = 4, 7$; and $N = 100$. The variance of the random error σ^2 is kept equal to unity for all cases. For each experiment, we generated 1,000 samples of N independent observations of $(y_{i1}, \ldots, y_{iT})$ from the process

$$y_{i1} = (1-\alpha)^{-1}\eta_i + (1-\alpha^2)^{-1/2} v_{i1} \qquad (30)$$

and

$$y_{it} = \alpha y_{i(t-1)} + \eta_i + v_{it}, \qquad t = 2, \ldots, T, \qquad (31)$$

with $v_i = (v_{i1}, \ldots, v_{iT})' \sim \text{N}(0, I)$ and $\eta_i \sim \text{N}(0, \sigma_\eta^2)$ independent of v_i.

Tables 1 and 2 (pp. 39–40) report sample medians, percentage biases, interquantile ranges, and median absolute errors (MAE's) for GMM, SNM, and LIML estimators for Model 1 (means and standard deviations are not reported because the symmetrically normalized estimators can be expected to have infinite moments). Table 1 contains the results for the nonrobust estimators and Table 2 for the robust ones. Table 2 also reports the results for the MDE, which is also robust. Whereas LIML2 and MDE are one-step estimators, however, GMM2 and SNM2 are calculated in two steps. The weighting matrices of GMM2 and SNM2 are based on GMM1 residuals. SNM1 and LIML1 always have a smaller bias and a larger dispersion than GMM1. When $\sigma_\eta^2 = 0$, all estimators perform well, but when $\sigma_\eta^2 = .2$

Table 4. Model 1: Nonrobust Estimates, Quantiles of the t Statistics

	$T = 4$						$T = 7$					
	$\alpha = .5$			$\alpha = .8$			$\alpha = .5$			$\alpha = .8$		
	GMM1	*SNM1*	*LIML1*	*GMM1*	*SNM1*	*LIML1*	*GMM1*	*SNM1*	*LIML1*	*GMM1*	*SNM1*	*LIML1*
$\sigma_\eta^2 = 0$												
.05	−1.97	−1.84	−1.87	−2.16	−1.90	−2.03	−2.04	−1.66	−1.84	−2.26	−1.62	−1.95
.10	−1.54	−1.42	−1.44	−1.74	−1.46	−1.56	−1.65	−1.27	−1.46	−1.87	−1.25	−1.51
.25	−.86	−.74	−.75	−.98	−.73	−.78	−1.01	−.64	−.79	−1.23	−.61	−.82
.50	−.13	−.02	−.01	−.25	.00	−.01	−.32	.04	−.08	−.53	.06	−.07
.75	.53	.62	.64	.41	.59	.64	.37	.74	.64	.17	.73	.68
.90	1.08	1.17	1.22	.93	1.06	1.15	.98	1.33	1.26	.75	1.29	1.30
.95	1.41	1.48	1.53	1.20	1.30	1.41	1.33	1.70	1.65	1.10	1.61	1.67
$\sigma_\eta^2 = .2$												
.05	−2.05	−1.89	−1.95	−2.39	−2.00	−2.38	−2.12	−1.65	−1.92	−2.51	−1.57	−2.35
.10	−1.63	−1.47	−1.52	−1.95	−1.55	−1.88	−1.74	−1.27	−1.51	−2.13	−1.19	−1.86
.25	−.91	−.77	−.79	−1.22	−.79	−.99	−1.08	−.63	−.82	−1.51	−.56	−1.02
.50	−.18	−.04	−.03	−.44	−.03	−.06	−.39	.06	−.10	−.81	.09	−.13
.75	.48	.61	.64	.25	.47	.64	.30	.73	.62	−.12	.69	.71
.90	1.03	1.13	1.19	.71	.82	1.07	.90	1.33	1.27	.48	1.19	1.43
.95	1.33	1.42	1.50	.92	.99	1.27	1.24	1.65	1.61	.80	1.47	1.79
$\sigma_\eta^2 = 1$												
.05	−2.20	−1.98	−2.13	−2.68	−2.16	−2.83	−2.19	−1.62	−2.03	−2.74	−1.47	−3.18
.10	−1.74	−1.52	−1.64	−2.20	−1.64	−2.30	−1.83	−1.25	−1.62	−2.40	−1.11	−2.66
.25	−1.04	−.81	−.88	−1.52	−.89	−1.46	−1.18	−.61	−.91	−1.79	−.51	−1.52
.50	−.27	−.05	−.05	−.74	−.12	−.39	−.49	.07	−.13	−1.10	.12	−.28
.75	.40	.57	.66	−.01	.27	.55	.20	.73	.62	−.40	.65	.85
.90	.91	1.00	1.16	.46	.56	.95	.79	1.29	1.27	.20	1.05	1.69
.95	1.17	1.23	1.41	.65	.71	1.17	1.11	1.61	1.63	.49	1.27	2.10

NOTE. 10,000 replications $N = 100$, $\sigma_v^2 = 1$ The 5th, 10th, 25th, 50th, 75th, 90th, and 95th quantiles for the standard normal distribution are, respectively, −1.64, −1.28, −.67, 0, .67, 1.28, and 1.64

or 1, the differences in the distributions of GMM1 and the symmetrically normalized estimators become apparent: The higher σ_η^2 or α, the larger the negative bias of GMM1 for a given T, whereas SNM1 remains essentially median unbiased. The behavior of LIML1 is similar to that of SNM1, although in some cases it shows somewhat larger biases and dispersion. SNM1 and LIML1 have a larger interquartile range than GMM1, but the differences are small except in the almost unidentified cases (with $\alpha = .8$ and $T = 4$). The MAE's of the three estimators are of a similar magnitude, although those for GMM1 tend to be smaller than those for SNM1 or LIML1 with $T = 4$ and larger with $T = 7$.

Turning to Table 2, GMM2 and SNM2 exhibit a very similar behavior to GMM1 and SNM1, respectively. LIML2, which is the robust continuously updated GMM estimator, is virtually median unbiased in all the experiments, although it tends to have a larger MAE than SNM2. LIML2 was calculated by numerical optimization, and we found some instances of nonconvergence. Out of 1,000 replications, we found 86 cases of nonconvergence for the experiment with $\alpha = .8, \sigma_\eta^2 = 1$, and $T = 4$, and 7 cases in each of the experiments with $\alpha = .8, \sigma_\eta^2 = .2, T = 4$, and $\alpha = .8, \sigma_\eta^2 = 1, T = 7$.

The MDE has a smaller interquartile range than GMM2, SNM2, or LIML2, a difference that is especially noticeable for $T = 4$ (with $\sigma_\eta^2 = 0$ and $\alpha = .8$, the interquartile range of the MDE is about three times smaller than that of the other estimators). As far as median bias is concerned, the MDE is practically unbiased when $\alpha = .5$, but exhibits some larger biases when σ_η^2 is not 0 and $\alpha = .8$. In common with LIML2, however, we also found several cases of nonconvergence for MDE, with all the cases arising almost exclusively in the experiments with $\alpha = .8$. Specifically, with $\alpha = .8$ and $T = 4$, we encountered 36, 46, and 86 cases of nonconvergence for $\sigma_\eta^2 = 0, .2$, and 1, respectively, whereas, with $T = 7$, the number of cases, given in the same order, were 22, 35, and 118.

With $T = 7$, Tables 1 and 2 clearly indicate that when $N = 100$ there is information in the data to estimate α with sufficient precision but that, contrary to SNM or LIML, GMM estimates may still be substantially biased.

The evidence from Tables 1 and 2 suggests that Hillier's basic results for ordinary and symmetrically normalized 2SLS estimators may have a wider applicability. In effect, GMM2 and SNM2, unlike 2SLS, are not only functions of the second moments of the data but also of the fourth-order moments that enter the weighting matrix of the moment conditions.

Model 1 is the leading case from the point of view that IV estimators of structural equations with predetermined instruments tend to rely on orthogonality conditions that are similar to those in Model 1.

Table 3 (p. 41) presents the results for Model 2, which makes use of the restrictions derived from Assumptions A and B. This model incorporates the quadratic orthogonality conditions given in (42). By adding the stationarity restrictions, however, the entire list of moment conditions admits a linear representation (Ahn and Schmidt 1995), so that GMM2 in Table 3 is a linear IV estimator (as proposed by Arellano and Bover 1995). All the estimators in this ta-

Table 5. Model 1: Robust Estimates, Quantiles of the t Statistics

	T = 4						T = 7					
	$\alpha = .5$			$\alpha = .8$			$\alpha = .5$			$\alpha = .8$		
	GMM2	SNM2	LIML2	GMM2	SNM2	LIML2	GMM2	SNM2	LIML2	GMM2	SNM2	LIML2
						$\sigma_\eta^2 = 0$						
.05	−2.04	−1.97	−1.91	−2.25	−2.12	−2.07	−2.49	−2.24	−2.34	−2.74	−2.24	−2.45
.10	−1.61	−1.54	−1.47	−1.80	−1.62	−1.55	−2.01	−1.73	−1.82	−2.28	−1.79	−1.90
.25	−.87	−.78	−.73	−1.00	−.80	−.75	−1.22	−.91	−.92	−1.47	−.94	−.92
.50	−.11	.01	.06	−.22	.02	.05	−.33	.00	.08	−.57	−.03	.09
.75	.58	.71	.76	.45	.72	.73	.56	.91	1.05	.28	.85	1.06
.90	1.18	1.32	1.35	1.00	1.28	1.26	1.30	1.67	1.89	1.03	1.62	1.89
.95	1.54	1.69	1.71	1.30	1.61	1.55	1.76	2.12	2.42	1.46	2.05	2.37
						$\sigma_\eta^2 = .2$						
.05	−2.15	−2.08	−2.00	−2.68	−2.71	−2.48	−2.62	−2.31	−2.42	−3.28	−2.53	−2.98
.10	−1.71	−1.62	−1.55	−2.15	−2.02	−1.84	−2.11	−1.79	−1.86	−2.73	−1.97	−2.22
.25	−.93	−.83	−.76	−1.28	−1.01	−.88	−1.30	−.93	−.95	−1.88	−1.05	−1.11
.50	−.17	.02	.05	−.43	−.05	.04	−.41	−.02	.06	−.97	−.11	.05
.75	.54	.71	.77	.29	.75	.73	.45	.87	1.04	−.05	.81	1.15
.90	1.13	1.31	1.34	77	1.32	1.15	1.24	1.68	1.90	.70	1.60	2.01
.95	1.44	1.65	1.66	.98	1.76	1.37	1.69	2.13	2.44	1.13	2.06	2.46
						$\sigma_\eta^2 = 1$						
.05	−2.36	−2.35	−2.26	−3.17	−4.44	−3.01	−2.76	−2.41	−2.55	−3.82	−3.10	−3.72
.10	−1.83	−1.78	−1.67	−2.58	−3.22	−2.26	−2.27	−1.88	−1.96	−3.26	−2.37	−2.77
.25	−1.09	−.95	−.82	−1.68	−1.67	−1.14	−1.44	−.98	−1.01	−2.35	−1.31	−1.39
.50	−.25	−.05	.03	−.78	−.33	.00	−.56	−.05	.03	−1.37	−.19	.00
.75	.46	.73	.77	.01	.70	.70	.32	.87	1.07	−.43	.82	1.26
.90	.98	1.31	1.30	.50	1.51	1.11	1.09	1.66	1.94	.35	1.68	2.14
.95	1.28	1.63	1.56	.70	2.52	1.40	1.51	2.11	2.46	.76	2.14	2.59

NOTE See note to Table 4.

Table 6. Employment Equations: Robust Estimates From the U.K. Sample

Independent variables	Model A				Model B		
	GMM2	*SNM2*	*LIML2*	*Indirect GMM2**	*GMM2*	*SNM2*	*LIML2*
$\Delta n_{i(t-1)}$	.800	1.596	1.900	1.214	.825	2.186	.836
	(.048)	(.105)	(.173)		(.056)	(.216)	(.060)
$\Delta n_{i(t-2)}$	−.116	−.384	.105	−.282	−.074	−.455	.344
	(.021)	(.045)	(.053)		(.020)	(.077)	(.038)
Δw_{it}	−.640	−1.897	.507	−4.638			
	(.054)	(.160)	(.224)				
$\Delta w_{i(t-1)}$	.564	2.138	.487	1.567	.431	2.841	.615
	(.066)	(.142)	(.222)		(.076)	(.312)	(.080)
Δk_{it}	.219	.238	−1.353	.604			
	(.051)	(.089)	(.198)				
$\Delta k_{i(t-1)}$					−.077	−.787	−.235
					(.045)	(.126)	(.049)
Δys_{it}	.890	1.747	.674	3.105			
	(.098)	(.204)	(.228)				
$\Delta ys_{i(t-1)}$	−.874	−2.897	−.006	−4.101	−.115	−2.438	−.427
	(.105)	(.229)	(.312)		(.100)	(.358)	(.112)
$\Delta ys_{i(t-2)}$					.095	1.511	.126
					(.091)	(.266)	(.101)
Sargan test (df)	63.0 (50)	67.1 (50)	44.5 (50)	62.8 (50)	68.3 (51)	66.5 (51)	57.8 (51)
				R^2's for IV's			
$\Delta n_{i(t-1)}$	.271				.269		
$\Delta w_{it)}$	.193						
$\Delta w_{i(t-1)}$	.309				.289		
Δk_{it}	.108						
$\Delta k_{i(t-1)}$					.158		

*Dependent variable is Δw_{it}

NOTE The dependent variable is Δn_{it} The sample period is 1979–1984 (140 companies) Time dummies are included in all equations. Asymptotic standard errors robust to heteroscedasticity are reported in parentheses. Model A treats $\Delta n_{i(t-1)}$, Δw_{it}, $\Delta w_{i(t-1)}$, and Δk_{it} as endogenous. Model B treats $\Delta n_{i(t-1)}$, $\Delta w_{i(t-1)}$, and $\Delta k_{i(t-1)}$ as endogenous The instrument set for Models A and B includes lags of employment dated ($t-2$) and earlier, lags of wages and capital dated ($t-2$) and ($t-3$), and the levels and first differences of firm real sales and firm real stocks dated ($t-2$). The instrument set for all the AR(2) models includes lags of employment dated ($t-2$) and earlier, and for those in the first three columns also lags of wages dated ($t-2$) and earlier The R^2's for the IV's denote the partial R^2 between the instruments and each endogenous explanatory variable once the exogenous variables included in the equation have been partialled out.

ble exhibit small median biases and dispersions, although when there is a difference in MAE it favors the MDE. The differences between GMM2, SNM2, and LIML2 are small in most cases without a clear pattern in the relation, except for the fact that LIML2 tended to have a smaller bias and it was the estimator with the highest dispersion in all the experiments.

Both GMM2 and SNM2 are two-step estimators based on one-step GMM residuals that use all the orthogonality conditions from Model 2, and the inverse of the second moments of the instruments as the weighting matrix. Notice that this one-step estimator is not asymptotically efficient, not even under classical errors. From calculations based on alternative residuals (not reported), we found that the results for GMM2 and SNM2 were sensitive to the choice of one-step residuals, an issue which does not arise for LIML2 or MDE because they are calculated in one step. (We obtained results for GMM2 and SNM2 estimates based on GMM1 residuals from Model 1 and one-step residuals from Model 2, but using an identity as the weighting matrix. As expected, the impact of using Model 1 residuals was more important when Model 1 estimates were highly imprecise.)

Table 7. Employment Equations: Robust Estimates From the U.K. Sample

Independent variables	AR(2) Models					
	GMM2	*SNM2*	*LIML2*	*GMM2*	*SNM2*	*LIML2*
$\Delta n_{i(t-1)}$	.691	1.635	1.412	.320	.827	.092
	(.051)	(.074)	(.067)	(.053)	(.065)	(.047)
$\Delta n_{i(t-2)}$	−.114	−.439	−.348	.022	−.094	.218
	(.026)	(.039)	(.025)	(.022)	(.032)	(.019)
$\Delta w_{i(t-1)}$	.598	1.958	.297			
	(.070)	(.095)	(.073)			
$\Delta w_{i(t-2)}$	.013	−.075	−.163			
	(.036)	(.053)	(.041)			
Sargan test (df)	65.9 (50)	71.3 (50)	48.8 (50)	32.8 (25)	31.3 (25)	31.7 (25)
			R^2's for IV's			
$\Delta n_{i(t-1)}$	.216			.152		

NOTE. See note to Table 6

Finally, it is possible to make comparisons across tables. The interquartile ranges become smaller if we move from Tables 1 and 2 to Table 3. Indeed, the efficiency gains from enforcing stationarity restrictions are always substantial for all the estimators, but they are particularly important in the cases with $\alpha = .8$ and $\sigma_\eta^2 = .2$ or 1.

We also investigated the finite-sample distributions of the standardized one- and two-step GMM, SNM and LIML "t statistics" for Model 1 of the form $t = \hat{v}^{-1/2}(\hat{\alpha} - \alpha)$, where $\hat{\alpha}$ is an estimator and $\hat{v}$ is the corresponding estimated asymptotic variance. The t statistics are asymptotically N(0,1). Because the usual tests of hypotheses and confidence intervals rely on this approximation, it is useful to check the accuracy of the approximation for the sample sizes and parameter values considered previously.

Tables 4 and 5 (pp. 42–43) report finite-sample quantiles of the t statistics based on 10,000 replications for nonrobust and robust estimates, respectively. We use a larger number of replications because in this case the .90 and .95 quantiles in the upper tail of the distribution are of special interest. The median shows that the distributions of the GMM t statistics are shifted to the left, with the absolute value of the shift increasing with α, σ_η^2, and T. In contrast, the distributions of the SNM and LIML t statistics are centered at values that are most of the time very close to 0. Turning to the .90 and .95 quantiles, when $T = 4$ the differences with the corresponding N(0,1) quantiles are always smaller for the SNM and LIML t statistics than for the GMM, sometimes by a wide margin. This is true for both nonrobust and robust t ratios, although the latter show higher interquantile ranges. When $T = 7$, the contrast between robust and nonrobust t ratios becomes more marked. Although the normal approximation works reasonably well for SNM1 and LIML1, the distributions of SNM2 and LIML2 exhibit thick tails. The distributions of the GMM t ratios with $T = 7$ remain skewed, but whereas the .95 quantiles are very low for GMM1, those for GMM2 tend to be closer to the normal values than those from SNM2 or LIML2.

3. EMPIRICAL ILLUSTRATIONS

Our first illustration of the previous methods proceeds by reestimating the employment equations presented by Arellano and Bond (1991) using symmetrically normalized and indirect GMM estimators. The Arellano–Bond dataset consists of an unbalanced panel of 140 quoted companies from the United Kingdom, whose main activity is manufacturing and for which seven, eight, or nine continuous annual

Table 8. VAR Estimates for Employment and Wage Equations From the Spanish Sample

Independent variables	"Model 1" restrictions					
	GMM2	*SNM2*	*LIML2*	*GMM2*	*SNM2*	*LIML2*
			Δn_{it} equation			
$\Delta n_{i(t-1)}$	.842	1.087	1.004	.748	.813	.832
	(.669; 1.015)	(.894; 1.280)	(.830; 1.178)	(.575; .921)	(.636; .988)	(.661; 1.002)
	[.712; 1.209]	[.959; 1.485]		[.505; .976]	[.629; 1.092]	
$\Delta n_{i(t-2)}$	−.003	−.074	−.049	.038	.030	.027
	(−.060; .054)	(−.140; −.008)	(−.110; .012)	(−.005; .081)	(−.015; .075)	(−.018; .072)
	[−.146; .028]	[- .244; −.039]		[−.027; .084]	[−.046; .073]	
$\Delta w_{i(t-1)}$	.078	.222	.177			
	(−.086; .242)	(.046; .398)	(.016; .338)			
	[−.006; .412]	[.124; .624]				
$\Delta w_{i(t-2)}$	−.053	−.074	−.068			
	(−.102; −.004)	(−.127; −.021)	(−.121; −.015)			
	[−.116; −.002]	[−.138; −.020]				
Sargan test (df)	36.9 (36)	37.2 (36)	35.5 (36)	14.4 (18)	13.5 (18)	13.0 (18)
			R^2's for IV's			
$\Delta n_{i(t-1)}$	.033			.022		
$\Delta w_{i(t-1)}$	.031					
			Δw_{it} equation			
$\Delta w_{i(t-1)}$	.178	.228	.063	.178	.228	.063
	(−.042; .398)	(−.008; .464)	(−.176; .302)	(−.042; .398)	(−.008; .464)	(−.176; .302)
	[−.075; .405]	[−.100; .482]		[−.144; .429]	[−.232; .519]	
$\Delta w_{i(t-2)}$	−.012	−.002	−.039	−.012	−.002	−.039
	(−.081; .049)	(−.066; .062)	(−.102; .024)	(−.081; .049)	(−.066; .062)	(−.102; .024)
	[−.076; .042]	[−.077; .052]		[−.089; .045]	[−.100; .060]	
Sargan test (df)	12.7 (18)	12.9 (18)	12.2 (18)	12.7 (18)	12.9 (18)	12.2 (18)
			R^2's for IV's			
$\Delta w_{i(t-1)}$	.019					

NOTE. The sample period is 1983–1990 (738 companies). Time dummies are included in all equations The instrument set for all the employment equations includes lags of employment dated ($t-2$) and earlier, and for those in the first three columns also lags of wages dated ($t-2$) and earlier. The instrument set for the wage equation includes lags of wages dated ($t-2$) and earlier The R^2's for the IV's denote the partial R^2 between the instruments and each endogenous explanatory variable once the exogenous variables included in the equation have been partialled out 95% asymptotic confidence intervals based on heteroscedasticity-robust standard errors are in parentheses, 95% moment-restricted bootstrap confidence intervals are in brackets The bootstrap confidence intervals for the equations in the first three columns are based on a distribution that satisfies a larger set of moment conditions than those in the last three columns The reason is that the former include lagged wages as instruments for the employment equation, which are absent from the latter.

observations are available for the period 1976–1984. The models are all log-linear relationships between the number of employees, the average real wage, the stock of capital, a measure of industry output, lagged values of the previous variables, time dummies, and company effects. The reader is referred to the Arellano and Bond article for a detailed description of the models and the data.

Table 6 (pp. 44) contains the results for two different models estimated in first differences using IV's. Model A includes contemporaneous wage and capital variables, which are treated as endogenous along with the first lag of employment. In this model, lagged sales and stocks are used as outside instruments in addition to lags of the endogenous variables included in the equation. Model B only includes lagged values of wages and capital, and it could be interpreted as an approximated Euler equation for employment with quadratic adjustment costs. Columns labeled GMM2 reproduce some of the results obtained by Arellano and Bond. The SNM2 and LIML2 estimates are calculated as described in Section 1, and for Model A there is an additional column containing indirect GMM2 estimates that were obtained by normalizing to unity the coefficient of contemporaneous wages. Finally, Table 7 (p. 44) presents GMM2, SNM2, and LIML2 estimates of some simple second-order autoregressive [AR(2)] models for employment with and without the inclusion of lagged wages.

As Tables 6 and 7 show, SNM2, LIML2 and indirect GMM2 estimates are mostly far apart from the direct GMM2 estimates. These results uncover the fact that the GMM2 estimates from the dataset of U.K. firms are probably much less reliable than what their estimated asymptotic standard errors would suggest.

Our second empirical illustration is based on a similar but larger balanced panel of 738 Spanish manufacturing companies, for which there are available annual observations for the period 1983–1990 (see the Appendix for a description of these data). We consider a bivariate VAR model for the logarithms of employment and wages. The employment equation contains both lagged employment and lagged wages, but the wage equation only includes its own lags. This model can be regarded as the reduced form of an intertemporal model of employment determination under rational expectations (see Sargent 1978). To obtain the reduced form, an AR(2) process for log wages is assumed, and the Euler equation in the log of employment for the optimal contingency plans is solved.

Table 8 (p. 45) presents GMM2, SNM2, and LIML2 estimates of the two equations, using only lagged variables in levels as instruments for equations in first-differences (the basic set of moment conditions that we called "Model 1"), and Table 9 contains the estimates that add lagged variables in first-differences as instruments for equations in levels (i.e., including the stationarity restrictions of "Model 2"). We also report estimates of a univariate AR(2) process for employment for the two models (nonrobust estimates are not reported but are available on request).

In addition to asymptotic confidence intervals, for GMM2 and SNM2 we calculated 95% semiparametric bootstrap confidence intervals based on 1,000 replications from the empirical distribution function of the data subject to the moment restrictions (Back and Brown 1993). Following Brown and Newey (1992), we drew the bootstrap samples from the mass-point distribution that estimated the probability of the ith observation as $\hat{p}_i = 1/[1 + \hat{\mu}'\psi(y_i, \hat{\delta})]N$, where

$$\hat{\mu} = \arg\min_{\mu} N^{-1} \sum_{i=1}^{N} \log[1 + \mu'\psi(y_i, \hat{\delta})]^2 \qquad (32)$$

and $\psi(y_i, \hat{\delta})$ is the vector of orthogonality conditions for observation i evaluated at the appropriate parameter estimates. (We were unable to obtain bootstrap confidence intervals for LIML2 due to computing limitations, because each evaluation of LIML2 required numerical optimization over a larger parameter space including time dummies.)

Table 8 (p. 45) contains some interesting results. GMM2 estimates of Model 1 are still different from SNM2 and LIML2 estimates but by a smaller margin than the corresponding estimates for the U.K. panel. The differences become even smaller for the univariate employment estimates that are based on half the number of moments used for the estimates in the first three columns. On the other hand, the estimates of Model 2 in Table 9 appear to be more precise, presumably because the additional orthogonality conditions are highly informative. In this case, GMM2 and SNM2 estimates provide very similar results. The Sargan statistics,

Table 9. VAR Estimates for Employment and Wage Equations From the Spanish Sample

Independent variables	"Model 2" restrictions		
	GMM2	SNM2	LIML2
	Δn_{it} equation		
$\Delta n_{i(t-1)}$	1.163	1.208	1.624
	(1.112; 1.214)	(1.137; 1.279)	(1.424; 1.824)
	[1.132; 1.218]	[1.143; 1.229]	
$\Delta n_{i(t-2)}$	−.135	−.142	−.160
	(−.172; −.098)	(−.185; −.099)	(−.231; −.089)
	[−.197; −.108]	[−.206; −.117]	
$\Delta w_{i(t-1)}$	.121	.116	.058
	(.086; .156)	(.077; .155)	(−.001; .117)
	[.091; .161]	[.094; .164]	
$\Delta w_{i(t-2)}$	−.132	−.151	−.242
	(−.171; −.093)	(−.194; −.108)	(−.313; −.171)
	[−.173; −.101]	[−.177; −.101]	
Sargan test (df)	80.1 (48)	69.1 (48)	50.3 (48)
	Δw_{it} equation		
$\Delta w_{i(t-1)}$	.854	.873	.869
	(.815; .893)	(.834; .912)	(.828; .911)
	[.825; .902]	[.828; .905]	
$\Delta w_{i(t-2)}$	.152	.138	.141
	(.105; .199)	(.089; .187)	(.090; .192)
	[.099; .186]	[.094; .183]	
Sargan test (df)	71.4 (24)	72.2 (24)	71.4 (24)

NOTE: The sample period is 1983–1990 (738 companies). Time dummies are included in all equations. The instrument set for the employment equations includes lags of employment and wages dated ($t - 2$) and earlier for errors in first differences, and lags of employment and wages in first differences dated ($t - 1$) for errors in levels. The instrument set for the wage equations is similar, but excludes lagged employment in levels and first differences. GMM2 and SNM2 are two-step estimates based on one-step GMM residuals that use all the orthogonality restrictions from Model 2 and the inverse of the second moments of the instruments as the weighting matrix. 95% asymptotic confidence intervals based on heteroscedasticity-robust standard errors are in parentheses; 95% moment-restricted bootstrap confidence intervals are in brackets.

Table 10. VAR Estimates for Employment and Wage Equations From the Spanish Sample

Independent variables	*GMM2*	*SNM2*	*LIML2*	*GMM2*	*SNM2*	*LIML2*
			Δn_{it} *equation*			
$\Delta n_{i(t-1)}$	.788	1.160	1.002	.441	.815	1.517
	(.610; .966)	(.888; 1.432)	(.777; 1.227)	(.167; .715)	(.509; 1.121)	(1.081; 1.952)
	[.528; 1.248]	[.932; 1.903]		[.217; 0.983]	[.424; 1.214]	
$\Delta n_{i(t-2)}$	−.042	−.206	−.181	.063	.003	−.170
	(−.109; .025)	(−.306; −.106)	(−.271; −.091)	(.002; .124)	(−.062; .069)	(−.268; −.072)
	[−.265; −.008]	[−.567; −.120]		[−.060; .120]	[−.138; .090]	
$\Delta w_{i(t-1)}$	.337	.650	.675			
	(.151; .523)	(.371; .929)	(.452; .898)			
	[.099; .680]	[.300; 1.048]				
$\Delta w_{i(t-2)}$	.001	−.040	−.018			
	(−.065; .067)	(−.120; .040)	(−.098; .062)			
	[−.150; .059]	[−.261; .006]				
Sargan test (df)	30.2 (36)	23.0 (36)	24.8 (36)	23.3 (18)	24.3 (18)	16.5 (18)
			R^2*'s for IV's:*			
$\Delta n_{i(t-1)}$	.064			.040		
$\Delta w_{i(t-1)}$	.080					
			Δw_{it} *Equation*			
$\Delta w_{i(t-1)}$	−.612	−1.198	−1.246	−.612	−1.198	−1.246
	(−.984; −.240)	(−1.442; −.953)	(−1.509; −.983)	(−.984; −.240)	(−1.442; −.953)	(−1.509; −.983)
	[−.962; .359]	[−3.512; 2.492]		[−.954; .402]	[−4.893; 4.932]	
$\Delta w_{i(t-2)}$	−.120	−.270	−.231	−.120	−.270	−.231
	(−.231; −.009)	(−.349; −.191)	(−.319; −.143)	(−.231; −.009)	(−.349; −.191)	(−.319; −.143)
	[−.232; .102]	[−.627; .348]		[−.239; .183]	[−1.202; .993]	
Sargan test (df)	17.3 (18)	11.0 (18)	9.3 (18)	17.3 (18)	11.0 (18)	9.3 (18)
			R^2*'s for IV's*			
$\Delta w_{i(t-1)}$	.023					

NOTE: The sample period is 1983–1990 (random subsample of 200 companies). See note to Table 8.

however, indicate a clear rejection of the stationarity restrictions in both the employment and the wage equations. It is also noticeable that, although bootstrap confidence intervals are always larger than the asymptotic confidence intervals, the differences between the two are generally small. As for the LIML2 parameter estimates and Sargan statistics, they are similar to GMM2 and SNM2 for the wage equation but somewhat different for the employment equation. In particular, the first lagged employment coefficient estimate is higher, and the Sargan statistic turns out to be much smaller than those for the other estimators.

We reestimated Model 1 with a random subsample of 200 firms, which is similar to the size of the U.K. sample. Interestingly, some of the results (reported in Table 10) are closer to the U.K. results for similar specifications than those based on the full Spanish sample. In particular, the SNM2 estimates of the AR(2) model for employment are remarkably stable over the three datasets, but standard GMM2 estimates would be seriously downward biased in the smaller samples. Moreover, the discrepancies between asymptotic and bootstrap confidence intervals in the random subsample were greater than in the full sample. (Bootstrap standard errors for the U.K. unbalanced panel were not calculated because they would depend on a nontrivial specification of the empirical distribution function for the unbalanced observations.) In contrast, perhaps as a result of a higher probability of outliers in small samples, the LIML2 estimate of the leading coefficient in the AR(2) model for employment was a very small number in the U.K. sample and a very large one in the Spanish subsample of 200 firms, whereas it was similar to SNM2 for the full Spanish sample.

Finally, we simulated data as close as possible to the AR(2) employment equation to see if the findings that we obtained with the subsample of 200 companies were substantiated in the Monte Carlo simulations. Random errors and individual effects were generated from independent normal distributions with variances equal to the values estimated from the SNM2 residuals of the full Spanish sample. Because the estimated time effects showed very little variability, the constant was set to a common value for all periods given by the average estimated time effect in levels, although the estimates in the simulations included time dummies. As a consequence the model was stationary, and we generated (and discarded) 100 preliminary observations for each individual to minimize the impact of initial conditions. The results for GMM2 and SNM2 are reported in Table 11 and confirm the impression conveyed by the real data (unfortunately, we were unable to simulate LIML2 due to computing limitations). The SNM2 estimates are almost median unbiased, but GMM2 shows large downward biases, especially when $N = 200$. A comparison in terms of MAE's also favors SNM2 for both sample sizes and parameter estimates. Last, looking at the quantiles of the t ratios shown in the lower panel of Table 11, it appears that the N(0,1) approximation is reasonable for the SNM t ratios but not for the GMM t ratios.

Table 11. Monte Carlo Simulations for the AR(2) Model for Employment

		N = 738		N = 200	
		GMM2	SNM2	GMM2	SNM2
		Summary of estimates			
α_1	Median	.72	.82	.55	.82
	% bias	12.0	.3	32.2	.8
	iqr	.14	.15	.27	.28
	iq80	.28	.29	.56	.61
	MAE	.11	.08	.26	.14
α_2	Median	.01	.03	−.02	.02
	% bias	64.6	7.0	163.3	35.4
	iqr	.04	.04	.06	.08
	iq80	.07	.07	.11	.14
	MAE	.02	.02	.05	.04
		Quantiles of the t statistics			
α_1	.10	−2.44	−1.37	−3.61	−1.62
	.25	−1.75	−.74	−2.77	−.82
	.50	−1.01	.02	−1.84	.04
	.75	−.25	.77	−.97	.81
	.90	.41	1.33	−.21	1.42
α_2	.10	−2.22	−1.55	−2.93	−1.92
	.25	−1.48	−.82	−2.16	−1.05
	.50	−.78	−.08	−1.26	−.24
	.75	−.01	.60	−.45	.60
	.90	.62	1.19	.17	1.08

NOTE: α_1 = .813, α_2 = .030, γ = .777, σ_η^2 = .038, σ_v^2 = .01. 1,000 replications. % bias gives the percentage median bias for all estimates; iqr is the 75th–25th interquartile range; iq80 is the 90th–10th interquantile range; MAE denotes the median absolute error. The 10th, 25th, 50th, 75th, and 90th quantiles for the standard normal distribution are, respectively, −1.28, −.67, 0, .67, and 1.28.

4. CONCLUSIONS

There has recently been a renewed interest in the finite-sample properties of GMM estimators in various time series and cross-sectional contexts. Several works have emphasized the role of estimated weighting matrices for the properties of the estimators in small samples, and several alternative methods have been considered (Angrist and Krueger 1995; Angrist, Imbens, and Krueger 1995; Altonji and Segal 1996; Hansen et al. 1996; Imbens 1997). In contrast, in this article we have focused on the role of normalization rules for the finite-sample properties of GMM estimators that make use of standard two-step weighting matrices. Our work is motivated by the results of Hillier (1990), who argued that the alternative normalization rules adopted by LIML and 2SLS are at the basis of their different sampling behavior. Hillier showed that symmetrically normalized 2SLS has similar finite-sample properties to those of LIML. This result is interesting because, unlike LIML, symmetrically normalized 2SLS is a GMM estimator based on structural-form moment conditions, and therefore it can be easily extended to distribution-free environments and robust statistics.

In particular, symmetrically normalized 2SLS is well suited for application to the nonstandard IV situations that arise in linear panel-data models with predetermined variables, which are the models of interest in this article. These models are typically estimated in orthogonal deviations or first-differences using all the available lags as instruments. Usually, there are many instruments available, but they are of poor quality because they tend to be only weakly correlated with the first-differenced endogenous variables that appear in the equation.

In this article we have presented symmetrically normalized GMM (SNM) estimators for dynamic panel-data models that are asymptotically equivalent to ordinary optimal GMM estimators. A by-product of the estimation is a test statistic of overidentifying restrictions, based on a minimum eigenvalue calculation. We have also discussed the relation between robust and nonrobust SNM estimators and the LIML analogues. In our context, a nonrobust LIML analogue in orthogonal deviations is algebraically equivalent to an ordinary LIML estimator that solves a minimum eigenvalue problem. The robust LIML analogue, however, is the continuously updated GMM estimator proposed by Hansen et al. (1996), which no longer involves a simple minimum eigenvalue calculation.

We have reported Monte Carlo evidence on the performance of nonrobust and robust GMM, SNM, and LIML analogue estimates for an AR(1) model with individual effects. For this model we have considered two alternative sets of moment conditions, as discussed by Arellano and Bond (1991) and Arellano and Bover (1995). Because for these models the IV restrictions can be expressed as straightforward structures on the data covariance matrix, using these representations we have also calculated MD estimates for comparisons with the IV estimates. Our findings suggest that Hillier's basic results may have a wider applicability. In most cases, the differences in the behavior of SNM and LIML were small, and both had a smaller median bias and a larger interquartile range than GMM. The differences in dispersion with ordinary GMM were small, however, except in the almost unidentified cases.

Finally, as an empirical illustration, we have reported estimates of employment and wage equations from U.K. and Spanish firm panels. The results show that GMM estimates from the (smaller) U.K. panel can be very unreliable when the degree of overidentification is large. The results from the (larger) Spanish panel produce a closer agreement between ordinary and symmetrically normalized GMM estimates, although there is evidence that there can still be serious biases in GMM estimates. Some of these results are confirmed by simulating data as close as possible to the empirical data. Moment-restricted bootstrap confidence intervals show that asymptotic confidence intervals are often overoptimistic, and Sargan tests tend to reject the restrictions implied by the stationarity of initial conditions.

ACKNOWLEDGMENTS

We thank Richard Blundell, Stephen Bond, Gary Chamberlain, Guido Imbens, Whitney Newey, Enrique Sentana, Jim Stock, Ruey Tsay, an associate editor, three anonymous referees, and seminar audiences at Harvard, Northwestern, Nuffield College, Princeton, and University College London for valuable advice and helpful comments. An earlier version of this article was presented at the ESRC Econometric Study Group Annual Conference, Bristol, July 1994, and at the Econometric Society European Meeting in Maastricht, August 1994. The first author acknowledges research fund-

Table A.1. Descriptive Statistics

Variable	Mean	Median	Std. deviation	Minimum	Maximum
Employment	310.4	124.0	702.4	10.0	11,004.0
Real wage	1.86	1.75	.67	.32	6.66

ing from a CEMFI Ph.D. scholarship and from the Spanish DGES, Grant PB95-0292.

APPENDIX: DATA DESCRIPTION

The Spanish dataset is a balanced panel of 738 manufacturing companies recorded in the database of the Bank of Spain's Central Balance Sheet Office from 1983 to 1990. This survey contains information on firms' balance sheets and other complementary information, including data on employment and total wage bill. This survey started in 1982 with the collection of data from large companies with a tendency in subsequent years toward the addition of smaller companies. The database includes both quoted and nonquoted firms. The manufacturing firms included in this dataset represent more than 40% of the Spanish value added in manufacturing in 1985.

We selected firms reporting information during the whole period 1983–1990 that fulfilled several coherency conditions. All companies with negative values for net worth, capital stock, accumulated depreciation, accounting depreciation, labor costs, employment, sales, or output, or those whose book value of capital stock jumped by a factor greater than 3 from one year to the next were dropped from the sample. Finally, we concentrated on nonenergy manufacturing companies with a public share lower than 50%.

Variable Construction

Employment. Number of employees is disaggregated into permanent employees (those with long-term contracts) and temporary employees (those with short-term contracts). Total employment is calculated as the number of permanent employees, plus the average annual number of temporary employees (number of temporary employees during the year times the average number of weeks worked by temporary employees divided by 52).

Real Wage. The measure of the firm's annual average labor costs per employee is computed as the ratio of total wages and salaries (in million Spanish pesetas) to total number of employees. This measure was deflated using retail price indexes for each of the industries of the manufacturing sector (Source: Spain's Institute of National Statistics). Table A.1 shows some descriptive statistics for the employment and real-wage variables.

[Received July 1996. Revised June 1998.]

REFERENCES

Ahn, S., and Schmidt, P. (1995), "Efficient Estimation of Models for Dynamic Panel Data," *Journal of Econometrics*, 68, 5–27.

Altonji, J., and Segal, L. (1996), "Small-Sample Bias in GMM Estimation of Covariance Structures," *Journal of Business & Economic Statistics*, 14, 353–366.

Anderson, T. W. (1976), "Estimation of Linear Functional Relationships: Approximate Distributions and Connections with Simultaneous Equations in Econometrics," *Journal of the Royal Statistical Society*, Ser. B, 38, 1–20.

Anderson, T. W., Kunitomo, N., and Sawa, T. (1982), "Evaluation of the Distribution Function of the Limited Information Maximum Likelihood Estimator," *Econometrica*, 50, 1009–1027.

Angrist, J. D., Imbens, G. W., and Krueger, A. (1995), "Jackknife Instrumental Variables Estimation," Technical Working Paper 172, National Bureau of Economic Research, Cambridge, MA.

Angrist, J. D., and Krueger, A. B. (1995), "Split Sample Instrumental Variables Estimates of the Return to Schooling," *Journal of Business & Economic Statistics*, 13, 225–235.

Arellano, M., and Bond, S. R. (1991), "Some Tests of Specification for Panel Data: Monte Carlo Evidence and an Application to Employment Equations," *Review of Economic Studies*, 58, 277–297.

Arellano, M., and Bover, O. (1995), "Another Look at the Instrumental-Variable Estimation of Error-Components Models," *Journal of Econometrics*, 68, 29–51.

Back, K., and Brown, D. P. (1993), "Implied Probabilities in GMM Estimators," *Econometrica*, 61, 971–975.

Bekker, P. A. (1994), "Alternative Approximations to the Distributions of Instrumental Variable Estimators," *Econometrica*, 62, 657–681.

Blundell, R., and Bond, S. (1998), "Initial Conditions and Moment Restrictions in Dynamic Panel Data Models," *Journal of Econometrics*, 87, 115–143.

Bound, J., Jaeger, D. A., and Baker, R. (1995), "Problems With Instrumental Variables Estimation When the Correlation Between the Instruments and the Endogenous Explanatory Variable is Weak," *Journal of the American Statistical Association*, 90, 443–450.

Brown, B. W., and Newey, W. K. (1992), "Bootstrapping for GMM," unpublished manuscript.

Chamberlain, G. (1982), "Multivariate Regression Models for Panel Data," *Journal of Econometrics*, 18, 5–46.

——— (1992), "Comment: Sequential Moment Restrictions in Panel Data," *Journal of Business & Economic Statistics*, 10, 20–26.

Goldberger, A. S., and Olkin, I. (1971), "A Minimum-Distance Interpretation of Limited-Information Estimation," *Econometrica*, 39, 635–639.

Hansen, L. P. (1982), "Large Sample Properties of Generalized Method of Moments Estimators," *Econometrica*, 50, 1029–1054.

Hansen, L. P., Heaton, J., and Yaron, A. (1996), "Finite-Sample Properties of Some Alternative GMM Estimators," *Journal of Business & Economic Statistics*, 14, 262–280.

Hillier, G. H. (1990), "On the Normalization of Structural Equations: Properties of Direction Estimators," *Econometrica*, 58, 1181–1194.

Holtz-Eakin, D., Newey, W., and Rosen, H. (1988), "Estimating Vector Autoregressions With Panel Data," *Econometrica*, 56, 1371–1395.

Imbens, G. (1997), "One-Step Estimators for Over-identified Generalized Method of Moments Models," *Review of Economic Studies*, 64, 359–383.

Keller, W. J. (1975), "A New Class of Limited-Information Estimators for Simultaneous Equation Systems," *Journal of Econometrics*, 3, 71–92.

Kunitomo, N. (1980), "Asymptotic Expansions of the Distributions of Estimators in a Linear Functional Relationship and Simultaneous Equations," *Journal of the American Statistical Association*, 75, 693–700.

Malinvaud, E. (1970), *Statistical Methods of Econometrics*, Amsterdam: North-Holland.

Morimune, K. (1983), "Approximate Distributions of k-Class Estimators When the Degree of Overidentifiability Is Large Compared With the Sample Size," *Econometrica*, 51, 821–841.

Phillips, P. C. B. (1983), "Exact Small Sample Theory in the Simultaneous Equations Model," in *Handbook of Econometrics* (vol. I), eds. Z. Griliches and M. D. Intriligator, Amsterdam: North-Holland, pp. 449–516.

Qin, J., and Lawless, J. (1994), "Empirical Likelihood and General Estimating Equations," *The Annals of Statistics*, 22, 300–325.

Sargent, T. J. (1978), "Estimation of Dynamic Labor Demand Schedules Under Rational Expectations," *Journal of Political Economy*, 86, 1009–1044.

Staiger, D., and Stock, J. H. (1997), "Instrumental Variables Regression With Weak Instruments," *Econometrica*, 65, 557–586.

White, H. (1982), "Instrumental Variables Regression With Independent Observations," *Econometrica*, 50, 483–499.

[4]

ELSEVIER

Journal of Econometrics 68 (1995) 29–51

JOURNAL OF
Econometrics

Another look at the instrumental variable estimation of error-components models

Manuel Arellano*,[a], Olympia Bover[b]

[a]*CEMFI, 28014 Madrid, Spain*
[b]*Research Department, Bank of Spain, 28014 Madrid, Spain*

Abstract

This article develops a framework for efficient IV estimators of random effects models with information in levels which can accommodate predetermined variables. Our formulation clarifies the relationship between the existing estimators and the role of transformations in panel data models. We characterize the valid transformations for relevant models and show that optimal estimators are invariant to the transformation used to remove individual effects. We present an alternative transformation for models with predetermined instruments which preserves the orthogonality among the errors. Finally, we consider models with predetermined variables that have constant correlation with the effects and illustrate their importance with simulations.

Key words: Dynamic panel data; Predetermined instrumental variables; Orthogonal deviations; Unrestricted covariance matrix; Unit roots
JEL classification: C23

1. Introduction

The static error components model with both time-invariant and time-varying explanatory variables allowing for the correlation of some of these

* Corresponding author.

An earlier version of this paper was presented at the World Congress of the Econometric Society in Barcelona, August 1990, and at the Canadian Econometrics Study Group in Guelph, September 1990. It circulated as Centre for Economic Performance Discussion Paper No. 7 (London School of Economics, August 1990). We thank Steve Bond, David Card, Gary Chamberlain, Franco Peracchi, and specially Peter Schmidt for useful comments. All remaining errors are our own.

SSDI 0 3 0 4 4 0 7 6 9 4 0 1 6 4 2 D

variables with the unobservable individual effects was first considered by Hausman and Taylor (1981) – hereafter HT. Bhargava and Sargan (1983) – hereafter BS – studied the estimation of dynamic error components models, and also considered a model which contained a lagged dependent variable and allowed for correlation between some of the regressors and the effects. Subsequently, Amemiya and MaCurdy (1986) – hereafter AM – and Breusch, Mizon, and Schmidt (1989) – hereafter BMS – developed alternative instrumental variable (IV) estimators of the HT model that are more efficient than the original HT estimator. On the other hand, Anderson and Hsiao (1982), Holtz-Eakin, Newey, and Rosen (1988), and Arellano and Bond (1991), amongst others, considered the estimation of models with predetermined but no strictly exogenous variables by IV methods using lagged values of the predetermined variables as instruments for the equations in first differences. In these models it is usually maintained that all the explanatory variables are potentially correlated with the individual effects and therefore only estimators based on deviations of the original observations can be consistent. However, if there are instruments available that are not correlated with the effects, the levels of the variables contain information concerning the parameters of interest which if exploited could improve, sometimes crucially, the efficiency of the resulting estimates. In addition, this information in the levels may be sufficient to identify the coefficients of time-invariant explanatory variables that are correlated with the effects.

The purpose of this paper is to develop a framework for efficient IV estimators with information in levels which is capable of accommodating models with lagged dependent variables and other predetermined variables. In Section 2 we present a generalised method of moments formulation of HT, AM, and BMS-like estimators. Each particular model gives rise to a set of orthogonality restrictions on which estimation is to be based. We follow Amemiya and MaCurdy in exploiting transformations of the original equations in order to obtain convenient expressions of these restrictions. However, we formulate the matrices of instruments as block-diagonal matrices with as many blocks as the total number of time periods. In this way we can show that the optimal estimators are invariant to the choice of transformation. Another advantage of proceeding in this way is that we can obtain HT, AM, and BMS estimators with nonstandard or unrestricted covariance matrix without having to specify the appropriate GLS transformation and subsequent changes to the instrument set to avoid inconsistencies. As noted by AM, since different instruments are only valid for subsets of equations, GLS transformations are sensitive in this context: a particular IV matrix that is valid for some GLS transformation of the model may be invalid under a different GLS transformation. By specifying an IV matrix that effectively lists all the individual moment restrictions available we avoid this problem. We also calculate the Fisher information bound for the parameters of a conditional moment specification of the model in order to assess the efficiency of the class of GMM estimators formulated in Section 2.

Section 3 shows how the previous framework can easily accommodate dynamic models, and other models with predetermined variables and information in levels. We discuss an IV estimator which is asymptotically equivalent to the limited information maximum likelihood (LIML) estimator with unrestricted covariance matrix and correlated exogenous variables of BS. This clarifies the relationship between HT/AM/BMS and BS. We also extend these estimators to include lags of predetermined variables as additional instruments. We characterise the class of valid transformations in this context and show the invariance of the optimal estimators to a particular choice of transformation. We argue that a computationally convenient transformation for these models is forward orthogonal deviations. A closely related transformation has been used by Hayashi and Sims (1983) for time series models. This transformation leads to simple expressions of the estimators in terms of the vectors of instruments corresponding to individual time periods, and so it avoids the need to operate with the full block-diagonal IV matrix which may have an excessively large number of columns. Section 3 also formulates a GMM estimator for a general model with predetermined variables and information in levels.

Section 4 considers a model with predetermined variables that have constant correlation with the individual effects. As an illustration of the potential of these constraints, we report Monte Carlo simulations of IV estimators of a first-order stationary autoregression with random effects that exploit the orthogonality restrictions in levels. An estimator that only uses the restrictions in first differences is also simulated for comparisons. The section concludes with some remarks on the usefulness of predetermined variables that have constant correlation with the effects for the testing of unit roots in short panels. Finally, Section 5 contains the conclusions of the paper.

2. A method of moments formulation of Hausman–Taylor and related estimators with unrestricted covariance matrix

Let us consider the model

$$y_{it} = \beta' x_{it} + \gamma' f_i + u_{it}, \qquad t = 1, \dots, T, \quad i = 1, \dots, N,$$

$$u_{it} = \eta_i + v_{it},$$

$$\mathrm{E}(v_{it} | x_{i1}, \dots, x_{iT}, f_i, \eta_i) = 0. \tag{1}$$

So that the variables x_{it} and f_i are assumed to be strictly exogenous given the unobservable individual effect η_i. Under standard conditions, this assumption identifies β but not γ. The identification of γ is based on the following assumption:

$$\mathrm{E}(\eta_i | x_{1i1}, \dots, x_{1iT}, f_{1i}) = 0, \tag{2}$$

where we are using the partitions $x_{it} = (x'_{1it}, x'_{2it})'$ and $f_i = (f'_{1i}, f'_{2i})'$. Throughout, T is small and N is large. This model can be regarded as an intermediate case between the 'fixed effects' model in which all the explanatory variables are potentially correlated with the effects and therefore only estimators based on deviations of the observations can be consistent, and the standard uncorrelated 'random effects' model in which $x_{1it} = x_{it}$ and $f_{1i} = f_i$.

It is convenient to re-write (1) in the form

$$y_i = W_i\delta + u_i, \tag{3}$$

where $y_i = (y_{i1}, \dots, y_{iT})'$, $u_i = (u_{i1}, \dots, u_{iT})'$, $\delta = (\beta', \gamma')'$, $W_i = (X_i | \iota f_i')$, $X_i = (x_{i1}, \dots, x_{iT})'$ and ι is a $T \times 1$ vector of ones. Below, we also make use of the notation $\bar{x}_i' = T^{-1}\iota' X_i = (\bar{x}'_{1i}, \bar{x}'_{2i})$ and the vectors $v_i = (v_{i1}, \dots, v_{iT})'$, $x_i = (x'_{i1}, \dots, x'_{iT})'$, and $w_i = (x_i', f_i')'$.

In general, the matrix $E(u_i u_i' | w_i)$ will be unrestricted and depend on w_i:

$$E(u_i u_i' | w_i) = E(v_i v_i' | w_i) + E(\eta_i^2 | w_i)\iota\iota' = \Omega(w_i).$$

However, here we emphasize two cases with cross-sectional homoskedasticity in the sense that $E(u_i u_i' | w_i) = E(u_i u_i')$.[1] Firstly, the case of a constant unrestricted Ω, which allows for the possibility of autocorrelation and time series heteroskedasticity of arbitrary form in the v_{it}. Secondly, the traditional error components specification given by $\Omega = \sigma^2 I_T + \sigma_\eta^2 \iota\iota'$, where I_T is the identity matrix of order T.

We then transform the system of T equations using a nonsingular $T \times T$ transformation matrix,

$$H = \begin{bmatrix} K \\ T^{-1}\iota' \end{bmatrix},$$

where K is any $(T-1) \times T$ matrix of rank $(T-1)$ such that $K\iota = 0$. For example, K could be the first difference operator or the first $(T-1)$ rows of the within-group operator. The transformed errors are given by

$$u_i^+ = Hu_i = \begin{bmatrix} Ku_i \\ \bar{u}_i \end{bmatrix}. \tag{4}$$

This class of transformations performs a decomposition between 'within-group' and 'between-group' variation which is helpful in order to implement

[1] We assume that $E(\eta_i) = E(E(\eta_i | w_i)) = 0$. Notice that, provided the model contains a constant term, there is no loss of generality in this assumption. Thus, although it is always true that $E(u_i u_i') = \text{var}(u_i) = \text{var}(v_i) + \text{var}(\eta_i)\iota\iota'$, in general $E(u_i u_i' | w_i)$ and $\text{var}(u_i | w_i) = \text{var}(y_i | w_i)$ will differ as follows:

$$E(u_i u_i' | w_i) = \text{var}(u_i | w_i) + (E(\eta_i | w_i))^2 \iota\iota'.$$

orthogonality restrictions implied by the model. Specifically, since the first $(T-1)$ errors do not contain η_i, all exogenous variables (as well as nonlinear functions of those variables) are valid instruments for the first $(T-1)$ equations. Then, if m_i denotes a vector of a subset of variables of w_i (or linear combinations of those variables) assumed to be uncorrelated in levels and such that $\dim(m_i) \geqslant \dim(\gamma)$, a valid IV matrix for the complete transformed system is

$$Z_i = \begin{bmatrix} w_i' & & & 0 \\ & \ddots & & \\ & & w_i' & \\ 0 & & & m_i' \end{bmatrix}.$$

We can now write down the optimal GMM estimator of δ with constant Ω based on the moment equations,

$$\mathrm{E}(Z_i' H u_i) = 0,$$

which is given by

$$\hat{\delta} = [W'\bar{H}'Z(Z'\bar{H}\bar{\Omega}\bar{H}'Z)^{-1}Z'\bar{H}W]^{-1}W'\bar{H}'Z(Z'\bar{H}\bar{\Omega}\bar{H}'Z)^{-1}Z'\bar{H}y, \quad (5)$$

where $W = (W_1' \dots W_N')'$, $y = (y_1' \dots y_N')'$, $Z = (Z_1' \dots Z_N')'$, $\bar{H} = I_N \otimes H$, and $\bar{\Omega} = I_N \otimes \Omega$. In practice, the covariance matrix of the transformed system $\Omega^+ = H\Omega H'$ will be replaced by a consistent estimator. An unrestricted estimator of Ω^+ takes the form

$$\hat{\Omega}^+ = \frac{1}{N}\sum_{i=1}^{N} \hat{u}_i^+ \hat{u}_i^{+\prime},$$

where the $\hat{u}_i^+$ are residuals based on consistent preliminary estimates. Alternatively, we consider a restricted estimate $\tilde{\Omega}^+ = H\tilde{\Omega}H'$ with $\tilde{\Omega} = \tilde{\sigma}^2 I_T + \tilde{\sigma}_\eta^2 \imath\imath'$, where $\tilde{\sigma}^2$ and $\tilde{\sigma}_\eta^2$ denote consistent estimates of σ^2 and σ_η^2.

The estimator of HT is $\hat{\delta}$ with $\tilde{\Omega}^+$ and

$$m_i = (f_{1i}', \bar{x}_{1i}')',$$

whereas the estimator of AM is $\hat{\delta}$ with $\tilde{\Omega}^+$ and

$$m_i = (f_{1i}'\ x_{1i1}' \dots x_{1iT}')'.$$

BS and BMS also exploited the additional moment restrictions that arise if it is assumed that the correlation between x_{2it} and η_i is constant over time. In this case, the deviations from time means $\tilde{x}_{2it} = x_{2it} - \bar{x}_{2i}$ are valid instruments for the last equation of the transformed system. A stronger conditional expectation version of this assumption along the lines of (2) is

$$\mathrm{E}(\eta_i \mid x_{1i}, f_{1i}, \tilde{x}_{2i}) = 0. \quad (6)$$

Setting

$$m_i = (f'_{1i}\ x'_{1i1} \dots x'_{1iT}\ \tilde{x}'_{2i2} \dots \tilde{x}'_{2iT})'$$

and using $\tilde{\Omega}^+$, $\hat{\delta}$ gives the estimator of BMS. Moreover, if all variables are uncorrelated with the effects, we can set $m_i = w_i$ in which case $\hat{\delta}$ with $\tilde{\Omega}^+$ becomes the GLS estimator of Balestra and Nerlove (1966). On the other hand, if all variables are correlated with the effects, the levels equation drops out, the coefficients γ are unidentified and estimation of β is based on $\mathrm{E}(Z'_{di}Ku_i) = 0$ with $Z_{di} = I_{(T-1)} \otimes w'_i$. In the case of restricted Ω since $K\Omega K' = \sigma^2 KK'$, letting $\bar{K} = I_N \otimes K$, $X = (X'_1 \dots X'_N)'$, and $Z_d = (Z'_{d1} \dots Z'_{dN})'$, the resulting estimator is

$$\hat{\beta} = [X'\bar{K}'Z_d(Z'_d\bar{K}\bar{K}'Z_d)^{-1}Z'_d\bar{K}X]^{-1}X'\bar{K}'Z_d(Z'_d\bar{K}\bar{K}'Z_d)^{-1}Z'_d\bar{K}y,$$

which can be shown to coincide with the within-group estimator.

It is interesting to notice that having chosen a block-diagonal form for Z_i, $\hat{\delta}$ is invariant to the choice of transformation K. To prove this assertion we can use the following simple fact in GMM estimation. The optimal estimator of θ based on $\mathrm{E}[\xi_i(\theta)] = 0$ minimizes

$$s = (\Sigma_i \xi_i)' \hat{A}^{-1} (\Sigma_i \xi_i),$$

where $\hat{A}$ is a consistent estimator of $\mathrm{E}(\xi_i \xi'_i)$. If we now consider $\xi^*_i = F\xi_i$ where F is a nonsingular transformation matrix, it turns out that the optimal estimator of θ based on ξ^*_i that minimizes

$$s^* = (\Sigma_i \xi^*_i)' \hat{A}^{*-1} (\Sigma_i \xi^*_i)$$

is numerically the same estimator as the one based on ξ_i provided that $\hat{A}^* = F\hat{A}F'$ since $s = s^*$. In our case

$$\xi_i = Z'_i H u_i = \begin{bmatrix} Ku_i \otimes w_i \\ \bar{u}_i m_i \end{bmatrix} = \begin{bmatrix} K \otimes I_{p_1} & 0 \\ 0 & T^{-1}\iota' \otimes I_{p_2} \end{bmatrix} \begin{bmatrix} \mathrm{vec}(u_i w'_i) \\ \mathrm{vec}(u_i m'_i) \end{bmatrix}, \quad (7)$$

where p_1 and p_2 are the number of elements in w_i and m_i, respectively, and the vec operator stacks the elements of a matrix by rows. Suppose that an alternative transformation $H^* = (K^{*\prime}\ k^*\iota')'$ is used. Letting $K^* = \Phi K$ and $k^* = \varphi T^{-1}$ we can write

$$\xi^*_i = Z'_i H^* u_i = F\xi_i,$$

where

$$F = \begin{bmatrix} \Phi \otimes I_{p_1} & 0 \\ 0 & \varphi I_{p_2} \end{bmatrix}.$$

So that any valid transformation leads to the same estimator.

This is useful because in this way we can obtain HT, AM, and BMS-like estimators easily with various specifications for Ω without having to specify the appropriate $\Omega^{-1/2}$ transformation and subsequent changes to the instrument set to avoid inconsistencies. It also provides a natural framework to extend the HT-type of estimators to cases where there are predetermined variables as we shall see below.

If Ω^+ is estimated as $\tilde{\Omega}^+$, straightforward manipulations reveal that (5) can be written as

$$\hat{\delta} = [\Sigma_i W_i' Q W_i + \tilde{\theta}^2 T \Sigma_i \bar{w}_i m_i' (\Sigma_i m_i m_i')^{-1} \Sigma_i m_i \bar{w}_i']^{-1} \times [\Sigma_i W_i' Q y_i + \tilde{\theta}^2 T \Sigma_i \bar{w}_i m_i' (\Sigma_i m_i m_i')^{-1} \Sigma_i m_i \bar{y}_i]^{-1}, \quad (8)$$

which produces more familiar expressions of the HT, AM, and BMS estimators for the corresponding choices of m_i (details available in the Appendix).[2] In this expression Q is the within-group operator:

$$Q = I_T - \iota\iota'/T = K'(KK')^{-1}K,$$

$$\bar{w}_i = W_i'\iota/T \quad \text{and} \quad \tilde{\theta}^2 = \tilde{\sigma}^2/(\tilde{\sigma}^2 + T\tilde{\sigma}_\eta^2).$$

As explained in the Appendix, in this case it is possible to simplify the form of Z_i without changing the estimator.

The obvious advantage of the formulation (5) is that if we replace the error components estimator $\tilde{\Omega}^+$ by an unrestricted estimator $\hat{\Omega}^+$, we obtain alternative HT, AM, or BMS-type estimators which are as efficient asymptotically as the versions in (8) when $E(v_i v_i') = \sigma^2 I_T$ and strictly more efficient when $E(v_i v_i') \neq \sigma^2 I_T$. Moreover, with cross-sectional heteroskedasticity further efficiency can be achieved using a GMM estimator of the type discussed by Chamberlain (1982), Hansen (1982), and White (1982) which would replace the term $(\Sigma_i Z_i' \Omega^+ Z_i)$ in (5) by a term of the form $(\Sigma_i Z_i' \hat{u}_i^+ \hat{u}_i^{+\prime} Z_i)$.

The efficiency bound for δ

In order to assess the efficiency of the class of GMM estimators given in (5), it is useful to compare the inverse of the asymptotic variance matrix of $\hat{\delta}$ with the Fisher information bound for δ based on the conditional moment restrictions (1) and (2). Chamberlain (1992a), using a specification that includes (1) as a special case, shows that the bound for β based on (1) is identical to the bound for β based on the conditional moment restriction

$$E(K(y_i - X_i\beta) | w_{1i}, w_{2i}) = 0, \quad (9)$$

[2] A derivation of the estimators of HT, AM, and BMS as GMM estimators, in the case that noise is iid, has been obtained independently by Ahn and Schmidt (1995).

where $w_{ji} = (x'_{ji}, f'_{ji})'$, $j = 1, 2$, so that $(w'_{1i}, w'_{2i})'$ is just a permutation of w_i. In addition, (2) can be written as

$$E(y_i - W_i\delta \,|\, w_{1i}) = 0. \tag{10}$$

The Fisher information bound for δ based on (9) and (10) can be obtained as an application of Theorem 1 of Chamberlain (1992b) for sequential conditional moment restrictions.[3] The bound will be the sum of the bounds corresponding to each of the conditional moments (see the Appendix for the details):

$$E(Ku_i \,|\, w_i) = 0, \tag{11}$$

$$E[(\iota'\Omega_i^{-1}\iota)^{-1}\,\iota'\Omega_i^{-1}u_i \,|\, w_{1i}] = 0, \tag{12}$$

where $\Omega_i = \Omega(w_i)$. Direct application of Chamberlain's theorem gives the following expression for the bound:

$$J = E(W_i'K'(K\Omega_iK')^{-1}KW_i + [E((\iota'\Omega_i^{-1}\iota)^{-1} \,|\, w_{1i})]^{-1} \times E(\bar{\bar{w}}_i \,|\, w_{1i})\,E(\bar{\bar{w}}_i' \,|\, w_{1i})), \tag{13}$$

where $\bar{\bar{w}}_i' = q'_iW_i$ and $q_i' = (\iota'\Omega_i^{-1}\iota)^{-1}\iota'\Omega_i^{-1}$. With a constant unrestricted Ω, J becomes

$$J = E\big(W_i'K'(K\Omega K')^{-1}KW_i + (\iota'\Omega^{-1}\iota)E(W_i' \,|\, w_{1i})qq'E(W_i \,|\, w_{1i})\big). \tag{14}$$

None of the GMM estimators of this section will attain the bound even in the absence of cross-sectional heteroskedasticity, since $E(W_i \,|\, w_{1i})$ could be a nonlinear function of w_{1i}. However, if $E(W_i \,|\, w_{1i})$ is linear, we have

$$E(W_i'q \,|\, w_{1i}) = E(\bar{\bar{w}}_i \,|\, w_{1i}) = E(\bar{\bar{w}}_i \,|\, w_{1i}')\,[E(w_{1i}w_{1i}')]^{-1}w_{1i}$$

and

$$J = E\big(W_i'K'(K\Omega K')^{-1}KW_i + (\iota'\Omega^{-1}\iota)E(\bar{\bar{w}}_i w_{1i}')\,[E(w_{1i}w_{1i}')]^{-1}\,E(w_{1i}\bar{\bar{w}}_i')\big). \tag{15}$$

Finally, if $\Omega = \sigma^2 I_T + \sigma_\eta^2\iota\iota'$, we have that $q = T^{-1}\iota$, $\iota'\Omega^{-1}\iota = \theta^2T/\sigma^2$, and $K'(K\Omega K')^{-1}K = (1/\sigma^2)Q$, so that

$$J = (1/\sigma^2)\,E\big(W_i'QW_i + \theta^2T\,E(\bar{w}_i w_{1i}')\,[E(w_{1i}w_{1i}')]^{-1}E(w_{1i}\bar{w}_i')\big), \tag{16}$$

which equals the inverse of the asymptotic covariance matrix of the AM estimator.

Notice that the assumptions of linearity of $E(W_i \,|\, w_{1i})$ and of a constant error components structure for Ω would imply further conditional moment restrictions that may lower the information bound for δ. Here, we merely particularize

[3] This theorem applies to the case where the joint distribution of the data is multinomial but it could be extended to a general distribution by using the approximation argument of Chamberlain (1987).

the bound for δ based on (11) and (12) to the case where these additional restrictions happen to occur in the population but are not used in the calculation of the bound.

We now turn to show that the inverse of the asymptotic covariance matrix of the GMM estimator given in (5) with unrestricted Ω and the AM choice of instruments for the average equation $m_i = w_{1i}$, V^{-1} say, coincides with the information bound given in (15). Under standard regularity conditions

$$V^{-1} = \mathrm{E}(W_i'H'Z_i)\,[\mathrm{E}(Z_i'H\Omega H'Z_i)]^{-1}\mathrm{E}(Z_i'HW_i).$$

On the other hand, since KX_i equals the block $I_{T-1} \otimes w_i'$ of Z_i multiplied by a constant selection matrix, after straightforward manipulations (15) can be written as

$$J = \mathrm{E}(W_i'H^{*\prime}Z_i)\,[\mathrm{E}(Z_i'H^{*}\Omega H^{*\prime}Z_i)]^{-1}\mathrm{E}(Z_i'H^{*}W_i),$$

with

$$H^{*} = \begin{bmatrix} K \\ \iota'\Omega^{-1} \end{bmatrix}.$$

We prove that $V^{-1} = J$ by showing that

$$Z_i'H^{*} = F(Z_i'H), \tag{17}$$

where F is a nonsingular matrix of constants. Firstly, notice that $H^{*} = \Phi H$ with

$$\Phi = \begin{bmatrix} I_{T-1} & 0 \\ \iota'\Omega^{-1}K'(KK')^{-1} & \iota'\Omega^{-1}\iota \end{bmatrix}.$$

Next, we consider a permutation of the columns of $Z_i = Z_i^{*}P'$ such that

$$Z_i^{*} = \begin{bmatrix} I_T \otimes w_{1i}' & \begin{matrix} I_{T-1} \otimes w_{2i}' \\ 0 \end{matrix} \end{bmatrix}.$$

Hence notice

$$Z_i^{*\prime}H = \begin{bmatrix} (I_T \otimes w_{1i})H \\ (I_T \otimes w_{2i})K \end{bmatrix} = \begin{bmatrix} H \otimes I & 0 \\ 0 & K \otimes I \end{bmatrix} \begin{bmatrix} I_T \otimes w_{1i} \\ I_T \otimes w_{2i} \end{bmatrix},$$

and similarly

$$Z_i^{*\prime}H^{*} = \begin{bmatrix} H^{*} \otimes I & 0 \\ 0 & K \otimes I \end{bmatrix} \begin{bmatrix} I_T \otimes w_{1i} \\ I_T \otimes w_{2i} \end{bmatrix},$$

which proves (17) with

$$F = P\begin{bmatrix} \Phi \otimes I & 0 \\ 0 & I \end{bmatrix} P^{-1}.$$

Remark that the previous result depends crucially on the fact that the variables in the instrument set for the between-group equation are linear combinations of the instruments used for the within-group equations. This means, for example, that in the block $I_{T-1} \otimes w_i'$ of Z_i we cannot replace w_i with $\text{vec}(KX_i)$, hence excluding f_{1i} and $\bar{x}_{1i}$, without altering the estimator and its asymptotic variance, contrary to the situation in the case that the noise is iid as explained in the Appendix. Nevertheless, some of the instruments used for the within-group equations are redundant in the sense that their omission would not alter the GMM estimator. Specifically, the situation is that for HT, AM, and BMS choices of m_i with unrestricted Ω, the submatrix $I_{T-1} \otimes w_i'$ of Z_i could be replaced by $I_{T-1} \otimes ([\text{vec}(KX_i)]', f_{1i}', \bar{x}_{1i}')$ leaving the estimator unaltered. Another remark is that the difference between the asymptotic covariance matrix of the HT estimator with unrestricted Ω and V will be a nonnegative matrix, except if $E^*(W_i | w_{1i})$ coincides with $E(W_i | \bar{x}_{1i}, f_{1i})$ where E^* denotes a best linear predictor, in which case the two estimators have the same asymptotic variances.

One last remark concerns BMS-type estimators. Clearly, our analysis can be repeated for BS/BMS models by using the conditional moment restriction (6) in place of (2). The previous discussion applies provided the vectors of conditioning variables are suitably redefined. In this case, the vector of IV for the between-group equation is $m_i = (f_{1i}' \; x_{1i}' \; \tilde{x}_{2i2}' \; \dots \; \tilde{x}_{2iT}')'$. However, for this choice of m_i the rows of KX_i are linear combinations of m_i. This means that the same instrument set is valid for all the equations and we can use $Z_i = I_T \otimes m_i'$ without altering the estimator. The consequence is that the transformation is unnecessary and the estimator can be obtained by simple application of three-stage least squares (3SLS) to the original system of equations using m_i as the vector of instruments for all equations:

$$\hat{\delta} = [\Sigma_i (W_i \otimes m_i)' (\hat{\Omega} \otimes \Sigma_i m_i m_i')^{-1} \Sigma_i (W_i \otimes m_i)]^{-1} \Sigma_i (W_i \otimes m_i)' \times (\hat{\Omega} \otimes \Sigma_i m_i m_i')^{-1} \Sigma_i (y_i \otimes m_i). \quad (18)$$

3. Models with predetermined variables and a useful transformation

We begin by considering a model of the type given in (1) with the addition of the dependent variable lagged one period:

$$y_{it} = \alpha y_{i(t-1)} + \beta' x_{it} + \gamma' f_i + u_{it}, \qquad u_{it} = \eta_i + v_{it}, \quad (19)$$

$$E(v_{it} | x_{i0}, \dots, x_{iT}, f_i, \eta_i) = 0. \quad (20)$$

Assuming that $t = 0$ is observed and redefining the symbols in (3) as $\delta = (\alpha, \beta', \gamma')'$ and $W_i = (y_{i(-1)}, X_i, \iota f_i')$ with $y_{i(-1)} = (y_{i0}, \ldots, y_{i(T-1)})'$, the expression given in (5) remains a consistent GMM estimator of δ for this model, provided there are enough valid instruments to ensure identification. The form of the IV matrix Z_i is the same as in Section 2, adjusting for the fact that $t = 0$ is now observed, so that $w_i = (x_{i0}', \ldots, x_{iT}', f_i')$ (notice the exclusion of $y_{i(-1)}$ despite its presence in W_i). The same range of choices for m_i are available depending on the assumptions concerning the dependence between η_i and subsets of the explanatory variables.

In particular, if $m_i = (f_{1i}', x_{1i}', \tilde{x}_{2i1}', \ldots, \tilde{x}_{2iT}')$, in view of the reasons explained for BMS-type cases above, the resulting estimator coincides with 3SLS and is therefore asymptotically equivalent to the LIML procedure with Ω unrestricted developed by Bhargava and Sargan. BS obtained their estimator as an application of subsystem LIML to the T equations (19), having completed the system with the reduced form equations,

$$y_{i0} = \pi_0' m_i + \varepsilon_{i0}, \quad f_{2i} = \Pi_1 m_i + \varepsilon_{i1}, \quad \bar{x}_{2i} = \Pi_2 m_i + \varepsilon_{i2},$$

and the identities

$$x_{2it} = \tilde{x}_{2it} + \bar{x}_{2i}, \qquad t = 0, \ldots, T-1.$$

It is well-known that subsystem LIML is asymptotically equivalent to subsystem 3SLS when Ω is unrestricted.

As in the static model, one polar case is the uncorrelated random effects specification with $\mathrm{E}(\eta_i | x_i, f_i) = 0$, so that $m_i = w_i$, which corresponds to the basic model of BS. At the other end, η_i would be potentially correlated with all explanatory variables and there would be no instruments for the levels equation, which would drop out. This corresponds to the model and the 3SLS estimator discussed by Chamberlain (1984, pp. 1266–1267).

In the previous model, regardless of the existence of individual effects, unrestricted serial correlation in v_{it} implies that $y_{i(t-1)}$ is an endogenous variable. A different model, in which $y_{i(t-1)}$ is a predetermined variable given η_i, replaces (20) by the following assumption:

$$\mathrm{E}(v_{it} | x_i, f_i, \eta_i, y_{i0}, \ldots, y_{i(t-1)}) = 0. \tag{21}$$

Notice that (21) implies lack of serial dependence in the sense that $\mathrm{E}(v_{it} | v_{i1} \ldots v_{i(t-1)}) = 0$. Orthogonality restrictions implied by this model can be easily incorporated in an estimator of the form of (5) provided that the transformation matrix K is upper-triangular in addition to the previous requirements. In effect, with lack of autocorrelation in v_{it} and K upper-triangular it turns out that the transformed error in the equation for period t is independent of η_i and $(v_{i1}, \dots, v_{i(t-1)})$ so that $(y_{i0}, \dots, y_{i(t-1)})$ are additional valid instruments for this equation. Hence giving rise to the following Z_i matrix:

$$Z_i = \begin{bmatrix} w_i' \; y_{i0} & & & & 0 \\ & w_i' \; y_{i0} \; y_{i1} & & & \\ & & \ddots & & \\ & & & w_i' \; y_{i0} \cdots y_{i(T-2)} & \\ 0 & & & & m_i' \end{bmatrix}. \tag{22}$$

Estimators that rely on these types of restrictions have been discussed by Anderson and Hsiao (1982), Holtz-Eakin, Newey, and Rosen (1988), and Arellano and Bond (1991). These authors transformed the data using first differences and disregarded the levels in the absence of valid instruments for this equation (Arellano and Bond (p. 280) did, however, present a discussion of models with predetermined and strictly exogenous variables that contain information in levels). Further discussion of these models is contained in Ahn and Schmidt (1995), who exploit the additional quadratic moment restrictions implied by lack of serial correlation and the restrictions derived from the assumption of homoskedasticity. A model may contain predetermined variables other than lags of the dependent variable, but their treatment would be similar to the one described for $y_{(t-1)}$. Moreover, it is often the case that instruments arising from assumptions on predetermined variables and lack of autocorrelation are the only ones available in the model, so that sequential moment restrictions like (21) become crucial for the identification of the parameters of interest.

As in the previous section, the GMM estimator (5) that uses (22) as the matrix of instruments is invariant to the choice of K provided K satisfies the required conditions. This is an example of a more general result: let z_{is} be the $r_s \times 1$ vector of instruments that are valid in the transformed equations for periods $s, s+1, \dots, (T-1)$ [for example, in (22) $z_{i1} = (w_i' \; y_{i0})'$ and $z_{is} = y_{i(s-1)}$ for $s > 1$], and let K_s be the $(T-s-1) \times T$ submatrix that results when the first s rows of K are eliminated. Then the moment restrictions available for estimation are

$$\mathrm{E}(\xi_i) = \mathrm{E} \begin{bmatrix} K u_i \otimes z_{i1} \\ K_1 u_i \otimes z_{i2} \\ \vdots \\ K_{T-2} u_i \otimes z_{i(T-1)} \\ T^{-1} \iota' u_i m_i \end{bmatrix} = 0. \tag{23}$$

Since ξ_i can be written as

$$\xi_i = \begin{bmatrix} K \otimes I_{r_1} & & & 0 \\ & \ddots & & \\ & & K_{T-2} \otimes I_{r_{T-1}} & \\ 0 & & & T^{-1}\iota' \otimes I_{p_2} \end{bmatrix} \begin{bmatrix} \text{vec}(u_i z'_{1i}) \\ \vdots \\ \text{vec}(u_i z'_{i(T-1)}) \\ \text{vec}(u_i m'_i) \end{bmatrix},$$

it turns out that for any other valid $K^* = \Phi K$ the resulting ξ_i^* will be of the form $F\xi_i$ with F having the following block-diagonal structure:

$$F = \text{diag}(\Phi \otimes I_{r_1}, \ldots, \Phi_1 \otimes I_{r_2}, \ldots, \Phi_{T-2} \otimes I_{r_{T-1}}, I_{p_2}),$$

where $K_s^* = \Phi_s K_s$. As a consequence, all the estimators of the form (5) with K upper-triangular, $K\iota = 0$ and Z_i given by

$$Z_i = \begin{bmatrix} z'_{i1} & & & & 0 \\ & z'_{i1}\, z'_{i2} & & & \\ & & \ddots & & \\ & & & z'_{i1} \ldots z'_{i(T-1)} & \\ 0 & & & & m'_i \end{bmatrix},$$

are identical.

However, as pointed out by Schmidt, Ahn, and Wyhowski (1992) who stress the point that filtering does not improve efficiency of estimation if all available instruments are used, this does not mean that filtering is useless, since in practice it may not be desirable to use all of the available instruments for computational reasons or if their number is excessive for the actual sample size, given the finite-sample properties of the estimators.

Orthogonal deviations

An alternative to first differencing which is very useful in the context of models with predetermined variables is the following Helmert's transformation:

$$u_{it}^* = c_t \left[u_{it} - \frac{1}{(T-t)}(u_{i(t+1)} + \cdots + u_{iT}) \right], \qquad t = 1, \ldots, T-1, \tag{24}$$

where $c_t^2 = (T-t)/(T-t+1)$. That is, to each of the first (T − 1) observations we subtract the mean of the remaining future observations available in the sample. The weighting c_t is introduced to equalise the variances. The choice of

K that produces this transformation is the forward orthogonal deviations operator:

$$A = \mathrm{diag}\left[\frac{T-1}{T}, \dots, \frac{1}{2}\right]^{1/2} \times$$

$$\begin{bmatrix} 1 & -(T-1)^{-1} & -(T-1)^{-1} & \cdots & -(T-1)^{-1} & -(T-1)^{-1} & -(T-1)^{-1} \\ 0 & 1 & -(T-2)^{-1} & \cdots & -(T-2)^{-1} & -(T-2)^{-1} & -(T-2)^{-1} \\ \vdots & \vdots & \vdots & & \vdots & \vdots & \vdots \\ 0 & 0 & 0 & \cdots & 1 & -\frac{1}{2} & -\frac{1}{2} \\ 0 & 0 & 0 & \cdots & 0 & 1 & -1 \end{bmatrix} \tag{25}$$

which clearly has rows whose elements add up to zero (so that the permanent effects are eliminated) and is upper-triangular (so that lags of predetermined variables are valid instruments in the transformed equations). In addition, it preserves the orthogonality among the transformed errors – if the original v_{it} are not autocorrelated and have constant variance, so are the transformed errors, and indeed it can be verified by direct multiplication that $AA' = I_{(T-1)}$ and $A'A = Q$. Hence, $A = (KK')^{-1/2}K$ for any upper-triangular K, so that for example transforming by A can be regarded as doing first differences to eliminate the effects plus a GLS transformation to remove the serial correlation induced by differencing.

A useful feature of this transformation when $\Omega = \sigma^2 I + \sigma_\eta^2 \iota\iota'$ is that since it diagonalises $H\Omega H'$ it is possible to calculate $\hat{\delta}$ in the following way:

$$\begin{aligned} \hat{\delta} = {} & \Bigg[\sum_{t=1}^{T-1} (\Sigma_i w_{it}^* z_{it}')(\Sigma_i z_{it} z_{it}')^{-1}(\Sigma_i z_{it} w_{it}^{*\prime}) \\ & + \tilde{\theta}^2 T(\Sigma_i \bar{w}_i m_i')(\Sigma_i m_i m_i')^{-1}(\Sigma_i m_i \bar{w}_i')\Bigg]^{-1} \\ & \times \Bigg[\sum_{t=1}^{T-1} (\Sigma_i w_{it}^* z_{it}')(\Sigma_i z_{it} z_{it}')^{-1}(\Sigma_i z_{it} y_{it}^*) \\ & + \tilde{\theta}^2 T(\Sigma_i \bar{w}_i m_i')(\Sigma_i m_i m_i')^{-1}(\Sigma_1 m_i \bar{y}_i)\Bigg], \end{aligned} \tag{26}$$

where w_{it}^* is the tth row of $W_i^* = AW_i$ and y_{it}^* is the tth element of Ay_i. This is of importance in practice because if Z_i has a large number of columns it may be difficult to compute expression (5) directly.

Finally, notice that since $A'A = Q$, the OLS regression of y_{it}^* on x_{it}^* (that is, least squares applied to the first $(T-1)$ equations of the system) will give the within-group estimator, whereas OLS applied to the complete system of T equations with $H = (A', \tilde{\theta} T^{-1/2}\iota)'$ will give the GLS estimator.

A general model with predetermined variables and information in levels

Combining together the various ingredients that have appeared so far, the form of a general model with predetermined variables and information in levels is as follows:

$$y_{it} = w_{it}'\delta + \eta_i + v_{it}, \tag{27}$$

$$\mathrm{E}(v_{it} | x_{i1}, \ldots, x_{iT}, f_i, p_{i1}, \ldots, p_{it}, \eta_i) = 0, \tag{28}$$

$$\mathrm{E}(\eta_i | x_{1i1}, \ldots, x_{1iT}, f_{1i}, p_{1i1}, \ldots, p_{1iT}) = 0. \tag{29}$$

The vector of right-hand-side variables w_{it} may include lags of y_{it}, time-invariant variables f_i, plus other strictly exogenous, predetermined, or endogenous variables. The variables f_i, x_{it}, and p_{it} refer to time-invariant, strictly exogenous, and predetermined variables, respectively. For each category we introduce the partitions $f_i = (f_{1i}', f_{2i}')'$, $x_{it} = (x_{1it}', x_{2it}')'$, and $p_{it} = (p_{1it}', p_{2it}')'$, with the first subsets denoting the variables that are uncorrelated to η_i according to (29).

Notice that (28) and (29) imply that

$$\mathrm{E}(y_{it} - w_{it}'\delta | x_{1i1}, \ldots, x_{1iT}, f_{1i}, p_{1i1}, \ldots, p_{1it}) = 0, \tag{30}$$

so that in the presence of p_{1it} variables there are different instruments available for different equations in levels, what precludes the use of the average equation in constructing GMM estimators.[4] Following Arellano and Bond (1991), we can define a $(2T-1) \times T$ transformation $H = (K', I_T)'$ and

$$Z_i = \begin{bmatrix} Z_{di} & 0 \\ 0 & Z_{li} \end{bmatrix}, \tag{31}$$

where Z_{di} is block-diagonal and has the tth block given by $(x_{1i}', \ldots, x_{iT}', f_i', p_{i1}', \ldots, p_{i(t-1)}')$, which are the instruments available for the tth equation transformed by K. The matrix Z_{li} is also block-diagonal and will contain the instruments available for the equations in levels. In principle, in the equation

[4] Chamberlain (1992b) obtained the Fisher information bound for δ in a model similar to (27) and (28), with the exclusion of (29). However, the addition of (29) breaks the sequential moment structure of the problem with the implication that Chamberlain's results are not directly applicable to this case.

for period t, the vector of valid instruments is $(x'_{1i1}, \ldots, x'_{1iT}, f'_{1i}, p'_{1i1}, \ldots, p'_{1it})$. However, given Z_{di}, some of these moment restrictions will be redundant. To see this, taking K to be the first difference operator without loss of generality, notice that

$$\mathrm{E}(u_{it}p_{i(t-s)}) = \sum_{j=0}^{s-1} \mathrm{E}(\Delta u_{i(t-j)}p_{i(t-s)}) + \mathrm{E}(u_{i(t-s)}p_{i(t-s)}). \tag{32}$$

Therefore, we specify Z_{li} as

$$Z_{li} = \begin{bmatrix} x'_{1i1} \ldots x'_{1iT} \quad f'_{1i} \quad p'_{1i1} & & & 0 \\ & p'_{1i2} & & \\ & & \ddots & \\ 0 & & & p'_{1iT} \end{bmatrix}. \tag{33}$$

We can construct optimal GMM estimators of δ based on the moment equations

$$\mathrm{E}(Z_i'Hu_i) = \mathrm{E}\begin{bmatrix} Z'_{di}Ku_i \\ Z'_{li}u_i \end{bmatrix} = 0. \tag{34}$$

So we are replacing the 'between-group' errors in (4) by the complete set of errors in levels in addition to those transformed by K. Individual equations in levels rather than an average equation are now required since we have different instruments valid for different equations in levels. The next section presents a model of special interest which contains predetermined variables that are valid instruments in the equations in levels.

Note that the estimators of HT, AM, and BMS can also be written in this way, for example selecting $Z_{di} = I_{T-1} \otimes w_i'$ and $Z_{li} = I_T \otimes m_i'$ and using expression (5). The only modification that (5) requires is the replacement of the inverse of $\Sigma_i Z_i' \Omega^+ Z_i$ by a Moore–Penrose generalised inverse, since this matrix will be singular due to repetitions of the same moments.

4. Additional moment restrictions using predetermined variables

The models of BS and BMS included strictly exogenous variables that had constant correlation with the individual effects. That is, variables such that

$$\mathrm{E}(x_{it}\eta_i) = \mathrm{E}(x_{is}\eta_i), \tag{35}$$

$$\mathrm{E}(x_{it}v_{is}) = 0, \tag{36}$$

for all t and s. Here we consider a model with predetermined variables that have constant correlation with the effects. These variables will therefore satisfy (35) for all t and s, but (36) will only be true for $t \leqslant s$.[5] This type of restrictions could be justified on the grounds of stationarity, and in many instances its validity or otherwise can be regarded as an empirical issue. Moreover, in models without strictly exogenous variables, like vector autoregressions and some rational expectations models, these additional restrictions may play a crucial role in substantially improving the precision of the estimates, especially when T is very small.

Estimation can proceed as a special case of the general model with predetermined variables and information in levels discussed in the previous section. Suppose for simplicity of presentation that in (1) all the x_{it} are predetermined variables that satisfy (35) and that all the f_i are correlated with η_i. Therefore in the equation in first differences for period t $(x_{i1}, x_{i2}, \dots, x_{i(t-1)})$ are valid instruments while in the equation in levels $(\Delta x_{i2}, \dots, \Delta x_{it})$ are valid. Some of these moment restrictions are redundant. To see this note that

$$E(u_{it}\Delta x_{i(t-1)}) - E(u_{i(t-1)}\Delta x_{i(t-1)}) = E(\Delta u_{it} x_{i(t-1)}) - E(\Delta u_{it} x_{i(t-2)}),$$

so that given three restrictions that equate three of these four terms to zero the equality of the fourth term to zero is redundant. Thus, given the instruments for the first difference equations, (35) contributes the additional constraints

$$E(u_{it}\Delta x_{it}) = 0, \qquad t = 1, \dots, T.$$

Redefining H as the $2(T-1)\times T$ transformation $H = (K', I_0')'$ with $I_0 = (0|I_{T-1})$ and choosing $Z_{di} = \mathrm{diag}[x_{i1}', \dots, (x_{i1}' \dots x_{i(T-1)}')]$ and $Z_{li} = \mathrm{diag}(\Delta x_{i2}', \dots, \Delta x_{iT}')$, we can construct optimal GMM estimators of β and γ based on the moment equations $E(Z'Hu_i) = 0$.

Monte Carlo results

Finally, we have carried out simulations concerning a well-known simple model: a first-order autoregression with random effects observed three time periods. The purpose of the experiments is to illustrate the potential of exploiting moment restrictions in levels equations using predetermined variables in first differences. For each experiment we generated 1000 samples of N independent observations of (y_{i0}, y_{i1}, y_{i2}) from the process

$$y_{i0} = (1-\alpha)^{-1}\eta_i + (1-\alpha^2)^{-1/2} v_{i0},$$

$$y_{i1} = \alpha y_{i0} + \eta_i + v_{i1},$$

$$y_{i2} = \alpha y_{i1} + \eta_i + v_{i2}, \qquad i = 1, \dots, N,$$

with $v_i = (v_{i0}\ v_{i1}\ v_{i2})' \sim N(0, I)$ and $\eta_i \sim N(0, \sigma_\eta^2)$ independent of v_i.

[5] A stronger conditional mean version of this situation would assume that x_{it} can be written as $x_{it} = g(\eta_i) + x_{it}^+$ and $E(\eta_i | x_{i1}^+ \dots x_{iT}^+) = 0$. If x_{it} is strictly exogenous, $E(v_{it} | x_{i1} \dots x_{iT}) = 0$, whereas if it is predetermined, $E(v_{it} | x_{i1} \dots x_{it}) = 0$.

The Anderson–Hsiao estimator of α is based on the restriction

$$\mathrm{E}[(\Delta y_{i2} - \alpha \Delta y_{i1}) y_{io}] = 0, \tag{37}$$

and is given by

$$\hat{\alpha}_{AH} = \frac{\Sigma_i y_{io} \Delta y_{i2}}{\Sigma_i y_{io} \Delta y_{i1}}. \tag{38}$$

Moreover we are also interested in exploiting the levels restriction

$$\mathrm{E}[(y_{i2} - \alpha y_{i1}) \Delta y_{i1}] = 0, \tag{39}$$

so that we consider the system of two equations

$$\begin{bmatrix} \Delta y_{i2} \\ y_{i2} \end{bmatrix} = \alpha \begin{bmatrix} \Delta y_{i1} \\ y_{i1} \end{bmatrix} + \begin{bmatrix} \Delta u_{i2} \\ u_{i2} \end{bmatrix},$$

with the matrix of instruments

$$Z_i = \begin{bmatrix} y_{io} & 0 \\ 0 & \Delta y_{i1} \end{bmatrix}.$$

Let $y_{it}^{+} = (\Delta y_{it}\ y_{it})'$. We simulate two estimators of the form

$$\hat{\alpha}_L = \frac{(\Sigma_i y_{i1}^{+\prime} Z_i) A_N (\Sigma_i Z_i' y_{i2}^{+})}{(\Sigma_i y_{i1}^{+\prime} Z_i) A_N (\Sigma_i Z_i' y_{i1}^{+})}. \tag{40}$$

The one-step estimator $\hat{\alpha}_{L1}$ sets $A_N = (\Sigma_i Z_i' Z_i)^{-1}$, while the two-step estimator $\hat{\alpha}_{L2}$ uses $A_N = (\Sigma_i Z_i' \hat{u}_i^{+} \hat{u}_i^{+\prime} Z_i)^{-1}$ where $\hat{u}_i^{+} = y_{i2}^{+} - \hat{\alpha}_{L1} y_{i1}^{+}$.

Table 1 reports Monte Carlo means and standard deviations of the three estimators for $\alpha = 0.2, 0.5, 0.8$, $\sigma_\eta^2 = 0, 0.2, 1$, and $N = 100, 500$. σ^2 is kept equal to unity for all the experiments (with $\sigma_\eta^2 = 0$ all three estimators are invariant to the value of σ^2). With $\sigma_\eta^2 = 0.2$, the variation due to the permanent effect represents 23, 37.5, and 57 percent of the total variance of y_{io} for $\alpha = 0.2, 0.5, 0.8$, respectively. While for $\sigma_\eta^2 = 1$ the corresponding percentages of variation are 60, 75, and 90.

As can be seen in the table, *L1* and *L2* always outperform *AH* both in terms of having a smaller standard deviation and a smaller bias. The gap in precision between *AH* and the estimators that also use the restrictions in levels widens for larger values of σ_η^2 and α. With $N = 100$ and $\alpha = 0.8$, *AH* is a useless estimator whereas *L1* and *L2* behave reasonably well. Even with $N = 500$, for $\alpha = 0.8$, the standard deviation of *AH* is twice that of *L1* and *L2* with $\sigma_\eta^2 = 0$, three times bigger with $\sigma_\eta^2 = 0.2$, and one hundred times bigger with $\sigma_\eta^2 = 1$! The same pattern still applies to $\alpha = 0.5$, with large efficiency gains and reductions in biases obtained by using the restriction in levels. On the other hand, there is not

Table 1
Means and standard deviations of the estimators, 1000 replications

	$\alpha = 0.2$			$\alpha = 0.5$			$\alpha = 0.8$		
	AH	*L1*	*L2*	*AH*	*L1*	*L2*	*AH*	*L1*	*L2*
$N = 100$									
$\sigma_\eta^2 = 0$									
Mean	0.2315	0.2147	0.2018	0.5571	0.5095	0.4953	0.9683	0.7841	0.7795
S.d.	0.1852	0.1460	0.1776	0.2827	0.1729	0.1720	0.8203	0.2027	0.2109
$\sigma_\eta^2 = 0.2$									
Mean	0.2353	0.2128	0.2009	0.5814	0.5001	0.4884	1.3701	0.7496	0.7482
S.d.	0.2134	0.1572	0.1556	0.4088	0.1895	0.1900	17.1953	0.2516	0.2667
$\sigma_\eta^2 = 1$									
Mean	0.2588	0.2065	0.2011	0.7980	0.4762	0.4748	0.0390	0.7526	0.7574
S.d.	0.3389	0.1948	0.1898	2.9516	0.2431	0.2409	15.9819	0.3309	0.3727
$N = 500$									
$\sigma_\eta^2 = 0$									
Mean	0.2056	0.2038	0.2011	0.5097	0.5031	0.4999	0.8248	0.7976	0.7984
S.d.	0.0768	0.0635	0.0622	0.1093	0.0765	0.0734	0.1949	0.0900	0.0870
$\sigma_\eta^2 = 0.2$									
Mean	0.2059	0.2041	0.2012	0.5120	0.5022	0.4983	0.8596	0.7887	0.7886
S.d.	0.0856	0.0695	0.0689	0.1356	0.0864	0.0849	0.3660	0.1105	0.1153
$\sigma_\eta^2 = 1$									
Mean	0.2089	0.2040	0.2019	0.5262	0.4963	0.4917	1.8560	0.7597	0.7600
S.d.	0.1189	0.0906	0.0891	0.2262	0.1155	0.1145	21.1516	0.1775	0.1813

Each sample consists of N independent observations of (y_{io}, y_{i1}, y_{i2}) generated from the process:

$$y_{io} = (1-\alpha)^{-1}\eta_i + (1-\alpha^2)^{-1/2}v_{io}, \qquad y_{i1} = \alpha y_{io} + \eta_i + v_{i1}, \qquad y_{i2} = \alpha y_{i1} + \eta_i + v_{i2},$$

with $v_i = (v_{io}, v_{i1}, v_{i2})' \sim N(0, I)$ and $\eta_i \sim N(0, \sigma_\eta^2)$ independent of v_i.

much difference between the behaviour of *L1* and *L2*. There seems to be a tendency of *L2* to have a smaller standard deviation than *L1* but the gain is negligible.

A specially interesting case is when the coefficient α in

$$y_{it} = \alpha y_{i(t-1)} + \eta_i + v_{it}$$

is allowed to take the value of unity. If $\eta_i = (1-\alpha)\eta_i^*$, where η_i^* represents the individual specific mean of y_{it} assumed to have a constant variance, with $\alpha = 1$ we have

$$y_{it} = y_{i(t-1)} + v_{it}.$$

The alternative specification of the model with $\alpha = 1$ would be a random walk with an individual drift η_i. In the former case, with $\alpha = 1$, $E(y_{i0} \Delta y_{i1}) = 0$ and as a consequence the Anderson–Hsiao restriction (37) fails to identify α. However, the level restriction (39) still applies and could be exploited in order to test the stationary autoregressive model against the random walk model without drift.

5. Conclusions

Models with predetermined variables for panel data are typically estimated in first differences using instruments in levels. In these models, the absence of information about the parameters of interest in the levels of the variables results in the loss of what sometimes is a very substantial part of the total variation in the data. In this article, we are concerned with panel data models that specify valid instruments for the equations in levels, in addition to those available for the equations in first differences or deviations from individual means. Static models of this kind, but using exclusively strictly exogenous explanatory variables, were first considered by Hausman and Taylor (1981) and, with the addition of a lagged dependent variable, by Bhargava and Sargan (1983). The impact of these models in applied work has been limited, partly due to the difficulty in finding exogenous variables that can be convincingly regarded a priori as being uncorrelated with the individual effects, and partly due to the difficulty in finding strictly exogenous variables at all.

This paper considers models with predetermined instrumental variables that are uncorrelated with the effects. The particular type of variables of this kind that we emphasize are first differences of predetermined variables that have a constant correlation with the effects. A similar assumption for strictly exogenous variables was previously exploited by Bhargava and Sargan (1983) and Breusch, Mizon, and Schmidt (1989). Thus, in addition to using instruments in levels for equations in first differences, we propose to use instruments in first differences for equations in levels. The potential gains in precision from using these constraints are illustrated by means of simulations of alternative estimators of an autoregressive model. Moreover, we also explain how the assumption of constant correlation with the effects can be exploited to test for unit roots in short panels against a stationary autoregressive model.

The paper presents a GMM formulation of Hausman–Taylor (HT) and related estimators with unrestricted covariance matrix, together with a derivation of the information bound for these models. We use this framework to extend HT-type estimators to models with predetermined variables. In doing this we unify a large literature in a coherent way. We propose a GMM estimator for a general model that includes time-invariant, strictly exogenous, and predetermined variables, a subset of which are uncorrelated with the effects. We also show that optimal estimators are invariant to the transformation used to remove the effects. Finally, we propose a new transformation, forward orthogonal deviations, which is a computationally convenient alternative for models with predetermined variables since it preserves the orthogonality among the errors.

Appendix

A.1. GMM formulation of HT, AM, and BMS estimators

Let

$$W_i^+ = HW_i = \begin{bmatrix} KW_i \\ \bar{w}_i' \end{bmatrix} \quad \text{and} \quad Z_i = \begin{bmatrix} Z_{di} & 0 \\ 0 & m_i' \end{bmatrix},$$

so that

$$W_i^{+\prime} Z_i = (W_i' K' Z_{di} \,|\, \bar{w}_i m_i').$$

Now using that $K\iota = 0$ we have $KW_i = (KX_i|0)$ and with $\Omega = \sigma^2 I_T + \sigma_\eta^2 \iota\iota'$,

$$\Omega^+ = H\Omega H' = \begin{bmatrix} K \\ T^{-1}\iota' \end{bmatrix} (\sigma^2 I_T + \sigma_\eta^2 \iota\iota')(K' \;\; T^{-1}\iota) = \sigma^2 \begin{bmatrix} KK' & 0 \\ 0 & (\theta^2 T)^{-1} \end{bmatrix}.$$

Therefore

$$Z_i' \Omega^+ Z_i = \sigma^2 \begin{bmatrix} Z_{di}' KK' Z_{di} & 0 \\ 0 & (0^2 T)^{-1} m_i m_i' \end{bmatrix},$$

and

$$\begin{aligned} & W'\bar{H}'Z(Z'\bar{H}\bar{\Omega}\bar{H}'Z)^{-1}Z'\bar{H}W \\ &= \Sigma_i W_i^{+\prime} Z_i (\Sigma_i Z_i' \Omega^+ Z_i)^{-1} \Sigma_i Z_i' W_i^+ \\ &= \frac{1}{\sigma^2}\left[\begin{bmatrix} M_d & 0 \\ 0 & 0 \end{bmatrix} + \theta^2 T \Sigma_i \bar{w}_i m_i' (\Sigma_i m_i m_i')^{-1} \Sigma_i m_i \bar{w}_i' \right], \end{aligned} \tag{A.1}$$

where

$$M_d = \Sigma_i X_i' K' Z_{di} (\Sigma_i Z_{di}' KK' Z_{di})^{-1} \Sigma_i Z_{di}' K' X_i. \tag{A.2}$$

Now with $Z_{di} = I_{T-1} \otimes w_i'$, M_d equals

$$M_d = \Sigma_i X_i' (I_T \otimes w_i') \,[K'(KK')^{-1} K \otimes (\Sigma_i w_i w_i')^{-1}]\, \Sigma_i (I_T \otimes w_i) X_i.$$

Moreover, since $K'(KK')^{-1}K = Q = A'A$, where A is the orthogonal deviations operator defined in Section 3, and the columns of AX_i are linear combinations of the columns of Z_{di}, M_d becomes

$$M_d = \Sigma_i X_i' A' Z_{di} (\Sigma_i Z_{di}' Z_{di})^{-1} \Sigma_i Z_{di}' A X_i = \Sigma_i X_i' A' A X_i,$$

so that (A.1) equals

$$(1/\sigma^2)\,(\Sigma_i W_i' Q W_i + \theta^2 T \Sigma_i \bar{w}_i m_i' \,(\Sigma_i m_i m_i')^{-1}\, \Sigma_i m_i \bar{w}_i').$$

The derivation of the second term of (8) follows along the same lines.

Note that this result only requires that the columns of AX_i are linear combinations of the columns of Z_{di} provided Z_{di} has the Kronecker structure. Thus, the estimators of the form given in (5) that use $\tilde{\Omega}$ remain unaltered if instead of $Z_{di} = I \otimes w_i'$ we use

$$Z_{di} = I \otimes [\mathrm{vec}(KX_i)]'.$$

In addition, if we choose $K = A$, the block-diagonal specification of Z_{di} could be replaced by simply AX_i without changing the estimator, as apparent from expression (A.2).

A.2. The information bound for Hausman–Taylor models

The model specifies the conditional moment restrictions

$$\mathrm{E}(u_i | w_{1i}) = 0 \quad \text{and} \quad \mathrm{E}(Ku_i | w_{1i}, w_{2i}) = 0.$$

Let us introduce the notation

$$\rho_{1i} = y_i - W_i \delta = u_i,$$

$$\rho_{2i} = K(y_i - W_i \delta) = Ku_i,$$

where $\rho_{ji} = \rho_j(y_i, w_i, \delta)$, $j = 1, 2$. Following Chamberlain (1992b) we consider a forward transformation of ρ_{1i} of the form

$$\rho_{1i}^* = \rho_{1i} - \Gamma(w_i)\, \rho_{2i},$$

which given sequential conditioning ensures that $\mathrm{E}(\rho_{1i}^* | w_{1i}) = 0$.

We wish to choose $\Gamma(w_i)$ such that $\mathrm{E}(\rho_{1i}^* \rho_{2i}' | w_i) = 0$. Since

$$\mathrm{E}(\rho_{1i}^* \rho_{2i}' | w_i) = \Omega_i K' - \Gamma(w_i)\, K \Omega_i K',$$

the condition is satisfied if

$$\Gamma(w_i) = \Omega_i K' (K \Omega_i K')^{-1},$$

where $\Omega_i = \Omega(w_i)$. Thus

$$\rho_{1i}^* = u_i - \Omega_i K' (K \Omega_i K')^{-1} K u_i = \iota(\iota' \Omega_i^{-1} \iota)^{-1}\, \iota' \Omega_i^{-1} u_i.$$

Therefore, the bound for δ will be the sum of the bounds corresponding to each of the conditional moments

$$E(Ku_i | w_i) = 0,$$

$$E[(\iota'\Omega_i^{-1}\iota)^{-1}\iota'\Omega_i^{-1}u_i | w_{1i}] = 0.$$

References

Ahn, S. and P. Schmidt, 1995, Efficient estimation of models for dynamic panel data, this issue.

Amemiya, T. and T.E. MaCurdy, 1986, Instrumental-variable estimation of an error-components model, Econometrica 54, 869–881.

Anderson, T.W. and C. Hsiao, 1982, Formulation and estimation of dynamic models using panel data, Journal of Econometrics 18, 47–82.

Arellano, M. and S.R. Bond, 1991, Some tests of specification for panel data: Monte Carlo evidence and an application to employment equations, Review of Economic Studies 58, 277–297.

Balestra, P. and M. Nerlove, 1966, Pooling cross section and time series data in the estimation of a dynamic model: The demand for natural gas, Econometrica 34, 585–612.

Bhargava, A. and J.D. Sargan, 1983, Estimating dynamic random effects models from panel data covering short time periods, Econometrica 51, 1635–1659.

Breusch, T.S., G.E. Mizon, and P. Schmidt, 1989, Efficient estimation using panel data, Econometrica 57, 695–700.

Chamberlain, G., 1982, Multivariate regression models for panel data, Journal of Econometrics 18, 5–46.

Chamberlain, G., 1984, Panel data, in: Z. Griliches and M.D. Intriligator, eds., Handbook of econometrics, Vol. 2 (Elsevier, Amsterdam) 1247–1313.

Chamberlain, G., 1987, Asymptotic efficiency in estimation with conditional moment restrictions, Journal of Econometrics 34, 305–334.

Chamberlain, G., 1992a, Efficiency bounds for semiparametric regression, Econometrica 60, 567–596.

Chamberlain, G., 1992b, Comment: Sequential moment restrictions in panel data, Journal of Business and Economic Statistics 10, 20–26.

Hansen, L.P., 1982, Large sample properties of generalized method of moments estimators, Econometrica 50, 1029–1054.

Hausman, J.A. and W.E. Taylor, 1981, Panel data and unobservable individual effects, Econometrica 49, 1377–1398.

Hayashi, F. and C. Sims, 1983, Nearly efficient estimation of time series models with predetermined, but not exogenous, instruments, Econometrica 51, 783–798.

Holtz-Eakin, D., W. Newey, and H. Rosen, 1988, Estimating vector autoregressions with panel data, Econometrica 56, 1371–1395.

Schmidt, P., S.C. Ahn, and D. Wyhowski, 1992, Comment, Journal of Business and Economic Statistics 10, 10–14.

White, H., 1982, Instrumental variables regression with independent observations, Econometrica 50, 483–499.

[5]

JOURNAL OF
Econometrics

ELSEVIER Journal of Econometrics 87 (1998) 115–143

Initial conditions and moment restrictions in dynamic panel data models

Richard Blundell[a,*], Stephen Bond[b]

[a] *Institute for Fiscal Studies and Department of Economics, University College London, London WC1E 6BT, UK*

[b] *Institute for Fiscal Studies and Nuffield College, Oxford OX1 1NF, UK*

Received 1 October 1995; received in revised form 1 November 1997

Abstract

Estimation of the dynamic error components model is considered using two alternative linear estimators that are designed to improve the properties of the standard first-differenced GMM estimator. Both estimators require restrictions on the initial conditions process. Asymptotic efficiency comparisons and Monte Carlo simulations for the simple AR(1) model demonstrate the dramatic improvement in performance of the proposed estimators compared to the usual first-differenced GMM estimator, and compared to non-linear GMM. The importance of these results is illustrated in an application to the estimation of a labour demand model using company panel data.

JEL classification: C23

Keywords: Dynamic panel data; Error components; Weak instruments; Initial conditions; GMM

1. Introduction

In dynamic panel data models where the autoregressive parameter is moderately large and the number of time series observations is moderately small, the widely used linear generalised method of moments (GMM) estimator obtained after first differencing has been found to have large finite sample bias and poor precision in simulation studies (see Alonso-Borrego and Arellano, 1996). Lagged

* Corresponding author. E-mail: mailbox@ifs.org.uk

0304-4076/98/$ – see front matter
PII S0304-4076(97)00009-8

levels of the series provide weak instruments for first differences in this case. Here we consider two alternative estimators that impose further restrictions on the initial conditions process, designed to improve the properties of the standard first-differenced GMM estimator.

The first type of restriction justifies the use of an extended linear GMM estimator that uses lagged *differences* of y_{it} as instruments for equations in levels, in addition to lagged *levels* of y_{it} as instruments for equations in first differences (see Arellano and Bover, 1995). Monte Carlo simulations and asymptotic variance calculations show that this extended GMM estimator offers dramatic efficiency gains in the situations where the basic first-differenced GMM estimator performs poorly. This estimator is also shown to encompass the GMM estimator based on the non-linear moment conditions available in the dynamic error components model (see Ahn and Schmidt, 1995), and we find substantial asymptotic efficiency gains relative to this non-linear GMM estimator.

The second type of restriction validates the use of the error components GLS estimator on an extended model that conditions on the observed initial values. This provides a consistent estimator under homoskedasticity which, under normality, is asymptotically equivalent to conditional maximum likelihood (see Blundell and Smith, 1991). A Monte Carlo analysis also suggests that this estimator has good finite sample properties. However, the conditional GLS estimator requires homoskedasticity, and only extends to a model with regressors if the regressors are strictly exogenous. This is not the case for the GMM estimators.

Both types of restrictions are satisfied under stationarity but both are also valid under weaker assumptions. The gain in precision that results from exploiting these initial condition restrictions in these two alternative estimators is shown to increase for higher values of the autoregressive parameter and as the number of time series observations gets smaller. Our Monte Carlo analysis finds both a large downward bias and very low precision for the standard first-differenced estimator in these cases. The initial condition information not only greatly improves the precision but also greatly reduces the finite sample bias.

The main contributions of the paper are: to characterise the weak instruments problem for the first-differenced GMM estimator in terms of the concentration parameter (cf. Staiger and Stock, 1997); to demonstrate that the levels restrictions suggested by Arellano and Bover (1995) remain informative in the cases where the first-differenced instruments become weak; to relate these restrictions explicitly to the initial conditions process; to evaluate the asymptotic efficiency gains that result from exploiting these restrictions compared to both the differenced GMM estimator and the non-linear GMM estimator of Ahn and Schmidt (1995); to relate the conditions needed for consistency of the Blundell and Smith (1991) conditional GLS estimator to the initial conditions process; and finally to evaluate the performance of these estimators using both Monte Carlo simulations and an application to company panel data.

The layout of the paper is as follows. In Section 2 we briefly review the standard moment conditions for the autoregressive error components model, in the framework of Anderson and Hsiao (1981), Holtz-Eakin et al. (1988), Arellano and Bond (1991), and Ahn and Schmidt (1995). In Section 3 we evaluate the problem of weak instruments in the first-differenced instrumental variable estimator. Section 4 goes on to consider restrictions on the initial condition process that render lagged values of Δy_{it} valid as instruments for the levels equations and discusses the extended GMM estimator which is available when these restrictions are satisfied. In Section 5 we consider the conditional GLS estimator in which initial conditions are explicitly added to the model. Section 6 presents the results of Monte Carlo simulations which highlight the potential importance of exploiting the extra moment restrictions relating to the properties of the initial condition process for the efficiency of the AR coefficient estimators. Section 7 discusses the extensions to models with strictly exogenous and predetermined regressors. An application to a panel data model of labour demand is presented which illustrates the usefulness of the extended GMM estimator in practice. Section 8 concludes.

2. The model

We consider an autoregressive panel data model of the form

$$y_{it} = \alpha y_{i,t-1} + \beta_1' x_{it} + \beta_2' x_{it-1} + \eta_i + v_{it} \tag{2.1}$$

for $i = 1, \ldots, N$ and $t = 2, \ldots, T$, where $u_{it} \equiv \eta_i + v_{it}$ is the usual 'fixed effects' decomposition of the error term; N is large, T is fixed and $|\alpha| < 1$.[1] This has the corresponding 'common factor' restricted ($\beta_2 = -\alpha\beta_1$) form

$$y_{it} = \beta_1' x_{it} + f_i + \zeta_{it}$$

with

$$\zeta_{it} = \alpha\zeta_{i,t-1} + v_{it} \quad \text{and} \quad \eta_i = (1-\alpha) f_i. \tag{2.2}$$

In our application to panel data employment equations presented in Section 7 we allow for the inclusion of x_{it} regressors, but for the evaluation of the various estimators we use an AR(1) model with unobserved individual-specific effects

$$y_{it} = \alpha y_{i,t-1} + \eta_i + v_{it} \tag{2.3}$$

[1] All of the estimators discussed below and their properties extend in an obvious fashion to higher-order autoregressive models.

for $i = 1, \ldots, N$ and $t = 2, \ldots, T$. Since our focus is on the role of initial conditions we will assume that η_i and v_{it} are independently distributed across i and have the familiar error components structure in which

$$\mathrm{E}(\eta_i) = 0.\ \mathrm{E}(v_{it}) = 0,\ \mathrm{E}(v_{it}\eta_i) = 0 \quad \text{for } i = 1, \ldots, N \text{ and } t = 2, \ldots, T \qquad (2.4)$$

and

$$\mathrm{E}(v_{it}v_{is}) = 0 \quad \text{for } i = 1, \ldots, N \text{ and } \forall t \neq s. \qquad (2.5)$$

In addition, there is the standard assumption concerning the initial conditions y_{i1} (see Ahn and Schmidt, 1995, for example)

$$\mathrm{E}(y_{i1}v_{it}) = 0 \quad \text{for } i = 1, \ldots, N \text{ and } t = 2, \ldots, T. \qquad (2.6)$$

Conditions (2.4), (2.5) and (2.6) imply moment restrictions that are sufficient to (identify and) estimate α for $T \geqslant 3$.

3. Estimation in first differences

3.1. The standard moment conditions

In the absence of any further restrictions on the process generating the initial conditions, the autoregressive error components model (2.3)–(2.6) implies the following $m = 0.5(T-1)(T-2)$ orthogonality conditions which are linear in the α parameter

$$\mathrm{E}(y_{i,t-s}\Delta v_{it}) = 0 \quad \text{for } t = 3, \ldots, T \text{ and } s \geqslant 2 \qquad (3.1)$$

where $\Delta v_{it} = v_{it} - v_{i,t-1}$. These depend only on the assumed absence of serial correlation in the time-varying disturbances v_{it}, together with the restriction in Eq. (2.6).

The moment restrictions in Eq. (3.1) can be expressed more compactly as

$$\mathrm{E}(\boldsymbol{Z}_i'\bar{\boldsymbol{u}}_i) = \boldsymbol{0}$$

where $\boldsymbol{Z}_i$ is the $(T-2) \times m$ matrix given by (omitting the i subscripts)

$$\boldsymbol{Z}_i = \begin{bmatrix} y_1 & 0 & 0 & \ldots & 0 & \ldots & 0 \\ 0 & y_1 & y_2 & \ldots & 0 & \ldots & 0 \\ . & . & . & \ldots & . & \ldots & . \\ 0 & 0 & 0 & \ldots & y_1 & \ldots & y_{T-2} \end{bmatrix},$$

and $\bar{\boldsymbol{u}}_i$ is the $(T-2)$ vector $(\Delta v_{i3}, \Delta v_{i4}, \ldots, \Delta v_{iT})'$.

The generalised method of moments estimator based on these moment conditions minimises the quadratic distance $(\bar{\boldsymbol{u}}'\boldsymbol{Z}\boldsymbol{A}_N\boldsymbol{Z}'\bar{\boldsymbol{u}})$ for some metric $\boldsymbol{A}_N$, where $\boldsymbol{Z}'$ is the $m \times N(T-2)$ matrix $(\boldsymbol{Z}_1', \boldsymbol{Z}_2', \ldots, \boldsymbol{Z}_N')$ and $\bar{\boldsymbol{u}}'$ is the $N(T-2)$

vector $(\bar{u}'_1, \bar{u}'_2, \ldots, \bar{u}'_N)$. This gives the GMM estimator for α as

$$\hat{\alpha}_{\text{dif}} = (\bar{y}'_{-1} Z A_N Z' \bar{y}_{-1})^{-1} \bar{y}'_{-1} Z A_N Z' \bar{y}. \tag{3.2}$$

where $\bar{y}_i$ is the $(T-2)$ vector $(\Delta y_{i3}, \Delta y_{i4}, \ldots, \Delta y_{iT})$, $\bar{y}_{i,-1}$ is the $(T-2)$ vector $(\Delta y_{i2}, \Delta y_{i3}, \ldots, \Delta y_{i,T-1})$, and $\bar{y}$ and $\bar{y}_{-1}$ are stacked across individuals in the same way as $\bar{u}$.

Alternative choices for the weights A_N give rise to a set of GMM estimators based on the moment conditions in Eq. (3.1), all of which are consistent for large N and finite T, but which differ in their asymptotic efficiency.[2] In general the optimal weights are given by

$$A_N = \left(N^{-1} \sum_{i=1}^{N} Z'_i \hat{\bar{u}}_i \hat{\bar{u}}'_i Z_i \right)^{-1},$$

where $\hat{\bar{u}}_i$ are residuals from an initial consistent estimator. We refer to this as the *two-step* GMM estimator.[3] In the absence of any additional knowledge about the process for the initial conditions, this estimator is asymptotically efficient in the class of estimators based on the linear moment conditions [Eq. (3.1)] (see Hansen, 1982; Chamberlain, 1987).

3.1.1. Homoskedasticity

Ahn and Schmidt (1995) show that additional linear moment conditions are available if the v_{it} disturbances are homoskedastic through time, i.e. if

$$\mathrm{E}(v_{it}^2) = \sigma_i^2 \quad \text{for } t = 2, \ldots, T. \tag{3.3}$$

This implies $T-3$ orthogonality restrictions of the form

$$\mathrm{E}(y_{i,t-2}\Delta v_{i,t-1} - y_{i,t-1}\Delta v_{it}) = 0 \quad \text{for } t = 4, \ldots, T. \tag{3.4}$$

[2] These estimators are all based on the normalisation (2.3). Alonso-Borrego and Arellano (1996) consider a symmetrically normalised instrumental variable estimator based on the normalisation invariance of the standard LIML estimator.

[3] As a choice of A_N to yield the initial consistent estimator, Arellano and Bond (1991) suggest

$$A_N = \left(N^{-1} \sum_{i=1}^{N} Z'_i H Z_i \right)^{-1},$$

where H is the $(T-2)\times(T-2)$ matrix given by

$$H = \begin{pmatrix} 2 & -1 & 0 & \ldots & 0 \\ -1 & 2 & -1 & \ldots & 0 \\ 0 & -1 & 2 & \ldots & 0 \\ \ldots & \ldots & \ldots & \ldots & . \\ 0 & 0 & 0 & \ldots & 2 \end{pmatrix}$$

which can be calculated in one step. Note that when the v_{it} are i.i.d., the one-step and two-step estimators are asymptotically equivalent in this model.

and allows a further $T-3$ columns to be added to the instrument matrix Z_i.[4] Calculation of the one-step and two-step GMM estimators then proceeds exactly as described above.

3.2. The problem of weak instruments

The instruments used in the standard first-differenced GMM estimator become less informative in two important cases. First, as the value of α increases towards unity, and second, as the relative variance of the fixed effects η_i increases. To examine this further consider the case with $T=3$. For $T=3$, moment conditions (3.1) reduce to a single orthogonality condition, so that α is just-identified. The corresponding method of moments estimator $\hat{\alpha}_{\text{dif}}$ in Eq. (3.2) reduces to a simple instrumental variable (IV) estimator with reduced form (instrumental variable regression) equation

$$\Delta y_{i2} = \pi y_{i1} + r_i \quad \text{for } i = 1,\ldots,N. \tag{3.5}$$

For sufficiently high α or variance of η_i, the least-squares estimate of the reduced form coefficient π can be made arbitrarily close to zero. In this case the instrument y_{i1} is only weakly correlated with Δy_{i2}. To see this notice that the model (2.3) implies that

$$\Delta y_{i2} = (\alpha - 1)y_{i1} + \eta_i + v_{i2} \quad \text{for } i = 1,\ldots,N. \tag{3.6}$$

The least-squares estimator of $(\alpha - 1)$ in Eq. (3.6) is generally biased upwards, towards zero, since we expect $E(y_{i1}\eta_i) > 0$. Assuming stationarity and letting $\sigma_\eta^2 = \text{var}(\eta_i)$ and $\sigma_v^2 = \text{var}(v_{it})$, the plim of $\hat{\pi}$ is given by

$$\text{plim}\,\hat{\pi} = (\alpha - 1)\frac{k}{(\sigma_\eta^2/\sigma_v^2) + k} \quad \text{with } k = \frac{(1-\alpha)^2}{(1-\alpha^2)}.$$

The bias term effectively scales the estimated coefficient on the instrumental variable y_{i1} toward zero. We find that $\text{plim}\,\hat{\pi} \to 0$ as $\alpha \to 1$ or as $(\sigma_\eta^2/\sigma_v^2) \to \infty$, which are the cases in which the first stage F-statistic is $O_p(1)$. A graph showing both $\text{plim}\,\hat{\pi}$ and $\alpha - 1$ against α is given in Fig. 1, for $\sigma_\eta^2 = \sigma_v^2 = 1$, $T = 3$.

Here we have considered taking α towards unity with σ_η^2 fixed $(=\sigma_v^2)$. This seems reasonable for the case where we are asking what happens to the properties of this IV estimator for specific values of α. An alternative is to

[4] The additional columns Z_{Hi} are

$$Z'_{Hi} = \begin{pmatrix} y_2 & -y_3 & 0 & \cdots & 0 & 0 \\ 0 & y_3 & -y_4 & \cdots & 0 & 0 \\ . & . & . & \cdots & . & . \\ 0 & 0 & 0 & \cdots & y_{T-2} & -y_{T-1} \end{pmatrix}.$$

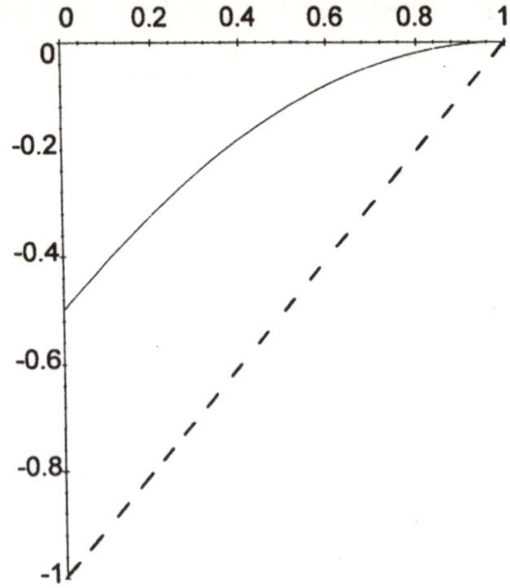

Fig. 1. plim $\hat{\pi}$ and $\alpha - 1, \sigma_\eta^2$ fixed.

analyse the limiting sequence of $\alpha \to 1$ keeping $\sigma_\eta^2/(1-\alpha)^2$ fixed.[5] In this case the plim $\hat{\pi}$ has the form illustrated in Fig. 2, and although there is still substantial bias towards zero, it is less serious than in Fig. 1.[6]

We are interested in inferences using this differenced IV estimator when π is local to zero, that is where the instrument y_{i1} is only weakly correlated with Δy_{i2}. Following Nelson and Startz (1990a,b) and Staiger and Stock (1997) we characterise this problem of weak instruments using the concentration parameter. First note that the F-statistic for the first stage instrumental variable regression converges to a noncentral chi-squared with one degree of freedom. The concentration parameter is then the corresponding noncentrality parameter which we label τ in this case. The IV estimator performs poorly when τ approaches zero. Assuming stationarity, τ has the following simple characterisation in terms of the parameters of the AR model

$$\tau = \frac{(\sigma_v^2 k)^2}{\sigma_\eta^2 + \sigma_v^2 k} \quad \text{where } k = \frac{(1-\alpha)^2}{(1-\alpha^2)}. \tag{3.7}$$

The performance of the $\hat{\alpha}_{\text{dif}}$ estimator in this AR(1) specification can therefore be seen to deteriorate as $\alpha \to 1$, as well as for decreasing values of σ_v^2 and for increasing values of σ_η^2. To examine this further, Fig. 3 provides a plot of

[5] This would be equivalent to fixing the variance of f_i in the common factor specification of the model (2.2).

[6] Fig. 2 shows the case where $\sigma_\eta^2/(1-\alpha)^2 = \sigma_v^2 = 1$, $T = 3$.

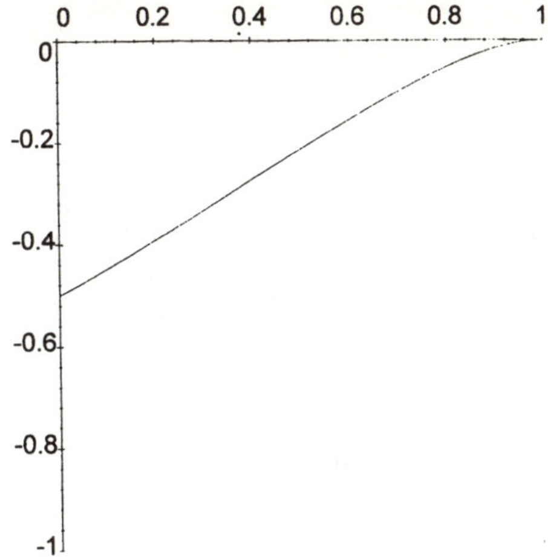

Fig. 2. plim $\hat{\pi}, \sigma_\eta^2/(1-\alpha)^2$ fixed.

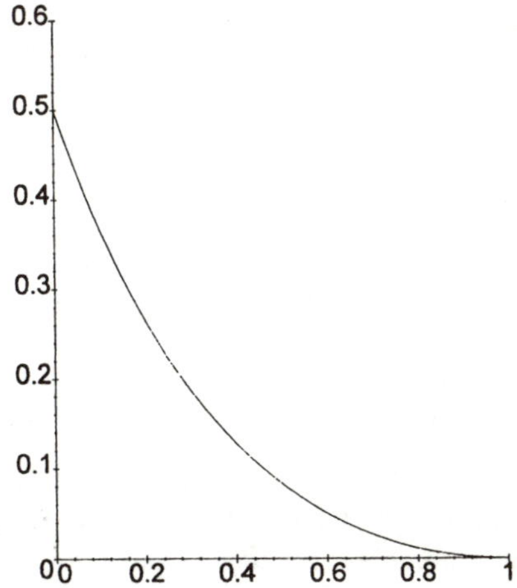

Fig. 3. Concentration parameter τ for $T = 3$.

τ against α for the case $\sigma_\eta^2 = \sigma_v^2 = 1$, $T = 3$. We further investigate the finite sample properties of the differenced GMM estimator using Monte Carlo experiments in Section 6.

In this special case, it is also interesting to note the following simple relationship between the asymptotic standard error of $\hat{\alpha}_{\text{dif}}$ and the concentration parameter

$$\text{asyse}(\hat{\alpha}_{\text{dif}}) = \frac{\sigma_v}{\sqrt{2\tau\sigma_r^2}}$$

where σ_r^2 is the reduced form error variance $E(r_i^2)$ in Eq. (3.5). We see that the asymptotic variance of the $\hat{\alpha}_{\text{dif}}$ estimator explodes as $\tau \to 0$. For higher values of T the precision of $\hat{\alpha}_{\text{dif}}$ will also be shown to deteriorate as $\alpha \to 1$, although at a slower rate. A comparison of asymptotic variances is given in more detail in the following section.

4. Non-linear moment conditions and restrictions on the initial conditions process

Introduction & Motivation For GMM.

In this section we consider an additional, but in many cases relatively mild, restriction on the initial conditions process which allows the use of additional linear moment conditions for the levels equations in the GMM framework. This allows the use of lagged differences of y_{it} as instruments in the levels equations. These additional moment conditions are likely to be important in practice when α is close to unity or when σ_η^2/σ_v^2 is high, since we have seen that lagged levels will be weak instruments in the differenced equations in these cases.

4.1. Non-linear moment conditions Just read.

A number of authors have previously suggested using the additional T-3 non-linear moment conditions (see, for example, Ahn and Schmidt, 1995, Eq. (4))

$$E(u_{it}\Delta u_{i,t-1}) = 0 \quad \text{for } t = 4,5,\ldots,T. \tag{4.1}$$

which are implied by Eqs. (2.4)–(2.6) and which could be expected to improve efficiency. These conditions relate directly to the absence of serial correlation in v_{it} and do not require homoskedasticity. Under the homoskedasticity through time restriction (3.3), Ahn and Schmidt (1995, Eq. (11b)) show the existence of an additional non-linear moment condition

$$E(\bar{u}_i\Delta u_{i3}) = 0 \quad \text{where } \bar{u}_i = \frac{1}{T-1}\sum_{t=2}^{T} u_{it}. \tag{4.2}$$

Asymptotic efficiency comparisons reported in Ahn and Schmidt (1995) confirm that these non-linear moments are particularly informative in cases where α is close to unity and/or where σ_η^2/σ_v^2 is high.

4.2. Initial conditions

In contrast to the non-linear moment restrictions (4.1), we consider the following T-3 linear moment conditions:[7]

$$\mathrm{E}(u_{it}\Delta y_{i,t-1}) = 0 \quad \text{for } t = 4,5,\ldots,T. \tag{4.3}$$

The use of lagged differences as possible instruments for equations in levels was proposed by Arellano and Bover (1995). Clearly, Eq. (4.3) does not imply Eq. (4.1). However, notice that since Δy_{i2} is observed, there is an additional restriction available, namely

$$\mathrm{E}(u_{i3}\Delta y_{i2}) = 0. \tag{4.4}$$

Note also that the validity of this extra moment condition depends on a restriction on the initial conditions process generating y_{i1}. Condition (4.4) has two important implications. First, combining Eq. (4.4) with the model for periods $2,\ldots,T$ set out in Eqs. (2.3)–(2.6) implies the validity of the linear moment restrictions in Eq. (4.3).[8] Second, combining Eq. (4.3) and Eq. (4.4) implies the non-linear restrictions in Eq. (4.1), and renders these redundant for estimation. Thus, the complete set of second-order moment restrictions implied by Eqs. (2.3)–(2.6) and Eq. (4.4) can be implemented as a linear GMM estimator.

To examine the conditions under which Eq. (4.4) will hold, we write y_{i1} as

$$y_{i1} = \frac{\eta_i}{1-\alpha} + u_{i1}. \tag{4.5}$$

The model specifies a convergent level for y_{it} from $t = 2$ onwards for each individual, and u_{i1} is simply the initial deviation from this convergent level. Noting that Eq. (4.4) is equivalent to $\mathrm{E}[(\eta_i + v_{i3})(v_{i2} + (\alpha - 1)u_{i1})] = 0$, necessary conditions for Eq. (4.4) are then

$$\mathrm{E}(u_{i1}\eta_i) = \mathrm{E}(u_{i1}v_{i3}) = 0 \quad \text{for } i = 1,\ldots,N. \tag{4.6}$$

The key requirement is therefore that the *deviations* of the initial conditions from $\eta_i/(1-\alpha)$ are uncorrelated with the *level* of $\eta_i/(1-\alpha)$ itself.

This condition is clearly satisfied in the fully stationary model, where u_{i1} will be the infinite weighted sum $\sum_{s=-1}^{\infty}(\alpha^{s+1}v_{i,-s})$, and where assumptions (2.4) and (2.5) are maintained for all s and t. However, stationarity is not necessary for the

---

[7] In this section we focus on moment conditions that remain valid under heteroskedasticity.

[8] Given Eqs. (2.3)–(2.6), we can write

$$\Delta y_{it} = \alpha^{t-2}\Delta y_{i2} + \sum_{s=0}^{t-3}\alpha^{s}\Delta v_{i,t-s} \quad \text{for } t = 3,4,\ldots,T$$

and the $\Delta v_{i,t-s}$ are uncorrelated with η_i. Hence $\mathrm{E}(\Delta y_{it}\eta_i) = \alpha^{t-2}\mathrm{E}(\Delta y_{i2}\eta_i)$.

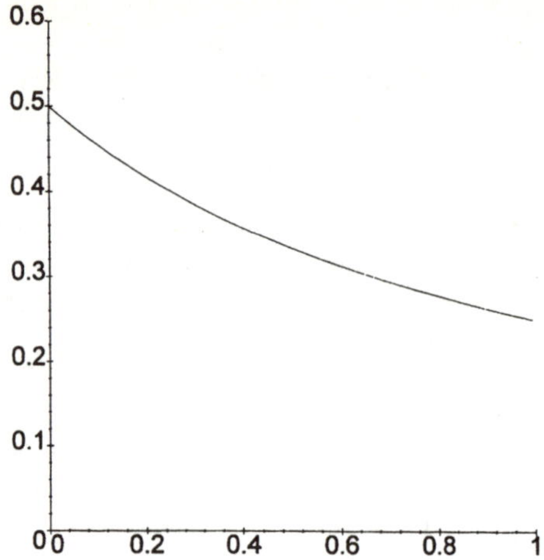

Fig. 4. plim $\hat{\pi}$.

validity of the extra linear moment conditions (4.3) and (4.4). Condition (4.6) imposes no restriction on the variance of u_{i1}, and any entry period 'disequilibrium' from $\eta_i/(1-\alpha)$ which is randomly distributed across agents will preserve condition (4.4). Other departures from stationarity such as $y_{i1} = k \forall i$ or $y_{i1} \sim$ i.i.d.$(0, \sigma^2_{y_1})$ will violate Eq. (4.6) however, so this restriction is not without content.

To show that the moment conditions (4.3) and (4.4) remain informative when α approaches unity or σ^2_η/σ^2_v becomes large, we again consider the case of $T = 3$. Here we can use one equation in levels

$$y_{i3} = \alpha y_{i2} + (\eta_i + v_{i3})$$

for which the instrument available is Δy_{i2}, and the reduced form equation is

$$y_{i2} = \pi \Delta y_{i2} + r_i.$$

In this case the plim $\hat{\pi}$ is given by

$$\text{plim}\,\hat{\pi} = \frac{1}{2}\left(\frac{1-\alpha}{1-\alpha^2}\right)$$

which is illustrated in Fig. 4.

As was the case for $\hat{\alpha}_{\text{dif}}$, the performance of the GMM estimator based on this levels equation can be seen to deteriorate as $\alpha \to 1$. However, with $|\alpha| < 1$, this moment condition stays informative in clear contrast to the $\hat{\alpha}_{\text{dif}}$ estimator. The efficient GMM estimator will combine both sets of orthogonality restrictions, to which we turn next.

4.3. A system GMM estimator

Calculation of the GMM estimators using conditions (4.3) and (4.4) can be based on a stacked system comprising all $(T-2)$ equations in first differences and the $(T-2)$ equations in levels corresponding to periods $3,\ldots,T$, for which instruments are observed. The instrument matrix for this system can be written

$$Z_i^+ = \begin{bmatrix} \boldsymbol{Z}_i & 0 & 0 & \cdots & 0 \\ 0 & \Delta y_{i2} & 0 & \cdots & 0 \\ 0 & 0 & \Delta y_{i3} & \cdots & 0 \\ \cdot & \cdot & \cdot & \cdots & 0 \\ 0 & 0 & 0 & \cdots & \Delta y_{i,T-1} \end{bmatrix} \tag{4.7}$$

Matrix of Instruments for S-GMM estimator.

where $\boldsymbol{Z}_i$ is as defined in Section 3. The calculation of the two-step GMM estimator is then analogous to that described above.[9]

4.4. Asymptotic variance comparisons

To quantify the gains in asymptotic efficiency that result from exploiting the linear moment conditions (4.3) and (4.4), Table 1 reports the ratio of the asymptotic variance of the standard first-differenced GMM estimator described in Section 3.1 to the asymptotic variance of the system GMM estimator described in Section 4.3. These asymptotic variance ratios are calculated assuming both stationarity and homoskedasticity. They are presented for $T = 3$ and $T = 4$, for two fixed values of σ_η^2/σ_v^2, and for a range of values of the autoregressive parameter α. For comparison, we also reproduce from Ahn and Schmidt (1995) the corresponding asymptotic variance ratios comparing first-differenced GMM to the non-linear GMM estimator which uses the quadratic moment conditions (4.1), but *not* the extra linear moment conditions (4.3) and (4.4). In the $T = 3$ case there are no quadratic moment restrictions available. These calculations suggest that exploiting conditions (4.3) and (4.4) can result in dramatic efficiency gains when $T = 3$, particularly at high values of α and high values of σ_η^2/σ_v^2. These are indeed the cases where we find the instruments used to obtain the first-differenced estimator to be weak.

In the $T = 4$ case we still find dramatic efficiency gains at high values of α. Comparison to the results for the non-linear GMM estimator also shows that the gains from exploiting conditions (4.3) and (4.4) can be much larger than the gains from simply exploiting the non-linear restrictions (4.1).

[9] In this case, though, there is no one-step GMM estimator that is asymptotically equivalent to the two-step estimator, even in the special case of i.i.d. disturbances.

In Blundell and Bond (1998) S-GMM exploiting the extra additional moment restrictions leads to significant efficiency gains, where it increase with value of α (i.e high persistence) and σ_η^2/σ_v^2. (see Table 1).

Table 1
Asymptotic variance ratios

	System	Non-linear	System	Non-linear
	$\sigma_\eta^2/\sigma_v^2 = 1$	$\sigma_\eta^2/\sigma_v^2 = 1$	$\sigma_\eta^2/\sigma_v^2 = 0.25$	$\sigma_\eta^2/\sigma_v^2 = 0.25$
α	$T = 3$		$T = 3$	
0.0	1.33	n/a	1.33	n/a
0.3	2.15		1.89	
0.5	4.00		2.91	
0.8	28.00		13.10	
0.9	121.33		47.91	
α	$T = 4$		$T = 4$	
0.0	1.75	1.67	1.40	1.29
0.3	2.31	1.91	1.77	1.33
0.5	3.26	2.10	2.42	1.35
0.8	13.97	2.42	8.88	1.41
0.9	55.40	2.54	30.90	1.45

In the Monte Carlo simulations presented in Section 6 we investigate whether similar improvements are found in finite samples.

4.5. Homoskedasticity

In the case where the initial conditions satisfy restriction (4.4) and the v_{it} satisfy restriction (3.3), Ahn and Schmidt (1995), (Eq. (12b)) show that the $T-2$ homoskedasticity restrictions (3.4) and (4.2) can be replaced by a set of $T-2$ moment conditions

$$\mathrm{E}(y_{it}u_{it} - y_{i,t-1}u_{i,t-1}) = 0 \quad \text{for } t = 3,\ldots,T \tag{4.8}$$

which are all linear in the parameter α. The non-linear condition (4.2) is again redundant for estimation given Eq. (4.4), and the complete set of second-order moment restrictions implied by Eqs. (2.3)–(2.6), (3.3) and (4.4) can be implemented in a linear GMM estimator.

5. The conditional GLS estimator

In the autoregressive error components model with homoskedasticity across *both* individuals and time,[10] restrictions on the initial conditions process can be used to derive a consistent *conditional* GLS (CGLS) estimator by including y_{i1} in

[10] In this section we require $\mathrm{E}(v_{it}^2) = \sigma_v^2$ and $\mathrm{E}(\eta_i^2) = \sigma_\eta^2$ for $i = 1,\ldots,N$ and $t = 2,\ldots,T$.

each of the $T-1$ levels equations and then applying the standard error components GLS estimator. Under joint normality, this is the conditional ML estimator (CMLE) proposed by Blundell and Smith (1991).[11]

To examine this estimator we write the model for each i as a $T-1$ equation system

$$\boldsymbol{y}_i = \alpha \boldsymbol{y}_{i,-1} + \boldsymbol{u}_i = \alpha \boldsymbol{y}_{i,-1} + \boldsymbol{l}\eta_i + \boldsymbol{v}_i \tag{5.1}$$

where $\boldsymbol{y}'_i = (y_{i2}, \dots, y_{i,T})$, $\boldsymbol{y}'_{i,-1} = (y_{i1}, \dots, y_{i,T-1})$, $\boldsymbol{l}$ is the $T-1$-unit vector, $\boldsymbol{u}'_i = (u_{i2}, \dots, u_{iT})$ and $\boldsymbol{v}'_i = (v_{i2}, \dots, v_{iT})$. The error component assumptions imply

$$\mathrm{E}(\boldsymbol{u}_i \boldsymbol{u}'_i) = \boldsymbol{\Omega} = \sigma_\eta^2 \boldsymbol{J}_{T-1} + \sigma_v^2 \boldsymbol{I}_{T-1}. \tag{5.2}$$

where $\boldsymbol{J}_{T-1}$ is the $(T-1)\times(T-1)$ unit matrix $\boldsymbol{ll}'$ and $\boldsymbol{I}_{T-1}$ the $(T-1)\times(T-1)$ identity matrix.

The presence of the fixed effect η_i in u_{it} not only implies

$$\mathrm{E}(\boldsymbol{y}'_{i,-1}\boldsymbol{u}_i) \neq \boldsymbol{0} \tag{5.3}$$

but also

$$\mathrm{E}(\boldsymbol{y}'_{i,-1}\boldsymbol{\Omega}^{-1}\boldsymbol{u}_i) \neq \boldsymbol{0}. \tag{5.4}$$

As a result the standard OLS, Within Groups and GLS estimators are all inconsistent (see Hsiao, 1986; Nickell, 1981 and Sevestre and Trognon, 1985, respectively).

Notice, however, that the system may be written

$$\boldsymbol{A}\boldsymbol{y}_i = \boldsymbol{a} y_{i1} + \boldsymbol{l}\eta_i + \boldsymbol{v}_i \tag{5.5}$$

with $\boldsymbol{A}$ a $(T-1)\times(T-1)$ lower triangular matrix and $\boldsymbol{a}' = (\alpha, 0, \dots, 0)$. Since $\boldsymbol{A}$ is lower triangular the inconsistency of the GLS estimator can be seen to depend on $\mathrm{E}(y_{i1}\eta_i) \neq 0$. That is, although diagonalising the $(T-1)\times(T-1)$ error covariance matrix, premultiplying the $T-1$ system (5.5) by $\boldsymbol{\Omega}^{-1/2}$ introduces y_{i1} into all $T-1$ equations of the transformed system and induces a correlation with η_i. The aim of the *conditional* GLS estimator is to eliminate this correlation.

Given Eq. (2.6), we have that $\mathrm{E}(y_{i1}u_{it}) = \mathrm{E}(y_{i1}\eta_i)$ for $t = 2, \dots, T$. We then make the following assumption

$$\mathrm{E}(\eta_i | y_{i1}) = \phi y_{i1} \quad \text{with } \mathrm{E}(y_{i1}^2) = \sigma_1^2 \quad \text{for } i = 1, \dots, N. \tag{5.6}$$

Including y_{i1} in each equation of the system (5.5) gives an *extended* system

$$\boldsymbol{A}\boldsymbol{y}_i = \boldsymbol{a} y_{i1} + \boldsymbol{l}\phi y_{i1} + \boldsymbol{l}\tilde{\eta}_i + \boldsymbol{v}_i \tag{5.7}$$

[11] Blundell and Smith (1991) consider a range of CMLE estimators, from the case without the full error components restrictions, to the fully stationary error components model (which is equivalent to the ML estimator in Bhagarva and Sargan (1983)).

in which $\tilde{\eta}_i = \eta_i - \phi y_{i1}$. From Eq. (5.6) we have $E(y_{i1}\tilde{\eta}_i) = 0$ and $\text{var}(\tilde{\eta}_i)$ is common across individuals. The conditional model (5.7) therefore retains an error components structure with homoskedastic errors.

Defining $\tilde{\Omega}$ to be the $(T-1)\times(T-1)$ error covariance matrix for the errors $\tilde{\boldsymbol{u}}_i = \boldsymbol{l}\tilde{\eta}_i + \boldsymbol{v}_i$ in system (5.7), we then have the following moment condition:

$$E(\boldsymbol{y}'_{i,-1}\tilde{\Omega}^{-1}\tilde{\boldsymbol{u}}_i) = \boldsymbol{0}. \tag{5.8}$$

As a result error components GLS will be consistent for α in the conditional model (5.7).[12] The parameter ϕ is identified for $T \geqslant 3$ through the restrictions between $\boldsymbol{A}$ and $\boldsymbol{a}$. Under the normality assumption

$$\boldsymbol{u}_i \sim N(\boldsymbol{l}\eta_i, \boldsymbol{\Omega}) \quad \text{for all } i = 1,\ldots,N \tag{5.9}$$

this CGLS estimator is equivalent to the conditional MLE. For the autoregressive error components model with homoskedastic normal disturbances and satisfying assumption (5.6), this CGLS estimator is therefore efficient for α provided there are no cross equation restrictions between α and ϕ.[13]

6. Monte Carlo results

In this section we report the results of a Monte Carlo study which investigates the potential gains from exploiting the moment conditions (4.3) and (4.4) in finite samples, as well as the potential gains from using the conditional GLS estimator.

6.1. Design

We consider two data generation processes for y_{it}.

Model A:

$$y_{it} = \alpha y_{i,t-1} + \eta_i + v_{it}$$

Model B:

$$y_{it} = \alpha y_{i,t-1} + (1-\alpha)\eta_i + v_{it}$$

α→1, y_{it} approaches random walk and η_i become less important

[12] Note that it remains the case that $E(\boldsymbol{y}'_{i,-1}\tilde{\boldsymbol{u}}_i) \neq \boldsymbol{0}$. The orthogonality condition (5.8) is an example of a GLS transformation which is necessary for consistency and not just efficiency. As a result, although consistency does not require normality, it does require imposing the correct restrictions on $\tilde{\Omega}$. As indicated in Prucha (1984), this is a situation when the asymptotic covariance matrix for the *feasible* conditional GLS estimator of α depends on the distribution of the estimated $\tilde{\Omega}$. Bootstrap methods would, however, be applicable in this parametric autoregressive model, as described in Horowitz (1997).

[13] See Blundell and Smith (1991).

for $i = 1,2,\dots,N$ and $t = 2, 3,\dots,T$, where in each case the η_i and v_{it} are drawn as mutually independent i.i.d. N(0,1) random variables. In model B, the contribution of the time-invariant component of the error term becomes less important as the autoregressive parameter α increases.

In both cases we generate the initial conditions y_{i1} as:

$$y_{i1} = \frac{\eta_i}{1-\alpha} + u_{i1}$$

where u_{i1} is an i.i.d. $N(0,\sigma_{u1}^2)$ random variable, independent of both η_i and v_{it}, and with the variance of u_{i1} chosen to satisfy stationarity. Some models with non-stationary initial conditions, and non-normal and heteroskedastic disturbances, are considered in the appendix. All results are based on 1000 Monte Carlo replications, with new values for the initial conditions drawn in each replication.

We present results for three GMM estimators:

DIF: The standard first-differenced GMM estimator, based on moment conditions (3.1) only.

SYS: The system GMM estimator, based on moment conditions (3.1), (4.3) and (4.4).

ALL: The system GMM estimator which also exploits the further $T-2$ moment restrictions (4.8) that follow from assumption (4.4) and the homoskedasticity through time of v_{it}.

Note that the linear GMM (ALL) estimator exploits the complete set of second-order moment restrictions implied by assumptions (2.3)–(2.6), (3.3) and (4.4).

The results reported below are for conventional two-step GMM estimators. For GMM (DIF), the choice of A_N to yield an initial consistent estimator is that discussed in footnote 3. In our Monte Carlo designs, these one-step and two-step GMM (DIF) estimators are asymptotically equivalent, and their finite sample distributions were found to be similar in our simulations. For GMM (SYS) and GMM (ALL), the choice of A_N to yield an initial consistent estimator is $A_N = (N^{-1}\sum_{i=1}^{N} Z_i^{+\prime} Z_i^{+})^{-1}$, which is asymptotically inefficient relative to the two-step estimators.[14] However the finite sample distributions of the one- and two-step system GMM estimators were found to be similar in most of our simulations. This is discussed further in the appendix. For comparison, we also report results for a feasible conditional GLS estimator, which uses residuals from the one-step GMM (SYS) estimator to estimate the required variance components.

[14] Without prior knowledge of, for example, σ_η^2/σ_v^2, there is no one-step weight matrix that is asymptotically equivalent to two-step GMM in these cases.

6.2. Results

The main results are presented in Table 2. We consider sample sizes with $N = 100$, 200 and 500, and values of α varying from 0.0 to 0.9. Table 2a reports results for model A with $T = 4$, Table 2b reports results for model B with $T = 4$, and Table 2c reports further results for model A with $T = 11$.

Our main findings concern the poor performance of the first-differenced GMM estimator at high values of α, and the dramatic improvement that results from exploiting the additional moment conditions (4.3) and (4.4) in these cases.

Table 2
(a) Stationary model A, $T = 4$

N	α		GMM2 (DIF)		GMM2 (SYS)		GMM2 (ALL)		CGLS
		Mean	RMSE *SD*	Mean	RMSE *SD*	Mean	RMSE *SD*	Mean	RMSE *SD*
100	0.0	− 0.0044	0.1227	0.0100	0.0994	0.0060	0.0970	0.0157	0.0986
			0.1227		*0.0990*		*0.0969*		*0.0974*
	0.3	0.2865	0.1853	0.3132	0.1221	0.3100	0.1216	0.3188	0.1228
			0.1849		*0.1215*		*0.1213*		*0.1215*
	0.5	0.4641	0.2693	0.5100	0.1333	0.5100	0.1356	0.5182	0.1353
			0.2674		*0.1330*		*0.1353*		*0.1342*
	0.8	0.4844	0.8805	0.8101	0.1620	0.8169	0.1541	0.8365	0.1396
			0.8224		*0.1618*		*0.1533*		*0.1349*
	0.9	0.2264	1.0659	0.9405	0.1615	0.9422	0.1415	0.9572	0.1121
			0.8264		*0.1564*		*0.1351*		*0.0964*
200	0.0	− 0.0037	0.0854	0.0051	0.0670	0.0028	0.0651	0.0083	0.0700
			0.0854		*0.0669*		*0.0651*		*0.0696*
	0.3	0.2919	0.1272	0.3092	0.0838	0.3061	0.0812	0.3120	0.0895
			0.1270		*0.0833*		*0.0810*		*0.0887*
	0.5	0.4828	0.1828	0.5098	0.0941	0.5079	0.0925	0.5135	0.1015
			0.1821		*0.0936*		*0.0922*		*0.1006*
	0.8	0.6362	0.5468	0.8050	0.1196	0.8112	0.1143	0.8259	0.1115
			0.5219		*0.1195*		*0.1138*		*0.1085*
	0.9	0.3731	1.1000	0.9235	0.1499	0.9308	0.1243	0.9431	0.1022
			0.9661		*0.1481*		*0.1205*		*0.0927*
500	0.0	− 0.0033	0.0557	0.0012	0.0434	0.0001	0.0421	0.0025	0.0462
			0.0556		*0.0434*		*0.0422*		*0.0461*
	0.3	0.2936	0.0827	0.3025	0.0552	0.3008	0.0530	0.3030	0.0607
			0.0824		*0.0552*		*0.0530*		*0.0606*
	0.5	0.4887	0.1177	0.5021	0.0632	0.5006	0.0612	0.5025	0.0710
			0.1172		*0.0632*		*0.0612*		*0.0710*
	0.8	0.7386	0.3144	0.7939	0.0781	0.7942	0.0770	0.8007	0.0853
			0.3085		*0.0779*		*0.0769*		*0.0853*
	0.9	0.5978	0.7081	0.9043	0.1000	0.9038	0.0884	0.9172	0.0880
			0.6407		*0.0999*		*0.0883*		*0.0863*

(b) Stationary model B. $T = 4$

N	α		GMM2 (DIF)		GMM2 (SYS)		GMM2 (ALL)		CGLS
		Mean	RMSE *SD*	Mean	RMSE *SD*	Mean	RMSE *SD*	Mean	RMSE *SD*
100	0.0	− 0.0044	0.1227	0.0100	0.0994	0.0060	0.0970	0.0157	0.0986
			0.1227		*0.0990*		*0.0969*		*0.0974*
	0.3	0.2895	0.1589	0.3042	0.1134	0.3018	0.1141	0.3075	0.1140
			0.1586		*0.1134*		*0.1141*		*0.1138*
	0.5	0.4833	0.1901	0.4939	0.1194	0.4931	0.1212	0.4944	0.1200
			0.1895		*0.1193*		*0.1211*		*0.1199*
	0.8	0.7586	0.2844	0.7737	0.1336	0.7762	0.1326	0.7638	0.1294
			0.2816		*0.1311*		*0.1305*		*0.1242*
	0.9	0.8115	0.4033	0.8626	0.1494	0.8670	0.1426	0.8505	0.1361
			0.3936		*0.1447*		*0.1388*		*0.1268*
200	0.0	− 0.0037	0.0854	0.0051	0.0670	0.0028	0.0651	0.0083	0.0700
			0.0854		*0.0669*		*0.0651*		*0.0696*
	0.3	0.2939	0.1087	0.3046	0.0775	0.3027	0.0764	0.3060	0.0830
			0.1086		*0.0774*		*0.0764*		*0.0828*
	0.5	0.4915	0.1280	0.5003	0.0816	0.4995	0.0816	0.5003	0.0877
			0.1278		*0.0816*		*0.0817*		*0.0877*
	0.8	0.7808	0.1842	0.7926	0.0890	0.7927	0.0898	0.7850	0.0920
			0.1833		*0.0887*		*0.0896*		*0.0908*
	0.9	0.8607	0.2488	0.8883	0.0967	0.8885	0.0967	0.8768	0.0966
			0.2458		*0.0960*		*0.0961*		*0.0938*
500	0.0	− 0.0033	0.0557	0.0012	0.0434	0.0001	0.0421	0.0025	0.0462
			0.0556		*0.0434*		*0.0422*		*0.0461*
	0.3	0.2943	0.0708	0.2999	0.0513	0.2991	0.0502	0.3004	0.0563
			0.0706		*0.0513*		*0.0502*		*0.0564*
	0.5	0.4920	0.0831	0.4969	0.0539	0.4966	0.0535	0.4969	0.0604
			0.0828		*0.0538*		*0.0534*		*0.0604*
	0.8	0.7851	0.1201	0.7938	0.0550	0.7937	0.0553	0.7888	0.0615
			0.1192		*0.0547*		*0.0549*		*0.0605*
	0.9	0.8759	0.1619	0.8932	0.0563	0.8930	0.0567	0.8850	0.0619
			0.1602		*0.0559*		*0.0563*		*0.0600*

(c) Stationary model A, ***T*** = ***11***

N	α		GMM2 (DIF)		GMM2 (SYS)		GMM2 (ALL)		CGLS
		Mean	RMSE *SD*	Mean	RMSE *SD*	Mean	RMSE *SD*	Mean	RMSE *SD*
100	0.0	− 0.0138	0.0483	− 0.0183	0.0468	− 0.0153	0.0467	− 0.0071	0.0364
			0.0463		*0.0431*		*0.0441*		*0.0358*
	0.3	0.2762	0.0591	0.2728	0.0558	0.2795	0.0545	0.2832	0.0424
			0.0541		*0.0487*		*0.0506*		*0.0389*
	0.5	0.4629	0.0725	0.4689	0.0618	0.4794	0.0592	0.4761	0.0490
			0.0623		*0.0535*		*0.0555*		*0.0428*
	0.8	0.6812	0.1576	0.7925	0.0655	0.8043	0.0624	0.8025	0.0595
			0.1036		*0.0651*		*0.0623*		*0.0595*
	0.9	0.6455	0.2996	0.9259	0.0522	0.9302	0.0523	0.9422	0.0623
			0.1581		*0.0453*		*0.0428*		*0.0459*
200	0.0	− 0.0070	0.0358	− 0.0059	0.0310	− 0.0057	0.0313	− 0.0037	0.0272
			0.0352		*0.0304*		*0.0307*		*0.0270*
	0.3	0.2883	0.0427	0.2914	0.0345	0.2925	0.0348	0.2907	0.0318
			0.0411		*0.0335*		*0.0340*		*0.0304*
	0.5	0.4815	0.0503	0.4899	0.0373	0.4922	0.0373	0.4858	0.0369
			0.0468		*0.0359*		*0.0365*		*0.0340*
	0.8	0.7373	0.0971	0.8025	0.0421	0.8075	0.0430	0.8039	0.0449
			0.0742		*0.0420*		*0.0423*		*0.0448*
	0.9	0.7256	0.2152	0.9231	0.0435	0.9263	0.0445	0.9345	0.0506
			0.1261		*0.0369*		*0.0359*		*0.0370*
500	0.0	− 0.0025	0.0201	− 0.0010	0.0172	− 0.0012	0.0173	− 0.0016	0.0169
			0.0200		*0.0172*		*0.0173*		*0.0168*
	0.3	0.2959	0.0237	0.2986	0.0182	0.2984	0.0183	0.2960	0.0196
			0.0233		*0.0181*		*0.0182*		*0.0192*
	0.5	0.4934	0.0276	0.4984	0.0189	0.4983	0.0190	0.4937	0.0228
			0.0268		*0.0189*		*0.0190*		*0.0220*
	0.8	0.7695	0.0536	0.8019	0.0244	0.8027	0.0249	0.8008	0.0316
			0.0441		*0.0243*		*0.0248*		*0.0316*
	0.9	0.8110	0.1168	0.9120	0.0306	0.9135	0.0312	0.9206	0.0361
			0.0757		*0.0280*		*0.0282*		*0.0296*

This is particularly the case for model A, where the permanent effects remain important even at high values of α, and when only a small number of time-series observations are available.

Consider first the experiments where α is 0.8 or 0.9 in Table 2a. For GMM (DIF) we find both a huge downward bias and very imprecise estimates. This is consistent with our analysis in Section 3.2, where we showed that there was a serious problem of weak instruments for the GMM (DIF) estimator at values of α around 0.8 and above, particularly in model A. In contrast, we find both a much smaller bias and much improved precision for either of the system

GMM estimators. For example, at $\alpha = 0.8$ and $N = 200$ the root mean squared error (RMSE) for GMM (SYS) is only 20% of the RMSE for GMM (DIF). These gains from using conditions (4.3) and (4.4) remain very impressive, even at $N = 500$.

Consistent with our theoretical analysis, the finite-sample bias of the first-differenced GMM estimator is less serious in model B, as shown in Table 2b. The weak instruments problem depends on the persistence in the level of the series, which decreases both with α *and* with the importance of the permanent effects. Even in this case, though, there remain substantial efficiency gains from exploiting conditions (4.3) and (4.4). For example, at $\alpha = 0.8$ and $N = 200$ the RMSE for GMM (SYS) is still 50% of the RMSE for GMM (DIF).

Similarly the poor performance of GMM (DIF) improves with the number of time periods available, as shown for model A in Table 2c. Nevertheless, for high values of α there remain impressive gains in bias, precision and RMSE, even at $T = 11$. For example, at $\alpha = 0.8$ and $N = 200$ the RMSE for GMM (SYS) remains less than half of the RMSE for GMM (DIF).

The gains from exploiting the homoskedasticity restrictions (4.8) are found to be much smaller. The biggest gains are found for highly persistent series and low values of T. At $\alpha = 0.9$ and $T = 4$, the RMSE for GMM (ALL) is around 85% of the RMSE for GMM (SYS) in model A. However at $T = 11$ we find that there is no gain from exploiting the homoskedasticity restrictions, and the same is found in model B even at $T = 4$.

Conditional GLS also offers much better performance than the first-differenced GMM estimator. At $N = 500$, the variance of conditional GLS is generally found to be higher than the variance of the system GMM estimators.[15] However at $N = 100$ the finite sample performance of conditional GLS is generally found to be better than that of the system GMM estimators.[16]

Table 3 summarises the gains in precision found in Table 2, in the same format as the asymptotic efficiency comparisons presented in Ahn and Schmidt (1995, Table 1) and used in Table 1 in Section 4.4. The figures in Table 3 show the ratio of the empirical variance of the two-step GMM (DIF) estimator in our simulations to the empirical variance of the two-step GMM (SYS) estimator. High values of this ratio imply large efficiency gains when the additional moment conditions (4.3) and (4.4) are exploited.[17] As would be expected from the discussion of Table 1, the efficiency gains are largest at high values of α, low values of T, and at higher values of the variance of the permanent effects (relative to the variance of v_{it}). The empirical variance ratios found at $N = 500$ in

[15] Exceptions are found for $\alpha = 0.9$ in Table 2a and for $\alpha = 0.0$ in Table 2c.

[16] At $T = 4$ this is particularly found at high values of α, although this is not repeated when $T = 11$.

[17] Notice that by neglecting the reductions in bias, these ratios tend to underestimate the improvement in root mean squared error.

Table 3
Empirical variance ratios

N	α	(a) $T = 4$ Model A	(b) $T = 4$ Model B	(c) $T = 11$ Model B
		$\frac{\text{var}(GMM-DIF)}{\text{var}(GMM-SYS)}$	$\frac{\text{var}(GMM-DIF)}{\text{var}(GMM-SYS)}$	$\frac{\text{var}(GMM-DIF)}{\text{var}(GMM-SYS)}$
100	0.0	1.54	1.54	1.15
	0.3	2.32	1.96	1.23
	0.5	4.04	2.52	1.36
	0.8	25.84	4.61	2.53
	0.9	27.92	7.40	12.18
200	0.0	1.63	1.63	1.34
	0.3	2.32	1.97	1.51
	0.5	3.79	2.45	1.70
	0.8	19.07	4.27	3.12
	0.9	42.55	6.56	11.68
500	0.0	1.64	1.64	1.35
	0.3	2.29	1.89	1.66
	0.5	3.44	2.37	2.01
	0.8	14.91	4.75	3.29
	0.9	41.13	8.21	7.31

Table 3a are reasonably close to the corresponding asymptotic variance ratios given in the $T = 4$, $\sigma_\eta^2/\sigma_v^2 = 1$ results of Table 1.

Further Monte Carlc results presented in the appendix investigate the reliability of inference based on the usual asymptotic variance formulae for the GMM estimators. The main result is that whilst asymptotic t-tests based on the one-step GMM estimators are found to have the correct empirical level in our simulations, the asymptotic t-tests based on the two-step GMM estimators can be seriously misleading, and tend to reject too frequently. This tendency is exaggerated when the errors are non-normal or heteroskedastic.

7. An application to employment equations

7.1. The model

In this section we illustrate the benefits of exploiting the additional linear moment restrictions (4.3) and (4.4) in an application using real data. We consider a simple dynamic labour demand equation of the form

$$n_{it} = \alpha n_{i,t-1} + \beta_0 w_{it} + \beta_1 w_{i,t-1} + \gamma_0 k_{it} + \gamma_1 k_{i,t-1} + (\eta_i + v_{it}),$$

where n_{it} is the log of employment in firm i in year t, w_{it} is the log of the wage rate and k_{it} is the log of the capital stock. This log-linear model can be derived as the static conditional labour demand equation for a competitive firm with Cobb–Douglas technology, with the dynamics resulting from an AR(1) disturbance as in model (2.2). However, we do not impose the implied common factor restrictions, and alternatively the dynamics may be thought of as an empirical approximation to some more general adjustment process.

In the context of model (2.1) with regressors x_{it}, the precise set of moment conditions available will depend on assumptions made about the correlation between x_{it} and u_{it}. To exploit the linear moment conditions in Eqs. (4.3) and (4.4) an additional requirement is that $\mathrm{E}(\Delta x_{it}\eta_i) = 0$, which is clearly weaker than requiring the levels of x_{it} to be uncorrelated with the individual effects. This is precisely the case considered in Arellano and Bover (1995). Together with the restriction (4.4) on the initial conditions process this allows the use of both lagged Δy_{it} and lagged Δx_{it} as instruments in levels equations.

As we do not expect wages and capital to be strictly exogenous in our employment application, we focus here on moment conditions of the type $\mathrm{E}(u_{it}\Delta y_{i,t-1}) = 0$ and $\mathrm{E}(u_{it}\Delta x_{i,t-1}) = 0$. Stricter exogeneity restrictions on the x_{it} would allow the use of further instruments, as detailed in Arellano and Bond (1991), Ahn and Schmidt (1995) and Arellano and Bover (1995). For the same reason we do not consider conditional GLS results here. Extension of conditional GLS to models with regressors requires strict exogeneity, as discussed in Blundell and Smith (1991).

7.2. Data

The data we use is taken from Arellano and Bond (1991). Briefly, this is an unbalanced panel of 140 UK listed manufacturing companies with between 7 and 9 annual observations over the period 1976–1984. The data starts in 1976 only because Datastream did not report employment in earlier years. Hence, there is nothing special about the first observation on the firms in this sample, and we might expect the initial conditions restriction (4.4) to be valid here.

7.3. Results for a short sample period

We first consider omitting the first 3 observations for each firm, leaving an unbalanced panel with between 4 and 6 observations between 1979 and 1984. The first two columns of Table 4 report the results for GMM (DIF) and GMM (SYS) respectively.[18] These are the one-step GMM estimators, for which we

[18] Both wages and capital are treated as potentially endogenous variables, so that for GMM (DIF) the instrument set contains observations on (n, w, k) dated t-2 and earlier. For GMM (SYS) the instruments used in the levels equations are the observations on (Δn, Δw, Δk) dated t-1. The results are obtained using DPD98 for GAUSS, which can be obtained by email from steve.bond@nuffield.ox.ac.uk.

Table 4
Employment equations

	1979–84 GMM-DIF	1979–84 GMM-SYS	1976–84 GMM-DIF	1976–84 GMM-SYS
$n_{i,t-1}$	0.4046	0.8596	0.7075	0.8103
	(0.1363)	(0.0680)	(0.0842)	(0.0578)
w_{it}	− 1.1073	− 1.0255	− 0.7088	− 0.7968
	(0.3888)	(0.1807)	(0.1171)	(0.1002)
$w_{i,t-1}$	0.3947	0.7705	0.5000	0.5488
	(0.1643)	(0.1527)	(0.1113)	(0.1488)
k_{it}	0.5463	0.5625	0.4660	0.4268
	(0.2571)	(0.2229)	(0.1010)	(0.0771)
$k_{i,t-1}$	− 0.4216	− 0.4769	− 0.2151	− 0.2786
	(0.2821)	(0.2420)	(0.0859)	(0.0784)
*m*1	− 2.24	− 3.94	− 5.60	− 6.50
*m*2	1.13	1.04	− 0.14	− 0.08
Sargan	15.34	43.43	88.80	116.05
(df)	(25)	(37)	(79)	(100)

Notes.
1. Year dummies are included in all specifications.
2. Asymptotic standard errors, asymptotically robust to heteroskedasticity, are reported in parentheses.
3. m1 and m2 are tests for first-order and second-order serial correlation in the first-differenced residuals, asymptotically distributed as N(0,1) under the null of no serial correlation.
4. Sargan is a test of the over-identifying restrictions, asymptotically distributed as χ^2 under the null of instrument validity, with degrees of freedom reported in parentheses.
5. The instruments used in each equation are
GMM (DIF) – $n_{i,t-2}, n_{i,t-3}, \ldots, n_{i1}$; $w_{i,t-2}, w_{i,t-3}, \ldots, w_{i1}$; $k_{i,t-2}, k_{i,t-3}, \ldots, k_{i1}$.
GMM (SYS) – differenced equations – as GMM (DIF); levels equations – $\Delta n_{i,t-1}$, $\Delta w_{i,t-1}$, $\Delta k_{i,t-1}$.

believe inference based on the asymptotic variance matrix to be more reliable.[19] Using the first-differenced GMM estimator in this short panel, the coefficient on the lagged dependent variable is only 0.4, and the elasticity of employment with respect to capital is only 0.2, suggesting implausibly low returns to scale. Using the system GMM estimator which exploits the moment conditions (4.3) and (4.4), the coefficient on the lagged dependent variable is 0.86, and the elasticity of employment with respect to capital is a more plausible 0.6. We also find a substantial improvement in precision, and the extended set of moment restrictions is not rejected by the Sargan/Hansen test of over-identifying

[19] See Section 6.2 and the appendix for further discussion. The reported standard errors are asymptotically robust to heteroskedasticity.

restrictions. The tests of serial correlation in the first-differenced residuals are in both cases consistent with the maintained assumption of no serial correlation in v_{it}.

7.4. Results for a longer sample period

The last two columns of Table 4 report the results for the same estimators, but using the full sample period from 1976 to 1984 as originally used in the Arellano and Bond (1991) study. The main difference is that the GMM (DIF) estimates are now much closer to the GMM (SYS) estimates: the coefficient on the lagged dependent variable is now 0.71, and the elasticity of employment with respect to capital is found to be around 0.8 for both estimators. There remains a gain in precision from exploiting the additional moment restrictions, and their validity is not rejected in this example.

The results of this section appear to be consistent with our earlier analysis. With short sample periods and persistent series, we find important small sample biases and imprecision using the standard first-differenced GMM estimator. These biases can be substantially reduced, and more precise parameter estimates can be obtained, if restriction (4.4) is satisfied and we exploit the extra moment conditions that this implies.

8. Summary and conclusions

In this paper we have discussed the importance of exploiting initial condition information in generating efficient estimators for dynamic panel data models where the number of time-series observations is small. We have focused on the individual effects autoregressive model $y_{it} = \alpha y_{i,t-1} + \eta_i + v_{it}$ although our results extend naturally to dynamic models with regressors.

We considered two estimators that can improve the precision of the standard first-differenced GMM estimator for this model. One approach imposes an additional restriction on the initial conditions process, under which all the moment conditions available can be exploited by a linear GMM estimator in a system of first-differenced and levels equations. The second approach conditions on the observed initial values to obtain a system that under certain conditions can be estimated consistently by error components GLS.

The finite sample properties of these estimators were studied using Monte Carlo simulations. Both can improve dramatically on the performance of the usual first-differenced GMM estimator when the autoregressive parameter is moderately high and the number of time-series observations is moderately small. In addition, asymptotic variance comparisons suggest that the system GMM estimator can be considerably more efficient than non-linear GMM in this case.

Acknowledgements

An earlier version of this paper was read to the Econometric Society Meetings in San Francisco January 1996. We are grateful to participants at that meeting, Seung Ahn, Manuel Arellano, Andrew Chesher, Zvi Griliches, Jinyong Hahn, Bronwyn Hall, Bo Honore, Joel Horowitz, Ekaterini Kyriazidou, Jacques Mairesse, Whitney Newey, Neil Shephard, Richard Smith, Richard Spady, Alain Trognon, Frank Windmeijer, three anonymous referees and seminar participants at Berkeley, INSEE, Manchester, MIT and Nuffield for helpful comments. Financial support from the ESRC is gratefully acknowledged. This research is part of the programme of research at the ESRC Centre for the Micro-Economic Analysis of Fiscal Policy at IFS.

Appendix A.

In this appendix we present some further Monte Carlo results, which consider designs with non-stationary initial conditions, non-normal and heteroskedastic disturbances; and we investigate the reliability of inference based on the usual asymptotic variance formulae for the GMM estimators. We focus on the case with $T = 4$, $N = 200$, $\alpha = 0.5$, $\sigma_\eta^2 = 1$ and $\sigma_v^2 = 1$.

Table 5 reproduces the base case results for this configuration from Table 2a. Here we present the one-step GMM estimators as well as the two-step GMM estimators, and we present OLS levels, within groups and standard error components GLS results for comparison. As expected in this i.i.d. design, the one-step GMM(DIF) estimator performs as well as the two-step GMM(DIF) estimator. More interestingly, the loss in efficiency from using the one-step GMM(SYS) and GMM(ALL) estimators is quite modest.

For the GMM estimators, we also report the number of rejections (from 1000 replications) of a Wald test of the null hypothesis that $\alpha = 0.5$, and of the standard Sargan/Hansen test of over-identifying restrictions. The one-step Wald tests appear to have the correct empirical level, but the two-step Wald tests tend to reject too frequently, particularly for the system estimators where there are more over-identifying restrictions. This is primarily because the asymptotic standard errors for the two-step GMM estimators tend to underestimate the true dispersion of these estimators in finite samples. For example, the mean asymptotic standard error (ASE) of the two-step GMM(ALL) estimator is only 89% of its empirical standard deviation.

Table 6 reports an experiment with non-stationary initial conditions, in which the initial values are mean zero noise. This results in serious biases for the system GMM estimators. The conventional Sargan test has power to detect these biases.

Table 7 presents a stationary design but with non-normal errors. The v_{it} disturbances are drawn from a skewed $\chi^2(1)$ distribution, then centred and

Table 5
Stationary, normal, homoskedastic base case

Estimator	Mean	Std. Dev.	Mean ASE	RMSE
OLS	0.8745	0.0185		0.3749
Within	− 0.0346	0.0467		0.5366
GLS	0.6684	0.0961		0.1944
GMM1(DIF)	0.4809	0.1783	0.1822	0.1792
GMM2(DIF)	0.4828	0.1821	0.1798	0.1828
GMM1(SYS)	0.5040	0.1079	0.1104	0.1079
GMM2(SYS)	0.5098	0.0936	0.0892	0.0941
GMM1(ALL)	0.5118	0.1073	0.1106	0.1079
GMM2(ALL)	0.5079	0.0922	0.0820	0.0925
CGLS	0.5135	0.1006		0.1015

Rejection frequencies

Estimator	One-Step Wald			Two-Step Wald			Two-Step Sargan		
	10%	5%	1%	10%	5%	1%	10%	5%	1%
DIF	83	49	15	97	64	18	110	54	8
SYS	99	56	11	153	95	34	97	59	11
ALL	100	56	14	167	106	43	98	50	13

$y_{i1} = 2\eta_i + u_{i1}$ with $u_{i1} \sim$ i.i.d. N(0,4/3).
$\sigma_\eta^2 = 1$, $\sigma_v^2 = 1$, $\alpha = 0.5$, $T = 4$, $N = 200$.

Table 6
Non-stationary initial conditions

Estimator	Mean	Std. Dev.	Mean ASE	RMSE
OLS	0.7000	0.0331		0.2028
Within	0.2852	0.0356		0.2177
GLS	0.4997	0.0396		0.0396
GMM1(DIF)	0.4972	0.0555	0.0567	0.0555
GMM2(DIF)	0.4972	0.0563	0.0561	0.0564
GMM1(SYS)	0.7006	0.0726	0.0602	0.2133
GMM2(SYS)	0.6866	0.1041	0.0542	0.2137
GMM1(ALL)	0.7032	0.0759	0.0600	0.2169
GMM2(ALL)	0.6852	0.1017	0.0523	0.2113
CGLS	0.5020	0.0482		0.0482

Rejection Frequencies

Estimator	One-Step Wald			Two-Step Wald			Two-Step Sargan		
	10%	5%	1%	10%	5%	1%	10%	5%	1%
DIF	91	49	15	98	52	18	110	55	7
SYS	927	883	728	832	791	672	1000	1000	1000
ALL	923	875	731	838	801	679	1000	1000	1000

$y_{i1} \sim$ i.i.d. N(0,16/3).
$\sigma_\eta^2 = 1$, $\sigma_v^2 = 1$, $\alpha = 0.5$, $T = 4$, $N = 200$.

Table 7
Non-normal errors

Estimator	Mean	Std Dev	Mean ASE	RMSE
OLS	0.8740	0.0203		0.3746
Within	− 0.0343	0.0565		0.5373
GLS	0.6659	0.0965		0.1919
GMM1(DIF)	0.4867	0.1844	0.1775	0.1848
GMM2(DIF)	0.4911	0.1840	0.1700	0.1841
GMM1(SYS)	0.4999	0.1082	0.1068	0.1081
GMM2(SYS)	0.5032	0.0938	0.0825	0.0938
GMM1(ALL)	0.5067	0.1109	0.1078	0.1111
GMM2(ALL)	0.5045	0.0981	0.0762	0.0981
CGLS	0.5124	0.1030		0.1037

Rejection frequencies

Estimator	One-Step Wald			Two-Step Wald			Two-Step Sargan		
	10%	5%	1%	10%	5%	1%	10%	5%	1%
DIF	103	55	10	124	65	12	94	44	8
SYS	105	59	19	171	102	41	84	45	4
ALL	108	70	25	228	155	75	116	55	8

$v_{it} = (\varepsilon_{it} - 1)/\sqrt{2}$ where $\varepsilon_{it} \sim \chi^2(1)$.
$\sigma_\eta^2 = 1$, $\sigma_v^2 = 1$, $\alpha = 0.5$, $T = 4$, $N = 200$.

Table 8
Heteroskedastic errors across individuals

Estimator	Mean	Std Dev	Mean ASE	RMSE
OLS	0.8748	0.0228		0.3754
Within	− 0.0351	0.0537		0.5378
GLS	0.6644	0.1117		0.1988
GMM1(DIF)	0.4585	0.2410	0.2368	0.2444
GMM2(DIF)	0.4715	0.2388	0.2253	0.2404
GMM1(SYS)	0.5011	0.1248	0.1258	0.1248
GMM2(SYS)	0.5127	0.1116	0.0976	0.1122
GMM1(ALL)	0.5145	0.1254	0.1266	0.1262
GMM2(ALL)	0.5148	0.1076	0.0868	0.1086
CGLS	0.5114	0.1161		0.1166

Rejection frequencies

Estimator	One-Step Wald			Two-Step Wald			Two-Step Sargan		
	10%	5%	1%	10%	5%	1%	10%	5%	1%
DIF	114	64	19	127	71	25	114	56	5
SYS	118	62	18	194	125	58	101	48	4
ALL	118	66	25	214	156	69	114	50	10

$v_{it} \sim N(0,\sigma_i^2)$ where $\sigma_i^2 = 0.5 + 0.5(y_{i1}^2 \text{ var}(y_{i1}))$.
$\sigma_\eta^2 = 1$, $\alpha = 0.5$. $T = 4$, $N = 200$.

Table 9
Heteroskedastic err^rs over time

Estimator	Mean	Std Dev	Mean ASE	RMSE
OLS	0.8998	0.0199		0.4003
Within	0.1214	0.0683		0.3798
GLS	0.7502	0.0755		0.2613
GMM1(DIF)	0.4478	0.2165	0.2111	0.2226
GMM2(DIF)	0.4636	0.1952	0.1894	0.1985
GMM1(SYS)	0.5023	0.1157	0.1158	0.1157
GMM2(SYS)	0.5182	0.0804	0.0754	0.0824
GMM1(ALL)	0.4313	0.1199	0.1117	0.1382
GMM2(ALL)	0.5854	0.0999	0.0732	0.1314
CGLS	0.6110	0.0903		0.1430

Rejection Frequen es

Estimator	One-Step Wald			Two-Step Wald			Two-Step Sargan		
	10%	5%	1%	10%	5%	1%	10%	5%	1%
DIF	102	41	6	95	54	11	108	54	10
SYS	102	55	20	148	78	28	103	47	10
ALL	157	85	11	403	311	180	1000	1000	1000

$v_{it} \sim N(0,\sigma_t^2)$ where $\sigma_2^2 = 0.2$, $\sigma_3^2 = 1$ and $\sigma_4^2 = 1.8$.
$\sigma_\eta^2 = 1$, $\alpha = 0.5$, $T = 4$. $N = 200$.

scaled to have mean zero and variance one. Comparing Tables 5 and 7 suggest that this non-normality has little impact on the means and standard deviations of these estimators. However, there is a further deterioration in the quality of inference based on the asymptotic standard errors for the two-step GMM estimators. The mean ASE for the two-step GMM(ALL) estimator falls to just 78% of its empirical standard deviation in this design.

Table 8 presents a design with heteroskedasticity across individuals, in which the variance of v_{it} is dependent on y_{i1}^2. These disturbances are again scaled such that they have variance one across the whole sample. This form of heteroskedasticity considerably increases the variance of the GMM(DIF) estimators, but has a smaller impact on the variance of the system GMM estimators. There is a small improvement in the precision of the two-step GMM estimators relative to the one-step GMM estimators. More striking again is the downward bias in the (heteroskedasticity consistent) asymptotic standard errors for the two-step GMM estimators. Inference based on the one-step GMM estimators appears to be much more reliable when either non-normality or heteroskedasticity is suspected.

Finally, Table 9 presents a design with heteroskedasticity over time. As expected, this results in serious biases for both the GMM(ALL) estimator and for conditional GLS. In the former case, the conventional Sargan test has power to detect the invalidity of the overidentifying restrictions in this design.

References

Ahn, S.C., Schmidt, P., 1995. Efficient estimation of models for dynamic panel data. Journal of Econometrics 68, 5–28.

Alonso-Borrego, C., Arellano, M., 1996. Symmetrically normalised instrumental variable estimation using panel data. CEMFI Working Paper No. 9612, September.

Anderson, T.W., Hsiao, C., 1981. Estimation of dynamic models with error components. Journal of the American Statistical Association 76, 598–606.

Arellano, M., Bond, S.R., 1991. Some tests of specification for panel data: Monte Carlo evidence and an application to employment equations. Review of Economic Studies 58, 277–297.

Arellano, M., Bover, O., 1995. Another look at the instrumental-variable estimation of error-components models. Journal of Econometrics 68, 29–52.

Bhagarva, A., Sargan, J.D., 1983. Estimating dynamic random effects models from panel data covering short time periods. Econometrica 51, 1635–1659.

Blundell, R.W., Smith, R.J., 1991. Initial conditions and efficient estimation in dynamic panel data models. Annales d'Economie et de Statistique 20/21, 109–123.

Chamberlain, G., 1987. Asymptotic efficiency in estimation with conditional moment restrictions. Journal of Econometrics 34, 305–334.

Hansen, L.P., 1982. Large sample properties of generalised method of moment estimators. Econometrica 50, 1029–1054.

Holtz-Eakin, D., Newey, W., Rosen, H.S., 1988. Estimating vector autoregressions with panel data. Econometrica 56, 1371–1396.

Horowitz, J.L., 1997. Bootstrap methods in econometrics: theory and numerical performance, in: Kreps, D.M., Wallis, K.F. (Eds.). Advances in Economics and Econometrics: Thoery and Applications vol. III, Chapter 8, Econometric Society Monograph No. 28. Cambridge University Press, Cambridge.

Hsiao, C., 1986. Analysis of Panel Data. Cambridge University Press, Cambridge.

Nelson, C.R., Startz, R., 1990a. Some further results on the exact small sample properties of the instrumental variable estimator. Econometrica 58, 967–976.

Nelson, C.R., Startz, R., 1990b. The distribution of the instrumental variable estimator and its t-ratio when the instrument is a poor one. Journal of Business Economics and Statistics 63, 5125–5140.

Nickell, S.J., 1981. Biases in dynamic models with fixed effects. Econometrica 49, 1417–1426.

Prucha, I.R., 1984. On the asymptotic efficiency of feasible aitken estimators for seemingly unrelated regression models with error components. Econometrica 52, 203–207.

Sevestre, P., Trognon, A., 1985. A note on autoregressive error components models. Journal of Econometrics 29, 231–245.

Staiger, D., Stock, J.H., 1997. Instrumental variables regression with weak instruments. Econometrica 65. 557–586.

[6]

ELSEVIER

Journal of Econometrics 82 (1997) 135–156

JOURNAL OF Econometrics

Parameters of interest, nuisance parameters and orthogonality conditions An application to autoregressive error component models

Bruno Crepon[a], Francis Kramarz[*,b] Alain Trognon[c]

[a] *Direction de la Prévision*
[b] *Insee – Crest – Département Recherche*
[c] *Insee – Genes*

Received 1 April 1994; received in revised form 1 August 1996

Abstract

In general, when one considers a set of orthogonality conditions, the parameters can be divided into parameters of interest that the econometrician wants to estimate – the coefficient of the lagged endogenous variable in the case of an autoregressive error component (AREC) model, for instance, – and nuisance parameters – most of the second-order terms in an AREC model. We demonstrate that the elimination of such nuisance parameters using their empirical counterpart does not entail an efficiency loss when only the parameters of interest are estimated. Applications of our results to both autoregressive error component models and time-varying individual fixed effects models are discussed at length. They show the nature of the efficiency losses when some orthogonality conditions are left aside.
© 1997 Elsevier Science S.A.

Key words: Panel data; Nuisance parameters; Orthogonality conditions
JEL classification: C13; C23; C33

1. Introduction

A characterization of an econometric model in terms of orthogonality conditions is an appealing procedure for modern econometricians who are looking for

* Correspondence address: 15 boulevard Gabriel Péri, 92245 Malakoff Cedex, France.

A first version of this paper was presented at the CREST-D3E-Recherche seminar at INSEE, at the panel data conference 1994 at Université Paris-XII, and at the ESEM 1994 in Maastricht. We would like to thank Richard Blundell, Steve Bond, Emmanuel Guerre, Guy Laroque, David Margolis, Alain Monfort and an anonymous referee for stimulating remarks. Any error remains ours.

PII S0304-4076(97)00054-7

simple and less restrictive specifications. This is because, in general, moments are less demanding than distributions. For instance, the estimation of autoregressive models (AR models) with serially correlated errors relies essentially on the instrumental variable (IV) framework. More recent treatments rely upon the generalized method of moments (GMM), which makes use of such orthogonality conditions.[1]

In general, the set of parameters contained in the orthogonality conditions can be divided into parameters of interest that the econometrician wants to estimate and nuisance parameters. An example of parameters of interest might be the coefficient of the lagged endogenous variable in the case of an autoregressive error component (AREC) model while most of the second-order terms in the AREC model would be considered nuisance parameters.

The distinction between parameters of interest and nuisance parameters remains implicit in the econometrics literature since the set of orthogonality conditions that is used for estimation purposes is obtained from the complete set by eliminating some conditions that include nuisance parameters without paying attention to the potential consequences on efficiency.[2] This article will show that the elimination of nuisance parameters has no effect on the efficiency of the corresponding estimators of the parameters of interest as long as the nuisance parameters are replaced by their empirical counterparts.

Proposition 1, in Section 2, shows that the efficiency properties of GMM run on the complete model are still valid in a model in which nuisance parameters have been replaced by their empirical counterparts. Proposition 2 of Section 2, on the other hand, gives the conditions under which GMM estimation of a model in which nuisance parameters have been replaced by their theoretical expressions in terms of the parameters of interest may be sometimes less efficient, sometimes more efficient than estimation in the original system. In the third section, applications to both AREC models and time-varying fixed effects for panel data are provided. They show, using simple examples, why both first- and second-order empirical moments are important when one wants to estimate the parameters of interest with full efficiency.

2. Implicit and active orthogonality conditions

2.1. The estimation of the parameters of interest

Consider a problem of inference about $(\theta, \gamma) \in \mathbb{R}^p \times \mathbb{R}^q$ where θ is the parameter of interest and γ is a nuisance parameter. The statistical problem is characterized

[1] See Hansen (1982) for the presentation of the method and Newey (1985) for specification tests.

[2] See, for instance, Arellano–Bond (1991) and Ahn–Schmidt (1995a, b) for the AREC model.

by a certain set of orthogonality conditions:[3]

$$\mathrm{E}m_i(\theta_0,\gamma_0)=0$$

with

$$m:\mathbb{R}^p\times\mathbb{R}^q\rightarrow\mathbb{R}^n \quad \text{and } n\geqslant p+q,$$

where θ_0 and γ_0 are the true values of the parameters.

These conditions are supposed to be identifying equations in the sense that

$$\mathrm{E}m_i(\theta,\gamma)=0 \Leftrightarrow \theta=\theta_0, \qquad \gamma=\gamma_0.$$

For ease of presentation, we will make use of the following definition:

Definition 1. $\hat{\Psi}$ is the efficient GMM estimator of Ψ based on the identifiying orthogonality conditions:

$$\mathrm{E}m_i(\Psi)=0$$

if $\hat{\Psi}=\arg\min_{\Psi}\bar{m}_n(\Psi)'S_n^{-1}\bar{m}_n(\Psi)$ with $\bar{m}_n(\Psi)=n^{-1}\sum_i m_i(\Psi)$ and $S_n=n^{-1}\sum_i m_i(\tilde{\Psi})m_i(\tilde{\Psi})'$, where $\tilde{\Psi}$ is a first stage consistent estimator of Ψ_0, the true value of Ψ (an example would be using the identity matrix instead of S_n at the first stage).

Suppose now that

$$\mathrm{E}m_i(\theta,\gamma)'=\mathrm{E}[h_i(\theta,\gamma)',g_i(\theta,\gamma)'],$$

where $g_i:\mathbb{R}^p\times\mathbb{R}^q\rightarrow\mathbb{R}^q$. The dimension of the set of orthogonality conditions based upon the subvector g_i of m_i is not sufficient to produce identifying equations. The empirical equivalent of the above equation is

$$\bar{m}_n(\theta,\gamma)=n^{-1}\sum_i m_i(\theta,\gamma).$$

If we want to eliminate γ, there is a 'choice' between an empirical and a theoretical method. In the empirical method, γ is replaced by its sample analog (in Manski, 1994 terminology) (Proposition 1). In the theoretical method, an analytical expression of γ in terms of θ is needed (Proposition 2).

Proposition 1. Suppose $(\hat{\theta},\hat{\gamma})$ *is the efficient GMM estimator of* (θ,γ) *which solves*

$$\arg\min_{\theta,\gamma}\bar{m}_n(\theta,\gamma)'S_n^{-1}\bar{m}_n(\theta,\gamma)$$

[3] If y and x are the sets of endogenous and exogenous variables, we denote $m_i(\theta,\gamma)$ for $\bar{m}(y_i,x_i,\theta,\gamma)$ and E will stand for the expectation relative to the true distribution of y_i,x_i which depends upon θ_0 and γ_0, the true values of the parameters.

with

$$\bar{m}_n(\theta,\gamma)=n^{-1}\sum_i m_i(\theta,\gamma)$$

and

$$S_n=n^{-1}\sum_i m_i(\bar{\theta},\bar{\gamma})m_i(\bar{\theta},\bar{\gamma})',$$

where $(\bar{\theta},\bar{\gamma})$ *is a first stage consistent estimator of* (θ_0,γ_0).

If $m_i(\theta,\gamma)'=[h_i(\theta,\gamma)',g_i(\theta,\gamma)']$ *and* g_i *has same dimension as* γ, *and*

$$n^{-1}\sum_i g_i(\theta,\gamma)=0 \Leftrightarrow \gamma=\varphi_n(\theta). \tag{1}$$

Then, θ^*, *the estimator of* θ *that solves*

$$\arg\min_\theta \bar{h}_n(\theta,\varphi_n(\theta))'Q_n^{-1}\bar{h}_n(\theta,\varphi_n(\theta)), \tag{2}$$

where

$$\bar{h}_n(\theta,\varphi_n(\theta))=n^{-1}\sum_i h_i(\theta,\varphi_n(\theta))$$

and

$$Q_n=n^{-1}\sum_i h_i^\varphi(\bar{\theta},\varphi_n(\bar{\theta}))h_i^\varphi(\bar{\theta},\varphi_n(\bar{\theta}))'$$

in which

$$h^\varphi=h_i(\bar{\theta},\varphi_n(\bar{\theta}))-\left(\frac{1}{n}\sum_i\frac{\partial h_i}{\partial\gamma'}(\bar{\theta},\bar{\gamma})\right)\left(\frac{1}{n}\sum_i\frac{\partial g_i}{\partial\gamma'}(\bar{\theta},\bar{\gamma})\right)^{-1}g_i(\bar{\theta},\varphi_n(\bar{\theta}))$$

is asymptotically equivalent to $\hat{\theta}$.

Furthermore, γ^*, *the solution of*

$$\arg\min_\gamma \bar{m}_n(\theta^*,\gamma)'\Omega^{-1}\bar{m}_n(\theta^*,\gamma)$$

with

$$m_i(\theta^*,\gamma)'=[h_i(\theta^*,\gamma)',g_i(\theta^*,\gamma)'],$$

$$\bar{m}_n(\theta^*,\gamma)=n^{-1}\sum_i m_i(\theta^*,\gamma),$$

$$\Omega=Vm_i(\theta_0,\gamma_0)$$

is asymptotically equivalent to the $\hat{\gamma}$ *obtained using GMM on the complete set of orthogonality conditions.*

Proof. See Appendix A.

Remark 1. From a technical point of view, the above proposition is related to the notion of concentration in maximum likelihood estimation. Here, the result seems more flexible since the conditions given by (1) devoted to the elimination of γ can be chosen from a set of several candidates.

Remark 2. The last part of the proposition shows that one can estimate the nuisance parameters as the second stage of the procedure in a fully efficient fashion. Hence, our method also bears some resemblance to the Frish–Waugh theorem.

Remark 3. θ^* in the above proposition is not strictly speaking a GMM estimator since $\varphi_n(\theta)$ is empirically defined. This explains why the optimal weighting matrix Q_n does not have the usual form.

Notice that in Remark 3, the elimination of the nuisance parameter is based on some empirical counterpart. One may ask whether Proposition 1 holds in the case where the relationship between γ and θ solves the following orthogonality condition:

$$\mathrm{E}g_i(\theta,\gamma)=0 \Leftrightarrow \gamma=\varphi(\theta).$$

In general, this is not true.

Proposition 2. Suppose that a set of orthogonality conditions on a parameter vector (θ,γ) *can be decomposed into*

$$\mathrm{E}h_i(\theta,\gamma)=0, \tag{3a}$$

$$\mathrm{E}g_i(\theta,\gamma)=0, \tag{3b}$$

where g_i *has the same dimension as* γ. *Denote* φ *the function that solves* (3b) *for* γ *as a function of* θ *in a neighbourhood of* (θ_0,γ_0) : $\mathrm{E}g_i(\theta,\gamma)=0 \Leftrightarrow \gamma=\varphi(\theta)$. *In this case, the GMM estimate of* θ *based on the following orthogonality condition:*

$$\mathrm{E}h_i(\theta,\varphi(\theta))=0 \tag{3c}$$

is not in general asymptotically equivalent to the GMM estimate of θ *based on* (3a) *and* (3b).

A necessary and sufficient condition for asymptotic equivalence is

$$\mathrm{E}\frac{\partial h_i}{\partial \gamma'}(\theta_0,\gamma_0)=0.$$

Proof. See Appendix A.e

Remark 4. Notice that, depending on structure of the problem, all cases are possible. The GMM estimate of θ based on (3c) may be more, equally, or less efficient than the one based on (3a) and (3b). For instance, if

$$\mathrm{Cov}[h_i(\theta_0,\gamma_0), g_i(\theta_0,\gamma_0)] = 0$$

the former estimate of θ is asymptotically more efficient than the latter estimate of θ.

Remark 5. Why should we be interested in this last proposition. We believe that, in a situation in which analytical expressions of the nuisance parameters are available, the general intuition would be to replace these parameters using such expressions. Proposition 2 serves as a warning against using this intuition.

3. Applications to panel data models

3.1. The framework and its application to the AREC(1) model

The autoregressive error component (AREC) model presents various singularities which justify the constant interest of the econometricians (see Chamberlain, 1982, 1984). The pure AREC model without exogenous variables is, in a sense, self-contained. The second-order assumptions of the classical definition of this model have been translated into orthogonality conditions by Arellano and Bond (1991), and Ahn and Schmidt (1995a, b) have recently added new conditions to achieve a certain degree of efficiency. The first conditions are linear in the parameters of interest while the second ones involve nonlinear specifications.

Even if the approach adopted by Ahn and Schmidt seems to be complete, it is not sufficiently systematic to provide the complete set of conditions embedded in the first- and second-order moments specification of the AREC model. The previous section demonstrates that, if we are interested in all of the parameters of the model which appear in the first and second-order specification, there is an estimation and an efficiency loss where one considers only a subset of these moments while making inference on the parameters of interest and the nuisance parameters.

In order to be more specific, let us consider the pure AREC(1):[4]

$$\begin{aligned} y_{it} &= \alpha y_{it-1} + \varepsilon_{it}, \\ \varepsilon_{it} &= u_i + \eta_{it}, \quad i=1,2,\ldots,N, \ t=1,2,\ldots,T, \end{aligned} \tag{4}$$

where u_i and η_{it}, $i=1,2,\ldots,N$, $t=1,2,\ldots,T$ are zero mean uncorrelated second-order random variables with respective variances σ_u^2 and σ_η^2.

[4] An AREC(n) is a model with n lags on the dependent variable.

This is what is called 'the classical definition' of the pure AREC(1) model. Implicitly (4) describes the time series $(y_{i1},\dots,y_{iT})$ up to the second order as a function of $\alpha,\sigma_u^2,\sigma_\eta^2$ and the initial condition y_{i0}:

$$y_{it}=\alpha^t y_{i0}+\frac{1-\alpha^t}{1-\alpha}u_i+\sum_{\tau=0}^{t-1}\alpha^\tau\eta_{it-\tau}. \tag{5}$$

If y_{i0} is a second-order variable the time series $(y_{i1},\dots,y_{iT})$ is also a second-order vector.[5]

For the sake of simplicity and because of the general agreement about the following hypothesis, we will assume that the vectors $\boldsymbol{y}_i'=(y_{i0},y_{iT},\dots,y_{i1})$, $i=1,2,\dots,N$ are iid second-order vectors fully specified by their first- and second-order moments $\mu=\mathrm{E}\boldsymbol{y}_i$ and $\Sigma=V\boldsymbol{y}_i$ where μ is a $(T+1)\times 1$ vector and Σ is a $(T+1)\times(T+1)$ matrix.

If no underlying structure is driving the expectation and the variance of $\boldsymbol{y}_i$, μ and Σ are completely free. Consequently, without any model restrictions $\boldsymbol{y}_i$ is characterized up to the second order by the $(T+1)$ elements of μ and $(T+1)(T+2)/2$ distinct elements of the symmetric matrix Σ.

The explicit specification (5) of the AREC(1) model makes $\boldsymbol{y}_i$ a function not only of α,σ_u^2 and σ_η^2, but also of the first and second moments of y_{i0}. If, as usual, y_{i0} is characterized by its expectation m, its variance σ_0^2, its covariance c with u_i, and assuming no correlation between y_{i0} and $\eta_{it},\forall i,\forall t$, the vector $\boldsymbol{y}_i$ depends upon 6 specific parameters. In what follows, m and σ_0^2 are considered to be pure nuisance parameters. If, for example, stationarity is assumed, m would be equal to zero while

$$\sigma_0^2=\frac{\sigma_u^2}{(1-\alpha)^2}+\frac{\sigma_\eta^2}{(1-\alpha^2)}\quad\text{and}\quad c=\frac{\sigma_u^2}{(1-\alpha)}.$$

From an operational point of view, it can be said that the AREC(1) model is derived from the more general specification of the second order variable $\boldsymbol{y}_i$ via $(T+1)+\frac{1}{2}(T+1)(T+2)-6$ restrictions on the expectation μ and the distinct elements of Σ.

To highlight the link between the above conditions and the approaches of Arellano and Bond (1991) and of Ahn and Schmidt (1995a, b), let us define the vector $\zeta_i(\alpha)'=(y_{iT}-\alpha y_{iT-1},y_{iT-1}-\alpha y_{iT-2},\dots,y_{i1}-\alpha y_{i0},y_{i0})$.[6]

With this notation, and in order to make appropriate comparisons, we can rewrite the general set of implicit orthogonality conditions for the pure AREC(1)

---

[5] For comments about the influence of the initial observations on the various statistics used for inference, see Barghava and Sargan (1983), Anderson and Hsiao (1981), Sevestre and Trognon (1985), Blundell and Smith (1991), Blundell and Bond (1995), etc.

[6] One should add $\mathrm{E}\zeta_{i0}(\alpha)=m$, $\mathrm{E}(\zeta_{i0}(\alpha)-m)^2=\sigma_0^2$, but these initial conditions are useless as long as m and σ_0^2 are independent of α, the parameter of interest.

model as in Arellano and Bond (1991) for (6a) and as given in Ahn and Schmidt (1995a, b) for (6b) and (6c):

$$\mathrm{E}y_{it-s}\Delta\zeta_{it}(\alpha)=0, \quad t=2,\dots,T, \ s\geqslant 2, \tag{6a}$$

$$\mathrm{E}[y_{it-2}\Delta\zeta_{it-1}(\alpha)-y_{it-1}\Delta\zeta_{it}(\alpha)]=0, \quad t=3,\dots,T, \tag{6b}$$

$$\mathrm{E}\Delta\zeta_{it}\left(\sum_{\tau=1}^{T}\zeta_{i\tau}(\alpha)\right)=0, \quad t=2,\dots,T, \tag{6c}$$

$$\mathrm{E}\zeta_{it}(\alpha)=0, \quad t=1,\dots,T. \tag{6d}$$

Eqs. (6a), (6b) and (6d) are linear conditions on α, while (6c) is nonlinear. These last nonlinear conditions prevent the econometricians from giving an interpretation of the GMM estimations in terms of instrumental variable estimators and lead to more complicated, although not particularly cumbersome, computations, as will be shown later.

The propositions of Section 2 are now illustrated using simple examples so that one can see how they apply (Section 3.2) and how important are the gains in estimability and efficiency derived from using (6d) in addition to (6a)–(6c) (Section 3.3). Finally, we analyze the case with time-varying fixed effects (Section 3.4).

3.2. On the elimination of nuisance parameters

As an illustration of the differences between Propositions 1 and 2, we consider two situations. First, we look at the case in which the orthogonality conditions used to eliminate the nuisance parameters are linear in these nuisance parameters. Second, we consider the case when these conditions are nonlinear in the nuisance parameters.

Case a. First, consider the simplest case of an AREC(1) model when $T=2$. The first and the second moments of $\boldsymbol{y}_i=(y_{i2},y_{i1},y_{i0})$ produce the following 9 identifying equations:

$$\mathrm{E}(y_{i2}-\alpha y_{i1})=0, \tag{7a}$$

$$\mathrm{E}(y_{i1}-\alpha y_{i0})=0, \tag{7b}$$

$$\mathrm{E}(y_{i0}-m)=0, \tag{7c}$$

$$\mathrm{E}(y_{i2}-\alpha y_{i1})^2=\sigma_u^2+\sigma_\eta^2, \tag{7d}$$

$$\mathrm{E}(y_{i1}-\alpha y_{i0})^2=\sigma_u^2+\sigma_\eta^2, \tag{7e}$$

$$\mathrm{E}[(y_{i1}-\alpha y_{i0})(y_{i2}-\alpha y_{i1})]=\sigma_u^2, \tag{7f}$$

$$\mathrm{E}y_{i0}(y_{i2} - \alpha y_{i1}) = c, \tag{7g}$$

$$\mathrm{E}y_{i0}(y_{i1} - \alpha y_{i0}) = c, \tag{7h}$$

$$\mathrm{E}(y_{i0} - m)^2 = \sigma_0^2. \tag{7i}$$

The elimination of the five nuisance parameters $(m, c, \sigma_0^2, \sigma_u^2, \sigma_\eta^2)$ leads to four active equations for α:

$$\mathrm{E}y_{i0}[(y_{i2} - \alpha y_{i1}) - (y_{i1} - \alpha y_{i0})] = 0 \tag{8a}$$

(elimination of c in (7g) and (7h))

$$\mathrm{E}[(y_{i2} - \alpha y_{i1})^2 - (y_{i1} - \alpha y_{10})^2] = 0 \tag{8b}$$

(elimination of $\sigma_u^2, \sigma_\eta^2$ in (7e) and (7f) using (7d))

$$\mathrm{E}(y_{i2} - \alpha y_{i1}) = 0, \tag{8c}$$

$$\mathrm{E}(y_{i1} - \alpha y_{i0}) = 0. \tag{8d}$$

The conditions (7c) and (7i) concern only m and σ_0^2 which are not present in the other conditions. According to Propositions 1 and 2 they can be discarded (both Propositions 1 and 2 apply here – see Remark 7 below). Eqs. (8a)–(8d) are our active orthogonality conditions.

Remark 6. The estimation of the nuisance parameters $\hat{\gamma} = \varphi(\hat{\alpha})$ is not as efficient as the GMM estimator of γ that comes from (7a)–(7i). For example, in the case where $T = 2$; $\hat{m} = \bar{y}_{.0}, \hat{\sigma}_0^2 = (1/n)\sum_{i=1}^n (y_{i0} - \bar{y}_{.0})^2$ are efficient estimators of m, σ_0^2 but $\hat{c} = (1/n)\sum_{i=1}^n y_{i0}(y_{i1} - \hat{\alpha} y_{i0}), \hat{\sigma}_u^2 = (1/n)\sum_{i=1}^n (y_{i1} - \hat{\alpha} y_{i0})(y_{i2} - \hat{\alpha} y_{i1})$ and $\hat{\sigma}_\eta^2 = (1/n)\sum_{i=1}^n (y_{i1} - \hat{\alpha} y_{i0})^2 - \hat{\sigma}_u^2$ are not as efficient as the corresponding estimators based upon (7d)–(7h)!

Case b: Suppose $m = 0$, $c = \sigma_u^2/(1-\alpha)$ and $\sigma_0^2 = \sigma_u^2/(1-\alpha)^2 + (\sigma_\eta^2/(1-\alpha^2))$. Now, the active orthogonality conditions look quite different since, in this case, (8a)–(8c) are not complete; the full set of conditions (7a)–(7i) is needed. However, using Remark 6, and rewriting (7i) as

$$\mathrm{E}y_{i0}^2 = \frac{\sigma_u^2}{(1-\alpha)^2} + \frac{\sigma_\eta^2}{1-\alpha^2}, \tag{7i*}$$

we can eliminate nuisance parameters from (7a)–(7i*). This gives us the new active conditions, (8a)–(8d) together with $\mathrm{E}y_{i0} = 0$ (7c) and

$$\mathrm{E}\left[y_{i0}^2 - \left[(y_{i1} - \alpha y_{i0})\frac{(y_{i2} - \alpha y_{i1})}{(1-\alpha)^2}\right]\right.$$
$$\left. - \left[(y_{i2} - \alpha y_{i1})\frac{((y_{i2} - \alpha y_{i1}) - (y_{i1} - \alpha y_{i0}))}{(1-\alpha^2)}\right]\right] = 0. \tag{8e}$$

Condition (8e) is included in Ahn and Schmidt (1995a, b) but condition (7c), which comes from first-order moments, must also be taken into account to attain full efficiency.

The specification of the initial conditions plays an important role in the structure of the orthogonality conditions as Blundell and Bond (1995) shows. The choice of $y_{i0} = u_i/(1-\alpha) + \eta_{i0}$ allows to transform the nonlinear conditions (6c) into linear orthogonality conditions.

Remark 7. Proposition 2, which generalizes Ahn and Schmidt (1995a), is *not* a justification of the practice found in Ahn and Schmidt (1995b) or Arellano and Bond (1991) in which they use their orthogonality conditions for estimation purposes. In Proposition 1, the nuisance parameters are eliminated by using the empirical counterpart based on the parameters of interest. In Proposition 2, the nuisance parameters are expressed in terms of the parameters of interest using the theoretical model. These two techniques lead to identical estimates (in terms of efficiency) only under very specific conditions (given in Proposition 2). It is important to note that the conditions of Proposition 2 are met for neither the Ahn and Schmidt (1995b) nor the Arellano and Bond (1991) approaches when they consider exclusively linear conditions for the nuisance parameters (the variance-covariance coefficients).

As in cases (a) and (b) that we have just presented, their orthogonality conditions are of the following form:

$$h_i(\theta,\gamma) = h_i^*(\theta) - H\gamma,$$

$$g_i(\theta,\gamma) = g_i^*(\theta) - G\gamma,$$

where H and G are two non-stochastic matrices of order $(n-q)\times q$ and $q \times q$, respectively. This situation is illustrated in Eqs. (7d) to (7f) or when one assumes that the sequence $(y_{i0},\dots,y_{iT})$ is stationary.[7]

Hence, if G is non-singular, $\varphi(\theta) = G^{-1}\mathrm{E}g_i^*(\theta)$, $\varphi_n(\theta) = G^{-1}(1/n)\sum_i g_i^*(\theta)$. The corresponding active orthogonality conditions are

$$h_i(\theta,\varphi(\theta)) = h_i^*(\theta) - HG^{-1}\mathrm{E}g_i^*(\theta),$$

$$h_i(\theta,\varphi_n(\theta)) = h_i^*(\theta) - HG^{-1}\frac{1}{n}\sum_i g_i^*(\theta).$$

Therefore, strictly speaking, Proposition 2 adresses the case of a 'mixed' empirical counterpart $((1/n)\sum_i[h_i^*(\theta) - HG^{-1}\mathrm{E}g_i^*(\theta)])$ and Proposition 1 adresses

[7] In this latter case, H and G may depend on the parameter of interest as in case (b).

the case of the 'pure' empirical counterpart $((1/n)\sum_i[h_i^*(\theta)-HG^{-1}g_i^*(\theta)])$. The two propositions are not equivalent in the linear case.

Both Arellano and Bond (1991) and Ahn and Schmidt (1995b) use the following active orthogonality conditions:

$$\mathrm{E}[h_i^*(\theta)-HG^{-1}g_i^*(\theta)]=0$$

which have the following 'pure' empirical counterpart:

$$\frac{1}{n}\sum_i[h_i^*(\theta)-HG^{-1}g_i^*(\theta)]=0.$$

Furthermore, the optimal weighting matrix (Q_n) is based on

$$h_i(\theta,\varphi_n(\theta))-\left(\frac{1}{n}\sum_i\frac{\partial h_i}{\partial\gamma'}(\theta,\gamma)\right)\left(\frac{1}{n}\sum_i\frac{\partial g_i}{\partial\gamma'}(\theta,\gamma)\right)^{-1}g_i(\theta,\varphi_n(\theta))$$

which is, only in this linear case, equal to

$$h_i^*(\theta)-HG^{-1}\frac{1}{n}\sum_i g_i^*(\theta).$$

Hence, this last fact together with the use of the above active conditions come under Proposition 1 and therefore produce a GMM estimator of θ which is asymptotically equivalent to the GMM estimator based on both $\mathrm{E}h_i=0$ and $\mathrm{E}g_i=0$.

However, this practice is inefficient in the case of nonlinear restrictions in the nuisance parameters.

Remark 8. Another favorable case, related to Ahn and Schmidt (1995a), is the following. Suppose that there exists K, a non-stochastic squared invertible matrix $(n\times n)$, such that

$$K\mathrm{E}m_i(\theta,\gamma)=\mathrm{E}Km_i(\theta,\gamma)=\mathrm{E}(\tilde{h}_i(\theta),\tilde{g}_i(\theta,\gamma))',$$

where $\tilde{g}_i$ has the same dimension as γ. Now, the optimal GMM estimate of θ can be based only on $\mathrm{E}(\tilde{h}_i(\theta))=0$. In this situation, $\mathrm{E}\partial\tilde{h}_i/\partial\gamma'=0$.

3.3. The need for first-order conditions

First, when comparing our approach with approaches that only include (6a), (6b), and/or (6c), the inclusion of (6d) allows the econometrician to identify all of the time dummies. Thus, the proposed approach entails an estimation gain. Furthermore, we show in the following paragraphs the nature of the efficiency loss stemming from failure to consider the first-order conditions. This follows directly from the above propositions, but will give the intuition for the inefficiency of the Ahn and Schmidt and Arellano and Bond techniques for pure AREC(1) models.

Consider the AREC model with $T=2$. As in Arellano and Bond (1991) we exploit only the following orthogonality condition: [8]

$$(ab)\quad \mathrm{E}y_{i0}[(y_{i2}-y_{i1})-\alpha(y_{i1}-y_{i0})]=0.$$

In this case α is estimated by $\hat{\alpha}=\bar{m}_{120}/\bar{m}_{010}$ where $\bar{m}_{120}=(1/N)\sum_{i=1}^{N} y_{i0}(y_{i2}-y_{i1})$ and $\bar{m}_{010}=(1/N)\sum_{i=1}^{N} y_{i0}(y_{i1}-y_{i0})$.

The asymptotic variance of $\hat{\alpha}$ is $v_0=2(m^2+\sigma_0^2)\sigma_\eta^2/(c-(1-\alpha)(m^2+\sigma_0^2))^2$

If we add the following two conditions to condition (ab):

$$(ckt_1)\mathrm{E}(y_{i2}-\alpha y_{i1})=0,$$

$$(ckt_2)\mathrm{E}(y_{i1}-\alpha y_{i0})=0.$$

The empirical counterpart of (ckt_1), (ckt_2), (ab) leads to an asymptotic model of the following form:

$$\bar{y}_2-\alpha\bar{y}_1=\bar{u}+\bar{\eta}_2:=\zeta_2,$$
$$\bar{y}_1-\alpha\bar{y}_0=\bar{u}+\bar{\eta}_1:=\zeta_1,$$
$$\bar{m}_{120}-\alpha\bar{m}_{010}=\frac{1}{N}\sum_{i=1}^{n} y_{i0}(\eta_{i2}-\eta_{i1}):=\zeta_3,$$

with $\bar{u}=(1/N)\sum_i u_i$, $\bar{\eta}_j=(1/N)\sum \eta_{ij}$, $j=1,2$.

From the central limit theorem

$$\sqrt{N}\begin{pmatrix}\zeta_1\\ \zeta_2\\ \zeta_3\end{pmatrix}\xrightarrow{\mathrm{D}}\mathrm{N}(0,S),$$

where

$$S=\begin{pmatrix}\sigma_u^2+\sigma_\eta^2 & \sigma_u^2 & m\sigma_\eta^2\\ \sigma_u^2 & \sigma_u^2+\sigma_\eta^2 & -m\sigma_\eta^2\\ m\sigma_\eta^2 & -m\sigma_\eta^2 & 2(m^2+\sigma_0^2)\sigma_\eta^2\end{pmatrix}.$$

The estimator of α in the above asymptotic model is asymptotically equivalent to the GMM estimator and is of the following form:

$$\tilde{\alpha}=\left[(\bar{y}_1,\bar{y}_0,\bar{m}_{010})\hat{S}^{-1}\begin{pmatrix}\bar{y}_1\\ \bar{y}_0\\ \bar{m}_{010}\end{pmatrix}\right]^{-1}\left[(\bar{y}_1,\bar{y}_0,\bar{m}_{010})\hat{S}^{-1}\begin{pmatrix}\bar{y}_1\\ \bar{y}_0\\ \bar{m}_{120}\end{pmatrix}\right].$$

[8] We know from Ahn and Schmidt that there exists a second orthogonality condition (nonlinear in α). For clarity, we do not consider it here.

Its asymptotic variance is

$$v_1 = \left[(\alpha m, m, c-(1-\alpha)(m^2+\sigma_0^2)) S^{-1} \begin{pmatrix} \alpha m \\ m \\ c-(1-\alpha)(m^2+\sigma_0^2) \end{pmatrix} \right]^{1}.$$

Given the general properties of GLS estimators, it is straightforward that $v_1 \leqslant v_0$. The efficiency gain can be significant. For example, if

$$\operatorname{cov}(y_{i0},(y_{i1}-y_{i0})) = c-(1-\alpha)(m^2+\sigma_0^2)$$

goes to 0, then v_0 goes to infinity as v_1 remains finite. Furthermore, y_{i0} is not a valid instrument in this situation.

If $m=0$, simple algebra shows that

$$v_1 = \frac{2\sigma_\eta^2[\sigma_0^2((\sigma_u^2+\sigma_\eta^2)^2-(\sigma_u^2)^2)]}{[(\sigma_u^2+\sigma_\eta^2)^2-(\sigma_u^2)^2)](c-(1-\alpha)\sigma_0^2)^2}.$$

Hence,

$$v_1 = v_0 = \frac{2\sigma_\eta^2\sigma_0^2}{(c-(1-\alpha)\sigma_0^2)^2}.$$

Consider now the AREC(1) with fixed time specific effects (but without exogenous regressors):

$$y_{it} = \delta_t + \alpha y_{it-1} + u_i + \eta_{it}, \quad i=1,2,\dots,N, \ t=1,2,$$
$$y_{i0} = \delta_0 + \varepsilon_{i0}, \delta_0 = m.$$

Aside from the conditions related to $m=\delta_0$ and σ_0^2, when $T=2$ there are 7 orthogonality conditions for $(\delta_1,\delta_2,\alpha,\sigma_u^2,\sigma_\eta^2,c)$:

$$\mathrm{E}(y_{i2}-\delta_1-\alpha y_{i1})=0 \quad (*\mathrm{a}),$$

$$\mathrm{E}(y_{i1}-\delta_2-\alpha y_{i0})=0 \quad (*\mathrm{b}),$$

$$\mathrm{E}(y_{i2}-\delta_2-\alpha y_{i1})^2=\sigma_u^2+\sigma_\eta^2,$$

$$\mathrm{E}(y_{i1}-\delta_1-\alpha y_{i0})^2=\sigma_u^2+\sigma_\eta^2,$$

$$\mathrm{E}(y_{i2}-\delta_2-\alpha y_{i1})(y_{i1}-\delta_1-\alpha y_{i0})=\sigma_u^2,$$

$$\mathrm{E}y_{i0}(y_{i2}-\delta_2-\alpha y_{i1})=c,$$

$$\mathrm{E}y_{i0}(y_{i1}-\delta_1-\alpha y_{i0})=c.$$

The first two conditions are used to eliminate δ_1 and δ_2 in order to produce 5 conditions in which the 'starred' variables are measured in difference from their means:

$$\mathrm{E}(y_{i2}^* - \alpha y_{i1}^*)^2 = \sigma_u^2 + \sigma_\eta^2,$$
$$\mathrm{E}(y_{i1}^* - \alpha y_{i0}^*)^2 = \sigma_u^2 + \sigma_\eta^2,$$
$$\mathrm{E}(y_{i2}^* - \alpha y_{i1}^*)(y_{i1}^* - \alpha y_{i0}^*) = \sigma_u^2,$$
$$\mathrm{E}y_{i0}(y_{i2}^* - \alpha y_{i1}^*) = 0,$$
$$\mathrm{E}y_{i0}(y_{i1}^* - \alpha y_{i0}^*) = 0.$$

The 5 conditions produce 2 active conditions for α:

$$\mathrm{E}y_{i0}[(y_{i2}^* - y_{i1}^*) - \alpha(y_{i1}^* - y_{i0}^*)] = 0,$$
$$\mathrm{E}[(y_{i2}^* - \alpha y_{i1}^*)^2 - (y_{i1}^* - \alpha y_{i0}^*)^2] = 0.$$

If, as in Arellano and Bond (1991), we concentrate on linear conditions, α is estimated by

$$\alpha_2^1 = \sum_i y_{i0}(y_{i2}^* - y_{i1}^*) \Big/ \sum_i y_{i0}(y_{i1}^* - y_{i0}^*).$$

It is clear that α_2^1 is not equal to $\hat{\alpha}$. Furthermore, $\hat{\alpha}$ is not consistent when $\delta_1 \neq \delta_2$. This simple example shows that first-order conditions have to be taken into account. Furthermore, if in this model with time dumies, the first two conditions ($*$a), ($*$b) are discarded, there are only 5 conditions left for 6 parameters.

If $\mu = \delta_1 = \delta_2$, there is a constant drift in the autoregressive model and there are still 7 conditions as above. The final active conditions for α in this last case also depend on the first-order conditions.

All of these examples show that first-order conditions have to be taken into account. However, note that an efficient – in the sense of our propositions of Section 2 – elimination procedure of such first-order moments can work on deviations from time means i.e. on $\bar{y}_{it} = y_{it} - y_{.t}$ where $y_{.t} = \sum_i y_{it}$. Notice also that, as soon as an intercept is included as an additional regressor (as suggested by Arellano and Bond as well as by Ahn and Schmidt), the induced orthogonality conditions generate our first-order orthogonality conditions.

3.4. An application to time-varying fixed effects

As in Ahn et al. (1994), we consider the following panel data model with both time-varying parameters and individual effects, first proposed by Kiefer (1980):

$$y_{it} = b_t x_{it} + \theta_t \alpha_i + \varepsilon_{it}, \quad i = 1, \ldots, N, \quad t = 1, \ldots, T.$$

Here the θ_t's are fixed parameters and the α_i are individual random effects possibly correlated with x_{it}. However, the x_{it} are assumed to be uncorrelated with $u_{it} - \theta_t u_{i1}$ (where $u_{it} = \theta_t \alpha_i + \varepsilon_{it}$).

If all the disturbances have zero means, the set of orthogonality conditions can be written as

$$E[y_{it} - b_t x_{it}] = 0, \quad t = 1, \ldots, T$$
$$E[x_{is}((y_{it} - b_t x_{it}) - \theta_t(y_{i1} - b_1 x_{i1}))] = 0, \quad s, t \geqslant 2, \ s \neq t,$$

with $\theta_1 = 1$ as an identification constraint.

The direct application of our propositions imply:

First step: Compute b_t, which can be seen as a nuisance parameter, using

$$b_{t_0,n} = \frac{\sum_i y_{it_0}}{\sum_i x_{it_0}}$$

for every t_0.

Second step: Estimate the θ_t's using the second group of orthogonality conditions, where b_t has been replaced using the first step computation. This is a direct application of our Proposition 1. Hence, all orthogonality conditions that include the θ_t's have to be used in this second step but none of the first group are necessary. Notice that all orthogonality conditions used at this step are linear in the parameters of interest, hence a GLS procedure using the appropriate covariance matrix is sufficient.

Third step: Estimate the b_t's making use of the whole set of orthogonality conditions, using the estimated θ_t's. This is a direct application of our Proposition 2. Once more, the orthogonality conditions at this step are linear in the parameters of interest.

Remark 9. To apply our elimination method, the number of orthogonality conditions that can be discarded at the second step cannot be greater than the dimension of the nuisance parameters (see Proposition 1).

Remark 10. On the contrary, suppose that our model assumes a constant nuisance parameter b for all t. Then, $b_{1,n}$ is an appropriate estimator of b for the second step of the elimination procedure. However, the remaining orthogonality conditions:

$$E[y_{it} - b_t x_{it}] = 0, \quad t = 2, \ldots, T \tag{9a}$$

have to be included within the so-called active orthogonality conditions since these conditions are correlated with the remaining set of active conditions:

$$E[x_{is}((y_{it} - b x_{it}) - \theta_t(y_{i1} - b x_{i1}))] = 0, \quad s, t \geqslant 2, \ s \neq t \tag{9b}$$

Remark 11. In the model with a constant nuisance parameter, Theorem 1 of Ahn and Schmidt (1995a), which allows one to consider a subset of the orthogonality conditions, only applies for $T=2$ since the set of orthogonality conditions generated by Eq. (4b) has to be of the same dimension as the θ_t's. For $T>2$, their theorem does not apply in this model. Our proposition states that, for $T>2$, efficient estimation of θ_t has to be performed on both (9a) and (9b).

Finally, if for some good reason there exists extra orthogonality conditions due to a set of exogenous and/or instrumental variables, and if these conditions do not contain the nuisance parameters but only the parameter of interest, then these conditions are not changed in the removal of the nuisance parameters. More generally, if a set of orthogonality conditions concerns only the parameter of interest, this set is not modified by elimination of nuisance parameters.

In a more general set-up of the dynamic panel data model, the distribution terms ε_{it} can be specified in a framework other than the error component model. AR, MA or some other serially correlated disturbances are good candidates for a second order specification of the model. The same approach can be used in such cases to produce convenient orthogonality conditions for the parameter of interest α. Thus, we will obtain active conditions which will be, in general, highly nonlinear in the parameters of interest. It seems clear that it would typically be inefficient to concentrate only on the linear orthogonality conditions, even if the estimation procedure is much more simple in this case. Moreover, since there is no real theoretical reason to distinguish linear and nonlinear conditions, computation is the only difficulty.

4. Conclusion

In this article, we show an appropriate manner to eliminate nuisance parameters in order to obtain active orthogonality conditions in line with Arellano–Bond (1991) and Ahn–Schmidt (1995a, b). We also show why their practice cannot be extended to the case of nonlinear orthogonality conditions in the nuisance parameters. In such nonlinear cases, active orthogonality conditions are 'mixed' conditions where theoretical expectations and empirical means coexist, and this takes us beyond the GMM framework.

Most difficulties can be solved if, instead of using the theoretical orthogonality conditions $Em_i(\theta,\gamma)=0$, we base the GMM approach on 'ergodic' orthogonality conditions such as $P\lim(1/n)\sum_i m_i(\theta,\gamma)=0$. In this new framework, our Propositions 1 and 2 are identical; nevertheless, the active 'ergodic' orthogonality conditions are non-standard since the efficient estimate of θ relies on $(1/n)\sum_i h_i(\theta,\varphi_n(\theta))$!

Appendix. Proof of Propositions 1 and 2

(a) Consider a set of orthogonality conditions for a parameter $\theta \in \mathbb{R}^p$

$$\mathrm{E}h_i(\theta)=0, \quad i=1,2,\ldots,n, h_i : \mathbb{R}^p \to \mathbb{R}^q, \ q \geqslant p. \tag{A.1}$$

Let $\hat{\theta}$ be the GMM estimator.

A first-order expansion of $h_i(\theta)$ in a neighbourhood of the true value θ_0 yields

$$h_i(\theta)=h_i(\theta_0)+\frac{\partial h_i}{\partial \theta'}(\theta_0)(\theta-\theta_0)+0((\theta-\theta_0)^2). \tag{A.2}$$

If we set $h_i^e(\theta)=h_i(\theta_0)+(\partial h_i/\partial\theta')(\theta_0)(\theta-\theta_0)$, the GMM-method based on the above approximate expansion produces a GMM estimator θ^* asymptotically equivalent to $\hat{\theta}$ (see Gouriéroux and Monfort, 1989). This approximate GMM-optimal method is clearly equivalent to an ALS method (see Gouriéroux et al., 1985) based on the auxiliary asymptotic model:

$$\frac{1}{n}\sum_i\left[-h_i(\theta_0)+\frac{\partial h_i}{\partial \theta'}(\theta_0)\theta_0\right]=\frac{1}{n}\sum_i\frac{\partial h_i}{\partial \theta'}(\theta_0)\theta+\varepsilon_n, \ E\varepsilon_n=0, \ V\varepsilon_n=S_n. \tag{A.3}$$

In other words $\theta^*=\theta_0+(X_n'S_n^{-1}X_n)^{-1}X_n'S_n^{-1}\varepsilon_n$ with $\varepsilon_n=-(1/n)\Sigma_i h_i^0$, $X_n=(1/n)\Sigma_i\partial h_i^0/\partial\theta'$, in which θ^* can be also defined as the minimum distance estimator of θ in the linear model:

$$y_n=X_n\theta+u_n, \ \mathrm{E}u_n=0, \ Vu_n=S_n \quad \text{with } y_n=X_n\theta_0+\varepsilon_n.$$

The optimal choice of S_n is $\Sigma_0=V\varepsilon_n=\mathrm{E}h_i(\theta_0)h_i(\theta_0)'$ or any consistent estimator of Σ_0 such as $(1/n)\sum_i h_i(\tilde{\theta})h_i(\tilde{\theta})'$ where $\tilde{\theta}$ is a consistent estimator of θ_0.

(b) We assume now that the orthogonality conditions can be decomposed into

$$\mathrm{E}h_i(\theta,\gamma)=0, \qquad \mathrm{E}g_i(\theta,\gamma)=0, \tag{A.4}$$

where $\theta\in\mathbb{R}^p, \gamma\in\mathbb{R}^m, h_i:\mathbb{R}^{p+m}\to\mathbb{R}^q, g_i:\mathbb{R}^{p+m}\to\mathbb{R}^m$.

From above, the GMM estimators $\hat{\theta},\hat{\gamma}$ with the $q+m$ orthogonality conditions are equivalent to the approximate GMM estimator $\hat{\theta}^V,\hat{\gamma}^V$ based on the auxiliary asymptotic model

$$\frac{1}{n}\sum_i\left[-h_i(\theta_0,\gamma_0)+\frac{\partial h_i}{\partial\theta'}(\theta_0,\gamma_0)\theta_0+\frac{\partial h_i}{\partial\gamma'}(\theta_0,\gamma_0)\gamma_0\right]$$

$$=\frac{1}{n}\sum_i\frac{\partial h_i}{\partial\theta'}(\theta_0,\gamma_0)\theta+\frac{1}{n}\sum_i\frac{\partial h_i}{\partial\gamma'}(\theta_0,\gamma_0)\gamma+\varepsilon_n^1, \tag{A.5a}$$

$$\frac{1}{n}\sum_i\left[-g_i(\theta_0,\gamma_0)+\frac{\partial g}{\partial\theta'}(\theta_0,\gamma_0)\theta_0+\frac{\partial g_i}{\partial\gamma'}(\theta_0,\gamma_0)\gamma_0\right]$$

$$=\frac{1}{n}\sum_i\frac{\partial g_i}{\partial\theta'}(\theta_0,\gamma_0)\theta+\frac{1}{n}\sum_i\frac{\partial g_i}{\partial\gamma'}(\theta_0,\gamma_0)\gamma+\varepsilon_n^2. \tag{A.5b}$$

For notational convenience we set

$$y_1=\frac{1}{n}\sum_i\left[-h_i(\theta_0,\gamma_0)+\frac{\partial h_i}{\partial\theta'}(\theta_0,\gamma_0)\theta_0+\frac{\partial h_i}{\partial\gamma'}(\theta_0,\gamma_0)\gamma_0\right],$$

$$y_2=\frac{1}{n}\sum_i\left[-g_i(\theta_0,\gamma_0)+\frac{\partial g_i}{\partial\theta'}(\theta_0,\gamma_0)\theta_0+\frac{\partial g_i}{\partial\gamma'}(\theta_0,\gamma_0)\gamma_0\right],$$

$$X_1=\frac{1}{n}\sum_i\frac{\partial h_i}{\partial\theta'}(\theta_0,\gamma_0),\qquad Z_1=\frac{1}{n}\sum_i\frac{\partial h_i}{\partial\gamma'}(\theta_0,\gamma_0),$$

$$X_2=\frac{1}{n}\sum_i\frac{\partial g_i}{\partial\theta'}(\theta_0,\gamma_0),\qquad Z_2=\frac{1}{n}\sum_i\frac{\partial g_i}{\partial\gamma'}(\theta_0,\gamma_0).$$

Thus $\hat{\theta}^V,\hat{\gamma}^V$ are the GLS estimators of θ,γ in the linear model:

$$\begin{cases}y_1=X_1\theta+Z_1\gamma+\varepsilon_n^1\\ y_2=X_2\theta+Z_2\gamma+\varepsilon_n^2\end{cases}\begin{pmatrix}\varepsilon_n^1\\ \varepsilon_n^2\end{pmatrix}\sim(0,\Sigma_0). \tag{A.6}$$

Z_2 is an invertible $m\times m$ matrix, and γ can be eliminated from (A.6):

$$y_1-Z_1Z_2^{-1}y_2=(X_1-Z_1Z_2^{-1}X_2)\theta+\varepsilon_n^1-Z_1Z_2^{-1}\varepsilon_n^2. \tag{A.7}$$

If $\tilde{\theta}$ is the GLS estimator of θ on (A.7), it follows from Gouriéroux and Monfort (1980) that $\tilde{\theta}=\hat{\theta}^V$!

(c) Consider the following linear model:

$$y_1=X_1b+Z_1c+u_1, \tag{A.8a}$$

$$y_2=X_2b+Z_2c+u_2 \tag{A.8b}$$

with X_1 $(n_1\times k)$, X_2 $(p\times k)$, Z_1 $(n_1\times p)$, Z_2 $(p\times p)$, $v(u_1)=\Omega_{11}$, $v(u_2)=\Omega_{22}$, and $cov(u_1,u_2)=\Omega_{12}$. Assuming that the model is identifiable (i.e. $n_1+p\geqslant k+p$) and that $\operatorname{rk}Z_2=p$, (A.8a) and (A.8b) are equivalent to

$$y_1-Z_1Z_2^{-1}y_2=(X_1-Z_1Z_2^{-1}X_2)b+u_1-Z_1Z_2^{-1}u_2, \tag{A.9a}$$

$$y_2=X_2b+Z_2c+u_2. \tag{A.9b}$$

Let $u_1^* = u_1 - Z_1 Z_2^{-1} u_2$ and u_2^* be the vector residual of the probabilistic regression of u_2 on to u_1^*. Then, $u_2 = Au_1^* + u_2^*$ with $A = cov(u_2, u_1^*) v(u_1^*)^{-1}$. Hence, u_1^* and u_2^* are orthogonal and the system

$$y_1^* = X_1^* b + u_1^*, \tag{A.10a}$$

$$y_2^* = X_2^* b + Z_2 c + u_2^* \tag{A.10b}$$

in which $y_1^* = y_1 - Z_1 Z_2^{-1} y_2$, $X_1^* = X_1 - Z_1 Z_2^{-1} X_2$, $y_2^* = y_2 - Ay_1^*$, and $X_2^* = X_2 - AX_1^*$, is equivalent to both (A.8a), (A.8b) and (A.9a), (A.9b).

It is also clear that the GLS estimator $\hat{b}$ of b in either (A.8), (A.9), or (A.10) is the GLS estimator of b in the sub-model (A.10a), while the GLS of c is $\hat{c} = Z_2^{-1}(y_2^* - X_2^* b)$.

(d) Define $\gamma = \varphi_n(\theta)$ as in (1). Let θ^V be the GMM estimator based on the remaining empirical counterpart $\frac{1}{n}\sum_i h_i(\theta, \varphi_n(\theta))$. Let θ^* be the GMM estimator of θ based on these two criteria, and θ^{V*} be the approximate GMM estimator based on the first-order expansion:

$$h_i(\theta, \varphi_n(\theta)) = h_i^0 + \frac{\partial h_i^0}{\partial \theta'}(\theta - \theta_0) + \frac{\partial h_i^0}{\partial \gamma'}(\varphi_n(\theta) - \gamma_0) + o(\theta - \theta_0). \tag{A.11}$$

Since

$$\begin{aligned} 0 &= \frac{1}{n}\sum_i g_i(\theta, \varphi_n(\theta)) \\ &= \frac{1}{n}\sum_i g_i^0 + \frac{1}{n}\sum_i \frac{\partial g_i^0}{\partial \theta'}(\theta - \theta_0) + \frac{1}{n}\sum_i \frac{\partial g_i^0}{\partial \gamma'}(\varphi_n(\theta) - \gamma_0) + o(\theta - \theta_0), \end{aligned} \tag{A.12}$$

we deduce that

$$\begin{aligned} &\frac{1}{n}\sum_i h_i(\theta, \varphi_n(\theta)) \\ &= \frac{1}{n}\sum_i h_i^0 - \left(\frac{1}{n}\sum_i \frac{\partial h_i^0}{\partial \gamma'}\right)\left(\frac{1}{n}\sum_i \frac{\partial g_i^0}{\partial \gamma'}\right)^{-1}\left(\frac{1}{n}\sum_i g_i^0\right) \\ &\times \left(\frac{1}{n}\sum_i \frac{\partial h_i^0}{\partial \theta'} - \left(\frac{1}{n}\sum_i \frac{\partial h_i^0}{\partial \gamma'}\right)\left(\frac{1}{n}\sum_i \frac{\partial g_i^0}{\partial \gamma'}\right)^{-1}\left(\frac{1}{n}\sum_i \frac{\partial h_i^0}{\partial \theta'}\right)\right) \\ &\times (\theta - \theta_0) + o(\theta - \theta_0). \end{aligned} \tag{A.13}$$

Along with (A.3), (A.13) shows that θ^{V*} is the GLS estimator of θ in the asymptotic generalized linear model:

$$y_1 - Z_1 Z_2^{-1} y_2 = (X_1 - Z_1 Z_2^{-1} X_2)\theta + \varepsilon_n^1 - Z_1 Z_2^{-1} \varepsilon_n^2. \tag{A.14}$$

Thus, by our previous result (part (c)), $\theta^{V*} = \hat{\theta}^V$. Therefore, θ^* and θ^V are asymptotically equivalent. This is the first part of Proposition 1.

(e) **Proof of Proposition 2**. Suppose that $\gamma = \varphi(\theta)$ solves $\mathrm{E}g_i(\theta, \gamma) = 0$. In this case, the first-order expansion of the criterion would be

$$\frac{1}{n}\sum_i h_i(\theta, \varphi(\theta))$$

$$= \frac{1}{n}\sum_i h_i^0 + \frac{1}{n}\sum_i \frac{\partial h_i^0}{\partial \theta'}(\theta - \theta_0) + \frac{1}{n}\sum_i \frac{\partial h_i^0}{\partial \gamma'}(\varphi(\theta) - \gamma_0) + \cdots$$

with

$$0 = \mathrm{E}g_i(\theta, \varphi(\theta)) = \mathrm{E}g_i(\theta_0, \varphi(\theta_0) + \mathrm{E}\frac{\partial g_i}{\partial \theta'}(\theta_0, \varphi(\theta_0)(\theta - \theta_0)$$

$$+\mathrm{E}\frac{\partial g_i}{\partial \gamma'}(\theta_0, \varphi(\theta_0)(\varphi(\theta) - \varphi(\theta_0)) + \cdots.$$

Since $\gamma_0 = \varphi(\theta_0)$, $\mathrm{E}g_i(\theta_0, \varphi(\theta_0)) = 0$, one has

$$\varphi(\theta) - \varphi(\theta_0) = -\left[\mathrm{E}\frac{\partial g_i}{\partial \gamma'}(\theta_0, \varphi(\theta_0))\right]\left[\mathrm{E}\frac{\partial g_i}{\partial \theta'}(\theta_0, \varphi(\theta_0))\right](\theta - \theta_0).$$

We conclude that the GMM estimator $\tilde{\theta}$ of θ of Proposition 2 is asymptotically equivalent to the GLS estimator $\tilde{\theta}^V$ of θ in the approximate generalized linear model:

$$y_1 = (X_1 - Z_1 Z_2^{-1} X_2)\theta + \varepsilon_n^1.$$

Now, inspection of (A.14) shows that, if $\lim Z_1 = 0$, i.e. $\mathrm{E}\partial h_i/\partial\gamma' = 0$, then $\tilde{\theta}^V$ and θ^{V*} are asymptotically equivalent. And, if

$$cov(\varepsilon_n^1, \varepsilon_n^2) = cov(h_i(\theta_0, \gamma_0), g_i(\theta_0, \gamma_0)) = 0$$

then $\tilde{\theta}^V$ is asymptotically more efficient than θ^{V*}. □

(f) **Proof of the second part of Proposition 1**. First notice that the estimator is consistent. First-order conditions of the program

$$\arg\min_\gamma \bar{m}_n(\hat{\theta}, \gamma)'\Omega^{-1}\bar{m}_n(\hat{\theta}, \gamma)$$

yield

$$\bar{m}_n(\hat{\theta}, \hat{\gamma})'\Omega^{-1}\frac{\partial \bar{m}_n}{\partial \gamma'}(\hat{\theta}, \hat{\gamma}) = 0.$$

Thus, using a first-order expansion around (θ_0, γ_0), we see that the true values give

$$\begin{aligned}
0 \approx\, & \bar{m}_n(\theta_0, \gamma_0)'\Omega^{-1}\frac{\partial \bar{m}_n}{\partial \gamma'}(\theta_0, \gamma_0) \\
& + (\hat{\theta} - \theta_0)\left[\frac{\partial \bar{m}_n}{\partial \theta}(\theta_0, \gamma_0)\Omega^{-1}\frac{\partial \bar{m}_n}{\partial \gamma'}(\theta_0, \gamma_0)\right] \\
& + \left[\bar{m}_n(\theta_0, \gamma_0)'\Omega^{-1}\frac{\partial}{\partial \theta}\left(\frac{\partial \bar{m}_n}{\partial \gamma'}(\theta_0, \gamma_0)\right)\right](\hat{\theta} - \theta_0) \\
& + (\hat{\gamma} - \gamma_0)\left[\frac{\partial \bar{m}_n}{\partial \gamma}(\theta_0, \gamma_0)\Omega^{-1}\frac{\partial \bar{m}_n}{\partial \gamma'}(\theta_0, \gamma_0)\right] \\
& \times \left[\bar{m}_n(\theta_0, \gamma_0)'\Omega^{-1}\frac{\partial}{\partial \gamma}\left(\frac{\partial \bar{m}_n}{\partial \theta'}(\theta_0, \gamma_0)\right)\right](\hat{\gamma} - \gamma_0).
\end{aligned}$$

Multiplying by $\sqrt{n}$ and remembering that $\bar{m}_n(\theta_0, \gamma_0)$ converges to zero, one obtains

$$\begin{aligned}
0 \approx\, & \sqrt{n}\bar{m}_n(\theta_0, \gamma_0)'\Omega^{-1}\mathrm{E}\left(\frac{\partial m_i}{\partial \gamma'}(\theta_0, \gamma_0)\right) \\
& + \sqrt{n}(\hat{\theta} - \theta_0)\left[\mathrm{E}\frac{\partial m_i}{\partial \theta}(\theta_0, \gamma_0)\Omega^{-1}\mathrm{E}\frac{\partial m_i}{\partial \gamma'}(\theta_0, \gamma_0)\right] \\
& + \sqrt{n}(\hat{\gamma} - \gamma_0)\left[\mathrm{E}\frac{\partial m_i}{\partial \gamma}(\theta_0, \gamma_0)\Omega^{-1}\mathrm{E}\frac{\partial m_i}{\partial \gamma'}(\theta_0, \gamma_0)\right].
\end{aligned}$$

This approximation is also satisfied by $(\tilde{\theta}, \tilde{\gamma})$, which is the GMM estimator of the complete system. Thus, taking the difference between the two expressions, one obtains

$$\sqrt{n}M(\hat{\theta} - \tilde{\theta}) + \sqrt{n}N(\hat{\gamma} - \tilde{\gamma}) \approx 0.$$

Therefore, since $\hat{\theta}$ and $\tilde{\theta}$ are equivalent (see Propositions 1a to 1c) and since the matrix N is invertible (locally), $\hat{\gamma}$ and $\tilde{\gamma}$ are asymptotically equivalent. □

References

Ahn, S.C., Schmidt, P., 1993. Efficient estimation of dynamic panel data models under alternative sets of assumptions. Mimeo, Michigan State University.

Ahn, S.C., Schmidt, P., 1995a. A separability result for GMM estimation, with applications to GLS predictions and conditional moment test. Econometric Reviews 14(1), 19–34.

Ahn, S.C., Schmidt, P., 1995b. Efficient estimation of models for dynamic panel data. Journal of Econometrics 68(1), 5–28.

Ahn, S.C., Lee, Y.H., Schmidt, P., 1994. GMM estimation of panel data regression models with time-varying individual effects. Mimeo, Michigan State University, Paper presented at the 1994 panel data Conference, Université Paris-XII.

Anderson, T.W., Hsiao, C., 1981. Estimation of dynamic models with error components. Journal of the American Statistical Association 76, 598–606.

Arellano, M., Bond, S.R., 1991. Some tests of specification for panel data: Monte Carlo evidence and an application to employment equations. Review of Economic Studies 58, 277–297.

Bhargava, A., Sargan. J.D., 1983. Estimation dynamic random effects models from panel data covering short time periods. Econometrica 51, 1635–1659.

Blundell, R.W., Smith, R.J., 1991. Initial conditions and efficient estimation in dynamic panel data models. Discussion Paper 91/4, University College London (also in Annales d'Economie et de Statistique).

Blundell, R.W., Bond, S., 1995. Initial conditions and moment restriction in dynamic panel data models. IFS working paper, 95/17.

Chamberlain, G., 1982. Multivariate regression models for panel data. Journal of Econometrics 18, 5–46.

Chamberlain, G., 1984. Panel Data. In: Griliches, Z., Intriligator, M. (Eds.), Handbook of Econometrics, vol. II, Chapter 22, North-Holland, Amsterdam.

Gouriéroux, C., Monfort, A., 1980. Sufficient linear structures: economic applications. Econometrica 48, 1083–1097.

Gouriéroux, C., Monfort, A., 1989. Statistiques et Modèles Econométriques, vol. 1. Economica, Paris.

Gouriéroux, C., Monfort, A., Trognon, A., 1985. Moindres Carrés Asymptotiques. Annales de l'INSEE 58, 91–121.

Hansen, L.P., 1982. Large sample properties of generalized method of moment estimators. Econometrica 50, 1029–1054.

Kiefer, N.M., 1980. A time series cross-section model with fixed-effects with an intertemporal factor structure. Unpublished manuscript, Cornell University.

Manski, C.F., 1994. Analog estimation of econometric models. In: Engle, R.F., McFadden, D.L. (Eds.), Handbook of Econometrics, vol. IV, pp. 2559–2582.

Newey, W.K., 1985. Generalized method of moments specification testing. Journal of Econometrics 29, 229–256.

Sevestre, P., Trognon, A., 1985. A note on autoregressive error components models. Journal of Econometrics 29, 231–245.

[7]

ELSEVIER Journal of Econometrics 93 (1999) 309–326

JOURNAL OF Econometrics

www.elsevier.nl/locate/econbase

How informative is the initial condition in the dynamic panel model with fixed effects?

Jinyong Hahn*

Department of Economics, University of Pennsylvania, 3718 Locust Walk, Philadelphia, PA 19104-6297, USA

Received 1 October 1997; accepted 1 November 1998

Abstract

I consider estimation of the autoregressive panel model with fixed effects $y_{it} = c_i + \beta y_{i,t-1} + \varepsilon_{it}$. I investigate the estimation method developed by Blundell and Bond (1998), which makes use of the stationarity of the initial levels. I do it by numerically comparing the semiparametric information bounds for the case that incorporates the stationarity of the initial condition and for the case that does not. It is found that the efficiency gain can be substantial. © 1999 Elsevier Science S.A. All rights reserved.

JEL classification: C14; C33

Keywords: Dynamic panel model; Initial condition; Semiparametric information bound

1. Introduction

The purpose of this paper is to examine the role of initial condition in a dynamic panel model with fixed effects as a potential source of efficiency gain. I consider efficient semiparametric estimation of the autoregressive parameter

* Corresponding author. Tel.: + 1-215-898-5652.

E-mail address: hahn@ssc.upenn.edu (J. Hahn)

0304-4076/99 $ - see front matter
PII: S0304-4076(99)00013-5

β in a dynamic panel model with fixed effects

$$y_{it} = c_i + \beta y_{i,t-1} + \varepsilon_{it}, \quad t = 1, 2, \ldots, T; \, i = 1, \ldots, n,$$

where n is relatively large, and T is moderately small. I make a standard sequential conditional moment restriction that

$$\mathrm{E}[\varepsilon_t \,|\, c, y_0, \ldots, y_{t-1}] = 0, \quad t = 1, 2, \ldots, T \tag{1}$$

(I omit the i subscript whenever obvious.) Nonparametric component of this model is the distribution of ε_ts and c.

It is fairly common in the panel literature to disregard the potentially informative role of the distribution of y_0 for the estimation of β. This practice is understandable because misspecification of the distribution of y_0 would result in the inconsistency of the resultant estimator. Perhaps because of this concern, efficiency in dynamic panel literature has been discussed in the framework where y_0 was assumed to be ancillary for the parameter of interest. Various efficient estimators have been developed in this limited context. Holtz-Eakin et al. (1988), Arellano and Bond (1991), and Hahn (1997) developed linear GMM estimators, which use the lagged levels of the series as instruments to the first differences. Ahn and Schmidt (1995) discovered additional (nonlinear) moment conditions for efficiency gain.

Recently, Blundell and Bond (1998) suggested an alternative linear GMM estimator based on additional moment restrictions, which are valid if we have

$$y_0 = \frac{c}{1-\beta} + u = \frac{c}{1-\beta} + \sum_{t=0}^{\infty} \beta^t \varepsilon_{-t}, \tag{2}$$

where ε_t are i.i.d. mean-zero random variables. Observe that the stationarity assumption (2) is not implied by the sequential conditional moment restrictions (1). In their Monte Carlo study, they report good finite sample properties. The purpose of this paper is to investigate the source of the efficiency gain by comparing the semiparametric information bound for the case which makes use of the initial condition with the one which does not: I do *not* compare a particular estimator with another.

To compute the additional information due to the stationarity (2), it would be ideal to have a semiparametric information bound in the model (1). Unfortunately, such a bound does not exist in the literature. The only available bound in the literature is Chamberlain's (1992) bound, which is based on

$$\mathrm{E}[\varepsilon_t \,|\, y_0, \ldots, y_{t-1}] = 0, \quad t = 1, 2, \ldots, T. \tag{3}$$

It is obvious that (3) does not imply (1): Although the moment restrictions

$$\mathrm{E}[y_{t-2}(\varepsilon_t - \varepsilon_{t-1})] = \cdots = \mathrm{E}[y_0(\varepsilon_t - \varepsilon_{t-1})] = 0, \quad t = 2, 3, \ldots, T \tag{4}$$

used by the usual linear GMM estimator are implied by (3), the nonlinear moment restriction

$$\mathrm{E}[(c + \varepsilon_T)(\varepsilon_t - \varepsilon_{t-1})] = 0, \quad t = 2, \ldots, T-1 \tag{5}$$

used by Ahn and Schmidt (1995) does not follow as a consequence of (3).

Because the semiparametric information bound for (1) is not available in the literature, and because it is most convenient to impose stationarity on initial levels when the error ε_t is i.i.d. normal, I assume that the DGP follows

$$\varepsilon_t | c, y_0, \ldots, y_{t-1} \sim \mathrm{N}(0, \sigma^2), \quad t = 1, 2, \ldots, T \tag{6}$$

and

$$y_0 | c \sim \mathrm{N}\left(\frac{c}{1-\beta}, \frac{\sigma^2}{1-\beta^2}\right). \tag{7}$$

The model is still semiparametric because the distribution of c is not parametrically specified. I compute the semiparametric information bound for β under (6) only, and the one under (6) and(7). Adding information clearly cannot hurt, and therefore, the latter information is expected to be strictly larger than the former on theoretical grounds.

In order to quantify the marginal information due to (7), I assume that c has a normal distribution, and numerically evaluate the bounds under various parameter combinations. One finds that the efficiency gain can be quite substantial even when the observation per individual $T + 1$ is moderately big.[1] To compare the stationarity related efficiency gain with the nonlinear-moment-restriction related efficiency gain, I numerically evaluate Chamberlain's (1992) semiparametric information bound under the same parameter combinations. Numerical comparison reveals that the stationarity related efficiency gain substantially dominates the other.

[1] This exercise is similar in spirit to Ahn and Schmidt (1995), who evaluated the efficiency gain due to the nonlinear-moment-restriction by numerically comparing the asymptotic variances of various estimators.

The layout of the paper is as follows. In Section 2, I briefly review the standard moment restrictions for the autoregressive panel model with fixed effects. In Section 3, I compute the semiparametric information bounds under (6) only, and under (6) along with (7). In Section 4, I present various information bounds under various parameter combinations. Section 5 concludes.

2. Semiparametric information bounds

In order to assess the marginal contribution of stationarity assumption (2), it is useful to compare the marginal information in the stationarity assumption in relation to the standard sequential moment restrictions. Information in a panel model with fixed effects is by definition semiparametric information: Distribution of the fixed effects is nonparametrically specified.

I focus on the case where semiparametric information bounds can be computed. I thus make an important restrictive assumption regarding the data generating process. I assume that

Assumption 1. $\varepsilon_t | y_{t-1}, \ldots, y_0, c \sim \mathrm{N}(0, \sigma^2)$, $t = 1, \ldots, T$, where σ^2 is unknown.

Assumption 2. $y_0 | c \sim \mathrm{N}(\frac{c}{1-\beta}, \frac{\sigma^2}{1-\beta^2})$.

Observe that the model is semiparametric even with Assumption 2 because the distribution of the individual specific effect c is nonparametrically specified.

To assess the marginal contribution of the stationarity assumption, I first compute the semiparametric information bound assuming that the stationarity is not part of our knowledge even though the data generating process follows the stationarity assumption. Under this assumption, we have another nonparametric component in the information calculation. We now have the distribution of y_0 nonparametrically specified. Furthermore, y_0 is ancillary β because the distribution of y_0 does not exhibit any dependence on β under our ignorance of the stationarity. For an excellent survey on semiparametric information bound, see Bickel et al. (1993) or Newey (1990). Semiparametric information bound is the expected value of the square of the efficient score.

Theorem 1. Under Assumption 1, the efficient score for β equals

$$\ell_\beta^* - \frac{\mathrm{E}[\ell_\beta^* \ell_{\sigma^2}^*]}{\mathrm{E}[(\ell_{\sigma^2}^*)^2]} \ell_{\sigma^2}^*,$$

where

$$\ell_\beta^* = -\frac{1}{\sigma^2}\left(\sum_{t=1}^{T-1} y_t - \mathrm{E}\left[\sum_{t=1}^{T-1} y_t \middle| y_0, S^*\right]\right)\mathrm{E}[c \mid y_0, S^*]$$

$$+ \frac{1}{\sigma^2}\left(\sum_{t=1}^{T} y_{t-1}(y_t - \beta y_{t-1}) - \mathrm{E}\left[\sum_{t=1}^{T} y_{t-1}(y_t - \beta y_{t-1}) \middle| y_0, S^*\right]\right), \quad (8)$$

$$\ell_{\sigma^2}^* = \frac{1}{2(\sigma^2)^2}\left(\sum_{t=1}^{T} (y_t - \beta y_{t-1})^2 - \mathrm{E}\left[\sum_{t=1}^{T} (y_t - \beta y_{t-1})^2 \middle| y_0, S^*\right]\right) \quad (9)$$

and

$$S^* \equiv \sum_{t=1}^{T} (y_t - \beta y_{t-1}).$$

Proof. See Appendix A. □

Now assume that the stationarity is part of our knowledge. We then know that Assumption 2 holds. Notice that y_0 is no longer ancillary. Furthermore, the only nonparametric component under this situation is the distribution of c.

Theorem 2. Under Assumptions 1 and 2, the efficient score for β equals

$$\ddot{\ell}_\beta - \frac{\mathrm{E}[\ddot{\ell}_\beta \ddot{\ell}_{\sigma^2}]}{\mathrm{E}[(\ddot{\ell}_{\sigma^2})^2]}\ddot{\ell}_{\sigma^2},$$

where

$$\ddot{\ell}_\beta = -\frac{1}{\sigma^2}\left(\sum_{t=1}^{T-1} y_t - \mathrm{E}\left[\sum_{t=1}^{T-1} y_t \middle| \ddot{S}\right]\right)\mathrm{E}[c \mid \ddot{S}]$$

$$+ \frac{1}{\sigma^2}\left(\sum_{t=1}^{T} (y_t - \beta y_{t-1})y_{t-1} - \mathrm{E}\left[\sum_{t=1}^{T} (y_t - \beta y_{t-1})y_{t-1} \middle| \ddot{S}\right]\right)$$

$$+ \frac{\beta}{\sigma^2}(y_0^2 - \mathrm{E}[y_0^2 \mid \ddot{S}]), \quad (10)$$

$$\ddot{\ell}_{\sigma^2} = \frac{1}{2(\sigma^2)^2}\left(\sum_{t=1}^{T}(y_t - \beta y_{t-1})^2 - \mathrm{E}\left[\sum_{t=1}^{T}(y_t - \beta y_{t-1})^2 \middle| \ddot{S}\right]\right)$$

$$+ \frac{1-\beta^2}{2(\sigma^2)^2}(y_0^2 - \mathrm{E}[y_0^2 \mid \ddot{S}]) \qquad (11)$$

and

$$\ddot{S} \equiv \sum_{t=1}^{T}(y_t - \beta y_{t-1}) + (1+\beta)y_0.$$

Proof. See Appendix B. □

It is easy to conjecture that the information bound in Theorem 2 is bigger than the one in Theorem 1. For a formal proof that it is indeed so, see Appendix C.

3. Numerical comparison

To assess the efficiency gain quantitatively, we need to condition on a particular distribution on c. To simplify the analytic calculation, I further assume that

Assumption. $c \sim \mathrm{N}(0, \omega^2)$.

The fact that the fixed effects follow a normal distribution is assumed unknown to an econometrician. Although this data generating process is restrictive due to the homoscedasticity and normality assumption, the quantitative result is at least suggestive that the initial condition can be quite informative about β. I then go on to compute the ratio of information bounds computed in Theorems 1 and 2. Such comparison would be meaningful only if both bounds are achievable.[2] It turns out that both are. Pfanzagl (1990) considered general mixture models, and suggested a sample-splitting-based efficient estimator construction strategy.

Given that the calculations are performed for normal c, comparisons with the Cramer–Raó lower bound for the parametric model with normal c may be deemed useful. Such comparisons do not seem to be necessary. Suppose first that stationarity is not assumed. The Fisher information in the parametric model with normal c should be greater than or equal to the one in the

[2] I am grateful to Oliver Linton for pointing this out.

Table 1
Stationarity-related efficiency gain ($T = 3$)

	ω^2/σ^2					
β	0	0.25	0.5	1	2	4
− 0.99	1.12	5.20	12.59	30.18	69.42	156.46
− 0.9	1.08	1.54	2.40	4.72	11.11	30.17
− 0.8	1.05	1.30	1.77	3.16	7.41	21.42
− 0.5	1.01	1.09	1.27	1.88	3.97	11.56
− 0.3	1.03	1.05	1.13	1.43	2.51	6.50
0	1.13	1.10	1.09	1.08	1.08	1.08
0.3	1.48	1.79	2.40	4.52	12.34	42.15
0.5	2.40	5.21	10.75	30.26	102.65	380.46
0.8	20.09	218.66	649.14	2207.43	8109.04	31 047.41
0.9	106.44	3472.83	11 371.84	40 550.06	152 253.32	588 886.27
0.99	14 462.97	0.3×10^8	0.1×10^9	0.4×10^9	0.1×10^{10}	0.6×10^9

semiparametric model derived in Theorem 1. On the other hand, the information in the semiparametric models should be greater than or equal to the one in models where the only restriction is given in the expression of (unconditional) second moments of $y_0, \ldots, y_T$ as functions of underlying parameters. Now, the information in models with second moment restriction should be equal to the information in the parametric models with normally distributed fixed effects because second moments exhausts information in general normal models. Similar reasoning applies to the case where stationarity is assumed. Therefore, the semiparametric information bounds in Theorems 1 and 2 will in fact coincide with the Cramer–Rao lower bounds for the particular DGP I consider.[3]

The numbers in Tables 1–3 are the ratio of information bounds computed in Theorems 1 and 2. I picked the parameter combinations according to the choice in Ahn and Schmidt (1995). It is clear that the marginal information contained in the initial condition is substantial even when the number of observations per individual is relatively large. We find some interesting patterns. First, the marginal gain tends to be larger for $|\beta|$ close to one. Intuitively, this can be explained by the alternative expression of y_t

$$y_t = \beta^t y_0 + \frac{1-\beta^t}{1-\beta} c + \sum_{j=0}^{t-1} \beta^j \varepsilon_{t-j}.$$

[3] In this sense, parametric models with normally distributed fixed effects are expected to be the 'worst' parametric models: Models with normally distributed fixed effects contain the least information. I am grateful to Gary Chamberlain for providing me with this insight.

Table 2
Stationarity-related efficiency gain ($T = 4$)

	ω^2/σ^2					
β	0	0.25	0.5	1	2	4
− 0.99	1.00	4.15	9.47	21.65	48.25	106.72
− 0.9	1.00	1.34	1.96	3.59	8.02	21.12
− 0.8	1.00	1.17	1.52	2.52	5.50	15.29
− 0.5	1.01	1.06	1.19	1.62	3.08	8.34
− 0.3	1.01	1.03	1.09	1.29	2.01	4.66
0	1.07	1.05	1.04	1.04	1.03	1.03
0.3	1.28	1.43	1.75	2.87	6.94	22.35
0.5	1.80	3.18	5.87	15.14	49.09	178.37
0.8	10.75	99.06	279.13	911.37	3260.49	12 294.00
0.9	54.89	1508.28	4657.70	15 879.71	57 926.95	220 363.77
0.99	7664.72	0.1×10^8	0.4×10^8	0.2×10^9	0.6×10^9	0.2×10^{10}

The coefficient β^t of y_0 indicates that the importance of initial condition in y_t is an increasing function of $|\beta|$.[4] Second, the marginal gain seen as a function of β is asymmetric around zero. Comparing the $\beta = 0.8$ case with the $\beta = -0.8$ case reveals that the marginal gain is larger when β is positive rather than negative. This is probably because of the differential effects of β on the conditional expectation and variance of y_0 given c. Observe that

$$y_0|c \sim \mathrm{N}\left(\frac{c}{1-\beta}, \frac{\sigma^2}{1-\beta^2}\right).$$

The conditional expectation $c/(1-\beta)$ increases in absolute value as β increases, whereas the conditional variance $\sigma^2/(1-\beta^2)$ increases as $|\beta|$ increases. It therefore seems natural that the marginal effect of β is the bigger when it is positive. Third, the marginal gain tends to be small when ω is small relative to σ. This could probably be explained by the same intuition as before. When ω is small, the fixed effect c is close to being constant, and the conditional expectation $c/(1-\beta)$ of y_0 given c would have a small variation. Hence, the effect of stationarity via the conditional expectation would be small. On the other hand, the conditional variance $\sigma^2/(1-\beta^2)$ does not depend on c, and the effect of stationarity via the conditional variance would still remain. Therefore, even when $\omega = 0$, the stationarity implies some marginal gain.

[4] I am grateful to an anonymous referee for providing me with this intuition.

Table 3
Stationarity-related efficiency gain ($T = 10$)

β	ω^2/σ^2 0	0.25	0.5	1	2	4
− 0.99	1.00	2.79	5.22	10.35	21.15	44.60
− 0.9	1.00	1.19	1.46	2.13	3.89	9.04
− 0.8	1.00	1.10	1.25	1.64	2.80	6.57
− 0.5	1.00	1.03	1.08	1.24	1.77	3.67
− 0.3	1.00	1.01	1.03	1.11	1.35	2.26
0	1.01	1.00	1.00	1.00	1.00	1.00
0.3	1.05	1.08	1.16	1.43	2.38	5.98
0.5	1.14	1.40	1.90	3.58	9.67	32.66
0.8	2.41	11.91	29.84	90.69	312.17	1154.14
0.9	8.05	132.14	369.57	1180.05	4142.32	15431.30
0.99	1120.29	907028.06	0.3×10^7	0.9×10^7	0.3×10^8	0.1×10^9

Table 4
Nonlinear-moment-restriction-related efficiency gain ($T = 3$)

β	ω^2/σ^2 0	0.25	0.5	1	2	4
− 0.99	1.00	1.01	1.01	1.01	1.01	1.01
− 0.9	1.05	1.05	1.06	1.07	1.09	1.12
− 0.8	1.08	1.09	1.11	1.14	1.18	1.25
− 0.5	1.14	1.20	1.26	1.35	1.51	1.71
− 0.3	1.15	1.25	1.35	1.51	1.77	2.11
0	1.14	1.31	1.49	1.80	2.27	2.86
0.3	1.11	1.39	1.67	2.18	2.95	3.91
0.5	1.08	1.45	1.84	2.53	3.58	4.87
0.8	1.03	1.64	2.26	3.34	4.96	6.97
0.9	1.01	1.76	2.49	3.75	5.62	7.96
0.99	1.00	1.94	2.78	4.21	6.35	9.03

To assess the efficiency gain due to the initial condition in perspective, I also compute the ratios of information bound in Theorem 1 with the one computed by Chamberlain's (1992) and summarized them in Tables 4–6. It is important to note that Chamberlain's (1992) bound is based only on the moment restriction (3): Normality is not part of his model. Observe that, although the efficiency gain is substantial, it is in general tiny compared with the information contained in the initial condition. On the other hand, the gain due to stationarity is rather small for small values of $|\beta|$.

Table 5
Nonlinear-moment-restriction-related efficiency gain ($T = 4$)

	$\omega^2\ \sigma^2$					
β	0	0.25	0.5	1	2	4
– 0.99	1.00	1.00	1.00	1.00	1.01	1.01
– 0.9	1.03	1.04	1.04	1.05	1.07	1.10
– 0.8	1.06	1.07	1.09	1.11	1.15	1.21
– 0.5	1.12	1.12	1.23	1.30	1.41	1.55
– 0.3	1.15	1.25	1.34	1.47	1.64	1.84
0	1.17	1.37	1.53	1.78	2.10	2.43
0.3	1.16	1.50	1.79	2.23	2.79	3.35
0.5	1.13	1.61	2.03	2.66	3.46	4.26
0.8	1.06	1.89	2.62	3.74	5.12	6.50
0.9	1.03	2.07	2.96	4.31	6.00	7.67
0.99	1.00	2.33	3.41	5.02	7.03	9.04

Table 6
Nonlinear-moment-restriction-related efficiency gain ($T = 10$)

	$\omega^2\ \sigma^2$					
β	0	0.25	0.5	1	2	4
– 0.99	1.00	1.00	1.00	1.00	1.00	1.01
– 0.9	1.02	1.03	1.03	1.03	1.04	1.05
– 0.8	1.04	1.05	1.06	1.07	1.08	1.10
– 0.5	1.07	1.12	1.15	1.78	1.21	1.25
– 0.3	1.10	1.18	1.22	1.27	1.32	1.37
0	1.15	1.30	1.38	1.47	1.55	1.62
0.3	1.19	1.49	1.65	1.81	1.94	2.05
0.5	1.21	1.71	1.96	2.22	2.43	2.57
0.8	1.17	2.42	3.06	3.71	4.22	4.56
0.9	1.11	2.96	3.92	4.89	5.65	6.16
0.99	1.01	3.94	5.42	6.89	8.07	8.86

Although the marginal gain due to stationarity can be substantial, it cannot be too much emphasized that such gain is feasible only under correct specification. Violation of stationarity assumption would lead to inconsistency for most estimators, and the resultant bias-variance trade-offs in finite samples would necessitate some decision scientific choice. Analysis of such trade-offs in finite samples is possible only for a given set of estimators, which is beyond the scope of this paper. In any case, the numbers in Tables 1–6 indicate that *correct* specification of the distribution of initial condition can in principle lead to a substantial efficiency gain.

We have an interesting by-product in this numerical exercise. We can assess the marginal information due to conditioning on c as in (1). Also, we can conclude that Ahn and Schmidt's (1995) additional moment restriction (5) virtually exhausts all the marginal information due to such conditioning. This can be explained as follows. Under the particular DGP that I consider, it can analytically be shown that the linear IV approach as used by Arellano and Bond (1991) achieves Chamberlain's (1992) bound. Therefore, under my particular DGP, Ahn and Schmidt's (1995) Table 1, which compares the information contained in Arellano and Bond's (1991) estimator with the one contained in theirs, can be reinterpreted as a comparison of the information in the moment restriction (3) with the one contained in both (3) and (5). Comparison of Ahn and Schmidt's (1995) Table 1 with Tables 4–6 reveals that the stronger form of the sequential moment restriction (1) is not too informative compared with the two moment restrictions (3) and (5). We can therefore conclude that Ahn and Schmidt's (1995) estimator is almost efficient in the sense that it almost achieves the semiparametric information bound for the model (1).

4. Summary

In this paper, I computed the information bounds for panel autoregressive model with fixed effects with and without incorporating the distribution of initial condition implied by stationarity assumption. Numerical comparison under various parameter combination suggests that the efficiency gain due to the stationarity assumption can be quite substantial. This result suggests that future research may be more productive if more attention is given to the stationarity assumption or initial condition in general.

Acknowledgements

I am grateful to Seung C. Ahn, Gary Chamberlain, A. Ronald Gallant, Oliver Linton, anonymous referees and seminar participants of Harvard/MIT and Yale econometrics workshops for their valuable comments. All errors are mine.

Appendix A. Proof of Theorem 1

Drop the i subscript, and calculate the conditional density given (y_0, c)

$$p(y_T, \ldots, y_1 \mid c, y_0; \beta, \sigma^2) = \left(\frac{1}{\sigma\sqrt{2\pi}}\right)^T \exp\left[-\frac{1}{2\sigma^2}\sum_{t=1}^{T}(y_t - c - \beta y_{t-1})^2\right].$$

Observe that

$$\log p(y_T, \ldots, y_1 \mid c, y_0; \beta, \sigma^2)$$

$$= \frac{T}{2}\log\sigma^2 + \frac{T}{2}\log(2\pi) - \frac{1}{2\sigma^2}\sum_{t=1}^{T}(y_t - c - \beta y_{t-1})^2$$

$$= \frac{\sum_{t=1}^{T}(y_t - \beta y_{t-1})}{\sigma^2}c - \frac{T}{2\sigma^2}c^2 + \frac{T}{2}\log\sigma^2 + \frac{T}{2}\log(2\pi)$$

$$-\frac{1}{2\sigma^2}\sum_{t=1}^{T}(y_t - \beta y_{t-1})^2.$$

Tentatively assume that (β, σ^2) is known, and treat c as a 'parameter'. We then recognize that $p(y_T, \ldots, y_1 \mid c, y_0; \beta, \sigma^2)$ form an exponential family with a complete sufficient statistic $(\sum_{t=1}^{T}(y_t - \beta y_{t-1}))/\sigma^2$. Our information bound calculation is based on this observation.

Now, compute the conditional density given y_0

$$p(y_T, \ldots, y_1 \mid y_0; \beta, \sigma^2)$$

$$= \int p(y_T, \ldots, y_1 \mid c, y_0; \beta, \sigma^2)\,\mathrm{d}\Gamma(c \mid y_0)$$

$$= \int\left(\frac{1}{\sigma\sqrt{2\pi}}\right)^T \exp\left[-\frac{1}{2\sigma^2}\sum_{t=1}^{T}(y_t - c - \beta y_{t-1})^2\right]\mathrm{d}\Gamma(c \mid y_0), \qquad \text{(A.1)}$$

where $\Gamma(\cdot \mid y_0)$ denotes the conditional distribution of c given y_0.

Observe that the log-likelihood given (y_0, c) of a parametric submodel equals[5]

$$\log p(y_T, \ldots, y_1 \mid c, y_0; \beta, \sigma^2, \delta)$$

$$= \frac{c}{\sigma^2}\sum_{t=1}^{T}(y_t - \beta y_{t-1}) - \frac{1}{2\sigma^2}\sum_{t=1}^{T}(y_t - \beta y_{t-1})^2 - \frac{Tc^2}{2\sigma^2} - \frac{T}{2}\log\sigma^2$$

$$+ \log g(c \mid y_0, \delta). \qquad \text{(A.2)}$$

[5] Ignore the constant $-(T/2)\log(2\pi)$.

Here, $g(c \mid y_0, 0) = \gamma(c \mid y_0)$, where $\gamma(c \mid y_0)$ is the density of $\Gamma(c \mid y_0)$. Note that (A.2) corresponds to the parametric submodel of (A.1):

$$p_G(y_T, \ldots, y_1 \mid y_0; \beta, \sigma^2, \delta)$$

$$= \int \left(\frac{1}{\sigma\sqrt{2\pi}}\right)^T \exp\left[-\frac{1}{2\sigma^2}\sum_{t=1}^{T}(y_t - c - \beta y_{t-1})^2\right] g(c \mid y_0, \delta)\, \mathrm{d}c. \qquad \text{(A.3)}$$

Calculation of Scores. Let $\tilde{\ell}_\theta = \partial \log p_G / \partial \theta$. We then have

$$\tilde{\ell}_\beta = -\frac{c}{\sigma^2}\sum_{t=1}^{T} y_{t-1} + \frac{1}{\sigma^2}\sum_{t=1}^{T} y_{t-1}(y_t - \beta y_{t-1}),$$

$$\tilde{\ell}_{\sigma^2} = -\frac{c}{(\sigma^2)^2}\sum_{t=1}^{T}(y_t - \beta y_{t-1}) + \frac{1}{2(\sigma^2)^2}\sum_{t=1}^{T}(y_t - \beta y_{t-1})^2 + \frac{Tc^2}{2(\sigma^2)^2} - \frac{T}{2\sigma^2},$$

$$\tilde{\ell}_\delta = \frac{g_\delta(c \mid y_0, 0)}{g(c \mid y_0, 0)}. \qquad \text{(A.4)}$$

Getting back to (A.3), we have the scores by Ibragimov and Has'minskii (1981)

$$\ell = \mathrm{E}[\tilde{\ell} \mid y_0, y_1, \ldots, y_T],$$

where

$$\ell = (\ell_\beta\ \ell_{\sigma^2}\ \ell_\delta)' \quad \text{and} \quad \tilde{\ell} = (\tilde{\ell}_\beta\ \tilde{\ell}_{\sigma^2}\ \tilde{\ell}_\delta)'.$$

Because of the sufficient statistic structure, for any measurable function $f(c)$, we have

$$\mathrm{E}[f(c) \mid y_0, y_1, \ldots, y_T] = \mathrm{E}[f(c) \mid y_0, S^*], \qquad \text{(A.5)}$$

where

$$S^* = \sum_{t=1}^{T}(y_t - \beta y_{t-1}).$$

Thus, we have

$$\ell_\beta = -\frac{\sum_{t=1}^{T} y_{t-1}}{\sigma^2}\,\mathrm{E}[c\,|\,y_0, S^*] + \frac{1}{\sigma^2}\sum_{t=1}^{T} y_{t-1}(y_t - \beta y_{t-1}),$$

$$\ell_{\sigma^2} = -\frac{S^*}{(\sigma^2)^2}\,\mathrm{E}[c\,|\,y_0, S^*] + \frac{1}{2(\sigma^2)^2}\sum_{t=1}^{T} (y_t - \beta y_{t-1})^2$$

$$+\frac{T}{2(\sigma^2)^2}\,\mathrm{E}[c^2\,|\,y_0, S^*] - \frac{T}{2\sigma^2}.$$

Now, the nonparametric tangent space **K** is calculated. From (A.4) and (A.5), it follows that **K** is the closure of the space consisting of functions of the form

$$(y_0, y_1, \ldots, y_T) \mapsto \frac{\int k(c, y_0) p_0(S^*(y_0, y_1, \ldots, y_T, \beta), c)\,\mathrm{d}\Gamma(c\,|\,y_0)}{\int p_0(S^*(y_0, y_1, \ldots, y_T, \beta), c)\,\mathrm{d}\Gamma(c\,|\,y_0)},$$

where

$$\int k(c, y_0)\,\mathrm{d}\Gamma(c\,|\,y_0) = 0.$$

Here, $p_0(S^*(y_0, y_1, \ldots, y_T, \beta), c)$ denotes the conditional density of $S^*(y_0, y_1, \ldots, y_T, \beta)$ for some fixed y_0 given c. Let $\mathbf{K}_{y_0}$ denote the closure of the space consisting of functions of the form

$$(y_1, \ldots, y_T) \mapsto \frac{\int k(c, y_0) p_0(S^*(y_0, y_1, \ldots, y_T, \beta), c)\,\mathrm{d}\Gamma(c\,|\,y_0)}{\int p_0(S^*(y_0, y_1, \ldots, y_T, \beta), c)\mathrm{d}\Gamma(c\,|\,y_0)},$$

where

$$\int k(c, y_0)\,\mathrm{d}\Gamma(c\,|\,y_0) = 0.$$

It will be shown that

$$\left\{ s \mapsto \frac{\int k(c, y_0) p_0(s, c)\,\mathrm{d}\Gamma(c\,|\,y_0)}{\int p_0(s, c)\,\mathrm{d}\Gamma(c\,|\,y_0)} : \int k(c, y_0)\,\mathrm{d}\Gamma(c\,|\,y_0) = 0 \right\} = L_*(R_{\Gamma, y_0}), \quad \text{(A.6)}$$

where $L_*(R_{\Gamma,y_0})$ denotes the set of zero mean functions in $L_2(R_{\Gamma,y_0})$. Here, R_{Γ,y_0} denotes the conditional distribution of S^* given y_0. Because $\subset$ is obvious, only the other implication is proved. Assume that $h(s) \in L_*(R_{\Gamma,y_0})$ is orthogonal to

$$s \mapsto \frac{\int k(c, y_0) p_0(s, c) \, d\Gamma(c \mid y_0)}{\int p_0(s, c) \, d\Gamma(c \mid y_0)}.$$

Then,

$$\int h(s) \cdot \frac{\int k(c, y_0) p_0(s, c) \, d\Gamma(c \mid y_0)}{\int p_0(s, c) \, d\Gamma(c \mid y_0)} R_{\Gamma,y_0}(ds)$$

$$= \int k(c, y_0) \left[\int h(s) p_0(s, c) \, ds \right] d\Gamma(c \mid y_0)$$

$$= 0.$$

If this holds for all $k(c, y_0)$, then

$$\Gamma\left\{c: \int h(s) p_0(s, c) \, ds = 0\right\} = 1.$$

But because S^* is complete and sufficient statistic for c, we should have $h = 0$. (A.6) is thus proved.

From (A.6), it follows that the projection on **K** is equivalent to the conditional expectation given S^* and y_0. The efficient score is the residual in the projection.

Appendix B. Proof of Theorem 2

From the likelihood of the parametric submodel of $y_0, y_1, \ldots, y_T, c$ under consideration

$$\left(\frac{1}{\sigma\sqrt{2\pi}}\right)^T \exp\left[-\frac{1}{2\sigma^2} \sum_{t=1}^{T} (y_t - c - \beta y_{t-1})^2 \right] \times \frac{\sqrt{1-\beta^2}}{\sigma\sqrt{2\pi}}$$

$$\exp\left[-\frac{1-\beta^2}{2\sigma^2} \left(y_0 - \frac{c}{1-\beta} \right)^2 \right],$$

which delivers the log-likelihood (again, ignoring irrelevant constants)

$$\frac{1}{2}\log(1-\beta^2) - \frac{T+1}{2}\log\sigma^2 + \frac{\sum_{t=1}^{T}(y_t - \beta y_{t-1}) + (1+\beta)y_0}{\sigma^2}c$$

$$-\frac{1}{2\sigma^2}\sum_{t=1}^{T}(y_t - \beta y_{t-1})^2 - \frac{1-\beta^2}{2\sigma^2}y_0^2 - \frac{1}{2\sigma^2}\left(T + \frac{1+\beta}{1-\beta}\right)c^2 + \log g(c,\delta)$$

,

we obtain

$$\tilde{\ell}_\beta = -\frac{\beta}{1-\beta^2} + \frac{-\sum_{t=1}^{T}y_{t-1} + y_0}{\sigma^2}c$$

$$+\frac{1}{\sigma^2}\sum_{t=1}^{T}(y_t - \beta y_{t-1})y_{t-1} + \frac{\beta}{\sigma^2}y_0^2 - \frac{c^2}{\sigma^2(1-\beta)^2},$$

$$\tilde{\ell}_{\sigma^2} = -\frac{T+1}{2\sigma^2} - \frac{\sum_{t=1}^{T}(y_t - \beta y_{t-1}) + (1+\beta)y_0}{(\sigma^2)^2}c + \frac{1}{2(\sigma^2)^2}\sum_{t=1}^{T}(y_t - \beta y_{t-1})^2$$

$$+\frac{1-\beta^2}{2(\sigma^2)^2}y_0^2 + \frac{1}{2(\sigma^2)^2}\left(T + \frac{1+\beta}{1-\beta}\right)c^2$$

and

$$\ell_\beta = \mathrm{E}[\tilde{\ell}_\beta \mid y_0, y_1, \ldots, y_T]$$

$$= -\frac{\beta}{1-\beta^2} + \frac{-\sum_{t=1}^{T}y_{t-1} + y_0}{\sigma^2}\mathrm{E}[c|\ddot{S}]$$

$$+\frac{1}{\sigma^2}\sum_{t=1}^{T}(y_t - \beta y_{t-1})y_{t-1} + \frac{\beta}{\sigma^2}y_0^2 - \frac{1}{\sigma^2(1-\beta)^2}\mathrm{E}[c^2 \mid \ddot{S}],$$

$$\ell_{\sigma^2} = \mathrm{E}[\tilde{\ell}_{\sigma^2} \mid y_0, y_1, \ldots, y_T]$$

$$= -\frac{T+1}{2\sigma^2} - \frac{\ddot{S}}{(\sigma^2)^2}\mathrm{E}[c \mid \ddot{S}] + \frac{1}{2(\sigma^2)^2}\sum_{t=1}^{T}(y_t - \beta y_{t-1})^2 + \frac{1-\beta^2}{2(\sigma^2)^2}y_0^2$$

$$+\frac{1}{2(\sigma^2)^2}\left(T + \frac{1+\beta}{1-\beta}\right)\mathrm{E}[c^2 \mid \ddot{S}]$$

for

$$\ddot{S} = \sum_{t=1}^{T} (y_t - \beta y_{t-1}) + (1+\beta)y_0.$$

By the same reasoning as in the previous section, we obtain the efficient score by

$$\ddot{\ell}_\beta = \ell_\beta - \mathrm{E}[\ell_\beta \mid \ddot{S}], \qquad \ddot{\ell}_{\sigma^2} = \ell_{\sigma^2} - \mathrm{E}[\ell_{\sigma^2} \mid \ddot{S}].$$

Appendix C. Theoretical comparison of bounds

Observe that

$$\mathrm{E}[f(c) \mid \ddot{S}] = E[(c) \mid y_0, S^*]$$

for any measurable function $f(\cdot)$ if

$$y_0 | c \sim \mathrm{N}\left(\frac{c}{1-\beta}, \frac{\sigma^2}{1-\beta^2}\right). \tag{C.1}$$

This is due to the sufficiency of $\ddot{S}$ for c under (C.1). With this in mind, we can rewrite

$$\begin{bmatrix} \ell^*_\beta \\ \ell^*_{\sigma^2} \end{bmatrix} = \begin{bmatrix} (\varphi_1 - \mathrm{E}[\varphi_1 \mid y_0, S^*])\mathrm{E}[c \mid \ddot{S}] + (\varphi_2 - \mathrm{E}[\varphi_2 \mid y_0, S^*]) \\ \varphi_3 - \mathrm{E}[\varphi_3 \mid y_0, S^*] \end{bmatrix},$$

$$\begin{bmatrix} \ddot{\ell}_\beta \\ \ddot{\ell}_{\sigma^2} \end{bmatrix} = \begin{bmatrix} (\varphi_1 - \mathrm{E}[\varphi_1 \mid \ddot{S}])\mathrm{E}[c \mid \ddot{S}] + (\varphi_2 - \mathrm{E}[\varphi_2 \mid \ddot{S}]) \\ \varphi_3 - \mathrm{E}[\varphi_3 \mid \ddot{S}] \end{bmatrix},$$

where

$$\varphi_1 = -\frac{1}{\sigma^2}\left(\sum_{t=1}^{T-1} y_t - \beta y_0^2\right),$$

$$\varphi_2 = \frac{1}{\sigma^2}\sum_{t=1}^{T} y_{t-1}(y_t - \beta y_{t-1}),$$

$$\varphi_3 = \frac{1}{2(\sigma^2)^2}\left(\sum_{t=1}^{T} (y_t - \beta y_{t-1})^2 + (1-\beta^2)y_0^2\right).$$

Observe that

$$\begin{bmatrix} \ddot{\ell}_{\beta} - \ell^*_{\beta} \\ \ddot{\ell}_{\sigma^2} - \ell^*_{\sigma^2} \end{bmatrix}$$

$$= \begin{bmatrix} (\mathrm{E}[\varphi_1 \mid y_0, S^*] - \mathrm{E}[\varphi_1 \mid \ddot{S}])\mathrm{E}[c \mid \ddot{S}] + \mathrm{E}[\varphi_2 \mid y_0, S^*] - \mathrm{E}[\varphi_2 \mid \ddot{S}] \\ \mathrm{E}[\varphi_3 \mid y_0, S^*] - \mathrm{E}[\varphi_3 \mid \ddot{S}] \end{bmatrix}$$

is orthogonal to $(\ell^*_{\beta}, \ell^*_{\sigma^2})'$, from which we can easily verify that the information contained in $(\ddot{\ell}_{\beta}, \ddot{\ell}_{\sigma^2})$ is bigger than the one contained in $(\ell^*_{\beta}, \ell^*_{\sigma^2})$.

References

Ahn, S., Schmidt, P., 1995. Efficient estimation of models for dynamic panel data. Journal of Econometrics 68, 5–28.

Arellano, M., Bond, S., 1991. Some tests of specification for panel data: Monte Carlo evidence and an application to employment equations. Review of Economic Studies 58, 277–297.

Bickel, P., Klaassen, C.A.J., Ritov, Y., Wellner, J.A., 1993. Efficient and Adaptive Estimation for Semiparametric Models. Johns Hopkins University Press, Baltimore.

Blundell, R., Bond, S., 1998. Initial conditions and moment restrictions in dynamic panel data models. Journal of Econometrics 87, 115–143.

Chamberlain, G., 1992. Comment: sequential moment restrictions in panel data. Journal of Business and Economic Statistics 10, 20–26.

Hahn, J., 1997. Efficient estimation of panel data models with sequential moment restrictions. Journal of Econometrics 79, 1–21.

Holtz-Eakin, D., Newey, W., Rosen, H., 1988. Estimating vector autoregressions with panel data. Econometrica 56, 1371–1396.

Ibragimov, I., Has'minskii, R., 1981. Statistical Estimation: Asymptotic Theory. Springer, New York.

Newey, W.K., 1990. Semiparametric efficiency bounds. Journal of Applied Econometrics 5, 99–135.

Pfanzagl, J., 1990. Estimation in Semiparametric Models: Some Recent Developments. Springer, New York.

[8]

ELSEVIER

Journal of Econometrics 68 (1995) 53–78

JOURNAL OF
Econometrics

On bias, inconsistency, and efficiency of various estimators in dynamic panel data models

Jan F. Kiviet

Tinbergen Institute and Faculty of Economics and Econometrics, University of Amsterdam, 1018 WB Amsterdam, The Netherlands

Abstract

When a model for panel data includes lagged dependent explanatory variables, then the habitual estimation procedures are asymptotically valid only when the number of observations in the time dimension (T) gets large. Usually, however, such datasets have substantial sample size in the cross-section dimension (N), whereas T is often a single-digit number. Results on the asymptotic bias ($N \to \infty$) in this situation have been published a decade ago, but, hence far, analytic small sample assessments of the actual bias have not been presented. Here we derive a formula for the bias of the Least-Squares Dummy Variable (LSDV) estimator which has a $O(N^{-1}T^{-3/2})$ approximation error. In a simulation study this is found to be remarkably accurate. Due to the small variance of the LSDV estimator, which is usually much smaller than the variance of consistent (Generalized) Method of Moments estimators, a very efficient procedure results when we remove the bias from the LSDV estimator. The simulations contain results for a particular operational corrected LSDV estimation procedure which in many situations proves to be (much) more efficient than various instrumental variable type estimators.

Key words: Bias correction; Dummy variables estimator; Dynamic panel data model; GMM estimators; Monte Carlo simulation; Unobserved heterogeneity
JEL classification: C13; C23

I am indebted to two anonymous referees and to the editor of this volume for various valuable suggestions. This paper was presented at the 1993 Far-Eastern Meeting of the Econometric Society, 25–27 June, Taipei, Taiwan. It benefited also from the comments by seminar participants at Texas A&M (USA), and the Universities of Amsterdam (The Netherlands), Tartu (Estonia), and Aarhus (Denmark).

SSDI 0304407694016 43 E

1. Introduction

Inference in dynamic regression equations is typically based on large-sample asymptotics, i.e., for $T \to \infty$, where T indicates the number of sample observations of the time-series variables involved. In econometrics the modelling of dynamic relationships usually requires inclusion of lagged dependent explanatory variables. If such dynamic models are estimated from a small (or only moderately large) sample of time-series data, then the standard asymptotic approximations can be very poor (see, for instance, Nankervis and Savin, 1987). The standard approach leads to estimators which (although consistent and asymptotically efficient) are often seriously biased in small samples, and yields test procedures that (although asymptotically valid) are afflicted with an actual type I error probability which differs considerably from the nominal size.

In the case of dynamic panel data models, the asymptotic approximations can be for $T \to \infty$ or for $N \to \infty$ or for both, where N indicates the number of units in each cross-section of the longitudinal sample. In practice T is often very small and N moderate or reasonably large. The accuracy and efficiency of various types of estimators in dynamic error-components models and in dynamic fixed-effects models have been the central issue of a vast number of theoretical and Monte Carlo studies, see *inter alia* Balestra and Nerlove (1966), Nerlove (1971), Maddala (1971), and Arellano and Bond (1991). Here we shall review some of this literature. Next we approximate the small sample bias (for finite N *and* finite T) of the within-group or Least-Squares Dummy Variables (LSDV) estimator for the coefficients of a first-order dynamic panel data model with strongly exogenous explanatory variables and unobserved (random) individual effects. As is well-known, this estimator is *in*consistent for $N \to \infty$ and finite T (see Hsiao, 1986, p.72). Here, we find its small sample bias by applying techniques which have been used so far (as it seems) exclusively in the context of pure time-series dynamic multivariate regression models, see Kiviet and Phillips (1993, 1994). The present results extend findings by Trognon (1978), Nickell (1981), and Sevestre and Trognon (1983, 1985), who derived expressions for the inconsistency (for $N \to \infty$) under alternative situations, such as absence or presence of exogenous explanatory variables, and under various special assumptions concerning the starting values of the dynamic data-generating process.

The approximating formula we derive depends on conditioning variables, but also on the unknown true parameter values. In a Monte Carlo study, where we assess the bias and mean squared error of a whole range of estimators, we find that our approximation (when evaluated at the true parameter values) is very accurate for relevant data generating processes and (small) finite values of N and T. From the same simulations we find, and it also appears from earlier Monte Carlo studies (notably Arellano and Bond, 1991), that the LSDV estimator, although severely biased, has a relatively small dispersion in comparison to various consistent (for $N \to \infty$) estimators. Its standard deviation is often much smaller than obtained for the simple Anderson–Hsiao Instrumental Variables (IV) estimators of the model in first differences and for various Generalized Method of Moments (GMM) estimators. This opens up promising perspectives to exploit an estimate of the LSDV bias for correcting that estimator. If the resulting corrected estimation procedure has minor bias and still a relatively small standard deviation, then, on a mean squared error criterion, this corrected LSDV estimator can be more efficient in finite samples than instrumental variable estimators and possibly even better than (asymptotically efficient) GMM estimators. A particular implementation of the bias assessment is examined, and the resulting operational estimation procedure is compared with other methods. Due to differences in the simulation design, we obtain results which are less favourable for GMM estimators than those presented by Arellano and Bond (1991), and which at the same time illustrate the effectiveness of bias correction of the LSDV estimator.

First, in Section 2, we introduce the model and various estimation techniques, whose small sample behaviour will be examined and compared in later sections. In Section 3 we give an overview of particular relevant earlier results on estimator inconsistency and bias. In Section 4 we derive the approximation to the small sample bias of the LSDV estimator, which has an approximation error of $O(N^{-1}T^{-3/2})$. Section 5 presents Monte Carlo results, and Section 6 concludes.

2. The state dependence model

We consider a dynamic model for panel data with both observed and unobserved exogenous heterogeneity. The unobserved individual effects, which are modelled as random, are possibly correlated with the included exogenous variables, and hence, they cannot simply be dealt with by GLS error-component techniques. The individual effects are to be eliminated by transformations of the model and data, and we consider both taking deviations from group averages (i.e., including dummies) and taking first differences. Both these transformations lead to correlation between the transformed lagged dependent variable and the transformed error term. Nerlove and Balestra (1992) argue that in panel data analysis simpler specifications, for instance static models or models where the unobserved individual effects are uncorrelated with the included explanatory variables, will seldomly be realistic. Also, in cases where the N individuals are a real sample (and not a census), they argue in favour of the random effects specification. See also Hsiao (1985) on this matter.

The present model can be denoted as follows:

$$y_{it} = \gamma y_{i,t-1} + x_{it}'\beta + \eta_i + \varepsilon_{it}, \qquad i = 1, \dots, N, \quad t = 1, \dots, T, \tag{1}$$

where y_{it} is the observation on the dependent variable for unit i at time period t, x_{it} is a $K \times 1$ vector of explanatory variables (the observed heterogeneity) with unknown $K \times 1$ coefficient vector β, η_i denotes the individual effect (unobserved heterogeneity), and ε_{it} is the unobserved disturbance term. The model is dynamic due to the presence of the lagged dependent explanatory variable $y_{i,t-1}$, which has unknown coefficient γ. Probably, the x_{it} vector includes lags of exogenous explanatories too, but such 'finite distributed lag' dynamics does not raise any extra special inference problems, and is therefore left implicit. We make the following further assumptions:

$$\eta_i \sim \mathrm{N}(0, \sigma_\eta^2), \qquad \sigma_\eta^2 \geqslant 0, \tag{2}$$

$$\varepsilon_{it} \sim \mathrm{N}(0, \sigma_\varepsilon^2), \qquad \sigma_\varepsilon^2 > 0. \tag{3}$$

with

(i) $\mathrm{E}\varepsilon_{it}\varepsilon_{js} = 0, \qquad i \neq j \text{ or } t \neq s,$ (4)

(ii) $\mathrm{E}\eta_i\eta_j = 0, \qquad i \neq j.$

(iii) $\mathrm{E}\eta_i\varepsilon_{jt} = 0, \qquad \forall i,j,t.$

(iv) $\mathrm{E}x_{it}\varepsilon_{js} = 0, \qquad \forall i,j,t,s,$

(v) $\mathrm{E}x_{it}\eta_j = \text{unknown}, \qquad \forall i,j,t.$

The normality assumptions made in (2) and (3) are not essential for all results to follow, but, as usual, they are convenient. The assumptions in (4) state that: (i) the homoscedastic error terms are mutually uncorrelated (over units and over time periods); the unobserved heterogeneity, if present ($\sigma_\eta^2 > 0$), is random and (ii) uncorrelated between individuals and (iii) exogenous (uncorrelated with the error terms); the observed heterogeneity is (iv) strongly exogenous but (v) possibly correlated with the unobserved individual effects. The generality of (v) leads to a situation where appropriate estimators have the same form as in the case of fixed effects, i.e., where the N elements $(\eta_1, \dots, \eta_N)$ are individual coefficients; therefore, error components estimation techniques (see the recent review in Baltagi and Raj, 1992) are ruled out.

In situations where Eq. (1) is a behavioural relationship we usually presuppose dynamic stability, i.e.,

$$|\gamma| < 1. \tag{5}$$

Note that at this stage we do not exclude nonstationarity of the variables x_{it} and y_{it}; they may be integrated, and hence unit roots may occur in univariate models for these variables. By (5) we only restrict relationship (1) in such a way that we suppose the (possibly nonstationary) variables y_{it} and x_{it} to have a stable long-run relationship.

Finally, contrary to the rule in the econometric analysis of pure (nonpanel) time-series relationships, we assume that y_{i0} is random, with

$$\begin{aligned} &\text{(vi)} \quad \mathrm{E}y_{i0}\varepsilon_{jt} = 0, \qquad \forall i,j,t, \\ &\text{(vii)} \quad \mathrm{E}y_{i0}\eta_j = \text{unknown}, \quad \forall ij. \end{aligned} \tag{6}$$

We again refer to arguments given in Nerlove and Balestra (1992), which basically rule out the possibility of fixed y_{i0} in the presence of random individual effects, except for cases where the start of the data-generating process precisely coincides with the start of actual data collection for the sample under study. Otherwise, y_{i0} will naturally be correlated with η_i, but predetermined with respect to the errors ε_{it}.

Under the assumptions made in (2) through (5) model (1) is labelled the 'state dependence model' by Anderson and Hsiao (1982, p. 61). They distinguish it from the model where the presence of a lagged dependent variable is merely due to serial correlation of the error term (common factor dynamics), and they present estimators and their consistency properties (for $N \to \infty$ or $T \to \infty$ or both) under the stationarity assumption:

$$\frac{1}{N \cdot T} \sum_{i=1}^{N} \sum_{t=1}^{T} x_{it} x_{it}' \quad \text{converges to a nonsingular constant matrix.} \tag{7}$$

They also define the latent variable

$$v_{it} = y_{it} - \frac{1}{1-\gamma} \eta_i, \qquad i = 1, \dots, N, \quad t = 0, \dots, T. \tag{8}$$

From substitution in (1) of

$$y_{it} = v_{it} + \frac{1}{1-\gamma} \eta_i, \tag{9}$$

$$v_{it} = \gamma v_{i,t-1} + x_{it}'\beta + \varepsilon_{it}, \qquad i = 1, \dots, N, \quad t = 1, \dots, T, \tag{10}$$

is obtained. From (4), (6), and (8) it follows that

$$\mathrm{E}v_{i0}\varepsilon_{jt} = 0, \qquad \forall i,j,t. \tag{11}$$

For further discussion on the treatment of initial observations see, for instance, Bhargava and Sargan (1983) and Blundell and Smith (1991).

We need to introduce a more succinct notation in order to give simple expressions for the various estimators to be compared. In our derivations to follow it will prove to be convenient to stack the T time period observations for the ith individual's characteristics into T element columns, so we write

$$y_i = \begin{bmatrix} y_{i1} \\ \vdots \\ y_{iT} \end{bmatrix}, \quad y_i^{(-1)} = \begin{bmatrix} y_{i0} \\ \vdots \\ y_{iT-1} \end{bmatrix}, \quad X_i = \begin{bmatrix} x'_{i1} \\ \vdots \\ x'_{iT} \end{bmatrix}, \quad \varepsilon_i = \begin{bmatrix} \varepsilon_{i1} \\ \vdots \\ \varepsilon_{iT} \end{bmatrix}, \quad \iota_T = \begin{bmatrix} 1 \\ \vdots \\ 1 \end{bmatrix}. \tag{12}$$

Now (1) can be written as

$$y_i = \gamma y_i^{(-1)} + X_i\beta + \eta_i\iota_T + \varepsilon_i, \tag{13}$$

or as

$$y = \gamma y^{(-1)} + X\beta + (I_N \otimes \iota_T)\eta + \varepsilon, \tag{14}$$

after defining

$$y = \begin{bmatrix} y_1 \\ \vdots \\ y_T \end{bmatrix}, \quad y^{(-1)} = \begin{bmatrix} y_1^{(-1)} \\ \vdots \\ y_N^{(-1)} \end{bmatrix}, \quad X = \begin{bmatrix} X_1 \\ \vdots \\ X_N \end{bmatrix}, \quad \eta = \begin{bmatrix} \eta_1 \\ \vdots \\ \eta_N \end{bmatrix}, \quad \varepsilon = \begin{bmatrix} \varepsilon_1 \\ \vdots \\ \varepsilon_N \end{bmatrix}. \tag{15}$$

Here y, $y^{(-1)}$, and ε are $NT \times 1$ vectors, X is a $NT \times K$ matrix, and η is a $N \times 1$ vector. Introducing also

$$W = [y^{(-1)} \;\vdots\; X] \quad \text{and} \quad \delta' = (\gamma, \beta'), \tag{16}$$

the model can compactly be written as

$$y = W\delta + (I_N \otimes \iota_T)\eta + \varepsilon. \tag{17}$$

Upon defining

$$A_T = I_T - \frac{1}{T}\iota_T\iota_T' \quad \text{and} \quad A = I_N \otimes A_T, \tag{18}$$

the LSDV estimator of δ, which is called the CV (covariance estimator) by Anderson and Hsiao (1981, p. 599), and is also often indicated as the fixed effects or the within-group estimator, can simply be expressed as

$$\hat{\delta} = (W'AW)^{-1}W'Ay. \tag{19}$$

This estimator is well-known to be inconsistent for finite T and $N \to \infty$, and so is the maximum likelihood estimator (see Anderson and Hsiao, 1982, p. 74). Although consistent estimators can be obtained by instrumental variables, we are nevertheless still interested in the inconsistent LSDV estimator. This is because it can be used to construct exact inference on γ, (see van den Doel and Kiviet, 1993), and also because it has a relatively small variance. Below, we shall derive an approximation to its small sample bias, and then show that a bias-corrected LSDV estimator can be constructed which compares favourably with other consistent ($N \to \infty$, fixed T) estimators.

Various implementations of IV (instrumental variable) estimators have been suggested which are consistent for either $T \to \infty$ or $N \to \infty$ or both. Anderson and Hsiao suggested the following procedure. Assuming that, next to y_{i0}, data are available for time period $t = 0$ for x_{it} too, we can define

$$\dot{y}_{it} = y_{it} - y_{i,t-1}, \quad \dot{x}_{it} = x_{it} - x_{i,t-1}, \qquad t = 1, \dots, T, \quad \forall i. \tag{20}$$

Assuming that data collection started at $t = 0$ and $T \geqslant 2$, we define

$$\dot{y}_i = \begin{bmatrix} \dot{y}_{i2} \\ \vdots \\ \dot{y}_{iT} \end{bmatrix}, \quad \dot{y}_i^{(-1)} = \begin{bmatrix} \dot{y}_{i1} \\ \vdots \\ \dot{y}_{iT-1} \end{bmatrix}, \quad \dot{X}_i = \begin{bmatrix} \dot{x}'_{i2} \\ \vdots \\ \dot{x}'_{iT} \end{bmatrix}, \quad \dot{\varepsilon}_i = \begin{bmatrix} \dot{\varepsilon}_{i2} \\ \vdots \\ \dot{\varepsilon}_{iT} \end{bmatrix}, \tag{21}$$

where $\dot{y}_i$, $\dot{y}_i^{(-1)}$, and $\dot{\varepsilon}_i$ are $(T-1) \times 1$ vectors and $\dot{X}_i$ is a $(T-1) \times K$ matrix. Upon stacking this information on all N individuals, we obtain the $N(T-1) \times 1$ vectors $\dot{y}$, $\dot{y}^{(-1)}$, and $\dot{\varepsilon}$ and the $N(T-1) \times K$ matrix $\dot{X}$, which are related according to

$$\dot{y} = \gamma \dot{y}^{(-1)} + \dot{X}\beta + \dot{\varepsilon} = \dot{W}\delta + \dot{\varepsilon} \quad \text{where} \quad \dot{W} = [\dot{y}^{(-1)} \;\vdots\; \dot{X}]. \tag{22}$$

A particular IV estimator suggested by Anderson and Hsiao uses instrumental variable set $Z_l = [y_l \;\vdots\; \dot{X}]$, where the first $N(T-1) \times 1$ instrumental vector is defined as

$$y_l = (y_{10}, \dots, y_{1,T-2}, y_{20}, \dots, y_{2,T-2}, \dots, y_{N0}, \dots, y_{N,T-2})'. \tag{23}$$

Below, we shall indicate this estimation procedure by $AH\mathscr{L}$. The same authors also suggest an IV estimator where the (twice) lagged first difference $\dot{y}^{(-2)}$ is used as an instrument instead of y_l (note that this can only be performed by dropping another observation in the time dimension, so it requires $T \geqslant 3$). We indicate this procedure by $AH\Delta$. However, Arellano (1989) showed that this estimator will suffer often from identification problems which will lead to a poor efficiency, so we will not pay much further attention to it.

Estimators which exploit more orthogonality conditions by employing more instrumental variables have been suggested *inter alia* by Holtz-Eakin et al. (1988), Arellano and Bond (1991), and Ahn and Schmidt (1993). Asymptotically the GMM (Generalized Method of Moments) estimators have optimal properties for particular classes of models. We shall only consider IV estimators which exploit particular linear moment restrictions. Following Arellano and Bond (1991) we examine in the Monte Carlo the procedures GMM1 and GMM2. Having $T + 1$ time-series observations available, these procedures use $K + T(T-1)/2$ instrumental variables for estimating (22); the two-step GMM2 estimator is robust with respect to correlated and heteroscedastic disturbances. In the context of our assumptions these estimators are not asymptotically optimal. However, this does not necessarily imply that their small sample behaviour will be inferior to the methods discussed in Ahn and Schmidt (1993).

Arellano and Bond find a small negative bias in the estimator for γ obtained by the GMM procedures. $AH\mathcal{L}$ shows a performance which is often similar to GMM, but can also be very imprecise, and even worse than $AH\Delta$. Arellano and Bond suppose this happens when γ is high; in Section 5 we come to somewhat different conclusions, which are less favourable for GMM.

When IV estimates are obtained from using as many instruments as regressors in the equation (just identification), such (indirect least-squares) estimators, as a rule, have no finite moments. In that light the unstable mean (squared) errors of both $AH\Delta$ and $AH\mathcal{L}$ are no surprise. Perhaps we can improve their performance by adding just one or a few instruments. Therefore, in the simulations in Section 5, we shall also examine results, indicated by $AHX\mathcal{L}$ and $AHX\Delta$, where apart from $\dot{X}$ and y_l or $\dot{y}^{(-2)}$ also the level of X is used as an instrument. As far as we know the actual existence of the moments of the estimators employed in this study has not yet been established. Any serious problems of this kind may emerge from the simulation results. For curiosity we shall also examine estimators where the untransformed original equation is estimated. Not only the inconsistent OLS estimator which neglects the individual effects will be calculated, but also IV estimators where we confront the original equation in levels with instruments which are in first differences or in deviation form (from individual means). From these instruments the individual effects have been removed, and therefore they are valid (except $Ay^{(-1)}$) and yield consistent estimators. We examine $IV\Delta X$ and $IVAX$. In the former, the instruments are first differences and conform to $\dot{W}$ given in (22). In the latter, the instruments $\dot{X}$ in $\dot{W}$ are replaced by AX.

3. The inconsistency of the LSDV estimator

The asymptotic bias of the LSDV estimator has been examined by Nickell (1981) in the fixed effects model, where he focusses on the case with random start-up (no conditioning on y_{i0}). For the model with no exogenous regressor variables he finds:

$$\operatorname*{plim}_{N\to\infty}(\hat{\gamma}-\gamma) = -\frac{1+\gamma}{T-1}\left[1-\frac{(1-\gamma^T)}{T(1-\gamma)}\right] \times\left\{1-\frac{2\gamma}{(1-\gamma)(T-1)}\left[1-\frac{(1-\gamma^T)}{T(1-\gamma)}\right]\right\}^{-1}, \tag{24}$$

which clearly shows that the inconsistency is $O(T^{-1})$ and negative for positive γ (if $T > 1$); moreover, it does not depend on σ_ε^2. Even for small N it has been found to approximate the true bias, as assessed from Monte Carlo studies, pretty close, except for large values of γ. Similar results have been found by Sevestre and Trognon (1985). They consider the situation where the individual effects are random and examine the consequences of various assumptions regarding the initial observations. They do not consider just the LSDV estimator, but the class of λ-type estimators (see Maddala, 1971) which includes LSDV and OLS as special cases.

Earlier results on inconsistency in Trognon (1978) and Sevestre and Trognon (1983) also concern the case of dynamic panel data models with random exogenous individual effects, and include the case of a model with exogenous explanatory variables. Like Nickell (1981, p. 1424) they find that in this situation the asymptotic bias of $\hat{\gamma}$ is related to result (24) in such a way that it has to be multiplied now by

$$\left[\operatorname*{plim}_{N\to\infty}\frac{1}{N\cdot T}y^{(-1)\prime}Ay^{(-1)}\right]\left[\operatorname*{plim}_{N\to\infty}\frac{1}{N\cdot T}y^{(-1)\prime}AMAy^{(-1)}\right]^{-1}, \tag{25}$$

where $M = I - AX(X'AX)^{-1}X'A$, whereas

$$\operatorname*{plim}_{N\to\infty}(\hat{\beta}-\beta) = -\left[\operatorname*{plim}_{N\to\infty}(X'AX)^{-1}X'Ay^{(-1)}\right]\cdot\operatorname*{plim}_{N\to\infty}(\hat{\gamma}-\gamma). \tag{26}$$

Nickell remarks that the factor (25) is greater than (or equal to) unity, so the presence of exogenous regressors aggravates the bias (although this is denied by Sevestre and Trognon).

Formulas (25) and (26) are not very helpful in providing a clearcut insight into the asymptotic bias, and they may even be very inaccurate as far as the actual magnitude of the bias of the LSDV estimator in small samples is concerned. Nickell (1981, p. 1423) gives an indication on how a more accurate approximation might be obtained. A comparable suggestion to approximate the bias to $O(N^{-1}T^{-1})$ is put forward by Beggs and Nerlove (1988), but they do not pursue this line of approach. Moreover, their suggestion seems only applicable for the approximation of the bias in $\hat{\gamma}$, and not for the complete coefficient vector $\hat{\delta}$. In the next section, however, we shall derive an approximating formula for the bias of the full vector of LSDV coefficient estimates in the model with exogenous regressors. As we shall show its magnitude can be evaluated and exploited easily.

4. An approximation to the bias of the LSDV estimator

Upon substituting (17), the bias of the LSDV estimator given in (19) can be expressed as (below expectations are always conditional on X and v_0):

$$\begin{aligned}\mathrm{E}(\hat{\delta}-\delta) &= \mathrm{E}(W'AW)^{-1}W'A[W\delta + (I_N\otimes\iota_T)\eta + \varepsilon] - \delta\\ &= \mathrm{E}(W'AW)^{-1}W'A\varepsilon.\end{aligned} \tag{27}$$

Here we made use of $A(I_N \otimes \iota_T) = (I_N \otimes A_T \iota_T) = 0$, since $A_T \iota_T = 0$. The expectation (27) is not easily evaluated since W is stochastic and hence the expression is nonlinear. In order to approximate this expectation it is helpful to expose the stochastic nature of W more explicitly by introducing a notation which clearly distinguishes between the fixed elements of W, viz. $\mathrm{E}(W)$, and the zero-mean random elements of W, i.e., $W - \mathrm{E}(W)$; we label them $\bar{W}$ and $\tilde{W}$, respectively. So, we introduce the following notational convention:

For any stochastic or nonstochastic $m_1 \times m_2$ matrix M we define $\bar{M} = \mathrm{E}(M)$ and $\tilde{M} = M - \mathrm{E}(M)$, and hence $M = \bar{M} + \tilde{M}$, where $\bar{M}$ is nonrandom and $\mathrm{E}(\tilde{M}) = 0$.

We thus have

$$W = \bar{W} + \tilde{W} \quad \text{where} \quad \bar{W} = [\bar{y}^{(-1)} \vdots X], \quad \tilde{W} = [\tilde{y}^{(-1)} \vdots 0]. \tag{28}$$

For further analysis of (27) we concentrate on AW, i.e., on $A\bar{W}$ and $A\tilde{W}$, and more in particular on $A\tilde{y}^{(-1)}$. We obtain

$$A\tilde{y}^{(-1)} = (I_N \otimes A_T) \begin{bmatrix} \tilde{y}_1^{(-1)} \\ \vdots \\ \tilde{y}_N^{(-1)} \end{bmatrix} = \begin{bmatrix} A_T \tilde{y}_1^{(-1)} \\ \vdots \\ A_T \tilde{y}_N^{(-1)} \end{bmatrix} = \begin{bmatrix} A_T \tilde{v}_1^{(-1)} \\ \vdots \\ A_T \tilde{v}_N^{(-1)} \end{bmatrix}, \tag{29}$$

where we made use of (15) and (9), which is expressed now as

$$y_i = v_i + \frac{1}{1-\gamma} \eta_i \iota_T. \tag{30}$$

Note that again the dummy variables (i.e., the within operation) removes the individual effects η_i, and hence the stochastic nature of AW originates fully from $\tilde{v} = (\tilde{v}_1, \ldots, \tilde{v}_N)'$. Since $\tilde{x}_{it} = 0$ and $\tilde{\varepsilon}_{it} = \varepsilon_{it}$, it follows straightforwardly from (10) that

$$\tilde{v}_{it} = \gamma \tilde{v}_{i,t-1} + \varepsilon_{it}, \qquad i = 1, \ldots, N, \quad t = 1, \ldots, T. \tag{31}$$

With $\tilde{v}_{i0} = 0$, since $\bar{v}_{i0} = v_{i0}$, relation (31) gives

$$\tilde{v}_i^{(-1)} = L\tilde{v}_i, \quad \Gamma \tilde{v}_i = \varepsilon_i \quad \text{and thus} \quad \tilde{v}_i^{(-1)} = L\Gamma^{-1}\varepsilon_i = C\varepsilon_i, \tag{32}$$

where L, Γ, and C are $T \times T$ matrices, viz.

$$L = \begin{bmatrix} 0 & 0 & \cdot & \cdot & \cdot & \cdot & 0 \\ 1 & 0 & & & & & \cdot \\ 0 & 1 & 0 & & & & \cdot \\ \cdot & \cdot & 1 & \cdot & & & \cdot \\ \cdot & & \cdot & \cdot & \cdot & & \cdot \\ \cdot & & & \cdot & \cdot & \cdot & \cdot \\ 0 & 0 & \cdot & \cdot & 0 & 1 & 0 \end{bmatrix}, \qquad \Gamma = \begin{bmatrix} 1 & 0 & \cdot & \cdot & \cdot & \cdot & 0 \\ -\gamma & 1 & 0 & & & & \cdot \\ 0 & -\gamma & 1 & & & & \cdot \\ \cdot & \cdot & \cdot & \cdot & & & \cdot \\ \cdot & & & \cdot & \cdot & & \cdot \\ \cdot & & & \cdot & \cdot & \cdot & \cdot \\ 0 & 0 & \cdot & \cdot & 0 & -\gamma & 1 \end{bmatrix},$$

$$C = \begin{bmatrix} 0 & \cdot & \cdot & \cdot & \cdot & \cdot & 0 \\ 1 & 0 & & & & & \cdot \\ \gamma & 1 & 0 & & & & \cdot \\ \gamma^2 & \gamma & 1 & \cdot & & & \cdot \\ \cdot & \cdot & \cdot & \cdot & \cdot & & \cdot \\ \cdot & & & \cdot & \cdot & \cdot & \cdot \\ \gamma^{T-2} & \cdot & \cdot & \cdot & \gamma & 1 & 0 \end{bmatrix}.$$

Hence, from (29) and (35) we find

$$A\tilde{y}^{(-1)} = A\tilde{v}^{(-1)} = (I_N \otimes A_T)(I_N \otimes C)\varepsilon = (I_N \otimes A_T C)\varepsilon. \tag{33}$$

So, according to (28), we obtain for $A\tilde{W}$ (the stochastic elements of AW)

$$A\tilde{W} = (I_N \otimes A_T C)\varepsilon q', \tag{34}$$

where q is the $(K+1)\times 1$ unit vector

$$q = (1, 0, \ldots, 0)'. \tag{35}$$

Note that (34) shows that the stochastic characteristics of AW are linear in the disturbance vector ε.

Formula (34) enables to find an approximation to the bias (27) when use is made of the following lemma (for proofs see Appendix A).

Lemma. Let D be a $m \times m$ stochastic matrix, such that $\bar{D} = \mathrm{E}(D)$ exists with $\bar{D}$ nonsingular, and

$$D = \sum_{j=1}^{n} d_j d_j',$$

where the d_j are $m \times 1$ vectors such that

$$\bar{D} = \mathrm{O}(n), \qquad D = \mathrm{O}_p(n), \qquad (D - \bar{D}) = \mathrm{O}_p(n^{1/2}),$$

then we have

$$D^{-1} = (\bar{D})^{-1} - (\bar{D})^{-1}(D - \bar{D})(\bar{D})^{-1} + O_p(n^{-2}).$$

We also make use of the well-known result that for general nonstochastic $m \times m$ matrices Q_1 and Q_2 and a random m-element vector $\xi \sim N(0, \sigma_\varepsilon^2 I_m)$ we have

$$E(\xi' Q_1 \xi)(\xi' Q_2 \xi) = \sigma_\varepsilon^4 [\mathrm{tr}(Q_1) \cdot \mathrm{tr}(Q_2) + \mathrm{tr}(Q_1 Q_2 + Q_1' Q_2)]. \tag{36}$$

For ease of reference, we now state the following:

Assumption 1. Let (1) through (7) hold, i.e., model (17) is a valid specification of the relationship between observations y and X (including the assumption that the regressors are stationary).

In Appendix A we prove:

Theorem 1. Under Assumption 1 we find for the LSDV estimator $\hat{\delta}$ of (19):

$$\begin{aligned} E(\hat{\delta} - \delta) = & -\sigma_\varepsilon^2 (\bar{D})^{-1} \Bigg(\frac{N}{T}(\iota_T' C \iota_T)[2q - \bar{W}' A \bar{W} (\bar{D})^{-1} q] \\ & + \mathrm{tr}\{\bar{W}'(I_N \otimes A_T C A_T) \bar{W} (\bar{D})^{-1}\} q \\ & + \bar{W}'(I_N \otimes A_T C A_T) \bar{W} (\bar{D})^{-1} q + \sigma_\varepsilon^2 N q' (\bar{D})^{-1} q \\ & \times \left[-\frac{N}{T}(\iota_T' C \iota_T) \mathrm{tr}\{C' A_T C\} + 2\,\mathrm{tr}\{C' A_T C A_T C\} \right] q \Bigg) \\ & + O(N^{-1} T^{-3/2}), \end{aligned}$$

where $\bar{D} = \bar{W}' A \bar{W} + \sigma_\varepsilon^2 N \mathrm{tr}\{C' A_T C\} q q'$ and $A\bar{W} = E(AW)$, with W, A, A_T, ι_T, q, and C given in (16), (18), (12), (35), and *(32) respectively.*

The approximation consists of terms which are either $O(1/T)$ or $O(1/NT)$.

We also want to cover the case where assumption (7) is relaxed, and where we allow regressors to be either stationary or nonstationary. To that end we can formulate:

Assumption 2. Let (1) through (6) hold, and let $\Lambda = (\lambda_{ii})$ be a $(K+1) \times (K+1)$ diagonal matrix of normalizing factors, with $\lambda_{ii} = (T^{-1/2})^{d(i)}$ and the integer $d(i) \geq 0$ $(i = 1, \ldots, K+1)$, such that for $B = \Lambda W' A W \Lambda$ we have $B = O_P(NT)$, $\bar{B} = O(NT)$, and $(B - \bar{B}) = O_p(N^{1/2} T^{1/2})$.

Obviously, the diagonal elements of Λ which correspond with stationary regressors are taken unity, and the others are typically $T^{-1/2}$ or T^{-1} etc. We have:

Theorem 2. Under Assumption 2 the bias of the LSDV estimator $\hat{\delta}$ of (19) can be approximated by the same first term as given in Theorem 1, but now the remainder term for the ith element ($i = 1, \ldots, K + 1$) of the coefficient estimate $\hat{\delta}_i$ is $O(N^{-1}T^{-3/2-d(i)})$.

The approximation obtained in Theorems 1 and 2 is used below in two ways. Firstly, we perform simulations in order to assess the actual small sample bias of the LSDV estimator, and then check the accuracy of the approximative formula. The latter can only be evaluated in a situation where the true parameters δ and σ_ε^2 and v_{i0} are known, as is the case in a simulation study. Secondly, however, we also examine in the simulation study the performance of an operational corrected LSDV estimation procedure, labelled LSDVc. Here, an estimate of the approximation formula is subtracted from the original LSDV estimator. For this estimate we will use the GMM1 results. This new estimation procedure will be compared with GMM1 and the various other estimation methods mentioned in Section 2. We assess the bias, the true standard error, and the root mean-squared error of the various estimators of the coefficients γ and β from 1000 Monte Carlo experiments for a few relevant designs.

5. Simulation experiments

In our simulation design we have to make a balanced and relevant choice on the various characteristics of model (1). From the result in Theorem 1 it is obvious that N, T, σ_ε^2, and γ (which appears in C) are important. The matrix X and its coefficients β affect the bias of the LSDV esimator through $A\bar{W} = [A\bar{y}^{(-1)} : AX]$; its first column can be established from (30) which yields $A\bar{y}_i = A\bar{v}_i$, where $\bar{v}_{it} = \gamma\bar{v}_{i,t-1} + x_{it}'\beta$. Obviously v_{i0} is important. Some estimators, viz. *LSDV*, *AHΔ*, and *AHXΔ*, are invariant with respect to η (and hence to σ_η^2); others are not. We perform the Monte Carlo simulation study on a design that closely corresponds to the experiments presented in Arellano and Bond (1991)–AB henceforth. However, our design is different in four respects.

Firstly, we do not fix $y_{i0} = 0$ while discarding the first ten cross-sections. We generate the data exactly according to the specifications, avoiding any slow convergence problems and waste of random numbers (see Appendix B).

Like AB we shall use σ_ε^2 as the normalization parameter, i.e., $\sigma_\varepsilon^2 = 1$, but a second difference with AB is that we do not siply choose $\sigma_\eta^2 = \sigma_\varepsilon^2$, but

$$\sigma_\eta = \mu\sigma_\varepsilon(1 - \gamma), \qquad \mu \geq 0. \tag{37}$$

The reason for including the factor $(1 - \gamma)$ follows from (9). By choosing $\mu = 1$ the impact on y_{it} of the disturbance and the individual effect have equal magnitudes. For $\mu = 2$ the impact of the effect is double (irrespective of any changes in γ). In AB changes in the dynamics through γ also affect the impact ratio of the two error components ε_{it} and η_i, which then obscures to establish the separate effects of γ and μ.

Like AB we include only one regressor variable, but a third difference is that we do not fix $\beta = 1$, but vary β (like σ_η) with γ such that the long-run multiplier of x with respect to y is unity, hence we choose

$$\beta = 1 - \gamma. \tag{38}$$

Now a change in γ only changes the dynamics of the relationship, and not at the same time the equilibrium causal relationship between y and x. The multiplier of unity does not lead to any loss of generality, since the contribution of βx_{it} in the relationship can also be varied by changing the scale of the regressor variable.

The generating equation for the exogenous explanatory variable is

$$x_{it} = \rho x_{i,t-1} + \xi_{it} \quad \text{with} \quad \xi_{it} \sim \text{i.i.d. N}(0, \sigma_\xi^2). \tag{39}$$

Therefore, apart from the coefficients β (which is linked to γ here) and ρ, it is also σ_ξ^2 which determines the signal-to-noise ratio of the relationship. AB give little or no attention to this ratio, although it will be of great significance for the magnitude of bias and the general performance of the various estimation techniques. Even if the only concern is the relative bias and efficiency of the estimators under investigation then, through nonlinear dependencies, the signal-to-noise ratio may still be of considerable importance. Therefore, we shall separately choose values for σ_ε^2, σ_η^2 (via μ), and the signal σ_s^2, which we define as the variance of the right-hand side of (10) minus the (independent) contribution of the disturbance. Upon using (B.3) and (B.7) we find:

$$\begin{aligned} \sigma_s^2 &= \text{var}(v_{it} - \varepsilon_{it}) \\ &= \beta^2 \sigma_\xi^2 \left[1 + \frac{(\gamma + \rho)^2}{1 + \gamma\rho} [\gamma\rho - 1] - (\gamma\rho)^2 \right]^{-1} + \frac{\gamma^2}{1 - \gamma^2} \sigma_\varepsilon^2. \end{aligned} \tag{40}$$

When varying γ (and thus β) in the simulations, we shall also adapt the value of σ_ξ^2 in such a way that we control the signal. It follows from (40) that a signal with variance σ_s^2 is obtained by taking

$$\sigma_\xi^2 = \left[\sigma_s^2 - \frac{\gamma^2}{1 - \gamma^2} \sigma_\varepsilon^2 \right] \left[1 + \frac{(\gamma + \rho)^2}{1 + \gamma\rho} [\gamma\rho - 1] - (\gamma\rho)^2 \right] \frac{1}{\beta^2}. \tag{41}$$

This choice is the fourth difference from the AB design, who have $\sigma_\xi^2 = 0.9$. From the first factor in square brackets of (41) we see that not all values of γ, σ_ε^2, and σ_s^2 are compatible (lead to positive σ_ξ^2).

By (41) the signal will be controlled only to a limited degree since the generation of the x_{it} is not replicated in every simulation run; they are generated only once (like in AB), and hence, in this design the exogenous variable x_{it} is independent of the individual effects η_i. Many of the techniques investigated here, however, are designed for the situation where the observed and the

Table 1
Monte Carlo design, 14 different parameter combinations

	T	γ	β	ρ	σ_s^2	μ	σ_η	σ_ξ	σ_X	R^2
I	6	0.0	1.0	0.8	2	1	1.0	0.85	1.41	0.78
II	6	0.4	0.6	0.8	2	1	0.6	0.88	1.47	0.79
III	6	0.8	0.2	0.8	2	1	0.2	0.40	0.66	0.81
IV	6	0.0	1.0	0.99	2	1	1.0	0.20	1.41	0.62
V	6	0.4	0.6	0.99	2	1	0.6	0.19	1.35	0.66
VI	6	0.8	0.2	0.99	2	1	0.2	0.07	0.48	0.81
VII	3	0.4	0.6	0.8	2	1	0.6	0.88	1.47	0.84
VIII	3	0.4	0.6	0.8	8	1	0.6	1.84	3.06	0.97
IX	3	0.4	0.6	0.8	2	5	3.0	0.88	1.47	0.98
X	3	0.4	0.6	0.8	8	5	3.0	1.84	3.06	0.99
XI	3	0.4	0.6	0.99	2	1	0.6	0.19	1.35	0.76
XII	3	0.4	0.6	0.99	8	1	0.6	0.40	2.81	0.83
XIII	3	0.4	0.6	0.99	2	5	3.0	0.19	1.35	0.98
XIV	3	0.4	0.6	0.99	8	5	3.0	0.40	2.81	0.98

unobserved individual heterogeneity are correlated. Note that $LSDV$ (and also $AH\Delta$) are invariant with respect to η. The effects on other techniques may be substantial, but will not be examined here.

To sum up, we will pay special attention to the parameter values:

$$\gamma = 0.0,\ 0.4,\ 0.8, \tag{42}$$

$$\rho = 0.8,\ 0.99,$$

$$\mu = 1,\ 5,$$

$$\sigma_\varepsilon^2 = 1, \qquad \sigma_s^2 = 2,\ 8.$$

The latter values are feasible and may differ sharply from those in the design of AB. For the design parameter values of their table 1 ($\gamma = 0.2, 0.5, 0.8$, $\rho = 0.8$, $\beta = 1$, $\sigma_\xi^2 = 0.9$), signal variances are found of 3.6, 8.1, 33.4, with $\mu = 1.25, 2, 5$, respectively. Hence, slower adjustment is conflated with more substantial signal and individual effects.

We investigate samples of size:

$$N = 100 \quad \text{and} \quad T = 3,\ 6. \tag{43}$$

(AB have $N = 100$, $T = 7$, but their T denotes the total number of observations available.) Choices (42) and (43) yield 48 combinations. Here we present results on only 14 of these (a copy of all computer output is available upon request). Table 1 presents the design parameter value combinations of these 14 selected

Table 2
Monte Carlo results for $\rho = 0.8$, $\sigma_s^2 = 2$, $\mu = 1$, $T = 6$

		Bias γ	Bias β	Std γ	Std β	Rmse γ	Rmse β
I	*GMM1*	– 0.036	– 0.015	0.058	0.070	0.068	0.071
	GMM2	– 0.033	– 0.026	0.065	0.074	0.073	0.078
	AHΔ	0.002	– 0.004	0.117	0.083	0.117	0.083
	AHXΔ	0.009	– 0.003	0.101	0.083	0.102	0.083
	AH𝓛	– 0.021	– 0.009	0.064	0.073	0.067	0.073
	AHX𝓛	0.218	0.287	0.094	0.104	0.238	0.305
	IVAX	0.001	0.005	0.061	0.067	0.061	0.067
	IVΔX	– 0.009	0.060	0.052	0.131	0.053	0.144
	OLS	0.370	– 0.345	0.046	0.055	0.373	0.349
	OLSι	0.368	– 0.342	0.046	0.055	0.371	0.346
	LSDV	– 0.111	0.020	0.035	0.054	0.117	0.058
	LSDVb	– 0.004	– 0.023	0.034	0.054	0.035	0.059
	LSDVc	– 0.019	– 0.018	0.038	0.054	0.043	0.057
II	*GMM1*	– 0.050	– 0.002	0.079	0.067	0.093	0.067
	GMM2	– 0.045	– 0.011	0.088	0.071	0.099	0.072
	AHΔ	0.022	0.000	0.273	0.082	0.274	0.082
	AHXΔ	0.013	0.001	0.166	0.079	0.166	0.079
	AH𝓛	– 0.018	– 0.004	0.092	0.070	0.094	0.070
	AHX𝓛	0.599	0.184	0.187	0.115	0.627	0.216
	IVAX	– 0.000	0.003	0.072	0.058	0.072	0.058
	IVΔX	– 0.007	0.026	0.061	0.102	0.061	0.105
	OLS	0.204	– 0.171	0.033	0.039	0.207	0.176
	OLSι	0.203	– 0.169	0.033	0.039	0.206	0.174
	LSDV	– 0.187	0.039	0.039	0.052	0.191	0.065
	LSDVb	– 0.003	– 0.008	0.039	0.052	0.039	0.052
	LSDVc	– 0.038	– 0.002	0.045	0.052	0.059	0.052
III	*GMM1*	– 0.065	0.000	0.099	0.155	0.118	0.155
	GMM2	– 0.065	– 0.006	0.112	0.166	0.129	0.166
	AHΔ	0.235	0.023	4.706	0.819	4.712	0.819
	AHXΔ	0.037	0.007	0.600	0.193	0.601	0.193
	AH𝓛	– 0.002	– 0.001	0.131	0.159	0.131	0.159
	AHX𝓛	2.109	0.176	1.891	0.521	2.832	0.550
	IVAX	– 0.009	0.006	0.085	0.119	0.086	0.119
	IVΔX	– 0.012	0.053	0.085	0.230	0.085	0.236
	OLS	0.049	– 0.068	0.021	0.058	0.054	0.090
	OLSι	0.048	– 0.067	0.021	0.058	0.053	0.089
	LSDV	– 0.360	0.005	0.042	0.117	0.362	0.117
	LSDVb	– 0.005	0.007	0.042	0.113	0.042	0.113
	LSDVc	– 0.125	– 0.011	0.049	0.113	0.135	0.114

Table 3
Monte Carlo results for $\rho = 0.99$, $\sigma_s^2 = 2$, $\mu = 1$, $T = 6$

		Bias γ	Bias β	Std γ	Std β	Rmse γ	Rmse β
IV	*GMM1*	− 0.018	0.004	0.062	0.311	0.065	0.311
	GMM2	− 0.018	− 0.016	0.070	0.335	0.073	0.335
	AHΔ	0.002	0.003	0.115	0.352	0.115	0.352
	AHXΔ	0.003	0.003	0.115	0.352	0.115	0.352
	AH$\mathscr{L}$	− 0.004	0.006	0.069	0.318	0.069	0.318
	AHX$\mathscr{L}$	0.015	0.277	0.088	0.407	0.089	0.492
	IVAX	− 0.009	0.083	0.076	0.234	0.076	0.248
	IVΔX	− 0.036	0.982	0.102	0.739	0.108	1.229
	OLS	0.498	− 0.872	0.047	0.040	0.500	0.873
	OLSι	0.495	− 0.870	0.048	0.041	0.498	0.871
	LSDV	− 0.164	0.087	0.039	0.226	0.168	0.242
	LSDVb	− 0.029	0.022	0.039	0.224	0.049	0.225
	LSDVc	− 0.017	0.005	0.047	0.217	0.050	0.217
V	*GMM1*	− 0.033	0.009	0.078	0.326	0.084	0.326
	GMM2	− 0.030	− 0.005	0.088	0.351	0.093	0.351
	AHΔ	0.013	0.006	0.220	0.371	0.220	0.371
	AHXΔ	0.014	0.006	0.216	0.370	0.216	0.370
	AH$\mathscr{L}$	− 0.004	0.009	0.091	0.333	0.091	0.333
	AHX$\mathscr{L}$	0.466	0.176	0.285	0.505	0.546	0.535
	IVAX	− 0.011	0.054	0.084	0.222	0.084	0.229
	IVΔX	− 0.029	0.601	0.106	0.634	0.110	0.874
	OLS	0.271	− 0.517	0.034	0.032	0.273	0.518
	OLSι	0.270	− 0.516	0.034	0.033	0.272	0.517
	LSDV	− 0.249	0.104	0.042	0.242	0.253	0.263
	LSDVb	− 0.040	0.049	0.042	0.238	0.057	0.243
	LSDVc	− 0.042	0.019	0.052	0.230	0.067	0.231
VI	*GMM1*	− 0.062	0.031	0.098	0.914	0.115	0.914
	GMM2	− 0.061	0.014	0.110	0.984	0.126	0.984
	AHΔ	0.621	0.101	12.032	7.892	12.048	7.892
	AHXΔ	0.045	− 0.009	1.014	1.297	1.015	1.297
	AH$\mathscr{L}$	0.000	0.034	0.129	0.941	0.129	0.942
	AHX$\mathscr{L}$	3.055	− 0.021	4.653	4.975	5.567	4.975
	IVAX	− 0.008	0.039	0.088	0.579	0.089	0.580
	IVΔX	− 0.008	0.262	0.102	1.574	0.103	1.595
	OLS	0.050	− 0.180	0.021	0.082	0.054	0.198
	OLSι	0.049	− 0.180	0.021	0.084	0.053	0.199
	LSDV	− 0.365	0.089	0.042	0.668	0.367	0.674
	LSDVb	− 0.008	0.100	0.041	0.643	0.042	0.650
	LSDVc	− 0.127	0.050	0.049	0.641	0.136	0.643

experiments. It also gives the resulting values of σ_η, σ_ξ, $\sigma_x = [\text{var}(x_{it})]^{1/2}$; the R^2 column contains the simulation average of this coefficient as obtained in the LSDV regressions. Note that LSDV produces biased and inconsistent estimates; nevertheless the R^2 values give some indication of the fit. The number of simulation replications was set at 1000.

Tables 2, 3, and 4 present the bias, the standard error (std), and the root mean squared error (rmse) of the various estimation techniques for both γ and β. Table 2 gives results for design parameter values $\rho = 0.8$, $\sigma_s^2 = 2$, $\mu = 1$ at $T = 6$. We see that GMM is virtually unbiased as far as β is concerned, but the γ estimate has a negative bias which is over 50% of its standard deviation. $AH\Delta$ is much less biased in designs I and II, at the expense of a loss in efficiency, but it breaks down for $\gamma = 0.8$, whereas $AHX\Delta$ seems more stable, as far as the bias is concerned, but the efficiency loss at $\gamma = 0.8$ is substantial. $AH\mathscr{L}$ shows smaller biases than GMM and its efficiency compares quite favourably. $AHX\mathscr{L}$, however, seems a waster. $IVAX$ is found to have remarkable capabilities. In these designs it beats GMM. It is virtually unbiased, and its efficiency is favourable, especially for the higher γ value. $IV\Delta X$ proves to have problems with estimating β, but as far as γ is concerned it beats GMM as well. It has already been established in many earlier studies, that OLS estimates γ with positive bias in this situation. Moreover, we find here that it has impressingly small standard deviation, and therefore, when the bias is moderate (which it is for the higher γ value) it has an attractive mean squared error and, in this situation, GMM is beaten again. The results are more or less the same when an intercept is included in the regressions ($OLS\iota$).

We now turn to the results on LSDV and its bias corrected variants. That the LSDV γ estimator has negative (asymptotic) bias is well-known from the literature. We see that this bias gets extremely large when γ increases (whereas the bias in β remains moderate). Hence, for slower dynamic adjustment processes, the bias is more serious (this regularity could not be established from the Arellano and Bond design). Although the standard deviation of the LSDV estimators is not as attractive as the OLS dispersion, for γ it is smaller than achieved by any of the consistent estimators. By LSDVb we indicate results which are obtained by subtracting from the LSDV estimator the bias approximation formula evaluated for the true values of the parameters and $\bar{W}$. Since LSDVb shows hardly any bias, we learn that at these parameter values the approximation is amazingly accurate. Since v_{i0} differs in each replication, the bias approximation varies for each replication, and so both estimators (LSDV and LSDVb) do not necessarily have equivalent standard deviations. LSDVb has the highest efficiency of all estimators considered here, but, as we know, it is not an operational technique. An operational variant is LSDVc, where GMM1 results are used to assess the bias formula. Obviously, whenever GMM1 shows noticable bias, the bias correction will be less accurate, and therefore LSDVc can be much more biased than LSDVb, and also than, for instance, $AH\mathscr{L}$. However,

Table 4
Monte Carlo results for $\gamma = 0.4$, $T = 3$

		Bias γ	Bias β	Std γ	Std β	Rmse γ	Rmse β
VII	*GMM1*	– 0.049	– 0.006	0.181	0.108	0.188	0.109
	LSDV	– 0.395	0.012	0.061	0.091	0.400	0.092
	LSDVb	– 0.010	0.006	0.058	0.088	0.059	0.088
	LSDVc	– 0.205	0.004	0.081	0.093	0.220	0.093
VIII	*GMM1*	0.255	0.073	0.147	0.062	0.295	0.096
	LSDV	– 0.175	0.051	0.036	0.045	0.178	0.068
	LSDVb	– 0.029	0.029	0.036	0.044	0.046	0.053
	LSDVc	– 0.033	0.061	0.069	0.048	0.077	0.077
IX	*GMM1*	– 0.096	– 0.008	0.389	0.112	0.401	0.112
	LSDV	– 0.395	0.012	0.061	0.091	0.400	0.092
	LSDVb	– 0.010	0.006	0.058	0.088	0.059	0.088
	LSDVc	– 0.211	0.007	0.105	0.094	0.236	0.094
X	*GMM1*	0.175	0.063	0.249	0.067	0.305	0.092
	LSDV	– 0.175	0.051	0.036	0.045	0.178	0.068
	LSDVb	– 0.029	0.029	0.036	0.044	0.046	0.053
	LSDVc	– 0.052	0.059	0.082	0.048	0.097	0.076
XI	*GMM1*	– 0.026	0.005	0.167	0.506	0.169	0.506
	LSDV	– 0.495	0.101	0.066	0.430	0.499	0.442
	LSDVb	– 0.086	0.070	0.065	0.409	0.108	0.415
	LSDVc	– 0.249	0.055	0.083	0.430	0.263	0.433
XII	*GMM1*	– 0.041	0.003	0.192	0.243	0.196	0.243
	LSDV	– 0.484	0.087	0.065	0.207	0.488	0.224
	LSDVb	– 0.159	0.057	0.065	0.198	0.172	0.206
	LSDVc	– 0.248	0.046	0.087	0.207	0.263	0.212
XIII	*GMM1*	– 0.060	0.008	0.341	0.512	0.346	0.512
	LSDV	– 0.495	0.101	0.066	0.430	0.499	0.442
	LSDVb	– 0.086	0.070	0.065	0.409	0.108	0.415
	LSDVc	– 0.263	0.061	0.102	0.432	0.282	0.437
XIV	*GMM1*	– 0.064	0.005	0.349	0.246	0.355	0.246
	LSDV	– 0.484	0.087	0.065	0.207	0.488	0.224
	LSDVb	– 0.159	0.057	0.065	0.198	0.172	0.206
	LSDVc	– 0.258	0.052	0.103	0.208	0.278	0.215

since its standard deviation is still close to the original favourable LSDV dispersion, LSDVc has a mean squared error which, although not uniformly superior, can compete with any other of the operational techniques. It seems worthwhile to investigate other variants of LSDVc, where we do not stick to the GMM results for the bias assessment.

Table 3 contains the same experiments with the only difference that the exogenous regressor is extremely smooth now (although still stationary). At particular coefficient values $AH\Delta$, $AHX\mathscr{L}$, and $IV\Delta X$ break down. $AH\mathscr{L}$ compares well with GMM, and $IVAX$ is even better. Oddly enough OLS works quite well in design VI. LSDVc is usually better than GMM and than most other techniques.

On the whole, the Anderson-Hsiao and the IV estimates of the equation in levels are found to be very vulnerable with respect to the parameter values. In the final Table 4 we focus on GMM1 and LSDV correction. We find that even for very small T the bias approximation is often very accurate and the efficiency of LSDVb is always superior; on balance LSDVc seems more attractive than GMM1.

6. Conclusions

From this study it is found that for dynamic panel data models the use of instrumental variables estimation methods may lead to poor finite sample efficiency. In particular situations it seems that valid orthogonality restrictions can better not be employed when composing a set of instrumental variables. It is difficult to find clues on when which instrumental variables are better put aside in order to avoid serious small sample bias or relatively large standard deviations, which both entail poor estimator efficiency. As yet, no technique is available that has shown uniform superiority in finite samples over a wide range of relevant situations as far as the true parameter values and the further properties of the data generating mechanism are concerned. Perhaps such a technique is just impossible. However, from our Monte Carlo experiments it follows that in many circumstances a bias corrected version of the (inconsistent) LSDV estimator is surprisingly efficient in comparison to the established consistent estimation methods, whereas this property seems rather robust. This is a result of the fact that the LSDV estimator usually has a much smaller dispersion than IV estimators, whilst the bias correction of this estimator hardly enhances its variance.

The assessment of the bias via the approximation formula derived in this paper can be extremely accurate, despite the mostly very substantial bias in LSDV. Frequently, however, there seems to be room for some further improvements (occasionally the bias correction has actually produced a larger bias). Such improvements might be achieved by either using a different (perhaps iterated) initial estimate of the parameters than one obtained from the sometimes pretty inefficient GMM estimator, or by further analytical work which would yield a more accurate approximation. The concomitant errors of the present approach are $O(N^{-1}T^{-3/2})$, hence the corrected estimator (LSDVc) is now consistent not just for $T \to \infty$, but also for finite T and $N \to \infty$. However, substantial further analytical derivations may reduce the errors to $o(N^{-1}T^{-1})$ which then would yield corrected estimators which require also a less substantial value of N.

The results in Kiviet and Phillips (1994) show that a generalization for the model with higher-order lags is feasible. At this stage the major conclusion about the present bias approximation formula is that the corrected LSDV estimator is reasonably easy to calculate and was never outclassed in our simulations by any of the other estimators, whereas most of these standard IV or GMM estimation techniques have been found to produce very poor results in particular customary finite sample situations. Whether this will also be the case for asymptotically efficient GMM estimators and in situations where regressors and effects are correlated is still an unanswered question.

Appendix A

Proof of the Lemma. See Kiviet and Phillips (1994, Lemma 2).

Proof of Theorem 1. In the derivation of the approximation we take $D = W'AW$, when applying the Lemma. We first obtain some results on this matrix in order to check whether the conditions of the lemma are satisfied. We find

$$\begin{aligned} \mathrm{E}(W'AW) &= \mathrm{E}(\bar{W}'A\bar{W} + \tilde{W}'A\bar{W} + \bar{W}'A\tilde{W} + \tilde{W}'A\tilde{W}) \\ &= \bar{W}'A\bar{W} + \mathrm{E}(\tilde{W}'A\tilde{W}), \end{aligned} \tag{A.1}$$

and using (34),

$$\begin{aligned} \mathrm{E}(\tilde{W}'A\tilde{W}) &= \mathrm{E}q\varepsilon'(I_N \otimes C'A_T)(I_N \otimes A_T C)\varepsilon q' \\ &= qq'\mathrm{E}\varepsilon'(I_N \otimes C'A_T)(I_N \otimes A_T C)\varepsilon \\ &= \sigma_\varepsilon^2 \operatorname{tr}\{I_N \otimes C'A_T C\} qq' \\ &= \sigma^2 N \operatorname{tr}\{C'A_T C\} qq' \\ &= O(NT). \end{aligned} \tag{A.2}$$

Moreover, employing (36) we find

$$\begin{aligned} \operatorname{var}[\varepsilon'(I_N \otimes C'A_T)(I_N \otimes A_T C)\varepsilon] &= \mathrm{E}\varepsilon'(I_N \otimes C'A_T C)\varepsilon\varepsilon'(I_N \otimes C'A_T C)\varepsilon \\ &\quad - [\sigma_\varepsilon^2 N \operatorname{tr}\{C'A_T C\}]^2 \\ &= 2\sigma_\varepsilon^4 \operatorname{tr}\{(I_N \otimes C'A_T CC'A_T C)\} \\ &= O(NT), \end{aligned}$$

giving, with (A.2),

$$\tilde{W}'A\tilde{W} - \mathrm{E}(\tilde{W}'A\tilde{W}) = \mathrm{O}_p(N^{1/2}T^{1/2}). \tag{A.3}$$

Because of (5) and (7) all regressors, including the lagged dependent variable, are assumed to be stationary, hence:

$$W'AW = \mathrm{O}_p(NT) \quad \text{and} \quad \mathrm{E}(W'AW) = \mathrm{O}(NT). \tag{A.4}$$

We also have

$$\bar{W}'A\tilde{W} = \mathrm{O}_p(N^{1/2}T^{1/2}), \tag{A.5}$$

which follows from $\mathrm{E}(\bar{W}'A\tilde{W}) = 0$, and

$$\begin{aligned} \mathrm{var}(\bar{W}'A\tilde{y}^{(-1)}) &= \sigma_\varepsilon^2 \bar{W}'A(I_N \otimes CC')A\bar{W} \\ &= \mathrm{O}(NT). \end{aligned} \tag{A.6}$$

Hence, from (A.3) and (A.5), we find

$$\begin{aligned} D - \bar{D} &= \tilde{W}'A\bar{W} + \bar{W}'A\tilde{W} + [\tilde{W}'A\tilde{W} - \mathrm{E}(\tilde{W}'A\tilde{W})] \\ &= \mathrm{O}_p(N^{1/2}T^{1/2}), \end{aligned} \tag{A.7}$$

and from (A.4) and (A.7) it follows that we can invoke the lemma for $(W'AW)^{-1}$ in the bias expression, with $n = NT$.

Before we do so, we first consider the remaining part of the bias expression, viz. $W'A\varepsilon$. It is easily found now that

$$\begin{aligned} \mathrm{E}(W'A\varepsilon) &= \mathrm{E}(\bar{W}'A\varepsilon + \tilde{W}'A\varepsilon) \\ &= 0 + q\mathrm{E}\varepsilon'(I_N \otimes C'A_T)\varepsilon \\ &= \sigma_\varepsilon^2 N \cdot \mathrm{tr}\{A_T C\} q \\ &= -\sigma^2(\iota_T' C \iota_T)\frac{N}{T} q \\ &= \mathrm{O}(N), \end{aligned} \tag{A.8}$$

and

$$\begin{aligned} \mathrm{var}(W'A\varepsilon) &= \mathrm{E}(\bar{W}'A\varepsilon + \tilde{W}'A\varepsilon)(\varepsilon'A\bar{W} + \varepsilon'A\tilde{W}) - [\sigma_\varepsilon^2 N \cdot \mathrm{tr}\{A_T C\}]^2 qq' \\ &= \sigma_\varepsilon^2 \bar{W}'A\bar{W} + \mathrm{E}(\bar{W}'A\varepsilon\varepsilon'A\tilde{W} + \tilde{W}'A\varepsilon\varepsilon'A\bar{W} + \tilde{W}'A\varepsilon\varepsilon'A\tilde{W}) \\ &\quad - [\sigma_\varepsilon^2 N \cdot \mathrm{tr}\{A_T C\}]^2 qq'. \end{aligned}$$

Of these five terms, the second and third terms are zero, since they involve the third moment of normal variables. Thus,

$$\begin{aligned}\operatorname{var}(W'A\varepsilon) &= \sigma_\varepsilon^2 \bar{W}'A\bar{W} + qq'\{\mathrm{E}\varepsilon'(I_N \otimes C'A_T)\varepsilon\varepsilon'(I_N \otimes A_T C)\varepsilon \\ &\quad - [\sigma_\varepsilon^2 N \cdot \operatorname{tr}\{A_T C\}]^2\} \\ &= \sigma_\varepsilon^2 \bar{W}'A\bar{W} + qq'\sigma_\varepsilon^4 N[\operatorname{tr}\{C'A_T C\} + \operatorname{tr}\{A_T C A_T C\}] \\ &= \mathrm{O}(NT), \end{aligned} \tag{A.9}$$

and it follows that

$$W'A\varepsilon - \mathrm{E}(W'A\varepsilon) = \mathrm{O}_p(N^{1/2} \cdot T^{1/2}). \tag{A.10}$$

Finally we turn to the expression for the estimation error

$$\hat{\delta} - \delta = (W'AW)^{-1}\mathrm{E}(W'A\varepsilon) + (W'AW)^{-1}[W'A\varepsilon - \mathrm{E}(W'A\varepsilon)]. \tag{A.11}$$

When writing $D = W'AW$ and applying the lemma, the approximation of $(D)^{-1}$ by $[(\bar{D})^{-1} - (\bar{D})^{-1}(D - \bar{D})(\bar{D})^{-1}]$ leads to the omission of terms of $\mathrm{O}_p(N^{-2}T^{-2})$. Hence, by replacing $(D)^{-1}$ in the two terms of (A.11) we have an approximation of $(\hat{\delta} - \delta)$, where terms are omitted which are $\mathrm{O}_p(N^{-1}T^{-2})$ and $\mathrm{O}_p(N^{-3/2}T^{-3/2})$, respectively. Thus, the overall approximation error is $\mathrm{O}_p(N^{-1}T^{-3/2})$. A more accurate result, where, for instance, the approximation is correct up to $\mathrm{O}_p(N^{-1}T^{-1})$ terms can be obtained (at the expense of substantial analytic problems) by using a higher-order approximation for $(D)^{-1}$. This will not be pursued here. We use

$$\mathrm{E}(\hat{\delta} - \delta) = \mathrm{E}[(\bar{D})^{-1} - (\bar{D})^{-1}(D - \bar{D})(\bar{D})^{-1}]W'A\varepsilon + \mathrm{O}(N^{-1}T^{-3/2}), \tag{A.12}$$

and so our approximation to the bias equals

$$\begin{aligned}&\mathrm{E}[(\bar{D})^{-1} - (\bar{D})^{-1}(D - \bar{D})(\bar{D})^{-1}]W'A\varepsilon \\ &= 2(\bar{D})^{-1}\mathrm{E}W'A\varepsilon - (\bar{D})^{-1}\mathrm{E}[D(\bar{D})^{-1}W'A\varepsilon] \\ &= -2\sigma_\varepsilon^2(\iota_T' C \iota_T)\frac{N}{T}(\bar{D})^{-1}q - (\bar{D})^{-1}\mathrm{E}[D(\bar{D})^{-1}W'A\varepsilon], \end{aligned} \tag{A.13}$$

where we made use of (A.8). For the expression in square brackets in the second term we find that its expectation, i.e.,

$$\begin{aligned}\mathrm{E}[D(\bar{D})^{-1}W'A\varepsilon] = \mathrm{E}(&\bar{W}'A\bar{W} + \tilde{W}'A\bar{W} + \bar{W}'A\tilde{W} \\ &+ \tilde{W}'A\tilde{W})(\bar{D})^{-1}(\bar{W}'A\varepsilon + \tilde{W}'A\varepsilon),\end{aligned}$$

is the sum of the expectations of eight separate terms, viz.:

(i) $\mathrm{E}\bar{W}'A\bar{W}(\bar{D})^{-1}\bar{W}'A\varepsilon = 0,$

(ii) $$\begin{aligned}\mathrm{E}\tilde{W}'A\bar{W}(\bar{D})^{-1}\bar{W}'A\varepsilon &= \mathrm{E}q\varepsilon'(I_N \otimes C'A_T)\bar{W}(\bar{D})^{-1}\bar{W}'A\varepsilon \\ &= \sigma_\varepsilon^2 \operatorname{tr}\{\bar{W}'(I_N \otimes A_T C A_T)\bar{W}(\bar{D})^{-1}\}q,\end{aligned}$$

(iii) $$\mathrm{E}\bar{W}'A\tilde{W}(\bar{D})^{-1}\bar{W}'A\varepsilon = \mathrm{E}\bar{W}'(I_N \otimes A_T C)\varepsilon q'(\bar{D})^{-1}\bar{W}'A\varepsilon = \mathrm{E}\bar{W}'(I_N \otimes A_T C)\varepsilon\varepsilon' A'\bar{W}(\bar{D})^{-1}q = \sigma_\varepsilon^2 \bar{W}'(I_N \otimes A_T C A_T)\bar{W}(\bar{D})^{-1}q,$$

(iv) $$\mathrm{E}\tilde{W}'A\bar{W}(\bar{D})^{-1}\bar{W}'A\varepsilon = 0 \qquad \text{(third moment)},$$

(v) $$\mathrm{E}\bar{W}'A\bar{W}(\bar{D})^{-1}\tilde{W}'A\varepsilon = -\sigma_\varepsilon^2(\iota_T' C\iota_T)\frac{N}{T}\bar{W}'A\bar{W}(\bar{D})^{-1}q,$$

(vi) $$\mathrm{E}\tilde{W}'A\bar{W}(\bar{D})^{-1}\tilde{W}'A\varepsilon = 0 \qquad \text{(third moment)},$$

(vii) $$\mathrm{E}\bar{W}'A\tilde{W}(\bar{D})^{-1}\tilde{W}'A\varepsilon = 0 \qquad \text{(third moment)},$$

(viii) $$\mathrm{E}\tilde{W}'A\tilde{W}(\bar{D})^{-1}\tilde{W}'A\varepsilon = \mathrm{E}q\varepsilon'(I_N \otimes C'A_T)(I_N \otimes A_T C)\varepsilon q'(\bar{D})^{-1} \times q\varepsilon'(I_N \otimes C'A_T)\varepsilon = \sigma_\varepsilon^4 N q'(\bar{D})^{-1}q\left[-\frac{N}{T}(\iota_T' C\iota_T)\mathrm{tr}\{C'A_T C\} + 2\mathrm{tr}\{C'A_T C A_T C\}\right]q.$$

Substitution of these terms in (A.13) and (A.12) respectively yields the result of the theorem. ■

Proof of Theorem 2. We have

$$\begin{aligned}\mathrm{E}\Lambda^{-1}(\hat{\delta}-\delta) &= \mathrm{E}(\Lambda W'AW\Lambda)^{-1}\Lambda W'A\varepsilon \\ &= \mathrm{E}[(\bar{B})^{-1} - (\bar{B})^{-1}(B-\bar{B})(\bar{B})^{-1}]\Lambda W'A\varepsilon + \mathrm{O}(N^{-1}T^{-3/2}) \\ &= -\sigma_\varepsilon^2\Lambda^{-1}(\bar{D})^{-1}\Bigg(\frac{N}{T}(\iota_T' C\iota_T)[2q - \bar{W}'A\bar{W}(\bar{D})^{-1}q] \\ &\quad + \mathrm{tr}\{\bar{W}'(I_N \otimes A_T C A_T)\bar{W}(\bar{D})^{-1}\}q + \bar{W}'(I_N \otimes A_T C A_T)\bar{W}(\bar{D})^{-1}q \\ &\quad + \sigma_\varepsilon^2 N q'(\bar{D})^{-1}q\left[-\frac{N}{T}(\iota_T' C\iota_T)\mathrm{tr}\{C'A_T C\} \right. \\ &\quad \left. + 2\mathrm{tr}\{C'A_T C A_T C\}\right]q\Bigg) + \mathrm{O}(N^{-1}T^{-3/2}).\end{aligned}$$

Premultiplication by Λ shows the [for $d(i) > 0$ increased] accuracy of the same approximation for $\mathrm{E}(\hat{\delta}-\delta)$ as given in Theorem 1. ■

Appendix B

Data according to (1) through (7), where the scalar x_{it} ($K = 1$) follows an AR(1) process, are simulated as follows. First we generate the latent variables v_{it} given in (10). Since data for all individuals are generated equivalently (but independently) we omit the index i, hence:

$$v_t = \gamma v_{t-1} + \beta x_t + \varepsilon_t, \qquad t = 1, \dots, T, \tag{B.1}$$

$$x_t = \rho x_{t-1} + \xi_t, \qquad t = 1, \dots, T, \tag{B.2}$$

where ε_t and ξ_t are mutually independent white noise series, with $\varepsilon_t \sim \mathrm{N}(0, \sigma_\varepsilon^2)$ and $\xi_t \sim \mathrm{N}(0, \sigma_\xi^2)$. Initial observations v_0 and x_0 are obtained from a procedure as in Kiviet (1986), which avoids 'warming-up' truncation errors.

Let $\mathscr{L}$ denote the lag operator then, upon substituting (B.2) in (B.1), we have $(1 - \gamma\mathscr{L})v_t = \beta(1 - \rho\mathscr{L})^{-1}\xi_t + \varepsilon_t$ or

$$\begin{aligned} v_t &= \beta[(1 - \gamma\mathscr{L})(1 - \rho\mathscr{L})]^{-1}\xi_t + (1 - \gamma\mathscr{L})^{-1}\varepsilon_t \\ &= \beta\varphi_t + \psi_t. \end{aligned} \tag{B.3}$$

Hence, v_t is the weighted sum of mutually independent stationary processes φ_t and ψ_t, which are an AR(2) and an AR(1) process, respectively.

Data for x_t and v_t (i.e., φ_t and ψ_t) can be obtained (from $t = 0$ onwards) from drawings $(\xi_0, \dots, \xi_T)$ and $(\varepsilon_0, \dots, \varepsilon_T)$ as follows:

$$x_0 = \xi_0(1 - \rho^2)^{-1/2}, \quad x_t = \rho x_{t-1} + \xi_t; \qquad t = 1, \dots, T, \tag{B.4}$$

$$\psi_0 = \varepsilon_0(1 - \gamma^2)^{-1/2}, \quad \psi_t = \gamma\psi_{t-1} + \varepsilon_t, \qquad t = 1, \dots, T. \tag{B.5}$$

In a similar way the AR(2) series is obtained from the scheme

$$\begin{aligned} \varphi_0 &= \xi_0[\mathrm{var}(\varphi^t)]^{1/2}, \\ \varphi_1 &= \varphi_0 \mathrm{cor}(\varphi_t, \varphi_{t-1}) + \xi_1[\mathrm{var}(\varphi_t)]^{1/2}\{1 - [\mathrm{cor}(\varphi_t, \varphi_{t-1})]^2\}^{1/2}, \\ \varphi_t &= (\gamma + \rho)\varphi_{t-1} - \gamma\rho\varphi_{t-2} + \xi_t, \qquad t = 2, \dots, T, \end{aligned} \tag{B.6}$$

where

$$\begin{aligned} \mathrm{cor}(\varphi_t, \varphi_{t-1}) &= \mathrm{cov}(\varphi_t, \varphi_{t-1})/\mathrm{var}(\varphi_t) = (\gamma + \rho)/(1 + \gamma\rho), \\ \mathrm{cor}(\varphi_t, \varphi_{t-2}) &= \mathrm{cov}(\varphi_t, \varphi_{t-2})/\mathrm{var}(\varphi_t) = (\gamma + \rho)^2/(1 + \gamma\rho) - \gamma\rho, \\ \mathrm{var}(\varphi_t) &= \sigma_\xi^2[1 - (\gamma + \rho)\mathrm{cor}(\varphi_t, \varphi_{t-1}) + \gamma\rho\,\mathrm{cor}(\varphi_t, \varphi_{t-2})]^{-1}. \end{aligned} \tag{B.7}$$

From (9) and (B.3) we find

$$y_t = \beta\varphi_t + \psi_t + \eta/(1 - \gamma), \tag{B.8}$$

and the dependent variable can be generated according to this scheme, upon using (B.5) through (B.7).

References

Ahn, S.C. and P. Schmidt, 1993, Efficient estimation of models for dynamic panel data, Mimeo.

Anderson, T.W. and C. Hsiao, 1981, Estimation of dynamic models with error components, Journal of the American Statistical Association 76, 589–606.

Anderson, T.W. and C. Hsiao, 1982, Formulation and estimation of dynamic models using panel data, Journal of Econometrics 18, 47–82.

Arellano, M., 1989, A note on the Anderson–Hsiao estimator for panel data, Economics Letters 31, 337–341.

Arellano, M. and S. Bond, 1991, Some tests of specification for panel data: Monte Carlo evidence and an application to employment equations, Review of Economic Studies 58, 277–297.

Balestra, P. and M. Nerlove, 1966, Pooling cross section and time series data in the estimation of a dynamic model: The demand for natural gas, Econometrica 34, 585–612.

Baltagi, B.H. and B. Raj, 1992, A survey of recent theoretical developments in the econometrics of panel data, Empirical Econometrics 17, 85–109.

Beggs, J.J. and M. Nerlove, 1988, Biases in dynamic models with fixed effects, Economics Letters 26, 29–31.

Bhargava, A. and J.D. Sargan, 1983, Estimating dynamic random effects models from panel data covering short time periods, Econometrica 51, 1635–1659.

Blundell, R. and R.J. Smith, 1991, Conditions initiales et estimation efficace dans les modèles dynamiques sur données panel: Une application au comportement d'investissement des entreprises, Annales d'Economie et de Statistique 20/21, 109–123.

Doel, I.T. van den and J.F. Kiviet, 1993, Neglected dynamics in panel data models: Consequences and detection in finite samples, Statistica Neerlandica, forthcoming.

Holtz-Eakin, D., W. Newey, and H. Rosen, 1988, Estimating vector autoregressions with panel data, Econometrica 56, 1371–1395.

Hsiao, C., 1985, Benefits and limitations of panel data, Econometric Reviews 4, 121–174 (with comments and reply, 175–189).

Hsiao, C., 1986, Analysis of panel data (Cambridge University Press, Cambridge).

Kiviet, J.F., 1986, On the rigour of some misspecification tests for modelling dynamic relationships, Review of Economic Studies LIII, 241–261.

Kiviet, J.F. and G.D.A. Phillips, 1993, Alternative bias approximations in regressions with a lagged dependent variable, Econometric Theory 9, 62–80.

Kiviet, J.F. and G.D.A. Phillips, 1994, Bias assessment and reduction in linear error-correction models, Journal of Econometrics 63, 215–243.

Maddala, G.S., 1971, The use of variance components models in pooling cross section and time series data, Econometrica 39, 341–358.

Nankervis, J.S. and N.E. Savin, 1987, Finite sample distributions of t and F statistics in an AR(1) model with an exogenous variable, Econometric Theory 3, 387–408.

Nerlove, M., 1971, Further evidence on the estimation of dynamic economic relations from a time series of cross-sections, Econometrica 39, 359–387.

Nerlove, M. and P. Balestra, 1992, Formulation and estimation of econometric models for the analysis of panel data, in: L. Màtyàs and P. Sevestre, eds., The econometrics of panel data (Kluwer Academic Publishers, Dordrecht).

Nickell, S., 1981, Biases in dynamic models with fixed effects, Econometrica 49, 1417–1426.

Sevestre, P. and A. Trognon, 1983, Propriétés de grands echantillons d'une classe d'estimateurs des modèles autorégressifs à erreurs composées, Annales de l'INSEE 50, 25–48.

Sevestre, P. and A. Trognon, 1985, A note on autoregressive error-components models, Journal of Econometrics 29, 231–245.

Trognon, A, 1978, Miscellaneous asymptotic properties of OLS and ML estimators in dynamic error components models, Annales de l'INSEE 30, 631–658.

[9]

ELSEVIER Journal of Econometrics 104 (2001) 259–268

JOURNAL OF Econometrics

www.elsevier.com/locate/econbase

GMM estimation in panel data models with measurement error

Tom Wansbeek*

Department of Economics, University of Groningen, P.O. Box 800, 9700 AV Groningen, The Netherlands

Received 5 June 1996; revised 28 February 2001; accepted 30 April 2001

Abstract

Griliches and Hausman (J. Econom. 32 (1986) 93) have introduced GMM estimation in panel data models with measurement error. We present a simple, systematic approach to derive moment conditions for such models under a variety of assumptions. © 2001 Elsevier Science S.A. All rights reserved.

JEL classification: C13; C23; G12

Keywords: Panel data; GMM; Measurement error; Tobin's q; Weak exogeneity; Weak instruments

1. Introduction

In regression analysis, the issue of the potential presence of measurement error is habitually neglected. Although measurement error, if present, will bias the OLS results and hence severely affect the quality of a regression analysis, identification problems may hamper consistent estimation. This no doubt contributes to the neglect of measurement error. A recent treatment of many aspects regarding measurement error in econometrics is provided by Wansbeek and Meijer (2000).

As has been shown by Griliches and Hausman (1986), one of the important aspects of panel data is that they allow to control the measurement error, to a certain extent at least. They consider the simplest situation of a single,

* Tel.: +31-50-633803; fax: +31-50-633720.
E-mail address: t.j.wansbeek@eco.rug.nl (T. Wansbeek).

PII: S0304-4076(01)00079-3

error-ridden, time-varying regressor, and discuss the asymptotic behavior of various estimators and present a GMM approach to consistent estimation. Wansbeek and Koning (1991) and especially Biørn (1992a, b) have extended this work in various directions.

Since the publication of the Griliches–Hausman paper, there have been a fair number of empirical applications. We mention a few. One of these is Himmelberg and Petersen (1994), who analyze a model of the 'permanent income' type. They are concerned with explaining R&D expenditures of firms by their 'permanent' cash flow. What is observed is the actual cash flow, which equals the permanent cash flow plus a transitory component. They allow for an MA(1) structure on the transitory component.

The most frequent application of measurement error techniques in panel data has to do with estimating investment models using Tobin's q (Tobin, 1969; Berndt, 1991). This variable is the ratio of the market valuation of a firm and the replacement value of its assets. Firms with a high value of q are considered attractive as to the investment opportunities, whereas a low value of q indicates the opposite. Since the operationalization of q is not clear-cut and unambiguous, estimation obviously poses a measurement error problem. Cummins et al. (1994) apply the methods proposed by Griliches and Hausman (1986) to an unbalanced data set with $T=36$, 1953–1988, and in total around 20,000 observations. In an earlier paper, Fazzari et al. (1988) analyze a data set with $T=15$ and N around 400. They compare the estimator based on first-differenced data with the estimator based on differences 2 years apart and find more or less similar results. They interpret this as indicating a lack of measurement error. Fazzari and Petersen (1993) and Blundell et al. (1992) extend the simple measurement error formulation of the q-model in a variety of ways.

In this paper, we consider the case of a single mismeasured variable. This simplification is justified since it covers the leading situation met in practice, as was recently argued by Meijer and Wansbeek (2000). We derive moment conditions by considering the covariances between the dependent variable and the regressors, projecting out nuisance parameters. This appears to be simple, and the approach is easily adapted for a variety of assumptions on endogeneity and measurement error structure. The model is described in Section 2. In Section 3, we derive consistent estimators. Sections 4 and 5 discuss adaptations of the assumptions on endogeneity and measurement error structure, respectively. Section 6 concludes the paper.

2. Measurement error in panel data

We consider a linear panel data model where one regressor is measured with error. For a typical observation, indexed by $n(=1,\ldots,N)$, the model is

$$y_n = \xi_n\beta + Z_n\gamma + \iota_T\alpha_n + u_n,$$
$$x_n = \xi_n + v_n,$$

where y_n, ξ_n, u_n and v_n are T-vectors; Z_n, of order $T \times k$ is a set of strongly exogenous variables; ι_T is a T-vector of ones; $\mathrm{E}(u_n) = \mathrm{E}(v_n) = 0$; ξ_n, u_n and v_n are mutually uncorrelated. The observables are y_n, x_n and Z_n; ξ_n is a regressor measured with measurement error v_n, which is i.i.d. with variance $\Sigma_v \equiv \mathrm{E}(v_n v_n')$; β is an unknown scalar parameter and γ is an unknown k-vector of parameters. Note that ξ_n and α_n may be correlated; u_n is i.i.d. with an unspecified covariance structure.

The assumption that the measurement error is uncorrelated with the true value is obviously a simplification. We note that there is evidence to the contrary in some cases. Bound and Krueger (1991) compare large-scale Current Population Survey data to Social Security payroll tax records and find a negative correlation between measurement error and true earnings. Bound et al. (1994) analyze the results of the PSID Valuation Study, a small-scale comparison between wage incomes as reported by individuals and the payroll information supplied by their employer, an unnamed large company. The sample size is around 350. They find that the individual reports were 'fairly accurate', and also that the errors are negatively related to true earnings. Notwithstanding this evidence on the particular case of earnings, we maintain the assumption of no correlation. However, the derivations to be given below will appear to be such that a relaxation of this assumption is straightforward.

A consistent estimator for β and γ may be obtained if we are willing to impose sufficient structure on Σ_v. We consider a structure of the form

$$\operatorname{vec} \Sigma_v = R_0\lambda, \tag{1}$$

where R_0 is a matrix of order $T^2 \times m$, say, of known elements, and λ is a vector with m parameters that may be functionally related.

3. Consistent estimation

Since ξ_n and α_n may be correlated we have what is commonly called a fixed effects model, which implies the use of estimation methods based on the elimination of the individual effects. The within transformation eliminating the effects is performed through the centering operator,

$$A_T \equiv I_T - \frac{1}{T}\iota_T\iota_T'.$$

In order to derive moment conditions we write the model in 'generic' variables omitting individual subscripts. Then

$$y = \xi\beta + Z\gamma + \iota_T\alpha + u,$$
$$x = \xi + v$$

and the within transformation gives

$$A_T y = A_T\xi\beta + A_T Z\gamma + A_T u,$$
$$A_T x = A_T\xi + A_T v$$

or, letting a tilde denote a T-vector in deviation from its mean over time,

$$\tilde{y} = \tilde{\xi}\beta + \tilde{Z}\gamma + \tilde{u},$$
$$\tilde{x} = \tilde{\xi} + \tilde{v}.$$

Let

$$R \equiv (I_T \otimes A_T)R_0, \tag{2}$$

then because of (1) the following holds:

$$\begin{aligned} \mathrm{E}(v \otimes \tilde{v}) &= (I_T \otimes A_T)\mathrm{E}(v \otimes v) \\ &= (I_T \otimes A_T)R_0\lambda \\ &= R\lambda. \end{aligned}$$

Hence,

$$\begin{aligned} \mathrm{E}(x \otimes \tilde{\xi}) &= \mathrm{E}(x \otimes \tilde{x}) - \mathrm{E}((\xi + v) \otimes \tilde{v}) \\ &= \mathrm{E}(x \otimes \tilde{x}) - R\lambda. \end{aligned}$$

The first set of moment conditions can be derived from the covariance between x and $\tilde{y}$:

$$\begin{aligned} \mathrm{E}(x \otimes \tilde{y}) &= \mathrm{E}(x \otimes \tilde{\xi})\beta + \mathrm{E}(x \otimes \tilde{Z})\gamma \\ &= \mathrm{E}(x \otimes \tilde{x})\beta + \mathrm{E}(x \otimes \tilde{Z})\gamma - R\lambda\beta. \end{aligned} \tag{3}$$

To eliminate the nuisance parameter λ, let $M_R \equiv I_{T^2} - R(R'R)^{-1}R'$, to obtain

$$M_R\mathrm{E}(x \otimes (\tilde{y} - (\tilde{x}, \tilde{Z})\delta)) = 0 \tag{4}$$

with

$$\delta \equiv \begin{bmatrix} \beta \\ \gamma \end{bmatrix}.$$

The second set of moment conditions follows directly from the exogeneity of Z, so, $\mathrm{E}(Z'\tilde{u}) = 0$, and the independence of Z and v. Hence,

$$\mathrm{E}(Z'(\tilde{y} - (\tilde{x}, \tilde{Z})\delta)) = 0. \tag{5}$$

The observable counterpart of the two sets of conditions (4) and (5) can now be given as follows. Let

$$M \equiv \begin{bmatrix} M_R & 0 \\ 0 & I_k \end{bmatrix},$$

$$B_n \equiv \begin{bmatrix} x_n \otimes I_T \\ Z_n' \end{bmatrix},$$

$$C_n \equiv B_n(\tilde{x}_n, \tilde{Z}_n),$$

$$d_n \equiv B_n \tilde{y}_n$$

and let $\bar{C}$ and $\bar{d}$ denote sample averages. Then the moment conditions imply that δ should be chosen such that $g(\delta) \equiv M(\bar{d} - \bar{C}\delta)$ is close to zero. This leads to a GMM approach, producing a consistent estimator if the model is identified. The identification condition is that $\partial g(\delta)/\partial\delta' = M\bar{C}$ be a full column rank.

If this condition is met, a consistent GMM estimator is

$$\hat{\delta} = (\bar{C}'M\bar{C})^{-1}\bar{C}'M\bar{d},$$

whose asymptotic variance is consistently estimated by

$$\frac{1}{N}(\bar{C}'M\bar{C})^{-1}\bar{C}'M\hat{W}M\bar{C}(\bar{C}'M\bar{C})^{-1},$$

with

$$\hat{W} \equiv \frac{1}{N}\sum_n (d_n - C_n\hat{\delta})(d_n - C_n\hat{\delta})'.$$

A GMM estimator that optimally exploits the moment conditions is given by

$$\hat{\hat{\delta}} = (\bar{C}'M\hat{W}^{-1}M\bar{C})^{-1}\bar{C}'M\hat{W}^{-1}M\bar{d},$$

with asymptotic variance consistently estimated by $(\bar{C}'M\hat{W}^{-1}M\bar{C})^{-1}/N$.

4. Measurement error structures

Up till now we left the specification of the structure on Σ_v open. We now consider various cases.

As the simplest case, assume that Σ_v is diagonal with equal diagonal elements. Then $m = 1$ and $R_0 = \operatorname{vec} I_T$, and for R as defined in (2) there holds $R = (I_T \otimes A_T)\operatorname{vec} I_T = \operatorname{vec} A_T$, $R'R = \operatorname{tr} A_T = T - 1$, and $M_R = I_{T^2} - (1/(T-1))\operatorname{vec} A_T(\operatorname{vec} A_T)'$. When we allow the various diagonal elements of Σ_v to be different, there now holds $m = T$ and

$$R_0 = \sum_{t=1}^{T} e_t e_t' \otimes e_t,$$

where e_t is the tth unit vector of order T. Then $M_R = I_{T^2} - (T/(T-1))RR'$ since $R'R = R_0'(I_T \otimes A_T)R_0 = I_T * A_T = ((T-1)/T)I_T$.

We now consider the correlation of the measurement error over time. Duncan and Hill (1989) emphasize the importance of a careful analysis of the extent of such correlation. Bound and Krueger (1991) report correlation over time of measurement error in reported earnings.

To start with, let time dependence of the measurement error follow an MA-process. Again, we need an adaptation of R but we now have to expand its number of columns. For example, if $T = 4$ and v is MA(1), then Σ_v has the following symbolic structure:

$$\Sigma_v = \begin{bmatrix} a & c & & \\ c & b & c & \\ & c & b & c \\ & & c & a \end{bmatrix},$$

the letters a, b, c indicating the three different parameters in Σ_v. The three are functionally dependent on two underlying parameters, but this structure is neglected. So $m = 3$ and $\operatorname{vec} \Sigma_v = R_0 \lambda$ with

$$R_0 = \begin{bmatrix} 1&0&0&0&0&0&0&0&0&0&0&0&0&0&0&1 \\ 0&0&0&0&0&1&0&0&0&0&1&0&0&0&0&0 \\ 0&1&0&0&1&0&1&0&0&1&0&1&0&0&1&0 \end{bmatrix}'$$

and $\lambda = (a, b, c)'$. The expression for Σ_v for general values of T is cumbersome, but for any given value of T the expressions are simple to derive.

A generalization is a structure with correlation in measurement error between successive observations. Then,

$$\Sigma_v = \begin{bmatrix} a & e & & \\ e & b & f & \\ & f & c & g \\ & & g & d \end{bmatrix},$$

so now $\lambda = (a, b, c, d, e, f, g)'$ and

$$R_0 = \begin{bmatrix} 1&0&0&0&0&0&0&0&0&0&0&0&0&0&0&0 \\ 0&0&0&0&0&1&0&0&0&0&0&0&0&0&0&0 \\ 0&0&0&0&0&0&0&0&0&0&1&0&0&0&0&0 \\ 0&0&0&0&0&0&0&0&0&0&0&0&0&0&0&1 \\ 0&1&0&0&1&0&0&0&0&0&0&0&0&0&0&0 \\ 0&0&0&0&0&0&1&0&0&1&0&0&0&0&0&0 \\ 0&0&0&0&0&0&0&0&0&0&0&1&0&0&1&0 \end{bmatrix}'.$$

Another interesting alternative is obtained when Σ_v is a (symmetric) Toeplitz matrix, i.e. a matrix S, say, with elements s_{ij} satisfying $s_{ij} = s_{i+k,j+k}$ for all

i, j, k. This is the basic structure for covariance stationary models. For example, for the case of $T=4$,

$$\Sigma_v = \begin{bmatrix} a & b & c & d \\ b & a & b & c \\ c & b & a & b \\ d & c & b & a \end{bmatrix}. \tag{6}$$

A symmetric $T \times T$ Toeplitz matrix has T parameters. This structure generalizes an AR(1)-process, where the T free parameters are nonlinear functions of two underlying parameters. So it is also simple to derive moment conditions when the measurement error follows an AR(1)-process, at least if one is willing to sacrifice efficiency gains that can be obtained when the nonlinear restrictions are exploited in addition to the linear restrictions derived from the Toeplitz structure.

When there is correlation over time of either the MA(1) or the AR(1) type and the choice is not clear, both specifications can easily be subsumed under an encompassing formulation. All that is needed is to replace the upper left and the lower right element of Σ_v in (6) by e, say, a fifth parameter.

5. Varying the assumptions on endogeneity

When an assumption of no correlation between ξ_n and α_n is justified, the more efficient random effects approach can be followed. This requires little adaptation of the derivations given in Section 3. The individual effects α_n can be neglected since they can be subsumed under the general disturbance term u_n, whose covariance structure was left unspecified. To adapt for this case, the within transformation is no longer needed, R has to be replaced by R_0, while the tildes can be omitted.

Another adaptation of the assumptions given in Section 2 appropriate in many cases like rational expectations and feedback models is to allow for a correlation between ξ and the previous u. This type of weak exogeneity can also be easily incorporated; for clarity, we do so in the random effects context. (See e.g. Keane and Runkle (1992) or Schmidt et al. (1992) for an analysis of such models without measurement error.) Let

$$\Sigma_{u\xi} \equiv \mathrm{E}(u_n \xi_n') = \mathrm{E}(u_n x_n'),$$

which in this case is a strictly upper triangular matrix. We assume that its elements are functionally independent (if this assumption does not hold some efficiency loss will be incurred) and we write, analogous to (1),

$$\operatorname{vec} \Sigma_{u\xi} = \mathrm{E}(\xi_n \otimes u_n) = L_0 \theta,$$

say, with θ the vector of nonzero elements in $\Sigma_{u\xi}$ and L_0 a matrix with zeros and ones. As an example, let $T = 3$. Then, $\Sigma_{u\xi}$ has the symbolic structure

$$\Sigma_{u\xi} = \begin{bmatrix} 0 & a & b \\ 0 & 0 & c \\ 0 & 0 & 0 \end{bmatrix}$$

and $\theta = (a, b, c)'$ and

$$L_0 = \begin{bmatrix} 0 & 0 & 0 & 1 & 0 & 0 & 0 & 0 & 0 \\ 0 & 0 & 0 & 0 & 0 & 0 & 1 & 0 & 0 \\ 0 & 0 & 0 & 0 & 0 & 0 & 0 & 1 & 0 \end{bmatrix}'.$$

Let $L \equiv (I_T \otimes A_T)L_0$, then (3) is adapted to

$$\begin{aligned} \mathrm{E}(x \otimes \tilde{y}) &= \mathrm{E}(x \otimes \tilde{x})\beta + \mathrm{E}(x \otimes \tilde{Z})\gamma - R\lambda + \mathrm{E}(\xi_n \otimes \tilde{u}_n) \\ &= \mathrm{E}(x \otimes \tilde{x})\beta + \mathrm{E}(x \otimes \tilde{Z})\gamma + (-R, L)\begin{bmatrix} \lambda \\ \theta \end{bmatrix}. \end{aligned}$$

So, handling a weakly endogenous regressor of this kind can be done by projection orthogonal to both R and L.

6. Concluding remarks

In this paper, we have derived moment conditions for a panel data model with measurement error in a straightforward way. The essence is in stacking the matrix of covariances between the vector of dependent variables over time and the regressors, and projecting out nuisance parameters. This approach is a simplification relative to the existing literature and is moreover shown to be flexible since it is easily adapted for different model assumptions. Further variations can be obtained, e.g. by exploiting any structure that one is willing to impose on the covariance structure of the regressor ξ or the disturbance term u. It is very simple to program the estimators for all these kinds of linear structures in a matrix language like Gauss or Matlab.

The approach proposed in the paper does not exploit all moment restrictions implied by the model. In particular, the covariance matrix of y contains an exploitable structure, leading to moment restrictions that are quadratic in the regression coefficients. Simulation experiments (not reported here) for the case where there is only a single regressor (so without Z) suggest that using these additional moment conditions hardly improves the small-sample quality of the estimator and is in some cases even detrimental. This may be another instance of the phenomenon of weak instruments, see e.g. Nelson and Startz (1990a, b).

This points to a topic for further research. The small-sample properties of the estimators for the present model are not known and in particular it is unknown whether the asymptotic distributions are a good reflection of the exact distributions. To the extent to which this will appear to be a problem, LIML estimation may offer an improvement; see Wansbeek and Meijer (2000), Section 6.6, for an introduction and Bekker (1994) for an extensive treatment.

Also, additional moments follow from the assumed strong exogeneity of Z. This translates into the moment conditions $\mathrm{E}(\operatorname{vec} Z \otimes \tilde{u}) = 0$. These conditions imply the conditions $\mathrm{E}(Z'\tilde{u}) = 0$ as used in Section 3. It can be shown that the moment conditions added by this last set are not redundant in the sense of Breusch et al. (1999), and their inclusion reduces the asymptotic variance of the GMM estimator. Again, these moments are helpful to reduce the asymptotic variance of the GMM estimator, but may not improve its quality in small samples.

Acknowledgements

Extremely helpful comments from Erik Meijer and three anonymous referees are gratefully acknowledged.

References

Bekker, P.A., 1994. Alternative approximations to the distributions of instrumental variable estimators. Econometrica 62, 657–681.

Berndt, E.R., 1991. The Practice of Econometrics. Addison-Wesley, Reading, MA.

Biørn, E., 1992a. Panel data with measurement errors. In: Mátyás, L., Sevestre, P. (Eds.), The Econometrics of Panel Data. Kluwer, Dordrecht.

Biørn, E., 1992b. The bias of some estimators for panel data models with measurement errors. Empirical Economics 17, 51–66.

Blundell, R., Bond. S., Devereux, M., Schiantarelli, F., 1992. Investment and Tobin's Q: evidence from company panel data. Journal of Econometrics 51, 233–257.

Bound, J., Brown, C., Duncan, G.J., Rodgers, W.L., 1994. Evidence on the validity of crosss-sectional and longitudinal labor market data. Journal of Labor Economics 12, 345–368.

Bound, J., Krueger, A.B., 1991. The extent of measurement error in longitudinal earnings data: do two wrongs make a right? Journal of Labor Economics 9, 1–24.

Breusch, T., Qian, H., Schmidt, P., Wyhowski, D.J., 1999. Redundancy of moment conditions. Journal of Econometrics 91, 89–111.

Cummins, J.G., Hassett, K.A., Hubbard, R.G., 1994. A reconsideration of investment behavior using tax reforms as natural experiments. Brookings Papers on Economic Activity 2, 1–74.

Duncan, G.J., Hill, D.H., 1989. Assessing the quality of household panel data: the case of the Panel Study of Income Dynamics. Journal of Business and Economic Statistics 7, 441–452.

Fazzari, S.M., Hubbard, R.G., Petersen, B.C., 1988. Financing constraints and corporate investment. Brookings Papers on Economic Activity 1, 141–195.

Fazzari, S.M., Petersen, B.C., 1993. Working capital and fixed investment: new evidence on financing constraints. Rand Journal of Economics 24, 328–342.

Griliches, Z., Hausman, J.A., 1986. Errors in variables in panel data. Journal of Econometrics 32, 93–118.

Himmelberg, C.P., Petersen, B.C., 1994. R&D and internal finance: a panel study of small firms in high-tech industries. The Review of Economics and Statistics 76, 38–51.

Keane, M.P., Runkle, D.E., 1992. On the estimation of panel-data models with serial correlation when instruments are not strictly exogenous. Journal of Business & Economic Statistics 10, 1–9.

Meijer, E., Wansbeek, T.J., 2000. Measurement error in a single regressor. Economics Letters 69, 277–284.

Nelson, C.R., Startz, R., 1990a. The distribution of the instrumental variables and its *t*-ratio when the instrument is a poor one. Journal of Business 63, 125–140.

Nelson, C.R., Startz, R., 1990b. Some further results on the exact small sample properties of the instrumental variables estimator. Econometrica 58, 967–976.

Schmidt, P., Ahn, S.C., Wyhowski, D.J., 1992. Comment. Journal of Business and Economic Statistics 10, 10–14.

Tobin, J., 1969. A general equilibrium approach to monetary theory. Journal of Money, Credit and Banking 1, 15–29.

Wansbeek, T.J., Koning, R.H., 1991. Measurement error and panel data. Statistica Neerlandica 45, 85–92.

Wansbeek, T.J., Meijer, E., 2000. Measurement Error and Latent Variables in Econometrics. North-Holland, Amsterdam.

[10]

Efficient Estimation With Panel Data When Instruments Are Predetermined: An Empirical Comparison of Moment-Condition Estimators

James P. Ziliak
Department of Economics, University of Oregon, Eugene, OR 97403-1285

I examine the empirical performance of instrumental variables estimators with predetermined instruments in an application to life-cycle labor supply under uncertainty. The estimators studied are two-stage least squares, generalized method-of-moments (GMM), forward filter, independently weighted GMM, and split-sample instrumental variables. I compare the bias/efficiency trade-off for the estimators using bootstrap algorithms suggested by Freedman and by Brown and Newey. Results indicate that the downward bias in GMM is quite severe as the number of moment conditions expands, outweighing the gains in efficiency. The forward-filter estimator, however, has lower bias and is more efficient than two-stage least squares.

KEY WORDS: Bootstrap; Life-cycle labor supply; Overidentifying restrictions; Split samples.

The panel-data literature offers little guidance on the relative empirical performance of instrumental variables (IV) estimators when applied to samples of the size typically encountered in practice. For example, when the number of observations is large (say, greater than 500), are the small-sample concerns of a bias/efficiency trade-off in generalized method-of-moments (GMM) raised by Tauchen (1986) and Altonji and Segal (1994) binding? Moreover, if bias is present, is it due to a correlation between the sample moments and the sample weight matrix (Altonji and Segal 1994) or to instruments weakly correlated with the endogenous regressor as recently discussed by Bound, Jaeger, and Baker (1995) and Angrist and Krueger (1995)? The latter issue is crucial for efficiency considerations because the optimal number of moments may contain instruments dated far into the past, possibly weakening the correlation between the instruments and the endogenous regressor(s). In this article, I examine the sample properties of several panel-data IV estimators first by applying them to a well-known life-cycle labor-supply model and then comparing the estimators in terms of the bias/efficiency trade-off via a bootstrap Monte Carlo.

For many panel-data applications, GMM is the obvious estimator of choice: It does not require a full specification of the stochastic process (Hansen and Singleton 1982), it is consistent asymptotically under a variety of situations including when the only instruments available are predetermined rather than strictly exogenous (Anderson and Hsiao 1982; Arellano and Bond 1991), and it attains the efficiency bound in the class of IV estimators (Chamberlain 1987; Ahn and Schmidt 1995; Arellano and Bover 1995). Tauchen (1986) demonstrated, however, that in samples typically encountered in time series applications ($N = 50$ or 75) GMM is biased as the number of moment conditions expands, leading to a bias/efficiency trade-off, and thus he recommended the use of "suboptimal" instrument sets.

Altonji and Segal (1994) extended the small-sample analysis of Tauchen to least squares optimal minimum-distance (OMD) estimation of covariance structures. They demonstrated via Monte Carlo simulation that the bias in OMD is quite severe, the source of which, like feasible general least squares, is due to a correlation between the sample moments and the estimated weight matrix used in optimally minimizing the distance between population and sample moments. They attempted to correct for the bias by developing a split-sample estimator, called independently weighted OMD (IW-OMD) but found that both OMD and IW-OMD are dominated in terms of lower bias and root mean squared error (RMSE) by equally weighted minimum distance. Although the findings of bias in GMM by Tauchen and by Altonji and Segal seem conclusive, they are for small samples, and there is no a priori expectation that comparable results exist in a large panel-data setting. If comparable negative results against GMM do exist, then a case could be made for less efficient estimators such as two-stage least squares (2SLS) or Keane and Runkle's (1992) forward-filter (FF) estimator.

Parallel to the time series research on IV estimators of Altonji and Segal (1994), Nelson and Startz (1990), and Tauchen (1986) is cross-sectional research on the properties of IV estimators when the correlation between the instruments and the endogenous regressor is weak (Bekker 1994; Staiger and Stock 1994; Angrist and Krueger 1995; Bound et al. 1995). As pointed out by Bound et al., a weak correlation between the instruments and the endogenous regressor can lead to (1) a large standard error, (2) a bias in IV even if a weak correlation exists between the instruments and the structural error, and (3) a bias in IV toward ordinary least squares (OLS) as the explanatory power of the instruments approaches 0. They demonstrated that the returns-to-schooling results from the overidentified models reported by Angrist and Krueger (1991) are biased toward OLS due to weakly correlated instruments and, worse still,

Journal of Business & Economic Statistics
October 1997, Vol. 15, No. 4

that similar IV results are found by using instruments from a uniform random-number generator.

Addressing the criticisms of Bound et al., Angrist and Krueger (1995) developed a computationally convenient split-sample IV (SSIV) estimator as an alternative to 2SLS. SSIV is not biased toward OLS; however, the estimator is biased toward 0, so they proposed to "inflate" the SSIV estimates with a bias-correction factor, giving unbiased SSIV (USSIV). They concluded that USSIV gives results comparable to 2SLS but at a substantial loss of efficiency due to the smaller samples used in estimation. Because panel data with a long time series present the opportunity for many (possibly weakly correlated) instruments, SSIV and USSIV may be viable alternatives to standard 2SLS or GMM.

In this article, I focus on panel-data IV estimators that are consistent asymptotically when only predetermined instruments are available. Applications that fall within this class of estimators include dynamic models, rational-expectations models, and simultaneous-equations models. Predetermined instruments complicate the estimation of such models because certain transformations that eliminate the model's temporally persistent latent heterogeneity, such as deviations from time-means (the "within" estimator), are inconsistent when instruments are predetermined (Keane and Runkle 1992). The estimators considered here include 2SLS, GMM, FF, SSIV, USSIV, and an IV analog to IW-OMD that I refer to as IW-GMM.

I study the sample properties of the estimators in a realistic setting using data from the Panel Study of Income Dynamics (PSID). The empirical model employed is MaCurdy's (1985) life-cycle labor-supply model under uncertainty. MaCurdy's model is pertinent to the issues studied here because uncertainty suggests a rational-expectations solution to the consumer's problem, thereby making the instrument set predetermined. In addition, the model produces estimates of the intertemporal substitution elasticity, a key parameter used in understanding the comovements in earnings and hours over the business cycle. For each estimator, I sequentially build up the moment matrix by adding extra years as instruments, and I test the specification with Sargan's test of the overidentifying restrictions (Godfrey 1988).

I complement the empirical investigation with a bootstrap Monte Carlo as developed by Efron (1979) and extended to IV by Freedman (1984) and Freedman and Peters (1984). The bootstrap is used to compare the estimators in terms of bias, efficiency, RMSE, median absolute error (MAE), and asymptotic coverage rates. The strength of the bootstrap over standard Monte Carlo analysis lies in the fact that, like the IV estimators themselves, the researcher simply approximates the empirical distribution of the estimator with a nonparametric estimate of the underlying error distribution. Although Freedman's method is asymptotically valid for bootstrapping estimators from overidentified models (Hahn in press), Brown and Newey (1995) and Hall and Horowitz (in press) showed that the Freedman algorithm does not yield an improvement in terms of coverage rates over asymptotic theory, and more importantly, it gives the wrong size asymptotically for the overidentifying restrictions test. Because each algorithm is asymptotically valid for the estimator, I compare bootstrap results from the approaches of both Freedman and Brown and Newey.

From a 10-year balanced panel of men, I find the following results of note. The downward bias in GMM is quite severe as the number of moment conditions expands, outweighing the gains in efficiency. The bias is due to a correlation between the sample moments used in estimation and the estimated weight matrix. The IW-GMM estimator is generally successful at eliminating the bias in GMM parameter estimates using Freedman's bootstrap algorithm; however, the standard errors from asymptotic theory seem to understate the true sampling variation, and the overidentifying-restrictions test tends to overreject. The levels distortion in the overidentifying-restrictions test persists in models with many moments, even after recentering the distribution using Brown and Newey's (1995) algorithm. Finally, the bias in FF parameter estimates is less than GMM and 2SLS, and it is more efficient than 2SLS.

1. ESTIMATION AND PREDETERMINED INSTRUMENTS

I begin with a brief overview of the IV estimators used in the empirical application and bootstrap simulations. Consider the linear regression for individual i $(i = 1, \ldots, N)$ in time t $(t = 1, \ldots, T)$

$$y_{it} = \alpha_i + x_{it}\beta + \varepsilon_{it}, \tag{1}$$

where α_i represents fixed latent heterogeneity, x_{it} is a $(1 \times K)$ vector of predetermined explanatory variables, β is a $(K \times 1)$ vector of parameters to estimate, and ε_{it} is a random error that varies over i and t and is assumed distributed iid $(0, \sigma_\varepsilon^2)$. Under the assumption of fixed effects, the latent heterogeneity is correlated with the explanatory variables for all periods; that is, $E[\alpha_i|x_{it}] \neq 0$ for all t.

A common practice in panel data is to eliminate the fixed effect by taking deviations from the individual's time series means, known as the within transformation. In IV estimation with predetermined instruments, however, the within transformation is inconsistent. In particular, for the within transformation to be consistent it is necessary for the instrument set to be strictly exogenous to the model's error term for all periods, $E[\varepsilon_{is}|W_{it}] = 0$ for all s, t; however, predetermined instruments only guarantee weak exogeneity, $E[\varepsilon_{is}|W_{it}] = 0$ for all $s \geq t$. This inconsistency carries over into the class of endogenous random-effects estimators studied by Hausman and Taylor (1981). The first-difference (Anderson and Hsiao 1982; Keane and Runkle 1992; Schmidt, Ahn, and Wyhowski 1992) and orthogonal-deviations (Arellano and Bover 1995) transformations are consistent when applied with lagged levels of predetermined (or endogenous) regressors as instruments. Orthogonal deviations may offer efficiency gains over first differences because differencing exacerbates measurement errors-in-variables (Maeshiro and Vali 1988). Each transformation will be applied to the estimators.

1.1 Method-of-Moments Estimators

The first estimator I consider is 2SLS, which minimizes the distance between the sample moments and the population moments, giving equal weight to each observation. The 2SLS estimator produces consistent parameter estimates for either the first-difference or orthogonal-deviations transformations and is given as

$$\hat{\beta}_{2SLS} = (X'P(W)X)^{-1}(X'P(W)y), \qquad (2)$$

where W is an $(N(T-1) \times L)$ matrix of instruments, $P(W) = W(W'W)^{-1}W'$ is the projection matrix of instruments, ε is the stacked $(N(T-1) \times 1)$ vector of residuals, X is the stacked $(N(T-1) \times K)$ matrix of regressors, and y is the stacked $(N(T-1) \times 1)$ dependent variable. Under the assumption of conditional homoscedasticity, $E[\varepsilon^2|W] = 0$, inference for the estimated 2SLS parameters is conducted with the variance–covariance matrix

$$\begin{aligned} \mathrm{var}(\hat{\beta}_{2SLS}) &= \hat{\sigma}_{\varepsilon}^2(X'P(W)X)^{-1} \\ \hat{\sigma}_{\varepsilon}^2 &= \left(\frac{1}{NT-N-K}\right)(y - X\hat{\beta}_{2SLS})^2. \end{aligned} \qquad (3)$$

As noted by White (1982), 2SLS standard errors are inconsistent when the conditional homoscedasticity assumption is violated; thus, he proposed a robust covariance matrix estimated as

$$\mathrm{var}(\hat{\beta}_{2SLS}) = (X'P(W)X)^{-1}X'P(W) \times \hat{\Omega}P(W)X(X'P(W)X)^{-1}, \qquad (4)$$

where $\hat{\Omega}$ is a diagonal matrix of squared residuals.

Because the number of instruments typically exceeds the number of parameters estimated ($L > K$), one can test the overidentifying restrictions with the Sargan test as $\varepsilon(\hat{\beta}_{2SLS})'P(W)\varepsilon(\hat{\beta}_{2SLS})/\hat{\sigma}_{\varepsilon}^2$, which is asymptotically distributed χ^2 with $L-K$ df (Godfrey 1988). In the case of conditional heteroscedasticity, Hansen's (1982) robust variant of the overidentifying-restrictions test given later is necessary for consistent inference.

1.1.1 Generalized Method-of-Moments. Hansen (1982) and White (1982) showed that improvements in efficiency over 2SLS are possible by optimally weighting the distance between the sample and population moments, with the weight being the inverse of the covariance matrix of sample moments. The ensuing GMM estimator typically relies on residuals from the 2SLS estimator for an initial consistent estimate of the covariance matrix. The GMM estimator is

$$\hat{\beta}_{gmm} = (X'P(W(\hat{S}))X)^{-1}(X'P(W(\hat{S}))y), \qquad (5)$$

where $P(W(\hat{S})) = W(\hat{S})^{-1}W'$ is the projection matrix of instruments and $\hat{S} = W'\hat{\Omega}W$ is the optimal weight matrix that permits both conditional heteroscedasticity and autocorrelation in the covariance matrix $\hat{\Omega}$. The variance–covariance matrix for the GMM estimator is

$$\mathrm{var}(\hat{\beta}_{gmm}) = (X'P(W(\hat{S}))X)^{-1}, \qquad (6)$$

and Hansen's version of the overidentifying-restrictions test is $\varepsilon(\hat{\beta}_{gmm})'P(W(\hat{S}))\varepsilon(\hat{\beta}_{gmm})$, which is distributed asymptotically χ^2 with $(L-K)$ df.

1.1.2 Forward Filtering. As an alternative to 2SLS and GMM, Keane and Runkle (1992) proposed an estimator called the forward-filter (FF) estimator. The FF estimator eliminates all forms of serial correlation while still maintaining orthogonality between the initial instrument set, which contains lagged values of predetermined/endogenous variables, and the structural error. There is a similarity between forward-filtering and the orthogonal-deviations transformation developed by Arellano and Bover (1995) in that both methods demean the variables with only current and future values; however, filtering is likely to be superior because it eliminates all forms of serial correlation. Although Schmidt et al. (1992) argued that filtering is irrelevant if one exploits all sample moments during estimation, filtering may be a desirable alternative to GMM in practice. First, because the dimension of the GMM moment matrix grows exponentially as the number of time periods and regressors expands, it can be computationally intractable and the overidentifying restrictions are less likely to be satisfied, possibly due to a weak correlation between instruments and endogenous regressors. Second, if the small-sample evidence from Tauchen (1986) and Altonji and Segal (1994) carries over to the panel-data setting, a bias/efficiency trade-off will arise with the optimal GMM estimator.

Similar to GMM the FF estimator is a two-step estimator. In the first step, the first-differenced equation is estimated by 2SLS. The $((T-1) \times 1)$ vector of first-difference residuals for individual i from the 2SLS regression, $\hat{\varepsilon}_{i,2SLS}$, are used in constructing a $(T-1) \times (T-1)$ covariance matrix, $\hat{\Sigma}_{FD} = \frac{1}{N}\sum_{i=1}^{N}\hat{\varepsilon}_{i,2SLS}\hat{\varepsilon}'_{i,2SLS}$. The inverse of the covariance matrix is then filtered by a Cholesky decomposition, $\hat{C}_{FF} = \mathrm{Chol}(\hat{\Sigma}_{FD}^{-1})$, that eliminates serial correlation in the differenced errors. The second step involves transforming the original stacked $N(T-1)$ first-difference observations by $\hat{Q}_{FF} = I_N \otimes \hat{C}_{FF}$, leading to the FF estimator

$$\hat{\beta}_{FF} = (X'\hat{Q}_{FF}P(W)\hat{Q}_{FF}X)^{-1}(X'\hat{Q}_{FF}P(W)\hat{Q}_{FF}y), \qquad (7)$$

with variance–covariance matrix $\mathrm{var}(\hat{\beta}_{FF}) = \hat{\sigma}_{\varepsilon}^2(X'\hat{Q}_{FF}P(W)\hat{Q}_{FF}X)^{-1}$. As noted by Hayashi (1992), inference with the FF estimator is inconsistent if the conditional homoscedasticity assumption is violated; however, heteroscedasticity-robust variants of the variance and the overidentifying restrictions test are easy to compute.

1.1.3 Independently Weighted Generalized Method-of-Moments. In an attempt to mitigate the finite-sample bias in OMD, Altonji and Segal (1994) developed a new estimator called independently weighted OMD. I extend their idea to the case of IV with panel data. The motivation behind IW-GMM is to break the correlation between the sample moments used in estimation, $(1/N)[W'\varepsilon]$, and the estimated weight matrix, $\hat{S} = W'\hat{\Omega}W$, that is constructed with the same data. The procedure is to randomly split the sample into independent groups (g), say two ($g = 1, 2$), with group 1 used in constructing the weight matrix, $\hat{S}_1 = W_1'\hat{\Omega}_1W_1$, and group 2 used in constructing the sample moments to estimate, $(1/N)[W_2'\varepsilon_2]$. The sample split must occur on the cross-sectional dimension of the data because each cross-sectional unit retains its own time series for instruments. Each group is used alternately in constructing the weight matrix and the sample moments so that the resulting IW-GMM estimator is the average of the independent estimations:

$$\hat{\beta}_{\text{IW-GMM}} = \frac{1}{G}\sum_{g=1}^{G}(X_g'W_g(W_{-g}'\hat{\Omega}_{-g}W_{-g})^{-1}W_g'X_g)^{-1} \times (X_g'W_g(W_{-g}'\hat{\Omega}_{-g}W_{-g})^{-1}W_g'y_g), \quad (8)$$

where $-g$ refers to the excluded group. Because the sampling errors of the population moments and weight matrix are independent, the average is a consistent estimator. The variance of the estimated average is constructed as $\text{var}(\hat{\beta}_{\text{IW-GMM}}) = (1/G^2)[\text{var}(\hat{\beta}_1) + \cdots + \text{var}(\hat{\beta}_G)]$, where the covariance between ith and jth sample split is 0 by construction. The IW-GMM estimator is expected to be less efficient than GMM because of the loss in degrees of freedom. In the application to follow, I fix $G = 2$ for the IW-GMM estimator.

1.1.4 Split-Sample Instrumental Variables. Angrist and Krueger (1995) confronted the problem of a weak correlation between the instruments and regressors in their earlier work by developing the split-sample IV (SSIV) estimator. Recall that if the instruments and the endogenous regressor(s) are weakly correlated and there exists a (weak) correlation between the error from the first-stage fitted value and the structural error, then IV is biased. SSIV breaks the correlation between the two errors by randomly splitting the sample in half and using one-half to estimate the first-stage equation and the other half to estimate the structural parameters. Let sample 2 estimate the first-stage equation and combine that with W_1 to form the fitted value for X_1, which is then regressed on y_1, yielding the SSIV estimator

$$\hat{\beta}_{\text{SSIV}} = (X_2'W_2(W_2'W_2)^{-1}W_1'W_1(W_2'W_2)^{-1}W_2'X_2)^{-1} \times X_2'W_2(W_2'W_2)^{-1}W_1'y_1, \quad (9)$$

which under conditional homoscedasticity has an asymptotic covariance matrix of $\text{var}(\hat{\beta}_{\text{SSIV}}) = \hat{\sigma}_\varepsilon^2(X_2'W_2(W_2'W_2)^{-1}W_2'X_2)^{-1}$. A loss of efficiency relative to 2SLS is expected with SSIV because only one-half of the observations are used in estimation. This divergence in efficiency may be exacerbated when heteroscedasticity-robust covariance matrices of Equation (4) are employed.

Because SSIV is biased toward 0, Angrist and Krueger (1995) inflated the SSIV estimator with a bias-correction factor, resulting in a just-identified 2SLS estimator in sample 1. USSIV is consistent under group asymptotics and is given by the formula

$$\hat{\beta}_{\text{USSIV}} = (X_1'W_{21}'(W_{21}'W_{21})^{-1}W_{21}'X_1)^{-1} \times X_1'W_{21}'(W_{21}'W_{21})^{-1}W_{21}y_1, \quad (10)$$

where $W_{21} = W_1(W_2'W_2)^{-1}W_2'X_2$. The asymptotic covariance matrix takes the usual form as 2SLS under conditional homoscedasticity as $\hat{\sigma}_{\varepsilon_1}^2(X_1'W_{21}(W_{21}'W_{21})^{-1}W_{21}'X_1)^{-1}$ and the robust covariance matrix is the same as in Equation (4) with W_{21} replacing W. For obvious reasons, there is no test of the overidentifying restrictions in this case.

1.2 Choice of Instrument Set

To this point, little attention has been given to the specification of the instrument set other than the overidentifying-restrictions test. When the matrix of explanatory variables is predetermined, the first-difference and orthogonal-deviations transformations make instruments dated $t-1$ and earlier valid for estimation. In the standard IV estimator, choosing one-period lagged instruments, $W = X_{(t-1)}$, leaves the system just identified ($L = K$), whereas choosing instruments dated $t-1$ and $t-2$ imposes $p = 2K - K$ overidentifying restrictions but sacrifices an extra period of data for each observation.

Schmidt et al. (1992) argued that efficiency gains are possible if, instead of the usual instrument set, one exploits all of the linear moments available as implied by the orthogonality conditions $E[W_i'\varepsilon_{i,d}] = 0$, where W_i is the matrix of instruments for individual i and $\varepsilon_{i.d}$ is the vector of first-difference or orthogonal deviations residuals. The Schmidt et al. approach uses levels of instruments from different time periods for different observations. The instrument set for individual i when all the regressors are predetermined is constructed as

$$W_i = \begin{bmatrix} x_1 & 0 & 0 & 0 & \cdot & \cdot & 0 & 0 & \cdot & 0 & 0 \\ 0 & x_1 & x_2 & 0 & \cdot & \cdot & 0 & 0 & \cdot & 0 & 0 \\ \cdot & 0 & 0 & 0 & \cdot & \cdot & \cdot & \cdot & \cdot & \cdot & \cdot \\ \cdot & \cdot & \cdot & \cdot & \cdot & \cdot & \cdot & \cdot & \cdot & \cdot & \cdot \\ \cdot & \cdot & \cdot & \cdot & \cdot & \cdot & x_1 & x_2 & \cdot & \cdot & x_{T-1} \end{bmatrix}, \quad (11)$$

which has dimension $(T-1) \times (T)(T-1)(K)/2$ and where $x_t (t = 1, \ldots, T-1)$ are the lagged levels of the explanatory variables. For example, in period 2 variables from period 1 are valid instruments, in period 3 variables from both periods 1 and 2 are valid, and so on until period T, where variables from periods 1 to $T-1$ are valid instruments. When T and K are both large, say $T = 15$ and $K = 10$, there are 1,040 overidentifying restrictions, highlighting the computational burden of the Schmidt et al. approach. In the application to follow, I compare the efficiency of the standard instrument set to the stacked instrument set in Equation (11).

2. AN APPLICATION TO LIFE-CYCLE LABOR SUPPLY UNDER UNCERTAINTY

A focal point of interest in the labor-supply literature is consistent and efficient estimation of the intertemporal substitution elasticity (ISE). The ISE measures intertemporal changes in hours of work due to an anticipated change in the real wage and aids in understanding comovements in earnings and hours over the business cycle. Consequently, reliable estimates of the ISE are of import to public policy in labor markets. The life-cycle labor-supply model developed by MaCurdy (1985) and Altonji (1986) forms the basis of the empirical exercise.

Based on a utility function that is additively separable between consumption and leisure, the double-log life-cycle labor-supply function for individual i ($i = 1, \ldots, N$) in time t ($t = 1, \ldots, T$) is

$$\ln h_{it} = \lambda_{i0} + \delta \ln \omega_{it} + z_{it}\gamma + \varepsilon_{it}, \tag{12}$$

where ln is the natural log operator; h_{it} is annual hours of work; λ_{i0} is the marginal utility of initial wealth that is a function of all future wages, assets, prices, and tastes and is correlated with the explanatory variables; z_{it} is a vector of time-varying demographics; and δ is the ISE parameter. The assumptions between the regressors and structural random error are $E[\varepsilon_{is}|\ln \omega_{it}] = 0$ for all $s > t$ and $E[\varepsilon_{is}|z_{it}] = 0$ for all $s \geq t$. Wages are assumed to be endogenous rather than predetermined to account for the possible presence of nonlinear income taxes and/or human capital considerations, or possibly measurement error.

Estimation proceeds by taking first differences or orthogonal deviations on Equation (12) to eliminate the unobserved marginal utility of wealth and then using the estimators outlined in Section 1. Because of the endogeneity of wages and the desire to use lagged values of wages as instruments, an extra year of data is lost; consequently, there are a maximum of $(T - 2) \times (T - 2)[(K - 1)(T + 1) + T]/2$ linear moment conditions to exploit in estimation. The stacked instrument matrix in Equation (11) for the labor-supply model contains, in period 3, wages from period 1 along with demographics in periods 1 and 2 as instruments, wages from periods 1 and 2 along with demographics from periods 1 to 3 are instruments in period 4, and so on until period T when there are $(T - 2)$ lagged wages and $(K - 1)(T - 1)$ lagged demographic variables as instruments.

2.1 Data

The data used to estimate the life-cycle labor-supply parameters come from Waves XII–XXI (calendar years 1978–1987) of the PSID. The sample is selected on many dimensions and is similar to other research studying life-cycle models of labor supply. The sample is restricted to continuously married, continuously working, prime-age men aged 22–51 in 1978 from the Survey Research Center random subsample of the PSID. In addition the individual must either be paid an hourly wage rate or must be salaried, and he cannot be a piece-rate worker or self-employed. This selection process resulted in a balanced panel of 532 men over 10 years or 5,320 observations. The real wage rate, ω_{it}, is the hourly wage reported by the panel participant rather than the average wage (annual earnings over annual hours) to minimize division bias (Borjas 1981). The predetermined time-varying taste shifters, z_{it}, include a quadratic in age, the number of children in the household, and a dummy variable for bad health.

2.2 Results

In Table 1 I report the results from 101 regressions, 55 based on the first-difference transformation and 46 based on the orthogonal-deviations transformation. The FF estimator is not included under orthogonal deviations because filtering would be redundant in this case. I begin with the standard instrument set with z_{it}'s from $t-1$ and $t-2$, along with lagged wages from $t - 2$. I then sequentially build up the stacked instrument set from Equation (11). Because the ISE is the parameter of primary interest, I only present results for the ISE in Table 1. The efficiency pattern in the demographic variables with changes in moment conditions is similar to the pattern in the ISE. The weighting matrix for the first-difference GMM estimator that corrected for a first-order moving average error failed to be positive definite in the stacked-moment models, even with modified Bartlett weights; hence, the results reported only correct for conditional heteroscedasticity. As a point of departure, I present OLS estimates at the bottom of Table 1. The OLS first-difference ISE is .111 with a heteroscedasticity-robust standard error of .079, and the orthogonal-deviations ISE is .176 with a heteroscedasticity-robust standard error of .074.

2.2.1 Base-Case Results. In the base case with demographic variables from $t - 1$ and $t - 2$ and wages from $t - 2$ as instruments for the contemporaneous period, the first-difference 2SLS and GMM estimates of the ISE are .21 and .52, respectively; however, neither estimate is significant even at the 10% level. As a benchmark to judge the first-difference base-case results, Altonji (1986) estimated a range of values from .01 to .45, most of which are imprecisely estimated. The orthogonal-deviations 2SLS estimates are more efficient than their first-difference counterparts, possibly due to reduced measurement error relative to differencing; however, there is no general pattern of efficiency gains across the other orthogonal-deviations estimators. The IW-GMM estimates vary across the first-difference and orthogonal-deviations transformations in that the former inflate the corresponding GMM estimate by about 40% and the latter deflate it by about 40%. Of course, the objective of IW-GMM is to correct for bias in GMM, whether it be positive or negative bias. On the contrary, SSIV and USSIV uniformly inflate their 2SLS counterparts across specifications, although there is a substantial loss in efficiency due to smaller sample sizes. Interestingly, under conditional homoscedasticity, the FF estimator performs best on efficiency grounds in the base case, even surpassing GMM; however, once one accounts for heteroscedasticity, GMM and IW-GMM improve on the FF estimates.

The results from the Sargan overidentifying-restrictions tests are mixed across the models. The conditionally homoscedastic p values of .02 and .01 from the first-difference 2SLS and FF estimators do not lend much support to the choice of instruments; however, the GMM and orthogonal-deviations versions do not reject the overidentifying restrictions. The test rejects the IW-GMM specifications under first differences but does not reject SSIV models. Two important findings that emerge in the base case and are magnified in the stacked-moment results to follow are that (1) once the Sargan test is modified for the presence of heteroscedasticity, the overidentifying restrictions are not rejected in any of the 2SLS or FF specifications and (2) as

Table 1. Intertemporal Substitution Elasticities Under Alternative Moment-Condition Estimators

	First difference						Orthogonal deviations				
Moments	*2SLS*	*GMM*	*FF*	*IW-GMM*	*SSIV*	*USSIV*	*2SLS*	*GMM*	*IW-GMM*	*SSIV*	*USSIV*
Base case:											
$T-1$, $T-2$	.2091	.5192	.1350	.7161	.7158	1.7491	.2552	.4506	.2603	.8931	1.1224
	(.4155)	(.3638)	(.3163)	(.3498)	(.6183)	(2.0709)	(.3773)	(.4011)	(.4044)	(.6427)	(.7987)
	(.4231)	[.4482]	(.3857)	[.0059]	(.7109)	(1.8272)	(.4488)	[.6431]	[.0392]	(.8237)	(.8270)
{9}	[.0234]		[.0138]		[.3447]		[.1361]			[.5862]	
	[.3147]		[.1925]		[.4356]		[.5744]			[.8326]	
Stacked cases:											
$T-1$ to $T-2$	.5428	.3942	.5422	.3971	.6752	6.0887	.7130	.6158	.5069	.4289	8.2390
	(.1808)	(.1504)	(.1525)	(.0846)	(.2120)	(7.3626)	(.1719)	(.1586)	(.0908)	(.1764)	(19.205)
	(.2259)	[.4248]	(.2007)	[.0000]	(.4878)	(7.1342)	(.2119)	[.2040]	[.0000]	(.4880)	(18.444)
{72}	[.0700]		[.0284]		[.0000]		[.0697]			[.8188]	
	[.3837]		[.2778]		[.0002]		[.1185]			[.9315]	
$T-1$ to $T-3$	.5620	.3916	.5093	.2868	.3768	−3.4139	.5885	.3768	.3724	.1070	−2.4665
	(.1436)	(.1158)	(.1225)	(.0584)	(.1609)	(3.6721)	(.1353)	(.1156)	(.0626)	(.1342)	(6.1924)
	(.1817)	[.4560]	(.1779)	[.0000]	(.3564)	(4.2839)	(.1792)	[.2209]	[.0000]	(.3406)	(7.2017)
{107}	[.0632]		[.0089]		[.0017]		[.0109]			[.3946]	
	[.3932]		[.2096]		[.0065]		[.0959]			[.4759]	
$T-1$ to $T-4$	.3774	.1933	.4568	.1832	.0881	.6702	.5432	.2778	.2819	−.0489	.3272
	(.1279)	(.1013)	(.1118)	(.0462)	(.1168)	(.8119)	(.1242)	(.1031)	(.0497)	(.1064)	(.9251)
	(.1780)	[.3192]	(.1711)	[.0000]	(.2886)	(1.2464)	(.1733)	[.2363]	[.0000]	(.3007)	(1.4420)
{137}	[.0000]		[.0003]		[.0000]		[.0002]			[.0000]	
	[.2211]		[.2715]		[.0002]		[.0772]			[.0000]	
$T-1$ to $T-5$	.3123	.1186	.3108	.3170	.0218	−.1169	.4006	.1714	.2838	−.0898	.5920
	(.1179)	(.0878)	(.1008)	(.0346)	(.1044)	(.5247)	(.1133)	(.0898)	(.0412)	(.0972)	(.7368)
	(.1742)	[.1393]	(.1829)	[.0000]	(.2389)	(.7319)	(.2000)	[.0480]	[.0000]	(.2779)	(1.1203)
{162}	[.0000]		[.0927]		[.0000]		[.0000]			[.0000]	
	[.0705]		[.0824]		[.0000]		[.0125]			[.0000]	
$T-1$ to $T-6$	.3502	.1524	.3517	.3615	.0299	−.2473	.4051	.1448	.4031	−.0754	.7449
	(.1084)	(.0802)	(.0927)	(.0311)	(.0940)	(.6665)	(.1044)	(.0799)	(.0346)	(.0910)	(.9966)
	(.1772)	[.3509]	(.1778)	[.0000]	(.2242)	(.9609)	(.1860)	[.1303]	[.0000]	(.2550)	(1.4588)
{182}	[.0000]		[.0000]		[.0000]		[.0000]			[.0000]	
	[.1927]		[.1383]		[.0000]		[.0253]			[.0000]	
$T-1$ to $T-7$	.2763	.1017	.3069	.3444	.0158	−.2577	.3650	.1413	.3082	−.0654	.7629
	(.1028)	(.0741)	(.0893)	(.0247)	(.0849)	(.7653)	(.1005)	(.0743)	(.0287)	(.0850)	(1.1336)
	(.1758)	[.3510]	(.1677)	[.0000]	(.2109)	(1.0709)	(.1799)	[.1849]	[.0000]	(.2331)	(1.6145)
{197}	[.0000]		[.0000]		[.0000]		[.0000]			[.0000]	
	[.2051]		[.2126]		[.0000]		[.0505]			[.0000]	
$T-1$ to $T-8$	.2653	.0659	.2781	.3479	.0017	−.1355	.3408	.1051	.2781	−.0800	.8239
	(.1003)	(.0691)	(.0869)	(.0237)	(.0834)	(.7492)	(.0984)	(.0679)	(.0262)	(.0825)	(.9977)
	(.1686)	[.3562]	(.1592)	[.0000]	(.2035)	(.9927)	(.1738)	[.1709]	[.0000]	(.2270)	(1.3779)
{207}	[.0000]		[.0000]		[.0000]		[.0000]			[.0000]	
	[.1663]		[.1593]		[.0000]		[.0364]			[.0000]	
$T-1$ to $T-9$	.2814	.0931	.2961	.3173	.0046	−.1808	.3512	.1227	.2544	−.0824	.7825
	(.0987)	(.0674)	(.0856)	(.0228)	(.0827)	(.7238)	(.0971)	(.0661)	(.0255)	(.0822)	(.9308)
	(.1623)	[.3787]	(.1540)	[.0000]	(.1949)	(.9267)	(.1694)	[.1926]	[.0000]	(.2207)	(1.2813)
{212}	[.0000]		[.0000]		[.0000]		[.0000]			[.0000]	
	[.1875]		[.1793]		[.0000]		[.0431]			[.0000]	
OLS	.1115						.1755				
	(.0247)						(.0224)				
	(.0791)						(.0743)				

NOTE: Standard errors are in parentheses and p values for the null hypothesis of correct overidentifying restrictions are in square brackets. The second values in parentheses and square brackets for the 2SLS, FF, SSIV, and USSIV estimators refer to heteroscedasticity-robust standard errors and p values. $N = 532$ and $T = 8$. The numbers between { } are the number of instruments used in estimation.

the ratio of instruments to *cross-sectional* sample size rises, Hansen's test seems to overreject. This will become evident in Subsection 2.2.2 when one compares GMM to IW-GMM and 2SLS to SSIV.

2.2.2 Stacked Moment Results. Turning now to the stacked moment-condition results reveals a striking change in the efficiency of the ISE. With 72 moment conditions in the stacked $t-1$ and $t-2$ case, significant efficiency gains are achieved for all the estimators, with the average reduction in standard errors around 50%. The FF estimator outperforms 2SLS in efficiency in all cases, but GMM is more efficient than FF in all of the stacked-moment specifications. No clear efficiency pattern emerges between orthogonal deviations and first-difference GMM, nor with heteroscedasticity-robust 2SLS across the transformations. Quite remarkably, IW-GMM outperforms GMM across the

Table 2. First-Stage F and Wald Tests for Wage Changes

Moments	First-difference F test	First-difference Wald Test	Orthogonal-deviations F test	Orthogonal-deviations Wald Test
Base case:				
$T-1, T-2$ {9}	2.541 [.007]	20.095 [.017]	3.979 [.000]	30.293 [.000]
Stacked cases:				
$T-1$ to $T-2$ {72}	1.182 [.141]	92.589 [.052]	1.382 [.019]	104.331 [.008]
$T-1$ to $T-3$ {107}	1.197 [.084]	129.862 [.066]	1.303 [.021]	150.497 [.004]
$T-1$ to $T-4$ {137}	1.098 [.208]	160.540 [.083]	1.154 [.109]	187.569 [.003]
$T-1$ to $T-5$ {162}	1.074 [.251]	210.043 [.007]	1.092 [.205]	245.218 [.000]
$T-1$ to $T-6$ {182}	1.138 [.104]	241.216 [.002]	1.120 [.134]	286.980 [.000]
$T-1$ to $T-7$ {197}	1.149 [.080]	271.128 [.000]	1.097 [.175]	309.148 [.000]
$T-1$ to $T-8$ {207}	1.146 [.079]	291.226 [.000]	1.079 [.214]	326.667 [.000]
$T-1$ to $T-9$ {212}	1.160 [.061]	325.604 [.000]	1.080 [.210]	362.342 [.000]

NOTE: The null hypothesis is that the instruments jointly explain none of the variation in the wage changes. P values are given in brackets. For the F test, the numerator degrees of freedom are (# of moments − 1) and the denominator degrees of freedom are $NT - N -$ #moments, where $N = 532$ and $T = 8$. The degrees of freedom for the Wald test are the number of moment conditions.

board on efficiency grounds. This result is surprising given that IW-GMM only uses half of the sample for each estimation and may point to some small-sample advantages of IW-GMM over GMM. Likewise, SSIV standard errors under homoscedasticity dominate 2SLS and FF; however, 2SLS and FF are far superior once one controls for heteroscedasticity. Proceeding down the columns, note that, as additional moments are added to the instrument set. the ISE is estimated more precisely as predicted. For example, exploiting all moments (212) reduces the 2SLS and FF standard errors by at least 45% and the GMM standard errors by at least 55% compared to the suboptimal matrix with 72 moments.

The efficiency gains of extra instruments, nonetheless, come at a cost. A clear pattern of downward bias in the first-difference and orthogonal-deviations GMM and SSIV estimators emerges in the stacked-moment results of Table 1. With 72 moments imposed, the first-difference 2SLS and GMM ISE parameters differ by 27%, but the difference is 67% with 212 moments. The bias is even more severe under orthogonal deviations. Unlike GMM, the finding that the SSIV parameter estimates converge toward 0 as the number of overidentifying restrictions expands is an expected property of the estimator (Angrist and Krueger 1995). What is not expected is the erratic and puzzling behavior of the USSIV estimator. The estimated ISE ranges from 8.239 in the 72-moment orthogonal-deviations case to −3.414 in the 107-moment first-difference case. No obvious explanation emerges for the disappointing USSIV results, but the findings indicate that "forcing" exact identification through the bias-correction factor may be undesirable with many overidentifying restrictions. The FF estimator from Keane and Runkle (1992) does not appear to suffer from the same bias as in GMM and yet is more efficient than 2SLS.

2.2.3 Tests for Weak Instruments. An obvious question arises: Is the bias in GMM due to instruments weakly correlated with the wage or due to a correlation between the sample moments and the estimated weight matrix? Several corroborating facts suggest that a correlation between the sample moments and the estimated weight matrix is the source of the bias. In Table 2 I report first-stage F tests and Wald tests with their associated p values for the endogenous wage regressor. I present the Wald test because the F test is inconsistent when there is heteroscedasticity. As seen in Table 2, the F test frequently leads to the incorrect conclusion that there are weakly correlated instruments when the Wald test does not, suggesting that when heteroscedasticity is present the Wald test is the more appropriate test for the correlation between instruments and regressors. The conclusion that the instruments are not weak is strengthened by noting that the overidentifying-restrictions test does not reject the model under heteroscedasticity-robust GMM, 2SLS, or FF.

Potentially the strongest piece of evidence that the bias comes from the estimated weight matrix is the IW-GMM parameter estimates. Beginning with 162 moments, the IW-GMM estimates are at least twice as large as GMM on average and are comparable to 2SLS and FF estimates, a result that would not arise if there were no correlation between the GMM sample moments and estimated weight matrix or if the instruments are weak. Unfortunately, Hansen's overidentifying-restrictions test rejects all of the IW-GMM specifications (and all SSIV models beginning with 137 moments). This "overrejection" as the ratio of moments to cross-sectional sample size increases, which reaches a maximum of 212/266 under IW-GMM compared to 212/532 under GMM, may indicate a weakness in the test.

2.2.4 Summary. The results of Tables 1 and 2 suggest that GMM is biased downward relative to 2SLS and FF as the number of moment conditions expands because of a correlation between the estimated weight matrix and the sample moments. Moreover, IW-GMM is successful in correcting the bias in GMM; however, the IW-GMM parameter estimates are more variable than 2SLS and FF and the overidentifying restrictions are rejected in each specification. SSIV is biased toward 0 as the number of instruments expands and USSIV performs poorly. Finally, inference, whether it be standard errors, overidentifying restrictions, or first-stage F tests, can be quite misleading when the assumption of conditional homoscedasticity is incorrect.

3. BOOTSTRAPPING OVERIDENTIFIED MODELS

To investigate the sample properties of the estimators such as the potential bias/efficiency trade-off in GMM, more deeply, I now turn to the bootstrap. The bootstrap, recently surveyed by Efron and Tibshirani (1993) and Jeong and Maddala (1993), is a powerful statistical technique for the computation of measures of variability, confidence intervals, and bias of an estimator. In the current application, the bootstrap is a natural alternative to standard Monte Carlo analysis because it is based on a nonparametric estimate of the underlying error distribution. Recall that a strength of each of the IV estimators considered in Section 2 emanates from their lack of dependence on an a priori specified small-sample distribution. Moreover, the parametric Monte Carlo is difficult to implement because the labor-supply literature offers little help in the way of the joint small-sample distribution of wages and hours, making the choice of a distribution a dubious exercise at best. Consequently, the bootstrap maintains the semiparametric, empirical-based spirit of the article.

The typical regression-based bootstrap is a multistep procedure whereby the researcher resamples with replacement the estimated residuals, constructs a new dependent variable as the sum of the fitted value from the regression plus the bootstrapped residual, reestimates the model, and repeats the exercise B times ($b = 1, \ldots, B$). There are then B observations from which to compute measures of bias, variability, or confidence intervals. This approach is consistent only under the assumptions of conditional homoscedasticity, no serial dependence, and nonstochastic regressors.

When the regressors are stochastic or there is conditional heteroscedasticity as is typical in IV estimation, Freedman (1984) and Freedman and Peters (1984) suggested an alternative procedure. Instead of resampling the residuals, one resamples simultaneously the estimated residuals along with the regressors and instruments. More specifically, one resamples with replacement from $(\hat{\varepsilon}, X, W)$, where $\hat{\varepsilon}$ is the vector of estimated first-difference or orthogonal-deviations residuals, X is the matrix of first-difference or orthogonal-deviations regressors, and W is the matrix of instruments. Call the constructed "pseudodata" $(\hat{\varepsilon}^*, X^*, W^*)$. The new dependent variable is $\hat{y}^* = X^*\hat{\beta} + \hat{\varepsilon}^*$, which is regressed on X^* with W^* as instruments to generate a new $\hat{\beta}^*$, and the procedure is repeated B times. This approach, in which each observation has equal probability weight $1/N$ of being drawn from the discrete empirical distribution function, is an asymptotically valid method of bootstrapping an IV estimator, even when the model is overidentified, and provides asymptotic coverage rates equal to their nominal rates (Hahn in press).

Brown and Newey (1995) and Hall and Horowitz (in press), however, showed that the Freedman method does not yield an improvement in terms of coverage rates over first-order asymptotic theory, and more importantly, it gives the wrong size, even asymptotically, for the overidentifying-restrictions test. The problem lies in the fact that when the model is overidentified the sample moments are typically not 0, and thus one bootstraps from an empirical distribution that is a poor approximation to the true underlying distribution. Hall and Horowitz attempted to mitigate this problem by recentering the moments at their sample values, and Brown and Newey suggested recentering the empirical distribution by imposing the moment conditions on the data.

Because Brown and Newey showed that their approach is efficient in the class of bootstrap methods, I use their resampling algorithm as an alternative to Freedman's method. The idea is to resample from the multinomial distribution in which each observation receives a different probability weight, $\hat{p}_i$, such that the sample moments, $\hat{g}_i = g(\hat{\varepsilon}, X, W)$, are satisfied by construction, $\sum_{i=1}^{N} \hat{p}_i \hat{g}_i = 0$. In general, $\hat{p}_i$ is solved numerically from a linear programming problem; however, Brown and Newey suggested a closed-form solution for the probability given as $\hat{p}_i = (1 - \bar{g}'\hat{V}^{-1}\hat{g}_i)/[N * (1 - \bar{g}'\hat{V}^{-1}\bar{g})]$, where $\bar{g} = 1/N \sum_{i=1}^{N} \hat{g}_i$ and $\hat{V} = 1/N \sum_{i=1}^{N} \hat{g}_i \hat{g}_i'$. The estimated probabilities are expected to satisfy the usual regularity conditions such as $\hat{p}_i > 0$ and $\sum_{i=1}^{N} \hat{p}_i = 1$.

For each experiment, I compute the bias as $(1/B) \sum_{b=1}^{B} \hat{\delta}_b - \hat{\delta}$, where $\hat{\delta}_b$ is the bth bootstrap estimate of the ISE and $\hat{\delta}$ is the pseudotrue value of the ISE defined later, the average heteroscedasticity-consistent standard error constructed from the asymptotic formulas in Section 1 (SE-A), the bootstrap standard error as $[(\sum_{b=1}^{B} (\hat{\delta}_b - \sum_{b=1}^{B} \hat{\delta}_b/B)^2)/(B - 1)]^{1/2}/\sqrt{B}$ (SE-B), the RMSE defined as the square root of the sum of bias squared and the average variance constructed from asymptotic formulas (RMSE-A), the RMSE defined as the square root of the sum of bias squared and boot SE squared (RMSE-B), and the MAE. In addition, I report a measure of reliability of asymptotic inference by constructing the coverage rates on a 95% two-tailed confidence interval as the fraction of times the pseudotrue value of the ISE falls within the interval based on asymptotic standard-error formulas and asymptotic critical values.

Because the t distribution does not adjust confidence intervals for the presence of skewness in the underlying population, I also construct bootstrap-t critical values that have the ability to account for skewness (Efron and Tibshirani 1993, pp. 159–162). The idea is to approximate the asymptotic pivotal t statistic from the bootstrap as $\hat{t}(b) = (\hat{\delta}_b - \hat{\delta})/\widehat{\text{se}}(b)$, where $\widehat{\text{se}}(b)$ is the bth estimated asymptotic standard error. The α and $1 - \alpha$ critical values are found by ordering the $\hat{t}(b)$'s for the entire bootstrap sample and are then used in constructing bootstrap-t confidence intervals. The bootstrap-t may offer asymptotic refinements over critical values from first-order asymptotic theory (Brown and Newey 1995; Hall and Horowitz in press). Finally, to gauge the potential gains in the Brown and Newey algorithm over Freedman's for correcting the size of the overidentifying-restrictions test, I report the fraction of times the bootstrap value of the overidentifying-restrictions test exceeds the asymptotic critical χ^2 value at the .05 level (Boot-J).

3.1 Results

To make relative comparisons of bias, RMSE, and MAE across the estimators I need to "prime" the bootstrap (i.e., construct $\hat{\varepsilon}$) with a common vector of parameters. This approach of choosing a common set of starting values mimics the parametric Monte Carlo and has been applied to the bootstrap by Freedman and Peters (1984). Because the focus is on the ISE, I use the estimated ISE most often encountered in male labor-supply studies as the pseudotrue value of δ. Pencavel (1986) noted that the ISE has a cen-

Table 3. Bootstrap Comparisons of First-Difference Moment-Condition Estimators Where Observations Are Drawn With Probability 1/N

Estimators	*Bias*	*SE-A*	*SE-B*	*RMSE-A*	*RMSE-B*	*MAE*	*95% asym-t coverage*	*95% boot-t critical values*	*Boot-J rejection rate: 5%*
				9 moments					
2SLS	−.108	.485	.474	.497	.486	.263	.99	−1.59, 1.71	.29
GMM	.174	.360	.330	.400	.373	.280	.95	−1.35, 2.15	.13
FF	−.097	.351	.309	.365	.324	.183	.98	−1.93, 1.29	.44
IW-GMM	.189	.459	.565	.497	.596	.336	.88	−1.48, 3.99	.66
SSIV	.208	.854	.909	.879	.932	.451	1.00	−1.63, 1.67	.29
USSIV	.828	15.621	6.082	15.643	6.138	1.683	.99	−1.04, 1.53	—
				72 moments					
2SLS	.128	.169	.199	.212	.236	.145	.85	−1.53, 3.27	.99
GMM	−.093	.097	.108	.134	.142	.108	.81	−3.34, .98	.99
FF	.055	.142	.156	.152	.168	.136	.87	−1.79, 2.63	.99
IW-GMM	.013	.070	.337	.071	.337	.149	.47	−7.28, 8.06	1.00
SSIV	.137	.310	.273	.339	.306	.160	.95	−2.13, 1.95	.63
USSIV	−1.107	3.4E2	42.527	3.4E2	42.541	4.965	1.00	−1.19, 1.69	—
				162 moments					
2SLS	.022	.131	.219	.132	.220	.147	.74	−3.73, 4.05	.99
GMM	−.169	.055	.077	.178	.186	.179	.21	−5.62, −.2	1.00
FF	−.046	.119	.128	.128	.136	.090	.87	−3.74, 1.49	1.00
IW-GMM	−.020	.029	.229	.035	.230	.156	.19	−15.1, 19.1	1.00
SSIV	−.216	.188	.124	.286	.249	.211	.84	−3.07, .31	.90
USSIV	−.932	11.598	5.707	11.636	5.782	.927	.96	−2.26, 1.79	—
				212 moments					
2SLS	−.014	.124	.166	.125	.166	.084	.79	−4.50, 3.12	1.00
GMM	−.175	.043	.047	.180	.181	.172	.04	−6.0, −1.74	1.00
FF	−.037	.100	.106	.107	.112	.069	.85	−3.69, 1.84	1.00
IW-GMM	.044	.018	.219	.047	.224	.144	.14	−27.4, 32.5	1.00
SSIV	−.209	.175	.096	.273	.231	.192	.83	−2.86, −.31	.95
USSIV	−.372	13.467	5.783	13.472	5.794	1.099	.99	−1.58, 1.41	—

NOTE: All calculations are based on 100 bootstrap replications. The pseudotrue value of the ISE is fixed at .21 for all calculations. Bias is computed as the difference between the average bootstrap estimate and the pseudotrue ISE, SE-A is the average standard error computed from asymptotic theory, SE-B is the average standard error constructed from the bootstrap, RMSE-A is the root mean squared error computed with the variance from asymptotic theory, RMSE-B is the root mean squared error computed with the variance from the bootstrap, MAE is the median absolute error, 95% asym-*t* coverage is the fraction of times the pseudotrue value of the ISE falls within the 95% confidence interval based on standard errors and critical values from asymptotic theory, 95% boot-*t* critical values are the .025 and .975 values from the bootstrap *t* statistic, and boot-*J* rejection rate is the fraction of times the bootstrap value of the overidentifying restrictions test exceeds the critical χ^2 value at the .05 level.

tral tendency of .20, which, coincidentally, is consistent with the 2SLS 9-moment model of Table 1; thus, the 2SLS 9-moment parameters form the starting values. I present 100 bootstrap replications for the 9-, 72-, 162-, and 212-moment cases for both the first-difference and orthogonal-deviations transformations. The small number of bootstrap Monte Carlo draws is sufficient for measures of bias and variability for most sample sizes but is sufficient for confidence intervals only in larger samples (Hall 1986; Efron and Tibshirani 1993, p. 161). All experiments were conducted in Gauss with a Pentium-90, where the models with 212 moments took at least 48 hours to compute. I present the results from the Freedman algorithm in Tables 3 and 4 and from Brown and Newey's algorithm in Tables 5 and 6. I focus on the first-difference results because the implications from orthogonal deviations are largely the same.

3.1.1 Results From Freedman Algorithm. Beginning with the base case of 9 moments in Table 3, 2SLS and FF tend to be biased toward OLS ($\hat{\delta}_{\text{OLS}} = .11$), which is consistent with the presence of a finite-sample bias in IV estimators. The absolute value of bias in GMM exceeds both 2SLS and FF, whereas GMM dominates all three of the split-sample estimators in terms of lower bias. Comparing the average asymptotic standard error (SE-A) to the bootstrap standard error (SE-B) suggests that there is little difference for 2SLS, FF, and GMM standard errors, but the asymptotic and bootstrap standard errors diverge for IW-GMM, SSIV, and USSIV. FF dominates all of the estimators in terms of lower RMSE and MAE, but GMM does better than 2SLS in terms of RMSE but not for MAE. Moreover, GMM dominates all of the split-sample estimators for lower RMSE and MAE. In terms of asym-*t* coverage rates, GMM performs best, 2SLS, FF, SSIV, and USSIV tend to underreject, and IW-GMM overrejects. The bootstrap-*t* critical values suggest that there is a slight departure from symmetry for each of the estimators and that asymptotic critical values are too large. The boot-*J* rejection rates, however, reveal that there is a serious level distortion in the overidentifying-restrictions test computed with Freedman's algorithm. Overall, Keane and Runkle's FF estimator performs best in the base case.

The most obvious trend arising in the stacked-moment cases is the increasing bias in GMM as the number of moment conditions expands. The bias in the GMM ISE rises (i.e., becomes more negative) from −.093 under 72 moments to −.175 with 212 moments. This finding, reenforc-

Table 4. Bootstrap Comparisons of Orthogonal-Deviations Moment-Condition Estimators Where Observations Are Drawn With Probability 1/N

Estimators	Bias	SE-A	SE-B	RMSE-A	RMSE-B	MAE	95% asym-t coverage	95% boot-t critical values	Boot-J rejection rate: 5%
					9 moments				
2SLS	.099	.432	.440	.443	.452	.259	.96	−1.85, 2.16	.30
GMM	.303	.370	.366	.478	.475	.317	.87	−1.68, 2.67	.16
IW-GMM	.068	.444	.451	.450	.457	.285	.90	−1.72, 2.63	.73
SSIV	.419	.753	.647	.862	.771	.494	.99	−1.61, 1.69	.12
USSIV	.312	5.992	3.793	5.999	3.806	1.079	.97	−1.05, 2.11	—
					72 moments				
2SLS	.280	.165	.219	.325	.356	.270	.62	−.80, 4.40	1.00
GMM	.011	.096	.113	.097	.114	.080	.88	−2.36, 2.62	1.00
IW-GMM	.124	.069	.264	.142	.292	.160	.45	−8.95, 11.5	1.00
SSIV	.058	.292	.168	.298	.178	.130	.99	−1.78, 1.39	.42
USSIV	.355	31.512	12.082	31.512	12.087	3.825	1.00	−1.17, 1.28	—
					162 moments				
2SLS	.112	.141	.209	.180	.238	.160	.77	−2.24, 7.36	1.00
GMM	−.141	.053	.074	.150	.159	.140	.27	−5.21, .12	1.00
IW-GMM	.042	.031	.248	.052	.252	.184	.20	−17.3, 17.3	1.00
SSIV	−.252	.222	.134	.336	.286	.255	.83	−3.11, .07	.85
USSIV	−1.458	83.064	10.147	83.077	10.252	1.220	.91	−2.23, 2.32	—
					212 moments				
2SLS	.087	.123	.175	.151	.196	.121	.84	−2.49, 7.62	1.00
GMM	−.154	.041	.056	.159	.164	.150	.07	−6.62, −1.21	1.00
IW-GMM	.009	.019	.251	.021	.251	.155	.13	−23.7, 40.5	1.00
SSIV	−.239	.186	.101	.302	.259	.243	.71	−2.81, −.01	.90
USSIV	−.039	17.758	6.229	17.759	6.230	1.274	.98	−1.49, 2.32	—

NOTE: See note to Table 3.

ing the results of Table 1, extends Tauchen's (1986) and Altonji and Segal's (1994) finding of bias in GMM in small samples to the large-sample case of panel data. The 2SLS and FF estimators are not biased toward OLS as in the base case, while IW-GMM has negligible bias in each of the stacked-moment simulations. Consistent with the results of Table 1 is the bias toward 0 in SSIV and USSIV as the number of moment conditions increases. The USSIV estimator does not succeed in its primary function to "inflate" the SSIV estimates.

In terms of statistical inference, there appears to be little difference between the bootstrap standard error and the average asymptotic standard error for the FF and GMM estimators. On the contrary, the standard errors do diverge for the other estimators, especially IW-GMM and USSIV. This suggests that the small IW-GMM standard errors in Table 1 may understate the true sampling variability in the estimator, making the bootstrap useful for correctly estimating IW-GMM standard errors. Examining the 95% asym-t coverage rates indicates that all of the estimators except USSIV tend to overreject the event that the pseudotrue ISE lies in the confidence region, with the overrejection being particularly acute for both GMM and IW-GMM. In GMM, the asymptotic confidence region is distorted because of the bias in the parameter estimates toward 0, coupled with a tight standard error. IW-GMM, on the other hand, has little bias in the estimated ISE's relative to GMM, but because the asymptotic standard errors are estimated tightly, the confidence interval is short, excluding the pseudotrue ISE too frequently. Moreover, inspecting the boot-t critical values reveals that GMM does not even include 0 in the critical region in the 162- and 212-moment cases. This suggests that the bootstrap-t confidence interval is useful for GMM and IW-GMM to capture the skewness in the underlying distribution. The FF estimator continues to outperform 2SLS in coverage rates; meanwhile, given the bias in the estimated ISE, the SSIV and USSIV estimators give relatively good coverage.

Comparing the omnibus measures of estimator performance (RMSE and MAE) for the stacked-moment bootstrap simulations reveals that FF dominates 2SLS in all cases and both FF and 2SLS always dominate GMM except with 72 moments. Highlighting the problems noted by Brown and Newey (1995) and Hall and Horowitz (in press), however, the overidentifying-restrictions test is distorted severely, resulting in 100% rejection rates when the nominal rejection rate is 5%. It must be stressed that, as established by Hahn (in press), overrejection of the overidentifying restrictions does not invalidate the other bias/efficiency results in Tables 3 and 4—the estimators and overidentifying restrictions are separate.

3.1.2 Results From Brown and Newey Algorithm. Tables 5 and 6 contain the bootstrap results for the first-difference and orthogonal-deviations transformations using Brown and Newey's (1995) algorithm. The USSIV estimator is not presented because the motivation for Brown and Newey's method is to get a correct overidentifying-restrictions test, which by definition does not exist for the USSIV. Compared to Table 3, the most striking result in

Table 5. Bootstrap Comparisons of First-Difference Moment-Condition Estimators Where Observations Are Drawn With Probability $\hat{p}_i$

Estimators	Bias	SE-A	SE-B	RMSE-A	RMSE-B	MAE	95% asym-t coverage	95% boot-t critical values	Boot-J rejection rate: 5%
					9 moments				
2SLS	−.045	.383	.306	.385	.309	.197	.99	−1.86, 1.09	.03
GMM	−.034	.316	.268	.317	.270	.161	.96	−2.07, 1.42	.00
FF	−.034	.316	.323	.316	.325	.210	.95	−2.06, 2.03	.12
IW-GMM	−.041	.251	.264	.254	.267	.143	.96	−1.99, 2.17	.03
SSIV	−.043	.460	.351	.462	.353	.220	.97	−2.35, .99	.00
					72 moments				
2SLS	−.086	.117	.123	.145	.150	.121	.84	−2.96, 1.61	.45
GMM	−.120	.074	.093	.141	.151	.130	.57	−3.65, 1.08	.31
FF	−.115	.101	.105	.153	.156	.118	.73	−3.83, .84	.58
IW-GMM	−.141	.034	.188	.145	.235	.116	.24	−22.4, 2.95	.96
SSIV	−.081	.078	.082	.112	.115	.088	.81	−3.37, 1.12	.00
					162 moments				
2SLS	−.099	.061	.082	.116	.128	.099	.58	−4.99, .84	.45
GMM	−.108	.039	.049	.115	.119	.111	.25	−5.55, −.4	.71
FF	−.103	.051	.061	.115	.120	.111	.43	−4.91, .50	.84
IW-GMM	—	—	—	—	—	—	—	—	—
SSIV	−.127	.056	.054	.138	.138	.120	.33	−4.79, .29	.00
					212 moments				
2SLS	−.134	.051	.068	.143	.150	.142	.30	−5.39, .36	.93
GMM	−.131	.031	.040	.135	.137	.136	.03	−6.6, −1.83	.74
FF	−.125	.045	.049	.133	.134	.129	.23	−5.45, −.16	.96
IW-GMM	—	—	—	—	—	—	—	—	—
SSIV	−.144	.046	.035	.152	.149	.144	.08	−5.35, −1.33	.03

NOTE: See note to Table 3.

the base case of 9 moments is the dramatic improvement in boot-J rejection rates. This is exemplified by 2SLS in which the boot-J rejection rate falls from .29 to .03. The test still overrejects with the FF estimator but 70% fewer times than under the Freedman method. In addition, the Brown and Newey algorithm improves on the efficiency of the bootstrap estimates, especially for 2SLS, IW-GMM, and SSIV. In terms of bias, FF and GMM are identical, but GMM dominates 2SLS and FF in terms of lower MAE and RMSE-B. IW-GMM, however, performs best overall in the

Table 6. Bootstrap Comparisons of Orthogonal-Deviations Moment-Condition Estimators Where Observations Are Drawn With Probability $\hat{p}_i$

Estimators	Bias	SE-A	SE-B	RMSE-A	RMSE-B	MAE	95% asym-t coverage	95% boot-t critical values	Boot-J rejection rate: 5%
					9 moments				
2SLS	−.009	.396	.454	.396	.454	.319	.92	−2.11, 2.21	.10
GMM	−.044	.341	.338	.344	.341	.240	.96	−2.27, 1.68	.02
IW-GMM	−.081	.291	.390	.302	.399	.230	.86	−2.74, 2.45	.03
SSIV	.011	.438	.424	.438	.425	.254	.98	−1.94, 1.25	.00
					72 moments				
2SLS	−.101	.096	.112	.140	.151	.109	.76	−3.74, 1.46	.32
GMM	−.108	.071	.072	.129	.130	.109	.62	−3.72, .38	.20
IW-GMM	−.090	.032	.138	.095	.138	.089	.33	−9.86, 3.71	.77
SSIV	−.119	.098	.101	.155	.156	.142	.56	−4.16, 1.33	.03
					162 moments				
2SLS	−.130	.053	.068	.140	.147	.126	.41	−5.82, −.11	.32
GMM	−.122	.037	.042	.127	.129	.119	.13	−6.01, −.99	.75
IW-GMM	—	—	—	—	—	—	—	—	—
SSIV	−.142	.046	.041	.149	.147	.140	.12	−6.75, −.67	.00
					212 moments				
2SLS	−.138	.049	.058	.147	.149	.136	.30	−5.52, −.37	.94
GMM	−.136	.030	.037	.140	.141	.139	.05	−7.15, −1.56	.85
IW-GMM	—	—	—	—	—	—	—	—	—
SSIV	−.167	.048	.029	.174	.170	.171	.04	−6.38, −1.86	.03

NOTE: See note to Table 3.

base case in terms of lower RMSE and MAE. Because of the gains in efficiency and in levels of the boot-J test, the Brown and Newey method seems to be preferable to the Freedman method with few moments.

On the other hand, problems arise with the Brown and Newey algorithm, especially in the many-moment models. First, some of the bootstrap probabilities ($\hat{p}_i$), although summing to one overall, are negative. This problem increased with the number of moment conditions, ranging from a low of .5% of the observations with 9 moments in 2SLS and GMM to over 40% with IW-GMM with 212 moments. I considered several methods to deal with this, and the method I chose was to redistribute a fraction of the negative probabilities to each observation and then assign a small positive probability (1/100th of the smallest positive probability) to those observations with negative probabilities, making sure the probabilities sum to 1. The results are not sensitive to the method used. Second, because so much weight (i.e., a "high" probability) is given to a subset of the observations for the IW-GMM estimators with 162 and 212 moments, the estimators are singular. Recall that in sampling with replacement an observation can be drawn more than once, which can occur with greater probability under the Brown and Newey algorithm. This singularity problem persisted with every bootstrap sample over a four-day period and with different random sample splits of the original data as well. Consequently, I am unable to report on the IW-GMM estimator for these cases. Brown and Newey also reported difficulties due to a singularity problem in their empirical application.

With the exception of SSIV, the boot-J test overrejects in the stacked-moment cases just as in Tables 3 and 4. The distortion in levels, although less than the Freedman method, becomes more severe as additional moments are appended to the instrument set. It is important to note that both Hall and Horowitz, with their Monte Carlo, and Brown and Newey, with their empirical application, found that level distortions persist in the test even after recentering the distribution. In terms of bias, the estimators do not distinguish themselves as in the Freedman method, and each tends to center on the OLS estimate. However, 2SLS and FF continue to dominate GMM in terms of lower bias. Moreover, asym-t coverage is worse for each estimator, suggesting that boot-t critical values may improve on coverage over first-order asymptotics. The central conclusion from the previous bootstrap results remains the same though: namely, in comparing the estimators across all criteria, the FF estimator continues to be preferred in this application.

4. SUMMARY AND CONCLUSIONS

In this article I compared several IV estimators for panel-data models with predetermined instruments. The empirical results from the life-cycle labor-supply model, in conjunction with results from two separate bootstrap Monte Carlo experiments, are summarized as follows. First, and most important, the GMM estimator is biased downward relative to the 2SLS and FF estimators as the number of moment conditions approaches the optimal number of moments because of a correlation between the estimated weight matrix and the sample moments. This leads to poor coverage rates for confidence intervals based on asymptotic critical values but provides a clear role for the bootstrap-t confidence interval as a basis of inference under GMM. GMM performs reasonably well with suboptimal instruments but is not recommended for panel-data applications when all of the moments are exploited for estimation.

Second, the IW-GMM estimator is generally successful at eliminating the bias in GMM parameter estimates using Freedman's bootstrap algorithm; however, the standard errors from asymptotic theory seem to understate the true sampling variation and the overidentifying-restrictions test is biased toward rejection, possibly due to the high ratio of moments to cross-section sample size. Further research on both the asymptotic and small-sample properties of this estimator is needed. In the meantime, the bootstrap is likely to be useful in IW-GMM for the construction of both standard errors and confidence intervals. Third, the USSIV estimator tends to be highly unstable and inefficient, in contrast to the SSIV estimator which works fairly well in models with few overidentifying restrictions.

Fourth, caution is warranted when conducting inference under the assumption of conditional homoscedasticity. On several occasions, incorrectly assuming homoscedasticity led to the rejection of the overidentifying restrictions and to the conclusion of weakly correlated instruments. When heteroscedasticity is present, one should use robust variants of the test of overidentifying restrictions and the Wald test for first-stage tests of correlation between instruments and regressors. In addition, after adjusting for conditional heteroscedasticity, there is no obvious efficiency gain of using orthogonal deviations rather than first-differences.

Fifth, further research is needed on improving methods of bootstrapping estimators from overidentified models. The levels distortion in the overidentifying-restrictions test persisted in models with many moments, even after recentering the distribution using Brown and Newey's (1995) algorithm. Moreover, complications arose in the implementation of their algorithm, notably negative probabilities and singularity problems. Hence, if the model has numerous moment restrictions and the focus is solely on the estimator and consistent confidence intervals and not on the overidentifying-restrictions test, then Freedman's (1984) method of giving equal weight to each observation is recommended.

Finally, although 2SLS is still a reliable method of estimation, the FF estimator performs best in terms of the bias/efficiency trade-off. It offers more efficient estimation than 2SLS but does not have the problem of excess bias found in GMM parameter estimates. Consequently, the FF estimator is attractive relative to the other estimators considered here.

ACKNOWLEDGMENTS

I thank the editor, an associate editor, and an anonymous referee for many helpful comments that have improved this article substantially. I also have benefited from discussions with George Evans, Tom Kniesner, Larry Singell, and Wes

Wilson. Most especially, I am indebted to Carlos Martins-Filho and Mark Thoma for their insightful advice. I alone am responsible for any remaining errors.

[Received December 1994. Revised July 1996.]

REFERENCES

Ahn, S. C., and Schmidt, P. (1995), "Efficient Estimation of Models for Dynamic Panel Data," *Journal of Econometrics*, 68, 5–27.

Altonji, J. G. (1986), "Intertemporal Substitution in Labor Supply: Evidence From Micro Data," *Journal of Political Economy*, 94, S176–S215.

Altonji, J. G., and Segal, L. M. (1994), "Small Sample Bias in GMM Estimation of Covariance Structures," Technical Working Paper 156, National Bureau of Economic Research, Cambridge, MA.

Anderson, T. W., and Hsiao, C. (1982), "Formulation and Estimation of Dynamic Models Using Panel Data," *Journal of Econometrics*, 18, 47–82.

Angrist, J. D., and Krueger, A. B. (1991), "Does Compulsory School Attendance Affect Schooling and Earnings?" *The Quarterly Journal of Economics*, 106, 979–1014.

——— (1995), "Split-Sample Instrumental Variables Estimates of the Return to Schooling," *Journal of Business & Economic Statistics*, 13, 225–235.

Arellano, M., and Bond, S. R. (1991), "Some Tests of Specification for Panel Data: Monte Carlo Evidence and an Application to Employment Equations," *Review of Economic Studies*, 58, 277–297.

Arellano, M., and Bover, O. (1995), "Another Look at the Instrumental Variable Estimation of Error-Components Models," *Journal of Econometrics*, 68, 29–51.

Bekker, P. A. (1994), "Alternative Approximations to the Distributions of Instrumental Variables Estimators," *Econometrica*, 62, 657–682.

Borjas, G. J. (1981), "The Relationship Between Wages and Weekly Hours of Work: The Role of Division Bias," *Journal of Human Resources*, 15, 409–423.

Bound, J., Jaeger, D. A., and Baker, R. M. (1995), "Problems With Instrumental Variables Estimation When the Correlation Between the Instruments and the Endogenous Explanatory Variable Is Weak," *Journal of the American Statistical Association*, 90, 443–450.

Brown, B. W., and Newey, W. K. (1995), "Bootstrapping for GMM," unpublished manuscript, Rice University, Dept. of Economics.

Chamberlain, G. (1987), "Asymptotic Efficiency in Estimation With Conditional Moment Restrictions," *Journal of Econometrics*, 34, 305–334.

Efron, B. (1979), "Bootstrap Methods: Another Look at the Jackknife," *The Annals of Statistics*, 7, 1–26.

Efron, B., and Tibshirani, R. J. (1993), *An Introduction to the Bootstrap*, New York: Chapman & Hall.

Freedman, D. A. (1984), "On Bootstrapping Two-Stage Least-Squares Estimates in Stationary Linear Models," *The Annals of Statistics*, 12, 827–842.

Freedman, D. A., and Peters, S. C. (1984), "Bootstrapping an Econometric Model: Some Empirical Results," *Journal of Business & Economic Statistics*, 2, 150–158.

Godfrey, L. G. (1988), *Misspecification Tests in Econometrics*, Cambridge, U.K.: Cambridge University Press.

Hahn, J. (in press), "A Note on Bootstrapping Generalized Method-of-Moments Estimators," *Econometric Theory*, 12.

Hall, P. (1986), "On the Bootstrap and Confidence Intervals," *The Annals of Statistics*, 14, 1431–1452.

Hall, P., and Horowitz, J. L. (in press), "Bootstrap Critical Values for Tests Based on Generalized Method-of-Moments Estimators," *Econometrica*, 65.

Hansen, L. P. (1982), "Large Sample Properties of Generalized Method-of-Moments Estimators," *Econometrica*, 50, 1029–1054.

Hansen, L. P., and Singleton, K. J. (1982), "Generalized Instrumental Variables Estimation of Nonlinear Rational Expectations Models," *Econometrica*, 50, 1269–1286.

Hausman, J. A., and Taylor, W. E. (1981), "Panel Data and Unobservable Individual Effects," *Econometrica*, 49, 1377–1398.

Hayashi, F. (1992), Comment on "On the Estimation of Panel-Data Models With Serial Correlation When Instruments Are Not Strictly Exogenous," by M. Keane and D. Runkle, *Journal of Business & Economic Statistics*, 10, 15–17.

Jeong, J., and Maddala, G. S. (1993), "A Perspective on Application of Bootstrap Methods in Econometrics," in *Handbook of Statistics: Econometrics* (Vol. 11), eds. G. S. Maddala, C. R. Rao, and H. D. Vinod, Amsterdam: North-Holland, pp. 573–610.

Keane, M., and Runkle, D. (1992), "On the Estimation of Panel-Data Models With Serial Correlation When Instruments Are Not Strictly Exogenous," *Journal of Business & Economic Statistics*, 10, 1–9.

MaCurdy, T. E. (1985), "Interpreting Empirical Models of Labor Supply in an Intertemporal Framework With Uncertainty," in *Longitudinal Analysis of Economic Data*, eds. J. Heckman and B. Singer, Cambridge, U.K.: Cambridge University Press, pp. 111–155.

Maeshiro, A., and Vali, S. (1988), "Pitfalls in the Estimation of a Differenced Model," *Journal of Business & Economic Statistics*, 6, 511–515.

Nelson, C., and Startz, R. (1990), "The Distribution of the Instrumental Variables Estimator and its *t*-ratio When the Instrument Is a Poor One," *Journal of Business*, 63, S125–S140.

Pencavel, J. (1986), "Labor Supply of Men," in *Handbook of Labor Economics* (Vol. 1), eds. O. Ashenfelter and R. Layard, Amsterdam: North-Holland, pp. 3–102.

Schmidt, P., Ahn, S., and Wyhowski, D. (1992), Comment on "On the Estimation of Panel-Data Models With Serial Correlation When Instruments Are Not Strictly Exogenous," by M. Keane and D. Runkle, *Journal of Business & Economic Statistics*, 10, 10–14.

Staiger, D., and Stock, J. H. (1994), "Instrumental Variables Regression With Weak Instruments," Technical Working Paper 151, National Bureau of Economic Research, Cambridge, MA.

Tauchen, G. (1986), "Statistical Properties of Generalized Method-of-Moments Estimators of Structural Parameters Obtained From Financial Market Data," *Journal of Business & Economic Statistics*, 4, 397–416.

White, H. (1982), "Instrumental Variables Regression With Independent Observations," *Econometrica*, 50, 483–500.

Part II
Heterogeneous Panels

[11]

ELSEVIER Journal of Econometrics 77 (1997) 303–327

JOURNAL OF Econometrics

Pooled estimators vs. their heterogeneous counterparts in the context of dynamic demand for gasoline

Badi H. Baltagi*, James M. Griffin

Department of Economics, Texas A&M University, College Station, TX 77843-4228, USA

(Received December 1994; final version received January 1996)

Abstract

This paper utilizes an international panel data set and a dynamic demand specification for gasoline to compare the performance of homogeneous and heterogeneous parameter estimators. In addition to comparing the plausibility of the various estimates, a forecast performance comparison is performed to examine differences in predictions over one-, five-, and ten-year horizons.

Key words: Panel data; Gasoline demand; Error components; Shrinkage estimators
JEL classification: C23

1. Introduction

Applied researchers face a wide choice of theoretically acceptable estimators when confronted with a panel data set and a dynamic demand model. Examples include the pioneering study of Balestra and Nerlove (1966), the more recent work by Anderson and Hsiao (1982), Ahn and Schmidt (1995), and Arellano and Bover (1995) to mention a few. Typically, the theoretical literature mitigates against some standard estimators on the basis of inconsistency or inefficiency of the estimates. For example, in the popular one-way error component model, the standard GLS estimator is often not recommended in a dynamic model because it yields biased and inconsistent estimators. Nevertheless, the standard GLS estimator as well as the within estimator are frequently applied.

* Corresponding author.

The authors wish to thank Weiwen Xiong for exceptional research assistance and two anonymous referees for their helpful comments.

PII S0304-4076(96)01802-7

Even amongst pooled instrumental variable estimators, choices abound. These options include the standard 2SLS pooled model, a 2SLS fixed effects model, a first-differenced 2SLS model, or 2SLS with a general variance–covariance matrix that allows for a general form of serial correlation (see, e.g., Keane and Runkle, 1992). Depending on the types of unobservable time and country effects, the choice of instruments, and the presence of serial correlation, each pooled estimator has certain strengths and weaknesses.

More recently, the fundamental assumption underlying pooled models – homogeneous parameters – has been called into question and alternative estimators proposed.[1] Maddala et al. (1994) propose a Shrinkage estimator based on the individual country estimates shrunk towards the pooled model estimates. Alternatively, Pesaran and Smith (1995) advocate abandoning the pooled approach altogether because of inherent parameter heterogeneity and relying upon average responses from individual country regressions. Despite the proliferation of these heterogeneous estimators, relatively little is known about their performance in applied work. Furthermore, if heterogeneous parameter models outperform the more traditional pooled estimators, which posit homogeneous parameters, much of recent work on pooling is called into question.

Our objective here is to compare the performance of both these homogeneous and heterogeneous estimators applying them to a common data set (pooled OECD data), a well-researched product (gasoline consumption), and the routinely applied dynamic demand specification. By selecting a generic data set and specification, we hope to provide insights into how these estimators perform for a general class of empirical studies. Building on our earlier gasoline demand study (Baltagi and Griffin, 1983), we utilize a panel data set for 18 OECD countries with annual observations for the period 1960–1990. Since gasoline demand has been studied extensively,[2] strong priors exist as to the plausibility of price and income effects, providing a useful plausibility check to the results of this study.

In comparing pooled homogeneous estimators and their heterogeneous rivals, we examine the suitability of these estimators by three different metrics. First, in Section 2 we describe each estimator, noting the types of situations in which on a priori grounds one would expect the estimator to fare either well or poorly. Next, in Section 3, we compare the plausibility of alternative estimates of the price and income elasticities as well as the speed of the adjustment path to long-run equilibrium. We find considerable variability in the parameter

[1] See, for example, Robertson and Symons (1992) who warned about the bias obtained from panel data methods when the estimated model is dynamic and homogeneous, when in fact the true model is static and heterogeneous.

[2] To name just a few, see Houthakker, Verleger, and Sheehan (1974), Sweeney (1978), Griffin (1979), Bohi and Zimmerman (1984), and more recently Dahl and Sterner (1991).

estimates even amongst the homogeneous pooled estimators. Some estimators can be ruled out as providing implausible results. Third, we compare the forecast performance of these alternative approaches using the model to provide 10-year forecasts of gasoline consumption. Section 4 summarizes the results of forecast experiments paying particular attention to the ability of the model to capture long-run price and income responses. These results show surprising variability in the forecast performance of various estimators. Section 5 recapitulates the major conclusions.

2. Description of the model and estimators

2.1. Model specification

For comparison purposes, we adopt the familiar flow adjustment model (Houthakker and Taylor, 1970), which has been applied extensively for gasoline consumption (see the recent survey by Dahl and Sterner, 1991). In such models, the stock of energy-using equipment is assumed to be fixed in the short run, and its utilization is assumed to be a function of normal economic influences. Over time, observed utilization is adopted to desired utilization through the familiar flow adjustment mechanism. Specifically, desired gasoline consumption per auto $(GAS/CAR)^*$ is posited to be a log-linear function of the real price of gasoline (P_{MG}/P_{GDP}), real income per capita (Y/N), and cars per capita[3] (CAR/N):

$$\left(\frac{GAS}{CAR}\right)^* = \alpha\left(\frac{P_{MG}}{P_{GDP}}\right)^{\beta}\left(\frac{Y}{N}\right)^{\gamma}\left(\frac{CAR}{N}\right)^{\delta}. \tag{1}$$

Adjustment to desired consumption per auto is assumed to follow the simple process:

$$\left(\frac{GAS}{CAR}\right)_t \Big/ \left(\frac{GAS}{CAR}\right)_{t-1} = \left(\left(\frac{GAS}{CAR}\right)^*_t \Big/ \left(\frac{GAS}{CAR}\right)_{t-1}\right)^{\theta}. \tag{2}$$

Adding the country and time subscripts, the resulting standard dynamic demand equation is

$$\begin{aligned}\ln\left(\frac{GAS}{CAR}\right)_{it} &= \theta\ln\alpha + \theta\beta\ln\left(\frac{P_{MG}}{P_{GDP}}\right)_{it} + \theta\gamma\ln\left(\frac{Y}{N}\right)_{it}\\ &\quad + \theta\delta\ln\left(\frac{CAR}{N}\right)_{it} + (1-\theta)\ln\left(\frac{GAS}{CAR}\right)_{it-1} + u_{it}.\end{aligned} \tag{3}$$

[3] This stock of (CAR/N) is included to capture the likely effect of reduced auto utilization, say, by a two-car family which does not necessarily drive twice the miles of a one-car family.

Although, the simple flow adjustment model has been applied extensively to gasoline consumption, it may be overly restrictive in that the lagged effects of price, income, and cars per capita are assumed a priori to have identical lags. For example, Baltagi and Griffin (1983) find that price effects work through the vintage of automobiles and thus have long lags whereas income and cars per capita work primarily through the short-run utilization of the auto fleet. Accordingly, we generalize Eq. (3) to allow for differential lag structures by adding lagged variables for cars per capita and income as follows:

$$\begin{aligned}\ln\left(\frac{GAS}{CAR}\right)_{it} &= \theta\ln\alpha + \theta\beta\ln\left(\frac{P_{\text{MG}}}{P_{\text{GDP}}}\right)_{it} + \theta\gamma\ln\left(\frac{Y}{N}\right)_{it} + \theta\gamma^*\ln\left(\frac{Y}{N}\right)_{i,t-1} \\ &+ \theta\delta\ln\left(\frac{CAR}{N}\right)_{it} + \theta\delta^*\ln\left(\frac{CAR}{N}\right)_{i,t-1} \\ &+ (1-\theta)\ln\left(\frac{GAS}{CAR}\right)_{i,t-1} + u_{it}. \qquad (4)\end{aligned}$$

Under this formulation, the short- and long-run income and cars per capita responses are identical when $\gamma^* = -\gamma(1-\theta)$ and $\delta^* = -\delta(1-\theta)$.

The data set consists of a panel of 18 OECD countries covering the period 1960–1990. This extends our earlier period of observation by 12 years from 1979 to 1990. This is a rich data set that incorporates wide variation in relative gasoline prices, per capita incomes, and cars per capita in both the cross-section as well as the time-series dimensions.[4]

The disturbances are assumed to follow a one-way error component model,

$$u_{it} = \mu_i + \nu_{it}, \qquad i = 1, 2, \ldots, N, \qquad t = 1, 2, \ldots, T, \qquad (5)$$

where μ_i denotes a country-specific effect which could be either fixed or random. In the latter case, μ_i is $\text{IID}(0, \sigma_\mu^2)$ and ν_{it} is the remainder disturbances which is $\text{IID}(0, \sigma_\nu^2)$ with μ_i independent of ν_{it}.

2.2. Standard pooled estimators

First, we consider the five standard pooled estimators, assuming the exogeneity of all the regressors. These include (i) OLS which ignores the country effects, (ii) Within estimator which allows for fixed country effects, (iii) first-difference estimator which wipes out any country specific effects, (iv) GLS which assumes that the country effects are random, and (v) GLS-AR(1) which in addition to allowing the country effects to be random assumes that the remainder disturbances follow an AR(1) process. Since our model is dynamic, even if all the

[4] For a more detailed description of the data, see the Appendix in Baltagi and Griffin (1983).

explanatory variables are uncorrelated with the error components, the presence of serial correlation in the remainder error term or the presence of a random country effect renders the lagged dependent variable correlated with the error term and leads to inconsistent least squares estimates. Even the Within estimator, which eliminates the country-specific effects, is biased unless T tends to infinity (see Nickell, 1981; and more recently, Kiviet, 1995).[5]

2.3. Instrumental variables pooled estimators

Next, we also focus on pooled estimators employing two-stage least squares (2SLS) using as instruments the exogenous variables and their lagged values. In particular, we examine five alternative 2SLS pooled estimators. First, we consider a standard 2SLS estimator, making no attempt to improve efficiency by taking into account the random country effects. The 2SLS estimator is consistent but not efficient. Second, the Within 2SLS estimator, which transforms the data about country means and thereby eliminates any country fixed effects, is reported.[6] Because the Within 2SLS estimator eliminates the fixed country effects, it avoids altogether the potential bias arising if a country-specific effect is correlated with one of the exogenous variables. The third estimator is the first-difference 2SLS model proposed by Anderson and Hsiao (1982). By first-differencing each country's time series, the fixed or random country effects in (5) are eliminated. However, first-differencing introduces autocorrelation in the remainder error term ($v_{it} - v_{i,t-1}$), and thus inefficiency problems. Nevertheless, consistency is preserved by the use of exogenous variables as instruments for this first-differenced equation.[7]

Fourth, we apply a two-stage least squares procedure that assumes a one-way error component model, i.e., (EC2SLS); see Baltagi (1981). This method transforms the error by $\hat{\Omega}^{-1/2}$, where $\hat{\Omega}$ is a consistent estimator of the variance–covariance matrix of the disturbances and then applies 2SLS using between and within variations in the exogenous variables and their lagged values as instruments. Fifth, to allow for the possibility of an AR(1) process on the remainder disturbances (v_{it} in Eq. (5)) and still preserve the one-way error component structure on the disturbances, we report an error component AR(1) model using 2SLS (EC-AR(1) 2SLS). See Baltagi and Li (1991) for the

[5] Kiviet (1995) showed that the Within estimator in a dynamic panel data model has an $O(N^{-1}T^{-3/2})$ approximation error.

[6] A test for the significance of country fixed effects yielded an F-value of 31.68. This is distributed as $F(17,498)$ under the null and is significant at the 5% level.

[7] More instrumental variables can be obtained if the v_{it}'s are not serially correlated by using predetermined instruments that are not correlated with the error term; see Arellano and Bover (1995) or Ahn and Schmidt (1995).

corresponding $\Omega^{-1/2}$ transformation in this context. Compared to the EC2SLS estimator, EC-AR(1) 2SLS is potentially more efficient since it allows for first-order serial correlation.[8]

A priori, the error component estimators (EC2SLS and EC-AR(1) 2SLS) would be expected to outperform the other pooled estimators on efficiency grounds since, unlike the Within 2SLS and first-difference 2SLS (FD2SLS) estimators, intercountry variation is not omitted altogether. On the other hand EC2SLS and EC-AR(1) 2SLS may be preferred to 2SLS because the latter typically places too great an importance on the between country variation. The only caveat to these a priori expectations arises if the random country effects are correlated with the regressors.[9]

2.4. Heterogeneous estimators

Implicitly, all the pooled estimators assume homogeneity of the parameters across countries enabling the poolability of the model across these countries. Nevertheless, even though formal tests for homogeneity are rejected as is the case here,[10] like most researchers we proceed to estimate pooled models. Recently, Pesaran and Smith (1995) argued that the dynamic pooled model could be biased because of heterogeneity in the parameters across each country. They argued that an average of the individual country regressions can lead to consistent estimates of the parameters as long as N and T tend to infinity. We therefore computed individual country regressions and the Pesaran and Smith average estimates to compare homogeneous as well as heterogeneous estimates of the regression coefficients.[11] Using a quite different approach, Maddala,

[8] Keane and Runkle (1992) suggested a modification of 2SLS that allows a general serially correlated error structure on the disturbances that is the same for all countries. This procedure requires $N > T$. Since $T > N$ in our case, we applied a variant of this method that allows for a general correlation structure across countries that is stable over time. This estimation procedure gave essentially the same results as the corresponding 2SLS, but with more robust standard errors.

[9] A Hausman-type test for the exogeneity of the regressors based on the difference between FD2SLS and Within 2SLS yields a χ^2-value of 9.63. This is distributed as χ^2_6 under the null and is insignificant at the 5% level. Another Hausman-type test for the significance of individual country effects is based on the difference between FD2SLS and 2SLS. This yields a χ^2-value of 15.97. This is distributed as χ^2_6 under the null and is significant at the 5% level.

[10] A Chow test for the equality of slope coefficients across countries yields an F-value of 10.99. The numerator of this F-statistic is based on the second-stage regression of 2SLS allowing for varying intercepts and common slopes under its restricted version, and varying intercepts and slopes under its unrestricted version. The denominator of this F-statistic is based on the unrestricted 2SLS residuals sums of squares; see Wooldridge (1990). Under the null hypothesis, this is distributed as $F(102,396)$. The null is rejected at the 5% level.

[11] The Wu–Hausman test was performed on the individual country regressions. None rejected the null hypothesis of exogeneity of the regressors at the 5% level.

Srivastava, and Li (1994) argue that Shrinkage estimators are superior to either the individual country (heterogeneous) estimates or the pooled (homogeneous) estimates especially for prediction purposes. In this case, one shrinks the individual estimates towards the pooled estimate using weights depending on their corresponding variance–covariance matrices. Thus, depending on the extent of intercountry heterogeneity in parameters, researchers may prefer either individual country regressions, or the Pesaran and Smith average, or the shrinkage estimates to the traditional pooled, homogeneous parameter estimates.

3. Comparison of parameter estimates

One obvious basis for comparison among estimators is differences in the plausibility of the parameter estimates vis-a-vis the existing literature. Both a priori experience as well as a voluminous set of gasoline demand studies provide evidence as to a range of plausible income, price, and cars per capita elasticities. Our specification focuses on gasoline consumption per car, so that gasoline consumption is affected both by the utilization as well as the efficiency of automobiles. Utilization is essentially a short-run decision, while the fuel efficiency of autos occurs, very roughly, over a 10-year period as the auto fleet is turned over. In the short run, the fuel efficiency is fixed and consumers vary their utilization of the auto fleet in response to current prices, income, and cars per capita. But over time the fuel efficiency of the auto fleet is modified in response to these variables, and the coefficient on the lagged dependent variable should reflect long lags corresponding to the turnover of the auto fleet over an approximate 10- to 12-year period.

Most econometric estimates show that the short-run price and income elasticities tend to be very inelastic, but with much greater long-run responsiveness. For example, in the Dahl and Sterner (1991) survey, the long-run response is 3.3 times the short-run response. According to Dahl and Sterner, for the price elasticity, the average of various studies places the short-run price elasticity at -0.26 and the long-run at -0.86. Bohi and Zimmerman's (1984) survey finds corresponding estimates of -0.26 and -0.70.

Estimates of income elasticities differ depending on whether the stock of autos is introduced explicitly, being lower in the latter case, because income augments the auto stock. Models explicitly introducing the vehicle stock show average long-run elasticities in the 0.6 to 0.87 range, whereas specifications omitting the vehicle stock estimate the income elasticity in the 1.3 range.

Specifications that allow for nonconstant returns to increases in the auto stock place the long-run vehicle stock elasticity in the $+0.5$ range (Dahl and Sterner, 1991, Table 1). Since in Eq. (1), the stock of cars enters as both a dependent and independent variable, the transformed elasticity is $\delta + 1$, which based on previous estimates is 0.5. Therefore, we would expect $\delta = -0.5$.

Table 1 summarizes both the homogeneous and the heterogeneous elasticity estimates utilizing the various estimators set forth in Section 2. The actual estimates and their standard errors are given in the Appendix. To summarize the individual country OLS and 2SLS estimates, Table 1 shows the maximum, minimum, and median estimates for the price, income, and cars per capita elasticities. These estimates reveal the wide variability of individual country estimates. For example, individual country OLS estimates of the long-run price elasticity range from -23.15 to $+0.05$. Likewise, the long-run income elasticity estimates range from -42.84 to 1.24, while the long-run elasticity estimates of cars per capita range from -1.69 to $+18.70$. Even though the individual country 2SLS estimates appear to exhibit somewhat less variability, the range is still wide. Such variation is particularly distressing when it is recognized that all 18 countries are OECD countries and should share considerable commonalities. Furthermore, for each country there are 31 years of data.

Pesaran and Smith's suggestion of using a simple average of the individual country estimates to obtain long-run elasticity estimates, implies that the long-run 2SLS elasticities are -0.43 for price, -0.21 for income, and -0.32 for cars per capita, while the corresponding average OLS elasticities are, respectively, -0.46, -0.21 and -0.32. This approach would appear to considerably understate the long-run price and income elasticities.

The shrinkage estimator suggested by Maddala et al. (1994) substantially reduces the wide dispersion of estimates found in the individual countries, demonstrating that the effect of pulling individual estimates towards a common mean profoundly affects the estimates. Even using the 2SLS Shrinkage estimates, individual country long-run price elasticities range from -1.30 to 0.05, with a median estimate of -0.57. The long-run income elasticities show less cohesiveness, ranging from -4.43 to $+1.22$. Considerable variation in estimates of the cars per capita coefficient is also apparent.

Turning to the pooled estimators, which posit homogeneous parameters across countries, we note that the short-run price elasticity estimates are all quite similar, yet the long-run price elasticity estimates vary widely from -0.24 to -1.42. Clearly, the estimators differ in their ability to characterize the long-run adjustment process. For example, the coefficient $(1-\theta)$ in Eq. (4) is 0.95 for OLS, while for FD it implies instantaneous adjustment (0.04). Generally, the 2SLS pooled estimates of $1-\theta$ are much lower than those models treating the lagged dependent variable as predetermined. The standard interpretation of such results is that the 2SLS estimators avoid biasing $1-\theta$ toward one. But the comparison of the standard Within versus the Within 2SLS estimators shows a considerable difference (0.87 vs. 0.55), not necessarily attributable to substantial bias. Indeed, except for the FD and FD2SLS, the standard pooled estimators imply substantially larger long-run price elasticities than their 2SLS counterpart. One intriguing alternative explanation is that the use of lagged values of the regressors as 2SLS instruments results in a poor estimation

Table 1
Comparison of elasticity estimates: Heterogeneous vs. homogeneous models estimates

	Short run			Long run		
	Price	Income	*CAR/N*	Price	Income	*CAR/N*
Heterogeneous parameter models						
Individual countries OLS						
Maximum	0.03	0.83	0.37	0.05	1.24	18.70
	(0.41)	(2.50)	(0.64)	(0.43)	(8.18)	(0.18)
Median	−0.15	0.05	−0.84	−0.71	−0.43	−0.16
	(2.01)	(0.17)	(6.73)	(3.02)	(1.12)	(0.46)
Minimum	−0.37	−0.65	−1.69	−23.15	−42.84	−1.69
	(4.76)	(1.47)	(3.21)	(0.18)	(0.18)	(1.02)
Average	−0.18	0.16	−0.67	−0.46	−0.21	−0.32
	(11.66)	(1.87)	(8.28)	(9.19)	(1.44)	(4.50)
Shrinkage OLS						
Maximum	0.01	0.48	0.14	0.01	1.22	7.05
	(0.10)	(3.86)	(0.44)	(0.10)	(0.09)	(0.39)
Median	−0.15	0.17	−0.63	−0.68	−0.47	−0.33
	(7.01)	(0.77)	(3.87)	(1.82)	(2.55)	(2.00)
Minimum	−0.30	−0.38	−1.46	−9.88	−16.96	−1.54
	(5.25)	(1.53)	(4.94)	(0.42)	(0.41)	(1.50)
Individual countries 2SLS						
Maximum	0.00	0.80	0.35	0.01	1.25	2.31
	(0.04)	(2.04)	(0.58)	(0.04)	(10.34)	(0.98)
Median	−0.17	−0.22	−0.53	−0.40	−0.52	−0.28
	(1.92)	(0.80)	(1.28)	(2.00)	(0.40)	(1.63)
Minimum	−0.38	−0.70	−2.47	−1.28	−4.91	−0.90
	(2.79)	(1.47)	(3.41)	(1.16)	(1.08)	(0.66)
Average	−0.19	0.10	−0.69	−0.43	−0.21	−0.32
	(10.66)	(1.12)	(7.43)	(6.58)	(0.03)	(3.97)
Shrinkage 2SLS						
Maximum	−0.29	0.73	0.07	0.05	1.22	2.02
	(3.88)	(3.85)	(5.87)	(0.31)	(7.53)	(1.04)
Median	−0.15	0.32	−0.76	−0.57	−0.50	−0.30
	(3.56)	(1.71)	(0.22)	(3.32)	(3.33)	(1.53)
Minimum	−0.12	−0.35	−1.97	−1.30	−4.43	−0.85
	(0.33)	(1.39)	(5.46)	(1.32)	(1.19)	(1.26)

Table 1 (continued)

	Short run			Long run		
	Price	Income	*CAR/N*	Price	Income	*CAR/N*
Homogeneous models						
Exogenous regressors						
OLS	−0.07	0.55	−0.66	−1.42	−0.46	−0.38
	(7.38)	(6.88)	(15.7)	(8.9)	(1.8)	(2.7)
Within	−0.11	0.39	−0.74	−0.86	−0.35	−0.51
	(9.52)	(5.00)	(15.4)	(7.6)	(2.1)	(8.0)
FD	−0.23	0.33	−0.83	−0.24	0.27	−0.54
	(13.07)	(4.79)	(21.0)	(11.6)	(3.1)	(18.7)
GLS	−0.08	0.53	−0.67	−1.42	−0.43	−0.42
	(8.00)	(6.64)	(15.6)	(8.8)	(1.7)	(4.1)
GLS-AR(1)	−0.09	0.50	−0.68	−1.39	−0.42	−0.45
	(8.56)	(6.38)	(15.5)	(8.4)	(1.7)	(4.7)
Endogenous regressors						
2SLS	−0.29	0.36	−0.91	−0.96	0.33	−0.63
	(7.34)	(2.46)	(10.74)	(2.40)	(4.8)	(2.16)
Within 2SLS	−0.20	0.19	−0.65	−0.44	0.11	−0.53
	(8.88)	(1.70)	(9.92)	(11.02)	(1.83)	(2.25)
FD2SLS	−0.23	0.31	−0.86	−0.30	0.18	−0.53
	(12.92)	(4.22)	(20.29)	(7.5)	(1.55)	(11.8)
EC2SLS	−0.17	0.26	−0.68	−0.50	0.07	−0.53
	(9.51)	(2.70)	(12.05)	(12.5)	(0.2)	(2.3)
EC-AR(1) 2SLS	−0.20	0.20	−0.92	−0.56	−0.21	−0.54
	(11.20)	(2.62)	(19.94)	(6.8)	(1.81)	(10.8)

Numbers in parentheses denote t-statistics.

of lagged gasoline consumption per car and thus coefficients of $1-\theta$ closer to zero.

The 2SLS estimator implies a long-run price elasticity of -0.96, whereas the remaining 2SLS estimates are in a -0.3 to -0.56 range. Differences of this magnitude provide sharply conflicting views of how price impacts gasoline consumption. If price primarily affects the utilization rate of existing autos and to a lesser extent the fleet efficiency, then the dynamics implied by the Within 2SLS, EC2SLS, and EC-AR(1) 2SLS estimates seem appropriate. In contrast, if short-term utilization effects are minor compared to the effects of modifying the fleet efficiency of autos and the road infrastructure, then the between country variation emphasized in the 2SLS estimates is better suited for explaining this phenomena. Baltagi and Griffin (1983) emphasize that pooled estimators dependent primarily on within country variation are not likely to capture these very long-run effects, whereas estimators relying on between variation provide much higher elasticities. Compared to other studies, the short-run price elasticity estimates are in virtual agreement, whereas the long-run 2SLS price elasticity estimate of -0.96 falls close to the average of -1.05. Likewise, some of the standard pooled estimators, ignoring possible endogeneity of the regressors, imply potentially even more elastic responses (e.g., GLS (-1.42), GLS-AR(1) (-1.39), and OLS (-1.42)).

The income elasticities implied by the various pooled estimators are generally positive and statistically significant in the short run, but frequently insignificant in the long run, suggesting that income effects primarily impact short-term utilization. Most studies indicate much higher long-run income elasticities but the stock of cars is frequently absent from such a regression.

The estimates of both the short-run and long-run elasticities with respect to cars per capita are surprisingly robust and stable, ranging in the short-run from -0.65 to -0.92. Indeed, the long-run estimates are almost identical and conform closely to other estimates. These estimates confirm that increased penetration of cars results in diminished auto utilization so that gasoline consumption per auto declines. For example, a -0.53 elasticity would suggest quite plausibly that when a family purchases a second auto, total gasoline consumption increases by 47%, not 100%.

In summary, the heterogeneous estimators (the individual 2SLS, the Pesaran and Smith average, and the Maddala et al. (1994) Shrinkage estimator) have the desirable property of allowing for differences among countries, but the range of individual 2SLS estimates suggests that the individual country estimates are highly unstable and unreliable. The Pesaran and Smith suggestion of using a simple average of these estimates is not entirely satisfactory given the likelihood of substantially understated income and price elasticities. Compared to individual country 2SLS estimates, the Shrinkage estimator seems to provide a smaller, more plausible range of estimates. In contrast, the pooled estimators, which implicitly posit homogeneous coefficients, appear to provide on balance much more plausible estimates. There are appreciable differences among these estimators about the implied path of dynamic adjustment. The first-difference (FD and FD2SLS) estimators imply rapid adjustment to the long run and can be ruled out. Not surprisingly, as a group, the standard pooled estimators yield substantially larger long-run elasticities than their 2SLS counterparts. While bias may account for part of this, we suspect that low estimates of $1 - \theta$ may simply be due to poor instruments. Also, it should be noted that the 2SLS estimator, which places more weight on the between country variation, implies a longer adjustment period and a larger more plausible long-run price elasticity than the other 2SLS estimators.

4. Forecast properties

An important and frequently underutilized criteria is the forecast properties of alternative estimators. Given the large data set of 18 countries for 31 years, it is natural to estimate the above models for truncated data sets and then apply each model to an out-of-sample forecast period. Since the models imply very different long-run elasticities, it seems particularly useful to contrast their forecast performance over a relatively long period.

Table 2 gives a comparison of various predictors obtained by estimating the model without the last 10 years of data and then applying these models to forecast gasoline consumption over these 10 years. The root mean square error (RMSE) are calculated for the resulting predictions. A total of 17 predictors are ranked according to RMSE performance.

Since at issue is the ability of an estimator to characterize long-run as well as short-run responses, the average root mean square error is calculated across the 18 countries at different forecast horizons. Specifically, each model was applied to each OECD country and out-of-sample forecasts for 10 years were calculated. The relative forecast rankings are reported in Table 2 after 1 year, after 5 years, and after 10 years.[12] The overall average ranking for the full 10-year period is also reported. To provide some relative comparison basis, we also include a naive model that sequentially forecasted 'no change' in a country's gasoline consumption per car. Fortunately, all of the models, both homogeneous and heterogeneous, outperform the 'no change' model for the first- and fifth-year forecasts and all but one (individual 2SLS) outperforms the 'no change' model for the 10-year average.

In comparing the relative performance of the various estimators, one can analyze these results from the following three perspectives: heterogeneous versus homogeneous, 2SLS versus an assumed exogenous lagged dependent variable, and one-year-ahead forecasts versus long-run forecasts. We begin by comparing the 2SLS estimators versus their conventional counterparts and conclude that there is a clear tendency for the 2SLS estimators to deteriorate relatively more the longer the forecast horizon. Note that for one-year-ahead forecasts, 6 of the top 8 estimators utilized 2SLS. However, for the 10th-year forecast, only two estimators using 2SLS corrections appear in the top 8. For the 10-year average, only one 2SLS correction (FD2SLS) appears in the top 8, and it ranks 6 with a RMSE of 11.775 compared to the top performer, GLS-AR(1), with a RMSE of 9.088. Our explanation for the relatively poor performance of the 2SLS type estimators in capturing long-run dynamics is the quality of the instruments. Current and lagged values of the exogenous variables produce instruments

[12] These predictions were intercept adjusted for each country. Additionally, all estimators have zero forecast errors for 1980.

Table 2
Comparison of forecast performance (RMSE × 10^2)

	1st year		5th year		10th year		10-year average	
Ranking	Estimator	RMSE	Estimator	RMSE	Estimator	RMSE	Estimator	RMSE
1.	Average 2SLS	2.889	Within	8.490	GLS-AR(1)	15.378	GLS-AR(1)	9.088
2.	Average OLS	2.902	GLS-AR(1)	8.644	GLS	15.684	GLS	9.263
3.	FD2SLS	2.991	GLS	9.062	OLS	15.708	OLS	9.287
4.	Within 2SLS	2.996	OLS	9.138	Within	17.122	Within	9.656
5.	EC2SLS	3.090	Shrinkage OLS	10.050	FD2SLS	18.788	Shrinkage OLS	11.298
6.	FD	3.349	2SLS	10.076	FD	19.125	FD2SLS	11.775
7.	EC-AR(1) 2SLS	3.583	Indiv. OLS	10.871	Shrinkage OLS	19.228	FD	12.171
8.	2SLS	3.652	Shrinkage 2SLS	11.208	EC-AR(1) 2SLS	20.154	Indiv. OLS	12.694
9.	Within	3.720	EC2SLS	12.082	Average OLS	20.746	EC2SLS	12.868
10.	GLS-AR(1)	4.199	FD2SLS	12.117	Average 2SLS	21.143	Average OLS	13.154
11.	GLS	4.224	FD	12.746	Indiv. OLS	21.343	Average 2SLS	13.262
12.	OLS	4.233	Average 2SLS	13.168	No change	21.924	Shrinkage 2SLS	13.376
13.	Shrinkage OLS	4.310	Average OLS	13.252	EC2SLS	23.099	2SLS	13.684
14.	Shrinkage 2SLS	4.534	Within 2SLS	13.571	Within 2SLS	23.826	Within 2SLS	13.772
15.	Indiv. OLS	5.464	EC-AR(1) 2SLS	14.463	2SLS	25.338	EC-AR(1) 2SLS	14.022
16.	Indiv. 2SLS	5.951	Indiv. 2SLS	15.784	Shrinkage 2SLS	26.874	No change	14.472
17.	No change	6.134	No change	16.324	Indiv. 2SLS	52.423	Indiv. 2SLS	22.601

that do not closely explain the lagged dependent variable. This is particularly evident in the relative poor performance in the 5th- and 10th-year forecasts, which depend critically on the lagged dependent variable to capture long-run dynamics.

Now turning to a comparison of the heterogeneous versus homogeneous estimators, we see some very interesting patterns. Of the heterogeneous estimators, individual OLS and individual 2SLS perform uniformly poorly vis-a-vis both the homogeneous and other heterogeneous estimators, confirming the gains from pooling. Indeed, individual 2SLS has the distinction of being the only estimator to perform worse than the naive, 'no change' model for the full 10-year period. The performance by the other heterogeneous estimators is more mixed. Pesaran's average 2SLS and OLS estimators rank 1st and 2nd, respectively, in one-year-ahead forecasts. Yet by the 10th year, they have dropped to 10th and 9th and overall rank 11th and 10th. It seems clear that these average estimators do well in capturing short-run responses but for long-term forecasts are not particularly adapted probably due to the fact that his procedure does not utilize the between variation which we have argued elsewhere is important for describing long-run responses.[13] The shrinkage estimator appears to have the reverse problem of the 'Average' estimator. For one-year forecasts, these shrinkage estimators rank 13th and 14th – only slightly better than the naive, 'no change' estimator. Yet for the 10-year average, the shrinkage OLS estimator ranks 5th overall, while the shrinkage 2SLS estimator ranks 12th overall.

The overall RMSE forecast rankings offer a strong endorsement for the traditional homogeneous models. GLS-AR(1) ranks 1st, followed closely by the GLS, OLS, and Within estimators. All four have RMSEs in the 9.09 to 9.66 range – well below the shrinkage OLS estimator. Interestingly, these estimators do not dominate for the one-year forecasts, but they do dominate for the 5th- and 10th-year forecasts. The finding that the GLS-AR(1) model is the best overall suggests that there are some additional gains vis-a-vis the standard GLS model. Just as in an individual time series, the AR(1) adjustment coupled with a Prais–Winsten adjustment that 'anchors' the regression leads to good performance in Monte Carlo exercises, it appears to offer some advantage in forecasting in a panel data setting. On the other hand, the more traditional GLS, OLS, and Within models also perform quite well, especially compared both to other rival estimators and the naive, 'no change' model.

5. Summary and conclusions

The results of this paper confirm the value of panel data sets and justify the emphasis given to pooled estimators. Even with a relatively long time series,

[13] See Baltagi and Griffin (1983).

heterogeneous models for individual countries tend to produce less plausible estimates which offer inferior overall forecast performance. Among the class of heterogeneous estimators, the shrinkage estimator appears the most promising, but even it is dominated by the traditional homogeneous pooled estimators. Our explanation for why pooled models, which posit homogeneous parameters, outperform their heterogeneous counterparts centers on the relative variability of the data between the individual time series and panels. Using a root mean square error criterion, the efficiency gains from pooling appear to more than offset the biases due to intercountry heterogeneities. Interestingly, even with 31 years of data and dynamic demand goods with substantial lags, individual time series perform poorly.

But having opted for a homogeneous model, the researcher faces a choice of which pooled estimator. The results here show significant differences in parameter estimates and forecast performance. The gains from correcting for possible endogeneity in the lagged dependent variable are disappointing as the 2SLS estimators performed worse than their counterparts assuming all variables are exogenous. We hesitate to generalize on this result because we believe it is simply a matter of the poor information content of the instruments selected. The traditional GLS, OLS, and Within estimators yield substantial differences in parameter estimates, yet in overall forecast performance perform quite similarly. The strong performance of the GLS-AR(1) estimator would seem to suggest it has very desirable properties.

References

Ahn, S.C. and P. Schmidt. 1995, Efficient estimation of models for dynamic panel data, Journal of Econometrics 68, 5–27.

Anderson, T.W. and C. Hsiao, 1982, Formulation and estimation of dynamic models using panel data, Journal of Econometrics 18, 47–82.

Arellano, M. and O. Bover, 1995, Another look at the instrumental variables estimation of error-component models, Journal of Econometrics 68, 29–51.

Balestra, P. and M. Nerlove, 1966, Pooling cross-section and time-series data in the estimation of a dynamic model: The demand for natural gas, Econometrica 34, 585–612.

Baltagi, B.H., 1981, Simultaneous equations with error components, Journal of Econometrics 17, 189–200.

Baltagi, B.H. and J.M. Griffin, 1983, Gasoline demand in the OECD: An application of pooling and testing procedures, European Economic Review 22, 117–137.

Baltagi, B.H. and Q. Li, 1991, A transformation that will circumvent the problem of autocorrelation in an error component model, Journal of Econometrics 48, 385–393.

Bohi, D.R. and M. Zimmerman, 1984, An update on econometric studies of energy demand, Annual Review of Energy 9, 105–154.

Dahl, Carol and Thomas Sterner, 1991, Analyzing gasoline demand elasticities: A survey, Energy Economics 11, 203–210.

Griffin, J.M., 1979, Energy conservation in the OECD: 1980 to 2000 (Ballinger, Cambridge, MA).

Houthakker, H.S. and D. Taylor, 1970, Consumer demand in the United States, analyses and projections (Harvard University Press, Cambridge, MA).

Appendix

Table A.1
OLS estimates for individual countries (*t*-statistics given in parentheses)

	$\ln(GAS/CAR)_{-1}$	$\ln(Y/N)$	$\ln(P_{MG}/P_{GDP})$	$\ln(CAR/N)$	$\ln(Y/N)_{-1}$	$\ln(CAR/N)_{-1}$	Const.	S.E.
Canada	0.89	0.77	−0.17	−1.13	−0.63	0.94	0.6	0.011
	(16.0)	(5.4)	(5.9)	(8.3)	(5.1)	(8.2)	(0.8)	
U.S.	0.88	−0.01	−0.10	−0.10	−0.25	0.22	0.84	0.021
	(10.9)	(0.1)	(2.7)	(0.2)	(1.0)	(0.5)	(1.4)	
Japan	0.42	0.43	−0.02	−0.75	−0.34	0.37	1.37	0.027
	(1.8)	(1.4)	(0.3)	(4.3)	(1.1)	(1.4)	(2.5)	
Austria	0.85	−0.32	−0.07	0.37	−0.35	−0.06	0.06	0.033
	(10.7)	(0.6)	(1.2)	(0.6)	(0.7)	(0.1)	(0.1)	
Belgium	0.80	−0.63	−0.28	−0.90	−0.08	1.13	0.38	0.038
	(8.9)	(1.4)	(3.9)	(3.3)	(0.2)	(4.3)	(0.8)	
Denmark	0.37	0.26	−0.17	−0.13	−0.55	−0.04	2.07	0.025
	(2.7)	(0.9)	(3.4)	(0.3)	(2.1)	(0.1)	(5.0)	
France	0.99	−0.47	−0.22	−0.48	0.07	0.66	0.12	0.017
	(19.1)	(1.4)	(4.6)	(1.4)	(0.2)	(2.2)	(0.3)	
Germany	0.80	−0.15	−0.12	−0.15	−0.03	0.17	0.91	0.029
	(8.5)	(0.4)	(2.5)	(0.3)	(0.1)	(0.4)	(1.5)	

Greece	0.02 (0.1)	0.83 (2.5)	−0.33 (4.3)	−0.84 (6.7)	0.39 (0.8)	0.1 (0.5)	9.06 (5.4)	0.038
Ireland	0.69 (5.7)	0.46 (1.6)	−0.19 (2.8)	−0.62 (2.9)	−0.87 (3.1)	0.74 (3.8)	1.57 (2.0)	0.029
Italy	0.58 (3.8)	−0.03 (0.1)	−0.15 (2.0)	−0.53 (1.2)	−0.15 (0.4)	0.39 (1.0)	1.16 (2.8)	0.038
Netherlands	0.87 (10.8)	0.05 (0.2)	0.31 (2.8)	−0.56 (1.8)	−0.50 (1.7)	0.59 (2.0)	−0.19 (0.3)	0.038
Norway	0.47 (3.4)	0.35 (2.7)	−0.37 (4.8)	−0.89 (4.2)	0.02 (0.2)	0.51 (2.6)	4.0 (5.0)	0.023
Spain	0.67 (5.9)	−0.65 (1.5)	−0.24 (2.8)	−0.36 (1.1)	0.40 (1.0)	0.25 (0.7)	0.71 (0.5)	0.031
Sweden	−0.02 (0.1)	0.56 (1.7)	−0.13 (2.3)	−1.69 (3.2)	−0.10 (0.3)	1.18 (3.5)	6.02 (5.6)	0.023
Switzerland	0.42 (2.3)	0.8 (2.4)	0.03 (0.4)	−1.28 (4.3)	0.17 (0.5)	0.86 (3.0)	4.13 (2.6)	0.030
Turkey	0.6 (5.7)	−0.1 (0.2)	0.34 (4.9)	−1.01 (5.5)	−0.50 (0.8)	0.95 (5.2)	−0.28 (0.2)	0.065
U.K.	0.76 (7.1)	0.66 (3.2)	−0.05 (1.5)	−1.03 (6.0)	−0.59 (3.1)	0.92 (6.6)	1.44 (2.0)	0.017

Table A.2
2SLS estimates for individual countries (t-statistics given in parentheses)

	$\ln(GAS/CAR)_{-1}$	$\ln(Y/N)$	$\ln(P_{MG}/P_{GDP})$	$\ln(CAR/N)$	$\ln(Y/N)_{-1}$	$\ln(CAR/N)_{-1}$	Const.	S.E.
Canada	0.85	0.72	−0.19	−1.09	−0.64	0.95	1.08	0.011
	(10.4)	(4.4)	(4.8)	(7.0)	(5.1)	(8.1)	(1.0)	
U.S.	0.73	−0.28	−0.11	0.34	−0.12	−0.15	1.78	0.023
	(6.2)	(0.8)	(2.7)	(0.6)	(0.4)	(0.3)	(2.1)	
Japan	0.60	0.34	−0.04	−0.81	−0.28	0.54	0.96	0.027
	(1.3)	(0.9)	(0.5)	(3.7)	(0.8)	(1.2)	(0.9)	
Austria	0.87	−0.32	−0.07	0.35	−0.33	−0.04	0.00	0.033
	(5.6)	(0.6)	(1.2)	(0.6)	(0.7)	(0.1)	(0.0)	
Belgium	0.67	−0.70	−0.30	−0.86	−0.07	1.07	0.96	0.040
	(3.7)	(1.5)	(3.7)	(2.9)	(0.2)	(3.7)	(1.2)	
Denmark	0.20	0.22	−0.19	−0.23	−0.62	0.01	2.37	0.026
	(1.2)	(0.8)	(3.6)	(0.6)	(2.3)	(0.0)	(5.1)	
France	0.83	−0.50	−0.21	−0.53	0.12	0.66	0.98	0.021
	(6.1)	(1.2)	(3.8)	(1.3)	(0.3)	(1.9)	(1.2)	
Germany	0.88	−0.20	−0.12	−0.07	0.02	0.10	0.52	0.030
	(4.5)	(0.5)	(2.4)	(0.1)	(0.1)	(0.2)	(0.5)	
Greece	−0.01	0.80	−0.34	−0.83	0.46	0.07	9.37	0.038
	(0.0)	(2.0)	(3.0)	(6.4)	(0.6)	(0.2)	(3.1)	

Ireland	0.74	0.51	−0.16	−0.63	−0.88	0.73	1.25	0.029
	(3.9)	(1.6)	(1.9)	(2.9)	(3.1)	(3.6)	(1.0)	
Italy	0.48	−0.07	−0.16	−0.49	−0.19	0.36	1.30	0.038
	(1.6)	(0.2)	(2.0)	(1.1)	(0.5)	(0.9)	(2.3)	
Netherlands	0.65	0.14	−0.38	−0.49	−0.54	0.48	−0.10	0.043
	(3.7)	(0.4)	(2.8)	(1.4)	(1.6)	(1.4)	(0.1)	
Norway	0.32	0.33	−0.37	−0.92	0.08	0.48	4.80	0.024
	(1.7)	(2.5)	(4.7)	(4.2)	(0.5)	(2.4)	(4.5)	
Spain	0.62	−0.63	−0.24	−0.31	0.43	0.18	1.09	0.031
	(2.5)	(1.4)	(2.6)	(0.8)	(1.0)	(0.4)	(0.5)	
Sweden	−0.52	0.77	−0.18	−2.47	0.09	1.56	8.71	0.026
	(1.6)	(2.0)	(2.6)	(3.4)	(0.2)	(3.6)	(4.8)	
Switzerland	0.62	0.71	0.00	−1.22	−0.35	0.95	2.48	0.031
	(1.3)	(1.8)	(0.0)	(3.7)	(0.7)	(2.8)	(0.6)	
Turkey	0.48	−0.38	0.37	−1.05	−0.13	0.89	0.36	0.067
	(3.1)	(0.6)	(4.8)	(5.5)	(0.2)	(4.6)	(0.2)	
U.K.	0.77	0.67	−0.05	−1.03	−0.60	0.93	1.35	0.017
	(3.5)	(3.1)	(1.5)	(5.8)	(2.4)	(6.5)	(0.9)	

Table A.3
Shrinkage OLS estimates for individual countries (*t*-statistics given in parentheses)

	$\ln(GAS/CAR)_{-1}$	$\ln(Y/N)$	$\ln(P_{MG}/P_{GDP})$	$\ln(CAR/N)$	$\ln(Y/N)_{-1}$	$\ln(CAR/N)_{-1}$	Const.
Canada	0.90	0.72	−0.15	−1.02	−0.62	0.87	0.54
	(24.8)	(6.5)	(7.0)	(9.6)	(6.3)	(9.2)	(1.2)
U.S.	0.89	0.11	−0.09	−0.23	−0.32	0.32	0.72
	(17.3)	(0.6)	(3.6)	(0.8)	(2.0)	(1.2)	(1.9)
Japan	0.54	0.46	−0.03	−0.73	−0.39	0.43	1.13
	(4.2)	(2.3)	(0.7)	(5.7)	(2.0)	(2.6)	(3.3)
Austria	0.87	−0.12	−0.07	0.13	−0.40	0.10	0.12
	(14.9)	(0.4)	(1.6)	(0.4)	(1.7)	(0.4)	(0.3)
Belgium	0.84	−0.36	−0.23	−0.85	−0.19	1.01	0.37
	(11.8)	(1.5)	(4.4)	(4.2)	(0.8)	(5.3)	(1.0)
Denmark	0.50	0.32	−0.14	−0.25	−0.55	0.12	1.67
	(6.0)	(1.7)	(3.9)	(1.0)	(3.1)	(0.6)	(5.4)
France	0.98	−0.24	−0.18	−0.52	−0.08	0.65	0.16
	(22.3)	(1.0)	(5.0)	(2.2)	(0.4)	(3.1)	(0.6)
Germany	0.84	0.01	−0.11	−0.27	−0.16	0.27	0.78
	(11.4)	(0.0)	(2.9)	(0.9)	(0.7)	(1.1)	(1.6)
Greece	0.24	0.76	−0.27	−0.80	0.17	0.23	7.06
	(2.0)	(3.9)	(5.5)	(7.4)	(0.6)	(1.7)	(6.5)

Ireland	0.75	0.48	−0.16	−0.63	−0.80	0.72	1.28
	(10.1)	(2.5)	(3.4)	(3.9)	(4.3)	(4.8)	(2.7)
Italy	0.67	0.10	−0.13	−0.56	−0.25	0.45	0.97
	(7.1)	(0.5)	(2.5)	(2.3)	(1.2)	(2.1)	(3.0)
Netherlands	0.89	0.17	−0.25	−0.58	−0.52	0.60	−0.08
	(14.6)	(0.8)	(3.5)	(2.7)	(2.6)	(3.0)	(0.2)
Norway	0.58	0.40	−0.30	−0.84	−0.11	0.54	3.13
	(5.5)	(3.8)	(5.2)	(4.8)	(1.1)	(3.5)	(5.0)
Spain	0.74	−0.38	−0.20	−0.43	0.18	0.34	0.62
	(8.7)	(1.5)	(3.9)	(2.0)	(0.8)	(1.6)	(0.7)
Sweden	0.20	0.56	−0.12	−1.46	−0.21	1.05	4.71
	(1.5)	(2.5)	(2.9)	(4.9)	(1.0)	(4.7)	(6.0)
Switzerland	0.54	0.74	0.00	−1.14	−0.26	0.81	3.26
	(4.2)	(3.4)	(0.1)	(5.3)	(1.2)	(4.1)	(3.1)
Turkey	0.68	0.05	−0.28	−0.93	−0.52	0.88	−0.15
	(8.7)	(0.2)	(5.9)	(7.2)	(2.0)	(6.2)	(0.2)
U.K.	0.80	0.63	−0.06	−0.95	−0.58	0.86	1.19
	(9.7)	(4.0)	(2.0)	(6.9)	(4.0)	(7.6)	(2.1)

Table A.4
Shrinkage 2SLS estimates for individual countries (t-statistics given in parentheses)

	$\ln(GAS/CAR)_{-1}$	$\ln(Y/N)$	$\ln(P_{MG}/P_{GDP})$	$\ln(CAR/N)$	$\ln(Y/N)_{-1}$	$\ln(CAR/N)_{-1}$	Const.
Canada	0.88	0.67	−0.15	−0.97	−0.62	0.86	0.86
	(21.0)	(5.7)	(6.6)	(8.8)	(6.3)	(9.0)	(1.8)
U.S.	0.79	−0.05	−0.10	0.06	−0.25	0.07	1.36
	(12.0)	(0.2)	(3.8)	(0.2)	(1.5)	(0.3)	(3.1)
Japan	0.70	0.40	−0.05	−0.76	−0.36	0.56	0.76
	(4.7)	(2.1)	(1.1)	(5.9)	(1.8)	(3.3)	(2.0)
Austria	0.89	−0.08	−0.07	0.07	−0.40	0.15	0.08
	(10.3)	(0.3)	(1.5)	(0.2)	(1.7)	(0.5)	(0.2)
Belgium	0.75	−0.35	−0.24	−0.80	−0.21	0.95	0.77
	(6.3)	(1.4)	(4.3)	(3.9)	(1.0)	(4.8)	(1.4)
Denmark	0.41	0.32	−0.16	−0.35	−0.61	0.19	1.78
	(3.8)	(1.7)	(4.2)	(1.4)	(3.4)	(0.9)	(5.4)
France	0.87	−0.21	−0.17	−0.56	−0.07	0.66	0.78
	(8.9)	(0.9)	(4.3)	(2.1)	(0.3)	(2.8)	(1.4)
Germany	0.90	0.01	0.11	−0.24	−0.15	0.25	0.45
	(7.3)	(0.0)	(2.6)	(0.7)	(0.7)	(0.9)	(0.6)
Greece	0.26	0.73	−0.26	−0.78	0.17	0.23	6.83
	(1.6)	(3.8)	(4.9)	(7.1)	(0.6)	(1.4)	(4.9)

Ireland	0.80	0.52	−0.14	0.63	−0.79	0.70	0.97
	(8.9)	(2.6)	(2.6)	(3.8)	(4.3)	(4.5)	(1.7)
Italy	0.62	0.10	−0.13	−0.54	−0.3	0.43	1.01
	(5.0)	(0.4)	(2.4)	(2.1)	(1.6)	(2.0)	(2.8)
Netherlands	0.74	0.05	−0.29	−0.53	−0.55	0.52	0.00
	(7.1)	(0.2)	(3.9)	(2.3)	(2.7)	(2.4)	(0.0)
Norway	0.50	0.40	−0.29	−0.85	−0.11	0.53	3.54
	(3.7)	(3.8)	(5.1)	(4.7)	(0.9)	(3.3)	(4.6)
Spain	0.72	−0.30	−0.19	−0.41	0.15	0.31	0.86
	(5.7)	(1.2)	(3.6)	(2.0)	(0.6)	(1.4)	(0.8)
Sweden	−0.11	0.72	−0.15	−1.97	−0.1	1.30	6.36
	(0.6)	(3.1)	(3.5)	(5.5)	(0.5)	(5.2)	(5.8)
Switzerland	0.71	0.66	−0.02	−1.06	−0.41	0.86	1.86
	(3.6)	(3.1)	(0.3)	(4.4)	(1.7)	(4.2)	(1.2)
Turkey	0.61	−0.12	−0.28	−0.94	−0.26	0.82	0.33
	(6.1)	(0.4)	(5.7)	(7.3)	(1.0)	(5.7)	(0.4)
U.K.	0.82	0.63	−0.06	−0.93	−0.59	0.85	1.05
	(6.0)	(4.0)	(1.9)	(6.3)	(3.6)	(7.4)	(1.1)

Table A.5
Pooled estimates (t-statistics given in parentheses)

Estimation techniques	$\ln(GAS/CAR)_{-1}$	$\ln(Y/N)$	$\ln(P_{MG}/P_{GDP})$	$\ln(CAR/N)$	$\ln(Y/N)_{-1}$	$\ln(CAR/N)_{-1}$	Const.	$\bar{R}^2$	S.E.
OLS	0.95	0.55	−0.07	−0.66	−0.57	0.64	0.32	0.993	0.042
	(122.7)	(6.9)	(7.4)	(15.7)	(7.1)	(16.0)	(5.0)		
Within	0.87	0.39	−0.11	−0.74	−0.44	0.67	—	0.994	0.039
	(53.5)	(5.0)	(9.5)	(15.4)	(5.5)	(14.3)			
FD	0.04	0.33	−0.23	−0.83	−0.08	0.31		0.619	0.038
	(1.1)	(4.8)	(13.1)	(21.0)	(1.1)	(6.7)			
GLS	0.94	0.53	−0.08	−0.67	−0.55	0.64	0.36	0.977	0.041
	(108.9)	(6.6)	(8.0)	(15.6)	(6.9)	(15.7)	(5.0)		
GLS-AR(1)	0.94	0.50	−0.09	−0.68	−0.53	0.65	0.39	0.989	0.040
	(96.3)	(6.4)	(8.6)	(15.5)	(6.7)	(15.4)	(4.9)		
2SLS	0.69	0.36	−0.29	−0.91	−0.26	0.72	2.23	0.974	0.074
	(15.8)	(2.5)	(7.3)	(10.7)	(1.7)	(9.9)	(6.7)		
Within 2SLS	0.55	0.19	−0.20	−0.65	−0.14	0.41	—	0.989	0.052
	(8.6)	(1.7)	(8.9)	(9.9)	(1.2)	(5.2)			
FD2SLS	0.22	0.31	−0.23	−0.86	−0.17	0.45	—	0.610	0.039
	(2.8)	(4.2)	(12.9)	(20.3)	(2.1)	(6.2)			
EC2SLS	0.65	0.26	−0.17	−0.68	−0.23	0.50	0.12	0.972	0.045
	(13.8)	(2.7)	(9.5)	(12.0)	(2.3)	(7.7)	(6.5)		
EC-AR(1) 2SLS	0.64	0.20	−0.20	−0.92	−0.28	0.73	0.07	0.947	0.040
	(13.3)	(2.6)	(11.2)	(19.9)	(3.6)	(13.4)	(6.5)		

Houthakker, H.S., P.K. Verleger, and D. Sheehan, 1974, Dynamic demand for gasoline and residential electricity, American Journal of Agricultural Economics 56, 412–418.

Hsiao, C., 1986, Analysis of panel data (Cambridge University Press, Cambridge).

Keane, M.P. and D.E. Runkle, 1992, On the estimation of panel-data models with serial correlation when instruments are not strictly exogenous, Journal of Business and Economics Statistics 10, 1–9.

Kiviet, J.F., 1995, On bias, inconsistency and efficiency of some estimators in dynamic panel data models, Journal of Econometrics 68, 53–78.

Maddala, G.S., V.K. Srivastava, and H. Li, 1994, Shrinkage estimators for the estimation of short-run and long-run parameters from panel data models, Working paper (Ohio State University, Columbus, OH).

Nickell, S., 1981, Biases in dynamic models with fixed effects, Econometrica 49, 1417–1426.

Pesaran, M.H. and R. Smith, 1995, Estimating long-run relationships from dynamic heterogeneous panels, Journal of Econometrics 68, 79–113.

Robertson, D. and J. Symons, 1992, Some strange properties of panel data estimators, Journal of Applied Econometrics 7, 175–189.

Sweeney, J., 1978, The demand for gasoline in the United States: A vintage capital model, in: Workshops on energy and supply and demand (International Energy Agency, Paris) 240–277.

Wooldridge, J.M., 1990, A note on the Lagrange multiplier and *F* statistics for two stage least squares regressions, Economics Letters 34, 151–155.

[12]

A Panel Analysis of Liquidity Constraints and Firm Investment

Cheng HSIAO and A. Kamil TAHMISCIOGLU

The issue of financial constraints on company investment is revisited using the U.S. panel data of 561 firms from 1971–1992. A number of economically meaningful factors are discovered to partition firms into relatively homogeneous groups. A mixed fixed- and random-coefficients framework is then used to capture unobserved heterogeneity within groups. The prediction criterion is used to select the final specification and evaluate the importance of financial constraints on firm's investment decisions.

1. INTRODUCTION

The pendulum frequently swings in economic debates. This is nowhere more obvious than in the literature on the effects of financial constraints on company investment. Although early econometric work of Meyer and Kuh (1957) showed that internal funds were an important determinant of investment, this result was largely dismissed by economists following the neoclassical tradition. Jorgenson (1971) claimed that "the evidence clearly favors the Modigliani–Miller theory. Internal liquidity is not an important determinant of investment, given the level of output and external funds." The Modigliani–Miller (1958, 1961) theory continued to have a profound influence on economists' thinking about investment behavior for many years. However, this consensus began to evaporate in the 1980s and 1990s as researchers demonstrated the implications of asymmetric information problems for the functioning of capital markets (see, e.g. Myers and Majluf 1984 and Stiglitz and Weiss 1981). One theme that emerges from this literature is that because of imperfections in the capital markets, costs of internal and external finance will diverge, and internal and external funds generally will not be perfect substitutes for each other. The recent empirical investment literature confirms these observations by finding extreme sensitivity of company investment to the availability of internal funds (see Bond and Meghir 1994, Chirinko and Schaller 1995, Devereux and Schianterelli 1990, Fazzari, Hubbard, and Petersen 1988, Hoshi, Kashyap, and Scharfstein 1991, Oliner and Rudebusch 1992, and Whited 1992).

Recent econometric work on company investment has used panel datasets to test whether a representative firm model has the power to explain investment behavior. Fazzari et al. (1988) tested for the importance of internal finance by studying the effects of cash flow across different groups of companies. These authors identified a group of firms deemed more likely to face asymmetric information problems in the capital market according to company retention practices. They claimed that companies with low dividend payout rates are more likely to be constrained in their investment. After dividing their sample according to dividend payout rates, they estimated their investment equations and compared the effects of the liquidity variable for different groups of companies. If the null hypothesis of perfect capital markets is correct, then no difference should be found in the coefficient of cash flow variable for different companies. However, Fazzari et al. found that cash flow coefficient was larger for companies with low payout rates. This study has been replicated by other authors for other countries. In a similar study, Hoshi et al. (1991) divided a sample of Japanese companies according to whether or not a company has a close relationship with a bank. They found that companies with close affiliation with banks suffer less from cash flow constraints. Devereux and Schianterelli (1990) used size to split a sample of U.K. companies into groups. Although they found that larger firms have larger cash flow coefficients, their results did not turn out to be significant. In other studies various firm characteristics have been used to distinguish the effects of liquidity for groups of firms: Bond and Meghir (1994) used dividend–capital stock ratio, Chirinko and Schaller (1995) used age, membership to an industrial group, and ownership structure; Oliner and Rudebusch (1992) used age, exchange listing, and pattern of insider trading; and Whited (1992) used debt–assets ratio, interest coverage ratio, and bond rating.

Although recent research has made important contributions to the knowledge base, important issues remain deserving further investigation. First, the controversy regarding what cash flow variable really represents continues (see, e.g., Sims 1988). Sims and others have argued that even when capital markets are perfect, cash flow may explain investment, because it is a variable that conveys information about the future profitability of a company. Cash flow effects may be different across firms not because of financial considerations but because of the differences in the information content of cash flow variable. Second, there are also disagreements about the choice of variables used to classify companies into separate groups and the interpretation of empirical results. For instance, when dividend payout rate is used to group firms, it is assumed that dividends are determined as a residual after all the profitable investment

Cheng Hsiao is Professor, Department of Economics, University of Southern California, Los Angeles, CA 90089. A. Kamil Tahmiscioglu is Assistant Professor, Department of Economics, University of Wisconsin, Milwaukee, WI 53201. This work was supported in part by National Science Foundation grant SBR 94-09540 and SBR 96-19330. The authors would like to thank Diane Lambert, an associate editor, and two referees for very helpful comments and suggestions. They also thank Tim Cason, Harrison Cheng, Moshe Fridman, Vai-Lam Mui, and Hashem Pesaran for helpful discussions and suggestions.

Journal of the American Statistical Association
June 1997, Vol. 92, No. 438, Applications and Case Studies

opportunities are taken, and thus a variety of reasons for paying dividends, including the role of dividends in solving information and agency cost problems, are ignored. (See Easterbrook 1984 for a discussion of the role that dividends play in monitoring managers and Miller and Rock 1985 for a signaling model.) There is no sound theoretical basis for assuming that only low-payout companies are subject to financial constraints. The empirical results are also sometimes puzzling. The finding that larger companies have larger cash flow coefficients is inconsistent with both the transaction costs and asymmetric information explanations of liquidity constraints. It is possible that using a single indicator variable to split a sample without controlling for different determinants of financial constraints may lead to misleading inferences. Third, whether firm heterogeneity can be captured by grouping firms according to some exogenous criteria remains open to question. The previous literature either assumes that firms within groups are homogeneous or that heterogeneity among firms can be captured by firm-specific intercepts and slope coefficients are homogeneous across firms. If homogeneity across firms is not a legitimate assumption, then the resulting estimates may be seriously misleading (see, e.g. Hsiao 1986 and Pesaran and Smith 1995).

The objectives of this article are threefold. First, we use panel data on 561 firms to investigate whether it is feasible to pool the data to draw some general conclusions about firm investment behavior. Although panel data offer many potential benefits, such as improving the accuracy of parameter estimates and the possibility of testing richer hypotheses (see, e.g., Hsiao 1985, 1986), panel data by nature tend to focus on individual outcomes. Factors affecting individual outcomes are numerous, yet we want a model to capture only the essential factors. To reach a compromise between simplicity of model specification and consistency of parameter estimates, various approaches have been suggested to capture the heterogeneity of individual units not represented by included explanatory variables—for example, the variable intercept model (Kuh 1963), the error components model (Balestra and Nerlove 1966), the random coefficients model (Hsiao 1974, 1975; Lindley and Smith 1972; Swamy 1971), and the mixed fixed and random coefficients model (Hsiao 1995). Estimates derived from these different approaches can be very different and hence lead to very different inferences. In this article we document the severity of heterogeneity in our data and discuss the manner in which the data may be pooled. We demonstrate that the extremely large adjustment cost parameters and underestimation of the impact of explanatory variables in previous studies may be the consequence of using inappropriate estimation techniques in a situation where a mixed fixed and random coefficients model may be more appropriate.

Second, we try to identify the causes of heterogeneity in liquidity coefficients. Liquidity coefficients appear to be larger for capital-intensive and high-growth firms. Because firms with these characteristics are expected to rely more on capital markets, our results point to the direction of possibly significant capital market imperfections.

Third, we assess the importance of liquidity constraints by comparing the predictive performance of the internal funds model against alternative investment models. Although investment may be determined by capacity and profitability considerations in the long run, the prediction comparison in this article shows that liquidity is an important determinant of investment at least in the short run for a subset of the universe of firms.

In Section 2 we present the results based on the analysis of individual firm investment behavior and explore the issues of poolability. In Section 3 we give a general framework for pooled data analysis and suggest a recursive predictive density criterion for model selection. We present the results based on pooled data analysis in Section 4, and conclusions in Section 5.

2. ANALYSIS OF INDIVIDUAL FIRM INVESTMENT BEHAVIOR

Most of the literature on investment studies assumes either that there exists a common investment function for a group of firms or that heterogeneity among firms can be captured by firm-specific intercepts. In this section we explore the feasibility of these assumptions by performing firm-by-firm analysis. The data sources for this study are various COMPUSTAT annual industrial files. From these files, we chose companies in the manufacturing sector with two-digit Standard Industrial Classification (SIC) codes between 20 and 40. Appendix B discusses other sample selection criteria and the construction of the variables used in this study. Our sample consists of 561 companies. We have data on about 90% of the firms for the period 1971–1992 and for the remaining firms for 1973–1992.

Three investment equations that use the liquidity variable as an explanatory variable are specified:

$$\left(\frac{I}{K}\right)_{it} = \alpha_i + \beta_{i1}\left(\frac{I}{K}\right)_{i,t-1} + \beta_{i2}\left(\frac{\text{LIQ}}{K}\right)_{i,t-1} + \varepsilon_{it}, \quad (1)$$

$$\left(\frac{I}{K}\right)_{it} = \alpha_i + \beta_{i1}\left(\frac{I}{K}\right)_{i,t-1} + \beta_{i2}\left(\frac{\text{LIQ}}{K}\right)_{i,t-1} + \beta_{i3}q_{it} + \varepsilon_{it}, \quad (2)$$

and

$$\left(\frac{I}{K}\right)_{it} = \alpha_i + \beta_{i1}\left(\frac{I}{K}\right)_{i,t-1} + \beta_{i2}\left(\frac{\text{LIQ}}{K}\right)_{i,t-1} + \beta_{i3}\left(\frac{S}{K}\right)_{i,t-1} + \varepsilon_{it}, \quad (3)$$

where I_t is capital investment; LIQ_t is a liquidity variable (defined as cash flow minus dividends); S_t is sales; q_t is Tobin's q (Brainard and Tobin 1968, Tobin 1969), defined as the ratio of the market value of the firm to the replacement value of capital; and K_t is the beginning-of-period capital stock. The subscript i denotes companies, and t denotes time. These equations are variants of commonly specified investment equations using liquidity as an explanatory variable (see, e.g., Coen 1971 and Fazzari et al. 1988). In the analysis we use the lagged values of the variables as explanatory variables to avoid endogeneity problems. We add the lagged investment capital ratio to all regressions, to capture the dynamics of the investment process. This variable helps substantially reduce the extent of serial correlation present in the static models. The coefficient β_{i2} measures the short-run impact of liquidity variable on firm i's investment in each of these three specifications.

In addition, we also consider two popular variants of investment equations that do not use the liquidity variable as an explanatory variable to compare their performance against the internal funds model: the q model (see, e.g., Hayashi 1982, Summers 1981, and von Furstenberg 1977),

$$\left(\frac{I}{K}\right)_{it} = \alpha_i + \theta_{i1}\left(\frac{I}{K}\right)_{i,t-1} + \theta_{i2}q_{it} + \varepsilon_{it}, \quad (4)$$

and the sales capacity (i.e., flexible accelerator) model (see, e.g., Chenery 1952, Koyck 1954, and Kuh 1963),

$$\left(\frac{I}{K}\right)_{it} = \alpha_i + \theta_{i1}\left(\frac{I}{K}\right)_{i,t-1} + \theta_{i2}\left(\frac{S}{K}\right)_{i,t-1} + \varepsilon_{it}. \quad (5)$$

The sales variable can be regarded as a proxy for future demand for the firm's output. The q theory relates investment to marginal q, which is defined as the ratio of the market value of new investment goods to their replacement cost. If a firm has unexploited profit opportunities, then an increase of its capital stock price of \$1 will increase its market value by more than \$1. Therefore, firm managers can be expected to increase investment until marginal q equals 1. On the other hand, if a firm already has more than adequate capital, then an increase in capital stock by \$1 will increase its market value by less than \$1. Hence the firm can be expected to forego the marginal project. Thus investment will be an increasing function of marginal q. Because marginal q is unobservable. it is common in empirical work to substitute it with average or Tobin's q.

Table 1. Individual Firm Regressions (Percentage of Firms With Significant Coefficients)

	Model				
	1	2	3	4	5
$\left(\frac{LIQ}{K}\right)_{t-1}$	46	36	31		
q_t		31		38	
$\left(\frac{S}{K}\right)_{t-1}$			27		44
Actual F	2.47	2.98	2.01	2.66	2.11
Critical F	1.08	1.08	1.08	1.06	1.06
Percentage with significant autocorrelation	14	12	13	20	15

NOTE The number of firms is 561. The significance level is 5% for a one-tailed test Actual F is the F statistic for testing the equality of slope coefficients across firms. For the F test, the 5% significance level is chosen To detect serial correlation, Durbin's t-test at the 5% significance level is used.

Table 2. Coefficient Heterogeneity

	Slope estimates at 1st and 3rd quartiles across a sample of 561 firms			
	$(\frac{I}{K})_{i,t-1}$	$(\frac{LIQ}{K})_{i,t-1}$	q_{it}	$(\frac{S}{K})_{i,t-1}$
Model 1	.026, .405	.127, .529		
Model 2	−.028, .359	.062, .464	0, .039	
Model 3	−.100, .295	.020, .488		−.005, .057
Model 4	.110, .459		.007, .048	
Model 5	−.035, .367			.012, .077

We estimate these five models firm by firm. Tables 1 and 2 present some summary information from these regressions. In general, all these models appear to explain investment behavior fairly well. However, the range and the significance of each coefficient vary widely. Table 1 shows the percentage of significant coefficients for the different models at the 5% significance level for a one-tailed test. Table 2 shows the first and third quartiles of the estimated coefficients. In terms of significant coefficients, the liquidity model ranks first, closely followed by the flexible accelerator model. When sales is added to liquidity, the percentage of significant coefficients drops by approximately one-third. To a lesser degree, the same feature is observed when liquidity and q are included together. Overall, there are indications of multicollinearity between the variables. The bottom row of Table 1 provides evidence about the degree of serial correlation. Durbin's t-test is used to detect serial correlation. The extent of serial correlation varies across models, with the q model exhibiting the highest serial correlation. When the number of explanatory variables is increased, autocorrelation is slightly reduced. However, these numbers do not seem to be practically significant.

These sets of explanatory variables appear to capture the variation of investment expenditure with some success. Adding further lags of the variables provides little additional explanatory power but increases multicollinearity and the degrees of freedom needed to fit the model. Therefore, we restrict our investment studies to these sets of explanatory variables. However, as Table 2 shows, the estimated coefficients vary widely from firm to firm. Therefore, we first test whether a common specification can be used to represent a group of firms' investment behavior by testing for slope homogeneity across firms while representing firm heterogeneity by firm-specific intercepts. The resulting F statistics are highly significant (see Table 1), indicating the rejection of the homogeneity hypothesis.

We then explore whether the variation of β_{i2} can be explained by certain firm characteristics. We run

$$\beta_{i2} = \gamma + \mathbf{W}_i\boldsymbol{\delta} + u_i \quad (6)$$

where W_i includes some of the variables used in previous studies and other variables possibly useful in this context. Specifically, we use dividend payout rate, company size, sales growth, capital intensity, standard deviation of retained earnings, debt–equity ratio, measures of liquidity stocks from the balance sheet (e.g., working capital–to–capital stock ratio), number of shareholders, and industry dummies. Dividend payout rate is the ratio of cash dividends to earnings. Because it takes a negative value in years when earnings are negative, we exclude the negative values when calculating the median value. We use the logarithm of the capital stock in 1973 as our measure of size. Using a size measure from the middle of the sample period does not change the results.

Capital intensity is defined as the minimum value of the ratio of capital stock to sales over the sample period. Our conclusions do not change when an average of the smallest three–five values of this ratio is used instead of the minimum value. Using capital sales ratio as a proxy for capital output ratio may be questionable. In principle, it is possible to obtain an output measure by combining sales with finished goods inventories, but about 40% of the companies in our sample do not report data on finished goods inventories. Instead of dealing with so much missing data, we check the accuracy of our capital intensity measure by ranking the firms that have data on finished goods inventories according to capital output ratio and comparing this ranking with our original ranking. There is very little difference in the results. We choose capital intensity because capital-intensive companies tend to rely on capital markets more than other companies due to the scale of their investments. Moreover, the evidence of Scherer (1980) indicates that firms in capital-intensive industries tend to have lower profitability because of high fixed costs and breakdowns in pricing discipline. Thus it is reasonable to expect the investment of capital-intensive companies to be sensitive to fluctuations in internal finance.

We define sales growth as the percentage change in real sales per year. Industry-specific price indices from the 1993 "Economic Report of the President" are used to deflate the nominal sales figures. Faster-growing companies are likely to be more dependent on capital markets, because a firm can grow only so much by using its internal funds alone. Standard deviation of retained earnings is the ratio of the standard deviation of retentions deflated by capital stock to the mean retentions of each company. This variable is introduced to capture the differences in uncertainty faced by companies. Companies with high volatility in their retained earnings are expected to change their investment more cautiously than companies with more stable earnings in response to increases in liquidity. Debt–equity ratio is constructed as the ratio of book value of debt to market value of equity. The median values of the variables (with the exception of size, capital intensity, and standard deviation of retentions) are calculated for each company. Medians are preferable to means, because they are less sensitive to outliers. Industry dummies at two-digit SIC codes are also included as explanatory variables. We try a large number of specifications using all the aforementioned variables and different subsets of variables separately as explanatory variables.

Table 3 presents the regression results of (6). We note that W_i as a whole does not explain the variation in the estimated liquidity coefficient β_{2i} well. Although the coefficients generally have the expected signs, many are not significant. The variables that are most often significant are capital intensity, real sales growth, and standard deviation of retained earnings. Although other authors have found that investment of larger companies is extremely sensitive to fluctuations in internal finance when companies are grouped solely on the basis of size (Devereux and Schianterelli 1990), our coefficient of the size variable is negative and not statistically significant. The coefficient of the dividend payout variable is negative, confirming the findings of Fazzari et al. (1988). However, its significance varies considerably, depending on whether sales growth is included in the regressions. Although a few of the industry dummies are statistically significant, their significance is erratic. They are not included in the regressions reported in Table 3 to aid in the detection of the changes in estimates of other variables across different specifications. None of the other variables turn out to be statistically significant in all specifications.

Many of the firm characteristics in our model affect the liquidity coefficients in the direction predicted by most of the empirical research on investment and financing constraints. But we cannot substitute (6) into models 1, 2, and 3 and estimate the coefficients directly because of perfect multicollinearity. Therefore, following standard prac-

Table 3. Regressions of Liquidity Coefficients on Firm Characteristics

	Dependent variable from model								
	1			*2*			*3*		
Intercept	.252	.264	.276	.199	.207	.218	.164	.238	.218
	(.045)	(.046)	(.048)	(.049)	(.051)	(.053)	(.058)	(.060)	(.062)
Capital intensity	.486	.443	.479	.487	.446	.481	.376	.423	.360
	(.088)	(.075)	(.088)	(.096)	(.082)	(.097)	(.114)	(.097)	(.113)
Sales growth	1.398	1.332	1.316	.829	.781	.766	1.117	.905	.932
	(.351)	(.356)	(.357)	(.387)	(.392)	(.393)	(.456)	(.461)	(.461)
Std. dev. of retentions	−.060	−.062	−.062	−.057	−.058	−.059	−.063	−.069	−.068
	(.015)	(.015)	(.015)	(.017)	(.017)	(.017)	(.020)	(.020)	(.013)
Size	−.014		−.008	−.012		−.008	−.001		.014
	(.009)		(.010)	(.010)		(.011)	(.012)		(.013)
Dividend payout rate		−.172	−.137		−.140	−.107		−.249	−.310
		(.095)	(.104)		(.104)	(.115)		(.122)	(.135)
$\bar{R}^2$	.111	.113	.113	.076	.077	.076	.056	.063	.063

NOTE. The dependent variable in columns 2–4, 5–7, and 8–10 is $\hat{\beta}_{i2}$ from models 1, 2 and 3. Capital intensity is the minimum value of the ratio of capital stock to sales. Sales growth is the growth rate of real sales. Standard deviation of retentions is the standard deviation of retentions–capital stock ratio as a percentage of mean retentions–capital stock ratio. Size is the logarithm of capital stock in 1973. Dividend payout rate is the ratio of dividends to earnings. The number of observations is 561. Standard errors are in parentheses.

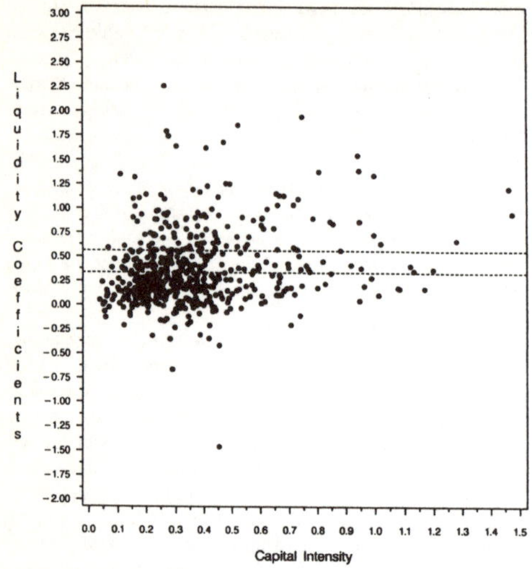

Figure 1. Scatterplot of Liquidity Coefficients and Their Respective Means for Less- and More-Capital Intensive Firms. The lower and upper dashed lines show the mean coefficients for firms with capital–sales ratio less than and greater than .55.

tice, we use these variables to classify firms into reasonably homogeneous groups. Because capital intensity appears to be the most statistically significant and most stable variable under different specifications, we group our sample according to capital intensity to see whether homogeneity within group can be established. Plotting the mean liquidity coefficients of the capital intensity variable at .1 intervals, it appears that .55 is a reasonable cut-off point. Figure 1 provides the scatterplot of the coefficient estimates of the liquidity variable of model 1 against capital intensity. A simple test of the hypothesis that the coefficients have a common mean against the alternative of a different mean for firms with capital–sales ratio less than or greater than .55 rejects the null with an F value of 24.10. Therefore, we group firms using .55 as the cutoff point. A small number of firms with capital–sales ratio less than .15 are not included in the less–capital-intensive group, because the mean of their liquidity coefficients appears to be somewhat different from the mean of the less–capital-intensive group.

Table 4 presents firm characteristics according to this grouping. There are substantial differences between the two groups. The more–capital-intensive group has a much lower median cash flow–capital stock ratio and investment rate relative to the less–capital-intensive group. Moreover, the ratio of the median investment to retentions is close to 1 and is substantially larger than the value of the same ratio for the less–capital-intensive group. The lower cash flow–capital stock ratio of more–capital-intensive firms is consistent with the findings of Scherer, as discussed earlier. The lower working capital–capital stock ratio of more–capital-intensive companies also portrays an overall weak financial position and can be considered a direct result of their low profitability. The ability of more–capital-intensive firms to finance their investment may also be adversely affected by their lack of working capital and other liquid assets, as pointed out by Fazzari and Petersen (1993).

Table 4. Summary of Firm Characteristics (Sample Split by Capital Intensity)

	Median values	
Firm characteristics	Less–capital-intensive firms	More–capital-intensive firms
Number of firms	418	86
Sales growth (%)	3.7	1.5
Investment growth (%)	3.9	3.1
Cash flow/capital stock (%)	27.5	12.9
Investment/capital stock (%)	15.0	11.9
Investment/retentions (%)	68.1	106.0
Dividends/profits (%)	30.2	37.4
Debt/equity (%)	19.7	36.6
Working capital/capital stock (%)	17.8	1.2
% change in stock price	9.8	6.5
Capital stock in 1973 ($million)	40.2	658.6
Capital stock in 1992 ($million)	248.7	2,958.0

Table 5 presents the within-group estimates for the groups of less– and more–capital-intensive firms. Three variants of the liquidity model are estimated. The liquidity variable is highly significant in all specifications, and there are significant differences in the coefficients of the liquidity variable across the two groups. Sales and q variables also enter the regressions significantly. However, although these results are encouraging, the null hypothesis of the equality of slope coefficients conditioning on the firm-specific effects are strongly rejected for all specifications for both groups. In other words, using the capital-to-sales ratio of .55 as a cut-off point, there is still substantial heterogeneity within the groups.

Because we are not able to find a set of explanatory variables that adequately explains the variation of β_{i2}, nor are

Table 5. Within Estimation of Models for Less– and More–Capital-Intensive Firms

	Less–capital-intensive firms			More–capital-intensive firms		
$(\frac{I}{K})_{i,t-1}$	.265	.198	.248	.392	.363	.384
	(.011)	(.012)	(.011)	(.022)	(.023)	(.022)
$(\frac{LIQ}{K})_{i,t-1}$	.161	.110	.119	.308	.253	.278
	(.007)	(.007)	(.007)	(.024)	(.027)	(.025)
$(\frac{S}{K})_{i,t-1}$		.023			.025	
		(.001)			(.006)	
q_{it}			.011			.009
			(.0006)			(.002)
Actual F	2.04	1.84	2.22	2.50	2.19	2.10
Critical F	1.09	1.07	1.07	1.20	1.17	1.17
Numerator df	834	1,251	1,251	170	255	255
Denominator df	6,592	6,174	6,174	1,368	1,282	1,282
Number of firms	418	418	418	86	86	86

NOTE: The dependent variable is $(I/K)_{it}$. Less–capital-intensive firms are those with minimum (K/S) between .15 and .55 over the sample period. For more–capital-intensive firms, the minimum (K/S) is greater than .55. The regressions include company-specific intercepts. Actual F is the F statistic for testing the homogeneity of slope coefficients. For the F test, a 5% significance level is chosen. The estimation period is 1974–1992. Standard errors are in parentheses.

we able to obtain homogeneity by classifying firms into groups, we are left with either treating β_{i2} as fixed and different or treating β_{i2} as random draws from a common distribution (i.e., fixed-effects vs. random-effects specification). One view is that there is really no distinction in the "nature of effect." It is assumed at the outset that the effects are random. The fixed-effects approach is viewed as one where investigators make inferences conditional on the effects in the sample. The random-effects approach is viewed as one in which investigators make unconditional or marginal inferences with respect to the population of all effects. It is up to the investigator to decide whether to consider the conditional likelihood or the marginal likelihood function (see, e.g., Box and Tiao 1973). Within the random-effects framework, individual differences are viewed as random draws from a population with constant mean and variance. Therefore, it is appropriate to pool the data and try to draw some generalization about the population. The unconditional, or random-effects inference generally is more efficient than the conditional, or fixed-effects inference.

On the other hand, if individual differences reflect fundamental heterogeneity or if individual response coefficients depend on the values of the included explanatory variables, then estimation of the model parameters based on the conventional random-effects formulation can be misleading. To avoid this bias, heterogeneity among individuals must be treated as fixed. In other words, one must investigate investment behavior firm by firm, and there is no advantage to pooling. Without pooling, though, the shortage of degrees of freedom and multicollinearity can render the resulting estimates meaningless and make drawing general conclusions difficult.

3. A FRAMEWORK FOR POOLED DATA ANALYSIS

We start with an unrestricted model by writing the model for each company as

$$\mathbf{y}_i = \mathbf{X}_i\beta_i + \mathbf{Z}_i\gamma_i + \mathbf{u}_i, \qquad i = 1, 2, \ldots, N, \tag{7}$$

where $\mathbf{y}_i$ is a $T\times 1$ vector of observations for the dependent variable and $\mathbf{X}_i$ and $\mathbf{Z}_i$ are matrices of explanatory variables with dimensions $T \times k_1$ and $T \times k_2$ for the ith individual. When (7) is stacked together for all firms, we get

$$\mathbf{y} = \mathbf{X}\beta + \mathbf{Z}\beta + \mathbf{u}, \tag{8}$$

where

$$\begin{aligned}
\mathbf{y} &= (\mathbf{y}_1', \mathbf{y}_2', \ldots, \mathbf{y}_N')', \\
\mathbf{X} &= \operatorname{diag}(\mathbf{X}_1, \mathbf{X}_2, \ldots, \mathbf{X}_N), \\
\mathbf{Z} &= \operatorname{diag}(Z_1, Z_2, \ldots, Z_N), \\
\mathbf{u} &= (\mathbf{u}_1', \mathbf{u}_2', \ldots, \mathbf{u}_N')', \\
\beta &= (\beta_1', \beta_2', \ldots, \beta_N')',
\end{aligned}$$

and

$$\gamma = (\gamma_1', \gamma_2', \ldots, \gamma_N')'.$$

The dimensions of $\mathbf{y}$, $\mathbf{X}$, $\mathbf{Z}$, $\mathbf{u}$, β, and γ are $NT \times 1$, $NT \times Nk_1$, $NT \times Nk_2$, $NT \times 1$, $Nk_1 \times 1$, and $Nk_2 \times 1$. It is also assumed that $E\mathbf{u} = 0$ and $E\mathbf{uu}' = \mathbf{\Omega}$.

We consider two types of constraints for this model; stochastic and fixed. We suppose that β is subject to a stochastic constraint of the form

$$\beta = \mathbf{A}_1\bar{\beta} + \varepsilon, \tag{9}$$

where $\mathbf{A}_1$ is an $Nk_1 \times m$ matrix with known elements, $\bar{\beta}$ is an $m \times 1$ vector of constants,

$$\varepsilon \sim N(0, \mathbf{C}). \tag{10}$$

and the variance–covariance matrix $\mathbf{C}$ is nonsingular. In addition, we assume that the coefficients γ are subject to exact constraints of the form

$$\gamma = \begin{pmatrix} \gamma_1 \\ \vdots \\ \gamma_N \end{pmatrix} = \mathbf{A}_2\bar{\gamma}, \tag{11}$$

where $\mathbf{A}_2$ is an $Nk_2 \times n$ matrix with known elements.

Because $\mathbf{A}_2$ is a known matrix, instead of working with (8), we treat the model

$$\mathbf{y} = \mathbf{X}\beta + \tilde{\mathbf{Z}}\bar{\gamma} + \mathbf{u} \tag{12}$$

subject to (9)–(11) as the maintained hypothesis, where $\tilde{\mathbf{Z}} = \mathbf{ZA}_2$ and $\mathbf{u}$ is normally distributed with mean $\mathbf{0}$ and covariance matrix $\mathbf{\Omega}$. This formulation encompasses many widely used panel data models as special cases. For instance, the two extreme cases of a common model for all firms and different models for different firms can be obtained by letting $\mathbf{X} = 0$ and $\mathbf{A}_2 = \mathbf{e}_N \otimes \mathbf{I}_{k_2}$ for the former and by letting $\mathbf{X} = 0$ and $\mathbf{A}_2 = \mathbf{I}_N \otimes \mathbf{I}_{k_2}$ for the latter, where $\mathbf{e}_N$ is an $N \times 1$ vector with each element equal to 1, $\mathbf{I}_{k_2}$ is a $k_2 \times k_2$ identity matrix, and $\otimes$ denotes the Kronecker product. The intermediate case of variable-intercept models (see, e.g., Kuh 1963) can be obtained by letting $\mathbf{X} = 0$, the first column of $\mathbf{Z}_i$ be a $T \times 1$ vector of 1s, $\mathbf{e}_T$, $\mathbf{A}_2 = (\mathbf{I}_N \otimes i_{k_2}, \mathbf{e}_N \otimes \mathbf{I}^*_{k_2-1})$, $\bar{\gamma}' = (\gamma_{11}, \ldots, \gamma_{1N}, \bar{\gamma}_2 \ldots \bar{\gamma}_{k_2})$, and

$$i_{k_2} = \begin{pmatrix} 1 \\ 0 \\ \vdots \\ 0 \end{pmatrix}, \qquad \mathbf{I}^*_{k_2-1} = \begin{pmatrix} \mathbf{0}' \\ \mathbf{I}_{k_2-1} \end{pmatrix}.$$

The error components model (see, e.g., Balestra and Nerlove 1966 and Wallace and Hussain 1969) is obtained by letting $\mathbf{X}_i = \mathbf{e}_T$, $\beta' = (\beta_{11}, \ldots, \beta_{1N})$, $\mathbf{A}_1 = \mathbf{e}_N$, $\mathbf{C} = \sigma^2_{\beta_1}\mathbf{I}_N$, and $\bar{\beta}_1 = 0$ if z_{it} contains the intercept term. The random-coefficients model (see, e.g., Swamy 1971) is obtained by letting $\mathbf{Z} = 0$, $\mathbf{A}_1 = \mathbf{e}_N \otimes \mathbf{I}_{k_1}$, $\varepsilon' = (\beta_1' - \bar{\beta}', \ldots, \beta_N' - \bar{\beta}')$, and $\mathbf{C} = \mathbf{I}_N \otimes \Delta$, where $\mathbf{\Delta}$ is a $k_1 \times k_1$ constant matrix. Moreover, (9) and (12) are simply the mixed fixed- and random-coefficients model used by Hsiao, Mountain, Tsui, and Chan (1989).

The framework (9)–(12) can be viewed as having prior knowledge about β—namely, normally distributed with mean $\mathbf{A}_1\bar{\beta}$ and covariance $\mathbf{C}$—but no prior knowledge about $\bar{\gamma}$. Substituting (9) into (12), we have

$$\mathbf{y} = \mathbf{X}\mathbf{A}_1\bar{\beta} + \tilde{\mathbf{Z}}\bar{\gamma} + \mathbf{v}, \quad (13)$$

where

$$\mathbf{v} = \mathbf{u} + \mathbf{X}\boldsymbol{\varepsilon}.$$

In a classical framework, the focus is on deriving the efficient estimators for the common mean $\bar{\beta}$ and $\bar{\gamma}$ of (13) based on this prior information. The prediction of the random variable β_i is not of great interest. However, in many panel studies not just the mean coefficients are of interest. Often, we are also interested in knowing the individual-specific coefficients β_i. In a Bayesian framework, the interest is in deriving the posterior distribution of β_i, $\bar{\beta}$, and $\bar{\gamma}$ given the prior and the data. Therefore, we take a Bayes approach to derive the estimators of β, $\bar{\beta}$, and $\bar{\gamma}$.

Suppose that the following assumptions hold:

A1. Given β, $\bar{\gamma}$ and $\boldsymbol{\Omega}$, $\mathbf{y} \sim N(\mathbf{X}\beta + \tilde{\mathbf{Z}}\bar{\gamma}, \boldsymbol{\Omega})$.
A2. The prior distributions of β and $\bar{\gamma}$ are independent.
A3. $\beta \sim N(\mathbf{A}_1\bar{\beta}, \mathbf{C})$.
A4. $\bar{\beta}$ and $\bar{\gamma}$ are independent and $p(\bar{\beta}) \propto$ constant and $p(\bar{\gamma}) \propto$ constant.

The posterior distributions of $\bar{\beta}$ and $\bar{\gamma}$ and the joint posterior distributions of β and $\bar{\gamma}$ given $\mathbf{y}$ are given in the Appendix.

As mentioned in Section 2, if the coefficients are fixed and different or the random components of the coefficients are correlated with the explanatory variables, then a fixed-effects model is more appropriate. However, instead of testing the correlation between random effects and variables (as in Hausman 1978), we propose to treat the fixed-effects and random-effects models as different models and use a model selection criterion based on Friedman and Schwarz's (1991, p. 48) suggestion that "the real proof of the pudding is whether it (i.e., a model) produces a satisfactory explanation of data not used in baking it—data for subsequent or earlier years, for other countries, or for other variables." Therefore, we divide the sample into two periods. The first period comprises observations from 1 to T_1, denoted by $\mathbf{y}_1$; the second period, observations from $T_1 + 1$ to T, denoted by $\mathbf{y}_2$. We use $\mathbf{y}_1$ to obtain the distribution of $\boldsymbol{\theta}$ ($\boldsymbol{\theta}' = (\beta', \bar{\gamma}')$) under different configurations of the fixed- (H_{FC}) and random-coefficient (H_{RC}) models. The posterior densities are denoted by $p(\theta_{\mathrm{FC}}|y_1)$ and $p(\boldsymbol{\theta}_{\mathrm{RC}}|\mathbf{y}_1)$. Then the predictive density is defined as

$$p_j(\mathbf{y}_2|\mathbf{y}_1) = \int p(\mathbf{y}_2|\boldsymbol{\theta}_j, \mathbf{y}_1)p(\boldsymbol{\theta}_j|\mathbf{y}_1)\, d\boldsymbol{\theta}_j, \quad j = \mathrm{FC}, \mathrm{RC}. \quad (14)$$

The model with a higher predictive density is favored.

If T_1 is small, then the estimated β and $\bar{\gamma}$ are likely to have large variances. If T_1 is close to T, then there are not many observations left for prediction, and the model comparison may be highly variable. To balance the precision of the estimates and reliability of prediction comparison, we follow Min and Zellner (1993) and compute the predictive density (14) with recursive updating using the formula

$$\int p(\mathbf{y}_T|\boldsymbol{\theta}_j, \mathbf{y}_{T-1})p(\boldsymbol{\theta}_j|\mathbf{y}_{T-1})\, d\boldsymbol{\theta}_j \times \int p(\mathbf{y}_{T-1}|\boldsymbol{\theta}_j, \mathbf{y}_{T-2})p(\boldsymbol{\theta}_j|\mathbf{y}_{T-2})\, d\boldsymbol{\theta}_j \cdots \int p(\mathbf{y}_{T_1+1}|\boldsymbol{\theta}_j, \mathbf{y}_1)p(\boldsymbol{\theta}_j|\mathbf{y}_1)\, d\boldsymbol{\theta}_j, \quad (15)$$

with the following Bayesian updating formula:

$$\tilde{\boldsymbol{\theta}}_t = \tilde{\mathbf{V}}_t(\mathbf{W}_t'\boldsymbol{\Omega}^{-1}\mathbf{y}_t + \tilde{\mathbf{V}}_{t-1}^{-1}\tilde{\boldsymbol{\theta}}_{t-1})$$

and

$$\tilde{\mathbf{V}}_t = (\mathbf{W}_t'\boldsymbol{\Omega}^{-1}\mathbf{W}_t + \tilde{\mathbf{V}}_{t-1}^{-1})^{-1}, \qquad t = T_1 + 1, \ldots, T.$$

Here $\mathbf{y}_t' = (\mathbf{y}_{1t}, \mathbf{y}_{2t}, \ldots, \mathbf{y}_{Nt})$, $\mathbf{W}_t = (\mathbf{X}_t, \mathbf{Z}_t)$, and $\tilde{\boldsymbol{\theta}}_t$ and $\tilde{\mathbf{V}}_t$ are the posterior mean and variance of θ based on the first t observations. Also, if $p(\boldsymbol{\theta}|\mathbf{y}_t)$ is $N(\tilde{\boldsymbol{\theta}}_t, \tilde{\mathbf{V}}_t)$, then

$$p(\mathbf{y}_{t+1}|\mathbf{y}_t) = \int p(\mathbf{y}_{t+1}|\boldsymbol{\theta}, \mathbf{y}_t)p(\boldsymbol{\theta}|\mathbf{y}_t)\, d\boldsymbol{\theta} \sim N(\mathbf{W}_{t+1}\tilde{\boldsymbol{\theta}}_t, \boldsymbol{\Omega} + \mathbf{W}_{t+1}\tilde{\mathbf{V}}_t\mathbf{W}_{t+1}'). \quad (16)$$

Formulas (A.2)–(A.4) in Appendix A can be used as the initial estimates for updating.

The formulas are derived conditionally on $\boldsymbol{\Omega}$ and $\boldsymbol{\Delta}$. Unconditional Bayes estimators can be derived by introducing the prior distributions of $\boldsymbol{\Omega}$ and $\boldsymbol{\Delta}$, but these are computationally burdensome. Monte Carlo studies (Hsiao et al. 1995) appear to indicate that not much information loss is entailed in using consistent estimates of $\boldsymbol{\Omega}$ and $\boldsymbol{\Delta}$ instead of prior distribution. Therefore, we take an empirical Bayes approach, assume that

$$\boldsymbol{\Omega} = \mathrm{diag}(\sigma_1^2\mathbf{I}_T, \sigma_2^2\mathbf{I}_T, \ldots, \sigma_N^2\mathbf{I}_T),$$

and use the following as consistent estimates of $\boldsymbol{\Delta}$ and σ_i^2:

$$\hat{\boldsymbol{\Delta}} = \frac{1}{N}\sum_{i=1}^{N}\left(\hat{\beta}_i - \frac{1}{N}\sum_{i=1}^{N}\hat{\beta}_i\right)\left(\hat{\beta}_i - \frac{1}{N}\sum_{i=1}^{N}\hat{\beta}_i\right)'$$

and

$$\hat{\sigma}_i^2 = \frac{\hat{\mathbf{u}}_i'\hat{\mathbf{u}}_i}{T - k},$$

where $\hat{\beta}_i$ and $\hat{\mathbf{u}}_i$ are obtained from ordinary least squares (OLS) estimation for each company and $k = k_1 + k_2$.

4. POOLED ANALYSIS OF INVESTMENT BEHAVIOR

In this section we reestimate the investment functions using a fixed-coefficient model and a mixed fixed- and random-coefficients model. The fixed-coefficient model assumes that each company has different coefficients or that the variation of coefficients is correlated with the explanatory variables. The mixed fixed- and random-coefficient model assumes that, conditional on company-specific effects, the remaining slope coefficients are randomly distributed around a certain mean within each of these groups. To see which model is more appropriate, we compute the recursive predictive density for three variants of the liquidity model. We split the sample into two groups using the

Table 6. Prediction Comparison of Fixed-Coefficients and Mixed Fixed and Random-Coefficients Models for Less– and More–Capital-Intensive Firms (Recursive Predictive Density)

Sample	Model	Liquidity	Liquidity with q	Liquidity with sales
Less–capital-intensive firms	Fixed-slope coefficients	2.244	2,178	2,172
	Random-slope coefficients	2.299	2,272	2,266
More–capital-intensive firms	Fixed-slope coefficients	587	544	557
	Random-slope coefficients	589	556	576

NOTE The recursive predictive density is the logarithm of (15) in the text Columns 3, 4, and 5 correspond to models 1, 2 and 3 The fixed-coefficients model assumes different coefficients for each firm The random-coefficients model assumes randomly distributed slope coefficients with constant mean conditional on fixed firm-specific effects The prediction period is 1990–1992

capital–sales ratio of .55 as a cut-off point, and calculate the recursive predictive density for each group separately. In implementing the prediction criterion, we divide observations into pre- and post-1989 periods. Approximately 10% of the companies have continuous data starting with 1976; we exclude these companies from the model selection comparisons. We report the results in Table 6. The numbers reported in the table are the logarithms of (15).

We find that the mixed fixed- and random-coefficients model is favored over the fixed-coefficient model for both groups. Similar results are obtained when the absolute value of the forecast error for the median firm is used to choose between models. Because a mixed fixed- and random-coefficients approach appears better able to predict individual firm outcome than a fixed-coefficient approach, and also allows us to draw some general conclusions about a firm's investment behavior, we focus our discussion based on the results of a mixed fixed- and random-coefficients approach.

Table 7 presents the estimation results of models 1–3 by the mixed fixed- and random-coefficients approach. The mean coefficient of the liquidity variable is highly significant. Moreover, the mean coefficient of the liquidity variable turns out to be 60%–80% larger for the more capital-intensive group than for the less-capital intensive group, a statistically significant difference. The implied long-run relationships between the liquidity variable and the fixed investment variable are also statistically significant. For instance, for model 1, a 10% increase in liquidity capital ratio leads to a 4% increase in fixed investment capital ratio in the long run for the less–capital-intensive group compared to a 7% increase in this ratio for the more–capital-intensive group. We also note that the mixed fixed- and random-coefficients approach yields substantially different coefficient estimates of the liquidity variable than those derived by the conventional within estimates (see Table 5). In general, the coefficients of the liquidity variable based on the mixed fixed- and random-coefficients model are almost 100% larger than the coefficients estimated using the within estimation technique for the less–capital-intensive group and 60% larger for the more–capital-intensive group, whereas the coefficients for the lagged dependent variable are smaller. If the coefficients are indeed randomly distributed and the explanatory variables are positively serially correlated, then this is precisely what one would expect from the within estimates (Pesaran and Smith 1995).

Table 7. Estimation of Mixed Fixed and Random-Coefficients Models for Less– and More–Capital-Intensive Firms

	Less–capital-intensive firms			More–capital-intensive firms		
$(\frac{I}{K})_{i,t-1}$	.230	.183	.121	.321	.302	.236
	(.018)	(.017)	(.019)	(.036)	(.037)	(.041)
$(\frac{LIQ}{K})_{i,t-1}$	.306	.252	.239	.488	.449	.416
	(.021)	(.023)	(.027)	(.065)	(.067)	(.079)
$(\frac{S}{K})_{i,t-1}$			.024			.038
			(.003)			(.015)
q_{it}		.019			.022	
		(.003)			(.008)	
Number of firms	418	418	418	86	86	86

NOTE The dependent variable is $(I/K)_{it}$. The regressions include fixed firm-specific effects The estimation period is 1974–1992. Standard errors are in parentheses

To further assess the robustness of the results to specification changes, we estimated three different models for each group. According to Leamer (1983), "an inference is not believable if it is fragile, if it can be reversed by minor changes in assumptions." Leamer and Leonard (1983) argued that the extreme values of the coefficients and their ranges can be used to delineate the ambiguity in the inferences. If the range of coefficient estimates is "short," then the ambiguity in the model will be irrelevant, because all models lead to essentially the same inferences. When sales and q are added to the regressions, the liquidity coefficient decreases only slightly (10%–25%). We think that the robustness of the coefficient estimates of the liquidity variable to alterations in the conditioning set of information satisfactorily addresses the concerns expressed by Leamer and others. The negligible collinearity between liquidity and sales and q also confirms our belief that the liquidity variable is fundamentally a measure of internal finance.

To compare the performance of the liquidity model with those appearing in the investment literature, we also ran a number of horse races of our own between alternative investment models. We used the recursive predictive density to evaluate the forecasting performance of the liquidity, sales-accelerator, and q models. A priori, we would expect the liquidity model to forecast the investment of the high–capital-intensive group better than other models. Table 8 supports our conjectures. For this group, the liquidity model performs the best. This result is also reinforced by other prediction criteria. Although the recursive predictive density favors the flexible accelerator model to the liquidity

Table 8. Prediction Comparison of Investment Models (Recursive Predictive Density)

Sample	Model: Liquidity	q	Sales-accelerator
Less–capital-intensive firms	2,299	2,274	2,314
More–capital-intensive firms	589	536	580

NOTE The recursive predictive density is the logarithm of Equation (15). Columns 2, 3, and 4 correspond to models 1, 4, and 5 The prediction period is 1990–1992

Table 9. Sensitivity of Estimates of the Liquidity Model to the Cut-Off Point

	Less-capital-intensive firms		More-capital-intensive firms	
	$.15 < (\frac{K}{S}) < .45$	$.15 < (\frac{K}{S}) < .65$	$(\frac{K}{S}) > .45$	$(\frac{K}{S}) > .65$
$(\frac{I}{K})_{i,t-1}$	.222	.230	.315	.349
	(.019)	(.017)	(.030)	(.043)
$(\frac{LIQ}{K})_{i,t-1}$	.298	.317	.452	.485
	(.021)	(.021)	(.053)	(.068)

NOTE: The dependent variable is $(I/K)_{it}$. The regressions include fixed firm-specific effects. The estimation period is 1974–1992. Standard errors are in parentheses.

model for the less–capital-intensive group, the difference in predictive ability does not seem great. We have also tried some more complicated specifications; however, these do not improve predictive performance. For instance, the addition of sales–capital ratio and q actually reduces the predictive ability of the base model.

The prediction comparisons between the liquidity model, Tobin's q, and sales-accelerator models appear to favor liquidity as an important explanatory variable. Insofar as investment decisions are largely determined by potential profit, this result would imply that liquidity could actually be a better proxy for potential profit than Tobin's q or sales. However, we believe instead that liquidity is not acting as a proxy for potential profit. Although investment decisions may be affected by potential profit, the actual appropriation or investment expenditure may be affected by firm's liquidity positions. If liquidity is simply a proxy for potential profit, then one would expect the different estimates of the liquidity coefficients between less– and more–capital-intensive firms to be due to the fact that more–capital-intensive firms are more profitable. On the other hand, if liquidity position does play a role in actual investment expenditures, then one would expect more–capital-intensive firms to have larger coefficients, because their capital requirement tends to be higher. However, the information summarized in Table 4 indicates that less–capital-intensive firms have higher sales growth, higher percentage changes in stock price, and higher cash flow–capital stock ratio than more–capital-intensive firms.

In short, the data appear to support a mixed fixed- and random-coefficients formulation of company investment behavior. The estimated liquidity coefficients show statistically significant differences across different classes of companies. However, because our classification scheme effectively groups companies according to their liquidity positions, we think that the statistically significant differences in the coefficient of the liquidity variable reflects more the degree of financial constraints rather than the differential information content of the liquidity variable for different groups of companies, as suggested by Sims (1988).

The foregoing inference is drawn from the analysis of classifying firms into two groups using capital intensity ratio of .55 as a cut-off point. We note that if firms can indeed be classified into two groups, but .55 is not the appropriate cut-off point, then some of the firms are falsely classified into the wrong group, and the analysis is contaminated. To examine the robustness of our inference, we use two criteria: the sensitivity of parameter estimates and the predictive performance of our model when other cut-off points are used.

Table 7 shows that the coefficients of the lagged investment and liquidity variables are larger for more–capital-intensive firms than for less–capital-intensive firms. If .55 is close to the right cut-off point, then using a cut-off point larger than .55 would misclassify some of the firms that should belong to the more–capital-intensive group into the less–capital-intensive group. The implication would be that the estimates of the parameters of the more–capital-intensive group will not change much, but the coefficients of the less–capital-intensive group will increase somewhat. Alternatively, using a cut-off point less than .55 would misclassify some of the firms that should belong to the less–capital-intensive group into the more–capital-intensive group. Thus we would see little change in the estimates of the less–capital-intensive groups, but somewhat reduced estimates of the more–capital-intensive group. Similarly, if an incorrect cut-off point is used, we would expect the prediction performance of the model to worsen. Table 9 presents the estimates of the liquidity model using .45 and .65 as cut-off points. Comparing this table with Table 7, it is clear that the directions of changes in the coefficients are precisely those predicted assuming that .55 is close to the correct cut-off point. The sums of the logarithm of the recursive predictive densities for the less– and more–capital-intensive groups using .45 and .65 are 2,864 and 2,861, smaller than those obtained using .55 as a cut-off point. The root mean-square prediction error is also smaller for models using .55 rather than .45 and .65 as cut-off points. Therefore, we feel reasonably confident that our results are insensitive to our possible misclassification of firms that results from using .55 as a cut-off point.

Finally, as the associate editor pointed out, capital stock variables are notorious for measurement errors. Therefore, instead of using the book value of capital, we construct the replacement value. We also check this conjecture using Casson's (1973) correction formula for the least squares estimates when the deflator is measured with error. The correlations between the corrected and uncorrected least squares estimates exceed 99% for all the variables. Moreover, because all of the models are deflated by the same capital stock variable, we expect that the general qualitative conclusion about different models would remain valid. Of course, the implication of measurement errors can be a serious one and deserves further study.

5. CONCLUSIONS

Two principal conclusions can be drawn from this study. First, there are substantial differences across firms in their investment behavior, and these differences cannot be completely captured by the included explanatory variables. When these differences are ignored by constraining the parameters to be identical across firms, the impact of liquidity variable on firm investment is seriously underestimated. When parameters are allowed to vary across firms, the issue of whether to pool the data may be resolved by using a mixed fixed- and random-coefficients framework. The recursive predictive density criteria appear to favor a mixed model over a fixed-coefficient model. The mixed model fit to the data allows pooling and allows some general conclusions to be drawn about a group of firms. Second. estimation results and prediction tests show that financial constraints affect investment, at least for a subset of U.S. companies. We find that the investment of capital-intensive companies is particularly sensitive to fluctuations in internal funds. Finally, the classification scheme used in this article lessens the criticism that differences in the coefficients of the liquidity variable reflect the information content of this variable rather than financial considerations.

APPENDIX A: DERIVATION OF BAYES ESTIMATOR

The following posterior distributions can be derived. as shown by Hsiao (1995) and Hsiao et al. (1993):

a. the posterior distribution of $\bar{\beta}$ and $\bar{\gamma}$ given $\mathbf{y}$ is

$$N\left[\begin{pmatrix} \bar{\beta}^{**} \\ \bar{\gamma}^{**} \end{pmatrix}, \mathbf{V}\right],$$

where

$$\begin{pmatrix} \bar{\beta}^{**} \\ \bar{\gamma}^{**} \end{pmatrix} = \begin{pmatrix} \mathbf{A}_1'\mathbf{X}'(\boldsymbol{\Omega} + \mathbf{XCX}')^{-1}\mathbf{XA}_1 & \mathbf{A}_1'\mathbf{X}'(\boldsymbol{\Omega} + \mathbf{XCX}')^{-1}\bar{\mathbf{Z}} \\ \bar{\mathbf{Z}}'(\boldsymbol{\Omega} + \mathbf{XCX}')^{-1}\mathbf{XA}_1 & \bar{\mathbf{Z}}'(\boldsymbol{\Omega} + \mathbf{XCX}')^{-1}\bar{\mathbf{Z}} \end{pmatrix}^{-1} \times \begin{pmatrix} \mathbf{A}_1'\mathbf{X}'(\boldsymbol{\Omega} + \mathbf{XCX}')^{-1}\mathbf{y} \\ \bar{\mathbf{Z}}'(\boldsymbol{\Omega} + \mathbf{XCX}')^{-1}\mathbf{y} \end{pmatrix} \quad (A.1)$$

$$\mathbf{V} = \begin{pmatrix} \mathbf{A}_1'\mathbf{X}'(\boldsymbol{\Omega} + \mathbf{XCX}')^{-1}\mathbf{XA}_1 & \mathbf{A}_1'\mathbf{X}'(\boldsymbol{\Omega} + \mathbf{XCX}')^{-1}\bar{\mathbf{Z}} \\ \bar{\mathbf{Z}}'(\boldsymbol{\Omega} + \mathbf{XCX}')^{-1}\mathbf{XA}_1 & \bar{\mathbf{Z}}'(\boldsymbol{\Omega} + \mathbf{XCX}')^{-1}\bar{\mathbf{Z}} \end{pmatrix}^{-1}$$

b. The joint posterior distribution of β, $\bar{\gamma}$ given $\mathbf{y}$ is

$$N\left[\begin{pmatrix} \beta^{**} \\ \bar{\gamma}^{**} \end{pmatrix}, \mathbf{V}^*\right],$$

where

$$\beta^{**} = \mathbf{D}_1(\mathbf{X}'\boldsymbol{\Sigma}_1\mathbf{y}), \quad (A.2)$$

$$\bar{\gamma}^{**} = \mathbf{D}_2(\mathbf{Z}'\boldsymbol{\Sigma}_2\mathbf{y}), \quad (A.3)$$

and

$$\mathbf{V}^* = \begin{pmatrix} \mathbf{X}'\boldsymbol{\Omega}^{-1}\mathbf{X} + \mathbf{C}^{-1} - \mathbf{C}^{-1}\mathbf{A}_1(\mathbf{A}_1'\mathbf{C}^{-1}\mathbf{A}_1)^{-1}\mathbf{A}_1'\mathbf{C}^{-1} & \mathbf{X}'\boldsymbol{\Omega}^{-1}\bar{\mathbf{Z}} \\ \bar{\mathbf{Z}}'\boldsymbol{\Omega}^{-1}\mathbf{X} & \bar{\mathbf{Z}}'\boldsymbol{\Omega}^{-1}\bar{\mathbf{Z}} \end{pmatrix}^{-1} \quad (A.4)$$

and

$$\mathbf{D}_1 = (\mathbf{X}'\boldsymbol{\Sigma}_1\mathbf{X} + \mathbf{C}^{-1} - \mathbf{C}^{-1}\mathbf{A}_1(\mathbf{A}_1'\mathbf{C}^{-1}\mathbf{A}_1)^{-1}\mathbf{A}_1'\mathbf{C}^{-1})^{-1},$$

$$\mathbf{D}_2 = (\tilde{\mathbf{Z}}'\boldsymbol{\Sigma}_2\tilde{\mathbf{Z}})^{-1},$$

$$\boldsymbol{\Sigma}_1 = \boldsymbol{\Omega}^{-1} - \boldsymbol{\Omega}^{-1}\tilde{\mathbf{Z}}(\tilde{\mathbf{Z}}'\boldsymbol{\Omega}^{-1}\tilde{\mathbf{Z}})^{-1}\tilde{\mathbf{Z}}'\boldsymbol{\Omega}^{-1},$$

and

$$\boldsymbol{\Sigma}_2 = \boldsymbol{\Omega}^{-1} - \boldsymbol{\Omega}^{-1}\mathbf{X}(\mathbf{X}'\boldsymbol{\Omega}^{-1}\mathbf{X} + \mathbf{C}^{-1} - \mathbf{C}^{-1}\mathbf{A}_1(\mathbf{A}_1'\mathbf{C}^{-1}\mathbf{A}_1)^{-1}\mathbf{A}_1'\mathbf{C}^{-1})^{-1}\mathbf{X}'\boldsymbol{\Omega}^{-1}.$$

Many of the well-known estimators, such as the generalized least squares estimators of variable intercepts, error components, and random-coefficients models, are special cases of (1) with appropriate definitions of $\mathbf{A}_1$, $\mathbf{X}$, and $\mathbf{Z}$ (see, e.g., Hsiao, Appelbe, and Dineen 1993). Moreover, the Bayes estimator (1) is consistent even when X contains lagged dependent variables if both N and $T \rightarrow \infty$. Monte Carlo studies also indicate that even when T is finite, the Bayes estimator possesses good properties (Hsiao, Pesaran, and Tahmiscioglu 1996).

APPENDIX B: DATA DESCRIPTION

The individual company data are obtained from Compustat annual industrial tapes. We combined the 1993 tape, which contains data for the 20-year period from 1973–1992, with an earlier tape to expand the sample period to 1971–1992. We constructed the sample following these guidelines:

- Companies in the manufacturing sector were chosen.
- Companies that do not have time series data going back to early 1970s were excluded.
- Companies that have missing data on the variables necessary for this study were excluded.
- Firms involved in significant mergers and acquisitions were excluded. Because we do not have reliable data on mergers, we use the excessive values of annual changes in gross capital stock to identify mergers. Companies whose gross property, plant, and equipment increased by more than 100% at any given year were excluded from the sample. Companies whose capital stocks showed decreases of more than 50% were also excluded.

The final sample comprises 561 companies. Construction of the replacement value of the capital stock and lags caused the loss of the first three observations. The number of observations on each company varies from 17 to 19.

We constructed the replacement value of the capital stock (K) using the perpetual inventory method (see, e.g., Fazzari et al. 1988). We set the replacement value of the capital stock equal to the book value for the year that the firm entered the dataset. To update the capital stock, we used the implicit price deflator for nonresidential investment from the 1993 "Economic Report of the President". We calculated the useful life of assets using the procedure outlined by Salinger and Summers (1983). Economic depreciation is assumed to be double-declining balance. The investment variable (I) is the expenditure on property, plant, and equipment; it does not include spending on acquisitions. The liquidity variable (LIQ) is defined as income after taxes and interest plus depreciation minus dividends. The q variable, the beginning-of-period q, is defined as $[(E + B - INV)/K] - 1$, where E is the market value of equity, B is the book value of debt, and INV is the market value of inventories. We obtained the market value of equity as the sum of the market value of common and preferred stock. We calculated the market value of common stock by multiplying the stock price with common shares outstanding. We computed the value of preferred stock by dividing preferred stocks by the preferred stock yield from the Standard and Poor's. Finally, we calculated the market value of inventories using the Salinger and Summers procedure.

[Received October 1995. Revised December 1996.]

REFERENCES

Balestra, P., and Nerlove, M. (1966), "Pooling Cross-Section and Time Series Data in the Estimation of a Dynamic Model: The Demand for Natural Gas," *Econometrica*, 34, 585–612.

Bond, S., and Meghir, C. (1994), "Dynamic Investment Models and the Firm's Financial Policy," *Review of Economic Studies*, 61, 197–222.

Box, G. E. P., and Tiao, G. C. (1973), *Bayesian Inference in Statistical Analysis*, Menlo Park, NJ: Addison-Wesley.

Brainard, W. C., and Tobin, J. (1968), "Pitfalls in Financial Model Building," *American Economic Review*, 58, 99–122.

Breusch, T. S., and Pagan, A. R. (1979), "A Simple Test for Heteroscedasticity and Random Coefficient Variation," *Econometrica*, 47, 1287–1294.

Casson, M. C. (1973), "Linear Regression With Error in the Deflating Variable," *Econometrica*, 41, 751–759.

Chenery, H. (1952), "Overcapacity and the Acceleration Principle," *Econometrica*, 20, 1–28.

Chirinko, R. S., and Schaller, H. (1995), "Why Does Liquidity Matter in Investment Equations?," *Journal of Money, Credit and Banking*, 27, 527–548.

Coen, R. M. (1971), "The Effect of Cash Flow on the Speed of Adjustment," in *Tax Incentives and Capital Spending*, ed. G. Fromm, Washington, DC: Brookings Institution, pp. 131–196.

De Finetti, B. (1964), "Foresight: Its Logical Laws, Its Subjective Sources," in *Studies in Subjective Probability*, eds. H. E. Kyburg Jr. and H. E. Smokler, New York: Wiley, pp. 93–158.

Devereux, M., and Schianterelli, F. (1990), "Investment, Financial Factors, and Cash Flow: Evidence From U.K. Panel Data," in *Asymmetric Information, Corporate Finance and Investment*, ed. R. G. Hubbard, Chicago: University of Chicago Press, pp. 279–306.

Easterbrook, F. (1984), "Two Agency Cost Explanations of Dividends," *American Economic Review*, 74, 221–230.

Fazzari, S. M., Hubbard, R. G., and Petersen, B. C. (1988), "Financing Constraints and Corporate Investment," *Brookings Papers on Economic Activity*, 1, 141–195.

Fazzari, S. M., and Petersen, B. C. (1993), "Working Capital and Fixed Investment: New Evidence on Financing Constraints," *Rand Journal of Economics*, 24, 328–342.

Friedman, M., and Schwartz, A. J. (1991), "Alternative Approaches to Analyzing Economic Data," *American Economic Review*, 81, 39–50.

Hausman, J. A. (1978), "Specification Tests in Econometrics," *Econometrica*, 46, 1251–1271.

Hayashi, F. (1982), "Tobin's Marginal q and Average q: A Neoclassical Interpretation," *Econometrica*, 50, 213–224.

Hoshi, T., Kashyap, A., and Scharfstein, D. (1991), "Corporate Structure, Liquidity, and Investment: Evidence From Japanese Industrial Groups," *Quarterly Journal of Economics*, 106, 33–60.

Hsiao, C. (1974), "Statistical Inference for a Model With Both Random Cross-Sectional and Time Effects," *International Economic Review*, 15, 12–30.

——— (1975), "Some Estimation Methods for a Random Coefficients Model," *Econometrica*, 43, 305–325.

——— (1985), "Benefits and Limitations of Panel Data," *Econometric Reviews*, 4, 121–174.

——— (1986), *Analysis of Panel Data*, Cambridge, U.K.: Cambridge University Press.

——— (1995), "Panel Analysis for Metric Data," in *Handbook of Statistical Modeling in the Social and Behavioral Sciences*, eds. G. Arminger, C. C. Clogg, and M. E. Sobel, New York: Plenum Press, pp. 361–400.

Hsiao, C., Appelbe, T. W., and Dineen, C. R. (1993), "A General Framework for Panel Data Analysis With an Application to Canadian Customer-Dialed Long-Distance Service," *Journal of Econometrics*, 59, 63–86.

Hsiao, C., Mountain, D. C., Tsui, K. Y., and Luke Chan, M. W. (1989), "Modeling Ontario Regional Electricity System Demand Using a Mixed Fixed and Random Coefficients Approach," *Regional Science and Urban Economics*, 19, 567–587.

Hsiao, C., Pesaran, M. H., and Tahmiscioglu, A. K. (1996), "Estimation of Dynamic Panel Data Models," unpublished manuscript.

Hsiao, C., Sun, B. H., and Lightwood, J. (1995), "Fixed vs. Random Effects—Specification for Panel Data Analysis," unpublished manuscript.

Jorgenson, D. W. (1971), "Econometric Studies of Investment Behavior: A Survey," *Journal of Economic Literature*, 9, 1111–1147.

Koyck, L. M. (1954), *Distributed Lags and Investment Analysis*, Amsterdam: North-Holland.

Kuh, E. (1963), *Capital Stock Growth: A Micro-Econometric Approach*, Amsterdam: North-Holland.

Leamer, E. E. (1983), "Let's Take the Con out of Econometrics," *American Economic Review*, 73, 31–43.

Leamer, E. E., and Leonard, H. (1983), "Reporting the Fragility of Regression Estimates," *Review of Economics and Statistics*, 65, 306–317.

Lindley, D. V., and Smith, A. F. M. (1972), "Bayes Estimates for the Linear Model," *Journal of the Royal Statistical Society*, 34, 1–41.

Meyer, J. R., and Kuh, E. E. (1957), *The Investment Decision: An Empirical Study*, Cambridge, MA: Harvard University Press.

Miller, M. H., and Modigliani, F. (1961), "Dividend Policy, Growth and the Valuation of Shares," *Journal of Business*, 34, 411–433.

Miller, M. H., and Rock, K. (1985), "Dividend Policy Under Asymmetric Information," *Journal of Finance*, 40, 1031–1051.

Min, C., and Zellner, A. (1993), "Bayesian and Non-Bayesian Methods for Combining Models With Applications to Forecasting International Growth Rates," *Journal of Econometrics*, 56, 89–118.

Modigliani, F., and Miller, M. H. (1958), "The Cost of Capital, Corporation Finance and the Theory of Investment," *American Economic Review*, 48, 261–297.

Myers, S. C., and Majluf, N. S. (1984), "Corporate Financing and Investment Decisions When Firms Have Information That Investors Do Not Have," *Journal of Financial Economics*, 13, 187–221.

Oliner, S., and Rudebusch, G. (1992), "Sources of the Financing Hierarchy for Business Investment," *Review of Economics and Statistics*, 74, 643–654.

Pesaran, M. H., and Smith, R. (1995), "Estimating Long-Run Relationships From Dynamic Heterogeneous Panels," *Journal of Econometrics*, 68, 79–113.

Salinger, M. A., and Summers, L. H. (1983), "Tax Reform and Corporate Investment: A Microeconomic Simulation Study," in *Behavioral Simulation Methods in Tax Policy Analysis*, ed. M. Feldstein, Chicago: University of Chicago Press, 247–281.

Scherer, F. M. (1980), *Industrial Market Structure and Economic Performance*, New York: Houghton Mifflin.

Sims, C. (1988), Comment on "Financing Constraints and Corporate Investment," by S. M. Fazzari, R. G. Hubbard, and B. G. Petersen, *Brookings Papers on Economic Activity*, 1, 204–205.

Stiglitz, J. E., and Weiss, A. (1981), "Credit Rationing in Markets With Imperfect Information," *American Economic Review*, 71, 393–410.

Summers, L. H. (1981), "Taxation and Corporate Investment: A q-Theory Approach," *Brookings Papers on Economic Activity*, 1, 67–127.

Swamy, P. A. V. B. (1971), *Statistical Inference in Random Coefficient Regression Models*, Berlin: Springer-Verlag.

Tobin, J. (1969), "A General Equilibrium Approach to Monetary Theory," *Journal of Money, Credit and Banking*, 1, 15–29.

von Furstenberg, G. M. (1977), "Corporate Investment: Does Market Valuation Matter in the Aggregate?," *Brookings Papers on Economic Activity*, 347–397.

Wallace, T. D., and Hussain, A. (1969), "The Use of Error Components Models in Combining Cross-Section With Time Series Data," *Econometrica*, 37, 55–72.

Whited, T. M. (1992), "Debt, Liquidity Constraints, and Corporate Investment: Evidence From Panel Data," *Journal of Finance*, 47, 1425–1460.

[13]

Estimation of Short-Run and Long-Run Elasticities of Energy Demand From Panel Data Using Shrinkage Estimators

G. S. MADDALA
Department of Economics, The Ohio State University, Columbus, OH 43210-1172

Robert P. TROST
Department of Economics, The George Washington University, Washington, DC 20052

Hongyi LI
Department of Management, The Chinese University of Hong Kong, Shatin N.T., Hong Kong

Frederick JOUTZ
Department of Economics, The George Washington University, Washington, DC 20052

This article discusses the problem of obtaining short-run and long-run elasticities of energy demand for each of 49 states in the United States using data for 21 years. Estimation using the time series data by each state gave several wrong signs for the coefficients. Estimation using pooled data was not valid because the hypothesis of homogeneity of the coefficients was rejected. Shrinkage estimators gave more reasonable results. The article presents in a unified framework the classical, empirical Bayes, and Bayes approaches for deriving these estimators.

KEY WORDS: Bayesian shrinkage estimator; Random-coefficient model; Stein-rule estimator.

In the analysis of panel data, it is customary to pool the observations, with or without individual-specific dummies. These dummy variables are assumed to be fixed (fixed-effects models) or random (random-effects or variance-components models). In these models the slope coefficients are assumed to be equal. The homogeneity of the slope coefficients is often an unreasonable assumption, and one can allow for cross-sectional heterogeneity and/or heterogeneity over time. A commonly used model to allow for cross-sectional heterogeneity is the random-coefficient model, in which the parameters are assumed to come from a common distribution. A commonly used model to allow for heterogeneity over time is the time-varying parameter model, which can be estimated by state-space methods. In any case, one needs to impose some structure on the coefficients if one allows for parameter heterogeneity.

In this article we will concentrate on cross-sectional heterogeneity only. The article considers several shrinkage-type estimators and illustrates their use in the estimation of short-run and long-run price and income elasticities of residential demand for electricity and natural gas in the United States based on a panel data on 49 states over 21 years (1970–1990). Robertson and Symons (1992) and Pesaran and Smith (1995) discussed the biases that are likely to occur in the estimation of long-run elasticities if parameter heterogeneity is ignored and the data are pooled. They assumed a random-coefficient model and were interested in the mean of the coefficients. The focus of this article is on the estimation of the individual parameters for each cross-section under parameter heterogeneity of the form considered by these authors. The framework used is the random-coefficient model, and even if interest centers on the mean of the coefficients, it will be pointed out that there are some problems with the use of two-step procedures in the general least squares (GLS) estimation, a procedure that is most commonly used. Moreover, an iterative procedure will be suggested and illustrated with the empirical example.

Because a review of the estimation of energy-demand models can be found in the book by Berndt (1991), we will not elaborate on the derivation of the demand model estimated. The model we use is a standard dynamic linear regression (DLR) model derived by taking account of error-correction and partial-adjustment mechanisms. For a review of these, see Nickell (1985) and Alogoskoufis and Smith (1991).

1. ALTERNATIVE ESTIMATION METHODS FOR THE ESTIMATION OF THE INDIVIDUAL HETEROGENEOUS PARAMETERS

Consider the linear model

$$y_i \sim N(X_i\beta_i, \sigma_i^2 I), \qquad i = 1, 2, \ldots, N. \tag{1}$$

where y_i is a $T \times 1$ vector, X_i is a $T \times k$ matrix of observations for the ith cross-section, and β_i is a $k \times 1$ vector of parameters. Unlike pure cross-section data, panel data allow us to take care of the dynamic structure. We will, therefore, assume that X_i include lagged values of y_i. This

Journal of Business & Economic Statistics
January 1997, Vol. 15, No. 1

creates problems when we consider the random-coefficient model later. In this case the assumption of strict exogeneity of X_i is no longer valid, and the results we discuss are valid only asymptotically under the usual regularity conditions assumed in dynamic regression models.

With panel data, however, there is the question of whether to pool the data and obtain a single estimate from the whole sample or to estimate the equations separately for each cross-section. The implicit assumption in both the fixed-effects and random-effects models for pooling the data is that the slope coefficients are all the same for all the cross-section units. This may not be a tenable assumption. In practice, the null hypothesis of constancy of slope parameters across the different cross-section units is often rejected. This implies that the equations should be estimated separately for each cross-section rather than obtaining an overall pooled estimate.

The problem with the two usual estimation methods of either pooling the data or obtaining separate estimates for each cross-section is that both are based on extreme assumptions. If the data are pooled, it is assumed that the parameters are all the same. If separate estimates are obtained for each cross-section, it is assumed that the parameters are all different in each cross-section. The truth probably lies somewhere in between. The parameters are not exactly the same, but there is some similarity between them. One way of allowing for the similarity is to assume that the parameters all come from a joint distribution with a common mean and a nonzero covariance matrix. It will be shown later that the resulting parameter estimates will be a weighted average of the overall pooled estimate and the separate time series estimates based on each cross-section. Thus, each cross-section estimate is "shrunk" toward the overall pooled estimate.

The idea of shrinkage occurs frequently in the literature on prediction (e.g., see Copas 1983; Rao 1987). Rubin (1980) also provided evidence on better predictions with shrinkage estimators [although Scott (1980) in her discussion of the article, disputed their usefulness]. He applied an empirical Bayes technique for law-school validation studies. The studies are primarily concerned with the prediction of first-year grades in law school from the LSAT score and undergraduate grade-point average. Traditionally, a separate admitting equation is estimated for each law school by the method of least squares by using data for students who attended that school in recent years. These least squares estimates can fluctuate wildly from year to year. The study by Rubin argued that the estimation of the admitting equations by the empirical Bayes methods provides more stable estimates and better predictions.

A shrinkage estimator sometimes suggested is the so-called Stein-rule estimator defined by

$$\tilde{\beta}_i = \left(1 - \frac{c}{F}\right)\hat{\beta}_i + \frac{c}{F}\hat{\beta}_p, \tag{2}$$

where $\hat{\beta}_i$ is the ordinary least squares (OLS) estimator and $\hat{\beta}_p$ is the estimator from the pooled regression. F is the test statistic to test the null hypothesis

$$\beta_1 = \beta_2 = \cdots = \beta_N = \beta. \tag{3}$$

Under the null hypothesis (3), F has an F distribution with degrees of freedom $(N-1)k$ and $N(T-k)$, where k is the dimension of β. The optimal value of the constant c suggested by Judge and Bock (1978, pp. 190–198) is

$$c = \frac{(N-1)k - 2}{NT - Nk + 2}. \tag{4}$$

This rule has, however, been derived for the case of strictly exogenous X's. Zeimer and Wetzstein (1983) applied the Stein-rule estimator to a wilderness-demand model and argued that the Stein rule gives better forecasts than the pooled or the individual cross-section estimators. The Stein rule shrinks the estimators $\hat{\beta}_i$ toward the pooled estimator $\hat{\beta}_p$. The factor c in (4) is roughly $k/(T-k)$ for large n. Thus, the higher the number of explanatory variables k relative to T, the smaller will be the shrinkage factor $(1 - c/F)$ for given F.

1.1 The Random-Coefficient Model

For ease of exposition, in the following presentation we will assume that X_i does not include lagged dependent variables. In the presence of lagged dependent variables, the results hold only asymptotically.

In the random-coefficient model

$$y_i = X_i\beta_i + u_i. \tag{5}$$

we assume that

$$\beta_i \sim IN(\mu, \Sigma). \tag{6}$$

We can write this as

$$\beta_i = \mu + v_i. \tag{7}$$

where $v_i \sim N(0, \Sigma)$.

In the classical random-coefficient model, Equations (5) and (7) imply that

$$y_i = X_i\mu + w_i. \tag{8}$$

where $w_i \sim IN(0, \Omega_i)$ with $\Omega_i = (X_i\Sigma X_i' + \sigma_i^2 I)$. Assuming that the u_i are independent across the N equations, we get the GLS estimator μ^* of μ as

$$\mu^* = \left(\sum_{i=1}^{N} X_i'\Omega_i^{-1}X_i\right)^{-1}\left(\sum_{i=1}^{N} X_i'\Omega_i^{-1}y_i\right).$$

Using the matrix identity

$$(A + BDB')^{-1} = A^{-1} - A^{-1}B(B'A^{-1}B + D^{-1})^{-1}B'A^{-1}$$

(see Rao 1973, p. 33) to decompose Ω_i, Swamy (1970) showed that

$$\mu^* = \sum_{i=1}^{N} W_i\hat{\beta}_i,$$

where $\hat{\beta}_i = (X_i'X_i)^{-1}X_i'y_i$ is the OLS estimator of β_i and

$$W_i = \left(\sum_{j=1}^{N} P_j^{-1}\right)^{-1} P_i^{-1} \tag{9}$$

with

$$P_i = (\sigma_i^2(X_i'X_i)^{-1} + \Sigma). \tag{10}$$

Two obstacles in applying the GLS procedure are the unknown parameters Σ and σ_i^2 in Ω. Swamy (1970) proposed a two-step procedure that uses the least squares estimators $\hat{\beta}_i$ of β_i and the least squares residuals to obtain unbiased estimators of Σ and σ_i^2. Of course, in dynamic models with lagged dependent variables, the unbiasedness property does not hold. We have to appeal to the consistency property. These estimators were also used by Rao (1975) in the empirical Bayes procedure. The Swamy (1970) method for estimating Σ and σ_i^2 is

$$\hat{\Sigma} = \frac{1}{N-1}\sum_i \left(\hat{\beta}_i - \frac{1}{N}\sum_{i=1}^{N}\hat{\beta}_i\right) \times \left(\hat{\beta}_i - \frac{1}{N}\sum_{i=1}^{N}\hat{\beta}_i\right)' - \frac{1}{N}\sum_i (X_i'X_i)^{-1}\hat{\sigma}_i^2. \tag{11}$$

where $\hat{\sigma}_i^2 = [1/(T-k)](y_i - X_i\hat{\beta}_i)'(y_i - X_i\hat{\beta}_i)$ and $\hat{\beta}_i$ is the OLS estimator of β_i.

One potential problem with the estimator for Σ is that it may not be positive definite. In this case Swamy suggests using only the first part of Equation (11) to estimate Σ. Hsiao (1986) adopted the same strategy. The suggested estimator, which is consistent in this case, is

$$\hat{\Sigma} = \frac{1}{N-1}\sum_i \left(\hat{\beta}_i - \frac{1}{N}\sum_{i=1}^{N}\hat{\beta}_i\right)\left(\hat{\beta}_i - \frac{1}{N}\sum_{i=1}^{N}\hat{\beta}_i\right)'. \tag{12}$$

In the random-coefficient model, interest centers on the mean parameters μ and σ_i^2 and the measure of heterogeneity Σ. Pesaran and Smith (1995) were concerned with the estimation of μ. Mairesse and Griliches (1990) were concerned with the estimation of Σ as well. The traditional estimator of μ from the random-coefficient model is a GLS, but because Ω_i involves the unknown parameters σ_i^2 and Σ, we substitute the estimates from Equation (11) and use the "feasible" GLS. Thus, it is a two-step GLS estimator based on an estimated covariance matrix. This procedure, as discussed later (Sec. 2) gives asymptotically efficient estimates only if there are no lagged dependent variables.

In the classical model it makes no sense to talk about obtaining estimators for the individual parameters β_i because they are treated as random variables. Hence, inference is based entirely on the parameters μ, Σ, and σ_i^2. One can, however, talk of predictors for the random parameters β_i. Lee and Griffiths (1978) derived the best linear unbiased predictors for β_i based on the prior likelihood approach advocated by Edwards (1969). This amounts to estimating β_i, σ_i^2, μ, and Σ by maximizing the likelihood

$$L(\beta_i, \sigma_i^2, \mu, \Sigma | y, X) = \text{const.} - \frac{T}{2}\sum_{i=1}^{N} \ln \sigma_i^2 - \frac{1}{2}\sum_{i=1}^{N}\frac{1}{\sigma_i^2}(y_i - X_i\beta_i)'(y_i - X_i\beta_i) - \frac{N}{2}\ln|\Sigma| - \frac{1}{2}\sum_{i=1}^{N}(\beta_i - \mu)'\Sigma^{-1}(\beta_i - \mu). \tag{13}$$

The resulting estimates for β_i, σ_i^2, μ, and Σ are given as

$$\beta_i^* = \left(\frac{1}{\sigma_i^2}X_i'X_i + \Sigma^{*-1}\right)^{-1}\left(\frac{1}{\sigma_i^2}X_i'X_i\hat{\beta}_i + \Sigma^{*-1}\mu^*\right), \tag{14}$$

$$\mu^* = \frac{1}{N}\sum_{i=1}^{N}\beta_i^*. \tag{15}$$

$$\sigma_i^2 = \frac{1}{T}(y_i - X_i\beta_i^*)'(y_i - X_i\beta_i^*). \tag{16}$$

and

$$\Sigma^* = \frac{1}{N}\sum_{i=1}^{N}(\beta_i^* - \mu^*)(\beta_i^* - \mu^*)'. \tag{17}$$

where $\hat{\beta}_i$ is the OLS estimate of β_i. As will be shown next, these prior likelihood estimators are closely related to the Bayesian estimators.

1.2 An Iterative Bayesian Approach

In the Bayesian framework, Equation (6) specifies the prior distribution of β_i. Because this prior distribution involves the parameters μ and Σ, if they are not known priors must be specified for these hyperparameters. One can then derive the posterior distribution for the parameters β_i.

If μ, σ_i^2, and Σ are known, the posterior distribution of β_i is normal with mean β_i^* given by

$$\beta_i^* = \left(\frac{1}{\sigma_i^2}X_i'X_i + \Sigma^{-1}\right)^{-1}\left(\frac{1}{\sigma_i^2}X'X_i\hat{\beta}_i + \Sigma^{-1}\mu\right) \tag{18}$$

and variance

$$V(\beta_i^*) = \left(\frac{1}{\sigma_i^2}X_i'X_i + \Sigma^{-1}\right)^{-1}.$$

where $\hat{\beta}_i$ is the OLS estimate of β_i. Note that, with lagged dependent variables, the normality of the posterior distribution of β_i^* holds only asymptotically and under the usual regularity conditions assumed in dynamic regression models.

Assuming a noninformative prior for μ, the mean of the posterior distribution of μ is $\mu^* = (1/N)\sum_{i=1}^{N}\beta_i^*$. Because in general σ_i^2 and Σ will not be known, one needs to specify priors for these hyperparameters. Smith (1973) took the conjugate Wishart distribution for Σ^{-1} and the independent inverse χ^2 distributions for the σ_i^2. He suggested using the mode of the posterior distribution. His modal estimators are

$$\hat{\sigma}_i^2 = \frac{1}{T + v_i + 2}\,[v_i\lambda_i + (y_i - X_i\beta_i^*)'(y_i - X_i\beta_i^*)] \quad (19)$$

and

$$\Sigma^* = \frac{1}{N - k - 2 + \delta}\left[R + \sum_{i=1}^{N} (\beta_i^* - \mu^*)(\beta_i^* - \mu^*)'\right]. \quad (20)$$

As discussed by Smith (1973), v_i, λ_i, R, and δ are parameters arising from the specification of the prior distributions, and k is the dimension of β. Approximations to vague priors are obtained by setting $v_i = 0, \delta = 1$, and R to be a diagonal matrix with small positive entries (e.g., .001).

The estimators are then

$$\hat{\sigma}_i^2 = \frac{1}{T+2}\,(Y_i - X_i\beta_i^*)'(Y_i - X_i\beta_i^*) \quad (21)$$

and

$$\Sigma^* = \frac{1}{N-k-1}\sum_{i=1}^{N} (\beta_i^* - \mu^*)(\beta_i^* - \mu^*)'. \quad (22)$$

Equations (21) and (22) have to be solved iteratively along with the equations for β^* and μ^* given by

$$\beta_i^* = \left(\frac{1}{\hat{\sigma}_i^2}\,X_i'X_i + \Sigma^{*-1}\right)^{-1}\left(\frac{1}{\hat{\sigma}_i^2}\,X_i'X_i\hat{\beta}_i + \Sigma^{*-1}\mu^*\right) \quad (23)$$

and

$$\mu^* = \frac{1}{N}\sum_{i=1}^{N}\beta_i^*. \quad (24)$$

Note that in Equations (21)–(24) the prior mean μ^* is an average of β_i^*, the estimate of the prior variance Σ is obtained from deviations of β_i^* from their average μ^*, and the estimate of σ_i^2 is obtained from the residual sum of squares using β_i^*. Equations (21)–(24) have to be solved iteratively, with the initial iteration using the OLS estimator $\hat{\beta}_i$ to compute μ^*, σ_i^2, and Σ^*. We take μ^* as the simple average of $\hat{\beta}_i, \hat{\sigma}_i^2$ as the usual estimate of σ_i^2 from the ith cross-section, and Σ^* as given by Equation (12). Moreover, to improve the convergence with the iterative procedure, Σ^* is computed as

$$\Sigma^* = \frac{1}{N-k-1}\left[R + \sum_{i=1}^{N} (\beta_i^* - \mu^*)(\beta_i^* - \mu^*)'\right], \quad (22a)$$

where R is a diagonal matrix with small positive entries (e.g., .001).

Thus, as noted by Maddala (1991), many shrinkage estimators only differ on the basis of the overall estimators toward which the individual estimators are shrunk and the estimates of variances and covariance matrices. Smith (1973) showed with some matrix manipulations that the GLS estimator of μ is related to the Bayesian estimator β_i^* by the equation

$$\mu = \frac{1}{N}\sum_{i=1}^{N}\beta_i^*, \quad (25)$$

which is the same as the Bayesian estimator and the maximum likelihood estimator (MLE) for μ. Moreover, the MLE's given by Lee and Griffiths (1978) only differ from the GLS and Bayesian estimators in the divisors for σ_i^2 and Σ^*.

1.3 The Empirical Bayes Approach

In the empirical Bayes approach, we take Equation (18) and plug in sample-based estimates for μ, σ_i^2, and Σ. Rao (1975) suggested estimating them by

$$\hat{\mu} = \frac{1}{N}\sum_{i=1}^{N}\hat{\beta}_i,$$

$$\hat{\sigma}_i^2 = \frac{1}{T-k}\,(y_i'y_i - y_i'X_i\hat{\beta}_i),$$

and

$$\hat{\Sigma} = \frac{1}{N-1}\sum_i (\hat{\beta}_i - \hat{\mu})(\hat{\beta}_i - \hat{\mu})' - \frac{1}{N}\sum_i (X_i'X_i)^{-1}\hat{\sigma}_i^2.$$

All of these expressions are based on the least squares estimators, $\hat{\beta}_i$. The estimators for σ_i^2 and Σ are unbiased if X_i includes exogenous variables only. As pointed out in the preceding sections, the Bayesian approach gives a different set of estimators, based on the Bayes estimators, β_i^*. Kadiyala and Oberhelman (1986) used a modification of the estimators suggested by Rao (1975). They used μ^* as an average of β_i^* rather than $\hat{\beta}_i$ as in the Bayesian approach, but they still used the same estimator for Σ as that suggested by Rao.

Both of these empirical estimators are two-step estimators and do not involve any iteration. One can think of the following empirical Bayes estimator, which, however, has to be computed iteratively:

$$\begin{aligned} \mu^* &= \frac{1}{N}\sum_{i=1}^{N}\beta_i^* \\ \hat{\sigma}_i^2 &= \frac{1}{T-k}\,(y_i - X_i\beta_i^*)'(y_i - X_i\beta_i^*) \\ \hat{\Sigma} &= \frac{1}{N-1}\sum_i (\beta_i^* - \mu^*)(\beta_i^* - \mu^*)'. \end{aligned} \quad (26)$$

These expressions differ from the ones derived by Smith (1973) and by Lee and Griffiths (1978) only in the divisors in $\hat{\sigma}_i^2$ and Σ^*. In the preceding equations, the prior mean μ^* is an average of β_i^*, the estimate of the prior variance Σ^* is obtained from deviations of β_i^* from their average μ^*, and the estimate of σ_i^2 is obtained from the residual sum of squares using β_i^*, not the OLS estimator $\hat{\beta}_i$. The preceding equations are solved iteratively, with the initial iteration using the OLS estimator $\hat{\beta}_i$ to compute μ^*, σ_i^2, and Σ^* as described earlier. Moreover, to improve the convergence with the iterative procedure Σ^* is computed as

$$\Sigma^* = \frac{1}{N-1}\left[R + \sum_{i=1}^{N}(\beta_i^* - \mu^*)(\beta_i^* - \mu^*)'\right],$$

where R is a diagonal matrix as defined previously. Hu and Maddala (1994) presented some Monte Carlo evidence to suggest that the iterative procedures for the computation of Σ^* give better estimates (in the mean squared sense) for both the overall mean μ and the heterogeneity matrix Σ than the two-step procedures.

1.4 In Summary

We have discussed the classical, Bayesian, and empirical Bayesian approaches to the estimation of individual cross-section parameters. We have also discussed two-step versus iterative methods. These are summarized in a tabular form in Table 1. In Section 2, we will discuss the theoretical justification of the iterative procedure over the two-step procedure in dynamic models. To conserve space, we will present empirical results for only the Stein-rule and (the iterative) empirical Bayes estimators.

The most important points to note are the estimation of Σ, which is computed using Formula (26) and not (11) or (12), the computation of μ^* as $(1/N)\sum_{i=1}^{N}\beta_i^*$ and the computation of $\sigma_i^{2^*}$ using not least squares residuals but residuals based on β_i^*. Note that, incidentally, we get an estimator of μ, which is computed in an iterative fashion, not using the two-step procedure used by Swamy (1970) and Hsiao (1986). Even if our interest centers on μ, we suggest using the iterative procedure.

2. TWO-STEP VERSUS ITERATIVE ESTIMATORS

In Section 1, we discussed several estimators for the estimation of the overall mean μ and covariance matrix Σ as well as the individual parameters β_i. The estimators for μ and β_i can be classified into two categories, (1) two-step estimators based on initial consistent estimators of Σ and σ_i^2 and (2) iterative estimators in which all the parameters μ, β_i, Σ, and σ_i^2 are estimated jointly.

In the first category we have the two-step empirical Bayes estimator for β_i and the Swamy–Hsiao estimator for μ. In

Table 1. Different Estimators for σ_i^2, Σ, β_i, and μ

Method	*Estimator*	*Note*
	For σ_i^2	
Swamy–Hsiao and two-step empirical Bayesian	$\frac{1}{T-k}(y_i - X_i\hat{\beta}_i)'(y_i - X_i\hat{\beta}_i)$	1
Prior likelihood	$\frac{1}{T}(y_i - X_i\beta_i^*)'(y_i - X_i\beta_i^*)$	2
Iterative Bayesian (Smith)	$\frac{1}{T+2}(y_i - X_i\beta_i^*)'(y_i - X_i\beta_i^*)$	
Empirical Bayes (iterative)	$\frac{1}{T-k}(y_i - X_i\beta_i^*)'(y_i - X_i\beta_i^*)$	
	For Σ	
Swamy–Hsiao	$\hat{\Sigma}_1 = \frac{1}{N-1}\sum_i\left(\hat{\beta}_i - \frac{1}{N}\sum_{i=1}^N\hat{\beta}_i\right)\left(\hat{\beta}_i - \frac{1}{N}\sum_{i=1}^N\hat{\beta}_i\right)'$	
Swamy–Rao (unbiased)	$\hat{\Sigma} = \hat{\Sigma}_1 - \frac{1}{N}\sum_i(X_i'X_i)^{-1}\hat{\sigma}_i^2$	3
Prior likelihood	$\Sigma^* = \frac{1}{N}\sum_{i=1}^N(\beta_i^* - \mu^*)(\beta_i^* - \mu^*)'$	
Iterative Bayes (Smith)	$\Sigma^* = \frac{1}{N-k-1}\sum_{i=1}^N(\beta_i^* - \mu^*)(\beta_i^* - \mu^*)'$	
Iterative empirical Bayes	$\Sigma^* = \frac{1}{N-1}\sum_{i=1}^N(\beta_i^* - \mu^*)(\beta_i^* - \mu^*)'$	
	For β_i	
Swamy	No estimators	
Stein-rule	$\hat{\beta}_i = (1 - c/F)\hat{\beta}_i + (c/F)\hat{\beta}_p$	4
Prior likelihood and iterative Bayes	$\beta_i^* = \left(\frac{1}{\sigma_i^{*2}}X_i'X_i + \Sigma^{*-1}\right)^{-1}\left(\frac{1}{\sigma_i^{*2}}X_i'X_i\hat{\beta}_i + \Sigma^{*-1}\mu^*\right)$	
Two-step empirical Bayes	$\beta_i^* = \left(\frac{1}{\hat{\sigma}_i^2}X_i'X_i + \hat{\Sigma}^{-1}\right)^{-1}\left(\frac{1}{\hat{\sigma}_i^2}X_i'X_i\hat{\beta}_i + \hat{\Sigma}^{-1}\hat{\mu}\right)$	
	For μ	
Swamy	$\hat{\mu}_{\text{GLS}} = \sum_{i=1}^N W_i\hat{\beta}_i$	5
Prior likelihood and iterative Bayes	$\mu^* = \frac{1}{N}\sum_{i=1}^N\beta_i^*$	6

NOTE: (1) $\hat{\beta}_i$ is the OLS estimator of β. (2) β_i^* is defined later. (3) The two-step empirical Bayes method is based on these estimators of Σ. $\hat{\Sigma}_1$ is used if $\hat{\Sigma}$ is not positive definite. (4) $c = [(N-1)k - 2]/[NT - Nk + 2]$. $\hat{\beta}_p$ is the pooled estimator, and F is the F statistic to test equality of the coefficients (5) $W_i = (\Sigma P_j^{-1})^{-1}P_i^{-1}$ with $P_i = [\sigma_i^2(X_i'X_i)^{-1} + \Sigma]$. We first get $\hat{\sigma}_i^2$ and $\hat{\Sigma}$ and then substitute these for σ_i^2 and Σ in $\hat{\mu}_{GLS}$ It is thus a two-step method (6) Because β_i^* are computed iteratively, μ^* is an iterative estimator. If σ_i^2 and Σ are known, then $\mu^* = \hat{\mu}_{GLS}$

the second category we have the prior likelihood, iterative empirical Bayes, and iterative Bayesian (Smith) estimators.

As is evident from Equations (15) and (18), the expressions for estimation of the overall mean μ and the individual parameters β_i involve the unknown parameters σ_i^2 and Σ. We need estimators for these parameters to implement the procedures. This is where the difference between the two-step (based on initial consistent estimators of σ_i^2 and Σ) and iterative procedures lies. Essentially, what we have here is a problem similar to that of GLS estimation with an estimated covariance matrix. As pointed out by Amemiya and Fuller (1967), Maddala (1971), and Pagan (1986), in the case that the explanatory variables X_i include only exogenous variables, the two-step estimators based on any consistent estimators of parameters σ_i^2 and Σ are as asymptotically efficient as the estimators from the joint efficient estimation of all the parameters. If the variables X_i include lagged dependent variables, however, as in the case of dynamic models, the two-step estimators based on any consistent estimates of σ_i^2 and Σ are consistent but not efficient. This suggests that even if we are interested in the estimation of the overall mean μ, in the presence of lagged dependent variables, the Swamy or Hsiao estimators of Σ do not provide efficient estimates of μ. We have to use the iterative procedure suggested in Section 1. In the case, as in this article, our interest centers on the estimation of β_i, and we again should use the iterative procedures.

Many of the applications in the statistical literature, as well as the example on Grunfeld's investment function of Swamy (1970), have no lagged dependent variables. Hence, the GLS based on the Swamy or Hsiao estimator of Σ is asymptotically efficient. This is not the case, however, with dynamic models considered by, for instance, Pesaran and Smith (1995) even though their interest was in the overall mean μ. In the example to be discussed next, we have a dynamic demand model. Hence, we used the iterative procedure described in Section 1 for the estimation of β_i as well as μ.

3. AN EMPIRICAL EXAMPLE

There have been numerous studies on the price and income elasticities of residential natural-gas and electricity demand. Short-run price elasticity estimates of both residential natural-gas and electricity demand have ranged from −.05 to −.9, and long-run price elasticities estimates have ranged from −.2 to as high as −4.6. There is a similar diversity among short-run and long-run income elasticity estimates. For a partial review of these studies, see Al-Sahlawi (1989), Bohi (1981), Bohi and Zimmerman (1984), and Taylor (1975).

In this section we present new residential gas and electricity price and income elasticity estimates using pooled cross-section and time series data from 49 U.S. states. The state of Hawaii was excluded because we could not obtain annual weather data.

The annual state residential electricity and gas price data used in this study were obtained from *The State Energy Price and Expenditure System* of the U.S. Energy Information Administration (1993). Weather data are population-weighted heating and cooling degree days by state and were taken from the National Oceanic and Atmospheric Administration, U.S. Department of Commerce, Ashville, North Carolina. Annual state income data were drawn from the Bureau of Economic Affairs, and the annual Consumer Price Index for the United States was from CITIBASE. The sample period is from 1970 to 1990.

To estimate the short-run and long-run price and income demand elasticities for gas and electricity, we specified the following DLR(1, 1) model:

$$\begin{aligned} y_{it} = {} & \beta_{i0} + \beta_{i1} y_{i,t-1} + \beta_{i2} x_{1it} \\ & + \beta_{i3} x_{1i,t-1} + \beta_{i4} x_{2it} + \beta_{i5} x_{2i,t-1} \\ & + \beta_{i6} x_{3it} + \beta_{i7} x_{4it} + \beta_{i8} x_{5it} + u_{it}, \end{aligned} \tag{27}$$

where $i = 1, 2, 3, \ldots, 49$ (U.S. state subscript) and $t = 2, 3, \ldots, 21$ (year subscript).

The variables for the electricity regression are y_{it} = ln(residential electricity per capita consumption), x_{1it} = ln(real per capita personal income), x_{2it} = ln(real residential electricity price), x_{3it} = ln(real residential natural-gas price), x_{4it} = heating degree days (HDD), and x_{5it} = cooling degree days (CDD).

For the natural-gas regression, we have y_{it} = ln(residential natural gas per capita consumption), x_{1it} = ln(real per capita personal income), x_{2it} = ln(real residential natural-gas price), and x_{3it} = ln(real residential electricity price), with x_{4it} and x_{5it} unchanged.

From Equation (27) the following short-run and long-run elasticities can be derived for the ith state:

Short-run income elasticity:	$\mathrm{SR}\eta_y = \beta_{i2}$
Long-run income elasticity:	$\mathrm{LR}\eta_y = \frac{\beta_{i2}+\beta_{i3}}{1-\beta_{i1}}$
Short-run price elasticity:	$\mathrm{SR}\eta_p = \beta_{i4}$
Long-run price elasticity:	$\mathrm{LR}\eta_p = \frac{\beta_{i4}+\beta_{i5}}{1-\beta_{i1}}$
Short-run cross-price elasticity:	$\mathrm{SR}\eta_p^c = \beta_{i6}$
Long-run cross-price elasticity:	$\mathrm{LR}\eta_p^c = \frac{\beta_{i6}}{1-\beta_{i1}}$.

4. EMPIRICAL RESULTS

We here present 10 tables of results. The separate state regression coefficients will be presented in Tables 6–9. Tables 10 and 11 will present estimates of the short- and long-run elasticities.

Tables 2–5 summarize the estimates from the five approaches discussed. In Table 2 the parameter estimates from the electricity-demand regression and t statistics are presented. Column 1 contains the results from the fixed-effects model given by $y_{it} = \alpha_1 y_{i,t-1} + \alpha_2 x_{1it} + \alpha_3 x_{1i,t-1} + \alpha_4 x_{2it} + \alpha_5 x_{2i,t-1} + \alpha_6 x_{3it} + \alpha x_{4it} + \alpha_8 x_{5it} + \sum_{i=1}^{49} \delta_i + u_{it}$, and column 2 contains the pooled data model given by $y_{it} = \alpha_0 + \alpha_1 y_{i,t-1} + \alpha_2 x_{1it} + \alpha_3 x_{1i,t-1} + \alpha_4 x_{2it} + \alpha_5 x_{2i,t-1} + \alpha_6 x_{3it} + \alpha_7 x_{4it} + \alpha_8 x_{5it} + u_{it}$. The next column of Table 2 presents the average of the separate state regression estimates followed by columns with the results on the average of the Bayesian estimates and finally the average of the Stein-rule estimates.

Table 2. Parameter Estimate of the Electricity Regression (t values in parentheses)

Variables	Pooled with dummies	Pooled without dummies	OLS estimator (average)	Shrinkage estimator (average)	Stein-rule estimator (average)
$y_{i,t-1}$	.789	.903	.530	.629	.685
	(49.00)	(106.03)	(22.28)	(32.12)	(47.76)
x_{1it}	.137	.138	.429	.394	.308
	(3.25)	(3.12)	(7.80)	(11.39)	(8.32)
$x_{1i,t-1}$	−.013	−.134	−.040	−.064	−.079
	(−.31)	(−3.08)	(−.74)	(−1.80)	(−2.16)
x_{2it}	−.196	−.214	−.163	−.158	−.184
	(−7.96)	(−8.47)	(−6.19)	(−8.37)	(−9.88)
$x_{2i,t-1}$	.078	.113	.057	.061	.081
	(3.15)	(4.49)	(2.16)	(2.71)	(4.30)
x_{3it}	.035	.028	.017	.023	.022
	(4.48)	(4.86)	(1.43)	(1.80)	(2.93)
x_{4it}	.138	.084	.129	.142	.110
	(3.99)	(6.97)	(3.53)	(6.77)	(5.03)
x_{5it}	1.319	.398	1.561	1.069	1.077
	(12.58)	(9.87)	(2.75)	(10.02)	(3.24)

Table 3 contains the short- and long-run income elasticities (SRη_y and LRη_y), price elasticities (SRη_p and LRη_p), and cross-elasticities (SRη_p^c and LRη_p^c) for electricity demand in the columns. The average, maximum, and minimum estimates by different methods are provided in the rows. There is less variability in the short-run elasticities compared with the long-run elasticities. The second law of demand appears to hold; the long-run elasticities are higher than the short-run elasticities except in one case. This exception appears to be due to an outlier in the LRη_p using the state-specific regressions. The F statistic testing hypothesis (3) is 1.698, and the 5% critical value for the F distribution is 1. Thus, the Stein-rule estimator for the electricity regression is $\tilde{\beta}_i = .584\hat{\beta}_i + .416\hat{\beta}_p$. The constant in the regression is .706.

The average SRη_y elasticity estimates for electricity presented in Table 3 range from .137 to .429 with the two pooled model estimates being approximately the same, .137 and .138. The separate OLS estimates are much higher and have the greatest variability ranging from −.83 to 1.328. The average of the Bayesian shrinkage estimates is .394 and the average of the Stein estimates is .308. The Bayesian shrinkage estimates have a much smaller spread than the Stein estimates, reflecting the greater weight for heterogeneity across the states in the Stein estimator.

The average LRη_y, LRη_p, and LRη_p^c elasticities for electricity are presented in two ways. First we calculate the simple average of the elasticities for each state. Then the elasticities are calculated using the average based on the individual parameter estimates. The LRη_y elasticity estimates range from .044 with the pooled data model to 1.58 for the OLS estimator. The separate OLS regression results have by far the greatest variability (−1.229 to 33.033) followed by the Stein estimator (−7.771 to 2.82) and the Bayesian shrinkage estimator (.486 to 1.966). The Bayesian shrinkage estimator produces a tighter and more sensible range for LRη_y than the Stein estimator because the latter is influenced by the separate regression results that contain several negative long-run elasticities.

The adverse impact of ignoring cross-section specific effects is clear by comparing the pooled model with state intercept dummies to the pooled model without state inter-

Table 3. Short-Run and Long-Run Income and Price Elasticities of the Electricity Regression

Approaches	SRη_y	LRη_y	SRη_p	LRη_p	SRη_p^c	LRη_p^c
Pooled w/ dummies	.137	.584	−.196	−.561	.035	.166
Pooled w/o dummies	.138	.044	−.214	−1.031	.028	.290
OLS[a] average	.429	1.580	−.163	−.375	.017	−.135
maximum	1.328	33.033	.778	2.179	.648	.977
minimum	−.830	−1.229	−.916	−10.380	−.392	−6.454
OLS[b]	.429	.827	−.163	−.225	.017	.037
Shrk[a] average	.394	.921	−.158	−.239	.023	.054
maximum	.585	1.966	−.064	.242	.161	.447
minimum	.211	.486	−.281	−.873	−.108	−.263
Shrk[b]	.394	.890	−.158	−.263	.023	.062
Stein[a] average	.308	.609	−.184	−.276	.022	.083
maximum	.833	2.820	.365	1.526	.390	1.888
minimum	−.427	−7.771	−.624	−1.745	−.217	−.994
Stein[b]	.308	.727	−.184	−.329	.022	.069

[a] Calculated based on the individual elasticities for each state. The same is the case for maximum and minimum.

[b] Calculated by first taking the mean of the individual parameter estimates. Then the elasticities are calculated from this mean. The elasticities marked by [a] and [b] are the same for the short-run but not for the long-run.

Table 4. Parameter Estimate of the Natural-Gas Regression (t values in parentheses)

Variables	*Pooled with dummies*	*Pooled without dummies*	*OLS estimator (average)*	*Shrinkage estimator (average)*	*Stein-rule estimator (average)*
$y_{i,t-1}$	.628	.983	.173	.499	.440
	(25.49)	(195.83)	(5.77)	(19.67)	(21.83)
x_{1it}	.114	.048	.307	.280	.222
	(1.15)	(.45)	(2.63)	(3.42)	(2.58)
$x_{1i,t-1}$	−.075	−.040	−.583	−.314	−.404
	(−.79)	(−.38)	(−5.31)	(−4.12)	(−4.98)
x_{2it}	−.177	−.164	−.092	−.099	−.116
	(−4.68)	(−4.13)	(−2.46)	(−3.77)	(−4.08)
$x_{2i,t-1}$	.035	.141	−.073	−.041	−.003
	(.92)	(3.60)	(−1.92)	(−1.43)	(−.09)
x_{3it}	.016	.026	−.034	−.001	−.014
	(.49)	(1.74)	(−.73)	(−.03)	(−.45)
x_{4it}	.529	.027	.421	.424	.291
	(6.30)	(.96)	(4.63)	(7.91)	(4.72)
x_{5it}	−1.104	−.079	1.494	−.913	.976
	(−4.40)	(−.96)	(.42)	(−5.83)	(.41)

cept dummies. The electricity $LR\eta_y$ elasticity of .584 from the former is closer to what economic theory would suggest than the simple pooled estimate without state intercept dummies of .044. This can be explained by the near canceling of the income estimates in the pooled model without state intercept dummies. Moreover, by ignoring heterogeneity in the intercepts, the size and explanatory power of the lagged dependent variable is greatly increased in the pooled model without state intercept dummies.

The $SR\eta_p$ are very similar across the five methods (−.158 to −.214). The separate state Bayesian shrinkage estimates are closest to the average and numerically the most inelastic (−.158) and do not contain any positive elasticities as does the Stein estimator. The range for the $LR\eta_p$ is (−.239 to −1.031), and the higher estimates are from the two pooled models. This appears due to the "imposition" of homogeneity across the states.

Table 4 summarizes the parameter estimates from the five methods using the natural-gas models. The explanatory power is provided primarily by the lagged consumption term and contemporary natural-gas price. Evidence of heterogeneity across the states is again evident by the relatively large estimate for the lagged dependent variable in the pooled model with state intercept dummies (.628) and the pooled model without state intercept dummies (.983) relative to the average from the individual state OLS estimates (.173).

Short- and long-run elasticities for the natural gas models are presented in Table 5 and organized as in Table 3. The short-run price elasticity estimates are quite stable over the different estimation approaches, ranging from −.092 to −.177. The short-run income-elasticity estimates range from .048 to .307. As with electricity demand, the long-run income and price elasticity estimates for natural-gas demand vary quite a bit over the five estimation approaches. The $LR\eta_p$ estimates range from −.239 to −1.358, and the $LR\eta_y$ estimates range from −.425 to .491.

The null hypothesis in (7) is again rejected from the F statistic for the Stein-rule estimator; the statistic is 2.143 and the 5% critical value is 1. This implies that the Stein-rule estimator is given by $\tilde{\beta}_i = .671\hat{\beta}_i + .329\hat{\beta}_p$ and suggests that there is relatively greater heterogeneity in the natural-gas regression model compared with the electricity model.

One final note on the natural-gas elasticities is worth

Table 5. Short-Run and Long-Run Income and Price Elasticities of the Natural Gas Regression

Approaches	$SR\eta_y$	$LR\eta_y$	$SR\eta_p$	$LR\eta_p$	$SR\eta_p^c$	$LR\eta_p^c$
Pooled w/ dummies	.114	.104	−.177	−.381	.016	.044
Pooled w/o dummies	.048	.491	−.164	−1.358	.026	1.558
OLS[a] average	.307	−.425	−.092	−.239	−.034	.046
maximum	3.339	1.847	1.069	2.198	.783	5.506
minimum	−2.745	−5.132	−1.341	−2.454	−.963	−2.104
OLS[b]	.307	−.334	−.092	−.200	−.034	−.041
Shrk[a] average	.280	−.057	−.099	−.273	−.001	−.007
maximum	.356	.473	−.060	.085	.083	.151
minimum	.210	−.486	−.150	−.660	−.091	−.233
Shrk[b]	.280	−.068	−.099	−.280	−.001	−.002
Stein[a] average	.222	−.412	−.116	−.250	−.014	.057
maximum	2.255	1.816	.663	2.127	.534	5.185
minimum	−1.825	−5.020	−.953	−2.365	−.637	−2.031
Stein[b]	.222	−.326	−.116	−.212	−.014	−.025

[a] Calculated based on the individual elasticities for each state. The same is the case for maximum and minimum.
[b] Calculated by first taking the mean of the individual parameter estimates. Then the elasticities are calculated from this mean. The elasticities marked by [a] and [b] are the same for the short-run but not for the long-run.

Table 6. OLS Estimates and t Values of Individual States (electricity regression)

State	$y_{i,t-1}$	x_{1it}	$x_{1i,t-1}$	x_{2it}	$x_{2i,t-1}$	x_{3it}
CA	.581	.510	−.215	−.211	.087	−.036
	3.647	1.814	−.918	−2.076	1.367	−1.016
FL	.422	1.265	−.659	−.163	.009	−.073
	2.617	6.491	−2.688	−2.601	.125	−1.303
IL	.241	.558	.144	−.011	−.051	.019
	1.832	2.353	.605	−.090	−.423	.570
MI	.754	.285	−.126	−.040	.012	−.008
	6.475	2.404	−1.124	−.468	.128	−.452
NY	.810	.476	−.243	−.152	.191	−.053
	7.615	2.491	−1.194	−2.581	3.400	−1.715
OH	.637	.437	−.007	−.110	−.065	.055
	7.022	2.428	−.042	−1.271	−.602	1.613
PA	.521	.522	.034	−.207	.166	−.010
	5.632	2.788	.174	−2.686	2.137	−.653
TX	.688	.091	.028	−.444	.206	.103
	3.243	.188	.073	−2.955	1.470	.651

NOTE *t* values are presented in the second line for each state. Coefficients for cooling and heating degree days are not reported.

Table 8. OLS Estimates and t Values of Individual States (natural-gas regression)

State	$y_{i,t-1}$	x_{1it}	$x_{1i,t-1}$	x_{2it}	$x_{2i,t-1}$	x_{3it}
CA	−.179	−.223	−1.686	.193	−.310	−.160
	−1.009	−.326	−2.036	1.554	−2.520	−.908
FL	.172	2.733	−3.914	−.579	−.472	.423
	1.183	3.376	−4.470	−2.703	−1.399	2.578
IL	−.512	.947	−.877	.662	−.447	−.898
	−2.905	2.588	−2.513	4.108	−2.728	−4.037
MI	−.023	−.563	.463	.359	−.263	−.506
	−.088	−.990	1.106	1.282	−.937	−1.829
NY	.023	1.088	−.738	.006	−.128	.012
	.089	1.982	−1.481	.041	−1.008	.089
OH	−.441	−.136	−.920	−.067	−.191	−.025
	−2.041	−.286	−2.345	−.419	−1.271	−.111
PA	−.133	−.010	−.410	.103	−.090	−.557
	−.450	−.017	−.793	.645	−.567	−2.677
TX	.599	−.751	−1.304	1.069	−.189	−.843
	4.700	−.772	−1.555	3.134	−.812	−2.807

NOTE See note to Table 6

making. The long-run income elasticity for natural gas is persistently estimated as negative with the individual OLS regressions and is nearly 0 (−.057) with the shrunken estimates. Although it seems counterintuitive that the long-run natural-gas income elasticity is smaller than the short-run natural-gas elasticity, there are several explanations for this result. First, as incomes rise, households may buy microwave ovens and will substitute away from gas cooking into microwave cooking. Second, as incomes rise, households may convert their homes to central air conditioning and households that previously used gas for heating now have the option of converting to electric heating and cooling with a heat pump. Hence, a certain subset of these households will reduce their gas consumption dramatically as incomes rise. Third, as incomes rise, households will remodel their homes. In many cases the configuration of appliances such as ranges, clothing dryers, and water heaters after remodeling are not convenient to gas lines. Again a subset of households that previously used gas for these end uses will now convert to electricity as incomes rise. Finally, natural-gas price controls had an impact on the availability of supplies. The availability of natural gas for new homes fell from 50% in 1971 to 37% in 1979 (when prices were decontrolled) and has risen to 63% in 1993. Over the same period, electricity's share of heating in new homes rose from 43% in 1971 to 57% in 1985 and then fell to 33% in 1993. In addition, the U.S. Energy Information Administration in 1987 reported that among the 2.2 million new homes that used electricity as a primary heating source, 89.3 percent of the households stated that they did not have access to natural gas in their neighborhoods. The combination of these factors can explain the income elasticity results.

Tables 6–9 present the estimates of the individual state regression coefficients with the associated *t* statistics and Tables 10 and 11 present the corresponding price, income, and cross-price elasticities. To conserve space, only the results for the OLS and Bayesian shrinkage estimation methods are presented for the largest eight states—California, Florida, Illinois, Michigan, New York, Ohio, Pennsylvania,

Table 7. Shrinkage Estimates and t Values of Individual States (electricity regression)

State	$y_{i,t-1}$	x_{1it}	$x_{1i,t-1}$	x_{2it}	$x_{2i,t-1}$	x_{3it}
CA	.635	.441	−.205	−.208	.090	−.018
	12.035	6.022	−3.241	−4.450	1.944	−.726
FL	.647	.585	−.296	−.233	.139	−.016
	12.760	8.387	−6.103	−5.347	3.090	−.477
IL	.561	.359	.035	−.086	.006	.014
	12.572	4.993	.528	−1.553	.117	.476
MI	.621	.338	−.050	−.120	.024	.003
	14.291	5.482	−.957	−2.499	.469	.162
NY	.715	.453	−.121	−.136	.167	−.042
	20.162	6.369	−2.166	−3.699	4.033	−1.536
OH	.679	.395	−.043	−.152	.044	.034
	19.903	6.128	−.931	−3.298	.814	1.259
PA	.679	.476	−.129	−.172	.115	−.004
	19.702	7.240	−2.452	−3.827	2.830	−.266
TX	.625	.353	.009	−.197	.045	.023
	11.576	3.864	.116	−3.223	.591	.429

NOTE See note to Table 6

Table 9. Shrinkage Estimates and t Values of Individual States (natural-gas regression)

State	$y_{i,t-1}$	x_{1it}	$x_{1i,t-1}$	x_{2it}	$x_{2i,t-1}$	x_{3it}
CA	.451	.240	−.417	−.128	−.154	.052
	11.531	6.998	−7.651	−4.485	−4.080	1.349
FL	.502	.225	−.409	−.135	−.115	.018
	13.056	5.436	−5.650	−3.822	−1.793	.429
IL	.481	.299	−.295	−.078	−.024	.003
	13.546	9.473	−6.176	−2.757	−.739	.094
MI	.512	.322	−.235	−.067	.029	−.027
	14.520	10.533	−5.207	−2.352	.920	−.787
NY	.523	.324	−.229	−.074	.040	−.045
	16.409	11.847	−6.159	−2.792	1.526	−1.518
OH	.461	.270	−.352	−.099	−.073	.030
	12.174	8.384	−7.246	−3.614	−2.351	.843
PA	.489	.290	−.303	−.090	−.020	−.008
	14.073	9.693	−7.138	−3.246	−.726	−.226
TX	.480	.268	−.359	−.106	−.093	.033
	12.880	7.682	−6.459	−3.522	−2.215	.837

NOTE· See note to Table 6

Table 10. Short-Run and Long-Run Income Elasticities (η_y), Price Elasticities (η_p), and Cross-Price Elasticities (η_p^c) of Individual States (electricity regression)

Estimation methods	State	$SR\eta_y$	$LR\eta_y$	$SR\eta_p$	$LR\eta_p$	$SR\eta_p^c$	$LR\eta_p^c$
OLS							
	CA	.510	.703	−.211	−.297	−.036	−.085
	FL	1.265	1.048	−.163	−.265	−.073	−.125
	IL	.558	.925	−.011	−.082	.019	.025
	MI	.285	.648	−.040	−.117	−.008	−.032
	NY	.476	1.225	−.152	.202	−.053	−.281
	OH	.437	1.184	−.110	−.480	.055	.152
	PA	.522	1.160	−.207	−.085	−.010	−.022
	TX	.091	.382	−.444	−.765	.103	.329
Shrinkage							
	CA	.441	.647	−.208	−.324	−.018	−.049
	FL	.585	.820	−.233	−.265	−.016	−.046
	IL	.359	.898	−.086	−.181	.014	.031
	MI	.338	.760	−.120	−.253	.003	.007
	NY	.453	1.166	−.136	.109	−.042	−.147
	OH	.395	1.096	−.152	−.336	.034	.105
	PA	.476	1.083	−.172	−.176	−.004	−.013
	TX	.353	.965	−.197	−.406	.023	.063

and Texas. Detailed tables for all the 49 states as well as for the Stein-rule estimation method are available on request from us. The differences between the results from the OLS and Bayesian shrinkage methods are evident and have also been discussed earlier and hence will not be elaborated on.

5. CONCLUSIONS

The most common procedure used in the analysis of panel data is to pool with individual-specific dummies that are assumed to be fixed (fixed-effects model) or random (random-effects model). This procedure, however, assumes homogeneity of the slope coefficients. At the other extreme is the case of complete heterogeneity and separate estimation of cross-section coefficients β_i. An intermediate case between complete homogeneity and complete heterogeneity is the random-coefficient model. In this framework we would be interested in estimating (a) the mean μ and covariance matrix Σ of the cross-section coefficients β_i and (b) the coefficients β_i themselves. In the classical framework only μ and Σ are estimable; β_i are not. One can talk of predictors for β_i, however.

This article presents in a unified framework different procedures for the estimation of β_i. The Bayesian approach to this problem results in shrinkage estimators that shrink the individual OLS estimator $\hat{\beta}_i$ toward the estimator of the overall mean μ. Other shrinkage estimators have been suggested in the literature. For instance, the Stein-rule estimator shrinks the OLS estimator $\hat{\beta}_i$ toward the pooled estimator obtained under complete homogeneity. The estimator of μ is different from the pooled estimator.

Table 11. Short-Run and Long-Run Income Elasticities (η_y), Price Elasticities (η_p), and Cross-Price Elasticities (η_p^c) of Individual States (electricity regression)

Estimation methods	State	$SR\eta_y$	$LR\eta_y$	$SR\eta_p$	$LR\eta_p$	$SR\eta_p^c$	$LR\eta_p^c$
OLS							
	CA	−.223	−1.620	.193	−.099	−.160	−.136
	FL	2.733	−1.425	−.579	−1.270	.423	.511
	IL	.947	.046	.662	.142	−.898	−.593
	MI	−.563	−.097	.359	.095	−.506	−.494
	NY	1.088	.358	.006	−.125	.012	.012
	OH	−.136	−.733	−.067	−.179	−.025	−.018
	PA	−.010	−.370	.103	.011	−.557	−.491
	TX	−.751	−5.132	1.069	2.198	−.843	−2.104
Shrinkage							
	CA	.240	−.322	−.128	−.513	.052	.094
	FL	.225	−.368	−.135	−.500	.018	.037
	IL	.299	.008	−.078	−.197	.003	.007
	MI	.322	.178	−.067	−.077	−.027	−.056
	NY	.324	.199	−.074	−.073	−.045	−.095
	OH	.270	−.153	−.099	−.319	.030	.055
	PA	.290	−.025	−.090	−.216	−.008	−.015
	TX	.268	−.176	−.106	−.383	.033	.063

The article discusses the classical prediction approach as well as the empirical Bayes and Bayes approaches to this problem. It discusses two-step versus iterative estimation methods. It is argued that the latter methods should be preferred in the presence of lagged dependent variables.

The article applies these procedures to the problem of estimating short-run and long-run elasticities of residential demand for electricity and natural gas in the United States for each of 49 states. The separate estimates were hard to interpret and had several wrong signs. These are not presented here to conserve space but are available from us. The pooled estimator gave a very high coefficient of the lagged dependent variable implying long lags in adjustment. This estimator was rejected because it rests on the hypothesis of homogeneity of the coefficients, which was easily rejected by an F test. The shrinkage estimator gave much more reasonable parameter values. Because the model was dynamic, iterative estimation methods were used.

If our interest lies in obtaining the elasticity estimates for each state, as in this study, then there are three choices open:

1. Use the individual state data only—but this gave bad results.
2. Pool the data and use the estimates from the pooled estimates—but this is not valid because the hypothesis of homogeneity is convincingly rejected.
3. Use the procedure presented here of allowing some (but not complete) heterogeneity (or homogeneity), which is what the random-coefficient model implies.

In many applications, the experience of researchers will be similar to ours in this case. The comparative performance of the different procedures in the context of dynamic panel-data models is being studied by Monte Carlo experiments.

ACKNOWLEDGMENTS

This research was partially supported by the U.S. Energy Information Administration (EIA). All statements are our own and do not reflect the views of the EIA. Helpful comments of an anonymous referee, an associate editor, and the editor, George Tauchen, are gratefully acknowledged. Responsibility for any remaining errors is ours.

[Received May 1994. Revised January 1996.]

REFERENCES

Alogoskoufis, G., and Smith, R. (1991), "On Error Correction Models: Specification, Interpretation, Estimation," *Journal of Economic Surveys*, 5, 97–128.

Al-Sahlawi, M. A. (1989), "The Demand For Natural Gas: A Survey Of Price And Income Elasticities," *The Energy Journal*, 10, 77–87.

Amemiya, T., and Fuller, W. (1967), "A Comparative Study of Alternative Estimators in a Distributed Lag Model," *Econometrica*, 35. 509–529.

Berndt, E. R. (1991), *The Practice of Econometrics: Classic and Contemporary*, Reading, MA: Addison-Wesley.

Bohi, D. R. (1981), *Analyzing Demand Behavior: A Study of Energy Elasticities*, Baltimore: Johns Hopkins University Press for Resources for the Future.

Bohi, D. R., and Zimmerman, M. B. (1984), "An Update On Econometric Studies Of Energy Demand Behavior," *Annual Review of Energy*, 9, 105–154.

Copas, J. B. (1983), "Regression, Prediction, and Shrinkage" (with discussion), *Journal of the Royal Statistical Society*, Ser. B, 45, 311–354.

Edwards, A. W. F. (1969), "Statistical Methods in Scientific Inference," *Nature, Land*, 222, 1233–1237.

Hsiao, C. (1986), *Analysis of Panel Data*, Cambridge, U.K.: Cambridge University Press.

Hu, W., and Maddala, G. S. (1994), "Estimation and Prediction Problems in Dynamic Heterogeneous Panel Data Models," working paper, Ohio State University, Dept. of Economics.

Judge, G. G., and Bock, M. E. (1978), *The Statistical Implications of Pre-Test and Stein-Rule Estimators in Econometrics*, Amsterdam: North-Holland.

Kadiyala, K. R., and Oberhelman, D. (1986), "Estimation of Actual Realizations in Stochastic Parameter Models," in *Bayesian Inference and Decision Techniques*, eds. P. Goel and A. Zellner, Amsterdam: Elsevier, pp. 363–373.

Lee, L.-F., and Griffiths, W. E. (1978), "The Prior Likelihood and Best Linear Unbiased Prediction in Stochastic Coefficient Linear Models," unpublished manuscript, University of Minnesota, Dept. of Economics.

Maddala, G. S. (1971), "Generalized Least Squares With an Estimated Variance Covariance Matrix," *Econometrica*, 39, 23–33.

——— (1991), "To Pool or Not To Pool: That Is the Question," *Journal of Quantitative Economics*, 7, 255–264.

Mairesse, J., and Griliches, Z. (1990), "Heterogeneity in Panel Data: Are There Stable Production Functions?" in *Essays in Honor of Edmond Malinvaud* (Vol. 3), Cambridge, MA: MIT Press.

Nickell, S. (1985), "Error Correction, Partial Adjustment And All That: An Expository Note," *Oxford Bulletin of Economics and Statistics*, 47, 119–129.

Pagan, A. (1986), "Two Stage and Related Estimators and Their Application," *Review of Economics Studies*, 53, 517–538.

Pesaran, M. H., and Smith, R. (1995), "Estimating Long-Run Relationships From Dynamic Heterogeneous Panels," *Journal of Applied Econometrics*, 68, 79–113.

Rao, C. R. (1973), *Linear Statistical Inference and Its Applications* (2nd ed.), New York: John Wiley.

——— (1975), "Simultaneous Estimation of Parameters in Different Linear Models and Applications to Biometric Problems," *Biometrics*, 31, 545–554.

——— (1987), "Prediction of Future Observations in Growth Curve Models" (with discussion), *Statistical Science*, 2, 434–471.

Robertson, D., and Symons, J. (1992), "Some Strange Properties of Panel Data Estimators," *Journal of Applied Econometrics*, 7, 175–189.

Rubin, D. B. (1980), "Using Empirical Bayes Techniques in the Law School Validity Studies," *Journal of the American Statistical Association*, 75, 801–827.

Scott, E. L. (1980), Comment on "Using Empirical Bayes Techniques in the Law School Validity Studies," by D. B. Rubin, *Journal of the American Statistical Association*, 75, 821–823.

Smith, A. F. M. (1973), "A General Bayesian Linear Model," *Journal of the Royal Statistical Society*, Ser. B, 35, 67–75.

Swamy, P. A. V. B. (1970), "Efficient Inference in a Random Coefficient Regression Model," *Econometrica*, 38, 311–323.

Taylor, L. D. (1975), "The Demand For Electricity: A Survey," *Bell Journal of Economics*, 6, 74–110.

U.S. Energy Information Administration (1993a), *The State Energy Price and Expenditure System*, Washington, DC: Author.

——— (1993b), *State Energy Data System*, Washington, DC: Author.

Zeimer, R. F., and Wetzstein, M. E. (1983), "A Stein-rule Method for Pooling Data," *Economics Letters*, 11, 137–143.

[14]

JOURNAL OF
Econometrics

ELSEVIER Journal of Econometrics 68 (1995) 79–113

Estimating long-run relationships from dynamic heterogeneous panels

M. Hashem Pesaran*,[a], Ron Smith[b]

[a]Trinity College, Cambridge CB2 1TQ, UK
[b]Department of Economics, Birkbeck College, London W1P 1PA, UK

Abstract

In panel data four procedures are widely used: pooling, aggregating, averaging group estimates, and cross-section regression. In the static case, if the coefficients differ randomly, all four procedures give unbiased estimates of coefficient means. In the dynamic case, when the coefficients differ across groups, pooling and aggregating give inconsistent and potentially highly misleading estimates of the coefficients, though the cross-section can provide consistent estimates of the long-run effects. The theoretical results on the properties of the four procedures are illustrated by UK labour demand functions for 38 industries over 30 years.

Key words: Dynamic panels; Parameter heterogeneity; Data fields; Sectoral employment equations
JEL classification: C13; C21; C22; C23

1. Introduction

It is now quite common to have panels in which both N (the number of groups) and T (the number of time periods) are quite large. The groups may be firms, industries, regions, or countries (as in the Summers–Heston data set widely used to study growth). Quah (1990) calls such panels 'data fields' to distinguish them from the small T panels typical of micro-econometrics. Surveys

* Corresponding author.

Excellent research assistance by van Garderen is gratefully acknowledged. The authors wish to thank three anonymous referees for helpful comments. The first author also wishes to acknowledge partial financial support from the ESRC and the Isaac Newton Trust of Trinity College, Cambridge.

SSDI 030440769401644 F

of the literature on panel data are provided in Hsiao (1986) and Matyas and Sevestre (1992).

Suppose the parameter of interest is the average effect of some exogenous variable on a dependent variable. When T is large enough that it is sensible to run separate regressions for each group, there are four procedures that can be used to estimate this average effect. The first involves estimating separate regressions for each group and averaging the coefficients over groups. We will refer to this as the mean group estimator. The second involves combining the data by imposing common slopes, allowing for fixed or random intercepts, and estimating pooled regressions. This coefficient homogeneity assumption although very widely adopted seems implausible for many applications (e.g., see the discussion in Mairesse and Griliches, 1990). The third involves averaging the data over groups and estimating aggregate time-series regressions. The properties of time-series regressions on group averages are examined in more detail in Pesaran, Pierse, and Kumar (1989) and Lee, Pesaran, and Pierse (1990). The fourth involves averaging the data over time and estimating cross-section regressions on group means. Much of the recent work on endogenous growth has used this approach (e.g., Barro, 1991). All four procedures will provide an estimate of the average coefficient; the difference is that in the case of the first estimator the averaging is explicit, while in the others it is implicit.

In the static case, where the regressors are strictly exogenous and the coefficients differ randomly and are distributed independently of the regressors across groups, all four procedures provide consistent (and unbiased) estimates of the coefficient means (e.g., Zellner, 1969). It often seems to be assumed that a similar result holds for dynamic models, i.e., all four procedures give consistent estimators.[1] We show that this is not the case. The group mean estimator obtained by averaging the coefficients for each group is consistent for large N and T, and thus provides a standard of comparison. However, the pooled and aggregate estimators are not consistent in dynamic models, even for large N and T, and the biases can be very substantial. The problem arises because when the regressors are serially correlated, incorrectly ignoring coefficient heterogeneity induces serial correlation in the disturbance, which generates inconsistent estimates in models with lagged dependent variables, even as $T \to \infty$. Thus this inconsistency is quite distinct from that suffered by the fixed effect estimator in small T panels as $N \to \infty$ (e.g., Nickell, 1981), and the solutions proposed in that literature do not solve this problem. Interestingly, the cross-section regressions when based on long time averages do produce consistent estimates of the average long-run coefficients, confirming a widely believed piece of econometric

[1] Certainly Zellner believed this to be the case. Zellner (1969, footnote 5) says: 'if X contains lagged values of y, (13) $\{E\hat{\beta} = \beta\}$ would have to be reformulated to read plim $\hat{\beta} = \beta$, a point made by H. Theil in conversation with the author' (term in { } added).

folk wisdom (e.g., Baltagi and Griffin, 1984). However, it should be emphasised that the familiar practice of running cross-section regressions based on a single or a few years of observations is not likely to yield unbiased or consistent estimates.

Section 2 examines the properties of the four procedures when the regressors are stationary and the model includes a lagged dependent variable. Section 3 examines their properties when the regressors are integrated and each group relationship cointegrates. Section 4 applies the various procedures to the data used in Pesaran, Pierse, and Kumar (1989) and Lee, Pesaran, and Pierse (1990), henceforth referred to as PPK and LPP, respectively, who estimated labour demand functions for 38 industries in the U.K. over 29 years. The application confirms that the biases in the pooled and aggregate estimates can be very serious. Section 5 contains some concluding remarks.

2. Dynamic models of heterogeneous panels

We assume that the data are generated by a set of relationships which have coefficients that are constant over time but differ randomly across groups, and that the distribution of the coefficients is independent of the regressors.[2] The parameters of interest are the averages, over groups, of the coefficients. Consider the following simple heterogeneous dynamic model:[3]

$$y_{it} = \lambda_i y_{i,t-1} + \beta_i' x_{it} + \varepsilon_{it}, \qquad i = 1, 2, \ldots, N, \quad t = 1, 2, \ldots, T, \tag{2.1}$$

with its coefficients λ_i and β_i varying across groups according to the following random coefficient model:

$$\mathrm{H_a}: \quad \lambda_i = \lambda + \eta_{1i}, \quad \beta_i = \beta + \eta_{2i}, \tag{2.2}$$

where η_{1i} and η_{2i} are assumed to have zero means and constant covariances. We also assume that the higher-order moments of η_{1i} and η_{2i} and their cross-moments exist and are finite. This is the standard formulation of the Random Coefficients Model (RCM), and introduces parameter heterogeneity through the 'short-run' coefficients, β_i and λ_i. An alternative characterization would be to let the long-run effects, $\theta_i = \beta_i/(1 - \lambda_i)$, and the mean lags, $\psi_i = \lambda_i/(1 - \lambda_i)$, vary randomly across groups:

$$\mathrm{H_b}: \quad \psi_i = \psi + \xi_{1i}, \quad \theta_i = \theta + \xi_{2i}, \tag{2.3}$$

[2] The assumption of randomness is made for convenience. The main results, in particular the inconsistency of the pooled estimator, will hold in the case where the coefficients are fixed but differ across groups.

[3] For expositional simplicity we confine our attention to the simple specification (2.1), but the main results of the paper also apply to more complicated dynamic models.

where it is now assumed that ξ_{1i} and ξ_{2i} have zero means and constant covariances. The 'average' long-run effect of $\boldsymbol{x}$ on y can now be defined either in terms of the 'average' of the short-run coefficients, $\bar{\beta}/(1-\bar{\lambda})$, or the average of the long-run coefficients, $\bar{\theta}$, where

$$\bar{\beta} = N^{-1}\sum_{i=1}^{N}\beta_i, \quad \bar{\lambda} = N^{-1}\sum_{i=1}^{N}\lambda_i, \quad \bar{\theta} = N^{-1}\sum_{i=1}^{N}\theta_i.$$

As $N \to \infty$, these two estimates converge to $\mathrm{E}(\beta_i)/(1-\mathrm{E}(\lambda_i))$ and $\mathrm{E}(\beta_i/(1-\lambda_i)) = \mathrm{E}(\theta_i)$, respectively, which in general differ from one another, unless λ_i and θ_i are independently distributed, for all i. It turns out that $\bar{\theta}$ [or its limit as $N \to \infty$, namely $\mathrm{E}(\theta_i)$] is the appropriate measure of the average long-run effect of $\boldsymbol{x}$ on y, which is also the probability limit of the cross-section estimates obtained in Section 2.3.

Throughout the paper, unless specifically stated otherwise, we shall make use of the following assumptions:

Assumption 1. $\boldsymbol{x}_{it}$ and ε_{is} are independently distributed for all t and s (i.e., $\boldsymbol{x}_{it}$'s are strictly exogenous), and both set of variables are independently distributed of η_{1i} and η_{2i}, under $\mathrm{H_a}$, and of ξ_{i1} and ξ_{i2}, under $\mathrm{H_b}$. The disturbances ε_{it} have zero means and variances, σ_i^2, that are constant over time.

Assumption 2. $\boldsymbol{x}_{it}$'s are covariance-stationary and mean square ergodic processes with means $\underline{\mu}_i$.[4]

Assumption 3. The support of the random coefficients λ_i lie in the stable range $(-1, 1)$. Further, all the cross-moments of λ_i and β_i exist and are finite, and in particular $\mathrm{E}(\beta_i/(1-\lambda_i))$ and $\mathrm{E}(1/(1-\lambda_i))$ exist and are finite.

Assumption 4. The cross-product matrices $N^{-1}\sum_{i=1}^{N}\underline{\mu}_i\underline{\mu}_i'$ are nonsingular for a finite N, and converge to a finite nonsingular matrix as $N \to \infty$.

Under the above assumptions and when data fields (namely panels with N and T large) are available, separate regressions can be run for each group and

[4] The necessary and sufficient condition for a covariance stationary process $\{x_t\}$ to be mean square ergodic is given by

$$\lim_{T\to\infty}\left\{T^{-1}\sum_{s=0}^{T}\gamma(s)\right\} = 0,$$

where $\gamma(s)$ is the autocovariance function of the process. This condition ensures that time averages such as $\bar{\boldsymbol{x}}_i$ converge to the means of $\boldsymbol{x}_{it}$, namely μ_i in the mean square error sense as $T \to \infty$. See, for example, Karlin and Taylor (1975, § 9.5).

the estimates obtained can be averaged. Both the unweighted average and the Generalised Least Squares weighted average proposed by Swamy (1971) will yield consistent estimates of λ and β and of θ and ψ under both H_a and H_b, for both N and T large. Of course, for small T, the estimates β_i and λ_i will inevitably be biased because of the presence of the lagged dependent variable and this will give an inconsistent estimate of their mean even for large N. However, in empirical applications estimating N separate regressions is rather rare, it is much more common to pool or average the data. Given that they are very widely used, it is important to examine the properties of the other three estimation procedures discussed in Section 1 – pooled, aggregate time-series, and cross-section – to the dynamic heterogeneous panel model (2.1). For exposition, the pooled and aggregate time-series estimator will be examined just under H_a. The results under H_b are qualitatively similar, and the estimates remain inconsistent even when $T \to \infty$. However, the cross-section estimator will be examined under both random coefficient hypotheses H_a and H_b as far as the estimation of average long-run effects are concerned, the (asymptotic) results do not depend on the particular specification and the random coefficient model.

2.1. Pooled estimators

Suppose the micro relations are specified by (2.1) explicitly including an intercept term, with random parameters defined according to H_a in (2.2). The pooled regression is given by

$$y_{it} = \alpha_i + \lambda y_{i,t-1} + \beta' \boldsymbol{x}_{it} + v_{it}, \qquad (2.4)$$

$$i = 1, 2, \ldots, N, \quad t = 1, 2, \ldots, T,$$

$$v_{it} = \varepsilon_{it} + \eta_{1i} y_{i,t-1} + \eta'_{2i} \boldsymbol{x}_{it}. \qquad (2.5)$$

Different group-specific fixed or random effects can be included in the pooled regressions through the intercept term α_i. It is now easily seen that under Assumptions 1–3 $y_{i,t-1}$ and $\boldsymbol{x}_{it}$ are correlated with v_{it}, thus rendering the pooled estimators inconsistent. More specifically, in the case where $\boldsymbol{x}_{it}$ is a scalar with zero mean and autocovariance function $\gamma_i(s)$, we have

$$\mathrm{E}(\boldsymbol{x}_{it} v_{it}) = \sum_{j=0}^{\infty} \mathrm{E}(\eta_{1i} \beta_i \lambda_i^j) \gamma_i(|j+1|)$$

and

$$\mathrm{E}(y_{i,t-1} v_{it}) = \sum_{s=0}^{\infty} \sum_{r=0}^{\infty} \mathrm{E}(\eta_{1i} \beta_i^2 \lambda_i^{r+s}) \gamma_i(|r-s|) + \sigma_i^2 \sum_{s=1}^{\infty} \mathrm{E}(\eta_{1i} \lambda_i^{2s})$$
$$+ \sum_{s=0}^{\infty} \mathrm{E}(\eta_{2i} \beta_i \lambda_i^s) \gamma_i(|s+1|).$$

Even if $\boldsymbol{x}_{it}$'s are serially uncorrelated, $\mathrm{E}(y_{i,t-1}\, v_{it})$ does not vanish because of the second term. In addition, the problem is unlikely to be amenable to the usual solutions. Standard corrections for serial correlation are unlikely to work because of the complexity of the process generating v_{it}. Nor is estimation by the instrumental variables (IV) method likely to be successful either. Given the structure of the composite disturbances v_{it}, all variables that are correlated with $y_{i,t-1}$ or $\boldsymbol{x}_{it}$ will also be correlated with v_{it}. In general, only variables that are uncorrelated with lagged values of ε_{it} and $\boldsymbol{x}_{it}$ have a zero correlation with v_{it}. But such variables, assuming they exist, fail to yield a valid set of instruments, since they will also be uncorrelated with the regressors. The fact that the average effects in a dynamic model where the slope coefficients differ over groups cannot be consistently estimated from a pooled regression even when N and T are large is not a particular problem since they can be estimated directly by the mean group procedure. Of course, when T is small the bias of the pooled estimator is likely to be a serious problem.

Since the pooled estimators are widely used, it would be useful to have some idea of the size of the likely biases and what they depend on. In the case where the slope coefficients are homogeneous, it is well-known that the 'within', or the fixed-effect estimators, and the random-effect estimators (namely the GLS estimators of λ and β when α_i's are treated as random) are asymptotically equivalent for both N and T large (see, for example, Chapter 4 in Matyas and Sevestre, 1992). Consequently, here we focus on the fixed-effect estimators, and expect to obtain similar results when the random-effect estimators are considered. Also to simplify the exposition we analyze the case where the model contains only one exogenous variable ($k = 1$), generated according to the following simple stationary autoregressive process:

$$x_{it} = \mu_i(1-\rho) + \rho\, x_{i\,t-1} + u_{it}, \tag{2.6}$$

where μ_i is the (unconditional) mean of x_{it}, $|\rho| < 1$, and for each i, $u_{it} \sim \mathrm{iid}(0, \tau_i^2)$. The variations in σ_i^2 and τ_i^2 across groups are also supposed to be independent of λ_i and β_i. We shall denote the means of σ_i^2 and τ_i^2 by σ^2 and τ^2, respectively.[5]

The probability limits of the fixed-effect estimators, which we denote by $\hat{\lambda}$ and $\hat{\beta}$, are derived in Appendix A. It is shown that the fixed-effect estimators are generally inconsistent (for large N and T), and yield an inconsistent estimator of the 'average' long run effects of $\boldsymbol{x}$ on y. Furthermore, this inconsistency does not disappear even if variations in β_i across groups is the only source of slope heterogeneity in the model. For this relatively simple case (with $\lambda_i = \lambda$, and

[5] When σ_i^2 and τ_i^2 are nonstochastic but variable across groups, σ^2 and τ^2 can be viewed as the limits of their respective averages.

hence $\eta_{1i} = 0$ for all i) we have[6]

$$\operatorname*{plim}_{N \to \infty, T \to \infty} (\hat{\lambda}) = \lambda + \frac{\rho(1-\lambda\rho)(1-\lambda^2)\omega_{22}}{\Psi_1}, \tag{2.7}$$

$$\operatorname*{plim}_{N \to \infty, T \to \infty} (\hat{\beta}) = \beta - \frac{\beta\rho^2(1-\lambda^2)\omega_{22}}{\Psi_1}, \tag{2.8}$$

where

$$\Psi_1 = (\sigma^2/\tau^2)(1-\rho^2)(1-\lambda\rho)^2 + (1-\lambda^2\rho^2)\omega_{22} + (1-\rho^2)\beta, \tag{2.9}$$

and ω_{22} is the variance of β_i. Since $|\lambda| < 1$ and $|\rho| < 1$, then $\Psi_1 > 0$. The large sample bias of $\hat{\lambda}$ will be positive when $\rho > 0$, and *vice versa*, while $\operatorname{plim}(\hat{\beta}) < \beta$ for all parameter values. The size of the asymptotic bias of the fixed-effect estimators depends on ρ, λ, β, ω_{22}, and σ^2/τ^2. As to be expected, the larger the degree of parameter heterogeneity (i.e., the larger ω_{22}), the greater the bias. For $\omega_{22} > 0$, the asymptotic biases in $\hat{\lambda}$ and $\hat{\beta}$ disappears only if $\rho = 0$.[7] Turning to the fixed-effect estimator of the 'average' long-run impact of x on y, namely $\hat{\theta} = \hat{\beta}/(1-\hat{\lambda})$, using (2.7) and (2.8) we have

$$\operatorname*{plim}_{N \to \infty, T \to \infty} (\hat{\theta}) = \frac{\theta}{1-\rho\Psi_2}, \tag{2.10}$$

where

$$\Psi_2 = \frac{(1+\lambda)\omega_{22}}{(\sigma^2/\tau^2)(1+\rho)(1-\lambda\rho)^2 + (1+\rho)(\beta^2+\omega_{22})} > 0\,. \tag{2.11}$$

Therefore, the fixed-effect estimator of the long-run effect, θ, is also asymptotically biased, and overestimates the long-run effect when $\rho > 0$, and underestimates it when $\rho < 0$. The bias disappears either when $\rho = 0$ or $\omega_{22} = 0$.[8]

As ρ approaches unity from below ($|\rho| < 1$), we have the following important results:

$$\operatorname*{plim}_{\rho \to 1}(\hat{\lambda}) = 1 \quad \text{and} \quad \operatorname*{plim}_{\rho \to 1}(\hat{\beta}) = 0,$$

which hold irrespective of the true value of λ![9] Robertson and Symons (1992) also obtain a similar result by considering pooled OLS estimates in the context

[6] Derivations are given in Appendix A. The probability limits are obtained by first letting $T \to \infty$, and then $N \to \infty$.

[7] This result crucially depends on the assumed homogeneity of λ_i and ρ_i across groups.

[8] The consistency of $\hat{\theta}$ for θ when $\rho = 0$ does not carry-over to the more general dynamic model where (2.1) also contains lagged values of x_{it}.

[9] It is important to note that these results hold only for values of ρ approaching unity from below (i.e., when x_{it}'s are near integrated) and are not valid for $\rho = 1$.

of a dynamic heterogeneous panel when the true value of λ is zero. Our results show that Robertson and Symons' finding is more general and holds for *all* values of $|\lambda| < 1$. The tendency for the fixed-effect estimators to underestimate the average short-run effects and overestimate the average long-run effects can be clearly seen in the application considered in Section 4, even though the sectoral employment demand equations are specified to contain higher-order lags of the dependent and the explanatory variables. Finally, it is worth noting that for $\rho \neq 0$ and $\omega_{22} \neq 0$ the asymptotic biases of $\hat{\lambda}$ and $\hat{\beta}$ vanish only if the true value of λ approaches its upper limit of unity from below. Using (2.7) and (2.8), it is clear that when $\lambda \to 1$, $\text{plim}(\hat{\lambda})$ and $\text{plim}(\hat{\beta})$ tend to λ and β, respectively. Once again this result is not necessarily valid for $\lambda = 1$.

2.2. *The aggregate time-series estimator*

As with the pooled regression, if the $\boldsymbol{x}_{it}$ are serially correlated, then the error in the aggregate equation will also be serially correlated producing inconsistent estimates if a lagged dependent variable is included in the model. Consider the simple dynamic RCM defined by (2.1) and assume that the short-run coefficients λ_i and β_i are random (i.e., H_a holds). The case where the long-run coefficients are assumed to be random yields the same qualitative results and will not be dealt with here separately.

Aggregating (2.1) over the micro-units and utilizing (2.2) we obtain

$$\bar{y}_t = \lambda \bar{y}_{t-1} + \beta' \bar{\boldsymbol{x}}_t + \bar{v}_t, \tag{2.12}$$

where $\bar{y}_t$ and $\bar{\boldsymbol{x}}_t$ are sample means of y_{it} and $\boldsymbol{x}_{it}$ across i, and

$$\bar{v}_t = \bar{\varepsilon}_t + N^{-1} \sum_{i=1}^{N} (\eta_{1i} y_{i,t-1} + \eta'_{2i} \boldsymbol{x}_{it}).$$

The macro disturbances, $\bar{v}_t$, are now correlated with the regressors in the aggregate equation and the OLS estimators based on (2.12) will not be consistent even if both N and T are allowed to increase without bounds. (See Appendix B.) As with the pooled regression, the serial correlation pattern in $\bar{v}_t$ is also sufficiently complex that standard procedures for dealing with it are unlikely to work and estimation of (2.12) by the instrumental variables (IV) method is not likely to be successful either. For example, lagged $\bar{x}_t$'s cannot be used as instruments, since

$$\text{E}(\bar{\boldsymbol{x}}_{t-r} \bar{v}_t) = N^{-1} \sum_{i=1}^{N} \sum_{s=0}^{\infty} \text{E}(\eta_{1i} \lambda_i^s \beta'_i)\, \text{E}(\boldsymbol{x}_{i,t-s-1} \bar{\boldsymbol{x}}_{t-r}),$$

which is nonzero for all values of $r > 0$. In general, only variables that are uncorrelated with lagged values of ε_{it} and $\boldsymbol{x}_{it}$ have a zero correlation with $\bar{v}_t$. But such variables, assuming they exist, fail to yield a valid set of instruments, since they will also be uncorrelated with the regressors of (2.12), namely $\bar{y}_{t-1}$ and $\bar{x}_t$. Therefore, Zellner's (1969) ingenious solution of the aggregation problem in the context of linear models does not, unfortunately, extend to random coefficient micro-relations with lagged endogenous variables.

The difficulty in estimating λ and β from the above aggregate time-series specification partly stems from the fact that (2.12) is not an 'optimal' aggregate predictor of $\bar{y}_t$, given the available aggregate information set, $\Omega_t = (\bar{\boldsymbol{x}}_t, \bar{\boldsymbol{x}}_{t-1}, \ldots; \bar{y}_{t-1}, \bar{y}_{t-2}, \ldots)$. As one of us has shown elsewhere (Pesaran, 1995), the optimal aggregate time-series specification associated with the heterogeneous dynamic model (2.1) is given by

$$\bar{y}_t = \sum_{j=0}^{\infty} \boldsymbol{a}'_j \bar{\boldsymbol{x}}_{t-j} + \bar{\xi}_t, \tag{2.13}$$

where $\bar{\xi}_t$'s have zero means and are independently distributed of the current and lagged values of $\bar{\boldsymbol{x}}_t$; and

$$\boldsymbol{a}_j = \mathrm{E}(\beta_i \lambda_i^j) \quad \text{for} \quad j = 0, 1, 2, \ldots . \tag{2.14}$$

In general, $\bar{\xi}_t$'s will have a complicated pattern of serial correlation. Comparing (2.13) with (2.12) it is now clear that (2.12) is misspecified and cannot be used to obtain consistent estimators of λ and β. A special case of (2.13) is also derived by Lewbel (1994), under the assumption that β_i and λ_i are independently distributed [i.e., $\mathrm{cov}(\eta_{1i}, \eta_{2i}) = 0, \forall i$]. However, to obtain the 'average' long-run effect of $\boldsymbol{x}_{it}$ on y_{it}, one does not need to make the restrictive assumption that λ_i and β_i are independently distributed, and using (2.14), it is easily seen that

$$\sum_{j=0}^{\infty} \boldsymbol{a}_j = \mathrm{E}\left(\sum_{j=0}^{\infty} \beta_i \lambda_i^j\right) = \mathrm{E}\left(\frac{\beta_i}{1-\lambda_i}\right) = \mathrm{E}(\theta_i) = \theta. \tag{2.15}$$

Hence, to estimate θ consistently from an aggregate times specification one needs to consider an infinite distributed lag specification between $\bar{y}_t$ and $\bar{x}_t$, allowing for the possibility of a high degree of residual serial correlation.

2.3. The cross-section estimator

Aggregating (2.1) over time, we get

$$\tilde{y}_i = \beta'_i \tilde{\boldsymbol{x}}_i + \lambda_i \tilde{y}_{i.,-1} + \tilde{\varepsilon}_i, \tag{2.16}$$

where

$$\tilde{y}_{i.,-1} = T^{-1} \sum_{t=1}^{T} y_{i,t-1}, \qquad \tilde{\boldsymbol{x}}_i = T^{-1} \sum_{t=1}^{T} x_{it}, \qquad \tilde{\varepsilon}_i = T^{-1} \sum_{t=1}^{T} \varepsilon_{it}.$$

Under $\mathrm{H_a}$, defined by (2.2), (2.16) becomes

$$\tilde{y}_i = \beta' \tilde{\boldsymbol{x}}_i + \lambda \tilde{y}_{i.,-1} + \tilde{v}_i, \tag{2.17}$$

where

$$\tilde{v}_i = \eta_{1i}\tilde{y}_{i,-1} + \eta'_{2i}\tilde{x}_i + \tilde{\varepsilon}_i. \tag{2.18}$$

The regression defined by (2.17) is the 'between' regression for the dynamic model, and will produce inconsistent estimates of β and λ as $N, T \to \infty$, even if the intercept parameter in (2.1) is the *only* parameter that varies across groups. This is due to the fact that $\tilde{v}_i$ is correlated with $\tilde{y}_{i,-1}$ even for large T.

A more promising route is first to rewrite (2.16) as

$$\tilde{y}_i = \beta'_i\tilde{x}_i + \lambda_i(\tilde{y}_i - \Delta_T y_i) + \tilde{\varepsilon}_i, \tag{2.19}$$

where the growth term $\Delta_T y_i = (y_{iT} - y_{i0})/T$ captures the end effects. Then solve for $\tilde{y}_i$ to obtain

$$\tilde{y}_i = \frac{\beta'_i}{1-\lambda_i}\tilde{x}_i - \frac{\lambda_i}{1-\lambda_i}\Delta_T y_i + \frac{1}{1-\lambda_i}\tilde{\varepsilon}_i$$

$$= \theta'_i\tilde{x}_i - \psi_i\Delta_T y_i + \frac{1}{1-\lambda_i}\tilde{\varepsilon}_i.$$

Thus the coefficients $\tilde{x}_i$ in this cross-section regression are in fact the appropriate long-run averages. Given the structure of this equation, it is natural to assume that the randomness is introduced through the long-run coefficients. Thus, under H_b, the cross-section regression is

$$\tilde{y}_i = \theta'\tilde{x}_i - \psi\Delta_T y_i + \tilde{u}_i, \tag{2.20}$$

where

$$\tilde{u}_i = \frac{1}{1-\lambda_i}\tilde{\varepsilon}_i + \xi'_{2i}\tilde{x}_i - \xi_{1i}\Delta_T y_i, \tag{2.21}$$

and the cross-section estimates of the 'average' long-run coefficients are given by

$$\hat{\theta}^c = \left(\sum_{i=1}^{N}\tilde{x}_i\tilde{x}'_i\right)^{-1}\left(\sum_{i=1}^{N}\tilde{x}_i\tilde{y}_i\right). \tag{2.22}$$

It may appear that the usual cross-sections, estimated purely from levels, are misspecified to the extent that they omit the growth terms $\Delta_T y_i$. However, asymptotically the growth terms such as $\Delta_T y_i$ (and $\Delta_T x_i$ had $x_{i,t-1}$ appeared in the regression) are uncorrelated with the level terms, so omitting them is irrelevant to the consistency of the average long-run effects. This suggests that cross-section estimates of the average long-run effect, θ, will be robust to dynamic misspecification of the underlying micro-model. This robustness is clearly an important feature of cross-section estimates of θ, not enjoyed by pooled or aggregate time-series estimates.

Consider now the asymptotic bias of the cross-section estimate, $\hat{\theta}^c$, for large T. First, note that since $\psi_i = \lambda_i/(1-\lambda_i)$, then $1+\psi_i = 1/(1-\lambda_i)$, and using (2.21), we have

$$\tilde{u}_i = (1+\psi_i)\tilde{\varepsilon}_i + \tilde{x}_i'\xi_{2i} - \xi_{1i}\Delta_T y_i. \tag{2.23}$$

Also, under Assumption 3 and assuming that the processes generating y_{it} have started a long time ago, we have[10]

$$y_{it} = \sum_{j=0}^{\infty} x_{i,t-j}'\beta_i\lambda_i^j + \sum_{j=0}^{\infty}\lambda_i^j\varepsilon_{i,t-j}, \tag{2.24}$$

and, therefore,

$$\begin{aligned}\Delta_T y_i &= T^{-1}(y_{iT}-y_{i0})T^{-1}\sum_{t=1}^{T}\Delta y_{it}\\ &= \sum_{j=0}^{\infty}(\tilde{x}_{i,-j}-\tilde{x}_{i,-j-1})'\beta_i\lambda_i^j + \sum_{j=0}^{\infty}\lambda_i^j(\tilde{\varepsilon}_{i,-j}-\tilde{\varepsilon}_{i,-j-1}).\end{aligned} \tag{2.25}$$

Substituting (2.20) for $\tilde{y}_i$ in (2.22) and making use of (2.23) and (2.25), we have

$$\begin{aligned}\hat{\theta}^c - \theta &= \boldsymbol{H}_N\sum_{i=1}^{N}(\tilde{x}_i\tilde{x}_i')\xi_{2i} + \boldsymbol{H}_N\sum_{i=1}^{N}(1+\psi_i)\tilde{x}_i\tilde{\varepsilon}_i - \boldsymbol{H}_N\\ &= \sum_{i=1}^{N}\sum_{j=0}^{\infty}\tilde{x}_i(\tilde{x}_{i,-j}-\tilde{x}_{i,-j-1})'\psi_i\beta_i\lambda_i^j\\ &\quad - \boldsymbol{H}_N\sum_{i=1}^{N}\sum_{j=0}^{\infty}\psi_i\lambda_i^j(\tilde{\varepsilon}_{i,-j}-\tilde{\varepsilon}_{i,-j-1}),\end{aligned}$$

where

$$\boldsymbol{H}_N = \left(\sum_{i=1}^{N}\tilde{x}_i\tilde{x}_i'\right)^{-1}.$$

Denote the set of observations on x_{it}'s by $x = (x_{11}, x_{12}, \ldots, x_{1T}; \ldots; x_{N1}, x_{N2}, \ldots, x_{NT})$, and take conditional expectations under Assumption 1 and hypothesis H_b, then

$$\mathrm{E}(\hat{\theta}^c|x) - \theta = -\boldsymbol{H}_N\sum_{j=0}^{\infty}\sum_{i=1}^{N}\tilde{x}_i(\tilde{x}_{i,-j}-\tilde{x}_{i,-j-1})'\,\mathrm{E}(\psi_i\beta_i\lambda_i^j).$$

Under our assumptions the moments $\mathrm{E}(\psi_i\beta_i\lambda_i^j) = \mathrm{E}\{\theta_i[\psi_i/(1+\psi_i)]^{j+1}\}$ exists and are finite for all j. It is also clear that, in general, they are nonzero. It therefore follows that for a *finite* T, the cross-section estimator, $\hat{\theta}^c$, yields

[10] The results are qualitatively unchanged if it is assumed that the initial values y_{i0} are fixed (nonstochastic).

a biased estimator of the mean of the long-run coefficients (i.e., $\theta = \mathrm{E}(\beta_i/(1-\lambda_i))$, and this bias does not vanish for large N. However, for large T (even when N is finite) under the assumption that $\boldsymbol{x}_{it}$'s are covariance-stationary, we have[11]

$$\tilde{\boldsymbol{x}}_i(\tilde{\boldsymbol{x}}_{i,-j} - \tilde{\boldsymbol{x}}_{i,-j-1})' = \mathrm{O}_p(T^{-1}) \quad \text{for} \quad j = 0, 1, 2, \ldots,$$

and the bias will be of order of T^{-1}. Thus for T and N large, the cross-section will provide a consistent estimate of the mean of the long-run coefficients.

2.4. Short-run coefficients and randomness

Consider now the case where the randomness is introduced through the short-run coefficients (i.e., under $\mathrm{H_a}$). Using (2.24), we have the following time averages of y_{it}'s in terms of the time averages of x_{it} and ε_{it}:

$$\tilde{y}_i = \sum_{j=0}^{\infty} \tilde{\boldsymbol{x}}_{i,-j}\boldsymbol{\beta}_i \lambda_i^j + \sum_{j=0}^{\infty} \lambda_i^j \tilde{\varepsilon}_{i,-j}, \qquad i = 1, 2, \ldots, N.$$

Substituting this result directly in (2.22) now yields

$$\hat{\theta}^c = \boldsymbol{H}_N^{-1}\left\{\sum_{j=0}^{\infty}\sum_{i=1}^{N} \tilde{\boldsymbol{x}}_i\tilde{\boldsymbol{x}}'_{i,-j}\boldsymbol{\beta}_i\lambda_i^j + \sum_{j=0}^{\infty}\sum_{i=1}^{N}(\tilde{\boldsymbol{x}}_i\tilde{\varepsilon}_{i,-j})\lambda_i^j\right\}.$$

Taking conditional expectations with respect to $\boldsymbol{x}$ (defined above), and noting that under Assumption 1 the distribution of $\boldsymbol{\beta}_i$, λ_i, and ε_{it} are distributed independently of $\boldsymbol{x}_{it}$'s, and under $\mathrm{H_a}$, ε_{it} and λ_i are also distributed independently, we have[12]

$$\mathrm{E_a}(\hat{\theta}^c\,|\,\boldsymbol{x}) = \boldsymbol{H}_N^{-1}\sum_{j=0}^{\infty}\sum_{i=1}^{N}\tilde{\boldsymbol{x}}_i\tilde{\boldsymbol{x}}'_{i,-j}\mathrm{E}(\boldsymbol{\beta}_i\lambda_i^j).$$

But $\mathrm{E}(\boldsymbol{\beta}_i\lambda_i^j) = \boldsymbol{a}_j$ is the same across groups, and hence

$$\mathrm{E_a}(\hat{\theta}^c\,|\,\boldsymbol{x}) = \sum_{j=0}^{\infty}\boldsymbol{H}_N^{-1}\left(\sum_{i=1}^{N}\tilde{\boldsymbol{x}}_i\tilde{\boldsymbol{x}}'_{i,-j}\right)\boldsymbol{a}_j. \tag{2.26}$$

Now for large T and under the assumption that $\boldsymbol{x}_{it}$'s are covariance-stationary, we have (Appendix C)

$$\tilde{\boldsymbol{x}}_i\tilde{\boldsymbol{x}}'_{i,-j} = \boldsymbol{\mu}_i\boldsymbol{\mu}'_i + \mathrm{O}_p(T^{-1}), \qquad j = 0, 1, 2, \ldots .$$

[11] A proof in the simple case where $\boldsymbol{x}_{it}$ is a scalar (i.e., when $k = 1$) is given in Appendix C.

[12] Note that $\mathrm{E}(\tilde{\boldsymbol{x}}_i\tilde{\varepsilon}_{i,-j}\lambda_i^j|\boldsymbol{x}) = \tilde{\boldsymbol{x}}_i\mathrm{E}(\tilde{\varepsilon}_{i,-j}\lambda_i^j) = \tilde{\boldsymbol{x}}_i\mathrm{E}(\tilde{\varepsilon}_{i,-j})\mathrm{E}(\lambda_i^j) = 0$, since $\mathrm{E}(\varepsilon_{it}) = 0$ for all i and t.

Therefore,

$$\boldsymbol{H}_N^{-1}\left(\sum_{i=1}^{N}\tilde{\boldsymbol{x}}_i\tilde{\boldsymbol{x}}'_{i,-j}\right)=\left(\sum_{i=1}^{N}\tilde{\boldsymbol{x}}_i\tilde{\boldsymbol{x}}'_i\right)^{-1}\left(\sum_{i=1}^{N}\tilde{\boldsymbol{x}}_i\tilde{\boldsymbol{x}}'_{i,-j}\right)$$

$$=\left\{\sum_{i=1}^{N}\underline{\mu}_i\underline{\mu}'_i+\mathrm{O}_p(T^{-1})\right\}^{-1}\left\{\sum_{i=1}^{N}\underline{\mu}_i\underline{\mu}'_i+\mathrm{O}_p(T^{-1})\right\},$$

and as $T\to\infty$,

$$\operatorname*{plim}_{T\to\infty}\boldsymbol{H}_N^{-1}\left(\sum_{i=1}^{N}\tilde{\boldsymbol{x}}_i\tilde{\boldsymbol{x}}'_{i,-j}\right)=\boldsymbol{I},$$

where $\boldsymbol{I}$ is an identity matrix of the same dimension as $\boldsymbol{x}_i$. Using this result in (2.26), we have [recall that $\boldsymbol{a}_j=\mathrm{E}(\beta_i\lambda_i^j)$]:

$$\operatorname*{plim}_{T\to\infty}\mathrm{E}(\hat{\theta}^c\,|\,\boldsymbol{x})=\sum_{j=0}^{\infty}\boldsymbol{a}_j=\mathrm{E}\left(\sum_{j=0}^{\infty}\beta_i\lambda_i^j\right)=\mathrm{E}\left(\frac{\beta_i}{1-\lambda_i}\right)=\theta.$$

Consequently,

$$\operatorname*{plim}_{T\to\infty}\mathrm{E}(\hat{\theta}^c)=\theta,$$

which establishes that for large T cross-section estimator, $\hat{\theta}^c$, is also an unbiased estimator of the average of the long-run coefficients under $\mathrm{H_a}$. Thus, the asymptotic unbiasedness of $\hat{\theta}^c$ does not depend on the particular specification of the random coefficient model.

3. Integrated variables

Suppose that the $\boldsymbol{x}_{it}$ are $I(1)$ and there is a single cointegrating relationship between y_{it} and $\boldsymbol{x}_{it}$ for each group, with the parameters differing randomly between groups. Then a simple static cointegrating regression of y_{it} on $\boldsymbol{x}_{it}$ will yield superconsistent estimates of θ_i, the cointegrating vector. These could then be averaged over groups. However, the pooled and aggregate time-series estimators will not provide consistent estimators of the mean effect. Suppose each micro-relationship cointegrates with different parameters. The pooled regression by imposing a common parameter on all the micro-relations generates a residual which has an $I(0)$ component, the residual from the cointegrating micro-relationship, and an $I(1)$ component, the product of the difference between the micro-coefficients and imposed common coefficient, and the $I(1)$ regressor. Thus the pooled regression will not constitute a cointegrating regression and the parameter estimates will not be consistent.

Consider now aggregating the micro-relations

$$y_{it}=\beta_i x_{it}+\varepsilon_{it},\tag{3.1}$$

where y_{it} and x_{it} are each $I(1)$ and are pairwise cointegrated; namely ε_{it} is $I(0)$.[13] Under the random coefficient specification, $\beta_i = \beta + \eta_i$, $\eta_i \sim \text{iid}(0,\ \omega^2)$, the corresponding time-series aggregate model is given by

$$\bar{y}_t = \beta \bar{x}_t + \bar{v}_t, \tag{3.2}$$

$$\bar{v}_t = \bar{\varepsilon}_t + N^{-1} \sum_{i=1}^{N} \eta_i x_{it}. \tag{3.3}$$

Suppose now

$$x_{it} = x_{i,t-1} + u_{it}, \qquad u_{it} \sim (0, \tau_i^2),$$

and for expositional simplicity assume that x_{i0} are fixed. In this case we have

$$\text{cov}(\bar{v}_t, \bar{v}_{t-s}) = \text{cov}(\bar{\varepsilon}_t, \bar{\varepsilon}_{t-s}) + \frac{\omega^2 \tau^2}{N}(t-s), \qquad t > s,$$

and $V(\bar{v}_t) = V(\bar{\varepsilon}_t) + (\tau^2 \omega^2 / N)t$, where as before $\tau^2 = N^{-1} \sum_{i=1}^{N} \tau_i^2$. Hence, for a fixed N, $\{\bar{v}_t\}$ will eventually behave as a random walk and $\bar{y}_t$ and $\bar{x}_t$ need not be cointegrated. even though *all* the underlying micro-relations are by assumption cointegrated. For a further analysis of cointegration and aggregation see Gonzalo (1993), where the conditions under which cointegration at micro-levels implies cointegration at the macro level, and *vice versa*, are discussed.

3.1. Cross-section estimates with integrated variables

We now examine the impact of nonstationary variables on the cross-section estimates. Once again consider the micro-relations (3.1). Here for simplicity of exposition we are considering the case where x_{it} is a scalar variable. Averaging the data across time periods and assuming random coefficients as above the OLS regression from the cross-section yields

$$\hat{\beta}^c = \frac{\sum_{i=1}^{N} \bar{y}_i \bar{x}_i}{\sum_{i=1}^{N} \bar{x}_i^2} = \beta + \frac{\sum_{i=1}^{N} \eta_i \bar{x}_i^2}{\sum_{i=1}^{N} \bar{x}_i^2} + \frac{\sum_{i=1}^{N} \bar{\varepsilon}_i \bar{x}_i}{\sum_{i=1}^{N} \bar{x}_i^2}. \tag{3.4}$$

Suppose x_{it} is a random walk with drift

$$x_{it} = x_{i,t-1} + \mu_i + u_{it}, \qquad u_{it} \sim (0, \tau_i^2). \tag{3.5}$$

[13] An intercept term can be readily allowed for in this model by regarding y_{it} and x_{it} being measured as deviations from their initial values x_{i0} and y_{i0}, treating these as fixed and assuming that $\varepsilon_{i0} = 0$.

Then

$$x_{it} = x_{i0} + \mu_i t + \sum_{j=1}^{t} u_{ij},$$

and the time averages, measured as deviations from the initial values x_{i0}, are given by

$$\tilde{x}_i = \mu_i + \left(\frac{T+1}{2}\right) + \sum_{j=1}^{T} (T+1-j)u_{ij}/T,$$

and hence

$$\mathrm{E}\left(N^{-1}\sum_{i=1}^{N}\tilde{x}_i^2\right) = \left(\frac{T+1}{2}\right)^2\left(\sum_{i=1}^{N}\mu_i^2/N\right) + \sum_{i=1}^{N}\sum_{j=1}^{T}\sum_{k=1}^{T}(T+1-j)(T+1-k)\,\mathrm{E}(u_{ij}u_{ik})/NT^2,$$

which under (3.5) yields

$$\mathrm{E}\left(N^{-1}\sum_{i=1}^{N}\tilde{x}_i^2\right) = \left(\sum_{i=1}^{N}\mu_i^2/N\right)\left(\frac{T+1}{2}\right)^2 + \frac{\tau^2}{T^2}\sum_{j=1}^{T}(T+1-j)^2.$$

Now taking limits as $N \to \infty$ for a fixed T, we have[14]

$$\lim_{N\to\infty}\mathrm{E}\left(\sum_{i=1}^{N}\tilde{x}_i^2/N\right) = \left(\frac{T+1}{2}\right)^2\lim_{N\to\infty}\left(\sum_{i=1}^{N}\mu_i^2/N\right) + \frac{T(T+1)(2T+1)}{6T^2}\lim_{N\to\infty}\left(\sum_{i=1}^{N}\tau_i^2/N\right),$$

which is finite for a finite T. Also under the assumption that x_{it}'s are strictly exogenous we have

$$\mathrm{E}\left(\sum_{i=1}^{N}\tilde{x}_i^2\eta_i/N\right) = 0, \qquad \mathrm{E}\left(\sum_{i=1}^{N}\tilde{x}_i^2\tilde{\varepsilon}_i/N\right) = 0.$$

Hence as $N \to \infty$, $\hat{\beta}^c \xrightarrow{p} \beta$, for a finite T.

This result indicates that the spurious correlation problem does not arise in the case of cross-section regressions, even if the underlying variables x_{it} and y_{it} contain a unit root. Under the above assumptions $\hat{\beta}^c$ is also an unbiased estimator of β, though the usual standard error formulae for the estimates are no longer valid.

[14] Note that $\sum_{j=1}^{T}(T+1-j)^2 = T(T+1)(2T+1)/6$.

The disturbance term in the cross-section regression is given by

$$\tilde{v}_i = \tilde{y}_i - \beta\tilde{x}_i = \tilde{\varepsilon}_i + \eta_i\tilde{x}_i,$$

with variance

$$V(\tilde{v}_i\,|\,\boldsymbol{x}) = V(\tilde{\varepsilon}_i) + \omega^2\tilde{x}_i^2,$$

where ω^2 is the variance of η_i. The first term is likely to be small, particularly if T is large, thus consistent estimates of the conditional variances of the cross-section coefficients can be obtained using White's procedure. It is, however, important to note that the above results are valid under the rather strong assumption that x_{it}'s are strictly exogenous, and do not hold in the standard case discussed in the time-series literature of cointegrated variables where possible dependence of x_{it} on $\varepsilon_{it'}$ (for some t and t') is not ruled out.

4. An application: Labour demand functions

The various procedures discussed above will be illustrated by an application previously used to examine the aggregation problem in linear models in PPK (1989) and LPP (1990). Employment functions will be estimated for a panel of 38 industries over the 29 years, 1956–84.[15] The logarithm of industry employment (e_{it}), measured in man-hours, is explained by current and lagged values of the logarithms of industry output (y_{it}), real product wage (w_{it}), and aggregate output ($\bar{y}_t$); together with two lags of log employment, an intercept, and a time trend.

This data set is used for illustration, primarily because it has already been documented and analyzed in previous papers. But in the light of the theory developed above it has a particular feature that may also make it relevant to the analysis of other large N, large T panels. For almost every industry the hypothesis that the output, employment, and real wage variables have unit roots cannot be rejected according to Augmented Dickey–Fuller statistics with zero, one, and two lagged changes. Only for output in industry 37 (business services) is there a unanimous rejection of the unit root hypothesis. There is one other case (industry 18) where there is conflict between the test statistics for output. There is one case of conflict for employment and five industries where one or two of the ADF statistics suggest rejection of the unit root null for real wages.

The primary parameters of interest are the long-run elasticities with respect to real wages and output. In the case of output, since an industry's employment is affected by its own output as well as by aggregate output, there are two possible measures of the long-run output elasticity: the response to its own output only,

[15] The full data set has 41 industries. For comparability with PPK and LPP we exclude the oil industry, where the data are zero for half the period and shipbuilding and tobacco where the common specification chosen for all the industries did not yield sensible results.

or the total response to both its own and aggregate output. Since aggregate output at any moment in time does not vary over industries, the parameters that can be recovered differ between procedures. The aggregate time-series can only give an estimate of the elasticity with respect to all output. The cross-sections can only give an estimate of the elasticity with respect to own output, and the aggregate effect, being the same for all groups, gets picked up in the intercept.

The long-run coefficients can be estimated by four basic methods: group means, aggregate time-series, pooled, and cross-section.

4.1. Group mean estimates

In this case the average long-run coefficients can be obtained in three ways:
1) from the mean of the long-run industry-specific coefficients,
2) from the average of industry specific short-run coefficients,
3) from the mean coefficients in the industry-specific cointegrating regressions.

In each case the means can be unweighted/weighted using the Swamy (1971) GLS procedure. The various estimates together with their standard errors are given in Table 1. In the case of the cointegrating regressions the reported standard errors, which are based on inappropriate estimates of the variances are given only for completeness. Our assumption that between industry disturbance covariances are zero can be relaxed. More specifically, the equation estimated for each industry has the autoregressive distributed lag (ADRL) form

$$e_{it} = \alpha_{1i} + \alpha_{2i}t + \beta_{1i}y_{it} + \beta_{2i}y_{i,t-1} + \beta_{3i}\bar{y}_t + \beta_{4i}\bar{y}_{t-1} + \gamma_{1i}w_{it} + \gamma_{2i}w_{i,t-1} + \lambda_{1i}e_{i,t-1} + \lambda_{2i}e_{it-2} + \varepsilon_{it}, \qquad (4.1)$$

$$i = 1, 2, \dots, 38, \quad t = 1956, \dots, 1984,$$

e_{it} is employment, y_{it} output, w_{it} real wage, and $\bar{y}_t$ aggregate output, all in logarithms. If we define the long-run elasticities for industry i as:

with respect to the real wage, $\hat{\phi}_i = (\hat{\gamma}_{1i} + \hat{\gamma}_{2i})/(1 - \hat{\lambda}_{1i} - \hat{\lambda}_{2i})$,

with respect to all output, $\hat{\theta}_{1i} = (\hat{\beta}_{1i} + \hat{\beta}_{2i} + \hat{\beta}_{3i} + \hat{\beta}_{4i})/(1 - \hat{\lambda}_{1i} - \hat{\lambda}_{2i})$,

and with respect to own output, $\hat{\theta}_{2i} = (\hat{\beta}_{1i} + \hat{\beta}_{2i})/(1 - \hat{\lambda}_{1i} - \hat{\lambda}_{2i})$,

the mean of the long runs (panel A(i) in Table 1) are computed as[16]

$$\hat{\phi} = \sum_{i=1}^{N} \hat{\phi}_i/N,$$

similarly for $\hat{\theta}_1$ and $\hat{\theta}_2$. The long-run estimates calculated from the means of the

[16]Notice that the estimators of the long-run parameters $\hat{\phi}_i$, $\hat{\theta}_{1i}$, $\hat{\theta}_{2i}$, and the mean group estimators based on them are also superconsistent when the regressors are $I(1)$. See Pesaran and Shin (1995).

Table 1
Heterogeneous panel estimates of mean long-run labour demand elasticities

		Output	
	Wages ($\hat{\phi}$)	Total ($\hat{\theta}_1$)	Own ($\hat{\theta}_2$)
(A) Based on dynamic industry regressions Eq. (4.1)			
(i) Means of industry long-run estimates			
Unweighted	– 0.33	0.85	0.42
	(0.27)	(0.25)	(0.19)
Weighted (Swamy estimates)	– 0.36	0.83	0.58
	(0.22)	(0.21)	(0.14)
(ii) Long-runs from means of industry short-run estimates			
Unweighted	– 0.45	1.03	0.57
	(0.10)	(0.18)	(0.11)
Weighted (Swamy estimates)	– 0.45	0.99	0.61
	(0.11)	(0.19)	(0.11)
(B) Based on cointegrating industry regressions, Eq. (4.2)			
Unweighted	– 0.30	0.64	0.36
	(0.05)	(0.11)	(0.07)
Weighted (Swamy estimates)	– 0.31	0.68	0.39
	(0.04)	(0.10)	(0.06)

Based on separate regressions on 38 industries, 1956–84 ($T = 29$). The standard errors of the estimates are given in parentheses, and computed assuming that regression coefficients are independently distributed across industries.

short-run coefficients use

$$\bar{\gamma}_1 = \sum_{i=1}^{N} \hat{\gamma}_{1i}/N, \quad \bar{\gamma}_2 = \sum_{i=1}^{N} \hat{\gamma}_{2i}/N, \quad \bar{\lambda}_1 = \sum_{i=1}^{N} \hat{\lambda}_{1i}/N, \quad \text{etc.}$$

to give the estimates in panel A(ii), namely

$$\bar{\phi} = (\bar{\gamma}_1 + \bar{\gamma}_2)/(1 - \bar{\lambda}_1 - \bar{\lambda}_2).$$

The cointegrating regressions have the form

$$e_{it} = \alpha_{1i} + \alpha_{2i} t + \theta_{2i} y_{it} + (\theta_{1i} + \theta_{2i}) \bar{y}_t + \phi_i w_{it} + u_{it}, \tag{4.2}$$
$$i = 1, 2, \ldots, 38, \quad t = 1956, \ldots, 1984,$$

and the average long-run effects are computed as

$$\bar{\phi} = \sum_{i=1}^{N} \hat{\phi}_i/N, \quad \bar{\theta}_1 = \sum_{i=1}^{N} \hat{\theta}_{1i}/N, \quad \text{etc.,}$$

given in panel B.

Table 2
Aggregate time-series estimates of long-run labour demand elasticities

		Output	
	Wages ($\hat{\phi}$)	Total ($\hat{\theta}_1$)	Own ($\hat{\theta}_2$)
(A) Based on dynamic regression Eq. (4.3)	− 1.22 (0.34)	1.51 (0.30)	N/A
(B) Based on cointegrating regression Eq. (4.4)	− 0.33 (0.13)	0.71 (0.10)	N/A

Based on a single regression, over 1956–84 ($T = 29$) using the averages for each year over 38 industries. The standard errors of the estimates are given in parentheses.

It is clear from the results in Table 1 that the estimates of the average long-run effects do differ. The weighting has the largest influence on the mean of the long runs, A(i). The individual estimates of the long-run effect have a large dispersion and a large variation in the accuracy of their estimates. Whether all the estimates of (4.2) constitute cointegrating relations may be questioned. The mean and standard deviation of the ADF(1) statistics on the residuals were − 3.37 and 0.86, respectively. The individual industry equations showed little sign of mis-specification. The full results can be found in PPK's Table 1. The results presented here differ a little from PPK, because they used restricted versions of the equations, whereas we used the unrestricted equation for all industries.

The estimates used to derive panel A(ii) are given in the first column of Table 4.

4.2. Aggregate time-series estimates

The results for the aggregate model are presented in Table 2. The aggregate equation was estimated in a full dynamic form:

$$\bar{e}_t = \alpha_1 + \alpha_2 t + \beta_3 \bar{y}_t + \beta_4 \bar{y}_{t-1} + \gamma_1 \bar{w}_t + \gamma_2 \bar{w}_{t-1} + \lambda_1 \bar{e}_{t-1} + \lambda_2 \bar{e}_{t-2} + \bar{v}_t, \tag{4.3}$$

Row A in Table 2 shows the long-run wage elasticity $\hat{\phi} = (\hat{\gamma}_1 + \hat{\gamma}_2)/(1 - \hat{\lambda}_1 - \hat{\lambda}_2)$ and the total output elasticity $\hat{\theta}_1 = (\hat{\beta}_3 + \hat{\beta}_4)/(1 - \hat{\lambda}_1 - \hat{\lambda}_2)$ (the own output elasticity not being identified). Row B gives the estimates from the cointegrating regression

$$\bar{e}_t = \alpha_1 + \alpha_2 t + \theta_1 \bar{y}_t + \phi \bar{w}_t + \bar{u}_t. \tag{4.4}$$

Again the hypothesis of cointegration might be questioned, since the ADF(1) statistic at − 3.23 would not quite reject the null that the residuals from the cointegrating regression are $I(1)$.

Table 3
Pooled estimates of long-run labour demand elasticities

		Output	
	Wages ($\hat{\phi}$)	Total ($\hat{\theta}_1$)	Own ($\hat{\theta}_2$)
(A) Based on dynamic regression, Eq. (4.6)[a]			
Assuming industry intercepts:			
(i) are the same	− 3.28	24.63	3.15
	(5.60)	(45.55)	(4.37)
(ii) differ randomly	− 1.83	10.18	1.68
	(1.52)	(9.06)	(0.82)
(iii) differ and are fixed	− 0.74	1.65	0.87
	(0.17)	(0.40)	(0.13)
(B) Based on static regression, Eq. (4.5)[a]			
Assuming industry intercepts:			
(i) are the same	− 0.53	0.84	0.87
	(0.04)	(0.28)	(0.02)
(ii) differ randomly	− 0.42	0.76	0.61
	(0.02)	(0.05)	(0.02)
(iii) differ and are fixed	− 0.41	0.76	0.60
	(0.02)	(0.05)	(0.02)
(C) Based on first-differenced regression[b]			
(i) Static[c]	− 0.24	0.44	0.28
	(0.02)	(0.04)	(0.02)
(ii) Dynamics[d]	− 0.35	1.02	0.56
	(0.03)	(0.08)	(0.04)
(iii) Dynamic IV[e]	− 0.36	1.08	0.58
	(0.05)	(0.10)	(0.05)

The standard errors of the estimates are given in parentheses.

[a]Using 1102 observations, $t = 1956$–84 ($T = 29$) with $N = 38$.

[b]Using 1026 observations, $t = 1958$–84 ($T = 27$) with $N = 38$.

[c]Δe_{it} on Δy_{it}, $\Delta \bar{y}_t$, Δw_{it}, and an intercept.

[d]As footnote c plus $\Delta y_{i,t-1}$, $\Delta \bar{y}_{t-1}$, $\Delta w_{i,t-1}$, $\Delta e_{i,e-1}$, $\Delta e_{i,t-2}$.

[e]The same specification as in footnote d, using Δy_{it}, $\Delta \bar{y}_t$, Δw_{it}, $\Delta y_{i,t-1}$, $\Delta \bar{y}_{t-1}$, $\Delta w_{i,t-1}$, $\Delta y_{i,t-2}$, $\Delta \bar{y}_{t-2}$, $\Delta w_{i,t-2}$, $e_{i,t\ \ 3}$, $e_{i,t\ \ 4}$, and ones as instruments.

It is noticeable that the aggregate 'cointegrating' regression gives results close to the means of the cointegrating micro-regression. This is what we would expect from the Zellner (1969) argument, given that no lagged dependent variables are included and the coefficients appear to be independent of the

Table 4
Alternative estimates of the dynamic labour demand equation

	Swamy estimates[a]	Pooled estimates[b]	Anderson–Hsiao estimates[c]
Intercept	−0.59	—	—
	(0.73)		
y_{it}	0.29	0.24	0.25
	(0.04)	(0.02)	(0.02)
$y_{i,t-1}$	−0.07	−0.20	0.11
	(0.05)	(0.02)	(0.04)
w_{it}	−0.23	−0.23	−0.23
	(0.03)	(0.01)	(0.01)
$w_{i,t-1}$	0.07	0.20	0.01
	(0.03)	(0.02)	(0.04)
$\bar{y}_t$	0.14	0.16	0.18
	(0.07)	(0.04)	(0.04)
$\bar{y}_{t-1}$	−0.001	−0.12	0.12
	(0.06)	(0.04)	(0.05)
$e_{i,t-1}$	0.79	1.16	0.22
	(0.06)	(0.03)	(0.14)
$e_{i,t-2}$	−0.14	−0.21	0.16
	(0.05)	(0.03)	(0.09)
t (coefficient × 100)	−0.60	0.15	−1.33
	(0.17)	(0.03)	(0.17)

The standard errors of the estimates are given in parentheses.
[a]Described in Table 1, panel A(ii).
[b]Described in Table 3, panel A(iii), assuming intercepts are different and fixed.
[c]Described in Table 3, panel C(iii).

regressors. As the results in PPK showed, the aggregate estimates are a very long way from the average of the industry coefficients. Given that the regressors are positively serially correlated, aggregation induces positive serial correlation in the residuals of the aggregate equation. We might expect this to bias the coefficient of the lagged dependent variable upwards, exaggerating the estimate of the long-run effect. The coefficients of the lagged dependent variables are 0.49 and 0.16 in the aggregate and 0.79 and −0.14 in the case of the Swamy estimates, so the sum is close though the pattern is not. It is also noticeable when comparing the aggregate with the Swamy estimators, that $\bar{w}_{t-1}$ and $\bar{y}_{t-1}$, in addition to $\bar{e}_{t-2}$ have opposite signs. Thus the impression of the dynamics given by the aggregate and averages are quite different. In addition, $\bar{y}_{t-1}$ and $y_{i,t-1}$ are insignificant in the average, but significant in the aggregate.

4.3. The pooled estimates

Table 3 provides estimates on the basis of the pooled regression. A static version is estimated, for comparison with the cointegrating regressions and the cross-sections (set B),

$$e_{it} = \alpha_{1i} + \alpha_2 t + \theta_2 y_{it} + (\theta_1 - \theta_2)\bar{y}_t + \phi w_{it}, \tag{4.5}$$

where the long-run coefficients are just θ_1, θ_2, and ϕ. Then a dynamic version is estimated (set A),

$$\begin{aligned} e_{it} = \alpha_{1i} + \alpha_2 t + \beta_1 y_{it} + \beta_2 y_{it-1} + \beta_3 \bar{y}_t + \beta_4 \bar{y}_{t-1} \\ + \gamma_1 w_{it} + \gamma_2 w_{i,t-1} + \lambda_1 e_{i,t-1} + \lambda_2 e_{i,t-2}, \end{aligned} \tag{4.6}$$

where the long-run coefficients are

$$\hat{\phi} = (\hat{\gamma}_1 + \hat{\gamma}_2)/(1 - \hat{\lambda}_1 - \hat{\lambda}_2), \quad \hat{\theta}_1 = (\hat{\beta}_1 + \hat{\beta}_2)/(1 - \hat{\lambda}_1 - \hat{\lambda}_2), \quad \text{etc.}$$

For each set three estimators are used which differ in the assumption about α_{1i}:

$\alpha_{1i} = \alpha_1$, constant,

$\alpha_{1i} = \alpha_1 + \mu_{1i}$, group-specific random effects, where μ_{1i} are the random components,

$\alpha_{1i} = \alpha_{1i}$, group-specific fixed effects.

The most obvious feature of the results is the erratic performance of the dynamic pooled model, whose estimates are very sensitive to specification. The estimates for the dynamic model with fixed industry effects are given in Table 4. Just as the theory predicts, the sum of the coefficients of the lagged dependent variable is very close to unity and the coefficients of the lagged exogenous variables are roughly equal and opposite in sign to the coefficients of their current values. Thus the estimate of the long-run coefficients are the ratios of two numbers which are tending to zero, and are likely to be computationally unstable. For example, the estimator of the income elasticity for the pooled estimates with industry-specific dummies is 0.04004/(1 − 0.95406) = 0.87 with a standard error of 0.13. Although this is not too far from the Swamy estimator of the long run from means 0.61 (0.11), the Swamy estimates suggest that the denominator should be 0.36 rather than 0.05 and the numerator 0.22 rather than 0.04. Note also that the fact that the pooled result looks like a first difference equation cannot be attributed to the need to remove group-specific intercepts, since these are included.

Although the fixed effect model is inconsistent with lagged dependent variables for fixed T even if N goes to infinity, this should not be a problem here, since T is relatively large. To investigate this effect, the model was also estimated using the Anderson–Hsiao procedure (e.g., Hsiao, 1986, p. 89). The dynamic equation is differenced to remove the fixed effects and then estimated by Instrumental Variables (IV) to deal with the correlation between the disturbances and the regressors caused by the induced MA(1) error. The instruments used were the current and two lags of the changes in the exogenous variables and the third and fourth lags of the dependent variable. Use of the extra two lags reduces the sample to 27×38 observations. The estimates of the long-run coefficients are given in Table 3 and the full results in Table 4. The differenced equation was also estimated by OLS which, as can be seen from Table 3, gives almost exactly the same results, and was estimated without the lags. When the equation is differenced before estimation, some of the serial correlation induced by the inappropriate imposition of homogeneity on the slope coefficients is removed. The coefficients on the current exogenous variables are very similar to the pooled and Swamy estimates as the theory predicts, but they do not suffer such extreme biases in the coefficients of the lagged exogenous variables as do the undifferenced pooled estimates. The coefficient of the lagged dependent variable seems to be seriously underestimated.

4.4. Cross-section estimates

The cross-section estimates using means for each industry over all 29 years are

$$\tilde{e} = \underset{\substack{(1.675)\\ [2.653]}}{-\,1.273} + \underset{\substack{(0.106)\\ [0.103]}}{0.876}\,\tilde{y}_i - \underset{\substack{(0.266)\\ [0.439]}}{0.523}\,\tilde{w}_i,$$

$$R^2 = 0.71, \qquad \hat{\sigma} = 0.641, \qquad N = 38.$$

The OLS standard errors of the estimates are given in parentheses, White's heteroscedasticity-consistent standard errors in brackets. The argument at the end of Section 3.1 suggests that the latter are appropriate. Note that the output coefficient is an estimate of the own elasticity θ_2. The cross-section was also estimated recursively, using first the data for 1954, then the averages for 1954 and 1955, extending the window till all 29 years were included. In this case the estimates seem quite robust to variations in the number of years used to form averages. The output elasticities all lie between 0.84 and 0.88, the wage elasticities between -0.58 and -0.42.

In this particular application, the cross-section provides quite reasonable point estimates of the mean of the long-run coefficients, although these estimates are rather poorly determined. However, it is important to be clear about the conditions under which this will be true. The coefficients and regressors appear to be independent, and the cross-section only provides an estimate of the own-output effect, not the total effect. Where macro-influences on individual decisions are important, because of interaction effects between groups for instance, the cross-section estimates will not reveal them.

5. Conclusions

The main conclusion of this paper is that the random coefficient argument of Zellner (1969), which seems to have been widely accepted in the literature, does not extend to dynamic models. Thus aggregating or pooling dynamic heterogeneous panels can produce very misleading estimates, as our applied example illustrates. Given the prevalence of aggregation and pooling in applied work, these results are of some importance, and indicate that the common assumption of homogeneity in dynamic models is far from innocuous. Our theoretical and empirical results provided some qualified support for the belief that cross-section estimates will provide estimates of long-run effects, which are robust to dynamic misspecification of the underlying time-series model. One can only make limited inferences from our particular applied example because there are specific features of the data which are important. In particular, in our application, it seems that the regressors are $I(1)$, the variables cointegrate, and the coefficients are independent of the regressors. All these features are important for the results. As the theory indicated the pooled and aggregated time-series regressions can give very misleading results for the dynamic model. First differencing appeared to reduce the problem somewhat for the pooled model, since it seemed to remove the serial correlation which was the primary source of the inconsistency, but it is not clear how general this result is. Simple static regressions also did quite well, perhaps because the argument for random coefficients with exogenous regressors can be approximately applied to the cointegrating regressions characteristic of this data, but our theoretical results showed this will not, in general, be true.

The lesson for applied work is that when large T panels are available, the individual micro-relations should be estimated separately and the averages of the estimated micro-parameters and their standard errors calculated explicitly. With modern computational facilities this is very easy to do. The hypothesis of homogeneity, common slope coefficients, can then be tested. Our experience is that it is almost always rejected, even when the size of the test is adjusted to take account of the large number of observations. The statistical relationship between the coefficients and the group means can then be examined. If coefficients are related to explanatory variables, which they were not in our data, these will cause the cross-section estimates to differ from the average of the time-series. Such correlated effects can then be investigated. Our applied example also brought out the importance of being explicit about variables which differ over time but not over groups, like aggregate output, and which differ across groups but not over time.

Although we have tried to be fairly comprehensive, we have only been able to present a representative selection of results, there are a range of other specifications of the model which could be considered. For instance, our results on the consistency of the cross-section estimates and cointegration relations required the regressors to be strictly exogenous, a much stronger assumption than is usually employed. The assumption of independence of the coefficients and regressors is crucial and appropriate tests for this assumption are required.

Appendix A

Inconsistency of the pooled estimators in the context of a heterogeneous dynamic panel

Consider the heterogeneous dynamic model (2.1), explicitly including a random intercept,

$$y_{it} = \alpha_i + \lambda_i y_{i,t-1} + \beta_i x_{it} + \varepsilon_{it}, \qquad i = 1,2,\ldots,N, \quad t = 1,2,\ldots,T, \tag{A.1}$$

and suppose that the parameters λ_i and β_i are random with means λ and β, respectively, variances ω_{11} and ω_{22}, and the covariance $\omega_{12} = \omega_{21}$. To simplify the exposition we consider the case where β_i is a scalar coefficient, and the process generating x_{it} can be characterized by the simple stationary AR(1) process

$$x_{it} = \mu_i(1-\rho) + \rho x_{i,t-1} + u_{it},$$

where μ_i is the (unconditional) mean of x_{it}, $|\rho| < 1$, and for each i, $u_{it} \sim \text{iid}(0, \tau_i^2)$.

Suppose that λ and β are estimated by the fixed-effect (or 'within') estimators using the pooled regression

$$y_{it} = \alpha_i + \lambda y_{i,t-1} + \beta x_{it} + v_{it}. \tag{A.2}$$

Here we derive the probability limits of the fixed-effect estimators of λ and β, which we denote by $\hat{\lambda}$ and $\hat{\beta}$, in the case where v_{it} is given by

$$v_{it} = \varepsilon_{it} + \eta_{1i} y_{i,t-1} + \eta_{2i} x_{it}. \tag{A.3}$$

This formulation allows for the randomness in the slope coefficients through the terms involving η_{1i} and η_{2i}, the random components of λ_i and β_i, respectively. In deriving the probability limits we first let $T \to \infty$ and then let $N \to \infty$. The same limiting expressions obtain if this order is reversed.

Using standard notations, the fixed effect estimators of λ and β in (A.2) are given by

$$\begin{pmatrix} \hat{\lambda} \\ \hat{\beta} \end{pmatrix} = \begin{pmatrix} \mathbf{y}'_{-1} \mathbf{W}_n \mathbf{y}_{-1} & \mathbf{y}'_{-1} \mathbf{W}_n \mathbf{x} \\ \mathbf{x}' \mathbf{W}_n \mathbf{y}_{-1} & \mathbf{x}' \mathbf{W}_n \mathbf{x} \end{pmatrix}^{-1} \begin{pmatrix} \mathbf{y}'_{-1} \mathbf{W}_n \mathbf{y} \\ \mathbf{x}' \mathbf{W}_n \mathbf{y} \end{pmatrix}, \tag{A.4}$$

where $\boldsymbol{y}$ and $\boldsymbol{x}$ are $NT \times 1$ vectors of observations on y_{it}'s and x_{it}'s, $\boldsymbol{y}_{-1}$ is $NT \times 1$ vector of observations on $y_{i,t-1}$, $i = 1, 2, \dots, N$, $t = 1, 2, \dots, T$. $\boldsymbol{W}_n$ is the 'within' transformation matrix operator,

$$\boldsymbol{W}_n = \boldsymbol{I}_{NT} - \boldsymbol{D}(\boldsymbol{D}(\boldsymbol{D}'\boldsymbol{D})^{-1}\boldsymbol{D}', \tag{A.5}$$

where

$$\boldsymbol{D} = \boldsymbol{I}_N \otimes \tau_T, \tag{A.6}$$

$\boldsymbol{I}_N$ is the identity matrix, τ_T is a $T \times 1$ unit vector, $\tau_T = (1, 1, \dots, 1)'$, and $\otimes$ stands for matrix Kroneker product (see, for example, Chapter 4 in Matyas and Sevestre, 1992). Under (A.2) and (A.3) we have

$$\begin{pmatrix} \hat{\lambda} - \lambda \\ \hat{\beta} - \beta \end{pmatrix} = \begin{Bmatrix} \dfrac{\boldsymbol{y}'_{-1}\boldsymbol{W}_n\boldsymbol{y}_{-1}}{NT} & \dfrac{\boldsymbol{y}'_{-1}\boldsymbol{W}_n\boldsymbol{x}}{NT} \\ \dfrac{\boldsymbol{x}'\boldsymbol{W}_n\boldsymbol{y}_{-1}}{NT} & \dfrac{\boldsymbol{x}'\boldsymbol{W}_n\boldsymbol{x}}{NT} \end{Bmatrix}^{-1} \begin{Bmatrix} \dfrac{\boldsymbol{y}'_{-1}\boldsymbol{W}_n\boldsymbol{v}}{NT} \\ \dfrac{\boldsymbol{x}'\boldsymbol{W}_n\boldsymbol{v}}{NT} \end{Bmatrix}, \tag{A.7}$$

where $\boldsymbol{v}$ is $NT \times 1$ vector of the 'composite errors' with typical elements given by (A.3). We have $\boldsymbol{v} = (\boldsymbol{v}'_1, \boldsymbol{v}'_2, \dots, \boldsymbol{v}'_N)'$, where $\boldsymbol{v}_i$ are $T \times 1$ vectors,

$$\boldsymbol{v}_i = \varepsilon_i + \eta_{1i}\boldsymbol{y}_{i,-1} + \eta_{i2}\boldsymbol{x}_i. \tag{A.8}$$

Now using $\boldsymbol{W}_n$ (see (A.5)), it is easily seen that

$$\boldsymbol{x}'\boldsymbol{W}_n\boldsymbol{x} = \sum_{i=1}^{N} \boldsymbol{x}'_i\boldsymbol{H}_T\boldsymbol{x}_i,$$

where

$$\boldsymbol{H}_T = \boldsymbol{I}_T - \tau_T(\tau'_T\tau_T)^{-1}\tau'_T.$$

Similarly,

$$\boldsymbol{y}'_{-1}\boldsymbol{W}_n\boldsymbol{y}_{-1} = \sum_{i=1}^{N} \boldsymbol{y}'_{i,-1}\boldsymbol{H}_T\boldsymbol{y}_{i,-1}, \quad \boldsymbol{x}'\boldsymbol{W}_n\boldsymbol{y}_{-1} = \sum_{i=1}^{N} \boldsymbol{x}'_i\boldsymbol{H}_T\boldsymbol{y}_{i,-1}, \quad \text{etc.}$$

This type of decomposition now allows us, for example, to write

$$\operatorname*{plim}_{N\to\infty,\, T\to\infty} \left(\frac{\boldsymbol{x}'\boldsymbol{W}_n\boldsymbol{x}}{NT}\right) = \operatorname*{plim}_{N\to\infty} \left\{\frac{1}{N}\sum_{i=1}^{N} \operatorname*{plim}_{T\to\infty} \left(\frac{\boldsymbol{x}'_i\boldsymbol{H}_T\boldsymbol{x}_i}{T}\right)\right\}, \tag{A.9}$$

where the limits are taken first letting $T \to \infty$ and then $N \to \infty$. As another example, note that

$$\underset{N\to\infty,\ T\to\infty}{\text{plim}} \left(\frac{\boldsymbol{y}'_{-1}\boldsymbol{W}_n\boldsymbol{v}}{NT}\right) = \underset{N\to\infty}{\text{plim}} \left\{\frac{1}{N}\sum_{i=1}^{N} \underset{T\to\infty}{\text{plim}} \left(\frac{\boldsymbol{y}'_{i,-1}\boldsymbol{H}_T\boldsymbol{v}_i}{T}\right)\right\}, \tag{A.10}$$

To obtain the probability limits of the various terms in (A.7) we first write (A.1) in vector notations as

$$\boldsymbol{y}_i = \alpha_i \tau_T + \lambda_i \boldsymbol{y}_{i,-1} + \boldsymbol{x}_i \beta_i + \varepsilon_i,$$

and under Assumption 3 in the text, and assuming that the process (A.1) generating y_{it} has started a long time ago we have

$$\boldsymbol{y}_i = \left(\frac{\alpha_i}{1-\lambda_i}\right)\tau_T + \sum_{j=0}^{\infty} \lambda_i^j \beta_i \boldsymbol{x}_{i,-j} + \sum_{j=0}^{\infty} \lambda_i^j \varepsilon_{i,-j}, \tag{A.11}$$

where $\boldsymbol{x}_{i,-j}$ and $\varepsilon_{i,-j}$ are $T\times 1$ vector of observations on the jth-order lags of x_i and ε_i.

Consider now the probability limit of $(\boldsymbol{y}'_{-1}\boldsymbol{W}_n{}^m \boldsymbol{v})/NT$. First using (A.8) in (A.10) we have

$$\underset{T\to\infty}{\text{plim}} \left(\frac{\boldsymbol{y}'_{i,-1}\boldsymbol{H}_T v_i}{T}\right) = \underset{T\to\infty}{\text{plim}} \left(\frac{\boldsymbol{y}'_{i,-1}\boldsymbol{H}_T \varepsilon_i}{T}\right) + \eta_{1i}\, \underset{T\to\infty}{\text{plim}} \left(\frac{\boldsymbol{y}'_{i,-1}\boldsymbol{H}_T \boldsymbol{y}_{i,-1}}{T}\right)$$
$$+ \eta_{2i}\, \underset{T\to\infty}{\text{plim}} \left(\frac{\boldsymbol{y}_{i,-1}\boldsymbol{H}_T \boldsymbol{x}_i}{T}\right). \tag{A.12}$$

Substituting from (A.11) in the above expressions and taking probability limits under Assumptions 1–4 (with $T \to \infty$) we have

$$\underset{T\to\infty}{\text{plim}} \left(\frac{\boldsymbol{y}'_{i,-1}\boldsymbol{H}_T \varepsilon_i}{T}\right) = \left(\frac{\alpha_i}{1-\lambda_i}\right) \underset{T\to\infty}{\text{plim}} \left(\frac{\tau'_T \boldsymbol{H}_T \varepsilon_i}{T}\right)$$
$$+ \sum_{j=0}^{\infty} \lambda_i^j \beta_i\, \underset{T\to\infty}{\text{plim}} \left(\frac{\boldsymbol{x}'_{i,-j-1}\boldsymbol{H}_T \varepsilon_i}{T}\right)$$
$$+ \sum_{j=0}^{\infty} \lambda_i^j\, \underset{T\to\infty}{\text{plim}} \left(\frac{\varepsilon'_{i,-j-1}\boldsymbol{H}_T \varepsilon_i}{T}\right). \tag{A.13}$$

But $\boldsymbol{H}_T \tau_T = 0$, and under Assumption 1 (in the text)

$$\underset{T\to\infty}{\text{plim}} \left(\frac{\boldsymbol{x}'_{i,-j-1}\boldsymbol{H}_T \varepsilon_i}{T}\right) = 0, \quad \forall i. \tag{A.14}$$

Also

$$T^{-1}(\varepsilon_{i,-j}' \boldsymbol{H}_T \varepsilon_i) = T^{-1}\sum_{t=1}^{T}(\varepsilon_{it}-\bar{\varepsilon}_{i0})'(\varepsilon_{i,t-j}-\bar{\varepsilon}_{i,-j}),$$

where $\bar{\varepsilon}_{i,-j} = T^{-1}\sum_{t=1}^{T}\varepsilon_{i,t-j}$ are time averages. Hence using results in Appendix C we also have

$$\operatorname*{plim}_{T\to\infty}\left(\frac{\varepsilon_{i,-j}'\boldsymbol{H}_T\varepsilon_i}{T}\right) = 0, \qquad j = 1,2,\ldots, \quad i = 1,2,\ldots,N. \tag{A.15}$$

$$\operatorname*{plim}_{T\to\infty}\left(\frac{\varepsilon_i'\boldsymbol{H}_T\varepsilon_i}{T}\right) = \sigma_i^2, \qquad i = 1,2,\ldots,N, \tag{A.16}$$

where $\sigma_i^2 = V(\varepsilon_{it})$. Using (A.14) and (A.15) in (A.13), we therefore have

$$\operatorname*{plim}_{T\to\infty}\left(\frac{\boldsymbol{y}_{i,-1}'\boldsymbol{H}_T\varepsilon_i}{T}\right) = 0. \tag{A.17}$$

Similarly, and after some algebra it can be shown that

$$\operatorname*{plim}_{T\to\infty}\left(\frac{\boldsymbol{y}_{i,-1}'\boldsymbol{H}_T\boldsymbol{y}_{i,-1}}{T}\right) = \left(\frac{\sigma_i^2}{1-\lambda_i^2}\right) + \sum_{j'=0}^{\infty}\sum_{j=0}^{\infty}\frac{\lambda_i^{j+j'}\beta_i^2\rho^{|j-j'|}\tau_i^2}{1-\rho^2}, \tag{A.18}$$

$$\operatorname*{plim}_{T\to\infty}\left(\frac{\boldsymbol{y}_{i,-1}'\boldsymbol{H}_T\boldsymbol{x}_i}{T}\right) = \sum_{j=0}^{\infty}\frac{\lambda_i^j\rho^{j+1}\beta_i\tau_i^2}{1-\rho^2}. \tag{A.19}$$

Substituting (A.17)–(A.19) back in (A.12) we have

$$\operatorname*{plim}_{T\to\infty}\left(\frac{\boldsymbol{y}_{i,-1}'\boldsymbol{H}_T\boldsymbol{v}_i}{T}\right) = \left(\frac{\sigma_i^2\eta_{1i}}{1-\lambda_i^2}\right) + \left(\frac{\tau_i^2\eta_{1i}\beta_i^2}{1-\rho^2}\right)\sum_{j'=0}^{\infty}\sum_{j=0}^{\infty}\lambda_i^{j+j'}\rho^{|j-j'|}$$
$$+ \left(\frac{\tau_i^2\eta_{2i}\beta_i}{1-\rho^2}\right)\sum_{j=0}^{\infty}\lambda_i^j\rho^{j+1}.$$

Finally, substituting this result in (A.10) yields

$$\operatorname*{plim}_{N\to\infty,\,T\to\infty}\left(\frac{\boldsymbol{y}_{-1}'\boldsymbol{W}_n\boldsymbol{v}}{NT}\right) = \operatorname*{plim}_{N\to\infty}\left\{\frac{1}{N}\sum_{i=1}^{N}\left(\frac{\sigma_i^2\eta_{1i}}{1-\lambda_i^2}\right)\right\}$$
$$+ \sum_{j'=0}^{\infty}\sum_{j=0}^{\infty}\frac{\rho^{|j-j'|}}{1-\rho^2}\operatorname*{plim}_{N\to\infty}\left(\frac{1}{N}\sum_{i=1}^{N}\eta_{1i}\tau_i^2\beta_i^2\lambda_i^{j+j'}\right)$$
$$+ \sum_{j=0}^{\infty}\frac{\rho^{j+1}}{1-\rho^2}\operatorname*{plim}_{T\to\infty}\left(\frac{1}{N}\sum_{i=1}^{N}\beta_i\eta_{2i}\tau_i^2\lambda_i^j\right),$$

and since by assumption λ_i, β_i, σ_i^2 and τ_i^2 are identically and independently distributed across i, and have moments of all orders, (see Assumption 3) by the law of large numbers, the probability limits as $N \to \infty$ converge to their respective means, and we have

$$\operatorname*{plim}_{N\to\infty,\,T\to\infty}\left(\frac{y'_{-1}W_n v}{NT}\right) = \mathrm{E}\left(\frac{\sigma_i^2\eta_{1i}}{1-\lambda_i^2}\right) + \sum_{j'=0}^{\infty}\sum_{j=0}^{\infty}\frac{\rho^{|j-j'|}}{1-\rho^2}\mathrm{E}(\eta_{1i}\tau_i^2\beta_i^2\lambda_i^{j+j'}) + \sum_{j=0}^{\infty}\frac{\rho^{j+1}}{1-\rho^2}\mathrm{E}\left(\beta_i\eta_{2i}\tau_i^2\lambda_i^j\right), \tag{A.20}$$

where the expectations are taken with respect to the joint distribution of η_{1i}, η_{2i}, τ_i^2, and σ_i^2. Recall that $\lambda_i = \lambda + \eta_{1i}$ and $\beta_i = \beta + \eta_{2i}$. The inconsistency of the fixed-effect estimators of λ and β in a dynamic heterogeneous model now follows from the fact that the above probability limit is, in general, nonzero even for N and T large. It vanishes only in the case where $\rho = 0$ and $\lambda_i = \lambda$ for all i (and hence $\eta_{1i} = 0$).[17]

Turning to the other terms in (A.7) and following a similar approach as above, we have

$$\operatorname*{plim}_{N\to\infty,\,T\to\infty}\left(\frac{x'W_n v}{NT}\right) = \sum_{j=0}^{\infty}\left(\frac{\rho^{j+1}}{1-\rho^2}\right)\mathrm{E}(\eta_{1i}\beta_i\tau_i^2\lambda_i^j), \tag{A.21}$$

$$\operatorname*{plim}_{N\to\infty,\,T\to\infty}\left(\frac{x'W_n x}{NT}\right) = \frac{\mathrm{E}(\tau_i^2)}{1-\rho^2}, \tag{A.22}$$

and using (A.18) and (A.19)

$$\operatorname*{plim}_{N\to\infty,\,T\to\infty}\left(\frac{y'_{-1}W_n y_{-1}}{NT}\right) = \mathrm{E}\left(\frac{\sigma_i^2}{1-\lambda_i^2}\right) + \sum_{j'=0}^{\infty}\sum_{j=0}^{\infty}\frac{\rho^{|j-j'|}}{1-\rho^2}\mathrm{E}(\tau_i^2\beta_i^2\lambda_i^{j+j'}), \tag{A.23}$$

$$\operatorname*{plim}_{N\to\infty,\,T\to\infty}\left(\frac{y'_{-1}W_n x}{NT}\right) = \sum_{j=0}^{\infty}\left(\frac{\rho^{j+1}}{1-\rho^2}\right)\mathrm{E}(\beta_i\tau_i^2\lambda_i^j). \tag{A.24}$$

[17] Notice that even this result depends on the assumed homogeneity of the autoregressive coefficient of the $\{x_{it}\}$ process for all i.

Using the probability limits (A.20) to (A.24) in (A.7), *explicit* expressions for the inconsistency of the fixed-effect estimators can now be readily obtained. The resultant expressions, however, would still be rather complicated and for pedagogic purposes it is worth considering the relatively simple case where $\lambda_i = \lambda$ for all. In this case, apart from the intercept terms, the only remaining source of parameter variations across groups is through β_i. Using (A.20)–(A.24) and setting $\eta_{1i} = 0$, and $\lambda_i = \lambda$ for all i, and denoting the variance of β_i by ω_{22} we have[18]

$$\operatorname*{plim}_{N\to\infty,\,T\to\infty}\begin{pmatrix}\hat{\lambda}-\lambda\\ \hat{\beta}-\beta\end{pmatrix} = \begin{bmatrix}\dfrac{\sigma^2}{1-\lambda^2}+\dfrac{\delta\tau^2(\beta^2+\omega_{22})}{1-\rho^2} & \dfrac{\beta\rho\tau^2}{(1-\rho^2)(1-\lambda\rho)}\\ \dfrac{\beta\rho\tau^2}{(1-\rho^2)(1-\lambda\rho)} & \dfrac{\tau^2}{1-\rho^2}\end{bmatrix}$$

$$\times\begin{bmatrix}\dfrac{\rho\omega_{22}\tau^2}{(1-\rho^2)(1-\lambda\rho)}\\ 0\end{bmatrix}, \tag{A.25}$$

which in turn yield (2.7) and (2.8) in the text.

Appendix B

Error properties of aggregate time-series models obtained from dynamic heterogeneous panels

Consider the micro-relations

$$y_{it} = \lambda_i y_{i,t-1} + \beta_i x_{it} + \varepsilon_{it}, \qquad i = 1,2,\ldots,N, \quad t = 1,2,\ldots,T, \tag{B.1}$$

where

$$\lambda_i = \lambda + \eta_{1i}, \qquad \beta_i = \beta + \eta_{2i},$$

[18] Variations in σ_i^2 and τ_i^2 across groups does not pose any difficulties so long as they are assumed to be independently distributed of β_i (and of λ_i, when λ_i is random). The same results also follow when $\sigma_i^2 = \sigma^2$, $\tau_i^2 = \tau^2$, for all i.

and Assumptions 1–3 in the text hold. Also assume for simplicity that x_{it}'s have zero means and that ε_{it}'s are serially uncorrelated. Here to simplify the exposition we shall confine the analysis to the case of a scalar x_{it}. The aggregate model associated with the above micro-specifications is given by

$$\bar{y}_t = \lambda \bar{y}_{t-1} + \beta \bar{x}_t + \bar{v}_t, \tag{B.2}$$

where

$$\bar{v}_t = \bar{\varepsilon}_t + N^{-1} \sum_{i=1}^{N} (\eta_{1i} x_{it} + \eta_{2i} y_{i,t-1}). \tag{B.3}$$

We now show that the aggregate time-series estimates of λ and β obtained by the OLS regression of $\bar{y}_t$ on $\bar{y}_{t-1}$ and $\bar{x}_t$ will be biased, and that this bias does not disappear even if both N and T tend to infinity.

The OLS estimator of β in (B.2), which we denote by $\hat{\beta}^a$, is given by

$$\hat{\beta}^a - \beta = \frac{\left(\sum_{t=1}^{T} \bar{y}_{t-1}^2\right)\left(\sum_{t=1}^{T} \bar{x}_t \bar{v}_t\right) - \left(\sum_{t=1}^{T} \bar{x}_t \bar{y}_{t-1}\right)\left(\sum_{t=1}^{T} \bar{y}_{t-1} \bar{v}_t\right)}{\left(\sum_{t=1}^{T} \bar{x}_t^2\right)\left(\sum_{t=1}^{T} \bar{y}_{t-1}^2\right) - \left(\sum_{t=1}^{T} \bar{x}_t \bar{y}_{t-1}\right)^2}. \tag{B.4}$$

Under Assumptions 1–3 and using (3.6) we have

$$\mathrm{E}(\bar{x}_t \bar{v}_t) = N^{-1} \sum_{i=1}^{N} \sum_{s=1}^{\infty} \mathrm{E}(\eta_{2i} \beta_i \lambda_i^s)\, \mathrm{E}(\bar{x}_t x_{i,t-s-1})$$

and

$$\mathrm{E}(\bar{y}_{t-1} \bar{v}_t) = N^{-1} \sum_{i=1}^{N} \{\mathrm{E}(\eta_{1i} x_{it} \bar{y}_{t-1}) + \mathrm{E}(\eta_{2i} y_{i,t-1} \bar{y}_{t-1})\},$$

where

$$\mathrm{E}(\eta_{1i} x_{it} \bar{y}_{t-1}) = N^{-1} \sum_{s=0}^{\infty} \mathrm{E}(\eta_{1i} \beta_i \lambda_i^s)\, \mathrm{E}(\bar{x}_{it} x_{i,t-s-1}),$$

$$\mathrm{E}(\eta_{2i} y_{i,t-1} \bar{y}_{t-1}) = N^{-1} \sum_{j=1}^{N} \mathrm{E}(\eta_{2i} y_{i,t-1} y_{j,t-1}),$$

where

$$\mathrm{E}(\eta_{2i} y_{i,t-1} \lambda_{j,t-1}) = \sum_{s=0}^{\infty} \sum_{s'=0}^{\infty} \mathrm{E}(\eta_{2i} \beta_i \lambda_i^s)\, \mathrm{E}(\beta_j \lambda_j^{s'})\, \mathrm{E}(x_{i,t-s-1}\, x_{j,t-s'-1})$$
$$+ \sum_{s=0}^{\infty} \mathrm{E}(\eta_{2i} \lambda_i^s)\, \mathrm{E}(\lambda_j^s)\, \mathrm{E}(\varepsilon_{i,t-s-1}\, \varepsilon_{j,t-s-1}).$$

Moreover,

$$\mathrm{E}(\eta_{ji}\beta_i\lambda_i^s) = \mathrm{E}[\eta_{ji}(\beta + \eta_{2i})(\lambda + \eta_{1i})^s], \qquad j = 1, 2,$$

and $\mathrm{E}(\eta_{2i}\lambda_i^s) = \mathrm{E}[\eta_{2i}(\lambda + \eta_{1i})^s]$ are all nonzero and, therefore, under the standard assumptions of the random coefficient model the regressors in (B.2) and the composite aggregate disturbance term $\bar{v}_t$ will be correlated. In the absence of parameter homogeneity, the correlation between $\bar{x}_t$ and $\bar{v}_t$ vanishes only if x_{it}'s are serially uncorrelated. The conditions under which $\mathrm{E}(\bar{v}_t\bar{y}_{t-1}) = 0$ are more stringent and also require that x_{it} and ε_{it} to be distributed independently of x_{jt} and ε_{jt}, respectively, for all $i \neq j$.

For a finite N, as $T \to \infty$ we have

$$\operatorname*{plim}_{T\to\infty}(\hat{\beta}^a - \beta) = \frac{\mathrm{E}(\bar{y}_{t-1}^2)\mathrm{E}(\bar{x}_t\bar{v}_t) - \mathrm{E}(\bar{x}_t\bar{y}_{t-1})\mathrm{E}(\bar{y}_{t-1}\bar{v}_t)}{\mathrm{E}(\bar{x}_t^2)\mathrm{E}(\bar{y}_{t-1}^2) - \mathrm{E}(\bar{x}_t\bar{y}_{t-1})\mathrm{E}(\bar{x}_t\bar{y}_{t-1})}, \tag{B.5}$$

which in view of the above results is in general nonzero. It is also easily seen that when the infinite sums

$$\sum_{s=0}^{\infty} \mathrm{E}(\eta_{2i}\beta_i\lambda_i^s)\mathrm{E}(\bar{x}_{jt}x_{i,t-s-1}), \quad \sum_{s=0}^{\infty} \mathrm{E}(\eta_{1i}\beta_i\lambda_i^s)\mathrm{E}(\bar{x}_{it}x_{i,t-s-1}), \quad \text{etc.,}$$

that appear in the expressions for $\mathrm{E}(\bar{x}_t\bar{v}_t)$ and $\mathrm{E}(\bar{y}_{t-1}\bar{v}_t)$ converge to finite limits, then all the terms in (C.5) are of order N^{-1} and increasing N does not eliminate the inconsistency in the aggregate time-series estimators. We have

$$\lim_{N\to\infty}\operatorname*{plim}_{T\to\infty}(\hat{\beta}^a - \beta) \neq 0,$$

and similarly,

$$\lim_{N\to\infty}\operatorname*{plim}_{T\to\infty}(\hat{\lambda}^a - \lambda) \neq 0.$$

The macro-disturbances, $\bar{v}_t$, are also serially correlated even if the micro-disturbances are white noise processes. In this case assuming for simplicity that the ε_{it}'s are serially and contemporaneously independently distributed, and that x_{it} and x_{jt} are also distributed independently we have

$$\mathrm{E}(\bar{v}_t\bar{v}_{t-s}) = N^{-2}(A + B + C + D + E + F),$$

where

$$A = \sum_{i=1}^{N}\sum_{l=0}^{\infty}\sum_{k=0}^{\infty} \mathrm{E}(\eta_{1i}^2\lambda_i^{l+k})\mathrm{E}(\beta_i^2)\gamma_i(|s + l - k|)$$

$$+ \sum_{i=1}^{N}\sum_{k=0}^{\infty} \sigma_i^2\mathrm{E}(\eta_{1i}^2\lambda_i^{2k+s}),$$

$$B = \sum_{i=1}^{N} \sum_{k=0}^{\infty} \mathrm{E}(\eta_{1i}\eta_{2i}\beta_i\lambda_i^k)\,\gamma_i(|s-k-1|),$$

$$C = \sum_{i=1}^{N} \sum_{k=0}^{\infty} \mathrm{E}(\eta_{1i}\eta_{2i}\beta_i\lambda_i^k)\,\gamma_i(|s+k+1|),$$

$$D = \sum_{i=1}^{N} \mathrm{E}(\eta_{2i}^2)\gamma_i(|s|),$$

$$E = \begin{cases} \sum_{i=1}^{N} \sigma_i^2, & s = 0, \\ 0 & s \neq 0, \end{cases}$$

$$F = \begin{cases} 0 & s = 0, \\ \sum_{i=1}^{N} \sigma_i^2\, \mathrm{E}(\eta_{1i}\lambda_i^{s-1}), & s \geqslant 1, \end{cases}$$

where $\sigma_i^2 = \mathrm{E}(\varepsilon_{it}^2)$ and $\gamma_i(|s|) = \mathrm{E}(x_{it}x_{i,t-s})$.

Unless one is prepared to make further strong assumptions about the autocovariance function of x_{it}, the above expressions do not simplify further. But it is clear that the serial correlation pattern of $\bar{v}_t$, in the case of micro-relations with lagged dependent variables, are highly complex and depend on higher-order moments of η_{1i} and η_{2i}. Notice that terms such as

$$\mathrm{E}(\eta_{1i}\beta_i\lambda_i^k) = \mathrm{E}\{\eta_{1i}(\lambda + \eta_{1i})^k(\beta + \eta_{2i})\},$$

$$\mathrm{E}(\eta_{1i}\eta_{2i}\beta_i\lambda_i^k) = \mathrm{E}\{\eta_{1i}\eta_{2i}(\beta + \eta_{2i})(\lambda + \eta_{1i})^k\}$$

depend on higher moments of the random variables η_{1i} and η_{2i} and in general do not vanish even when η_{1i} and η_{2i} can be assumed to be distributed independently.

Appendix C

Derivation of the autocorrelation function of time averages

Let $\{x_t\}$ be convariance-stationary process with mean μ and the autocovariance function $\mathrm{E}(x_t - \mu)(x_{t-s} - \mu) = \gamma_s = \gamma_{-s}$ and consider time averages $\bar{x}_{-j} = T^{-}\sum_{t=1}^{T} x_{t-j}$. We are interested in the autocovariance function of the

$\{\tilde{x}_{ij}\}$ process. We have

$$\psi_j = \mathrm{E}[(\tilde{x}_0 - \mu)(\tilde{x}_{-j} - \mu)]$$

$$= \frac{1}{T^2} \sum_{t=1}^{T} \sum_{t'=1}^{T} \gamma_{t-t'+j}$$

$$= \frac{1}{T}\left\{\gamma_j + \sum_{s=1}^{T-1}\left(1 - \frac{s}{T}\right)(\gamma_{j+s} + \gamma_{j-s})\right\}. \tag{C.1}$$

However,

$$\left|\sum_{s=1}^{T-1}\left(1 - \frac{s}{T}\right)\gamma_{j+s}\right| \leqslant \sum_{s=1}^{T-1} |\gamma_{j+s}|,$$

which is bounded since it is assumed that $\{x_t\}$ is covariance-stationary and mean square ergodic. Hence it follows that $\mathrm{E}(\tilde{x}_0 \tilde{x}_{-j}) = \mu^2 + \mathrm{O}(T^{-1})$, for all j.

Consider now the term

$$\phi_j = \mathrm{E}\{\tilde{x}_0(\tilde{x}_{-j} - \tilde{x}_{-j-1}\} = \psi_j - \psi_{j+1}.$$

Using (C.1) and after some algebraic manipulations we have

$$\phi_j = \frac{1}{T^2}\left\{\sum_{i=1}^{T} \gamma_{i-j-1} - \sum_{i=1}^{T} \gamma_{i+j}\right\}. \tag{C.2}$$

Once again since $\{x_t\}$ is stationary it follows that the term in { } is finite and that $\phi_j = \mathrm{O}(T^{-2})$. It is also worth noting that

$$\phi_0 = \frac{1}{T^2}(\gamma_0 - \gamma_T),$$

$$\phi_j = \phi_{j-1} + \frac{1}{T^2}\{(\gamma_j - \gamma_{T+j}) + (\gamma_{j-1} - \gamma_{T-j})\}, \qquad j = 1, 2, \ldots .$$

References

Baltagi, B.H. and J.M. Griffin, 1984, Short and long run effects in pooled models, International Economic Review 25, 631–645.

Barro, R.J., 1991, Economic growth in a cross section of countries, Quarterly Journal of Economics 106, 407-443.

Engle, R.F. and C.W.J. Granger, eds., 1991, Long-run economic relationships: Readings in cointegration (Oxford University Press, Oxford).

Gonzalo, J., 1993, Cointegration and aggregation, Mimeo. (Department of Economics, Boston University, Boston, MA).

Hsiao, C., 1986, Analysis of panel data (Cambridge University Press, Cambridge).

Hsiao, C., 1992, Random coefficients models, in: L. Matyas and P. Sevestre (1992, Ch. 5, pp. 71–93).

Karlin, S. and H.M. Taylor, 1975, A first course in stochastic processes, 2nd ed. (Academic Press, London).

Lee, K.C., M.H. Pesaran, and R.G. Pierse, 1990, Testing for aggregation bias in linear models. Economic Journal 100, 137–150.

Lewbel, A., 1994, Aggregation and simple dynamics, American Economic Review 84, 905–918.

Mairesse, J. and Z. Griliches, 1990, Heterogeneity in panel data: Are there stable production functions?, in: Champsaur et al., eds., Essays in honour of Edmund Malinvaud (M.I.T. Press, Cambridge, MA).

Matyas, L. and P. Sevestre, eds., 1992, The econometrics of panel data (Kluwer Academic Publishers, Boston, MA).

Nickell, S., 1981, Biases in dynamic models with fixed effects, Econometrica 49, 1399–1416.

Pesaran, M.H., 1995, Cross-sectional aggregation of linear dynamic models: Some new results, Under preparation.

Pesaran, M.H. and Y. Shin, 1995, An autoregressive distributed lag modelling approach to cointegration analysis, Paper presented at the Symposium for the Centennial of Ragnar Frisch, Oslo, March 3–5, 1995.

Pesaran, M.H., R.G. Pierce, and M.S. Kumar, 1989, Econometric analysis of aggregation in the context of linear prediction models, Econometrica 57, 861–888.

Quah, D., 1990, International patterns of growth: I. Persistence in cross-country disparities, Mimeo. (Economics Department, M.I.T., Cambridge, MA).

Robertson, D. and J. Symons, 1992, Some strange properties of panel data estimators, Journal of Applied Econometrics 7, 175–189.

Sevestre, P. and A. Trognon, 1992, Linear dynamic models, in: L. Matyas and P. Sevestre (1992, Ch. 6, pp. 94–116).

Swamy, P.A.V.B., 1971, Statistical inference in random coefficient regression models, Lecture notes in operations research and mathematical systems 55 (Springer-Verlag, Berlin).

Zellner, A., 1969, On the aggregation problem: A new approach to a troublesome problem, in: K.A. Fox et al., eds., Economic models, estimation and risk programming: Essays in honor of Gerhard Tintner (Springer-Verlag, Berlin) 365–378.

Part III
Non-Stationary Panels

[15]

Econometrics Journal (2000), volume **3**, pp. 148–161.

Testing for stationarity in heterogeneous panel data

KADDOUR HADRI

Department of Economics & Accounting, The University of Liverpool, Liverpool, L69 7ZA, UK
E-mail: Hadri@liv.ac.uk

Received: October 1999

Summary This paper proposes a residual-based Lagrange multiplier (LM) test for a null that the individual observed series are stationary around a deterministic level or around a deterministic trend against the alternative of a unit root in panel data. The tests which are asymptotically similar under the null, belong to the locally best invariant (LBI) test statistics. The asymptotic distributions of the statistics are derived under the null and are shown to be normally distributed. Finite sample sizes and powers are considered in a Monte Carlo experiment. The empirical sizes of the tests are close to the true size even in small samples. The testing procedure is easy to apply, including, to panel data models with fixed effects, individual deterministic trends and heterogeneous errors across cross-sections. It is also shown how to apply the tests to the more general case of serially correlated disturbance terms.

Keywords: *Panel data, Unit roots, LBI test, LM test, Central limit theorem, Brownian bridge.*

1. INTRODUCTION

There is a vast literature on testing for unit root in time series data but it is only recently that some procedures have been suggested for panel data models. The most noticeable studies in this field are Breitung and Meyer (1994), Quah (1994), Levin and Lin (1993), Im *et al.* (1995), and Maddala and Wu (1999). In all these studies the unit root is the null hypothesis to be tested, and it is a well known fact that the way in which classical hypothesis testing is carried out ensures that the null hypothesis is accepted unless there is strong evidence to the contrary. This is confirmed in the time series literature by the fact that it has been found that standard unit root tests are not very powerful against relevant alternatives and fail to reject the null hypothesis for many economic series. It should be noted that in these comparisons the tests suggested by Elliott *et al.* (1996) are not included. Working from the Bayesian perspective, DeJong and Whiteman (1991) found only two of the Nelson–Plosser series to have stochastic trends instead of 13 out of 14 using the Dickey–Fuller tests. These studies suggest that, in trying to decide by classical methods whether economic data are stationary or integrated, it would be useful to perform tests of the null hypothesis of stationarity as well as tests of the null hypothesis of a unit root. Kwiatkowski *et al.* (1992) suggested tests of the null hypothesis of stationarity against the alternative of a unit root for time series data with stationary error. In this paper we extend their tests to panel data with *i.i.d.* disturbance terms across i and over t. We also show how our results can accommodate the case of heterogeneous disturbance terms across i. Moreover, we indicate how to extend our present results to the case of heterogeneous and temporally serially correlated disturbance terms.

The main motivation for testing for stationarity in a panel data instead of single time series is the same as the one generally invoked for panel unit root tests. It is found that the power of the test increases with an increase in the number of cross-sections. Another positive by-product of using panel data instead of single time series in this context is that the asymptotic distributions of the test statistics are asymptotically normally distributed instead of following nonconventional distributions and are approximately normally distributed for samples with size generally encountered in Econometrics. Another point in favour of our tests is that the moments of our asymptotic distributions are derived exactly whereas for the tests of a unit root cited above, simulation is needed. Our tests are applicable to panel data with large T and moderate N. Some of these panel data sets including the widely used Penn World Tables, have time series components that are nonstationary.

It is not possible using the Dickey–Fuller test to test the null hypothesis of stationarity against the alternative of a unit root. In this paper we use a parametrization which provides an adequate representation of both stationary and nonstationary variables and permits a test of stationarity to be formulated easily. More precisely, we adopt a components representation in which an individual time series is written for the general case as a sum of a deterministic trend, a random walk and a white noise disturbance term. The null hypothesis of trend stationarity corresponds to the hypothesis that the variance of the random walk equals zero. Under the additional assumptions that the random walk is normal and that the stationary error is normal white noise, the one-sided Langrange multiplier (LM) statistics for the level and trend stationary hypotheses are locally best invariant (LBI) tests as shown by Nabeya and Tanaka (1988). The suggested tests belong to the class of tests proposed by King and Hillier (1985) for testing the variance–covariance matrix of the error term in a linear regression model. This class of tests has been very useful in the pure time series context. Kwiatkowski *et al.* (1992), Nyblom and Harvey (1999), Saikkonen and Luukonen (1993), and Tanaka (1990) have tested for stationarity within this framework; Harris and Inder (1994) and Shin (1994) have used the test for testing the null of cointegration. It has been recently utilized to test for the null of cointegration in panel data by McCoskey and Kao (1998). It should be noted that recently Larsson *et al.* (1999) proposed a likelihood-based cointegration test in panels. This procedure has the advantage over the residual-based one to estimate and test for the presence of multiple cointegrating vectors.

The tests we are proposing in this paper are shown to have an asymptotic normal distribution. In all the above papers, either the critical values of the tests or the moments of the asymptotic distributions were evaluated using Monte Carlo simulations and in one case using numerical integration. The novelty in our paper is that the moments of the asymptotic distribution are calculated exactly.

The layout of this paper is as follows. Section 2 outlines the models under consideration and the assumptions required for the construction of the proposed tests. The formulation of the tests and their limiting distributions are given in Section 3. Section 4 investigates the finite sample properties of the suggested panel stationarity tests by means of Monte Carlo simulation. Finally, Section 5 provides some concluding remarks. Some of the mathematical proofs are in the Appendix.

For notational simplicity we use $\xrightarrow{p}$ to denote the weak convergence in probability, and $\Rightarrow$ to indicate the weak convergence in distribution. We write integrals such as $\int_0^1 V(r)dr$ as $\int V$ when there is no ambiguity over limits.

2. PANEL MODELS AND LM STATISTICS

We consider the following two models:

$$y_{it} = r_{it} + \epsilon_{it}, \tag{1}$$

and

$$y_{it} = r_{it} + \beta_i t + \epsilon_{it}. \tag{2}$$

Here r_{it} is a random walk:

$$r_{it} = r_{it-1} + u_{it},$$

where y_{it}, $t = 1, \dots, T$ and $i = 1, \dots, N$ are the observed series for which we wish to test stationarity for all i, the ϵ_{it} and u_{it} are mutually independent normals and *i.i.d.* across i and over t with $E[\epsilon_{it}] = 0$, $E[\epsilon_{it}^2] = \sigma_\epsilon^2 > 0$, $E[u_{it}] = 0$ and $E[\sigma_u^2] = \sigma_u^2 \geq 0$. We show below (see Remark 3) how to apply the tests to the more realistic cases where the ϵ_{it} are serially correlated. The initial values r_{i0} are treated as fixed unknowns and play the role of heterogeneous intercepts. Model 2 includes fixed effects and individual trends. The stationary hypothesis is simply $\sigma_u^2 = 0$. Since the ϵ_{it}'s are assumed *i.i.d.*, then under the null hypothesis y_{it} is stationary around a level in model 1 and trend stationary in model 2.

Using back substitution, model 2 can be written as:

$$\begin{aligned} y_{it} &= r_{i0} + \beta_i t + \sum_{t=1}^{t} u_{it} + \epsilon_{it}, \\ &= r_{i0} + \beta_i t + e_{it}, \end{aligned} \tag{3}$$

where $e_{it} = \sum_{t=1}^{t} u_{it} + \epsilon_{it}$. We deduce that

$$E[e_{it}] = 0,$$

and

$$\begin{aligned} E[e_{it}e_{js}] &= \min(t, s)\sigma_u^2 + \sigma_\epsilon^2 \qquad i = j,\ t = s, \\ &= \min(t, s)\sigma_u^2 \qquad i = j,\ t \neq s, \\ &= 0 \qquad i \neq j,\ t = s, \\ &= 0 \qquad i \neq j,\ t \neq s. \end{aligned} \tag{4}$$

In a matrix form model 2 becomes:

$$y_i = X_i\beta_i + e_i, \qquad i = 1, \dots, N, \tag{5}$$

where

$$\begin{aligned} y_i' &= (y_{i1}, \dots, y_{iT}), \\ e_i' &= (e_{i1}, \dots, e_{iT}), \end{aligned}$$

and

$$X_i = (\iota_T, a_T),$$

where $\beta_i = (r_{i0}, \beta_i)'$ is a 2×1 vector of parameters, X_i is $T \times 2$ vector where ι_T is a $T \times 1$ vector of ones and a_T is a $T \times 1$ vector of consecutive natural numbers starting at one. Equation (5) can also be written as

$$y = \begin{bmatrix} X_1 & 0 & \cdots & 0 \\ 0 & X_2 & \cdots & 0 \\ \vdots & \vdots & \ddots & \vdots \\ 0 & 0 & \cdots & X_N \end{bmatrix} \begin{bmatrix} \beta_1 \\ \beta_2 \\ \vdots \\ \beta_N \end{bmatrix} + e,$$
$$= X\beta + e, \tag{6}$$

where

$$y' = (y_{11}, \ldots, y_{1T}, y_{21}, \ldots, y_{2T}, \ldots, y_{N1}, \ldots, y_{NT}),$$
$$e' = (e_{11}, \ldots, e_{1T}, e_{21}, \ldots, e_{2T}, \ldots, e_{N1}, \ldots, e_{NT}).$$

The other elements are self-explanatory. It follows that

$$E[ee'] = I_N \otimes (\sigma_u^2 A_T + \sigma_\epsilon^2 I_T),$$
$$= \sigma_\epsilon^2 I_N \otimes \{(\sigma_u^2/\sigma_\epsilon^2) A_T + I_T\},$$

where I_T is the $T \times T$ identity matrix and A_T is a $T \times T$ matrix where the ijth element equals $\min(i, j)$

$$A_T = \begin{bmatrix} 1 & 1 & \cdots & 1 \\ 1 & 2 & \cdots & 2 \\ \vdots & \vdots & \ddots & \vdots \\ 1 & 2 & \cdots & T \end{bmatrix}.$$

For model 1 we have only to replace $X_i = (\iota_T, a_T)$ in (5) by $X_i = (\iota_T)$. Equation (3) for model 1 becomes:

$$y_{it} = r_{i0} + \sum_{t=1}^{t} u_{it} + \epsilon_{it},$$
$$= r_{i0} + e_{it}. \tag{7}$$

It should be noted that if $\sigma_u^2 = 0$, then e_{it} is reduced to be identical to ϵ_{it} and is *ipso facto* stationary (r_{it} reduces to a constant), whereas if $\sigma_u^2 \neq 0$, then e_{it} is nonstationary (r_{it} is a random walk). This shows that our testing procedure fits the general framework of Nabeya and Tanaka (1988) which can be used to obtain an LBI test. More specifically, the test takes the following form:

$$H_0 : \lambda = 0, \qquad \text{against } H_1 : \lambda > 0,$$

where $\lambda = \frac{\sigma_u^2}{\sigma_\epsilon^2}$. Hence, the statistic we will use is both the one-sided LM statistic and the LBI test statistic for the hypothesis $\lambda = 0$.

Let $\hat{e}_{it}$ be the residuals from the regression y on an intercept for model 1 (see (7)) and on an intercept plus a time trend for model 2 (see (3)). The LM (and LBI) statistic is then (see Nabeya and Tanaka (1988, p. 220) for the single time series case):

$$LM = \frac{\frac{1}{N}\sum_i^N \frac{1}{T^2}\sum_{t=1}^T S_{it}^2}{\hat{\sigma}_\epsilon^2}, \tag{8}$$

where S_{it} is the partial sum of the residuals,

$$S_{it} = \sum_{j=1}^{t} \hat{\epsilon}_{ij},$$

and $\hat{\sigma}_\epsilon^2$ is a consistent estimator of σ_ϵ^2 under H_0. A possible candidate is given by:

$$\hat{\sigma}_\epsilon^2 = \frac{1}{NT} \sum_{i=1}^{N} \sum_{t=1}^{T} \hat{\epsilon}_{it}^2. \tag{9}$$

However, the simulations showed that for finite samples we should correct (9) for the degrees of freedom.

3. ASYMPTOTIC DISTRIBUTION OF THE TEST STATISTIC

In this section we consider the asymptotic distribution of the LM statistic given in (8) for each of the two models we are dealing with. In Assumption 1 below we gather all the assumptions we are making.

Assumption 1.

(i) $E[u_{it}] = E[\epsilon_{it}] = 0$,
(ii) u_{it} and ϵ_{it} are mutually independent normal $i.i.d.$ across i and over t,
(iii) $E[u_{it}^2] = \sigma_u^2 \geq 0$, $E[\epsilon_{it}^2] > \sigma_\epsilon^2$,
(iv) $\{r_{it}\}$ starts with r_{i0} which is assumed to be an unknown constant for each i.

In two remarks below we show how to relax the conditions on u_{it} to apply the tests to the more general and interesting case of serially correlated over t and heteroscedastic across i disturbance terms.

The tests are asymptotically similar in the sense that the distribution under the null is invariant with respect to the nuisance parameters of the data-generating process. In particular, similarity with respect to the initial conditions of the generating process is obtained by the inclusion of fixed effects in the regression model, while similarity with respect to the individual deterministic trends is achieved by the inclusion of individual deterministic trends. The similarity is asymptotic in the sense that in order to obtain the invariance of the distribution under the null with respect to the variance of the data-generating process, we divide the statistic of the tests by a consistent estimator of the variance instead of the true variance which is assumed to be unknown to the researcher.

All our limits use a sequential asymptotic in which $T \to \infty$ followed by $N \to \infty$ (see Phillips and Moon (1999)). The sequential limit may be justified in the situation where the panel data set has much more time series components than cross-section components. As Phillips and Moon (1999) pointed out, the sequential limit is relatively easy to derive and so gives a more rapid result than the joint limit which allows both N and T to tend to infinity simultaneously. In Remark 2 below, following Phillips and Moon (1999), the condition under which the sequential limit becomes the joint limit is given.

We shall derive the test for model 1 first. Let us call η_μ the numerator of the test statistic in (8), then we obtain:

$$\eta_\mu = \frac{1}{N}\sum_{i=1}^{N}\frac{1}{T^2}\sum_{t=1}^{T}S_{it}^2. \tag{10}$$

The index μ indicates that the residuals come from model 1.

Lemma 1. *If Assumption 1 holds then:*

$$\eta_\mu \xrightarrow{p} \sigma_\epsilon^2 E\left[\int_0^1 V(r)^2 dr\right] = \sigma_\epsilon^2 \xi_\mu. \tag{11}$$

Here $V(r)$ is a standard Brownian bridge $V(r) = W(r) - rW(1)$, where $W(r)$ is a standard Wiener process. As in (8), we now divide η_μ by a consistent estimate of σ_ϵ^2 to obtain:

$$\widehat{LM}_\mu = \frac{\eta_\mu}{\hat{\sigma}_\epsilon^2}, \tag{12}$$

then,

$$\widehat{LM}_\mu \xrightarrow{p} E\left[\int_0^1 V(r)^2 dr\right] = \xi_\mu. \tag{13}$$

Theorem 1. *Assume Assumption 1 holds. Then the test statistic in* (12) *for the null of level stationary has the following limiting distribution:*

$$Z_\mu = \frac{\sqrt{N}(\widehat{LM}_\mu - \xi_\mu)}{\zeta_\mu} \Rightarrow N(0, 1), \tag{14}$$

where $\zeta_\mu^2 = \mathrm{var}(\int V^2)$.

To compute ξ_μ and ζ_μ^2 we shall use the characteristic function (c.f.) of the random variable $\int V^2$. This characteristic function which is also the c.f. for the limiting distribution of the Cramér-von-Mises statistic is given by Anderson and Darling (1952).

$$\phi_\mu(\theta) = \{\sqrt{2i\theta}/\sin(\sqrt{2i\theta})\}^{1/2}, \tag{15}$$

where $i = \sqrt{-1}$. It is well known that cumulants are given by the expansion of $\log\{\phi_\mu(\theta)\}$ as a power series in $i\theta$:

$$\log\{\phi_\mu(\theta)\} = \frac{1}{6}\frac{i\theta}{1!} + \frac{1}{45}\frac{(i\theta)^2}{2!} + \frac{40}{4725}\frac{(i\theta)^3}{3!} + O(i\theta)^4. \tag{16}$$

The first and second cumulants, κ_1 and κ_2, give, respectively, the mean and the variance of the random variable $\int V^2$:

$$\kappa_1 = \xi_\mu = \frac{1}{6} \quad \text{and} \quad \kappa_2 = \zeta_\mu^2 = \frac{1}{45}. \tag{17}$$

Now, the statistic Z_μ can be used to test the null hypothesis of level stationary against the alternative of unit root after replacing the mean and variance by their numerical values from (17). For model 2 we obtain the residuals from the regression of y on an intercept and a time trend. Then as above:

Lemma 2. *If Assumption* 1 *holds then:*

$$\eta_\tau \xrightarrow{p} \sigma_\epsilon^2 E\left[\int_0^1 V_2(r)^2 dr\right] = \sigma_\epsilon^2 \xi_\mu, \tag{18}$$

where $V_2(r)$ is the so-called second-level Brownian bridge.

The expression of $V_2(r)$ is given by Kwiatkowski *et al.* (1992). We reproduce it here for completeness sake:

$$V_2(r) = W(r) + (2r - 3r^2)W(1) + 6r(r-1)\int_0^1 W(s)ds. \tag{19}$$

As above, we divide η_τ by a consistent estimator of σ_ϵ^2 to obtain:

$$\widehat{LM}_\tau = \frac{\eta_\tau}{\hat{\sigma}_\epsilon^2}, \tag{20}$$

then,

$$\widehat{LM}_\tau \xrightarrow{p} E\left[\int_0^1 V_2(r)^2 dr\right] = \xi_\tau. \tag{21}$$

Theorem 2. *Assume Assumption* 1 *holds. Then the test statistic in* (20) *for the null of trend stationary has the following limiting distribution:*

$$Z_\tau = \frac{\sqrt{N}(\widehat{LM}_\tau - \xi_\tau)}{\zeta_\tau} \Rightarrow N(0,1), \tag{22}$$

where $\zeta_\tau^2 = \mathrm{var}(\int V_2^2)$.

To compute ξ_τ and ζ_τ^2 we shall use as before the characteristic function of the random variable $\int {V_2}^2$. This characteristic function has been derived by Nabeya and Tanaka (1988) using the Fredholm determinants technique:

$$\phi_\tau(\theta) = \left\{\frac{12}{(2i\theta)^2}(2 - \sqrt{2i\theta}\sin\sqrt{2i\theta} - 2\cos\sqrt{2i\theta})\right\}^{-1/2}. \tag{23}$$

The cumulants are extracted from the following expansion of $\log\{\phi_\tau(\theta)\}$:

$$\log\{\phi_\tau(\theta)\} = \frac{1}{15}\frac{i\theta}{1!} + \frac{11}{6300}\frac{(i\theta)^2}{2!} + \frac{1}{6750}\frac{(i\theta)^3}{3!} + O(i\theta)^{7/2}. \tag{24}$$

Hence, the mean and the variance of the random variable $\int {V_2}^2$ are:

$$\kappa_1 = \xi_\tau = \frac{1}{15} \quad \text{and} \quad \kappa_2 = \zeta_\tau^2 = \frac{11}{6300}. \tag{25}$$

The statistic Z_τ is now operational for testing the null hypothesis of trend stationary against the alternative of nonstationarity after replacing the mean and variance by their numerical values in (22). As stated above, in related literature, similar moments are derived by Monte Carlo simulation. It can be shown, following similar steps as Kwiatkowski *et al.* (1992), that the above tests are consistent.

Table 1. Empirical size of Z_μ test.

	$N = 1$	$N = 15$	$N = 25$	$N = 50$	$N = 100$
$T = 5$	0.0015	0.0113	0.0086	0.0060	0.0031
$T = 10$	0.0544	0.0381	0.0350	0.0319	0.0260
$T = 15$	0.0565	0.0475	0.0457	0.0409	0.0381
$T = 25$	0.0627	0.0536	0.0538	0.0498	0.0465
$T = 50$	0.0655	0.0586	0.0589	0.0531	0.0539
$T = 100$	0.0660	0.0612	0.0562	0.0573	0.0548

Note: $\alpha_i \sim U[0, 10]$. Size based on one-sided $N(0, 1)$, critical value 1.645.

Remark 1. It is worthwhile to note that the $\widehat{LM}$ statistic can be written as

$$\widehat{LM} = \frac{1}{N}\sum_{i=1}^{N}\left(\frac{\frac{1}{T^2}\sum_{t=1}^{T} S_{it}^2}{\hat{\sigma}_\epsilon^2}\right). \tag{26}$$

Then, it is evident from (26) that we can allow the disturbance terms to be heteroscedastic across i. We have simply to compute σ_ϵ^2 for each individual time series i, say $\sigma_{\epsilon,i}^2$, and then apply the following formula:

$$\widehat{LM} = \frac{1}{N}\sum_{i=1}^{N}\left(\frac{\frac{1}{T^2}\sum_{t=1}^{T} S_{it}^2}{\hat{\sigma}_{\epsilon,i}^2}\right). \tag{27}$$

Remark 2. Following Phillips and Moon (1999), under Assumption 1 and the rate condition $N/T \to 0$, the sequential results obtained above imply joint convergence. This result has been more formally proven recently by Shin and Snell (1999). In the joint limit theory, T and N are allowed to pass to infinity simultaneously. As noted by Phillips and Moon (1999), the rate condition indicates that the joint limit theory is going to be applicable to cases where N is moderate and T is allowed to be large. Examples of this type of data configuration are industries, regions and countries observed during a long span of time. A well known example of this type of data is the Penn World Tables where the time series components are found to be nonstationary.

Remark 3. We can also relax the assumption on the errors ϵ_{it} being $i.i.d.$ $N(0, \sigma_\epsilon^2)$ over t to accommodate serial dependence cases. To allow for quite general forms of temporal dependence over t, we may assume either that ϵ_{it} satisfy the strong mixing regularity conditions of Phillips and Perron (1988) or the linear process conditions of Phillips and Solo (1992). In both cases we have to replace in (11) and (18) σ_ϵ^2 by the long-run variance σ^2 defined as:

$$\sigma^2 = \frac{1}{N}\sum_{i=1}^{N}\lim_{T\to\infty} T^{-1}(S_{iT}^2). \tag{28}$$

A consistent estimator of σ^2 can be obtained using one of the HAC estimators in the market. The most recent ones are: Andrews and Monahan (1992), Den Haan and Levin (1996), Lee and Phillips (1994), and Newey and West (1994).

Table 2. Power of Z_μ test.

	$\lambda = \sigma_u^2/\sigma_\epsilon^2$	0.0001	0.001	0.01	0.1	1	100	10000
$N = 1$	$T = 15$	0.0604	0.0612	0.0825	0.2572	0.5905	0.7258	0.7289
	$T = 25$	0.0708	0.0776	0.1447	0.4569	0.7738	0.8700	0.8716
	$T = 50$	0.0756	0.1056	0.3439	0.7469	0.9261	0.9696	0.9700
$N = 15$	$T = 15$	0.0477	0.0549	0.1393	0.9052	0.9999	1.0	1.0
	$T = 25$	0.0566	0.0844	0.4258	0.9996	1.0	1.0	1.0
	$T = 50$	0.0697	0.1826	0.9715	1.0	1.0	1.0	1.0
$N = 25$	$T = 15$	0.0463	0.0522	0.1693	0.9813	1.0	1.0	1.0
	$T = 25$	0.0557	0.0845	0.5763	1.0	1.0	1.0	1.0
	$T = 50$	0.0622	0.2294	0.9965	1.0	1.0	1.0	1.0
$N = 50$	$T = 15$	0.0454	0.0582	0.2529	0.9994	1.0	1.0	1.0
	$T = 25$	0.0591	0.1003	0.7999	1.0	1.0	1.0	1.0
	$T = 50$	0.0807	0.3803	1.0	1.0	1.0	1.0	1.0
$N = 100$	$T = 15$	0.0356	0.0528	0.3625	1.0	1.0	1.0	1.0
	$T = 25$	0.0517	0.1154	0.9638	1.0	1.0	1.0	1.0
	$T = 50$	0.0802	0.5298	1.0	1.0	1.0	1.0	1.0

Table 3. Empirical size of Z_τ test.

	$N = 1$	$N = 15$	$N = 25$	$N = 50$	$N = 100$
$T = 10$	0.0220	0.0119	0.0078	0.0044	0.0014
$T = 15$	0.0391	0.0233	0.0212	0.0180	0.0117
$T = 25$	0.0502	0.0417	0.0372	0.0369	0.0311
$T = 50$	0.0593	0.0524	0.0492	0.0470	0.0434
$T = 100$	0.0630	0.0567	0.0537	0.0528	0.0496

Note: $\alpha_i \sim U[0, 10]$, $\beta_i \sim U[0, 2]$. Size based on one-sided $N(0, 1)$, critical value 1.645.

4. MONTE CARLO SIMULATION RESULTS

In this section we use Monte Carlo experiments to examine finite properties of Z_μ and Z_τ. The simulations using 20000 replications (see Hadri and Phillips (1999) for the importance of the number of replications in simulations) each, are based on GAUSS RNDN procedure. The data-generating process for model 1 is:

$$y_{it} = \alpha_i + \epsilon_{it},$$

and for model 2 we have:

$$y_{it} = \alpha_i + \beta_i t + \epsilon_{it},$$

where ϵ_{it} are *i.i.d.* $N(0, 1)$ under H_0.

It is evident that the distributions of both statistics under the null do not depend neither on the scale factor σ_ϵ^2, which without loss of generality can be fixed to take the value of one, nor on α_i.

Table 4. Power of Z_τ test.

	$\lambda = \sigma_u^2/\sigma_\epsilon^2$	0.0001	0.001	0.01	0.1	1	100	10000
$N = 1$	$T = 15$	0.0415	0.0418	0.0454	0.0843	0.3193	0.5516	0.5537
	$T = 25$	0.0500	0.0526	0.0666	0.2040	0.6291	0.8305	0.8344
	$T = 50$	0.0536	0.0617	0.1372	0.5693	0.9219	0.9798	0.9815
$N = 15$	$T = 15$	0.0237	0.0248	0.0339	0.2542	0.9934	1.0	1.0
	$T = 25$	0.0401	0.0448	0.1004	0.8531	1.0	1.0	1.0
	$T = 50$	0.0480	0.0737	0.4783	1.0	1.0	1.0	1.0
$N = 25$	$T = 15$	0.0230	0.0244	0.0370	0.3512	0.9999	1.0	1.0
	$T = 25$	0.0427	0.0477	0.1310	0.9685	1.0	1.0	1.0
	$T = 50$	0.0439	0.0729	0.6362	1.0	1.0	1.0	1.0
$N = 50$	$T = 15$	0.0206	0.0220	0.0397	0.5705	1.0	1.0	1.0
	$T = 25$	0.0389	0.0464	0.1814	0.9996	1.0	1.0	1.0
	$T = 50$	0.0566	0.1084	0.8655	1.0	1.0	1.0	1.0
$N = 100$	$T = 15$	0.0135	0.0151	0.0370	0.8089	1.0	1.0	1.0
	$T = 25$	0.0285	0.0365	0.2317	1.0	1.0	1.0	1.0
	$T = 50$	0.0466	0.1184	0.9871	1.0	1.0	1.0	1.0

The size of the test depends on T and N. We generated α_i from $U[0, 10]$ and β_i from $U[0, 2]$, where U stands for uniform distribution.

Table 1 presents the estimates of the empirical size of Z_μ at the 5% level when the asymptotic critical value of 1.645 is used. The size of the test is quite close to the theoretical size 0.05 for samples with $T > 10$. For instance, when $T = 15$ and $N = 15$ the empirical size is 0.0475. For the largest sample simulated, $T = 100$ and $N = 100$ it is equal to 0.0548. As T and N get larger, the test becomes more accurate but not always in a monotonic fashion. To correct for degrees of freedom in finite samples, we used $\hat{\sigma}_\epsilon^2 = \frac{1}{N(T-1)} \sum_i^N \sum_{t=1}^T \hat{\epsilon}_{it}^2$ as an estimator of σ_ϵ^2.

Table 2 presents simulated results giving the power of the test Z_μ in the presence of *i.i.d.* errors, as a function of T, N, λ. Where λ is equal to the ratio $\sigma_u^2/\sigma_\epsilon^2$. Thus $\lambda = 0\,(\sigma_u^2 = 0)$ means that y is stationary whereas $\lambda = \infty$ entails that y comprises a random walk (see Kwiatkowski *et al.* (1992, p. 163)). By varying the value of λ we can see how the power of the test changes as we approach the two polar cases (stationary versus nonstationary y). In general, the power increases as T or N or both grow.

Table 3 gives the estimates of the empirical size of Z_τ at the 5% level when the asymptotic critical value of 1.645 is used. The test has approximately correct size for $T > 25$. Like for Z_μ as T and N increase the test becomes more accurate. As in model 1, it should be noted that we used $\hat{\sigma}_\epsilon^2 = \frac{1}{N(T-2)} \sum_i^N \sum_{t=1}^T \hat{\epsilon}_{it}^2$ as an estimator of σ_ϵ^2.

Table 4 shows the power of the test Z_τ. As above, in general, the power of the test increases with λ for all T and N. For $\lambda > 0.01$ the power increases monotonically as T or N or both grow.

5. CONCLUSIONS

In this paper, we presented statistical tests of the hypothesis of stationarity, either around a level or around a linear trend, against the alternative of a unit root in panel data. The tests proposed are LM-LBI tests when we assume that the disturbance terms are normally distributed instead of being only *i.i.d.*. The most general panel data model to which these tests can be applied is a panel data model with fixed effects, individual deterministic trend and heterogeneous across i but serially uncorrelated errors over t. However, it is shown how to apply the tests in cases where the disturbance terms are heteroscedastic and serially correlated. The tests may be used in conjunction with panel data tests testing the null of a unit root. By testing both the unit root hypothesis and the stationarity hypothesis, we can distinguish series that appear to be stationary, series that appear to have a unit root, and series for which we are unsure whether they are stationary or integrated. The asymptotic distribution of each test is shown to be normal. The empirical application of the tests is straightforward and do not necessitate, as in previous similar studies, the use of moments estimated through Monte Carlo simulation. The moments of the asymptotic distributions of our tests are derived exactly.

Monte Carlo simulations are used to assess the small sample properties of our tests. We found that the empirical size is close to the nominal five percent level for T and N sufficiently large.

ACKNOWLEDGEMENTS

I would like to thank Karim M. Abadir, Simon James and Jan Kiviet for useful comments. This research was supported by ESRC grant R000236627 and by the Humanities Research Board of the British Academy.

REFERENCES

Anderson, T. W. and J. Darling (1952). Asymptotic theory of certain "goodness of fit" criteria based on stochastic processes. *Annals of Mathematical Statistics 23*, 193–212.

Andrews, D. W. K. and J. C. Monahan (1992). An improved heteroscedasticity and autocorrelation consistent covariance matrix estimator. *Econometrica 60*, 953–66.

Breitung, J. and W. Meyer (1994). Testing for unit roots in panel data: Are wages on different bargaining levels cointegrated? *Applied Economics 26*, 353–61.

Dejong, D. N. and C. H. Whiteman (1991). Reconsidering 'Trends and random walks in macroeconomic time series'. *Journal of Monetary Economics 28*, 221–54.

Den Haan, W. J. and A. Levin (1996). Inferences from parametric and non-parametric covariance matrix estimation procedures. Manuscript, UCSD and Federal Reserve Board.

Elliot, G., T. Rothenberg, and J. H. Stock (1996). Efficient tests for autoregressive unit root. *Econometrica 64*, 813–36.

Hadri, K. and G. D. A. Phillips (1999). The accuracy of the higher order bias approximation for the *2SLS* estimator. *Economic Letters 62*, 167–74.

Harris, D. and B. Inder (1994). A test of the null hypothesis of cointegration. In C. P. Hargreaves (ed.), *Nonstationary Time Series Analysis and Cointegration*. New York, Oxford University Press.

Im, K., M. H. Pesaran and Y. Shin (1995). Testing for unit roots in heterogeneous panels. Unpublished Manuscript, Department of Applied Economics, University of Cambridge.

Kao, C. (1997). Spurious regression and residual-based tests for cointegration in panel data. *Journal of Econometrics 90*, 1–44.

King, M. A. and G. H. Hillier (1985). Locally best invariant tests of the error covariance matrix of the linear regression model. *Journal of the Royal Statistical Society B 47*, 98–102.

Kwiatkowski, D., P. C. B. Phillips, P. Schmidt and Y. Shin (1992). Testing the null hypothesis of stationarity against the alternative of a unit root. *Journal of Econometrics 54*, 91–115.

Larsson, R., J. Lyhagen and M. Löthgren (1999). Likelihood-based cointegration tests in heterogeneous panels. Manuscript, Stockholm School of Economics.

Lee, C. C. and P. C. B. Phillips (1994). An ARMA prewhitened long-run variance estimator. Manuscript, Yale University.

Levin, A. and C. F. Lin (1993). Unit root tests in panel data: New results. Discussion Paper, Department of Economics (UC-San Diego).

Leybourne, S. J. and B. P. M. McCabe (1989). On the distribution of some test statistics for parameter constancy. *Biometrika 76*, 169–77.

Mac Neill, I. (1978). Properties of sequences of partial sums of polynomial regression residuals with applications to tests for change of regression at unknown times. *Annals of Statistics 6*, 422–33.

Maddala, G. S. and S. Wu (1999). A comparative study of unit root tests with panel data and a new simple test. *Oxford Bulletin of Economics and Statistics 61*, 631–52.

McCabe, B. P. M. and S. J. Leybourne (1988). Testing for variation in multivariate random coefficient regression models. Unpublished Manuscript, University of Sydney, Sydney, NSW.

McCoskey, S. and C. Kao (1998). A residual based test of the null of cointegration in panel data. *Econometric Reviews 17*, 57–84.

Nabeya, S. and K. Tanaka (1988). Asymptotic theory of a test for the constancy of regression coefficients against the random walk alternative. *Annals of Statistics 16*, 218–35.

Newey, W. K. and K. D. West (1994). Automatic lag selection in covariance matrix estimation. *Review of Economic Studies 61*, 631–53.

Nyblom, J. (1986). Testing for deterministic linear trend in time series. *Journal of the American Statistical Association 81*, 545–49.

Nyblom, J. and A. Harvey (1999). Tests of common stochastic trends. Working Paper 9902, Department of Applied Economics, University of Cambridge.

Nyblom, J. and T. Makelainen (1983). Comparison of tests for the presence of random walk coefficients in a simple linear model. *Journal of the American Statistical Association 78*, 856–64.

Pedroni, P. (1995). Panel cointegration: Asymptotic and finite sample properties of pooled time series tests with an application to the PPP hypothesis. Manuscript, Department of Economics, Indiana University.

Pedroni, P. (1996). Fully modified OLS for heterogeneous cointegrated panel and the case of Purchasing Power Parity. Manuscript, Department of Economics, Indiana University.

Phillips, P. C. B. (1987). Time series regression with unit roots. *Econometrica 55*, 277–301.

Phillips, P. C. B. and H. Moon (1999). Linear regression limit theory and nonstationary panel data. *Econometrica 67*, 1057–1111.

Phillips, P. C. B. and P. Perron (1988.) Testing for a unit root in times series regression. *Biometrika 75*, 335–46.

Phillips, P. C. B. and V. Solo (1992). Asymptotics for linear processes. *Annals of Statistics 20*, 971–1001.

Quah, D. (1994). Exploiting cross section variation for unit root inference in dynamic data. *Economics Letters 44*, 9–19.

Saikkonen, P. and R. Luukonen (1993). Testing for a moving average unit root in autoregressive integrated moving average models. *Journal of the American Statistical Association 88*, 596–601.

Shin, Y. (1994). A residual based test of the null of cointegration against the alternative of no cointegration. *Econometric Theory 10*, 91–115.

Shin, Y. and A. Snell (1999). Testing for stationarity in heterogenous panels with serially correlated errors. Manuscript, University of Edinburgh.

Tanaka, K. (1983). Non-normality of the Lagrange multiplier statistic for testing the constancy of regression coefficients. *Econometrica 51*, 1577–82.

Tanaka, K. (1990). Testing for a moving average unit root. *Econometric Theory 6*, 445–58.

Tanaka, K. (1996). *Time Series Analysis*. New York: John Wiley & Sons.

APPENDIX

A Proof of Lemma 1. We note that

$$\frac{1}{T^2}\sum_{t=1}^{T} S_{it}^2 = \frac{1}{T^2}\sum_{t=1}^{T}\Big(\sum_{j=1}^{t}\hat{e}_{ij}\Big)^2 \Rightarrow \sigma_\epsilon^2 \int_0^1 V^2,$$

from Leybourne and McCabe (1989), as $T \to \infty$ for fixed N, where V is a functional of Brownian motions. The distribution and the characteristic function of $\int_0^1 V^2$ are given by Anderson and Darling (1952). Then, if we apply the law of large numbers to $\frac{1}{N}\sum_{i=1}^{N}(\sigma_\epsilon^2 \int_0^1 V_i^2)$, we obtain as $N \to \infty$

$$\frac{1}{N}\sum_{i=1}^{N}\Big(\sigma_\epsilon^2 \int_0^1 V_i^2\Big) \xrightarrow{p} \sigma_\epsilon^2 E\Big[\int_0^1 V^2\Big].$$

Hence, we have shown that

$$\frac{1}{N}\sum_{i=1}^{N}\frac{1}{T^2}\sum_{t=1}^{T} S_{it}^2 \xrightarrow{p} \sigma_\epsilon^2 E\Big[\int_0^1 V^2\Big],$$

as $T \to \infty$ first and then $N \to \infty$ by the sequential limit theory. It follows that

$$\widehat{LM}_\mu = \frac{\frac{1}{N}\sum_{i=1}^{N}\frac{1}{T^2}\sum_{t=1}^{T} S_{it}^2}{\hat{\sigma}_\epsilon^2} \xrightarrow{p} \frac{\sigma_\epsilon^2 E\Big[\int_0^1 V^2\Big]}{\sigma_\epsilon^2} = \xi_\mu.$$

The proof of Lemma 2 follows the same lines. However, we use here the Mac Neill (1978) result which gives

$$\frac{1}{T^2}\sum_{t=1}^{T} S_{it}^2 = \frac{1}{T^2}\sum_{t=1}^{T}\Big(\sum_{j=1}^{t}\hat{e}_{ij}\Big)^2 \Rightarrow \sigma_\epsilon^2 \int_0^1 V_2^2,$$

where V_2 is the second-level Brownian bridge and the residuals are obtained from the regression of y on an intercept and a time trend. The characteristic function of $\int_0^1 V_2^2$ is given by Mac Neill (1978) and Nabeya and Tanaka (1988).

Proof of Theorem 1. In Lemma 1 we found that

$$\widehat{LM}_\mu = \frac{\frac{1}{N}\sum_{i=1}^{N}\frac{1}{T^2}\sum_{t=1}^{T} S_{it}^2}{\hat{\sigma}_\epsilon^2} \xrightarrow{p} \xi_\mu.$$

Now we have to find an appropriate normalization of $\widehat{LM}_\mu$ to make sure it converges to a proper random variable. For fixed N as $T \to \infty$ we obtain

$$\sqrt{N}\Bigg(\frac{\frac{1}{N}\sum_{i=1}^{N}\frac{1}{T^2}\sum_{t=1}^{T} S_{it}^2}{\hat{\sigma}_\epsilon^2} - \xi_\mu\Bigg) \Rightarrow \frac{1}{\sqrt{N}}\sum_{i=1}^{N}\Big(\int V_i^2 - \xi_\mu\Big),$$

which will converge to a normal variable by the Lindeberg–Lévy central limit theorem as $N \to \infty$:

$$\frac{1}{\sqrt{N}}\sum_{i=1}^{N}\Big(\frac{\int V_i^2 - \xi_\mu}{\zeta_\mu}\Big) \Rightarrow N(0, 1),$$

where $\zeta_\mu^2 \equiv \text{var}(\int V^2)$. Then by the sequential limit theory we obtain the following result

$$\sqrt{N}\left(\frac{\widehat{LM}_\mu - \xi_\mu}{\zeta_\mu}\right) \Rightarrow N(0, 1),$$

as $T \to \infty$ then $N \to \infty$ proving Theorem 1.

The proof of Theorem 2 follows the same line as above. The only difference is to replace $\int V^2$, ξ_μ and ζ_μ by $\int V_2^2$, ξ_τ and ζ_τ, respectively.

[16]

ELSEVIER

Journal of Econometrics 91 (1999) 201–226

JOURNAL OF
Econometrics

www.elsevier.nl/locate/econbase

Inference for unit roots in dynamic panels where the time dimension is fixed

Richard D.F. Harris, Elias Tzavalis*

Department of Economics, University of Exeter, Exeter EX4 4PU, UK

Received 1 April 1996; received in revised form 1 May 1998

Abstract

This paper derives similar, asymptotic unit root tests for first-order autoregressive panel data models, assuming that the time dimension of the panel is fixed. It is shown that the limiting distributions of the test statistics are normal. The assumption that the time dimension is fixed allows us to derive analytical expressions for the moments of the distributions. Similarity with respect to the initial conditions of the data generating process is achieved by including fixed effect dummy variables in the regression model, while similarity with respect to fixed effects in the data generating process is achieved by including a linear deterministic trend for each individual unit of the panel. When fixed effects or individual trends are included as regressors the *least squares* estimator of the autoregressive parameter is inconsistent and thus the test statistics must be appropriately adjusted. Monte Carlo evidence suggests that the proposed tests have empirical size that is very close to the nominal five percent level and substantially more power than the corresponding unit root tests for the single time series case. © 1999 Elsevier Science S.A. All rights reserved.

JEL classification: C22; C23

Keywords: Panel data; Unit roots; Fixed effects; Central limit theorem

1. Introduction

Substantial research effort has now been devoted to developing inference techniques for detecting the presence of a unit autoregressive root in time series

* Corresponding author. E-mail: e.tzavalis@exeter.ac.uk

0304-4076/99/$-see front matter
PII: S0304-4076(98)00076-1

data. The extension of these techniques to the analysis of panel data is of considerable interest in order to study the dynamic behaviour of a number of economic units (such as individuals, firms or countries) over time (Hsiao, 1986; Baltagi, 1995). Unit root testing procedures for dynamic panel data models have been recently suggested by Quah (1992, 1994), Levin and Lin (1993), and Im et al. (1995).

The tests of Quah (1992, 1994) are limited to the case of panel data without fixed effects, and assume that both the cross-section dimension (N) and the time dimension (T) of the panel go to infinity ($\to \infty$) at the same rate, that is the ratio N/T is constant. Levin and Lin (1993) consider the more general model with fixed effects and individual deterministic trends, and allow for heterogeneous serially correlated errors. They assume that both N and T go to infinity, but that T increases faster than N, with $N/T \to 0$. They show that the inclusion of fixed effects or individual trends in the regression model creates a downward bias in the least squares estimator of the autoregressive parameter, and thus the tests statistics must be appropriately adjusted. Finally, Im et al. (1995) consider the same class of models and propose a test based on the average of N individual Augmented Dickey–Fuller statistics. They assume that both N and T go to infinity, but with the weaker assumption that $\sqrt{N}/T \to 0$. For the case that the error term is serially uncorrelated and independent across N, Im et al. (1995) demonstrate that their tests are also valid for the case that T is fixed.[1] All these test statistics have normal limiting distributions, whose analytical moments can be derived under the assumption that N and T go to infinity. However, in order for the more general tests of Levin and Lin (1993) and Im et al. (1995) to be made operational in small T samples, the authors suggest the use of simulated, rather than analytical values of the distribution moments.

In this paper, we develop asymptotic unit root tests for first-order autoregressive panel data models with serially uncorrelated errors, under the assumption that $N \to \infty$, while T is fixed. The assumption that T is fixed seems natural considering that in most empirical studies the number of cross-section units is typically large relative to the number of time series observations for each cross-section unit (see, for instance, Chamberlain, 1984). In contrast with the unit root tests discussed above, this assumption enables us to derive analytical expressions of the moments of the distributions of the tests by applying standard (classical) asymptotic theory across N (Anderson, 1978).

The tests derived in this paper are based on the normalised least squares (LS) estimators of the autoregressive coefficient and allow for fixed effects and

[1] The t-ratio test of Im et al. (1995) is valid for T greater than five when only an intercept is included in each Dickey–Fuller regression and for T greater than six when a trend is added. Their likelihood ratio test is valid for T greater than nine and T greater than ten, respectively.

individual deterministic trends. The tests are similar in the sense that their distribution under the null hypothesis is invariant with respect to the nuisance parameters of the data generating process (DGP) even in finite samples (Kiviet and Phillips, 1990, 1992). Similarity with respect to the initial conditions of the data generating process is achieved by the inclusion of fixed effects in the regression model, while similarity with respect to the fixed effects of the data generating process is achieved by the inclusion of the individual deterministic trends.

We show that the limiting distributions of the test statistics are normal and that their convergence rate is the same as for the case of stationary panel data, namely $\sqrt{N}$. The normality result does not require T to grow large. When fixed effects or individual deterministic trends are included in the regression the LS estimators are asymptotically biased downwards, as in the much studied case of stationary dynamic panels (see, inter alia, Nickell, 1981; Hsiao, 1986; Blundell and Smith, 1991; Sevestre and Trognon, 1992). In contrast with the stationary case, however, the bias remains even as T grows large (see also Levin and Lin, 1993). Where appropriate, the normalised coefficient statistic must be first corrected for the inconsistency of the LS estimator in order to yield a test statistic with a standard normal density.[2] We derive analytical expressions for both the inconsistency of the LS estimators when fixed effects or individual deterministic trends are included in the regression model, and the asymptotic variance of the resulting test statistics. Comparisons are made with the corresponding moments of the test statistics introduced by Quah (1994) and Levin and Lin (1993), who derive analogous results for the case that T grows large.

Monte Carlo experiments are used to evaluate the finite sample performance of the proposed tests, and to investigate the consequences for inference in finite samples of assuming that T is asymptotic rather than fixed. The results of these experiments indicate that the normal distribution accurately approximates the empirical distribution of the test statistics. Furthermore the proposed tests have substantially more power to discriminate between stationary and non-stationary processes than the corresponding unit root tests using single time series. It is shown that when fixed effects or individual trends are included in the regression model, the assumption that T is asymptotic yields a test which has substantially reduced power in small T samples.

The paper is organised as follows. Section 2 derives the test statistics based on the LS estimators of the autoregressive coefficient, and their limiting

[2] In the stationary case, generalised method of moments estimation is frequently employed to give consistent estimates of the autoregressive coefficient. However, this approach is not appropriate in the non-stationary case as the necessary moment conditions (over time) between the level of the series and the disturbance term are not satisfied (see, for instance, Ahn and Schmidt, 1995).

distributions. Section 3 investigates the finite sample size and power of the proposed panel unit root tests by means of Monte Carlo simulation. Finally, Section 4 offers some concluding remarks.

2. The test statistics and their limiting distributions

Following single time series unit root testing procedures (see Dickey and Fuller (1981), Phillips and Perron (1988), or for a survey, Stock (1994)), we consider the following three models.[3]

$$y_{it} = \varphi y_{it-1} + v_{it}, \qquad i = 1, \ldots, N; \quad t = 1, \ldots, T, \tag{1a}$$

$$y_{it} = \alpha_i + \varphi y_{it-1} + v_{it}, \tag{1b}$$

$$y_{it} = \alpha_i + \beta_i t + \varphi y_{it-1} + v_{it}. \tag{1c}$$

For each model, the null hypothesis is that there is a unit root present in the DGP, that is $\varphi = 1$. Under the alternative hypothesis, it is assumed that $|\varphi| < 1$. The appropriateness of each model depends, in part, on what is known about the DGP, and therefore how the null and alternative hypotheses are to be formulated. Model (1a) is the simple case of the homogeneous panel. Model (1b) is a unit root process with heterogeneous drift parameters under the null hypothesis, and a stationary process with heterogeneous intercepts under the alternative hypothesis. Model (1c), which includes heterogeneous fixed effects and individual trends, provides a test with better power to distinguish between the null hypothesis that each series follows a random walk with drift, and the alternative hypothesis that each series is stationary around a deterministic trend (Phillips and Perron, 1988). It will be seen that a second consideration in the choice between the Models (1a)–(1c) is that of similarity with respect to the nuisance parameters of the DGP.

Unit root test statistics have typically taken two forms in the single time series context. The first is the normalised coefficient statistic, which is based directly on the LS estimate of the autoregressive coefficient. The other is the t-ratio statistic. In this paper, we concentrate on the normalised coefficient statistic.

[3] These models correspond to those used by Levin and Lin (1993) and require that the autoregressive coefficient is homogeneous under both the null and alternative hypotheses, since they pool the data over the cross-section dimension. Im et al. (1995), who consider Models (1b) and (1c), do not pool the data, but instead base their test on N separate unit root regressions. This allows for heterogeneity in the autoregressive parameter under the alternative hypothesis. Quah (1994) considers only Model (1a) and assumes that the autoregressive parameter is homogeneous.

Under the null hypothesis that $\varphi = 1$, the LS estimators of φ in Models (1a)–(1c) satisfy

$$\hat{\varphi} - 1 = \left[\sum_{i=1}^{N} y'_{i,-1} Q_T y_{i,-1}\right]^{-1} \cdot \left[\sum_{i=1}^{N} y'_{i,-1} Q_T v_i\right] \tag{2}$$

where $y'_{i,-1} = (y_{i0}, \ldots, y_{iT-1})$, $v'_i = (v_{i1}, \ldots, v_{iT})$ and Q_T is the appropriate $(T \times T)$ indempotent transformation matrix. For Model (1a), $Q_T = I_T$, where I_T is the $(T \times T)$ identity matrix. For Model (1b), $Q_T = M_T = (I_T - (1/T)e_T e'_T)$ and e_T is the unit column vector of length T. For Model (1c), $Q_T = I_T - Z_T(Z'_T Z_T)^{-1} Z'_T$ with $Z_T = (e_T, \tau_T)$ and $\tau'_T = (1, 2, \ldots, T)$. The three LS estimators of φ corresponding to regression Models (1a)–(1c) are the least squares pooled estimator ($\hat{\varphi}_{\text{LSP}}$), the least squares dummy variable estimator ($\hat{\varphi}_{\text{LSDV}}$) and the least squares dummy variable with trend estimator ($\hat{\varphi}_{\text{LSDVT}}$).

In order to derive the limiting distribution of the test statistics we must be precise about the nature of the series $\{v_{it}\}$, the initial conditions, y_{i0}, and the individual effects, α_i. In what follows, we maintain the following assumptions.

Assumptions. (a) $\{v_{it}; i = 1, \ldots, N, t = 1, \ldots, T\}$ is a series of independently and identically normally distributed (n.i.i.d.) random variables having $\mathrm{E}(v_{it}) = 0$ and $\mathrm{Var}(v_{it}) = \sigma_v^2 < \infty$, for all i and t; (b) the initial values, y_{i0}, are fixed; (c) the individual effects, α_i, are fixed.

Assumptions (a)–(c) imply that v_{it} and $y_{i,t-1}$, and their product $y_{i,t-1}v_{it}$, are independent across i.[4] This enables us to derive the limiting distributions of the normalised coefficient statistics for Models (1a)–(1c) by applying a Law of Large Numbers (LLN) and the Linderberg-Levy version of the Central Limit Theorem (CLT).[5] Assumption (a) implies that v_{it} is serially uncorrelated and thus makes the test comparable with the Dickey–Fuller test for single time series.

Assumption (b) requires that the initial conditions are observable constants, which implies that y_{i0} is uncorrelated with the sequence $\{v_{it}\}$. This is a reasonable assumption when the decision to start sampling is not arbitrary and

[4] The independence assumption can be relaxed to allow for time-varying aggregate effects in the data. These effects can be removed by including time-specific dummy variables in each regression model, or equivalently, by first subtracting the cross-section mean from the data. Removing aggregate effects in this way does not affect the LS estimators or the limiting distributions of the test statistics (O'Connell, 1997; Levin and Lin, 1993).

[5] Note that the normality assumption is not required to satisfy the conditions of the Linderberg–Levy CLT. However, this assumption greatly simplifies the testing procedure. As can be seen from the Appendix, the limiting distributions of the test statistics can be derived by relaxing the assumption of normality, but this requires a consistent estimator of the kurtosis coefficient of v_{it}.

therefore reflects the initial conditions of the panel at that particular point in time. It is also an appropriate assumption when the regression model includes fixed effects (see, for instance, Anderson and Hsiao, 1981, 1982). Evans and Savin (1984) also note that this assumption is suitable when the model is non-stable and thus does not converge in probability towards an unconditional mean. Similarly, Assumption (c) implies that α_i is uncorrelated with the sequence $\{v_{it}\}$.

We now present the limiting distributions of the normalised coefficient statistics for Models (1a)–(1c). In order to compare our results with those of Quah (1994) and Levin and Lin (1993), we assume that $y_{i0} = 0$ in Model (1a).

Theorem 1. If Assumption (a) holds and $y_{i0} = 0$ for all i, then under the null hypothesis that $\varphi = 1$,

$$\sqrt{N}(\hat{\varphi}_{\mathrm{LSP}} - 1) \xrightarrow{L} N(0, C_1) \tag{3}$$

where $C_1 = 2\{T(T-1)\}^{-1}$, and $\xrightarrow{L}$ denotes convergence in distribution.

The proof of Theorem 1 is given in the appendix, but it is instructive to sketch its outline here. The limiting distribution of $\sqrt{N}(\hat{\varphi}_{\mathrm{LSP}} - 1)$ is obtained by writing Eq. (2) as

$$(\hat{\varphi}_{\mathrm{LSP}} - 1) = \sum_{i=1}^{N} \sum_{t=1}^{T} y_{it-1} v_{it} \Big/ \sum_{i=1}^{N} \sum_{t=1}^{T} y_{it-1}^2 \tag{4}$$

and noting that for fixed T, $\sum_{t=1}^{T} y_{iT-1} v_{it}$ is a random variable, independently and identically distributed across i by Assumptions (a) and (b), with zero mean and finite variance given by $(T(T-1)/2)\sigma_v^4$. As $N \to \infty$, with T fixed, the numerator of Eq. (4) converges at the rate $\sqrt{N}$ to a normal random variable by the Linderberg–Levy CLT. The denominator converges in probability at the rate N to a non-stochastic scalar, and so the result of Theorem 1 follows by appropriately scaling the numerator and denominator of Eq. (4) and applying the Cramer–Wold lemma. It should be noted that the normality result does not require T to grow large.

Theorem 1 shows that the limiting distribution of the normalised coefficient statistic $\sqrt{N}(\hat{\varphi}_{\mathrm{LSP}} - 1)$ is normal with zero mean and variance given by C_1, which is decreasing in T. Therefore $\sqrt{N}(\hat{\varphi}_{\mathrm{LSP}} - 1)$, scaled by its asymptotic standard deviation, $C_1^{1/2}$, yields a test statistic which depends only on the estimated parameter and the known values of N and T, and thus can be readily used for statistical inference employing the critical values of the standard normal distribution.

The result of Theorem 1 is consistent with Breitung and Meyer (1994) who show that $\hat{\varphi}_{LSP}$ is a $\sqrt{N}$ consistent estimator. Theorem 1 can also be compared with Quah (1994) and Levin and Lin (1993), both of whom analyse the limiting distribution of analogous statistics in the case that both N and T grow large. For sufficiently large T, Eq. (3) becomes $T\sqrt{N}(\hat{\varphi}_{LSP} - 1) \xrightarrow{L} N(0, 2)$, which is the distribution given by Quah's Theorem 1 when the initial conditions are zero for all i, and by Theorem 4.7 of Levin and Lin for their test statistic Z_3^* in the case that the error process is i.i.d. This asymptotic result implies that $\hat{\varphi}_{LSP}$ converges at the rate $T\sqrt{N}$, which is higher than the convergence rate of the LS estimator in the stationary case. The higher convergence rate is due to the fact that as T grows large the time variability of y_{it} dominates its cross-section variability. The higher convergence rate with respect to T is known as 'super-consistency'.

It is interesting to note the consequences for inference in finite samples of assuming that T is asymptotic rather than fixed. It can be seen that the variance of the test statistic when T is assumed to be fixed is greater than its variance when T is assumed to be asymptotic by a factor of $T/(T-1)$. In small samples, therefore, the test based on the standardised test statistic assuming that T is asymptotic, using the nominal critical values of the standard normal distribution, will tend to reject the null hypothesis of a unit root too often, and hence the test will be oversized. The extent of this size distortion is investigated using Monte Carlo simulation in Section 3.

The results of Theorem 1 are specific to the case that y_{i0} is zero for all i, and thus may have limited practical application. Furthermore, if this assumption is relaxed the limiting distribution of Theorem 1 is no longer invariant to the nuisance parameters of the DGP, namely y_{i0} and σ_v^2.[6] However, a similar test statistic for the autoregressive parameter of Model (1a), which is invariant to the nuisance parameters of the DGP under the null hypothesis, even for finite samples, can be achieved by including N fixed effect dummy variables as redundant regressors in the regression model, that is by estimating, instead, Model (1b). The limiting distribution of the normalised bias statistic of $\hat{\varphi}_{LSDV}$ is given by the following theorem.

Theorem 2. If Assumption (a) holds and $\alpha_i = 0$ for all i, then under the null hypothesis that $\varphi = 1$,

$$\sqrt{N}(\hat{\varphi}_{LSDV} - 1 - B_2) \xrightarrow{L} N(0, C_2) \tag{5}$$

where $B_2 = \text{plim}_{N\to\infty}(\hat{\varphi}_{LSDV} - 1) = -3(T+1)^{-1}$ *and* $C_2 = \{3(17T^2 - 20T + 17)\}\{5(T-1)(T+1)^3\}^{-1}$.

[6] Harris and Tzavalis (1996) give the limiting distribution of $\hat{\varphi}_{LSP}$ for the more general case that $y_{i0} \neq 0$.

The proof of Theorem 2 is given in Appendix.

Theorem 2 demonstrates that for $N \to \infty$ with T fixed, $\hat{\varphi}_{\mathrm{LSDV}}$ is an inconsistent estimator, as in the stationary case that $|\varphi| < 1$. The inconsistency of $\hat{\varphi}_{\mathrm{LSDV}}$, given by B_2, is negative and depends only on T. The inconsistency arises from the elimination of an unknown constant from each observation of the panel, which yields a correlation between the mean of $y_{i,\,t-1}$ and v_{it} for each i (Hsiao, 1986). Correcting for the inconsistency of $\hat{\varphi}_{\mathrm{LSDV}}$ yields a statistic which has a normal limiting distribution with asymptotic variance, C_2.

For sufficiently large T, Eq. (5) implies that $T\sqrt{N}(\hat{\varphi}_{\mathrm{LSDV}} - 1) + 3\sqrt{N} \xrightarrow{L} \mathrm{N}(0, \frac{51}{5})$, which is consistent with the distribution of the test statistic Z_δ^* given by Theorem 4.1 of Levin and Lin (1993) for $\alpha_i = 0$.[7] The term $3\sqrt{N}$ is a necessary adjustment for the inconsistency of $\hat{\varphi}_{\mathrm{LSDV}}$ as N and T go to infinity.[8] The inconsistency remains since it is not influenced by the cross-section dimension of the panel and the convergence rate (with respect to T) of C_2 is bigger than that of B_2. Thus, as noted by Levin and Lin (1993), in contrast to the case of stationary panel data, the presence of a unit root causes the fixed effects to influence the asymptotic distribution of the panel autoregressive estimator, even as both N and T become large.

As with Theorem 1, we can analyse the consequences for inference in finite samples of assuming that T is asymptotic rather than fixed. When T is assumed to be asymptotic, the adjustment term required for the inconsistency of φ_{LSDV} is larger than when T is assumed to be fixed (by a factor of $(T+1)/T$). The variance of the statistic $\sqrt{N}(\hat{\varphi}_{\mathrm{LSDV}} - 1 - B_2)$, when T is assumed to be asymptotic, is also larger (by a factor of $17(T-1)(T+1)^3/T^2(17T^2 - 20T + 17)$), and so the variance of the *standardised* test statistic, $C^{-1/2}\sqrt{N}(\hat{\varphi}_{\mathrm{LSDV}} - 1 - B_2)$, is smaller. Together, these have the effect of shifting the distribution of the standardised test statistic to the left, relative to when T is assumed to be fixed, by

$$3\sqrt{N}\left[\left(\frac{5(T-1)(T+1)^3}{3(T+1)^2(17T^2-20T+7)}\right)^{1/2} - \left(\frac{5}{51}\right)^{1/2}\right],$$

[7] To obtain this result, and the corresponding result for Model (1c), the limiting distribution of the test statistic Z_δ^* of Levin and Lin must be adjusted for the inconsistency of the LS estimator of the autoregressive coefficient, rather than by the asymptotic mean of the numerator of the estimator. Then the variance of the limiting distribution of Z_δ^* becomes

$$\frac{\sigma_{m1}^2}{\mu_{m2}^2} + \left(\frac{\mu_{m1}}{\mu_{m2}}\right)^2 \frac{\sigma_{m2}^2}{\mu_{m2}^2},$$

where the moments for each model are computed by Levin and Lin (see their Table 1).

[8] This result is consistent with Bernard and Jones (1996) who consider panel data unit root tests when the a_i are random effects. Note that in this case the bias disappears as $N \to \infty$ and $T \to \infty$.

which increases the size of the test over the nominal level. However, since the variance of the standardised statistic is smaller when T is assumed to be asymptotic, the tails of the distribution are drawn in, which decreases the empirical size of the test. If the first of these effects dominates the second, then the test will be oversized and will reject the null hypothesis of a unit root too often when using the nominal critical values of the standard normal distribution. If the second effect is dominant, then the test will be undersized and hence have low power to reject the null hypothesis. The relative importance of these effects are investigated using Monte Carlo simulation in Section 3.

The results of Theorem 2 are specific to the case that $\alpha_i = 0$ for all i. In the more general case that $\alpha_i \neq 0$, the test statistic given by Theorem 2 will depend on the nuisance parameters of the DGP, namely α_i and σ_v^2.[9] However, similarity with respect to these nuisance parameters can be achieved by including individual deterministic trends in the regression model, that is by estimating instead regression Model (1c). In this case, the limiting distribution of the test statistic is given by the following theorem.

Theorem 3. If Assumption (a) holds and $\beta_i = 0$ for all i, then under the null hypothesis that $\varphi = 1$

$$\sqrt{N}(\hat{\varphi}_{\mathrm{LSDVT}} - 1 - B_3) \xrightarrow{L} \mathrm{N}(0, C_3) \tag{6}$$

where $B_3 = \mathrm{plim}_{N\to\infty}(\hat{\varphi}_{\mathrm{LSDVT}} - 1) = -15\{2(T+2)\}^{-1}$ *and* $C_3 = \{15(193T^2 - 728T + 1147)\}\{112(T+2)^3(T-2)\}^{-1}$.

The proof of Theorem 3 is given in Appendix.

The inconsistency of $\hat{\varphi}_{\mathrm{LSDVT}}$, given by B_3, is larger than in the case of Theorem 2. This is due to the fact that now, in addition to an unknown constant, a linear trend is subtracted from each observation which leads to greater correlation between the mean of $y_{i,t-1}$ and v_{it} for each i.

For T sufficiently large, Eq. (8) implies that $T\sqrt{N}(\hat{\varphi}_{\mathrm{LSDV}} - 1) + 7.5\sqrt{N} \xrightarrow{L} \mathrm{N}(0, 2895/112)$, which is consistent with the distribution of the test statistic Z_δ^* given by Theorem 4.1 of Levin and Lin (1993) for $\alpha_i \neq 0$ (see footnote 7). Note that in this case, since $B_3 > B_2$, the adjustment factor that is required for the inconsistency which remains as N and T go to infinity is bigger than that corresponding to Theorem 2.

[9] Harris and Tzavalis (1996) consider the case that $\alpha_i \neq 0$. When $N = 1$ and $T \to \infty$, this corresponds to Theorem 3.1 of West (1988).

We can again consider the consequences for inference in finite samples of assuming that T is asymptotic rather than fixed. As with Theorem 2, using the moments based on asymptotic T rather than fixed T to compute the test statistic has two counteracting effects on the size of the test. When T is assumed to be asymptotic, the magnitude of the adjustment for the inconsistency of φ_{LSDVT} is larger (by a factor of $(T+2)/T$). The variance of the statistic $\sqrt{N}(\hat{\varphi}_{\text{LSDVT}} - 1 - B_2)$ is larger (by a factor of $15T^2(193T^2 - 728T + 1147)/2895(T-2)(T+2)^3$) and so the variance of the *standardised* test statistic, $C^{-1/2}\sqrt{N}(\hat{\varphi}_{\text{LSDVT}} - 1 - B_2)$ is smaller. Together, these have the effect of shifting the distribution of the standardised statistic to the left by

$$7.5\sqrt{N}\left[\left(\frac{112(T-2)(T+2)^3}{15(T+2)^2(193T^2 - 728T + 1147)}\right)^{1/2} - \left(\frac{112}{2895}\right)^{1/2}\right],$$

which increases the size of the test over the nominal level. On the other hand, since the variance of the standardised statistic is smaller when T is assumed to be asymptotic, the tails of the distribution are drawn in, which decreases the empirical size of the test.

3. Simulation experiments

In this section we present two sets of Monte Carlo experiments. The first assesses the finite sample accuracy of the limiting distributions and the power of the test statistics derived in this paper. We perform these experiments for the normalised coefficient statistic corresponding to the simple case of Theorem 1 and the similar tests suggested by Theorems 2 and 3. The second set of experiments investigates the consequences for inference in finite samples of using the test statistics based on asymptotic T, rather than fixed T. This enables us to judge the appropriate size of T that can be reasonably considered to be asymptotic.

The empirical quantiles of the tests and their size for different combinations of N and T, using 5000 replications, are reported in Table 1a–c. The last column of the table gives the true size of a one-sided test with critical values taken from the standard normal distribution at the nominal 5% level of significance. For comparison, we also include in the tables the corresponding quantiles of the standard normal distribution. The null model is given in each table. In each experiment, the data are generated according to the null model with disturbance terms drawn independently from the standard normal distribution.

Table 1a–c show that the standard normal distribution accurately approximates the empirical distribution of the test statistics for the cases where N is large relative to T, which is typical in most dynamic panels, or for sufficiently large N. Consequently, for these cases the tests have empirical size very close to the nominal 5% level. On the other hand, for panels of very small N and relatively large T the empirical distribution approaches the Dickey–Fuller density (Dickey and Fuller, 1981). This is because the time dimension of the panel in this case dominates the cross-section dimension. The slight size deterioration observed in Table 1a for small T and N (such as $\{T, N\} = \{5, 5\}$) may be due to the fact that for $\hat{\varphi}_{\text{LSP}}$, finite ($T$) sample results depend on y_{i0} (Abadir, 1993).

The empirical power of the tests is reported in Table 2a–c. We generate data according to the three alternative hypotheses that $\varphi = 0.8$, $\varphi = 0.9$ and $\varphi = 0.95$ respectively, and tabulate both the size-adjusted power using the actual 5% critical values taken from Table 1a–c and the nominal power using the 5% critical values of the standard normal distribution. In all experiments y_{i0} was set to zero (as in Im et al., 1995). Using the size adjusted power enables us to better judge the relative performance of the three tests for small N, where the actual

Table 1a
Empirical quantiles of $C_1^{-1/2}\sqrt{N}(\hat{\varphi}_{\text{LSP}} - 1)$ for $(y_{i0}, \varphi) = (0, 1)$

T	N	1%	5%	10%	50%	90%	95%	99%	Size
5	5	− 3.76	− 2.52	− 1.92	− 0.14	1.03	1.34	1.91	0.13
5	10	− 3.31	− 2.23	− 1.71	− 0.12	1.10	1.39	2.03	0.10
5	25	− 2.88	− 1.95	− 1.49	− 0.05	1.14	1.46	2.06	0.08
5	50	− 2.89	− 1.84	− 1.39	− 0.04	1.17	1.48	2.07	0.07
5	100	− 2.60	− 1.82	− 1.38	− 0.01	1.18	1.51	2.16	0.07
10	5	− 4.37	− 2.71	− 2.04	− 0.21	0.95	1.20	1.71	0.14
10	10	− 3.75	− 2.27	− 1.71	− 0.11	1.02	1.31	1.80	0.11
10	25	− 3.06	− 2.00	− 1.54	− 0.07	1.10	1.40	1.95	0.08
10	50	− 2.86	− 1.91	− 1.45	− 0.04	1.14	1.47	2.04	0.07
10	100	− 2.60	− 1.83	− 1.43	− 0.04	1.18	1.49	2.08	0.07
25	5	− 4.45	− 2.85	− 2.06	− 0.24	0.92	1.18	1.60	0.15
25	10	− 3.77	− 2.43	− 1.82	− 0.15	1.00	1.31	1.81	0.12
25	25	− 3.10	− 2.05	− 1.55	− 0.09	1.07	1.38	1.91	0.09
25	50	− 2.82	− 1.95	− 1.51	− 0.06	1.15	1.44	2.00	0.08
25	100	− 2.60	− 1.84	− 1.43	− 0.05	1.17	1.47	2.02	0.07
50	5	− 4.94	− 2.94	− 2.14	− 0.22	0.90	1.17	1.62	0.15
50	10	− 3.99	− 2.41	− 1.79	− 0.13	1.02	1.26	1.72	0.12
50	25	− 3.13	− 2.18	− 1.60	− 0.09	1.09	1.38	1.86	0.09
50	50	− 2.67	− 1.85	− 1.44	− 0.09	1.10	1.40	1.95	0.07
50	100	− 2.72	− 1.78	− 1.35	− 0.05	1.15	1.49	2.11	0.06
$N(0, 1)$		− 2.33	− 1.65	− 1.28	0.00	1.28	1.65	2.33	

Table 1b
Empirical quantiles of $C_2^{-1/2}\sqrt{N}(\hat{\phi}_{\text{LSDV}} - 1 - B_2)$ for $(\alpha_i, \varphi) = (0, 1)$

T	N	1%	5%	10%	50%	90%	95%	99%	Size
5	5	− 2.82	− 2.03	− 1.62	− 0.14	1.14	1.50	2.14	0.09
5	10	− 2.83	− 1.97	− 1.54	− 0.09	1.14	1.51	2.06	0.08
5	25	− 2.60	− 1.85	− 1.44	− 0.06	1.21	1.54	2.12	0.07
5	50	− 2.55	− 1.79	− 1.40	− 0.04	1.26	1.60	2.20	0.07
5	100	− 2.45	− 1.77	− 1.40	− 0.04	1.22	1.57	2.27	0.06
10	5	− 3.27	− 2.24	− 1.68	− 0.19	1.03	1.33	1.88	0.10
10	10	− 2.97	− 2.02	− 1.57	− 0.12	1.09	1.40	1.96	0.09
10	25	− 2.81	− 1.98	− 1.51	− 0.09	1.18	1.52	2.13	0.08
10	50	− 2.66	− 1.88	− 1.48	− 0.05	1.22	1.60	2.18	0.07
10	100	− 2.60	− 1.82	− 1.44	− 0.04	1.24	1.60	2.18	0.06
25	5	− 3.44	− 2.36	− 1.81	− 0.21	0.95	1.24	1.67	0.12
25	10	− 3.14	− 2.14	− 1.66	− 0.12	1.08	1.35	1.86	0.10
25	25	− 3.00	− 1.97	− 1.55	− 0.06	1.19	1.51	2.99	0.08
25	50	− 2.75	− 1.96	− 1.52	− 0.06	1.24	1.57	2.11	0.08
25	100	− 2.68	− 1.81	− 1.44	− 0.05	1.23	1.60	2.33	0.07
50	5	− 3.58	− 2.41	− 1.83	− 0.17	0.98	1.25	1.67	0.12
50	10	− 3.15	− 2.09	− 1.65	− 0.15	1.00	1.32	1.85	0.10
50	25	− 3.02	− 1.99	− 1.53	− 0.10	1.14	1.44	2.17	0.08
50	50	− 2.64	− 1.86	− 1.44	− 0.07	1.19	1.53	2.12	0.07
50	100	− 2.67	− 1.84	− 1.43	− 0.06	1.25	1.61	2.20	0.07
$N(0, 1)$		− 2.33	− 1.65	− 1.28	0.00	1.28	1.65	2.33	

bias of the LS estimators may not be well approximated by the inconsistency given by Theorems 1–3. As N grows large, the size adjusted power tends to the nominal power. For the test given by Theorem 2 the data are generated assuming that the intercept, α_i, is set to zero for all i under both the null and alternative hypotheses, ensuring that the mean of Δy_{it} is the same in both cases. For the test given by Theorem 3 the data are generated according to $y_{it} = \alpha_i + \beta_i t + \varphi y_{it-1} + u_{it}$, where α_i is drawn once for each i from the standard normal distribution and $\beta_i = \alpha_i(1 - \varphi)$. This specification ensures that the intercept parameter is the same under both the null and the alternative hypotheses and thus enables us to evaluate the ability of the test to reject the null hypothesis of a unit root against the trend stationary alternative, where the rate of trend is the same under both the null and alternative hypotheses.

As expected, the estimated power of the tests is very low for values of φ very close to unity and increases monotonically with both N and T. For all three

Table 1c

Empirical quantiles of $C_3^{-1/2}\sqrt{N}(\hat{\varphi}_{\mathrm{LSDVT}} - 1 - B_3)$ for $(\beta_i, \varphi) = (0, 1)$ and α_i drawn from $N(0, 1)$ once for each i

T	N	1%	5%	10%	50%	90%	95%	99%	Size
5	5	− 2.37	− 1.71	− 1.36	− 0.12	1.21	1.58	2.48	0.06
5	10	− 2.28	− 1.65	− 1.30	− 0.09	1.24	1.62	2.33	0.05
5	25	− 2.31	− 1.67	− 1.36	− 0.05	1.24	1.55	2.31	0.05
5	50	− 2.43	− 1.66	− 1.30	− 0.03	1.25	1.61	2.23	0.05
5	100	− 2.29	− 1.63	− 1.26	− 0.02	1.23	1.60	2.30	0.05
10	5	− 2.61	− 1.84	− 1.45	− 0.14	1.10	1.45	2.01	0.07
10	10	− 2.48	− 1.77	− 1.41	− 0.10	1.15	1.46	2.05	0.06
10	25	− 2.45	− 1.78	− 1.39	− 0.06	1.19	1.52	2.18	0.06
10	50	− 2.49	− 1.76	− 1.36	− 0.05	1.21	1.57	2.17	0.06
10	100	− 2.47	− 1.71	− 1.33	− 0.05	1.22	1.59	2.21	0.05
25	5	− 2.92	− 2.02	− 1.58	− 0.14	1.00	1.30	1.81	0.09
25	10	− 2.80	− 1.95	− 1.52	− 0.08	1.08	1.40	1.87	0.08
25	25	− 2.63	− 1.77	− 1.40	− 0.06	1.14	1.46	2.00	0.06
25	50	− 2.57	− 1.76	− 1.38	− 0.06	1.17	1.51	2.09	0.06
25	100	− 2.44	− 1.75	− 1.40	− 0.03	1.26	1.57	2.21	0.06
50	5	− 3.03	− 2.06	− 1.57	− 0.16	0.97	1.30	1.84	0.09
50	10	− 2.82	− 1.97	− 1.54	− 0.09	1.09	1.37	1.96	0.09
50	25	− 2.61	− 1.81	− 1.42	− 0.06	1.13	1.44	2.01	0.07
50	50	− 2.46	− 1.72	− 1.35	− 0.05	1.19	1.52	2.15	0.06
50	100	− 2.48	− 1.73	− 1.33	0.04	1.22	1.57	2.18	0.06
$N(0, 1)$		− 2.33	− 1.65	− 1.28	0.00	1.28	1.65	2.33	

tests, as N grows large the power approaches its maximum value of unity even for very small T. The power improves faster as T increases (with N given) than as N increases (with T given). It is also interesting to note that the power achieves its maximum value for sizes of T which are much smaller than for the corresponding single time series Dickey–Fuller tests (see, for instance, Dickey and Fuller, 1981), suggesting that for given T, the power is an increasing function of N due to the increased information content of the sample arising from its cross-section variation.

The deterioration of the estimated power of the normalised coefficient statistics associated with Theorems 2 and 3, compared with Theorem 1, is a consequence of including redundant regressors in the unit root regressions to achieve test similarity with regard to the nuisance parameters of the DGP (Kiviet and Phillips, 1992). The loss in power is the price paid for the property of similarity.

Table 2a
Empirical power of $C_1^{-1/2}\sqrt{N}(\hat{\varphi}_{LSP} - 1)$

		$\varphi = 0.8$		$\varphi = 0.9$		$\varphi = 0.95$	
T	N	Size adjusted	Nominal	Size adjusted	Nominal	Size adjusted	Nominal
5	5	0.24	0.47	0.12	0.26	0.08	0.19
5	10	0.47	0.64	0.19	0.33	0.10	0.19
5	25	0.86	0.92	0.39	0.49	0.16	0.23
5	50	0.99	0.99	0.65	0.72	0.25	0.31
5	100	1.00	1.00	0.90	0.93	0.40	0.47
10	5	0.63	0.88	0.25	0.52	0.12	0.31
10	10	0.94	0.98	0.49	0.68	0.20	0.34
10	25	1.00	1.00	0.89	0.94	0.40	0.53
10	50	1.00	1.00	0.99	0.99	0.67	0.76
10	100	1.00	1.00	1.00	1.00	0.93	0.95
25	5	0.99	1.00	0.79	0.96	0.33	0.66
25	10	1.00	1.00	0.99	0.99	0.64	0.84
25	25	1.00	1.00	1.00	1.00	0.97	0.99
25	50	1.00	1.00	1.00	1.00	1.00	1.00
25	100	1.00	1.00	1.00	1.00	1.00	1.00
50	5	1.00	1.00	0.99	1.00	0.77	0.96
50	10	1.00	1.00	1.00	1.00	0.99	0.99
50	25	1.00	1.00	1.00	1.00	1.00	1.00
50	50	1.00	1.00	1.00	1.00	1.00	1.00
50	100	1.00	1.00	1.00	1.00	1.00	1.00

The results of the second set of experiments are reported in Table 3. The table gives the size and power of the tests suggested by Theorems 1–3 using the 5% critical values of the standard normal distribution. The test statistics are constructed under the assumption that T is large. The power is considered against the alternative hypothesis that $\varphi = 0.95$.[10] The data are generated in the same way as for the first set of experiments.

For the test statistic implied by Theorem 1, Table 3 indicates that the assumption that T is asymptotic rather than fixed leads to a test that is oversized (cf. Table 1a). The size distortion is much more serious for small T, such as $T = \{5, 10\}$, but becomes negligible once T reaches about 25 observations, where both tests have approximately the same size. Consistent with the increase

[10] The estimates of the power for the other values of φ are not reported for reasons of space.

Table 2b
Empirical power of $C_2^{-1/2}\sqrt{N}(\hat{\varphi}_{\mathrm{LSDV}} - 1 - B_2)$

		$\varphi = 0.8$		$\varphi = 0.9$		$\varphi = 0.95$	
T	N	Size adjusted	Nominal	Size adjusted	Nominal	Size adjusted	Nominal
5	5	0.18	0.29	0.10	0.18	0.07	0.13
5	10	0.30	0.41	0.15	0.22	0.09	0.14
5	25	0.62	0.69	0.28	0.39	0.13	0.17
5	50	0.90	0.91	0.47	0.51	0.20	0.23
5	100	1.00	1.00	0.72	0.76	0.31	0.35
10	5	0.30	0.50	0.15	0.30	0.09	0.19
10	10	0.58	0.70	0.28	0.40	0.14	0.23
10	25	0.90	0.94	0.54	0.64	0.24	0.34
10	50	0.99	0.99	0.82	0.87	0.40	0.48
10	100	1.00	1.00	0.98	0.98	0.66	0.71
25	5	0.80	0.93	0.37	0.59	0.18	0.36
25	10	0.98	0.99	0.66	0.79	0.31	0.47
25	25	1.00	1.00	0.96	0.97	0.63	0.73
25	50	1.00	1.00	1.00	1.00	0.88	1.00
25	100	1.00	1.00	1.00	1.00	0.99	0.99
50	5	1.00	1.00	0.76	0.92	0.35	0.58
50	10	1.00	1.00	0.98	0.99	0.66	0.78
50	25	1.00	1.00	1.00	1.00	0.95	0.97
50	50	1.00	1.00	1.00	1.00	1.00	1.00
50	100	1.00	1.00	1.00	1.00	1.00	1.00

in size, for small T the power of the test is greater than when T is assumed to be fixed (cf. Table 2a).

For the test statistics associated with Theorems 2 and 3, Table 3 shows that the assumption that T is asymptotic rather than fixed yields a test which is substantially undersized (cf. Table 1b and c). It was noted in Section 2 that this assumption has two counteracting effects on the size of the test : the distribution of the standardised test statistic is shifted to the left (increasing the size of the test), but the variance of the standardised statistic is smaller (reducing the size of the test). The results of Table 3 indicate that the variance effect dominates the mean shift effect, resulting in a net reduction in the size of the test. The consequence of this is a considerable decrease in the power of the test to reject the null hypothesis (cf. Table 2b and c). The differences in the size and the power of the tests based on fixed T and asymptotic T disappear for values of T greater than about 50 observations.

Table 2c
Empirical power of $C_3^{-1/2}\sqrt{N}(\hat{\varphi}_{LSDVT} - 1 - B_3)$

		$\varphi = 0.8$		$\varphi = 0.9$		$\varphi = 0.95$	
T	N	Size adjusted	Nominal	Size adjusted	Nominal	Size adjusted	Nominal
5	5	0.05	0.06	0.05	0.05	0.05	0.05
5	10	0.05	0.05	0.04	0.05	0.04	0.04
5	25	0.07	0.08	0.05	0.06	0.05	0.06
5	50	0.08	0.08	0.05	0.06	0.05	0.08
5	100	0.11	0.11	0.06	0.06	0.05	0.05
10	5	0.08	0.11	0.06	0.08	0.05	0.07
10	10	0.12	0.14	0.07	0.08	0.06	0.07
10	25	0.17	0.20	0.08	0.09	0.06	0.07
10	50	0.26	0.30	0.08	0.10	0.06	0.07
10	100	0.44	0.47	0.11	0.13	0.06	0.07
25	5	0.30	0.43	0.10	0.17	0.06	0.11
25	10	0.51	0.61	0.14	0.21	0.07	0.11
25	25	0.91	0.92	0.27	0.31	0.09	0.11
25	50	0.99	0.99	0.44	0.48	0.12	0.14
25	100	1.00	1.00	0.69	0.72	0.17	0.19
50	5	0.89	0.95	0.30	0.43	0.10	0.17
50	10	0.99	0.99	0.50	0.62	0.15	0.21
50	25	1.00	1.00	0.89	0.92	0.26	0.31
50	50	1.00	1.00	0.99	0.99	0.44	0.47
50	100	1.00	1.00	1.00	1.00	0.68	0.71

4. Conclusions

This paper introduces similar, asymptotic unit root tests for first order autoregressive panel data models where the time dimension of the panel is fixed, allowing for fixed effects and individual deterministic trends. The tests are based on the normalised LS estimator of the autoregressive coefficient, corrected where appropriate for its inconsistency. The inconsistency arises as a result of the inclusion of fixed effects and individual trends in the regression model, and is influenced only by T. The limiting distributions of the tests are shown to be normal. Comparisons are made with the limiting distributions of the corresponding test statistics given by Quah (1994) and Levin and Lin (1993), who consider the case that both N and T grow large. Monte Carlo experiments suggest that the standard normal density accurately approximates the empirical distributions of the tests, and that for sufficiently large N the tests have an empirical size very close to the nominal 5% level. The power performance of the tests against local alternatives is found to be considerably better than that of the

Table 3
Size and power of the tests at the nominal level 5% ($\varphi = 0.95$), assuming that T is large

		Statistic 1		Statistic 2		Statistic 3	
T	N	Size	Power	Size	Power	Size	Power
5	5	0.15	0.22	0.01	0.02	0.01	0.00
5	10	0.12	0.23	0.01	0.02	0.00	0.00
5	25	0.10	0.28	0.00	0.01	0.00	0.00
5	50	0.09	0.37	0.00	0.00	0.00	0.00
5	100	0.08	0.54	0.00	0.00	0.00	0.00
10	5	0.15	0.32	0.05	0.10	0.02	0.02
10	10	0.11	0.37	0.03	0.10	0.01	0.01
10	25	0.09	0.56	0.02	0.14	0.01	0.01
10	50	0.08	0.79	0.01	0.19	0.01	0.02
10	100	0.08	0.95	0.00	0.27	0.01	0.01
25	5	0.15	0.67	0.09	0.30	0.06	0.07
25	10	0.12	0.85	0.07	0.39	0.05	0.07
25	25	0.09	0.99	0.05	0.64	0.04	0.07
25	50	0.08	1.00	0.04	0.86	0.03	0.09
25	100	0.07	1.00	0.02	0.98	0.03	0.12
50	5	0.15	0.96	0.11	0.56	0.07	0.15
50	10	0.11	0.99	0.08	0.75	0.06	0.18
50	25	0.09	1.00	0.06	0.96	0.05	0.27
50	50	0.07	1.00	0.05	1.00	0.04	0.42
50	100	0.06	1.00	0.05	1.00	0.04	0.68

Statistic 1 is $2^{-1/2}T\sqrt{N}(\hat{\phi}_{\mathrm{LSP}} - 1)$, corresponding to Theorem 1.
Statistic 2 is $(5/51)^{-1/2}(T\sqrt{N}(\hat{\phi}_{\mathrm{LSDV}} - 1) + 3\sqrt{N})$, corresponding to Theorem 2.
Statistic 3 is $(112/2895)^{-1/2}(T\sqrt{N}(\hat{\phi}_{\mathrm{LSDVT}} - 1) + 7.5\sqrt{N})$, corresponding to Theorem 3.

single time series Dickey–Fuller tests and increases monotonically with both T and N. Furthermore, it is shown that the assumption that T is asymptotic yields a test which has substantially reduced power in small T samples.

Acknowledgements

The authors thank C. Hsiao (the editor), three anonymous referees, K. Abadir, K. Hadri, M. Magdalinos, M.H. Pesaran, G.D.A. Phillips, Z. Psaradakis, D. Quah, R. Smith, the participants at the Sixth Biennial International Conference on Panel Data, Amsterdam 1996, and at the Econometric Society European Meeting, Istanbul 1996, for helpful discussions and comments.

Appendix A.

This appendix contains the proofs of the theorems that are given in the main text. The derivations of the results are based on the Linderberg–Levy version of the Central Limit Theorem, the Strong Law of Large Numbers (SLLN), and the results of the following Lemma.

Lemma A.1. Let $\varepsilon_{it} = \sum_{t=1}^{t} v_{it}$, then

(a) $\sum_{t=1}^{T} \varepsilon_{it-1} = \sum_{t=1}^{T} (T-t) v_{it}$,

(b) $\sum_{t=1}^{T} \varepsilon_{it-1}^2 = \sum_{t=1}^{T} (T-t) v_{it}^2 + 2\sum_{t=1}^{T-1} \sum_{s=t+1}^{T} (T-s) v_{it} v_{is}$,

(c) $\sum_{t=1}^{T} \varepsilon_{it-1} v_{it} = \sum_{t=1}^{T-1} \sum_{s=t+1}^{T} v_{it} v_{is}$,

(d) $\sum_{t=1}^{T} t\varepsilon_{it-1} = \sum_{t=1}^{T} ((T+t+1)(T-t)/2) v_{it}$,

(e) $\sum_{t=1}^{T} \varepsilon_{it-1} \sum_{t=1}^{T} v_{it} = \sum_{t=1}^{T} (T-t) v_{it}^2 + \sum_{t=1}^{T-1} \sum_{s=t+1}^{T} (2T-s-t) v_{it} v_{is}$,

(f)
$$\sum_{t=1}^{T} t\varepsilon_{it-1} \sum_{t=1}^{T} v_{it} = \sum_{t=1}^{T} ((T+t+1)(T-t)/2) v_{it}^2 + \sum_{t=1}^{T-1} \sum_{s=t+1}^{T} ((T+t+1)(T-t) + (T+s+1)(T-s)/2) v_{it} v_{is},$$

(g)
$$\sum_{t=1}^{T} t\varepsilon_{it-1} \sum_{t=1}^{T} t v_{it} = \sum_{t=1}^{T} ((T+t+1)(T-t)t/2) v_{it}^2 + \sum_{t=1}^{T-1} \sum_{s=t+1}^{T} ((T+t+1)(T-t)s + (T+s+1)(T-s)t/2) v_{it} v_{is},$$

(h)
$$\sum_{t=1}^{T} t\varepsilon_{it-1} \sum_{t=1}^{T} \varepsilon_{it-1} = \sum_{t=1}^{T} ((T+t+1)(T-t)^2/2) v_{it}^2 + \sum_{t=1}^{T-1} \sum_{s=t+1}^{T} ((T-t)(T-s) \times (2T+t+s+2)/2) v_{it} v_{is}.$$

Proof. Results (a)–(d) follow immediately from the definition of ε_{it}, while results (e)–(h) follow by using (a)–(d) and the general result that, for any functions $f(\cdot)$ and $g(\cdot)$

$$\sum_{t=1}^{T} f(t)v_{it} \sum_{t=1}^{T} g(t)v_{it} = \sum_{t=1}^{T} f(t)g(t)v_{it}^2 + \sum_{t=1}^{T-1} \sum_{s=t+1}^{T} [f(t)g(s) + f(s)g(t)]v_{it}v_{is}.$$

Proof of Theorem 1. Define $w_{iT} = \sum_{t=1}^{T} \varepsilon_{it-1} v_{it}$. Since by Assumption (a), v_{it} and ε_{it-1} are independent across i, and v_{it} are i.i.d. across i and t, $\{w_{iT}\}$ is an independent random sequence across i with mean zero and constant variance, given by $\sigma_{w_T}^2 = \sigma_v^4 \sum_{t=1}^{T}(t-1) = \sigma_v^4 T(T-1)/2 < \infty$. Applying the CLT, for $N \to \infty$, to the sum of $\{w_{iT}\}$ yields

$$\frac{1}{\sqrt{N}} \sum_{i=1}^{N} \frac{w_{iT}}{\sigma_{w_T}} \xrightarrow{L} \mathrm{N}(0, 1) \tag{A.1}$$

The numerator of Eq. (4) can be expanded by recursive substitution to yield

$$\sum_{i=1}^{N} \sum_{t=1}^{T} y_{it-1} v_{it} = \sum_{i=1}^{N} \sum_{t=1}^{T} y_{i0} v_{it} + \sum_{i=1}^{N} w_{i,T} \tag{A.2}$$

which using Eq. (A.1) implies

$$\frac{1}{\sqrt{N}} \sum_{i=1}^{N} \frac{1}{\sigma_{w_T}} \sum_{t=1}^{T} y_{it-1} v_{it} \xrightarrow{L} \mathrm{N}(0, 1) \tag{A.3}$$

since $y_{i0} = 0$. Note that the last result implies that $\hat{\varphi}_{\mathrm{LSP}}$ is $\sqrt{N}$ consistent. Expanding the denominator in a similar fashion, and noting that v_{it} are independent across i, implies that

$$\operatorname*{plim}_{N \to \infty} \frac{1}{N} \sum_{i=1}^{N} \sum_{t=1}^{T} y_{it-1}^2 = \sum_{t=1}^{T} (T-t) \operatorname*{plim}_{N \to \infty} \frac{1}{N} \sum_{i=1}^{N} v_{it}^2 = \frac{T(T-1)}{2} \sigma_v^2 \tag{A.4}$$

where

$$\operatorname*{plim}_{N \to \infty} \frac{1}{N} \sum_{i=1}^{N} v_{it}^2 = \sigma_v^2$$

by the SLLN. Theorem 1 follows by scaling Eqs. (A.3) and (A.4) appropriately and applying the Cramer–Wold lemma.

Proof of Theorem 2. In order to prove Theorem 2, we proceed in two stages. We first show that $\hat{\varphi}_{\mathrm{LSDV}}$ is an inconsistent estimator, and derive the inconsistency for $N \to \infty$. We then construct a normalised coefficient statistic corrected for the inconsistency and derive its limiting distribution.

Decompose the vector $y_{i,-1}$ under the null hypothesis that $\varphi = 1$ and $a_i = 0$, as

$$y_{i,-1} = e_T y_{i0} + C_T v_i$$

where C_T is the $(T \times T)$ matrix

$$C_T = \begin{bmatrix} 0 & . & . & 0 \\ 1 & 0 & . & 0 \\ . & . & . & . \\ 1 & 1 & . & 0 \end{bmatrix}$$

and note that, since $Q_T e_T = 0$ (where $Q_T = M_T$), it follows that $Q_T y_{i,-1} = Q_T C_T v_i$. Then Eq. (2) can be written as the ratio

$$\hat{\varphi}_{\mathrm{LSDV}} - 1 = \left[\sum_{i=1}^{N} v_i' C_T' Q_T C_T v_i\right]^{-1} \left[\sum_{i=1}^{N} v_i' C_T' Q_T v_i\right]. \tag{A.5}$$

Dividing both terms of this ratio by σ_v^2 yields a ratio of two summands consisting of quadratic forms in standardised variables which are invariant to y_{i0} and σ_v^2, even in finite samples, thus implying that $\hat{\varphi}_{\mathrm{LSDV}}$ can be used to construct a similar test with respect to the nuisance parameters of Model (1a).

The inconsistency of $\hat{\varphi}_{\mathrm{LSDV}}$ can be derived by writing Eq. (2) based on Eq. (A.5) as

$$\hat{\varphi}_{\mathrm{LSDV}} - 1 = \sum_{i=1}^{N} w_{iT}' \Big/ \sum_{i=1}^{N} D_{iT}' \tag{A.6}$$

where

$$\begin{aligned} w_{iT}' &= \sum_{t=1}^{T} \varepsilon_{it-1} v_{it} - \frac{1}{T} \sum_{t=1}^{T} \varepsilon_{it-1} \sum_{t=1}^{T} v_{it} \\ &= \sum_{t=1}^{T-1} \sum_{s=t+1}^{T} v_{it} v_{is} - \frac{1}{T}\left[\sum_{t=1}^{T} (T-t) v_{it}^2 \right. \\ &\quad \left. + \sum_{t=1}^{T-1} \sum_{s=t+1}^{T} (2T - s - t) v_{it} v_{is}\right] \end{aligned}$$

$$= \sum_{t=1}^{T} \omega_1'(t) v_{iT}^2 + \sum_{t=1}^{T-1} \sum_{s=t+1}^{T} \omega_2'(t,s) v_{it} v_{is}$$

$$D_{iT}' = \sum_{t=1}^{T} \varepsilon_{it-1}^2 - \frac{1}{T}\left(\sum_{t=1}^{T} \varepsilon_{it-1}\right)^2$$

$$= \sum_{t=1}^{T} \delta_1'(t) v_{it}^2 + \sum_{t=1}^{T-1} \sum_{s=t+1}^{T} \delta_2'(t,s) v_{it} v_{is},$$

$$\omega_1'(t) = -(T-t)/T, \quad \omega_2'(t,s) = -(T-s-t)/T,$$

$$\delta_1'(t) = t(T-t)/T \quad \text{and} \quad \delta_2'(t,s) = 2t(T-s)/T.$$

The probability limit of the numerator of Eq. (A.6) is

$$\operatorname*{plim}_{N\to\infty} \frac{1}{N} \sum_{i=1}^{N} w_{iT}' = \sum_{t=1}^{T} \omega_1'(t)\left(\operatorname*{plim}_{N\to\infty} \frac{1}{N} \sum_{i=1}^{N} v_{it}^2\right) + \sum_{t=1}^{T-1} \sum_{s=t+1}^{T} \omega_2'(t,s)\left(\operatorname*{plim}_{N\to\infty} \frac{1}{N} \sum_{t=1}^{N} v_{it} v_{is}\right) = -\frac{(T-1)\sigma_v^2}{2}.$$

The probability of the denominator of Eq. (A.6) is

$$\operatorname*{plim}_{N\to\infty} \frac{1}{N} \sum_{i=1}^{N} D_{iT}' = \sum_{t=1}^{T} \delta_1'(t)\left(\operatorname*{plim}_{N\to\infty} \frac{1}{N} \sum_{i=1}^{N} v_{it}^2\right) - \frac{1}{T} \sum_{t=1}^{T-1} \sum_{s=t+1}^{T} \delta_2'(t,s)\left(\operatorname*{plim}_{N\to\infty} \frac{1}{N} \sum_{i=1}^{N} v_{it} v_{is}\right) = \frac{(T^2-1)\sigma_v^2}{6}$$

and so by the Slutzky theorem, the inconsistency of $\hat{\varphi}_{\mathrm{LSDV}}$ is

$$B_2 = \operatorname*{plim}_{N\to\infty} (\hat{\varphi}_{\mathrm{LSDV}} - 1) = \frac{\operatorname{plim}_{N\to\infty} \frac{1}{N} \sum_{i=1}^{N} w_{iT}'}{\operatorname{plim}_{N\to\infty} \frac{1}{N} \sum_{i=1}^{n} D_{iT}'} = \frac{-3}{T+1}. \tag{A.7}$$

Subtracting the inconsistency given by Eq. (A.7) from both sides of Eq. (A.6) yields

$$\hat{\varphi}_{\mathrm{LSDV}} - 1 - B_2 = \frac{\sum_{i=1}^{N} w_{iT}'}{\sum_{i=1}^{N} D_{iT}'} - B_2 = \frac{\sum_{i=1}^{N} x_{iT}'}{\sum_{i=1}^{N} D_{iT}'} \tag{A.8}$$

where $x'_{iT} = w'_{iT} - B_2 D'_{iT}$ is an i.i.d. process, with zero mean, and variance given by

$$\mathrm{Var}(x'_{iT}) = \frac{(T-1)(T-2)(2T-1)}{15T(T+1)}k + \frac{(T-1)(17T^3-44T^2+77T-24)}{60T(T+1)}\sigma_v^4$$

where $\mathrm{Var}(x'_{iT})$ is derived by writing

$$\mathrm{Var}(x'_{iT}) = \mathrm{E}(w'^2_{iT}) + B_2^2\mathrm{E}(D'^2_{iT}) - 2B_2\mathrm{E}(w'_{iT}D'_{iT})$$

and using the following results:

$$\mathrm{E}(w'^2_{iT}) = \frac{(2T-1)(T-1)}{6T}k + \frac{(T-1)(2T^2-4T+3)}{6T}\sigma_v^4,$$

$$\mathrm{E}(D'^2_{iT}) = \frac{(T^2-1)(T^2+1)}{30T}k + \frac{(T^2-1)(T-2)(T^2+1)}{20T}\sigma_v^4,$$

$$\mathrm{E}(w'_{iT}D'_{iT}) = -\frac{(T^2-1)}{12}k - \frac{(T^2-1)(T-2)}{12}\sigma_v^4,$$

where $k = \mathrm{E}(v_{it}^4)$ exists by Assumption (a).

The result of Theorem 2 follows by scaling Eq. (A.8) appropriately, performing manipulations similar to those in Theorem 1, and noting that for the normal distribution, $k/\sigma^4 = 3$.[11]

Proof of Theorem 3. The proof of Theorem 3 follows the same steps as that of Theorem 2. Decompose the vector $y_{i,-1}$, under the null hypothesis that $\beta_i = 0$ and $\varphi = 1$, as

$$y_{i,-1} = e_T y_{i0} + C_T e_T \alpha_i + C_T v_i$$

[11] Relaxing the normality assumption requires the existence of the fourth moment $\mathrm{E}(v_{it}^4)$ in order to derive a limiting distribution of the test statistic given by Theorem 2. Implementation of the test then requires consistent estimation of the kurtosis coefficient under the null hypothesis.

and note that $Q_T Z_T = Q_T(e_T, C_T e_T) = 0$. Then Eq. (2) can be written as

$$\hat{\varphi}_{\text{LSDVT}} - 1 = \left[\sum_{i=1}^{N} v_i' C_T' Q_T C_T v_i \right]^{-1} \cdot \left[\sum_{i=1}^{N} v_i' C_T' Q_T v_i \right]. \tag{A.9}$$

Dividing both the numerator and the denominator of Eq. (A.9) by σ_v^2, yields a ratio of two summands consisting of quadratic forms in standardised variables which are independent of y_{i0}, σ_v^2 and α_i and so $\hat{\varphi}_{\text{LSDVT}}$ can be used to construct a similar test with respect to the nuisance parameters of Model (1b).

The inconsistency of $\hat{\varphi}_{\text{LSDVT}}$ can be derived by writing Eq. (2), according to Eq. (A.9), as

$$\hat{\varphi}_{\text{LSDTV}} - 1 = \sum_{i=1}^{N} w_{iT}'' \bigg/ \sum_{i=1}^{N} D_{iT}'' \tag{A.10}$$

where

$$w_{iT}'' = (\tau_T' M_T \tau_T)(\varepsilon_{i,-1}' M_T v_i) - (\varepsilon_{i,-1}' M_T \tau_T)(\tau_T' M_T \varepsilon_{i,-1})$$
$$= \sum_{t=1}^{T} \omega_1''(t) v_{it}^2 + \sum_{t=1}^{T-1} \sum_{s=t+1}^{T} \omega_2''(t, s) v_{it} v_{is},$$

$\varepsilon_i' = (\varepsilon_{i0}, \ldots, \varepsilon_{iT-1})$ with $\varepsilon_{i0} = 0$,

$$D_{iT}'' = (\tau_T' M_T \tau_T)(\varepsilon_{i,-1}' M_T \varepsilon_{i,-1}) - (\varepsilon_{i,-1}' M_T \tau_T)(\tau_T' M_T \varepsilon_{i,-1})\cdot$$
$$= \sum_{t=1}^{T} \delta_1''(t) v_{it}^2 + \sum_{t=1}^{T-1} \sum_{s=t+1}^{T} \delta_2''(t, s) v_{it} v_{is},$$

$$\omega_1''(t) = -\frac{(T-t)(T^2 - 3Tt + 6t^2 - 3t - 1)}{12},$$

$$\omega_2''(t, s) = -\tfrac{1}{12}(T^2 - 1)(T - t - s)$$
$$+ \tfrac{1}{4}(T+1)[t(T-t) + s(T-s)] - \tfrac{1}{2}ts(2T - t - s),$$

$$\delta_1''(t) = \frac{t(T-t)(T^2 + 3t^2 - 3tT - 1)}{12}$$

and

$$\delta_2''(t,s) = -\tfrac{1}{6}t(T-s)(T^2-3Ts+3ts-1).$$

The probability limit of the numerator of Eq. (A.10) is

$$\begin{aligned}\operatorname*{plim}_{N\to\infty}\frac{1}{N}\sum_{i=1}^{N} w_{iT}'' &= \sum_{t=1}^{T}\omega_1''(t)\left(\operatorname*{plim}_{N\to\infty}\frac{1}{N}\sum_{i=1}^{N} v_{it}^2\right)\\ &\quad+\sum_{t=1}^{T-1}\sum_{s=t+1}^{T}\omega_2''(t,s)\left(\operatorname*{plim}_{N\to\infty}\frac{1}{N}\sum_{t=1}^{N} v_{it}v_{is}\right)\\ &= -\frac{T(T^2-1)(T-2)\sigma_v^2}{24}.\end{aligned}$$

The probability limit of the denominator of Eq. (A.10) is

$$\begin{aligned}\operatorname*{plim}_{N\to\infty}\frac{1}{N}\sum_{i=1}^{N} D_{iT}'' &= \sum_{t=1}^{T}\delta_1''(t)\left(\operatorname*{plim}_{N\to\infty}\frac{1}{N}\sum_{i=1}^{N} v_{it}^2\right)\\ &\quad-\frac{1}{T}\sum_{t=1}^{T-1}\sum_{s=t+1}^{T}\delta_2''(t,s)\left(\operatorname*{plim}_{N\to\infty}\sum_{i=1}^{N} v_{it}v_{is}\right)\\ &= \frac{T(T^2-1)(T^2-2)\sigma_v^2}{180}\end{aligned}$$

and so by the Slutzky theorem, the inconsistency of $\hat{\varphi}_{\text{LSDVT}}$ is

$$B_3 = \operatorname*{plim}_{N\to\infty}(\hat{\varphi}_{\text{LSDVT}}-1) = \frac{\text{plim}_{N\to\infty}(1/N)\sum_{i=1}^{N} w_{iT}''}{\text{plim}_{N\to\infty}(1/N)\sum_{i=1}^{N} D_{iT}''} = -\frac{15}{2(T+2)}. \tag{A.11}$$

Subtracting Eq. (A.11) from both sides of Eq. (A.10) yields

$$\hat{\varphi}_{\text{LSDVT}} - 1 - B_3 = \frac{\sum_{i=1}^{N} w_{iT}''}{\sum_{i=1}^{N} D_{iT}''} - B_3 = \frac{\sum_{i=1}^{N} x_{iT}''}{\sum_{i=1}^{N} D_{iT}''} \tag{A.12}$$

where $x_{iT}'' = w_{iT}'' - B_3 D_{iT}''$ is an i.i.d. process, with zero mean, and variance given by

$$\text{Var}(x_{iT}'') = \frac{T(T^2-1)(T-2)(37T^4-302T^3+384T^2+1934T-2701)}{120{,}960(T+2)}k$$

$$+\frac{T(T^2-1)(T-2)(193T^5-950T^4-2766T^3-1576T^2-12751T+16206)}{241{,}920(T+2)}\sigma_V^4$$

where $\mathrm{Var}(x''_{iT})$ is derived by writing

$$\mathrm{Var}(x''_{iT}) = \mathrm{E}(w''^2_{iT}) + B_3^2\mathrm{E}(D''^2_{iT}) - 2B_3\mathrm{E}(w''_{iT}D''_{iT})$$

and using the following results

$$\mathrm{E}(w''^2_{iT}) = \sum_{t=1}^{T} \omega''_1(t)^2 k + \sum_{t=1}^{T-1}\sum_{s=t+1}^{T} [2\omega''_1(t)\omega''_1(s) + \omega''_2(t,s)^2]\sigma_v^4$$

$$= \frac{T(T-2)(T^2-1)(29T^3-47T^2-23T+59)}{15{,}120}k$$

$$+ \frac{T(T^2-1)(T-2)(56T^4-167T^3-226T^2+131T-354)}{30{,}240}\sigma_v^4,$$

$$\mathrm{E}(D''^2_{iT}) = \sum_{t=1}^{T} \delta''_1(t)^2 k + \sum_{t=1}^{T-1}\sum_{s=t+1}^{T} [2\delta''_1(t)\delta''_1(s) + \delta''_2(t,s)^2]\sigma_v^4$$

$$= \frac{T(T^2-1)(T^2-2)(T^2-5)(T^2+5)}{30{,}240}k$$

$$+ \frac{T(T^2-1)(T^2-2)(13T^5-30T^4+10T^3-23T+750)}{302{,}400}\sigma_v^4,$$

and

$$\mathrm{E}(w''_{iT}D''_{iT}) = \sum_{t=1}^{T} \omega''_1(t)\delta''_1(t)k + \sum_{t=1}^{T-1}\sum_{s=t+1}^{T} [\omega''_1(t)\delta''_1(s)$$

$$+ \omega''_1(s)\delta''_1(t) + \omega''_2(t,s)\delta''_2(t,s)]\sigma_v^4$$

$$= -\frac{T(T^2-1)(T^2-2)(14T^3-15T^2-14T-33)}{60{,}480}k$$

$$- \frac{T(T^2-1)(T^2-2)(14T^4-42T^3+31T^2+42T+99)}{60{,}480}\sigma_v^4.$$

The result of Theorem 3 follows by the same arguments as in Theorem 2. □

References

Abadir, K.M., 1993. OLS Bias in a nonstationary autoregression. Econometric Theory 9, 81–93.

Ahn, S.C., Schmidt, P., 1995. Efficient estimation of models for dynamic panel data. Journal of Econometrics 68, 5–27.

Anderson, T.W., 1978. Repeated measurements on autoregressive processes. Journal of the American Statistical Association 73, 362.

Anderson, T.W., Hsiao, C., 1981. Estimation of dynamic models with error components. Journal of the American Statistical Association 76, 598–606.

Anderson, T.W., Hsiao, C., 1982. Formulation and estimation of dynamic models using panel data. Journal of Econometrics 18, 47–82.

Baltagi, B.H., 1995. Econometric Analysis of Panel Data. Wiley, Chichester.

Bernard, A.B., Jones, C.I., 1996. Productivity across industries and countries; time series theory and evidence. The Review of Economics and Statistics 135–146.

Breitung, J., Meyer, W., 1994. Testing for unit roots using panel data; are wages on different bargaining levels cointegrated. Applied Economics 26, 353–361.

Blundell, R., Smith, R.J., 1991. Conditions initiales et estimation efficase dans les modeles dynamiques sur donees panel: use application au comportement d'investissement des entreprises. Annales d'Economie et de Statistique 20/21, 109–123.

Chamberlain, G., 1984. Panel data. In: Griliches, Z., Intriligator, M.D. (Eds.), Handbook of Econometrics, vol. II, Elsevier, Amsterdam, pp. 1247–1318.

Dickey, D.A., Fuller, W.A., 1981. Likelihood ratio statistics for autoregressive time series with a unit root. Econometrica 49, 1057–1072.

Evans, G.B.A., Savin, N.E., 1984. Testing for unit roots: 2. Econometrica 52, 1241–1269.

Harris, R.D.F., Tzavalis, E., 1996. Inference for unit roots in dynamic panels. Discussion Paper in Economics 96/04, University of Exeter.

Hsiao, C., 1986. Analysis of Panel Data, Econometric Society Monographs No. 11. Cambridge University Press, Cambridge.

Im, K.S., Pesaran, M.H., Shin, Y., 1995. Testing for unit roots in heterogeneous panels. DAE Working Paper 9526, University of Cambridge, Cambridge.

Kiviet, J.F., Phillips, G.D.A., 1990. Exact similar tests for the root of a first-order autoregressive regression model. Unpublished manuscript, University of Amsterdam.

Kiviet, J.F., Phillips, G.D.A., 1992. Exact similar tests for unit roots and cointegration. Oxford Bulletin of Economics and statistics 54, 349–366.

Levin, A., Lin, C.F., 1993. Unit root tests in panel data: asymptotic and finite-sample properties. Unpublished manuscript, University of California, San Diego.

Nickell, S., 1981. Biases in dynamic models with fixed effects. Econometrica 6, 1417–1426.

O'Connell, P.G.J., 1997. The overvaluation of purchasing power parity. Journal of International Economics, forthcoming.

Phillips, P.C.B., Perron, P., 1988. Testing for a unit root in time series resgression. Biometrica 75, 335–346.

Quah, D., 1992. International patterns of growth: I. persistency in cross-country disparities. Unpublished manuscript, London School of Economics, London.

Quah, D., 1994. Exploiting cross-section variations for unit root inference in dynamic data. Economics Letters 44, 9–19.

Sevestre, P., Trognon, A., 1992. Linear dynamic models. In: Matyas, Sevestre, P. (Eds), The Econometrics of Panel Data, Chapter 6. pp. 94–116.

Stock, J.H., 1994. Unit roots, structural breaks and trends. In: Engle, R.F., McFadden, D.L. (Eds.), Handbook of Econometrics, vol. IV, North-Holland, Amsterdam.

West, K., 1988. Asymptotic normality when regressors have a unit root. Econometrica 56, 1397–1418.

[17]

ELSEVIER Journal of Econometrics 90 (1999) 1–44

JOURNAL OF Econometrics

Spurious regression and residual-based tests for cointegration in panel data

Chihwa Kao*

Center for Policy Research and Department of Economics, Syracuse University, Syracuse, NY 13244-1020, USA

Received 10 January 1995; received in revised form 9 December 1997

Abstract

In the first half of the paper I study spurious regressions in panel data. Asymptotic properties of the least-squares dummy variable (LSDV) estimator and other conventional statistics are examined. The asymptotics of LSDV estimator are different from those of the spurious regression in the pure time-series. This has an important consequence for residual-based cointegration tests in panel data, because the null distribution of residual-based cointegration tests depends on the asymptotics of LSDV estimator.

In the second half of the paper I study residual-based tests for cointegration regression in panel data. I study Dickey–Fuller (DF) tests and an augmented Dickey–Fuller (ADF) test to test the null of no cointegration. Asymptotic distributions of the tests are derived and Monte Carlo experiments are conducted to evaluate finite sample properties of the proposed tests. © 1999 Elsevier Science S.A. All rights reserved.

JEL classification: C22; C23

Keywords: Panel data; Spurious regression; LSDV; Sequential limit theory; Residual-based tests; ADF; DF

1. Introduction

Although there is immense interest in testing for unit roots and cointegration in time-series data, not much attention has been paid to testing the unit roots and cointegration of panel data at either empirical or theoretical levels.

* E-mail: cdkao@maxwell.syr.edu.

PII: S0304-4076(98)00023-2

Apparently, the only theoretical studies in this area are Breitung and Meyer (1994), Quah (1994), Levin and Lin (1993), Im, Pesaran and Shin (1997), Kao and Chen (1995a,b), Kao and Chiang (1997), McCoskey and Kao (1998), Pedroni (1995), and Phillips and Moon (1997). Breitung and Meyer (1994) derived the asymptotic normality of the Dickey–Fuller test statistic for panel data with a large cross-section dimension and a small time-series dimension. Quah (1994) studied the unit roots tests for panel data that have simultaneous extensive cross-section and time-series variation. Levin and Lin (1993) recently derived the limiting distributions for unit roots on panel data and showed that the power of these tests increases dramatically as the cross-section dimension increases. Im et al. (1997) critiqued the Levin and Lin panel unit root statistics and proposed alternatives. Kao and Chen (1995a) and Kao and Chiang (1997) studied the asymptotic results for a least-squares dummy variable (LSDV) estimator, a fully modified estimator and a dynamic least-squares estimator in a cointegrated regression in panel data. Kao and Chen (1995b) proposed residual-based tests for cointegration under a set of restricted assumptions. McCoskey and Kao (1998) proposed further tests for the null hypothesis of cointegration in panel data. Another paper dealing with residual-based tests in the presence of spurious regression is the paper by Pedroni (1995). In it, Pedroni allows different assumptions of the homogeneity and heterogeneity of the panel data. In particular, Pedroni introduces a model which allows for different intercepts and different slopes and heterogeneous long-run variance covariance matrices. Phillips and Moon (1997) developed a sequential limit theory for nonstationary panel data. Pesaran and Smith (1995) are not directly concerned with cointegration but do touch on a number of related issues, including the potential problems of homogeneity misspecification for cointegrated panels.

The first half of this paper examines a spurious regression in panel data. Asymptotic properties of the LSDV estimator and other conventional statistics are examined. I show that the LSDV estimator, $\hat{\beta}$, is consistent for its true value, but the t-statistic, t_{β}, diverges so that inferences about the regression coefficient, β, are wrong with the probability that goes to one asymptotically. The asymptotics of $\hat{\beta}$ are also different from those of the spurious regression in the pure time-series. This has an important consequence for residual-based cointegration tests in panel data, because the null distribution of residual-based cointegration tests depends on the asymptotics of $\hat{\beta}$. The second half of the paper examines the asymptotic null distribution of residual-based cointegration tests in panel data. I study Dickey–Fuller (DF) tests and an augmented Dickey–Fuller (ADF) test to test the null of no cointegration. Asymptotic distributions of the tests are derived and Monte Carlo experiments are conducted to evaluate finite sample properties of the proposed tests. The simulation results suggest that the DF_{ρ}^{*} and DF_{t}^{*} tests have better size and power properties than the DF_{ρ},DF_{t}, and ADF tests when σ is small. However, when σ is large, ADF clearly dominates the rest.

Section 2 introduces the model and derives the asymptotic distributions of the LSDV estimator and various conventional statistics from the spurious regression in panel data. Section 3 derives the asymptotic distributions for the residual-based tests for the cointegration. Section 4 describes the estimation of long-run variances. Section 5 reports the simulation results. An extension to allow nonzero drifts for the regressors is discussed in Section 6. Concluding remarks are given in Section 7. The proofs in the text are collected in the Appendix.

A word on notation. We write the integral $\int_0^1 W(s)\,ds$ as $\int W$ when there is no ambiguity over limits. We define $\Omega^{1/2}$ to be any matrix such that $\Omega = (\Omega^{1/2})(\Omega^{1/2})'$. We use $\Rightarrow$ to denote weak convergence, $\xrightarrow{p}$ to denote convergence in probability, $[x]$ to denote the largest integer $\leqslant x$, $I(0)$ and $I(1)$ to signify a time-series that is integrated of order zero and one, respectively, and $BM(\Omega)$ to denote Brownian motion with covariance matrix Ω.

2. The model and assumptions

Suppose that $w_{it} = (u_{it}, \varepsilon_{it})'$ is a bivariate process with zero mean vector and the long-run covariance matrix of w_{it}:

$$\Omega = \lim_{T\to\infty} \frac{1}{T}\mathrm{E}\left(\sum_{t=1}^{T} w_{it}\right)\left(\sum_{t=1}^{T} w_{it}\right)' = \Sigma + \Gamma + \Gamma' = \begin{bmatrix} \sigma_{0u}^2 & \sigma_{0u\varepsilon} \\ \sigma_{0u\varepsilon} & \sigma_{0\varepsilon}^2 \end{bmatrix}, \tag{1}$$

where

$$\Gamma = \lim_{T\to\infty} \frac{1}{T}\sum_{k=1}^{T-1}\sum_{t=k+1}^{T} \mathrm{E}(w_{it}w_{it-k}') = \begin{bmatrix} \Gamma_u & \Gamma_{u\varepsilon} \\ \Gamma_{\varepsilon u} & \Gamma_\varepsilon \end{bmatrix} \tag{2}$$

and

$$\Sigma = \lim_{T\to\infty} \frac{1}{T}\sum_{t=1}^{T} \mathrm{E}(w_{it}w_{it}') = \begin{bmatrix} \sigma_u^2 & \sigma_{u\varepsilon} \\ \sigma_{u\varepsilon} & \sigma_\varepsilon^2 \end{bmatrix}. \tag{3}$$

Let $y_{it} = \sum_{s=1}^{t} u_{is}$ and $x_{it} = \sum_{s=1}^{t} \varepsilon_{is}$ in which $u_{i0} = \varepsilon_{i0} = O_p(1)$. Suppose y_{it} and x_{it}, are incorrectly estimated by least squares for all i using panel data; the spurious LSDV regression model is

$$y_{it} = \alpha_i + \beta x_{it} + e_{it}, \quad i = 1,\dots,N, \; t = 1,\dots,T, \tag{4}$$

where e_{it} is $I(1)$. The LSDV estimator of β is

$$\hat{\beta} = \frac{\sum_{i=1}^{N}\sum_{t=1}^{T} y_{it}(x_{it} - \bar{x}_i)}{\sum_{i=1}^{N}\sum_{t=1}^{T}(x_{it} - \bar{x}_i)^2}. \tag{5}$$

Assumption 1. The asymptotic theory employed in this paper is a sequential limit theory established by Phillips and Moon (1997) in which $T \to \infty$ followed by $N \to \infty$ sequentially.

Remark 1. One of main issues in deriving the asymptotic distribution of the double indexed model is how to treat the two indices, T and N. In general, there are three types of convergence: (i) sequential limit, $T \to \infty$ first and then $N \to \infty$, (ii) pairwise limit, assuming $N(T)$ where $N(T) \to \infty$ as $T \to \infty$, and (iii) joint limit, N and $T \to \infty$. The joint limit is the strongest concept among the three. Some of the results in this paper will continue to hold for a pairwise limit or a joint limit theory if additional assumptions are imposed, e.g., one needs to restrict the rate at which N grows relative to T so as to guarantee that the appropriate terms do not diverge as N grows large.

Assumption 2. The $(u_{it}, \varepsilon_{it})'$ are assumed to be independent across i.

Remark 2. It is true that the assumption of independence across i is rather strong. However, the assumption of independence across i is needed in order to satisfy the requirement of the Lindeberg–Levy central limit theorem. Moreover, as pointed out by Quah (1994), modeling cross-sectional dependence is involved because individual observations in cross-section have no natural ordering. It is possible to extend the current model to allow a degree of dependency across i using the approaches adapted by Im et al. (1995) and Pedroni (1995). However, it goes beyond the scope of this paper.

Remark 3. Indeed, assuming constant variances across i is also restrictive. The real job is how to verify the Lindeberg condition. The Lemma 4.2 (a version of the central limit theorem for triangular arrays) presented by Levin and Lin (1993) is not ready to derive the asymptotics when the variances are not constant across i. The difficulty is that uniform integrability is not guaranteed from the moment conditions in their lemma. Moreover, their conditions in the lemma do not yield the Lindeberg condition. Hence, before technical issues can be resolved, I think the assumption of constant variance across i is an acceptable compromise for the purpose of this paper.

Assumption 3. For each i, we assume

1. $E[w_{it}] = 0$,
2. $\sup_t E|w_{it}|^p$ for some $2 \leqslant p < \infty$,
3. $\{w_{it}\}_1^\infty$ is strong mixing with mixing number η_m satisfying $\sum_{m=1}^{\infty} \eta_m^{1-2/p} < \infty$.

It follows that w_{it} satisfies the invariance principle so that

$$\frac{1}{\sqrt{T}} \sum_{t=1}^{[Tr]} w_{it} \Rightarrow \Omega^{1/2} W_i(r) \quad \text{as } T \to \infty, \tag{6}$$

for all i, where $W_i(r)$ is a 2×1 dimensional standard Wiener process with

$$W_i(r) = \begin{bmatrix} V_i(r) \\ W_i(r) \end{bmatrix}.$$

All limits in Theorems 1–4 and Corollaries 1 and 2 are taken as $T \to \infty$ and followed by $N \to \infty$ sequentially by Assumption 1. The asymptotic properties of the LSDV estimator and other conventional statistics are given in the following theorem:

Theorem 1. Assume that Assumptions 1–3 are satisfied; *then*

(a) $\hat{\beta} \xrightarrow{p} \sigma_{0u\varepsilon}/\sigma_{0\varepsilon}^2$,
(b) $\sqrt{N}(\hat{\beta} - \sigma_{0u\varepsilon}/\sigma_{0\varepsilon}^2) \Rightarrow N(0, 2\sigma_{0v}^2/5\sigma_{0\varepsilon}^2)$,
(c) $T^{-1/2} t_\beta - T^{-1/2} \sigma_{0\varepsilon}^{-2} \sigma_{0u\varepsilon} \sqrt{\sum_{i=1}^{N} \sum_{t=1}^{T} (x_{it} - \bar{x}_i)^2} / s \Rightarrow N(0, 2/5)$,
(d) $R^2 \xrightarrow{p} \dfrac{\sigma_{0u\varepsilon}^2}{\sigma_{0v}^2 \sigma_{0\varepsilon}^2 + \sigma_{0u\varepsilon}^2}$,
(e) $DW = O_p(T^{-1})$,
(f) $TDW \xrightarrow{p} 6$,

where

$$s = \sqrt{\frac{1}{NT} \sum_{i=1}^{N} \sum_{t=1}^{T} \{(y_{it} - \bar{y}_i) - \hat{\beta}(x_{it} - \bar{x}_i)\}^2}.$$

Remark 4. Theorem 1 shows that the LSDV estimator, $\hat{\beta}$, is consistent for its true value, $\sigma_{0u\varepsilon}/\sigma_{0\varepsilon}^2$. It is known that if a time-series regression for give i is performed in model (4), then the ordinary least squares (OLS) estimator of β is spurious (It is due to that the noise, e_{it}, is as strong as the signal, x_{it}, since both e_{it} and x_{it} are $I(1)$.) In the panel regression (4) with a large number of cross-section data, the strong noise of e_{it} is attenuated by pooling the data and a consistent estimate of the signal can be extracted. However, the t-statistic, t_β, diverges so that inferences about the regression coefficient, β, are wrong with the probability that goes to one asymptotically.

If we assume strong exogeneity and no serial correlation, then Theorem 1 is reduced to the following corollary which was investigated by Kao and Chen (1995b):

Corollary 1. If $u_{it} \sim iid(0, \sigma_u^2)$, $\varepsilon_{it} \sim iid(0, \sigma_\varepsilon^2)$, $E(u_{it}^4) < \infty$, $E(\varepsilon_{it}^4) < \infty$, *and* u_{it} *and* ε_{it} *are independent, then*

(a) $\hat{\beta} \xrightarrow{p} 0$,
(b) $\sqrt{N}\hat{\beta} \Rightarrow N\left(0, \dfrac{2\sigma_u^2}{5\sigma_\varepsilon^2}\right)$ or $\hat{\beta} = O_p(N^{-1/2})$,
(c) $T^{-1/2} t_\beta \Rightarrow N(0, \frac{2}{5})$ or $t_\beta = O_p(T^{1/2})$,
(d) $R^2 \xrightarrow{p} 0$,
(e) $DW = O_p(T^{-1})$,
(f) $TDW \xrightarrow{p} 6$.

Remark 5. The results of Theorem 1 can also be extended to multiple regression, provided that $\{x_{it}\}$ are not cointegrated.

The asymptotics of $\hat{\beta}$ are different from those of a spurious regression in the pure time-series, and this difference has an important consequence for residual-based cointegration tests using panel data, because the null distribution of residual-based cointegration tests depends on the asymptotics of $\hat{\beta}$. This point is explained further in the next section.

3. Residual-based tests for cointegration

In this section we derive the limiting distributions of residual-based cointegration tests using DF tests and ADF when applied to the model (4) in Section 2.

3.1. Dickey–Fuller (DF) test

The DF test can be applied to the residuals using

$$\hat{e}_{it} = \rho \hat{e}_{it-1} + v_{it}, \qquad (7)$$

where $\hat{e}_{it}$ is the estimate of e_{it} from Eq. (4). The OLS of ρ, $\hat{\rho}$, is

$$\hat{\rho} = \frac{\sum_{i=1}^{N}\sum_{t=2}^{T}\hat{e}_{it}\hat{e}_{it-1}}{\sum_{i=1}^{N}\sum_{t=2}^{T}\hat{e}_{it-1}^{2}}. \tag{8}$$

The null hypothesis that $\rho = 1$ in regression (7) is tested by

$$\begin{aligned}\sqrt{N}T(\hat{\rho}-1) &= \frac{\frac{1}{\sqrt{N}}\sum_{i=1}^{N}\frac{1}{T}\sum_{t=2}^{T}\hat{e}_{it-1}\Delta\hat{e}_{it}}{\frac{1}{N}\sum_{i=1}^{N}\frac{1}{T^2}\sum_{t=2}^{T}\hat{e}_{it-1}^{2}} \\ &= \frac{\frac{1}{\sqrt{N}}\sum_{i=1}^{N}\frac{1}{T}\sum_{t=2}^{T}\hat{e}_{it-1}^{*}\Delta\hat{e}_{it}^{*}}{\frac{1}{N}\sum_{i=1}^{N}\frac{1}{T^2}\sum_{t=2}^{T}(\hat{e}_{it-1}^{*})^{2}} \\ &= \frac{\sqrt{N}\frac{1}{N}\sum_{i=1}^{N}\zeta_{3iT}}{\frac{1}{N}\sum_{i=1}^{N}\zeta_{4iT}} \\ &= \frac{\sqrt{N}\breve{\zeta}_{3NT}}{\breve{\zeta}_{4NT}},\end{aligned}$$

where $\hat{e}_{it}^{*}$ is defined in Eq. (A.3), $\zeta_{3iT} = (1/T)\sum_{t=2}^{T}\hat{e}_{it-1}^{*}\Delta\hat{e}_{it}^{*}$, $\zeta_{4iT} = (1/T^2)\sum_{t=2}^{T}\hat{e}_{it-1}^{*2}$, $\breve{\zeta}_{3NT} = (1/N)\sum_{i=1}^{N}\zeta_{3iT}$, and $\xi_{4NT} = (1/N)\sum_{i=1}^{N}\zeta_{4iT}$. The t-statistic to test $\rho = 1$, t_ρ, is

$$t_\rho = \frac{(\hat{\rho}-1)\sqrt{\sum_{i=1}^{N}\sum_{t=2}^{T}\hat{e}_{it-1}^{*2}}}{s_e},$$

where $s_e^2 = (1/NT)\sum_{i=1}^{N}\sum_{t=2}^{T}(\hat{e}_{it}^{*} - \hat{\rho}\hat{e}_{it-1}^{*})^2$.

Theorem 2. Suppose Assumptions 1–3 *hold. Then,*

$$\sqrt{N}T(\hat{\rho}-1) - \frac{\sqrt{N}\mu_{3T}}{\mu_{4T}} \Rightarrow \mathrm{N}\left(0,\, 3 + \frac{36}{5}\frac{\sigma_v^4}{\sigma_{0v}^4}\right)$$

and

$$t_\rho - \frac{\sqrt{N}\mu_{3T}}{s_e\sqrt{\mu_{4T}}} \Rightarrow \mathrm{N}\left(0, \frac{\sigma_{0v}^2}{2\sigma_v^2} + \frac{3\sigma_v^2}{10\sigma_{0v}^2}\right),$$

where $\mu_{3T} = \mathrm{E}[\zeta_{3iT}]$ *and* $\mu_{4T} = \mathrm{E}[\zeta_{4iT}]$.

Remark 6. Theorem 2 shows that the asymptotic distributions test statistics, $\sqrt{N}T(\hat{\rho}-1)$ and t_ρ depend on the nuisance parameters: μ_{3T}, μ_{4T}, σ_v^2 and σ_{0v}^2. First we note that μ_{3T} and μ_{4T} can be approximated by $\mu_3 = -\sigma_v^2/2$ and $\mu_4 = \sigma_{0v}^2/6$, respectively. It is necessary to construct new statistics whose limiting distributions are not dependent on $\mu_{3T}, \mu_{4T}, \sigma_v^2$ and σ_{0v}^2. We now define

$$DF_\rho^* = \frac{\sqrt{N}T(\hat{\rho}-1) + \dfrac{3\sqrt{N}\hat{\sigma}_v^2}{\hat{\sigma}_{0v}^2}}{\sqrt{3 + \dfrac{36\hat{\sigma}_v^4}{5\hat{\sigma}_{0v}^4}}},$$

and

$$DF_t^* = \frac{t_\rho + \dfrac{\sqrt{6N}\hat{\sigma}_v}{2\hat{\sigma}_{0v}}}{\sqrt{\dfrac{\hat{\sigma}_{0v}^2}{2\hat{\sigma}_v^2} + \dfrac{3\hat{\sigma}_v^2}{10\hat{\sigma}_{0v}^2}}},$$

where $\hat{\sigma}_v^2$ and $\hat{\sigma}_{0v}^2$ are consistent estimates of σ_v^2 and σ_{0v}^2. The limiting distributions of DF_ρ^* and DF_t^*, by construction, do not depend on σ_v^2 and σ_{0v}^2. It can be shown easily that $DF_\rho^* \Rightarrow \mathrm{N}(0,1)$ and $DF_\rho^* \Rightarrow \mathrm{N}(0,1)$ by the sequential limit theory.

Remark 7. Alternatively, we could define a bias-corrected serial correlation coefficient estimate,

$$\hat{\rho}^* = \frac{\sum_{i=1}^N \sum_{t=2}^T (\hat{e}_{it}\hat{e}_{it-1} - \mu_3)}{\sum_{i=1}^N \sum_{t=2}^T \hat{e}_{it-1}^2}$$

then it can be shown that the bias-corrected test statistics are

$$\sqrt{N}T(\hat{\rho}^* - 1) \Rightarrow \mathrm{N}(0,3)$$

and

$$t_\rho^* \Rightarrow \mathrm{N}\left(0, \frac{\sigma_{0v}^2}{2\sigma_v^2}\right)$$

by following Eqs. (C.8) and (C.14).

Note that with strong exogeneity and in the absence of serial correlation we have $\sigma_u^2 = \sigma_{0u}^2 = \sigma_v^2 = \sigma_{0v}^2$. This case was previously studied by Kao and Chen (1995b). We then have the following corollary:

Corollary 2. Suppose strong exogeneity holds and there is no serial correlation. Then,

$$\sqrt{N}T(\hat{\rho} - 1) - \frac{\sqrt{N}\mu_{5T}}{\mu_{6T}} \Rightarrow N\left(0, \frac{51}{5}\right)$$

and

$$\sqrt{5/4}\left\{t_\rho - \frac{\sqrt{N}\mu_{5T}}{\sqrt{\mu_{6T}}}\right\} \Rightarrow N(0, 1).$$

3.2. Augmented Dickey–Fuller (ADF) test

The DF test in Section 3.1 was based on a simple OLS regression of $\hat{e}_{it}$ on its own lagged value. Correction for serial correlation was made to the OLS and t-statistic. Alternatively, the lagged changes in the residuals can be added to the regression of (7):

$$\hat{e}_{it} = \rho\hat{e}_{it-1} + \sum_{j=1}^{p} \varphi_j \Delta\hat{e}_{it-j} + v_{itp}, \tag{9}$$

where p is chosen so that the residuals v_{itp} are serially uncorrelated. The ADF test statistic discussed in this section is the usual t-statistic of $\rho = 1$ in regression (9). Let X_{ip} and X_{ip}^* be the matrices of observation on the p regressors $(\Delta\hat{e}_{it-1}, \Delta\hat{e}_{it-2}, \dots, \Delta\hat{e}_{it-p})$ and $(\Delta\hat{e}_{it-1}^*, \Delta\hat{e}_{it-2}^*, \dots, \Delta\hat{e}_{it-p}^*)$ respectively, e_i and e_i^* equal the vector of observations of $\hat{e}_{it-1}$ and $\hat{e}_{it-1}^*$, respectively, v_i equal the vector of observations of v_{itp}, $Q_i = I - X_{ip}(X_{ip}'X_{ip})^{-1}X_{ip}'$, $Q_i^* = I - X_{ip}^*(X_{ip}^{*\prime}X_{ip}^*)^{-1}X_{ip}^{*\prime}$, and $s_v^2 = (1/NT)\sum_{i=1}^{N}\sum_{t=1}^{T}\hat{v}_{itp}^2$, where $\hat{v}_{itp}$ is an estimate of v_{itp}. Under the null hypothesis of no cointegration, the *ADF* test takes the form

$$t_{ADF} = \frac{(\hat{\rho} - 1)[\sum_{i=1}^{N}(e_i'Q_ie_i)]^{1/2}}{s_v},$$

where $\hat{\rho}$ is the OLS estimate of ρ. Note that

$$(\hat{\rho} - 1) = \left[\sum_{i=1}^{N}(e_i'Q_ie_i)\right]^{-1}\left[\sum_{i=1}^{N}(e_i'Q_iv_i)\right].$$

Now,

$$t_{ADF} = \frac{\sum_{i=1}^{N} (e_i' Q_i v_i)}{s_v \sqrt{\sum_{i=1}^{N} (e_i' Q_i e_i)}}$$

$$= \frac{\sqrt{N} \frac{1}{N} \sum_{i=1}^{N} \frac{1}{T} (e_i' Q_i v_i)}{s_v \sqrt{\frac{1}{N} \sum_{i=1}^{N} \frac{1}{T^2} (e_i' Q_i e_i)}}$$

$$= \frac{\sqrt{N} \frac{1}{N} \sum_{i=1}^{N} \frac{1}{T} (e_i^{*\prime} Q_i^* v_i)}{s_v \sqrt{\frac{1}{N} \sum_{i=1}^{N} \frac{1}{T^2} (e_i^{*\prime} Q_i^* e_i^*)}}$$

$$= \frac{\sqrt{N} \xi_{5NT}}{s_v \sqrt{\xi_{6NT}}},$$

where $\xi_{5NT} = (1/N) \sum_{i=1}^{N} \zeta_{5iT}$, $\zeta_{5iT} = (1/T)(e_i^{*\prime} Q_i^* v_i)$, $\xi_{6NT} = (1/N) \sum_{i=1}^{N} \zeta_{6iT}$, and $\zeta_{6iT} = (1/T^2)(e_i^{*\prime} Q_i^* e_i^*)$.

Theorem 3. Suppose that the assumptions of Theorem 2 are satisfied. Then, we have

$$t_{ADF} - \frac{\sqrt{N} \mu_{5T}}{s_v \sqrt{\mu_{6T}}} \Rightarrow \mathrm{N}\left(0, \frac{\sigma_{0v}^2}{2\sigma_v^2} + \frac{3\sigma_v^2}{10\sigma_{0v}^2}\right),$$

provided $p \to \infty$ *as* $T \to \infty$ *such that* $p = o(T^{1/3})$, *where* $\mu_{5T} = E[\zeta_{5iT}]$ *and* $\mu_{6T} = E[\zeta_{6iT}]$.

Remark 8. Similarly, we can define

$$ADF = \frac{t_{ADF} + \sqrt{6N} \hat{\sigma}_v / 2\hat{\sigma}_{0u}}{\sqrt{\hat{\sigma}_{0v}^2 / 2\hat{\sigma}_v^2 + 3\hat{\sigma}_v^2 / 10\hat{\sigma}_{0v}^2}}$$

which does not depend on the nuisance parameters. We thus have $ADF \Rightarrow$ N(0,1) by the sequential limit theory.

Remark 9. Alternatively, we could follow Pedroni (1995) to remove the nuisance parameters in the limiting distribution of t_{ADF} as follows:

$$\frac{\sigma_v}{s_v}\left(t_{ADF} - \frac{\sqrt{N}\lambda}{\sigma_{ov}\sqrt{\xi_{6NT}}} + \frac{\sqrt{6N}}{2}\right) \Rightarrow \mathrm{N}(0, \tfrac{4}{5}),$$

where $\lambda = (\sigma_{ov}^2 - \sigma_v^2)/2$.

Remark 10. This paper is related to recent work by Pedroni (1995) that came to my attention when this work was completed. Pedroni (1995) derived asymptotic distributions for residual-based tests of cointegration for both homogenous and heterogeneous panels. This paper discusses the fixed effect model, which Pedroni (1995) does not discuss. Using a pooled unstandardized version of the Phillips–Perron statistics, Pedroni finds that models with common slopes and homogeneous errors produce statistics which converge in distribution to normal random variables. This result is analogous to the results in Theorem 2, except that Pedroni's results (see his Proposition 2) are based on the overly restrictive assumption that the regressors are strictly exogenous.

4. Estimation of long-run parameters

The asymptotic distributions given in Theorems 2 and 3 depend on unknown parameters ($\sigma_u^2, \sigma_\varepsilon^2, \sigma_{u\varepsilon}, \sigma_{0\varepsilon}^2, \sigma_{0u}^2$ and $\sigma_{0u\varepsilon}$). Once the estimates of $w_{it} = (u_{it}, \varepsilon_{it})'$, $\hat{w}_{it}$, are obtained, we can use

$$\hat{\Sigma} = \begin{pmatrix} \hat{\sigma}_u^2 & \hat{\sigma}_{u\varepsilon} \\ \hat{\sigma}_{u\varepsilon} & \hat{\sigma}_\varepsilon^2 \end{pmatrix} = \frac{1}{NT}\sum_{i=1}^{N}\sum_{t=1}^{T} \hat{w}_{it}\hat{w}_{it}' \tag{10}$$

to estimate Σ. Ω can be estimated by

$$\hat{\Omega} = \begin{pmatrix} \hat{\sigma}_{0u}^2 & \hat{\sigma}_{0u\varepsilon} \\ \hat{\sigma}_{0u\varepsilon} & \hat{\sigma}_{0\varepsilon}^2 \end{pmatrix} \tag{11}$$

$$= \frac{1}{N}\sum_{i=1}^{N}\left\{\frac{1}{T}\sum_{t=1}^{T} \hat{w}_{it}\hat{w}_{it}' + \frac{1}{T}\sum_{\tau=1}^{l} \varpi_{\tau l} \sum_{t=\tau+1}^{T} (\hat{w}_{it}\hat{w}_{it-\tau}' + \hat{w}_{it-\tau}\hat{w}_{it}')\right\} \tag{12}$$

where $\varpi_{\tau l}$ is a weight function or a kernel. Usually kernels are truncated by the bandwidth parameter l so that $\varpi_{\tau l} = 0$ for $\tau > l$. Using Phillips and Durlauf (1986), a law of large numbers and the sequential limit theory, $\hat{\Sigma}$ and $\hat{\Omega}$ can be shown to be consistent for Σ and Ω.

Remark 11. The distribution results for DF_ρ^*, DF_t^*, and ADF may require $N = o(T^{2\gamma})$ if a pairwise limit or a joint limit theory is used, where γ is the convergence rate of the spectral density estimator (e.g., $\gamma = 1/5$ for the Barlett kernel, 1/3 for the quadratic spectral kernel, and up to 1/2 for parametric kernel estimators). For example, for the quadratic spectral kernel with optimal selection of the bandwidth parameter, $\hat{\Omega}$ has bias of order $O(T^{-1/3})$. Since this bias is due to the declining weights assigned by the kernel to the true autocovariances, the bias does not shrink with the cross-sectional dimension N. Thus the asymptotic distributions presented in this paper will be appropriate if either one treats the asymptotics sequentially or one restricts the rate at which N grows relative to T so to guarantee that $\sqrt{N}(\hat{\Omega} - \Omega)$, for example, does not diverge as N grows large. If the sequential limit theory is used then the difference between $\hat{\Omega}$ and Ω will be eliminated in the first step when $T \to \infty$.

5. Some Monte Carlo results

5.1. Spurious regression

In this section, I report some results from Monte Carlo experiments that examined the finite-sample properties of the LSDV estimator, $\hat{\beta}$, t_β, R^2, and DW. The simulations were performed by a Sun SparcServer 1000 using the software GAUSS 3.27. The results I report are based on 10 000 replications. The data were generated by creating $T + 1000$ observations and discarding the first 1000 observations to remove the effect of the initial conditions.

The data generating process (DGP) was $y_{it} = y_{it-1} + u_{it}$ and $x_{it} = x_{it-1} + \varepsilon_{it}$ for $i = 1, \ldots, N$ and $t = 1, \ldots, T$, where the innovation sequences $(u_{it}, \varepsilon_{it})$ were generated from a bivariate normal with independence across both individuals and time periods, i.e.,

$$\begin{bmatrix} u_{it} \\ \varepsilon_{it} \end{bmatrix} \overset{\text{iid}}{\sim} N\left(\begin{bmatrix} 0 \\ 0 \end{bmatrix}, \begin{bmatrix} 1 & 0 \\ 0 & 2 \end{bmatrix}\right). \tag{13}$$

Eq. (13) assumes strong exogeneity and no serial correlation. Random numbers for $(u_{it}, \varepsilon_{it})$ were generated by the GAUSS procedure RNDNS. For each experiment, we calculated the mean values of $\hat{\beta}$, t_β, R^2, DW, the mean estimated standard error (ESE), $P(|t| > 1.96)$ (the rejection frequency of the t-test of H_0: $\beta = 0$), and the sample standard deviation (SSD) of $\hat{\beta}$ where

$$SSD(\hat{\beta}) = \left\{\frac{1}{M-1} \sum_{i=1}^{M} [\hat{\beta}_i - \bar{\beta}]^2\right\}^{1/2},$$

$\bar{\beta} = (1/M)\sum_{i=1}^{M}\hat{\beta}_i$, and M was the number of replications. For sample size, I considered different settings for T and N.

The Monte Carlo results are reported in Tables 1–3. In the case where $N = T = 30$, the probability of rejecting H_0, $P(|t_\beta| > 1.96)$ is approximately 0.5723, which is far from the 'conventional' value of 0.05. Similar discrepancies exist for all our other values of N and T. This means that even when the null hypothesis is true, we will wrongly reject it most of the time.

We know from Table 1 that the mean values of $\hat{\beta}$ almost always stay constant around zero, but $\bar{\beta} \pm 2 \times SSD$ converges to the mean value as panel size increases. Unlike in the pure time-series case, $\hat{\beta}$ converges to zero in probability instead of being a random variable. Table 1 also reveals some discrepancy between the SSD and the ESE. However, the discrepancy between these two measures is not as severe as the discrepancy in the pure time-series because both the SSD and the ESE diminish as T increases in panel data.

The mean value of the t-statistic changes little as $T(N)$ grows from 10 to 70, but the SSD increases rapidly. The likelihood of $|t_\beta| > 1.96$ becomes higher and higher so that the critical value at the 5% significance level increases as T increases. Therefore, as in a pure time-series, the spurious regression problem becomes worse as the panel size grows. This is confirmed by Table 1, which records the rejection frequency of the t-test for the sample sizes from 10 to 80. The rejection rate of the null hypothesis of no relationship between x_{it} and y_{it} increases steadily with T. At $N = T = 50$; the rejection rate is as high as 66%.

I also examine how the finite sample properties of the spurious LSDV regression change if N and T are different. I first fix N at 30 and change T. Then, I let T be fixed at 30 and change N. Table 2 summarizes the results for different time-series dimensions with $N = 30$. Table 3 summarizes the results for different cross-section dimensions with $T = 30$. We find that an increase in cross-section

Table 1
LSDV regression with $N = T$

$N(T)$	$\bar{\beta}$	$SSD(\hat{\beta})$	$ESE(\hat{\beta})$	$\bar{t}_\beta$	$SSD(t_\beta)$	$P(\lvert t_\beta\rvert > 1.96)$	$\bar{R}^2$	$\overline{DW}$
10	− 0.0028	0.2865	0.1495	− 0.0185	1.9603	0.3150	0.0384	0.6184
20	0.0024	0.2039	0.0727	0.0339	2.8375	0.4889	0.0200	0.3057
30	0.0012	0.1652	0.0479	0.0248	3.4693	0.5723	0.0133	0.2033
40	0.0006	0.1423	0.0358	0.0160	4.0065	0.6166	0.0100	0.1519
50	0.0001	0.1265	0.0286	0.0060	4.4392	0.6598	0.0079	0.1212
60	0.0004	0.1160	0.0237	0.0207	4.8987	0.6894	0.0066	0.1009
70	− 0.0006	0.1072	0.0203	− 0.0365	5.3014	0.7096	0.0057	0.0864
80	− 0.0001	0.1002	0.0178	− 0.0057	5.6369	0.7264	0.0049	0.0755

Note: (a) $\bar{\beta} = (1/M)\sum_{i=1}^{M}\hat{\beta}_i$. (b) $\bar{t}_\beta = (1/M)\sum_{i=1}^{M}t_{\beta_i}$. (c) $\overline{R^2} = (1/M)\sum_{i=1}^{M}R_i^2$. (d) $\overline{DW} = (1/M)\sum_{i=1}^{M}DW_i$. (e) The number of replications = 10,000.

Table 2
LSDV regression with $N = 30$

T	$\bar{\beta}$	$SSD(\hat{\beta})$	$ESE(\hat{\beta})$	$\bar{t}_\beta$	$SSD(t_\beta)$	$P(\lvert t_\beta\rvert > 1.96)$	$\bar{R}^2$	$\overline{DW}$
10	0.0006	0.1669	0.0861	0.0104	1.9546	0.3130	0.0136	0.5686
20	0.0022	0.1660	0.0593	0.0397	2.8192	0.4858	0.0134	0.2991
30	0.0012	0.1652	0.0479	0.0248	3.4693	0.5723	0.0133	0.2033
40	0.0004	0.1639	0.0413	0.0131	3.9855	0.6218	0.0131	0.1538
50	– 0.0001	0.1651	0.0368	– 0.0074	4.5078	0.6651	0.0133	0.1238
60	0.0013	0.1643	0.0336	0.0381	4.9167	0.6889	0.0131	0.1033
70	– 0.0012	0.1647	0.0310	– 0.0419	5.3318	0.7103	0.0132	0.0890
100	0.0026	0.1634	0.0259	0.1072	6.3427	0.7548	0.0130	0.0626
150	0.0002	0.1647	0.0211	0.0802	7.8426	0.8022	0.0132	0.0418

Note: (a) $\bar{\beta} = (1/M)\sum_{i=1}^{M}\hat{\beta}_{i}$. (b) $\bar{t}_\beta = (1/M)\sum_{i=1}^{M}t_{\beta_i}$. (c) $\overline{R^2} = (1/M)\sum_{i=1}^{M}R_i^2$. (d) $\overline{DW} = (1/M)\sum_{i=1}^{M}DW_i$. (e) The number of replications = 10,000.

Table 3
LSDV Regression with $T = 30$

N	$\bar{\beta}$	$SSD(\hat{\beta})$	$ESE(\hat{\beta})$	$\bar{t}_\beta$	$SSD(t_\beta)$	$P(\lvert t_\beta\rvert > 1.96)$	$\bar{R}^2$	$\overline{DW}$
10	0.0029	0.2848	0.0832	0.0261	3.5000	0.5732	0.0378	0.2232
20	0.0037	0.2005	0.0588	0.0567	3.4577	0.5788	0.0195	0.2080
30	0.0012	0.1652	0.0479	0.0248	3.4693	0.5723	0.0133	0.2033
40	0.0009	0.1425	0.0415	0.0195	3.4532	0.5692	0.0099	0.2007
50	0.0001	0.1265	0.0371	0.0259	3.4306	0.5699	0.0109	0.1993
60	0.0017	0.1163	0.0339	0.0444	3.4478	0.5635	0.0067	0.1983
70	0.0020	0.1080	0.0313	0.0588	3.4613	0.5745	0.0058	0.1976

Note: (a) $\bar{\beta} = (1/M)\sum_{i=1}^{M}\hat{\beta}_{i}$. (b) $\bar{t}_\beta = (1/M)\sum_{i=1}^{M}t_{\beta_i}$. (c) $\overline{R^2} = (1/M)\sum_{i=1}^{M}R_i^2$. (d) $\overline{DW} = (1/M)\sum_{i=1}^{M}DW_i$. (e) The number of replications = 10,000.

decreases the SSD of $\hat{\beta}$; varying cross-section size has little effect on the t-statistic; and the t-statistic is closely related to the time-series dimension. The reason why the t-statistic does not converge to the standard normal distribution is that the t-statistic does not have a zero mean even when T is fixed (at 30). Hence, increasing N will not help the t-statistic converge to a meaningful distribution (here a standard normal distribution) without some sort of normalization. When T grows, the SSD of the t-statistic and the rejection rate of the null hypothesis based on the conventional critical value increase significantly.

The results obtained from the pure time-series tell us that R^2 may be quite high in the spurious regression. However, this is not the case using panel data. Tables 1 and 2 reveal that R^2 remains very low and decreasing, which is consistent with the result in Corollary 1. Corollary 1 also demonstrates that the

$DW \to 0$ and $TDW \to 6$ as $T \to \infty$ and then $N \to \infty$. The results on the Durbin–Watson statistic are also what we expected. Clearly, as shown in Table 1, DW converges to zero in probability. Furthermore, TDW stays constant at about 6 on average.

5.2. Residual-based tests

To examine the finite sample properties of the proposed tests, I conducted Monte Carlo experiments which are similar to the design of Engle and Granger (1987) and are used in Gonzalo (1994) and Haug (1996). The data generating process (DGP) was

$$y_{it} - \alpha_i - \beta x_{it} = z_{it},$$

$$a_1 y_{it} - a_2 x_{it} = w_{it}, \qquad z_{it} = \rho z_{it-1} + e_{zit},$$

$$w_{it} = w_{it-1} + e_{wit}, \qquad e_{wit} = \phi_{it} + \pi \phi_{it-1},$$

and

$$\begin{bmatrix} e_{zit} \\ \phi_{it} \end{bmatrix} \overset{\text{iid}}{\sim} \mathrm{N}\left(\begin{bmatrix} 0 \\ 0 \end{bmatrix}, \begin{bmatrix} 1 & \theta\sigma \\ \theta\sigma & \sigma^2 \end{bmatrix} \right).$$

The RNDN procedure in GAUSS was used to generate the random numbers. The data were generated by creating $T + 1000$ observations and discarding the first 1000 observations to remove the effect of the initial conditions. The results I report are based on 10 000 replications. I generate α_i from a uniform distribution, $U[0,10]$, and set $\beta = 2$.

For the purposes of the this paper, I consider the following values for the parameters in the DGP: $a_1 = 1$, $a_2 = -1$, $\rho = (0.95,1)$, $\sigma = (0.25,1,4)$, $\pi = (-0.8,0,0.8)$, and $\theta = (-0.5,0,0.5)$. When $\rho = 1$, y_{it} and x_{it} are not cointegrated, and when $|\rho| < 1$, they are cointegrated.

The estimate of the long-run covariance matrix

$$\hat{\Omega} = \begin{pmatrix} \hat{\sigma}_{0u}^2 & \hat{\sigma}_{0u\varepsilon} \\ \hat{\sigma}_{0u\varepsilon} & \hat{\sigma}_{0\varepsilon}^2 \end{pmatrix}$$

and the long-run conditional variance, $\hat{\sigma}_{0v}^2 = \hat{\sigma}_{0u}^2 - \hat{\sigma}_{0u\varepsilon}^2 \hat{\sigma}_{0\varepsilon}^{-2}$, were obtained by using the procedure KERNEL in COINT 2.0 with a Bartlett window of lag length 5.

Define the following bias-corrected test statistics:

$$DF_\rho = \frac{\sqrt{N}T(\hat{\rho} - 1) + 3\sqrt{N}}{\sqrt{51/5}},$$

and

$$DF_t = \sqrt{\frac{5t_\rho}{4}} + \sqrt{\frac{15N}{8}}.$$

DF^*_ρ, DF^*_t, and ADF are defined in Remarks 5 and 6. We expect that DF^*_ρ, DF^*_t, and ADF converge to N(0,1) asymptotically. I also put DF_ρ and DF_t here for comparison and the two lags are selected for ADF.

Table 4 contains estimates of the size of tests at the 5% level when the asymptotic critical value, 1.645, from the N(0,1) distribution was used. Five different tests are considered – DF_ρ, DF_t, DF^*_ρ, DF^*_t, and ADF – for different sample sizes with $\theta = 0$, no moving average component ($\pi = 0.0$), $\sigma = 1$, and endogenous x_{it} ($a_1 = 1.0$). We note that all tests have a large size distortion when T is small (e.g., $T = 10$) even at $N = 300$, but the size distortion begins to disappear quickly when the T is increased to 25 for all N. The empirical sizes of DF^*_ρ and DF^*_t are close to 0.05 when T and N are both large. But the empirical size of the ADF test is greater than 0.09 at each sample size for T and N. Overall, it is found that DF^*_ρ and DF^*_t outperform the rest in terms of the size distortion.

Table 5 reports the unadjusted powers of the five tests when the asymptotic critical value is used and $\rho = 0.90$ for different sample sizes with 0 contemporaneous correlation ($\theta = 0$), no moving average component ($\pi = 0.0$), $\sigma = 1$ and endogenous x_{it} ($a_1 = 1.0$). All tests have little power when $T = 10$ and N is small, as one would expect. However, DF^*_ρ displays little power even when N is large. When T is increased to 25 and above, DF^*_ρ dominates DF^*_t, and the ADF tests for all N. Interestingly, DF_ρ and DF_t, though they are misspecified, perform pretty well in terms of size distortion and power.

To provide further insight into other specifications, I consider the size and power of these five tests for three different values of θ,π, and σ in Tables 6–8. With negative π, all five tests are severely distorted, as one would expect. In fact, with $\pi = -0.8$, all tests except ADF reject no cointegration 100% of the time for a nominal 5% level for sample sizes $T = 50$ and $N = 50$. The empirical sizes of the DF_ρ and DF_t tests are smaller than the nominal sizes of the tests (at 5%) when $\pi = 0.8$ at $N = T = 50$. For $\pi = 0.8$, the size distortion of all five tests begins to improve as σ is increased from 0.25 to 1 and 4. For $\pi = 0.0$, all five tests

Table 4
The empirical size at 5% for $a_1 = 1$, $\sigma = 1$, $\rho = 1$, $\pi = 0.0$, and $\theta = 0$

	$T = 10$					$T = 25$				
N	DF_ρ	DF_t	DF_ρ^*	DF_t^*	ADF	DF_ρ	DF_t	DF_ρ^*	DF_t^*	ADF
1	0.350	0.282	0.034	0.075	0.139	0.435	0.239	0.157	0.098	0.137
2	0.257	0.233	0.028	0.079	0.138	0.307	0.180	0.130	0.092	0.125
5	0.182	0.191	0.021	0.084	0.167	0.195	0.139	0.088	0.089	0.115
10	0.149	0.179	0.018	0.096	0.210	0.142	0.114	0.068	0.079	0.113
15	0.142	0.179	0.021	0.099	0.272	0.135	0.118	0.059	0.080	0.123
20	0.144	0.193	0.023	0.115	0.315	0.121	0.109	0.054	0.078	0.123
25	0.149	0.212	0.024	0.121	0.367	0.115	0.110	0.052	0.078	0.129
50	0.178	0.270	0.041	0.192	0.575	0.119	0.122	0.053	0.089	0.161
75	0.208	0.320	0.068	0.255	0.722	0.117	0.126	0.054	0.095	0.185
100	0.242	0.372	0.098	0.314	0.829	0.121	0.139	0.061	0.106	0.214
150	0.318	0.472	0.173	0.433	0.939	0.132	0.154	0.070	0.123	0.265
200	0.378	0.551	0.269	0.535	0.979	0.142	0.170	0.079	0.138	0.308
250	0.446	0.623	0.372	0.630	0.993	0.153	0.187	0.091	0.156	0.356
300	0.513	0.682	0.473	0.708	0.998	0.171	0.212	0.105	0.177	0.407
	$T = 50$					$T = 100$				
1	0.461	0.218	0.354	0.145	0.167	0.467	0.213	0.429	0.179	0.184
2	0.322	0.159	0.249	0.115	0.135	0.319	0.152	0.291	0.133	0.139
5	0.202	0.118	0.153	0.093	0.107	0.209	0.115	0.187	0.103	0.113
10	0.149	0.101	0.106	0.079	0.092	0.150	0.092	0.129	0.082	0.093
15	0.127	0.091	0.087	0.075	0.090	0.127	0.083	0.105	0.078	0.085
20	0.121	0.093	0.084	0.076	0.093	0.116	0.084	0.098	0.077	0.087
25	0.113	0.091	0.077	0.074	0.094	0.108	0.078	0.090	0.071	0.084
50	0.105	0.090	0.072	0.075	0.098	0.095	0.076	0.079	0.071	0.081
75	0.093	0.085	0.065	0.075	0.107	0.087	0.073	0.073	0.067	0.079
100	0.092	0.093	0.064	0.077	0.114	0.085	0.070	0.071	0.062	0.081
150	0.094	0.094	0.069	0.084	0.127	0.084	0.075	0.069	0.067	0.085
200	0.098	0.098	0.069	0.086	0.141	0.085	0.076	0.068	0.068	0.091
250	0.098	0.104	0.072	0.091	0.149	0.079	0.078	0.069	0.071	0.096
300	0.104	0.113	0.075	0.096	0.166	0.079	0.076	0.065	0.069	0.095

Note: (a) The number of replications = 10,000. (b) All rejection frequencies are based on the asymptotic critical value 1.645.

show little variation in size across the various values of θ and σ. Note that some of the results in Table 6 have extremely severe size distortions. Pedroni (1995) also observed this; it is probably due to more challenging experimental designs employed in this section.

For $\sigma \geqslant 1$, we note that the unadjusted power of tests is extremely high for all values of θ, and π. For $\sigma = 0.25$ and $\pi = 0$, the power of all tests is very low. When σ is increased to 1 and 4, the power increases dramatically.

Table 8 reports the size-adjusted powers with $\rho = 0.85$ such that each test has the same rejection frequency of 5% when the null hypothesis is true. For $\sigma = 0.25$ and $\pi = -0.8$, the power of all tests is low and the null

Table 5
The power at 5% for $a_1 = 1$, $\sigma = 1$, $\rho = 0.90$, $\pi = 0$, and $\theta = 0$

	$T = 10$					$T = 25$				
N	DF_ρ	DF_t	DF_ρ^*	DF_t^*	ADF	DF_ρ	DF_t	DF_ρ^*	DF_t^*	ADF
1	0.359	0.283	0.028	0.068	0.137	0.496	0.255	0.135	0.084	0.139
2	0.296	0.252	0.022	0.073	0.136	0.451	0.234	0.154	0.091	0.145
5	0.270	0.249	0.017	0.077	0.184	0.465	0.261	0.185	0.115	0.176
10	0.286	0.277	0.014	0.090	0.248	0.569	0.341	0.255	0.163	0.225
15	0.329	0.317	0.017	0.100	0.323	0.674	0.421	0.334	0.205	0.276
20	0.375	0.358	0.018	0.112	0.373	0.756	0.488	0.406	0.248	0.321
25	0.419	0.405	0.019	0.121	0.435	0.823	0.559	0.484	0.291	0.368
50	0.626	0.581	0.027	0.195	0.665	0.966	0.799	0.774	0.507	0.566
75	0.773	0.714	0.040	0.264	0.811	0.994	0.914	0.913	0.674	0.715
100	0.870	0.809	0.054	0.325	0.899	1.00	0.967	0.972	0.793	0.822
150	0.958	0.919	0.093	0.464	0.974	1.00	0.996	0.998	0.922	0.934
200	0.988	0.964	0.143	0.583	0.993	1.00	1.00	1.00	0.977	0.977
250	0.998	0.988	0.195	0.679	0.998	1.00	1.00	1.00	0.995	0.992
300	0.999	0.995	0.266	0.758	0.000	1.00	1.00	1.00	0.998	0.997
	$T = 50$					$T = 100$				
1	0.622	0.293	0.458	0.179	0.197	0.845	0.471	0.781	0.391	0.355
2	0.569	0.341	0.255	0.163	0.225	0.939	0.667	0.898	0.601	0.518
5	0.798	0.471	0.657	0.340	0.324	0.999	0.949	0.994	0.922	0.843
10	0.936	0.698	0.853	0.561	0.496	1.00	1.00	1.00	0.998	0.985
15	0.983	0.841	0.944	0.724	0.630	1.00	1.00	1.00	1.00	0.998
20	0.997	0.922	0.982	0.835	0.735	1.00	1.00	1.00	1.00	1.00
25	0.999	0.995	0.995	0.905	0.818	1.00	1.00	1.00	1.00	1.00
50	1.00	1.00	1.00	0.996	0.977	1.00	1.00	1.00	1.00	1.00
75	1.00	1.00	1.00	1.00	0.997	1.00	1.00	1.00	1.00	1.00
100	1.00	1.00	1.00	1.00	1.00	1.00	1.00	1.00	1.00	1.00
150	1.00	1.00	1.00	1.00	1.00	1.00	1.00	1.00	1.00	1.00
200	1.00	1.00	1.00	1.00	1.00	1.00	1.00	1.00	1.00	1.00
250	1.00	1.00	1.00	1.00	1.00	1.00	1.00	1.00	1.00	1.00
300	1.00	1.00	1.00	1.00	1.00	1.00	1.00	1.00	1.00	1.00

Note: (a) The number of replications = 10,000. (b) All rejection frequencies are based on the asymptotic critical value 1.645.

hypothesis of no cointegration is often not rejected. With $\pi = 0$, ADF has the lowest power for all θ and, on the other hand, DF_ρ^* has the highest power. With $\pi = 0$, the power of all tests except ADF is high. When σ is increased to 1, the power of all tests increases to virtually 1 except when $\theta = -0.8$. In fact, the power of all tests remains very low, zeros for most cases when $\theta = -0.8$. Interestingly and to my surprise, ADF became very powerful when $\sigma = 4$ and $\theta \geqslant 0$.

The results in Tables 4–8 suggest that the DF_ρ^* and DF_t^* tests have better size and power properties than the DF_ρ, DF_t, and ADF tests when σ is small. However, when σ is large, ADF clearly dominates the rest.

Table 6
The empirical size of 5% of tests with the null hypothesis of no cointegration

	$\sigma = 0.25$			$\sigma = 1$			$\sigma = 4$		
θ	−0.5	0	0.5	−0.5	0	0.5	−0.5	0	0.5
$\pi = -0.8$									
DF_ρ	1.00	1.00	1.00	1.00	1.00	1.00	1.00	1.00	1.00
DF_t	1.00	1.00	1.00	1.00	1.00	1.00	1.00	1.00	1.00
DF_ρ^*	1.00	1.00	1.00	1.00	1.00	1.00	1.00	1.00	1.00
DF_t^*	1.00	1.00	1.00	1.00	1.00	1.00	1.00	1.00	1.00
ADF	0.814	0.038	0.062	1.00	0.985	0.998	0.993	0.672	0.466
$\pi = 0$									
DF_ρ	0.100	0.102	0.102	0.104	0.105	0.104	0.104	0.104	0.101
DF_t	0.089	0.089	0.089	0.087	0.090	0.088	0.089	0.088	0.088
DF_ρ^*	0.069	0.069	0.069	0.073	0.072	0.073	0.073	0.070	0.075
DF_t^*	0.072	0.072	0.072	0.077	0.090	0.088	0.074	0.076	0.073
ADF	0.097	0.096	0.096	0.099	0.098	0.100	0.099	0.099	0.100
$\pi = 0.8$									
DF_ρ	0.005	0.000	0.000	0.145	0.020	0.067	0.287	0.086	0.306
DF_t	0.014	0.000	0.000	0.113	0.028	0.064	0.206	0.078	0.215
DF_ρ^*	0.287	0.095	0.041	0.208	0.163	0.273	0.101	0.076	0.089
DF_t^*	0.161	0.070	0.048	0.149	0.116	0.174	0.098	0.078	0.088
ADF	0.519	0.615	0.416	0.157	0.317	0.269	0.049	0.113	0.044

Note: (a) The number of replications = 10,000. (b) $N = 50$ and $T = 50$. (c) All rejection frequencies are based on the asymptotic critical value 1.645. (d) $a_1 = 1$.

6. Extension to models with deterministic trends

It was assumed in the previous sections that y_{it} and x_{it} have zero drifts. It is known that many macroeconomic variables, such as GNP, could be described as $I(1)$ with drift, which is the sum of an $I(1)$ process with zero-mean increments and a linear trend. It is therefore important to study data generating processes which allow for some drift over time. In this section, I extend the results obtained in the previous sections to allow non-zero drifts for y_{it} and x_{it}. The treatment of nonzero drifts in this section follows Hansen (1992) and Hamilton (1994, pp. 591–601). Suppose that

$$\Delta x_{it} = \gamma_i + \varepsilon_{it}, \tag{14}$$

where $\gamma_i \neq 0$. Then $x_{it} = \gamma_i t + \sum_{s=1}^{t} \varepsilon_{is}$, where $\sum_{s=1}^{t} \varepsilon_{is}$ is in fact a trendless random walk.

Note that the stochastic part, $\sum_{s=1}^{t} \varepsilon_{is}$, is asymptotically dominated by the deterministic part, t. For example, the term $(x_{it} - \bar{x}_i)$ consists of the deterministic part, $\gamma_i(t - (T+1)/2)$, and the stochastic part, $\kappa_{it} - \bar{\kappa}_i$, i.e., $(x_{it} - \bar{x}_i) =$

Table 7
The power of 5% of tests with the null hypothesis of no cointegration and the alternative hypothesis of cointegration ($\rho = 0.90$)

	$\sigma = 0.25$			$\sigma = 1$			$\sigma = 4$		
θ	-0.5	0	0.5	-0.5	0	0.5	-0.5	0	0.5
$\pi = -0.8$									
DF_ρ	1.00	1.00	1.00	1.00	1.00	1.00	1.00	1.00	1.00
DF_t	1.00	1.00	1.00	1.00	1.00	1.00	1.00	1.00	1.00
DF_ρ^*	1.00	1.00	1.00	1.00	1.00	1.00	1.00	1.00	1.00
DF_t^*	1.00	1.00	1.00	1.00	1.00	1.00	1.00	1.00	1.00
ADF	0.198	0.021	0.012	0.882	0.781	0.877	0.986	0.991	0.999
$\pi = 0$									
DF_ρ	0.100	0.487	0.215	0.998	1.00	1.00	1.00	1.00	1.00
DF_t	0.044	0.298	0.165	0.907	1.00	1.00	1.00	1.00	1.00
DF_ρ^*	0.127	0.424	0.293	0.997	1.00	1.00	1.00	1.00	1.00
DF_t^*	0.054	0.251	0.206	0.812	0.996	1.00	0.999	1.00	1.00
ADF	0.095	0.259	0.224	0.813	0.977	0.997	0.988	0.998	0.998
$\pi = 0.8$									
DF_ρ	0.665	0.369	0.111	1.00	1.00	1.00	1.00	1.00	1.00
DF_t	0.324	0.186	0.076	1.00	1.00	1.00	1.00	1.00	1.00
DF_ρ^*	0.998	0.995	0.973	1.00	1.00	1.00	1.00	1.00	1.00
DF_t^*	0.888	0.855	0.738	1.00	1.00	1.00	1.00	1.00	1.00
ADF	0.844	0.993	0.996	0.987	1.00	1.00	0.982	0.999	0.988

Note: (a) The number of replications = 10,000. (b) $N = 50$ and $T = 50$. (c) All rejection frequencies are based on asymptotic critical value: 1.645. (d) $a_1 = 1$.

$\gamma_i(t-(T+1)/2) + (\kappa_{it} - \bar{\kappa}_i)$, where $\kappa_{it} = \sum_{s=1}^{t} \varepsilon_{is}$ and $\bar{\kappa}_i = (1/T)\sum_{t=1}^{T} \kappa_{it}$. For the deterministic part we note that

$$\gamma_i^2 \sum_{t=1}^{T} \left(t - \frac{T+1}{2}\right)^2 = O(T^3).$$

For the stochastic part we know that $\sum_{t=1}^{T}(\kappa_{it} - \bar{\kappa}_i)^2 = O(T^2)$. Thus within $\sum_{t=1}^{T}(x_{it} - \bar{x}_i)^2$ the deterministic part dominates the stochastic part.

x_{it} behaves asymptotically as if it were $\gamma_i t$. Thus the residuals from the LSDV estimation of Eq. (4) behave like the residuals from a regression of y_{it} on a time trend. Also, the dominance of the deterministic trend of x_{it} over the stochastic trend makes the correlation between u_{it} and ε_{it} irrelevant. It implies that the unit root test for $\hat{e}_{it}$ the residual from LSDV estimation of Eq. (4), has the same asymptotic distribution as the unit root test for testing $\rho = 1$ in the following regression:

$$y_{it} = \rho y_{it-1} + \alpha_i + \gamma_i t + \varepsilon_{it} \tag{15}$$

for an error term ε_{it}.

Table 8
The size-adjusted power of 5% of tests with the null hypothesis of no cointegration and the alternative hypothesis of cointegration ($\rho = 0.85$)

	$\sigma = 0.25$			$\sigma = 1$			$\sigma = 4$		
θ	-0.5	0	0.5	-0.5	0	0.5	-0.5	0	0.5
$\pi = -0.8$									
DF_ρ	0.001	0.027	0.012	0.000	0.000	0.000	0.000	0.001	0.010
DF_t	0.002	0.026	0.011	0.000	0.000	0.000	0.000	0.000	0.003
DF_ρ^*	0.000	0.012	0.004	0.000	0.000	0.000	0.000	0.000	0.000
DF_t^*	0.000	0.014	0.106	0.000	0.000	0.000	0.000	0.000	0.000
ADF	0.000	0.026	0.004	0.000	0.000	0.000	0.073	0.925	1.00
$\pi = 0$									
DF_ρ	0.297	0.732	0.508	1.00	1.00	1.00	1.00	1.00	1.00
DF_t	0.128	0.446	0.334	1.00	1.00	1.00	1.00	1.00	1.00
DF_ρ^*	0.388	0.751	0.728	1.00	1.00	1.00	1.00	1.00	1.00
DF_t^*	0.128	0.458	0.464	1.00	1.00	1.00	1.00	1.00	1.00
ADF	0.128	0.299	0.336	0.991	0.999	1.00	1.00	1.00	1.00
$\pi = 0.8$									
DF_ρ	1.00	1.00	1.00	1.00	1.00	1.00	1.00	1.00	1.00
DF_t	0.998	0.997	0.993	1.00	1.00	1.00	1.00	1.00	1.00
DF_ρ^*	1.00	1.00	1.00	1.00	1.00	1.00	1.00	1.00	1.00
DF_t^*	0.990	0.995	0.992	1.00	1.00	1.00	1.00	1.00	1.00
ADF	0.582	0.974	0.996	1.00	1.00	1.00	1.00	1.00	0.988

Note: (a) The number of replications = 10,000. (b) $N = 50$ and $T = 50$. (c) All rejection frequencies are based on the 5th percentile of the empirical distribution. (d) $a_1 = 1$.

Remark 12. Similarly, Eq. (15) will continue to hold when there is more than one regressor if all the regressors have nonzero drifts. Let us consider the case where there are two regressors, x_{1it} and x_{2it}, without loss of generality. Suppose that the regressors are generated by

$$\begin{bmatrix} \Delta x_{1it} \\ \Delta x_{2it} \end{bmatrix} = \begin{bmatrix} \gamma_{1i} \\ \gamma_{2i} \end{bmatrix} + \begin{bmatrix} \varepsilon_{1i} \\ \varepsilon_{2i} \end{bmatrix}. \tag{16}$$

Then Eq. (4) can be written as

$$y_{it} = \alpha_i + \beta_1 x_{1it} + \beta_2 x_{2it} + e_{it} \tag{17}$$

for an error term e_{it}. From Eqs. (16) and (17) we note the unit root test for $\hat{e}_{it}$, the residual from LSDV estimator of Eq. (17), again has the same asymptotic distribution as the unit root test for testing $\rho = 1$ in the following regression:

$$y_{it} = \rho y_{it-1} + \alpha_i + (\beta_1 \gamma_{1i} + \beta_2 \gamma_{2i})t + \varepsilon_{it}. \tag{18}$$

Obviously, Eq. (18) is identical to Eq. (15) with $\gamma_i = (\beta_1\gamma_{1i} + \beta_2\gamma_{2i})$.

Remark 13. If there is a drift in y_{it}, i.e., $\Delta y_{it} = \delta_i + u_{it}$. Then we simply replace y_{it} by $y_{it} - (\delta_i/\gamma_i)x_{it}$ in Eq. (15).

Remark 14. Testing $\rho = 1$ in Eq. (15) has been studied by Levin and Lin (1993) with i.i.d. error terms.

The asymptotic distributions of *DF* tests and an *ADF* test for Eq. (15) can be obtained analogously with Theorems 2 and 3.

Theorem 4. Suppose $\mathrm{E}(\Delta x_{it}) \neq 0$ *and Assumptions* 1–3 *are satisfied. Then*

$$\sqrt{N}\left[T(\hat{\rho}-1) - \frac{\mu_{7T}}{\mu_{8T}}\right] \Rightarrow \mathrm{N}\left(0, \frac{15}{4} + \frac{\sigma_u^4}{\sigma_{0u}^4}\frac{2475}{112}\right),$$

$$t_\rho - \frac{\sqrt{N}\mu_{7T}}{s_e\sqrt{\mu_{8T}}} \Rightarrow \mathrm{N}\left(0, \frac{1}{4}\frac{\sigma_{0u}^2}{\sigma_u^2} + \frac{165}{448}\frac{\sigma_u^2}{\sigma_{0u}^2}\right),$$

and

$$t_{ADF} - \frac{\sqrt{N}\mu_{7T}}{s_v\sqrt{\mu_8}} \Rightarrow \mathrm{N}\left(0, \frac{1}{4}\frac{\sigma_{0u}^2}{\sigma_u^2} + \frac{165}{448}\frac{\sigma_u^2}{\sigma_{0u}^2}\right),$$

where s_v *is defined in a similar fashion as in Section 3.2 and* s_e, μ_{7T} *and* μ_{8T} *are defined in Eqs.* (*E.10*), (*E.8*) *and* (*E.9*), *respectively.*

Remark 15. From Theorem 4 we find that inclusion of drifts in the regressors does not affect the asymptotic distributions of the tests of cointegration in panel data although the asymptotic variances and asymptotic biases are different from the ones in Theorems 2 and 3. That is, allowing drifts for the regressors only affects the precision of the testing and the main results given in Section 3 continue to hold.

7. Conclusion

The first half of this paper develops a framework for understanding the behavior of spurious panel regression. I have provided an asymptotic theory for the behavior of the LSDV estimator in a model which attempts to estimate the panel regression when the dependent variable and independent variable are actually independent $I(1)$ processes. In particular, the t-statistic diverges in spite of the fact that the LSDV estimator converges to its true value in probability. The asymptotic results and simulation results in this paper are useful beyond explaining the spurious effects on panel regression. Asymptotic distributions of residual-based tests depend on the LSDV estimator from the spurious regression because residual-based tests for cointegration in panel data take the spurious regression as the null hypothesis.

In the second half of this paper, I propose tests for the null hypothesis of no cointegration in panel data and derive asymptotic distributions for each test. The simulations show that the distributions of DF_ρ^*, DF_t^*, and ADF can be far different from N(0, 1) suggested by the theory when the underlying process contains an MA component. From the Monte Carlo results, it is apparent that the DF_ρ and DF_t tests are substantially robust despite the model misspecification. The results in Tables 4–8 suggest that the DF_ρ^* and DF_t^* tests have better size and power properties than the DF_ρ, DF_t, and ADF tests.

Acknowledgements

I thank Suzanne McCoskey, Biing-Shen Kuo, two referees, an associate editor and a coeditor, Richard Blundell, for helpful comments. I also thank participants of workshop seminars at Syracuse University, Hong Kong University of Science and Technology, Academia Sinica, and SUNY-Albany for helpful comments and suggestions. I thank Bangtian Chen for his research assistance on an earlier draft of this paper. Thanks also go to Jodi Woodson and Martha Bonney for correcting my English and carefully checking the manuscript to enhance its readability.

Appendix A. Lemma 1

Before we derive the asymptotics of Theorem 1 we need to summarize some limit theory for the LSDV estimator. Note that

$$\hat{\beta} = \frac{\frac{1}{N}\sum_{i=1}^{N}\frac{1}{T^2}\sum_{t=1}^{T}(x_{it}-\bar{x}_i)y_{it}}{\frac{1}{N}\sum_{i=1}^{N}\frac{1}{T^2}\sum_{t=1}^{T}(x_{it}-\bar{x}_i)^2} = \frac{\frac{1}{N}\sum_{i=1}^{N}\zeta_{1iT}}{\frac{1}{N}\sum_{i=1}^{N}\zeta_{2iT}} = \frac{\xi_{1NT}}{\xi_{2NT}}, \tag{A.1}$$

where $\bar{x}_i = (1/T)\sum_{t=1}^{T}x_{it}$, $\bar{y}_i = (1/T)\sum_{t=1}^{T}y_{it}$, $\zeta_{1iT} = (1/T^2)\sum_{t=1}^{T}(x_{it}-\bar{x}_i)y_{it}$, $\zeta_{2iT} = (1/T^2)\sum_{t=1}^{T}(x_{it}-x_i)^2$, $\xi_{1NT} = (1/N)\sum_{i=1}^{N}\zeta_{1iT}$, and $\xi_{2NT} = (1/N)\sum_{i=1}^{N}\zeta_{2iT}$.

Remark A.1. We need to require that ζ_{1iT} and ζ_{1i} (ζ_{2iT} and ζ_{2i}) are defined on the same probability space so that $\sum_{i=1}^{N}\zeta_{1i}(\sum_{i=1}^{N}\zeta_{2i})$ can be used to derive the sequential asymptotics. The requirement that ζ_{1iT} and ζ_{1i} are defined on the same probability space can be done by suitably enlarging the underlying space by using the Skorohod's theorem in Billingsley (1986, p. 399) and Phillips and Moon (1997, p. 8).

All limits in Lemma 1 are taken as $T \to \infty$, for all i, except (j) and (k). We use $V_i(x)$ to denote $\sum_{t=1}^{T}(x_{it} - \bar{x}_i)^2$, use $V(x)$ to denote $\sum_{i=1}^{N}\sum_{t=1}^{T}(x_{it} - \bar{x}_i)^2$, use $V_i(x,y)$ to denote $\sum_{t=1}^{T} y_{it}(x_{it} - \bar{x}_i)$, and use $V(x,y)$ to denote $\sum_{i=1}^{N}\sum_{t=1}^{T} y_{it}(x_{it} - \bar{x}_i)$ to simplify the excessive notation.

Lemma A.1. If Assumptions 1–3 hold, then

(a) $\zeta_{1iT} \Rightarrow \int W_i^* V_i^* - \int W_i^* \int V_i^* = \zeta_{1i}$,
(b) $\zeta_{2iT} \Rightarrow \int W_i^{*2} - (\int W_i^*)^2 = \zeta_{2i}$,
(c) $\mathrm{E}[\zeta_{1iT}] = \mu_{1T} = \mathrm{E}[\zeta_{1i}] = \mu_1 = 0$,
(d) $\mathrm{E}[\zeta_{2i}] = \mu_2 = \frac{1}{6}$,
(e) $\mathrm{E}[\zeta_{2iT}] = \mu_{2T} = \mu_2 + \mathrm{O}(T^{-1})$,
(f) $Var[\zeta_{1iT}] = \sigma_{1T}^2 = \frac{1}{90} + \mathrm{O}(T^{-1})$,
(g) $Var[\zeta_{2iT}] = \sigma_{2T}^2 = \frac{1}{45} + \mathrm{O}(T^{-1})$,
(h) $Var[\zeta_{1i}] = \sigma_1^2 = \frac{1}{90}$,
(i) $Var[\zeta_{2i}] = \sigma_2^2 = \frac{1}{45}$,
(j) $\xi_{1NT} \xrightarrow{p} \mu_1 = 0$,
(k) $\xi_{2NT} \xrightarrow{p} \mu_2 = \frac{1}{6}$.

Proof. Let

$$y_{it}^* = y_{it} - \sigma_{0u\varepsilon}\sigma_{0\varepsilon}^{-2} x_{it}, \tag{A.2}$$

$$x_{it}^* = \sigma_{0\varepsilon}^{-1} x_{it},$$

with

$$\hat{e}_{it}^* = y_{it}^* - \hat{\alpha}_i^* - \hat{\beta}^* x_{it}^*. \tag{A.3}$$

The residuals from LSDV estimation of Eq. (4) are identical to those from LSDV of Eq. (A.2) in that

$$\begin{aligned} y_{it} - \hat{\alpha}_i - \hat{\beta} x_{it} &= y_{it}^* - \hat{\alpha}_i^* - \hat{\beta}^* x_{it}^* \\ &= y_{it} - \sigma_{0u\varepsilon}\sigma_{0\varepsilon}^{-2} x_{it} - \hat{\alpha}_i^* - \hat{\beta}^*(\sigma_{0\varepsilon}^{-1/2} x_{it}) \\ &= y_{it} - \hat{\alpha}_i^* - (\hat{\beta}^*\sigma_{0\varepsilon}^{-1} + \sigma_{0u\varepsilon}\sigma_{0\varepsilon}^{-2}) x_{it} \end{aligned} \tag{A.4}$$

with $\hat{\alpha}_i = \hat{\alpha}_i^*$ and $\hat{\beta} = \hat{\beta}^*\sigma_{0\varepsilon}^{-1} + (\sigma_{0\varepsilon}^{-2})\sigma_{0u\varepsilon}$. This implies that $\hat{\beta}^* = \sigma_{0\varepsilon}\hat{\beta} - \sigma_{0\varepsilon}^{-1}\sigma_{0u\varepsilon}$. Define

$$\sigma_{0v}^2 = \sigma_{0u}^2 - \sigma_{0u\varepsilon}^2\sigma_{0\varepsilon}^{-2} \tag{A.5}$$

and $\sigma_v^2 = \sigma_u^2 - \sigma_{u\varepsilon}^2\sigma_\varepsilon^{-2}$. Notice that

$$\begin{bmatrix} y_{it}^*/\sigma_{0v} \\ x_{it}^* \end{bmatrix} = L'\begin{bmatrix} y_{it} \\ x_{it} \end{bmatrix},$$

where

$$L' = \begin{bmatrix} \frac{1}{\sigma_{0v}} & -\frac{1}{\sigma_{0v}}\sigma_{0u\varepsilon}\sigma_{0\varepsilon}^{-2} \\ 0 & \frac{1}{\sigma_{0\varepsilon}} \end{bmatrix}.$$

It follows that (e.g., Hamilton, 1994) $W_i^*(r) = L'\Omega^{1/2}W_i(r)$ is a Wiener process with an identity covariance, I, with

$$W_i^*(r) = \begin{bmatrix} V_i^*(r) \\ W_i^*(r) \end{bmatrix}.$$

Therefore

$$\begin{aligned}
\frac{1}{\sqrt{T}}\sum_{t=1}^{[Tr]} L'w_{it} &= \frac{1}{\sqrt{T}}\sum_{t=1}^{[Tr]}\begin{bmatrix} \frac{1}{\sigma_{0v}} & -\frac{1}{\sigma_{0v}}\sigma_{0u\varepsilon}\sigma_{0\varepsilon}^{-2} \\ 0 & \sigma_{0\varepsilon}^{-1} \end{bmatrix}\begin{bmatrix} u_{it} \\ \varepsilon_{it} \end{bmatrix} \\
&= \frac{1}{\sqrt{T}}\sum_{t=1}^{[Tr]}\begin{bmatrix} \frac{u_{it}}{\sigma_{0v}} - \frac{\varepsilon_{it}}{\sigma_{0v}}\sigma_{0u\varepsilon}\sigma_{0\varepsilon}^{-2} \\ \frac{\varepsilon_{it}}{\sigma_{0\varepsilon}} \end{bmatrix} \\
&= \frac{1}{\sqrt{T}}\sum_{t=1}^{[Tr]}\begin{bmatrix} \frac{u_{it}^*}{\sigma_{0v}} \\ \varepsilon_{it}^* \end{bmatrix} \\
&\Rightarrow W_i^*(r) \quad \text{as } T \to \infty,
\end{aligned}$$

where $u_{it}^* = u_{it} - \varepsilon_{it}\sigma_{0u\varepsilon}\sigma_{0\varepsilon}^{-2}$ and $\varepsilon_{it}^* = \varepsilon_{it}/\sigma_{0\varepsilon}$. Define

$$\sqrt{N}\frac{\hat{\beta}^*}{\sigma_{0v}} = \frac{\sqrt{N}\xi_{1NT}}{\xi_{2NT}},$$

where $\zeta_{1iT} = (1/T^2)\sum_{t=1}^{T}(x_{it}^* - \bar{x}_i^*)(y_{it}^*/\sigma_{0v}) = (1/T^2\sigma_{0v})V_i(x^*,y^*)$, $\zeta_{2iT} = (1/T^2)\sum_{t=1}^{T}(x_{it}^* - \bar{x}_i^*)^2 = (1/T^2)V_i(x^*)$, $\xi_{1NT} = (1/N)\sum_{i=1}^{N}\zeta_{1iT}$, and $\xi_{2NT} = (1/N)\sum_{i=1}^{N}\zeta_{4iT}$.

First we note that

$$\begin{bmatrix} T^{-3/2}\sum_{t=1}^{T}\frac{y_{it}^*}{\sigma_{0\varepsilon}} \\ T^{-3/2}\sum_{t=1}^{T}x_{it}^* \end{bmatrix} = T^{-3/2}\sum_{t=1}^{T} L'\begin{bmatrix} y_{it} \\ x_{it} \end{bmatrix} \Rightarrow \int W_i^*, \tag{A.6}$$

and

$$\begin{bmatrix} \frac{1}{T^2}\sum_{t=1}^{T}\frac{(y_{it}^*)^2}{\sigma_{0\varepsilon}^2} & \frac{1}{T^2}\sum_{t=1}^{T}\frac{y_{it}^*x_{it}^*}{\sigma_{0\varepsilon}} \\ \frac{1}{T^2}\sum_{t=1}^{T}\frac{x_{it}^*y_{it}^*}{\sigma_{0\varepsilon}} & \frac{1}{T^2}\sum_{t=1}^{T}(x_{it}^*)^2 \end{bmatrix}$$

$$= L'\left(\frac{1}{T^2}\sum_{t=1}^{T}\begin{bmatrix} y_{it} \\ x_{it} \end{bmatrix}[y_{it}\ x_{it}]\right)L \Rightarrow \int W_i^* W_i^{*\prime}$$

$$= \begin{bmatrix} \int V_i^{*2} & \int V_i^* W_i^* \\ \int W_i^* V_i^* & \int W_i^{*2} \end{bmatrix}. \tag{A.7}$$

It follows that

$$\xi_{2iT} \Rightarrow \int W_i^{*2} - \left\{\int W_i^*\right\}^2 = \int \bar{W}_i^2,$$

for all i, where $\bar{W}_i$ is the demeaned standard Wiener process $\bar{W}_i = W_i^* - \int W_i^*$, proving (b). Recall that

$$\zeta_{1iT} = \frac{1}{T^2\sigma_{0v}}V_i(x^*,y^*) = \frac{1}{T^2}\sum_{t=1}^{T} x_{it}^*\frac{y_{it}^*}{\sigma_{0v}} - (T^{-1/2}\bar{x}_i^*)\left(T^{-1/2}\frac{\bar{y}_i^*}{\sigma_{0v}}\right).$$

Using Eqs. (A.6) and (A.7), we have

$$\frac{1}{T^2}\sum_{t=1}^{T} x_{it}^*\frac{y_{it}^*}{\sigma_{0v}} \Rightarrow \int W_i^* V_i^*,$$

$$T^{-1/2}\bar{x}_i^* \Rightarrow \int W_i^*,$$

and $T^{-1/2}(\bar{y}_i/\sigma_{0v}) \Rightarrow \int V_i^*$. Hence,

$$\zeta_{1iT} \Rightarrow \int W_i^* V_i^* - \int W_i^* \int V_i^* = \int \bar{W}_i \bar{V}_i,$$

for all i, where $\bar{V}_i = V_i^* - \int V_i^*$. This proves (a).

To prove (c), we use the fact that $\mathrm{E}[\int W_i^* V_i^*] = 0$ and $\mathrm{E}[\int W_i^*] = \mathrm{E}[\int V_i^*] = 0$, and, therefore, $\mathrm{E}[\zeta_{1i}] = \mu_1 = 0$. Also, $\mathrm{E}[\zeta_{1iT}] = \mu_{1T} = 0$ because of the independence of x_{it}^* and y_{it}^*.

Parts (d) and (g) can be shown easily as follows: $\mathrm{E}[\zeta_{2i}] = \frac{1}{6} = \mu_2$ and $Var[\zeta_{2i}] = \frac{1}{45} = \sigma_2^2$.

To prove (e), we note that

$$\begin{aligned}
\mu_{2T} &= \mathrm{E}[\zeta_{2iT}] \\
&= \frac{1}{T^2}\left\{\sum_{t=1}^{T} \mathrm{E}[x_{it}^*]^2 - \frac{1}{T}\mathrm{E}\left(\sum_{t=1}^{T} x_{it}^*\right)^2\right\} \\
&= \frac{1}{T^2}\left\{\frac{T(T+1)}{2} - \frac{T(T+1)(2T+1)}{6T}\right\} \\
&= \tfrac{1}{6} + \mathrm{O}(T^{-1}) = \mu_2 + \mathrm{O}(T^{-1}).
\end{aligned}$$

To prove (f), we first rewrite

$$\begin{aligned}
\mathrm{Var}(\zeta_{1iT}) &= \frac{1}{\sigma_{0v}^2} Var\left(\frac{1}{T^2} V_i(x^*, y^*)\right) \\
&= \frac{1}{\sigma_{0v}^2}\frac{1}{T^4}\mathrm{E}\left[\left(\sum_{t=1}^{T} x_{it}^* y_{it}^*\right)^2\right] \\
&\quad - \frac{1}{\sigma_{0v}^2}\frac{2}{T^5}\mathrm{E}\left[\left(\sum_{t=1}^{T} x_{it}^* y_{it}^*\right)\left(\sum_{t=1}^{T} x_{it}^*\right)\left(\sum_{t=1}^{T} y_{it}^*\right)\right] \\
&\quad + \frac{1}{\sigma_{0v}^2}\frac{1}{T^6}\mathrm{E}\left[\left(\sum_{t=1}^{T} x_{it}^*\right)^2\left(\sum_{t=1}^{T} y_{it}^*\right)^2\right].
\end{aligned}$$

After some tedious algebra, we can show that

$$\frac{1}{\sigma_{0v}^2}\frac{1}{T^4}\mathrm{E}\left[\left(\sum_{t=1}^{T} x_{it}^* y_{it}^*\right)^2\right] = \frac{1}{6} + \mathrm{O}(T^{-1}),$$

$$\frac{1}{\sigma_{0v}^2}\frac{2}{T^5}\mathrm{E}\left[\left(\sum_{t=1}^{T} x_{it}^* y_{it}^*\right)\left(\sum_{t=1}^{T} x_{it}^*\right)\left(\sum_{t=1}^{T} y_{it}^*\right)\right] = \frac{4}{15} + \mathrm{O}(T^{-1}),$$

and

$$\frac{1}{\sigma_{0v}^2}\frac{1}{T^6}\mathrm{E}\left[\left(\sum_{t=1}^{T} x_{it}^*\right)^2\left(\sum_{t=1}^{T} y_{it}^*\right)^2\right]=\frac{1}{9}+\mathrm{O}(T^{-1}).$$

It follows that

$$Var(\zeta_{1iT})=\frac{1}{\sigma_{0v}^2}\left(\frac{1}{6}-\frac{4}{15}+\frac{1}{9}\right)+\mathrm{O}(T^{-1})=\frac{1}{90}+\mathrm{O}(T^{-1}),$$

proving (f). Next, we prove (h). First,

$$\begin{aligned}\mathrm{Var}(\zeta_{1i})&=\frac{1}{\sigma_{0v}^2}\mathrm{E}\left[\left(\int W_i^*V_i^*-\int W_i^*\int V_i^*\right)^2\right]\\&=\frac{1}{\sigma_{0v}^2}\left\{\mathrm{E}\left[\left(\int W_i^*V_i^*\right)^2\right]+\frac{1}{\sigma_{0v}^2}\mathrm{E}\left[\left(\int W_i^*\int V_i^*\right)^2\right]\right.\\&\left.\quad-\frac{2}{\sigma_{0v}^2}\mathrm{E}\left[\left(\int W_i^*V_i^*\right)\left(\int W_i^*\int V_i^*\right)\right]\right\}.\end{aligned}$$

Again we can show, after tedious algebra,

$$\frac{1}{\sigma_{0v}^2}\mathrm{E}\left[\left(\int W_i^*V_i^*\right)^2\right]=\frac{1}{6},$$

$$\frac{1}{\sigma_{0v}^2}E\left[\left(\int W_i^*\int V_i^*\right)^2\right]=\frac{1}{9},$$

and

$$\frac{1}{\sigma_{0v}^2}\mathrm{E}\left[\left(\int W_i^*V_i^*\right)\left(\int W_i^*\int V_i^*\right)\right]=\frac{2}{15}.$$

Hence, $Var(\zeta_{1i})=\frac{1}{90}$, establishing (h).

Part (i) is easy. Finally, by a law of large numbers $(1/N)\sum_{i=1}^{N}\zeta_{1i}\xrightarrow{p}\mu_1$ and $(1/N)\sum_{i=1}^{N}\zeta_{2i}\xrightarrow{p}\mu_2$ as $N\to\infty$. It follows that

$$\breve{\zeta}_{1NT}=\frac{1}{N}\sum_{i=1}^{N}\zeta_{1iT}\xrightarrow{p}\mu_1=0$$

and

$$\xi_{2NT} = \frac{1}{N}\sum_{i=1}^{N} \zeta_{2iT} \xrightarrow{p} \mu_2 = \frac{1}{6}$$

as required for (j) and (k) by the sequential limit theory. □

Appendix B. Proof of Theorem 1

Proof. Using (j) and (k) in Lemma A.1 we know that $\hat{\beta}^* \xrightarrow{p} 0$. Recall that $\hat{\beta} = \hat{\beta}^* \sigma_{0\varepsilon}^{-1} + \sigma_{0\varepsilon}^{-2}\sigma_{0u\varepsilon}$. Then we obtain $\hat{\beta} \xrightarrow{p} \sigma_{0u\varepsilon}/\sigma_{0\varepsilon}^2$, proving (a).

We note that, unlike the pure time-series case, $\hat{\beta}$ does converge in probability to its true value here. Next we show that $\sqrt{N}\hat{\beta}^* \Rightarrow N(0, 2\sigma_{0v}^2/5)$. First, we note that $E[\zeta_{1i}] = 0$ and $Var[\zeta_{1i}] = \frac{1}{90}$ from Lemma 1. Then from the Lindeberg–Levy central limit theorem and combing this the limit of $(1/N)\sum_{i=1}^{N}\zeta_{2i}$ we have

$$\frac{\frac{1}{\sqrt{N}}\sum_{i=1}^{N}\zeta_{1i}}{\frac{1}{N}\sum_{i=1}^{N}\zeta_{2i}} \Rightarrow N\left(0, \frac{2}{5}\right).$$

Then we obtain

$$\sqrt{N}\hat{\beta}^* - \sigma_{0v}\frac{\sqrt{N}\xi_{1NT}}{\xi_{2NT}} \Rightarrow N\left(0, \frac{2}{5}\sigma_{0v}^2\right)$$

by the sequential limit theory. Hence

$$\sqrt{N}\left(\hat{\beta} - \frac{\sigma_{0u\varepsilon}}{\sigma_{0\varepsilon}^2}\right) \Rightarrow N\left(0\frac{2\sigma_{0v}^2}{5\sigma_{0\varepsilon}^2}\right) \tag{B.1}$$

establishes (b). Thus, after rescaling by $\sqrt{N}$, $\hat{\beta}$ converges in distribution to a normal random variable for all i as $T \to \infty$. Note that

$$\begin{aligned}\frac{1}{\sigma_{0v}^2}\frac{1}{T}s^2 &= \frac{1}{N}\sum_{i=1}^{N}\frac{1}{T^2}\sum_{t=1}^{T}\frac{1}{\sigma_{0v}^2}\hat{e}_{it}^2 \\ &= \frac{1}{N}\sum_{i=1}^{N}\frac{1}{T^2}\sum_{t=1}^{T}\frac{1}{\sigma_{0v}^2}\hat{e}_{it}^{*2}\end{aligned}$$

$$= \frac{1}{N}\sum_{i=1}^{N}\left[\frac{1}{T^2}\sum_{t=1}^{T}\left(\frac{y_{it}^* - \bar{y}_i^*}{\sigma_{0v}}\right)^2 - (\hat{\beta}^*)^2\frac{1}{\sigma_{0v}^2}\frac{1}{T^2}(x_{it}^* - \bar{x}_i^*)^2\right]$$

$$\xrightarrow{p} \frac{1}{6}, \tag{B.2}$$

where $\hat{e}_{it}^* = y_{it}^* - \hat{\alpha}_i^* - \hat{\beta}^* x_{it}^*$, $(1/N)\sum_{i=1}^{N}\sum_{t=1}^{T} 1/T^2(x_{it}^* - \bar{x}_i^*)^2 = O_p(1)$, and $\hat{\beta}^* = o_p(1)$.

Observe that

$$T^{-1/2}t_\beta = \frac{T^{-1/2}\hat{\beta}V(x)}{s}$$

$$= \frac{\sqrt{N}\hat{\beta}\frac{1}{\sigma_{0v}}\sqrt{\frac{1}{N}\sum_{i=1}^{N}\frac{1}{T^2}V_i(x)}}{\sqrt{\frac{1}{\sigma_{0v}^2}\frac{1}{T}s^2}}$$

$$= \frac{\sqrt{N}(\hat{\beta}^*\sigma_{0\varepsilon}^{-1} + \sigma_{0\varepsilon}^{-2}\sigma_{0u\varepsilon})\frac{\sigma_{0\varepsilon}}{\sigma_{0v}}\sqrt{\frac{1}{N}\sum_{i=1}^{N}\frac{1}{T^2}V_i(x^*)}}{\sqrt{\frac{1}{\sigma_{0v}^2}\frac{1}{T}s^2}}$$

$$= \frac{\frac{\sqrt{N}}{\sigma_{0v}}\left(\hat{\beta}^* + \frac{\sigma_{0u\varepsilon}}{\sigma_{0\varepsilon}}\right)\sqrt{\frac{1}{N}\sum_{i=1}^{N}\frac{1}{T^2}V_i(x^*)}}{\sqrt{\frac{1}{\sigma_{0v}^2}\frac{1}{T}s^2}}.$$

It follows that

$$T^{-1/2}t_\beta - \frac{T^{-1/2}\sigma_{0\varepsilon}^{-2}\sigma_{0u\varepsilon}V(x)}{s}$$

$$= \frac{T^{-1/2}\hat{\beta}\sqrt{V(x)} - T^{-1/2}\sigma_{0\varepsilon}^{-2}\sigma_{0u\varepsilon}\sqrt{V(x)}}{s}$$

$$= \frac{T^{-1/2}(\hat{\beta} - \sigma_{0\varepsilon}^{-2}\sigma_{0u\varepsilon})\sqrt{V(x)}}{s}$$

$$= \frac{T^{-1/2}(\hat{\beta}^*\sigma_{0\varepsilon}^{-1})\sqrt{V(x)}}{s}$$

$$= \frac{\frac{\sqrt{N}}{\sigma_{0v}}(\hat{\beta}^*)\sqrt{\frac{1}{N}\sum_{i=1}^{N}\frac{1}{T^2}V(x^*)}}{\sqrt{\frac{1}{\sigma_{0v}^2}\frac{1}{T}s^2}}$$

$$\Rightarrow \frac{\mathrm{N}(0,2/5)\cdot\sqrt{1/6}}{\sqrt{1/6}} = \mathrm{N}(0,\tfrac{2}{5}),$$

proving (c). It is easy to show that

$$\frac{1}{N}\sum_{i=1}^{N}\frac{1}{T^2}V_i(x) = \sigma_{0\varepsilon}^2\frac{1}{N}\sum_{i=1}^{N}\frac{1}{T^2}V_i(x^*) = \sigma_{0\varepsilon}^2\frac{1}{N}\sum_{i=1}^{N}\zeta_{4iT} \xrightarrow{p} \frac{\sigma_{0\varepsilon}^2}{6}, \tag{B.3}$$

and

$$\frac{1}{N}\sum_{i=1}^{N}\frac{1}{T^2}V_i(y)$$

$$= \frac{1}{N}\sum_{i=1}^{N}\frac{1}{T^2}\sum_{t=1}^{T}\left(y_{it}^* + \frac{\sigma_{0u\varepsilon}}{\sigma_{0\varepsilon}}x_{it}^* - \bar{y}_{it}^* - \frac{\sigma_{0u\varepsilon}}{\sigma_{0\varepsilon}}\bar{x}_{it}^*\right)^2$$

$$= \frac{1}{N}\sum_{i=1}^{N}\frac{1}{T^2}\sum_{t=1}^{T}\left[(y_{it}^* - \bar{y}_{it}^*)^2 + \left(\frac{\sigma_{0u\varepsilon}}{\sigma_{0\varepsilon}}\right)^2(x_{it}^* - \bar{x}_{it}^*)^2\right.$$

$$\left. - 2\frac{\sigma_{0u\varepsilon}}{\sigma_{0\varepsilon}}(y_{it}^* - \bar{y}_{it}^*)(x_{it}^* - \bar{x}_{it}^*)\right]$$

$$\xrightarrow{p} \frac{\sigma_{0v}^2}{6} + \left(\frac{\sigma_{0u\varepsilon}}{\sigma_{0\varepsilon}}\right)^2\frac{1}{6}. \tag{B.4}$$

To prove (d), we use Eqs. (B.3) and (B.4) to obtain

$$R^2 = \frac{\sum_{i=1}^{N}\sum_{t=1}^{T}(\hat{y}_{it} - \bar{y}_i)^2}{\sum_{i=1}^{N}\sum_{t=1}^{T}(y_{it} - \bar{y}_i)^2}$$

$$= \frac{\hat{\beta}^2\frac{1}{N}\sum_{i=1}^{N}\frac{1}{T^2}V_i(x)}{\frac{1}{N}\sum_{i=1}^{N}\frac{1}{T^2}V_i(y)}$$

$$\xrightarrow{p} \frac{\left(\dfrac{\sigma_{0u\varepsilon}}{\sigma_{0\varepsilon}^2}\right)^2 \dfrac{\sigma_{0\varepsilon}^2}{6}}{\dfrac{\sigma_{0v}^2}{6} + \left(\dfrac{\sigma_{0u\varepsilon}}{\sigma_{0\varepsilon}}\right)^2 \dfrac{1}{6}} = \frac{\sigma_{0u\varepsilon}^2}{\sigma_{0v}^2\sigma_{0\varepsilon}^2 + \sigma_{0u\varepsilon}^2}.$$

Again using Eq. (A.4) gives

$$DW = \frac{\sum_{i=1}^N \sum_{t=2}^T (\hat{e}_{it} - \hat{e}_{it-1})^2}{\sum_{i=1}^N \sum_{t=1}^T \hat{e}_{it}^2} = \frac{\sum_{i=1}^N \sum_{t=2}^T (\hat{e}_{it}^* - \hat{e}_{it-1}^*)^2}{\sum_{i=1}^N \sum_{t=1}^T \hat{e}_{it}^{*\,2}}$$

$$= \frac{1}{T} \frac{\dfrac{1}{N}\sum_{i=1}^N \dfrac{1}{T}\sum_{t=2}^T (u_{it}^* - \hat{\beta}\varepsilon_{it}^*)^2}{\dfrac{1}{N}\sum_{i=1}^N \dfrac{1}{T^2}\sum_{t=1}^T \hat{e}_{it}^{*2}}.$$

Now,

$$\frac{1}{N}\sum_{i=1}^N \frac{1}{T}\sum_{t=2}^T (u_{it}^* - \hat{\beta}^*\varepsilon_{it}^*)^2$$

$$= \frac{1}{N}\sum_{i=1}^N \left\{\frac{1}{T}\sum_{t=2}^T u_{it}^{*2} - \hat{\beta}^*\frac{1}{T}\sum_{t=2}^T u_{it}^*\varepsilon_{it}^* + \frac{1}{T}(\hat{\beta}^*)^2 \sum_{t=2}^T \varepsilon_{it}^{*2}\right\}$$

$$= \frac{1}{N}\sum_{i=1}^N \left\{\frac{1}{T}\sum_{t=2}^T u_{it}^{*2}\right\} - \hat{\beta}^*\frac{1}{N}\sum_{i=1}^N \left\{\frac{1}{T}\sum_{t=2}^T u_{it}^*\varepsilon_{it}^*\right\} + \hat{\beta}^{*2}\frac{1}{N}\sum_{i=1}^N \frac{1}{T}\sum_{t=2}^T \varepsilon_{it}^{*2}$$

$$\xrightarrow{p} \sigma_{0v}^2$$

because

$$\frac{1}{N}\sum_{i=1}^N \left\{\frac{1}{T}\sum_{t=2}^T u_{it}^{*2}\right\} \xrightarrow{p} \sigma_{0v}^2,$$

$\hat{\beta}^* = o_p(1)$, $(1/N)\sum_{i=1}^N\{(1/T)\sum_{t=2}^T u_{it}^*\varepsilon_{it}^*\} = o_p(1)$, and $(1/N)\sum_{i=1}^N(1/T)\sum_{t=2}^T\varepsilon_{it}^{*2} = O_p(1)$.

From Eq. (B.2),

$$\frac{1}{N}\sum_{i=1}^N \frac{1}{T^2}\sum_{t=1}^T \hat{e}_{it}^{*2} \xrightarrow{p} \frac{\sigma_{0v}^2}{6}.$$

Thus, $DW = O_p(T^{-1})$ or $DW \xrightarrow{p} 0$. It also follows that $TDW \xrightarrow{p} 6$. Therefore, we establish parts (e) and (f). □

Appendix C. Proof of Theorem 2

Proof. First, we note that

$$\hat{e}^*_{it-1} = y^*_{it-1} - \hat{\alpha}^*_i - \hat{\beta}^* x^*_{it-1} = y^*_{it-1} - \bar{y}^*_i - \hat{\beta}^*(x^*_{it-1} - \bar{x}^*_i)$$

and $\Delta\hat{e}^*_{it} = u^*_{it} - \hat{\beta}^*\varepsilon^*_{it}$, where $u^*_{it} = u_{it} - (\sigma_{0u\varepsilon}/\sigma^2_{0\varepsilon})\varepsilon_{it}$ and $\varepsilon^*_{it} = \varepsilon_{it}/\sigma_{0\varepsilon}$. It follows that

$$\begin{aligned}
\zeta_{4NT} &= \frac{1}{N}\sum_{i=1}^{N}\left\{\frac{1}{T^2}\sum_{t=2}^{T}\hat{e}^{*2}_{it-1}\right\} \\
&= \frac{1}{N}\sum_{i=1}^{N}\left\{\frac{1}{T^2}\sum_{t=2}^{T}(y^*_{it-1} - \bar{y}^*_i)^2\right\} - \hat{\beta}^{*2}\frac{1}{N}\sum_{i=1}^{N}\left\{\frac{1}{T^2}\sum_{t=2}^{T}(x^*_{it-1} - \bar{x}^*_i)^2\right\} \\
&= \frac{1}{N}\sum_{i=1}^{N}\left\{\frac{1}{T^2}\sum_{t=2}^{T}(y^*_{it-1} - \bar{y}^*_i)^2\right\} + o_p(1), \qquad \text{(C.1)}
\end{aligned}$$

since $(1/N)\sum_{i=1}^{N}\{(1/T^2)\sum_{t=2}^{T}(x^*_{it-1} - \bar{x}^*_i)^2\} = O_p(1)$ and $\hat{\beta}^{*2} = o_p(1)$. We also note that

$$\frac{1}{T^2}\sum_{t=2}^{T}(y^*_{it-1} - \bar{y}^*_i)^2 \Rightarrow \sigma^2_{0v}\left[\int V^{*2}_i - \left\{\int V^*_i\right\}^2\right] = \zeta_{4i}, \qquad \text{(C.2)}$$

$$E[\zeta_{4i}] = \frac{\sigma^2_{0v}}{6} = \mu_4,$$

and $Var[\zeta_{4i}] = \sigma^4_{0v}/45 = \sigma^2_4$. Thus,

$$\frac{1}{N}\sum_{i=1}^{N}\left\{\frac{1}{T^2}\sum_{t=2}^{T}(y^*_{it} - \bar{y}^*_i)^2\right\} \xrightarrow{p} \frac{\sigma^2_{0v}}{6} = \mu_4 \qquad \text{(C.3)}$$

and $\zeta_{4NT} \xrightarrow{p} \sigma^2_{0v}/6 = \mu_4$ by a law of large numbers and the sequential limit theory. Moreover,

$$\begin{aligned}
&\sqrt{N}\frac{1}{N}\sum_{i=1}^{N}\frac{1}{T}\sum_{t=2}^{T}\hat{e}^*_{it-1}\Delta\hat{e}^*_{it} \\
&= \sqrt{N}\frac{1}{N}\sum_{i=1}^{N}\frac{1}{T}\sum_{t=2}^{T}[y^*_{it-1} - \bar{y}^*_i - \hat{\beta}^*(x^*_{it-1} - \bar{x}^*_i)][u^*_{it} - \hat{\beta}^*\varepsilon^*_{it}]
\end{aligned}$$

$$= \sqrt{N}\frac{1}{N}\sum_{i=1}^{N}\frac{1}{T}\sum_{t=2}^{T}[(y_{it-1}^{*}-\bar{y}_{i}^{*})u_{it}^{*}-\hat{\beta}^{*}(x_{it-1}^{*}-\bar{x}_{i}^{*})u_{it}^{*}-\hat{\beta}^{*}(y_{it-1}^{*}-\bar{y}_{i}^{*})\varepsilon_{it}^{*}$$

$$+\hat{\beta}^{*2}(x_{it-1}^{*}-\bar{x}_{i}^{*})]\varepsilon_{it}^{*} = \sqrt{N}\frac{1}{N}\sum_{i=1}^{N}\frac{1}{T}\sum_{t=2}^{T}(y_{it-1}^{*}-\bar{y}_{i}^{*})u_{it}^{*}+o_{p}(1),$$

since

$$\frac{1}{N}\sum_{i=1}^{N}\left\{\frac{1}{T}\sum_{t=2}^{T}(x_{it-1}^{*}-\bar{x}_{i}^{*})\varepsilon_{it}^{*}\right\}\overset{p}{\to}-\frac{1}{2},$$

$$\frac{1}{N}\sum_{i=1}^{N}\left\{\frac{1}{T}\sum_{t=2}^{T}(y_{it-1}^{*}-\bar{y}_{i}^{*})\varepsilon_{it}^{*}\right\}=o_{p}(1),$$

and

$$\frac{1}{N}\sum_{i=1}^{N}\left\{\frac{1}{T}\sum_{t=2}^{T}(x_{it-1}^{*}-\bar{x}_{i}^{*})u_{it}^{*}\right\}=o_{p}(1)$$

by a law of large numbers and the sequential limit theory. Hence,

$$\sqrt{N}T(\hat{\rho}-1)=\frac{\sqrt{N}\xi_{3NT}}{\xi_{4NT}}$$

$$=\frac{\sqrt{N}\frac{1}{N}\sum_{i=1}^{N}\left\{\frac{1}{T}\sum_{t=2}^{T}(y_{it-1}^{*}-\bar{y}_{i}^{*})u_{it}^{*}\right\}}{\frac{1}{N}\sum_{i=1}^{N}\left\{\frac{1}{T^{2}}\sum_{t=2}^{T}(y_{it-1}^{*}-\bar{y}_{i}^{*})^{2}\right\}}+o_{p}(1). \tag{C.4}$$

Next, we derive the asymptotic distribution of

$$\frac{\sqrt{N}\frac{1}{N}\sum_{i=1}^{N}\left\{\frac{1}{T}\sum_{t=2}^{T}(y_{it-1}^{*}-\bar{y}_{i}^{*})u_{it}^{*}\right\}}{\frac{1}{N}\sum_{i=1}^{N}\left\{\frac{1}{T^{2}}\sum_{t=2}^{T}(y_{it-1}^{*}-\bar{y}_{i}^{*})^{2}\right\}}=\frac{\sqrt{N}\xi'_{3NT}}{\xi_{4NT}}=\frac{\sqrt{N}\frac{1}{N}\sum_{i=1}^{N}\zeta'_{3iT}}{\frac{1}{N}\sum_{i=1}^{N}\zeta_{4iT}},$$

where $\zeta'_{3iT} = (1/T)\sum_{t=2}^{T}(y^*_{it-1} - \bar{y}^*_i)u^*_{it}$ and $\xi'_{3NT} = (1/N)\sum_{i=1}^{N}\zeta'_{3iT}$. But

$$\frac{1}{T}\sum_{t=2}^{T}(y^*_{it-1} - \bar{y}^*_i)u^*_{it} = T^{-1}\sum_{t=2}^{T} y^*_{it-1}u^*_{it} - \left(T^{-3/2}\sum_{t=2}^{T} y^*_{it}\right)\left(T^{-1/2}\sum_{t=2}^{T} u^*_{it}\right),$$

$$T^{-1}\sum_{t=2}^{T} y^*_{it-1}u^*_{it} \Rightarrow \frac{\sigma^2_{0v}}{2}\left[V^*_i(1)^2 - \frac{\sigma^2_v}{\sigma^2_{0v}}\right],$$

$$T^{-3/2}\sum_{t=2}^{T} y^*_{it} \Rightarrow \sigma_{0v}\int V^*_i,$$

and $T^{-1/2}\sum_{t=2}^{T} u^*_{it} \Rightarrow \sigma_{0v}V^*_i(1)$. Clearly,

$$\frac{1}{T}\sum_{t=2}^{T}(y^*_{it-1} - \bar{y}^*_i)u^*_{it} \Rightarrow \frac{\sigma^2_{0v}}{2}\left[V^*_i(1)^2 - \frac{\sigma^2_v}{\sigma^2_{0v}}\right] - \sigma^2_{0v}V^*_i(1)\int V^*_i = \zeta_{3i}, \tag{C.5}$$

$$\mathrm{E}[\zeta_{3i}] = -\sigma^2_v/2 = \mu_3,$$

and $Var[\zeta_{3i}] = \sigma^4_{0v}/12 = \sigma^2_3$, since $\mathrm{E}[V^*_i(1)\int V^*_i] = \frac{1}{2}$ and $\mathrm{E}[V^*_i(1)^2] = 1$.

Let $\mu_{3T} = \mathrm{E}[\zeta'_{3iT}] = \mu_3 + \mathrm{O}(T^{-1})$ and $\mu_{4T} = \mathrm{E}[\zeta_{4iT}] = \mu_4 + \mathrm{O}(T^{-1})$. The next step is to find an appropriate normalization of $(\xi'_{3NT}/\xi_{4NT} - \mu_{3T}/\mu_{4T})$ to make sure it converges to a proper random variable. For this purpose, we note the following standardization:

$$\frac{\sqrt{N}\xi'_{3NT}}{\xi_{4NT}} - \frac{\sqrt{N}\mu_{3T}}{\mu_{4T}} = \frac{\sqrt{N}(\zeta'_{3NT} - \mu_{3T})}{\xi_{4NT}} + \xi'_{3NT}\sqrt{N}\left[\frac{1}{\xi_{4NT}} - \frac{1}{\mu_{4T}}\right]. \tag{C.6}$$

Since $\{\xi_{3i}\}$ satisfies the conditions of the Lindeberg–Levy central limit theorem, we can readily see that the

$$\frac{1}{\sqrt{N}}\sum_{i=2}^{N}(\xi_{3i} - \mu_3) \Rightarrow \mathrm{N}(0, \sigma^2_3)$$

and the $(1/N)\sum_{i=2}^{N}\xi_{4i}$ will converge to μ_4 in probability as $N \to \infty$. Using the Slutsky theorem, we obtain

$$\frac{\frac{1}{\sqrt{N}}\sum_{i=2}^{N}(\xi_{3i} - \mu_3)}{\frac{1}{N}\sum_{i=2}^{N}\xi_{4i}} \Rightarrow \mathrm{N}\left(0, \frac{\sigma^2_3}{\mu^2_4}\right). \tag{C.7}$$

It follows that

$$\frac{\sqrt{N}(\zeta'_{3NT}-\mu_{3T})}{\xi_{4NT}} \Rightarrow \mathrm{N}\left(0,\frac{\sigma_3^2}{\mu_4^2}\right) \tag{C.8}$$

by the sequential limit theory. Similarly,

$$\xi'_{3NT}\sqrt{N}\left[\frac{1}{\xi_{4NT}}-\frac{1}{\mu_{4T}}\right] \Rightarrow \mathrm{N}\left(0,\frac{\mu_3^2}{\mu_4^4}\sigma_4^2\right), \tag{C.9}$$

since it can be shown that $cov(\zeta'_{3iT},\zeta_{4iT})=O(T^{-1})$ and $\sqrt{N}[\xi'_{3NT}-\mu_{3T}]$ and $\sqrt{N}[\xi_{4NT}-\mu_{4T}]$ are asymptotically uncorrelated. We, therefore, conclude

$$\sqrt{N}\left[\frac{\sqrt{N}\xi'_{3NT}}{\xi_{4NT}}-\frac{\mu_{3T}}{\mu_{4T}}\right] \Rightarrow \mathrm{N}\left(0,\frac{\sigma_3^2}{\mu_4^2}+\frac{\mu_3^2}{\mu_4^4}\sigma_4^2\right), \tag{C.10}$$

where

$$\frac{\sigma_3^2}{\mu_4^2}=\frac{\sigma_{0v}^4/12}{(\sigma_{0v}^2/6)^2}=3 \quad \text{and} \quad \frac{\mu_3^2}{\mu_4^4}\sigma_4^2=\frac{(\sigma_v^2/2)^2}{(\sigma_{0v}^2/6)^4}\frac{\sigma_{0v}^4}{45}=\frac{36}{5}\frac{\sigma_v^4}{\sigma_{0v}^4}.$$

Thus,

$$\sqrt{N}T(\hat{\rho}-1)-\frac{\sqrt{N}\mu_{3T}}{\mu_{4T}} \Rightarrow \mathrm{N}\left(0,3+\frac{36\sigma_v^4}{5\sigma_{0v}^4}\right). \tag{C.11}$$

The t-statistic is

$$t_\rho=\frac{(\hat{\rho}-1)\sqrt{\sum_{i=1}^N\sum_{t=2}^T\hat{e}_{it-1}^{*2}}}{s_e}=\frac{\sqrt{N}T(\hat{\rho}-1)\sqrt{\frac{1}{N}\sum_{i=1}^N\frac{1}{T^2}\sum_{t=2}^T\hat{e}_{it-1}^{*2}}}{s_e}$$

$$=\frac{\sqrt{N}T(\hat{\rho}-1)\sqrt{\xi_{4NT}}}{s_e}=\frac{\dfrac{\sqrt{N}\xi_{3NT}}{\zeta_{4NT}}\sqrt{\xi_{4NT}}}{s_e}$$

$$=\frac{\sqrt{N}\zeta_{3NT}}{s_e\sqrt{\xi_{4NT}}}=\frac{\sqrt{N}\xi'_{3NT}}{s_e\sqrt{\xi_{4NT}}}+o(1), \tag{C.12}$$

where $s_e^2 = (1/NT)\sum_{i=1}^{N}\sum_{t=2}^{T}(\hat{e}_{it}^* - \hat{\rho}\hat{e}_{it-1}^*)^2$. It follows that

$$s_e^2 = \frac{1}{NT}\sum_{i=1}^{N}\sum_{t=2}^{T}\{(u_{it}^* - \beta^*\varepsilon_{it}^*)\}^2 + o_p(1)$$

$$= \frac{1}{NT}\sum_{i=1}^{N}\sum_{t=2}^{T}(u_{it}^{*2} - 2\beta^* u_{it}^*\varepsilon_{it}^* + \beta^{*2}\varepsilon_{it}^{*2}) + o_p(1) \xrightarrow{p} \sigma_v^2.$$

That is, s_e^2 is a consistent estimator of σ_v^2. Next, we derive the asymptotic distribution of $\sqrt{N}\xi'_{3NT}/s_e\sqrt{\xi_{4NT}}$.

We use the same approach for the asymptotic distribution of $\sqrt{N}\xi'_{3NT}/s\sqrt{\xi_{4NT}}$ as we used for $\sqrt{NT}(\hat{\rho}-1)$. We make the following normalization:

$$\frac{N\xi'_{3NT}}{s_e\sqrt{\xi_{4NT}}} - \frac{N\mu_{3T}}{s_e\mu_{4T}}$$

$$= \frac{N\xi'_{3NT}}{s_e\xi_{4NT}} - \frac{N\mu_{3T}}{s_e\mu_{4T}} = \frac{N[\xi'_{3NT} - \mu_{3T}]}{s_e\xi_{4NT}} + \frac{\mu_{3T}}{s_e}N\left[\frac{1}{\xi_{4NT}} - \frac{1}{\mu_{4T}}\right]. \quad \text{(C.13)}$$

Since

$$\frac{N[\xi'_{3NT} - \mu_{3T}]}{s_e\xi_{4NT}} \Rightarrow \mathrm{N}\left(0, \frac{\sigma_3^2}{\mu_4\sigma_v^2}\right), \quad \text{(C.14)}$$

$$\frac{\mu_{3T}}{s_e}\sqrt{N}[\sqrt{1/\xi_{4NT}} - \sqrt{1/\mu_{4T}}] \Rightarrow \mathrm{N}\left(0, \frac{1}{4}\frac{\mu_3^2\sigma_4^2}{\mu_4^3\sigma_v^2}\right),$$

and $\sqrt{N}[\xi'_{3NT} - \mu_{3T}]$ and $\sqrt{N}[\xi_{4NT} - \mu_{4T}]$ are asymptotically uncorrelated, we note that

$$\frac{N\xi'_{3NT}}{s_e\xi_{4NT}} - \frac{N\mu_{3T}}{s_e\sqrt{\mu_{4T}}} \Rightarrow \mathrm{N}\left(0, \frac{\sigma_3^2}{\mu_4\sigma_v^2} + \frac{1}{4}\frac{\mu_3^2\sigma_4^2}{\mu_4^3\sigma_v^2}\right)$$

where

$$\frac{\sigma_3^2}{\mu_4\sigma_v^2} = \frac{\dfrac{\sigma_{0v}^4}{12}}{\dfrac{\sigma_{0v}^2}{6}\sigma_v^2} = \frac{\sigma_{0v}^2}{2\sigma_v^2} \quad \text{and} \quad \frac{1}{4}\frac{\mu_3^2\sigma_4^2}{\mu_4^3\sigma_v^2} = \frac{1}{4}\frac{\left(\dfrac{\sigma_v^2}{2}\right)^2\dfrac{\sigma_{0v}^4}{45}}{\left(\dfrac{\sigma_{0v}^2}{6}\right)^3\sigma_v^2} = \frac{3\sigma^2 v}{10\sigma_{0v}^2}.$$

Thus,

$$t_\rho - \frac{\sqrt{N}\mu_{3T}}{s_e\sqrt{\mu_{4T}}} \Rightarrow \mathrm{N}\left(0, \frac{\sigma_{0v}^2}{2\sigma_v^2} + \frac{3\sigma_v^2}{10\sigma_{0v}^2}\right).$$

Therefore, we established Theorem 3. □

Appendix D. Proof of Theorem 3

Proof. Observe that

$$\xi_{6NT} = \frac{1}{N}\sum_{i=1}^{N} \zeta_{6iT} = \frac{1}{N}\sum_{i=1}^{N} \frac{1}{T^2}(e_i^{*\prime}Q_i^* e_i^*)$$
$$= \frac{1}{N}\sum_{i=1}^{N} \frac{1}{T^2}(e_i^{*\prime}e_i^*) + \mathrm{o_p}(1) = \frac{1}{N}\sum_{i=1}^{N} \frac{1}{T^2}\sum_{t=2}^{T} (\hat{e}_{it-1}^{*2})$$
$$+ \mathrm{o_p}(1) = \frac{1}{N}\sum_{i=1}^{N} \left\{\frac{1}{T^2}\sum_{t=2}^{T} (y_{it}^* - \bar{y}_i^*)^2\right\} + \mathrm{o_p}(1).$$

We also note that

$$\frac{1}{T^2}\sum_{t=2}^{T} (y_{it}^* - \bar{y}_i^*)^2 \Rightarrow \sigma_{0v}^2\left[\int V_i^{*2} - \left\{\int V_i^*\right\}^2\right] = \zeta_{6i}, \tag{D.1}$$

$$\mathrm{E}[\zeta_{6i}] = \frac{\sigma_{0v}^2}{6} = \mu_6,$$

and

$$Var[\zeta_{6i}] = \sigma_{0v}^4/45 = \sigma_6^2.$$

Under the null hypothesis that $\rho = 1$, expression (9) can be written as

$$d(L)\Delta\hat{e}_{it}^* = v_{it}, \tag{D.2}$$

where $d(L) = (1 - \varphi_1 L - \varphi_2 L^2 - \cdots + \varphi_p L^p)$ and L is the backshift operator. Moreover,

$$\sqrt{N}\xi_{5NT} = \sqrt{N}\frac{1}{N}\sum_{i=1}^{N} \zeta_{5NT} = \sqrt{N}\frac{1}{N}\sum_{i=1}^{N} \frac{1}{T}(e_i^{*\prime}Q_i^* v_i)$$

$$= \sqrt{N}\frac{1}{N}\sum_{i=1}^{N}\frac{1}{T}(e_i^{*\prime}v_i) + o_p(1) = \sqrt{N}\frac{1}{N}\sum_{i=1}^{N}\frac{1}{T}\sum_{t=2}^{T}(\hat{e}_{it-1}^{*}v_{it})$$

$$+ o_p(1) = \sqrt{N}\frac{1}{N}\sum_{i=1}^{N}\left\{\frac{1}{T}\sum_{t=2}^{T}(y_{it}^{*} - \bar{y}_i^{*})d(L)u_{it}^{*}\right\} + o_p(1).$$

Since

$$\sqrt{N}\frac{1}{N}\sum_{i=1}^{N}\frac{1}{T}\sum_{T=2}^{T}\hat{e}_{it-1}^{*}v_{it}$$

$$= \sqrt{N}\frac{1}{N}\sum_{i=1}^{N}\frac{1}{T}\left[\sum_{t=2}^{T}\hat{e}_{it-1}^{*}(1 - \varphi_1 L - \varphi_2 L^2 - \cdots - \varphi_p L^p)\Delta\hat{e}_{it}^{*}\right]$$

$$= \sqrt{N}\frac{1}{N}\sum_{i=1}^{N}\frac{1}{T}\left[\sum_{t=2}^{T}\hat{e}_{it-1}^{*}\Delta\hat{e}_{it}^{*} - \varphi_1\hat{e}_{it-1}^{*}\Delta\hat{e}_{it-1}^{*}\right.$$

$$\left. - \varphi_2\hat{e}_{it-1}^{*}\Delta\hat{e}_{it-2}^{*} - \cdots - \varphi_p\hat{e}_{it-1}^{*}\Delta\hat{e}_{it-p}^{*}\right]$$

$$= \frac{1}{\sqrt{N}T}\sum_{i=1}^{N}\sum_{t=2}^{T}[(y_{it-1}^{*} - \bar{y}_i^{*})(u_{it} - \varphi_1 u_{it-1}$$

$$- \varphi_2 u_{it-2} - \cdots - \varphi_p u_{it-p})] + o_p(1),$$

it follows that

$$\sqrt{N}\xi_{5NT} = \sqrt{N}\frac{1}{N}\sum_{i=1}^{N}\frac{1}{T}\sum_{t=2}^{T}\hat{e}_{it-1}^{*}v_{it} + o_p(1)$$

$$= \frac{1}{NT}\sum_{i=1}^{N}\sum_{t=2}^{T}(y_{it-1}^{*} - \bar{y}_i^{*})(u_{it} - \varphi_1 u_{it-1} - \varphi_2 u_{it-2} - \cdots$$

$$- \varphi_p u_{it-p}) + o_p(1).$$

Hence,

$$t_{ADF} = \frac{\sqrt{N}\xi_{5NT}}{s_v\sqrt{\xi_{6NT}}} = \frac{\sqrt{N}\frac{1}{N}\sum_{i=1}^{N}\left\{\frac{1}{T}\sum_{t=2}^{T}(y_{it-1} - \bar{y}_i)d(L)u_{it}^{*}\right\}}{s_v\sqrt{\xi_{6NT}}} + o_p(1)$$

$$= \frac{\sqrt{N}\xi_{5NT}'}{s_v\sqrt{\xi_{6NT}}} + o_p(1),$$

where

$$\zeta'_{5iT} = \frac{1}{T}\sum_{t=2}^{T} (y^*_{it-1} - \bar{y}^*_i) d(L) u^*_{it} \quad \text{and} \quad \xi'_{5NT} = \frac{1}{N}\sum_{i=1}^{N} \zeta'_{5iT}.$$

Assume that the sequence $\{u^*_{it}\}$ satisfies condition (C2) in Phillips and Ouliaris (1990) so that

$$\frac{1}{T}\sum_{t=2}^{[rT]} d(L) u^*_{it} \Rightarrow d(1)\sigma_{0v} V^*_i(r)$$

for all i. Consequently,

$$\frac{1}{T}\sum_{t=2}^{T} y^*_{it-1} d(L) u^*_{it} \Rightarrow d(1)\sigma^2_{0v} \int V^*_i \, \mathrm{d}V^*_i$$

and

$$\frac{1}{T}\sum_{t=2}^{T} \bar{y}^*_i d(L) u^*_{it} \Rightarrow d(1)\sigma^2_{0v} V^*_i(1) \int V^*_i .$$

for all i. Clearly,

$$\frac{1}{T}\sum_{t=2}^{T} (y^*_{it-1} - \bar{y}^*_i) \mathrm{d}(L) u^*_{it} \Rightarrow d(1)\sigma^2_{0v} \int V^*_i \, \mathrm{d}V^*_i - d(1)\sigma^2_{0v} V^*_i(1) \int V^*_i = \zeta_{5i}$$

for all i, with $\mathrm{E}(\zeta_{5i}) = -d(1)\sigma^2_{0v}/2$ and $Var(\zeta_{5i}) = d^2(1)\sigma^4_{0v}/12$. Let

$$s^2_v = \frac{1}{NT}\sum_{i=1}^{N}\sum_{t=2}^{T} \{(\hat{e}^*_{it} - \hat{\rho}^* \hat{e}_{it-1}) - (\hat{\varphi}_1 L + \hat{\varphi}_2 L^2 + \cdots + \hat{\varphi}_p L^p)\Delta \hat{e}^*_{it}\}^2.$$

Observe that $\{\hat{e}^*_{it}\}$ are linear combinations of $u^*_{it}$and ε^*_{it}. Those linear combinations are in general ARMA processes. Therefore, we need to have $p \to \infty$ as $T \to \infty$ such that $p = \mathrm{o}(T^{1/3})$ to capture the true structure of v_{it}. As a result of $p \to \infty$, $\hat{\rho} \overset{\mathrm{p}}{\to} 1$ and the estimated coefficients $\{\hat{\varphi}_i\}$ may well represent $\{\varphi_i\}$:

$$s^2_v = \frac{1}{NT}\sum_{i=1}^{N}\sum_{t=2}^{T} \{(1 - \varphi_1 L - \varphi_2 L^2 - \cdots - \varphi_p L^p)(u^*_{it} - \hat{\beta}^* \varepsilon^*_{it})\}^2 + \mathrm{o}_p(1)$$

$$= \frac{1}{NT}\sum_{i=1}^{N}\sum_{t=2}^{T} d^2(L)(u^{*2}_{it} - 2\hat{\beta}^* u^*_{it}\varepsilon^*_{it} + \hat{\beta}^{*2}\varepsilon^{*2}_{it}) + \mathrm{o}_p(1) \overset{\mathrm{p}}{\to} d^2(1)\sigma^2_v = \sigma^2$$

by the sequential limit theory. We are now in a position to derive the asymptotic distribution of $\sqrt{N}\xi'_{5NT}/s_v\sqrt{\xi_{6NT}}$. Define

$$\mu_{5T} = \mathrm{E}(\zeta'_{5iT}) = \mathrm{E}(\zeta'_{5i}) + \mathrm{o_p}(1)$$

and

$$\mu_{6T} = \mathrm{E}(\zeta_{6iT}) = \mathrm{E}(\zeta_{6i}) + \mathrm{o_p}(1).$$

Then, we make the following normalization:

$$t_{ADF} - \frac{\sqrt{N}\mu_{5T}}{s_v\mu_{6T}} = \frac{\sqrt{N}\xi'_{5NT}}{s_v\sqrt{\xi_{6NT}}} - \frac{\sqrt{N}\mu_{5T}}{s_v\sqrt{\mu_{6T}}} = \frac{\sqrt{N}(\xi'_{5NT} - \mu_{5T})}{s_v\sqrt{\xi_{6NT}}}$$

$$+ \frac{\mu_{5T}}{s_v}\sqrt{N}(\sqrt{1/\zeta_{6NT}} - \sqrt{1/\mu_{6T}}).$$

Since

$$\frac{\sqrt{N}(\xi'_{5NT} - \mu_{5T})}{s_v\sqrt{\xi_{6NT}}} \Rightarrow \mathrm{N}\left(0, \frac{\frac{d^2(1)\sigma_{0v}^4}{12}}{\frac{\sigma^2\sigma_{0v}^2}{6}}\right) = \mathrm{N}\left(0, \frac{d^2(1)\sigma_{0v}^2}{2\sigma^2}\right)$$

$$\frac{\mu_{5T}}{s_v}\sqrt{N}\left(\sqrt{\frac{1}{\xi_{6NT}}} - \sqrt{\frac{1}{\mu_{6T}}}\right) \Rightarrow \mathrm{N}\left(0, \frac{1}{4}\frac{\left(-d(1)\frac{\sigma_v^2}{2}\right)^2\frac{\sigma_{0v}^4}{45}}{\sigma^2\left(\frac{\sigma_{0v}^2}{6}\right)^3}\right)$$

$$= \mathrm{N}\left(0, \frac{3d^2(1)\sigma_v^4}{10\sigma^2\sigma_{0v}^2}\right)$$

and $\sqrt{N}(\xi_{5NT} - \mu_{5T})$ and $\sqrt{N}(\xi_{6NT} - \mu_{6T})$ are asymptotically uncorrelated, we conclude that

$$t_{ADF} - \frac{\sqrt{N}\mu_{5T}}{s_v\sqrt{\mu_{6T}}} \Rightarrow \mathrm{N}\left(0, \frac{d^2(1)\sigma_{0v}^2}{2d^2(1)\sigma_v^2} + \frac{3d^2(1)\sigma_v^4}{10d^2(1)\sigma_v^2\sigma_{0v}^2}\right)$$

$$= \mathrm{N}\left(0, \frac{\sigma_{0v}^2}{2\sigma_v^2} + \frac{3\sigma_v^2}{10\sigma_{0v}^2}\right). \quad \square$$

Appendix E. Proof of Theorem 4

Proof. The OLS of ρ of Eq. (15) is

$$\hat{\rho} = \frac{\sum_{i=1}^{N}\sum_{t=1}^{T}\tilde{y}_{it}\tilde{y}_{it-1}}{\sum_{i=1}^{N}\sum_{t=1}^{T}\tilde{y}_{it-1}^{2}}, \tag{E.1}$$

where $\tilde{y}_{it} = y_{it} - \bar{y}_i - d_i$, $d_i = \sum_{t=1}^{T}(t-\bar{t})y_{it}/\sum_{t=1}^{T}(t-\bar{t})^2$, $\bar{t} = (T+1)/2$, and $\bar{y}_i = (1/T)\sum_{t=1}^{T}y_{it}$. Under the null of no cointegration, $\rho = 1$, we have

$$\sqrt{N}T(\hat{\rho}-1) = \frac{\sum_{i=1}^{N}\sum_{t=1}^{T}\tilde{y}_{it-1}\varepsilon_{it}}{\sum_{i=1}^{N}\sum_{t=1}^{T}\tilde{y}_{it-1}^{2}} = \frac{\sqrt{N}\frac{1}{N}\sum_{i=1}^{N}\frac{1}{T}\sum_{t=1}^{T}\tilde{y}_{it-1}\varepsilon_{it}}{\frac{1}{N}\sum_{i=1}^{N}\frac{1}{T^2}\sum_{t=1}^{T}\tilde{y}_{it-1}^{2}}. \tag{E.2}$$

Consider the denominator in Eq. (E.2) from Phillips and Perron (1988):

$$\frac{1}{T^2}\sum_{t=1}^{T}\tilde{y}_{it-1}^{2} \Rightarrow \sigma_{0u}^{2}\int\tilde{V}^2, \tag{E.3}$$

where $\tilde{V}(r)$ is the standard demeaned and detrended Wiener process

$$\tilde{V}(r) = V(r) + (6r-4)\int V + (-12r+6)\int sV. \tag{E.4}$$

Note that $\mathrm{E}[\sigma_{0u}^2\int\tilde{V}^2] = \sigma_{0u}^2/15 = \mu_8$ and $Var[\sigma_{0u}^2\int\tilde{V}^2] = 11\sigma_{0u}^4/6300$. It follows that

$$\frac{1}{N}\sum_{i=1}^{N}\frac{1}{T^2}\sum_{t=1}^{T}\tilde{y}_{it-1}^{2} \xrightarrow{p} \frac{\sigma_{0u}^{2}}{15}$$

by a law of large numbers and the sequential limit theory. Next consider the numerator from Phillips and Perron (1988):

$$\frac{1}{T}\sum_{t=1}^{T}\tilde{y}_{it-1}\varepsilon_{it} \Rightarrow \sigma_{0u}^{2}\int\tilde{V}\,\mathrm{d}V + \lambda \tag{E.5}$$

where $\lambda = \frac{1}{2}(\sigma_{0u}^2 - \sigma_u^2)$. It can be shown that

$$\mathrm{E}\left[\int\tilde{V}\,dV\right] = -\frac{\sigma_{0u}^{2}}{2} + \lambda = -\frac{\sigma_{u}^{2}}{2} = \mu_9 \tag{E.6}$$

and $Var[\int \tilde{V}\, dV] = \sigma_{0u}^4/60$. Then

$$\sqrt{N}\left[T(\hat{\rho}-1) - \frac{\mu_{7T}}{\mu_{8T}}\right] \Rightarrow N\left(0, \frac{15}{4} + \frac{\sigma_u^4}{\sigma_{0u}^4}\frac{2475}{112}\right), \tag{E.7}$$

by the Lindeberg–Levy central limit theorem and the sequential limit theory, where

$$\mu_{7T} = E\left[\frac{1}{T}\sum_{t=1}^{T} \tilde{y}_{it-1}\varepsilon_{it}\right] \tag{E.8}$$

and

$$\mu_{8T} = E\left[\frac{1}{T^2}\sum_{t=1}^{T} \tilde{y}_{it-1}^2\right]. \tag{E.9}$$

The t-statistic to test $\rho = 1$, t_ρ, is

$$t_\rho = \frac{(\hat{\rho}-1)\sqrt{\sum_{i=1}^{N}\sum_{t=1}^{T}\tilde{y}_{it-1}^2}}{s_e},$$

where

$$s_e^2 = \frac{1}{NT}\sum_{i=1}^{N}\sum_{t=2}^{T}(\hat{\varepsilon}_{it})^2. \tag{E.10}$$

The asymptotic distribution of t_ρ can be found using the same approach as in Eqs. (E.2), (E.3), (E.4), (E.5), (E.6), (E.7), (E.8) and (E.9)

$$t_\rho - \frac{\sqrt{N}\mu_{7T}}{s_e\sqrt{\mu_{8T}}} \Rightarrow N\left(0, \frac{1}{4}\frac{\sigma_{0u}^2}{\sigma_u^2} + \frac{165}{448}\frac{\sigma_u^2}{\sigma_{0u}^2}\right). \tag{E.11}$$

Finally, it can be shown that the ADF test, t_{ADF}, has the same asymptotic distribution as the t_ρ using the same approach as in Section 3.2. Therefore, we have established Theorem 4. □

References

Billingsley, P., 1986. Probability and Measure. John Wiley, New York.

Breitung, J., Meyer, W., 1994. Testing for unit roots in panel data: Are wages on different bargaining levels cointegrated? Applied Economics 26, 353–361.

Engle, R.F., Granger, C.W.J., 1987. Co-integration and error correction: Representation, estimation, and testing. Econometrica 55, 251–276.

Gonzalo, J., 1994. Five alternative methods of estimating long-run equilibrium relationships. Journal of Econometrics 60, 203–233.

Hansen, B., 1992. Efficient estimation and testing of cointegrating vectors in the presence of deterministic trends. Journal of Econometrics 53, 87–121.

Haug, A., 1996. Tests for cointegration: A Monte Carlo comparison. Journal of Econometrics 71, 89–115.

Im K., Pesaran, H., Shin, Y., 1997. Testing for unit roots in heterogeneous panels. Manuscript, Department of Applied Economics, University of Cambridge.

Kao, C., Chen, B., 1995a. On the estimation and inference of a cointegrated regression in panel data when the cross-section and time-series dimensions are comparable. Manuscript, Department of Economics, Syracuse University.

Kao, C., Chen, B., 1995b. Residual-based tests for cointegration in panel data when the cross-section and time-series dimensions are comparable. Manuscript, Department of Economics, Syracuse University.

Kao, C., Chiang, M.-H., 1997. On the estimation and inference of a cointegrated regression in panel data. Econometric Theory, Under Revision.

Levin, A., Lin, C.-F., 1993. Unit root tests in panel data: New results. Discussion Paper, Department of Economics, UC-San Diego.

McCoskey, S., Kao, C., 1998. A residual-based test of the null of cointegration in panel data. Econometric Reviews 17, 57–84.

Pedroni, P., 1995. Panel cointegration: Asymptotic and finite sample properties of pooled time series tests with an application to the PPP hypothesis. Indiana University Working Papers in Economics, No. 95–013.

Pesaran, H., Smith, R., 1995. Estimating long-run relationships from dynamic heterogeneous panels. Journal of Econometrics 68, 79–113.

Phillips, P.C.B., Moon, H., 1997. Linear regression limit theory for nonstationary panel data. Cowles Foundation Discussion Paper.

Phillips, P.C.B., Ouliaris, S., 1990. Asymptotic properties of residual based test for cointegration. Econometrica 58, 165–193.

Phillips, P.C.B., Perron, P., 1988. Testing for unit root in time series regression. Biometrika 75, 335–346.

Quah, D., 1994. Exploiting cross section variation for unit root inference in dynamic data. Economics Letters 44, 9–19.

OXFORD BULLETIN OF ECONOMICS AND STATISTICS, SPECIAL ISSUE (1999)
0305-9049

A COMPARATIVE STUDY OF UNIT ROOT TESTS WITH PANEL DATA AND A NEW SIMPLE TEST

*G. S. Maddala and Shaowen Wu**

Simplicity, simplicity, simplicity: I say let your affairs be as two or three and not a hundred or thousand.
Simplify, simplify.

(H. D. Thoreau: *Walden*)

I. INTRODUCTION

Since the appearance of the papers by Levin and Lin (1992, 1993), the use of panel data unit root tests has become very popular among empirical researchers with access to a panel data set. It is by now a generally accepted argument that the commonly used unit root tests like the Dickey–Fuller (DF), augmented Dickey–Fuller (ADF) and Phillips–Perron (PP) tests lack power in distinguishing the unit root null from stationary alternatives, and that using panel data unit root tests is one way of increasing the power of unit root tests based on a single time series. See, for example, the arguments in Oh (1996), Wu (1996), MacDonald (1996) and Frankel and Rose (1996), who try to resurrect the purchasing power parity (*PPP*) theory using panel data unit root tests.

Such use of panel unit root tests may not be meaningful because different null hypotheses are being tested in each case. For instance, consider the simplified model

$$\Delta y_{i,t} = \rho_i y_{i,t-1} + \varepsilon_{i,t},\ i = 1, 2, \ldots, N,\ t = 1, 2, \ldots, T.$$

Suppose we are interested in testing $\rho_1 = 0$ vs. $\rho_1 < 0$, we apply a single equation unit root for the first time series. The panel data unit root test tests a different hypothesis:

$$H_0\colon \rho_i = 0 \text{ vs.} H_1\colon \rho_i < 0, \text{ for } i = 1, 2, \ldots, N.$$

Furthermore, there are now more powerful tests available even in the single equation context. See, for example, Elliott, Rothenberg and Stock (1996) and also Perron and Ng (1996) who suggest modifications of the PP test to increase power.

*An earlier version of this paper was presented at the Econometric Society meetings in New Orleans, January 1997. We would like to thank Anindya Banerjee for helpful comments.

In the following sections, we shall present a review of the Levin–Lin tests, their extension by Im, Pesaran and Shin (1997), which will be referred to as the IPS test, and a simple alternative due to Fisher (1932) which will be referred to as the Fisher test. We then present some results from Monte Carlo experiments comparing these three tests and some evidence from the bootstrap which allows for correlation in the errors. Finally, we consider a test based on the Bonferroni inequality and conduct a Monte Carlo experiment to compare this test with the Fisher test.

II. PANEL DATA UNIT ROOT TESTS

Some early papers on testing for unit roots based on panel data are by Quah (1992, 1994) and Breitung and Mayer (1994). Since these have been superseded by the papers by Levin and Lin (1992, 1993), they are not discussed here.

2.1. The Levin–Lin (LL) Tests

Levin and Lin (1992) conduct an exhaustive study and develop unit root tests for the model:

$$\Delta y_{i,t} = \rho y_{i,t-1} + \alpha_0 + \delta t + \alpha_i + \theta_t + \varepsilon_{i,t},\ i = 1, 2, \ldots, N,\ t = 1, 2, \ldots, T.$$

Thus, the model incorporates a time trend as well as individual and time-specific effects. Initially, they assume that $\varepsilon_{i,t} \sim IID(0, \sigma^2)$ but they state that under serial correlation, with the inclusion of lagged first differences as in the ADF test, the test statistics have the same limiting distributions as mentioned subsequently, provided the number of lagged differences increase with sample size. Levin and Lin consider several subcases of this model. In all cases the limiting distributions are as $N \to \infty$ and $T \to \infty$. Also in all cases, the equation is estimated by *OLS* as a pooled regression model. The submodels are:

Model 1: $\Delta y_{i,t} = \rho y_{i,t-1} + \varepsilon_{i,t}$ $\quad H_0$: $\rho = 0$
Model 2: $\Delta y_{i,t} = \rho y_{i,t-1} + \alpha_0 + \varepsilon_{i,t}$ $\quad H_0$: $\rho = 0$
Model 3: $\Delta y_{i,t} = \rho y_{i,t-1} + \alpha_0 + \delta t + \varepsilon_{i,t}$ $\quad H_0$: $\rho = 0,\ \delta = 0$
Model 4: $\Delta y_{i,t} = \rho y_{i,t-1} + \theta_t + \varepsilon_{i,t}$ $\quad H_0$: $\rho = 0$
Model 5: $\Delta y_{i,t} = \rho y_{i,t-1} + \alpha_i + \varepsilon_{i,t}$ $\quad H_0$: $\rho = 0,\ \alpha_i = 0$ for all i
Model 6: $\Delta y_{i,t} = \rho y_{i,t-1} + \alpha_i + \delta_i t + \varepsilon_{i,t}$ $\quad H_0$: $\rho = 0,\ \delta_i = 0$ for all i.

For models 1–4, they show that

(a) $T\sqrt{N}\hat{\rho} \Rightarrow N(0, 2)$
(b) $t_{\rho=0} \Rightarrow N(0, 1)$.

For model 5, if $\sqrt{N}/T \to 0$, then

(a) $T\sqrt{N}\hat{\rho}+3\sqrt{N}\Rightarrow N(0,\,10.2)$

(b) $\sqrt{1.25}t_{\rho=0}+\sqrt{1.875N}\Rightarrow N\left(0,\dfrac{645}{112}\right).$

In model 6, both intercept and time trend vary with individuals.

In the empirical applications, Oh (1996) uses only models 1 and 5. Wu (1996) uses the complete model with trend, and individual and time-specific effects but uses the distributions derived for model 5. Papell (1997) uses model 5 with lagged first differences added but computes his own exact finite sample critical values using Monte Carlo methods and finds them 3 to 15 percent higher than those tabulated in Levin and Lin (1992).

Levin and Lin argue that in contrast to the standard distributions of unit root test statistics for a single time series, the panel test statistics have limiting normal distributions. However, the convergence rates are faster as $T\to\infty$ (superconsistency) than as $N\to\infty$.

The paper by Levin and Lin (1993) provides some new results on panel unit root tests. These tests are designed to take care of the problem of heteroscedasticity and autocorrelation. They involve the following steps.

(i) Subtract cross-section averages from the data to eliminate the influence of aggregate effects.

(ii) Apply the augmented Dickey–Fuller (ADF) test to each individual series and normalize the disturbances. For illustration, we use model 5. The ADF regression

$$\Delta y_{i,t}=\rho_i y_{i,t-1}+\sum_{j=1}^{p_i}\theta_{ij}\Delta y_{i,t-j}+\alpha_i+\varepsilon_{i,t} \tag{1}$$

is equivalent to performing two auxiliary regressions of Δy_{it} and $y_{i,t-1}$ on the remaining variables in equation (1). Let the residuals from these two auxiliary regressions be $\hat{e}_{i,t}$ and $\hat{V}_{i,t-1}$ respectively. Now regress $\hat{e}_{i,t}$ on $\hat{V}_{i,t-1}$:

$$\hat{e}_{i,t}=\rho_i\hat{V}_{i,t-1}+\varepsilon_{i,t}$$

to get $\hat{\rho}_i$ which is equivalent to the *OLS* estimator of ρ_i in (1) directly. Since there is heteroscedasticity in $\varepsilon_{i,t}$, they suggest the following normalization to control it:

$$\hat{\sigma}^2_{e_i}=\frac{1}{T-p_i-1}\sum_{t=p_i+2}^{T}(\hat{e}_{i,t}-\hat{\rho}_i\hat{V}_{i,t-1})^2$$

$$\tilde{e}_{i,t}=\frac{\hat{e}_{i,t}}{\hat{\sigma}_{e_i}}$$

$$\tilde{V}_{i,t-1}=\frac{\hat{V}_{i,t-1}}{\hat{\sigma}_{e_i}}.$$

Asymptotically, $\tilde{e}_{i,t}$ will be i.i.d. for all individual i.

(iii) Estimate the ratio of long-run to short-run standard deviation for each individual series and then calculate the average ratio for the panel as:

$$\hat{S}_{NT} = \frac{1}{N}\sum_{i=1}^{N}\frac{\hat{\sigma}_{y_i}}{\hat{\sigma}_{e_i}}$$

where the long-run variance $\hat{\sigma}^2_{y_i}$ is estimated by

$$\hat{\sigma}^2_{y_i} = \frac{1}{T-1}\sum_{t=2}^{T}\Delta y^2_{i,t} + 2\sum_{L=1}^{\overline{K}} w_{\overline{K}L}\left(\frac{1}{T-1}\sum_{t=L+2}^{T}\Delta y_{i,t}\Delta y_{i,t-L}\right).$$

$\overline{K}$ is the lag truncation parameter and $w_{\overline{K}L}$ is some lag window.

(iv) Compute the panel test statistic. Then consider the following regression:

$$\tilde{e}_{i,t} = \rho\tilde{V}_{i,t-1} + \tilde{\varepsilon}_{i,t}$$

using all i and t. The resulting t-statistic is

$$t_{\rho=0} = \frac{\hat{\rho}}{RSE(\hat{\rho})}$$

where

$$RSE(\hat{\rho}) = \hat{\sigma}_{\varepsilon}\left[\sum_{i=1}^{N}\sum_{t=2+p_i}^{T}\hat{V}^2_{i,t-1}\right]^{-1/2}$$

$$\hat{\sigma}^2_{\varepsilon} = \frac{1}{N\tilde{T}}\sum_{i=1}^{N}\sum_{t=2+p_i}^{T}(\tilde{e}_{i,t} - \hat{\rho}\tilde{V}_{i,t-1})^2$$

$$\tilde{T} = T - p - 1 \text{ and } \overline{p} = \frac{1}{N}\sum_{i=1}^{N}p_i$$

is the average lag length used in the individual ADF regression.

Since the test statistic is not centered at zero, Levin and Lin suggest using the following adjusted t-statistic:

$$t^*_{\rho} = \frac{t_{\rho=0} - N\tilde{T}\hat{S}_{NT}\hat{\sigma}^{-2}_{\varepsilon}RSE(\hat{\rho})\mu^*_{\tilde{T}}}{\sigma^*_{\tilde{T}}}$$

where $\mu^*_{\tilde{T}}$ and $\sigma^*_{\tilde{T}}$ are the mean and the standard deviation adjustment terms which are obtained from Monte Carlo simulation and tabulated in their paper. Under

$$H_0: \rho = 0,\ t^*_{\rho} \Rightarrow N(0, 1).$$

In the simulations reported later we used this procedure.

The major limitation of the Levin–Lin tests is that ρ is the same for all observations. Thus, if we denote by ρ_i the value of ρ for the ith cross-section unit then the Levin–Lin test specifies the null H_0 and alternative H_1 as:

$$H_0: \rho_1 = \rho_2 = \ldots = \rho_N = \rho = 0$$
$$H_1: \rho_1 = \rho_2 = \ldots = \rho_N = \rho < 0.$$

The null makes sense under some circumstances, but the alternative is too strong to be held in any interesting empirical cases. For example, in testing the convergence hypothesis in growth models, one can formulate the null as implying that none of the economies under study converges and thus $\rho = 0$ for all countries. But it does not make any sense to assume that all the countries will converge at the same rate if they do converge.

2.2. *The Im–Pesaran–Shin (IPS) Test (1997)*

IPS relax the assumption that $\rho_1 = \rho_2 = \ldots = \rho_N$ under H_1. The basic idea of the test is very simple. Take model 5 in Levin and Lin and substitute ρ_i for ρ. Essentially what we have is a model with a linear trend for each of the N cross-section units. Thus, instead of pooling the data, we use separate unit root tests for the N cross-section units. Consider the t-test for each cross-section unit based on T observations. Let $t_{i,T}$ $(i = 1, 2, \ldots, N)$ denote the t-statistics for testing unit roots, and let $E(t_{i,T}) = \mu$ and $V(t_{i,T}) = \sigma^2$. Then

$$\sqrt{N}\frac{(\bar{t}_{N,T} - \mu)}{\sigma} \Rightarrow N(0,\ 1), \quad \text{where } \bar{t}_{N,T} = \frac{1}{N}\sum_{i=1}^{N} t_{i,T}.$$

The problem is computing μ and σ^2. This they do by Monte Carlo methods and tabulate them for ready reference (Tables 3 and 4 of their paper).

Although IPS talk of their test as a generalization of the LL tests, the important thing to note is that the IPS test is a way of combining the evidence on the unit root hypothesis from the N unit root tests performed on the N cross-section units. Note that implicit in the test is the assumption that T is the same for all cross-section units and hence $E(t_{i,T})$ and $V(t_{i,T})$ are the same for all i. Thus, we are considering only balanced panel data. In practice, if unbalanced data are used, more simulations have to be carried out to get critical values.

In the case of serial correlation, IPS propose using the ADF t-test for individual series. However, $E(t_{i,T})$ and $V(t_{i,T})$ will vary as the lag length included in the ADF regression varies. They tabulate $E(t_{i,T})$ and $V(t_{i,T})$ for different lag lengths. In practice, however, to make use of their tables, we are restricted implicitly to using the same lag length for all the ADF regressions for individual series.

IPS also suggest an *LR*-bar test based on likelihood ratio statistics, but we shall concentrate our discussion on their t-bar test. The same arguments apply to the LR-bar test.

2.3. Fisher's (p_λ) Test

It should be noted that the IPS test is for testing the significance of the results from N independent tests of a hypothesis. There is a large amount of literature on this issue dating back to Tippett (1931) and Fisher (1932). This problem has been studied under the title 'Meta Analysis' and the different tests are reviewed in Hedges and Olkin (1985, Chapter 3). All these procedures depend on different ways of combining the observed significance levels (p-values) from the different tests. If the test statistics are continuous, the significance levels π_i ($i = 1, 2, \ldots, N$) are independent uniform (0, 1) variables, and $-2\log_e \pi_i$ has a χ^2 distribution with two degrees of freedom. Using the additive property of the χ^2 variables, we get $\lambda = -2\sum_{i=1}^{N} \log_e \pi_i$ has a χ^2 distribution with $2N$ degrees of freedom. This is the test suggested by Fisher (1932). Pearson suggested a slight modification of this and the Fisher test goes under the name of p_λ test. It is discussed in Rao (1952, p. 44) and by Maddala (1977, p. 47) but there have not been many econometric applications of this test.

Tippett suggested using the distribution of the smallest of the p-values, π_i. There have been several other suggestions about the p-value combinations. Becker (1977) lists 16 of them, but no p-value combination is most powerful. However, the Fisher test based on the sum of the log-p-values has been widely recommended. In this paper, we shall use the Fisher test. (We tried the Tippett test as well but it was not as powerful as the Fisher test, and hence the results are not reported.)

The advantage of this test is that it does not require a balanced panel as in the case of the IPS test. Also, one can use different lag lengths in the individual ADF regression. Another advantage of the Fisher test is that it can also be carried out for any unit root test derived. The disadvantage is that the p-values have to be derived by Monte Carlo simulation. The IPS test is easy to use because there are ready tables available in the paper for $E(t_{i,T})$ and $V(t_{i,T})$. However, these are valid only for the ADF test.

III. A COMPARISON OF THE DIFFERENT TESTS

Some broad comments on the merits and demerits of the three tests would be useful in interpreting the results to be presented later. Hence we shall go through these first.

(1) The LL tests test a very restrictive hypothesis that is rarely of practical interest.

(2) The IPS test is claimed to be a generalization of the LL tests. However, it is better viewed as a way of combining the evidence of several independent unit root tests.

(3) Im–Pesaran–Shin present a power comparison of the LL and IPS tests and argue that the IPS test is more powerful than the LL test. However, strictly speaking, the power comparison is not valid. Although the null hypothesis is the same in the two tests, the alternative hypothesis is different. The LL tests are based on homogeneity of the autoregressive parameter (although there is heterogeneity in the error variances and the serial correlation structure of the errors). Thus the tests are based on pooled regressions. The IPS test, on the other hand, is based on heterogeneity of the autoregressive parameter. As argued earlier, the test amounts to a combination of different independent tests. There is no pooling of data involved as in the LL tests. In the following sections, we shall also present power comparisons with the LL test but it should be borne in mind that the LL test will necessarily come out worse because the LL test has to use the panel estimation method which is not valid if there is no need for pooling.

(4) The Fisher test and the IPS test *are* directly comparable. The aim of both tests is a combination of the significance of different *independent tests*. The Fisher test is non-parametric; whatever test statistic we use for testing for a unit root for each sample, we can get the p-values π_i and then $-2\sum \log_e \pi_i \sim \chi^2$ with $2N$ d.f., where N is the number of separate samples. The IPS test, on the other hand, is parametric. The distribution of the t-bar statistic involves the mean and variance of the t-statistics used. IPS compute this for the ADF test statistic for different values of the number of lags used and different sample sizes. However, these tables are valid *only* if the ADF test is used for the unit root tests. Also, if the length of the time series for the different samples is different, there is a problem using the tables prepared by IPS. The Fisher test does not have any such limitations. It can be used with any unit root test and even if the ADF test is used, the choice of the lag length for each sample can be separately determined. Also, there is no restriction of the sample sizes for different samples (they can vary according to availability of the data).

(5) The Fisher test is an exact test. The IPS test is an asymptotic test. Note that this does not lead to a huge difference in finite sample results, since the adjustment terms in the IPS test are derived from simulations while the p-values in the Fisher test are also derived from simulations. However, the asymptotic validity of the tests depends on different conditions. For the IPS test the asymptotic results depend on N going to infinity while for the Fisher test they depend on T going to infinity.

(6) The crucial element that distinguishes the two tests is that the Fisher test is based on combining the *significance levels* of the different tests, and the IPS test is based on combining the *test statistics*. Which is better is the question. We conducted Monte Carlo studies with these issues in mind.

(7) Both the Fisher test and IPS test are based on combining independent tests. So if there is contemporaneous correlation, then there are correlations

among the individual test statistics. Both tests will need modifications in this case.

IV. DESIGN OF THE MONTE CARLO STUDIES

In this section, we present details on the designs of Monte Carlo simulations. Basically, there are two experiments. The first one studies the size and power performances of the three unit root tests under the general setup of the null and the alternative hypotheses, i.e., H_0: $\rho_i = \rho = 0$ for all i, and H_1: $\rho_i = \rho < 0$ for all i. In the second experiment, we change the alternative to H_1: $\rho_i = 0$ for some i, and $\rho_i < 0$ for the other i. We do so due to the following consideration. In reality, some series in a panel under study might be stationary while the others are non-stationary. We expect the null to be rejected for such panels. But due to the masking problems, power might be relatively low for panel unit root tests. Thus we want to investigate the powers of the three panel unit root tests in this circumstance. Details of these two designs are as follows.

4.1. *Basic Monte Carlo Simulation Design*

In this experiment, we use the following data-generating process (*DGP*) for a dynamic panel containing group and time-specific effects. The coefficient on the lagged dependent variable is denoted by ϕ_i in the *DGP*. Thus,

$$\text{Drift model: } \Delta y_{i,t} = -\phi_i\mu_i + \phi_i y_{i,t-1} + u_{i,t}$$

$$\text{Trend model: } \Delta y_{i,t} = \mu_i - \phi_i\mu_i t + \phi_i y_{i,t-1} + u_{i,t}$$

where $i = 1, 2, \ldots, N$ and $t = 1, 2, \ldots, T$, and $y_{i,0}$ is random.

The error term $u_{i,t}$ contains a time-specific effect θ_t and random component $\varepsilon_{i,t}$:

$$u_{i,t} = \theta_t + \varepsilon_{i,t}$$

where $\theta_t = 0.9\theta_{t-1} + \omega_t$, $\omega_t \sim N(0, 1)$ and $\varepsilon_{i,t} = \lambda_i\varepsilon_{i,t-1} + e_{i,t}$, λ_i's are randomly generated on $U[0.2, 0.4]$ and different for each i where U denotes the uniform distribution. We assume $e_{i,t}$ to be jointly normal distributed with

$$E(e_{i,t}) = 0,\ E(e_{i,t}, e_{j,s}) = \begin{cases} \sigma_{ij} & \text{for } t = s \\ 0 & \text{for } t \neq s. \end{cases}$$

If we let Σ denote $(\sigma_{ij})_{i,j=1}^{N}$, then non-zero terms on the off-diagonal terms in Σ represents the existence of cross-correlations. Here we randomly generate some positive definite matrices for Σ.

In the simulation, μ_i is generated randomly from $N(0, 1)$ and then fixed for each model. The randomness of $y_{i,0}$ is achieved by generating extra y's and discarding some initial observations.

This experiment is very similar to IPS's experiments. The biggest difference is that we allow contemporaneous correlation in $\varepsilon_{i,t}$.

After the data have been generated, we apply the LL, IPS and Fisher tests. For the Fisher test, we apply the ADF(p) test for each individual series. The following two models are estimated.

$$\text{Drift model: } \Delta y_{i,t} = \alpha_i + \rho_i y_{i,t-1} + \sum_{j=1}^{p} \gamma_{ij} \Delta y_{i,t-j} + \text{residual}$$

$$\text{Trend model: } \Delta y_{i,t} = \alpha_i + \delta_i t + \rho_i y_{i,t} + \sum_{j=1}^{p} \gamma_{ij} \Delta y_{i,t-j} + \text{residual}$$

where $p = 0, 1, 2$ are used and p-values using the Dickey–Fuller t-distributions generated by 100,000 simulations for the corresponding ADF t-test statistics are computed. Consequently, $p_\lambda = (-2\sum \log_e \pi_i)$ is calculated. For the LL and IPS tests, we follow the procedures described in their papers.

In each experiment, we consider the cases of $N = 10, 25, 50, 100$ and $T = 10, 25, 50, 100$. A total of 2000 trials are used in computing the empirical size and power of the tests. In analyzing the size, ϕ_i is set to be 0, and in calculating the power, ϕ_i is set to be -0.1 for all i. The results are presented in Tables 1 and 2.

Table 1 reports the simulation results of the model with constant term only. Overall, the performance of the LL test is the worst but it should be noted that as argued earlier, the power comparison between the LL test and the other two tests is not valid. The IPS and the Fisher tests are directly comparable because they are tests of the same hypothesis. When reading Table 1, it should be kept in mind that the power comparisons are not appropriate because there are significant size distortions. However, we have not computed size-adjusted power because some broad conclusions can be drawn from the figures presented, without looking at the size-adjusted power.

The major conclusion that one can draw is that for high values of T (50 or 100) and values of $N = 50$ and 100 the Fisher test dominates the IPS test in the sense that the Fisher test has smaller size distortions and comparable power. The same conclusions follow from Table 2, the case with trend. We shall see that this conclusion about the dominance of the Fisher test is reinforced in the results presented in Table 3 later.

Another observation in Tables 1 and 2 is the effect of selection of order of the ADF regressions. We generate the error terms according to an $AR(1)$ model thus using ADF(1) is appropriate. From the results we can see the danger of under-selecting the order of ADF regression which is also pointed out by IPS. Meanwhile, over-selecting the order of ADF regression, i.e.,

TABLE 1
Size and Power of the Unit Root Tests (Constant Term Only)

			ADF(0)		*ADF(1)*		*ADF(2)*	
N	*T*		*Size*	*Power*	*Size*	*Power*	*Size*	*Power*
25	25	IPS	0.0065	0.0095	0.1060	0.4235	0.0590	0.2535
		Fisher	0.0060	0.0005	0.0440	0.1910	0.0250	0.0875
		LL	0.0230	0.0245	0.1585	0.4760	0.0880	0.2575
	50	IPS	0.0025	0.0650	0.0880	0.9000	0.0645	0.8085
		Fisher	0.0075	0.0175	0.0845	0.7575	0.0665	0.6300
		LL	0.0165	0.0205	0.1415	0.7660	0.1030	0.5550
	100	IPS	0.0010	0.7725	0.1050	1.0000	0.0920	0.9995
		Fisher	0.0015	0.1090	0.0230	0.9975	0.0175	0.9925
		LL	0.0220	0.0265	0.1440	0.9905	0.1300	0.9525
50	25	IPS	0.0000	0.0060	0.1040	0.6520	0.0400	0.3705
		Fisher	0.0040	0.0025	0.1070	0.4945	0.0575	0.2695
		LL	0.0115	0.0170	0.1805	0.6950	0.0840	0.3555

	50	IPS	0.0015	0.0690	0.1035	0.9920	0.0715	0.9620
		Fisher	0.0025	0.0040	0.0730	0.9355	0.0510	0.8250
		LL	0.0080	0.0105	0.1550	0.9400	0.1030	0.7865
	100	IPS	0.0000	0.9880	0.0905	1.0000	0.0745	1.0000
		Fisher	0.0005	0.6970	0.0545	1.0000	0.0410	1.0000
		LL	0.0025	0.0800	0.1410	1.0000	0.1130	0.9990
100	25	IPS	0.0000	0.0030	0.0985	0.8615	0.0235	0.5415
		Fisher	0.0000	0.0005	0.1315	0.7080	0.0495	0.4040
		LL	0.0040	0.0070	0.1950	0.8760	0.0660	0.5085
	50	IPS	0.0000	0.0830	0.0945	1.0000	0.0545	0.9995
		Fisher	0.0005	0.0025	0.0740	0.9970	0.0415	0.9780
		LL	0.0010	0.0075	0.1770	0.9990	0.0990	0.9495
	100	IPS	0.0000	1.0000	0.0875	1.0000	0.0645	1.0000
		Fisher	0.0000	0.9010	0.0460	1.0000	0.0345	1.0000
		LL	0.0005	0.0790	0.1575	1.0000	0.1225	1.0000

TABLE 2
Size and Power of the Unit Root Tests (Time Trend)

			ADF(0)		*ADF(1)*		*ADF(2)*	
N	*T*		*Size*	*Power*	*Size*	*Power*	*Size*	*Power*
25	25	IPS	0.0010	0.0005	0.1145	0.2000	0.0450	0.0900
		Fisher	0.0010	0.0000	0.1060	0.1805	0.0535	0.0765
		LL	0.0015	0.0020	0.1090	0.2285	0.0150	0.0320
	50	IPS	0.0000	0.0015	0.1055	0.4895	0.0655	0.3340
		Fisher	0.0000	0.0000	0.0940	0.3670	0.0525	0.2305
		LL	0.0000	0.0030	0.1180	0.5635	0.0365	0.2430
	100	IPS	0.0000	0.0190	0.1015	0.9895	0.0780	0.9620
		Fisher	0.0000	0.0040	0.0435	0.9210	0.0335	0.8390
		LL	0.0000	0.0130	0.1250	0.9665	0.0650	0.8420
50	25	IPS	0.0000	0.0000	0.1320	0.2635	0.0365	0.0790
		Fisher	0.0000	0.0000	0.1340	0.2295	0.0465	0.0780
		LL	0.0000	0.0005	0.1135	0.2850	0.0065	0.0195
	50	IPS	0.0000	0.0000	0.1155	0.6920	0.0705	0.4775
		Fisher	0.0000	0.0000	0.0705	0.4560	0.0385	0.2625
		LL	0.0000	0.0010	0.1165	0.7420	0.0235	0.3170

	100	IPS	0.0000	0.0275	0.0975	1.0000	0.0720	0.9990
		Fisher	0.0000	0.0005	0.0420	0.9970	0.0285	0.9830
		LL	0.0000	0.0100	0.1210	0.9990	0.0530	0.9710
100	25	IPS	0.0000	0.0000	0.1265	0.3305	0.0185	0.0700
		Fisher	0.0000	0.0000	0.1570	0.2850	0.0360	0.0785
		LL	0.0000	0.0000	0.0925	0.3335	0.0010	0.0085
	50	IPS	0.0000	0.0000	0.1105	0.9015	0.0470	0.6930
		Fisher	0.0000	0.0000	0.0645	0.7100	0.0260	0.4215
		LL	0.0000	0.0000	0.1155	0.9220	0.0130	0.4525
	100	IPS	0.0000	0.0240	0.0900	1.0000	0.0645	1.0000
		Fisher	0.0000	0.0005	0.0355	1.0000	0.0265	0.9995
		LL	0.0000	0.0030	0.1255	1.0000	0.0440	0.9990

Note: Empirical size is reported when the nominal size is 5%. Power is reported when ϕ is set to be -0.1.

$p = 2$, seems to alleviate the size distortions for all three tests, the price is the decline in power, as has been observed often.

4.2. *Simulation with a Mixture of Stationary and Non-stationary Alternatives*

In this experiment we generate the data according to the *DGP* described in the last section except that we set $\phi_i = 0$ for some of the individual series and $\phi_i < 0$ for the others as our maintained hypothesis. We study the case of $N = 25$ and $T = 50$. First, we consider the case where there is only one stationary process in the group, and we then increase the number of stationary processes (k) to 2, 4, 8, 10 and 12. For the cases of $k = 1, 2, 4$, we set $\phi_i = -0.2$, while for cases of $k = 8, 10, 12$, ϕ_i is generated from $U[-0.3, -0.1]$ and is different for each series. The powers of the three tests are reported in Table 3. The general result is that the Fisher test has the highest power in all cases. The more the number of stationary processes included, the stronger the relative advantage. Thus if only part of the panel is stationary, the Fisher test is the most likely one to point it out.

Broadly speaking, our conclusions are as follows:

1. In general, when there is no cross-sectional correlation in the errors, the IPS test is slightly more powerful than the Fisher test, in the sense that the IPS test has higher power when the two have the same size. Both tests are more powerful than the LL test.
2. As for the issues of heteroscedasticity and serial correlation in the errors, all the tests can take care of these problems. But when the errors in the different samples (or cross-section units) are cross-correlated (as would often be the case in empirical work) none of the tests can handle this problem well. However, the Monte Carlo evidence suggests that this problem is less severe with the Fisher test than with the LL or the IPS test. More specifically, when T is large but N is not very large, the size distortion with the Fisher test is small. But for

TABLE 3

*Power Comparison: Design 2 ($N = 25$, $T = 50$)**

Number of Stationary Units	*IPS*	*Fisher*	*LL*
1	0.0785	0.1085	0.0885
2	0.1270	0.1875	0.1040
4	0.1835	0.2490	0.1350
8	0.4685	0.5900	0.2545
10	0.6165	0.6840	0.3240
12	0.7385	0.8145	0.4045

* In the Monte Carlo simulation design, for the cases of stationary units included is 1, 2, 4, 8, we set ϕ_i to -0.2. In the cases of 10 and 12, the ϕ_i are generated at $U[-0.3, -0.1]$.

medium values of T and large N, the size distortion of the Fisher test is of the same level as that of the IPS test.

3. For the cases that we include a mixture of stationary and non-stationary series in the group as an alternative hypothesis, the Fisher test is the best because it has the highest power in distinguishing the null and the alternative.

Overall, we can conclude from these results that the Fisher test is better than the IPS and LL tests.

V. CORRELATED ERRORS AND THE BOOTSTRAP ALTERNATIVE

Recall that the properties of all three tests are based on the assumption that the error terms are not cross-correlated. When this assumption is violated the derived distributions for these test statistics are no longer valid. They all suffer from nuisance parameter problems. More specifically, if there is cross-correlation in the data, as noted earlier, the distributions of the test statistics are not the same as before and are not known. For the t-bar test in IPS, the t-statistics are correlated and hence the t-bar statistic does not have the stated variance in its (asymptotic) normal distribution, and for the Fisher test, too, we do not have independent tests and hence the p_λ criterion does not have the χ^2 distribution. Im, Pesaran and Shin (1997) consider a special case of correlated errors. They assume that the cross-correlations are caused by common time-specific effects, i.e. in the model $\Delta y_{i,t} = \rho_i y_{i,t-1} + u_{i,t}$ we have $u_{i,t} = \theta_t + \varepsilon_{i,t}$. They suggest eliminating θ_t by subtracting out the mean $\bar{y} = (1/N)\sum_{i=1}^{N} y_{i,t}$ from $y_{i,t}$ before applying the unit root tests and the t-bar test. In many practical applications the cross-correlation is not likely to be of this simple form. In fact they suggest that if

$$u_{i,t} = r_i\theta_t + \varepsilon_{i,t}$$

this procedure of demeaning would not work.

O'Connell (1998) assumes cross-sectional dependence of the form

$$\Omega = \begin{bmatrix} 1 & \omega & \dots & \omega \\ \omega & 1 & \dots & \omega \\ . & . & . & . \\ \omega & \omega & \dots & 1 \end{bmatrix} \qquad \omega < 1$$

but $E(u_{i,t}, u_{j,s}) = 0\ \forall i, j \text{ if } s \neq t$.

This sort of covariance matrix would arise with random time effects as in random effects models, i.e. $u_{i,t} = \theta_t + \varepsilon_{i,t}$ where θ_t are i.i.d., $\varepsilon_{i,t}$ are i.i.d., θ_t and $\varepsilon_{i,t}$ are mutually independent.

One way out of this problem of cross-correlated errors is to use the bootstrap method to get the empirical distributions of the test statistics to make inferences. In what follows, we shall illustrate the bootstrap method by using an empirical example of testing convergence in real GDPs of 17

European countries. Please refer to Maddala and Wu (1999) for motivation of the problem and detailed discussion of the data. We shall discuss the bootstrap method briefly and then present the results. The bootstrap method for univariate time series is well developed. Readers are referred to Li and Maddala (1996) for a good introduction. Meanwhile the bootstrap method for panel data is in its infancy. We shall discuss our proposed method in detail.

The problem here is to generate the bootstrap distributions of the test statistics. The bootstrap data were generated using the sampling scheme S_3 described in Li and Maddala (1996). Generally speaking, if the null hypothesis is H_0: $\beta = \beta_0$, the sampling scheme S_3 suggests generating bootstrap sample y^* as $y^* = x\beta_0 + \varepsilon^*$ where ε^* is the bootstrap sample from $\varepsilon^0 = y - x\beta_0$. Since we have panel data here, we should also take care of special problems arising from the serial correlation. So we get the bootstrap sample of the error term ε^0 from

$$\Delta y_{i,t} = \eta_i \Delta y_{i,t-1} + \varepsilon^0_{i,t} \tag{2}$$

since under the null hypothesis $y_{i,t}$ has a unit root. Since there are cross-correlations among $\varepsilon^0_{i,t}$, we cannot resample $\varepsilon^0_{i,t}$ directly. We propose resampling $\varepsilon^0_{i,t}$ with the cross-section index fixed, i.e. instead of resampling $\varepsilon^0_{i,t}$, we resample $\varepsilon^0_t = [\varepsilon^0_{1,t}, \varepsilon^0_{2,t}, \ldots, \varepsilon^0_{N,t}]'$ to get ε^*_t. In this way, we can preserve the cross-correlation structure of the error term. Then the bootstrap sample y^* is generated as

$$y^*_{i,t} = y^*_{i,t-1} + u^*_{i,t} \text{ with } y^*_{i,0} = 0$$

$$u^*_{i,t} = \hat{\eta}_i u^*_{i,t-1} + \varepsilon^*_{i,t} \text{ with } u^*_{i,0} = \sum_{j=0}^{m} \hat{\eta}_i^j \varepsilon^*_{-j}$$

where $\hat{\eta}_i$'s are from estimation results of (2). The method to get the initial value of $u^*_{i,0}$ is suggested by Rayner (1990). Here ε^*_{-j}'s are drawn as an independent bootstrap sample and m is selected as 30. A total of 2000 replications are used to generate the empirical distributions.

We can get the critical values at the 5 percent level based on these empirical distributions. For the sample of the 17 European countries under study, these critical values are -0.518, 42.61 and -1.157 for the IPS, Fisher and LL tests respectively. Now, the test statistics for the same sample are -0.950, 48.912 and -1.078. In contrast to the non-rejection results based on the usual critical values (derived from standard normal for the IPS and LL tests and χ^2 for the Fisher test), we can now strongly reject the unit root null for the data set by using the critical values at the 5 percent level for the IPS and the Fisher tests, although for the LL test we fail marginally to reject the null.

In general, the conclusions from the bootstrap experiments are: In the case of cross-correlated errors there are substantial size distortions in using the conventional test statistics for the IPS, Fisher and LL tests, although the size distortions are less serious for the Fisher test than for the IPS test. Using the bootstrap method results in a decrease of these size distortions, although it does not eliminate them. The Fisher test does better than the IPS test overall using the bootstrap method.

The size distortions with the Levin–Lin test in the case of cross-correlated errors have also been discussed in O'Connell (1998). He talks of dramatic size distortions, the actual size being 50 percent when the nominal size is 5 percent. The size distortions that we observed with the panel data unit root tests (including the LL test), under cross-correlations, were not as dramatic as those noted by O'Connell. It is possible that his results are a consequence of the equi-correlational error structure he assumed.

VI. TESTS BASED ON BONFERRONI INEQUALITY

For the correlated errors case we argued that, for both the Fisher test statistic and the IPS test statistic, the distribution involves nuisance parameters, but bootstrap methods could be used to make inferences. There is, however, one test statistic that is equally applicable in both the uncorrelated and correlated cases. This is the statistic based on the Bonferroni inequality (see Alt, 1982) and discussed in Dufour and Torres (1996). These tests have also been discussed earlier in Savin (1984) and Dufour (1990).

The idea behind this test is to break up the hypothesis H_0: $\rho_i = 0$ for all i, $i = 1, 2, \ldots, N$ into a set of sub-hypotheses H_{0i}: $\rho_i = 0$ and noting that H_0 is wrong if and only if any of its components H_{0i} is wrong. Suppose we choose the significance level π_i for the ith test. Then if we follow the rule that we reject H_0 if at least one of the sub-hypotheses H_{0i} is rejected at significance level π_i for H_{0i}, then the Bonferroni inequality says that the significance level π for H_0 is given by

$$\pi \leqslant \sum_{i=1}^{N} \pi_i.$$

One simple rule that Dufour and Torres suggest is to take $\pi_i = \pi/N$, unless there is an *a priori* compelling reason that some tests ought to be rejected at lower (or higher) significance level than the others.

We shall now compare this test with the Fisher test for both the cases of independent tests and correlated tests. Since the tables of significance values for unit root tests are readily available at the 1 percent significance level, we chose $N = 5$ in our investigation, so that $\pi_i = 0.01$ and $\pi = 0.05$. Note that the case of small N is favorable to the test based on the Bonferroni inequality (see p. 299 of Alt, 1982).

We consider four cases of *DGP*. The basic *DGP* is

$$\Delta y_{i,t} = \alpha_i + \rho_i y_{i,t-1} + \varepsilon_{i,t}$$

$$\alpha_i \sim U[0, 1]$$

$$\rho_i = \begin{cases} -0.1 & \text{for power} \\ 0 & \text{for size} \end{cases}$$

where assumptions on $\varepsilon_{i,t}$ are different in each case as follows:

Case 1: No serial correlation and contemporaneous correlation

$$\varepsilon_{i,t} \sim N(0, \sigma_i^2), \text{ where } \sigma_i^2 \sim U[0.5, 1.5].$$

Case 2: There is serial correlation, but no contemporaneous correlation

$$\varepsilon_{i,t} = \lambda_i \varepsilon_{i,t-1} + e_{i,t}, \text{ where } \lambda_i \sim U[0.2, 0.4]$$

and

$$e_{i,t} \sim N(0, \sigma_i^2), \text{ with } \sigma_i^2 \sim U[0.5, 1.5].$$

Case 3: There is contemporaneous correlation but no serial correlation

$$\varepsilon_t = [\varepsilon_{1,t}, \varepsilon_{2,t}, \ldots, \varepsilon_{N,t}]' \sim N(0, \Sigma),$$
$$\text{where } \Sigma = \Psi'\Psi \text{ with} \Psi_{N\times N} \sim U[-1, 1]$$

Case 4: There are both serial correlation and contemporaneous correlation

$$\varepsilon_{i,t} = \lambda_i \varepsilon_{i,t-1} + e_{i,t}, \text{ where } \lambda_i \sim U[0.2, 0.4]$$

and

$$e_t = [e_{1,t}, e_{2,t}, \ldots, e_{N,t}]' \sim N(0, \Sigma),$$
$$\text{where } \Sigma = \Psi'\Psi \text{ with } \Psi_{N\times N} \sim U[-1, 1].$$

Table 4 presents the results from the Monte Carlo studies based on 4000 simulations. The results clearly suggest that the power of the Dufour–Torres (DT) test is substantially lower than that of the Fisher test, although there is a slight size distortion for the Fisher test in the case of correlated tests.

VII. PANEL DATA TESTS WITH STATIONARITY AS NULL

Although the use of the Fisher test has been outlined in the previous sections with reference to the ADF test, to compare it with the IPS test, it can be used with *any* of the efficient unit root tests suggested in the literature, such as the Elliott *et al.* (1996) test or the Perron-Ng (1996) test. It can also be used for tests of stationarity as the null, like the test by Kwiatkowski *et al.* (1992) or Leybourne and McCabe (1994). We suggest the same procedure of combining the p-values to get a χ^2 test statistic and using the bootstrap method for obtaining the critical values, to account for the correlations among the test statistics for the individual cross-section units.

TABLE 4

Size and Power Comparison of the Fisher Test with the Dufour–Torres (DT) Test

Case No.	*Test*	*Size*	*Power*
Case 1	Fisher	0.0505	0.1180
$T = 25$	DT	0.0460	0.0693
Case 1	Fisher	0.0473	0.3142
$T = 50$	DT	0.0467	0.1232
Case 2	Fisher	0.0560	0.1135
$T = 25$	DT	0.0565	0.0760
Case 2	Fisher	0.0480	0.2802
$T = 50$	DT	0.0493	0.1185
Case 3	Fisher	0.0785	0.1630
$T = 25$	DT	0.0480	0.0683
Case 3	Fisher	0.0750	0.3448
$T = 50$	DT	0.0432	0.1215
Case 4	Fisher	0.0858	0.1530
$T = 25$	DT	0.0578	0.0767
Case 4	Fisher	0.0825	0.3073
$T = 50$	DT	0.0462	0.1143

VIII. THE CASE OF PANEL COINTEGRATION TESTS

Again the methodology we suggest is applicable to panel cointegration tests, whether they are tests using no cointegration as null, or cointegration as null. (There are several tests in each category – see Chapter 6 of Maddala and Kim (1998) for a review.) The procedure we suggest is simple and universally applicable. There is no need for a separate theory for each type of test. The only problem is the correlation among the test statistics for the different cross-section units, for which we suggest using the bootstrap method to get critical values for the χ^2 test. This is the procedure used by Wu (1998, Chapter 5) for deriving panel data cointegration tests to test the PPP (purchasing power parity) hypothesis. There have been several panel data cointegration tests suggested in the literature. See Pedroni (1995, 1997), Kao (1999) and McCoskey and Kao (1998a). They all allow for heterogeneity in the cointegrating coefficients. But the null and alternatives imply that either *all* the relationships are cointegrated or *all* the relationships are not cointegrated. There is no allowance for some relationships to be cointegrated and others not (the Fisher test allows for this – the p-values can be different).

Pedroni (1997) suggests seven test statistics. There is a lot of complicated algebra in the derivations which depend on the construction of LR covariance matrices of the errors, whose small sample properties are known to be questionable. His tests are for no cointegration as null.

Kao (1999) suggests tests for no cointegration as the null and McCoskey and Kao (1998a) suggest tests for the null of cointegration. The methodology for the derivation of the test statistics in the two cases is different.

We have outlined briefly the deficiencies of these alternative tests for cointegration in panel data. A detailed discussion of these tests is beyond the scope of our paper. This can be found in McCoskey and Kao (1998b) who present a detailed Monte Carlo study of the tests by Kao, Pedroni and McCoskey and Kao. Limit theory for non-stationary panel data can be found in Phillips and Moon (1999).

IX. CONCLUSIONS

The paper compares the Levin–Lin and Im–Pesaran–Shin (IPS) panel data unit root tests with the Fisher test which was suggested over 60 years ago by R. A. Fisher and has a celebrated history in the statistical literature. The main conclusion of the paper is that the Fisher test is simple and straightforward to use and is a better test than the LL and IPS tests. Some other conservative tests (applicable in the case of correlated tests) based on the Bonferroni bounds have also been found to be inferior to the Fisher test. Our arguments also apply to tests using stationarity as null and to panel cointegration tests testing the null of no cointegration as well as testing the null of cointegration. The essential problem there is again one of combining the evidence from several tests. Also, the same problems of correlated tests have to be addressed, using bootstrap methods.

One major problem with the literature on unit root and cointegration tests in panel data is that there is an urge to generalize the tests used in univariate data to panel data under assumptions that are not likely to be meaningful in practice. There is more concentration on technical details and less on the questions being answered. This makes them not very useful in practice. For instance, the tests are almost all tests for the hypothesis that *all* series are stationary vs. *all* series are non-stationary, or that *all* series are cointegrated vs. that *none* is cointegrated. This is almost always a hypothesis of questionable value to test.

It is very important to bear in mind Thoreau's admonition quoted at the beginning of our paper.

The Ohio State University
SUNY at Buffalo

Date of Receipt of Final Manuscript: July 1999

REFERENCES

Alt, F. B. (1982). 'Bonferroni Inequalities and Intervals', in Johnson, N. L. and Kotz, S. (eds.) *Encyclopedia of Statistical Sciences*, Vol. I, 294-301, Wiley, New York.

Becker, B. J. (1997). '*P*-Values: Combination', in Kotz, S. and Read, C. B. (eds.) *Encyclopedia of Statistical Sciences: Update*, Vol. I, 448-453, Wiley, New York.

Breitung, J. and Mayer, W. (1994). 'Testing for Unit Roots in Panel Data: Are Wages on Different Bargaining Levels Cointegrated?', *Applied Economics*, 26, 353-361.

Cavanagh, C. L., Elliott, G. and Stock, J. H. (1995). 'Inference in Models with Nearly Nonstationary Regressors', *Econometric Theory*, 11, 1131-1147.

Dufour, J. M. (1990). 'Exact Tests and Confidence Sets in Linear Regressions with Autocorrelated Errors', *Econometrica*, 58, 479-494.

Dufour, J. M. and Torres, O. (1996). 'Union-Intersection and Sample-Split Methods in Econometrics with Application to MA and SURE Models', Paper presented at the summer meetings of the Econometric Society, Iowa City.

Elliott, G., Rothenberg, T. J. and Stock, J. H. (1996). 'Efficient Tests for an Autoregressive Unit Root', *Econometrica*, 64, 813-836.

Fisher, R. A. (1932). *Statistical Methods for Research Workers*, Oliver & Boyd, Edinburgh, 4th Edition.

Frankel, J. A. and Rose, A. K. (1996). 'A Panel Project on Purchasing Power Parity: Mean Reversion Within and Between Countries', *Journal of International Economics*, 40, 209-224.

Hedges, L. V. and Olkin, I. (1985). *Statistical Methods for Meta Analysis*, Academic Press, New York.

Im, K. S., Pesaran, M. H. and Shin, Y. (1997). 'Testing for Unit Roots in Heterogeneous Panels', Mimeo, Department of Applied Economics, University of Cambridge.

Kao, C. (1999). 'Spurious Regression and Residual-Based Tests for Cointegration in Panel Data', *Journal of Econometrics*, 90, 1-44.

Kwiatkowski, D., Phillips, P. C. B., Schmidt, P. and Shin, Y. (1992). 'Testing for the Null of Stationarity Against the Alternative of a Unit Root', *Journal of Econometrics*, 54, 159-178.

Levin, A. and Lin, C. F. (1992). 'Unit Root Test in Panel Data: Asymptotic and Finite Sample Properties', University of California at San Diego, Discussion Paper No. 92-93.

Levin, A. and Lin, C. F. (1993). 'Unit Root Test in Panel Data: New Results', University of California at San Diego, Discussion Paper No. 93-56.

Leybourne, S. J. and McCabe, B. P. M. (1994). 'A Consistent Test for a Unit Root', *Journal of Business and Economic Statistics*, 12, 157-166.

Li, H. and Maddala, G. S. (1996). 'Bootstrapping Time Series Models' (with discussion), *Econometric Reviews*, 15, 115-195.

McCoskey, S. and Kao, C. (1998a). 'A Residual-Based Test for the Null of Cointegration in Panel Data', *Econometric Reviews*, 17, 57-84.

McCoskey, S. and Kao, C. (1998b). 'A Monte Carlo Comparison of Tests for Cointegration in Panel Data', Mimeo, Center for Policy Research, Syracuse University, February.

MacDonald, R. (1996). 'Panel Unit Root Tests and Real Exchange Rates', *Economics Letters*, 50, 7-11.

Maddala, G. S. (1977). *Econometrics*, McGraw-Hill, New York.

Maddala, G. S. and Wu, S. (1999). 'Cross-country Growth Regressions: Problems of Heterogeneity, Stability and Interpretation', forthcoming in *Applied Economics*.

Maddala, G. S. and Kim, I. M. (1998). *Unit Roots, Cointegration and Structural Change*, Cambridge University Press, Cambridge.

O'Connell, P. (1998). 'The Overvaluation of Purchasing Power Parity', *Journal of International Economics*, 44, 1-19.

Oh, K. Y. (1996). 'Purchasing Power Parity and Unit Root Tests using Panel Data', *Journal of International Money and Finance*, 15, 405-418.

Papell, D. H. (1997). 'Searching for Stationarity: Purchasing Power Parity under the Current Float', *Journal of International Economics*, 43, 313-332.

Pedroni, P. (1995). 'Panel Cointegration: Asymptotic and Finite Sample Properties of Pooled Time Series Tests with an Application to the *PPP* Hypothesis', Indiana University Working Paper in Economics No. 95-013.

Pedroni, P. (1997). 'Panel Cointegration: Asymptotic and Finite Sample Properties of Pooled Time Series Tests with an Application to the *PPP* Hypothesis: New Results', Indiana University Working Paper in Economics.

Perron, P. and Ng, S. (1996). 'Useful Modifications to some Unit Root Tests with Dependent Errors and their Local Asymptotic Properties', *Review of Economic Studies*, 63, 435-465.

Phillips, P. C. B. and Moon, H. (1999). 'Linear Regression Limit Theory for Nonstationary Panel Data', *Econometrica*, 67, 1057–1111.

Quah, D. (1992). 'International Patterns of Growth I: Persistence in Cross-Country Disparities', LSE Working Paper.

Quah, D. (1994). 'Exploiting Cross-Section Variation for Unit Root Inference in Dynamic Data', *Economics Letters*, 44, 9-19.

Rao, C. R. (1952). *Advanced Statistical Methods in Biometric Research*, Wiley, New York.

Rayner, R. K. (1990). 'Bootstrapping P-values and Power in the First-Order Autoregression: A Monte Carlo Investigation', *Journal of Business & Economic Statistics*, 8, 251-263.

Savin, N. E. (1984). 'Multiple Hypothesis Testing', *Handbook of Econometrics*, eds. Griliches, Z. and Intriligator, M. D., Chapter 14, North-Holland, Amsterdam.

Tippett, L. H. C. (1931). *The Methods of Statistics*, Williams & Norgate, London, 1st Edition.

Wu, S. (1998). 'Nonstationary Panel Data Analysis', Thesis, Ohio State University.

Wu, Y. (1996). 'Are Real Exchange Rates Stationary? Evidence from a Panel Data Test', *Journal of Money, Credit and Banking*, 28, 54-63.

[19]

OXFORD BULLETIN OF ECONOMICS AND STATISTICS, SPECIAL ISSUE (1999)
0305-9049

MAXIMUM LIKELIHOOD ESTIMATION IN PANELS WITH INCIDENTAL TRENDS*

*Hyungsik R. Moon and Peter C. B. Phillips**

I. INTRODUCTION

In recent non-stationary time series applications, it has been extremely common to model time series with roots near unity using the device of an autoregressive root that is local to unity. Some early studies of near unit root non-stationary time series include developments of local alternatives to unit root specifications (Bobkoski, 1983; Phillips, 1987), derivations of power functions and power envelopes of unit root tests (e.g., Cavanagh, 1985; Phillips, 1987; Johansen, 1991), and the construction of confidence intervals for the long-run autoregressive coefficient (Stock, 1991). More recent research on near unit root non-stationary time series investigates the efficient extraction of deterministic trends (Phillips and Lee, 1996; Canjels and Watson, 1997), and the construction of point optimal invariant tests for a unit root (Elliott, Rotherberg and Stock, 1996) and cointegrating rank (Xiao and Phillips, 1999). For further examples, readers can refer to recent surveys on unit root processes (e.g., Stock, 1994; Phillips and Xiao, 1998).

Like other parameters in econometric models, localizing parameters in near integrated processes are not usually observable. But, implementation of some methods in the aforementioned studies requires knowledge of the localizing parameter or a consistent estimate of it. For example, it is well known that efficiency gains in the estimation of deterministic trends can be obtained by quasi-differencing the data using the unknown localizing parameter (e.g. Phillips and Lee, 1996; Canjels and Watson, 1997). However, if we implement this procedure using inconsistent estimates of the localizing parameter, then the limit distribution of the resulting trend coefficient estimator is highly non-standard, which introduces new difficulties, for example, in constructing confidence intervals for the trend coefficient. Largely because of this problem, Cavanagh, Elliott and Stock (1995) and Canjels and Watson (1997) suggested the use of Bonferroni-type confidence intervals, which are often very conservative.

Finding a consistent estimate of the localizing parameter is not straight-

*Moon thanks the Academic Research Committee of UCSB for research support and Phillips thanks the NSF for research support under Grant No. SBR97-30295.

forward. Obvious procedures like the use of least squares are well known to be inconsistent (Phillips, 1987); and, even in the simplest framework, consistent estimation inevitably involves the introduction of additional information. In view of its potential applications in both estimation and inference, the problem of consistent estimation of the localizing parameter in local to unity models poses an interesting problem with important implications. Two recent studies that consider the subject are Moon and Phillips (1998) and Phillips, Moon and Xiao (1998).

The main purpose of this paper is to investigate the asymptotic properties of the Gaussian maximum likelihood estimators (*MLE*) of the localizing parameter in local to unity dynamic panel regression models. The model we consider here allows for the panel to be generated with deterministic and stochastic trends, and a common localizing parameter is assumed to apply across individuals. Commonality of the localizing parameter is restrictive, but is no more restrictive than the conventional assumption of common *AR* parameters in stationary dynamic panels (e.g., Nickell, 1981). Two different models are considered: a homogeneous trend model in which the deterministic trends are homogeneous across the individuals in the panel; and a heterogeneous trend model where the deterministic trends may vary across individuals, much like fixed individual effects. In the homogeneous trend model we show that the Gaussian *MLE* of the common localizing parameter is $\sqrt{N}$-consistent and has a limiting normal distribution that is the same as that in the case where the trends are known. In the heterogeneous trends model it is shown that the Gaussian *MLE* of the localizing parameter is inconsistent.

The inconsistency of the *MLE* of the localizing parameter in the heterogeneous trend model is an instance of the so-called incidental parameter problem originally explored by Neyman and Scott (1948). In this model, the heterogenous trend coefficients correspond to incidental parameters whose number goes to infinity as the cross-section dimension $N \to \infty$. Such problems frequently appear in panel data models with fixed effects, a well-known example being the dynamic panel regression model with fixed effects. In this case, the *MLE* of the lagged dependent variable coefficient that is common over individuals is inconsistent if $N \to \infty$ while the sample size dimension, T, is fixed (Nickell, 1981). In most panel data situations this incidental parameter problem disappears when T passes to infinity also (e.g., Alvarez and Arellano, 1998; Hahn, 1998). A particularly interesting aspect of the incidental parameter problem discovered in this paper is that the inconsistency of the *MLE* of the localizing parameter does not disappear even when both N and T tend to infinity.

The paper is organized as follows. Section 2 lays out the model and assumptions, and shows that when the deterministic components are known, the Gaussian *MLE* of the localizing parameter is consistent. Section 3 studies asymptotic properties of the Gaussian *MLE* of the panel regression model with unknown deterministic trends. Section 4 reports some Monte

Carlo simulations that investigate the magnitude of the inconsistency. Section 5 concludes and offers some suggestions for dealing with the inconsistency. Proofs and technical derivations are collected in the Appendix in the last section.

Our notation is mostly standard. We use '$\rightarrow_p$' and '$\Rightarrow$' to denote convergence in probability and convergence in distribution, respectively. The notation $(N, T \rightarrow \infty)$ implies that N and T tend to infinity together, while $(N, T \rightarrow \infty)_{\text{seq}}$ means that the indices pass to infinity sequentially (first T and then N). Standard Brownian motion is denoted by $W(r)$.

II. NEAR INTEGRATED PANELS: PRELIMINARY THEORY

We start by introducing a panel regression model where data $z_{i,t}$ are generated by deterministic trends $G_i(t)$ and near integrated stochastic trends $y_{i,t}$ as follows:

$$z_{i,t} = G_i(t) + y_{i,t}, \qquad t = 1, \ldots, T; i = 1, \ldots, N, \tag{1}$$

$$y_{i,t} = ay_{i,t-1} + \varepsilon_{i,t}, \qquad a = \exp\left(\frac{c}{T}\right) \sim \left(1 + \frac{c}{T}\right).$$

The parameter c in (1) is a local to unity parameter that is common to all individuals in the panel. The main purpose of this paper is to investigate asymptotic properties of the *MLE* of the localizing parameter c.

To provide some intuition, we first consider the simple case where $y_{i,t} = z_{i,t} - G_i(t)$ is observable, abstracting from the problem of fitting the deterministic component in (1). Assume that the errors $\varepsilon_{i,t}$ are i.i.d. $N(0, \sigma^2)$, and, for simplicity in this section, that σ^2 is known and that the initial observations $y_{i,0} = 0$ for all i. Under these assumptions the standardized log-likelihood function of the panel data $y^{N,T} = (y_{1,1}, \ldots, y_{N,T})'$ is

$$L_{N,T}(y^{N,T}; c) = -\frac{1}{2\sigma^2 N}\sum_{i=1}^{N}\sum_{t=1}^{T}\left(\Delta y_{i,t} - \frac{c}{T}y_{i,t-1}\right)^2 + \text{constant}. \tag{2}$$

Let c_0 denote the true localizing parameter, and assume that c_0 is an element of the interior of a convex set of $\mathbb{R}$. Define $\varepsilon_{i,t}(c_0) = \Delta y_{i,t} - (c_0/T)y_{i,t-1}$. Then, the *MLE* of c is obtained by maximizing the standardized log-likelihood

$$
\begin{aligned}
&L_{N,T}(y^{N,T}; c) - L_{N,T}(y^{N,T}; c_0) \\
&= -\frac{1}{2\sigma^2 N}\sum_{i=1}^{N}\sum_{t=1}^{T}\left(\Delta y_{i,t} - \frac{c}{T}y_{i,t-1}\right)^2 + \frac{1}{2\sigma^2 N}\sum_{i=1}^{N}\sum_{t=1}^{T}\varepsilon_{i,t}(c_0)^2 \\
&= -\frac{1}{2}(c-c_0)^2\frac{1}{\sigma^2 N}\sum_{i=1}^{N}\frac{1}{T^2}\sum_{t=1}^{T}y_{i,t-1}^2 \\
&\quad -(c-c_0)\frac{1}{\sigma^2 N}\sum_{i=1}^{N}\frac{1}{T}\sum_{t=1}^{T}y_{i,t-1}\varepsilon_{i,t}(c_0),
\end{aligned}
$$

which is quadratic in c.

According to Lemma 6(c) and (d) in the Appendix, as $(N, T \to \infty)$, we have

$$\frac{1}{\sigma^2 N}\sum_{i=1}^{N}\frac{1}{T^2}\sum_{t=1}^{T}y_{i,t-1}^2 \to_p \int_0^1\int_0^r e^{2c_0(r-s)}\,ds\,dr$$

and

$$\frac{1}{\sigma^2 N}\sum_{i=1}^{N}\frac{1}{T}\sum_{t=1}^{T}y_{i,t-1}\varepsilon_{i,t}(c_0) \to_p 0.$$

It follows that

$$
\begin{aligned}
&L_{N,T}(y^{N,T}; c) - L_{N,T}(y^{N,T}; c_0) \\
&\to_p -\frac{1}{2}(c-c_0)^2\left(\int_0^1\int_0^r e^{2c_0(r-s)}\,ds\,dr\right) = l(c, c_0),
\end{aligned}
$$

say for each c, as $(N, T \to \infty)$. Note that the objective function $L_{N,T}(y^{N,T}; c) - L_{N,T}(y^{N,T}; c_0)$ is concave in c over $\mathbb{R}$ and the limit function $l(c, c_0)$ has a unique maximum at c_0 and is continuous and concave in c over $\mathbb{R}$. Thus, the *MLE* $\hat{c}$ is consistent for c_0 by standard theory for extremum estimator (e.g., Theorem 2.7 in Newey and McFadden, 1994).

In this particular case, the *MLE* has the closed form

$$\hat{c} = T(\hat{a} - 1),$$

where

$$\hat{a} = \left(\sum_{i=1}^{N}\sum_{t=1}^{T}y_{i,t-1}^2\right)^{-1}\left(\sum_{i=1}^{N}\sum_{t=1}^{T}y_{i,t-1}y_{i,t}\right).$$

Using Lemma 6(a) and Lemma 6(c) in the Appendix, we can show that as $(N, T \to \infty)$

$$\sqrt{N}(\hat{c} - c_0) \Rightarrow N\left(0, \frac{\sigma^2}{\left(\int_0^1 \int_0^r e^{2c_0(r-s)} ds\, dr\right)}\right). \tag{3}$$

Therefore, when $y_{i,t}$ is observable (i.e., when $G_i(t)$ in model (1) is known), the Gaussian *MLE* $\hat{c}$ of the common localizing parameter c is $\sqrt{N}$-consistent and weakly convergent to the normal distribution (3).

The question to be explored in the present paper is whether these asymptotic properties (particularly, the consistency and asymptotic normality of the Gaussian *MLE* of c) continue to hold in panel models with unknown deterministic trends. It is known from Moon and Phillips (1998) that the *OLS* estimator of c is inconsistent under these circumstances, viz. when the deterministic trends are estimated and eliminated by prior regression.

Before proceeding further, we introduce the following three assumptions which will be maintained throughout the paper.

Assumption 1 ***(Error Normality).*** *The $\varepsilon_{i,t}$ are i.i.d. $N(0, \sigma_0^2)$ across i and over t.*

Assumption 2 ***(Parameter Set)***

(a) The localizing parameter c and the variance parameter σ^2 of $\varepsilon_{i,t}$ take values in a compact subset $\mathbb{C} \times \mathbb{V}$ of $\mathbb{R}^2$.
(b) The true localizing parameter c_0 and the true variance parameter σ_0^2 are in interior of the parameter subsets $\mathbb{C}$ and $\mathbb{V}$, respectively.

Assumption 3 ***(Initial Conditions).*** $y_{i,0} = 0$ *for all i.*

Assumption 3 on the initial condition is made mainly to simplify the arguments that follow. When the initial errors $y_{i,0}$ are random, the corresponding log-likelihood is obtained by conditioning on the initial errors. Some changes in the limit theory are to be expected in the case of distant initial conditions, as in Phillips and Lee (1996) and Canjels and Watson (1997), but otherwise this assumption has little bearing on the main results.

III. ESTIMATION WHEN THE TRENDS ARE UNKNOWN

This section studies the realistic situation of the panel model (1) when the trend functions are unknown. The following two subsections investigate the two cases of homogeneous deterministic trends and heterogeneous deterministic trends.

3.1. Homogeneous Trends

Suppose $G_i(t)$ in (1) is linear and homogeneous across i. Specifically, let us impose the following condition.

Assumption 4 *(Homogeneous Trends).* $G_i(t) = \delta t$.

The linear trend assumption is relevant for much empirical work and it simplifies formulae and derivations. However, the main thrust of the theory in this section continues to hold for general polynomial trends.

Let δ_0 denote the true value of δ. Then the data $z_{i,t}$ are generated by

$$z_{i,t} = \delta_0 t + y_{i,t}$$

$$y_{i,t} = \left(1 + \frac{c_0}{T}\right) y_{i,t-1} + \varepsilon_{i,t}.$$

Let $z^{N,T} = (z_{1,1}, \ldots, z_{N,T})'$, and define $y_{i,t}(\delta) = z_{i,t} - \delta t$, and $\varepsilon_{i,t}(\delta, c) = y_{i,t}(\delta) - (1 + [c/T])y_{i,t-1}(\delta)$. Let Δ_c be the quasi-differencing operator, $\Delta_c = 1 - aL$, where L is the lag operator and $a = 1 + (c/T)$.

Under the Gaussian assumption, the log-likelihood function of the panel data $z^{N,T}$ is

$$L_{N,T}(c, \delta, \sigma^2; z^{N,T})$$
$$= -\frac{NT}{2}\log\sigma^2 - \frac{1}{2\sigma^2}\sum_{i=1}^{N}\sum_{t=1}^{T}\left(\Delta_c z_{i,t} - \delta\left(1 - c\frac{t-1}{T}\right)\right)^2.$$

Since the parameter c is our main interest, we focus on the concentrated log-likelihood. For fixed c and σ^2, the log-likelihood $L_{N,T}(c, \delta, \sigma^2; z^{N,T})$ is maximized by $\hat{\delta}(c)$, where

$$\hat{\delta}(c) = \frac{\frac{1}{N}\sum_{i=1}^{N}\sum_{t=1}^{T}\left(1 - c\frac{t-1}{T}\right)\left(\Delta z_{i,t} - \frac{c}{T} z_{i,t-1}\right)}{\sum_{t=1}^{T}\left(1 - c\frac{t-1}{T}\right)^2}$$

$$= \delta_0 + \frac{\frac{1}{N}\sum_{i=1}^{N}\sum_{t=1}^{T}\left(1 - c\frac{t-1}{T}\right)\left(\varepsilon_{i,t}(\delta_0, c_0) - (c - c_0)\frac{y_{i,t-1}(\delta_0)}{T}\right)}{\sum_{t=1}^{T}\left(1 - c\frac{t-1}{T}\right)^2}. \quad (4)$$

Substituting $\hat{\delta}(c)$ in $L_{N,T}(c, \delta, \sigma^2; z^{N,T})$ gives the following concentrated log-likelihood function:

$$L_{N,T}(c,\hat{\delta}(c),\sigma^2;z^{N,T})$$
$$=-\frac{NT}{2}\log\sigma^2-\frac{1}{2\sigma^2}\sum_{i=1}^{N}\sum_{t=1}^{T}\left(\Delta_c z_{i,t}-\hat{\delta}(c)\left(1-c\frac{t-1}{T}\right)\right)^2.$$

Maximizing $L_{N,T}(c,\hat{\delta}(c),\sigma^2;z^{N,T})$, we find the *MLE* of σ^2 as

$$\hat{\sigma}^2(c)=\frac{1}{N}\sum_{i=1}^{N}\frac{1}{T}\sum_{t=1}^{T}\left(\Delta_c z_{i,t}-\hat{\delta}(c)\left(1-c\frac{t-1}{T}\right)\right)^2.$$

Plugging $\hat{\sigma}^2(c)$ into $L_{N,T}(c,\hat{\delta}(c),\sigma^2;z^{N,T})$ leads to the following concentrated log-likelihood:

$$L_{N,T}(c,\hat{\delta}(c),\hat{\sigma}^2(c);z^{N,T})$$
$$=-\frac{NT}{2}\log\left(\frac{1}{N}\sum_{i=1}^{N}\frac{1}{T}\sum_{t=1}^{T}\left(\Delta_c z_{i,t}-\hat{\delta}(c)\left(1-c\frac{t-1}{T}\right)\right)^2\right)-\frac{NT}{2}$$
$$=-\frac{NT}{2}\log\left(\frac{1}{N}\sum_{i=1}^{N}\sum_{t=1}^{T}\left(\Delta_c z_{i,t}-\hat{\delta}(c)\left(1-c\frac{t-1}{T}\right)\right)^2\right)-\frac{NT}{2}$$
$$+\frac{NT}{2}\log T.$$

The *MLE* $\hat{c}$ is obtained by maximizing the concentrated log-likelihood $L_{N,T}(c,\hat{\delta}(c),\hat{\sigma}^2(c);z^{N,T})$, so that

$$L_{N,T}(\hat{c},\hat{\delta}(\hat{c}),\hat{\sigma}^2(\hat{c});z^{N,T})=\max_{c\in\mathbb{C}}L_{N,T}(c,\hat{\delta}(c),\hat{\sigma}^2(c);z^{N,T}),\qquad(5)$$

which is equivalent to maximizing[1]

$$\max_{c\in\mathbb{C}}l_{N,T}(c,\hat{\delta}(c),\hat{\sigma}^2(c);z^{N,T}),$$

where

$$l_{N,T}(c,\hat{\delta}(c),\hat{\sigma}^2(c);z^{N,T})$$
$$=-\frac{1}{2N}\sum_{i=1}^{N}\sum_{t=1}^{T}\left(\Delta_c z_{i,t}-\hat{\delta}(c)\left(1-c\frac{t-1}{T}\right)\right)^2$$
$$+\frac{1}{2N}\sum_{i=1}^{N}\sum_{t=1}^{T}\left(\Delta_{c_0}z_{i,t}-\hat{\delta}(c_0)\left(1-c_0\frac{t-1}{T}\right)\right)^2.\qquad(6)$$

[1]Notice that the second term, $(1/N)\sum_{i=1}^{N}\sum_{t=1}^{T}(\Delta_{c_0}z_{i,t}-\hat{\delta}(c^0)(1-c^0[t-1/T]))^2$, in (6) below is not a function of c.

To investigate the consistency of the *MLE* $\hat{c}$ as $(N, T \to \infty)$, we write

$$
\begin{aligned}
&l_{N,T}(c, \hat{\delta}(c), \hat{\sigma}^2(c); z^{N,T}) \\
&= -\frac{1}{2N}\sum_{i=1}^{N}\sum_{t=1}^{T}\left(\varepsilon_{i,t}(\delta_0, c_0) - (c - c_0)\frac{y_{i,t}(\delta_0)}{T}\right. \\
&\left. - \left(\hat{\delta}(c) - \delta_0\right)\left(1 - c\frac{t-1}{T}\right)\right)^2 \\
&+ \frac{1}{2N}\sum_{i=1}^{N}\sum_{t=1}^{T}\left\{\varepsilon_{i,t}(\delta_0, c_0) - (\hat{\delta}(c_0) - \delta_0\left(1 - c_0\frac{t-1}{T}\right)\right\}^2.
\end{aligned} \tag{7}
$$

It then follows that as $(N, T \to \infty)$

$$
l_{N,T}(c, \hat{\delta}(c), \hat{\sigma}^2(c); z^{N,T}) \to_p -\frac{1}{2}(c - c_0)^2\int_0^1\int_0^r e^{2c_0(r-s)}ds\, dr \tag{8}
$$

uniformly in c. The proof of (8) is given in the Appendix. Note that the limit function $-\frac{1}{2}(c - c_0)^2 \int_0^1 \int_0^r e^{2c_0(r-s)}ds\, dr$, is continuous and concave over $\mathbb{R}$ and is uniquely maximized at the true parameter $c = c_0$. Therefore, the *MLE* $\hat{c}$ that maximizes the objective function $l_{N,T}(c, \hat{\delta}(c), \hat{\sigma}^2(c); z^{N,T})$ is consistent for the localizing parameter c_0 as $(N, T \to \infty)$ by standard asymptotic theory (e.g., Theorem 2.1 in Newey and McFadden, 1994). Summarizing, we have the following result.

Theorem 1. *Under Assumptions* 1–4, $\hat{c} \to_p c_0$ *as* $(N, T \to \infty)$.

Next, we derive the limit distribution of $\hat{c}$. Since the log-likelihood function $L_{N,T}(c, \hat{\delta}(c), \hat{\sigma}^2(c); z^{N,T})$ is differentiable with respect to c and since $\hat{c}$ is consistent for c_0, a point in an interior of the parameter set $\mathbb{C}$, the *MLE* $\hat{c}$ solves the following first-order condition with probability one;

$$0 = \frac{dL_{N,T}(\hat{c}, \hat{\delta}(\hat{c}), \hat{\sigma}^2(\hat{c}); z^{N,T})}{dc} = \frac{\partial L_{N,T}(\hat{c}, \hat{\delta}(\hat{c}), \hat{\sigma}^2(\hat{c}); z^{N,T})}{\partial c}$$

$$= \left[\frac{1}{N}\sum_{i=1}^{N}\sum_{t=1}^{T}\left\{\Delta z_{i,t} - \hat{\delta}(\hat{c}) - \hat{c}\left(\frac{z_{i,t-1}}{T} - \hat{\delta}(\hat{c})\frac{t-1}{T}\right)\right\}^2\right]^{-1}$$

$$\times \frac{1}{N}\sum_{i=1}^{N}\sum_{t=1}^{T}\left\{\left(\Delta z_{i,t} - \hat{\delta}(\hat{c}) - \hat{c}\left(\frac{z_{i,t-1}}{T} - \hat{\delta}(\hat{c})\frac{t-1}{T}\right)\right)\right.$$

$$\left.\times \left(\frac{z_{i,t-1}}{T} - \hat{\delta}(\hat{c})\frac{t-1}{T}\right)\right\}, \tag{9}$$

where the second equality holds by the Envelope Function Theorem.

Theorem 2. *Under Assumptions* 1–4,

$$\sqrt{N}(\hat{c} - c_0) \Rightarrow N\left(0, \frac{1}{\sigma_0^2 \int_0^1\int_0^r e^{2c_0(r-s)}\,ds\,dr}\right)$$

as $(N, T \to \infty)$.

In view of (4), the *MLE* of the homogeneous trend coefficient $\hat{\delta}$ is found to be

$$\hat{\delta}(\hat{c}) = \frac{\frac{1}{N}\sum_{i=1}^{N}\sum_{t=1}^{T}\left(1 - \hat{c}\frac{t-1}{T}\right)\left(\Delta z_{i,t} - \frac{\hat{c}}{T}z_{i,t-1}\right)}{\sum_{t=1}^{T}\left(1 - \hat{c}\frac{t-1}{T}\right)^2}, \tag{10}$$

and as $(N, T \to \infty)$, it is possible to show that

$$\sqrt{NT}(\hat{\delta}(\hat{c}) - \delta_0) \Rightarrow N\left(0, \frac{\sigma_0^2}{\int_0^1 (1 - c_0 r)^2\,dr}\right). \tag{11}$$

The proof of (11) is straightforward using the results in Lemmas 6 and 7 and the consistency of $\hat{c}$ and is therefore omitted. Summarizing, we have:

Theorem 3. *Under Assumptions* 1–4,

$$\sqrt{NT}(\hat{\delta}(\hat{c}) - \delta_0) \Rightarrow N\left(0, \frac{\sigma_0^2}{\int_0^1 (1 - c_0 r)^2 dr}\right)$$

as $(N, T \to \infty)$.

Remarks

(a) When the trends in the panel regression model (1) are homogeneous, the Gaussian *MLE* $\hat{c}$ is $\sqrt{N}$-consistent and has an asymptotic normal limit distribution that is equivalent to the normal limit distribution in (3), a result that continues to hold in a model with general polynomial deterministic trends.

(b) Since $\hat{\delta}(c)$ is a non-linear function of c in general, it is not easy to find a closed-form solution of the first-order condition (9). In this case, to solve the first-order condition (9), it would be common to employ an iteration involving the use of a preliminary $\sqrt{N}$-consistent estimator, $\tilde{c}$, say, which leads to a second-stage estimator via suitable numerical optimization, such as Newton–Raphson. In the model (1), a natural candidate for the preliminary estimator would be

$$\tilde{c} = \left(\sum_{i=1}^{N}\sum_{t=1}^{T}\left(\frac{z_{i,t-1}}{T} - \hat{\delta}(c)\frac{t-1}{T}\right)^2\right)^{-1} \times \left(\sum_{i=1}^{N}\sum_{t=1}^{T}(\Delta z_{i,t} - \hat{\delta}(c))\left(\frac{z_{i,t-1}}{T} - \hat{\delta}(c)\frac{t-1}{T}\right)\right), \tag{12}$$

where c is arbitrarily chosen. Then, using the first step estimator $\tilde{c}$, we may construct the following second step estimator;

$$\check{c} = \left(\sum_{i=1}^{N}\sum_{t=1}^{T}\left(\frac{z_{i,t-1}}{T} - \hat{\delta}(\tilde{c})\frac{t-1}{T}\right)^2\right)^{-1} \times \left(\sum_{i=1}^{N}\sum_{t=1}^{T}(\Delta z_{i,t} - \hat{\delta}(\tilde{c}))\left(\frac{z_{i,t-1}}{T} - \hat{\delta}(\tilde{c})\frac{t-1}{T}\right)\right). \tag{13}$$

An important feature of the first step estimator $\tilde{c}$ is that it is asymptotically as efficient as the *MLE* $\hat{c}$, because

$$\sqrt{N}(\tilde{c} - c_0) \Rightarrow N\left(0, \frac{1}{\sigma_0^2 \int_0^1\int_0^r e^{2c_0(r-s)} ds\, dr}\right), \tag{14}$$

the proof of which is provided in the Appendix.

(c) From Theorem 2 we see that the asymptotic variance of $\sqrt{N}(\hat{c} - c_0)$ depends on the true parameter c_0. Figure 1 graphs the asymptotic variance of $\sqrt{N}(\hat{c} - c_0)$. As is apparent in the graph, the asymptotic variance of $\sqrt{N}(\hat{c} - c_0)$ decreases rather rapidly to zero as c_0 increases.

3.2. Heterogeneous Trends

Here we study the asymptotic properties of the *MLE* of the panel regression model (1) with heterogeneous deterministic trends specified as follows.

Assumption 5 *(Heterogeneous Trends).* $G_i(t) = \delta_i t$.

Suppose that the true trend coefficients are $\{\delta_{0,i}: i = 1, \ldots, N\}$. Then, the data $z_{i,t}$ are generated by the following parametric model:

$$z_{i,t} = \delta_{0,i} t + y_{i,t}$$

$$y_{i,t} = \left(1 + \frac{c_0}{T}\right) y_{i,t-1} + \varepsilon_{i,t}. \tag{15}$$

Let $\delta^{N,0} = (\delta_{0,1}, \ldots, \delta_{0,N})'$ and $z^{N,T} = (z_{1,1}, \ldots, z_{N,T})'$. Define $y_{i,t}(\delta_i) = z_{i,t} - \delta_i t$ and $\varepsilon_{i,t}(\delta_i, c) = y_{i,t}(\delta_i) - (1 + [c/T]) y_{i,t-1}(\delta_i)$.

Under Gaussianity, the standardized log-likelihood function is

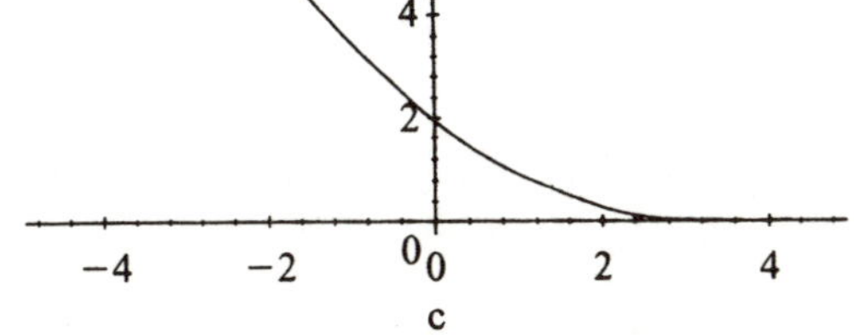

Figure 1. Graph of the Asymptotic Variance of the *MLE* $\hat{c}$

$$L_{N,T}(c,\, \delta^N,\, \sigma^2;\, z^{N,T})$$

$$= -\frac{NT}{2}\log\sigma^2 - \frac{1}{2\sigma^2}\sum_{i=1}^{N}\sum_{t=1}^{T}\left(\Delta_c z_{i,t} - \delta_i\left(1 - c\frac{t-1}{T}\right)\right)^2.$$

Given c, the *MLE* for δ_i is

$$\hat{\delta}_i(c) = \left(\sum_{t=1}^{T}\left(1 - c\frac{t-1}{T}\right)^2\right)^{-1}\left(\sum_{t=1}^{T}\Delta_c z_{i,t}\left(1 - c\frac{t-1}{T}\right)\right),$$

leading to the concentrated log-likelihood function

$$L_{N,T}(c,\, \hat{\delta}(c)^N,\, \sigma^2;\, z^{N,T})$$

$$= -\frac{NT}{2}\log\sigma^2 - \frac{1}{2\sigma^2}\sum_{i=1}^{N}\sum_{t=1}^{T}\left(\Delta_c z_{i,t} - \hat{\delta}_i(c)\left(1 - c\frac{t-1}{T}\right)\right)^2, \qquad (16)$$

where $\hat{\delta}(c)^N = (\hat{\delta}_1(c), \ldots, \hat{\delta}_N(c))'$.

We seek to show that $\hat{c}$, the *MLE* of c maximizing $L_{N,T}(c,\, \hat{\delta}(c)^N,\, \sigma^2;\, z^{N,T})$, is inconsistent. To do so, it is simplest to assume that the variance of $\varepsilon_{i,t}$, σ^2, is known. By definition

$$\Delta_c z_{i,t} = \delta_{0,i}\Delta_c t + \Delta_c y_{i,t}(\delta_{0,i}) = \delta_{0,i}\Delta_c t + \Delta_{c_0} y_{i,t}(\delta_{0,i}) + (\Delta_c - \Delta_{c_0})y_{i,t}(\delta_{0,i})$$

$$= \delta_{0,i}\left(1 - c\frac{t-1}{T}\right) + \varepsilon_{i,t}(\delta_{0,i},\, c_0) - (c - c_0)\frac{y_{i,t-1}(\delta_{0,i})}{T},$$

so we can write

$$\frac{1}{N}[L(z^{N,T};\, \hat{\delta}^N(c),\, c) - L(z^{N,T};\, \hat{\delta}^N(c_0),\, c_0)]$$

$$= -\frac{1}{2\sigma^2 N}\sum_{i=1}^{N}\sum_{t=1}^{T}\left\{\varepsilon_{i,t}(\delta_{0,i},\, c_0) - (c - c_0)\frac{y_{i,t-1}(\delta_{0,i})}{T}\right.$$

$$\left. - (\hat{\delta}_i(c) - \delta_{0,i})\left(1 - c\frac{t-1}{T}\right)\right\}^2$$

$$+ \frac{1}{2\sigma^2 N}\sum_{i=1}^{N}\sum_{t=1}^{T}\left\{\varepsilon_{i,t}(\delta_{0,i},\, c_0) - (\hat{\delta}_i(c_0) - \delta_{0,i})\left(1 - c_0\frac{t-1}{T}\right)\right\}^2. \qquad (17)$$

Lemma 4 *Suppose Assumptions* 1–3 *and* 5 *hold and that the variance of* $\varepsilon_{i,t}$, σ^2 *is known. Then, as* $(N,\, T \to \infty)$,

$$\frac{1}{N}[L(z^{N,T}; \hat{\delta}^N(c), c) - L(z^{N,T}; \delta^{0,N}, c_0)]$$

$$\to_p \frac{(c-c_0)^2 \int_0^1\int_0^1 (1-cr)(1-cs)\int_0^{r\wedge s} e^{c_0(r+s-2p)}\,dp\,ds\,dr}{2\int_0^1 (1-cr)^2 dr}$$

$$- \frac{2(c-c_0)\int_0^1\int_0^r e^{c_0(r-s)}(1-cr)(1-cs)\,ds\,dr}{2\int_0^1 (1-cr)^2 dr}$$

$$- \frac{1}{2}(c-c_0)^2 \int_0^1\int_0^r e^{2c_0(r-s)}\,ds\,dr$$

$$= G(c; c_0), \textit{ say, uniformly in } c.$$

According to this lemma, the standardized concentrated log-likelihood function, $(1/N)[L(z^{N,T}; \hat{\delta}^N(c), c) - L(z^{N,T}; \delta^{0,N}, c_0)]$, has the uniform limit $G(c; c_0)$, a function that is continuous on the parameter set $\mathbb{C}$. Hence, the *MLE* $\hat{c}$ that maximizes $(1/N)[L(z^{N,T}; \hat{\delta}^N(c), c) - L(z^{N,T}; \delta^{0,N}, c_0)]$ converges in probability to the point that maximizes the limit function $G(c; c_0)$. For the *MLE* $\hat{c}$ to be consistent, the true parameter c_0 must maximize $G(c; c_0)$; and, conversely, if some point $\bar{c} \neq c_0$ maximizes $G(c; c_0)$, then the *MLE* $\hat{c}$ is not consistent.

We proceed to differentiate $G(c; c_0)$ with respect to c and evaluate the derivative at $c = c_0$. Since the true parameter c_0 is in an interior of the parameter set $\mathbb{C}$ and the limit function $G(c; c_0)$ is differentiable, if c_0 maximizes $G(c; c_0)$, its first derivative at $c = c_0$ must necessarily be zero. However, direct calculation shows that

$$\left.\frac{dG(c; c_0)}{dc}\right|_{c=c_0}$$

$$= \left.\frac{\left\{-\int_0^1\int_0^r e^{c_0(r-s)}(1-cr)(1-cs)\,ds\,dr\right\}\left\{\int_0^1 (1-cr)^2 dr\right\}}{\left(\int_0^1 (1-cr)^2 dr\right)^2}\right|_{c=c_0}$$

$$= \frac{-3+2c_0}{6(1-c_0+\frac{1}{3}(c_0)^2)} \neq 0 \qquad (18)$$

if $c_0 \neq \frac{3}{2}$. Therefore, for all $c_0 \neq \frac{3}{2}$ the limit function $G(c; c_0)$ cannot attain a maximum at $c = c_0$. For $c_0 = \frac{3}{2}$, we graph the function $G(c; \frac{3}{2})$ in Figure 2. As the figure shows, the limit function $G(c; \frac{3}{2})$ has a local minimum at $c = \frac{3}{2}$, and so $G(c; c_0)$ does not attain a maximum at $c = c_0$ for any value of c_0.

In summary, we have the following result.

Theorem 5 *(Inconsistency)*. *Suppose Assumptions* 1–3 *and* 5 *hold. Then, the MLE* $\hat{c}$ *is inconsistent when* $(N, T \to \infty)$.

Remarks

(a) From (18), it is apparent that $[dG(c; c_0)/dc]|_{c=c_0}$ tends to zero as $|c_0|$ increases to infinity. So when the absolute value of c_0 is large, we may expect the limit function to be maximized at a value close to c_0. In such cases, the probability limit of the *MLE* can be expected to be close to the true parameter c_0, even though the *MLE* is inconsistent. To investigate, we present graphs of the limit functions $G(c, 4)$ and $G(c, -8)$ in Figures 3 and 4, respectively. When the true parameter $c_0 = 4$, the limit of the standardized concentrated log-likelihood $G(c, 4)$ is maximized around $c = 4.057$, which is close to the true parameter value, involving only a 1 percent bias. On the other hand, when the true parameter $c_0 = -8$, $G(c, -8)$ is maximized around $c = -10.27$, giving a 28 percent asymptotic bias. These results indicate that we can expect the inconsistency of the *MLE* to be greater when c_0 is negative.

(b) The inconsistency of the *MLE* $\hat{c}$ in the above theorem is an instance of the so-called incidental parameter problem (Neyman and Scott, 1948). Incidental parameter problems are known to arise in other panel data regression models, the celebrated example being the

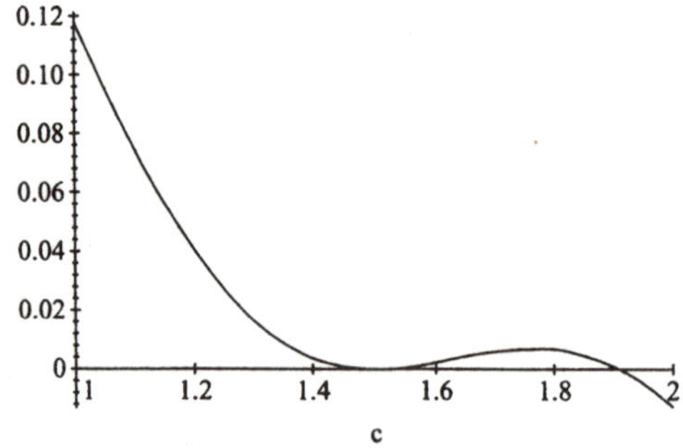

Figure 2. Graph of $G(c, \frac{3}{2})$

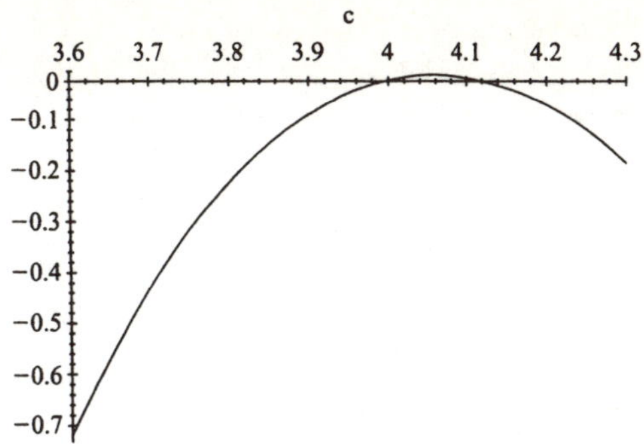

Figure 3. Graph of $G(c, 4)$

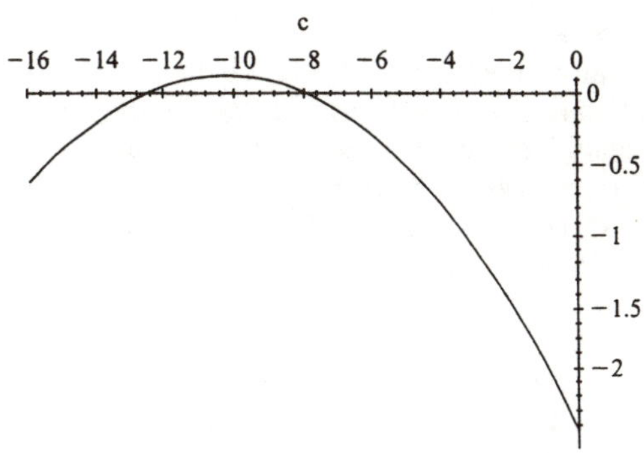

Figure 4. Graph of $G(c, -8)$

dynamic panel regression model with fixed effects. In that case, the panel data $z_{i,t}$ are generated by the autoregression

$$z_{i,t} = \delta_i + az_{i,t-1} + \varepsilon_{i,t},$$

where $|a| < 1$ and the $\varepsilon_{i,t}$ are i.i.d. $N(0, \sigma^2)$. The individual intercept terms δ_i enter the model to account for individual effects in the panel data $z_{i,t}$. The main focus of interest in this model is the estimation of the common parameter a, and the individual effects δ_i are incidental parameters. For simplicity, assume that $z_{i,0} = 0$ for all i. Then, the *MLE* of a is equivalent to the within estimator, defined as:

$$\hat{a} = \frac{\sum_{i=1}^{N}\sum_{t=1}^{T}(z_{i,t-1} - \bar{z}_{i,-})(z_{i,t} - \bar{z}_{i,.})}{\sum_{i=1}^{N}\sum_{t=1}^{T}(z_{i,t-1} - \bar{z}_{i,-})^2}$$

$$= a + \frac{\sum_{i=1}^{N}\sum_{t=1}^{T}(z_{i,t-1} - \bar{z}_{i,-})(\varepsilon_{i,t} - \bar{\varepsilon}_{i,.})}{\sum_{i=1}^{N}\sum_{t=1}^{T}(z_{i,t-1} - \bar{z}_{i,-})^2}, \tag{19}$$

where $\bar{z}_{i,-} = (1/T)\sum_{t=1}^{T} z_{i,t-1}$, $\bar{z}_{i,.} = (1/T)\sum_{t=1}^{T} z_{i,t}$, and $\bar{\varepsilon}_{i,.} = (1/T)\sum_{t=1}^{T}\varepsilon_{i,t}$. In this case, when $N \to \infty$ for fixed T, we know that $\hat{a} \not\to_p a$, due to the correlation between $z_{i,t-1} - \bar{z}_{i,-}$ and $\varepsilon_{i,t} - \bar{\varepsilon}_{i,.}$. So, in this case with $N \to \infty$ and T fixed, the *MLE* $\hat{a}$ is inconsistent (Nickell, 1981).

(c) An especially interesting aspect of the model (15) is that the incidental parameter problem leading to the inconsistency of the *MLE* $\hat{c}$ continues to be present even though $T \to \infty$ as well as $N \to \infty$. In contrast, the incidental parameter problem that gives rise to the inconsistency of $\hat{a}$ in (19) disappears if $T \to \infty$ fast enough when $N \to \infty$.

IV. MONTE CARLO SIMULATIONS

This section reports some simulations designed to explore the finite sample properties of the maximum likelihood estimators studied in the previous section. First, to investigate the homogeneous trend model, data $z_{i,t}$ were generated by the system

$$z_{i,t} = \delta_0 t + y_{i,t}, \quad \delta_0 = 3,$$

$$y_{i,t} = \left(1 + \frac{c_0}{T}\right) y_{i,t-1} + \varepsilon_{i,t}, \quad c_0 \in \{-4, -2, 0, 2, 4\}, \tag{20}$$

where the $\varepsilon_{i,t}$ are i.i.d. $N(0, 1)$ across i and over t, and the initial values of $y_{i,0}$ are zeros. Following the notation used in the previous section, we let $\hat{c}$ denote the *MLE* of the localizing parameter and $\hat{\delta}(\hat{c})$ to be the *MLE* of the homogeneous trend coefficient in (10). Also, let $\tilde{c}$ denote the first step estimator in (12), and $\check{c}$ denote the second step estimator in (13).

The main goals of the simulation experiment with model (12) are as follows: (i) to examine the finite sample properties of the *MLE*'s $\hat{\delta}(\hat{c})$ and $\hat{c}$ by comparing their mean squared errors for various parameter configurations; and (ii) to compare the asymptotic efficiencies of the three estimators considered in Section 3.1—the *MLE* $\hat{c}$, the first step estimator $\tilde{c}$, and the second step estimator $\breve{c}$. From the *DGP* (20), we generate panels of 16 different sizes, with $N \in \{25, 50, 75, 100\}$ and $T \in \{25, 50, 75, 100\}$. The estimates $\hat{\delta}(\hat{c})$, $\hat{c}$, $\tilde{c}$, and $\breve{c}$ are computed and 1000 replications used to calculate their mean squared errors. Table 1 reports the mean squared errors of $\hat{\delta}(\hat{c})$ and $\hat{c}$. The first column of the table contains the sample size, the top element of each column contains the true parameter value, and the first and second elements in the table are the *MSE* of $\hat{\delta}(\hat{c})$ and the *MSE* of $\hat{c}$, respectively.

Several features of the results are notable. First, the *MSE* of $\hat{c}$ is much more sensitive to the sample size than the *MSE* of $\hat{\delta}(\hat{c})$. Second, the *MSE* of $\hat{c}$ decreases more as T increases than when N increases. For example, when $(\delta_0, c_0) = (3, -4)$ and the sample size changes from $(N, T) = (50, 75)$ to $(N, T) = (50, 100)$, the *MSE* of $\hat{c}$ decreases from 1.034 to 0.204. On the other hand, when the sample size changes from $(N, T) = (50, 75)$ to $(N, T) = (75, 75)$, the *MSE* of $\hat{c}$ decreases from 1.034 to 1.021. A more interesting feature is that when the sample size is small, increases in N sometimes lead to a deterioration in the finite sample properties of $\hat{c}$. For example, when $(\delta_0, c_0) = (3, -4)$ again, and the sample size changes from $(N, T) = (50, 50)$ to $(N, T) = (75, 50)$, the *MSE* of $\hat{c}$ increases from 3.887 to 3.911. Third, when $c_0 = 0$, the finite sample performance of $\hat{c}$ is

TABLE 1
MSE of $\hat{\delta}(\hat{c})$ *and* $\hat{c}$

	(δ_0, c_0)				
(N, T)	(3, −4)	(3, −2)	(3, 0)	(3, 2)	(3, 4)
(25, 25)	0.010, 8.486	0.010, 2.084	0.011, 0.125	0.012, 2.583	0.014, 9.411
(25, 50)	0.009, 3.779	0.009, 0.968	0.010, 0.117	0.012, 1.160	0.012, 4.042
(25, 75)	0.009, 1.064	0.009, 0.344	0.010, 0.114	0.011, 0.318	0.010, 1.032
(25, 100)	0.009, 0.421	0.009, 0.249	0.009, 0.106	0.010, 0.020	0.010, 0.019
(50, 25)	0.009, 8.803	0.010, 2.189	0.010, 0.052	0.010, 2.380	0.012, 9.146
(50, 50)	0.009, 3.887	0.009, 0.971	0.009, 0.046	0.010, 1.079	0.010, 4.038
(50, 75)	0.009, 1.034	0.009, 0.290	0.009, 0.049	0.010, 0.282	0.009, 1.019
(50, 100)	0.009, 0.204	0.009, 0.116	0.009, 0.047	0.010, 0.012	0.009, 0.017
(75, 25)	0.009, 8.817	0.009, 2.184	0.010, 0.036	0.010, 2.361	0.011, 9.142
(75, 50)	0.009, 3.911	0.009, 0.974	0.009, 0.034	0.010, 1.061	0.010, 4.034
(75, 75)	0.009, 1.021	0.009, 0.273	0.009, 0.030	0.010, 0.273	0.009, 1.017
(75, 100)	0.009, 0.145	0.009, 0.081	0.009, 0.032	0.009, 0.009	0.009, 0.016
(100, 25)	0.009, 8.920	0.009, 2.224	0.009, 0.023	0.010, 2.312	0.010, 9.078
(100, 50)	0.009, 3.981	0.009, 0.999	0.009, 0.022	0.010, 1.033	0.010, 4.014
(100, 75)	0.009, 1.047	0.009, 0.280	0.009, 0.023	0.010, 0.264	0.009, 1.013
(100, 100)	0.009, 0.107	0.009, 0.059	0.009, 0.022	0.009, 0.008	0.009, 0.016

apparently far better than it is for $c_0 < 0$. Also, as implied by the form of the asymptotic variance (see Theorem 2 and Remark (c) following Theorem 3), the *MSE* of $\hat{c}$ decreases as c_0 increases.

Table 2 reports the mean squared errors of the first step estimator $\tilde{c}$ and the second step estimator $\breve{c}$. The simulations cover the same 16 panel data sizes and use the same number of replications as before. The layout of the table is the same as Table 1. To calculate $\tilde{c}$ we use $c = 0$ for quasi-differencing the data. This experiment focuses on comparing the finite sample properties of three asymptotically equivalent estimators, the *MLE* $\hat{c}$, the first step estimator $\tilde{c}$, and the second step estimator $\breve{c}$. As is apparent from comparison of Tables 1 and 2, there are apparently no major differences in the mean squared errors of the three asymptotically equivalent estimators. So, finite sample effects are not important in this case.

The next simulation experiment involves the heterogeneous trend model, for which the generating process is taken to be

$$z_{i,t} = \delta_{0,i}t + y_{i,t}, \quad \delta_{0,i} \sim \text{i.i.d. } \textit{Uniform } [0, 4],$$

$$y_{i,t} = \left(1 + \frac{c_0}{T}\right) y_{i,t-1} + \varepsilon_{i,t}, \quad c_0 \in \{-4, 0, 4\}, \tag{21}$$

TABLE 2
MSE of $\tilde{c}$ and $\breve{c}$

	(δ_0, c_0)				
(N, T)	(3, −4)	(3, −2)	(3, 0)	(3, 2)	(3, 4)
(25, 25)	8.505, 8.486	2.086, 2.084	0.125, 0.125	2.585, 2.583	9.449, 9.412
(25, 50)	3.825, 3.780	0.972, 0.968	0.117, 0.117	1.173, 1.161	4.157, 4.042
(25, 75)	1.098, 1.064	0.346, 0.344	0.113, 0.114	0.336, 0.318	1.124, 1.034
(25, 100)	0.398, 0.412	0.242, 0.249	0.105, 0.106	0.022, 0.020	0.056, 0.012
(50, 25)	8.812, 8.803	2.190, 2.189	0.052, 0.052	2.381, 2.380	9.169, 9.147
(50, 50)	3.906, 3.887	0.973, 0.971	0.046, 0.046	1.085, 1.079	4.090, 4.038
(50, 75)	1.054, 1.034	0.292, 0.290	0.049, 0.049	0.291, 0.282	1.062, 1.019
(50, 100)	0.200, 0.204	0.115, 0.116	0.047, 0.047	0.012, 0.012	0.025, 0.017
(75, 25)	8.822, 8.817	2.184, 2.184	0.036, 0.036	2.362, 2.361	9.156, 9.142
(75, 50)	3.926, 3.911	0.975, 0.974	0.034, 0.034	1.065, 1.061	4.068, 4.034
(75, 75)	1.034, 1.021	0.274, 0.273	0.030, 0.030	0.279, 0.273	1.046, 1.017
(75, 100)	0.143, 0.145	0.080, 0.081	0.032, 0.032	0.010, 0.009	0.020, 0.016
(100, 25)	8.924, 8.920	2.224, 2.224	0.023, 0.023	2.313, 2.312	9.087, 9.078
(100, 50)	3.991, 3.981	1.000, 0.999	0.022, 0.022	1.036, 1.033	4.039, 4.014
(100, 75)	1.057, 1.047	0.281, 0.280	0.023, 0.023	0.268, 0.264	1.034, 1.013
(100, 100)	0.106, 0.107	0.058, 0.059	0.022, 0.022	0.008, 0.008	0.018, 0.016

where $\varepsilon_{i,t}$ are i.i.d. $N(0, 1)$ across i and over t, and $y_{i,0} = 0$ for all i. The main purpose of this simulation is to explore the finite sample manifestation of the inconsistency of the *MLE* $\hat{c}$. For this, we generated a panel data set with size dimensions $N = 300$, $T = 300$, and found the Gaussian *MLE* $\hat{c}$ by a grid search method. The grid used in the simulation is 0.075; 1000 replications were employed. Estimated density functions of the Gaussian *MLE* $\hat{c}$ of the panel models with $c_0 \in \{-4, 0, 4\}$ are shown in Figures 5–7.

As is apparent in Figures 5 and 6, the density of $\hat{c}$ is concentrated in a region substantially removed from the true parameter value when $c = -4$ and $c = 0$. On the other hand, in Figure 7, when $c_0 = 4$, the density of the $\hat{c}$ appears to be concentrated around 4.16, a value that is quite near the true value. This outcome corroborates the asymptotic analysis of the previous section, where it was shown that when $c_0 = 4$, the standardized Gaussian log-likelihood converges in probability to the limit function $G(c, 4)$ whose maximum is close to the true value $c_0 = 4$.

V. CONCLUSION

This paper explores the asymptotic properties of the Gaussian maximum likelihood estimator of the localizing parameter in a panel model with

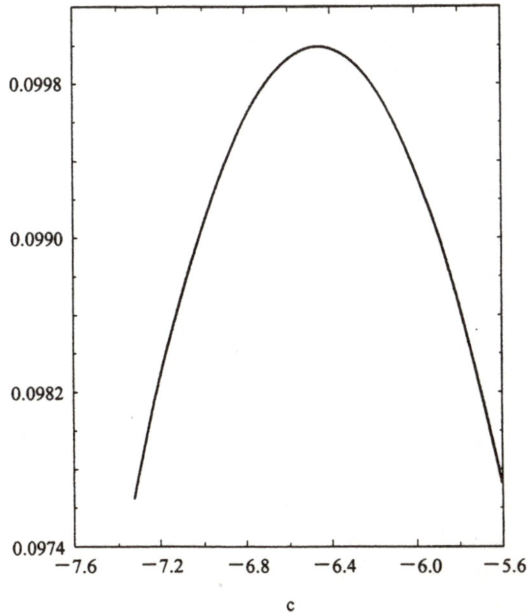

Figure 5. Density of $\hat{c}$ when the true $c_0 = -4$

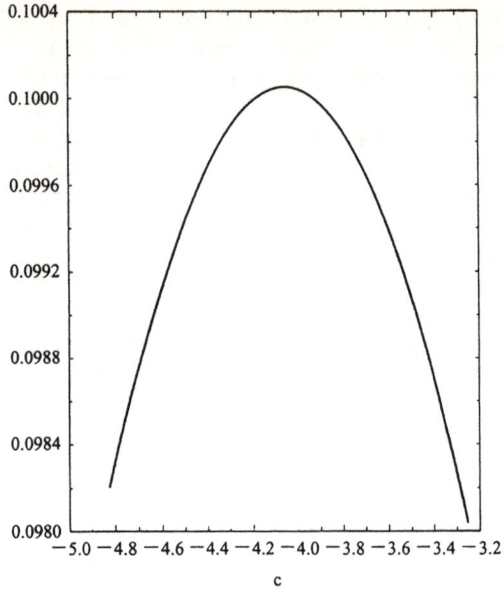

Figure 6. Density of $\hat{c}$ when the true $c_0 = 0$

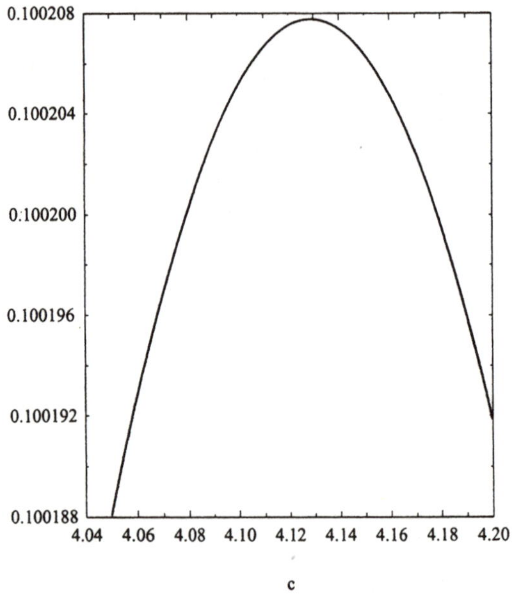

Figure 7. Density of $\hat{c}$ when the true $c_0 = 4$

deterministic and stochastic trends. Several new findings emerge. First, when the trends are homogeneous across individuals in the panel, the Gaussian *MLE* of the common localizing parameter is $\sqrt{N}$-consistent and has a limiting normal distribution that is equivalent to the asymptotic distribution of the Gaussian *MLE* of the model in which the deterministic trends are known. So, in this case, trend elimination carries no cost in the limit, just as in the case of a stationary autoregression with trend. However, when the trends are heterogeneous across individuals, the Gaussian *MLE* of the localizing parameter is shown to be inconsistent. The inconsistency is due to the presence of an infinite number of incidental parameters for the individual trends. Procedures for resolving this manifestation of the incidental parameter problem in panel regression are now being explored by the authors and will be reported in later work.

University of California, Santa Barbara
Cowles Foundation for Research in Economics, Yale University

Date of Receipt of Final Manuscript: July 1999

REFERENCES

Alvarez, J. and Arellano, M. (1998). 'The Time Series and Cross-Section Asymptotics of Dynamic Panel Data Estimators', Mimeo.

Billingsley, P. (1968). *Convergence of Probability Measures*, Wiley, New York.

Bobkoski, M. J. (1983). 'Hypothesis Testing in Nonstationary Time Series', Ph.D thesis, Department of Statistics, University of Winsconsin.

Canjels, N. and Watson, M. (1997). 'Estimating Deterministic Trends in the Presence of Serially Correlated Errors', *Review of Economics and Statistics*, 79, 184–200.

Cavanagh, C. (1985). 'Roots Local to Unity', manuscript, Department of Ecomonics, Harvard University.

Cavanagh, C., Elliott, G. and Stock, J. H. (1995). 'Inference in Models with Nearly Integrated Regressors', *Econometric Theory*, 11, 1131–1147.

Elliott, G., Rothenberg, T. J. and Stock, J. H. (1995). 'Efficient tests of an autoregressive unit root', *Econometrica*, 64, 813–836.

Hahn, J. (1998). 'Asymptotically Unbiased Inference of Dynamic Panel Model with Fixed Effects when Both *n* and *T* are Large', Mimeo.

Hansen, L. P. (1982). 'Large Sample Properties of Generalized Method of Moments Estimators', *Econometrica*, 50, 1029–1054.

Johansen, S. (1991). 'Estimation and Hypothesis Testing of Cointegration Vectors in Gaussian Vector Autoregressive Models', *Econometrica*, 59, 1551–1580.

Moon, H. R. and Phillips, P. C. B. (1998) 'Consistent Estimation of Autoregressive Roots near Unity using Panel Data', Mimeo, Yale University.

Newey, W. and MacFadden D. (1994), 'Large Sample Estimation and Hypothesis Testing', in Engle R. F. and McFadden, D. L. (eds.) *Handbook of Econometrics, Vol. 4*. North-Holland, Amsterdam, 2111–2245.

Neyman, J. and Scott, E. (1948). 'Consistent Estimates Based on Partially Consistent Observations', *Econometrica*, 16, 1–32.

Nickell, S. (1981). 'Biases in Dynamic Models with Fixed Effects', *Econometrica*, 49, 1417–1426.

Phillips, P. C. B. (1987). 'Towards a Unified Asymptotic Theory for Autoregression', *Biometrika*, 74, 535–547.

Phillips, P. C. B. and Lee, C. C. (1996). 'Efficiency Gains from Quasi-Differencing under Nonstationarity', in Robinson, P. M. and Rosenblatt, M. (eds.) *Athens Conference on Applied Probability and Time Series: Essays in Memory of E. J. Hannan*, Springer-Verlag, New York.

Phillips, P. C. B. and Moon, H. R. (1999). 'Linear Regression Limit Theory for Nonstationary Panel Data', *Econometrica*, 67, 1057–1111.

Phillips, P. C. B. and Xiao, Z. (1998). 'A Primer on Unit Root Testing', *Journal of Economic Surveys*, 12, 423–469.

Phillips, P. C. B., Moon, H. R. and Xiao, Z. (1998). 'How to Estimate Autoregressive Roots Near Unity', Mimeo, Yale University.

Stock, J. H. (1991). 'Confidence Intervals for the Largest Autoregressive Root in US Macroeconomic Time Series', *Journal of Monetary Economics*, 28, 435–460.

Stock, J. H. (1994). 'Unit Roots, Structure Breaks and Trends', in Engle, R. F. and McFadden, D. L. (eds.) *Handbook of Econometrics, Vol. 4*, North-Holland, Amsterdam, 2739–2841.

Xiao, Z. and Phillips, P. C. B. (1999). 'Efficient Detrending in Cointegrating Regression', forthcoming in *Econometric Theory*.

APPENDIX

Lemma 6. *Suppose that* $\mathbb{C}$ *is a compact subset of* $\mathbb{R}$. *Assume that, for* $k = 1, \ldots, K$, $h_k(c, \tilde{c})$ *is a real-valued continuous function on* $\mathbb{C} \times C$ *with* $h_k(c, c) = 0$, *and* $l_k(x, y)$ *is a real-valued continuous function on* $[0, 1] \times [0, 1]$. *Also, assume that* $f(x, c)$ *and* $g(x, c)$ *are continuous functions from* $[0, 1] \times \mathbb{C}$ *to* $\mathbb{R}$ *such that* $f(x, c)g(y, c) - f(x, \tilde{c})g(y, \tilde{c}) = \sum_{k=1}^{K} h_k(c, \tilde{c})l_k(x, y)$. *Suppose that* $y_{i,t} = \exp(c_0/T)y_{i,t-1} + \varepsilon_{i,t}$, *where* $\varepsilon_{i,t}$ *are i.i.d.* $(0, \sigma_0^2)$ *across i and over t and* $y_{i,0} = 0$. *Then, as* $(N, T \to \infty)$, *the following hold.*

(a) $$\frac{1}{N}\sum_{i=1}^{N}\frac{1}{T^2}\sum_{t=1}^{T} y_{i,t-1}^2 \to_p \sigma_0^2 \int_0^1\int_0^r e^{2c_0(r-s)}ds\,dr.$$

(b) $$\frac{1}{N}\sum_{i=1}^{N}\left(\frac{1}{\sqrt{T}}\sum_{t=1}^{T}\varepsilon_{i,t}f\left(\frac{t}{T}, c\right)\right)\left(\frac{1}{T\sqrt{T}}\sum_{t=1}^{T} y_{i,t-1}g\left(\frac{t}{T}, c\right)\right)$$
$$\to_p \sigma_0^2 \int_0^1\int_0^r e^{c_0(r-s)}g(r, c)f(s, c)d \text{ uniformly in } c.$$

(c) $$\frac{1}{N}\sum_{i=1}^{N}\left(\frac{1}{T\sqrt{T}}\sum_{t=1}^{T}y_{i,t-1}f\left(\frac{t}{T},c\right)\right)\left(\frac{1}{T\sqrt{T}}\sum_{t=1}^{T}y_{i,t-1}g\left(\frac{t}{T},c\right)\right)$$

$$\rightarrow_p \sigma_0^2\int_0^1\int_0^1 f(r,c)g(s,c)\int_0^{r\wedge s}e^{c_0(r+s-2p)}\,dp\,ds \text{ uniformly in } c.$$

(d) $$\frac{1}{N}\sum_{i=1}^{N}\left(\frac{1}{\sqrt{T}}\sum_{t=1}^{T}\varepsilon_{i,t}f\left(\frac{t}{T},c\right)\right)\left(\frac{1}{\sqrt{T}}\sum_{t=1}^{T}\varepsilon_{i,t}g\left(\frac{t}{T},c\right)\right)$$

$$\rightarrow_p \sigma_0^2\int_0^1\int_0^1 f(r,c)g(s,c)\,ds\,dr \text{ uniformly in } c.$$

Proof

Part (a). This holds by Lemma 9(a) in Moon and Phillips (1998). ■

Part (b). First, using Corollary 1 in Phillips and Moon (1999), we establish Part (b) for fixed c (pointwise convergence). Note that

$$\frac{1}{N}\sum_{i=1}^{N}\left(\frac{1}{\sqrt{T}}\sum_{t=1}^{T}\varepsilon_{i,t}f\left(\frac{t}{T},c\right)\right)\left(\frac{1}{T\sqrt{T}}\sum_{t=1}^{T}y_{i,t-1}g\left(\frac{t}{T},c\right)\right)$$

$$\Rightarrow \frac{1}{N}\sum_{i=1}^{N}\sigma_0^2\left(\int_0^1 f(s,c)dW_i(s)\right)\left(\int_0^1 g(r,c)J_{c,i}(r)dr\right)$$

as $T\rightarrow\infty$ for fixed N and c

$$\rightarrow_p \sigma_0^2\int_0^1\int_0^r e^{c_0(r-s)}g(r,c)f(s,c)\,ds\,dr \text{ as } N\rightarrow\infty \text{ for fixed c.}$$

According to Corollary 1 in Phillips and Moon (1999), this sequential limit becomes the joint limit if

$$Q_{i,T}(c)=\left(\frac{1}{\sqrt{T}}\sum_{t=1}^{T}\varepsilon_{i,t}f(t/T,c)\right)\left(\frac{1}{T\sqrt{T}}\sum_{t=1}^{T}y_{i,t-1}g(t/T,c)\right)$$

is uniformly integrable in T for fixed c, which holds if

$$Q_{1,i,T}(c)=\left(\frac{1}{\sqrt{T}}\sum_{t=1}^{T}\varepsilon_{i,t}f\left(\frac{t}{T},c\right)\right)^2$$

and

$$Q_{2,i,T}(c) = \left(\frac{1}{T\sqrt{T}}\sum_{t=1}^{T} y_{i,t-1}\, g\left(\frac{t}{T}, c\right)\right)^2$$

are uniformly integrable in T for fixed c. Notice that $Q_{1,i,T}(c) \Rightarrow Q_{1,i}(c) = \sigma_0^2(\int_0^1 f(r,c)dW_i(r))^2$, and $EQ_{1,i,T}(c) = \sigma_0^2(1/T)\sum_{t=1}^{T} f(t/T,c)^2 \rightarrow \sigma_0^2\int_0^1 f(r,c)^2 dr = EQ_{1,i}(c)$ as $T\rightarrow\infty$ for all i. Then, by Theorem 5.4 in Billingsley (1968), $Q_{1,i,T}(c)$ are uniformly integrable in T for fixed c. By similar fashion, $Q_{2,i,T}(c)$ is also uniformly integrable in T for fixed c. Therefore, Part (b) is just established for fixed c.

Next, define $R_{N,T}(c) = (1/N)\sum_{i=1}^{N} Q_{i,T}(c)$. To complete the proof, we need to show that $R_{N,T}(c)$ is stochastically equi-continuous, that is, for given $\varepsilon > 0$ and $\eta > 0$, there exists $\delta > 0$ such that

$$\limsup_{(N,T\rightarrow\infty)} P\left\{\sup_{|c-\bar{c}|<\delta,\ c,\ \bar{c}\in\mathbb{C}} |R_{N,T}(c) - R_{N,T}(\bar{c})| > \varepsilon\right\} < \eta.$$

Then, since the index set $\mathbb{C}$ is hypothesized to be compact, the pointwise convergence of $R_{N,T}(c)$ and the stochastic equi-continuity of $R_{N,T}(c)$ imply uniform convergence.

To show the stochastic equi-continuity of $R_{N,T}(c)$, first observe that

$$\sup_{|c-\bar{c}|<\delta,\ c,\ \bar{c}\in\mathbb{C}} |R_{N,T}(c) - R_{N,T}(\bar{c})|$$

$$= \sup_{|c-\bar{c}|<\delta,\ c,\ \bar{c}\in\mathbb{C}} \left|\frac{1}{N}\sum_{i=1}^{N}\frac{1}{T^2}\sum_{t=1}^{T}\sum_{s=1}^{T}\varepsilon_{i,t}y_{i,s-1}\right.$$

$$\left.\times\left\{f\left(\frac{t}{T}, c\right)g\left(\frac{s}{T}, c\right) - f\left(\frac{t}{T}, \bar{c}\right)g\left(\frac{s}{T}, \bar{c}\right)\right\}\right|$$

$$= \sup_{|c-\bar{c}|<\delta,\ c,\ \bar{c}\in\mathbb{C}} \left|\frac{1}{N}\sum_{i=1}^{N}\frac{1}{T^2}\sum_{t=1}^{T}\sum_{s=1}^{T}\varepsilon_{i,t}y_{i,s-1}\left\{\sum_{k=1}^{K} h_k(c,\bar{c})l_k\left(\frac{t}{T}, \frac{s}{T}\right)\right\}\right|$$

$$\leqslant \sup_{1\leqslant k\leqslant K}\ \sup_{|c-\bar{c}|<\delta,\ c,\ \bar{c}\in\mathbb{C}} |h_k(c,\bar{c})|\frac{1}{N}\sum_{i=1}^{N}\left|\frac{1}{T^2}\sum_{t=1}^{T}\sum_{s=1}^{T}\varepsilon_{i,t}y_{i,s-1}\right.$$

$$\left.\times\left\{\sum_{k=1}^{K} l_k\left(\frac{t}{T}, \frac{s}{T}\right)\right\}\right|.$$

Since $h_k(c, \bar{c})$ is continuous on a compact set with $h_k(c, c) = 0$ for all $k = 1, \ldots, K$, we can make $\sup_{1\leqslant k\leqslant K}\sup_{|c-\bar{c}|<\delta,c,\bar{c}\in\mathbb{C}}|h_k(c, \bar{c})|$ arbitrarily small by choosing a small $\delta > 0$. Also, under the assumptions in the lemma, it is not difficult to show that

$$\frac{1}{N}\sum_{i=1}^{N}\left|\frac{1}{T^2}\sum_{t=1}^{T}\sum_{s=1}^{T}\varepsilon_{i,t}y_{i,s-1}\left\{\sum_{k=1}^{K}l_k\left(\frac{t}{T},\frac{s}{T}\right)\right\}\right| = O_p(1).$$

Therefore, $R_{N,T}(c)$ is stochastically equicontinuous. ■

Part (c) and Part (d). The proofs of Parts (c) and (d) are similar to that of Part (b) and they are omitted.

Lemma 7. *Suppose that $f(x, c)$ and $g(x, c)$ are continuous functions from $[0, 1] \times \mathbb{C}$ to $\mathbb{R}$. Assume that $y_{i,t} = \exp(c_0/T)y_{i,t-1} + \varepsilon_{i,t}$, where $\varepsilon_{i,t}$ are i.i.d. $(0, \sigma_0^2)$ across i and over t and $y_{i,0} = 0$.*

Then, as $(N, T \to \infty)$, the following hold.

(a) $$\frac{1}{\sqrt{N}}\sum_{i=1}^{N}\frac{1}{\sqrt{T}}\sum_{t=1}^{T}\varepsilon_{i,t}f\left(\frac{t}{T},c\right) \Rightarrow N\left(0, \sigma_0^2\int_0^1 f(r)^2dr\right).$$

(b) $$\frac{1}{\sqrt{N}}\sum_{i=1}^{N}\frac{1}{T\sqrt{T}}\sum_{t=1}^{T}y_{i,t-1}f\left(\frac{t}{T},c\right) \Rightarrow$$

$$N\left(0, \sigma_0^2\int_0^1\int_0^1\int_0^{r\wedge s} e^{c_0(r+s-2p)}dp\, f(r)f(s)dr\, ds\right).$$

(c) $$\frac{1}{\sqrt{N}}\sum_{i=1}^{N}\frac{1}{T}\sum_{t=1}^{T}\varepsilon_{i,t} \Rightarrow N\left(0, \sigma_0^2\int_0^1\int_0^r e^{2c_0(r-s)}ds\, dr\right).$$

Proof. The proofs verify the conditions of Theorem 3 in Phillips and Moon (1999).

Part (a). Following the notation in Phillips and Moon (1999), we let

$$Q_{i,T} = \frac{1}{\sqrt{T}}\sum_{t=1}^{T}\varepsilon_{i,t}f\left(\frac{t}{T}\right).$$

Then, $Q_{i,T}$ are i.i.d. $(0, \Sigma_T)$ across i with

$$\Sigma_T = \sigma_0^2\frac{1}{T}\sum_{t=1}^{T}f\left(\frac{t}{T}\right)^2.$$

Since $Q_{i,T} \Rightarrow Q_i = \sigma_0\int_0^1 f(r)dW_i(r)$ and $E(Q_{i,T}^2) = \Sigma_T \to \Sigma = E(Q_i^2) =$

$\sigma_0^2 \int_0^1 f(r)^2 dr > 0$ as $T \to \infty$ for fixed i, it follows that $Q_{i,T}^2$ are uniformly integrable in T. Then, by Theorem 3 in Phillips and Moon (1999), we have the desired result. ■

Part (b). By similar fashion, we let

$$Q_{i,T} = \frac{1}{T\sqrt{T}} \sum_{t=1}^{T} y_{i,t-1} f\left(\frac{t}{T}\right)$$

and

$$Q_i = \sigma_0 \int_0^1 f(r) J_{c_0,i}(r) dr.$$

Then, we know that $Q_{i,T} \Rightarrow Q_i$ and

$$E(Q_{i,T}^2) = E\left(\frac{1}{T\sqrt{T}} \sum_{t=1}^{T} y_{i,t-1} f\left(\frac{t}{T}\right)\right)^2$$

$$= \frac{1}{T^3} \sum_{t=1}^{T} \sum_{s=1}^{T} E(y_{i,t-1} y_{i,s-1}) f\left(\frac{t}{T}\right) f\left(\frac{s}{T}\right)$$

$$\to \sigma_0^2 \int_0^1 \int_0^1 \int_0^{r \wedge s} e^{c_0(r+s-2p)} dp\, f(r) f(s) ds\, dr = E(Q_i^2),$$

as $T \to \infty$ for all i. Therefore, $Q_{i,T}^2$ are uniformly integrable in T, and by Theorem 3 in Phillips and Moon (1999), we have the desired result. ■

Part (c) holds by the similar fashion, and we omit the proof. ■

Lemma 8. *$\sqrt{N}\sqrt{T}(\hat{\delta}(c) - \delta_0) = O_p(1)$ uniformly in c as $(N, T \to \infty)$, where $\hat{\delta}(c)$ is defined in* (4).

Proof. By definition,

$$\sqrt{N}\sqrt{T}(\hat{\delta}(c) - \delta_0)$$

$$= \frac{\frac{1}{\sqrt{N}} \sum_{i=1}^{N} \frac{1}{\sqrt{T}} \sum_{t=1}^{T} \left(1 - c\frac{t-1}{T}\right) \left(\varepsilon_{i,t}(\delta_0, c_0) - (c - c_0) \frac{y_{i,t-1}(\delta_0)}{T}\right)}{\frac{1}{T} \sum_{t=1}^{T} \left(1 - c\frac{t-1}{T}\right)^2}.$$

Then, we have

$$\sup_{c\in\mathbb{C}}\left|\sqrt{N}\sqrt{T}(\hat{\delta}(c)-\delta_0)\right|$$

$$\leqslant \frac{\sup_{c\in\mathbb{C}}\left|\frac{1}{\sqrt{N}}\sum_{i=1}^{N}\frac{1}{\sqrt{T}}\sum_{t=1}^{T}\left(1-c\frac{t-1}{T}\right)\left(\varepsilon_{i,t}(\delta_0, c_0)-(c-c_0)\frac{y_{i,t-1}(\delta_0)}{T}\right)\right|}{\inf_{c\in\mathbb{C}}\frac{1}{T}\sum_{t=1}^{T}\left(1-c\frac{t-1}{T}\right)^2}.$$

First, note that

$$\inf_{c\in\mathbb{C}}\frac{1}{T}\sum_{t=1}^{T}\left(1-c\frac{t-1}{T}\right)^2$$

$$=1-2\left(\inf_{c\in\mathbb{C}}c\right)\frac{1}{T}\sum_{t=1}^{T}\frac{t-1}{T}+\left(\inf_{c\in\mathbb{C}}c\right)^2\frac{1}{T}\sum_{t=1}^{T}\left(\frac{t-1}{T}\right)^2$$

$$=\frac{1}{T}\sum_{t=1}^{T}\left(\frac{t-1}{T}\right)^2\left(\inf_{c\in\mathbb{C}}c-\frac{\frac{1}{T}\sum_{t=1}^{T}\frac{t-1}{T}}{\frac{1}{T}\sum_{t=1}^{T}\left(\frac{t-1}{T}\right)^2}\right)^2+1-\frac{\left(\frac{1}{T}\sum_{t=1}^{T}\frac{t-1}{T}\right)^2}{\frac{1}{T}\sum_{t=1}^{T}\left(\frac{t-1}{T}\right)^2}$$

$$\geqslant 1-\frac{\left(\frac{1}{T}\sum_{t=1}^{T}\frac{t-1}{T}\right)^2}{\frac{1}{T}\sum_{t=1}^{T}\left(\frac{t-1}{T}\right)^2}\to 1-\tfrac{3}{4}=\tfrac{1}{4}>0.$$

Next, note that

$$\sup_{c\in\mathbb{C}}\left|\frac{1}{\sqrt{N}}\sum_{i=1}^{N}\frac{1}{\sqrt{T}}\sum_{t=1}^{T}\left(1-c\frac{t-1}{T}\right)\left(\varepsilon_{i,t}(\delta_0,c_0)-(c-c_0)\frac{y_{i,t-1}(\delta_0)}{T}\right)\right|$$

$$\leqslant\left|\frac{1}{\sqrt{N}}\sum_{i=1}^{N}\frac{1}{\sqrt{T}}\sum_{t=1}^{T}\varepsilon_{i,t}(\delta_0,c_0)\right|$$

$$+\sup_{c\in\mathbb{C}}|c|\left|\frac{1}{\sqrt{N}}\sum_{i=1}^{N}\frac{1}{\sqrt{T}}\sum_{t=1}^{T}\frac{t-1}{T}\varepsilon_{i,t}(\delta_0,c_0)\right|$$

$$+\sup_{c\in\mathbb{C}}|c-c_0|\left|\frac{1}{\sqrt{N}}\sum_{i=1}^{N}\frac{1}{T\sqrt{T}}\sum_{t=1}^{T}y_{i,t-1}(\delta_0)\right|$$

$$+\sup_{c\in\mathbb{C}}|c(c-c_0)|\frac{1}{\sqrt{N}}\sum_{i=1}^{N}\frac{1}{T\sqrt{T}}\sum_{t=1}^{T}\frac{t-1}{T}y_{i,t-1}(\delta_0).$$

Recall that $\sup_{c\in\mathbb{C}}|c|$ is finite. In view of Lemma 7(a) and (b), each term in the above display is $O_p(1)$ as $(N, T\to\infty)$. Therefore, we have $\sup_{c\in\mathbb{C}}|\sqrt{N}\sqrt{T}(\hat{\delta}(c)-\delta_0)|=O_p(1)$ as $(N, T\to\infty)$. ■

Derivation of (8). Recall that

$$l_{N,T}(c,\hat{\delta}(c),\hat{\sigma}^2(c);z^{N,T})$$

$$=-\frac{1}{2N}\sum_{i=1}^{N}\sum_{t=1}^{T}\left(\varepsilon_{i,t}(\delta_0,c_0)-(c-c_0)\frac{y_{i,t-1}(\delta_0)}{T}\right.$$

$$\left.-(\hat{\delta}(c)-\delta_0)\left(1-c\frac{t-1}{T}\right)\right)^2$$

$$+\frac{1}{2N}\sum_{i=1}^{N}\sum_{t=1}^{T}\left\{\varepsilon_{i,t}(\delta_0,c_0)-(\hat{\delta}(c_0)-\delta_0)\left(1-c_0\frac{t-1}{T}\right)\right\}^2.$$

In view of (4), we have

$$-\frac{1}{2N}\sum_{i=1}^{N}\sum_{t=1}^{T}\left\{\varepsilon_{i,t}(\delta_0, c_0) - (c - c_0)\frac{y_{i,t-1}(\delta_0)}{T} - (\hat{\delta}(c) - \delta_0)\left(1 - c\frac{t-1}{T}\right)\right\}^2$$

$$= -\frac{1}{2N}\sum_{i=1}^{N}\sum_{t=1}^{T}\varepsilon_{i,t}(\delta_0, c_0)^2 + 2T(\hat{\delta}(c) - \delta_0)^2\frac{1}{T}\sum_{t=1}^{T}\left(1 - c\frac{t-1}{T}\right)^2$$

$$-\tfrac{1}{2}(c - c_0)^2\left(\frac{1}{N}\sum_{i=1}^{N}\frac{1}{T}\sum_{t=1}^{T}\frac{y_{i,t-1}(\delta_0)^2}{T}\right)$$

$$+(c - c_0)\left(\frac{1}{N}\sum_{i=1}^{N}\frac{1}{T}\sum_{t=1}^{T}y_{i,t-1}(\delta_0)\varepsilon_{i,t}(\delta_0, c_0)\right),$$

and

$$\frac{1}{2N}\sum_{i=1}^{N}\sum_{t=1}^{T}\left\{\varepsilon_{i,t}(\delta_0, c_0) - (\hat{\delta}(c_0) - \delta_0)\left(1 - c_0\frac{t-1}{T}\right)\right\}^2$$

$$= \frac{1}{2N}\sum_{i=1}^{N}\sum_{t=1}^{T}\varepsilon_{i,t}(\delta_0, c_0)^2 - \frac{1}{2}T(\hat{\delta}(c_0) - \delta_0)^2\frac{1}{T}\sum_{t=1}^{T}\left(1 - c_0\frac{t-1}{T}\right)^2,$$

which yields

$$l_{N,T}(c, \hat{\delta}(c), \hat{\sigma}^2(c); z^{N,T})$$

$$= \tfrac{1}{2}T(\hat{\delta}(c) - \delta_0)^2\frac{1}{T}\sum_{t=1}^{T}\left(1 - c\frac{t-1}{T}\right)^2 - \tfrac{1}{2}(c - c_0)^2\left(\frac{1}{N}\sum_{i=1}^{N}\frac{1}{T}\sum_{t=1}^{T}\frac{y_{i,t-1}(\delta_0)^2}{T}\right)$$

$$+(c - c_0)\left(\frac{1}{N}\sum_{i=1}^{N}\frac{1}{T}\sum_{t=1}^{T}y_{i,t-1}(\delta_0)\varepsilon_{i,t}(\delta_0, c_0)\right)$$

$$-\tfrac{1}{2}T(\hat{\delta}(c_0) - \delta_0)^2\frac{1}{T}\sum_{t=1}^{T}\left(1 - c_0\frac{t-1}{T}\right)^2.$$

Note by Lemma 8 that $\sqrt{T}(\hat{\delta}(c) - \delta_0) = o_p(1)$ uniformly in c, and by Lemma 6(a) and Lemma 7(c) that

$$\frac{1}{N}\sum_{i=1}^{N}\frac{1}{T}\sum_{t=1}^{T}\frac{y_{i,t-1}(\delta_0)^2}{T} \to_p \sigma_0^2\int_0^1\int_0^r e^{2c_0(r-s)}ds\,dr$$

and

$$\frac{1}{N}\sum_{i=1}^{N}\frac{1}{T}\sum_{t=1}^{T} y_{i,t-1}(\delta_0)\varepsilon_{i,t}(\delta_0, c_0) = o_p(1),$$

respectively. Also recall that parameter set $\mathbb{C}$ is compact. Therefore, as $(N, T \to \infty)$,

$$\begin{aligned} &l_{N,T}(c, \hat{\delta}(c), \hat{\sigma}^2(c); z^{N,T}) \\ &= -\tfrac{1}{2}(c-c_0)^2\left(\frac{1}{N}\sum_{i=1}^{N}\frac{1}{T}\sum_{t=1}^{T}\frac{y_{i,t-1}(\delta_0)^2}{T}\right) + o_p(1) \\ &\to_p -(\sigma_0^2/2)(c-c_0)^2\int_0^1\int_0^r e^{2c_0(r-s)}ds\,dr \text{ uniformly in } c. \end{aligned}$$

Proof of Theorem 2. By the first-order Taylor expansion of the first-order condition (9) around the true parameter c_0, we have

$$0 = \frac{dL(c, \hat{\delta}(c), \hat{\sigma}^2(c); z^{N,T})}{dc} + \left\{\frac{d^2L(c^*, \hat{\delta}(c^*), \hat{\sigma}^2(c^*); z^{N,T})}{dc^2}\right\}(\hat{c}-c_0),$$

where c^* lies between c_0 and $\hat{c}$. From this, we write

$$\begin{aligned} \sqrt{N}(\hat{c}-c_0) = &-\left(\frac{d^2L(c^*, \hat{\delta}(c^*), \hat{\sigma}^2(c^*); z^{N,T})}{dc^2}\right)^{-1} \\ &\times\left(\sqrt{N}\frac{dL(c_0, \hat{\delta}(c_0), \hat{\sigma}^2(c_0); z^{N,T})}{dc}\right). \end{aligned} \tag{22}$$

Define

$$Q_{N,T}(c, \hat{\delta}(c)) = \frac{1}{N}\sum_{i=1}^{N}\frac{1}{T}\sum_{t=1}^{T}\left(\Delta_c z_{i,t} - \hat{\delta}(c)\left(1 - c\frac{t-1}{T}\right)\right)^2.$$

Then, (22) is written as

$$\begin{aligned} &\sqrt{N}(\hat{c}-c_0) \\ &= -\left(\frac{\dfrac{d^2Q_{N,T}(c^*, \hat{\delta}(c^*))}{d^2c}}{Q_{N,T}(c^*, \hat{\delta}(c^*))} - \left(\frac{\dfrac{dQ_{N,T}(c^*, \hat{\delta}(c^*))}{dc}}{Q_{N,T}(c^*, \hat{\delta}(c^*))}\right)^2\right)^{-1} \\ &\quad\times\left(\frac{\sqrt{N}\dfrac{dQ_{N,T}(c_0, \hat{\delta}(c_0))}{dc}}{Q_{N,T}(c_0, \hat{\delta}(c_0))}\right). \end{aligned} \tag{23}$$

Note that

$$\sqrt{N}\frac{dQ_{N,T}(c_0, \hat{\delta}(c_0))}{dc}$$

$$= \frac{1}{\sqrt{N}}\sum_{i=1}^{N}\frac{1}{T}\sum_{t=1}^{T} y_{i,t-1}(\delta_0)\varepsilon_{i,t}(\delta_0, c_0)$$

$$- \sqrt{N}\sqrt{T}(\hat{\delta}(c_0) - \delta_0)\frac{1}{N}\sum_{i=1}^{N}\frac{1}{T\sqrt{T}}\sum_{t=1}^{T} y_{i,t-1}\left(1 - c_0\frac{t-1}{T}\right)$$

$$- \sqrt{N}\sqrt{T}(\hat{\delta}(c_0) - \delta_0)\frac{1}{N}\sum_{i=1}^{N}\frac{1}{\sqrt{T}}\sum_{t=1}^{T} \varepsilon_{i,t}\frac{t-1}{T}$$

$$+ NT(\hat{\delta}(c_0) - \delta_0)^2\frac{1}{\sqrt{N}T}\sum_{t=1}^{T}\frac{t-1}{T}\left(1 - c_0\frac{t-1}{T}\right)$$

$$= \frac{1}{\sqrt{N}}\sum_{i=1}^{N}\frac{1}{T}\sum_{t=1}^{T} y_{i,t-1}(\delta_0)\varepsilon_{i,t}(\delta_0, c_0) + o_p(1),$$

where the last line holds because

$$\sqrt{N}\sqrt{T}(\hat{\delta}(c_0) - \delta_0) = O_p(1) \text{ by Lemma 8,}$$

$$\frac{1}{N}\sum_{i=1}^{N}\frac{1}{T\sqrt{T}}\sum_{t=1}^{T} y_{i,t-1}\left(1 - c_0\frac{t-1}{T}\right) = o_p(1) \text{ by Lemma 7(b)}$$

$$\frac{1}{N}\sum_{i=1}^{N}\frac{1}{\sqrt{T}}\sum_{t=1}^{T} \varepsilon_{i,t}\frac{t-1}{T} = o_p(1) \text{ by Lemma 7(a),}$$

$$\text{and } \frac{1}{\sqrt{N}T}\sum_{t=1}^{T}\frac{t-1}{T}\left(1 - c_0\frac{t-1}{T}\right) = O\left(\frac{1}{\sqrt{N}}\right).$$

From Lemma 7(c), as $(N, T \to \infty)$ we have

$$\frac{1}{\sqrt{N}}\sum_{i=1}^{N}\frac{1}{T}\sum_{t=1}^{T} y_{i,t-1}(\delta_0)\varepsilon_{i,t}(\delta_0, c_0) \Rightarrow N\left(0, \sigma_0^2\int_0^1\int_0^r e^{2c_0(r-s)}ds\,dr\right),$$

and so

$$\sqrt{N}\frac{dQ_{N,T}\left(c_0, \hat{\delta}(c_0)\right)}{dc} \Rightarrow N\left(0, \sigma_0^2\int_0^1\int_0^r e^{2c_0(r-s)}ds\,dr\right). \quad (24)$$

Also, since $\hat{\delta}(c_0)$ is consistent for δ_0, we have

$$Q_{N,T}(c, \hat{\delta}(c)) = \frac{1}{N}\sum_{i=1}^{N}\frac{1}{T}\sum_{t=1}^{T}\left(\Delta_c z_{i,t} - \hat{\delta}(c)\left(1 - c\frac{t-1}{T}\right)\right)^2 \to_p \sigma_0^2. \quad (25)$$

Combining (24) and (25), as $(N, T \to \infty)$, we have

$$\frac{\sqrt{N}\dfrac{dQ_{N,T}(c_0, \hat{\delta}(c_0))}{dc}}{Q_{N,T}(c_0, \hat{\delta}(c_0))} \Rightarrow N\left(0, \frac{1}{\sigma_0^2}\int_0^1\int_0^r e^{2c_0(r-s)}ds\,dr\right). \quad (26)$$

Next, by the envelope function theorem and the chain rule, it follows that

$$\frac{d^2Q_{N,T}(c, \hat{\delta}(c))}{d^2c} = \frac{\partial^2Q_{N,T}(c, \hat{\delta}(c))}{\partial c^2} + \frac{\partial^2Q_{N,T}(c, \hat{\delta}(c))}{\partial\delta\partial c}\frac{d\hat{\delta}(c)}{dc}. \quad (27)$$

A short calculation yields

$$\begin{aligned}
&\frac{\partial^2Q_{N,T}(c^*, \hat{\delta}(c^*))}{\partial c^2}\\
&= \frac{1}{N}\sum_{i=1}^{N}\frac{1}{T^2}\sum_{t=1}^{T}y_{i,t-1}^2(\delta_0)\\
&\quad - 2\sqrt{T}(\hat{\delta}(c^*) - \delta_0)\frac{1}{N}\sum_{i=1}^{N}\frac{1}{T\sqrt{T}}\sum_{t=1}^{T}y_{i,t-1}(\delta_0)\frac{t-1}{T}\\
&\quad + T(\hat{\delta}(c^*) - \delta_0)^2\frac{1}{T}\sum_{t=1}^{T}\left(\frac{t-1}{T}\right)^2.
\end{aligned}$$

Since $\sqrt{T}(\hat{\delta}(c) - \delta_0) = o_p(1)$ uniformly in c by Lemma 8 and $c^* \to_p c_0$, it follows that $\sqrt{T}(\hat{\delta}(c^*) - \delta_0) = o_p(1)$ as $(N, T \to \infty)$. Also, we know

$$\frac{1}{N}\sum_{i=1}^{N}\frac{1}{T\sqrt{T}}\sum_{t=1}^{T}y_{i,t-1}(\delta_0)\frac{t-1}{T} = o_p(1) \text{ as } (N, T \to \infty).$$

From these and Lemma 6(a), we have

$$-\frac{\partial^2 Q_{N,T}(c^*, \hat{\delta}(c^*))}{\partial c^2}$$
$$= \frac{1}{N}\sum_{i=1}^{N}\frac{1}{T^2}\sum_{t=1}^{T} y_{i,t-1}^2(\delta_0) + o_p(1) \rightarrow_p \sigma_0^2 \int_0^1\int_0^r e^{2c_0(r-s)}\,ds\,dr. \quad (28)$$

In similar fashion, using the facts that $\sqrt{T}(\hat{\delta}(c^*) - \delta_0) = o_p(1)$ and $c^* \rightarrow_p c_0$, and the results in Lemmas 6 and 7, it is not difficult to show that

$$\frac{1}{\sqrt{T}}\frac{\partial^2 Q_{N,T}(c^*, \hat{\delta}(c^*))}{\partial\delta\,\partial c},\ \sqrt{T}\frac{d\hat{\delta}(c^*)}{dc} = o_p(1). \quad (29)$$

Since

$$Q_{N,T}(c^*, \hat{\delta}(c^*)) \rightarrow_p \sigma_0^2,$$

the first term in the numerator of (23)

$$\frac{\dfrac{d^2 Q_{N,T}(c^*, \hat{\delta}(c^*))}{d^2 c}}{Q_{N,T}(c^*, \hat{\delta}(c^*))} \rightarrow_p \int_0^1\int_0^r e^{2c_0(r-s)}\,ds\,dr. \quad (30)$$

For limits of the second term in the numerator of (23), notice that

$$\frac{dQ_{N,T}(c^*, \hat{\delta}(c^*))}{dc} = \frac{\partial Q_{N,T}(c^*, \hat{\delta}(c^*))}{\partial c} \rightarrow_p 0$$

as $(N, T \rightarrow \infty)$ since $c^* \rightarrow_p c_0$ and $\partial Q_{N,T}(c, \hat{\delta}(c))/\partial c = O_p(1/\sqrt{N})$ uniformly in c. Therefore,

$$\left(\frac{\dfrac{dQ_{N,T}(c^*, \hat{\delta}(c^*))}{dc}}{Q_{N,T}(c^*, \hat{\delta}(c^*))}\right) \rightarrow_p 0. \quad (31)$$

From (30) and (31) we have

$$-\left(\frac{d^2 L(z^{N,T}; \hat{\delta}(c^*), c^*)}{dc^2}\right) \rightarrow_p \int_0^1\int_0^r e^{2c_0(r-s)}\,ds\,dr,$$

and combining this with (24), we have the desired result,

$$\sqrt{N}(\hat{c} - c_0) \Rightarrow N\left(0, \frac{1}{\sigma_0^2\displaystyle\int_0^1\int_0^r e^{2c_0(r-s)}\,ds\,dr}\right).$$

■

Proof of (14).

By definition, we have

$$\sqrt{N}(\tilde{c} - c_0)$$

$$= \frac{\frac{1}{\sqrt{N}}\sum_{i=1}^{N}\sum_{t=1}^{T}\left\{(\Delta z_{i,t} - \hat{\delta}(c))\left(\frac{z_{i,t-1}}{T} - \hat{\delta}(c)\frac{t-1}{T}\right) - c_0\left(\frac{z_{i,t-1}}{T} - \hat{\delta}(c)\frac{t-1}{T}\right)^2\right\}}{\frac{1}{N}\sum_{i=1}^{N}\sum_{t=1}^{T}\left(\frac{z_{i,t-1}}{T} - \hat{\delta}(c)\frac{t-1}{T}\right)^2}$$

First, note that

$$\frac{1}{N}\sum_{i=1}^{N}\sum_{t=1}^{T}\left(\frac{z_{i,t-1}}{T} - \hat{\delta}(c)\frac{t-1}{T}\right)^2$$

$$= \frac{1}{N}\sum_{i=1}^{N}\frac{1}{T^2}\sum_{t=1}^{T} y_{i,t-1}(\delta_0)^2$$

$$- 2\sqrt{T}\left(\hat{\delta}(c) - \delta_0\right)\frac{1}{N}\sum_{i=1}^{N}\frac{1}{T\sqrt{T}}\sum_{t=1}^{T} y_{i,t-1}(\delta_0)\frac{t-1}{T}$$

$$+ T\left(\hat{\delta}(c) - \delta_0\right)^2\frac{1}{T}\sum_{t=1}^{T}\left(\frac{t-1}{T}\right)^2$$

$$= \frac{1}{N}\sum_{i=1}^{N}\frac{1}{T^2}\sum_{t=1}^{T} y_{i,t-1}(\delta_0)^2 + o_p(1) \to_p \sigma_0^2\int_0^1\int_0^r e^{2c_0(r-s)}ds\,dr.$$

where the last equality holds because $\sqrt{T}(\hat{\delta}(c) - \delta_0) = o_p(1)$ and

$$\frac{1}{N}\sum_{i=1}^{N}\frac{1}{T\sqrt{T}}\sum_{t=1}^{T} y_{i,t-1}(\delta_0)\frac{t-1}{T} = o_p(1).$$

Next, for the numerator, we write

$$\frac{1}{\sqrt{N}}\sum_{i=1}^{N}\sum_{t=1}^{T}\left\{(\Delta z_{i,t}-\hat{\delta}(c))\left(\frac{z_{i,t-1}}{T}-\hat{\delta}(c)\frac{t-1}{T}\right)-c_0\left(\frac{z_{i,t-1}}{T}-\hat{\delta}(c)\frac{t-1}{T}\right)^2\right\}$$

$$=\frac{1}{\sqrt{N}}\sum_{i=1}^{N}\sum_{t=1}^{T}\left\{(\Delta z_{i,t}-\delta_0)\left(\frac{z_{i,t-1}}{T}-\delta_0\frac{t-1}{T}\right)-c_0\left(\frac{z_{i,t-1}}{T}-\delta_0\frac{t-1}{T}\right)^2\right\}$$

$$-\sqrt{T}(\hat{\delta}(c)-\delta_0)\frac{1}{\sqrt{N}}\sum_{i=1}^{N}\frac{1}{T\sqrt{T}}\sum_{t=1}^{T}y_{i,t-1}(\delta_0)$$

$$-\sqrt{T}(\hat{\delta}(c)-\delta_0)\frac{1}{\sqrt{N}}\sum_{i=1}^{N}\frac{1}{\sqrt{T}}\sum_{t=1}^{T}\left(c_0\frac{y_{i,t}(\delta_0)}{T}+\varepsilon_{i,t}(\delta_0,c_0)\right)\frac{t-1}{T}$$

$$+\sqrt{N}T(\hat{\delta}_0(c)-\delta_0)^2\frac{1}{T}\sum_{t=1}^{T}\frac{t-1}{T}$$

$$+2c_0\sqrt{T}(\hat{\delta}(c)-\delta_0)\frac{1}{\sqrt{N}}\sum_{i=1}^{N}\frac{1}{T\sqrt{T}}\sum_{t=1}^{T}y_{i,t-1}(\delta_0)\frac{t-1}{T}$$

$$-c_0\sqrt{T}T(\hat{\delta}(c)-\delta_0)^2\frac{1}{T}\sum_{t=1}^{T}\frac{t-1}{T}$$

$$=I+II+III+IV+V+VI,\ \text{say.}$$

Recall that $\sqrt{N}\sqrt{T}(\hat{\delta}(c)-\delta_0)=O_p(1)$ by Lemma 8. Then, in view of Lemmas 6 and 7, it is not difficult to find that $II, III, IV, V, VI = o_p(1)$. For I, we have

$$\frac{1}{\sqrt{N}}\sum_{i=1}^{N}\sum_{t=1}^{T}\left\{(\Delta z_{i,t}-\delta_0)\left(\frac{z_{i,t-1}}{T}-\delta_0\frac{t-1}{T}\right)-c_0\left(\frac{z_{i,t-1}}{T}-\delta_0\frac{t-1}{T}\right)^2\right\}$$

$$=\frac{1}{\sqrt{N}}\sum_{i=1}^{N}\sum_{t=1}^{T}\left\{\Delta y_{i,t}(\delta_0)\frac{y_{i,t-1}(\delta_0)}{T}-c_0\frac{y_{i,t-1}(\delta_0)^2}{T^2}\right\}$$

$$=\frac{1}{\sqrt{N}}\sum_{i=1}^{N}\frac{1}{T}\sum_{t=1}^{T}y_{i,t-1}(\delta_0)\varepsilon_{i,t}(\delta_0,c_0)$$

$$\Rightarrow N\left(0,\sigma_0^2\int_0^1\int_0^r e^{2c_0(r-s)}ds\,dr\right)$$

as $(N,\ T \to \infty)$. Then we have the desired result. ■

Proof of Lemma 4. In view of

$$\sqrt{T}(\hat{\delta}_i(c) - \delta_{i,0})$$
$$= \left(\frac{1}{T}\sum_{t=1}^{T}\left(1 - c\frac{t-1}{T}\right)^2\right)^{-1}\left\{\sum_{t=1}^{T}\left(1 - c\frac{t-1}{T}\right)\frac{\varepsilon_{i,t}(\delta_{0,i},\ c_0)}{\sqrt{T}}\right.$$
$$\left. -\ (c - c_0)\frac{1}{T}\sum_{t=1}^{T}\left(1 - c\frac{t-1}{T}\right)\frac{y_{i,t-1}(\delta_{0,i})}{\sqrt{T}}\right\}, \qquad (32)$$

we write (17) as

$$L(z^{N,T};\ \hat{\delta}^N(c),\ c) - L(z^{N,T};\ \hat{\delta}^N(c_0),\ c_0)$$
$$= \frac{1}{2N}\sum_{i=1}^{N}T\left(\hat{\delta}_i(c) - \delta_{0,i}\right)^2\frac{1}{T}\sum_{t=1}^{T}\left(1 - c\frac{t-1}{T}\right)^2$$
$$-\frac{1}{2}(c - c_0)^2\left(\frac{1}{N}\sum_{i=1}^{N}\frac{1}{T}\sum_{t=1}^{T}\frac{y_{i,t-1}(\delta_{0,i})^2}{T}\right)$$
$$+(c - c_0)\left(\frac{1}{N}\sum_{i=1}^{N}\frac{1}{T}\sum_{t=1}^{T}y_{i,t-1}(\delta_{0,i})\varepsilon_{i,t}(\delta_{0,i},\ c_0)\right)$$
$$-\frac{1}{2N}\sum_{i=1}^{N}T\left(\hat{\delta}_i(c_0) - \delta_{0,i}\right)^2\frac{1}{T}\sum_{t=1}^{T}\left(1 - c_0\frac{t-1}{T}\right)^2,$$
$$= I + II + III + IV, \quad \text{say.}$$

Now we find limits of I, II, III, and IV. In view of (32) and by Lemma 6, and Assumption 2, we have

$$I = \left(\frac{1}{T}\sum_{t=1}^{T}\left(1 - c\frac{t-1}{T}\right)^2\right)^{-1}$$

$$\times \frac{1}{2N}\sum_{i=1}^{N}\left(\sum_{t=1}^{T}\left(1 - c\frac{t-1}{T}\right)\frac{\varepsilon_{i,t}(\delta_0, i, c_0)}{\sqrt{T}}\right.$$

$$\left. - (c - c_0)\frac{1}{T}\sum_{t=1}^{T}\left(1 - c\frac{t-1}{T}\right)\frac{y_{i,t-1}(\delta_{0,i})}{\sqrt{T}}\right)^2 \to_p \frac{1}{2}\left(\int_0^1 (1 - cr)^2 dr\right)^{-1}$$

$$\times \left(\begin{array}{c}\int_0^1 (1 - cr)^2 dr - 2(c - c_0)\int_0^1\int_0^s e^{c_0(s-r)}(1 - cr)(1 - cs)dr\,ds \\ +(c - c_0)^2\int_0^1\int_0^1 (1 - cr)(1 - cs)\int_0^{r\wedge s} e^{c_0(r+s-+p)}dp\,ds\,dr\end{array}\right) \quad (33)$$

uniformly in c as $(N, T \to \infty)$. Similarly, using Lemma 6(a) and Lemma 7(c), we can show that, as $(N, T \to \infty)$

$$II = -\tfrac{1}{2}(c - c_0)^2\left(\frac{1}{N}\sum_{i=1}^{N}\frac{1}{T}\sum_{t=1}^{T}\frac{y_{i,t-1}(\delta_{0,i})^2}{T}\right)$$

$$\to_p -\tfrac{1}{2}(c - c_0)^2\int_0^1\int_0^r e^{2c_0(r-s)}ds\,dr \text{ uniformly in } c, \quad (34)$$

and

$$III = (c - c_0)\left(\frac{1}{N}\sum_{i=1}^{N}\frac{1}{T}\sum_{t=1}^{T} y_{i,t-1}(\delta_{0,i})\varepsilon_{i,t}(\delta_{0,i}, c_0)\right) \to_p 0 \text{ uniformly in } c. \quad (35)$$

Also, it is not difficult to derive that as $(N, T \to \infty)$

$$IV = -\frac{1}{2N}\sum_{i=1}^{N} T(\hat{\delta}_0(c_0) - \delta_{0,i})^2\frac{1}{T}\left(1 - c_0\frac{t-1}{T}\right)^2 \to_p -\tfrac{1}{2}. \quad (36)$$

Combining (33)–(36), we finally have the desired result.

[20]

FULLY MODIFIED OLS FOR HETEROGENEOUS COINTEGRATED PANELS

Peter Pedroni

ABSTRACT

This chapter uses fully modified OLS principles to develop new methods for estimating and testing hypotheses for cointegrating vectors in dynamic panels in a manner that is consistent with the degree of cross sectional heterogeneity that has been permitted in recent panel unit root and panel cointegration studies. The asymptotic properties of various estimators are compared based on pooling along the 'within' and 'between' dimensions of the panel. By using Monte Carlo simulations to study the small sample properties, the group mean estimator is shown to behave well even in relatively small samples under a variety of scenarios.

I. INTRODUCTION

In this chapter we develop methods for estimating and testing hypotheses for cointegrating vectors in dynamic time series panels. In particular we propose methods based on fully modified OLS principles which are able to accommodate considerable heterogeneity across individual members of the panel. Indeed, one important advantage to working with a cointegrated panel approach of this type is that it allows researchers to selectively pool the long run information contained in the panel while permitting the short run dynamics

Nonstationary Panels, Panel Cointegration and Dynamic Panels, Volume 15, pages 93–130.

ISBN: 0-7623-0688-2

and fixed effects to be heterogeneous among different members of the panel. An important convenience of the fully modified approach that we propose here is that in addition to producing asymptotically unbiased estimators, it also produces nuisance parameter free standard normal distributions. In this way, inferences can be made regarding common long run relationships which are asymptotically invariant to the considerable degree of short run heterogeneity that is prevalent in the dynamics typically associated with panels that are composed of aggregate national data.

A. *Nonstationary Panels and Heterogeneity*

Methods for nonstationary time series panels, including unit root and cointegration tests, have been gaining increased acceptance in a number of areas of empirical research. Early examples include Canzoneri, Cumby & Diba (1996), Chinn & Johnson (1996), Chinn (1997), Evans & Karras (1996), Neusser & Kugler (1998), Obstfeld & Taylor (1996), Oh (1996), Papell (1997), Pedroni (1996b), Taylor (1996) and Wu (1996), with many more since. These studies have for the most part been limited to applications which simply ask whether or not particular series appear to contain unit roots or are cointegrated. In many applications, however, it is also of interest to ask whether or not common cointegrating vectors take on particular values. In this case, it would be helpful to have a technique that allows one to test such hypothesis about the cointegrating vectors in a manner that is consistent with the very general degree of cross sectional heterogeneity that is permitted in such panel unit root and panel cointegration tests.

In general, the extension of conventional nonstationary methods such as unit root and cointegration tests to panels with both cross section and time series dimensions holds considerable promise for empirical research considering the abundance of data which is available in this form. In particular, such methods provide an opportunity for researchers to exploit some of the attractive theoretical properties of nonstationary regressions while addressing in a natural and direct manner the small sample problems that have in the past often hindered the practical success of these methods. For example, it is well known that superconsistent rates of convergence associated with many of these methods can provide empirical researchers with an opportunity to circumvent more traditional exogeneity requirements in time series regressions. Yet the low power of many of the associated statistics has often impeded the ability to take full advantage of these properties in small samples. By allowing data to be pooled in the cross sectional dimension, nonstationary panel methods have the potential to improve upon these small sample limitations. Conversely, the use of nonstationary time series asymptotics provides an opportunity to make panel methods more amenable to pooling aggregate level data by allowing researchers to selectively pool the long run information contained in the panel, while allowing the short run dynamics to be heterogeneous among different members of the panel.

Initial methodological work on nonstationary panels focused on testing for unit roots in univariate panels. Quah (1994) derived standard normal asymptotic distributions for testing unit roots in homogeneous panels as both the time series and cross sectional dimensions grow large. Levin & Lin (1993) derived distributions under more general conditions that allow for heterogeneous fixed effects and time trends. More recently, Im, Pesaran & Shin (1995) study the small sample properties of unit root tests in panels with heterogeneous dynamics and propose alternative tests based on group mean statistics. In practice however, empirical work often involves relationships within multivariate systems. Toward this end, Pedroni (1993, 1995) studies the properties of spurious regressions and residual based tests for the null of no cointegration in dynamic heterogeneous panels. This chapter continues this line of research by proposing a convenient method for estimating and testing hypotheses about common cointegrating vectors in a manner that is consistent with the degree of heterogeneity permitted in these panel unit root and panel cointegration studies.

In particular, we address here two key sources of cross member heterogeneity that are particularly important in dealing with dynamic cointegrated panels. One such source of heterogeneity manifests itself in the familiar fixed effects form. These reflect differences in mean levels among the variables of different individual members of the panel and we model these by including individual specific intercepts. The second key source of heterogeneity in such panels comes from differences in the way that individuals respond to short run deviations from equilibrium cointegrating vectors that develop in response to stochastic disturbances. In keeping with earlier panel unit root and panel cointegration papers, we model this form of heterogeneity by allowing the associated serial correlation properties of the error processes to vary across individual members of the panel.

B. Related Literature

Since the original version of this paper, Pedroni (1996a),[1] many more papers have contributed to our understanding of hypothesis testing in cointegrating panels. For example, Kao & Chiang (1997) extended their original paper on the least squares dummy variable model in cointegrated panels, Kao & Chen

(1995), to include a comparison of the small sample properties of a dynamic OLS estimator with other estimators including a FMOLS estimator similar to Pedroni (1996a). Specifically, Kao & Chiang (1997) demonstrated that a panel dynamic OLS estimator has the same asymptotic distribution as the type of panel FMOLS estimator derived in Pedroni (1996a) and showed that the small sample size distortions for such an estimator were often smaller than certain forms of the panel FMOLS estimator. The asymptotic theory in these earlier papers were generally based on sequential limit arguments (allowing the sample sizes T and N to grow large sequentially), whereas Phillips & Moon (1999) subsequently provided a rigorous and more general study of the limit theory in nonstationary panel regressions under joint convergence (allowing T and N to grow large concurrently). Phillips & Moon (1999) also provided a set of regularity conditions under which convergence in sequential limits implies convergence in joint limits, and considered these properties in the context of a FMOLS estimator, although they do not specifically address the small sample properties of feasible versions of the estimators. More recently, Mark & Sul (1999) also study a similar form of the panel dynamic OLS estimator first proposed by Kao & Chiang (1997). They compare the small sample properties of a weighted versus unweighted version of the estimator and find that the unweighted version generally exhibits smaller size distortion than the weighted version.

In this chapter we report new small sample results for the group mean panel FMOLS estimator that was originally proposed in Pedroni (1996a). An advantage of the group mean estimator over the other pooled panel FMOLS estimators proposed in the Pedroni (1996a) is that the t-statistic for this estimator allows for a more flexible alternative hypothesis. This is because the group mean estimator is based on the so called 'between dimension' of the panel, while the pooled estimators are based on the 'within dimension' of the panel. Accordingly, the group mean panel FMOLS provides a consistent test of a common value for the cointegrating vector under the null hypothesis against values of the cointegrating vector that need not be common under the alternative hypothesis, while the pooled within dimension estimators do not. Furthermore, as Pesaran & Smith (1995) argue in the context of OLS regressions, when the true slope coefficients are heterogeneous, group mean estimators provide consistent point estimates of the sample mean of the heterogeneous cointegrating vectors, while pooled within dimension estimators do not. Rather, as Phillips & Moon (1999) demonstrate, when the true cointegrating vectors are heterogeneous, pooled within dimension estimators provide consistent point estimates of the average regression coefficient, not the sample mean of the cointegrating vectors. Both of these features of the group mean estimator are often important in practical applications.

Finally, the implementation of the feasible form of the between dimension group mean estimator also has advantages over the other estimators in the presence of heterogeneity of the residual dynamics around the cointegrating vector. As was demonstrated in Pedroni (1996a), in the presence of such heterogeneity, the pooled panel FMOLS estimator requires a correction term that depends on the true cointegrating vector. For a specific null value for a cointegrating vector, the t-statistic is well defined, but of course this is of little use per se when one would like to estimate the cointegrating vector. One solution is to obtain a preliminary estimate of the cointegrating vector using OLS. However, although the OLS estimator is superconsistent, it still contains a second order bias in the presence of endogeneity, which is not eliminated asymptotically. Accordingly, this bias leads to size distortion, which is not necessarily eliminated even when the sample size grows large in the panel dimension. Consequently, this type of approach based on a first stage OLS estimate was not recommended in Pedroni (1996a), and it is not surprising that Monte Carlo simulations have shown large size distortions for such estimators. Even when the null hypothesis was imposed without using an OLS estimator, the size distortions for this type of estimator were large as reported in Pedroni (1996a). Similarly, Kao & Chiang (1997) also found large size distortions for such estimators when OLS estimates were used in the first stage for the correction term. By contrast, the feasible version of the between dimension group mean based estimator does not suffer from these difficulties, even in the presence of heterogeneous dynamics. As we will see, the size distortions for this estimator are minimal, even in panels of relatively modest dimensions.

The remainder of the chapter is structured as follows. In Section 2, we introduce the econometric models of interest for heterogeneous cointegrated panels. We then present a number of theoretical results for estimators designed to be asymptotically unbiased and to provide nuisance parameter free asymptotic distributions which are standard normal when applied to heterogeneous cointegrated panels and can be used to test hypotheses regarding common cointegrating vectors in such panels. In Section 3 we study the small sample properties of these estimators and propose feasible FMOLS statistics that perform relatively well in realistic panels with heterogeneous dynamics. In Section 4 we enumerate the algorithm used to construct these statistics and briefly describe a few examples of their uses. Finally, in Section 5 we offer conclusions and discuss a number of related issues in the ongoing research on estimation and inference in cointegrated panels.

II. ASYMPTOTIC RESULTS FOR FULLY MODIFIED OLS IN HETEROGENEOUS COINTEGRATED PANELS

In this section we study asymptotic properties of cointegrating regressions in dynamic panels with common cointegrating vectors and suggest how a fully modified OLS estimator can be constructed to deal with complications introduced by the presence of parameter heterogeneity in the dynamics and fixed effects across individual members. We begin, however, by discussing the basic form of a cointegrating regression in such panels and the problems associated with unmodified OLS estimators.

A. Cointegrating Regressions in Heterogeneous Panels

Consider the following cointegrated system for a panel of $i=1,\ldots,N$ members,

$$\begin{aligned} y_{it} &= \alpha_i + \beta x_{it} + \mu_{it} \\ x_{it} &= x_{it-1} + \varepsilon_{it} \end{aligned} \tag{1}$$

where the vector error process $\xi_{it}=(\mu_{it}, \varepsilon_{it})'$ is stationary with asymptotic covariance matrix Ω_i. Thus, the variables x_i, y_i are said to cointegrate for each member of the panel, with cointegrating vector β if y_{it} is integrated of order one. The term α_i allows the cointegrating relationship to include member specific fixed effects. In keeping with the cointegration literature, we do not require exogeneity of the regressors. As usual, x_i can in general be an m dimensional vector of regressors, which are not cointegrated with each other. In this case, we partition $\xi_{it}=(\mu_{it}, \varepsilon_{it}')$ so that the first element is a scalar series and the second element is an m dimensional vector of the differences in the regressors $\varepsilon_{it}=x_{it}-x_{it-1}=\Delta x_{it}$, so that when we construct

$$\Omega_i = \begin{bmatrix} \Omega_{11i} & \Omega_{21i}' \\ \Omega_{21i} & \Omega_{22i} \end{bmatrix} \tag{2}$$

then Ω_{11i} is the scalar long run variance of the residual μ_{it}, and Ω_{22i} is the $m \times m$ long run covariance among the ε_{it}, and Ω_{21i} is an $m \times 1$ vector that gives the long run covariance between the residual μ_{it} and each of the ε_{it}. However, for simplicity and convenience of notation, we will refer to x_i as univariate in the remainder of this chapter. Each of the results of this study generalize in an obvious and straightforward manner to the vector case, unless otherwise indicated.[2]

In order to explore the asymptotic properties of estimators as both the cross sectional dimension, N, and the time series dimension, T, grow large, we will make assumptions similar in spirit to Pedroni (1995) regarding the degree of dependency across both these dimensions. In particular, for the time series dimension, we will assume that the conditions of the multivariate functional central limit theorems used in Phillips & Durlauf (1986) and Park & Phillips (1988), hold for each member of the panel as the time series dimension grows large. Thus, we have

Assumption 1.1 (invariance principle): *The process ξ_{it} satisfies a multivariate functional central limit theorem such that the convergence as $T \rightarrow \infty$ for the partial sum $\frac{1}{\sqrt{T}} \sum_{t=1}^{[Tr]} \xi_{it} \rightarrow B_i(r, \Omega_i)$ holds for any given member, i, of the panel, where $B_i(r, \Omega_i)$ is Brownian motion defined over the real interval $r \in [0,1]$, with asymptotic covariance Ω_i.*

This assumption indicates that the multivariate functional central limit theorem, or invariance principle, holds over time for any given member of the panel. This places very little restriction on the temporal dependency and heterogeneity of the error process, and encompasses for example a broad class of stationary ARMA processes. It also allows the serial correlation structure to be different for individual members of the panel. Specifically, the asymptotic covariance matrix, Ω_i varies across individual members, and is given by $\Omega_i \equiv \lim_{T \rightarrow \infty} E[T^{-1}(\Sigma_{t=1}^{T} \xi_{it})(\Sigma_{t=1}^{T} \xi_{it})']$, which can also be decomposed as $\Omega_i = \Omega_i^o + \Gamma_i + \Gamma_i'$, where Ω_i^o is the contemporaneous covariance and Γ_i is a weighted sum of autocovariances. The off-diagonal terms of these individual Ω_{21i} matrices capture the endogenous feedback effect between y_{it} and x_{it}, which is also permitted to vary across individual members of the panel. For several of the estimators that we propose, it will be convenient to work with a triangularization of this asymptotic covariance matrix. Specifically, we will refer to this lower triangular matrix of Ω_i as L_i, whose elements are related as follows

$$L_{11i} = (\Omega_{11i} - \Omega_{21i}^2/\Omega_{22i})^{1/2}, \; L_{12i} = 0, \; L_{21i} = \Omega_{21i}/\Omega_{22i}^{1/2}, \; L_{22i} = \Omega_{22i}^{1/2} \qquad (3)$$

Estimation of the asymptotic covariance matrix can be based on any one of a number of consistent kernel estimators such as the Newey & West (1987) estimator.

Next, for the cross sectional dimension, we will employ the standard panel data assumption of independence. Hence we have:

Assumption 1.2 (cross sectional independence): *The individual processes are assumed to be independent cross sectionally, so that $E[\xi_{it}, \xi_{jt}'] = 0$ for all $i \neq j$.*

More generally, the asymptotic covariance matrix for a panel of dimension $N \times T$ is block diagonal with the ith diagonal block given by the asymptotic covariance for member i.

This type of assumption is typical of our panel data approach, and we will be using this condition in the formal derivation of the asymptotic distribution of our panel cointegration statistics. For panels that exhibit common disturbances that are shared across individual members, it will be convenient to capture this form of cross sectional dependency by the use of a common time dummy, which is a fairly standard panel data technique. For panels with even richer cross sectional dependencies, one might think of estimating a full non-diagonal $N \times N$ matrix of Ω_{ij} elements, and then premultiplying the errors by this matrix in order to achieve cross sectional independence. This would require the time series dimension to grow much more quickly than the cross sectional dimension, and in most cases one hopes that a common time dummy will suffice.

While the derivation of most of the asymptotic results of this chapter are relegated to the mathematical appendix, it is worth discussing briefly here how we intend to make use of assumptions 1.1 and 1.2 in providing asymptotic distributions for the panel statistics that we consider in the next two subsections. In particular, we will employ here simple and somewhat informal sequential limit arguments by first evaluating the limits as the T dimension grows large for each member of the panel in accordance with assumption 1.1 and then evaluating the sums of these statistics as the N dimension grows large under the independence assumption of 1.2.[3] In this manner, as N grows large we obtain standard distributions as we average the random functionals for each member that are obtained in the initial step as a consequence of letting T grow large. Consequently, we view the restriction that first $T \rightarrow \infty$ and then $N \rightarrow \infty$ as a relatively strong restriction that ensures these conditions, and it is possible that in many circumstances a weaker set of restrictions that allow N and T to grow large concurrently, but with restrictions on the relative rates of growth might deliver similar results. In general, for heterogeneous error processes, such restrictions on the rate of growth of N relative to T can be expected to depend in part on the rate of convergence of the particular kernel estimators used to eliminate the nuisance parameters, and we can expect that our iterative $T \rightarrow \infty$ and then $N \rightarrow \infty$ requirements proxy for the fact that in practice our asymptotic approximations will be more accurate in panels with relatively large T dimensions as compared to the N dimension. Alternatively, under a more pragmatic interpretation, one can simply think of letting $T \rightarrow \infty$ for fixed N reflect the fact that typically for the panels in which we are interested, it is the time series dimension which can be expected to grow in actuality rather than the cross sectional dimension, which is in practice fixed. Thus, $T \rightarrow \infty$ is in a sense the true asymptotic feature in which we are interested, and this leads to statistics which are characterized as sums of i.i.d. Brownian motion functionals. For practical purposes, however, we would like to be able to characterize these statistics for the general case in which N is large, and in this case we take $N \rightarrow \infty$ as a convenient benchmark for which to characterize the distribution, provided that we understand $T \rightarrow \infty$ to be the dominant asymptotic feature of the data.

B. Asymptotic Properties of Panel OLS

Next, we consider the properties of a number of statistics that might be used for a cointegrated panel as described by (1) under assumptions 1.1 and 1.2 regarding the time series and cross dimensional dependencies in the data. The first statistic that we examine is a standard panel OLS estimator of the cointegrating relationship. It is well known that the conventional single equation OLS estimator for the cointegrating vector is asymptotically biased and that its standardized distribution is dependent on nuisance parameters associated with the serial correlation structure of the data, and there is no reason to believe that this would be otherwise for the panel OLS estimator. The following proposition confirms this suspicion.[4]

Proposition 1.1 (Asymptotic Bias of the Panel OLS Estimator). *Consider a standard panel OLS estimator for the coefficient* β *of panel (1), under assumptions 1.1 and 1.2, given as*

$$\hat{\beta}_{NT} = \left(\sum_{i=1}^{N} \sum_{t=1}^{T} (x_{it} - \bar{x}_i)^2 \right)^{-1} \sum_{i=1}^{N} \sum_{t=1}^{T} (x_{it} - \bar{x}_i)(y_{it} - \bar{y}_i)$$

where $\bar{x}_i$ *and* $\bar{y}_i$ *refer to the individual specific means. Then,*

(a) The estimator is asymptotically biased and its asymptotic distribution will be dependent on nuisance parameters associated with the dynamics of the underlying processes.

(b) Only for the special case in which the regressors are strictly exogenous and the dynamics are homogeneous across members of the panel can valid inferences be made from the standardized distribution of $\hat{\beta}_{NT}$ *or its associated t-statistic.*

As the proof of proposition 1.1 given in the appendix makes clear, the source of the problem stems from the endogeneity of the regressors under the usual assumptions regarding cointegrated systems. While an exogeneity assumption is common in many treatments of cross sectional panels, for dynamic cointegrated panels such strict exogeneity is by most standards not acceptable. It is stronger than the standard exogeneity assumption for static panels, as it implies the absence of any dynamic feedback from the regressors at all frequencies. Clearly, the problem of asymptotic bias and data dependency from the endogenous feedback effect can no less be expected to diminish in the context of such panels, and Kao & Chen (1995) document this bias for a panel of cointegrated time series for the special case in which the dynamics are homogeneous. For the conventional time series case, a number of methods have been devised to deal with the consequences of such endogenous feedback effects, and in what follows we develop an approach for cointegrated panels based on fully modified OLS principles similar in spirit to those used by Phillips & Hanson (1990).

C. Pooled Fully Modified OLS Estimators for Heterogeneous Panels

Phillips & Hansen (1990) proposed a semi-parametric correction to the OLS estimator which eliminates the second order bias induced by the endogeneity of the regressors. The same principle can also be applied to the panel OLS estimator that we have explored in the previous subsection. The key difference in constructing our estimator for the panel data case will be to account for the heterogeneity that is present in the fixed effects as well as in the short run dynamics. These features lead us to modify the form of the standard single equation fully modified OLS estimator. We will also find that the presence of fixed effects has the potential to alter the asymptotic distributions in a non-trivial manner.

The following proposition establishes an important preliminary result which facilitates intuition for the role of heterogeneity and the consequences of dealing with both temporal and cross sectional dimensions for fully modified OLS estimators.

Proposition 1.2 (Asymptotic Distribution of the Pooled Panel FMOLS Estimator). *Consider a panel FMOLS estimator for the coefficient* β *of panel (1) given by*

$$\hat{\beta}^*_{NT} - \beta = \left(\sum_{i=1}^{N} \hat{L}_{22i}^{-2} \sum_{t=1}^{T} (x_{it} - \bar{x}_i)^2 \right)^{-1} \sum_{i=1}^{N} \hat{L}_{11i}^{-1} \hat{L}_{22i}^{-1} \left(\sum_{t=1}^{T} (x_{it} - \bar{x}_i)\mu^*_{it} - T\hat{\gamma}_i \right)$$

where

$$\mu^*_{it} = \mu_{it} - \frac{\hat{L}_{21i}}{\hat{L}_{22i}} \Delta x_{it}, \; \hat{\gamma}_i \equiv \hat{\Gamma}_{21i} + \hat{\Omega}^o_{21i} - \frac{\hat{L}_{21i}}{\hat{L}_{22i}} (\hat{\Gamma}_{22i} + \hat{\Omega}^o_{22i})$$

and $\hat{L}_i$ *is a lower triangular decomposition of* $\hat{\Omega}_i$ *as defined in (2) above. Then, under assumptions 1.1 and 1.2, the estimator* $\hat{\beta}^*_{NT}$ *converges to the true value at rate* $T\sqrt{N}$*, and is distributed as*

$$T\sqrt{N}(\hat{\beta}^*_{NT} - \beta) \rightarrow N(0, v) \text{ where } v = \begin{cases} 2 \text{ iff } \bar{x}_i = \bar{y}_i = 0 \\ 6 \text{ else} \end{cases}$$

as $T \rightarrow \infty$ *and* $N \rightarrow \infty$.

As the proposition indicates, when proper modifications are made to the estimator, the corresponding asymptotic distribution will be free of the nuisance parameters associated with any member specific serial correlation patterns in the data. Notice also that this fully modified panel OLS estimator is asymptotically unbiased for both the standard case without intercepts as well as the fixed effects model with heterogeneous intercepts. The only difference is in the size of the variance, which is equal to 2 in the standard case, and 6 in the case with heterogeneous intercepts, both for x_{it} univariate. More generally, when x_{it} is an m-dimensional vector, the specific values for v will also be a function of the dimension m. The associated t-statistics, however, will not depend on the specific values for v, as we shall see.

The fact that this estimator is distributed normally, rather than in terms of unit root asymptotics as in Phillips & Hansen (1990), derives from the fact that these unit root distributions are being averaged over the cross sectional dimension. Specifically, this averaging process produces normal distributions whose variance depends only on the moments of the underlying Brownian motion functionals that describe the properties of the integrated variables. This is achieved by constructing the estimator in a way that isolates the idiosyncratic components of the underlying Wiener processes to produce sums of standard and independently distributed Brownian motion whose moments can be computed algebraically, as the proof of the proposition makes clear. The estimators $\hat{L}_{11i}$ and $\hat{L}_{22i}$, which correspond to the long run standard errors of conditional process μ_{it}, and the marginal process Δx_{it} respectively, act to purge the contribution of these idiosyncratic elements to the endogenous feedback and serial correlation adjusted statistic $\sum_{t=1}^{T} (x_{it} - \bar{x}_i) y^*_{it} - T\hat{\gamma}_i$.

The fact that the variance is larger for the fixed effects model in which heterogeneous intercepts are included stems from the fact that in the presence of unit roots, the variation from the cross terms of the sample averages $\bar{x}_i$ and $\bar{y}_i$ grows large over time at the same rate T, so that their effect is not eliminated asymptotically from the distribution of $T\sqrt{N}(\hat{\beta}^*_{NT} - \beta)$.[5] However, since the contribution to the variance is computable analytically as in the proof of proposition 1.2, this in itself poses no difficulties for inference. Nevertheless, upon consideration of these expressions, it also becomes apparent that there should exist a metric which can directly adjust for this effect in the distribution and consequently render the distribution standard normal. In fact, as the following proposition indicates, it is possible to construct a t-statistic from this fully modified panel OLS estimator whose distribution will be invariant to this effect.

Corollary 1.2 (Asymptotic Distribution of the Pooled Panel FMOLS t-statistic). *Consider the following t-statistic for the FMOLS panel estimator of β as defined in proposition 1.2 above. Then under the same assumptions as in proposition 1.2, the statistic is standard normal,*

$$t_{\hat{\beta}^*_{NT}} = (\hat{\beta}^*_{NT} - \beta)\left(\sum_{i=1}^{N} \hat{L}^{-2}_{22i} \sum_{t=1}^{T} (x_{it} - \bar{x}_i)^2\right)^{1/2} \to N(0, 1)$$

as $T \to \infty$ and $N \to \infty$ for both the standard model without intercepts as well as the fixed effects model with heterogeneous estimated intercepts.

Again, as the derivation in the appendix makes apparent, because the numerator of the fully modified estimator $\hat{\beta}^*_{NT}$ is a sum of mixture normals with zero mean whose variance depends only on the properties of the Brownian motion functionals associated with the quadratic $\sum_{t=1}^{T} (x_{it} - \bar{x}_i)^2$, the t-statistic constructed using this expression will be asymptotically standard normal. This is regardless of the value of v associated with the distribution of $T\sqrt{N}(\hat{\beta}^*_{NT} - \beta)$ and so will also not depend on the dimensionality of x_{it} in the general vector case.

Note, however, that in contrast to the conventional single equation case studied by Phillips & Hansen (1990), in order to ensure that the distribution of this t-statistic is free of nuisance parameters when applied to heterogeneous panels, the usual asymptotic variance estimator of the denominator is replaced with the estimator $\hat{L}^{-2}_{22i}$. By construction, this corresponds to an estimator of the asymptotic variance of the differences for the regressors and can be estimated accordingly. This is in contrast to the t-statistic for the conventional single equation fully modified OLS, which uses an estimator for the conditional asymptotic variance from the residuals of the cointegrating regression. This distinction may appear puzzling at first, but it stems from the fact that in heterogeneous panels the contribution from the conditional variance of the residuals is idiosyncratic to the cross sectional member, and must be adjusted for directly in the construction of the numerator of the $\hat{\beta}^*_{NT}$ estimator itself before averaging over cross sections. Thus, the conditional variance has already been implicitly accounted for in the construction of $\hat{\beta}^*_{NT}$, and all that is required is that the variance from the marginal process Δx_{it} be purged from the quadratic $\sum_{t=1}^{T}(x_{it}-\bar{x}_i)^2$. Finally, note that proposition 1.2 and its corollary 1.2 have been specified in terms of a transformation, μ^*_{it}, of the true residuals. In Section 3 we will consider various strategies for specifying these statistics in terms of observables and consider the small sample properties of the resulting feasible statistics.

D. A Group Mean Fully Modified OLS t-Statistic

Before preceding to the small sample properties, we first consider one additional asymptotic result that will be of use. Recently Im, Pesaran & Shin (1995) have proposed using a group mean statistic to test for unit roots in panel data. They note that under certain circumstances, panel unit root tests may suffer from the fact that the pooled variance estimators need not necessarily be asymptotically independent of the pooled numerator and denominator terms of the fixed effects estimator. Notice, however, that the fully modified panel OLS statistics in proposition 1.2 and corollary 1.2 here have been constructed without the use of a pooled variance estimator. Rather, the statistics of the numerator and denominator have been purged of any influence from the nuisance parameters prior to summing over N. Furthermore, since asymptotically the distribution for the numerator is centered around zero, the covariance between the summed terms of the numerator and denominator also do not play a role in the asymptotic distribution of $T\sqrt{N}(\hat{\beta}^*_{NT}-\beta)$ or $t_{\hat{\beta}^*_{it}}$ as they would otherwise.

Nevertheless, it is also interesting to consider the possibility of a fully modified OLS group mean statistic in the present context. In particular, the group mean t-statistic is useful because it allows one to entertain a somewhat broader class of hypotheses under the alternative. Specifically, we can think of the distinction as follows. The t-statistic for the true panel estimator as described in corollary 1.2 can be used to test the null hypothesis $H_o: \beta_i = \beta_o$ *for all i* versus the alternative hypothesis $H_a: \beta_i = \beta_a \neq \beta_o$ *for all i* where β_o is the hypothesized common value for β under the null, and β_a is some alternative value for β which is also common to all members of the panel. By contrast, the group mean fully modified t-statistic can be used to test the null hypothesis $H_o: \beta_i = \beta_o$ for all i versus the alternative hypothesis $H_a: \beta_i \neq \beta_o$ for all i, so that the values for β are not necessarily constrained to be homogeneous across different members under the alternative hypothesis.

The following proposition gives the precise form of the panel fully modified OLS t-statistic that we propose and gives its asymptotic distributions.

Proposition 1.3 (Asymptotic Distribution of the Panel FMOLS Group Mean t-Statistic). *Consider the following group mean FMOLS t-statistic for* β *of the cointegrated panel (1). Then under assumptions 1.1 and 1.2, the statistic is standard normal, and*

$$\bar{t}_{\hat{\beta}^*_{NT}} = \frac{1}{\sqrt{N}} \sum_{i=1}^{N} \hat{L}^{-1}_{11i} \left(\sum_{t=1}^{T} (x_{it} - \bar{x}_i)^2 \right)^{-1/2} \left(\sum_{t=1}^{T} (x_{it} - \bar{x}_i) y^*_{it} - T\hat{\gamma}_i \right) \rightarrow N(0, 1)$$

where

$$y^*_{it} = (y_{it} - \bar{y}_i) - \frac{\hat{L}_{21i}}{\hat{L}_{22i}} \Delta x_{it}, \; \hat{\gamma}_i \equiv \hat{\Gamma}_{21i} + \hat{\Omega}^o_{21i} - \frac{\hat{L}_{21i}}{\hat{L}_{22i}} (\hat{\Gamma}_{22i} + \hat{\Omega}^o_{22i})$$

and $\hat{L}_i$ *is a lower triangular decomposition of* $\hat{\Omega}_i$ *as defined in (2) above, as* $T \rightarrow \infty$ *and* $N \rightarrow \infty$ *for both the standard model without intercepts as well as the fixed effects model with heterogeneous intercepts.*

Note that the asymptotic distribution of this group mean statistic is also invariant to whether or not the standard model without intercepts or the fixed effects model with heterogeneous intercepts has been estimated. Just as with the previous t-statistic of corollary 1.2, the asymptotic distribution of this panel group mean t-statistic will also be independent of the dimensionality of x_{it} for the more general vector case. Thus; we have presented two different types of t-statistics, a pooled panel OLS based fully modified t-statistic based on the 'within' dimension of the panel, and a group mean fully modified OLS t-statistic based on the 'between' dimension of the panel, both of which are asymptotically unbiased, free of nuisance parameters, and invariant to whether or not idiosyncratic fixed effects have been estimated. Furthermore, we have characterized the asymptotic distribution of the fully modified panel OLS estimator itself, which is also asymptotically unbiased and free of nuisance parameters, although in this case one should be aware that while the distribution will be a centered normal, the variance will depend on whether heterogeneous intercepts have been estimated and on the dimensionality of the vector of regressors. In the remainder of this chapter we investigate the small sample properties of feasible statistics associated with these asymptotic results and discuss examples of their application.

III. SMALL SAMPLE PROPERTIES OF FEASIBLE PANEL FULLY MODIFIED OLS STATISTICS

In this section we investigate the small sample properties of the pooled and group mean panel FMOLS estimators that were developed in the previous section. We discuss two alternative feasible estimators associated with the panel FMOLS estimators of proposition 1.2 and its t-statistic, which were defined only in terms of the true residuals. While these estimators perform reasonably well in idealized situations, more generally, size distortions for these estimators have the potential to be fairly large in small samples, as was reported in Pedroni (1996a). By contrast, we find that the group mean test statistics do very well and exhibit relatively little size distortion even in relatively small panels even in the presence of substantial cross sectional heterogeniety of the error process associated with the dynamics around the cointegrating vector. Consequently, after discussing some of the basic properties of the feasible versions of the pooled estimators and the associated difficulties for small samples, we focus here on reporting the small sample properties of the group mean test statistics, which are found to do extremely well provided that the time series dimension is not smaller than the cross sectional dimension.

A. General Properties of the Feasible Estimators

First, before reporting the results for the between dimension group mean test statistic, we discuss the general properties of various feasible forms of the within dimension pooled panel fully modified OLS statistics and consider the consequences of these properties in small samples. One obvious candidate for a feasible estimator based on proposition 1.2 would be to simply construct the statistic in terms of estimated residuals, which can be obtained from the initial N single equation OLS regressions associated with the cointegrating regression for (1). Since the single equation OLS estimator is superconsistent, one might hope that this produces a reasonably well behaved statistic for the panel FMOLS estimator. The potential problem with this reasoning stems from the fact that although the OLS regression is superconsistent it is also asymptotically biased in general. While this is a second order effect for the conventional single series estimator, for panels, as N grows large, the effect has the potential to become first order.

Another possibility might appear to be to construct the feasible panel FMOLS estimator for proposition 1.2 in terms of the original data series $y^*_{it}=(y_{it}-\bar{y}_i)-\frac{\hat{L}_{21i}}{\hat{L}_{22i}}\Delta x_{it}$ along the lines of how it is often done for the conventional single series case. However, this turns out to be correct only in very specialized cases. More generally, for heterogeneous panels, this will introduce an asymptotic bias which depends on the true value of the cointegrating relationship and the relative volatility of the series involved in the regression. The following makes this relationship precise.

Proposition 2.1 (Regarding Feasible Pooled Panel FMOLS) *Under the conditions of proposition 1.2 and corollary 1.2, consider the panel FMOLS estimator for the coefficient* β *of panel (1) given by*

$$\hat{\beta}^*_{NT}=\left(\sum_{i=1}^{N}\hat{L}_{22i}^{-2}\sum_{t=1}^{T}(x_{it}-\bar{x}_i)^2\right)^{-1}\sum_{i=1}^{N}\hat{L}_{11i}^{-1}\hat{L}_{22i}^{-1}\left(\sum_{t=1}^{T}(x_{it}-\bar{x}_i)y^*_{it}-T\hat{\gamma}_i\right)$$

where

$$y^*_{it}=(y_{it}-\bar{y}_i)-\frac{\hat{L}_{21i}}{\hat{L}_{22i}}\Delta x_{it}+\frac{\hat{L}_{11i}-\hat{L}_{22i}}{\hat{L}_{22i}}\beta(x_{it}-\bar{x}_i)$$

and $\hat{L}_i$ *and* $\hat{\gamma}_i$ *are defined as before. Then the statistics* $T\sqrt{N}(\hat{\beta}^*_{NT}-\beta)$ *and* $t_{\hat{\beta}^*_{NT}}$ *constructed from this estimator are numerically equivalent to the ones defined in proposition 1.2 and corollary 1.2.*

This proposition shows why it is difficult to construct a reliable point estimator based on the naive FMOLS estimator simply by using a transformation of y^*_{it} analogous to the single equation case. Indeed, as the proposition makes explicit, such an estimator would in general depend on the true value of the parameter that it is intended to estimate, except in very specialized cases, which we discuss below. On the other hand, this does not necessarily prohibit the usefulness of an estimator based on proposition 2.1 for the purposes of testing a particular hypothesis about a cointegrating relationship in heterogeneous panels. By using the hypothesized null value for β in the expression for y^*_{it}, proposition 2.1 can at least in principle be employed to construct a feasible FMOLS statistics to test the null hypothesis that $\beta_i=\beta$ for all i. However, as was reported in Pedroni (1996a), even in this case the small sample performance of the statistic is often subject to relatively large size distortion.

Proposition 2.1 also provides us with an opportunity to examine the consequences of ignoring heterogeneity associated with the serial correlation dynamics for the error process for this type of estimator. In particular, we notice that the modification involved in this estimator relative to the convential time series fully modified OLS estimator differs in two respects. First, it includes the estimators $\hat{L}_{11i}$ and $\hat{L}_{22i}$ that premultiply the numerator and denominator terms to control for the idiosyncratic serial correlation properties of individual cross sectional members prior to summing over N. Secondly, and more importantly, it includes in the transformation of the dependent variable y^*_{it} an additional term $\frac{\hat{L}_{11i} - \hat{L}_{22i}}{\hat{L}_{22i}} \beta(x_{it} - \bar{x}_i)$. This term is eliminated only in two special cases: (1) The elements L_{11i} and L_{22i} are identical for all members of the panel, and do not need to be indexed by i. This corresponds to the case in which the serial correlation structure of the data is homogeneous for all members of the panel. (2) The elements L_{11i} and L_{22i} are perhaps heterogeneous across members of the panel, but for each panel $L_{11i} = L_{22i}$. This corresponds to the case in which asymptotic variances of the dependent and independent variables are the same. Conversely, the effect of this term increases as (1) the dynamics become more heterogeneous for the panel, and (2) as the relative volatility becomes more different between the variables x_{it} and y_{it} for any individual members of the panel. For most panels of interest, these are likely to be important practical considerations. On the other hand, if the data are known to be relatively homogeneous or simple in its serial correlation structure, the imprecise estimation of these elements will decrease the attractiveness of this type of estimator relative to one that implicitly imposes these known restrictions.

B. Monte Carlo Simulation Results

We now study small sample properties in a series of Monte Carlo simulations. Given the difficulties associated with the feasible versions of the within dimension pooled panel fully modified OLS estimators discussed in the previous subsection based on proposition 2.1, it is not surprising that these tend to exhibit relatively large size distortions in certain scenarios, as reported in the Pedroni (1996a). Kao & Chiang (1997) subsequently also confirmed the poor small sample properties of the within dimension pooled panel fully modified estimator based on a version in which a first stage OLS estimate was used for the adjustment term. Indeed, such results should not be surprising given that the first stage OLS estimator introduces a second order bias in the presence of endogeneity, which is not eliminated asymptotically. Consequently, this bias leads to size distortion for the panel which is not necessarily eliminated even when the sample size grows large. By contrast, the feasible version of the between dimension group mean estimator does not require such an adjustment term even in the presence of heterogeneous serial correlation dynamics, and does not suffer from the same size distortion.[6] Consequently, we focus here on reporting the small sample Monte Carlo results for the between dimension group mean estimator and refer readers to Pedroni (1996a) for simulation results for the feasible versions of the within dimension pooled estimators.

To facilitate comparison with the conventional time series literature, we use as a starting point a few Monte Carlo simulations analogous to the ones studied in Phillips & Loretan (1991) and Phillips & Hansen (1990) based on their original work on FMOLS estimators for conventional time series. Following these studies, we model the errors for the data generating process in terms of a vector MA(1) process and consider the consequences of varying certain key parameters. In particular, for the purposes of the Monte Carlo simulations, we model our data generating process for the cointegrated panel (1) under assumptions 1.1 and 1.2 as

$$y_{it} = \alpha_i + \beta x_{it} + \mu_{it}$$

$$x_{it} = x_{it-1} + \varepsilon_{it}$$

$i = 1, \ldots, N$, $t = 1, \ldots, T$, for which we model the vector error process $\xi_{it} = (\mu_{it}, \varepsilon_{it})$ in terms of a vector moving average process given by

$$\xi_{it} = \eta_{it} - \theta_i \eta_{it-1};\ \eta_{it} \sim i.i.d.\ N(0, \Psi_i) \tag{3}$$

where θ_i is a 2×2 coefficient matrix and Ψ_i is a 2×2 contemporaneous covariance matrix. In order to accommodate the potentially heterogeneous nature of these dynamics among different members of the panel, we have indexed these parameters by the subscript i. We will then allow these parameters to be drawn from uniform distributions according to the particular experiment. Likewise, for each of the experiments we draw the fixed effects α_i from a uniform distribution, such that $\alpha_i \sim U(2.0, 4.0)$.

We consider first as a benchmark case an experiment which captures much of the richness of the error process studied in Phillips & Loretan (1991) and yet also permits considerable heterogeneity among individual members of the panel. In their study, Phillips & Loretan (1991), following Phillips & Hansen (1990), fix the following parameters $\theta_{11i} = 0.3$, $\theta_{12i} = 0.4$, $\theta_{22i} = 0.6$, $\Psi_{11i} = \Psi_{22i} = 1.0$, $\beta = 2.0$ and then permit θ_{21i} and Ψ_{21i} to vary. The coefficient θ_{21i} is particularly interesting since a non-zero value for this parameter reflects an absence of even weak exogeneity for the regressors in the cointegrating regression associated with (1), and is captured by the term L_{21i} in the panel FMOLS statistics. For our heterogeneous panel, we therefore set $\Psi_{11i} = \Psi_{22i} = 1.0$, $\beta = 2.0$ and draw the remaining parameters from uniform distributions which are centered around the parameter values set by Phillips & Loretan (1991), but deviate by up to 0.4 in either direction for the elements of θ_i and by up to 0.85 in either direction for Ψ_{21i}. Thus, in our first experiment, the parameters are drawn as follows: $\theta_{11i} \sim U(-0.1, 0.7)$, $\theta_{12i} \sim (0.0, 0.8)$, $\theta_{21i} \sim U(0.0, 0.8)$, $\theta_{22i} \sim U(0.2, 1.0)$ and $\Psi_{21i} \sim U(-0.85, 0.85)$. This specification achieves considerable heterogeneity across individual members and also allows the key parameters θ_{21i} and Ψ_{21i} to span the set of values considered in Phillips and Loretan's study. In this first experiment we restrict the values of θ_{21i} to span only the positive set of values considered in Phillips and Loretan for this parameter. In several cases Phillips and Loretan found negative values for θ_{21i} to be particularly problematic in terms of size distortion for many of the conventional test statistics applied to pure time series, and in our subsequent experiments we also consider the consequences of drawing negative values for this coefficient. In each case, the asymptotic covariances were estimated individually for each member i of the cross section using the Newey-West (1987) estimator. In setting the lag length for the band width, we employ the data dependent scheme recommended in Newey & West (1994), which is to set the lag truncation to the nearest integer given by $K = 4\left(\frac{T}{100}\right)^{2/9}$, where T is the number of sample observations over time. Since we consider small sample results for panels ranging in dimension from $T = 10$ to $T = 100$ by increments of 10, this implies that the lag truncation ranges from 2 to 4. For the cross sectional dimension, we consider small sample results for $N = 10$, $N = 20$ and $N = 30$ for each of these values of T.

Results for the first experiment, with $\theta_{21i} \sim U(0.0, 0.8)$ are reported in Table I of Appendix B. The first column of results reports the bias of the point estimator and the second column reports the associated standard error of the sampling distribution. Clearly, the biases are small at –0.058 even in extreme cases when both the N and T dimensions are as small as $N = 10$, $T = 10$ and become minuscule as the T dimension grows larger. At $N = 10$, $T = 30$ the bias is already down to –0.009, and at $T = 100$ it goes to –0.001. This should be anticipated, since the estimators are superconsistent and converge at rate $T\sqrt{N}$, so that even for relatively small dimensions the estimators are extremely precise. Furthermore, the Monte Carlo simulations confirm that the bias is reduced more quickly with respect to growth in the T dimension than with respect to growth in the N dimension. For example, the biases are much smaller for $T = 30$, $N = 10$ than for $T = 10$, $N = 30$ for all of the experiments. The standard errors in column two confirm that the sampling variance around these biases are also very small. Similar results continue to hold in subsequent experiments with negative moving average coefficients, regardless of the data generating process for the serial correlation processes. Consequently, the first thing to note is that these estimators are extremely accurate even in panels with very heterogeneous serial correlation dynamics, fixed effects and endogenous regressors.

Of course these findings on bias should not come as a surprise given the superconsistency results presented in the previous section. Instead, a more central concern for the purposes of inference are the small sample properties of the associated t-statistic and the possibility for size distortion. For this, we consider the performance of the small sample sizes of the test under the null hypothesis for various nominal sizes based on the asymptotic distribution. Specifically, the last two columns report the Monte Carlo small sample results for the nominal 5% and 10% p-values respectively for a two sided test of the null hypothesis $\beta = 2.0$. As a general rule, we find that the size distortions in these small samples are remarkably small provided that the time series dimension, T, is not smaller than the cross sectional dimension, N. The reason for this condition stems primarily as a consequence of the estimation of the fixed effects. The number of fixed effects, α_i, grows with the N dimension of the panel. On the other hand, each of these N fixed effects are estimated consistently as T grows large, so that $\hat{\alpha}_i - \alpha_i$ goes to zero only as T grows large. Accordingly, we require T to grow faster than N in order to eliminate this effect asymptotically for the panel. As a practical consequence, small sample size distortion tends to be high when N is large relative to T, and decreases as T becomes large relative to N, which can be anticipated in any fixed effects model. As we can see from the results in Table I, in cases when N exceeds T, the size distortions are large, with actual sizes exceeding 30 and 40% when $T = 10$ and N grows from 10 to 20 and 30. This represents an unattractive scenario, since in this case, the tests are likely to report rejections of the null hypothesis when in fact it is not warranted. However, these represent extreme cases, as the techniques are designed to deal with the opposite case, where the T dimension is reasonably large relative to the N dimension. In these cases, even when the T dimension is only slightly larger than the N dimension, and even in cases where it is comparable, we find that the size distortion is remarkably small. For example, in the results reported in Table I we find that with $N = 20$, $T = 40$ the size of the nominal 5% and 10% tests becomes 4.5% and 9.3% respectively. Similarly, for $N = 10$, $T = 30$ the sizes for the Monte Carlo sample become 6.1% and 11% respectively, and for $N = 30$, $T = 60$, they become 4.7% and 9.6%. As the T dimension grows even larger for a fixed N dimension, the tests tend to become slightly undersized, with the actual size becoming slightly smaller than the nominal size. In this case the small sample tests actually become slightly more conservative than one would anticipate based on the asymptotic critical values.

Next, we consider the case in which the values for θ_{21i} span negative numbers, and for the experiment reported in Table II of Appendix B we draw this coefficient from $\theta_{21i} \sim U(-0.8, 0.0)$. Large negative values for moving average coefficients are well known to create size distortion for such estimators, and we anticipate this to be a case in which we have higher small sample distortion. It is interesting to note that in this case the biases for the point estimate become slightly positive, although as mentioned before, they continue to be very small. The small sample size distortions follow the same pattern in that they tend to be largest when T is small relative to N and decrease as T grows larger. In this case, as anticipated, they tend to be higher than for the case in which θ_{21i} spans only positive values. However, the values still fall within a fairly reasonable range considering that we are dealing with all negative values for θ_{21i}. For example, with $N=10$, $T=100$ we have values of 6.3% and 12% for the 5% and 10% nominal sizes respectively. For $N=20$, $T=100$ they become 9% and 15.6% respectively. These are still remarkably small compared to the size distortions reported in Phillips & Loretan (1991) for the conventional time series case.

Finally, we ran a third experiment in which we allowed the values for θ_{21i} to span both positive and negative values so that we draw the values from $\theta_{21i} \sim U(-0.4, 0.4)$. We consider this to be a fairly realistic case, and this corresponds closely to the range of moving average coefficients that were estimated in the purchasing power parity study contained in Pedroni (1996a). We find the group mean estimator and test statistic to perform very well in this situation. The Monte Carlo simulation results for this case are reported in Table III of Appendix B. Whereas the biases for the case with large positive values of θ_{21i} in Table I were negative, and for the case with large negative values in Table II were positive, here we find the biases to be positive and often even smaller in absolute value than either of the first two cases. Most importantly, we find the size distortions for the t-statistic to be much smaller here than in the case where we have exclusively negative values for θ_{21i}. For example, with $N=30$, and T as small as $T=60$, we find the nominal 5% and 10% sizes to be 5.4% and 10.5%. Again, generally the small sample sizes for the test are quite close to the asymptotic nominal sizes provided that the T dimension is not smaller than the N dimension. Consequently, it appears to be the case that even when some members of the panel exhibit negative moving average coefficients, as long as other members exhibit positive values, the distortions tend to be averaged out so that the small sample sizes for the group mean statistic stay very close to the asymptotic sizes. Thus, we conclude that in general when the T dimension is not smaller than the N dimension, the asymptotic normality result appears to provide a very good benchmark for the sampling distribution under the null hypothesis, even in relatively small samples with heterogeneous serial correlation dynamics.

Finally, although power is generally not a concern for such panel tests, since the power is generally quite high, it is worth mentioning the small sample power properties of the group mean estimator. Specifically, we experimented by checking the small sample power of the test against the alternative hypothesis by generating the 10,000 draws for the DGP associated with case 3 above with $\beta = 1.9$. For the test of the null hypothesis that $\beta = 2.0$ against the alternative hypothesis that $\beta = 1.9$, we found that the power for the 10% p-value test reached 100% for $N = 10$ when T was 40 or more (or 98.2% when $T = 30$) and reached 100% for $N = 20$ when T was 30 or more, and for $N = 30$ the power reached 100% already when T was 20 or more. Consequently, considering the high power and the relatively small size distortion, we find the small sample properties of the estimator and associated t-statistic to be extremely well behaved in the cases for which it was designed.

IV. ESTIMATION ALGORITHM AND SOME EXAMPLES OF APPLICATIONS[7]

In this section we describe the algorithm for computing the panel FMOLS estimators and their associated test statistics and then discuss a few examples of their use. In summary, we can compute any one the desired statistics by performing the following steps:

1. *Estimate the panel regression and collect the residuals.* Specifically one should estimate the desired panel cointegration regression, making sure to include any desired intercepts, or common time dummies in the regression, and then collect the residuals $\hat{\mu}_{i,t}$ for each of the members of the panel. If the slopes are homogeneous, the common time dummy effects can be eliminated more simply by first demeaning the data over the time dimension prior to estimating the regression. Thus, construct $y_{it} - \bar{y}_t$, $x_{it} - \bar{x}_t$ for each variable, where $\bar{y}_t = N^{-1} \sum_{i=1}^{N} y_{it}$, $\bar{x}_t = N^{-1} \sum_{i=1}^{N} x_{it}$ prior to estimating the regression, and prior to the following steps.
2. *Estimate the long run covariances and autocovariances of the errors.* Use the estimated residuals from part (1) plus the differences of each of the regressors to construct a vector error series $\xi_{it} = (\mu_{it}, \varepsilon_{it}')'$. Note that the second element is a vector of dimension m, where m corresponds to the number of regressors. Now use any long run covariance matrix estimator,

such as the Newey-West (1987) estimator to estimate the elements of the long run covariance Ω_i and the autocovariances Γ_i. This can be done by applying the estimator to the entire $m+1$ vector $\xi_{it}=(\mu_{it}, \varepsilon'_{it})'$ to produce an $(m+1)\times(m+1)$ long run covariance matrix and autocovariances matrix. The elements of Ω_i and Γ_i then correspond to partitions of the $(m+1)\times(m+1)$ long run covariance matrix and autocovariance matrix respectively. Specifically, the far upper right scalar element of the $(m+1)\times(m+1)$ long run covariance matrix corresponds to Ω_{11i}. The lower $m\times m$ partition corresponds to Ω_{22i}, which is an $m\times m$ matrix representing the long run covariance among the regressors, and the remaining m elements in the column below the far upper right scalar element correspond to Ω_{21i}. Since the covariance matrix is symmetric, $\Omega_{12i}=\Omega_{21i}$. The same mapping corresponds the partitions of the $(m+1)\times(m+1)$ autocovariance matrix and the elements of Γ_i, except that unlike Ω_i, the autocovariance matrix Γ_i is not symmetric, so $\Gamma_{12i}\neq\Gamma'_{21i}$, and these elements must be extracted from the corresponding column and row partitions separately. Once Ω_i has been constructed, apply a Cholesky style triangularization to obtain the elements of the matrix L_i. Finally, we will use an estimate of the standard contemporaneous covariance matrix, Ω^o_i, for the elements of $\xi_{it}=(\mu_{it}, \varepsilon'_{it})'$, similarly partitioned.

3. *Construct the estimator.* Now we have all of the pieces required to construct the estimators. Each estimator uses a serial correlation correction term, γ_i, which can be constructed from the pieces obtained in part (2) above, as

$$\hat{\gamma}_i \equiv \hat{\Gamma}_{21i}+\hat{\Omega}^o_{21i}-\frac{\hat{L}_{21i}}{\hat{L}_{22i}}(\hat{\Gamma}_{22i}+\hat{\Omega}^o_{22i})$$

Next, using the elements of L_i, the expression for $y^*_{it}=(y_{it}-\bar{y}_i)-\frac{\hat{L}_{21i}}{\hat{L}_{22i}}\Delta x_{it}$ can be constructed from the original data. Then the final step is to construct the cross product terms between y^*_{it} and $(x_{it}-x_i)$. This is sufficient now to compute either the point estimators or the associated t-statistics for any of the statistics.

It is worth noting two points here. The difference between the panel 'within' dimension estimators and the group mean 'between' dimension estimators is in the way in which the cross product terms are computed. For the 'within' dimension statistics, the cross product terms are computed by summing over the T and N dimensions separately for the numerator and the denominator. For the group mean 'between' dimension statistics, the cross product terms are computed by summing over the T dimension for the numerator and denominator separately, and then summing over the N dimension for the entire ratio. Consequently, the first point to note is that the algorithm as applied to the group mean estimator describes the same steps that one would take if one were estimating N different conventional FMOLS estimators and then taking the average of these. The same is true for the group mean t-statistic. Thus, if one already has a routine to estimate the conventional time series FMOLS estimator, then the group mean panel FMOLS estimator is extremely simple and convenient to estimate. The second point to note is that for the panel FMOLS 'within' dimension estimator we have used the estimates of Ω_i, Γ_i, Ω_i^o and γ_i to compute the weighted panel variances. But it is equally feasible to compute the unweighted panel variances by first averaging the values Ω_i, Γ_i, Ω_i^o before applying the transformations. Whether or not the two different treatments has much consequence for the estimate is likely to depend on how heterogeneous the values of Ω_i are across individual members.

Next, we briefly describe a few examples of the use of these panel FMOLS estimators. One obvious application is to the exchange rate literature, and in particular the purchasing power parity literature. Long run *absolute* or strong purchasing power parity predicts that nominal exchange rates and aggregate price ratios among countries should be cointegrated with a unit cointegrating vector, so that the real exchange rate is stationary. However, panel unit root tests based on Levin & Lin (1993) have generally found mixed results. See for example Oh (1996) and Papell (1997) and Wu (1996) among others. On the other hand, panel cointegration tests based on Pedroni (1995, 1997a) have generally rejected the null of no cointegration. See for example Canzoneri, Cumby & Diba (1996), Chinn (1997) and Taylor (1996) among others for these. By contrast, long run *relative* or weak purchasing power parity simply predicts that the nominal exchange rate and aggregate price ratios will be cointegrated, though not necessarily with a unit cointegrating vector. The panel FMOLS estimators presented in this paper are an obvious way to distinguish between these two hypothesis, and Pedroni (1996a, 1999) uses these panel FMOLS estimators to show that only the relative, weak form of purchasing power parity holds for a panel of post Bretton Woods period floating exchange rates. The latter paper contrasts results for both a parametric group mean DOLS estimator and nonparametric group mean FMOLS estimator for the weak purchasing power parity test. In a similar spirit, Alexius & Nilson (2000), Canzoneri, Cumby & Diba (1996), Chinn (1997) apply these panel FMOLS tests from Pedroni (1996a) to test the Samuelson-Balassa hypothesis that long run movements of real exchange rates are driven by differences in long run relative productivities among countries.

Other examples of the use of these panel FMOLS tests have been to the growth literature. Neusser & Kugler (1998) use the tests from Pedroni (1996a) to investigate the connection between financial development and growth. Kao,

Chiang & Chen (1999) use a panel FMOLS estimator and compare it to a panel DOLS estimator to investigate the connection between research and development expenditure and growth. Keller & Pedroni (1999) use the group mean panel estimator presented in this chapter to study the mechanism by which imported R&D impacts growth at the industry level and demonstrate the attractiveness of the more flexible form of the group mean estimator. Canning & Pedroni (1999) use the same group mean panel FMOLS test as a first step estimator to construct a test for the direction of long run causality between public infrastructure and long run growth. Finally Pedroni & Wen (2000) make use of the group mean panel FMOLS estimator as a first step estimator in an overlapping generations model to identify the position of the U.S., Japanese and European economies relative to the golden rule, and the extent to which social security transfer programs can move economies closer to this position.

This is just a brief summary of the application of these estimators to two literatures, the exchange rate and growth literatures. Needless to say, many potential applications exist beyond these two literatures.

V. DISCUSSION OF FURTHER RESEARCH AND CONCLUDING REMARKS

We have explored in this chapter methods for testing and making inferences about cointegrating vectors in heterogeneous panels based on fully modified OLS principles. When properly constructed to take account of potential heterogeneity in the idiosyncratic dynamics and fixed effects associated with such panels, the asymptotic distributions for these estimators can be made to be centered around the true value and will be free of nuisance parameters. Furthermore, based on Monte Carlos simulations we have shown that in particular the t-statistic constructed from the between dimension group mean estimator performs very well in that in exhibits relatively little small sample size distortion. To date, the techniques developed in this study have been employed successfully in a number of applications, and it will be interesting to see if the panel FMOLS methods developed in this paper fare equally well in other scenarios.

The area of research and application of nonstationary panel methods is rapidly expanding, and we take this opportunity to remark on a few further issues of current and future research as they relate to the subject of this chapter. As we have already discussed, the between dimension group mean estimator has an advantage over the within dimension pooled estimators presented in this chapter in that it permits a more flexible alternative hypothesis that allows for heterogeneity of the cointegrating vector. In many cases it is not known a priori whether heterogeneity of the cointegrating vector can be ruled out, and it would be particularly nice to test the null hypothesis that the cointegrating vectors are heterogeneous in such panels with heterogeneous dynamics. In this context, Pedroni (1998) provides a technique that allows one to test such a null hypothesis against the alternative hypothesis that they are homogeneous and demonstrates how the technique can be used to test whether convergence in the Solow growth model occurs to distinct versus common steady states for the Summers and Heston data set.

Another important issue that is often raised for these types of panels pertains to the assumption of cross sectional independence as per assumption 1.2 in this chapter. The standard approach is to use common time dummies, which in many cases is sufficient to deal with cross sectional dependence. However, in some cases, common time dummies may not be sufficient, particularly when the cross sectional dependence is not limited to contemporaneous effects and is dynamic in nature. Pedroni (1997b) proposes an asymptotic covariance weighted GLS approach to deal with such dynamic cross sectional dependence for the case in which the time series dimension is considerably larger than the cross sectional dimension, and applies the panel fully modified form of the test to the purchasing power parity hypothesis using monthly OECD exchange rate data. It is interesting to note, however, that for this particular application, taking account of such cross sectional dependencies does not appear to impact the conclusions and it is possible that in many cases cross sectional dependence does not play as large a role as one might anticipate once common time dummies have been included, although this remains an open question.

Another important issue is parameteric versus non-parametric estimation of nuisance parameters. Clearly, any of the estimators presented here can be implemented by taking care of the nuisance parameter effects either nonparameterically using kernel estimators, or parametrically, as for example using dynamic OLS corrections. Generally speaking, non-parametric estimation tends to be more robust, since one does not need to assume a specific parametric form. On the other hand, since non-parametric estimation relies on fewer assumptions, it generally requires more data than parametric estimation. Consequently, for conventional time series tests, when data is limited it is often worth making specific parameteric assumptions. For panels, on the other hand, the greater abundance of data suggests an opportunity to take advantage of the greater robustness of nonparametric methods, though ultimately the choice may simply be a matter of taste. The Monte Carlo simulation results provided here demonstrate that even in the presence of considerable heterogeneity, non-parametric correction methods do very well for the group mean estimator and the corresponding t-statistic.

NOTES

1. The results in section 2 and appendix A first appeared in Pedroni (1996a). The Indiana University working paper series is available at http://www.indiana.edu/ iuecon/ workpaps/

2. In fact the computer program which accompanies this paper also allows one to implement these tests for any arbitrary number of regressors. It is available upon request from the author at ppedroni@indiana.edu

3. See Phillips & Moon (1999) for a recent formal study of the regularity conditions required for the use of sequential limit theory in panel data and a set of conditions under which sequential limits imply joint limits, including the case in which the long run variances differ among members of the panel.

4. These results are for the OLS estimator when the variables are cointegrated. A related stream of the literature studies the properties of the panel OLS estimator when the variables are not cointegrated and the regression is spurious. See for example Entorf (1997), Kao (1999), Phillips & Moon (1999) and Pedroni (1993, 1997a) on spurious regression in nonstationary panels.

5. A separate issue pertains to differences between the sample averages and the true population means. Since we are treating the asymptotics sequentially, this difference goes to zero as T grows large prior to averaging over N, and thus does not impact the limiting distribution. Otherwise, more generally we would require that the ratio N/T goes to zero as N and T grow large in order to ensure that these differences do not impact the limiting distribution. We return to this point in the discussion of the small sample properties in section 3.2.

6. Of course this is not to say that all within dimension estimators will necessarily suffer from this particular form of size distortion, and it is likely that some forms of the pooled FMOLS estimator will be better behaved than others. Nevertheless, given the other attractive features of the between dimension group mean estimator, we focus here on reporting the very attractive small sample properties of this estimator.

7. I am grateful to an anonymous referee for suggesting this section.

ACKNOWLEDGMENTS

I thank especially Bob Cumby, Bruce Hansen, Roger Moon, Peter Phillips, Norman Swanson and Pravin Trivedi and two anonymous referees for helpful comments and suggestions on various earlier versions, and Maria Arbatskaya for research assistance. The paper has also benefitted from presentations at the June 1996 North American Econometric Society Summer Meetings, the April 1996 Midwest International Economics Meetings, and workshop seminars at Rice University-University of Houston, Southern Methodist University, The Federal Reserve Bank of Kansas City, U. C. Santa Cruz and Washington University. The current version of the paper was completed while I was a visitor at the Department of Economics at Cornell University, and I thank the members of the Department for their generous hospitality. A computer program which implements these tests is available upon request from the author at ppedroni@indiana.edu

REFERENCES

Alexius, A., & Nilson, J. (2000). Real Exchange Rates and Fundamentals: Evidence from 15 OECD Countries. *Open Economies Review*, forthcoming.

Canning, D., & Pedroni, P. (1999). *Infrastructure and Long Run Economic Growth*. CAE Working paper, No. 99–09, Cornell University.

Canzoneri M., Cumby, R., & Diba, B. (1996). *Relative Labor Productivity and the Real Exchange Rate in the Long Run: Evidence for a Panel of OECD Countries*. NBER Working paper No. 5676.

Chinn, M. (1997). *Sectoral Productivity, Government Spending and Real Exchange Rates: Empirical Evidence for OECD Countries*. NBER Working paper No. 6017.

Chinn, M., & Johnson, L. (1996). *Real Exchange Rate Levels, Productivity and Demand Shocks: Evidence from a Panel of 14 Countries*. NBER Working paper No. 5709.

Entorf, H. (1997). Random Walks and Drifts: Nonsense Regression and Spurious Fixed-Effect Estimation'. *Journal of Econometrics*, *80*, 287–96.

Evans, P., & Karras, G. (1996). Convergence Revisited. *Journal of Monetary Economics*, *37*, 249–265.

Im, K., Pesaran, H., & Shin, Y. (1995). *Testing for Unit Roots in Heterogeneous Panels*. Working paper, Department of Economics, University of Cambridge.

Kao, C. (1999). Spurious Regression and Residual-Based Tests for Cointegration in Panel Data'. *Journal of Econometrics*, *90*, 1–44.

Kao, C., & Chen, B. (1995). *On the Estimation and Inference of a Cointegrated Regression in Panel Data When the Cross-section and Time-series Dimensions Are Comparable in Magnitude*. Working paper, Department of Economics, Syracuse University.

Kao, C., & Chiang, M. (1997). *On the Estimation and Inference of a Cointegrated Regression In Panel Data*. Working paper, Department of Economics, Syracuse University.

Kao, C., Chiang, M., & Chen, B. (1999). International R&D Spillovers: An Application of Estimation and Inference in Panel Cointegration. *Oxford Bulletin of Economics and Statistics*, *61*(4), 691–709.

Keller, W., & Pedroni, P. (1999). *Does Trade Affect Growth? Estimating R&D Driven Models of Trade and Growth at the Industry Level*. Working paper, Department of Economics, Indiana University and University of Texas.

Levin, A., & Lin, F. (1993). *Unit Root Tests in Panel Data; Asymptotic and Finite-sample Properties*. Working paper, Department of Economic, U. C. San Diego.

Mark, N., & Sul, D. (1999). *A Computationally Simple Cointegration Vector Estimator for Panel Data*. Working paper, Department of Economics, Ohio State University.

Neusser, K., & Kugler, M. (1998). Manufacturing Growth and Financial Development: Evidence from OECD Countries. *Review of Economics and Statistics*, *80*, 638–646.

Newey, W., & West, K. (1987). A Simple, Positive Semi-Definite, Heteroskedasticity and Autocorrelation Consistent Coariance Matrix. *Econometrica*, *55*, 703–708.

Newey, W., & West, K. (1994). Autocovariance Lag Selection in Covariance Matrix Estimation'. *Review of Economic Studies*, *61*, 631–653.

Obstfeld M., & Taylor, A. (1996). *International Capital-Market Integration over the Long Run: The Great Depression as a Watershed.* Working paper, Department of Economics, U. C. Berkeley.

Oh, K. (1996). Purchasing Power Parity and Unit Root Tests Using Panel Data'. *Journal of International Money and Finance, 15*, 405–418.

Papell, D. (1997). Searching for Stationarity: Purchasing Power Parity Under the Current Float'. *Journal of International Economics, 43*, 313–32.

Pedroni, P. (1993). Panel Cointegration. Chapter 2 in *Panel Cointegration, Endogenous Growth And Business Cycles in Open Economies*, Columbia University Dissertation, Ann Arbor, MI: UMI Publishers.

Pedroni, P. (1995). *Panel Cointegration; Asymptotic and Finite Sample Properties of Pooled Time Series Tests, With an Application to the PPP Hypothesis.* Working paper, Department of Economics, No. 95–013, Indiana University.

Pedroni, P. (1996a). *Fully Modified OLS for Heterogeneous Cointegrated Panels and the Case of Purchasing Power Parity.* Working paper No. 96–020, Department of Economics, Indiana University.

Pedroni, P. (1996b). *Human Capital, Endogenous Growth, & Cointegration for Multi-Country Panels.* Working paper, Department of Economics, Indiana University.

Pedroni, P. (1997a). *Panel Cointegration; Asymptotic and Finite Sample Properties of Pooled Time Series Tests, With an Application to the PPP Hypothesis; New Results.* Working paper, Department of Economics, Indiana University.

Pedroni, P. (1997b). *On the Role of Cross Sectional Dependency in Dynamic Panel Unit Root and Panel Cointegration Exchange Rate Studies.* Working paper, Department of Economics, Indiana University.

Pedroni, P. (1998). *Testing for Convergence to Common Steady States in Nonstationary Heterogeneous Panels.* Working paper, Department of Economics, Indiana University.

Pedroni, P. (1999). *Purchasing Power Parity Tests in Cointegrated Panels.* Working paper, Department of Economics, Indiana University.

Pedroni, P., & Wen, Y. (2000). *Government and Dynamic Efficiency.* Working paper, Department of Economics, Cornell University and Indiana University.

Pesaran, H., & Smith, R. (1995). Estimating Long Run Relationships from Dynamic Heterogeneous Panels. *Journal of Econometrics, 68*, 79–114.

Phillips, P., & Durlauf, S. (1986). Multiple Time Series Regressions with Integrated Processes'. *Review of Economic Studies, 53*, 473–495.

Phillips, P., & Hansen, B. (1990). Statistical Inference in Instrumental Variables Regression with I(1) Processes. *Review of Economic Studies, 57*, 99–125.

Phillips, P., & Loretan, M. (1991). Estimating Long-run Economic Equilibria. *Review of Economic Studies, 58*, 407–436.

Phillips, P., & Moon, H. (1999). Linear Regression Limit Theory for Nonstationary Panel Data'. *Econometrica, 67*, 1057–1112.

Quah, D. (1994). Exploiting Cross-Section Variation for Unit Root Inference in Dynamic Data'. *Economics Letters, 44*, 9–19.

Taylor, A. (1996). *International Capital Mobility in History: Purchasing Power Parity in the Long-Run.* NBER Working paper No. 5742.

Wu, Y. (1996). Are Real Exchange Rates Nonstationary? Evidence from a Panel-Data Test. *Journal of Money Credit and Banking, 28*, 54–63.

MATHEMATICAL APPENDIX A

Proposition 1.1: *We establish notation here which will be used throughout the remainder of the appendix. Let* $Z_{it} = Z_{it-1} + \xi_{it}$ *where* $\xi_{it} = (\mu_{it}, \varepsilon_{it})'$. *Then by virtue of assumption 1.1 and the functional central limit theorem,*

$$T^{-1} \sum_{t=1}^{T} \tilde{Z}_{it}\xi'_{it} \rightarrow \int_{r=0}^{1} \tilde{B}(r, \Omega_i)\, d\tilde{B}(r, \Omega_i)' + \Gamma_i + \Omega_i^o \tag{A1}$$

$$T^{-2} \sum_{t=1}^{T} \tilde{Z}_{it}\tilde{Z}'_{it} \rightarrow \int_{r=0}^{1} \tilde{B}(r, \Omega_i)\tilde{B}(r, \Omega_i)'\, dr \tag{A2}$$

for all i, where $\tilde{Z}_{it} = Z_{it} - \bar{Z}_i$ *refers to the demeaned discrete time process and* $\tilde{B}(r, \Omega_i)$ *is demeaned vector Brownian motion with asymptotic covariance* Ω_i. *This vector can be decomposed as* $\tilde{B}(r, \Omega_i) = L'_i \tilde{W}_i(r)$ *where* $L_i = \Omega_i^{1/2}$ *is the lower triangular decomposition of* Ω_i *and* $\tilde{W}(r) = \left(W_1(r) - \int_0^1 W_1(r)\, dr,\ W_2(r) - \int_0^1 W_2(r)\, dr \right)'$ *is a vector of demeaned standard Brownian motion, with* W_{1i} *independent of* W_{2i}. *Under the null hypothesis, the statistic can be written in these terms as*

$$T\sqrt{N}(\hat{\beta}_{NT} - \beta) = \frac{\frac{1}{\sqrt{N}} \sum_{i=1}^{N} \left(T^{-1} \sum_{t=1}^{T} \tilde{Z}_{it}\xi'_{it} \right)_{21}}{\frac{1}{N} \sum_{i=1}^{N} \left(T^{-2} \sum_{t=1}^{T} \tilde{Z}_{it}\tilde{Z}'_{it} \right)_{22}} \tag{A3}$$

Based on (A1), as $T \rightarrow \infty$, *the bracketed term of the numerator converges to*

$$\left(\int_{r=0}^{1} \tilde{B}(r, \Omega_i)\, d\tilde{B}(r, \Omega_i)' \right)_{21} + \Gamma_{21i} + \Omega_{21i}^o \tag{A4}$$

the first term of which can be decomposed as

$$\left(\int_{r=0}^{1} \tilde{B}(r, \Omega_i)\, d\tilde{B}(r, \Omega_i)' \right)_{21} = L_{11i}L_{22i}\left(\int W_{2i}\, dW_{1i} - W_{1i}(1) \int W_{2i} \right)$$

$$+ L_{21i}L_{22i}\left(\int W_{2i}\, dW_{2i} - W_{2i}(1) \int W_{2i} \right) \tag{A5}$$

In order for the distribution of the estimator to be unbiased, it will be necessary that the expected value of the expression in (A4) be zero. But although the expected value of the first bracketed term in (A5) is zero, the expected value of the second bracketed term is given as

$$E\left[L_{21i}L_{22i}\left(\int W_{2i}\,dW_{2i} - W_{2i}(1)\int W_{2i}\right)\right] = \frac{1}{2}L_{21i}L_{22i} \qquad \text{(A6)}$$

Thus, given that the asymptotic covariance matrix, Ω_i, must have positive diagonals, the expected value of the expression (A4) will be zero only if $L_{21i} = \Gamma_{21i} = \Omega^o_{21i} = 0$, which corresponds to strict exogeneity of regressors for all members of the panel. Finally, even if such strict exogeneity does hold, the variance of the numerator will still be influenced by the parameters L_{11i}, L_{22i} which reflect the idiosyncratic serial correlation patterns in the individual cross sectional members. Unless these are homogeneous across members of the panel, they will lead to non-trivial data dependencies in the asymptotic distribution.

Proposition 1.2: *Continuing with the same notation as above, the fully modified statistic can be written under the null hypothesis as*

$$T\sqrt{N}(\hat{\beta}^*_{NT} - \beta) = \frac{\frac{1}{\sqrt{N}}\sum_{i=1}^{N}\hat{L}^{-1}_{11i}\hat{L}^{-1}_{22i}\left((0,1)\left(T^{-1}\sum_{t=1}^{T}\tilde{Z}_{it}\xi'_{it}\right)\left(1, \frac{\hat{L}_{21i}}{\hat{L}_{22i}}\right)' - \hat{\gamma}_i\right)}{\frac{1}{N}\sum_{i=1}^{N}\hat{L}^{-2}_{22i}\left(\left(T^{-2}\sum_{t=1}^{T}\tilde{Z}_{it}\tilde{Z}'_{it}\right)_{22}\right)} \qquad \text{(A7)}$$

Thus, based on (A1), as $T \to \infty$, the bracketed term of the numerator converges to

$$\left(\int_{r=0}^{1}\tilde{B}(r,\Omega_i)\,d\tilde{B}(r,\Omega_i)'\right)_{21} - \frac{\hat{L}_{21i}}{\hat{L}_{22i}}\left(\int_{r=0}^{1}\tilde{B}(r,\Omega_i)\,d\tilde{B}(r,\Omega_i)'\right)_{22}$$

$$+\Gamma_{21i} + \Omega^o_{21i} - \frac{\hat{L}_{21i}}{\hat{L}_{22i}}(\Gamma_{22i} + \Omega^o_{22i}) \qquad \text{(A8)}$$

which can be decomposed into the elements of $\tilde{W}_i$ such that

$$\left(\int_{r=0}^{1} \tilde{B}(r, \Omega_i)\, d\tilde{B}(r, \Omega_i)'\right)_{21} = L_{11i}L_{22i}\left(\int W_{2i}\, dW_{1i} - W_{1i}(1)\int W_{2i}\right)$$

$$+ L_{21i}L_{22i}\left(\int W_{2i}\, dW_{2i} - W_{2i}(1)\int W_{2i}\right) \quad \text{(A9)}$$

$$\left(\int_{r=0.}^{1} \tilde{B}(r, \Omega_i)\, d\tilde{B}(r, \Omega_i)'\right)_{22} = L_{22i}^{2}\left(\int W_{2i} dW_{2i} - W_{2i}(1)\int W_{2i}\right) \quad \text{(A10)}$$

where the index r has been omitted for notational simplicity. Thus, if a consistent estimator of Ω_i *is employed, so that* $\hat{\Omega}_i \to \Omega_i$ *and consequently* $\hat{L}_i \to L_i$ *and* $\hat{\gamma}_i \to \gamma$, *then*

$$\hat{L}_{11i}^{-1}\hat{L}_{22i}^{-1}\left((0,1)(T^{-1}\sum_{t=1}^{T} \tilde{Z}_{it}\xi_{it}')\left(1, \frac{\hat{L}_{21i}}{\hat{L}_{22i}}\right)' - \hat{\gamma}_i\right)$$

$$\to \int_{0}^{1} W_{2i}(r)\, dW_{1i}(r) - W_{1i}(1)\int_{0}^{1} W_{2i}(r)\, dr \quad \text{(A11)}$$

where the mean and variance of this expression are given by

$$E\left[\int W_{2i} dW_{1i} - W_{1i}(1)\int W_{2i} dr\right] = 0 \quad \text{(A12)}$$

$$E\left[\left(\int W_{2i}\, dW_{1i}\right)^2 - 2W_{1i}(1)\int W_{2i} dr \int W_{2i} dW_{1i} + W_{1i}(1)^2\left(\int W_{2i} dr\right)^2\right]$$

$$= \frac{1}{2} - 2\left(\frac{1}{3}\right) + \frac{1}{3} = \frac{1}{6} \quad \text{(A13)}$$

respectively. Now that this expression has been rendered void of any idiosyncratic components associated with the original $\tilde{B}(r, \Omega_i)$, *then by virtue of assumption 1.2 and a standard central limit theorem argument,*

$$\frac{1}{\sqrt{N}}\sum_{i=1}^{N}\left(\int_{0}^{1} W_{2i}(r)\, dW_{1i}(r) - W_{1i}(1)\int_{0}^{1} W_{2i}(r)\, dr\right) \to N(0, 1/6) \quad \text{(A14)}$$

as $N \rightarrow \infty$. Next, consider the bracketed term of the denominator of (A3), which based on (A1), as $T \rightarrow \infty$, converges to

$$\left(\int_{r=0}^{1} \tilde{B}(r, \Omega_i)\tilde{B}(r, \Omega_i)'\right)_{22} = L_{22i}^{2}\left(\int_0^1 W_{2i}(r)^2\,dr - \left(\int_0^1 W_{2i}(r)\,dr\right)^2\right) \quad \text{(A15)}$$

Thus,

$$\hat{L}_{22i}^{-2}\left((T^{-2}\sum_{t=1}^{T} \tilde{Z}_{it}\tilde{Z}_{it}')\right)_{22} \rightarrow \int_0^1 W_{2i}(r)^2dr - \left(\int_0^1 W_{2i}(r)\,dr\right)^2 \quad \text{(A16)}$$

which has finite variance, and a mean given by

$$E\left[\int_0^1 W_{2i}(r)^2dr - \left(\int_0^1 W_{2i}(r)\,dr\right)^2\right] = \frac{1}{2} - \frac{1}{3} = \frac{1}{6} \quad \text{(A18)}$$

Again, since this expression has been rendered void of any idiosyncratic components associated with the original $\tilde{B}(r, \Omega_i)$, then by virtue of assumption 1.2 and a standard law of large numbers argument,

$$\frac{1}{N}\sum_{i=1}^{N}\left(\int_0^1 W_{2i}(r)^2\,dr - \left(\int_0^1 W_{2i}(r)\,dr\right)^2\right) \rightarrow \frac{1}{6} \quad \text{(A18)}$$

as $N \rightarrow \infty$. Thus, by iterated weak convergence and an application of the continuous mapping theorem, $T\sqrt{N}(\hat{\beta}^*_{NT} - \beta) \rightarrow N(0, 6)$ for this case where heterogeneous intercepts have been estimated. Next, recognizing that $T^{-1/2}\bar{y}_{i\cdot}$ $\rightarrow \int_0^1 W_{1i}(r)\,dr$ and $T^{-1/2}\bar{x}_i \rightarrow \int_0^1 W_{2i}(r)\,dr$ as $T \rightarrow \infty$, and setting $\int W_{1i} = \int W_{2i} = 0$ for the case where $\bar{y}_i = \bar{x}_{i=0}$ gives as a special case of (A13) and (A17) the results for the distribution in the case with no estimated *intercepts. In this case the mean given by* (A12) *remains zero, but the variance in* (A13) *become* $\frac{1}{2}$ *and the mean in* (A17) *also becomes* $\frac{1}{2}$. *Thus,* $T\sqrt{N}(\hat{\beta}^*_{NT} - \beta) \rightarrow N(0, 2)$ *for this case.*

Corollary 1.2: *In terms of earlier notation, the statistic can be rewritten as:*

$$t_{\hat{\beta}^*_{NT}} = \frac{\frac{1}{\sqrt{N}} \sum_{i=1}^{N} \hat{L}_{11i}^{-1} \hat{L}_{22i}^{-1} \left((0,1) \left(T^{-1} \sum_{t=1}^{T} \tilde{Z}_{it} \xi'_{it} \right) \left(1, \frac{\hat{L}_{21i}}{\hat{L}_{22i}} \right)' - \hat{\gamma}_i \right)}{\sqrt{\frac{1}{N} \sum_{i=1}^{N} \hat{L}_{22i}^{-2} \left(\left(T^{-2} \sum_{t=1}^{T} \tilde{Z}_{it} \tilde{Z}'_{it} \right)_{22} \right)}} \quad \text{(A19)}$$

where the numerator converges to the same expression as in proposition 1.2, and the root term of the denominator converges to the same value as in proposition 1.2. Since the distribution of the numerator is centered around zero, the asymptotic distribution of $t_{\hat{\beta}^*_{NT}}$ *will simply be the distribution of the numerator divided by the square root of this value from the denominator. Since*

$$E\left[\left(\int W_{2i}\, dW_{1i} \right)^2 - 2W_{1i}(1) \int W_{2i} \int W_{2i}\, dW_{1i} + W_{1i}(1)^2 \left(\int W_{2i} \right)^2 \right]$$

$$= E\left[\int W_{2i}^2 - \left(\int W_{2i} \right)^2 \right] \quad \text{(A20)}$$

by (A13) and (A17) regardless of whether or not $\int W_{1i}$, $\int W_{2i}$ *are set to zero, then* $t_{\hat{\beta}^*_{NT}} \rightarrow N(0, 1)$ *irrespective of whether* $\bar{x}_i$, $\bar{y}_i$ *are estimated or not.*

Proposition 1.3: *Write the statistic as:*

$$\bar{t}_{\hat{\beta}^*_{NT}} = \frac{1}{\sqrt{N}} \sum_{i=1}^{N} \hat{L}_{11i}^{-2} \left((0, 1) \left(T^{-1} \sum_{t=1}^{T} \tilde{Z}_{it} \xi'_{it} \right) \left(1, \frac{\hat{L}_{21i}}{\hat{L}_{22i}} \right)' - \hat{\gamma}_i \right)$$

$$\times \left((T^{-2} \sum_{t=1}^{T} \tilde{Z}_{it} \tilde{Z}'_{it})_{22} \right)^{-1/2}. \quad \text{(A21)}$$

Then the first bracketed term converges to

$$L_{11i}L_{22i}\left(\int_0^1 W_{2i}(r)\,dW_{1i}(r) - W_{1i}(1)\int_0^1 W_{2i}(r)\,dr\right)$$

$$\sim N\left(0, L_{11i}L_{22i}\int_0^1 W_{2i}(r)^2\,dr - \left(\int_0^1 W_{2i}(r)\,dr\right)^2\right) \tag{A22}$$

by virtue of the independence of $W_{21i}(r)$ *and* $dW_{1i}(r)$. *Since the second bracketed term converges to*

$$L_{22i}\left(\int_0^1 W_{2i}(r)^2\,dr - \left(\int_0^1 W_{2i}(r)\,dr\right)^2\right)^{-1/2} \tag{A23}$$

then, taken together, for $\hat{L}_i \to L_i$, *(A21) becomes a standardized sum of i.i.d. standard normals regardless of whether or not* $\int W_{1i}, \int W_{2i}$ *are set to zero, and thus* $\bar{t}_{\beta^*_{NT}} \to N(0, 1)$ *by a standard central limit theorem argument irrespective of whether* $\bar{x}_i, \bar{y}_i$ *are estimated or not.*

Proposition 2.1: *Insert the expression for* y^*_{it} *into the numerator and use* $y_{it} - \bar{y}_i = \beta(x_{it} - \bar{x}_i) + \mu_{it}$ *to give*

$$\hat{\beta}^*_{NT} = \frac{\sum_{i=1}^{N} \hat{L}_{11i}^{-1}\hat{L}_{22i}^{-1}\left(\sum_{t=1}^{T}(x_{it} - \bar{x}_i)(\mu_{it} - \frac{\hat{L}_{21i}}{\hat{L}_{22i}}\Delta x_{it}) - T\hat{\gamma}_i\right)}{\sum_{i=1}^{N}\hat{L}_{22i}^{2}\sum_{t=1}^{T}(x_{it} - \bar{x}_i)^2}$$

$$+ \frac{\sum_{i=1}^{N}\hat{L}_{11i}^{-1}\hat{L}_{22i}^{-1}\left(1 + \frac{\hat{L}_{11i} - \hat{L}_{22i}}{\hat{L}_{22i}}\right)\beta\sum_{t=1}^{T}(x_{it} - \bar{x}_i)^2}{\sum_{i=1}^{N}\hat{L}_{22i}^{-2}\sum_{t=1}^{T}(x_{it} - \bar{x}_i)^2} \tag{A24}$$

Since $\hat{L}_{22i}^{-2} = \hat{L}_{11i}^{-1}\hat{L}_{22i}^{-1}\left(1 + \frac{\hat{L}_{11i} - \hat{L}_{22i}}{\hat{L}_{22i}}\right)$, *the last term in (A24) reduces to* β, *thereby giving the desired result.*

APPENDIX B

Table I. Small Sample Performance of Group Mean Panel FMOLS with Heterogeneous Dynamics

Case 1: $\theta_{21i} \sim (0.0, 0.8)$

N	*T*	bias	std error	5% size	10% size
10	10	–0.058	0.115	0.282	0.362
	20	–0.018	0.047	0.084	0.145
	30	–0.009	0.029	0.061	0.110
	40	–0.006	0.020	0.035	0.076
	50	–0.004	0.016	0.027	0.062
	60	–0.003	0.012	0.020	0.049
	70	–0.002	0.010	0.016	0.044
	80	–0.002	0.009	0.014	0.040
	90	–0.002	0.008	0.014	0.038
	100	–0.001	0.007	0.014	0.037
20	10	–0.034	0.079	0.291	0.378
	20	–0.012	0.033	0.100	0.166
	30	–0.006	0.020	0.076	0.132
	40	–0.004	0.014	0.045	0.093
	50	–0.003	0.011	0.039	0.081
	60	–0.003	0.009	0.028	0.066
	70	–0.002	0.007	0.026	0.059
	80	–0.002	0.006	0.021	0.055
	90	–0.002	0.006	0.020	0.050
	100	–0.001	0.005	0.018	0.052
30	10	–0.049	0.061	0.386	0.470
	20	–0.017	0.025	0.156	0.234
	30	–0.009	0.015	0.107	0.177
	40	–0.006	0.011	0.072	0.133
	50	–0.004	0.008	0.059	0.118
	60	–0.003	0.007	0.047	0.096
	70	–0.003	0.006	0.039	0.086
	80	–0.002	0.005	0.035	0.073
	90	–0.002	0.004	0.032	0.077
	100	–0.002	0.004	0.030	0.076

Notes: Based on 10,000 independent draws of the cointegrated system (1)–(3), with $\beta = 2.0$, $\alpha_{1i} \sim U(2.0, 4.0)$, $\Psi_{11i} = \Psi_{22i} = 1.0$, $\Psi_{21i} \sim U(-0.85, 0.85)$ and $\theta_{11i} \sim U(-0.1, 0.7)$, $\theta_{12i} \sim U(0.0, 0.8)$, $\theta_{21i} \sim U(0.0, 0.8)$, $\theta_{22i} \sim U(0.2, 1.0)$.

Table II. Small Sample Performance of Group Mean Panel FMOLS with Heterogeneous Dynamics

Case 2: $\theta_{21i} \sim U(-0.8, 0.0)$

N	*T*	bias	std error	5% size	10% size
10	10	0.082	0.132	0.422	0.498
	20	0.041	0.058	0.234	0.324
	30	0.025	0.037	0.187	0.268
	40	0.016	0.027	0.137	0.213
	50	0.012	0.021	0.115	0.185
	60	0.009	0.017	0.091	0.155
	70	0.007	0.014	0.087	0.151
	80	0.006	0.012	0.078	0.140
	90	0.005	0.011	0.072	0.135
	100	0.005	0.010	0.063	0.120
20	10	0.093	0.092	0.581	0.648
	20	0.043	0.042	0.352	0.447
	30	0.026	0.027	0.265	0.361
	40	0.017	0.020	0.205	0.294
	50	0.012	0.015	0.158	0.242
	60	0.009	0.012	0.130	0.211
	70	0.007	0.010	0.117	0.194
	80	0.006	0.009	0.109	0.181
	90	0.005	0.008	0.103	0.170
	100	0.004	0.007	0.090	0.156
30	10	0.070	0.071	0.563	0.630
	20	0.033	0.032	0.339	0.433
	30	0.020	0.020	0.259	0.352
	40	0.013	0.015	0.196	0.289
	50	0.009	0.011	0.152	0.236
	60	0.007	0.009	0.131	0.211
	70	0.006	0.008	0.113	0.190
	80	0.005	0.007	0.103	0.175
	90	0.004	0.006	0.096	0.164
	100	0.003	0.005	0.087	0.156

Notes: Based on 10,000 independent draws of the cointegrated system (1)–(3), with $\beta = 2.0$, $\alpha_{1i} \sim U(2.0, 4.0)$, $\Psi_{11i} = \Psi_{22i} = 1.0$, $\Psi_{21i} \sim U(-0.85, 0.85)$ and $\theta_{11i} \sim U(-0.1, 0.7)$, $\theta_{12i} \sim U(-0.8, 0.0)$, $\theta_{21i} \sim U(-0.8, 0.0)$, $\theta_{22i} \sim U(0.2, 1.0)$.

Table III. Small Sample Performance of Group Mean Panel FMOLS with Heterogeneous Dynamics

Case 3: $\theta_{21i} \sim U(-0.4, 0.4)$

N	T	bias	std error	5% size	10% size
10	10	0.009	0.129	0.284	0.367
	20	0.011	0.052	0.113	0.179
	30	0.008	0.033	0.086	0.150
	40	0.005	0.023	0.058	0.113
	50	0.004	0.018	0.048	0.093
	60	0.003	0.014	0.039	0.083
	70	0.002	0.012	0.037	0.077
	80	0.002	0.011	0.031	0.072
	90	0.002	0.009	0.029	0.068
	100	0.001	0.008	0.028	0.062
20	10	0.028	0.090	0.346	0.430
	20	0.014	0.037	0.145	0.222
	30	0.009	0.024	0.106	0.179
	40	0.006	0.017	0.077	0.138
	50	0.004	0.013	0.060	0.114
	60	0.003	0.010	0.048	0.093
	70	0.002	0.009	0.040	0.085
	80	0.002	0.008	0.037	0.083
	90	0.001	0.007	0.035	0.079
	100	0.001	0.006	0.035	0.078
30	10	0.008	0.069	0.317	0.402
	20	0.006	0.028	0.122	0.194
	30	0.004	0.018	0.095	0.155
	40	0.003	0.013	0.068	0.122
	50	0.002	0.010	0.054	0.105
	60	0.001	0.008	0.044	0.088
	70	0.001	0.007	0.038	0.082
	80	0.001	0.006	0.036	0.076
	90	0.001	0.005	0.033	0.073
	100	0.001	0.005	0.036	0.074

Notes: Based on 10,000 independent draws of the cointegrated system (1)–(3), with $\beta = 2.0$, $\alpha_{1i} \sim U(2.0, 4.0)$, $\Psi_{11i} = \Psi_{22i} = 1.0$, $\Psi_{21i} \sim U(-0.85, 0.85)$ and $\theta_{11i} \sim U(-0.1, 0.7)$, $\theta_{12i} \sim U(-0.4, 0.4)$, $\theta_{21i} \sim U(-0.4, 0.4)$, $\theta_{22i} \sim U(0.2, 1.0)$.

[21]

Pooled Mean Group Estimation of Dynamic Heterogeneous Panels

M. Hashem PESARAN, Yongcheol SHIN, and Ron P. SMITH

It is now quite common to have panels in which both T, the number of time series observations, and N, the number of groups, are quite large and of the same order of magnitude. The usual practice is either to estimate N separate regressions and calculate the coefficient means, which we call the mean group (MG) estimator, or to pool the data and assume that the slope coefficients and error variances are identical. In this article we propose an intermediate procedure, the pooled mean group (PMG) estimator, which constrains long-run coefficients to be identical but allows short-run coefficients and error variances to differ across groups. We consider both the case where the regressors are stationary and the case where they follow unit root processes, and for both cases derive the asymptotic distribution of the PMG estimators as T tends to infinity. We also provide two empirical applications: aggregate consumption functions for 24 Organization for Economic Cooperation and Development economies over the period 1962–1993, and energy demand functions for 10 Asian developing economies over the period 1974–1990.

KEY WORDS: Consumption functions; Energy demand; Heterogeneous dynamic panels; $I(0)$ and $I(1)$ regressors; Pooled mean group estimator.

1. INTRODUCTION

Recent years have brought increasing interest in dynamic panel data models, where the number of time series observations, T, is relatively large and of the same order of magnitude as N, the number of groups. Such panels arise particularly in cross-country analyses. In most applications of this type, the parameters of interest are the long-run effects and the speed of adjustment to the long run. An example is the large literature on testing purchasing power parity in panels, where according to economic theory the long-run coefficients of the logarithms of domestic prices, foreign prices, and exchange rates should be $(1, -1, -1)$, with the speed of adjustment being of central policy concern. (A recent review of this literature was provided in Rogoff 1996; some of the related econometric issues were discussed in Boyd and Smith 1998.) Another prominent example is the Fisher equation, which postulates a unit coefficient for the long-run effect of (expected) inflation on the nominal rate of interest, but is silent as to the magnitude of the short-run effects of changes in inflation on interest rates.

There are two procedures commonly used for such panels. At one extreme, one can estimate separate equations for each group and examine the distribution of the estimated coefficients across groups. Of particular interest will be the mean of the estimates, which we call the mean group (MG) estimator. In earlier work, Pesaran and Smith (1995) we showed that the MG estimator will produce consistent estimates of the average of the parameters. This estimator, however, does not take account of the fact that certain parameters may be the same across groups. At the other extreme are the traditional pooled estimators, such as the fixed and random effects estimators, where the intercepts are allowed to differ across groups while all other coefficients and error variances are constrained to be the same. In this paper, we consider an intermediate estimator, which we call the pooled mean group (PMG) estimator because it involves both pooling and averaging. This estimator allows the intercepts, short-run coefficients, and error variances to differ freely across groups, but constrains the long-run coefficients to be the same. There are often good reasons to expect the long-run equilibrium relationships between variables to be similar across groups, due to budget or solvency constraints, arbitrage conditions, or common technologies influencing all groups in a similar way. The reasons for assuming that short-run dynamics and error variances should be the same tend to be less compelling. Not imposing equality of short-run slope coefficients also allows the dynamic specification (e.g., the number of lags included) to differ across groups.

We use two important empirical examples to compare the MG, PMG, and dynamic fixed effect (DFE) estimators. The first is the consumption function in Organization for Economic Cooperation and Development (OECD) countries. Determination of saving rates is an important policy issue and, as with the example of purchasing power parity mentioned earlier, the theory makes strong predictions: The long-run income elasticity of consumption should be unity in all countries, despite their important institutional and cultural differences. Otherwise, national (private) saving rates will be rising or falling indefinitely. The PMG estimator allows us to estimate this common long-run coefficient without making the less plausible assumption of identical dynamics in each country. In this application, both $N = 24$ and $T = 32$ are quite large. The second example is

M. Hashem Pesaran is Professor, Faculty of Economics and Politics, Trinity College, University of Cambridge CB3 9DD, U.K., and University of Southern California (E-mail: *hashem.pesaran@econ.cam.ac.uk*). Yongcheol Shin is Lecturer, Department of Economics, University of Edinburgh, EH8 9JY, U.K. (E-mail: *Yongcheol.Shin@ed.ac.uk*). Ron P. Smith is Professor, Department of Economics, Birkbeck College, University of London, W1P 1PA, U.K. (E-mail: *R.Smith@bbk.ac.uk*). Partial financial support from the ESRC (grant H519255003) and the Isaac Newton Trust of Trinity College, Cambridge is gratefully acknowledged. The first author also acknowledges the hospitality of the IMF Research Department while some of the ideas behind this article were formalized. The authors are also grateful for the efforts of Sunil Sharma and Mansour Gill in compiling the OECD dataset; for helpful discussions with Michael Binder, Nadeem U. Haque, Robert MacKay, Sunil Sharma, and Richard Smith; and for valuable comments on an earlier version from the editors and a referee.

Journal of the American Statistical Association
June 1999, Vol. 94, No. 446, Theory and Methods

energy demand in developing Asian economies. Prior to the financial crises of the summer of 1997, this was the world's fastest growing region, and the growth in its energy demand will have serious implications both for world energy markets and greenhouse gas emissions. As with the consumption function example, long-run responses of energy demand to income and relative energy prices are likely to be similar across countries, although short-run adjustments in energy demand, depending on patterns of investment in energy using equipment and supply constraints, is unlikely to be homogeneous across countries. Again, the PMG estimator allows us to investigate long-run homogeneity without imposing parameter homogeneity in the short run. In this example, both $N = 10$ and $T = 17$ are quite small. Thus there is a contrast in the panel dimensions in the two examples.

The article is organized as follows: Section 2 provides a brief review of alternative panel data estimators and discusses how the PMG estimator is related to them. Section 3 sets out the model and its underlying assumptions, and derives the log-likelihood function. Section 4 develops the general theory of PMG estimation, in both stationary regressors and unit root processes. Section 5 discusses a number of modeling issues and presents the empirical applications, and Section 6 contains some concluding remarks. Mathematical proofs are provided in an Appendix.

The following notation is used throughout: The symbol $\xrightarrow{p}$ signifies convergence in probability; $\Rightarrow$, weak convergence in probability measure; $\overset{a}{\sim}$, asymptotic equality in distributions; MN, mixture normal distribution; $\mathbf{I}_m$, an identity matrix of order m; diag[·], a diagonal matrix; and $I(d)$, an integrated variable of order d.

2. ALTERNATIVE ESTIMATORS OF DYNAMIC PANELS

Numerous dynamic panel data estimators exist. To see the relationship of the PMG estimator advanced in this article to the ones proposed in the literature, it is convenient to divide the latter into three categories, differing in their assumptions about the relative magnitudes of N and T. First, there is the "small N, large T" time-series literature devoted to estimating long-run effects. In the case of individual time-series where $N = 1$, the traditional approach was to estimate an autoregressive distributed lag (ARDL) model. In recent years, the emphasis has shifted to estimating cointegrating relationships from a single time series. The relation between these two approaches has been discussed in earlier work (Pesaran and Shin 1999). For $N > 1$, following Zellner (1962), the seemingly unrelated regression equation (SURE) procedure is often used. The main attraction of the SURE procedure is that it allows the contemporaneous error covariances to be freely estimated. But this is possible only when N is reasonably small relative to T. When N is of the same order of magnitude as T—the case we are interested in—SURE is not feasible. (It is also worth noting that most of the SURE literature is concerned with linear cross-equation restrictions, whereas our concern with common long-run coefficients implies nonlinear restrictions across the different equations.) Other approaches must be sought. It is often likely that the cause of nonzero error covariances may be due to omitted common effects that impact all groups; an indication of misspecification rather than error correlation. In such cases it is more appropriate to model the effects that account for between-group nonzero error covariances explicitly. This can be done in a number of ways. One possibility is to include cross-sectional means of the included regressors as additional regressors in the model. For instance, in an earlier work (Pesaran and Smith 1995), aggregate output was included in addition to industry output in industry employment equations. A second possibility is to express all of the variables as deviations from their respective cross-sectional means in each period. In the special case where the slope coefficients are identical across groups, the common time-period effects will be completely eliminated by this (cross-sectional) demeaning procedure. In cases where the slope coefficients differ, such demeaning will reduce (but not eliminate) the common time-specific effects. A third possibility is using explicit spatial models of the interactions between neighbors. In what follows, we assume that the use of such procedures has made it reasonable to assume that the errors are independent between groups.

Second, there is the "small T, large N" dynamic panel literature. In the case where T is small, we (Pesaran and Smith 1995) have shown that under certain assumptions, the cross-section regression based on time-averages of the variables will provide consistent estimates of the long-run coefficients. However, these assumptions are quite strong. In particular, they require that the group-specific parameters are distributed independently of the regressors, and that the regressors are strictly exogenous. For larger T, we (Pesaran and Smith 1995) showed that the traditional procedures for estimation of pooled models, such as the fixed effects, instrumental variables, and generalized method-of-moments (GMM) estimators proposed, by among others, Ahn and Schmidt (1995), Anderson and Hsiao (1981, 1982), Arellano (1989), Arellano and Bover (1995), and Keane and Runkle (1992) can produce inconsistent, and potentially very misleading estimates of the average values of the parameters in dynamic panel data models unless the slope coefficients are in fact identical. (This result holds in the case of dynamic random coefficient models even if it is assumed that the random coefficients and the regressors are independently distributed.) But tests on most panels of this sort, indicate that these parameters differ significantly across groups. Thus an estimator that imposes weaker homogeneity assumptions would be useful.

The third literature, and the one closest to our concerns, is the Bayes and empirical Bayes estimators proposed by Hsiao and Tahmiscioglu (1997) and Hsiao, Pesaran and Tahmiscioglu (1999). These estimators build on the early work of Lindley and Smith (1972) and Swamy (1970). Hsiao et al. (1999) considered Bayes estimation of short-run coefficients in dynamic heterogenous panels, and established the asymptotic equivalence of the Bayes estimator and the MG estimator. In particular, they showed that the MG estimator is asymptotically normal for large N and large T as long as $\sqrt{N}/T \to 0$ as both N and $T \to \infty$. Using Monte Carlo experiments, they also showed that although the MG estimator is consistent, it is unlikely to be a good estimator when either N or T is small. The main difference between the approach adopted in this article and the literature on Bayes estimation is that whereas we regard the parameters as fixed, this literature regards them as random: drawn from some distribution with a finite number of parameters. Given that the possibility of random parameters is admitted, the issue is not primarily one of classical versus Bayesian approaches, as classical estimators can be given a Bayesian interpretation. For example, the Swamy (1970) estimator for random coefficient models, motivated by classical generalized least squares arguments, can also be viewed as an empirical Bayes estimator.

The choice between fixed- and random-effects formulations, which has been extensively discussed in the literature, depends on a number of related considerations. First, the purpose of the exercise matters, as the two approaches try to answer distinctly different questions. Hsiao (1996, pp. 93–94) gave a number of examples in which the purpose of analysis will determine the choice between the two formulations. Stoker (1993, p. 1848) pointed out that if one wishes to make inference about macro relationships from micro estimates based on a subset of the population—a common problem—then the effects must be treated as random.

Second, the perceived degree of commonality in the parameters matters. There is a continuum, with at one extreme fixed and common parameters and the other extreme fixed and heterogenous parameters, with the random coefficient model fitting somewhere in between (see, e.g., Maddala and Hu 1996). In practice, it is often difficult to determine where on this continuum a particular case lies. The examples that we use are not samples, but rather almost the whole population of countries in a particular category: members of the OECD or Asian developing countries. This suggests treating their parameters as fixed. The difficulty of making the distinction precise was illustrated by Hsiao et al. (1995), who proposed a procedure for choosing between fixed- and random-effects models, which they evaluated by Monte Carlo methods. But in the simulations, the fixed effects are actually generated randomly either as a mixture of normal distributions or as a function of the regressors. Although this design effectively captures the situations where traditional random-effects estimators do badly, the fact that there is no obvious way to generate fixed-effects data for heterogenous panels indicates the conceptual difficulty.

Third are considerations of estimation. The fixed-effects approach uses the conditional likelihood (conditional on the particular effects); the random approach uses the unconditional or marginal likelihood. Given the correct specification, the latter will be more efficient. When N is large relative to T, the fixed-effects approach can be very inefficient.

Fourth, and an important practical issue, is whether the effects are independent of the regressors and this is the basis of a number of tests between the two specifications.

Dynamic models add further complications. The initial conditions can also be treated as fixed or random, and the long-run parameters are nonlinear functions of the short-run parameters. Thus, when using the random coefficient approach, one must ensure that the joint distribution for the short-run parameters implies a meaningful joint distribution for the long-run parameters, or vice versa. In the case that we consider—homogenous long-run parameters—the long-run parameters across the groups have a degenerate distribution, which raises some technical difficulties in treating the heterogenous short-run parameters as random. Although a number of issues remain to be resolved, and there is unlikely to be a single estimator that is appropriate for all dynamic heterogenous panel problems, we believe that the PMG estimator that we propose may be useful in a number of cases that are important in practice.

3. THE MODEL

Suppose that given data on time periods, $t = 1, 2, \ldots, T$, and groups, $i = 1, 2, \ldots, N$, we wish to estimate an ARDL$(p, q, q, \ldots, q)$ model,

$$y_{it} = \sum_{j=1}^{p} \lambda_{ij} y_{i,t-j} + \sum_{j=0}^{q} \boldsymbol{\delta}'_{ij} \mathbf{x}_{i,t-j} + \mu_i + \varepsilon_{it}, \quad (1)$$

where $\mathbf{x}_{it}$ $(k \times 1)$ is the vector of explanatory variables (regressors) for group i; μ_i represent the fixed effects; the coefficients of the lagged dependent variables, λ_{ij}, are scalars; and $\boldsymbol{\delta}_{ij}$ are $k \times 1$ coefficient vectors. T must be large enough such that we can estimate the model for each group separately. For notational convenience, we use a common T and p across groups and a common q across groups and regressors, but this is not necessary. Similarly, time trends or other types of fixed regressors, such as seasonal dummies, can be included in (1). But to keep the notations simple, we do not allow for such effects.

It is convenient to work with the following reparameterization of (1):

$$\Delta y_{it} = \phi_i y_{i,t-1} + \boldsymbol{\beta}'_i \mathbf{x}_{it} + \sum_{j=1}^{p-1} \lambda^*_{ij} \Delta y_{i,t-j} + \sum_{j=0}^{q-1} \boldsymbol{\delta}^{*\prime}_{ij} \Delta \mathbf{x}_{i,t-j} + \mu_i + \varepsilon_{it}, \quad (2)$$

$i = 1, 2, \ldots, N$, and $t = 1, 2, \ldots, T$, where $\phi_i = -(1 - \sum_{j=1}^{p} \lambda_{ij})$, $\boldsymbol{\beta}_i = \sum_{j=0}^{q} \boldsymbol{\delta}_{ij}$,

$$\lambda^*_{ij} = -\sum_{m=j+1}^{p} \lambda_{im}, \qquad j = 1, 2, \ldots, p-1,$$

and

$$\boldsymbol{\delta}^*_{ij} = -\sum_{m=j+1}^{q} \boldsymbol{\delta}_{im}, \qquad j = 1, 2, \ldots, q-1. \quad (3)$$

If we stack the time-series observations for each group, then (2) can be written as

$$\Delta \mathbf{y}_i = \phi_i \mathbf{y}_{i,-1} + \mathbf{X}_i \beta_i + \sum_{j=1}^{p-1} \lambda_{ij}^* \Delta \mathbf{y}_{i,-j} + \sum_{j=0}^{q-1} \Delta \mathbf{X}_{i,-j} \delta_{ij}^* + \mu_i \iota + \varepsilon_i, \quad (4)$$

$i = 1, 2, \ldots, N$, where $\mathbf{y}_i = (y_{i1}, \ldots, y_{iT})'$ is a $T \times 1$ vector of the observations on the dependent variable of the ith group, $\mathbf{X}_i = (\mathbf{x}_{i1}, \ldots, \mathbf{x}_{iT})'$ is a $T \times k$ matrix of observations on the regressors that vary both across groups and time periods, $\iota = (1, \ldots, 1)'$ is a $T \times 1$ vector of 1s, $\mathbf{y}_{i,-j}$ and $\mathbf{X}_{i,-j}$ are j period lagged values of $\mathbf{y}_i$ and $\mathbf{X}_i$, and $\Delta \mathbf{y}_i = \mathbf{y}_i - \mathbf{y}_{i,-1}, \Delta \mathbf{X}_i = \mathbf{X}_i - \mathbf{X}_{i,-1}, \Delta \mathbf{y}_{i,-j}$ and $\Delta \mathbf{X}_{i,-j}$ are j period lagged values of $\Delta \mathbf{y}_i$ and $\Delta \mathbf{X}_i$, and $\varepsilon_i = (\varepsilon_{i1}, \ldots, \varepsilon_{iT})'$.

We make the following assumptions.

Assumption 1. The disturbances $\varepsilon_{it}, i = 1, 2, \ldots, N, t = 1, 2, \ldots, T$, in (1) are independently distributed across i and t, with means 0, variances $\sigma_i^2 > 0$, and finite fourth-order moments. They are also distributed independently of the regressors, $\mathbf{x}_{it}$.

The assumption that the disturbances ε_{it} are distributed independently across groups was discussed in Section 2. The assumption that they are independent across time is also not very restrictive, and can be satisfied in most applications by increasing the distributed lag orders on y_{it} and $\mathbf{x}_{it}$. The independence of the disturbances and the regressors is needed for the consistent estimation of the short-run coefficients, but, as shown by Pesaran (1997), it is relatively straightforward to allow for the possible dependence of $\mathbf{x}_{it}$ on ε_{it} when estimating the long-run coefficients, as long as $\mathbf{x}_{it}$ have finite-order autoregressive representations.

Assumption 2. The ARDL$(p, q, q, \ldots, q)$ model (1) is stable in that the roots of

$$\sum_{j=1}^{p} \lambda_{ij} z^j = 1, \qquad i = 1, 2, \ldots, N,$$

lie outside the unit circle.

This assumption ensures that $\phi_i < 0$, and hence there exists a long-run relationship between y_{it} and $\mathbf{x}_{it}$ defined by

$$y_{it} = -(\beta_i'/\phi_i)\mathbf{x}_{it} + \eta_{it},$$

for each $i = 1, 2, \ldots, N$, where η_{it} is a stationary process. Pesaran, Shin, and R. J. Smith (1999) provide a general framework for testing assumption 2, irrespective of whether the regressors, $\mathbf{x}_{it}$, are $I(1)$ or $I(0)$. Assumption 2 also ensures that the order of integration of y_t is at most equal to that of $\mathbf{x}_{it}$.

Assumption 3 (Long-Run Homogeneity). The long-run coefficients on $\mathbf{X}_i$, defined by $\boldsymbol{\theta}_i = -\beta_i/\phi_i$, are the same across the groups, namely

$$\boldsymbol{\theta}_i = \boldsymbol{\theta}, \qquad i = 1, 2, \ldots, N. \qquad (5)$$

Under Assumptions 2 and 3, relation (4) can be written more compactly as

$$\Delta \mathbf{y}_i = \phi_i \boldsymbol{\xi}_i(\boldsymbol{\theta}) + \mathbf{W}_i \boldsymbol{\kappa}_i + \varepsilon_i, \qquad i = 1, 2, \ldots, N, \quad (6)$$

where

$$\boldsymbol{\xi}_i(\boldsymbol{\theta}) = \mathbf{y}_{i,-1} - \mathbf{X}_i \boldsymbol{\theta}, \qquad i = 1, 2, \ldots, N, \qquad (7)$$

is the error correction component, $\mathbf{W}_i = (\Delta \mathbf{y}_{i,-1}, \ldots, \Delta \mathbf{y}_{i,-p+1}, \Delta \mathbf{X}_i, \Delta \mathbf{X}_{i,-1}, \ldots, \Delta \mathbf{X}_{i,-q+1}, \iota)$, and $\boldsymbol{\kappa}_i = (\lambda_{i1}^*, \ldots, \lambda_{i,p-1}^*, \boldsymbol{\delta}_{i0}^{*\prime}, \boldsymbol{\delta}_{i1}^{*\prime}, \ldots, \boldsymbol{\delta}_{i,q-1}^{*\prime}, \mu_i)'$. The group-specific equations in the panel (6) are nonlinear in ϕ_i and $\boldsymbol{\theta}$, and since $\boldsymbol{\theta}$ is common across groups the panel is subject to cross-equation parameter restrictions. In what follows we also allow the error variances, $\mathrm{var}(\varepsilon_{it}) = \sigma_i^2$, to differ across groups.

To estimate the model, we adopt a likelihood approach and initially assume that the disturbances ε_{it} are normally distributed, though this assumption is not required for the asymptotic results. Under Assumption 1, the likelihood of the panel data model can be written as the product of the likelihoods for each group. Because the parameters of interest are the long-run effects and adjustment coefficients, we work directly with the concentrated log-likelihood function. Given normality, we have

$$l_T(\boldsymbol{\varphi}) = -\frac{T}{2} \sum_{i=1}^{N} \ln 2\pi\sigma_i^2 - \frac{1}{2} \sum_{i=1}^{N} \frac{1}{\sigma_i^2} (\Delta \mathbf{y}_i - \phi_i \boldsymbol{\xi}_i(\boldsymbol{\theta}))' \mathbf{H}_i (\Delta \mathbf{y}_i - \phi_i \boldsymbol{\xi}_i(\boldsymbol{\theta})). \quad (8)$$

where $\mathbf{H}_i = \mathbf{I}_T - \mathbf{W}_i(\mathbf{W}_i'\mathbf{W}_i)^{-1}\mathbf{W}_i', \boldsymbol{\varphi} = (\boldsymbol{\theta}', \boldsymbol{\phi}', \boldsymbol{\sigma}')', \boldsymbol{\phi} = (\phi_1, \phi_2, \ldots, \phi_N)'$, and $\boldsymbol{\sigma} = (\sigma_1^2, \sigma_2^2, \ldots, \sigma_N^2)'$.

For the proof of consistency and asymptotic normality of the PMG estimators, we also require the following additional assumptions.

Assumption 4. $\boldsymbol{\varphi} \in \Theta_\varphi = \Theta_\theta \times \Theta_\phi \times \Theta_\sigma$, where Θ_φ is a compact subset of $\mathbb{R}^{n_\varphi}$ with $n_\varphi = k + 2N$. The true value of $\boldsymbol{\varphi}$, denoted by $\boldsymbol{\varphi}_0 = (\boldsymbol{\theta}_0', \boldsymbol{\phi}_0', \boldsymbol{\sigma}_0')'$, is an interior point of Θ_φ.

Assumption 5.

a. For a given sample size, T, and all values of $\boldsymbol{\varphi} \in \Theta_\varphi$, the redefined observation matrix $\mathbf{Z}(\boldsymbol{\varphi}) = [\check{\mathbf{X}}(\boldsymbol{\phi}, \boldsymbol{\sigma}), \check{\boldsymbol{\xi}}(\boldsymbol{\theta}, \boldsymbol{\sigma}), \check{\mathbf{W}}(\boldsymbol{\sigma})]$ has a full column rank, where

$$\check{\mathbf{X}}(\boldsymbol{\phi}, \boldsymbol{\sigma}) = -[(\phi_1/\sigma_1)\mathbf{X}_1', (\phi_2/\sigma_2)\mathbf{X}_2', \ldots, (\phi_N/\sigma_N)\mathbf{X}_N']'$$

and $\check{\mathbf{W}}(\boldsymbol{\sigma})$ and $\check{\boldsymbol{\xi}}(\boldsymbol{\theta}, \boldsymbol{\sigma})$ are block diagonal matrices with their ith blocks given by $\mathbf{W}_i/\sigma_i$ and $\boldsymbol{\xi}_i(\boldsymbol{\theta})/\sigma_i$.

b. When $\mathbf{x}_{it}$ are stationary, $T^{-1}\mathbf{Z}'(\boldsymbol{\varphi})\mathbf{Z}(\boldsymbol{\varphi})$ converges in probability to a positive definite matrix as $T \to \infty$.

c. When $\mathbf{x}_{it}$ are $I(1)$, as $T \to \infty, \mathbf{K}_z\mathbf{Z}'(\boldsymbol{\varphi})\mathbf{Z}(\boldsymbol{\varphi})\mathbf{K}_z$ weakly converges in probability to a positive definite random matrix with probability 1, where $\mathbf{K}_z = \mathrm{diag}(T^{-1}\mathbf{I}_k, T^{-1/2}\mathbf{I}_N, T^{-1/2}\mathbf{I}_{N(p+kq)})$.

Assumption 5 sets out standard identification conditions and rules out the possibility of exact multicollinearity. In the case where $\mathbf{x}_{it}$ are $I(1)$, part c of this assumption ensures that $\mathbf{x}_{it}$ are not themselves cointegrated. Notice also that this assumption is weaker than is needed for identification of the group-specific long-run coefficients, $\boldsymbol{\theta}_i$, if the long-run homogeneity assumption 3 is not imposed.

Necessary conditions for parts b and c of assumption 5 to hold are given in the Appendix, Section A.1. In the case where $\mathbf{x}_{it}$ are $I(0)$, the pooled cross-product observation matrix on the regressors, $N^{-1}\sum_{i=1}^{N}(\phi_i^2/\sigma_i^2)T^{-1}\mathbf{X}_i'\mathbf{H}_i\mathbf{X}_i$, must converge in probability to a fixed positive definite matrix as $T \rightarrow \infty$. In the case where $\mathbf{x}_{it}$ are $I(1)$, $N^{-1}\sum_{i=1}^{N}(\phi_i^2/\sigma_i^2)T^{-2}\mathbf{X}_i'\mathbf{H}_i\mathbf{X}_i$ must weakly converge to a random positive definite matrix with probability 1 as $T \rightarrow \infty$. These conditions also cover the case where both T and N are large. The conditions should hold for all feasible values of ϕ_i and σ_i^2.

4. THE POOLED MEAN GROUP ESTIMATOR

Maximum likelihood (ML) estimation of the long-run coefficients, $\boldsymbol{\theta}$, and the group-specific error-correction coefficients, ϕ_i, can be computed by maximizing (8) with respect to φ. These ML estimators (MLEs) are termed the *pooled mean group* (PMG) estimators to highlight both the pooling implied by the homogeneity restrictions on the long-run coefficients and the averaging across groups used to obtain means of the estimated error-correction coefficients and the other short-run parameters of the model.

The PMG estimators can be computed by the familiar Newton–Raphson algorithm, which makes use of both the first and second derivatives. Alternatively, they can be computed by a "back-substitution" algorithm that makes use of only the first derivatives of (8). In this case, setting the first derivatives of the concentrated log-likelihood function with respect to φ to 0 yields the following relations in $\hat{\boldsymbol{\theta}}, \hat{\phi}_i$, and $\hat{\sigma}_i^2$, which need to be solved iteratively:

$$\hat{\boldsymbol{\theta}} = -\left\{\sum_{i=1}^{N} \frac{\hat{\phi}_i^2}{\hat{\sigma}_i^2}\mathbf{X}_i'\mathbf{H}_i\mathbf{X}_i\right\}^{-1} \times \left\{\sum_{i=1}^{N} \frac{\hat{\phi}_i}{\hat{\sigma}_i^2}\mathbf{X}_i'\mathbf{H}_i(\Delta\mathbf{y}_i - \hat{\phi}_i\mathbf{y}_{i,-1})\right\}, \quad (9)$$

$$\hat{\phi}_i = (\hat{\boldsymbol{\xi}}_i'\mathbf{H}_i\hat{\boldsymbol{\xi}}_i)^{-1}\hat{\boldsymbol{\xi}}_i'\mathbf{H}_i\Delta\mathbf{y}_i, \qquad i = 1, 2, \ldots, N, \quad (10)$$

and

$$\hat{\sigma}_i^2 = T^{-1}(\Delta\mathbf{y}_i - \hat{\phi}_i\hat{\boldsymbol{\xi}}_i)'\mathbf{H}_i(\Delta\mathbf{y}_i - \hat{\phi}_i\hat{\boldsymbol{\xi}}_i), \qquad i = 1, 2, \ldots, N, \quad (11)$$

where $\hat{\boldsymbol{\xi}}_i = \mathbf{y}_{i,-1} - \mathbf{X}_i\hat{\boldsymbol{\theta}}$. To simplify the notations, we denote $\boldsymbol{\xi}_i(\hat{\boldsymbol{\theta}})$ by $\hat{\boldsymbol{\xi}}_i$. Starting with an initial estimate of $\boldsymbol{\theta}$, say $\hat{\boldsymbol{\theta}}^{(0)}$, estimates of ϕ_i and σ_i^2 can be computed using (10) and (11), which can then be substituted in (9) to obtain a new estimate of $\boldsymbol{\theta}$, say $\hat{\boldsymbol{\theta}}^{(1)}$, and so on until convergence is achieved.

In order to derive the asymptotic distribution of the PMG estimators we distinguish between the cases of stationary and nonstationary regressors, $\mathbf{x}_{it}$. Although in principle the same algorithm can be used to compute the PMG estimators irrespective of whether the regressors are $I(0)$ or $I(1)$, the underlying asymptotic theories for these two cases are fundamentally different and their derivations require separate treatments.

4.1 The Case of Stationary Regressors

In this case, under fairly standard conditions, the consistency and the asymptotic normality of the ML estimators of the parameters in (8) can be easily established. We set out the consistency and the asymptotic distribution of the MLEs of φ, denoted by $\hat{\varphi} = (\hat{\boldsymbol{\theta}}', \hat{\boldsymbol{\phi}}', \hat{\boldsymbol{\sigma}}')'$, in the following theorem.

Theorem 1. Under assumptions 1–4, and 5(a) and (b), and assuming that the regressors $\mathbf{x}_{it}$ are stationary, the MLE of φ in the dynamic heterogeneous panel data model (6) is consistent. Furthermore, as $T \rightarrow \infty$ for a fixed N, the PMG estimator of $\boldsymbol{\psi} = (\boldsymbol{\theta}', \boldsymbol{\phi}')'$ has the following asymptotic distribution:

$$\sqrt{T}(\hat{\boldsymbol{\psi}} - \boldsymbol{\psi}_0) \overset{a}{\sim} \mathrm{N}\{\mathbf{0}, \mathbf{J}^{-1}(\boldsymbol{\psi}_0)\}, \quad (12)$$

where $\mathbf{J}(\boldsymbol{\psi}_0)$ is the $(k+N) \times (k+N)$ information matrix given by

$$\mathbf{J}(\boldsymbol{\psi}_0) \equiv \begin{bmatrix} \sum_{i=1}^{N}\frac{\phi_{i0}^2}{\sigma_{i0}^2}\mathbf{Q}_{X_iX_i} & -\frac{\phi_{10}}{\sigma_{10}^2}\mathbf{Q}_{X_1\xi_{10}} & \cdots & -\frac{\phi_{N0}}{\sigma_{N0}^2}\mathbf{Q}_{X_N\xi_{N0}} \\ -\frac{\phi_{10}}{\sigma_{10}^2}\mathbf{Q}_{X_1\xi_{10}}' & \frac{1}{\sigma_{10}^2}q_{\xi_{10}\xi_{10}} & \cdots & 0 \\ \vdots & \vdots & \vdots & \vdots \\ -\frac{\phi_{N0}}{\sigma_{N0}^2}\mathbf{Q}_{X_N\xi_{N0}}' & 0 & \cdots & \frac{1}{\sigma_{N0}^2}q_{\xi_{N0}\xi_{N0}} \end{bmatrix}, \quad (13)$$

with $\mathbf{Q}_{X_iX_i}, \mathbf{Q}_{X_i\xi_{i0}}$, and $q_{\xi_{i0}\xi_{i0}}$ being the probability limits of $T^{-1}\mathbf{X}_i'\mathbf{H}_i\mathbf{X}_i$, $T^{-1}\mathbf{X}_i'\mathbf{H}_i\boldsymbol{\xi}_{i0}$, and $T^{-1}\boldsymbol{\xi}_{i0}'\mathbf{H}_i\boldsymbol{\xi}_{i0}$.

Proof. In this case the proof can be established using familiar results. (Details can be found in Pesaran, Shin, and Smith 1997, appendix.)

Remark 1. Focusing on the long-run coefficients, for a fixed N as $T \rightarrow \infty$ the pooled MLE $\hat{\boldsymbol{\theta}}$, defined by (9), is asymptotically distributed as

$$\sqrt{T}(\hat{\boldsymbol{\theta}} - \boldsymbol{\theta}_0) \overset{a}{\sim} \mathrm{N}\left\{\mathbf{0}, \left[\sum_{i=1}^{N}\frac{\phi_{i0}^2}{\sigma_{i0}^2}\left(\mathbf{Q}_{X_iX_i} - \mathbf{Q}_{X_i\xi_{i0}}q_{\xi_{i0}\xi_{i0}}^{-1}\mathbf{Q}_{X_i\xi_{i0}}'\right)\right]^{-1}\right\}. \quad (14)$$

4.2 The Case of Nonstationary Regressors

Here the underlying regressors are assumed to follow integrated processes of order 1, namely $I(1)$. The asymptotic analysis in this case is more complicated, due to the fact that the MLEs of the long-run and the short-run parameters, $\boldsymbol{\theta}$ and $(\boldsymbol{\phi}', \boldsymbol{\sigma}')'$, converge to their true values at different rates, and the mere consistency of the MLEs is not sufficient to guarantee the weak convergence of the sample information matrix to its true value. In particular, to ensure such a convergence, the sample information matrix should satisfy the stochastic equicontinuity condition. (For a general treatment of these issues, see Pesaran and Shin 1999; Saikkonen 1995.)

The following theorem establishes the consistency, the relative rates of convergence, and the asymptotic distribution of the MLE of φ.

Theorem 2. Under Assumptions 1–4 and 5(a) and (c), and assuming that $\mathbf{x}_{it}$ are $I(1)$, the MLE of the short-run coefficients $\boldsymbol{\phi}$ and $\boldsymbol{\sigma}$ in the dynamic heterogeneous panel data model (6) are $\sqrt{T}$ consistent and the MLE of $\boldsymbol{\theta}$ is T consistent, namely

$$\hat{\boldsymbol{\theta}} - \boldsymbol{\theta}_0 = o_p(T^{-1/2}), \qquad \hat{\boldsymbol{\phi}} - \boldsymbol{\phi}_0 = o_p(1$$

and

$$\hat{\boldsymbol{\sigma}} - \boldsymbol{\sigma}_0 = o_p(1). \tag{15}$$

Furthermore, for a fixed N and as $T \to \infty$, the MLE of $\boldsymbol{\psi} = (\boldsymbol{\theta}', \boldsymbol{\phi}')'$ asymptotically has the mixture-normal distribution

$$\mathbf{D}_{\psi}^{-1}(\hat{\boldsymbol{\psi}} - \boldsymbol{\psi}_0) \overset{a}{\sim} \mathrm{MN}\{\mathbf{0}, \mathcal{I}^{-1}(\boldsymbol{\psi}_0)\}, \tag{16}$$

where $\mathbf{D}_{\psi} = \mathrm{diag}(T^{-1}\mathbf{I}_k, T^{-1/2}\mathbf{I}_N)$ and $\mathcal{I}(\boldsymbol{\psi}_0)$ is the random information matrix defined by (A.20).

Proof. See the Appendix, Section A.2.

Remark 2. More specifically, the pooled MLE $\hat{\boldsymbol{\theta}}$, defined by (9), has the following large T asymptotic distribution:

$$T(\hat{\boldsymbol{\theta}} - \boldsymbol{\theta}_0) \overset{a}{\sim} \mathrm{MN}\left\{\mathbf{0}, \left(\sum_{i=1}^{N} \frac{\phi_{i0}^2}{\sigma_{i0}^2} \mathbf{R}_{X_i X_i}\right)^{-1}\right\}, \tag{17}$$

where $\mathbf{R}_{X_i X_i}, i = 1, 2, \ldots, N$, are the random probability limits defined by (A.1). Notice that it is not required that all the matrices $\mathbf{R}_{X_i X_i}$ be positive definite. It is, however, easily seen that by part (c) of Assumption 5, $\sum_{i=1}^{N}(\phi_{i0}^2/\sigma_{i0}^2)\mathbf{R}_{X_i X_i}$ is a positive definite matrix with probability 1. Also note that in the case of $I(1)$ regressors, the MLEs of the long-run and short-run parameters are asymptotically distributed independently of each other. [For a proof of (17), see Section A.3 in the Appendix.]

Once the pooled MLE of the long-run parameters, $\hat{\boldsymbol{\theta}}$, is successfully computed, the short-run coefficients, including the group-specific error-correction coefficients, ϕ_i can be consistently estimated by running the individual ordinary least squares (OLS) regressions of $\Delta \mathbf{y}_i$ on $(\hat{\boldsymbol{\xi}}_i, \mathbf{W}_i), i = 1, \ldots, N$, where $\hat{\boldsymbol{\xi}}_i = \mathbf{y}_{i,-1} - \mathbf{X}_i\hat{\boldsymbol{\theta}}$. The covariance matrix of the MLEs, $(\hat{\boldsymbol{\theta}}', \hat{\phi}_1, \ldots, \hat{\phi}_N, \hat{\boldsymbol{\kappa}}_1', \ldots, \hat{\boldsymbol{\kappa}}_N')'$, is then consistently estimated by the inverse of

$$\begin{bmatrix} \sum_{i=1}^{N} \frac{\hat{\phi}_i^2 \mathbf{X}_i'\mathbf{X}_i'}{\hat{\sigma}_i^2} & \frac{-\hat{\phi}_1 \mathbf{X}_1'\hat{\boldsymbol{\xi}}_1}{\hat{\sigma}_1^2} & \cdots & \frac{-\hat{\phi}_N \mathbf{X}_N'\hat{\boldsymbol{\xi}}_N}{\hat{\sigma}_N^2} & \frac{-\hat{\phi}_1 \mathbf{X}_1'\mathbf{W}_1}{\hat{\sigma}_1^2} & \cdots & \frac{-\hat{\phi}_1 \mathbf{X}_N'\mathbf{W}_N}{\hat{\sigma}_N^2} \\ & \frac{\hat{\boldsymbol{\xi}}_1'\hat{\boldsymbol{\xi}}_1}{\hat{\sigma}_1^2} & \cdots & 0 & \frac{\hat{\boldsymbol{\xi}}_1'\mathbf{W}_1}{\hat{\sigma}_1^2} & \cdots & 0 \\ & & \vdots & \vdots & & \vdots & \vdots \\ & & & \frac{\hat{\boldsymbol{\xi}}_N'\hat{\boldsymbol{\xi}}_N}{\hat{\sigma}_N^2} & 0 & \cdots & \frac{\hat{\boldsymbol{\xi}}_N'\mathbf{W}_N}{\hat{\sigma}_N^2} \\ & & & & \frac{\mathbf{W}_1'\mathbf{W}_1}{\hat{\sigma}_1^2} & \cdots & 0 \\ & & & & & \vdots & \vdots \\ & & & & & & \frac{\mathbf{W}_N'\mathbf{W}_N}{\hat{\sigma}_N^2} \end{bmatrix}.$$

4.3 The Case of Large *T* and Large *N*

In this case the mean of the error correction coefficients and the other short-run parameters can be estimated consistently by the unweighted average of the individual coefficients (or the MG estimators):

$$\hat{\phi}_{\mathrm{MG}} = N^{-1}\sum_{i=1}^{N}\hat{\phi}_i, \qquad \hat{\boldsymbol{\kappa}}_{\mathrm{MG}} = N^{-1}\sum_{i=1}^{N}\hat{\boldsymbol{\kappa}}_i.$$

The variance of these estimators can be consistently estimated along the lines suggested by Pesaran, Smith, and Im (1996). For example, in the case of $\hat{\phi}_{\mathrm{MG}}$, a consistent estimator of the variance of $\hat{\phi}_{\mathrm{MG}}$ is given by

$$\hat{\Delta}_{\hat{\phi}} = \frac{1}{N-1}\sum_{i=1}^{N}(\hat{\phi}_i - \hat{\phi}_{\mathrm{MG}})^2.$$

Alternatively, one can use the weighted estimator proposed by Swamy (1970) in the context of the static random coefficient models. But as was shown by Hsiao, Pesaran, and Tahmiscioglu (1999) and noted earlier in this article, the Swamy estimator (also known as the empirical Bayes estimator) and the MG estimator are asymptotically equivalent as $T \to \infty$ and $N \to \infty$ such that $\sqrt{N}/T \to 0$. Under these conditions, the asymptotic distribution of $\hat{\phi}_{\mathrm{MG}}$, for example, is given by

$$\sqrt{N}(\hat{\phi}_{MG} - \phi) \overset{a}{\sim} N(0, \Delta_\phi),$$

where $\phi = E(\phi_i)$ and $\Delta_\phi = \text{var}(\phi_i)$.

For the common long-run coefficients, $\boldsymbol{\theta}$, the pooled MLE is consistent as long as $T \to \infty$, irrespective of whether N is large or not. To obtain the asymptotic distribution of $\hat{\boldsymbol{\theta}}$ when N is large, we need to assume that N is a monotonic function of T, say $N(T)$, such that $N \to \infty$ *only* as $T \to \infty$. In this setting the rate of convergence of $\hat{\boldsymbol{\theta}}$ toward its true value is given by $\sqrt{NT}$ in the case where the regressors are $I(0)$. For this result to hold, the limit of

$$N^{-1}\sum_{i=1}^{N}\frac{\phi_{i0}^2}{\sigma_{i0}^2}\left(\mathbf{Q}_{X_iX_i} - \mathbf{Q}_{X_i\xi_{i0}}q_{\xi_{i0}\xi_{i0}}^{-1}\mathbf{Q}'_{X_i\xi_{i0}}\right)$$

as $N \to \infty$ must be a positive definite matrix [see (14)]. When the regressors are $I(1)$, the rate of convergence of $\hat{\boldsymbol{\theta}}$ is given by $T\sqrt{N}$ as long as

$$N^{-1}\sum_{i=1}^{N}\frac{\phi_{i0}^2}{\sigma_{i0}^2}\mathbf{R}_{X_iX_i}$$

tends to a positive definite matrix with probability 1, as $N \to \infty$ [see (17)]. Notice that $\hat{\boldsymbol{\theta}}$ will not be consistent for finite T, even if $N \to \infty$.

5. EMPIRICAL APPLICATIONS

Before considering the two examples, we briefly discuss three modeling issues. The first issue is that although the aforementioned theory assumes that all long-run coefficients are the same across groups, it is straightforward to adapt the PMG estimator to allow only a subset of the long-run coefficients to be the same while the others differ. Details have been given in the earlier version of this article (Pesaran, Shin, and Smith 1997). The second issue is that we need to choose between the alternative specifications. Tests of homogeneity of error variances and/or short- or long-run slope coefficients can be easily carried out using likelihood ratio and other classical statistical tests, because the PMG and fixed-effects estimators are restricted versions of the set of individual group equations. Although it is common to use pooled estimators without testing the implied restrictions, in the case of cross-country studies the likelihood ratio tests usually reject equality of error variances and/or slopes (short-run or long-run) at conventional significance levels. This is the case in both of our examples. The interpretation of this feature has been discussed extensively by Pesaran, Smith, and Akiyama (1998), and we return to this work in our conclusion. An alternative to likelihood ratio tests would be to use Hausman (1978)-type tests. The MG estimator provides consistent estimates of the mean of the long-run coefficients, though these will be inefficient if slope homogeneity holds. Under long-run slope homogeneity, the pooled estimators are consistent and efficient. Therefore, the effect of heterogeneity on the means of the coefficients can be determined by a Hausman-type test applied to the difference between the MG and the PMG or the fixed-effects estimators. (The details of such tests were discussed in Pesaran, Smith and Im 1996.) The third issue is that although the MG estimator is consistent for large N and T, for small T the familiar lagged dependent variable bias causes the estimates of λ_i and $\phi_i = (\lambda_i - 1)$ to underestimate their true values. Large N does not help with this problem, as all of the estimates are biased in the same direction. Pesaran and Zhao (1999) proposed a bias-corrected MG estimator that directly adjusts the long-run coefficient by an estimate of its bias. In the case of the pooled estimators, the downward-lagged dependent variable bias, which they also suffer, may offset the upward heterogeneity bias discussed by Pesaran and Smith (1995). In empirical applications it may be difficult to judge the relative effect of the two biases, making inference about the speed of adjustment difficult. This is a feature of both of our examples.

5.1 The Consumption Function in the OECD

The first example that we examine is a standard consumption function of the Davidson et al. (1978) type for a sample of OECD countries. Similar specifications have also been estimated for a number of developing countries by Haque and Montiel (1989). We assume that the long-run consumption function is given by

$$c_{it} = \theta_{0i} + \theta_{1i}y_{it}^d + \theta_{2i}\pi_{it} + u_{it},$$
$$i = 1, 2, \ldots, N, \qquad t = 1, 2, \ldots, T,$$

where c_{it} is the logarithm of real consumption per capita, y_{it}^d is the logarithm of real per capita disposable income, and π_{it} is the rate of inflation. Most theories of aggregate consumption would suggest that $\theta_{1i} = 1$. The PMG estimation procedure allows us to estimate a common long-run coefficient and test whether it is unity. The inflation variable, π_{it}, is a proxy for various wealth effects, and we would expect $\theta_{2i} < 0$. We assume that all of these variables are $I(1)$ and cointegrated, making u_{it} an $I(0)$ process for all i. In this application we take the maximum lag as being 1; thus the autoregressive distributed lag (ARDL) $(1,1,1)$ equation is

$$c_{it} = \mu_i + \delta_{10i}y_{it}^d + \delta_{11i}y_{i,t-1}^d + \delta_{20i}\pi_{it} + \delta_{21i}\pi_{i,t-1} + \lambda_i c_{i,t-1} + \varepsilon_{it},$$

and the error correction equation is

$$\Delta c_{it} = \phi_i(c_{i,t-1} - \theta_{0i} - \theta_{1i}y_{it} - \theta_{2i}\pi_{it}) - \delta_{11i}\Delta y_{it}^d - \delta_{21i}\Delta\pi_{it} + \varepsilon_{it}.$$

where

$$\theta_{0i} = \frac{\mu_i}{1-\lambda_i}, \qquad \theta_{1i} = \frac{\delta_{10i} + \delta_{11i}}{1-\lambda_i},$$

$$\theta_{2i} = \frac{\delta_{20i} + \delta_{21i}}{1-\lambda_i}, \qquad \phi_i = -(1-\lambda_i).$$

The foregoing error correction equations are written in terms of current, rather than lagged levels of the exogenous regressors. This allows an ARDL$(1,0,0)$ as a special case.

We measure consumption by the logarithm of total real private consumption per capita and inflation by the change in the logarithm of the consumption deflator. The initial measure of income that we use is national disposable per capita income deflated by the consumption deflator, NDI. (The data are taken from the OECD National Accounts Statistics and were collected as part of an IMF project on international saving rates.) Using 1960 and 1961 to create lags, we have data for 32 years (1962–1993) for 23 countries and 31 years (1962–1992) for Belgium.

First, a common ARDL$(1, 1, 1)$ was run for each country separately. The results are given in the earlier version of this article (Pesaran, Shin, and Smith 1997). For a long-run relationship to exist, we require that $\phi_i \neq 0$. It is clear that in a number of countries, the hypothesis of no long-run relation would not be rejected. (Pesaran, Shin, and R. J. Smith [1999] develop a test for the existence of a long-run relationship in ARDLs of this form.) The long-run income elasticities range from .62 in Switzerland to 1.19 in the United States and are significantly less than unity in nine countries and significantly greater than unity in three (Italy, the United Kingdom, and the United States). The long-run inflation coefficient is more dispersed, ranging between 1.46 in Germany and −1.25 in Canada. However, it is negative in all but four countries. More than 60% of the change in the logarithm of per capita consumption is explained in all but three countries: Luxembourg, Norway, and Austria. The standard error of regression varies from .5% in France to 3.3% in Turkey, and the equality of error variances does not seem to be an appropriate assumption—a result born out by formal statistical tests. At the 5% level, there is evidence of serial correlation in the equations for two of the 24 countries, and of functional form misspecification in three, nonnormal errors in two, and heteroscedasticity in one. The tests have been described by Pesaran and Pesaran (1997). The RESET tests for functional form and the test of heteroscedasticity are based on the fitted values for the changes in the logarithm of per capita consumption. The fact that 17 of the 24 country-specific equations show no evidence of misspecification is reassuring.

Table 1 presents the alternative pooled estimates: MG, which imposes no restrictions; PMG, which imposes common long-run effects; and DFE, which constrains all of the slope coefficients and error variances to be the same. The PMG computations were carried out using the Newton-Raphson algorithm in a program written in Gauss. The program and data are available on *http://www.econ.cam.ac.uk/faculty/pesaran*. The program

Table 1. Alternative Pooled Estimates for ARDL(1, 1, 1) Consumption Functions for OECD Countries Over the Period 1962–1993 Using National Disposable Income

	MG	PMG	DFE
Income elasticity, θ_1	.918 (.027)	.904 (.010)	.912 (.045)
Inflation effect, θ_2	−.353 (.117)	−.466 (.063)	−.266 (.099)
Speed of adjustment, ϕ	−.306 (.030)	−.200 (.032)	−.179 (.042)
Maximized log likelihood	2,390	2,247	1,999
Number of parameters estimated	168	122	30

NOTE: Figures in parentheses are asymptotic standard errors. In the case of the dynamic fixed effects estimates the standard errors are corrected for possible heteroscedasticity in the cross-sectional error variances.

allows the user to start the iterations with different sets of initial values, depending on the nature of the ARDL specification across the groups. When the same ARDL is estimated across the countries, the MG and DFE estimates of the long-run coefficients can be used as initial values. In the examples considered here, these resulted in the same maximum for the pooled log-likelihood function. This has not been the case in some other examples.

The DFE standard errors are corrected for the heteroscedasticity of error variances across countries; the uncorrected ones are substantially smaller. The heteroscedasticity robust standard errors are computed allowing for a general covariance matrix of the disturbances ε_{it} across i (see, e.g., Baltagi 1995, pp. 12–13). The three estimates of the long-run income elasticities are very similar, close to .91 and significantly less than unity. The long-run inflation coefficients are all significantly negative, though the estimates differ somewhat. As the econometric theory suggests, imposing homogeneity causes an upward bias in the coefficient of the lagged dependent variable, and the MG estimate suggests much faster adjustment than the PMG or DFE. The MG estimate of the adjustment coefficient also has the smallest standard error.

Imposing long-run homogeneity reduces the standard errors of the long-run coefficients, but does not change the estimates very much. This is confirmed by the Hausman test statistic of 1.19, which is $\chi^2(2)$ under the null hypothesis of no difference between the MG and PMG estimators. As is clear from Table 1, likelihood ratio tests at conventional significance levels, on the other hand, would strongly reject all of the restrictions, including homogeneity of long-run coefficients. This is true for both income and inflation. If homogeneity of just the long-run income elasticities is imposed (23 restrictions), then the maximized log-likelihood (MLL) falls from 2,390 to 2,270. If homogeneity of both income and inflation long-run effects is imposed (46 restrictions), then the MLL falls to 2,247.

One advantage of the PMG over the traditional DFE model is that it can allow the short-run dynamic specification to differ from country to country. The lag order was first chosen in each country on the unrestricted model by the Schwarz Bayesian criterion (SBC), subject to a maximum lag of 1. Then, using these SBC-determined lag orders, homogeneity was imposed. The most common choice, in half of the countries, was an ARDL$(1, 1, 0)$, one lag of consumption and income but only current inflation. Performance on the misspecification tests and estimates of the long-run effects were very similar to those obtained using an ARDL$(1, 1, 1)$ model. Again, the Hausman test statistic does not reject equality between the MG and PMG estimates, whereas the likelihood ratio test statistic of 281 rejects equality of all of the long-run coefficients. Notice that under the null hypothesis, this statistic is asymptotically distributed as $\chi^2(46)$. In this example, estimates of the long-run coefficients are robust to the order of the ARDL. This is partly because T is large; as shown in the next example, when T is small, the choice of lag order is more important.

Although data for national disposable income is widely available, it is not the most appropriate theoretical measure of income. Thus we also estimated an equation using a better measure, private disposable labor income (interest and dividend income are excluded). Data availability reduces the sample to 15 countries, with some countries having as few as 8 observations (the Netherlands). The characteristics of these data allow us to investigate the sensitivity of the estimators to a number of interesting features. The panel is very unbalanced, with T very small in some cases; in these cases, choosing lag order by the SBC is more reliable than using a common ARDL(1, 1, 1), which tends to show misspecification. There is also an extreme outlier. In Sweden, where the SBC chose ARDL(1, 1, 0), the speed of adjustment was −.03 (.154), the long-run income elasticity was −3.74 (25.22), and the long-run inflation coefficient was −7.768 (40.36). Although this equation passes the four misspecification tests, the fit is very poor, and it distorts the MG estimates.

Table 2 presents the alternative pooled estimates of the long-run income elasticity for three groups of countries ($N = 15, 14$, and 9), for three ARDL specifications. The $N = 15$ group includes all the countries for which there are data on private disposable labor income. The $N = 14$ group excludes Sweden. The $N = 9$ group also excludes countries for which T is 13 or less (Italy, Netherlands, New Zealand, Portugal, Spain). The effect of Sweden on the MG estimator in the $N = 15$ group is very obvious, completely distorting the ARDL$(1, 1, 1)$ estimate and severely biasing the SBC estimate. The PMG estimates are much less sensitive, as one would expect, given the large standard errors on the Swedish estimates. Dropping Sweden from the sample hardly changes the PMG estimate, but changes the MG substantially. Again, the Hausman test statistic does not reject equality between the MG and PMG, whereas the likelihood ratio test statistic rejects equality of all of the long-run coefficients.

These results indicate that the PMG seems quite robust to outliers and to choice of lag order. Overall the estimates suggest that the average long-run income elasticity is rather larger than .9, but significantly less than unity on PMG standard errors. However, these standard errors may be underestimates. The average long-run inflation effect is significantly less than 0. These general conclusions seem robust to lag order, sample, and estimation method. The average adjustment coefficient seems to be significantly less than 0 and greater than −.5, but the estimates of the adjustment coefficients tend to show more sensitivity to the choice of the estimation method. The example of the consumption function was chosen to demonstrate the PMG estimator because of its familiarity and importance. However, it should be recognized that modeling consumption raises many difficult issues not captured by this simple model. Clearly, some important variables are omitted, including initial wealth, real interest rate effects, credit regulations, government budget surpluses (deficits), and demographics. This type of equation has proved structurally unstable in a number of the countries in our sample. In many of the countries one would not be able to reject the null hypothesis of no long-run relationship, though these tests have low power. The MG estimates are also subject to small T bias because of the familiar lagged dependent variable problem.

Table 2. Alternative Pooled Estimates of the Long-Run Consumption Income Elasticity Using per Capita Real Private Disposable Labor Income

N	ARDL	MG	PMG	DFE
15	1, 0, 0	.948 (.070)	.933 (.010)	.936 (.022)
15	1, 1, 1	−12.8 (13.8)	.918 (.016)	.935 (.023)
15	SBC	.669 (.319)	.938 (.013)	
14	1, 0, 0	.999 (.052)	.934 (.010)	.94 (.012)
14	1, 1, 1	.918 (.066)	.919 (.016)	.943 (.021)
14	SBC	.985 (.054)	.939 (.013)	
9	1, 0, 0	.993 (.060)	.926 (.011)	.931 (.014)
9	1, 1, 1	.916 (.100)	.927 (.015)	.925 (.025)
9	SBC	.995 (.059)	.941 (.013)	

NOTE: Figures in parentheses are asymptotic standard errors. In the case of the dynamic fixed effects estimates the standard errors are corrected for possible heteroscedasticity in the cross-sectional error variances.

5.2 Energy Demand in Asian Developing Countries

Our second example involves explaining the logarithm of energy consumption (measured in tons of oil equivalents [TOE] per capita), e_{it}, by the logarithm of real per capita output in international prices taken from the Penn World Tables, y_{it}, and by the logarithm of real energy prices (average energy prices per TOE in local currency, deflated by the consumer price index), p_{it}. The data are for 10 Asian developing countries for the years 1974–1990; thus both N and T are small. This example is drawn from Pesaran, Smith, and Akiyama (1998), who discussed the data in more detail and investigated functional form, dynamics, disaggregation, and various other issues.

The initial unrestricted model is a partial adjustment (ARDL(1, 0, 0)) model:

$$\Delta e_{it} = \phi_i(e_{it-1}-\theta_{0i}-\theta_{1i}y_{it}-\theta_{2i}p_{it})+\varepsilon_{it}, \quad i = 1, 2, \ldots, 10.$$

Partial adjustment and homogeneity of degree zero in prices were not rejected in all but one of the 10 countries (Taiwan). In the country-specific regressions, the long-run income and price elasticity estimates for Malaysia, Sri Lanka, and Bangladesh are implausible, which could be due to data inadequacies and the high level of aggregation. Apart from these, the estimates are reasonable. The long-run income elasticity ranges from .835 to 1.564, with an average of 1.12; the long-run price elasticities range from .05 to −.488, with an average estimate of −.22. All of the estimates of the adjustment coefficients, ϕ_i, are negative and fall in the range −.132 to −.825. The standard error of the regression varies from 1.7% in the case of Thailand to 6.3% in Sri Lanka; so again, the assumption of constant error variances across countries seems inappropriate. Diagnostic tests reveal few problems: one failure for serial correlation and one for normality at the 5% level. When the order of each lag is chosen by the SBC for each country, starting with a general ARDL(1, 1, 1) specification, the ARDL(1, 0, 0) is chosen for seven countries, a static model is chosen for India and Sri Lanka, and an unstable ARDL(1, 0, 1) is chosen for Taiwan.

The alternative pooled estimators for the ARDL(1, 0, 0) specification are presented in Table 3. The table presents es-

Table 3. Alternative Pooled Estimators for ARDL(1, 0, 0) Energy Demand Function for 10 Asian Economies Over the Period 1974–1990

	MG estimators	PMG estimators	DFE estimators	Static fixed-effects estimators
Output	1.228	1.184	1.301	1.009
Elasticity ($\hat{\theta}_1$)	(.183)	(.039)	(.109)	(.037)
Price	−.261	−.339	−.365	−.067
Elasticity ($\hat{\theta}_2$)	(.118)	(.033)	(.097)	(.030)
Adjustment	−.524	−.298	−.235	−1
Coefficient ($\hat{\phi}$)	(.070)	(.063)	(.040)	(N/A)
Log-likelihood	347.12	322.79	288.36	186.95
$N \times T$	170	170	170	170
No. of estimated parameters	50	32	15	13

NOTE: Figures in parentheses are asymptotic standard errors. In the case of the dynamic fixed effects estimates the standard errors are corrected for possible heteroscedasticity in the cross-sectional error variances.

Table 4. Alternative Pooled Estimators for ARDL-SBC Energy Demand Function

	MG estimators	PMG estimators	DFE estimators ARDL(1, 1, 1)
Output	1.277	1.171	1.181
Elasticity ($\hat{\theta}_1$)	(.182)	(.036)	(.147)
Price	−.160	−.301	−.324
Elasticity ($\hat{\theta}_2$)	(.164)	(.028)	(.0137)
Adjustment	−.502	−.417	−.153
Coefficient ($\hat{\phi}$)	(.113)	(.121)	(.042)
Log-likelihood	356.81	315.41	300.27
$N \times T$	170	170	170
No. of estimated parameters	51	33	17

NOTE: Figures in parentheses are asymptotic standard errors. In the case of the dynamic fixed effects estimates the standard errors are corrected for possible heteroscedasticity in the cross-sectional error variances.

timates of the long-run output and price elasticities and the adjustment coefficients, together with the MLL, the number of observations, and the number of parameters estimated (including the error variances). As in the previous example, likelihood ratio tests reject the hypothesis of equality of long-run coefficients, whereas Hausman tests do not reject this hypothesis when the PMG and MG estimators are compared. Because the MG estimates have large standard errors, the Hausman test is likely to have low power. If the focus of the analysis is on average (across countries) income and price elasticities, then the PMG estimates are probably preferable to the MG estimates on the grounds of their better precision and the fact that they are less sensitive to outlier estimates. In this context, the Hausman test can be seen as providing formal statistical evidence that we are not in gross violation of the data by relying on PMG estimates rather than the MG estimates. The estimates suggest a long-run income elasticity of 1.18 (.039) and a price elasticity of −.34 (.033). The PMG estimates are close to the MG estimates, and the DFE estimates are rather larger. The dynamics clearly matter, and the static fixed-effects estimator has an insignificant price effect. The standard errors of both the PMG and the DFE are very much smaller than those of the MG: pooling sharpens the estimates considerably. As before, pooling also leads to a much smaller estimated speed of adjustment; the MG estimates suggest speeds of convergence to equilibrium of around 50% per year; the PMG, 30%; and the DFE, about 20%.

Table 4 gives MG and PMG estimates when the order of the specification in the individual countries is chosen by the SBC. This procedure cannot be used with the fixed-effects estimator; the ARDL(1, 1, 1) estimates are given instead. Again, the PMG estimates of the long-run price and income elasticities hardly change, though the estimated speed of adjustment is rather higher, partly because the SBC chooses the static model, with instantaneous adjustment, in the case of some countries. Using the SBC gives a substantial improvement in the MLL for the MG estimator (at 357 it is close to the ARDL(1, 1, 1) MLL of 362, with far fewer parameters) but less for the PMG, where the SBC MLL is worse than the ARDL(1, 0, 0) MLL. It is clear that homogeneity restrictions and dynamic specification interact in a complex way. What might be the optimal order for the country-specific estimates may not be the optimal order when cross-country homogeneity restrictions are imposed. The rather serious policy implications of an income elasticity around 1.2 and a price elasticity around −.3 have been discussed by Pesaran, Smith, and Akiyama (1998).

6. CONCLUDING REMARKS

The PMG estimator, which assumes homogeneous long-run coefficients, provides a useful intermediate alternative between estimating separate regressions, which allows all coefficients and error variances to differ across the groups, and conventional fixed-effects estimators, which assume that all slope coefficients and error variances are the same. It has the practical advantage in allowing the short-run dynamics to be data determined for each country, taking into account the number of time series observations available in each case. A number of unresolved issues remain, however. For small T, all of the estimators (group-specific, MG, PMG, and fixed-effects) will be subject to the familiar downward bias on the coefficient of the lagged dependent variable. Because the bias is in the same direction for each group, averaging or pooling does not reduce this bias. Bias corrections are available in the literature (e.g., Kiviet and Phillips 1993), but these apply to the short-run coefficients. Because the long-run coefficient is a nonlinear function of the short-run coefficients, procedures that remove the bias in the short-run coefficients can leave the long-run coefficient biased. Pesaran and Zhao (1999) discussed how the bias in the long-run coefficient can be reduced. The MG estimator used in this article is a simple unweighted mean of the coefficients. Weighted means are an obvious alternative; Hsiao et al. (1999) have considered Bayes estimation of the means of short-run coefficients in dynamic panel data models. Estimation in this article was conducted under the assumption that a long-run relationship existed. It would be useful to have a panel test for the existence of a long-run relationship when the variables are $I(1)$, similar to the panel unit root test suggested by Im, Pesaran, and Shin (1997).

Perhaps the most important issue is interpretation of the heterogeneity. Most studies that estimate separate relationships for a number of groups find differences in coefficients that are not only statistically significant, but also economically implausible. In our empirical examples such cases were the income elasticity of consumption out of labor income in Sweden and the income elasticity of demand for energy in Sri Lanka. Despite this, the MG and PMG estimates of the long-run coefficients tend to be sensible. One explanation is that the group-specific estimates are biased because of sample-specific omitted variables or measurement errors correlated with the regressors. If one is estimating an equation for a single group, then one might experiment with different specifications or alternative data until plausible estimates are obtained. When estimating equations for large numbers of groups, where no other data is available in many cases, this is not an option. If the coefficients really are the same and the bias-inducing correlations are not systematic (i.e., they average to 0 over groups), then pooled estimation will be appropriate despite the homogeneity restrictions being rejected. However, there is no obvious way of determining from the data that this is the case. This raises obvious problems for inference that require further analysis.

APPENDIX: MATHEMATICAL PROOFS

To save space, we give the proofs only for cases where the regressors are $I(1)$. Proof for the $I(0)$ case is given in the appendix to the earlier version of this article (Pesaran et al. 1997).

A.1 Preliminary Results

A.1.1 Some Useful Probability Limits

To simplify the notations in what follows, we denote $\boldsymbol{\xi}_i(\boldsymbol{\theta})$ by $\boldsymbol{\xi}_i$ and $\boldsymbol{\xi}_i(\boldsymbol{\theta}_0)$ by $\boldsymbol{\xi}_{i0}$. When $\mathbf{x}_{it}$ are all $I(1)$, the following probability limits exist as $T \to \infty$, for each i:

$$T^{-2}\mathbf{X}_i'\mathbf{H}_i\mathbf{X}_i \Rightarrow \mathbf{R}_{X_iX_i}, \qquad T^{-1}\mathbf{X}_i'\mathbf{H}_i\boldsymbol{\xi}_{i0} \Rightarrow \mathbf{R}_{X_i\xi_{i0}},$$
$$T^{-1}\mathbf{X}_i'\mathbf{H}_i\boldsymbol{\varepsilon}_i = O_p(1), \tag{A.1}$$

where $\mathbf{R}_{X_iX_i}$ and $\mathbf{R}_{X_i\xi_{i0}}$ are $O_p(1)$ random matrices. We also have

$$T^{-1/2}\boldsymbol{\xi}_{i0}'\mathbf{H}_i\boldsymbol{\varepsilon}_i = O_p(1), \qquad T^{-1}\boldsymbol{\xi}_{i0}'\mathbf{H}_i\boldsymbol{\xi}_{i0} \xrightarrow{p} q_{\xi_{i0}\xi_{i0}},$$

and

$$T^{-1}\boldsymbol{\varepsilon}_i'\mathbf{H}_i\boldsymbol{\varepsilon}_i = \sigma_{i0}^2 + o_p(1), \qquad i = 1, \ldots, N. \tag{A.2}$$

A.1.2 Decomposition of the Log-Likelihood Ratio

Using (8), it is easily seen that

$$T^{-1}[l_T(\boldsymbol{\varphi}_0) - l_T(\boldsymbol{\varphi})] = \frac{1}{2}(\mathcal{A}_T + \mathcal{B}_T), \tag{A.3}$$

where

$$\mathcal{A}_T = \mathcal{A}_\sigma + \mathcal{C}_T, \tag{A.4}$$

$$\mathcal{A}_\sigma = \sum_{i=1}^N \left(\frac{\sigma_{i0}^2}{\sigma_i^2} - \ln\frac{\sigma_{i0}^2}{\sigma_i^2} - 1\right),$$

$$\mathcal{C}_T = \sum_{i=1}^N \left(\frac{1}{\sigma_i^2} - \frac{1}{\sigma_{i0}^2}\right)\left(\frac{\boldsymbol{\varepsilon}_i'\mathbf{H}_i\boldsymbol{\varepsilon}_i}{T} - \sigma_{i0}^2\right), \tag{A.5}$$

and

$$\mathcal{B}_T = T^{-1}\sum_{i=1}^N \frac{1}{\sigma_i^2}[(\Delta\mathbf{y}_i - \phi_i\boldsymbol{\xi}_i)'\mathbf{H}_i(\Delta\mathbf{y}_i - \phi_i\boldsymbol{\xi}_i) - \boldsymbol{\varepsilon}_i'\mathbf{H}_i\boldsymbol{\varepsilon}_i]. \tag{A.6}$$

Also, using the result

$$\begin{aligned}\phi_i\boldsymbol{\xi}_i &= (\phi_i - \phi_{i0} + \phi_{i0})(\boldsymbol{\xi}_i - \boldsymbol{\xi}_{i0} + \boldsymbol{\xi}_{i0}) \\ &= -\phi_i\mathbf{X}_i(\boldsymbol{\theta} - \boldsymbol{\theta}_0) + (\phi_i - \phi_{i0})\boldsymbol{\xi}_{i0} + \phi_{i0}\boldsymbol{\xi}_{i0},\end{aligned}$$

and noting that $\Delta\mathbf{y}_i = \phi_{i0}\boldsymbol{\xi}_{i0} + \mathbf{W}_i\boldsymbol{\kappa}_{i0} + \boldsymbol{\varepsilon}_i$, we have

$$\Delta\mathbf{y}_i - \phi_i\boldsymbol{\xi}_i = \boldsymbol{\varepsilon}_i + \mathbf{W}_i\boldsymbol{\kappa}_{i0} + \phi_i\mathbf{X}_i(\boldsymbol{\theta} - \boldsymbol{\theta}_0) - (\phi_i - \phi_{i0})\boldsymbol{\xi}_{i0}. \tag{A.7}$$

[See (6), and note that under the data-generating process, $\boldsymbol{\varphi} = \boldsymbol{\varphi}_0$.] Substituting (A.7) in (A.6), and after some algebra, we have

$$\begin{aligned}\mathcal{B}_T &= (\boldsymbol{\theta} - \boldsymbol{\theta}_0)'\left(\sum_{i=1}^N \frac{\phi_i^2}{\sigma_i^2}\frac{\mathbf{X}_i'\mathbf{H}_i\mathbf{X}_i}{T}\right)(\boldsymbol{\theta} - \boldsymbol{\theta}_0) \\ &\quad + \sum_{i=1}^N \left[\frac{(\phi_i - \phi_{i0})^2}{\sigma_i^2}\right]\left(\frac{\boldsymbol{\xi}_{i0}'\mathbf{H}_i\boldsymbol{\xi}_{i0}}{T}\right) \\ &\quad - 2\sum_{i=1}^N \left[\frac{\phi_i(\phi_i - \phi_{i0})}{\sigma_i^2}\right]\left(\frac{\boldsymbol{\xi}_{i0}'\mathbf{H}_i\mathbf{X}_i(\boldsymbol{\theta} - \boldsymbol{\theta}_0)}{T}\right) \\ &\quad + 2(\boldsymbol{\theta} - \boldsymbol{\theta}_0)'\left(\sum_{i=1}^N \frac{\phi_i}{\sigma_i^2}\frac{\mathbf{X}_i'\mathbf{H}_i\boldsymbol{\varepsilon}_i}{T}\right) \\ &\quad - 2\sum_{i=1}^N \left[\frac{(\phi_i - \phi_{i0})}{\sigma_i^2}\right]\left(\frac{\boldsymbol{\xi}_{i0}'\mathbf{H}_i\boldsymbol{\varepsilon}_i}{T}\right),\end{aligned} \tag{A.8}$$

which can also be written more compactly as [recall that $\boldsymbol{\psi} = (\boldsymbol{\theta}', \boldsymbol{\phi}')'$]

$$\mathcal{B}_T = (\boldsymbol{\psi} - \boldsymbol{\psi}_0)'\mathbf{G}_T(\boldsymbol{\psi} - \boldsymbol{\psi}_0) + 2(\boldsymbol{\psi} - \boldsymbol{\psi}_0)'\mathbf{f}_T, \tag{A.9}$$

where

$\mathbf{G}_T$

$$= \begin{bmatrix} \sum_{i=1}^N \frac{\phi_i^2}{\sigma_i^2}\frac{\mathbf{X}_i'\mathbf{H}_i\mathbf{X}_i}{T} & -\frac{\phi_1}{\sigma_1^2}\frac{\mathbf{X}_1'\mathbf{H}_1\boldsymbol{\xi}_{10}}{T} & \cdots & -\frac{\phi_N}{\sigma_N^2}\frac{\mathbf{X}_N'\mathbf{H}_N\boldsymbol{\xi}_{N0}}{T} \\ -\frac{\phi_1}{\sigma_1^2}\frac{\boldsymbol{\xi}_{10}'\mathbf{H}_1\mathbf{X}_1}{T} & \frac{1}{\sigma_1^2}\frac{\boldsymbol{\xi}_{10}'\mathbf{H}_1\boldsymbol{\xi}_{10}}{T} & \cdots & 0 \\ -\frac{\phi_2}{\sigma_2^2}\frac{\boldsymbol{\xi}_{20}'\mathbf{H}_2\mathbf{X}_2}{T} & 0 & \cdots & 0 \\ \vdots & \vdots & \vdots & \vdots \\ -\frac{\phi_N}{\sigma_N^2}\frac{\boldsymbol{\xi}_{N0}'\mathbf{H}_N\mathbf{X}_N}{T} & 0 & \cdots & \frac{1}{\sigma_N^2}\frac{\boldsymbol{\xi}_{N0}'\mathbf{H}_N\boldsymbol{\xi}_{N0}}{T} \end{bmatrix},$$

$$\mathbf{f}_T = \begin{bmatrix} \sum_{i=1}^N \frac{\phi_i}{\sigma_i^2}\frac{\mathbf{X}_i'\mathbf{H}_i\boldsymbol{\varepsilon}_i}{T} \\ -\frac{1}{\sigma_1^2}\frac{\boldsymbol{\xi}_{10}'\mathbf{H}_1\boldsymbol{\varepsilon}_1}{T} \\ \vdots \\ -\frac{1}{\sigma_N^2}\frac{\boldsymbol{\xi}_{N0}'\mathbf{H}_N\boldsymbol{\varepsilon}_N}{T} \end{bmatrix}. \tag{A.10}$$

In terms of the matrix notations used in Section 3, $\mathbf{G}_T$ can also be written as

$$\mathbf{G}_T = \mathbf{Z}_1'(\varphi)[\mathbf{I} - \check{\mathbf{W}}(\sigma)(\check{\mathbf{W}}'(\sigma)\check{\mathbf{W}}(\sigma))^{-1}\check{\mathbf{W}}'(\sigma)]\mathbf{Z}_1(\varphi), \quad \text{(A.11)}$$

where $\mathbf{Z}_1(\varphi) = [\bar{\mathbf{X}}(\phi,\sigma)\vdots\boldsymbol{\xi}(\theta,\sigma)]$, $\bar{\mathbf{X}}(\phi,\sigma) = -[(\phi_1/\sigma_1)\mathbf{X}_1', (\phi_2/\sigma_2)\mathbf{X}_2', \ldots, (\phi_N/\sigma_N)\mathbf{X}_N']'$, and $\check{\mathbf{W}}(\sigma)$ and $\check{\boldsymbol{\xi}}(\theta,\sigma)$ are block diagonal matrices with their ith blocks given by $\mathbf{W}_i/\sigma_i$ and $\xi_i(\theta)/\sigma_i$, with $\theta = \theta_0$. Therefore, $\mathbf{G}_T$ is the partitioned inverse of the upper left-hand corner of

$$\mathbf{Z}'(\varphi)\mathbf{Z}(\varphi) = \begin{pmatrix} \mathbf{Z}_1'(\varphi)\mathbf{Z}_1(\varphi) & \mathbf{Z}_1'(\varphi)\check{\mathbf{W}}(\sigma) \\ \check{\mathbf{W}}'(\sigma)\mathbf{Z}_1(\varphi) & \check{\mathbf{W}}'(\sigma)\check{\mathbf{W}}(\sigma) \end{pmatrix},$$

with $\varphi = \varphi_0$. Hence, under assumption 5, $\mathbf{G}_T$ is also a positive definite matrix.

A.2 Proof of Theorem 2: The Case of I(1) Regressors

Partition $\varphi = (\theta', \rho')'$ into the long-run parameters, θ, and the short-run parameters, $\rho = (\phi', \sigma')'$. Define the open ball $B(\theta_0, \delta_\theta) = \{\theta \in \Theta_\theta\colon \|\theta - \theta_0\| < \delta_\theta\}$ and its complement $\bar{B}(\theta_0, \delta_\theta) = \{\theta \in \Theta_\theta\colon \|\theta - \theta_0\| \geq \delta_\theta\}$.

To prove the consistency of the MLE of θ (denoted by $\hat{\theta}$), it is sufficient to show that for all values of $\rho \in \Theta_\rho = \Theta_\phi \times \Theta_\sigma$ and for every $\delta_\theta > 0$, (see, e.g., Saikkonen 1995, p. 903),

$$\lim_{T\to\infty} \Pr\{\inf_{\varphi \in \bar{B}(\theta_0,\delta_\theta)\times\Theta_\rho} T^{-1}[l_T(\varphi_0) - l_T(\varphi)] > 0\} = 1. \quad \text{(A.12)}$$

Using the results in (A.1) and (A.2) and under assumption 4, it is easily seen that except for the first term in (A.8), the inf over $\varphi \in \bar{B}(\theta_0, \delta_\theta) \times \Theta_\rho$ of all of the other terms are at most $O_p(1)$. Therefore,

$$\begin{aligned} &\inf_{\varphi \in \bar{B}(\theta_0,\delta_\theta)\times\Theta_\rho} T^{-1}[l_T(\varphi_0) - l_T(\varphi)] \\ &\geq T \inf_{\varphi \in \bar{B}(\theta_0,\delta_\theta)\times\Theta_\rho} \left\{(\theta - \theta_0)' \left(\sum_{i=1}^{N} \frac{\phi_i^2}{\sigma_i^2} \frac{\mathbf{X}_i'\mathbf{H}_i\mathbf{X}_i}{T^2}\right)(\theta - \theta_0)\right\} \\ &\quad + O_p(1), \\ &\geq T\delta_\theta^2 \lambda_{\min}(\mathbf{R}_T) + O_p(1), \end{aligned} \quad \text{(A.13)}$$

where $\lambda_{\min}(\mathbf{R}_T)$ is the smallest eigenvalue of $\mathbf{R}_T = \sum_{i=1}^{N} (\phi_i^2/\sigma_i^2)(\mathbf{X}_i'\mathbf{H}_i\mathbf{X}_i/T^2)$ defined over Θ_ρ. As $T \to \infty$, $\mathbf{R}_T$ converges to $\mathbf{R} = \sum_{i=1}^{N} (\phi_i^2/\sigma_i^2)\mathbf{R}_{X_iX_i}$ with probability 1, where $\mathbf{R}_{X_iX_i}$ is given by (A.1). But under assumptions 4 and 5, $\sum_{i=1}^{N} (\phi_i^2/\sigma_i^2)\mathbf{R}_{X_iX_i}$ is a positive definite matrix with probability 1 for all values of $\rho \in \Theta_\rho$. Hence, as $T \to \infty$, $\lambda_{\min}(\mathbf{R}_T)$ also weakly converges to $\lambda_{\min}(\mathbf{R}) > 0$, and the right side of (A.13) will increase without bounds with probability 1, which establishes the consistency of $\hat{\theta}$.

To prove the superconsistency of $\hat{\theta}$, and the consistency of the MLEs of the other parameters, we define $B(\rho_0, \delta_\rho) = \{\rho \in \Theta_\rho\colon \|\rho - \rho_0\| < \delta_\rho\}$, $B(\phi_0, \delta_\phi) = \{\phi \in \Theta_\phi\colon \|\phi - \phi_0\| < \delta_\phi\}$, $B(\sigma_0, \delta_\sigma) = \{\sigma \in \Theta_\sigma\colon \|\sigma - \sigma_0\| < \delta_\sigma\}$ and their complements, $\bar{B}(\rho_0, \delta_\rho)$, $\bar{B}(\phi_0, \delta_\phi)$, and $\bar{B}(\sigma_0, \delta_\sigma)$, and follow Saikkonen (1995) and define the open shrinking ball $\mathrm{N}_T(\theta_0, \delta_d) = \{\theta \in \Theta_\theta\colon T^{1/2}\|\theta - \theta_0\| < \delta_d\}$ for θ and its complement $\bar{\mathrm{N}}_T(\theta_0, \delta_d) = \{\theta \in \Theta_\theta\colon T^{1/2}\|\theta - \theta_0\| \geq \delta_d\}$. Because the consistency of $\hat{\theta}$ is already established, we focus our analysis on values of θ close to θ_0, defined by $\theta = \theta_0 + T^{-1/2}\mathbf{d}$, where we take $\mathbf{d}$ to be a $k \times 1$ vector of fixed constants defined on a compact set. The case where elements of $\mathbf{d}$ are allowed to increase without bound has already been covered. Notice that on $\bar{\mathrm{N}}_T(\theta_0, \delta_d)$, we also have $\|\mathbf{d}\| \geq \delta_d$.

Let $C(\varphi_0, \delta_\rho, \delta_d) = \cup_{\delta_d,\delta_\rho} (\bar{N}_T(\theta_0, \delta_d) \times \bar{B}(\rho_0, \delta_\rho))$, where the union is taken over all values of δ_d and δ_ρ such that $\delta_\varphi = (\delta_d^2 + \delta_\rho^2)^{1/2}$ and $\delta_\rho = (\delta_\phi^2 + \delta_\sigma^2)^{1/2}$. We now prove that for every $\delta_\varphi > 0$,

$$\lim_{T\to\infty} \Pr\{\inf_{\varphi \in C(\varphi_0,\delta_\rho,\delta_d)} T^{-1}[l_T(\varphi_0) - l_T(\varphi)] > 0\} = 1. \quad \text{(A.14)}$$

Using (A.4) and (A.9) in (A.3), we first note that

$$\begin{aligned} &2 \inf T^{-1}[l_T(\varphi_0) - l_T(\varphi)] \\ &\geq \inf(\mathcal{A}_\sigma) + \inf(\mathcal{C}_T) + \inf[(\psi - \psi_0)'\mathbf{G}_T(\psi - \psi_0)] \\ &\quad + 2\inf[(\psi - \psi_0)'\mathbf{f}_T], \end{aligned} \quad \text{(A.15)}$$

where it is now assumed that all of the inf operations are taken over the set $\varphi \in C(\varphi_0, \delta_\rho, \delta_d)$. But

$$(\psi - \psi_0)'\mathbf{f}_T = \mathbf{d}' \sum_{i=1}^{N} \frac{\phi_i}{\sigma_i^2} \frac{\mathbf{X}_i'\mathbf{H}_i\varepsilon_i}{T^{3/2}} - \sum_{i=1}^{N} \frac{(\phi_i - \phi_{i0})}{\sigma_i^2} \frac{\boldsymbol{\xi}_{i0}'\mathbf{H}_i\varepsilon_i}{T}. \quad \text{(A.16)}$$

Therefore, using the results in (A.1) and (A.2), and recalling that $\mathbf{d}$ and ρ are defined on compact sets, it then follows that $\inf[(\psi - \psi_0)'\mathbf{f}_T] = o_p(1)$. Also from (A.2), it is easily seen that $\mathcal{C}_T = o_p(1)$. Using these results in (A.15), we now have

$$\begin{aligned} 2 \inf T^{-1}[l_T(\varphi_0) - l_T(\varphi)] &\geq \inf(\mathcal{A}_\sigma) \\ &\quad + \inf[(\psi - \psi_0)'\mathbf{G}_T(\psi - \psi_0)] + o_p(1), \end{aligned} \quad \text{(A.17)}$$

where it is again assumed that all of the inf operations are taken over the set $\varphi \in C(\varphi_0, \delta_\rho, \delta_d)$. But the ith term in $\mathcal{A}_\sigma$—namely, $(\sigma_{i0}^2/\sigma_i^2) - \ln(\sigma_{i0}^2/\sigma_i^2) - 1$—attains its unique minimum at $(\sigma_{i0}^2/\sigma_i^2) = 1$ and is strictly positive for all feasible values of σ_i^2 not equal to σ_{i0}^2, for all $i = 1, 2, \ldots, N$. Hence $\inf(\mathcal{A}_\sigma) > 0 \Leftrightarrow \delta_\sigma > 0$. To establish (A.14), it thus is sufficient to prove that even if $\delta_\sigma = 0$, there exists $\delta_\varphi > 0$ such that

$$\lim_{T\to\infty} \Pr\{\inf\{(\psi - \psi_0)'\mathbf{G}_T(\psi - \psi_0)\} > 0\} = 1.$$

To this end, first note that

$$(\psi - \psi_0)'\mathbf{G}_T(\psi - \psi_0) = [\mathbf{K}_\psi(\psi - \psi_0)]'\mathcal{G}_T[\mathbf{K}_\psi(\psi - \psi_0)],$$

where $\mathbf{K}_\psi = \mathrm{diag}(T^{1/2}\mathbf{I}_k, \mathbf{I}_N)$, $\mathbf{K}_\psi(\psi - \psi_0) = \vartheta = (\mathbf{d}', (\phi - \phi_0)')'$, and $\mathcal{G}_T = \mathbf{K}_\psi^{-1}\mathbf{G}_T\mathbf{K}_\psi^{-1}$. Hence

$$\inf\{(\psi - \psi_0)'\mathbf{G}_T(\psi - \psi_0)\} \geq \delta_\vartheta^2 \lambda_{\min}(\mathcal{G}_T),$$

where $\lambda_{\min}(\mathcal{G}_T)$ is the smallest eigenvalue of $\mathcal{G}_T$, and $\delta_\vartheta = (\delta_d^2 + \delta_\phi^2)^{1/2} > 0$. (Notice that for $\delta_\sigma = 0$, we have $\delta_\vartheta = \delta_\varphi > 0$. In the case where $\delta_\sigma > 0$, (A.17) will be satisfied even if $\delta_\vartheta = 0$.) As $T \to \infty$, $\lambda_{\min}(\mathcal{G}_T)$ converges weakly to $\lambda_{\min}(\mathcal{G}) > 0$, which is the smallest eigenvalue of $\mathcal{G}$, where

$$\mathcal{G} = \begin{bmatrix} \sum_{i=1}^{N} \frac{\phi_i^2}{\sigma_i^2} \mathbf{R}_{X_iX_i} & 0 & \cdots & 0 \\ 0 & \frac{1}{\sigma_1^2} q_{\xi_{10}\xi_{10}} & \cdots & 0 \\ \vdots & \vdots & \vdots & \vdots \\ 0 & 0 & \cdots & \frac{1}{\sigma_N^2} q_{\xi_{N0}\xi_{N0}} \end{bmatrix},$$

and $\mathbf{R}_{X_iX_i}$ and $q_{\xi_{i0}\xi_{i0}}$, $i = 1, 2, \ldots, N$, are defined in (A.1) and (A.2). But under assumptions 1, 4, and 5(a) and (b) $\mathcal{G}$ is positive definite with probability 1, and hence $\lambda_{\min}(\mathcal{G}) > 0$ with probability 1. Hence for sufficiently large T, $\inf\{(\psi - \psi_0)'\mathbf{G}_T(\psi -$

$\psi_0)\} > 0$. This completes the proof and establishes the desired consistency and superconsistency results given by (4.7).

To derive the asymptotic distribution of the MLEs of $\boldsymbol{\theta}$ and $\varphi_i, i = 1, \ldots, N$, we now allow for the fact that in this case the different components of the score vector and the sample information matrix converge to their true values at different rates. Let $\mathbf{D}_\psi = \text{diag}(T^{-1}\mathbf{I}_k, T^{-1/2}\mathbf{I}_N)$, and define

$$\begin{aligned} \mathbf{d}_T(\psi) &= \mathbf{D}_\psi[\partial l_T(\varphi)/\partial\psi], \\ \mathcal{I}_T(\psi) &= \mathbf{D}_\psi[-\partial^2 l_T(\varphi)/\partial\psi\partial\psi']\mathbf{D}_\psi. \end{aligned} \quad \text{(A.18)}$$

Then, using standard results from the unit root literature, it can be established that (see, e.g., Phillips and Durlauf 1986) that

$$\mathbf{d}_T(\psi_0) \overset{a}{\sim} \text{MN}\{0, \mathcal{I}(\psi_0)\}, \qquad \mathcal{I}_T(\psi_0) \Rightarrow \mathcal{I}(\psi_0), \quad \text{(A.19)}$$

where the $(k+N) \times (k+N)$ matrix,

$$\mathcal{I}(\psi_0) \equiv \begin{bmatrix} \sum_{i=1}^N \frac{\phi_{i0}^2}{\sigma_{i0}^2} \mathbf{R}_{X_i X_i} & 0 & \cdots & 0 \\ 0 & \frac{1}{\sigma_{10}^2} q_{\xi_{10}\xi_{10}} & \cdots & 0 \\ \vdots & \vdots & \vdots & \vdots \\ 0 & 0 & \cdots & \frac{1}{\sigma_{N0}^2} q_{\xi_{N0}\xi_{N0}} \end{bmatrix}$$

(A.20)

is the random information matrix, which is positive definite with probability 1.

Now using the mean-value expansion of $\partial l_T(\hat{\varphi})/\partial\psi$ around ψ_0 and standardizing the result by $\mathbf{D}_\psi$, we have

$$\mathbf{D}_\psi^{-1}(\hat{\psi} - \psi_0) = \mathcal{I}_T(\bar{\psi})^{-1}\mathbf{d}_T(\psi_0), \quad \text{(A.21)}$$

where the (i,j) element of $\partial^2 l_T(\bar{\varphi})/\partial\psi\partial\psi'$ is evaluated at $(\bar{\varphi}_i, \bar{\varphi}_j)$ and $\bar{\varphi}_i$ is a convex combination of φ_{i0} and $\hat{\varphi}_i$.

Notice, however, that in the case of the models with unit root regressors the sample information matrix $\mathcal{I}_T(\bar{\psi})$ need not converge weakly to $\mathcal{I}(\psi_0)$ even when $\bar{\psi}$ converges to ψ_0. To ensure that such a convergence occurs, the sample information matrix $\mathcal{I}_T(\psi)$ should satisfy the stochastic equicontinuity condition (see, e.g., Saikkonen 1995, condition SE_o, p. 894). This result is summarized in the following lemma.

Lemma A.1. Under assumptions 1–4, and 5(a) and (c), and assuming that the regressors $\mathbf{x}_{it}$ in the dynamic heterogeneous panel data model (6) are $I(1)$, the sample information matrix, $\mathcal{I}_T(\psi)$, defined by (A.18), satisfy the stochastic equicontinuity condition such that

$$\sup_{\psi_* \in B(\phi_0,\delta) \times N_T(\theta_0,\delta)} \|\mathcal{I}_T(\psi_*) - \mathcal{I}_T(\psi_0)\| \le O_p(1), \quad \text{(A.22)}$$

where $B(\boldsymbol{\phi}, \delta) = \{\boldsymbol{\phi}_* \in \Theta_o\colon \|\boldsymbol{\phi}_* - \boldsymbol{\phi}\| < \delta\}$ and $N_T(\boldsymbol{\theta}, \delta) = \{\boldsymbol{\theta}_* \in \Theta_\theta\colon T^{1/2}\|\boldsymbol{\theta}_* - \boldsymbol{\theta}\| < \delta\}$, with δ a common positive real number.

Proof. See the Appendix in the earlier version of this article (Pesaran et al. 1997).

In view of the relative orders of consistency of the MLEs established in (15) and the fact that the sample information matrix satisfies the stochastic equicontinuity condition, (A.22), it also follows that (see Saikkonen, 1995, prop. 3.2)

$$\mathcal{I}_T(\bar{\psi}) = \mathcal{I}(\psi_0) + o_p(1). \quad \text{(A.23)}$$

Using this result in (A.21) now yields

$$\mathbf{D}_\psi^{-1}(\hat{\psi} - \psi_0) = \mathcal{I}_T(\psi_0)^{-1}O_T(\psi_0) + o_p(1). \quad \text{(A.24)}$$

Using (A.19) in (A.24) and by the continuous mapping theorem, we obtain (16).

A.3 Asymptotic Distribution of the Long-Run Coefficients: The Case of I(1) Regressors

First, note that

$$\hat{\boldsymbol{\xi}}_i = \mathbf{y}_{i,-1} - \mathbf{X}_i\hat{\boldsymbol{\theta}} = \boldsymbol{\xi}_{i0} - \mathbf{X}_i(\hat{\boldsymbol{\theta}} - \boldsymbol{\theta}_0) \quad \text{(A.25)}$$

and

$$\mathbf{H}_i(\Delta\mathbf{y}_i - \hat{\phi}_i\mathbf{y}_{i,-1}) = \mathbf{H}_i[-\mathbf{X}_i\boldsymbol{\theta}_0\phi_{i0} - (\hat{\phi}_i - \phi_{i0})\mathbf{y}_{i,-1} + \boldsymbol{\varepsilon}_i]. \quad \text{(A.26)}$$

Using (6) and (A.25) in (10), we have

$$\hat{\phi}_i - \phi_{i0} = (\hat{\boldsymbol{\xi}}_i'\mathbf{H}_i\hat{\boldsymbol{\xi}}_i)^{-1}[\hat{\boldsymbol{\xi}}_i'\mathbf{H}_i\mathbf{X}_i(\hat{\boldsymbol{\theta}} - \boldsymbol{\theta}_0)\phi_{i0} + \hat{\boldsymbol{\xi}}_i'\mathbf{H}_i\boldsymbol{\varepsilon}_i]. \quad \text{(A.27)}$$

Moreover, using (A.26) in (9),

$$\hat{\boldsymbol{\theta}} - \boldsymbol{\theta}_0 = \left\{\sum_{i=1}^N \frac{\hat{\phi}_i^2}{\hat{\sigma}_i^2}\mathbf{X}_i'\mathbf{H}_i\mathbf{X}_i\right\}^{-1} \times \left\{\sum_{i=1}^N \frac{\hat{\phi}_i}{\hat{\sigma}_i^2}\mathbf{X}_i'\mathbf{H}_i\boldsymbol{\xi}_i(\hat{\phi}_i - \phi_{i0}) - \sum_{i=1}^N \frac{\hat{\phi}_i}{\hat{\sigma}_i^2}\mathbf{X}_i'\mathbf{H}_i\boldsymbol{\varepsilon}_i\right\} \quad \text{(A.28)}$$

Substituting (A.27) in (A.28), and solving for $\hat{\boldsymbol{\theta}} - \boldsymbol{\theta}_0$, we obtain

$$\hat{\boldsymbol{\theta}} - \boldsymbol{\theta}_0 = \mathbf{S}_{NT}^{-1}\mathbf{s}_{NT}, \quad \text{(A.29)}$$

where

$$\mathbf{S}_{NT} = \sum_{i=1}^N \frac{\hat{\phi}_i^2}{\hat{\sigma}_i^2}\mathbf{X}_i'\mathbf{H}_i\mathbf{X}_i - \sum_{i=1}^N \frac{\hat{\phi}_i\phi_{i0}}{\hat{\sigma}_i^2}\mathbf{X}_i'\mathbf{H}_i\boldsymbol{\xi}_{i0}(\hat{\boldsymbol{\xi}}_i'\mathbf{H}_i\hat{\boldsymbol{\xi}}_i)^{-1}\hat{\boldsymbol{\xi}}_i'\mathbf{H}_i\mathbf{X}_i \quad \text{(A.30)}$$

and

$$\mathbf{s}_{NT} = -\sum_{i=1}^N \frac{\hat{\phi}_i}{\hat{\sigma}_i^2}\mathbf{X}_i'\mathbf{H}_i\boldsymbol{\varepsilon}_i + \sum_{i=1}^N \frac{\hat{\phi}_i}{\hat{\sigma}_i^2}\mathbf{X}_i'\mathbf{H}_i\boldsymbol{\xi}_{i0}(\hat{\boldsymbol{\xi}}_i'\mathbf{H}_i\hat{\boldsymbol{\xi}}_i)^{-1}\hat{\boldsymbol{\xi}}_i'\mathbf{H}_i\boldsymbol{\varepsilon}_i. \quad \text{(A.31)}$$

Using the consistency of $\hat{\boldsymbol{\theta}}$; $\hat{\phi}_1, \ldots, \hat{\phi}_N; \hat{\sigma}_1^2, \ldots, \hat{\sigma}_N^2$, it is also easily seen that

$$T^{-1}\hat{\boldsymbol{\xi}}_i'\mathbf{H}_i\mathbf{X}_i \Rightarrow \mathbf{R}_{X_i\xi_{i0}}', \qquad T^{-1}\hat{\boldsymbol{\xi}}_i'\mathbf{H}_i\hat{\boldsymbol{\xi}}_i \Rightarrow q_{\xi_{i0}\xi_{i0}},$$

$$T^{-1/2}\hat{\boldsymbol{\xi}}_i'\mathbf{H}_i\boldsymbol{\varepsilon}_i \Rightarrow T^{-1/2}\boldsymbol{\xi}_{i0}'\mathbf{H}_i\boldsymbol{\varepsilon}_i, \quad \text{(A.32)}$$

where $\mathbf{R}_{X_i\xi_{i0}}$ and $q_{\xi_{i0}\xi_{i0}}$ are defined by (A.1) and (A.2).

Using (A.1), (A.32), and the consistency of $\hat{\phi}_i$ and $\hat{\sigma}_i^2, i = 1, 2, \ldots, N$, in (A.30) and (A.31), we now have

$$T^{-2}\mathbf{S}_{NT} \Rightarrow \sum_{i=1}^N \frac{\phi_{i0}^2}{\sigma_{i0}^2}\mathbf{R}_{X_iX_i},$$

$$T^{-1}\mathbf{s}_{NT} \sim \text{MN}\left\{0, \sum_{i=1}^N \frac{\phi_{i0}^2}{\sigma_{i0}^2}\mathbf{R}_{X_iX_i}\right\},$$

where $\mathbf{R}_{X_iX_i}$ is defined by (A.1). Using these results in (A.29) and by the continuous mapping theorem, we obtain (17).

[Received August 1997. Revised December 1998.]

REFERENCES

Ahn, S. C., and Schmidt, P. (1995), "Efficient Estimation of Models for Dynamic Panel Data," *Journal of Econometrics*, 68, 29–52.

Anderson, T. W., and Hsiao, C. (1981), "Estimation of Dynamic Models With Error Components," *Journal of the American Statistical Association*, 76, 598–606.

——— (1982), "Formation and Estimation of Dynamic Models Using Panel Data," *Journal of Econometrics*, 18, 47–82.

Arellano, M. (1989), "A Note on the Anderson–Hsiao Estimator for Panel Data," *Economics Letters*, 31, 337–341.

Arellano, M., and Bover, O. (1995), "Another Look at the Instrumental Variable Estimation of Error-Components Models," *Journal of Econometrics*, 68, 29–52.

Baltagi, B. H. (1995), *Econometric Analysis of Panel Data*, New York: Wiley.

Boyd, D. A. C., and Smith, R. P. (in press), "Testing for Purchasing Power Parity: Econometric Issues and an Application to Developing Countries," unpublished manuscript, *Manchester School*.

Davidson, J. E. H., Hendry, D. F., Srba, F., and Yeo, S. (1978), "Econometric Modelling of the Aggregate Time-Series Relationship Between Consumers' Expenditure and Income in the United Kingdom," *Economic Journal*, 88, 661–692.

Haque, N. U., and Montiel, P. (1989), "Consumption in Developing Countries: Tests for Liquidity Constraints and Finite Horizons," *Review of Economics and Statistics*, 71, 408–415.

Hausman, J. (1978), "Specification Tests in Econometrics," *Econometrica*, 46, 1251–1271.

Hsiao, C. (1996), "Random Coefficient Models," in *The Economics of Panel Data: A Handbook of Theory With Applications* (2nd rev. ed.), eds. L. Mátyás and P. Sevestre, Dordrecht: Kluwer, chap. 5.

Hsiao, C., Pesaran, M. H., and Tahmiscioglu, A. K. (1999), "Bayes Estimation of Short-Run Coefficients in Dynamic Panel Data Models," in *Analysis of Panels and Limited Dependent Variables: A Volume in Honour of G. S. Maddala*, eds. C. Hsiao, K. Lahiri, L-F. Lee, and M. H. Pesaran, Cambridge, U.K.: Cambridge University Press.

Hsiao, C., Sun, B. H., and Lightwood, J. (1995), "Fixed Versus Random Effects Specification for Panel Data Analysis," unpublished manuscript, University of Southern California.

Hsiao, C., and Tahmiscioglu, A. K. (1997), "A Panel Analysis of Liquidity Constraints and Firm Investment," *Journal of the American Statistical Association*, 92, 455–465.

Im, K. S., Pesaran, M. H., and Shin, Y. (1997), "Testing for Unit Roots in Heterogeneous Panels," unpublished manuscript, University of Cambridge (*http://www.econ.cam.ac.uk/faculty/pesaran*).

Keane, M., and Runkle, D. (1992), "On the Estimation of Panel Data Models With Serial Correlation When Instruments Are Not Strictly Exogenous," *Journal of Business and Economic Statistics*, 10, 1–9.

Kiviet, J. F., and Phillips, G. D. A. (1993), "Alternative Bias Approximations With a Lagged Dependent Variable," *Econometric Theory*, 9, 62–80.

Lindley, D. V., and Smith, A. F. M. (1972), "Bayes Estimates for the Linear Model," *Journal of the Royal Statistical Society*, Ser. B, 34, 1–41.

Maddala, G. S., and Hu, W. (1996), "The Pooling Problem," in *The Economics of Panel Data: A Handbook of Theory With Applications*, (2nd rev. ed.), eds. L. Mátyás and P. Sevestre, Dordrecht: Kluwer, chap. 13.

Mátyás, L., and Sevestre, P. (Eds.) (1996), *The Econometrics of Panel Data: A Handbook of Theory With Applications*, (2nd rev. ed.), Dordrecht: Kluwer.

Pesaran, M. H. (1997), "The Role of Economic Theory in Modelling the Long-Run," *The Economic Journal*, 107, 178–191.

Pesaran, M. H., and Pesaran, B. (1997), *Microfit 4.0: Interactive Econometric Analysis*. Oxford, U.K.: Oxford University Press.

Pesaran, M. H., and Shin, Y. (1999), "Long-Run Structural Modelling," unpublished manuscript, University of Cambridge. (*http://www.econ.cam.ac.uk/faculty/pesaran/*).

——— (1999), "An Autoregressive Distributed Lag Modelling Approach to Cointegration Analysis," in *Econometrics and Economic Theory in the 20th Century: The Ragnar Frisch Centennial Symposium*, ed. S. Strom, Cambridge, U.K.: Cambridge University Press.

Pesaran, M. H., Shin, Y., and Smith, R. J. (1999), "Bounds Testing Approaches to the Analysis of Long Run Relationships," Unpublished manuscript, University of Cambridge (*http://www.econ.cam.ac.uk/faculty/pesaran*).

Pesaran, M. H., Shin, Y., and Smith, R. P. (1997), "Pooled Estimation of Long-Run Relationships in Dynamic Heterogenous Panels," DAE Working Papers Amalgamated Series 9721, University of Cambridge.

Pesaran, M. H., and Smith, R. P. (1995), "Estimating Long-Run Relationships From Dynamic Heterogeneous Panels," *Journal of Econometrics*, 68, 79–113.

Pesaran, M. H., Smith, R. P., and Akiyama, T. (1998), *Energy Demand in Asian Economies*, Oxford, U.K.: Oxford University Press.

Pesaran, M. H., Smith, R. P., and Im, K. S. (1996), "Dynamic Linear Models for Heterogeneous Panels," in *The Economics of Panel Data: A Handbook of Theory With Applications*, (2nd rev. ed.), eds. L. Mátyás and P. Sevestre, Dordrecht: Kluwer, chap. 8.

Pesaran, M. H., and Zhao, Z. (1999), "Bias Reduction in Estimating Long-Run Relationships From Dynamic Heterogeneous Panels," in *Analysis of Panels and Limited Dependent Variables: A Volume in Honour of G. S. Maddala*, eds. C. Hsiao, K. Lahiri, L-F. Lee, and M. H. Pesaran, Cambridge, U.K.: Cambridge University Press.

Phillips, P. C. B., and Durlauf, S. (1986), "Multiple Time Series With Integrated Variables," *Review of Economic Studies*, 53, 473–496.

Rogoff, K. (1996), "The Purchasing Power Parity Puzzle," *Journal of Economic Literature*, 34, 647–668.

Saikkonen, P. (1995), "Problems With the Asymptotic Theory of Maximum Likelihood Estimation in Integrated and Cointegrated Systems," *Econometric Theory*, 11, 888–911.

Stoker, T. M. (1993), "Empirical Approaches to the Problem of Aggregation Over Individuals," *Journal of Economic Literature*, 31, 1827–1874.

Swamy, P. A. V. B. (1970), "Efficient Inference in a Random Coefficient Regression Model," *Econometrica*, 38, 311–323.

Zellner, A. (1962), "An Efficient Method of Estimating Seemingly Unrelated Regressions and Test for Aggregation Bias," *Journal of the American Statistical Association*, 57, 348–368.

[22]

Econometrica, Vol. 67, No. 5 (September, 1999), 1057–1111

LINEAR REGRESSION LIMIT THEORY FOR NONSTATIONARY PANEL DATA[1]

BY PETER C. B. PHILLIPS AND HYUNGSIK R. MOON[2]

This paper develops a regression limit theory for nonstationary panel data with large numbers of cross section (n) and time series (T) observations. The limit theory allows for both sequential limits, wherein $T \to \infty$ followed by $n \to \infty$, and joint limits where $T, n \to \infty$ simultaneously; and the relationship between these multidimensional limits is explored. The panel structures considered allow for no time series cointegration, heterogeneous cointegration, homogeneous cointegration, and near-homogeneous cointegration. The paper explores the existence of long-run average relations between integrated panel vectors when there is no individual time series cointegration and when there is heterogeneous cointegration. These relations are parameterized in terms of the matrix regression coefficient of the long-run average covariance matrix. In the case of homogeneous and near homogeneous cointegrating panels, a panel fully modified regression estimator is developed and studied. The limit theory enables us to test hypotheses about the long run average parameters both within and between subgroups of the full population.

KEYWORDS: Nonstationary panel data, long-run average relations, multidimensional limits, panel cointegration regression, panel spurious regression.

1. INTRODUCTION

THERE HAS BEEN MUCH RECENT EMPIRICAL econometric work on economic models that uses panel data for which the time series component is nonstationary. Testing growth convergence theories in macroeconomics and estimating long-run relations between international financial series such as relative prices and exchange rates, and spot and future exchange rates are a few examples. This work has been facilitated by the construction and availability of a number of important panel data sets covering different individuals, regions, and countries over a relatively long time period, a notable example being the Penn World table. For such cases a new nonstationary panel data limit theory which allows for large n and large T asymptotics is useful. Much past panel data research has focused on identifying and estimating effects from stationary panels with a large cross section data dimension (n) but with few time series (T) observations. In

[1]An earlier version of this paper, Phillips and Moon (1997a), hereafter PM^a, was presented at the inaugural meeting of the New Zealand Econometric Society Group in Auckland, February 1997, while Phillips was visiting the University of Auckland. Some of the results were also presented in a training course on panel cointegration given by the first author at the EMBA meetings in Palm Cove, Australia, August 1996. The present paper is a shortened version of Phillips and Moon (1997b), hereafter PM^b, to which readers will be frequently referred for a full development of the algebra and limit theory given here.

[2]The authors thank a co-editor and three referees for comments on the paper, and Donald Andrews, David Pollard, and Oliver Linton for helpful discussions. Phillips thanks the NSF for research support under Grant No. SBR 94-22922, and Moon gratefully acknowledges financial support from a C.A. Anderson Prize Fellowship. The paper was typed by the authors in Scientific Word 2.5.

such cases a large n, fixed T limit theory is natural and Chamberlain (1984), Hsiao (1986), Matyas and Sevestre (1992), and Baltagi (1995) review much of this research.

The purpose of the present contribution is to investigate regressions with nonstationary panel data for which the time series component is an integrated process and where both T and n are large. In such cases, panel regressions can behave very differently from time series regressions. It has long been recognized by econometricians that panel data can distinguish effects that time series or cross section data alone cannot identify, and nonstationary panels provide a further instance of this phenomenon.

Suppose that we have two $I(1)$ random vectors, say $Y_{i,t}$ and $X_{i,t}$. When there is no cointegrating relation between $Y_{i,t}$ and $X_{i,t}$, and a time series regression for given i is performed, then the regression coefficient is well known to have a nondegenerate limit distribution and the regression is characterized as spurious (Granger and Newbold (1974) and Phillips (1986)). Now suppose that there are panel observations of $Y_{i,t}$ and $X_{i,t}$ with large cross sectional and time series components. In this case, even if the noise in the time series regression is strong, the noise can often be characterized as independent across individuals. Hence, by pooling the cross section and time series observations, we may attenuate the strong effect of the residuals in the regression while retaining the strength of the signal ($X_{i,t}$). In such a case, we can expect a panel-pooled regression to provide a consistent estimate of some long-run regression coefficient.

The present paper is concerned with developing a limit theory that is helpful in understanding and interpreting regressions of this type. In particular, we show the existence of an interesting long-run relation between panel vectors like $Y_{i,t}$ and $X_{i,t}$ that have no individual time series cointegrating relation. The new relation is a long-run *average* relationship over the cross section and it is parameterized in terms of a matrix regression coefficient derived from the cross section long-run average covariance matrix.

The following sections consider four possible panel structures for $Y_{i,t}$ and $X_{i,t}$: (i) no cointegrating relation, (ii) a heterogeneous cointegrating relation, (iii) a homogeneous cointegrating relation, and (iv) a near-homogeneous relation. Our analysis shows that in all four cases the pooled estimator is consistent and has a normal limit distribution. In the no cointegration and heterogeneous cointegration cases, we also study a limiting cross section estimator and prove that it is consistent and has a normal limit distribution, but that it is less efficient than the pooled estimator. In addition, in the case of homogeneous cointegration and near-homogeneous cointegration, we can construct a consistent estimator for the long-run regression coefficient, which we call a pooled FM (fully modified) estimator. This estimator has a faster coefficient convergence rate than the simple cross section and time series estimators.

Since the beginning of the 1990's there has been some ongoing research on nonstationary panel data that connects to our work here. Quah (1994), Levin and Lin (1993), and recently Im et al. (1996) considered unit root time series regressions with nonstationary panel data and proposed test statistics for unit roots. In addition, Pedroni (1995) studied some properties of cointegration statistics in pooled time series panels, and Robertson and Symons (1992) studied the biases that are likely to arise in practice with both stationary and nonstationary panel data. More closely related to our work is Pesaran and Smith (1995), who examined the impact of nonstationary variables on cross section regression estimates. They showed that spurious correlation between two $I(1)$ variables does not arise in the case of cross section regression with a finite number of time series observations under conditions such as exogenous regressors and iid disturbances. Our paper extends that result to a very general setting and provides a limit theory as $T \to \infty$ and $n \to \infty$ in panel regressions. The long-run relation defined in Pesaran and Smith (1995) is an average of randomly different cointegrating coefficients and they suggested cross section regression with time averaged data for consistent estimation. By contrast, our long run relation is the regression relation associated with the long run average covariance matrix and it is this regression that is the natural limit of a pooled panel regression. Further, we show that both pooled panel regression and limiting cross section regression estimators are consistent for this long-run average relation.

The limit theory developed here allows for both sequential limits, wherein $T \to \infty$ followed by $n \to \infty$, and joint limits where $T, n \to \infty$ simultaneously. A detailed discussion of multi-index asymptotic theory is provided and some general theorems for laws of large numbers and central limit theory are given. Sequential limit theory is easy to derive and generally leads to quick results for a variety of model configurations. Under some strengthening of the conditions, the results obtained under sequential limits are shown to apply also when $T, n \to \infty$ simultaneously. For a limit distribution theory we need the rate condition $n/T \to 0$. The latter condition indicates that the limit theory here is most likely to be useful in practice when n is moderate and T is large. We can expect such data configurations in multi-country macreconomic data, for example, when we restrict attention to groups of countries like OECD nations or developing countries. The limit theory enables us to test hypotheses about the long-run average parameters both within and between such subgroups of the full population.

The paper is organized as follows. Section 2 introduces the basic model, lays out assumptions, and gives some preliminary results including a multidimensional Beveridge Nelson (BN) decomposition. Section 3 develops a framework for asymptotics for double indexed processes that is used in the paper for both sequential and joint limit theories. Section 4 assumes that there is no cointegration among the $I(1)$ variable across all the individuals and gives asymptotic theories for a pooled regression estimator and a limiting cross section estimator. Section 5 assumes that there exists a cointegrating relation in the $I(1)$ variables across all the individuals and derives limit theories for the pooled estimators in three cases—heterogenous, homogeneous, and near-homogeneous cointegration. Section 6 indicates some extensions of this theory to allow for models with individual specific effects. Section 7 concludes the paper. Five appendices are included to develop the multidimensional limit theory, provide some technical background, relevant lemmas, and proofs of results in the paper.

Notation is fairly standard. The symbol "$\Rightarrow$" signifies weak convergence, "$:=$" is definitional equivalence, "$\equiv$" signifies equivalence in distribution, "$\xrightarrow{p}$" is convergence in probability, and "$\xrightarrow{a.s.}$" is convergence almost surely. The inequality ">0" signifies positive definiteness when applied to matrices. Stochastic processes such as Brownian motion $W(r)$ on $[0,1]$ are usually written as W, integrals such as $\int_0^1 W(r)\,dr$ as $\int W$, and stochastic integrals like $\int_0^1 W(r)\,dW(r)$ as $\int W dW$. Also $\text{vec}(A)$ denotes vectorization of the matrix A by stacking columns, and $\|A\|$ is the Euclidean norm $(\text{tr}(A'A))^{1/2}$.

2. ASSUMPTIONS, LARGE T ASYMPTOTICS, AND THE LONG-RUN AVERAGE COVARIANCE MATRIX

We start with a panel data model based on the vector integrated process

$$Z_{i,t} = Z_{i,t-1} + U_{i,t} \qquad (t=1,\ldots,T;\ i=1,\ldots,n) \tag{2.1}$$

with common initialization at $t=0$ satisfying

$$Z_{i,0} \text{ is iid across } i \text{ with } E\|Z_{i,0}\|^4 < \infty. \tag{2.2}$$

We partition the m-vectors $Z_{i,t}$ and $U_{i,t}$ in (2.1) into m_y and m_x components ($m = m_y + m_x$) as $Z_{i,t} = (Y'_{i,t}, X'_{i,t})'$ and $U_{i,t} = (U'_{y_i,t}, U'_{x_i,t})'$. Condition (2.2) is made for convenience and could be generalized to allow for remote past initialization at the cost of some further complications (e.g., Phillips and Lee (1996)). The error $U_{i,t}$ is assumed to be generated by the random coefficient linear process

$$U_{i,t} = \sum_{s=0}^{\infty} C_{i,s} V_{i,t-s}, \tag{2.3}$$

where: (i) $\{C_{i,t}\}$ is a double sequence of $(m \times m)$ random matrices across i and over t; (ii) the m-vectors $V_{i,t}$ are iid across i and over t with $E(V_{i,t}) = 0$, $E(V_{i,t}V'_{i,t}) = I_m$, and, letting $V_{a,i,t}$ be the ath element of $V_{i,t}$, the $V_{a,i,t}$ are assumed to be independent across $a = 1,\ldots,m$ with $E(V^4_{a,i,t}) = \upsilon^4$ for all i and t; (iii) $C_{i,s}$ and $V_{j,t}$ are independent for all i, j, t, and s.

We make two further assumptions about the random coefficients in (2.3). The first involves moment conditions and the second is a set of summability conditions on the moments of the random coefficients.

ASSUMPTION 1 (Random Coefficient Conditions):
(i) $\{C_{i,s}\}_i$ *is iid across* i *for all* s.
(ii) $E\|C_{i,s}\|^4 < \infty$ *for all* s.

Thus, $C_{i,s}$ is assumed to be iid across individuals and to have finite fourth moments that may vary over time. We allow $C_{i,s}$ to be dependent over s. This is important, because whenever $U_{i,t}$ is generated by a finite-parameter time series model like an autoregression, the coefficients in the Wold decomposition (2.3) will be nonlinear functions of these parameters that are lag (s) dependent and will therefore inevitably be dependent over s. Let $C_{a,i,s}$ be the ath element of $\mathrm{vec}(C_{i,s})$. Also let $E(C_{a,i,s}^k) = \sigma_{k,a,s}$. Then we make the following assumption:

ASSUMPTION 2 (Summability Conditions): *The following hold for all* $a = 1,\dots,m^2$:

(i) $\sum_{s=0}^{\infty} s^2 \sigma_{2,a,s} < \infty$.
(ii) $\sum_{s=0}^{\infty} s^4 (\sigma_{4,a,s})^{1/4} < \infty$.

Suppose the $U_{i,t}$ in (2.1) are generated by a random coefficient ARMA process whose characteristic equation has roots $\{\lambda_{ij}: j = 1,\dots,J\}$. Then the coefficients $C_{i,s}$ in the Wold decomposition (2.3) are all linear combinations of powers of these characteristic roots. Under weak conditions on the distribution of the roots we can now verify Assumptions 1 and 2. Suppose, for instance, that the support of the distribution of the moduli of these roots is a compact set inside the stable region, so that $|\lambda_{ij}| \le M_\lambda < 1$ a.s. Then all moments of $\|C_{i,s}\|$ are finite for all s, and series such as those in Assumption 2 are easily seen to be majorized by convergent series. For example, $\sum_{s=0}^{\infty} s^2 \sigma_{2,a,s} \le M \sum_{s=0}^{\infty} s^2 M_\lambda^{2s} < \infty$ for some constant M. Similar conditions will ensure the validity of the alternative Assumptions 4 and 5 that are used later on in the paper.

The following lemma establishes the integrability of terms that appear frequently in our development.

LEMMA 1: *Let* $C_i(1) = \sum_{s=0}^{\infty} C_{i,s}$, $\tilde{C}_{i,s} = \sum_{t=s+1}^{\infty} C_{i,t}$, *and* $\tilde{U}_{i,t} = \sum_{s=0}^{\infty} \tilde{C}_{i,s} V_{i,t-s}$. *Under Assumptions* 1 *and* 2, *the following hold*:

(a) $E[\sum_{s=0}^{\infty} s^2 \|C_{i,s}\|^2] < \infty$.
(b) $E\|U_{i,t}\|^2 < M$ *for some* $M < \infty$.
(c) $E\|\tilde{U}_{i,t}\|^4 < M$ *for some* $M < \infty$.
(d) $E\|C_i(1)\|^4 < \infty$.

The temporal shift operator generating the iid sequence $\{V_{i,t}\}_t$ defines a measure preserving map on the product probability space induced by the independent sequences $\{V_{i,t}\}_t$ and $\{C_{i,t}\}_t$ and it generates the sequence $\{U_{i,t}\}_t$. Also the random coefficient sequence $\{C_{i,t}\}_t$ is square summable a.s. since $\sum_{t=0}^{\infty} \|C_{i,t}\|^2 < \infty$ a.s. by Lemma 1(a). Hence, the time series sequence $\{U_{i,t}\}_t$ is square integrable (Lemma 1(b)) and strictly stationary for all i. However, the sequence $\{U_{i,t}\}_t$ is not ergodic. This is because $\mathcal{F}_{c_i} = \sigma(C_{i,0},\dots,C_{i,t},\dots)$, the sigma field generated by the sequence $\{C_{i,t}\}_{t=0}^{\infty}$, is an invariant sigma field with respect to the temporal shift operator and generates events with probability between zero and unity.

The following lemma shows that, for each i, $U_{i,t}$ satisfies a time series BN decomposition (see Phillips and Solo (1992)) almost surely.

LEMMA 2 (Panel BN decomposition): *Under Assumptions* 1 *and* 2 *the processes* $U_{i,t} = \Sigma_{s=0}^{\infty} C_{i,s} V_{i,t-s}$ *in* (2.3) *admit the following BN decomposition*:

$$U_{i,t} = C_i(1)V_{i,t} + \tilde{U}_{i,t-1} - \tilde{U}_{i,t} \qquad a.s. \tag{2.4}$$

Note that $C_i(1) = \Sigma_{s=0}^{\infty} C_{i,s} < \infty$ a.s. in view of Lemma 1(d), and $\tilde{U}_{i,t}$ are well defined square integrable random vectors by Lemma 1(c). Following Phillips and Solo (1992), partial sums of $U_{i,t}$ can be written as

$$\frac{1}{\sqrt{T}} \sum_{t=1}^{[Tr]} U_{i,t} \overset{\text{a.s.}}{=} C_i(1) \frac{1}{\sqrt{T}} \sum_{t=1}^{[Tr]} V_{i,t} + \frac{1}{\sqrt{T}} \tilde{U}_{i,0} - \frac{1}{\sqrt{T}} \tilde{U}_{i,[Tr]}, \tag{2.5}$$

where $[Tr]$ denotes the integer part of Tr and it is a simple matter to establish that these partial sum processes satisfy functional laws. Indeed, we have the following large T result.

LEMMA 3 (Panel Functional CLT): *Under Assumptions* 1 *and* 2,

$$\frac{1}{\sqrt{T}} \sum_{t=1}^{[Tr]} U_{i,t} \Rightarrow C_i(1) W_i(r) \qquad \text{as } T \to \infty \text{ for all } i.$$

Let $M_i(r) = (M_{y_i}(r)', M_{x_i}(r)')' = C_i(1)W_i(r) = (C_{y_i}(1)', C_{x_i}(1)')'W_i(r)$. Here, $M_i(r)$ is a randomly scaled (or mixed) Brownian Motion with conditional covariance matrix $C_i(1)C_i(1)'$, whose expectation is well defined because $\| EC_i(1)C_i(1)' \| < \infty$ in view of Lemma 1(d).

By the continuous mapping theorem and initial condition (2.2) we have

$$\frac{1}{T^2} \sum_{t=1}^{T} Z_{i,t} Z'_{i,t} \Rightarrow C_i(1) \int W_i W'_i C_i(1)' = \int M_i M'_i,$$

as $T \to \infty$ for all i. Then, averaging over $i = 1, \ldots, n$, we have

$$\frac{1}{n} \sum_{i=1}^{n} \frac{1}{T^2} \sum_{t=1}^{T} Z_{i,t} Z'_{i,t} \Rightarrow \frac{1}{n} \sum_{i=1}^{n} C_i(1) \int W_i W'_i C_i(1)' = \frac{1}{n} \sum_{i=1}^{n} \int M_i M'_i, \tag{2.6}$$

as $T \to \infty$ for any fixed n. Integrability of the summands in (2.6) follows readily under the given summability and moment conditions.

LEMMA 4: *Under Assumptions* 1 *and* 2, $E \| \int M_i M'_i \|^2 < \infty$.

In consequence, a strong law of large numbers applies to (2.6) as $n \to \infty$ and so

$$\frac{1}{n} \sum_{i=1}^{n} \int M_i M'_i \overset{\text{a.s.}}{\to} E\left(\int M_i M'_i \right). \tag{2.7}$$

The limit here depends not on the covariance matrix of $Z_{i,t}$, but on a parameter matrix that measures the long-run (over t) covariance of $Z_{i,t}$ averaged over i. This parameter matrix is constructed as follows.

Let Ω_i be the long-run conditional covariance matrix of $Z_{i,t} = (Y_{i,t}, X_{i,t})'$ conditioned on $\mathscr{F}_{c_i}$, i.e.,

$$\Omega_i = \begin{pmatrix} \Omega_{y_iy_i} & \Omega_{y_ix_i} \\ \Omega_{x_iy_i} & \Omega_{x_ix_i} \end{pmatrix} = C_i(1)C_i(1)' = \begin{pmatrix} C_{y_i}(1)C_{y_i}(1)' & C_{y_i}(1)C_{x_i}(1)' \\ C_{x_i}(1)C_{y_i}(1)' & C_{x_i}(1)C_{x_i}(1)' \end{pmatrix},$$

where the partitions of Ω_i and $C_i(1)C_i(1)'$ are conformable. By Lemma 1(d), Ω_i is integrable and we denote

$$\Omega = \begin{pmatrix} \Omega_{yy} & \Omega_{yx} \\ \Omega_{xy} & \Omega_{xx} \end{pmatrix} = E(\Omega_i) = E(C_i(1)C_i(1)').$$

We call Ω the *long-run average covariance* matrix of $Z_{i,t}$.

It is now apparent from (2.6) that $E(\int M_iM_i') = E[C_i(1)E(\int W_iW_i')C_i(1)']$. A simple calculation reveals that $E(\int W_iW_i') = \frac{1}{2}I_m$, so that (2.7) becomes

$$\text{(2.8)} \qquad \frac{1}{n}\sum_{i=1}^{n}\int M_iM_i' \overset{\text{a.s.}}{\to} \frac{1}{2}\Omega,$$

showing that the limit of the second moment matrix of the data depends on the long-run average covariance matrix Ω. Taken together, (2.6) and (2.7) give us an instance of an asymptotic development in which $T \to \infty$, followed by $n \to \infty$, leading to the sequence of limits

$$\text{(2.9)} \qquad X_{n,T} := \frac{1}{n}\sum_{i=1}^{n}\left(\frac{1}{T^2}\sum_{i=1}^{T} Z_{i,t}, Z_{i,t}'\right) \Rightarrow \frac{1}{n}\sum_{i=1}^{n}\int M_iM_i' \overset{\text{a.s.}}{\to} \frac{1}{2}\Omega$$

for the double indexed process $X_{n,T}$. The next section discusses this type of sequential asymptotic theory in relation to more general joint asymptotics.

3. LIMIT THEORY FOR MULTIDIMENSIONAL PROCESSES

Throughout this paper, attention is focused on deriving the limit behavior of a double indexed process $X_{n,T}$, such as that given in (2.9). In general, the limit of $X_{n,T}$ depends on the treatment of the two indices, n and T, and the properties that link the rows and columns of the process. Several approaches are possible. One approach is to fix one of the indexes, say n, and allow the other (T) to pass to infinity, giving an intermediate limit. By letting n pass to infinity subsequently, a *sequential* limit theory is obtained. We write this type of limit process in the form $(T, n \to \infty)_{\text{seq}}$, where the order of the indices is critical to the meaning. While they often lead to tractable deviations, sequential limits can give asymptotic results that are misleading in cases where both indexes pass to infinity simultaneously. A second approach is to pass to infinity along a specific diagonal path (in the two dimensional array) determined by a monotonically increasing function relation of the type $T = T(n)$ while the index $n \to \infty$. (This approach really requires specificity about the functional dependence only in the limit, so it includes cases such as those where we assume that $(T/n) \to c \neq 0$, in which case we simply have $T(n) = cn$.) We write this type of limit process in the form $(T(n), n \to \infty)_{\text{diag}}$. This approach also simplifies the asymptotic theory by replacing $X_{n,T}$ with the single indexed process $X_{n,T(n)}$. The drawback of *diagonal path* limit theory is that the assumed expansion path $(T(n), n) \to \infty$ is highly specific and may not provide an appropriate approximation for a given (T,n) situation. Moreover, the limit theory can depend on the specific functional relation $T = T(n)$ that is used in the asymptotic development. (A recent econometric example of this situation is analyzed in Phillips and Lee (1996).) A third approach is to allow both indexes to pass to infinity simultaneously without placing specific diagonal path restrictions on the divergence. We write this type of limit process in the form $(T, n \to \infty)$. Generally speaking, such *joint* limit theory requires stronger conditions (linking the rows and columns of the joint array, and on the moments of the component variates) to establish than sequential convergence or diagonal path convergence. But, by the same token, the results are also stronger and may be expected to be relevant to a wider range of circumstances, provided the conditions hold.

The asymptotic development in this paper will involve both sequential limit theory and joint limit theory arguments. The sequential limits are especially helpful in extracting quick asymptotics and they are useful because they bring into play all of the key elements in our final limit theory in a straightforward way. The joint limit theory is more difficult to derive and applies under stronger conditions. Fortunately, these conditions do not seem to exclude cases of major importance for the type of large T and moderate n empirical applications that we have in mind for our methods.

The following subsections define the convergence concepts that we need and give some conditions that assure joint convergence.

3.1. *Definitions and Some Relations between Sequential and Joint Limits*

A typical double index process of the type that occurs in this paper has the linear form

$$X_{n,T} = \frac{1}{k_n} \sum_{i=1}^{n} Y_{i,T}, \tag{3.1}$$

where $Y_{i,T}$ are independent m-component random vectors across i defined on a probability space $(\Omega, \mathcal{F}, P)$. A typical $Y_{i,T}$ component in our case has the form of a standardized sum

$$(3.2) \qquad Y_{i,T} = \frac{1}{d_T} \sum_{t=1}^{T} f(Z_{i,t=[Tr]}),$$

where the $Z_{i,[Tr]}$ are random elements in the space[3] $D[0,1]^h$, for some integer h, within the space $(\Omega, \mathscr{F}, P)$, d_T is a standardizing factor, and f is a continuous functional from $D[0,1]^h$ to $\mathbb{R}^m$. We alert the reader that the meaning of the notation $X_{n,T}$ and $Y_{i,T}$ in (3.1) and (3.2) above is different from that of the symbols $Y_{i,t}$ and $X_{i,t}$ which represent components of $Z_{i,t}$ given in (2.1) that appear in other sections of this paper. The differences in meaning should be obvious from the context.

DEFINITION 1: (a) A sequence of m-vectors $\{X_{n,T}\}$ on $(\Omega, \mathscr{F}, P)$ is said to *converge in probability to X sequentially*, written $X_{n,T} \to_p X$ in sequential limit as $(T, n \to \infty)_{\text{seq}}$, if

$$\lim_{n\to\infty} \lim_{T\to\infty} P\{\|X_{n,T} - X\| > \varepsilon\} = 0 \qquad \forall \varepsilon > 0.$$

(b) $X_{n,T}$ converges in distribution sequentially to the m-vector X, written $X_{n,T} \Rightarrow X$ in sequential limit as $(T, n \to \infty)_{\text{seq}}$, if

$$\lim_{n\to\infty} \lim_{T\to\infty} |Ef(X_{n,T}) - Ef(X)| = 0 \qquad \forall f \in \mathscr{C},$$

where $\mathscr{C}$ is the class of all bounded, continuous, real functions on $\mathbb{R}^m$.

In practice, we can find the sequential limits of $X_{n,T}$ in (3.1) as follows. Using time series limit theory we find the limit behavior of $Y_{i,T}$. Suppose, for example, that as $T \to \infty$

$$(3.3) \qquad Y_{i,T} \Rightarrow Y_i$$

or

$$(3.4) \qquad Y_{i,T} \overset{p}{\to} Y_i \qquad \text{for all } i.$$

Then, by the independence of $Y_{i,T}$ across i for all T, we have $X_{n,T} \Rightarrow X_n$ or $X_{n,T} \to_p X_n$ as $T \to \infty$ for all n, where $X_n = (1/k_n)\Sigma_{i=1}^n Y_i$.

By enlarging the underlying probability space if necessary, we can take it in the case of (3.3) that all the Y_i's are defined on the same probability space.

[3] $D[0,1]^h$ is a product metric space of h independent copies of $D[0,1]$, the space of the all real valued functions on the interval $[0,1]$ that are right continuous and have finite left limits. $D[0,1]^h$ is endowed with the metric $\rho_h(f,g) = \max_i\{\rho(f_i, g_i)$: $i \in \{1,\dots,h\}$, $f_i, g_i \in D[0,1]\}$, where ρ is the modified Skorohod metric (see Billingsley (1968, p. 112)) under which $D[0,1]$ is separable and complete.

Hence, the sum of the limit random variables $\Sigma_{i=1}^n Y_i$ is well defined on the same space. Next, we allow $n \to \infty$ and apply a limit theory to the standardized sum

$$(3.5) \qquad X_n = \frac{1}{k_n} \sum_{i=1}^{n} Y_i.$$

Under some regularity conditions, we can now find the sequential limit, X, or X_n. For example, if $k_n = n$, we can apply a law of large numbers (LLN) to X_n and if $k_n = \sqrt{n}$ we can use an appropriate central limit theorem (CLT).

The requirement that the Y_i's in (3.3) are defined on the same probability space is important, especially when we apply an LLN to X_n in the second stage (3.5). The reason is as follows. The weak convergence $X_{n,T} \Rightarrow X_n$ as $T \to \infty$ involves only the implication that the distribution of the $X_{n,T}$ converges to the distribution of the X_n, not any properties of the probability space where the X_n are defined. Indeed, if the weak convergence is mixing (e.g., see Hall and Heyde (1980)), then X_n escapes from the underlying probability space when $T \to \infty$. However, to employ an LLN to the sequence of X_n, these variates need to be defined on the same probability space. The requirement that the Y_i's in (3.3) are defined on the same probability space can be accommodated by suitably enlarging the underlying space. The construction of such a probability space is provided in Appendix B.

Next, we define the concepts of joint convergence in probability and joint weak convergence.

Definition 2: (a) Suppose that the m-vector random sequence $X_{n,T}$ and X are defined on a probability space $(\Omega, \mathcal{F}, P)$. $X_{n,T}$ is said to *converge in probability jointly to* X, written $X_{n,T} \to_p X$ as $(T, n \to \infty)$, if

$$(3.6) \qquad \lim_{T,n\to\infty} P\{\|X_{n,T} - X\| > \varepsilon\} = 0 \qquad \forall \varepsilon > 0.$$

(b) $X_{n,T}$ is said to converge in distribution jointly to a $(m \times 1)$ random vector X, written $X_{n,T} \Rightarrow X$ as $(T, n \to \infty)$, if

$$(3.7) \qquad \lim_{T,n\to\infty} |Ef(X_{n,T}) - Ef(X)| = 0 \qquad \forall f \in \mathcal{C},$$

where $\mathcal{C}$ is the class of all bounded, continuous real functions on $\mathbb{R}^m$.

Remarks: (a) Evidently, joint convergence implies diagonal convergence on all monotonic diagonal paths. Moreover, a version of the converse is also true, namely that $X_{n,T} \to_p X$ (or $X_{n,T} \Rightarrow X$) as $(T, n \to \infty)$ if $X_{n,T(n)} \to_p X$ as $(T(n), n \to \infty)_{\text{diag}}$ for all $T(n) \to \infty$ monotonically as $n \to \infty$.

(b) In some of our results, we need to place a condition on the indexes in joint convergence of the form $n/T \to 0$. Joint convergence as $(T, n \to \infty)$ is then said to apply subject to this condition. The definitional limits given in (3.6) and (3.7) above are naturally subject to the same condition regarding the passage of the indexes to infinity in this case.

Sequential limits are by no means always the same as joint limits or diagonal path limits. Sometimes, different normalizations even are required to obtain nondegenerate limits. PM[b] gives several examples. Nevertheless, under some circumstances we can establish a relationship between sequential limits and joint limits. The following two lemmas give some elementary conditions.

LEMMA 5 (Conditions for Joint Convergence to Imply Sequential Convergence): (a) *Suppose there exist random vectors* X_n *on the same probability space as* $X_{n,T}$ *satisfying, for all n,* $X_{n,T} \to_p X_n$ *as* $T \to \infty$. *If* $X_{n,T} \to_p X$ *as* $(T, n \to \infty)$, *then* $X_{n,T} \to_p X$ *sequentially as* $(T, n \to \infty)_{\text{seq}}$.

(b) *Suppose there exist random vectors* X_n *such that, for any fixed n,* $X_{n,T} \Rightarrow X_n$ *as* $T \to \infty$. *If* $X_{n,T} \Rightarrow X$ *as* $n, T \to \infty$, *then* $X_{n,T} \Rightarrow X$ *sequentially as* $(T, n \to \infty)_{\text{seq}}$.

LEMMA 6 (Conditions for Sequential Convergence to Imply Joint Convergence): (a) *Suppose there exist random vectors* X_n *and X on the same probability space as* $X_{n,T}$ *satisfying, for all n,* $X_{n,T} \to_p X_n$ *as* $T \to \infty$ *and* $X_n \to_p X$ *as* $n \to \infty$. *Then,* $X_{n,T} \to_p X$ *as* $(n, T \to \infty)$ *if and only if,*

$$\limsup_{n,T} P\{\|X_{n,T} - X_n\| > \varepsilon\} = 0 \qquad \forall \varepsilon > 0. \tag{3.8}$$

(b) *Suppose there exist random vectors* X_n *such that, for any fixed n,* $X_{n,T} \Rightarrow X_n$ *as* $T \to \infty$ *and* $X_n \Rightarrow X$ *as* $n \to \infty$. *Then,* $X_{n,T} \Rightarrow X$ *as* $(n, T \to \infty)$ *if and only if,*

$$\limsup_{n,T} | E(f(X_{n,T})) - E(f(X_n)) | = 0 \qquad \forall f \in \mathscr{C}. \tag{3.9}$$

3.2. *Joint Convergence in Probability*

Consider a double indexed process $X_{n,T}$ whose typical form is an average of $(m \times 1)$ random vectors $Y_{i,T}$,

$$X_{n,T} = \frac{1}{n} \sum_{i=1}^{n} Y_{i,T}, \tag{3.10}$$

where the $Y_{i,T}$ are independent across i for all T. The concern is to establish conditions under which a probability limit of $X_{n,T}$ in (3.10) exists and to develop methods of finding this probability limit.

Suppose the $X_{n,T}$ are integrable and let

$$\mu_X = \lim_{n,T \to \infty} EX_{n,T} = \lim_{n,T \to \infty} \frac{1}{n} \sum_{i=1}^{n} EY_{i,T} \quad \text{be finite}. \tag{3.11}$$

By definition it is sufficient for $X_{n,T} \to_p \mu_X$ as $(n, T \to \infty)$ to show that

$$\lim_{n,T \to \infty} P\left\{ \left\| \frac{1}{n} \sum_{i=1}^{n} (Y_{i,T} - EY_{i,T}) \right\| > \varepsilon \right\} = 0 \qquad \text{for all } \varepsilon > 0. \tag{3.12}$$

In some applications (3.12) can be verified by showing that

$$\text{(3.13)} \qquad \lim_{n,T\to\infty} E\left\| \frac{1}{n}\sum_{i=1}^{n}(Y_{i,T}-EY_{i,T})\right\| = 0$$

using the Markov inequality. Or, if the $X_{n,T}$ are square integrable, (3.12) follows by Chebychev's inequality when

$$\text{(3.14)} \qquad \lim_{n,T\to\infty} E\left\| \frac{1}{n}\sum_{i=1}^{n}(Y_{i,T}-EY_{i,T})\right\|^2 = \lim_{n,T\to\infty} \frac{1}{n^2}\sum_{i=1}^{n} E\|Y_{i,T}-EY_{i,T}\|^2 = 0,$$

where the first equality holds because the $Y_{i,T}$ are independent across i for all T.

Sequential probability limits can also be derived. From time series limit theory we may obtain the limit behavior of $Y_{i,T}$ when $T\to\infty$. Suppose, for instance, that as $T\to\infty$

$$\text{(3.15)} \qquad Y_{i,T} \Rightarrow Y_i \qquad \forall i$$

or

$$\text{(3.16)} \qquad Y_{i,T} \overset{p}{\to} Y_i \qquad \forall i$$

so that, by the independence of $Y_{i,T}$ across i for all T, it follows $X_{n,T}\Rightarrow X_n$ or $X_{n,T}\to_p X_n$ as $T\to\infty$ for all n, where $X_n=(1/n)\Sigma_{i=1}^{n}Y_i$.

Suppose also, in the case of (3.15), that the Y_i are defined on the same probability space for all i so that the sum of the limit random variables $(1/n)\Sigma_{i=1}^{n}Y_i$ is meaningful. Appendix B(1) provides a construction for doing this and, hereafter, we assume that the random vectors Y_i in (3.15) exist on the same probability space whenever we use sequential limit arguments. By allowing $n\to\infty$ and applying a standard strong law for independent random variables to

$$\text{(3.17)} \qquad X_n = \frac{1}{n}\sum_{i=1}^{n} Y_i,$$

under some regularity conditions,[4] we may find the sequential limit X. Let

$$\text{(3.18)} \qquad \tilde{\mu}_X = \lim_n \frac{1}{n}\sum_{i=1}^{n} EY_i.$$

Then

$$X_n = \frac{1}{n}\sum_{i=1}^{n} Y_i \overset{\text{a.s.}}{\to} \tilde{\mu}_X = \lim_n \frac{1}{n}\sum_{i=1}^{n} EY_i.$$

A fundamental question is whether the joint probability limit μ_X in (3.11) is equivalent to the sequential probability limit $\tilde{\mu}_X$ in (3.18). Lemma 6 provides

[4]Simple sufficient conditions are that the Y_i are independent with $\sup_i E\|Y_i - EY_i\|^2 < \infty$.

one solution. According to Lemma 6, it is enough to verify condition (3.9) with $X_{n,T} = (1/n)\Sigma_{i=1}^{n} Y_{i,T}$ and $X_n = (1/n)\Sigma_{i=1}^{n}\Sigma_{i=1}^{n} Y_i$ to conclude that $X_{n,T} \to_p \tilde{\mu}_X$ as $n, T \to \infty$, where $\tilde{\mu}_X = \lim_n (1/n)\Sigma_{i=1}^{n} EY_i$. The following theorem gives a set of sufficient conditions under which condition (3.9) is satisfied, so that the probability limits μ_X in (3.11) and $\tilde{\mu}_X$ in (3.18) are equivalent.

THEOREM 1 (Joint Probability Limits): *Suppose the* $(m \times 1)$ *random vectors* $Y_{i,T}$ *are independent across i for all T and integrable. Assume that* $Y_{i,T} \Rightarrow Y_i$ *as* $T \to \infty$ *for all i. Let the following hold*:

(i) $\limsup_{n,T}(1/n)\Sigma_{i=1}^{n} E\|Y_{i,T}\| < \infty$;
(ii) $\limsup_{n,T}(1/n)\Sigma_{i=1}^{n}\|EY_{i,T} - EY_i\| = 0$;
(iii) $\limsup_{n,T}(1/n)\Sigma_{i=1}^{n} E\|Y_{i,T}\|1\{\|Y_{i,T}\| > n\varepsilon\} = 0\ \forall \varepsilon > 0$; *and*
(iv) $\limsup_{n}(1/n)\Sigma_{i=1}^{n} E\|Y_i\|1\{\|Y_i\| > n\varepsilon\} = 0\ \forall \varepsilon > 0$.
(a) *Then condition* (3.9) *holds*.
(b) *If* $\lim_{n\to\infty}(1/n)\Sigma_{i=1}^{n} EY_i (:= \tilde{\mu}_X)$ *exists and* $X_n \to_p \tilde{\mu}_X$ *as* $n \to \infty$, *then* $X_{n,T} \to_p \tilde{\mu}_X$ *as* $(n, T \to \infty)$.

In establishing the existence of a joint probability limit of $(1/n)\Sigma_{i=1}^{n} Y_{i,T}$, Theorem 1 requires only first moment assumptions on $Y_{i,T}$ and is, in this respect, less demanding than (3.14), which uses second moments of $Y_{i,T}$. Theorem 1 is particularly useful when the first moment condition (3.13) is not so easy to establish.

An important special case arises when the $Y_{i,T}$ are a scaled version of some iid random vectors $Q_{i,T}$.[5] Suppose that $Y_{i,T} = C_i Q_{i,T}$, where the $\{Q_{i,T}\}_i$ are iid for all T and the C_i are $(m \times m)$ nonrandom matrices for all i. Suppose that $Q_{i,T} \Rightarrow Q_i$ as $T \to \infty$ for all i, so that $Y_i = C_i Q_i$. In general, the $Y_{i,T}$ are heterogenous across i unless the C_i are the same for all i. The source of the heterogeneity of $Y_{i,T}$ is the scale effect C_i, and then the heterogeneity from C_i is smoothed by letting $n \to \infty$. We have the following result for this special case.

COROLLARY 1: *Suppose that* $Y_{i,T} = C_i Q_{i,T}$, *where the* $Q_{i,T}$ *are iid across i for all T, and the* C_i *are* $(m \times m)$ *nonrandom matrices for all i. Assume that the* $Q_{i,T}$ *are integrable for all T and* $Q_{i,T} \Rightarrow Q_i$ *as* $T \to \infty$. *Assume that* $C = \lim_n (1/n)\Sigma_{i=1}^{n} C_i$ *exists. If* $\|Q_{i,T}\|$ *is uniformly integrable in T for all i, and if* $\sup_i \|C_i\| < \infty$, *then* $(1/n)\Sigma_{i=1}^{n} Y_{i,T} \to_p CE(Q_i)$ *as* $(n, T \to \infty)$.

[5] In many applications, an $I(1)$ process $Z_{i,t}$ can be decomposed into a scaled random walk process plus an error term, that is, $Z_{i,t} = C_i(1)S_{i,t} + \tilde{U}_{i,0} - \tilde{U}_{i,t}$, where $S_{i,t} = S_{i,t-1} + U_{i,t}$ and $C_i(1)$ is the long-run moving average coefficient of $\Delta Z_{i,t}$ (see Phillips and Solo (1992)). Then, the scale factor C_i is $C_i(1)$ and $Q_{i,T}$ corresponds to $f(S_{i,t}/\sqrt{T})$, where f is a continuous functional on some metric space.

3.3. *Joint Central Limit Theory*

This section considers joint convergence in distribution of the $\sqrt{n}$-standardized double sequence $X_{n,T}$,

$$X_{n,T} = \frac{1}{\sqrt{n}} \sum_{i=1}^{n} Y_{i,T}, \tag{3.19}$$

where the $Y_{i,T}$ are independent $(m \times 1)$ random vectors across i with $EY_{i,T} = 0$ and $EY_{i,T}Y_{i,T}' = \Omega_{i,T}$.

One approach to the limit distribution of $X_{n,T}$ is to attempt to use a multivariate CLT directly. This approach is particularly appropriate in the case of diagonal path limits where we have $X_{n,T(n)} = (1/\sqrt{n})\Sigma_{i=1}^{n} Y_{i,T(n)}$ and a suitable multivariate CLT for triangular arrays can be applied. This idea was employed by Quah (1994) and Levin and Lin (1993) in their work on panel unit root tests. But, in general, when n and T go to infinity and no specific expansion relation between n and T is assumed, we cannot use traditional CLT's in this way. In what follows, therefore, we develop a joint CLT for $(n, T \to \infty)$, using a Lindeberg condition for a double indexed process.

First, take the case where the $Y_{i,T}$ in (3.19) are scalar random variables. Let $s_{n,T}^2 = \Sigma_{i=1}^{n} \Omega_{i,T}$ and define $\xi_{i,n,T} = Y_{i,T}/s_{n,T}$. Then we have the following result.

THEOREM 2 (Joint Limit CLT): *Suppose that for* $\forall \varepsilon > 0$,

$$\lim_{n,T \to \infty} \sum_{i=1}^{n} E\left[\xi_{i,n,T}^2 1\{|\xi_{i,n,T}| > \varepsilon\}\right] = 0. \tag{3.20}$$

Then, as $(n, T \to \infty)$,

$$\sum_{i=1}^{n} \xi_{i,n,T} \Rightarrow N(0,1).$$

There are some interesting special cases of this joint CLT. The following result, which is related to a theorem of Eicker (1963), arises when the $(m \times 1)$ random vectors $Y_{i,T}$ are scaled versions of iid random vectors $Q_{i,T}$.

THEOREM 3 (Joint Limit CLT for Scaled Variates): *Suppose that* $Y_{i,T} = C_i Q_{i,T}$, *where the* $(m \times 1)$ *random vectors* $Q_{i,T}$ *are* iid$(0, \Sigma_T)$ *across i for all T and the* C_i *are* $(m \times m)$ *nonzero and nonrandom matrices. Assume the following conditions hold*:

(i) *Let* $\sigma_T^2 = \lambda_{\min}(\Sigma_T)$ *and* $\liminf_T \sigma_T^2 > 0$;
(ii) $\max_{i \le n} \|C_i\|^2 / \lambda_{\min}(\Sigma_{i=1}^{n} C_i C_i') = O(1/n)$ *as* $n \to \infty$;
(iii) $\|Q_{i,T}\|^2$ *are uniformly integrable in* T;
(iv) $\lim_{n,T} (1/n) \Sigma_{i=1}^{n} C_i \Sigma_T C_i' = \Omega > 0$.

Then,

$$X_{n,T} = \frac{1}{\sqrt{n}} \sum_{i=1}^{n} Y_{i,T} \Rightarrow N(0, \Omega) \qquad \textit{as } n, T \to \infty.$$

Sequential weak convergence of $(1/\sqrt{n})\Sigma_{i=1}^{n} Y_{i,T}$ can be derived in the same way as the sequential probability limit of $(1/n)\Sigma_{i=1}^{n} Y_{i,T}$ considered earlier. Suppose that, for each i as $T \to \infty$, the random variables $Y_{i,T}$ converge in distribution to Y_i, where the Y_i are independent with mean zero and variance Ω_i. Then, $(1/\sqrt{n})\Sigma_{i=1}^{n} Y_i \Rightarrow N(0, \Omega)$ if for all $\varepsilon > 0$ as $n \to \infty$

$$(3.21) \qquad E \frac{Y_i^2}{s_n^2} 1\left\{\left|\frac{Y_i^2}{s_n^2}\right| > \varepsilon\right\} \to 0,$$

and

$$(3.22) \qquad \frac{1}{n} s_n^2 = \frac{1}{n} \sum_{i=1}^{n} \Omega_i \to \Omega.$$

In many econometric applications Y_i is a Gaussian random variable or a function of the Gaussian process. So the Y_i usually possess higher moments. Second moment requirements then follow automatically, and the Lindeberg condition (3.21) for $(1/\sqrt{n})\Sigma_{i=1}^{n} Y_i$ may be verified directly using a Liapounov condition.

Additional Remarks

(a) Sequential weak convergence of $(1/\sqrt{n})\Sigma_{i=1}^{n} Y_{i,T}$ to $N(0, \Omega)$ under conditions (3.21) and (3.22) does not imply that $(1/\sqrt{n})\Sigma_{i=1}^{n} Y_{i,T}$ converges in distribution jointly to $N(0, \Omega)$ as $(n, T \to \infty)$. According to Lemma 6(ii), condition (3.9) is a necessary and sufficient condition for $(1/\sqrt{n})\Sigma_{i=1}^{n} Y_{i,T}$ to converge in distribution jointly to the sequential limit distribution $N(0, \Omega)$. In this case, therefore, condition (3.20) and the condition that $(1/n)\Sigma_{i=1}^{n} \Omega_{i,T} \to \Omega$ as $(n, T \to \infty)$ provide sufficient conditions for condition (3.9).

(b) When $Y_{i,T}$ in (3.19) does not have mean zero, but instead has mean zero asymptotically as $T \to \infty$ for each i, joint CLT's such as Theorem 2 or Corollary 3 cannot be applied. In this case, T needs to increase fast enough to make the $\sqrt{n}$-standardized sum of the biases small. That is, $(1/\sqrt{n})\Sigma_{i=1}^{n} EY_{i,T}$ should go to zero as $(n, T \to \infty)$. In this case, asymptotic normality of $(1/\sqrt{n})\Sigma_{i=1}^{n} Y_{i,T}$ will continue to hold provided the expansion rate between n and T allows the bias to go to zero. The next section gives an example where this problem arises (e.g., see Theorem 4).

4. SPURIOUS PANEL REGRESSION

This section considers the case where the two component random vectors $Y_{i,t}$ and $X_{i,t}$ of $Z_{i,t}$ in (2.1) have no cointegrating relation for any i. This case is covered by the following assumption.

Assumption 3 (Spurious Regression): *The random matrices Ω_i are positive definite almost surely.*

Suppose that we perform a time series regression of $Y_{i,t}$ on $X_{i,t}$:

$$(4.1) \qquad Y_{i,t} = \hat{\beta}_i X_{i,t} + \hat{U}_{i,t},$$

where $\hat{\beta}_i = \Sigma_{t=1}^T Y_{i,t} X'_{i,t} (\Sigma_{t=1}^T X_{i,t} X'_{i,t})^{-1}$. As is well known (e.g., Phillips (1986)), under Assumption 3 the regression coefficient estimator $\hat{\beta}_i$ has the following nondegenerate limit distribution, as $T \to \infty$:

$$(4.2) \qquad \hat{\beta}_i \Rightarrow \int M_{y_i} M'_{x_i} \left(\int M_{x_i} M'_{x_i} \right)^{-1} \qquad \text{for all } i.$$

The weak convergence result (4.2) implies that regression (4.1) is spurious in the sense that the regression of $Y_{i,t}$ on $X_{i,t}$ does not identify any fixed long-run relation between $Y_{i,t}$ and $X_{i,t}$. By contrast, the main result in what follows is that, in a panel data set, such regressions are no longer spurious and do, in fact, distinguish a long-run average relation between $Y_{i,t}$ and $X_{i,t}$.

Consider the following linear least-squares regression of $Y_{i,t}$ on $X_{i,t}$ with pooled panel data:

$$(4.3) \qquad Y_{i,t} = \hat{\beta}_{n,T} X_{i,t} + \hat{U}_{i,t},$$

where

$$(4.4) \qquad \hat{\beta}_{n,T} = \left(\sum_{i=1}^{n} \sum_{t=1}^{T} Y_{i,t} X'_{i,t} \right) \left(\sum_{i=1}^{n} \sum_{t=1}^{T} X_{i,t} X'_{i,t} \right)^{-1}.$$

We now proceed to develop an asymptotic theory for $\hat{\beta}_{n,T}$. The approach we adopt is to derive the limit under sequential convergence of the indices (T, n), and then show that the limit continues to hold under joint convergence $(T, n \to \infty)$ provided certain conditions hold. In many cases, this is the simplest way to proceed.

Indeed, for estimators like $\hat{\beta}_{n,T}$, asymptotic results are readily obtained using sequential asymptotics such as $(T, n \to \infty)_{\text{seq}}$. According to (2.6) in first stage asymptotics, the pooled estimator $\hat{\beta}_{n,T}$ has the following limit distribution:

$$\hat{\beta}_{n,T} \Rightarrow \left(\frac{1}{n} \sum_{i=1}^{n} \int M_{y_i} M'_{x_i} \right) \left(\frac{1}{n} \sum_{i=1}^{n} \int M_{x_i} M'_{x_i} \right)^{-1}$$

as $T \to \infty$ for any fixed n. From Lemma 4 we know that $\int M_{y_i} M'_{x_i}$ and $\int M_{x_i} M'_{x_i}$ have finite second moments. Also, as in (2.8) above, by direct calculation we get $E(\int M_i M'_i) = \frac{1}{2} E(\Omega_i) = \frac{1}{2}\Omega$. And then, applying the strong law of large numbers as in (2.7), we have

$$\frac{1}{n} \sum_{i=1}^{n} \int M_{y_i} M'_{x_i} \overset{\text{a.s.}}{\to} \frac{1}{2} \Omega_{yx} \qquad \text{and} \qquad \frac{1}{n} \sum_{i=1}^{n} \int M_{x_i} M'_{x_i} \overset{\text{a.s.}}{\to} \frac{1}{2} \Omega_{xx},$$

as $n \to \infty$. By Assumption 3, $\Omega_{x_i x_i}$ is positive definite a.s., and $c'\Omega_{x_i x_i} c > 0$ a.s. for any $c \neq 0$ in $\mathbb{R}^{m_x}$. Thus, $Ec'\Omega_{x_i x_i} c = c'\Omega_{xx} c > 0$, which implies that Ω_{xx} is positive definite. Hence Ω_{xx}^{-1} exists, and so we have as $(T, n \to \infty)_{\text{seq}}$:

$$\hat{\beta}_{n,T} \xrightarrow{p} \Omega_{yx} \Omega_{xx}^{-1}.$$

Let $\beta = \Omega_{yx}\Omega_{xx}^{-1}$. We will call the parameter β the *long-run average* regression coefficient. It is the matrix regression coefficient (of y on x) associated with the long-run average covariance matrix Ω. To find the limit distribution of $\hat{\beta}_{n,T}$ we rescale the centered estimator $(\hat{\beta}_{n,T} - \beta)$ by $\sqrt{n}$ and let $T \to \infty$ for fixed n. For all fixed n as $T \to \infty$ we have

$$\sqrt{n}\left(\hat{\beta}_{n,T} - \beta\right) \Rightarrow \frac{1}{\sqrt{n}} \sum_{i=1}^{n} \left(\int M_{y_i} M_{x_i}' - \beta \int M_{x_i} M_{x_i}' \right) \left(\frac{1}{n} \sum_{i=1}^{n} \int M_{x_i} M_{x_i}' \right)^{-1}. \tag{4.5}$$

Note that

$$E\left(\int M_{y_i} M_{x_i}' - \beta \int M_{x_i} M_{x_i}'\right) = E\left[E\left(\int M_{y_i} M_{x_i}' - \beta \int M_{x_i} M_{x_i}' \middle| \mathcal{F}_{c_i} \right)\right]$$
$$= \tfrac{1}{2} E\left(\Omega_{y_i x_i} - \Omega_{yx} \Omega_{xx}^{-1} \Omega_{x_i x_i} \right) = 0,$$

where the conditional expectation exists because $\int M_{y_i} M_{x_i}' - \beta \int M_{x_i} M_{x_i}'$ is square integrable by Lemma 4. Thus, the numerator of (4.5) has mean zero. Also, we know that the numerator has finite second moments from Lemma 4, and with a straightforward calculation the variance matrix is found[6] to be

$$E\left(\operatorname{vec}\left(\int M_{y_i} M_{x_i}' - \beta \int M_{x_i} M_{x_i}' \right) \operatorname{vec}\left(\int M_{y_i} M_{x_i}' - \beta \int M_{x_i} M_{x_i}' \right)' \right) \tag{4.6}$$
$$= \tfrac{1}{6} E\left(\Omega_{x_i x_i} \otimes \left(\Omega_{y_i y_i} - \beta \Omega_{x_i y_i} - \Omega_{y_i x_i} \beta' + \beta \Omega_{x_i x_i} \beta' \right) \right)$$
$$+ \tfrac{1}{6} E\left(\left(\Omega_{x_i y_i} - \Omega_{x_i x_i} \beta' \right) \otimes \left(\Omega_{y_i x_i} - \beta \Omega_{x_i x_i} \right) K_{m_y m_x} \right)$$
$$+ \tfrac{1}{4} E\left(\operatorname{vec}\left(\Omega_{y_i x_i} - \beta \Omega_{x_i x_i} \right) \left(\operatorname{vec}\left(\Omega_{y_i x_i} - \beta \Omega_{x_i x_i} \right) \right)' \right)$$
$$= \Theta, \quad \text{say}$$

where $K_{m_y m_x}$ is the $(m_y m_x \times m_y m_x)$ commutation matrix (e.g., see Magnus and Neudecker (1988)). The sequence of random matrices $\{\int M_{y_i} M_{x_i}' - \beta \int M_{x_i} M_{x_i}'\}_i$ in the numerator of the matrix quotient (4.5) is iid $(0, \Theta)$ across i. From the multivariate Lindeberg-Levy theorem, we then get as $n \to \infty$

$$\frac{1}{\sqrt{n}} \sum_{i=1}^{n} \left(\int M_{y_i} M_{x_i}' - \beta \int M_{x_i} M_{x_i}' \right) \Rightarrow N(0, \Theta). \tag{4.7}$$

[6] The calculations are given in Appendix C of PM[b].

Combining (4.7) with the limit

$$\frac{1}{n}\sum_{i=1}^{n}\int M_{x_i}M_{x_i}' \overset{\text{a.s.}}{\to} \frac{1}{2}\Omega_{xx} \qquad \text{as} \qquad n\to\infty,$$

we have the following limit distribution of the pooled estimator $\hat{\beta}_{n,T}$ as $(T,n\to\infty)_{\text{seq}}$

$$\sqrt{n}\left(\hat{\beta}_{n,T}-\beta\right)\Rightarrow N\left(0,4\left(\Omega_{xx}^{-1}\otimes I_{m_y}\right)\Theta\left(\Omega_{xx}^{-1}\otimes I_{m_y}\right)\right). \tag{4.8}$$

Theorem 4 below shows that these results continue to hold in joint asymptotics as $(T,n\to\infty)$. For the limit distribution (4.8) to hold in this case we need the additional requirement that $n/T\to 0$. No additional condition is required for consistency.

THEOREM 4: *Suppose Assumptions* 1, 2, *and* 3 *hold.*
(a) *Then, as* $(n,T\to\infty)$, *we have* $\hat{\beta}_{n,T}\to_p \beta$.
(b) *If* $(n,T\to\infty)$ *and* $n/T\to 0$, *then*

$$\sqrt{n}\left(\hat{\beta}_{n,T}-\beta\right)\Rightarrow N\left(0,4\left(\Omega_{xx}^{-1}\otimes I_{m_y}\right)\Theta\left(\Omega_{xx}^{-1}\otimes I_{m_y}\right)\right).$$

REMARKS: (a) The restriction $(n/T)\to 0$ in Theorem 4 controls the effects of bias in the panel regression. Under the assumptions on the DGP given in Section 2, the expectation of the components in the numerator of $\sqrt{n}(\hat{\beta}_{n,T}-\beta)$ is generally nonzero, i.e.,

$$E\left(\frac{1}{T^2}\sum_{t=1}^{T}(Y_{i,t}X_{i,t}'-\beta X_{i,t}X_{i,t}')\right)\neq 0,$$

whereas

$$E\left(\frac{1}{T^2}\sum_{t=1}^{T}(Y_{i,t}X_{i,t}'-\beta X_{i,t}X_{i,t}')\right)\to 0,$$

as $T\to\infty$ for all i. In this case, the condition $(n/T)\to 0$ prevents the bias from having a dominating asymptotic effect on the standardized quantity $\sqrt{n}(\hat{\beta}_{n,T}-\beta)$. But, when $(n/T)\nrightarrow 0$, the bias can dominate and the asymptotic behavior can be very different. For example, suppose that

$$\frac{1}{\sqrt{n}}\sum_{i=1}^{n}E\left(\frac{1}{T^2}\sum_{t=1}^{T}(Y_{i,t}X_{i,t}'-\beta X_{i,t}X_{i,t}')\right)\to b$$

along some diagonal limit $(T(n),n\to\infty)_{\text{diag}}$. In this event, we can expect to have a limit distribution with an asymptotic bias b. Further, the required restriction on the expansion rate between n and T will change depending on the underlying assumptions about the DGP. For example, if the shocks $U_{i,t}(=\Delta Z_{i,t})$ are iid over t and $Z_{i,0}=0$ for all i, then our results hold as $(n,T\to\infty)$ without imposing any restriction on the expansion rate between n and T.

(b) Theorem 4 holds for any partition of $Z_{i,t}$. If the panel data form a vector unit root model such as (2.1), then we can estimate the average long-run relation between any two subvectors. In effect, therefore, there is an average long-run relationship between any two subvector components of an integrated process over a cross section population.

(c) A key factor in determining these results is that panel data provide iid cross section information that is unavailable in a simple time series context. In consequence, we may expect some version of these results to apply when the regression utilizes only a fraction of the time series data. Suppose we regress $Y_{i,t}$ on $X_{i,t}$ using the cross section observations at time period $t=[Tr]$ with $0<r\leq 1$. The cross section OLS estimator $\tilde{\beta}_{n,[Tr]}$ is then defined by

$$(4.9)\qquad \tilde{\beta}_{n,[Tr]}=\left(\sum_{i=1}^{n} Y_{i,t}X_{i,t}'\right)\left(\sum_{i=1}^{n} X_{i,t}X_{i,t}'\right)^{-1}.$$

Using similar arguments to those employed above, we can show that, in sequential asymptotics as $(T,n\to\infty)_{\text{seq}}$, we have

$$\tilde{\beta}_{n,[Tr]}\xrightarrow{p}\beta,\qquad\text{and}$$

$$\sqrt{n}\left(\tilde{\beta}_{n,[Tr]}-\beta\right)\Rightarrow N\left(0,\left(\Omega_{xx}^{-1}\otimes I_{m_y}\right)\tilde{\Theta}\left(\Omega_{xx}^{-1}\otimes I_{m_y}\right)\right),$$

where

$$\begin{aligned}\tilde{\Theta}=&\,E\left(\Omega_{x_ix_i}\otimes(\Omega_{y_iy_i}-\beta\Omega_{x_ix_i}-\Omega_{x_ix_i}\beta'+\beta\Omega_{x_ix_i}\beta')\right)\\&+E\left((\Omega_{x_iy_i}-\Omega_{x_ix_i}\beta')\otimes(\Omega_{y_ix_i}-\beta\Omega_{x_ix_i})K_{m_ym_x}\right)\\&+E\left(\text{vec}(\Omega_{y_ix_i}-\beta\Omega_{x_ix_i})\left(\text{vec}(\Omega_{y_ix_i}-\beta\Omega_{x_ix_i})\right)'\right).\end{aligned}$$

(d) Since $(\Omega_{xx}^{-1}\otimes I_{m_y})\tilde{\Theta}(\Omega_{xx}^{-1}\otimes I_{m_y})-4(\Omega_{xx}^{-1}\otimes I_{m_y})\Theta(\Omega_{xx}^{-1}\otimes I_{m_y})>0$, the cross section estimator $\tilde{\beta}_n$ is asymptotically less efficient than the pooled estimator $\hat{\beta}_{n,T}$. This is to be expected because the pooled estimator $\hat{\beta}_{n,T}$ uses all the time series information while the cross section estimator $\tilde{\beta}_{n,[Tr]}$ uses only single time period information. It is therefore interesting to note that, although time series regression may be spurious, use of all the time series data does reduce the limiting variance in a panel regression. Heuristically, this is because when we pool the data we average the limiting information and quantities like $\int_0^1 M_{y_i}$ and $\int_0^1 M_{y_i}M_{x_i}'$ have less variation than $M_{y_i}(1)$ and $M_{y_i}(1)M_{x_i}(1)$. For example, $W(1)\equiv N(0,1)$, whereas $\int_0^1 W\equiv N(0,\frac{1}{3})$.

5. PANEL COINTEGRATION

This section considers the case where the variables in $Z_{i,t}$ are cointegrated. As discussed in Phillips (1986), there exists a cointegrating relation among the variables in $Z_{i,t}$ if the conditional long-run variance matrix Ω_i of $Z_{i,t}$ has deficient rank. We will discuss three particular types of model: (i) heterogeneous panel cointegration, where there exist different cointegrating relations among the variables in $Z_{i,t}$ across individuals; (ii) homogeneous panel cointegration, where the cointegration relation is the same for all the individuals; and (iii) near-homogeneous panel cointegration, where there exist slightly different cointegrating relations across the individuals.

5.1. *Heterogeneous Panel Cointegration*

We start by strengthening the moment conditions of the random coefficients $C_{i,t}$ in (2.3) and the summability conditions as follows. These conditions help to ensure the existence of a valid BN decomposition for the equation errors in the panel cointegration model (5.2) given below.

ASSUMPTION 4 (Random Coefficient Conditions′):
(i) *Assumption* 1(*i*) *holds.*
(ii) $EC_{a,i,t}^{16}(=\sigma_{16,a,t})<\infty$ *for all* $a=1,\dots,m^2$.

ASSUMPTION 5 (Summability Condition′): *For all* $a=1,\dots,m^2$:
(i) $\Sigma_{t=0}^{\infty} t^2\sigma_{2,a,t}<\infty$;
(ii) $\Sigma_{t=0}^{\infty} t^4(\sigma_{4,a,t})^{1/4}<\infty$;
(iii) $\Sigma_{t=0}^{\infty} t^2(\sigma_{8,a,t})^{1/8}<\infty$;
(iv) $\Sigma_{t=0}^{\infty}(\sigma_{16,a,t})^{1/16}<\infty$.

The previous section assumes that the conditional long-run covariance matrix Ω_i of the integrated vector $Z_{i,t}$ in (2.1) is positive definite. When Ω_i is singular, important differences arise in the time series case, as is well known, and a different large T time theory applies for each i.

ASSUMPTION 6: *The following conditions hold almost surely.*
(i) Ω_i *has rank* m_x.
(ii) *Each* $(m_x\times m_x)$ *leading submatrix* $\Omega_{x_ix_i}$ *is positive definite.*

In this case the generating mechanism (2.1) has a deficient set of unit roots and the vector $Z_{i,t}$ is cointegrated almost surely. To see this, take an arbitrary element of the probability space for which (i) and (ii) of Assumption 6 hold. Then we have $\Omega_{y_iy_i}=\Omega_{y_ix_i}\Omega_{x_ix_i}^{-1}\Omega_{x_iy_i}$. Let $\alpha_i=(I_{m_y},-\beta_i)$ and $\beta_i=\Omega_{y_ix_i}\Omega_{x_ix_i}^{-1}$. The $(m_y\times m)$ random matrix α_i is well defined because $\Omega_{x_ix_i}$ is positive definite. Since $\Omega_i=C_i(1)C_i(1)'$, the equality $\Omega_{y_iy_i}-\Omega_{y_ix_i}\Omega_{x_ix_i}^{-1}\Omega_{x_iy_i}=0$ can be written as

$$\alpha_iC_i(1)C_{y_i}(1)'=0, \tag{5.1}$$

so that α_i is in the row null space of the matrix $C_i(1)$.

Define $E_{i,t}=\alpha_iZ_{i,t}=Y_{i,t}-\beta_iX_{i,t}$. Note that $\Delta E_{i,t}=\alpha_i\,\Delta Z_{i,t}=\alpha_iU_{i,t}=\alpha_iC_i(1)V_{i,t}-\Delta\alpha_i\tilde{U}_{i,t}$, where the last equality comes from the BN decomposition of $U_{i,t}$. Then, since $\alpha_i C_i(1)=0$, $\Delta E_{i,t} = -\Delta\alpha_i \tilde{U}_{i,t}$, that is $E_{i,t} = -\alpha_i \tilde{U}_{i,t} = -\alpha_i \Sigma_{s=0}^{\infty} \tilde{C}_{i,s} V_{i,t-s}$. Lemma 15 in Appendix D shows that $E_{i,t}$ is square integrable and that the random coefficients $\{-\alpha_i \tilde{C}_{i,s}\}_s$ are summable. Hence, Assumption 6 implies the existence of the following panel cointegration model with probability one:

$$(5.2) \qquad Y_{i,t} \overset{\text{a.s.}}{=} \beta_i X_{i,t} + E_{i,t},$$
$$X_{i,t} = X_{i,t-1} + U_{x_i,t},$$

where

$$(5.3) \qquad F_{i,t} = \begin{pmatrix} E_{i,t} \\ U_{x_i,t} \end{pmatrix} = \sum_{s=0}^{\infty} G_{i,s} V_{i,t-s},$$

$$G_{i,s} = \begin{pmatrix} -\alpha_i \tilde{C}_{i,s} \\ \Gamma C_{i,s} \end{pmatrix}, \qquad \text{and} \qquad \Gamma = (0 \vdots I_{m_x})(m_x \times m).$$

The coefficient β_i in model (5.2) is random. This means that β_i differs randomly across i and so the cointegrating relation between $Y_{i,t}$ and $X_{i,t}$ is heterogenous. Also, the random coefficients $G_{i,s}$ in the linear process generating $(E'_{i,t}, U'_{x_i,t})'$ in model (5.2) each involve the cointegrating matrix α_i whose main component is $\beta_i = \Omega_{y_i x_i} \Omega_{x_i x_i}^{-1}$, which depends on the inverse of $\Omega_{x_i x_i}$. From Assumption 6, $\Omega_{x_i x_i}^{-1}$ exists almost surely. But, additionally, we need some moment conditions on $\Omega_{y_i x_i} \Omega_{x_i x_i}^{-1}$ to ensure the existence of moments of the random coefficients $G_{i,s}$, which help in establishing the validity of a panel BN decomposition. Assumptions 1 and 2 alone do not assure the existence of moments of $\Omega_{x_i x_i}^{-1}$. Hence, to avoid heavy tails in the density of $\Omega_{x_i x_i}^{-1}$, we make the following assumption about the distribution of $\Omega_{x_i x_i}$.

ASSUMPTION 7: *The random matrix $\Omega_{x_i x_i}$ has continuous density function f with the following properties.*

(i) $f(\Omega) = O(\text{etr}(-c\Omega))$ *for some* $c > 0$ *when* $\text{tr}(\Omega) \to \infty$, *where* $\text{etr}(-c\Omega)$ *denotes* $\exp\{\text{tr}(-c\Omega)\}$.

(ii) $f(\Omega) = O((\det \Omega)^{\gamma})$ *for some* $\gamma > 7$ *when* $\det(\Omega) \to 0$.

REMARKS: (a) Condition (i) implies that the tail of the density f is exponentially small as $\text{tr}(\Omega) \to \infty$. Condition (ii) restricts the behavior of the density f when $\det \Omega \to 0$. Taken together (i) and (ii) ensure that $(\det \Omega)^s f(\Omega)$ is integrable for $s \geq -8$.

(b) An example of a density f satisfying conditions (i) and (ii) is the Wishart distribution $W_{m_x}(J, I_{m_x})$ whose probability element is

$$f(\Omega)(d\Omega) = \frac{1}{2^{m_x(J/2)}\Gamma_{m_x}(J/2)} \text{etr}\left(-\frac{1}{2}\Omega\right) \det \Omega^{(J-m_x-1)/2}(d\Omega),$$

with degrees of freedom parameter $J > m_x + 15$ and where

$$\Gamma_{m_x}\left(\frac{J}{2}\right) = \int_{\Omega>0} \operatorname{etr}(-\Omega) \det \Omega^{J-m_x-1/2}(d\Omega).$$

In this case, Ω^{-1} has an inverse Wishart distribution with $(J+m_x+1)$ degrees of freedom and $(m_x \times m_x)$ parameter matrix $I_{m_x}, W_{m_x}^{-1}(J+m_x+1, I_{m_x})$ (e.g., see Muirhead (1982, p. 113).

In view of Lemma 15(a) in Appendix D, $\sum_{s=1}^{\infty} s^2 \|G_{i,s}\|^2 < \infty$. a.s. Then, as in Lemma 2, it follows from Phillips and Solo (1992) that $F_{i,t}$ has a valid panel BN decomposition of the form

$$F_{i,t} \overset{\text{a.s.}}{=} G_i(1)V_{i,t} + \tilde{F}_{i,t-1} - \tilde{F}_{i,t}, \tag{5.4}$$

where $G_i(1)V_{i,t}$ and $\tilde{F}_{i,t}$ are well defined square integrable random vectors in view of Lemma 15. Using (5.4), the partial sum process of $F_{i,t}$ can be written as

$$\frac{1}{\sqrt{T}} \sum_{t=1}^{[Tr]} F_{i,t} \overset{\text{a.s.}}{=} G_i(1) \frac{1}{\sqrt{T}} \sum_{t=1}^{[Tr]} V_{i,t} + \frac{1}{\sqrt{T}} \tilde{F}_{i,0} - \frac{1}{\sqrt{T}} \tilde{F}_{i,[Tr]}. \tag{5.5}$$

With this BN decomposition in place, we can use the Phillips-Solo approach to deduce a functional law for partial sums of $F_{i,t}$. In particular, we have the following lemma:

LEMMA 7: *If Assumptions 4–7 hold, then*

$$\frac{1}{\sqrt{T}} \sum_{t=1}^{[Tr]} F_{i,t} \Rightarrow G_i(1)W_i(r) \qquad \text{as } T \to \infty \text{ for all } i, \tag{5.6}$$

where $W_i(r)$ is a standard vector Brownian motion independent of $\mathscr{F}_{c_i}$.

Thus, $(1/\sqrt{T})\sum_{t=1}^{[Tr]} F_{i,t}$ converges in distribution to a randomly scaled (or mixed) Brownian motion $G_i(1)W_i(r)$ as $T \to \infty$ for all i. Let $S_{i,t} = \sum_{s=1}^{t} F_{i,s} + S_{i,0}$, where $S_{i,0}$ are iid across i with $E\|S_{i,0}\|^4 < \infty$. The next lemma shows that $(1/T)\sum_{t=1}^{T} S_{i,t}F'_{i,t}$ converges in distribution to a matrix stochastic integral plus an $\mathscr{F}_{c_i}$-measurable random matrix.

LEMMA 8: *Suppose the assumptions in Lemma 7 hold. Then,*

$$\frac{1}{T} \sum_{t=1}^{T} F_{i,t} S'_{i,t} \Rightarrow G_i(1) \int dW_i \, W_i' G_i(1)' + \Lambda_i \qquad \text{as } T \to \infty, \tag{5.7}$$

where $\Lambda_i = \sum_{k=0}^{\infty} E(F_{i,k} F'_{i,0} | \mathscr{F}_{c_i}) = \sum_{k=0}^{\infty} \sum_{s=0}^{\infty} G_{i,s+k} G'_{i,s}$.

Partition $G_i(1)$, Λ_i, and $G_i(1)W_i(r)$ conformably as follows:

$$G_i(1) = \begin{pmatrix} G_{e_i}(1) \\ G_{x_i}(1) \end{pmatrix} \begin{matrix} m_y \\ m_x \end{matrix}, \qquad \Lambda_i = \begin{pmatrix} \Lambda_{e_i e_i} & \Lambda_{e_i x_i} \\ \Lambda_{x_i e_i} & \Lambda_{x_i x_i} \end{pmatrix},$$

$$G_i(1)W_i(r) = \begin{pmatrix} G_{e_i}(1)W_i(r) \\ G_{x_i}(1)W_i(r) \end{pmatrix} = \begin{pmatrix} M_{e_i}(r) \\ M_{x_i}(r) \end{pmatrix}.$$

Consider the time series regression of $Y_{i,t}$ on $X_{i,t}$. Using (5.6), (5.7), and the continuous mapping theorem, we find the following large T limit distribution for the OLS estimator of the (random) coefficient β_i:

(5.8)
$$T(\hat{\beta}_i - \beta_i) \overset{\text{a.s.}}{=} \left(\frac{1}{T}\sum_{t=1}^{T} E_{i,t}X'_{i,t}\right)\left(\frac{1}{T^2}\sum_{t=1}^{T} X_{i,t}X'_{i,t}\right)^{-1}$$
$$\Rightarrow \left(G_{e_i}(1)\int dW_i\, W_i' G_{x_i}(1)' + \Lambda_{e_i x_i}\right)\left(G_{x_i}(1)\int W_i W_i' G_{x_i}(1)'\right)^{-1}$$
$$= \left(\int dM_{e_i} M'_{x_i} + \Lambda_{e_i x_i}\right)\left(\int M_{x_i} M'_{x_i}\right)^{-1} \qquad \text{as } T \to \infty \text{ for all } i.$$

The bias term $\Lambda_{e_i x_i}$ arises in the usual way from the temporal correlation between $E_{i,t}$ and $U_{x_i,t}$ (c.f., Phillips and Durlauf (1986)). Thus, time series regression produces a consistent estimator of the cointegrating matrix β_i, and thereby distinguishes the randomly differing individual long-run relations between $Y_{i,t}$ and $X_{i,t}$.

When both dimensions of the panel data are utilized, a long-run average coefficient β is also identified. This can be accomplished as in the previous section, by means of a pooled panel regression or a limiting cross section regression. The following sections concentrate on pooled panel regression and discuss limiting cross section estimators only briefly.

In the heterogeneous panel cointegration model (5.2) the pooled estimator $\hat{\beta}_{n,T}$ has the same form as that defined in (4.4). The limit theory for this pooled estimator is as follows.

THEOREM 5: *Let the assumptions of Lemma* 15 *hold. Then*:
(a) *as* $(n,T \to \infty)$, $\hat{\beta}_{n,T} \to_p \beta = \Omega_{yx}\Omega_{xx}^{-1}$;
(b) *as* $(n,T\to\infty)$ *with* $n/T \to 0$,

$$\sqrt{n}\left(\hat{\beta}_{n,T} - \beta\right) \Rightarrow N\left(0, 4\left(\Omega_{xx}^{-1} \otimes I_{m_y}\right)\Theta\left(\Omega_{xx}^{-1} \otimes I_{m_y}\right)\right),$$

where

$$\Theta = \tfrac{1}{6}\left(\Omega_{x_i x_i} \otimes (\Omega_{y_i y_i} - \beta\Omega_{x_i x_i} - \Omega_{x_i x_i} - \Omega_{x_i x_i}\beta' + \beta\Omega_{x_i x_i}\beta')\right)$$
$$+ \tfrac{1}{6}E\left((\Omega_{x_i y_i} - \Omega_{x_i x_i}\beta') \otimes (\Omega_{y_i x_i} - \beta\Omega_{x_i x_i})\right)K_{m_x m_y}$$
$$+ \tfrac{1}{4}E\left(\operatorname{vec}(\Omega_{y_i x_i} - \beta\Omega_{x_i x_i})\operatorname{vec}(\Omega_{y_i x_i} - \beta\Omega_{x_i x_i})'\right).$$

REMARKS: (a) Define $\tilde{E}_{i,t} = (\beta_i - \beta)X_{i,t} + E_{i,t}$. Then the heterogeneous panel cointegration model (5.2) becomes

$$(5.9) \qquad Y_{i,t} = \beta X_{i,t} + \tilde{E}_{i,t}.$$

The pooled estimator $\hat{\beta}_{n,T}$ is a least squares estimator of the regression coefficient in (5.9) and consistently estimates the long-run average coefficient β between $Y_{i,t}$ and $X_{i,t}$. Note that the noise, $\tilde{E}_{i,t}$, in this regression involves the integrated random vector $X_{i,t}$. By the same logic as that of the spurious regression case, the long-run coefficient β is consistently estimated by pooling the panel data because cross section pooling attenuates the strength of the noise $\tilde{E}_{i,t}$ relative to the signal in the regression (5.9).

(b) As seen in Theorem 5, the pooled estimator $\hat{\beta}_{n,T}$ is $\sqrt{n}$ consistent for the average long-run regression coefficient β and has a normal limit distribution. Observe that the limit variance matrix for the heterogeneous pooled panel regression estimator in Theorem 5, viz., $4(\Omega_{xx}^{-1} \otimes I_{m_y})(\Omega_{xx}^{-1} \otimes I_{m_y})$ has precisely the same form as the limit variance matrix of the spurious regression pooled panel regression estimator in Theorem 4. This equivalence in form is especially interesting because the individual long-run covariance matrix Ω_i is singular in the heterogeneous cointegration case but nonsingular in the spurious regression case, so that these individual component matrices must be different between the two models. Nevertheless, and in spite of these differences, the average long-run covariance matrix Ω may well be nonsingular in the heterogeneous cointegration model, in which case there is a basis for direct comparison between the two results. Obviously, the effect of the heterogeneity in the cointegration parameter is to slow down the rate of convergence of the pooled estimator. In particular, the convergence rate is $\sqrt{n}$ and, interestingly, this rate is uninfluenced by the time series sample size in spite of the fact that the individual time series regressions are themselves T-consistent (see (5.8)). Thus, there is a correspondence in the limit theory between the heterogeneous cointegration model and the pooled spurious regression model after pooling the data.

(c) In general, of course, $E[\Omega_{y_i x_i}\Omega_{x_i x_i}^{-1}] \neq E[\Omega_{y_i x_i}](E[\Omega_{x_i x_i}])^{-1}$, so there is no reason why the limit of the average of the cointegrating relation $(1/n)\Sigma_{i=1}^{n} \beta_i$ should equal β, the average long-run regression coefficient. As we have seen, it is the latter parameter that is the limit of the pooled regression estimator in the heterogeneous cointegration model. One situation where $\lim_{n\to\infty}(1/n)\Sigma_{i=1}^{n} \beta_i = \beta$ does hold is when $\Omega_{x_i x_i}$ has a degenerate distribution, namely, $\Omega_{x_i x_i} = \Omega_{xx}$ almost surely. Thus, in the heterogeneous panel cointegration case, the parameter being estimated is *not* the average cointegrating coefficient, but the average long-run regression coefficient, just as in the spurious panel regression case. Again, the two models are much closer than they might appear.

(d) As discussed in (a), the heterogeneous panel cointegration model can be reinterpreted in the form of the panel model (5.9). As such, we may be interested in constructing statistical tests about the long-run coefficients β. For example, to test $\mathbb{H}_0$: $\varphi(\beta) = 0$, where $\varphi(\cdot)$ is a p-vector of smooth functions on a subset of $\mathbb{R}^{m_y \times m_x}$ such that $\partial\varphi/\partial\beta'$ has full rank $p(\leq m_y m_x)$, we may use the Wald statistic

$$W_\varphi = n\varphi\left(\hat{\beta}_{n,T}\right)'\hat{V}_\varphi^{-1}\varphi\left(\hat{\beta}_{n,T}\right),$$

where $\hat{V}_\varphi = (\partial\varphi(\hat{\beta}_{n,T})/\partial\beta')(\partial\varphi(\hat{\beta}_{n,T})'/\partial\beta)$, $\hat{V}_\beta = 4(\hat{\Omega}_{xx}^{-1} \otimes I_{m_y})\hat{\Theta}(\hat{\Omega}_{xx}^{-1} \otimes I_{m_y})$,

$$\hat{\Theta} = \frac{1}{n}\sum_{i=1}^{n}\left\{\frac{1}{T^4}\sum_{s,t=1}^{T} X_{i,t}X_{i,s}' \otimes \hat{E}_{i,t}\hat{E}_{i,s}'\right\},$$

$$\hat{\Omega}_{xx}^{-1} = \left[\frac{1}{n}\sum_{i=1}^{n}\left\{\frac{2}{T^2}\sum_{t=1}^{T} X_{i,t}X_{i,t}'\right\}\right]^{-1},$$

and $\hat{E}_{it} = Y_{i,t} - \hat{\beta}_{n,T}X_{i,t}$. Some simple manipulations in the case of sequential asymptotics show that this statistic leads to a standard asymptotic χ^2 test as $(T, n \to \infty)_{\text{seq}}$. This limit theory also holds very generally under joint limits as $(T, n \to \infty)$ as the next result reveals.

THEOREM 6: *Under* $\mathbb{H}_0$: $\varphi(\beta) = 0$ *and Assumptions* 4–7, $W_\varphi \Rightarrow \chi_p^2$, *as* $(n, T \to \infty)$ *with* $n/T \to 0$.

(e) We may also be interested in testing hypotheses about the coefficients in generalizations of model (5.9) of the following form:

$$(5.10) \qquad Y_{i,t} = \beta_\mu X_{i,t} + \tilde{E}_{i,t} \qquad \text{with} \qquad \begin{cases} \beta_\mu = \beta_a \text{ for } i \in I_a, \\ \beta_\mu = \beta_b \text{ for } i \in I_b, \end{cases}$$

where I_a and I_b are index sets corresponding to subgroups of the cross section population for which the long-run average covariance matrices are Ω_a and Ω_b, respectively, leading to long-run average regression coefficients $\beta_a = \Omega_{a,yx}\Omega_{a,xx}^{-1}$ and $\beta_b = \Omega_{b,yx}\Omega_{b,xx}^{-1}$ that may differ between the two populations. Models like (5.10) can be readily extended to multi-category models and will be empirically relevant, for example, in cross country panel regressions where countries are partitioned into classes of similar category like developed (OECD) nations and developing and undeveloped nations. Note that in such cases the model (5.10) allows for intra-class variation (i.e., the regression coefficients β_i for $i \in I_a$ will differ) but our primary interest lies in the inter-class difference $\beta_a - \beta_b$. A natural hypothesis is then: $\mathbb{H}_0$: $\beta_a = \beta_b$. Let $n_a = \#(I_a)$ and $n_b = \#(I_b)$, respectively. Suppose that $n_b/n_a \to \kappa < \infty$ as $n_a, n_b \to \infty$. The null hypothesis can be tested by constructing pooled regression coefficients $\hat{\beta}_a$, $\hat{\beta}_b$ in each class and computing the Wald statistic

$$W_{a,b} = n_b\left\{\text{vec}\left(\hat{\beta}_a - \hat{\beta}_b\right)'\hat{V}_{a-b}^{-1}\,\text{vec}\left(\hat{\beta}_a - \hat{\beta}_b\right)\right\},$$

where $\hat{V}_{a-b} = (n_a/n_b)\hat{V}_a + \hat{V}_b, \hat{V}_\mu = 4(\hat{\Omega}_{\mu,xx}^{-1} \otimes I_{m_x})\hat{\Theta}_\mu(\hat{\Omega}_{\mu,xx}^{-1} \otimes I_{m_x})$,

$$\hat{\Theta}_\mu = \frac{1}{n_\mu} \sum_{i \in I_\mu} \left\{ \frac{1}{T^4} \sum_{s,t=1}^{T} X_{i,t} X'_{i,s} \otimes \hat{E}_{i,t} \hat{E}'_{i,s} \right\},$$

$$\hat{\Omega}_{\mu,xx}^{-1} = \left[\frac{1}{n_\mu} \sum_{i \in I_\mu} \left\{ \frac{1}{T^2} \sum_{t=1}^{T} X_{i,t} X'_{i,t} \right\} \right]^{-1},$$

and $\hat{E}_{it} = Y_{i,t} - \hat{\beta}_\mu X_{i,t}$ with $\mu \in \{a, b\}$. Again, this leads to an asymptotic χ^2 test. The following result gives the limit theory under joint limits as $(n_a, n_b, T \to \infty)$ and can be obtained in a simple way from Theorems 5 and 6.

THEOREM 7: *Under* $\mathbb{H}_0$: $\beta_a = \beta_b$ *and Assumptions* 4–7, $W_{a,b} \Rightarrow \chi^2_{m_y m_x}$, *as* $(n_a, n_b, T \to \infty)$ *with* $n_a/T, n_b/T \to 0$.

5.2. *Homogeneous Panel Cointegration and Pooled FM Estimation*

This section considers a homogeneous panel cointegration model, where the cointegrating relations are the same across individuals, and develops an asymptotic theory for a pooled FM estimator. We start with the following simplifying assumption.

ASSUMPTION 8: $C_{i,t} =_{\text{a.s.}} C_t$, *where* C_t *is an* $(m \times m)$ *nonrandom matrix for all* t.

Then, under Assumption 6, the panel cointegration model (5.2) becomes

$$(5.11) \qquad Y_{i,t} \overset{\text{a.s.}}{=} \beta X_{i,t} + E_{i,t}, \qquad X_{i,t} = X_{i,t-1} + U_{x_i,t},$$

where

$$\beta = \Omega_{yx}\Omega_{xx}^{-1}, \qquad \alpha = \left(I_{m_y}, -\beta\right), \qquad \begin{pmatrix} E_{i,t} \\ U_{x_i,t} \end{pmatrix} = \sum_{s=0}^{\infty} G_s V_{i,t-s},$$

$$G_s = \begin{pmatrix} G_{e,s} \\ G_{x,s} \end{pmatrix} = \begin{pmatrix} -\alpha \tilde{C}_s \\ \gamma C_s \end{pmatrix}, \qquad \text{and} \qquad \tilde{C}_s = \sum_{j=s+1}^{\infty} C_j.$$

In this model the same long-run relation between $Y_{i,t}$ and $X_{i,t}$ applies for all i. Unlike previous models, the error term in model (5.11) is generated by a linear process with nonrandom coefficients $\{G_s\}$, on which we impose the following summability condition.

ASSUMPTION 9: $\Sigma_{s=0}^{\infty} s^3 \|C_s\| < \infty$.

Define $\tilde{G}_s = \Sigma_{j=s+1}^{\infty} G_j$. Under Assumption 9, $G(1) = \Sigma_{s=0}^{\infty} G_s < \infty$ and $\Sigma_{s=0}^{\infty} s^2 \|\tilde{G}_s\| = \Sigma_{s=0}^{\infty} s^2 \|\Sigma_{j=s+1}^{\infty} G_j\|^2 < \infty$. Write $F_{i,t} = (E'_{i,t}, U'_{x_i,t})'$. Then, as $T \to \infty$, we have the functional law $(1/\sqrt{T})\Sigma_{t=1}^{[Tr]} F_{i,t} \Rightarrow B_i(r) \equiv BM(\Omega_F)$, where $\Omega_F = G(1)G(1)'$ (Theorem 3.4 in Phillips and Solo (1992)). The following assumption is conventional in time series cointegration analysis, although it could be relaxed with some consequential changes in the asymptotics, including changes in convergence rates in directions determined by the singularity.

ASSUMPTION 10: *Ω_F is positive definite.*

Partition $B_i(r) = (B_{e_i}(r)', B_{x_i}(r)')'$ conformably with $F_{i,t}$. Set $S_{i,t} = \Sigma_{s=1}^{t} F_{i,s} + S_{i,0}$, where $S_{i,0}$ are iid across i with $E\|S_{i,0}\|^4 < \infty$. Then, in the usual way (Phillips (1988)), as $T \to \infty$

$$\frac{1}{T}\sum_{t=1}^{T} F_{i,t} S'_{i,t} \Rightarrow \int dB_i\, B'_i + \Lambda_F,$$

where $\Lambda_F = \Sigma_{k=0}^{\infty} E(F_{i,k} F'_{i,0}) = \Sigma_{k=0}^{\infty} \Sigma_{s=0}^{\infty} G_{s+k} G'_s$. Again, conformably partition Ω_F and Λ_F as

$$\begin{pmatrix} \Omega_{ee} & \Omega_{ex} \\ \Omega_{xe} & \Omega_{xx} \end{pmatrix} \quad \text{and} \quad \begin{pmatrix} \Lambda_{ee} & \Lambda_{ex} \\ \Lambda_{xe} & \Lambda_{xx} \end{pmatrix}, \quad \text{respectively}.$$

For each i, model (5.11) is a time series cointegrating regression. The least squares estimator

$$\hat{\beta}_i = \sum_{t=1}^{T} Y_{i,t} X'_{i,t} \left(\sum_{t=1}^{T} X_{i,t} X'_{i,t} \right)^{-1}$$

$$\overset{\text{a.s.}}{=} \beta + \sum_{t=1}^{T} E_{i,t} X'_{i,t} \left(\sum_{t=1}^{T} X_{i,t} X'_{i,t} \right)^{-1}$$

has the following asymptotic distribution (Phillips and Durlauf (1986)):

$$(5.12) \qquad T(\hat{\beta}_i - \beta) \Rightarrow \left(\int dB_{e_i} B'_{x_i} + \Lambda_{ex} \right) \left(\int B_{x_i} B'_{x_i} \right)^{-1} \quad \text{as} \quad T \to \infty.$$

The time series estimator $\hat{\beta}_i$ is therefore consistent for β, the common long-run coefficient for all i, although there may be a second order bias effect entering through the term Λ_{ex} in (5.12) arising from the correlation between $E_{i,t}$ and $X_{i,s}$.

When the panel observations are pooled, as in the estimator $\hat{\beta}_{n,T}$ defined in (4.4), we get

$$\hat{\beta}_{n,T} \overset{\text{a.s.}}{=} \beta + \sum_{i=1}^{n}\sum_{t=1}^{T} E_{i,t}X'_{i,t}\left(\sum_{i=1}^{n}\sum_{t=1}^{T} X_{i,t}X'_{i,t}\right)^{-1}.$$

When $\Lambda_{ex} = 0$, the limit theory of this estimator is as follows.

THEOREM 8: *Suppose that Assumptions* 6, 8–10 *hold. If* $\Lambda_{ex} = 0$, *then as* $(n, T \to \infty)$ *with* $n/T \to 0$,

$$\sqrt{n}\,T\left(\hat{\beta}_{n,T} - \beta\right) \Rightarrow N\left(0, 2(\Omega_{xx}^{-1} \otimes \Omega_{ee})\right).$$

Thus, if $E_{i,t}$ and $U_{x_i,s}$ are uncorrelated, so that the one sided long-run covariance $\Lambda_{ex} = 0$, the pooled estimator $\hat{\beta}_{n,T}$ is $\sqrt{n}\,T$ consistent and has a limiting normal distribution in joint asymptotics as $(n, T \to \infty)$ when $n/T \to 0$.

When $\Lambda_{ex} \neq 0$, we do not attain $\sqrt{n}\,T$ consistency with the pooled least squares estimator $\hat{\beta}_{n,T}$, because of the persistence of bias effects. However, we may 'fully modify' the regressor $Y_{i,t}$ to eliminate the serial correlation Λ_{ex}. Originally, the fully modified (FM) regression method was introduced in Phillips and Hansen (1990) to correct for the presence of endogeneity (the correlation between B_{e_i} and B_{x_i}) and serial correlation in the OLS estimator $\hat{\beta}_i$ of the individual cointegration regression model. Their construction calls for consistent time series estimators $\hat{\Omega}_F$ and $\hat{\Lambda}_F$ of Ω_F and Λ_F. In our case, consistent estimates may be constructed using averages (over $i = 1, \ldots, n$) of the usual consistent (as $T \to \infty$) nonparametric kernel estimates of the corresponding long-run quantities for each i. More specifically, let $\hat{\Gamma}_i(j) = (1/T)\Sigma_t F_{i,t+j}F'_{i,t}$, where the summation is over $1 \leq t, t+j \leq T$, and define the averaged kernel estimators

$$(5.13) \qquad \hat{\Omega}_F = \frac{1}{n}\sum_{i=1}^{n} \hat{\Omega}_{F,i}, \qquad \hat{\Omega}_{F,i} = \sum_{j=-T+1}^{T-1} w\left(\frac{j}{K}\right)\hat{\Gamma}_i(j),$$

$$\hat{\Lambda}_F = \frac{1}{n}\sum_{i=1}^{n} \hat{\Lambda}_{F,i}, \qquad \hat{\Lambda}_{F,i} = \sum_{j=0}^{T-1} w\left(\frac{j}{K}\right)\hat{\Gamma}_i(j),$$

where $w(x)$ is a lag kernel for which $w(0) = 1$, $w(x) = w(-x)$, $\int_{-\infty}^{\infty} w(x)^2\,dx < \infty$, and with Parzen's exponent $q \in (0, \infty)$ such that $k_q = \lim_{x \to \infty}(1 - w(x))/|x|^q < \infty$ (e.g., see Hannan (1970) or Andrews (1991)).[7] As is well know in the nonparametric literature, the choice of the bandwidth K is important in the limit

[7] In determining asymptotic properties of kernel estimates of the long-run variance we usually also impose a smoothness restriction on the spectral density at the origin. This smoothness condition can be formulated as a summability condition on the autocovariance sequence $\Gamma(h) = E(F_{i,t}F'_{i,t+h})$. The summability conditions in Assumption 9 ensure that $\Sigma_{h=0}^{\infty} h^2 \|\Gamma(h)\| < \infty$, and provide sufficient smoothness for our results here.

behavior of $\hat{\Omega}_F$. Under the summability condition given in Assumption 9, it is known that $\hat{\Omega}_{F,i} \to \Omega_F$ if $K, T \to \infty$ with $K/T \to 0$. However, later in this section (e.g., for Theorem 9) we need the stronger result that $\sqrt{n}(\hat{\Omega}_F - \Omega_F), \sqrt{n}(\hat{\Lambda}_F - \Lambda_F) = o_p(1)$ as $(n, T \to \infty)$ with $n/T \to 0$. The following Assumption about bandwidth choice is made so that these conditions apply.

ASSUMPTION 11: *The lag kernel $w(\cdot)$ in (5.13) has Parzen exponent $q > 1/2$, and the bandwidth parameter K tends to infinity with $K/T \to 0$ and $K^{2q}/T \to \epsilon > 0$.*

Define

$$(5.14) \qquad Y_{i,t}^{+} = Y_{i,t} - \hat{\Omega}_{ex}\hat{\Omega}_{xx}^{-1}\,\Delta X_{i,t}$$

and

$$(5.15) \qquad \hat{\Lambda}_{ex}^{+} = \hat{\Lambda}_{ex} - \hat{\Omega}_{ex}\hat{\Omega}_{xx}^{-1}\hat{\Lambda}_{xx}.$$

Equation (5.14) gives the endogeneity correlation and equation (5.15) gives the serial correlation correction.

Using these corrections, a pooled FM (PFM) estimator can be defined as follows:

$$(5.16) \qquad \hat{\beta}_{PFM} = \left(\sum_{i=1}^{n}\sum_{t=1}^{T} Y_{i,t}^{+}X_{i,t}' - nT\hat{\Lambda}_{ex}^{+}\right)\left(\sum_{i=1}^{n}\sum_{t=1}^{T} X_{i,t}X_{i,t}'\right)^{-1}$$

$$\overset{\text{a.s.}}{=} \beta + \left(\sum_{i=1}^{n}\left(\sum_{t=1}^{T}\hat{E}_{i,t}^{+}X_{i,t}' - T\hat{\Lambda}_{ex}^{+}\right)\right)\left(\sum_{i=1}^{n}\sum_{t=1}^{T} X_{i,t}X_{i,t}'\right)^{-1},$$

where $\hat{E}_{i,t}^{+} = E_{i,t} - \hat{\Omega}_{ex}\hat{\Omega}_{xx}^{-1}\,\Delta X_{i,t}$. Rescaling $\hat{\beta}_{FPM} - \beta$ by $\sqrt{n}\,T$ and letting $T \to \infty$ for fixed n, we have

$$\sqrt{n}\,T(\hat{\beta}_{PFM} - \beta) \Rightarrow \left(\frac{1}{\sqrt{n}}\sum_{i=1}^{n}\int dB_{e_i.x_i}B_{x_i}'\right)\left(\frac{1}{n}\sum_{i=1}^{n}\int B_{x_i}B_{x_i}'\right)^{-1},$$

where $B_{e_i,x_i}(r) \equiv BM(\Omega_{e.x})$ and $\Omega_{e.x} = \Omega_{ee} - \Omega_{ex}\Omega_{xx}^{-1}\Omega_{xe}$.

Note that $B_{e_i.x_i}(r)$ and $B_{x_i}(r)$ are independent, so $E\int dB_{e_i.x_i}B_{x_i}' = 0$ and

$$E\left(\text{vec}\int dB_{e_i.x_i}B_{x_i}'\right)\left(\text{vec}\int dB_{e_i.x_i}B_{x_i}'\right)' = \tfrac{1}{2}(\Omega_{xx} \otimes \Omega_{e.x}).$$

Thus, applying the multivariate Lindeberg-Levy theorem to

$$(1/\sqrt{n})\Sigma_{i=1}^{n}\int dB_{e_i.x_i}B_{x_i}'$$

and combining this with the limit of $(1/n)\Sigma_{i=1}^{n}\int B_{x_i}B_{x_i}'$, we find that as $n \to \infty$

$$\left(\frac{1}{\sqrt{n}}\sum_{i=1}^{n}\int dB_{e_i.x_i}B_{x_i}'\right)\left(\frac{1}{n}\sum_{i=1}^{n}\int B_{x_i}B_{x_i}'\right)^{-1} \Rightarrow N(0, 2(\Omega_{xx}^{-1} \otimes \Omega_{e.x})).$$

Thus, $\sqrt{n}\,T(\hat{\beta}_{FPM} - \beta) \Rightarrow N(0, 2(\Omega_{xx}^{-1} \otimes \Omega_{e.x}))$ in sequential limit as $(T, n \to \infty)_{\text{seq}}$. The following theorem shows that these asymptotics also hold for joint limits.

THEOREM 9: *Under Assumptions* 6, 8–11 *we have*

$$\sqrt{n}\,T\left(\hat{\beta}_{PFM} - \beta\right) \Rightarrow N\left(0, 2(\Omega_{xx}^{-1} \otimes \Omega_{e.x})\right)$$

as $(n, T \to \infty)$ *with* $n/T \to 0$.

REMARKS: (a) The pooled FM estimator $\hat{\beta}_{PFM}$ is $\sqrt{n}\,T$ consistent and has a normal limit distribution.

(b) When $\Lambda_{ex} = 0$, observe that $\hat{\beta}_{PFM}$ is more efficient than $\hat{\beta}_{n,T}$ because $\Omega_{e.x} < \Omega_{ee}$. The efficiency gain in $\hat{\beta}_{PFM}$ is obtained from the endogeneity correction that adjusts $Y_{i,t}$ in the fully modified estimator. This effectively reduces the long-run variance of the noise in the panel cointegrating equation.

(c) Asymptotic χ^2 tests follow from Theorem 9 in the usual way. A consistent estimate of the covariance matrix, $2(\hat{\Omega}_{xx}^{-1} \otimes \hat{\Omega}_{e.x})$, can be constructed from $\hat{\Omega}$ in (5.13) by defining $\hat{\Omega}_{e.x} = \hat{\Omega}_{ee} - \hat{\Omega}_{ex}\hat{\Omega}_{xx}^{-1}\hat{\Omega}_{xe}$. A Wald test of $\mathbb{H}_0$: $\varphi(\beta) = 0$, where $\varphi(\cdot)$ is a p-vector of smooth functions such that $\partial\varphi/\partial\beta'$ has full rank p, can then be formulated in the usual way as

$$W_{\varphi} = nT^2\varphi\left(\hat{\beta}_{PFM}\right)'\hat{V}_{\varphi}^{-1}\varphi\left(\hat{\beta}_{PFM}\right), \tag{5.17}$$

where

$$\hat{V}_{\varphi} = \left(\partial\varphi\left(\hat{\beta}_{PFM}\right)/\partial\beta'\right)\left[2\hat{\Omega}_{xx}^{-1} \otimes \hat{\Omega}_{e.x}\right]\left(\partial\varphi\left(\hat{\beta}_{PFM}\right)'/\partial\beta\right).$$

(d) As in Remark (e) following Theorem 6, it may be of interest to generalize model 5.11 to allow for subgroups of the population in which the regression coefficient is the same. In effect, we may replace model (5.11) with

$$Y_{i,t} \overset{\text{a.s.}}{=} \beta_{\mu}X_{i,t} + E_{i,t} \qquad \text{with} \qquad \begin{cases} \beta_{\mu} = \beta_a & \text{for } i \in I_a, \\ \beta_{\mu} = \beta_b & \text{for } i \in I_b, \end{cases} \tag{5.18}$$

$$X_{i,t} = X_{i,t-1} + U_{x_i,t}.$$

It is then possible to test hypotheses about the vectors β_a and β_a in the generalized model (5.18). For example, to test $\mathbb{H}_0$: $\beta_a = \beta_b$, letting $n_a = \#(I_a)$ and $n_b = \#(I_b)$, respectively, and assuming that $n_b/n_a \to \kappa \to \infty$ as $n_a, n_b \to \infty$, we may construct pooled FM regression coefficients $\hat{\beta}_{a,PFM}, \hat{\beta}_{b,PFM}$ in each class and then the Wald statistic

$$W_{a-b,PFM} = n_bT^2\left\{\text{vec}\left(\hat{\beta}_{a,PFM} - \hat{\beta}_{b,PFM}\right)' \times \hat{V}_{a-b,PFM}^{-1}\,\text{vec}\left(\hat{\beta}_{a,PFM} - \hat{\beta}_{b,PFM}\right)\right\}.$$

Here, $\hat{V}_{a-b,PFM} = \kappa \hat{V}_{a,PFM} + \hat{V}_{b,PFM}$, $\hat{V}_{\mu,PFM} = 2\hat{\Omega}^{-1}_{\mu,xx} \otimes \hat{\Omega}_{\mu,e.x}$, and $\hat{\Omega}_{\mu,xx}$, $\hat{\Omega}_{\mu,e.x}$ are the respective estimates of the long-run conditional covariance matrices of the regressors and the fully modified error processes in the classes I_μ with $n_\mu = \#(I_\mu)$ where $\mu \in \{a, b\}$. As in the earlier case of heterogeneous cointegration, this leads to an asymptotic χ^2 test based on the null distribution $W_{a-b,PFM} \Rightarrow \chi^2_{m_y m_x}$, which follows in a manner analogous to that of Theorem 7.

5.3. *Near-Homogeneous Panels*

The homogeneous panel model (5.11) discussed above is somewhat unrealistic because it assumed that each individual has exactly the same cointegrating relation. Here we study briefly a panel cointegration model with nearly homogeneous cointegrating vectors of the form

$$(5.19) \qquad \beta_i = \beta + \frac{\theta_i}{\sqrt{n}\,T},$$

where the sequence of $(m_y \times m_x)$ random matrices θ_i is iid across i with mean θ and finite variance.

ASSUMPTION 12: *θ_i is independent of $(E_{i,t}, U_{x_i,t})$ for all i and t.*

We again consider the pooled FM estimator $\hat{\beta}_{PFM}$ given in (5.16) and the limit theory follows in Theorem 9 above.

THEOREM 10: *Suppose there exists near-homogeneous panel cointegration of the form* (5.19). *Let Assumptions* 9–12 *hold. Then, as* $(n, T \to \infty)$ *with* $n/T \to 0$

$$(5.20) \qquad \sqrt{n}\,T\left(\hat{\beta}_{PFM} - \beta\right) \Rightarrow N\left(\theta, 2(\Omega^{-1}_{xx} \otimes \Omega_{e.x})\right).$$

Theorem 5.20 is useful in calculating the asymptotic local power of the test statistic for the null hypothesis

$$(5.21) \qquad H_0\colon \beta_i = \beta_0 \qquad \forall i.$$

According to remark (c) of the previous subsection, the Wald statistic in (5.17) for the null hypothesis in (5.21) is W_φ with $\varphi(\beta) = \mathrm{vec}(\beta - \beta_0)$ and its limit distribution is $\chi^2_{m_y m_x}$. A sequence of local alternatives to the null (5.21) can be formulated as

$$(5.22) \qquad H_{LA}\colon \beta_i = \beta_0 + \frac{\theta_i}{\sqrt{n}\,T},$$

where the θ_i are iid across i with mean $\theta \neq 0$, have finite variance and satisfy Assumption 12. In this case, under the local alternative hypothesis (5.22) and the assumptions of Theorem 5.20, the Wald statistic W_φ has an asymptotic noncentral chi-square distribution as $(n, T \to \infty)$ with $n/T \to 0$, i.e.,

$$W_\varphi \Rightarrow \chi^2_{m_y m_x}(\lambda),$$

where the noncentrality parameter is $\lambda = \mathrm{vec}(\theta)' V_\varphi^{-1} \mathrm{vec}(\theta)/2$.

6. MODELS WITH INDIVIDUAL EFFECTS

Much of the preceding asymptotic theory can be extended in a straightforward way to panel models with individual specific effects and time trends. We illustrate what is involved in these extensions by taking the case of primary importance where the panel regression equation involves individual special effects. To motivate the analysis, consider the following model of heterogeneous panel cointegration in place of (5.2):

$$\text{(6.1)} \qquad \begin{aligned} Y_{i,t} &\overset{\text{a.s.}}{=} \gamma_i + \beta_i X_{i,t} + E_{i,t}, \\ X_{i,t} &= X_{i,t-1} + U_{x_i,t}. \end{aligned}$$

Here, the γ_i are individual effects in the cointegrating equation. They could be fixed or random effects. We can also allow for individual effects in the equation for $X_{i,t}$ in (6.1). In that case, the $X_{i,t}$ have individual deterministic trends as well as stochastic trends and in what follows we would proceed using detrended rather than demeaned data in the pooled panel regression, with some associated change in the final formulae.

The individual effect in (6.1) can be eliminated in the usual way by removing individual specific means, i.e., $\bar{Y}_{i,\cdot} = (1/T)\Sigma_{t=1}^T Y_{i,t}$ and $\bar{X}_{i,\cdot} = (1/T)\Sigma_{t=1}^T X_{i,t}$. Then pooled panel regression leads to the estimator

$$\tilde{\beta}_{n,T} = \left(\sum_{i=1}^{n} \sum_{t=1}^{T} \tilde{Y}_{i,t} \tilde{X}'_{i,t} \right) \left(\sum_{i=1}^{n} \sum_{t=1}^{T} \tilde{X}_{i,t} \tilde{X}'_{i,t} \right)^{-1},$$

where $\tilde{Y}_{i,t} = Y_{i,t} - \bar{Y}_{i,\cdot}$, and $\tilde{X}_{i,t} = X_{i,t} - \bar{X}_{i,\cdot}$.

As in our earlier theory, some quick asymptotic results for $\tilde{\beta}_{n,T}$ can be obtained using sequential limits. First consider the case where there is no cointegration and the true data generating mechanism is (2.1), even though it is model (6.1) that is estimated. Define the demeaned limiting process $\tilde{M}_i(r) = (\tilde{M}'_{y_i}(r), \tilde{M}'_{x_i}(r))' = M_i(r) - \int M_i(s)\,ds$. According to (2.6) and the continuous mapping theorem, under Assumptions 1–3, the pooled estimator $\tilde{\beta}_{n,T}$ has the following limit distribution as $T \to \infty$ for any fixed n:

$$\tilde{\beta}_{n,T} \Rightarrow \left(\frac{1}{n} \sum_{i=1}^{n} \int \tilde{M}_{y_i} \tilde{M}'_{x_i} \right) \left(\frac{1}{n} \sum_{i=1}^{n} \int \tilde{M}_{x_i} \tilde{M}'_{x_i} \right)^{-1}.$$

A simple calculation shows that $E(\int \tilde{M}_i \tilde{M}'_i) = E(\int M_i M'_i) - E(\int M_i \int M'_i) = \frac{1}{6}\Omega$. Thus, applying the strong law of large numbers to $(1/n)\Sigma_{i=1}^n \int \tilde{M}_{y_i} \tilde{M}'_{x_i}$ and

$(1/n)\Sigma_{i=1}^{n}\tilde{M}_{x_i}\tilde{M}_{x_i}'$, we get $(1/n)\Sigma_{i=1}^{n}\int\tilde{M}_{y_i}\tilde{M}_{x_i}' \rightarrow_{\text{a.s.}} \frac{1}{6}\Omega_{yx}$, and $(1/n)\Sigma_{i=1}^{n}\int\tilde{M}_{x_i}\tilde{M}_{x_i}' \rightarrow_{\text{a.s.}} \frac{1}{6}\Omega_{xx}$. It follows that $\tilde{\beta}_{n,T} \rightarrow_p \beta = \Omega_{yx}\Omega_{xx}^{-1}$ as $(T, n \rightarrow \infty)_{\text{seq}}$.

The asymptotic normality of $\tilde{\beta}_{n,T}$ follows by arguments analogous to those of Section 4. Rescaling the centered estimator $(\tilde{\beta}_{n,T} - \beta)$ by $\sqrt{n}$ and letting $T \rightarrow \infty$ for fixed n, we have

$$\sqrt{n}\left(\tilde{\beta}_{n,T} - \beta\right) \Rightarrow \frac{1}{\sqrt{n}}\sum_{i=1}^{n}\left(\int\tilde{M}_{y_i}\tilde{M}_{x_i}' - \beta\int\tilde{M}_{x_i}\tilde{M}_{x_i}'\right)\left(\frac{1}{n}\sum_{i=1}^{n}\int\tilde{M}_{x_i}\tilde{M}_{x_i}'\right)^{-1}.$$

Note that $E(\int\tilde{M}_{y_i}\tilde{M}_{x_i}' - \beta\int\tilde{M}_{x_i}\tilde{M}_{x_i}') = 0$, so demeaning the data does not affect the asymptotic centering. After some lengthy calculations, we find the variance matrix

$$\begin{aligned}
&E\left(\operatorname{vec}\left(\int\tilde{M}_{y_i}\tilde{M}_{x_i}' - \beta\int\tilde{M}_{x_i}\tilde{M}_{x_i}'\right)\operatorname{vec}\left(\int\tilde{M}_{y_i}\tilde{M}_{x_i}' - \beta\int\tilde{M}_{x_i}\tilde{M}_{x_i}'\right)'\right)\\
&\quad= \tfrac{1}{90}E\left(\Omega_{x_ix_i} \otimes (\Omega_{y_iy_i} - \beta\Omega_{x_iy_i} - \Omega_{y_ix_i}\beta' + \beta\Omega_{x_ix_i}\beta')\right)\\
&\qquad+ \tfrac{1}{90}E\left((\Omega_{x_iy_i} - \Omega_{x_ix_i}\beta') \otimes (\Omega_{y_ix_i} - \beta\Omega_{x_ix_i})K_{m_ym_x}\right)\\
&\qquad+ \tfrac{1}{36}E\left(\operatorname{vec}(\Omega_{y_ix_i} - \beta\Omega_{x_ix_i})(\operatorname{vec}(\Omega_{y_ix_i} - \beta\Omega_{x_ix_i}))'\right)\\
&\quad= \Theta_f, \qquad \text{say.}
\end{aligned}$$

Note that this covariance matrix differs in the coefficients of its components from the earlier matrix Θ given in (4.6) for the case where there is no demeaning to remove possible individual effects. As is clear from the formulae for these two cases (see (6.2) below), $\Theta_f < \Theta$, so one effect of demeaning is to reduce time series variability.

Applying the multivariate Lindeberg-Levy Theorem to $(1/\sqrt{n})\Sigma_{i=1}^{n}(\int\tilde{M}_{y_i}\tilde{M}_{x_i}' - \beta\int\tilde{M}_{x_i}\tilde{M}_{x_i}')$ and combining this with the limit of $((1/n)\Sigma_{i-1}^{n}\int\tilde{M}_{x_i}\tilde{M}_{x_i}')^{-1}$ as $n \rightarrow \infty$, we have

$$\begin{aligned}
&\frac{1}{\sqrt{n}}\sum_{i=1}^{n}\left(\int\tilde{M}_{y_i}\tilde{M}_{x_i}' - \beta\int\tilde{M}_{x_i}\tilde{M}_{x_i}'\right)\left(\frac{1}{n}\sum_{i=1}^{n}\int\tilde{M}_{x_i}\tilde{M}_{x_i}'\right)^{-1}\\
&\qquad\Rightarrow N\left(0, 36\left(\Omega_{xx}^{-1} \otimes I_{m_y}\right)\Theta_f\left(\Omega_{xx}^{-1} \otimes I_{m_y}\right)\right).
\end{aligned}$$

Hence, as $(T, n \rightarrow \infty)_{\text{seq}}$ we have

$$\sqrt{n}\left(\tilde{\beta}_{n,T} - \beta\right) \Rightarrow N\left(0, 36\left(\Omega_{xx}^{-1} \otimes I_{m_y}\right)\Theta_f\left(\Omega_{xx}^{-1} \otimes I_{m_y}\right)\right).$$

These sequential limit results can be extended to joint limit results, just as in the proof of Theorem 4, and we merely state the final results here.

THEOREM 11: *Suppose Assumptions* 1, 2, *and* 3 *hold and the data generating mechanism is* (2.1). *Then*:

(a) *as* $(n, T \to \infty)$, *we have* $\tilde{\beta}_{n,T} \to_p \beta$;

(b) *if* $(n, T \to \infty)$ *and* $n/T \to 0$,

$$\sqrt{n}\left(\tilde{\beta}_{n,T} - \beta\right) \Rightarrow N\left(0, 36\left(\Omega_{xx}^{-1} \otimes I_{m_y}\right)\Theta_f\left(\Omega_{xx}^{-1} \otimes I_{m_y}\right)\right).$$

REMARKS: (a) Comparing the limit variance of $\tilde{\beta}_{n,T}$ in Theorem 11 to that of $\hat{\beta}_{n,T}$ in Theorem 4, we find that $\tilde{\beta}_{n,T}$ has the smaller asymptotic covariance. In fact, it is apparent from the formulae that

$$(6.2) \quad 4\Theta - 36\Theta_f = \tfrac{4}{15}\left(\Omega_{x_i x_i} \otimes (\Omega_{y_i y_i} - \beta\Omega_{x_i y_i} - \Omega_{y_i x_i}\beta' + \beta\Omega_{x_i x_i}\beta')\right)$$
$$+ \tfrac{4}{15}E\left((\Omega_{x_i y_i} - \Omega_{x_i x_i}\beta') \otimes (\Omega_{y_i x_i} - \beta\Omega_{x_i x_i})K_{m_y m_x}\right)$$
$$= \tfrac{4}{15}E\left\{\left(C_{x_i}(1) \otimes \left(C_{y_i}(1) - \beta C_{x_i}(1)\right)\right)(I_{m^2} + K_m)\right.$$
$$\left. \times \left(C_{x_i}(1) \otimes \left(C_{y_i}(1) - \beta C_{x_i}(1)\right)\right)'\right\}$$
$$(6.3) \quad > 0.$$

As remarked above, this reduction in variance occurs because demeaning the data by removing individual effects reduces time series variability. Similar effects occur when higher order time trends are removed from the data in the construction of pooled panel estimators.

(b) In the heterogenous panel cointegration case, the data are generated by (6.1). The individual effects γ_i can now be consistently estimated by time series regression on (6.1) leading to $\hat{\gamma}_i = \overline{Y}_{i,\cdot} - \tilde{\beta}_i \overline{X}_{i,\cdot}$ and $\tilde{\beta}_i = (\Sigma_{t=1}^T \tilde{Y}_{i,t}\tilde{X}_{i,t}')(\Sigma_{t=1}^T \tilde{X}_{i,t}\tilde{X}_{i,t}')^{-1}$. These least squares estimates and their fully modified variants have asymptotic properties that are well known (Phillips and Hansen (1990)). Following the same line of argument as in Section 5.1, the pooled panel estimator $\tilde{\beta}_{n,T}$ can be shown to have the same limit distribution as that given in Theorem 11 for the spurious regression case, although the long run covariance matrices Ω_i are now singular, just as in Section 5.1. Under the assumptions of Theorem 5, the asymptotic theory holds for joint limits as $(n, T \to \infty)$ and $n/T \to 0$, as well as sequential limits. Again $\tilde{\beta}_{n,T}$ estimates the long run average coefficient $\beta = \Omega_{yx}\Omega_{xx}^{-1}$. Wald tests like those discussed in Section 5 can now be constructed with obvious modifications to the estimated covariance matrix formulae that allow for elimination of the individual effects by demeaning.

(c) In the homogeneous panel cointegration case, the data are generated by (6.1) with $\beta_i = \beta = \Omega_{yx}\Omega_{xx}^{-1}$ a.s. We can eliminate individual effects by removing individual specific means as above, and may proceed with FM estimation as in Section 5.2. The data are now corrected according to the formula $\tilde{Y}_{i,t}^{+} = \tilde{Y}_{i,t} -$

$\hat{\Omega}_{ex}\hat{\Omega}_{xx}^{-1}\,\Delta\tilde{X}_{i,t}$ rather than as in (5.14). The pooled FM estimator in this case is given by

$$\tilde{\beta}_{PFM} = \left(\sum_{i=1}^{n}\sum_{t=1}^{T}\tilde{Y}_{i,t}^{+}\tilde{X}_{i,t}' - nT\tilde{\Lambda}_{ex}^{+}\right)\left(\sum_{i=1}^{n}\sum_{t=1}^{T}\tilde{X}_{i,t}\tilde{X}_{i,t}'\right)^{-1}.$$

Under the same assumptions as Theorem 9, we find that $\sqrt{n}\,T(\tilde{\beta}_{PFM}-\beta)\Rightarrow N(0,6(\Omega_{xx}^{-1}\otimes\Omega_{e.x}))$ as $(n,T\to\infty)$ with $n/T\to 0$. Note that in this case, the effect of eliminating individual specific means is to increase the limit variance matrix in comparison with Theorem 9. Wald tests can be constructed as described in Section 5.2 with obvious modifications for the use of demeaned data, and a noncentral limit theory follows as in Section 5.3.

7. CONCLUSION

This paper has developed a linear regression limit theory for nonstationary panel data with large numbers of cross section and time series observations. A central result is the existence of interesting long-run relations between two integrated panel vectors where there is no individual time series cointegration or where there are heterogeneous cointegrating relations. The new relations are characterized as long-run average relationships over the cross section and are parameterized in terms of the matrix regression coefficient, $\Omega_{yx}\Omega_{xx}^{-1}$, of the cross section long-run average covariance matrix, Ω. They are analogous to population regression coefficients in conventional cross section regression of iid variates. The limit theory can be used to construct tests of hypotheses about the long-run average regression coefficients and to compare these coefficients in subgroups of the cross section population. These tests are given explicitly for the two cases of heterogeneous panel cointegration and homogeneous panel cointegration, which seem to be the important cases for empirical applications. The local asymptotic power function for these tests is also derived.

The limit theory developed in this paper is designed for two dimensional arrays where both time series and cross section sample sizes pass to infinity. It allows for both sequential limits as $T\to\infty$ and $n\to\infty$ in that sequence, and joint limits where $T,n\to\infty$ jointly. As the proofs in the Appendices demonstrate, convergence for joint limit is more difficult to obtain. However, apart from some stricter moment and summability conditions, the only additional requirement we use in the development of this theory is the rate condition that $n/T\to 0$. This condition indicates that the limit theory given herein is likely to be most useful in cases where T is large and n is moderately large. The usefulness of this asymptotic theory in describing finite sample behavior in panel regressions now needs to be systematically explored in simulation experiments.

An important assumption that is common in panel data work and is used here in deriving asymptotics is cross section independence. For many nonstationary panel data applications, this independence condition is restrictive and it is an important limitation of our theory. For instance, multi-country GDP series, exchange rates, and financial assets prices all involve cross section dependence arising from global shocks and complicated interdependencies among the variables. As is apparent from our approach, certain strong laws and central limit results will continue to apply when the cross sectional dependence is of the weak memory variety, but in this case the limit variance matrices will change according to the dependence. More significantly, when there are strong correlations in a cross section (as there will be in the face of global shocks) we can expect failures in the strong laws and central limit theory arising from the nonergodicity. However, even in this event, theorems like the ergodic theorem will still apply but the limits will be random and measurable with respect to the invariant algebra generated by the global shocks.

In the present case and, indeed, quite commonly in panel data theory, cross section independence is assumed in part because of the difficulties of characterizing and modeling cross section dependence. In general, finding a natural ordering for cross section indices in economic data is not easy, and this has been a serious obstacle in the development of a satisfactory approach. While some recent research has attempted to resolve the difficulty by employing a framework for spatial data based on the economic distance between individuals (e.g. Conley (1997)), the successful simultaneous modeling of both cross section dependence and time series dependence remains a challenging problem and is a major area for future research in multi-index asymptotics of the type considered here.

Cowles Foundation for Research in Economics, Yale University, Box 208281, New Haven, CT 06520-8281, U.S.A., and University of Auckland; peter.phillips@yale.edu

and

Dept. of Economics, University of California, Santa Barbara, CA 93106, U.S.A.; rmoon@econ.ucsb.edu

Manuscript received April, 1997; final revision received September, 1998.

APPENDICES

Appendix A: Preliminary Lemmas and Proofs

We start with some lemmas that are useful in following arguments. The results are straightforward and proofs are omitted here, but are available in PM[b].

Lemma 9: (a) *For any $p \geq 1$ and any $m \times n$ matrix A, there exists a constant $M > 0$ such that*

$$\|A\|^p \leq M \sum_{i=1}^{m} \sum_{j=1}^{n} |a_{i,j}|^p, \tag{8.1}$$

where $a_{i,j}$ is the (i,j)th element of A.

(b) *For any $m \times m$ matrix A*

$$(\text{tr}(A))^2 \leq m\|A\|^2. \tag{8.2}$$

LEMMA 10: *Suppose that* $A\ (=\{a_{i,j}\}_{i,j})$ *and* $B\ (=\{b_{i,j}\}_{i,j})$ *are* $(m \times m)$ *matrices and* K_m *is the commutation matrix. Then,*

$$tr[(A \otimes B)K_m] \leq \|A\|\,\|B\|.$$

If A is symmetric, then

$$tr[(A \otimes A)K_m] = \|A\|^2.$$

LEMMA 11: (a) *Under Assumptions* 1 *and* 2

$$E\left\|\sum_{t=0}^{\infty} C_{i,t}\right\|^4 < \infty. \tag{8.3}$$

(b) *Under Assumptions* 4 *and* 5

$$E\left\|\sum_{t=0}^{\infty} tC_{i,t}\right\|^8 < \infty. \tag{8.4}$$

(c) *Under Assumptions* 4 *and* 5

$$E\left\|\sum_{t=0}^{\infty} C_{i,t}\right\|^{16} < \infty. \tag{8.5}$$

1. PROOF OF LEMMA 2: The panel BN decomposition

$$U_{i,t} = C_i(1)V_{i,t} + \tilde{U}_{i,t-1} - \tilde{U}_{i,t} \qquad \text{a.s.} \tag{8.6}$$

follows directly from Phillips and Solo (1992) provided $Y_i = \Sigma_{s=0}^{\infty} s^2\|C_{i,s}\|^2 < \infty$ a.s. This condition holds if $E(Y_i) < \infty$, which holds by Lemma 1(a). *Q.E.D.*

2. PROOF OF LEMMA 1: See PM[b]. *Q.E.D.*

3. PROOF OF LEMMA 2: It is enough to show that

$$\left|\frac{1}{\sqrt{T}}\tilde{U}_{a,i,0}\right| \xrightarrow{p} 0 \quad \text{and}$$

$$\sup_r \left|\frac{1}{\sqrt{T}}\tilde{U}_{a,i,[Tr]}\right| \xrightarrow{p} 0 \quad \text{as } T \to \infty \text{ for all } a, i.$$

But, these follow because $\tilde{U}_{a,i,t}$ is strictly stationary in t and square integrable by Lemma 1, so that the results hold by the same argument as that given in Phillips and Solo (1992, p. 978). The functional law follows directly. *Q.E.D*

4. PROOF OF LEMMA 4: Substituting $M_i = C_i(1)W_i$, we have

$$E\left\|\int M_i M_i'\right\|^2 = E\left\|\text{vec}\int M_i M_i'\right\|^2 = E\left\|(C_i(1) \otimes C_i(1))\text{vec}\int W_i W_i'\right\|^2$$

$$\leq E\|C_i(1) \otimes C_i(1)\|^2 E\left\|\text{vec}\int W_i W_i'\right\|^2,$$

where the last inequality holds because $\|AB\| \leq \|A\|\,\|B\|$ and because $C_i(1)$ is independent of W_i. We know $E\|\text{vec} \int W_i W_i'\|^2 < \infty$ and $E\|C_i(1) \otimes C_i(1)\|^2 = E\|C_i(1)\|^4 < \infty$ by Lemma 1. Therefore, $E\| \int M_i M_i' \|^2 < \infty$, as required. *Q.E.D.*

APPENDIX B: PROOFS FOR SECTION 3—MULTIDIMENSIONAL LIMIT THEORY

1. CONSTRUCTION OF RANDOM VECTORS Y_i IN (3.3) TO EXIST ON THE SAME PROBABILITY SPACE: According to Skorohod's Theorem in $\mathbb{R}^m$, Theorem 29.6 in Billingsley (1986),[8] we can construct a probability space $(\Omega_i^*, \mathcal{F}_i^*, P_i^*)$ where there exist random vectors $Y_{i,T}^*$ and Y_i^* such that $Y_{i,T} \equiv Y_{i,T}^*$, $Y_i \equiv Y_i^*$, and $Y_{i,T}^* \to_{\text{a.s.}} Y_i^*$ as $T \to \infty$ for all i. Also, we can choose independent Y_i^* because the $Y_{i,T}$ are independent across i for all T. Now we define $\Omega^* = \prod_{i=1}^{\infty} \Omega_i^*$, the Cartesian product of Ω_i^*, and let π_i be the natural projection of Ω^* onto Ω_i^* for each i. Let $\mathcal{F}^*$ be the smallest σ-field containing all the sets $\pi_i^{-1}(F)$ for all i and $F \in \mathcal{F}_i^*$. Define $\mathcal{R}$ to be the collection of all finite dimensional rectangles, $\prod_{i=1}^{\infty} F_i$ where $F_i \in \mathcal{F}_i^*$ for all i and $F_i = \Omega_i^*$, except for at most finite many values of i. Now define $P^*(\prod_{i=1}^{\infty} F_i) = \prod_{i=1}^{\infty} P_i^*(F_i)$. Then, by Theorem 8.2.2 (p. 201) in Dudley (1989), P^* on $\mathcal{R}$ extends uniquely to a probability measure on $\mathcal{F}^*$. Let $\tilde{Y}_i(\omega) = Y_i^*(\pi_i^{-1}(\omega))$ for all $\omega \in \Omega^*$. By the way of their construction, the $\tilde{Y}_i(\omega)$ are random vectors on the probability space $(\Omega^*, \mathcal{F}^*, P^*)$ and $\tilde{Y}_i \equiv Y_i^* \equiv Y_i$. Choose Y_i in (3.3) to be $\tilde{Y}_i$ and we have the desired result. *Q.E.D.*

2. PROOF OF LEMMA 5: We prove part (b). Then part (a) holds by the same principle. Suppose that $f \in \mathcal{C}$ is given. From $X_{n,T} \Rightarrow X$ as $n, T \to \infty$, for any given $\varepsilon > 0$, we can chosen n_0 and T_1 such that whenever $n \geq n_0$ and $T \geq T_1$, the following inequality holds:

$$|Ef(X_{n,T}) - Ef(X)| < \frac{\varepsilon}{2}. \tag{8.7}$$

From $X_{n,T} \Rightarrow X_n$ as $T \to \infty$ $\forall_n$, we can choose T_2 depending on n and ε such that

$$|Ef(X_{n,T}) - Ef(X_n)| < \frac{\varepsilon}{2} \quad \text{if } T \geq T_2. \tag{8.8}$$

For each $n \geq n_0$ choose $T_2(n, \varepsilon)$, and choose a fixed T_0 greater than both T_1 and T_2. Then both (8.7) and (8.8) hold and therefore

$$|Ef(X_n) - Ef(X)| < \varepsilon \quad \text{if } n \geq n_0$$

and $X_{n,T} \Rightarrow X$ sequentially as $(T, n \to \infty)_{\text{seq}}$. *Q.E.D.*

3. PROOF OF LEMMA 6: We show part (b). Part (a) can be established by similar arguments.

Suppose that $f \in \mathcal{C}$ is given. Assume that (3.9) holds. From (3.9) and $X_n \Rightarrow X$ as $n \to \infty$, for any given $\varepsilon > 0$, we can choose n_0 and T_0 such that whenever $n \geq n_0$ and $T \geq T_0$, we have

$$\sup_{n \geq n_0, T \geq T_0} |Ef(X_{n,T}) - Ef(X_n)| < \frac{\varepsilon}{2},$$

and

$$|Ef(X_n) - Ef(X)| < \frac{\varepsilon}{2}.$$

[8]For Skorohod's theorem on function spaces refer to the representation theorem in Pollard (1984) or Theorem 4 on p. 47 in Shorack and Wellner (1986).

Thus, if $n \geq n_0$ and $T \geq T_0$,

$$|Ef(X_{n,T}) - Ef(X)| \leq \sup_{n \geq n_0, T \geq T_0} |Ef(X_{n,T}) - Ef(X_n)| + |Ef(X_n) - Ef(X)| < \varepsilon.$$

Hence, $X_{n,T} \Rightarrow X$ as $(n, T \to \infty)$.

Now assume that $X_{n,T} \Rightarrow X$ and $X_n \Rightarrow X$ as $(n, T \to \infty)$. The necessity of the condition follows because

$$\limsup_{n,T} |Ef(X_{n,T}) - Ef(X_n)|$$
$$\leq \limsup_{n,T} |Ef(X_{n,T}) - Ef(X)| + \limsup_{n} |Ef(X_n) - Ef(X)| = 0. \qquad Q.E.D.$$

Before starting the proof of Theorem 1 we give the following lemma.

LEMMA 12: *Suppose $Y_{i,T}$ are independent across i. Assume that $Y_{i,T} \Rightarrow Y_i$ as $T \to \infty$ for all i. Then,* $\limsup_{n\to\infty}(1/n)\Sigma_{i=1}^n E|Y_{i,T}| < \infty$ *implies* $\limsup_{n\to\infty}(1/n)\Sigma_{i=1}^n E|Y_i| < \infty$.

PROOF: Note that, since $|Y_{i,T}| \Rightarrow |Y_i|$ as $T \to \infty$ by the continuous mapping theorem, it follows that $E|Y_i| \leq \liminf_T E|Y_{i,T}|$ (see Theorem 5.3 in Billingsley (1968)). Thus,

$$\limsup_{n\to\infty} \frac{1}{n} \sum_{i=1}^{n} E|Y_i| \leq \limsup_{n\to\infty} \liminf_{T\to\infty} \frac{1}{n} \sum_{i=1}^{n} E|Y_{i,T}|$$
$$\leq \limsup_{n,T\to\infty} \frac{1}{n} \sum_{i=1}^{n} E|Y_{i,T}| < \infty. \qquad Q.E.D.$$

4. PROOF OF THEOREM 1: Part (b) follows easily from Lemma 6 and part (a). In particular, from the assumptions of the theorem we know that $X_{n,T} = (1/n)\Sigma_{i=1}^n Y_{i,T} \Rightarrow X_n = (1/n)\Sigma_{i=1}^n Y_i$ as $T \to \infty$ for all n and $X_n = (1/n)\Sigma_{i=1}^n Y_i \to_p \bar{\mu}_X = \lim_n (1/n)\Sigma_{i=1}^n EY_i$. Then, since condition (3.9) holds from part (a), the desired result $X_{n,T} \to_p \bar{\mu}_X$ as $(n, T \to \infty)$ follows by Lemma 6.

Now, we prove part (a). First, we establish condition (3.9) in the scalar class. It is sufficient for condition (3.9) to restrict $\mathscr{C}$ to $\mathscr{C}^\infty$, the class of all the bounded, continuous real functions with bounded, continuous derivatives of all orders (see Theorem 7.1 in Billingsley (1968) or Theorem 12 in Pollard (1984)). Without loss of generality, let the functions be such that $|f^{(k)}(x)| \leq 1$, $\forall k$, where $f^{(k)}(x)$ denotes the kth derivative function of $f(x)$.

Before proceeding, we need to ensure that the probability space on which the variates are defined is large enough to permit the arguments that follow. Limits such as $X_{n,T} = (1/n)\Sigma_{i=1}^n Y_{i,T} \Rightarrow X_n = (1/n)\Sigma_{i=1}^n Y_i$ as $T \to \infty$ involve the joint distributions of the random vectors $(Y_{1,T}, \ldots, Y_{n,T})'$ and $(Y_1, \ldots, Y_n)'$, not any properties of the probability space on which they are defined. However, we need to ensure that we can relate these variates on the same space. This can be accomplished by passing to a new probability space, using Skorohod's Theorem in $\mathbb{R}^m$ (e.g., Theorem 29.6 in Billingsley (1986)), in which they are defined new random variables $(\tilde{Y}_{1,T}, \ldots, \tilde{Y}_{n,}, \tilde{Y}_1, \ldots, \tilde{Y}_n)'$ such that $\tilde{Y}_{i,T} \equiv Y_{i,T}$ and $\tilde{Y}_i \equiv Y_i$ for all i and the $2n$ random variables $\tilde{Y}_{1,T}, \ldots, \tilde{Y}_{n,T}, \tilde{Y}_1, \ldots, \tilde{Y}_n$ are independent. Without loss of generality, we can assume that $\tilde{Y}_{i,T} = Y_{i,T}$ and $\tilde{Y}_i = Y_i$ for all i and T.[9]

[9]As in Appendix B(1) above, we can construct an infinite dimensional probability space where the two independent random vectors $(Y_{1,T}, \ldots, Y_{n,T})'$ and $(Y_1, \ldots, Y_n)'$ coexist. However, the argument given is enough for the proof that follows.

Now we can define the quantities $\zeta_{k,n,T} = \Sigma_{k>i\geq 1} Y_{i,T} + \Sigma_{k<i\leq n} Y_i$, for $1 \leq k \leq n$, all on the same probability space. By virtue of the definitions of $X_{n,T}$, X_n, and $\zeta_{k,n,T}$, we have

$$f\left(\frac{1}{n}\sum_{i=1}^{n} Y_{i,T}\right) - f\left(\frac{1}{n}\sum_{i=1}^{n} Y_i\right) = f\left(\frac{1}{n}(\zeta_{n,n,T} + Y_{n,T})\right) - f\left(\frac{1}{n}(\zeta_{1,n,T} + Y_1)\right)$$

$$= \sum_{k=1}^{n}\left\{f\left(\frac{1}{n}(\zeta_{k,n,T} + Y_{k,T})\right) - f\left(\frac{1}{n}(\zeta_{k,n,T} + Y_k)\right)\right\}.$$

It follows that

$$(8.9)\qquad \limsup_{n,T\to\infty} |Ef(X_{n,T}) - Ef(X_n)|$$

$$= \limsup_{n,T\to\infty}\left|Ef\left(\frac{1}{n}\sum_{i=1}^{n} Y_{i,T}\right) - Ef\left(\frac{1}{n}\sum_{i=1}^{n} Y_i\right)\right|$$

$$= \limsup_{n,T\to\infty}\left|\sum_{k=1}^{n} E\left\{\begin{array}{l} f\left(\frac{1}{n}(\zeta_{k,n,T} + Y_{k,T})\right) - f\left(\frac{1}{n}\zeta_{k,n,T}\right) \\ +f\left(\frac{1}{n}\zeta_{k,n,T}\right) - f\left(\frac{1}{n}(\zeta_{k,n,T} + Y_k)\right)\end{array}\right\}\right|.$$

Let $g(h) = \sup_x |f(x+h) - f(x) - f'(x)h|$. Take $x = \zeta_{k,n,T}/n$ and $h = Y_{k,T}/n$ in the case of $f((1/n)(\zeta_{k,n,T} + Y_{k,T})) - f((1/n)\zeta_{k,n,T})$, and take $x = \zeta_{k,n,T}/n$ and $h = Y_k/n$ in the case of $f((1/n)(\zeta_{k,n,T} + Y_i)) - f((1/n)\zeta_{k,n,T})$. By the triangle inequality, it follows that (8.9) is bounded above by

$$(8.10)\qquad \limsup_{n,T\to\infty}\left|\sum_{i=1}^{n} E\left\{f'\left(\frac{\zeta_{i,n,T}}{n}\right)\left(\frac{Y_{i,T}}{n} - \frac{Y_i}{n}\right)\right\}\right|$$

$$+ \limsup_{n,T\to\infty}\sum_{i=1}^{n} Eg\left(\frac{Y_{i,T}}{n}\right) + \limsup_{n,T\to\infty}\sum_{i=1}^{n} Eg\left(\frac{Y_i}{n}\right).$$

By the triangle inequality, the first term in (8.10) is less than

$$\limsup_{n,T\to\infty}\sum_{i=1}^{n}\left|E\left\{f'\left(\frac{\zeta_{i,n,T}}{n}\right)\left(\frac{Y_{i,T}}{n} - \frac{Y_i}{n}\right)\right\}\right|$$

$$= \limsup_{n,T\to\infty}\sum_{i=1}^{n}\left|Ef'\left(\frac{\zeta_{i,n,T}}{n}\right)E\left(\frac{Y_{i,T}}{n} - \frac{Y_i}{n}\right)\right|$$

$$\leq \limsup_{n,T\to\infty}\sum_{i=1}^{n}\left|E\left(\frac{Y_{i,T}}{n} - \frac{Y_i}{n}\right)\right| = 0.$$

The first line above uses the fact that $\zeta_{i,n,T}/n$, $Y_{i,T}/n$ and Y_i/n are independent, the inequality in the second line holds because $|f'| \leq 1$, and the third line follows directly from condition (ii).

For the second term in (8.10), note by the mean value theorem that $g(h) \le M_1 \min\{|h|, h^2\}$ for some constant M_1 which depends on f alone. Then, for any $\varepsilon > 0$

$$\begin{aligned}
\limsup_{n,T\to\infty} \sum_{i=1}^{n} Eg\left(\frac{Y_{i,T}}{n}\right) &\le \limsup_{n,T\to\infty} \sum_{i=1}^{n} E\left[g\left(\frac{Y_{i,T}}{n}\right)1\left\{\left|\frac{Y_{i,T}}{n}\right| \le \varepsilon\right\}\right] \\
&\quad + \limsup_{n,T\to\infty} \sum_{i=1}^{n} E\left[g\left(\frac{Y_{i,T}}{n}\right)1\left\{\left|\frac{Y_{i,T}}{n}\right| > \varepsilon\right\}\right] \\
&\le \varepsilon M_1^2 \limsup_{n,T\to\infty} \sum_{i=1}^{n} E\left|\frac{Y_{i,T}}{n}\right| + M_1 \limsup_{n,T\to\infty} \sum_{i=1}^{n} E\left[\left|\frac{Y_{i,T}}{n}\right|1\left\{\left|\frac{Y_{i,T}}{n}\right| > \varepsilon\right\}\right] = \varepsilon M_2,
\end{aligned}$$

where the first inequality holds by applying $g(h) \le M_1 h^2$ on $1\{|Y_{i,T}/n| \le \varepsilon\}$ and $g(h) \le M_1|h|$ on $1\{|Y_{i,T}/n| > \varepsilon\}$ and the last inequality holds by conditions (i) and (iii) with $M_2 = M_1^2 \limsup_{n,T}\Sigma_{i=1}^{n} E|Y_{i,T}/n|$.

By Lemma 12, condition (i) implies

$$\limsup_{n,T} \frac{1}{n}\sum_{i=1}^{n} E|Y_i| < \infty,$$

and by condition (iv) we have

$$\limsup_{n,T} \frac{1}{n}\sum_{i=1}^{n} E|Y_i|1\{|Y_i| > \varepsilon n\} < \infty.$$

Thus, applying the same arguments as those used for $\limsup_{n,T}\Sigma_{i=1}^{n} Eg(Y_{i,T}/n)$ to $\limsup_{n,T}\Sigma_{i=1}^{n} Eg(Y_i/n)$, we have $\limsup_{n,T}\Sigma_{i=1}^{n} Eg(Y_i/n) = 0$. It follows from (8.9) and (8.10) that condition (3.9) holds.

When the $Y_{i,T}$ are m-vectors, the Cramér-Wold device can be used. That is, using the above argument, we obtain $s'X_{n,T} \to_p s'\bar{\mu}_X$ as $(n, T \to \infty)$ $\forall s \in \mathbb{R}^m$, and it follows that $X_{n,T} \to_p \bar{\mu}_X$ as $n, T \to \infty$. *Q.E.D.*

5. Proof of Corollary 1: Define $X_{n,T} = (1/n)\Sigma_{i=1}^{n} Y_{i,T} = (1/n)\Sigma_{i=1}^{n} C_i Q_{i,T}$ and $X_n = (1/n)\Sigma_{i=1}^{n} Y_i = (1/n)\Sigma_{i=1}^{n} C_i Q_i$. Assume $\sup_i\|C_i\| > 0$, for if this does not hold, the result is trivial. We know that $X_{n,T} \Rightarrow X$ as $T \to \infty$ for all n by the conditions in the corollary. By assumption the $Q_{i,T}$ are uniformly integrable and $Q_{i,T} \Rightarrow Q_i$, so $E\|Q_i\| < \infty$. Also, $C = \lim_n (1/n)\Sigma_{i=1}^{n} C_i$ exists, so we have $X_n \to_p CE(Q_i)$ as $n \to \infty$. Hence, if we establish conditions (i)–(iv) of Theorem 1, then $X_{n,T} \to_p CE(Q_i)$ as $(n, T \to \infty)$.

By the uniform integrability of $\|Q_{i,T}\|$ and $\sup_i\|C_i\| < \infty$, we have

$$\limsup_{n,T} \frac{1}{n}\sum_{i=1}^{n} E\|Y_{i,T}\| \le \left(\sup_i\|C_i\|\right)\sup_T E\|Q_{i,T}\| < \infty,$$

verifying condition (i), and

$$\limsup_{n,T} \frac{1}{n}\sum_{i=1}^{n} \|EY_{i,T} - EY_i\| \le \left(\sup_i\|C_i\|\right)\limsup_T \|EQ_{i,T} - EQ_i\| = 0.$$

Condition (iii) is satisfied since

$$\frac{1}{n}\sum_{i=1}^{n} E[\|Y_{i,T}\|1\{\|Y_{i,T}\| > n\varepsilon\}] \le \left(\sup_i \|C_i\|\right) \sup_T E\left[\|Q_{i,T}\|1\left\{\|Q_{i,T}\| > \frac{n\varepsilon}{\sup_i\|C_i\|}\right\}\right] \tag{8.11}$$

which converges to zero as $n \to \infty$, again by virtue of uniform integrability and $\sup_i\|C_i\| < \infty$.

Condition (iv) of Theorem 1 holds because

$$\frac{1}{n}\sum_{i=1}^{n} E\|Y_i\|1\{\|Y_i\| > n\varepsilon\} \le \left(\sup_i \|C_i\|\right) E\left[\|Q_i\|1\left\{\|Q_i\| > \frac{n\varepsilon}{\sup_i\|C_i\|}\right\}\right] \to 0$$

by $\sup_i\|C_i\| < \infty$ and dominated convergence since $E\|Q_i\| < \infty$. *Q.E.D.*

6. Proof of Theorem 2: The proof follows that of Lindeberg's theorem given in Billingsley (1968, Theorem 7.2). The only change is that the additional index T appears in the component variates $\xi_{i,n,T}$ and limits are taken as $(n, T \to \infty)$. The fact that T passes to infinity with n is incidental to the main argument. For example, we still have

$$\frac{\Omega_{i,T}}{s_{n,T}^2} \le \varepsilon^2 + E[\xi_{i,n,T}^2 1\{|\xi_{i,n,T}| > \varepsilon\}]$$

and, as a consequence of the Lindeberg condition (3.20),

$$\max_{i \le n} \frac{\Omega_{i,T}}{s_{n,T}^2} \to 0$$

as $(n, T \to \infty)$. *Q.E.D.*

7. Proof of Theorem 3: Define

$$\xi_{i,n,T} = \Omega_{n,T}^{-1/2} C_i Q_{i,T},$$

where $\Omega_{n,T} = \Sigma_{i=1}^n C_i \Sigma_T C_i'$. By the Cramér-Wold device, $\Sigma_{i=1}^n \xi_{i,n,T} \Rightarrow N(0, I_m)$ as $(n, T \to \infty)$, if $\forall t \in \mathbb{R}^m$ with $\|t\| = 1$

$$t' \sum_{i=1}^{n} \xi_{i,n,T} \Rightarrow N(0,1) \quad \text{as} \quad n, T \to \infty. \tag{8.12}$$

Then, by condition (iv) $(1/n)\Sigma_{i=1}^n Y_{i,T} \Rightarrow N(0, \Omega)$ as $(n, T \to \infty)$.

To establish (8.12), it is sufficient to verify condition (3.20). For given $\varepsilon > 0$ and $t \in \mathbb{R}^m$ with $\|t\| = 1$, we have

$$t' \sum_{i=1}^{n} E[\xi_{i,n,T}\xi_{i,n,T}' 1\{|t'\xi_{i,n,T}\xi_{i,n,T}' t| > \varepsilon\}]t \tag{8.13}$$

$$= t'\Omega_{n,T}^{-1/2} \sum_{i=1}^{n} E[C_i Q_{i,T} Q_{i,T}' C_i' 1\{|t'\Omega_{n,T}^{-1/2} C_i Q_{i,T} Q_{i,T}' C_i' \Omega_{n,T}^{-1/2} t| > \varepsilon\}] \Omega_{n,T}^{-1/2} t.$$

Take the indicator function first. Note that

$$\begin{aligned}
&1\{|t'\Omega_{n,T}^{-1/2}C_iQ_{i,T}Q_{i,T}'C_i'\Omega_{n,T}^{-1/2}t|>\varepsilon\}\\
&\le 1\left\{\max_{\|t\|=1}|t'\Omega_{n,T}^{-1/2}C_iQ_{i,T}Q_{i,T}'C_i'\Omega_{n,T}^{-1/2}t|>\varepsilon\right\}\\
&=1\{\lambda_{\max}(\Omega_{n,T}^{-1/2}C_iQ_{i,T}Q_{i,T}'C_i'\Omega_{n,T}^{-1/2})>\varepsilon\}\\
&\le 1\left\{\lambda_{\max}(\Omega_{n,T}^{-1})\left(\max_{j\le n}\|C_j\|^2\right)\|Q_{i,T}\|^2>\varepsilon\right\}\\
&=1\left\{\|Q_{i,T}\|^2>\varepsilon\frac{\lambda_{\min}(\Omega_{n,T})}{\max_{j\le n}\|C_j\|^2}\right\}\le 1\left\{\|Q_{i,T}\|^2>\varepsilon\frac{\sigma_T^2\lambda_{\min}(\Sigma_{j=1}^nC_jC_j')}{\max_{j\le n}(\|C_j\|^2)}\right\}.
\end{aligned}$$

Next, expression (8.13) is bounded above by

$$\text{(8.14)}\qquad \max_{\|t\|=1}\left[t'\Omega_{n,T}^{-1/2}\sum_{i=1}^nE\left[C_iQ_{i,T}Q_{i,T}'C_i'1\left\{\|Q_{i,T}\|^2>\varepsilon\frac{\sigma_T^2\lambda_{\min}(\Sigma_{j=1}^nC_jC_j')}{\max_{j\le n}\|C_j\|^2}\right\}\right]\Omega_{n,T}^{-1/2}t\right]$$

$$\begin{aligned}
&\le \lambda_{\min}^{-1}(\Omega_{n,T})\sum_{i=1}^nE\left[\|C_iQ_{i,T}\|^21\left\{\|Q_{i,T}\|^21>\varepsilon\frac{\sigma_T^2\lambda_{\min}(\Sigma_{j=1}^nC_jC_j')}{\max_{j\le n}(\|C_j\|^2)}\right\}\right]\\
&\le\frac{\Sigma_{i=1}^n\|C_i\|^2}{\lambda_{\min}(\Omega_{n,T})}E\left[\|Q_{1,T}\|^21\left\{\|Q_{1,T}\|^2>\varepsilon\frac{\sigma_T^2\lambda_{\min}(\Sigma_{j=1}^nC_jC_j')}{\max_{j\le n}(\|C_j\|^2)}\right\}\right]\\
&\le\frac{n\max_i\|C_i\|^2}{\sigma_T^2\lambda_{\min}(\Sigma_{i=1}^nC_iC_i')}E\left[\|Q_{1,T}\|^21\left\{\|Q_{1,T}\|^2>\varepsilon\frac{\sigma_T^2\lambda_{\min}(\Sigma_{i=1}^nC_iC_i')}{\max_{i\le n}(\|C_i\|^2)}\right\}\right].
\end{aligned}$$

By conditions (i) and (ii),

$$\frac{n\max_i\|C_i\|^2}{\sigma_T^2\lambda_{\min}(\Sigma_{i=1}^nC_iC_i')}=O(1)\qquad\text{and}\qquad\frac{\sigma_T^2\lambda_{\min}(\Sigma_{i=1}^nC_iC_i')}{\max_{i\le n}(\|C_i\|^2)}\to\infty,$$

as $(n,T\to\infty)$. Then, since $\|Q_{i,T}\|^2$ is uniformly integrable in T by condition (iii), it follows that (8.14) $\to 0$ as $(n,T\to\infty)$. *Q.E.D.*

APPENDIX C: PROOFS FOR SECTION 4—SPURIOUS PANEL REGRESSION LIMIT THEORY

The next lemma gives the joint limit theory needed for Theorem 4.

LEMMA 13: *Suppose that Assumptions* 1–3 *hold.*
(a) *As* $(n,T\to\infty)$,

$$\frac{1}{n}\sum_{i=1}^n\frac{1}{T^2}\sum_{t=1}^TZ_{i,t}Z_{i,t}'\xrightarrow{p}\frac{1}{2}E\Omega_i=\frac{1}{2}\Omega.$$

(b) *If* $(n, T \to \infty)$ *and* $n/T \to 0$, *then*

$$\frac{1}{\sqrt{n}} \sum_{i=1}^{n} \frac{1}{T} \sum_{t=1}^{T} (Y_{i,t} X'_{i,t} - \beta X_{i,t} X'_{i,t}) \Rightarrow N(0, \Theta).$$

PROOF OF LEMMA 13: (a) From the BN decomposition of $U_{i,t}$ in (2.4) we have

$$Z_{i,t} \overset{\text{a.s.}}{=} C_i(1) P_{i,t} + \tilde{U}_{i,0} - \tilde{U}_{i,t} + Z_{i,0},$$

where $P_{i,t} = \Sigma_{s=1}^{t} V_{i,s}$, which leads to

$$\frac{1}{n} \sum_{i=1}^{n} \frac{1}{T^2} \sum_{t=1}^{T} Z_{i,t} Z'_{i,t} \overset{\text{a.s.}}{=} \frac{1}{n} \sum_{i=1}^{n} (Q_{i,T} + R_{i,T}),$$

where

$$Q_{i,T} = \frac{1}{T^2} \sum_{t=1}^{T} C_i(1) P_{i,t} P'_{i,t} C_i(1),$$

$$R_{i,T} = R_{1,i,T} + R'_{1,i,T} + R_{2,i,T},$$

$$R_{1,i,T} + \frac{1}{T^2} \sum_{t=1}^{T} C_i(1) P_{i,t} (\tilde{U}_{i,0} - \tilde{U}_{i,t} + Z_{i,0})', \quad \text{and}$$

$$R_{2,i,T} = \frac{1}{T^2} \sum_{t=1}^{T} (\tilde{U}_{i,0} - \tilde{U}_{i,t} + Z_{i,0})(\tilde{U}_{i,0} - \tilde{U}_{i,t} + Z_{i,0})'.$$

We show that as $(n, T \to \infty)$, $(1/n)\Sigma_{i=1}^{n} Q_{i,T} \to_p \frac{1}{2}\Omega$ and $(1/n)\Sigma_{i=1}^{n} R_{k,i,T} \to_p 0$, for $k = 1, 2$.

The $Q_{i,T}$ are iid across i for all T. Also, as $T \to \infty$, $Q_{i,T} \Rightarrow Q_i = C_i(1) \int W_i W_i' C_i(1)'$ and $(1/n)\Sigma_{i=1}^{n} Q_i \to_{\text{a.s.}} \frac{1}{2}\Omega$. That is, in sequential asymptotics such as $(T, n \to \infty)_{\text{seq}} (1/n)\Sigma_{i=1}^{n} Q_{i,T} \to_p \frac{1}{2}\Omega$. According to Corollary 1 (set $C_i = I_m$ so that the second condition is automatically satisfied), if we show that $\|Q_{i,T}\|$ is uniformly integrable in T, then it follows that

$$\frac{1}{n} \sum_{i=1}^{n} Q_{i,T} \overset{p}{\to} \frac{1}{2}\Omega \tag{8.15}$$

as $(n, T \to \infty)$.

By $\|AB\| \leq \|A\| \, \|B\|$ and the triangle inequality

$$\|Q_{i,T}\| \leq \|C_i(1)\|^2 \frac{1}{T^2} \sum_{t=1}^{T} \|P_{i,t}\|^2. \tag{8.16}$$

Also, as $T \to \infty$

$$\frac{1}{T^2} \sum_{t=1}^{T} \|P_{i,t}\|^2 \Rightarrow \int \|W_i\|^2,$$

and we have

$$E\left(\frac{1}{T^2} \sum_{t=1}^{T} \|P_{i,t}\|^2\right) = \text{tr}\left(\frac{1}{T^2} \sum_{t=1}^{T} E(P_{i,t}, P'_{i,t})\right) \to E\left(\int \|W_i\|^2\right) = \frac{1}{2}\text{tr}(I_m).$$

It follows (e.g., Billingsley (1968, Theorem 5.4)) that $(1/T^2)\Sigma_{t=1}^{T} \|P_{i,t}\|^2$ is uniformly integrable in T. Since $E\|C_i(1)\|^2 < \infty$ by Lemma 1, we deduce that $\|C_i(1)\|^2 (1/T^2) \Sigma_{t=1}^{T} \|P_{i,t}\|^2$ is uniformly integrable in T. Thus, $\|Q_{i,T}\|$ is uniformly integrable in T, and (8.15) follows.

Next, $(1/n)\Sigma_{i=1}^{n} R_{1,i,T}$ and $(1/n)\Sigma_{i=1}^{n} R_{2,i,T}$ converge in probability to zero if $E\|R_{1,i,T}\|$, $E\|R_{2,i,T}\| \to 0$ as $(n, T \to \infty)$. Note that

(8.17)
$$E\|R_{1,i,T}\| \le \frac{1}{T^2}\sum_{t=1}^{T} E[\|C_i(1)P_{i,t}\| \|\tilde{U}_{i,0} - \tilde{U}_{i,t} + Z_{i,0}\|]$$
$$\le \frac{1}{\sqrt{T}}\frac{1}{T}\sum_{t=1}^{T}\sqrt{E\left\|C_i(1)\frac{P_{i,t}}{\sqrt{T}}\right\|^2 E\|\tilde{U}_{i,0} - \tilde{U}_{i,t} + Z_{i,0}\|^2}$$
$$= \frac{1}{\sqrt{T}}O(1),$$

where the first inequality holds by the triangle inequality and $\|AB\| \le \|A\|\,\|B\|$, the second inequality holds by the Cauchy-Schwarz inequality and the last line holds because $E\|C_i(1)(P_{i,t}/\sqrt{T})\|^2 = O(1)$, $E\|Z_{i,0}\|^2 < M_1$, and $E\|\tilde{U}_{i,t}\|^2 < M_2$ $\forall t$ and for some $M_1, M_2 < \infty$ by Lemma 1(c). Thus, $E\|R_{1,i,T}\| \to 0$, as $(n, T \to \infty)$.

Similar arguments show that $E\|R_{2,i,T}\| = (1/T)O(1)$. So, all the desired results hold and part (a) is proved.

(b) Write $C_i(1) = (C_{y_i}(1)', C_{x_i}(1)')'$, and $\tilde{U}_{i,t} = (\tilde{U}'_{y_i,t}, \tilde{U}'_{x_i,t})'$, conformably with the partition of $Z_{i,t}$ into $Y_{i,t}$ and $X_{i,t}$. Using the BN decomposition of $U_{i,t}$ in (2.4), we have

$$\frac{1}{\sqrt{n}}\sum_{i=1}^{n}\frac{1}{T^2}\sum_{t=1}^{T}(Y_{i,t}X'_{i,t} - \beta X_{i,t}X'_{i,t}),$$
$$= \frac{1}{\sqrt{n}}\sum_{i=1}^{n}(Q_{i,T} + R_{1,i,T} + R_{2,i,T} + R_{3,i,T} + R_{4,i,T} + R_{5,i,T}),$$

where

$$Q_{i,T} = \frac{1}{T^2}\sum_{t=1}^{T}\{C_{y_i}(1)P_{i,t}P'_{i,t}C_{x_i}(1)' - \beta C_{x_i}(1)P_{i,t}P'_{i,t}C_{x_i}(1)'\},$$

$$R_{1,i,T} = \frac{1}{T^2}\sum_{t=1}^{T}\left\{C_{y_i}(1)P_{i,t}\left(\tilde{U}_{x_i,0} - \tilde{U}_{x_i,t} + X_{i,0}\right)'\right\},$$

$$R_{2,i,T} = \frac{1}{T^2}\sum_{t=1}^{T}\left\{\left(\tilde{U}_{y_i,0} - \tilde{U}_{y_i,t} + Y_{i,0}\right)P'_{i,t}C_{x_i}(1)'\right\},$$

$$R_{3,i,T} = \frac{1}{T^2}\sum_{t=1}^{T}\left\{\left(\tilde{U}_{y_i,0} - \tilde{U}_{y_i,t} + Y_{i,0}\right)\left(\tilde{U}_{x_i,0} - \tilde{U}_{x_i,t} + X_{i,0}\right)'\right\},$$

$$R_{4,i,T} = \frac{1}{T^2}\sum_{t=1}^{T}\left\{\beta C_{x_i}(1)P_{i,t}\left(\tilde{U}_{x_i,0} - \tilde{U}_{x_i,t} + X_{i,0}\right)' + \beta\left(\tilde{U}_{x_i,0} - \tilde{U}_{x_i,t} + X_{i,0}\right)P'_{i,t}C_{x_i}(1)'\right\},$$

$$R_{5,i,T} = \frac{1}{T^2}\sum_{t=1}^{T}\left\{\beta\left(\tilde{U}_{x_i,0} - \tilde{U}_{x_i,t} + X_{i,0}\right)\left(\tilde{U}_{x_i,0} - \tilde{U}_{x_i,t} + X_{i,0}\right)'\right\}.$$

We show that as $(n, T \to \infty)$

(8.18)
$$\frac{1}{\sqrt{n}}\sum_{i=1}^{n} Q_{i,T} \Rightarrow N(0, \Theta)$$

and as $(n, T \to \infty)$ with $n/T \to 0$,

$$\text{(8.19)} \qquad \frac{1}{\sqrt{n}} \sum_{i=1}^{n} R_{k,i,T} \xrightarrow{p} 0 \qquad (k = 1, \ldots, 5).$$

Note that

$$EQ_{i,T} = \frac{1}{T^2} \sum_{t=1}^{T} t(E[C_{y_i}(1) C_{x_i}(1)'] - \beta E[C_{x_i}(1) C_{x_i}(1)']) = 0.$$

Also,

$$\text{(8.20)} \qquad \frac{1}{T^4} \sum_{t=1}^{T} \sum_{s=1}^{T} E[\text{vec}(P_{i,t} P_{i,t}') \text{vec}(P_{i,s} P_{i,s}')']$$

$$= \frac{1}{T^4} \sum_{t=1}^{T} \sum_{s=1}^{T} E[P_{i,t} P_{i,s}' \otimes P_{i,t} P_{i,s}']$$

$$= \frac{1}{T^2} \sum_{t=1}^{T} \sum_{s=1}^{T} \left\{ \begin{array}{l} \left(\dfrac{t \wedge s}{T}\right)^2 (I_{m^2} + K_m + \text{vec}\, I_m (\text{vec}\, I_m)') \\ \quad + \left(\dfrac{t \wedge s}{T}\right) \left(\left(\dfrac{t \vee s}{T}\right) - \left(\dfrac{t \wedge s}{T}\right) \right) \text{vec}\, I_m (\text{vec}\, I_m)' \end{array} \right\} + O\left(\frac{1}{T}\right)$$

$$= \Xi_T + O\left(\frac{1}{T}\right), \qquad \text{say,}$$

and

$$\text{(8.21)} \qquad E(\text{vec}(Q_{i,T}) \text{vec}(Q_{i,T})')$$

$$= E\left[(C_{x_i}(1) \otimes (C_{y_i}(1) - \beta C_{x_i}(1))) \frac{1}{T^4} \sum_{t=1}^{T} \sum_{s=1}^{T} E[\text{vec}(P_{i,t} P_{i,t}') \text{vec}(P_{i,s} P_{i,s}')'] \right.$$

$$\left. \times (C_{x_i}(1)' \otimes (C_{y_i}(1) - \beta C_{x_i}(1))') \right.$$

$$= E\left[(C_{x_i}(1) \otimes (C_{y_i}(1) - \beta C_{x_i}(1))) \left(\Xi_T + O\left(\frac{1}{T}\right) \right) \right.$$

$$\left. \times (C_{x_i}(1)' \otimes (C_{y_i}(1) - \beta C_{x_i}(1))') \right]$$

$$= \Xi_T, \qquad \text{say.}$$

It is easy to see that $\Theta_T \to \Theta$ as $T \to \infty$. So $\{Q_{i,T}\}_i$ is an iid sequence with mean zero and covariance matrix Θ_T.

Next, apply Theorem 3 with $C_i = I_{m_y m_x}$ to establish that $(1/\sqrt{n}) \Sigma_{i=1}^{n} Q_{i,T} \Rightarrow N(0, \Theta)$ as $(n, T \to \infty)$. Conditions (i), (ii), and (iv) of the theorem are obviously satisfied in view of the fact that $C_i = I_{m_y m_x}$ and $\Theta_T \to \Theta$ as $T \to \infty$. For the uniform integrability of $\|Q_{i,t}\|^2$, note by the continuous mapping that as $T \to \infty$

$$\|Q_{i,T}\|^2 \Rightarrow \|Q_i\|^2 = \left\| \int \{ C_{y_i}(1) W_i W_i' C_{x_i}(1)' - \beta C_{x_i}(1) W_i W_i C_{x_i}(1)' \} \right\|^2.$$

Then, $\|Q_{i,T}\|^2$ is uniformly integrable in T because

$$E\|Q_{i,T}\|^2 = \operatorname{tr}(E(\operatorname{vec}(Q_{i,T})\operatorname{vec}(Q_{i,T})')) = \operatorname{tr}(\Theta_T)$$
$$\to \operatorname{tr}(\Theta) = \operatorname{tr}(E(\operatorname{vec}(Q_i)\operatorname{vec}(Q_i)')) = E\|Q_i\|^2.$$

Next, to prove $(1/\sqrt{n})\Sigma_{i=1}^{n} R_{k,i,T} \to_p 0$ as $(n,T\to\infty)$ with $n/T\to 0$, we simply show that $\sqrt{n}\,E\|R_{k,i,T}\|\to 0$ as $n,T\to\infty$ with $n/T\to 0$ for $k=1,\ldots,5$. Note that

$$\sqrt{n}\,E\|R_{1,i,T}\| \le \sqrt{n}\,\frac{1}{T^2}\sum_{t=1}^{T} E\left\{\|C_{y_i}(1)P_{i,t}\|\,\|\tilde{U}_{x_i,0} - \tilde{U}_{x_i,t} + X_{i,0}\|\right\}$$
$$= \sqrt{\frac{n}{T}}\,O(1) \to 0,$$

where the first inequality holds by the triangle inequality and $\|AB\| \le \|A\|\,\|B\|$ and the last line holds in view of (8.17) above. Similarly we can show that $\sqrt{n}\,E\|R_{2,i,T}\|$, $\sqrt{n}\,E\|R_{4,i,T}\| = \sqrt{n/T}\,O(1)$ and $\sqrt{n}\,E\|R_{3,i,T}\|$, $\sqrt{n}\,E\|R_{5,i,T}\| = (\sqrt{n}/T)O(1)$. So we have the desired limits and part (b) follows. *Q.E.D.*

PROOF OF THEOREM 4: By Lemma 13(a), it is easy to see that as $(n,T\to\infty)$

$$\hat{\beta}_{n,T} = \frac{1}{n}\sum_{i=1}^{n}\frac{1}{T^2}\sum_{t=1}^{T} Y_{i,t}X_{i,t}'\left(\frac{1}{n}\sum_{i=1}^{n}\frac{1}{T^2}\sum_{t=1}^{T} X_{i,t}X_{i,t}'\right)^{-1} \xrightarrow{p} \Omega_{yx}\Omega_{xx}^{-1} = \beta.$$

Also, when $(n,T\to\infty)$ with $n/T\to 0$, from Lemma 13(a) and (b) we have

$$\sqrt{n}\,(\hat{\beta}_{n,T} - \beta) = \left(\frac{1}{\sqrt{n}}\sum_{i=1}^{n}\frac{1}{T^2}\sum_{t=1}^{T}(Y_{i,t}X_{i,t}' - \beta X_{i,t}X_{i,t}')\right)\left(\frac{1}{n}\sum_{i=1}^{n}\frac{1}{T^2}\sum_{t=1}^{T} X_{i,t}X_{i,t}'\right)^{-1}$$
$$\Rightarrow N\left(0, 4\left(\Omega_{xx}^{-1}\otimes I_{m_y}\right)\Theta\left(\Omega_{xx}^{-1}\otimes I_{m_y}\right)\right),$$

giving the required result. *Q.E.D.*

8.4. APPENDIX D: PROOFS FOR SECTION 5.1—HETEROGENEOUS PANEL COINTEGRATION LIMIT THEORY

The following two lemmas give some useful results on the existence of moments of the heterogeneous coefficients β_i in (5.2) and the random coefficients in the linear process representation (5.3). Both results are proved in PM[b].

LEMMA 14: *Under Assumptions* 4, 5, *and* 7, $E\|\beta_i\|^8 < \infty$.

LEMMA 15: *Let* $G_i(1) = \Sigma_{s=0}^{\infty} G_{i,s}$, $\tilde{G}_{i,s} = \Sigma_{t=s+1}^{\infty} G_{i,t}$, *and* $\tilde{F}_{i,t} = \Sigma_{s=0}^{\infty}\tilde{G}_{i,s}V_{i,t-s}$. *Suppose that Assumptions* 4–7 *hold. Then*:

(a) $E(\Sigma_{s=0}^{\infty} s^2\|G_{i,s}\|^2) < \infty$.
(b) $E\|F_{i,t}\|^2 < M$ *for some constant* $M < \infty$.
(c) $E\|G_i(1)\|^4 < \infty$.
(d) $E\|\tilde{F}_{i,t}\|^4 < M$ *for some constant* $M < \infty$.

2. PROOF OF LEMMA 7: As in the proof of Lemma 3, since $\{\tilde{F}_{i,t}\}_t$ is strictly stationary and $\tilde{F}_{i,t}$ is square integrable from Lemma 15(d), it follows that

$$\sup_{0 \le r \le 1} \left| \frac{1}{\sqrt{T}} \tilde{F}_{a,i,[Tr]} \right| \xrightarrow{p} 0 \quad \text{as } T \to \infty \quad \text{for all } a, i, \tag{8.22}$$

where $\tilde{F}_{a,i,[Tr]}$ is the ath element of $\tilde{F}_{i,[Tr]}$. The functional law follows directly from (5.5) and Donsker's theorem applied to $(1/\sqrt{T})\Sigma_{t=1}^{[Tr]}V_{i,t}$. *Q.E.D.*

3. PROOF OF LEMMA 8: The proof follows the same lines as Phillips (1988) and is omitted here (details are available in PM[b]). *Q.E.D.*

4. PROOF OF THEOREM 5: The proof follows similar lines to that of Lemma 13 and Theorem 4 above but makes use of the bounds established in Lemmas 14 and 15 and the panel BN decomposition (5.4). The details are lengthy and to save space they are not repeated here. They are given in full in PM[b]. *Q.E.D.*

5. PROOF OF THEOREM 6: The proof proceeds by showing that as $(n, T \to \infty)$ with $n, T \to 0$,

$$\hat{\Theta} = \frac{1}{n} \sum_{i=1}^{n} \left\{ \frac{1}{T^4} \sum_{t=1}^{T} \sum_{s=1}^{T} X_{i,t}X_{i,s}' \otimes \hat{E}_{i,t}\hat{E}_{i,x}' \right\} \xrightarrow{p} \Theta,$$

and

$$\hat{\Omega}_{xx}^{-1} = \left[\frac{1}{n} \sum_{i=1}^{n} \left\{ \frac{2}{T^2} \sum_{t=1}^{T} X_{i,t}X_{i,t}' \right\} \right]^{-1} \xrightarrow{p} \Omega_{xx}^{-1}.$$

Then, by Theorem 5 and the delta method, the proof is complete. From Lemma 13, we know that $(1/n)\Sigma_{i=1}^{n}\{(2/T^2)\Sigma_{t=1}^{T}X_{i,t}X_{i,t}'\} \to_p \Omega_{xx}$ as $(n, T \to \infty)$. In consequence, $\hat{\Omega}_{xx}^{-1} \to_p \Omega_{xx}^{-1}$ as $(n, T \to \infty)$ since $\Omega_{xx} > 0$. Again, full details are available in PM[b]. *Q.E.D.*

6. PROOF OF THEOREM 7: Under the null hypothesis, using the cross section independence and applying Theorem 5, we have

$$\begin{aligned} \sqrt{n_b}(\hat{\beta}_a - \hat{\beta}_b) &= \sqrt{n_a}(n_b/n_a)^{1/2}(\hat{\beta}_a - \beta_a) - \sqrt{n_b}(\hat{\beta}_b - \beta_b) \\ &\Rightarrow N(0, \kappa V_a + V_b), \end{aligned}$$

when $(T, n_a, n_b \to \infty)$ and $n_a/T, n_b/T \to 0$, and where $V_\mu = 4(\Omega_{\mu,xx}^{-1} \otimes I_{m_x})\Theta_\mu(\Omega_{\mu,xx}^{-1} \otimes I_{m_x})$ for $\mu = a, b$.

As in the proof of Theorem 6, we can show that as $(T, n_a, n_b \to \infty)$ with $n_a/T, n_b/T \to 0$, we have

$$\hat{\Theta}_\mu = \frac{1}{n_\mu} \sum_{i \in I_\mu} \left\{ \frac{1}{T^4} \sum_{t=1}^{T} \sum_{s=1}^{T} X_{i,t}X_{i,s}' \otimes \hat{E}_{i,t}\hat{E}_{i,s}' \right\} \xrightarrow{p} \Theta_\mu,$$

and

$$\hat{\Omega}_{\mu,xx}^{1} = \left[\frac{1}{n_\mu} \sum_{i \in I_\mu} \left\{ \frac{2}{T^2} \sum_{t=1}^{T} X_{i,t}X_{i,t}' \right\} \right]^{-1} \xrightarrow{p} \Omega_{\mu,xx}^{-1}.$$

Consequently, $\hat{V}_\mu \to_p V_\mu$, and $\hat{V}_{a-b} = (n_b/n_a)\hat{V}_a + \hat{V}_b \to_p \kappa V_a + V_b$. It follows that

$$W_{a,b} = n_b\{\text{vec}(\hat{\beta}_a - \hat{\beta}_b)'\hat{V}_{a-b}^{-1}\text{vec}(\hat{\beta}_a - \hat{\beta}_b)\} \Rightarrow \chi^2_{m_y m_x},$$

giving the required result.

APPENDIX E: PROOFS FOR SECTION 5.2—HOMOGENEOUS PANEL COINTEGRATION LIMIT THEORY

Before we start the proof of Theorem 9, we give the following useful lemma.

THEOREM 16: *Let $F_{i,t} = (E'_{i,t}, U'_{x_i,t})' = \Sigma_{s=0}^{\infty} G_s V_{i,t-s}$ be the panel process defined in Model* (5.11). *Also, let $S_{i,t} = \Sigma_{i=1}^{T} F_{i,t} + S_{i,0}$, where $S_{i,0}$ are iid with $E\|S_{i,0}\|^4 < \infty$, $\Omega_F = G(1)G(1)'$, $\Lambda_F = \Sigma_{k=0}^{\infty}\Sigma_{s=0}^{\infty} G_{s+k}G'_s$, and $G(1) = \Sigma_{s=0}^{\infty} G_s$. Then, under the summability condition Assumption 9 and positive definiteness condition Assumption* 10, *as $(n, T \to \infty)$ with $n/T \to 0$,*

$$\frac{1}{\sqrt{n}}\sum_{i=1}^{n}\left(\frac{1}{T}\sum_{t=1}^{T} F_{i,t}S'_{i,t} - \Lambda_F\right) \Rightarrow N\left(0, \frac{1}{2}\Omega_F \otimes \Omega_F\right).$$

PROOF OF LEMMA 16: Using the BN decomposition as in the proof of Lemma 8, we have

$$\begin{aligned}
&\frac{1}{\sqrt{n}}\sum_{i=1}^{n}\left(\frac{1}{T}\sum_{t=1}^{T} F_{i,t}S'_{i,t} - \Lambda_F\right)\\
&= \frac{1}{\sqrt{n}}\sum_{i=1}^{n}\left(\frac{1}{T}\sum_{t=1}^{T} G(1)(V_{i,t}P'_{i,t} - I_m)G(1)'\right)\\
&\quad + \frac{1}{\sqrt{n}}\sum_{i=1}^{n}\left(\frac{1}{T}\sum_{t=1}^{T-1}\left(\tilde{F}_{i,t}F'_{i,t+1} - \sum_{s=0}^{\infty}\tilde{G}_s G'_{s+1}\right)\right) + \frac{\sqrt{n}}{T}\sum_{s=0}^{\infty}\tilde{G}_s G'_{s+1}\\
&\quad - \frac{1}{\sqrt{n}}\sum_{i=1}^{n}\left(\frac{1}{T}\sum_{t=1}^{T}(G(1)V_{i,t}\tilde{F}'_{i,t} - G(1)\tilde{G}'_0)\right)\\
&\quad + \frac{1}{\sqrt{n}}\sum_{i=1}^{n}\left(\frac{1}{T}\sum_{t=1}^{T} G(1)V_{i,t}(\tilde{F}_{i,0} + S_{i,0})'\right)\\
&\quad - \frac{1}{\sqrt{n}}\sum_{i=1}^{n}\frac{1}{T}\tilde{F}_{i,T}S'_{i,T} + \frac{1}{\sqrt{n}}\sum_{i=1}^{n}\frac{1}{T}\tilde{F}_{i,0}S'_{i,1} \qquad \text{a.s.}\\
&= \frac{1}{\sqrt{n}}\sum_{i=1}^{n}(Q_{1,i,T} + R_{1,i,T} + R_{2,i,T} + R_{3,i,T} + R_{4,i,T} + R_{5,i,T})\\
&\quad + O\left(\frac{\sqrt{n}}{T}\right) \qquad \text{a.s., say.}
\end{aligned}$$

We show that $(1/\sqrt{n})\Sigma_{i=1}^{n} Q_{i,T} \Rightarrow N(0, \frac{1}{2}\Omega_F \otimes \Omega_F)$, and $(1/\sqrt{n})\Sigma_{i=1}^{n} R_{k,i,T} \to_p 0$, $k = 1, \ldots, 5$, as $(n, T \to \infty)$ with $n/T \to 0$.

Note that

$$\frac{1}{\sqrt{n}}\sum_{i=1}^{n} Q_{i,T} = \frac{1}{\sqrt{n}}\sum_{i=1}^{n}\left(\frac{1}{T}\sum_{t=2}^{T} G(1)V_{i,t}P'_{i,t-1}G(1)'\right)$$

$$+\frac{1}{\sqrt{n}}\sum_{i=1}^{n}\left(\frac{1}{T}\sum_{i=1}^{T} G(1)(V_{i,t}V'_{i,t}-I_m)G(1)'\right)$$

$$=\frac{1}{\sqrt{n}}\sum_{i=1}^{n}(Q_{1,i,T}+Q_{2,i,T}), \qquad \text{say.}$$

Since $E((1/T)\Sigma_{t=1}^{T}G(1)(V_{i,t}V'_{i,t}-I_m)G(1)')=0$, we have

$$E\left\|\frac{1}{\sqrt{n}}\sum_{i=1}^{n}Q_{2,i,T}\right\|^2$$

$$=E\left\|\frac{1}{T}\sum_{t=1}^{T}G(1)(V_{i,t}V'_{i,t}-I_m)G(1)'\right\|^2$$

$$\leq \|G(1)\|^4 \operatorname{tr}\left[\frac{1}{T^2}\sum_{t=1}^{T}\sum_{s=1}^{T}E\{(V_{i,t}V'_{i,s}\otimes V_{i,t}V'_{i,s})-\operatorname{vec}(I_m)(\operatorname{vec}(I_m))'\}\right]$$

$$=O\left(\frac{1}{T}\right).$$

Thus, $(1/\sqrt{n})\Sigma_{i=1}^{n}Q_{2,i,T}=o_p(1)$. Next, observe that

$$E[\operatorname{vec}(Q_{1,i,T})(\operatorname{vec}(Q_{1,i,T}))']$$

$$=\frac{1}{T^2}\sum_{t=2}^{T}\sum_{s=2}^{T}(G(1)\otimes G(1))E(P_{i,t-1}P'_{i,s-1}\otimes V_{i,t}V'_{i,s})(G(1)'\otimes G(1)')$$

$$=\frac{1}{T}\sum_{t=2}^{T}\left(\frac{t-1}{T}\right)(G(1)G(1)'\otimes G(1)G(1)')\equiv \Xi_T^* \qquad \text{(say)}$$

$$\to\frac{1}{2}(G(1)G(1)'\otimes G(1)G(1)')=\frac{1}{2}(\Omega_F\otimes\Omega_F)\equiv\Xi^*, \qquad \text{say.}$$

Also, note that $\frac{1}{2}(\Omega_F\otimes\Omega_F)>0$. These verify conditions (i), (ii), and (iv) of Theorem 3. Condition (iii) of Theorem 3 holds because

$$\|Q_{i,T}\|^2\Rightarrow\|Q_i\|^2=\left\|G(1)\int dW_i\, W_i' G(1)'\right\|^2$$

and

$$Q_{i,T}^2=\operatorname{tr}(\Xi_T^*)\to\operatorname{tr}(\Xi^*)=E\|Q_i\|^2$$

so that the $\|Q_{i,T}\|^2$ are uniformly integrable in T. By Theorem 3, $(1/\sqrt{n})\Sigma_{i=1}^{n}Q_{1,i,T}\Rightarrow N(0,\frac{1}{2}\Omega_F\otimes\Omega_F)$.

Next, we show that $(1/\sqrt{n})\Sigma_{i=1}^{n} R_{1,i,T} \to_p 0$ by proving $E\|(1/\sqrt{n})\Sigma_{i=1}^{n} R_{1,i,T}\|^2 \to 0$ as $(n, T \to \infty)$. Note that

$$
\begin{aligned}
E&\left\| \frac{1}{\sqrt{n}} \sum_{i=1}^{n} R_{1,i,T} \right\|^2 \\
&= \operatorname{tr}[E(\operatorname{vec}(R_{1,i,T})(\operatorname{vec}(R_{1,i,T}))')] \text{ since } E(R_{1,i,T}) = 0 \\
&= \operatorname{tr}\left[\frac{1}{T^2} \sum_{t=1}^{T-1} \sum_{s=1}^{T-1} E \left\{ \begin{array}{l} \operatorname{vec}\left(\sum_{j=0}^{\infty} \sum_{k=0}^{\infty} \tilde{G}_j V_{i,t-j} V'_{i,t+1-k} G'_k \right) \\ \times \left(\operatorname{vec}\left(\sum_{p=0}^{\infty} \sum_{q=0}^{\infty} \tilde{G}_p V_{i,s-p} V'_{i,s+1-q} G'_q \right) \right)' \\ -\operatorname{vec}\left(\sum_{s=0}^{\infty} \tilde{G}_s G'_{s+1} \right) \left(\operatorname{vec}\left(\sum_{s=0}^{\infty} \tilde{G}_s G'_{s+1} \right) \right)' \end{array} \right\} \right] \\
&= \operatorname{tr}\left[\frac{1}{T} \sum_{h=-T+2}^{T-2} \left(\frac{T-1-|h|}{T} \right) \right. \\
&\qquad \left. \times \left(\begin{array}{l} \sum_{j=0}^{\infty} \sum_{k=0}^{\infty} \sum_{p=0}^{\infty} \sum_{q=0}^{\infty} (G_k \otimes \tilde{G}_j) \\ \times E(V_{i,t+1-k} V'_{i,t+h+1-q} \otimes V_{i,t-j} V'_{i,t+h-p})(G_q \otimes \tilde{G}_p)' \\ -\operatorname{vec}\left(\sum_{s=0}^{\infty} \tilde{G}_s G'_{s+1} \right) \left(\operatorname{vec}\left(\sum_{s=0}^{\infty} \tilde{G}_s G'_{s+1} \right) \right)' \end{array} \right) \right].
\end{aligned}
$$

If we show

$$
\operatorname{tr} \sum_{h=0}^{\infty} \left(\begin{array}{l} \sum_{j=0}^{\infty} \sum_{k=0}^{\infty} \sum_{p=0}^{\infty} \sum_{q=0}^{\infty} (G_k \otimes \tilde{G}_j) \\ \times E(V_{i,t+1-k} V'_{i,t+h+1-q} \otimes V_{i,t-j} V'_{i,t+h-p})(G_q \otimes \tilde{G}_p)' \\ -\operatorname{vec}\left(\sum_{s=0}^{\infty} \tilde{G}_s G'_{s+1} \right) \left(\operatorname{vec}\left(\sum_{s=0}^{\infty} \tilde{G}_s G'_{s+1} \right) \right)' \end{array} \right) < \infty,
$$

then, by Cesaro summability, it follows that $E\|(1/\sqrt{n})\Sigma_{i=1}^{n} R_{1,i,T}\|^2 = O(1/T)$. Observe that

$$
\begin{aligned}
(8.23) \qquad &= \sum_{h=0}^{\infty} \left(\sum_{j=0}^{\infty} \sum_{k=0}^{\infty} \operatorname{tr}\left(G_k G'_{k+h} \otimes \tilde{G}_j \tilde{G}'_{j+h} \right) \right) \\
&\quad + \sum_{h=0}^{\infty} \left(\sum_{j=0}^{\infty} \sum_{k=(0 \vee (1-h))}^{\infty} \operatorname{tr}\left(G_k \tilde{G}'_{k+h-1} \otimes \tilde{G}_j G'_{j+h+1} \right) K_m \right) \\
&\quad + (\upsilon^4 - 3) \sum_{h=0}^{\infty} \sum_{j=0}^{\infty} \operatorname{tr}\left((G_{j+1} \otimes \tilde{G}_j) \left(\sum_{l=1}^{m} e_{\ell,\ell} \otimes e_{\ell,\ell} \right) (G'_{j+h+1} \otimes \tilde{G}'_{j+h}) \right) \\
&= I + II + III, \qquad \text{say.}
\end{aligned}
$$

Since $\mathrm{tr}(A \otimes B) = \mathrm{tr}(A)\mathrm{tr}(B)$ and $\mathrm{tr}(A) \le \mathrm{rows}((A))^{1/2}\|A\|$ from (8.2) in Lemma 9, we have

$$I = \sum_{h=0}^{\infty} \mathrm{tr}\left(\sum_{k=0}^{\infty} G_k G'_{k+h} \right) \mathrm{tr}\left(\sum_{j=0}^{\infty} \tilde{G}_j \tilde{G}'_{j+h} \right)$$

$$\le \left[\sum_{h=0}^{\infty} \left| \mathrm{tr}\left(\sum_{k=0}^{\infty} G_k G'_{k+h} \right) \right| \right] \left[\sum_{h=0}^{\infty} \left| \mathrm{tr}\left(\sum_{j=0}^{\infty} \tilde{G}_j \tilde{G}'_{j+h} \right) \right| \right]$$

$$\le m \left(\sum_{k=0}^{\infty} \|G_k\| \right)^2 \left(\sum_{k=0}^{\infty} \|\tilde{G}_k\| \right)^2 < \infty \qquad \text{by Assumption 9.}$$

By Lemma 10,

$$II \le \sum_{k=1}^{\infty} \sum_{j=0}^{\infty} \|G_k\| \|\tilde{G}_{k-1}\| \|\tilde{G}_j\| \|G_{j+1}\| + \sum_{h=1}^{\infty} \left(\sum_{k=0}^{\infty} \sum_{j=0}^{\infty} \|G_k\| \|\tilde{G}_{k+h-1}\| \|\tilde{G}_j\| \|G_{j+h+1}\| \right)$$

$$\le \left(\sum_{j=0}^{\infty} \|G_j\| \right)^4 + \left(\sum_{h=0}^{\infty} \sum_{k=0}^{\infty} \|G_k\| \|\tilde{G}_{k+h}\| \right) \left(\sum_{h=0}^{\infty} \sum_{j=0}^{\infty} \|\tilde{G}_j\| \|G_{j+h}\| \right)$$

$$\le \left(\sum_{j=0}^{\infty} \|G_j\| \right)^4 + \left(\sum_{j=0}^{\infty} j\|G_j\| \right)^2 \left(\sum_{j=0}^{\infty} \|G_j\| \right)^2 < \infty.$$

Similarly, we can show that for some $M > 0$

$$III \le M \left(\sum_{j=0}^{\infty} \|G_j\| \right)^4 < \infty.$$

Also, we can show by modifying the arguments used above that

$$E\left\| \frac{1}{\sqrt{n}} \sum_{i=1}^{n} R_{2,i,T} \right\|^2, \qquad E\left\| \frac{1}{\sqrt{n}} \sum_{i=1}^{n} R_{3,i,T} \right\|^2 = O\left(\frac{1}{T} \right),$$

and

$$E\left\| \frac{1}{\sqrt{n}} \sum_{i=1}^{n} R_{4,i,T} \right\| = O\left(\sqrt{\frac{n}{T}} \right), \qquad E\left\| \frac{1}{\sqrt{n}} \sum_{i=1}^{n} R_{5,i,T} \right\| = O\left(\frac{\sqrt{n}}{T} \right),$$

so all the desired results are proved and the lemma follows. *Q.E.D.*

PROOF OF THEOREM 9: To establish joint limit normality of the PFM estimator $\hat{\beta}_{PFM}$, it is enough to show that, as $(n, T \to \infty)$ with $n/T \to 0$,

$$\frac{1}{\sqrt{n}} \sum_{i=1}^{n} \left(\frac{1}{T} \sum_{t=1}^{T} (\hat{E}^+_{i,t} X'_{i,t} - \hat{\Lambda}^+_{ex}) \right) \Rightarrow N(0, \tfrac{1}{2}(\Omega_{xx} \otimes \Omega_{e.x})),$$

and

$$\left[\frac{1}{n} \sum_{i=1}^{n} \left\{ \frac{1}{T^2} \sum_{t=1}^{T} X_{i,t} X'_{i,t} \right\} \right]^{-1} \xrightarrow{p} 2\Omega_{xx}^{-1}.$$

The proof of the latter result is similar to the proof of Lemma 13(a), so we concentrate on the former.

Let $\Lambda_{ex}^{+} = \Lambda_{ex} - \Omega_{ex}\Omega_{xx}^{-1}\Lambda_{xx}$ and $E_{i,t}^{+} = E_{i,t} - \Omega_{ex}\Omega_{xx}^{-1}\,\Delta X_{i,t}$. Then

$$\frac{1}{\sqrt{n}}\sum_{i=1}^{n}\left(\frac{1}{T}\sum_{t=1}^{T}(\hat{E}_{i,t}^{+}X_{i,t}' - \hat{\Lambda}_{ex}^{+})\right)$$

$$= \frac{1}{\sqrt{n}}\sum_{i=1}^{n}\left(\frac{1}{T}\sum_{t=1}^{T}(E_{i,t}^{+}X_{i,t}' - \Lambda_{ex}^{+})\right)$$

$$-(\hat{\Omega}_{ex}\hat{\Omega}_{xx}^{-1} - \Omega_{ex}\Omega_{xx}^{-1})\frac{1}{\sqrt{n}}\sum_{i=1}^{n}\left(\frac{1}{T}\sum_{t=1}^{T}(\Delta X_{i,t}X_{i,t}' - \Lambda_{xx})\right)$$

$$-\sqrt{n}(\hat{\Lambda}_{ex} - \Lambda_{ex}) + \hat{\Omega}_{ex}\hat{\Omega}_{xx}^{-1}\sqrt{n}(\hat{\Lambda}_{xx} - \Lambda_{xx}).$$

First, $(\hat{\Omega}_{ex}\hat{\Omega}_{xx}^{-1} - \Omega_{ex}\Omega_{xx}^{-1})(1/\sqrt{n})\Sigma_{i=1}^{n}((1/T)\Sigma_{t=1}^{T}(\Delta X_{i,t}X_{i,t}' - \Lambda_{xx})) = o_p(1)$ because $\hat{\Omega}_{ex}\hat{\Omega}_{xx}^{-1} - \Omega_{ex}\Omega_{xx}^{-1} = o_p(1)$ and $(1/\sqrt{n})\Sigma_{i=1}^{n}((1/T)\Sigma_{t=1}^{T}(\Delta X_{i,t}X_{i,t}' - \Lambda_{xx})) = O_p(1)$ by Lemma 16 and $E\|X_{i,0}\|^4 < M$ for some constant M. Next, according to Theorems 9 and 10 in Hannan (1970, pp. 280–283) (or Proposition 1 in Andrews (1991)), we know that $E\|\hat{\Omega}_{F,i} - E\hat{\Omega}_{F,i}\|^2 = (K/T)O(1)$, and $\|E\hat{\Omega}_{F,i} - \Omega_F\|^2 = (1/K^{2q})O(1)$. Thus,

$$E\|\sqrt{n}(\hat{\Omega}_F - \Omega_F)\|^2 = E\left\|\frac{1}{\sqrt{n}}\sum_{i=1}^{n}(\hat{\Omega}_{F,i} - E\hat{\Omega}_{F,i} + E\hat{\Omega}_{F,i} - \Omega_F)\right\|^2$$

$$= E\|\hat{\Omega}_{F,i} - E\hat{\Omega}_{F,i}\|^2 + n\|E\hat{\Omega}_{F,i} - \Omega_F\|^2$$

$$= \left(\frac{K}{T} + \frac{n}{K^{2q}}\right)O(1).$$

Since the bandwidth parameter $K \to \infty$ with $K/T \to 0$ and $K^{2q}/T \to \epsilon > 0$ for some $q > \frac{1}{2}$ by Assumption 11, it follows that $E\|\sqrt{n}(\hat{\Omega}_F - \Omega_F)\|^2 \to 0$ as $(n, T \to \infty)$ with $n/T \to 0$. The same argument can be applied to $\hat{\Lambda}_F$. In consequence, we have

$$\sqrt{n}(\hat{\Lambda}_{ex} - \Lambda_{ex}),\ \hat{\Omega}_{ex}\hat{\Omega}_{xx}^{-1}\sqrt{n}(\hat{\Lambda}_{xx} - \Lambda_{xx}) = o_p(1).$$

The remainder of the proof involves showing that

$$\frac{1}{\sqrt{n}}\sum_{i=1}^{n}\left(\frac{1}{T}\sum_{t=1}^{T}(E_{i,t}^{+}X_{i,t}' - \Lambda_{ex}^{+})\right) \Rightarrow N\left(0, \frac{1}{2}(\Omega_{xx}\otimes\Omega_{e.x})\right),$$

and this is entirely analogous to the proof of Lemma 16. The main contribution of $(1/\sqrt{n})\Sigma_{i=1}^{n}((1/T)\Sigma_{t=1}^{T}(E_{i,t}^{+}X_{i,t}' - \Lambda_{ex}^{+}))$ from the BN decomposition is

$$\frac{1}{\sqrt{n}}\sum_{i=1}^{n}\left(\frac{1}{T}\sum_{t=1}^{T}(G_e(1) - \Omega_{ex}\Omega_{xx}^{-1}C_x(1))V_{i,t}P_{i,t-1}'C_x(1)'\right) = \frac{1}{\sqrt{n}}\sum_{i=1}^{n}Q_{i,T},$$

and it is easy to see that

$$E[\text{vec}(Q_{i,T})(\text{vec}(Q_{i,T}))'] = \left(\frac{1}{T}\sum_{t=1}^{T}\frac{t-1}{T}\right)(\Omega_{xx}\otimes\Omega_{e.x})$$

$$\to \frac{1}{2}(\Omega_{xx}\otimes\Omega_{e.x}) = E[\text{vec}(Q_i)(\text{vec}(Q_i))'],$$

where $Q_i = (G_e(1) - \Omega_{ex}\Omega_{xx}^{-1}C_x(1))\int dW_i\, W_i'C_x(1)'$. Thus, by Theorem 3, we have the desired result. All the remainder terms in the BN decomposition of $(1/\sqrt{n})\Sigma_{i=1}^{n}((1/T)\Sigma_{t=1}^{T}(E_{i,t}^{+}X_{i,t}' - \Lambda_{ex}^{+}))$ converge in probability to zero by Lemma 16 and the moment bound $E\|X_{i,0}\|^4 < M$, for some constant M. *Q.E.D.*

REFERENCES

ANDREWS, D. W. K. (1991): "Heteroskedasticity and Autocorrelation Consistent Covariance Matrix Estimation," *Econometrica*, 59, 817–858.

BALTAGI, B. (1995): *Econometric Analysis of Panel Data*. New York: Wiley.

BILLINGSLEY, P. (1968): *Convergence of Probability Measures*. New York: Wiley.

——— (1986): *Probability and Measure*. New York: Wiley.

CHAMBERLAIN, G. (1984): "Panel Data," in *Handbook of Econometrics*, Vol. 2, ed. by Z. Griliches and M. Intriligator. Amsterdam: North-Holland.

CONLEY, T. (1997): "Econometric Modelling of Cross Sectional Dependence," Mimeo.

DUDLEY, R. (1989): *Real Analysis and Probability*. Pacific Grove: Wadsworth & Brooks/Cole Mathematics Series.

EICKER, F. (1963): "Central Limit Theorems for Families of Sequences of Random Variables," *Annals of Mathematical Statistics*, 34, 439–446.

GRANGER, C. W. J., AND P. NEWBOLD (1974): "Spurious Regressions in Econometrics," *Journal of Econometrics*, 2, 111–120.

HSIAO, C. (1986): *Analysis of Panel Data*. Cambridge: Cambridge University Press.

HALL, P., AND C. HEYDE (1980): *Martingale Limit Theory and its Applications*. New York: Academic Press.

HANNAN, E. (1970): *Multiple Time Series*. New York: Wiley.

IM, K., H. PESARAN, AND Y. SHIN (1996): "Testing for Unit Roots in Heterogeneous Panels," Mimeo.

LEVIN, A., AND C. LIN (1993): "Unit Root Tests in Panel Data: New Results," UC San Diego Working Paper.

MAGNUS, J., AND H. NEUDECKER (1988): *Matrix Differential Calculus*. New York: Wiley.

MATYAS, L., AND P. SEVESTRE (EDS.) (1992): *The Econometrics of Panel Data*. Boston, MA: Kluwer Academic Publishers.

MUIRHEAD, R. (1982): *Aspects of Multivariate Statistical Theory*. New York: Wiley.

PEDRONI, P. (1995): "Panel Cointegration; Asymptotic and Finite Sample Properties of Pooled Time Series Tests with an Application to the PPP Hypothesis," Indiana University Working Papers in Economics No. 95-013.

PESARAN, H., AND R. SMITH (1995): "Estimating Long-Run Relationships from Dynamic Heterogeneous Panels," *Journal of Econometrics*, 68, 79–113.

PHILLIPS, P. C. B. (1986): "Understanding Spurious Regressions in Econometrics," *Journal of Econometrics*, 33, 311–340.

——— (1988): "Weak Convergence of Sample Covariance Matrices to Stochastic Integrals via Martingale Approximations," *Econometric Theory*, 4, 528–533.

PHILLIPS, P. C. B., AND S. DURLAUF (1986): "Multiple Time Series Regression with Integrated Processes," *Review of Economic Studies*, 53, 473–495.

PHILLIPS, P. C. B., AND B. HANSEN (1990): "Statistical Inference in Instrumental Variables Regression with $I(1)$ Processes," *Review of Economic Studies*, 57, 99–125.

PHILLIPS, P. C. B., AND C. LEE (1996): "Efficiency Gains from Quasi-Differerencing under Nonstationarity," in *Athens Conference on Applied Probability and Time Series: Volume II, Time Series Analysis in Memory of E. J. Hannan*, ed. by P. M. Robinson and M. Rosenblatt. New York: Springer-Verlag.

PHILLIPS, P. C. B., AND H. MOON (1997a): "Linear Regression Limit Theory for Nonstationary Panel Data," University of Auckland Discussion Paper in Economics.

——— (1997b): "Linear Regression Limit Theory for Nonstationary Panel Data," Yale University, Mimeographed.

PHILLIPS, P. C. B., AND V. SOLO (1992): "Asymptotics for Linear Processes," *Annals of Statistics*, 20, 971–1001.

POLLARD, D. (1984): *Convergence of Stochastic Processes*. New York: Springer Verlag.

QUAH, D. (1994): "Exploiting Cross-Section Variations for Unit Root Inference in Dynamic Data," *Economic Letters*, 44, 9–19.

ROBERTSON, D., AND J. SYMONS (1992): "Some Strange Properties of Panel Data Estimators," *Journal of Applied Econometrics*, 7, 175–189.

SHORACK, G., AND J. WELLNER (1986): *Empirical Processes with Applications to Statistics*. New York: Wiley.

Name Index